MW01258526

UNIVERSITY CASEBOOK SERIES®

THE U.S. CONSTITUTION:

CREATION, RECONSTRUCTION, THE PROGRESSIVES, AND THE MODERN ERA

STEVEN GOW CALABRESI
Clayton J. and Henry R. Barber Professor of Law,
Northwestern Pritzker School of Law

GARY LAWSON
Philip S. Beck Professor of Law,
Boston University School of Law

444 Cedar Street, Suite 700
St. Paul, MN 55101
1-877-888-1330

Printed in the United States of America

ISBN: 978-1-64242-909-1

Professor Calabresi dedicates his work on this casebook to the Yale Law School faculty members from whom he has learned constitutional law:

Joseph Goldstein

Robert H. Bork

Bruce Ackerman

and

Akhil Reed Amar

Professor Lawson dedicates his work on this casebook, as with all things, to Patty, Nathaniel, and Noah.

PREFACE

Constitutional law is too big a subject for a constitutional law course. Everyone knows this. Law schools accordingly parcel out study of constitutional law among many courses. Separation of powers is often delegated to courses in Administrative Law or Federal Courts. Criminal procedure goes to courses in Constitutional Criminal Procedure. Freedom of speech and freedom of religion often get their own specialized courses, as does much of the law under the Reconstruction Amendments. Procedural due process is often the province of Administrative Law. And so on. Amidst all of this dispersion and specialization, what is the role of the introductory survey course in Constitutional Law?

We think its role is to study the Constitution and the law and practices that have emerged under it over the last (as of this writing) 232 years—the *whole* Constitution, and not just isolated parts of it. The Constitution is an integrated document, whose original pieces were designed in 1787 to work together. Some transformative amendments have occurred, primarily at two distinct periods of time (Reconstruction and the Progressive Era); and those transformations, in turn, can only be understood in light of what they were trying to transform. We think an introductory look at the Constitution and constitutional law needs to be panoramic in scope. Accordingly, we have structured this book to cover the *entire* Constitution and the *entire* history of the law resulting from it, including the vital history that preceded the Constitution's adoption.

Can we really do that in a single book for a single course?

That is for the reader to judge. We have tried, in this book, to provide materials on every provision of the Constitution, from the Preamble to the Twenty-Seventh Amendment. Obviously, some parts of the Constitution get, and deserve, more attention than others, and a few key provisions, such as the Eleventh Amendment, end up (after hundreds of pages of painful cuts) getting only a passing mention. But we try to keep in context everything that happens in the document and in the more than two centuries of cases, practices, decisions, and wars that have occurred in the Constitution's name.

Can a one-semester survey course assign and cover everything in this book? Of course not. But we think that the full menu of options, along with materials that can be treated as background, needs to be available to students and professors alike. We have divided the material into eighty-two "assignments." Those divisions are only recommendations, based on our own judgments about logical groupings of materials and/or likely allocations of time. Users naturally may have their own ideas about coverage and emphasis; we hope that our structure makes it easy to adapt the material in the book to those ideas.

Substantively, both of us are notorious advocates of a jurisprudence of original meaning. It would make no sense to try to hide that fact in constructing this book, so we made no effort to do so. Indeed, we are perhaps more open about sharing our own—sometimes conflicting—views on doctrine than is conventional in casebook construction. That is not because we expect users of this book to share our own methodological commitments. Rather, we think it will be stimulating, engaging, and (perish the thought in a law school course) maybe even *fun* for users who disagree with us to take our comments as challenges and as spurs for discussion and debate. If students (and professors) can figure out *why* they think we are full of hot gas, that may help them sort out their own views on the complex questions posed by constitutional law. Indeed, notwithstanding our shared commitment to originalism, we disagree with each other on some important points of doctrine, and we freely share those disagreements in the ensuing materials. Perhaps airing those differences may also encourage students to think through their own positions.

In any event, this book presents extensive materials on original meaning, in addition to extensive materials—meaning pretty much the entire history of Supreme Court caselaw—employing other modalities of interpretation and application. That is not just because both of us happen to be fans of original meaning. We think this approach is sound pedagogy. Originalism has become, in recent decades, an increasingly important modality of interpretation on the Supreme Court and the lower federal courts. (We suspect that the same is true even at the state court level.) There is some reason to think that this trend will accelerate, perhaps substantially, in coming years. The kinds of arguments that will be successful in constitutional litigation will need at least to take account of original meaning for some time to come. One purpose of this book is thus to give students some of the tools that they will need to make successful constitutional arguments in the coming years. Arguments that would have worked forty years ago, when the two of us started law school, are not likely to have the same success rate today.

In the end, our main objective is to promote *understanding* of the Constitution and constitutional doctrine. We spend a lot of time and space in this book on history—not just because history is interesting and important, but because history is vital for *understanding* why doctrine is shaped in particular ways (and how one can try to mold that shape going forward). We harp extensively on getting students to think about modalities of interpretation—not just because interpretative theory is interesting and important, but because it explains much of what happens in the world of constitutional law. Method matters. We emphasize structural constitutionalism—not just because it has been a scholarly focus for both of us, but because the Constitution is mostly about structure, and one can understand neither the document nor the practices under it without thinking about almost everything in structural terms. And we emphasize the Reconstruction Amendments (and the almost-as-important Progressive-Era Amendments) because the Constitution we have today is not, even in a formal sense, the Constitution that was adopted in 1788. We try to treat Reconstruction like the Second Founding that it truly was.

This book thus addresses constitutional law, constitutional history, constitutional method, and constitutional theory. All of those elements are essential for understanding the remarkable document that is the Constitution of the United States.

Much, though by no means all, of the material in this book consists of cases, primarily from the United States Supreme Court. No surprise there. The problem with cases in constitutional law, however, is that they tend to be very long—much longer than in many other subjects. With multiple opinions, it is not uncommon for leading cases to consume one hundred or even two hundred or more pages in the United States Reports. This means that editing must be brutal, and whenever editing of that magnitude takes place, there is always the risk that important elements of meaning are lost. We see no solution to this problem other than to be aware of it.

As a matter of form: Textual omissions from quoted material are indicated by three asterisks. Citations, footnotes, and formatting such as headings and subheadings are generally omitted from quoted material without indication. Footnotes in quoted material retain their original numbering. Editors' footnotes are numbered consecutively in each chapter. Editors' footnotes that appear in quoted material are clearly identified, in brackets and italicized. We have used the official versions of Supreme Court opinions as they appear in the United States Reports. Accordingly, if the spelling, grammar, or punctuation in the opinions seems odd, it is nearly certain that it is so in the original. In our own text, we have tried to capitalize the word "State" when it is used as a noun but not when it is used as an adjective. We generally capitalize adjectives such as "Northern" and "Southern" for emphasis. We do not generally capitalize terms such as "senate," "house," or "justice" unless we are speaking of a specific entity or person. We make no promises of consistency in these practices.

STEVEN GOW CALABRESI
GARY LAWSON

March 2020

ACKNOWLEDGEMENTS

Professor Calabresi would like to thank his two law school Deans, Kim Yuracko at Northwestern Pritzker School of Law and Heather Gerken at Yale Law School, where Professor Calabresi visited in the Fall of 2019, for their unstinting and generous financial and personal support of all of his scholarly endeavors, including the writing of this casebook.

Professor Calabresi would also like to express his deeply held gratitude to the four Yale Law School faculty members to whom he dedicated his work on this casebook and from whom he has been taught constitutional law: Joseph Goldstein, Robert H. Bork, Bruce Ackerman, and Akhil Reed Amar.

Professor Goldstein brilliantly taught Professor Calabresi constitutional law in his 1-L fall semester small group. Professor Calabresi loved his small group, took two additional courses from Professor Joseph Goldstein, and relied on him as a critical job reference when Professor Calabresi was hired in 1990 by the Northwestern Pritzker School of Law. Professor Goldstein was an indispensable mentor to Professor Calabresi.

Professor Calabresi, along with Professor Akhil Amar, took the last class which then-Judge Robert H. Bork taught at Yale Law School. It was a brilliantly taught seminar on Constitutional Theory. Professor Calabresi went on to clerk for Judge Bork and then to work as a research assistant to him on his book, THE TEMPTING OF AMERICA: THE POLITICAL SEDUCTION OF THE LAW (1990). Judge Bork was also an indispensable mentor to Professor Calabresi, to whom he taught the critical importance to judges of deciding cases by adhering to the original public meaning of texts.

Professor Calabresi did not take a course in constitutional law from Professor Bruce Ackerman, but Professor Ackerman's writings in WE THE PEOPLE VOLUME I: FOUNDATIONS (1993), WE THE PEOPLE, VOLUME 2: TRANSFORMATIONS (2000), and WE THE PEOPLE, VOLUME 3: THE CIVIL RIGHTS REVOLUTION (2018) have forever shaped Professor Calabresi's thoughts on constitutional law. This is also true with respect to a book review of THE TEMPTING OF AMERICA, which Professor Ackerman wrote and published.

Finally, Professor Calabresi wants to thank Professor Akhil Reed Amar, who he has known since Professor Amar's freshman year in Yale College. Professor Calabresi values his friendship with Professor Amar beyond what words can convey! Professor Amar helped Professor Calabresi when he was on the academic teaching market in 1989–1990, and he walked Professor Calabresi day by day through the first course which Professor Calabresi taught on Federal Jurisdiction. Beyond that, Professor Calabresi has been deeply influenced by two of Professor Amar's many spectacular books: THE BILL OF RIGHTS: CREATION AND RECONSTRUCTION (2000) and AMERICA'S CONSTITUTION: A BIOGRAPHY (2006). Professor Amar is also a wonderful friend and mentor.

Professor Calabresi's work on this casebook has also been critically shaped by Justice Antonin Scalia's writing and mentorship of Professor Calabresi, starting in 1982, when they first met, continuing through Professor Calabresi's clerkship with Justice Scalia in 1987–1988, and then in many, many conversations between 1988 and the justice's death in 2016. While Justice Scalia would have disagreed with some of the conclusions intimated in this casebook, Professor Calabresi is certain that he would have found it a valuable contribution to the U.S. constitutional law casebook literature.

Professor Calabresi's work on this casebook has also been shaped by three other individuals who he wants to acknowledge. First, former Attorney General Edwin Meese III has affected Professor Calabresi's views in a whole host of ways. Second, Justice Clarence Thomas's originalist opinions for the Supreme Court have had a huge impact on Professor Calabresi's views. And, third, Professor John Harrison of the University of Virginia School of Law helped Professor Calabresi refine and develop his understanding of constitutional law and of the Fourteenth Amendment in particular, both when Professors Calabresi and Harrison worked together for Attorney General Meese on his personal staff and via Professor Harrison's stunning law review article on the original meaning of Section 1 of the Fourteenth Amendment published in 1992.

Professor Calabresi's last and deepest gratitude goes to Professors Michael Stokes Paulsen, Michael W. McConnell, Samuel L. Bray, and William Baude, with whom Professor Calabresi has previously co-edited a casebook in three editions from 2010 to 2017. Professor Calabresi has learned an immense amount about constitutional law from all four of these individuals, as well as a great amount about how to write a casebook. In writing this casebook with Professor Gary Lawson, Professor Calabresi stands on the shoulders of Professors Paulsen, McConnell, Bray, and Baude.

Professor Lawson, for his part, is grateful to Philip S. Beck for endowing a chair that helped make this book possible, to Boston University School of Law and Dean Angela Onwuachi-Willig (and former Deans Ron Cass and Maureen O'Rourke) for unwavering support of scholarship, to just about everyone mentioned by Professor Calabresi for inspiration and guidance, to Robert G. Natelson and Guy Seidman for opening his eyes to many wondrous things, and, most of all, to Steve Calabresi for including him in this project.

We are both grateful to Ryan Pfeiffer, Laura Holle, Whitney Esson, and the staff at Foundation Press.

COPYRIGHT ACKNOWLEDGEMENTS

We acknowledge with appreciation the following publishers, authors, and journals who have granted permission to reprint excerpts from their publications:

Steven G. Calabresi & Lucy D. Bickford, *Federalism and Subsidiarity: Perspectives from Law, in* FEDERALISM AND SUBSIDIARITY: NOMOS LV 123 (James E. Fleming & Jacob T. Levy ed., 2014). Republished with permission of New York University Press; permission conveyed through Copyright Clearance Center, Inc.

DOUGLAS W. KMIEC & STEPHEN B. PRESSER, THE AMERICAN CONSTITUTIONAL ORDER: HISTORY, CASES, AND PHILOSOPHY 958–59 (1998). Copyright 1998 Matthew Bender & Company, Inc., a LexisNexis company. All rights reserved.

Gary Lawson, *Take the Fifth . . . Please! The Original Insignificance of the Fifth Amendment's Due Process of Law Clause,* 2017 BYU L. Rev. 611. Republished with permission of Brigham Young University Law Review.

Gary Lawson, *Interpretative Equality as a Structural Imperative (Or: Pucker Up and Settle* This), 20 CONST. COMMENTARY 379 (2003). Republished with permission of Constitutional Commentary.

Gary Lawson & Guy Seidman, *Originalism as a Legal Enterprise,* 23 CONST. COMMENTARY 47 (2006). Republished with permission of Constitutional Commentary.

"A Great Power of Attorney": Understanding the Fiduciary Constitution, by Gary Lawson and Guy Seidman, published by the University Press of Kansas, ©2017. www.kansaspress.ku.edu.

SUMMARY OF CONTENTS

TABLE OF CONTENTS

TABLE OF CASES

The principal cases are in bold type.

UNIVERSITY CASEBOOK SERIES®

THE U.S. CONSTITUTION:

CREATION, RECONSTRUCTION, THE PROGRESSIVES, AND THE MODERN ERA

INTRODUCTION TO THE CONSTITUTION OF THE UNITED STATES

[Assignment 1]

I. THE FOUNDATIONS OF THE CONSTITUTION OF THE UNITED STATES

A. THE HISTORICAL IMPORTANCE OF THE U.S. CONSTITUTION

When the Constitution of the United States went into full effect in the spring of 1789, it was the only document of its kind to be found anywhere in the world. To be sure, eleven of the thirteen original States adopted written constitutions—and often multiple iterations of written constitutions—between 1776 and 1787. (Rhode Island and Connecticut continued to use their colonial charters as their constitutions into the early nineteenth century.) The thirteen original States, however, while technically nations as a matter of international law, were not effectively functional nations, and the U.S. Constitution of 1787[1] is thus the first truly national constitution. The British Empire, the French Empire, the Holy Roman Empire, the Spanish Empire, the Portuguese Empire, the Dutch Empire, the Russian Empire, the Chinese Empire, and all the other nations of Europe, Asia, Africa, and Latin America lacked: 1) written constitutions, 2) popular sovereignty, 3) republican systems of governance, and 4) a system of checks and balances backed up by judicial review by life-tenured judges whose job was to enforce the written Constitution even against the people's President and their Congress. Constitutional democratic government existed only in the United States of America, a small country of 3 million people then living mostly near the Atlantic coast of North America. While not every adult could yet vote, a defect that would systematically be remedied in time, the level of popular participation in the formation of the government was unprecedented. No other regime rested so extensively on the consent of the governed, expressed in a written social contract of the kind that John Locke and Thomas Hobbes had theorized about. The United States, in 1789, was a *novus ordo seclorum*—a new order of the ages—without parallel either in human history or in the then-existing governmental systems of the world.[2]

---

[1] It is conventional to refer to the original Constitution as "the Constitution of 1787" because that is the year in which it was written. The Constitution, however, became effective for nine ratifying states on June 21, 1788, and did not become fully effective, with a functioning Congress and President who could enact legislation and make treaties, until the spring of 1789, so "the Constitution of 1788" or "the Constitution of 1789" is probably more descriptively accurate. Nonetheless, we often follow the standard convention. If you are interested in the niceties of the Constitution's proper dates of effectiveness (which actually turn out to be important in some significant cases), see Gary Lawson & Guy Seidman, *When Did the Constitution Become Law?*, 77 NOTRE DAME L. REV. 1 (2001).

[2] *See* FORREST MCDONALD, NOVUS ORDO SECLORUM: THE INTELLECTUAL ORIGINS OF THE CONSTITUTION (1985); GORDON S. WOOD, THE CREATION OF THE AMERICAN REPUBLIC (1969).

Today, virtually every country in the world has a written constitution and bill of rights backed up by judicial review, in emulation of the U.S. example.[3] This is true not only of the fifteen of the G-20 nations that are now constitutional democracies, but even of such dictatorships as those that exist in China, Russia, Iran, and Turkey, all of which in form have written constitutions which they *pretend* to follow. Most of the G-20 nations, which together account for 85% of the world's gross domestic product (GDP), have written constitutions, written bills of rights, and systems of judicial review of the constitutionality of executive and legislative acts. This is true of the United Kingdom, France, Germany, Japan, Italy, India, Canada, Australia, South Korea, Brazil, South Africa, Indonesia, Mexico, the European Union, and Argentina. Many other nations have highly successful systems of written constitutionalism and judicial review, including Spain, Israel, Austria, Belgium, the Philippines, and Colombia. If the first shot fired in the battles of Lexington and Concord was "[t]he shot heard round the world," the U.S. Constitution is, as George Athan Billias puts it, "The Constitution Heard Round the World." Professor Billias writes that:

> we are left to ponder the prophecy of America's founders, who claimed that their work would exert an influence beyond America's shores for years to come and that they had created a "New Order for the Ages." To a remarkable extent, they have been proved right! Within the framework of Western constitutionalism, American constitutionalism was * * * heard round the world for more than two centuries * * *. For those two hundred years, no matter what the future might hold, the United States merited Abraham Lincoln's praise as "the last, best hope on earth."[4]

The U.S. traditions of popular sovereignty, written constitutions and bills of rights, systems of checks and balances, and judicial review of the constitutionality of legislation and executive action have been quite literally "heard" and copied all over the world. American constitutionalism is our greatest, if least remunerative, export!

B. FIRST THINGS FIRST: UNDERSTANDING CONSTITUTIONALISM

Because this is a course in Constitutional Law, you are probably expecting now to become immersed in the constitutional text, or at least to become immersed in important cases or decisions applying the Constitution. All of that is coming. But the Constitution, and the cases and other decisions involving it, did not and do not exist in a vacuum. In order to *understand* the Constitution and the practices that have emerged under it, one must first understand from where the Constitution came and what it tries to do. If you jump in too fast without that crucial context, you are likely to miss some very important features of the Constitution and the government and society that have grown up under it. A great many scholars and judges have made (and continue to make) precisely that mistake. We hope to help you avoid it.

The arrangements of powers and rights contained in the Constitution grew out of many sources: a long English historical background and unwritten constitutional

---

[3] *See* GEORGE ATHAN BILLIAS, AMERICAN CONSTITUTIONALISM HEARD ROUND THE WORLD, 1776–1989: A GLOBAL PERSPECTIVE (2009).

[4] *Id.* at 371. *See also* CONSTITUTIONALISM AND RIGHTS: THE INFLUENCE OF THE UNITED STATES CONSTITUTION ABROAD (Louis Henkin & Albert J. Rosenthal eds., 1990). For a discussion of the historiography of the U.S. Constitution and its global influence, see WALTER MURPHY, CONSTITUTIONAL DEMOCRACY: CREATING AND MAINTAINING A JUST POLITICAL ORDER (2007).

tradition dating back at least to the reign of King Edward the Confessor (1042–1066)[5]; the colonial experience with government charters that were the prototypes of the first written constitutions, judicially enforced by the King's Privy Council sitting in London, England;[6] the ideologically transforming crucible of the American Revolution of 1776–1783;[7] theories of popular sovereignty and representative, republican government and the experiments of the first written *state* constitutions; and, finally, the lessons of a (largely) failed federated government under the Articles of Confederation, our nation's first "constitution," proposed by the Continental Congress in 1777 but not ratified until 1781. All of these sources need to be examined at least cursorily before you plunge into the Constitution.

C. THE ENGLISH HISTORICAL BACKGROUND

From the founding of Jamestown in 1607 to the American Revolution in 1776, most Americans considered themselves Englishmen—heirs to a largely unwritten, unsystematized, and customary constitutional tradition that had emerged over centuries of history. Sir Edward Coke, a great seventeenth-century English legal thinker who was known and admired in the American colonies,[8] described that tradition of venerable customs and enactments as the "auntient and undoubted patrimony and birthright" of English subjects. It later came to be called England's "Ancient Constitution."[9] That "Ancient Constitution" was less a fixed set of rules than a symbol of liberty under law and of the idea that society's most basic law is prior to government rather than vice versa. This last idea—that government gains its authority from fundamental law rather than fundamental law gaining its authority from government—is perhaps the most important feature of the "Ancient Constitution": "Under this conception of an 'Ancient Constitution,' law derives its authority not from the sovereign's command but from its historical pedigree, particularly its role as the organic expression of the centuries-old customs of a particular people." Gregory Ablavsky, *Empire States: The Coming of Dual Federalism,* 128 YALE L.J. 1792, 1803 (2019). As Lord Coke put it in 1608 in one of his most famous judicial decisions: "this Law of nature is part of the Laws of England * * * [and] the law of nature was before any judicial or municipal Law in the world." *Calvin's Case, or the Case of the* Postnati (1608), 77 Eng. Rep. 377; 7 Co. Rep. 1 b. The broad principle of *Calvin's Case*—that fundamental law is prior to any particular governmental institutions—is historically more important than the specific context

---

[5] Indeed, a full treatment of the Constitution's origins would require going back several millennia to events in ancient Greece and Rome—events with which the founding generation was intimately familiar as a result of a firmly classical education. *See* CARL J. RICHARD, THE FOUNDERS AND THE CLASSICS: GREECE, ROME, AND THE AMERICAN ENLIGHTENMENT (1994).

[6] *See* JOSEPH HENRY SMITH, APPEALS TO THE PRIVY COUNCIL FROM THE AMERICAN PLANTATIONS (1965); MARY SARAH BILDER, THE TRANSATLANTIC CONSTITUTION: COLONIAL LEGAL CULTURE AND THE EMPIRE (2004).

[7] *See* GORDON S. WOOD, THE RADICALISM OF THE AMERICAN REVOLUTION (1991).

[8] For Coke's fascinating life story, see CATHERINE DRINKER BOWEN, THE LION AND THE THRONE: THE LIFE AND TIMES OF SIR EDWARD COKE: 1552–1634 (1956).

[9] THE ROOTS OF LIBERTY: MAGNA CARTA, ANCIENT CONSTITUTION, AND THE ANGLO-AMERICAN TRADITION OF RULE OF LAW (Ellis Sandoz ed., 1993); David J. Hulseboch, *The Ancient Constitution and the Expanding Empire: Sir Edward Coke's British Jurisprudence*, 21 L. & HIST. REV. 439, 445 (2003) ("Coke's 'frame of the ancient common laws of this realm' was a canon of iconic common law institutions (preeminently the jury), core rules (like an heir's right to inherit property), and historic statutes (the most famous being Magna Carta) * * *. By the middle of the seventeenth century, this canon was known as the ancient constitution—though Coke never used that term.")

in which the principle was applied in that case, which was to claim that subjects naturally owe allegiance to their King. Indeed, Coke's principle was later used by many seventeenth-century thinkers to justify deposing, and even waging war against, a king who violated the liberties of the Ancient Constitution. *See* JANELLE GREENBERG, THE RADICAL FACE OF THE ANCIENT CONSTITUTION: ST. EDWARD'S "LAWS" IN EARLY MODERN POLITICAL THOUGHT (2001).

Sir Edward Coke decided two important cases—the *Case of the Proclamations,* (1610) 77 Eng. Rep. 1352, and *Dr. Bonham's Case*, (1610) 77 Eng. Rep. 638, in which he held that both the King and the Parliament were bound by law. The *Case of the Proclamations* held that the monarch could make law only through Parliament. Coke held that King James I could only impose duties on customs that Parliament had already authorized, and he held that the King could not prohibit new buildings in the City of London on the ground that it was overcrowded. "The king cannot change any part of the common law, nor create any offense, by his proclamation, which was not an offense before, without Parliament * * *. The King has no prerogative but that which the law of the land allows him." *Id.* at 1353–54. King James I and his successor King Charles I did not acquiesce in Sir Edward Coke's opinions, and the matter was not fully settled until the English Civil War in the 1640s and even until the Glorious Revolution of 1688.

In *Dr. Bonham's Case*, Sir Edward Coke said in dictum that "in many cases, the common law will controul Acts of Parliament." 77 Eng. Rep. at 652. He held specifically that no man can be a judge in his own case. Colonial Americans cited *Dr. Bonham's Case* during the campaigns against the writs of assistance issued in Massachusetts in the 1760s and the 1765 Stamp Act, saying that King George III and Parliament were violating England's Ancient Constitution.

Sir Edward Coke also attained notoriety for reporting the *Case of the Monopolies*, also known as *Darcy v. Allein*, (1602) 74 Eng. Rep. 1131, which held that Queen Elizabeth I did not have the right to give a royal monopoly on the selling of playing cards to her favorite, Edward Darcy. Allein went on producing playing cards and was sued by Darcy for violating his monopoly. The Court of Queen's Bench ruled against Darcy, saying that: 1) monopolies prevent people from pursuing their trades and promote idleness, 2) monopolists raise prices and reduce the quality of what they produce, and 3) royally issued monopolies were contrary to the common law and to liberty itself. That liberty was guaranteed by the Ancient Constitution. This antimonopoly sentiment, as we will later see, played a large, and often overlooked, role in American constitutional development. *See infra* pages 1182–1187.

To be sure, some historians claim that this notion of an "Ancient Constitution" was a myth concocted by Sir Edward Coke and others from dubious, and in some cases obviously fabricated, sources. *See*, e.g., J.G.A. POCOCK, THE ANCIENT CONSTITUTION AND THE FEUDAL LAW: A STUDY OF ENGLISH HISTORICAL THOUGHT IN THE SEVENTEENTH CENTURY (1987). That might be right as a matter of English historiography. But for the *legal* purpose of understanding the U.S. Constitution, what matters is *what the American people in the seventeenth and eighteenth centuries believed* about the English legal history, not whether what they believed was historically correct. When one is trying to understand, rather than to evaluate or critique, a set of institutions or practices, you want to know how institutions and practices are shaped by what people think, whether or not they are right to think it. And the key ideas behind the "Ancient Constitution," whatever their actual historical pedigree, played a role in shaping eighteenth-century American thought. As one scholar describes it, revolutionary Americans "were 'looking backward' * * * to government by the rule of law, to a sovereign that did not grant rights but was limited by rights, a sovereign that was, like liberty, created by law, the guardian of liberty. Perhaps they were not looking back to the ancient constitution, but they were looking back to the constitution of Sir Edward Coke, to the constitution that had triumphed over Charles I and James II." JOHN PHILLIP REID, THE ANCIENT CONSTITUTION AND THE ORIGINS OF ANGLO-AMERICAN LIBERTY 52–53 (2005). Thus, to understand American legal history, one must look to Coke's account for a description of the rights that colonial Americans thought they had as Englishmen.

So, what did those (Cokean) rights of Englishmen look like to an eighteenth-century American? That is a very difficult question to answer, because the phrase "the rights of Englishmen," like the concept of an "Ancient Constitution," may have been as much a symbol as it was a concept with clearly defined content. But one can say this much: Colonial Americans thought that royal and parliamentary power was limited by law and that where there was no positive law, they were free to act. This was very different from the situation in France, which followed the Divine Right of Kings and where King Louis XIV could famously say—"*L'Etat, cest Moi*—I am the law and the government."

The English legal history, which Americans believed that they had inherited, included some important *written* texts or documents, which had, over time, generated certain settled understandings of the rightful powers of both kings and parliaments and of the many rights of individuals under the "Ancient Constitution." A few of those texts deserve special mention.

(1) One of the most revered of all English kings was King Edward "the Confessor," who ruled from 1042–1066. Whether or not Edward ever actually promulgated, collected, or codified any laws while he was king, he came to be associated with a collection of laws later called the *Leges Edwardi Confessori*, named after a twelfth-century work with that title purporting to represent a collection of good laws that Edward had set forth. Whatever the actual history may have been, "according to informed opinion from the middle ages to the nineteenth century, the laws came into existence when, in the words of Edward's eleventh-century biographer, 'this goodly king abrogated bad laws, with his witan [i.e., council of advisers] established good ones, and filled with joy all of Britain . . . .' " GREENBERG, *supra*, at 55. The actual content of the *Leges Edwardi Confessori* was hardly inspiring, *see id.* at 61–62, but, as with much that we discuss in this chapter, the eighteenth-century perception is far more important than the eleventh-century reality. The perception was that Edward's laws were an ancient (and hence admirable) representation of responsible government under law, and that perception became dominant shortly after Edward's death on January 5, 1066.

(2) The day after Edward died, Harold Godwinson was crowned King of England. Duke William of Normandy, who had supposedly been promised the throne by the childless Edward some years earlier, staked his claim by invading England. On October 14, 1066, Duke William's army defeated Harold's forces and killed Harold at the Battle of Hastings. William and Harold both had had plausible claims to the English throne, and the battle settled those claims decisively on behalf of William, who has since come to be known as "William the Conqueror," though that title begs the debatable question about whose claim to the throne was better. William,

although he was Edward's cousin, was seen as a foreigner by his English subjects, as he had lived his life in what we now call France. If there had been strong resistance to his reign, it is hard to see how he could maintain control over both his home turf in Normandy and the vast expanse of England across the Channel. William had about 10,000 Norman soldiers, who spoke French, with which to govern an English population of some two million people. Accordingly, when William was crowned King of England on Christmas Day 1066, he promised in his coronation oath "that he would so well govern this nation as any before him best did, if they would be faithful to him." THE ANGLO-SAXON CHRONICLE (Rev. James Ingram trans., 1823), http://mcllibrary.org/Anglo/part5.html. This was understood as a promise to govern in accordance with the laws of King Edward; indeed, the *Leges Edwardi Confessori* was supposedly assembled on the orders of King William so that he and others could better know those ancient laws. William reaffirmed his commitment to the laws of Edward in 1072, swearing "a personal oath . . . that he would from thenceforth observe and keep the good and ancient approved laws of the realm . . ., namely those of S[t]. Edward." MATTHEW PARIS, HISTORIA ANGLORUM (quoted in GREENBERG, *supra,* at 67). This coronation oath came to be seen as a symbol of law's supremacy over rulers. William's son, King Henry I, also pledged in 1101 to maintain Edward's laws; his coronation oath containing that promise to rule in accordance with the ancient laws came to be called "The Charter of Liberties."

On June 15, 1215, a civil war between King John I and a group of rebellious barons was settled at Runnymede by a document called the Magna Carta, or "Great Charter." Magna Carta purported to be no "new thing," but merely a restoration of the laws of King Edward, which bad King John had violated. Versions of the Magna Carta were repeatedly reissued by subsequent monarchs, the most famous reissuance occurring just ten years later in 1225. The document, in all of its incarnations, primarily involved the rights of barons and the Church against the King, but over time it acquired a legendary status as a bastion of citizens' rights. Once again, for purposes of understanding what happened in the seventeenth and eighteenth century, perception is more important than reality. As one scholar writes: "by the second half of the eighteenth century Magna Carta could be accurately described as an instrument containing 'the common rights of mankind,' even if none of those rights had ever occurred to the barons who confronted King John . . . . [W]hat was important about Magna Carta in the eighteenth century was not what it said but what it had come to mean." JOHN PHILLIP REID, THE ANCIENT CONSTITUTION AND THE ORIGINS OF ANGLO-AMERICAN LIBERTY 83 (2005). At least one thing that Magna Carta actually said, however, has proved of enduring significance. Article 39 of Magna Carta proclaimed: "No free man shall be taken or imprisoned or disseised [i.e., deprived of his lands] or outlawed or exiled or in any way ruined, nor will we go against him, except by the lawful judgment of his peers or by the law of the land." This was a significant denial of royal authority; "here the King acknowledged that his mere dictates are not the law." Timothy Sandefur, Lex Terrae *800 Years On: The Magna Carta's Legacy Today*, 9 N.Y.U. J.L. & LIBERTY 759, 760 (2015). You will hear more about this provision, which is the ancestor of our Due Process of Law Clauses, later in the course.

(3) Now we jump ahead four centuries to the early 1600s. King Charles I needed money for his military ambitions, and Parliament would not give it to him. At that point in English legal history in the 1620s, it was firmly settled that kings or

queens could not unilaterally impose taxes without Parliament, so King Charles got creative about finding sources of money. He forced citizens, at their own expense, to house his soldiers (a practice called "billeting"), and he ordered wealthy citizens to "loan" him money. Five knights who refused to grant the King these "loans" were imprisoned and held without bail. The knights sued for bail, and in order to adjudicate the case, the courts needed to know why they were being held, as there were some offenses (such as treason) for which no bail was available. The King's lawyers simply said that the knights were being held for "reasons of state," with no more detailed legal explanation. If that was enough to hold the knights without bail, then couldn't the King just jail anyone and hold them without bail, with no legal recourse?

The knights lost in court in *Darnell's Case*, 3 How St. Tr. 1 (K.B. 1627) (known as *The Case of the Five Knights*), but the principle for which they argued prevailed the next year. In 1628, Parliament, led by Sir Edward Coke, about whom we have already spoken, responded to the King's forced loans, billeted soldiers, and the use of martial law to try people for crimes without proper legal procedures by issuing the "Petition of Right." This is perhaps the most famous and important English legal text since Magna Carta. Like Magna Carta, it purported to restore the traditional rights of Englishmen and not to create new rights. After enumerating the threats to liberty in a manner that foreshadows the American Declaration of Independence written a century and a half later, the Petition of Right declared:

> that no man hereafter be compelled to make or yield any gift, loan, benevolence, tax, or such like charge, without common consent by act of parliament * * *; and that no freeman, in any such manner as is before mentioned, be imprisoned or detained [without due process of law]; and that your Majesty would be pleased to remove the said [billeted] soldiers and mariners, and that your people may not be so burdened in time to come; and that the aforesaid commissions, for proceeding by martial law, may be revoked and annulled; and that hereafter no commissions of like nature may issue forth to any person or persons whatsoever to be executed as aforesaid, lest by color of them any of your Majesty's subjects be destroyed or put to death contrary to the laws and franchise of the land.

Although King Charles believed that he had a right to rule, and to tax and imprison, without resort to Parliament or the law courts, he nonetheless was forced to agree to the Petition of Right, which became a cornerstone of the English Constitution and the "rights of Englishmen."

The House of Commons, for its part, later claimed the power unilaterally to try the King for treason—a power that was denied by the House of Lords and by the chief justices of all three English courts. The House of Commons nonetheless, after a long and bloody civil war in England, convened its own "court," tried and convicted King Charles I, and executed him in 1649. The House of Commons also claimed—successfully, since its forces had won the civil war—the power to govern the country unilaterally, without a House of Lords or a separate executive. After a dozen unhappy years of rule first by a single legislative House and then by a "protectorate" run by Oliver Cromwell, England in 1660 returned to a constitutional monarchy, with an executive (the King), an upper legislative body (the House of Lords), and a lower, or popular, legislative body (the House of Commons), as it had been governed for centuries beforehand.

(4) The principle that every person who is arrested should be able to challenge in court the legality of their confinement, and thus to know for what reasons they are being confined, was confirmed and strengthened by statutes in 1641 and 1679. The 1679 Habeas Corpus Act, in particular, "rejected outright the proposition that the royal command, standing alone, sufficed as lawful cause to detain." Amanda L. Tyler, *A "Second Magna Carta": The English Habeas Corpus Act and the Statutory Origins of the Habeas Privilege*, 91 NOTRE DAME L. REV. 1949, 1958 (2016).

(5) The English Bill of Rights of 1689 does not necessarily read like what today we think of as a Bill of Rights. The document is full of (and was driven by) anti-Catholic religious intolerance, and indeed one of the chief causes of the document was King James II's refusal to enforce the "Test Acts" which made membership in the Protestant Church of England a precondition to government and military service. The English people, in 1688, were terrified by King Louis XIV's expulsion of 400,000 French Protestants, known as Huguenots, from France three years earlier in 1685. Louis XIV was a close military ally of English King James II. Englishmen feared that, since King James II was a practicing Roman Catholic himself, he would hire a Catholic mercenary army to drive English Protestants out of England. James required all English bishops to read his Declaration of Indulgence suspending the Test Act from the pulpit at Sunday services. Seven bishops petitioned the King to be absolved of this duty, and the King had them thrown in the Tower of London to be tried for seditious libel. The jury acquitted the bishops in an act of jury nullification, but by that time James had acquired a son from his second wife, who was Catholic. Faced with the prospect of a Catholic monarchy for all time to come, the people rose up in the Glorious Revolution of 1688 and installed James' Protestant daughter by his first wife Mary, and James' Protestant nephew and son-in-law, William of Orange, as monarchs in his place.

(6) To guard against the Divine Right of Kings, the English people adopted the 1689 Bill of Rights, which was a crucial step in the development of the separation of powers; and while some of its motivations may not have been the most admirable, it contains important statements of what eighteenth-century Americans regarded as the "rights of Englishmen." As noted, King James II claimed the power to "suspend" through executive decree the operation of laws of which he did not approve—most notably the anti-Catholic Test Act. After the Glorious Revolution, the English people adopted a Bill of Rights, which William and Mary were compelled to sign, and which proclaimed:

> That the pretended power of suspending the laws or the execution of laws by regal authority without consent of Parliament is illegal;
>
> That the pretended power of dispensing with laws or the execution of laws by regal authority, as it hath been assumed and exercised of late, is illegal;
>
> That the commission for erecting the late Court of Commissioners for Ecclesiastical Causes, and all other commissions and courts of like nature, are illegal and pernicious;
>
> That levying money for or to the use of the Crown by pretence of prerogative, without grant of Parliament, for longer time, or in other manner than the same is or shall be granted, is illegal;

> That it is the right of the subjects to petition the king, and all commitments and prosecutions for such petitioning are illegal;
>
> That the raising or keeping a standing army within the kingdom in time of peace, unless it be with consent of Parliament, is against law;
>
> That the subjects which are Protestants may have arms for their defence suitable to their conditions and as allowed by law;
>
> That election of members of Parliament ought to be free;
>
> That the freedom of speech and debates or proceedings in Parliament ought not to be impeached or questioned in any court or place out of Parliament;
>
> That excessive bail ought not to be required, nor excessive fines imposed, nor cruel and unusual punishments inflicted;
>
> That jurors ought to be duly impanelled and returned, and jurors which pass upon men in trials for high treason ought to be freeholders;
>
> That all grants and promises of fines and forfeitures of particular persons before conviction are illegal and void;
>
> And that for redress of all grievances, and for the amending, strengthening and preserving of the laws, Parliaments ought to be held frequently.

There was much more to the events of 1688–89 than we have let on or can discuss in this book. Here is how eighteenth-century American colonists were likely to look back on and interpret the events of a century beforehand: Protestant Englishmen had risen up in popular outrage to overthrow the Catholic Stuart dynasty of King James II, which had tried to assert the then-new doctrine of the Divine Rights of Kings. The English people responded by reestablishing parliamentary, constitutional supremacy over the English monarchy according to the "Ancient Constitution." The Glorious Revolution of 1688 thus (to compress drastically) (a) restored fundamental individual rights against executive authority; (b) reestablished constitutional government in England; (c) established the supremacy of parliamentary government and of law over the king; and, perhaps even more significantly, (d) established the principle that legitimate government ultimately must depend on the consent of the governed. The long battle between seventeenth-century English monarchs who claimed to be able to rule by executive commands and Parliament ended, after two civil wars and the forcible deposing of two kings, with the 1689 Bill of Rights.

(7) Thus far we have described ongoing battles between the Crown and Parliament. Where were the courts in these disputes?

In a few landmark cases decided or reported by Sir Edward Coke, who was the most revered judge of both the seventeenth century and of all of English history—the *Case of Proclamations,* the *Case of the Monopolies,* and *Dr. Bonham's Case*—the English courts held that the common law, in effect, contained a presumption of liberty. For the most part, however, as was illustrated by *The Case of the Five Knights*, the courts either stood aside or ruled for the Crown. That is not surprising, as courts in those days were arms of the executive. Stuart kings could and did remove judges that they did not like or (if this was any different) who they thought would rule against them. Sir Edward Coke was removed in 1616 by King James I from his position as Chief Justice of England, and King James II removed numerous judges who would not recognize his claimed power of suspending laws. In 1701, the Act of Settlement, which was primarily about preventing Catholics from ever ascending to the English throne, provided that judges would serve during the full lives of the monarchs who appointed them unless they were removed by Parliament, thus securing judges a measure of independence from the Crown. In 1761, on the eve of the American Revolution, a statute gave the judges tenure for life (subject to removal by Parliament), even beyond the life of the monarch who appointed them. Importantly, however, this provision did not apply to *colonial* judges, who were subject to absolute removal by the King.

(8) Also on the eve of the American Revolution, the English courts had something important to say on a matter that very much concerned the colonies. A Virginia slave trader brought one of his slaves to England and then sought to take him back to be sold in Jamaica. The slave sought habeas corpus, claiming that slavery was not recognized by either statutory or common law in England and was so contrary to natural law that only express legal provisions (if anything) could sustain such a relationship; and that by bringing him to England, the "master" thereby lost any claim that could have been sustained under the laws of Virginia or Jamaica. In *Somerset v. Stewart*, 98 Eng. Rep. 499 (1772), Lord Mansfield ruled in favor of the (no longer) slave:

> The state of slavery is of such a nature, that it is incapable of being introduced on any reasons, moral or political; but only positive law, which preserves its force long after the reasons, occasion, and time itself from whence it was created, is erased from memory: it's so odious, that nothing can be suffered to support it, but positive law. Whatever inconveniences, therefore, may follow from a decision, I cannot say this case [to reclaim the slave] is allowed or approved by the law of England; and therefore the black must be discharged.

Id. at 510. Here too, an English court held that the common law presumed liberty, as Sir Edward Coke had done in reporting the *Case of the Monopolies*, and in deciding the *Case of the Proclamations* and *Dr. Bonham's Case*. Did that mean that if a slave in, for example, Virginia, escaped to a colony that did not recognize slavery, the person would be free? As we will see, this question looms very large in American constitutional and political history.

These acquired traditions—individual rights to be governed by law, to trial by jury, to habeas corpus, limitations on the power of government, the right to be represented in any legislative body that possessed the power to enact taxes, the right to independent life-tenured judges, and even the right to revolution to preserve these other rights—were all features of the English constitution as it had become known to the generation of *American* Englishmen in the eighteenth century.

D. COLONIES IN THE ENGLISH CONSTITUTIONAL STRUCTURE

While "federalism," a device (which you will study at some length later in this course) for dividing power across different governmental entities, is often considered a unique feature of American constitutional government, it owes something to the British colonial experience. The British Empire was, in fact, from 1607 to 1776, a "federal" entity. Some powers were exercised centrally, in London by the King's Privy

Council (also called the Board of Trade), while others devolved to the various colonial enterprises, of which the thirteen North American colonies were only a part of a greater whole that included Canada, British islands in the Caribbean, and parts of India. The King's imperial government in London handled foreign policy, defense policy, and the regulation of colonial trade. Eighteenth-century Americans, before 1776, thus had first-hand experience with power-sharing arrangements between the whole and the parts, but while they acknowledged King George III as their king, they denied that the British Parliament, in which they were not represented, could tax them or legislate for them.[10]

The King of England's prerogative power—the power to wage war, declare peace, or rule without the authorization of Parliament—had been eliminated in Great Britain domestically by statute in 1641 at the start of the English Civil War. The King's prerogative power, however, remained intact in the Channel Islands, the Isle of Mann, and England's overseas colonies. The King's Privy Council thus heard and decided appeals from the highest courts of the thirteen North American colonies, and it also reviewed and disallowed some colonial laws or executive actions where they were deemed to be "repugnant to the laws of England." Thus, from 1607 until 1776, the North Americans were part of a federal imperial entity whose power over the colonies came exclusively from the royal prerogative. *See* MARY SARAH BILDER, THE TRANSATLANTIC CONSTITUTION: COLONIAL LEGAL CULTURE AND THE EMPIRE (2004).

E. THE AMERICAN INNOVATION OF WRITTEN CONSTITUTIONALISM: COLONIAL CHARTERS AND ELECTED LOWER HOUSES OF COLONIAL ASSEMBLIES WITH THE SOLE POWER OF TAXATION

The pre-Revolutionary historical background of the American colonies is no less complex and difficult to distill.[11] Colonial corporate charters, marking the powers of governors and proprietors and the rights of the colonists, were antecedents to written constitutions, judicially enforced by the King's Privy Council sitting 3,000 miles away in London, England. The Lords who sat on the Privy Council were appointed by the English King. The King handled foreign affairs and taxed colonial trade by assessing customs fees, but the colonies governed themselves domestically. From 1607 until 1765, Parliament made no effort itself to tax or legislate for the thirteen North American colonies.

The governments of the thirteen North American colonies were divided into three types: provincial governments; proprietary governments; and charter governments.[12]

The provincial governments were, in theory, wholly under the government of the King and depended on the instructions the King gave his Royal Governors from

---

10 *See* JACK P. GREENE, PERIPHERIES AND CENTER: CONSTITUTIONAL DEVELOPMENT IN THE EXTENDED POLITIES OF THE BRITISH EMPIRE AND THE UNITED STATES 1607–1788 (1986).

11 For excellent treatments of the first steps toward distinctively American constitutionalism during the colonial period, see GORDON WOOD, THE AMERICAN REVOLUTION: A HISTORY 65–70 (2002); GORDON WOOD, THE CREATION OF THE AMERICAN REPUBLIC 1776–1787, 125–256 (1969).

12 JOSEPH STORY, A FAMILIAR EXPOSITION OF THE CONSTITUTION OF THE UNITED STATES 33 (Regnery Gateway, Inc. 1986).

time to time in their commissions, although in practice the lower Houses of the colonial legislative assemblies exercised significant power. The commissions issued to each Royal Governor specified that there would a governor appointed by the king; an elite council of notable colonial aristocrats, which would assist the governor in carrying out his powers; and an elected representative lower house of the colonial legislature, convened by the governor, to represent the freeholders and planters and to exercise the sole power of taxation, as did the House of Commons in England. The governor and his council served at the pleasure of the King, and the governor had the power to appoint and remove judges and executive magistrates while sitting in council. Colonial legislatures faced off stiffly against royal governors, as when colonial legislatures refused to enact an annual salary for the royal governor. The lower houses of the colonial legislatures preferred instead to pay the royal governor a salary on a year by year basis depending on how well the royal governor had behaved during the prior twelve months. The King and his men in London were furious about the colonies' refusal to appropriate a set annual salary for the royal governor, but, in practice, they could do nothing about this. Provincial governments of this kind were in place in New Hampshire, New York, Virginia, North Carolina, South Carolina, and Georgia, and English royal power was at its apogee in these colonies.[13]

Proprietary governments were "grants by letters patent * * * from the Crown to one or more persons as Proprietary of Proprietaries, conveying to them not only the rights of the soil, but also the general powers of government within the territory so granted, in the nature of feudatory principalities, or dependent royalties."[14] The proprietors were as powerful in their colonies as the King was in his domain, and they appointed the governor and convened an elected colonial legislature with the power of taxation. Three proprietary governments existed in 1776: Maryland, which had been held by Lord Baltimore; and Pennsylvania and Delaware, which had been held by William Penn.[15]

Finally, three charter governments existed in the colonies of Massachusetts, Rhode Island, and Connecticut, which were political corporations created by the King and which "contained, in fact, a fundamental constitution for the Colony, distribut[ing] the powers of government into three great departments, legislative, executive, and judicial [and providing] for the mode in which these powers should be vested and exercised" as well as "securing to [the] inhabitants certain political privileges and rights."[16] These colonial charters were, in effect, proto-type State constitutions.

"Notwithstanding these differences in their original and actual political organization, the Colonies, at the time of the American Revolution, in most respects, enjoyed the same general rights and privileges. In all of them, there existed a Governor, a Council, and [a lower House of the colonial assembly], composed of delegates chosen by the People."[17] The lower houses of the colonial assemblies had all the powers of the House of Commons in England. In all of the North American colonies, court decisions could be and were frequently appealed to the King's Privy

13 Id., at 33–34

14 Id. at 33.

15 Id., at 35.

16 Id.

17 Id. 35–36.

Council in London, which could overrule any colonial law, executive action, or court opinion, which was "repugnant to the laws of England." Vertical federalism judicial review of colonial laws, executive actions, and court opinions was thus vigorous and included determination as to whether colonial actions taken were *ultra vires* of the colonial charter. The existence of these written colonial charters laid the groundwork for America's love of and fascination with comprehensive, written constitutionalism. *See* Mary Sarah Bilder, *The Corporate Origins of Judicial Review*, 116 YALE L.J. 502 (2006).

F. THE AMERICAN REVOLUTION

The thirteen North American English colonies originally had no formal connection to one another, but this began to change when the British Parliament enacted the Stamp Act tax in 1765. The British thought these taxes were reasonable because they would help pay for the conquest of Quebec and the defense of territorial boundaries resulting from the French and Indian War of 1754–1763. The American Colonists in the 1760s and 1770s, however, thought that, like the Electorate of Hanover, in Germany, they shared a king with Great Britain but not a legislature, because the colonists were represented in the colonial legislatures but not in the British Parliament's House of Commons. Parliament had never taxed the colonies prior to 1765, and the colonists denied that Parliament had any power over them. The Stamp Tax of 1765 produced such outrage in the thirteen North American colonies that Parliament was forced to repeal it.

Indeed, Parliament accommodated the thirteen North American colonies by eliminating all its taxes on the colonies except for one symbolic tax—a tax on tea, which was assessed not for the revenue it would generate but as a symbol of the British Parliament's claimed constitutional power to tax the colonists. On December 16, 1773, a large group of men from Boston boarded all the British ships in Boston Harbor that had tea on board, and they dumped all of the British tea into the ocean in an act called "The Boston Tea Party." Parliament responded to the Boston Tea Party severely, in 1774, by passing "The Coercive Acts," which ended colonial self-government in Massachusetts and closed Boston's harbor to commerce, thereby trying to starve the colony into submission and make it an example to the twelve other North American colonies. The citizens of Massachusetts labelled this legislation "The Intolerable Acts," and they called for a Continental Congress to be held in Philadelphia with representatives from all thirteen of the North American British colonies.

To be sure, Parliament was not the only, or even necessarily the chief, object of colonial complaint. While the colonists recognized in principle the power of the British Crown to govern them, they chafed under what they regarded as abuses of that power, such as trying persons in admiralty courts without juries, appointing heavy-handed colonial governors who interfered with colonial self-governance, and engaging in intrusive searches under "general" warrants that allowed executive agents to search anywhere and for anything without fear of subsequent legal action. These general warrants were objected to by James Otis, citing Sir Edward Coke, in the writs of assistance cases in the 1760s. Thus, colonial objections were on two fronts: objections to *assertions* of power by Parliament and objections to *exercises* of power by the King.

In 1774, a First Continental Congress was held in Philadelphia, which was attended by representatives from all thirteen of the British North American colonies—an extraordinary feat considering the limited transportation of the times! The Congress met from September 5 to October 26, 1774, with each colony having one vote. The First Continental Congress drew up and unanimously adopted articles of association and a declaration of the rights of the Colonies, and it called on all of the British colonies to boycott all British goods in response to "The Intolerable Acts" beginning on December 1, 1774. Imports from Great Britain to North America dropped by an astonishing 97%, in 1775, due to this action of the First Continental Congress!

On April 19, 1775, the British Army marched in their redcoats from Boston to Lexington, Massachusetts in an effort to seize a colonial arsenal rumored to be in nearby Concord, Massachusetts. The first shots were fired at sunrise, and eight Americans were killed in the Battle of Lexington as was one Englishmen. The soldiers then proceeded to Concord, Massachusetts, where 400 militiamen attacked 100 British redcoats at the Old North Bridge. The combined force of 1,700 British soldiers then was forced to retreat under heavy gunfire from American militiamen hiding behind every tree and stone wall on the long, long way back to Boston. Seventy-three British soldiers were killed, twenty-six were missing, and one hundred and seventy-four were wounded as a result of the Battle of Concord. On the American side, forty-nine were killed, five were missing, and thirty-nine were wounded. The battle was considered to be a great American victory, and the British never again dared to leave the City of Boston and go out into the Massachusetts countryside. All of Massachusetts outside of Boston was effectively free of British control. The American Revolution had begun.

G. THE DECLARATION OF INDEPENDENCE

In May 1775, a Second Continental Congress was convened with delegates chosen by popular conventions in the Colonies. On July 4, 1776, the Second Continental Congress adopted the Declaration of Independence, which is one of the most remarkable legal documents in human history. It proclaimed that "All men are created equal" and that there existed "self-evident" natural rights to "life, liberty, and the pursuit of happiness" bestowed by the Creator, which it was the function and duty of governments to protect. Most importantly, the Declaration of Independence proclaimed the natural right of people to alter or abolish any form of government that becomes destructive of those ends and to establish a government conducive to those ends. The Declaration severed all ties between We the People of North America and the British authorities, most notably King George III. The Declaration of Independence held that the American people no longer consented to British rule.

The Declaration of Independence

In Congress, July 4, 1776

The unanimous Declaration of the thirteen united States of America,

When in the Course of human events, it becomes necessary for one people to dissolve the political bands which have connected them with another, and to assume among the powers of the earth, the separate and equal station to which the Laws of

Nature and of Nature's God entitle them, a decent respect to the opinions of mankind requires that they should declare the causes which impel them to the separation.

We hold these truths to be self-evident, that all men are created equal, that they are endowed by their Creator with certain unalienable Rights, that among these are Life, Liberty and the pursuit of Happiness.—That to secure these rights, Governments are instituted among Men, deriving their just powers from the consent of the governed,—That whenever any Form of Government becomes destructive of these ends, it is the Right of the People to alter or to abolish it, and to institute new Government, laying its foundation on such principles and organizing its powers in such form, as to them shall seem most likely to effect their Safety and Happiness. Prudence, indeed, will dictate that Governments long established should not be changed for light and transient causes; and accordingly all experience hath shewn, that mankind are more disposed to suffer, while evils are sufferable, than to right themselves by abolishing the forms to which they are accustomed. But when a long train of abuses and usurpations, pursuing invariably the same Object evinces a design to reduce them under absolute Despotism, it is their right, it is their duty, to throw off such Government, and to provide new Guards for their future security.—Such has been the patient sufferance of these Colonies; and such is now the necessity which constrains them to alter their former Systems of Government. The history of the present King of Great Britain is a history of repeated injuries and usurpations, all having in direct object the establishment of an absolute Tyranny over these States. To prove this, let Facts be submitted to a candid world.

He has refused his Assent to Laws, the most wholesome and necessary for the public good.

He has forbidden his Governors to pass Laws of immediate and pressing importance, unless suspended in their operation till his Assent should be obtained; and when so suspended, he has utterly neglected to attend to them.

He has refused to pass other Laws for the accommodation of large districts of people, unless those people would relinquish the right of Representation in the Legislature, a right inestimable to them and formidable to tyrants only.

He has called together legislative bodies at places unusual, uncomfortable, and distant from the depository of their Public Records, for the sole purpose of fatiguing them into compliance with his measures.

He has dissolved Representative Houses repeatedly, for opposing with manly firmness his invasions on the rights of the people.

He has refused for a long time, after such dissolutions, to cause others to be elected; whereby the Legislative powers, incapable of Annihilation, have returned to the People at large for their exercise; the State remaining in the mean time exposed to all the dangers of invasion from without, and convulsions within.

He has endeavoured to prevent the population of these States; for that purpose obstructing the Laws for Naturalization of Foreigners; refusing to pass others to encourage their migrations hither, and raising the conditions of new Appropriations of Lands.

He has obstructed the Administration of Justice, by refusing his Assent to Laws for establishing Judiciary Powers.

He has made Judges dependent on his Will alone, for the tenure of their offices, and the amount and payment of their salaries.

He has erected a multitude of New Offices, and sent hither swarms of Officers to harass our people, and eat out their substance.

He has kept among us, in times of peace, Standing Armies without the Consent of our legislatures.

He has affected to render the Military independent of and superior to the Civil power.

He has combined with others to subject us to a jurisdiction foreign to our constitution, and unacknowledged by our laws; giving his Assent to their Acts of pretended Legislation:

For Quartering large bodies of armed troops among us:

For protecting them, by a mock Trial, from punishment for any Murders which they should commit on the Inhabitants of these States:

For cutting off our Trade with all parts of the world:

For imposing Taxes on us without our Consent:

For depriving us in many cases, of the benefit of Trial by Jury:

For transporting us beyond Seas to be tried for pretended offences:

For abolishing the free System of English Laws in a neighbouring Province, establishing therein an Arbitrary government, and enlarging its Boundaries so as to render it at once an example and fit instrument for introducing the same absolute rule into these Colonies:

For taking away our Charters, abolishing our most valuable Laws, and altering fundamentally the Forms of our Governments:

For suspending our own Legislatures, and declaring themselves invested with power to legislate for us in all cases whatsoever.

He has abdicated Government here, by declaring us out of his Protection and waging War against us.

He has plundered our seas, ravaged our Coasts, burnt our towns, and destroyed the lives of our people.

He is at this time transporting large Armies of foreign Mercenaries to compleat the works of death, desolation, and tyranny, already begun with circumstances of Cruelty & perfidy scarcely paralleled in the most barbarous ages, and totally unworthy the Head of a civilized nation.

He has constrained our fellow Citizens taken Captive on the high Seas to bear Arms against their Country, to become the executioners of their friends and Brethren, or to fall themselves by their Hands.

He has excited domestic insurrections amongst us, and has endeavoured to bring on the inhabitants of our frontiers, the merciless Indian Savages whose known rule of warfare, is an undistinguished destruction of all ages, sexes and conditions.

In every stage of these Oppressions We have Petitioned for Redress in the most humble terms: Our repeated Petitions have been answered only by repeated injury.

A Prince whose character is thus marked by every act which may define a Tyrant, is unfit to be the ruler of a free people.

Nor have We been wanting in attentions to our British brethren. We have warned them from time to time of attempts by their legislature to extend an unwarrantable jurisdiction over us. We have reminded them of the circumstances of our emigration and settlement here. We have appealed to their native justice and magnanimity, and we have conjured them by the ties of our common kindred to disavow these usurpations, which, would inevitably interrupt our connections and correspondence. They too have been deaf to the voice of justice and of consanguinity. We must, therefore, acquiesce in the necessity, which denounces our Separation, and hold them, as we hold the rest of mankind, Enemies in War, in Peace Friends.

We, therefore, the Representatives of the united States of America, in General Congress, Assembled, appealing to the Supreme Judge of the world for the rectitude of our intentions, do, in the Name, and by Authority of the good People of these Colonies, solemnly publish and declare, That these united Colonies are, and of Right ought to be Free and Independent States; that they are Absolved from all Allegiance to the British Crown, and that all political connection between them and the State of Great Britain, is and ought to be totally dissolved; and that as Free and Independent States, they have full Power to levy War, conclude Peace, contract Alliances, establish Commerce, and to do all other Acts and Things which Independent States may of right do. And for the support of this Declaration, with a firm reliance on the protection of divine Providence, we mutually pledge to each other our Lives, our Fortunes and our sacred Honor.

H. THE ARTICLES OF CONFEDERATION AND THE FIRST STATE DECLARATIONS OF RIGHTS AND CONSTITUTIONS

When the Declaration asserted independence and the power of these "Free and Independent States" to "levy War, conclude Peace, contract Alliances, establish Commerce, and to do all other Acts and Things which Independent States may of right do," this meant that these governmental powers could be exercised by *each* of the thirteen newly independent nation-states individually. An actual framework for a common, continental government was not proposed until 1777—"the Act of Confederation of the United States of America," commonly referred to as the Articles of Confederation—and did not receive the approval of all of the new states until 1781, after British General Cornwallis had already surrendered to American General George Washington at Yorktown, Virginia. Independence was not recognized formally until the Treaty of Paris was signed in 1783 and ratified by the Continental Congress in January 1784.

Meanwhile, acting at the prodding of the Continental Congress in May 1776 and continuing throughout the revolutionary period, the several States engaged in the first American enterprise of constitution-writing, adapting English forms to American revolutionary ideology to varying degrees. Most of the new States began by adopting Declarations of Rights, and eleven States eventually adopted written state constitutions, many of which went through several iterations, setting out in some detail the frames of government. (The Massachusetts constitution of 1780 is still in force.) Connecticut and Rhode Island decided to be governed by their colonial charters, which they treated as being their state constitutions with all references to the King of England excised.

In an ideal world, one would study those pre-1787 state constitutions very carefully before undertaking a study of the United States Constitution. In a law school world of limited time, one can only summarize the central themes of those vitally important state constitutions. Any summary must be approached with caution, because the pace of constitutional development and adoption was often rapid; the constitutions of 1776 and 1777 did not always resemble the constitutions of 1780. But one can fairly say that a distrust of executive power, and of government power generally, led to: 1) the predominance of legislative authority[18]; 2) bicameralism, which was urged on all by John Adams in his *Thoughts on Government, see infra* pages 65–67, and which had been the practice in all of the colonies except for Pennsylvania; 3) term limitations for representatives; 4) rotation in office; and 5) declarations of rights that operated as essential restrictions on the authority of government.

In addition, the American States all adopted, to some degree, systems of separation of powers, which was also urged by John Adams in his *Thoughts on Government*. The separation of powers in the eleven new state constitutions, however, was no longer rooted in the now-repugnant British idea that each of the separate hereditary "estates"—the King (monarchy), the House of Lords (aristocracy), and the House of Commons (democracy) needed to be represented in a "Mixed Government" (also referred to as a "balanced" government by the One, the Few, and the Many). Political philosophers from Aristotle to Polybius to Cicero to St. Thomas Aquinas to Machiavelli had all argued for such Mixed Regimes[19] because they realized, as Lord Acton would later say, that "Power tends to corrupt, and absolute power corrupts absolutely."[20] It was also hoped that a Mixed Regime would have the energy of a monarchy; the wisdom of an aristocracy; and the love of liberty and commonsense of a democracy. The American colonial governments from 1607 to 1776 had been Mixed Regimes with a royally appointed governor; an aristocratic governor's council; and a democratically elected lower house of the legislature, which alone had the power to tax and spend.[21] In 1776, Americans embraced the Enlightenment principle that all men are created equal, and they thus abandoned hereditary monarchy and aristocracy as they had existed in Great Britain. In their place, Americans endorsed new ideas of popular sovereignty and republicanism in declaring independence, and the separation of powers and bicameralism were endorsed as replacements for "Mixed Regimes."

Instead of the One, the Few, and the Many, the categories of American governance were the legislative power, the executive power, and the judicial power—the latter now separated from the executive and legislative powers as a distinct aspect of government. Many States expressly incorporated these new ideas; the Massachusetts Constitution of 1780, for example, wrote: "In the government of this

---

[18] *See* CHARLES C. THACH, THE CREATION OF THE PRESIDENCY, 1775–1789: A STUDY IN CONSTITUTIONAL HISTORY (1922).

[19] *See* Steven G. Calabresi et al., *The Rise and Fall of the Separation of Powers* 106 NW. U.L. REV.527 (2012).

[20] Letter from Lord Acton to Mandell Creighton (Apr. 5, 1887) IN LORD ACTON, ESSAYS ON FREEDOM AND POWER 329, 335 (Gertrude Himmelfarb ed., 1972).

[21] *See* JACK P. GREENE, THE QUEST FOR POWER: THE ROLE OF THE LOWER HOUSES OF ASSEMBLY IN THE SOUTHERN ROYAL COLONIES, 1689–1776 (1972).

Commonwealth, the legislative department shall never exercise the executive and judicial powers, or either of them: The executive shall never exercise the legislative and judicial powers, or either of them: The judicial shall never exercise the legislative and executive powers, or either of them: to the end it may be a government of laws and not of men." MASS. CONST. OF 1780, pt. 1, art. XXX. The Virginia Constitution of 1776 similarly declared that "[t]he legislative, executive, and judiciary department[s], shall be separate and distinct, so that neither exercise the powers properly belonging to the other," VA. CONST. OF 1776, ¶ 3, and the Georgia Constitution of 1777 and the Vermont Constitution of 1786 used the same language. Constitutions that did not expressly contain these separation-of-powers provisions did so implicitly.

To be sure, old "Mixed Regime" ideas about the power of the King or the Royal Governor, in practice, informed the new idea of the executive power, while old "Mixed Regime" ideas about the power of the two Houses of Parliament came to inform, in practice, new ideas about the legislative power. But instead of a traditional "Mixed Regime," Americans adopted *republican government* as the key principle: representative government, divided into separate institutions with distinctive tasks and responsibilities, accountable to the people. Old forms, such as bicameral legislatures, were adapted to new structures with new justifications. The energy of the King became the energy of the President. The wisdom of the aristocracy became the wisdom of the Senate and of the Supreme Court. And, the democracy of the House of Commons applied not only to the House of Representatives, but eventually to the President and the Senators, who are now popularly elected and who indirectly pick the Supreme Court. The American republic is a regime of the One, the Few, and the Many in which the Many get to pick the One and the Few.

The complaints about heavy-handed rule by the King and his royal governors, of course, were fresh in everyone's mind. Most of the eleven States that wrote state constitutions between 1776 and 1787 gave their governors only one-year terms, under the cry that "where annual election ends, tyranny begins." State governors were stripped of their appointment and pardon power and often of their veto power as well. The States were determined that they would not have governors with the power of King George III or his appointees. An exception was New York, which had an unusually (for the times) strong governor.

The experimental and evolving state constitutions were the first step. The second step was the Articles of Confederation, which was the first effort to create a truly national governing body. As you read the Articles of Confederation, consider whether they actually constitute a government at all.

The Articles of Confederation

To all to whom these Presents shall come, we the undersigned Delegates of the States affixed to our Names send greeting.

Articles of Confederation and perpetual Union between the states of New Hampshire, Massachusetts-bay Rhode Island and Providence Plantations, Connecticut, New York, New Jersey, Pennsylvania, Delaware, Maryland, Virginia, North Carolina, South Carolina and Georgia.

I.

The Stile of this Confederacy shall be

"The United States of America".

II.

Each state retains its sovereignty, freedom, and independence, and every power, jurisdiction, and right, which is not by this Confederation expressly delegated to the United States, in Congress assembled.

III.

The said States hereby severally enter into a firm league of friendship with each other, for their common defense, the security of their liberties, and their mutual and general welfare, binding themselves to assist each other, against all force offered to, or attacks made upon them, or any of them, on account of religion, sovereignty, trade, or any other pretense whatever.

IV.

The better to secure and perpetuate mutual friendship and intercourse among the people of the different States in this Union, the free inhabitants of each of these States, paupers, vagabonds, and fugitives from justice excepted, shall be entitled to all privileges and immunities of free citizens in the several States; and the people of each State shall free ingress and regress to and from any other State, and shall enjoy therein all the privileges of trade and commerce, subject to the same duties, impositions, and restrictions as the inhabitants thereof respectively, provided that such restrictions shall not extend so far as to prevent the removal of property imported into any State, to any other State, of which the owner is an inhabitant; provided also that no imposition, duties or restriction shall be laid by any State, on the property of the United States, or either of them.

If any person guilty of, or charged with, treason, felony, or other high misdemeanor in any State, shall flee from justice, and be found in any of the United States, he shall, upon demand of the Governor or executive power of the State from which he fled, be delivered up and removed to the State having jurisdiction of his offense.

Full faith and credit shall be given in each of these States to the records, acts, and judicial proceedings of the courts and magistrates of every other State.

V.

For the most convenient management of the general interests of the United States, delegates shall be annually appointed in such manner as the legislatures of each State shall direct, to meet in Congress on the first Monday in November, in every year, with a power reserved to each State to recall its delegates, or any of them, at any time within the year, and to send others in their stead for the remainder of the year.

No State shall be represented in Congress by less than two, nor more than seven members; and no person shall be capable of being a delegate for more than three years in any term of six years; nor shall any person, being a delegate, be capable of holding any office under the United States, for which he, or another for his benefit, receives any salary, fees or emolument of any kind.

Each State shall maintain its own delegates in a meeting of the States, and while they act as members of the committee of the States.

In determining questions in the United States in Congress assembled, each State shall have one vote.

Freedom of speech and debate in Congress shall not be impeached or questioned in any court or place out of Congress, and the members of Congress shall be protected in their persons from arrests or imprisonments, during the time of their going to and from, and attendence on Congress, except for treason, felony, or breach of the peace.

VI.

No State, without the consent of the United States in Congress assembled, shall send any embassy to, or receive any embassy from, or enter into any conference, agreement, alliance or treaty with any King, Prince or State; nor shall any person holding any office of profit or trust under the United States, or any of them, accept any present, emolument, office or title of any kind whatever from any King, Prince or foreign State; nor shall the United States in Congress assembled, or any of them, grant any title of nobility.

No two or more States shall enter into any treaty, confederation or alliance whatever between them, without the consent of the United States in Congress assembled, specifying accurately the purposes for which the same is to be entered into, and how long it shall continue.

No State shall lay any imposts or duties, which may interfere with any stipulations in treaties, entered into by the United States in Congress assembled, with any King, Prince or State, in pursuance of any treaties already proposed by Congress, to the courts of France and Spain.

No vessel of war shall be kept up in time of peace by any State, except such number only, as shall be deemed necessary by the United States in Congress assembled, for the defense of such State, or its trade; nor shall any body of forces be kept up by any State in time of peace, except such number only, as in the judgement of the United States in Congress assembled, shall be deemed requisite to garrison the forts necessary for the defense of such State; but every State shall always keep up a well-regulated and disciplined militia, sufficiently armed and accoutered, and shall provide and constantly have ready for use, in public stores, a due number of filed pieces and tents, and a proper quantity of arms, ammunition and camp equipage.

No State shall engage in any war without the consent of the United States in Congress assembled, unless such State be actually invaded by enemies, or shall have received certain advice of a resolution being formed by some nation of Indians to invade such State, and the danger is so imminent as not to admit of a delay till the United States in Congress assembled can be consulted; nor shall any State grant commissions to any ships or vessels of war, nor letters of marque or reprisal, except it be after a declaration of war by the United States in Congress assembled, and then only against the Kingdom or State and the subjects thereof, against which war has been so declared, and under such regulations as shall be established by the United States in Congress assembled, unless such State be infested by pirates, in which case vessels of war may be fitted out for that occasion, and kept so long as the danger shall continue, or until the United States in Congress assembled shall determine otherwise.

VII.

When land forces are raised by any State for the common defense, all officers of or under the rank of colonel, shall be appointed by the legislature of each State respectively, by whom such forces shall be raised, or in such manner as such State shall direct, and all vacancies shall be filled up by the State which first made the appointment.

VIII.

All charges of war, and all other expenses that shall be incurred for the common defense or general welfare, and allowed by the United States in Congress assembled, shall be defrayed out of a common treasury, which shall be supplied by the several States in proportion to the value of all land within each State, granted or surveyed for any person, as such land and the buildings and improvements thereon shall be estimated according to such mode as the United States in Congress assembled, shall from time to time direct and appoint.

The taxes for paying that proportion shall be laid and levied by the authority and direction of the legislatures of the several States within the time agreed upon by the United States in Congress assembled.

IX.

The United States in Congress assembled, shall have the sole and exclusive right and power of determining on peace and war, except in the cases mentioned in the sixth article—of sending and receiving ambassadors—entering into treaties and alliances, provided that no treaty of commerce shall be made whereby the legislative power of the respective States shall be restrained from imposing such imposts and duties on foreigners, as their own people are subjected to, or from prohibiting the exportation or importation of any species of goods or commodities whatsoever—of establishing rules for deciding in all cases, what captures on land or water shall be legal, and in what manner prizes taken by land or naval forces in the service of the United States shall be divided or appropriated—of granting letters of marque and reprisal in times of peace—appointing courts for the trial of piracies and felonics commited on the high seas and establishing courts for receiving and determining finally appeals in all cases of captures, provided that no member of Congress shall be appointed a judge of any of the said courts.

The United States in Congress assembled shall also be the last resort on appeal in all disputes and differences now subsisting or that hereafter may arise between two or more States concerning boundary, jurisdiction or any other causes whatever; which authority shall always be exercised in the manner following. Whenever the legislative or executive authority or lawful agent of any State in controversy with another shall present a petition to Congress stating the matter in question and praying for a hearing, notice thereof shall be given by order of Congress to the legislative or executive authority of the other State in controversy, and a day assigned for the appearance of the parties by their lawful agents, who shall then be directed to appoint by joint consent, commissioners or judges to constitute a court for hearing and determining the matter in question: but if they cannot agree, Congress shall name three persons out of each of the United States, and from the list of such persons each party shall alternately strike out one, the petitioners beginning, until the number shall be reduced to thirteen; and from that number not less than seven, nor more than nine names as Congress shall direct, shall in the presence of Congress be drawn out by lot, and the persons whose names shall be so drawn or any five of them, shall be commissioners or judges, to hear and finally determine the controversy, so always as a major part of the judges who shall hear the cause shall agree in the determination: and if either party shall neglect to attend at the day appointed, without showing reasons, which Congress shall judge sufficient, or being present shall refuse to strike, the Congress shall proceed to nominate three persons out of each State, and the secretary of Congress shall strike in behalf of such party absent or refusing; and the judgement and sentence of the court to be appointed, in the manner before prescribed, shall be final and conclusive; and if any of the parties shall refuse to submit to the authority of such court, or to appear or defend their claim or cause, the court shall nevertheless proceed to pronounce sentence, or judgement, which shall in like manner be final and decisive, the judgement or sentence and other proceedings being in either case transmitted to Congress, and lodged among the acts of Congress for the security of the parties concerned: provided that every commissioner, before he sits in judgement, shall take an oath to be administered by one of the judges of the supreme or superior court of the State, where the cause shall be tried, 'well and truly to hear and determine the matter in question, according to the best of his judgement, without favor, affection or hope of reward': provided also, that no State shall be deprived of territory for the benefit of the United States.

All controversies concerning the private right of soil claimed under different grants of two or more States, whose jurisdictions as they may respect such lands, and the States which passed such grants are adjusted, the said grants or either of them being at the same time claimed to have originated antecedent to such settlement of jurisdiction, shall on the petition of either party to the Congress of the United States, be finally determined as near as may be in the same manner as is before presecribed for deciding disputes respecting territorial jurisdiction between different States.

The United States in Congress assembled shall also have the sole and exclusive right and power of regulating the alloy and value of coin struck by their own authority, or by that of the respective States—fixing the standards of weights and measures throughout the United States—regulating the trade and managing all affairs with the Indians, not members of any of the States, provided that the legislative right of any State within its own limits be not infringed or violated—establishing or regulating post offices from one State to another, throughout all the United States, and exacting such postage on the papers passing through the same as may be requisite to defray the expenses of the said office—appointing all officers of the land forces, in the service of the United States, excepting regimental officers—appointing all the officers of the naval forces, and commissioning all officers whatever in the service of the United States—making rules for the government and regulation of the said land and naval forces, and directing their operations.

The United States in Congress assembled shall have authority to appoint a committee, to sit in the recess of Congress, to be denominated 'A Committee of the States', and to consist of one delegate from each State; and to appoint such other committees and civil officers as may be necessary for managing the general affairs of the United States under their direction—to appoint one of their members to preside, provided that no person be allowed to serve in the office of president more than one year in any term of three years; to ascertain the necessary sums of money to be raised for the service of the United States, and to appropriate and apply the same for defraying the public expenses—to borrow money, or emit bills on the credit of the United States, transmitting every half-year to the respective States an account of the sums of money so borrowed or emitted—to build and equip a navy—to agree upon the number of land forces, and to make requisitions from each State for its quota, in proportion to the number of white inhabitants in such State; which requisition shall be binding, and thereupon the legislature of each State shall appoint the regimental officers, raise the men and cloath, arm and equip them in a solid-like manner, at the expense of the United States; and the officers and men so cloathed, armed and equipped shall march to the place appointed, and within the time agreed on by the United States in Congress assembled. But if the United States in Congress assembled shall, on consideration of circumstances judge proper that any State should not raise men, or should raise a smaller number of men than the quota thereof, such extra number shall be raised, officered, cloathed, armed and equipped in the same manner as the quota of each State, unless the legislature of such State shall judge that such extra number cannot be safely spread out in the same, in which case they shall raise, officer, cloath, arm and equip as many of such extra number as they judge can be safely spared. And the officers and men so cloathed, armed, and equipped, shall march to the place appointed, and within the time agreed on by the United States in Congress assembled.

The United States in Congress assembled shall never engage in a war, nor grant letters of marque or reprisal in time of peace, nor enter into any treaties or alliances, nor coin money, nor regulate the value thereof, nor ascertain the sums and expenses necessary for the defense and welfare of the United States, or any of them, nor emit bills, nor borrow money on the credit of the United States, nor appropriate money, nor agree upon the number of vessels of war, to be built or purchased, or the number of land or sea forces to be raised, nor appoint a commander in chief of the army or navy, unless nine States assent to the same: nor shall a question on any other point, except for adjourning from day to day be determined, unless by the votes of the majority of the United States in Congress assembled.

The Congress of the United States shall have power to adjourn to any time within the year, and to any place within the United States, so that no period of adjournment be for a longer duration than the space of six months, and shall publish the journal of their proceedings monthly, except such parts thereof relating to treaties, alliances or military operations, as in their judgement require secrecy; and the yeas and nays of the delegates of each State on any question shall be entered on the journal, when it is desired by any delegates of a State, or any of them, at his or their request shall be furnished with a transcript of the said journal, except such parts as are above excepted, to lay before the legislatures of the several States.

X.

The Committee of the States, or any nine of them, shall be authorized to execute, in the recess of Congress, such of the powers of Congress as the United States in Congress assembled, by the consent of the nine States, shall from time to time think expedient to vest them with; provided that no power be delegated to the said Committee, for the exercise of which, by the Articles of Confederation, the voice of nine States in the Congress of the United States assembled be requisite.

XI.

Canada acceding to this confederation, and adjoining in the measures of the United States, shall be admitted into, and entitled to all the advantages of this Union; but no other colony shall be admitted into the same, unless such admission be agreed to by nine States.

XII.

All bills of credit emitted, monies borrowed, and debts contracted by, or under the authority of Congress, before the assembling of the United States, in pursuance of the present confederation, shall be deemed and considered as a charge against the United States, for payment and satisfaction whereof the said United States, and the public faith are hereby solemnly pleged.

XIII.

Every State shall abide by the determination of the United States in Congress assembled, on all questions which by this confederation are submitted to them. And the Articles of this Confederation shall be inviolably observed by every State, and the Union shall be perpetual; nor shall any alteration at any time hereafter be made in any of them; unless such alteration be agreed to in a Congress of the United States, and be afterwards confirmed by the legislatures of every State.

And Whereas it hath pleased the Great Governor of the World to incline the hearts of the legislatures we respectively represent in Congress, to approve of, and to authorize us to ratify the said Articles of Confederation and perpetual Union. Know Ye that we the undersigned delegates, by virtue of the power and authority to us given for that purpose, do by these presents, in the name and in behalf of our respective constituents, fully and entirely ratify and confirm each and every of the said Articles of Confederation and perpetual Union, and all and singular the matters and things therein contained: And we do further solemnly plight and engage the faith of our respective constituents, that they shall abide by the determinations of the United States in Congress assembled, on all questions, which by the said Confederation are submitted to them. And that the Articles thereof shall be inviolably observed by the States we respectively represent, and that the Union shall be perpetual.

In Witness whereof we have hereunto set our hands in Congress. Done at Philadelphia in the State of Pennsylvania the ninth day of July in the Year of our Lord One Thousand Seven Hundred and Seventy-Eight, and in the Third Year of the independence of America.

Agreed to by Congress 15 November 1777. In force after ratification by Maryland, 1 March 1781

[Assignment 2]

II. THE EFFECT OF THE ARTICLES OF CONFEDERATION

Whether or not the Articles of Confederation created a true "government," they clearly created some kind of association among the States. As of 1781 at the latest, there was a legal entity that one could call "the United States." Technically, that legal entity was a *corporation,* though that term meant something different in 1781 than it means today. Eighteenth-century corporations were public, governmental bodies. Even when they were business organizations with private stockholders, they received specific charters from the government to perform public functions such as building bridges or running orphanages. All governmental bodies were—and for centuries had been—considered corporations. As Justice James Iredell wrote in 1793: "The word 'corporations,' in its largest sense, has a more extensive meaning than people generally are aware of. Any body politic (sole or aggregate) whether its power be restricted or transcendant, is in this sense 'a corporation.' The King, accordingly, in England is called a corporation. 10 Co. 29. b. So also, by a very respectable author (Sheppard, in his abridgement, 1 Vol. 431.) is the Parliament itself. In this extensive sense, not only each State singly, but even the *United States* may without impropriety be termed 'corporations.' " *Chisholm v. Georgia*, 2 U.S. (2 Dall.) 419, 447 (1793). The legal consequence of being a corporation was (and is) that the "United States" was (and is) a juridical entity capable of suing and being sued, having a seal, making contracts, and owning and holding property. Those attributes of corporate entities were clearly identified in many governmental charters in the seventeenth and eighteenth centuries, and those charters would have been well known to the founding generation. *See* GARY LAWSON & GUY SEIDMAN, "A GREAT POWER OF ATTORNEY": UNDERSTANDING THE FIDUCIARY CONSTITUTION 64–66 (2017). This is important, because once we get to the Constitution, we see that it *did not create the United States* but rather altered and empowered an entity that already existed.

Article I of the Articles of Confederation declares that "[t]he Stile of this Confederacy shall be 'The United States of America.' " ART. OF CONFEDERATION art. I. On several occasions, the Articles speak of the United States as an entity separate and apart from the constituent States. *See id.* art. VI (forbidding "any office of profit or trust under the United States, or any of them"); *id.* (forbidding "the United States in congress assembled, or any of them" from granting titles of nobility); *id.* art. IX (precluding the Confederation Congress from ascertaining "the sums and expenses necessary for the defense and welfare of the United States, or any of them" without the assent of nine States). Indeed, the corporate existence of the United States was recognized—though not necessarily correctly—by Pennsylvania courts as early as 1779 in *Respublica v. Cornelius Sweers,* 1 U.S. (1 Dall.) 41 (Pa. S. Ct. 1779), several years before the Articles of Confederation were ratified. Cornelius Sweers, a commissary clerk in the United States Army during the Revolutionary War, was convicted for forging false receipts and thus defrauding the United States. Sweers' counsel objected that there could be no such offense against the United States because " 'at the time of the offence charged, the United States were not a body corporate known in law.' " *Id.* at 44. This was a clever argument: If there was no such thing as a United States that was a legal entity capable of contracting, then there would be no such thing as a United States that was a legal entity capable of being defrauded in a contract. The Pennsylvania Supreme Court rejected that position, even though no formal documents establishing a "United States" were then in force: "From the moment of their association, the United States necessarily became a body corporate; for, there was no superior from whom that character could otherwise be derived. In England, the king, lords, and commons, are certainly a body corporate; and yet there never was any charter or statute, by which they were expressly so created." *Id.* Whether or not the Pennsylvania Supreme Court was right about the United States in 1779, by 1781 the United States was unambiguously an entity capable of contracting, suing, and holding property. Indeed, the United States under the Articles of Confederation held, in its name, an enormous amount of property: The cessions of western lands from various states, most notably Virginia.

A. THE DEFICIENCIES OF THE ARTICLES OF CONFEDERATION

Throughout the American Revolutionary War and the fight for independence, the deficiencies of the U.S. central government, first under the Continental Congress and then under the Articles of Confederation, were well known. The rule that each State had a single vote made the Congress more like the European Union—an assembly of independent nations rather than a representative legislature for one nation. Combined with the requirement that nine out of thirteen States agree on most significant matters, this meant that the Congress could be at the mercy of a small minority and often could not act. Moreover, there was little practical authority of the central government to enforce its enactments even where Congress could agree on measures; the government of the whole was completely dependent on the independent actions of the separate States, where the real powers lay. The Articles were *not* "inviolably observed by every State" but were frequently disregarded. Congress was dependent on the thirteen States to raise tax money for the federal government, and almost all the States failed to provide the money for which Congress asked. As a result, the federal government was always bankrupt. Congress lacked the power to regulate interstate or foreign commerce, and so protectionist tariffs sprang up at state borders, leading to an economic depression in the 1780s. The economic tensions created by the sinking economy led to incidents of violence over debts and taxes, such as Shays' Rebellion in Massachusetts (1786–1787), which state governments seemed powerless to control. Finally, as provided in Article XIII, no changes in the Articles could be made without approval by Congress *and* unanimous approval of all thirteen state legislatures. An amendment to the Articles of Confederation that would have given the Continental Congress the power to regulate commerce was passed by twelve States, but was vetoed by Rhode Island, a State full of merchants who did not want to pay tariffs. Rhode Island had 1/65th of the population of Virginia—the most populous State. As Joseph Story, one the country's most eminent Justices and legal scholars, wrote in 1840:

> It was remarked by an eminent statesman, that by this political compact the Continental Congress has exclusive power for the following purposes, without being able to execute one of them:—It may make and conclude treaties; but it can only recommend the observance of them. It may appoint ambassadors; but it cannot defray even the expense of their tables. It may borrow money in its own name, or the faith of the Union; but it cannot pay a dollar. It may coin money; but it cannot import an ounce of bullion. It may make war, and determine what number of troops are necessary; but it cannot raise a single soldier. In short, it may declare everything, but it can do nothing.

JOSEPH STORY, A FAMILIAR EXPOSITION OF THE CONSTITUTION OF THE UNITED STATES 48 (1840).

Many recognized these problems, but the exigencies of the Revolutionary War meant that little was done about them during those years. After independence was finally won in 1783, concerns mounted in many quarters about the inadequacies of the Articles of Confederation, the impotence of the central government, the weakness and vulnerability to foreign military threats to which it continued to expose the United States, the breakdown of trade and commerce among the States, and the inability or unwillingness of the state governments to provide stable government and protect individual rights. By 1786—a mere decade after the Declaration of Independence of 1776—it seemed that the experiment of American independence was on the verge of abject failure. Many were worried that the thirteen States might be reconquered by the British Empire or by some other European power. The national credit and currency were in shambles. These concerns became so prevalent that Congress agreed to call for a special convention of representatives from each of the States to consider revisions to the Articles of Confederation. The call led to a convention that met in Philadelphia in the summer of 1787.

B. THE ROLE OF THE DYSTOPIAS OF 1776 AND 1787 IN THE WRITING OF THE CONSTITUTION

The government under the Articles of Confederation proved strong enough to win the Revolutionary War, but it rapidly became clear by the 1780s that the people had gone too far after 1776 in weakening national and executive power in response to the absolute, imperial power of King George III. This was the Dystopia of 1776—an evil empire headed up by a tyrant Darth Vader-like King.

In contrast, the government under the Articles of Confederation suffered from what we will call the Dystopia of 1787 because it was constantly bankrupt, the States refused to provide the funds that Congress requisitioned, and the paper money which the national government printed was so subject to inflation that the phrase emerged that something was "not worth a Continental (dollar bill)." Moreover, the American Revolution had taken the United States out of the free trade zone of the British Empire, and the Confederation Congress lacked power to regulate commerce with foreign nations, so new trade treaties could not be negotiated on a large scale. Congress also lacked the power to guarantee free trade among the thirteen States, and States began assessing tariffs against other States' goods. As a result of all of these problems, an economic depression occurred in the 1780s that was aggravated by the fact that many States printed paper money freely, leading to inflation. This, in turn, led in 1786–87 to Shays' Rebellion in Massachusetts in which four thousand indebted farmers threatened to overturn the Massachusetts state government, terrifying property owners in other States (such as George Washington and James Madison in Virginia). These men began to worry more about village tyrants and mob chaos than about imperial, royal tyrants like King George III.

Meanwhile, the state governments were experiencing huge frustration with their overly weak governors. Thomas Jefferson was exasperated with his one-year term as Governor of Virginia. Vesting the appointment power in state legislatures instead of governors led to factionalism and log-rolling behavior with respect to appointments to office, with which no one was satisfied. By 1787, many Americans concluded that they not only needed a stronger national government, but that they also needed stronger executive power. Whereas in 1776 Americans associated their colonial Royal Governors with oppression and their decentralized state legislatures with liberty, by 1787 the tide had turned, so that James Madison could write:

> In a government where numerous and extensive prerogatives are placed in the hands of an hereditary monarch, the executive department is

> very justly regarded as the source of danger, and watched with all the jealousy which a zeal for liberty ought to inspire. In a democracy, where a multitude of people exercise in person the legislative functions, and are continually exposed, by their incapacity for regular deliberation and concerted measures, to the ambitious intrigues of their executive magistrates, tyranny may well be apprehended, on some favorable emergency, to start up in the same quarter. But in a representative republic, where the executive magistracy is carefully limited; both in the extent and the duration of its power; and where the legislative power is exercised by an assembly, which is inspired, by a supposed influence over the people, with an intrepid confidence in its own strength; which is sufficiently numerous to feel all the passions which actuate a multitude, yet not so numerous as to be incapable of pursuing the objects of its passions, by means which reason prescribes; it is against the enterprising ambition of this department that the people ought to indulge all their jealousy and exhaust all their precautions.

THE FEDERALIST No. 48 (James Madison).

In short, 1776 had seen a dystopia of overly strong imperial and executive power, whereas by 1787 the Framers were concerned about a dystopia of overly weak national and executive power. When the Framers gathered in Philadelphia from May until September of 1787, they wanted to correct the dystopia of 1787 without returning to the dystopia of 1776.

C. THE CALLING OF THE PHILADELPHIA CONVENTION OF 1787

The Constitution of the United States was drafted by a distinguished convention of fifty-five citizens assembled in Philadelphia during the hot summer of 1787. Rhode Island boycotted the Convention because it opposed a federal commerce power, and New York ominously sent only one delegate—the very young Alexander Hamilton—to represent its powerful State. The Philadelphia Convention was chaired by (retired) General George Washington, who threw the critical weight of his prestige behind the effort to draft and then ratify the new Constitution. It is safe to say that without Washington's backing the effort to draft a new Constitution would never have gotten off the ground. The presence of Washington also played a critical role in the designing of the new office of President of the United States. Everyone believed that Washington would be the first President, and it was only because of confidence in him that the office was given the broad powers it was.

The Philadelphia Convention agreed to keep its proceedings secret—something that would be almost inconceivable in the modern era—in part to enable wide-open debate, and in part to present a façade of consensus to the public by not advertising the delegates' many disagreements. Accordingly, what we know about the Convention's proceedings comes from a few journals kept by those present, including (most importantly) the notes of James Madison. The authoritative collection of these journals and records is Max Farrand's four-volume THE RECORDS OF THE FEDERAL CONVENTION OF 1787 (Max Farrand ed. 1911). Madison and the other Framers at Philadelphia believed the text of the Constitution should speak for itself and be judged on its own terms—and that their subjective intentions as draftsmen should not matter. Accordingly, Madison's *Notes* were not published until after his death, nearly fifty years later, in 1836.

The Convention was called for the seemingly narrow purpose of proposing *revisions* to the Articles of Confederation. The delegates, however, quickly set about drafting a new Constitution rather than amending the Articles of Confederation (which, keep in mind, required unanimous consent among the States to amend). James Madison and the Virginia delegation arrived with an ambitious "Virginia Plan" to create a new very powerful national government with a two-house Congress chosen on the basis of population, which would have benefitted Virginia, which was then the most populous State in the Union. The Virginia Plan was met by a "New Jersey plan" put forward by the less populous States, which gave much less power to Congress and had both Houses of Congress representing the States equally. Ultimately, the two sides reached a Great Compromise in which the States are equally represented in the Senate while representation in the House of Representatives is based on population and in which the new national government was not given plenary power but only limited and enumerated powers of varying breadth.

Another issue that vexed, and nearly wrecked, the Philadelphia Convention was how the Constitution should treat the slave states. Southerners wanted slaves to count fully as persons for the purpose of representation in the House of Representatives and Electoral College for the election of the President, even while those States themselves treated slaves as property rather than persons. Northerners like Gouverneur Morris, Alexander Hamilton, and Benjamin Franklin thought this was outrageous and that southern slaves ought not be counted at all in determining representation in the House and Electoral College. A compromise, which nobody liked, was worked out. Southern slaves were counted as three-fifths of a person for the purpose of determining a state's representation and in the assessment of direct taxes, and—with the 1772 English decision in *Somerset v. Stewart* fresh in mind—a Fugitive Slave Clause was added to the Constitution requiring that free States return fugitive slaves to their owners—a clause which had not appeared in the Articles of Confederation. For good measure, southerners also insisted on forbidding Congress from abolishing the international slave trade until 1808. Northerners opposed to slavery concluded that the government of the United States under the Articles of Confederation was much too weak to abolish slavery. They thought that the abolition of slavery in North America would first require setting up a more powerful national government and then using that government to uproot slavery in the South, where it was deeply embedded in state culture and economics. With great reluctance, Morris, Hamilton, Franklin, and others accepted the slavery accommodations as being the price they would have to pay to create the U.S. government we know today. With all of this background in mind (including the thousand-year-old background of the "Ancient Constitution"), please now read (even if it seems tedious to do so) the originally ratified text of the U.S. Constitution, written in 1787, as it went into effect in 1788 and 1789.

The Constitution of the United States of America

PREAMBLE

We the People of the United States, in Order to form a more perfect Union, establish Justice, insure domestic Tranquillity, provide for the common defence, promote the general Welfare, and secure the Blessings of Liberty to ourselves and our Posterity, do ordain and establish this Constitution for the United States of America.

ARTICLE I

Section 1. All legislative Powers herein granted shall be vested in a Congress of the United States, which shall consist of a Senate and House of Representatives.

Section 2. The House of Representatives shall be composed of Members chosen every second Year by the People of the several States, and the Electors in each State shall have the Qualifications requisite for Electors of the most numerous Branch of the State Legislature.

No Person shall be a Representative who shall not have attained to the age of twenty five Years, and been seven Years a Citizen of the United States, and who shall not, when elected, be an Inhabitant of that State in which he shall be chosen.

Representatives and direct Taxes shall be apportioned among the several States which may be included within this Union, according to their respective Numbers, which shall be determined by adding to the whole Number of free Persons, including those bound to Service for a Term of Years, and excluding Indians not taxed, three fifths of all other Persons. The actual Enumeration shall be made within three Years after the first Meeting of the Congress of the United States, and within every subsequent Term of ten Years, in such Manner as they shall by Law direct. The Number of Representatives shall not exceed one for every thirty Thousand, but each State shall have at Least one Representative; and until such enumeration shall be made, the State of New Hampshire shall be entitled to chuse three, Massachusetts eight, Rhode-Island and Providence Plantations one, Connecticut five, New-York six, New Jersey four, Pennsylvania eight, Delaware one, Maryland six, Virginia ten, North Carolina five, South Carolina five, and Georgia three.

When vacancies happen in the Representation from any State, the Executive Authority thereof shall issue Writs of Election to fill such Vacancies.

The House of Representatives shall chuse their Speaker and other Officers; and shall have the sole Power of Impeachment.

Section 3. The Senate of the United States shall be composed of two Senators from each State, chosen by the Legislature thereof, for six Years; and each Senator shall have one Vote.

Immediately after they shall be assembled in Consequence of the first Election, they shall be divided as equally as may be into three Classes. The Seats of the Senators of the first Class shall be vacated at the Expiration of the second Year, of the second Class at the Expiration of the fourth Year, and of the third Class at the Expiration of the sixth Year, so that one third may be chosen every second Year; and if Vacancies happen by Resignation, or otherwise, during the Recess of the

Legislature of any State, the Executive thereof may make temporary Appointments until the next Meeting of the Legislature, which shall then fill such Vacancies.

No Person shall be a Senator who shall not have attained to the Age of thirty Years, and been nine Years a Citizen of the United States, and who shall not, when elected, be an Inhabitant of that State for which he shall be chosen.

The Vice President of the United States shall be President of the Senate but shall have no Vote, unless they be equally divided.

The Senate shall chuse their other Officers, and also a President pro tempore, in the Absence of the Vice President, or when he shall exercise the Office of President of the United States.

The Senate shall have the sole Power to try all Impeachments. When sitting for that Purpose, they shall be on Oath or Affirmation. When the President of the United States is tried the Chief Justice shall preside: And no Person shall be convicted without the Concurrence of two thirds of the Members present.

Judgment in Cases of Impeachment shall not extend further than to removal from Office, and disqualification to hold and enjoy any Office of honor, Trust or Profit under the United States: but the Party convicted shall nevertheless be liable and subject to Indictment, Trial, Judgment and Punishment, according to Law.

Section 4. The Times, Places and Manner of holding Elections for Senators and Representatives, shall be prescribed in each State by the Legislature thereof; but the Congress may at any time by Law make or alter such Regulations, except as to the Places of chusing Senators.

The Congress shall assemble at least once in every Year, and such Meeting shall be on the first Monday in December, unless they shall by Law appoint a different Day.

Section 5. Each House shall be the Judge of the Elections, Returns and Qualifications of its own Members, and a Majority of each shall constitute a Quorum to do Business; but a smaller Number may adjourn from day to day, and may be authorized to compel the Attendance of absent Members, in such Manner, and under such Penalties as each House may provide.

Each House may determine the Rules of its Proceedings, punish its Members for disorderly Behaviour, and, with the Concurrence of two thirds, expel a Member.

Each House shall keep a Journal of its Proceedings, and from time to time publish the same, excepting such Parts as may in their Judgment require Secrecy; and the Yeas and Nays of the Members of either House on any question shall, at the Desire of one fifth of those Present, be entered on the Journal.

Neither House, during the Session of Congress, shall, without the Consent of the other, adjourn for more than three days, nor to any other Place than that in which the two Houses shall be sitting.

Section 6. The Senators and Representatives shall receive a Compensation for their Services, to be ascertained by Law, and paid out of the Treasury of the United States. They shall in all Cases, except Treason, Felony and Breach of the Peace, be privileged from Arrest during their Attendance at the Session of their respective Houses, and in going to and returning from the same; and for any Speech or Debate in either House, they shall not be questioned in any other Place.

No Senator or Representative shall, during the Time for which he was elected, be appointed to any civil Office under the Authority of the United States, which shall have been created, or the Emoluments whereof shall have been encreased during such time; and no Person holding any Office under the United States, shall be a Member of either House during his Continuance in Office.

Section 7. All Bills for raising Revenue shall originate in the House of Representatives; but the Senate may propose or concur with amendments as on other Bills.

Every Bill which shall have passed the House of Representatives and the Senate, shall, before it become a law, be presented to the President of the United States: If he approve he shall sign it, but if not he shall return it, with his Objections to that House in which it shall have originated, who shall enter the Objections at large on their Journal, and proceed to reconsider it. If after such Reconsideration two thirds of that House shall agree to pass the Bill, it shall be sent, together with the Objections, to the other House, by which it shall likewise be reconsidered, and if approved by two thirds of that House, it shall become a Law. But in all such Cases the Votes of both Houses shall be determined by Yeas and Nays, and the Names of the Persons voting for and against the Bill shall be entered on the Journal of each House respectively. If any Bill shall not be returned by the President within ten Days (Sundays excepted) after it shall have been presented to him, the Same shall be a Law, in like Manner as if he had signed it, unless the Congress by their Adjournment prevent its Return, in which Case it shall not be a Law.

Every Order, Resolution, or Vote to which the Concurrence of the Senate and House of Representatives may be necessary (except on a question of Adjournment) shall be presented to the President of the United States; and before the Same shall take Effect, shall be approved by him, or being disapproved by him, shall be repassed by two thirds of the Senate and House of Representatives, according to the Rules and Limitations prescribed in the Case of a Bill.

Section 8. The Congress shall have Power To lay and collect Taxes, Duties, Imposts and Excises, to pay the Debts and provide for the common Defence and general Welfare of the United States; but all Duties, Imposts and Excises shall be uniform throughout the United States;

To borrow Money on the credit of the United States;

To regulate Commerce with foreign Nations, and among the several States, and with the Indian Tribes;

To establish an uniform Rule of Naturalization, and uniform Laws on the subject of Bankruptcies throughout the United States;

To coin Money, regulate the Value thereof, and of foreign Coin, and fix the Standard of Weights and Measures;

To provide for the Punishment of counterfeiting the Securities and current Coin of the United States;

To establish Post Offices and post Roads;

To promote the Progress of Science and useful Arts, by securing for limited Times to Authors and Inventors the exclusive Right to their respective Writings and Discoveries;

To constitute Tribunals inferior to the supreme Court;

To define and punish Piracies and Felonies committed on the high Seas, and Offences against the Law of Nations;

To declare War, grant Letters of Marque and Reprisal, and make Rules concerning Captures on Land and Water;

To raise and support Armies, but no Appropriation of Money to that Use shall be for a longer Term than two Years;

To provide and maintain a Navy;

To make Rules for the Government and Regulation of the land and naval Forces;

To provide for calling forth the Militia to execute the Laws of the Union, suppress Insurrections and repeal Invasions;

To provide for organizing, arming, and disciplining, the Militia, and for governing such Part of them as may be employed in the Service of the United States, reserving to the States respectively, the Appointment of the Officers, and the Authority of training the Militia according to the discipline prescribed by Congress;

To exercise exclusive Legislation in all Cases whatsoever, over such District (not exceeding ten Miles square) as may, by Cession of Particular States, and the Acceptance of Congress, become the Seat of the Government of the United States, and to exercise like Authority over all Places purchased by the Consent of the Legislature of the State in which the Same shall be, for the Erection of Forts, Magazines, Arsenals, dock-Yards and other needful Buildings;—And

To make all Laws which shall be necessary and proper for carrying into Execution the foregoing Powers and all other Powers vested by this Constitution in the Government of the United States, or in any Department or Officer thereof.

Section 9. The Migration or Importation of such Persons as any of the States now existing shall think proper to admit, shall not be prohibited by the Congress prior to the Year one thousand eight hundred and eight, but a Tax or duty may be imposed on such Importation, not exceeding ten dollars for each Person.

The Privilege of the Writ of Habeas Corpus shall not be suspended, unless when in Cases or Rebellion or Invasion the public Safety may require it.

No Bill of Attainder or ex post facto Law shall be passed.

No Capitation, or other direct, Tax shall be laid, unless in Proportion to the Census of Enumeration herein before directed to be taken.

No Tax or Duty shall be laid on Articles exported from any State.

No Preference shall be given by any Regulation of Commerce or Revenue to the Ports of one State over those of another: nor shall Vessels bound to, or from, one State, be obliged to enter, clear or pay Duties in another.

No Money shall be drawn from the Treasury, but in Consequence of Appropriations made by Law; and a regular Statement and Account of the Receipts and Expenditures of all public Money shall be published from time to time.

No Title of Nobility shall be granted by the United States: And no Person holding any Office of Profit or Trust under them, shall, without the Consent of the Congress, accept of any present, Emolument, Office, or Title, of any kind whatever, from any King, Prince or foreign State.

Section 10. No State shall enter into any Treaty, Alliance, or Confederation; grant Letters of Marque and Reprisal; coin Money; emit Bills of Credit; make any Thing but gold and silver Coin a Tender in Payment of Debts; pass any Bill of Attainder, ex post facto Law, or Law impairing the Obligation of Contracts, or grant any Title of Nobility.

No State shall, without the Consent of the Congress, lay any Imposts or Duties on Imports or Exports, except what may be absolutely necessary for executing it's inspection Laws: and the net Produce of all Duties and Imposts, laid by any State on Imports or Exports, shall be for the Use of the Treasury of the United States; and all such Laws shall be subject to the Revision and Controul of the Congress.

No State shall, without the Consent of Congress, lay any Duty of Tonnage, keep Troops, or Ships of War in time of Peace, enter into any Agreement or Compact with another State, or with a foreign Power, or engage in War, unless actually invaded, or in such imminent Danger as will not admit of delay.

ARTICLE II

Section 1. The executive Power shall be vested in a President of the United States of America. He shall hold his Office during the Term of four Years, and, together with the Vice President, chosen for the same Term, be elected, as follows:

Each State shall appoint, in such Manner as the Legislature thereof may direct, a Number of Electors, equal to the whole Number of Senators and Representatives to which the State may be entitled in the Congress: but no Senator or Representative, or Person holding an Office of Trust or Profit under the United States, shall be appointed an Elector.

The Electors shall meet in their respective States, and vote by Ballot for two Persons, of whom one at least shall not be an Inhabitant of the same State with themselves. And they shall make a List of all the Persons voted for, and of the Number of Votes for each; which List they shall sign and certify, and transmit sealed to the Seat of the Government of the United States, directed to the President of the Senate. The President of the Senate shall, in the Presence of the Senate and House of Representatives, open all the Certificates, and the Votes shall then be counted. The Person having the greatest Number of Votes shall be the President, if such Number be a Majority of the whole Number of Electors appointed; and if there be more than one who have such Majority, and have an equal Number of Votes, then the House of Representatives shall immediately chuse by Ballot one of them for President; and if no Person have a Majority, then from the five highest on the List the said House shall in like Manner chuse the President. But in chusing the President, the Votes shall be taken by States, the Representatives from each State having one Vote; a quorum for this Purpose shall consist of a Member or Members from two thirds of the States, and a Majority of all the States shall be necessary to a Choice. In every Case, after the Choice of the President, the Person having the greatest Number of Votes of the Electors shall be the Vice President. But if there should remain two or more who have equal Votes, the Senate shall chuse from them by Ballot the Vice President.

The Congress may determine the Time of chusing the Electors, and the Day on which they shall give their Votes; which Day shall be the same throughout the United States.

No Person except a natural born Citizen, or a Citizen of the United States, at the time of the Adoption of this Constitution, shall be eligible to the Office of President; neither shall any person be eligible to that Office who shall not have attained to the Age of thirty five Years, and been fourteen Years a Resident within the United States.

In Case of the Removal of the President from Office, or of his Death, Resignation, or Inability to discharge the Powers and Duties of the said Office, the Same shall devolve on the Vice President, and the Congress may by Law provide for the Case of Removal, Death, Resignation or Inability, both of the President and Vice President, declaring what Officer shall then act as President, and such Officer shall act accordingly, until the Disability be removed, or a President shall be elected.

The President shall, at stated Times, receive for his Services, a Compensation, which shall neither be encreased nor diminished during the Period for which he shall have been elected, and he shall not receive within that Period any other Emolument from the United States, or any of them.

Before he enter on the Execution of his Office, he shall take the following Oath or Affirmation:—"I do solemnly swear (or affirm) that I will faithfully execute the Office of President of the United States, and will to the best of my Ability, preserve, protect and defend the Constitution of the United States."

Section 2. The President shall be Commander in Chief of the Army and Navy of the United States, and of the Militia of the several States, when called into the actual Service of the United States; he may require the Opinion, in writing, of the principal Officer in each of the executive Departments, upon any Subject relating to the Duties of their respective Offices, and he shall have Power to Grant Reprieves and Pardons for Offences against the United States, except in Cases of Impeachment.

He shall have Power, by and with the Advice and Consent of the Senate, to make Treaties, provided two thirds of the Senators present concur; and he shall nominate, and by and with the Advice and Consent of the Senate, shall appoint Ambassadors, other public Ministers and Consuls, Judges of the supreme Court, and all other Officers of the United States, whose Appointments are not herein otherwise provided for, and which shall be established by Law: but the Congress may by Law vest the Appointment of such inferior Officers, as they think proper, in the President alone, in the Courts of Law, or in the Heads of Departments.

The President shall have Power to fill up all Vacancies that may happen during the Recess of the Senate, by granting Commissions which shall expire at the End of their next Session.

Section 3. He shall from time to time give to the Congress Information on the State of the Union, and recommend to their Consideration such Measures as he shall judge necessary and expedient; he may, on extraordinary Occasions, convene both Houses, or either of them, and in Case of Disagreement between them, with Respect to the Time of Adjournment, he may adjourn them to such Time as he shall think proper; he shall receive Ambassadors and other public Ministers; he shall take Care that the Laws be faithfully executed, and shall Commission all the Officers of the United States.

Section 4. The President, Vice President and all Civil Officers of the United States, shall be removed from Office on Impeachment for and Conviction of, Treason, Bribery, or other high Crimes and Misdemeanors.

ARTICLE III

Section 1. The judicial Power of the United States, shall be vested in one supreme Court, and in such inferior Courts as the Congress may from time to time ordain and establish. The Judges, both of the supreme and inferior Courts, shall hold their Offices during good Behaviour, and shall, at stated Times, receive for their Services, a Compensation, which shall not be diminished during their Continuance in Office.

Section 2. The judicial Power shall extend to all Cases, in Law and Equity, arising under this Constitution, the Laws of the United States, and Treaties made, or which shall be made, under their Authority;—to all Cases affecting Ambassadors, other public ministers and Consuls;—to all Cases of admiralty and maritime Jurisdiction;—to Controversies to which the United States shall be a Party;—to Controversies between two or more States;—between a State and Citizens of another State;—between Citizens of different States;—between Citizens of the same State claiming Lands under Grants of different States, and between a State, or the Citizens thereof, and foreign States, Citizens or Subjects.

In all Cases affecting Ambassadors, other public Ministers and Consuls, and those in which a State shall be Party, the supreme Court shall have original Jurisdiction. In all the other Cases before mentioned, the supreme Court shall have appellate Jurisdiction, both as to Law and Fact, with such Exceptions, and under such Regulations as the Congress shall make.

The Trial of all Crimes, except in Cases of Impeachment, shall be by Jury; and such Trial shall be held in the State where the said Crimes shall have been committed; but when not committed within any State, the Trial shall be at such Place or Places as the Congress may by Law have directed.

Section 3. Treason against the United States, shall consist only in levying War against them, or in adhering to their Enemies, giving them Aid and Comfort. No Person shall be convicted of Treason unless on the Testimony of two Witnesses to the same overt Act, or on Confession in open Court.

The Congress shall have Power to declare the Punishment of Treason, but no Attainder of Treason shall work Corruption of Blood, or Forfeiture except during the Life of the Person attainted.

ARTICLE IV

Section 1. Full Faith and Credit shall be given in each State to the public Acts, Records, and judicial Proceedings of every other State. And the Congress may by general Laws prescribe the Manner in which such Acts, Records and Proceedings shall be proved, and the Effect thereof.

Section 2. The Citizens of each State shall be entitled to all Privileges and Immunities of Citizens in the several States.

A Person charged in any State with Treason, Felony, or other Crime, who shall flee from Justice, and be found in another State, shall on Demand of the executive Authority of the State from which he fled, be delivered up, to be removed to the State having Jurisdiction of the Crime.

No Person held to Service or Labour in one State, under the Laws thereof, escaping into another, shall, in Consequence of any Law or Regulation therein, be discharged from such Service or Labour, but shall be delivered up on Claim of the Party to whom such Service or Labour may be due.

Section 3. New States may be admitted by the Congress into this Union; but no new State shall be formed or erected within the Jurisdiction of any other State; nor any State be formed by the Junction of two or more States, or Parts of States, without the Consent of the Legislatures of the States concerned as well as of the Congress.

The Congress shall have Power to dispose of and make all needful Rules and Regulations respecting the Territory or other Property belonging to the United States; and nothing in this Constitution shall be so construed as to Prejudice any Claims of the United States, or of any particular State.

Section 4. The United States shall guarantee to every State in this Union a Republican Form of Government, and shall protect each of them against Invasion; and on Application of the Legislature, or of the Executive (when the Legislature cannot be convened) against domestic Violence.

ARTICLE V

The Congress, whenever two thirds of both Houses shall deem it necessary, shall propose Amendments to this Constitution, or, on the Application of the Legislatures of two thirds of the several States, shall call a Convention for proposing Amendments, which, in either Case, shall be valid to all Intents and Purposes, as Part of this Constitution, when ratified by the Legislatures of three fourths of the several States, or by Conventions in three fourths thereof, as the one or the other Mode of Ratification may be proposed by the Congress; Provided that no Amendment which may be made prior to the Year One thousand eight hundred and eight shall in any Manner affect the first and fourth Clauses in the Ninth Section of the first Article; and that no State, without its Consent, shall be deprived of its equal Suffrage in the Senate.

ARTICLE VI

All Debts contracted and Engagements entered into, before the Adoption of this Constitution, shall be as valid against the United States under this Constitution, as under the Confederation.

This Constitution, and the Laws of the United States which shall be made in Pursuance thereof; and all Treaties made, or which shall be made, under the Authority of the United States, shall be the supreme Law of the Land; and the Judges in every State shall be bound thereby, any Thing in the Constitution or Laws of any state to the Contrary notwithstanding.

The Senators and Representatives before mentioned, and the Members of the several State Legislatures, and all executive and judicial Officers, both of the United States and of the several States, shall be bound by Oath or Affirmation, to support this Constitution; but no religious Test shall ever be required as a Qualification to any Office or public Trust under the United States.

ARTICLE VII

The Ratification of the Conventions of nine States, shall be sufficient for the Establishment of this Constitution between the States so ratifying the same.

D. THE RATIFICATION OF THE CONSTITUTION

Article VII above declares how the Constitution will become effective as law: through ratification by nine state conventions. (Whether the Constitution could, in fact, bootstrap itself into effectiveness this way is the subject of the next section.) Conventions were held in 1787 and 1788 in every State except Rhode Island.

The proposal of the new Constitution naturally spurred an extended debate in the thirteen States over whether it should be adopted. This debate is well presented in PAULINE MAIER, RATIFICATION: THE PEOPLE DEBATE THE CONSTITUTION, 1787–1788 (2011). The advocates of ratification came to be known as the *Federalists* because they favored replacing the treaty-like arrangements of the Articles of Confederation with a whole new federal government. The opponents of ratification came to be known as the *Anti-Federalists,* most of whom feared the new central government would come to be tyrannical. *See* HERBERT J. STORING, WHAT THE ANTI-FEDERALISTS WERE FOR: THE POLITICAL THOUGHT OF THE OPPONENTS OF THE CONSTITUTION (1981).

Delaware was the first State to ratify the Constitution, on December 7, 1787, and Pennsylvania, New Jersey, Georgia, and Connecticut all followed by January 9, 1788. These state conventions ratified the Constitution unanimously or by very large majorities. The really difficult work lay ahead.

The next State to ratify, on February 6, 1788, was the big State of Massachusetts, where the Constitution was extremely controversial. The Anti-Federalists had actually won a majority in the elections for the Massachusetts ratifying convention. Eventually, leading Anti-Federalists like John Hancock and Samuel Adams and eight others agreed to support the Constitution—but only if a Bill of Rights was added to it, and even then the vote to ratify was only 187 to 168.

Four of the next States to ratify followed Massachusetts by also insisting on the promised addition of a federal Bill of Rights as a condition of ratification. Maryland and South Carolina became the seventh and eighth States to ratify in the Spring of 1788, and New Hampshire became the critical ninth State to ratify on June 21, 1788 by the close vote of 57 to 47. The Constitution itself said that it would go into effect once nine States ratified, so as a formal matter the Constitution became law—at least for nine States—on that date. Few people, however, believed that the Constitution would actually go into effect until it was ratified by Virginia and New York. The French Minister Plenipotentiary, upon learning of New Hampshire's ratification, wrote that "without Virginia and New York the new Government will exist more in name than in fact." Letter from Comte de Moustier to Comte do Montmorin (June 25, 1788), *reprinted in* 18 DOCUMENTARY HISTORY OF THE RATIFICATION OF THE CONSTITUTION 189, 192 (John P. Kaminski & Gaspare J. Saladino eds., 1995). Ezra Stiles of Connecticut said virtually the same thing in his diary: "Adoption of the new foederal Constitution by the State of New Hampshire . . . . So now the new Constitution is ratified, ie, literally—but if N York, Virga. & No Caro should not accede, it will yet be some time before the Ratification may be considered as completely established." Ezra Stiles Diary, June 25, 1788, *in id.* at 194

Virginia was by far the largest and most populous of the thirteen States—at least counting its slaves as part of the population. James Madison and John Marshall led the Federalists in the state convention, while Patrick Henry led the Anti-Federalists. The vote on June 25, 1788 was 89 in favor and 79 opposed, with a recommendation that a federal Bill of Rights be added to the document. Patrick Henry remained so opposed to the new government that he turned down offers to serve either as Secretary of State or as a U.S. Supreme Court Justice after the new Constitution had gone into effect.

From June 25th until July 26th, the fate of the new nation lay in New York's hands. The Anti-Federalists in New York were led by the State's very powerful Governor, George Clinton. The Federalists were led by the young but charismatic Alexander Hamilton, and by future Chief Justice John Jay. In order to persuade New York (and Virginia beforehand) to ratify the federal Constitution, Hamilton, Jay, and James Madison wrote a series of 85 articles and essays under the pen-name of "Publius," which came to be known collectively as *The Federalist Papers*. These articles and essays include some of the most important works in political science ever written. *The Federalist Papers* continue to be consulted down to the present day both in interpreting the U.S. Constitution and in providing advice to other countries about constitution writing. Perhaps they are responsible for the government we have today, because on July 26, 1788, New York ratified the Constitution by the close vote of 30 to 27, also insisting on the addition of a Bill of Rights.

Once Virginia and New York had ratified the Constitution in the summer of 1788, eleven of the original thirteen States had ratified. The only dissenters were Rhode Island and North Carolina. The 1788 convention in the latter neither ratified nor rejected the Constitution. North Carolina eventually ratified a year later, on November 21, 1789 (with a *lengthy* declaration of rights and suggestions for amendments); and Rhode Island followed on May 29, 1790—on its third try—by a one-vote margin (with merchant John Brown having reportedly bribed the key vote and several major ports threatening to secede from the State absent ratification).

The first session of Congress under the new Constitution began on March 4, 1789, though the body did not have a quorum until April 6, 1789. George Washington was sworn in as President on April 30, 1789. At that point, the new country was capable of enacting laws, forming treaties, and appointing judges and other officers.

E. THE LEGALITY OF THE RATIFICATION OF THE CONSTITUTION

Was the Constitution legally ratified under existing law in place in the United States in 1787 and 1788? There are two bodies of constitutional law that were disregarded by the ratification of the U.S. Constitution: (1) the Articles of Confederation and (2) the existing eleven state constitutions and the colonial charters of Rhode Island and Connecticut, which functioned as those States' constitutions.

The Articles of Confederation explicitly provided both that they could only be amended by the unanimous consent of all thirteen sovereign States and that they were Articles of "perpetual" Union. Thus, the U.S. Constitution, which purportedly went into effect when nine out of thirteen States ratified it, was seemingly illegal under the Articles of Confederation.

On the other hand, the Articles of Confederation also explicitly say that the thirteen States retained their full and unimpaired sovereignty, implying that the "government" under the Articles was a treaty organization, like the United Nations or the European Union. It was well understood in 1787 that parties to a treaty could withdraw from the treaty, especially when other treaty partners were failing to live up to their obligations by, for example, not providing the funds which the Continental Congress had asked them to requisition. *See* Akhil Reed Amar, *Philadelphia Revisited: Amending the Constitution Outside Article V*, 55 U. CHI. L. REV. 1043, 1048 (1988).

Complaints were also made at the time that the Philadelphia Convention had exceeded its mandate from the Continental Congress to draft amendments to the Articles by instead proposing a whole new constitution. But the Continental Congress had accepted what the Philadelphia Convention had done, and it had submitted the document to the States, all thirteen of which ultimately ratified it by popularly elected ratifying conventions held in those States. Did ratification by those popular assemblies cure any procedural defects? Consider James Madison's answer in *The Federalist* to doubts about the Constitutional Convention's power to propose the Constitution for ratification as it did:

> [I]t shall be granted for a moment that the convention were neither authorized by their commission, nor justified by circumstances in proposing a Constitution for their country: does it follow that the Constitution ought, for that reason alone, to be rejected? If, according to the noble precept, it be lawful to accept good advice even from an enemy, shall we set the ignoble example of refusing such advice even when it is offered by our friends? The prudent inquiry, in all cases, ought surely to be not so much *from whom* the advice comes, as whether the advice be *good*.

THE FEDERALIST No. 40 (James Madison). Is that a legally convincing answer?

Before you decide, reflect on an even more serious legal question concerning ratification: Whether the U.S. Constitution was lawfully adopted under the state constitutional amendment rules that were in place in 1787 and 1788? The Constitution was obviously amending, by supercession, provisions in all of the state constitutions (or corporate charters), and the U.S. Constitution's ratification process obviously did *not* comply with state constitutional amending procedures; no state constitution permitted legal action by the kinds of popular conventions contemplated by Article VII. This objection was squarely raised at the Constitutional Convention in connection with an early draft of Article VII; a delegate from Maryland "mentioned the mode of altering the Constitution of Maryland pointed out therein, and that no other mode could be pursued in that State." Consider James Madison's response, and then—in light of that response—reconsider his response above to the objection to the Convention's authority to propose a new Constitution:

> The difficulty in Maryland was no greater than in other States, where no mode of change was pointed out by the constitution, and all officers were under oath to support it. *The people were in fact, the fountain of all power, and by resorting to them, all difficulties were got over.* They could alter constitutions as they pleased. It was a principle in the Bill of rights, that first principles might be resorted to.

2 THE RECORDS OF THE FEDERAL CONVENTION OF 1787, at 476 (emphasis added). The "Bill of rights" to which Madison referred was *not* the U.S. Constitution's Bill of Rights, since neither it nor the Constitution yet existed. It was the "Declaration of Rights" in the Maryland Constitution of 1776, which said that "all government of right originates from the people, is founded in compact only, and instituted solely for the good of the whole * * * [and] the people of this State ought to have the sole and

exclusive right of regulating the internal government and police thereof." Is that the final answer? Was the Constitution thus the product of the Lockean right of revolution, going back to seventeenth-century English notions of the "Ancient Constitution" and the right to depose unfaithful kings? Did the ratification of the Constitution simply overthrow existing institutions the same way that the American Revolution of 1776 simply overthrew British rule?

There is, of course, one obvious difference between 1776 and 1788: the British fought back while defenders of the state constitutional amendment processes did not. Is that legally relevant?

> One of the most remarkable features of the Constitution was its quick acceptance by former opponents upon ratification. The ratification process was hard fought, with strong accusations flung by both sides. Opponents of the Constitution feared tyranny; from their standpoint, adoption of the Constitution would essentially undo the effects of the American Revolution * * *. People who were inclined to fight against what they perceived as a new tyranny had plenty of intellectual resources on which to draw. Shays' Rebellion demonstrated that the material resources for armed uprisings were readily present as well. The new federal government could not possibly have an overwhelming military force until the government had been up and running for some time. Recent events cast great doubt on the Constitution's durability: The Articles of Confederation had failed within a very short time, and state constitutions were changing with astonishing rapidity. The process by which the Constitution was brought into being seemed to contain the ingredients of a very bloody civil war.
>
> It never happened. Almost uniformly, the opponents of the Constitution quickly and publicly assented to the new regime, and many of them took positions in the federal government or the old state governments that required constitutionally-mandated oaths—and oaths actually meant something to politicians in those days—to preserve the new constitutional order. The ordinary citizens who opposed the Constitution, including those who dominated certain regions of the country, did not take up arms against those who they regarded as usurpers and enemies of liberty, even though the new government had either no or a very weak army for much of this time. The transition from the Articles of Confederation to the Constitution was spectacularly peaceful and smooth.

Gary Lawson & Guy Seidman, *Originalism as a Legal Enterprise*, 23 CONST. COMMENTARY 47, 68–69 (2006) (footnotes omitted). Was Madison's argument in *The Federalist* therefore much stronger than it might seem at first glance to modern eyes? For an important study of why the Anti-Federalists gave up without a fight, see DAVID J. SIEMERS, RATIFYING THE REPUBLIC: ANTIFEDERALISTS AND FEDERALISTS IN CONSTITUTIONAL TIME (2002).

[Assignment 3]

III. THE ADDITION OF THE BILL OF RIGHTS

One of the most contentious issues surrounding the ratification of the Constitution was the absence in the document of a comprehensive Bill of Rights.

Article I, section 9 contained a number of categorical prohibitions on action by institutions of the national government, and Article I, section 10 added a small number of restrictions on the States, but on its face the Constitution seems relatively unconcerned about declaring the rights of the people against their government. Ratification of the Constitution had been conditioned in many States upon the addition of a federal Bill of Rights. Indeed, ratification of the Constitution would have stalled at the sixth State without the "Massachusetts Compromise" of ratifying the Constitution but insisting that a Bill of Rights be added to it. Ratification in Virginia and New York was almost certainly attributable to the solemn promises of James Madison and Alexander Hamilton that a Bill of Rights would be added to the Constitution after ratification. Most of the eleven States which had written new state constitutions, between 1776 and 1787 had also written state declarations of rights, which had sometimes actually preceded the adoption of the respective state constitutions. Many people asked to ratify the Constitution simply could not fathom why the Framers of the Federal Constitution had failed to include a Bill of Rights, and they wondered whether the absence of a Bill of Rights was due to some tyrannical purpose.

In order to understand why the Federalists had originally thought a Bill of Rights was unnecessary, it is essential to consider Alexander Hamilton's and James Wilson's arguments against a Bill of Rights below.

A. THE FEDERALIST POSITION

1. THE FEDERALIST NO. 84 (HAMILTON)

To the People of the State of New York:

* * * The most considerable of the remaining objections is that the plan of the convention contains no bill of rights * * *.

It has been several times truly remarked that bills of rights are, in their origin, stipulations between kings and their subjects, abridgements of prerogative in favor of privilege, reservations of rights not surrendered to the prince. Such was MAGNA CHARTA, obtained by the barons, sword in hand, from King John. Such were the subsequent confirmations of that charter by succeeding princes. Such was the *petition of right* assented to by Charles I., in the beginning of his reign. Such, also, was the Declaration of Right presented by the Lords and Commons to the Prince of Orange in 1688, and afterwards thrown into the form of an act of parliament called the Bill of Rights. It is evident, therefore, that, according to their primitive signification, they have no application to constitutions professedly founded upon the power of the people, and executed by their immediate representatives and servants. Here, in strictness, the people surrender nothing; and as they retain every thing they have no need of particular reservations. "WE, THE PEOPLE of the United States, to secure the blessings of liberty to ourselves and our posterity, do ORDAIN and ESTABLISH this Constitution for the United States of America." Here is a better recognition of popular rights, than volumes of those aphorisms which make the principal figure in several of our State bills of rights, and which would sound much better in a treatise of ethics than in a constitution of government.

But a minute detail of particular rights is certainly far less applicable to a Constitution like that under consideration, which is merely intended to regulate the general political interests of the nation, than to a constitution which has the regulation of every species of personal and private concerns.

I go further, and affirm that bills of rights, in the sense and to the extent in which they are contended for, are not only unnecessary in the proposed Constitution, but would even be dangerous. They would contain various exceptions to powers not granted; and, on this very account, would afford a colorable pretext to claim more than were granted. For why declare that things shall not be done which there is no power to do? Why, for instance, should it be said that the liberty of the press shall not be restrained, when no power is given by which restrictions may be imposed? I will not contend that such a provision would confer a regulating power; but it is evident that it would furnish, to men disposed to usurp, a plausible pretense for claiming that power. They might urge with a semblance of reason, that the Constitution ought not to be charged with the absurdity of providing against the abuse of an authority which was not given, and that the provision against restraining the liberty of the press afforded a clear implication, that a power to prescribe proper regulations concerning it was intended to be vested in the national government. This may serve as a specimen of the numerous handles which would be given to the doctrine of constructive powers, by the indulgence of an injudicious zeal for bills of rights.

* * *

There remains but one other view of this matter to conclude the point. The truth is, after all the declamations we have heard, that the Constitution is itself, in every rational sense, and to every useful purpose, A BILL OF RIGHTS. The several bills of rights in Great Britain form its Constitution, and conversely the constitution of each State is its bill of rights. And the proposed Constitution, if adopted, will be the bill of rights of the Union. Is it one object of a bill of rights to declare and specify the political privileges of the citizens in the structure and administration of the government? This is done in the most ample and precise manner in the plan of the convention; comprehending various precautions for the public security, which are not to be found in any of the State constitutions. Is another object of a bill of rights to define certain immunities and modes of proceeding, which are relative to personal and private concerns? This we have seen has also been attended to, in a variety of cases, in the same plan. Adverting therefore to the substantial meaning of a bill of rights, it is absurd to allege that it is not to be found in the work of the convention. It may be said that it does not go far enough, though it will not be easy to make this appear; but it can with no propriety be contended that there is no such thing. It certainly must be immaterial what mode is observed as to the order of declaring the rights of the citizens, if they are to be found in any part of the instrument which establishes the government. And hence it must be apparent, that much of what has been said on this subject rests merely on verbal and nominal distinctions, entirely foreign from the substance of the thing.

2. SPEECH OF JAMES WILSON

Pennsylvania, October 6, 1787

It will be proper . . . to mark the leading discrimination between the State constitutions and the constitution of the United States. When the people established the powers of legislation under their separate governments, they invested their representatives with every right and authority which they did not in explicit terms reserve; and therefore upon every question respecting the jurisdiction of the House of Assembly, if the frame of government is silent, the jurisdiction is efficient and complete. But in delegating federal powers, another criterion was necessarily introduced, and the congressional power is to be collected, not from tacit implication, but from the positive grant expressed in the instrument of the union. Hence, it is evident, that in the former case everything which is not reserved is given; but in the latter the reverse of the proposition prevails, and everything which is not given is reserved.

This distinction being recognized, will furnish an answer to those who think the omission of a bill of rights a defect in the proposed constitution; for it would have been superfluous and absurd to have stipulated with a federal body of our own creation, that we should enjoy those privileges of which we are not divested, either by the intention or the act that has brought the body into existence. For instance, the liberty of the press, which has been a copious source of declamation and opposition—what control can proceed from the Federal government to shackle or destroy that sacred palladium of national freedom? If, indeed, a power similar to that which has been granted for the regulation of commerce had been granted to regulate literary publications, it would have been as necessary to stipulate that the liberty of the press should be preserved inviolate, as that the impost should be general in its operation * * *. In truth, then, the proposed system possesses no influence whatever upon the press, and it would have been merely nugatory to have introduced a formal declaration upon the subject—nay, that very declaration might have been construed to imply that some degree of power was given, since we undertook to define its extent.

B. THE BILL OF RIGHTS TO THE FEDERAL CONSTITUTION

(Ratified December 15, 1791)

Articles in addition to, and amendments of, the Constitution of the United States of America, proposed by Congress, and ratified by the legislatures of the several states, pursuant to the Fifth Article of the original Constitution.

Structural

AMENDMENT I (1791)

Congress shall make no law respecting an establishment of religion, or prohibiting the free exercise thereof; or abridging the freedom of speech, or of the press; or the right of the people peaceably to assemble, and to petition the Government for a redress of grievances.

AMENDMENT II (1791)

A well regulated Militia, being necessary to the security of a free State, the right of the people to keep and bear Arms, shall not be infringed.

AMENDMENT III (1791)

No Soldier shall, in time of peace be quartered in any house, without the consent of the Owner, nor in time of war, but in a manner to be prescribed by law.

AMENDMENT IV (1791)

The right of the people to be secure in their persons, houses, papers, and effects, against unreasonable searches and seizures, shall not be violated, and no Warrants shall issue, but upon probable cause, supported by Oath or affirmation, and particularly describing the place to be searched, and the persons or things to be seized.

AMENDMENT V (1791)

No person shall be held to answer for a capital, or otherwise infamous crime, unless on a presentment or indictment of a Grand Jury, except in cases arising in the land or naval forces, or in the Militia, when in actual service in time of War or public danger; nor shall any person be subject for the same offence to be twice put in jeopardy of life or limb; nor shall be compelled in any criminal case to be a witness against himself, nor be deprived of life, liberty, or property, without due process of law; nor shall private property be taken for public use, without just compensation.

AMENDMENT VI (1791)

In all criminal prosecutions, the accused shall enjoy the right to a speedy and public trial, by an impartial jury of the State and district wherein the crime shall have been committed, which district shall have been previously ascertained by law, and to be informed of the nature and cause of the accusation; to be confronted with the witnesses against him; to have compulsory process for obtaining witnesses in his favor, and to have the Assistance of Counsel for his defence.

AMENDMENT VII (1791)

In Suits at common law, where the value in controversy shall exceed twenty dollars, the right of trial by jury shall be preserved, and no fact tried by a jury, shall be otherwise re-examined in any Court of the United States, than according to the rules of the common law.

AMENDMENT VIII (1791)

Excessive bail shall not be required, nor excessive fines imposed, nor cruel and unusual punishments inflicted.

AMENDMENT IX (1791)

The enumeration in the Constitution, of certain rights, shall not be construed to deny or disparage others retained by the people.

AMENDMENT X (1791)

The powers not delegated to the United States by the Constitution, nor prohibited by it to the States, are reserved to the States respectively, or to the people.

NOTES AND QUESTIONS ON THE ADDITION OF THE BILL OF RIGHTS

1. Is the argument that a Bill of Rights was unnecessary and inappropriate in a government of limited and specifically enumerated powers persuasive? Why or why not? Recall that Alexander Hamilton insisted in two vitriolic paragraphs above that the Constitution gives the Congress no enumerated power whatsoever to infringe upon the freedom of the press, and he therefore contended that the First Amendment's Freedom of the Press Clause was not needed. Ten years later, in 1798, Alexander Hamilton and his allies caused a major constitutional crisis by shepherding a Sedition Act through Congress protecting Federalist President John Adams and the Federalist majority in the Senate and in the House of Representatives from published statements calling their reputations into disrepute. *See* ch. 74, § 2, 1 Stat. 596, 596–97 (1798). The Sedition Act made it a federal crime punishable by imprisonment and fines to criticize President Adams, but not Vice President Jefferson, by calling President Adams pompous or fussy!

Congress actually passed the Sedition Act into law; President Adams signed the law and ordered that prosecutions be brought under it; and Federalist District Judges upheld the Sedition Act as constitutional notwithstanding the First Amendment or Hamilton's contention that Congress has no power to regulate the press. People were fined and sent to jail under that statute.

Thomas Jefferson and James Madison won the next presidential election; the Sedition Act sunsetted out of existence, Jefferson pardoned everyone convicted under the Sedition Act, and Congress appropriated funds to repay the fines that those prosecuted under the Sedition Act had had to pay.

Is the lesson that a Bill of Rights was, as the Federalists claimed, pointless or harmful (since the Sedition Act was enacted and enforced in the face of the First Amendment) or that the Anti-federalists were right about the dangers of tyranny and the Constitution's drafters therefore should have paid much more attention to the protection of rights by putting into the original Constitution something even stronger than the First Amendment? Or was Madison right that these are all "parchment barriers" and one should just concentrate on checks and balances?

2. Think about the history leading up to the Constitution. Which provisions in the Bill of Rights are direct responses to specific historical events or concerns, either in England or in colonial America? Do any of the provisions seem to come out of nowhere? In Congress, James Madison took principal responsibility for drafting the Bill of Rights. Madison included two clauses which no State ratifying convention asked for: the Freedom of Speech Clause of the First Amendment and the Takings Clause of the Fifth Amendment. Between 1789 and 1791, only one State—Pennsylvania—had a Freedom of Speech Clause, though Freedom of the Press Clauses were ubiquitous; Madison joined protections of speech to those of the press in the First Amendment, and the idea took hold. Today, all fifty States protect freedom of speech in their constitutions. Does that mean that Madison was right to include it? Madison also inserted the Takings Clause into the Fifth Amendment with no obvious prompting or source, and since no one objected, it stayed in. For purposes of interpretation of the Bill of Rights, does it matter how the various provisions got there?

3. Congress originally proposed *twelve* amendments for ratification, not ten. The first two proposed amendments failed in 1791 to secure ratification from the necessary three-fourths of the States, though the original second amendment failed at that time by only one vote. The original first amendment was an elaborate formula setting minimum and maximum sizes for the House of Representatives. The original second amendment provided that "No law, varying the compensation for the services of Senators and Representatives, shall take effect, until an election of Representatives shall have intervened." In other words, members of Congress—who the Constitution of 1787 flatly forbids from taking executive or judicial offices that they created or whose salary they helped increase—cannot give themselves pay raises until the public has had a chance to vote them out of office for doing so. While this amendment failed by a single vote in 1791, it was eventually ratified by the necessary number of States—in *1992*, more than two centuries after it was proposed by Congress. The original proposed second amendment is now the actual Twenty-Seventh Amendment. And the actual First Amendment was the original proposed third amendment. That is a warning not to spend too much time worrying about the possible significance of the numbering or sequencing of the provisions in the Bill of Rights.

4. The First Amendment says that "Congress shall make no law" abridging various rights. The other provisions in the Bill of Rights, however, are silent about which institutions of the national government they bind. Does that mean that they bind all

institutions of the national government? Does that mean that the First Amendment binds only Congress and does not bind the President or the courts? *See American Legion v. American Humanist Ass'n,* 139 S.Ct. 2067, 2095 n.1 (2019) (Thomas, J., concurring in the judgment). Think carefully about which government actors are the likely targets of the various amendments. *See* Nicholas Quinn Rosencranz, *The Subjects of the Constitution*, 62 STAN. L. REV. 1209 (2010); Nicholas Quinn Rosencranz, *The Objects of the Constitution*, 63 STAN. L. REV. 1005 (2011).

5. Scan the first ten amendments, which are generally thought to comprise "The Bill of Rights." How do the Ninth and Tenth Amendments fit with the other provisions in the Bill of Rights? What work do they actually do? You will have many occasions later in this course to think about that question.

6. For that matter, what work do the first eight amendments actually do? The Federalists, remember, thought that the Constitution did not give agents of the federal government the enumerated power to violate the rights of the people. If they are right, how different was the legal world after the Bill of Rights was ratified on December 15, 1791?

> Suppose that on December 14, 1791, Congress passed a statute forbidding the publication of any pamphlets that were deemed by a government censorship board to be unduly critical of Congress. In order to enforce the statute and effectively ferret out offending material, courts were authorized to issue to Treasury Department agents general warrants to seize and search shipments of goods without particularized cause or identification. Finally, the statute specified that charges brought under the statute, including charges implicating the death penalty, shall be by information rather than indictment and trials of offenses under the statute shall be by judges without juries.
>
> * * * On December 15, 1791, [t]he Bill of Rights would lay waste to this statute.
>
> But is the statute unconstitutional *only* because of the Bill of Rights? Was the statute constitutional on December 14, 1791, before the Bill of Rights ever existed? The Federalist supporters of the Constitution in the late eighteenth century uniformly would have said "no" to both questions.
>
> Consider the provision restricting the publication of antigovernment pamphlets. During the ratification debates, when opponents of the Constitution raised the specter of precisely such laws—and the absence of a Bill of Rights to prevent them—as a reason to vote down the proposed Constitution, the Federalists countered that any such laws would be unconstitutional *even without* a Bill or Rights or a First Amendment because of the fundamental principle of enumerated federal powers * * *. [A] parade of Federalist heavyweights were quick to point out that the federal Constitution does not enumerate any power that would permit Congress to restrict the liberties ultimately identified in the First Amendment. As Hugh Williamson memorably put it in a ratification-era letter: "[E]xamine the Plan [of the Constitution], and you will find that the Liberty of the Press and the laws of Mahomet are equally affected by it" * * *. Similar statements during the ratification debates came from such notables as [James Wilson,] Oliver Ellsworth, James Iredell, Charles Cotesworth Pinckney, Edmund Randolph, and Roger Sherman. The same response was made to claims by Antifederalists that freedom of religion, freedom from general warrants, and rights to jury trial were in danger without a Bill of Rights to safeguard them. As Edmund Randolph put it, "No part of the

> Constitution, even if strictly construed, will justify a conclusion that the general government can take away or impair the freedom of religion"—and he was seconded (and more) during the ratification debates by, inter alia, Iredell, Richard Spaight, and Wilson. Randolph made the same point with respect to general warrants * * *. Hamilton extended the argument to jury trials, and "An Impartial Citizen" denied that the Constitution gave Congress enumerated power to impose cruel and unusual punishments. The Federalists' consistent line was that the original, unamended Constitution, by virtue of the structure of enumerated powers, already prohibited virtually any law that would run afoul of what ultimately became the Bill of Rights.
>
> * * *
>
> Thus, if Congress tries to outlaw publication of pamphlets critical of the government, the most basic constitutional problem with that statute is the absence of any congressional power to enact it. The First Amendment ("Congress shall make no law") emphasizes, clarifies, and amplifies that absence. There may, however, be circumstances in which it is more convenient—easier, clearer, and simpler—to invoke the First Amendment as the ground for invalidation of the law rather than to go "beneath" the First Amendment to the scheme of enumerated powers. In that respect, it makes good sense to speak of laws that violate the First Amendment, and even to speak of a broader First Amendment doctrine which describes the set of laws concerning speech and religion that exceed the enumerated powers of Congress. Even though it would be conceptually possible to reach precisely the same results * * * without mentioning the First Amendment, the existence of a First Amendment can add conceptual clarity to the inquiry and can focus attention on instances of federal overreaching that might otherwise escape notice. That is precisely the original function of the Bill of Rights, and it is not a function to dismiss lightly.

Gary Lawson, *A Truism with Attitude: The Tenth Amendment in Constitutional Context,* 83 NOTRE DAME L. REV. 469, 475–78, 487, 491 (2008). This approach obviously depends on the Federalists being right about the scope of the federal government's enumerated powers. While the enumerations of congressional power in Article I, section 8 do not include a "Press Clause," a "General Warrants Clause," or an "Abolish Juries Clause," could the Necessary and Proper Clause be a source of federal power to regulate speech, issue general warrants, and abolish juries that the Bill of Rights needs to limit? Stay tuned (or see *id.* at 479–84 if you are itchy). What would be the purpose and content of the Ninth and Tenth Amendments if the Federalists were right about enumerated powers? Do those provisions have different purposes and contents if the Federalists were wrong about enumerated powers?

7. As you will see later in the course, modern law treats the Bill of Rights (or at least most of the Bill of Rights) as something very far from a truism. Modern law also rejects (as the Anti-Federalists feared) much of the Federalist vision of the scope of enumerated federal powers. Would it make sense to adhere to the Federalist vision of the Bill of Rights while rejecting its vision of enumerated powers? In constitutional theory, do two wrongs sometimes make a right? *See* Peter B. McCutchen, *Mistakes, Precedent, and the Rise of the Administrative State: Toward a Constitutional Theory of the Second Best*, 80 CORNELL L. REV. 1 (1994).

8. Many modern bills of rights in countries other than the United States are not (or not just) shields against government harm but entitlements to government transfer payments. Thus, many modern constitutions contain a right to healthcare, a job, housing,

and so forth. Courts, however, typically lack the power of the purse—the legislature's powers to tax and spend. *See*, e.g., U.S. CONST. art. I, § 9, cl. 7. This often renders judicially enforced rights to entitlement programs unenforceable. Is that an argument against having them? If you consider those kinds of provisions to be truisms in the same way that the Federalists thought of the Bill of Rights as truisms, is there value in stating them in a constitution? *See* Lawrence Gene Sager, *Fair Measure: The Legal Status of Underenforced Constitutional Norms*, 91 HARV. L. REV. 1212 (1978). In fact, some major figures have urged the need for a second Bill of Rights devoted to positive rather than negative rights. In his 1944 State of the Union Address, President Franklin Roosevelt claimed that such a Bill of Rights has essentially become part of the United States' constitutional tradition:

> This Republic had its beginning, and grew to its present strength, under the protection of certain inalienable political rights—among them the right of free speech, free press, free worship, trial by jury, freedom from unreasonable searches and seizures. They were our rights to life and liberty.
>
> As our Nation has grown in size and stature, however—as our industrial economy expanded—these political rights proved inadequate to assure us equality in the pursuit of happiness.
>
> We have come to a clear realization of the fact that true individual freedom cannot exist without economic security and independence. "Necessitous men are not free men." People who are hungry and out of a job are the stuff of which dictatorships are made.
>
> In our day these economic truths have become accepted as self-evident. We have accepted, so to speak, a second Bill of Rights under which a new basis of security and prosperity can be established for all regardless of station, race, or creed.
>
> Among these are:
>
> The right to a useful and remunerative job in the industries or shops or farms or mines of the Nation;
>
> The right to earn enough to provide adequate food and clothing and recreation;
>
> The right of every farmer to raise and sell his products at a return which will give him and his family a decent living;
>
> The right of every businessman, large and small, to trade in an atmosphere of freedom from unfair competition and domination by monopolies at home or abroad;
>
> The right of every family to a decent home;
>
> The right to adequate medical care and the opportunity to achieve and enjoy good health;
>
> The right to adequate protection from the economic fears of old age, sickness, accident, and unemployment;
>
> The right to a good education.
>
> All of these rights spell security. And after this war is won we must be prepared to move forward, in the implementation of these rights, to new goals of human happiness and well-being.

What does it mean, in the legal sense, to call something a right? What does it mean, in the legal sense, to call something a constitutional right? Was President Roosevelt saying that his list of rights were constitutional rights? Did they become constitutional rights because President Roosevelt convincingly won re-election—three times—by emphasizing them?

9. James Madison initially wanted the provisions of the Bill of Rights to be added to Article I, Section 9, which prohibits Congress from doing various things. Had this been done, the Bill of Rights might arguably have applied only to Congress and not to the President and the federal courts. The decision to list the amendments at the end of the document with each new amendment marking a new ending point stresses that a constitutional amendment affects, and must be synthesized with, the entire constitutional text that precedes it. The Bill of Rights is also a more powerful document because it stands alone and was not interwoven into the text of the original Constitution.

10. You will hear much more about specific provisions in the Bill of Rights—and in the Constitution of 1787—later in this course. For now, our focus has been on abstract features of the Constitution. You may have noticed, for example, that you have not yet read a single case. That is about to change.

C. DID THE BILL OF RIGHTS ORIGINALLY BIND THE STATES?

The Bill of Rights at first bound only institutions of the federal government. It did not originally bind the States. This is understandable, given its birth in Anti-Federalist concerns about the powers of the new *national* government infringing on individual rights or the role of the state governments. It was not until long after the adoption of the Fourteenth Amendment in 1868, after the Civil War, that provisions of the Bill of Rights were made applicable to actions taken by state governments. From the end of the nineteenth century to the present day, the Supreme Court has slowly "incorporated" the Bill of Rights into the Fourteenth Amendment so that, today, almost all of the provisions in the Bill of Rights limit the States as well as the federal government. You will study that crucial process of "incorporation" later in the course.

Even before the adoption of the Fourteenth Amendment, some argued that the provisions of the Bill of Rights applied to state governments. The argument was not necessarily that the Bill of Rights literally applied to the States (though that argument is textually possible for every provision except the First Amendment), but rather that it had liquidated the content of certain natural rights, inherent in the Ancient Constitution, that bound all levels of government as a matter of first principles. That is essentially the issue presented in *Barron v. Baltimore*, decided by the U.S. Supreme Court in 1833.

Barron is the first judicial "case" in this book, and it provides a good time to think about the question of *how* to interpret and apply the Constitution. Following the case, we present an extended note on the "modalities" or methods of constitutional interpretation. As you read Chief Justice John Marshall's opinion, watch for how he uses and prioritizes arguments from (1) the words of the Constitution's *text*; (2) inferences derived from the Constitution's *structure* and the *relationship* of various provisions to one another; (3) the *historical understanding, purpose, or original intention* underlying a provision of the text; (4) prior *precedent* (if any) or consistent *practice* interpreting the provision at issue; and (5) general *policy* or pragmatic considerations. Which of these modalities properly count in constitutional interpretation? How much do they count? How do they relate to one another? If they point in different directions, which modalities are most important?

1. BARRON V. BALTIMORE

32 U.S. (7 Pet.) 243 (1833)

■ MR. CHIEF JUSTICE MARSHALL delivered the opinion of the Court.

[*Editors' Note: John Barron owned a commercial wharf in the City of Baltimore harbor. His ability to make money from that wharf was impaired by the City of Baltimore when it took actions that rendered the water near Brown's wharf too shallow for most ships. Barron sued the City in the Maryland state courts, claiming that the state and city had taken his property without just compensation, in violation of the Fifth Amendment to the U.S. Constitution, which provides, in relevant part: "nor shall private property be taken for public use, without just compensation." Barron won $4,500 in the trial court but that judgment was reversed on appeal. Barron then appealed again, to the U.S. Supreme Court.*]

* * *

The plaintiff in error contends that * * * [this case] comes within that clause in the fifth amendment to the constitution, which inhibits the taking of private property for public use, without just compensation. He insists that this amendment, being in favour of the liberty of the citizen, ought to be so construed as to restrain the legislative power of a state, as well as that of the United States. If this proposition be untrue, the court can take no jurisdiction of the cause.

The question thus presented is, we think, of great importance, but not of much difficulty.

The constitution was ordained and established by the people of the United States for themselves, for their own government, and not for the government of the individual states. Each state established a constitution for itself, and, in that constitution, provided such limitations and restrictions on the powers of its particular government as its judgment dictated. The people of the United States framed such a government for the United States as they supposed best adapted to their situation, and best calculated to promote their interests. The powers they conferred on this government were to be exercised by itself; and the limitations on power, if expressed in general terms, are naturally, and, we think, necessarily applicable to the government created by the instrument. They are limitations of power granted in the instrument itself; not of distinct governments, framed by different persons and for different purposes.

If these propositions be correct, the fifth amendment must be understood as restraining the power of the general government, not as applicable to the states * * *.

The counsel for the plaintiff in error insists that the constitution was intended to secure the people of the several states against the undue exercise of power by their respective state governments; as well as against that which might be attempted by their general government. In support of this argument he relies on the inhibitions contained in the tenth section of the first article.

We think that section affords a strong if not a conclusive argument in support of the opinion already indicated by the court.

The preceding section contains restrictions which are obviously intended for the exclusive purpose of restraining the exercise of power by the departments of the general government. Some of them use language applicable only to congress: others are expressed in general terms. The third clause, for example, declares that "no bill of attainder or ex post facto law shall be passed." No language can be more general; yet the demonstration is complete that it applies solely to the government of the United States. In addition to the general arguments furnished by the instrument itself, some of which have been already suggested, the succeeding section, the avowed purpose of which is to restrain state legislation, contains in terms the very prohibition. It declares that "no state shall pass any bill of attainder or ex post facto law." This provision, then, of the ninth section, however comprehensive its language, contains no restriction on state legislation.

The ninth section having enumerated, in the nature of a bill of rights, the limitations intended to be imposed on the powers of the general government, the tenth proceeds to enumerate those which were to operate on the state legislatures. These restrictions are brought together in the same section, and are by express words applied to the states. "No state shall enter into any treaty," &c. Perceiving that in a constitution framed by the people of the United States for the government of all, no limitation of the action of government on the people would apply to the state government, unless expressed in terms; the restrictions contained in the tenth section are in direct words so applied to the states.

It is worthy of remark, too, that these inhibitions generally restrain state legislation on subjects entrusted to the general government, or in which the people of all the states feel an interest.

A state is forbidden to enter into any treaty, alliance or confederation. If these compacts are with foreign nations, they interfere with the treaty making power which is conferred entirely on the general government; if with each other, for political purposes, they can scarcely fail to interfere with the general purpose and intent of the constitution. To grant letters of marque and reprisal, would lead directly to war; the power of declaring which is expressly given to congress. To coin money is also the exercise of a power conferred on congress. It would be tedious to recapitulate the several limitations on the powers of the states which are contained in this section. They will be found, generally, to restrain state legislation on subjects entrusted to the government of the union, in which the citizens of all the states are interested. In these alone were the whole people concerned. The question of their application to states is not left to construction. It is averred in positive words.

If the original constitution, in the ninth and tenth sections of the first article, draws this plain and marked line of discrimination between the limitations it imposes on the powers of the general government, and on those of the states; if in every inhibition intended to act on state power, words are employed which directly express that intent; some strong reason must be assigned for departing from this safe and judicious course in framing the amendments, before that departure can be assumed.

We search in vain for that reason.

Had the people of the several states, or any of them, required changes in their constitutions; had they required additional safeguards to liberty from the apprehended encroachments of their particular governments: the remedy was in their own hands, and would have been applied by themselves. A convention would have been assembled by the discontented state, and the required improvements would have been made by itself. The unwieldy and cumbrous machinery of procuring a recommendation from two-thirds of congress, and the assent of three-fourths of their sister states, could never have occurred to any human being as a mode of doing that which might be effected by the state itself. Had the framers of these amendments intended them to be limitations on the powers of the state governments, they would have imitated the framers of the original constitution, and have expressed that intention. Had congress engaged in the extraordinary occupation of improving the constitutions of the several states by affording the people additional protection from the exercise of power by their own governments in matters which concerned themselves alone, they would have declared this purpose in plain and intelligible language.

But it is universally understood, it is a part of the history of the day, that the great revolution which established the constitution of the United States, was not effected without immense opposition. Serious fears were extensively entertained that those powers which the patriot statesmen, who then watched over the interests of our country, deemed essential to union, and to the attainment of those invaluable objects for which union was sought, might be exercised in a manner dangerous to liberty. In almost every convention by which the constitution was adopted, amendments to guard against the abuse of power were recommended. These amendments demanded security against the apprehended encroachments of the general government—not against those of the local governments.

In compliance with a sentiment thus generally expressed, to quiet fears thus extensively entertained, amendments were proposed by the required majority in congress, and adopted by the states. These amendments contain no expression indicating an intention to apply them to the state governments. This court cannot so apply them.

We are of opinion that the provision in the fifth amendment to the constitution, declaring that private property shall not be taken for public use without just compensation, is intended solely as a limitation on the exercise of power by the government of the United States, and is not applicable to the legislation of the states. We are therefore of opinion that there is no repugnancy between the several acts of the general assembly of Maryland, given in evidence by the defendants at the trial of this cause, in the court of that state, and the constitution of the United States * * *.

* * *

NOTES AND QUESTIONS

1. *The "Modalities" of Constitutional Interpretation*: How should one go about the task of interpreting the Constitution? What method(s) should the various units of government, including the courts, use in construing and carrying out the Constitution? Are different methods appropriate for different units of government? Are "construing" and "carrying out" the Constitution distinct tasks that call for distinct, and possibly varying, methods? These are recurring themes of this casebook. Even a minimally adequate treatment of those themes would require a course in itself; interpretative theory is a major subject of debate, within and without the academy. We aim here only to identify

the principal fault lines that have shown up in more than two centuries of American constitutional law.

Throughout this course (and the rest of your legal life), you will persistently encounter at least six main types of constitutional arguments, each of which is the locus of a great many sub-debates about how those types of arguments function. We do not suggest that every argument that one encounters or can make must slot into one of these categories. But as an empirical matter, most arguments that one will encounter or make will likely do so. The classic treatment of these so-called "modalities" of constitutional interpretation is PHILIP BOBBITT, CONSTITUTIONAL INTERPRETATION (1991), and we adapt our list from his seminal categorization of argument forms.

First, we will encounter arguments based on the *text* of the Constitution. That seems simple, and even simplistic. The Constitution is a written legal instrument, so of course the text matters. But what is actually meant by "the text"? If you look only at the bare words of the Fifth Amendment, they say nothing about which levels of government must abide by them. Does that mean that there is a strong "textual" argument for Barron's position that Maryland was bound by the Takings Clause? On that reasoning, does the Fifth Amendment's Takings Clause also purport to bind the governments of, say, Norway and Argentina? Does it purport to bind private actors and thus render common theft unconstitutional? And when Article II vests "[t]he executive Power," with no explicit "textual" qualification, in the President, does that grant include the "executive Power" of Virginia and Wyoming (and Norway and Argentina) and not just the "executive Power" of the United States federal government? Chief Justice Marshall thought it clear that the Constitution refers only to the federal government unless the document expressly says otherwise. But that point is not clear just from the bare words of the "text," divorced from some fairly complex assumptions about what that "text" actually is and is trying to accomplish as an act of communication. Any text only has meaning when it is understood in *context*, against a whole set of background understandings about language, assumed states of affairs, and probable communicative intentions. So "textual" arguments are really *contextual* arguments, and the real work comes when you try to fix the appropriate context.

Importantly, the appropriate context depends very much on what kind of text you are dealing with.

> One approaches interpretation of a poem very differently from interpretation of a spouse's shopping list * * * or a power of attorney granting another person authority over one's health care or financial decisions.
>
> If one is interpreting a poem, for example, one will presumably not be hyper-focused on the literal, semantic meaning of the sentences (or sentence fragments) in the poem. One will likely be on the lookout for metaphors, similes, exaggerations, sarcasm, irony, and a host of other literary devices that typically are employed in poems. Of course, in any particular instance, one might fail to find any such devices. Perhaps a straightforward semantic interpretation is precisely what the author of a poem had in mind. The point is only that if one knows that one is reading a poem, that knowledge triggers certain expectations about the way in which language is likely to be used * * *.
>
> If the document is a shopping list from one's spouse, interpretation guided by metaphor or irony is likely to lead to trouble. "Yes, the list said 'four apples,' but since apples are associated with sin, I bought four boxes of double-stuffed Oreos instead." Again, perhaps there are individual cases in which * * * the spouse intends that the shopping list be the occasion for a culinary adventure

> and just wants to see what you will bring back. But over a wide range of cases, the background assumptions that one might bring to interpretation of a poem will not suit the interpretation of a shopping list * * *.
>
> * * *
>
> If one is reading a power of attorney, one would likely approach the process * * * with attention directed to the possibility of encountering technical terms of art keyed to the subject matter. One does not expect instructions on end-of-life decisions or investments of life savings to be written using metaphor or irony or to contain private codes, but one does expect to encounter a fair amount of "legalese," including terms that might be accessible only to someone with advanced training in the law * * *. Those assumptions do not guarantee interpretative success, but they are the tools that a capable and honest interpreter is likely to bring to the job.

GARY LAWSON & GUY SEIDMAN, "A GREAT POWER OF ATTORNEY": UNDERSTANDING THE FIDUCIARY CONSTITUTION 9–10 (2017). What kind of instrument is the Constitution? How does that characterization affect how one should understand the "text" of the document? Those questions will come up repeatedly in this course.

The Constitution of the United States is obviously a legal instrument of some kind. Normally, legal instruments are addressed to a wide public, because a wide public will normally need to know what those instruments, as part of the larger network of legal rights and obligations, say. That is why textual arguments in law ordinarily (though not exclusively) refer to the *public meaning* of the text rather than to a private meaning that might be held only by a few people involved in producing the legal text.

Because all documents are forms of communication, and all communication is ultimately grounded in communicative intentions (otherwise it is random symbols or sounds and not communication at all), any kind of meaning, including public meaning, has to refer to some kind of communication intentions. When Chief Justice Marshall ended the opinion in *Barron* by saying that the Takings Clause "is intended solely as a limitation on the exercise of power by the government of the United States," who does he think "intended" that result? The people who actually wrote the words of the Constitution, meaning the Constitutional Convention (or perhaps even just the five distinguished Framers on the Committee of Detail who did most of the drafting)? The people whose actions gave the document legal effect, meaning the people at the various state ratifying conventions? The people who gave the document practical effect by not starting another revolution in 1788? Or is the "intention" of a document something entirely separate from the actual thoughts inside the heads of any specific people? The "reasonable person" that you encounter in your Torts class is not any specific person; it is a hypothetical legal construct. But that legal construct is capable of providing grounds for decision in countless cases. Similarly, the "intending" agent for purposes of understanding the Constitution might also be a hypothetical legal construct, so that the "public meaning" of the document is not ascertained by counting up in some fashion what actual people thought but instead by ascertaining what a hypothetical reasonable person thinks or would have thought. Isn't that pretty clearly what Chief Justice Marshall was doing in *Barron* when he talked about what the Constitution "intended"? Indeed, if the meaning of the constitutional text is found inside the heads of actual historical figures, wouldn't that mean that historians, psychologists, and linguists rather than lawyers are the right people to be interpreting the Constitution? *See* Gary Lawson & Guy Seidman, *Originalism as a Legal Enterprise*, 23 CONST. COMMENTARY 47 (2006).

Even a focus on an objective public meaning grounded in the hypothetical thoughts of a reasonable person, however, does not fully tell you what a "textual" argument must look like. Language often changes meaning over time; the word "liberty," for example, may mean one thing to a reasonable public observer in 1787 and something quite different to a reasonable public observer in 2020. When interpreting a text, does one look for the public meaning *when the text was promulgated* or *when the text is interpreted*—keeping in mind that centuries can separate those two times? In other words, textual arguments can be based on the original public meaning of the constitutional text at the time when it was adopted or on the public meaning the text seems to have today (understanding that "today" is a moving target).

And all of this assumes that we have correctly identified the language in which the text was written. The word "gift" means one thing in English and quite a different thing in German. But of course the Constitution is written in English, isn't it? Yes, but English, as with many languages, has dialects and variants. The Constitution contains many words that are part of any English variant, but it also contains some technical terms that would not be part of the vocabulary of most people. As a result, one can say (though professional linguists might well dispute this) that the Constitution is written in a particular variant of English that one might call "legal English." *See* John O. McGinnis & Michael B. Rappaport, *The Constitution and the Language of the Law*, 59 WM. & MARY L. REV. 1321 (2018). The way that one reads a text naturally depends on the language in which one reads it. Does that mean that to be a good constitutional interpreter, you must be fluent not only in English but in "legal English"?

This note could go on for much longer and could easily turn into a technical discourse on the philosophy of language. We don't want that (though it would not necessarily be the worst thing for law students to grapple with). The point is only that when you see or think of something that looks to be a "textual" argument, there are a *lot* of quite complex issues lurking behind even the seemingly simplest such argument. Unsurprisingly, courts and other legal actors do not always, or even often, identify or recognize those issues. The assumptions behind textual arguments often need to be excavated.

Second, in addition to textual arguments, we will also encounter arguments based on the *structure* or *internal logic* of the document. At their best, such arguments are a sophisticated form of textual argument that attempts to draw sound inferences from the usages of identical or similar words across constitutional provisions, the presence or absence of particular words across provisions, the relationship of provisions to each other, their location and context within the constitutional text, and the structures of government necessarily framed by the document as a whole. The first two kinds of arguments are sometimes call *intratextual* arguments, *see* Akhil Reed Amar, *Intratextualism*, 112 HARV. L. REV. 747 (1999), while the other kinds are often called arguments from *structure and relation. See* CHARLES L. BLACK, STRUCTURE AND RELATIONSHIP IN CONSTITUTIONAL LAW (1968); Steven G. Calabresi, *The Vesting Clauses as Power Grants*, 88 NW. U.L. REV.1377 (1993). At their worst, structural arguments can try to "connect the dots" of a mass of constitutional provisions, whose dots do not actually connect very much, in order to derive some overarching principle that can yield results far removed from anything fairly derivable from the text. Suppose, for example, that Barron had argued, "Article I, section 10 forbids States from impairing the obligation of contracts and printing paper money. Those provisions are obviously designed to protect property rights from action by States. Therefore, the Constitution contains a general principle that forbids States from abridging property rights in any respect, so I win." Would that be a good argument?

Third, we will frequently encounter arguments from *"original intent"* or *"history"* or, in a slightly different formulation, about the perceived *"purpose"* or *"function"* of a provision. These kinds of arguments can be made in conjunction with, instead of, or even in opposition to directly "textual" arguments. *"Purposivist"* or *"functional"* arguments look for evidence of either specific historical or general philosophical *intentions* or *purposes* underlying a provision, as evidenced by statements of its drafters or ratifiers (or occasionally opponents). Persons making such arguments thus often cite *The Federalist* or statements made in the records of the debates at the Philadelphia Constitutional Convention or the subsequent State ratification processes. If one thinks about how American colonial or English history might bear on understanding the Constitution, is one making this kind of argument? If one is looking for the intentions or purposes of actual, concrete historical actors, which actors' intentions should one look at? In the case of the Constitution, should one look to the intentions of its drafters? (Does that mean the Constitutional Convention that guided the document's direction or the five-person Committee of Detail that actually wrote most of the document's words?) Or should one look to the intentions of the ratifiers who made the Constitution law in form? Or should one instead look to the intentions of the broad (and armed) general public, whose acquiescence in the Constitution made it law in fact?

Fourth, we will encounter arguments based on *precedent* or *practice*—that is, past judicial (or other governmental) interpretations, where those interpretations have become sufficiently settled essentially to "fix" the meaning of constitutional provisions that otherwise might be thought ambiguous or unclear. There is a good case that we should have put this set of arguments first in our list, as a very high percentage of constitutional (and statutory) cases do not really focus on the text or purposes of the Constitution (or statutes) at all but are concerned almost entirely with figuring out the meaning and implications of prior constitutional decisions, usually (but not always) meaning Supreme Court decisions. In other words, constitutional law is often about interpreting the texts and purposes of Supreme Court opinions far more than it is about interpreting the text and purposes of the Constitution. The standard argument for precedent claims that it promotes certainty and stability in the law and that the costs of overruling precedent and upsetting settled expectations will often exceed the benefits of deciding an issue the right way. *See* RANDY J. KOZEL, SETTLED VERSUS RIGHT: A THEORY OF PRECEDENT (2017). What if either of the democratically elected departments of the national government—the President or Congress—disagrees with the federal courts' pragmatic cost-benefit analysis on whether to follow a precedent? The Supreme Court has consistently said that the practice of adhering to precedent—the doctrine of "*stare decisis*"—is a rule of policy and not one of constitutional law. Are the President and Congress better situated institutionally to assess policy costs and benefits than are life-tenured judges? *See* Steven G. Calabresi, *Text, Precedent, and the Constitution: Some Originalist and Normative Arguments for Overruling* Planned Parenthood of Southeastern Pennsylvania v. Casey, 22 CONST. COMMENTARY 1044 (2005). Is the Burkean "tradition" in the United States one of exalting the original meaning of the text of the Constitution over all else? If so, American Burkeans should all be originalists. Steven G. Calabresi, *The Tradition of the Written Constitution: Text, Precedent, and Burke*, 57 ALA. L. REV. 635 (2006). Indeed, if the doctrine of *stare decisis* is merely a matter of policy and practice, should a court *ever* follow precedent when otherwise persuaded that the correct interpretation of the Constitution dictates a result contrary to precedent? *See* Gary Lawson, *The Constitutional Case Against Precedent,* 17 HARV. J. L. & PUB. POL'Y 23 (1994); Gary Lawson, *Mostly Unconstitutional: The Case Against Precedent Revisited,* 5 AVE MARIA L. REV. 1 (2007). One (but only one) modern Supreme Court Justice has openly called for abandonment of all but some very modest uses of precedent in constitutional cases. *See Gamble v. United States*, 139 S.Ct. 1960, 1982 (2019) (Thomas, J., concurring); *infra* pages 1100–1103.

Fifth, we will encounter arguments based on *policy, natural law* or *pragmatic considerations*. In such cases, interpreters ask what interpretation produces the "better" or "best" results from the standpoint of social policy or specific notions of justice. *See* STEPHEN BREYER, ACTIVE LIBERTY: INTERPRETING OUR DEMOCRATIC CONSTITUTION (2006). Sometimes it is possible to synthesize arguments from policy and practice, perhaps using practice as the baseline but then interpreting that practice in light of views of morality or policy. *See,* e.g., JAMES E. FLEMING, FIDELITY TO OUR IMPERFECT CONSTITUTION: FOR MORAL READINGS AND AGAINST ORIGINALISMS (2015). Are these kinds of arguments "legal" arguments? What makes an argument "legal"? Does the Constitution encourage, or even mandate, this kind of argument by saying in the Preamble that one of the aims of the Constitution is to "establish Justice"?

Sixth, and finally, we will encounter arguments that the courts should engage in "judicial restraint" and that they ought to defer to the democratic branches of the government unless their actions are irrational and a clear mistake. These are not really arguments about how to interpret a text; they are arguments about how courts should resolve cases.  But because courts resolve cases by pronouncing on the meanings of texts, arguments of this sort feed back into the interpretative process, so that interpretations that would be deemed "correct" using, for example, textual and structural arguments are deemed "incorrect" if they lead to the conclusion that a law is unconstitutional (unless that conclusion is absolutely inescapable). This approach of strong judicial deference to legislative and executive acts is most famously associated with James Bradley Thayer, *The Origin and Scope of the American Doctrine of Constitutional Law,* 7 HARV. L. REV. 129 (1893), who said that courts "can only disregard the Act when those who have the right to make laws have not merely made a mistake, but have made a very clear one,—so clear that it is not open to rational question," *id.* at 144, and that a rule of clear mistake "recognizes that, having regard to the great, complex, ever-unfolding exigencies of government, much which will seem unconstitutional to one man, or body of men, may reasonably not seem so to another; that the constitution often admits of different interpretations; that there is often a range of choice and judgment; that in such cases the constitution does not impose upon the legislature any one specific opinion, but leaves open this range of choice; and that whatever choice is rational is constitutional." *Id.* Thayer thought that this rule was both desirable and a descriptively accurate account of court practice in actual cases. As you will see throughout this course, courts from the founding era forward have often said—though have not necessarily acted as though they said—that democratically enacted laws come to court with a "presumption of constitutionality." Is any such presumption derivable from textual arguments? From any of the other kinds of arguments described above? Is it a desirable approach for a scheme of judicial review? For critical accounts of Thayer's rule of clear mistake, see Steven G. Calabresi, *Originalism and James Bradley Thayer,* 113 NW. U.L. REV. 1419 (2019); Gary Lawson & Christopher D. Moore, *The Executive Power of Constitutional Interpretation,* 81 IOWA L. REV. 1267, 1274–79 (1996): Gary Lawson, *Thayer Versus Marshall,* 88 NW. U.L. REV. 221 (1993). And if Thayer is simply prescribing a role for courts, what does that mean for constitutional interpretation performed by non-court actors, such as executives and legislators?

If this all seems like a lot to digest before one even begins to dig into constitutional doctrine, take a deep breath, because the "modalities" of interpretation are just the tip of the interpretative iceberg. The first five modalities involve determining *what counts* when ascertaining constitutional meaning. In a sense, those modalities and other methods of interpretation establish what is "admissible" for determining constitutional meaning (though we do not normally use formalized rules of evidence or formal procedures of proof when deciding questions of legal meaning.) Once you know what counts, or what is "admissible" as evidence of meaning, you also need to know *how much* it counts. Even after you have settled on which modalities are useable in which circumstances, you need to know how to weigh the results from application of those modalities if they point in different directions. (If everything points in the same direction, you have an easy case.) People can agree on which of the modalities to use but disagree on how to prioritize them.

And to make matters even more complicated, the sixth modality that we identified above—the presumption of constitutionality or rule of clear mistake—is a different creature altogether. It concerns, not what counts towards constitutional meaning or how much it counts, but *how much of whatever you choose to count* you need in order to reach a particular result. The presumption of constitutionality, in the abstract, is agnostic about how you apply the other modalities to determine constitutional meaning. It concerns the *standard of proof* (very high) and the *burden of proof* (on the person challenging government action) for claims about meaning rather than the *principles of admissibility (or relevance)* or the *principles of significance (or weight)* of an interpretative theory, just like the "beyond a reasonable doubt" standard for criminal convictions concerns *how much* evidence the prosecution must produce rather than *what kind of evidence is admissible*.

Thus, whenever you approach an interpretative question, you need to consider (1) what counts towards establishing meaning, (2) how much it counts, (3) how much of whatever counts you need to find in order to reach a conclusion, (4) what happens when your best answer is "I don't know," and (5) when to stop looking for more evidence and just make the best decision you can with the information you have. *See* GARY LAWSON, EVIDENCE OF THE LAW: PROVING LEGAL CLAIMS (2017). Legal decision-makers (and legal scholars) almost never break down their reasoning process into these component parts—or even necessarily recognize that all of these component parts are present. So one tricky task in the law is to figure out when people are arguing about what counts, when they are arguing about how much it counts, when they are arguing about who has the burden of proof, when they are arguing about how heavy that burden should be, and/or when they are arguing about whether people have looked hard enough for evidence to meet that burden.

One more point to ponder: When you are thinking about constitutional theory, are you asking how to *interpret the Constitution* or how to *decide constitutional cases*? If you think that this is a silly question, because of course constitutional cases should be decided in light of constitutional meaning, think again. Questions about how to *interpret* the Constitution involve the ascertainment of a text's meaning. Questions about how to decide a case involve real-world action in real time, in a world of limited resources. What if to decide a case "correctly," using whatever mode of ascertainment of meaning you think is "correct," would take years of careful research? Should the court hold the case until it gets the perfect answer? Or should it decide the case, perhaps using rough "rules of thumb" that everyone knows will probably not be the ideally perfect answer but which allow the court to move on to the next case? In other words, to what extent should constitutional *decisionmaking* be driven by constitutional *meaning,* even after you have figured out how to ascertain constitutional meaning? Is that a "legal" question or a "moral" question? If the latter, do you think law school is likely to help you answer it?

If all of this seems overly abstract and far removed from what you thought a course in Constitutional Law would be about, we ask for patience. As you get into the doctrine, ask yourself which modalities, and which of the five aspects of proving legal claims, are in play in any dispute. Most of the time, the cases will not tell you and you will have to tease out on your own (hopefully with some help from us and/or your professor) what is going on.

2. *An Overview of Marshall's Interpretive Method in Barron v. Baltimore.* With all of the foregoing in mind: What was Chief Justice Marshall's interpretive method in *Barron v. Baltimore*? Which of the modalities of interpretation listed above does Chief Justice Marshall use? Interestingly, Marshall begins by stating Barron's argument that the Takings Clause of the Fifth Amendment, "being in favour of the liberty of the citizen, ought to be so construed as to restrain the legislative power of a state, as well as that of the United States." Marshall never specifically addresses this argument, which hearkens back to arguments invoking the "Ancient Constitution." Does Marshall regard the argument as inadmissible? As admissible but of little weight? As getting wrong the proper assignment of the burden of proof for claims of unconstitutionality? Does the Constitution contain, as Barron evidently claimed, a generalized "presumption of liberty" good against all governments, state and federal? *See* RANDY E. BARNETT, RESTORING THE LOST CONSTITUTION: THE PRESUMPTION OF LIBERTY (2004).

Nor, as we indicated earlier, does Marshall start with the unadorned language of the Takings Clause itself, which does not say on its face whether it applies only to the federal government or also to the States. The exact words of the text are: "Nor shall private property be taken for public use, without just compensation." The clause itself is written in the passive voice—"shall be taken" (by whom?)—a writing style often frowned upon by legal writing instructors precisely because it can create ambiguity.

Instead, Marshall begins with the first principles of the enactment of the Constitution itself (as he understands them): The Constitution was established by the people of the United States for the government of the United States as a whole, and not for the government of the individual States. The powers the Constitution confers are conferred on this government of the nation; and the limitations on those powers, where expressed in general terms, are naturally understood to be limits imposed on the government of the nation, not of the States. In a sense, this is an argument from the Constitution's *text,* but in the enlarged sense of seeking to ascertain the meaning of the words within the larger context of the document as a whole. One might just as readily characterize the argument as one from the Constitution's *structure* or *purpose*—an enlarged (and somewhat less definite) type of textual argument.

Next, Marshall turns one of Barron's arguments around on him—and this becomes a specific and highly sophisticated *textual* (and *intratextual*) argument. Barron had said (in effect): "look here, the Constitution *sometimes does* limit state governments; look at Article I, Section 10." Marshall responds by pointing out the differences in wording between Article I, Section 9 and Article I, Section 10. Section 9 limits the powers of the national government; it is a miniature bill of rights in the original constitution. Several times, its prohibitions are stated in general terms. But each time, they limit the power of only the national government. Marshall points out that some of the same limitations are repeated in Article I, Section 10, as limitations on the powers of the States. *But whenever the limitations are meant to apply to the States, the Constitution says so specifically,* by using the "*No State shall . . .*" language of Article I, Section 10. If you re-read Article I, Sections 9 and 10, you will see what Marshall is talking about.

Note how, in making this (intra)textual argument, Marshall does not read the words of the Fifth Amendment in isolation, but takes into account their linguistic and structural relationship to other provisions of the Constitution. He reads the words *holistically,* in the context of the overall structure of the document. The textual argument is ingenious and insightful. It is not (quite) "literal"—because Article I, Section 9 does not in terms *say* that it applies only to the national government—but it is a serious textual argument about the meaning of the words of the document and *how they function within the overall text and structure* of the Constitution.

Marshall also turns to evidence of *history and intent* to buttress his textual and structural arguments. It is "part of the history of the day," well understood by all, he relates, that the immediate intentions of the Framers of the Bill of Rights was to limit the power of the *national* government, *not* that of the States. This is true, but why should we give any weight to what a lawmaker "intends" or to "the history of the day" as opposed to what the laws "say." Isn't the law the enacted text rather than the (perhaps conflicting) intentions of the many people who wrote and ratified it? And the Bill of Rights was ratified more than forty years—essentially two generations—before the decision in *Barron*. Why should the present be bound by not only the laws of people who are dead and gone but also by their unenacted opinions and intentions? Group intent is a notoriously slippery concept—as the criminal law governing conspiracy shows—so in what sense is it even meaningful to talk about the intentions of the Framers? Could we say that the Framers of the original Constitution showed an intent that we look only at the words of the text and not at their intent when they voted to keep the debates at Philadelphia in 1787 secret until after James Madison's death in 1836? *See* H. Jefferson Powell, *The Original Understanding of Original Intent,*98 HARV. L. REV. 885 (1985).

Largely absent from *Barron* is any argument from *precedent*. There are no arguments from case law in *Barron* because it appears to have presented a question of first impression in 1833. Of course, the mere fact that no one tried to argue that the Bill of Rights bound the States during the first forty-two years of its existence strongly suggests that it did not do so as a matter of longstanding practice. For this reason, Chief Justice Marshall does discuss whether applying the Bill of Rights to the States would be a bigger change in practice to people's expectations than holding that it applies only to the federal government.

In general, to what extent does consistent *practice* change (or "settle," or "liquidate") the meaning of the text of the Constitution? Does *longstanding practice* by executives and/or legislatures under the Constitution have any different status than *judicial precedent* as prior constitutional interpretation? Is there a difference between a very recent 5–4 Supreme Court decision and a view that has been widely held for a long time, and on which many institutions have been constructed, such as the belief held by virtually all Americans and all three departments of our national government since 1884 that the federal government has the power to print paper money in peacetime?

What if the practice in question fills out the meaning of an "open-ended" concept like the scope of the President's "executive power" or the meaning of the "case" or "controversy" limitation on the jurisdiction of the federal courts? Is practice more valuable in structural constitutional cases—cases addressing the scope of the separation of powers and federalism—than in determining the extent of the Constitution's protection of individual rights? Or may practice just as properly establish, or settle, the meaning of open-ended "rights" provisions like the Fourteenth Amendment guarantee of the "equal protection of the laws"? (Careful: It was long considered "settled" that the Equal Protection Clause permitted racial segregation by law.)

The proper role of *practice and precedent* in constitutional interpretation is a recurrent theme of this book.

Chief Justice Marshall in *Barron* also makes a policy argument. It would be cumbersome, Marshall says, to have state officials bound by the federal Bill of Rights because the whole country would have to agree pursuant to Article V if a State changed its mind about wanting to be bound by a right. How much simpler, Marshall said, to let each State be bound only by its own bill of rights. Such a system encourages the States to compete and experiment with one another to produce optimal levels and kinds of protections for liberty. (As we shall see, Chief Justice Marshall's policy argument in *Barron* has not been widely accepted. The conventional wisdom in constitutional law is that fundamental rights must be uniformly protected all over the country.) Ought the Supreme Court to pay any attention to policy considerations of this kind? Judges are unelected and life tenured, and they have only limited abilities to gather and systematically evaluate information. Moreover, the Supreme Court can change course only when private litigants bring an issue before them. Is this particular institution well suited to being a pragmatic policy-maker? Should real pragmatists want the federal courts to stay far away from this kind of decision-making?

What about the proposition that the federal courts should apply *natural law*? *Barron v. Baltimore* was rendered in the 1830s when John Austin's theories of legal positivism—the notion that law is a social fact independent of moral considerations—were in full sway. Half a century earlier, in the 1770s and 1780s, when the eleven States which wrote their new constitutions added "Declarations of Rights" to them, the standard assumption was that the declarations of rights did not themselves create the rights in question, but were "declaratory" of pre-existing natural rights. Even before the Civil War, there were so-called *Barron* contrarians" who thought that, while the Taking Clause did not literally apply to Maryland, it did not need to do so because it was simply *declaratory* of a great natural right which bound the government of Maryland along with all other governments. *See infra* page 1552. Did Chief Justice Marshall respond at all to this argument?

The problem with natural-law constitutional arguments, even for many people who believe in some form of natural law, is that there are as many different versions of natural law as there are people. One is tempted to ask how judges are supposed to choose as between the Catholic natural law of St. Thomas Aquinas, the teachings of Martin Luther and John Calvin, the Islamic Sharia, and the beliefs as to natural law of Orthodox Judaism. What about the proposition that the courts should apply and enforce the Deistic secular natural law of the Enlightenment (or the atheistic natural law of Ayn Rand)? Does that present essentially the same problem? If rights—including what many might consider "natural rights"—appear in the text of the Constitution (or have been recognized as embraced by the texts as part of a body of rights established by long-standing, uncontroverted practice), then there is a textual basis for arguing that they may be enforced as part of the law of the Constitution. But if the text does *not* embrace such a right, is there any warrant for displacing democratically enacted laws and official actions because they violate judges' notions of natural law—especially when the "natural law" thus discovered tends to be suspiciously similar to what judges think amounts to good public policy? Are Supreme Court Justices more skilled in discerning natural law moral truths than the mass of citizens in our American democracy? Do you think that your training as a lawyer is giving you unique insight into the contents of natural law?

3. *Final Thoughts on Barron v. Baltimore.* Was Chief Justice Marshall correct in concluding that the provisions of the Bill of Rights (including the Takings Clause of the Fifth Amendment), did not limit the actions of state governments? Were his interpretive methodological choices and moves the right ones? Which moves would you make? Would you write an opinion in *Barron* that looked significantly different from Marshall's?

[Assignment 4]

IV. REASONS FOR HAVING A WRITTEN CONSTITUTION—AND THE NATURE OF THE U.S. CONSTITUTION

Now that you have seen the U.S. Constitution, it is time to ask some basic questions about the enterprise of constitutionalism. What is the purpose or purposes of having a constitution at all? If a constitution is desirable, should it be written or unwritten? If a written constitution is adopted, should it be a short one or a long and detailed document? What consequences might follow from adopting a written constitution? How long should a constitution last before it is replaced? How easy should it be to change the constitution? Why have a written constitution that sometimes stifles (at least for a time) majoritarian choices in a democracy or a republic where the underlying norm is one of majority rule?

Keep in mind that "constitutionalism" is not necessarily synonymous with democracy, republicanism, or any other governmental form. A written constitution could, in theory, vest all governmental power in: 1) a president, a monarch, or a dictator, 2) an aristocracy, an oligarchy, or life-tenured judges, 3) representatives, or 4) a direct democracy of initiatives and referenda or a system of mob rule. Or it could combine these forms in any way imaginable. England, for example, was a constitutional monarchy from 1689 until the writing of the U.S. Constitution, but it could not plausibly be called a constitutional democracy until at least after the nineteenth-century suffrage reforms of 1832 and 1867, and arguably not until the elimination of the House of Lords' absolute veto over legislation, which did not occur until 1911. Constitutional government is thus limited government (what would be the point of a constitution that simply says "anything goes"?), but it is not necessarily democratic or republican government. The American Constitution is republican, but that is a product of the unique historical forces that we have discussed thus far.

The following readings discuss the nature and purposes of constitutionalism, at an abstract level, from an American perspective and thus sometimes discuss both constitutionalism and republicanism without distinguishing the two ideas. Try to see when the authors are talking about constitutionalism as such and when they are talking about distinctively *republican* constitutionalism. Also, reflect back on the Declaration of Independence and the U.S. Constitution as you read these materials. Ask yourselves what each of those documents presupposes about the nature and purposes of constitutionalism. The centrality of the consent of the governed is a key theme, but the overarching purpose of American constitutionalism is found in the bedrock principle that "We hold these truths to be self-evident, that all men are created equal, that they are endowed by their Creator with certain unalienable Rights, that among these are Life, Liberty and the pursuit of Happiness." How successful was America's first constitution, the Articles of Confederation, in reflecting the consent of the governed or in securing equality, life, liberty, or the pursuit of happiness? Does the U.S. Constitution do a better job? Are these even the right questions to ask about whether or not to have a constitution?

A. JOHN ADAMS, THOUGHTS ON GOVERNMENT

(1776)

My Dear Sir,—If I was equal to the task of forming a plan for the government of a colony, I should be very flattered with your request, and very happy to comply with it; because, as the divine science of politics is the science of social happiness, and as the blessings of society depend entirely on the constitutions of government, which are generally institutions that last for many generations, there can be no employment more agreeable to a benevolent mind than a research after the best.

Pope flattered tyrants too much when he said,

"For forms of government let fools contest, That which is best administered is best."

Nothing can be more fallacious than this. But poets read history to collect flowers, not fruits; they attend to fanciful images, not the effects of social institutions. Nothing is more certain, from the history of nations and nature of man, than that some forms of government are better fitted for being well administered than others.

We ought to consider what is the end of government, before we determine which is the best form. Upon this point all speculative politicians will agree, that the happiness of society is the end of government, as all divines will agree that the happiness of the individual is the end of man. From this principle it will follow, that the form of government which communicates ease, comfort, security, or, in one word, happiness, to the greatest number of persons, and in the greatest degree, is the best.

All sober inquiries after truth, ancient and modern, pagan and Christian, have declared that the happiness of man, as well as his dignity, consists in virtue. Confucius, Zoroaster, Socrates, Mahomet, not to mention authorities really sacred, have agreed in this.

If there is a form of government then, whose principle and foundation is virtue, will not every sober man acknowledge it better calculated to promote the general happiness than any other form?

Fear is the foundation of most governments; but it is so sordid and brutal a passion, and renders men in whose breasts it predominates so stupid and miserable, that Americans will not be likely to approve of any political institutions which is founded on it.

Honor is truly sacred, but holds a lower rank in the scale of moral excellence than virtue. Indeed, the former is but a part of the latter, and consequently has not equal pretensions to support a frame of government productive of human happiness. The foundation of every government is some principle or passion in the minds of the people. The noblest principles and most generous affections in our nature, then, have the fairest chance to support the noblest and most generous models of government.

* * * [T]here is no good government but what is republican * * *. [T]he very definition of a republic is "an empire of laws, and not of men." * * * [A]s a republic is the best of governments, so that particular arrangement of the powers of society, or, in other words, that form of government which is best contrived to secure an exact and impartial execution of the laws, is the best of republics.

Of republics there is an inexhaustible variety, because the possible combinations of the powers of society are capable of innumerable variations.

As good government is an empire of laws, how shall your laws be made? In a large society, inhabiting an extensive country, it is impossible that the whole should assemble to make laws. The first necessary step, then, is to depute power from the many to a few of the most wise and good. But by what rules shall you choose your representatives? Agree upon the number and qualifications of persons who shall have the benefit of choosing, or annex the privilege to the inhabitants of a certain extent of ground.

The principle difficulty lies, and the greatest care should be employed in constituting this representative assembly. It should be in miniature an exact portrait of the people at large. It should think, reason, and act like them. That it may be the interest of this assembly to do strict justice at all times, it should be an equal representation, or, in other words, equal interests among the people should have equal interests in it * * *.

A representation of the people in one assembly being obtained, a question arises, whether all the powers of government, legislative, executive, and judicial, shall be left in this body? I think a people cannot be long free, nor ever happy, whose government is in one assembly. My reasons for this opinion are as follow:—

1. A single assembly is liable to all the vices, follies, and frailties of an individual; subject to fits of humor, starts of passion, flights of enthusiasm, partialities, or prejudice, and consequently productive of hasty results and absurd judgments. And all these errors ought to be corrected and defects supplied by some controlling power.

2. A single assembly is apt to be avaricious, and in time will not scruple to exempt itself from burdens, which it will lay, without compunction, on its constituents.

3. A single assembly is apt to grow ambitious, and after a time will not hesitate to vote itself perpetual. This was one fault of the Long Parliament; but more remarkably of Holland, whose assembly first voted themselves from annual to septennial, then for life, and after a course of years, that all vacancies happening by death or otherwise, should be filled by themselves, without any application to constituents at all.

4. A representative assembly, although extremely well qualified, and absolutely necessary, as a branch of the legislative, is unfit to exercise the executive power for want of two essential properties, secrecy and dispatch.

5. A representative assembly is still less qualified for the judicial power, because it is too numerous, too slow, and too little skilled in the laws.

6. Because a single assembly, possessed of all the powers of government, would make arbitrary laws for their own interest, execute all laws arbitrarily for their own interest, and adjudge all controversies in their own favor.

[John Adams concludes by recommending a separation of the legislative, executive, and judicial functions into independent departments and by insisting that the legislature had to be bicameral—contrary to the teaching of Condorcet, the philosophes in France, and the practice of Pennsylvania and Georgia, which initially adopted unicameral assemblies. John Adams' advice carried the day in New Hampshire, Massachusetts, Rhode Island, Connecticut, New York, New Jersey, Maryland, Delaware, Virginia, and North and South Carolina. After Adams' views

formed the mainstay of the U.S. Constitution, Pennsylvania and Georgia switched to the federal model of having a bicameral legislature.]

B. LETTER FROM THOMAS JEFFERSON TO JAMES MADISON

6 Sept. 1789, 15 THE PAPERS OF THOMAS JEFFERSON 392–99 (Julian P. Boyd ed., 1958)

I sit down to write to you without knowing by what occasion I shall send my letter. I do it because a subject comes into my head which I would wish to develop a little more than is practicable in the hurry of the moment of making up general dispatches.

The question Whether one generation of men has a right to bind another, seems never to have been started either on this or our side of the water. Yet it is a question of such consequences as not only to merit decision, but place also, among the fundamental principles of every government. The course of reflection in which we are immersed here on the elementary principles of society has presented this question to my mind; and that no such obligation can be so transmitted I think very capable of proof.—I set out on this ground, which I suppose to be self evident, *"that the earth belongs in usufruct to the living"*: that the dead have neither powers nor rights over it. The portion occupied by an individual ceases to be his when himself ceases to be, and reverts to the society. If the society has formed no rules for the appropriation of its lands in severality, it will be taken by the first occupants. These will generally be the wife and children of the decedent. * * *

On similar ground it may be proved that no society can make a perpetual constitution, or even a perpetual law. The earth belongs to the living generation. They may manage it then, and what proceeds from it, as they please, during their usufruct. They are masters too of their own persons, and consequently may govern them as they please. But persons and property make the sum of the objects of government. The constitution and the laws of their predecessors extinguished them, in their natural course, with those whose will gave them being. This could preserve that being till it ceased to be itself, and no longer. Every constitution, then, and every law, naturally expires at the end of 19 years. If it be enforced longer, it is an act of force and not of right. * * *

What is true of a generation all arriving to self-government on the same day, and dying all on the same day, is true of those in a constant course of decay and renewal, with this only difference. A generation coming in and going out entire, as in the first case, would have a right in the 1st. year of their self-dominion to contract a debt for 33. years, in the 10th. for 24. in the 20th. for 14. in the 30th. for 4. whereas generations, changing daily by daily deaths and births, have one constant term, beginning at the date of their contract, and ending when a majority of those of full age at that date shall be dead. The length of that term may be estimated from the tables of mortality, corrected by the circumstances of climate, occupation & c. peculiar to the country of the contractors.

C. LETTER FROM JAMES MADISON TO THOMAS JEFFERSON

4 February 1790, 5 THE WRITINGS OF JAMES MADISON 437–40 (Gaillard Hunt ed., 1904)

Your [letter] of Jan 9 inclosing one of [September] last did not get to hand till a few days ago. The idea which the latter evolves is a great one; and suggests many interesting reflections to Legislators; particularly when contracting and providing for public debts. Whether it can be received in the extent to which your reasonings carry it, is a question which I ought to turn more in my thoughts than I have yet been able to do, before I should be justified in making up a full opinion on it. My first thoughts lead me to view the doctrine as not *in all respects* compatible with the course of human affairs. I will endeavor to sketch the grounds of my skepticism. "As the Earth belongs to the living, not to the dead, a living generation can bind itself only; in every Society the will of the majority binds the whole; according to the laws of mortality, a majority of those ripe for the exercise of their will do not live beyond the term of 19 years: To this term then is limited the validity of every act of the Society; or can any act be continued beyond this term without an *express* declaration of the public will." This I understand to be the outline of the argument.

The Acts of a political Society may be divided into three classes.

1. the fundamental constitution of the Government.

2. laws involving some stipulation, which renders them irrevocable at the will of the Legislature.

3. laws involving no such irrevocable quality.

1. However applicable in theory the doctrine may be to a Constitution, it seems liable in practice to some weighty objections.

Would not a Government ceasing of necessity at the end of a given term, unless prolonged by some Constitutional Act, previous to its expiration, be too subject to the casualty and consequences of an interregnum?

Would not a Government so often revised become too mutable & novel to retain that share of prejudice in its favor which is a salutary aid to the most rational Government?

Would not such a periodical revision engender pernicious factions that might not otherwise come into existence; and agitate the public mind more frequently and more violently than might be expedient?

2. In the second class of acts involving stipulations, must not exceptions at least to the doctrine, be admitted?

If the earth be the gift of *nature* to the living, their title can extend to the earth in its *natural* state only. The *improvements* made by the dead form a debt against the living, who take the benefit of them. This charge cannot be otherwise discharged then by a proportionate obedience to the will of the Authors of the improvements.

* * * Debts may be incurred with a direct view to the interests of the unborn as well as of the living. Such are debts for repelling a Conquest, the evils of which descend through many generations. Debts may even be incurred principally for the benefit of posterity: Such perhaps is debt incurred by the U. States. In these instances the debts might not be dischargeable within the term of 19 years.

There seems, then, to be some foundation in the nature of things; in the relation which one generation bears to another, for the *descent* of obligations from one to another. Equity may require it. Mutual good may be promoted by it. And all that seems indispensable in stating the account between the dead and the living, is to see that the debts against the latter do not exceed the advances made by the former. Few of the incumbrances entailed on nations by their predecessors would bear a liquidation even on this principle.

3. Objections to the doctrine, as applied to the third class of Acts must be merely practical. But in that view alone they appear to be material.

Unless such temporary laws should be kept in force by acts regularly anticipating their expiration, all the rights depending on positive laws, that is most of the rights of property would become absolutely defunct, and the most violent struggles ensue between the parties interested in reviving & those interested in reforming the antecedent state of property. Nor does it seem improbable that such an event might be suffered to take place. The checks & difficulties opposed to the passage of laws which render the power of repeal inferior to an opportunity to reject, as a security against oppression, would here render the latter an insecure provision against anarchy. Add to this that the very possibility of an event so hazardous to the rights of property could not but depreciate its value; that the approach of the crisis wd. increase the effect; that the frequent return of periods superseding all the obligations dependent on antecedent laws & usages, must by weakening the sense of them, co-operate with motives to licentiousness already too powerful; and that the general uncertainty & vicissitudes of such a state of things would, on one side, discourage every useful effort of steady industry pursued under the sanction of existing laws, and on the other, give an immediate advantage to the more sagacious over the less sagacious part of the Society.

I can find no relief from such embarrassments but in the received doctrine that a *tacit* assent may be given to established Governments & laws, and that this assent is to be inferred from the omissions of an express revocation. It seems more practicable to remedy by well-constituted Governments the pestilent operation of this doctrine, in the unlimited sense in which it as at present recd., than it is to find a remedy for evils necessarily springing from an unlimited admission to the contrary doctrine.

Is it not doubtful whether it be possible to exclude wholly the idea of an implied or tacit assent, without subverting the very foundation of Civil Society?

On what principle is it that the voice of the majority binds the minority? It does not result I conceive from a law of nature but from compact founded on utility. A greater proportion might be required by the fundamental Constitution of Society, if under any particular circumstances it were judged eligible. Prior therefore to the establishment of this principle, *unanimity* was necessary; and rigid Theory, accordingly presupposes the assent of every individual to the rule, which subjects the minority to the will of the majority. If this assent cannot be given tacitly, or be not implied where no positive evidence forbids, no person born in Society, could on attaining ripe age, be bound by any acts of the majority, and either a unanimous renewal of every law would be necessary, as often as a new member should be added to the Society, or the express consent of every new member be obtained to the rule by which the majority decides for the whole.

NOTES AND QUESTIONS

1. On the debate between Jefferson and Madison, see ILAN WURMAN, A DEBT AGAINST THE LIVING: AN INTRODUCTION TO ORIGINALISM (2017). On contractarianism, see RUSSELL HARDIN, LIBERALISM, CONSTITUTIONALISM, AND DEMOCRACY (1999); RUSSELL HARDIN, COLLECTIVE ACTION (1982).

2. The U.S. Constitution, of course, is not simply *a* constitution. It is a constitution with a specific structure, purpose, and history. For purposes of constitutional law, and therefore for purposes of this course, it is *the* Constitution. (That would not be true in a course on comparative constitutional law or on political theory.) Arguments for constitutionalism in the abstract are not necessarily arguments for the particular kind of constitution that the U.S. adopted. Consider the following arguments, which are openly normative rather than being contractual or coordination/conventional, in favor of key features of the U.S. Constitution.

D. STEVEN G. CALABRESI & LIVIA FINE, *TWO CHEERS FOR PROFESSOR BALKIN'S ORIGINALISM*

103 Nw. U. L. Rev. 663 (2009)[22]

A. * * * Consider the following ten purposes that could be argued as an historical matter to underlie the U.S. Constitution.

1. Set up or Constitute the Institutions of the National Government.—A first purpose that clearly underlies the U.S. Constitution as an historical matter was to set up or constitute the institutions of the national government. * * * Before 1789, there was no presidency, no Senate or House of Representatives, and no Supreme or inferior federal courts. By creating *ex nihilo* these institutions, the Framers did get constitutional politics going, but they also did quite a bit more to constrain and channel the constitutional politics they started. The Framers in 1787 put in place powerful institutional actors who would become constitutional interpreters, and they set rules on when and how those actors could be selected. The Framers' decision in 1787 to establish a six-year electoral cycle with House elections every two years, presidential elections every four years, and Senate elections every six years with one third of the Senate turning over in two-year intervals completely shapes our public life to the present day. This basic electoral framework rule guarantees that we do not have one winner-take-all election in the U.S. roughly every five years as Britain does. It guarantees that for a political movement to prevail nationally, it must win more than one election. * * * To achieve constitutional change by replacing a majority of the Supreme Court, political movements in the U.S. may have to win three to six elections over a six- to twelve-year time period. In Britain or Canada, in contrast, constitutional change can occur by winning just one election.

The Framers' choice of electoral rules, not standards, allows for no judicial or other build-outs, and it is absolutely fundamental. It sets a circadian rhythm to our politics and promotes gradualism and Burkean change rather than French revolutionary style changes. In this respect, we think a better metaphor for the Constitution than a skeletal framework is that of a sea anchor. A sea anchor is a large parachute filled with water that drags behind an ocean-liner and slows

[22] Footnotes omitted. A version of this material was initially published with the U.S. Constitution Center. Steven G. Calabresi, *On Originalism in Constitutional Interpretation*, NAT'L CONST. CTR. http://constitutioncenter.org/interactive-constitution/about#?what-is-the-interactive-constitution.

enormously its movement in any direction even though the anchor never touches bottom. It can hence be used in the middle of the ocean where the water is too deep for a normal anchor. A first purpose of the U.S. Constitution is to set up the electoral cycle to slow change the way a sea anchor does in the middle of the ocean.

The six-year electoral cycle set up by the Constitution serves other purposes as well as slowing down change. It guarantees that the popular will in the U.S. is sampled not in one election every five or so years but in multiple elections held every two years over a six-year cycle. The U.S. method of sampling the popular will is superior to the British method in the same way that a daily tracking poll is superior to a one-time only poll. Multiple samplings lead to greater accuracy. The fact that the U.S. samplings of the popular will occur in geographically different congressional districts, states (for the Senate), and the nation (for the presidency) adds to the accuracy of our system. * * *

* * *

2. *Divide and Allocate Power.*—A second obvious purpose of the U.S. Constitution is to divide and allocate power in four different ways. First, the Constitution divides and allocates power between We the People, who are sovereign, and the government, which is given only limited and enumerated powers. Second, the Constitution divides power horizontally among the Congress, the President, and the federal courts. Third, the Constitution divides power vertically between the national government and the states. And finally, the Constitution protects certain enumerated and unenumerated individual rights from government intrusion at all levels.

This function of dividing and allocating power in so many different ways again goes somewhat beyond just the creation of a skeletal framework or the getting going of politics. The Framers' Constitution set in motion a whole Newtonian system of planets orbiting around the sun of the sovereign people, each exerting gravitational force on one another. The Madisonian system of checks and balances is, as Michael Kammen has described it, "a machine that would go of itself." * * * At the margins, presidential, congressional, and federal judicial power have been made concrete by practice * * *. One cannot understand presidential power in foreign affairs, or the political question doctrine, or the case and controversy limitation without making reference to practice. The gloss of history * * * and of two centuries of tradition does matter a lot [in structural constitutional law cases], and some institutions like the presidency and the federal courts have clearly turned out to be more powerful than the Framers anticipated. But again, the basic divisions and allocations of power made in the period between 1787 and 1791 still govern with the vital additions of the Reconstruction and Progressive Era Amendments. Presidents still have the veto power, the pardon power, the treaty-making power, and the appointment power because of what happened [231] years ago. There are grey areas to be sure where build-outs (or repairs) have been made, but they are dwarfed by how much has stayed the same * * *. The Framers' system of checks and balances reinforces the sea anchor-like qualities of the Constitution discussed above. It slows down change and provides for certainty which in turn promotes investment and economic growth. * * * For this reason, the Constitution of the Framers has helped make the United States the most prosperous nation on earth * * *.

3. *Serve as a Gag Rule.*—A third purpose served by the U.S. Constitution is that it functions as a gag rule: it takes certain subjects off the table of discussion in ordinary politics * * *. The Framers of the Constitution meant to do this at the national level when they forbade a national established church, protected the free exercise of religion, and forbade religious tests for holding office. These three prohibitions were meant to prevent a repeat of the English civil wars of the seventeenth century by taking the subject of religion and removing it entirely from ordinary politics. The Framers' effort was a complete success. Religious strife has been greatly reduced. The authors of the Reconstruction Amendments, perhaps inspired by the Framers' success, tried to take the subject of racial discrimination off the table by forbidding laws that distinguish citizens by race. Their effort was less successful—in our opinion in part because the language they used was somewhat more equivocal * * *.

* * *

4. *Restrain the Passions of the Moment.*—A fourth purpose of the U.S. Constitution historically was that it was meant to restrain the passions of the moment. Tying ourselves to the constitutional text was to be like Ulysses lashing himself to the mast of his ship so he could listen to, but not heed, the alluring and deadly songs of the sirens * * *. The Framers themselves made it quite clear that they designed the Madisonian system of checks and balances to prevent temporary passions, which might engulf the body politic, from being legislated immediately into law * * *. They guaranteed, as we have said above, that change would be slow and incremental, and that social movements would have to win many elections and not just one to get their way on constitutional changes * * *.

5. *A Framework for Private Ordering.*—* * * It is not just hard to amend the Constitution; it is also very hard to pass an ordinary law. The U.S. legal system is thus super-entrenched and that leaves people a lot of room to make their own choices in terms of economics and personal liberties. One goal of a constitution is to guarantee credibly that if you write a book today you will not be prosecuted for what you said in it twenty years from now. Similarly, if you start a business or build a factory today, it will not be taken away from you without just compensation being paid twenty years from now. The U.S. Constitution accomplishes these goals of promoting private ordering because it is so hard to pass laws and because it is almost impossible to amend the Constitution. This is why, in our opinion, we are the freest and most prosperous nation on earth. The Framers did not say in so many words that they wanted to promote private ordering, but they did make it clear that they wanted to protect life, liberty, and property. Obviously, they succeeded beyond their wildest expectations * * *.

6. *A System of Intergenerational Lawmaking.*—A sixth purpose of the Constitution is one that the Framers could only have hoped for rather than expected: the successful creation of a real working system of intergenerational lawmaking. Law can create a freedom or power in people that would not exist if it were not there. This insight is at the bottom of contract law. By giving up the "freedom" to breach their contracts, citizens gain a power to make more certain arrangements in the future, which is liberty- and prosperity-enhancing. Ironically, perhaps, agreeing to be bound by a contract is empowering.

The same thing occurs in constitutional law as to intergenerational lawmaking. There are some problems that are just so big that no one generation can or should have to deal with them on its own. Thus, for example, the U.S. government borrowed a lot of money from future generations to win World War II and the Cold War. The generations that won those wars could not have won them without borrowing from the future. And it made sense to borrow from future generations because those very future citizens would themselves benefit from winning the wars in question. The Constitution similarly allows us, in exchange for giving up our freedom to scrap it, the security of being bound by some pretty sensible rules that have persisted over two hundred years. By agreeing to be bound by our great-great-grandparents' Fourteenth Amendment, we also gain the power to bind our great-great-grandchildren with some new amendment. Constitutional originalism thus acknowledges that the present has obligations both to the past and to the future, and that just as every individual is not an island all by himself, every generation is not an island all by itself. We honor our parents when we give their laws a presumption of validity while reserving the means to change them in a consensus-based way. * * *

7. *Promote the Rule of Law.*—A seventh purpose of the Constitution is to promote the rule of law and not of individual men or women. As Robert's Rules of Order say at the outset, "where there is no law and where every man does what is right in his own eyes there is the least of real liberty." * * * The original Constitution is an ingenious effort to promote the rule of law because, as James Madison explained in *The Federalist No. 51*, it does not rely on mere parchment barriers for enforcement, but instead sets in play a mechanism by which ambition is made to counteract ambition * * *.

8. *Promote Democracy.*—An eighth purpose of the Constitution is to promote democracy. As much as they believed in and talked about checks and balances, the Framers were determined to set up a democratic system of government and not an English-style monarchy or aristocracy. The Constitution provides for popular ratification and for popular election of representatives, senators, and, indirectly, Presidents. Judges, whose selection is removed from the people, are picked by the President and Senate and thus indirectly by the people. The Constitution itself commands that Congress shall guarantee to each state a republican form of government, * * * and the Framers must have thought that was the form of government they had prescribed at the federal level. Even the six-year electoral cycle, described above as a series of biannual tracking polls, is an effort to discern what the people *really* want, as opposed to what they might impulsively vote for in one election * * *. On balance, the Constitution is a very democratic document in the true sense of the word "democracy." * * *

9. *Certainty from Getting Things in Writing.*—A ninth purpose of the Constitution is to make it easier to find the law by getting it down in writing. The Framers grew up with the British unwritten constitution, and they obviously thought it was very important to get constitutional constraints in writing so as to eliminate uncertainty about the law and, in Jefferson's words, to bind down government officials in the chains of the Constitution * * *. The Framers were skeptical about the ability of people to agree on unwritten constitutional commands, and this skepticism seems well warranted. The writtenness of the Constitution reflects the Framers' desire to make concrete the meaning of our fundamental law * * *.

10. Lead to Good Consequences.—The tenth and final purpose of the Constitution is aspirational and consequential. The Constitution itself describes its purposes aspirationally and consequentially in the Preamble. The Framers say the purposes of the Constitution include forming a more perfect Union, establishing Justice, ensuring domestic tranquility, providing for the common defense, and securing the Blessings of Liberty to ourselves and our posterity * * *. The Constitution aspires to promote these ends so as to produce good consequences, and the Preamble describes the promotion of these ends as being a purpose of the document. The Preamble is, along with the Declaration of Independence, a statement of national aspirations or hopes. The rest of the document is quite legalistic compared with twentieth-century constitutions in other countries, which often express aspirations to provide equal healthcare and welfare rights and other entitlements of that kind * * *. Our Constitution eschews these kinds of positive entitlements in favor of more limited ambitions.

NOTES AND QUESTIONS

1. To what extent should constitutions impede democratic lawmaking by creating "gag rules" on certain issues, thereby taking them off the table permanently? For a discussion, see the useful little book CONSTITUTIONALISM AND DEMOCRACY (STUDIES IN RATIONALITY AND SOCIAL CHANGE) (Jon Elster & Rune Slagstad, eds., 1993). Should questions on the legality of abortion be made in the constitution or be left up to future generations to decide on their own? How about affirmative action or same-sex marriage? For another provocative discussion about the purposes of constitutionalism, see CASS R. SUNSTEIN, DESIGNING DEMOCRACY: WHAT CONSTITUTIONS DO (2001).

2. The U.S. Constitution establishes the essential structure of our government. Should Congress be able to alter that structure if it thinks that certain important tasks are best performed by entities, such as administrative agencies, that the Constitution may not accommodate? What if the President thinks that he or she needs more power than the Constitution confers in order to, for example, wage a war or respond to an economic downturn? Does it matter if those actors get elected or re-elected after announcing or implementing those extra-constitutional plans? *See* ADRIAN VERMEUELE, LAW'S ABNEGATION: FROM LAW'S EMPIRE TO THE ADMINISTRATIVE STATE (2016).

3. Is the high level of constitutional entrenchment in the U.S.—a result of the difficulty of passing constitutional amendments, or even of passing statutes—a good thing or a bad thing? *See* John O. McGinnis & Michael B. Rappaport, *Our Supermajoritarian Constitution*, 80 TEX. L. REV. 703 (2002) Does the answer depend on the empirical question how important certainty and predictability are to economic growth?

4. Thomas Jefferson, in his letter to James Madison quoted above, argued that the U.S. Constitution should sunset out of existence every nineteen years. Jefferson argued that the Earth belongs to the living and not to the dead, and so each new generation ought to write its own constitution rather than being bound by the dead hand of the past. James Madison was appalled by Jefferson's idea and thought that it would lead to constant turmoil. Who has the better argument?

5. The English political philosopher David Hume argued for what he called a coordination rather than a Lockean, or contractarian, theory of constitutional legitimacy. Russell Hardin has called into question whether Americans ever really meaningfully consented to the Constitution in the 1780s or to the Fourteenth Amendment in 1868, and he asks why Americans today ought to feel bound by what a few of our (or likely someone

else's) ancestors did back then. *See* RUSSELL HARDIN, LIBERALISM, CONSTITUTIONALISM, AND DEMOCRACY (1999); Russell Hardin, *Why a Constitution?, in* SOCIAL AND POLITICAL FOUNDATIONS OF CONSTITUTIONS (Denis J. Galligan & Mila Versteed eds., 2013).

But, consider how easy it is to emigrate out of the United States, unlike the former Soviet Union, which forbade emigration (and built a wall in Berlin to keep people in). If Americans do not like our Constitution, they can in theory emigrate to Western Europe, Africa, Asia, Latin America, Canada, Australia, or New Zealand. Yet those who have immigrated to or have been transported to the United States have almost never chosen to leave the country. Italian and Irish immigrants have not generally chosen to go back to Europe (or anywhere else), nor have Asian-Americans widely chosen to go back to China, Japan, India, or Vietnam (or anywhere else), nor have even the descendants of African-Americans, whose ancestors were kidnapped and brought unwillingly to these shores, chosen in large numbers to leave for Africa (or anywhere else). Instead, America is a magnet for immigrants. By choosing to stay in the United States, do we consent to and acquiesce in the legitimacy of our constitutional regime? The question is as old as philosophy. *See* PLATO, CRITO.

6. The purposes of the Constitution as set forth in the Preamble were obviously unrealized for the millions of people held as slaves before the Civil War. The Constitution, as we noted earlier, made a number of important concessions to the slave States. Were Morris, Hamilton, and Franklin right in retrospect to sign the Constitution in light of its accommodations of slavery? Do those accommodations so poison the document that all other arguments that might be mustered for it become irrelevant? *See* JACK M. BALKIN, CONSTITUTIONAL REDEMPTION: POLITICAL FAITH IN AN UNJUST WORLD (2011); SANFORD LEVINSON, CONSTITUTIONAL FAITH (2011)

Consider that the Constitution produced a powerful U.S. government which, after seventy-two years, fought a Civil War between the North and the South, which ended slavery in North America. Would slavery have ended sooner if the Constitution was not ratified and the Articles of Confederation had remained in force? Do criticisms of people like Morris, Hamilton, and Franklin commit what economists call the "grass is greener" or "nirvana" fallacy of comparing a defective real world with a non-existent, imaginary perfect one?

But consider in turn that the three-fifths rule allowed the slave-owning South to "win" all but two presidential elections between 1800 and 1856, even though "winners" like Thomas Jefferson, in 1800, actually *lost* the popular vote of free Americans to John Adams, an opponent of slavery. *See* GARY WILLS, "NEGRO PRESIDENT": JEFFERSON AND THE SLAVE POWER (2005).This was possible because the slave States counted their slaves as three-fifths of a person for determining their representatives in the Electoral College, but slaves could not vote so their white masters voted for them. If Thomas Jefferson *himself* did not win a majority of the popular vote in the critical election of 1800, it may be that some of the lesser Jeffersonian and Jacksonian presidents who followed him, and who did not have Thomas Jefferson's or Andrew Jackson's charisma, probably lost the popular vote among free persons as well. This feature of the Three-Fifths Clause explains what Northern abolitionists meant when they said there was such a thing as the "Slave Power," LEONARD L. RICHARDS, THE SLAVE POWER: THE FREE NORTH AND SOUTHERN DOMINATION 1780–1860 (2000), and that, as abolitionist publisher William Lloyd Garrison said: "The Constitution was a Covenant with Death, an Agreement with Hell."

Fifteen men served as President between George Washington and Abraham Lincoln. Ten of them owned slaves at one point in their lives and eight of them owned slaves while they served as President. Two Presidents, Franklin Pierce and James Buchanan, were shills for slavery. Of the first fifteen Presidents, only two men—John Adams and his son

John Quincy Adams—were opposed to slavery. Of the thirty-six Supreme Courts justices appointed by the first fifteen Presidents, only four were appointed by John Adams and John Quincy Adams. The other thirty-two pre-1860 Supreme Court justices were appointed either by slave owners or those shilling for the Slave Power.

Thus, the Constitution the Framers produced at Philadelphia was a deeply *structurally* problematic document. It was designed to over-represent slave holders in the House of Representatives, in the Electoral College, and in the selection of U.S. Supreme Court justices.

On the other hand, on July 13, 1787, the Continental Congress, acting under the Articles of Confederation, passed the Northwest Ordinance outlawing slavery in the huge Northwest Territories of the United States, which ultimately became the free states of Ohio, Indiana, Illinois, Michigan, Wisconsin, and part of Minnesota. *See* An Ordinance for the Government of the Territory of the United States Northwest of the River Ohio art. IV (1787) ("There shall be neither slavery nor involuntary servitude in the said territory, otherwise than in the punishment of crimes whereof the party shall have been duly convicted."). This move effectively guaranteed that free state senators and States would eventually outnumber slave state senators and States, and it also reflected a widely held belief in the 1780s that slavery was morally wrong and economically foolish. Northern States, even before the Constitution, systematically abolished slavery: Pennsylvania (1780), New Hampshire and Massachusetts (1783); Connecticut and Rhode Island (1784), and Vermont when it joined the Union in 1791. By 1804, both New York and New Jersey had banned slavery, completing its abolition in the North (apart from Delaware).

In the 1790s, a group of Quakers and Abolition of Slavery Committees formed in Philadelphia by Benjamin Franklin and in New York by Alexander Hamilton petitioned Congress to take whatever steps it could to lead toward an abolition of slavery, triggering an angry sectional debate. In 1794, Congress actually passed a federal law, which President Washington signed, that prevented American citizens from themselves engaging in the African slave trade. The outlawing of importation of slaves into the United States from other countries passed Congress in 1807, was signed by President Jefferson, and went into effect in 1808, on the earliest possible date under the Constitution.

Alexander Stephens, the future Vice President of the Confederacy and a vicious defender of slavery, said the following about the Framers of the Constitution and slavery:

> The prevailing ideas entertained by [Thomas Jefferson] and most of the leading statesmen at the time of the formation of the old Constitution were, that the enslavement of the African was in violation of the laws of nature; that it was wrong in principle, socially, morally and politically. It was an evil they knew not well how to deal with; but the general opinion of the men of that day was, that, somehow or other, in the order of Providence, the institution would be evanescent and pass away.

Alexander Stephens, The Cornerstone Address, Athenaeum, Savanah, Georgia, on March 21, 1861.

While the anti-slavery actions and attitudes of the founding generation may today seem feeble given the enormity of the underlying moral horror, it is hard from the present day to fathom the context in which those attitudes and actions were formed. The Constitution entered a world in which slavery was the norm and its abolition in countries like England and France (but *not* in those country's colonies, one should be clear[23]) was the rare exception. The Atlantic slave trade started in the early 1500s, as Spanish and Portuguese traders forcibly brought to the Western Hemisphere people who had already been enslaved in Africa. "Slavery had not been excluded from the ideal societies of Plato and Thomas More, nor from the social experiments of Las Casas, the English Puritans, or William Penn." DAVID BRION DAVIS, THE PROBLEM OF SLAVERY IN WESTERN CULTURE 146 (1966). "Enlightenment" thinkers, including such notables as Hugo Grotius and John Locke, either endorsed slavery or criticized it faintly (with Adam Smith as a notable exception offering a full-throated objection to slavery). *See id.* at 114–21, 433–35. As the lawyer defending the slaveowner in *Somerset v. Stewart* accurately described matters in 1772, on the eve of the Constitution: "[Slavery [t]'is found in three quarters of the globe, and in part of the fourth. In Asia the whole people; in Africa and America far the greater part; in Europe great numbers of the Russians and Polanders." 99 Eng. Rep. at 503. As an eighteenth-century legal document, is the Constitution more noteworthy for its concessions to slavery or for the modesty of those concessions?

If one thinks that accommodating slavery was a fatal defect in the Constitution of 1787, was that defect cured after the Civil War when slavery was legally abolished by the Thirteenth, Fourteenth, and Fifteenth Amendments? *See* JOHN O. MCGINNIS & MICHAEL B. RAPPAPORT, ORIGINALISM AND THE GOOD CONSTITUTION 107–08 (2013). Whatever your answer may be at this point, take up the question again after you have studied the materials on Reconstruction.

V. THE NATURE AND CONTENT OF THE CONSTITUTION: THEN AND NOW

A. A "REPUBLICAN FORM OF GOVERNMENT"

According to a possibly apocryphal story, when Benjamin Franklin emerged at the conclusion of the closed-door Constitutional Convention: "A lady asked Dr. Franklin Well Doctor what have we got a republic or a monarchy—a Republic replied the Doctor if you can keep it." 3 THE RECORDS OF THE FEDERAL CONVENTION OF 1787, Appendix A, at 85 (Max Farrand ed. 1911). The idea of republicanism is explicitly written into the document; the United States must guarantee to each State "a Republican Form of Government." U.S. CONST. art. IV, § 4. What does it mean for a government to be "Republican" in form?

A full answer to that question—if there is a full answer to that question to be found—would be the subject of a graduate-level curriculum in political theory. Here, we can offer not much more than one paragraph (plus one sentence) from James Madison:

> What, then, are the distinctive characters of the republican form * * *?
>
> If we resort for a criterion to the different principles on which different forms of government are established, we may define a republic to be, or at least may bestow that name on, a government which derives all its powers directly or indirectly from the great body of the people, and is administered by persons holding their offices during pleasure, for a limited period, or during good behavior. It is *essential* to such a government that it be derived

[23] Somerset, the slave who was freed by an English court in *Somerset v. Stewart*, was going to be sold in Jamaica, a British colony. Slavery thrived elsewhere in the Caribbean in Haiti, a French colony.

> from the great body of the society, not from an inconsiderable proportion, or a favored class of it; otherwise a handful of tyrannical nobles, exercising their oppressions by a delegation of their powers, might aspire to the rank of republicans, and claim for their government the honorable title of republic. It is *sufficient* for such a government that the persons administering it be appointed, either directly or indirectly, by the people; and that they hold their appointments by either of the tenures just specified; otherwise every government in the United States, as well as every other popular government that has been or can be well organized or well executed, would be degraded from the republican character * * *.

THE FEDERALIST No. 39 (Madison). Obviously, that is not much to go on. But it is enough to pose the following problem: An important class of people, African-American slaves, played no role at all in electing federal officers, thanks in part to James Madison's own defense of slavery at the Philadelphia Convention. Worse still, slaves were counted as being three-fifths of a person for purposes of apportioning members of the House of Representatives and the Electoral College, thus allowing slave-owners to vote on behalf of their slaves. The Constitution of 1788 rather plainly fails James Madison's own test for republicanism. Did it become republican in 1870, after the ratification of the last of the three post-Civil War amendments (which you will read elsewhere in this section)? After the Constitution was amended in 1920 to assure women the right to vote? Was the Constitution aristocratic in 1788 but republican a century later (or aristocratic in 1919 but republican a year later)? Does the Guarantee Clause ("The United States shall guarantee to every State in this Union a Republican Form of Government"), enacted when half the States recognized slavery, prove that, for constitutional purposes, a slave society can still be "republican" in form? Or did the Guarantee Clause mandate the abolition of slavery from 1788 onward and people at the time simply did not recognize the fact?

One more point: In the entirety of *The Federalist* No. 39, in which Madison discusses the essential character of the federal government under the Constitution, the word "democracy" never appears. Does that surprise you at all?

B. THE U.S. CONSTITUTION AND THE ENDS OF GOVERNMENT

The Constitution's Preamble declares its purposes to be "to form a more perfect Union, establish Justice, insure domestic Tranquility, provide for the common defence, promote the general Welfare, and secure the Blessings of Liberty to ourselves and our Posterity." The Declaration of Independence says that governments are instituted to secure to people their rights to "Life, Liberty, and the pursuit of Happiness"—and that if a government fails in those ends, it is "the Right of the People to alter or abolish it." John Adams, you may recall from an earlier excerpt, wrote: "Upon this point all speculative politicians will agree, that the happiness of society is the end of government, as all divines will agree that the happiness of the individual is the end of man. From this principle it will follow, that the form of government which communicates ease, comfort, security, or in one word happiness, to the greatest number of persons, and in the greatest degree, is the best."

Such accounts of the ends of government were commonplace in eighteenth-century American constitutions. The Massachusetts Constitution of 1780 declares:

> Art. I.—All men are born free and equal, and have certain natural, essential, and unalienable rights; among which may be reckoned the right of enjoying and defending their lives and liberties; that of acquiring, possessing, and protecting property; in fine, that of seeking and obtaining their safety and happiness.

The Pennsylvania Constitution of 1776 began by saying:

> I. That all men are born equally free and independent, and have certain natural, inherent and inalienable rights, amongst which are, the enjoying and defending life and liberty, acquiring, possessing and protecting property, and pursuing and obtaining happiness and safety.

And George Mason's 1776 draft of the Virginia Declaration of Rights said:

> SECTION I. That all men are by nature equally free and independent and have certain inherent rights, of which, when they enter into a state of society, they cannot, by any compact, deprive or divest their posterity; namely, the enjoyment of life and liberty, with the means of acquiring and possessing property, and pursuing and obtaining happiness and safety.

Indeed, Thomas Jefferson may have derived his most famous lines in the Declaration of Independence from George Mason's Virginia draft, which was published in May 1776. *See* PAULINE MAIER, AMERICAN SCRIPTURE: MAKING THE DECLARATION OF INDEPENDENCE (1998).

The boldest clause stating the purposes of government appears in the Vermont Territories Constitution of 1786:

> I. THAT all men are born equally free and independent, and have certain natural, inherent and unalienable rights; amongst which are, the enjoying and defending life and liberty-acquiring, possessing and protecting property-and pursuing and obtaining happiness and safety. Therefore, no male person, born in this country, or brought from over sea, ought to be holden by law to serve any person, as a servant, slave, or apprentice, after he arrives to the age of twenty one Years; nor female, in like manner, after she arrives to the age of eighteen years; unless they are bound by their own consent after they arrive to such age; or bound by law for the payment of debts, damages, fines, costs, or the like.

This "born free and equal" clause outlaws slavery *ab initio*! (How can you have a "born free and equal" clause *without* outlawing slavery *ab initio*?) All in all, six of the twelve States that wrote new constitutions between 1776 and 1791 adopted "born free and equal" clauses. Twenty-four of the thirty-seven States had such clauses, in 1868, when the Fourteenth Amendment was ratified; and thirty-nine out of fifty States have such clauses in their state constitutions today. Steven G. Calabresi, James Lindgren; Hannah M. Begley; Katherine L. Dore; and Sarah E. Agudo, *Individual Rights under State Constitutions in 2018: What Rights are Deeply Rooted in a Modern Day Consensus of the States?;* 94 NOTRE DAME L. REV. 49–153 (2018). These clauses essentially show that the language of the Declaration of Independence about all men having been created equal with natural and inherent rights to life, liberty, and the pursuit of happiness is today codified in an Article V majority of more than three-quarters of the States. You will see repeatedly throughout this course that the Declaration of Independence is the cornerstone on which the Constitution rests.

How much does it help in *interpreting* the Constitution to understand its *goals* or *ends*? Does it follow that, if the Constitution is set up to pursue certain ends, it *must* confer sufficient power on government to achieve those ends? *See* John Mikhail, *Is the Constitution a Power of Attorney or a Corporate Charter?*, 17 GEO. J.L. & PUB. POL'Y 407, 429 (2019) ("it seems plausible to hold that the Constitution vests the Government of the United States with the implied power to fulfill every purpose for which that government was established, including the six great objects of the Preamble"). Or is it an open question how well and to what extent the Constitution structures institutions to achieve its stated goals?

Suppose that Article I, section 8 of the Constitution said (as a proposal from the Constitutional Convention did actually say) that Congress would have power to legislate in "those Cases to which the States are separately incompetent," 2 THE RECORDS OF THE FEDERAL CONVENTION OF 1787, at 131–32, with no further enumeration or specification. In that instance, it would be clear that the *purpose* identified in the Constitution determined the *powers* that Congress possesses. It is possible to draft legal instruments creating institutions in which the institutions' purposes effectively define their powers. It is also possible to draft legal instruments creating institutions in which the institutions' powers effectively define their purposes.

> Consider the 1781 federal charter for the Bank of North America. The document is very sparse. It grants (or confirms) to the corporation all of the basic powers of perpetuity and legal personhood, appoints initial directors, and provides for the appointment of officers and future directors. The powers of the corporation are defined starkly as follows:
>
>> And be it further ordained, that the said corporation are hereby declared and made able and capable in law, to have, purchase, receive, possess, enjoy, and retain lands, rents, tenements, hereditaments, goods, chattels and effects, of what kind, nature or quality soever, to the amount of ~~thirty~~ ten millions of Spanish silver milled dollars and no more; and also to sell, grant, demise, alien, or dispose of the same lands, rents, tenements, hereditaments, goods, chattels and effects . . . .
>>
>> And be it further ordained, that the said corporation may make, ordain, establish, and put in execution such laws, ordinances and regulations as shall seem necessary and convenient [for] the government of the said corporation.
>>
>> * * *
>
> In essence, the statute says to the bank, "go forth and be a bank to the extent of ten million Spanish silver milled dollars." The purpose of the corporation—"the support which the finances of the United States would receive from the establishment of a national bank"—effectively constitutes and defines the bank's powers. The [1791] statute establishing the first Bank of the United States was to similar effect * * *; indeed, the language describing powers is almost identical in the two enactments. In 1791, as in 1781, the purposes behind the corporation—promoting "the successful conducting of the national finances," "the obtaining of loans, for the use of the government, in sudden emergencies," and producing "advantages to

> trade and industry in general"—do much of the work in defining the corporation's powers.
>
> The United States Constitution is a very different instrument * * *. [T]he document does not broadly define the powers of the government by means of the purposes. Rather, the powers define and cabin the means by which, and the extent to which, the purposes are to be pursued. The Constitution * * * is not a document that says, "go forth and be a government." It is a document that says, "go forth and be a government as defined in this instrument, using the means specified in this instrument." The Constitution could have been written along the lines of the charter for the Bank of North America. There likely were people who wanted the Constitution to be written along the lines of the charter for the Bank of North America. It was not written that way.

Gary Lawson & Guy Seidman, *Authors' Response: An Enquiry Concerning Constitutional Understanding*, 17 GEO. J.L. & PUB. POL'Y 491, 513–14 (2019) (footnotes omitted). The question whether the Constitution's powers define its purposes or vice versa is fundamental. We think the powers define the purposes. What do you think, and why?

C. COMMON BENEFITS AND PUBLIC TRUSTS

Other important clauses in state constitutional law that shed light on the purposes of eighteenth-century constitution-writers include what might be called "Common Benefit Clauses." One example is Article V of the Pennsylvania Declaration of Rights of 1776, which says:

> V. That government is, or ought to be, instituted for the common benefit, protection and security of the people, nation or community; and not for the particular emolument or advantage of any single man, family, or set of men, who are a part only of that community.

Another such clause appears in Vermont's 1786 territorial Constitution and provides:

> VII. That government is, or ought to be, instituted for the common benefit, protection and security of the people, nation, or community: and that the community hath an indubitable, unalienable, single man, family, or set of men, who are a part only of that community: and that the community hath an indubitable, unalienable, and indefeasible right, to reform or alter government, in such manner as shall be, by that community, judged to be most conducive to the public weal.

Finally, consider Articles VI and VII from John Adams' famous Massachusetts Constitution of 1780:

> VI.—No man, nor corporation, or association of men, have any other title to obtain advantages, or particular and exclusive privileges, distinct from those of the community, than what arises from the consideration of services rendered to the public; and this title being in nature neither hereditary, nor transmissible to children, or descendants, or relations by blood, the idea of a man born a magistrate, lawgiver, or judge, is absurd and unnatural.

> VII.—Government is instituted for the common good; for the protection, safety, prosperity and happiness of the people; and not for the profit, honor, or private interest of any one man, family, or class of men.

The eighteenth-century language of constitution writing generally posits: 1) that all men are born free and equal; 2) that class legislation or feudalism is unconstitutional; and 3) that the end of government is to protect life, liberty, property, safety, and the pursuit of happiness, subject nevertheless to just laws enacted for the general good of the whole people. Why did the Framers think that the best way to accomplish these goals was not by listing people's individual rights but instead by constitutionalizing the separation of powers, checks and balances, and federalism?

Part of the answer may lie in the Framers' concern with *factions*. The Framers saw a special threat to safety and happiness from the tendency of the State governments, between 1776 and 1787, to form factions in the legislature, which enacted (notwithstanding constitutional prohibitions) special laws for the good of only a portion of the whole people. The Framers were convinced that the problem of factions was the principal cause of the failure of republican governments. James Madison, in *The Federalist* No. 10, explained the problem of factions, which he said inhered in human nature and in the various differences in the ability and ingenuity of men in acquiring different and unequal amounts of property. Madison argued that a large, extended commercial federal republic would reduce the mischiefs of faction by filtering factional views through representatives, which would moderate and mitigate them, and by *expanding* the number and range of factions and thereby inducing interest groups to compete rather than cooperation with each other, making it less likely that some coercive, majority coalition would form at the federal level. We will excerpt and discuss this crucial essay at the beginning of Chapter 3 below.

Another set of clauses that appeared prominently in eighteenth-century constitutions was "fiduciary" clauses. A fiduciary is someone who is entrusted with responsibility for the affairs of another, such as a guardian, the executor of a will, a business agent, or a health-care proxy. Fiduciary agents must act for the benefit of the principal rather than for the fiduciaries' own interests and must comply with basic "fiduciary duties," such as the duty to remain within the scope of granted authority and follow instructions from the principal, the duty to act with loyalty and good faith toward the principal, the duty to act with reasonable care in carrying out delegated functions, the duty personally to exercise discretion that was entrusted by the principal, the duty to act impartially towards multiple principals if the fiduciary is acting on behalf of more than one person, and the duty to account for resources managed or expended by the fiduciary agent. *See* Robert G. Natelson, *The Legal Origins of the Necessary and Proper Clause, in* GARY LAWSON, GEOFFREY P. MILLER, ROBERT G. NATELSON & GUY I. SEIDMAN, THE ORIGINS OF THE NECESSARY AND PROPER CLAUSE 57, 57–59 (2010). By the eighteenth century, there was a long tradition, stretching back millennia, of conceiving of government officials as fiduciary agents for their citizens. *See* GARY LAWSON & GUY SEIDMAN, "A GREAT POWER OF ATTORNEY": UNDERSTANDING THE FIDUCIARY CONSTITUTION 31–43 (2017). It was therefore not surprising to see those ideas cropping up frequently in State constitutions. On June 29, 1776, Virginia adopted a constitution that provided, among other things, that "all power is vested in, and consequently derived from, the people; that magistrates are their *trustees and servants*, and at all times amenable to them." VA. CONST. OF 1776, § 2 (emphasis added). On September 28, 1776,

Pennsylvania's constitution said that "all power being originally inherent in, and consequently derived from, the people; therefore all officers of government, whether legislative or executive, are their *trustees and servants*, and at all times accountable to them." PA. CONST. OF 1776, art. IV (emphasis added). On November 11, 1776, Maryland also provided in its constitution that "all persons invested with the legislative or executive powers of government are the *trustees* of the public, and, as such, accountable for their conduct." MD. CONST. OF 1776, art. IV (emphasis added). On June 15, 1780, the Massachusetts constitution provided: "All power residing originally in the people, and being derived from them, the several magistrates and officers of government, vested with authority, whether legislative, executive, or judicial, are their substitutes and *agents*, and are at all times accountable to them." MASS. CONST. OF 1780, Part the First, art. V (emphasis added). These provisions were surely declaratory of understandings that existed as part of the legal background whether or not they were stated expressly.

Is the United States Constitution a fiduciary instrument? If so, what does that mean for its interpretation? (Recall our earlier discussion of how the character of a document affects how you approach its interpretation.) Do Members of Congress, the President, and federal judges have duties of care, loyalty, and impartiality to American citizens? Do they have an obligation personally to exercise the authority that has been entrusted to them? Are those obligations, if they exist, legally enforceable? These questions will recur throughout the course.

D. THE PROBLEM OF DEFENSIBLE BORDERS AND OF STANDING ARMIES

One key reason for the formation of the U.S. Constitution was the desire to create a nation that would not be conquered by a European imperial power like Britain. Similarly, a key goal of the Framers was to eliminate the need for a standing army, which was a threat to liberty at home. These goals are admirably expressed in the following two essays.

1. THE FEDERALIST NO. 5 (JOHN JAY)

(Nov. 10, 1787)

It was remarked in the preceding paper, that weakness and divisions at home would invite dangers from abroad; and that nothing would tend more to secure us from them than union, strength, and good government within ourselves. This subject is copious and cannot easily be exhausted.

The history of Great Britain is the one with which we are in general the best acquainted, and it gives us many useful lessons. We may profit by their experience without paying the price which it cost them. Although it seems obvious to common sense that the people of such an island should be but one nation, yet we find that they were for ages divided into three, and that those three were almost constantly embroiled in quarrels and wars with one another. Notwithstanding their true interest with respect to the continental nations was really the same, yet by the arts and policy and practices of those nations, their mutual jealousies were perpetually kept inflamed, and for a long series of years they were far more inconvenient and troublesome than they were useful and assisting to each other.

Should the people of America divide themselves into three or four nations, would not the same thing happen? Would not similar jealousies arise, and be in like manner cherished? Instead of their being "joined in affection" and free from all apprehension of different "interests," envy and jealousy would soon extinguish confidence and affection, and the partial interests of each confederacy, instead of the general interests of all America, would be the only objects of their policy and pursuits. Hence, like most other BORDERING nations, they would always be either involved in disputes and war, or live in the constant apprehension of them.

The most sanguine advocates for three or four confederacies [among the thirteen North Americas States] cannot reasonably suppose that they would long remain exactly on an equal footing in point of strength, even if it was possible to form them so at first; but, admitting that to be practicable, yet what human contrivance can secure the continuance of such equality? Independent of those local circumstances which tend to beget and increase power in one part and to impede its progress in another, we must advert to the effects of that superior policy and good management which would probably distinguish the government of one above the rest, and by which their relative equality in strength and consideration would be destroyed. For it cannot be presumed that the same degree of sound policy, prudence, and foresight would uniformly be observed by each of these confederacies for a long succession of years * * *.

They who well consider the history of similar divisions and confederacies will find abundant reason to apprehend that those in contemplation would in no other sense be neighbors than as they would be borderers; that they would neither love nor trust one another, but on the contrary would be a prey to discord, jealousy, and mutual injuries; in short, that they would place us exactly in the situations in which some nations doubtless wish to see us, viz., FORMIDABLE ONLY TO EACH OTHER * * *.

Let candid men judge, then, whether the division of America into any given number of independent sovereignties would tend to secure us against the hostilities and improper interference of foreign nations.

2. THE FEDERALIST NO. 8 (ALEXANDER HAMILTON)

(Nov. 20, 1787)

* * * Standing armies, it is said, are not provided against in the new Constitution; and it is therefore inferred that they may exist under it * * *. Their existence, however, from the very terms of the proposition, is, at most, problematical and uncertain. But standing armies, it may be replied, must inevitably result from a dissolution of the Confederacy. Frequent war and constant apprehension, which require a state of as constant preparation, will infallibly produce them. The weaker States or confederacies would * * * at the same time, be necessitated to strengthen the executive arm of government, in doing which their constitutions would acquire a progressive direction toward monarchy. It is of the nature of war to increase the executive at the expense of the legislative authority * * *. Thus, we should, in a little time, see established in every part of this country the same engines of despotism which have been the scourge of the Old World * * *.

The kingdom of Great Britain falls within [this] description. An insular situation, and a powerful marine, guarding it in a great measure against the possibility of foreign invasion, supersede the necessity of a numerous army within the kingdom. A sufficient force to make head against a sudden descent, till the militia could have time to rally and embody, is all that has been deemed requisite. No motive of national policy has demanded, nor would public opinion have tolerated, a larger number of troops upon its domestic establishment * * *. [Great Britain's insular geography has led to a strong navy and a weak army all of which has contributed vitally to the growth of liberty in that country. Navies cannot suppress political dissent at home, but armies can].

If we are wise enough to preserve the Union we may for ages enjoy an advantage similar to that of an insulated situation. Europe is at a great distance from us. Her colonies in our vicinity will be likely to continue too much disproportioned in strength to be able to give us any dangerous annoyance. Extensive military establishments cannot, in this position, be necessary to our security. But if we should be disunited, and the integral parts should either remain separated, or, which is most probable, should be thrown together into two or three confederacies, we should be, in a short course of time, in the predicament of the continental powers of Europe—our liberties would be a prey to the means of defending ourselves against the ambition and jealousy of each other.

NOTES AND QUESTIONS

1. Are John Jay and Alexander Hamilton right that the thirteen American States would have been taken over by European powers or fought wars with one another had the Constitution not been ratified? Note here that the United States shares a border with Mexico and Canada and that we fought a war with Mexico in the 1840s, acquiring a huge amount of land in the process. At the same time, one of the purposes of the War of 1812 was to annex Canada to the Union. The continental European powers of France, Germany, and Russia had land borders, and they have repeatedly fought wars with one another. The island nation of Great Britain, with its powerful navy, escaped this fate for a millennium after 1066.

2. Nations that have land borders with hostile powers, such as France, Germany, and Russia, have always maintained large standing armies to defend themselves. Such armies, once assembled, are easily used to squash political dissent at home. Great Britain, in contrast, had an all-powerful navy to defend the island nation and, from 1689 on, Britain had no standing army. Navies cannot be used to squash political dissent at home. As a consequence, Britain was much freer than were France under King Louis XIV, Germany under Kaiser Wilhelm, and Russia under the Czars, the Communists, and now under Vladimir Putin—a fact the British attributed to their status as an island nation with a navy, but not an army. A key argument for the ratification of the Constitution, in 1787 and 1788, was that it would eliminate any need in the new United States for a standing army, which could be abused to suppress liberty at home. The new United States, like Great Britain, would need a navy, and eventually an air force and intercontinental ballistic missiles, but no standing army, at least not on the home front. Note that the Constitution gives Congress power "[t]o raise and support Armies," U.S. CONST. art. I, § 8, cl. 12, but stipulates that "no Appropriation of Money to that Use shall be for a longer Term than two Years." *Id.* (There is no such two-year proviso for *naval* appropriations. *See id.* at art. I, § 8, cl. 13.) To the American people, this was a recipe for political freedom. It was not until the end of World War II that it was thought necessary for the United States to maintain a large standing army, which is mostly kept in bases overseas.

3. The United States, Great Britain, and ancient Athens were all commercial societies located on the water that traded constantly with other nations and whose ports were filled with foreigners. This led to a vibrant intellectual life. The humming ports of Athens, London, and New York City were full of interesting people from exotic lands with new wisdom to share. In contrast, France, Germany, Russia, and ancient Sparta were largely land-locked regimes with no major port cities. Paris, Berlin, Moscow, and Sparta were inland cities with no ports and no bustling community of foreigners with new and exciting ideas. Sparta, for example, was a farmer community that had land borders with its enemies and had a standing army. No wonder Sparta was neither as free nor as intellectually vibrant as Athens. The United States borders the Atlantic Ocean on the east, the Gulf of Mexico on the south, and the Pacific Ocean on the west. The huge Great Lakes and Mississippi River have rendered even the city of Chicago a major port. Geography is destiny, and the geography of the United States has contributed mightily to the intellectually vibrant nation we have become. For further discussion, see Akhil Reed Amar, *Some New World Lessons for the Old World*, 58 U. CHI. L. REV. 483 (1991).

E. CONSTITUTIONAL AMENDMENTS FROM 1791 TO THE PRESENT

The Framers knew even in 1787 that their handiwork was not flawless, and so they provided for a process under Article V of the Constitution whereby constitutional amendments can be add, as happened with the Bill of Rights, by approval of two-thirds of both Houses of Congress and ratification by three quarters of the States. Since 1791, seventeen constitutional amendments have been ratified, some of them creating new rights, and others adding to federal power. We list Amendments 11 through 27 here with reference to the historical period which gave rise to them. Think about how these amendments promote, fail to promote, or change the purposes of constitutionalism that drove development of the Constitution of 1787. We will have many occasions to explore these issues in subsequent chapters.

The first two constitutional amendments are from the Founding Era and were ratified in 1798 and in 1804. The Eleventh Amendment restored the States' common law sovereign immunity in cases seeking money damages from state legislatures. It has given rise to a large and surprising doctrine of so-called state sovereign immunity, and it was the first constitutional amendment to overturn a Supreme Court decision, *Chisholm v. Georgia*, 2 U.S. 419 (1793), which had allowed lawsuits to proceed in federal courts against state governments. The Twelfth Amendment altered presidential elections by providing for separate election on one ticket of the President and the Vice President instead of having the Vice President be the person with the second-most votes in the electoral college. This change inadvertently helped to give birth to the American two-party system—a development that the framing generation would have universally abhorred. *See* BRUCE ACKERMAN, THE FAILURE OF THE FOUNDING FATHERS: JEFFERSON, MARSHALL, AND THE RISE OF PRESIDENTIAL DEMOCRACY (2005).

1. FOUNDING ERA

AMENDMENT XI (1798)

The Judicial power of the United States shall not be construed to extend to any suit in law or equity, commenced or prosecuted against one of the United States by Citizens of another State, or by Citizens or Subjects of any Foreign State.

AMENDMENT XII (1804)

The Electors shall meet in their respective states, and vote by ballot for President and Vice-President, one of whom, at least, shall not be an inhabitant of the same state with themselves; they shall name in their ballots the person voted for as President, and in distinct ballots the person voted for as Vice-President, and they shall make distinct lists of all persons voted for as President, and of all persons voted for as Vice-President, and of the number of votes for each, which lists they shall sign and certify, and transmit sealed to the seat of the government of the United States, directed to the President of the Senate;—The President of the Senate shall, in the presence of the Senate and House of Representatives, open all the certificates and the votes shall then be counted;—The person having the greatest number of votes for President, shall be the President, if such number be a majority of the whole number of Electors appointed; and if no person have such majority, then from the persons having the highest numbers not exceeding three on the list of those voted for as President, the House of Representatives shall choose immediately, by ballot, the President. But in choosing the President, the votes shall be taken by states, the representation from each state having one vote; a quorum for this purpose shall consist of a member or members from two-thirds of the states, and a majority of all the states shall be necessary to a choice. And if the House of Representatives shall not choose a President whenever the right of choice shall devolve upon them, before the fourth day of March next following, then the Vice-President shall act as President, as in the case of the death or other constitutional disability of the President.—The person having the greatest number of votes as Vice-President, shall be the Vice-President, if such number be a majority of the whole number of Electors appointed, and if no person have a majority, then from the two highest numbers on the list, the Senate shall choose the Vice-President; a quorum for the purpose shall consist of two-thirds of the whole number of Senators, and a majority of the whole number shall be necessary to a choice. But no person constitutionally ineligible to the office of President shall be eligible to that of Vice-President of the United States.

2. THE CIVIL WAR AND RECONSTRUCTION: 1861–1877

The second set of constitutional amendments are the three great post-Civil War Amendments. These amendments are so transformative that we devote an entire chapter to them later in this book. Of the three Reconstruction Amendments, the Thirteenth Amendment abolishes slavery and indentured servitude by either state or private actors and empowers Congress to enforce those prohibitions. The Fourteenth Amendment overturns the Supreme Court's decision in *Dred Scott v. Sandford*, 60 U.S. 393 (1857) and makes "All persons born or naturalized in the United States" citizens of both the United States and of the State wherein they reside. The Fourteenth Amendment also contains powerful restrictions on actions by state governments and also gives Congress power to enforce its provisions. Today, virtually all attention is paid to the first and fifth sections of the Fourteenth Amendment, but sections two through four were considered vital in 1868. The Fifteenth Amendment forbids race discrimination with respect to voting rights either in elections or (we think) on juries. All three Reconstruction Amendments empower Congress to enforce them by passing "appropriate" legislation.

AMENDMENT XIII (1865)

Section 1. Neither slavery nor involuntary servitude, except as a punishment for crime whereof the party shall have been duly convicted, shall exist within the United States, or any place subject to their jurisdiction.

Section 2. Congress shall have power to enforce this article by appropriate legislation.

AMENDMENT XIV (1868)

Section 1. All persons born or naturalized in the United States, and subject to the jurisdiction thereof, are citizens of the United States and of the State wherein they reside. No State shall make or enforce any law which shall abridge the privileges or immunities of citizens of the United States; nor shall any State deprive any person of life, liberty, or property, without due process of law; nor deny to any person within its jurisdiction the equal protection of the laws.

Section 2. Representatives shall be apportioned among the several States according to their respective numbers, counting the whole number of persons in each State, excluding Indians not taxed. But when the right to vote at any election for the choice of electors for President and Vice President of the United States, Representatives in Congress, the Executive and Judicial officers of a State, or the members of the Legislature thereof, is denied to any of the male inhabitants of such State, being twenty-one years of age, and citizens of the United States, or in any way abridged, except for participation in rebellion, or other crime, the basis of representation therein shall be reduced in the proportion which the number of such male citizens shall bear to the whole number of male citizens twenty-one years of age in such State.

Section 3. No person shall be a Senator or Representative in Congress, or elector of President and Vice President, or hold any office, civil or military, under the United States, or under any State, who, having previously taken an oath, as a member of Congress, or as an officer of the United States, or as a member of any State legislature, or as an executive or judicial officer of any State, to support the Constitution of the United States, shall have engaged in insurrection or rebellion against the same, or given aid or comfort to the enemies thereof. But Congress may by a vote of two-thirds of each House, remove such disability.

Section 4. The validity of the public debt of the United States, authorized by law, including debts incurred for payment of pensions and bounties for services in suppressing insurrection or rebellion, shall not be questioned. But neither the United States nor any State shall assume or pay any debt or obligation incurred in aid of insurrection or rebellion against the United States, or any claim for the loss or emancipation of any slave; but all such debts, obligations and claims shall be held illegal and void.

Section 5. The Congress shall have power to enforce, by appropriate legislation, the provisions of this article.

AMENDMENT XV (1870)

Section 1. The right of citizens of the United States to vote shall not be denied or abridged by the United States or by any State on account of race, color, or previous condition of servitude.

Section 2. The Congress shall have power to enforce this article by appropriate legislation.

3. THE PROGRESSIVE ERA: 1890–1933

The Progressive Era Amendments grew out of the Progressive movement championed by Theodore Roosevelt, Woodrow Wilson, and Franklin D. Roosevelt. *See infra* pages 189–191. They transformed the Constitution almost as dramatically as did Reconstruction. While it is always treacherous to generalize about any large social movement: Progressives typically believed in government by independent agencies of experts and widely disliked James Madison's system of checks and balances, and they also wanted (and ultimately got) a much larger and more powerful federal government than any the Framers had ever dreamed of. Core Progressive Era amendments were the Sixteenth Amendment constitutionalizing the federal income tax, the Seventeenth Amendment creating direct election of U.S. Senators, the Nineteenth Amendment giving women the right to vote, and the Eighteenth Amendment enacting Prohibition, followed by the Twenty-First Amendment repealing Prohibition. The Twentieth Amendment made minor changes to governmental structures.

AMENDMENT XVI (1913)

The Congress shall have power to lay and collect taxes on incomes, from whatever source derived, without apportionment among the several States, and without regard to any census or enumeration.

AMENDMENT XVII (1913)

The Senate of the United States shall be composed of two Senators from each State, elected by the people thereof, for six years; and each Senator shall have one vote. The electors in each State shall have the qualifications requisite for electors of the most numerous branch of the State legislatures.

When vacancies happen in the representation of any State in the Senate, the executive authority of such State shall issue writs of election to fill such vacancies: Provided, That the legislature of any State may empower the executive thereof to make temporary appointments until the people fill the vacancies by election as the legislature may direct.

This amendment shall not be so construed as to affect the election or term of any Senator chosen before it becomes valid as part of the Constitution.

AMENDMENT XVIII (1919)

Section 1. After one year from the ratification of this article the manufacture, sale, or transportation of intoxicating liquors within, the importation thereof into, or the exportation thereof from the United States and all territory subject to the jurisdiction thereof for beverage purposes is hereby prohibited.

Section 2. The Congress and the several States shall have concurrent power to enforce this article by appropriate legislation.

Section 3. This article shall be inoperative unless it shall have been ratified as an amendment to the Constitution by the legislatures of the several States, as provided in the Constitution, within seven years from the date of the submission hereof to the States by the Congress.

AMENDMENT XIX (1920)

The right of citizens of the United States to vote shall not be denied or abridged by the United States or by any State on account of sex.

Congress shall have power to enforce this article by appropriate legislation.

AMENDMENT XX (1933)

Section 1. The terms of the President and Vice President shall end at noon on the 20th day of January, and the terms of Senators and Representatives at noon on the 3d day of January, of the years in which such terms would have ended if this article had not been ratified; and the terms of their successors shall then begin.

Section 2. The Congress shall assemble at least once in every year, and such meeting shall begin at noon on the 3d day of January, unless they shall by law appoint a different day.

Section 3. If, at the time fixed for the beginning of the term of the President, the President elect shall have died, the Vice President elect shall become President. If a President shall not have been chosen before the time fixed for the beginning of his term, or if the President elect shall have failed to qualify, then the Vice President elect shall act as President until a President shall have qualified; and the Congress may by law provide for the case wherein neither a President elect nor a Vice President elect shall have qualified, declaring who shall then act as President, or the manner in which one who is to act shall be selected, and such person shall act accordingly until a President or Vice President shall have qualified.

Section 4. The Congress may by law provide for the case of the death of any of the persons from whom the House of Representatives may choose a President whenever the right of choice shall have devolved upon them, and for the case of the death of any of the persons from whom the Senate may choose a Vice President whenever the right of choice shall have devolved upon them.

Section 5. Sections 1 and 2 shall take effect on the 15th day of October following the ratification of this article.

Section 6. This article shall be inoperative unless it shall have been ratified as an amendment to the Constitution by the legislatures of three-fourths of the several States within seven years from the date of its submission.

AMENDMENT XXI (1933)

Section 1. The eighteenth article of amendment to the Constitution of the United States is hereby repealed.

Section 2. The transportation or importation into any State, Territory, or possession of the United States for delivery or use therein of intoxicating liquors, in violation of the laws thereof, is hereby prohibited.

Section 3. This article shall be inoperative unless it shall have been ratified as an amendment to the Constitution by conventions in the several States, as provided in the Constitution, within seven years from the date of the submission hereof to the States by the Congress.

4. THE MODERN ERA: 1945 TO THE PRESENT

The Modern Era constitutional amendments have two themes. The first is a modest, but critically important and desirable, pruning of national and presidential power by limiting the President, who presides over the huge modern administrative state, to no more than ten years in office, which almost always means only two four-year terms in office. Thanks to the Twenty-Second Amendment, all second term Presidents are now lame ducks with limited power. The second power-limiting amendment is the Twenty-Seventh Amendment, which requires that an intervening congressional election occur before congressional pay raises can go into effect. This was originally proposed as the "second amendment" among the twelve proposals in the Bill of Rights that were went to the States for ratification in 1791; it failed ratification by one vote in 1791 but secured the necessary votes in 1992.

The second big theme of the Modern Era constitutional amendments is expanding suffrage and political rights. Amendments were adopted giving the residents of the District of Columbia three electoral votes, banning the use of poll taxes in federal elections, and reducing the voting age in federal and state elections to 18.

Finally, the Twenty-Fifth Amendment is an effort at constitutional house-cleaning, which requires that the President nominate a new Vice President, subject to confirmation by both Houses of Congress whenever there is a vacancy in the office of Vice President. This Amendment also provide that whenever there is a vacancy in the office of President, the Vice President "becomes" President. Finally, the Twenty-Fifth Amendment provides a mechanism for transferring power away from the President when he or she is incapacitated.

AMENDMENT XXII (1951)

Section 1. No person shall be elected to the office of the President more than twice, and no person who has held the office of President, or acted as President, for more than two years of a term to which some other person was elected President shall be elected to the office of the President more than once. But this article shall not apply to any person holding the office of President when this article was proposed by the Congress, and shall not prevent any person who may be holding the office of President, or acting as President, during the term within which this article becomes operative from holding the office of President or acting as President during the remainder of such term.

Section 2. This article shall be inoperative unless it shall have been ratified as an amendment to the Constitution by the legislatures of three-fourths of the several states within seven years from the date of its submission to the states by the Congress.

AMENDMENT XXIII (1961)

Section 1. The District constituting the seat of government of the United States shall appoint in such manner as the Congress may direct:

A number of electors of President and Vice President equal to the whole number of Senators and Representatives in Congress to which the District would be entitled if it were a state, but in no event more than the least populous state; they shall be in addition to those appointed by the states, but they shall be considered, for the purposes of the election of President and Vice President, to be electors appointed by a state; and they shall meet in the District and perform such duties as provided by the twelfth article of amendment.

Section 2. The Congress shall have power to enforce this article by appropriate legislation.

AMENDMENT XXIV (1964)

Section 1. The right of citizens of the United States to vote in any primary or other election for President or Vice President, for electors for President or Vice President, or for Senator or Representative in Congress, shall not be denied or abridged by the United States or any state by reason of failure to pay any poll tax or other tax.

Section 2. The Congress shall have power to enforce this article by appropriate legislation.

AMENDMENT XXV (1967)

Section 1. In case of the removal of the President from office or of his death or resignation, the Vice President shall become President.

Section 2. Whenever there is a vacancy in the office of the Vice President, the President shall nominate a Vice President who shall take office upon confirmation by a majority vote of both Houses of Congress.

Section 3. Whenever the President transmits to the President pro tempore of the Senate and the Speaker of the House of Representatives his written declaration that he is unable to discharge the powers and duties of his office, and until he transmits to them a written declaration to the contrary, such powers and duties shall be discharged by the Vice President as Acting President.

Section 4. Whenever the Vice President and a majority of either the principal officers of the executive departments or of such other body as Congress may by law provide, transmit to the President pro tempore of the Senate and the Speaker of the House of Representatives their written declaration that the President is unable to discharge the powers and duties of his office, the Vice President shall immediately assume the powers and duties of the office as Acting President.

Thereafter, when the President transmits to the President pro tempore of the Senate and the Speaker of the House of Representatives his written declaration that no inability exists, he shall resume the powers and duties of his office unless the Vice President and a majority of either the principal officers of the executive department or of such other body as Congress may by law provide, transmit within four days to the President pro tempore of the Senate and the Speaker of the House of Representatives their written declaration that the President is unable to discharge the powers and duties of his office. Thereupon Congress shall decide the issue, assembling within forty-eight hours for that purpose if not in session. If the Congress, within twenty-one days after receipt of the latter written declaration, or, if Congress is not in session, within twenty-one days after Congress is required to assemble, determines by two-thirds vote of both Houses that the President is unable to discharge the powers and duties of his office, the Vice President shall continue to discharge the same as Acting President; otherwise, the President shall resume the powers and duties of his office.

AMENDMENT XXVI (1971)

Section 1. The right of citizens of the United States, who are 18 years of age or older, to vote, shall not be denied or abridged by the United States or any state on account of age.

Section 2. The Congress shall have the power to enforce this article by appropriate legislation.

AMENDMENT XXVII (1992)

No law varying the compensation for the services of the Senators and Representatives shall take effect until an election of Representatives shall have intervened.

[Assignment 5]

VI. JUDICIAL REVIEW

Who decides what the Constitution means? Suppose that Congress passes a bill, which is signed by the President and thus becomes a "law" under Article I, section 7. Congress and the President both conclude (either expressly or by implication from having enacted the law) that the law is constitutional. You disagree and challenge the law in a federal court. Can the court disagree with Congress and the President and find the law unconstitutional? Or is the court conclusively bound by the prior determinations of constitutionality made by Congress and the President?

Today those questions seem odd. Courts routinely second-guess the constitutional decisions of Congress and the President. Indeed, today it seems odd when Congress and the President purport to disagree with the courts on constitutional matters rather than vice versa. But in 1787 the role of the courts in constitutional adjudication was not settled—for the simple reason that there was relatively little experience with written constitutions. Nonetheless, by 1787, the Framers could draw on the practices under their state constitutions, as well as 150 years of review of colonial actions by the Privy Council in London. Consider now the arguments put forward by Alexander Hamilton in *The Federalist* No. 78 for the proposition that courts do and must stand ready to pass judgment on the constitutionality of actions by Congress and the President.

A. THE FEDERALIST NO. 78 (ALEXANDER HAMILTON)

(June 14, 1788)

The complete independence of the courts of justice is peculiarly essential in a limited Constitution. By a limited Constitution, I understand one which contains certain specified exceptions to the legislative authority; such, for instance, as that it shall pass no bills of attainder, no *ex post facto* laws, and the like. Limitations of this kind can be preserved in practice no other way than through the medium of courts of justice, whose duty it must be to declare all acts contrary to the manifest tenor of the Constitution void. Without this, all the reservations of particular rights or privileges would amount to nothing.

Some perplexity respecting the rights of the courts to pronounce legislative acts void, because contrary to the Constitution, has arisen from an imagination that the doctrine would imply a superiority of the judiciary to the legislative power. It is urged that the authority which can declare the acts of another void, must necessarily be superior to the one whose acts may be declared void. As this doctrine is of great importance in all the American constitutions, a brief discussion of the ground on which it rests cannot be unacceptable.

There is no position which depends on clearer principles, than that every act of a delegated authority, contrary to the tenor of the commission under which it is exercised, is void. No legislative act, therefore, contrary to the Constitution, can be valid. To deny this, would be to affirm, that the deputy is greater than his principal; that the servant is above his master; that the representatives of the people are superior to the people themselves; that men acting by virtue of powers, may do not only what their powers do not authorize, but what they forbid.

If it be said that the legislative body are themselves the constitutional judges of their own powers, and that the construction they put upon them is conclusive upon the other departments, it may be answered, that this cannot be the natural presumption, where it is not to be collected from any particular provisions in the Constitution. It is not otherwise to be supposed, that the Constitution could intend to enable the representatives of the people to substitute their *will* to that of their constituents. It is far more rational to suppose, that the courts were designed to be an intermediate body between the people and the legislature, in order, among other things, to keep the latter within the limits assigned to their authority. The interpretation of the laws is the proper and peculiar province of the courts. A constitution is, in fact, and must be regarded by the judges, as a fundamental law. It therefore belongs to them to ascertain its meaning, as well as the meaning of any particular act proceeding from the legislative body. If there should happen to be an irreconcilable variance between the two, that which has the superior obligation and validity ought, of course, to be preferred; or, in other words, the Constitution ought to be preferred to the statute, the intention of the people to the intention of their agents.

Nor does this conclusion by any means suppose a superiority of the judicial to the legislative power. It only supposes that the power of the people is superior to both; and that where the will of the legislature, declared in its statutes, stands in opposition to that of the people, declared in the Constitution, the judges ought to be governed by the latter rather than the former. They ought to regulate their decisions by the fundamental laws, rather than by those which are not fundamental.

This exercise of judicial discretion, in determining between two contradictory laws, is exemplified in a familiar instance. It not uncommonly happens, that there are two statutes existing at one time, clashing in whole or in part with each other, and neither of them containing any repealing clause or expression. In such a case, it is the province of the courts to liquidate and fix their meaning and operation. So far as they can, by any fair construction, be reconciled to each other, reason and law conspire to dictate that this should be done; where this is impracticable, it becomes a matter of necessity to give effect to one, in exclusion of the other. The rule which has obtained in the courts for determining their relative validity is, that the last in order of time shall be preferred to the first. But this is a mere rule of construction, not derived from any positive law, but from the nature and reason of the thing. It is a rule not enjoined upon the courts by legislative provision, but adopted by themselves, as consonant to truth and propriety, for the direction of their conduct as interpreters of the law. They thought it reasonable, that between the interfering acts of an EQUAL authority, that which was the last indication of its will should have the preference.

But in regard to the interfering acts of a superior and subordinate authority, of an original and derivative power, the nature and reason of the thing indicate the converse of that rule as proper to be followed. They teach us that the prior act of a superior ought to be preferred to the subsequent act of an inferior and subordinate authority; and that accordingly, whenever a particular statute contravenes the Constitution, it will be the duty of the judicial tribunals to adhere to the latter and disregard the former.

B. THE HISTORICAL CONTEXT IN WHICH *MARBURY V. MADISON* AROSE

Fifteen years after Hamilton addressed the subject, the Supreme Court took up the topic of judicial review of congressional legislation. Before you read the opinion in *Marbury v. Madison*, some background information is essential to understanding what happened in the case.

Under the original Constitution, before the Twelfth Amendment, the runner-up for the presidency became the Vice President. Accordingly, John Adams, an arch-Federalist, had to put up with Thomas Jefferson, his chief political rival, as Vice President from 1797–1800. Adams and Jefferson faced off in the election of 1800, with Jefferson heading the new Democratic-Republican Party. The election was one of the most contentious in American history, coming on the heels of the Federalist-sponsored Sedition Act. The stakes were high, because the emerging political parties (which just a few years earlier would have struck everyone as anathema) had well developed and starkly contrasting ideologies. "Republicans were for revolutionary France and against monarchical England; Federalists were against atheistic France and for a realistic accommodation with England. Republicans were for a strictly limited central government; Federalists advanced an ambitious national agenda of economic and social development." BRUCE ACKERMAN, THE FAILURE OF THE FOUNDING FATHERS: JEFFERSON, MARSHALL, AND THE RISE OF PRESIDENTIAL DEMOCRACY 19 (2005). Adams likely would have won but for the Three-Fifths Clause, which increased the voting power of the South. As it was, Jefferson ended up tying in electoral votes with his intended Vice President Aaron Burr, throwing the election into the (Federalist-controlled) House of Representatives. Jefferson won in the House—on the *thirty-sixth* ballot. The Jeffersonian Democratic-Republicans were also set to take control of Congress from the Federalists after that election. But there was a four-month gap between the election and the transfer of power. It was an eventful four months.

Jefferson and his new Congress were due to take office on March 4, 1801. In the days after the November 1800 election but before the transfer of power, the still-Federalist-dominated Congress enacted the Judiciary Act of 1801, which created sixteen new circuit court judgeships, widely expanded the jurisdiction of the federal courts (so the new Federalist-appointed judges would have more power), and abolished circuit-riding by Supreme Court justices (so the Federalist-appointed justices would not have to travel the country on horseback for six months every year). *See* Steven G. Calabresi & David C. Presser, *Reintroducing Circuit Riding: A Timely Proposal,* 90 U. Minn. L. Rev. 1386 (2006). And just to be safe, the statute reduced the size of the Supreme Court from six to five upon the next vacancy. *See* Act of Feb. 3, 1801, ch. IV, § 3, 2 Stat. 89, 89. Jefferson famously commented on this court-packing plan that the Federalists "have retired into the judiciary as a stronghold. There the remains of federalism are to be preserved and fed from the treasury, and from that battery all the works of republicanism are to be beaten down and erased."

Letter from Thomas Jefferson to John Dickinson, Dec. 19, 1801, *in* 10 THE WRITINGS OF THOMAS JEFFERSON 301, 301 (Albert Ellery Bergh ed., 1907).

In addition to the new circuit judges, President Adams nominated John Marshall to be Chief Justice of the Supreme Court (replacing the retiring Oliver Ellsworth) on January 20, 1801, and the Federalist Senate confirmed Marshall in two weeks. This was the most important single thing John Adams did as President. It was John Marshall who built up the power and prestige of the Supreme Court, and of the entire federal government, during his record thirty-five-year long tenure as Chief Justice. Marshall will come in for a drumbeat of criticism in this casebook for his sometimes slippery misreading of statutory and constitutional texts, but it must be acknowledged that he suffered through a bitter cold winter as George Washington's right-hand man at Valley Forge during a time when the Continental Congress could not even raise the money to pay General Washington's soldiers. Marshall no doubt determined that the federal government would never be that weak again, and he may have done his work too well. In any event, remember Valley Forge when we criticize John Marshall.

The new circuit judges, with their jurisdiction extending (for the first time) over all federal question cases, *see* Act of Feb. 3, 1801, at § 11, 2 Stat. at 92, were only the beginning. Just before President Jefferson took office, Congress enacted a statute for the government of the District of Columbia which authorized the appointment of "such number of discreet persons to be justices of the peace, as the President of the United States shall from time to time think expedient * * *." Act of Feb. 27, 1801, ch. XV, § 11, 2 Stat. 103, 107. To make sure that these last-second Adams appointees would not be removed by the new president, the statute added that the justices of the peace would "continue in office five years." *Id.* Two days before Jefferson was to take office, President Adams nominated forty-two justices of the peace for the District of Columbia (including, as it was misspelled in the Senate journal, William "Marberry"). *See* 1 J. Exec. Proceedings of the Senate of the U.S. 388. The Senate confirmed all of the nominees the next day. *See id.* at 389.

Now things get interesting. John Adams had just appointed, and the Senate had confirmed, John Marshall as Chief Justice. On March 3, 1801, just before Thomas Jefferson was to take office, the U.S. Secretary of State was (wait for it)—John Marshall. He held both positions for the last month of the Adams Administration, which the Constitution permits, as there is no disqualification on simultaneously holding executive and judicial positions. President Adams signed all of the commissions for the new justices of the peace, and it was left to Marshall and his brother, James Marshall (who was confirmed as a circuit court judge on March 3, 1801) to deliver the commissions to the appointees. About half the appointees were in Virginia and the other half were in Maryland, and the two Marshalls simply could not get them all delivered in the short time available. When President Jefferson and his new Secretary of State, James Madison, took office, Jefferson instructed Madison not to deliver any of the still-undelivered commissions remaining in the Secretary of State's office.

Marbury and three other appointees sued for a writ of mandamus to compel delivery of their commissions. While they possibly could have sued in the District of Columbia circuit court, they chose to sue in the Supreme Court under its original jurisdiction. *See* Susan Low Bloch, *The Marbury Mystery: Why Did William Marbury Sue in the Supreme Court?*, 18 CONST. COMMENTARY 607 (2001).

The Jeffersonians were outraged about President Adams' "midnight judges," and they repealed the Judiciary Act of 1801, thus eliminating altogether the sixteen circuit court judgeships created in February 1801. There was a real constitutional question as to whether life-tenured Article III judgeships could simply be abolished as the Jeffersonians had done. In addition, the Jeffersonians restored the obligation of the Supreme Court justices to ride circuit. The nation waited with bated breath to see if the Federalist Marshall Court would hold unconstitutional the abolition of the sixteen life-tenured circuit judges, triggering a constitutional crisis, with Jefferson highly likely to refuse to enforce the Supreme Court's order if it went against him.

In the end, the Supreme Court accepted the constitutionality of both the abolition of the sixteen circuit court judgeships and the reimposition of the obligation of Supreme Court justices to ride circuit. *See Stuart v. Laird*, 5 U.S. 299 (1803). This decision upholding the actions of the Jeffersonian Congress and presidency was issued five days after the blockbuster opinion in *Marbury v. Madison* (though there is a good argument that *Laird* was the real blockbuster).

With this background in mind, you should now read the (heavily edited) opinion in *Marbury*.

C. MARBURY V. MADISON

5 U.S. (1 Cranch) 137 (1803)

■ MR. CHIEF JUSTICE MARSHALL delivered the opinion of the Court.

At the last term, on the affidavits then read and filed with the clerk, a rule was granted in this case requiring the Secretary of State to shew cause why a mandamus should not issue directing him to deliver to William Marbury his commission as a justice of the peace for the county of Washington, in the District of Columbia.

No cause has been shewn, and the present motion is for a mandamus. The peculiar delicacy of this case, the novelty of some of its circumstances, and the real difficulty attending the points which occur in it require a complete exposition of the principles on which the opinion to be given by the Court is founded.

These principles have been, on the side of the applicant, very ably argued at the bar. In rendering the opinion of the Court, there will be some departure in form, though not in substance, from the points stated in that argument.

In the order in which the Court has viewed this subject, the following questions have been considered and decided.

1st. Has the applicant a right to the commission he demands?

2dly. If he has a right, and that right has been violated, do the laws of his country afford him a remedy?

3dly. If they do afford him a remedy, is it a mandamus issuing from this court?

The first object of inquiry is:

1st. Has the applicant a right to the commission he demands?

His right originates in an act of Congress passed in February, 1801, concerning the District of Columbia.

After dividing the district into two counties, the eleventh section of this law enacts, "that there shall be appointed in and for each of the said counties such number of discreet persons to be justices of the peace as the President of the United States shall, from time to time, think expedient, to continue in office for five years."

It appears from the affidavits that, in compliance with this law, a commission for William Marbury as a justice of peace for the County of Washington, was signed by John Adams, then President of the United States; after which the seal of the United States was affixed to it; but the commission has never reached the person for whom it was made out.

In order to determine whether he is entitled to this commission, it becomes necessary to inquire whether he has been appointed to the office. For if he has been appointed, the law continues him in office for five years, and he is entitled to the possession of those evidences of office, which, being completed, became his property.

The second section of the second article of the Constitution declares that, "The President shall nominate, and, by and with the advice and consent of the Senate, shall appoint ambassadors, other public ministers and consuls, and all other officers of the United States, whose appointments are not otherwise provided for."

The third section declares, that "he shall commission all the officers of the United States."

An act of congress directs the secretary of state to keep the seal of the United States, "to make out and record, and affix the said seal to all civil commissions to officers of the United States to be appointed by the President, by and with the consent of the Senate, or by the President alone; provided that the said seal shall not be affixed to any commission before the same shall have been signed by the President of the United States."

These are the clauses of the constitution and laws of the United States which affect this part of the case. They seem to contemplate three distinct operations:

1st. The nomination. This is the sole act of the President, and is completely voluntary.

2dly. The appointment. This is also the act of the President, and is also a voluntary act, though it can only be performed by and with the advice and consent of the Senate.

3dly. The commission. To grant a commission to a person appointed might perhaps be deemed a duty enjoined by the Constitution. "He shall," says that instrument, "commission all the officers of the United States."

* * *

The last act to be done by the President is the signature of the commission. He has then acted on the advice and consent of the senate to his own nomination. The time for deliberation has then passed. He has decided. His judgment, on the advice and consent of the senate concurring with his nomination, has been made, and the officer is appointed. This appointment is evidenced by an open, unequivocal act, and, being the last act required from the person making it, necessarily excludes the idea of its being, so far as it respects the appointment, an inchoate and incomplete transaction.

* * *

The commission being signed, the subsequent duty of the secretary of state is prescribed by law, and not to be guided by the will of the President. He is to affix the seal of the United States to the commission, and is to record it.

This is not a proceeding which may be varied if the judgment of the executive shall suggest one more eligible, but is a precise course accurately marked out by law, and is to be strictly pursued. It is the duty of the secretary of state to conform to the law, and in this he is an officer of the United States, bound to obey the laws. He acts, in this respect, as has been very properly stated at the bar, under the authority of law, and not by the instructions of the President. It is a ministerial act which the law enjoins on a particular officer for a particular purpose.

* * *

It is therefore decidedly the opinion of the Court that, when a commission has been signed by the President, the appointment is made; and that the commission is complete when the seal of the United States has been affixed to it by the secretary of state.

Where an officer is removable at the will of the executive, the circumstance which completes his appointment is of no concern, because the act is at any time revocable, and the commission may be arrested if still in the office. But when the officer is not removable at the will of the executive, the appointment is not revocable, and cannot be annulled. It has conferred legal rights which cannot be resumed.

The discretion of the executive is to be exercised until the appointment has been made. But having once made the appointment, his power over the office is terminated in all cases, where, by law, the officer is not removeable by him. The right to the office is *then* in the person appointed, and he has the absolute, unconditional power of accepting or rejecting it.

Mr. Marbury, then, since his commission was signed by the President, and sealed by the secretary of state, was appointed; and as the law creating the office gave the officer a right to hold for five years, independent of the executive, the appointment was not revocable; but vested in the officer legal rights, which are protected by the laws of his country.

To withhold the commission, therefore, is an act deemed by the court not warranted by law, but violative of a vested legal right.

This brings us to the second inquiry; which is,

2dly. If he has a right, and that right has been violated, do the laws of his country afford him a remedy?

The very essence of civil liberty certainly consists in the right of every individual to claim the protection of the laws, whenever he receives an injury. One of the first duties of government is to afford that protection. In Great Britain, the king himself is sued in the respectful form of a petition, and he never fails to comply with the judgment of his court.

* * *

The Government of the United States has been emphatically termed a government of laws, and not of men. It will certainly cease to deserve this high appellation, if the laws furnish no remedy for the violation of a vested legal right.

If this obloquy is to be cast on the jurisprudence of our country, it must arise from the peculiar character of the case.

It behooves us, then, to inquire whether there be in its composition any ingredient which shall exempt from legal investigation, or exclude the injured party from legal redress. In pursuing this inquiry the first question which presents itself, is, whether this can be arranged with that class of cases which come under the description of *damnum absque injuria*—a loss without an injury.

This description of cases never has been considered, and it is believed never can be considered, as comprehending offices of trust, of honour or of profit. The office of justice of peace in the district of Columbia is such an office; it is therefore worthy of the attention and guardianship of the laws. It has received that attention and guardianship. It has been created by special act of congress, and has been secured, so far as the laws can give security to the person appointed to fill it, for five years. It is not then on account of the worthlessness of the thing pursued that the injured party can be alleged to be without remedy.

Is it in the nature of the transaction? Is the act of delivering or withholding a commission to be considered as a mere political act, belonging to the executive department alone, for the performance of which entire confidence is placed by our Constitution in the supreme executive; and for any misconduct respecting which, the injured individual has no remedy?

That there may be such cases is not to be questioned; but that every act of duty, to be performed in any of the great departments of government, constitutes such a case, is not to be admitted.

By the act concerning invalids, passed in June, 1794, the secretary at war is ordered to place on the pension list all persons whose names are contained in a report previously made by him to congress. If he should refuse to do so, would the wounded veteran be without remedy? Is it to be contended that where the law, in precise terms, directs the performance of an act, in which an individual is interested, the law is incapable of securing obedience to its mandate? Is it on account of the character of the person against whom the complaint is made? Is it to be contended that the heads of departments are not amenable to the laws of their country?

* * *

It is not believed that any person whatever would attempt to maintain such a proposition.

It follows then that the question whether the legality of an act of the head of a department be examinable in a court of justice or not, must always depend on the nature of that act.

If some acts be examinable, and others not, there must be some rule of law to guide the Court in the exercise of its jurisdiction.

In some instances there may be difficulty in applying the rule to particular cases; but there cannot, it is believed, be much difficulty in laying down the rule.

By the constitution of the United States, the President is invested with certain important political powers, in the exercise of which he is to use his own discretion, and is accountable only to his country in his political character, and to his own conscience. To aid him in the performance of these duties, he is authorized to appoint certain officers, who act by his authority and in conformity with his orders.

In such cases, their acts are his acts; and whatever opinion may be entertained of the manner in which executive discretion may be used, still there exists, and can exist, no power to control that discretion. The subjects are political. They respect the nation, not individual rights, and, being entrusted to the executive, the decision of the executive is conclusive. The application of this remark will be perceived by adverting to the act of Congress for establishing the department of foreign affairs. This officer, as his duties were prescribed by that act, is to conform precisely to the will of the President. He is the mere organ by whom that will is communicated. The acts of such an officer, as an officer, can never be examinable by the courts.

But when the legislature proceeds to impose on that officer other duties; when he is directed peremptorily to perform certain acts; when the rights of individuals are dependent on the performance of those acts; he is so far the officer of the law; is amenable to the laws for his conduct; and cannot at his discretion sport away the vested rights of others.

The conclusion from this reasoning is, that, where the heads of departments are the political or confidential agents of the executive, merely to execute the will of the President, or rather to act in cases in which the executive possesses a constitutional or legal discretion, nothing can be more perfectly clear than that their acts are only politically examinable. But where a specific duty is assigned by law, and individual rights depend upon the performance of that duty, it seems equally clear that the individual who considers himself injured, has a right to resort to the laws of his country for a remedy.

If this be the rule, let us inquire how it applies to the case under the consideration of the court.

The power of nominating to the senate, and the power of appointing the person nominated, are political powers, to be exercised by the President according to his own discretion. When he has made an appointment, he has exercised his whole power, and his discretion has been completely applied to the case. If, by law, the officer be removable at the will of the President; then a new appointment may be immediately made, and the rights of the officer are terminated. But as a fact which has existed cannot be made never to have existed, the appointment cannot be annihilated; and consequently if the officer is by law not removable at the will of the President, the rights he has acquired are protected by the law, and are not resumable by the President. They cannot be extinguished by executive authority, and he has the privilege of asserting them in like manner as if they had been derived from any other source.

* * *

It is then the opinion of the Court:

1st. That, by signing the commission of Mr. Marbury, the president of the United States appointed him a justice of peace for the county of Washington in the district of Columbia; and that the seal of the United States, affixed thereto by the secretary of state, is conclusive testimony of the verity of the signature, and of the completion of the appointment; and that the appointment conferred on him a legal right to the office for the space of five years.

2dly. That, having this legal title to the office, he has a consequent right to the commission; a refusal to deliver which is a plain violation of that right, for which the laws of his country afford him a remedy.

It remains to be inquired whether,

3dly. He is entitled to the remedy for which he applies. This depends on:

1st. The nature of the writ applied for, and

2dly. The power of this court.

1st. The nature of the writ.

Blackstone, in the 3d volume of his commentaries, page 110, defines a mandamus to be "a command issuing in the king's name from the court of king's bench, and directed to any person, corporation, or inferior court of judicature within the king's dominions requiring them to do some particular thing therein specified, which appertains to their office and duty, and which the court of king's bench has previously determined, or at least supposes, to be consonant to right and justice."

* * *

Still, to render the mandamus a proper remedy, the officer to whom it is to be directed, must be one to whom, on legal principles, such writ may be directed; and the person applying for it must be without any other specific and legal remedy.

1st. With respect to the officer to whom it would be directed. The intimate political relation, subsisting between the president of the United States and the heads of departments, necessarily renders any legal investigation of the acts of one of those high officers peculiarly irksome, as well as delicate; and excites some hesitation with respect to the propriety of entering into such investigation. Impressions are often received without much reflection or examination, and it is not wonderful that, in such a case as this, the assertion, by an individual of his legal claims in a court of justice; to which claims it is the duty of that court to attend; should at first view be considered by some as an attempt to intrude into the cabinet, and to intermeddle with the prerogatives of the executive.

It is scarcely necessary for the court to disclaim all pretensions to such a jurisdiction. An extravagance so absurd and excessive, could not have been entertained for a moment. The province of the court is, solely, to decide on the rights of individuals, not to inquire how the executive or executive officers, perform duties in which they have a discretion. Questions, in their nature political, or which are, by the constitution and laws, submitted to the executive, can never be made in this court.

But, if this be not such a question; if so far from being an intrusion into the secrets of the cabinet, it respects a paper which, according to law, is upon record, and to a copy of which the law gives a right, on the payment of ten cents; if it be no intermeddling with a subject, over which the executive can be considered as having exercised any control; what is there in the exalted station of the officer which shall bar a citizen from asserting, in a court of justice, his legal rights, or shall forbid a court to listen to the claim; or to issue a mandamus directing the performance of a duty, not depending on executive discretion, but on particular acts of congress and the general principles of law?

If one of the heads of departments commits any illegal act, under colour of his office, by which an individual sustains an injury, it cannot be pretended that his office alone exempts him from being sued in the ordinary mode of proceeding, and being compelled to obey the judgment of the law. How then can his office exempt him from this particular mode of deciding on the legality of his conduct, if the case be such a case as would, were any other individual the party complained of, authorize the process?

It is not by the office of the person to whom the writ is directed, but the nature of the thing to be done, that the propriety or impropriety of issuing a mandamus is to be determined. Where the head of a department acts in a case, in which executive discretion is to be exercised; in which he is the mere organ of xecutive will; it is again repeated, that any application to a court to control, in any respect, his conduct, would be rejected without hesitation.

But where he is directed by law to do a certain act affecting the absolute rights of individuals, in the performance of which he is not placed under the particular direction of the President, and the performance of which, the President cannot lawfully forbid, and therefore is never presumed to have forbidden; as, for example, to record a commission, or a patent for land, which has received all the legal solemnities; or to give a copy of such record; in such cases, it is not perceived on what ground the courts of the country are further excused from the duty of giving judgment, that right to be done to an injured individual, than if the same services were to be performed by a person not the head of a department.

* * *

This, then, is a plain case of a mandamus, either to deliver the commission, or a copy of it from the record; and it only remains to be inquired,

Whether it can issue from this court.

[Editors' Note: Here begins Chief Justice Marshall's explanation of why the Supreme Court lacked jurisdiction or power to decide this case. Everything you have read up to this point is dicta.]

The act to establish the judicial courts of the United States authorizes the Supreme Court "to issue writs of mandamus, in cases warranted by the principles and usages of law, to any courts appointed, or persons holding office, under the authority of the United States."

The secretary of state, being a person, holding an office under the authority of the United States, is precisely within the letter of the description; and if this court is not authorized to issue a writ of mandamus to such an officer, it must be because the law is unconstitutional, and therefore absolutely incapable of conferring the authority, and assigning the duties which its words purport to confer and assign.

The constitution vests the whole judicial power of the United States in one supreme court, and such inferior courts as congress shall, from time to time, ordain and establish. This power is expressly extended to all cases arising under the laws of the United States; and consequently, in some form, may be exercised over the present case; because the right claimed is given by a law of the United States.

In the distribution of this power. it is declared that "The supreme court shall have original jurisdiction in all cases affecting ambassadors, other public ministers and consuls, and those in which a state shall be a party. In all other cases, the supreme court shall have appellate jurisdiction."

It has been insisted, at the bar, that, as the original grant of jurisdiction to the supreme and inferior courts, is general, and the clause, assigning original jurisdiction to the supreme court, contains no negative or restrictive words; the power remains to the legislature, to assign original jurisdiction to that court in other cases than those specified in the article which has been recited; provided those cases belong to the judicial power of the United States.

If it had been intended to leave it in the discretion of the legislature to apportion the judicial power between the supreme and inferior courts according to the will of that body, it would certainly have been useless to have proceeded further than to have defined the judicial power, and the tribunals in which it should be vested. The subsequent part of the section is mere surplusage, is entirely without meaning, if such is to be the construction. If congress remains at liberty to give this court appellate jurisdiction, where the constitution has declared their jurisdiction shall be original; and original jurisdiction where the constitution has declared it shall be appellate; the distribution of jurisdiction, made in the constitution, is form without substance.

Affirmative words are often, in their operation, negative of other objects than those affirmed; and, in this case, a negative or exclusive sense must be given to them or they have no operation at all.

It cannot be presumed that any clause in the constitution is intended to be without effect; and therefore such construction is inadmissible, unless the words require it.

If the solicitude of the convention respecting our peace with foreign powers, induced a provision that the supreme court should take original jurisdiction in cases which might be supposed to affect them; yet the clause would have proceeded no further than to provide for such cases, if no further restriction on the powers of congress had been intended. That they should have appellate jurisdiction in all other cases, with such exceptions as congress might make, is no restriction; unless the words be deemed exclusive of original jurisdiction.

When an instrument organizing fundamentally, a judicial system, divides it into one supreme, and so many inferior courts as the legislature may ordain and establish; then enumerates its powers, and proceeds so far to distribute them as to define the jurisdiction of the supreme court by declaring the cases in which it shall take original jurisdiction, and that in others it shall take appellate jurisdiction; the plain import of the words seems to be, that in one class of cases its jurisdiction is original, and not appellate; in the other it is appellate, and not original. If any other construction would render the clause inoperative, that is an additional reason for rejecting such other construction, and for adhering to the obvious meaning.

To enable this court then to issue a mandamus, it must be shewn to be an exercise of appellate jurisdiction, or to be necessary to enable them to exercise appellate jurisdiction.

It has been stated at the bar that the appellate jurisdiction may be exercised in a variety of forms, and that if it be the will of the legislature that a mandamus should be used for that purpose, that will must be obeyed. This is true, yet the jurisdiction must be appellate, not original.

It is the essential criterion of appellate jurisdiction, that it revises and corrects the proceedings in a cause already instituted, and does not create that case. Although, therefore, a mandamus may be directed to courts, yet to issue such a writ to an officer for the delivery of a paper, is in effect the same as to sustain an original action for that paper, and therefore seems not to belong to appellate, but to original jurisdiction. Neither is it necessary in such a case as this, to enable the court to exercise its appellate jurisdiction.

The authority, therefore, given to the supreme court, by the act establishing the judicial courts of the United States, to issue writs of mandamus to public officers, appears not to be warranted by the constitution; and it becomes necessary to inquire whether a jurisdiction, so conferred, can be exercised.

The question, whether an act, repugnant to the constitution, can become the law of the land, is a question deeply interesting to the United States; but, happily, not of an intricacy proportioned to its interest. It seems only necessary to recognise certain principles, supposed to have been long and well established, to decide it.

That the people have an original right to establish, for their future government, such principles as, in their opinion, shall most conduce to their own happiness, is the basis, on which the whole American fabric has been erected. The exercise of this original right is a very great exertion; nor can it nor ought it to be frequently repeated. The principles, therefore, so established, are deemed fundamental. And as the authority, from which they proceed, is supreme, and can seldom act, they are designed to be permanent.

This original and supreme will organizes the government, and assigns, to different departments, their respective powers. It may either stop here; or establish certain limits not to be transcended by those departments.

The government of the United States is of the latter description. The powers of the legislature are defined and limited; and that those limits may not be mistaken, or forgotten, the constitution is written. To what purpose are powers limited, and to what purpose is that limitation committed to writing, if these limits may, at any time, be passed by those intended to be restrained? The distinction between a government with limited and unlimited powers, is abolished, if those limits do not confine the persons on whom they are imposed, and if acts prohibited and acts allowed, are of equal obligation. It is a proposition too plain to be contested, that the constitution controls any legislative act repugnant to it; or that the legislature may alter the constitution by an ordinary act.

Between these alternatives there is no middle ground. The constitution is either a superior, paramount law, unchangeable by ordinary means, or it is on a level with ordinary legislative acts, and like other acts, is alterable when the legislature shall please to alter it.

If the former part of the alternative be true, then a legislative act contrary to the constitution is not law; if the latter part be true, then written constitutions are absurd attempts, on the part of the people, to limit a power, in its own nature illimitable.

Certainly all those who have framed written constitutions contemplate them as forming the fundamental and paramount law of the nation, and consequently the theory of every such government must be, that an act of the legislature, repugnant to the constitution, is void.

This theory is essentially attached to a written constitution, and is consequently to be considered, by this court, as one of the fundamental principles of our society. It is not therefore to be lost sight of in the further consideration of this subject.

If an act of the legislature, repugnant to the constitution, is void, does it, notwithstanding its invalidity, bind the courts, and oblige them to give it effect? Or, in other words, though it be not law, does it constitute a rule as operative as if it was a law? This would be to overthrow in fact what was established in theory; and would seem, at first view, an absurdity too gross to be insisted on. It shall, however, receive a more attentive consideration.

It is emphatically the province and duty of the judicial department to say what the law is. Those who apply the rule to particular cases, must of necessity expound and interpret that rule. If two laws conflict with each other, the courts must decide on the operation of each.

So if a law be in opposition to the constitution; if both the law and the constitution apply to a particular case, so that the court must either decide that case conformably to the law, disregarding the constitution; or conformably to the constitution, disregarding the law; the court must determine which of these conflicting rules governs the case. This is of the very essence of judicial duty.

If then the courts are to regard the constitution; and the constitution is superior to any ordinary act of the legislature; the constitution, and not such ordinary act, must govern the case to which they both apply.

Those then who controvert the principle that the constitution is to be considered, in court, as a paramount law, are reduced to the necessity of maintaining that courts must close their eyes on the constitution, and see only the law.

This doctrine would subvert the very foundation of all written constitutions. It would declare that an act, which, according to the principles and theory of our government, is entirely void; is yet, in practice, completely obligatory. It would declare, that, if the legislature shall do what is expressly forbidden, such act, notwithstanding the express prohibition, is in reality effectual. It would be giving to the legislature a practical and real omnipotence, with the same breath which professes to restrict their powers within narrow limits. It is prescribing limits, and declaring that those limits may be passed at pleasure.

That it thus reduces to nothing what we have deemed the greatest improvement on political institutions—a written constitution—would of itself be sufficient, in America, where written constitutions have been viewed with so much reverence, for rejecting the construction. But the peculiar expressions of the constitution of the United States furnish additional arguments in favour of its rejection.

The judicial power of the United States is extended to all cases arising under the constitution.

Could it be the intention of those who gave this power, to say that, in using it, the constitution should not be looked into? That a case arising under the constitution should be decided without examining the instrument under which it arises?

This is too extravagant to be maintained.

In some cases then, the constitution must be looked into by the judges. And if they can open it at all, what part of it are they forbidden to read, or to obey?

There are many other parts of the constitution which serve to illustrate this subject.

It is declared that "no tax or duty shall be laid on articles exported from any state." Suppose a duty on the export of cotton, of tobacco, or of flour; and a suit instituted to recover it. Ought judgment to be rendered in such a case? ought the judges to close their eyes on the constitution, and only see the law?

The constitution declares that "no bill of attainder or *ex post facto* law shall be passed."

If, however, such a bill should be passed and a person should be prosecuted under it; must the court condemn to death those victims whom the constitution endeavours to preserve?

"No person," says the constitution, "shall be convicted of treason unless on the testimony of two witnesses to the same overt act, or on confession in open court."

Here. the language of the constitution is addressed especially to the courts. It prescribes, directly for them, a rule of evidence not to be departed from. If the legislature should change that rule, and declare *one* witness, or a confession *out* of court, sufficient for conviction, must the constitutional principle yield to the legislative act?

From these and many other selections which might be made, it is apparent, that the framers of the constitution contemplated that instrument, as a rule for the government of *courts*, as well as of the legislature.

Why otherwise does it direct the judges to take an oath to support it? This oath certainly applies, in an especial manner, to their conduct in their official character. How immoral to impose it on them, if they were to be used as the instruments, and the knowing instruments, for violating what they swear to support!

* * * If such be the real state of things, this is worse than solemn mockery. To prescribe, or to take this oath, becomes equally a crime.

It is also not entirely unworthy of observation, that in declaring what shall be the *supreme* law of the land, the *constitution* itself is first mentioned; and not the laws of the United States generally, but those only which shall be made *in pursuance* of the constitution, have that rank.

Thus, the particular phraseology of the constitution of the United States confirms and strengthens the principle, supposed to be essential to all written constitutions, that a law repugnant to the Constitution is void; and that *courts*, as well as other departments, are bound by that instrument.

The rule must be discharged.

NOTES AND QUESTIONS

Marbury v. Madison is surely the most famous case in American legal history. It is therefore remarkable how many apparent (and in some cases obvious) errors it contains.

1. Marbury did not have his commission because John Marshall, while serving as Secretary of State, failed to deliver it. Marshall's brother, James, was also at fault in the waning days of the Adams Administration, and James Marshall testified as a witness before the Supreme Court. Should John Marshall have recused himself from hearing the case? Today, there is no doubt that Chief Justice Marshall would have been recused, but standards were looser in the early nineteenth century, when appellate judges who presided over trials would actually sit on appeals from their own decisions.

2. The *Marbury* opinion addresses, at interminable length (much of which we have edited out), the lawfulness of the Jefferson Administration's refusal to deliver William Marbury's commission—in a case where it concluded it lacked jurisdiction, or power, to act at all. If the Court had no power to act, shouldn't it have started, rather than ended, with that observation and then said no more? Was the first two-thirds of the opinion really a judicial opinion or more like an op-ed?

3. *Marbury* says in dicta, on five separate occasions, that Congress can create offices, such as the Justice of the Peace for the District of Columbia, with a fixed term of five years from which the President cannot immediately fire people at will. This cavalierly addresses one of the most important and long-lived controversies in American constitutional law. STEVEN G. CALABRESI & CHRISTOPHER S. YOO, THE UNITARY EXECUTIVE: PRESIDENTIAL POWER FROM WASHINGTON TO BUSH (2008). At first glance, Marshall's dicta seem entirely wrong; the Constitution specifies that *judicial* officers have tenure during good behavior; doesn't this imply that *executive* officers have no such tenure and can be fired at will? This dicta in *Marbury* was specifically rejected in *Myers v. United States*, 272 U.S. 52 (1926), though it has since been resurrected in substance. *See Humphrey's Executor v. United States,* 295 U.S. 602 (1935); *infra* pages 430–445. (And if you think that Marbury was a judicial rather than an executive official, how could he have a five-year term of office rather than tenure during good behavior?)

4. *Marbury* fairly obviously misreads Section 13 of the Judiciary Act of 1789 as purporting to add to the original jurisdiction of the Supreme Court. The Act does not such thing. It simply says that in cases over which the Supreme Court already has jurisdiction, it can issue writs of mandamus.

5. Even if Congress had tried to add to the Supreme Court's original jurisdiction (which it did not), *Marbury v. Madison* misreads Article III in finding such action unconstitutional. Article III says in full context:

> Section 1.
>
> The judicial Power of the United States, shall be vested in one Supreme Court, and in such inferior Courts as the Congress may from time to time ordain and establish * * *.
>
> Section 2.
>
> The judicial Power shall extend to all Cases, in Law and Equity, arising under this Constitution, the Laws of the United States, and Treaties made, or which shall be made, under their Authority * * *.
>
> In all Cases affecting Ambassadors, other public Ministers and Consuls, and those in which a State shall be Party, the Supreme Court shall have original Jurisdiction. In all the other Cases before mentioned, the Supreme Court shall have appellate Jurisdiction, both as to Law and Fact, with such Exceptions, and under such Regulations as the Congress shall make.

Under Marshall's reading of the Original Jurisdiction Clause as being exclusive and as comprehending only the "Cases affecting Ambassadors, other public Ministers [and cases] in which a State shall be a Party," the next sentence allowing Congress to make exceptions to the Supreme Court's appellate jurisdiction would allow Congress to take cases arising under federal law entirely away from the U.S. Supreme Court, leaving them to be decided by the state supreme courts. But this runs counter to the language in Article III, which expressly vests *the* "judicial Power of the United States" in the Supreme Court" and which expressly says the judicial power "shall extend to all Cases, in Law and Equity, arising under this Constitution, the Laws of the United States, and Treaties made, or which shall be made, under their Authority." The correct way to read the second paragraph of Article III, Section 2 is that it grants—or, more precisely, recognizes—Congress's power to move cases back and forth between the Supreme Court's original and appellate jurisdiction, so that an "exception" to appellate jurisdiction *places the case in the Supreme Court's original jurisdiction instead. See* Steven G. Calabresi & Gary Lawson, *The Unitary Executive, Jurisdiction Stripping, and the* Hamdan *Opinions: A Textualist Response to Justice Scalia*, 107 COLUM. L. REV.1002, 1036–42 (2007). (The power to make such a move comes from the Necessary and Proper Clause in Article I; the so-called "Exceptions Clause" cross-references but does not create or grant that power. *See* David E. Engdahl, *Intrinsic Limits of Congress' Power Regarding the Judicial Branch*, 1999 B.Y.U. L. REV. 75, 119–26.)

6. Thus, much of the opinion in *Marbury v Madison* is riddled with errors. But what of the discussion concerning judicial review? Here Marshall's argument parallels Alexander Hamilton's arguments in *The Federalist* No. 78. Marshall treats judicial review as a species of *conflict of laws*. Courts have the "judicial Power," which is quintessentially the power to decide cases within their jurisdiction pursuant to governing law. In order to carry out that function, courts must identify the law that governs the cases before them. Duly enacted congressional statutes are obviously law—Article I, section 7 says so—but the Constitution is also law. Just as a statute takes precedence over an administrative regulation if the two sources of law conflict, the Constitution takes precedence over a statute if the two sources of law conflict. The only remaining question is whether the courts are conclusively bound by the prior judgments of Congress and the President regarding the meaning of the Constitution, and the Constitution's obvious scheme of separation of powers (and express insulation of judges from direct political control) suggests that courts must make their own judgments about legal meaning. So stated, Marshall's argument for judicial review seems unanswerable. For whatever this is worth, we both think it is unanswerable. Since most of the rest of this course involves instances of judicial review, it is probably a good thing if we are right.

7. At least one prominent thinker has criticized Chief Justice Marshall's argument for judicial review on the ground that it does not adequately recognize the political role of courts. James Bradley Thayer, who we have encountered before, objected in 1893 that Marshall's argument in *Marbury* "took no notice of the remarkable peculiarities of the situation; it went forward as smoothly as if the constitution were a private letter of attorney, and the court's duty under it were precisely like any of its most ordinary operations." James B. Thayer, *The Origin and Scope of the American Doctrine of Constitutional Law,* 7 HARV. L. REV. 129, 139 (1893). Marshall's framing "easily results in the wrong kind of disregard of legislative considerations; not merely in refusing to let them directly operate as grounds of judgment, but in refusing to consider them at all. Instead of taking them into account and allowing for them as furnishing possible grounds of legislative action, there takes place a pedantic and academic treatment of the texts of the constitution and the laws. And so we miss that combination of a lawyer's rigor with a statesman's breadth of view which should be found in dealing with this class of questions in constitutional law." *Id.* at 138. Should judges try to behave like statesmen? *See* James E. Bond, *The Perils of Judicial Statesmanship,* 7 OKLA. CITY U. L. REV. 399 (1982). If judges are really statesmen, what is the rationale for judicial review? Are lawyers especially likely to be good statesmen?

8. Perhaps the most famous line in *Marbury v. Madison* is the declaration that "[i]t is emphatically the province and duty of the judicial department to say what the law is." Does that mean that the judicial department has the final word on constitutional

meaning and that all other actors must defer to the Supreme Court's interpretations of the Constitution?

That was obviously *not* what Marshall was saying in *Marbury*. Marshall was defending the *power* of courts to decide on constitutional meaning without being conclusively bound by the prior interpretations of Congress and the President; he was not making the much stronger claim that Congress and the President are conclusively bound by the prior interpretations of the Court. The very next line in *Marbury* is: "Those who apply the rule to particular cases must, of necessity, expound and interpret that rule." That principle applies to legislative and executive as well as judicial actors. *Marbury* is all about judicial *equality* with the political branches of the federal government and was not about judicial *supremacy* over them.

The Court asserted judicial supremacy in 1958, when it announced that:

> *Marbury* declared the basic principle that the federal judiciary is supreme in the exposition of the law of the Constitution, and that principle has ever since been respected by this Court and the Country as a permanent and indispensable feature of our constitutional system. It follows that *the interpretation of the Fourteenth Amendment enunciated by this Court* in the *Brown* case is the supreme law of the land, and Art. VI of the Constitution makes it of binding effect on the States 'any Thing in the Constitution or Laws of any State to the Contrary notwithstanding.'

Cooper v. Aaron, 358 U.S. 1, 18 (1958) (emphasis added). *Cooper*, for the first time, equated decisions of the Supreme Court with the actual text of the Constitution as "the supreme law of the land." This was an obvious misinterpretation of *Marbury,* but one that is perhaps understandable given the context. As you will later read, *see infra* pages 1314–1317, in 1954 the Supreme Court declared segregated public schools unconstitutional under the Fourteenth Amendment. The result was massive resistance in some Southern States, including refusals by state executive officials to comply with *specific judgments* issued by federal courts in particular cases. The Court's pronouncement in *Cooper* was prompted by that kind of open defiance of federal court orders.

But even if the Court's claim was understandable, was it correct as a general proposition about the Constitution's allocation of interpretative authority? As it happens, political actors have frequently found it expedient to yield interpretative authority to the Supreme Court, for complex reasons that have been well studied by political scientists. *See* KEITH E. WHITTINGTON, POLITICAL FOUNDATIONS OF JUDICIAL SUPREMACY: THE PRESIDENCY, THE SUPREME COURT, AND CONSTITUTIONAL LEADERSHIP IN U.S. HISTORY (2007). Nonetheless, consistently throughout U.S. history, people have asserted the co-equal power and duty of non-judicial actors to interpret and apply the Constitution as they best understand it. After all, the Constitution does not contain a "judicial review" clause or any kind of "interpretative power" clause. All powers of interpretation are inferences from other granted powers, such as the "judicial Power." Why isn't a power of interpretation equally an inference from, say, the "executive Power"? *See* Frank Easterbrook, *Presidential Review,* 40 CASE WESTERN L. REV. 905 (1989); Gary Lawson & Christopher D. Moore, *The Executive Power of Constitutional Interpretation,* 81 IOWA L. REV. 1267 (1996); Steven G. Calabresi, *Originalism and James Bradley Thayer*, 113 NW. U. L. REV. 1419 (2019). The idea that all units of government have the same power and duty independently to construe the Constitution is called "departmentalism." Virtually all departmentalists believe that specific judgments of courts must be enforced, but they doubt whether abstract pronouncements by courts in aid of those judgments are equivalent to the Constitution itself. We close out this chapter with some materials on constitutional interpretation outside the courts.

D. LETTER FROM THOMAS JEFFERSON TO ABIGAIL ADAMS

September 11, 1804, 11 THE WRITINGS OF THOMAS JEFFERSON 49, 50–51 (Albert Ellery Bergh ed., 1905)

You seem to think it devolved on the judges to decide on the validity of the sedition law. But nothing in the Constitution has given them a right to decide for the Executive, more than to the Executive to decide for them. Both magistrates are equally independent in the sphere of action assigned to them. The judges, believing the law to be constitutional, had a right to pass a sentence of fine and imprisonment; because the power was placed in their hands by the Constitution. But the executive, believing the law to be unconstitutional, were bound to remit the execution of it; because that power has been confided to them by the Constitution. That instrument meant that its coordinate branches should be checks on each other. But the opinion which gives to the judges the right to decide what law are constitutional, and what are not, not only for themselves in their own sphere of action, but for the legislature and the executive also, in their spheres, would make the judiciary a despotic branch.

E. JAMES MADISON, LETTER WRITTEN IN 1834

4 LETTERS AND OTHER WRITINGS OF JAMES MADISON 349, 349–50 (1865)

Having alluded to the Supreme Court of the United States as a constitutional resort in deciding questions of jurisdiction between the United States and the individual States, a few remarks may be proper, showing the sense and degree in which that character is more particularly ascribed to that department of the Government.

As the Legislative, Executive, and Judicial departments of the United States are co-ordinate, and each equally bound to support the Constitution, it follows that each must, in the exercise of its functions, be guided by the text of the Constitution according to its own interpretation of it; and, consequently, that in the event of irreconciliable interpretations, the prevalence of one or the other department must depend on the nature of the case, as receiving its final decision from the one or the other, and passing from that decision into effect, without involving the functions of any other.

It is certainly due from the functionaries of the several departments to pay much respect to the opinions of each other; and, as far as official independence and obligation will permit, to consult the means of adjusting differences and avoiding practical embarrassments growing out of them, as must be done in like cases between the different coordinate branches of the Legislative department.

But notwithstanding this abstract view of the co-ordinate and independent right of the three departments to expound the Constitution, the Judicial department most familiarizes itself to the public attention as the expositor, by the *order* of its functions in relation to the other departments; and attracts most the public confidence by the composition of the tribunal.

It is the Judicial department in which questions of constitutionality, as well as of legality, generally find their ultimate discussion and operative decision: and the public deference to and confidence in in the judgement of the body are peculiarly inspired by the qualities implied in its members; by the gravity and deliberation of their proceedings; and by the advantage their plurality gives them over the unity of the Executive department, and their fewness over the multitudinous composition of the Legislative department.

Without losing sight, therefore, of the co-ordinate relations of the three departments to each other, it may always be expected that the judicial bench, when happily filled, will, for the reasons suggested, most engage the respect and reliance of the public as the surest expositor of the Constitution, as well in questions within its cognizance concerning the boundaries between the several departments of the Government as in those between the Union and its members.

F. ABRAHAM LINCOLN, FIRST INAUGURAL ADDRESS

March 4, 1861

I do not forget the position assumed by some that constitutional questions are to be decided by the Supreme Court, nor do I deny that such decisions must be binding in any case upon the parties to a suit as to the object of that suit, while they are also entitled to very high respect and consideration in all parallel cases by all other departments of the Government. And while it is obviously possible that such decision may be erroneous in any given case, still the evil effect following it, being limited to that particular case, with the chance that it may be overruled and never become a precedent for other cases, can better be borne than could the evils of a different practice. At the same time, the candid citizen must confess that if the policy of the Government upon vital questions affecting the whole people is to be irrevocably fixed by decisions of the Supreme Court, the instant they are made in ordinary litigation between parties in personal actions the people will have ceased to be their own rulers, having to that extent practically resigned their Government into the hands of that eminent tribunal."

G. ATTORNEY GENERAL EDWIN MEESE III, THE TULANE SPEECH, October 21, 1986 in MAJOR POLICY STATEMENTS OF THE ATTORNEY GENERAL, EDWIN MEESE III

45–51 (1989)

Tonight I would like to look at * * * [the distinction between the Constitution and constitutional law] from yet another perspective * * *. Specifically, I would like to consider a distinction that is essential to maintaining our form of government.

The Constitution is—to put it simply * * * a document of our most fundamental law. It begins "We the People of the United States in Order to form a more perfect Union. . ." and ends up, some 6,000 words later, with the 26th Amendment * * *.

Constitutional law, on the other hand, is that body of law which has resulted from the Supreme Court's adjudications involving disputes over constitutional provisions or doctrines. To put it a bit more simply, constitutional law is what the Supreme Court says about the Constitution in its decisions resolving the cases and controversies that come before it * * *. And in its limited role of offering judgment, the Court has had a good deal to say. In almost two hundred years, it has produced nearly 500 volumes of reports of cases. While not all of these opinions deal with constitutional issues, of course, a good many do * * *.

Once we understand the distinction between constitutional law and the Constitution, once we see that constitutional decisions need not be seen as the last words in constitutional construction, once we comprehend that these decisions do not necessarily determine future public policy—once we see all of this, we can grasp a correlative point: that constitutional interpretation is not the business of the [Supreme] Court only, but also, and properly the business of all branches of government.

The Supreme Court, then, is not the only interpreter of the Constitution. Each of the three coordinate branches created and empowered by the Constitution—the executive and legislative no less than the judicial—has a duty to interpret the Constitution in the performance of its official functions. In fact, every official takes an oath precisely to that effect.

H. GARY LAWSON, INTERPRETATIVE EQUALITY AS A STRUCTURAL IMPERATIVE (OR: PUCKER UP AND SETTLE *THIS*)

20 CONST. COMMENTARY 379, 382–84 (2003)

Consider the more general case for a regime that divides governmental power through separation of powers and bicameralism. Separation of powers, as its critics are quick to point out, is very messy. The American system of separation of powers and bicameralism, which provides for the possibility, and even likelihood, of divided government, is especially messy. The lawmaking process is slow, cumbersome, and difficult. The laws that emerge from such a divided regime are likely to lack coherence, and thus likely to lack some of the characteristics that make law valuable. The separation of execution from lawmaking increases the cumbersomeness, unpredictability, and incoherence of the system: the actual effect of laws will vary enormously across space and time with variations in enforcement regimes. Throw in a separate judicial body and the problems of predictability and coherence multiply. Separation of powers and bicameralism significantly threaten the settlement function of law. The same arguments can be made about federalism. The dispersion of authority among distinct governmental actors creates the possibility of conflicts among jurisdictions and reduces the clarity of signals sent by any one jurisdiction to its subjects. Federalism significantly threatens the settlement function of law.

Separation of powers, bicameralism, and federalism are all mechanisms for dispersing power that make it more difficult for wise lawmakers to produce and enforce a stable, coherent body of law * * *. If one was confident that the governmental masters were likely to be wise and benevolent rulers who would do the right thing a substantial percentage of the time, it is hard to imagine why one would ever adopt a regime containing these structural features. That may be why many countries have not in fact adopted such a regime and why modern America has effectively abandoned it through adoption of administrative mechanisms that mostly dispense with the structural niceties of the Constitution.

But there is nonetheless a powerful normative case for an eighteenth-century-American style system of separated powers, bicameralism, and federalism. Quite simply, separation of powers works better than more concentrated systems, whether parliamentary or dictatorial, if governments are likely to reach a lot of wrong results—whether through corruption, stupidity, disinterest, or lack of knowledge. Put bluntly, separation of powers reduces the amount of damage that any particular bad people can do * * *. It doesn't take very much risk aversion to think that dividing power is, all things considered, likely to work better across a broad range of real-world scenarios than concentrating it in one authority.

Interpretative power is a kind of governmental power—a very potent and important kind of governmental power. Concentrating it in one place furthers some important values that go to the very core of law. But it is a very risky strategy. If the supreme interpreter is in fact likely to be bad at the job, then one must face the costs of imposing bad decisions on a whole country. The same arguments that justify dividing the power of substantive lawmaking among different bodies also justify dividing the power of interpretation among different bodies. It does not take very much risk aversion to justify departmentalism.

* * *

In sum, the case for dividing interpretative authority is no different than the case for dividing legislative authority horizontally or vertically, for separating legislative from executive authority, or for dividing power geographically among distinct units.

CHAPTER 1

THE PREAMBLE

[Assignment 6]

We the People of the United States, in Order to form a more perfect Union, establish Justice, insure domestic Tranquility, provide for the common defense, promote the general Welfare, and secure the Blessings of Liberty to ourselves and our Posterity, do ordain and establish this Constitution for the United States of America.

I. THE GLOBAL SIGNIFICANCE OF THE PREAMBLE

The Preamble is hugely important in U.S. constitutional law, as we shall see, but it is also important because its principal of popular sovereignty has been copied so widely all over the world. Constitutional preambles are commonplace, though most such preambles are much longer than the single sentence that appears in the U.S. Constitution, and some reflect fundamentally different principles of government and human relations. Consider below a sampling of excerpts from a few preambles from countries all over the world and compare them to the Framers' terse but dense eighteenth-century statement.

A. GERMANY

Preamble to the Basic Law for the Federal Republic of Germany

(Approved 8 May 1949, took effect 23 May 1949)

Conscious of their responsibility before God and man, Inspired by the determination to promote world peace as an equal partner in a united Europe, the German people, in the exercise of their constituent power, have adopted this Basic Law. Germans in the Länder of Baden-Württemberg, Bavaria, Berlin, Brandenburg, Bremen, Hamburg, Hesse, Lower Saxony, Mecklenburg-Western Pomerania, North Rhine-Westphalia, Rhineland-Palatinate, Saarland, Saxony, Saxony-Anhalt, Schleswig-Holstein and Thuringia have achieved the unity and freedom of Germany in free self-determination. This Basic Law thus applies to the entire German people.

B. JAPAN

Preamble to the Constitution of Japan

(Promulgated on Nov. 3, 1946, took effect on May 3, 1947)

We, the Japanese people, acting through our duly elected representatives in the National Diet, determined that we shall secure for ourselves and our posterity the fruits of peaceful cooperation with all nations and the blessings of liberty throughout this land, and resolved that never again shall we be visited with the horrors of war through the action of government, do proclaim that sovereign power resides with the people and do firmly establish this Constitution. Government is a sacred trust of the people, the authority for which is derived from the people, the powers of which are exercised by the representatives of the people, and the benefits of which are enjoyed by the people. This is a universal principle of mankind upon which this Constitution is founded. We reject and revoke all constitutions, laws, ordinances, and rescripts in conflict herewith.

C. INDIA

Preamble to the Constitution of the Republic of India

(Adopted on 26 Nov. 1949, took effect on 26 Jan. 1950)

WE, THE PEOPLE OF INDIA, having solemnly resolved to constitute India into a SOVEREIGN SOCIALIST SECULAR DEMOCRATIC REPUBLIC and to secure to all its citizens:

JUSTICE, social, economic and political;

LIBERTY, of thought, expression, belief, faith and worship;

EQUALITY of status and of opportunity;

and to promote among them all

FRATERNITY assuring the dignity of the individual and the unity and integrity of the Nation;

IN OUR CONSTITUENT ASSEMBLY this twenty-sixth day of November, 1949, DO HEREBY ADOPT, ENACT AND GIVE TO OURSELVES THIS CONSTITUTION.

D. CANADA

The Canadian Constitution Act of 1867

30–31 Vict., c. 3 (1867) (U.K.). Amended by the U.K. Parliament in 1982

An Act of Queen Victoria in Parliament with the Lords Spiritual and Temporal and with the Commons of the Kingdom of Great Britain and Ireland for the Union of Canada, Nova Scotia, and New Brunswick, and the Government thereof; and for Purposes connected therewith. *[29th March 1867]*

WHEREAS the Provinces of Canada, Nova Scotia, and New Brunswick have expressed their Desire to be federally united into One Dominion under the Crown of the United Kingdom of Great Britain and Ireland, with a Constitution similar in Principle to that of the United Kingdom:

And whereas such a Union would conduce to the Welfare of the Provinces and promote the Interests of the British Empire:

And whereas on the Establishment of the Union by Authority of Parliament it is expedient, not only that the Constitution of the Legislative Authority in the Dominion be provided for, but also that the Nature of the Executive Government therein be declared:

And whereas it is expedient that Provision be made for the eventual Admission into the Union of other Parts of British North America: * * *

It shall be lawful for the Queen, by and with the Advice of Her Majesty's Most Honourable Privy Council, to declare by Proclamation that, on and after the passing of this Act, the Provinces of Canada, Nova Scotia, and New Brunswick shall form and be One Dominion under the Name of Canada; and on and after that Day those Three Provinces shall form and be One Dominion under that Name accordingly.

E. AUSTRALIA

Preamble to the Commonwealth of Australia Constitution Act 1900

(Became law on 9 July 1900, took effect on 1 Jan. 1901)
(Achieved full independence in 1986)

Whereas the people of New South Wales, Victoria, South Australia, Queensland, and Tasmania, humbly relying on the blessing of Almighty God, have agreed to unite in one indissoluble Federal Commonwealth under the Crown of the United Kingdom of Great Britain and Ireland, and under the Constitution hereby established:

And whereas it is expedient to provide for the admission into the Commonwealth of other Australasian Colonies and possessions of the Queen:

Be it therefore enacted by the Queen's most Excellent Majesty, by and with the advice and consent of the Lords Spiritual and Temporal, and Commons of the Kingdom of Great Britain and Ireland, in this present Parliament assembled, and by the authority of the same, as follows: * * *

F. THE REPUBLIC OF KOREA

Preamble to the Constitution of the Republic of Korea

(Promulgated on July 17, 1948, revised Oct. 29, 1987)

We, the people of Korea, proud of a resplendent history and traditions dating from time immemorial, upholding the cause of the Provisional Republic of Korea Government born of the March First Independence Movement of 1919 and the democratic ideals of the April Nineteenth Uprising of 1960 against injustice, having assumed the mission of democratic reform and peaceful unification of our homeland * * * Do hereby amend, through national referendum following a resolution by the National Assembly, the Constitution, ordained and established on the Twelfth Day of July anno Domini Nineteen hundred and forty-eight, and amended eight times subsequently.

G. THE FEDERATIVE REPUBLIC OF BRAZIL

Preamble to the Constitution of the Federal Republic of Brazil

(Ratified on Oct. 5, 1988)

We, the representatives of the Brazilian People, convened in the national constituent assembly to institute a democratic state for the purpose of ensuring the exercise of social and individual rights, liberty, security, well-being, development, equality and justice as supreme values of a fraternal, pluralist and unprejudiced society, founded on social harmony and committed, in the internal and international orders, to the peaceful settlement of disputes, promulgate, under the protection of God, this Constitution of the Federative Republic of Brazil.

H. THE REPUBLIC OF SOUTH AFRICA

Preamble to the Constitution of South Africa

(Approved on 4 Dec. 1996, took effect on 4 Feb. 1997)

We, the people of South Africa,

Recognise the injustices of our past;

Honour those who suffered for justice and freedom in our land;

Respect those who have worked to build and develop our country; and

Believe that South Africa belongs to all who live in it, united in our diversity.

We therefore, through our freely elected representatives, adopt this Constitution as the supreme law of the Republic so as to

- Heal the divisions of the past and establish a society based on democratic values, social justice and fundamental human rights;
- Lay the foundations for a democratic and open society in which government is based on the will of the people and every citizen is equally protected by law;
- Improve the quality of life of all citizens and free the potential of each person; and
- Build a united and democratic South Africa able to take its rightful place as a sovereign state in the family of nations.

May God protect our people.

Nkosi Sikelel' iAfrika. Morena boloka setjhaba sa heso.

God seën Suid-Afrika. God bless South Africa.

Mudzimu fhatutshedza Afurika. Hosi katekisa Afrika

I. THE CONSTITUTION OF SAUDI ARABIA

Basic Law of the Kingdom of Saudi Arabia

(Adopted on 1 Mar. 1992)

CHAPTER ONE: GENERAL PRINCIPLES

Article 1: The Kingdom of Saudi Arabia is a sovereign Arab Islamic State. Its religion is Islam. Its constitution is Almighty God's Book, The Holy Qur'an, and the Sunna (Traditions) of the Prophet. Arabic is the language of the Kingdom. The City of Riyadh is the capital.

Article 2: The State public holidays are Eid Al Fitr (the Feast of Ramadan) and Eid Al Adha (The Feast of the Sacrifice). Its calendar follows the Hijri year (the lunar year).

Article 3: The flag of the State is as follows:

(a) Its color is green

(b) Its width equals two thirds of its length

The words: "There is no god but God and Mohammed is His Messenger" are inscribed in the center, with a drawn sword underneath. The flag should never be inverted. The Law will specify the rules pertaining to the flag.

Article 4: The State's Emblem represents two crossed swords with a palm tree in the middle of the upper space between them. The Law will define the State's Anthem and medals. * * *

Article 39 [Expression]:

Information, publication, and all other media shall employ courteous language and the state's regulations, and they shall contribute to the education of the nation and the bolstering of its unity. All acts that foster sedition or division or harm the state's security and its public relations or detract from man's dignity and rights shall be prohibited. The statutes shall define all that.

J. THE CONSTITUTION OF THE EUROPEAN UNION

The Treaty of Lisbon

(Signed on 13 Dec. 2007, entered into force on 1 Dec. 2009)

PREAMBLE

HIS MAJESTY THE KING OF THE BELGIANS, THE PRESIDENT OF THE CZECH REPUBLIC, HER MAJESTY THE QUEEN OF DENMARK, THE PRESIDENT OF THE FEDERAL REPUBLIC OF GERMANY, THE PRESIDENT OF THE REPUBLIC OF ESTONIA, THE PRESIDENT OF THE HELLENIC REPUBLIC, HIS MAJESTY THE KING OF SPAIN, THE PRESIDENT OF THE FRENCH REPUBLIC, THE PRESIDENT OF IRELAND, THE PRESIDENT OF THE ITALIAN REPUBLIC, THE PRESIDENT OF THE REPUBLIC OF CYPRUS, THE PRESIDENT OF THE REPUBLIC OF LATVIA, THE PRESIDENT OF THE REPUBLIC OF LITHUANIA, HIS ROYAL HIGHNESS THE GRAND DUKE OF LUXEMBOURG, THE PRESIDENT OF THE REPUBLIC OF HUNGARY, THE

PRESIDENT OF MALTA, HER MAJESTY THE QUEEN OF THE NETHERLANDS, THE FEDERAL PRESIDENT OF THE REPUBLIC OF AUSTRIA, THE PRESIDENT OF THE REPUBLIC OF POLAND, THE PRESIDENT OF THE PORTUGUESE REPUBLIC, THE PRESIDENT OF THE REPUBLIC OF SLOVENIA, THE PRESIDENT OF THE SLOVAK REPUBLIC, THE PRESIDENT OF THE REPUBLIC OF FINLAND, THE GOVERNMENT OF THE KINGDOM OF SWEDEN, HER MAJESTY THE QUEEN OF THE UNITED KINGDOM OF GREAT BRITAIN AND NORTHERN IRELAND,

DRAWING INSPIRATION from the cultural, religious and humanist inheritance of Europe, from which have developed the universal values of the inviolable and inalienable rights of the human person, freedom, democracy, equality and the rule of law,

BELIEVING that Europe, reunited after bitter experiences, intends to continue along the path of civilisation, progress and prosperity, for the good of all its inhabitants, including the weakest and most deprived; that it wishes to remain a continent open to culture, learning and social progress; and that it wishes to deepen the democratic and transparent nature of its public life, and to strive for peace, justice and solidarity throughout the world, * * *

GRATEFUL to the members of the European Convention for having prepared the draft of this Constitution on behalf of the citizens and States of Europe,

HAVE DESIGNATED AS THEIR PLENIPOTENTIARIES: * * *

K. THE UNITED NATIONS

Charter of the United Nations

(Signed on 26 June 1945, took effect on 24 Oct. 1945)

WE THE PEOPLE OF THE UNITED NATIONS DETERMINED

- to save succeeding generations from the scourge of war, which twice in our lifetime has brought untold sorrow to mankind, and
- to reaffirm faith in fundamental human rights, in the dignity and worth of the human person, in the equal rights of men and women and of nations large and small, and
- to establish conditions under which justice and respect for the obligations arising from treaties and other sources of international law can be maintained, and
- to promote social progress and better standards of life in larger freedom,

AND FOR THESE ENDS

- to practice tolerance and live together in peace with one another as good neighbours, and
- to unite our strength to maintain international peace and security, and
- to ensure, by the acceptance of principles and the institution of methods, that armed force shall not be used, save in the common interest, and

- to employ international machinery for the promotion of the economic and social advancement of all peoples,

HAVE RESOLVED TO COMBINE OUR EFFORTS TO ACCOMPLISH THESE AIMS * * *

NOTES AND QUESTIONS

1. It is striking and inspiring to see how the Framers' words "We the People of the United States" have echoed down now for more than two centuries in constitution-writing.

2. Consider the Preamble of the German Constitution, which, unlike the eighteenth-century American Constitution, explicitly invokes God. (There are also explicit references to God in the Australian, Brazilian, South African, Argentinian, and Saudi Arabian preambles.) What explains this, and what do you think of the German Preamble. Why do you think there is the reference to all the German states? Why do you think the Preamble says it applies to "the entire German people"? The German Basic Law, as its Constitution is called, was ratified by all the elected parliaments of the German states, which were elected with women having the right to vote for the first time in German history. There were no special constitutional ratifying conventions like those held in each of the thirteen original United States.

3. The Preamble of the Japanese Constitution is ironic because Americans forced Japan to adopt its Constitution, and the Japanese government in recent years has been desperate to rewrite it, especially to get rid of freedom of speech and to place the Emperor above the law. Japanese elites have been foiled, however, by the amending rules of Japan's Constitution, which require majority popular approval in a referendum of any constitutional changes. Public opinion polls have showed for decades that the people of Japan oppose making any changes to General Douglas MacArthur's Constitution. The Japanese Constitution was published in outline form before a bicameral legislature was elected in an election in which women were allowed to vote in Japan for the first time. The new Constitution was adopted in the form prescribed for amending Japan's previous Meiji Constitution. The Emperor Hirohito submitted the draft to both Houses of the legislature. Revisions were made, and an identical draft was passed by a two-thirds vote of both Houses of the legislature and signed by the Emperor. There was no special ratifying convention as there had been in the thirteen United States.

4. The Preamble of the Indian Constitution was written by Mr. B.R. Ambedkar, an untouchable, who received graduate degrees in both the United Kingdom and from Columbia University in the United States. Ambedkar was a big admirer of the U.S. Constitution and its preamble, and he single-handedly introduced both a written Bill of Rights and judicial review of the constitutionality of federal and state legislation into the Constitution of India. Note that India's constituent assembly *gave* the Constitution to India. It was never submitted for ratification by the people of India in any way, either by referendum or by elected ratifying conventions. The Indian Preamble contrasts with the German Preamble in that India establishes a "secular republic" while the German Preamble refers to "God." The U.S. Preamble, unlike the opening lines of the Declaration of Independence, is silent on the subject of religion.

5. Consider the Constitutions of Canada and Australia, which were enacted as statutes of the U.K. Parliament in 1867 and 1901. Those two countries became at that time "Dominions" of the British Empire and acquired full self-governing status with the adoption of the Statute of Westminster in 1931. From 1867 to 1949, decisions of the highest courts in Canada could be and were often appealed to His Majesty's Judicial

Committee of the Privy Council, which decided Canadian cases using British judges in London who had never been to Canada. From 1901 to 1986, decisions of some of the highest courts in Australia were also appealable to the Judicial Committee of the Privy Council in London. Canada and Australia evolved toward democracy and independence and never rebelled against the British Empire the way the U.S. did. This evolution is reflected today in their constitutional preambles. It is also reflected in the fact that Queen Elizabeth II is not only the Queen of the United Kingdom but is also the Queen of Canada and of Australia. No ratifying conventions of either the Canadian or the Australian Constitutions were ever held in any of the Canadian provinces or the Australian states, although there was substantial informal popular input in both cases. Quebec Province, in particular, has never ratified *any* Canadian constitutional document.

6. Consider the Preamble of South Africa's Constitution, which peacefully and bloodlessly ended decades of racist apartheid government by the white Afrikaner minority. The fact that *all* of "We the People of South Africa" made the new constitution is poignant and significant as a milestone. South Africans did freely elect a constitutional convention, which ratified its Constitution.

7. Brazil, also begins its Constitution with the magic words from Philadelphia: "We the People." This is striking because Brazil, the fifth most populous and fifth largest country on the earth, is a complex multi-racial society. The Brazilian Constitution was ratified by both a special constitutional convention elected to write Brazil's Constitution and by voters in a national referendum who voted for a presidential separation of power system and against either a parliamentary system or a constitutional monarchy.

8. Saudi Arabia's Constitution has no formal Preamble, but the "General Principles" of its "Basic Law" serve many of the functions of a preamble. There is no separation of God's law and man's law in Saudi Arabia. Not only is there no protection of freedom of expression, but there is actually a clause in the Saudi Arabian Constitution denying any right to freedom of expression. The Constitution was adopted by royal decree and presumably could be repealed the same way.

9. The Preamble to the European Union Constitution proclaims that the document issues, not from "We the People of the European Union," but from the ceremonial heads of states of the contracting parties. It is similar in this respect to the Preamble of the U.S. Articles of Confederation, which, of course, proved to be a failure.

10. Finally, consider the "We the People" Preamble to the treaty setting up the United Nations. It, too, is inspired by the U.S. example. More than two centuries after its adoption, the U.S. Constitution, which was ratified by special ratifying conventions in all of the States, stands out as a beacon of liberty and equality. It is now time to give that Preamble a closer look.

II. "A MORE PERFECT UNION": THE CONSTITUTIONALITY OF SECESSION AND THE CIVIL WAR

Justice Joseph Story, A Familiar Exposition of the Constitution of the United States, Chapter VII: Exposition of the Constitution—The Preamble

* * * [W]e are now prepared to enter upon an examination of the actual structure and organization of that Constitution, and the powers belonging to it. We shall treat it, not as a mere compact, or league, or confederacy, existing at the mere will of any

one or more of the States, during their good pleasure; but, (as it purports on its face to be,) as a Constitution of Government, framed and adopted by the people, in the manner pointed out in the instrument itself. It is to be interpreted, as all solemn instruments are, by endeavoring to ascertain the true sense and meaning of all its terms; and we are neither to narrow them, nor to enlarge them, by straining them from their just and natural import, for the purpose of adding to, or diminishing its powers, or bending them to any favorite theory or dogma of party. It is the language of the people, to be judged of according to common sense, and not by mere theoretical reasoning. It is not an instrument for the mere private interpretation of any particular men. The people have established it and spoken their will; and their will, thus promulgated, is to be obeyed as the supreme law. Every department of the Government must, of course, in the first instance, in the exercise of its own powers and duties, necessarily construe the instrument. But, if the case admits of judicial cognizance, every citizen has a right to contest the validity of that construction before the proper judicial tribunal; and to bring it to the test of the Constitution. And, if the case is not capable of judicial redress, still the people may, through the acknowledged means of new elections, or proposed amendments, check any usurpation of authority, whether wanton, or unintentional, and thus relieve themselves from any grievances of a political nature.

NOTES AND QUESTIONS

1. In this excerpt, Justice Story says that the Constitution is written in "the language of the people, to be judged of according to common sense * * *." In other words, the Constitution means what a reasonable person versed in its language would understand it to mean. Does that interpretative principle follow from the Preamble's declaration that the Constitution is the product of "We the People"? *See* Michael Stokes Paulsen, *Captain James T. Kirk and the Enterprise of Constitutional Interpretation: Some Modest Proposals from the Twenty-Third Century,* 59 ALBANY L. REV. 671 (1995). Are other principles of interpretation therefore "unconstitutional"?

2. Perhaps surprisingly, the Preamble was not much discussed or employed in the Founding Era. Indeed, James Wilson "is the only one of the Founders to treat the Preamble as a statement of the principles underlying the Constitution." William Ewald, *James Wilson and the American Founding,* 17 GEO. J.L. & PUB. POL'Y 1, 21 (2019). (For a more optimistic view of the influence of the Preamble in early America, see John W. Welch & James A. Heilpern, *Recovering Our Forgotten Preamble,* 91 SO. CAL. L. REV. 1021 (2018).) On the other hand, Abraham Lincoln, three quarters of a century after the founding, made extensive use of the Preamble—and of the Declaration of Independence that anticipated it. Perhaps that is because the events faced by President Lincoln, when eleven of the Southern slave States attempted to secede from the Union, called up the principles of the Preamble and Declaration in a fashion that the country had never before faced.

3. The roots of secession lay in the idea that the Constitution was a "contract among the States" rather than a national government founded by "We the People of the United States." According to the first view, sovereignty laid in the States. According to the second view, sovereignty laid in a majority of the people in nine of the thirteen States (and thereafter in a majority in three quarters of the States).

4. The "contract among the States" idea was first publicly discussed in 1798 after the Federalist Congress and President Adams passed the Sedition Act of 1798, which made it a federal crime to criticize President Adams or either House of Congress but not

Vice President Jefferson. The Adams Administration brought numerous prosecutions under the Sedition Act, the federal courts upheld the constitutionality of the Act, and a number of people were jailed and fined accordingly. James Madison and Thomas Jefferson responded to Sedition Act prosecutions in the only way they could by getting the state legislatures of Virginia and Kentucky, respectively, to pass resolutions condemning the Sedition Act as unconstitutional and mobilizing public opinion against it. Jefferson and Madison were right on the merits, but they chose an unfortunate framework for expressing their ideas. Mobilizing public opinion against federal action is clearly a proper state function; one might call this approach "interposition," as it interposes the State between the people and the national government but without challenging the legal authority of the United States. This risk is that interposition can morph into *nullification,* in which a State claims the right to declare federal laws unconstitutional and unenforceable. That latter idea depends on the view that the U.S. Constitution was "a contract among the States" and that the States were the final judges of whether the contract had been broken. Interposition might also, but need not, depend on that "contract among the States" idea. Examine Madison's Virginia Resolution and Jefferson's Kentucky Resolution to see what assumptions they make about the nature of the Union and its origins in "We the People."

A. VIRGINIA RESOLUTION OF 1798 IN RE THE SEDITION ACT (MADISON)

RESOLVED,

* * *

That this Assembly doth explicitly and peremptorily declare, that it views the powers of the federal government, as resulting from the compact, to which the states are parties; as limited by the plain sense and intention of the instrument constituting the compact; as no further valid that they are authorized by the grants enumerated in that compact; and that in case of a deliberate, palpable, and dangerous exercise of other powers, not granted by the said compact, the states who are parties thereto, have the right, and are in duty bound, to interpose for arresting the progress of the evil, and for maintaining within their respective limits, the authorities, rights and liberties appertaining to them.

* * *

That the good people of this commonwealth, having ever felt, and continuing to feel, the most sincere affection for their brethren of the other states; the truest anxiety for establishing and perpetuating the union of all; and the most scrupulous fidelity to that constitution, which is the pledge of mutual friendship, and the instrument of mutual happiness; the General Assembly doth solemnly appeal to the like dispositions of the other states, in confidence that they will concur with this commonwealth in declaring, as it does hereby declare, that the acts aforesaid, are unconstitutional; and that the necessary and proper measures will be taken by each, for co-operating with this state, in maintaining the Authorities, Rights, and Liberties, referred to the States respectively, or to the people.

B. KENTUCKY RESOLUTION OF 1798 IN RE THE SEDITION ACT (JEFFERSON)

1. *Resolved*, That the several States composing, the United States of America, are not united on the principle of unlimited submission to their general government; but that, by a compact under the style and title of a Constitution for the United States, and of amendments thereto, they constituted a general government for special purposes—delegated to that government certain definite powers, reserving, each State to itself, the residuary mass of right to their own self-government; and that whensoever the general government assumes undelegated powers, its acts are unauthoritative, void, and of no force: that to this compact each State acceded as a State, and is an integral part, its co-States forming, as to itself, the other party: that the government created by this compact was not made the exclusive or final judge of the extent of the powers delegated to itself; since that would have made its discretion, and not the Constitution, the measure of its powers; but that, as in all other cases of compact among powers having no common judge, each party has an equal right to judge for itself, as well of infractions as of the mode and measure of redress.

C. JOHN C. CALHOUN

Note that Madison's Virginia Resolution described the Constitution as a compact "to which the states are parties," and Jefferson's Kentucky Resolution said that "they"—meaning "the States", and not "We the People"—"constituted a general government." While that characterization of the relationship between the national government, the States, and We the People may have served to mobilize opposition to the Sedition Act, which was eventually repealed, it laid the groundwork for something much more consequential.

The father of Southern secession was John C. Calhoun of South Carolina, who wrote the document below while serving as Vice President to Andrew Jackson. Calhoun was also Vice President under John Quincy Adams, served as Secretary of War and Secretary of State, and for many years was a Representative and Senator from South Carolina, where he tirelessly advanced the cause of slavery. He died on March 31, 1850, but he is for all practical purposes the key theorist of the subsequent Southern secession. Does Calhoun's theory of "nullification" follow logically from the premises of Madison and Jefferson's 1798 Resolves? Does a right of secession follow from those premises as well?

Mr. Calhoun's Letter to [South Carolina Governor] General Hamilton on the Subject of State Interposition *IN* John C. Calhoun, Speeches of John C. Calhoun Delivered in the Congress of the United States from 1811 to the Present Time

44–46, 55 (1843)

* * * [T]he first and most important point is to ascertain distinctly who are the real authors of the Constitution of the United States—whose powers created it—whose voice clothed it with authority; and whose agent the government it formed in reality is * * *.

* * * [I]f it be true, indeed, that the Constitution is the work of the American people collectively; if it originated with them, and derives its authority from their will, then there is an end of the argument. The right claimed for a state of defending her reserved powers against the General Government would be an absurdity. Viewing the American people collectively as the source of political power, the rights of the states would be mere concessions—concessions from the common majority, and to be revoked by them with the same facility that they were granted * * *. But, fortunately, the supposition is entirely destitute of truth. So far from the Constitution being the work of the American people collectively, no such political body either now, or ever did, exist. In that character the people of this country never performed a single political act, nor, indeed, can, without an entire revolution in all our political relations.

* * * [I]t is declared in the preamble of the Constitution to be ordained **by** the people of the *United States,* and in the article of ratification, when ratified, it is declared *"to be binding between the states so ratifying."* The conclusion is inevitable, that the Constitution is the work of the people of the states, considered as separate and independent political communities; that they are its authors—their power created it, their voice clothed it with authority—that the government formed is, in reality, their agent; and that the Union, of which the Constitution is the bond, is a union of states, and not of individuals * * *.

* * *

* * * [I]t was only by the ratification of the state that its citizens became subject to the control of the General Government. The ratification of any other, or all the other states, without its own, could create no connexion between them and the General Government, nor impose on them the slightest obligation * * *. It follows * * * that, on a question whether a particular power exercised **by** the General Government be granted by the Constitution, it belongs to the state as a member of the Union, in her sovereign capacity in convention, to determine definitively, as far as her citizens are concerned, the extent of the obligation which she contracted; and if. in her opinion, the act exercising the power be unconstitutional, to declare it null and void * * *. In coming to this conclusion, it may be proper to remark, to prevent misrepresentation, that I do not claim for a state the right to abrogate an act of the General Government. It is the Constitution that annuls an unconstitutional act. Such an act is of itself void and of no effect * * *.

* * *

D. THE IMMEDIATE CAUSES OF SOUTHERN SECESSION

In order to understand the immediate causes of Southern secession from the Union in 1860 and 1861, it is necessary to review briefly the relevant history of the United States from 1787 to 1860.

In 1787, the Continental Congress, acting under the Articles of Confederation, banned slavery in the Northwest Territories, which became the free States of Ohio, Indiana, Illinois, Michigan, Wisconsin, and Minnesota. No one in the South or elsewhere questioned the Continental Congress's power to ban slavery in the Northwest Territory. Moreover, in 1787, Article IV of the Articles of Confederation provided that "The better to secure and perpetuate mutual friendship and intercourse among the people of the different States in this Union, *the free inhabitants of each of these States,* paupers, vagabonds, and fugitives from justice excepted, shall be entitled to all privileges and immunities of free citizens in the several States." (emphasis added). This provision makes it crystal clear that, in 1787, free African-Americans were citizens of the United States, and nothing in the new federal Constitution deprived them of that status. In the 1780s, slavery was widely regarded as a dying institution repugnant to the principle of the American Revolution that "All men are created Equal." The Northwest Ordinance banning slavery in the territories was thus uncontroversial, and the leading Framer, President George Washington, freed all his slaves upon the death of his wife Martha. Participation in the international slave trade by U.S. citizens was made a federal crime by Congress and President Washington in 1794. The international slave trade itself was outlawed in 1808, at the earliest possible date allowed by the Constitution. Slavery was abolished in all of the New England States in the 1780s and in all the Northern States by 1820. The development of the cotton gin, however, in the 1790s made growing cotton on Southern plantations with slave labor highly profitable, and so slavery in the South became entrenched.

In 1820, the slave State of Missouri sought admission to the Union. At the time, there was an even number of slave and free State senators, and the admission of a new slave State would have tipped the balance. An uproar occurred, but the problem was solved by what came to be known as the Missouri Compromise. Maine was carved out of Massachusetts and admitted as a free State and Missouri was admitted as a slave State. The even balance of free and slave State senators was preserved. The question remained, however, what ought to be the status of slavery in the vast Western territories acquired by President Thomas Jefferson in 1803 through the Louisiana Purchase, encompassing essentially all the lands between the Rocky Mountains and the Mississippi River and from Canada to the Mexican border, plus territory acquired by treaty from England that eventually became the States of Oregon and Washington. A compromise was adopted whereby all remaining lands from the Louisiana Purchase north of the 36 degrees, 30 minutes parallel would be free territories, while all lands south of that line would be slave territories. This bitterly-arrived-at Missouri Compromise lasted for thirty-seven years until the Supreme Court, absurdly and incautiously, held it unconstitutional in the case of *Dred Scott v. Sandford,* 60 U.S. 393 (1857). *See infra* pages 932–954.

By the 1850s, the slavery issue had become all consuming. The slave State of Texas had been added to the Union, while the Mexican War added to the Union territories including the present States of New Mexico, Arizona, California, Nevada, and Utah. Southerners were desperate to maintain their parity in the Senate with free State senators, and so they worked actively, but with limited success, to spread slavery to the newly acquired Southern and Southwestern territories. In the meantime, the Northern States made their abolition of slavery absolute, so that if a slave-owner voluntarily brought a slave with him into a free State, while he was in route to another slave State, that slave became instantly free upon setting foot on free state soil. Moreover, the Northern States were increasingly lax and grudging in enforcing the Fugitive Slave Clause, which obligated them to return fugitive slaves to the South. Mobs often formed around federal courthouses adjudicating whether a particular African-American was a free man or a runaway slave. The mobs demanded that such men be freed at once. (Was this a form of Calhounian nullification?)

In the Compromise of 1850, the South agreed to admit California as a free State; the territories of New Mexico, Arizona, and Utah were to be allowed to decide in a popular referendum, when they became States, whether they wished to be slave States or free States; and the slave trade was banned in the District of Columbia. The slave states of the South thus lost their equality in the Senate. The South gained, in return, a new and more stringent fugitive slave law in the Compromise of 1850, under which federal commissioners deciding whether an African-American, apprehended in the North, was a slave or a free person received $10 if they ruled the person was a slave and only $5 if they ruled the person was free. (This feature of the statute was a plain violation of the Due Process of Law Clause of the Fifth Amendment.) To an even greater degree than before 1850, huge mobs gathered outside of federal courthouses in the North every time an alleged fugitive slave's status was adjudicated. Many Northerners defied federal law by nobly running an under-ground railroad, transporting fugitive slaves from the South to Canada, where they were beyond the reach of the new fugitive slave law.

In 1857, the U.S. Supreme Court issued its opinion in *Dred Scott v. Sandford*, 60 U.S. 393 (1857). The case, which we will read later in this casebook, is by most accounts (including ours) the worst opinion the Supreme Court ever issued, not only because it was a direct cause of the Civil War, but also because it was so badly and duplicitously reasoned. The Court held: 1) that Congress lacked the power under the Territories Clause of Article IV to ban slavery in any of the federal territories, even though the far weaker Continental Congress had banned slavery in the Northwest Territories in 1787; and 2) that even free African-Americans in the North were not citizens of the United States because the Framers of the Constitution were so racist that they could not have imagined free African-Americans being a part of "We the People of the United States" who made the Constitution. This argument overlooks, inter alia, the fact that Article IV of the Articles of Confederation expressly made "all the free inhabitants" of the thirteen original States citizens. We will say much more about *Dred Scott* later.

The *Dred Scott* opinion declared that the platform of the newly created Republican Party, which pledged to abolish slavery in all of the federal Territories, both North and South, was unconstitutional. The *Dred Scott* opinion was extremely controversial, and it engulfed in flames the four-year presidency of the feckless and weak President James Buchanan. In the 1858 midterm elections, the Republican Party won control of the House of Representative but not the Senate. In 1860, Abraham Lincoln, a Republican, was elected President, ending the Slave Power's seventy-one-year long, Three-Fifths-Clause-generated lock on the presidency. The Republican Party in 1860 also won a majority in both the Senate and the House of Representatives. Lincoln pledged loudly that he had no intention of interfering with slavery in the States where it existed—and that he thought the federal government had no power to do that in any event. He also pledged to support a constitutional amendment that would be unamendable which would allow slavery in the slave States.

The South was unmoved by Lincoln's pledges and was terrified that he had been elected President at all. The South saw the ban on slavery in all the federal territories and the ban on Southerners travelling with their slaves through Northern States as the forming of a noose around slavery, which would be gradually tightened until the South's "peculiar" institution was abolished. The Slave Power was especially terrified by the loss of its strangle-hold on the Electoral College. (For a fuller description of what was meant by "The Slave Power" see LEONARD L. RICHARDS, THE SLAVE POWER: THE FREE NORTH AND SOUTHERN DOMINATION 1780–1860 (2000).) Southerners appealed to the "Spirit of 1798" and the Virginia and Kentucky Resolutions as support for what they were about to do. As a result, beginning in December of 1860 and continuing through April of 1861, eleven of the fifteen slave States, out of thirty-four States then in the Union, seceded unilaterally without seeking Congress's permission. They purported to accomplish this by electing constitutional conventions in the same way as had been done in 1787 and 1788 to ratify the Constitution, and those elected conventions rescinded their ratifications of the Constitution. The eleven slave States then formed a federal government, which they called the Confederate States of America, or the Confederacy, with its capitol in Richmond, Virginia. They adopted their own Constitution, modeled, with some important modifications, on the U.S. Constitution.

Four slave States remained in the Union: Maryland, Delaware, Kentucky, and Missouri. Given how closely fought the Civil War was, it is quite possible that if all four of these loyal Unionist slave States had seceded, the South might have beaten the North.

Consider below one argument, building on Jefferson's, Madison's, and Calhoun's idea that the Constitution was a compact among the sovereign States which any State could repeal. Please then read President Abraham Lincoln's First Inaugural Address, which responds to the South's arguments.

E. SENATOR JUDAH BENJAMIN'S SPEECH TO THE U.S. SENATE

December 31, 1860, *in* 5 GREAT DEBATES IN AMERICAN HISTORY, 384–387 (1913)

The wrongs under which the South is now suffering, and for which she seeks redress, seem chiefly to arise from a difference in our construction of the Constitution. You, Senators of the Republican Party, assert and your people whom you represent assert, that, under a just and fair interpretation of the Federal Constitution, it is right that you deny our slaves, which directly and indirectly involve a value of more than four thousand million dollars, are property at all, or entitled to protection in Territories owned by the common Government. You assume the interpretation that it is right to encourage, by all possible means, directly and indirectly, the robbery of this property and to legislate so as to render its recovery as difficult and dangerous as possible; that it is right and proper and justifiable, under the Constitution, to provide a mere transit across a sister State, to embark with our property on a lawful voyage, without openly being despoiled of it. You assert, and practice upon the assertion, that it is right to hold us up to the ban of mankind in speech, writing, and print with every possible appliance of publicity, as thieves, robbers, murderers, villains, and criminals of the blackest dye, because we continue to own property which we owned at the time that we all signed the compact; that it is right that we should be exposed to spend our treasure in the purchase, or shed our blood in the conquest, of foreign territory, with no right to enter it for settlement without leaving behind our most valuable property, under penalty of its confiscation. You practically interpret the instrument to be that it is eminently in accordance with the assurance that our tranquility and welfare were to be preserved and promoted;

that our sister States should combine to prevent our growth and development; that they should surround us with a cordon of hostile communities for the express and avowed purpose of accumulating in dense masses, and within restricted limits, a population which you believe to be dangerous, and thereby force the sacrifice of property nearly sufficient to pay the public debt of every nation in Europe.

This is the construction of the instrument that was to preserve our safety, promote our welfare, and which we signed on your assurance that that was its object. You tell us that this is a fair construction—not all, some say one thing, some say another; but you act, or your people do, upon this principle. You do not propose to enter into our States, you say, and what do we complain of? You do not pretend to enter into our States to kill or destroy our institutions by force. Oh no. You imitate the faith of Rhadamistus, who according to Tacitus's account, having sworn to Mithradites that he would not employ either poison or steel against him, caused him to be smothered under a heap of clothes. You propose simply to close us in an embrace that will suffocate us. You do not propose to fell the tree; you promised not. You merely propose to girdle it, that it dies. And then, when we tell you that we did not understand this bargain this way, that your acting upon it in this spirit releases us from the obligations that accompany it; that under no circumstances can we consent to live together under that interpretation and say: "we will go from you; let us go in peace"; we are answered by your leading spokesmen: "Oh, no; you cannot do that; we have no objection to it personally, but we are bound by our oaths; if you attempt it, your people will be hanged for treason. We have examined this Constitution thoroughly; we have searched it out with a fair spirit, and we can find warrant in it for releasing ourselves from the obligation of giving you any of its benefits, but our oaths force us to tax you; we can dispense with everything else; but our consciences, we protest upon our souls, will be sorely worried if we do not take your money." That is the proposition of the Senator from Ohio, in plain language. He can avoid everything else under the Constitution, in the way of secession; but how is he to get rid of the duty of taking our money he cannot see,

Now, Senators, this picture is not placed before you with any idea that it will act upon any one of you, or change your plans, or alter your conduct. All hope of that is gone. Our committee has reported this morning that no possible scheme of adjustment can be devised by them all combined. The day for the adjustment has passed. If you would give it now, you are too late.

And now, Senators, within a few weeks we part to meet as Senators in one common council chamber of the nation no more forever. We desire, we beseech you, let this parting be in peace. I conjure you to indulge in no vain delusion that duty or conscience, interest or honor, imposes upon you the necessity of invading our States or shedding the blood of our people. You have no possible justification for it. I trust it is in no craven spirit, and with no sacrifice of the honor or dignity of my own State, that I make this last appeal, but from far higher and holier motives. If, however, it shall prove vain, if you are resolved to pervert the Constitution framed by the fathers for the protection of our rights into an instrument for subjugating and enslaving us, then appealing to the Supreme Judge of the universe for the rectitude of our intentions, we must meet the issue that you force upon us as best becomes freemen defending all that is dear to man.

What may be the fate of this horrible contest, no man can tell, none pretend to foresee; but this much I will say: the fortunes of war may be adverse to our arms; you may carry desolation into our peaceful land, and with torch and fire you may set all our cities in flames; you may even emulate the atrocities of those who, in the war of the Revolution, hounded on the blood thirsty savage to attack upon the defenceless frontier; you may under the protection of your advancing armies, give shelter to the furious fanatics who desire, and profess to desire, nothing more than to add all the horrors of a servile insurrection to the calamaties of a civil war; you may do all this—and more, too, if there be—but you can never subjugate us; you can never convert the free sons of the soil into vassals, paying tribute to your power; and you can never, never can degrade them to the level of an inferior and servile race. Never! Never!

F. President Abraham Lincoln's First Inaugural Address

Monday, March 4th, 1861

Fellow citizens of the United States:

In compliance with a custom as old as the Government itself, I appear before you to address you briefly, and to take, in your presence, the oath prescribed by the Constitution of the United States to be taken by the President "before he enters on the execution of this office."

I do not consider it necessary, at present, for me to discuss those matters of administration about which there is no special anxiety or excitement.

Apprehension seems to exist among the people of the Southern States, that by the accession of a Republican Administration, their property, and their peace, and personal security, are to be endangered. There has never been any reasonable cause for such apprehension. Indeed, the most ample evidence to the contrary has all the while existed, and been open to their inspection. It is found in nearly all the published speeches of him who now addresses you. I do but quote from one of those speeches when I declare that "I have no purpose, directly or indirectly, to interfere with the institution of slavery in the States where it exists. I believe I have no lawful right to do so, and I have no inclination to do so." Those who nominated and elected me did so with full knowledge that I had made this, and many similar declarations, and had never recanted them. And more than this, they placed in the platform for my acceptance, and as a law to themselves and to me, the clear and emphatic resolution which I now read:

"*Resolved*, That the maintenance inviolate of the rights of the States, and especially the right of each State to order and control its own domestic institutions according to its own judgment exclusively, is essential to that balance of power on which the perfection and endurance of our political fabric depend; and we denounce the lawless invasion by armed force of the soil of any State or Territory, no matter what pretext, as among the gravest of crimes."

I now reiterate these sentiments, and in doing so I only press upon the public attention the most conclusive evidence of which the case is susceptible, that the property, peace, and security of no section are to be in anywise endangered by the now incoming Administration. I add too, that all the protection which, consistently with the Constitution and the laws, can be given will be cheerfully given to all the States when lawfully demanded, for whatever cause—as cheerfully to one section, as to another.

There is much controversy about the delivering up of fugitives from service or labor. The clause I now read is as plainly written in the Constitution as any other of its provisions:

"No person held to service or labor in one State, under the laws thereof, escaping into another, shall in consequence of any law or regulation therein be discharged from such service or labor, but shall be delivered up on claim of the party to whom such service or labor may be due."

It is scarcely questioned that this provision was intended by those who made it, for the reclaiming of what we call fugitive slaves; and the intention of the law-giver is the law. All members of Congress swear their support to the whole Constitution—to this provision as much as to any other. To the proposition, then, that slaves whose cases come within the terms of this clause "shall be delivered up," their oaths are unanimous. Now, if they would make the effort in good temper, could they not, with nearly equal unanimity, frame and pass a law by means of which to keep good that unanimous oath?

There is some difference of opinion whether this clause should be enforced by national or by state authority; but surely that difference is not a very material one. If the slave is to be surrendered, it can be of but little consequence to him, or to others, by which authority it is done. And should anyone, in any case, be content that his oath shall go unkept, on a merely unsubstantial controversy as to how it shall be kept?

Again, in any law upon this subject, ought not all the safeguards of liberty known in civilized and humane jurisprudence to be introduced, so that a free man be not, in any case, surrendered as a slave? And might it not be well at the same time to provide by law for the enforcement of that clause in the Constitution which guarantees that "the citizens of each State shall be entitled to all privileges and immunities of citizens in the several States"?

I take the official oath to-day with no mental reservations, and with no purpose to construe the Constitution or laws, by any hypercritical rules. And while I do not choose now to specify particular acts of Congress as proper to be enforced, I do suggest, that it will be much safer for all, both in official and private stations, to conform to, and abide by, all those acts which stand unrepealed, than to violate any of them, trusting to find impunity in having them held to be unconstitutional.

It is seventy-two years since the first inauguration of a President under our national Constitution. During that period fifteen different and greatly distinguished citizens, have, in succession, administered the executive branch of the government. They have conducted it through many perils, and generally with great success. Yet, with all this scope of precedent, I now enter upon the same task for the brief constitutional term of four years under great and peculiar difficulty. A disruption of the Federal Union, heretofore only menaced, is now formidably attempted.

I hold, that in contemplation of universal law, and of the Constitution, the Union of these States is perpetual. Perpetuity is implied, if not expressed, in the fundamental law of all national governments. It is safe to assert that no government proper, ever had a provision in its organic law for its own termination. Continue to execute all the express provisions of our national Constitution, and the Union will endure forever—it being impossible to destroy it, except by some action not provided for in the instrument itself.

Again, if the United States be not a government proper, but an association of States in the nature of contract merely, can it, as a contract, be peaceably unmade, by less than all the parties who made it? One party to a contract may violate it—break it, so to speak; but does it not require all to lawfully rescind it?

Descending from these general principles, we find the proposition that, in legal contemplation, the Union is perpetual, confirmed by the history of the Union itself. The Union is much older than the Constitution. It was formed, in fact, by the Articles of Association in 1774. It was matured and continued by the Declaration of Independence in 1776. It was further matured, and the faith of all the then thirteen States expressly plighted and engaged that it should be perpetual, by the Articles of Confederation in 1778. And finally, in 1787, one of the declared objects for ordaining and establishing the Constitution was "*to form a more perfect Union.*"

But if destruction of the Union, by one, or by a part only, of the States, be lawfully possible, the Union is *less* perfect than before the Constitution, having lost the vital element of perpetuity.

It follows from these views that no State, upon its own mere motion, can lawfully get out of the Union,—that *resolves* and *ordinances* to that effect are legally void; and that acts of violence, within any State or States, against the authority of the United States, are insurrectionary or revolutionary, according to circumstances.

I therefore consider, that in view of the Constitution and the laws, the Union is unbroken; and to the extent of my ability, I shall take care, as the constitution itself expressly enjoins upon me, that the laws of the Union be faithfully executed in all the States. Doing this I deem to be only a simple duty on my part, and I shall perform it so far as practicable, unless my rightful masters, the American people, shall withhold the requisite means, or in some authoritative manner direct the contrary. I trust this will not be regarded as a menace, but only as the declared purpose of the Union that it will constitutionally defend, and maintain itself.

In doing this there needs to be no bloodshed or violence; and there shall be none unless it be forced upon the national authority. The power confided to me, will be used to hold, occupy, and possess the property and places belonging to the government, and to collect the duties and imposts; but beyond what may be necessary for these objects, there will be no invasion—no using of force against, or among the people anywhere. Where hostility to the United States, in any interior locality, shall be so great and universal, as to prevent competent resident citizens from holding the Federal offices, there will be no attempt to force obnoxious strangers among the people for that object. While the strict legal right may exist in the government to enforce the exercise of these offices, the attempt to do so would be so irritating, and so nearly impracticable with all, that I deem it better to forego, for the time, the uses of such offices.

The mails, unless repelled, will continue to be furnished in all parts of the Union. So far as possible, the people everywhere shall have that sense of perfect security which is most favorable to calm thought and reflection. The course here indicated will be followed, unless current events and experience, shall show a modification or change to be proper; and in every case and exigency my best discretion will be exercised, according to circumstances actually existing, and with a view and a hope of a peaceful solution of the national troubles and the restoration of fraternal sympathies and affections.

That there are persons in one section or another who seek to destroy the Union at all events, and are glad of any pretext to do it, I will neither affirm nor deny; but if there be such, I need address no word to them. To those, however, who really love the Union, may I not speak?

Before entering upon so grave a matter as the destruction of our national fabric, with all its benefits, its memories, and its hopes, would it not be wise to ascertain precisely why we do it? Will you hazard so desperate a step, while there is any possibility that any portion of the ills you fly from, have no real existence? Will you, while the certain ills you fly to are greater than all the real ones you fly from? Will you risk the commission of so fearful a mistake?

All profess to be content in the Union if all constitutional rights can be maintained. Is it true, then, that any right, plainly written in the Constitution, has been denied? I think not. Happily the human mind is so constituted that no party can reach to the audacity of doing this. Think, if you can, of a single instance in which a plainly written provision of the Constitution has ever been denied. If, by the mere force of numbers, a majority should deprive a minority of any clearly written constitutional right, it might, in a moral point of view, justify revolution—certainly would, if such right were a vital one. But such is not our case. All the vital rights of minorities, and of individuals, are so plainly assured to them, by affirmations and negations, guaranties and prohibitions, in the Constitution, that controversies never arise concerning them. But no organic law can ever be framed with a provision specifically applicable to every question which may occur in practical administration. No foresight can anticipate, nor any document of reasonable length contain express provisions for all possible questions. Shall fugitives from labor be surrendered by national or by State authority? The Constitution does not expressly say. *May* Congress prohibit slavery in the Territories? The Constitution does not expressly say. *Must* Congress protect slavery in the Territories? The Constitution does not expressly say.

From questions of this class spring all our constitutional controversies, and we divide upon them into majorities and minorities. If the minority will not acquiesce, the majority must, or the government must cease. There is no other alternative; for continuing the government, is acquiescence on one side or the other. If a minority, in such case, will secede rather than acquiesce, they make a precedent which, in turn, will divide and ruin them; for a minority of their own will secede from them whenever a majority refuses to be controlled by such minority. For instance, why may not any portion of a new confederacy, a year or two hence, arbitrarily secede again, precisely as portions of the present Union now claim to secede from it. All who cherish disunion sentiments are now being educated to the exact temper of doing this.

Is there such perfect identity of interests among the States to compose a new Union, as to produce harmony only, and prevent renewed secession?

Plainly, the central idea of secession is the essence of anarchy. A majority held in restraint by constitutional checks and limitations, and always changing easily, with deliberate changes of popular opinions and sentiments, is the only true sovereign of a free people. Whoever rejects it, does, of necessity, fly to anarchy or to despotism. Unanimity is impossible; the rule of a minority, as a permanent arrangement, is wholly inadmissible; so that, rejecting the majority principle, anarchy, or despotism in some form, is all that is left.

I do not forget the position assumed by some, that constitutional questions are to be decided by the Supreme Court; nor do I deny that such decisions must be binding in any case, upon the parties to a suit as to the object of that suit, while they are also entitled to very high respect and consideration in all parallel cases, by all other departments of the government. And while it is obviously possible that such decision may be erroneous in any given case, still the evil effect following it, being limited to that particular case, with the chance that it may be over-ruled, and never become a precedent for other cases, can better be borne than could the evils of a different practice. At the same time the candid citizen must confess that if the policy of the government upon vital questions affecting the whole people is to be irrevocably fixed by decisions of the Supreme Court, the instant they are made, in ordinary litigation between parties, in personal actions, the people will have ceased to be their own rulers, having to that extent practically resigned their government into the hands of that eminent tribunal. Nor is there, in this view, any assault upon the Court, or the judges. It is a duty, from which they may not shrink, to decide cases properly brought before them; and it is no fault of theirs if others seek to turn their decisions to political purposes.

One section of our country believes slavery is *right* and ought to be extended, while the other believes it is *wrong* and ought not to be extended. This is the only substantial dispute. The fugitive slave clause of the Constitution, and the law for the suppression of the foreign slave trade, are each as well enforced, perhaps, as any law can ever be in a community where the moral sense of the people imperfectly supports the law itself. The great body of the people abide by the dry legal obligation in both cases, and a few break over in each. This, I think, cannot be perfectly cured; and it would be worse in both cases *after* the separation of the sections than before. The foreign slave trade, now imperfectly suppressed, would be ultimately revived without restriction, in one section; while fugitive slaves, now only partially surrendered, would not be surrendered at all, by the other.

Physically speaking, we can not separate. We can not remove our respective sections from each other, nor build an impassable wall between them. A husband and wife may be divorced, and go out of the presence and beyond the reach of each other; but the different parts of our country can not do this. They cannot but remain face to face; and intercourse, either amicable or hostile, must continue between them. Is it possible, then, to make that intercourse more advantageous, or more satisfactory, *after* separation than *before*? Can aliens make treaties easier than friends can make laws? Can treaties be more faithfully enforced between aliens, than laws can among friends? Suppose you go to war, you can not fight always; and when, after much loss on both sides and no gain on either, you cease fighting, the identical old questions, as to terms of intercourse, are again upon you.

This country, with its institutions, belongs to the people who inhabit it. Whenever they shall grow weary of the existing government, they can exercise their *constitutional* right of amending it, or their *revolutionary* right to dismember, or overthrow it. I can not be ignorant of the fact that many worthy and patriotic citizens are desirous of having the national constitution amended. While I make no recommendation of amendments, I fully recognize the rightful authority of the people over the whole subject, to be exercised in either of the modes prescribed in the instrument itself; and I should, under existing circumstances, favor, rather than oppose, a fair opportunity being afforded the people to act upon it. I will venture to add that, to me, the convention mode seems preferable, in that it allows amendments to originate with the people themselves, instead of only permitting them to take, or reject, propositions originated by others, not especially chosen for the purpose, and which might not be precisely such, as they would wish to either accept or refuse. I understand a proposed amendment to the Constitution, which amendment, however, I have not seen, has passed Congress, to the effect that the federal government, shall never interfere with the domestic institutions of the States, including that of persons held to service. To avoid misconstruction of what I have said, I depart from my purpose not to speak of particular amendments, so far as to say that, holding such a provision to now be implied constitutional law, I have no objection to its being made express and irrevocable.

The Chief Magistrate derives all his authority from the people, and they have referred none upon him to fix terms for the separation of the States. The people themselves can do this if also they choose; but the executive, as such, has nothing to do with it. His duty is to administer the present government, as it came to his hands, and to transmit it, unimpaired by him, to his successor.

Why should there not be a patient confidence in the ultimate justice of the people? Is there any better or equal hope, in the world? In our present differences, is either party without faith of being in the right? If the Almighty Ruler of nations, with his eternal truth and justice, be on your side of the North, or on yours of the South, that truth, and that justice, will surely prevail, by the judgment of this great tribunal of the American people.

By the frame of the government under which we live, this same people have wisely given their public servants but little power for mischief; and have, with equal wisdom, provided for the return of that little to their own hands at very short intervals.

While the people retain their virtue and vigilance, no administration, by any extreme of wickedness or folly, can very seriously injure the government in the short space of four years.

My countrymen, one and all, think calmly and well upon this whole subject. Nothing valuable can be lost by taking time. If there be an object to hurry any of you, in hot haste, to a step which you would never take deliberately, that object will be frustrated by taking time; but no good object can be frustrated by it. Such of you as are now dissatisfied still have the old Constitution unimpaired, and, on the sensitive point, the laws of your own framing under it; while the new administration will have no immediate power, if it would, to change either. If it were admitted that you who are dissatisfied, hold the right side in the dispute, there still is no single good reason for precipitate action. Intelligence, patriotism, Christianity, and a firm reliance on Him, who has never yet forsaken this favored land, are still competent to adjust, in the best way, all our present difficulty.

In your hands, my dissatisfied fellow countrymen, and not in mine, is the momentous issue of civil war. The government will not assail you. You can have no conflict without being yourselves the aggressors. *You* have no oath registered in Heaven to destroy the government, while *I* shall have the most solemn one to "preserve, protect, and defend it."

I am loath to close. We are not enemies, but friends. We must not be enemies. Though passion may have strained, it must not break our bonds of affection. The mystic chords of memory, stretching from every battlefield and patriot grave, to every living heart and hearthstone, all over this broad land, will yet swell the chorus of the Union, when again touched, as surely they will be, by the better angels of our nature.

NOTES AND QUESTIONS ON LINCOLN'S FIRST INAUGURAL ADDRESS

1. Lincoln's First Inaugural Address lays out a legal argument as to why the unilateral secession of the Southern States was unconstitutional. He builds on Justice Story's arguments, which you read above, and he rejects the idea that the Constitution is a mere "compact among the States." Senator Benjamin could counter that, even if the Southern States lacked a formal constitutional right to secede, the Constitution no longer enjoyed the consent of the governed in the Confederacy and that, pursuant to the Declaration of Independence, the Confederacy had a right "to alter and abolish their forms of government." Why was the secession of the thirteen original States legitimate in the Revolutionary War but the secession of the eleven Confederate states in the Civil War illegitimate? It is true, of course, that there was a large disenfranchised minority of enslaved African-Americans in the South who opposed slavery and secession, but one-third of the colonists in the thirteen original United States were Tories who opposed the American Revolution. Who do you think gets the better of the argument and why?

2. Lincoln's theory was that secession was illegal—unconstitutional—and thus of no effect. Accordingly, the Civil War was not a "war" in the constitutional sense but was instead an "insurrection" or a "rebellion. Accordingly, Lincoln did not think that Congress needed to declare war in 1861. He referred to the conflict as the War of the Rebellion, and Northern troops referred to their Southern adversaries as rebels. The well-known phrase "Johnny Rebel" refers to Confederate troops. The Civil War in Lincoln's eyes was a massive domestic insurrection, subject to the Guarantee Clause power of the national government to assure republican government (presumably, republican government under the Constitution and the Union created thereby) and to the duty of the national government to protect each state from "domestic violence."

3. Consider Lincoln's statement that geographically the North and the South cannot split. They are unlike a divorced couple where the ex-husband can live in one city and the ex-wife in another, and they will not run into each other. Lincoln knows, as a citizen of Illinois, that all of his home State's crops, and all the crops from other nearby States, are shipped to market via the Mississippi River, at the mouth of which lies the Southern port city of New Orleans. The South would be able to strangle the Midwest in 1861 if it were a separate country.

4. Lincoln holds in his First Inaugural Address that the Supreme Court's 1857 decision in *Dred Scott v. Sandford*, 60 U.S. 393 (1857) was wrongly decided and that it did not bind him in his actions as President, except that he had to execute the judgment as to Dred Scott. Note that Lincoln says "I hold" that secession and *Dred Scott v. Sandford* are unconstitutional, thus issuing a "holding" like a court of law. The Supreme Court, in *Dred Scott*, had held that free African-Americans could not be citizens of the United States nor could Southerners be prohibited from bringing slaves into the federal territories. President Lincoln ordered that passports be issued to free African-Americans, and he forbade slavery in the federal territories, although slavery continued in the four slave States that remained loyal to the Union during the Civil War: Maryland; Delaware; Kentucky; and Missouri. Lincoln did not believe that he, or any other national institution, had the constitutional power to end slavery in Union States before 1865.

5. Several years after the War, a (somewhat) reconstituted Supreme Court considered a case in which the outcome turned in part on whether Texas had or had not left the Union—and ceased to be a State of the United States—during the period of the Civil War when Texas purported to secede. Prior to the Civil War, Texas had obtained some United States bonds, which under Texas state law could not be sold without the endorsement (signature) of the governor. Once Texas seceded, the rebel government repealed the state statute requiring the governor's endorsement and sold the bonds to acquire war supplies. After the war, the Reconstruction government imposed by Congress tried to recover the bonds on the ground that the rebel government was unlawful, its purported repeal of the law regarding bond sales was ineffective, and the absence of the governor's endorsement therefore voided the sale. In *Texas v. White*, 74 U.S. (7 Wall.) 700 (1868), in an opinion by Chief Justice Salmon P. Chase (who had been Lincoln's Secretary of Treasury and at one time a rival for the presidency), the Court held that Texas was a "State" for purposes of the clauses in Article III extending federal jurisdiction to "controversies * * * between a State and citizens of another State" and giving the Supreme Court original jurisdiction over cases "in which a State shall be a Party," even though Texas at that time had no representation in Congress or in the electoral college (and was being administered by federal officials). The Court held, in other words, that the Reconstruction government was valid enough to make Texas after the Civil War a constitutional "State," even though it would not at that time be entitled to all of the rights that go along with being a constitutional State, such as representation in Congress. The case sets forth, in a Supreme Court decision, the essential legal theory of the Lincoln Administration on secession, national authority to combat secession, and reconstruction.

G. TEXAS V. WHITE

74 U.S. (7 Wall.) 700 (1868)

* * *

The Republic of Texas was admitted into the Union, as a State, on the 27th of December, 1845. By this act the new State, and the people of the new State, were invested with all the rights, and became subject to all the responsibilities and duties of the original States under the Constitution.

From the date of admission, until 1861, the State was represented in the Congress of the United States by her senators and representatives, and her relations as a member of the Union remained unimpaired. In that year, acting upon the theory that the rights of a State under the Constitution might be renounced, and her obligations thrown off at pleasure, Texas undertook to sever the bond thus formed, and to break up her constitutional relations with the United States.

On the 1st of February, a convention, called without authority, but subsequently sanctioned by the legislature regularly elected, adopted an ordinance to dissolve the union between the State of Texas and the other States under the Constitution of the United States, whereby Texas was declared to be "a separate and sovereign State," and "her people and citizens" to be "absolved from all allegiance to the United States, or the government thereof."

It was ordered by a vote of the convention and by an act of the legislature, that this ordinance should be submitted to the people, for approval or disapproval, on the 23d of February, 1861.

* * *

* * * [T]he vote upon the ratification or rejection of the ordinance of secession was taken on the 23d of February. It was ratified by a majority of the voters of the State.

* * *

In all respects, so far as the object could be accomplished by ordinances of the convention, by acts of the legislature, and by votes of the citizens, the relations of Texas to the Union were broken up, and new relations to a new government were established for them.

* * *

Did Texas, in consequence of these acts, cease to be a State? Or, if not, did the State cease to be a member of the Union?

It is needless to discuss, at length, the question whether the right of a State to withdraw from the Union for any cause, regarded by herself as sufficient, is consistent with the Constitution of the United States.

The Union of the States never was a purely artificial and arbitrary relation. It began among the Colonies, and grew out of common origin, mutual sympathies, kindred principles, similar interests, and geographical relations. It was confirmed and strengthened by the necessities of war, and received definite form, and character, and sanction from the Articles of Confederation. By these the Union was solemnly declared to "be perpetual." And when these Articles were found to be inadequate to the exigencies of the country, the Constitution was ordained "to form a more perfect Union." It is difficult to convey the idea of indissoluble unity more clearly than by these words. What can be indissoluble if a perpetual Union, made more perfect, is not?

But the perpetuity and indissolubility of the Union, by no means implies the loss of distinct and individual existence, or of the right of self-government by the States. Under the Articles of Confederation each State retained its sovereignty, freedom, and independence, and every power, jurisdiction, and right not expressly delegated to the United States. Under the Constitution, though the powers of the States were much restricted, still, all powers not delegated to the United States nor prohibited to the States, are reserved to the States respectively, or to the people * * *. Not only, therefore, can there be no loss of separate and independent autonomy to the States, through their union under the Constitution, but it may be not unreasonably said that the preservation of the States, and the maintenance of their governments, are as much within the design and care of the Constitution as the preservation of the Union and the maintenance of the National government. The Constitution, in all its provisions, looks to an indestructible Union, composed of indestructible States.

When, therefore, Texas became one of the United States, she entered into an indissoluble relation. All the obligations of perpetual union, and all the guaranties of republican government in the Union, attached at once to the State. The act which consummated her admission into the Union was something more than a compact; it was the incorporation of a new member into the political body. And it was final. The union between Texas and the other States was as complete, as perpetual and indissoluble as the union between the original States. There was no place for reconsideration, or revocation, except through revolution, or through consent of the States.

Considered therefore as transactions under the Constitution, the ordinance of secession, adopted by the convention and ratified by a majority of the citizens of Texas, and all the acts of her legislature intended to give effect to that ordinance, were absolutely null. They were utterly without operation in law. The obligations of the State, as a member of the Union, and of every citizen of the State, as a citizen of the United States, remained perfect and unimpaired. It certainly follows that the States did not cease to be a State, nor her citizens to be citizens of the Union. If this were otherwise, the State must have become foreign, and her citizens foreigners. The war must have ceased to be a war for the suppression of rebellion, and must have become a war for conquest and subjugation.

Our conclusion therefore is, that Texas continued to be a State, and a State of the Union, notwithstanding the transactions to which we have referred * * *.

* * *

* * * [I]t is by no means a logical conclusion * * * that the governmental relations of Texas to the Union remained unaltered. Obligations often remained unimpaired, while relations are greatly changed * * *. No one has been bold enough to contend that, while Texas was controlled by a government hostile to the United States, and in affiliation with a hostile confederation, waging war upon the United States, senators chosen by her legislature, or representatives elected by her citizens, were entitled to seats in Congress; or that any suit, instituted in her name, could be entertained in this court. All admit that, during this condition of civil war, the rights of the State as a member, and of her people as citizens of the Union, were suspended. The government and the citizens of the State, refusing to recognize their constitutional obligations, assumed the character of enemies, and incurred the consequences of rebellion.

These new relations imposed new duties upon the United States. The first was that of suppressing the rebellion. The next was that of re-establishing the broken relations of the State with the Union. The first of these duties having been performed, the next necessarily engaged the attention of the National government.

The authority for the performance of the first had been found in the power to suppress insurrection and carry on war; for the performance of the second, authority was derived from the obligation of the United States to guarantee to every State in the Union a republican form of government. The latter, indeed, in the case of a rebellion which involves the government of a State * * * seems to be a necessary complement to the former.

Of this, the case of Texas furnishes a striking illustration * * *.

* * *

There being then no government in Texas in constitutional relations with the Union, it became the duty of the United States to provide for the restoration of such a government. But the restoration of the government which existed before the rebellion, without a new election of officers, was obviously impossible; and before any such election could be properly held, it was necessary that the old constitution should receive such amendments as would conform its provisions to the new conditions created by emancipation, and afford adequate security to the people of the State.

In the exercise of the power conferred by the guaranty clause, as in the exercise of every other constitutional power, a discretion in the choice of means is * * * allowed. It is essential only that the means must be necessary and proper for carrying into execution the power conferred, through the restoration of the State to its constitutional relations, under a republican form of government, and that no acts be done, and no authority exerted, which is either prohibited or unsanctioned by the Constitution.

* * *

What has thus been said generally describes, with sufficient accuracy, the situation of Texas. A provisional governor of the State was appointed by the President in 1865; in 1866 a governor was elected by the people under the constitution of that year; at a subsequent date a governor was appointed by the commander of the district. Each of the three exercised executive functions and actually represented the State in the executive department.

In the case before us each has given his sanction to the prosecution of the suit, and we find no difficulty, without investigating the legal title of either to the executive office, in holding that the sanction thus given sufficiently warranted the action of the solicitor and counsel in behalf of the State. The necessary conclusion is that the suit was instituted and is prosecuted by competent authority.

* * *

NOTES AND QUESTIONS

1. Three justices dissented, on the ground that if Texas was not a "State" for purposes of representation in Congress (and everyone agreed that it was not), it was also not a "State" for purposes of the jurisdictional provisions in Article III. If Texas was really a "State" in 1865, why wasn't it immediately entitled to two senators and representation in Congress? For what constitutional purposes was Texas under Reconstruction not a State? Could the Reconstruction government impair the obligation of contracts or enter into foreign treaties or alliances?

2. It was of course, the "adjudication" of the Civil War itself, not the decision in *Texas v. White*, that authoritatively "held" the Union under the Constitution to be indestructible. Still, *Texas v. White* is interesting for its judicial discussion of the unlawfulness of secession and the indestructibility of both the Union and the States. The case stands for the proposition that the Constitution creates "An indestructible Union of indestructible States."

3. If the rebel "government" from 1861–65 was not really a government, and its repeal of the State's law concerning bonds was invalid, as the Court went on to hold after finding that it had jurisdiction over the case, does that mean that all acts sanctioned by that "government" were invalid? That all private contracts made under its authority were invalid? That all marriages performed under its authority were invalid? The Court in *Texas v. White* had this to say:

> It is not necessary to attempt any exact definitions, within which the acts of such a State government must be treated as valid, or invalid. It may be said, perhaps with sufficient accuracy, that acts necessary to peace and good order among citizens, such for example, as acts sanctioning and protecting marriage and the domestic relations, governing the course of descents, regulating the conveyance and transfer of property, real and personal, and providing remedies for injuries to person and estate, and other similar acts, which would be valid if emanating from a lawful government, must be regarded in general as valid

> when proceeding from an actual, though unlawful government; and that acts in furtherance or support of rebellion against the United States, or intended to defeat the just rights of citizens, and other acts of like nature, must, in general, be regarded as invalid and void.

74 U.S. (7 Wall.) at 733. On this reasoning, were taxes levied by the rebel government to fund the war effort invalid?

4. Article IV, Clause 3 provides a way for new States to join the Union, but it does not provide for any mechanism for States to leave, whether unilaterally or with Congress's consent. Does this mean that before a State—say Alaska or Hawaii—could leave the Union, the Constitution would first have to be amended to provide a way out? *Expressio unius, exclusion alterius*: the specification of way to enter without the specification of a way to leave implies that leaving has not been authorized. *See* Gary Lawson, *One(?) Nation Overextended,* 94 B.U. L. REV. 1109, 1120–24 (2014).

5. The Canadian Supreme Court was asked by the government in the 1990s to render an advisory opinion on whether Quebec could unilaterally secede from Canada if the people of that province voted for secession in a popular referendum (as they almost did). The Court concluded, in *Reference re Secession of Quebec,* 2 S.C.R. 217 (Supreme Court of Canada 1998), that if the people of Quebec voted for secession the central government would be obligated to enter into negotiations with it on the terms of secession, including how to apportion the national debt and where to draw the new nation's boundary lines as well as how effectively to protect the rights of English speakers in Quebec. The opinion makes for fascinating reading for anyone interested in constitutionalism or secession. It also shows what it might be like to live under a constitutional regime where courts can issue advisory opinions. On the topic of constitutionalism and secession generally, see Andrei Kreptul, *The Constitutional Right of Secession in Political Theory and History,* 17 J. LIBERTARIAN STUD. 39 (2003); Glenn Harlan Reynolds, *Splitsylvania: State Secession and What to Do About It,* 94 NOTRE DAME L. REV. ONLINE 90 (2019); Cass R. Sunstein, *Constitutionalism and Secession,* 58 U. CHI. L. REV. 633 (1991).

CHAPTER 2

THE SEPARATION OF POWERS AND THE FEDERAL GOVERNMENT: A SYSTEM OF CHECKS AND BALANCES

[Assignment 7]

The first thing a reader of the Constitution notices upon looking at that document is the majesty of the Preamble. The second thing he or she will notice is the separation of legislative, executive, and judicial powers among Articles I, II, and III. There is good reason for the Constitution's emphasis on the centrality of the separation of powers.

The Massachusetts Constitution of 1780, the oldest constitution still in force in the world today, actually declares that: "In the government of this Commonwealth, the legislative department shall never exercise the executive and judicial powers, or either of them: The executive shall never exercise the legislative and judicial powers, or either of them; The judicial shall never exercise the legislative and executive powers, or either of them: To the end it may be a government of laws and not of men." MASS. CONST. OF 1780, pt. I, art. 30. Other state constitutions had previously employed express "separation of powers" clauses; the Virginia Constitution of 1776 and the Georgia Constitution of 1777 both said that "[t]he legislative, executive, and judicial departments, shall be distinct, so that neither exercise the powers properly belonging to the other," VA. CONST. OF 1776, § 3; GEORGIA CONSTITUTION OF 1777, art. I. Today, such express separation-of-powers clauses appear in forty state constitutions. *See* Steven Gow Calabresi, James Lindgren, Hannah M. Begley, Kathryn L. Dore & Sarah E. Agudo, *What Rights Are Deeply Rooted in a Modern-Day Consensus of the States?*, 94 NOTRE DAME L. REV. 49, 141–43 (2018).

The U.S. Constitution contains no such express separation-of-powers clause. Does that mean that the U.S. Constitution is unconcerned with the separation of powers? Of course not. It simply means that the U.S. Constitution, as with the States whose constitutions lack such a clause, chooses a different strategy for securing a separation of governmental powers. To understand the U.S. Constitution's strategy, one has to start with something even more basic.

I. INTRODUCTION: FINDING FEDERAL POWERS

The text of the Constitution begins with an emphatic declaration of popular sovereignty: "We the People of the United States * * * do ordain and establish this Constitution for the United States of America." Whether for purposes of political theory one regards this statement as an historic and profound expression or as an arrogant pretention, for *interpretative* purposes it is clear that the Constitution regards itself as resulting from an act by a power higher than and prior to itself. It is conventional to refer to the ultimate ground of political power in a society by the slippery and vague, but unavoidable, term "sovereignty." According to the Constitution, sovereignty lies with "We the People." Recall from the Introduction how James Madison responded to complaints that the Constitutional Convention had exceeded its authority and that the Constitution's ratification process illegally sidestepped state constitutional rules. *See supra* at page 41. And recall how opponents of the Constitution responded—or, more precisely, failed to respond—to Madison's defense of the legality of the Constitution. Whatever its merits as a matter of abstract normative political theory, the Constitution's assertion of popular sovereignty was taken as social fact in the founding era.

The Constitution thus makes it clear that, whereas in England the King-in-Parliament—the combination of the King, the House of Lords, and the House of Commons acting in a legislative capacity—was sovereign, in America sovereignty rests with We the People of the United States. The Constitution went into effect after nine of the twelve States that sent delegates to the Philadelphia Convention ratified it in special conventions elected for that purpose. Once in effect, the Constitution can only be amended by three-quarters of the States. Sovereignty thus lies in a majority of the people in three quarters of the States (directly if ratification is by convention, indirectly if ratification is by state legislatures); it does not lie in the federal government or the States (notwithstanding what you will read in some subsequent Supreme Court opinions).

In 1788, the sovereign We the People granted to the United States certain powers (and duties). This sovereign act of delegation is the ground for the fundamental constitutional idea of enumerated powers: the agent (the government) only has those powers granted to it by the principal (We the People). And the idea of enumerated powers, in turn, is the ground for the Constitution's regime of separated powers.

Read through the Constitution again and mark out all clauses that grant power to the federal government. Okay, we will save you the trouble: *There are none!* The only clause that even arguably grants power to the federal government *as an entity* is the Article IV, section 4 Guarantee Clause. The Constitution is certainly full of power-granting clauses, but those clauses do not grant power to "the federal government" or "the national government" or "the United States." They grant power to *particular institutions or actors* within the federal governmental structure created by the Constitution: Congress, the President, the Vice President, the federal courts, members of the Electoral College, and so forth.

Each actor can only claim from the Constitution the specific powers granted to them by the instrument, though some of those actors, such as States or voters, may have powers that pre-exist and thus do not stem from the Constitution. (Indeed, as we saw in the Introduction, the United States, as a pre-existing corporate entity, even has a few powers that do not come from the Constitution but are inherent in corporate status, such has the power to make contracts, hold property, and sue and be sued.) This idea of limited and enumerated grants of power to specific institutions or actors is the Constitution's strategy for separating governmental powers.

Congress cannot exercise executive power because Congress is not granted executive power by the Constitution; that power goes to the President in Article II. The President and the courts cannot exercise legislative power because "[a]ll legislative Powers herein granted" are vested in Congress. Congress and the President cannot exercise judicial power because "[t]he judicial Power of the United States" is vested in federal judges with tenure during good behavior and guarantees against diminishment of salary while in office and is not vested in Congress or the President. The Constitution did not need an express "separation of powers" clause because the scheme of enumerated institutional power secures that separation by giving to each institution and actor only a certain subset of the total mass of potential governmental powers. That is why when James Madison tried to introduce an express separation-of-powers clause as part of the Bill of Rights, *see* 1 ANNALS OF CONG. 453 (1789), it was rejected as "altogether unnecessary, inasmuch as the constitution assigned the business of each branch of the Government to a separate department." *Id.* at 789 (statement of Rep. Sherman).

The separation of powers secured by the Constitution through this mechanism of enumerated institutional powers is a very *specific* separation of powers. The principle of enumerated institutional power limits each constitutional actor to its own sphere, but those spheres are defined by the actual terms of the grants of power rather than by abstract theories about ideal governmental structures.

If the Constitution wants to give the Vice President the tie-breaking vote in the Senate, let the President have a qualified veto over legislation, and give the Senate a role in appointments and treaty-making, that is the Constitution's business, whether or not those assignments conform to someone's idealized model of separated powers. Those blendings of theoretical roles do not mean that the Constitution fails to separate powers, though it may mean that it fails to separate them the way that some external critic would prefer them to be separated.

The Constitution grants three categories of power to various actors: "[a]ll legislative Powers herein granted" go to Congress; "[t]he executive Power" is vested in the President, and "[t]he judicial Power" is vested in the federal courts. Each actor can only exercise those powers which they have been delegated by We the People. But what are those powers? What defines a power as legislative, executive, or judicial within the meaning of the Constitution?

The Constitution does not expressly define those categories of power. Neither do any of the state constitutions, now or in the founding era, which contain express separation-of-powers clauses. This lack of definition was *not* because everyone in the eighteenth century thought the categories of legislative, executive, and judicial powers were clear. They most certainly did not think that. Madison memorably said in *The Federalist*: "Experience has instructed us, that no skill in the science of government has yet been able to discriminate and define, with sufficient certainty, its three great provinces, the legislative, executive, and judiciary * * *. Questions daily occur in the course of practice, which prove the obscurity which reigns in these subjects, and which puzzle the greatest adepts in political science." THE FEDERALIST No. 37 (James Madison). Indeed, the three-part categorization that today we take for granted was relatively new in 1788, having originated in 1748 with Montesquieu's publication of *The Spirit of the Laws*.

For most of English legal history before that point, judicial power was not a distinct category of governmental power at all; it was considered part and parcel of executive power. English judges were removable at will by the King until 1701 and did not acquire what we think of as life tenure until 1761. And kings and parliaments had battled—sometimes literally—for centuries over the boundaries of their respective powers. The conceptual lines among legislative, executive, and judicial powers were hardly clear in 1788.

Nonetheless:

> That adept-puzzling obscurity * * * did not stop Madison from categorically declaring that various powers of government are "*in their nature* . . . legislative, executive, or judiciary." Nor did it stop John Adams from stating that the "three branches of power have an unalterable foundation in nature; that they exist in every society natural and artificial . . .; that the legislative and executive authorities are naturally distinct; and that liberty and the laws depend entirely on a separation of them in the frame of government." Nor did it prevent many state constitutions of the founding era from including separation-of-powers clauses that expressly distinguished, again without express definitions, legislative, executive, and judicial powers. Nor did it prevent the United States Constitution from basing its entire scheme of governance on the distinctions between those powers. However difficult it may be at the margins to distinguish the categories of power from each other, the founding generation assumed that there was a fact of the matter about those distinctions and that one could discern that fact in at least a large range of cases. The communicative meaning of the Constitution of 1788 cannot be ascertained without reference to some such distinction, even if legal scholars or political scientists (adept or otherwise) find the distinction unhelpful or confusing * * *.

Gary Lawson, *Take the Fifth . . . Please! The Original Insignificance of the Fifth Amendment's Due Process of Law Clause*, 2017 B.Y.U. L. REV. 611, 623–25 (emphasis added) (footnotes omitted).

The task of defining the limits of the three classes of power delegated by the Constitution has bedeviled governmental actors and scholars for more than two centuries. Moreover, the Constitution does not simply delegate three classes of power and move on. Instead, it also contains an intricate network of specific grants of power to various actors, many of which are precisely calibrated to counterbalance or offset other grants of power in the document. One cannot truly appreciate the Constitution's separation of powers without considering the entire structure as a whole. A study of the Constitution's unique scheme of separated powers requires back-and-forth movements and counter-movements among some very abstract and some very specific and technical provisions. Make no mistake—it is often tough sledding. But, as two authors who have spent much of their professional lives studying the Constitution's separation of powers, we promise you that it is also some of the most rewarding and interesting sledding that you will undertake in your legal education.

In this Chapter, we consider the structure, nature, and functions of Congress, the President, and the federal courts, and the relationships among them. We reserve (in the main) questions of "Federalism"—the quantum of the combined power of federal institutions vis-à-vis the state governments and the people—for the next chapter. This chapter is addressed primarily to the "separation of powers"—the division and distribution of power among the legislative, executive, and judicial departments—or branches, as we call them today[1]—of the national government.

Before getting into the details of the Constitution's scheme of separated powers, however, we present some materials on the rationale behind and operational function of the Constitution's separation of powers, beginning with the most important statement ever made about the American system of separation of powers and checks and balances.

The Federalist No. 51 (James Madison)

TO WHAT expedient, then, shall we finally resort, for maintaining in practice the necessary partition of power among the several departments, as laid down in the Constitution? The only answer that can be given is, that as all these exterior provisions are found to be inadequate, the defect must be supplied, by so contriving the interior structure of the government as that its several constituent parts may, by their mutual relations, be the means of keeping each other in their proper places * * *.

In order to lay a due foundation for that separate and distinct exercise of the different powers of government, which to a certain extent is admitted on all hands to be essential to the preservation of liberty, it is evident that each department should have a will of its own; and consequently should be so constituted that the members of each should have as little agency as possible in the appointment of the members of the others. Were this principle rigorously adhered to, it would require that all the appointments for the supreme executive, legislative, and judiciary magistracies should be drawn from the same fountain of authority, the people, through channels having no communication whatever with one another. Perhaps such a plan of constructing the several departments would be less difficult in practice than it may in contemplation appear. Some difficulties, however, and some additional expense would attend the execution of it. Some deviations, therefore, from the principle must be admitted. In the constitution of the judiciary department in particular, it might be inexpedient to insist rigorously on the principle: first, because peculiar qualifications being essential in the members, the primary consideration ought to be to select that mode of choice which best secures these qualifications; secondly, because the permanent tenure by which the appointments are held in that department, must soon destroy all sense of dependence on the authority conferring them.

It is equally evident, that the members of each department should be as little dependent as possible on those of the others, for the emoluments annexed to their offices. Were the executive magistrate, or the judges, not independent of the legislature in this particular, their independence in every other would be merely nominal. But the great security against a gradual concentration of the several powers in the same department, consists in giving to those who administer each department

---

[1] In the founding era, the legislative, executive, and judicial bodies were usually called "departments," as they were in the Massachusetts, Virginia, and Georgia constitutions quoted above. The term "branches" was generally reserved for the different bodies in a multicameral legislature. Thus, the House and Senate are *branches* of the legislative *department*. Today, people freely speak of the "legislative branch," the "executive branch," and the "judicial branch." We often—not always, but often—follow that modern practice simply because it is familiar.

the necessary constitutional means and personal motives to resist encroachments of the others. The provision for defense must in this, as in all other cases, be made commensurate to the danger of attack. Ambition must be made to counteract ambition. The interest of the man must be connected with the constitutional rights of the place. It may be a reflection on human nature, that such devices should be necessary to control the abuses of government. But what is government itself, but the greatest of all reflections on human nature? If men were angels, no government would be necessary. If angels were to govern men, neither external nor internal controls on government would be necessary. In framing a government which is to be administered by men over men, the great difficulty lies in this: you must first enable the government to control the governed; and in the next place oblige it to control itself.

A dependence on the people is, no doubt, the primary control on the government; but experience has taught mankind the necessity of auxiliary precautions. This policy of supplying, by opposite and rival interests, the defect of better motives, might be traced through the whole system of human affairs, private as well as public. We see it particularly displayed in all the subordinate distributions of power, where the constant aim is to divide and arrange the several offices in such a manner as that each may be a check on the other that the private interest of every individual may be a sentinel over the public rights. These inventions of prudence cannot be less requisite in the distribution of the supreme powers of the State. But it is not possible to give to each department an equal power of self-defense. In republican government, the legislative authority necessarily predominates. The remedy for this inconveniency is to divide the legislature into different branches; and to render them, by different modes of election and different principles of action, as little connected with each other as the nature of their common functions and their common dependence on the society will admit. It may even be necessary to guard against dangerous encroachments by still further precautions. As the weight of the legislative authority requires that it should be thus divided, the weakness of the executive may require, on the other hand, that it should be fortified * * *.

There are, moreover, two considerations particularly applicable to the federal system of America, which place that system in a very interesting point of view. First. In a single republic, all the power surrendered by the people is submitted to the administration of a single government; and the usurpations are guarded against by a division of the government into distinct and separate departments. In the compound republic of America, the power surrendered by the people is first divided between two distinct governments, and then the portion allotted to each subdivided among distinct and separate departments. Hence a double security arises to the rights of the people. The different governments will control each other, at the same time that each will be controlled by itself. Second. It is of great importance in a republic not only to guard the society against the oppression of its rulers, but to guard one part of the society against the injustice of the other part. Different interests necessarily exist in different classes of citizens. If a majority be united by a common interest, the rights of the minority will be insecure.

There are but two methods of providing against this evil: the one by creating a will in the community independent of the majority that is, of the society itself; the other, by comprehending in the society so many separate descriptions of citizens as will render an unjust combination of a majority of the whole very improbable, if not impracticable. The first method prevails in all governments possessing an hereditary or self-appointed authority. This, at best, is but a precarious security; because a power independent of the society may as well espouse the unjust views of the major, as the rightful interests of the minor party, and may possibly be turned against both parties. The second method will be exemplified in the federal republic of the United States. Whilst all authority in it will be derived from and dependent on the society, the society itself will be broken into so many parts, interests, and classes of citizens, that the rights of individuals, or of the minority, will be in little danger from interested combinations of the majority.

II. AN OVERVIEW OF THE SEPARATION OF POWERS AND OF CHECKS AND BALANCES

The Constitution's separation-of-powers scheme is designed to create practical checks and balances among the institutions of government, rather than to conform to an idealized theoretical model, so that the Constitution will be, as James Madison argued, effectively self-enforcing. The American idea of the separation of powers is thus critically different from the way the doctrine is understood in the Civil Law tradition in continental Europe, Latin America, and in parts of Asia and Africa. *See* JOHN HENRY MERRYMAN & ROGELIO PEREZ-PERDOMO, THE CIVIL LAW TRADITION: AN INTRODUCTION TO THE LEGAL SYSTEMS OF WESTERN EUROPE AND OF LATIN AMERICA (3d. ed. 2007). Continental Europeans today (and the eighteenth-century French revolutionaries who first designed the dominant Continental framework) understand the separation of powers to mean that the legislature has total power over policy-making; the executive has total power over law execution including administrative law courts, which are part of the executive branch; and the ordinary judiciary lacks the power of judicial review because that would involve it in policy-making. Continental European and Asian democracies typically have a special fourth branch of government, called a Constitutional Court, which alone has the "policy-making" powers of judicial review.

In Latin America, the separation of powers is typically understood as giving the President the power to make law by presidential decree. The U.S. understanding of the phrase "the separation of powers" is thus fundamentally and radically different from Continental European, Asian, and Latin American understandings of that phrase. Different people around the world use the same term to convey very different ideas, so you always need to be aware of the context when you see a term such as "separation of powers." And the "separation of powers" that you will find in any particular State in the U.S. will not necessarily mirror the distinctive structure of the U.S. Constitution.

In the U.S. Constitution, legislative, executive, and judicial institutions and powers are intermingled in certain specific ways so as to make the whole system of checks and balances work. Some powers that Englishmen considered to be legislative, like the veto, are given to the President. And some powers that Englishmen considered to be executive, like advising and consenting to nominees for executive or judicial office or ratifying treaties, are given to the Senate. The Constitution thus does not create a perfect separation of powers even as Englishmen understood that subject. Instead, the Constitution intermingles powers to create a regime of checks and balances. This is what James Madison was defending in

Federalist No. 51, which you just read. Consider just a few of the checks and balances among the three branches of the federal government.

The most important check on the President comes from the vesting of legislative power in Congress. Under the Constitution, there cannot be any enacted laws without action from both houses of Congress, *see* U.S. CONST. art. I, § 7, and without enacted laws there is not much for the President to execute. Congress can also check the President with its most formidable power—the Power of the Purse, expressed by the constitutional command that "[n]o Money shall be drawn from the Treasury, but in Consequence of Appropriations made by Law," U.S. CONST. art. I, § 9, cl. 7, and enforced by statutory provisions making it a federal crime for government officials to spend money beyond appropriations. *See* 31 U.S.C. §§ 1341(a), 1350 (2018). (This is why government agencies literally have to shut down during "shut-downs" when the President and Congress cannot agree on budgets.)

Congress can effectively use its Power of the Purse to stop a war, or the building of a wall on the U.S.-Mexican border, simply by cutting off or refusing to appropriate funding. Congress can make or unmake executive departments and other agencies; Congress, not the Constitution itself or the President, dictates the architecture of the executive branch. Congress can also check the President by passing bills by a two-thirds majority over his or her veto. The Senate, through its constitutional role in the appointments and treaty processes, can hobble the President's administration of the government by refusing to confirm his or her nominees or to ratify by a two-thirds vote any treaties the President makes. Both houses of Congress can and do hold oversight hearings of the executive branch through their committees, which can consume time and resources and lead to unwanted publicity. Moreover, U.S. bureaucrats or civil servants know that Presidents, and their political appointees, come and go every four or eight years, while the members of the congressional oversight committees may sit on those committees for many decades. As a result, it is debatable (and political scientists actively debate) whether the executive bureaucracy really works for the President, the committees of Congress, both, or neither.

Congress's power to control the courts is more complex. In theory, Congress has many of the same formal powers over courts as it has with executive agents. While Congress cannot constitutionally decrease the salaries of federal judges, it can check the Supreme Court and the lower federal courts by denying them salary increases, as it is doing now. (Congress can neither increase nor decrease the President's salary while the President is in office. *See* U.S. CONST. art. II, § 1, cl. 6.) Congress has sweeping power to alter the jurisdiction and remedial powers of the lower federal courts and some power over the jurisdiction of even the Supreme Court. Congress has the power to either eliminate the lower federal courts or to double their judges in number at any point in time. Congress can also increase or decrease the size of the Supreme Court, if public opinion supports it in doing that. In theory, Congress could hold the same kinds of oversight hearings over the activities of courts that it holds over executive actions; in practice, it has generally not done so. Congress can overturn presidential or Supreme Court constructions of statutes by passing new legislation, which it frequently does. It can try to overturn Supreme Court constructions of the Constitution by proposing constitutional amendments, which it has successfully done four times in American history to date.

Finally, Congress can impeach and remove any executive or judicial officer, including the President and the Justices of the Supreme Court, by a majority of the House of Representatives and a two-thirds majority of the Senate.

All of these congressional powers, as with any powers, can be used abusively or vindictively to try to force presidents or judges to bend to Congress's will. The Constitution anticipates precisely this possibility (likelihood?), *see* Gary Lawson, *The Constitution's Congress,* 89 B.U. L. REV. 399 (2009), and accordingly gives the President and the courts some defensive mechanisms.

The President can check Congress by vetoing its bills, which veto can be overridden only by a two-thirds vote of both houses. Vetoes are seldom overridden. The President can also check Congress by setting priorities in law enforcement and law execution. Congress may outlaw something, but if the President does not bring many or any prosecutions and enforcement actions, Congress's lawmaking will be only symbolic (which, to be sure, is all that Congress sometimes hopes for when it passes laws). The President has broad power to direct, control, and remove policy-making subordinates in the executive branch, thereby counter-balancing the power of the congressional oversight committees. The President can also check Congress in the foreign affairs area where the Commander in Chief power, the treaty-negotiating power, and other inherent executive powers make the President the lead player. The Constitution guarantees the President a salary that can be neither increased nor decreased by Congress during the President's term.

The President and Senate jointly have a powerful check over the federal courts because they appoint new federal judges and even Supreme Court justices. The President also influences what issues are litigated by controlling litigation in which the U.S. is a party and through influencing the government's amicus participation.

The federal courts can check and balance both Congress and the President with the formidable power of judicial review. The Court can invalidate actions and laws on constitutional grounds, or it can "reinterpret" them either in light of constitutional difficulties or simply to make them say what the courts want them to say. The courts have not traditionally been subject to the congressional oversight process (except, once a year, when two justices present the budget for the federal judiciary). No Supreme Court justice has ever been successfully impeached and removed from office in 230 years of constitutional history, and only thirteen lower federal court judges have been impeached and removed, and every single impeached and removed federal judge had previously been convicted of some federal crime.

In sum, each of the three branches has powerful checks and balances, written into the Constitution and resulting from more than two centuries of practice, on the actions of the other two. The net result is that change of any kind is generally very hard to accomplish, and it usually requires a consensus of the whole people—expressed consistently in at least two or three national elections—before significant change occurs. This is why people who want quick change often find the Constitution's separation of powers frustrating. It makes it harder for bad ideas to get through, but it also makes it harder to impose what you think are good ideas on others through the power of government. Normative assessments of the Constitution's scheme of separated powers thus often turn on the assessor's degree of risk aversion—and on who the assessor imagines will likely bear the risks and reap the rewards of removing structural brakes on governmental action.

One more point of introduction that we think is crucial for understanding the Constitution before we get to the document's concrete provisions. The idea of a function-based separation of powers was something of an innovation in 1787 when the Constitution was written. The French political philosopher Montesquieu developed the idea in its modern form in 1748, in a famous book called *De L'esprit des Lois ("On the Spirit of the Laws")*. Montesquieu built on the writings of seventeenth-century political philosophers who no longer accepted an Aristotelian Mixed Regime of the King, the Aristocrats, and the People—the One, the Few, and the Many—each of whom belonged to a different social class. This Mixed Regime was the type of regime that was thought to have existed in England from 1689 to 1776, with the hereditary King representing the One, the hereditary House of Lords representing the Few, and the elected House of Commons representing the Many.

Hereditary monarchs and lords were out of the question both for Montesquieu and for the Framers of the U.S. Constitution. The Enlightenment and the Declaration of Independence were committed to the idea that "All men are created equal." No one could be born a king, a noble, or a commoner. Everyone was born equal to everyone else; the Constitution even specifically proclaims that "[n]o Title of Nobility shall be granted by the United States." U.S. CONST. art. I, § 9, cl. 8. In place of the classical Mixed Regime, Montesquieu argued instead for a functional separation of legislative, executive, and judicial power. One purpose of the Mixed Regime had been to divide power among the three classes of society because, as Lord Acton would later say, "Power tends to corrupt, and absolute power corrupts absolutely." Once the Enlightenment had ruled out Mixed Regimes, Montesquieu hit upon the idea of a functional separation of legislative and executive and judicial power as an alternative vehicle for protecting against "absolute power corrupting absolutely." The difficulty for the Framers of the U.S. Constitution was that no regime had tried to set up a separation of powers system nationwide prior to 1787.

Moreover, many of the most sophisticated Framers, like John Adams, Alexander Hamilton, and Gouverneur Morris, still believed that the eighteenth-century Mixed Regime Constitution of Britain, with its king, lords, and commoners, was the best constitution in the world in the 1780s, even if its hereditary components were anathema in the U.S. They, and some others, set out to create a republican version of the Mixed Regime of the One, the Few, and the Many. The advantage to having some power in the One was energy in the executive and military and foreign policy prowess. The advantage to having some power in the Few was the expertise of a natural aristocracy of talents in the government. And, the advantage in placing most power ultimately with the Many was that one would get the common sense of liberty and good judgment in the government.

Mixed Regimes gave the power of the One to a hereditary monarch who served for life, but the Constitution hemmed that power in greatly by giving it to one democratically elected President—who, after the enactment of the Twenty-Second Amendment in 1951, can serve no more than two four-year terms. Major powers of the King of England were shorn from the President, including the power to declare war, to create new executive departments and officers, and unilaterally to make appointments and treaties. The President is also subject to impeachment, unlike the King, and he or she can be prosecuted like any ordinary citizen once he or she leaves office for crimes committed while President. This represents what political philosopher Harvey Mansfield has called *The Taming of the Prince* (1989).

Mixed Regimes gave the power of the Few to a House of Lords and Bishops in England, most of whom inherited their seats from their fathers, and to English barristers who were drawn only from the upper class of society. The Constitution substituted for this feudal aristocracy a republican aristocracy of merit, with a Senate consisting of an equal number of senators from each State. Senators serve lengthy terms (six years), with only a third of the seats being open every two years. The name "the Senate" comes from the aristocratic body equivalent to the House of Lords in the ancient Roman Republic. The class differences that the name suggests still persist: more than half of senators are millionaires (compared to fewer than 5% of American households), fifty-six senators hold law degrees, and all have been to college (only 25% of Americans are college graduates). The Senate is an elected body, and it responds quickly to shifts in public opinion, but it is also an elite body that fits, however unevenly, into the mold of the Few.

Moreover, the Few in the Senate (100) share power with the Few who are Supreme Court justices (currently nine) and inferior federal court judges (currently approximately 1000), all of whom, as a matter of practice and tradition even if not of formal legal requirement, must be not only college graduates but also law school graduates—and usually "elite" law school graduates. The present (2020) Supreme Court has four graduates of Yale Law School, four graduates of Harvard Law School, and one graduate of Columbia Law School. The present Supreme Court is thus fairly characterized in eighteenth-century terms as a natural aristocracy of talent, even though two of its members—Justices Clarence Thomas and Sonia Sotomayor—grew up dirt poor. The "aristocratic" Senate plays a large role in selecting life-tenured federal judges, a considerable number of whom are also millionaires. Whether the judges and the senators in the U.S. today are more aristocratic (rule by the "best") than oligarchic (rule by a corrupt few) is a matter of some debate. What seems indisputable is that, as descriptive matter, there is in practice an aristocratic/oligarchic element to the current U.S. constitutional regime.

Mixed Regimes, like eighteenth-century Britain's, purported to give the power of the Many to a severely malapportioned House of Commons. The Constitution gave that power to the House of Representatives, with representatives allocated to States on the basis of census-based population numbers, and to the States who would select presidential electors for the Electoral College. But, since the early nineteenth century, the States have allowed the people in each State to pick directly those state's presidential electors, so today the Many in America pick the One. In addition, the Many have directly elected the Few U.S. senators since the Seventeenth Amendment was ratified in 1913 (and a large number of States had already moved towards direct election of senators before that amendment). The U.S. Constitution thus gives We the People a say in choosing the One (President), the Few (in the Senate), and the Many (in the House) and a say, indirectly, in choosing those who choose the Few who are federal judges (presidential nomination and senatorial confirmation). Thus, as James Madison said quite presciently in *The Federalist No. 51*, "all the appointments for the supreme executive, legislative, and judiciary magistracies [are] drawn from the same fountain of authority, the people."

As you read the cases and materials in this chapter (and throughout the rest of this course), ask yourself whether the Mixed Regime of the One, the Few, and the Many was really abandoned by the U.S. Constitution of 1787 or whether it was brought back in a new guise with the One President, the Few senators and Supreme

Court justices, and the Many members of the House of Representatives, with the Many also electing the One and the Few. Does our Constitution really have its roots in the constitutional ideas and practices of Aristotle, Polybius, Sparta, Carthage, the Roman Republic, and the Republic of Venice? (Remember that serious education in the eighteenth century uniformly included close study of Greek, Latin, and classical history.) Or is it radically different because in the U.S. the Many get to pick the One and the Few? Is it a Constitution that you would recommend to emerging democracies?

We start with perhaps the most difficult problem in separation-of-powers law: Distinguishing the three classes of power vested by the Constitution in legislative, executive, and judicial actors. It is obviously impossible to approach that problem without generating some ideas regarding the core meanings of legislative, executive, and judicial power, and the cases and materials to follow introduce some of the most important settings in which those powers have been defined (or left undefined). In the subsequent section, we will elaborate on those core meanings and see how both the Constitution's text and the nation's history flesh out the roles assigned to each governmental institution.

III. DEFINING GOVERNMENTAL POWERS

A. THE BOUNDARY BETWEEN LEGISLATIVE AND EXECUTIVE POWER

We turn now to the first three words of Article I, Section 1 which vest "All legislative powers" herein granted by the Constitution in a bicameral Congress of the United States, which consists of a Senate and a House of Representatives. What exactly is a "legislative power"?

One often hears of presidents issuing "executive orders"—as of 2020, there have been approximately 14,000 such orders. Almost all of those orders govern the internal relations within the executive branch. They are just a formalized way for the President to give instructions to subordinates; the President could accomplish the same goals on a piecemeal basis by sending individualized text messages to agency officials or by calling people into the Oval Office for a chat. To emphasize the internal, managerial character of these orders, executive orders almost always specify that they are not meant to be enforceable in court or to create rights or obligations for private parties. The penalty for violating an executive order is usually the President's displeasure and perhaps a presidential firing (more on the President's power to fire subordinates is coming later). Some presidential executive orders indirectly affect third parties by, for example, forbidding executive branch officers from discriminating based on a forbidden basis in hiring or contracting.

On some occasions, presidents take actions by executive order that purport to have real-world legal effects outside the executive branch. Where those actions merely implement duly enacted statutes, they are the quintessential exercise of "executive Power"—the power (and duty, given the Constitution's Take Care Clause) of the President to carry into effect the laws. But what if the President, by unilateral action in the absence of statutory authority, alters people's rights and responsibilities? Does the "executive Power" (or the "judicial Power") include some inherent power to govern independently of statutes? Does it matter if a war is going on (and does it matter whether Congress has declared war)? When does action by a President become a forbidden exercise of "legislative Power"?

These questions were posed starkly—though not remotely for the first time in American history—during the Korean War. Consider the multivariant answers provided in the following case, which is surely among the most important cases ever decided by the U.S. Supreme Court. As you read the opinions, consider what modalities of argument each opinion employs.

B. YOUNGSTOWN SHEET & TUBE CO. V. SAWYER

343 U.S. 579 (1952)

■ MR. JUSTICE BLACK delivered the opinion of the Court.

We are asked to decide whether the President was acting within his constitutional power when he issued an order directing the Secretary of Commerce to take possession of and operate most of the Nation's steel mills. The mill owners argue that the President's order amounts to lawmaking, a legislative function which the Constitution has expressly confided to the Congress and not to the President. The Government's position is that the order was made on findings of the President that his action was necessary to avert a national catastrophe which would inevitably result from a stoppage of steel production, and that in meeting this grave emergency the President was acting within the aggregate of his constitutional powers as the Nation's Chief Executive and the Commander in Chief of the Armed Forces of the United States. The issue emerges here from the following series of events:

In the latter part of 1951, a dispute arose between the steel companies and their employees over terms and conditions that should be included in new collective bargaining agreements. Long-continued conferences failed to resolve the dispute On December 18, 1951, the employees' representative, United Steelworkers of America, C.I.O., gave notice of an intention to strike when the existing bargaining agreements expired on December 31 * * *. On April 4, 1952, the Union gave notice of a nation-wide strike called to begin at 12:01 a.m. April 9. The indispensability of steel as a component of substantially all weapons and other war materials led the President to believe that the proposed work stoppage would immediately jeopardize our national defense and that governmental seizure of the steel mills was necessary in order to assure the continued availability of steel. Reciting these considerations for his action, the President, a few hours before the strike was to begin, issued Executive Order 10340 * * *. The order directed the Secretary of Commerce to take possession of most of the steel mills and keep them running. The Secretary immediately issued his own possessory orders, calling upon the presidents of the various seized companies to serve as operating managers for the United States. They were directed to carry on their activities in accordance with regulations and directions of the Secretary. The next morning the President sent a message to Congress reporting his action. Twelve days later he sent a second message.

Obeying the Secretary's orders under protest, the companies brought proceedings against him in the District Court. Their complaints charged that the seizure was not authorized by an act of Congress or by any constitutional provisions. The District Court was asked to declare the orders of the President and the Secretary invalid and to issue preliminary and permanent injunctions restraining their enforcement. Opposing the motion for preliminary injunction, the United States asserted that a strike disrupting steel production for even a brief period would so endanger the well-being and safety of the Nation that the President had "inherent power" to do what he had done—power "supported by the Constitution, by historical precedent, and by court decisions." Holding against the Government on all points, the District Court on April 30 issued a preliminary injunction restraining the Secretary from "continuing the seizure and possession of the plant . . . and from acting under the purported authority of Executive Order No. 10340." On the same day the Court of Appeals stayed the District Court's injunction. Deeming it best that the issues raised be promptly decided by this Court, we granted certiorari on May 3 and set the cause for argument on May 12.

* * *

The President's power, if any, to issue the order must stem either from an act of Congress or from the Constitution itself. There is no statute that expressly authorizes the President to take possession of property as he did here. Nor is there any act of Congress to which our attention has been directed from which such a power can fairly be implied. Indeed, we do not understand the Government to rely on statutory authorization for this seizure. There are two statutes which do authorize the President to take both personal and real property under certain conditions. However, the Government admits that these conditions were not met and that the President's order was not rooted in either of the statutes. The Government refers to the seizure provisions of one of these statutes (s 201(b) of the Defense Production Act) as "much too cumbersome, involved, and time-consuming for the crisis which was at hand."

Moreover, the use of the seizure technique to solve labor disputes in order to prevent work stoppages was not only unauthorized by any congressional enactment; prior to this controversy, Congress had refused to adopt that method of settling labor disputes. When the Taft-Hartley Act was under consideration in 1947, Congress rejected an amendment which would have authorized such governmental seizures in cases of emergency. Apparently it was thought that the technique of seizure, like that of compulsory arbitration, would interfere with the process of collective bargaining. Consequently, the plan Congress adopted in that Act did not provide for seizure under any circumstances * * *.

It is clear that if the President had authority to issue the order he did, it must be found in some provisions of the Constitution. And it is not claimed that express constitutional language grants this power to the President. The contention is that presidential power should be implied from the aggregate of his powers under the Constitution. Particular reliance is placed on provisions in Article II which say that "the executive Power shall be vested in a President . . ."; that "he shall take Care that the Laws be faithfully executed"; and that he "shall be Commander in Chief of the Army and Navy of the United States."

The order cannot properly be sustained as an exercise of the President's military power as Commander in Chief of the Armed Forces. The Government attempts to do so by citing a number of cases upholding broad powers in military commanders engaged in day-to-day fighting in a theater of war. Such cases need not concern us here. Even though "theater of war" be an expanding concept, we cannot with faithfulness to our constitutional system hold that the Commander in Chief of the Armed Forces has the ultimate power as such to take possession of private property in order to keep labor disputes from stopping production. This is a job for the Nation's lawmakers, not for its military authorities.

Nor can the seizure order be sustained because of the several constitutional provisions that grant executive power to the President. In the framework of our Constitution, the President's power to see that the laws are faithfully executed refutes the idea that he is to be a lawmaker. The Constitution limits his functions in the lawmaking process to the recommending of laws he thinks wise and the vetoing of laws he thinks bad. And the Constitution is neither silent nor equivocal about who shall make laws which the President is to execute. The first section of the first article says that "All legislative Powers herein granted shall be vested in a Congress of the United States . . . ." After granting many powers to the Congress, Article I goes on to provide that Congress may "make all Laws which shall be necessary and proper for carrying into Execution the foregoing Powers and all other Powers vested by this Constitution in the Government of the United States, or in any Department or Officer thereof."

The President's order does not direct that a congressional policy be executed in a manner prescribed by Congress—it directs that a presidential policy be executed in a manner prescribed by the President. The preamble of the order itself, like that of many statutes, sets out reasons why the President believes certain policies should be adopted, proclaims these policies as rules of conduct to be followed, and again, like a statute, authorizes a government official to promulgate additional rules and regulations consistent with the policy proclaimed and needed to carry that policy into execution. The power of Congress to adopt such public policies as those proclaimed by the order is beyond question. It can authorize the taking of private property for public use. It can make laws regulating the relationships between employers and employees, prescribing rules designed to settle labor disputes, and fixing wages and working conditions in certain fields of our economy. The Constitution did not subject this law-making power of Congress to presidential or military supervision or control.

It is said that other Presidents without congressional authority have taken possession of private business enterprises in order to settle labor disputes. But even if this be true, Congress has not thereby lost its exclusive constitutional authority to make laws necessary and proper to carry out the powers vested by the Constitution "in the Government of the United States, or in any Department or Officer thereof."

The Founders of this Nation entrusted the law making power to the Congress alone in both good and bad times. It would do no good to recall the historical events, the fears of power and the hopes for freedom that lay behind their choice. Such a review would but confirm our holding that this seizure order cannot stand.

The judgment of the District Court is

Affirmed.

■ MR. JUSTICE FRANKFURTER, concurring.

* * * The issue before us can be met, and therefore should be, without attempting to define the President's powers comprehensively * * *.

* * *

* * * The powers of the President are not as particularized as are those of Congress. But unenumerated powers do not mean undefined powers. The separation

of powers built into our Constitution gives essential content to undefined provisions in the frame of our government.

To be sure, the content of the three authorities of government is not to be derived from an abstract analysis. The areas are partly interacting, not wholly disjointed. The Constitution is a framework for government. Therefore the way the framework has consistently operated fairly establishes that it has operated according to its true nature. Deeply embedded traditional ways of conducting government cannot supplant the Constitution or legislation, but they give meaning to the words of a text or supply them. It is an inadmissibly narrow conception of American constitutional law to confine it to the words of the Constitution and to disregard the gloss which life has written upon them. In short, a systematic, unbroken, executive practice, long pursued to the knowledge of the Congress and never before questioned, engaged in by Presidents who have also sworn to uphold the Constitution, making as it were such exercise of power part of the structure of our government, may be treated as a gloss on "executive Power" vested in the President by s[ection] 1 of Art. II.

Such was the case of *United States v. Midwest Oil Co.*, 236 U.S. 459 * * *. In the *Midwest Oil* case lands which Congress had opened for entry were, over a period of 80 years and in 252 instances, and by Presidents learned and unlearned in the law, temporarily withdrawn from entry so as to enable Congress to deal with such withdrawals. No remotely comparable practice can be vouched for executive seizure of property at a time when this country was not at war, in the only constitutional way in which it can be at war. It would pursue the irrelevant to reopen the controversy over the constitutionality of some acts of Lincoln during the Civil War * * *.

* * *

* * * We need not split hairs in comparing those actions to the one before us, though much might be said by way of differentiation * * *. [T]hese * * * instances do not add up, either in number, scope, duration or contemporaneous legal justification, to the kind of executive construction of the Constitution revealed in the *Midwest Oil* case. Nor do they come to us sanctioned by long-continued acquiescence of Congress giving decisive weight to a construction by the Executive of its powers.

* * *

■ MR. JUSTICE DOUGLAS, concurring.

There can be no doubt that the emergency which caused the President to seize these steel plants was one that bore heavily on the country. But the emergency did not create power; it merely marked an occasion when power should be exercised * * *.

* * *

* * * We therefore cannot decide this case by determining which branch of government can deal most expeditiously with the present crisis. The answer must depend on the allocation of powers under the Constitution * * *.

* * *

The legislative nature of the action taken by the President seems to me to be clear. When the United States takes over an industrial plant to settle a labor controversy, it is condemning property * * *.

The power of the Federal Government to condemn property is well established * * *. But there is a duty to pay for all property taken by the Government. The command of the Fifth Amendment is that no "private property be taken for public use, without just compensation." * * *

The President has no power to raise revenues. That power is in the Congress by Article I, Section 8 of the Constitution. The President might seize and the Congress by subsequent action might ratify the seizure. But until and unless Congress acted, no condemnation would be lawful. The branch of government that has the power to pay compensation for a seizure is the only one able to authorize a seizure or make lawful one that the President had effected * * *.

* * *

We pay a price for our system of checks and balances, for the distribution of power among the three branches of government. It is a price that today may seem exorbitant to many. Today a kindly President uses the seizure power to effect a wage increase and to keep the steel furnaces in production. Yet tomorrow another President might use the same power to prevent a wage increase, to curb trade unionists, to regiment labor as oppressively as industry thinks it has been regimented by this seizure.

■ MR. JUSTICE JACKSON, concurring in the judgment and opinion of the court.

That comprehensive and undefined presidential powers hold both practical advantages and grave dangers for the country will impress anyone who has served as legal adviser to a President in time of transition and public anxiety. [*Editors' Note: Prior to his appointment to the Supreme Court, Justice Jackson served as both Solicitor General and Attorney General in the Roosevelt Administration. In those capacities, he authored several executive branch legal opinions taking a broad view of presidential authority.*] While an interval of detached reflection may temper teachings of that experience, they probably are a more realistic influence on my views than the conventional materials of judicial decision which seem unduly to accentuate doctrine and legal fiction * * *.

A judge, like an executive adviser, may be surprised at the poverty of really useful and unambiguous authority applicable to concrete problems of executive power as they actually present themselves. Just what our forefathers did envision, or would have envisioned had they foreseen modern conditions, must be divined from materials almost as enigmatic as the dreams Joseph was called upon to interpret for Pharaoh. A century and a half of partisan debate and scholarly speculation yields no net result but only supplies more or less apt quotations from respected sources on each side of any question. They largely cancel each other. And court decisions are indecisive because of the judicial practice of dealing with the largest questions in the most narrow way.

The actual art of governing under our Constitution does not and cannot conform to judicial definitions of the power of any of its branches based on isolated clauses or even single Articles torn from context. While the Constitution diffuses power the better to secure liberty, it also contemplates that practice will integrate the dispersed powers into a workable government. It enjoins upon its branches separateness but interdependence, autonomy but reciprocity. Presidential powers are not fixed but fluctuate, depending upon their disjunction or conjunction with those of Congress.

We may well begin by a somewhat over-simplified grouping of practical situations in which a President may doubt, or others may challenge, his powers * * *.

1. When the President acts pursuant to an express or implied authorization of Congress, his authority is at its maximum, for it includes all that he possesses in his own right plus all that Congress can delegate. In these circumstances, and in these only, may he be said (for what it may be worth), to personify the federal sovereignty. If his act is held unconstitutional under these circumstances, it usually means that the Federal Government as an undivided whole lacks power. A seizure executed by the President pursuant to an Act of Congress would be supported by the strongest of presumptions and the widest latitude of judicial interpretation, and the burden of persuasion would rest heavily upon any who might attack it.

2. When the President acts in absence of either a congressional grant or denial of authority, he can only rely upon his own independent powers, but there is a zone of twilight in which he and Congress may have concurrent authority, or in which its distribution is uncertain. Therefore, congressional inertia, indifference or quiescence may sometimes, at least as a practical matter, enable, if not invite, measures on independent presidential responsibility. In this area, any actual test of power is likely to depend on the imperatives of events and contemporary imponderables rather than on abstract theories of law.

3. When the President takes measures incompatible with the expressed or implied will of Congress, his power is at its lowest ebb, for then he can rely only upon his own constitutional powers minus any constitutional powers of Congress over the matter. Courts can sustain exclusive Presidential control in such a case only be disabling the Congress from acting upon the subject. Presidential claim to a power at once so conclusive and preclusive must be scrutinized with caution, for what is at stake is the equilibrium established by our constitutional system.

Into which of these classifications does this executive seizure of the steel industry fit? It is eliminated from the first by admission, for it is conceded that no congressional authorization exists for this seizure. That takes away also the support of the many precedents and declarations which were made in relation, and must be confined, to this category.

Can it then be defended under flexible tests available to the second category? It seems clearly eliminated from that class because Congress has not left seizure of private property an open field but has covered it by three statutory policies inconsistent with this seizure * * *.

This leaves the current seizure to be justified only by the severe tests under the third grouping, where it can be supported only by any remainder of executive power after subtraction of such powers as Congress may have over the subject. In short, we can sustain the President only by holding that seizure of such strike-bound industries is within his domain and beyond control by Congress. Thus, this Court's first review of such seizures occurs under circumstances which leave Presidential power most vulnerable to attack and in the least favorable of possible constitutional postures.

I did not suppose, and I am not persuaded, that history leaves it open to question, at least in the courts, that the executive branch, like the Federal Government as a whole, possesses only delegated powers. The purpose of the Constitution was not only to grant power, but to keep it from getting out of hand.

However, because the President does not enjoy unmentioned powers does not mean that the mentioned ones should be narrowed by a niggardly construction. Some clauses could be made almost unworkable, as well as immutable, by refusal to indulge some latitude of interpretation for changing times. I have heretofore, and do now, give to the enumerated powers the scope and elasticity afforded by what seem to be reasonable practical implications instead of the rigidity dictated by a doctrinaire textualism.

The Solicitor General seeks the power of seizure in three clauses of the Executive Article, the first reading, "The executive Power shall be vested in a President of the United States of America." Lest I be thought to exaggerate, I quote the interpretation which his brief puts upon it: "In our view, this clause constitutes a grant of all the executive powers of which the Government is capable." If that be true, it is difficult to see why the forefathers bothered to add several specific items, including some trifling ones.

The example of such unlimited executive power that must have most impressed the forefathers was the prerogative exercised by George III, and the description of its evils in the Declaration of Independence leads me to doubt that they were creating their new Executive in his image. Continental European examples were no more appealing. And if we seek instruction from our own times, we can match it only from the executive powers in those governments we disparagingly describe as totalitarian. I cannot accept the view that this clause is a grant in bulk of all conceivable executive power but regard it as an allocation to the presidential office of the generic powers thereafter stated.

The clause on which the Government next relies is that "The President shall be Commander in Chief of the Army and Navy of the United States . . . ." These cryptic words have given rise to some of the most persistent controversies in our constitutional history. Of course, they imply something more than an empty title. But just what authority goes with the name has plagued Presidential advisers who would not waive or narrow it by nonassertion yet cannot say where it begins or ends. It undoubtedly puts the Nation's armed forces under Presidential command. Hence, this loose appellation is sometimes advanced as support for any Presidential action, internal or external, involving use of force, the idea being that it vests power to do anything, anywhere, that can be done with an army or navy.

* * *

I cannot foresee all that it might entail if the Court should indorse this argument. Nothing in our Constitution is plainer than that declaration of a war is entrusted only to Congress. Of course, a state of war may in fact exist without a formal declaration. But no doctrine that the Court could promulgate would seem to me more sinister and alarming than that a President whose conduct of foreign affairs is so largely uncontrolled, and often even is unknown, can vastly enlarge his mastery over the internal affairs of the country by his own commitment of the Nation's armed forces to some foreign venture. I do not, however, find it necessary or appropriate to consider the legal status of the Korean enterprise to discountenance argument based on it.

Assuming that we are in a war *de facto*, whether it is or is not a war *de jure*, does that empower the Commander-in-Chief to seize industries he thinks necessary to supply our army? The Constitution expressly places in Congress power "to raise and *support* Armies" and "to *provide* and *maintain* a Navy." (Emphasis supplied.) This certainly lays upon Congress primary responsibility for supplying the armed forces. Congress alone controls the raising of revenues and their appropriation and may determine in what manner and by what means they shall be spent for military and naval procurement. I suppose no one would doubt that Congress can take over war supply as a Government enterprise. On the other hand, if Congress sees fit to rely on free private enterprise collectively bargaining with free labor for support and maintenance of our armed forces can the Executive because of lawful disagreements incidental to that process, seize the facility for operation upon Government-imposed terms?

There are indications that the Constitution did not contemplate that the title Commander-in-Chief *of the Army and Navy* will constitute him also Commander-in-Chief of the country, its industries and its inhabitants * * *.

That military powers of the Commander-in-Chief were not to supersede representative government of internal affairs seems obvious from the Constitution and from elementary American history * * *.

* * *

The third clause in which the Solicitor General finds seizure powers is that "he shall take Care that the Laws be faithfully executed . . . ." That authority must be matched against words of the Fifth Amendment that "No person shall be . . . deprived of life, liberty, or property, without due process of law . . . ." One gives a governmental authority that reaches so far as there is law, the other gives a private right that authority shall go no farther. These signify about all there is of the principle that ours is a government of laws, not of men, and that we submit ourselves to rulers only if under rules.

The Solicitor General lastly grounds support of the seizure upon nebulous, inherent powers never expressly granted but said to have accrued to the office from the customs and claims of preceding administrations. The plea is for a resulting power to deal with a crisis or an emergency according to the necessities of the case, the unarticulated assumption being that necessity knows no law.

Loose and irresponsible use of adjectives colors all non-legal and much legal discussion of presidential powers. "Inherent" powers, "implied" powers, "incidental" powers, "plenary" powers, "war" powers and "emergency" powers are used, often interchangeably and without fixed or ascertainable meanings.

The vagueness and generality of the clauses that set forth presidential powers afford a plausible basis for pressures within and without an administration for presidential action beyond that supported by those whose responsibility it is to defend his actions in court * * *.

* * *

The appeal * * * that we declare the existence of inherent powers *ex necessitate* to meet an emergency asks us to do what many think would be wise, although it is something the forefathers omitted. They knew what emergencies were, knew the pressures they engender for authoritative action, knew, too, how they afford a ready pretext for usurpation. We may also suspect that they suspected that emergency powers would tend to kindle emergencies. Aside from suspension of the privilege of the writ of habeas corpus in time of rebellion or invasion, when the public safety may require it, they made no express provision for exercise of extraordinary authority because of a crisis. I do not think we rightfully may so amend their work, and, if we could, I am not convinced it would be wise to do so, although many modern nations have forthrightly recognized that war and economic crises may upset the normal balance between liberty and authority. Their experience with emergency powers may not be irrelevant to the argument here that we should say that the Executive, of his own volition, can invest himself with undefined emergency powers.

Germany, after the First World War, framed the Weimar Constitution, designed to secure her liberties in the Western tradition. However, the President of the Republic, without concurrence of the Reichstag, was empowered temporarily to suspend any or all individual rights if public safety and order were seriously disturbed or endangered. This proved a temptation to every government, whatever its shade of opinion, and in 13 years suspension of rights was invoked on more than 250 occasions. Finally, Hitler persuaded President Von Hindenberg to suspend all such rights, and they were never restored.

* * *

In view of the ease, expedition and safety with which Congress can grant and has granted large emergency powers, certainly ample to embrace this crisis, I am quite unimpressed with the argument that we should affirm possession of them without statute. Such power either has no beginning or it has no end. If it exists, it need submit to no legal restraint. I am not alarmed that it would plunge us straightway into dictatorship, but it is at least a step in that wrong direction.

* * *

* * * With all its defects, delays and inconveniences, men have discovered no technique for long preserving free government except that the Executive be under the law, and that the law be made by parliamentary deliberations.

Such institutions may be destined to pass away. But it is the duty of the Court to be last, not first, to give them up.

* * *

■ MR. JUSTICE BURTON, concurring in both the opinion and judgment of the Court. [Omitted.]

■ MR. JUSTICE CLARK, concurring in the judgment of the Court.

* * *

I conclude that where Congress has laid down specific procedures to deal with the type of crisis confronting the President, he must follow those procedures in meeting the crisis; but that in the absence of such action by Congress, the President's independent power to act depends upon the gravity of the situation confronting the nation. I cannot sustain the seizure in question because * * * Congress had prescribed methods to be followed by the President in meeting the emergency at hand. * * *.

■ MR. CHIEF JUSTICE VINSON, with whom MR. JUSTICE REED and MR. JUSTICE MINTON join, dissenting.

* * *

In passing upon the question of Presidential powers in this case, we must first consider the context in which those powers were exercised.

Those who suggest that this is a case involving extraordinary powers should be mindful that these are extraordinary times. A world not yet recovered from the devastation of World War II has been forced to face the threat of another and more terrifying global conflict.

Accepting in full measure its responsibility in the world community, the United States was instrumental in securing adoption of the United Nations Charter, approved by the Senate by a vote of 89 to 2. The first purpose of the United Nations is to "maintain international peace and security, and to that end: to take effective collective measures for the prevention and removal of threats to the peace, and for the suppression of acts of aggression or other breaches of the peace . . . ." In 1950, when the United Nations called upon member nations "to render every assistance" to repel aggression in Korea, the United States furnished its vigorous support. For almost two full years, our armed forces have been fighting in Korea, suffering casualties of over 108,000 men. Hostilities have not abated. The "determination of the United Nations to continue its action in Korea to meet the aggression" has been reaffirmed. Congressional support of the action in Korea has been manifested by provisions for increased military manpower and equipment and for economic stabilization * * *.

* * *

The President has the duty to execute the foregoing legislative programs. Their successful execution depends upon continued production of steel and stabilized prices for steel. Accordingly, when the collective bargaining agreements between the Nation's steel producers and their employees, represented by the United Steel Workers, were due to expire on December 31, 1951, and a strike shutting down the entire basic steel industry was threatened, the President acted to avert a complete shutdown of steel production * * *.

* * *

Secretary of Defense Lovett swore that "a work stoppage in the steel industry will result immediately in serious curtailment of production of essential weapons and munitions of all kinds." He illustrated by showing that 84% of the national production of certain alloy steel is currently used for production of military-end items and that 35% of total production of another form of steel goes into ammunition, 80% of such ammunition now going to Korea. The Secretary of Defense stated that: "We are holding the line (in Korea) with ammunition and not with the lives of our troops."

* * *

Plaintiffs do not remotely suggest any basis for rejecting the President's finding that *any* stoppage of steel production would immediately place the Nation in peril * * *.

* * *

* * * The whole of the "executive Power" is vested in the President * * *.

This comprehensive grant of the executive power to a single person was bestowed soon after the country had thrown the yoke of monarchy. Only by instilling initiative and vigor in all of the three departments of Government, declared Madison, could tyranny in any from be avoided. Hamilton added: "Energy in the Executive is a leading character in the definition of good government * * *." It is thus apparent that the Presidency was deliberately fashioned as an office of power and independence. Of course, the Framers created no autocrat capable of arrogating any power unto himself at any time. But neither did they create an automaton impotent to exercise the powers of Government at a time when the survival of the Republic itself may be at stake.

* * *

A review of executive action demonstrates that our Presidents have on many occasions exhibited the leadership contemplated by the Framers * * *. With or without explicit statutory authorization, Presidents have at such times dealt with national emergencies by acting promptly and resolutely to enforce legislative programs, at least to save those programs until Congress could act. Congress and the courts have responded to such executive initiative with consistent approval.

[*Editors' Note: Chief Justice Vinson described at great length numerous presidential actions without statutory authority, including President Washington's Neutrality Proclamation, President Jefferson's Louisiana Purchase, and emergency measures taken by President Lincoln.*]

* * *

This is but a cursory summary of executive leadership. But it amply demonstrates that Presidents have taken prompt action to enforce the laws and protect the country whether or not Congress happened to provide in advance for the particular method of execution. At the minimum, the executive actions reviewed herein sustain the action of the President in this case. And many of the cited examples of Presidential practice go far beyond the extent of power necessary to sustain the President's order to seize the steel mills. The fact that temporary executive seizures of industrial plants to meet an emergency have not been directly tested in this Court furnishes not the slightest suggestion that such actions have been illegal. Rather, the fact that Congress and the courts have consistently recognized and given their support to such executive action indicates that such a power of seizure has been accepted throughout our history * * *.

Focusing now on the situation confronting the President on the night of April 8, 1952, we cannot but conclude that the President was performing his duty under the Constitution to "take Care that the Laws be faithfully executed" * * *.

* * *

* * * [T]he single Presidential purpose disclosed on this record is to faithfully execute the laws by acting in an emergency to maintain the status quo, thereby preventing collapse of the legislative programs until Congress could act. The President's action served the same purposes as a judicial stay entered to maintain the status quo in order to preserve the jurisdiction of a court * * *.

* * * The Framers knew, as we should know in these times of peril, that there is real danger in Executive weakness. There is no cause to fear Executive tyranny so long as the laws of Congress are being faithfully executed. Certainly there is no basis for fear of dictatorship when the Executive acts, as he did in this case, only to save the situation until Congress could act * * *.

As the District Judge stated, this is no time for "timorous" judicial action. But neither is this a time for timorous executive action. Faced with the duty of executing the defense programs which Congress had enacted and the disastrous effects that any stoppage in steel production would have on those programs, the President acted to preserve those programs by seizing the steel mills. There is no question that the possession was other than temporary in character and subject to congressional direction—either approving, disapproving or regulating the manner in which the mills were to be administered and returned to the owners. The President immediately informed Congress of his action and clearly stated his intention to abide by the legislative will. No basis for claims of arbitrary action, unlimited powers or dictatorial usurpation of congressional power appears from the facts of this case. On the contrary, judicial, legislative and executive precedents throughout our history demonstrate that in this case the President acted in full conformity with his duties under the Constitution. Accordingly, we would reverse the order of the District Court.

NOTES AND QUESTIONS

1. The Steel Seizure crisis arose shortly after World War II, a mere three years after the formation of the government of Communist China under Mao Zedong, and at a time when Joseph Stalin was alive and well as the dictator of the Soviet Union. Americans feared communist aggression and expansion; they also feared government by a dictator. Some Americans were appalled that Franklin D. Roosevelt ran for, and won, four terms as President. Was that part of the backdrop of the Court's decision? Should it have been?

2. As a textual matter, could the phrase the "executive power" refer to all the powers possessed by King George III except for those powers, like the power to declare war, which were specifically reassigned to Congress by the Framers? Alexander Hamilton made precisely this argument in a series of 1793 essays written under the pseudonym *Pacificus*, *see infra* pages 469–471, which defended a Neutrality Proclamation of 1793 issued by President George Washington that read in relevant part:

> WHEREAS it appears that a state of war exists between Austria, Prussia, Sardinia, Great Britain, and the United Netherlands of the one part, and France on the other, and the duty and interest of the United States require that they should with sincerity and good faith adopt and pursue a conduct friendly and impartial toward the belligerent powers:
>
> I have therefore thought fit, by these presents, to declare the disposition of the United States to observe the conduct aforesaid towards those powers respectively; and to exhort and warn the citizens of the United States carefully to avoid all acts and proceedings whatsover, which may in any manner tend to contravene such disposition.
>
> And I do hereby also make known that whosoever of the citizens of the United States shall render himself liable to punishment or forfeiture under the law of nations, by committing, aiding or abetting hostilities against any of the said powers, or by carrying to any of them those articles which are deemed contraband by the modern usage of nations, will not receive the protection of the United States, against such punishment or forfeiture; and further, that I have given instructions to those officers, to whom it belongs, to cause prosecutions to be instituted against all persons who shall, within the cognizance of the courts of the United States, violate the law of nations, with respect to the powers at war, or any of them.

11 Stat. 753 (App. 1859). Does this proclamation purport to create any new legal duties for American citizens? Does it claim any kind of legislative power for the President? Is it precedent for President Truman's seizure of steel mills?

3. Justice Black's opinion is often described, and sometime derided, as "formalistic," because it tries to match governmental functions with the categories of legislative, executive, and judicial power. Commentators have been much more admiring of Justice Jackson's opinion, praising it as being "sophisticated" or "practical" because it does not put powers into categories or boxes. But isn't Justice Jackson's opinion just as categorical? Justice Jackson lists three categories of presidential action—1) with Congress's support, 2) when Congress is silent, and 3) when the President acts over Congress's disapproval. The answer in the case at hand depended on which box Justice Jackson used. He chose to put *Youngstown's* facts into box 3, although they were arguably better slotted into box 2. Is Justice Jackson's approach really more "sophisticated" than Justice Black's? Is it better for an approach to be sophisticated or to be the best reading of the Constitution? Is Justice Jackson's opinion the best reading of the Constitution?

4. Both Justice Frankfurter and Chief Justice Vinson rely heavily on past practice in their *Youngstown* opinions, but it leads them to different conclusions. How useful is past practice as a guide, in 1952, when nuclear weapons were first used only seven years earlier and when the world seemed to be teetering on the edge of World War III?

5. Courts often defer to executive officials on matters of war and foreign policy, at least partly because courts often lack information that is available to the President. *See* ERIC. A. POSNER & ADRIAN VERMEULE, TERROR IN THE BALANCE: SECURITY, LIBERTY, AND THE COURTS (2007). Should that sort of consideration be relevant to constitutional interpretation? What might President Truman have known that a court would not know?

6. As the dissenting opinion explained at great length in a discussion that we have edited out, this was far from the first time that questions had arisen about presidential action that seems, on its face, to be "legislative" in character. Consider whether any of the following events—and this is just a handful—shed light on the issues in *Youngstown*:

(a) In 1799, the United States was in a state of naval hostilities with France but with no formal declaration of war. As a result of this so-called "quasi-war," Congress enacted a statute forbidding American-owned ships from trading with France and authorizing the President to search and seize vessels "bound or sailing *to any or place* within the territory of the French republic or her dependencies." As written, the statute only authorized seizures of American vessels heading *to* French ports, not vessels heading *from* French ports. Since the purpose of the trade embargo would obviously be undermined if ships could conduct trade *from* French ports, the President instructed American naval officers "to prevent all intercourse, whether direct or circuitous, between the ports of the United States and those of France or her dependencies." An American naval ship under the command of Captain George Little seized a ship sailing *from* a French port, and the owner of the seized ship sued Captain Little as a tortfeasor. Today, Captain Little would be protected by a doctrine called "qualified immunity," in which government officials can only be held personally liable for violating "clearly established" legal norms—a standard that is very difficult for plaintiffs to meet. That doctrine, however, did not emerge until the middle of the twentieth century. In 1799, the case depended solely on whether or not Captain Little acted in accordance with valid legal authorization; if he had no such authorization, he was no more entitled to seize someone's ship than was any random private person. If he had seized a vessel heading *to* a French port, the statute would have provided the necessary authorization to shield him from liability as a tortfeasor. Could the President's extra-statutory order, issued to naval commanders engaged in undeclared but very real hostilities, serve as authorization? The

Supreme Court, in an opinion by Chief Justice Marshall, held that the President's "instructions cannot change the nature of the transaction, or legalize an act which without those instructions would have been a plain trespass." *Little v. Barreme,* 6 U.S. (2 Cranch) 170, 179 (1804). Captain Little was held personally liable for about $8,500 in damages—a tidy sum in 1804 money. (Really? Yes, really, although Congress chose to indemnify Captain Little with a private bill, so the taxpayers ended up paying the judgment. *See* Act for the Relief of George Little, ch. 4, 6 Stat. 63 (1807).) Should that decision have determined the outcome in *Youngstown*?

(b) United States territory that is not part of a State, such as the Northwest Territory in 1788 or Puerto Rico or Guam today, is governed pursuant to Article IV's Territories Clause, which gives *"Congress* * * * Power to dispose of and make all needful Rules and Regulations respecting the Territory or other Property belonging to the United States." U.S. CONST. art. IV, § 3, cl. 2 (emphasis added). During wartime, American troops might occupy some extent of foreign territory. That occupied territory is not "Territory * * * belonging to the United States" until and unless it is transferred to the U.S. by the foreign power in a formal instrument of transfer, usually a peace treaty concluding the war. Wartime-occupied territory is governed by the President, under his "executive Power" and power as "Commander in Chief," as part of the conduct of the war, pursuant to the international laws of war that both authorize and require occupiers to maintain law and order in occupied territory. If the territory is transferred to the U.S. after the war, it then becomes "Territory * * * belonging to the United States," and governance authority shifts to Congress under Article IV. *See* GARY LAWSON & GUY I. SEIDMAN, THE CONSTITUTION OF EMPIRE: TERRITORIAL EXPANSION AND AMERICAN LEGAL HISTORY 151–52 (2004).

But what if a war ends, the presidential war power ends with it, territory is transferred to the U.S., but Congress passes no statute for governance of the now-American territory? Exactly this happened in 1848 after the Mexican-American War ended, and California was transferred to the U.S. in the peace treaty. Congress was so deadlocked over slavery that it could not agree on a statute for the governance of the territory of California—not even a statute saying that the wartime military government should stay in force as a civilian government. Indeed, no statute for governance of California was ever passed before California became a State in 1850. Lacking either statutes or direction, the military commander, who had been "governor" during the war, kept the former military government going even in peacetime from 1848–50, including collecting tariffs on imports into San Francisco notwithstanding the absence of a congressional statute authorizing those tariffs. An importer sued to get back the tariffs.

Secretary of State James Buchanan (who later became one of the country's most infamous presidents) and President James Polk both issued formal statements endorsing the continuance of the military government and insisting that it was lawful. Secretary Buchanan wrote: "The termination of the war left an existing government, a government de facto, in full operation, and this will continue, with the presumed consent of the people, until Congress shall provide for them a territorial government. The great law of necessity justifies this conclusion." Letter from James Buchanan, Secretary of State, to William V. Voorhies (Oct. 7, 1848). President Polk said much the same thing in a State of the Union address. *See* Cong. Globe, 30th Cong., 2d Sess. 5 (1848). Could executive officials really operate, entirely on their own initiative, a military government in American territory during peacetime? The Supreme Court said "yes" in *Cross v. Harrison*, 57 U.S. (16 How.) 164 (1854), in reasoning that can fairly be called cryptic and conclusory. *See id* at 193–94; LAWSON & SEIDMAN, *supra*, at 152–87. Does this serve as precedent for the seizure of the steel mills in *Youngstown*? Is it distinguishable from *Little v. Barreme*?

(c) During the Civil War, President Lincoln exercised, unilaterally, a wide range of powers that seem legislative, ranging from substituting military commissions for courts in theaters of battle to suspending the writ of habeas corpus to issuing the Emancipation Proclamation. *See infra* pages 496–496, 508–509. Congress eventually ratified these actions, but when taken they were done without statutory authorization. Do emergencies expand the range of "executive Power" to include seemingly legislative actions? If so, what kinds of emergencies do the trick? *See* Gary Lawson, *Ordinary Powers in Extraordinary Times: Common Sense in Times of Crisis,* 87 B.U. L. REV. 289 (2007).

7. Is it relevant that from 1607 to 1776 colonial executives and English monarchs had some inherent power to respond to emergencies (at least to preserve the ability of the legislature to address the emergency)? John Locke called this power "The Prerogative Power." Does the President have such a power, given the Declaration of Independence's denunciation of prerogative powers exercised by King George III?

8. Justice Jackson's three-part framework has been very influential and is often relied upon in modern Supreme Court separation-of-powers cases and executive department memoranda. On some occasions, interpreters will stretch mightily to (mis)interpret statutes to provide authorization for presidential action, thus putting the action into "Category 1," which likely means that the action stands.

One dramatic example is *Dames & Moore v. Regan*, 453 U.S. 654 (1981), in which the Supreme Court upheld a unilateral presidential property seizure, plus a unilateral presidential order to federal courts to dismiss pending lawsuits, as part of an elaborate settlement to the Iranian Hostage Crisis which lasted from the fall 1979 to the winter of 1981. The actions in *Dames & Moore* were not specifically authorized by statute, but the Court read some available statutes generously enough to "authorize" the action (while stating openly that this was a one-time decision and should not be used as precedent for anything in the future). A similarly generous reading of statutes has "authorized" military action against ISIS. The Authorization for Use of Military Force enacted by Congress in the aftermath of September 11, 2001 only authorizes military action "against those nations, organizations, or persons he [the President] determines planned, authorized, committed, or aided the terrorist attacks that occurred on September 11, 2001, or harbored such organizations or persons." 115 Stat. 224 (2001). ISIS did not exist on 9/11. For a study of the machinations by which the statute has been (mis)used to justify essentially all of the American military operations in the Middle East and Africa for the past two decades, see Rebecca Ingber, *Co-Belligerency*, 42 YALE J. INT'L L. 67 (2017).

[Assignment 8]

C. THE BOUNDARY BETWEEN LEGISLATIVE AND JUDICIAL POWER

James Wilson—who was one of the most learned legal scholars of the founding era, a key figure in the drafting and ratification of the Constitution, and a Supreme Court justice—defined the judicial power as "applying, according to the principles of right and justice, the constitution and laws to facts and transactions in cases, in which the manner or principles of this application are disputed by the parties interested in them." 1 James Wilson, *Of Government*, in THE WORKS OF JAMES WILSON 343, 363 (James DeWitt Andrews ed., 1896). The judicial power, in other words, is the power to decide cases in accordance with governing law. Does it also include the power to *make* governing law?

Today, that question seems quaint. It is commonplace to think of courts as lawmaking institutions, especially the common-law courts that you study in your

Contracts, Torts, and Property classes. But for the federal Constitution of 1788, the idea of courts as lawmakers seems as dubious as the idea of presidents as lawmakers. Courts can of course construe or misconstrue legal texts to authorize all manner of questionable actions (their own or those of other actors), but so can presidents and congresses. The question here is whether courts can literally make law on their own.

The founding-era answer would surely have been "no." That does not mean that courts could only properly decide cases based on statutes or the Constitution. The "law" that courts could use to decide cases was always broader than that. It included, at a minimum, broad legal principles of contract, tort, property, and procedure that today we call "common law" but which in earlier times was called "general law." *See* John Harrison, *The Power of Congress over the Rules of Precedent*, 50 DUKE L.J. 503, 525–31 (2000). The Constitution makes specific reference to "the Law of Nations." U.S. Const. art. I, § 8, cl. 10. Whether the "law" a also included natural law was and is a matter of dispute, as was the hierarchy among those sources when they came into conflict. But those legal norms, whether general or natural, were considered part of the legal background to be *discovered and applied* by courts, not something to be *created or invented* by courts. To be sure, some of those norms were vague enough to accommodate, or even require, some element of judicial creativity, but that is equally true of statutes or constitutional provisions. At least as a formal matter, courts applying, for example, general law were not thought of as making law, even if that was the functional result. Making law is an exercise of legislative power, not an exercise of judicial power.

This was confirmed early in the Nation's history in *United States v. Hudson and Goodwin*, 11 U.S. (7 Cranch) 32 (1812). A newspaper accused the President and Congress of secretly bribing Napoleon Bonaparte, and the government responded with a criminal libel suit. The Federalist-era Sedition Acts of 1798 had long since expired, so the newspaper violated no federal statute even if its reporting was libelous. The lower federal court divided on whether federal courts could try something as a crime without a congressional statute making it a crime. The Supreme Court said no:

> The only ground on which it has ever been contended that this jurisdiction could be maintained is, that, upon the formation of any political body, an implied power to preserve its own existence and promote the end and object of its creation, necessarily results to it * * *.
>
> But if admitted as applicable to the state of things in this country, the consequence would not result from it which is here contended for. If it may communicate certain implied powers to the general Government, it would not follow that the Courts of that Government are vested with jurisdiction over any particular act done by an individual in supposed violation of the peace and dignity of the sovereign power. The legislative authority of the Union must first make an act a crime, affix a punishment to it, and declare the Court that shall have jurisdiction of the offence.
>
> Certain implied powers must necessarily result to our Courts of justice from the nature of their institution. But jurisdiction of crimes against the state is not among those powers. To fine for contempt—imprison for contumacy—inforce the observance of order, &c. are powers which cannot be dispensed with in a Court, because they are necessary to the exercise of

> all others: and so far our Courts no doubt possess powers not immediately derived from statute; but all exercise of criminal jurisdiction in common law cases we are of opinion is not within their implied powers.

Id. at 33–34. Thus, federal courts cannot fashion non-statutory criminal law.

What about tort law rather than criminal law? Federal courts hear tort cases through several jurisdictional vehicles. First, they can hear tort cases brought against federal officials who claim authorization for their actions under federal law; *Little v. Barreme* is a good illustration of this kind of case. Second, after 1948, the Federal Tort Claims Act authorizes certain kinds of claims to be brought directly against the United States rather than against the official who acted on behalf of the government. (Absent that statute, sovereign immunity prevents direct suit against the United States.) Third, courts can hear common-law tort claims when the plaintiff and defendant are citizens of different states (so-called "diversity" jurisdiction). In those diversity cases, federal courts are supposed to apply the law of whichever State's law governs, under the rule of *Erie R. Co. v. Tompkins,* 304 U.S. 64 (1938). The extent to which courts can make, and are making, law when deciding these cases has consumed the attention of federal courts scholars for quite some time. Similar questions obviously arise when courts deal with federal contracts. In this course, we can only note the question without attempting to explore it. *See* Caleb Nelson, *The Legitimacy of (Some) Federal Common Law,* 101 VA. L. REV. 1 (2015).

Can legislators ever act in a way that looks like the exercise of "judicial Power"? We take up that question later in this chapter, in connection with some clauses of the Constitution that specifically anticipate exactly such an occurrence. *See infra* pages 309–328. Congress has, as you will see below, occasionally held individuals in contempt of Congress, and it has imprisoned them even though the executive branch has brought no prosecution and even though the Article III courts have not found them guilty of contempt. This is a congressional usurpation of judicial as well as of executive power. We will discuss the caselaw on this below.

In addition, Congress has on occasion passed laws naming an individual or a few individuals to be guilty of crimes. Such laws are called bills of attainder, and they too are unconstitutional. We will discuss bills of attainder further below, along with their cousin *ex post facto* laws.

D. THE BOUNDARY BETWEEN EXECUTIVE AND JUDICIAL POWER

For most of the millennium prior to the U.S. Constitution, Anglo-American law did not recognize "judicial Power" as a distinct category of governmental power. Judicial power was simply an aspect of the executive power, and judges were arms of the monarch. Judges in England did not acquire any kind of permanent tenure until 1701 and did not acquire tenure longer than the life of the monarch who appointed them until 1761. Colonial judges *never* had any kind of tenure protections against executive control. This was one of the complaints in the Declaration of Independence, which objected that King George III "has obstructed the Administration of Justice by refusing his Assent to Laws for establishing Judiciary Powers" and "has made Judges dependent on his Will alone for the tenure of their offices, and the amount and payment of their salaries." A quarter century before the Declaration, Montesquieu had identified judicial power as a distinct head of governmental power. In light of these developments and the colonial experience, the

U.S. Constitution, as had state constitutions preceding it, created a separate department of government—the judicial department—vested with the "judicial Power of the United States," staffed by judges who "shall hold their Offices during good Behaviour, and shall, at stated Times, receive for their Services, a Compensation, which shall not be diminished during their Continuance in Office." U.S. CONST. art. III, § 1. Thus, by 1788, "judicial Power" was understood as a distinct governmental power, but there was very little history or practice to distinguish it from executive power.

The line between executive and judicial power is thus perhaps the most difficult constitutional line among the constitutional powers to draw, because much of what executives do is functionally very similar to what courts do. Courts apply law to particular sets of facts. Executive actors applying statutes or the Constitution do the same thing, whether they are administering a veterans' benefits program, deciding whether to prosecute someone for a suspected crime, or imposing fines for violating pollution control laws. All of these activities are functionally adjudicative in nature. Executive officials do not enjoy tenure during good behavior, nor do they (other than the President) have constitutional guarantees against diminishment in salary. Does that make all executive adjudication unconstitutional?

The answer is obviously "no"; applying law to facts is precisely what "executive Power" involves. Does that mean that executive officials can do anything that courts can do? The answer again is obviously "no"; executive officials cannot, for example, preside over the trial of a criminal defendant. (Is there anything in the Constitution that expressly says this?) So what kinds of adjudication involve exercises of "judicial Power" and what involve exercises of "executive Power"—keeping open the possibility that at least some governmental functions might fall within *both* conceptual categories and thus be performable by either executive or judicial actors?

As a matter of original meaning, there is a fairly straightforward answer: Governmental action that results in a deprivation of someone's life, liberty, or property requires *judicial* adjudication, while governmental action that disburses or confers benefits can be done either judicially or through executive action, as Congress so directs. *See* Gary Lawson, *Appointments and Illegal Adjudication: The America Invents Act Through a Constitutional Lens*, 26 GEO. MASON L. REV. 26, 35–51 (2018). For reasons that are better explained in a course on Administrative Law, a number of twentieth-century developments make that easy resolution doctrinally impossible today. At a minimum, that resolution depends on a distinction between action that violates *rights* ("life, liberty, or property") and that adjudicates *privileges*, and from the 1960s onward "the Court has fully and finally rejected the wooden distinction between 'rights' and 'privileges' " * * *. *Board of Regents of State Colleges v. Roth*, 408 U.S. 564, 571 (1972). Modern doctrine thus needs another way to sort out what, if anything, belongs exclusively to the "judicial Power." (For whatever it is worth, we both believe there is no solution to this problem other than returning to the traditional rights/benefits distinction.)

Even before the twentieth century, the problem of distinguishing executive from judicial power was recognized as difficult. Consider William Marbury and his fellow Justices of the Peace for the District of Columbia.[2] Those officials had both civil and

---

[2] The ensuing paragraphs are adapted from GARY LAWSON, FEDERAL ADMINISTRATIVE LAW 279–89 (8th ed. 2019).

criminal jurisdiction, comparable to the power of state-court judges in Virginia or Maryland. If Marbury thereby exercised the "judicial Power of the United States," he would need to have life tenure and a salary guarantee in accordance with the terms of Article III. As Chief Justice Marshall pointed out five different times in *Marbury v. Madison*, Marbury was appointed under a statute providing for a five-year term of office rather than for tenure during good behavior, and Congress frequently changed the terms of compensation for Justices of the Peace. Were these tenure and compensation statutes unconstitutional? Or did Marbury exercise something other than federal "judicial Power"?

In 1803—the same year that *Marbury v. Madison* was decided—a federal circuit court held, by a 2–1 vote, that the District of Columbia Justices of the Peace exercised federal "judicial Power" and that the statutes changing their forms of compensation were unconstitutional diminishments of the salaries of federal judges. *See United States v. More,* 7 U.S. (3 Cranch) 159, 160 n* (1805) (reporting the 1803 circuit court opinion). Presumably, that meant that the Justices of the Peace also constitutionally held office during good behavior, though the court (in a perhaps extravagant bit of judicial restraint) declined to comment on that issue. The decision was appealed to the Supreme Court, which reversed on jurisdictional grounds without reaching the merits of the constitutional claim.

A quarter-century later, however, the Supreme Court said, in powerful and influential language, that territorial judges—adjudicatory officials in federal territories who exercise, among other things, admiralty jurisdiction—do not possess Article III judicial power but are instead "legislative Courts" exercising power granted by Congress under its Article IV power to govern federal territory. *See American Insurance Co. v. 356 Bales of Cotton,* 26 U.S. (1 Pet.) 511 (1828). The same reasoning would apply to judges such as Marbury in the District of Columbia, which is governed by Congress under the Article I District Clause. The upshot of this decision was to validate a class of federal officials who look like federal judges, act like federal judges, and rule like federal judges (including handing out death sentences in appropriate cases) but who do not constitutionally count as Article III federal judges. For constitutional purposes, according to the Supreme Court, they are executive officials exercising executive power. A wide range of scholars across a breadth of modalities has vigorously criticized this decision, *see, e.g.,* Gary Lawson & Guy Seidman, The Constitution of Empire: Territorial Expansion and American Legal History 139–50 (2004)), but it remains a cornerstone of constitutional doctrine.

Another quarter-century later, the Court further held that military courts martial, which can hand out death penalties in extreme cases, involved the exercise of Article I congressional power and Article II presidential power to regulate and govern the military rather than Article III "judicial Power." *See Dynes v. Hoover,* 61 U.S. (20 How.) 65 (1857). And shortly thereafter, Congress created a federal tribunal, without life tenure or salary guarantees, to rule on money claims against the federal government. This latter form of non-Article III adjudication was validated on the ground of sovereign immunity: The federal government does not have to provide *any* forum for claims against it, so no one has a right to complain about the kind of forums that Congress does choose to provide. *See United States v. Sherwood,* 312 U.S. 584 (1941).

None of these forms of non-Article III adjudication—territorial tribunals, military courts martial, or suits against the United States—encompasses executive agencies resolving claims by one person against another, such as a claim by a shipper that a railroad has charged an unlawful rate or a claim by a maritime worker that he or she is owed compensation from an employer under a federal workers' compensation statute. The latter issue came up in 1932 in *Crowell v. Benson,* 285 U.S. 22 (1932). The Longshoremen's and Harbor Workers' Compensation Act of 1927 ("LHWCA") required (and still requires) employers to compensate employees for certain injuries "occurring upon the navigable waters of the United States." 33 U.S.C. § 903 (2018). Claims under the act in 1932 were to be adjudicated by executive department Deputy Commissioners of the United States Employees' Compensation Commission, subject to judicial review. The question was whether federal courts would review the executive decisions deferentially, reversing only in the event of *extreme* error, or *de novo* with no deference to the administrative decision. For ordinary fact-finding which does not determine the agency's very jurisdiction to decide the case at all, the Court held that it would not impinge on the Article III "judicial Power" for Congress to commit most of the fact-finding in these cases to executive agencies:

> There is no requirement that, in order to maintain the essential attributes of the judicial power, all determinations of fact in constitutional courts shall be made by judges * * *. In cases of equity and admiralty, it is historic practice to call to the assistance of the courts, without the consent of the parties, masters, and commissioners or assessors, to pass upon certain classes of questions, as, for example, to take and state an account or to find the amount of damages. While the reports of masters and commissioners in such cases are essentially of an advisory nature, it has not been the practice to disturb their findings when they are properly based upon evidence, in the absence of errors of law, and the parties have no right to demand that the court shall redetermine the facts thus found * * *.
>
> * * *
>
> In deciding whether the Congress, in enacting the statute under review, has exceeded the limits of its authority to prescribe procedure in cases of injury upon navigable waters, regard must be had, as in other cases where constitutional limits are invoked, not to mere matters of form, but to the substance of what is required. The statute has a limited application, being confined to the relation of master and servant, and the method of determining the questions of fact, which arise in the routine of making compensation awards to employees under the act, is necessary to its effective enforcement. The act itself, where it applies, establishes the measure of the employer's liability, thus leaving open for determination the questions of fact as to the circumstances, nature, extent, and consequences of the injuries sustained by the employee for which compensation is to be made in accordance with the prescribed standards. Findings of fact by the deputy commissioner upon such questions are closely analogous to the findings of the amount of damages that are made according to familiar practice by commissioners or assessors, and the reservation of full authority to the court to deal with matters of law provides for the appropriate exercise of the judicial function in this class of cases. For the purposes stated, we are unable to find any constitutional obstacle to the action of the Congress in availing itself of a method shown by experience to

> be essential in order to apply its standards to the thousands of cases involved, thus relieving the courts of a most serious burden while preserving their complete authority to insure the proper application of the law.

285 U.S. at 50–54. According to *Crowell,* courts fully exercise the "judicial Power" in private lawsuits by making sure that executive officials who find facts do so within the bounds of reason, even if they do so incorrectly. Does the same hold true if courts also give way to executive officials on questions of law? Does it matter if the courts *choose* to give way to executive officials on questions of law rather than (as is generally true of administrative fact-finding) Congress orders them to do so by statute?

The modern administrative state is largely built on the foundations of *Crowell v. Benson.* Modern government is full of executive officials essentially like the Deputy Commissioners in *Crowell,* though today we usually call them "administrative law judges" (or "ALJs"). They are not Article III judges; they are executive actors who adjudicate people's rights and responsibilities, on matters ranging from labor law to securities law to workplace safety to patent validity, subject only to very deferential judicial review on matters of both fact and law. We will hear more about those ALJs later in this chapter. Consider now one of the leading modern cases concerning the permissible limits of congressional assignment of adjudicatory powers to executive officials, keeping in mind that these materials are just the tip of a large iceberg that can easily consume much of a course on Federal Courts or Administrative Law.

Commodity Futures Trading Comm'n v. Schor

478 U.S. 833 (1986)

■ JUSTICE O'CONNOR delivered the opinion of the Court.

[*Editors' Note: The Commodity Futures Trading Commission (CFTC) is an independent agency that enforces the Commodity Exchange Act (CEA), which regulates commodity futures transactions. The CFTC is authorized by statute to adjudicate claims for damages, or reparations, brought by customers of commodity brokers for the brokers' violations of the CEA or of CFTC regulations. The CFTC additionally promulgated a regulation permitting itself to adjudicate counterclaims brought by brokers in reparations proceedings when the counterclaim arises out of the transaction(s) giving rise to the customer's complaint.*

Schor sought reparations for numerous alleged violations of the CEA by his broker, ContiCommodity Services of America, Inc. (Conti), which Schor maintained was responsible for the debit (negative) balance in his trading account with Conti. Conti counterclaimed for the debit balance, which was a simple common-law action for recovery of a contractual debt, in the CFTC reparations proceeding. The agency ruled in favor of Conti on all counts, and Schor then questioned the statutory authority for the agency's regulation permitting it to adjudicate Conti's common-law counterclaim. The agency rejected the challenge to its authority, and Schor appealed. The Court of Appeals reversed, on the ground that construing the CEA to deny the agency power to adjudicate ordinary contract-law counterclaims "avoids significant constitutional questions" that would be raised by such agency authority.]

* * *

Article III, § 1, directs that the "judicial Power of the United States shall be vested in one supreme Court and in such inferior Courts as the Congress may from time to time ordain and establish," and provides that these federal courts shall be staffed by judges who hold office during good behavior, and whose compensation shall not be diminished during tenure in office. Schor claims that these provisions prohibit Congress from authorizing the initial adjudication of common law counterclaims by the CFTC, an administrative agency whose adjudicatory officers do not enjoy the tenure and salary protections embodied in Article III.

Although our precedents in this area do not admit of easy synthesis, they do establish that the resolution of claims such as Schor's cannot turn on conclusory reference to the language of Article III. Rather, the constitutionality of a given congressional delegation of adjudicative functions to a non-Article III body must be assessed by reference to the purposes underlying the requirements of Article III. This inquiry, in turn, is guided by the principle that "practical attention to substance rather than doctrinaire reliance on formal categories should inform application of Article III." *Thomas* [*v. Union Carbide Agricultural Products Co.,* 473 U.S. 568, 587 (1985)] * * *.

* * *

In determining the extent to which a given congressional decision to authorize the adjudication of Article III business in a non-Article III tribunal impermissibly threatens the institutional integrity of the Judicial Branch, the Court has declined to adopt formalistic and unbending rules. Although such rules might lend a greater degree of coherence to this area of the law, they might also unduly constrict Congress' ability to take needed and innovative action pursuant to its Article I powers. Thus, in reviewing Article III challenges, we have weighed a number of factors, none of which has been deemed determinative, with an eye to the practical effect that the congressional action will have on the constitutionally assigned role of the federal judiciary. Among the factors upon which we have focused are the extent to which the "essential attributes of judicial power" are reserved to Article III courts, and, conversely, the extent to which the non-Article III forum exercises the range of jurisdiction and powers normally vested only in Article III courts, the origins and importance of the right to be adjudicated, and the concerns that drove Congress to depart from the requirements of Article III.

An examination of the relative allocation of powers between the CFTC and Article III courts in light of the considerations given prominence in our precedents demonstrates that the congressional scheme does not impermissibly intrude on the province of the judiciary. The CFTC's adjudicatory powers depart from the traditional agency model in just one respect: the CFTC's jurisdiction over common law counterclaims. While wholesale importation of concepts of pendent or ancillary jurisdiction into the agency context may create greater constitutional difficulties, we decline to endorse an absolute prohibition on such jurisdiction out of fear of where some hypothetical "slippery slope" may deposit us * * *.

* * *

* * * The risk that Congress may improperly have encroached on the federal judiciary is obviously magnified when Congress "[withdraws] from judicial cognizance any matter which, from its nature, is the subject of a suit at the common law, or in equity, or admiralty" and which therefore has traditionally been tried in

Article III courts, and allocates the decision of those matters to a non-Article III forum of its own creation. *Murray's Lessee v. Hoboken Land & Improvement Co.*, 18 How. 272, 284 (1856). Accordingly, where private, common law rights are at stake, our examination of the congressional attempt to control the manner in which those rights are adjudicated has been searching. In this litigation, however, "[looking] beyond form to the substance of what" Congress has done, we are persuaded that the congressional authorization of limited CFTC jurisdiction over a narrow class of common law claims as an incident to the CFTC's primary, and unchallenged, adjudicative function does not create a substantial threat to the separation of powers.

It is clear that Congress has not attempted to "withdraw from judicial cognizance" the determination of Conti's right to the sum represented by the debit balance in Schor's account. Congress gave the CFTC the authority to adjudicate such matters, but the decision to invoke this forum is left entirely to the parties and the power of the federal judiciary to take jurisdiction of these matters is unaffected. In such circumstances, separation of powers concerns are diminished, for it seems self-evident that just as Congress may encourage parties to settle a dispute out of court or resort to arbitration without impermissible incursions on the separation of powers, Congress may make available a quasi-judicial mechanism through which willing parties may, at their option, elect to resolve their differences. This is not to say, of course, that if Congress created a phalanx of non-Article III tribunals equipped to handle the entire business of the Article III courts without any Article III supervision or control and without evidence of valid and specific legislative necessities, the fact that the parties had the election to proceed in their forum of choice would necessarily save the scheme from constitutional attack. But this case obviously bears no resemblance to such a scenario, given the degree of judicial control saved to the federal courts, as well as the congressional purpose behind the jurisdictional delegation, the demonstrated need for the delegation, and the limited nature of the delegation.

* * *

It also bears emphasis that the CFTC's assertion of counterclaim jurisdiction is limited to that which is necessary to make the reparations procedure workable. The CFTC adjudication of common law counterclaims is incidental to, and completely dependent upon, adjudication of reparations claims created by federal law, and in actual fact is limited to claims arising out of the same transaction or occurrence as the reparations claim.

In such circumstances, the magnitude of any intrusion on the Judicial Branch can only be termed *de minimis*. Conversely, were we to hold that the Legislative Branch may not permit such limited cognizance of common law counterclaims at the election of the parties, it is clear that we would "defeat the obvious purpose of the legislation to furnish a prompt, continuous, expert and inexpensive method for dealing with a class of questions of fact which are peculiarly suited to examination and determination by an administrative agency specially assigned to that task." *Crowell v. Benson*, [285 U.S. 22 (1932)] at 46. See also *Thomas*, *supra*, at 583–584. We do not think Article III compels this degree of prophylaxis.

* * *

* * * [O]ur Article III precedents * * * counsel that bright-line rules cannot effectively be employed to yield broad principles applicable in all Article III inquiries.

Rather, due regard must be given in each case to the unique aspects of the congressional plan at issue and its practical consequences in light of the larger concerns that underlie Article III. We conclude that the limited jurisdiction that the CFTC asserts over state law claims as a necessary incident to the adjudication of federal claims willingly submitted by the parties for initial agency adjudication does not contravene separation of powers principles or Article III.

* * *

■ JUSTICE BRENNAN, with whom JUSTICE MARSHALL joins, dissenting.

* * *

On its face, Article III, § 1, seems to prohibit the vesting of any judicial functions in either the Legislative or the Executive Branch. The Court has, however, recognized three narrow exceptions to the otherwise absolute mandate of Article III: territorial courts, courts-martial, and courts that adjudicate certain disputes concerning public rights. See generally *Northern Pipeline Construction Co. v. Marathon Pipe Line Co.,* 458 U.S. 50 (1982) (opinion of Brennan, J.). Unlike the Court, I would limit the judicial authority of non-Article III federal tribunals to these few, long-established exceptions and would countenance no further erosion of Article III's mandate.

* * *

The Framers knew that "[the] accumulation of all powers, Legislative, Executive, and Judiciary, in the same hands, whether of one, a few, or many, and whether hereditary, self-appointed, or elective, may justly be pronounced the very definition of tyranny." The Federalist No. 46, p. 334 (H. Dawson ed. 1876) (J. Madison) * * *. The federal judicial power, then, must be exercised by judges who are independent of the Executive and the Legislature in order to maintain the checks and balances that are crucial to our constitutional structure.

The Framers also understood that a principal benefit of the separation of the judicial power from the legislative and executive powers would be the protection of individual litigants from decisionmakers susceptible to majoritarian pressures. Article III's salary and tenure provisions promote impartial adjudication by placing the judicial power of the United States "in a body of judges insulated from majoritarian pressures and thus able to enforce [federal law] without fear of reprisal or public rebuke." *United States v. Raddatz,* 447 U.S. 667, 704 (1980) (Marshall, J., dissenting) * * *.

These important functions of Article III are too central to our constitutional scheme to risk their incremental erosion. The exceptions we have recognized for territorial courts, courts-martial, and administrative courts were each based on "certain exceptional powers bestowed upon Congress by the Constitution or by historical consensus." *Northern Pipeline, supra*, at 70 (opinion of Brennan, J.). Here, however, there is no equally forceful reason to extend further these exceptions to situations that are distinguishable from existing precedents * * *.

* * *

* * * The Court requires that the legislative interest in convenience and efficiency be weighed against the competing interest in judicial independence. In doing so, the Court pits an interest the benefits of which are immediate, concrete, and easily understood against one, the benefits of which are almost entirely

prophylactic, and thus often seem remote and not worth the cost in any single case. Thus, while this balancing creates the illusion of objectivity and ineluctability, in fact the result was foreordained, because the balance is weighted against judicial independence. The danger of the Court's balancing approach is, of course, that as individual cases accumulate in which the Court finds that the short-term benefits of efficiency outweigh the long-term benefits of judicial independence, the protections of Article III will be eviscerated.

Perhaps the resolution of reparations claims such as respondents' may be accomplished more conveniently under the Court's decision than under my approach, but the Framers foreswore this sort of convenience in order to preserve freedom * * *.

NOTES AND QUESTIONS

1. *Schor* spends much time telling us what *not* to consider when drawing lines between executive and judicial power: "reference to the language of Article III," "formalistic and unbending rules," "factors * * * deemed determinative," "bright-line rules," and so forth. What does it want us consider instead?

2. The caselaw since *Schor* has not been much clearer, especially with regard to what counts as a "public right" that can be adjudicated by executive officials with only limited court review. In *Stern v. Marshall,* 564 U.S. 462 (2011), the Court split 5–4 (and essentially 4–1–4 on the reasoning) in holding that non-Article III bankruptcy courts could not enter final orders on common law tort claims as part of bankruptcy proceedings. The Court discussed at length the "public rights" doctrine at issue in *Schor,* distinguishing those cases because, inter alia, the right to relief in a common law tort claim "does not flow from a federal statutory scheme." 564 U.S. at 493. The Court summarized the principles underlying its cases as follows:

> We recognize that there may be instances in which the distinction between public and private rights—at last as framed by some of our recent cases—fails to provide concrete guidance as to whether, for example, a particular agency can adjudicate legal issues under a substantive regulatory scheme. Given the extent to which this case is so markedly distinct from the agency cases discussing the public rights exception in the context of such a regime, however, we do not in this opinion express any view on how the doctrine might apply in that different context.

Id. at 494. The four dissenting justices thought that the majority's approach was unduly formalistic and paid insufficient attention to *Crowell v. Benson.* They wrote:

> This case law * * * requires us to determine pragmatically whether a congressional delegation of adjudicatory authority to a non-Article III judge violates the separation-of-powers principles inherent in Article III. That is to say, we must determine through an examination of certain relevant factors whether that delegation constitutes a significant encroachment by the Legislative or Executive Branches of Government upon the realm of authority that Article III reserves for exercise by the Judicial Branch of Government. Those factors include (1) the nature of the claim to be adjudicated; (2) the nature of the non-Article III tribunal; (3) the extent to which Article III courts exercise control over the proceeding; (4) the presence or absence of the parties' consent; and (5) the nature and importance of the legislative purpose served by the grant of adjudicatory authority to a tribunal with judges who lack Article III's tenure and compensation protections. The presence of "private rights" does

not automatically determine the outcome of the question but requires a more "searching" examination of the relevant factors.

Id. at 512–13 (Breyer, J., dissenting).

3. Can Congress allow an executive agency to cancel a patent that has already been issued? Seven justices said "yes" in *Oil States Energy Services, LLC v. Greene's Energy Group, LLC,* 138 S.Ct. 1365 (2018), reasoning that a patent is a "public right" under the caselaw. Can executive agencies similarly undo land patents issued by the federal government?

4. Some of the country's best minds in the field of federal courts have tried to synthesize and rationalize the caselaw and practice concerning non-Article III adjudication. *See* Richard H. Fallon, Jr., *Of Legislative Courts, Administrative Agencies, and Article III,* 101 Harv. L. Rev. 915 (1988); Caleb Nelson, *Adjudication in the Political Branches,* 107 Colum. L. Rev. 559 (2007); James E. Pfander, *Article I Tribunals, Article III Courts, and the Judicial Power of the United States,* 118 Harv. L. Rev. 643 (2004). For a short introduction from the original meaning perspective, see Jennifer L. Mascott, *Constitutionally Conforming Agency Adjudication,* 2 Loy. U. Chi. J. Reg. Compliance 22 (2017).

5. The closeness of the executive and judicial power is further illustrated by the long-standing, but now frowned upon, practice of judges holding executive offices simultaneously with their judicial offices. As we said above, members of Congress are barred by Article I, Section 6 from simultaneously holding executive or judicial offices, but there is no constitutional incompatibility clause that bans the simultaneous holding of judicial and executive offices. Thus, Chief Justice Jay held an executive office when he negotiated Jay's Treaty between the United States and the United Kingdom in 1794. Chief Justice Oliver Ellsworth served as the executive envoy to France, where he signed the Convention of 1800 to settle the hostilities of the Quasi-War between the United States and France. Chief Justice John Marshall served for a month in 1801 as John Adams' Secretary of State. Justice Robert Jackson served as Chief United States Prosecutor in 1945 at the Nuremburg Trials of Nazi war criminals after the end of World War II. And, Chief Justice Earl Warren served as the Chairman of the Warren Commission—an executive branch criminal investigation into who shot and killed President John F. Kennedy and who aided or abetted the murderer. As a general matter, dual judicial and executive office holding has over time come to be seen as inappropriate and unethical even if it is technically constitutional. The very existence of the practice shows how hard it is to draw a line between the judicial and the executive power. For a full discussion, see Steven G. Calabresi & Joan L. Larsen, *One Person, One Office: Separation of Powers or Separation of Personnel?,* 79 CORNELL L. REV. 1045 (1994).

[Assignment 9]

IV. ARTICLE I: CONGRESS AND THE POWER OF THE PURSE

All legislative Powers herein granted shall be vested in a Congress of the United States . . .

A. LEGISLATION AND DELEGATION

The problem of drawing lines among the legislative, executive, and judicial powers can sometimes arise when one branch unilaterally tries to exercise authority that arguably goes beyond its enumerated powers and bleeds into power entrusted to another branch, as in *Youngstown* or *United States v. Hudson and Goodwin*. Far more often, however, the line-drawing problem arises when, Congress specifically grants authority to some governmental actor that arguably belongs exclusively to another actor. Perhaps the most common example is when Congress (so critics of the action claim) attempts to transfer *its own legislative authority* to executive or judicial actors. If Congress, for example, creates an administrative agency and then instructs it to "go forth and do good," and the agency then promulgates "goodness regulations" which have the force and effect of law (and please keep in mind that administrative agency regulations pursuant to valid authorization do have the force and effect of law, even to the extent of justifying criminal penalties or preempting state laws), is the agency exercising "executive Power" or "legislative Power[ ]"? One could say that the agency is simply doing exactly what Congress instructed it to do in the statute, which is the essence of "executive Power." *See* Eric A. Posner & Adrian Vermeuele, *Interring the Nondelegation Doctrine,* 69 U. CHI. L. REV. 1721 (2002) (arguing that Congress only delegates legislative power if it tries to delegate the formal right to vote on bills). Or one could say that the terms "legislative Power[ ]," "executive Power," and "judicial Power" have substantive meaning, so that deciding what is "good," without more statutory specification about what it means to be "good," simply cannot be an executive or judicial function. *See* Gary Lawson, *Delegation and Original Meaning,* 88 VA. L. REV. 327 (2002).

If one says the latter, how carefully does Congress have to spell out what counts as "good"? What determines when Congress has granted "too much" discretion to executive or judicial agents? At what point does the formal act of "interpreting" a law turn into *making* a law, because the "interpreter" is effectively giving the law its content? Are courts really supposed to try to figure out precisely how much guidance to executives and courts Congress has to provide in its statutes?

The founding era came out squarely on the side of trying to give substance to the meaning of legislative, executive, and judicial powers, however difficult that task may be. John Locke, writing nearly a century before the U.S. came into existence, wrote:

> [The Legislative Power] being but a delegated Power from the People, they who have it, cannot pass it over to others * * *. And, when the people have said, We will submit to rules, and be govern'd by Laws made by such Men, and in such Forms, no Body else can say other Men shall make Laws for them; nor can the people be bound by any Laws but such as are Enacted by those, whom they have Chosen, and Authorized to make Laws for them. The power of the Legislative being derived from the People by a positive voluntary Grant and Institution, can be no other, than what the positive Grant conveyed, which being only to make Laws, and not to make Legislators, the Legislature can have no power to transfer their Authority of making laws, and place it in other hands.

JOHN LOCKE, SECOND TREATISE ON GOVERNMENT ¶ 141 (1690). A conception of government in which legislative power (and other governmental power) is "but a delegated Power from the People" is a *fiduciary* conception. The principal (the People) delegates a measure of power to the agent (the government), and the agent must then act in accordance with the best interests of the principal and conform to background norms of fiduciary conduct. Government was uniformly described in such fiduciary, or agency, terms in the founding era. *See supra* pages 82–83. Under well settled eighteenth-century principles of agency law—governing trustees, factors, guardians, stewards, and every other kind of agent known to the law—agents could not freely delegate, or more precisely *subdelegate*, their delegated discretionary powers, exactly as John Locke described it for legislators.

Matthew Bacon's 1730 *New Abridgement of the Law*, which was among the best known and most widely used legal resources in the eighteenth century, said: "One who has an Authority to do an Act for another, must execute it himself, and cannot transfer it to another; for this being a Trust and Confidence reposed in the Party, cannot be assigned to a Stranger whose Ability and Integrity were not so well thought of by him for whom the Act was done * * *. 1 MATTHEW BACON, A NEW ABRIDGEMENT OF THE LAW 203 (1730). Leading treatises on agency law in the early nineteenth century said the same thing. *See, e.g.,* 1 SAMUEL LIVERMORE, A TREATISE ON THE LAW OF PRINCIPAL AND AGENT AND OF SALES BY AUCTION 54 (1818); JOSEPH STORY, COMMENTARIES ON THE LAW OF AGENCY § 13, at 4 (1844). The U.S. Congress under the Constitution is obviously an entity in which the People have reposed their "Trust and Confidence" when granting powers.

The Constitution goes into hyper-technical detail about the election of members of Congress. In terms of numbers and lengths of provisions, the mechanisms and processes for selection of those who will serve in government is *by far* the single most dominant topic in the Constitution; it matters a great deal to the Constitution who holds the offices in which legislative power is vested. The Constitution thus slots perfectly into the world of eighteenth-century fiduciary instruments that do not permit free subdelegation of discretionary authority.

The eighteenth-century fiduciary norm against subdelegation, however, was not absolute. Power conferred in trust was *presumptively* not subject to subdelegation, but the agent was permitted to transfer some measure of authority to others when (1) the authorizing instrument expressly permitted it, (2) there was a custom or usage in the relevant trade that assumed subdelegation, or (3) the nature of the task required subdelegation, as when the task called for filing of legal documents and the agent was not a lawyer. As Joseph Story summarized the law of agency subdelegation in 1844: "the true doctrine, which is to be deduced from the decisions, is (and it is entirely coincident with the dictates of natural justice) that the authority is exclusively personal, unless, from the express language used, or from the fair presumptions, growing out of the particular transaction, or of the usage of trade, a broader power was intended to be conferred on the agent." STORY, *supra*, at 16–17.

The U.S. Constitution contains no clause expressly authorizing subdelegation of Congress's power, nor could there be a relevant custom or usage given the novelty of the Constitution's arrangements. The real question is when the nature of certain tasks so obviously calls for subdelegation that authority to transfer power to others must be presumed.

That question is as old as the country. From the start, Congress had to determine what kind of power to grant to executive and judicial agents and how much discretion it could give those agents in carrying out congressionally specified tasks. For example, Congress wanted to provide benefits for wounded or disabled Revolutionary War veterans, but rather than fix precisely the terms of those benefits, it said that wounded veterans "shall be placed on the list of the invalids of the United States, at such rate of pay, and under such regulations as shall be directed by the

President," Act of April 30, 1790, ch. 20, § 11, 1 Stat. 119, 121, subject only to some statutory limitations on how high the benefits could ever be. *See id.* Congress wanted to regulate trade with the Indian tribes; its solution was to require traders to be licensed, to authorize the executive to give a license "to any proper person," Act of July 22, 1790, ch. 33, § 1, 1 Stat. 137, 137, with no specification of what made a person "proper," and to provide that licensees must be "governed in all things touching the said trade and intercourse, by such rules and regulations as the President shall prescribe." *Id.* Were these unconstitutional subdelegations of legislative authority or simply authorizations to exercise core "executive Power"? Is it relevant that both of these statutes involved military or foreign affairs rather than garden-variety domestic matters? *See* Michael B. Rappaport, *The Selective Nondelegation Doctrine and the Line Item Veto: A New Approach to the Nondelegation Doctrine and Its Implications for* Clinton v. City of New York, 76 TUL. L. REV. 265 (2001).

There were plenty of garden-variety domestic matters to be addressed as well in the Nation's first years. In early 1791, Congress imposed an excise tax on liquor. Federal agents would have to police the transactions and collect the tax. For that purpose, Congress divided the U.S. into collection districts, so that officers charged with collection would have defined geographic areas of administration (think about the problems of communication and transportation in 1791 and you will see why this was a vital part of the tax system). The statute made each State a collection district, "but subject to alterations by the President of the United States, from time to time, by adding to the smaller such portions of the greater as shall in his judgment best tend to secure and facilitate the collection of the revenue; which districts it shall be lawful for the President of the United States to subdivide into surveys of inspection, and the same to alter at his discretion." Act of Mar. 3, 1791, ch. 15, § 4, 1 Stat. 199. 200. No one raised any concerns about subdelegation of legislative authority in this statute.

Those concerns arose in a big way, however, shortly thereafter in 1791 when Congress debated the bill establishing the Post Office. The Constitution gives Congress power "[t]o establish Post Offices and post Roads." U.S. CONST. art. I, § 8, cl. 7. Does Congress "establish" post roads by passing a law saying, "There shall be post roads wherever the President thinks a post road is needed," or does Congress actually have to specify where the post roads must be? The original draft of the bill specified, town by town, the path of the post roads. Representative Sedgwick "moved to strike out all that clause of the bill which designated the roads, and to insert, instead thereof, these words, '*by such route as the President of the United States shall, from time to time, cause to be established.*'" 2 Annals of Cong. 229 (1791). That set off a major debate about the proper form for the exercise of the postal power—and, by extension, Congress's other powers as well.

Representative Livermore was the first to object on constitutional grounds:

> Mr. Livermore observed that the Legislative body being empowered by the Constitution "to establish post offices and post roads," it is as clearly their duty to designate the roads as to establish the offices; and he did not think they could with propriety delegate that power, which they were themselves appointed to exercise. Some gentlemen, he knew, were of the opinion that the business of the United States could be better transacted by a single person than by many; but this was not the intention of the

> Constitution. It was provided that the Government should be administered by Representatives of the people's choice * * *.

Id. Representative Hartley added: "The Constitution seems to have intended that we should exercise all the powers respecting the establishing of post roads we are capable of * * *. We represent the people, we are constitutionally vested with the power of determining upon the establishment of post roads; and, as I understand at present, ought not to delegate the power to any other person." *Id.* at 231. James Madison agreed: "However difficult it may be to determine with precision the exact boundaries of the Legislative and Executive powers, he was of opinion that those arguments [in favor of subdelegation to the President] were not well founded, for they admit of such construction as will lead to blending those powers so as to leave no line of separation whatever." *Id.* at 238. Representative Vining opined that no affirmative authorization for subdelegation was provided by the Constitution: "The Constitution has certainly given us the power of establishing posts and roads, and it is not even implied that it should be transferred to the President * * *." *Id.* at 235. And Representative Page topped everyone when he remarked: "If the motion before the committee succeeds, I shall make one which will save a deal of time and money, by making a short session of it; for if this House can, with propriety, leave the business of the post office to the President, it may leave to him any other business of legislation; and I may move to adjourn and leave all the objects of legislation to his sole consideration and direction." *Id.* at 233.

Many representatives, on the other hand, doubted whether there was any constitutional problem with letting the President fix the location of post roads. Representative Sedgwick, who proposed the amendment in question, wondered where the constitutional argument against such authorization would end:

> Congress, he observed, are authorized not only to establish post offices and post roads, but also to borrow money; but is it understood that Congress are to go in a body to borrow every sum that may be requisite? Is it not rather their office to determine the principle on which the business is to be conducted, and then delegate the power of carrying their resolves into execution? They are also empowered to coin money, and if no part of their power be delegable, he did not know but that they might be obliged to turn coiners, and work in the Mint themselves. Nay, they must even act the part of executioners, in punishing piracies committed on the high seas. In the delegation of power, the whole purpose, in his opinion, is answered, when the rules by which the business is to be conducted are pointed out by law * * *.

Id. at 230–31. Representative Bourne invoked the very recent precedent of the excise districts, noting that "[i]n passing the excise law, the House, not thinking themselves possessed of sufficient information, empowered the President to mark out the districts and surveys; and if they had a right to delegate such power to the Executive, the further delegation of the power of marking out the roads for the conveyance of the mail, could hardly be thought dangerous." *Id.* at 232. Representative Sedgwick also invoked the example of the excise law: "Nothing more was in that instance done, than to define the powers and duties annexed to the offices, but the limits to which their authority was to extend, and their number, was very properly left with the Executive. In that instance, such a delegation was indispensably necessary; nor was it, in his opinion, less necessary in the multifarious arrangements of post offices." *Id.* at 239.

James Madison countered that there was a necessity in the case of the excise law that did not exist with respect to the post office: "The reference to the appointments and arrangements made by the Executive, pursuant to the powers delegated to the Executive by the excise law, cannot be considered as a parallel case; no similar exigency exists to justify a similar delegation * * *. Where is the necessity of departing from the principles of the Constitution in respect to the post office and post roads, more than in all other cases? The subject is expressly committed to Legislative determination by the Constitution." *Id.* at 238. Representative Hartley added: "If, upon experience, we find ourselves incompetent to the duty, we must (if the Constitution will admit) grant the power to the Executive; or, if the Constitution will not allow such a delegation, submit the article for amendment in a constitutional way." *Id.* at 232.

The amendment was defeated, and the law as enacted laid out, town by town from Maine all the way to Georgia, the path that the post roads must take. *See* Act of Feb. 20, 1792, ch. VII, § 1, 1 Stat. 232. Does this prove that there was no strict necessity for subdelegation? The law specified every city and town through which the post roads must travel, but it did not specify the precise physical path from one town to the next. Was there strict necessity for entrusting that decision to the President? For entrusting to the President which contractors to hire to build the roads? Does enactment of the final law show that the opponents of subdelegation won that particular constitutional battle? (Keep in mind that the power to designate the location of a post road was the eighteenth-century version of an earmark, because having a town on a post road was a significant commercial benefit, so Congress's final decision may have been motivated as much by pork-barrel politics as by high constitutional theory.)

Suppose that Congress wants to place an embargo on trade with countries that are interfering with American commerce (for example, by boarding U.S. ships and seizing the sailors), leaving it up to the President (or the courts) to determine which countries meet that criterion. Can Congress make the effect of a law conditional on fact-finding by some other body? In 1813, the Supreme Court thought the answer was obviously yes. According to an 1810 statute, a prior statute imposing a trade embargo on Great Britain and France would be revived unless those countries "revoke or modify her edicts as that they shall cease to violate the neutral commerce of the United States, which fact the President of the United States shall declare by proclamation * * *. Act of May 1, 1810, ch. 39, § 4, 2 Stat. 605, 606. The law was challenged because, according to counsel, "Congress could not transfer the legislative power to the President. To make the revival of a law depend upon the President's proclamation, is to give to that proclamation the force of a law." *Cargo of the Brig Aurora v. United States*, 11 U.S. (7 Cranch) 382, 386 (1813) (argument of Joseph P. Ingersoll). The Court dismissed the challenge in one sentence: "we can see no sufficient reason, why the legislature should not exercise its discretion in reviving the act * * *, either expressly or conditionally, as their judgment should direct." *Id.* at 388. In other words, ascertaining whether the statutory conditions for a law's effectiveness are met is a proper exercise of executive power. That makes a measure of sense if one thinks about it. Suppose that Congress sets a specific calendar date for the effectiveness of a law ("this law shall take effect 30 days after enactment").

Someone has to decide whether that date has arrived. Is it improper subdelegation to let executive or judicial agents make that call? That example seems simplistic, but is it any different in principle from deciding whether any event in the world other than the celestial motions that fix calendar dates has occurred? Keep that thought open for the time being.

It took considerably more than one sentence for the Court, in 1825, to address the subdelegation challenge in the next case to raise one. Interestingly, the claimed subdelegation was to the federal courts rather than to the federal executive. A Kentucky statute provided that plaintiffs must accept state bank notes in satisfaction of judicial judgments (which seems like a plain violation of the constitutional rule that "[n]o State shall * * * make any Thing but gold and silver Coin a Tender in Payment of Debts," U.S. CONST. art. I, § 10, cl. 1, but that argument was not pressed). The Supreme Court held that this statute did not apply to the execution of *federal* court judgments in Kentucky, which was instead governed by a federal statute which provided that the "forms of writs, executions, and other processes" would be "subject * * * to such alterations and additions as the * * * [federal] Courts * * * shall, in their discretion, deem expedient, or to such regulations as the Supreme Court of the United States shall think proper, from time to time, by rule, to prescribe to any Circuit or District Court concerning the same." Act of May 8, 1792, ch. 36, § 2, 1 Stat. 275, 276. The defendant, who wanted to pay off his judgment debt with worthless state bank notes, argued that this federal statute unconstitutionally subdelegated legislative power to the courts. The Supreme Court disagreed and upheld the law. As you read the rest of the materials in this section, ask yourself whether any court decision in the past two centuries has come up with a more sophisticated analysis of subdelegation than Chief Justice Marshall's opinion:

> It will not be contended that Congress can delegate to the Courts, or to any other tribunals, powers which are strictly and exclusively legislative. But Congress may certainly delegate to others, powers which the legislature may rightfully exercise itself * * *. [Under the Judiciary Act, which authorizes the federal courts to regulate their practice,] [t]he Courts, for example, may make rules, directing the returning of writs and processes, the filing of declarations and other pleadings, and other things of the same description. It will not be contended, that these things might not be done by the legislature, without the intervention of the Courts; yet it is not alleged that the power may not be conferred on the judicial department.
>
> The line has not been exactly drawn which separates those important subjects, which must be entirely regulated by the legislature itself, from those of less interest, in which a general provision may be made, and power given to those who are to act under such general provisions to fill up the details * * *.
>
> * * *
>
> * * * The power given to the Court to vary the mode of proceeding * * * [concerning such matters as the proper notice to be given a judgment debtor before his or her property is seized for sale and the manner in which the property is held before sale] is a power to vary minor regulations, which are within the great outlines marked out by the legislature in directing the

> execution. To vary the terms on which a sale is to be made, and declare whether it shall be on credit, or for ready money, is certainly a more important exercise of the power of regulating the conduct of the officer, but is one of the same principle. It is, in all its parts, the regulation of the conduct of the officer of the Court in giving effect to its judgments. A general superintendence over this subject seems to be properly within the judicial province, and has been always so considered. It is, undoubtedly, proper for the legislature to prescribe the manner in which these ministerial offices shall be performed, and this duty will never be devolved on any other department without urgent reasons. But, in the mode of obeying the mandate of a writ issuing from a Court, so much of that which may be done by the judiciary, under the authority of the legislature, seems to be blended with that for which the legislature must expressly and directly provide, that there is some difficulty in discerning the exact limits within which the legislature may avail itself of the agency of the Courts.
>
> The difference between the departments undoubtedly is, that the legislature makes, the executive executes, and the judiciary construes the law; but the maker of the law may commit something to the discretion of the other departments, and the precise boundary of this power is a subject of delicate and difficult inquiry, into which a Court will not enter unnecessarily.

Wayman v. Southard, 23 U.S. (10 Wheat.) 1, 42–43, 45–46 (1825). Is the correct constitutional rule really that Congress can give executive and judicial actors power to make decisions on matters of "less interest" while Congress has to decide "important matters"? Is how a plaintiff gets paid a matter of "less interest"? If Congress passed no statute at all, would the "judicial Power" include the power to set the terms of payment of judgments?

For more than a century after *Wayman,* the Court decided a steady stream of cases raising subdelegation challenges to congressional statutes. Prior to 1935, it only found two unconstitutional subdelegations: one to the courts to fill in the meaning of a criminal statute (which today we would describe as the "void for vagueness" doctrine), *see United States v. L. Cohen Grocery Store Co.,* 255 U.S. 81 (1921) (holding unconstitutional a criminal statute prohibiting "unjust or unreasonable" charges for any "necessaries"), and one to the States to fill in the content of federal admiralty law. *See Knickerbocker Ice Co. v. Stewart,* 253 U.S. 149 (1920) (holding unconstitutional federal statutes that made state workmen's compensation laws applicable in admiralty cases). No case before 1935 found a federal statute unconstitutional because it improperly subdelegated legislative power to an executive agent.

The most important of those pre-1935 cases involved tariff laws. In *Field v. Clark,* 143 U.S. 649 (1892), Congress had provided for duty-free importation of certain goods but said that the free-trade provisions could be suspended by the President for any country which he determined imposed "reciprocally unequal and unreasonable" trade restrictions on American goods. By a 7–2 vote, the Supreme Court determined: "Legislative power was exercised when Congress declared that the suspension should take effect upon a named contingency. What the President was required to do was simply in execution of the act of Congress. It was not the making of law. He was the mere agent of the law-making department to ascertain and declare the event upon which its expressed will was to take effect." *Id.* at 505. Is that just another way of saying that Congress has to decide "important" matters but can leave matters of "less interest" to others? Is the President deciding something of "less interest" under this statute, and do the terms "simply" and "mere" accurately describe the President's authority? Two justices in 1892 thought not, finding that the statute "certainly extends to the executive the exercise of those discretionary powers which the Constitution has vested in the law-making department." *Id.* at 699–700 (Lamar, J., dissenting). Is letting the President determine whether there are "reciprocally unequal and unreasonable" trade restrictions different in principle from letting the President determine whether Great Britain or France is violating the neutral commerce of the United States? Are either or both different from letting the President determine whether thirty days have passed since enactment of a law?

Three and a half decades later, Congress let the President alter the amounts of duties on certain imports in order to "equalize the * * * costs of production" between the U.S. and the origin country. Chief Justice Taft's 1928 opinion upholding the statute has been remarkably influential, as we will see:

> * * * It seems clear what Congress intended by section 315. Its plan was to secure by law the imposition of customs duties on articles of imported merchandise which should equal the difference between the cost of producing in a foreign country the articles in question and laying them down for sale in the United States, and the cost of producing and selling like or similar articles in the United States, so that the duties not only secure revenue, but at the same time enable domestic producers to compete on terms of equality with foreign producers in the markets of the United States. It may be that it is difficult to fix with exactness this difference, but the difference which is sought in the statute is perfectly clear and perfectly intelligible. Because of the difficulty in practically determining what that difference is, Congress seems to have doubted that the information in its possession was such as to enable it to make the adjustment accurately, and also to have apprehended that with changing conditions the difference might vary in such a way that some readjustments would be necessary to give effect to the principle on which the statute proceeds. To avoid such difficulties, Congress adopted in section 315 the method of describing with clearness what its policy and plan was and then authorizing a member of the executive branch to carry out its policy and plan and to find the changing difference from time to time and to make the adjustments necessary to conform the duties to the standard underlying that policy and plan. As it was a matter of great importance, it concluded to give by statute to the President, the chief of the executive branch, the function of determining the difference as it might vary * * *.
>
> * * *
>
> * * * [I]t is a breach of the national fundamental law if Congress gives up its legislative power and transfers it to the President, or to the judicial branch, or if by law it attempts to invest itself or its members with either executive power or judicial power. This is not to say that the three branches are not co-ordinate parts of one government and that each in the field of its duties may not invoke the action of the two other branches in so far as the action invoked shall not be an assumption of the constitutional field of

action of another branch. In determining what it may do in seeking assistance from another branch, the extent and character of that assistence must be fixed according to common sense and the inherent necessities of the governmental co-ordination. * * *

It is conceded by counsel that Congress may use executive officers in the application and enforcement of a policy declared in law by Congress and authorize such officers in the application of the congressional declaration to enforce it by regulation equivalent to law. But it is said that this never has been permitted to be done where Congress has exercised the power to levy taxes and fix customs duties. The authorities make no such distinction. The same principle that permits Congress to exercise its rate-making power in interstate commerce by declaring the rule which shall prevail in the legislative fixing of rates, and enables it to remit to a rate-making body created in accordance with its provisions the fixing of such rates, justifies a similar provision for the fixing of customs duties on imported merchandise. If Congress shall lay down by legislative act an intelligible principle to which the person or body authorized to fix such rates is directed to conform, such legislative action is not a forbidden delegation of legislative power.

J.W. Hampton, Jr. & Co. v. United States, 276 U.S. 394, 404–05, 406, 409 (1928).

By the time *Hampton* was decided in 1928, the U.S. had experienced almost half a century of a new political movement and ideology known as Progressivism. While this is a course in Constitutional Law rather than U.S. History, and we are lawyers rather than historians, it is impossible to understand modern developments in the subdelegation doctrine, and in separation of powers law in general, without some background in the rise and meaning of Progressivism.

An initial problem is that there is no single meaning of "Progressivism," either as an ideology or as a political movement. Nonetheless, one can identify a few common themes.

Progressivism was both *historicist* and *scientistic*. Historicism means that Progressives generally believed that human values and institutions were products of particular times and places. They were accordingly suspicious of universal principles (such as those that begin the Declaration of Independence), theories of natural rights, or institutional arrangements that were supposed to endure across changing social conditions, most notably the idea of an enduring Constitution. Progressives found public support for the original Constitution of 1788 frustrating and inexplicable. In the lamenting words of Frank Goodnow, an influential Progressive theorist of government, in 1911: "For one reason or another the people of the United States came soon to regard with an almost superstitious reverence the document into which this general scheme of government was incorporated, and many considered, and even now consider, that scheme, as they conceive it, to be the last word which can be said as to the proper form of government—a form believed to be suited to all times and conditions." FRANK J. GOODNOW, SOCIAL REFORM AND THE CONSTITUTION 9–10 (1911). According to Progressivism, governmental organization must fit current perceptions of how to solve problems rather than, as originalist constitutionalism would have it, vice versa.

Scientism means that Progressives believed that the great successes of the physical sciences could be duplicated by the social sciences, including the "sciences" of politics and government. The purpose of government, for Progressives, was to identify and solve social problems. The people best suited to that task were not We the People or the politicians that they would elect. Rather, the ideal problem solvers were *experts*, identified as such by their credentials and training. (As an aside: For at least some Progressives, breeding was also an important aspect of fitness to rule. Progressivism had a strong element of classism, racialism, and flat-out racism, which led many prominent Progressives, from Theodore Roosevelt to Margaret Sanger, to embrace eugenics and compulsory sterilization, so that people from the "wrong" stock would not reproduce or intermingle. *See* Steven G. Calabresi & Gary Lawson, *The Depravity of the 1930s and the Modern Administrative State*, 94 NOTRE DAME L. REV. 821, 832–34 (2018).) This idea is illustrated by ALDOUS HUXLEY, BRAVE NEW WORLD (1932), a dystopian novel about a society divided into different classes based on the intelligence of each individual. At the extreme, Progressivism "posited that educated, trained, expert administrators could fashion scientific solutions to any public policy problem." Paul J. Larkin, Jr. & Elizabeth H. Slatterly, *The World After* Seminole Rock *and* Auer, 42 HARV. J.L. & PUB. POL'Y 625, 636 & n.64 (2019).

One thing that unified virtually all Progressives was a profound dislike of the Constitution of 1788. That document places restrictions on governmental power, both by granting only limited power and, perhaps even more importantly, by dispersing those limited power grants among a multitude of actors, all of whose cooperation is necessary in order to get things done. For those who thought that experts could come up with indisputably right answers to social problems, in the same way that engineers could come up with indisputably right answers about metal stresses for bridge struts, it was not clear why those experts should have to convince multiple and overlapping majorities of their lessers, who surely do not understand the complex bodies of learning involved in the engineering of human activity, to accept the experts' solutions. The biggest enemy of Progressivism was the constitutional separation of powers. As one scholar puts it, "While difficult to define, progressivism shared a belief that the old constitutional system was inadequate, and that a significant empowerment of government (at whatever level) was needed." PAUL D. MORENO, THE AMERICAN STATE FROM THE CIVIL WAR TO THE NEW DEAL: THE TWILIGHT OF CONSTITUTIONALISM AND THE TRIUMPH OF PROGRESSIVISM 49 (2013).

Woodrow Wilson, who was a leading Progressive academic political scientist for decades before he became President, said of the American constitutional system of separated powers: "It is, therefore, manifestly a radical defect in our federal system that it parcels out power and confuses responsibility as it does. The main purpose of the Convention of 1787 seems to have been to accomplish this grievous mistake." WOODROW WILSON, CONGRESSIONAL GOVERNMENT: A STUDY IN AMERICAN POLITICS 284 (1885). Wilson was a champion of parliamentary government rather than a system of separated powers, because parliamentary governments could act in a unified and decisive manner to enact and implement the programs designed by the experts.

The Constitution flatly forbids parliamentary government by making active members of Congress constitutionally ineligible to serve in the executive or judicial departments. *See* U.S. CONST. art. I, § 6, cl. 2. (Woodrow Wilson despised this provision and urged its repeal. *See* RONALD J. PESTRITTO, WOODROW WILSON AND THE ROOTS OF MODERN LIBERALISM 125 (2005).) Even the loosest interpretation of the Constitution cannot get around that provision. So how would one implement a program of energetic, unitary, expert-driven government without moving directly to a parliamentary system?

Step one would be to delegate as much power as possible to expert administrators. The ideal statute, on this model, is a statute that creates an agency, gives it a budget, tells it to go find and solve problems using expertise, and then gets out of the way. Step two would be to insulate the experts as much as possible from influence by elected politicians, whether legislative or executive, by giving them employment security through fixed tenures of office. Step three would be to allow those experts to implement their visions of the good without having to enlist the support of other governmental actors such as the federal courts, which means combining within single administrative agencies the (legislative) power to formulate rules of conduct, the (executive) power to enforce those rules, and the (judicial) power to adjudicate violations.

That is precisely the vision of government that developed, not just in the United States but worldwide, from the last quarter of the nineteenth century up to the 1930s. When the Great Depression hit the world—not just the United States but the entire world—in 1929, this vision of government stood ready to frame the response. Legislatures were primed to cede vast power to supposedly expert executive agents, subject to minimal, if any, formal legal controls. This was true across the globe. *See* Peter L. Lindseth, *The Paradox of Parliamentary Supremacy: Delegation, Democracy, and Dictatorship in Germany and France, 1920s–1950s*, 113 YALE L.J. 1341 (2004). Consider first the most sweeping and final delegation of legislative power that any democracy has ever made in human history:

1. THE ENABLING ACT OF 1933

[Editors' Note: The Enabling Act of March 1933 was an act of the German parliament that gave Chancellor Adolf Hitler and his Cabinet the power to enact laws without the involvement of the parliament (or "Reichstag"). The Act passed in both the Reichstag and the Reischrat on March 23, 1933 and was signed into law by President Paul Von Hindenburg later that day. The vote was held with the Communist delegates not counting for purposes of a quorum and with Hitler's thugs surrounding the building. The final vote in the Reichstag was 444 in favor and 94 Social Democrats against. The translation used here comes from UNITED STATES DEP'T OF STATE, DIV. OF EUROPEAN AFFAIRS, NATIONAL SOCIALISM: BASIC PRINCIPLES, THEIR APPLICATION BY THE NAZI PARTY'S FOREIGN ORGANIZATION, AND THE USE OF GERMANS ABROAD FOR NAZI AIMS 217–18 (1943).]

Law to Remedy the Distress of People and State

Article 1. National laws can be enacted by the National Cabinet as well as in accordance with the procedure established in the Constitution. This applies also to the laws referred to in article 85, paragraph 2, and in article 87 of the Constitution.

Article 2. The national laws enacted by the National Cabinet may deviate from the Constitution so far as they do not affect the position of the Reichstag and the National Council. The powers of the President remain undisturbed.

Article 3. The national laws enacted by the National Cabinet are prepared by the Chancelor and published in the *Reichsgeseztblatt*. They come into effect, unless otherwise specified, upon the day following their publication. Articles 68 to 77 of the Constitution do not apply to the laws enacted by the National Cabinet.

Article 4. Treaties of the Reich with foreign states which concern matters of national legislation do not require the consent of the bodies participating in legislation. The National Cabinet is empowered to issue the necessary provisions for the execution of these treaties.

Article 5. This law becomes effective on the day of its publication. It becomes invalid on April 1, 1937; it further becomes invalid when the present National Cabinet is replaced by another.

NOTES AND QUESTIONS

1. In the wake of the Enabling Act, the Reichstag never met again, and when President Von Hindenburg died on August 2, 1934, Adolf Hitler declared that the Weimar Republic of Germany was dead and had been replaced by a new Third Reich, of which he was the head as Fuhrer.

2. Three months after the Enabling Act was passed in Germany, the United States Congress enacted the National Industrial Recovery Act ("NIRA"). This statute was part of the "100 days" of President Franklin D Roosevelt's first administration, which saw a flurry of legislative activity in response to the Great Depression. New government programs and agencies were created at a pace unheard of in the Nation's history. The NIRA, and the National Recovery Administration ("NRA") that was to implement it, was the centerpiece of this activity, because while other agencies were given significant responsibilities, those responsibilities were confined to particular economic sectors, such as agriculture or the issuance of securities. The NIRA covered the entire economy. It called for "codes of fair competition," drawn up initially by businesses but subject to approval, amendment, or substitution by the President, that could regulate the affairs of every firm and worker in the country. Two years after its enactment, challenges to that law led to two of the most famous cases in American legal history, which remain (for now) the only two times that the Supreme Court has found congressional grants of authority to executive agents to be unconstitutional subdelegations of legislative power. The first of those cases, *Panama Refining Co v. Ryan,* 293 U.S. 388 (1935), invalidated one small portion of the statute that dealt only with interstate shipments of oil. The case was decided in the lower courts and briefed in the Supreme Court based on a much wider challenge to the law, but it turns out that most of the code of fair competition for the petroleum industry had been accidentally amended out of existence by sloppy drafting, leaving only the portion of the code resulting from the narrow provision invalidated by the Court in *Panama Refining*. Because there was no formalized mechanism for reporting or compiling official versions of the codes, the accidental amendment was not discovered until the eve of oral argument before the Supreme Court. (These comical sounding but legally troubling events led to the passage of the Federal Register Act in 1935, which now requires all legally binding government rules to be published in an official volume called the *Federal Register*.) The next case, however, squarely addressed the central structure of the NIRA. It was decided unanimously and with the background history of Germany adopting Hitler's Enabling Act firmly in mind.

2. A.L.A. SCHECHTER POULTRY CORP. V. UNITED STATES

295 U.S. 495 (1935)

■ MR. CHIEF JUSTICE HUGHES delivered the opinion of the Court.

Petitioners in No. 854 were convicted in the District Court of the United States for the Eastern District of New York on eighteen count of an indictment charging violations of what is known as the "Live Poultry Code,"* * * and on an additional count for conspiracy to commit such violations. By demurrer to the indictment and appropriate motions on the trial, the defendants contended * * * that the Code had been adopted pursuant to an unconstitutional delegation by Congress of legislative power * * *.

* * *.

* * * A. L. A. Schechter Poultry Corporation and Schechter Live Poultry Market are corporations conducting wholesale poultry slaughterhouse markets in Brooklyn, New York City. Joseph Schechter operated the latter corporation and also guaranteed the credits of the former corporation which was operated by Martin, Alex and Aaron Schechter. Defendants ordinarily purchase their live poultry from commission men at the West Washington Market in New York City or at the railroad terminals serving the City, but occasionally they purchase from commission men in Philadelphia. They buy the poultry for slaughter and resale. After the poultry is trucked to their slaughterhouse markets in Brooklyn, it is there sold, usually within twenty-four hours, to retail poultry dealers and butchers who sell directly to consumers. The poultry purchased from defendants is immediately slaughtered, prior to delivery, by schochtim in defendants' employ. Defendants do not sell poultry in interstate commerce.

The "Live Poultry Code" was promulgated under § 3 of the National Industrial Recovery Act.

That section * * * authorizes the President to approve "codes of fair competition." Such a code may be approved for a trade or industry, upon application by one or more trade or industrial associations or groups, if the President finds (1) that such associations or groups "impose no inequitable restrictions on admission to membership therein and are truly representative," and (2) that such codes are not designed to promote monopolies or to eliminate or oppress small enterprises and will not operate to discriminate against them, and will tend to effectuate the policy of Title I of the Act. Such codes "shall not permit monopolies or monopolistic practices." As a condition of his approval, the President may "impose such conditions (including requirements for the making of reports and the keeping of accounts) for the protection of consumers, competitors, employees, and others, and in furtherance of the public interest, and may provide such exceptions to and exemptions from the provisions of such code, as the President in his discretion deems necessary to effectuate the policy herein declared." Where such a code has not been approved, the President may prescribe one, either on his own motion or on complaint. Violation of any provision of a code (so approved or prescribed) "in any transaction in or affecting interstate or foreign commerce" is made a misdemeanor punishable by a fine of not more than $500 for each offense, and each day the violation continues is to be deemed a separate offense.

The "Live Poultry Code" was approved by the President on April 13, 1934. Its divisions indicate its nature and scope. The Code has eight articles entitled (1) purposes, (2) definitions, (3) hours, (4) wages, (5) general labor provisions, (6) administration, (7) trade practice provisions, and (8) general.

The declared purpose is "To effect the policies of title I of the National Industrial Recovery Act." The Code is established as "a code of fair competition for the live poultry industry of the metropolitan area in and about the City of New York." That area is described as embracing the five boroughs of New York City, the counties of Rockland, Westchester, Nassau and Suffolk in the State of New York, the counties of Hudson and Bergen in the State of New Jersey, and the county of Fairfield in the State of Connecticut.

The "industry" is defined as including every person engaged in the business of selling, purchasing for resale, transporting, or handling and/or slaughtering live poultry, from the time such poultry comes into the New York metropolitan area to the time it is first sold in slaughtered form, and such "related branches" as may from time to time be included by amendment. Employers are styled "members of the industry," and the term employee is defined to embrace "any and all persons engaged in the industry, however compensated," except "members."

* * *

Provision is made for administration through an "industry advisory committee," to be selected by trade associations and members of the industry, and a "code supervisor," to be appointed, with the approval of the committee, by agreement between the Secretary of Agriculture and the Administrator for Industrial Recovery. The expenses of administration are to be borne by the members of the industry proportionately upon the basis of volume of business, or such other factors as the advisory committee may deem equitable, "subject to the disapproval of the Secretary and/or Administrator."

The seventh article, containing "trade practice provisions," prohibits various practices which are said to constitute "unfair methods of competition." The final article provides for verified reports, such as the Secretary or Administrator may require, "(1) for the protection of consumers, competitors, employees, and others, and in furtherance of the public interest, and (2) for the determination by the Secretary or Administrator of the extent to which the declared policy of the act is being effectuated by this code." The members of the industry are also required to keep books and records which "will clearly reflect all financial transactions of their respective business and the financial condition thereof," and to submit weekly reports showing the range of daily prices and volume of sales for each kind of produce.

The President approved the Code by an executive order in which he found that the application for his approval had been duly made in accordance with the provisions of Title I of the National Industrial Recovery Act, that there had been due notice and hearings, that the Code constituted "a code of fair competition" as contemplated by the Act, and complied with its pertinent provisions, including clauses (1) and (2) of subsection (a) of § 3 of Title I, and that the Code would tend "to effectuate the policy of Congress as declared in section 1 of Title I" * * *.

* * *

Of * * * six counts, one charged the sale to a butcher of an unfit chicken; two counts charged the making of sales without having the poultry inspected or approved in accordance with regulations or ordinances of the City of New York; two counts charged the making of false reports or the failure to make report relating to the range of daily prices and volume of sales for certain periods, and the remaining count was for sales to slaughterers or dealers who were without licenses required by the ordinances and regulations of the city of New York.

First. Two preliminary points are stressed by the Government with respect to the appropriate approach to the important questions presented. We are told that the provision of the statute authorizing the adoption of codes must be viewed in the light of the grave national crisis with which Congress was confronted. Undoubtedly, the conditions to which power is addressed are always to be considered when the exercise of power is challenged. Extraordinary conditions may call for extraordinary remedies. But the argument necessarily stops short of an attempt to justify action which lies outside the sphere of constitutional authority. Extraordinary conditions do not create or enlarge constitutional power. The Constitution established a national government with powers deemed to be adequate, as they have proved to be both in war and peace, but these powers of the national government are limited by the constitutional grants. Those who act under these grants are not at liberty to transcend the imposed limits because they believe that more or different power is necessary. Such assertions of extraconstitutional authority were anticipated and precluded by the explicit terms of the Tenth Amendment—"The powers not delegated to the United States by the Constitution, nor prohibited by it to the States, are reserved to the States respectively, or to the people."

The further point is urged that the national crisis demanded a broad and intensive cooperative effort by those engaged in trade and industry, and that this necessary cooperation was sought to be fostered by permitting them to initiate the adoption of codes. But the statutory plan is not simply one for voluntary effort. It does not seek merely to endow voluntary trade or industrial associations or groups with privileges or immunities. It involves the coercive exercise of the lawmaking power. The codes of fair competition which the state attempts to authorize are codes of laws. If valid, they place all persons within their reach under the obligation of positive law, binding equally those who assent and those who do not assent. Violations of the provisions of the codes are punishable as crimes.

Second. The question of the delegation of legislative power. We recently had occasion to review the pertinent decisions and the general principles which govern the determination of this question. *Panama Refining Co. v. Ryan,* 293 U.S. 388. The Constitution provides that "All legislative powers herein granted shall be vested in a Congress of the United States, which shall consist of a Senate and House of Representatives."

Art I, § 1. And the Congress is authorized "To make all laws which shall be necessary and proper for carrying into execution" its general powers. Art. I, 8, par. 18. The Congress is not permitted to abdicate or to transfer to others the essential legislative functions with which it is thus vested. We have repeatedly recognized the necessity of adapting legislation to complex conditions involving a host of details with which the national legislature cannot deal directly. We pointed out in the *Panama Company* case that the Constitution has never been regarded as denying to Congress the necessary resources of flexibility and practicality which will enable it to perform its function in laying down policies and establishing standards while leaving to selected instrumentalities the making of subordinate rules within prescribed limits, and the determination of facts to which the policy, as declared by the legislature, is to apply. But we said that the constant recognition of the necessity and validity of such provisions, and the wide range of administrative authority which has been developed by means of them, cannot be allowed to obscure the limitations of the authority to delegate, if our constitutional system is to be maintained. *Id.*, p. 421.

Accordingly, we look to the statute to see whether Congress has overstepped these limitations—whether Congress, in authorizing "codes of fair competition," has itself established the standards of legal obligation, thus performing its essential legislative function, or, by the failure to enact such standards, has attempted to transfer that function to others.

* * *

What is meant by "fair competition" as the term is used in the Act? Does it refer to a category established in the law, and is the authority to make codes limited accordingly? Or is it used as a convenient designation for whatever set of laws the formulators of a code for a particular trade or industry may propose and the President may approve (subject to certain restrictions), or the President may himself prescribe, as being wise and beneficent provisions for the government of the trade or industry in order to accomplish the broad purposes of rehabilitation, correction and expansion which are stated in the first section of Title I?

The Act does not define "fair competition." "Unfair competition," as known to the common law, is a limited concept. Primarily, and strictly, it relates to the palming off of one's goods as those of a rival trader. In recent years, its scope has been extended. It has been held to apply to misappropriation as well as misrepresentation, to the selling of another's goods as one's own—to misappropriation of what equitably belongs to a competitor. *International News Service v. Associated Press,* 248 U.S. 215, 241, 242. Unfairness in competition has been predicated of acts which lie outside the ordinary course of business and are tainted by fraud, or coercion, or conduct otherwise prohibited by law. *Id.,* p. 258. But it is evident that in its widest range, "unfair competition," as it has been understood in the law, does not reach the objectives of the codes which are authorized by the National Industrial Recovery Act. The codes may, indeed, cover conduct which existing law condemns, but they are not limited to conduct of that sort. The Government does not contend that the Act contemplates such a limitation. It would be opposed both to the declared purposes of the Act and to its administrative construction.

* * *

For a statement of the authorized objectives and content of the "codes of fair competition," we are referred repeatedly to the "Declaration of Policy" in section one of Title I of the Recovery Act. Thus, the approval of a code by the President is conditioned on his finding that it "will tend to effectuate the policy of this title." § 3(a). The President is authorized to impose such conditions for the protection of consumers, competitors, employees, and others, and in furtherance of the public interest, and may provide such exceptions to and exemptions from the provisions of such code as the President in his discretion deems necessary to effectuate the policy herein declared. *Id.* The "policy herein declared" is manifestly that set forth in section one. That declaration embraces a broad range of objectives. Among them we find the elimination of "unfair competitive practices." But even if this clause were to be taken to relate to practices which fall under the ban of existing law, either common law or statute, it is still only one of the authorized aims described in section one. It is there declared to be "the policy of Congress"—

> "to remove obstructions to the free flow of interstate and foreign commerce which tend to diminish the amount thereof, and to provide for the general welfare by promoting the organization of industry for the purpose of cooperative action among trade groups, to induce and maintain united action of labor and management under adequate governmental sanctions

and supervision, to eliminate unfair competitive practices, to promote the fullest possible utilization of the present productive capacity of industries, to avoid undue restriction of production (except as may be temporarily required), to increase the consumption of industrial and agricultural products by increasing purchasing power, to reduce and relieve unemployment, to improve standards of labor, and otherwise to rehabilitate industry and to conserve natural resources."

Under § 3, whatever "may tend to effectuate" these general purposes may be included in the "codes of fair competition." We think the conclusion is inescapable that the authority sought to be conferred by § 3 was not merely to deal with "unfair competitive practices" which offend against existing law, and could be the subject of judicial condemnation without further legislation, or to create administrative machinery for the application of established principles of law to particular instances of violation. Rather, the purpose is clearly disclosed to authorize new and controlling prohibitions through codes of laws which would embrace what the formulators would propose, and what the President would approve, or prescribe, as wise and beneficent measures for the government of trades and industries in order to bring about their rehabilitation, correction and development, according to the general declaration of policy in section one. Codes of laws of this sort are styled "codes of fair competition."

* * *

The Government urges that the codes will "consist of rules of competition deemed fair for each industry by representative members of that industry—by the persons most vitally concerned and most familiar with its problems." Instances are cited in which Congress has availed itself of such assistance; as, *e.g.,* in the exercise of its authority over the public domain with respect to the recognition of local customs or rules of miners as to mining claims, or, in matters of a more or less technical nature, as in designating the standard height of drawbar. But would it be seriously contended that Congress could delegate its legislative authority to trade or industrial associations or groups so as to empower them to enact the laws they deem to be wise and beneficent for the rehabilitation and expansion of their trade or industries? Could trade or industrial associations or groups be constituted legislative bodies for that purpose because such associations or groups are familiar with the problems of their enterprises? And, could an effort of that sort be made valid by such a preface of generalities as to permissible aims as we find in section 1 of title I? The answer is obvious. Such a delegation of legislative power is unknown to our law, and is utterly consistent with the constitutional prerogatives and duties of Congress.

The question, then, turns upon the authority which § 3 of the Recovery Act vests in the President to approve or prescribe. If the codes have standing as penal statutes, this must be due to the effect of the executive action. But Congress cannot delegate legislative power to the President to exercise an unfettered discretion to make whatever laws he thinks may be needed or advisable for the rehabilitation and expansion of trade or industry. *See Panama Refining Co. v. Ryan, supra,* and cases there reviewed.

Accordingly, we turn to the Recovery Act to ascertain what limits have been set to the exercise of the President's discretion. *First,* the President, as a condition of approval, is required to find that the trade or industrial associations or groups which propose a code, "impose no inequitable restrictions on admission to membership," and are "truly representative." That condition, however, relates only to the status of the initiators of the new laws, and not to the permissible scope of such laws. *Second,* the President is required to find that the code is not "designed to promote monopolies or to eliminate or oppress small enterprises, and will not operate to discriminate against them." And to this is added a proviso that the code "shall not permit monopolies or monopolistic practices." But these restrictions leave virtually untouched the field of policy envisaged by section one, and, in that wide field of legislative possibilities, the proponents of a code, refraining from monopolistic designs, may roam at will, and the President may approve or disapprove their proposals as he may see fit. That is the precise effect of the further finding that the President is to make—that the code "will tend to effectuate the policy of this title." While this is called a finding, it is really but a statement of an opinion as to the general effect upon the promotion of trade or industry of a scheme of laws. These are the only findings which Congress has made essential in order to put into operation a legislative code having the aims described in the "Declaration of Policy."

Nor is the breadth of the President's discretion left to the necessary implication of this limited requirement as to his findings. As already noted, the President, in approving a code, may impose his own conditions, adding to or taking from what is proposed as, "in his discretion," he thinks necessary "to effectuate the policy" declared by the Act. Of course, he has no less liberty when he prescribes a code on his own motion or on complaint, and he is free to prescribe one if a code has not been approved. The Act provides for the creation by the President of administrative agencies to assist him, but the action or reports of such agencies, or of his other assistants—their recommendations and findings in relation to the making of codes—have no sanction beyond the will of the President, who may accept, modify, or reject them as he pleases. Such recommendations or findings in no way limit the authority which § 3 undertakes to vest in the President with no other conditions than those there specified. And this authority relates to a host of different trades and industries, thus extending the President's discretion to all the varieties of laws which he may deem to be beneficial in dealing with the vast array of commercial and industrial activities throughout the country.

Such a sweeping delegation of legislative power finds no support in the decisions upon which the Government especially relies. By the Interstate Commerce Act, Congress has itself provided a code of laws regulating the activities of the common carriers subject to the Act in order to assure the performance of their services upon just and reasonable terms, with adequate facilities and without unjust discrimination. Congress, from time to time, has elaborated its requirements as needs have been disclosed. To facilitate the application of the standards prescribed by the Act, Congress has provided an expert body. That administrative agency, in dealing with particular cases, is required to act upon notice and hearing, and its orders must be supported by findings of fact which, in turn, are sustained by evidence. *Interstate Commerce Comm'n v. Louisville & Nashville R. Co.,* 227 U.S. 88; *Florida v. United States,* 282 U.S. 194; *United States v. Baltimore & Ohio R. Co.,* 293 U.S. 454. When the Commission is authorized to issue, for the construction, extension or abandonment of lines, a certificate of "public convenience and necessity," or to permit the acquisition by one carrier of the control of another, if that is found to be "in the public interest," we have pointed out that these provisions are not left without standards to guide determination. The authority conferred has direct relation to the standards prescribed for the service of common carriers, and can be exercised only upon findings, based upon evidence, with respect to particular conditions of transportation. *New York Central Securities Co. v. United States,* 287 U.S. 12, 24, 25; *Texas & Pacific Railway Co. v. Gulf, Colorado & Santa Fe Ry. Co.,* 270 U.S. 266, 273; *Chesapeake & Ohio Ry. Co. v. United States,* 283 U.S. 35, 42.

Similarly, we have held that the Radio Act of 1927 established standards to govern radio communications, and, in view of the limited number of available broadcasting frequencies, Congress authorized allocation and licenses. The Federal Radio Commission was created as the licensing authority in order to secure a reasonable equality of opportunity in radio transmission and reception. The authority of the Commission to grant licenses "as public convenience, interest or necessity requires" was limited by the nature of radio communications and by the scope, character, and quality of the services to be rendered and the relative advantages to be derived through distribution of facilities. These standards established by Congress were to be enforced upon hearing, and evidence, by an administrative body acting under statutory restrictions adapted to the particular activity. *Federal Radio Comm'n v. Nelson Brothers Co.,* 289 U.S. 266.

In *Hampton & Co. v. United States,* 276 U.S. 394, the question related to the "flexible tariff provision" of the Tariff Act of 1922. We held that Congress had described its plan "to secure by law the imposition of customs duties on articles of imported merchandise which should equal the difference between the cost of producing in a foreign country the articles in question and laying them down for sale in the United States, and the cost of producing and selling like or similar articles in the United States." As the differences cost might vary from time to time, provision was for the investigation and determination of these differences by the executive branch, so as to make "the adjustments necessary to conform the duties to the standard underlying that policy and plan." *Id.* pp. 404, 405. The Court found the same principle to be applicable in fixing customs duties as that which permitted Congress to exercise its ratemaking power in interstate commerce, "by declaring the rule which shall prevail in the legislative fixing of rates" and then remitting "the fixing of such rates" in accordance with its provisions "to a ratemaking body." *Id.*, p. 409. The Court fully recognized the limitations upon the delegation of legislative power. *Id.* pp. 408–411.

To summarize and conclude upon this point: Section 3 of the Recovery Act is without precedent. It supplies no standards for any trade, industry or activity. It does not undertake to prescribe rules of conduct to be applied to particular states of fact determined by appropriate administrative procedure. Instead of prescribing rules of conduct, it authorizes the making of codes to prescribe them. For that legislative undertaking, § 3 sets up no standards, aside from the statement of the general aims of rehabilitation, correction and expansion described in section one. In view of the scope of that broad declaration, and of the nature of the few restrictions that are imposed, the discretion of the President in approving or prescribing codes, and thus enacting laws for the government of trade and industry throughout the country, is virtually unfettered. We think that the code-making authority this conferred is an unconstitutional delegation of legislative power.

* * *

* * * [W]e hold the code provisions here in question to be invalid and that the judgment of conviction must be reversed.

■ MR. JUSTICE CARDOZO, concurring.

The delegated power of legislation which has found expression in this code is not canalized within banks that keep it from overflowing. It is unconfined and vagrant, if I may borrow my own words in an earlier opinion. *Panama Refining Co. v. Ryan,* 293 U.S. 388, 440.

This court has held that delegation may be unlawful, though the act to be performed is definite and single, if the necessity, time and occasion of performance have been left in the end to the discretion of the delegate. *Panama Refining Co. v. Ryan, supra.* I thought that ruling went too far. I pointed out in an opinion that there had been "no grant to the Executive of any roving commission to inquire into evils and then, upon discovering them, do anything he pleases." 293 U.S. at p. 435. Choice, though within limits, had been given him "as to the occasion, but none whatever as to the means." *Ibid.* Here, in the case before us, is an attempted delegation not confined to any single act nor to any class or group of acts identified or described by reference to a standard. Here, in effect, is a roving commission to inquire into evils and, upon discovery, correct them.

I have said that there is no standard, definite or even approximate, to which legislation must conform. Let me make my meaning more precise. If codes of fair competition are codes eliminating "unfair" methods of competition ascertained upon inquiry to prevail in one industry or another, there is no unlawful delegation of legislative functions when the President is directed to inquire into such practices and denounce them when discovered. For many years, a like power has been committed to the Federal Trade Commission with the approval of this court in a long series of decisions. *Cf. Federal Trade Comm'n v. Keppel & Bro.,* 291 U.S. 304, 312; *Federal Trade Comm'n v. Raladam Co.,* 283 U.S. 643, 648; *Federal Trade Comm'n v. Gratz,* 253 U.S. 421. Delegation in such circumstances is born of the necessities of the occasion * * *.

But there is another conception of codes of fair competition, their significance and function, which leads to very different consequences, though it is one that is struggling now for recognition and acceptance. By this other conception, a code is not to be restricted to the elimination of business practices that would be characterized by general acceptation as oppressive or unfair. It is to include whatever ordinances may be desirable or helpful for the wellbeing or prosperity of the industry affected. In that view, the function of its adoption is not merely negative, but positive—the planning of improvements as well as the extirpation of abuses. What is fair, as thus conceived, is not something to be contrasted with what is unfair or fraudulent or tricky. The extension becomes as wide as the field of industrial regulation. If that conception shall prevail, anything that Congress may do within the limits of the commerce clause for the betterment of business may be done by the President upon the recommendation of a trade association by calling it a code. This is delegation running riot. No such plenitude of power is susceptible of transfer. The statute, however, aims at nothing less, as one can learn both from its terms and from the administrative practice under it. Nothing less is aimed at by the code now submitted to our scrutiny.

The code does not confine itself to the suppression of methods of competition that would be classified as unfair according to accepted business standards or accepted norm of ethics. It sets up a comprehensive body of rules to promote the welfare of the industry, if not the welfare of the nation, without reference to standards, ethical or commercial, that could be known or predicted in advance of its adoption. One of the new rules, the source of ten counts in the indictment, is aimed at an established practice, not unethical or oppressive, the practice of selective buying. Many others could be instanced as open to the same objection if the sections of the code were to be examined one by one. The process of dissection will not be traced in all its details. Enough at this time to state what it reveals. Even if the statute itself had fixed the meaning of fair competition by way of contrast with practices that are oppressive or unfair, the code outruns the bounds of the authority conferred. What is excessive is not sporadic or superficial. It is deep-seated and pervasive. The licit and illicit sections are so combined and welded as to be incapable of severance without destructive mutilation.

* * *

I am authorized to State that MR. JUSTICE STONE joins in this opinion.

NOTES AND QUESTIONS

1. The NIRA was unique among New Deal agencies in the *scope* of the power that it granted to executive agents and to private individuals. If left in place, the NIRA would have cartelized the entire American economy and ended the free market. This is part of the reason why the Supreme Court was unanimous in holding it unconstitutional. The NIRA was not at all unique, however, in the *vagueness* of the statutory guidance offered to those agents. For example, the Communications Act of 1934 provided (and still provides) that the Federal Communications Commission shall grant broadcast licenses to applicants "if public convenience, interest, or necessity will be served thereby * * *." 47 U.S.C. § 307 (2018); and the 1934 Securities Exchange Act provided (and still provides) that it shall be unlawful in certain securities transactions "[t]o use or employ * * * any manipulative or deceptive device or contrivance in contravention of such rules and regulations as the Commission may prescribe as necessary or appropriate in the public interest or for the protection of investors." 15 U.S.C. § 10(b) (2018). All of these statutes were written in accordance with the Progressive model, in which the ideal statute creates an agency, tells it to solve problems, and moves on. Under that model, detailed guidance from Congress would surely be a bad thing, because a largely ignorant and politically motivated Congress would be telling the educated and impartial experts what to do. Consider in this regard the views of James Landis, who was possibly the single most important intellectual figure in the New Deal. He was a member of the Federal Trade Commission and the Securities and Exchange Commission and one of the principal authors of the Securities Exchange Act of 1934. For nearly a decade, he was Dean of the Harvard Law School. He was in many ways the intellectual architect of the modern administrative state. In 1938, Landis gave the Storrs Lectures at Yale Law School, which were issued as a book called *The Administrative Process*. The book is a paean to, and blueprint for, the New Deal adaptation of the Progressive model of government. Landis wrote that agencies in the modern state need to have "not merely legislative power or simply executive power, but whatever power might be required to achieve the desired results." JAMES LANDIS, THE ADMINISTRATIVE PROCESS 10 (1938). Accordingly, he continued, the administrative state "vests the necessary powers with the administrative authority it creates, not too greatly concerned with the extent to which such action does

violence to the traditional tripartite theory of government." *Id.* at 12. For Landis, the ideal executive agent did not worry about whether Congress had provided adequate guidance in the statute. To the contrary, he said, "[o]ne of the ablest administrators that it was my good fortune to know, I believe, never read, at least more than casually, the statutes that he translated into reality. He assumed that they gave him power to deal with the broad problems of an industry and, upon that understanding, he sought his own solutions." *Id.* at 75. With this model driving governmental design, if the real problem in *Schechter* was that Congress had not provided detailed enough guidance to the President, virtually every New Deal agency-empowering statute would be unconstitutional. Did the Court in *Schechter* think that lack of guidance was the real problem with the NIRA? If not, what was the real problem?

2. *Schechter* was the last hurrah for the subdelegation doctrine for quite some time. The change in outlook and composition of the Supreme Court that began in 1937 and accelerated through the rest of the New Deal resulted in effective non-enforcement of the subdelegation doctrine, and of separation of powers doctrine generally, for decades to come. In short order, the Court began routinely and dismissively rejecting subdelegation challenges to statutes. In 1943, the Court upheld as constitutionally adequate the "public interest" standard in the Communications Act of 1934. *See National Broadcasting Co. v. United States*, 319 U.S. 190 (1943). In 1944, it found constitutional the Emergency Price Control Act of 1942, a World War II price control statute, that let a federal Price Administrator set prices for commodities which "in his judgment will be generally fair and equitable." *See Yakus v. United States*, 321 U.S. 414 (1944). Two years later, the Court rejected a subdelegation challenge to a 1935 statute charging the Securities and Exchange Commission with assuring that certain corporate financial structures would not "unduly or unnecessarily complicate the structure, or unfairly and inequitably distribute voting power among security holders." *See American Power & Light Co. v. SEC*, 329 U.S. 90 (1946). One could multiply this list of examples several times over.

3. Only a few justices on rare occasions raised any concerns about subdelegation. In 1963, Justices Hugo Black and William O. Douglas objected to the Court's adoption of amendments to the Federal Rules of Civil Procedure without congressional action, pursuant to a subdelegation in the Rules Enabling Act:

> MR. JUSTICE BLACK and MR. JUSTICE DOUGLAS are opposed to the submission of these rules to the Congress under a statute which permits them to "take effect" and to repeal "all laws in conflict with such rules" without requiring any affirmative consideration, action, or approval of the rules by Congress or the President. We believe that while some of the Rules of Civil Procedure are simply housekeeping details, many determine matters so substantially affecting the rights of litigants in lawsuits that in practical effect they are the equivalent of new legislation which, in our judgment, the Constitution requires to be initiated in and enacted by the Congress and approved by the President. The Constitution, as we read it, provides that all laws shall be enacted by the House, the Senate, and the President, not by the mere failure of Congress to reject proposals of an outside agency.

Statement of MR. JUSTICE BLACK and MR. JUSTICE DOUGLAS, 361 U.S. 865–66 (1963). And Justice William Rehnquist, joined in one case by Chief Justice Warren Burger, twice objected on subdelegation grounds to a statute which instructed the Secretary of Labor (through the Occupational Safety and Health Administration) to set the standard for workplace exposure to toxic substances "which most adequately assures, to the extent feasible, on the basis of the best available evidence, that no employee will suffer material impairment of health or functional capacity even if such employee has regular exposure to the hazard * * *." *See Industrial Union Dep't, AFL-CIO v. American Petroleum Inst.,* 448 U.S. 607, 671 (1980) (Rehnquist, J., concurring in the judgment); *American Textile Manuf. Inst., Inc. v. Donovan,* 452 U.S. 490, 543 (1981) (Rehnquist, J., dissenting). Justice Rehnquist never again repeated those concerns in connection with any statute in his remaining time on the Court.

More than half a century of case law was aptly summarized and applied in 1989 in *Mistretta v. United States,* 488 U.S. 361 (1989), in which the Court upheld a grant of power to the United States Sentencing Commission to prescribe sentencing ranges for federal crimes that would bind federal judges. The Court described the statutory constraints on the Commission's discretion as follows:

> To guide the Commission in its formulation of offense categories, Congress directed it to consider seven factors: the grade of the offense; the aggravating and mitigating circumstances of the crime; the nature and degree of the harm caused by the crime; the community view of the gravity of the offense; the public concern generated by the crime; the deterrent effect that a particular sentence may have on others; and the current incidence of the offense. * * * Congress set forth 11 factors for the Commission to consider in establishing categories of defendants. These include the offender's age, education, vocational skills, mental and emotional condition, physical condition (including drug dependence), previous employment record, family ties and responsibilities, community ties, role in the offense, criminal history, and degree of dependence upon crime for a livelihood. * * * Congress also prohibited the Commission from considering the "race, sex, national origin, creed, and socioeconomic status of offenders," * * * and instructed that the guidelines should reflect the "general inappropriateness" of considering certain other factors, such as current unemployment, that might serve as proxies for forbidden factors. * * *

Id. at 375–76. Invoking half a century of precedents, which left the Court with "no doubt that Congress's delegation of authority to the Sentencing Commission is sufficiently specific and detailed to meet constitutional requirements," *id.* at 374, the Court said, in oft-quoted language: "our jurisprudence has been driven by a practical understanding that in our increasingly complex society, replete with ever changing and more technical problems, Congress simply cannot do its job absent an ability to delegate power under broad general directives * * *." *Id.* at 372. Justice Scalia dissented because of a technical feature of the Sentencing Commission (it had no adjudicative authority to sustain the fiction that it was executing rather than making law), but on the larger question of the adequacy of the statutory guidance to the agency, he went even further than did the majority:

> But while the doctrine of unconstitutional delegation is unquestionably a fundamental element of our constitutional system, it is not an element readily enforceable by the courts. Once it is conceded, as it must be, that no statute can be entirely precise, and that some judgments, even some judgments involving policy considerations, must be left to the officers executing the law and to the judges applying it, the debate over unconstitutional delegation becomes a debate not over a point of principle but over a question of degree* * *.
>
> In short, I fully agree with the Court's rejection of petitioner's contention that the doctrine of unconstitutional delegation of legislative authority has been violated because of the lack of intelligible, congressionally prescribed standards to guide the Commission * * *.

Id. at 415–16 (Scalia, J., dissenting).

Mistretta was a very strong statement issuing from (with respect to this point) a unanimous Court that challenges to statutes on the ground that they give insufficient guidance to those who implement the statute would not be well received. The statement had less effect than one might think from reading it. Lawyers continued to raise subdelegation challenges, looking for some angle or avenue that would avoid the wave of precedents that crested with *Mistretta.* Were there perhaps stricter rules against subdelegation for taxes, or laws with criminal penalties, or instances in which the agency did not constrain its own discretion with clear administrative rules? On some occasions, lower courts agreed with those challenges, but the Supreme Court consistently did not. *See Skinner v. Mid-America Pipeline Co.*, 490 U.S. 212 (1989) (no special subdelegation rules for tax cases); *Touby v. United States,* 500 U.S. 160 (1991) (no special subdelegation rules for criminal cases (dictum); *Whitman v. American Trucking Ass'ns,* 531 U.S. 457 (2001) (no special subdelegation rules when the agency fails to constrain its own discretion). *But cf. U.S. Dep't of Transportation v. Ass'n of American Railroads,* 575 U.S. 43 (2015) (leaving open the possibility of a stricter subdelegation rule when the subdelegee is a private party). Indeed, in a series of cases from 1989 to 2001, the combined vote in the Supreme Court on the merits of subdelegation challenges was 53–0 against the challenges. Of course, the fact that the justices had to cast 53 votes during that time indicates that if *Mistretta* was trying to take the subdelegation issue off the table, it did not succeed.

From 2001 onward, the only change in the firmament was Justice Thomas declaring, on several occasions, that he thought that the Court's subdelegation jurisprudence was wrong as an original matter and should be reconsidered. He was a lone voice until 2017, when Neil Gorsuch joined the Court. As a lower court judge, Justice Gorsuch had expressed some sympathy for reviving the subdelegation doctrine. *See Gutierrez-Brizuela v. Lynch*, 834 F.3d 1142, 1154 (10th Cir. 2016) (Gorsuch, J., concurring). Nonetheless, almost no one saw coming what happened next.

4. In 2006, Congress enacted the Sex Offender Registration and Notification Act ("SORNA"), Pub. L No. 109–248, Title I, § 113 (a), 120 Stat. 593 (2006) (codified at 34 U.S.C. § 20913(a) (2018)), which requires convicted sex offenders to register with local governments Registration involves providing extensive information on the registrant's whereabouts and activities to government and the general public, and failing to register properly is a federal crime carrying up to a ten-year sentence, which can be considerably longer than the sentence for any underlying sex offense. One very large question was whether the registration requirements should apply to people who were convicted of qualifying offenses *before* the effective date of the act; there are hundreds of thousands of such people. The statute's answer to that question is: "The Attorney General shall have the authority to specify the applicability of the requirements of this subchapter to sex offenders convicted before the enactment of this chapter or its implementation in a particular jurisdiction, and to prescribe rules for the registration of any such sex offenders * * *." 34 U.S.C. § 20913(d) (2018). There are no criteria identified in the statute for the Attorney General to apply. Does this statute violate the subdelegation doctrine?

Every lower federal court to consider the matter—encompassing eleven out of the twelve federal circuits with criminal jurisdiction—said no. In 2017, the Second Circuit rejected Herman Gundy's subdelegation claim against SORNA in a dismissive footnote in an unpublished opinion that relied on prior circuit precedent from 2010. *See United States v. Gundy*, 695 Fed. Appx. 639, 641 n.2 (2d Cir.2017). The defendant petitioned for certiorari in the Supreme Court. The government waived its right to respond to the petition, which the government often does when it thinks that the petition for certiorari is so obviously meritless that it does not require a response and that the Court will surely refuse to take the case. To the surprise of almost everyone (including us), the Court asked for a government response and then took the case, indicating that at least four justices thought the subdelegation issue regarding SORNA worthy of consideration. Here is the intriguing (we cannot think of a more appropriate word) result:

3. GUNDY V. UNITED STATES

588 U.S. ___, 139 S.Ct. 2116 (2019)

■ JUSTICE KAGAN announced the judgment of the Court and delivered an opinion, in which JUSTICE GINSBURG, JUSTICE BREYER, and JUSTICE SOTOMAYOR join.

The nondelegation doctrine bars Congress from transferring its legislative power to another branch of Government. This case requires us to decide whether 34 U.S.C. § 20913(d), enacted as part of the Sex Offender Registration and Notification Act (SORNA), violates that doctrine. We hold it does not. Under § 20913(d), the Attorney General must apply SORNA's registration requirements as soon as feasible to offenders convicted before the statute's enactment. That delegation easily passes constitutional muster * * *.

The basic registration scheme works as follows. A "sex offender" is defined as "an individual who was convicted of" specified criminal offenses: all offenses "involving a sexual act or sexual contact" and additional offenses "against a minor." 34 U.S.C. §§ 20911(1), (5)(A), (7). Such an individual must register—provide his name, address, and certain other information—in every State where he resides, works, or studies. See §§ 20913(a), 20914. And he must keep the registration current, and periodically report in person to a law enforcement office, for a period of between fifteen years and life (depending on the severity of his crime and his history of recidivism). See §§ 20915, 20918.

Section 20913—the disputed provision here—elaborates the "[i]nitial registration" requirements for sex offenders. §§ 20913(b), (d). Subsection (b) sets out the general rule: An offender must register "before completing a sentence of imprisonment with respect to the offense giving rise to the registration requirement" (or, if the offender is not sentenced to prison, "not later than [three] business days after being sentenced"). Two provisions down, subsection (d) addresses (in its title's words) the "[i]nitial registration of sex offenders unable to comply with subsection (b)." The provision states:

> "The Attorney General shall have the authority to specify the applicability of the requirements of this subchapter to sex offenders convicted before the enactment of this chapter . . . and to prescribe rules for the registration of any such sex offenders and for other categories of sex offenders who are unable to comply with subsection (b)."

Subsection (d), in other words, focuses on individuals convicted of a sex offense before SORNA's enactment—a group we will call pre-Act offenders. Many of these individuals were unregistered at the time of SORNA's enactment, either because pre-existing law did not cover them or because they had successfully evaded that law (so were "lost" to the system). And of those potential new registrants, many or most could not comply with subsection (b)'s registration rule because they had already completed their prison sentences. For the entire group of pre-Act offenders, once again, the Attorney General "shall have the authority" to "specify the applicability" of SORNA's registration requirements and "to prescribe rules for [their] registration."

Under that delegated authority, the Attorney General issued an interim rule in February 2007, specifying that SORNA's registration requirements apply in full to "sex offenders convicted of the offense for which registration is required prior to the enactment of that Act." 72 Fed. Reg. 8897. The final rule, issued in December 2010, reiterated that SORNA applies to all pre-Act offenders. 75 Fed. Reg. 81850. That rule has remained the same to this day.

Petitioner Herman Gundy is a pre-Act offender. The year before SORNA's enactment, he pleaded guilty under Maryland law for sexually assaulting a minor. After his release from prison in 2012, Gundy came to live in New York. But he never registered there as a sex offender. A few years later, he was convicted for failing to register, in violation of § 2250. He argued below (among other things) that Congress unconstitutionally delegated legislative power when it authorized the Attorney General to "specify the applicability" of SORNA's registration requirements to pre-Act offenders. § 20913(d). The District Court and Court of Appeals for the Second Circuit rejected that claim, see 695 Fed.Appx. 639 (2017), as had every other court (including eleven Courts of Appeals) to consider the issue. We nonetheless granted certiorari. Today, we join the consensus and affirm.

II

Article I of the Constitution provides that "[a]ll legislative Powers herein granted shall be vested in a Congress of the United States." § 1. Accompanying that assignment of power to Congress is a bar on its further delegation. Congress, this Court explained early on, may not transfer to another branch "powers which are strictly and exclusively legislative." *Wayman v. Southard*, 23 U.S. (10 Wheat.) 1, 42–43 (1825). But the Constitution does not "deny[ ] to the Congress the necessary resources of flexibility and practicality [that enable it] to perform its function[s]." *Yakus v. United States*, 321 U.S. 414, 425 (1944) (internal quotation marks omitted). Congress may "obtain[ ] the assistance of its coordinate Branches"—and in particular, may confer substantial discretion on executive agencies to implement and enforce the laws. *Mistretta v. United States*, 488 U.S. 361, 372 (1989). "[I]n our increasingly complex society, replete with ever changing and more technical problems," this Court has understood that "Congress simply cannot do its job absent an ability to delegate power under broad general directives." *Ibid.* So we have held, time and again, that a statutory delegation is constitutional as long as Congress "lay[s] down by legislative act an intelligible principle to which the person or body authorized to [exercise the delegated authority] is directed to conform." *Ibid.* (quoting *J. W. Hampton, Jr., & Co. v. United States*, 276 U.S. 394, 409 (1928); brackets in original).

Given that standard, a nondelegation inquiry always begins (and often almost ends) with statutory interpretation. The constitutional question is whether Congress has supplied an intelligible principle to guide the delegee's use of discretion. So the answer requires construing the challenged statute to figure out what task it delegates and what instructions it provides. Only after a court has determined a challenged statute's meaning can it decide whether the law sufficiently guides executive discretion to accord with Article I. And indeed, once a court interprets the statute, it may find that the constitutional question all but answers itself.

That is the case here, because § 20913(d) does not give the Attorney General anything like the "unguided" and "unchecked" authority that Gundy says. Brief for Petitioner 37, 45. The provision, in Gundy's view, "grants the Attorney General plenary power to determine SORNA's applicability to pre-Act offenders—to require them to register, or not, as she sees fit, and to change her policy for any reason and at any time." *Id.*, at 42. If that were so, we would face a nondelegation question. But it is not. This Court has already interpreted § 20913(d) to say something different—to require the Attorney General to apply SORNA to all pre-Act offenders as soon as feasible. *See Reynolds* [*v. United States*], 565 U.S. [432,] 442–443 [2012]. And revisiting that issue yet more fully today, we reach the same conclusion. The text, considered alongside its context, purpose, and history, makes clear that the *2124 Attorney General's discretion extends only to considering and addressing feasibility issues. Given that statutory meaning, Gundy's constitutional claim must fail. Section 20913(d)'s delegation falls well within permissible bounds.

A

This is not the first time this Court has had to interpret *Reynolds* § 20913(d). In *Reynolds*, the Court considered whether SORNA's registration requirements applied of their own force to pre-Act offenders or instead applied only once the Attorney General said they did. We read the statute as adopting the latter approach. But even as we did so, we made clear how far SORNA limited the Attorney General's authority. And in that way, we effectively resolved the case now before us.

Everything in *Reynolds* started from the premise that Congress meant for SORNA's registration requirements to apply to pre-Act offenders * * *.

But * * * "[I]nstantaneous registration" of pre-Act offenders "might not prove feasible," or "[a]t least Congress might well have so thought." *Id.*, at 440–441, 443 * * *. Some pre-Act offenders (as defined by SORNA) had never needed to register before; others had once had to register, but had fulfilled their old obligations. And still others (the "lost" or "missing" offenders) should have registered, but had escaped the system. As a result, SORNA created a "practical problem[ ]": It would require "newly registering or reregistering a large number of pre-Act offenders." *Reynolds*, 565 U.S. at 440 (internal quotation marks omitted). And attached to that broad feasibility concern was a more technical one. Recall that under SORNA "a sex offender must initially register before completing his 'sentence of imprisonment.' " *Id.*, at 439 (quoting § 20913(b)). But many pre-Act offenders were already out of prison, so could not comply with that requirement. That inability raised questions about "how[ ] the new registration requirements applied to them." 565 U.S. at 441. "Congress['s] solution" to both those difficulties was the same: Congress "[a]sk[ed] the Department of Justice, charged with responsibility for implementation, to examine [the issues] and to apply the new registration requirements accordingly." *Ibid.*

On that understanding, the Attorney General's role under § 20913(d) was important but limited: It was to apply SORNA to pre-Act offenders as soon as he thought it feasible to do so * * * Reasonably read, SORNA enabled the Attorney General only to address (as appropriate) the "practical problems" involving pre-Act offenders before requiring them to register. *Id.*, at 440. The delegation was a stopgap, and nothing more * * *.

* * * [*Editors' Note: After a lengthy discussion of SORNA's language, legislative history, and purpose, the Court reaffirms what it thinks was previously held in* Reynolds:] the whole of § 20913(d) joins the rest of SORNA in giving the Attorney General only time-limited latitude to excuse pre-Act offenders from the statute's requirements. Under the law, he had to order their registration as soon as feasible * * *.

Now that we have determined what § 20913(d) means, we can consider whether it violates the Constitution. The question becomes: Did Congress make an impermissible delegation when it instructed the Attorney General to apply SORNA's registration requirements to pre-Act offenders as soon as feasible? Under this Court's long-established law, that question is easy. Its answer is no.

As noted earlier, this Court has held that a delegation is constitutional so long as Congress has set out an "intelligible principle" to guide the delegee's exercise of authority. *J. W. Hampton, Jr., & Co.*, 276 U.S. at 409. Or in a related formulation, the Court has stated that a delegation is permissible if Congress has made clear to the delegee "the general policy" he must pursue and the "boundaries of [his] authority." *American Power & Light*, 329 U.S. at 105. Those standards, the Court has made clear, are not demanding * * *. Only twice in this country's history (and that in a single year) have we found a delegation excessive—in each case because "Congress had failed to articulate *any* policy or standard" to confine discretion. *Mistretta*, 488 U.S. at 373, n. 7 (emphasis added). By contrast, we have over and over upheld even very broad delegations. Here is a sample: We have approved delegations to various agencies to regulate in the "public interest." We have sustained authorizations for agencies to set "fair and equitable" prices and "just and reasonable" rates. We more recently affirmed a delegation to an agency to issue whatever air quality standards are "requisite to protect the public health." And so forth.

In that context, the delegation in SORNA easily passes muster * * *. The statute conveyed Congress's policy that the Attorney General require pre-Act offenders to register as soon as feasible. Under the law, the feasibility issues he could address were administrative—and, more specifically, transitional—in nature * * *. That statutory authority, as compared to the delegations we have upheld in the past, is distinctly small-bore. It falls well within constitutional bounds.

Indeed, if SORNA's delegation is unconstitutional, then most of Government is unconstitutional—dependent as Congress is on the need to give discretion to executive officials to implement its programs * * *. Among the judgments often left to executive officials are ones involving feasibility. In fact, standards of that kind are ubiquitous in the U.S. Code. See, e.g., 12 U.S.C. § 1701z–2(a) (providing that the Secretary of Housing and Urban Development "shall require, to the greatest extent feasible, the employment of new and improved technologies, methods, and materials in housing construction[ ] under [HUD] programs"); 47 U.S.C. § 903(d)(1) (providing that "the Secretary of Commerce shall promote efficient and cost-effective use of the spectrum to the maximum extent feasible" in "assigning frequencies for mobile radio services"). In those delegations, Congress gives its delegee the flexibility to deal with real-world constraints in carrying out his charge. So too in SORNA.

It is wisdom and humility alike that this Court has always upheld such "necessities of government." *Mistretta,* 488 U.S. at 416 (Scalia, J., dissenting) (internal quotation marks omitted) We therefore affirm the judgment of the Court of Appeals.

It is so ordered.

■ JUSTICE KAVANAGH took no part in the consideration or decision of this case.

■ JUSTICE ALITO, concurring in the judgment.

The Constitution confers on Congress certain "legislative [p]owers," Art. I, § 1, and does not permit Congress to delegate them to another branch of the Government. Nevertheless, since 1935, the Court has uniformly rejected nondelegation arguments and has upheld provisions that authorized agencies to adopt important rules pursuant to extraordinarily capacious standards.

If a majority of this Court were willing to reconsider the approach we have taken for the past 84 years, I would support that effort. But because a majority is not willing to do that, it would be freakish to single out the provision at issue here for special treatment.

Because I cannot say that the statute lacks a discernable standard that is adequate under the approach this Court has taken for many years, I vote to affirm.

■ JUSTICE GORSUCH, with whom THE CHIEF JUSTICE and JUSTICE THOMAS join, dissenting.

The Constitution promises that only the people's elected representatives may adopt new federal laws restricting liberty. Yet the statute before us scrambles that design. It purports to endow the nation's chief prosecutor with the power to write his own criminal code governing the lives of a half-million citizens. Yes, those affected are some of the least popular among us. But if a single executive branch official can write laws restricting the liberty of this group of persons, what does that mean for the next?

Today, a plurality of an eight-member Court endorses this extraconstitutional arrangement but resolves nothing. Working from an understanding of the Constitution at war with its text and history, the plurality reimagines the terms of the statute before us and insists there is nothing wrong with Congress handing off so much power to the Attorney General. But Justice ALITO supplies the fifth vote for today's judgment and he does not join either the plurality's constitutional or statutory analysis, indicating instead that he remains willing, in a future case with a full Court, to revisit these matters. Respectfully, I would not wait.

I

For individuals convicted of sex offenses after Congress adopted the Sex Offender Registration and Notification Act (SORNA) in 2006, the statute offers detailed instructions * * *.

But what about those convicted of sex offenses before the Act's adoption? At the time of SORNA's enactment, the nation's population of sex offenders exceeded 500,000, and Congress concluded that something had to be done about these "pre-Act" offenders too. But it seems Congress couldn't agree what that should be. The treatment of pre-Act offenders proved a "controversial issue with major policy significance and practical ramifications for states." Among other things, applying SORNA immediately to this group threatened to impose unpopular and costly burdens on States and localities by forcing them to adopt or overhaul their own sex offender registration schemes. So Congress simply passed the problem to the Attorney General. For all half-million pre-Act offenders, the law says only this, in 34 U.S.C. § 20913(d):

> "The Attorney General shall have the authority to specify the applicability of the requirements of this subchapter to sex offenders convicted before the enactment of this chapter . . . and to prescribe rules for the registration of any such sex offender."

Yes, that's it. The breadth of the authority Congress granted to the Attorney General in these few words can only be described as vast * * *. Congress thus gave the Attorney General free rein to write the rules for virtually the entire existing sex offender population in this country—a situation that promised to persist for years or decades until pre-Act offenders passed away or fulfilled the terms of their registration obligations and post-Act offenders came to predominate * * *.

These unbounded policy choices have profound consequences for the people they affect. Take our case. Before SORNA's enactment, Herman Gundy pleaded guilty in 2005 to a sexual offense. After his release from prison five years later, he was arrested again, this time for failing to register as a sex offender according to the rules the Attorney General had then prescribed for pre-Act offenders. As a result, Mr. Gundy faced an additional 10-year prison term—10 years more than if the Attorney General had, in his discretion, chosen to write the rules differently.

II

A

Our founding document begins by declaring that "We the People . . . ordain and establish this Constitution." At the time, that was a radical claim, an assertion that sovereignty belongs not to a person or institution or class but to the whole of the people. From that premise, the Constitution proceeded to vest the authority to exercise different aspects of the people's sovereign power in distinct entities. In Article I, the Constitution entrusted all of the federal government's legislative power to Congress. In Article II, it assigned the executive power to the President. And in Article III, it gave independent judges the task of applying the laws to cases and controversies.

To the framers, each of these vested powers had a distinct content. When it came to the legislative power, the framers understood it to mean the power to adopt generally applicable rules of conduct governing future actions by private persons—the power to "prescrib[e] the rules by which the duties and rights of every citizen are to be regulated," or the power to "prescribe general rules for the government of society." * * *

Why did the framers insist on this particular arrangement? They believed the new federal government's most dangerous power was the power to enact laws restricting the people's liberty. An "excess of law-making" was, in their words, one of "the diseases to which our governments are most liable." To address that tendency, the framers went to great lengths to make lawmaking difficult. In Article I, by far the longest part of the Constitution, the framers insisted that any proposed law must win the approval of two Houses of Congress—elected at different times, by different constituencies, and for different terms in office—and either secure the President's approval or obtain enough support to override his veto. Some occasionally complain about Article I's detailed and arduous processes for new legislation, but to the framers these were bulwarks of liberty.

Nor was the point only to limit the government's capacity to restrict the people's freedoms. Article I's detailed processes for new laws were also designed to promote deliberation. "The oftener the measure is brought under examination," Hamilton explained, "the greater the diversity in the situations of those who are to examine it," and "the less must be the danger of those errors which flow from want of due deliberation, or of those missteps which proceed from the contagion of some common passion or interest."

Other purposes animated the framers' design as well. Because men are not angels and majorities can threaten minority rights, the framers insisted on a legislature composed of different bodies subject to different electorates as a means of ensuring that any new law would have to secure the approval of a supermajority of the people's representatives. This, in turn, assured minorities that their votes would often decide the fate of proposed legislation. Indeed, some even thought a Bill of Rights would prove unnecessary in light of the Constitution's design; in their view, sound structures forcing "[a]mbition [to] . . . counteract ambition" would do more than written promises to guard unpopular minorities from the tyranny of the majority. Restricting the task of legislating to one branch characterized by difficult and deliberative processes was also designed to promote fair notice and the rule of law, ensuring the people would be subject to a relatively stable and predictable set of rules. And by directing that legislating be done only by elected representatives in a public process, the Constitution sought to ensure that the lines of accountability would be clear: The sovereign people would know, without ambiguity, whom to hold accountable for the laws they would have to follow.

If Congress could pass off its legislative power to the executive branch, the "[v]esting [c]lauses, and indeed the entire structure of the Constitution," would "make no sense." Without the involvement of representatives from across the country or the demands of bicameralism and presentment, legislation would risk becoming nothing more than the will of the current President. And if laws could be simply declared by a single person, they would not be few in number, the product of widespread social consensus, likely to protect minority interests, or apt to provide stability and fair notice. Accountability would suffer too. Legislators might seek to take credit for addressing a pressing social problem by sending it to the executive for resolution, while at the same time blaming the executive for the problems that attend whatever measures he chooses to pursue. In turn, the executive might point to Congress as the source of the problem. These opportunities for finger-pointing might prove temptingly advantageous for the politicians involved, but they would also threaten to " 'disguise . . . responsibility for . . . the decisions.' "

* * * The framers knew * * * that the job of keeping the legislative power confined to the legislative branch couldn't be trusted to self-policing by Congress; often enough, legislators will face rational incentives to pass problems to the executive branch * * *. So when a case or controversy comes within the judicial competence, the Constitution does not permit judges to look the other way; we must call foul when the constitutional lines are crossed. Indeed, the framers afforded us independence from the political branches in large part to encourage exactly this kind of "fortitude . . . to do [our] duty as faithful guardians of the Constitution."

B

Accepting, then, that we have an obligation to decide whether Congress has unconstitutionally divested itself of its legislative responsibilities, the question follows: What's the test? Madison acknowledged that "no skill in the science of government has yet been able to discriminate and define, with sufficient certainty, its three great provinces—the legislative, executive, and judiciary." Chief Justice Marshall agreed that policing the separation of powers "is a subject of delicate and difficult inquiry." Still, the framers took this responsibility seriously and offered us important guiding principles.

First, we know that as long as Congress makes the policy decisions when regulating private conduct, it may authorize another branch to "fill up the details." In *Wayman v. Southard* * * * Chief Justice Marshall distinguished between those "important subjects, which must be entirely regulated by the legislature itself," and "those of less interest, in which a general provision may be made, and power given to those who are to act . . . to fill up the details." The Court upheld the statute before it because Congress had announced the controlling general policy when it ordered federal courts to follow state procedures, and the residual authority to make "alterations and additions" did no more than permit courts to fill up the details * * *.

Second, once Congress prescribes the rule governing private conduct, it may make the application of that rule depend on executive fact-finding * * *. In *Cargo of Brig Aurora v. United States*, this Court explained that it could "see no sufficient reason, why the legislature should not exercise its discretion [to impose an embargo] either expressly or conditionally, as their judgment should direct." Half a century later, Congress likewise made the construction of the Brooklyn Bridge depend on a finding by the Secretary of War that the bridge wouldn't interfere with navigation of the East River. The Court held that Congress "did not abdicate any of its authority" but "simply declared that, upon a certain fact being established, the bridge should be deemed a lawful structure, and employed the secretary of war as an agent to ascertain that fact."

Third, Congress may assign the executive and judicial branches certain non-legislative responsibilities. While the Constitution vests all federal legislative power in Congress alone, Congress's legislative authority sometimes overlaps with authority the Constitution separately vests in another branch. So, for example, when a congressional statute confers wide discretion to the executive, no separation-of-powers problem may arise if "the discretion is to be exercised over matters already within the scope of executive power." Though the case was decided on different grounds, the foreign-affairs-related statute in *Cargo of the Brig Aurora* may be an example of this kind of permissible lawmaking, given that many foreign affairs powers are constitutionally vested in the president under Article II. *Wayman* itself might be explained by the same principle as applied to the judiciary: Even in the absence of any statute, courts have the power under Article III "to regulate their practice."

C

Before the 1930s, federal statutes granting authority to the executive were comparatively modest and usually easily upheld. But then the federal government began to grow explosively. And with the proliferation of new executive programs

came new questions about the scope of congressional delegations. Twice the Court responded by striking down statutes for violating the separation of powers * * *.

After *Schechter Poultry* and *Panama Refining*, Congress responded by writing a second wave of New Deal legislation more "[c]arefully crafted" to avoid the kind of problems that sank these early statutes. And since that time the Court hasn't held another statute to violate the separation of powers in the same way. Of course, no one thinks that the Court's quiescence can be attributed to an unwavering new tradition of more scrupulously drawn statutes. Some lament that the real cause may have to do with a mistaken "case of death by association" because *Schechter Poultry* and *Panama Refining* happened to be handed down during the same era as certain of the Court's now-discredited substantive due process decisions. But maybe the most likely explanation of all lies in the story of the evolving "intelligible principle" doctrine.

This Court first used that phrase in 1928 in *J. W. Hampton, Jr., & Co. v. United States*, where it remarked that a statute "lay[ing] down by legislative act an intelligible principle to which the [executive official] is directed to conform" satisfies the separation of powers. No one at the time thought the phrase meant to effect some revolution in this Court's understanding of the Constitution. While the exact line between policy and details, lawmaking and fact-finding, and legislative and non-legislative functions had sometimes invited reasonable debate, everyone agreed these were the relevant inquiries. And when Chief Justice Taft wrote of an "intelligible principle," it seems plain enough that he sought only to explain the operation of these traditional tests; he gave no hint of a wish to overrule or revise them. Tellingly, too, he wrote the phrase seven years before *Schechter Poultry* and *Panama Refining*, and it did nothing to alter the analysis in those cases, let alone prevent those challenges from succeeding by lopsided votes * * *.

* * * [I]t's undeniable that the "intelligible principle" remark eventually began to take on a life of its own. We sometimes chide people for treating judicial opinions as if they were statutes, divorcing a passing comment from its context, ignoring all that came before and after, and treating an isolated phrase as if it were controlling. But that seems to be exactly what happened here. For two decades, no one thought to invoke the "intelligible principle" comment as a basis to uphold a statute that would have failed more traditional separation-of-powers tests. In fact, the phrase sat more or less silently entombed until the late 1940s. Only then did lawyers begin digging it up in earnest and arguing to this Court that it had somehow displaced (sub silentio of course) all prior teachings in this area.

This mutated version of the "intelligible principle" remark has no basis in the original meaning of the Constitution, in history, or even in the decision from which it was plucked * * *.

* * * To determine whether a statute provides an intelligible principle, we must ask: Does the statute assign to the executive only the responsibility to make factual findings? Does it set forth the facts that the executive must consider and the criteria against which to measure them? And most importantly, did Congress, and not the Executive Branch, make the policy judgments? Only then can we fairly say that a statute contains the kind of intelligible principle the Constitution demands * * *.

III

A

Returning to SORNA with this understanding of our charge in hand, problems quickly emerge. Start with this one: It's hard to see how SORNA leaves the Attorney General with only details to fill up. Of course, what qualifies as a detail can sometimes be difficult to discern and, as we've seen, this Court has upheld statutes that allow federal agencies to resolve even highly consequential details so long as Congress prescribes the rule governing private conduct. But it's hard to see how the statute before us could be described as leaving the Attorney General with only details to dispatch * * *. Because members of Congress could not reach consensus on the treatment of pre-Act offenders, it seems this was one of those situations where they found it expedient to hand off the job to the executive and direct there the blame for any later problems that might emerge.

Nor can SORNA be described as an example of conditional legislation subject to executive fact-finding. To be sure, Congress could have easily written this law in that way. It might have required all pre-Act offenders to register, but then given the Attorney General the authority to make case-by-case exceptions for offenders who do not present an " 'imminent hazard to the public safety' " comparable to that posed by newly released post-Act offenders. It could have set criteria to inform that determination, too, asking the executive to investigate, say, whether an offender's risk of recidivism correlates with the time since his last offense, or whether multiple lesser offenses indicate higher or lower risks than a single greater offense.

But SORNA did none of this * * *. Far from deciding the factual predicates to a rule set forth by statute, the Attorney General himself acknowledges that the law entitles him to make his own policy decisions.

Finally, SORNA does not involve an area of overlapping authority with the executive. Congress may assign the President broad authority regarding the conduct of foreign affairs or other matters where he enjoys his own inherent Article II powers. But SORNA stands far afield from any of that. It gives the Attorney General the authority to "prescrib[e] the rules by which the duties and rights" of citizens are determined, a quintessentially legislative power * * *.

It would be easy enough to let this case go. After all, sex offenders are one of the most disfavored groups in our society. But the rule that prevents Congress from giving the executive carte blanche to write laws for sex offenders is the same rule that protects everyone else. Nor is it hard to imagine how the power at issue in this case—the power of a prosecutor to require a group to register with the government on pain of weighty criminal penalties—could be abused in other settings. To allow the nation's chief law enforcement officer to write the criminal laws he is charged with enforcing—to " 'unit[e]' " the " 'legislative and executive powers . . . in the same person' "—would be to mark the end of any meaningful enforcement of our separation of powers and invite the tyranny of the majority that follows when lawmaking and law enforcement responsibilities are united in the same hands.

Nor would enforcing the Constitution's demands spell doom for what some call the "administrative state." The separation of powers does not prohibit any particular policy outcome, let alone dictate any conclusion about the proper size and scope of government. Instead, it is a procedural guarantee that requires Congress to assemble a social consensus before choosing our nation's course on policy questions like those implicated by SORNA. What is more, Congress is hardly bereft of options to accomplish all it might wish to achieve. It may always authorize executive branch officials to fill in even a large number of details, to find facts that trigger the generally applicable rule of conduct specified in a statute, or to exercise non-legislative powers. Congress can also commission agencies or other experts to study and recommend legislative language. Respecting the separation of powers forecloses no substantive outcomes. It only requires us to respect along the way one of the most vital of the procedural protections of individual liberty found in our Constitution.

[*Editors' Note: In a lengthy discussion, Justice Gorsuch disagreed that SORNA could be interpreted to contain an unexpressed requirement that the Attorney General register all pre-Act offenders as soon as feasible.*] * * *

* * * In a future case with a full panel, I remain hopeful that the Court may yet recognize that, while Congress can enlist considerable assistance from the executive branch in filling up details and finding facts, it may never hand off to the nation's chief prosecutor the power to write his own criminal code. That "is delegation running riot."

NOTES AND QUESTIONS

1. If Justice Kavanaugh had participated in the case and joined Justice Gorsuch's dissenting opinion, would Justice Alito have joined as well? Did Justice Alito say that he would have joined Justice Gorsuch's opinion?

2. Consider Justice Gorsuch's proposed test for identifying unconstitutional subdelegations. Is it any different from Chief Justice Marshall's distinction between "important subjects" and matters of "less interest"? Is a better formulation than Chief Justice Marshall's available? Neither of us thinks so:

> I have elsewhere proposed as the appropriate nondelegation principle: "Congress must make whatever policy decisions are sufficiently important to the statutory scheme at issue so that Congress must make them." In other words, Chief Justice Marshall's circular formulation was right all along, and rather than wind our way back to it indirectly, we might as well take the freeway. The line between legislative and executive power (or between legislative and judicial power) must be drawn in the context of each particular statutory scheme. In every case, Congress must make the central, fundamental decisions, but Congress can leave ancillary matters to the President or the courts. One can try to find alternative ways to express the distinction between fundamental and ancillary matters, such as focusing on case-resolving power or demonstration of political commitment or choices among salient alternatives, but in the end, one cannot really get behind or beneath the fact that law execution and application involve discretion in matters of "less interest" but turn into legislation when that discretion extends to "important subjects." That is the line that the Constitution draws, and there is no escape from it.

Gary Lawson, *Delegation and Original Meaning,* 88 VA. L. REV. 327, 376–77 (2002).

3. Go back to *Mistretta* and our Note preceding it and look at the agency-empowering statutes that have been upheld over the past eight decades. Then re-read Justice Gorsuch's dissenting opinion in *Gundy*. How many of those statutes from the discussion in *Mistretta* would survive Justice Gorsuch's test for constitutionality? How many of those statutes, some of which are central to the modern administrative state,

does Justice Gorsuch specifically address in his opinion? We heavily edited his opinion, but we did not edit out any discussion relevant to this question.

[Assignment 10]

V. THE CONGRESS OF THE UNITED STATES

Article I, Section 1: All legislative Powers herein granted shall be vested in a Congress of the United States, which shall consist of a Senate and House of Representatives.

A. BICAMERALISM AND CONGRESSIONAL STRUCTURE

Article I vests all legislative powers herein granted "in a Congress of the United States, which shall consist of a Senate and House of Representatives." The Constitution thus creates a bicameral—or two-chambered—Congress. The Framers had grown accustomed to bicameralism between 1607 and 1776. Twelve of the thirteen colonies had a popularly elected lower assembly, and an aristocratic upper house (the Governor's council). In his very influential *Thoughts on Government* in 1776, John Adams urged the drafters of new state constitutions to opt for bicameralism. *See supra* pages 65–67. John Adams favored bicameralism because he thought it would guard against decisions being made precipitously, in the heat and passions of the moment. Ninc of the eleven States which wrote new constitutions between 1776 and 1787 opted for a bicameral legislature. Pennsylvania and Georgia initially opted for unicameral legislatures. Pennsylvania did so in part because Benjamin Franklin thought it was desirable, based on the dubious advice of the French philosophes, and in part because Pennsylvania's colonial legislature had been unicameral. In 1791, Pennsylvania adopted a new state constitution with a bicameral state legislature, as had Georgia in 1789, and today every State except Nebraska has a bicameral state legislature.

Bicameral legislatures are common in federations all over the world. Most bicameral legislatures follow what Yale Law Professor Bruce Ackerman calls the "one and one-half house" solution of having a lower house which elects the Prime Minister and an upper house with limited powers. *See* Bruce Ackerman, *The New Separation of Powers*, 113 Harv. L. Rev. 633, 635 (2000). This is true of the bicameral legislatures of the United Kingdom, France, Germany, Japan, India, Canada, Australia, and the European Union. The United States Constitution, as we shall see, is unique in making the smaller and longer-serving Senate (the "upper" house) more powerful than the larger and more popularly responsive House of Representatives (the "lower" house).

The two houses of Congress must cooperate in order to enact legislation, *see* U.S. CONST. art. I, § 7, cls. 2–3, but each chamber has its own constitutional role as well. The Senate, but not the House of Representatives, participates in the treaty-making and appointment process. *See id.* art. II, § 2, cl. 2. The House, but not the Senate, can impeach executive and judicial officials. *See id.* art. I, § 2, cl. 5. The Senate, but not the House, can convict impeached officials and remove them from office. *See id.* art. I, § 3, cl. 6. The House, but not the Senate, can originate tax legislation. *See id.* art. I, § 7, cl. 1. Importantly, the two chambers are also differently constructed and differently elected.

The House "shall be composed of Members chosen every second Year by the People of the several States," *id.* art. I, § 2, cl. 1, and representation in the House is based on state population, though with each State guaranteed at least one representative. *See id.* art. I, § 2, cl. 3; Amend. XIV § 2. The Constitution of 1788 specified an initial distribution among the States of sixty-five representatives, with future distributions to be based on the census every ten years. *See id.* art. I, § 2, cl. 3. The decennial census thus becomes a major political and legal event, as it can substantially affect the political influence of States by changing their representation in Congress.

The number of representatives grew as additional States were added to the country. Since 1913, the number of representatives has been statutorily fixed at 435, except for one brief period from 1958–60 when the number was 436–37, as Alaska and Hawaii were admitted with one representative each in addition to the 435 already-existing representatives. The number was restored to 435 after the 1960 census. (Why 435? Because in 1911, when the number 435—really 433 plus one for each of two new States about to be added—was picked, it was the lowest number that would accommodate the newly added States but not result in the reduction of any existing State's delegation. *See* Pamela S. Karlan, *Reapportionment, Nonapportionment, and Recovering Some Lost History of One Person, One Vote*, 59 WM. & MARY L. REV. 1921, 1934 (2018).)

The Senate "shall be composed of two Senators from each State." *Id.* art. I, § 3, cl. 1. Initially, the Senators from each State were "chosen by the Legislature thereof, for six years." *Id.* The six-year term—three times as long as the two-year term of House members—and the mandate of two senators for each State, no matter the size of the State, are still in force, but in 1913 the Seventeenth Amendment provided that a State's two senators shall be "elected by the people thereof." *Id.* amend. XVII, § 1. One might also consider the Vice President to be a quasi-member of the Senate: "The Vice President of the United States shall be President of the Senate, but shall have no Vote, unless they be equally divided." *Id.* art. I, § 3, cl. 4. The powers to preside over and break ties in the Senate are the *only* powers conferred by the Constitution on the Vice President when he or she is acting as Vice President rather than as Acting President, *see id.* amend. XX, § 3 & XXV, §§ 3–4, or as the President following the death, resignation, or removal of the prior President. *See id.* art. II, § 1, cl. 6 & amend. XXV. The Vice President is not literally a senator, so provisions of the Constitution addressed to senators, such as their method of election, do not apply to the Vice President. But neither does the Vice President have any constitutionally vested executive functions outside of being in the line of succession to the presidency; the constitutionally vested functions all involve the Senate.

For both representatives and senators, the state electorate consists of whoever elects the most numerous branch of the state legislature; whatever rules for voting the State uses for its own legislature apply as well to elections for the federal legislative offices, subject to the many constitutional and statutory rules forbidding voting discrimination on the basis of race, sex, and age. Thus, all members of Congress are elected by the people of their States. Senators, however, are elected "at large" by the entire voting population of the State, while representatives, under current practice, are elected locally by district. Nothing in the Constitution prevents House elections from also being at large, but since 1842 election of House members in States that have more than one representative has been by district. *See* Act of

June 25, 1842, ch. 47, § 2, 5 Stat. 491, 491. Thus, members of the House and Senate have somewhat different constituencies within their States.

The structure of Congress—including the size of the houses, the lengths of terms of representatives and senators, and the rules for apportionment and elections—was a major, and arguably *the* major, topic of discussion during the drafting and ratification of the Constitution. In particular, many people worried that two-year and six-year terms of office were much too long and that all legislators should stand for election every year at least; some States had elections for their legislatures every six months. Consider the following passages from *The Federalist* about the rationale for having two distinct houses (the founding generation would have called them "branches") of Congress and the distinctive features of each house.

B. FEDERALIST NO. 53 (MADISON)

* * * Where no Constitution, paramount to the government, either existed or could be obtained, no constitutional security, similar to that established in the United States, was to be attempted. Some other security, therefore, was to be sought for * * *. [H]ence the doctrine has been inculcated by a laudable zeal, to erect some barrier against the gradual innovations of an unlimited government, that the advance towards tyranny was to be calculated by the distance of departure from the fixed point of annual elections. But what necessity can there be of applying this expedient to a government limited, as the federal government will be, by the authority of a paramount Constitution? Or who will pretend that the liberties of the people of America will not be more secure under biennial elections, unalterably fixed by such a Constitution, than those of any other nation would be, where elections were annual, or even more frequent, but subject to alterations by the ordinary power of the government?

* * *

No man can be a competent legislator who does not add to an upright intention and a sound judgment a certain degree of knowledge of the subjects on which he is to legislate. A part of this knowledge may be acquired by means of information which lie within the compass of men in private as well as public stations. Another part can only be attained, or at least thoroughly attained, by actual experience in the station which requires the use of it. The period of service, ought, therefore, in all such cases, to bear some proportion to the extent of practical knowledge requisite to the due performance of the service. The period of legislative service established in most of the States for the more numerous branch is, as we have seen, one year. The question then may be put into this simple form: does the period of two years bear no greater proportion to the knowledge requisite for federal legislation than one year does to the knowledge requisite for State legislation? The very statement of the question, in this form, suggests the answer that ought to be given to it.

In a single State, the requisite knowledge relates to the existing laws which are uniform throughout the State, and with which all the citizens are more or less conversant * * *. The great theatre of the United States presents a very different scene * * *. [T]he public affairs of the Union are spread throughout a very extensive region, and are extremely diversified by the local affairs connected with them, and can with difficulty be correctly learnt in any other place than in the central councils to which a knowledge of them will be brought by the representatives of every part of the empire * * *.

C. FEDERALIST NO. 55 (MADISON)

THE number of which the House of Representatives is to consist, forms another and a very interesting point of view, under which this branch of the federal legislature may be contemplated.

Scarce any article, indeed, in the whole Constitution seems to be rendered more worthy of attention, by the weight of character and the apparent force of argument with which it has been assailed.

The charges exhibited against it are, first, that so small a number of representatives will be an unsafe depositary of the public interests; secondly, that they will not possess a proper knowledge of the local circumstances of their numerous constituents; thirdly, that they will be taken from that class of citizens which will sympathize least with the feelings of the mass of the people, and be most likely to aim at a permanent elevation of the few on the depression of the many; fourthly, that defective as the number will be in the first instance, it will be more and more disproportionate, by the increase of the people, and the obstacles which will prevent a correspondent increase of the representatives. In general it may be remarked on this subject, that no political problem is less susceptible of a precise solution than that which relates to the number most convenient for a representative legislature * * *. In all very numerous assemblies, of whatever character composed, passion never fails to wrest the sceptre from reason.

Had every Athenian citizen been a Socrates, every Athenian assembly would still have been a mob.

It is necessary also to recollect here the observations which were applied to the case of biennial elections. For the same reason that the limited powers of the Congress, * * * justify less frequent elections than the public safely might otherwise require, the members of the Congress need be less numerous than if they possessed the whole power of legislation, and were under no other than the ordinary restraints of other legislative bodies. With these general ideas in our mind, let us weigh the objections which have been stated against the number of members proposed for the House of Representatives. It is said, in the first place, that so small a number cannot be safely trusted with so much power. The number of which this branch of the legislature is to consist, at the outset of the government, will be sixty five. Within three years a census is to be taken, when the number may be augmented to one for every thirty thousand inhabitants; and within every successive period of ten years the census is to be renewed, and augmentations may continue to be made under the above limitation. It will not be thought an extravagant conjecture that the first census will, at the rate of one for every thirty thousand, raise the number of representatives to at least one hundred * * *. At the expiration of twenty-five years, according to the computed rate of increase, the number of representatives will amount to two hundred, and of fifty years, to four hundred. This is a number which, I presume, will put an end to all fears arising from the smallness of the body * * *.

NOTES AND QUESTIONS

1. Much of the founding generation worried that a two-year term for the House was too long. If Madison was right about the importance of on-the-job knowledge to the proper functioning of the House, is two years too *short* a term in this day and age? Is there any evidence that people elected to Congress, even for a very long time, acquire knowledge and wisdom from being on the job? If Madison is right, does that mean that imposing term limits on elected representatives is a bad idea? We will take up that topic shortly, so keep the question in mind.

2. As we noted before, the number of representatives for the House in the First Congress was set by the Constitution at sixty-five. As predicted by Madison, the number gradually climbed up to 243 in 1869, and it sits today at 435, where by statute it will remain after each census unless Congress specifically says otherwise. *See* Act of June 18, 1929, ch. 28, 46 Stat. 21. James Madison assumed that the number would increase with each census to provide essentially one representative for every 30,000 people. If that formula applied today, the House would have more than 10,000 representatives. As it happens, the Constitution contains a maximum size for the House ("the number of Representatives shall not exceed one for every thirty thousand"), but it contains no numerical *minimum* size for the House. A minimum was proposed at the Convention in an early draft of the Constitution which would have required at least one representative for every 40,000 people. 2 THE RECORDS OF THE FEDERAL CONVENTION OF 1787 178 (Max Farrand ed. 1911). Madison objected because "[t]he future increase of population if the Union shd. be permanent, will render the number of Representatives excessive," *id.* at 221, and the proposal was rejected in favor of a maximum rather than minimum size requirement. *See id.* The original "First Amendment" proposed in 1791 as part of the twelve amendments sent to the States for ratification also would have imposed a minimum size requirement for the House, but it failed to get the necessary votes for ratification. Today, each Member of the House represents about 700,000 citizens—a huge change from the Framers' widespread belief that there ought to be one representative for every 30,000 or 40,000 people.

3. When Madison suggested that capping the number of constituents that any House member can represent would lead to an impossibly large House, Nathaniel Gorham, who served as Chairman of the Committee of the Whole at the Convention and was one of five members of the Committee of Detail that was responsible for drafting the Constitution's final language, memorably answered Madison by saying: "It is not to be supposed that the Gov't will last so long as to produce this effect. Can it be supposed that this vast Country including the Western territory will 150 years hence remain one nation?" *Id.* A quick glance at any atlas will verify that Gorham was wrong. But as a functional matter, is the real problem with the House simply that the country has gotten too big for a single legislature? Is there an optimal size for an extended republic that the U.S. has overshot? *See* Gary Lawson, *One(?) Nation Over-Extended,* 94 B.U. L. REV. 1109 (2014).

4. Is a House in which each representative has more than 700,000 constituents consistent with a republican form of government?

D. THE SENATE

We turn now to the U.S. Senate, which is the world's most powerful upper house of a legislature. The Senate has the sole power to advise and consent to presidential nominations for appointments to federal offices, and it has the sole power to ratify, by a two-thirds majority, treaties made by the President. The Senate is the only legislative body in the world where the passage of legislation requires 60 votes rather than a majority because of the filibuster rule. *See infra* pages 255–258. The Senate is also unique because a single senator can often put a hold on a presidential nomination and tie it up for a long period of time. Consider the purposes which the Senate serves, and remember that the President and the Senate together appoint the Supreme Court justices and all other federal judges of the United States.

E. THE FEDERALIST NO. 62 (MADISON)

* * * The number of senators, and the duration of their appointment, come next to be considered. In order to form an accurate judgment on both of these points * * *, it will be necessary to review the inconveniences which a republic must suffer from the want of such an institution.

First. It is a misfortune incident to republican government, though in a less degree than to other governments, that those who administer it may forget their obligations to their constituents, and prove unfaithful to their important trust. In this point of view, a senate, as a second branch of the legislative assembly, distinct from, and dividing the power with, a first, must be in all cases a salutary check on the government. It doubles the security to the people, by requiring the concurrence of two distinct bodies in schemes of usurpation or perfidy, where the ambition or corruption of one would otherwise be sufficient * * *.

Second. The necessity of a senate is not less indicated by the propensity of all single and numerous assemblies to yield to the impulse of sudden and violent passions, and to be seduced by factious leaders into intemperate and pernicious resolutions. Examples on this subject might be cited without number; and from proceedings within the United States, as well as from the history of other nations. But a position that will not be contradicted, need not be proved. All that need be remarked is, that a body which is to correct this infirmity ought itself to be free from it, and consequently ought to be less numerous. It ought, moreover, to possess great firmness, and consequently ought to hold its authority by a tenure of considerable duration.

Third. Another defect to be supplied by a senate lies in a want of due acquaintance with the objects and principles of legislation. It is not possible that an assembly of men called for the most part from pursuits of a private nature, continued in appointment for a short time, and led by no permanent motive to devote the intervals of public occupation to a study of the laws, the affairs, and the comprehensive interests of their country, should, if left wholly to themselves, escape a variety of important errors in the exercise of their legislative trust. It may be affirmed, on the best grounds, that no small share of the present embarrassments of America is to be charged on the blunders of our governments; and that these have proceeded from the heads rather than the hearts of most of the authors of them. What indeed are all the repealing, explaining, and amending laws, which fill and disgrace our voluminous codes, but so many monuments of deficient wisdom; so many impeachments exhibited by each succeeding against each preceding session; so many admonitions to the people, of the value of those aids which may be expected from a well-constituted senate? * * *

Fourth. The mutability in the public councils arising from a rapid succession of new members, however qualified they may be, points out, in the strongest manner, the necessity of some stable institution in the government. Every new election in the States is found to change one half of the representatives. From this change of men must proceed a change of opinions; and from a change of opinions, a change of measures. But a continual change even of good measures is inconsistent with every rule of prudence and every prospect of success. The remark is verified in private life, and becomes more just, as well as more important, in national transactions * * *.

The internal effects of a mutable policy are still more calamitous. It poisons the blessing of liberty itself. It will be of little avail to the people, that the laws are made by men of their own choice, if the laws be so voluminous that they cannot be read, or so incoherent that they cannot be understood; if they be repealed or revised before they are promulgated, or undergo such incessant changes that no man, who knows what the law is to-day, can guess what it will be to-morrow. Law is defined to be a rule of action; but how can that be a rule, which is little known, and less fixed?

Another effect of public instability is the unreasonable advantage it gives to the sagacious, the enterprising, and the moneyed few over the industrious and uniformed mass of the people. Every new regulation concerning commerce or revenue, or in any way affecting the value of the different species of property, presents a new harvest to those who watch the change, and can trace its consequences; a harvest, reared not by themselves, but by the toils and cares of the great body of their fellow-citizens. This is a state of things in which it may be said with some truth that laws are made for the *few*, not for the *many*.

In another point of view, great injury results from an unstable government. The want of confidence in the public councils damps every useful undertaking, the success and profit of which may depend on a continuance of existing arrangements. What prudent merchant will hazard his fortunes in any new branch of commerce when he knows not but that his plans may be rendered unlawful before they can be executed? What farmer or manufacturer will lay himself out for the encouragement given to any particular cultivation or establishment, when he can have no assurance that his preparatory labors and advances will not render him a victim to an inconstant government? In a word, no great improvement or laudable enterprise can go forward which requires the auspices of a steady system of national policy.

F. FEDERALIST NO. 63 (HAMILTON OR MADISON)

* * * A FIFTH desideratum, illustrating the utility of a senate, is the want of a due sense of national character. Without a select and stable member of the government, the esteem of foreign powers will not only be forfeited by an unenlightened and variable policy, proceeding from the causes already mentioned, but the national councils will not possess that sensibility to the opinion of the world, which is perhaps not less necessary in order to merit, than it is to obtain, its respect and confidence.

* * * Yet however requisite a sense of national character may be, it is evident that it can never be sufficiently possessed by a numerous and changeable body. It can only be found in a number so small that a sensible degree of the praise and blame of public measures may be the portion of each individual; or in an assembly so durably invested with public trust, that the pride and consequence of its members may be sensibly incorporated with the reputation and prosperity of the community * * *.

I add, as a SIXTH defect the want, in some important cases, of a due responsibility in the government to the people, arising from that frequency of elections which in other cases produces this responsibility * * *. The objects of government may be divided into two general classes: the one depending on measures which have singly an immediate and sensible operation; the other depending on a succession of well-chosen and well-connected measures, which have a gradual and perhaps unobserved operation. The importance of the latter description to the collective and permanent welfare of every country, needs no explanation. And yet it is evident that an assembly elected for so short a term as to be unable to provide more than one or two links in a chain of measures, on which the general welfare may essentially depend, ought not to be answerable for the final result, any more than a steward or tenant, engaged for one year, could be justly made to answer for places or improvements which could not be accomplished in less than half a dozen years * * *.

The proper remedy for this defect must be an additional body in the legislative department, which, having sufficient permanency to provide for such objects as require a continued attention, and a train of measures, may be justly and effectually answerable for the attainment of those objects.

It adds no small weight to all these considerations, to recollect that history informs us of no long-lived republic which had not a senate. Sparta, Rome, and Carthage are, in fact, the only states to whom that character can be applied * * *. I am not unaware of the circumstances which distinguish the American from other popular governments, as well ancient as modern; and which render extreme circumspection necessary, in reasoning from the one case to the other. But after allowing due weight to this consideration, it may still be maintained, that there are many points of similitude which render these examples not unworthy of our attention * * *.

In answer to all these arguments, suggested by reason, illustrated by examples, and enforced by our own experience, the jealous adversary of the Constitution will probably content himself with repeating, that a senate appointed not immediately by the people, and for the term of six years, must gradually acquire a dangerous pre-eminence in the government, and finally transform it into a tyrannical aristocracy.

To this general answer, the general reply ought to be sufficient, that liberty may be endangered by the abuses of liberty as well as by the abuses of power; that there are numerous instances of the former as well as of the latter; and that the former, rather than the latter, are apparently most to be apprehended by the United States * * *.

Besides the conclusive evidence resulting from this assemblage of facts, that the federal Senate will never be able to transform itself, by gradual usurpations, into an independent and aristocratic body, we are warranted in believing, that if such a revolution should ever happen from causes which the foresight of man cannot guard against, the House of Representatives, with the people on their side, will at all times be able to bring back the Constitution to its primitive form and principles. Against the force of the immediate representatives of the people, nothing will be able to maintain even the constitutional authority of the Senate, but such a display of enlightened policy, and attachment to the public good, as will divide with that branch of the legislature the affections and support of the entire body of the people themselves.

NOTES AND QUESTIONS

1. In the modern era, the Senate has by far been the most functional of the two Houses of Congress. The House of Representatives is bitterly partisan; the minority in the House plays almost no role greater than do private citizens, and the House seems permanently divided into 40% radical conservatives from safe districts who only fear a primary challenge from the right and 40% radical progressives from safe districts who only fear a primary challenge from the left. The remaining 20% hold swing seats that can put either of the two major parties in power, but they lack the political leverage to get very much done.

2. The Senate tends to be more moderate than the House, for a quite simple reason: senators have to win in a statewide election in which, in most States, millions of people vote, whereas representatives must only win in a district, where, on average, 700,000 people vote. The median State has a population of 4,700,000 people. On balance, a larger population will, as James Madison argued in *The Federalist* No. 10, be divided into more factions and interest groups than will be a smaller population. Assembling a 51% majority will often require more moderation in a State with 4,700,000 people than in a congressional district with 700,000 people who perhaps share distinctive urban, suburban, or rural outlooks. The net result is that both Republican and Democratic senators are, on average, more moderate than are Republican and Democratic members of the House of Representatives. This explains why sixteen former or sitting U.S. senators have been elected President. If one excludes, as one should, members of the House of Representatives who have also served as Vice President, as a senator, as a governor, or as a general, only one former member of the House of Representatives has been elected President of the United States: Abraham Lincoln.

3. In 1788, the ratio of representatives to senators was 2.5/1 (65/26). Today the ratio is 4.35/1. Is that ratio significant? As an absolute matter, the Senate today is almost four times the size of the Senate in 1788. Do the advantages of small size envisioned by the Founders apply to the modern Senate?

4. The English House of Lords was an openly aristocratic body whose function was to preserve the interests of large property owners. Is the Senate, which surely represents the republican incarnation of the Few in classical governmental theory, materially different from the House of Lords? Would *The Federalist's* arguments for a Senate equally support a House of Lords?

[Assignment 11]

G. ARTICLE I, SECTIONS 2, 3, AND 5: QUALIFICATIONS TO BE A MEMBER OF THE SENATE OR THE HOUSE

Section 2, Clause 2: No Person shall be a Representative who shall not have attained to the Age of twenty five Years, and been seven Years a Citizen of the United States, and who shall not, when elected, be an Inhabitant of that State in which he shall be chosen.

Section 3, Clause 3: No Person shall be a Senator who shall not have attained to the age of thirty Years, and been nine Years a Citizen of the United States and who shall not, when elected, be an Inhabitant of that State for which he shall be chosen.

Section 5: Each House shall be the Judge of the Elections, Returns and Qualifications of its own Members * * *. Each House

may determine the Rules of its Proceedings, punish its Members for disorderly Behavior, and, with the Concurrence of two thirds, expel a Member.

Article I, section 1 consists of a single sentence that vests all legislative powers herein granted in a Congress of the United States, which shall consist of a House of Representatives and a Senate. Article I, section 2, by contrast, contains five distinct clauses, some of which perform more than one function.

The first two clauses address the length of terms and eligibility requirements for members of the House, and the first three clauses of Article I, section 3 contain parallel provisions for the Senate. The constitutional text is clear on term lengths: fixed terms of two years for representatives and six years for senators. Importantly, the Constitution diverges dramatically from the Articles of Confederation's conception of the legislature, under which members of the Continental Congress were paid, and could be recalled, by their States. The Constitution also rejects term limits whereas the Articles of Confederation explicitly embraced them. The Constitution's fixed terms of office prevent recall, and Article I, Section 6 provides that senators and representatives "shall receive a Compensation for their Services, to be ascertained by Law, and *paid out of the Treasury of the United States*" (emphasis added).

After providing for the terms of office, and defining the electorate for congressional elections,[3] the Constitution next addresses the qualifications for congressional office-holding, again with a parallel provision for the Senate in Article I, section 3 and an important provision concerning Congress's power over its membership in Article I, section 5. Read carefully the constitutional text concerning who can serve in Congress, which appears above.

While these provisions would seem to be clear cut, they do pose some very intriguing interpretative questions. First, are the three listed qualifications the *exclusive* qualifications for congressional office-holding? In other words, can either Congress or the States add *additional* qualifications for holding office? Second, does Congress's power to "expel a Member" contain any limitations on the grounds for expulsion? Can Congress expel a Member because a two-thirds majority does not like his or her policy views (or his or her race, sex, or religion)? Third, do federal courts have any power to adjudicate either of these questions? For example, the Constitution says point-blank in Article VI that "no religious Test shall ever be required as a Qualification to any Office or public Trust under the United States." If Congress expels a Member for being Catholic, can the courts hear a challenge to that action?

---

3 After ratification of the Seventeenth Amendment in 1913, the electorate for both the House and Senate is the electorate for "the most numerous Branch of the State Legislature." Whatever voting qualifications a State provides for election of its own lower chamber apply as well to elections for Congress. That certainly forbids States from having *stricter* voting rules for Congress than for its own legislature. But does it also forbid States from having *looser* voting rules for Congress than for its own elected offices? A simple reading of the text would suggest "yes," because the Constitution seems straightforwardly to call for complete equivalence in voter qualifications. Indeed, it is hard to imagine how one could write the provision more clearly to require complete equivalence. Nonetheless, in one of its oddest decisions ever, the Supreme Court has held that States can have different electorates for the state legislature and Congress so long as the state-office rules are stricter. *See* Tashjian v. Republican Party of Connecticut, 479 U.S. 208 (1987).

Recall from *Marbury v. Madison* that Chief Justice Marshall described cases in which "the President is invested with certain important political powers, in the exercise of which he is to use his own discretion, and is accountable only to his country in his political character and to his own conscience." There are, in other words, certain governmental decisions which "can never be examinable by the Courts." As we will see later in the course, a body of doctrine has arisen over the past two centuries that tries to identify so-called "political questions" over which courts simply have no jurisdiction, no matter how egregious the governmental decision may be. *See infra* pages 556–576. For now, it is enough to know that the governing doctrinal test says that a case presents a nonjusticiable "political question" when there is "a textually demonstrable constitutional commitment of the issue to a coordinate political department; or a lack of judicially discoverable and manageable standards for resolving it; or the impossibility of deciding without an initial policy determination of a kind clearly for nonjudicial discretion; or the impossibility of a court's undertaking independent resolution without expressing lack of the respect due coordinate branches of government; or an unusual need for unquestioning adherence to a political decision already made; or the potentiality of embarrassment from multifarious pronouncements by various departments on one question." *Baker v. Carr,* 369 U.S. 186, 217 (1962). Courts very seldom conclude that constitutional cases present "political questions" that courts have no power to address. (Should *Youngstown* have been nonjusticiable under this standard?) Consider whether the following case concerning Congress's powers over its membership presented one.

H. POWELL V. MCCORMACK

395 U.S. 486 (1969)

■ MR. CHIEF JUSTICE WARREN delivered the opinion of the Court.

In November 1966, petitioner Adam Clayton Powell, Jr., was duly elected from the 18th Congressional District of New York to serve in the United States House of Representatives for the 90th Congress. However, pursuant to a House resolution, he was not permitted to take his seat. Powell * * * filed suit in Federal District Court, claiming that the House could exclude him only if it found he failed to meet the standing requirements of age, citizenship, and residence contained in Art. I, § 2, of the Constitution—requirements the House specifically found Powell met—and thus had excluded him unconstitutionally. We have determined that * * * petitioner Powell is entitled to a declaratory judgment that he was unlawfully excluded from the 90th Congress.

During the 89th Congress, a Special Subcommittee on Contracts of the Committee on House Administration conducted an investigation into the expenditures of the Committee on Education and Labor, of which petitioner Adam Clayton Powell, Jr., was chairman. The Special Subcommittee issued a report concluding that Powell and certain staff employees had deceived the House authorities as to travel expenses. The report also indicated there was strong evidence that certain illegal salary payments had been made to Powell's wife at his direction. No formal action was taken during the 89th Congress. However, prior to the organization of the 90th Congress, the Democratic members-elect met in caucus and voted to remove Powell as chairman of the Committee on Education and Labor.

When the 90th Congress met to organize in January 1967, Powell was asked to step aside while the oath was administered to the other members-elect. Following the administration of the oath to the remaining members, the House discussed the procedure to be followed in determining whether Powell was eligible to take his seat. After some debate, by a vote of 363 to 65 the House adopted House Resolution No. 1, which provided that the Speaker appoint a Select Committee to determine Powell's eligibility. Although the resolution prohibited Powell from taking his seat until the House acted on the Select Committee's report, it did provide that he should receive all the pay and allowances due a member during the period.

* * *

[After extensive proceedings, the Select Committee] recommended that Powell be sworn and seated as a member of the 90th Congress but that he be censured by the House, fined $40,000 and be deprived of his seniority.

The report was presented to the House on March 1, 1967, and the House debated the Select Committee's proposed resolution. At the conclusion of the debate, by a vote of 222 of 202 the House rejected a motion to bring the resolution to a vote. An amendment to the resolution was then offered; it called for the exclusion of Powell and a declaration that his seat was vacant. The Speaker ruled that a majority vote of the House would be sufficient to pass the resolution if it were so amended. After further debate, the amendment was adopted by a vote of 248 to 176. Then the House adopted by a vote of 307 to 116 House Resolution No. 278 in its amended form, thereby excluding Powell and directing that the Speaker notify the Governor of New York that the seat was vacant.

Powell and 13 voters of the 18th Congressional District of New York subsequently instituted this suit in the United States District Court for the District of Columbia. Five members of the House of Representatives were named as defendants individually and "as representatives of a class of citizens who are presently serving * * * as members of the House of Representatives." John W. McCormack was named in his official capacity as Speaker, and the Clerk of the House of Representatives, the Sergeant at Arms and the Doorkeeper were named individually and in their official capacities. The complaint alleged that House Resolution No. 278 violated the Constitution, specifically Art. I, § 2, cl. 1, because the resolution was inconsistent with the mandate that the members of the House shall be elected by the people of each state, and Art. I, § 2, cl. 2, which, petitioners alleged, sets forth the exclusive qualifications for membership * * *.

* * *

The District Court granted respondents' motion to dismiss the complaint "for want of jurisdiction of the subject matter." The Court of Appeals for the District of Columbia Circuit affirmed on somewhat different grounds, with each judge of the panel filing a separate opinion. We granted certiorari. While the case was pending on our docket, the 90th Congress officially terminated and the 91st Congress was seated. In November 1968, Powell was again elected as the representative of the 18th Congressional District of New York, and he was seated by the 91st Congress. The resolution seating Powell also fined him $25,000 * * *.

The resolution excluding petitioner Powell was adopted by a vote in excess of two-thirds of the 434 Members of Congress. Article I, § 5, grants the House authority to expel a member "with the Concurrence of two thirds." Respondents assert that the

House may expel a member for any reason whatsoever and that, since a two-thirds vote was obtained, the procedure by which Powell was denied his seat in the 90th Congress should be regarded as an expulsion, not an exclusion * * *.

Although respondents repeatedly urge this Court not to speculate as to the reasons for Powell's exclusion, their attempt to equate exclusion with expulsion would require a similar speculation that the House would have voted to expel Powell had it been faced with that question. Powell had not been seated at the time House Resolution No. 278 was debated and passed. After a motion to bring the Select Committee's proposed resolution to an immediate vote had been defeated, an amendment was offered which mandated Powell's exclusion. Mr. Celler, chairman of the Select Committee, then posed a parliamentary inquiry to determine whether a two-thirds vote was necessary to pass the resolution if so amended "in the sense that it might amount to an expulsion." The Speaker replied that "action by a majority vote would be in accordance with the rules." Had the amendment been regarded as an attempt to expel Powell, a two-thirds vote would have been constitutionally required. The Speaker ruled that the House was voting to exclude Powell, and we will not speculate what the result might have been if Powell had been seated and expulsion proceedings subsequently instituted.

Nor is the distinction between exclusion and expulsion merely one of form. The misconduct for which Powell was charged occurred prior to the convening of the 90th Congress. On several occasions the House has debated whether a member can be expelled for actions taken during a prior Congress and the House's own manual of procedure applicable in the 90th Congress states that "both Houses have distrusted their power to punish in such cases." The House rules manual reflects positions taken by prior Congresses * * *. Members of the House having expressed a belief that such strictures apply to its own power to expel, we will not assume that two-thirds of its members would have expelled Powell for his prior conduct had the Speaker announced that House Resolution No. 278 was for expulsion rather than exclusion.

* * *

* * * [W]e turn to the question whether the case is justiciable * * *. [W] e must determine whether the structure of the Federal Government renders the issue presented a "political question"-that is, a question which is not justiciable in federal court because of the separation of powers provided by the Constitution.

* * *

Respondents first contention is that this case presents a political question because under Art. I, § 5, there has been a 'textually demonstrable constitutional commitment' to the House of the 'adjudicatory power' to determine Powell's qualifications. Thus it is argued that the House, and the House alone, has power to determine who is qualified to be a member.

* * *

If examination of § 5 disclosed that the Constitution gives the House judicially unreviewable power to set qualifications for membership and to judge whether prospective members meet those qualifications, further review of the House determination might well be barred by the political question doctrine. On the other hand, if the Constitution gives the House power to judge only whether elected members possess the three standing qualifications set forth in the Constitution, further consideration would be necessary to determine whether any of the other formulations of the political question doctrine are "inextricable from the case at bar."

In order to determine the scope of any "textual commitment" under Art. I, § 5, we necessarily must determine the meaning of the phrase to "be the Judge of the Qualifications of its own Members." Petitioners argue that the records of the debates during the Constitutional Convention; available commentary from the post-Convention, pre-ratification period, and early congressional applications of Art. I, § 5, support their construction of the section. Respondents insist, however, that a careful examination of the pre-Convention practices of the English Parliament and American colonial assemblies demonstrates that, by 1787, a legislature's power to judge the qualifications of its members was generally understood to encompass exclusion or expulsion on the ground that an individual's character or past conduct rendered him unfit to serve. When the Constitution and the debates over its adoption are thus viewed in historical perspective, argue respondents, it becomes clear that the "qualifications" expressly set forth in the Constitution were not meant to limit the long-recognized legislative power to exclude or expel at will, but merely to establish "standing incapacities," which could be altered only by a constitutional amendment. Our examination of the relevant historical materials leads us to the conclusion that petitioners are correct, and that the Constitution leaves the House without authority *to exclude* any person, duly elected by his constituents, who meets all the requirements for membership expressly prescribed in the Constitution.

a. The Pre-Convention Precedents.

Since our rejection of respondents' interpretation of § 5 results in significant measure from a disagreement with their historical analysis, we must consider the relevant historical antecedents in considerable detail. As do respondents, we begin with the English and colonial precedents.

The earliest English exclusion precedent appears to be a declaration by the House of Commons in 1553 "that Alex. Nowell, being Prebendary [i.e., a clergyman] in Westminster, and thereby having voice in the Convocation House, cannot be a member of this House. . . ." J. Tanner, Tudor Constitutional Documents: A.D. 1485–1603, p. 596 (2d ed.1930). This decision, however, was consistent with a long-established tradition that clergy who participated in their own representative assemblies or convocations were ineligible for membership in the House of Commons. See 1 E. Porritt, The Unreformed House of Commons 125 (1963); T. Taswell-Langmead's English Constitutional History 14143 (11th ed. T. Plucknett 1960). The traditional ineligibility of clergymen was recognized as a standing incapacity. See 1 W. Blackstone's Commentaries *175. Nowell's exclusion, therefore, is irrelevant to the present case, for petitioners concede—and we agree—that, if Powell had not met one of the standing qualifications set forth in the Constitution, he could have been excluded under Art. I, § 5. The earliest colonial exclusions also fail to support respondents' theory.

Respondents' remaining 16th and 17th century English precedents all are cases of expulsion, although some were for misdeeds not encompassed within recognized standing incapacities existing either at the time of the expulsions or at the time the Constitution was drafted in 1787. Although these early expulsion orders occasionally contained statements suggesting that the individual expelled was thereafter ineligible for reelection, at least for the duration of the Parliament from which he was expelled, there is no indication that any were reelected and thereafter excluded. Respondents' colonial precedents during this period follow a similar pattern.

Apparently the reelection of an expelled member first occurred in 1712. The House of Commons had expelled Robert Walpole for receiving kickbacks for contracts relating to "foraging the Troops," 17 H.C.Jour. 28, and committed him to the Tower. Nevertheless, two months later, he was reelected. The House thereupon resolved "[t]hat Robert Walpole, Esquire, having been, this Session of Parliament, committed a Prisoner to the *Tower of London*, and expelled [from] this House, . . . is incapable of being elected a Member to serve *in this present Parliament*. . . ." Id. at 128. (Second emphasis added.) A new election was ordered, and Walpole was not reelected. At least two similar exclusions after an initial expulsion were effected in the American colonies during the first half of the 18th century.

Respondents urge that the Walpole case provides strong support for their conclusion that the pre-Convention English and colonial practice was that members-elect could be excluded for their prior misdeeds at the sole discretion of the legislative body to which they had been elected. However, this conclusion overlooks an important limiting characteristic of the Walpole case and of both the colonial exclusion cases on which respondents rely: the excluded member had been previously expelled * * *. [N]one of these cases supports respondents' contention that, by the 18th century the English Parliament and colonial assemblies had assumed absolute discretion to exclude any member-elect they deemed unfit to serve. Rather, they seem to demonstrate that a member could be excluded only if he had first been expelled.

Even if these cases could be construed to support respondents' contention, their precedential value was nullified prior to the Constitutional Convention. By 1782, after a long struggle, the arbitrary exercise of the power to exclude was unequivocally repudiated by a House of Commons resolution which ended the most notorious English election dispute of the 18th century—the John Wilkes case. While serving as a member of Parliament in 1763, Wilkes published an attack on a recent peace treaty with France, calling it a product of bribery and condemning the Crown's ministers as " 'the tools of despotism and corruption.' " R. Postgate, That Devil Wilkes 53 (1929). Wilkes and others who were involved with the publication in which the attack appeared were arrested. Prior to Wilkes' trial, the House of Commons expelled him for publishing "a false, scandalous, and seditious libel." 15 Parl.Hist.Eng. 1393 (1764). Wilkes then fled to France, and was subsequently sentenced to exile. 9 L. Gipson, The British Empire Before the American Revolution 37 (1956).

Wilkes returned to England in 1768, the same year in which the Parliament from which he had been expelled was dissolved. He was elected to the next Parliament, and he then surrendered himself to the Court of King's Bench. Wilkes was convicted of seditious libel and sentenced to 22 months' imprisonment. The new Parliament declared him ineligible for membership and ordered that he be "expelled this House." 16 Parl. Hist. Eng. 545 (1769). Although Wilkes was reelected to fill the vacant seat three times, each time the same Parliament declared him ineligible and refused to seat him. See 11 Gipson, *supra*, at 207–215.

Wilkes was released from prison in 1770, and was again elected to Parliament in 1774. For the next several years, he unsuccessfully campaigned to have the resolutions expelling him and declaring him incapable of reelection expunged from the record. Finally, in 1782, the House of Commons voted to expunge them, resolving that the prior House actions were "subversive of the rights of the whole body of electors of this kingdom." 22 Parl.Hist.Eng. 1411 (1782).

With the successful resolution of Wilkes' long and bitter struggle for the right of the British electorate to be represented by men of their own choice, it is evident that, on the eve of the Constitutional Convention, English precedent stood for the proposition that "the law of the land had regulated the qualifications of members to serve in parliament" and those qualifications were "not occasional, but fixed." 16 Parl.Hist.Eng. 589, 590 (1769). Certainly English practice did not support, nor had it ever supported, respondents' assertion that the power to judge qualifications was generally understood to encompass the right to exclude members-elect for general misconduct not within standing qualifications. With the repudiation in 1782 of the only two precedents for excluding a member-elect who had been previously expelled, it appears that the House of Commons also repudiated any "control over the eligibility of candidates, except in the administration of the laws which define their [standing] qualifications." T. May's Parliamentary Practice 66 (13th ed. T. Webster 1924). See Taswell-Langmead, supra, at 585.

* * *

Wilkes' struggle and his ultimate victory had a significant impact in the American colonies. His advocacy of libertarian causes and his pursuit of the right to be seated in Parliament became a cause *célèbre* for the colonists. "[T]he cry of 'Wilkes and Liberty' echoed loudly across the Atlantic Ocean as wide publicity was given to every step of Wilkes' public career in the colonial press. . . . The reaction in America took on significant proportions. Colonials tended to identify their cause with that of Wilkes. They saw him as a popular hero and a martyr to the struggle for liberty. . . . They named towns, counties, and even children in his honour." 11 Gipson, *supra*, at 222. It is within this historical context that we must examine the Convention debates in 1787, just five years after Wilkes' final victory.

b. Convention Debates.

* * * [T]he records of the [Convention] debates, viewed in the context of the bitter struggle for the right to freely choose representatives which had recently concluded in England and in light of the distinction the Framers made between the power to expel and the power to exclude, indicate that petitioner ultimate conclusion is correct.

* * *

The debates at the state [ratification] conventions also demonstrate the Framers' understanding that the qualifications for members of Congress had been fixed in the Constitution * * *.

c. Post-Ratification.

* * *

* * * In 1868, the House voted for the first time in its history to exclude a member-elect. It refused to seat two duly elected representatives for giving aid and comfort to the Confederacy. "This change was produced by the North's bitter enmity toward those who failed to support the Union cause during the war, and was effected by the Radical Republican domination of Congress. It was a shift brought about by the naked urgency of power and was given little doctrinal support." From that time

until the present, congressional practice has been erratic; and on the few occasions when a member-elect was excluded although he met all the qualifications set forth in the Constitution, there were frequently vigorous dissents. Even the annotations to the official manual of procedure for the 90th Congress manifest doubt as to the House's power to exclude a member-elect who has met the constitutionally prescribed qualifications.

* * *

Had the intent of the Framers emerged from these materials with less clarity, we would nevertheless have been compelled to resolve any ambiguity in favor of a narrow construction of the scope of Congress' power to exclude members-elect. A fundamental principle of our representative democracy is, in Hamilton's words, "that the people should choose whom they please to govern them." 2 Elliot's Debates 257. As Madison pointed out at the Convention, this principle is undermined as much by limiting whom the people can select as by limiting the franchise itself. In apparent agreement with this basic philosophy, the Convention adopted his suggestion limiting the power to expel. To allow essentially that same power to be exercised under the guise of judging qualifications, would be to ignore Madison's warning, borne out in the Wilkes case and some of Congress' own post-Civil War exclusion cases, against "vesting an improper & dangerous power in the Legislature." 2 Farrand 249. Moreover, it would effectively nullify the Convention's decision to require a two-thirds vote for expulsion * * *. In short, both the intention of the Framers, to the extent it can be determined, and an examination of the basic principles of our democratic system persuade us that the Constitution does not vest in the Congress a discretionary power to deny membership by a majority vote.

For these reasons, we have concluded that Art. I, § 5, is at most a 'textually demonstrable commitment' to Congress to judge only the qualifications expressly set forth in the Constitution. Therefore, the 'textual commitment' formulation of the political question doctrine does not bar federal courts from adjudicating petitioners' claims.

2. Other Considerations

Respondents' alternate contention is that the case presents a political question because judicial resolution of petitioners' claim would produce a "potentially embarrassing confrontation between coordinate branches" of the Federal Government. But, as our interpretation of Art. I, § 5, discloses, a determination of petitioner Powell's right to sit would require no more than an interpretation of the Constitution. Such a determination falls within the traditional role accorded courts to interpret the law, and does not involve a "lack of the respect due (a) coordinate (branch) of government," nor does it involve an "initial policy determination of a kind clearly for nonjudicial discretion." Our system of government requires that federal courts on occasion interpret the Constitution in a manner at variance with the construction given the document by another branch. The alleged conflict that such an adjudication may cause cannot justify the courts' avoiding their constitutional responsibility.

Nor are any of the other formulations of a political question "inextricable from the case at bar." Petitioners seek a determination that the House was without power to exclude Powell from the 90th Congress, which, we have seen, requires an interpretation of the Constitution—a determination for which clearly there are "judicially . . . manageable standards." Finally, a judicial resolution of petitioners' claim will not result in "multifarious pronouncements by various departments on one question." For, as we noted in *Baker v. Carr*, *supra*, at 211, it is the responsibility of this Court to act as the ultimate interpreter of the Constitution. *Marbury v. Madison*, 1 Cranch (5 U.S.) 137 (1803). Thus, we conclude that petitioners' claim is not barred by the political question doctrine, and, having determined that the claim is otherwise generally justiciable, we hold that the case is justiciable.

* * *

■ MR. JUSTICE DOUGLAS. [Omitted.]

[*Editors' Note: Justice Stewart dissented on the ground that the case was moot because the 90th Congress that refused to seat Powell no longer existed and had been replaced by the 91st Congress.*]

NOTES AND QUESTIONS

1. The vast bulk of the opinion in *Powell v. McCormack* was devoted to pre- and post-constitutional history—*much* more than we have included in this edited version of the case. Near the end of its opinion, the Court essentially says that it would have decided the case in favor of Powell even if the history had been different. Why, then, did the Court spend so much time and energy on history? What modalities of interpretation were at work here? Is *Powell v. McCormack* an originalist opinion written by Chief Justice Earl Warren?

2. The constitutional text seems very clear that each house of Congress cannot add additional qualifications beyond the three enumerated in Article I, Sections 2 and 3. *Expressio unius est exclusion alterius* ("the expression of one thing is the exclusion of the other"). The text of the Constitution speaks directly to the issues raised by this case. So too does the structure of the document. Should those considerations ever give way to history, purposes, or past practice? What policy concerns are implicated here and how much weight would you give them? Should the voters in one district ever have their choice of representative overridden by members elected from other districts?

3. Suppose a house of Congress expels a member by a two-thirds vote under Article I, Section 5. Can the expelled member appeal to the Supreme Court, claiming that the expulsion was a punishment for political views in violation of the First Amendment? Or would that raise a political question? Why is *Powell v. McCormack* any different?

4. Is this case an example of judicial supremacy or departmentalism in constitutional interpretation? Can one be a departmentalist and think *Powell v. McCormack* was rightly decided? Ought the Supreme Court to more generally police the holding of elections and the democratic process in the United States? See JOHN HART ELY, DEMOCRACY AND DISTRUST (1980).

5. The Warren Court decided *Powell v. McCormack* in 1969. The Democratic caucus in the House at that time was dominated by Southern Democrats. Adam Clayton Powell represented Harlem in New York City and was the first African-American member of Congress from the State of New York. Is any of that relevant?

I. STATE POWER TO ADD QUALIFICATIONS FOR SENATORS AND REPRESENTATIVES

In *Powell v. McCormack*, the House was effectively seeking to add qualifications for office-holding in addition to those specified in the Constitution. Can a *State*—

through its constitution, its legislature, or a citizen referendum—impose qualifications on its congressional representatives beyond those specified in the Constitution? Could a State, for example, require its representatives to have longer residence in the State than the Constitution requires? Or, more pointedly, could a State make it a requirement for service in Congress that you not already have served in Congress for a certain time? Before reading the next case, read again the Qualifications Clauses and consider the following textual provision:

> **Amendment X: The powers not delegated to the United States by the Constitution, nor prohibited by it to the States, are reserved to the States respectively, or to the people.**

U.S. Term Limits, Inc. v. Thornton, et al.

514 U.S. 779 (1995)

■ JUSTICE STEVENS delivered the opinion of the Court.

The Constitution sets forth qualifications for membership in the Congress of the United States. Article I, § 2, cl. 2, which applies to the House of Representatives, provides:

> "No Person shall be a Representative who shall not have attained to the Age of twenty five Years, and been seven Years a Citizen of the United States, and who shall not, when elected, be an Inhabitant of that State in which he shall be chosen."

Article I, § 3, cl. 3, which applies to the Senate, similarly provides:

> "No Person shall be a Senator who shall not have attained to the Age of thirty Years, and been nine Years a Citizen of the United States, and who shall not, when elected, be an Inhabitant of that State for which he shall be chosen."

Today's cases present a challenge to an amendment to the Arkansas State Constitution that prohibits the name of an otherwise-eligible candidate for Congress from appearing on the general election ballot if that candidate has already served three terms in the House of Representatives or two terms in the Senate. The Arkansas Supreme Court held that the amendment violates the Federal Constitution. We agree with that holding. Such a state-imposed restriction is contrary to the "fundamental principle of our representative democracy," embodied in the Constitution, that "the people should choose whom they please to govern them." *Powell v. McCormack*, 395 U.S. 486, 547 (1969). Allowing individual States to adopt their own qualifications for congressional service would be inconsistent with the Framers' vision of a uniform National Legislature representing the people of the United States. If the qualifications set forth in the text of the Constitution are to be changed, that text must be amended.

At the general election on November 3, 1992, the voters of Arkansas adopted Amendment 73 to their State Constitution. Proposed as a "Term Limitation Amendment," its preamble stated:

> "The people of Arkansas find and declare that elected officials who remain in office too long become preoccupied with reelection and ignore their duties as representatives of the people. Entrenched incumbency has

reduced voter participation and has led to an electoral system that is less free, less competitive, and less representative than the system established by the Founding Fathers. Therefore, the people of Arkansas, exercising their reserved powers, herein limit the terms of elected officials."

* * * Section 3, the provision at issue in these cases, applies to the Arkansas Congressional Delegation. It provides:

> "(a) Any person having been elected to three or more terms as a member of the United States House of Representatives from Arkansas shall not be certified as a candidate and shall not be eligible to have his/her name placed on the ballot for election to the United States House of Representatives from Arkansas.
>
> (b) Any person having been elected to two or more terms as a member of the United States Senate from Arkansas shall not be certified as a candidate and shall not be eligible to have his/her name placed on the ballot for election to the United States Senate from Arkansas."

* * *

On November 13, 1992, respondent Bobbie Hill, on behalf of herself, similarly situated Arkansas "citizens, residents, taxpayers and registered voters," and the League of Women Voters of Arkansas, filed a complaint in the Circuit Court for Pulaski County, Arkansas, seeking a declaratory judgment that § 3 of Amendment 73 is "unconstitutional and void" * * *.

* * *

* * * [The state courts held that § 3 of Amendment 73 violated Article I of the Federal Constitution.] We now affirm.

* * * [T]he constitutionality of Amendment 73 depends critically on the resolution of two distinct issues. The first is whether the Constitution forbids States to add to or alter the qualifications specifically enumerated in the Constitution. The second is, if the Constitution does so forbid, whether the fact that Amendment 73 is formulated as a ballot access restriction rather than as an outright disqualification is of constitutional significance. Our resolution of these issues draws upon our prior resolution of a related but distinct issue: whether Congress has the power to add to or alter the qualifications of its Members.

Twenty-six years ago, in *Powell v. McCormack,* we reviewed the history and text of the Qualifications Clauses in a case involving an attempted exclusion of a duly elected Member of Congress * * *.

* * *

* * * [We concluded] that the House of Representatives has no "authority to *exclude* any person, duly elected by his constituents, who meets all the requirements for membership expressly prescribed in the Constitution." * * *

* * *

Powell * * * establishes two important propositions: first, that the "relevant historical materials" compel the conclusion that, at least with respect to qualifications imposed by Congress, the Framers intended the qualifications listed in the Constitution to be exclusive; and second, that that conclusion is equally compelled by an understanding of the "fundamental principle of our representative democracy . . . 'that the people should choose whom they please to govern them.' "

* * *

* * * [A]fter examining *Powell's* historical analysis and its articulation of the "basic principles of our democratic system," we reaffirm that the qualifications for service in Congress set forth in the text of the Constitution are "fixed," at least in the sense that they may not be supplemented by Congress.

Our reaffirmation of *Powell* does not necessarily resolve the specific questions presented in these cases. For petitioners argue that whatever the constitutionality of additional qualifications for membership imposed by Congress, the historical and textual materials discussed in *Powell* do not support the conclusion that the Constitution prohibits additional qualifications imposed by States. In the absence of such a constitutional prohibition, petitioners argue, the Tenth Amendment and the principle of reserved powers require that States be allowed to add such qualifications.

Before addressing these arguments, we find it appropriate to take note of the striking unanimity among the courts that have considered the issue. None of the overwhelming array of briefs submitted by the parties and *amici* has called to our attention even a single case in which a state court or federal court has approved of a State's addition of qualifications for a Member of Congress. To the contrary, an impressive number of courts have determined that States lack the authority to add qualifications. Courts have struck down state-imposed qualifications in the form of term limits, district residency requirements, loyalty oath requirements, and restrictions on those convicted of felonies. Prior to *Powell,* the commentators were similarly unanimous * * *. This impressive and uniform body of judicial decisions and learned commentary indicates that the obstacles confronting petitioners are formidable indeed.

Petitioners argue that the Constitution contains no express prohibition against state-added qualifications, and that Amendment 73 is therefore an appropriate exercise of a State's reserved power to place additional restrictions on the choices that its own voters may make. We disagree for two independent reasons. First, we conclude that the power to add qualifications is not within the "original powers" of the States, and thus is not reserved to the States by the Tenth Amendment. Second, even if States possessed some original power in this area, we conclude that the Framers intended the Constitution to be the exclusive source of qualifications for Members of Congress, and that the Framers thereby "divested" States of any power to add qualifications.

The "plan of the convention" as illuminated by the historical materials, our opinions, and the text of the Tenth Amendment draws a basic distinction between the powers of the newly created Federal Government and the powers retained by the pre-existing sovereign States. As Chief Justice Marshall explained, "it was neither necessary nor proper to define the powers retained by the States. These powers proceed, not from the people of America, but from the people of the several States; and remain, after the adoption of the constitution, what they were before, except so far as they may be abridged by that instrument." *Sturges v. Crowninshield,* 4 Wheat. 122, 193 (1819).

* * * The text of the Tenth Amendment unambiguously confirms this principle: "The powers not delegated to the United States by the Constitution, nor prohibited by it to the States, are reserved to the States respectively, or to the people."

As we have frequently noted, "[t]he States unquestionably do retain a significant measure of sovereign authority. They do so, however, *only to the extent that the Constitution has not divested them of their original powers* and transferred those powers to the Federal Government".

Contrary to petitioners' assertions, the power to add qualifications is not part of the original powers of sovereignty that the Tenth Amendment reserved to the States. Petitioners' Tenth Amendment argument misconceives the nature of the right at issue because that Amendment could only "reserve" that which existed before. As Justice Story recognized, "the states can exercise no powers whatsoever, which exclusively spring out of the existence of the national government, which the constitution does not delegate to them. . . . No state can say, that it has reserved, what it never possessed." 1 Story § 627.

* * *

With respect to setting qualifications for service in Congress, no such right existed before the Constitution was ratified. The contrary argument overlooks the revolutionary character of the Government that the Framers conceived. Prior to the adoption of the Constitution, the States had joined together under the Articles of Confederation. In that system, "the States retained most of their sovereignty, like independent nations bound together only by treaties." *Wesberry v. Sanders,* 376 U.S. 1, 9 (1964). After the Constitutional Convention convened, the Framers were presented with, and eventually adopted a variation of, "a plan not merely to amend the Articles of Confederation but to create an entirely new National Government with a National Executive, National Judiciary, and a National Legislature." *Id.*, at 10. In adopting that plan, the Framers envisioned a uniform national system, rejecting the notion that the Nation was a collection of States, and instead creating a direct link between the National Government and the people of the United States. In that National Government, representatives owe primary allegiance not to the people of a State, but to the people of the Nation. As Justice Story observed, each Member of Congress is "an officer of the union, deriving his powers and qualifications from the constitution, and neither created by, dependent upon, nor controllable by, the states. . . . Those officers owe their existence and functions to the united voice of the whole, not of a portion, of the people." 1 Story § 627. Representatives and Senators are as much officers of the entire Union as is the President. States thus "have just as much right, and no more, to prescribe new qualifications for a representative, as they have for a president. . . . It is no original prerogative of state power to appoint a representative, a senator, or president for the union." *Ibid.*

We believe that the Constitution reflects the Framers' general agreement with the approach later articulated by Justice Story. For example, Art. I, § 5, cl. 1, provides: "Each House shall be the Judge of the Elections, Returns and Qualifications of its own Members." The text of the Constitution thus gives the representatives of all the people the final say in judging the qualifications of the representatives of any one State. For this reason, the dissent falters when it states that "the people of Georgia have no say over whom the people of Massachusetts select to represent them in Congress."

Two other sections of the Constitution further support our view of the Framers' vision. First, consistent with Story's view, the Constitution provides that the salaries of representatives should "be ascertained by Law, and paid out of the Treasury of the United States," Art. I, § 6, rather than by individual States. The salary provisions reflect the view that representatives owe their allegiance to the people, and not to the States. Second, the provisions governing elections reveal the Framers' understanding that powers over the election of federal officers had to be delegated to, rather than reserved by, the States. It is surely no coincidence that the context of federal elections provides one of the few areas in which the Constitution expressly requires action by the States, namely that "[t]he Times, Places and Manner of holding Elections for Senators and Representatives, shall be prescribed in each State by the Legislature thereof." Art. I, § 4, cl. 1. This duty parallels the duty under Article II that "Each State shall appoint, in such Manner as the Legislature thereof may direct, a Number of Electors." Art. II, § 1, cl. 2. These Clauses are express delegations of power to the States to act with respect to federal elections.

* * *

In short, as the Framers recognized, electing representatives to the National Legislature was a new right, arising from the Constitution itself * * *. In the absence of any constitutional delegation to the States of power to add qualifications to those enumerated in the Constitution, such a power does not exist.

Even if we believed that States possessed as part of their original powers some control over congressional qualifications, the text and structure of the Constitution, the relevant historical materials, and, most importantly, the "basic principles of our democratic system" all demonstrate that the Qualifications Clauses were intended to preclude the States from exercising any such power and to fix as exclusive the qualifications in the Constitution.

Much of the historical analysis was undertaken by the Court in *Powell*. There is, however, additional historical evidence that pertains directly to the power of the States. That evidence, though perhaps not as extensive as that reviewed in *Powell,* leads unavoidably to the conclusion that the States lack the power to add qualifications.

* * *

We * * * find compelling the complete absence in the ratification debates of any assertion that States had the power to add qualifications * * *.

* * *

Congress' subsequent experience with state-imposed qualifications provides further evidence of the general consensus on the lack of state power in this area * * *. [D]uring the first 100 years of its existence, "Congress strictly limited its power to judge the qualifications of its members to those enumerated in the Constitution." Congress first confronted the issue in 1807 when it faced a challenge to the qualifications of William McCreery, a Representative from Maryland who allegedly did not satisfy a residency requirement imposed by that State. In recommending that McCreery be seated, the Report of the House Committee on Elections noted:

> "The committee proceeded to examine the Constitution, with relation to the case submitted to them, and find that *qualifications of members are therein determined, without reserving any authority to the State*

Legislatures to change, add to, or diminish those qualifications; and that, by that instrument, Congress is constituted the sole judge of the qualifications prescribed by it, and are obliged to decide agreeably to the Constitutional rules. . . ."*Powell,* 395 U.S., at 542, quoting 17 Annals of Cong. 871 (1807) (emphasis added). * * *

Though the House Debate may be inconclusive, commentators at the time apparently viewed the seating of McCreery as confirmation of the States' lack of power to add qualifications * * *.

* * *

The Senate experience with state-imposed qualifications further supports our conclusions. In 1887, for example, the Senate seated Charles Faulkner of West Virginia, despite the fact that a provision of the West Virginia Constitution purported to render him ineligible to serve. The Senate Committee on Privileges and Elections unanimously concluded that "no State can prescribe any qualification to the office of United States Senator in addition to those declared in the Constitution of the United States." S.Rep. No. 1, 50th Cong., 1st Sess., 4 (1887) * * *.

We recognize * * * that "congressional practice has been erratic" and that the precedential value of congressional exclusion cases is "quite limited." *Powell,* 395 U.S., at 545–546. Nevertheless, those incidents lend support to the result we reach today.

Our conclusion that States lack the power to impose qualifications vindicates the same "fundamental principle of our representative democracy" that we recognized in *Powell,* namely, that "the people should choose whom they please to govern them." *Id.,* at 547.

* * *

Finally, state-imposed restrictions, unlike the congressionally imposed restrictions at issue in *Powell,* violate a third idea central to this basic principle: that the right to choose representatives belongs not to the States, but to the people. From the start, the Framers recognized that the "great and radical vice" of the Articles of Confederation was "the principle of LEGISLATION for STATES or GOVERNMENTS, in their CORPORATE or COLLECTIVE CAPACITIES, and as contradistinguished from the INDIVIDUALS of whom they consist." The Federalist No. 15, at 108 (Hamilton). Thus the Framers, in perhaps their most important contribution, conceived of a Federal Government directly responsible to the people, possessed of direct power over the people, and chosen directly, not by States, but by the people * * *.

* * *

Permitting individual States to formulate diverse qualifications for their representatives would result in a patchwork of state qualifications, undermining the uniformity and the national character that the Framers envisioned and sought to ensure. Such a patchwork would also sever the direct link that the Framers found so critical between the National Government and the people of the United States.

Petitioners attempt to overcome this formidable array of evidence against the States' power to impose qualifications by arguing that the practice of the States immediately after the adoption of the Constitution demonstrates their understanding that they possessed such power. One may properly question the extent to which the States' own practice is a reliable indicator of the contours of restrictions that the Constitution imposed on States, especially when no court has ever upheld a state-imposed qualification of any sort. But petitioners' argument is unpersuasive even on its own terms. At the time of the Convention, "[a]lmost all the State Constitutions required members of their Legislatures to possess considerable property." Despite this near uniformity, only one State, Virginia, placed similar restrictions on Members of Congress, requiring that a representative be, *inter alia*, a "freeholder." Just 15 years after imposing a property qualification, Virginia replaced that requirement with a provision requiring that representatives be only "qualified according to the constitution of the United States." Moreover, several States, including New Hampshire, Georgia, Delaware, and South Carolina, revised their Constitutions at around the time of the Federal Constitution. In the revised Constitutions, each State retained property qualifications for its own state elected officials yet placed no property qualification on its congressional representatives.

The contemporaneous state practice with respect to term limits is similar. At the time of the Convention, States widely supported term limits in at least some circumstances. The Articles of Confederation contained a provision for term limits. As we have noted, some members of the Convention had sought to impose term limits for Members of Congress. In addition, many States imposed term limits on state officers, four placed limits on delegates to the Continental Congress, and several States voiced support for term limits for Members of Congress. Despite this widespread support, no State sought to impose any term limits on its own federal representatives. Thus, a proper assessment of contemporaneous state practice provides further persuasive evidence of a general understanding that the qualifications in the Constitution were unalterable by the States.

* * *

Petitioners argue that, even if States may not add qualifications, Amendment 73 is constitutional because it is not such a qualification, and because Amendment 73 is a permissible exercise of state power to regulate the "Times, Places and Manner of holding Elections." We reject these contentions.

Unlike §§ 1 and 2 of Amendment 73, which create absolute bars to service for long-term incumbents running for state office, § 3 merely provides that certain Senators and Representatives shall not be certified as candidates and shall not have their names appear on the ballot. They may run as write-in candidates and, if elected, they may serve * * *.

* * *

* * * [E]ven if petitioners are correct that incumbents may occasionally win reelection as write-in candidates, there is no denying that the ballot restrictions will make it significantly more difficult for the barred candidate to win the election. In our view, an amendment with the avowed purpose and obvious effect of evading the requirements of the Qualifications Clauses by handicapping a class of candidates cannot stand. To argue otherwise is to suggest that the Framers spent significant time and energy in debating and crafting Clauses that could be easily evaded. More importantly, allowing States to evade the Qualifications Clauses by "dress[ing] eligibility to stand for Congress in ballot access clothing" trivializes the basic principles of our democracy that underlie those Clauses. Petitioners' argument treats the Qualifications Clauses not as the embodiment of a grand principle, but rather as

empty formalism. " 'It is inconceivable that guaranties embedded in the Constitution of the United States may thus be manipulated out of existence.' "

* * *

The merits of term limits, or "rotation," have been the subject of debate since the formation of our Constitution, when the Framers unanimously rejected a proposal to add such limits to the Constitution * * *. It is not our province to resolve this longstanding debate.

We are, however, firmly convinced that allowing the several States to adopt term limits for congressional service would effect a fundamental change in the constitutional framework. Any such change must come not by legislation adopted either by Congress or by an individual State, but rather—as have other important changes in the electoral process—through the amendment procedures set forth in Article V * * *.

The judgment is affirmed.

It is so ordered.

■ JUSTICE KENNEDY, concurring.

I join the opinion of the Court.

The majority and dissenting opinions demonstrate the intricacy of the question whether or not the Qualifications Clauses are exclusive. In my view, however, it is well settled that the whole people of the United States asserted their political identity and unity of purpose when they created the federal system. The dissent's course of reasoning suggesting otherwise might be construed to disparage the republican character of the National Government, and it seems appropriate to add these few remarks to explain why that course of argumentation runs counter to fundamental principles of federalism.

Federalism was our Nation's own discovery. The Framers split the atom of sovereignty. It was the genius of their idea that our citizens would have two political capacities, one state and one federal, each protected from incursion by the other. The resulting Constitution created a legal system unprecedented in form and design, establishing two orders of government, each with its own direct relationship, its own privity, its own set of mutual rights and obligations to the people who sustain it and are governed by it. It is appropriate to recall these origins, which instruct us as to the nature of the two different governments created and confirmed by the Constitution.

A distinctive character of the National Government, the mark of its legitimacy, is that it owes its existence to the act of the whole people who created it. It must be remembered that the National Government, too, is republican in essence and in theory * * *.

In one sense it is true that "the people of each State retained their separate political identities, for the Constitution takes care both to preserve the States and to make use of their identities and structures at various points in organizing the federal union. It does not at all follow from this that the sole political identity of an American is with the State of his or her residence. It denies the dual character of the Federal Government which is its very foundation to assert that the people of the United States do not have a political identity as well, one independent of, though consistent with, their identity as citizens of the State of their residence. It must be recognized that " '[f]or all the great purposes for which the Federal government was formed, we are one people, with one common country.' " *Shapiro v. Thompson,* 394 U.S. 618, 630 (1969) (quoting *Passenger Cases,* 7 How. 283, 492 (1849) (Taney, C.J., dissenting).

* * *

* * * There can be no doubt, if we are to respect the republican origins of the Nation and preserve its federal character, that there exists a federal right of citizenship, a relationship between the people of the Nation and their National Government, with which the States may not interfere. Because the Arkansas enactment intrudes upon this federal domain, it exceeds the boundaries of the Constitution.

■ JUSTICE THOMAS, with whom THE CHIEF JUSTICE, JUSTICE O'CONNOR, and JUSTICE SCALIA join, dissenting.

It is ironic that the Court bases today's decision on the right of the people to "choose whom they please to govern them." Under our Constitution, there is only one State whose people have the right to "choose whom they please" to represent Arkansas in Congress. The Court holds, however, that neither the elected legislature of that State nor the people themselves (acting by ballot initiative) may prescribe any qualifications for those representatives. The majority therefore defends the right of the people of Arkansas to "choose whom they please to govern them" by invalidating a provision that won nearly 60% of the votes cast in a direct election and that carried every congressional district in the State.

I dissent. Nothing in the Constitution deprives the people of each State of the power to prescribe eligibility requirements for the candidates who seek to represent them in Congress. The Constitution is simply silent on this question. And where the Constitution is silent, it raises no bar to action by the States or the people.

Because the majority fundamentally misunderstands the notion of "reserved" powers, I start with some first principles. Contrary to the majority's suggestion, the people of the States need not point to any affirmative grant of power in the Constitution in order to prescribe qualifications for their representatives in Congress, or to authorize their elected state legislators to do so.

Our system of government rests on one overriding principle: All power stems from the consent of the people. To phrase the principle in this way, however, is to be imprecise about something important to the notion of "reserved" powers. The ultimate source of the Constitution's authority is the consent of the people of each individual State, not the consent of the undifferentiated people of the Nation as a whole.

The ratification procedure erected by Article VII makes this point clear. The Constitution took effect once it had been ratified by the people gathered in convention in nine different States. But the Constitution went into effect only "between the States so ratifying the same," Art. VII; it did not bind the people of North Carolina until they had accepted it * * *.

* * *

These basic principles are enshrined in the Tenth Amendment, which declares that all powers neither delegated to the Federal Government nor prohibited to the States "are reserved to the States respectively, or to the people." With this careful last phrase, the Amendment avoids taking any position on the division of power between the state governments and the people of the States: It is up to the people of each State to determine which "reserved" powers their state government may exercise. But the Amendment does make clear that powers reside at the state level except where the Constitution removes them from that level. All powers that the Constitution neither delegates to the Federal Government nor prohibits to the States are controlled by the people of each State.

* * * The Constitution simply does not recognize any mechanism for action by the undifferentiated people of the Nation. Thus, the amendment provision of Article V calls for amendments to be ratified not by a convention of the national people, but by conventions of the people in each State or by the state legislatures elected by those people. Likewise, the Constitution calls for Members of Congress to be chosen State by State, rather than in nationwide elections. Even the selection of the President—surely the most national of national figures—is accomplished by an electoral college made up of delegates chosen by the various States, and candidates can lose a Presidential election despite winning a majority of the votes cast in the Nation as a whole.

In short, the notion of popular sovereignty that undergirds the Constitution does not erase state boundaries, but rather tracks them * * *. [T]he people of each State retained their separate political identities * * *.

* * * If we are to invalidate Arkansas' Amendment 73, we must point to something in the Federal Constitution that deprives the people of Arkansas of the power to enact such measures.

* * *

The majority begins by announcing an enormous and untenable limitation on the principle expressed by the Tenth Amendment. According to the majority, the States possess only those powers that the Constitution affirmatively grants to them or that they enjoyed before the Constitution was adopted; the Tenth Amendment "could only 'reserve' that which existed before" * * *.

* * * But it was not the state governments that were doing the reserving. The Constitution derives its authority instead from the consent of *the people* of the States. Given the fundamental principle that all governmental powers stem from the people of the States, it would simply be incoherent to assert that the people of the States could not reserve any powers that they had not previously controlled.

* * *

The majority is therefore quite wrong to conclude that the people of the States cannot authorize their state governments to exercise any powers that were unknown to the States when the Federal Constitution was drafted. Indeed, the majority's position frustrates the apparent purpose of the Amendment's final phrase. The Amendment does not pre-empt any limitations on state power found in the state constitutions, as it might have done if it simply had said that the powers not delegated to the Federal Government are reserved to the States. But the Amendment also does not prevent the people of the States from amending their state constitutions to remove limitations that were in effect when the Federal Constitution and the Bill of Rights were ratified.

* * *

The majority * * * suggests that it would be inconsistent with the notion of "national sovereignty" for the States or the people of the States to have any reserved powers over the selection of Members of Congress * * *.

Political scientists can debate about who commands the "primary allegiance" of Members of Congress once they reach Washington. From the framing to the present, however, the *selection* of the Representatives and Senators from each State has been left entirely to the people of that State or to their state legislature. See Art. I, § 2, cl. 1 (providing that Members of the House of Representatives are chosen "by the People of the several States"); Art. I, § 3, cl. 1 (originally providing that the Senators from each State are "chosen by the Legislature thereof"); Amdt. 17 (amending § 3 to provide that the Senators from each State are "elected by the people thereof"). The very name "congress" suggests a coming together of representatives from distinct entities. In keeping with the complexity of our federal system, once the representatives chosen by the people of each State assemble in Congress, they form a national body and are beyond the control of the individual States until the next election. But the selection of representatives in Congress is indisputably an act of the people of each State, not some abstract people of the Nation as a whole.

* * *

In a final effort to deny that the people of the States enjoy "reserved" powers over the selection of their representatives in Congress, the majority suggests that the Constitution expressly delegates to the States certain powers over congressional elections. Such delegations of power, the majority argues, would be superfluous if the people of the States enjoyed reserved powers in this area.

Only one constitutional provision—the Times, Places and Manner Clause of Article I, § 4—even arguably supports the majority's suggestion. It reads:

> "The Times, Places and Manner of holding Elections for Senators and Representatives, shall be prescribed in each State by the Legislature thereof; but the Congress may at any time by Law make or alter such Regulations, except as to the Places of chusing Senators."

Contrary to the majority's assumption, however, this Clause does not delegate any authority to the States. Instead, it simply imposes a duty upon them * * *.

Of course, the second part of the Times, Places and Manner Clause does grant a power rather than impose a duty. [H]owever, the Clause grants power exclusively to Congress, not to the States. If the Clause did not exist at all, the States would still be able to prescribe the times, places, and manner of holding congressional elections; the deletion of the provision would simply deprive Congress of the power to override these state regulations.

* * *

I take it to be established, then, that the people of Arkansas do enjoy "reserved" powers over the selection of their representatives in Congress. Purporting to exercise those reserved powers, they have agreed among themselves that the candidates covered by § 3 of Amendment 73—those whom they have already elected to three or more terms in the House of Representatives or to two or more terms in the Senate—should not be eligible to appear on the ballot for reelection, but should nonetheless be returned to Congress if enough voters are sufficiently enthusiastic about their candidacy to write in their names. Whatever one might think of the wisdom of this arrangement, we may not override the decision of the people of Arkansas unless something in the Federal Constitution deprives them of the power to enact such measures.

The majority settles on "the Qualifications Clauses" as the constitutional provisions that Amendment 73 violates. * * * [T]he Qualifications Clauses are merely straightforward recitations of the minimum eligibility requirements that the Framers thought it essential for every Member of Congress to meet. They restrict state power only in that they prevent the States from *abolishing* all eligibility requirements for membership in Congress.

* * *

* * * To the extent that they bear on this case, the records of the Philadelphia Convention affirmatively support my unwillingness to find hidden meaning in the Qualifications Clauses, while the surviving records from the ratification debates help neither side. As for the postratification period, five States supplemented the constitutional disqualifications in their very first election laws. The historical evidence thus refutes any notion that the Qualifications Clauses were generally understood to be exclusive. Yet the majority must establish just such an understanding in order to justify its position that the Clauses impose unstated prohibitions on the States and the people. In my view, the historical evidence is simply inadequate to warrant the majority's conclusion that the Qualifications Clauses mean anything more than what they say.

* * *

I agree with the majority that Congress has no power to prescribe qualifications for its own Members. This fact, however, does not show that the Qualifications Clauses contain a hidden exclusivity provision. The reason for Congress' incapacity is not that the Qualifications Clauses deprive Congress of the authority to set qualifications, but rather that nothing in the Constitution grants Congress this power. In the absence of such a grant, Congress may not act. But deciding whether the Constitution denies the qualification-setting power to the States and the people of the States requires a fundamentally different legal analysis.

* * *

It is radical enough for the majority to hold that the Constitution implicitly precludes the people of the States from prescribing any eligibility requirements for the congressional candidates who seek their votes. This holding, after all, does not stop with negating the term limits that many States have seen fit to impose on their Senators and Representatives. Today's decision also means that no State may disqualify congressional candidates whom a court has found to be mentally incompetent, see, *e.g.*, Fla.Stat. §§ 97.041(2), 99.021(1)(a) (1991), who are currently in prison, see, *e.g.*, Ill.Comp.Stat.Ann., ch. 10, §§ 5/3–5, 5/7–10, 5/10–5 (1993 and West Supp.1995), or who have past vote-fraud convictions, see, *e.g.*, Ga.Code Ann. §§ 21–2–2(25), 21–2–8 (1993 and Supp.1994). Likewise, after today's decision, the people of each State must leave open the possibility that they will trust someone with their vote in Congress even though they do not trust him with *a* vote in the election for Congress. See, *e.g.*, R.I.Gen.Laws § 17–14–1.2 (1988) (restricting candidacy to people "qualified to vote").

In order to invalidate § 3 of Amendment 73, however, the majority must go further. The bulk of the majority's analysis * * * addresses the issues that would be raised if Arkansas had prescribed "genuine, unadulterated, undiluted term limits." But as the parties have agreed, Amendment 73 does not actually create this kind of disqualification. *See* Tr. of Oral Arg. 53–54. It does not say that covered candidates may not serve any more terms in Congress if reelected, and it does not indirectly achieve the same result by barring those candidates from seeking reelection. It says only that if they are to win reelection, they must do so by write-in votes.

* * *

I am not sure why the intent behind a law should affect our analysis under the Qualifications Clauses. If a law does not in fact add to the constitutional qualifications, the mistaken expectations of the people who enacted it would not seem to affect whether it violates the alleged exclusivity of those Clauses * * *.

* * *

* * * Current federal law (enacted, of course, by congressional incumbents) confers numerous advantages on incumbents, and these advantages are widely thought to make it "significantly more difficult" for challengers to defeat them . For instance, federal law gives incumbents enormous advantages in building name recognition and good will in their home districts. See, *e.g.,* 39 U.S.C. § 3210 (permitting Members of Congress to send "franked" mail free of charge); 2 U.S.C. §§ 61–1, 72a, 332 (permitting Members to have sizable taxpayer-funded staffs); 2 U.S.C. § 123b (establishing the House Recording Studio and the Senate Recording and Photographic Studios) * * *.

* * *

At the same time that incumbents enjoy the electoral advantages that they have conferred upon themselves, they also enjoy astonishingly high reelection rates * * *.

The voters of Arkansas evidently believe that incumbents would not enjoy such overwhelming success if electoral contests were truly fair—that is, if the government did not put its thumb on either side of the scale. The majority offers no reason to question the accuracy of this belief. Given this context, petitioners portray § 3 of Amendment 73 as an effort at the state level to offset the electoral advantages that congressional incumbents have conferred upon themselves at the federal level.

* * *

I do not mean to suggest that States have unbridled power to handicap particular classes of candidates, even when those candidates enjoy federally conferred advantages that may threaten to skew the electoral process. But laws that allegedly have the purpose and effect of handicapping a particular class of candidates traditionally are reviewed under the First and Fourteenth Amendments rather than the Qualifications Clauses * * *.

* * *

* * * [T]oday's decision reads the Qualifications Clauses to impose substantial implicit prohibitions on the States and the people of the States. I would not draw such an expansive negative inference from the fact that the Constitution requires Members of Congress to be a certain age, to be inhabitants of the States that they represent, and to have been United States citizens for a specified period. Rather, I would read the Qualifications Clauses to do no more than what they say. I respectfully dissent.

NOTES AND QUESTIONS

1. No justice in *Thornton* argued that the case presented a political question beyond the capacity of the courts to decide. Why not? Should someone have made that argument?

2. Under the Articles of Confederation, members of the Continental Congress were subject to term limits. As the majority notes, the Framers of the U.S. Constitution explicitly decided that term limits for members of Congress were a bad idea, and so the Constitution deliberately omits them. Can the States undo this founding era decision by manipulating its ballot access laws?

3. The upholding of Arkansas's term limits of Members of Congress in this case would have had a negative external effect on other States, because a House of Congress half of whose members are subject to term limits would never agree to a seniority system for distributing Committee Chairmanships or seats on congressional committees. Term-limited Members of Congress would vote down seniority systems. Professor Calabresi thinks congressional seniority systems are valuable, preserve institutional and foreign policy knowledge, and help check presidential power. He also thinks the Qualifications Clauses of the federal Constitution preempt Arkansas's ballot placement law.

4. In the wake of *Term Limits v. Thornton,* can the States constitutionally disqualify felons from being elected to and serving in Congress? If not, can the States prohibit felons from voting given that they are eligible to be elected to Congress? What if a felon is still in prison and cannot perform the duties of being a member of Congress?

5. Robert G. Natelson, *The Original Scope of the Congressional Power to Regulate Elections,* U. Pa. J. Const. L. 1 (2010), argues that Arkansas did not actually impose term limits, or place any other qualifications, on its federal legislators. It just placed limits on whose name could appear on a printed ballot. Anyone who met the three constitutional qualifications, including any long-standing incumbent member of Congress, was free to run for and serve in Congress. That implicates yet another constitutional provision dealing with federal elections that appears in Article I, section 4, clause 1 and that played a role in *Thornton*:

> **The Times, Places, and Manner of holding Elections for Senators and Representatives, shall be prescribed in each State by the Legislature thereof; but the Congress may at any time by Law make or alter such Regulations, except as to the Places of chusing Senators.**

Natelson argues that the Constitution explicitly places the default responsibility for election machinery with the States, subject to congressional override. The forms of ballots would seem to be a "Manner of holding Elections" within the constitutional power of the States, and Arkansas Amendment 73 was framed as a matter of ballot form. No congressional statute overturned that state ballot regulation. Was the Qualifications Clause even relevant to this case? The majority thought so because changing the State's ballot-access regulations might have the same *effect* as imposing direct qualifications for office even if, as a formal matter, they do not actually impose additional qualifications for office. Is that the right way to think about the Constitution in general? About structural provisions specifically? If the Court was right, does that mean that a State has to include on its ballots every single person who meets the three constitutional requirements who wants to run for office? What if ten thousand people who meet the three requirements want to run for a single congressional seat? How far does congressional power under the Times, Places, and Manner Clause extend? That clause is, for example, the source of power for the congressional statute that since 1842 has required congressional elections to be held by district rather than at large. *See* Act of June 25,1842, ch. 47, 5 Stat. 491.

Does it allow Congress to force States to allow people to register to vote whenever they apply for a driver's license? *See* 52 U.S.C. § 20504(a)(1) (2018) ("Each State motor vehicle driver's license application (including any renewal application) submitted to the appropriate State motor vehicle authority under State law shall serve as an application for voter registration with respect to elections for Federal office unless the applicant fails to sign the voter registration application.") Does it allow Congress to regulate how much money can be spent on federal elections and by whom it can be spent?

[Assignment 12]

J. IMPEACHMENT

Most of Article I, section 2 is concerned with the structure of the House of Representatives. As we saw, clause 1 concerns terms and election, and clause 2 concerns qualifications for holding office. Clause 3 sets out the initial apportionment of representatives (and direct taxes!) among the States, provides for recalibration of that apportionment every ten years in light of the census, and contains the infamous clause giving slaveowners three-fifths of an extra vote for each of their slaves—a provision that was amended away following the Civil War. Clauses 4 and 5 are brief:

> **When vacancies happen in the Representation from any State, the Executive Authority thereof shall issue Writs of Election to fill such Vacancies.**
>
> **The House of Representatives shall choose their Speaker and other Officers; and shall have the sole Power of Impeachment.**

Clause 4 is straightforward and has a slightly more complicated counterpart in the Seventeenth Amendment for filling Senate vacancies. *See* Zachary D. Clopton & Steven E. Art, *The Meaning of the Seventeenth Amendment and a History of State Defiance,* 107 NW. U.L REV. 1181 (2013). Clause 5 guarantees the House the right to choose its own officers—a perhaps overly cautious guard against the President and Senate claiming that power under the Appointments Clause. There is again a parallel clause for Senate officers, *see* U.S. CONST. art. I, § 3, cl. 5 ("The Senate shall chuse their other Officers, and also a President pro tempore, in the Absence of the Vice President, or when he shall exercise the Office of President of the United States"), subject to the constitutional designation of the Vice President as the President of the Senate. *See id.* art. I § 3, cl. 4 ("The Vice President of the United States shall be President of the Senate, but shall have no Vote, unless they be equally divided"). Then, in a seemingly discordant note from these internal structural matters, clause 5 adds that the House "shall have the sole power of impeachment."

That is the first of six provisions in the Constitution dealing with impeachment. Two of those provisions, in Article I, section 3, clauses 6–7, concern the role of the Senate and the Chief Justice of the Supreme Court:

> **The Senate shall have the sole Power to try all Impeachments. When sitting for that Purpose, they shall be on Oath or Affirmation. When the President of the United States is tried, the Chief Justice shall preside: And no Person shall be convicted without the Concurrence of two thirds of the Members present.**
>
> **Judgment in Cases of Impeachment shall not extend further than to removal from Office, and disqualification to hold and enjoy**

any Office of honor, Trust or Profit under the United States: but the Party convicted shall nevertheless be liable and subject to Indictment, Trial, Judgment and Punishment, according to Law.

Another provision specifies that all civil officers, including the President, are subject to impeachment and identifies the permissible grounds for impeachment and removal: **"The President, Vice President and all civil Officers of the United States, shall be removed from Office on Impeachment for, and Conviction of, Treason, Bribery, or other high Crimes and Misdemeanors."** *Id.* art. II, § 4. Other provisions clarify that the President's pardon power does not extend to cases of impeachment, *see id.* art. II, § 2, cl. 1, and that constitutional guarantees of trial by jury do not apply to impeachment proceedings. *See id.* art. III, § 2, cl. 3. Impeachment is obviously a topic that that Constitution takes very seriously.

Impeachment thus requires two steps by two distinct bodies. First, the House must decide (by a majority vote) whether to impeach. If it does, then the Senate must decide (by a two-thirds majority vote) to convict or else nothing happens as a result of the House's action. The House thus acts, in essence, as an executive prosecutor, and the Senate acts in a judicial or adjudicative capacity. Justice Story says that these clauses of the Constitution "respect the judicial power of the Senate to try impeachments", and he observes that the Senate rather than a court of law is the appropriate tribunal because "[i]n the first place, the offences to be tried are generally of a political character * * *." JOSEPH STORY, A FAMILIAR EXPOSITION OF THE CONSTITUTION OF THE UNITED STATES 102 (1986). As one scholar frames it, "The framers and ratifiers chose Congress as the federal impeachment authority because they believed that the special power to sanction executive and judicial misconduct should be exercised by an electorally accountable body that was not subject to the control of those whom it was attempting to discipline." MICHAEL J. GERHARDT, THE FEDERAL IMPEACHMENT PROCESS: A CONSTITUTIONAL AND HISTORICAL ANALYSIS 1 (3d ed. 2019).

Alexander Hamilton addressed the subject of impeachment ably in the following essay.

K. FEDERALIST NO. 65 (HAMILTON)

* * *A well-constituted court for the trial of impeachments is an object not more to be desired than difficult to be obtained in a government wholly elective. The subjects of its jurisdiction are those offenses which proceed from the misconduct of public men, or, in other words, from the abuse or violation of some public trust. They are of a nature which may with peculiar propriety be denominated POLITICAL, as they relate chiefly to injuries done immediately to the society itself. The prosecution of them, for this reason, will seldom fail to agitate the passions of the whole community, and to divide it into parties more or less friendly or inimical to the accused. In many cases it will connect itself with the pre-existing factions, and will enlist all their animosities, partialities, influence, and interest on one side or on the other; and in such cases there will always be the greatest danger that the decision will be regulated more by the comparative strength of parties, than by the real demonstrations of innocence or guilt.

The delicacy and magnitude of a trust which so deeply concerns the political reputation and existence of every man engaged in the administration of public affairs, speak for themselves. The difficulty of placing it rightly, in a government resting entirely on the basis of periodical elections, will as readily be perceived, when it is considered that the most conspicuous characters in it will, from that circumstance, be too often the leaders or the tools of the most cunning or the most numerous faction, and on this account, can hardly be expected to possess the requisite neutrality towards those whose conduct may be the subject of scrutiny.

The convention, it appears, thought the Senate the most fit depositary of this important trust. Those who can best discern the intrinsic difficulty of the thing, will be least hasty in condemning that opinion, and will be most inclined to allow due weight to the arguments which may be supposed to have produced it.

What, it may be asked, is the true spirit of the institution itself? Is it not designed as a method of NATIONAL INQUEST into the conduct of public men? If this be the design of it, who can so properly be the inquisitors for the nation as the representatives of the nation themselves? It is not disputed that the power of originating the inquiry, or, in other words, of preferring the impeachment, ought to be lodged in the hands of one branch of the legislative body. Will not the reasons which indicate the propriety of this arrangement strongly plead for an admission of the other branch of that body to a share of the inquiry? The model from which the idea of this institution has been borrowed, pointed out that course to the convention. In Great Britain it is the province of the House of Commons to prefer the impeachment, and of the House of Lords to decide upon it. Several of the State constitutions have followed the example. As well the latter, as the former, seem to have regarded the practice of impeachments as a bridle in the hands of the legislative body upon the executive servants of the government. Is not this the true light in which it ought to be regarded?

Where else than in the Senate could have been found a tribunal sufficiently dignified, or sufficiently independent? What other body would be likely to feel CONFIDENCE ENOUGH IN ITS OWN SITUATION, to preserve, unawed and uninfluenced, the necessary impartiality between an INDIVIDUAL accused, and the REPRESENTATIVES OF THE PEOPLE, HIS ACCUSERS?

Could the Supreme Court have been relied upon as answering this description? It is much to be doubted, whether the members of that tribunal would at all times be endowed with so eminent a portion of fortitude, as would be called for in the execution of so difficult a task; and it is still more to be doubted, whether they would possess the degree of credit and authority, which might, on certain occasions, be indispensable towards reconciling the people to a decision that should happen to clash with an accusation brought by their immediate representatives. A deficiency in the first, would be fatal to the accused; in the last, dangerous to the public tranquillity. The hazard in both these respects, could only be avoided, if at all, by rendering that tribunal more numerous than would consist with a reasonable attention to economy. The necessity of a numerous court for the trial of impeachments, is equally dictated by the nature of the proceeding. This can never be tied down by such strict rules, either in the delineation of the offense by the prosecutors, or in the construction of it by the judges, as in common cases serve to limit the discretion of courts in favor of personal security. There will be no jury to stand between the judges who are to pronounce the sentence of the law, and the party who is to receive or suffer it. The awful discretion which a court of impeachments must necessarily have, to doom to honor or to infamy the most confidential and the most distinguished characters of the community, forbids the commitment of the trust to a small number of persons.

These considerations seem alone sufficient to authorize a conclusion, that the Supreme Court would have been an improper substitute for the Senate, as a court of impeachments. There remains a further consideration, which will not a little strengthen this conclusion. It is this: The punishment which may be the consequence of conviction upon impeachment, is not to terminate the chastisement of the offender. After having been sentenced to a perpetual ostracism from the esteem and confidence, and honors and emoluments of his country, he will still be liable to prosecution and punishment in the ordinary course of law. Would it be proper that the persons who had disposed of his fame, and his most valuable rights as a citizen in one trial, should, in another trial, for the same offense, be also the disposers of his life and his fortune? Would there not be the greatest reason to apprehend, that error, in the first sentence, would be the parent of error in the second sentence? That the strong bias of one decision would be apt to overrule the influence of any new lights which might be brought to vary the complexion of another decision? Those who know anything of human nature, will not hesitate to answer these questions in the affirmative; and will be at no loss to perceive, that by making the same persons judges in both cases, those who might happen to be the objects of prosecution would, in a great measure, be deprived of the double security intended them by a double trial * * *.

NOTES AND QUESTIONS

1. Is impeachment a legislative power (because it oversees both executive and judicial officers), an executive power (because it involves a prosecutorial element), a judicial power (because of the adjudicative role of the Senate), or something that defies categorization? Because the Constitution specifically allocates the various functions involved in impeachment to specific institutions, it is not necessary to use the abstract categories of legislative, executive, and judicial power in order to identify the constitutional rules for impeachment. Or is it? Is it relevant that when the Senate tries impeachments, it describes itself as a Court of Impeachment?

2. In defending the decision to lodge the power to convict and remove impeached officers in the Senate rather than a court, Hamilton claimed: "The awful discretion which a court of impeachments must necessarily have, to doom to honor or to infamy the most confidential and the most distinguished characters of the community, forbids the commitment of the trust to a small number of persons." Is "nine" a small number of persons? Is "eighteen" (the number of Senators if only nine States had ratified the Constitution) a small number? People get sent to jail by single judges or, at most, twelve-person juries. Is losing your office in an impeachment proceeding worse than getting life in prison or the death penalty, so that a large adjudicative body is necessary for the former but not the latter? Is the overturning of a presidential election or a Supreme Court appointment a momentous matter? Or does Hamilton really mean that you need a larger body for removal of an executive or judicial official for the same reasons that James Madison thought that an effective republic needed a larger territory—*i.e.,* to minimize the influence of faction? In that case, why not let the Senate impeach and the House convict and remove? The answer is because House members are up for re-election every two years whereas Senators are up for re-election every six years. Senators, who are elected statewide, are more moderate than congressmen and are more likely to take a long run view of things.

3. Early proposals at the Constitutional Convention uniformly would have placed impeachment with the judiciary—either the federal judiciary or a panel composed of the highest judge in each State. *See* GERHARDT, *supra,* at 5–7. James Madison, in particular, objected to giving the Senate a role because he thought it would make the President too dependent on the Senate. *See id.* at 7. The Convention ultimately settled on the Senate as the final authority because it "posed the fewest problems of any of the proposed trial courts." *Id.*

4. Article II concludes in Section 4 by declaring that the president, vice president and all civil officers of the United States "shall be removed from Office on Impeachment for, and Conviction of, Treason, Bribery, or other high Crimes and Misdemeanors." This makes clear that the President of the United States is removable from office by impeachment, unlike the King of England. The only ways to get rid of the King were to kill him, force him to abdicate, or drive him into exile. These things were done from time to time, but it was an expensive way of getting rid of a king.

5. The permissible constitutional grounds for impeachment are "Treason, Bribery, or other high Crimes and Misdemeanors." With regard to the meaning of "high Crimes and Misdemeanors": Some people at the Constitutional Convention wanted impeachment limited only to treason and bribery. Others, such as James Madison and George Mason, thought those two grounds excessively narrow.

> Mason then moved to add "maladministration" in order to permit impeachment upon less conventionally defined common-law offenses. [Eldridge] Gerry seconded the motion. Madison objected that "[s]o vague a term will be equivalent to a tenure during pleasure of the Senate" * * *. Mason thereupon withdrew his motion and substituted as the grounds for impeachment "bribery and other high crimes and misdemeanors," which he evidently understood as including maladministration. The motion carried without any further discussion of the new phrase by a vote of eight to three.

GERHARDT, *supra,* at 8–9. Does this mean that executive officials can be impeached and removed because Congress thinks they are doing a lousy job? Can judges be impeached and removed because Congress thinks they are deciding cases incorrectly?

6. When people think about impeachment, they normally think about impeachment of presidents. In pre-U.S. England, impeachment was largely about removing executive ministers since kings were not subject to impeachment. All too often, Parliament would execute the King's favorite ministers in the process, which is why the Constitution takes pains to specify that removal and disqualification from office are the only penalties for impeachment. As a matter of practice in the U.S., impeachment has almost always been about judges. Under the Constitution, federal judges serve "during good Behaviour," so impeachment is the only way to get rid of them. The most important Supreme Court decision on the impeachment process involved a federal judge. *See (Walter) Nixon v. United States,* 506 U.S. 224 (1993). Judge Nixon had been convicted of lying to a grand jury and was sent to prison. He continued to draw his salary as a judge, because federal judges are not removed from office simply because they are felons; they can only be removed from office through impeachment. The House accordingly adopted articles of impeachment, and the case moved to the Senate, which employed the following procedure:

> After the House presented the articles to the Senate, the Senate voted to invoke its own Impeachment Rule XI, under which the presiding officer appoints a committee of Senators to "receive evidence and take testimony." Senate Impeachment Rule XI. The Senate committee held four days of

> hearings, during which 10 witnesses, including Nixon, testified. Pursuant to Rule XI, the committee presented the full Senate with a complete transcript of the proceeding and a Report stating the uncontested facts and summarizing the evidence on the contested facts. Nixon and the House impeachment managers submitted extensive final briefs to the full Senate and delivered arguments from the Senate floor during the three hours set aside for oral argument in front of that body. Nixon himself gave a personal appeal, and several Senators posed questions directly to both parties. The Senate voted by more than the constitutionally required two-thirds majority to convict Nixon on the first two articles. The presiding officer then entered judgment removing Nixon from his office as United States District Judge.

Id., at 227–28. Judge Nixon claimed that in order to "try" an impeachment within the meaning of the Constitution, *all* senators must participate in the evidentiary hearing and that the Senate cannot "try" an impeachment by delegating fact-finding to a committee. The Supreme Court concluded that the case presented a non-justiciable political question, both because the Constitution gives the "sole" power to convict to the Senate and because "the word 'try' in the Impeachment Trial Clause does not provide an identifiable textual limit on the authority which is committed to the Senate." *Id.* at 238. Of course, if the first reason is adequate to divest the courts of jurisdiction, the second is superfluous. Does that mean that the Court was reserving the right to intervene in future impeachments when it *did* think that it could discern a textual limit? Several justices expressly wanted to reserve that right. *See id.* at 239 (White, J., concurring in the judgment); *id.* at 252 (Souter, J., concurring in the judgment). Does having the "sole" power of impeachment mean that the Senate can do literally anything it wishes once the House votes articles of impeachment?

7. In 1789, when the Constitution went into full effect, there were twenty-two senators. Today there are one hundred senators. Is it feasible to have a fact-finding process in which one hundred people simultaneously participate? Federal grand juries "consist of not less than sixteen nor more than twenty-three persons." 18 U.S.C. § 3321 (2018). Is delegation of investigatory fact-finding to a Senate committee unavoidable?

8. The Constitution specifically says that two features of federal criminal trials—trial by jury and the possibility of a presidential pardon—do not apply to impeachments. Does that establish by implication that other essential features of criminal trials, such as confrontation of witnesses and general notions of due process of law, do apply to impeachments? Could Congress impeach and remove someone based on closed-door testimony that is never revealed either to the public or to the official who is impeached and removed? Would that action be judicially reviewable after *Nixon*? Note that the Sixth Amendment applies "[i]n all criminal prosecutions" and that Article III, Section 2, Clause 3 says that: "[t]he Trial of all Crimes, except in Cases of Impeachment, shall be by Jury."

9. Walter Nixon was impeached and removed *after* he had been convicted of serious federal crimes. Suppose he had been impeached and removed for issuing poorly reasoned opinions, or for delegating too much of the work to his law clerks, or for telling inappropriate jokes. Or suppose that a judge declares, "I do not believe in law and do not feel bound by it." *See* RICHARD POSNER, OVERCOMING LAW (1995). Are those constitutionally permissible grounds for impeachment? The question is not entirely hypothetical. In the early 1800s, district judge John Pickering was impeached and removed for alleged drunkenness and insanity. *See* Adam A. Perlin, *The Impeachment of Samuel Chase: Redefining Judicial Independence,* 62 RUTGERS L. REV. 725, 741–42 (2010. Supreme Court Samuel Chase was impeached in 1804 in large measure because congressional Jeffersonian Democrats did not like his decisions (nor his obvious

Federalist party bias in giving jury instructions), *see id.* at 742–46, but he was acquitted by the Senate in a decision that has long been taken as a legislative precedent against removing judges based on their decision-making. *See* WILLIAM H. REHNQUIST, GRAND INQUESTS: THE HISTORIC IMPEACHMENTS OF JUSTICE SAMUEL CHASE AND PRESIDENT ANDREW JOHNSON (1992). *But see* Michael Stokes Paulsen, *Checking the Court,* 10 N.Y.U. J. L. & LIBERTY 18, 67–90 (2016) (arguing that impeachment of judges based on bad decisions can be justified). Does *Nixon* establish that all questions about the appropriate grounds for impeachment are non-justiciable?

10. There might be a resolution to the justiciability question that has largely escaped notice. Article III gives the federal courts jurisdiction to hear: 1) cases in law, 2) cases in equity, 3) cases in admiralty, and 4) six party-based kinds of controversies. Note that in England and Wales in 1787: 1) cases in law were heard by the Court of King's Bench, the Court of Common Pleas, or the Court of Exchequer; 2) cases in equity were heard by the Court of Chancery; and 3) cases in admiralty were heard by special admiralty courts and were decided without a jury. Cases in impeachment, in England and Wales in 1787, were heard by Parliament. The U.S. Constitution thus actually assigns jurisdiction over "Cases in Impeachment" to the House of Representative and the Senate rather than the federal courts. Impeachment is a political question—or, more precisely, not a judicial question—because the Article III federal courts quite literally do not have jurisdiction over it. It is not a case in law, equity, or admiralty.

11. Three presidents have been impeached: Andrew Johnson in 1868, Bill Clinton in 1998, and Donald Trump in 2020. Andrew Johnson's fate was very much in the air; indeed, his acquittal (by one vote in the Senate) was something of a surprise. On the other hand, given the party alignment in the Senate in 1998 and 2020 and the public reactions to the Clinton and Trump impeachments, there was no chance at all that the Senate was going to vote to remove President Clinton or President Trump from office. Everyone in the House of Representatives knew this in both instances. Should the House ever impeach an executive or judicial officer when it is clear that the Senate will not remove the official? *See* Congressional Record—House 105th Congress, 2nd Session, 144 Cong. Rec. H 11975 (statement of Rep. Charles Canady) ("I believe that we have an independent responsibility, under the Constitution, to make a judgment concerning the conduct of the president, and whether he should be impeached or not. And it would be in derogation of our constitutional responsibility to attempt to count noses in the Senate.").

L. CONGRESSIONAL MEETINGS

Article I, Section 4, Clause 2: The Congress shall assemble at least once in every Year, and such Meeting shall be on the first Monday in December, unless they shall by Law appoint a different Day.

Article I, Section 5, Clause 4: Neither House, during the Session of Congress, shall, without the Consent of the other, adjourn for more than three days, nor to any other Place than that in which the two Houses shall be sitting.

Article II, Section 3: [The President] may, on extraordinary Occasions, convene both Houses, or either of them, and in Case of Disagreement between them, with Respect to the Time of Adjournment, he may adjourn them to such Time as he shall think proper.

Under England's founding-era parliamentary system, the King could call and dismiss Parliament at will (though as a practical matter he needed to call it whenever he needed money). Sometimes as much as eleven years would go by before the King called Parliament into session. Article I, Section 4 prevents this from occurring in the United States. The Twentieth Amendment, ratified in 1933, repeats and clarifies the fixed obligation of Congress to meet and also sets the dates on which presidential and congressional terms begin and end:

> **Section 1. The terms of the President and Vice President shall end at noon on the 20th day of January, and the terms of Senators and Representatives at noon on the 3d day of January, of the years in which such terms would have ended if this article had not been ratified; and the terms of their successors shall then begin.**
>
> **Section 2. The Congress shall assemble at least once in every year, and such meeting shall begin at noon on the 3d day of January, unless they shall by law appoint a different day.**

U.S. CONST. amend. XX, §§ 1–2. The provision for the President to call special sessions of Congress was very important in early days, when Congress met only for short times and quick congressional action was sometimes needed to deal with wars and other crises. Note that the Constitution only allows the President to create *additional* meeting times; the Constitution sets an unavoidable floor for congressional sessions.

The adjournment provisions similarly avoid the traditional executive power to dismiss (or "prorogue") the legislature at will. The President's limited power to adjourn Congress only comes into play when Congress itself cannot agree, and the power "to adjourn them to such Time as he shall think proper" is constrained by the requirement of annual sessions.

If these provisions seem arcane and pointless, take a few minutes to re-read the Declaration of Independence and see how many of the colonists' complaints about the King relate to matters addressed by these provisions. It is (in our opinion) a sign of the Constitution's genius that we do not even think about these provisions anymore. They function silently, like the operating system of the computer in the background—though we will later address a few important modern issues regarding congressional adjournments and recesses. *See infra* pages 412–430.

M. ARTICLE I, SECTION 5: "EACH HOUSE MAY DETERMINE THE RULES OF ITS PROCEEDINGS"

Article I, Section 5 grants to the Senate and the House the power to determine the rules of their own proceedings. This is one of the few areas where each body can act alone. Both the Senate and the House of Representatives have adopted rules to govern their proceedings and at least some of those rules are of constitutional magnitude. The most obvious example is the Senate rule that debates (and thus "filibusters") can be stopped only by a three-fifths majority of the Senate, which today means sixty votes. *See* Rules of the Senate XXII. Without a successful "cloture" motion approved by three-fifths of the body, the Senate will not vote on the substance of matters before it, whether it be legislation, appointments, or treaties. The U.S.

Senate is, as far as we know, the only legislative body in the world where most important decisions require a super-majority. The Senate rule establishing the three-fifths threshold to end filibusters is thus of constitutional magnitude. It affects the entire operation of the Congress in lawmaking and the President's ability to have nominees confirmed.

While Rule XXII is framed (in very obscure language) as a rule about cutting of debate, it has the practical effect of imposing a sixty-vote requirement for virtually all Senate action—especially since under modern practice the Senate leaders no longer make filibustering senators actually talk for hours on end but simply treat the threat of a filibuster as sufficient grounds to move on to other business if sixty votes for cloture are not at hand. Moreover, Rule XXII states that the three-fifths rule governs "except on a measure or motion to amend the Senate rules, in which case the necessary affirmative vote shall be two-thirds of the Senators present and voting." In other words, Rule XXII purports to make itself (and all other Senate rules) unamendable by a simple majority vote of the Senate.

The Constitution says, quite simply, that "[e]ach House may determine the Rules of its Proceedings." Can one Senate adopt rules for subsequent senates and then make those rules effectively unamendable (if Rule XXII can require a two-thirds vote for amendments, it can presumably require unanimity as well)? This raises an ancient question, long preceding the Constitution, about the extent to which one legislative body can bind its successors. *See* John O. McGinnis & Michael B. Rappaport, *Symmetric Entrenchment: A Constitutional and Normative Theory,* 89 VA. L. REV. 385 (2003). Consider the arguments made in the following testimony before the Senate Judiciary Committee.

Testimony of Professor Steven G. Calabresi

Senate Judiciary Committee Hearing on Judicial Nominations and Filibusters (May 6, 2003)

* * * The U.S. Constitution was written to establish majority rule. The historical reasons for this are clear. A major defect with the Constitution's precursor, the Articles of Confederation, was that it required super majorities for making many important decisions. The Framers deliberately set out to remedy this defect by empowering Congress to make most decisions by a simple majority. The only exceptions to this principle are in seven express situations where a two-thirds vote is required. Each house of Congress does have the power by majority vote to establish the rules of its proceedings but there's no evidence this clause was originally meant to authorize filibusters. From 1789 to 1806, the Senate's rules allowed for cutting off debate by moving the previous question, a motion which required only a simple majority to pass.

The filibuster of legislation did not originate until 1841, when it was employed by Senator John C. Calhoun to defend slavery and an extreme vision of minority rights. Calhoun was called a filibusterer from a Dutch word for pirate, or as we would say today terrorist, because he was subverting majority rule. From 1841 to the present, the principle use of the filibuster has been to defend Jim Crow laws oppressing African Americans. Now for the first time in 214 years a minority of senators are seeking to extend filibustering from legislation to the whole new area of judicial nominees—nominees who they know enjoy the support of a majority of the Senate.

This is a bad idea * * *. First, such filibusters weaken the power of the president, who is one of only two officers of government who is elected to represent all of the American people. Second, filibusters of judges undermine judicial independence by giving a minority of senators led by special interest groups a veto over who can become a judge. It's already hard enough for talented and capable individuals to be appointed judges without a minority of senators imposing a litmus test * * *.

The Senate can always change its rules by majority vote. To the extent that Senate Rule Twenty-Two purports to require a two-thirds majority for rules changes, Rule Twenty-Two is unconstitutional. It is an ancient principle of Anglo-American constitutional law that one session of a legislature cannot bind a succeeding session of the same legislature. This principle goes back to the great William Blackstone, who said in his commentaries "Acts of Parliament derogatory from the power of subsequent parliaments be naught." Three vice presidents of the United States presiding over the Senate, Richard Nixon, Hubert Humphrey, and Nelson Rockefeller, have all ruled that the Senate rules can be changed by a simple majority of the Senate. Lloyd Cutler, White House Counsel to Presidents Jimmy Carter and Bill Clinton, has written in the "Washington Post" that Senate Rule Twenty-Two is plainly unconstitutional. The Senate can and should now amend Rule Twenty-Two by simple majority vote to ban filibusters of judicial nominations.

NOTES AND QUESTIONS

1. If you consult the Constitution, you will see that the text provides for a two-thirds majority for: (1) the passage of constitutional amendments by both the House and the Senate; (2) the overriding of a presidential veto by both the House and the Senate; (3) the ratification of a treaty by the Senate only; (4) the conviction of an official by the Senate only when that official has been impeached by a majority of the House of Representatives; (5) the expulsion of a member either of the Senate or of the House of Representatives; (6) the lifting by either the Senate or the House of the ineligibility for service of an individual who, despite having taken an oath to uphold the Constitution, has "engaged in insurrection or rebellion against the same, or given aid or comfort to the enemies thereof"; and (7) the Senate and the House acting together to remove from office a president who is disabled, upon the petition of the Vice President and a majority of the Cabinet. In *all* other instances, the presumption seems to be a presumption of majority rule. This is the case for law-making pursuant to Article I, Section 7; for admitting new States to the union pursuant to Article IV, Section 3; and even for calling a new constitutional convention pursuant to Article V. There is an ancient canon of construing written texts which you have already encountered called *expressio unius est exclusio alterius*: the writing down of some things excludes all others not mentioned. Does the Constitution's requirement of a super-majority in seven instances prove that in all other instances a simple majority is enough? Most important decisions under the Articles of Confederation required the support of a super-majority of nine States to pass. The Framers of the Constitution hated this super-majority rule, which they blamed for the weakness of the Continental Congress. They deliberately departed from it by creating a presumption of majority decision-making in the Constitution except where the text explicitly provided otherwise.

2. Are super-majority rules a good idea as a matter of policy? Is the Senate filibuster a good idea as a matter of policy? We already have bicameralism, the presidential veto, and judicial review to slow down the making of new laws. Do we really need or want Senate filibusters as well? See John O. McGinnis & Michael B. Rappaport, *The Condorcet Case for Supermajority Rules*, SUP. CT. ECON. REV. (2008). On the other

hand, a key factor in promoting economic growth is certainty and stability in the law, which allows people to invest and plan for the future more readily. Rules that promote stability—even perhaps the Senate filibuster?—can reduce risk and thus encourage investment in the United States.

3. Is there a stronger or a weaker case for super-majority rules when confirming federal judges, especially Supreme Court justices? The U.S. Senate in recent years has eliminated filibusters of both lower federal court judges (in 2013, with a Democratic President and Democratic Senate) and Supreme Court justices (in 2017, with a Republican President and Republican Senate) through a parliamentary maneuver that assumes that Rule XXII, as with all other rules, can be overridden by a majority vote on a point of order. This reduces from sixty to fifty the number of Senators needed to confirm a nominee (assuming that the Vice President will break a 50–50 tie in favor of the President's nominee). Was this reform a good idea or a bad idea? The Federal Republic of Germany requires a two-thirds vote of a committee of the lower house of its legislature to pick half the justices on the German Constitutional Court, while the other half are picked by a two-thirds vote of the upper house of the legislature which represents the German states. Is the function of constitutional interpretation best entrusted to those who can muster a legislative super-majority or will such a rule produce a bland and overly cautious court? Even if such a rule were to be employed for nominees to the U.S. Supreme Court, is it desirable to use filibusters in responding to lower court judicial nominations or to executive branch nominations?

4. Right after the rulemaking provision, the Constitution says: "Each House shall keep a Journal of its Proceedings, and from time to time publish the same, excepting such Parts as may in their Judgment require Secrecy; and the Yeas and Nays of the Members of either House on any question shall, at the Desire of one fifth of those Present, be entered on the Journal." U.S. CONST. art. I, § 5, cl. 3. From 1873 onward, the *Congressional Record* has served as the official reporter for affairs in Congress. (Private services published reports of congressional debates before 1873, with wildly varying degrees of accuracy.) Members can insert anything they wish into the *Congressional Record,* including remarks or speeches that they never made on the floor of Congress. In theory, according to internal congressional rules, any changes or additions to the actual remarks made are supposed to be clearly indicated. In practice, the results are mixed, though Congress's control of the content of its journal, including whether or not it chooses to enforce its own rules about marking added content, has been deemed a political question not subject to judicial review. *See Gregg v. Barrett,* 772 F.2d 539 (D.C.Cir.1985).

N. CONGRESSIONAL COMMITTEES AND THE POWER TO INVESTIGATE

Another set of rules with constitutional significance adopted by both the Senate and the House of Representatives is the division of each body into numerous committees and sub-committees that deal with every issue of law-making, oversight, and investigation. Membership on these committees is partially the result of a seniority system and partially the result of member preferences. Usually, members ask to be appointed to, and eventually (if they acquire enough seniority) are appointed to, committees whose business is a special concern of the member's home state or congressional district. Thus, farm state members of Congress typically gravitate toward the Agriculture Committees, while members from New York and other commercial centers prefer to be on the Finance or Ways and Means Committees. The combination of interest and seniority poses significant risks that a small number of members of Congress can exert outsized influence on behalf of their favored constituencies. Some scholars think that the danger of special interest capture can be offset only by officers who are accountable to the nationally elected President. See, e.g., Steven G. Calabresi, *Some Normative Arguments for the Unitary Executive*, 48 Ark. L. Rev. 23 (1995).

The congressional committees serve as gate keepers for new bills in their respective areas, and they conduct "oversight" of their respective sections of the executive branch. Appropriations sub-committees, which have the power of the purse, play an especially important role, but all committees can exert (or at least try to exert) influence over the executive agencies that fall within their purview (and any given agency might have to deal with numerous committees). As a result of these constant and close contacts between executive officials and the congressional committees, and especially the chairpersons of those committees, who oversee them,

The congressional committees are effectively the stunted growth of a parliamentary government in the United States. The growth is stunted by the Constitution. The committees might want to displace the President's Cabinet, but consider the limitations placed on congressional committees by the Incompatibility Clause of Article I, Section 6. It forbids anyone from serving in any executive or judicial office while being a member of Congress. The Incompatibility Clause was adopted as an eighteenth-century ethics rule to prevent the President from bribing members of Congress to support his policies by dangling federal offices in front of them the way British monarchs were thought to have bribed members of Parliament to build up a Court Party. *See* Steven G. Calabresi & Joan L. Larsen, *One Person, One Office: Separation of Powers or Separation of Personnel?*, 79 CORNELL L. REV. 1045 (1994) (discussing the historical origins of the Incompatibility Clause). *See also* Michael Stokes Paulsen, *Is Lloyd Bentsen Unconstitutional?*, 46 STAN. L. REV. 907 (1994) (discussing the Ineligibility Clause). This eighteenth-century ethics rule produced the American system of separation of personnel as well as separation of powers. But that was all an unintended consequence.

One of the most formidable powers of the congressional committees is their ability to conduct investigations either of other branches of the government or of private industries, groups, or even individuals. The rules of each House authorize committees to issue subpoenas to compel attendance of witnesses and production of materials. *See* Rule of the Senate 26.1; Rules of the House of Representatives 2(m)(1)(B). Noncompliance with a subpoena can result in a prosecution for criminal contempt. *See* 2 U.S.C. § 194 (2018). The investigative power of Congress has triggered fascinating caselaw, and we offer you the two foundational cases below. As you read them, ask whether the Article I, Section 5 rules that authorize these investigations allow the committees to go too far.

The first case below, *Kilbourn v. Thompson*, arose when Hallet Kilbourn was subpoenaed by the House of Representatives, which was investigating the bankruptcy of Jay Cooke & Company. The company was a major bank that had sold millions of dollars in U.S. government bonds and then went bankrupt in the Panic of 1873. A bankruptcy proceeding had begun in federal district court; the United States was a major creditor of the firm. Simultaneously, a congressional committee began investigating. Kilbourn refused to testify before the congressional committee, and he was taken into custody by John Thompson, the Sergeant-at-Arms of the House of

Representatives. The House voted to hold Kilbourn in custody for contempt until he testified.

Kilbourn v. Thompson

103 U.S. 168 (1880)

■ MR. JUSTICE MILLER, after stating the case, delivered the opinion of the court.

The argument before us has assumed a very wide range, and includes the discussion of almost every suggestion that can well be conceived on the subject. The two extremes of the controversy are the proposition on the part of the plaintiff that the House of Representatives has no power whatever to punish for a contempt of its authority, and, on the part of defendants, that such power undoubtedly exists, and when that body has formally exercised it, it must be presumed that it was right fully exercised * * *.

* * *

The powers of Congress itself, when acting through the concurrence of both branches, are dependent solely on the Constitution. Such as are not conferred by that instrument, either expressly or by fair implication from what is granted, are "reserved to the States respectively, or to the people." * * * No general power of inflicting punishment by the Congress of the United States is found in that instrument. It contains in the provision [of the Fifth Amendment] that no "person shall be deprived of life, liberty, or property, without due process of law" the strongest implication against punishment by order of the legislative body. It has been repeatedly decided by this court, and by others of the highest authority, that this means a trial in which the rights of the party shall be decided by a tribunal appointed by law, which tribunal is to be governed by rules of law previously established. An act of Congress which proposed to adjudge a man guilty of a crime and inflict the punishment would be conceded by all thinking men to be unauthorized by anything in the Constitution. That instrument, however, is not wholly silent as to the authority of the separate branches of Congress to inflict punishment. It authorizes each House to punish its own members. By the second clause of the fifth section of the first article, each House may determine the rules of its proceedings, punish its members for disorderly behavior, and, with the concurrence of two-thirds, expel a member * * *. These provisions are equally instructive in what they authorize and in what they do not authorize. There is no express power in that instrument conferred on either House of Congress to punish for contempts.

The advocates of this power have, therefore, resorted to an implication of its existence founded on two principal arguments. These are, 1, its exercise by the House of Commons of England, from which country we, it is said, have derived our system of parliamentary law; and 2d, the necessity of such a power to enable the two Houses of Congress to perform the duties and exercise the power which the Constitution has conferred on them.

That the power to punish for contempt has been exercised by the House of Commons in numerous instances is well known to the general student of history, and is authenticated by the rolls of the Parliament. And there is no question but that this has been upheld by the courts of Westminster Hall * * *.

It is important, however, to understand on what principle this power in the House of Commons rests, that we may see whether it is applicable to the two Houses of Congress, and, if it be, whether there are limitations to its exercise.

While there is, in the adjudged cases in the English courts, little agreement of opinion as to the extent of this power and the liability of its exercise to be inquired into by the courts, there is no difference of opinion as to its origin. This goes back to the period when the bishops, the lords, and the knights and burgesses met in one body, and were, when so assembled, called the High Court of Parliament.

They were not only called so, but the assembled Parliament exercised the highest function of a court of judicature, representing in that respect the judicial authority of the king in his Court of Parliament. While this body enacted laws, it also rendered judgments in matters of private right which, when approved by the king, were recognized as valid. Upon the separation of the Lords and Commons into two separate bodies, holding their sessions in different chambers, and hence called the House of Lords and the House of Commons, the judicial function of reviewing by appeal the decisions of the courts of Westminster Hall passed to the House of Lords, where it has been exercised without dispute ever since. To the Commons was left the power of impeachment, and perhaps others of a judicial character, and jointly they exercised, until a very recent period, the power of passing bills of attainder for treason and other high crimes which are in their nature punishment for crime declared judicially by the High Court of Parliament of the Kingdom of England.

It is upon this idea that the two Houses of Parliament were each courts of judicature originally which, though divested by usage and by statute, probably, of many of their judicial functions, have yet retained so much of that power as enables them, like any other court, to punish for a contempt of these privileges and authority that the power rests.

* * *

* * * [T]he powers and privileges of the House of Commons of England, on the subject of punishment for contempts, rest on principles which have no application to other legislative bodies, and certainly can have none to the House of Representatives of the United States—a body which is in no sense a court, which exercises no functions derived from its once having been a part of the highest court of the realm, and whose functions, so far as they partake in any degree of that character, are limited to punishing its own members and determining their election * * *.

We are of opinion that the right of the House of Representatives to punish the citizen for a contempt of its authority or a breach of its privileges can derive no support from the precedents and practices of the two Houses of the English Parliament, nor * * * is much aid given to the doctrine that this power exists as one necessary to enable either House of Congress to exercise successfully their function of legislation.

This latter proposition is one which we do not propose to decide in the present case, because we are able to decide it without passing upon the existence or non-existence of such a [contempt] power in aid of the legislative function.

As we have already said, the Constitution expressly empowers each House to punish its own members for disorderly behavior. We see no reason to doubt that this punishment may, in a proper case, be imprisonment, and that it may be for refusal to obey some rule on that subject made by the House for the preservation of order.

* * *

Whether the power of punishment in either House by fine or imprisonment goes beyond this or not, we are sure that no person can be punished for contumacy as a witness before either House unless his testimony is required in a matter into which that House has jurisdiction to inquire, and we feel equally sure that neither of these bodies possesses the general power of making inquiry into the private affairs of the citizen.

It is believed to be one of the chief merits of the American system of written constitutional law that all the powers intrusted to government, whether State or national, are divided into the three grand departments, the executive, the legislative, and the judicial. That the functions appropriate to each of these branches of government shall be vested in a separate body of public servants, and that the perfection of the system requires that the lines which separate and divide these departments shall be broadly and clearly defined. It is also essential to the successful working of this system that the persons intrusted with power in any one of these branches shall not be permitted to encroach upon the powers confided to the others, but that each shall, by the law of its creation, be limited to the exercise of the powers appropriate to its own department, and no other * * *.

* * *

In looking to the preamble and resolution under which the committee acted, before which Kilbourn refused to testify, we are of opinion that the House of Representatives not only exceeded the limit of its own authority, but assumed a power which could only be properly exercised by another branch of the government, because it was, in its nature, clearly judicial.

* * *

* * * [W]e do not concede that the Houses of Congress possess [a] general power of punishing for contempt. The cases in which they can do this are very limited, as we have already attempted to show. If they are proceeding in a matter beyond their legitimate cognizance, we are of opinion that this can be shown, and we cannot give our assent to the principle that, by the mere act of asserting a person to be guilty of a contempt, they thereby establish their right to fine and imprison him, beyond the power of any court or any other tribunal whatever to inquire into the grounds on which the order was made * * *.

* * *

But we have found no better expression of the true principle on this subject than in the following language of Mr. Justice Hoar, in the Supreme Court of Massachusetts, in the case of *Burnham* v. *Morrissey*, 14 Gray, 226. That was a case in which the plaintiff was imprisoned under an order of the House of Representatives of the Massachusetts legislature for refusing to answer certain questions as a witness and to produce certain books and papers. The opinion, or statement rather, was concurred in by all the court, including the venerable Mr. Chief Justice Shaw.

"The house of representatives is not the final judge of its own power and privileges in cases in which the rights and liberties of the subject are concerned, but the legality of its action may be examined and determined by this court. That house is not the legislature, but only a part of it, and is therefore subject in its action to the laws, in common with all other bodies, officers, and tribunals within the

Commonwealth. Especially is it competent and proper for this court to consider whether its proceedings are in conformity with the Constitution and laws, because, living under a written constitution, no branch or department of the government is supreme; and it is the province and duty of the judicial department to determine in cases regularly brought before them, whether the powers of any branch of the government, and even those of the legislature in the enactment of laws, have been exercised in conformity to the Constitution; and if they have not, to treat their acts as null and void. The house of representatives has the power under the Constitution to imprison for contempt; but the power is limited to cases expressly provided for by the Constitution, or to cases where the power is necessarily implied from those constitutional functions and duties, to the proper performance of which it is essential."

In this statement of the law, and in the principles there laid down, we fully concur.

We must, therefore, hold * * * that the resolution of the House of Representatives finding Kilbourn guilty of contempt, and the warrant of its speaker for his commitment to prison, are not conclusive in this case, and, in fact, are no justification, because, as the whole plea shows, the House was without authority in the matter.

* * *

McGrain v. Daugherty

273 U.S. 135 (1927)

■ MR. JUSTICE VAN DEVANTER delivered the opinion of the Court.

This is an appeal from the final order in a proceeding in habeas corpus discharging a recusant witness held in custody under process of attachment issued from the United States Senate in the course of an investigation which it was making of the administration of the Department of Justice. A full statement of the case is necessary.

The Department of Justice is one of the great executive departments established by congressional enactment * * *. The Attorney General is the head of the department, and its functions are all to be exercised under his supervision and direction.

Harry M. Daugherty became the Attorney General March 5, 1921, and held that office until March 28, 1924, when he resigned. Late in that period various charges of misfeasance and nonfeasance in the Department of Justice after he became its supervising head were brought to the attention of the Senate by individual senators and made the basis of an insistent demand that the department be investigated to the end that the practices and deficiencies which, according to the charges, were operating to prevent or impair its right administration might be definitely ascertained and that appropriate and effective measures might be taken to remedy or eliminate the evil * * *.

* * *

In the course of the investigation the committee issued and caused to be duly served on Mally S. Daugherty—who was a brother of Harry M. Daugherty and president of the Midland National Bank of Washington Court House, Ohio—a subpoena commanding him to appear before the committee * * *. The witness failed to appear.

* * *

* * * [T]he Senate adopted a resolution * * * as follows:

* * *

> "Resolved, that the president of the Senate pro tempore issue his warrant commanding the sergeant at arms or his deputy to take into custody the body of the said M. S. Daugherty wherever found, and to bring the said M. S. Daugherty before the bar of the Senate, then and there to answer such questions pertinent to the matter under inquiry as the Senate may order the President of the Senate pro tempore to propound, and to keep the said M. S. Daugherty in custody to await the further order of the Senate."

It will be observed from the terms of the resolution that the warrant was to be issued in furtherance of the effort to obtain the personal testimony of the witness * * *.

The warrant was issued agreeably to the resolution and was addressed simply to the sergeant at arms. That officer, on receiving the warrant, indorsed thereon a direction that it be executed by John J. McGrain, already his deputy, and delivered it to him for execution.

The deputy, proceeding under the warrant, took the witness into custody at Cincinnati, Ohio, with the purpose of bringing him before the bar of the Senate as commanded, whereupon the witness petitioned the federal District Court in Cincinnati for a writ of *habeas corpus* * * *.

We have given the case earnest and prolonged consideration because the principal questions involved are of unusual importance and delicacy. They are (a) whether the Senate—or the House of Representatives, both being on the same plane in this regard—has power, through its own process, to compel a private individual to appear before it or one of its committees and give testimony needed to enable it efficiently to exercise a legislative function belonging to it under the Constitution; and (b) whether it sufficiently appears that the process was being employed in this instance to obtain testimony for that purpose.

* * *

* * * [T]here is no provision expressly investing either house with power to make investigations and exact testimony, to the end that it may exercise its legislative function advisedly and effectively. So the question arises whether this power is so far incidental to the legislative function as to be implied.

In actual legislative practice, power to secure needed information by such means has long been treated as an attribute of the power to legislate. It was so regarded in the British Parliament and in the Colonial legislatures before the American Revolution; and a like view has prevailed and been carried into effect in both houses of Congress and in most of the state legislatures.

This power was both asserted and exerted by the House of Representatives in 1792, when it appointed a select committee to inquire into the St. Clair expedition and authorized the committee to send for necessary persons, papers and records. Mr. Madison, who had taken an important part in framing the Constitution only five years before, and four of his associates in that work, were members of the House of Representatives at the time, and all voted for the inquiry. 3 Cong. Ann. 494. Other exertions of the power by the House of Representatives, as also by the Senate, are shown * * *.

* * *

The state courts quite generally have held that the power to legislate carries with it by necessary implication ample authority to obtain information needed in the rightful exercise of that power, and to employ compulsory process for the purpose.

* * *

* * * [*Kilbourn v Thompson*] has been cited at times, and is cited to us now, as strongly intimating, if not holding, that neither house of Congress has power to make inquires and exact evidence in aid of contemplated legislation. There are expressions in the opinion which, separately considered, might bear such an interpretation; but that this was not intended is shown by the immediately succeeding statement (page 189) that "This latter proposition is one which we do not propose to decide in the present case, because we are able to decide it without passing upon the existence or nonexistence of such a power in aid of the legislative function."

* * *

We are of opinion that the power of inquiry—with process to enforce it—is an essential and appropriate auxiliary to the legislative function. It was so regarded and employed in American Legislatures before the Constitution was framed and ratified. Both houses of Congress took this view of it early in their history—the House of Representatives with the approving votes of Mr. Madison and other members whose service in the convention which framed the Constitution gives special significance to their action—and both houses have employed the power accordingly up to the present time * * *. So, when their practice in the matter is appraised according to the circumstances in which it was begun and to those in which it has been continued, it falls nothing short of a practical construction, long continued, of the constitutional provisions respecting their powers, and therefore should be taken as fixing the meaning of those provisions, if otherwise doubtful.

* * * A legislative body cannot legislate wisely or effectively in the absence of information respecting the conditions which the legislation is intended to affect or change; and where the legislative body does not itself possess the requisite information—which not infrequently is true—recourse must be had to others who do possess it. Experience has taught that mere requests for such information often are unavailing, and also that information which is volunteered is not always accurate or complete; so some means of compulsion are essential to obtain what is needed. All this was true before and when the Constitution was framed and adopted * * *.

The contention is earnestly made on behalf of the witness that this power of inquiry, if sustained, may be abusively and oppressively exerted. If this be so, it affords no ground for denying the power. The same contention might be directed against the power to legislate, and of course would be unavailing. We must assume, for present purposes, that neither houses will be disposed to exert the power beyond its proper bounds, or with out due regard to the rights of witnesses. But if, contrary to this assumption, controlling limitations or restrictions are disregarded, * * * a witness rightfully may refuse to answer where the bounds of the power are exceeded or the questions are not pertinent to the matter [under] inquiry.

* * *.

It is quite true that the resolution directing the investigation does not in terms avow that it is intended to be in aid of legislation; but it does show that the subject to be investigated was the administration of the Department of Justice—whether its functions were being properly discharged or were being neglected or misdirected, and particularly whether the Attorney General and his assistants were performing or neglecting their duties in respect of the institution and prosecution of proceedings to punish crimes and enforce appropriate remedies against the wrongdoers; specific instances of alleged neglect being recited. Plainly the subject was one on which legislation could be had and would be materially aided by the information which the investigation was calculated to elicit. This becomes manifest when it is reflected that the functions of the Department of Justice, the powers and duties of the Attorney General, and the duties of his assistants are all subject to regulation by congressional legislation, and that the department is maintained and its activities are carried on under such appropriations as in the judgment of Congress are needed from year to year.

The only legitimate object the Senate could have in ordering the investigation was to aid it in legislating, and we think the subject-matter was such that the presumption should be indulged that this was the real object. An express avowal of the object would have been better; but in view of the particular subject-matter was not indispensable * * *.

* * *

We conclude that the investigation was ordered for a legitimate object; that the witness wrongfully refused to appear and testify before the committee and was lawfully attached; that the Senate is entitled to have him give testimony pertinent to the inquiry, either at its bar or before the committee; and that the district court erred in discharging him from custody under the attachment.

* * *

NOTES AND QUESTIONS

1. What enumerated power is Congress relying on in the two cases which you have just read? If it is Congress's power to adopt rules to govern its own proceedings, then why does that grant of limited and enumerated power enable Congress to subpoena witnesses and hold them in contempt? Surely Congress can adopt the equivalent of Robert's Rules of Order without itself prosecuting, humiliating, exposing, or jailing those whom it subpoenas to appear as sworn witnesses before congressional committees. What do you make of the claim in *Kilbourn v. Thompson* that just because the House of Lords and the House of Commons had adjudicative as well as legislative powers in seventeenth and eighteenth century England, it does not follow that Congress or any other body that is given only the "function" of legislating has such powers? Does the fact revealed by *McGrain v. Daugherty* that Congress de facto has an almost adjudicative investigatory power today suggest that the Framers' effort to divide and separate power functionally has not completely succeeded? Do the Senate and the House, in effect, have at least some of the adjudicative powers once exercised in England by the Few in the House of Lords and the Many in the House of Commons? If so, is this not another instance in which the

Framers' effort to create a functional separation of powers has led in practice to a Mixed Regime with all of the components being selected democratically? See the discussion below on the Bill of Attainder Clause.

2. An Act of Congress first passed in 1857 gives the two houses of Congress the power to subpoena witnesses and compel them to testify under oath on pain of criminal prosecution. *See* 2 U.S.C. § 192 (2018). Like all federal criminal laws, this statute is enforced only by a U.S. attorney's office bringing a prosecution and securing a conviction in an Article III court. Is this statute constitutional? Are all constitutional concerns eliminated so long as contempt of Congress is prosecuted by the executive branch and adjudicated by the judiciary? Since World War II, Congress has abandoned its efforts to prosecute contempt of Congress itself and has instead referred any such cases to the U.S. Attorneys' offices pursuant to this statute.

3. Justice Joseph Story appears to agree with the outcome of *McGrain v. Dougherty*. In his treatise on the Constitution, Story writes: "[O]ther incidental powers [of the two Houses of Congress] may well be presumed to exist. Among these, the power to punish contempts, committed against either House by strangers, has been generally admitted, and insisted upon in practice, as indispensable to the freedom, the deliberative functions, and the personal safety of the members." JOSEPH STORY, A FAMILIAR EXPOSITION OF THE CONSTITUTION OF THE UNITED STATES § 140 (1840). Justice Story, writing half a century before *Kilbourn,* was surely referring to *Anderson v. Dunn*, 19 U.S. (6 Wheat.) 204 (1821). A member of Congress accused John Anderson of attempted bribery. Instead of referring the matter to federal prosecutors, the House ordered its Sergeant-at-Arms to arrest and imprison Anderson for "breach of the privileges of the said House, and of a high contempt of the dignity and authority of the same." *Id.* at 208. Anderson contested the House's power unilaterally to arrest and hold him. The Supreme Court upheld the power of Congress unilaterally to punish people for contempt of Congress:

> It is certainly true, that there is no power given by the constitution to either House to punish for contempts, except when committed by their own members. Nor does the judicial or criminal power given to the United States, in any part, expressly extend to the infliction of punishment for contempt of either House, or any one co-ordinate branch of the government. Shall we, therefore, decide, that no such power exists?
>
> * * *
>
> * * * The argument obviously leads to the total annihilation of the power of the House of Representatives to guard itself from contempts, and leaves it exposed to every indignity and interruption that rudeness, caprice, or even conspiracy, may meditate against it. This result is fraught with too much absurdity not to bring into doubt the soundness of any argument from which it is derived. That a deliberate assembly, clothed with the majesty of the people, and charged with the care of all that is dear to them; composed of the most distinguished citizens, selected and drawn together from every quarter of a great nation; whose deliberations are required by public opinion to be conducted under the eye of the public, and whose decisions must be clothed with all that sanctity which unlimited confidence in their wisdom and purity can inspire; that such an assembly should not possess the power to suppress rudeness, or repel insult, is a supposition too wild to be suggested. And, accordingly, to avoid the pressure of these considerations, it has been argued, that the right of the respective Houses to exclude from their presence, and their absolute control within their own walls, carry with them the right to punish

> contempts committed in their presence; while the absolute legislative power given to Congress within this District, enables them to provide by law against all other insults against which there is any necessity for providing.
>
> * * *
>
> In reply to the suggestion that, on this same foundation of necessity, might be raised a superstructure of implied powers in the executive, and every other department, and even ministerial officer of the government, it would be sufficient to observe, that neither analogy nor precedent would support the assertion of such powers in any other than a legislative or judicial body. Even corruption any where else would not contaminate the source of political life. In the retirement of the cabinet, it is not expected that the executive can be approached by indignity or insult; nor can it ever be necessary to the executive, or any other department, to hold a public deliberative assembly. These are not arguments; they are visions which mar the enjoyment of actual blessings, with the attack or feint of the harpies of imagination.

Id. at 225, 228–29, 233–34. Do you find this argument convincing? Does it seem consistent with the idea of separation of powers? Does it support a congressional power to issue and enforce subpoenas?

4. Both *Kilbourn* and *McGrain* assume that any congressional subpoena power can only be exercised in connection with some proper legislative function, such as oversight of an executive agency. In an era in which Congress's legislative powers were construed fairly narrowly, that was a potentially significant limitation on the scope of Congress's compulsory investigatory powers. As you will see later in this course, after the 1930s Congress's legislative powers have been given a much broader scope, so that they now encompass virtually anything in the country. Do the implied investigatory powers recognized in *McGrain* grow along with Congress's legislative powers?

These questions became very real in the 1940s and 1950s. In 1938, the House established the House Un-American Activities Committee (or "HUAC"):

> *Resolved,* That the Speaker of the House of Representatives be, and he is hereby, authorized to appoint a special committee to be composed of seven members for the purpose of conducting an investigation of (1) the extent, character, and objects of un-American propaganda activities in the United States, (2) the diffusion within the United States of subversive and un-American propaganda that is instigated from foreign countries or of a domestic origin and attacks the principle of the form of government as guaranteed by our Constitution, and (3) all other questions in relation thereto that would aid Congress in any necessary remedial legislation.
>
> That said special committee, or any subcommittee thereof, is hereby authorized to sit and act during the present Congress at such times and places within the United States, whether or not the House is sitting, has recessed, or has adjourned, to hold such hearings, to require the attendance of such witnesses and the production of such books, papers, and documents, by subpena or otherwise, and to take such testimony as it deems necessary * * *. Every person who, having been summoned as a witness by authority of said committee, or any subcommittee thereof, willfully makes default, or who, having appeared, refuses to answer any question pertinent to the investigation heretofore authorized, shall be held to the penalties provided by section 102 of the Revised Statutes of the United States (U. S. C., title 2, sec. 192).

H. Res. 282, 83 CONG. REC. 7568 (May 26, 1938). The Committee was relatively dormant for a time, but after World War II it became an aggressive force for seeking information on Communist influence in American institutions. In the other branch of Congress, Joseph McCarthy became (in)famous for Senate investigations of Communist penetration into the U.S. government, but on the House side much of HUAC's activity was focused on nongovernmental institutions such as the movie industry and education. *See* MARTIN H. REDISH, THE LOGIC OF PERSECUTION: FREE EXPRESSION AND THE MCCARTHY ERA 137–40 (2005). The famous line, "Are you now or have you even been a member of the Communist Party?," was a question posed by HUAC to numerous private citizens called to testify. And numerous private citizens who refused to answer the question, or to identify people that they knew to be Communists, were prosecuted for contempt.

One such person was John T. Watkins, a union official who freely admitted to his own past Communist associations but would not identify people who he thought in the past might have been involved in Communist activities. Watkins explained:

> "I am not going to plead the fifth amendment, but I refuse to answer certain questions that I believe are outside the proper scope of your committee's activities. I will answer any questions which this committee puts to me about myself. I will also answer questions about those persons whom I knew to be members of the Communist Party and whom I believe still are. I will not, however, answer any questions with respect to others with whom I associated in the past. I do not believe that any law in this country requires me to testify about persons who may in the past have been Communist Party members or otherwise engaged in Communist Party activity but who to my best knowledge and belief have long since removed themselves from the Communist movement.
>
> "I do not believe that such questions are relevant to the work of this committee nor do I believe that this committee has the right to undertake the public exposure of persons because of their past activities. I may be wrong, and the committee may have this power, but until and unless a court of law so holds and directs me to answer, I most firmly refuse to discuss the political activities of my past associates."

Watkins v. United States, 354 U.S. 178, 185 (1957). Watkins was criminally prosecuted under 2 U.S.C. § 192, and he appealed the conviction. The en banc D.C. Circuit divided on the legality of the conviction, and the case went to the Supreme Court, which reversed the conviction. The Court acknowledged Congress's power to conduct compulsory investigations in pursuit of legitimate legislative goals while affirming that "[t]here is no general authority to expose the private affairs of individuals without justification in terms of the functions of the Congress." 354 U.S. at 187. *See also id.* at 200 ("We have no doubt that there is no congressional power to expose for the sake of exposure. The public is, of course, entitled to be informed concerning the workings of its government. That cannot be inflated into a general power to expose where the predominant result can only be an invasion of the private rights of individuals."). In an opinion that relied as much on notions of due process of law as on separation of powers, it concluded that HUAC's mandate was too broadly framed to allow either the Court or a witness to ascertain whether the questions posed to Watkins were a proper inquiry. *See* 354 U.S. at 203–06; *id.* at 216, 217 (Frankfurter, J., concurring). The Court concluded:

> We are mindful of the complexities of modern government and the ample scope that must be left to the Congress as the sole constitutional depository of legislative power. Equally mindful are we of the indispensable function, in the exercise of that power, of congressional investigations. The conclusions we have reached in this case will not prevent the Congress, through its committees, from

> obtaining any information it needs for the proper fulfillment of its role in our scheme of government. The legislature is free to determine the kinds of data that should be collected. It is only those investigations that are conducted by use of compulsory process that give rise to a need to protect the rights of individuals against illegal encroachment. That protection can be readily achieved through procedures which prevent the separation of power from responsibility and which provide the constitutional requisites of fairness for witnesses. A measure of added care on the part of the House and the Senate in authorizing the use of compulsory process and by their committees in exercising that power would suffice. That is a small price to pay if it serves to uphold the principles of limited, constitutional government without constricting the power of the Congress to inform itself.

Id. at 215–16.

Two years later, a 5–4 Court ruling sharply limited the holding in *Watkins*. Lloyd Barenblatt was a university teaching fellow and instructor from 1947–54. Barenblatt refused to answer questions from HUAC about his participation in Communist organizations and was convicted of contempt. The Court upheld his conviction. The Court said that the committee's subject matter—Communist involvement in American education—was clearly enough identified to satisfy the due process of law concerns voiced in *Watkins*. As to why Congress had any plausible legislative business investigating the politics of higher education, the Court said:

> That Congress has wide power to legislate in the field of Communist activity in this Country, and to conduct appropriate investigations in aid thereof, is hardly debatable * * *. In the last analysis this power rests on the right of self-preservation, "the ultimate value of any society," *Dennis v. United States*, 341 U.S. 494, 509, 71 S.Ct. 857, 867, 95 L.Ed. 1137. Justification for its exercise in turn rests on the long and widely accepted view that the tenets of the Communist Party include the ultimate overthrow of the Government of the United States by force and violence, a view which has been given formal expression by the Congress.
>
> * * *
>
> We think that investigatory power in this domain is not to be denied Congress solely because the field of education is involved * * *. Indeed we do not understand petitioner here to suggest that Congress in no circumstances may inquire into Communist activity in the field of education. Rather, his position is in effect that this particular investigation was aimed not at the revolutionary aspects but at the theoretical classroom discussion of communism.
>
> In our opinion this position rests on a too constricted view of the nature of the investigatory process, and is not supported by a fair assessment of the record before us * * *. Nor can it fairly be concluded that this investigation was directed at controlling what is being taught at our universities rather than at overthrow. The statement of the Subcommittee Chairman at the opening of the investigation evinces no such intention, and so far as this record reveals nothing thereafter transpired which would justify our holding that the thrust of the investigation later changed * * *.
>
> Nor can we accept the further contention that this investigation should not be deemed to have been in furtherance of a legislative purpose because the true objective of the Committee and of the Congress was purely "exposure." So

long as Congress acts in pursuance of its constitutional power, the Judiciary lacks authority to intervene on the basis of the motives which spurred the exercise of that power * * *. Certainly this is not a case like *Kilbourn v. Thompson*, 103 U.S. 168, 192, where "the House of Representatives not only exceeded the limit of its own authority, but assumed a power which could only be properly exercised by another branch of the government, because it was in its nature clearly judicial." *See McGrain v. Daugherty*, 273 U.S. 135, 171. The constitutional legislative power of Congress in this instance is beyond question.

Barenblatt v. United States, 360 U.S. 109, 127–33 (1959). If Congress concluded that it was unacceptable to have Communists teaching college courses, what legislation could it enact and pursuant to what enumerated constitutional powers? Keep that question in mind in the next chapter when we examine the scope of Congress's enumerated powers. You might also ask whether the answer to that question today would have been different in either 1880 or 1927 and whether *Kilbourn* or *McGrain* would have been written differently had the Court in either case anticipated a nearly limitless scope to Congress's legislative powers.

O. ARTICLE I, SECTION 6

The Senators and Representatives shall receive a compensation for their services, to be ascertained by law, and paid out of the treasury of the United States. They shall in all cases, except treason, felony and breach of the peace, be privileged from arrest during their attendance at the session of their respective Houses, and in going to and returning from the same; and for any speech or debate in either House, they shall not be questioned in any other place.

No Senator or Representative shall, during the time for which he was elected, be appointed to any civil office under the authority of the United States, which shall have been created, or the emoluments whereof shall have been increased during such time: and no person holding any office under the United States, shall be a member of either House during his continuance in office.

The two clauses in Article I, section 6 contain five distinct provisions. The first, which we have already discussed to some extent, concerns compensation: Members of Congress are paid as national officers, not as State officers. Congress sets the terms of its own pay, but as of 1992 that power is subject to the Twenty-Seventh Amendment, which delays the effectiveness of any congressional pay increases until after the next election. This amendment was first proposed in 1791 as part of the Bill of Rights, but it fell one vote short of ratification at that time.

The second provision establishes a privilege for senators and representatives from civil arrest during, and on the way to and from, attendance at sessions of Congress. The Articles of Confederation contained a nearly identical provision. The clause *does not* provide any immunity from eventual prosecution or civil liability, or even from service of process in civil suits. *See Long v. Ansell*, 293 U.S. 76 (1934) (no legislative immunity from service of process in civil cases during sessions of Congress). It is *only* a limited privilege against arrest, and it *only* extends to civil arrest, not to arrest for any crimes. (What is a "civil arrest"? It is an archaic procedure that was mostly used to stop debtors from fleeing the jurisdiction with their property. Today, "[c]ivil arrest is prohibited in most states," BLACK'S LAW DICTIONARY, *Arrest* (11th ed. 2019), but "[w]hen the Constitution was adopted, arrests in civil suits were still common in America." 293 U.S. at 83.). The excepting phrase "treason, felony and breach of the peace" in connection with legislative privilege was a legal term of art at the time of the framing that was understood to cover all crimes. The Supreme Court in 1908, in the course of upholding the arrest (and imprisonment) of a sitting representative on federal subornation of perjury charges, held that "it has been recognized from the beginning that the convention which framed the Constitution, in adopting the words 'treason, felony, and breach of peace' as applicable to the privileges of a parliamentary body, used those words in the sense which the identical words had been settled to mean in England," *Williamson v. United States,* 207 U.S. 425, 443 (1908), which included all indictable crimes whatever their character or severity.

Third, is the Speech or Debate Clause. The Speech or Debate Clause of Article I, Section 6 broadly protects members of Congress from being made to answer in any other place, including state or federal courts, for comments made during a speech or debate in either house or in committee. This is a privilege against liability and not merely against (civil) arrest. It thus protects against federal or state prosecution or against a libel action. The Speech or Debate Clause is of enormous practical importance given the voluminous Congressional Record and the testimony and proceedings of all of Congress's many committees and subcommittees. The ability of members of Congress to say or publish anything free of consequence both in the *Congressional Record* and in committee helps to guarantee, along with the First Amendment, that there will be a free flow of information to the public. The Speech or Debate Clause in the English Bill of Rights of 1689 allowed Members of Parliament to speak freely with all the other Members of King-in-Parliament who were sovereign. In the U.S., We the People are sovereign. Does that mean that in the U.S., as Senator Gravel contended in a famous argument, picked up by Justice William O. Douglas, a senator could freely disseminate the classified Pentagon Papers among the American people?

The Speech or Debate Clause, read narrowly, would appear to apply only to members of Congress themselves. But the Supreme Court has read the Clause more broadly to apply to legislative aides. *See Gravel v. United States,* 408 U.S. 606 (1972):

> It is true that the Clause itself mentions only "Senators and Representatives," but prior cases have plainly not taken a literalistic approach in applying the privilege. The Clause also speaks only of "Speech or Debate," but the Court's consistent approach has been that to confine the protection of the Speech or Debate Clause to words spoken in debate would be an unacceptably narrow view. Committee reports, resolutions, and the act of voting are equally covered * * *. Rather than giving the Clause a cramped construction, the Court has sought to implement its fundamental purpose of freeing the legislator from executive and judicial oversight that realistically threatens to control his conduct as a legislator. We have little doubt that we are neither exceeding our judicial powers nor mistakenly construing the Constitution by holding that the Speech or Debate Clause applies not only to a Member but also to his aides insofar as the conduct of the latter would be a protected legislative act if performed by the Member himself.

Id. at 617–18. The Speech or Debate Clause is also striking in that it applies only to Congress and not to the President, executive branch officers, Supreme Court justices, or other federal judges. As we will see later, the President and the Supreme Court have read an implied doctrine of executive privilege, as well as implied limited (or "qualified") immunities for executive officials, into the Constitution, which accomplishes, to a lesser degree, much the same object for the executive branch as the Speech or Debate Clause accomplishes for Congress.

Fourth is the Congressional Emoluments Clause, sometimes called the Sinecure Clause or the Ineligibility Clause, which prevents members of Congress from being appointed to any executive or judicial office which was created or the salary of which was increased while they were in Congress. This is a simple ethics rule to prevent members of Congress (who perhaps think they are about to be voted out of Congress) from creating lucrative offices to which they can get themselves appointed. Notwithstanding this clause, many members of Congress have taken executive and judicial positions whose benefits were increased while those members were in Congress, including (to name just a few) Justice Hugo Black, Attorney General William Saxbe, Circuit Judge Abner Mikva, United Nations Ambassador Bill Richardson, Secretary of Defense William Cohen, and Secretary of State Hillary Clinton. Administrations of both parties have devised several end-arounds the Emoluments Clause, including reasoning that pensions do not count as emoluments (used to validate Justice Black's appointment) and having the appointees decline to take the salary increase that Congress voted on when they were members of Congress or having Congress roll back the salary increase before the person takes office. This latter so-called "solution" to the Emoluments Clause "problem" is known as the "Saxbe Fix," after William Saxbe, who took office as Richard Nixon's final Attorney General but declined a pay increase that Congress had voted on when he was a Senator, though the mechanism had been used long before 1973. This fix does not satisfy textualists like ourselves because the Emoluments Clause establishes a clear rule that links ineligibility to a specific legislative action: if the emoluments for an office are increased at any time that a person is in Congress, that person cannot be appointed to that office during their elected term in Congress. Even if Congress subsequently reduces the salary for an office, in our view ineligibility attached at the moment that the increase took place and cannot be undone by anything other than running out the member's electoral term. The "Saxbe Fix" does satisfy constitutionalists who stress the purposes behind the text, because the "Saxbe Fix" eliminates the particular ethics problem that the Framers were concerned about—*i.e.*, it resolves the Framers' original expected application of the Emoluments Clause. With one exception, the Department of Justice has consistently endorsed the "Saxbe Fix." In 1987, the Office of Legal Counsel ("OLC") took our textualist position to conclude that Senator Orrin Hatch was ineligible at that time for appointment to the Supreme Court. In 2009, OLC rejected that view in favor of a purposive and historical analysis that endorsed the "Saxbe Fix." *See* Memorandum for Attorney General Eric Holder from David Barron, Assistant Attorney General, Office of Legal Counsel, *Validity of Statutory Rollbacks as a Means of Complying with the Ineligibility Clause* (May 20, 2009), https://www.justice.gov/file/18501/download. There have been a number of court challenges to actions of executive officials or judges who were appointed pursuant to some version of the "Saxbe Fix," but all of those cases have been dismissed for lack of standing, so there has never been a court ruling on whether the Emoluments Clause really means what it says.

Fifth, is the Incompatibility Clause of Article I, Section 6, which says that "no person holding any office under the United States, shall be a member of either House during his continuance in office." This clause is hugely consequential because it prevents, for example, the Chair of the Senate Foreign Relations Committee from demanding that he be appointed Secretary of State, or the Chair of the House Ways and Means Committee from demanding that she be appointed Secretary of the Treasury. The Incompatibility Clause significantly strengthens the presidency because it gives the President his own Cabinet. The congressional oversight committees are, as we said above, the stunted growths of parliamentary ministries, which can never formally take over the Cabinet departments and agencies, which they oversee because of the Incompatibility Clause.

Ironically, the Incompatibility Clause was inserted into the Constitution as an ethics rule to prevent presidents from bribing members of Congress to vote his way by offering them high offices, as the Hanoverian kings had done repeatedly in 18th Century Britain. The clause had the exact opposite effect from that intended. It strengthened the President and weakened the Congress by enhancing the separation of powers. Note that there is no Incompatibility Clause between holding an executive and a judicial office at the same time, and such dual service has happened many times in American history. It has, quite rightly, been deemed unethical and has not occurred in the last 50 years. Steven G. Calabresi & Joan L. Larsen, *One Person, One Office: Separation of Powers or Separation of Personnel?*, 79 CORNELL L. REV. 1045 (1994).

[Assignment 13]

P. ARTICLE I, SECTION 7: LAWMAKING THROUGH BICAMERALISM AND PRESENTMENT

Article I, Section 7, Clause 1: All Bills for raising Revenue shall originate in the House of Representatives; but the Senate may propose or concur with Amendments as on other Bills.

Article I, Section 7, Clause 2: Every Bill which shall have passed the House of Representatives and the Senate, shall, before it become a Law, be presented to the President of the United States; If he approve he shall sign it, but if not he shall return it, with his Objections to that House in which it shall have originated, who shall enter the Objections at large on their Journal, and proceed to reconsider it. If after such Reconsideration two thirds of that House shall agree to pass the Bill, it shall be sent, together with the Objections, to the other House, by which it shall likewise be reconsidered, and if approved by two thirds of that House, it shall become a Law. But in all such Cases the Votes of both Houses shall be determined by yeas and Nays, and the Names of the Persons voting for and against the Bill shall be entered on the Journal of each House respectively. If any Bill shall not be returned by the President within ten Days (Sundays excepted) after it shall have been presented to him, the Same shall be a Law, in like Manner as if he had signed it, unless the Congress by their Adjournment prevent its Return, in which Case it shall not be a Law.

Article I, Section 7, Clause 3: Every Order, Resolution, or Vote to which the Concurrence of the Senate and House of Representatives may be necessary (except on a question of Adjournment) shall be presented to the President of the United States; and before the Same shall take Effect, shall be approved by him, or being disapproved by him, shall be repassed by two thirds of the Senate and House of Representatives, according to the Rules and Limitations prescribed in the Case of a Bill.

Congress, unlike the Continental Congress under the Articles of Confederation, is a fully functioning legislative body, so providing the procedures for lawmaking was one of the Constitution's most important tasks. Article I, Section 7 lays out those procedures in considerable detail. Notwithstanding the seeming technical precision of the language, however, Article I, section 7 leaves some vital questions unanswered, as we shall see.

All legislation begins as a bill. *See* Schoolhouse Rock, "I'm Just a Bill," https://www.youtube.com/watch?v=FFroMQlKiag. In order to become a law, it must pass both Houses of Congress (and pass in identical form and language or else it will not be the same "bill"), be presented to the President, and either be signed by the President or re-passed by two-thirds supermajorities in both Houses. Clause 1, known as the Origination Clause, specifies that all tax legislation must start as a bill in the House, just as all such legislation in England must originate with the House of Commons. But because the Senate can offer amendments, including amendments that substitute a completely different text for the House version, and because not all bills that involve getting money for the government are considered "Bills for raising Revenue" (user fees, for example, don't count, *see United States v. Munoz-Flores,*495 U.S. 385 (1990)), the Origination Clause has relatively little bite.

Section 2 is the heart of the Constitution's lawmaking process. It embodies two crucial principles: (1) bicameralism, because both Houses must agree in order for anything to get done and (2) presentment, which places the President directly into the lawmaking process by requiring his or her agreement unless the House and Senate can both muster large supermajorities to override a veto. Alexander Hamilton in *The Federalist* well stated the framers' reasons for giving the President a qualified (meaning subject to override) veto over legislation:

> The propensity of the legislative department to intrude upon the rights, and to absorb the powers, of the other departments, has been already suggested and repeated; the insufficiency of a mere parchment delineation of the boundaries of each, has also been remarked upon; and the necessity of furnishing each with constitutional arms for its own defense, has been inferred and proved. From these clear and indubitable principles results the propriety of a negative, either absolute or qualified, in the Executive, upon the acts of the legislative branches * * *.
>
> But the power in question has a further use. It not only serves as a shield to the Executive, but it furnishes an additional security against the enaction of improper laws. It establishes a salutary check upon the legislative body, calculated to guard the community against the effects of faction, precipitancy, or of any impulse unfriendly to the public good, which may happen to influence a majority of that body.

* * *

> It may perhaps be said that the power of preventing bad laws includes that of preventing good ones; and may be used to the one purpose as well as to the other * * *. The injury which may possibly be done by defeating a few good laws, will be amply compensated by the advantage of preventing a number of bad ones.

THE FEDERALIST No. 73 (Hamilton).

Ordinarily, all of these formalities are readily satisfied and Article I, section 7 functions like an operating system in the background. But suppose that Congress enacts something that it calls a "resolution" or "declaration" or some other term and claims that it can be enacted without presentment to the President because it is not a "bill"? Can the constitutional lawmaking process be skirted so easily? Of course not, because Article I, section 7, clause 3—the Orders, Resolutions, or Votes Clause ("ORV")—makes *all* such measures, except motions to adjourn, subject to presidential presentment no matter what Congress chooses to call them. This was James Madison's objective in proposing what became the ORV: "if the negative of the President was confined to *bills;* it would be evaded by acts under the form and name of resolutions, votes, &c." 5 DEBATES ON THE ADOPTION OF THE FEDERAL CONSTITUTION 431 (Jonathan Elliott ed., 1907). Does a presentment requirement apply to congressional proposals for constitutional amendments under Article V? The text of the ORV says yes. The Supreme Court, in an early opinion that gave no reasoning, said no, *see Hollingsworth v. State of Virginia*, 3 U.S. (3 Dall.) 378 (1798), so "no" it has been for more than two centuries. For a thoughtful (though not necessarily convincing) defense of *Hollingsworth,* see Seth Barrett Tillman, *A Textualist Defense of Article I, Section 7, Clause 3: Why* Hollingsworth v. Virginia *Was Rightly Decided and Why* INS v Chadha *Was Wrongly Reasoned,* 83 TEX. L. REV. 1265 (2005). Does the ORV require Congress to present congressional subpoenas to the President for signature or veto? We both think so, *see* Gary Lawson, *Burning Down the House (and Senate): A Presentment Requirement for Legislative Subpoenas under the Orders, Resolutions, and Votes Clause,* 83 TEX. L. REV. 1373 (2005), though no President has advanced that position and no modern court would adopt it given the longstanding practice to the contrary.

The most dramatic challenge in the past century to the formal lawmaking process of Article I, section 7 was (and still is, in one important sense) the "legislative veto." We saw earlier how Congress routinely subdelegates enormous power to executive agencies and presidents using vague statutory language. *See supra* pages 180–216. Congress has available various tools, both formal and informal, to try to control or influence agency action; those tools are often studied in courses on Legislation or Administrative Law. *See, e.g.,* GARY LAWSON, FEDERAL ADMINISTRATIVE LAW 167–81 (8th ed. 2019). One tool that emerged contemporaneously with the explosion of subdelegation during the New Deal was statutory provisions that gave agencies broad discretion but allowed their actions to be nullified by votes of Congress, or even of single Houses of Congress, without presentment to the President. (Congress can, of course, always overturn agency action by passing Article I, section 7 legislation with presidential presentment.) These devices became routine parts of congressional subdelegations to agencies, eventually appearing in almost 200 statutes, including more than 100 statutes enacted between 1970 and 1975. Presidents consistently groused about these provisions, but no legal challenge to them was mounted until the mid-1970s. The case reached the Supreme Court in 1983.

Q. IMMIGRATION & NATURALIZATION SERVICE V. CHADHA

462 U.S. 919 (1983)

■ CHIEF JUSTICE BURGER delivered the opinion of the Court.

* * *

Chadha is an East Indian who was born in Kenya and holds a British passport. He was lawfully admitted to the United States in 1966 on a nonimmigrant student visa. His visa expired on June 30, 1972. On October 11, 1973, the District Director of the Immigration and Naturalization Service ordered Chadha to show cause why he should not be deported for having "remained in the United States for a longer time than permitted." Pursuant to § 242(b) of the Immigration and Nationality Act (Act), 8 U.S.C. § 1252(b), a deportation hearing was held before an immigration judge on January 11, 1974. Chadha conceded that he was deportable for overstaying his visa and the hearing was adjourned to enable him to file an application for suspension of deportation under § 244(a)(1) of the Act, 8 U.S.C. § 1254(a)(1). Section 244(a)(1) provides:

> "As hereinafter prescribed in this section, the Attorney General may, in his discretion, suspend deportation * * * in the case of an alien who applies to the Attorney General for suspension of deportation and—
>
> "(1) * * * has been physically present in the United States for a continuous period of not less than seven years immediately preceding the date of such application, and proves that during all of such period he was and is a person of good moral character; and is a person whose deportation would, in the opinion of the Attorney General, result in extreme hardship * * *."

* * * The Immigration Judge, on June 25, 1974, ordered that Chadha's deportation be suspended. The immigration judge found that Chadha met the requirements of § 244(a)(1): he had resided continuously in the United States for over seven years, was of good moral character, and would suffer "extreme hardship" if deported.

Pursuant to § 244(c)(1) of the Act, 8 U.S.C. § 1254(c)(1), the immigration judge suspended Chadha's deportation and a report of the suspension was transmitted to Congress. Section 244(c)(1) provides:

> "* * * If the deportation of any alien is suspended under the provisions of this subsection, a complete and detailed statement of the facts and pertinent provisions of law in the case shall be reported to the Congress with the reasons for such suspension. Such reports shall be submitted on the first day of each calendar month in which Congress is in session."

Once the Attorney General's recommendation for suspension of Chadha's deportation was conveyed to Congress, Congress had the power under § 244(c)(2) of the Act, 8 U.S.C. § 1254(c)(2), to veto the Attorney General's determination that Chadha should not be deported. Section 244(c)(2) provides:

"(2) In the case of an alien specified in paragraph (1) of subsection (a) of this subsection—

"if during the session of the Congress at which a case is reported, or prior to the close of the session of the Congress next following the session at which a case is reported, either the Senate or the House of Representatives passes a resolution stating in substance that it does not favor the suspension of such deportation, the Attorney General shall thereupon deport such alien or authorize the alien's voluntary departure at his own expense under the order of deportation in the manner provided by law. If, within the time above specified, neither the Senate nor the House of Representatives shall pass such a resolution, the Attorney General shall cancel deportation proceedings."

* * *

On December 12, 1975, Representative Eilberg, Chairman of the Judiciary Subcommittee on Immigration, Citizenship, and International Law, introduced a resolution opposing "the granting of permanent residence in the United States to [six] aliens", including Chadha. H. Res. 926, 94th Cong., 1st Sess.; 121 Cong Rec. 40247 (1975). The resolution was referred to the House Committee on the Judiciary. On December 16, 1975, the resolution was discharged from further consideration by the House Committee on the Judiciary and submitted to the House of Representatives for a vote * * *. The resolution was passed without debate or recorded vote. Since the House action was pursuant to § 244(c)(2), the resolution was not treated as an Article I legislative act; it was not submitted to the Senate or presented to the President for his action.

After the House veto of the Attorney General's decision to allow Chadha to remain in the United States, the immigration judge reopened the deportation proceedings to implement the House order deporting Chadha * * * On November 8, 1976, Chadha was ordered deported pursuant to the House action. * * *

* * * the [Ninth Circuit] Court of Appeals held that the House was without constitutional authority to order Chadha's deportation; accordingly it directed the Attorney General "to cease and desist from taking any steps to deport this alien based upon the resolution enacted by the House of Representatives." 634 F.2d 408, 436 (1980). The essence of its holding was that § 244(c)(2) violates the constitutional doctrine of separation of powers.

We granted certiorari * * * and we now affirm.

* * *

We turn now to the question whether action of one House of Congress under § 244(c)(2) violates strictures of the Constitution. We begin, of course, with the presumption that the challenged statute is valid. Its wisdom is not the concern of the courts; if a challenged action does not violate the Constitution, it must be sustained * * *.

By the same token, the fact that a given law or procedure is efficient, convenient, and useful in facilitating functions of government, standing alone, will not save it if it is contrary to the Constitution. Convenience and efficiency are not the primary objectives—or the hallmarks—of democratic government and our inquiry is sharpened rather than blunted by the fact that Congressional veto provisions are appearing with increasing frequency in statutes which delegate authority to executive and independent agencies * * *.

* * *

Explicit and unambiguous provisions of the Constitution prescribe and define the respective functions of the Congress and of the Executive in the legislative process. Since the precise terms of those familiar provisions are critical to the resolution of this case, we set them out verbatim. Art. I provides:

> "All legislative Powers herein granted shall be vested in a Congress of the United States, which shall consist of a Senate *and* a House of Representatives." Art. I, § 1. (Emphasis added).
>
> "Every Bill which shall have passed the House of Representatives *and* the Senate, *shall*, before it becomes a Law, be presented to the President of the United States; . . ." Art. I, § 7, cl. 2. (Emphasis added).
>
> "*Every* Order, Resolution, or Vote to which the Concurrence of the Senate and House of Representatives may be necessary (except on a question of Adjournment) *shall be* presented to the President of the United States; and before the Same shall take Effect, *shall be* approved by him, or being disapproved by him, *shall be* repassed by two thirds of the Senate and House of Representatives, according to the Rules and Limitations prescribed in the Case of a Bill." Art. I, § 7, cl. 3. (Emphasis added).

These provisions of Art. I are integral parts of the constitutional design for the separation of powers. We have recently noted that "[t]he principle of separation of powers was not simply an abstract generalization in the minds of the Framers: it was woven into the documents that they drafted in Philadelphia in the summer of 1787." *Buckley v. Valeo*, 424 U.S., at 124 * * *. The very structure of the Articles delegating and separating powers under Arts. I, II, and III exemplify the concept of separation of powers, and we now turn to Art. I.

The records of the Constitutional Convention reveal that the requirement that all legislation be presented to the President before becoming law was uniformly accepted by the Framers. Presentment to the President and the Presidential veto were considered so imperative that the draftsmen took special pains to assure that these requirements could not be circumvented. During the final debate on Art. I, § 7, cl. 2, James Madison expressed concern that it might easily be evaded by the simple expedient of calling a proposed law a "resolution" or "vote" rather than a "bill." As a consequence, Art. I, § 7, cl. 3 was added.

The decision to provide the President with a limited and qualified power to nullify proposed legislation by veto was based on the profound conviction of the Framers that the powers conferred on Congress were the powers to be most carefully circumscribed. It is beyond doubt that lawmaking was a power to be shared by both Houses and the President * * * [citing, inter alia, Alexander Hamilton and Joseph Story].

* * *

The bicameral requirement of Art. I, §§ 1, 7 was of scarcely less concern to the Framers than was the Presidential veto and indeed the two concepts are interdependent. By providing that no law could take effect without the concurrence of the prescribed majority of the Members of both Houses, the Framers reemphasized their belief, already remarked upon in connection with the Presentment Clauses, that legislation should not be enacted unless it has been carefully and fully considered by the Nation's elected officials * * *.

* * *

* * * [T]he Framers were acutely conscious that the bicameral requirement and the Presentment Clauses would serve essential constitutional functions. The President's participation in the legislative process was to protect the Executive Branch from Congress and to protect the whole people from improvident laws. The division of the Congress into two distinctive bodies assures that the legislative power would be exercised only after opportunity for full study and debate in separate settings. The President's unilateral veto power, in turn, was limited by the power of two-thirds of both Houses of Congress to overrule a veto thereby precluding final arbitrary action of one person. It emerges clearly that the prescription for legislative action in Art. I, §§ 1, 7 represents the Framers' decision that the legislative power of the Federal Government be exercised in accord with a single, finely wrought and exhaustively considered, procedure.

The Constitution sought to divide the delegated powers of the new Federal Government into three defined categories, Legislative, Executive and Judicial, to assure, as nearly as possible, that each branch of government would confine itself to its assigned responsibility. The hydraulic pressure inherent within each of the separate Branches to exceed the outer limits of its power, even to accomplish desirable objectives, must be resisted.

Although not "hermetically" sealed from one another, the powers delegated to the three Branches are functionally identifiable. When any Branch acts, it is presumptively exercising the power the Constitution has delegated to it. When the Executive acts, he presumptively acts in an executive or administrative capacity as defined in Art. II. And when, as here, one House of Congress purports to act, it is presumptively acting within its assigned sphere.

Beginning with this presumption, we must nevertheless establish that the challenged action under § 244(c)(2) is of the kind to which the procedural requirements of Art. I, § 7 apply. Not every action taken by either House is subject to the bicameralism and presentment requirements of Art. I. Whether actions taken by either House are, in law and fact, an exercise of legislative power depends not on their form but upon "whether they contain matter which is properly to be regarded as legislative in its character and effect." S. Rep. No. 1335, 54th Cong., 2d Sess., 8 (1897).

Examination of the action taken here by one House pursuant to § 244(c)(2) reveals that it was essentially legislative in purpose and effect. In purporting to exercise power defined in Art. I, § 8, cl. 4 to "establish an uniform Rule of Naturalization," the House took action that had the purpose and effect of altering the legal rights, duties and relations of persons, including the Attorney General, Executive Branch officials and Chadha, all outside the legislative branch * * *.

The legislative character of the one-House veto in this case is confirmed by the character of the Congressional action it supplants. Neither the House of Representatives nor the Senate contends that, absent the veto provision in § 244(c)(2), either of them, or both of them acting together, could effectively require the Attorney General to deport an alien once the Attorney General, in the exercise of legislatively delegated authority,[16] had determined the alien should remain in the United States. Without the challenged provision in § 244(c)(2), this could have been achieved, if at all, only by legislation requiring deportation * * *.

* * *

Finally, we see that when the Framers intended to authorize either House of Congress to act alone and outside of its prescribed bicameral legislative role, they narrowly and precisely defined the procedure for such action. There are but four provisions in the Constitution, explicit and unambiguous, by which one House may act alone with the unreviewable force of law, not subject to the President's veto:

(a) The House of Representatives alone was given the power to initiate impeachments. Art. I, § 2, cl. 6;

(b) The Senate alone was given the power to conduct trials following impeachment on charges initiated by the House and to convict following trial. Art. I, § 3, cl. 5;

(c) The Senate alone was given final unreviewable power to approve or to disapprove Presidential appointments. Art. II, § 2, cl. 2;

(d) The Senate alone was given unreviewable power to ratify treaties negotiated by the President. Art. II, § 2, cl. 2.

Clearly, when the Draftsmen sought to confer special powers on one House, independent of the other House, or of the President, they did so in explicit, unambiguous terms * * *.

Since it is clear that the action by the House under § 244(c)(2) was not within any of the express constitutional exceptions authorizing one House to act alone, and equally clear that it was an exercise of legislative power, that action was subject to the standards prescribed in Article I * * *. To accomplish what has been attempted by one House of Congress in this case requires action in conformity with the express procedures of the Constitution's prescription for legislative action: passage by a majority of both Houses and presentment to the President.

The veto authorized by § 244(c)(2) doubtless has been in many respects a convenient shortcut; the "sharing" with the Executive by Congress of its authority over aliens in this manner is, on its face, an appealing compromise. In purely practical terms, it is obviously easier for action to be taken by one House without

---

16 Congress protests that affirming the Court of Appeals in these cases will sanction "lawmaking by the Attorney General. . . . Why is the Attorney General exempt from submitting his proposed changes in the law to the full bicameral process?" To be sure, some administrative agency action—rule making, for example, may resemble "lawmaking" * * *. Clearly, however, "[i]n the framework of our Constitution, the President's power to see that the laws are faithfully executed refutes the idea that he is to be a lawmaker." *Youngstown Sheet & Tube Co. v. Sawyer*, 343 U.S. 579, 587 (1952). When the Attorney General performs his duties * * *, he does not exercise "legislative" power * * *. It is clear, therefore, that the Attorney General acts in his presumptively Art. II capacity when he administers the Immigration and Nationality Act. Executive action under legislatively delegated authority that might resemble "legislative" action in some respects is not subject to the approval of both Houses of Congress and the President for the reason that the Constitution does not so require. That kind of Executive action is always subject to check by the terms of the legislation that authorized it; and if that authority is exceeded it is open to judicial review as well as the power of Congress to modify or revoke the authority entirely. A one-House veto is clearly legislative in both character and effect and is not so checked; the need for the check provided by Art. I, §§ 1, 7 is therefore clear. Congress' authority to delegate portions of its power to administrative agencies provides no support for the argument that Congress can constitutionally control administration of the laws by way of a Congressional veto.

submission to the President; but it is crystal clear from the records of the Convention, contemporaneous writings and debates, that the Framers ranked other values higher than efficiency. The records of the Convention and debates in the states preceding ratification underscore the common desire to define and limit the exercise of the newly created federal powers affecting the states and the people. There is unmistakable expression of a determination that legislation by the national Congress be a step-by-step, deliberate and deliberative process.

The choices we discern as having been made in the Constitutional Convention impose burdens on governmental processes that often seem clumsy, inefficient, even unworkable, but those hard choices were consciously made by men who had lived under a form of government that permitted arbitrary governmental acts to go unchecked. There is no support in the Constitution or decisions of this Court for the proposition that the cumbersomeness and delays often encountered in complying with explicit Constitutional standards may be avoided, either by the Congress or by the President. With all the obvious flaws of delay, untidiness, and potential for abuse, we have not yet found a better way to preserve freedom than by making the exercise of power subject to the carefully crafted restraints spelled out in the Constitution.

We hold that the Congressional veto provision in § 244(c)(2) is severable from the Act and that it is unconstitutional. Accordingly, the judgment of the Court of Appeals is

Affirmed.

■ POWELL, J., concurring in the judgment. [Omitted.]

[*Editors' Note: Justice Powell thought that the power to override the Attorney General was judicial power that could not be exercised by a legislative body: "When Congress finds that a particular person does not satisfy the statutory criteria for permanent residence in this country, it has assumed a judicial function in violation of the principle of separation of powers. Accordingly, I concur only in the judgment."*]

■ WHITE, J. dissenting.

* * *

The prominence of the legislative veto mechanism in our contemporary political system and its importance to Congress can hardly be overstated. It has become a central means by which Congress secures the accountability of executive and independent agencies. Without the legislative veto, Congress is faced with a Hobson's choice: either to refrain from delegating the necessary authority, leaving itself with a hopeless task of writing laws with the requisite specificity to cover endless special circumstances across the entire policy landscape, or in the alternative, to abdicate its law-making function to the Executive Branch and independent agencies. To choose the former leaves major national problems unresolved; to opt for the latter risks unaccountable policymaking by those not elected to fill that role * * *.

* * *

* * * We should not find the lack of a specific constitutional authorization for the legislative veto surprising, and I would not infer disapproval of the mechanism from its absence. From the summer of 1787 to the present the Government of the United States has become an endeavor far beyond the contemplation of the Framers. Only within the last half century has the complexity and size of the Federal Government's responsibilities grown so greatly that the Congress must rely on the legislative veto

as the most effective if not the only means to insure its role as the Nation's lawmaker. But the wisdom of the Framers was to anticipate that the Nation would grow and new problems of governance would require different solutions. Accordingly, our Federal Government was intentionally chartered with the flexibility to respond to contemporary needs without losing sight of fundamental democratic principles * * *.

* * *

* * * The Court's holding today that all legislative-type action must be enacted through the lawmaking process ignores that legislative authority is routinely delegated to the Executive Branch, to the independent regulatory agencies, and to private individuals and groups * * *.

This Court's decisions sanctioning such delegations make clear that Art. I does not require all action with the effect of legislation to be passed as a law.

* * *

The wisdom and the constitutionality of these broad delegations are matters that still have not been put to rest. But for present purposes, these cases establish that by virtue of congressional delegation, legislative power can be exercised by independent agencies and Executive departments without the passage of new legislation. For some time, the sheer amount of law—the substantive rules that regulate private conduct and direct the operation of government—made by the agencies has far outnumbered the lawmaking engaged in by Congress through the traditional process. There is no question but that agency rulemaking is lawmaking in any functional or realistic sense of the term * * *. When agencies are authorized to prescribe law through substantive rulemaking, the administrator's * * * regulations bind courts and officers of the Federal Government, may pre-empt state law, and grant rights to and impose obligations on the public. In sum, they have the force of law.

If Congress may delegate lawmaking power to independent and Executive agencies, it is most difficult to understand Art. I as prohibiting Congress from also reserving a check on legislative power for itself * * *.

* * *

■ REHNQUIST, J., dissenting. [Omitted.]

[Editors' Note: Justice Rehnquist thought that no live case or controversy was presented, so that the Court had no jurisdiction to decide the case one way or the other, and he accordingly did not address the constitutionality of the legislative veto. We discuss his views below.]

NOTES AND QUESTIONS

1. Chief Justice Burger's majority opinion in *INS v. Chadha* is often described as being formalistic, like Justice Black's majority opinion in *Youngstown*, while Justice White's dissent in *Chadha* is openly functionalist or purposive, like Justice Jackson's *Youngstown* concurrence. Chief Justice Burger asks which of the three powers of government Congress is exercising when it adopts a legislative veto, whether that power was exercised by the proper institution, and whether the proper procedures were followed. Burger concludes that Congress is trying to exercise its legislative power, but it can only do that through bicameralism and presentment. Congress cannot in *Chadha* exercise executive power, since the Constitution gives all of the executive power to the

President. As Justice Powell, argues, Congress also cannot exercise judicial power, if that is the best characterization of what Congress was doing in *Chadha*. This kind of matching of governmental actions with powers, institutions, and procedures according to rigorous categorizations and close attention to constitutional text is often called *formalism*. The more flexible, purpose-based approach to accommodate modern practice is often called *functionalism,* though both terms are employed so loosely that precise definitions are treacherous. For a thoughtful discussion of formalism and functionalism in separation of powers cases, see Peter B. McCutchen, *Mistakes, Precedent, and the Rise of the Administrative State: Toward a Constitutional Theory of the Second Best,* 80 CORNELL L. REV. 1, 5–11 (1994). For the attempt by one of us to provide a roadmap for students through this methodological thicket, see Gary Lawson, *Prolegomenon to Any Future Administrative Law Course: Separation of Powers and the Transcendental Deduction,* 49 ST. LOUIS U.L. REV. 885 (2005).

2. Justice White says the Court's approval of broad subdelegations renders the majority's formalist analysis pointless and (without using the word) hypocritical. Does the demise of the subdelegation doctrine (but see *Gundy v. United States, supra* pages 205–215) really mean that anything goes? If so, can Congress give itself law execution power? Can it give such power to just the Senate or just the House? Why not delegate it to one committee or subcommittee of one of the two houses? Indeed, why not just delegate all the legislative power to the Speaker of the House of Representatives? What then is left of the separation of powers?

3. On the other hand, Justice White has a point when he says that delegations subject to congressional control are, in some sense, "closer" to the constitutional design than giving uncontrollable lawmaking authority to administrative agencies. Is it better—constitutionally better—to swallow subdelegation and then hold the line on other structural lines, such as Article I, section 7, or to try to adjust (or "re-center") the rest of the Constitution each time longstanding practice and precedent sanction a departure from the original design? Does forbidding legislative vetoes perhaps give Congress a modest incentive not to subdelegate legislative authority?

4. Congress has considered in recent years legislation that would lead to automatic fast-track voting in Congress, with no possibility of a filibuster in the Senate, of any agency rule imposing costs of more than $100,000,000. This would require approval pursuant to Article I, Section 7 before the regulation can become effective. Wouldn't this be a very good idea that would enhance the democratic legitimacy of the administrative state?

5. Justice Rehnquist did not think the Court should have decided *Chadha* at all. Chadha was facing deportation. He could avoid that fate only if the Attorney General exercised a discretionary statutory power to withhold deportation. The statute giving the Attorney General that power came with a legislative veto attached. If the legislative veto is unconstitutional, shouldn't that drag the Attorney General's power down with it, since the power and the veto were enacted together as one law? If that is right, then the Court had nothing to decide. If the legislative veto was invalid, Chadha lost because the Attorney General had no (valid) power to withhold deportation. If the legislative veto was valid, Chadha lost because Congress ordered his deportation. If Chadha was going to lose no matter how the case came out, how was there a live "case or controversy" for the Court to decide? In *United States v. Windsor*, 570 U.S. 744 (2013), the Court said that the House of Representatives had a justiciable legal right to litigate to protect its one-House veto power. The case is styled, however, as *INS v. Chadha* and not as *U.S. House of Representatives v.* either *INS or Chadha*. Does it matter as to justiciability how a case is

styled? Does it matter if the House of Representatives defended its position in an amicus brief?

The catch is that the law concerning when the unconstitutionality of one provision of a statute drags down the entire statute of which it is a part is very complicated. Congress often, as it did with the statutes in *Chadha,* specifies that it wants each provision to be "severable" from the others, so that if one provision is found unconstitutional, the other provisions should all stand. Both of us doubt whether those severability clauses should be given any effect. If Congress wants provisions in a statute to be "severable" in that fashion, it can pass each provision as a separate law. But if Congress bundles many provisions together into a single enacted law, that law as enacted is either constitutional or not; courts have no business crafting what amounts to a new law out of the remains of the old one. Or so at least so we both think. One justice agrees, *see Murphy v. National Collegiate Athletic Ass'n,* 138 S.Ct. 1461, 1485–86 (2018) (Thomas, J., concurring), but the doctrine is otherwise. It treats congressional severability provisions as *presumptively* allowing the rest of a law to stand when part of it is found unconstitutional, but that presumption can be overcome if the Court determines that Congress, notwithstanding its severability clause, really would not have enacted other parts of the law without the legislative veto. *See Executive Benefits Ins. Agency v. Arkison,* 573 U.S. 25, 36–37 (2014). Justice Rehnquist doubted whether Congress would have given the Attorney General authority to cancel deportations without a legislative veto as a backstop, so he thought that the authority would fall if the legislative veto fell. On that assumption, Justice Rehnquist was clearly right that the Court had no case to decide.

6. The legislative veto in *Chadha* was a "one-house" veto, because the House alone could, under the statute, overturn executive action. What if you needed both Houses to overturn executive action? That would solve the bicameralism problem from *Chadha,* but it would still leave the presentment problem. Shortly after *Chadha,* the Supreme Court, in a summary order without opinion, invalidated a two-house legislative veto, confirming that Article I, section 7 requires both bicameralism and presentment. *See Consumer Energy Council of America v. FERC,* 673 F.2d 425 (D.C.Cir.1982*), aff'd sub nom. Process Gas Consumers Group v. Consumer Energy Council of America*, 463 U.S. 1216 (1983).

7. Notwithstanding the clear holding in *Chadha,* Congress has continued to enact legislative veto provisions with some frequency. *See* LOUIS FISHER, RECONSIDERING JUDICIAL FINALITY: WHY THE SUPREME COURT IS NOT THE LAST WORD ON THE CONSTITUTION 217–21 (2019). Under existing severability doctrine, this is a classic instance of sound departmentalism in action: Congress disagrees with the Court, and while it cannot force the Court to enforce legislative veto provisions when they are challenged, by the same token the Court cannot tell Congress what laws it can pass. If the Court ever changes its mind about the constitutionality of legislative vetoes, the many enacted provisions, which currently lay dormant and unenforced, will spring back to life. Keep in mind that when courts find statutes unconstitutional, they do not, as the misleading metaphor suggests, "strike down" those laws. The laws still exist; we do not burn all copies of the United States Code that contain them. Courts simply do not give those laws any legal effect when they are challenged. *See* Jonathan F. Mitchell, *The Writ-of-Erasure Fallacy,* 104 VA. L. REV. 934 (2018). That does not forbid a legislature from enacting them. On the other hand, if both of us (and Justice Thomas) are right about nonseverability, enactment of an unconstitutional legislative veto renders the entire act of which it is a part unconstitutional.

8. The presentment requirement matters because the President's signature is ordinarily necessary before a bill becomes a law. Indeed, under the "pocket veto" provision

in Article I, section 7, if Congress passes a proposed law near the end of its session, the President sits on it without acting for ten days, and then the congressional term ends, the bill dies without need for a veto (and with no opportunity for an override). An actual veto prevents a bill from becoming law unless Congress can produce two-thirds majorities in each House for an override. That does happen on some occasions, but it is relatively rare. The veto is one of the President's most important powers. Under the terms of Article I, section 7, the object that is presented to the President is a bill, so the only object that the President can sign or veto (or pocket-veto) is the bill that was presented to him or her. If that bill happens to contain 12,000 pages of provisions, the President cannot pick and choose which provisions in the bill to sign or veto. The President must take or leave the whole package. Many state governors have so-called "line-item veto" power that lets them veto specific provisions of bills, but the Constitution does not seem to give the President any such power.

9. Can Congress give the President that power even when the Constitution does not? In 1996, Congress enacted a statute entitled "The Line Item Veto Act," though it is debatable—and was debated by the Court—whether the title accurately described the law. The statute gave the President power to "cancel in whole" "(1) any dollar amount of discretionary budget authority; (2) any item of new direct spending; or (3) any limited tax benefit." 2 U.S.C. § 691(a) (1994 ed. Supp. II). President Clinton used his authority under the Act to "cancel" some spending and tax benefit measures, and some anticipated beneficiaries sued to declare the cancellations unconstitutional. Six justices found the statute unconstitutional because, in effect, it allows the President to amend or repeal a law without going through the full Article I, Section 7 process. *See Clinton v. City of New York,* 524 U.S. 417, 438–39 (1998). The other three justices disagreed with the majority's characterization of the law's effects (and therefore with Congress's characterization of the law in its title). Three justices thought that the President was not amending or repealing anything; he was executing the law that Congress had enacted: "He simply *followed* the law, leaving the statutes, as they are literally written, intact." *See id.* at 474 (Breyer, J., dissenting). The same three justices also thought that more than two centuries of history had established that Congress could, without violating either Article I, Section 7 or the subdelegation doctrine, pass a statute whose execution gives the President a measure of spending discretion, even if such authority would be dubious as an original matter. *See id.* at 464 (Scalia, J., dissenting). And two of the three dissenting justices thought that modern conditions required allowance of presidential cancellation authority even if original meaning would forbid it. In an era when Congress's appropriation bills were literally one brief paragraph in length, "a Congress, wishing to give a President the power to select among appropriations, could simply have embodied each appropriation in a separate bill, each bill subject to a separate Presidential veto." *Id.* at 471 (Breyer, J., dissenting). But today, said Justices Breyer and O'Connor, "a typical budget appropriations bill may have a dozen titles, hundreds of sections, and spread across more than 500 pages of the Statutes at Large. Congress cannot divide such a bill into thousands, or tens of thousands, of separate appropriations bills, each one of which the President would have to sign, or to veto, separately." *Id.* (Why not? What stops them?) All of the justices appeared to agree that a pure line-item veto, allowing the President to prevent portions of an enacted bill from taking effect, would be unconstitutional.

10. The parties in *Clinton v. New York* briefed the case on the assumption that the Court might decide it based on the subdelegation doctrine. Indeed, the statutes in cases addressing contingent legislation, such as *The Brig Aurora* and *Field v. Clark, see supra* pages 185, 187–188, bear some similarity to the Line Item Veto Act: They make the effectiveness of a law depend on a presidential determination. The Court in *Clinton* did not think it needed to address the subdelegation issue, because it found the statute

unconstitutional on other grounds. *See* 524 U.S. at 448. The dissenting justices thought that subdelegation was the *key* issue (since they did not see a problem with Article I, Section 7), *see id.* at 465 (Scalia, J., dissenting), and they found the subdelegation doctrine satisfied as a matter of precedent and history. In *The Brig Aurora, Field v Clark,* and other cases of contingent legislation, however, the statutes prescribed some finding or determination that the President must make—whether it was ascertaining a calendar date, determining whether foreign countries are violating our neutral commerce, or deciding whether foreign tariffs are reciprocally unequal. What determination did the Line Item Veto Act require the President to make before cancelling an item? Congress can obviously make the effectiveness of legislation depend on all manner of external events and can give the President power to determine if those events have occurred. Can Congress make the effectiveness of legislation depend on the President's ascertainment of his or her own will or preferences? Is that any different in principle from making legislation depend on the President's ascertainment of whether England violates our neutral commerce? If Congress had said that the effectiveness of any spending bill or special tax benefit depends on a presidential finding that it is fair and equitable, would that solve all constitutional problems?

[Assignment 14]

R. ARTICLE I, SECTION 8 AND CONGRESS'S POWER OF THE PURSE

The first seven sections of Article I establish, define, and set up the structures for Congress. They describe the machinery through which Congress can exercise the "legislative Powers herein granted" by the Constitution. Section 8 identifies most of those "herein granted" legislative powers. Some important congressional powers, as we shall see, appear in subsequent articles of the Constitution, but the eighteen clauses in Article I, section 8 are the primary sources of federal legislative power.

Many of those enumerated powers define Congress's relationship to people and States. We address those powers in subsequent chapters. Many of the Article I, section 8 powers—almost a third of them—involve war and foreign affairs. We address those powers in the next section of this chapter. For the moment, our focus is on a small but vital set of powers in Article I, section 8 that directly deal with the structure of the national government:

> **The Congress shall have Power * * ***
>
> **To constitute Tribunals inferior to the Supreme Court; * * * And**
>
> **To make all Laws which shall be necessary and proper for carrying into Execution the foregoing Powers, and all other Powers vested by this Constitution in the Government of the United States, or in any Department or Officer thereof.**

U.S. CONST. art. I, § 8, cl. 9 & 18. Consider the context of these provisions. The Constitution, of its own force, creates very little of the national government. It creates the Congress, the President, the Vice President, and a Supreme Court that must have at least one member—and that is all. The Constitution assumes that there will likely be more than one Supreme Court justice, some inferior federal courts, and executive officials other than the President such as ambassadors, ministers, consuls, and heads of departments, but it does not actually create any of those positions. The Constitution does not create a Department of State, a Department of Treasury, or a

Department of War. It does not create the positions of Secretary of State, Attorney General, United States Marshal, and the like. The entire structure of the executive and judicial departments of the national government beyond the President, the Vice President, and a Supreme Court consisting of at least one person must be created after the Constitution comes into effect.

This situation is completely unlike the situation in the United Kingdom in 1787. In the U.K., King George III could create cabinet departments, agencies, officer, judges, and even enough new members of the House of Lords to pack that body, as Kings William IV and Edward VII did do when the House of Lords dragged its feet on crucial reform legislation in 1832 and in 1911. The President can do none of these things. It is up to Congress whether or not to create Cabinet departments, agencies, executive officers, or judgeships.

Take the federal judiciary. Article III vests the "judicial Power of the United States * * * in one supreme Court, and in such inferior Courts as the Congress may from time to time ordain and establish." *Id.* art. III, § 1. According to this provision, there *must* be a Supreme Court (and there *must* be a "Chief Justice" to preside over presidential impeachment trials in the Senate, *see id.* art. I, § 3, cl. 6), but there might or might not be any particular lower federal courts, depending on what Congress chooses to "ordain and establish." Laws creating lower federal courts would surely be laws "necessary and proper for carrying into Execution" the federal judicial power, so the Necessary and Proper Clause (which the founding generation almost uniformly called the "Sweeping Clause") provides constitutional authority for Congress to fill in the structure of the federal judiciary. The same provision allows Congress to define the number of seats on the Supreme Court, a subject on which the Constitution is silent. Over the course of the nation's history, the number of Supreme Court justices has included every digit between six and ten (inclusive), with the size of the Court fixed at nine for the past century and a half. The number of federal district judges, federal circuit judges, federal circuits, and whether there will even be federal districts and circuits are all matters left to Congress—and the President via presentment—by the Necessary and Proper Clause. There are today 1,000 inferior federal court judges. Congress could either double that number of cut it in half tomorrow if it wanted to do so.

Notice that the power to create federal judges comes from the Necessary and Proper Clause, not the Tribunals Clause that precedes it. You can see this by realizing that the Tribunals Clause cannot authorize the creation of Supreme Court justices. (Do you see why? It grants only the power to create judges inferior to the Supreme Court; it does not grant Congress the power to create judges or justices of the Supreme Court.) That power must come from elsewhere, and it plainly comes from the Necessary and Proper Clause. Once you see the Necessary and Proper Clause as the source of power to create federal offices, it follows that the power to create lower federal courts comes from that clause as well as from Congress's power to constitute tribunals inferior to the Supreme Court. Congress has since the Judiciary Act of 1789 constituted the state supreme courts as tribunals inferior to the Supreme Court when they decide against a claim made under federal law. Note the broad use of the word "tribunals." This encompasses elected state supreme courts, which the Framers might not have thought of as truly being courts. It is possible to read the Tribunals Clause as additional authorization for the creation of lower federal courts, but because the Necessary and Proper Clause is the source of power to create every other federal office, it would be odd if it was not also the source of power to create lower federal courts. So what function does the Tribunals Clause play if not to authorize the creation of lower federal courts?

Many cases involving federal law originate in state courts. As we will see later in this chapter, the Supreme Court can review and reverse state court judgments, including state supreme court judgments, involving federal law, but that does not make those state courts "inferior to" the Supreme Court—no more than the power of judicial review makes Congress and the President "inferior to" the Supreme Court. State courts can have their judgments reviewed by the Supreme Court, but they are not part of the federal judicial structure. The Supreme Court has no "supervisory" power over state courts, nor do state courts have to follow Supreme Court precedents—no more than state courts have to follow precedents from the International Court of Justice. But if they really were "inferior to" the Supreme Court, all of that would change. The Tribunals Clause permits Congress to bring state courts within the federal judicial hierarchy, with an accompanying obligation to follow Supreme Court precedent and a supervisory power, by "constitut[ing]" them as "inferior to the Supreme Court." Or so we think. *See* Steven G. Calabresi & Gary Lawson, *The Unitary Executive, Jurisdiction Stripping, and the* Hamdan *Opinions: A Textualist Response to Justice Scalia,* 107 COLUM. L. REV. 1002, 1028–34 (2007).

To be sure, we suspect that most scholars and judges, if asked, would locate the power to create lower federal courts in the Tribunals Clause. For reasons that we have just given, we doubt whether this is right, but because everyone agrees that the power exists, not much (other than constitutional fidelity) turns on precisely where the power is placed.

Now turn to the executive branch. In England, the King could create executive offices at will, without needing Parliamentary authorization. The Declaration of Independence bitterly complained that King George III "has erected a multitude of New Offices, and sent hither swarms of Officers to harass our people and eat out their substance." The Constitution gave the President no such power. Congress, and Congress alone (subject always to presentment), can create federal offices pursuant to the Necessary and Proper Clause. James Madison and Charles Pinckney at the Constitutional Convention tried to make this explicit by inserting "between 'laws' and 'necessary' [the phrase] 'and establish all offices' it appearing to them liable to cavil that the latter was not included in the former." 2 THE RECORDS OF THE FEDERAL CONVENTION OF 1787, at 345 (Max Farrand ed., 1911). An all-star chorus of framers insisted "that the amendment could not be necessary," because it was already too clear for cavil that the Necessary and Proper Clause gave Congress power to create federal offices, and the amendment was rejected 9–2. *See id.* The Appointments Clause, as we shall shortly see, refers to "Officers of the United States * * * which shall be *established by Law.*" U.S. CONST. art. II, § 2, cl. 2 (emphasis added). Under the Constitution, it takes a law to raise an office.

Congress thus determines the structure of the federal court system and the executive department. The only requirement is that any laws creating federal offices must be "necessary and proper for carrying into Execution" federal powers. We will soon explore what that vital phrase actually means.

There is another way in which Congress determines the structure of the national government: The Power of the Purse.

S. THE POWER OF THE PURSE

The history of England from 1066 to 1701 was punctuated by frequent battles between Parliament, which had the Power of the Purse, and the King, who had the Power of the Sword. (The ancient metaphors of the Purse and the Sword to represent legislative and executive powers frequently appeared in founding-era materials.) English kings often wished to wage warfare against the French, the Scots, and the Irish, and wars cost a lot of money. While the King had sources of revenue from royal lands available to him, he frequently needed more money, which could only be obtained from Parliament, which alone had the Power of the Purse in the form of the power to tax and spend. In the seventeenth century in particular, Kings James I and Charles I frequently called Parliament into session when they were broke and needed money. Since both monarchs were spendthrifts, they were often forced to call Parliament into session even though they knew it would pass laws revoking royal patents and imposing bills of attainder putting to death the King's favorites at court. The Framing generation was well aware of this history.

In the American colonies between 1607 and 1776, there was also a recognition by royal governors that only the popular lower house of the colonial assemblies had the Power of the Purse. This was most dramatically demonstrated in the Puritan, Congregationalist Colony of Massachusetts, which refused to pass a permanent salary for the royal governor. The Massachusetts Assembly insisted on paying each royal governor at the end of each year depending on how well he had behaved during the prior year. Suffice it to say that the idea that the legislature has the sole Power of the Purse was very deeply rooted in American and British history and tradition when the Philadelphia Constitutional Convention met in 1787.

The Constitution confirms that neither the President nor the federal courts can unilaterally spend money. It says flat-out: "**No Money shall be drawn from the Treasury, but in Consequence of Appropriations made by Law**." U.S. CONST. art. I, § 9, cl. 7. Congress thus not only can determine the structure of the executive and judicial departments by creating offices, but it can also control the extent of their operations by funding or not funding them. The President cannot so much as buy a paper clip without an appropriation from Congress. Unlike the King, the President has no royal lands to generate a stream of income independent of the legislature. And even if an independently rich President was inclined to fund government operations from his or her own private fortune, Congress has forbidden that by requiring all funds received by the government to go into the Treasury, from which, by constitutional command, they then cannot be withdrawn absent an appropriations law. *See* 31 U.S.C. § 3302(b) (2018). Nor can government agencies accept volunteer services without specific statutory authorization. *See id.* § 1342. Congress indeed holds the Power of the Purse.

So why, at the beginning of this section, didn't we include the Spending Clause as a provision that helps Congress structure the national government? We actually think that we did.

There is no express "Spending Clause" in the Constitution. The Appropriations Clause mentioned above obviously assumes that there will be "Appropriations made by Law," but it does not itself grant power to appropriate or spend. "This clause is a limitation on executive or judicial action rather than a grant of any power—which is why it appears in Article I, section 9, the portion of the original Constitution that is devoted to direct limitations on various federal actors." GARY LAWSON & GUY SEIDMAN, THE CONSTITUTION OF EMPIRE: TERRITORIAL EXPANSION AND AMERICAN LEGAL HISTORY 27 (2004). The power to spend must come from somewhere else.

Ever since 1936, and some dictum in *United States v. Butler,* 297 U.S. 1, 65 (1936), the Constitution's "Spending Clause" has been almost universally pegged as Article I, section 8, clause 1, which gives Congress "Power To lay and collect Taxes, Duties, Imposts and Excises, to pay the Debts and provide for the common Defence and general Welfare of the United States." The Court so held in *Steward Machine Co. v. Davis,* 301 U.S. 548 (1937), endorsing a view held by Alexander Hamilton that one could infer a power to spend, for the purposes identified in the Taxing Clause, from the power to tax. It is settled doctrine today that Congress has nearly unfettered power to spend for the "general Welfare," *see Agency for Int'l Development v. Alliance for Open Society Int'l, Inc.,* 570 U.S. 205, 213 (2013) ("The Spending Clause of the Federal Constitution grants Congress the power '[t]o lay and collect Taxes, Duties, Imposts and Excises, to pay the Debts and provide for the common Defence and general Welfare of the United States.' Art. I, § 8, cl. 1. The Clause provides Congress broad discretion to tax and spend for the 'general Welfare,' including by funding particular state or private programs or activities"), subject only to vague restrictions on using the spending power to coerce States into following federal dictates. *See National Federation of Independent Business v. Sebelius,* 567 U.S. 519, 575–85 (2012). James Madison disagreed, and so do we.

The Taxing Clause is—for lack of a better term—a Taxing Clause, not a Spending Clause. It is one of three (or four, if one considers the possibility that treaties might involve money payments) clauses that allow the government to raise revenue, along with the immediately following power to "borrow Money on the credit of the United States," U.S. CONST. art. I, § 8, cl. 2, and the Article IV power to "dispose of * * * Territory or other Property belonging to the United States." *Id.* art. IV, § 3, cl. 2. The Taxing Clause is immensely important, because it gives the federal government direct power to demand resources from individuals. Under the Articles of Confederation, only States had that power, and Congress had to ask States to exercise that power and then turn money over to the federal government, and there was no enforcement mechanism if States did not comply. The grant to the federal government of the power to tax, primarily to pay off the debts incurred during the Revolutionary War and to safeguard the country against European powers, was one of the principal reasons for adoption of the Constitution. Textually, grammatically, structurally, and historically, however, the Taxing Clause does not grant power to spend money; it only grants power to raise money. *See* Gary Lawson, *Making a Federal Case Out of It:* Sabri v. United States *and the Constitution of Leviathan,* 2003–2004 CATO SUP. CT. REV. 119, 133–39; Jeffrey T. Renz, *What Spending Clause? (Or the President's Paramour): An Examination of the Views of Hamilton, Madison, and Story on Article I, Section 8, Clause 1 of the United States Constitution*, 33 J. MARSHALL L. REV. 81, 136–40 (1999).

The phrase "to pay the Debts and provide for the common Defence and general Welfare of the United States" describes the permissible purposes for which taxes may be imposed but does not constitute authority for spending. Whether taxes could be imposed only for raising revenue or could also be used for regulatory purposes, such as to prop up domestic industry with protectionist tariffs, was a huge issue in founding-era political theory. By specifying that taxes could be imposed for the "general Welfare," the Taxing Clause resolved that issue in favor of the broader view. *See* Renz, *supra*. Hence, the first substantive statute passed by the First Congress was a tariff which identified its purposes as "for the support of the government, for the discharge of the debts of the United States, and the encouragement and protection of manufactures." Act of July 4, 1789, ch. 2, § 1, 1 Stat. 24.

If the Taxing Clause is the implicit source of federal spending power, does that mean that money raised through borrowing or land sales cannot be spent? After all, "the spending allusion in the Taxing Clause does not even colorably reach borrowed sums." David E. Engdahl, *The Basis of the Spending Power,* 18 SEATTLE U.L. REV. 215, 222 (1995). But of course Congress can spend borrowed money and sales receipts—which just proves that the source of the spending power is something other than the Taxing Clause.

Just as laws creating federal offices and departments can be "necessary and proper for carrying into Execution" federal powers, so can laws appropriating funds for governmental operations. The Necessary and Proper Clause is the true source of federal spending power, at least as a matter of original meaning. That was Madison's view, and Madison was right. As a matter of current doctrine, however, the Taxing Clause is considered the font of federal spending authority. That is good news for Congress, because a spending power derived from the Necessary and Proper Clause would likely be narrower than a power inferred from the Taxing Clause. If one uses the Taxing Clause as spending authorization and then takes a capacious enough view of what constitutes "Debts," "common Defense," and "general Welfare," Congress can justify spending money on virtually anything. If spending must be "necessary and proper for carrying into Execution" some identifiable federal power, the constitutional lines might be a bit stricter. *See* Gary Lawson, *A Truism with Attitude: The Tenth Amendment in Constitutional Context*, 83 NOTRE DAME L. REV. 469, 499–501 (2008).

Under any view of the source of and limits on the federal spending power, however, the power lies with Congress. We explain those limits, as they exist under current doctrine, in the next chapter. *See infra* pages 666–685.

T. CONGRESS'S POWER TO CARRY INTO EXECUTION THE PRESIDENT'S EXECUTIVE POWER AND THE FEDERAL COURTS JUDICIAL POWER

The Necessary and Proper Clause not only grants Congress the power to carry into execution its own federal powers. The clause also gives Congress the power to carry into execution the President's "executive Power" and the "judicial Power" of the Supreme Court and inferior federal courts ("all other Powers vested by this Constitution"). The First Congress carried the President's "executive Power" into execution by creating a Department of State, a Department of the Treasury, a Department of War, and an Attorney General (who lacked a Department to help him). President Washington then appointed Thomas Jefferson to be Secretary of State, Alexander Hamilton to be Secretary of the Treasury, Henry Knox to be Secretary of War, and Edmund Randolph to be Attorney General. Congress separately created an office of Postmaster General, and President Washington appointed Samuel Osgood to that office. All of Washington's nominations were confirmed unanimously by the Senate.

The creation of the first three Departments and of the offices of Attorney General and Postmaster General by the First Congress are classic instances of Congress using its Necessary and Proper Clause power to carry into execution "the executive Power" in a constitutional and proper way. Unlike King George III, American presidents do not have the power to create departments, agencies, or offices. Congressional action is required to accomplish all of these things. It is also Congress, both through legislation and appropriation, which determines how many people there will be on the White House staff or in any of the Cabinet[4] Departments or agencies, though Congress often passes general authorizations to agencies to make whatever hires they deem necessary given their budgetary limitations. These kinds of laws structuring the government are exactly what the Necessary and Proper Clause contemplates.

But there are limits on how Congress can employ its power to structure the government. What happens when Congress, in the guise of structuring the government, tries to *control* the activities of executive or judicial actors? Would it be "necessary and proper for carrying into Execution" the President's pardon power for Congress to pass a law requiring all pardons to be approved by a committee of Congress? Can Congress "carry[ ] into Execution" the judicial power by telling courts how they must decide cases?

The text of the Necessary and Proper Clause suggests three constraints on the power of Congress: Laws pursuant to that clause must be (1) necessary and (2) proper for (3) carrying into execution some federal power. In the next chapter, we will look closely at what it means for a law to be "necessary and proper." For the moment, we will focus on what it means to "carry[ ] into Execution" the executive or judicial power, though it is impossible to explore the application of the Necessary and Proper Clause without some attention to the words that give the clause its modern name.

A clearly dubious use of Congress's power to carry into execution the "executive Power" is the War Powers Resolution of 1973, which was passed during the Watergate scandal over President Nixon's veto. 50 U.S.C. §§ 1542–43 (2018). This Act, as we will later see *infra* pages 506–508, purports to carry into execution the President's "executive Power" and his "Commander in Chief power," *see id.* § 1541(b) (invoking the Necessary and Proper Clause as constitutional authorization), by *limiting* the situations in which they can be used. This is unconstitutional because Congress cannot "carry[ ] into Execution" a power by curtailing its usage. Every President since 1973, Democrats and Republicans alike, has treated the War Powers Resolution as advisory only.

Similar problems can occur with congressional efforts to carry into execution the "judicial Power" of the federal courts. The First Congress passed a framework statute, called the Judiciary Act of 1789, setting up a six-member Supreme Court and sixteen federal district courts with one judge each. Act of Sept. 4, 1789, ch. XX, 1 Stat. 73. As to the Supreme Court, Congress not only specified that the Court would

---

4 To call something a "Cabinet" department simply means that the head of that department is one of the President's top advisers. There is no formal legal role for the "Cabinet." It exists by custom, and the composition of the Cabinet often changes, even during the term of a single President. Congress will sometimes designate certain agencies as "Departments" (as when it converted the Veterans Administration into the Department of Veterans Affairs in 1989), which has the effect of making the heads of those agencies the default actors to determine presidential disability under the Twenty-Fifth Amendment, though Congress can designate non-Department heads to make disability determinations as well.

have six members, *see id.* § 1; it also required that the Court have two terms, "the one commencing the first Monday of February, and the other the first Monday of August," *id.* (this was changed to the present first Monday in October in 1916); it required that the Supreme Court justices ride circuit, *see id.* § 4; and it defined the jurisdiction of the Supreme Court, *see id.* § 13. Most of this obviously "carr[ies] into Execution" the judicial power, though one could raise questions about the requirement of circuit riding. *See Stuart v. Laird,* 5 U.S. (1 Cranch) 229 (1803) (upholding the requirement based on legislative precedent).

What about statutes that regulate the courts' process of decision-making? Can Congress prescribe rules of evidence for courts? Tell courts that they must decide cases in favor of the government unless the government is flagrantly wrong? Order courts to rule in favor of specific parties?

Statutes in the first two categories exist and are considered obviously constitutional by almost everyone. (Both of us idiosyncratically doubt Congress's ability to interfere in any way with the judicial decision-making process, including by specifying standards of proof and rules of evidence, *see* Gary Lawson, *Controlling Precedent: Congressional Regulation of Judicial Decision-Making,* 18 CONST. COMMENTARY 191 (2001), but that position is considered fringe even by our friends.) Congress has enacted the Federal Rules of Evidence that must be applied by federal courts, and a raft of statutes order federal courts to affirm executive agency decisions as long as they are not "arbitrary or capricious" or are supported by "substantial evidence." In other words, Congress routinely orders courts to rule in favor of the government even when the court thinks that the government is wrong, and almost no one doubts Congress's power to do this under the Necessary and Proper Clause.

Once we get to Congress ordering courts to rule in favor of specific parties, however, some limits start to come into focus. Fixing those limits, however, has proved exceedingly difficult as illustrated by the oft-overlooked but exceedingly important *Plaut v. Spendthrift Farm*, 514 U.S. 211 (1995).

U. PLAUT V. SPENDTHRIFT FARM

514 U.S. 211 (1995)

■ JUSTICE SCALIA delivered the opinion of the Court.

The question presented in this case is whether § 27A(b) of the Securities Exchange Act of 1934, to the extent that it requires federal courts to reopen final judgments in private civil actions under § 10(b) of the Act, contravenes the Constitution's separation of powers or the Due Process Clause of the Fifth Amendment.

In 1987, petitioners brought a civil action against respondents in the United States District Court for the Eastern District of Kentucky. The complaint alleged that in 1983 and 1984 respondents had committed fraud and deceit in the sale of stock in violation of § 10(b) of the Securities Exchange Act of 1934 and Rule 10b–5 of the Securities and Exchange Commission. The case was mired in pretrial proceedings in the District Court until June 20, 1991, when we decided *Lampf, Pleva, Lipkind, Prupis & Petigrow v. Gilbertson*, 501 U.S. 350 (1991). Lampf held that "litigation instituted pursuant to § 10(b) and Rule 10b–5 . . . must be commenced within one year after the discovery of the facts constituting the violation and within three years after such violation." *Id.*, at 364. We applied that holding to the plaintiff-respondents in *Lampf* itself, found their suit untimely, and reinstated a summary judgment previously entered in favor of the defendant-petitioners. On the same day we decided *James B. Beam Distilling Co. v. Georgia,* 501 U.S. 529 (1991), in which a majority of the Court held, albeit in different opinions, that a new rule of federal law that is applied to the parties in the case announcing the rule must be applied as well to all cases pending on direct review. The joint effect of *Lampf* and *Beam* was to mandate application of the 1-year/3-year limitations period to petitioners' suit. The District Court, finding that petitioners' claims were untimely under the *Lampf* rule, dismissed their action with prejudice on August 13, 1991. Petitioners filed no appeal; the judgment accordingly became final 30 days later.

On December 19, 1991, the President signed the Federal Deposit Insurance Corporation Improvement Act of 1991. Section 476 of the Act—a section that had nothing to do with FDIC improvements—became § 27A of the Securities Exchange Act of 1934, and was later codified as 15 U.S.C. 78aa–1 (1988 ed., Supp. V). It provides:

"(a) Effect on pending causes of action

"The limitation period for any private civil action implied under section 78j(b) of this title § 10(b) of the Securities Exchange Act of 1934 that was commenced on or before June 19, 1991, shall be the limitation period provided by the laws applicable in the jurisdiction, including principles of retroactivity, as such laws existed on June 19, 1991.

"(b) Effect on dismissed causes of action

"Any private civil action implied under section 78j(b) of this title that was commenced on or before June 19, 1991—

"(1) which was dismissed as time barred subsequent to June 19, 1991, and

"(2) which would have been timely filed under the limitation period provided by the laws applicable in the jurisdiction, including principles of retroactivity, as such laws existed on June 19, 1991,

"shall be reinstated on motion by the plaintiff not later than 60 days after December 19, 1991."

On February 11, 1992, petitioners returned to the District Court and filed a motion to reinstate the action previously dismissed with prejudice. The District Court found that the conditions set out in §§ 27A(b)(1) and (2) were met, so that petitioners' motion was required to be granted by the terms of the statute. It nonetheless denied the motion, agreeing with respondents that § 27A(b) is unconstitutional. The United States Court of Appeals for the Sixth Circuit affirmed. We granted certiorari * * *.

* * *

We conclude that in § 27A(b) Congress has exceeded its authority by requiring the federal courts to exercise "the judicial Power of the United States," U.S. Const., Art. III, § 1, in a manner repugnant to the text, structure and traditions of Article III.

Our decisions to date have identified two types of legislation that require federal courts to exercise the judicial power in a manner that Article III forbids. The first appears in *United States v. Klein*, 13 Wall. 128 (1872), where we refused to give effect to a statute that was said "to prescribe rules of decision to the Judicial Department of the government in cases pending before it." *Id.*, 13 Wall., at 146. Whatever the precise scope of *Klein*, however, later decisions have made clear that its prohibition does not take hold when Congress "amends applicable law." *Robertson v. Seattle Audubon Society*, 503 U.S. 429, 441 (1992). Section 27A(b) indisputably does set out substantive legal standards for the Judiciary to apply, and in that sense changes the law (even if solely retroactively). The second type of unconstitutional restriction upon the exercise of judicial power identified by past cases is exemplified by *Hayburn's Case*, 2 Dall. 409 (1792), which stands for the principle that Congress cannot vest review of the decisions of Article III courts in officials of the Executive Branch. Yet under any application of § 27A(b) only courts are involved; no officials of other departments sit in direct review of their decisions. Section 27A(b) therefore offends neither of these previously established prohibitions.

We think, however, that § 27A(b) offends a postulate of Article III just as deeply rooted in our law as those we have mentioned. Article III establishes a "judicial department" with the "province and duty . . . to say what the law is" in particular cases and controversies. *Marbury v. Madison*, 1 Cranch 137, 177 (1803). The record of history shows that the Framers crafted this charter of the judicial department with an expressed understanding that it gives the Federal Judiciary the power, not merely to rule on cases, but to decide them, subject to review only by superior courts in the Article III hierarchy—with an understanding, in short, that "a judgment conclusively resolves the case" because "a 'judicial Power' is one to render dispositive judgments." Easterbrook, *Presidential Review*, 40 Case W.Res.L.Rev. 905, 926 (1990). By retroactively commanding the federal courts to reopen final judgments, Congress has violated this fundamental principle.

The Framers of our Constitution lived among the ruins of a system of intermingled legislative and judicial powers, which had been prevalent in the colonies long before the Revolution, and which after the Revolution had produced factional strife and partisan oppression. In the 17th and 18th centuries colonial assemblies and legislatures functioned as courts of equity of last resort, hearing original actions or providing appellate review of judicial judgments. G. Wood, The Creation of the American Republic 1776–1787, pp. 154–155 (1969). Often, however, they chose to correct the judicial process through special bills or other enacted legislation. It was common for such legislation not to prescribe a resolution of the dispute, but rather simply to set aside the judgment and order a new trial or appeal. Thus, as described in our discussion of *Hayburn's Case*, such legislation bears not on the problem of interbranch review but on the problem of finality of judicial judgments.

The vigorous, indeed often radical, populism of the revolutionary legislatures and assemblies increased the frequency of legislative correction of judgments. Wood, *supra*, at 155–156, 407–408. "The period 1780–1787 . . . was a period of 'constitutional reaction' " to these developments, "which . . . leaped suddenly to its climax in the Philadelphia Convention." E. Corwin, The Doctrine of Judicial Review 37 (1914). Voices from many quarters, official as well as private, decried the increasing legislative interference with the private-law judgments of the courts * * *.

* * *

This sense of a sharp necessity to separate the legislative from the judicial power, prompted by the crescendo of legislative interference with private judgments of the courts, triumphed among the Framers of the new Federal Constitution. The Convention made the critical decision to establish a judicial department independent of the Legislative Branch * * *. Before and during the debates on ratification, Madison, Jefferson, and Hamilton each wrote of the factional disorders and disarray that the system of legislative equity had produced in the years before the framing; and each thought that the separation of the legislative from the judicial power in the new Constitution would cure them * * *.

If the need for separation of legislative from judicial power was plain, the principal effect to be accomplished by that separation was even plainer. As Hamilton wrote in his exegesis of Article III, § 1, in Federalist No. 81:

> "It is not true ... that the parliament of Great Britain, or the legislatures of the particular states, can rectify the exceptionable decisions of their respective courts, in any other sense than might be done by a future legislature of the United States. The theory neither of the British, nor the state constitutions, authorises the revisal of a judicial sentence, by a legislative act.... A legislature without exceeding its province cannot reverse a determination once made, in a particular case; though it may prescribe a new rule for future cases."

The essential balance created by this allocation of authority was a simple one. The Legislature would be possessed of power to "prescribe the rules by which the duties and rights of every citizen are to be regulated," but the power of "the interpretation of the laws" would be "the proper and peculiar province of the courts." The Federalist No. 78 * * *.

Judicial decisions in the period immediately after ratification of the Constitution confirm the understanding that it forbade interference with the final judgments of courts. In *Calder v. Bull*, 3 Dall. 386, 1 L.Ed. 648 (1798), the Legislature of Connecticut had enacted a statute that set aside the final judgment of a state court in a civil case. Although the issue before this Court was the construction of the Ex Post Facto Clause, Art. I, § 10, Justice Iredell (a leading Federalist who had guided the Constitution to ratification in North Carolina) noted that

> "the Legislature of Connecticut has been in the uniform, uninterrupted, habit of exercising a general superintending power over its courts of law, by granting new trials. It may, indeed, appear strange to some of us, that in any form, there should exist a power to grant, with respect to suits depending or adjudged, new rights of trial, new privileges of proceeding, not previously recognized and regulated by positive institutions.... The power ... is judicial in its nature; and whenever it is exercised, as in the present instance, it is an exercise of judicial, not of legislative, authority." Id., 3 Dall., at 398.

The state courts of the era showed a similar understanding of the separation of powers, in decisions that drew little distinction between the federal and state constitutions. To choose one representative example from a multitude: in *Bates v. Kimball*, 2 Chipman 77 (Vt.1824), a special Act of the Vermont Legislature authorized a party to appeal from the judgment of a court even though, under the general law, the time for appeal had expired. The court, noting that the unappealed judgment had become final, set itself the question "Have the Legislature power to vacate or annul an existing judgment between party and party?" Id., at 83. The answer was emphatic: "The necessity of a distinct and separate existence of the three great departments of government . . . had been proclaimed and enforced by . . . Blackstone, Jefferson and Madison," and had been "sanctioned by the people of the United States, by being adopted in terms more or less explicit, into all their written constitutions." Id., at 84. The power to annul a final judgment, the court held (citing *Hayburn's Case*, 2 Dall., at 410), was "an assumption of Judicial power," and therefore forbidden. *Bates v. Kimball*, supra, at 90. For other examples, see *Merrill v. Sherburne*, 1 N.H. 199 (1818) (legislature may not vacate a final judgment and grant a new trial); Lewis v. Webb, 3 Greenleaf 299 (Me.1825) (same); T. Cooley, Constitutional Limitations 95–96 (1868) (collecting cases); J. Sutherland, Statutory Construction 18–19 (J. Lewis ed. 1904) (same).

* * *

Section 27A(b) effects a clear violation of the separation-of-powers principle we have just discussed. It is, of course, retroactive legislation, that is, legislation that prescribes what the law was at an earlier time, when the act whose effect is controlled by the legislation occurred—in this case, the filing of the initial Rule 10b–5 action in the District Court. When retroactive legislation requires its own application in a case already finally adjudicated, it does no more and no less than "reverse a determination once made, in a particular case." The Federalist No. 81 * * *.

It is true, as petitioners contend, that Congress can always revise the judgments of Article III courts in one sense: When a new law makes clear that it is retroactive, an appellate court must apply that law in reviewing judgments still on appeal that were rendered before the law was enacted, and must alter the outcome accordingly. See *United States v. Schooner Peggy*, 1 Cranch 103 (1801); *Landgraf v. USI Film Products*, 511 U.S. ___, ___, 114 S.Ct. 1483, 1500–1508 (1994). Since that is so, petitioners argue, federal courts must apply the "new" law created by § 27A(b) in finally adjudicated cases as well; for the line that separates lower court judgments that are pending on appeal (or may still be appealed), from lower-court judgments that are final, is determined by statute, see, e.g., 28 U.S.C. 2107(a) (30-day time limit for appeal to federal court of appeals), and so cannot possibly be a constitutional line. But a distinction between judgments from which all appeals have been forgone or completed, and judgments that remain on appeal (or subject to being appealed), is implicit in what Article III creates: not a batch of unconnected courts, but a judicial department composed of "inferior Courts" and "one supreme Court." Within that hierarchy, the decision of an inferior court is not (unless the time for appeal has expired) the final word of the department as a whole. It is the obligation of the last court in the hierarchy that rules on the case to give effect to Congress's latest enactment, even when that has the effect of overturning the judgment of an inferior court, since each court, at every level, must "decide according to existing laws." *Schooner Peggy*, supra, 1 Cranch, at 109. Having achieved finality, however, a judicial decision becomes the last word of the judicial department with regard to a particular case or controversy, and Congress may not declare by retroactive legislation that the law applicable to that very case was something other than what the courts said it was * * *.

To be sure, § 27A(b) reopens (or directs the reopening of) final judgments in a whole class of cases rather than in a particular suit. We do not see how that makes any difference. The separation-of-powers violation here, if there is any, consists of depriving judicial judgments of the conclusive effect that they had when they were announced, not of acting in a manner—viz., with particular rather than general effect—that is unusual (though, we must note, not impossible) for a legislature. To be sure, a general statute such as this one may reduce the perception that legislative interference with judicial judgments was prompted by individual favoritism; but it is legislative interference with judicial judgments nonetheless. Not favoritism, nor even corruption, but power is the object of the separation-of-powers prohibition. The prohibition is violated when an individual final judgment is legislatively rescinded for even the very best of reasons, such as the legislature's genuine conviction (supported by all the law professors in the land) that the judgment was wrong; and it is violated 40 times over when 40 final judgments are legislatively dissolved.

* * * Apart from the statute we review today, we know of no instance in which Congress has attempted to set aside the final judgment of an Article III court by retroactive legislation. That prolonged reticence would be amazing if such interference were not understood to be constitutionally proscribed * * *.

* * *

Finally, petitioners liken § 27A(b) to Federal Rule of Civil Procedure 60(b), which authorizes courts to relieve parties from a final judgment for grounds such as excusable neglect, newly discovered evidence, fraud, or "any other reason justifying relief. . . ." We see little resemblance. Rule 60(b), which authorizes discretionary judicial revision of judgments in the listed situations and in other "extraordinary circumstances," *Liljeberg v. Health Services Acquisition Corp.*, 486 U.S. 847, 864 (1988), does not impose any legislative mandate-to-reopen upon the courts, but merely reflects and confirms the courts' own inherent and discretionary power, "firmly established in English practice long before the foundation of our Republic," to set aside a judgment whose enforcement would work inequity. *Hazel-Atlas Glass Co. v. Hartford-Empire Co.*, 322 U.S. 238, 244 (1944). Thus, Rule 60(b), and the tradition that it embodies, would be relevant refutation of a claim that reopening a final judgment is always a denial of property without due process; but they are irrelevant to the claim that legislative instruction to reopen impinges upon the independent constitutional authority of the courts * * *.

The dissent sets forth a number of hypothetical horribles flowing from our assertedly "rigid holding"—for example, the inability to set aside a civil judgment that has become final during a period when a natural disaster prevented the timely filing of a certiorari petition. That is horrible not because of our holding, but because the underlying statute *itself* enacts a "rigid" jurisdictional bar to entertaining untimely civil petitions. Congress could undoubtedly enact *prospective* legislation permitting, or indeed requiring, this Court to make equitable exceptions to an otherwise applicable rule of finality, just as district courts do pursuant to Rule 60(b). It is no indication whatever of the invalidity of the constitutional rule which we announce, that it produces unhappy consequences when a legislature lacks foresight, and acts belatedly to remedy a deficiency in the law. That is a routine result of constitutional rules.

* * *

Ultimately, the concurrence agrees with our judgment only "because the law before us embodies risks of the very sort that our Constitution's 'separation of powers' prohibition seeks to avoid." But the doctrine of separation of powers is a structural safeguard rather than a remedy to be applied only when specific harm, or risk of specific harm, can be identified. In its major features (of which the conclusiveness of judicial judgments is assuredly one) it is a prophylactic device, establishing high walls and clear distinctions because low walls and vague distinctions will not be judicially defensible in the heat of interbranch conflict * * *. Separation of powers, a distinctively American political doctrine, profits from the advice authored by a distinctively American poet: Good fences make good neighbors.

* * *

■ JUSTICE BREYER, concurring in the judgment.

I agree with the majority that § 27A(b) of the Securities Exchange Act of 1934 is unconstitutional. In my view, the separation of powers inherent in our Constitution means that at least *sometimes* Congress lacks the power under Article I to reopen an otherwise closed court judgment. And the statutory provision here at issue, § 27A(b), violates a basic "separation-of-powers" principle—one intended to protect individual liberty. Three features of this law—its exclusively retroactive effect, its application to a limited number of individuals, and its reopening of closed judgments—taken together, show that Congress here impermissibly tried to *apply,* as well as *make,* the law. Hence, § 27A(b) falls outside the scope of Article I. But, it is far less clear, and unnecessary for the purposes of this case to decide, that separation of powers "is violated" *whenever* an "individual final judgment is legislatively rescinded" * * *.

* * * Thus, it seems to me, if Congress enacted legislation that reopened an otherwise closed judgment but in a way that mitigated some of the here relevant "separation-of-powers" concerns, by also providing some of the assurances against "singling out" that ordinary legislative activity normally provides—say, prospectivity and general applicability—we might have a different case.* * *

Because the law before us embodies risks of the very sort that our Constitution's "separation-of-powers" prohibition seeks to avoid, and because I can find no offsetting legislative safeguards that normally offer assurances that minimize those risks, I agree with the Court's conclusion and I join its judgment.

■ JUSTICE STEVENS, with whom JUSTICE GINSBURG joins, dissenting.

* * *

The majority's rigid holding unnecessarily hinders the Government from addressing difficult issues that inevitably arise in a complex society. This Court, for example, lacks power to enlarge the time for filing petitions for certiorari in a civil case after 90 days from the entry of final judgment, no matter how strong the equities. See 28 U.S.C. § 2101(c). If an Act of God, such as a flood or an earthquake, sufficiently disrupted communications in a particular area to preclude filing for several days, the majority's reasoning would appear to bar Congress from addressing the resulting inequity. If Congress passed remedial legislation that retroactively granted movants from the disaster area extra time to file petitions or motions for extensions of time to file, today's holding presumably would compel us to strike down the legislation as an attack on the finality of judgments * * *.

* * *

The Court has drawn the wrong lesson from the Framers' disapproval of colonial legislatures' appellate review of judicial decisions. The Framers rejected that practice, not out of a mechanistic solicitude for "final judgments," but because they believed the impartial application of rules of law, rather than the will of the majority, must govern the disposition of individual cases and controversies. Any legislative interference in the adjudication of the merits of a particular case carries the risk that political power will supplant evenhanded justice, whether the interference occurs before or after the entry of final judgment. Section 27A(b) neither commands the reinstatement of any particular case nor directs any result on the merits * * *.

"We must remember that the machinery of government would not work if it were not allowed a little play in its joints." *Bain Peanut Co. of Tex. v. Pinson,* 282 U.S. 499, 501 (1931) (Holmes, J.). The three branches must cooperate in order to govern. We should regard favorably, rather than with suspicious hostility, legislation that enables the judiciary to overcome impediments to the performance of its mission of administering justice impartially, even when, as here, this Court has created the impediment. Rigid rules often make good law, but judgments in areas such as the review of potential conflicts among the three coequal branches of the Federal Government partake of art as well as science * * *.

* * *

NOTES AND QUESTIONS

1. Does any of this sound familiar? Strict adherence to definitional lines among the various governmental powers versus a pragmatic assessment of consequences in particular cases? A back-and-forth between "formalist" and "functionalist" modes of analysis has characterized separation of powers cases for a very long time. You will continue to see that tension in the materials to come.

2. If one is a functionalist concerned about consequences, such as making sure that laws are general and do not single out people for bad treatment, is it possible that the best way to accomplish those goals is with bright-line rules that minimize judicial discretion? Are there functionalist reasons to be formalistic? *See* MARTIN H. REDISH, THE CONSTITUTION AS POLITICAL STRUCTURE 125 (1995) (arguing that "reliance on simple-minded definitional approaches" can be justified "not because of the dictates of rigid and abstract principle[s] of legal formalism, but because the Constitution's drafters wisely concluded that a case-by-case analysis to determine 'undue accretions' of power was simply too speculative a method to provide effective protection against the incremental development of a threat of tyranny").

3. If one is a formalist, does the absence of clear definitions of legislative, executive, and judicial power, along with the textual need to give those terms meaning, force one to make hard judgments about the likely dynamics and effects of institutional allocations of power? Are there formalist reasons to be functionalist?

4. As we will shortly see, the Constitution contains some specific, and cabined, restrictions on the ability of Congress to legislative retroactively. Is the Court in *Plaut* adding new restrictions to those already prescribed by the Constitution?

5. Justice Scalia emphasizes that the federal courts—as a department—had rendered a final judgment in *Plaut* that Congress ordered reopened. If the federal courts—as a department—had not yet issued a final judgment, because there were still

levels of appeal yet to be pursued, he agreed that Congress could change the applicable law, and whatever court next decided the case would have to decide it in light of the new law. That principle is firmly established. *See, e.g., Bank Markazi v. Peterson,* 136 S.Ct. 1310 (2016); *Robertson v. Seattle Audubon Soc.,* 503 U.S. 429 (1992). What if that new law said, "decide the case in favor of Party A"? On multiple occasions, Congress has come very close to doing just that. In *Bank Markazi,* Congress systematically eliminated every defense that an Iranian bank was raising in a lawsuit brought by claimed victims of Iranian-sponsored terrorism, leaving very little for the courts to decide. "Very little" was evidently enough, because the Court, over the dissenting voices of Chief Justice Roberts and Justice Sotomayor, concluded that Congress had merely provided "a new standard clarifying that, if Iran owns certain assets, the victims of Iran-sponsored terrorist attacks will be permitted to execute against those assets. Applying laws implementing Congress' policy judgments, with fidelity to those judgments, is commonplace for the Judiciary." 136 S.Ct. at 1326.

[Assignment 15]

V. ARTICLE I, SECTIONS 9 & 10

SECTION 9

[1] The Migration or Importation of such Persons as any of the States now existing shall think proper to admit, shall not be prohibited by the Congress prior to the Year one thousand eight hundred and eight, but a Tax or duty may be imposed on such Importation, not exceeding ten dollars for each Person.

[2] The Privilege of the Writ of Habeas Corpus shall not be suspended, unless when in Cases of Rebellion or Invasion the public Safety may require it.

[3] No Bill of Attainder or ex post facto Law shall be passed.

[4] No Capitation, or other direct, Tax shall be laid, unless in Proportion to the Census or enumeration herein before directed to be taken.

[5] No Tax or Duty shall be laid on Articles exported from any State.

[6] No Preference shall be given by any Regulation of Commerce or Revenue to the Ports of one State over those of another: nor shall Vessels bound to, or from, one State, be obliged to enter, clear, or pay Duties in another.

[7] No Money shall be drawn from the Treasury, but in Consequence of Appropriations made by Law; and a regular Statement and Account of the Receipts and Expenditures of all public Money shall be published from time to time.

[8] No Title of Nobility shall be granted by the United States: And no Person holding any Office of Profit or Trust under them, shall, without the Consent of the Congress, accept of any present, Emolument, Office, or Title, of any kind whatever, from any King, Prince, or foreign State.

SECTION 10

[1] No State shall enter into any Treaty, Alliance, or Confederation; grant Letters of Marque and Reprisal; coin Money; emit Bills of Credit; make any Thing but gold and silver Coin a Tender in Payment of Debts; pass any Bill of Attainder, ex post facto Law, or Law impairing the Obligation of Contracts, or grant any Title of Nobility.

[2] No State shall, without the Consent of the Congress, lay any Imposts or Duties on Imports or Exports, except what may be absolutely necessary for executing its inspection Laws: and the net Produce of all Duties and Imposts, laid by any State on Imports or Exports, shall be for the Use of the Treasury of the United States; and all such Laws shall be subject to the Revision and Control of the Congress.

[3] No State shall, without the Consent of Congress, lay any Duty of Tonnage, keep Troops, or Ships of War in time of Peace, enter into any Agreement or Compact with another State, or with a foreign Power, or engage in War, unless actually invaded, or in such imminent Danger as will not admit of delay.

This chapter is primarily about the internal structure of the institutions of the national government, because most of the Constitution of 1788 is about the internal structure of the institutions of the national government. Specific rights of people or the States against the federal government, or of people against the States, are dealt with mostly in post-1788 amendments, primarily the 1791 Bill of Rights and the Thirteenth, Fourteenth, and Fifteenth Amendments that followed the Civil War. Those provisions are addressed later. But before the Constitution of 1788 addresses the executive and judicial departments in Articles II and III, it concludes Article I by listing some specific prohibitions on Congress and other federal actors (Article I, section 9) and the States (Article I, section 10). Because these provisions have the form of a "bill of rights," there is an argument for postponing discussion of them until the entire governmental structure is on the table. But the drafters of the Constitution placed them at the end of Article I, so we defer to their judgment about the proper order of consideration. Indeed, the framers' organization makes a measure of sense: In Article I, the rule of recognition for federal lawmaking (Section 7) is followed by a sweeping list of enumerated powers for the federal legislature (Section 8), which is followed, in turn, by limits on federal power (Section 9) and by partial clarification of which federal powers are exclusive, which are shared concurrently with the States, and which are forbidden to all governmental actors (Section 10).

W. ARTICLE I, SECTION 9

We start by quickly discussing some of the prohibitions on exercises of federal power in Article, I Section 9 that generate relatively few modern controversies. Then we will consider in more detail several of the most vibrant of those prohibitions. Finally, we will (too-) briefly examine Article I, section 10's prohibitions on action by States.

Tellingly, the first prohibition on federal action in the U.S. Constitution—Article I, section 9, clause 1—prohibited Congress from stopping the international slave trade with Africa until 1808. Along with the Three-Fifths Clause and the Fugitive Slave Clause (of which we will hear more later), this was part of the compromise between the free and slave States that infected the original Constitution. At its first opportunity in 1808, Congress did outlaw the international slave trade with Africa imposing, criminal penalties on those who conducted it. Act of Mar. 2, 1807, ch. XXII, 2 Stat. 426. Note that the international slave trade involved the buying and selling of human beings and thus, apart from the Slave Trade Clause, would seem to fall within the power of Congress to "regulate Commerce with foreign nations, and among the several States," U.S. CONST. art. I, § 8, cl. 3, though various early justices differed on the extent of congressional power over slave transactions, and the matter did not get resolved prior to the Reconstruction Amendments. *See Groves v. Slaughter,* 40 U.S. (15 Pet. 449) (1841); David P. Currie, *The Constitution in the Supreme Court: Contracts and Commerce, 1836–1864,* 1983 DUKE L.J. 471, 497–99. Voluntary transit to and from other countries, divorced from the buying and selling of persons, is not "Commerce," so any federal power to regulate either travel or immigration, as opposed to the slave trade, has to come from some source other than the Commerce Clause. We explore the general scope and limits of Congress's regulatory powers in the next chapter.

The next two clauses, the Suspension Clause and the Bill of Attainder or Ex Post Facto Clause, are two of the most important clauses in the Constitution. We discuss the latter in more detail below and the former in the materials on Article II.

The other clauses in Article I, section 9 are also vitally important, but they tend in most instances to function without controversy, again as part of the operating system whirring in the background. But every so often even these relatively obscure clauses rise to the forefront. Consider Article I, section 9, clause 4: "No Capitation, or other direct, Tax shall be laid, unless in Proportion to the Census or enumeration herein before directed to be taken." In other words, Congress cannot impose direct taxes unless the amount collected from each State's population is proportional to that population. This Clause was inserted at the insistence of the Southern States to make it impracticable, and politically impossible, for the federal government to impose: 1) head taxes counting slaves as more than three-fifths of a person, 2) federal taxes on real estate (there has never been a federal real estate tax), and 3) federal income and inheritance taxes, which fall directly on individuals. The founding generation assumed—correctly for quite some time—that the federal government would raise its revenue primarily through a combination of land sales and "Duties, Imposts and Excises," U.S. CONST. art. I, § 8, cl. 1, known as indirect taxes, which do not have to be apportioned based on state population, but which must "be uniform throughout the United States." *Id.* Thus, tariffs on goods shipped into the country or excises on rubber tires or telephone service do not have to be apportioned by population among the States, but you cannot have one tariff or excise rate in Massachusetts and a different rate in South Carolina. This distinction between direct and indirect taxes, which are subject to different constitutional constraints (apportionment versus uniformity), leads to some tricky questions about precisely what constitutes a "direct" tax. For contrasting views on how to resolve those tricky questions, compare Bruce Ackerman, *Taxation and the Constitution,* 99 COLUM. L. REV. 1 (1999) (arguing for a narrow construction of "direct" taxes because of the Capitation Clause's origins in slavery and Progressive Era popular rejections of limitations on federal taxation) with Erik M. Jensen, *The Apportionment of "Direct*

Taxes": Are Consumption Taxes Constitutional?, 97 COLUM. L. REV. 2334 (1997) (arguing for a broader construction of "direct" taxes on originalist textual and structural grounds). The stakes of those debates were lowered considerably in 1913 by the Sixteenth Amendment, which expressly provides that federal income and inheritance taxes—the two most important forms of plainly direct taxes—can be imposed even if they are not apportioned. *See* U.S. CONST. amend. XVI ("The Congress shall have power to lay and collect taxes on incomes, from whatever source derived, without apportionment among the several States, and without regard to any census or enumeration"). Nonetheless, even today, for any direct tax that does not count as a tax on "incomes," the Constitution's apportionment rule still governs.

The issue came to unexpected prominence in 2012. The Patient Protection and Affordable Care Act, colloquially known as "Obamacare," contained a so-called "individual mandate," which required every American (with some minor exceptions) to have government-approved health insurance or else pay a fine as a penalty. Five justices concluded that neither the Commerce Clause nor the Necessary and Proper Clause, nor the two put together, could give Congress power to force people to purchase a product that they did not want to buy. *See infra* pages 714–736. The individual mandate was nonetheless upheld as constitutional (only to be repealed by Congress in 2017) as a valid exercise of Congress's taxing power. This holding required two moves. First, one had to recharacterize the statute's penalty for not having government-approved health insurance as a tax, which was no mean feat given Congress's repeated insistence when passing it that it was not a tax. *See* Gary Lawson & David B. Kopel, *The PPACA in Wonderland,* 38 AM. J.L. & MED. 269, 278–81 (2012). Second, one had to characterize it as an indirect rather than direct tax to avoid the apportionment requirement. The Court did both, notwithstanding that the thorny issue of what constitutes a direct tax was not briefed or argued by the parties. Five justices maintained:

> Even if the taxing power enables Congress to impose a tax on not obtaining health insurance, any tax must still comply with other requirements in the Constitution. Plaintiffs argue that the shared responsibility payment does not do so, citing Article I, § 9, clause 4 * * *. According to the plaintiffs, if the individual mandate imposes a tax, it is a direct tax, and it is unconstitutional because Congress made no effort to apportion it among the States.
>
> Even when the Direct Tax Clause was written it was unclear what else, other than a capitation (also known as a "head tax" or a "poll tax"), might be a direct tax. See *Springer v. United States,* 102 U.S. 586, 596–598 (1881). Soon after the framing, Congress passed a tax on ownership of carriages, over James Madison's objection that it was an unapportioned direct tax. *Id.,* at 597. This Court upheld the tax, in part reasoning that apportioning such a tax would make little sense, because it would have required taxing carriage owners at dramatically different rates depending on how many carriages were in their home State. See *Hylton v. United States,* 3 Dall. 171, 174 (1796) (opinion of Chase, J.). The Court was unanimous, and those Justices who wrote opinions either directly asserted or strongly suggested that only two forms of taxation were direct: capitations and land taxes. See *id.,* at 175; *id.,* at 177 (opinion of Paterson, J.); *id.,* at 183 (opinion of Iredell, J.).

> That narrow view of what a direct tax might be persisted for a century. In 1880, for example, we explained that "*direct taxes,* within the meaning of the Constitution, are only capitation taxes, as expressed in that instrument, and taxes on real estate." *Springer, supra,* at 602. In 1895, we expanded our interpretation to include taxes on personal property and income from personal property, in the course of striking down aspects of the federal income tax. *Pollock v. Farmers' Loan & Trust Co.,* 158 U.S. 601, 618 (1895). That result was overturned by the Sixteenth Amendment, although we continued to consider taxes on personal property to be direct taxes. See *Eisner v. Macomber,* 252 U.S. 189, 218–219 (1920).
>
> A tax on going without health insurance does not fall within any recognized category of direct tax. It is not a capitation. Capitations are taxes paid by every person, "without regard to property, profession, or *any other circumstance.*" *Hylton, supra,* at 175 (opinion of Chase, J.) (emphasis altered). The whole point of the shared responsibility payment is that it is triggered by specific circumstances—earning a certain amount of income but not obtaining health insurance. The payment is also plainly not a tax on the ownership of land or personal property. The shared responsibility payment is thus not a direct tax that must be apportioned among the several States.

National Federation of Independent Businesses v. Sebelius, 567 U.S. 519, 570–71 (2012). The four dissenting justices did not address the direct/indirect tax issue because they did not believe that the individual mandate was a tax rather than a penalty; they said only that "[o]ne would expect this Court to demand more than fly-by-night briefing and argument before deciding a difficult constitutional question of first impression." *Id.* at 669 (Justice Scalia, Justice Kennedy, Justice Thomas, and Justice Alito, dissenting).

Recall that the Taxing Clause contains a national uniformity requirement that prohibits indirect taxes from discriminating for or against particular States. This requirement has been given a very narrow construction that allows Congress to tailor taxes geographically even if it benefits or burdens particular States. *See United States v. Ptasynski,* 462 U.S. 74 (1983) (upholding an excise tax on oil that exempted certain Alaskan oil from the tax). Two additional clauses also deal with intra-State equality and freedom of commerce: "No Tax or Duty shall be laid on Articles exported from any State," and "No Preference shall be given by any Regulation of Commerce or Revenue to the Ports of one State over those of another: nor shall Vessels bound to, or from, one State, be obliged to enter, clear, or pay Duties in another." The purposes of these Clauses are evident from reading them. Congress can tax imports but not exports (so exporting States cannot be disfavored through taxation), and maritime commercial regulations cannot discriminate among American ports. The federal regulatory laws for New York and Charleston have to be the same. As with the uniformity requirement in the Taxing Clause, the uniformity requirement for port regulation (which was, at one point in the Constitutional Convention, in the same clause as the uniformity requirement for indirect taxes) has been given a narrow construction:

> There are many acts of congress passed in the exercise of this power to regulate commerce, providing for a special advantage to the port or ports of one State, and which very advantage may incidentally operate to the

> prejudice of the ports in a neighboring State, which have never been supposed to conflict with this limitation upon its power. The improvement of rivers and harbors, the erection of light-houses, and other facilities of commerce, may be referred to as examples. It will not do to say that the exercise of an admitted power of congress conferred by the constitution is to be withheld, if it appears, or can be shown, that the effect and operation of the law may incidentally extend beyond the limitation of the power. Upon any such interpretation, the principal object of the framers of the instrument in conferring the power would be sacrificed to the subordinate consequences resulting from its exercise. These consequences and incidents are very proper considerations to be urged upon congress for the purpose of dissuading that body from its exercise, but afford no ground for denying the power itself, or the right to exercise it.

State of Pennsylvania v. Wheeling & Belmont Bridge Co, 59 U.S. (18 How.) 421, 433–34 (1856). Congress does not have to spend the same amount on every port nor make the same improvements (or impose the same obstructions) on every port. How uniform do you think the Constitution anticipated congressional laws would have to be?

We have already examined the Appropriations Clause and its vital role in securing congressional control over federal finances. *See supra* page 150. Lastly, Article I, Section 9 provides: "No Title of Nobility shall be granted by the United States: And no Person holding any Office of Profit or Trust under them, shall, without the Consent of the Congress, accept of any present, Emolument, Office, or Title, of any kind whatever, from any King, Prince, or foreign State." The clause is a slight reformulation of identical restrictions in Article VI, clause 1 of the Articles of Confederation. The first part of this clause makes it clear that the language of the Declaration of Independence saying that "All men are created equal" is constitutionalized and that feudalism cannot exist in the United States. It is a strong statement of republican sentiment against hereditary and aristocratic rule. It is a statement against hereditary and aristocratic rule that was incompatible with slavery, under which some were born masters and others were born slaves.

The second part, known as the Emoluments Clause, is a fairly obvious anti-corruption measure designed to prevent federal officers from going on the payroll of foreign countries. It went more than two centuries with little fanfare but acquired new prominence after the election of President Donald Trump, when multiple lawsuits claimed that President Trump's profits from extensive business interest overseas amounted to forbidden "Emolument[s]" from "foreign State[s]." As of this writing, none of these cases has yet resulted in a judgment on the merits. If they do (and there are serious questions about whether any of the plaintiffs in these cases have standing to sue), courts will have to address at least two significant, and thus far judicially unresolved, issues. First, they will have to decide whether an "Emolument" means only a direct payment made by virtue of public employment rather than any benefit received, however indirectly, from investments abroad. *See* Robert G. Natelson, *The Original Meaning of "Emoluments" in the Constitution*, 52 GA. L. REV. 1 (2017). Second, they will have to decide whether the Emoluments Clause applies at all to elected as well as appointed officials—that is, whether the presidency, the vice presidency, and Congress are "Office[s] of Profit or Trust" under this clause. *See* Seth Barrett Tillman, *The Original Public Meaning of the Foreign*

Emoluments Clause: A Reply to Professor Zephyr Teachout, 107 NW. U.L. REV. COLLOQUY 180 (2013). Constitutional law in the twenty-first century seldom presents courts with bona fide cases of first impression, but this might be one of them.

To be sure, while the meaning of the Emoluments Clause is a matter of first impression in the courts, the Justice Department and Congress deal with such issues regularly. In 2009, for example, two major issues involving the Emoluments Clause received executive and legislative constructions. President Obama received the Nobel Peace Prize, which is awarded by a committee selected by the parliament of Norway. The prize includes about $1.4 million (which President Obama donated to charity). Congress never consented to President Obama's receipt of the award. Was the Nobel Prize money an "Emolument" received from a "foreign State"? Relying on a history of prior presidents who received the Peace Prize (President Obama was the third) and a functional analysis of the current relationship between the Norwegian parliament and the Nobel Prize committee, the Department of Justice concluded that the Nobel committee did not count as a "foreign State." *See* Memorandum from Acting Assistant Attorney General David J. Barron to the Counsel for the President, *Applicability of the Emoluments Clause and the Foreign Gifts and Decorations Act to the President's Receipt of the Nobel Peace Prize* (Dec. 7, 2009). Meanwhile, in the same year, Senator Edward Kennedy was knighted by Queen Elizabeth II, which seems to constitute a "Title, of any kind whatever" from the head of a "foreign State." No formal congressional consent was given, but Congress uniformly celebrated Senator Kennedy's title when it was announced. Perhaps that approval without the formal consent required by the Constitution amounts to a congressional determination that congressional offices are not "Office[s] of Profit or Trust." That determination, if such it was, is correct as a matter of original meaning if, as Professor Seth Tillman has maintained for many years, the Emoluments Clause only applies to appointed officials, not to elected officials. The Department of Justice, however, in its opinion on President Obama's receipt of the Nobel Peace Prize, said, without any argument or supporting materials: "[t]he President surely 'hold[s] an[ ] Office of Profit or Trust." *See id.* at 4. Was the term "Office of Profit or Trust" a legal term of art in 1788? If you were a Department of Justice lawyer, would you want to know the answer to that question before you wrote an opinion for the President?

X. ARTICLE I, SECTION 10

The Constitution of 1788 contained very few restrictions on the actions of State governments. Some forms of legislation, however, were considered so heinous that the original Constitution banned them at both the state and federal level. Bills of attainer and ex post facto laws are banned at the national level by Article I, section 9, clause 3 and at the state level by Article I, section 10, clause 1. It is significant that Article I, Section 10 forbids the States from enacting bills of attainder or ex post facto laws because almost all of Article I, section 10 is concerned with forbidding the States from doing some of the things that Congress or other national institutions are *authorized* to do. Section 10 thus explains, in part, that national institutions have sole or principal power over: 1) making war, 2) raising armies and navies, 3) entering into treaties; 4) granting letters of marque and reprisal, 5) coining money; or 6) imposing tariffs to raise general revenue. Section 10 forbids the states from doing only three things that Article I, Section 9 also forbids Congress from doing: (1)

passing bills of attainder; (2) passing ex post facto laws; and (3) granting any title of nobility.

1. BILLS OF ATTAINDER

Start with bills of attainder. What is it about them that led the framers to forbid both Congress and the States from enacting them?

A bill of attainder is a legislative act targeted at only one or a few individuals that declares them to be guilty of a crime and specifies the punishment that they must suffer. A bill of attainder combined in Parliament the legislative, the executive, and the judicial powers, something which the Framers thought was inherently despotic. The history of bills of attainder is recounted at length in the opinions that follow, so we will not recount it here. We do wish to note, however, an important policy that underlies the Constitution's proscription of bills of attainder. Congress is responsive and democratically accountable to popular majorities—and sometimes to minority factions and special interest groups. It may not, however, be accountable in any meaningful way to the interests of one individual or a few individuals. It is rare for a handful of people to have the political clout that is necessary to prevent a legislature from voting to harm them. *See* JOHN HART ELY, DEMOCRACY AND DISTRUST (1980). The separation of powers generally works to protect liberty by requiring that the majority of legislators lay down some rule of general applicability, which a single prosecutor then executes in a case against an accused person, which is then adjudicated by a judge with the aid of a jury of the accused individual's peers. Bills of Attainder circumvent this separation of powers. They allow the legislature to be at the same time the lawmaker, the prosecutor, and the judge and jury. No wonder the Framers wanted to make clear that bills of attainder were never "necessary" or "proper" and that even the States ought to be forbidden from enacting them. No wonder that James Madison said: "Bills of attainder, *ex post facto* laws, and laws impairing the obligation of contracts, are contrary to the first principles of the social contract and to every principle of sound legislation." THE FEDERALIST No. 44.

Bills of attainder are thus the flip side of the subdelegation doctrine. The latter kicks in when Congress leaves *too much* to be decided by executive or judicial agents. The former kicks in when Congress leaves *too little* to be decided by the constitutionally proper actors. But, of course, courts and executives cannot decide everything, because Congress is the principal source of substantive law. It cannot be the case that every law that adversely affects a person, or some group of persons, constitutes a bill of attainder, can it? So how does one distinguish valid legislation from a constitutionally forbidden bill of attainder? The Bill of Attainder Clause plays a major role in maintaining the line between the legislative and the judicial power discussed above in assignment 8.

a. *United States v. Brown*

381 U.S. 437 (1965)

■ MR. CHIEF JUSTICE WARREN delivered the opinion of the Court.

In this case we review for the first time a conviction under § 504 of the Labor-Management Reporting and Disclosure Act of 1959, which makes it a crime for a member of the Communist Party to serve as an officer or (except in clerical or custodial positions) as an employee of a labor union * * *.

Respondent has been a working longshoreman on the San Francisco docks, and an open and avowed Communist, for more than a quarter of a century. He was elected to the Executive Board of Local 10 of the International Longshoremen's and Warehousemen's Union for consecutive one-year terms in 1959, 1960, and 1961. On May 24, 1961, respondent was charged * * * with "knowingly and willfully serv(ing) as a member of an executive board of a labor organization * * * while a member of the Communist Party, in willful violation of Title 29, United States Code, Section 504." It was neither charged nor proven that respondent at any time advocated or suggested illegal activity by the union, or proposed a political strike. The jury found respondent guilty, and he was sentenced to six months' imprisonment. The Court of Appeals for the Ninth Circuit, sitting *en banc*, reversed and remanded with instructions to set aside the conviction and dismiss the indictment, holding that § 504 violates the First and Fifth Amendments to the Constitution * * *.

Respondent urges—in addition to the grounds relied on by the court below—that the statute under which he was convicted is a bill of attainder, and therefore violates Art. I, § 9, of the Constitution. We agree that § 504 is void as a bill of attainder and affirm the decision of the Court of Appeals on that basis. We therefore find it unnecessary to consider the First and Fifth Amendment arguments.

The provisions outlawing bills of attainder were adopted by the Constitutional Convention unanimously, and without debate * * *. A logical starting place for an inquiry into the meaning of the prohibition is its historical background. The bill of attainder, a parliamentary act sentencing to death one or more specific persons, was a device often resorted to in sixteenth, seventeenth and eighteenth century England for dealing with persons who had attempted, or threatened to attempt, to overthrow the government. In addition to the death sentence, attainder generally carried with it a "corruption of blood," which meant that the attainted party's heirs could not inherit his property. The "bill of pains and penalties" was identical to the bill of attainder, except that it prescribed a penalty short of death, *e.g.*, banishment, deprivation of the right to vote, or exclusion of the designated party's sons from Parliament. Most bills of attainder and bills of pains and penalties named the parties to whom they were to apply; a few, however, simply described them * * *. The use of bills of attainder and bills of pains and penalties was not limited to England. During the American Revolution, the legislatures of all thirteen States passed statutes directed against the Tories; among these statutes were a large number of bills of attainder and bills of pains and penalties.

While history thus provides some guidelines, the wide variation in form, purpose and effect of ante-Constitution bills of attainder indicates that the proper scope of the Bill of Attainder Clause, and its relevance to contemporary problems, must ultimately be sought by attempting to discern the reasons for its inclusion in the Constitution, and the evils it was designed to eliminate. The best available evidence, the writings of the architects of our constitutional system, indicates that the Bill of Attainder Clause was intended not as a narrow, technical (and therefore soon to be outmoded) prohibition, but rather as an implementation of the separation of powers, a general safeguard against legislative exercise of the judicial function, or more simply—trial by legislature.

* * *

The authors of the Federalist Papers took the position that although under some systems of government (most notably the one from which the United States had just broken), the Executive Department is the branch most likely to forget the bounds of its authority, "in a representative republic * * * where the legislative power is exercised by an assembly * * * which is sufficiently numerous to feel all the passions which actuate a multitude; yet not so numerous as to be incapable of pursuing the objects of its passions * * *," barriers had to be erected to ensure that the legislature would not overstep the bounds of its authority and perform the functions of the other departments. The Bill of Attainder Clause was regarded as such a barrier * * *.

Thus the Bill of Attainder Clause * * * reflected the Framers' belief that the Legislative Branch is not so well suited as politically independent judges and juries to the task of ruling upon the blameworthiness, of, and levying appropriate punishment upon, specific persons * * *. By banning bills of attainder, the Framers of the Constitution sought to guard against such dangers by limiting legislatures to the task of rule-making. "It is the peculiar province of the legislature to prescribe general rules for the government of society; the application of those rules to individuals in society would seem to be the duty of other departments." *Fletcher v. Peck*, 6 Cranch 87, 136.

It is in this spirit that the Bill of Attainder Clause was consistently interpreted by this Court * * *. In 1810, Chief Justice Marshall, speaking for the Court in *Fletcher v. Peck*, 6 Cranch 87, stated that "(a) bill of attainder may affect the life of an individual, or may confiscate his property, or may do both." This means, of course, that what were known at common law as bills of pains and penalties are outlawed by the Bill of Attainder Clause. The Court's pronouncement therefore served notice that the Bill of Attainder Clause was not to be given a narrow historical reading (which would exclude bills of pains and penalties), but was instead to be read in light of the evil the Framers had sought to bar: legislative punishment, of any form or severity, of specifically designated persons or groups.

The approach which Chief Justice Marshall had suggested was followed in the twin post-Civil War cases of *Cummings v. State of Missouri*, 4 Wall. 277, and *Ex parte Garland*, 4 Wall. 333. *Cummings* involved the constitutionality of amendments to the Missouri Constitution of 1865 which provided that no one could engage in a number of specified professions (Cummings was a priest) unless he first swore that he had taken no part in the rebellion against the Union. At issue in *Garland* was a federal statute which required attorneys to take a similar oath before they could practice in federal courts. This Court struck down both provisions as bills of attainder on the ground that they were legislative acts inflicting punishment on a specific group: clergymen and lawyers who had taken part in the rebellion and therefore could not truthfully take the oath * * *.

The next extended discussion of the Bill of Attainder Clause came in 1946, in *United States v. Lovett*, 328 U.S. 303, where the Court invalidated § 304 of the Urgent Deficiency Appropriation Act, 1943, 57 Stat. 431, 450, which prohibited payment of further salary to three named federal employees, as a bill of attainder.

> "(L)egislative acts, no matter what their form, that apply either to named individuals or to easily ascertainable members of a group in such a way as to inflict punishment on them without a judicial trial are bills of attainder prohibited by the Constitution. * * * This permanent proscription

from any opportunity to serve the Government is punishment, and of a most severe type * * *. No one would think that Congress could have passed a valid law, stating that after investigation it had found Lovett, Dodd, and Watson 'guilty' of the crime of engaging in 'subversive activities,' defined that term for the first time, and sentenced them to perpetual exclusion from any government employment. Section 304, while it does not use that language, accomplishes that result." *Id.*, at 315–316.

Under the line of cases just outlined, § 504 of the Labor-Management Reporting and Disclosure Act plainly constitutes a bill of attainder. Congress undoubtedly possesses power under the Commerce Clause to enact legislation designed to keep from positions affecting interstate commerce persons who may use such positions to bring about political strikes. In § 504, however, Congress has exceeded the authority granted it by the Constitution. The statute does not set forth a generally applicable rule decreeing that any person who commits certain acts or possesses certain characteristics (acts and characteristics which, in Congress' view, make them likely to initiate political strikes) shall not hold union office, and leave to courts and juries the job of deciding what persons have committed the specified acts or possess the specified characteristics. Instead, it designates in no uncertain terms the persons who possess the feared characteristics and therefore cannot hold union office without incurring criminal liability—members of the Communist Party.

* * *

The Solicitor General points out that in *Board of Governors of Federal Reserve System v. Agnew*, 329 U.S. 441, this Court applied § 32 of the Banking Act of 1933, which provides:

> "No officer, director, or employee of any corporation or unincorporated association, no partner or employee of any partnership, and no individual, primarily engaged in the issue, flotation, underwriting, public sale, or distribution, at wholesale or retail, or through syndicate participation, of stocks, bonds, or other similar securities, shall serve the same time as an officer, director, or employee of any member bank * * *."

He suggests that for purposes of the Bill of Attainder Clause, such conflict-of-interest laws are not meaningfully distinguishable from the statute before us. We find this argument without merit. First, we note that § 504, unlike § 32 of the Banking Act, inflicts its deprivation upon the members of a political group thought to present a threat to the national security. As we noted above, such groups were the targets of the overwhelming majority of English and early American bills of attainder. Second, § 32 incorporates no judgment censuring or condemning any man or group of men. In enacting it, Congress relied upon its general knowledge of human psychology, and concluded that the concurrent holding of the two designated positions would present a temptation to *any* man—not just certain men or members of a certain political party. Thus insofar as § 32 incorporates a condemnation, it condemns all men. Third, we cannot accept the suggestion that § 32 constitutes an exercise in specification rather than rule-making. It seems to us clear that § 32 establishes an objective standard of conduct * * *.

It is argued, however, that in § 504 Congress did no more than it did in enacting § 32: it promulgated a general rule to the effect that persons possessing characteristics which make them likely to incite political strikes should not hold union office, and simply inserted in place of a list of those characteristics an alternative, shorthand criterion—membership in the Communist Party. Again, we cannot agree. The designation of Communists as those persons likely to cause political strikes is not the substitution of a semantically equivalent phrase; on the contrary, it rests * * * upon an empirical investigation by Congress of the acts, characteristics and propensities of Communist Party members. In a number of decisions, this Court has pointed out the fallacy of the suggestion that membership in the Communist Party, or any other political organization, can be regarded as an alternative, but equivalent, expression for a list of undesirable characteristics. For, as the Court noted in *Schneiderman v. United States*, 320 U.S. 118, 136, "under our traditions beliefs are personal and not a matter of mere association, and * * * men in adhering to a political party or other organization notoriously do not subscribe unqualifiedly to all of its platforms or asserted principles" * * *.

The Solicitor General argues * * * that the statute was enacted for preventive rather than retributive reasons—that its aim is not to punish Communists for what they have done in the past, but rather to keep them from positions where they will in the future be able to bring about undesirable events * * *.

* * *

* * * [I]t * * * clearly appears that § 504 inflicts "punishment" within the meaning of the Bill of Attainder Clause. It would be archaic to limit the definition of "punishment" to "retribution." Punishment serves several purposes; retributive, rehabilitative, deterrent—and preventive. One of the reasons society imprisons those convicted of crimes is to keep them from inflicting future harm, but that does not make imprisonment any the less punishment.

* * *

The Solicitor General urges us to distinguish *Lovett* on the ground that the statute struck down there "singled out three identified individuals." It is of course true that § 504 does not contain the words "Archie Brown," and that it inflicts its deprivation upon more than three people. However, the decisions of this Court, as well as the historical background of the Bill of Attainder Clause, make it crystal clear that these are distinctions without a difference. It was not uncommon for English acts of attainder to inflict their deprivations upon relatively large groups of people, sometimes by description rather than name * * *. We cannot agree that the fact that § 504 inflicts its deprivation upon the membership of the Communist Party rather than upon a list of named individuals takes it out of the category of bills of attainder.

We do not hold today that Congress cannot weed dangerous persons out of the labor movement, any more than the Court held in *Lovett* that subversives must be permitted to hold sensitive government positions. Rather, we make again the point made in *Lovett*: that Congress must accomplish such results by rules of general applicability. It cannot specify the people upon whom the sanction it prescribes is to be levied. Under our Constitution, Congress possesses full legislative authority, but the task of adjudication must be left to other tribunals.

* * *

The judgment of the Court of Appeals is

Affirmed.

■ MR. JUSTICE WHITE, with whom MR. JUSTICE CLARK, MR. JUSTICE HARLAN, and MR. JUSTICE STEWART join, dissenting.

"A bill of attainder is a legislative act which inflicts punishment without a judicial trial." *Cummings v. State of Missouri*, 4 Wall. 277, 323. When an enactment is challenged as an attainder, the central inquiry must be whether the disability imposed by the act is "punishment" (*i.e.*, is directed at an individual or a group of individuals) or is "regulation" (*i.e.*, is directed at controlling future conduct). Whether a punitive purpose would be inferred has depended in past cases on a number of circumstances, including the nature of the disability, whether it was traditionally regarded as punishment, whether it is rationally connected to a permissible legislative objective, as well as the specificity of the legislature's designation of the persons to be affected.

In this case, however, the Court discards this meticulous multifold analysis that has been deemed necessary in the past. Instead the Court places the burden of separating attainders from permissible regulation on an examination of the legislative findings implied by the nature of the class designated * * *.

At this point the Court implies that legislation is sufficiently general if it specifies a characteristic that makes it *likely* that individuals falling within the group designated will engage in conduct Congress may prohibit. But the Court then goes on to reject the argument that Communist Party membership is in itself a characteristic raising such a likelihood * * *. This sudden shift in analysis—from likelihood to certainty—must mean that the Bill of Attainder Clause proscribes legislative action with respect to any group smaller than the total class possessing the characteristic upon which legislative power is premised whenever the legislation is based only on a finding about the average characteristics of the subgroup. The legislature may focus on a particular group or class only when the group designation is a "shorthand phrase" for the feared characteristic—*i.e.*, when it is common knowledge that all, not just some, members of the group possess the feared characteristic and thus such legislative designation would require no legislative fact-finding about individuals.

* * *

It is not difficult to find some of the cases and statutes which the necessary implications of the Court's approach will overrule or invalidate.

* * *

Similarly invalidated are statutes denying positions of public importance to groups of persons identified by their business affiliations, commonly known as conflict-of-interest statutes * * *.

* * *

In terms of the Court's analysis of the Bill of Attainder Clause, no meaningful distinction may be drawn between § 32 of the Banking Act and § 504. Both sections disqualify a specifically described group, officers and employees of underwriting firms in the one case and members of the Communist Party in the other. Both sections may be said to be underinclusive: others besides underwriters may have business interests conflicting with the duties of a bank director and others than Communists may call political strikes. Equally, both sections may be deemed overinclusive: neither section finds that all members of the group affected would violate their obligations to the office from which they are disqualified; some members would and perhaps others would not. Both sections are based on a probability or likelihood that this would occur. Both sections leave to the courts the task of determining whether particular persons are members of the designated groups and occupy the specified positions.

* * *

Conflict-of-interest statutes are an accepted type of legislation. Indeed, our Constitution contains a conflict-of-interest provision in Art. I, § 6, cl. 2, which prohibits any Congressman from simultaneously holding office under the United States. If the Court would save the conflict-of-interest statutes, which apparently it would, it is difficult to understand why § 504 is stricken down as a bill of attainder.

Other legislative enactments relevant here are those statutes disqualifying felons from occupying certain positions * * *.

* * *

* * * By the same token, a statute disqualifying Communists (or authorizing the Executive Branch to do so) from holding sensitive positions in the Government would be automatically infirm, as would a requirement that employees of the Central Intelligence Agency or the National Security Agency disclaim membership in the Communist Party, unless in each case it is proved by evidence other than membership in the Communist Party, the nature of which has already been adjudicated, that the individual would commit acts of disloyalty or subordinate his official undertakings to the interests of the Party.

But how does one prove that a person would be disloyal? The Communist Party's illegal purpose and its domination by a foreign power have already been adjudicated, both administratively and judicially. If this does not in itself provide a sufficient probability with respect to the individual who persists in remaining a member of the Party, or if a probability is in any event insufficient, what evidence with regard to the individual will be sufficient to disqualify him? If he must be apprehended in the act of calling one political strike or in one act of disloyalty before steps can be taken to exclude him from office, there is little or nothing left of the preventive or prophylactic function of * * * [such] statutes * * *.

* * *

* * * [T]here are substantial reasons for concluding that the Bill of Attainder Clause may not be regarded as enshrining any general rule distinguishing between the legislative and judicial functions. Congress may pass legislation affecting specific persons in the form of private bills. It may also punish persons who commit contempt before it. So too, one may note that if Art. I, § 9, cl. 3, immortalizes some notion of the separation of powers at the federal level, then Art. I, § 10, necessarily does the same for the States. But it has long been recognized by this Court that "(w)hether the legislative, executive, and judicial powers of a state shall be kept altogether distinct and separate, or whether persons or collections of persons belonging to one department may, in respect to some matters, exert powers which, strictly speaking, pertain to another department of government, is for the determination of the state." *Dreyer v. Illinois*, 187 U.S. 71, 84.

* * *

In view of Congress' demonstrated concern in preventing future conduct—political strikes—and the reasonableness of the means adopted to that end, I cannot conclude that § 504 had a punitive purpose or that it constitutes a bill of attainder. I intimate no opinion on the issues that the Court does not reach.

NOTES AND QUESTIONS

1. *United States v. Brown* was a close decision (5–4), and the opinion of the Court was written by Chief Justice Earl Warren, with a spirited dissent by Justice Byron White. Warren is not particularly known for championing the modalities of text and history. Yet his opinion here is full of history, as was his opinion in *Powell v. McCormack*, which you read earlier. Can the objection be made, not that Warren fails to ground his work in history, but rather that he is too quick to identify a broad "purpose" that he thinks the history reveals?

2. One theme at the heart of the dispute between Chief Justice Warren and Justice White is the role of the courts when reviewing legislation. White was an ardent proponent of judicial restraint. There is a direct line of intellectual descent from Professor James Bradley Thayer, *see supra* page 59, to Justice Oliver Wendell Holmes, to Justice Felix Frankfurter, and on to Justice White. All accepted some form or another of the Thayerian rule of clear mistake—the idea that the courts ought only to invalidate the actions of the political branches when it is "clear" that they have made a mistake. What do you think of this idea and its employment in the context of this case? Warren, on the other hand, has a reputation as a proponent of "judicial activism," at least on behalf of causes that he thought were underrepresented in the political process. As it happens, one of Warren's law clerks in the October 1964 term was future law professor John Hart Ely, who as an academic urged a vigorous role for courts as protectors of the political process, and especially as protectors of minorities who were not part of powerful interest-group lobbies. *See* JOHN HART ELY, DEMOCRACY AND DISTRUST (1980). Indeed, several years before his clerkship, Ely wrote his Yale Law School student Note on the Bill of Attainder Clause, suggesting a broad (but not limitless) application of the clause. *See* John Hart Ely, *The Bounds of Legislative Specification: A Suggested Approach to the Bill of Attainder Clause*, 72 YALE L. J. 330 (1962). Targets of attainder-like laws, and certainly members of the Communist Party, obviously fit the description of persons who are likely to be thinly represented in the political process. Is this a sensible or attractive organizing tool for a scheme of judicial review? Is it a tool actually prescribed by the Constitution? Be prepared to revisit all of those questions later in connection with the Equal Protection Clause of the Fourteenth Amendment.

3. The Court in *Brown* relied heavily on its prior decision in *United States v. Lovett,* 328 U.S. 303 (1946), which struck down an appropriations rider which prohibited any federal funds from being used by the executive branch to pay a salary to three named individuals who Congress thought were communists. Is cutting off the salary of a few named federal officials who have been properly appointed to an office a de facto punishment? Remember that Article I, Section 9, Clause 7 provides that "No Money shall be drawn from the Treasury, but in Consequence of Appropriations made by Law * * *." In light of this Clause, was it even constitutional for the Supreme Court in *United States v. Lovett* to permit Lovett's salary to be paid out of the Treasury even if not doing so amounts to a bill of attainder? Should the Court have invalidated the whole of Congress's appropriations bill because of the unconstitutional bill of attainder rider rather than ordering that Lovett and the others be paid? Suppose in *Lovett* that Congress had simply eliminated the positions held by the three employees that it didn't like. Is that judicially reviewable?

4. Justice White's dissenting opinion in *Brown* worried that the majority's broad view of the Bill of Attainder Clause would threaten a wide range of federal and state statutes that turned on what the courts would regard as inadequate generalizations. A quick glance at the national reporter system shows that there have been relatively few cases brought under the two Bill of Attainder Clauses since 1965—and, as far as we can tell, no laws invalidated at the federal appellate level as bills of attainder since 1965—so Justice White's concerns have not materialized. To the contrary, subsequent decisions have taken what seems to be a much narrower view of bills of attainder than did the five-Justice majority in *Brown*.

5. The Court revisited the question of the proper scope of the Bill of Attainder Clauses in *Nixon v. General Services Administration,* 433 U.S. 425 (1977). This case involved control over 42 million pages of documentary material and 880 tape recordings that former President Richard Nixon had secretly made of himself and others while he was serving in the White House. A month after Nixon's resignation from the presidency, under threat of certain impeachment and removal by the Senate, the Administrator of the General Services Administration ("GSA") announced that he and Nixon had signed an agreement highly favorable to Nixon over the custody of these materials. The Administrator argued persuasively that all presidents prior to Nixon had been recognized as having total rights of ownership and custody of their personal papers accumulated during their presidencies. (After 1978, presidents no longer own their official papers. *See* Presidential Records Act of 1978, 44 U.S.C. § 2202 (2018).) Congress responded to news of the Nixon-GSA agreement by passing a new law, which President Gerald Ford signed, seizing all records that "(1) involve former President Richard M. Nixon or other individuals who, at the time of the conversation, were employed by the federal government; (2) were recorded in the White House or in the Office of the President in the Executive Office Buildings located in Washington, District of Columbia; Camp David, Maryland; Key Biscayne, Florida; or San Clemente, California; and (3) were recorded during the period beginning January 20, 1969, and ending August 9, 1974." Presidential Recordings and Materials Preservation Act, Pub. L. No. 93–526, 88 Stat. 1695 (1974). The law thus mentioned Nixon by name, identified precisely his and only his presidential term, and identified the locations where he and only he (in places like Key Biscayne and San Clemente) conducted presidential business. Nixon challenged the constitutionality of this law on multiple grounds, including that it was a constitutionally forbidden bill of attainder. Justice William J. Brennan, Jr., writing for a majority of the Court, disagreed:

> *Brown, Lovett,* and earlier cases unquestionably gave broad and generous meaning to the constitutional protection against bills of attainder. But appellant's proposed reading is far broader still. In essence, he argues that *Brown* establishes that the Constitution is offended whenever a law imposes undesired consequences on an individual or on a class that is not defined at a proper level of generality. The Act in question therefore is faulted for singling out appellant, as opposed to all other Presidents or members of the Government, for disfavored treatment.
>
> Appellant's characterization of the meaning of a bill of attainder obviously proves far too much. By arguing that an individual or defined group is attainted whenever he or it is compelled to bear burdens which the individual or group dislikes, appellant removes the anchor that ties the bill of attainder guarantee to realistic conceptions of classification and punishment. His view would cripple the very process of legislating, for any individual or group that is made the subject of adverse legislation can complain that the lawmakers could and should have defined the relevant affected class at a greater level of generality.

Furthermore, every person or group made subject to legislation which he or it finds burdensome may subjectively feel, and can complain, that he or it is being subjected to unwarranted punishment. However expansive the prohibition against bills of attainder, it surely was not intended to serve as a variant of the equal protection doctrine, invalidating every Act of Congress or the States that legislatively burdens some persons or groups but not all other plausible individuals * * *.

Thus, in the present case, the Act's specificity—the fact that it refers to appellant by name—does not automatically offend the Bill of Attainder Clause * * *. Congress' action to preserve only appellant's records is easily explained by the fact that at the time of the Act's passage, only his materials demanded immediate attention. The Presidential papers of all former Presidents from Hoover to Johnson were already housed in functioning Presidential libraries. Congress had reason for concern solely with the preservation of appellant's materials, for he alone had entered into a depository agreement * * * which by its terms called for the destruction of certain of the material. In short, appellant constituted a legitimate class of one, and this provides a basis for Congress' decision to proceed with dispatch with respect to his materials while accepting the status of his predecessors' papers and ordering the further consideration of generalized standards to govern his successors.

Moreover, even if the specificity element were deemed to be satisfied here * * *, we must inquire further whether Congress * * * "inflict(ed) punishment" within the constitutional proscription against bills of attainder.

* * *

* * * While it is true that Congress ordered the General Services Administration to retain control over records that appellant claims as his property, § 105 of the Act makes provision for an award by the District Court of "just compensation." This undercuts even a colorable contention that the Government has punitively confiscated appellant's property, for the "owner (thereby) is to be put in the same position monetarily as he would have occupied if his property has not been taken." Thus, no feature of the challenged Act falls within the historical meaning of legislative punishment.

* * *

We, of course, are not blind to appellant's plea that we recognize the social and political realities of 1974. It was a period of political turbulence unprecedented in our history. But this Court is not free to invalidate Acts of Congress based upon inferences that we may be asked to draw from our personalized reading of the contemporary scene or recent history. In judging the constitutionality of the Act, we may only look to its terms, to the intent expressed by Members of Congress who voted its passage, and to the existence or nonexistence of legitimate explanations for its apparent effect. We are persuaded that none of these factors is suggestive that the Act is a punitive bill of attainder, or otherwise facially unconstitutional.

433 U.S. at 469–85. Does this sound more like the majority opinion or the dissenting opinion in *Brown*? Did the majority in *Brown* take account of the "social and political realities" of 1965 (and the preceding decade) when it invalidated legislative action against communists? John Hart Ely's 1962 student Note on bills of attender concluded with: "This Comment has analyzed only legislation directed at members of the Communist Party. This emphasis results not from design or sympathy, but from necessity. For it is the

Communists who are the targets of today's bills of attainder." Ely, *supra,* at 366. Should the Court have taken account of "social and political realities" in *Brown, Nixon,* both, or neither?

6. Courts in other cases similarly have given a narrow application to the Bill of Attainder Clauses. In *SBC Communications, Inc. v. FCC,* 154 F.3d 226 (5th Cir.1998), a majority held that a statutory provision imposing specific and targeted legal disabilities on communications companies that were formerly part of the Bell System before it was broken up under the antitrust laws was not a bill of attainder:

> [I]f legislation has a legitimately nonpunitive function, purpose, and structure, it does not constitute punishment for purposes of the Bill of Attainder Clause, even where it imposes the historically punitive sanction of barring designated individuals from engaging in certain professions. This statement is consistent with the older, traditional lines of analysis in the Court's attainder jurisprudence, * * * including Justice Frankfurter's concurrence in *Lovett.* It is also not inconsistent with the more sweeping separation of powers theory espoused by Chief Justice Warren in his somewhat aberrant *Brown* opinion * * *. Although some portions of *Nixon* might be read to suggest that historical punishments are "inherently suspect" * * *, it simply cannot be convincingly maintained that employment bars are inherently historically punitive without reference to *Nixon*'s other consideration.

Id. at 241–42. A dissenting judge wrote: "En route to minting a 'regulatory exception' to the Bill of Attainder Clause, the majority holds that punishment is not punishment when it is inflicted with a 'prophylactic' intent. The majority reaches this cherished goal by stitching together a patchwork of concurrences and dissents and by brushing aside binding Supreme Court majority opinions as 'aberrant' and 'unsensible.'" *Id.* at 247 (Smith, J., dissenting).

7. Congress and Parliament have long passed and continue to pass special bills that benefit private individuals or small groups of individuals. There are no constitutional constraints on either Congress or any state legislature when it comes to benefiting one or a few individuals except the Constitution's rule that neither Congress nor a State can confer any "Titles of Nobility." Prior to the creation of the Court of Claims in 1855, all persons seeking compensation for a taking of property by the federal government or any other form of money damages had to get a private bill passed for their relief because the doctrine of sovereign immunity rendered the U.S. government immune from suit in court. Even today, Congress regularly passes "earmarks" which spend federal money for the benefit of one or a few individuals. Ought there to be any constitutional limit on the legislature, not only when it imposes bill-of-attainder-like burdens, but also when it confers benefits with insufficient generality? Is conferring benefits on some people but not others really any different from imposing burdens on some people but not others? Some state constitutions require that laws be "general" in scope but such requirements are practically unenforceable in court. Would a presidential or gubernatorial line item veto help?

[Assignment 16]

b. *Ex Post Facto Laws*

In addition to forbidding Congress and the States from passing any bills of attainder, Article I, Sections 9 and 10 also forbid Congress and the States from passing any "ex post facto Laws." This is another clause that plays a major role in delineating the line between legislative and judicial power described above in assignment 8. Article, I, Section 10 also adds that the States (although not the national government) are forbidden from passing any "Law impairing the Obligation of Contracts." What is an "ex post facto Law" for purposes of the Constitution? Does the ban forbid only retroactive criminal laws or also retroactive civil laws? A lot of the ordinary process of law making involves the making of retrospective civil laws. This question was thus of great interest early in our constitutional history, and it led to the decision of *Calder v. Bull*, 3 U.S. 386 (1798). As you read *Calder*, which appears below, you will be struck by the fact that it contains several seriatim opinions instead of one majority opinion of the court. This was the style in English and colonial American courts at that time. It was Chief Justice Marshall who persuaded his colleagues to speak with one voice, and with one opinion of the Court, after 1801—a time when the Court was under attack by Jeffersonian critics. As you read the opinions of Justice Chase and Justice Iredell, note the sharp debate over whether judges should decide cases on the basis of natural as opposed to positive law. The exchange is famous. The opinions draw on every single one of the modalities of constitutional interpretation. As you read them, ask whether you are more persuaded by the arguments from text, structure, history and purpose, practice, policy considerations, or natural law. *Calder v. Bull* construes the Ex Post Facto Laws Clause of Article I, Section 10, but in the process it also lays down a rule for the Ex Post Facto Laws Clause of Article I, Section 9, which constrains Congress. As you read the opinions, keep in mind the central question before the Court: To what kinds of laws do the Ex Post Facto Clauses apply? All laws, both civil and criminal? Only criminal laws? Some kinds of civil laws but less than all?

2. CALDER V. BULL

3 U.S. (3 Dall.) 386 (1798)

[*Editors' Note: Justice Chase's opinion contains a great deal of italicization that does not, in our judgment, contribute very much communicative value. Accordingly, for ease of exposition, we have deleted all italics from the opinions in this case.*]

In error from the State of Connecticut. The cause was argued at the last term, (in the absence of THE CHIEF JUSTICE) and now the court delivered their opinions seriatim.

■ CHASE, JUSTICE.

* * *

The Legislature of Connecticut, on the 2nd Thursday of May 1795, passed a resolution or law, which, for the reasons assigned, set aside a decree of the court of Probate for Harford, on the 21st of March 1793, which decree disapproved of the will of Normand Morrison (the grandson) made the 21st of August 1779, and refused to record the said will; and granted a new hearing by the said Court of Probate, with liberty of appeal therefrom, in six months. A new hearing was had, in virtue of this resolution, or law, before the said Court of Probate, who, on the 27th of July 1795, approved the said will, and ordered it to be recorded. At August 1795, appeal was then had to the superior court at Harford, who at February term 1796, affirmed the decree of the Court of Probate. Appeal was had to the Supreme Court of errors of Connecticut, who, in June 1796, adjudged, that there were no errors. More than 18 months elapsed from the decree of the Court of Probate (on the 1st of March 1793) and thereby Caleb Bull and wife were barred of all right of appeal, by a statute of Connecticut. There was no law of that State whereby a new hearing, or trial, before the said Court of Probate might be obtained. Calder and wife claim the premises in question, in right of his wife, as heiress of N. Morrison, physician; Bull and wife claim under the will of N. Morrison, the grandson.

The Council for the Plaintiffs in error [Calder], contend, that the said resolution or law of the Legislature of Connecticut, granting a new hearing, in the above case, is an ex post facto law, prohibited by the Constitution of the United States * * *.

* * *

The effect of the resolution or law of Connecticut, above stated, is to revise a decision of one of its Inferior Courts * * * and to direct a new hearing of the case by the same Court of Probate * * *. By the existing law of Connecticut a right to recover certain property had vested in Calder and wife (the appellants) in consequence of a decision of a court of justice, but, in virtue of a subsequent resolution or law, and the new hearing thereof, and the decision in consequence, this right to recover certain property was divested, and the right to the property declared to be in Bull and wife, the appellees. The sole enquiry is, whether this resolution or law of Connecticut, having such operation, is an ex post facto law, within the prohibition of the Federal Constitution?

Whether the Legislature of any of the States can revise and correct by law, a decision of any of its Courts of Justice * * * is a question of very great importance, and not necessary NOW to be determined; because the resolution or law in question does not go so far. I cannot subscribe to the omnipotence of a State Legislature, or that it is absolute and without controul; although its authority should not be expressly restrained by the Constitution, or fundamental law, of the State. The people of the United States erected their Constitutions, or forms of government, to establish justice, to promote the general welfare, to secure the blessings of liberty; and to protect their persons and property from violence. The purposes for which men enter into society will determine the nature and terms of the social compact; and as they are the foundation of the legislative power, they will decide what are the proper objects of it * * *. There are certain vital principles in our free Republican governments, which will determine and over-rule an apparent and flagrant abuse of legislative power; as to authorize manifest injustice by positive law; or to take away that security for personal liberty, or private property, for the protection whereof of the government was established. An ACT of the Legislature (for I cannot call it a law) contrary to the great first principles of the social compact, cannot be considered a rightful exercise of legislative authority * * *. A law that punished a citizen for an innocent action, or, in other words, for an act, which, when done, was in violation of no existing law; a law that destroys, or impairs, the lawful private contracts of citizens; a law that makes a man a Judge in his own cause; or a law that takes property from A. and gives it to B: It is against all reason and justice, for a people to entrust a Legislature with SUCH powers; and, therefore, it cannot be presumed that they have done it. The genius, the nature, and the spirit, of our State Governments, amount to a prohibition of such acts of legislation; and the general principles of law and reason forbid them. The Legislature may enjoin, permit, forbid, and punish; they may declare new crimes; and establish rules of conduct for all its citizens in future cases; they may command what is right, and prohibit what is wrong; but they cannot change innocence into guilt; or punish innocence as a crime; or violate the right of an antecedent lawful private contract; or the right of private property. To maintain that our Federal, or State, Legislature possesses such powers, if they had not been expressly restrained; would, in my opinion, be a political heresy, altogether inadmissible in our free republican governments.

* * *

The prohibition against [the States] making any ex post facto laws * * * very probably arose from the knowledge, that the Parliament of Great Britain claimed and exercised a power to pass such laws, under the denomination of bills of attainder, or bills of pains and penalties; the first inflicting capital, and the other less, punishment. These acts [by Parliament] were legislative judgments; and an exercise of judicial power * * *. With very few exceptions, the advocates of such laws were stimulated by ambition, or personal resentment, and vindictive malice. To prevent such, and similar, acts of violence and injustice, I believe, the Federal and State Legislatures, were prohibited from passing any bill of attainder; or any ex post facto law.

* * *

I shall endeavour to shew what law is to be considered an ex post facto law, within the words and meaning of the prohibition in the Federal Constitution * * *. [T]he plain and obvious meaning and intention of the prohibition is this; that the Legislatures of the several states, shall not pass laws, after a fact done by a subject, or citizen, which shall have relation to such fact, and shall punish him for having done it. The prohibition considered in this light, is an additional bulwark in favour of the personal security of the subject, to protect his person from punishment by legislative acts, having a retrospective operation. I do not think it was inserted to secure the citizen in his private rights, of either property, or contracts. The prohibitions not to make any thing but gold and silver coin a tender in payment of debts, and not to pass any law impairing the obligation of contracts, were inserted to secure private rights; but the restriction not to pass any ex post facto law, was to secure the person of the subject from injury, or punishment, in consequence of such law. If the prohibition against making ex post facto laws was intended to secure personal rights from being affected, or injured, by such laws, and the prohibition is sufficiently extensive for that object, the other restraints, I have enumerated, were unnecessary, and therefore improper; for both of them are retrospective.

I will state what laws I consider ex post facto laws, within the words and the intent of the prohibition. 1st. Every law that makes an action, done before the passing of the law, and which was innocent when done, criminal; and punishes such action. 2d. Every law that aggravates a crime, or makes it greater than it was, when committed. 3d. Every law that changes the punishment, and inflicts a greater punishment, than the law annexed to the crime, when committed. 4th. Every law that alters the legal rules of evidence, and receives less, or different, testimony, than the law required at the time of the commission of the offence, in order to convict the offender. All these, and similar laws, are manifestly unjust and oppressive. In my opinion, the true distinction is between ex post facto laws, and retrospective laws. Every ex post facto law must necessarily be retrospective; but every retrospective law is not an ex post facto law: The former, only, are prohibited. Every law that takes away, or impairs, rights vested, agreeably to existing laws, is retrospective, and is generally unjust; and may be oppressive; and it is a good general rule, that a law should have no retrospect: but there are cases in which laws may justly, and for the benefit of the community, and also of individuals, relate to a time antecedent to their commencement * * *. The expressions "ex post facto laws," are technical, they had been in use long before the Revolution, and had acquired an appropriate meaning, by Legislators, Lawyers, and Authors. The celebrated and judicious Sir William Blackstone, in his commentaries, considers an ex post facto law precisely in the same light I have done. His opinion is confirmed by his successor, Mr. Woodeson; and by the author of the Federalist, who I esteem superior to both, for his extensive and accurate knowledge of the true principles of Government.

I also rely greatly on the definition, or explanation of EX POST FACTO LAWS, as given by the Conventions of Massachusetts, Maryland, and North Carolina; in their several Constitutions, or forms of Government.

* * *

* * * In my judgment the case of the Plaintiffs in Error, is not within the letter of the prohibition; and, for the reasons assigned, I am clearly of opinion, that it is not within the intention of the prohibition; and if within the intention, but out of the letter, I should not, therefore, consider myself justified to continue it within the prohibition, and therefore that the whole was void.

* * *

If the term ex post facto law is to be construed to include and to prohibit the enacting any law after a fact, it will greatly restrict the power of the federal and state legislatures; and the consequences of such a construction may not be foreseen.

* * *

It was further urged, that if the provision does not extend to prohibit the making any law after a fact * * * rights vested may be divested at the will and pleasure of the state legislatures * * *.

It is not to be presumed, that the federal or state legislatures will pass laws to deprive citizens of rights vested in them by existing laws; unless for the benefit of the whole community; and on making full satisfaction. The restraint against making any ex post facto laws was not considered, by the framers of the constitution, as extending to prohibit the depriving a citizen even of a vested right to property; or the provision, "that private property should not be taken for PUBLIC use, without just compensation," was unnecessary.

* * *

* * * I will not decide any law to be void, but in a very clear case.

I am of opinion, that the decree of the Supreme Court of Errors of Connecticut be affirmed, with costs.

■ PATERSON, JUSTICE.

The Constitution of Connecticut is made up of usages[5], and it appears that its Legislature have, from the beginning, exercised the power of granting new trials * * *. This usage makes up part of the Constitution of Connecticut, and we are bound to consider it as such, unless it be inconsistent with the Constitution of the United

5 *[Editors' Note: Connecticut, along with Rhode Island, did not adopt a state constitution in the founding era. It relied on its corporate charter. Thus, the "constitution" of Connecticut, as with the British constitution, consisted largely of practices, or "usages" as Justice Paterson called them.]*

States. True it is, that the awarding of new trials falls properly within the province of the judiciary; but if the Legislature of Connecticut have been in the uninterrupted exercise of this authority, in certain cases, we must, in such cases, respect their decisions as flowing from a competent jurisdiction, or constitutional organ. And therefore we may, in the present instance, consider the Legislature of the state, as having acted in their customary judicial capacity. If so, there is an end of the question. For if the power, thus exercised, comes more properly within the description of a judicial than of a legislative power; and if by usage or the Constitution, which, in Connecticut, are synonimous terms, the Legislature of that state acted in both capacities; then in the case now before us, it would be fair to consider the awarding of a new trial, as an act emanating from the judiciary side of the department. But * * * [Calder] has contended * * * that the awarding of a new trial, was the effect of a legislative act, and that it is unconstitutional, because an ex post facto law. For the sake of ascertaining the meaning of these terms, I will consider the resolution of the General court of Connecticut, as the exercise of a legislative and not a judicial authority * * *. The words, ex post facto, when applied to a law, have a technical meaning, and, in legal phraseology, refer to crimes, pains, and penalties. Judge Blackstone's description of the terms is clear and accurate * * *. [T[he meaning, annexed to the terms ex post facto laws, unquestionably refers to crimes, and nothing else. The historic page abundantly evinces, that the power of passing such laws should be withheld from legislators; as it is a dangerous instrument in the hands of bold, unprincipled, aspiring, and party men, and has been two often used to effect the most detestable purposes.

On inspecting such of our state Constitutions, as take notice of laws made ex post facto, we shall find, that they are understood in the same sense.

* * *

I had an ardent desire [as a delegate to the Constitutional Convention] to have extended the provision in the Constitution to retrospective laws in general. There is neither policy nor safety in such laws; and, therefore, I have always had a strong aversion against them. It may, in general, be truly observed of retrospective laws of every description, that they neither accord with sound legislation, nor the fundamental principles of the social compact. But on full consideration, I am convinced, that ex post facto laws must be limited in the manner already expressed; they must be taken in their technical, which is also their common and general, acceptation, and are not to be understood in their literal sense.

■ IREDELL, JUSTICE.

Though I concur in the general result of the opinions, which have been delivered, I cannot entirely adopt the reasons that are assigned upon the occasion.

From the best information to be collected, relative to the Constitution of Connecticut, it appears, that the Legislature of that State has been in the uniform, uninterrupted, habit of exercising a general superintending power over its courts of law, by granting new trials. It may, indeed, appear strange to some of us * * *; but such is the established usage of Connecticut * * *. When Connecticut was settled, the right of empowering her Legislature to superintend the Courts of Justice, was, I presume, early assumed; and its expediency, as applied to the local circumstances and municipal policy of the State, is sanctioned by a long and uniform practice. The power, however, is judicial in its nature; and whenever it is exercised, as in the present instance, it is an exercise of judicial, not of legislative, authority.

But, let us, for a moment, suppose, that the resolution, granting a new trial, was a legislative act, it will by no means follow, that it is an act affected by the constitutional prohibition, that "no State shall pass any ex post facto law" * * *.

If * * * a government, composed of Legislative, Executive and Judicial departments, were established, by a Constitution, which imposed no limits on the legislative power, the consequence would inevitably be, that whatever the legislative power chose to enact, would be lawfully enacted, and the judicial power could never interpose to pronounce it void. It is true, that some speculative jurists have held, that a legislative act against natural justice must, in itself, be void; but I cannot think that, under such a government, any Court of Justice would possess a power to declare it so * * *.

In order, therefore, to guard against so great an evil, it has been the policy of all the American states, which have, individually, framed their state constitutions since the revolution, and of the people of the United States, when they framed the Federal Constitution, to define with precision the objects of the legislative power, and to restrain its exercise within marked and settled boundaries. If any act of Congress, or of the Legislature of a state, violates those constitutional provisions, it is unquestionably void; though, I admit, that as the authority to declare it void is of a delicate and awful nature, the Court will never resort to that authority, but in a clear and urgent case. If, on the other hand, the Legislature of the Union, or the Legislature of any member of the Union, shall pass a law, within the general scope of their constitutional power, the Court cannot pronounce it to be void, merely because it is, in their judgment, contrary to the principles of natural justice. The ideas of natural justice are regulated by no fixed standard: the ablest and the purest men have differed upon the subject; and all that the Court could properly say, in such an event, would be, that the Legislature (possessed of an equal right of opinion) had passed an act which, in the opinion of the judges, was inconsistent with the abstract principles of natural justice. There are then but two lights, in which the subject can be viewed: 1st. If the Legislature pursue the authority delegated to them, their acts are valid. 2d. If they transgress the boundaries of that authority, their acts are invalid. In the former case, they exercise the discretion vested in them by the people, to whom alone they are responsible for the faithful discharge of their trust: but in the latter case, they violate a fundamental law, which must be our guide, whenever we are called upon as judges to determine the validity of a legislative act.

Still, however, in the present instance, the act or resolution of the Legislature of Connecticut, cannot be regarded as an ex post facto law; for, the true construction of the prohibition extends to criminal, not to civil, cases. It is only in criminal cases, indeed, in which the danger to be guarded against, is greatly to be apprehended * * *.

The policy, the reason and humanity, of the prohibition, do not, I repeat, extend to civil cases, to cases that merely affect the private property of citizens. Some of the most necessary and important acts of Legislation are, on the contrary, founded upon the principle, that private rights must yield to public exigences. Highways are run through private grounds. Fortifications, Light-houses, and other public edifices, are necessarily sometimes built upon the soil owned by individuals. In such, and similar cases, if the owners should refuse voluntarily to accommodate the public, they must be constrained, as far as the public necessities require; and justice is done, by allowing them a reasonable equivalent. Without the possession of this power the operations of Government would often be obstructed, and society itself would be endangered. It is not sufficient to urge, that the power may be abused, for, such is the nature of all power,—such is the tendency of every human institution: and, it might as fairly be said, that the power of taxation, which is only circumscribed by the discretion of the Body, in which it is vested, ought not to be granted, because the Legislature, disregarding its true objects, might, for visionary and useless projects, impose a tax to the amount of nineteen shillings in the pound. We must be content to limit power where we can, and where we cannot, consistently with its use, we must be content to repose a salutary confidence. It is our consolation that there never existed a Government, in ancient or modern times, more free from danger in this respect, than the Governments of America.

Upon the whole, though there cannot be a case, in which an ex post facto law in criminal matters is requisite, or justifiable (for Providence never can intend to promote the prosperity of any country by bad means) yet, in the present instance the objection does not arise: Because, 1st. if the act of the Legislature of Connecticut was a judicial act, it is not within the words of the Constitution; and 2d. even if it was a legislative act, it is not within the meaning of the prohibition.

■ CUSHING, JUSTICE.

The case appears to me to be clear of all difficulty, taken either way. If the act is a judicial act, it is not touched by the Federal Constitution: and, if it is a legislative act, it is maintained and justified by the ancient and uniform practice of the state of Connecticut.

Judgment affirmed.

NOTES AND QUESTIONS

1. One of the most powerful arguments in *Calder v. Bull* is that if the "Ex Post Facto Laws Clause" of Section 10 already banned retroactive civil laws, then the Contracts Clause, which immediately follows it and which bans all "Law[s] impairing the Obligation of Contracts" would have been redundant. Is this a persuasive constitutional argument? Might not the document be redundant in places to make doubly sure that a right or grant of power is followed? What do you think about Justice Iredell's policy argument in favor of the occasional retroactive civil law? Is he right? Is this observation relevant as a matter of constitutional construction? Who gets the better of the debate between Justices Chase and Iredell over the possible relevance of natural law? All of the Justices who address the point seem to agree that legislation should only be found unconstitutional in cases of clear error. Does that suggest that Thayerian judicial restraint is correct as an original matter?

2. What do you think about the use of seriatim opinions in *Calder v. Bull*? Ought all the justices have to say what they think when a legislative act is struck down, or should there be an opinion of the Court? What are the advantages and disadvantages of seriatim opinions? Does a culture that requires judges to orally and publicly state the reasons for their decisions encourage accountability? Does it prevent incompetent or decrepit judges from hiding behind their law clerks? In civil law countries in continental Europe the tradition is for the judges not even to sign their opinions or indicate the courts' vote on a case since they are supposed to be impersonal oracles of the law. Is this a good

idea? Would it discourage judicial grandstanding? Would it lead to less openness and transparency in the courts?

3. *Calder* was decided in 1798. What does the modern law of the Ex Post Facto Law Clauses look like? The basic holding of *Calder* that the clauses apply only to criminal cases has survived intact, though Justice Thomas said in 1998: "Since *Calder v. Bull* * * *, this Court has considered the *Ex Post Facto* Clause to apply only in the criminal context. I have never been convinced of the soundness of this limitation * * *. In an appropriate case, therefore, I would be willing to reconsider *Calder* and its progeny." *Eastern Enterprises v. Apfel,* 524 U.S. 498, 538–39 (1998) (Thomas, J., concurring). A thorough study of founding-era materials suggests that *Calder* probably got the right answer as a matter of original meaning, though the matter is not entirely free from doubt, *see* Robert G. Natelson, *Statutory Retroactivity: The Founders' View*, 39 IDAHO L. REV. 489 (2003), and there is no indication that the Court is prepared to reconsider the reach of the clauses. But that limitation on the scope of the clauses requires courts to be able to distinguish civil from criminal laws, and that is not necessarily as simple as it sounds. Do you look just to the label given to the law by the legislature? To whether imprisonment is a possible penalty (remembering that there are such things as criminal fines)? To an all-things-considered assessment of the law's purposes and effects? Modern doctrine chooses the latter path.

In *Smith v. Doe,* 538 U.S. 84 (2003), the Supreme Court considered the constitutionality of an Alaska statute that required, *inter alia,* that people convicted of sex offenses register in the Alaska Sex Offender Registration Act—even people who were convicted *before* the Act was passed. (This was one of many state registration statutes that were the models for the federal statute at issue in *Gundy v. United States, supra* pages 204–215.) Under the terms of the Alaska Act, all sex offenders who moved to Alaska were required to register within one day of entering the State. The Act also required that information about the registered sex offenders—including their names, addresses, places of employment, and driver's license numbers—be posted on the internet. The Supreme Court upheld the Act against a challenge under the Ex Post Facto Laws Clause:

> This is the first time we have considered a claim that a sex offender registration and notification law constitutes retroactive punishment forbidden by the *Ex Post Facto* Clause. The framework for our inquiry, however, is well established. We must "ascertain whether the legislature meant the statute to establish 'civil' proceedings." *Kansas v. Hendricks,* 521 U.S. 346, 361 (1997). If the intention of the legislature was to impose punishment, that ends the inquiry. If, however, the intention was to enact a regulatory scheme that is civil and nonpunitive, we must further examine whether the statutory scheme is " 'so punitive either in purpose or effect as to negate [the State's] intention' to deem it 'civil.' " *Ibid.* Because we "ordinarily defer to the legislature's stated intent," " 'only the clearest proof' will suffice to override legislative intent and transform what has been denominated a civil remedy into a criminal penalty," *Hudson v. United States,* 522 U.S. 93, 100 (1997).
>
> * * *
>
> In analyzing the effects of the Act we refer to the seven factors noted in *Kennedy v. Mendoza-Martinez,* 372 U.S. 144, 168–169 (1963), as a useful framework * * *. Because the *Mendoza-Martinez* factors are designed to apply in various constitutional contexts, we have said they are "neither exhaustive nor dispositive," *United States v. Ward,* 448 U.S., at 249, but are "useful guideposts," *Hudson,* 522 U.S., at 99. The factors most relevant to our analysis are whether, in its necessary operation, the regulatory scheme: has been

> regarded in our history and traditions as a punishment; imposes an affirmative disability or restraint; promotes the traditional aims of punishment; has a rational connection to a nonpunitive purpose; or is excessive with respect to this purpose.

538 U.S. at 92, 97. Applying that framework, the majority concluded that the Alaska law was not punitive in intent or in effect and was therefore a civil law not covered by the Ex Post Facto Laws Clause. Justices Stevens, Ginsburg, and Breyer dissented, saying the law was punitive in effect (and possibly in intent as well) and thus violated the Ex Post Facto Laws Clause. *See id.* at 110 (Stevens, J., dissenting); *id.* at 114 (Ginsburg, J., dissenting). Justice Souter concurred in the judgment, saying the case was so difficult that he simply could not say that the State of Alaska had erred. In other words, for Justice Souter, the presumption of constitutionality carried the day. *See id.* at 107, 110 (Souter, J., concurring in the judgment) ("What tips the scale for me is the presumption of constitutionality normally accorded a State's law. That presumption gives the State the benefit of the doubt in close cases like this one, and on that basis alone I concur in the Court's judgment."). Based on this brief sketch, who has the better of the argument between Justice Kennedy and the dissenters? How would each of the justices who decided *Calder v. Bull* have decided this case? Does Justice Chase's opinion, with its concern about any retroactive law that makes harsher the effects of a prior conviction, suggest that the Court erred in *Smith v. Doe*?

4. Article I, Sections 9 and 10 forbid both Congress and the States from adopting bills of attainder and ex post facto laws, but they forbid only the States, not Congress, from enacting "Law[s that impair] the Obligation of Contracts." Why? Are federal laws that impair the obligation of contracts "necessary" and "proper" so long as they have a rational basis? Is there a higher threshold? Those questions lead into what the founding generation regarded as one of the most important provisions of the Constitution: The Contracts Clause.

a. *The Contract Clause*

The Supreme Court under Chief Justice John Marshall was famous for two things: first, for reading broadly the powers of the national government and, second, for vigorously enforcing the Contracts Clause of Article I, Section 10 to limit state power. The text of the Contract Clause provides: **"No State shall * * * pass any * * * Law impairing the Obligation of Contracts."**

The most obvious purpose of the Contracts Clause was to forbid States from enacting debtor-relief laws in response to popular pressure. The object was not just to protect creditors in general but also to protect out-of-state and foreign creditors from discriminatory laws. Notwithstanding this focus on debtor-relief laws, the clause's language is entirely general and seemingly applies to all impairments of all kinds of contracts.

All kinds of contracts? Land contracts? Contracts entered into by a State? These were precisely the questions which arose very early in the Nation's constitutional history and which consumed much of the energy of the Marshall Court.

The most famous of the Marshall Court's Contracts Clause opinions is *Fletcher v. Peck,* 10 U.S. (6 Cranch) 87 (1810). The case arose as a result of the seizure by the State of Georgia of Indian lands now in Alabama and Mississippi (the Yazoo Lands). Georgia sold the land to speculators in 1795 for the ridiculously low price of 1.4 cents per acre. It was revealed after the fact that some of the state legislators had been bribed, and there was a public outcry. At the next election, many incumbent legislators lost. The new session of the Georgia State Legislature passed a law revoking the sale of the land to the speculators and voiding the corrupt transactions. In the meantime, many of the speculators had sold parts of the land to innocent third parties. John Peck sold a parcel to Robert Fletcher. The deed contained promises that Peck had good title to the land because Georgia, its original owner, had properly conveyed it. Fletcher sued Peck for breach of those promises (or "covenants"), on the ground that Georgia had not validly transferred the land because of the Georgia Legislature's Act repealing the land grant. If the Georgia statute revoking its initial sale was a "Law impairing the Obligation of Contracts," it would be unconstitutional, Peck's covenants of good title would be fine, and Fletcher would have nothing to complain about.

The Supreme Court found the repealing act unconstitutional on two grounds. First, in his opinion for the Court, Chief Justice Marshall wondered whether the Georgia law purporting to rescind the land grant, and thereby to undo a legal (or "vested") right to the land, was a violation of natural law:

> It may well be doubted whether the nature of society and of government does not prescribe some limits to the legislative power; and, if any be prescribed, where are they to be found, if the property of an individual, fairly and honestly acquired, may be seized without compensation.
>
> To the legislature all legislative power is granted; but the question, whether the act of transferring the property of an individual to the public, be in the nature of the legislative power, is well worthy of serious reflection.

Id. at 135–36. Even without regard to first principles of government, said Chief Justice Marshall, the Constitution imposed a positive-law limitation on States through the Contracts Clause. The land grant was a fully executed contract, and to repeal that grant would be to impair the obligation of the contract: "A law annulling conveyances between individuals, and declaring that the grantors should stand seised of their former estates, notwithstanding those grants, would be as repugnant to the constitution as a law discharging the vendors of property from the obligation of executing their contracts by conveyances. It would be strange if a contract to convey was secured by the constitution, while an absolute conveyance remained unprotected." *Id.* at 137. The last question was whether the Contract Clause applied to contracts entered into by the State as well as to contracts between private parties. The Court said yes, both because "[t]he words [of the Contracts Clause] themselves contain no such distinction," *id.*, and because "[w]hatever respect might have been felt for the state sovereignties, it is not to be disguised that the framers of the constitution viewed, with some apprehension, the violent acts which might grow out of the feelings of the moment." *Id.* at 137–38. Thus, said Chief Justice Marshall, "the state of Georgia was restrained, either by general principles which are common to our free institutions, or by the particular provisions of the constitution of the United States, from passing a law whereby the estate of the plaintiff in the premises so purchased could be constitutionally and legally impaired and rendered null and void." *Id.* at 139. Evidently, either "general principles" or "the particular provisions of the constitution" would do the trick.

The key to *Fletcher v. Peck* was that the initial grant from the State created a "vested" right in the landowner, which right could then be transferred to other purchasers. Not every document that comes from the government creates a vested right of that kind. Governments often issue licenses that look similar to contracts. Is your state driver's license a contract with terms that the State cannot retroactively change without violating the Contracts Clause? Of course not. Licenses are and always have been revocable or alterable at the will of the government that issued them. But what is the difference between a license and a contract? The answer can only be determined by reasoning from historical practice and analogy. Are land grants revocable? Today, we would say they can be revoked only for a public purpose and if just compensation is paid, but in 1810 when *Fletcher v. Peck* was decided, the Fifth Amendment Takings Clause did not yet apply to the States. Indeed, Marshall himself said as much in *Barron v. Baltimore*.

The Marshall Court expanded further its aggressive construction of the Contracts Clause in a second major opinion, *Dartmouth College v. Woodward*, 17 U.S. (4 Wheat.) 518 (1819), where the Court considered the constitutionality of a New Hampshire law that altered the membership of Dartmouth College's Board of Trustees in an attempt to make the school a publicly controlled institution. Dartmouth had been issued its corporate charter in 1769 by King George III, and private investors had donated funds to it under the assumption it would be privately operated under the terms of its royal charter. New Hampshire claimed that a corporate charter is just a license from the government to do business and that such licenses can be revoked or altered by the State at any time. Dartmouth alumnus Daniel Webster argued and won the case in the Supreme Court. Marshall ruled that the corporate charter was a contract between the King and the trustees on which numerous private donors had relied and that the State could not alter it without violating the Contract Clause. This ruling was of immense importance because it established that state legislatures lacked the power to change the corporate charters of not only non-profit but also of for-profit corporations. *Dartmouth College* was thus vital to the enormous growth of commerce and business in nineteenth century America.

Was Marshall's construction of the Contract Clause as covering corporate charters correct? English monarchs revoked and altered corporate charters with some frequency. Of course, the legislature of New Hampshire—in a federal republic with a Contracts Clause in its constitution—is obviously not invested with all of the power King Charles II exercised in 1684, for example, when he revoked the corporate charter issued to the Massachusetts Bay colony by his father, King Charles I, in 1629. A corporate charter is in important respects like a license to do business or, say, a liquor license. Marshall's broad construction of the Contracts Clause as covering corporate charters was by no means foreordained, and it was controversial.

A third key Marshall Court Contracts Clause opinion came in the case of *Ogden v. Saunders*, 25 U.S. (12 Wheat.) 213 (1827). It was a 4–3 decision and was the only constitutional case in which Chief Justice Marshall ever dissented. *Ogden v. Saunders* involved a New York state contract that had been dissolved under New York bankruptcy law. When the contract was signed, the bankruptcy law was already in force. *Ogden v. Saunders* thus raised the question of whether the Contracts Clause protected "liberty of contract" prospectively and in the abstract or whether it protected only against state laws that retroactively impaired the obligations of contracts that had already been made before a challenged law was passed. The four justices in the majority ruled that the Contract Clause protected only against state laws that interfered with contracts already in place when the law was made. The Clause did not, they said, take away a state's power prospectively to limit future contracts by saying they would be dissolvable through state bankruptcy proceedings. The majority rested its decision in part on the claim that the text of the Clause indicates that it protected against any "Law impairing the *Obligation* of Contracts." Prospective impairments by adoption of state bankruptcy laws for future contracts did not impair any "obligations."

Chief Justice Marshall, in a dissent joined by Justice Joseph Story, seems to have thought that the Contracts Clause of Section 10 ought to be paired with the Commerce Clause of Article I, Section 8 and that—read together—these two clauses established that the whole field of commercial relations was exclusively the province of the federal government and not of the States. This construction finds a parallel in Section 10's bar on state war-making, treaty-making, and imposition of revenue-raising tariffs paired with the grant of all of those powers in Section 8 exclusively to the federal government. Marshall also revived his interest in natural law, which he expressed in *Fletcher v. Peck*. Much of Marshall's opinion was devoted to showing that the right to contract is a natural, pre-political right that governments of any kind can enforce but not redefine. If governments can alter contract law prospectively, they could presumably change the future "Obligation of Contracts" away from the natural-law baseline, and Marshall considered that unthinkable. *See* 25 U.S. (12 Wheat.) at 344–48.

The Supreme Court's vigorous enforcement of the Contracts Clause ended under Marshall's successor, Chief Justice Roger Taney, who was to go on to write the infamous *Dred Scott* opinion. The Taney Court's leading Contracts Clause precedent was *Charles River Bridge v. Warren Bridge,* 36 U.S. (11 Pet.) 420 (1837). In 1785, the Charles River Bridge Company had been granted the right by the Massachusetts legislature to build a bridge across the Charles River, and it did in fact build the bridge. Massachusetts then authorized the building of a second bridge across the river which would compete with the first bridge, thus harming the financial interests of the first bridge company. The first bridge company sued, claiming that authorization of a second bridge impaired its contractual rights to build the only bridge in the area. The Taney Court ruled 5 to 2, with Justice Story dissenting, that the Contracts Clause had not been violated. While the case largely turned on the absence of any express language in the contract guaranteeing freedom from competition, so that any such contractual right had to be implied from circumstances (which Justice Story, in a *very* long dissenting opinion, thought could be done in the case of royal grants), Taney made that point that public charters from the government to private citizens ought to be read narrowly so as not to create monopolies. Monopolies were originally granted by the monarch: only one seller would be licensed to sell a particular good, such as playing cards. The word *monopoly* comes from the Greek words *monos*, which means "one," and *polein*, which means "to sell." Economists agree that by far the most stable and successful monopolies are those that have exclusive government licenses. *See* ROBERT H. BORK, THE ANTITRUST PARADOX: A POLICY AT WAR WITH ITSELF (1978). It was a staple of Jacksonian orthodoxy to favor free markets and oppose government monopolies, because they could hurt consumers and favor a select few. Taney thought that the Massachusetts license to build a bridge would become a monopoly if the Contract Clause were read to foreclose the building of a second bridge.

Contracts Clause jurisprudence, as with much constitutional jurisprudence, took a major turn in the New Deal era. For the Contracts Clause, the fateful event was the Great Depression. In 1933, facing a wave of mortgage foreclosures as deflation raised the real value of mortgage payments (because debtors had to pay off loans with money that would now have higher purchasing power and be worth more), Minnesota passed a statute imposing a temporary moratorium on foreclosures. In other words, the statute prohibited creditors from enforcing rights reflected in their contracts—specifically the right to foreclose on property when debt payments are not made. It is hard to imagine a statute that more straightforwardly violates both the text and purposes of the Contracts Clause. A 5–4 Supreme Court nonetheless upheld the statute as constitutional. The opinion contains a trove of pithy and quotable lines: "While emergency does not create power, emergency may furnish the occasion for the exercise of power." *Id.* at 426. "[W]here constitutional grants and limitations of power are set forth in general clauses, which afford a broad outline, the process of construction is essential to fill in the details. That is true of the contract clause. *Id.* "[T]he prohibition is not an absolute one and is not to be read with literal exactness like a mathematical formula." *Id.* at 428. "The policy of protecting contracts against impairment presupposes the maintenance of a government by virtue of which contractual relations are worth while,—a government which retains adequate authority to secure the peace and good order of society." *Id.* at 435. "The economic interests of the state may justify the exercise of its continuing and dominant protective power notwithstanding interference with contracts." *Id.* at 437. "The question is not whether the legislative action affects contracts incidentally, or directly or indirectly, but whether the legislation is addressed to a legitimate end and the measures taken are reasonable and appropriate to that end." *Id.* at 438. "[C]onditions may * * * arise in which a temporary restraint of enforcement may be consistent with the spirit and purpose of the constitutional provision and thus be found to be within the range of the reserved power of the state to protect the vital interests of the community." *Id.* at 439. The key to the opinion, however, is the following passage:

> * * * [T]here has been a growing appreciation of public needs and of the necessity of finding ground for a rational compromise between individual rights and public welfare. The settlement and consequent contraction of the public domain, the pressure of a constantly increasing density of population, the interrelation of the activities of our people and the complexity of our economic interests, have inevitably led to an increased use of the organization of society in order to protect the very bases of individual opportunity. Where, in earlier days, it was thought that only the concerns of individuals or of classes were involved, and that those of the state itself were touched only remotely, it has later been found that the fundamental interests of the state are directly affected; and that the question is no longer merely that of one party to a contract as against another, but of the use of reasonable means to safeguard the economic structure upon which the good of all depends.
>
> It is no answer to say that this public need was not apprehended a century ago, or to insist that what the provision of the Constitution meant

to the vision of that day it must mean to the vision of our time. If by the statement that what the Constitution meant at the time of its adoption it means to-day, it is intended to say that the great clauses of the Constitution must be confined to the interpretation which the framers, with the conditions and outlook of their time, would have placed upon them, the statement carries its own refutation * * *. When we are dealing with the words of the Constitution, said this Court in *Missouri v. Holland*, 252 U.S. 416, 433, "we must realize that they have called into life a being the development of which could not have been foreseen completely by the most gifted of its begetters. * * * The case before us must be considered in the light of our whole experience and not merely in that of what was said a hundred years ago."

Nor is it helpful to attempt to draw a fine distinction between the intended meaning of the words of the Constitution and their intended application. When we consider the contract clause and the decisions which have expounded it in harmony with the essential reserved power of the states to protect the security of their peoples, we find no warrant for the conclusion that the clause has been warped by these decisions from its proper significance or that the founders of our government would have interpreted the clause differently had they had occasion to assume that responsibility in the conditions of the later day. The vast body of law which has been developed was unknown to the fathers, but it is believed to have preserved the essential content and the spirit of the Constitution. With a growing recognition of public needs and the relation of individual right to public security, the court has sought to prevent the perversion of the clause through its use as an instrument to throttle the capacity of the states to protect their fundamental interests. This development is a growth from the seeds which the fathers planted * * *.

Applying the criteria established by our decisions, we conclude:

1. An emergency existed in Minnesota which furnished a proper occasion for the exercise of the reserved power of the state to protect the vital interests of the community * * *. As the Supreme Court of Minnesota said (249 N.W. 334, 337), the economic emergency which threatened 'the loss of homes and lands which furnish those in possession the necessary shelter and means of subsistence' was a 'potent cause' for the enactment of the statute.

2. The legislation was addressed to a legitimate end; that is, the legislation was not for the mere advantage of particular individuals but for the protection of a basic interest of society.

3. In view of the nature of the contracts in question—mortgages of unquestionable validity—the relief afforded and justified by the emergency, in order not to contravene the constitutional provision, could only be of a character appropriate to that emergency, and could be granted only upon reasonable conditions.

4. The conditions upon which the period of redemption is extended do not appear to be unreasonable * * *. The relief afforded by the statute has regard to the interest of mortgagees as well as to the interest of

> mortgagors. The legislation seeks to prevent the impending ruin of both by a considerate measure of relief.

Id. at 442–46. The lengthy dissent, canvassing the history of the Contracts Clause, responded:

> A provision of the Constitution * * * does not mean one thing at one time and an entirely different thing at another time. If the contract impairment clause, when framed and adopted, meant that the terms of a contract for the payment of money could not be altered in invitum by a state statute enacted for the relief of hardly pressed debtors to the end and with the effect of postponing payment or enforcement during and because of an economic or financial emergency, it is but to state the obvious to say that it means the same now * * *.
>
> * * *
>
> The provisions of the Federal Constitution, undoubtedly, are pliable in the sense that in appropriate cases they have the capacity of bringing within their grasp every new condition which falls within their meaning. But, their meaning is changeless; it is only their application which is extensible."

Id. at 448–49, 451 (Sutherland, J., dissenting). Is it relevant to *Blaisdell* that economic conditions in Minnesota were so bad that rioting debtors made enforcement of the written contracts impossible? As with the Bill of Attainder Clauses, to what extent should courts in Contracts Clause cases take account of "social and political realities"?

For contrasting views on whether *Blaisdell* was a sharp departure from prior precedent, compare Samuel R. Olken, *Charles Evans Hughes and the* Blaisdell *Decision: A Historical Study of Contract Clause Jurisprudence*, 72 ORE. L. REV. 513, 516 (1993) (concluding that *Blaisdell* "fit within traditional inroads upon the Contract Clause that emanated in response to tensions within the federal system over the appropriate role of state governments in regulating private interests") with Douglas W. Kmiec & John O. McGinnis, *The Contract Clause: A Return to the Original Understanding,* 14 HASTINGS. CON. L.Q. 525, 541–42 (1987) ("In *Home Building & Loan Association v. Blaisdell*, the Court turned the meaning of the Contract Clause on its head"). An argument in support of the result in *Blaisdell* is that the Minnesota statute did not actually abolish, or even reduce, the amount of the debts. It simply removed one possible remedy—foreclosure—from the creditor's arsenal of remedies, and courts have long allowed legislatures to change procedures and remedies without having to let pre-existing contracts be litigated under old procedures and remedies. *See Sturges v. Crowninshield,* 17 U.S. (4 Wheat.) 122, 200 (1819) ("The distinction between the obligation of a contract, and the remedy given by the legislature to enforce that obligation, has been taken at the bar, and exists in the nature of things. Without impairing the obligation of the contract, the remedy may certainly be modified as the wisdom of the nation shall direct."). The counter is that in the case of a mortgage, the "remedy" of foreclosure is precisely what distinguishes mortgages from unsecured loans. In the absence of the possibility of foreclosure, the interest rate on the loans would be much higher, so the right to foreclose seems more like the obligation itself than the remedy. Is there a principled way to tell whether a law alters procedures or remedies (valid) or impairs the obligation of a contract (invalid)? If not, is that a reason for courts to withdraw from trying to enforce the Contracts Clause?

Whatever the correct answer to that last question may be, since *Blaisdell,* the Contracts Clause has been close to a dead letter. The governing doctrinal inquiry involves

> a two-step test. The threshold issue is whether the state law has "operated as a substantial impairment of a contractual relationship." In answering that question, the Court has considered the extent to which the law undermines the contractual bargain, interferes with a party's reasonable expectations, and prevents the party from safeguarding or reinstating his rights. If such factors show a substantial impairment, the inquiry turns to the means and ends of the legislation. In particular, the Court has asked whether the state law is drawn in an "appropriate" and "reasonable" way to advance "a significant and legitimate public purpose." *Energy Reserves Group, Inc. v. Kansas Power & Light Co.,* 459 U.S. 400, 411–412, 103 S.Ct. 697, 74 L.Ed.2d 569 (1983).

Sveen v. Melin, 138 S.Ct. 1815, 1821–22 (2018). Post-*Blaisdell,* it is virtually impossible for a challenge to a statute to clear both steps. Intriguingly given the history of Contracts Clause jurisprudence going back to *Fletcher v. Peck*, the Court today applies a *stricter* standard to laws that implicate a State's own contracts than to laws adjusting contractual rights among private parties. *See United States Trust Co. v. New Jersey,* 431 U.S. 1 (1977).

b. *Other Limitations on States*

In addition to the prohibitions on bills of attainder, ex post facto laws, impairments of obligations of contracts, and titles of nobility, Article I, section 10 contains a miscellany of prohibitions on actions by States. States categorically cannot "enter into any Treaty, Alliance, or Confederation; grant Letters of Marque and Reprisal; coin Money; emit Bills of Credit; [or] make any Thing but gold and silver Coin a Tender in Payment of Debts." States cannot, without the consent of Congress, "lay any Imposts or Duties on Imports or Exports, except what may be absolutely necessary for executing its inspection Laws * * * [or] lay any Duty of Tonnage, keep Troops, or Ships of War in time of Peace, enter into any Agreement or Compact with another State, or with a foreign Power, or engage in War, unless actually invaded, or in such imminent Danger as will not admit of delay." While this list may seem random, each prohibition has a purpose, and the group as a whole has a collective logic, as you will see more clearly at the beginning of the next chapter. The chief goal of these prohibitions is to ensure federal exclusivity over the powers of war and peace, monetary policy, and tariff policy. The experience with States in the post-Revolutionary era imposing interstate trade barriers, issuing economically destructive paper money, and angering foreign countries in a way that potentially threatened all of the States with new wars were very much on the minds of the Framers, and these prohibitions targeted the most obvious ways in which States could adversely affect the interests of the nation as a whole. Oddly enough, given the framers' keen focus on interstate trade barriers, the Supreme Court in 1869 held that the prohibition on taxing imports without congressional consent applied only to taxes on goods from *foreign countries,* not to taxes on goods from *other States. See Woodruff v. Parham,* 75 U.S. (8 Wall.) 123 (1869). That is almost surely wrong as an original matter, *see Camps Newfound/Owatonna, Inc. v. Town of Harrison,* 520 U.S. 564, 609 (1997) (Thomas, J., dissenting); Brannon P. Denning, *Justice Thomas, the Import-Export Clause, and* Camps Newfound/Owatonna v. Harrison, 70 COLO. L. REV. 155, 213–15 (1999), and it has led to interstate taxes being analyzed under the so-called Dormant Commerce Clause, which we examine in the next chapter. When you encounter that doctrine later, consider how much of it could be textually grounded in a combination of the Import/Export Clause and the Privileges and Immunities Clause of Article IV if *Woodruff* was overruled.

Another provision for which doctrine seems to have departed from original meaning is the prohibition, without congressional consent, on States entering into "any Agreement or Compact with another State." It is easy to see why the Constitution would look askance on state compacts with "a foreign Power," but why would the Constitution care if States cooperated with each other? The answer, very simply, is that "[t]his provision is obviously intended to guard the rights and interests of the other States, and to prevent any compact or agreement between any two States, which might affect injuriously the interest of the others." *Florida v. Georgia,* 58 (17 How.) 478, 494 (1854). One group of States might make a compact among themselves that disadvantages States that are outside the compact, so congressional approval of any such agreements makes sense. *See* MICHAEL S. GREVE, THE UPSIDE-DOWN CONSTITUTION 298–302 (2012). The Supreme Court, however, worried that a too-broad construction of the Compact Clause would require routine transactions among States to be submitted to Congress, so beginning in the mid-nineteenth century the Court limited the clause's scope only to interstate agreements that seemed to have national significance. In 1893, the Court declared in dictum that "the prohibition is directed to the formation of any combination tending to the increase of political power in the states, which may *encroach upon or interfere with the just supremacy of the United States.*" *Virginia v. Tennessee,* 148 U.S. 503, 519 (1893) (emphasis added). In other words, the Court would no longer worry about compacts that might advantage some States over others; it would look only at compacts that implicate important federal interests. That dictum has been endorsed by modern Courts. *See New Hampshire v. Maine,* 426 U.S. 363, 369 (1976): *U.S. Steel Corp. v. Multistate Tax Comm'n,* 434 U.S. 452, 471 (1978). Accordingly, many interstate agreements that would seem to fall squarely within the language of the Compact Clause do not today require congressional approval. *See* Michael S. Greve, *Compacts, Cartels, and Congressional Consent,* 68 MO. L. REV. 285 (2003).

[Assignment 17]

VI. ARTICLE II: THE PRESIDENT'S POWER OF THE SWORD

The executive Power shall be vested in a President of the United States.

"We come next to the second article of the Constitution, which provides the structure, organization, and powers of the Executive department. What is the best constitution for the executive department, and what are the powers, with which it should be intrusted, are problems among the most important, and probably the most difficult to be satisfactorily solved, of all, which are involved in the theory of free governments. No man, who has ever studied the subject with profound attention, has risen from the labor without an increased and almost overwhelming sense of its

intricate relations, and perplexing doubts. No man, who has ever deeply read the human history, and especially the history of republics, but has been struck with the consciousness, how little has been hitherto done to establish a safe depositary of power in any hands, and how often, in the hands of one, or a few, or many,—of an hereditary monarch, or an elective chief, or a national council, the executive power has brought ruin upon the state, or sunk under the oppressive burden of its own imbecility. Perhaps our own history has not, as yet, established that we shall wholly escape all the dangers; and that here will not be found, as has been the case in other nations, the vulnerable part of the republic."—JOSEPH STORY, A FAMILIAR EXPOSITION OF THE CONSTITUTION OF THE UNITED STATES 203 (1986).

The President of the United States is the most powerful person in the whole world, but he or she cannot buy a new light bulb for the Oval Office without Congress appropriating the funds. Although the President of the United States is not a king, the presidency is the most powerful office ever created in a republican government. The President's power is remarkable given that the Constitution establishing this office was written just eleven years after the formal start of the American Revolution, a revolution largely directed at grievances attributed to the tyranny of the British king. In this section, we address the major positions, issues, and cases concerning the constitutional powers and duties of the President of the United States.

A. ARTICLE II: THE EXECUTIVE POWER

Article II of the Constitution contains four sections. Section 1's first clause, out of eight clauses, assigns all of "[t]he executive Power" of the new national government to one "President of the United States." We will hear much more about that Delphic phrase "executive Power" shortly. The lengthy remainder of Article II, section 1 defines how that person and the Vice President are to be chosen, the term of service (four years), and the presidential oath of office.

The method of selection for the President and Vice President is unique. The President and Vice President are elected, but not by a direct popular vote (as with the House or, after the Seventeenth Amendment, the Senate) or by the vote of state legislatures (as with the original Senate). The President is chosen by a novel institution called the Electoral College: "Each State shall appoint, in such Manner as the Legislature thereof may direct, a Number of Electors, equal to the whole Number of Senators and Representatives to which the State may be entitled in the Congress," U.S. CONST. art. II, § 1, cl. 2, with the proviso that no member of Congress and no federal executive or judicial officer can serve as an elector. *See id.* Under the original Constitution, each elector voted for two different people; the person with the most votes became President and the runner-up became Vice President. In 1796, this resulted in John Adams having as "his" Vice President Thomas Jefferson, who was his most bitter political rival (and to whom he lost the presidency in 1800). The procedure was changed after that debacle with ratification of the Twelfth Amendment, which says that each elector votes once for President and once for Vice President. It is theoretically possible under this system for the President and Vice President to be at odds, but it is much less likely than under the original scheme, especially after the rise of party government in the 1830s in which presidential and vice-presidential candidates run as a joint "ticket." Both the original Constitution and the Twelfth Amendment prohibit electors from casting both of their votes for inhabitants of the electors' home States. Nothing in the Constitution, however, prohibits electors from voting contrary to the popular votes in their own States. (Indeed, nothing in the Constitution prevents a State from dispensing with a popular vote altogether and simply having the state legislature pick the electors.) Thus, what most people regard as presidential elections are not technically presidential elections at all. They are elections to *pick the presidential electors,* who then meet at a later date (chosen by Congress pursuant to Article II, section 1, clause 4) to choose the President. Electors almost always vote in accordance with the popular vote in their States, but every so often a "rogue" elector will go their own way. In 1972, for example, an elector from Virginia, a State which voted for Richard Nixon, cast his electoral votes for the then-fledgling Libertarian Party candidates John Hospers and Tonie Nathan, making Ms. Nathan the first woman ever to receive an electoral vote. A total of eighty-five electors (out of more than 23,000 electoral votes cast) have deviated from the election results in their States. *See* https://www.wsj.com/graphics/electoral-college-2016/. A number of States have passed statutes purporting to bind their electors to vote in accordance with state results. The Supreme Court has agreed to hear a case raising the constitutionality of state attempts to bind their electors. *See Chiafalo v. State of Washington,* 193 Wash.2d 380 (2019), *cert. granted,* 2020 WL 254167. For discussion, see Robert J. Delahunty, *Is the Uniform Faithful Presidential Electors Act Constitutional?*, 2016 CARDOZO L. REV. DE NOVO 165.

The Electoral College makes it possible for a President (and Vice President) to be elected with a minority of the popular votes, because landslide wins in big States run up popular vote totals but do not yield more electoral votes than do narrow victories. Some people find this anti-democratic element unacceptable, and calls for elimination of the Electoral College are accordingly commonplace. The desirability of the Electoral College is a normative rather than legal question, so we leave it for courses on American Government. We offer only this observation: A consequence of the Electoral College is to make it difficult—not impossible, but difficult—to win a presidential election solely by dominating one region of the country. To amass the necessary 270 electoral votes requires some measure of cross-regional consensus. As with much of the American governmental structure, this has a moderating influence on American politics. (Anyone who finds that statement startling in an age of polarization should examine carefully the political variance in other countries and compare it to the *relative* stability and moderation of American politics even today.)

A few other provisions in Article II, section 1 deserve a brief mention. First, the President must be at least thirty-five years old and "a natural born Citizen * * * of the United States." U.S. CONST. art. II, § 1, cl. 5. That is, immigrants who are citizens by virtue of naturalization are not eligible to be President. Who else might not count as a "natural born Citizen"? What if someone is borne of American parents overseas? One of the earliest federal statutes dealing with naturalization of immigrants added a provision declaring: "the children of citizens of the United States, that may be born beyond the sea, or out of the limits of the United States, shall be considered as natural born citizens." Act of Mar. 26, 1790, ch. III, § 1, 1 Stat. 103, 104. Does that statute fix the meaning of Article II of the Constitution? Is it relevant for determining the meaning of Article II of the Constitution? The law, both statutory and otherwise, governing citizenship is remarkably complicated, and the Constitution says very little about the subject. *See* JAMES H. KETTNER, THE DEVELOPMENT OF AMERICAN CITIZENSHIP 1608–1870 (1974). We will most definitely revisit the subject of American citizenship in another context in a later chapter.

Article II also provides: "The President shall, at stated Times, receive for his Services, a Compensation, which shall neither be increased nor diminished during the Period for which he shall be elected, and he shall not receive within that Period any other Emolument from the United States, or any of them." U.S. CONST. art. II, § 1, cl. 7. The provision makes the President independent of both Congress and the States. Does it supplant or supplement the Article I, section 9 Emoluments Clause which forbids holders of any federal "Office of Profit or Trust" from receiving emoluments from foreign countries? Is the presidency even an "Office of Profit or Trust"? *See supra* pages 307–308. Does a President who was a former state governor or other official have to give up his state pension if he or she becomes President? *See President Reagan's Ability to Receive Retirement Benefits from the State of California*, 5 OP. O.L.C. 187 (1981) (Justice Department memo saying "no" because receipt of vested pension rights that are not subject to alteration by the State does not implicate the purposes of the Emoluments Clause). Does a President who owns, for example, a small business in a State have to sell the business before becoming President (or insure that it loses money during his or her time in office) lest receipt of profits count as an "Emolument" from a State? Or does "Emolument" refer only to direct government benefits? *See supra* page 307.

Article II, section 1 concludes by specifying the exact form of the President's required oath of office: "Before he enter on the Execution of his Office, he shall take the following Oath or Affirmation:—'I do solemnly swear (or affirm) that I will faithfully execute the Office of President of the United States, and will to the best of my Ability, preserve, protect and defend the Constitution of the United States.' " U.S. CONST. art. II, § 1, cl. 8. Elsewhere, the Constitution requires all federal and state legislative, executive, and judicial officials to be "bound by Oath or Affirmation, to support this Constitution," *id.* art. VI, § 3, but the Constitution prescribes precise words only for the President.[6] "The Oath Clause had a profound, almost covenantal, significance for the framers—a significance that may be difficult for some fully to understand and appreciate today." Michael Stokes Paulsen, *The Most Dangerous Branch: Executive Power to Say What the Law Is*, 83 GEO. L.J. 217, 257 (1994). Chief Justice Marshall invoked the judicial oath of office in support of the argument for judicial review in *Marbury v. Madison*. Ask yourself throughout this section whether there are legal implications to the presidential oath as well.

Section 2 of Article II specifies, describes, and limits certain powers of the President, elaborating on the general assignment of "the executive Power" in Section 1 and sharing the appointment power and the treaty-making power between the President and the Senate. In England, both the appointment power and the treaty power had belonged exclusively to the king. Section 3 of Article II imposes a series of duties on the President, such as the duty to give a State of the Union Address and the duty to take care that the laws be faithfully executed. Section 4 then concludes Article II by providing that the President and Vice President, unlike the king of England, are subject to impeachment and removal from office along with all civil

[6] As an aside: The very first statute enacted by Congress under the Constitution prescribed the form of oath for officials other than the President. *See* Act of June 1, 1789, ch. I, § 1, 1 Stat. 23. It seems fairly obvious that, while Congress can prescribe the form of oath for federal officials under the Necessary and Proper Clause, Congress has no constitutional power to prescribe the specific form of oath for state officials—a fact of which at least some members of Congress were well aware in 1789. *See* Gary Lawson, *The Constitution's Congress*, 89 B.U. L. REV. 399, 403–06 (2009). Congress thus began its existence by passing a flagrantly unconstitutional law.

officers of the government of the United States. The Constitution thus puts the President under the law and not above it.

Prior to Montesquieu's characterization of the legislative, executive, and judicial powers as distinct aspects of government, Englishmen believed there were only two great powers of government: Parliament's Power of the Purse and the King's Power of the Sword. Under the Constitution, Congress has the Power of the Purse and the President has the Power of the Sword. (The federal courts, as Alexander Hamilton explained in a passage that you will read later, have the newly minted Power of Judgment.) In prosecuting federal crimes, maintaining the public peace, and waging war against foreign nations, the President is the chief law enforcement officer and the Commander-in-Chief of the executive branch and of the Armed Forces.

This Power of the Sword sounds both impressive and ominous. It is both of those things. But what exactly does it involve? How much power does the Constitution actually give to the President? What can he or she do with that power? What legal mechanisms (other than impeachment, which we have already discussed) does the Constitution, or history, put in place to rein in that power? You may (or may not) find it surprising that after more than two hundred years, those questions remain among the most hotly contested questions in American governance. People disagree not just about the answers, and not just about the proper modalities to employ to find those answers, but even about where in the Constitution to look for those answers. In this course, we can only touch on what we consider the most important issues concerning presidential power. The topic could be (and often is) the subject of entire courses.

We begin, as we often do, with some essays from *The Federalist,* which offer some of the most important observations ever made about the presidency. These essays were all written by Alexander Hamilton, who in the Washington Administration acquired a well-deserved reputation as a strong advocate of expansive presidential power. In *The Federalist,* however, Hamilton was trying to assuage the fears of New Yorkers in the aftermath of the overthrow of a royal regime. In particular, one of the big decisions regarding the executive was to create a single President rather than a council of governors, as was the practice in many States. Consider whether Hamilton's explanation of the values of unity are persuasive. Are they more or less persuasive today than they would have been in 1788?

1. EXCERPTS FROM THE FEDERALIST PAPERS

THE FEDERALIST NO. 67 (Alexander Hamilton)

(March 11, 1788)

THE constitution of the executive department of the proposed government, claims next our attention.

There is hardly any part of the system which could have been attended with greater difficulty in the arrangement of it than this; and there is, perhaps, none which has been inveighed against with less candor or criticised with less judgment.

Here the writers against the Constitution seem to have taken pains to signalize their talent of misrepresentation * * *. [T]he intended President of the United States * * * has been decorated [by Antifederalists] with attributes superior in dignity and splendor to those of a king of Great Britain. He has been shown to us with the diadem sparkling on his brow and the imperial purple flowing in his train. He has been seated on a throne surrounded with minions and mistresses, giving audience to the envoys of foreign potentates, in all the supercilious pomp of majesty * * *.

* * *

THE FEDERALIST NO. 69 (Alexander Hamilton)

(March 14, 1788)

I PROCEED now to trace the real characters of the proposed Executive, as they are marked out in the plan of the convention. This will serve to place in a strong light the unfairness of the representations which have been made in regard to it.

The first thing which strikes our attention is, that the executive authority, with few exceptions, is to be vested in a single magistrate. This will scarcely, however, be considered as a point upon which any comparison can be grounded; for if, in this particular, there be a resemblance to the king of Great Britain, there is not less a resemblance to the Grand Seignior, to the khan of Tartary, to the Man of the Seven Mountains, or to the governor of New York.

That magistrate is to be elected for FOUR years * * *. In these circumstances there is a total dissimilitude between HIM and a king of Great Britain, who is an HEREDITARY monarch, possessing the crown as a patrimony descendible to his heirs forever; but there is a close analogy between HIM and a governor of New York, who is elected for THREE years * * *.

The President of the United States would be liable to be impeached * * * and would afterwards be liable to prosecution and punishment in the ordinary course of law. The person of the king of Great Britain is sacred and inviolable; there is no constitutional tribunal to which he is amenable; no punishment to which he can be subjected without involving the crisis of a national revolution. In this delicate and important circumstance of personal responsibility, the President of Confederated America would stand upon no better ground than a governor of New York, and upon worse ground than the governors of Maryland and Delaware.

The President of the United States is to have power to return a bill, which shall have passed the two branches of the legislature, for reconsideration; and the bill so returned is to become a law, if, upon that reconsideration, it be approved by two thirds of both houses. The king of Great Britain, on his part, has an absolute negative upon the acts of the two houses of Parliament * * *. The qualified negative of the President * * * would be precisely the same with that of the governor of Massachusetts, whose constitution, as to this article, seems to have been the original from which the convention have copied.

The President is to be the "commander-in-chief of the army and navy of the United States, and of the militia of the several States, when called into the actual service of the United States. He is to have power to grant reprieves and pardons for offenses against the United States, EXCEPT IN CASES OF IMPEACHMENT; to recommend to the consideration of Congress such measures as he shall judge necessary and expedient; to convene, on extraordinary occasions, both houses of the legislature, or either of them * * *; to take care that the laws be faithfully executed; and to commission all officers of the United States." In most of these particulars, the power of the President will resemble equally that of the king of Great Britain and of the governor of New York * * *.

The President is to have power, with the advice and consent of the Senate, to make treaties, provided two thirds of the senators present concur. The king of Great Britain is the sole and absolute representative of the nation in all foreign transactions. He can of his own accord make treaties of peace, commerce, alliance, and of every other description. * * * In this respect, therefore, there is no comparison between the intended power of the President and the actual power of the British sovereign. The one can perform alone what the other can do only with the concurrence of a branch of the legislature * * *.

The President is also to be authorized to receive ambassadors and other public ministers. This, though it has been a rich theme of declamation, is more a matter of dignity than of authority * * *.

The President is to nominate, and, WITH THE ADVICE AND CONSENT OF THE SENATE, to appoint ambassadors and other public ministers, judges of the Supreme Court, and in general all officers of the United States established by law, and whose appointments are not otherwise provided for by the Constitution. The king of Great Britain is emphatically and truly styled the fountain of honor. He not only appoints to all offices, but can create offices. He can confer titles of nobility at pleasure; and has the disposal of an immense number of church preferments. There is evidently a great inferiority in the power of the President, in this particular, to that of the British king; nor is it equal to that of the governor of New York, if we are to interpret the meaning of the constitution of the State by the practice which has obtained under it * * *.

* * *

The President of the United States would be an officer elected by the people for FOUR years; the king of Great Britain is a perpetual and HEREDITARY prince. The one would be amenable to personal punishment and disgrace; the person of the other is sacred and inviolable. The one would have a QUALIFIED negative upon the acts of the legislative body; the other has an ABSOLUTE negative. The one would have a right to command the military and naval forces of the nation; the other, in addition to this right, possesses that of DECLARING war, and of RAISING and REGULATING fleets and armies by his own authority. The one would have a concurrent power with a branch of the legislature in the formation of treaties; the other is the SOLE POSSESSOR of the power of making treaties. The one would have a like concurrent authority in appointing to offices; the other is the sole author of all appointments. The one can confer no privileges whatever; the other can make denizens of aliens, noblemen of commoners; can erect corporations with all the rights incident to corporate bodies. The one can prescribe no rules concerning the commerce or currency of the nation; the other is in several respects the arbiter of commerce, and in this capacity can establish markets and fairs, can regulate weights and measures, can lay embargoes for a limited time, can coin money, can authorize or prohibit the circulation of foreign coin. The one has no particle of spiritual jurisdiction; the other is the supreme head and governor of the national church! What answer shall we give to those who would persuade us that things so unlike resemble each other? The same that ought to be given to those who tell us that a government, the whole power of which would be in the hands of the elective and periodical servants of the people, is an aristocracy, a monarchy, and a despotism.

THE FEDERALIST NO. 70 (Alexander Hamilton)

(March 15, 1788)

THERE is an idea, which is not without its advocates, that a vigorous Executive is inconsistent with the genius of republican government. The enlightened well-wishers to this species of government must at least hope that the supposition is destitute of foundation; since they can never admit its truth, without at the same time admitting the condemnation of their own principles. Energy in the Executive is a leading character in the definition of good government. It is essential to the protection of the community against foreign attacks; it is not less essential to the steady administration of the laws; to the protection of property against those irregular and high-handed combinations which sometimes interrupt the ordinary course of justice; to the security of liberty against the enterprises and assaults of ambition, of faction, and of anarchy. Every man the least conversant in Roman story, knows how often that republic was obliged to take refuge in the absolute power of a single man, under the formidable title of Dictator, as well against the intrigues of ambitious individuals who aspired to the tyranny, and the seditions of whole classes of the community whose conduct threatened the existence of all government, as against the invasions of external enemies who menaced the conquest and destruction of Rome.

There can be no need, however, to multiply arguments or examples on this head. A feeble Executive implies a feeble execution of the government. A feeble execution is but another phrase for a bad execution; and a government ill executed, whatever it may be in theory, must be, in practice, a bad government.

Taking it for granted, therefore, that all men of sense will agree in the necessity of an energetic Executive, it will only remain to inquire, what are the ingredients which constitute this energy? How far can they be combined with those other ingredients which constitute safety in the republican sense? And how far does this combination characterize the plan which has been reported by the convention?

The ingredients which constitute energy in the Executive are, first, unity; secondly, duration; thirdly, an adequate provision for its support; fourthly, competent powers.

The ingredients which constitute safety in the republican sense are, first, a due dependence on the people, secondly, a due responsibility.

Those politicians and statesmen who have been the most celebrated for the soundness of their principles and for the justice of their views, have declared in favor of a single Executive and a numerous legislature. They have with great propriety, considered energy as the most necessary qualification of the former, and have regarded this as most applicable to power in a single hand, while they have, with equal propriety, considered the latter as best adapted to deliberation and wisdom, and best calculated to conciliate the confidence of the people and to secure their privileges and interests.

That unity is conducive to energy will not be disputed. Decision, activity, secrecy, and despatch will generally characterize the proceedings of one man in a much more eminent degree than the proceedings of any greater number; and in proportion as the number is increased, these qualities will be diminished.

This unity may be destroyed in two ways: either by vesting the power in two or more magistrates of equal dignity and authority; or by vesting it ostensibly in one man, subject, in whole or in part, to the control and co-operation of others, in the capacity of counsellors to him * * *.

Wherever two or more persons are engaged in any common enterprise or pursuit, there is always danger of difference of opinion. If it be a public trust or office, in which they are clothed with equal dignity and authority, there is peculiar danger of personal emulation and even animosity. From either, and especially from all these causes, the most bitter dissensions are apt to spring. Whenever these happen, they lessen the respectability, weaken the authority, and distract the plans and operation of those whom they divide * * *.

* * *

Upon the principles of a free government, inconveniences from the source just mentioned must necessarily be submitted to in the formation of the legislature; but it is unnecessary, and therefore unwise, to introduce them into the constitution of the Executive. It is here too that they may be most pernicious. In the legislature, promptitude of decision is oftener an evil than a benefit. The differences of opinion, and the jarrings of parties in that department of the government, though they may sometimes obstruct salutary plans, yet often promote deliberation and circumspection, and serve to check excesses in the majority * * *. But no favorable circumstances palliate or atone for the disadvantages of dissension in the executive department * * *. They serve to embarrass and weaken the execution of the plan or measure to which they relate, from the first step to the final conclusion of it. They constantly counteract those qualities in the Executive which are the most necessary ingredients in its composition—vigor and expedition, and this without any counterbalancing good. In the conduct of war, in which the energy of the Executive is the bulwark of the national security, every thing would be to be apprehended from its plurality.

* * *

But one of the weightiest objections to a plurality in the Executive, and which lies as much against the last as the first plan, is, that it tends to conceal faults and destroy responsibility * * *.

It often becomes impossible, amidst mutual accusations, to determine on whom the blame or the punishment of a pernicious measure, or series of pernicious measures, ought really to fall * * *.

* * *

It is evident from these considerations, that the plurality of the Executive tends to deprive the people of the two greatest securities they can have for the faithful exercise of any delegated power, *first*, the restraints of public opinion, which lose their efficacy, as well on account of the division of the censure attendant on bad measures among a number, as on account of the uncertainty on whom it ought to fall; and, *second*, the opportunity of discovering with facility and clearness the misconduct of the persons they trust, in order either to their removal from office or to their actual punishment in cases which admit of it.

NOTES AND QUESTIONS

1. In *The Federalist* No. 69, Hamilton goes out of his way to assure New Yorkers that the President's powers are more analogous to those of their Governor than to the powers of King George III. Is Hamilton's argument persuasive? *See* HARVEY MANSFIELD, TAMING THE PRINCE (1989). As we will see, once the Constitution had been ratified Hamilton immediately began arguing that the President's executive power in foreign affairs was comparable to that of the king of England.

2. *The Federalist* No. 70 argues that *energy* in the executive is essential to good government. How important do you think energy in the executive is either in foreign affairs or in controlling powerful domestic factions and special interests that can tie up a legislature?

3. *Duration* in office through a fixed term is an essential attribute of the American presidency that gives it energy and power. In *The Federalist* No. 71, Hamilton defends the presidency's fixed four-year term on the ground that this would make the president independent:

> DURATION in office * * * has relation to two objects: to the personal firmness of the executive magistrate, in the employment of his constitutional powers; and to the stability of the system of administration which may have been adopted under his auspices. With regard to the first, it must be evident, that the longer the duration in office, the greater will be the probability of obtaining so important an advantage. It is a general principle of human nature, that a man will be interested in whatever he possesses, in proportion to the firmness or precariousness of the tenure by which he holds it * * *. The inference from it is, that a man acting in the capacity of chief magistrate, under a consciousness that in a very short time he *must* lay down his office, will be apt to feel himself too little interested in it to hazard any material censure or perplexity, from the independent exertion of his powers * * *. It cannot be affirmed, that a duration of four years, or any other limited duration, would completely answer the end proposed; but it would contribute towards it in a degree which would have a material influence upon the spirit and character of the government.

THE FEDERALIST No. 71 (Hamilton). Is four years too long or too short? Is the limitation that the President can serve only two consecutive terms—added in 1951 after four terms of Franklin D. Roosevelt—a good idea? Some have proposed that the President should serve a single six-year term with a ban on re-election. Wouldn't this make every President both a lame duck and an officer who was too unresponsive to public opinion? Professor Juan Linz, among the most distinguished political scientists of the past few generations, has criticized the American system of fixed terms, saying that elections should be held when there is a big issue for the public to decide and not at arbitrary, random intervals. Would such a system give excessive weight to the passions of the moment rather than the views the public expresses at regular intervals? Consider in this regard some more of Hamilton's comments on duration of office: "The republican principle demands that the deliberate sense of the community should govern the conduct of those to whom they intrust the management of their affairs; but it does not require an unqualified complaisance to every sudden breeze of passion, or to every transient impulse which the people may receive from the arts of men, who flatter their prejudices to betray their interests." *Id.*

4. How important do you think it is that the Framers chose to create a *unitary* executive instead of an executive council of two or three or more leaders? What are the

consequences of the Framers' decision? Are you persuaded by the argument for a unitary executive in *The Federalist* No. 70? What doctrinal implications flow from the Framers' decision to give all of the executive power to the President? Can one imply from this that the President must have the power to veto all actions taken by subordinate officers in the executive branch? To fire all subordinate officers in the executive branch? Those questions will loom large shortly.

5. After reading these essays, think back to President Harry Truman's claim in the *Youngstown* case that the President had an unenumerated power to seize steel mills, which were private property, in the absence of legislative approval simply because of a foreign policy emergency. How plausible does Truman's claim of power now seem to you?

2. INHERENT EXECUTIVE POWERS?

Article II, Section 1: The executive Power shall be vested in a President of the United States of America.

Article II, Section 3: [The President] . . . shall take Care that the Laws be faithfully executed . . . .

Start with a seemingly simple question: Which clauses in the Constitution grant power to the President? Article I, section 7 plainly grants to the President a qualified veto power over legislation, but what about Article II?

Article II, section 2 describes some specific functions of the President: Commander in Chief of the military, supervisor of the executive branch (able to demand opinions in writing from subordinates), dispenser of pardons, co-maker of treaties with the Senate, and co-appointer of executive and judicial officers with the Senate. Three of those provisions explicitly say that the President "shall have Power" to perform the relevant functions, which certainly makes it sound as though Article II, section 2 is granting powers to the President. Article II, section 3 is then framed in terms of presidential duties: to report on the state of the Union, to recommend measures to Congress, to convene and adjourn Congress on certain occasions, to receive ambassadors, to take care that the laws be faithfully executed, and to commission federal officers. At least some of these duties, such as the duty to receive ambassadors, can plausibly be read as implicitly conferring the necessary power as well. Taken collectively, this is an impressive but very limited list of presidential functions. Do those two sections, along with Article I, section 7, exhaust the constitutional powers vested in the President?

Before trying to answer, take a close look at the first sentence of Article II: "The executive Power shall be vested in a President of the United States." Article I, remember, vests "[a]ll legislative Powers *herein granted*" in Congress. Article II's declaration of vesting contains no qualification. Does that mean that Article II vests in the President the full quantum of a particular kind of power called "executive Power," in addition to anything else specified in the Constitution? If so, what might that power involve? And why would the Constitution bother listing specific powers of the President if it was simply granting to him or her a lump sum of power called "executive Power"?

The stakes in the resolutions of these questions are enormous. If the President is limited only to the specific functions identified in Article II, sections 2 and 3 (plus the veto), a good many separation of powers disputes become very easy to resolve—against the President. On the other hand, if the President has some reservoir of power called "executive Power," then one must carefully ascertain precisely what that power involves. Does it make the President the functional equivalent of the English king, contrary to Alexander Hamilton's assurances to the people of New York? Does it include only a subset of what English law would have regarded as "executive Power"? If so, which subset? These questions matter in the real world.

More than 230 years after the founding, there is no consensus in our legal system about the answer to that basic question of the sources of presidential power. The statement is remarkable enough to bear repetition: More than 230 years after the founding, there is no consensus in our legal system about the answer to that basic question of the sources of presidential power. It seems odd that a country could survive and prosper without knowing even which clauses in the Constitution give power to the President, but that is exactly what has happened.

In the interests of full disclosure, both of us have spent much of our professional lives arguing that the first sentence of Article II—the "Article II Vesting Clause"—is a grant of "executive Power" to the President. *See* Steven G. Calabresi, *The Vesting Clauses as Power Grants,* 88 NW. U.L. REV. 1377 (1994); Gary Lawson & Guy Seidman, *The Jeffersonian Treaty Clause,* 2006 U. ILL. L. REV. 1, 22–43. Some very distinguished scholars disagree. *See, e.g.,* Lawrence Lessig & Cass R. Sunstein, *The President and the Administration,* 94 COLUM. L. REV. 1 (1994); Curtis A. Bradley & Martin S. Flaherty, *Executive Power Essentialism and Foreign Affairs,* 102 MICH. L. REV. 545 (2004). The Supreme Court has never definitively pronounced on this question, though some justices have expressed (conflicting) views, as a quick review of the opinions in *Youngstown* and of many of the opinions yet to come in this section will show. A bit later, we will share some of the reasons why we endorse the "Vesting Clause Thesis," as many people call the claim that the Article II Vesting Clause grants power. *See infra* pages 363–364. In the end, you of course might conclude that we are all wet on this point (as we might be on many others). This is one of many vital issues in constitutional law on which you will have to make up your own minds. As we go through the materials to follow, we will try to point out the implications of accepting or rejecting the Vesting Clause Thesis for the resolution of concrete cases.

The Vesting Clause Thesis is often confused with something quite different: The "Unitary Executive." The latter term, properly employed, describes nothing more dramatic than the fact that whatever powers the Constitution grants to the federal executive are granted *to a single President*. The notion of the Unitary Executive is agnostic on whether the President gets powers from the Vesting Clause or only from sections 2 and 3 of Article II; it says simply that whatever powers exist are vested personally in the President. We do not see any plausible arguments for thinking that the U.S. Constitution's executive is anything other than unitary in this sense, so as an original matter we do not regard the Unitary Executive as a controversial point worthy of attention—though, as you will soon see, modern practice often allows for dispersal of executive authority to actors other than the President. But the term "Unitary Executive" is often carelessly used to describe the Vesting Clause Thesis, and sometimes even to describe particular versions of the Vesting Clause Thesis that give a broad reading to the "executive Power." We will try not to make that mistake here.

If one decides to accept the Vesting Clause Thesis and thus to view the first sentence of Article II as a grant of power to the President, the next question is what reservoir of power is encompassed by the term "executive Power." At a maximum, it would include all powers possessed by English monarchs in 1788. We frankly find that position wildly implausible in the context of the U.S. Constitution, though pay attention to how often it shows up in the materials to come and has already shown up in some of the materials thus far. At a minimum, the "executive Power" includes the power to execute—to carry into effect—federal laws. (What does it mean to have power to execute the laws? We will say more about that a bit later. *See infra* pages 362–381.) Those laws capable of execution certainly include congressional statutes and the Constitution. Do they also include general law and court decisions? The law of nations? Natural law? Those questions, of course, arise even for people who reject the Vesting Clause Thesis. No one doubts that the President can (and must) execute the laws; the only question is whether the power to do so stems from the Article II Vesting Clause or from some other source, such as an inference from the Take Care Clause, which imposes on the President a duty to "take Care that the Laws be faithfully executed." In either case, one needs to know what counts as laws to be executed. The source of the power to execute matters only if one thinks that perhaps something more than a bare power to execute the laws might come from the Article II Vesting Clause if it is an affirmative grant of power. So, is there anything in between a bare power to execute the laws and the royal prerogatives of the King of England? *See* Julian Davis Mortenson, *Article II Vests the Executive Power, Not the Royal Prerogative,* 119 COLUM. L. REV. 1169 (2019) (denying that anything more than a power to execute the laws can be derived from the Vesting Clause Thesis). You have already encountered that question in *Youngstown.* Consider it again in a context also fraught with peril but on a more localized scale than was at issue in *Youngstown.*

The United States Secret Service is authorized by statute to protect the President, the Vice President, their families, and certain candidates for the presidency. *See* 18 U.S.C. § 3056 (2018). The Attorney General is statutorily authorized to hire persons to protect himself or herself. *See* 28 U.S.C. § 533(3) (2018). And under a statute enacted in 2002, the Supreme Court Police are authorized by statute "in any State, to protect—(A) the Chief Justice, any Associate Justice of the Supreme Court, and any official guest of the Supreme Court; and (B) any officer or employee of the Supreme Court while that officer or employee is performing official duties." 40 U.S.C. § 6121(a)(2) (2018). But what if that last statute did not exist—as it did not exist in the late nineteenth century? Does the President have constitutional power to protect federal officials if Congress does not provide statutory authorization to do so? From where in the Constitution would such a power come if it existed? Think hard about those questions in the following case.

In re Neagle

135 U.S. 1 (1890)

■ MR. JUSTICE MILLER * * * delivered the opinion of the Court.

This is an appeal by Cunningham, sheriff of the County of San Joaquin, in the State of California, from a judgment of the Circuit Court of the United States for the Northern District of California, discharging David Neagle from the custody of said sheriff, who held him a prisoner on a charge of murder.

On the 16th day of August, 1889, there was presented to Judge Sawyer, the Circuit Judge of the United States for the Ninth Circuit, embracing the Northern

District of California, a petition signed, David Neagle, deputy United States Marshal * * *. This petition * * * state[d] that said Neagle was imprisoned, confined, and restrained of his liberty in the county jail in San Joaquin County, in the State of California, by Thomas Cunningham, sheriff of said county, upon a charge of murder [of David S. Terry] * * *.

The petition then recited the circumstances of a rencontre between said Neagle and David S. Terry, in which the latter was instantly killed by two shots from a revolver in the hands of the former * * *. The main allegation of this petition is that Neagle, as United States deputy marshal, acting * * * in pursuance of instructions from the Attorney General of the United States, had, in consequence of an anticipated attempt at violence on the part of Terry against the Honorable Stephen J. Field, a justice of the Supreme Court of the United States, been in attendance upon said justice, and was sitting by his side at a breakfast table when a murderous assault was made by Terry on Judge Field * * *. [T]he allegation is very distinct that Justice Field was engaged in the discharge of his duties as circuit justice of the United States for that circuit, having held court at Los Angeles, one of the places at which the court is by law held, and, having left that court, was on his way to San Francisco for the purpose of holding the Circuit Court at that place. The allegation is also very full * * * that Marshal Neagle, in killing Terry under the circumstances, was in the discharge of his duty as an officer of the United States, and was not, therefore, guilty of a murder, and that his imprisonment under the warrant held by Sheriff Cunningham is in violation of the laws and constitution of the United States, and that he was in custody for an act done in pursuance of the laws of the United States * * *. *[Editors' Note: The circuit court below ruled for Neagle and directed his release; this ruling was appealed to the U.S. Supreme Court.]*

* * *

Section 753 of the Revised Statutes * * * [provides for release on habeas corpus of a prisoner who] "is in custody for an act done or omitted in pursuance of a law of the United States" * * *.

* * *

The history of the incidents which led to the tragic event of the killing of Terry by the prisoner Neagle had its origin in a suit brought by William Sharon * * * in the Circuit Court of the United States for the District of California, against Sarah Althea Hill * * *, for the purpose of obtaining a decree adjudging a certain instrument in writing, possessed and exhibited by her, purporting to be a declaration of marriage between them, under the code of California, to be a forgery, and to have it set aside and annulled * * *. [A] decree was rendered granting the prayer of the bill. In that decree it was declared that the instrument purporting to be a declaration of marriage, set out and described in the bill of complaint, "was not signed or executed at any time by William Sharon, the complainant; that it is not genuine; that it is false, Counterfeited, Fabricated, forged, and fraudulent, and, as such, is utterly null and void. And it is further ordered and decreed that the respondent, Sarah Althea Hill, deliver up and deposit with the clerk of the court said instrument, to be endorsed 'cancelled' * * *."

The rendition of this decree was accompanied by two opinions * * *. They were very full in their statement of the fraud and forgery practiced by Miss Hill, and stated that it was also accompanied by perjury * * *. Mr. Sharon * * * died * * * [before the issuance of] this decision * * *.

Nothing was done under this decree. The defendant, Sarah Althea Hill, did not deliver up the instrument to the clerk to be cancelled, but she continued to insist upon its use in the state court. Under these circumstances, Frederick W. Sharon, as the executor of the will of his father, William Sharon, filed in the Circuit Court for the Northern district of California, on March 12, 1888, a bill of revivor, stating the circumstances of the decree, the death of his father, and that the decree had not been performed; alleging also the intermarriage of Miss Hill with David S. Terry, of the city of Stockton in California, and making the said Terry and wife parties to this bill of revivor. The defendants both demurred and answered, resisting the prayer of the plaintiff, and denying that the petitioner was entitled to any relief.

This case was argued in the circuit court before Field, Circuit Justice, Sawyer, Circuit Judge, and Sabin, District Judge. While the matter was held under advisement, Judge Sawyer * * * found himself on the train as it left Fresno, which is understood to have been the residence of Terry and wife, in a car in which he noticed that Mr. and Mrs. Terry were in a section behind him, on the same side. On this trip from Fresno to San Francisco, Mrs. Terry grossly insulted Judge Sawyer, and had her husband change seats so as to sit directly in front of the judge, while she passed him with insolent remarks, and pulled his hair with a vicious jerk, and then, in an excited manner, taking her seat by her husband's side, said: "I will give him a taste of what he will get by and by. Let him render this decision if he dares."—the decision being the one already mentioned, then under advisement. Terry then made some remark about too many witnesses being in the car, adding that "the best thing to do with him would be to take him out into the bay, and drown him." These incidents were witnessed by two gentlemen who knew all the parties, and whose testimony is found in the record before us.

This was August 14, 1888. On the 3d of September, the court rendered its decision * * * against Sarah Althea Terry and her husband, David S. Terry. The opinion was delivered by Mr. Justice Field, and during its delivery a scene of great violence occured in the court-room * * *. Mrs. Terry arose from her seat, and addressing the justice who was delivering the opinion, asked in an excited manner, whether he was going to order her to give up the marriage contract to be canceled. Mr. Justice Field said: "Be seated, madam." She repeated the question, and was again told to be seated. She then said, in a very excited and violent manner, that Justice Field had been bought, and wanted to know the price he had sold himself for * * *. Mr. Justice Field then directed the marshal to remove her from the court-room. She asserted that she would not go from the room, and that no one could take her from it.

Marshal Franks proceeded to carry out the order of the court by attempting to compel her to leave, when Terry, her husband, rose from his seat under great excitement, exclaiming that no man living should touch his wife, and struck the marshal a blow in his face so violent as to knock out a tooth. He then unbuttoned his coat, thrust his hand under his vest, apparently for the purpose of drawing a bowie-knife, when he was seized by persons present and forced down on his back. In the meantime Mrs. Terry was removed from the court-room by the marshal, and Terry was allowed to rise and was accompanied by officers to the door leading to the marshal's office. As he was about leaving the room, or immediately after being out of it, he succeeded in drawing a bowie-knife, when his arms were seized by a deputy marshal and others present to prevent him from using it, and they were able to wrench it from him only after a severe struggle. The most prominent person engaged in wresting the knife from Terry was Neagle, the prisoner now in court.

For this conduct both Terry and his wife were sentenced by the court to imprisonment for contempt, Mrs. Terry for one month, and Terry for six months, and these sentences were immediately carried into effect. Both the judgment of the court on the petition for the revival of the decree in the case of Sharon against Hill and the judgment of the Circuit Court imprisoning Terry and wife for contempt have been brought to this court for review; and in both cases the judgments have been affirmed. The report of the cases may be found in *Ex parte Terry*, 128 U S. 289 and *Terry v. Sharon*, 131 U. S. 40.

Terry and Mrs. Terry were separately indicted by the grand jury of the Circuit Court of the United States during the same term for their part in these transactions, and the cases were pending in said court at the time of Terry's death. It also appears that Mrs. Terry, during her part of this altercation in the court room, was making efforts to open a small satchel which she had with her, but through her excitement she failed. This satchel, which was taken from her, was found to have in it a revolving pistol.

From that time until his death the denunciations by Terry and his wife of Mr. Justice Field were open, frequent, and of the most vindictive and malevolent character. While being transported from San Francisco to Alameda, where they were imprisoned, Mrs. Terry repeated a number of times that she would kill both Judge Field and Judge Sawyer. Terry, who was present, said nothing to restrain her, but added that *he* was not through with Judge Field yet; and, while in jail at Alameda, Terry said that after he got out of jail he would horsewhip Judge Field; and that he did not believe he would ever return to California, but this earth was not large enough to keep him from finding Judge Field and horsewhipping him; and, in reply to a remark that this would be a dangerous thing to do, and that Judge Field would resent it, he said: "If Judge Field resents it, I will kill him." And while in jail Mrs. Terry exhibited to a witness Terry's knife, at which he laughed, and said, "Yes, I always carry that," and made a remark about judges and marshals, that "they were all a lot of cowardly curs,' and he would "see some of them in their graves yet." Mrs. Terry also said that she expected to kill Judge Field some day.

* * *

* * * Many of these matters were published in the newspapers, and the press of California was filled with the conjectures of a probable attack by Terry on Justice Field, as soon as it became known that he was going to attend the Circuit Court in that year.

So much impressed were the friends of Judge Field, and of public justice, both in California and in Washington, with the fear that he would fall a sacrifice to the resentment of Terry and his wife, that application was made to the Attorney General of the United States suggesting the propriety of his furnishing some protection to the judge while in California. This resulted in a correspondence between the Attorney General of the United States, the district attorney, and the marshal of the Northern District of California on that subject * * *.

"DEPARTMENT OF JUSTICE, WASHINGTON, April 27th, 1889. JOHN C. FRANKS, United States Marshal, San Francisco, Cal.—

"SIR: The proceedings which have heretofore been had in connection with the case of Mr. and Mrs. Terry in your United States Circuit Court have become matter of public notoriety, and I deem it my duty to call your attention to the propriety of exercising unusual caution, in case further proceedings shall be had in that case, for the protection of his Honor Justice Field or whoever may be called upon to hear and determine the matter. Of course, I do not know what may be the feelings or purpose of Mr. and Mrs. Terry in the premises, but many things which have happened indicate that violence on their part is not impossible. It is due to the dignity and independence of the court and the character of its judge that no effort on the part of the government shall be spared to make them feel entirely safe and free from anxiety in the discharge of their high duties.

"You will understand, of course, that this letter is not for the public, but to put you upon your guard. It will be proper for you to show it to the district attorney if deemed best.

"Yours, truly, W. H. H. MILLER, *Attorney General.*"

[Editors' Note: There was considerable additional correspondence back and forth between the U.S. Marshal and Attorney General Miller, with the latter making special funds available to hire extra help to protect Justice Field and other federal judges from the wrath of Mr. and Mrs. Terry.]

* * *

The result of this correspondence was that [the U.S.] Marshal Franks appointed Mr. Neagle a deputy marshal for the Northern District of California, and gave him special instructions to attend upon Judge Field both in court and while going from one court to another, and protect him from any assault that might be attempted upon him by Terry and wife. Accordingly, when Judge Field went from San Francisco to Los Angeles to hold the Circuit Court of the United States at that place, Mr. Neagle accompanied him, remained with him for the few days that he was engaged in the business of that court, and returned with him to San Francisco.

It appears from the uncontradicted evidence in the case that while the sleeping-car, in which were Justice Field and Mr. Neagle, stopped a moment in the early morning at Fresno, Terry and wife got on the train. The fact that they were on the train became known to Neagle, and he held a conversation with the conductor as to what peace officers could be found at Lathrop, where the train stopped for breakfast, and the conductor was requested to telegraph to the proper officers of that place to have a constable or some peace officer on the ground when the train should arrive, anticipating that there might be violence attempted by Terry upon Judge Field. It is sufficient to say that this resulted in no available aid to assist in keeping the peace. When the train arrived, Neagle informed Judge Field of the presence of Terry on the train, and advised him to remain and take his breakfast in the car. This the judge refused to do, and he and Neagle got out of the car, and went into the dining-room, and took seats beside each other in the place assigned them by the person in charge of the breakfast-room, and very shortly after this Terry and wife came into the room; and Mrs. Terry, recognizing Judge Field, turned and left in great haste, while Terry passed beyond where Judge Field and Neagle were and took his seat at another table.

It was afterwards ascertained that Mrs. Terry went to the car, and took from it a satchel in which was a revolver. Before she returned to the eating-room, Terry arose from his seat; and, passing around the table in such a way as brought him behind Judge Field, who did not see him or notice him, came up where he was sitting with his feet under the table, and struck him a blow on the side of his face, which was repeated on the other side. He also had his arm drawn back and his fist doubled up, apparently to strike a third blow, when Neagle, who had been observing him all this time, arose from his seat with his revolver in his hand, and in a very loud voice shouted out: "Stop! stop! I am an officer!" Upon this Terry turned his attention to Neagle, and, as Neagle testifies, seemed to recognize him, and immediately turned his hand to thrust it in his bosom, as Neagle felt sure, with the purpose of drawing a bowie-knife. At this instant Neagle fired two shots from his revolver into the body of Terry, who immediately sank down and died in a few minutes.

Mrs. Terry entered the room with the satchel in her hand just after Terry sank to the floor. She rushed up to the place where he was, threw herself upon his body, made loud exclamations and moans, and commenced inviting the spectators to avenge her wrong upon Field and Neagle. She appeared to be carried away by passion, and in a very earnest manner charged that Field and Neagle had murdered her husband intentionally, and shortly afterwards she appealed to the persons present to examine the body of Terry to see that he had no weapons. This she did once or twice. The satchel which she had, being taken from her, was found to contain a revolver.

These are the material circumstances produced in evidence before the Circuit Court on the hearing of this *habeas corpus* case. It is but a short sketch of a history which is given in over five hundred pages in the record, but we think it is sufficient to enable us to apply the law of the case to the question before us. Without a more minute discussion of this testimony, it produces upon us the conviction of a settled purpose on the part of Terry and his wife, amounting to a conspiracy, to murder Justice Field. And we are quite sure that if Neagle had been merely a brother or a friend of Judge Field, travelling with him, and aware of all the previous relations of Terry to the Judge,—as he was,—of his bitter animosity, his declared purpose to have revenge even to the point of killing him, he would have been justified in what he did in defense of Mr. Justice Field's life, and possibly of his own.

But such a justification would be a proper subject for consideration on a trial of the case for murder in the courts of the State of California, and there exists no authority in the courts of the United States to discharge the prisoner while held in custody by the State authorities for this offense, unless there be found in aid of the defense of the prisoner some element of power and authority asserted under the government of the United States.

This element is said to be found in the facts that Mr. Justice Field, when attacked, was in the immediate discharge of his duty as judge of the Circuit Courts of the United States within California; that the assault upon him grew out of the animosity of Terry and wife, arising out of the previous discharge of his duty as circuit justice in the case, for which they were committed for contempt of court; and that the deputy marshal of the United States, who killed Terry in defense of Field's life, was charged with a duty under the law of the United States to protect Field from the violence which Terry was inflicting, and which was intended to lead to Field's death.

To the inquiry whether this proposition is sustained by law and the facts which we have recited, we now address ourselves.

Mr. Justice Field was a member of the Supreme Court of the United States * * *.

* * *

* * * [Federal law] declares that it "shall be the duty of the chief justice and of each justice of the Supreme Court, to attend at least one term of the Circuit Court, in each district of the circuit to which he is allotted during every period of two years."

* * *

The justices of the Supreme Court have been members of the Circuit Courts of the United States ever since the organization of the government, and their attendance of the circuit and appearance at the places where the courts are held has always been thought to be a matter of importance. In order to enable him to perform this duty, Mr. Justice Field had to travel each year from Washington City, near the Atlantic coast, to San Francisco, on the Pacific coast. In doing this he was as much in the discharge of a duty imposed upon him by law as he was while sitting in court and trying causes. There are many duties which the judge performs outside of the court-room where he sits to pronounce judgment or to preside over a trial. The statutes of the United States, and the established practice of the courts, require that the judge perform a very large share of his judicial labors at what is called "chambers." This chamber work is as important as necessary, as much a discharge of his official duty as that performed in the court-house. Important cases are often argued before the judge at any place convenient to the parties concerned, and a decision of the judge is arrived at by investigations made in his own room, wherever he may be, and it is idle to say that this is not as much the performance of judicial duty as the filing of the judgment with the clerk, and the announcement of the result in open court.

So it is impossible for a justice of the Supreme Court of the United States, who is compelled by the obligations of duty to be so much in Washington City, to discharge his duties of attendance on the Circuit Courts * * * without travelling in the usual and most convenient modes of doing it to the place where the court is to be held. This duty is as much an obligation imposed by the law as if it had said in words: "The justices of the Supreme Court shall go from Washington City to the place where their terms are held every year."

Justice Field had not only left Washington, and travelled the three thousand miles or more which was necessary to reach his circuit, but he had entered upon the duties of that circuit, had held the court at San Francisco for some time; and, taking a short leave of that court, had gone down to Los Angeles, another place where a court was to be held, and sat as a judge there for several days, hearing cases and rendering decisions. It was in the necessary act of returning from Los Angeles to San Francisco, by the usual mode of travel between the two places, where his court was still in session, and where he was required to be, that he was assaulted by Terry in the manner which we have already described.

* * *

It is urged, however, that there exists no statute authorizing any such protection as that which Neagle was instructed to give Judge Field in the present case, and indeed no protection whatever against a vindictive or malicious assault growing out of the faithful discharge of his official duties; and that the language of [the relevant federal habeas corpus statute] * * * makes it necessary that upon this occasion it should be shown that the act for which Neagle is imprisoned was done by virtue of an act of Congress. It is not supposed that any special act of Congress exists which authorizes the marshals or deputy marshals of the United States in express terms to accompany the judges of the Supreme Court through their circuits, and act as a body-guard to them, to defend them against malicious assaults against their persons. But we are of opinion that this view of the statute is an unwarranted restriction of the meaning of a law designed to extend in a liberal manner the benefit of the writ of *habeas corpus* to persons imprisoned for the performance of their duty. And we are satisfied that, if it was the duty of Neagle, under the circumstances, a duty which could only arise under the laws of the United States, to defend Mr. Justice Field from a murderous attack upon him, he brings himself within the meaning of the [habeas law] * * *.

In the view we take of the Constitution of the United States, any obligation fairly and properly inferable from that instrument, or any duty of the marshal to be derived from the general scope of his duties under the laws of the United States, is a "law" * * *. It would be a great reproach to the system of government of the United States, declared to be within its sphere sovereign and supreme, if there is to be found within the domain of its powers no means of protecting the judges, in the conscientious and faithful discharge of their duties, from the malice and hatred of those upon whom their judgments may operate unfavorably.

* * *

If a person in the situation of Judge Field could have no other guaranty of his personal safety while engaged in the conscientious discharge of a disagreeable duty, than the fact that if he was murdered his murderer would be subject to the laws of a State and by those laws could be punished, the security would be very insufficient. The plan which Terry and wife had in mind, of insulting him and assaulting him, and drawing him into a defensive physical contest, in the course of which they would slay him, shows the little value of such remedies. We do not believe that the government of the United States is thus inefficient, or that its Constitution and laws have left the high officers of the government so defenseless and unprotected.

* * *

* * * Where, then, are we to look for the protection which we have shown Judge Field was entitled to when engaged in the discharge of his official duties? Not to the courts of the United States; because, as has been more than once said in this court, in the division of the powers of government between the three great departments, executive, legislative, and judicial, the judicial is the weakest for the purposes of self-protection and for the enforcement of the powers which it exercises. The ministerial officers through whom its commands must be executed are marshals of the United States, and belong emphatically to the executive department of the government. They are appointed by the President, with the advice and consent of the Senate. They are removable from office at his pleasure. They are subjected by act of Congress to the supervision and control of the Department of Justice, in the hands of one of the cabinet officers of the President, and their compensation is provided by acts of Congress. The same may be said of the district attorneys of the United States, who prosecute and defend the claims of the government in the courts.

The legislative branch of the government can only protect the judicial officers by the enactment of laws for that purpose, and the argument we are now combating assumes that no such law has been passed by Congress.

If we turn to the executive department of the government, we find a very different condition of affairs. The Constitution, section 3, Article 2, declares that the President "shall take care that the laws be faithfully executed;" and he is provided with the means of fulfilling this obligation by his authority to commission all the officers of the United States, and, by and with the advice and consent of the Senate, to appoint the most important of them and to fill vacancies. He is declared to be the commander-in-chief of the army and navy of the United States. The duties which are thus imposed upon him he is further enabled to perform by the recognition in the Constitution, and the creation by acts of Congress, of executive departments, which have varied in number from four or five to seven or eight, who are familiarly called cabinet ministers. These aid him in the performance of the great duties of his office, and represent him in a thousand acts to which it can hardly be supposed his personal attention is called, and thus he is enabled to fulfill the duty of his great department, expressed in the phrase that "he shall take care that the laws be faithfully executed."

Is this duty limited to the enforcement of acts of Congress or of treaties of the United States according to their *express terms*, or does it include the rights, duties, and obligations growing out of the Constitution itself, our international relations, and all the protection implied by the nature of the government under the Constitution?

One of the most remarkable episodes in the history of our foreign relations, and which has become an attractive historical incident, is the case of Martin Koszta, a native of Hungary, who, though not fully a naturalized citizen of the United States, had in due form of law made his declaration of intention to become a citizen. While in Smyrna he was seized by command of the Austrian consul general at that place, and carried on board the Hussar, an Austrian vessel, where he was held in close confinement. Captain Ingraham, in command of the American sloop of war St. Louis, arriving in port at that critical period, and ascertaining that Koszta had with him his naturalization papers, demanded his surrender to him, and was compelled to train his guns upon the Austrian vessel before his demands were complied with. It was, however, to prevent bloodshed, agreed that Koszta should be placed in the hands of the French consul subject to the result of diplomatic negotiations between Austria and the United States. The celebrated correspondence between Mr. Marcy, Secretary of State, and Chevalier Hulsemann, the Austrian minister at Washington, which arose out of this affair and resulted in the release and restoration to liberty of Koszta, attracted a great deal of public attention, and the position assumed by Mr. Marcy met the approval of the country and of Congress, who voted a gold medal to Captain Ingraham for his conduct in the affair. Upon what act of Congress then existing can any one lay his finger in support of the action of our government in this matter?

So, if the President or the Postmaster General is advised that the mails of the United States, possibly carrying treasure, are liable to be robbed and the mail carriers assaulted and murdered, in any particular region of country, who can doubt the authority of the President or of one of the executive departments under him to make an order for the protection of the mail and of the persons and lives of its carriers, by doing exactly what was done in the case of Mr. Justice Field, namely, providing a sufficient guard, whether it be by soldiers of the army or by marshals of the United States * * * to secure the safe performance of the duty of carrying the mail wherever it may be intended to go?

* * *

We cannot doubt the power of the President to take measures for the protection of a judge of one of the courts of the United States who, while in the discharge of the duties of his office, is threatened with a personal attack which may probably result in his death, and we think it clear that where this protection is to be afforded through the civil power, the Department of Justice is the proper one to set in motion the necessary means of protection. The correspondence, already recited in this opinion, between the marshal of the Northern District of California, and the Attorney General, and the district attorney of the United States for that district, although prescribing no very specific mode of affording this protection by the Attorney General, is sufficient, we think, to warrant the marshal in taking the steps which he did take, in making the provisions which he did make, for the protection and defense of Mr. Justice Field.

* * *

* * * [I]t is urged against the relief sought by this writ of *habeas corpus* that the question of the guilt of the prisoner of the crime of murder is a question to be determined by the laws of California * * *.

The enactments now found in the Revised Statutes of the United States on the subject of the writ of *habeas corpus* are the result of a long course of legislation forced upon Congress by the attempt of the States of the Union to exercise the power of imprisonment over officers and other persons asserting rights under the federal government or foreign governments, which the States denied * * *. [W]hen, during the controversy growing out of the nullification laws of South Carolina, officers of the United States were arrested and imprisoned for the performance of their duties in collecting the revenue of the United States in that State, and held by the state authorities, it became necessary for the Congress of the United States to take some action for their relief. Accordingly the act of Congress of March 2, 1833, 4 St. 634, among other remedies for such condition of affairs, provided, by its 7th section, that the federal judges should grant writs of *habeas corpus* in all cases of a prisoner in jail or confinement, where he should be committed or confined on or by any authority or law, for any act done or omitted to be done, in pursuance of a law of the United States, or any order, process, or decree of any judge or court thereof.

* * *

* * * [I]f the prisoner is held in the state court to answer for an act which he was authorized to do by the law of the United States, which it was his duty to do as marshal of the United States, and if, in doing that act he did no more than what was necessary and proper for him to do, he *cannot* be guilty of a crime under the law of the State of California. When these things are shown, it is established that he is innocent of any crime against the laws of the State, or of any other authority whatever. There is no occasion for any further trial in the state court, or in any court * * *.

* * * [I]n the protection of the person and the life of Mr. Justice Field while in the discharge of his official duties, Neagle was authorized to resist the attack of Terry

upon him * * * and * * * he is not liable to answer in the courts of California on account of his part in that transaction.

We therefore affirm the judgment of the Circuit Court authorizing his discharge from the custody of the sheriff of San Joaquin County.

■ FIELD, J., did not sit at the hearing of this case, and took no part in its decision.

■ MR. JUSTICE LAMAR (with whom concurred MR. CHIEF JUSTICE FULLER), dissenting.

The Chief Justice and myself are unable to assent to the conclusion reached by the majority of the court.

Our dissent is not based on any conviction as to the guilt or innocence of the appellee. The view which we take renders that question immaterial to the inquiry presented by this appeal. That inquiry is whether the appellee, Neagle, shall in this *ex parte* proceeding be discharged and delivered from any trial or further inquiry in any court, state or federal, for what he has been accused of in the forms prescribed by the constitution and laws of the state in which the act in question was committed * * *.

* * *

* * * [W]e deny that, upon the facts of this record * * * deputy marshal Neagle, or as private citizen Neagle, had any duty imposed on him by the laws of the United States growing out of the official character of Judge Field as a Circuit Justice. We deny that anywhere in this transaction, accepting throughout the appellee's version of the facts, he occupied in law any position other than what would have been occupied by any other person who should have interfered in the same manner, in any other assault of the same character, between any two other persons in that room. In short, we think that there was nothing whatever, in fact, of an official character in the transaction, whatever may have been the appellee's view of his alleged official duties and powers; and, therefore, we think that the courts of the United States have in the present state of our legislation no jurisdiction whatever in the premises, and that the appellee should have been remanded to the custody of the sheriff.

* * *.

* * * We must * * * call attention again to the formal and deliberate admission that it is not pretended that there is any *single* specific statute making it, in so many words, Neagle's duty to protect the justice * * *.

The Attorney General of the United States has appeared in this case for the appellee, in behalf of the government; and in order that the grounds upon which the government relies in support of its claim against the State of California that Neagle should be discharged on this writ may fully appear, it is proper to give some of his most important propositions in his own language * * *. "We insist that, by the Constitution of the United States, a government was created possessed of all the powers necessary to existence as an independent nation; that these powers were distributed in three great constitutional departments, and that each of these departments is, by that Constitution, invested with all of those governmental powers naturally belonging to such department which have not been expressly withheld by the terms of the Constitution. In other words, that Congress is invested not only with expressed but with implied, legislative powers; that the judiciary is invested not only with express powers granted in the Constitution as its share of the government, but with all the judicial powers which have not been expressly withheld from it; and that the President, in like manner, by the very fact that he is made the chief executive of the nation, and is charged to protect, preserve, and defend the Constitution, and to take care that the laws are faithfully executed, is invested with necessary and implied executive powers which neither of the other branches of the government can either take away or abridge; that many of these powers, pertaining to each branch of the government are self-executing, and in no way dependent, except as to the ways and means, upon legislation."

* * *

In reply to these propositions we have this to say: We recognize that the powers of the government * * * may be found not only in the express authorities conferred by the Constitution, but also in necessary and proper implications. But while that is all true, it is also true that the powers must be exercised, not only by the organs, but also in conformity with the modes, prescribed by the Constitution itself. These great federal powers, whose existence in all their plenitude and energy is incontestable, are not autocratic and lawless; they are organized powers, committed by the people to the hands of their servants for their own government, and distributed among the legislative, executive, and judicial departments; hey are not *extra* the Constitution * * *.

* * * [O]ne very prominent feature of the Constitution * * * is the closing paragraph of section 8, Art. 1, in which it is declared that "the Congress shall have power * * * to make all laws which shall be necessary and proper for carrying into execution the foregoing powers, and all other powers vested by this Constitution in the government of the United States, or in any department or officer thereof."

This clause * * * contains the germ of all the implication of powers under the Constitution * * *. And that clause alone, conclusively refutes the assertion of the Attorney General, that it was "the duty of the executive department of the United States to guard and protect, at any hazard, the life of Mr. Justice Field in the discharge of his duty, because such protection is essential to the existence of the government." Waiving the question of the essentiality of any such protection to the existence of the government, the manifest answer is, that the protection needed and to be given must proceed not from the President, but primarily from Congress. Again, while it is the President's duty to take care that the laws be faithfully executed, it is not his duty to *make* laws or a law of the United States. The laws he is to see executed are manifestly those contained in the Constitution, and those enacted by Congress, whose duty it is to make all laws necessary and proper for carrying into execution the powers of those tribunals * * *.

For these reasons the letters of the Attorney General * * * invested Neagle with no special powers whatever. They were, if so construed, without authority of law, and Neagle was then and there a simple deputy marshal,—no more and no less.

* * *

NOTES AND QUESTIONS

1. *In re Neagle* seems like an easy case for finding an implicit executive "protective power," if there is one. *See* Henry P. Monaghan, *The Protective Power of the Presidency*, 93 COLUM. L. REV. 1 (1993); How can the President execute the law if law enforcement and federal judicial personnel can be gunned down? But that begs the question whether

such a "protective power" exists in the Constitution. What is its source? What does the Court in *Neagle* say is its source? The *Neagle* Court never once mentions the Article II Vesting Clause as a potential source of executive power. Does that count against the Vesting Clause Thesis? Does a defender of the Vesting Clause Thesis have to believe that *Neagle* was rightly decided? If one thinks that the "executive Power" includes a "protective power" in addition, or as or an adjunct or incident, to the power to execute the laws, does that equate the President with the English king?

2. Does the President's oath "to preserve, protect, and defend the Constitution of the United States" mean that the President has a power to "protect" federal officials, instrumentalities, and (as Abraham Lincoln argued) the Union itself? *See* Michael Stokes Paulsen, *The Constitution of Necessity,* 79 NOTRE DAME L. REV. 1257 (2004). Does it seem reasonable to you to read the Oath Clause as a source of power?

3. If *Neagle* is based on a supervening, non-textual principle of necessity, does that mean that *Youngstown* was inconsistent with *Neagle?* That *Youngstown* was wrongly decided? Was the necessity for presidential action in the absence of a statute greater in *Neagle* or in *Youngstown*?

4. Suppose in *Neagle* that the Attorney General had no appropriated funds available to send guards. Could the Attorney General, or the President, send them anyway, even though "[n]o Money shall be drawn from the Treasury, but in Consequence of Appropriations made by Law"? If necessity generates power, who decides what kind of necessity and how much power? Suppose that the President or Attorney General decides that the state sheriff in San Joaquin County is corrupt, so that the life, liberty, and property of American citizens in that county are not secure. Can the federal executive displace the local government and set up its own law enforcement machinery—all without any statutory authorization? Could they do it for the entire State of California? This last hypothetical is not at all hypothetical: Precisely that set of events happened in 1848, forty years before *Neagle* was decided. In *Cross v. Harrison,* 57 U.S. (16 How.) 164 (1854), discussed *supra* at page 168, the Supreme Court upheld the constitutionality of almost two years' worth of peacetime military governance of California in the absence of any statutory authority. The *Neagle* Court did not cite *Cross v. Harrison*. Should it have? Could the President invade Iran to disable its nuclear weapons program without congressional authorization on the grounds that such an invasion "protects" New York City and other parts of the U.S. from nuclear incineration? If so, is anything left of the separation of powers?

3. THE PREROGATIVE POWER: JOHN LOCKE, TWO TREATISES ON GOVERNMENT, CHAPTER 14 (1689)

WHERE the legislative and executive power are in distinct hands, (as they are in all moderated monarchies, and well-framed governments) there the good of the society requires, that several things should be left to the discretion of him that has the executive power: for the legislators not being able to foresee, and provide by laws, for all that may be useful to the community, the executor of the laws having the power in his hands, has by the common law of nature a right to make use of it for the good of the society, in many cases, where the municipal law has given no direction, till the legislative can conveniently be assembled to provide for it. Many things there are, which the law can by no means provide for; and those must necessarily be left to the discretion of him that has the executive power in his hands, to be ordered by him as the public good and advantage shall require * * *.

NOTES AND QUESTIONS

1. The Declaration of Independence is a list of complaints about King George III's many abuses of the prerogative power in the thirteen British North American colonies. There can be no doubt that the U.S. President thus does not have a prerogative power like that of English Monarchs. But English monarchs claimed, and still claim, some prerogative power to act in emergencies, when the legislature cannot be assembled, or to deal with unusual threats, like the ones David Terry made about wanting to kill U.S. Supreme Court Justice Stephen Field. The protective power of the President described above is a vestige of the prerogative power in the United States. Would the Framers have been surprised or unhappy about the result in *In re Neagle*? Is the result consistent with Alexander Hamilton's representations to the people of New York in *The Federalist*?

2. The President is the only elected officer of the government who is on call 24 hours a day, 7 days a week. Sometimes the crisis involves foreign policy and sometimes it involves domestic lawlessness. Congress is usually not in session, and the federal courts hear cases only after some delay. Anything that needs an instant answer tends to fall in the President's in-box, and he or she has to respond to it. The Constitution to some extent accommodates this by providing that the President "may, on extraordinary Occasions, convene both Houses, or either of them." U.S. CONST. art. II, § 3. Does this provision for emergency convenings of Congress (or just the Senate if the emergency involves an appointment or a treaty) foreclose inferring any kind of substantive emergency powers in the President?

3. The result in *Neagle* flows very easily *if* (1) the Vesting Clause Thesis is correct *and* (2) the substantive content of the "executive Power" includes a protective power. Does it? Suppose that one adopts the Vesting Clause Thesis. The Constitution thereby grants to the President the "executive Power." But what exactly does that involve? To say that the President has been granted a particular kind of power does not say *how much* power the President has been granted. If the "executive Power" includes only the bare power to carry laws, created by sources external to the President, into effect according to their strict terms, it matters very little whether or not the Vesting Clause Thesis is true, because no one doubts that the President has that power and duty, from whatever source derived. If the "executive Power" includes a full-fledged Lockean royal prerogative, the Article II Vesting Clause becomes one of the most potent provisions in the Constitution. *Neagle* would surely be an easy case on that understanding, but *Youngstown* probably would be as well—in *favor* of the claimed presidential power. If that is really the consequence of the Vesting Clause Thesis, one can understand why so many people are reluctant to accept the Vesting Clause Thesis; a presidency with a full-fledged royal prerogative seems hard to square with either the text or history of the Constitution. A third option says that the "executive Power" includes only the power of law execution, but that there is nothing "bare" (or "only") about that power, because it carries in its wake certain ancillary, or incidental, powers. In other words, the "executive Power" is purely a power to implement pre-existing laws, but that power includes, as a necessary and customary incident, the power to direct and control subordinates, to promulgate regulations, to determine enforcement priorities, to select among a menu of means by which the laws get executed, and to protect the machinery of law execution (including the courts). One scholar aptly calls this a "thick" conception of executive power, *see* Ilan Wurman, *In Search of Prerogative,* 70 DUKE L.J. ___ (2020), as opposed to a bare power to follow instructions from others. And a fourth option falls somewhere between the "thick" understanding of law execution and the royal prerogative. That fourth option claims that by 1788, especially after more than a decade of experience with distinctively American state constitutions, a term such as "executive Power" would be understood to

include a modicum of powers beyond law execution and its incidents, though certainly far fewer powers than would be possessed by a European monarch in a non-republican system.

We will revisit this thorny question about the scope of the "executive Power" when we come to the subject of foreign affairs. For now, the moral of the story is that thinking through Article II requires keeping straight in one's mind a number of distinct questions: (1) Is the executive department unitary or plural? (2) Does the first sentence of Article II grant to the President the "executive Power"? (3) If the answer to the second question is yes, what does the "executive Power" encompass? We turn now to those last two questions.

[Assignment 18]

B. THE PRESIDENT'S POWER TO EXECUTE THE LAWS

Article II, Section 1: The executive Power shall be vested in a President of the United States of America.

Article II, Section 3: [The President] . . . shall take Care that the Laws be faithfully executed . . . .

The Article II Vesting Clause, at a minimum, makes real the Framers' decision at Philadelphia to create a unitary rather than plural executive. If the Vesting Clause Thesis is correct, this clause literally gives to the President alone the power to execute the Constitution, laws, and treaties of the United States. In contrast to the Article I Vesting Clause, which gives "[a]ll legislative Powers herein granted" to a bicameral Congress, the Article II Vesting Clause gives all of the "executive Power," not merely those executive powers *herein granted*, but anything encompassed by the phrase "executive Power," to a single President of the United States.

Of course, to say that the Article II Vesting Clause "gives" anything to the President begs the question in favor of the Vesting Clause Thesis. An alternative account claims that the Article II Vesting Clause is simply a *designation of the presidential office*, which "says who has the executive power, not what that power is, just as the Vesting Clause of Article I says who has the legislative power (a Congress), while section 8 says what that power is * * *." Lawrence Lessig and Cass R. Sunstein, *The President and the Administration*, 94 COLUM. L. REV. 1, 48 (1994). Especially given that sections 2 and 3 of Article II enumerate functions of the President, just as Article I, section 8 enumerates powers of Congress, why would anyone think (as we do) that the Article II Vesting Clause gives the President something as ill-defined as the "executive Power"?

If you come away from this course convinced that no one should ever think that, you will be in excellent company. In addition to the many scholars who have taken that view, you may remember that, for example, Justice Robert Jackson maintained, in his concurring opinion in the *Youngstown* case, that the Vesting Clause simply specified the President's title and reinforced the unity of the office. Because it is impossible to work through Article II sensibly without coming to some conclusion about the proper meaning of its first sentence, we share some of the considerations that persuade us to endorse the Vesting Clause Thesis—more as a spur to thought and an exercise in the modalities of interpretation than as an effort at persuasion (though we will not object if you are persuaded).

Start, as always(?), with the language of the clause. It says that the executive power "shall be *vested*" in the President, just as Article I says that all herein granted legislative powers "shall be vested" in Congress and Article III says that the federal judicial power "shall be vested" in the Supreme Court and such inferior courts as Congress ordains and establishes. Why the word "vested"? This word comes from the Latin word for "clothes" or "vestments," and it is used here in the Constitution to mean that the president is "clothed with," and therefore possesses, the executive power. When bishops or judges or executive officials assume their offices and the powers that go with them, the ceremony conferring those powers is called an "investiture." Indeed, bishops and judges literally put on the robes or clothes of their offices and assume their powers at this time. This substantive meaning of "vested" is confirmed intratextually by the term's other appearances in the Constitution. The Necessary and Proper Clause allows Congress to implement "all other Powers vested by this Constitution." It is easy to see how one can implement substantively granted powers. It is very hard to see how one can implement a designation of office. The Appointments Clause, which we will discuss shortly, allows Congress to "vest the appointment" of inferior officers in certain officials. Again, it is hard to see how "vest" in this context can mean anything other than "grant power to." Thus, by "vesting" the President with the executive power, Article II, section 1 clothes the President with all powers that are not legislative or judicial or specifically allocated to other actors (or specifically denied to the President). What those powers are has been the subject of great debate, but we think that is the right debate to have. More on that shortly.

A second argument, grounded in both intratextual and structure-and-relation reasoning, compares the Constitution's three Vesting Clauses. The comparison of Article II's Vesting Clause with Article I's Vesting Clause is apparent—one limits the empowered institution to those powers "herein granted" while the other does not. But the more telling comparison is with the Vesting Clause of Article III. We are going to address Article III in the next section, but for the moment go read Article III to try to see if there are any other clauses besides the Vesting Clause that could arguably empower the federal courts to decide cases. There are none. The various grants of jurisdiction *limit* the range of cases over which the "judicial Power" extends, but by their terms those jurisdictional clauses "extend" rather than grant power. One extends something that already exists; one does not grant power by extending it to something. And if the Vesting Clause of Article III is a grant of power to the federal courts, then the similarly worded Vesting Clause of Article II must be a grant of power to the President.

At this point opponents of the Vesting Clause Thesis usually raise an objection: if Article II, Section 1 is a grant of the executive power to the President, then why doesn't Article II just stop right there? Why declare that the President shall be commander in chief of the army and navy, shall have the power to pardon except in cases of impeachment, shall have the power to make treaties with the concurrence of two-thirds of the Senate and shall have the power of appointment subject to Senate confirmation? There are several answers to this question. Article II, section 2 defines, explicates, and limits the general grant of the executive power in the Article II Vesting Clause. It makes clear that the President does not have the executive powers that British monarchs had not only to command armies but also to raise them, to make treaties without legislative consent, and to appoint executive and judicial officers without a legislative confirmation process. Article II, Section 2 thus qualifies the general grant of the executive power in the Vesting Clause in some specific and important ways. (For a clause-by-clause account of how Article II, section 2, and section 3 as well, clarifies and qualifies the executive power, *see* Lawson & Seidman, *The Jeffersonian Treaty Clause,* 2006 U. ILL. L. REV. at 28–34.) But, Article II, Section 2 does not describe every one of the President's powers. It does not mention the President's powers to execute the laws and to regulate foreign affairs—powers that have been claimed and exercised by every President since 1789. Article II, Section 2 clarifies the *nature* of presidential power and it limits it sharply from the executive power claimed by King George III, but it is not, and it does not purport to be, a comprehensive list of presidential powers the way Article I, Section 8 is such a list of Congress's legislative powers.

Notice that we have not presented passages from any founding-era figures to support the Vesting Clause Thesis. We have not, in other words, made arguments from history or original intentions. We could do so, but we think them much weaker—both in general and in this particular case—than the textual, intratextual, and structural arguments presented above. We have also not made arguments here from policy or consequences, though one of us has done so elsewhere. *See* Steven G. Calabresi, *Some Normative Arguments for the Unitary Executive,* 48 ARK. L. REV. 23 (1995). And we have not made arguments from precedent, though, as we will see later, both sides in the debate over the Vesting Clause Thesis can find case-law support for their claims. This obviously reflects our own sense of what kinds of constitutional arguments are most persuasive. If your sense of what kinds of arguments are persuasive is different, do you read Article II differently than we do as a result?

What about Article II, Sections 3 and 4? What role do they play in the constitutional system? Section 3 imposes a series of duties on the President. The President "shall"—i.e., "must"—1) deliver a State of the Union message to Congress, 2) receive ambassadors and other public ministers, 3) commission federal officers, and 4) "take care that the laws be faithfully executed." (This last duty means that the President is not permitted to dispense with or suspend statutes the way King James II did before the Glorious Revolution of 1688 in Britain.) Where does the President's power to fulfill the "take care" duty come from? Presumably, it comes from the Vesting Clause of Article II, the clause which makes the President the chief law enforcement officer of the government. Because these duties qualify the grant of the "executive Power," they help explain why Article II is not only one sentence long.

Article II, Section 4 makes the President and Vice President impeachable from office and removable by the Senate for treason, bribery, and other high crimes and misdemeanors. British monarchs could not be impeached by Parliament; only the king's ministers could be impeached. Section 4 makes clear that the President is under the law.

On any view of Article II, the President's "executive Power"—whether derived from the Vesting Clause or from inferences from Sections 2 and 3—consists of two main branches: first, the law-executing power; and second, a power over foreign affairs that extends at least to treaty-making, diplomatic relations, and the direction and control of the nation's armed forces as "Commander in Chief." (Whether the President's foreign affairs power extends beyond those boundaries depends largely on the fate of the Vesting Clause Thesis, as we shall soon see.)

We start with the law execution power. What does it mean for the President to execute the laws or to take care that they be faithfully executed? Law execution is a classic instance of the Power of the Sword. One executes laws by carrying them into effect, by force if necessary. The executive monitors, investigates, sues, negotiates with, arrests, and prosecutes those suspected of not following the laws. The executive power is quintessentially a power of enforcement—of the Constitution, statutes, treaties, and court judgments. (And the law of nations? And general law? And natural law? Hold those thoughts.)

Obviously, the President does not personally conduct more than an insignificant fraction, if any, of the actual law execution activities conducted by the federal government (though the President could do so if he or she wishes, given the incontrovertible fact of the Unitary Executive in which all of the "executive Power" is vested in the President). Virtually all executive action is conducted through subordinates: the roughly two and a half million civilian employees of the national government and roughly two million military personnel. If the President is going to exercise executive power effectively, it is almost surely going to be through ordering or supervising subordinates.

The Constitution specifies only one form of presidential control over subordinates: "he may require the Opinion, in writing, of the principal Officer in each of the executive Departments, upon any Subject relating to the Duties of their respective Offices." U.S. CONST. art. II, § 2, cl. 1. This seems trivial, but it prevents Congress from using the Necessary and Proper Clause to create executive officers who report only to Congress. Is this the President's only means of controlling the process of law execution?

Of course not. But having said that, it is far from obvious what other means the Constitution provides by implication. What forms of presidential control over executive branch activity are packed into the "executive Power"? Suppose that the President gives an order regarding the execution of the laws and the subordinates who are supposed to effectuate that order fail to do so (whether out of laziness, insubordination, or incompetence does not matter here). What are the President's options? Can he or she fire the subordinates and replace them with people who will hopefully (for the President) be more compliant? Can the President personally exercise the function (though that is probably impractical in the real world)? Do the President's orders at least have the effect of legally nullifying any action by subordinates that are contrary to that order? The Constitution is silent on all of these possible mechanisms of presidential control. But a logical consequence, we think, of the Framers' decision to vest all of the executive power in one President of the United States is that the President must have *at least one* of these mechanisms of control—and it is possibly that the President gets all three.

Since the text (beyond the Opinions Clause) does not expressly address the President's methods of control, what might the other modalities of interpretation say? One argument from structure and relation says that the President must have the ability to nullify actions by subordinates contrary to his or her instructions, because otherwise subordinates will be able to exercise "executive Power" that is vested by the Constitution in the President. *See* Gary Lawson, *The Rise and Rise of the Administrative States,* 107 HARV. L. REV. 1231, 1241–45 (1994). A textual argument might maintain that the "executive Power," read as a legal term of art, necessarily includes a power to remove executive officials that operates alongside

Congress's power to remove such officials through impeachment. An argument from consequences might say that the President must have the power to remove officials because otherwise the values of the unitary executive articulated by Alexander Hamilton cannot be achieved. By the same token, a devotee of the Progressive Era might argue *against* a presidential power to remove or direct subordinates, on the ground that law execution is best left to technocratic experts free from the baleful political influence of elected officials, including the President. And a textual argument against a presidential power to remove even insubordinate underlings could point to the six constitutional provisions for impeachment and to Congress's power under the Necessary and Proper Clause to create the duties, salaries, and benefits of offices, so why not the method of removal as well. Do you find it odd that the Constitution expressly says so little about a subject as important as presidential control of law enforcement? Is that because the answer was so obvious that no express provision was necessary?

The last question suggests that perhaps history could prove to be a useful modality of argument in this instance. If we turn to history, we find that early presidential practice reflects the view that the President has, and has always had, some form of power to supervise the execution of the laws. For example, President George Washington took office on April 30, 1789, and he immediately asserted control over all the executive entities of the government of the United States, which had existed under the Articles of Confederation, even though Congress had not yet given him any statutory authority over those entities. Thus, President Washington issued directives to the acting secretary of war, the board of treasury, the acting postmaster general, and the acting secretaries of war and of foreign affairs. He continued throughout his presidency to issue hundreds of written communications approving plans and actions, conveying directions about administrative operations, and making requests. Specifically, Washington started and ended criminal prosecutions by federal district attorneys (the forerunners of today's U.S. attorneys). And his Neutrality Proclamation was a major exercise of presidential power, both guiding foreign policy and giving orders to law enforcement personnel.

Presidents John Adams (1797–1801) and Thomas Jefferson (1801–09), also exercised personal control over some prosecutions. Adams personally directed that a prosecution be brought against Jeffersonian newspaper editor William Duane under the Sedition Act of 1798 even though no statute purported to give Adams the power to do that. Adams must have thought that his power to start this case was conferred on him by the Constitution. The Senate asked Adams to see to it that Duane was prosecuted, thus confirming that senators also thought the President had the power to direct the district attorneys. On two other occasions Adams specifically ordered that prosecutions be dropped, just as Washington had also done.

When President Thomas Jefferson took office, he directed the district attorneys not to bring any new prosecutions under the Alien and Sedition Acts (which he thought unconstitutional). He also directed that the prosecution of Duane under the Sedition Act be dropped. He wrote:

> The President is to have the laws executed. He may order an offense then to be prosecuted. If he sees a prosecution put into a train which is not lawful, he may order it to be discontinued and put into a legal train * * *. There appears to be no weak part in any of these positions or inferences.

35 THE PAPERS OF THOMAS JEFFERSON, 1 AUGUST–30 NOVEMBER, 1801, at 544 (Barbara B. Oberg ed., 2008). Jefferson also urged his Treasury Secretary to bring a prosecution in a case involving a schooner called *Sally*, and he directed that all federal common law prosecutions for libel be discontinued because he thought them unconstitutional as well. Jefferson was minutely involved in controlling the government's prosecution of his first Vice President, Aaron Burr, for treason. In sum, the early practice shows that Presidents Washington, Adams, and Jefferson all believed that Article II made them the nation's prosecutor in chief. For a comprehensive discussion of all 230 years of presidential practice, see STEVEN G. CALABRESI & CHRISTOPHER S. YOO, THE UNITARY EXECUTIVE: PRESIDENTIAL PRACTICE FROM WASHINGTON TO BUSH (2008).

By the time of the Monroe Administration, it was well established that presidents could control their subordinates in the executive branch. Nonetheless, it was at this time that the first suggestions arose of some limits on presidential power to direct and control. Monroe's Attorney General, William Wirt, expressed some hesitance in a famous case involving presidential review and control of the decisions of accounting officers as to whether the President could direct and control quasi-adjudicative and ministerial acts taken by lower-level executive employees. *See The President and Accounting Officers,* 1 OP. ATT'Y GEN. 624 (1823). Wirt's opinion was rejected by some of his successors as limiting presidential powers of direction too much; it was embraced by others. In particular, President Andrew Jackson's Attorney General, the future Chief Justice Roger B. Taney, took the position that the President may order a prosecution stopped. *See The Jewels of the Princess of Orange,* 2 OP. ATT'Y GEN. 482 (1831). Is presidential direction of accounting officers different in any way from presidential direction to stop or start a prosecution or some other executive function?

Presidents today continue to exercise broad powers of direction and control of the executive department. For example, for more than half a century, presidents of both parties have issued executive orders forbidding discrimination in government hiring and contracting. Every president since 1976 has also issued executive orders directing and supervising executive branch subordinates involved in regulation. The Office of Management and Budget (OMB) was created in the 1920s to help reinforce the unitariness of the executive branch by making it easier for presidents to control what executive branch subordinates are doing.

Presidential direction and control occurs through several mechanisms: executive orders, proclamations, national security directives, casual conversations, and presidential signing statements. Signing statements are issued by the President when signing a bill into law; they explain how the President understands the bill, and they direct law enforcement subordinates on how to use their discretion in executing the new law. They have been controversial since the Reagan Administration, which first made wide use of them as tools of governance. Notwithstanding the controversy, which has much more to do with the substance and policy of specific presidential directives than with the practice of signing statements per se, signing statements have become common.

1. THE POWER TO DIRECT NON-PROSECUTION

Presidents have historically claimed the power to stop prosecutions as well as the power to start them. To some that may seem a heresy, and there is no doubt that a presidential power to stop criminal prosecutions, like the power to issue pardons (which can stop prosecutions by being granted before trial or even before indictment), could be abused. As an historical matter, presidential power to direct non-prosecution is generally not abused in the United States today because powerful and normatively desirable traditions of non-partisanship have grown up around the U.S. Attorneys' offices. Occasionally, however, even in modern times cases have arisen where presidents have directed non-prosecution and have been acclaimed for doing so. Before reading the next case, which involves one such episode, you need a bit of background on a crucial but oft-overlooked aspect of federal law enforcement.

Even under the strongest version of the Vesting Clause Thesis, there is one aspect of federal law enforcement over which presidents do not have complete control: The initiation of criminal prosecutions. The Fifth Amendment provides, in part: "No person shall be held to answer for a capital, or otherwise infamous crime, unless on a presentment or indictment of a Grand Jury," U.S. CONST. amend. V, except within the confines of the military justice system. By both case law, *see Stirone v. United States,* 361 U.S. 212 (1960), and federal rule, *see* Fed. R. Crim. P. 7(a)(1), an "infamous crime" includes at a minimum any crime punishable by more than one year in prison—and perhaps more besides. That describes virtually all federal crimes. The "Grand Jury," a gathering of between sixteen and twenty-three ordinary citizens, *see* 18 U.S.C. § 3321 (2018), is a centuries-old institution that serves both investigatory and prosecutorial functions:

> First, grand juries are supposed to serve a "screening function": they review the prosecutor's case and decide if the government has presented enough evidence to justify an indictment. In forcing the government to present its case to a panel of citizens at an early stage in the process, and in giving these citizens the ultimate charging power, the institution has been likened to a "shield" against ill-conceived or malicious prosecutions.
>
> Second, the grand jury acts as an investigative arm of the government. It helps the prosecutor gather evidence by calling witnesses and issuing subpoenas to compel production of documents. When acting in its investigative capacity, the grand jury has been called a "sword" in the hands of the prosecution in the fight against crime.

Andrew D. Leipold, *Why Grand Juries Do Not (and Cannot) Protect the Accused,* 80 CORNELL L. REV. 260, 262–63 (1995). Thus, no significant federal criminal prosecution can go forward, no matter how much the President wants it, without an indictment by a grand jury. (About half the States still retain the same procedure, though many have abolished it in favor of allowing prosecutors to proceed on their own initiative, called "information," and the Supreme Court has not interpreted the Fourteenth Amendment to require the use of grand juries.) In modern times, the investigative aspect of the grand jury has predominated over its screening function, as grand juries normally defer to prosecutors; New York state-court judge Sol Wachtel famously quipped in 1985: "If a district attorney wanted, a grand jury would indict a ham sandwich." But suppose that the grand jury wants to indict the ham sandwich but the prosecutor does not? The grand jury can clearly stop a federal executive decision to prosecute, but can a grand jury *compel* a federal prosecution if the President and his or her subordinates do not want one? The President can always grant pardons, but if you are a potential defendant, would you rather receive a presidential pardon or simply not be prosecuted at all?

With those thoughts in mind, consider the issues raised by the following case, decided by an en banc (the full bench rather than just a panel of three judges) federal court of appeals in 1965. Think about whether the case involves anything more than simple interpretation of a statutory rule of criminal procedure.

United States v. Cox

342 F.2d 167 (5th Cir. 1965)

■ Before TUTTLE, CHIEF JUDGE, and RIVES, JONES, BROWN, WISDOM, GEWIN and BELL, CIRCUIT JUDGES.

■ JONES, CIRCUIT JUDGE:

On October 22, 1964, an order of the United States District Court for the Southern District of Mississippi, signed by Harold Cox, a judge of that Court, was entered. The order, with caption and formal closing omitted, is as follows:

> "THE GRAND JURY, duly elected, impaneled and organized, for the Southern District of Mississippi, reconvened on order of the Court at 9:00 A.M., October 21, 1964, in Court Room Number 2 in Jackson, Mississippi, for the general dispatch of its business * * *.The United States Attorney (and one of his assistants) sat with the grand jury throughout the day on October 21 and explained in detail to the grand jury the perjury laws and the Court's construction of such laws for their information. The grand jury heard witnesses throughout the day on October 21, 1964. On the morning of October 22, 1964, the grand jury, through its foreman, made known to the Court in open court that they had requested Robert E. Hauberg, United States Attorney, to prepare certain indictments which they desired to bring against some of the persons under consideration and about which they had heard testimony, and the United States Attorney refused to draft or sign any such indictments on instructions of the Acting Attorney General of the United States; whereupon the Court ordered and directed said United States Attorney to draft such true bills or no bills as the grand jury may have duly voted and desired to report and to sign such instruments as required by law under penalty of contempt. The United States Attorney was afforded one hour within which to decide as to whether or not he would abide by the instructions and order of the Court in such respect. At the end of such time, the Court re-convened and the United States Attorney was specifically asked in open court as to whether or not he intended to conform with the order and direction of the Court in said respects whereupon the United States Attorney answered that he respectfully declined to do so on instructions from Nicholas deB. Katzenbach, Acting Attorney General. He was thereupon duly adjudged by the Court to be in civil contempt of the Court and was afforded an opportunity to make any statement which he desired to make to the Court before sentence; whereupon the United States Attorney reiterated his inability to comply with the order of the Court upon express and direct instructions from Nicholas deB. Katzenbach, Acting Attorney General of the United States.
>
> "WHEREFORE, IT IS ORDERED AND ADJUDGED by the Court that Robert E. Hauberg, United States Attorney, is guilty of civil contempt of this Court and in the presence of the Court for his said refusal to obey its said order

and he is ordered into custody of the United States Marshal to be confined by him in the Hinds County, Mississippi, jail, there to remain until he purges himself of this contempt by agreeing to conform to said order by performing his official duty for the grand jury as requested in the several (about five) pending cases before them on October 21 and October 22, 1964.

"IT IS FURTHER ORDERED by the Court that a citation issue to Nicholas deB. Katzenbach, Acting Attorney General of the United States, directing him to appear before this Court and show cause why he should not be adjudged guilty of contempt of this Court for his instructions and directions to the United States Attorney to disregard and disobey the orders of this Court in the respects stated.

"The United States Attorney requested a stay of enforcement of this order and further proceedings herein for five days after this date to enable him to apply to the United States Court of Appeals for the Fifth Circuit for a writ of prohibition and such request is granted; and these proceedings and enforcement of this order in its entirety is stayed for five days, subject to the further orders of the United States Court of Appeals on said application; and for the enforcement of all of which, let proper process issue."

The United States Attorney, Robert E. Hauberg, and the Acting Attorney General, Nicholas deB. Katzenbach, have appealed from the order and they, joined by the United States, seek a writ of prohibition against the District Judge from enforcing the Court's order, and from asserting jurisdiction to require the Attorney General or the United States Attorney "to institute criminal prosecutions or to take any steps in regard thereto." The facts recited in the order are uncontroverted. No further facts are essential to a decision of the issues before this Court. Although the issues here presented arose, in part at least, as an incident of a civil rights matter, no civil rights questions are involved in the rather broad inquiry which we are called upon to make.

The constitutional requirement of an indictment * * * as a predicate to a prosecution for capital or infamous crimes has for its primary purpose the protection of the individual from jeopardy except on a finding of probable cause by a group of his fellow citizens, and is designed to afford a safeguard against oppressive actions of the prosecutor or a court. The constitutional provision is not to be read as conferring on or preserving to the grand jury, as such, any rights or prerogatives * * *.

* * *

It is now provided by the Federal Rules of Criminal Procedure that the Attorney General or the United States Attorney may by leave of court file a dismissal of an indictment. Rule 48(a) Fed.Rules Crim.Proc. In the absence of the Rule, leave of court would not have been required. The purpose of the Rule is to prevent harassment of a defendant by charging, dismissing and re-charging without placing a defendant in jeopardy * * *. The Rule also provides that "It [the indictment] shall be signed by the attorney for the government." Rule 7(c).

The judicial power of the United States is vested in the federal courts, and extends to prosecutions for violations of the criminal laws of the United States. The executive power is vested in the President of the United States, who is required to take care that the laws be faithfully executed. The Attorney General is the hand of the President in taking care that the laws of the United States in legal proceedings and in the prosecution of offenses, be faithfully executed. The role of the grand jury is restricted to a finding as to whether or not there is probable cause to believe that an offense has been committed. The discretionary power of the attorney for the United States in determining whether a prosecution shall be commenced or maintained may well depend upon matters of policy wholly apart from any question of probable cause * * *. It follows, as an incident of the constitutional separation of powers, that the courts are not to interfere with the free exercise of the discretionary powers of the attorneys of the United States in their control over criminal prosecutions. The provision of Rule 7, requiring the signing of the indictment by the attorney for the Government, is a recognition of the power of Government counsel to permit or not to permit the bringing of an indictment. If the attorney refuses to sign, as he has the discretionary power of doing, we conclude that there is no valid indictment * * *.

If it were not for the discretionary power given to the United States Attorney to prevent an indictment by withholding his signature, there might be doubt as to the constitutionality of the requirement of Rule 48 for leave of court for a dismissal of a pending prosecution.

Because, as we conclude, the signature of the Government attorney is necessary to the validity of the indictment and the affixing or withholding of the signature is a matter of executive discretion which cannot be coerced or reviewed by the courts, the contempt order must be reversed. It seems that, since the United States Attorney cannot be required to give validity to an indictment by affixing his signature, he should not be required to indulge in an exercise of futility by the preparation of the form of an indictment which he is unwilling to vitalize with his signature. Therefore he should not be required to prepare indictments which he is unwilling and under no duty to sign.

* * *

■ RIVES, GEWIN and GRIFFIN B. BELL, CIRCUIT JUDGES (concurring in part and dissenting in part):

The question presented arose pointedly when the foreman of the grand jury, in the presence of the grand jurors in open court, requested help from the court as follows:

"BY FOREMAN COWAN:

> "Judge Cox, we have under consideration three different matters, two we have concluded, the third is in the process of being concluded. On yesterday we asked Mr. Hauberg, the United States District Attorney, to assist us in preparing true bills in the manner that we have been served here before handing us these bills. Mr. Hauberg said that he could not do so without permission being given from the Department in Washington. We concluded yesterday afternoon by asking him to secure that permission and to have those true bills ready for us this morning. Mr. Hauberg now tells us that he has been instructed on all three matters not so to do. In other words we are at the position now in the event that we should vote indictment why we don't know what to do with it after that may or may not be accomplished."

The court then asked the District Attorney if he wished to respond. The District Attorney stated that he had been instructed by the Acting Attorney General not to prepare the indictments. The record discloses that the grand jury had heard evidence about certain matters which the Attorney General's office had already investigated and determined did not warrant prosecution. The grand jury had also heard evidence about matters of which the Attorney General had no knowledge and had made no investigation. The District Attorney disclosed to the court that the Acting Attorney General had directed him to request the FBI to investigate such matters, but that he had likewise been directed not to proceed in assisting the grand jury. In this colloquy the court stated to the District Attorney that the court considered the grand jury to be within its province in hearing the matters under consideration and in passing upon them pursuant to their oath. Accordingly, the court directed the District Attorney to disregard his instructions from the Department of Justice and to serve the grand jury by preparing the true bills as had been requested. The court then recessed and requested the District Attorney to communicate further with the Department of Justice and to advise that Department of the instructions of the court. After the recess, the District Attorney reported to the court that he had conferred by telephone with the Acting Attorney General who instructed him as follows:

> "I have been instructed 'As United States Attorney neither you nor any of your assistants are authorized to prepare or to sign indictments in the matters being heard on October 21 and 22 by the Grand Jury and I direct you and your assistants to refrain from doing so in your official capacity. If the Court should direct you to disregard my instructions on pain of contempt you should inform the Court that the Department will immediately apply to the Court of Appeals for a writ prohibiting such an order. You should request the Court for a stay of further proceedings pending the application and decision with respect to the writ of prohibition.' "

The court further inquired whether the District Attorney was refusing to obey the court's order to prepare true bills and sign the same as requested by the grand jury "in these cases presently pending and being considered by the Grand Jury." The District Attorney stated to the court as follows:

> "If the Court please, because of instructions I have received I most humbly and respectfully have to refuse to comply."

Thus the basic issue before this Court is whether the controlling discretion as to the institution of a felony prosecution rests with the Attorney General or with the grand jury. The majority opinion would ignore the broad inquisitorial powers of the grand jury, and limit the constitutional requirement of Amendment V to the benefit of the accused.

We agree with Professor Orfield that:

> "The grand jury serves two great functions. One is to bring to trial persons accused of crime upon just grounds. The other is to protect persons against unfounded or malicious prosecutions by insuring that no criminal proceeding will be undertaken without a disinterested determination of probable guilt. The inquisitorial function has been called the more important."

* * *

The grand jury possesses plenary and independent inquisitorial powers * * *.

A federal grand jury has the unquestioned right to inquire into any matter within the jurisdiction involving violations of law and to return an indictment if it finds a reasonable probability that a crime has been committed. This it may do at the instance of the court, the District Attorney, the Attorney General or on its own initiative, from evidence it may gather or from knowledge of its members.

* * *

The United States Attorney cannot, except in an advisory capacity, inquire into the merits of whether indictments should be found and returned in particular cases being considered by the grand jury. Only the grand jurors themselves have that power * * *.

* * *

The Attorney General insists that the prosecution of offenses against the United States is an executive function of the Attorney General [derived] from the executive power vested in the President to "take care that the laws be faithfully executed." U.S. Const. art. II, § 3. The short answer is that one of the most fundamental and important of the laws so to be faithfully executed is the clear and explicit provision of the Fifth Amendment to the Constitution that "No person shall be held to answer for a capital, or otherwise infamous crime, unless on a presentment or indictment of a Grand Jury * * *."

The Fifth Amendment adopted the grand jury as it had then been developed in England over the course of many centuries, and made it a part of the fundamental law of the United States for the institution of prosecutions for crime. Thus the grand jury originated long before the doctrine of separation of powers was made the constitutional basis of our frame of government. The same Constitution which separated the three powers of government adopted the institution of the grand jury. It follows that no nice distinction need be drawn as to whether the grand jury may perform some function of the executive department. As well said by the Seventh Circuit:

> "While the grand jury is, in a sense, a part of our court system, when exercising its traditional functions it possesses an independence which is unique. Its authority is derived from none of the three basic divisions of our government, but rather directly from the people themselves."

In re April 1956 Term Grand Jury, 239 F.2d 263, 269 (7th Cir. 1956).

* * *

The grand jury may be permitted to function in its traditional sphere, while at the same time enforcing the separation of powers doctrine as between the executive and judicial branches of the government. This can best be done, indeed, it is mandatory, by requiring the United States Attorney to assist the grand jury in preparing indictments which they wish to consider or return, and by requiring the United States Attorney to sign any indictment that is to be returned. Then, once the indictment is returned, the Attorney General or the United States Attorney can refuse to go forward. That refusal will, of course, be in open court and not in the secret confines of the grand jury room. To permit the district court to compel the United States Attorney to proceed beyond this point would invest prosecutorial power in the judiciary, power which under the Constitution is reserved to the executive branch of the government. It may be that the court, in the interest of justice, may require a showing of good faith, and a statement of some rational basis for dismissal. In the unlikely event of bad faith or irrational action, not here present, it may be that the court could appoint counsel to prosecute the case. In brief, the court may have the same inherent power to administer justice to the government as it does to the defendant. That question is not now before us and may never arise. Except for a very limited discretion, however, the court's power to withhold leave to dismiss an indictment is solely for the protection of the defendant.

The United States Attorney is under an affirmative and mandatory duty to lend his assistance to a grand jury in making effective its decision to institute a criminal prosecution. When the grand jury insists on finding and returning an indictment, the Attorney General must acquiesce, even though its action may be contrary to the advice of the United States Attorney. The further prosecution of the case is another matter.

* * *

Looking beyond the present controversy, one can foresee the grave danger inherent in such a restriction of the powers of a grand jury. If a grand jury is prevented from returning an indictment * * *, the statute of limitations may permanently bar prosecution for the crime * * *. [T]he accused may flee or witnesses may get beyond the jurisdiction of the court. For all practical purposes, the case could be dead * * *. Worse still, this could be accomplished in the shadows of secrecy, with the Attorney General not being required to disclose his reasons. How much better is the constitutional system by which the grand jury can find and return an effective indictment upon which a prosecution for crime is instituted. At that point the power of the grand jury ceases. It is effectively checked and overbalanced by the power of the Attorney General, recognized in Rule 48(a), to move for a dismissal of the indictment. The court may then require such a motion to be heard in open court. Instead of a prevention in the shadows of secrecy, there would be a dismissal in a formal, public judicial proceeding * * *.

* * *

* * * [N]othing here said is intended to reflect upon the present Acting Attorney General, in whose integrity we have the utmost confidence. Memory goes back, however, to days when we had an Attorney General suspected of being corrupt. There is no assurance that that will never again happen. We are establishing a precedent for other cases; we are construing a Constitution; we should retain intact that great constitutional bulwark, the institution of the grand jury.

* * * We concur with the majority as to the dismissal of the appeal of the Acting Attorney General and as to the denial of the petition for writ of prohibition. [*Editors' note: We did not give you the majority's discussion of those essentially procedural matters, and you should not worry about them here.*] We would, however, affirm the judgment of civil contempt against the United States Attorney.

We therefore concur in part and dissent in part.

■ JOHN R. BROWN, CIRCUIT JUDGE (concurring specially):

* * * I do not agree that the District Attorney may ignore the efforts of the Grand Jury to the point of declining to prepare in proper legal form the indictment they have voted to return. On the contrary, I am of the view that the Court may properly

compel the District Attorney to act as legal scrivener to the Grand Jury. The Court may, therefore, order the District Attorney to prepare the indictment in legal form * * *.

* * * All must be aware now that there are times when the interests of the nation require that a prosecution be foregone. These instances will most often be in the area of state secrets and national security. With stakes so high, the safety of our country, and hence the security of the world, ought not to be imperiled by leaving the important decision to a body having no definitive political responsibility. And it is hardly realistic to suggest, as do the dissenters, that these factors may be evaluated by the Grand Jury. What will be the source of their information? How extensive will it be? How close will a Grand Jury session approach a presidential cabinet meeting? How will essential government secrets be kept when disclosed to persons none of whom as Grand Jurors will have been subjected to customary security clearance checks?

* * *

Putting to one side these factors which bear on the delicate nature of governmental decisions, there are technical reasons indigenous to criminal law which are equally compelling. Federal crimes are more and more for violation of highly complex statutes. Federal jurisdiction, indeed, whether the activity constitutes a federal crime, depend on intricate facts, many beyond the knowledge and experience of laymen composing the Grand Jury. The aim of the Grand Jury indictment as the means of protecting the citizen against the initiation of unfounded charges is hardly advanced by a rule that permits the Grand Jury on its own to initiate the prosecution when the conscientious District Attorney knows to a legal certainty that a federal crime cannot be established.

Finally, it seems to me incongruous to assert, as do the dissenters, that the signing of the indictment is a ministerial act having no function other than one of authentication * * *.

The fact is that the signature of the District Attorney has much more awesome consequence. Without a doubt that signature, together with that of the Grand Jury's foreman, is a formal, effective initiation of a prosecution. What it might be in the absence of the District Attorney's signature, we need not determine. With it, the whole prosecution has been started. And what was previously an unfettered discretionary right on the part of the executive not to initiate prosecution has now been set in motion and can be stopped only on the executive taking affirmative action for dismissal with all of the uncertainties which F.R.Crim.P. 48(a) generates.

But while I am firm that signature is a vital and significant act which reflects the exercise of an executive discretion to initiate prosecution—a thing here lacking—I am equally positive that the District Attorney has the duty to prepare the indictment when requested to do so by the Grand Jury. If this lacks logical consistency, I can only urge that an institution as old as the Grand Jury, implanted in the structure as idealistic as the Constitution, is one born, not out of logic, but out of the needs of history's rich experience. system not logical, rooted in history

* * *

There are a number of reasons why it is essential that the Grand Jury's conclusions be reflected in language which is legally sufficient and in proper form.

First, and perhaps foremost, in no other way can the Grand Jury effectively carry out its obligations as charged to it by the Judge. An important historical body, it ought not to have to cast about for recognition or, seemingly frustrated as it was in this case, mill around the courtroom or its environs in a sort of hat-in-hand helplessness * * *.

This leads to the second important reason. The powers of the Executive are so awesome in determining those whom it will not prosecute, that where there is a difference between the Grand Jury and the Executive, this determination and the resulting conflict of views should be revealed in open court. With great power comes great responsibility. Disclosure of this difference of view and the resulting impasse would subject this decision of the Executive to the scrutiny of an informed electorate * * *.

By following this middle course [of requiring the U.S. Attorney to draft but not to sign indictments at the request of a Grand Jury], we preserve fully the rightful independence of the Grand Jury in its inquisitorial role and the time-proved wisdom of the separation of powers which commits determination (and responsibility) to the Executive * * *.

For these reasons I concur specially in the reversal of the contempt order, the dismissal of the Acting Attorney General's appeal, and the denial of the writ of prohibition.

■ WISDOM, CIRCUIT JUDGE (concurring specially):

Too many opinion-writers are like too many cooks. I brave the danger of spoiling our broth only because the savory aroma of the competing dish the dissenters offer conceals its indigestible ingredients.

The dissenters show judicial craftsmanship of the highest order in writing persuasively about "the traditional sphere" of the grand jury while not turning up one case holding that a court may compel a prosecutor to prepare and sign a bill of indictment requested by a grand jury. Not one case in all the years between 1166 and 1965. I submit that the result reached in the dissent is the product of a misunderstanding of the historical meaning of "presentment and indictment," a failure to give effect to the difference between the sword and the shield of the grand jury, and an abstract approach that disregards the factual setting in which the issue is presented.

* * *

I

The Fifth Amendment requires the grand jury's "presentment or indictment" as a prerequisite to trial for a "capital, or otherwise infamous crime." This language provides no aid and comfort to the notion that either the grand jury or the court has the power to compel prosecution once the grand jury has exercised its accusatorial function. "In fact, confusion reigns as to just what a (federal) grand jury can do. Federal statutes are silent on the relationship which is to exist between a federal grand jury, the district court which summons it, and the United States attorney's office in the district. From 1789 to the present, Congress has made no definitive statement concerning grand jury powers." There is, however, "every reason to believe that our constitutional grand jury was intended to operate substantially like its English progenitor."

* * * The function of the early grand juries was "to discover and present facts in answer to enquiries addressed to them by the King" * * *. The "whole principle" of the early grand jury "was to get information useful to the Crown from those most likely to have it—the principle of the ancient inquisition" * * *.

From its beginning until its abolition by Parliament in 1933, the English common law presenting jury could act on its own knowledge, or on the information of others, or on the Crown's written bill of indictment. But only when this bill was preferred to the grand jury by the Crown and endorsed as a "true bill" was the accusation known as an indictment. This was the accepted usage when the Fifth Amendment was adopted * * *.

* * * Unless there is a bill of indictment preferred to the grand jury at the instance of the Government, there can be no indictment. It is entirely in the hands of the Government whether to submit an accusation to the grand jury leading to presentment in the form of an indictment and serving as the initial pleading in a criminal prosecution.

* * *

In sum, there is nothing in my view or in that of the other judges in the majority that would, as the dissenting judges assert, authorize Government counsel to "radically reduce the powers of the grand jury." The grand jury never had a plenary power to indict. It had a limited power to indict—after accusation by the Crown or the Government in the form of a bill of indictment preferred to the grand jury * * *.

The decision of the majority does not affect the inquisitorial power of the grand jury. No one questions the jury's plenary power to inquire, to summon and interrogate witnesses, and to present either findings and a report or an accusation in open court by presentment.

Finally, the decision does not affect the power of the grand jury to shield suspected law violators. By refusing to indict, the grand jury has the unchallengeable power to defend the innocent from government oppression by unjust prosecution. And it has the equally unchallengeable power to shield the guilty, should the whims of the jurors or their conscious or subconscious response to community pressures induce twelve or more jurors to give sanctuary to the guilty.

II

* * * If there is one aspect of the doctrine of Separation of Powers that the Founding Fathers agreed upon, it is the principle, as Montesquieu stated it: "To prevent the abuse of power, it is necessary that by the very disposition of things, power should be a check to power" * * * [T]he power of the executive not to prosecute, and therefore not to take steps necessarily leading to prosecution, is the appropriate curb on a grand jury in keeping with the constitutional theory of checks and balances * * *. The need [for such a curb] is rendered more acute if there is a possibility that community hostility against the suspected offenders, individually or as a race, may jeopardize justice before the petit jury * * *.

III

The prosecution of offenses against the United States is an executive function * * *.

* * *

The functions of prosecutor and judge are incompatible * * *.

* * *

The reason for vesting discretion to prosecute in the Executive, acting through the Attorney General is two-fold. First, in the interests of justice and the orderly, efficient administration of the law, some person or agency should be able to prevent an unjust prosecution. The freedom of the petit jury to bring in a verdict of not guilty and the progressive development of the law in the direction of making more meaningful the guarantees of an accused person's constitutional rights give considerable protection to the individual before and after trial. They do not protect against a baseless prosecution. This is a harassment to the accused and an expensive strain on the machinery of justice. The appropriate repository for authority to prevent a baseless prosecution is the chief law-enforcement officer whose duty, unlike the grand jury's duty, is to collect evidence on both sides of a case.

Second, when, within the context of law-enforcement, national policy is involved, because of national security, conduct of foreign policy, or a conflict between two branches of government, the appropriate branch to decide the matter is the executive branch. The executive is charged with carrying out national policy on law-enforcement and, generally speaking, is informed on more levels than the more specialized judicial and legislative branches * * *.

IV.

This brings me to the facts. They demonstrate, better than abstract principles or legal dicta, the imperative necessity that the United States, through its Attorney General, have uncontrollable discretion to prosecute.

The crucial fact here is that Goff and Kendrick, two Negroes, testified in a suit by the United States against the Registrar of Clarke County, Mississippi, and the State of Mississippi, to enforce the voting rights of Negroes under the Fourteenth Amendment and the Civil Rights Act. *United States v. Ramsey*, 331 F.2d 824 (5 Cir. 1964); *rev'd on reh'g*, 331 F.2d 838.

Goff and Kendrick testified that some seven years earlier at Stonewall, Mississippi, the registrar had refused to register them or give them application forms. They said that they had seen white persons registering, one of whom was a B. Floyd Jones. Ramsey, the registrar, testified that Jones had not registered at that time or place, but had registered the year before in Enterprise, Mississippi. He testified also that he had never discriminated against Negro applicants for registration.[20] Jones testified that he was near the registration table in Stonewall in 1955, had talked with the registrar, and had shaken hands with him. The presiding judge, Judge W. Harold Cox, stated from the bench that Goff and Kendrick should be "bound over to await the action of the grand jury for perjury."[21]

---

[20] Judge Cox found "as a fact from the evidence that negro citizens have been discriminated against by the registrar," although he found also that there was "no pattern or practice of discrimination." In its original opinion in the Ramsey case this Court noted the "testimony which witness by witness convicts Ramsey of palpable discrimination." United States v. Ramsey, 5 Cir. 1964, 331 F.2d 824, 826. In his opinion Judge Rives noted that "This case reveals gross and flagrant denials of the rights of Negro citizens to vote." 331 F.2d at 833. And on rehearing, this Court ruled that the finding that "there was no pattern or practice in the discrimination by the Registrar" was "clearly erroneous." 331 F.2d at 838. No one has suggested that Mr. Ramsey may have been guilty of perjury.

[21] When counsel for the State, Mr. Riddell, completed Mr. Ramsey's direct examination, and before his cross-examination, respondent Judge W. Harold Cox, who was presiding, stated:

In January 1963 attorneys of the Department of Justice requested the Federal Bureau of Investigation to investigate the possible perjury. The FBI completed a full investigation in March 1963 and referred the matter to the Department's Criminal Division. In June 1963 the Criminal Division advised the local United States Attorney, Mr. Hauberg, that the matter presented "no basis for a perjury prosecution." Mr. Hauberg informed Judge Cox of the Department's decision. Judge Cox stated that in his view the matter was clearly one for the grand jury and that he would be inclined, if necessary, to appoint an outside attorney to present the matter to the grand jury. (I find no authority for a federal judge to displace the United States Attorney by appointing a special prosecutor.) On receiving this information, the Criminal Division again reviewed its files and concluded that the charge of perjury could not be sustained. General Katzenbach, then Deputy Attorney General, after reviewing the files, concurred in the Criminal Division's decision. In September 1963 General Katzenbach called on Judge Cox as a courtesy to explain why the Department had arrived at the conclusion that no perjury was involved. Judge Cox, unconvinced, requested the United States Attorney to present to the grand jury the Goff and Kendrick cases, which he regarded as cases of "palpable perjury."

In October 1963 Goff and Kendrick were arrested, jailed for two days, and placed on a $3,000 bond for violations of State law for falsely testifying in federal court. After their indictment by a state grand jury, the Department of Justice filed suit against the State District Attorney, *United States v. Warner*, (Civ. No. 1219, S.D.Miss.), seeking to enjoin the state prosecution on the grounds that: (1) the States have no authority to prosecute for alleged perjury committed while testifying in a federal court; (2) the purpose and effect of the State's prosecution was to threaten and intimidate Goff and Kendrick and to inhibit them and other Negroes from registering to vote.

The Federal Grand Jury, originally convened on September 9, 1963, was reconvened on September 21, 1964. September 28, 1964, the Foreman of the Grand Jury advised the Government Attorney who was presenting matters to the Grand Jury that Judge Cox had asked the Foreman to hear several witnesses * * *.

* * *

October 20 Mr. Katzenbach talked with Judge Cox by telephone, reiterating the Department's position. He also instructed Mr. Hauberg not to prepare or sign indictments. October 22 the foreman of the grand jury in open court informed Judge Cox that Mr. Hauberg had declined to assist in preparing true bills. The United States Attorney stated that "the Department of Justice and the United States felt as

---

"I want to hear from the government about why this Court shouldn't require this Negro Reverend W. G. Goff and his companion Kendrick to show cause why they shouldn't be bound over to await the action of the grand jury for perjury. I want to hear from you on that.

"I think they ought to be put under about a $3,000.00 bond each to await the action of a grand jury. Unless I change my mind that is going to be the order.

"BY MR. STERN (Government counsel): I will be happy to reconcile their testimony.

"BY THE COURT: I just want these Negroes to know that they can't come into this Court and swear to something as important as that was and is and get by with it. I don't care who brings them here.

"BY MR. STERN: I understand.

"BY THE COURT: Yes sir. And I mean that for whites alike, but I am talking about the case at hand. I just don't intend to put up with perjury. That is something I will not tolerate. All right."

if that the law and the fact was not sufficient to constitute perjury and that an indictment thereon would be no good." Judge Cox said:

> "I here and now order and direct you to disregard your instructions from the Department of Justice and to prepare true bills or no bills as this Grand Jury may direct you to do and to sign those bills or no bills, as the Grand Jury may decide under penalty of contempt, * * *."

Judge Cox recessed court for one hour. During this recess Mr. Hauberg and Mr. Katzenbach conferred by telephone; the Attorney General directed the United States Attorney not to prepare or sign perjury indictments of Goff and Kendrick. Court reopened. Mr. Hauberg respectfully declined to comply with the court's order. Judge Cox forthwith adjudged him "guilty of civil contempt," ordered him confined to a jail in Hinds County, ordered the issuance of a citation to the Acting Attorney General to appear before the court to show cause why he should not be held in contempt; and stayed the order for a period of five days.

Against the backdrop of Mississippi versus the Nation in the field of civil rights, we have a heated but bona fide difference of opinion between Judge Cox and the Attorney General as to whether two Negroes, Goff and Kendrick, should be prosecuted for perjury. Taking a narrow view of the case, we would be justified in holding that the Attorney General's implied powers, by analogy to the express powers of Rule 48(a), give him discretion to prosecute. Here there was a bona fide, reasonable exercise of discretion made after a full investigation and long consideration of the case—both sides of the case, not just the evidence tending to show guilt. If the grand jury is dissatisfied with that administrative decision, it may exercise its inquisitorial power and make a presentment in open court. It could be said, that is all there is to the case. But there is more to the case.

This Court, along with everyone else, knows that Goff and Kendrick, if prosecuted, run the risk of being tried in a climate of community hostility. They run the risk of a punishment that may not fit the crime. The Registrar, who provoked the original litigation, runs no risk, notwithstanding the fact that the district court, in effect, found that Ramsay did not tell the truth on the witness stand. In these circumstances, the very least demands of justice require that the discretion to prosecute be lodged with a person or agency insulated from local prejudices and parochial pressures. This is not the hard case that makes bad law. This is the type of case that comes up, in one way or another, whenever the customs, beliefs, or interests of a region collide with national policy as fixed by the Constitution or by Congress. It is not likely that the men who devised diversity jurisdiction expected to turn over to local juries the discretionary power to bring federal prosecutions. This case is unusual only for the clarity with which the facts, speaking for themselves, illuminate the imperative necessity in American Federalism that the discretion to prosecute be lodged in the Attorney General of United States.

* * * As a matter of law, the Attorney General has concluded that there is not sufficient evidence to prove perjury. As a matter of fact, the Attorney General has concluded * * * that trial for perjury would have the effect of inhibiting not only Goff and Kendrick but other Negroes in Mississippi from registering to vote. There is a conflict, therefore, between society's interest in law enforcement (diluted in this case by the Attorney General's conclusion that the evidence does not support the charge of guilt) and the national policy, set forth in the Constitution and the Civil Rights

Acts, of outlawing racial discrimination. It is unthinkable that resolution of this important conflict affecting the whole Nation should lie with a majority of twenty-three members of a jury chosen from the Southern District of Mississippi. The nature of American Federalism, looking to the differences between the Constitution and the Articles of Confederation, requires that the power to resolve this question lie in the unfettered discretion of the President of United States or his deputy for law enforcement, the Attorney General.

My memory, too, goes back to the days, pointedly referred to by the dissenters, when we had "an Attorney General suspected of being corrupt." But I am not aware that we have had more lawless Attorneys General than lawless juries.

NOTES AND QUESTIONS

UNIQUE

1. Does a grand jury exercise judicial power or executive power or is it *sui generis*? What about a regular trial court petit jury? Juries of both kinds were developed by the Plantagenet kings of England only to advise them in criminal cases. Does that suggest that the majority is right in *United States v. Cox*? Think back to Alexander Hamilton's discussion of the executive power in *The Federalist*. How do you think Hamilton would come down in *United States v. Cox*? What are the constitutional arguments for a presidential power to veto the bringing of a prosecution? What policy arguments can be made on either side of this issue?

2. Did your view of the case change at all once you read Judge Wisdom's concurring opinion and understood what the trial judge and grand jury were doing? Does your answer to that question tell you anything about your own views of the appropriate modalities of interpretation? Under what modalities would those facts be relevant? Did Judge Wisdom present facts that should have been discussed in the other opinions as well? Are you surprised that those facts showed up in only one lone concurring opinion? Take all of this as a warning *not* to confuse court opinions—at any level of any court system—with history. Court opinions present truncated versions of facts—and those versions are not always accurate, much less complete.

[Assignment 19]

C. THE APPOINTMENT POWER: OFFICERS OR EMPLOYEES?

Article II, Section 2: [The President] shall nominate, and by and with the Advice and Consent of the Senate, shall appoint Ambassadors, other public Ministers and Consuls, Judges of the Supreme Court, and all other Officers of the United States, whose Appointments are not herein otherwise provided for, and which shall be established by Law: but the Congress may by Law vest the Appointment of such inferior Officers, as they think proper, in the President alone, in the Courts of Law, or in the Heads of Departments.

The President shall have Power to fill up all Vacancies that may happen during the Recess of the Senate, by granting Commissions which shall expire at the End of their next Session.

Virtually all executive actions are taken by one or more of the four-and-a-half million federal workers other than the President. The President may formally have some power of direction or control, but that formal power is useless if subordinates do not comply with presidential directives. It is therefore crucial to know how the government below the level of the President (and Vice President) gets staffed. Three constitutional clauses are crucial to that inquiry, only two of which appear above.

As we have already explained, *see supra* pages 287–289, the Constitution does not directly create the machinery of government other than the Congress, the President, the Vice President, and the federal courts. Instead, the Constitution leaves it to Congress to create positions in the federal government through its power under the Necessary and Proper Clause to make all laws "necessary and proper for carrying into Execution" all vested federal powers. Sometimes Congress creates those positions very specifically. *See, e.g.,* 31 U.S.C. § 301 (2018) (creating twenty-six key positions in the Department of the Treasury, including the Secretary of the Treasury); 28 U.S.C. §§ 503–06 (2018) (creating the Attorney General, Deputy Attorney General, Associate Attorney General, Solicitor General, and eleven Assistant Attorneys General). Sometimes Congress authorizes executive actors to create whatever positions they deem fit, subject to budgetary and other constraints imposed by legislation. *See, e.g.,* 7 U.S.C. § 610(a) (2018) (giving the Secretary of Agriculture power to "appoint such officers and employees * * * and such experts, as are necessary to execute the functions vested in him"). But in all events it is up to Congress either to create the positions or to provide necessary authorization for their creation.

That is a big change from the law of pre-Revolutionary England. One of the most formidable powers of the king of England in 1787 was his power to create offices with rents accruing to them and unilaterally to appoint individuals to those offices. English kings and queens could thus raise up individuals from nothing and make them great and important people by conferring offices upon them. Thus, the monarch was often described as being the "fountain of honors." He or she made and unmade "Great Men," like Sir Walter Raleigh. The English Revolution of 1688, while designed to limit monarchical power by the principle of parliamentary supremacy, led British monarchs from 1688 to 1776 to create lucrative offices and appoint members of Parliament to them to buy their favor. There grew up in the British Parliament, and in Great Britain itself, a corrupt Court Party, composed of officeholder members of Parliament, who could be counted on to do the king's bidding; and a Country Party, composed of those whose power came from outside of London, who had less money, and who opposed the king.

The American Revolutionaries were repulsed by the English practice of kings essentially bribing members of Parliament to vote their way on legislation. They came to see the royal appointment power as being primarily a tool for monarchical power in what they viewed as a systemic culture of corruption. The first American state constitutions, after 1776, thus took the appointment power away from the governors of the various states and vested it in either an executive council or in the state legislature. This led to weak, and ineffective, state governors and to all-powerful state legislative bodies. By the Dystopia of 1787, Americans had begun to think that their governors were too weak to keep the peace or to enforce the law. *Legislative* favoritism, and patronage in the making of appointments came to be seen as the key problem. Plural executive councils were viewed, by 1787, as being both too weak and too unaccountable to wield the appointment power.

The Philadelphia Constitutional Convention wrestled at length with the problem of the appointment power and considered vesting it in Congress, in the

Senate, and in the President alone, before settling on the compromise we are so familiar with today: presidential nomination and senatorial advice and consent. The Framers dealt with the problem of the executive "bribing" members of the legislature with appointments to executive office with the Incompatibility Clause and the Ineligibility Clause. *See supra* pages 273–274.

Obviously, the President does not nominate, and the Senate does not confirm, all four and a half million federal workers. That is because, for constitutional purposes, there are four categories of people who receive salaries from the federal government for working in the executive or judicial branches: 1) principal officers; 2) superior officers; 3) inferior officers; and 4) employees. The constitutional rules for appointment differ across those categories of executive and judicial officers. (The House and Senate get to "chuse" their own officers, *see supra* page 248, so legislative officers are not subject to the Appointments Clause.)

The Constitution only specifies an appointment procedure for "Officers of the United States." The vast majority of the people who work for and receive salaries from the federal government are not "Officers." They are *employees* whose appointments are not covered by the Appointments Clause. Collectively, they form the clerks, special assistants, secretaries, cafeteria workers, analysts, research staff, janitors, and so forth who together comprise all but a tiny fraction of the federal workforce. They may be appointed in any "necessary and proper" manner that Congress specifies by statute. They could all be hired by the President, as happened under the Jacksonian spoils system. They could be hired by other employees after doing well on a merit selection exam, as often happens under the various civil service statutes. Any responsible system (an irresponsible system would not be "necessary and proper") of appointment for employees is constitutionally permissible. Once appointed, employees can generally only be fired for cause under modern civil service laws and constitutional due process doctrine, which require articulated causes for dismissal or other discipline coupled with elaborate hearings and layers of appeal.

If a federal worker is an "Officer[ ] of the United States," however, their appointment is controlled by the Appointments Clause. The clause contemplates three different kinds of officers and three different kinds of appointment procedures.

The default method of appointment for all federal officers, of all descriptions, is presidential nomination and senatorial advice and consent. Absent a congressional statute saying otherwise, that is the only permissible form of appointment, other than the recess appointment process that we will address a bit later. For officers who are not "inferior" officers, this default mode of presidential nomination and senatorial advice and consent is the *only* permissible mode *regardless* of what Congress might say in a statute, again subject to the modest exception for recess appointments. If an officer is not "inferior," Congress has no choice regarding their mode of appointment. The Constitution makes the call.

If an officer is "inferior," the Constitution gives Congress an option. Congress can stick with the default mode of presidential nomination and senatorial advice and consent, or Congress can choose by statute ("by Law") to cut the Senate out of the process and allow appointment by *either* the President, the courts of law, or the heads of executive departments. Because this can only happen by statute, the Senate can never lose its default role in the appointment of inferior officers without its consent (though one Senate can effectively "consent" on behalf of future Senates by agreeing to legislation).

The Appointments Clause does not give a technical name to officers who are not inferior and who therefore *must* be appointed, regardless of congressional wishes, by presidential nomination and senatorial confirmation. The modern case law, as you will see shortly, calls them "principal" officers. This is very sloppy use of language that has the potential to work real mischief to the constitutional scheme. It assumes that there are two kinds of federal officers—principal and inferior—when in fact there are three.

Principal officers are the most powerful federal executive branch officers, and while the term "principal Officer" does not appear in the Appointments Clause, it does appear in two places in the Constitution, which both contemplate that principal officers are the heads of the Cabinet Departments. First, the Opinions Clause of Article II, Section 2 gives the President the power to "require the Opinion, in writing, of the principal Officer, in each of the executive Departments, upon any Subject relating to the Duties of their respective Offices." The language of the clause (*viz.*, "the") obviously assumes that there will be one and only "principal Officer" in each department. Second the 25th Amendment says:

> Whenever the Vice President and a majority of either principal officers of the executive departments or of such other body as Congress may by law provide, transmit to the President pro tempore of the Senate and the Speaker of the House of Representatives their written declaration that the President is unable to discharge the powers and duties of his office, the Vice President shall immediately assume the powers and duties of the office as Acting President.

U.S. CONST. amend. XXV, § 4, cl. 1. If the President disagrees with the decision regarding his or her disability, the issue of the President's fitness for office is resolved by Congress, with a two-thirds vote of both Houses being required to render the President unfit for office. *Id.* § 4, cl. 2. This provision does not strictly require that there be only one "principal officer" in each department, but that is the evident understanding. It thus seems clear that the "principal Officers" contemplated by the Opinions Clause and the Twenty Fifth Amendment are the "Heads of Departments" who are capable of receiving from Congress power to appoint inferior officers. One would not expect to see very many principal officers even in a large activist federal government.

The debates at the Constitutional Convention assumed that there would be a lot of non-inferior officers. The discussions of the Appointments Clause at the Convention were almost exclusively about the appointment of officers nominated by the President and confirmed by the Senate. For example, Gouverneur Morris said of appointment of officers on September 7, 1787 "that as the President was to nominate, there would be responsibility, and as the Senate was to concur, there would be security." 2 RECORDS OF THE FEDERAL CONVENTION 539 (Max Farrand ed., 1911). There was significant discussion at the Convention about the appointment process for non-inferior officers, but only one very brief meaningless and perfunctory conversation about the process for appointing inferior officers on September 15, 1787: "The motion being lost by the equal division of votes, It was urged that it be put a second time, some such provision being too necessary to be omitted, and on a second question it was agreed to ne, con." *Id.* at 627–28.

None of this makes sense if the only non-inferior officers are "principal Officers, so that virtually all of the officers in the federal government are inferior. But, of course, not all non-inferior officers are "principal Officers." Principal officers are a small, but constitutionally important, subset of the wider category of *superior officers.*

> The residual counterpart to an inferior officer is a *superior* officer, and many superior officers are not principal officers. This was very clear at the Constitutional Convention. When the inferior officers provision of the Appointments Clause was introduced by Gouverneur Morris on September 15, 1787, James Madison claimed: "It does not go far enough if it be necessary at all—Superior Officers *below Heads of Departments* ought in some cases to have the appointment of lesser offices." Madison clearly had the understanding that the class of "Superior Officers" was broader than the class of department heads (or "principal Officers"). This distinction * * * was recognized by others at the Constitutional Convention as well. Rufus King, in discussing the Senate's role in appointments, "did not suppose it was meant that all the *minute* officers were to be appointed by the Senate, or any other original source, but by the *higher* officers of the departments to which they belong." Whether one calls them "superior" or "higher" officers, the Framers distinguished more important from less important officers, and the scheme of appointment was based upon that distinction.

Steven G. Calabresi & Gary Lawson, *Why Robert Mueller's Appointment as Special Counsel Was Unlawful,* 95 NOTRE DAME L. REV. 86, 136–37 (2019) (first emphasis added).

A number of questions immediately leap from this scheme. First, how do you tell whether someone is an "Officer[ ]" who is subject to the Appointments Clause or an employee who is not? Second, what makes someone an "inferior" officer who can, if Congress so chooses, be appointed without senatorial confirmation? Third, who are the "Courts of Law" or "Heads of Departments" who are capable of appointing inferior officers if Congress chooses to give them that power? Fourth, once a person is appointed to an office, what actions can they perform without requiring a whole new appointments process? The following materials explore all of those questions. We begin with the distinction between officers and employees, which arose in 1976 in one of the most important separation of powers cases ever decided.

1. THE LINE BETWEEN OFFICERS AND EMPLOYEES

a. *Buckley v. Valeo*

424 U.S. 1 (1976)

■ PER CURIAM:

These appeals present constitutional challenges to the key provisions of the Federal Election Campaign Act of 1971 * * *.

* * *

The 1974 amendments to the Act create an eight-member Federal Election Commission (Commission), and vest in it primary and substantial responsibility for administering and enforcing the Act. The question that we address in this portion of the opinion is whether, in view of the manner in which a majority of its members are appointed, the Commission may under the Constitution exercise the powers conferred upon it * * *.

Chapter 14 of Title 2 makes the Commission the principal repository of the numerous reports and statements which are required by that chapter to be filed by those engaging in the regulated political activities * * *.

Beyond these recordkeeping, disclosure, and investigative functions, however, the Commission is given extensive rulemaking and adjudicative powers. Its duty under § 438(a)(10) is "to prescribe suitable rules and regulations to carry out the provisions of . . . chapter (14)." Under § 437d(a)(8) the Commission is empowered to make such rules "as are necessary to carry out the provisions of this Act." Section 437d(a)(9) authorizes it to "formulate general policy with respect to the administration of this Act" and enumerated sections of Title 18's Criminal Code, as to all of which provisions the Commission "has primary jurisdiction with respect to (their) civil enforcement." § 437c(b) * * *.

The Commission's enforcement power is both direct and wide ranging. It may institute a civil action for (i) injunctive or other relief against "any acts or practices which constitute or will constitute a violation of this Act," § 437g(a)(5); (ii) declaratory or injunctive relief "as may be appropriate to implement or con[s]true any provisions" of Chapter 95 of Title 26, governing administration of funds for Presidential election campaigns and national party conventions; and (iii) "such injunctive relief as is appropriate to implement any provision" of Chapter 96 of Title 26, governing the payment of matching funds for Presidential primary campaigns. If after the Commission's post-disbursement audit of candidates receiving payments under Chapter 95 or 96 it finds an overpayment, it is empowered to seek repayment of all funds due the Secretary of the Treasury. In no respect do the foregoing civil actions require the concurrence of or participation by the Attorney General; conversely, the decision not to seek judicial relief in the above respects would appear to rest solely with the Commission * * *. Finally, as "(a)dditional enforcement authority," § 456(a) authorizes the Commission, after notice and opportunity for hearing, to make "a finding that a person . . . while a candidate for Federal office, failed to file" a required report of contributions or expenditures. If that finding is made within the applicable limitations period for prosecutions, the candidate is thereby "disqualified from becoming a candidate in any future election for Federal office for a period of time beginning on the date of such finding and ending one year after the expiration of the term of the Federal office for which such person was a candidate."

The body in which this authority is reposed consists of eight members. The Secretary of the Senate and the Clerk of the House of Representatives are *ex officio* members of the Commission without the right to vote. Two members are appointed by the President *pro tempore* of the Senate "upon the recommendations of the majority leader of the Senate and the minority leader of the Senate." Two more are to be appointed by the Speaker of the House of Representatives, likewise upon the recommendations of its respective majority and minority leaders. The remaining two members are appointed by the President. Each of the six voting members of the

Commission must be confirmed by the majority of both Houses of Congress, and each of the three appointing authorities is forbidden to choose both of their appointees from the same political party.

* * *

Appellants urge that since Congress has given the Commission wide-ranging rulemaking and enforcement powers with respect to the substantive provisions of the Act, Congress is precluded under the principle of separation of powers from vesting in itself the authority to appoint those who will exercise such authority. Their argument is based on the language of Art. II, § 2, cl. 2, of the Constitution, which provides in pertinent part as follows:

> "[The President] shall nominate, and by and with the Advice and Consent of the Senate, shall appoint . . . all other Officers of the United States, whose Appointments are not herein otherwise provided for, and which shall be established by Law: but the Congress may by Law vest the Appointment of such inferior Officers, as they think proper, in the President alone, in the Courts of Law, or in the Heads of Departments."

Appellants' argument is that this provision is the exclusive method by which those charged with executing the laws of the United States may be chosen. Congress, they assert, cannot have it both ways. If the Legislature wishes the Commission to exercise all of the conferred powers, then its members are in fact "Officers of the United States" and must be appointed under the Appointments Clause. But if Congress insists upon retaining the power to appoint, then the members of the Commission may not discharge those many functions of the Commission which can be performed only by "Officers of the United States," as that term must be construed within the doctrine of separation of powers.

* * *

The majority of the Court of Appeals * * * described appellants' argument based upon Art. II, § 2, cl. 2, as "strikingly syllogistic," and concluded that Congress had sufficient authority under the Necessary and Proper Clause of Art. I of the Constitution not only to establish the Commission but to appoint the Commission's members * * *.

We do not think appellants' arguments * * * may be so easily dismissed * * *.

The Framers regarded the checks and balances that they had built into the tripartite Federal Government as a self-executing safeguard against the encroachment or aggrandizement of one branch at the expense of the other * * *.

This Court has not hesitated to enforce the principle of separation of powers embodied in the Constitution when its application has proved necessary for the decisions of cases or controversies properly before it. The Court has held that executive or administrative duties of a nonjudicial nature may not be imposed on judges holding office under Art. III of the Constitution. *United States v. Ferreira*, 54 U.S. 40 (1852); *Hayburn's Case*, 2 U.S. 409 (1792). The Court has held that the President may not execute and exercise legislative authority belonging only to Congress. *Youngstown Sheet & Tube Co. v. Sawyer*, supra * * *. More closely in point to the facts of the present case is this Court's decision in *Springer v. Philippine Islands*, 277 U.S. 189 (1928), where the Court held that the legislature of the

Philippine Islands could not provide for legislative appointment to executive agencies.

The principle of separation of powers was not simply an abstract generalization in the minds of the Framers: it was woven into the document that they drafted in Philadelphia in the summer of 1787. Article I, § 1, declares: "All legislative Powers herein granted shall be vested in a Congress of the United States." Article II, § 1, vests the executive power "in a President of the United States of America," and Art. III, § 1, declares that "The judicial Power of the United States, shall be vested in one supreme Court, and in such inferior Courts as the Congress may from time to time ordain and establish." The further concern of the Framers of the Constitution with maintenance of the separation of powers is found in the so-called "Ineligibility" and "Incompatibility" Clauses contained in Art. I, § 6 * * *:

It is in the context of these cognate provisions of the document that we must examine the language of Art. II, § 2, cl. 2 * * *.

The Appointments Clause could, of course, be read as merely dealing with etiquette or protocol in describing "Officers of the United States," but the drafters had a less frivolous purpose in mind * * *.

We think that the term "Officers of the United States" as used in Art. II * * * is a term intended to have substantive meaning. We think its fair import is that any appointee exercising significant authority pursuant to the laws of the United States is an "Officer of the United States," and must, therefore, be appointed in the manner prescribed by § 2, cl. 2, of that Article.

* * * If a postmaster first class, *Myers v. United States*, 272 U.S. 52 (1926), and the clerk of a district court, *Ex parte Hennen*, 38 U.S. 225 (1839), are inferior officers of the United States within the meaning of the Appointments Clause, as they are, surely the Commissioners before us are at the very least such "inferior Officers" within the meaning of that Clause.[162]

Although two members of the Commission are initially selected by the President, his nominations are subject to confirmation not merely by the Senate, but by the House of Representatives as well. The remaining four voting members of the Commission are appointed by the President *pro tempore* of the Senate and by the Speaker of the House. While the second part of the Clause authorizes Congress to vest the appointment of the officers described in that part in "the Courts of Law, or in the Heads of Departments," neither the Speaker of the House nor the President *pro tempore* of the Senate comes within this language.

The phrase "Heads of Departments," used as it is in conjunction with the phrase "Courts of Law," suggests that the Departments referred to are themselves in the Executive Branch or at least have some connection with that branch. While the Clause expressly authorizes Congress to vest the appointment of certain officers in the "Courts of Law," the absence of similar language to include Congress must mean that neither Congress nor its officers were included within the language "Heads of Departments" in this part of cl. 2.

---

162 "*Officers of the United States*" does not include all employees of the United States, but there is no claim made that the Commissioners are employees of the United States rather than officers. Employees are lesser functionaries subordinate to officers of the United States, whereas the Commissioners, appointed for a statutory term, are not subject to the control or direction of any other executive, judicial, or legislative authority.

Thus with respect to four of the six voting members of the Commission, neither the President, the head of any department, nor the Judiciary has any voice in their selection.

* * *

Appellee Commission and *amici* urge that because of what they conceive to be the extraordinary authority reposed in Congress to regulate elections, this case stands on a different footing than if Congress had exercised its legislative authority in another field. There is, of course, no doubt that Congress has express authority to regulate congressional elections * * *. But Congress has plenary authority in all areas in which it has substantive legislative jurisdiction, so long as the exercise of that authority does not offend some other constitutional restriction. We see no reason to believe that the authority of Congress over federal election practices is of such a wholly different nature from the other grants of authority to Congress that it may be employed in such a manner as to offend well-established constitutional restrictions stemming from the separation of powers.

The position that because Congress has been given explicit and plenary authority to regulate a field of activity, it must therefore have the power to appoint those who are to administer the regulatory statute is both novel and contrary to the language of the Appointments Clause. Unless their selection is elsewhere provided for, *all* Officers of the United States are to be appointed in accordance with the Clause. Principal officers are selected by the President with the advice and consent of the Senate. Inferior officers Congress may allow to be appointed by the President alone, by the heads of departments, or by the Judiciary. No class or type of officer is excluded because of its special functions * * *.

* * *

We are also told by appellees and *amici* that Congress had good reason for not vesting in a Commission composed wholly of Presidential appointees the authority to administer the Act, since the administration of the Act would undoubtedly have a bearing on any incumbent President's campaign for re-election. While one cannot dispute the basis for this sentiment as a practical matter, it would seem that those who sought to challenge incumbent Congressmen might have equally good reason to fear a Commission which was unduly responsive to members of Congress whom they were seeking to unseat. But such fears, however rational, do not by themselves warrant a distortion of the Framers' work.

Appellee Commission and *amici* finally contend, and the majority of the Court of Appeals agreed with them, that whatever shortcomings the provisions for the appointment of members of the Commission might have under Art. II, Congress had ample authority under the Necessary and Proper Clause of Art. I to effectuate this result. We do not agree. The proper inquiry when considering the Necessary and Proper Clause is not the authority of Congress to create an office or a commission, which is broad indeed, but rather its authority to provide that its own officers may make appointments to such office or commission.

So framed, the claim that Congress may provide for this manner of appointment under the Necessary and Proper Clause of Art. I stands on no better footing than the claim that it may provide for such manner of appointment because of its substantive authority to regulate federal elections. Congress could not, merely because it concluded that such a measure was "necessary and proper" to the discharge of its substantive legislative authority, pass a bill of attainder or *ex post facto* law contrary to the prohibitions contained in § 9 of Art. I. No more may it vest in itself, or in its officers, the authority to appoint officers of the United States when the Appointments Clause by clear implication prohibits it from doing so.

* * *

Insofar as the powers confided in the Commission are essentially of an investigative nature, falling in the same general category as those powers which Congress might delegate to one of its own committees, there can be no question that the Commission as presently constituted may exercise them * * *.

But when we go beyond this type of authority to the more substantial powers exercised by the Commission, we reach a different result. The Commission's enforcement power, exemplified by its discretionary power to seek judicial relief, is authority that cannot possibly be regarded as merely in aid of the legislative function of Congress * * *.

Congress may undoubtedly under the Necessary and Proper Clause create "offices" in the generic sense and provide such method of appointment to those "offices" as it chooses. But Congress' power under that Clause is inevitably bounded by the express language of Art. II, § 2, cl. 2, and unless the method it provides comports with the latter, the holders of those offices will not be "Officers of the United States." They may, therefore, properly perform duties only in aid of those functions that Congress may carry out by itself, or in an area sufficiently removed from the administration and enforcement of the public law as to permit their being performed by persons not "Officers of the United States."

* * *

We hold that these provisions of the Act, vesting in the Commission primary responsibility for conducting civil litigation in the courts of the United States for vindicating public rights, violate Art. II, § 2, cl. 2, of the Constitution. Such functions may be discharged only by persons who are "Officers of the United States" within the language of that section.

All aspects of the Act are brought within the Commission's broad administrative powers: rulemaking, advisory opinions, and determinations of eligibility for funds and even for federal elective office itself * * *. [E]ach of these functions also represents the performance of a significant governmental duty exercised pursuant to a public law * * *. These administrative functions may therefore be exercised only by persons who are "Officers of the United States."

* * *

■ MR. JUSTICE WHITE, concurring in part and dissenting in part. [omitted]

NOTES AND QUESTIONS

1. Look closely at the statute creating the FEC and providing for the appointment of its eight members. Now look again at the text of the Appointments Clause. If you set out to write a flagrantly unconstitutional statute, could you do a better job? How could Congress in 1974 possibly think that this was constitutional? And how could an en banc D.C. Circuit Court of Appeals possibly uphold the statute? As it happens, both the Congress of 1974 and the D.C. Circuit of 1975 had good reasons to be surprised, and even

astonished, that the Supreme Court ruled against them in 1976. This is the reason why *Buckley v. Valeo* is such an important case in modern separation of powers jurisprudence.

2. Remember that in 1935, the Supreme Court twice invalidated congressional statutes for violating the subdelegation doctrine. *See supra* pages 192–201. The next year, the Court invalidated another statute, primarily because it exceeded Congress's powers under the Commerce Clause but secondarily because it subdelegated legislative power to private parties. *See Carter v. Carter Coal Co.,* 298 U.S. 238, 311 (1936). That was the last time in forty years that the Supreme Court invalidated a congressional statute on separation of powers grounds. To be clear: From 1937–1975, the number of congressional statutes invalidated by the Supreme Court on separation of powers grounds was exactly zero. *Youngstown* and *Powell v. McCormack,* keep in mind, did not invalidate congressional statutes; they invalidated unilateral executive and House actions. Notice the cases cited by *Buckley* to show how "[t]his Court has not hesitated to enforce the principle of separation of powers." When were those cases decided? Not a one other than *Youngstown* was decided after 1936. Moreover, the four decades between 1936 and *Buckley* were a period of rapid growth in the federal government so the Court did not lack for opportunities to consider separation-of-powers cases. What happened?

The full story will emerge in the next chapter, but the short version for now is that in 1937, the Court began a major retreat from policing the boundaries of congressional power. That retreat primarily concerned Congress's power to regulate people and the States, but Congress's power to regulate the structure of the federal government was swept up as well in this judicial change of approach. That is why the D.C. Circuit dismissively described the Appointments Clause challenge in *Buckley* as "strikingly syllogistic." If you were taught that syllogisms are among the *strongest* arguments that you can form ("All men are mortal, Socrates is a man, therefore Socrates is mortal"), you were taught correctly, but *only* if you are dealing with a form of reasoning in which one moves from premises to conclusions in logical fashion. For forty years, that simply stopped being an acceptable form of reasoning in separation-of-powers law. During that time period, one just did not try to match up congressional statutes with the text of the Constitution. That kind of "formalism" had been, it was thought, buried in the 1930s. The question in these cases was simply whether Congress could reasonably think that it had good policy reasons to do what it did, and if so, that was the end of the matter. *Buckley* was a shock to the system less for its result (which was important in its own right) but for its *method.* The Court in *Buckley* paid close attention to the text and original meaning of the Appointments Clause, and it rather casually dismissed the policy arguments in favor of the law as irrelevant. That had not happened for a very long time.

Why did the Court change its mind about constitutional method in *Buckley*? We frankly do not know. As best we can tell, neither does anyone else. Indeed, it was not clear even after the decision in 1976 that *Buckley* was anything other than a random event. The next year, in 1977, the Court decided *Nixon v. Administrator of General Services,* 433 U.S. 425 (1977), briefly discussed earlier. *See supra* pages 317–319. In that case, decided just one term after *Buckley*, the Court said of Nixon's argument that Congress had violated the separation of powers by seizing his records:

> Appellants' argument is * * * based on an interpretation of the separation-of-powers doctrine inconsistent with the origins of that doctrine, recent decisions of the Court, and the contemporary realities of our political system * * *.
>
> * * *

> * * * [I]n determining whether the Act disrupts the proper balance between the coordinate branches, *the proper inquiry focuses on the extent to which it prevents the Executive Branch from accomplishing its constitutionally assigned functions. Only where the potential for disruption is present must we then determine whether that impact is justified by an overriding need to promote objectives within the constitutional authority of Congress.*

Id. at 441, 443 (emphasis added). Congress and the D.C. Circuit in 1976 had every reason to think that the Court would decide *Buckley* based on "recent decisions of the Court," which had consistently upheld congressional action for four decades, and "the contemporary realities of our political system" rather than the text of the Constitution (which did not warrant a mention in *Nixon's* discussion of appropriate modalities of interpretation).

Any thought that *Buckley* could be dismissed as a one-off decision, however, vanished in the next few years. In 1982, the Court, albeit without a majority opinion, invalidated Congress's scheme for bankruptcy courts because it lodged Article III "judicial Power" in persons other than Article III judges, *see Northern Pipeline Construction Co. v. Marathon Pipe Line Co.,* 458 U.S. 50 (1982); and in 1983 the Court invalidated the legislative veto on separation of powers grounds. *See INS v. Chadha*, 462 U.S. 919 (1983); *see supra* pages 277–283. These were major decisions affecting major components of the federal government. Both cases exhibited the kind of "formalistic" reasoning employed in *Buckley,* and in the ensuing nearly four decades, formalist and functionalist modes of reasoning have struggled for supremacy in separation of powers law. For the four decades before 1976, there was no struggle at all. *Buckley* thus represents the birth of modern separation of powers doctrine.

3. *Buckley* is importantly doctrinally as well as methodologically. It defines the line between employees and officers as turning on whether the person exercises "significant authority pursuant to the laws of the United States." How does one tell whether authority is "significant"? The Department of Justice's Office of Legal Counsel in 2007 wrote a forty-page memo addressing the question, with the observation that "the Supreme Court has not articulated the precise scope and application of the [Appointments] Clause's requirements; the Executive Branch * * * has adopted differing interpretations since *Buckley;* and questions about the Clause continue to arise regularly, both in the operation of the Executive branch and in proposed legislation." Office of Legal Counsel, U.S. Dep't of Justice, *Officers of the United States Within the Meaning of the Appointments Clause* 3 (Apr. 16, 2007). The analysis concluded that "a position, however labeled, is in fact a federal office if (1) it is invested by legal authority with a portion of the sovereign power of the federal Government, and (2) it is 'continuing.'" *Id.* at Sovereign power is considered "power lawfully conferred by the Government to bind third parties, or the Government itself," *id.* at 11, which entails the authority to administer, execute, or interpret the law," *id.*, or to perform certain other functions traditionally associated with the executive arm of the national government such as military affairs and diplomacy. *Id.* at 13–14. Does that represent an advance in clarity over just asking whether the authority is "significant"?

4. Recent scholarship suggests that the term "Officer" might have a broader original meaning than *Buckley* and ensuing authorities suggest, referring to anyone "whom the government entrusts with ongoing responsibility to perform a statutory duty of any level of importance." Jennifer Mascott, *Who Are "Officers of the United States"?*, 70 Stan. L. Rev.443 (2018). *See also* James C. Phillips, Benjamin Lee & Jacob Crump, *Corpus Linguistics and "Officers of the United States,"* 42 HARV. J.L. & PUB. POL'Y 871 (2019) (essentially confirming this finding). In other words, an officer is anyone exercising

non-trivial—rather than, as *Buckley* puts it, "significant"—authority. Under this test, many officials now chosen through competitive processes rather than through the Appointments Clause or appointed by officials below the level of department head would likely be unconstitutional in their current guises. Even under *Buckley's* less demanding inquiry, a decent amount of the federal government's structure is subject to challenge. For example, do team managers in the Internal Revenue Service's appeals office, who can approve or disapprove settlements with taxpayers and thus determine with finality their tax liability, exercise "significant" authority? *See Tucker v. Commissioner of Internal Revenue,* 676 F.3d 1129, 1133–35 (D.C.Cir.2012) (straining very hard to say "no").

5. Earlier in this chapter, we explored the line between executive and judicial power. *See supra* pages 171–180. Because that line is fuzzy, there are many executive officials who exercise adjudicative functions at many levels of the executive branch hierarchy, from lower-level staff in field offices who are obviously employees rather than officers to officials whose only real difference from Article III judges is their lack of tenure and salary guarantees. Which of these executive adjudicators are "Officers of the United States"? Some cases are very easy. The nineteen judges of the United States Tax Court, for instance, who hear appeals by taxpayers who want to challenge tax assessments without paying them and then suing for refunds in District Court, are appointed by the President with the advice and consent of the Senate. *See* 26 U.S.C. § 7443(b) (2018). No one doubts that they are "Officers of the United States." But what about Tax Court "special trial judges," who assist the Tax Court judges in their duties in much the way that magistrates assist District Court judges? In *Freytag v. Commissioner of Internal Revenue*, 501 U.S. 868 (1991), the Supreme Court held that special trial judges are "Officers of the United States" rather than mere employees for purposes of the Appointments Clause. Although special trial judges do not always render final decisions, they "perform more than ministerial tasks. They take testimony, conduct trials, rule on the admissibility of evidence, and have the power to enforce compliance with discovery orders." *Id.* at 881–82. Moreover, in a limited class of cases the special trial judges can actually render, with finality, the Tax Court's decisions. *Id.* at 882. Is that any different from IRS appeals office team managers?

Members of non-Article III "legislative courts," such as the Tax Court and the Court of Federal Claims, are not the only judge-like entities in the executive department. Administrative law judges, or ALJs, are a special breed of federal agency personnel who preside over many important agency adjudications (and a small handful of agency rulemakings). ALJs have most of the powers normally associated with trial judges, and their decisions become the final decisions of the agency for which they work if the decisions are not appealed. *See* 5 U.S.C. § 557(b) (2018). ALJs traditionally have not been appointed in the fashion prescribed in the Appointments Clause. In the case of the Securities and Exchange Commission before 2018, for example, "the SEC's Office of Administrative Law Judges, with input from the Chief Administrative Law Judge, human resources, and OPM, identifies and selects SEC ALJs. The SEC Commissioners are not involved in the appointment process in any way." Linda D. Jellum & Moses M. Tincher, *The Shadow of* Free Enterprise: *The Unconstitutionality of the Securities & Exchange Commission Administrative Law Judges*, 70 S.M.U. L. Rev. 3, 15–16 (2017). The lower-level staff members who chose the ALJs under this scheme are clearly not among the "Heads of Departments" capable of appointing inferior officers, so if those ALJs are "Officers of the United States," their appointment was flagrantly unlawful. The D.C. Circuit first considered the constitutional status of ALJs in 2000, holding, in a 2–1 decision, that ALJs generally were not constitutional officers. *See Landry v. FDIC*, 204 F.3d 1125 (D.C.Cir.2000). A decade later, the Dodd-Frank Wall Street Reform and Consumer Protection Act, Pub. L. No. 111–203, 124 Stat. 1376 (2010), allowed the SEC to pursue monetary penalty claims in administrative adjudications conducted by ALJs rather than in court. In 2018, the Supreme Court addressed whether those ALJs had to be appointed in conformance with the Appointments Clause.

b. Lucia v. Securities and Exchange Commission

585 U.S. ___, 138 S.Ct. 2044 (2018)

■ JUSTICE KAGAN delivered the opinion of the Court.

The Appointments Clause of the Constitution lays out the permissible methods of appointing "Officers of the United States," a class of government officials distinct from mere employees. This case requires us to decide whether administrative law judges (ALJs) of the Securities and Exchange Commission (SEC or Commission) qualify as such "Officers." In keeping with *Freytag v. Commissioner*, 501 U.S. 868 (1991), we hold that they do.

I

The SEC has statutory authority to enforce the nation's securities laws. One way it can do so is by instituting an administrative proceeding against an alleged wrongdoer. By law, the Commission may itself preside over such a proceeding. *See* 17 CFR § 201.110 (2017). But the Commission also may, and typically does, delegate that task to an ALJ. *See ibid.*; 15 U.S.C. § 78d–1(a). The SEC currently has five ALJs. Other staff members, rather than the Commission proper, selected them all.

An ALJ assigned to hear an SEC enforcement action has extensive powers—the "authority to do all things necessary and appropriate to discharge his or her duties" and ensure a "fair and orderly" adversarial proceeding. §§ 201.111, 200.14(a). Those powers "include, but are not limited to," supervising discovery; issuing, revoking, or modifying subpoenas; deciding motions; ruling on the admissibility of evidence; administering oaths; hearing and examining witnesses; generally "[r]egulating the course of" the proceeding and the "conduct of the parties and their counsel"; and imposing sanctions for "[c]ontemptuous conduct" or violations of procedural requirements. §§ 201.111, 201.180. As that list suggests, an SEC ALJ exercises authority "comparable to" that of a federal district judge conducting a bench trial. *Butz v. Economou*, 438 U.S. 478, 513 (1978).

After a hearing ends, the ALJ issues an "initial decision." § 201.360(a)(1). That decision must set out "findings and conclusions" about all "material issues of fact [and] law"; it also must include the "appropriate order, sanction, relief, or denial thereof." § 201.360(b). The Commission can then review the ALJ's decision, either upon request or sua sponte. *See* § 201.360(d)(1). But if it opts against review, the Commission "issue[s] an order that the [ALJ's] decision has become final." § 201.360(d)(2). At that point, the initial decision is "deemed the action of the Commission." § 78d–1(c).

This case began when the SEC instituted an administrative proceeding against petitioner Raymond Lucia and his investment company. Lucia marketed a retirement savings strategy called "Buckets of Money." In the SEC's view, Lucia used misleading slideshow presentations to deceive prospective clients. The SEC charged Lucia under the Investment Advisers Act, § 80b–1 et seq., and assigned ALJ Cameron Elliot to adjudicate the case. After nine days of testimony and argument, Judge Elliot issued an initial decision concluding that Lucia had violated the Act and imposing sanctions, including civil penalties of $300,000 and a lifetime bar from the investment industry. In his decision, Judge Elliot made factual findings about only one of the four ways the SEC thought Lucia's slideshow misled investors. The Commission thus remanded for factfinding on the other three claims, explaining that an ALJ's "personal experience with the witnesses" places him "in the best position to make findings of fact" and "resolve any conflicts in the evidence." App. to Pet. for Cert. 241a. Judge Elliot then made additional findings of deception and issued a revised initial decision, with the same sanctions.

On appeal to the SEC, Lucia argued that the administrative proceeding was invalid because Judge Elliot had not been constitutionally appointed. According to Lucia, the Commission's ALJs are "Officers of the United States" and thus subject to the Appointments Clause. Under that Clause, Lucia noted, only the President, "Courts of Law," or "Heads of Departments" can appoint "Officers." And none of those actors had made Judge Elliot an ALJ. To be sure, the Commission itself counts as a "Head[ ] of Department[ ]." *Ibid.; see Free Enterprise Fund v. Public Company Accounting Oversight Bd.*, 561 U.S. 477, 511–513 (2010). But the Commission had left the task of appointing ALJs, including Judge Elliot, to SEC staff members. As a result, Lucia contended, Judge Elliot lacked constitutional authority to do his job.

The Commission rejected Lucia's argument. It held that the SEC's ALJs are not "Officers of the United States." Instead, they are "mere employees"—officials with lesser responsibilities who fall outside the Appointments Clause's ambit. App. to Pet. for Cert. 87a. The Commission reasoned that its ALJs do not "exercise significant authority independent of [its own] supervision." *Id.*, at 88a. Because that is so (said the SEC), they need no special, high-level appointment.

Lucia's claim fared no better in the Court of Appeals for the D.C. Circuit. A panel of that court seconded the Commission's view that SEC ALJs are employees rather than officers, and so are not subject to the Appointments Clause. *See* 832 F.3d 277, 283–289 (2016). Lucia then petitioned for rehearing en banc. The Court of Appeals granted that request and heard argument in the case. But the ten members of the en banc court divided evenly, resulting in a per curiam order denying Lucia's claim. *See* 868 F.3d 1021 (2017). That decision conflicted with one from the Court of Appeals for the Tenth Circuit. *See Bandimere v. SEC*, 844 F.3d 1168, 1179 (2016).

Lucia asked us to resolve the split by deciding whether the Commission's ALJs are "Officers of the United States within the meaning of the Appointments Clause." Pet. for Cert. i. Up to that point, the Federal Government (as represented by the Department of Justice) had defended the Commission's position that SEC ALJs are employees, not officers. But in responding to Lucia's petition, the Government switched sides. So when we granted the petition, 583 U.S. ___ (2018), we also appointed an amicus curiae to defend the judgment below. We now reverse.

II

The sole question here is whether the Commission's ALJs are "Officers of the United States" or simply employees of the Federal Government. The Appointments Clause prescribes the exclusive means of appointing "Officers." Only the President, a court of law, or a head of department can do so. And as all parties agree, none of those actors appointed Judge Elliot before he heard Lucia's case; instead, SEC staff members gave him an ALJ slot. So if the Commission's ALJs are constitutional officers, Lucia raises a valid Appointments Clause claim. The only way to defeat his position is to show that those ALJs are not officers at all, but instead non-officer employees—part of the broad swath of "lesser functionaries" in the Government's workforce. *Buckley v. Valeo*, 424 U.S. 1, 126, n. 162 (1976) (per curiam). For if that is true, the Appointments Clause cares not a whit about who named them. *See United States v. Germaine*, 99 U.S. 508, 510 (1879).

Two decisions set out this Court's basic framework for distinguishing between officers and employees. *Germaine* held that "civil surgeons" (doctors hired to perform various physical exams) were mere employees because their duties were "occasional or temporary" rather than "continuing and permanent." *Id.*, at 511–512. Stressing "ideas of tenure [and] duration," the Court there made clear that an individual must occupy a "continuing" position established by law to qualify as an officer. *Id.*, at 511. *Buckley* then set out another requirement, central to this case. It determined that members of a federal commission were officers only after finding that they "exercis[ed] significant authority pursuant to the laws of the United States." 424 U.S., at 126. The inquiry thus focused on the extent of power an individual wields in carrying out his assigned functions.

Both the amicus and the Government urge us to elaborate on *Buckley's* "significant authority" test * * *. And maybe one day we will see a need to refine or enhance the test *Buckley* set out so concisely. But that day is not this one, because in *Freytag v. Commissioner*, 501 U.S. 868 (1991), we applied the unadorned "significant authority" test to adjudicative officials who are near-carbon copies of the Commission's ALJs. As we now explain, our analysis there (sans any more detailed legal criteria) necessarily decides this case.

The officials at issue in *Freytag* were the "special trial judges" (STJs) of the United States Tax Court. The authority of those judges depended on the significance of the tax dispute before them. In "comparatively narrow and minor matters," they could both hear and definitively resolve a case for the Tax Court. *Id.*, at 873. In more major matters, they could preside over the hearing, but could not issue the final decision; instead, they were to "prepare proposed findings and an opinion" for a regular Tax Court judge to consider. *Ibid.* The proceeding challenged in *Freytag* was a major one, involving $1.5 billion in alleged tax deficiencies. After conducting a 14-week trial, the STJ drafted a proposed decision in favor of the Government. A regular judge then adopted the STJ's work as the opinion of the Tax Court. The losing parties argued on appeal that the STJ was not constitutionally appointed.

This Court held that the Tax Court's STJs are officers, not mere employees. Citing *Germaine*, the Court first found that STJs hold a continuing office established by law. *See* 501 U.S., at 881. They serve on an ongoing, rather than a "temporary [or] episodic[,] basis"; and their "duties, salary, and means of appointment" are all specified in the Tax Code. *Ibid.* The Court then considered, as *Buckley* demands, the "significance" of the "authority" STJs wield. 501 U.S., at 881. In addressing that issue, the Government had argued that STJs are employees, rather than officers, in all cases (like the one at issue) in which they could not "enter a final decision." *Ibid.* But the Court thought the Government's focus on finality "ignore[d] the significance of the duties and discretion that [STJs] possess." *Ibid.* Describing the responsibilities involved in presiding over adversarial hearings, the Court said: STJs "take testimony, conduct trials, rule on the admissibility of evidence, and have the power to enforce compliance with discovery orders." *Id.*, at 881–882. And the Court observed that "[i]n the course of carrying out these important functions, the [STJs] exercise significant discretion." *Id.*, at 882. That fact meant they were officers, even when their decisions were not final.[4]

Freytag says everything necessary to decide this case. To begin, the Commission's ALJs, like the Tax Court's STJs, hold a continuing office established by law. Indeed, everyone here—Lucia, the Government, and the amicus—agrees on that point. Far from serving temporarily or episodically, SEC ALJs "receive[ ] a career appointment." 5 CFR § 930.204(a) (2018). And that appointment is to a position created by statute, down to its "duties, salary, and means of appointment." *Freytag*, 501 U.S., at 881; see 5 U.S.C. §§ 556–557, 5372, 3105.

Still more, the Commission's ALJs exercise the same "significant discretion" when carrying out the same "important functions" as STJs do. Both sets of officials have all the authority needed to ensure fair and orderly adversarial hearings—indeed, nearly all the tools of federal trial judges * * *. [T]he Commission's ALJs have equivalent duties and powers as STJs in conducting adversarial inquiries.

And at the close of those proceedings, ALJs issue decisions much like that in *Freytag*—except with potentially more independent effect. As the *Freytag* Court recounted, STJs "prepare proposed findings and an opinion" adjudicating charges and assessing tax liabilities. 501 U.S., at 873. Similarly, the Commission's ALJs issue decisions containing factual findings, legal conclusions, and appropriate remedies. *See* § 201.360(b). And what happens next reveals that the ALJ can play the more autonomous role. In a major case like *Freytag*, a regular Tax Court judge must always review an STJ's opinion. And that opinion counts for nothing unless the regular judge adopts it as his own. *See* 501 U.S., at 873. By contrast, the SEC can decide against reviewing an ALJ decision at all. And when the SEC declines review (and issues an order saying so), the ALJ's decision itself "becomes final" and is "deemed the action of the Commission." § 201.360(d)(2); 15 U.S.C. § 78d–1(c). That last-word capacity makes this an a fortiori case: If the Tax Court's STJs are officers, as *Freytag* held, then the Commission's ALJs must be too.

* * *

[*Editors' Note: The Court then held that Lucia was entitled to a new hearing before a different adjudicator than Judge Eliott, even if Eliott was subsequently given a proper appointment.*]

* * *

■ JUSTICE THOMAS, with whom JUSTICE GORSUCH joins, concurring.

I agree with the Court that this case is indistinguishable from *Freytag v. Commissioner*, 501 U.S. 868 (1991). If the special trial judges in *Freytag* were "Officers of the United States," Art. II, § 2, cl. 2, then so are the administrative law

---

[4] The Court also provided an alternative basis for viewing the STJs as officers. "Even if the duties of [STJs in major cases] were not as significant as we . . . have found them," we stated, "our conclusion would be unchanged." *Freytag*, 501 U.S., at 882. That was because the Government had conceded that in minor matters, where STJs could enter final decisions, they had enough "independent authority" to count as officers. And we thought it made no sense to classify the STJs as officers for some cases and employees for others. *See ibid.* Justice SOTOMAYOR relies on that back-up rationale in trying to reconcile *Freytag* with her view that "a prerequisite to officer status is the authority" to issue at least some "final decisions." But *Freytag* has two parts, and its primary analysis explicitly rejects Justice SOTOMAYOR's theory that final decisionmaking authority is a sine qua non of officer status. *See* 501 U.S., at 881–882. As she acknowledges, she must expunge that reasoning to make her reading work. See post, at 5 ("That part of the opinion[ ] was unnecessary to the result").

judges of the Securities and Exchange Commission. Moving forward, however, this Court will not be able to decide every Appointments Clause case by comparing it to *Freytag*. And, as the Court acknowledges, our precedents in this area do not provide much guidance. While precedents like *Freytag* discuss what is sufficient to make someone an officer of the United States, our precedents have never clearly defined what is necessary. I would resolve that question based on the original public meaning of "Officers of the United States." To the Founders, this term encompassed all federal civil officials " 'with responsibility for an ongoing statutory duty.' " *NLRB v. SW General, Inc.*, 580 U.S. ___, ___ (2017) (THOMAS, J., concurring) (slip op., at 4); Mascott, *Who Are "Officers of the United States"?* 70 Stan. L.Rev. 443, 564 (2018) (Mascott).

* * *

The Founders likely understood the term "Officers of the United States" to encompass all federal civil officials who perform an ongoing, statutory duty—no matter how important or significant the duty. *See* Mascott 454 * * *. The ordinary meaning of "officer" was anyone who performed a continuous public duty. *See id.*, at 484–507; e.g., *United States v. Maurice*, 26 F. Cas. 1211, 1214 (No. 15,747) (CC Va. 1823) (defining officer as someone in " 'a public charge or employment' " who performed a "continuing" duty); 8 Annals of Cong. 2304–2305 (1799) (statement of Rep. Harper) (explaining that the word officer "is derived from the Latin word *officium*" and "includes all persons holding posts which require the performance of some public duty"). For federal officers, that duty is "established by Law"—that is, by statute. Art. II, § 2, cl. 2. The Founders considered individuals to be officers even if they performed only ministerial statutory duties—including recordkeepers, clerks, and tidewaiters (individuals who watched goods land at a customhouse). *See* Mascott 484–507 * * *.

Applying the original meaning here, the administrative law judges of the Securities and Exchange Commission easily qualify as "Officers of the United States." These judges exercise many of the agency's statutory duties, including issuing initial decisions in adversarial proceedings. *See* 15 U.S.C. § 78d–1(a); 17 CFR §§ 200.14, 200.30–9 (2017). As explained, the importance or significance of these statutory duties is irrelevant. All that matters is that the judges are continuously responsible for performing them.

* * * Because the Court reaches the same conclusion by correctly applying *Freytag*, I join its opinion.

■ JUSTICE BREYER, with whom JUSTICE GINSBURG and JUSTICE SOTOMAYOR join as to Part III, concurring in the judgment in part and dissenting in part.

I agree with the Court that the Securities and Exchange Commission did not properly appoint the Administrative Law Judge who presided over petitioner Lucia's hearing. But I * * * would rest our conclusion upon statutory, not constitutional, grounds. I believe it important to do so because I cannot answer the constitutional question that the majority answers without knowing the answer to a different, embedded constitutional question, which the Solicitor General urged us to answer in this case: the constitutionality of the statutory "for cause" removal protections that Congress provided for administrative law judges. *Cf. Free Enterprise Fund v. Public Company Accounting Oversight Bd.*, 561 U.S. 477 (2010) * * *.

I

The relevant statute here is the Administrative Procedure Act. That Act governs the appointment of administrative law judges. It provides (as it has, in substance, since its enactment in 1946) that "[e]ach agency shall appoint as many administrative law judges as are necessary for" hearings governed by the Administrative Procedure Act. 5 U.S.C. § 3105. In the case of the Securities and Exchange Commission, the relevant "agency" is the Commission itself. But the Commission did not appoint the Administrative Law Judge who presided over Lucia's hearing. Rather, the Commission's staff appointed that Administrative Law Judge, without the approval of the Commissioners themselves.

I do not believe that the Administrative Procedure Act permits the Commission to delegate its power to appoint its administrative law judges to its staff * * *.

I have found no other statutory provision that would permit the Commission to delegate the power to appoint its administrative law judges to its staff * * *.

The analysis may differ for other agencies that employ administrative law judges. Each agency's governing statute is different, and some, unlike the Commission's, may allow the delegation of duties without a published order or rule. *See*, e.g., 42 U.S.C. § 902(a)(7) (applicable to the Social Security Administration). Similarly, other agencies' administrative law judges perform distinct functions, and their means of appointment may therefore not raise the constitutional questions that inform my reading of the relevant statutes here.

The upshot, in my view, is that for statutory, not constitutional, reasons, the Commission did not lawfully appoint the Administrative Law Judge here at issue. And this Court should decide no more than that.

The reason why it is important to go no further arises from the holding in a case this Court decided eight years ago, *Free Enterprise Fund, supra*. The case concerned statutory provisions protecting members of the Public Company Accounting Oversight Board from removal without cause. The Court held in that case that the Executive Vesting Clause of the Constitution, Art. II, § 1 ("[t]he executive Power shall be vested in a President of the United States of America"), forbade Congress from providing members of the Board with "multilevel protection from removal" by the President. *Free Enterprise Fund*, 561 U.S., at 484; *see id.*, at 514 ("Congress cannot limit the President's authority" by providing "two levels of protection from removal for those who . . . exercise significant executive power"). *But see id.*, at 514–549 (BREYER, J., dissenting). Because, in the Court's view, the relevant statutes (1) granted the Securities and Exchange Commissioners protection from removal without cause, (2) gave the Commissioners sole authority to remove Board members, and (3) protected Board members from removal without cause, the statutes provided Board members with two levels of protection from removal and consequently violated the Constitution. *Id.*, at 495–498.

* * *

If the *Free Enterprise Fund* Court's holding applies equally to the administrative law judges—and I stress the "if"—then to hold that the administrative law judges are "Officers of the United States" is, perhaps, to hold that their removal protections are unconstitutional. This would risk transforming administrative law judges from independent adjudicators into dependent decisionmakers, serving at the pleasure of the Commission * * *.

* * *

* * * [I]if a holding that administrative law judges are "inferior Officers" brings with it application of *Free Enterprise Fund's* limitation on "for cause" protections from removal, then a determination that administrative law judges are, constitutionally speaking, "inferior Officers" would directly conflict with Congress' intent, as revealed in the statute. In that case, it would be clear to me that Congress did not intend that consequence, and that it therefore did not intend to make administrative law judges "inferior Officers" at all.

Congress' intent on the question matters, in my view, because the Appointments Clause is properly understood to grant Congress a degree of leeway as to whether particular Government workers are officers or instead mere employees not subject to the Appointments Clause * * *.

The use of the words "by Law" to describe the establishment and means of appointment of "Officers of the United States," together with the fact that Article I of the Constitution vests the legislative power in Congress, suggests that (other than the officers the Constitution specifically lists) Congress, not the Judicial Branch alone, must play a major role in determining who is an "Office[r] of the United States." And Congress' intent in this specific respect is often highly relevant. Congress' leeway is not, of course, absolute—it may not, for example, say that positions the Constitution itself describes as "Officers" are not "Officers." But given the constitutional language, the Court, when deciding whether other positions are "Officers of the United States" under the Appointments Clause, should give substantial weight to Congress' decision.

How is the Court to decide whether Congress intended that the holder of a particular Government position count as an "Office[r] of the United States"? Congress might, of course, write explicitly into the statute that the employee "is an officer of the United States under the Appointments Clause," but an explicit phrase of this kind is unlikely to appear. If it does not, then I would approach the question like any other difficult question of statutory interpretation * * *.

* * *

* * * I would not answer the question whether the Securities and Exchange Commission's administrative law judges are constitutional "Officers" without first deciding * * * what effect that holding would have on the statutory "for cause" removal protections that Congress provided for administrative law judges. If, for example, *Free Enterprise Fund* means that saying administrative law judges are "inferior Officers" will cause them to lose their "for cause" removal protections, then I would likely hold that the administrative law judges are not "Officers," for to say otherwise would be to contradict Congress' enactment of those protections in the Administrative Procedure Act. In contrast, if *Free Enterprise Fund* does not mean that an administrative law judge (if an "Office[r] of the United States") would lose "for cause" protections, then it is more likely that interpreting the Administrative Procedure Act as conferring such status would not run contrary to Congress' intent. In such a case, I would more likely hold that, given the other features of the Administrative Procedure Act, Congress did intend to make administrative law judges inferior "Officers of the United States."

* * *

The Court's decision to address the Appointments Clause question separately from the constitutional removal question is problematic. By considering each question in isolation, the Court risks (should the Court later extend *Free Enterprise Fund*) unraveling, step-by-step, the foundations of the Federal Government's administrative adjudication system as it has existed for decades, and perhaps of the merit-based civil-service system in general. And the Court risks doing so without considering that potential consequence. For these reasons, I concur in the judgment in part and, with respect, I dissent in part.

[*Editors' Note: Part III of Justice Breyer's opinion, joined by Justices Ginsburg and Sotomayor, dissented from the majority's remedial holding that Judge Elliot could not hear Lucia's case on remand.*]

■ JUSTICE SOTOMAYOR, with whom JUSTICE GINSBURG joins, dissenting.

* * *

As the majority notes, this Court's decisions currently set forth at least two prerequisites to officer status: (1) an individual must hold a "continuing" office established by law, *United States v. Germaine*, 99 U.S. 508, 511–512 (1879), and (2) an individual must wield "significant authority," *Buckley v. Valeo*, 424 U.S. 1, 126 (1976) (per curiam). The first requirement is relatively easy to grasp; the second, less so. To be sure, to exercise "significant authority," the person must wield considerable powers in comparison to the average person who works for the Federal Government * * *. But this Court's decisions have yet to articulate the types of powers that will be deemed significant enough to constitute "significant authority."

To provide guidance to Congress and the Executive Branch, I would hold that one requisite component of "significant authority" is the ability to make final, binding decisions on behalf of the Government. Accordingly, a person who merely advises and provides recommendations to an officer would not herself qualify as an officer.

* * *

Confirming that final decisionmaking authority is a prerequisite to officer status would go a long way to aiding Congress and the Executive Branch in sorting out who is an officer and who is a mere employee. At the threshold, Congress and the Executive Branch could rule out as an officer any person who investigates, advises, or recommends, but who has no power to issue binding policies, execute the laws, or finally resolve adjudicatory questions.

* * *

* * *I would hold that Commission ALJs are not officers because they lack final decisionmaking authority * * *. Even where the Commission does not review an ALJ's initial decision, as in cases in which no party petitions for review and the Commission does not act sua sponte, the initial decision still only becomes final when the Commission enters a finality order. 17 CFR. § 201.360(d)(2). And by operation of law, every action taken by an ALJ "shall, for all purposes, . . . be deemed the action of the Commission." 15 U.S.C. § 78d–1(c) (emphasis added). In other words, Commission ALJs do not exercise significant authority because they do not, and cannot, enter final, binding decisions against the Government or third parties.

* * *

NOTES AND QUESTIONS

1. Isn't the Supreme Court clearly right that administrative law judges are, at least, inferior officers of the United States and not merely employees? Indeed, given the importance of the decision-making that administrative law judges do, isn't the real question whether they are superior officers of the United States who need to be nominated by the President, confirmed by the Senate, and then appointed by the President when he or she commissions them?

2. Justice Sotomayor would limit the category of "Officers" to those who exercise final decision-making authority. As you will shortly see, that is the key line between superior and inferior officers, not between officers and employees.

3. Justice Breyer's opinion worries about the consequences of the Court's holding when that holding is combined with doctrines regarding removal of executive officials. When we come to the removal doctrine shortly, be prepared to revisit Justice Breyer's concerns. Are his concerns, if valid, good grounds for constitutional decision-making?

4. Once someone is properly appointed, they can function as an "Officer of the United States." But what does that mean? Every appointment is to a specific office. The duties of that office are determined by statute. But statutes come and go, as do the duties of particular offices. Those duties are not likely to remain constant over time. If the office's duties change, does that mean that a new appointment is necessary because the official is now inhabiting a different office than the one to which they were appointed? This is especially pertinent when the office is subject to Senate confirmation; exactly to what did the Senate advise and consent? On the one hand, it seems absurd to think that a new appointment is necessary every time a new statute is passed affecting in any way the duties of an office. On the other hand, can someone appointed, for example, Secretary of Defense suddenly be given responsibility to administer the Clean Air Act, agricultural subsidies, and the federal banking laws just because the appointment as Secretary of Defense was valid? If Congress does not like the President's appointment to an office, can Congress just reassign that office's duties to someone else that Congress prefers? The Court largely ducked those difficult questions in *Weiss v. United States,* 510 U.S. 163, which involved whether persons who were properly appointed as military officers could serve on a military court without a new appointment. A previous case had suggested that appointment to a federal office generally allows the appointee to perform new duties that are "germane" to the positions to which they were appointed. *See Shoemaker v. United States,* 147 U.S. 282 (1893). The Court in *Weiss* declined to hold that only "germane" duties could be performed by an appointee without a new appointment, ruling that *even if* that was the right test, serving as a military judge was "germane" to serving as a military officer. Justices Scalia and Thomas concurred in the result but would have tackled the "germaneness" inquiry with more vigor.

5. How should one figure out what duties are "germane" to a particular office? Is it germane to the office of being a Supreme Court justice to ride circuit for six months of the year on horseback and try cases as a designated federal circuit court judge? The Framers apparently thought so, even though many justices privately disagreed. Is it germane to the office of Secretary of the Treasury to receive authority to spend $750 billion to buy whatever securities the Secretary thinks will promote financial stability? *See* Gary Lawson, *Burying the Constitution under a TARP,* 33 HARV. J.L. & PUB. POL'Y 55, 67–69 (2010). Scholars, as with the Court, have had a tough time explaining how to determine the germaneness of new duties. *See* David R. Stras & Ryan W. Scott, *Are Senior Judges Unconstitutional?*, 92 CORNELL L. REV. 453 (2007); Matthew H. Hunter,

Legislating Around the Appointments Clause, 91 B.U. L. REV. 753 (2011). Some constitutional questions are just plain hard, and this may be one of them.

6. One important variant on the problem of germaneness concerns the difference between inferior and superior officers. Could someone properly appointed as an inferior officer, without presidential nomination and senatorial confirmation, become improperly appointed if their duties change so significantly that they now hold a superior rather than inferior office? That can only happen, of course, if the line between inferior and superior offices depends to some degree on the kind of authority that the office possesses. If it seems obvious to you—as it does to us—that the scope of the office's powers *must* affect whether someone is a superior or inferior ("minute," as Rufus King put it) officer, chew on the following caselaw addressing the inferior/superior distinction (keeping in mind that the cases use the term "principal officer" to describe what we call a superior officer).

2. MORRISON V. OLSON

487 U.S. 654 (1988)

■ CHIEF JUSTICE REHNQUIST delivered the opinion of the Court.

* * * Title VI of the Ethics in Government Act (Title VI or the Act) allows for the appointment of an "independent counsel" to investigate and, if appropriate, prosecute certain high-ranking Government officials for violations of federal criminal laws. The Act requires the Attorney General, upon receipt of information that he determines is "sufficient to constitute grounds to investigate whether any person [covered by the Act] may have violated any Federal criminal law," to conduct a preliminary investigation of the matter. When the Attorney General has completed this investigation, or 90 days has elapsed, he is required to report to a special court (the Special Division) [consisting of three life tenured Article III judges appointed by the Chief Justice] created by the Act "for the purpose of appointing independent counsels." If the Attorney General determines that "there are no reasonable grounds to believe that further investigation is warranted," then he must notify the Special Division of this result. In such a case, "the division of the court shall have no power to appoint an independent counsel." § 592(b)(1). If, however, the Attorney General has determined that there are "reasonable grounds to believe that further investigation or prosecution is warranted," then he "shall apply to the division of the court for the appointment of an independent counsel." The Attorney General's application to the court "shall contain sufficient information to assist the [court] in selecting an independent counsel and in defining that independent counsel's prosecutorial jurisdiction." * * * Upon receiving this application, the Special Division "shall appoint an appropriate independent counsel and shall define that independent counsel's prosecutorial jurisdiction."

With respect to all matters within the independent counsel's jurisdiction, the Act grants the counsel "full power and independent authority to exercise all investigative and prosecutorial functions and powers of the Department of Justice, the Attorney General, and any other officer or employee of the Department of Justice." The functions of the independent counsel include conducting grand jury proceedings and other investigations, participating in civil and criminal court proceedings and litigation, and appealing any decision in any case in which the counsel participates in an official capacity. Under [the Act], the counsel's powers include "initiating and conducting prosecutions in any court of competent jurisdiction, framing and signing indictments, filing informations, and handling all aspects of any case, in the name of the United States." The counsel may appoint employees, may request and obtain assistance from the Department of Justice, and may accept referral of matters from the Attorney General if the matter falls within the counsel's jurisdiction as defined by the Special Division. The Act also states that an independent counsel "shall, except where not possible, comply with the written or other established policies of the Department of Justice respecting enforcement of the criminal laws." In addition, whenever a matter has been referred to an independent counsel under the Act, the Attorney General and the Justice Department are required to suspend all investigations and proceedings regarding the matter. An independent counsel has "full authority to dismiss matters within [his or her] prosecutorial jurisdiction without conducting an investigation or at any subsequent time before prosecution, if to do so would be consistent" with Department of Justice policy.

* * *

* * * The initial question is * * *whether appellant is an "inferior" or a "principal" officer. If she is the latter, as the Court of Appeals concluded, then the Act is in violation of the Appointments Clause.

The line between "inferior" and "principal" officers is one that is far from clear, and the Framers provided little guidance into where it should be drawn. We need not attempt here to decide exactly where the line falls between the two types of officers, because in our view appellant clearly falls on the "inferior officer" side of that line. Several factors lead to this conclusion.

First, appellant is subject to removal by a higher Executive Branch official. Although appellant may not be "subordinate" to the Attorney General (and the President) insofar as she possesses a degree of independent discretion to exercise the powers delegated to her under the Act, the fact that she can be removed by the Attorney General indicates that she is to some degree "inferior" in rank and authority. Second, appellant is empowered by the Act to perform only certain, limited duties. An independent counsel's role is restricted primarily to investigation and, if appropriate, prosecution for certain federal crimes. Admittedly, the Act delegates to appellant "full power and independent authority to exercise all investigative and prosecutorial functions and powers of the Department of Justice," but this grant of authority does not include any authority to formulate policy for the Government or the Executive Branch, nor does it give appellant any administrative duties outside of those necessary to operate her office. The Act specifically provides that in policy matters appellant is to comply to the extent possible with the policies of the Department.

Third, appellant's office is limited in jurisdiction. Not only is the Act itself restricted in applicability to certain federal officials suspected of certain serious federal crimes, but an independent counsel can only act within the scope of the jurisdiction that has been granted by the Special Division pursuant to a request by the Attorney General. Finally, appellant's office is limited in tenure. There is concededly no time limit on the appointment of a particular counsel. Nonetheless, the office of independent counsel is "temporary" in the sense that an independent counsel is appointed essentially to accomplish a single task, and when that task is over the office is terminated, either by the counsel herself or by action of the Special Division. Unlike other prosecutors, appellant has no ongoing responsibilities that extend beyond the accomplishment of the mission that she was appointed for and authorized by the Special Division to undertake. In our view, these factors relating to the "ideas of tenure, duration . . . and duties" of the independent counsel, are sufficient to establish that appellant is an "inferior" officer in the constitutional sense.

* * *

■ JUSTICE SCALIA, dissenting.

* * *

* * * [T]he Court does not attempt to "decide exactly" what establishes the line between principal and "inferior" officers, but is confident that, whatever the line may be, appellant "clearly falls on the 'inferior officer' side" of it. The Court gives three reasons: *First,* she "is subject to removal by a higher Executive Branch official," namely, the Attorney General. *Second,* she is "empowered by the Act to perform only certain, limited duties." *Third,* her office is "limited in jurisdiction" and "limited in tenure."

The first of these lends no support to the view that appellant is an inferior officer. Appellant is removable only for "good cause" or physical or mental incapacity. By contrast, most (if not all) *principal* officers in the Executive Branch may be removed by the President *at will.* I fail to see how the fact that appellant is more difficult to remove than most principal officers helps to establish that she is an inferior officer. And I do not see how it could possibly make any difference to her superior or inferior status that the President's limited power to remove her must be exercised through the Attorney General. If she were removable at will by the Attorney General, then she would be subordinate to him and thus properly designated as inferior; but the Court essentially admits that she is not subordinate. If it were common usage to refer to someone as "inferior" who is subject to removal for cause by another, then one would say that the President is "inferior" to Congress.

The second reason offered by the Court—that appellant performs only certain, limited duties—may be relevant to whether she is an inferior officer, but it mischaracterizes the extent of her powers. As the Court states: "Admittedly, the Act delegates to appellant [the] '*full power and independent authority to exercise all investigative and prosecutorial functions and powers of the Department of Justice.*' " Moreover, in addition to this general grant of power she is given a broad range of specifically enumerated powers, including a power not even the Attorney General possesses: to "contes[t] in court . . . any claim of privilege or attempt to withhold evidence on grounds of national security." Once all of this is "admitted," it seems to me impossible to maintain that appellant's authority is so "limited" as to render her an inferior officer. The Court seeks to brush this away by asserting that the independent counsel's power does not include any authority to "formulate policy for the Government or the Executive Branch." But the same could be said for all officers of the Government, with the single exception of the President. All of them only formulate policy within their respective spheres of responsibility—as does the independent counsel, who must comply with the policies of the Department of Justice only to the extent possible.

The final set of reasons given by the Court for why the independent counsel clearly is an inferior officer emphasizes the limited nature of her jurisdiction and tenure. Taking the latter first, I find nothing unusually limited about the independent counsel's tenure. To the contrary, unlike most high-ranking Executive Branch officials, she continues to serve until she (or the Special Division) decides that her work is substantially completed. * * * This particular independent prosecutor has already served more than two years, which is at least as long as many Cabinet officials. As to the scope of her jurisdiction, there can be no doubt that is small (though far from unimportant). But within it she exercises more than the full power of the Attorney General. The Ambassador to Luxembourg is not anything less than a principal officer, simply because Luxembourg is small. And the federal judge who sits in a small district is not for that reason "inferior in rank and authority." * * *

* * * [T]he text of the Constitution and the division of power that it establishes * * * demonstrate, I think, that the independent counsel is not an inferior officer because she is not *subordinate* to any officer in the Executive Branch (indeed, not even to the President). Dictionaries in use at the time of the Constitutional Convention gave the word "inferiour" two meanings which it still bears today: (1) "[l]ower in place, . . . station, . . . rank of life, . . . value or excellency," and (2) "[s]ubordinate." S. Johnson, Dictionary of the English Language (6th ed. 1785). In a document dealing with the structure (the constitution) of a government, one would naturally expect the word to bear the latter meaning—indeed, in such a context it would be unpardonably careless to use the word *unless* a relationship of subordination was intended. If what was meant was merely "lower in station or rank," one would use instead a term such as "lesser officers." At the only other point in the Constitution at which the word "inferior" appears, it plainly connotes a relationship of subordination. Article III vests the judicial power of the United States in "one supreme Court, and in such *inferior* Courts as the Congress may from time to time ordain and establish." U.S. Const., Art. III, § 1 (emphasis added). In Federalist No. 81, Hamilton pauses to describe the "inferior" courts authorized by Article III as inferior in the sense that they are "subordinate" to the Supreme Court.

To be sure, it is not a *sufficient* condition for "inferior" officer status that one be subordinate to a principal officer. Even an officer who is subordinate to a department head can be a principal officer. * * * But it is surely a *necessary* condition for inferior officer status that the officer be subordinate to another officer.

The independent counsel is not even subordinate to the President. The Court essentially admits as much, noting that "appellant may not be 'subordinate' to the Attorney General (and the President) insofar as she possesses a degree of independent discretion to exercise the powers delegated to her under the Act." In fact, there is no doubt about it. As noted earlier, the Act specifically grants her the "*full* power and *independent* authority to exercise *all* investigative and prosecutorial functions of the Department of Justice," and makes her removable only for "good cause," a limitation specifically intended to ensure that she be *independent* of, not *subordinate* to, the President and the Attorney General.

Because appellant is not subordinate to another officer, she is not an "inferior" officer and her appointment other than by the President with the advice and consent of the Senate is unconstitutional.

Edmond v. United States

520 U.S. 651 (1997)

[*Editors' Note: This case involved the question of whether Congress had authorized the Secretary of Transportation to appoint civilian members of the Coast Guard Court of Criminal Appeals, and if so, whether this authorization was constitutional under the Appointments Clause of Article II. The Coast Guard Court of Criminal Appeals is an intermediate court within the military justice system with both military and civilian judges. The appointment of the military judges was clearly constitutional under* Weiss v. United States, *510 U.S. 163 (1994), but the appointment of the two civilian judges by the Secretary of Transportation, a "Head[ ] of Department, was constitutional only if the judges were inferior officers within the meaning of the Appointments Clause.*]

■ JUSTICE SCALIA delivered the opinion of the Court:

* * *

Our cases have not set forth an exclusive criterion for distinguishing between principal and inferior officers for Appointment Clause purposes. Among the offices that we have found to be inferior are that of a district court clerk, an election supervisor, a vice-consul charged temporarily with the duties of the consul, and a "United States commissioner" in district court proceedings. Most recently, in *Morrison v. Olson*, 487 U.S. 654 (1988), we held that the independent counsel created by provisions of the Ethics in Government Act of 1978 was an inferior officer. In reaching that conclusion, we relied on several factors: that the independent counsel was subject to removal by a higher officer (the Attorney General), that she performed only limited duties, that her jurisdiction was narrow, and that her tenure was limited.

Petitioners are quite correct that the last two of these conclusions do not hold with regard to the office of military judge at issue here. It is not "limited in tenure," as that phrase was used in *Morrison* to describe "appoint[ment] essentially to accomplish a single task [at the end of which] the office is terminated." Nor are military judges "limited in jurisdiction," as used in *Morrison* to refer to the fact that an independent counsel may investigate and prosecute only those individuals, and for only those crimes, that are within the scope of jurisdiction granted by the special three judge appointing panel. However, *Morrison* did not purport to set forth a definitive test for whether an office is "inferior" under the Appointments Clause. To the contrary, it explicitly stated: "We need not attempt here to decide exactly where the line falls between the two types of officers, because in our view [the independent counsel] clearly falls on the 'inferior officer' side of the line." 487 U.S., at 671.

To support principal-officer status, petitioners emphasize the importance of the responsibilities that Court of Criminal Appeals judges bear. They review those court-martial proceedings that result in the most serious sentences, including those "in which the sentence, as approved, extends to death, dismissal . . ., dishonorable or bad-conduct discharge, or confinement for one year or more." Art. 66(b)(1), UCMJ, 10 U.S.C. § 866(b)(1). They must ensure that the court-martial's finding of guilt and its sentence are "correct in law and fact," *id.* Art. 66(c), § 866(c), which includes resolution of constitutional challenges. And finally, unlike most appellate judges, Court of Criminal Appeals judges are not required to defer to the trial court's factual findings, but may independently "weigh the evidence, judge the credibility of witnesses, and determine controverted questions of fact, recognizing that the trial court saw and heard the witnesses." *Ibid.* We do not dispute that military appellate judges are charged with exercising significant authority on behalf of the United States. This, however, is also true of offices that we have held were "inferior" within the meaning of the Appointments Clause. The exercise of "significant authority pursuant to the laws of the United States" marks, not the line between principal and inferior officer for Appointments Clause purposes, but rather, as we said in *Buckley*, the line between officer and non-officer. 424 U.S., at 126.

Generally speaking, the term "inferior officer" connotes a relationship with some higher ranking officer or officers below the President: Whether one is an "inferior" officer depends on whether he has a superior. It is not enough that other officers may be identified who formally maintain a higher rank, or possess responsibilities of a greater magnitude. If that were the intention, the Constitution might have used the phrase "lesser officer." Rather, in the context of a Clause designed to preserve political accountability relative to important Government assignments, we think it evident that "inferior officers" are officers whose work is directed and supervised at some level by others who were appointed by Presidential nomination with the advice and consent of the Senate.

* * *

Supervision of the work of Court of Criminal Appeals judges is divided between the Judge Advocate General (who in the Coast Guard is subordinate to the Secretary of Transportation) and the Court of Appeals for the Armed Forces. The Judge Advocate General exercises administrative oversight over the Court of Criminal Appeals. He is charged with the responsibility to "prescribe uniform rules of procedure" for the court, and must "meet periodically [with other Judge Advocates General] to formulate policies and procedure in regard to review of court-martial cases." * * * It is conceded by the parties that the Judge Advocate General may also remove a Court of Criminal Appeals judge from his judicial assignment without cause. The power to remove officers, we have recognized, is a powerful tool for control.

* * *

We conclude that 49 U.S.C. § 323(a) authorizes the Secretary of Transportation to appoint judges of the Coast Guard Court of Criminal Appeals; and that such appointment is in conformity with the Appointments Clause of the Constitution, since those judges are "inferior Officers" within the meaning of that provision, by reason of the supervision over their work exercised by the General Counsel of the Department of Transportation in his capacity as Judge Advocate General and the Court of Appeals for the Armed Forces. The judicial appointments at issue in this case are therefore valid.

Accordingly, we affirm the judgment of the Court of Appeals for the Armed Forces with respect to each petitioner.

■ SOUTER, J., concurring in part and concurring in the judgment.

* * *

Because the term "inferior officer" implies an official superior, one who has no superior is not an inferior officer. This unexceptionable maxim will in some instances be dispositive of status; it might, for example, lead to the conclusion that United

States district judges cannot be inferior officers, since the power of appellate review does not extend to them personally, but is limited to their judgments.

It does not follow, however, that if one is subject to some supervision and control, one is an inferior officer. Having a superior officer is necessary for inferior officer status, but not sufficient to establish it. * * * Thus, * * * the Solicitor General of the United States, for example, may well be a principal officer, despite his statutory "inferiority" to the Attorney General * * *.

In this case, as the Court persuasively shows, the Judge Advocate General has substantial supervisory authority over the judges of the Coast Guard Court of Criminal Appeals * * *. While these facts establish that the condition of supervision and control necessary for inferior officer status has been met, I am wary of treating them as sufficient to demonstrate that the judges of the Court of Criminal Appeals are actually inferior officers under the Constitution.

In having to go beyond the Court's opinion to decide that the criminal appeals judges are inferior officers, I do not claim the convenience of a single sufficient condition, and, indeed, at this stage of the Court's thinking on the matter, I would not try to derive a single rule of sufficiency. What is needed, instead, is a detailed look at the powers and duties of these judges to see whether reasons favoring their inferior officer status within the constitutional scheme weigh more heavily than those to the contrary * * *.

NOTES AND QUESTIONS

1. *Morrison* was a 7–1 decision. *Edmond* was unanimous in the judgment and 8–1 on the reasoning. Are they consistent? In two subsequent cases, the majority of the Supreme Court cited *Edmond* as being good law, but it did not cite the Appointments Clause holding of *Morrison v. Olson*. *See Free Enterprise Fund v. P.C.A.O.B.*, 561 U.S. 477 (2010); *Lucia v. SEC*, 585 U.S. ___, 138 S.Ct. 2044 (2018). Has *Morrison* been overruled *sub silentio,* or are there now two distinct tests operating side by side? If you were a lower court judge facing an Appointments Clause case, what would you do? A Court of Appeals opinion from October 2019 concluded that administrative judges on the Patent Trial and Appeal Board, who issue final decisions on the cancellation of patents, are superior officers, relying almost entirely on *Edmond,* with only a brief mention of *Morrison*. *See Arthrex, Inc. v. Smith & Nephew, Inc.*, 941 F.3d 1320 (Fed.Cir.2019).

2. Justice Souter's concurring opinion in *Edmond* suggests a possible reconciliation of *Edmond* and *Morrison*: If an officer's decision is not reviewable or reversible by anyone else in the executive branch other than the President (who, under a unitary executive theory, can review anything), that officer is necessarily a superior officer without need for further inquiry; but an officer whose decisions are internally reviewable but who exercises vast power can also be a superior officer, depending on the levels and kinds of supervision involved. This approach makes a lot of sense. If all that matters is internal reviewability, there will be one and only one superior officer in virtually every executive department, because the head of the department almost always has the final say. For example, the Attorney General is vested with "all functions of agencies and employees of the Department of Justice," 28 U.S.C. § 509 (2018), meaning that the Attorney General can make the decision for anyone in the Department of Justice. Under *Edmond,* does that make the Deputy Attorney General, the Solicitor General, the eleven Assistant Attorneys General, and the ninety-two U.S. Attorneys all inferior officers? That would be bizarre. It would almost wholly conflate the category of superior

officers with the much narrower category of "Heads of Departments." And are federal district and court of appeals judges inferior officers because the Supreme Court can reverse their decisions? Could Congress let the Supreme Court appoint lower federal judges? For an argument that Justice Souter is right on this point, *see* Steven Gow Calabresi & Gary Lawson, *Why Robert Mueller's Appointment as Special Counsel Was Unlawful*, 95 NOTRE DAME L. REV.87 (2019).

3. But then how does one explain the outcome in *Morrison*? The Independent Counsel had both independent decision-making authority *and* even more power within her scope of authority than is possessed by a U.S. Attorney. Or was *Morrison* just flat-out wrong, even on its own terms, as Justice Scalia argued in his dissent?

4. Once you determine that someone is an inferior officer, Congress can, if it wishes, vest the appointment, without Senate confirmation, "in the President alone, in the Courts of Law, or in the Heads of Departments." Who are the "Courts of Law" and "Heads of Departments" to whom the Appointments Clause refers? The "Courts of Law" would seem obviously to be the federal courts who exercise the "judicial Power of the United States" under Article III. The only problem is that the Supreme Court rejected that easy and obvious answer in 1991 in *Freytag v. Comm'r of Internal Revenue*, 501 U.S. 868 (1991), in which a five-justice majority concluded that the Chief Judge of the Tax Court—a non-Article III executive agency—could count as a "Court of Law" under the Appointments Clause and could therefore appoint Special Trial Judges as inferior officers:

> The text of the [Appointments] Clause does not limit the "Courts of Law" to those courts established under Article III of the Constitution. The Appointments Clause does not provide that Congress can vest appointment power only in "one Supreme Court" and other courts established under Article III, or only in tribunals that exercise broad common-law jurisdiction * * *. Petitioners * * * underestimate the importance of this Court's time-honored reading of the Constitution as giving Congress wide discretion to assign the task of adjudication in cases arising under federal law to legislative tribunals.

501 U.S. at 888–91. Justice Scalia, writing for himself and three other justices, concurred in the result but not the reasoning:

> The [Appointments] Clause does not refer generally to "Bodies exercising judicial Functions," or even to "Courts" generally, or even to "Courts of Law" generally. It refers to "*the* Courts of Law." Certainly this does not mean *any* "Cour[t] of Law" (the Supreme Court of Rhode Island would not do). The definite article "the" obviously narrows the class of eligible "Courts of Law" to those courts of law envisioned by the Constitution. Those are Article III courts, and the Tax Court is not one of them.

Id. at 902 (Scalia, J., concurring in part and concurring in the judgment). Justice Scalia thought that the Chief Judge of the Tax Court was a "Head[ ] of Department[ ]" and could appoint inferior officers for that reason. The majority resisted that conclusion because it thought that "Heads of Departments" had a much narrower meaning:

> This court for more than a century has held that the term "Departmen[t]" refers only to " 'a part or division of the executive government, as the Department of State, or of the Treasury,' " expressly "creat[ed]" and "giv[en] . . . the name of a department" by congress. *Germaine*, 99 U.S., at 510–511. Accordingly, the term "heads of departments" does not embrace "inferior commissioners and bureau officers." *Germaine*, 99 U.S., at 511 * * *. Confining the term "heads of Departments" in the appointments Clause to executive

> divisions like the Cabinet-level departments constrains the distribution of the appointment power just as the Commissioner's interpretation, in contrast, would diffuse it.

Id. at 886. Justice Scalia countered that trying to limit "Heads of Departments" to Cabinet officers

> * * * has no basis in text or precedent * * *. The term "Cabinet" does not appear in the Constitution * * *.
>
> * * *
>
> * * * I would give the term ["Departments"] its ordinary meaning * * *. As an American dictionary roughly contemporaneous with adoption of the Appointments Clause provided, and as remains the case, a department is "[a] separate allotment or part of business; a distinct province, in which a class of duties are allotted to a particular person. . ." 1 N. Webster, American Dictionary 58 (1828) * * *. [T]he Founders * * * chose the word "Departmen[t]," * * * not to connote size or function (much less Cabinet status), but separate organization—a connotation that still endures even in colloquial usage today ("that is not my department") * * *.

Id. at 915–16 (Scalia, J., concurring in part and concurring in the judgment).

This all came to a head twenty years later in *Free Enterprise Fund v. Public Company Accounting Oversight Board,* 561 U.S. 477 (2010), which we will examine in more detail shortly. In the wake of major corporate accounting scandals involving such firms as Enron, Congress in 2002 created the Public Company Accounting Oversight Board (PCAOB) to regulate corporate accounting practices. The PCAOB members are appointed by the Securities and Exchange Commission (SEC), a five-member administrative body created in 1934 to regulate the securities markets. Commissioners on multi-member regulatory agencies like the SEC have never been part of the President's Cabinet (though, since the Cabinet has no official legal definition, nothing forbids a President from changing that tradition). Relying on *Freytag's* narrow understanding of "Departments," challengers questioned whether the SEC could be given authority to appoint inferior officers. The Court in *Free Enterprise Fund* cited precisely the same dictionary definition and historical sources relied upon by Justice Scalia in his *Freytag* concurrence to conclude that the SEC could count as a "Department" under the Appointments Clause and that a multimember body can, as a collective unit, be the "Head[ ]" of a department. *See* 561 U.S. at 511–13. The durability of the majority opinion in *Freytag,* which seemed squarely to support the challengers' position, was the subject of an exchange at oral argument in *Free Enterprise Fund* between Justice Scalia, Chief Justice Roberts (who later wrote the majority opinion), and Mike Carvin, counsel for Free Enterprise Fund which was contesting the SEC's appointment authority:

> Mr. Carvin: * * * The SEC cannot be a department under *Freytag*, because it is an independent agency indistinguishable from the Tax Court. And—and what the *Freytag* majority opinion said was, if you are unlike a [C]abinet department because you are not subject to political oversight, then—
>
> Justice Scalia: I hope your case doesn't rest on *Freytag*.
>
> [Laughter.]
>
> Mr. Carvin: So do I. I want to take an opportunity to focus on the real point of *Freytag*, which was made very eloquently in the *Freytag* dissenting opinion, which was—
>
> [Laughter.]

Chief Justice Roberts: And the brief.

[Laughter.]

Https://www.supremecourt.gov/oral_arguments/argument_transcripts/2009/08-861.pdf, at 23–24. Deputy Solicitor General John Roberts argued *Freytag* on behalf of the United States in 1991 and presumably wrote the brief to which Chief Justice John Roberts referred in 2010. Has *Freytag* now been overruled by laughter at oral argument? Does the (apparent) rejection of *Freytag* extend to its view of what counts as "the Courts of Law" as well as what counts as "Heads of Departments"? If "Departments" is a term broad enough to include the SEC, what else might it include? Is the PCAOB, an entity located within the SEC, itself a "Department[ ]"? Is the FBI, an entity located within the Department of Justice, a "Department[ ]"? Is the American Battle Monuments Commission, which oversees maintenance of overseas American war memorials, a "Department[ ]"? And is the head of a "Department[ ]" by definition a principal officer?

5. As an aside, some closing thoughts on *Freytag:* When explaining why it thought that the Tax Court was not a "Department[ ]," the majority wrote: "The Tax Court exercises judicial, rather than executive, legislative, or administrative, power. It was established by Congress to interpret and apply the Internal Revenue Code in disputes between taxpayers and the Government. By resolving these disputes, the court exercises a portion of the judicial power of the United States." 501 U.S. at 891. Is the Court saying that anyone who adjudicates in any fashion exercises "judicial Power"? And when the Court distinguishes judicial power from "executive, legislative, or administrative power," what does it mean by "administrative power"? Which Article of the Constitution vests "administrative power"? Did the gallery at the oral argument in *Free Enterprise Fund* laugh at the wrong parts of *Freytag? But see* Lawrence Lessig & Cass R. Sunstein, *The President and the Administration,* 94 COLUM. L. REV. 1 (1994) (arguing that the Constitution really contains an "administrative" power). *But but see* Steven G. Calabresi & Saikrishna B. Prakash, *The President's Power to Execute the Laws,* 104 YALE L.J. 541, 559–70 (1994) (no, it really doesn't).

6. If someone is concededly an inferior officer, can Congress allow them to be appointed by *any* of the appointing authorities identified in the Appointments Clause? Can Congress allow the "Courts of Law" to appoint inferior executive officers and, for example, the Attorney General to appoint inferior judicial officers? In *Morrison v. Olson,* the Court held that the "interbranch" appointment of an executive prosecutor by the "Courts of Law" was not unconstitutional, but it left open the possibility that some "interbranch" appointments might cross a line "if there was some 'incongruity' between the functions normally performed by the courts and the performance of their duty to appoint." 487 U.S. at 676. That is as much guidance as the case law provides on that point.

[Assignment 20]

3. THE RECESS APPOINTMENT CLAUSE

Article II, Section 2, Clause 3: The President shall have Power to fill up all Vacancies that may happen during the Recess of the Senate, by granting Commissions which shall expire at the end of their next Session.

When the Constitution was ratified, travel and communication was difficult. Senators were generally not professional politicians. They had private lives to which they returned when they were not in session—and the sessions of Congress were very short. What would happen if, in the middle of war or some other crisis, the President needed a new Secretary of State, Secretary of War, or top general who could only be appointed with Senate confirmation, but the Senate was not in session? Yes, the Constitution allows the President to call the Senate into special session, *see* U.S. CONST. art. II, § 3, but that could take a lot of time in the eighteenth century. The solution was the Recess Appointments Clause, which allows temporary appointments even of superior, and even of principal, officers without Senate confirmation. That seems both sensible and simple.

Is it in fact neither? In 1789, there may have been a need for such a provision, but in 2019 or beyond does it still make any sense? Does that, or should that, matter for purposes of interpretation? There has been only a modest amount of caselaw on the Recess Appointments Clause, but the few cases have addressed—in split decisions—some major questions raised by the provision.

United States v. Woodley

751 F.2d 1008 (9th Cir. 1985)

■ BEEZER, CIRCUIT JUDGE, with whom BROWNING, CHIEF JUDGE, and SNEED, SKOPIL, FARRIS, ALARCON, and POOLE, CIRCUIT JUDGES, join concurring.

We take this case en banc to address the constitutionality of a practice followed by the Executive for nearly 200 years. The question before us is whether the President of the United States may constitutionally confer temporary federal judicial commissions during a recess of the Senate pursuant to article II, section 2 of the Constitution.

On February 28, 1980, Walter Heen was nominated to fill a judicial vacancy in the United States District Court for Hawaii. * * *. When the Senate recessed on December 16, 1980 * * * the nomination [had] not come before the full Senate for its advice and consent. During the Senate's recess, on December 31, 1980, President Carter conferred a commission on Judge Heen pursuant to the recess appointment clause of article II of the United States Constitution. Heen then took his oath and assumed his duties as district court judge * * * until December 16, 1981, when the 97th Congress ended its First Session.

* * * [W]hile Heen was sitting out his commission, * * * [he] presided over a bench trial [of Woodley on narcotics charges]. Woodley filed a motion to suppress evidence, which was denied by Heen. Judge Heen then presided over a bench trial on stipulated facts and found Woodley guilty as charged in the indictment.

Woodley appealed the denial of her motion to suppress * * *. [W]e hold that the recess appointment clause extends to judicial officers and that a recess appointee to the federal bench can exercise the judicial power of the United States.

The recess appointment clause provides that: "The President shall have Power to fill up all Vacancies that may happen during the Recess of the Senate, by granting Commissions which shall expire at the End of their next Session." U.S. Const. art. II, § 2, cl. 3. Article III, in turn, provides in relevant part that: "The Judges, both of the supreme and inferior Courts, shall hold their Offices during good Behaviour, and shall, at stated Times, receive for their Services a Compensation, which shall not be diminished during their Continuance in Office." U.S. Const. art. III, § 1.

Woodley contends that under generally accepted principles of statutory construction, the more specific language of article III governs over the general language of the recess appointment clause. She concludes therefore that article III forbids interim judicial recess appointments. We reject this argument.

The United States Supreme Court has unequivocally stated that "[t]he Constitution . . . must be regarded as one instrument, all of whose provisions are to be deemed of equal validity." *Prout v. Starr*, 188 U.S. 537, 543 (1903). Moreover, while article III speaks specifically about the tenure of federal judges, article II is equally specific in addressing the manner of their appointment. There is therefore no reason to favor one Article over the other.

The language of the recess appointment clause explicitly provides that the President has the power to fill *all* vacancies during the recess of the Senate. The *Federalist* papers clarify the meaning of the recess clause, stating that it "is to be considered as supplementary to the [clause] which precedes [it]" and that the vacancies referred to "must be construed to relate to the 'officers' described in the preceding [clause]." *The Federalist No. 67.* The preceding clause in question provides in relevant part that the President "shall nominate, and by and with the Advice and Consent of the Senate shall appoint . . . *Judges of the supreme Court, and all other Officers of the United States* . . . ." U.S. Const. art. II, § 2, cl. 2 (emphasis added). The language further underscores that there is no basis upon which to carve out an exception from the recess power for federal judges. Particularly relevant in this context is Alexander Hamilton's statement that "[a]s to the mode of appointing the judges: This is the same with that of appointing the officers of the union in general . . . ." *The Federalist No. 78.*

Woodley also argues that there is no historical evidence that the Framers intended the recess provision to apply to the judiciary. This argument is not only refuted by the express language of the recess clause, which, as previously noted, refers to *all* vacancies, but it is also refuted by legislative history, as well as historical practice, consensus, and acquiescence.

Although the recess appointment clause was adopted without debate, 2 Farrand, *Records of the Federal Convention* 533, 540 (1911), there is evidence that it was not entirely uncontroversial. Edmund Randolph, the governor of Virginia, initially declined to sign the Constitution, in part because the recess provision gave the Executive the power to confer judicial commissions during the recess of the Senate. 3 Farrand, *supra*, at 123, 127.

In 1789, shortly after ratification of the Constitution, George Washington, who had served as President of the Constitutional Convention, exercised his power under the recess provision. During the recess between the sessions of the First Congress, he conferred three recess district judge commissions. At the time of these appointments, Edmund Randolph and two contributors to *The Federalist*, Alexander Hamilton and John Jay, served as members of President Washington's Cabinet. There is no evidence that they doubted the constitutionality of the recess appointments. Moreover, the district court judges were confirmed upon the return of the Senate without objection to their recess appointments. It is further noteworthy that President Washington's recess appointments of Justice Johnson in 1791 and of Chief Justice Rutledge in 1795 went unchallenged. One commentator has aptly noted that "the most significant historical fact is that by the end of 1823, there had been five recess appointments to the Supreme Court. During this period, when those who wrote the Constitution were alive and active, not one dissenting voice was raised against the practice." Note, *Recess Appointments to the Supreme Court—Constitutional But Unwise?*, 10 Stan. L. Rev. 124, 132 (1957).

The actions of the three branches of our government have consistently confirmed the President's power to make recess appointments. The Executive Branch has made extensive use of the recess power. Approximately 300 judicial recess appointments have been made in our nation's history * * *.

The Legislative Branch has consistently confirmed judicial recess appointees without dissent. Moreover, Congress has passed legislation providing for the salaries of recess appointees, without excluding judges.

Finally, we turn to the Judicial Branch. The only direct challenge, prior to the present action, to the President's power to make judicial recess appointments was rejected by the Second Circuit in *United States v. Allocco*, 305 F.2d 704 (2d Cir. 1962), *cert. denied*, 371 U.S. 964 (1963). Although the United States Supreme Court has never passed on the issue, numerous Justices have been recess appointees * * *. Altogether, fifteen recess appointments have been made to the Supreme Court. Of these, at least four appointees sat on the Court prior to their confirmation. There is no evidence that any member of the Supreme Court ever objected to this practice on constitutional grounds.

Our historical review demonstrates that there is an unbroken acceptance of the President's use of the recess power to appoint federal judges by the three branches of government. Woodley argues, however, that the Supreme Court's recent decision in *INS v. Chadha*, 462 U.S. 919 (1983), teaches that historical patterns cannot save an unconstitutional practice.

* * * The legislative veto is, however, a recent practice, barely 50 years old. Its use does not reach back to the days of the Framers, such as the practice at issue * * *.

* * *

Even viewing the recess clause as an unwise constitutional provision, it is not for this court to redraft the Constitution. Changes in that great document must come through constitutional amendment, not through judicial reform based on policy arguments. Accordingly, we hold that Judge Heen, as a recess appointee to the federal bench, could exercise the judicial power of the United States.

* * *

■ NORRIS, CIRCUIT JUDGE, with whom FLETCHER, FERGUSON and REINHARDT, CIRCUIT JUDGES, join in the dissent.

Article III of the Constitution provides that "the judicial Power of the United States" shall be exercised by judges whose independence from the political branches of government is assured by guarantees of life tenure and undiminished compensation. Today, our Court carves out an exception to this explicit and unqualified constitutional command by holding that the judicial power of the United States may be exercised by judges who serve at the pleasure of the President and the Senate. As Professor Freund aptly commented, every recess appointee sits with "one eye over his shoulder on Congress." He has no assured tenure beyond the next session of the Senate.

* * *

My major point of disagreement with the majority is its reliance upon the executive's practice of making recess judicial appointments as virtually the sole basis for its conclusion that the practice is constitutional. In my view, the majority skips what I believe should be a crucial step in the constitutional inquiry: evaluating and balancing the competing constitutional values at stake * * *.

* * *

To be sure, the executive's practice of vesting recess appointees with Article III power has a long and impressive historical pedigree, but the majority indiscriminately defers to this practice as dispositive of its constitutionality * * *.

The Constitution presents us with two separate and contradictory clauses, one in Article II and one in Article III, each clear and unambiguous on its face * * *.

* * *

Hence, we face an extraordinary situation: a direct conflict between two provisions of the Constitution. No accommodation seems possible; one clause must yield to the other * * *.

* * *

The contemporaneous writings of the Framers are virtually barren of any references to the Recess Appointments Clause. Although the record contains a few scattered references to the Clause, it was never explained, debated or discussed in any meaningful way * * *.

* * *

In contrast to the paucity of comments on the Recess Appointments Clause by the Framers, the historical record is a cornucopia of references to the principle of life tenure enshrined in Article III. History makes absolutely clear the supreme importance the Framers attached to an independent judiciary as a vital corollary to the fundamental concept of the constitutional plan, the separation of powers * * *.

In my view, the majority simply fails to take [seriously enough] the institutional protections of Article III * * *; indeed, the majority denigrates the tenure and salary provisions when it argues that there are no examples of executive or legislative coercion of a recess appointee. This rationale implies that the institutional protections of Article III are of little consequence because we can rely on the integrity and courage of individual judges to assure judicial independence. The Framers, quite obviously, did not share that view. Rather, they were firm in their conviction that permanency of office and salary protection were crucial institutional safeguards against encroachment on the judicial power by the political branches * * *.

Moreover, we must preserve not only the reality but also the appearance of judicial independence. Public confidence in the integrity and independence of the courts is imperative, especially when a constitutional confrontation between the judiciary and the political branches creates a national crisis. Such confidence could be threatened if, for example, recess appointees were called upon to participate in a highly charged case involving the constitutional limits on presidential power. The facts of *Youngstown Sheet & Tube Co. v. Sawyer,* 343 U.S. 579 (1952) provide a thought provoking historical hypothetical. Imagine a recess appointee sitting on a Supreme Court that was otherwise divided, four to four, on the question of the constitutionality of President Truman's steel mill seizure. Imagine further that this hypothetical justice is courageous and intends to vote his conscience. Were he to believe the President's action in seizing the mills was unconstitutional, the recess appointee would confront the possibility that an infuriated President might withdraw his nomination. If, on the other hand, the justice were to believe the seizure was constitutional, he would find it difficult if not impossible to avoid the appearance that his tie breaking vote had been influenced by the President's power to cut short his tenure on the Court * * *.

* * *

* * * [T]he brute historical fact that the executive or legislature has engaged in a practice, even for an extended period, cannot by itself establish the constitutionality of the practice * * *.

* * *

Today we must choose between Article III and the Recess Appointments Clause. We must also choose between deference to the historical practice of many chief executives and vindication of the fundamental constitutional values of judicial independence and separation of powers. These choices are not easy, but they must be made * * *. The fundamental principle of separation of powers must prevail over a peripheral concern for governmental efficiency, and core constitutional values must prevail over uncritical acceptance of historical practice.

NOTES AND QUESTIONS

1. The dissenting opinion was much longer than the majority opinion and spent a great deal of time discussing why it thought the history was inconclusive; it noted, for example, that there was no indication that the Washington Administration, or anyone else, had thought carefully about the constitutional issues at stake. If the dissent thought that the history did not matter, why did it spend so much time discussing it? What modalities were at work in this case? What modalities make the most sense in this case?

2. Is two centuries of practice dispositive here? If so, why should practice govern in *Woodley* but not in *INS v. Chadha*? If, as the majority suggests, fifty years of practice are not enough, how many years are enough?

3. The majority began with lengthy discussions of executive and legislative practices, only later turning to judicial practices. Is that order in which you would proceed if you were deciding this case? Whose practices matter most? Or does practice only matter when all three branches agree for a long period of time?

4. Can this case be resolved on textual grounds? Do the purposes behind the Recess Appointments Clause apply to judicial officers the same way that they apply to executive officers such as the Secretary of State or the Secretary of War?

5. The Eleventh Circuit sitting en banc reached the same conclusion as the one reached in *United States v. Woodley* in a case challenging President George W. Bush's recess appointment of Judge William Pryor. *Evans v. Stephens*, 387 F.3d 1220 (11th Cir. 2004). In both *Woodley and Evans,* the vacancy in question occurred while the Senate was in session. The Recess Appointments Clause says that any vacancies filled under the clause must "*happen* during the Recess of the Senate." One dissenting judge in *Evans* thought that the timing of the vacancy invalidated the recess appointment in that case (and in *Woodley* as well). That issue, along with the question of what counts as a Senate "Recess," reached the Supreme Court in 2014.

National Labor Relations Board v. Noel Canning

573 U.S. 513 (2014)

■ JUSTICE BREYER delivered the opinion of the Court.

Ordinarily the President must obtain "the Advice and Consent of the Senate" before appointing an "Office[r] of the United States." U. S. Const., Art. II, § 2, cl. 2. But the Recess Appointments Clause creates an exception. It gives the President alone the power "to fill up all Vacancies that may happen during the Recess of the Senate, by granting Commissions which shall expire at the End of their next Session." Art. II, § 2, cl. 3. We here consider three questions about the application of this Clause.

The first concerns the scope of the words "recess of the Senate." Does that phrase refer only to an inter-session recess (*i.e.,* a break between formal sessions of Congress), or does it also include an intra-session recess, such as a summer recess in the midst of a session? We conclude that the Clause applies to both kinds of recess.

The second question concerns the scope of the words "vacancies that may happen." Does that phrase refer only to vacancies that first come into existence during a recess, or does it also include vacancies that arise prior to a recess but continue to exist during the recess? We conclude that the Clause applies to both kinds of vacancy.

The third question concerns calculation of the length of a "recess." The President made the appointments here at issue on January 4, 2012. At that time the Senate was in recess pursuant to a December 17, 2011, resolution providing for a series of brief recesses punctuated by "*pro forma* session[s]," with "no business . . . transacted," every Tuesday and Friday through January 20, 2012. S. J., 112th Cong., 1st Sess., 923 (2011) (hereinafter 2011 S. J.). In calculating the length of a recess are we to ignore the *pro forma* sessions, thereby treating the series of brief recesses as a single, month-long recess? We conclude that we cannot ignore these *pro forma* sessions.

Our answer to the third question means that, when the appointments before us took place, the Senate was in the midst of a 3-day recess. Three days is too short a time to bring a recess within the scope of the Clause. Thus we conclude that the President lacked the power to make the recess appointments here at issue.

I

The case before us arises out of a labor dispute. The National Labor Relations Board (NLRB) found that a Pepsi-Cola distributor, Noel Canning, had unlawfully refused to reduce to writing and execute a collective-bargaining agreement with a labor union. The Board ordered the distributor to execute the agreement and to make employees whole for any losses.

The Pepsi-Cola distributor * * * claimed that three of the five Board members had been invalidly appointed, leaving the Board without the three lawfully appointed members necessary for it to act. See 29 U.S.C. § 160(f) (providing for judicial review); § 153(a) (providing for a 5-member Board); § 153(b) (providing for a 3-member quorum); *New Process Steel, L.P. v. NLRB,* 560 U.S. 674, 687–688 (2010) (in the absence of a lawfully appointed quorum, the Board cannot exercise its powers).

The three members in question were Sharon Block, Richard Griffin, and Terence Flynn. In 2011 the President had nominated each of them to the Board. As of January 2012, Flynn's nomination had been pending in the Senate awaiting confirmation for approximately a year. The nominations of each of the other two had been pending for a few weeks. On January 4, 2012, the President, invoking the Recess Appointments Clause, appointed all three to the Board.

The distributor argued that the Recess Appointments Clause did not authorize those appointments. It pointed out that on December 17, 2011, the Senate, by unanimous consent, had adopted a resolution providing that it would take a series of brief recesses beginning the following day. Pursuant to that resolution, the Senate held *pro forma* sessions every Tuesday and Friday until it returned for ordinary business on January 23, 2012. The President's January 4 appointments were made between the January 3 and January 6 *pro forma* sessions * * *.

The Court of Appeals agreed that the appointments fell outside the scope of the Clause. But the court set forth different reasons. It held that the Clause's words "the recess of the Senate" do not include recesses that occur *within* a formal session of Congress, *i.e.,* intra-session recesses. Rather those words apply only to recesses *between* those formal sessions, *i.e.,* inter-session recesses. Since the second session of the 112th Congress began on January 3, 2012, the day before the President's appointments, those appointments occurred during an intra-session recess, and the appointments consequently fell outside the scope of the Clause. 705 F.3d 490, 499–507 (C.A.D.C.2013).

II

Before turning to the specific questions presented, we shall mention two background considerations that we find relevant to all three. First, *the Recess Appointments Clause sets forth a subsidiary, not a primary, method for appointing officers of the United States* * * *.

* * *

Second, *in interpreting the Clause, we put significant weight upon historical practice* * * *.

* * *

* * * As James Madison wrote, it "was foreseen at the birth of the Constitution, that difficulties and differences of opinion might occasionally arise in expounding terms & phrases necessarily used in such a charter . . . and that it might require a regular course of practice to liquidate & settle the meaning of some of them." Letter to Spencer Roane (Sept. 2, 1819), in 8 Writings of James Madison 450 (G. Hunt ed. 1908) * * *.

* * *

There is a great deal of history to consider here. Presidents have made recess appointments since the beginning of the Republic. Their frequency suggests that the Senate and President have recognized that recess appointments can be both necessary and appropriate in certain circumstances. We have not previously interpreted the Clause, and, when doing so for the first time in more than 200 years, we must hesitate to upset the compromises and working arrangements that the elected branches of Government themselves have reached.

III

The first question concerns the scope of the phrase *"the recess* of the Senate." Art. II, § 2, cl. 3 (emphasis added). The Constitution provides for congressional elections every two years. And the 2-year life of each elected Congress typically consists of two formal 1-year sessions, each separated from the next by an "inter-session recess." Congressional Research Service, H. Hogue, Recess Appointments: Frequently Asked Questions 2 (2013). The Senate or the House of Representatives announces an inter-session recess by approving a resolution stating that it will "adjourn *sine die*," *i.e.*, without specifying a date to return (in which case Congress will reconvene when the next formal session is scheduled to begin).

The Senate and the House also take breaks in the midst of a session. The Senate or the House announces any such "intra-session recess" by adopting a resolution stating that it will "adjourn" to a fixed date, a few days or weeks or even months later. All agree that the phrase "the recess of the Senate" covers inter-session recesses. The question is whether it includes intra-session recesses as well.

In our view, the phrase "the recess" includes an intra-session recess of substantial length. Its words taken literally can refer to both types of recess. Founding-era dictionaries define the word "recess," much as we do today, simply as "a period of cessation from usual work." 13 The Oxford English Dictionary 322–323 (2d ed. 1989) (hereinafter OED) (citing 18th- and 19th-century sources for that definition of "recess"); 2 N. Webster, An American Dictionary of the English Language (1828) ("[r]emission or suspension of business or procedure"); 2 S. Johnson, A Dictionary of the English Language 1602–1603 (4th ed. 1773) (hereinafter Johnson) (same). The Founders themselves used the word to refer to intra-session, as well as to inter-session, breaks. See, *e.g.,* 3 Records of the Federal Convention of 1787, p. 76 (M. Farrand rev. 1966) (hereinafter Farrand) (letter from George Washington to John Jay using "the recess" to refer to an intra-session break of the Constitutional Convention); *id.,* at 191 (speech of Luther Martin with a similar usage); 1 T. Jefferson, A Manual of Parliamentary Practice § LI, p. 165 (2d ed. 1812) (describing a "recess by adjournment" which did *not* end a session).

We recognize that the word "the" in "*the* recess" might suggest that the phrase refers to the single break separating formal sessions of Congress. That is because the word "the" frequently (but not always) indicates "a particular thing." 2 Johnson 2003. But the word can also refer "to a term used generically or universally." 17 OED 879. The Constitution, for example, directs the Senate to choose a President *pro tempore* "in *the* Absence of the Vice-President." Art. I, § 3, cl. 5 (emphasis added) * * *. Reading "the" generically in this way, there is no linguistic problem applying the Clause's phrase to both kinds of recess. And, in fact, the phrase "the recess" was used to refer to intra-session recesses at the time of the founding. See, *e.g.,* 3 Farrand 76 (letter from Washington to Jay); New Jersey Legislative-Council Journal, 5th Sess., 1st Sitting 70, 2d Sitting 9 (1781) (twice referring to a 4-month, intra-session break as "the Recess"); see also Brief for Petitioner 14–16 (listing examples).

The constitutional text is thus ambiguous. And we believe the Clause's purpose demands the broader interpretation. The Clause gives the President authority to make appointments during "the recess of the Senate" so that the President can ensure the continued functioning of the Federal Government when the Senate is away. The Senate is equally away during both an inter-session and an intra-session recess, and its capacity to participate in the appointments process has nothing to do with the words it uses to signal its departure.

History also offers strong support for the broad interpretation * * *.

In all, between the founding and the Great Depression, Congress took substantial intra-session breaks (other than holiday breaks) in four years: 1867, 1868, 1921, and 1929. And in each of those years the President made intra-session recess appointments.

Since 1929, and particularly since the end of World War II, Congress has shortened its inter-session breaks as it has taken longer and more frequent intra-session breaks; Presidents have correspondingly made more intra-session recess appointments. Indeed, if we include military appointments, Presidents have made thousands of intra-session recess appointments. President Franklin Roosevelt, for example, commissioned Dwight Eisenhower as a permanent Major General during an intra-session recess; President Truman made Dean Acheson Under Secretary of State; and President George H. W. Bush reappointed Alan Greenspan as Chairman of the Federal Reserve Board * * *.

* * *

* * * [N]either the Senate considered as a body nor its committees, despite opportunities to express opposition to the practice of intra-session recess appointments, has done so * * *.

* * *

The upshot is that restricting the Clause to inter-session recesses would frustrate its purpose. It would make the President's recess-appointment power dependent on a formalistic distinction of Senate procedure. Moreover, the President has consistently and frequently interpreted the word "recess" to apply to intra-session recesses, and has acted on that interpretation. The Senate as a body has done nothing to deny the validity of this practice for at least three-quarters of a century. And three-quarters of a century of settled practice is long enough to entitle a practice to "great weight in a proper interpretation" of the constitutional provision.

* * *

The greater interpretive problem is determining how long a recess must be in order to fall within the Clause. Is a break of a week, or a day, or an hour too short to count as a "recess"? The Clause itself does not say * * *.

* * *

* * * [T]he Solicitor General * * * acknowledges that there is a lower limit * * *. He argues that the lower limit should be three days by analogy to the Adjournments Clause of the Constitution. That Clause says: "Neither House, during the Session of Congress, shall, without the Consent of the other, adjourn for more than three days." Art. I, § 5, cl. 4.

We agree with the Solicitor General that a 3-day recess would be too short * * *. A Senate recess that is so short that it does not require the consent of the House is not long enough to trigger the President's recess-appointment power.

That is not to say that the President may make recess appointments during any recess that is "more than three days." Art. I, § 5, cl. 4. The Recess Appointments Clause seeks to permit the Executive Branch to function smoothly when Congress is unavailable. And though Congress has taken short breaks for almost 200 years, and there have been many thousands of recess appointments in that time, we have not found a single example of a recess appointment made during an intra-session recess that was shorter than 10 days * * *.

* * * We therefore conclude, in light of historical practice, that a recess of more than 3 days but less than 10 days is presumptively too short to fall within the Clause. We add the word "presumptively" to leave open the possibility that some very unusual circumstance—a national catastrophe, for instance, that renders the Senate unavailable but calls for an urgent response—could demand the exercise of the recess-appointment power during a shorter break * * *.

In sum, we conclude that the phrase "the recess" applies to both intra-session and inter-session recesses. If a Senate recess is so short that it does not require the consent of the House, it is too short to trigger the Recess Appointments Clause. See Art. I, § 5, cl. 4. And a recess lasting less than 10 days is presumptively too short as well.

IV

The second question concerns the scope of the phrase "vacancies *that may happen* during the recess of the Senate." Art. II, § 2, cl. 3 (emphasis added). All agree that the phrase applies to vacancies that initially occur during a recess. But does it also apply to vacancies that initially occur before a recess and continue to exist during the recess? In our view the phrase applies to both kinds of vacancy.

We believe that the Clause's language, read literally, permits, though it does not naturally favor, our broader interpretation. We concede that the most natural meaning of "happens" as applied to a "vacancy" (at least to a modern ear) is that the vacancy "happens" when it initially occurs. See 1 Johnson 913 (defining "happen" in relevant part as meaning "[t]o fall out; to chance; to come to pass"). But that is not the only possible way to use the word.

Thomas Jefferson wrote that the Clause is "certainly susceptible of [two] constructions." Letter to Wilson Cary Nicholas (Jan. 26, 1802), in 36 Papers of Thomas Jefferson 433 (B. Oberg ed., 2009). It "may mean 'vacancies that may happen to be' or 'may happen to fall' " during a recess. *Ibid.* * * *.

Similarly, when Attorney General William Wirt advised President Monroe to follow the broader interpretation, he wrote that the "expression seems not perfectly clear. It may mean 'happen to take place:' that is, '*to originate*,' " or it "may mean, also, without violence to the sense, 'happen to exist.' " 1 Op. Atty. Gen. 631, 631–632 (1823) * * *.

* * *

In any event, the linguistic question here is not whether the phrase can be, but whether it must be, read more narrowly. The question is whether the Clause is ambiguous. And the broader reading, we believe, is at least a permissible reading of a " 'doubtful' " phrase. We consequently go on to consider the Clause's purpose and historical practice.

The Clause's purpose strongly supports the broader interpretation. That purpose is to permit the President to obtain the assistance of subordinate officers when the Senate, due to its recess, cannot confirm them. Attorney General Wirt clearly described how the narrower interpretation would undermine this purpose:

"Put the case of a vacancy occurring in an office, held in a distant part of the country, on the last day of the Senate's session. Before the vacancy is made known to the President, the Senate rises. The office may be an important one; the vacancy may paralyze a whole line of action in some essential branch of our internal police; the public interests may imperiously demand that it shall be immediately filled. But the vacancy happened to occur during the session of the Senate; and if the President's power is to be limited to such vacancies only as happen to occur during the recess of the Senate, the vacancy in the case put must continue, however ruinous the consequences may be to the public." 1 Op. Atty. Gen., at 632.

* * *

Historical practice over the past 200 years strongly favors the broader interpretation. The tradition of applying the Clause to pre-recess vacancies dates at least to President James Madison * * *.

The next President, James Monroe, received and presumably acted upon Attorney General Wirt's advice, namely that "all vacancies which, from any casualty, happen to exist at a time when the Senate cannot be consulted as to filling them, may be temporarily filled by the President." 1 Op. Atty. Gen., at 633. Nearly every subsequent Attorney General to consider the question throughout the Nation's history has thought the same. *E.g.,* 2 Op. Atty. Gen. 525, 528 (1832); 7 Op. Atty. Gen. 186, 223 (1855); 10 Op. Atty. Gen. 356, 356–357 (1862); 12 Op. Atty. Gen. 32, 33 (1866); 12 Op. Atty. Gen., at 452; 14 Op. Atty. Gen. 562, 564 (1875); 15 Op. Atty. Gen. 207 (1877); 16 Op. Atty. Gen. 522, 524 (1880); 17 Op. Atty. Gen. 521 (1883); 18 Op. Atty. Gen. 29, 29–30 (1884); 19 Op. Atty. Gen. 261, 262 (1889); 26 Op. Atty. Gen. 234, 234–235 (1907); 30 Op. Atty. Gen. 314, 315 (1914); 41 Op. Atty. Gen. 463, 465 (1960); 3 Op. OLC 314 (1979); 6 Op. OLC 585, 586 (1982); 20 Op. OLC 124, 161 (1996); 36 Op. OLC ___ (2012) * * *.

* * *

Did the Senate object? Early on, there was some sporadic disagreement with the broad interpretation * * *. In any event, by 1862 Attorney General Bates could still refer to "the unbroken acquiescence of the Senate" in support of the broad interpretation. 10 Op. Atty. Gen., at 356.

Then in 1863 the Senate Judiciary Committee disagreed with the broad interpretation. It issued a report concluding that a vacancy "must have its inceptive point after one session has closed and before another session has begun." S. Rep. No. 80, 37th Cong., 3d Sess., p. 3. And the Senate then passed the Pay Act, which provided that "no money shall be paid . . . as a salary, to any person appointed during the recess of the Senate, to fill a vacancy . . . which . . . existed while the Senate was in session." Act of Feb. 9, 1863, § 2, 12 Stat. 646 * * *. Relying upon the floor statement of a single Senator, Justice Scalia suggests that the passage of the Pay Act indicates that the Senate as a whole endorsed the position in the 1863 Report. But the circumstances are more equivocal. During the floor debate on the bill, not a single Senator referred to the Report. Cong. Globe, 37th Cong., 3d Sess. 564–565 (1863). Indeed, Senator Trumbull, who introduced the Pay Act, acknowledged that there was disagreement about the underlying constitutional question. *Id.,* at 565 ("[S]ome other persons think he has that power"). Further, if a majority of the Senate had believed appointments to pre-recess vacancies were unconstitutional, it could have attempted to do far more than temporarily dock the appointees' pay. Cf. Tenure of Office Act of 1867, § 5, 14 Stat. 431 (making it a federal crime for "any person" to "accept any appointment" in certain circumstances).

In any event, the Senate subsequently abandoned its hostility * * *.

The upshot is that the President has consistently and frequently interpreted the Recess Appointments Clause to apply to vacancies that initially occur before, but continue to exist during, a recess of the Senate. The Senate as a body has not countered this practice for nearly three-quarters of a century, perhaps longer. The tradition is long enough to entitle the practice "to great regard in determining the true construction" of the constitutional provision * * *.

In light of some linguistic ambiguity, the basic purpose of the Clause, and the historical practice we have described, we conclude that the phrase "all vacancies" includes vacancies that come into existence while the Senate is in session.

V

The third question concerns the calculation of the length of the Senate's "recess." On December 17, 2011, the Senate by unanimous consent adopted a resolution to convene "*pro forma* session[s]" only, with "no business . . . transacted," on every Tuesday and Friday from December 20, 2011, through January 20, 2012. 2011 S. J. 923. At the end of each *pro forma* session, the Senate would "adjourn until" the following *pro forma* session. *Ibid.* During that period, the Senate convened and adjourned as agreed. It held *pro forma* sessions on December 20, 23, 27, and 30, and on January 3, 6, 10, 13, 17, and 20; and at the end of each *pro forma* session, it adjourned until the time and date of the next. *Id.,* at 923–924; 158 Cong. Rec. S1–S11.

The President made the recess appointments before us on January 4, 2012, in between the January 3 and the January 6 *pro forma* sessions. We must determine the significance of these sessions—that is, whether, for purposes of the Clause, we should treat them as periods when the Senate was in session or as periods when it was in recess. If the former, the period between January 3 and January 6 was a 3-day recess, which is too short to trigger the President's recess-appointment power, see *supra,* at 19–21. If the latter, however, then the 3-day period was part of a much longer recess during which the President did have the power to make recess appointments.

* * *

In our view, * * * the *pro forma* sessions count as sessions, not as periods of recess. We hold that, for purposes of the Recess Appointments Clause, the Senate is in session when it says it is, provided that, under its own rules, it retains the capacity to transact Senate business. The Senate met that standard here.

* * *

VI

The Recess Appointments Clause responds to a structural difference between the Executive and Legislative Branches: The Executive Branch is perpetually in operation, while the Legislature only acts in intervals separated by recesses. The purpose of the Clause is to allow the Executive to continue operating while the Senate is unavailable. We believe that the Clause's text, standing alone, is ambiguous. It does not resolve whether the President may make appointments during intra-session recesses, or whether he may fill pre-recess vacancies. But the broader reading better serves the Clause's structural function. Moreover, that broader reading is reinforced by centuries of history, which we are hesitant to disturb. We thus hold that the Constitution empowers the President to fill any existing vacancy during any recess—intra-session or inter-session—of sufficient length.

* * *

The foregoing discussion should refute Justice Scalia's claim that we have "embrace[d]" an "adverse-possession theory of executive power." *Post,* at 48. Instead, as in all cases, we interpret the Constitution in light of its text, purposes, and "our whole experience" as a Nation. *Missouri* v. *Holland*, 252 U. S. 416, 433 (1920). And we look to the actual practice of Government to inform our interpretation.

Given our answer to the last question before us, we conclude that the Recess Appointments Clause does not give the President the constitutional authority to make the appointments here at issue * * *.

■ JUSTICE SCALIA, with whom THE CHIEF JUSTICE, JUSTICE THOMAS, and JUSTICE ALITO join, concurring in the judgment.

* * * To prevent the President's recess-appointment power from nullifying the Senate's role in the appointment process, the Constitution cabins that power in two significant ways. First, it may be exercised only in "the Recess of the Senate," that is, the intermission between two formal legislative sessions. Second, it may be used to fill only those vacancies that "happen during the Recess," that is, offices that become vacant during that intermission. Both conditions are clear from the Constitution's text and structure, and both were well understood at the founding. * * *

* * *

The Court's decision transforms the recess-appointment power from a tool carefully designed to fill a narrow and specific need into a weapon to be wielded by future Presidents against future Senates. To reach that result, the majority casts aside the plain, original meaning of the constitutional text in deference to late-arising historical practices that are ambiguous at best * * *. I concur in the judgment only.

I. Our Responsibility

Today's majority disregards two overarching principles that ought to guide our consideration of the questions presented here.

First, the Constitution's core, government-structuring provisions are no less critical to preserving liberty than are the later adopted provisions of the Bill of Rights * * *.

Second and relatedly, when questions involving the Constitution's government-structuring provisions are presented in a justiciable case, it is the solemn responsibility of the Judicial Branch " 'to say what the law is.' " *Zivotofsky* v. *Clinton*, 566 U. S. ___, ___ (2012) (slip op., at 7) (quoting *Marbury* v. *Madison*, 1 Cranch 137, 177 (1803)). This Court does not defer to the other branches' resolution of such controversies * * *.

* * * Of course, where a governmental practice has been open, widespread, and unchallenged since the early days of the Republic, the practice should guide our interpretation of an ambiguous constitutional provision. But " '[p]ast practice does not, by itself, create power.' " *Medellín* v. *Texas*, 552 U. S. 491, 532 (2008) (quoting *Dames & Moore* v. *Regan*, 453 U. S. 654, 686 (1981)). That is a necessary corollary of the principle that the political branches cannot by agreement alter the constitutional structure. Plainly, then, a self-aggrandizing practice adopted by one branch well after the founding, often challenged, and never before blessed by this Court—in other words, the sort of practice on which the majority relies in this case—does not relieve us of our duty to interpret the Constitution in light of its text, structure, and original understanding.

* * *

II. Intra-Session Breaks

* * *

A sensible interpretation of the Recess Appointments Clause should start by recognizing that the Clause uses the term "Recess" in contradistinction to the term "Session." * * *

In the founding era, the terms "recess" and "session" had well-understood meanings in the marking-out of legislative time. The life of each elected Congress typically consisted (as it still does) of two or more formal sessions separated by adjournments "*sine die*," that is, without a specified return date. The period *between* two sessions was known as "the recess." As one scholar has thoroughly demonstrated, "in government practice the phrase 'the Recess' *always* referred to the gap between sessions." Natelson, The Origins and Meaning of "Vacancies that May Happen During the Recess" in the Constitution's Recess Appointments Clause, 37 Harv. J. L. & Pub. Pol'y 199, 213 (2014) (hereinafter Natelson); see *id.*, at 214–227 (providing dozens of examples). By contrast, other provisions of the Constitution use the verb "adjourn" rather than "recess" to refer to the commencement of breaks *during* a formal legislative session. See, *e.g.*, Art. I, § 5, cl. 1; *id.*, § 5, cl. 4.

To be sure, in colloquial usage both words, "recess" and "session," could take on alternative, less precise meanings. A session could include any short period when a legislature's members were "assembled for business," and a recess could refer to any brief "suspension" of legislative "business." 2 N. Webster, American Dictionary of the English Language (1828) * * *.

* * * [N]either the Solicitor General nor the majority argues that the Clause uses "session" in its loose, colloquial sense. And if "the next Session" denotes a *formal* session, then "the Recess" must mean the break *between* formal sessions * * *. It is linguistically implausible to suppose—as the majority does—that the Clause uses one of those terms ("Recess") informally and the other ("Session") formally in a single sentence, with the result that an event can occur during *both* the "Recess" *and* the "Session."

* * *

One way to avoid the linguistic incongruity of the majority's reading would be to read both "the Recess" and "the next Session" colloquially, so that the recess-appointment power would be activated during any temporary suspension of Senate proceedings, but appointments made pursuant to that power would last only until the beginning of the next suspension (which would end the next colloquial session). See, *e.g.*, Rappaport, The Original Meaning of the Recess Appointments Clause, 52 UCLA L. Rev. 1487, 1569 (2005) (hereinafter Rappaport, Original Meaning). That approach would be more linguistically defensible than the majority's. But it would not cure the most fundamental problem with giving "Recess" its colloquial, rather than its formal, meaning: Doing so leaves the recess-appointment power without a textually grounded principle limiting the time of its exercise.

* * *

* * * [T]he majority contends that the Clause's supposed purpose of keeping the wheels of government turning demands that we interpret the Clause to maintain its relevance in light of the "new circumstance" of the Senate's taking an increasing number of intra-session breaks that exceed three days. Even if I accepted the canard that courts can alter the Constitution's meaning to accommodate changed circumstances, I would be hard pressed to see the relevance of that notion here. The rise of intra-session adjournments has occurred in tandem with the development of modern forms of communication and transportation that mean the Senate "is always available" to consider nominations, even when its Members are temporarily dispersed for an intra-session break. Tr. of Oral Arg. 21 (Ginsburg, J.). The Recess Appointments Clause therefore is, or rather, should be, an anachronism—"essentially an historic relic, something whose original purpose has disappeared." *Id.*, at 19 (Kagan, J.). The need it was designed to fill no longer exists, and its only remaining use is the ignoble one of enabling the President to circumvent the Senate's role in the appointment process. That does not justify "read[ing] it out of the Constitution" and * * * I would not do so; but neither would I distort the Clause's original meaning, as the majority does, to ensure a prominent role for the recess-appointment power in an era when its influence is far more pernicious than beneficial.

To avoid the absurd results that follow from its colloquial reading of "the Recess," the majority is forced to declare that some intra-session breaks—though undisputedly within the phrase's colloquial meaning—are simply "too short to trigger the Recess Appointments Clause." *Ante,* at 21. But it identifies no textual basis whatsoever for limiting the length of "the Recess," nor does it point to any clear standard for determining how short is too short. It is inconceivable that the Framers would have left the circumstances in which the President could exercise such a significant and potentially dangerous power so utterly indeterminate * * *.

* * *

And what about breaks longer than three days? The majority says that a break of four to nine days is "presumptively too short" but that the presumption may be rebutted in an "unusual circumstance," such as a "national catastrophe . . . that renders the Senate unavailable but calls for an urgent response." The majority must hope that the *in terrorem* effect of its "presumptively too short" pronouncement will deter future Presidents from making any recess appointments during 4-to-9-day breaks and thus save us from the absurd spectacle of unelected judges evaluating (after an evidentiary hearing?) whether an alleged "catastrophe" was sufficiently "urgent" to trigger the recess-appointment power * * *.

* * *

* * * The majority, however, insists that history "offers strong support" for its interpretation. *Ante,* at 11. The historical practice of the political branches is, of course, irrelevant when the Constitution is clear. But even if the Constitution were thought ambiguous on this point, history does not support the majority's interpretation.

* * *

[*Editors' Note: Nine pages of history later . . .*]

What does all this amount to? In short: Intra-session recess appointments were virtually unheard of for the first 130 years of the Republic, were deemed unconstitutional by the first Attorney General to address them, were not openly defended by the Executive until 1921, were not made in significant numbers until after World War II, and have been repeatedly criticized as unconstitutional by Senators of both parties. It is astonishing for the majority to assert that this history lends "strong support," to its interpretation of the Recess Appointments Clause. * * *

* * *

III. Pre-Recess Vacancies

* * *

A. Plain Meaning

As the majority concedes, "the most natural meaning of 'happens' as applied to a 'vacancy' . . . is that the vacancy 'happens' when it initially occurs." The majority adds that this meaning is most natural "to a modern ear," but it fails to show that founding-era ears heard it differently. "Happen" meant then, as it does now, "[t]o fall out; to chance; to come to pass." 1 Johnson, Dictionary of the English Language 913. Thus, a vacancy that *happened* during the Recess was most reasonably understood as one that *arose* during the recess. It was, of course, possible in certain contexts for the word "happen" to mean "happen to be" rather than "happen to occur," as in the idiom "it so happens." But that meaning is not at all natural when the subject is a vacancy, a state of affairs that comes into existence at a particular moment in time.

In any event, no reasonable reader would have understood the Recess Appointments Clause to use the word "happen" in the majority's "happen to be" sense, and thus to empower the President to fill all vacancies that might *exist* during a recess, regardless of when they arose. For one thing, the Clause's language would have been a surpassingly odd way of giving the President that power. The Clause easily could have been written to convey that meaning clearly: It could have referred to "all Vacancies that may exist during the Recess," or it could have omitted the qualifying phrase entirely and simply authorized the President to "fill up all Vacancies during the Recess." Given those readily available alternative phrasings, the reasonable reader might have wondered, why would any intelligent drafter intending the majority's reading have inserted the words "that may happen"—words that, as the majority admits, make the majority's desired reading awkward and unnatural, and that must be effectively read out of the Clause to achieve that reading?

For another thing, the majority's reading not only strains the Clause's language but distorts its constitutional role, which was meant to be subordinate. As Hamilton explained, appointment with the advice and consent of the Senate was to be "the general mode of appointing officers of the United States." The Federalist No. 67, at

455. The Senate's check on the President's appointment power was seen as vital because " 'manipulation of official appointments' had long been one of the American revolutionary generation's greatest grievances against executive power." *Freytag*, 501 U. S., at 883. The unilateral power conferred on the President by the Recess Appointments Clause was therefore understood to be "nothing more than a supplement" to the "general method" of advice and consent. The Federalist No. 67, at 455.

If, however, the Clause had allowed the President to fill *all* pre-existing vacancies during the recess by granting commissions that would last throughout the following session, it would have been impossible to regard it—as the Framers plainly did—as a mere codicil to the Constitution's principal, power-sharing scheme for filling federal offices * * *.

* * *

B. Historical Practice

* * * [T]he majority says "[h]istorical practice" requires the broader interpretation. And again the majority is mistaken * * *.

* * *

[*Editors' Note: eleven pages of history later . . .*]

In sum: Washington's and Adams' Attorneys General read the Constitution to restrict recess appointments to vacancies arising during the recess, and there is no evidence that any of the first four Presidents consciously departed from that reading. The contrary reading was first defended by an executive official in 1823, was vehemently rejected by the Senate in 1863, was vigorously resisted by legislation in place from 1863 until 1940, and is arguably inconsistent with legislation in place from 1940 to the present. The Solicitor General has identified only about 100 appointments that have ever been made under the broader reading, and while it seems likely that a good deal more have been made in the last few decades, there is good reason to doubt that many were made before 1940 (since the appointees could not have been compensated). I can conceive of no sane constitutional theory under which this evidence of "historical practice"—which is actually evidence of a long-simmering inter-branch conflict—would require us to defer to the views of the Executive Branch.

IV. Conclusion

What the majority needs to sustain its judgment is an ambiguous text and a clear historical practice. What it has is a clear text and an at-best-ambiguous historical practice. Even if the Executive could accumulate power through adverse possession by engaging in a *consistent* and *unchallenged* practice over a long period of time, the oft-disputed practices at issue here would not meet that standard * * *.

* * *

The real tragedy of today's decision is not simply the abolition of the Constitution's limits on the recess-appointment power and the substitution of a novel framework invented by this Court. It is the damage done to our separation-of-powers jurisprudence more generally. It is not every day that we encounter a proper case or controversy requiring interpretation of the Constitution's structural provisions. Most of the time, the interpretation of those provisions is left to the political branches—which, in deciding how much respect to afford the constitutional text, often take their cues from this Court. We should therefore take every opportunity to affirm the primacy of the Constitution's enduring principles over the politics of the moment. Our failure to do so today will resonate well beyond the particular dispute at hand. Sad, but true: The Court's embrace of the adverse-possession theory of executive power (a characterization the majority resists but does not refute) will be cited in diverse contexts, including those presently unimagined, and will have the effect of aggrandizing the Presidency beyond its constitutional bounds and undermining respect for the separation of powers.

I concur in the judgment only.

NOTES AND QUESTIONS

1. Do you agree with Justice Breyer's majority opinion or with Justice Scalia's dissent on the question of whether the Recess Appointment Clause applies only to inter-session recesses or also to intra-session recesses? Note that from 1789 on Congress usually convened in December, when there was no farm work to be done, and the session ended in a recess where everyone went home to plant their crops. Those days are long since gone. How do we apply the Recess Appointments Clause in a world where plane travel has eliminated the sharp bifurcation between the session and the recess that existed in 1789 and, which no longer exists?

2. Do you agree with the majority or the dissent on the meaning of the "happen to occur" language? What modalities would you use to address that question?

3. Based on what you have seen thus far, is there any good way to predict when the Court will defer to executive and/or legislative practice and when it will go its own way?

[Assignment 21]

D. PRESIDENTIAL REMOVAL POWER

Article II, Section 1: The executive Power shall be vested in a President of the United States of America.

Article II, Section 3: [The President] . . . shall take Care that the Laws be faithfully executed . . . .

Elected officials are automatically removed from office once their terms of office expire (though they can be reelected to those positions). Congress can also remove its own members through expulsion and can remove executive or judicial officials through impeachment. The requirement in Article III that federal judges serve during "good Behaviour" establishes that impeachment is the only constitutionally permissible mode of removal for those judicial officers. But what about non-elected *executive* officials—which means everyone in the executive department except the President and the Vice President? The Constitution says nothing explicitly about their removal apart from the elaborate provisions for impeachment. There is no executive "Removal Clause" analogous to the Appointments Clause.

One could plausibly draw from the Constitution's text at least four different inferences about the removal of executive officials. First, one could say that because impeachment is the only mode of removal for executive officers specifically mentioned in the Constitution, it is the only permissible mode. Second, one could say that Article II gives the President the sole power of removal when it vests "[t]he executive Power * * * in a President of the United States of America," *id.* art. II, § 1, cl. 1, on the theory that removal is fundamentally an executive power (and that the impeachment clauses specifically confer a limited measure of that power on Congress). Third, one could say that the mode of removal ordinarily follows the mode of appointment, so that officials appointed, for example, by the President with the advice and consent of the Senate can be removed only by the same procedure. And finally, one could say that Congress can set whatever terms of removal it wishes (provided that they are "necessary and proper") whenever it uses the Necessary and Proper Clause to create offices.

All of these positions are textually and structurally plausible, and all of them were advanced with considerable vigor in the First Congress when the first executive departments and offices were created in 1789. The issue was addressed when members of the House of Representatives debated whether and how the statute creating the Secretary of the Department of Foreign Affairs should address that officer's removal. That debate remains to this day among the most spirited and sophisticated constitutional debates recorded in American history. Substantial arguments were made for the exclusivity of impeachment as a mode of removal, see 1 ANNALS OF CONG. 389 (1789) (statement of Rep. Jackson); *id.* at 477 (statement of Rep. Huntington); for a presidential removal power, *see, e.g.*, *id.* at 387, 479–82, 514–19 (statement of Rep. Madison); *id.* at 387–88, 525–27 (statement of Rep. Benson); *id.* at 388, 482–84, 531–32 (statement of Rep. Vining); *id.* at 393 (statement of Rep. Goodhue); *id.* at 397–98, 508–09 (statement of Rep. Clymer); *id.* at 478–79 (statement of Rep. Sedgwick); *id.* at 486–88, 548–50 (statement of Rep. Boudinot); *id.* at 492–96, 561–64 (statement of Rep. Ames); *id.* at 498–500 (statement of Rep. Hartley); for a removal power that follows the mode of appointment, *see, e.g.*, *id.* at 389–90 (statement of Rep. Bland); *id.* at 391, 473–74 (statement of Rep. White); *id.* at 393 (statement of Rep. Sylvester); *id.* at 395–96, 490–92 (statement of Rep. Gerry); *id.* at 509–10 (statement of Rep. Page); *id.* at 585–91 (statement of Rep. Stone); and for a congressional power to specify the mode of removal. *See, e.g.*, *id.* at 391 (statement of Rep. Thatcher); *id.* at 391–92 (statement of Rep. Jackson); *id.* at 393–92, 500–05 (statement of Rep. Lawrence); *id.* at 496–98 (statement of Rep. Livermore).

Alexander Hamilton in *The Federalist*, for his part, thought it obvious that the power of removal would follow the power of appointment. *See* THE FEDERALIST No. 77 (Hamilton): "IT HAS been mentioned as one of the advantages to be expected from the co-operation of the Senate, in the business of appointments, that it would contribute to the stability of the administration. The consent of that body would be necessary to displace as well as to appoint. A change of the Chief Magistrate, therefore, would not occasion so violent or so general a revolution in the officers of the government as might be expected, if he were the sole disposer of offices." Nonetheless, the House endorsed a provision that implied an inherent presidential removal power. The Senate divided evenly on the question (it did not keep a journal until 1795, so we have no information on the Senate's views beyond the bare vote), and Vice President John Adams broke the tie in favor of the House's—and the President's—position. This implicit legislative endorsement of a presidential power to remove executive officials is so important that it is known simply as "the decision of 1789." Reflect on all of the decisions that the First Congress made in 1789 and you will realize the significance of the label. For a thorough treatment of this historic constitutional event, see Saikrishna Prakash, *New Light on the Decision of 1789*, 91 CORNELL L. REV. 1021 (2006). For the next seventy years, presidents asserted that it was settled practice that Congress could not interfere with their power to remove at will executive branch subordinates. Congress did not always agree with the President on that point. President Andrew Jackson was "censured" by a politically hostile Senate for firing a Treasury Secretary who refused to obey Jackson's orders regarding the controversial Bank of the United States. President Jackson formally objected to the Senate's actions, and after Jackson decisively won the next election, the censure was expunged. President Andrew Johnson fared much worse. Johnson was Abraham Lincoln's Vice President but shared few of Lincoln's attitudes toward the Southern insurrection. After the Civil War, Johnson sought to undermine the Northern Republicans' Reconstruction plans by replacing Lincoln's holdover officials with his own people who would be less committed to Reconstruction. Congress responded with the Tenure of Office Act, discussed in the following opinion, which required senatorial consent to removal of certain key officials, such as the Secretary of War. Jackson defied the law, claiming that it was unconstitutional, and the House impeached him. The Senate fell one vote short of the two-thirds majority needed for conviction and removal, at least partly because some senators, who would have been happy to be rid of Johnson on policy grounds, agreed with Johnson that the Tenure of Office Act was likely unconstitutional, and they did not think it an impeachable offense to refuse to execute an unconstitutional law.

While Congress and the President vigorously debated the removal question—including in the context of a presidential impeachment trial—from the founding onward, the federal courts were mostly silent. It was almost 150 years before the Supreme Court took up the executive removal question in the following landmark decision, written by the only Supreme Court Justice to have previously served as President. The varied opinions in the case consume more than 240 pages of the United States Reports, but here is what we consider their gist.

Myers v. United States

272 U.S. 52 (1926)

■ MR. CHIEF JUSTICE TAFT delivered the opinion of the Court.

This case presents the question whether under the Constitution the President has the exclusive power of removing executive officers of the United States whom he has appointed by and with the advice and consent of the Senate.

Myers * * * was on July 21, 1917, appointed by the President, by and with the advice and consent of the Senate, to be a postmaster of the first class at Portland, Oregon, for a term of four years. On January 20, 1920, Myers' resignation was demanded. He refused the demand. On February 2, 1920, he was removed from office by order of the Postmaster General, acting by direction of the President * * *. On April 21, 1921, he brought this suit in the Court of Claims for his salary from the date of his removal, which, as claimed by supplemental petition filed after July 21, 1921, the end of his term, amounted to $8,838.71 * * *.

The Court of Claims gave judgment against Myers, and this is an appeal from that judgment * * *.

By the sixth section of the Act of Congress of July 12, 1876 under which Myers was appointed * * *, it is provided that:

"Postmasters of the first, second, and third classes shall be appointed and may be removed by the President by and with the advice and consent of the Senate, and shall hold their offices for four years unless sooner removed or suspended according to law."

The Senate did not consent to the President's removal of Myers during his term. If this statute in its requirement that his term should be four years unless sooner removed by the President by and with the consent of the Senate is valid, the appellant * * * is entitled to recover his unpaid salary for his full term, and the judgment of the Court of Claims must be reversed. The government maintains that the requirement is invalid, for the reason that under Article II of the Constitution the President's power of removal of executive officers appointed by him with the advice and consent of the Senate is full and complete without consent of the Senate * * *.

* * *

The question where the power of removal of executive officers appointed by the President by and with the advice and consent of the Senate was vested, was presented early in the first session of the First Congress. There is no express provision respecting removals in the Constitution, except as Section 4 of article II * * * provides for removal from office by impeachment. The subject was not discussed in the Constitutional Convention. Under the Articles of Confederation, Congress was given the power of appointing certain executive officers of the Confederation, and during the Revolution and while the Articles were given effect, Congress exercised the power of removal.

* * *

On June 16, 1789, the House resolved itself into a Committee of the Whole on a bill proposed by Mr. Madison for establishing an executive department to be denominated the Department of Foreign Affairs, in which the first clause, after stating the title of the officer and describing his duties, had these words" "to be removable from office by the President of the United States." 1 Annals of Congress, 455. After a very full discussion the question was put: shall the words "to be removable by the President" be struck out? It was determined in the negative-yeas 20, nays 34. 1 Annals of Congress, 576.

On June 22, in the renewal of the discussion: * * *

"Mr. Benson stated that his objection to the clause 'to be removable by the President' arose from an idea that the power of removal by the President hereafter might appear to be exercised by virtue of a legislative grant only, and consequently be subjected to legislative instability, when he was well satisfied in his own mind that it was fixed by a fair legislative construction of the Constitution." 1 Annals of Congress, 579.

"Mr. Benson * * * would move to strike out the words in the first clause, 'to be removable by the President,' which appeared somewhat like a grant. Now, the mode he took would evade that point and establish a legislative construction of the Constitution * * *." 1 Annals of Congress, 578.

Mr. Madison admitted the objection made by the gentleman near him (Mr. Benson) to the words in the bill. He said: "They certainly may be construed to imply a legislative grant of the power. He wished everything like ambiguity expunged, and the sense of the House explicitly declared, and therefore seconded the motion. Gentlemen have all along proceeded on the idea that the Constitution vests the power in the President; and what arguments were brought forward respecting the convenience or inconvenience of such disposition of the power were intended only to throw light upon what was meant by the compilers of the Constitution. Now, as the words proposed by the gentleman from New York expressed to his mind the meaning of the Constitution, he should be in favor of them, and would agree to strike out those agreed to in the committee." 1 Annals of Congress, 578, 579.

* * *

* * * Mr. Benson * * * moved to strike out in the first clause the words "to be removable by the President," * * * and this * * * motion of his was carried by a vote of thirty-one to nineteen. 1 Annals of Congress, 585.

* * *

* * * [T]here is not the slightest doubt, after an examination of the record, that the vote was, and was intended to be, a legislative declaration that the power to remove officers appointed by the President and the Senate vested in the President alone, and until the Johnson Impeachment trial in 1868, its meaning was not doubted even by those who questioned its soundness.

* * * The Senate divided by ten to ten, requiring the deciding vote of the Vice-President, John Adams, who voted * * * in favor of the passage of the bill as it had left the House. Ten of the Senators had been in the Constitutional Convention, and of them six voted that the power of removal was in the President alone. The bill having passed as it came from the House was signed by President Washington and became a law. Act July 27, 1789, 1 Stat. 28, c. 4.

The bill was discussed in the House at length and with great ability. The report of it in the Annals of Congress is extended. James Madison was then a leader in the House, as he had been in the Convention. His arguments in support of the President's constitutional power of removal independently of Congressional provision, and without the consent of the Senate, were masterly, and he carried the House.

It is convenient in the course of our discussion of this case to review the reasons advanced by Mr. Madison and his associates for their conclusion * * *.

First, Mr. Madison insisted that Article II by vesting the executive power in the President was intended to grant to him the power of appointment and removal of executive officers except as thereafter expressly provided in that Article. He pointed out that one of the chief purposes of the Convention was to separate the legislative from the executive functions * * *.

* * *

The vesting of the executive power in the President was essentially a grant of the power to execute the laws. But the President alone and unaided could not execute the laws. He must execute them by the assistance of subordinates. * * * [Since the President] is charged specifically to take care that the[ ] [laws] be faithfully executed, the reasonable implication, even in the absence of express words, was that as part of his executive power he should select those who were to act for him under his direction in the execution of the laws. The further implication must be, in the absence of any express limitation respecting removals, that as his selection of administrative officers is essential to the execution of the laws by him, so must be his power of removing those for whom he cannot continue to be responsible. * * * [T]he natural meaning of the term "executive power" granted the President included the appointment and removal of executive subordinates. If such appointments and removals were not an exercise of the executive power, what were they? They certainly were not the exercise of legislative or judicial power in government as usually understood.

* * *

* * * The executive power was given in general terms, strengthened by specific terms where emphasis was regarded as appropriate, and was limited by direct expressions where limitation was needed, and the fact that no express limit was placed on the power of removal by the Executive was convincing indication that none was intended * * *.

Second. The view of Mr. Madison and his associates was that not only did the grant of executive power to the President in the first section of Article II carry with it the power of removal, but the express recognition of the power of appointment in the second section enforced this view on the well approved principle of constitutional and statutory construction that the power of removal of executive officers was incident to the power of appointment. It was agreed by the opponents of the bill, with only one or two exceptions, that as a constitutional principle the power of appointment carried with it the power of removal. This principle as a rule of constitutional and statutory construction, then generally conceded, has been recognized ever since. Ex parte Hennen, 13 Pet. 230, 259; Reagan v. United States, 182 U. S. 419; Shurtleff v. United States, 189 U. S. 311, 315. The reason for the principle is that those in charge of and responsible for administering functions of government who select their executive subordinates need in meeting their responsibility to have the power to remove those whom they appoint.

Under section 2 of Article II, however, the power of appointment by the Executive is restricted in its exercise by the provision that the Senate, a part of the legislative branch of the Government, may check the action of the Executive by rejecting the officers he selects. Does this make the Senate part of the removing power? * * *

The history of the clause by which the Senate was given a check upon the President's power of appointment makes it clear that it was not prompted by any desire to limit removals. * * * [T]he important purpose of those who brought about the restriction was to lodge in the Senate, where the small States had equal representation with the larger States, power to prevent the President from making too many appointments from the larger states * * *.

* * *

* * * [T]he power of removal, though equally essential to the executive power, is different in its nature from that of appointment. A veto by the Senate—a part of the legislative branch of the Government—upon removals is a much greater limitation upon the executive branch and a much more serious blending of the legislative with the executive than a rejection of a proposed appointment. It is not to be implied. The rejection of a nominee of the President for a particular office does not greatly

embarrass him in the conscientious discharge of his high duties in the selection of those who are to aid him, because the President usually has an ample field from which to select for office * * *.

The power to prevent the removal of an officer who has served under the President is different from the authority to consent to or reject his appointment. When a nomination is made, it may be presumed that the Senate is, or may become, as well advised as to the fitness of the nominee as the President, but in the nature of things the defects in ability or intelligence or loyalty in the administration of the laws of one who has served as an officer under the President, are facts as to which the President, or his trusted subordinates, must be better informed than the Senate, and the power to remove him may, therefore, be regarded as confined for very sound and practical reasons, to the governmental authority which has administrative control. The power of removal is incident to the power of appointment, not to the power of advising and consenting to appointment, and when the grant of the executive power is enforced by the express mandate to take care that the laws be faithfully executed, it emphasizes the necessity for including within the executive power as conferred the exclusive power of removal.

* * *

Third. Another argument urged against the constitutional power of the President alone to remove executive officers appointed by him with the consent of the Senate is that, in the absence of an express power of removal granted to the President, power to make provision for removal of all such officers is vested in the Congress by section 8 of Article I.

* * *

It is reasonable to suppose also that, had it been intended to give to Congress power to regulate or control removals in the manner suggested, it would have been included among the specifically enumerated legislative powers in Article I, or in the specified limitations on the executive power in Article II * * *.

Fourth. Mr. Madison and his associates pointed out with great force the unreasonable character of the view that the Convention intended, without express provision, to give to Congress or the Senate, in case of political or other differences, the means of thwarting the Executive in the exercise of his great powers * * * by fastening upon him, as subordinate executive officers, men who by their inefficient service under him, by their lack of loyalty to the service, or by their different views of policy, might make his taking care that the laws be faithfully executed most difficult or impossible.

As Mr. Madison said in the debate in the First Congress:

"Vest this power in the Senate jointly with the President, and you abolish at once that great principle of unity and responsibility in the Executive department, which was intended for the security of liberty and the public good. If the President should possess alone the power of removal from office, those who are employed in the execution of the law will be in their proper situation, and the chain of dependence be preserved; the lowest officers, the middle grade, and the highest, will depend, as they ought, on the President, and the President on the community."

* * *

We have devoted much space to this discussion and decision of the question of the Presidential power of removal in the First Congress not because a Congressional conclusion on a constitutional issue is conclusive, but, first because of our agreement with the reasons upon which it was avowedly based; second, because this was the decision of the First Congress on a question of primary importance in the organization of the government, made within two years after the Constitutional Convention and within a much shorter time after its ratification; and, third, because that Congress numbered among its leaders those who had been members of the Convention. It must necessarily constitute a precedent upon which many future laws supplying the machinery of the new Government would be based, and, if erroneous, would be likely to evoke dissent and departure in future Congresses. It would come at once before the executive branch of the Government for compliance, and might well be brought before the judicial branch for a test of its validity * * *. [I]t was soon accepted as a final decision of the question by all branches of the Government.

* * *

[*Editors' Note:* Marbury v. Madison *had assumed—on at least five separate occasions—that officers such as Marbury could be given fixed terms of office and were not removable at will. Indeed, if Marbury was removable at will, it would not have mattered whether or not he was properly commissioned, because President Jefferson could simply fire him and be done with it. Chief Justice Taft addressed* Marbury *as follows: "While everything that the great Chief Justice said, whether obiter dictum or not, challenges the highest and most respectful consideration, it is clear that the mere statement of the conclusion made by him, without any examination of the discussion which went on in the First Congress, and without reference to the elaborate arguments there advanced to maintain the decision of 1789, cannot be regarded as authority in considering the weight to be attached to that decision, a decision which, as we shall see, he subsequently recognized as a well-established rule of constitutional construction." Taft then extensively discussed the history of the removal controversy up to the Civil War, concluding: "Summing up, then, the facts as to acquiescence by all branches of the Government in the legislative decision of 1789 as to executive officers, whether superior or inferior, we find that from 1789 until 1863, a period of 74 years, there was no act of Congress, no executive act, and no decision of this court at variance with the declaration of the First Congress; but there was, as we have seen, clear affirmative recognition of it by each branch of the Government."*]

We come now to a period in the history of the Government when both Houses of Congress attempted to reverse this constitutional construction and to subject the power of removing executive officers appointed by the President and confirmed by the Senate to the control of the Senate—indeed finally to the assumed power in Congress to place the removal of such officers anywhere in the Government.

This reversal grew out of the serious political difference between the two Houses of Congress and President Johnson. There was a two-thirds majority of the Republican party, in control of each House of Congress, which resented what it feared would be Mr. Johnson's obstructive course in the enforcement of * * * reconstruction. * * *

* * * [T]he chief legislation in support of the reconstruction policy of Congress was the Tenure of Office Act of March 2, 1867, providing that all officers appointed by and with the consent of the Senate should hold their offices until their successors

should have in like manner been appointed and qualified, and that certain heads of departments, including the Secretary of War, should hold their offices during the term of the President by whom appointed and one month thereafter subject to removal by consent of the Senate. The Tenure of Office Act was vetoed, but it was passed over the veto * * *.

* * *

The extreme provisions of all this legislation were a full justification for the considerations so strongly advanced by Mr. Madison and his associates in the First Congress for insisting that the power of removal of executive officers by the President alone was essential in the division of powers between the executive and the legislative bodies. It exhibited in a clear degree the paralysis to which a partisan Senate and Congress could subject the executive arm and destroy the principle of executive responsibility * * *. It was an attempt to re-distribute the powers and minimize those of the President.

* * *

* * * [I]t is contended that, since the passage of the Tenure of Office Act, there has been general acquiescence by the Executive in the power of Congress to forbid the President alone to remove executive officers—an acquiescence which has changed any formerly accepted constitutional construction to the contrary. Instances are cited of the signed approval by President Grant and other Presidents of legislation in derogation of such construction. We think these are all to be explained, not by acquiescence therein, but by reason of the otherwise valuable effect of the legislation approved * * *

* * *

The fact seems to be that all departments of the Government have constantly had in mind, since the passage of the Tenure of Office Act, that the question of power of removal by the President of officers appointed by him with the Senate's consent, has not been settled adversely to the legislative action of 1789, but, in spite of congressional action, has remained open until the conflict should be subjected to judicial investigation and decision.

* * *

For the reasons given, we must therefore hold that the provision of the law of 1876, by which the unrestricted power of removal of first-class postmasters is denied to the President, is in violation of the Constitution and invalid. This leads to an affirmance of the judgment of the Court of Claims.

■ MR. JUSTICE HOLMES, dissenting.

* * *

* * * We have to deal with an office that owes its existence to Congress and that Congress may abolish tomorrow. Its duration and the pay attached to it while it lasts depend on Congress alone. Congress alone confers on the President the power to appoint to it and at any time may transfer the power to other hands. With such power over its own creation, I have no more trouble in believing that Congress has power to prescribe a term of life for it free from any interference than I have in accepting the undoubted power of Congress to decree its end. I have equally little trouble in accepting its power to prolong the tenure of an incumbent until Congress or the Senate shall have assented to his removal. The duty of the President to see that the

laws be executed is a duty that does not go beyond the laws or require him to achieve more than Congress sees fit to leave within his power.

* * *

[Editors' Note: The lengthy dissenting opinion of Justice McReynolds is omitted. His key point: "I find no suggestion of the theory that "the executive power" of article 2, § 1, includes all possible federal authority executive in nature unless definitely excluded by some constitutional provision, prior to the well known House debate of 1789, when Mr. Madison seems to have given it support."]

■ MR. JUSTICE BRANDEIS, dissenting.

In 1833 Mr. Justice Story, after discussing in * * * his Commentaries on the Constitution the much debated question concerning the President's power of removal, said * * *:

"If there has been any aberration from the true constitutional exposition of the power of removal (which the reader must decide for himself), it will be difficult, and perhaps impracticable, after forty years' experience, to recall the practice to the correct theory. But, at all events, it will be a consolation to those who love the Union, and honor a devotion to the patriotic discharge of duty, that in regard to 'inferior officers' (which appellation probably includes ninety-nine out of a hundred of the lucrative offices in the government), the remedy for any permanent abuse is still within the power of Congress, by the simple expedient of requiring the consent of the Senate to removals in such cases."

Postmasters are inferior officers. Congress might have vested their appointment in the head of the department. * * * [The] statute [at issue in this case] has been in force unmodified for half a century. Throughout the period, it has governed a large majority of all civil officers to which appointments are made by and with the advice and consent of the Senate. May the President, having acted under the statute in so far as it creates the office and authorizes the appointment, ignore, while the Senate is in session, the provision which prescribes the condition under which a removal may take place?

It is this narrow question, and this only. which we are required to decide. We need not consider what power the President, being Commander in Chief, has over officers in the Army and the Navy. We need not determine whether the President, acting alone, may remove high political officers. We need not even determine whether, acting alone, he may remove inferior civil officers when the Senate is not in session. It was in session when the President purported to remove Myers, and for a long time thereafter * * *.

* * *

* * * The ability to remove a subordinate executive officer, being an essential of effective government, will, in the absence of express constitutional provision to the contrary, be deemed to have been vested in some person or body. But it is not a power inherent in a chief executive. * * * [T]he Constitution has confessedly granted to Congress the legislative power to create offices, and to prescribe the tenure thereof; and it has not in terms denied to Congress the power to control removals * * *.

It is also argued that the clauses in Article 2, § 3, of the Constitution, which declare that the President "shall take Care that the Laws be faithfully executed, and shall Commission all the Officers of the United States" imply a grant to the President of the alleged uncontrollable power of removal. I do not find in either clause anything which supports this claim * * *. There is no express grant to the President of incidental powers resembling those conferred upon Congress by clause 18 of Article 1, § 8 * * *.

To imply a grant to the President of the uncontrollable power of removal from statutory inferior executive offices involves an unnecessary and indefensible limitation upon the constitutional power of Congress to fix the tenure of the inferior statutory offices. That such a limitation cannot be justified on the ground of necessity is demonstrated by the practice of our governments, state and national. In none of the original thirteen States did the chief executive possess such power at the time of the adoption of the federal Constitution. In none of the forty-eight States has such power been conferred at any time since by a state constitution, with a single possible exception * * *.

* * *

The historical data submitted present a legislative practice, established by concurrent affirmative action of Congress and the President, to make consent of the Senate a condition of removal from statutory inferior, civil, executive offices to which the appointment is made for a fixed term by the President with such consent. They show that the practice has existed, without interruption, continuously for the last fifty-eight years; that, throughout this period, it has governed a great majority of all such offices; that the legislation applying the removal clause specifically to the office of postmaster was enacted more than half a century ago; and that recently the practice has, with the President's approval, been extended to several newly created offices. * * * A persistent legislative practice which involves a delimitation of the respective powers of Congress and the President, and which has been so established and maintained, should be deemed tantamount to judicial construction, in the absence of any decision by any court to the contrary. *United States v. Midwest Oil Co.*, 236 U. S. 459, 469.

* * * The action taken by Congress in 1789 after the great debate does not * * * [support the Court's holding]. The vote then taken did not involve a decision that the President had uncontrollable power. It did not involve a decision of the question whether Congress could confer upon the Senate the right, and impose upon it the duty, to participate in removals. It involved merely the decision that the Senate does not, in the absence of legislative grant thereof, have the right to share in the removal of an officer appointed with its consent; and that the President has, in the absence of restrictive legislation, the constitutional power of removal without such consent * * *.

* * *

NOTES AND QUESTIONS

1. Is there a stronger constitutional case for presidential power to remove superior officers than to remove inferior officers? Suppose the Tenure of Office Act had been in effect on January 20, 2021. Would a new President be stuck with former President Donald Trump's Cabinet and subcabinet officials unless sixty senators agreed to confirm replacements? Would this affect the way our democracy works or the meaningfulness of presidential elections?

2. In an omitted portion, Justice Brandeis's dissent claims that civil service laws would be nullified if the President could unilaterally fire inferior executive branch officers. Is this true if the only way in which new civil service officials could be hired is by passing exams and going through a merit-selection process? Is the key step in getting rid of the Jacksonian spoils system the adoption of merit-selection hiring rather than the tenuring of hundreds of thousands of subordinate executive branch personnel?

3. The majority and dissenting opinions in *Myers* both spend an enormous amount of space and energy—much more than we can present here—on practice, though they give very different interpretations to some of those practices. Are they opinions using different modalities of interpretation or just disagreeing about the evidence?

4. How broad is the holding of *Myers* as opposed to its dicta? Myers was a first-class postmaster for Portland, Oregon. Where does that sound like it slots in the executive hierarchy? Does that sound more or less important than a Federal Trade Commissioner or an Independent Counsel? Does the importance of the office matter on the reasoning of any of the opinions? Do all of the opinions, in the end, rest on contestable empirical claims about how government operates? Are those kinds of arguments good enough to overcome statutes?

5. Does the majority opinion in *Myers* presuppose the correctness of the Vesting Clause Thesis? Yes

6. *Myers* was decided just a few years before the Great Depression. During the preceding half-century, with the rise of Progressivism, Congress had created a number of regulatory agencies, such as the Interstate Commerce Commission and the Federal Reserve Board, whose heads were subject to removal only for statutorily specified "good cause." The Progressive ethos suggested that this was wise design, in order to insulate technocratic experts from the baneful influence of politics, including (and perhaps especially) presidential politics. Consider whether that ethos, a wariness of President Roosevelt, or both may have contributed to the next decision, issued less than a decade after *Myers*.

Humphrey's Executor v. United States

295 U.S. 602 (1935)

■ MR. JUSTICE SUTHERLAND delivered the opinion of the Court.

Plaintiff brought suit in the Court of Claims against the United States to recover a sum of money alleged to be due the deceased for salary as a Federal Trade Commissioner from October 8, 1933, when the President undertook to remove him from office, to the time of his death on February 14, 1934 * * *.

William E. Humphrey, the decedent, on December 10, 1931, was nominated by President Hoover to succeed himself as a member of the Federal Trade Commission, and was confirmed by the United States Senate. He was duly commissioned for a term of seven years, expiring September 25, 1938; and, after taking the required oath of office, entered upon his duties. On July 25, 1933, President Roosevelt addressed a letter to the commissioner asking for his resignation, on the ground "that the aims and purposes of the Administration with respect to the work of the Commission can be carried out most effectively with personnel of my own selection," but disclaiming any reflection upon the commissioner personally or upon his services. The commissioner replied, asking time to consult his friends. After some further correspondence upon the subject, the President on August 31, 1933, wrote the commissioner expressing the hope that the resignation would be forthcoming, and saying:

"You will, I know, realize that I do not feel that your mind and my mind go along together on either the policies or the administering of the Federal Trade Commission, and, frankly, I think it is best for the people of this country that I should have a full confidence."

The commissioner declined to resign; and on October 7, 1933, the President wrote him:

"Effective as of this date you are hereby removed from the office of Commissioner of the Federal Trade Commission."

Humphrey never acquiesced in this action, but continued thereafter to insist that he was still a member of the commission, entitled to perform its duties and receive the compensation provided by law at the rate of $10,000 per annum * * *.

* * *

[Editors' Note: The Court concluded—wrongly, in our view, for whatever that is worth—that the Federal Trade Commission Act intended to limit the President's power to remove FTC Commissioners to three specified statutory grounds, none of which was holding policy views with which the President disagreed. No one contended that Humphrey was removable under any of the statutorily specified grounds.]

* * * To support its contention that the removal provision of § 1, as we have just construed it, is an unconstitutional interference with the executive power of the President, the government's chief reliance is *Myers v. United States*, 272 U.S. 52. That case has been so recently decided, and the prevailing and dissenting opinions so fully review the general subject of the power of executive removal, that further discussion would add little of value to the wealth of material there collected * * *. Nevertheless, the narrow point actually decided was only that the President had power to remove a postmaster of the first class, without the advice and consent of the Senate as required by act of Congress. In the course of the opinion of the court, expressions occur which tend to sustain the government's contention, but these are beyond the point involved and, therefore, do not come within the rule of *stare decisis*. In so far as they are out of harmony with the views here set forth, these expressions are disapproved * * *.

* * *

The office of a postmaster is so essentially unlike the office now involved that the decision in the *Myers* Case cannot be accepted as controlling our decision here. A postmaster is an executive officer restricted to the performance of executive functions. He is charged with no duty at all related to either the legislative or judicial power. The actual decision in the *Myers* case finds support in the theory that such an officer is merely one of the units in the executive department and, hence, inherently subject to the exclusive and illimitable power of removal by the Chief Executive, whose subordinate and aid he is. Putting aside *dicta*, which may be followed if sufficiently persuasive but which are not controlling, the necessary reach of the decision goes far enough to include all purely executive officers. It goes no farther;—much less does it include an officer who occupies no place in the executive department and who exercises no part of the executive power vested by the Constitution in the President.

The Federal Trade Commission is an administrative body created by Congress to carry into effect legislative policies embodied in the statute in accordance with the legislative standard therein prescribed, and to perform other specified duties as a legislative or as a judicial aid. Such a body cannot in any proper sense be characterized as an arm or an eye of the executive. Its duties are performed without executive leave and, in the contemplation of the statute, must be free from executive control. In administering the provisions of the statute in respect of "unfair methods of competition"—that is to say, in filling in and administering the details embodied by that general standard—the commission acts in part quasi-legislatively and in part quasi-judicially. In making investigations and reports thereon for the information of Congress under § 6, in aid of the legislative power, it acts as a legislative agency. Under § 7, which authorizes the commission to act as a master in chancery under rules prescribed by the court, it acts as an agency of the judiciary. To the extent that it exercises any executive function,—as distinguished from executive power in the constitutional sense—it does so in the discharge and effectuation of its quasi-legislative or quasi-judicial powers, or as an agency of the legislative or judicial departments of the government.

If Congress is without authority to prescribe causes for removal of members of the trade commission and limit executive power of removal accordingly, that power at once becomes practically all-inclusive in respect of civil officers with the exception of the judiciary provided for by the Constitution. The Solicitor General, at the bar, apparently recognizing this to be true, with commendable candor, agreed that his view in respect of the removability of members of the Federal Trade Commission necessitated a like view in respect of the Interstate Commerce Commission and the Court of Claims. We are thus confronted with the serious question whether not only the members of these quasi-legislative and quasi-judicial bodies, but the judges of the legislative Court of Claims, exercising judicial power (*Williams v. United States*, 289 U.S. 553, 565–567), continue in office only at the pleasure of the President.

We think it plain under the Constitution that illimitable power of removal is not possessed by the President in respect of officers of the character of those just named. The authority of Congress, in creating quasi-legislative or quasi-judicial agencies, to require them to act in discharge of their duties independently of executive control cannot well be doubted; and that authority includes, as an appropriate incident, power to fix the period during which they shall continue in office, and to forbid their removal except for cause in the meantime. For it is quite evident that one who holds his office only during the pleasure of another cannot be depended upon to maintain an attitude of independence against the latter's will.

* * *

In the light of the question now under consideration, we have reexamined the precedents referred to in the *Myers* Case, and find nothing in them to justify a conclusion contrary to that which we have reached. The so-called "decision of 1789" had relation to a bill proposed by Mr. Madison to establish an executive Department of Foreign Affairs. * * * We shall not discuss the subject further, since it is so fully covered by the opinions in the *Myers* case, except to say that the office under consideration by Congress was not only purely executive, but the officer one who was responsible to the President, and to him alone, in a very definite sense. A reading of the debates shows that the President's illimitable power of removal was not considered in respect of other than executive officers. And it is pertinent to observe that when, at a later time, the tenure of office for the Comptroller of the Treasury was under consideration, Mr. Madison quite evidently thought that, since the duties of that office were not purely of an executive nature but partook of the judiciary quality as well, a different rule in respect of executive removal might well apply.

* * *

The result of what we now have said is this: Whether the power of the President to remove an officer shall prevail over the authority of Congress to condition the power by fixing a definite term and precluding a removal except for cause, will depend upon the character of the office; the *Myers* decision, affirming the power of the President alone to make the removal, is confined to purely executive officers; and as to officers of the kind here under consideration, we hold that no removal can be made during the prescribed term for which the officer is appointed, except for one or more of the causes named in the applicable statute.

To the extent that, between the decision in the *Myers* case, which sustains the unrestrictable power of the President to remove purely executive officers, and our present decision that such power does not extend to an office such as that here involved, there shall remain a field of doubt, we leave such cases as may fall within it for future consideration and determination as they may arise.

* * *

■ MR. JUSTICE MCREYNOLDS agrees [for reasons stated in his dissent in *Myers v. United States*] * * *.

NOTES AND QUESTIONS

1. What kind of constitutional power does the Court think that the Federal Trade Commission exercises? If it is legislative power, how can the agency, which is not Congress, exercise it? If it is judicial power, how can the agency, which is not an Article III court, exercise it? What does it mean, under the Constitution, to call a power "quasi" legislative or judicial? *Humphrey's Executor* is generally taken as constitutional validation of the administrative state as the so-called "Fourth Branch" of government. Under the majority's reasoning, could it be unconstitutional for Congress *not* to limit the President's removal power over members of the Federal Trade Commission?

2. We edited out literally hundreds of pages from *Myers*. We edited out almost nothing from *Humphrey's Executor*.

3. *Humphrey's Executor* was decided contemporaneously with *Panama Refining* and *Schechter Poultry*, which held that portions of the National Industrial Recovery Act gave too much unconstrained power to the President. The Federal Trade Commission administers a statute that prohibits "unfair or deceptive acts or practices," 15 U.S.C. § 45(a)(2) (2018), in interstate commerce. If the President could appoint, all at once, a full majority of the Federal Trade Commission, would the President need the NIRA in order to run the economy as he or she saw fit? Might that have been on the minds of the Court in 1935? Or is *Humphrey's Executor* simply the inevitable consequence of more than half a century of Progressive ideology? Consider the following comments by the Court in the portion of *Humphrey's Executor* dealing with interpretation of the statute:

> The commission is to be non-partisan; and it must, from the very nature of its duties, act with entire impartiality. It is charged with the enforcement of no policy except the policy of the law. Its duties are neither political nor executive, but predominantly quasi-judicial and quasi-legislative * * *. [I]ts

members are called upon to exercise the trained judgment of a body of experts * * *.

* * *

The debates in both houses demonstrate that the prevailing view was that the commission was not to be "subject to anybody in the government but . . . only to the people of the United States"; free from "political domination or control" or the "probability or possibility of such a thing"; to be "separate and apart from any existing department of the government—not subject to the orders of the President."

* * *

Thus, the language of the act, the legislative reports, and the general purposes of the legislation as reflected by the debates, all combine to demonstrate the Congressional intent to create a body of experts who shall gain experience by length of service; a body which shall be independent of executive authority, *except in its selection*, and free to exercise its judgment without the leave or hindrance of any other official or any department of the government.

295 U.S. at 623–26.

4. The line between "executive" and "quasi-legislative" or "quasi-judicial" officials seems odd, especially if it means that the Portland, Oregon postmaster must be subject to unlimited presidential removal while one of the five Federal Trade Commissioners must not. That line got tested, and shattered, in the most important removal case in the second half of the twentieth century.

Morrison v. Olson

487 U.S. 654 (1988)

[*Editors' note: Other portions of the case are presented supra at pages 403–406.*]

■ CHIEF JUSTICE REHNQUIST delivered the opinion of the Court.

This case presents us with a challenge to the independent counsel provisions of the Ethics in Government Act of 1978 * * *.

* * *

* * * Two related issues must be addressed: The first is whether the provision of the Act restricting the Attorney General's power to remove the independent counsel to only those instances in which he can show "good cause," taken by itself, impermissibly interferes with the President's exercise of his constitutionally appointed functions. The second is whether, taken as a whole, the Act violates the separation of powers by reducing the President's ability to control the prosecutorial powers wielded by the independent counsel.

Two Terms ago we had occasion to consider whether it was consistent with the separation of powers for Congress to pass a statute that authorized a Government official who is removable only by Congress to participate in what we found to be "executive powers." *Bowsher v. Synar,* 478 U.S. 714, 730 (1986). We held in *Bowsher* that "Congress cannot reserve for itself the power of removal of an officer charged with the execution of the laws except by impeachment." *Id.,* at 726. A primary antecedent for this ruling was our 1926 decision in *Myers v. United States,* 272 U.S. 52 (1926) * * *.

Unlike both *Bowsher* and *Myers,* this case does not involve an attempt by Congress itself to gain a role in the removal of executive officials other than its established powers of impeachment and conviction. The Act instead puts the removal power squarely in the hands of the Executive Branch; an independent counsel may be removed from office, "only by the personal action of the Attorney General, and only for good cause." * * * There is no requirement of congressional approval of the Attorney General's removal decision, though the decision is subject to judicial review. * * * In our view, the removal provisions of the Act make this case more analogous to *Humphrey's Executor,* 295 U.S. 602 (1935), and *Wiener v. United States,* 357 U.S. 349 (1958), than to *Myers* or *Bowsher.*

In *Humphrey's Executor,* the issue was whether a statute restricting the President's power to remove the Commissioners of the Federal Trade Commission (FTC) only for "inefficiency, neglect of duty, or malfeasance in office" was consistent with the Constitution * * *. [W]e found it "plain" that the Constitution did not give the President "illimitable power of removal" over the officers of independent agencies. Were the President to have the power to remove FTC Commissioners at will, the "coercive influence" of the removal power would "threate[n] the independence of [the] commission." * * *

Similarly, in *Wiener* we considered whether the President had unfettered discretion to remove a member of the War Claims Commission, which had been established by Congress in the War Claims Act of 1948, 62 Stat. 1240. The Commission's function was to receive and adjudicate certain claims for compensation from those who had suffered personal injury or property damage at the hands of the enemy during World War II. Commissioners were appointed by the President, with the advice and consent of the Senate, but the statute made no provision for the removal of officers, perhaps because the Commission itself was to have a limited existence. As in *Humphrey's Executor,* however, the Commissioners were entrusted by Congress with adjudicatory powers that were to be exercised free from executive control. In this context, "Congress did not wish to have hang over the Commission the Damocles' sword of removal by the President for no reason other than that he preferred to have on that Commission men of his own choosing." 357 U.S., at 356. Accordingly, we rejected the President's attempt to remove a Commissioner "merely because he wanted his own appointees on [the] Commission," stating that "no such power is given to the President directly by the Constitution, and none is impliedly conferred upon him by statute." *Ibid.*

Appellees contend that *Humphrey's Executor* and *Wiener* are distinguishable from this case because they did not involve officials who performed a "core executive function." They argue that our decision in *Humphrey's Executor* rests on a distinction between "purely executive" officials and officials who exercise "quasi-legislative" and "quasi-judicial" powers. In their view, when a "purely executive" official is involved, the governing precedent is *Myers,* not *Humphrey's Executor.* See *Humphrey's Executor, supra,* 295 U.S., at 628. And, under *Myers,* the President must have absolute discretion to discharge "purely" executive officials at will. See *Myers,* 272 U.S., at 132–134.

We undoubtedly did rely on the terms "quasi-legislative" and "quasi-judicial" to distinguish the officials involved in *Humphrey's Executor* and *Wiener* from those in *Myers,* but our present considered view is that the determination of whether the Constitution allows Congress to impose a "good cause"-type restriction on the

President's power to remove an official cannot be made to turn on whether or not that official is classified as "purely executive." * * * The analysis contained in our removal cases is designed not to define rigid categories of those officials who may or may not be removed at will by the President * * *, but to ensure that Congress does not interfere with the President's exercise of the "executive power" and his constitutionally appointed duty to "take care that the laws be faithfully executed" under Article II. *Myers* was undoubtedly correct in its holding, and in its broader suggestion that there are some "purely executive" officials who must be removable by the President at will if he is to be able to accomplish his constitutional role.[29] See 272 U.S., at 132–134. But as the Court noted in *Wiener*:

> "The assumption was short-lived that the *Myers* case recognized the President's inherent constitutional power to remove officials no matter what the relation of the executive to the discharge of their duties and no matter what restrictions Congress may have imposed regarding the nature of their tenure." 357 U.S., at 352.

At the other end of the spectrum from *Myers,* the characterization of the agencies in *Humphrey's Executor* and *Wiener* as "quasi-legislative" or "quasi-judicial" in large part reflected our judgment that it was not essential to the President's proper execution of his Article II powers that these agencies be headed up by individuals who were removable at will. We do not mean to suggest that an analysis of the functions served by the officials at issue is irrelevant. But the real question is whether the removal restrictions are of such a nature that they impede the President's ability to perform his constitutional duty, and the functions of the officials in question must be analyzed in that light.

Considering for the moment the "good cause" removal provision in isolation from the other parts of the Act at issue in this case, we cannot say that the imposition of a "good cause" standard for removal by itself unduly trammels on executive authority. There is no real dispute that the functions performed by the independent counsel are "executive" in the sense that they are law enforcement functions that typically have been undertaken by officials within the Executive Branch * * *. Although the counsel exercises no small amount of discretion and judgment in deciding how to carry out his or her duties under the Act, we simply do not see how the President's need to control the exercise of that discretion is so central to the functioning of the Executive Branch as to require as a matter of constitutional law that the counsel be terminable at will by the President.

Nor do we think that the "good cause" removal provision at issue here impermissibly burdens the President's power to control or supervise the independent counsel, as an executive official, in the execution of his or her duties under the Act. This is not a case in which the power to remove an executive official has been completely stripped from the President, thus providing no means for the President to ensure the "faithful execution" of the laws. Rather, because the independent

[29] The dissent says that the language of Article II vesting the executive power of the United States in the President requires that every officer of the United States exercising any part of that power must serve at the pleasure of the President and be removable by him at will. This rigid demarcation—a demarcation incapable of being altered by law in the slightest degree, and applicable to tens of thousands of holders of offices neither known nor foreseen by the Framers—depends upon an extrapolation from general constitutional language which we think is more than the text will bear. It is also contrary to our holding in *United States v. Perkins, supra,* decided more than a century ago.

counsel may be terminated for "good cause," the Executive, through the Attorney General, retains ample authority to assure that the counsel is competently performing his or her statutory responsibilities in a manner that comports with the provisions of the Act * * *. We do not think that this limitation as it presently stands sufficiently deprives the President of control over the independent counsel to interfere impermissibly with his constitutional obligation to ensure the faithful execution of the laws.

The final question to be addressed is whether the Act, taken as a whole, violates the principle of separation of powers by unduly interfering with the role of the Executive Branch * * *.

* * *

* * * [W]e do not think that the Act "impermissibly undermine[s]" the powers of the Executive Branch or "disrupts the proper balance between the coordinate branches [by] prevent [ing] the Executive Branch from accomplishing its constitutionally assigned functions," *Nixon v. Administrator of General Services,* 433 U.S., at 443. It is undeniable that the Act reduces the amount of control or supervision that the Attorney General and, through him, the President exercises over the investigation and prosecution of a certain class of alleged criminal activity. The Attorney General is not allowed to appoint the individual of his choice; he does not determine the counsel's jurisdiction; and his power to remove a counsel is limited. Nonetheless, the Act does give the Attorney General several means of supervising or controlling the prosecutorial powers that may be wielded by an independent counsel. Most importantly, the Attorney General retains the power to remove the counsel for "good cause," a power that we have already concluded provides the Executive with substantial ability to ensure that the laws are "faithfully executed" by an independent counsel. No independent counsel may be appointed without a specific request by the Attorney General, and the Attorney General's decision not to request appointment if he finds "no reasonable grounds to believe that further investigation is warranted" is committed to his unreviewable discretion. The Act thus gives the Executive a degree of control over the power to initiate an investigation by the independent counsel. In addition, the jurisdiction of the independent counsel is defined with reference to the facts submitted by the Attorney General, and once a counsel is appointed, the Act requires that the counsel abide by Justice Department policy unless it is not "possible" to do so. Notwithstanding the fact that the counsel is to some degree "independent" and free from executive supervision to a greater extent than other federal prosecutors, in our view these features of the Act give the Executive Branch sufficient control over the independent counsel to ensure that the President is able to perform his constitutionally assigned duties.

* * *

Reversed.

■ JUSTICE KENNEDY took no part in the consideration or decision of this case.

■ JUSTICE SCALIA, dissenting.

It is the proud boast of our democracy that we have "a government of laws and not of men." Many Americans are familiar with that phrase; not many know its derivation. It comes from Part the First, Article XXX, of the Massachusetts Constitution of 1780, which reads in full as follows:

> "In the government of this Commonwealth, the legislative department shall never exercise the executive and judicial powers, or either of them: The executive shall never exercise the legislative and judicial powers, or either of them: The judicial shall never exercise the legislative and executive powers, or either of them: to the end it may be a government of laws and not of men."

The Framers of the Federal Constitution similarly viewed the principle of separation of powers as the absolutely central guarantee of a just Government. In No. 47 of The Federalist, Madison wrote that "[n]o political truth is certainly of greater intrinsic value, or is stamped with the authority of more enlightened patrons of liberty." The Federalist No. 47, p. 301 (C. Rossiter ed. 1961) (hereinafter Federalist). Without a secure structure of separated powers, our Bill of Rights would be worthless, as are the bills of rights of many nations of the world that have adopted, or even improved upon, the mere words of ours.

* * *

* * * [T]his suit is about * * * [p]ower. The allocation of power among Congress, the President, and the courts in such fashion as to preserve the equilibrium the Constitution sought to establish—so that "a gradual concentration of the several powers in the same department," Federalist No. 51, p. 321 (J. Madison), can effectively be resisted. Frequently an issue of this sort will come before the Court clad, so to speak, in sheep's clothing: the potential of the asserted principle to effect important change in the equilibrium of power is not immediately evident, and must be discerned by a careful and perceptive analysis. But this wolf comes as a wolf.

* * *

If to describe this case is not to decide it, the concept of a government of separate and coordinate powers no longer has meaning. The Court devotes most of its attention to such relatively technical details as the Appointments Clause and the removal power, addressing briefly and only at the end of its opinion the separation of powers * * *. I think that has it backwards. Our opinions are full of the recognition that it is the principle of separation of powers, and the inseparable corollary that each department's "defense must . . . be made commensurate to the danger of attack," Federalist No. 51, p. 322 (J. Madison), which gives comprehensible content to * * * and determines the appropriate scope of the removal power. Thus, while I will subsequently discuss why our appointments and removal jurisprudence does not support today's holding, I begin with a consideration of the fountainhead of that jurisprudence, the separation and equilibration of powers.

* * *

* * * Article II, § 1, cl. 1, of the Constitution provides:

> "The executive Power shall be vested in a President of the United States."

* * * [T] his does not mean *some of* the executive power, but *all of* the executive power. It seems to me, therefore, that the decision of the Court of Appeals invalidating the present statute must be upheld on fundamental separation-of-powers principles if the following two questions are answered affirmatively: (1) Is the conduct of a criminal prosecution (and of an investigation to decide whether to prosecute) the exercise of purely executive power? (2) Does the statute deprive the

President of the United States of exclusive control over the exercise of that power? Surprising to say, the Court appears to concede an affirmative answer to both questions, but seeks to avoid the inevitable conclusion that since the statute vests some purely executive power in a person who is not the President of the United States it is void.

The Court concedes that "[t]here is no real dispute that the functions performed by the independent counsel are 'executive' " * * *. There is no possible doubt that the independent counsel's functions fit this description. She is vested with the "full power and independent authority to exercise all *investigative and prosecutorial* functions and powers of the Department of Justice [and] the Attorney General." 28 U.S.C. § 594(a) (1982 ed., Supp. V) (emphasis added). Governmental investigation and prosecution of crimes is a quintessentially executive function.

As for the second question, whether the statute before us deprives the President of exclusive control over that quintessentially executive activity: The Court does not, and could not possibly, assert that it does not. That is indeed the whole object of the statute. Instead, the Court points out that the President, through his Attorney General, has at least *some* control. That concession is alone enough to invalidate the statute, but I cannot refrain from pointing out that the Court greatly exaggerates the extent of that "some" Presidential control. "Most importan[t]" among these controls, the Court asserts, is the Attorney General's "power to remove the counsel for 'good cause.' " This is somewhat like referring to shackles as an effective means of locomotion. * * * What we in *Humphrey's Executor* found to be a means of eliminating Presidential control, the Court today considers the "most importan[t]" means of assuring Presidential control. Congress, of course, operated under no such illusion when it enacted this statute, describing the "good cause" limitation as "protecting the independent counsel's ability to act independently of the President's direct control" since it permits removal only for "misconduct."

Moving on to the presumably "less important" controls that the President retains * * * the Court points out that the Act directs the independent counsel to abide by general Justice Department policy, except when not "possible." * * *

As I have said, however, it is ultimately irrelevant *how much* the statute reduces Presidential control * * *. It is not for us to determine, and we have never presumed to determine, how much of the purely executive powers of government must be within the full control of the President. The Constitution prescribes that they *all* are.

* * *

Is it unthinkable that the President should have such exclusive power, even when alleged crimes by him or his close associates are at issue? No more so than that Congress should have the exclusive power of legislation, even when what is at issue is its own exemption from the burdens of certain laws. No more so than that this Court should have the exclusive power to pronounce the final decision on justiciable cases and controversies, even those pertaining to the constitutionality of a statute reducing the salaries of the Justices. A system of separate and coordinate powers necessarily involves an acceptance of exclusive power that can theoretically be abused. While the separation of powers may prevent us from righting every wrong, it does so in order to ensure that we do not lose liberty * * *.

The Court has, nonetheless, replaced the clear constitutional prescription that the executive power belongs to the President with a "balancing test." What are the standards to determine how the balance is to be struck, that is, how much removal of Presidential power is too much? Many countries of the world get along with an executive that is much weaker than ours—in fact, entirely dependent upon the continued support of the legislature. Once we depart from the text of the Constitution, just where short of that do we stop? The most amazing feature of the Court's opinion is that it does not even purport to give an answer. It simply *announces,* with no analysis, that the ability to control the decision whether to investigate and prosecute the President's closest advisers, and indeed the President himself, is not "so central to the functioning of the Executive Branch" as to be constitutionally required to be within the President's control. Apparently that is so because we say it is so. Having abandoned as the basis for our decision-making the text of Article II that "the executive Power" must be vested in the President, the Court does not even attempt to craft a *substitute* criterion—a "justiciable standard," however remote from the Constitution—that today governs, and in the future will govern, the decision of such questions. Evidently, the governing standard is to be what might be called the unfettered wisdom of a majority of this Court, revealed to an obedient people on a case-by-case basis. This is not only not the government of laws that the Constitution established; it is not a government of laws at all.

* * *

There is, of course, no provision in the Constitution stating who may remove executive officers, except the provisions for removal by impeachment. Before the present decision it was established, however, * * * that the President's power to remove principal officers who exercise purely executive powers could not be restricted, see *Myers v. United States,* 272 U.S. 52, 127 (1926) * * *.

* * *

* * * [In] our 1935 decision in *Humphrey's Executor v. United States,* 295 U.S. 602—which was considered by many at the time the product of an activist, anti-New Deal Court bent on reducing the power of President Franklin Roosevelt—it [was further] established that the line of permissible restriction upon removal of principal officers lies at the point at which the powers exercised by those officers are no longer purely executive * * *. It has often been observed, correctly in my view, that the line between "purely executive" functions and "quasi-legislative" or "quasi-judicial" functions is not a clear one or even a rational one. But at least it permitted the identification of certain officers, and certain agencies, whose functions were entirely within the control of the President. Congress had to be aware of that restriction in its legislation. Today, however, *Humphrey's Executor* is swept into the dustbin of repudiated constitutional principles * * *.

One can hardly grieve for the shoddy treatment given today to *Humphrey's Executor,* which, after all, accorded the same indignity (with much less justification) to Chief Justice Taft's opinion 10 years earlier in *Myers v. United States,* 272 U.S. 52 (1926)—gutting, in six quick pages devoid of textual or historical precedent for the novel principle it set forth, a carefully researched and reasoned 70-page opinion. It is in fact comforting to witness the reality that he who lives by the *ipse dixit* dies by the *ipse dixit.* But one must grieve for the Constitution. *Humphrey's Executor* at least had the decency formally to observe the constitutional principle that the President had to be the repository of *all* executive power, see 295 U.S., at 627–628, which, as *Myers* carefully explained, necessarily means that he must be able to discharge those who do not perform executive functions according to his liking * * *. By contrast, "our present considered view" is simply that *any* executive officer's removal can be restricted, so long as the President remains "able to accomplish his constitutional role." There are now no lines. If the removal of a prosecutor, the virtual embodiment of the power to "take care that the laws be faithfully executed," can be restricted, what officer's removal cannot? This is an open invitation for Congress to experiment. What about a special Assistant Secretary of State, with responsibility for one very narrow area of foreign policy, who would not only have to be confirmed by the Senate but could also be removed only pursuant to certain carefully designed restrictions? Could this possibly render the President "[un]able to accomplish his constitutional role"? Or a special Assistant Secretary of Defense for Procurement? The possibilities are endless, and the Court does not understand what the separation of powers, what "[a]mbition . . . counteract [ing] ambition," Federalist No. 51, p. 322 (Madison), is all about, if it does not expect Congress to try them. As far as I can discern from the Court's opinion, it is now open season upon the President's removal power for all executive officers, with not even the superficially principled restriction of *Humphrey's Executor* as cover. The Court essentially says to the President: "Trust us. We will make sure that you are able to accomplish your constitutional role." I think the Constitution gives the President—and the people—more protection than that.

The purpose of the separation and equilibration of powers in general, and of the unitary Executive in particular, was not merely to assure effective government but to preserve individual freedom. Those who hold or have held offices covered by the Ethics in Government Act are entitled to that protection as much as the rest of us, and I conclude my discussion by considering the effect of the Act upon the fairness of the process they receive.

Only someone who has worked in the field of law enforcement can fully appreciate the vast power and the immense discretion that are placed in the hands of a prosecutor with respect to the objects of his investigation * * *. Under our system of government, the primary check against prosecutorial abuse is a political one. The prosecutors who exercise this awesome discretion are selected and can be removed by a President, whom the people have trusted enough to elect. Moreover, when crimes are not investigated and prosecuted fairly, nonselectively, with a reasonable sense of proportion, the President pays the cost in political damage to his administration * * *.

That is the system of justice the rest of us are entitled to, but what of that select class consisting of present or former high-level Executive Branch officials? * * * An independent counsel is selected, and the scope of his or her authority prescribed, by a panel of judges. What if they are politically partisan, as judges have been known to be, and select a prosecutor antagonistic to the administration, or even to the particular individual who has been selected for this special treatment? There is no remedy for that, not even a political one. Judges, after all, have life tenure, and appointing a surefire enthusiastic prosecutor could hardly be considered an impeachable offense. So if there is anything wrong with the selection, there is effectively no one to blame. The independent counsel thus selected proceeds to assemble a staff. As I observed earlier, in the nature of things this has to be done by finding lawyers who are willing to lay aside their current careers for an indeterminate amount of time, to take on a job that has no prospect of permanence and little prospect for promotion. One thing is certain, however: it involves investigating and perhaps prosecuting a particular individual. Can one imagine a less equitable manner of fulfilling the executive responsibility to investigate and prosecute? What would be the reaction if, in an area not covered by this statute, the Justice Department posted a public notice inviting applicants to assist in an investigation and possible prosecution of a certain prominent person? * * * [And] even if it were entirely evident that unfairness was in fact the result—the judges hostile to the administration, the independent counsel an old foe of the President, the staff refugees from the recently defeated administration—*there would be no one accountable to the public to whom the blame could be assigned.*

* * *

Worse than what it has done, however, is the manner in which it has done it. A government of laws means a government of rules. Today's decision on the basic issue of fragmentation of executive power is ungoverned by rule, and hence ungoverned by law. It extends into the very heart of our most significant constitutional function the "totality of the circumstances" mode of analysis that this Court has in recent years become fond of. Taking all things into account, we conclude that the power taken away from the President here is not really *too* much. The next time executive power is assigned to someone other than the President we may conclude, taking all things into account, that it *is* too much. That opinion, like this one, will not be confined by any rule * * *.

The ad hoc approach to constitutional adjudication has real attraction, even apart from its work-saving potential. It is guaranteed to produce a result, in every case, that will make a majority of the Court happy with the law. The law is, by definition, precisely what the majority thinks, taking all things into account, it *ought* to be. I prefer to rely upon the judgment of the wise men who constructed our system, and of the people who approved it, and of two centuries of history that have shown it to be sound. Like it or not, that judgment says, quite plainly, that "[t]he executive Power shall be vested in a President of the United States."

NOTES AND QUESTIONS

1. The Ethics in Government Act was allowed to expire in 1999, since congressional Democrats and Republicans had both come to the conclusion that it was constitutionally flawed. Does this mean that Justice Scalia's lone dissent has been vindicated?

2. How should the problem of high-level executive branch malfeasance be addressed? Has the House of Representatives been lax in its constitutional duty to impeach high executive branch officials who are guilty of misconduct in office? Or is the House so polarized—now and/or in the past—that impeachment is (and perhaps always was) unreliable? Note that although in England impeachment was used almost exclusively against high-level executive officials, it has been never been used in the United States to try to force the resignation of a Cabinet secretary or under-secretary. Three Presidents and over a dozen federal judges have been impeached, but none of the various Cabinet officers who have eventually been convicted of felonies committed while they were in office were ever impeached. Should the House of Representatives set up a special committee on impeachments with a large staff of highly trained public integrity prosecutors to investigate, with House subpoenas if necessary, any evidence of Cabinet-level or White House "high crimes and misdemeanors?" Why do you think the House of

Representatives is so shy about its impeachment power? Do members want to "pass the buck" on investigating wrongdoing?

3. By the time *Morrison v. Olson* was litigated Olson had resigned from his position as an Assistant Attorney General and was a private citizen. Is it necessary or even appropriate for someone who is no longer in government to have his own specially appointed prosecutor? Was the creation of such a prosecutor for Olson a kind of bill of attainder?

4. As the Court has become more attuned to formalist separation-of-powers analysis over the past few decades, the status of *Morrison* has been a recurring question. The Court has not—yet—taken a case in which it was asked by the parties to reconsider *Morrison*. An interesting iteration of the removal problem arose in *Free Enterprise Fund v. Public Company Accounting Oversight Board*, 561 U.S. 477 (2010). The Securities and Exchange Commission ("SEC"), created in 1934, is an independent agency—or at least it has always been understood by everyone to be an independent agency, although its statute does not specifically say that its members can only be removed for specified or good causes. But taking it as an independent agency, its (implicit) restrictions on presidential removal are squarely within *Humphrey's Executor*. In 2002, the Sarbanes-Oxley Act created the Public Company Accounting Oversight Board ("PCAOB") to regulate corporate accounting practices. Members of the PCAOB can be removed by the SEC "for good cause shown." 15 U.S.C. § 7211(e)(6) (2018). The Court considered whether the "double for-cause" provision, in which the PCAOB members can only be removed from office for cause by officials who themselves can only be removed from office for cause, was constitutional. A 5–4 majority, in an opinion by Chief Justice Roberts, said "no":

> * * * [W]e have previously upheld limited restrictions on the President's removal power. In those cases, however, only one level of protected tenure separated the President from an officer exercising executive power. It was the President—or a subordinate he could remove at will—who decided whether the officer's conduct merited removal under the good-cause standard.
>
> The Act before us does something quite different. It not only protects Board members from removal except for good cause, but withdraws from the President any decision on whether that good cause exists. That decision is vested instead in other tenured officers—the [Securities and Exchange] Commissioners—none of whom is subject to the President's direct control. The result is a Board that is not accountable to the President, and a President who is not responsible for the Board.
>
> The added layer of tenure protection makes a difference. Without a layer of insulation between the Commission and the Board, the Commission could remove a Board member at any time, and therefore would be fully responsible for what the Board does. The President could then hold the Commission to account for its supervision of the Board, to the same extent that he may hold the Commission to account for everything else it does.
>
> A second level of tenure protection changes the nature of the President's review. Now the Commission cannot remove a Board member at will. The President therefore cannot hold the Commission fully accountable for the Board's conduct, to the same extent that he may hold the Commission accountable for everything else that it does. The Commissioners are not responsible for the Board's actions. They are only responsible for their own determination of whether the Act's rigorous good-cause standard is met. And even if the President disagrees with their determination, he is powerless to

> intervene—unless that determination is so unreasonable as to constitute "inefficiency, neglect of duty, or malfeasance in office." *Humphrey's Executor*, 295 U.S., at 620 (internal quotation marks omitted).
>
> This novel structure does not merely add to the Board's independence, but transforms it. Neither the President, nor anyone directly responsible to him, nor even an officer whose conduct he may review only for good cause, has full control over the Board. The President is stripped of the power our precedents have preserved, and his ability to execute the laws—by holding his subordinates accountable for their conduct—is impaired.
>
> That arrangement is contrary to Article II's vesting of the executive power in the President * * *.
>
> Indeed, if allowed to stand, this dispersion of responsibility could be multiplied. If Congress can shelter the bureaucracy behind two layers of good-cause tenure, why not a third? At oral argument, the Government was unwilling to concede that even *five* layers between the President and the Board would be too many. Tr. of Oral Arg. 47–48. The officers of such an agency—safely encased within a Matryoshka doll of tenure protections—would be immune from Presidential oversight, even as they exercised power in the people's name.
>
> * * *
>
> The diffusion of power carries with it a diffusion of accountability. The people do not vote for the "Officers of the United States." They instead look to the President to guide the "assistants or deputies * * * subject to his superintendence." The Federalist No. 72, p. 487 (J. Cooke ed.1961) (A. Hamilton) * * *.

561 U.S. at 495–98. Does this sound more like the majority opinion in *Morrison* or like Justice Scalia's dissent? Would the Justices who signed onto this opinion overrule *Morrison* if given the chance? They were not given the chance: Chief Justice Roberts noted right away that "[t]he parties do not ask us to reexamine any * * * precedents, and we do not do so." *Id.* at 484.

Justice Breyer wrote a lengthy four-Justice dissent:

> In answering the question presented, we cannot look to more specific constitutional text, such as the text of the Appointments Clause or the Presentment Clause, upon which the Court has relied in other separation-of-powers cases. That is because, with the exception of the general "vesting" and "take care" language, the Constitution is completely "silent with respect to the power of removal from office." *Ex parte Henne,* 13 Pet. 230, 258 (1839).
>
> Nor does history offer significant help * * *.
>
> Nor does this Court's precedent fully answer the question presented. At least it does not clearly invalidate the provision in dispute * * *.
>
> * * *
>
> When previously deciding this kind of nontextual question, the Court has emphasized the importance of examining how a particular provision, taken in context, is likely to function * * *.
>
> * * *
>
> * * * [A] functional approach permits Congress and the President the flexibility needed to adapt statutory law to changing circumstances * * *. [T]he

Federal Government at the time of the founding consisted of about 2,000 employees and served a population of about 4 million. Today, however, the Federal Government employs about *4.4 million workers* who serve a Nation of more than 310 million people living in a society characterized by rapid technological, economic, and social change.

* * *

The upshot is that today vast numbers of statutes governing vast numbers of subjects, concerned with vast numbers of different problems, provide for, or foresee, their execution or administration through the work of administrators organized within many different kinds of administrative structures, exercising different kinds of administrative authority, to achieve their legislatively mandated objectives. And, given the nature of the Government's work, it is not surprising that administrative units come in many different shapes and sizes.

The functional approach required by our precedents recognizes this administrative complexity and, more importantly, recognizes the various ways presidential power operates within this context—and the various ways in which a removal provision might affect that power * * *.

Id. at 516–21 (Breyer, J., dissenting). The majority responded:

One can have a government that functions without being ruled by functionaries, and a government that benefits from expertise without being ruled by experts. Our Constitution was adopted to enable the people to govern themselves, through their elected leaders. The growth of the Executive Branch, which now wields vast power and touches almost every aspect of daily life, heightens the concern that it may slip from the Executive's control, and thus from that of the people. This concern is largely absent from the dissent's paean to the administrative state.

Id. at 499. As we noted, no party in *Free Enterprise Fund* asked the Court to reconsider *Humphrey's Executor* or *Morrison* (though several amici did so). What if they had?

5. Return to *Lucia v. SEC, supra* pages 394–401. Administrative law judges are appointed by the agencies for which they work. Many of those ALJs are in independent agencies, where the appointing heads are removable only for cause. Does that mean that ALJs must be removable at will? Justice Breyer worried that the decision in *Lucia* mandated this result. The majority tried to leave that question open. Cases raising it are working their way through the courts as we write this note. Was Justice Breyer right that the result is now inevitable?

6. One more twist on removal: Virtually all federal statutes that limit the removability of officers concern people who are part of multi-member commissions, such as the Federal Reserve Board, the Federal Communications Commission, and the SEC. The few exceptions are all of relatively modern vintage: the independent counsel discussed in *Morrison v. Olson*; the Federal Housing Finance Agency, created in 2008; the Social Security Administration, which was converted (over the constitutional doubts of President Clinton) to an independent agency in 1994 after six decades as an executive agency; and the Consumer Financial Protection Bureau (CFPB), which was created in 2010 as part of the Dodd-Frank Act. Does an agency's internal organizational structure make any constitutional difference when it comes to congressional restrictions on removal of agency officials? The circuit courts have split on that question. In 2016, a panel of the D.C. Circuit held that the CFPB was unconstitutional because the CFPB is headed by a single director, and limitations on presidential removal of agency heads are permissible only when the agency is multi-membered. *See PHH Corp. v. CFPB*, 839 F.3d 1

(D.C.Cir.2016). The other single-headed independent agencies listed above were dismissed as anomalies or distinguished as not having direct regulatory authority over private parties. *See id.* at 18–21. The *en banc* D.C. Circuit overturned the panel decision and upheld the structure of the CFPB. *See PHH Corp. v. CFPB*, 881 F.3d 75 (D.C.Cir.2018). The plaintiff chose not to seek Supreme Court review of that decision. Shortly thereafter, however, a district judge in New York adopted the reasoning of the panel majority (which had been repeated in dissenting opinions in the D.C. Circuit's *en banc* proceeding) and held that the CFPB could not constitutionally pursue lawsuits. *See CFPB v. RD Legal Funding, LLC*, 332 F.Supp.3d 729 (S.D.N.Y. 2018). The Ninth Circuit held the agency constitutional, *see CFPB v. Seila Law LLC,* 923 F.3d 680 (9th Cir. 2019), and on October 18, 2019, the Supreme Court granted certiorari to resolve the split; oral argument was held on March 3, 2020. That Supreme Court decision will also surely resolve the status of the Federal Housing Finance Agency, one of the few other independent agencies headed by a single director, which was found (by a 2–1 vote) unconstitutional by the Fifth Circuit. *See Collins v. Mnuchin*, 896 F.3d 640 (5th Cir.2018). The Fifth Circuit panel, as had the D.C. Circuit panel that found the CFPB unconstitutional, relied in part on the absence of a multi-member board at the top of the agency, reasoning that presidents are likely to be able to appoint at least some members of such a board and thus exert a degree of control over its actions, whereas "the FHFA's single-Director leadership structure insulates the agency from presidential oversight." *Id.* at 667. The court also invoked a multiplicity of other factors as evidence that the agency's structure removed it too far from presidential control and direction to be constitutional. *See Collins*, 896 F.3d at 666 (grounding a finding of unconstitutionality on "(1) for-cause removal restriction; (2) single-Director leadership structure; (3) lack of a bipartisan leadership composition requirement; (4) funding stream outside the normal appropriations process; and (5) Federal Housing Finance Oversight Board's purely advisory oversight role"). The *en banc* Fifth Circuit approved and adopted this reasoning, *see Collins v. Mnuchin,* 938 F.3d 553, 587–88 (5th Cir.2019); a certiorari petition is pending.

7. Does it seem at all odd that, after 230 years, there is so little consensus about something as basic to governance as the President's constitutional relationship to administrative agencies?

[Assignment 22]

E. THE TAKE CARE CLAUSE

Article II, Section 1: The executive Power shall be vested in a President of the United States of America.

Article II, Section 3: [The President] . . . shall take Care that the Laws be faithfully executed . . . .

Article II, Section 3 imposes a series of duties on the President, including the duty to take care that the laws be faithfully executed. The Take Care Clause had its origins in the English Glorious Revolution of 1688. King James II had claimed an absolute power to dispense with, or suspend, the laws. When King James II was overthrown in 1688, part of the settlement that the English Revolutionaries insisted on was that James' successors William and Mary agree that no future monarch would ever have or claim a dispensing power. The Take Care Clause of Article II reflects this understanding. It was meant to make clear that the President would not have a power to suspend or dispense with acts of Congress. In this sense, the Clause was originally meant to limit, not to augment, the executive power of the President. Ironically, American presidents immediately began claiming the Take Care Clause implicitly granted them the power to direct and control executive branch subordinates and to remove them at will. Our view is that the President already had that power by virtue of the Vesting Clause of Article II, but if the Vesting Clause Thesis does not prevail at any given moment or in any given context, the Take Care Clause has been the fall-back provision of choice.

The existence of the Take Care Clause raises some problems in constitutional law that we have already encountered. If the President thinks a law is unconstitutional even though it has been upheld by federal courts, may the President decline to execute it? Thomas Jefferson did precisely this with the Sedition Act. Did he act unconstitutionally in "dispensing" with the Sedition Act? In general, presidents have been understandably skittish about not executing acts of Congress that they think are unconstitutional, but which Congress and/or the federal courts think pass constitutional muster. Congress has actually required notification from the Department of Justice whenever it fails to defend the constitutionality of an act of Congress in court, so Congress can hire its own counsel to defend the act.

One issue wending its way through the courts as we write concerns large-scale nonenforcement of certain laws (immigration laws in the case before the Supreme Court in 2020). The President undeniably has discretion not to prosecute any given lawbreaker. But can the President choose, on policy grounds, not to prosecute *anyone* who breaks a certain law? Is that a backdoor suspension or dispensation of that law in violation of the Take Care Clause? What if the President's explanation is that enforcement budgets are limited and something has to give? Can the Constitution really require enforcement resources to be distributed "equitably" (whatever that would mean) across the entire universe of federal laws? As it happens, the case now before the Court will surely be decided on administrative-law grounds without addressing the underlying constitutional question concerning large-scale non-enforcement. *See Regents of the Univ. of Cal. v. U.S. Dep't of Homeland Security,* 908 F.3d 476 (9th Cir. 2018), *cert. granted,* 139 S.Ct. 2779 (2019). For competing views on the President's power and how they apply in the large-scale immigration context, see Josh Blackman, *The Constitutionality of DAPA Part II: Faithfully Executing the Law,* 19 TEX. REV. L. & POL. 213 (2015); Louis W. Fisher, *Executive Enforcement Discretion and the Separation of Powers: A Case Study on the Constitutionality of DACA and DAPA,* 120 W. VA. L. REV. 131 (2017).

Another scenario arises when an act of Congress imposes a clear duty on an executive branch officer of a ministerial sort. Suppose Congress passes an act (like the one discussed in the *Kendall* case below) settling a claim against the United States and directing the postmaster general to pay a certain sum of money to the claimants against the government. Can executive officials or the President decline to execute such laws? Just as importantly, can federal judges order executive officials to perform ministerial acts, or would such an order involve a judge in law execution unconstitutionally? These questions were addressed in dicta in *Marbury*, but that dicta finally became a holding in the following famous and important case.

1. KENDALL V. UNITED STATES EX REL. STOKES

37 U.S. (12 Pet.) 524 (1838)

■ MR. JUSTICE THOMPSON delivered the opinion of the Court:

This case comes up on a writ of error from the circuit court of the United States for the District of Columbia, sitting for the county of Washington.

This case was brought before the court below by petition, setting out certain contracts made between the relators and the late postmaster general, upon which they claimed certain credits and allowances upon their contracts for the transportation of the mail. That credits and allowances were duly made by the late postmaster general. That the present postmaster general when he came into office, re-examined the contracts entered into with his predecessor, and the allowances made by him, and the credits and payments which had been made; and directed that the allowances and credits should be withdrawn, and the relators recharged with divers payments they had received. That the relators presented a memorial to congress on the subject, upon which a law was passed on the 21st of July, 1836, for their relief; by which the solicitor of the treasury was authorized and directed to settle and adjust the claims of the relators for extra-services performed by them; to inquire into and determine the equity of such claims; and to make the relators such allowance therefor, as upon full examination of all the evidence may seem right, according to the principles of equity. And that the postmaster general be, and he is hereby directed to credit the relators with whatever sum or sums of money, if any, the solicitor shall so decide to be due to them, for and on account of any such service or contract. And the petition further sets out, that the solicitor, Virgil Maxcy, assumed upon himself the performance of the duty and authority created and conferred upon him by the law, and did make out and communicate his decision and award to the postmaster general; by which award and decision the relators were allowed one hundred and sixty-one thousand five hundred and sixty-three dollars and eighty-nine cents. That the postmaster general, on being notified of the award, only so far obeyed and carried into execution the act of congress, as to direct, and cause to be carried to the credit of the relators, the sum of one hundred and twenty-two thousand one hundred and two dollars and forty-six cents. But that he has, and still does refuse and neglect to credit the relators with the residue of the sum so awarded by the solicitor, amounting to thirty-nine thousand four hundred and sixty-two dollars and forty-three cents. And the petition prayed the court, to award a mandamus directed to the postmaster general, commanding him fully to comply with, obey and execute the said act of congress, by crediting the relators with the full and entire sum awarded in their favour by the solicitor of the treasury.

Such proceedings were afterwards had in the case, that a peremptory mandamus was ordered commanding the said Amos Kendall, postmaster general, forthwith to credit the relators with the full amount awarded and decided by the solicitor of the treasury to be due to the relators.

The questions arising upon this case, may be considered under two general inquiries:

1. Does the record present a proper case for a mandamus; and if so, then,

2. Had the circuit court of this district jurisdiction of the case, and authority to issue the writ.

Under the first head of inquiry, it has been considered by the counsel on the part of the-postmaster general, that this is a proceeding against him to enforce the performance of an official duty. And the proceeding has been treated as an infringement upon the executive department of the government; which has led to a very extended range of argument on the independence and duties of that department; but which, according to the view taken by the Court of the case, is entirely misapplied. We do not think the proceedings in this case, interferes, in any respect whatever, with the rights or duties of the executive; or that it involves any conflict of powers between the executive and judicial departments of the government. The mandamus does not seek to direct or control the postmaster general in the discharge of any official duty, partaking in any respect of an executive character; but to enforce the performance of a mere ministerial act, which neither he nor the President had any authority to deny or control.

We shall not, therefore, enter into any particular examination of the line to be drawn between the powers of the executive and judicial departments of the government. The theory of the constitution undoubtedly is, that the great powers of the government are divided into separate departments; and so far as these powers are derived from the constitution, the departments may be regarded as independent of each other. But beyond that, all are subject to regulations by law, touching the discharge of the duties required to be performed.

The executive power is vested in a President; and as far as his powers are derived from the constitution, he is beyond the reach of any other department, except in the mode prescribed by the constitution through the impeaching power. But it by no means follows, that every officer in every branch of that department is under the exclusive direction of the President. Such a principle, we apprehend, is not, and certainly cannot be claimed by the President.

There are certain political duties imposed upon many officers in the executive department, the discharge of which is under the direction of the President. But it would be an alarming doctrine, that congress cannot impose upon any executive officer any duty they may think proper, which is not repugnant to any rights secured and protected by the constitution; and in such cases, the duty and responsibility grow out of and are subject to the control of the law, and not to the direction of the President. And this is emphatically the case, where the duty enjoined is of a mere ministerial character.

Let us proceed, then, to an examination of the act required by the mandamus to be performed by the postmaster general; and his obligation to perform, or his right to resist the performance, must depend upon the act of congress of the 2d of July, 1836. This is a special act for the relief of the relators, Stockton & Stokes; and was passed, as appears on its face, to adjust and settle certain claims which they had for extra services, as contractors for carrying the mail * * *. [T]he act directs the postmaster general to credit the relators with whatever sum, if any, the solicitor shall decide to be due to them, for or on account of any such service or contract.

* * *

Under this law the postmaster general is vested with no discretion or control over the decisions of the solicitor; nor is any appeal or review of that decision provided for by the act. The terms of the submission was a matter resting entirely in the discretion of congress; and if they thought proper to vest such a power in any one, and especially as the arbitrator was an officer of the government, it did not rest with the postmaster general to control congress, or the solicitor, in that affair * * *.

* * *

It was urged at the bar, that the postmaster general was alone subject to the direction and control of the President, with respect to the execution of the duty imposed upon him by this law, and this right of the President is claimed, as growing out of the obligation imposed upon him by the constitution, to take care that the laws be faithfully executed. This is a doctrine that cannot receive the sanction of this court. It would be vesting in the President a dispensing power, which has no countenance for its support in any part of the constitution; and is asserting a principle, which, if carried out in its results, to all cases falling within it, would be clothing the President with a power entirely to control the legislation of congress, and paralyze the administration of justice.

To contend that the obligation imposed on the President to see the laws faithfully executed, implies a power to forbid their execution, is a novel construction of the constitution, and entirely inadmissible * * *.

* * *

The right of the relators to the benefit of the award ought now to be considered as irreversibly established; and the question is whether they have any, and what remedy?

The act required by the law to be done by the postmaster general is simply to credit the relators with the full amount of the award of the solicitor. This is a precise, definite act, purely ministerial; and about which the postmaster general had no discretion whatever. The law upon its face shows the existence of accounts between the relators and the post office department. No money was required to be paid; and none could have been drawn out of the treasury without further legislative provision, if this credit should overbalance the debit standing against the relators. But this was a matter with which the postmaster general had no concern. He was not called upon to furnish the means of paying such balance, if any should be found. He was simply required to give the credit. This was not an official act in any other sense than being a transaction in the department where the books and accounts were kept; and was an official act in the same sense that an entry in the minutes of a court, pursuant to an order of the court, is an official act. There is no room for the exercise of any discretion, official or otherwise: all that is shut out by the direct and positive command of the law, and the act required to be done is, in every just sense, a mere ministerial act.

And in this view of the case, the question arises, is the remedy by mandamus the fit and appropriate remedy?

The common law, as it was in force in Maryland when the cession [of the land now comprising the District of Columbia] was made, remained in force in this district. We must, therefore, consider this writ as it was understood at the common law with respect to its object and purpose, and varying only in the form required by the different character of our government. It is a writ, in England, issuing out of the [court of] king's bench, in the name of the king, and is called a prerogative writ, but considered a writ of right; and is directed to some person, corporation or inferior court, requiring them to do some particular thing, therein specified, which appertains to their office or duty, and which is supposed to be consonant to right and justice, and where there is no other adequate specific remedy. Such a writ, and for such a purpose, would seem to be peculiarly appropriate to the present case. The right claimed is just and established by positive law; and the duty required to be performed is clear and specific, and there is no other adequate remedy.

The remedies suggested at the bar were, then, an application to congress; removal of the postmaster general from office; and an action against him for damages.

The first has been tried and failed. The second might not afford any certain relief, for his successors might withhold the credit in the same manner; and, besides, such extraordinary measures are not the remedies spoken of in the law which will supersede the right of resorting to a mandamus; and it is seldom that a private action at law will afford an adequate remedy * * *.

* * *

The next inquiry is, whether the court below [the United States Circuit Court for the District of Columbia] had jurisdiction of the case, and power to issue the mandamus?

* * *

The theory of the British government, and of the common law is, that the writ of mandamus is a prerogative writ, and is sometimes called one of the flowers of the crown, and is therefore confided only to the [court of] king's bench; where the king, at one period of the judicial history of that country, is said to have sat in person, and is presumed still to sit. And the power to issue this writ is given to the king's bench only, as having the general supervising power over all inferior jurisdictions and officers, and is coextensive with judicial sovereignty. And the same theory prevails in our state governments, where the common law is adopted, and governs in the administration of justice; and the power of issuing this writ is generally confided to the highest court of original jurisdiction. But, it cannot be denied but this common law principle may be modified by the legislature, in any manner that may be deemed proper and expedient. No doubt the British parliament might authorize the court of common pleas to issue this writ [as well as the court of king's bench]; or that the legislature of the states, where this doctrine prevails, might give the power to issue the writ to any judicial tribunal in the state, according to its pleasure: and in some of the states, this power is vested in other judicial tribunals than the highest court of original jurisdiction * * *.

* * * To consider the writ of mandamus, in use here, as it is in England, the issuing of it should be confined to this Court, as it is there to the King's bench. But, under the constitution, the power to issue this as an original writ, in the general sense of the common law, cannot be given to this Court, according to the decision in Marbury v. Madison.

* * *

* * * The third section [of the statute establishing the District of Columbia federal court], so far as it relates to the present inquiry, declares: "That there shall be a court in this district, which shall be called the circuit court of the District of Columbia; and the said court, and the judges thereof, shall have all the powers by law vested in the circuit courts and the judges of the circuit courts of the United States." And the fifth section declares: "That the said court shall have cognizance of

all cases, in law and equity, between parties, both or either of which shall be resident or be found within the district."

* * *

* * * That proceedings on an application to a court of justice for a mandamus, are judicial proceedings, cannot admit of a doubt; and that this is a case in law is equally clear. It is the prosecution of a suit to enforce a right secured by a special act of congress, requiring of the postmaster general the performance of a precise, definite, and specific act, plainly enjoined by the law. It cannot be denied but that congress had the power to command that act to be done; and the power to enforce the performance of the act must rest somewhere, or it will present a case which has often been said to involve a monstrous absurdity in a well organized government, that there should be no remedy, although a clear and undeniable right should be shown to exist. And if the remedy cannot be applied by the circuit court of this district, it exists nowhere. But, by the express terms of this act, the jurisdiction of this circuit court extends to all cases in law, & c. No more general language could have been used. An attempt at specification would have weakened the force and extent of the general words—all cases. Here, then, is the delegation, to this circuit court, of the whole judicial power in this district * * *.

* * *

The judgment of the court below is accordingly affirmed with costs, and the cause remanded for further proceedings.

■ MR. CHIEF JUSTICE TANEY:

* * *

* * * We all agree that by the act of July 2, 1836, it was the duty of the postmaster general to credit Stockton and Stokes with the amount awarded by the solicitor of the treasury; that no discretionary power in relation to the award, was given to the postmaster general; and that the duty enjoined upon him was merely ministerial.

These principles being agreed on, it follows, that this was a proper case for a mandamus; provided congress have conferred on the circuit court for the District of Columbia, the prerogative, jurisdiction and powers exercised by the court of king's bench, in England; for Stockton and Stokes are entitled to have the credit entered in the manner directed by the act of congress, and they have no other specific means provided by law, for compelling the performance of this duty. In such a case, the court of king's bench, in England, would undoubtedly issue the writ of mandamus to such an officer, commanding him to enter the credit. Have congress conferred similar jurisdiction and powers upon the circuit court for this district? This is the only question in the case. The majority of my brethren think that this jurisdiction and power has been conferred; and they have given their reasons for their opinion. I, with two of my brethren, think otherwise; and with the utmost respect for the opinion of the majority of this Court, I proceed to show the grounds on which I dissent from their judgment.

* * *

In England this writ can be issued by the king's bench only. It cannot be issued by the court of common pleas, or any other court known to the English law, except the court of king's bench * * *

These peculiar powers were possessed by the court of king's bench; because, the king originally sat there in person, and aided in the administration of justice * * *. And although the king has long since ceased to sit there in person, yet the sovereign is still there in construction of law so far as to enable the court to exercise its prerogative powers in his name; and hence its powers to issue the writ of mandamus * * *. It is, therefore, evident, that by the principles of the common law, this power would not be incident to any court which did not possess the general superintending power of the court of king's bench, in which the sovereignty might by construction of law be supposed to sit, and to exert there its prerogative powers in aid of the court, in order that a right might not be without a remedy.

* * *

Upon a view of the whole case, therefore, I cannot find the power which the circuit court has exercised either in the first section, or the third section, or the fifth section [of the statute]; and it is difficult to believe that congress meant to have given this high prerogative power in so many places, and yet, in every one of them, have left it, at best, so ambiguous and doubtful. And if we now sanction its exercise, we shall give to the court, by remote inferences and implications, a delicate and important power which I feel persuaded congress never intended to entrust to its hands.

* * *

[*Editors' Note: The dissenting opinion of Justice Barbour is omitted.*]

NOTES AND QUESTIONS

1. When a court uses the writ of mandamus to compel an executive officer to perform a ministerial act required by law, is it exercising judicial or executive power? In England this would have been done by the Court of King's Bench. The power of this court to issue writs of mandamus to executive officers stemmed from the fact that long ago in English history the king himself actually sat on the Court of King's Bench. Thus, ancient British monarchs possessed what we today would call both "judicial" and "executive" power. From this English history descends the power of federal courts to issue writs of mandamus directing executive officers to carry out ministerial duties. *Kendall* is a landmark in American administrative law because it establishes the power of American courts to order executive branch officials to follow the law—at least where the law is so clear that it imposes a "ministerial" duty. And by interpreting the statute creating the D.C. Circuit Court very generously, it helped generate a presumption that all inferior federal courts, like the United States Circuit Court for the District of Columbia, have the power to issue writs of mandamus, though the decision in *Kendall* relied on some special statutory features of the D.C. court.

2. What if a law gives an executive official discretion? Under *Kendall, Marbury,* and the Constitution, could a court exercising judicial power direct an executive official as to how to use her political discretion in executing the law? Can the president control subordinates in their exercises of such discretion but not where the law imposes a ministerial duty? How does one tell whether a duty is "ministerial"?

3. One interesting question is why Congress did not in the Judiciary Act of 1789 follow the English practice with the Court of King's Bench of having only one court, perhaps the U.S. Supreme Court, which could issue writs of mandamus and injunctions; one court, like the English Court of Chancery, which alone could issue injunctions and hear cases in equity; and all other courts, as being merely courts of law, like the English

of Common Please, which could only award money damages. Instead, the U.S. has ended up with a court system wherein the Supreme Court and 1,000 lower federal court judges *all* have the power to issue writs of mandamus; injunctions; and make awards of money damages. This development makes the U.S. federal court system radically more powerful than was the English court system, and it greatly hems in what the President can do.

4. The *Marbury* and *Kendall* idea—that federal courts can order the President and subordinate officials to execute the law in a particular way where the law imposes a ministerial duty on the executive branch—is a cornerstone of American administrative law and a major limitation on presidential power under our constitutional system. Of course, in whatever way one defines ministerial duties, many statutory grants of authority confer anything but ministerial duties. Discretion abounds throughout the executive department. Even statutes that do not raise colorable claims under an originalist subdelegation doctrine are likely to confer a great deal of discretion, in both interpretation and application, on the executive agents implementing them. Mandamus is not a remedy when discretion is involved. So what is? That is the chief subject of courses in Administrative Law, and we are not going to pursue the matter here, beyond these few thoughts: First, for most of the Nation's history, the normal way to get judicial review of adverse executive action was to sue the offending official in a common-law action—as Captain Little got sued in *Little v Barreme*. *See supra* pages 167–168. The officials would then interpose their official authorization as a defense, and the court would decide whether the authorization was legally valid. Since mandamus is only available when no ordinary remedy is possible, why couldn't Stokes have just sued in a common-law action and gone from there? The Court determined that such an action would not be adequate where, for instance, "the amount of damages is beyond the capacity of a party to pay." 37 U.S. (12 Pet.) at 615. Stokes was suing for a *lot* of money in 1838 terms. As a matter of the law of remedies, it is perhaps dubious whether the Court correctly applied the conditions for mandamus in that case, but certainly in cases with lower stakes damages against the officer rather than mandamus would be the proper form of action. This scheme has been displaced over the past seventy-five years by a combination of statutory provisions and judicial creations. A combination of numerous organic statutes plus one very large framework statute enacted in 1946, the Administrative Procedure Act, creates a thick network of substantive and procedural rules that executive agencies must follow, enforceable by an equally thick network of provisions for judicial review. That is why virtually every significant executive action these days winds up in court, usually on statutory rather than constitutional grounds. But while Congress has enormously expanded the range of legal forms for seeking review of executive action (and courts have creatively expanded the range even further through generous statutory interpretation), courts have simultaneously cut back on the traditional damages actions against officers through judicially crafted doctrines of official immunity that make it very difficult to win an old-fashioned common law suit against a federal agent's official acts. And to cap it off, a combination of statutory provisions and judge-made doctrines normally (not always, but normally) give enormous deference to executive agents—on matters of law as well as fact or policy. Some of those deference doctrines, especially on questions of law, are shifting even as we write this to allow for more active judicial oversight of executive action. But that is all just a teaser for a course on Administrative Law—a subject on which one of us has written another casebook. *See* GARY LAWSON, FEDERAL ADMINISTRATIVE LAW (8th ed. 2019).

2. THE PARDON POWER

Article II, Section 2: The President . . . shall have Power to grant Reprieves and Pardons for Offenses against the United States, except in Cases of Impeachment.

Under the theory of the unitary executive the President has the power to order that prosecutions be stopped as well as that they be commenced. In modern times this power is always (and should almost always be) filtered through the professional institution of a U.S. Attorney's office. Presidents who are seen to be politicizing the U.S. Attorneys' offices to get their political opponents or to let their supporters off lightly pay a terrible political price for this behavior.

There is a mechanism, however, in Article II by which the President is specifically empowered not only to stop prosecutions but to free those imprisoned for the commission of crimes or to guarantee that individuals will never be prosecuted for a crime. Article II, Section 2 gives the President sweeping power to grant pardons for all offenses against the United States. This reinforces the President's control of the executive branch: if a federal prosecutor decides to prosecute someone, and the President disapproves, even if the prosecutor succeeds in getting a conviction, the law enforcement priorities of the President can still be vindicated, without having to fire the prosecutor, through the pardon power.

The power to pardon all individuals who have violated federal law is without a doubt one of the most formidable powers of the President. The President can pardon people before they are even indicted, as was done for Richard Nixon, or after they have been unconstitutionally imprisoned, as was done for American Socialist Party leader Eugene V. Debs, who was pardoned by President Harding after he was sentenced to ten years imprisonment for allegedly urging workers to avoid the military draft during World War I. The Framers thought that a well-timed offer of a general pardon might be vital to ending rebellions or civil wars and that in individual cases the pardon power might temper the criminal law. Most pardons over the course of American history have been issued after rebellions (including the Civil War) or to draft evaders after a war (including the two World Wars and the Vietnam War). President Gerald Ford simultaneously pardoned both former President Richard Nixon and the Vietnam War draft evaders. President Andrew Johnson issued widespread pardons to Confederate loyalists after the Civil War—a policy Abraham Lincoln would probably also have followed had he lived to do so.

What reasons of state are sufficiently important to warrant a pardon? How broadly ought the federal courts to read the pardon power? Do the federal courts even have occasion to read the pardon power? Consider these questions as you read *The Federalist* No. 74.

THE FEDERALIST NO. 74 (Alexander Hamilton)

(March 25, 1788)

THE President of the United States * * * is also to be authorized to grant "reprieves and pardons for offenses against the United States, EXCEPT IN CASES OF IMPEACHMENT." Humanity and good policy conspire to dictate, that the benign prerogative of pardoning should be as little as possible fettered or embarrassed. The criminal code of every country partakes so much of necessary severity, that without an easy access to exceptions in favor of unfortunate guilt, justice would wear a countenance too sanguinary and cruel. As the sense of responsibility is always strongest, in proportion as it is undivided, it may be inferred that a single man would be most ready to attend to the force of those motives which might plead for a mitigation of the rigor of the law, and least apt to yield to considerations which were calculated to shelter a fit object of its vengeance * * *. On these accounts, one man appears to be a more eligible dispenser of the mercy of government, than a body of men.

* * *

* * * But the principal argument for reposing the power of pardoning in this case to the Chief Magistrate is this: in seasons of insurrection or rebellion, there are often critical moments, when a welltimed offer of pardon to the insurgents or rebels may restore the tranquillity of the commonwealth; and which, if suffered to pass unimproved, it may never be possible afterwards to recall. The dilatory process of convening the legislature, or one of its branches, for the purpose of obtaining its sanction to the measure, would frequently be the occasion of letting slip the golden opportunity. The loss of a week, a day, an hour, may sometimes be fatal * * *.

NOTES AND QUESTIONS

1. What protects against the President abusing the pardon power? Did Jefferson abuse the pardon power when he pardoned anyone convicted under the Sedition Act on the ground that it was unconstitutional? Is there any more reason to fear presidential abuse of the pardon power than there is to fear that since Congress can set its own salaries, the members may vote themselves huge pay raises? Does the fact that such abuses have not occurred over the last 230 years affect your view of this matter?

2. Reformers have occasionally proposed that the Constitution be amended to allow a two-thirds majority of both Houses of Congress to override a presidential pardon much as they can override a presidential veto. Is this a good idea? Doesn't the President need to be able, as Alexander Hamilton argued in *The Federalist*, to be able to offer pardons to subdue civil rebellions and end wars? Could the President credibly make such offers if the rebels in question knew that their pardons could be overridden by Congress?

3. Are there certain kinds of pardons—for example, to reward political friends or immunize subordinates from the consequences of following presidential orders of dubious legality—that are unlawful? Could they form the basis for impeachment proceedings? May a President pardon himself or herself? *See* Ethan J. Leib & Jed Handelsman Shugerman, *Fiduciary Constitutionalism: Implications for Self-Pardons and Non-Delegation,* 17 GEO. J.L. & PUB. POL'Y 463 (2019).

4. Courts seldom have occasion to consider the lawfulness of presidential pardons. One intriguing exception is *Ex parte Grossman,* 267 U.S. 87 (1925), in which the Court held that the President could grant pardons for criminal contempt orders entered by judges, rejecting the argument that judicial independence required judges to be able to protect their domains with contempt orders free of presidential pardons. Chief Justice (and former President) Taft wrote:

> The power of a court to protect itself and its usefulness by punishing contemnors is of course necessary, but it is one exercised without the restraining influence of a jury and without many of the guaranties which the bill of rights offers to protect the individual against unjust conviction. Is it unreasonable to provide for the possibility that the personal element may

> sometimes enter into a summary judgment pronounced by a judge who thinks his authority is flouted or denied? May it not be fairly said that in order to avoid possible mistake, undue prejudice or needless severity, the chance of pardon should exist at least as much in favor of a person convicted by a judge without a jury as in favor of one convicted in a jury trial? The pardoning by the President of criminal contempts has been practiced more than three-quarters of a century, and no abuses during all that time developed sufficiently to invoke a test in the federal courts of its validity.

267 U.S. at 122.

[Assignment 23]

F. EXECUTIVE POWER AND FOREIGN AFFAIRS

> **Article II, Section 1: The executive Power shall be vested in a President of the United States of America.**
>
> **Article II, Section 2: The President shall be Commander in Chief of the Army and Navy of the United States, and of the Militia of the several States, when called into the actual Service of the United States . . . .**
>
> **Article II, Section 3: [The President] shall receive Ambassadors and other public Ministers . . . .**

Where does the Constitution assign the power of foreign affairs? There is no generalized "foreign affairs" clause. There are numerous clauses that pertain to some aspect of foreign affairs, but there is no clause that expressly allocates authority over matters not covered by the specific clauses but which it seems inconceivable do not exist somewhere in the federal government. (Consider, for example, the power to break treaties.) We present above three powers vested solely in the President that involve foreign affairs. The power to make treaties is jointly vested in the President and the Senate; we will have much more to say about that power later in this section. Before the Constitution gives the President the foregoing executive, warmaking, and diplomatic powers, however, it first grants extensive foreign affairs powers to *Congress* in Article I, section 8, including some powers, such as the power to declare war, that traditionally had been an executive function:

> **The Congress shall have power . . .**
>
> **[10] To define and punish Piracies and Felonies committed on the high Seas, and Offences against the Law of Nations;**
>
> **[11] To declare War, grant Letters of Marque and Reprisal, and make Rules concerning Captures on Land and Water;**
>
> **[12] To raise and support Armies, but no Appropriation of Money to that Use shall be for a longer Term than two Years;**
>
> **[13] To provide and maintain a Navy;**
>
> **[14] To make Rules for the Government and Regulation of the land and naval Forces;**
>
> **[15] To provide for calling forth the Militia to execute the Laws of the Union, suppress Insurrections and repel Invasions;**

[16] To provide for organizing, arming, and disciplining, the Militia, and for governing such Part of them as may be employed in the Service of the United States, reserving to the States respectively, the Appointment of the Officers, and the Authority of training the Militia according to the discipline prescribed by Congress;

[18] To make all Laws which shall be necessary and proper for carrying into Execution the foregoing Powers, and all other Powers vested by this Constitution in the Government of the United States, or in any Department or Officer thereof

This is an impressive set of congressional powers. Given their depth and breadth, is Congress a plausible claimant for any residual foreign affairs powers that are not part of express clauses? Do the States have a plausible claim to those powers under the Tenth Amendment (other than those powers forbidden to them, such as the power to make treaties or to engage in war unless directly attacked)? Or are there simply certain powers that most governments possess that no American institution can exercise?

The scope of the foreign affairs powers of the various federal institutions (and the States) has been, quite understandingly, one of the most contentious topics in constitutional law and politics for more than two centuries. The stakes are very high, and the constitutional text leaves plenty of questions.

The scope of the President's foreign affairs powers arose early in the Nation's history. In April 1793, war had broken out in Europe between Revolutionary France and Great Britain and its various allies. The United States had signed a treaty of alliance with France during the American Revolution, when King Louis XVI was still alive and in power. France had overthrown its monarchy in 1792, and France had executed King Louis XVI on January 21, 1793. The question that arose in April of 1793, was whether the U.S. was bound by this old Franco-American treaty of alliance to come to Revolutionary France's aid or whether the treaty had become a dead letter because both the regime and French government, which had signed it, had been overthrown. President George Washington construed the treaty of alliance as being dead, and he issued the famous Neutrality Proclamation on April 22, 1793, which we reproduced earlier. *See supra* pages 166–167. Alexander Hamilton, writing as "Pacificus," and James Madison, writing as "Helvidius," exchanged essays on the validity of the President's power to issue the proclamation. History has mostly sided with Hamilton; see if you agree or disagree with history's verdict.

1. THE HAMILTON-MADISON DEBATE

Pacificus Essay (Alexander Hamilton)

(1793)

* * *

The inquiry then is—what department of the Government of the UStates is the prop[er] one to make a declaration of Neutrality in the cases in which the engagements [of] the Nation permit and its interests require such a declaration.

A correct and well informed mind will discern at once that it can belong neit[her] to the Legislature nor Judicial Department and of course must belong to the Executive.

The Legislative Department is not the organ of intercourse between the United States and foreign Nations. It is charged neither with making nor interpreting Treaties. It is therefore not naturally that Organ of the Government, which is to pronounce the existing condition of the Nation, with regard to foreign Powers, or to admonish the Citizens of their obligations and duties as founded upon that condition of things. Still less is it charged with execution and observance of those obligations and those duties.

It is equally obvious that the act in question is foreign to the Judiciary Department of Government. The province of that Department is to decide litigations in particular cases. It is indeed charged with the interpretation of treaties; but it exercises this function only in the litigated cases; that is where contending parties bring before it a specific controversy. It has no concern with pronouncing upon the external political relations of Treaties between Government and Government. This position is too plain to need being insisted upon.

It must then of necessity belong to the Executive Department to exercise the function in Question—when a proper case for the exercise of it occurs.

It appears to be connected with that department in various capacities, as the organ of intercourse between the Nation and foreign Nations—as the interpreter of the National Treaties, in those cases in which the Judiciary is not competent, that is in the cases between Government and Government—as the power, which is charged with the Execution of the Laws, of which Treaties form a part—as that Power which is charged with the command and application of the Public Force.

This view of the subject is so natural and obvious—so analogous to general theory and practice—that no doubt can be entertained of its justness, unless such doubt can be deduced from particular provisions of the Constitution of the UStates.

* * *

The general doctrine then of our Constitution is, that the EXECUTIVE POWER of the Nation is vested in the President; subject only to the exceptions and qu[a]lifications which are expressed in the instrument.

Two of these have been already noticed—the participation of the Senate in the appointment of Officers and in the making of Treaties. A third remains to be mentioned: the right of the Legislature "to declare war and grant letters of marque and reprisal."

With these exceptions the EXECUTIVE POWER of the Union is completely lodged in the President. This mode of construing the Constitution has indeed been recognized by Congress in formal acts, upon full consideration and debate. The power of removal from office is an important instance.

And since upon general principles for reasons already given, the issuing of a proclamation of neutrality is merely an Executive Act; since also the general Executive Power of the Union is vested in the President, the conclusion is, that the step, which has been taken by him, is liable to no just exception on the score of authority.

It may be observed that this Inference would be just if the power of declaring war had not been vested in the Legislature, but that power naturally includes the right of judge whether the Nation is under obligations to make war or not.

The answer to this is, that however true it may be, that the right of the Legislature to declare war includes the right of judging whether the Nation be under obligations to make War or not—it will not follow that the Executive is in any case excluded from a similar right of Judgment, in the execution of its own functions.

If the Legislature have a right to make war on the one hand—it is on the other the duty of the Executive to preserve Peace till war is declared; and in fulfilling that duty, it must necessarily possess a right of judging what is the nature of the obligations which the treaties of the Country impose on the Government; and when in pursuance of this right it has concluded that there is nothing in them inconsistent with a state of neutrality, it becomes both its province and its duty to enforce the laws incident to that state of the Nation. The Executive is charged with the execution of all laws, the law of Nations as well as the Municipal law, which recognises and adopts those laws. It is consequently bound, by faithfully executing the laws of neutrality, when that is the state of the Nation, to avoid giving a cause of war to foreign Powers.

* * *

Helvidius Essay (James Madison)

(1793)

If we consult for a moment, the nature and operation of the two powers to declare war and make treaties, it will be impossible not to see that they can never fall within a proper definition of executive powers. The natural province of the executive magistrate is to execute laws, as that of the legislature is to make laws. All his acts therefore, properly executive, must presuppose the existence of the laws to be executed. A treaty is not an execution of laws: it does not pre-suppose the existence of laws. It is, on the contrary, to have itself the force of a law, and to be carried into execution, like all other laws, by the executive magistrate. To say then that the power of making treaties which are confessedly laws, belongs naturally to the department which is to execute laws, is to say, that the executive department naturally includes a legislative power. In theory, this is an absurdity—in practice a tyranny.

The power to declare war is subject to similar reasoning. A declaration that there shall be war, is not an execution of laws: it does not suppose preexisting laws to be executed: it is not in any respect, an act merely executive. It is, on the contrary, one of the most deliberative acts that can be performed; and when performed, has the effect of repealing all the laws operating in a state of peace, so far as they are inconsistent with a state of war: and of enacting as a rule for the executive, a new code adapted to the relation between the society and its foreign enemy. In like manner a conclusion of peace annuls all the laws peculiar to a state of war, and revives the general laws incident to a state of peace.

These remarks will be strengthened by adding that treaties, particularly treaties of peace, have sometimes the effect of changing not only the external laws of the society, but operate also on the internal code, which is purely municipal, and to which the legislative authority of the country is of itself competent and compleat.

From this view of the subject it must be evident, that although the executive may be a convenient organ of preliminary communications with foreign governments, on the subjects of treaty or war; and the proper agent for carrying into execution the final determinations of the competent authority; yet it can have no pretensions from the nature of the powers in question compared with the nature of the executive trust, to that essential agency which gives validity to such determinations.

It must be further evident that, if these powers be not in their nature purely legislative, they partake so much more of that, than of any other quality, that under a constitution leaving them to result to their most natural department, the legislature would be without a rival in its claim.

* * *

It is a condition annexed to every treaty that an infraction even of an important article, on one side extinguishes the obligations on the other: and the immediate consequence of a dissolution of a treaty of peace is a restoration of a state of war. If the executive is "to decide on the obligation of the nation with regard to foreign nations"—"to pronounce the existing condition (in the sense annexed by the writer) of the nation with regard to them; and to admonish the citizens of their obligations and duties as founded upon that condition of things"—"to judge what are the reciprocal rights and obligations of the United States, and of all and each of the powers at war:"—add, that if the executive moreover possesses all powers relating to war not strictly within the power to declare war, which any pupil of political casuistry, could distinguish from a mere relapse into a war, that had been declared: With this store of materials and the example given of the use to be made of them, would it be difficult to fabricate a power in the executive to plunge the nation into war, whenever a treaty of peace might happen to be infringed?

* * *

* * * As the constitution has not permitted the Executive singly to conclude or judge that peace ought to be made, it might be inferred from that circumstance alone, that it never meant to give it authority, singly, to judge and conclude that war ought not to be made. The trust would be precisely similar and equivalent in the two cases. The right to say that war ought not to go on, would be no greater than the right to say that war ought to begin. Every danger of error or corruption, incident to such a prerogative in one case, is incident to it in the other. If the Constitution therefore has deemed it unsafe or improper in the one case, it must be deemed equally so in the other case.

NOTES AND QUESTIONS

1. The Treaty of Alliance between the executed King Louis XVI and the United States, which dated back to the American Revolution was a treaty and was therefore, under the Supremacy Clause of Article VI of the Constitution, part of the supreme law of the land. The President has the obligation to take care that the laws, which include treaties, be faithfully executed. In order to do this, the President must interpret the aforesaid laws and treaties. Wasn't President Washington merely "interpreting" the treaty of alliance with the executed King Louis XVI and informing his executive branch subordinates that it did not apply to Revolutionary France? As such, the issuance of the

Neutrality Proclamation was quintessentially an executive act of law interpretation pursuant to the President's duty to "take care that the laws be faithfully executed."

2. Madison argues the President's executive power is simply a power to carry into execution the laws and treaties made by Congress. But during the Decision of 1789, Madison argued that the King of England had the power to appoint and remove officers and the Constitution had given the Senate a role in confirming officers but that the royal power of removal, which was not shared by the Constitution with the Senate, was accordingly an executive power of the President alone. Is the power to interpret, or abrogate, treaties any different? Is Madison as Helvidius rejecting the Vesting Clause Thesis?

3. Madison denies that the power of making treaties is an executive power given that treaties can only be made if two-thirds of the Senate advises and consents to them. But absent the Treaty Clause, where would the power to make treaties lie? In the President by virtue of the Vesting Clause? If the latter, then the Treaty Clause clarifies and qualifies an executive power. *See* Gary Lawson & Guy Seidman, *The Jeffersonian Treaty Clause,* 2006 U. ILL. L. REV. 1, 43–45.

4. As an historical matter, treaties have sometimes been abrogated by Congress and sometimes by the President alone, but Presidents Carter, George W. Bush, and Trump have all abrogated major treaties and few have questioned their unilateral power to do so. President Jimmy Carter, for example, unilaterally abrogated a U.S. treaty with Taiwan following the normalization of relations with the Communist Chinese government. Senator Barry Goldwater then sued President Carter in federal court, arguing that the President had no right unilaterally to abrogate a treaty. Senator Goldwater lost his case in the federal courts. The United States Court of Appeals for the D.C. Circuit reached the merits, and it ruled that the President had a unilateral right to abrogate treaties. *Goldwater v. Carter,* 617 F.2d 697 (D.C. Cir. 1979). The case was then appealed to the Supreme Court, which held that it lacked jurisdiction. Four justices believed the case raised a political question and one justice thought the conflict between the President and Congress was not ripe for adjudication, because it was not at all clear that Senator Goldwater spoke for anyone other than himself. Justice William J. Brennan dissented from the order to dismiss the case and would have held that the President did have a unilateral right to abrogate treaties. *Goldwater v. Carter*, 444 U.S. 996 (1979). To the extent the issue has been litigated, to date Hamilton has won and Madison has lost.

2. THE FOREIGN AFFAIRS POWER: JUDICIAL CASELAW

There have been surprisingly few (given the importance of the question) major court decisions defining the President's foreign affairs powers. Indeed, the "leading" case addressed the subject only in dictum, but that dictum has had a profound effect on modern law and practice.

U.S. v. Curtiss-Wright Export Corporation

299 U.S. 304 (1936)

■ MR. JUSTICE SUTHERLAND delivered the opinion of the Court.

On January 27, 1936, an indictment was returned in the court below, the first count of which charges that appellees, beginning with the 29th day of May, 1934, conspired to sell in the United States certain arms of war, namely fifteen machine guns, to Bolivia, a country then engaged in armed conflict in the Chaco, in violation of the Joint Resolution of Congress approved May 28, 1934, and the provisions of a proclamation issued on the same day by the President of the United States pursuant to authority conferred by § 1 of the resolution * * *. The Joint Resolution (chapter 365, 48 Stat. 811) follows:

"* * *[I]f the President finds that the prohibition of the sale of arms and munitions of war in the United States to those countries now engaged in armed conflict in the Chaco may contribute to the reestablishment of peace between those countries, and if after consultation with the governments of other American Republics and with their cooperation, as well as that of such other governments as he may deem necessary, he makes proclamation to that effect, it shall be unlawful to sell, except under such limitations and exceptions as the President prescribes, any arms or munitions of war in any place in the United States to the countries now engaged in that armed conflict, or to any person, company, or association acting in the interest of either country, until otherwise ordered by the President or by Congress.

"Sec. 2. Whoever sells any arms or munitions of war in violation of section 1 shall, on conviction, be punished by a fine not exceeding $10,000 or by imprisonment not exceeding two years, or both."

The President's proclamation (48 Stat. 1744), after reciting the terms of the Joint Resolution, declares:

"Now, therefore, I, Franklin D. Roosevelt, President of the United States of America, acting under and by virtue of the authority conferred in me by the said joint resolution of Congress, do hereby declare and proclaim that I have found that the prohibition of the sale of arms and munitions of war in the United States to those countries now engaged in armed conflict in the Chaco may contribute to the reestablishment of peace between those countries * * *; and I do hereby admonish all citizens of the United States and every person to abstain from every violation of the provisions of the joint resolution above set forth, hereby made applicable to Bolivia and Paraguay, and I do hereby warn them that all violations of such provisions will be rigorously prosecuted."

* * *

Whether, if the Joint Resolution had related solely to internal affairs, it would be open to the challenge that it constituted an unlawful delegation of legislative power to the Executive, we find it unnecessary to determine. The whole aim of the resolution is to affect a situation entirely external to the United States, and falling within the category of foreign affairs * * *. In other words, assuming (but not deciding) that the challenged delegation, if it were confined to internal affairs, would be invalid, may it nevertheless be sustained on the ground that its exclusive aim is to afford a remedy for a hurtful condition within foreign territory?

It will contribute to the elucidation of the question if we first consider the differences between the powers of the federal government in respect of foreign or external affairs and those in respect of domestic or internal affairs. That there are differences between them, and that these differences are fundamental, may not be doubted.

The two classes of powers are different, both in respect of their origin and their nature. The broad statement that the federal government can exercise no powers except those specifically enumerated in the Constitution, and such implied powers as are necessary and proper to carry into effect the enumerated powers, is categorically true only in respect of our internal affairs. In that field, the primary purpose of the Constitution was to carve from the general mass of legislative powers *then possessed by the states* such portions as it was thought desirable to vest in the federal government, leaving those not included in the enumeration still in the states. That this doctrine applies only to powers which the states had, is self evident. And since the states severally never possessed international powers, such powers could not have been carved from the mass of state powers but obviously were transmitted to the United States from some other source. During the colonial period, those powers were possessed exclusively by and were entirely under the control of the Crown. By the Declaration of Independence, "the Representatives of the United States of America" declared the United [not the several] Colonies to be free and independent states, and as such to have "full Power to levy War, conclude Peace, contract Alliances, establish Commerce and to do all other Acts and Things which Independent States may of right do."

As a result of the separation from Great Britain by the colonies acting as a unit, the powers of external sovereignty passed from the Crown not to the colonies severally, but to the colonies in their collective and corporate capacity as the United States of America. Even before the Declaration, the colonies were a unit in foreign affairs, acting through a common agency—namely, the Continental Congress, composed of delegates from the thirteen colonies. That agency exercised the powers of war and peace, raised an army, created a navy, and finally adopted the Declaration of Independence. Rulers come and go; governments end and forms of government change; but sovereignty survives. A political society cannot endure without a supreme will somewhere. Sovereignty is never held in suspense. When, therefore, the external sovereignty of Great Britain in respect of the colonies ceased, it immediately passed to the Union. That fact was given practical application almost at once. The treaty of peace, made on September 3, 1783, was concluded between his Brittanic Majesty and the "United States of America."

The Union existed before the Constitution, which was ordained and established among other things to form "a more perfect Union." * * * The Framers' Convention was called and exerted its powers upon the irrefutable postulate that though the states were several their people in respect of foreign affairs were one * * *.

It results that the investment of the federal government with the powers of external sovereignty did not depend upon the affirmative grants of the Constitution. The powers to declare and wage war, to conclude peace, to make treaties, to maintain diplomatic relations with other sovereignties, if they had never been mentioned in the Constitution, would have vested in the federal government as necessary concomitants of nationality * * *. As a member of the family of nations, the right and power of the United States in that field are equal to the right and power of the other members of the international family. Otherwise, the United States is not completely sovereign. The power to acquire territory by discovery and occupation, the power to expel undesirable aliens, the power to make such international agreements as do not constitute treaties in the constitutional sense, none of which is expressly affirmed by the Constitution, nevertheless exist as inherently inseparable from the conception of nationality * * *.

* * *

Not only, as we have shown, is the federal power over external affairs in origin and essential character different from that over internal affairs, but participation in the exercise of the power is significantly limited. In this vast external realm, with its important, complicated, delicate and manifold problems, the President alone has the power to speak or listen as a representative of the nation. He *makes* treaties with the advice and consent of the Senate; but he alone negotiates. Into the field of negotiation the Senate cannot intrude; and Congress itself is powerless to invade it. As Marshall said in his great argument of March 7, 1800, in the House of Representatives, "The President is the sole organ of the nation in its external relations, and its sole representative with foreign nations." Annals, 6th Cong., col. 613 * * *.

It is important to bear in mind that we are here dealing not alone with an authority vested in the President by an exertion of legislative power, but with such an authority plus the very delicate, plenary and exclusive power of the President as the sole organ of the federal government in the field of international relations—a power which does not require as a basis for its exercise an act of Congress, but which, of course, like every other governmental power, must be exercised in subordination to the applicable provisions of the Constitution. It is quite apparent that if, in the maintenance of our international relations, embarrassment—perhaps serious embarrassment—is to be avoided and success for our aims achieved, congressional legislation which is to be made effective through negotiation and inquiry within the international field must often accord to the President a degree of discretion and freedom from statutory restriction which would not be admissible were domestic affairs alone involved. Moreover, he, not Congress, has the better opportunity of knowing the conditions which prevail in foreign countries, and especially is this true in time of war. He has his confidential sources of information. He has his agents in the form of diplomatic, consular and other officials. Secrecy in respect of information gathered by them may be highly necessary, and the premature disclosure of it productive of harmful results. Indeed, so clearly is this true that the first President refused to accede to a request to lay before the House of Representatives the instructions, correspondence and documents relating to the negotiation of the Jay Treaty—a refusal the wisdom of which was recognized by the House itself and has never since been doubted * * *.

* * *

Practically every volume of the United States Statutes contains one or more acts or joint resolutions of Congress authorizing action by the President in respect of subjects affecting foreign relations, which either leave the exercise of the power to his unrestricted judgment, or provide a standard far more general than that which has always been considered requisite with regard to domestic affairs * * *.

* * *

* * * A legislative practice such as we have here, evidenced not by only occasional instances, but marked by the movement of a steady stream for a century and a half of time, goes a long way in the direction of proving the presence of unassailable ground for the constitutionality of the practice, to be found in the origin and history of the power involved, or in its nature, or in both combined.

* * *

The judgment of the court below must be reversed and the cause remanded for further proceedings in accordance with the foregoing opinion * * *.

■ MR. JUSTICE MCREYNOLDS does not agree. He is of opinion that the court below reached the right conclusion and its judgment ought to be affirmed.

■ MR. JUSTICE STONE took no part in the consideration or decision of this case.

NOTES AND QUESTIONS

1. For purposes of determining whether the delegation of power to the executive in this case was excessive, what difference does it make whether sovereignty devolved upon the Union or upon the individual States upon independence? Even assuming the Court is correct that the powers of war and peace devolved upon the Union, why does that have any bearing on the allocation of powers between Congress and the executive?

2. Is it correct, in the context of the United States Constitution, to reason: "All respectable governments can do X; the United States has a respectable government; therefore, the United States government can do X"? This was a very popular argument in the Supreme Court for more than half a century before *Curtiss-Wright*. Of course, if one infers governmental powers that are not enumerated, one must figure out which federal institution(s) can exercise them. You will see that problem emerge in the case following these notes.

3. What modalities of interpretation drove this opinion? Practice? Policy? Structure and relation? How would you categorize the argument described in the previous note?

4. Review the questions raised in the discussion above of the Neutrality Proclamation of 1793. Where *does* the Constitution vest the power of foreign affairs? Is it an aspect of "the executive Power"? If so, may the President enact, on his or her own, a criminal prohibition on citizens' interference with the U.S. foreign policy of neutrality? Note that George Washington's Neutrality Proclamation of 1793 explicitly called on federal prosecutors to prosecute any American citizen who violated the law of nations by waging war when the United States was, as President Washington declared, neutral in the war between Britain and France. Did Washington exceed his powers here or was he simply acting as the nation's prosecutor in chief? Is the Due Process of Law Clause relevant here? It forbids depriving persons of liberty (such as throwing them in prison) without due process of *law*. Does "law" mean legislation? Or is the President's power over foreign affairs and his power to direct prosecutors under the Vesting Clause of Article II a part of American law?

5. Are you persuaded by the Court's argument that the federal government is vested with all foreign affairs powers, as an inherent attribute of sovereignty rather than by constitutional enumeration? What is the Court's evidence for this conclusion? Does it depend on the proposition that the terms "United Colonies" in the Declaration of Independence and "United States" in the Treaty of Paris were singular (referring to the government of the Union) rather than plural (referring to the States)? Is that so clear? What do you make of the fact that the Articles of Confederation declared that the several States were "sovereign"? If the States had no international status or foreign affairs powers at the Founding, why would Article I, section 10 need to deny the States some of those powers? *See* MICHAEL GLENNON & ROBERT D. SLOANE, FOREIGN AFFAIRS FEDERALISM: THE MYTH OF NATIONAL EXCLUSIVITY (2016); Michael D. Ramsey, *The Power of the States in Foreign Affairs: The Original Understanding of Foreign Policy Federalism*, 75 NOTRE DAME L. REV. 341 (1999).

6. Government litigators for decades have relied on *Curtiss-Wright* to defend all manner of presidential action in foreign affairs. "*Curtiss-Wright*; therefore, we're right"

is a quip often spoken by Department of Justice lawyers. What is the status of *Curtiss-Wright* after the following fascinating case? Note that the events in the case, which concern the recognition of Jerusalem as the capital of Israel, have been overtaken by events: On December 6, 2017, President Donald Trump reversed the long-standing executive policy that was being challenged. The case remains, however, one of the Court's most important statements on the allocation of foreign affairs powers.

Zivotofsky v. Kerry

576 U.S. 1 (2015)

■ JUSTICE KENNEDY delivered the opinion of the Court.

A delicate subject lies in the background of this case. That subject is Jerusalem. Questions touching upon the history of the ancient city and its present legal and international status are among the most difficult and complex in international affairs. In our constitutional system these matters are committed to the Legislature and the Executive, not the Judiciary. As a result, in this opinion the Court does no more, and must do no more, than note the existence of international debate and tensions respecting Jerusalem. Those matters are for Congress and the President to discuss and consider as they seek to shape the Nation's foreign policies.

The Court addresses two questions to resolve the interbranch dispute now before it. First, it must determine whether the President has the exclusive power to grant formal recognition to a foreign sovereign. Second, if he has that power, the Court must determine whether Congress can command the President and his Secretary of State to issue a formal statement that contradicts the earlier recognition. The statement in question here is a congressional mandate that allows a United States citizen born in Jerusalem to direct the President and Secretary of State, when issuing his passport, to state that his place of birth is "Israel."

Jerusalem's political standing has long been, and remains, one of the most sensitive issues in American foreign policy, and indeed it is one of the most delicate issues in current international affairs. In 1948, President Truman formally recognized Israel in a signed statement of "recognition." See Statement by the President Announcing Recognition of the State of Israel, Public Papers of the Presidents, May 14, 1948, p. 258 (1964). That statement did not recognize Israeli sovereignty over Jerusalem. Over the last 60 years, various actors have sought to assert full or partial sovereignty over the city, including Israel, Jordan, and the Palestinians. Yet, in contrast to a consistent policy of formal recognition of Israel, neither President Truman nor any later United States President has issued an official statement or declaration acknowledging any country's sovereignty over Jerusalem * * *.

* * * [President Barack Obama's] position on Jerusalem is reflected in State Department policy regarding passports and consular reports of birth abroad. Understanding that passports will be construed as reflections of American policy, the State Department's Foreign Affairs Manual instructs its employees, in general, to record the place of birth on a passport as the "country [having] present sovereignty over the actual area of birth." Dept. of State, 7 Foreign Affairs Manual (FAM) § 1383.4 (1987). If a citizen objects to the country listed as sovereign by the State Department, he or she may list the city or town of birth rather than the country. The FAM, however, does not allow citizens to list a sovereign that conflicts with Executive

Branch policy. Because the United States does not recognize any country as having sovereignty over Jerusalem [*Editors' Note: this changed on December 6, 2017, more than two years after this case was decided*], the FAM instructs employees to record the place of birth for citizens born there as "Jerusalem." *Id.*, § 1383.5–6 (emphasis deleted).

In 2002, Congress passed the Act at issue here, the Foreign Relations Authorization Act, Fiscal Year 2003, 116 Stat. 1350 * * *. § 214(d) states that "[f]or purposes of the registration of birth, certification of nationality, or issuance of a passport of a United States citizen born in the city of Jerusalem, the Secretary shall, upon the request of the citizen or the citizen's legal guardian, record the place of birth as Israel."

When he signed the Act into law, President George W. Bush issued a statement declaring his position that § 214 would, "if construed as mandatory rather than advisory, impermissibly interfere with the President's constitutional authority to formulate the position of the United States, speak for the Nation in international affairs, and determine the terms on which recognition is given to foreign states." Statement on Signing the Foreign Relations Authorization Act, Fiscal Year 2003, Public Papers of the Presidents, George W. Bush, Vol. 2, Sept. 30, 2002, p. 1698 (2005). The President concluded, "U. S. policy regarding Jerusalem has not changed." [*Editors' Note: U.S. policy remained the same under President Barack Obama, but it changed markedly, as to the status of Jerusalem, on December 6, 2017, when President Donald Trump officially recognized Jerusalem as the capital of Israel.*]

* * *

In 2002, petitioner Menachem Binyamin Zivotofsky was born to United States citizens living in Jerusalem. In December 2002, Zivotofsky's mother visited the American Embassy in Tel Aviv to request both a passport and a consular report of birth abroad for her son. She asked that his place of birth be listed as " 'Jerusalem, Israel.' " The Embassy clerks explained that, pursuant to State Department policy, the passport would list only "Jerusalem." Zivotofsky's parents objected and, as his guardians, brought suit on his behalf in the United States District Court for the District of Columbia, seeking to enforce § 214(d).

Pursuant to § 214(d), Zivotofsky claims the right to have "Israel" recorded as his place of birth in his passport * * *.

* * *

In considering claims of Presidential power this Court refers to Justice Jackson's familiar tripartite framework from *Youngstown Sheet & Tube Co.* v. *Sawyer*, 343 U. S. 579, 635–638 (1952) (concurring opinion). The framework divides exercises of Presidential power into three categories: First, when "the President acts pursuant to an express or implied authorization of Congress, his authority is at its maximum, for it includes all that he possesses in his own right plus all that Congress can delegate." *Id.*, at 635. Second, "in absence of either a congressional grant or denial of authority" there is a "zone of twilight in which he and Congress may have concurrent authority," and where "congressional inertia, indifference or quiescence may" invite the exercise of executive power. *Id.*, at 637. Finally, when "the President takes measures incompatible with the expressed or implied will of Congress . . . he can rely only upon his own constitutional powers minus any constitutional powers of Congress over the matter." *Ibid.* To succeed in this third category, the President's asserted power must be both "exclusive" and "conclusive" on the issue. *Id.*, at 637–638.

In this case the Secretary contends that § 214(d) infringes on the President's exclusive recognition power by "requiring the President to contradict his recognition position regarding Jerusalem in official communications with foreign sovereigns." Brief for Respondent 48. In so doing the Secretary acknowledges the President's power is "at its lowest ebb." *Youngstown*, 343 U. S., at 637. Because the President's refusal to implement § 214(d) falls into Justice Jackson's third category, his claim must be "scrutinized with caution," and he may rely solely on powers the Constitution grants to him alone. *Id.*, at 638.

To determine whether the President possesses the exclusive power of recognition the Court examines the Constitution's text and structure, as well as precedent and history bearing on the question.

Recognition is a "formal acknowledgement" that a particular "entity possesses the qualifications for statehood" or "that a particular regime is the effective government of a state." * * *

Legal consequences follow formal recognition. Recognized sovereigns may sue in United States courts, see *Guaranty Trust Co.* v. *United States*, 304 U. S. 126, 137 (1938), and may benefit from sovereign immunity when they are sued, see *National City Bank of N. Y.* v. *Republic of China*, 348 U. S. 356, 358–359 (1955). The actions of a recognized sovereign committed within its own territory also receive deference in domestic courts under the act of state doctrine. See *Oetjen* v. *Central Leather Co.*, 246 U. S. 297, 302–303 (1918). Recognition at international law, furthermore, is a precondition of regular diplomatic relations. 1 Moore § 27, at 72. Recognition is thus "useful, even necessary," to the existence of a state. *Ibid.*

Despite the importance of the recognition power in foreign relations, the Constitution does not use the term "recognition," either in Article II or elsewhere. The Secretary asserts that the President exercises the recognition power based on the Reception Clause, which directs that the President "shall receive Ambassadors and other public Ministers." Art. II, § 3. As Zivotofsky notes, the Reception Clause received little attention at the Constitutional Convention. See Reinstein, Recognition: A Case Study on the Original Understanding of Executive Power, 45 U. Rich. L. Rev. 801, 860–862 (2011). In fact, during the ratification debates, Alexander Hamilton claimed that the power to receive ambassadors was "more a matter of dignity than of authority," a ministerial duty largely "without consequence." The Federalist No. 69, p. 420 (C. Rossiter ed. 1961).

At the time of the founding, however, prominent international scholars suggested that receiving an ambassador was tantamount to recognizing the sovereignty of the sending state. See E. de Vattel, The Law of Nations § 78, p. 461 (1758) (J. Chitty ed. 1853) ("[E]very state, truly possessed of sovereignty, has a right to send ambassadors" and "to contest their right in this instance" is equivalent to "contesting their sovereign dignity"). It is a logical and proper inference, then, that a Clause directing the President alone to receive ambassadors would be understood to acknowledge his power to recognize other nations.

This in fact occurred early in the Nation's history when President Washington recognized the French Revolutionary Government by receiving its ambassador. See A. Hamilton, Pacificus No. 1, in The Letters of Pacificus and Helvidius 5, 13–14

(1845) (reprint 1976) (President "acknowledged the republic of France, by the reception of its minister"). After this incident the import of the Reception Clause became clear—causing Hamilton to change his earlier view. He wrote that the Reception Clause "includes th[e power] of judging, in the case of a revolution of government in a foreign country, whether the new rulers are competent organs of the national will, and ought to be recognised, or not." As a result, the Reception Clause provides support, although not the sole authority, for the President's power to recognize other nations.

The inference that the President exercises the recognition power is further supported by his additional Article II powers. It is for the President, "by and with the Advice and Consent of the Senate," to "make Treaties, provided two thirds of the Senators present concur." Art. II, § 2, cl. 2. In addition, "he shall nominate, and by and with the Advice and Consent of the Senate, shall appoint Ambassadors" as well as "other public Ministers and Consuls." *Ibid.*

As a matter of constitutional structure, these additional powers give the President control over recognition decisions. At international law, recognition may be effected by different means, but each means is dependent upon Presidential power. In addition to receiving an ambassador, recognition may occur on "the conclusion of a bilateral treaty," or the "formal initiation of diplomatic relations," including the dispatch of an ambassador * * *. The President, too, nominates the Nation's ambassadors and dispatches other diplomatic agents. Congress may not send an ambassador without his involvement * * *.

The text and structure of the Constitution grant the President the power to recognize foreign nations and governments. The question then becomes whether that power is exclusive. The various ways in which the President may unilaterally effect recognition—and the lack of any similar power vested in Congress—suggest that it is. So, too, do functional considerations. Put simply, the Nation must have a single policy regarding which governments are legitimate in the eyes of the United States and which are not * * *.

* * * Between the two political branches, only the Executive has the characteristic of unity at all times. And with unity comes the ability to exercise, to a greater degree, "[d]ecision, activity, secrecy, and dispatch." The Federalist No. 70, p. 424 (A. Hamilton). The President is capable, in ways Congress is not, of engaging in the delicate and often secret diplomatic contacts that may lead to a decision on recognition. See, *e.g., United States* v. *Pink*, 315 U. S. 203, 229 (1942). He is also better positioned to take the decisive, unequivocal action necessary to recognize other states at international law. These qualities explain why the Framers listed the traditional avenues of recognition—receiving ambassadors, making treaties, and sending ambassadors—as among the President's Article II powers.

* * *

In foreign affairs, as in the domestic realm, the Constitution "enjoins upon its branches separateness but interdependence, autonomy but reciprocity." *Youngstown,* 343 U.S., at 635 (Jackson, J., concurring). Although the President alone effects the formal act of recognition, Congress' powers, and its central role in making laws, give it substantial authority regarding many of the policy determinations that precede and follow the act of recognition itself. If Congress disagrees with the President's recognition policy, there may be consequences. Formal recognition may seem a hollow act if it is not accompanied by the dispatch of an ambassador, the easing of trade restrictions, and the conclusion of treaties. And those decisions require action by the Senate or the whole Congress.

In practice, then, the President's recognition determination is just one part of a political process that may require Congress to make laws. The President's exclusive recognition power encompasses the authority to acknowledge, in a formal sense, the legitimacy of other states and governments, including their territorial bounds. Albeit limited, the exclusive recognition power is essential to the conduct of Presidential duties. The formal act of recognition is an executive power that Congress may not qualify. If the President is to be effective in negotiations over a formal recognition determination, it must be evident to his counterparts abroad that he speaks for the Nation on that precise question.

* * *

No single precedent resolves the question whether the President has exclusive recognition authority and, if so, how far that power extends. In part that is because, until today, the political branches have resolved their disputes over questions of recognition * * *.

The Secretary * * * contends that under the Court's precedent the President has "exclusive authority to conduct diplomatic relations," along with "the bulk of foreign-affairs powers." Brief for Respondent 18, 16. In support of his submission that the President has broad, undefined powers over foreign affairs, the Secretary quotes *United States v. Curtiss-Wright Export Corp.*, which described the President as "the sole organ of the federal government in the field of international relations." 299 U.S., at 320. This Court declines to acknowledge that unbounded power. A formulation broader than the rule that the President alone determines what nations to formally recognize as legitimate—and that he consequently controls his statements on matters of recognition—presents different issues and is unnecessary to the resolution of this case.

The *Curtiss-Wright* case does not extend so far as the Secretary suggests. In *Curtiss-Wright,* the Court considered whether a congressional delegation of power to the President was constitutional * * *. Describing why such broad delegation may be appropriate, the opinion stated:

> "In this vast external realm, with its important, complicated, delicate and manifold problems, the President alone has the power to speak or listen as a representative of the nation. He *makes* treaties with the advice and consent of the Senate; but he alone negotiates. Into the field of negotiation the Senate cannot intrude; and Congress itself is powerless to invade it. As Marshall said in his great argument of March 7, 1800, in the House of Representatives, 'The President is the sole organ of the nation in its external relations, and its sole representative with foreign nations.' [10 Annals of Cong.] 613." *Id.,* at 319.

This description of the President's exclusive power was not necessary to the holding of *Curtiss-Wright*—which, after all, dealt with congressionally authorized action, not a unilateral Presidential determination. Indeed, *Curtiss-Wright* did not hold that the President is free from Congress' lawmaking power in the field of international relations. The President does have a unique role in communicating with foreign governments, as then-Congressman John Marshall acknowledged. See

10 Annals of Cong. 613 (1800) (cited in *Curtiss-Wright, supra,* at 319). But whether the realm is foreign or domestic, it is still the Legislative Branch, not the Executive Branch, that makes the law.

In a world that is ever more compressed and interdependent, it is essential the congressional role in foreign affairs be understood and respected. For it is Congress that makes laws, and in countless ways its laws will and should shape the Nation's course. The Executive is not free from the ordinary controls and checks of Congress merely because foreign affairs are at issue. It is not for the President alone to determine the whole content of the Nation's foreign policy.

That said, judicial precedent and historical practice teach that it is for the President alone to make the specific decision of what foreign power he will recognize as legitimate, both for the Nation as a whole and for the purpose of making his own position clear within the context of recognition in discussions and negotiations with foreign nations. Recognition is an act with immediate and powerful significance for international relations, so the President's position must be clear. Congress cannot require him to contradict his own statement regarding a determination of formal recognition.

* * *

As the power to recognize foreign states resides in the President alone, the question becomes whether § 214(d) infringes on the Executive's consistent decision to withhold recognition with respect to Jerusalem.

Section 214(d) requires that, in a passport or consular report of birth abroad, "the Secretary shall, upon the request of the citizen or the citizen's legal guardian, record the place of birth as Israel" for a "United States citizen born in the city of Jerusalem." 116 Stat. 1366. That is, § 214(d) requires the President, through the Secretary, to identify citizens born in Jerusalem who so request as being born in Israel. But according to the President, those citizens were not born in Israel. As a matter of United States policy, neither Israel nor any other country is acknowledged as having sovereignty over Jerusalem. In this way, § 214(d) "directly contradicts" the "carefully calibrated and longstanding Executive branch policy of neutrality toward Jerusalem." 725 F.3d, at 217, 216.

If the power over recognition is to mean anything, it must mean that the President not only makes the initial, formal recognition determination but also that he may maintain that determination in his and his agent's statements * * *.

* * *

It is true, as Zivotofsky notes, that Congress has substantial authority over passports. The Court does not question the power of Congress to enact passport legislation of wide scope * * *. This is consistent with the extensive lawmaking power the Constitution vests in Congress over the Nation's foreign affairs.

The problem with § 214(d), however, lies in how Congress exercised its authority over passports * * *. To allow Congress to control the President's communication in the context of a formal recognition determination is to allow Congress to exercise that exclusive power itself. As a result, the statute is unconstitutional.

* * *

The judgment of the Court of Appeals for the District of Columbia Circuit is *Affirmed.*

■ JUSTICE BREYER, concurring.

I continue to believe that this case presents a political question inappropriate for judicial resolution. See *Zivotofsky* v. *Clinton*, 566 U. S. ___, ___ (2012) (Breyer, J., dissenting). But because precedent precludes resolving this case on political question grounds, see *id.*, at ___ (majority opinion) (slip op., at 1), I join the Court's opinion.

■ JUSTICE THOMAS, concurring in the judgment in part and dissenting in part.

Our Constitution allocates the powers of the Federal Government over foreign affairs in two ways. First, it expressly identifies certain foreign affairs powers and vests them in particular branches, either individually or jointly. Second, it vests the residual foreign affairs powers of the Federal Government—*i.e.,* those not specifically enumerated in the Constitution—in the President by way of Article II's Vesting Clause.

Section 214(d) of the Foreign Relations Authorization Act, Fiscal Year 2003, ignores that constitutional allocation of power insofar as it directs the President, contrary to his wishes, to list "Israel" as the place of birth of Jerusalem-born citizens on their passports. The President has long regulated passports under his residual foreign affairs power, and this portion of § 214(d) does not fall within any of Congress' enumerated powers.

By contrast, § 214(d) poses no such problem insofar as it regulates consular reports of birth abroad. Unlike passports, these reports were developed to effectuate the naturalization laws, and they continue to serve the role of identifying persons who need not be naturalized to obtain U. S. citizenship. The regulation of these reports does not fall within the President's foreign affairs powers, but within Congress' enumerated powers under the Naturalization and Necessary and Proper Clauses.

* * *

The Constitution specifies a number of foreign affairs powers and divides them between the political branches * * *.

These specific allocations, however, cannot account for the entirety of the foreign affairs powers exercised by the Federal Government. Neither of the political branches is expressly authorized, for instance, to communicate with foreign ministers, to issue passports, or to repel sudden attacks. Yet the President has engaged in such conduct, with the support of Congress, since the earliest days of the Republic. Prakash & Ramsey, The Executive Power Over Foreign Affairs, 111 Yale L. J. 231, 298–346 (2001) (Prakash & Ramsey).

The President's longstanding practice of exercising unenumerated foreign affairs powers reflects a constitutional directive that "the President ha[s] primary responsibility—along with the necessary power—to protect the national security and to conduct the Nation's foreign relations." *Hamdi* v. *Rumsfeld*, 542 U. S. 507, 580 (2004) (THOMAS, J., dissenting). Specifically, the Vesting Clause of Article II provides that "[t]he executive Power shall be vested in a President of the United States." Art. II, § 1. This Clause is notably different from the Vesting Clause of Article I, which provides only that "[a]ll legislative Powers *herein granted* shall be vested in a Congress of the United States," Art. I, § 1 (emphasis added). By omitting the words "herein granted" in Article II, the Constitution indicates that the "executive Power" vested in the President is not confined to those powers expressly identified in the document. Instead, it includes all powers originally understood as falling within the "executive Power" of the Federal Government.

Founding-era evidence reveals that the "executive Power" included the foreign affairs powers of a sovereign State. See Prakash & Ramsey 253. John Locke's 17th-century writings laid the groundwork for this understanding of executive power. Locke described foreign affairs powers—including the powers of "war and peace, leagues and alliances, and all the transactions with all persons and communities without the commonwealth"—as "federative" power. Second Treatise of Civil Government § 146,p. 73 (J. Gough ed. 1947). He defined the "executive" power as "comprehending the execution of the municipal laws of the society within itself upon all that are parts of it." *Id.*, § 147, at 73. Importantly, however, Locke explained that the federative and executive powers must be lodged together, lest "disorder and ruin" erupt from the division of the "force of the public." *Id.*, § 148, at 73–74.

Subsequent thinkers began to refer to both of these powers as aspects of "executive power." William Blackstone, for example, described the executive power in England as including foreign affairs powers, such as the "power of sending embassadors to foreign states, and receiving embassadors at home"; making "treaties, leagues, and alliances with foreign states and princes"; "making war and peace"; and "issu[ing] letters of marque and reprisal." 1 Commentaries on the Laws of England 245, 249, 250, 242–252 (1765) (Blackstone). Baron de Montesquieu similarly described executive power as including the power to "mak[e] peace or war, sen[d] or receiv[e] embassies, establis[h] the public security, and provid[e] against invasions." The Spirit of the Laws bk. XI, ch. 6, p. 151 (O. Piest ed., T. Nugent transl. 1949). In fact, "most writers of [Montesquieu's] tim[e] w[ere] inclined to think of the executive branch of government as being concerned nearly entirely with foreign affairs." W. Gwyn, The Meaning of the Separation of Powers 103 (1965).

That understanding of executive power prevailed in America. Following independence, Congress assumed control over foreign affairs under the Articles of Confederation. See, *e.g.*, Articles of Confederation, Art. IX, cl. 1. At that time, many understood that control to be an exercise of executive power. See Prakash & Ramsey 272, 275–278. Letters among Members of the Continental Congress, for instance, repeatedly referred to the Department of Foreign Affairs, established under the control of the Continental Congress, as an "Executive departmen[t]" and to its officers as " 'Executives or Ministers.' " *Id.*, at 276, and nn. 194–196 * * *.

This view of executive power was widespread at the time of the framing of the Constitution * * *.

Given this pervasive view of executive power, it is unsurprising that those who ratified the Constitution understood the "executive Power" vested by Article II to include those foreign affairs powers not otherwise allocated in the Constitution * * *.

* * *

The statutory provision at issue implicates the President's residual foreign affairs power. Section 214(d) instructs the Secretary of State, upon request of a citizen born in Jerusalem (or that citizen's legal guardian), to list that citizen's place of birth as Israel on his passport and consular report of birth abroad, even though it is the undisputed position of the United States that Jerusalem is not a part of Israel. The President argues that this provision violates his foreign affairs powers generally and his recognition power specifically. Zivotofsky rejoins that Congress passed

§ 214(d) pursuant to its enumerated powers and its action must therefore take precedence.

Neither has it quite right. The President is not constitutionally compelled to implement § 214(d) as it applies to passports because passport regulation falls squarely within his residual foreign affairs power and Zivotofsky has identified no source of congressional power to require the President to list Israel as the place of birth for a citizen born in Jerusalem on that citizen's passport. Section 214(d) can, however, be constitutionally applied to consular reports of birth abroad because those documents do not fall within the President's foreign affairs authority but do fall within Congress' enumerated powers over naturalization.

In the Anglo-American legal tradition, passports have consistently been issued and controlled by the body exercising executive power—in England, by the King; in the colonies, by the Continental Congress; and in the United States, by President Washington and every President since.

* * *

Both safe conducts and passports were in use at the time of the founding. Passports were given "for greater security" "on ordinary occasions [to] persons who meet with no special interference in going and coming," whereas "safe-conduct[s]" were "given to persons who could not otherwise enter with safety the dominions of the sovereign granting it." 3 E. de Vattel, The Law of Nations § 265, p. 331 (1758 ed. C. Fenwick transl. 1916) (emphasis deleted). Both were issued by the person exercising the external sovereign power of a state. See *id.*, §§ 162, 275, at 69, 332. In the absence of a separate executive branch of government, the Continental Congress issued passports during the American Revolution, see, *e.g.*, Resolution (May 9, 1776), in 4 Journals of the Continental Congress 340–341; Resolution (May 24, 1776), in *id.*, at 385; as did the Congress under the Articles of Confederation, see, *e.g.*, 25 *id.*, at 859 (Jan. 24, 1783) (discussing its authority to issue passports under the war power).

After the ratification of the Constitution, President Washington immediately took responsibility for issuing passports * * *. The President has continued to designate and prescribe the rules for passports ever since.

That the President has the power to regulate passports under his residual foreign affairs powers does not, however, end the matter, for Congress has repeatedly legislated on the subject of passports * * *.

As with any congressional action, however, such legislation is constitutionally permissible only insofar as it is promulgated pursuant to one of Congress' enumerated powers. I must therefore address whether Congress had constitutional authority to enact § 214(d)'s regulation of passports.

[*Editors' Note: In a lengthy discussion, Justice Thomas considers and rejects various asserted sources of congressional power over passports and rejects all of them.*]

* * *

Although the consular report of birth abroad shares some features with a passport, it is historically associated with naturalization, not foreign affairs * * *.

The consular report of birth abroad is well suited to carrying into execution the power conferred on Congress in the Naturalization Clause. The report developed in response to Congress' requirement that children born abroad to U.S. citizens register with the consulate or lose their citizenship. And it continues to certify the acquisition of U.S. citizenship at birth by a person born abroad to a U.S. citizen. See 22 U.S.C. § 2705(2).

* * *

Because regulation of the consular report of birth abroad is justified as an exercise of Congress' powers under the Naturalization and Necessary and Proper Clauses and does not fall within the President's foreign affairs powers, § 214(d)'s treatment of that document is constitutional.

The majority * * * instead relies on a variation of the recognition power. That power is among the foreign affairs powers vested in the President by Article II's Vesting Clause, as is confirmed by Article II's express assignment to the President of the duty of receiving foreign Ambassadors, Art. II, § 3. But I cannot join the majority's analysis because no act of recognition is implicated here.

* * *

Assuming for the sake of argument that listing a non-recognized foreign sovereign as a citizen's place of birth on a U.S. passport could have the effect of recognizing that sovereign under international law, no such recognition would occur under the circumstances presented here. The United States has recognized Israel as a foreign sovereign since May 14, 1948. Statement by the President Announcing the Recognition of the State of Israel, Public Papers of the Presidents, Harry S. Truman, p. 258 (1964). That the United States has subsequently declined to acknowledge Israel's sovereignty over Jerusalem has not changed its recognition of Israel as a sovereign state. And even if the United States were to acknowledge Israel's sovereignty over Jerusalem, that action would not change its recognition of Israel as a sovereign state. That is because the United States has already afforded Israel the rights and responsibilities attendant to its status as a sovereign State. Taking a different position on the Jerusalem question will have no effect on that recognition.

* * *

Adhering to the Constitution's allocation of powers leads me to reach a different conclusion in this case from my colleagues: Section 214(d) can be constitutionally applied to consular reports of birth abroad, but not passports. I therefore respectfully concur in the judgment in part and dissent in part.

■ CHIEF JUSTICE ROBERTS, with whom JUSTICE ALITO joins, dissenting.

Today's decision is a first: Never before has this Court accepted a President's direct defiance of an Act of Congress in the field of foreign affairs. We have instead stressed that the President's power reaches "its lowest ebb" when he contravenes the express will of Congress, "for what is at stake is the equilibrium established by our constitutional system." *Youngstown Sheet & Tube Co.* v. *Sawyer*, 343 U. S. 579, 637–638 (1952) (Jackson, J., concurring).

JUSTICE SCALIA's principal dissent, which I join in full, refutes the majority's unprecedented holding in detail. I write separately to underscore the stark nature of the Court's error on a basic question of separation of powers.

The first principles in this area are firmly established. The Constitution allocates some foreign policy powers to the Executive, grants some to the Legislature, and enjoins the President to "take Care that the Laws be faithfully executed." Art. II, § 3. The Executive may disregard "the expressed or implied will of Congress" only if the Constitution grants him a power "at once so conclusive and preclusive" as to "disabl[e] the Congress from acting upon the subject." *Youngstown*, 343 U. S., at 637–638 (Jackson, J., concurring).

* * *

In this case, the President claims the exclusive and preclusive power to recognize foreign sovereigns. The Court devotes much of its analysis to accepting the Executive's contention. I have serious doubts about that position. The majority places great weight on the Reception Clause, which directs that the Executive "shall receive Ambassadors and other public Ministers." Art. II, § 3. But that provision, framed as an obligation rather than an authorization, appears alongside the *duties* imposed on the President by Article II, Section 3, not the *powers* granted to him by Article II, Section 2 * * *.

* * *

Ultimately, the only power that could support the President's position is the one the majority purports to reject: the "exclusive authority to conduct diplomatic relations." Brief for Respondent 18. The Government offers a single citation for this allegedly exclusive power: *United States v. Curtiss-Wright Export Corp.*, 299 U.S. 304, 319–320 (1936). But as the majority rightly acknowledges, *Curtiss-Wright* did not involve a claim that the Executive could contravene a statute; it held only that he could act pursuant to a legislative delegation.

The expansive language in *Curtiss-Wright* casting the President as the "sole organ" of the Nation in foreign affairs certainly has attraction for members of the Executive Branch. The Solicitor General invokes the case no fewer than ten times in his brief. Brief for Respondent 9, 10, 18, 19, 23, 24, 53, 54. But our precedents have never accepted such a sweeping understanding of executive power.

* * *

* * * It has not been necessary over the past 225 years to definitively resolve a dispute between Congress and the President over the recognition power. Perhaps we could have waited another 225 years. But instead the majority strains to reach the question based on the mere possibility that observers overseas might misperceive the significance of the birthplace designation at issue in this case. And in the process, the Court takes the perilous step—for the first time in our history—of allowing the President to defy an Act of Congress in the field of foreign affairs. I respectfully dissent.

■ JUSTICE SCALIA, with whom THE CHIEF JUSTICE and JUSTICE ALITO join, dissenting.

Before this country declared independence, the law of England entrusted the King with the exclusive care of his kingdom's foreign affairs. The royal prerogative included the "sole power of sending ambassadors to foreign states, and receiving them at home," the sole authority to "make treaties, leagues, and alliances with foreign states and princes," "the sole prerogative of making war and peace," and the "sole power of raising and regulating fleets and armies." 1 W. Blackstone, Commentaries *253, *257, *262. The People of the United States had other ideas when they organized our Government. They considered a sound structure of balanced powers essential to the preservation of just government, and international relations formed no exception to that principle.

The People therefore adopted a Constitution that divides responsibility for the Nation's foreign concerns between the legislative and executive departments * * *.

This case arises out of a dispute between the Executive and Legislative Branches about whether the United States should treat Jerusalem as a part of Israel. The Constitution contemplates that the political branches will make policy about the territorial claims of foreign nations the same way they make policy about other international matters: The President will exercise his powers on the basis of his views, Congress its powers on the basis of its views. That is just what has happened here.

* * *

The Court frames this case as a debate about recognition. Recognition is a sovereign's official acceptance of a status under international law * * *.

The Court holds that the Constitution makes the President alone responsible for recognition and that § 214(d) invades this exclusive power. I agree that the Constitution *empowers* the President to extend recognition on behalf of the United States, but I find it a much harder question whether it makes that power exclusive * * *. Neither text nor history nor precedent yields a clear answer to these questions. Fortunately, I have no need to confront these matters today—nor does the Court—because § 214(d) plainly does not concern recognition.

Recognition is more than an announcement of a policy. Like the ratification of an international agreement or the termination of a treaty, it is a formal legal act with effects under international law. It signifies acceptance of an international status, and it makes a commitment to continued acceptance of that status and respect for any attendant rights * * *.

To know all this is to realize at once that § 214(d) has nothing to do with recognition. Section 214(d) does not require the Secretary to make a formal declaration about Israel's sovereignty over Jerusalem * * *.

* * *

* * *[T]he law displays symbolic support for Israel's territorial claim. That symbolism may have tremendous significance as a matter of international diplomacy, but it makes no difference as a matter of constitutional law.

Even if the Constitution gives the President sole power to extend recognition, it does not give him sole power to make all decisions relating to foreign disputes over sovereignty. To the contrary, a fair reading of Article I allows Congress to decide for itself how its laws should handle these controversies. Read naturally, power to "regulate Commerce with foreign Nations," § 8, cl. 3, includes power to regulate imports from Gibraltar as British goods or as Spanish goods. Read naturally, power to "regulate the Value . . . of foreign Coin," § 8, cl. 5, includes power to honor (or not) currency issued by Taiwan * * *.

The Constitution likewise does not give the President exclusive power to determine which claims to statehood and territory "are legitimate in the eyes of the United States," *ante,* at 2086. Congress may express its own views about these matters by declaring war, restricting trade, denying foreign aid, and much else besides * * *.

* * *

In the final analysis, the Constitution may well deny Congress power to recognize—the power to make an international commitment accepting a foreign entity as a state, a regime as its government, a place as a part of its territory, and so on. But whatever else § 214(d) may do, it plainly does not make (or require the President to make) a commitment accepting Israel's sovereignty over Jerusalem.

* * *

In the end, the Court's decision does not rest on text or history or precedent. It instead comes down to "functional considerations"—principally the Court's perception that the Nation "must speak with one voice" about the status of Jerusalem. The vices of this mode of analysis go beyond mere lack of footing in the Constitution. Functionalism of the sort the Court practices today will *systematically* favor the unitary President over the plural Congress in disputes involving foreign affairs. It is possible that this approach will make for more effective foreign policy, perhaps as effective as that of a monarchy. It is certain that, in the long run, it will erode the structure of separated powers that the People established for the protection of their liberty.

JUSTICE THOMAS's concurrence deems § 214(d) constitutional to the extent it regulates birth reports, but unconstitutional to the extent it regulates passports. The concurrence finds no congressional power that would extend to the issuance or contents of passports. Including the power to regulate foreign commerce—even though passports facilitate the transportation of passengers, "a part of our commerce with foreign nations," *Henderson* v. *Mayor of New York,* 92 U. S. 259, 270 (1876). Including the power over naturalization—even though passports issued to citizens, like birth reports, "have the same force and effect as proof of United States citizenship as certificates of naturalization," 22 U. S. C. § 2705. Including the power to enforce the Fourteenth Amendment's guarantee that "[a]ll persons born or naturalized in the United States . . . are citizens of the United States"—even though a passport provides evidence of citizenship and so helps enforce this guarantee abroad. Including the power to exclude persons from the territory of the United States, see Art. I, § 9, cl. 1—even though passports are the principal means of identifying citizens entitled to entry. Including the powers under which Congress has restricted the ability of various people to leave the country (fugitives from justice, for example, see 18 U. S. C. § 1073)—even though passports are the principal means of controlling exit. Including the power to "make all needful Rules and Regulations respecting the Territory or other Property belonging to the United States," Art. IV, § 3, cl. 2—even though "[a] passport remains at all times the property of the United States," 7 FAM § 1317 (2013). The concurrence's stingy interpretation of the enumerated powers forgets that the Constitution does not "partake of the prolixity of a legal code," that "only its great outlines [are] marked, its important objects designated, and the minor ingredients which compose those objects [left to] be deduced from the nature of the objects themselves." *McCulloch*, 4 Wheat., at 407. It forgets, in other words, "that it is a *constitution* we are expounding." *Ibid.*

* * *

Whereas the Court's analysis threatens congressional power over foreign affairs with gradual erosion, the concurrence's approach shatters it in one stroke. The combination of (a) the concurrence's assertion of broad, unenumerated "residual powers" in the President; (b) its parsimonious interpretation of Congress's enumerated powers; and (c) its even more parsimonious interpretation of Congress's authority to enact laws "necessary and proper for carrying into Execution" the President's executive powers; produces (d) a presidency more reminiscent of George III than George Washington.

* * *

NOTES AND QUESTIONS

1. Does the majority opinion in this case adopt the Vesting Clause Thesis? Does it reject it?

2. Suppose that one agrees that the President has residual, unenumerated foreign policy powers. Precisely what presidential power does the Court think was at stake in this case? Precisely what power does the Court think that Congress was exercising? What was the precise *legal* effect, as a matter of foreign relations law, of section 214? Does the Court even ask those questions? How do you resolve a case like this without asking them?

3. Justices Thomas and Scalia definitely asked those questions, and they differ dramatically in their answers. Is that because they are employing different modalities of interpretation? We will revisit their dispute later, when we consider the scope of congressional powers under the Constitution.

4. To what extent does it matter what King George III would have been able to do in 1788?

5. Justice Thomas's views about the residual foreign affairs powers of the President relies heavily on scholarship defending that position. *See* Saikrishna B. Prakash & Michael D. Ramsey, *The Executive Power Over Foreign Affairs*, 111 YALE L. J. 231 (2001). For a response to that important and influential article, see Curtis A. Bradley & Martin S. Flaherty, *Executive Power Essentialism and Foreign Affairs,* 102 MICH. L. REV. 545 (2004).

6. *Zivotofsky* presented a circumstance where Congress was trying to constrain the actions of the President. *Curtiss-Wright* involved a circumstance in which Congress was trying to empower the President. The latter is much more common. Indeed, courts often avoid the kinds of legislative/executive conflicts represented by *Zivotofsky* by straining to find statutory authorization for presidential action that would be arguably, or even obviously, unconstitutional on its own. A classic illustration is *Dames & Moore v. Regan,* 453 U.S. 654 (1981). In 1979, the Iranian government seized and held hostage fifty-two diplomatic personnel in the American embassy in Tehran. The United States responded by freezing Iranian assets in the United States. On January 20, 1981, Iran released the hostages, and the United States and Iran agreed on procedures, including international arbitration, to settle claims against Iranian assets. Part of that agreement required the United States to terminate all domestic litigation against Iranian assets and transfer those cases to the arbitration tribunal. Executive orders by Presidents Carter and Reagan implemented the agreement by, among other things, declaring that pending suits in American courts against Iranian assets "shall have no legal effect in any action now pending in any court of the United States" but instead must be dealt with through arbitration. Dames & Moore had successfully prosecuted a breach-of-contract case in federal court against an Iranian instrumentality, obtaining a multi-million-dollar judgment. But after the executive orders, the court determined that it could not allow execution on the judgment or otherwise allow the case to proceed. Dames & Moore challenged the authority of the President to, in effect, order the dismissal of a federal lawsuit properly filed in the federal courts. The Supreme Court found statutory authority

for some portions of the executive orders, but it found no direct statutory authority for "the President's authority to suspend claims pending in American courts." *Id.* at 675. Nonetheless, the Court found *implicit* congressional authorization for the action, which obviated any need to plumb the edges of unilateral presidential power:

> Concluding that neither the IEEPA nor the Hostage Act constitutes specific authorization of the President's action suspending claims, however, is not to say that these statutory provisions are entirely irrelevant to the question of the validity of the President's action. We think both statutes highly relevant in the looser sense of indicating congressional acceptance of a broad scope for executive action in circumstances such as those presented in this case * * *.
>
> * * * W]e cannot ignore the general tenor of Congress' legislation in this area in trying to determine whether the President is acting alone or at least with the acceptance of Congress. * * * Congress cannot anticipate and legislate with regard to every possible action the President may find it necessary to take or every possible situation in which he might act. Such failure of Congress specifically to delegate authority does not, "especially . . . in the areas of foreign policy and national security," imply "congressional disapproval" of action taken by the Executive. On the contrary, the enactment of legislation closely related to the question of the President's authority in a particular case which evinces legislative intent to accord the President broad discretion may be considered to "invite" "measures on independent presidential responsibility," *Youngstown*, 343 U.S., at 637 (Jackson, J., concurring) * * *.
>
> * * *
>
> Crucial to our decision today is the conclusion that Congress has implicitly approved the practice of claim settlement by executive agreement * * *.
>
> * * *
>
> In light of all of the foregoing—the inferences to be drawn from the character of the legislation Congress has enacted in the area, such as the IEEPA and the Hostage Act, and from the history of acquiescence in executive claims settlement—we conclude that the President was authorized to suspend pending claims pursuant to Executive Order No. 12294. As Justice Frankfurter pointed out in *Youngstown*, 343 U.S., at 610–611, "a systematic, unbroken, executive practice, long pursued to the knowledge of the Congress and never before questioned . . . may be treated as a gloss on 'Executive Power' vested in the President by § 1 of Art. II." * * *

Id. at 677–79, 680, 686.

What legal authority gives the president the power to make binding international agreements that "settle" the property rights of U.S. citizens out from under them? See Michael Stokes Paulsen, *The Constitutional Power to Interpret International Law*, 118 YALE L.J. 1762, 1773–86 (2009). Did the Supreme Court really say that the President can halt federal court proceedings based on an inference that Congress, while not authorizing the action, has not expressly forbidden it?

7. After World War I, President Woodrow Wilson urged the creation of a global League of Nations, the predecessor to the United Nations. To Wilson's, and the United States', great embarrassment, the Republican Senate could not muster a two-thirds vote to ratify the treaty making the U.S. a member of the League of Nations. This destroyed, from the outset, the legitimacy of the League of Nations, and it contributed to the global climate that led to Adolf Hitler's coming to power in Germany in 1933. President Franklin

D. Roosevelt concluded that the Treaty Clause was a relic of the horse-and-buggy days, and so he started, as President, reaching executive agreements, with no approval from Congress or ratification by the Senate, which he argued had the force of law. The New Deal Supreme Court upheld the making of such agreements and their having the force of law. *See United States v. Belmont*, 301 U.S. 324 (1937); *United States v. Pink*, 315 U.S. 203 (1942). The Case-Zablocki Act of 1972 requires that the President inform the Senate within 60 days of the making of any executive agreements, but it does not bar the making of such agreements and appears in fact to acknowledge their legitimacy. Isn't it scary, and constitutionally dubious, for the President alone to have the power to enter into executive agreements which function like treaties and have the force of law? For a spirited (though we think unsuccessful) defense of the practice of executive agreements, see Bruce Ackerman & David Golove, *Is NAFTA Constitutional?,* 108 HARV. L. REV. 799 (1995). For an equally spirited (and we think much more successful) rebuttal, see Laurence H. Tribe, *Taking Text and Structure Seriously: Reflections on Free-Form Method in Constitutional Interpretation,* 108 HARV. L. REV. 1221 (1995).

8. How is President Carter's action (ratified by President Reagan) different in this regard from President Truman's actions in seizing the steel mills? In each case, the president took action on his own authority, without further participation by Congress, that had the effect of taking away the property of some U.S. citizens, in order to accomplish a stated foreign policy goal. Is *Dames & Moore* consistent with *Youngstown*? Is it because the relevant statutes in *Dames & Moore*, IEEPA and the Hostage Act, come close to authorizing the action the President? Is it because Congress has authorized similar actions in the past and has not refused to authorize them as in *Youngstown*? Is it because there is political support in Congress for the action? Are any of these good *legal* reasons as opposed to being merely good *policy* reasons?

[Assignment 24]

G. THE WAR POWER: EXECUTIVE, CONGRESSIONAL, OR MIXED?

How is the War Power allocated between Congress and the President and what role, if any, do judges have to play with respect to these questions? For answers, consider in order: 1) the text of the Constitution; 2) the historical aspirations and background of those who wrote it; and 3) our actual practice over the last 230 years. Never forget that the Philadelphia Constitutional Convention was chaired by the same man who had served as Commander-in-Chief during the Revolutionary War, and many of his top lieutenants, like Alexander Hamilton, were there as well. They all remembered the hardship of Valley Forge and the disastrous micro-managing of the Continental Congress. They knew their young nation needed a strong defense, that it should stay out of European Wars, that as a result it should be hard to start a war, but that once a war was started, the President needed to be given some leeway to successfully finish it.

1. TEXT

The Constitution gives both Congress and the President some role in foreign affairs, including specifically warmaking. Review at this point the list of clauses that bear on these questions. *See supra* page 468. And keep in mind that the Constitution specifically denies the States all but the most minor warmaking role. *See* U.S. CONST. art. I, § 10, cl. 3 ("No State shall, without the Consent of Congress, * * * keep Troops, or ships of War in time of Peace, * * * or engage in War, unless actually invaded, or in such imminent Danger as will not admit of delay"); *id* art. I, § 10, cl. 1 ("No State shall enter into any Treaty, Alliance, or Confederation").

2. ORIGINAL HISTORY AND BACKGROUND

The Framers' Constitution emerged in a world with a background understanding of "executive power" as including the power to start wars and the power to make peace. Thus, the Framers' favorite political philosopher, John Locke, thought that there were three inherent powers of government: (1) the federative power to wage war, make treaties, and conduct foreign policy; (2) the executive power to prosecute, and try in court, violations of the laws; and (3) the legislative power to make laws, impose taxes, and spend money. Locke assumed that the King, with his Power of the Sword, would exercise the federative and the executive powers; while the Parliament, with its Power of the Purse, would exercise the legislative power. JOHN LOCKE, SECOND TREATISE ON GOVERNMENT (1689).

Another of the Framers' favorite political philosophers, Montesquieu, writing in 1748 in *The Spirit of the Laws*, also thought the chief executive officer should have the power to start wars. Montesquieu envisioned three branches of government: 1) a legislative branch, which would make laws, impose taxes, and spend money; 2) an executive branch, which would make war or peace and prosecute crimes and execute the laws at home; and, 3) finally, a judicial branch, which would hear and decide impartial private lawsuits or cases brought by the government. Again, the expectation was that the chief executive officer would have the power to start wars.

The Framers of the Constitution in Philadelphia, meeting in 1787, parted ways with Locke, Montesquieu, and the British unwritten constitution by vesting the power to declare war firmly in Congress's hands. See generally Saikrishna B. Prakash & Michael D. Ramsey, *The Executive Power Over Foreign Affairs*, 111 YALE L.J. 231 (2001); Saikrishna Prakash, *Unleashing the Dogs of War: What the Constitution Means by "Declare War,"* 93 CORNELL L. REV. 45 (2007). It is one of the great disappointments of the last 230 years that this deliberate vesting of the war-making power in Congress has not worked. The U.S. has only declared war five times, but it has been engaged in more than 200 military deployments, many of which have universally been called wars, such as the Korean War, the Vietnam War, the First Gulf War, the War on Terror, and the Iraq War. Some of these "wars" have been authorized to some degree and some have not. In any event, Congress has paid for all of them. How did we so thoroughly disregard the constitutional text and purpose? This assignment will try to show how.

Consider, first, a portion of the debate at the Constitutional Convention at Philadelphia for some possible illumination. James Madison's notes of the debates at the Philadelphia Convention focused on a proposal to change the language from a grant of power to Congress to "*make* War" to a power to "*declare* War." Here is the most pertinent part of that brief and cryptic discussion:

> Mr. Madison and Mr. Gerry moved to insert "*declare*," striking out "*make*" war; leaving to the Executive the power to repel sudden attacks.
>
> Mr. Sharman thought it stood very well. The executive shd be able to repel and not to commence war. "Make" better than "declare" the latter narrowing the power too much.

> Mr. Gerry never expected to hear in a republic a motion to empower the Executive alone to declare war.
>
> Mr. Elseworth. there is a material difference between the cases of making *war* and making *peace*. It shd be more easy to get out of war, than into it. War also is a simple and overt declaration. peace attended with intricate & secret negociations.
>
> Mr. Mason was agst giving the power of war to the Executive, because not safely to be trusted with it; or to the Senate, because not so constructed as to be entitled to it. He was for clogging rather than facilitating war; but for facilitating peace. He preferred "*declare*" to "*make*."
>
> On the motion to insert *declare*—in place of *make*, it was agreed to.

JAMES MADISON, NOTES OF DEBATES IN THE FEDERAL CONVENTION OF 1787, at 475–76.

Debates in the state ratifying conventions, and early practice, seem to suggest that most people of the day understood the Declare War Clause to have vested in Congress, and not the President, the power to decide to take the nation into a condition of war. See Michael D. Ramsey, *Textualism and War Powers*, 69 U. CHI. L. REV. 1543 (2002); Charles A. Lofgren, *War-Making Under the Constitution: The Original Understanding*, 81 YALE L.J. 672 (1972). Others see the historical evidence differently, reading the text and history as preserving the executive power to wage war as an aspect of the President's foreign affairs power, with the Declare War Clause serving a lesser (but still crucial) role of providing formal recognition to such a state of affairs and triggering certain national and international legal relationships that come with a formal state of war. Under this view, it is Congress's power over appropriations that serves as a check on presidential war-making, not the Declare War Clause. See John C. Yoo, *The Continuation of Politics by Other Means: The Original Understanding of War Powers*, 84 CAL. L. REV. 167 (1996); John C. Yoo & Robert J. Delahunty, *The President's Constitutional Authority to Conduct Military Operations Against Terrorist Organizations and the Nations that Harbor or Support Them*, 25 HARV. J. L. & PUB. POL'Y 488 (2002).

Even on the view that sees Congress's power to declare war as mandating congressional authorization for the initiation of military hostilities, there remain the questions of whether the President may engage in use of military force *defensively*—to "repel sudden attacks" in the words of the Philadelphia Convention debate—and how far such a defensive power can be pushed (especially in a world where the technology permitting "sudden" attacks creates greater risks of imminent danger than in the eighteenth century). Also, there is the question of what kind of presidential uses of military power actually constitute "war" in the constitutional sense of the word. Traditionally, and increasingly so beginning in the early twentieth century, use of military force to rescue or protect Americans abroad was understood to be an executive power. Warfare is now expanding into cyber space, outer space, and to reliance on terrorism as a form of intimidation.

Are limited "rescue" operations or humanitarian or peacekeeping deployments of troops, or limited armed interventions to affect an arrest, governed by the Declare War Clause? Or are they part of the executive power? Remember that a great many major armed conflicts involving the United States were not authorized by a declaration of war. Indeed, there have been only five formal *declarations* of war in our nation's history: The War of 1812, the Mexican-American War, the Spanish-American War, World War I, and World War II. (Six, if one counts the American Declaration of Independence, part of the purpose of which was to attempt to clothe American forces with the status of legitimate armed belligerents entitled to the protections of the law of war.) Must Congress "declare" "war"—use those magic words—in order to exercise its war-initiating power under the Declare War Clause? The clause has never been thought to require the use of particular words. For a powerful dissenting view, see J. Gregory Sidak, *To Declare War*, 41 Duke L.J. 27 (1991). What is the value of "precedent"—in the sense of actual practice, not just judicial decisions—in resolving questions like these? The courts have rarely been involved in these disputes. Does practice "liquidate" the meaning of the Constitution, as Madison said in *The Federalist* No. 37? Or, if practice is inconsistent with the Constitution, must we conclude that a great deal of our Nation's practice with respect to war powers has been *unconstitutional*?

Intriguingly, some of the most important cases involving the war powers came in a context wildly different from anything contemplated by those powers: The Civil War.

3. PRACTICE AND "PRECEDENT"

President Lincoln was very careful *not* to fire the first shot in the Civil War. The citizens of South Carolina did that when they fired on the federal Fort Sumter in Charleston harbor, South Carolina on April 12, 1861. President Lincoln then took a series of emergency actions to preserve the Union, during which time he could not safely convene Congress in Washington, D.C., because Maryland, which was a slave State, was in a state of open rebellion since many of its citizens wanted Maryland to secede. President Lincoln could not safely call Congress into special session in Washington, D.C. until Maryland was secured, as the city would have been behind enemy lines.

Among the emergency actions President Lincoln took in the spring of 1861 were: 1) the blockading of all the Southern ports to shut down the South's economy and to prevent it from importing munitions; 2) unilaterally suspending the writ of habeas corpus in Maryland, so that he could prevent that State from seceding; 3) federalizing the state national guard units and calling them into active duty; and 4) finally, giving directions that 600,000 mercenary soldiers be hired. Once Maryland was secure, President Lincoln symbolically called Congress into special session on July 4, 1861 to ask it retroactively to approve of everything he had done.

The Supreme Court addressed the legality of President Lincoln's actions in the following case.

a. The Brig Amy Warwick (The Prize Cases)

67 U.S. (2 Black) 635 (1863)

These were cases in which the vessels named, together with their cargoes, were severally captured and brought in as prizes by public ships of the United States. The libels were filed by the proper District Attorneys, on behalf of the United States and on behalf of the officers and crews of the ships, by which the captures were respectively made. In each case the District Court pronounced a decree of condemnation, from which the claimants took an appeal.

The *Amy Warwick* was a merchant vessel, and belonged to Richmond * * *. Previous to her capture she had made a voyage from New York to Richmond, and thence to Rio de Janeiro, Brazil. At the last named port she shipped a cargo of coffee, 5,100 bags, to be delivered at New York, Philadelphia, Baltimore or Richmond, according to the orders which the master would receive at Hampton Roads. She was on her voyage from Rio to Hampton Roads and off Cape Henry when she was captured (July 10th, 1861) by the Quaker City. At the time of the capture the barque was sailing under American colors, and her commander was ignorant of the war. The Quaker City carried her into Boston, where she was libelled as enemy's property. The claimants [owners] of the vessel * * * denied any hostility on their part to the Government or Laws of the United States, averred that the master was ignorant of any blockade, embargo or other interdiction of commerce with the ports of Virginia, and asserted generally that the capture was unlawful.

The *Crenshaw* was captured by the United States Steamer *Star*, at the mouth of James River, on the 17th of May, 1861. She was bound for Liverpool with a cargo of tobacco from Richmond, and was owned by David and William Currie, who admitted the existence of an insurrection in Virginia against the Laws and Government of the United States, but averred that they were innocent of it * * *. She was condemned as prize on the ground that she had broken, or was attempting to break, the blockade at the time of her capture.

The *Hiawatha* was a British barque, and was on her voyage from Richmond to Liverpool with a cargo of tobacco. She left Richmond on the 17th of May, 1861, and was captured in Hampton Roads on the 20th by the Minnesota, and taken to New York. Her owners * * * denied her liability to capture and condemnation on the ground that no sufficient notice had been given of the blockade * * *.

The *Brilliante* was a Mexican schooner * * *. At New Orleans she took in her cargo of flour, part to be delivered at Sisal and part at Campeche, and took a clearance for both those places. On her homeward voyage she anchored in Biloxi Bay, intending to communicate with some vessel of the blockading fleet and get a permit to go to sea, and while so at anchor she was taken by two boats sent off from the Massachusetts. She was carried into Key West, where the legal proceedings against her were prosecuted in the District Court of the United States for the District of Florida.

■ MR. JUSTICE GRIER.

* * *

* * * Had the President a right to institute a blockade of ports in possession of persons in armed rebellion against the Government, on the principles of international law, as known and acknowledged among civilized States?

* * *

That a blockade *de facto* actually existed, and was formally declared and notified by the President on the 27th and 30th of April, 1861, is an admitted fact in these cases.

That the President, as the Executive Chief of the Government and Commander-in-chief of the Army and Navy, was the proper person to make such notification, has not been, and cannot be disputed.

The right of prize and capture has its origin in the "*jus belli*," and is governed and adjudged under the law of nations. To legitimate the capture of a neutral vessel or property on the high seas, a war must exist *de facto*, and the neutral must have a knowledge or notice of the intention of one of the parties belligerent to use this mode of coercion against a port, city, or territory, in possession of the other.

Let us enquire whether, at the time this blockade was instituted, a state of war existed which would justify a resort to these means of subduing the hostile force.

War has been well defined to be, "That state in which a nation prosecutes its right by force."

The parties belligerent in a public war are independent nations. But it is not necessary to constitute war, that both parties should be acknowledged as independent nations or sovereign States. A war may exist where one of the belligerents, claims sovereign rights as against the other.

Insurrection against a government may or may not culminate in an organized rebellion, but a civil war always begins by insurrection against the lawful authority of the Government. A civil war is never solemnly declared; it becomes such by its accidents—the number, power, and organization of the persons who originate and carry it on. When the party in rebellion occupy and hold in a hostile manner a certain portion of territory; have declared their independence; have cast off their allegiance; have organized armies; have commenced hostilities against their former sovereign, the world acknowledges them as belligerents, and the contest a *war*. *They* claim to be in arms to establish their liberty and independence, in order to become a sovereign State, while the sovereign party treats them as insurgents and rebels who owe allegiance, and who should be punished with death for their treason.

* * *

As a civil war is never publicly proclaimed, *eo nomine* against insurgents, its actual existence is a fact in our domestic history which the Court is bound to notice and to know.

* * *

By the Constitution, Congress alone has the power to declare a national or foreign war. It cannot declare was against a State, or any number of States, by virtue of any clause in the Constitution. The Constitution confers on the President the whole Executive power * * *. He has no power to initiate or declare a war either against a foreign nation or a domestic State. But * * * he is authorized to called out the militia and use the military and naval forces of the United States in case of invasion by foreign nations, and to suppress insurrection against the government of a State or of the United States.

If a war be made by invasion of a foreign nation, the President is not only authorized but bound to resist force by force. He does not initiate the war, but is bound to accept the challenge without waiting for any special legislative authority. And whether the hostile party be a foreign invader, or States organized in rebellion, it is none the less a war, although the declaration of it be "*unilateral*." * * *

* * *

This greatest of civil wars was not gradually developed by popular commotion, tumultuous assemblies, or local unorganized insurrections. However long may have been its previous conception, it nevertheless sprung forth suddenly from the parent brain, a Minerva in the full panoply of *war*. The President was bound to meet it in the shape it presented itself, without waiting for Congress to baptize it with a name; and no name given to it by him or them could change the fact.

It is not the less a civil war, with belligerent parties in hostile array, because it may be called an "insurrection" by one side, and the insurgents be considered as rebels or traitors. It is not necessary that the independence of the revolted province or State be acknowledged in order to constitute it a party belligerent in a war according to the law of nations. Foreign nations acknowledge it as war by a declaration of neutrality * * *.

* * *

The law of nations is also called the law of nature; it is founded on the common consent as well as the common sense of the world. It contains no such anomalous doctrine as that which this Court are now for the first time desired to pronounce, to wit: That insurgents who have risen in rebellion against their sovereign, expelled her Courts, established a revolutionary government, organized armies, and commenced hostilities, are not *enemies* because they are *traitors*; and a war levied on the Government by traitors, in order to dismember and destroy it, is not a *war* because it is an "insurrection."

Whether the President in fulfilling his duties, as Commander in-chief, in suppressing an insurrection, has met with such armed hostile resistance, and a civil war of such alarming proportions as will compel him to accord to them the character of belligerents, is a question to be decided *by him*, and this Court must be governed by the decisions and acts of the political department of the Government to which this power was entrusted * * *. The proclamation of blockade is itself official and conclusive evidence to the Court that a state of war existed which demanded and authorized a recourse to such a measure, under the circumstances peculiar to the case.

* * *

If it were necessary to the technical existence of a war, that it should have a legislative sanction, we find it in almost every act passed at the extraordinary session of the Legislature of 1861, which was wholly employed in enacting laws to enable the Government to prosecute the war with vigor and efficiency. And finally, in 1861, we find Congress * * * passing an act "approving, legalizing, and making valid all the acts, proclamations, and orders of the President, &c., as if they had *been issued and done under the previous express authority* and direction of the Congress of the United States."

* * *

* * * [W]e are of the opinion that the President had a right, *jure belli*, to institute a blockade of ports in possession of the States in rebellion, which neutrals are bound to regard.

* * *

[*Editors' Note: The Court then determined that once a state of war existed and the blockade was valid, the United States did not need to show that each individual ship or cargo owner was disloyal. The blockade would be valid, as a matter of the laws of war, even against "innocent" shipowners. The Court affirmed all of the seizures except for one small bit of cargo bought before the war by New York citizens.*]

■ MR. JUSTICE NELSON, dissenting.

* * *

In the case of a rebellion or resistance of a portion of the people of a country against the established government, there is no doubt, if in its progress and enlargement the government thus sought to be overthrown sees fit, it may by the competent power recognize, or declare the existence of a state of civil war, which will draw after it all the consequences and rights of war between the contending parties as in the case of a public war * * *. But before this insurrection against the established Government can be dealt with on the footing of a civil war, within the meaning of the law of nations and the Constitution of the United States, and which will draw after it belligerent rights, it must be recognized or declared by the war-making power of the Government. No power short of this can change the legal status of the Government or the relations of its citizens from that of peace to a state of war, or bring into existence all those duties and obligations to neutral third parties growing out of a state of war. The war power of the Government must be exercised before this changed condition of the Government and people and of neutral third parties can be admitted. There is no difference in this respect between a civil or a public war.

* * *

An idea seemed to be entertained that all that was necessary to constitute a war was organized hostility in the district of country in a state of rebellion—that conflicts on land and on sea—the taking of towns and capture of fleets—in fine, the magnitude and dimensions of the resistance against the Government—constituted war with all the belligerent rights belonging to civil war. With a view to enforce this idea, we had, during the argument, an imposing historical detail of the several measures adopted by the Confederate States to enable them to resist the authority of the general Government, and of many bold and daring acts of resistance and of conflict. It was said that war was to be ascertained by looking at the armies and navies or public force of the contending parties, and the battles lost and won * * *.

Now, in one sense, no doubt this is war, and may be a war of the most extensive and threatening dimensions and effects, but it is a statement simply of its existence in a material sense, and has no relevancy or weight when the question is what constitutes war in a legal sense, in the sense of the law of nations, and of the Constitution of the United States? For it must be a war in this sense to attach to it all the consequences that belong to belligerent rights. Instead, therefore, of inquiring after armies and navies, and victories lost and won, or organized rebellion against the general Government, the inquiry should be into the law of nations and into the municipal fundamental laws of the Government. For we find there that to constitute a civil war in the sense in which we are speaking, before it can exist, in contemplation of law, it must be recognized or declared by the sovereign power of the State, and which sovereign power by our Constitution is lodged in the Congress of the United States—civil war, therefore, under our system of government, can exist only by an act of Congress, which requires the assent of two of the great departments of the Government, the Executive and Legislative.

* * * But we are asked, what would become of the peace and integrity of the Union in case of an insurrection at home or invasion from abroad if this power could

not be exercised by the President in the recess of Congress, and until that body could be assembled?

The framers of the Constitution fully comprehended this question, and provided for the contingency. Indeed, it would have been surprising if they had not, as a rebellion had occurred in the State of Massachusetts while the Convention was in session, and which had become so general that it was quelled only by calling upon the military power of the State. The Constitution declares that Congress shall have power "to provide for calling forth the militia to execute the laws of the Union, suppress insurrections, and repel invasions." Another clause, "that the President shall be Commander-in-chief of the Army and Navy of the United States, and of the militia of the several States when called into the actual service of United States;" and, again, "He shall take care that the laws shall be faithfully executed." Congress passed laws on this subject in 1792 and 1795. 1 United States Laws, pp. 264, 424.

The last Act provided that whenever the United States shall be invaded or be in imminent danger of invasion from a foreign nation, it shall be lawful for the President to call forth such number of the militia most convenient to the place of danger, and in case of insurrection in any State against the Government thereof, it shall be lawful for the President, on the application of the Legislature of such State, if in session, or if not, of the Executive of the State, to call forth such number of militia of any other State or States as he may judge sufficient to suppress such insurrection.

The 2d section provides, that when the laws of the United States shall be opposed, or the execution obstructed in any State by combinations too powerful to be suppressed by the course of judicial proceedings, it shall be lawful for the President to call forth the militia of such State, or of any other State or States as may be necessary to suppress such combinations; and by the Act 3 March, 1807, (2 U. S. Laws, 443,) it is provided that in case of insurrection or obstruction of the laws, either in the United States or of any State of Territory, where it is lawful for the President to call forth the militia for the purpose of suppressing such insurrection, and causing the laws to be executed, it shall be lawful to employ for the same purpose such part of the land and naval forces of the United States as shall be judged necessary.

It will be seen, therefore, that ample provision has been made under the Constitution and laws against any sudden and unexpected disturbance of the public peace from insurrection at home or invasion from abroad * * *. It is the exercise of a power under the municipal laws of the country and not under the law of nations; and, as we see, furnishes the most ample means of repelling attacks from abroad or suppressing disturbances at home until the assembling of Congress, who can, if it be deemed necessary, bring into operation the war power, and thus change the nature and character of the contest. Then, instead of being carried on under the municipal law of 1795, it would be under the law of nations, and the Acts of Congress as war measures with all the rights of war.

* * *

Congress assembled on the call for an extra session the 4th of July, 1861, and among the first acts passed was one in which the President was authorized by proclamation to interdict all trade and intercourse between all the inhabitants of States in insurrection and the rest of the United States * * *.

* * *

This Act of Congress, we think, recognized a state of civil war between the Government and the Confederate States, and made it territorial. * * *

* * *

Upon the whole, after the most careful consideration of this case which the pressure of other duties has admitted, I am compelled to the conclusion that no civil war existed between this Government and the States in insurrection till recognized by the Act of Congress 13th of July, 1861; that the President does not possess the power under the Constitution to declare war or recognize its existence within the meaning of the law of nations, which carries with it belligerent rights, and thus change the country and all its citizens from a state of peace to a state of war; that this power belongs exclusively to the Congress of the United States, and, consequently, that the President had no power to set on foot a blockade under the law of nations, and that the capture of the vessel and cargo in this case, and in all cases before us in which the capture occurred before the 13th of July, 1861, for breach of blockade, or as enemies' property, are illegal and void, and that the decrees of condemnation should be reversed and the vessel and cargo restored.

■ MR. CHIEF JUSTICE TANEY, MR. JUSTICE CATRON and MR. JUSTICE CLIFFORD, concurred in the dissenting opinion of MR. JUSTICE NELSON.

NOTES AND QUESTIONS

1. Lincoln always called the struggle the War of the Rebellion and the Southerners Rebels. Southerners called the struggle the War Between the States or the War of Northern Aggression. The name "the Civil War" emerged long after the struggle was over, as Americans tried to put their country back together again. Are you persuaded that the Civil War was in fact a rebellion, and so there was no need to have Congress declare war because we were suppressing a domestic insurrection and not waging war against a sovereign State?

2. Does this case open the door to presidents claiming that other uses of force are not really "war" and thus do not require a congressional declaration? Or can its reasoning be confined to the facts of the Civil War?

3. Does it surprise you that the decision in this case was 5–4, meaning that four justices thought that President Lincoln's actions before July 13, 1861 were unlawful?

4. President Lincoln maintained that the South's attempt at secession was unlawful and that the rebel States remained part of the Union. If he had sought a formal declaration of war, would that have undercut his case against secession? Note that Congress did not declare war; it simply purported to ratify the President's actions.

4. FORMS OF CONGRESSIONAL "AUTHORIZATION" FOR WAR

Can Congress authorize military action by the President without declaring war? As we have repeatedly said, there have only been five declarations of war in American history. Those declarations tend to be very sparse. Here are the last two:

> **Declaration of War in World War I**
>
> WHEREAS, The Imperial German Government has committed repeated acts of war against the people of the United States of America; therefore, be it resolved by the Senate and House of Representatives of the United States of America in Congress assembled, That the state of war

between the United States and the Imperial German Government, which has thus been thrust upon the United States, is hereby formally declared; and that the President be, and he is hereby, authorized and directed to employ the entire naval and military forces of the United States and the resources of the Government to carry on war against the Imperial German Government; and to bring the conflict to a successful termination all the resources of the country are hereby pledged by the Congress of the United States.

Approved April 3, 1917

Declaration of War Against Japan in World War II

Joint Resolution. Declaring that a state of war exists between the Imperial Government of Japan and the Government and the people of the United States and making provisions to prosecute the same.

Whereas the Imperial Government of Japan has committed unprovoked acts of war against the Government and the people of the United States of America: Therefore be it Resolved by the Senate and House of Representatives of the United States of America in Congress assembled,

That the state of war between the United States and the Imperial Government of Japan which has thus been thrust upon the United States is hereby formally declared; and the President is hereby authorized and directed to employ the entire naval and military forces of the United States and the resources of the Government to carry on war against the Imperial Government of Japan; and, to bring the conflict to a successful termination, all of the resources of the country are hereby pledged by the Congress of the United States.

Approved December 8, 1941

Obviously, there have been a lot of military engagements since World War II. None, with the possible exception of the so-called "War on Terror," involved a direct attack on United States territory. What, if anything, legally justified those actions? The Vietnam War was congressionally "authorized" (after many years of United States involvement) in 1964 by the Gulf of Tonkin Resolution:

Gulf of Tonkin Resolution (August 7, 1964)

Resolved by the Senate and House of Representatives of the United States of America in Congress assembled,

[Section 1.] That the Congress approves and supports the determination of the President, as Commander in Chief, to take all necessary measures to repel any armed attack against the forces of the United States and to prevent further aggression.

Section 2. The United States regards as vital to its national interest and to world peace the maintenance of international peace and security in southeast Asia. Consonant with the Constitution of the United States and the Charter of the United Nations and in accordance with its obligations under the Southeast Asia Collective Defense Treaty, the United States is, therefore, prepared, as the President determines, to take all necessary steps, including the use of armed force, to assist any member or protocol state of the Southeast Asia Collective Defense Treaty requesting assistance in defense of its freedom.

Section 3. This resolution shall expire when the President shall determine that the peace and security of the area is reasonably assured by international conditions created by action of the United Nations or otherwise, except that it may be terminated earlier by concurrent resolution of the Congress.

Pub. L. No. 88–408, 78 Stat. 384 (1964). Do you think this is the legal equivalent of a declaration of war? If it isn't, what would legally justify the use of United States military force in Vietnam? Numerous lawsuits were filed challenging the legality of the Vietnam War, but the Supreme Court never ruled on the merits of the claims. Congress eventually turned against the Vietnam War, repealing the Gulf of Tonkin Resolution in 1971 and defunding the war. President Nixon had no choice but to begin withdrawing United States troops, and President Ford finished the withdrawal in 1975. Once the Gulf of Tonkin Resolution was repealed, what authorized the continued United States military involvement in Vietnam for the next four years? Did the Gulf of Tonkin Resolution ever do any legal work at all?

Virtually all United States military activity over the past two decades has occurred in the Middle East and Africa following the events of September 11, 2001. And virtually all of those activities have been justified by an Authorization for the Use of Military Force enacted by Congress a week after the 9/11 attacks. Consider what this document does and does not purport to authorize:

Authorization for the Use of Military Force (AUMF) (September 18, 2001)

Joint Resolution: To authorize the use of United States Armed Forces against those responsible for the recent attacks launched against the United States

Whereas, on September 11, 2001, acts of treacherous violence were committed against the United States and its citizens; and

Whereas, such acts render it both necessary and appropriate that the United States exercise its rights to self-defense and to protect United States citizens both at home and abroad; and

Whereas, in light of the threat to the national security and foreign policy of the United States posed by these grave acts of violence; and

Whereas, such acts continue to pose an unusual and extraordinary threat to the national security and foreign policy of the United States; and

Whereas, the President has authority under the Constitution to take action to deter and prevent acts of international terrorism against the United States:

Now, therefore, be it

Resolved by the Senate and House of Representatives of the United States of America in Congress assembled,

SECTION 1. SHORT TITLE.

* * * "Authorization for Use of Military Force."

SECTION 2. AUTHORIZATION FOR USE OF UNITED STATES ARMED FORCES.

(a) IN GENERAL—That the President is authorized to use all necessary and appropriate force against those nations, organizations, or persons he determines planned, authorized, committed or aided the terrorist attacks that occurred on September 11, 2001, or harbored such organizations or persons, in order to prevent any future acts of international terrorism against the United States by such nations, organizations, or persons.

(b) War Powers Resolution Requirements—

(1) SPECIFIC STATUTORY AUTHORIZATION.—Consistent with section 8(a)(1) of the War Powers Resolution, the Congress declares that this section is intended to constitute specific statutory authorization within the meaning of section 5(b) of the War Powers Resolution.

(2) APPLICABILITY OF OTHER REQUIREMENTS.—Nothing in this resolution supercedes any requirement of the War Powers Resolution.

Pub. L. No. 107–40, 115 Stat. 224 (2001). If Congress had wanted formally to declare war after 9/11, against whom would it have declared war? If the President wanted to respond unilaterally, without congressional authorization, could he have done so? Against whom or what?

These authorizing instruments do not come close to covering all United States military engagements in the last century. For example, in two instances—the Korean War and the 2011 overthrow by U.S. military force of the government of Libya—Congress did nothing at all to authorize the wars in question, although it did from year to year pay for them. The use of force in both of these cases was called for by the Security Council of the United Nations, of which the U.S. is a member. Presidents Truman and Obama claimed they were executing the treaty by which the U.S. entered the United Nations by following the call to arms of the U.N. Security Council. Do you buy this argument for war-making?

While these questions are all theoretically interesting and important (and difficult!), as a practical matter the various institutions of the federal government appear to have reached something of an accommodation. Apart from the Vietnam War, Congress has never failed to fund a presidentially driven military activity. Congress has not declared war since World War II. Presidents have universally asserted authority or project United States military power anywhere in the world, without tying the assertion to direct threats on the United States. Courts have stayed out of the way on this basic question of warmaking authority (though, as we will shortly see, they have involved themselves heavily in matters concerning the conduct of hostilities). If modern practice can liquidate constitutional meaning, the allocation of warmaking powers looks to be very one-sided in favor of the President.

A potentially important part of the allocational structure, however, is the War Powers Resolution ("WPR"), enacted by Congress in 1973 after it had repealed the Gulf of Tonkin Resolution. The WPR came at a time when the Vietnam War had become very unpopular and President Nixon had become politically weakened by the "Watergate" scandal. The WPR purports to set forth Congress's constitutional views concerning the respective war powers of Congress and the President, along with a framework for enforcing those views. As you read the materials on the WPR, ask yourself whether the WPR is constitutionally valid (in whole or in part) and whether, even if it is, it can be given meaningful enforcement by Congress, or perhaps by the courts. Every President from Nixon to George W. Bush took the position that the WPR is an unconstitutional attempt by Congress to limit the president's constitutional authority as Commander-in-Chief. At the same time, presidents generally report military actions to Congress in a manner consistent with the WPR's requirements, seeking to avoid (in the main) direct confrontations with Congress over the WPR.

The War Powers Resolution of 1973

Resolved by the Senate and House of Representatives of the United States of America in Congress assembled,

Section 1. This joint resolution may be cited as the "War Powers Resolution."

Section 2.

(a) It is the purpose of this joint resolution to fulfill the intent of the framers of the Constitution of the United States and insure that the collective judgment of both the Congress and the President will apply to the introduction of United States Armed Forces into hostilities, or into situations where imminent involvement in hostilities is clearly indicated by the circumstances, and to the continued use of such forces in hostilities or in such situations.

* * *.

(c) The constitutional powers of the President as Commander-in-Chief to introduce United States Armed Forces into hostilities, or into situations where imminent involvement in hostilities is clearly indicated by the circumstances, are exercised only pursuant to (1) a declaration of war, (2) specific statutory authorization, or (3) a national emergency created by attack upon the United States, its territories or possessions, or its armed forces.

Section 3. The President in every possible instance shall consult with Congress before introducing United States Armed Forces into hostilities or into situation where imminent involvement in hostilities is clearly indicated by the circumstances, and after every such introduction shall consult regularly with the Congress until United States Armed Forces are no longer engaged in hostilities or have been removed from such situations.

Section 4. * * * [Whenever military forces are deployed without a declaration of war, the President "shall submit within 48 hours to the Speaker of the House of Representatives and to the President pro tempore of the Senate a report, in writing, setting forth" the President's legal and policy justifications for the action and the expected scope and duration of the activity.]

Section 5.

* * *

> (b) Within sixty calendar days after a report is submitted or is required to be submitted pursuant to section 4(a)(1), whichever is earlier, the President shall terminate any use of United States Armed Forces with respect to which such report was submitted (or required to be submitted), unless the Congress (1) has declared war or enacted a specific authorization for such use of the United States Armed Forces, (2) has extended by law such sixty-day period, or (3) is physically unable to meet as a result of an armed attack upon the United States. Such sixty-day period shall be extended for not more than an additional thirty days if the President determines and certifies to the Congress in writing that unavoidable military necessity respecting the safety of United States Armed Forces requires the continued use of such armed forces in the course of bringing about a prompt removal of such forces.
>
> (c) Notwithstanding subsection (b), at any time that United States Armed Forces are engaged in hostilities outside the territory of the United States, its possessions and territories without a declaration of war or specific statutory authorization, such forces shall be removed by the President if the Congress so directs by concurrent resolution.
>
> * * *

Pub. L. No. 93–148, 87 Stat. 555 (1973) (codified at 50 U.S.C. §§ 1541–48 (2018)). The WPR goes on to say that authorization for military force should never be inferred from statutes or treaties absent specific statutory language providing the authorization.

Congress, of course, is free to express its views on anything, whether it is the scope of the President's constitutional war powers or the appropriate timing of National Potato Month. Is the WPR equivalent to a declaration of National Potato Month, or does it have real legal bite? Presidents have consistently maintained the former, starting with President Nixon's veto of the WPR. Most of the veto messages focused on practical and policy consequences of the WPR, but the message also noted, in rather conclusory fashion:

> House Joint Resolution 542 would attempt to take away, by a mere legislative act, authorities which the President has properly exercised under the Constitution for almost 200 years. One of its provisions would automatically cut off certain authorities after sixty days unless the Congress extended them. Another would allow the Congress to eliminate certain authorities merely by the passage of a concurrent resolution—an action which does not normally have the force of law, since it denies the President his constitutional role in approving legislation.
>
> I believe that both these provisions are unconstitutional. The only way in which the constitutional powers of a branch of the Government can be altered is by amending the Constitution—and any attempt to make such alterations by legislation alone is clearly without force.

President's Veto of War Powers Resolution, 9 Weekly Comp. Pres. Doc. 1285 (Oct. 24, 1973). President Nixon was clearly right that the provisions for congressional "action" without presentment to the President are invalid, as the Court held ten years after the WPR in *INS v. Chadha*. *See supra* pages 277–283. What about the substance of the WPR? Does the WPR impinge on the President's constitutional powers or modestly begin to (re)assert Congress's own authority? Presidents almost always have elected to comply with the WPR, so the courts have yet to weigh in consequentially. The most notable exception to compliance concerned the Obama Administration's military operations in Libya, which lasted long beyond the sixty-day period for unauthorized military action specified in the WPR. The Obama Administration claimed that the WPR did not apply because all of the military operations were airborne, so there were no "boots on the ground." Does that sound persuasive? *See* Bruce Ackerman, *Legal Acrobatics, Illegal War,* N.Y. Times, June 20, 2011, https://www.nytimes.com/2011/06/21/opinion/21Ackerman.html.

[Assignment 25]

H. THE NATURE OF THE POWER TO WAGE WAR: MILITARY COMMISSIONS AND EMERGENCY POWERS

Article II, Section 2, Clause 1: The President shall be Commander in Chief of the Army and Navy of the United States, and of the Militia of the several States, when called into the actual Service of the United States.

What "kind" of power is unleashed when the dogs of war are unchained? There is a perhaps surprising amount of caselaw on this question—surprising if one was expecting courts to find the extent of warmaking powers to be political questions beyond their jurisdiction. Courts have decided quite a number of important cases involving warmaking from the founding era to the present, though many of those cases involve a strong measure of deference to executive decisionmaking. *See* ERIC A. POSNER & ADRIAN VERMEULE, TERROR IN THE BALANCE: SECURITY, LIBERTY, AND THE COURTS (2007); Gary Lawson, *Ordinary Powers in Extraordinary Times: Common Sense in Times of Crisis,* 87 B.U. L. REV. 289 (2007). Indeed, there is far too much law in this area to address the subject in a survey course; international law, for example, plays a large role in this area. We present here only a few pieces of this story that are of especial historical interest.

The first is an exercise of the war power by President Abraham Lincoln that was never challenged in court. If it had been challenged (by whom?), ask yourself as you read this document if it was a legitimate use of the war power—or was even a use of the war power at all—which the President could engage in without consulting Congress. If it was not an exercise of the war power, what power was it exercising?

The Emancipation Proclamation

January 1, 1863

A Transcription

By the President of the United States of America:

A Proclamation.

Whereas, on the twenty-second day of September, in the year of our Lord one thousand eight hundred and sixty-two, a proclamation was issued by the President of the United States, containing, among other things, the following, to wit:

"That on the first day of January, in the year of our Lord one thousand eight hundred and sixty-three, all persons held as slaves within any State or designated part of a State, the people whereof shall then be in rebellion against the United States, shall be then, thenceforward, and forever free; and the Executive Government of the United States, including the military and naval authority thereof, will recognize and maintain the freedom of such persons, and will do no act or acts to repress such persons, or any of them, in any efforts they may make for their actual freedom."

* * * Now, therefore I, Abraham Lincoln, President of the United States, by virtue of the power in me vested as Commander-in-Chief, of the Army and Navy of the United States in time of actual armed rebellion against the authority and government of the United States, and as a fit and necessary war measure for suppressing said rebellion, do, on this first day of January, in the year of our Lord one thousand eight hundred and sixty-three, and in accordance with my purpose so to do publicly proclaimed for the full period of one hundred days, from the day first above mentioned, order and designate as the States and parts of States wherein the people thereof respectively, are this day in rebellion against the United States, the following, to wit:

Arkansas, Texas, Louisiana, (except the Parishes of St. Bernard, Plaquemines, Jefferson, St. John, St. Charles, St. James Ascension, Assumption, Terrebonne, Lafourche, St. Mary, St. Martin, and Orleans, including the City of New Orleans) Mississippi, Alabama, Florida, Georgia, South Carolina, North Carolina, and Virginia, (except the forty-eight counties designated as West Virginia, and also the counties of Berkley, Accomac, Northampton, Elizabeth City, York, Princess Ann, and Norfolk, including the cities of Norfolk and Portsmouth[)], and which excepted parts, are for the present, left precisely as if this proclamation were not issued.

And by virtue of the power, and for the purpose aforesaid, I do order and declare that all persons held as slaves within said designated States, and parts of States, are, and henceforward shall be free; and that the Executive government of the United States, including the military and naval authorities thereof, will recognize and maintain the freedom of said persons.

And I hereby enjoin upon the people so declared to be free to abstain from all violence, unless in necessary self-defence; and I recommend to them that, in all cases when allowed, they labor faithfully for reasonable wages.

And I further declare and make known, that such persons of suitable condition, will be received into the armed service of the United States to garrison forts, positions, stations, and other places, and to man vessels of all sorts in said service.

And upon this act, sincerely believed to be an act of justice, warranted by the Constitution, upon military necessity, I invoke the considerate judgment of mankind, and the gracious favor of Almighty God * * *.

NOTES AND QUESTIONS

1. President Lincoln believed that, as an historical matter, a nation fighting another nation or entity that maintained slaves had the right, under the laws of war, to offer freedom to that nation's slaves to incite them to rebel and to crush the slave power's domestic economy. By the end of the Civil War in 1865, 20% of the Union Army consisted

of freed African-Americans. The South's economy was also completely destroyed by emancipation, with slaves fleeing the Southern plantations and heading to cities or North.

2. By issuing the Emancipation Proclamation, President Lincoln turned the Civil War from a war about keeping the Union together, in the face of Southern secession, into a much broader war about ending slavery altogether in the United States. The Emancipation Proclamation freed about 3.5 million out of the 4 million African-Americans held in slavery on January 1, 1863. Because the Emancipation Proclamation was authorized by the war power, it did not—and constitutionally could not—apply to the four slave States which had stayed in the Union: Maryland, Delaware, Kentucky, and Missouri. Nor did it apply to the portions of the South which the North had reconquered by January 1, 1863. The remaining African-American slaves were freed by the adoption, on December 6, 1865, of the Thirteenth Amendment banning slavery anywhere in the United States.

3. Note that the slave owners, even in the States that had remained loyal to the Union, did not receive any just compensation for the deprivation of their so-called property interest in other human beings. At the same time, the freed African-Americans were given their freedom, but nothing else either in the way of reparations or a share of the land they had toiled on as slaves. Radical Reconstructionists called for every free African-American to receive "40 acres and a mule," but that did not happen.

4. Recent estimates are that 750,000 Americans, and possibly as many as 850,000 Americans, died in the Civil War. Of these casualties, it seems certain that at least 500,000 Union Army soldiers gave their lives to end slavery, and countless others were permanently maimed.

5. The spirit of the times is well captured in the Battle Hymn of the Republic, a song that was often sung when the editors were children, but which is no longer sung much, perhaps because it is so Christian. Every American ought to read the lyrics to the Battle Hymn of the Republic, written in 1861 by Julia Ward Howe, because it is a key part of our history.

Battle Hymn of the Republic

Mine eyes have seen the glory of the coming of the Lord;
He is trampling out the vintage where the grapes of wrath are stored;
He hath loosed the fateful lightning of His terrible swift sword:
His truth is marching on.

(Chorus)

Glory, Glory, hallelujah!
Glory, glory, hallelujah!
Glory, glory, hallelujah!
His truth is marching on.

I have seen Him in the watch-fires of a hundred circling camps,
They have builded Him an altar in the evening dews and damps;
I can read His righteous sentence by the dim and flaring lamps:
His day is marching on.

(Chorus)

I have read a fiery gospel writ in burnished rows of steel:
"As ye deal with my contemners, so with you my grace shall deal";

Let the Hero, born of woman, crush the serpent with his heel,
Since God is marching on.

(Chorus)

He has sounded forth the trumpet that shall never call retreat;
He is sifting out the hearts of men before His judgment-seat;
Oh, be swift, my soul, to answer Him! Be jubilant, my feet!
Our God is marching on.

(Chorus)

In the beauty of the lilies Christ was born across the sea,
With a glory in His bosom that transfigures you and me.
As He died to make men holy, let us die to make men free,
While God is marching on.

(Chorus)

1. WORLD WARS I AND II AND THE RULE OF LAW

During World War I, the federal government imposed a nationwide draft of all men over the age of 18, and many women took their jobs on the home front. This turned out to be a turning point in the emergence of sex equality and helped lead to the approval of the Nineteenth Amendment in 1920 giving women the right to vote in all federal and state elections. But as often happens with war, there was a cost—in law as well as in lives and treasure. The draft itself was of dubious constitutionality, and it was upheld by the Supreme Court on reasoning that could charitably be described as conclusory. *See Avery v. United States,* 245 U.S. 366 (1918) ("*Selective Draft Law Cases*"); *infra* pages 775–779. Moreover, President Woodrow Wilson pushed through Congress a blatantly unconstitutional statute called the Sedition Act of 1918 making it a crime, among other things to "willfully utter, print, write, or publish any disloyal, profane, scurrilous, or abusive language about the form of government of the United States, or the Constitution of the United States, or the military or naval forces of the United States, or the flag of the United States, or the uniform of the Army or Navy of the-United States, or any language intended, to bring the form of government of the United States, or the Constitution, or situation of the United States, or the military or naval forces of the United States, or the flag of the United States, or the uniform of the Army or Navy of the United States into contempt, scorn, contumely, or disrepute * * *." 40 Stat. 553. Combined with the Espionage Act of 1917, ch. 30, § 3, 40 Stat. 217, 219, which criminalized any "attempt to cause insubordination * * * in the military or naval forces of the United States" or obstruction of "the recruiting or enlistment service of the United States," the Sedition Act gave the government sweeping authority to prosecute people for speaking out against war. American Socialist leader Eugene Debs (among others), who had received nearly one million votes for President in 1912, was convicted under these statutes for giving anti-war speeches during World War I that would be commonplace in almost any public space in the country today in time of war. *See Debs v. United States* 249 U.S. 211 (1919); *Schenck v. United States,* 249 U.S. 47 (1919). Debs was sentenced to ten years in prison for expressing his views, though his sentence was commuted in 1921 by President Harding. In 1920, while in prison for these "crimes," Debs again ran for President and again received nearly one million votes.

World War II again brought the federal war power to bear on American territory. The United States was attacked, by surprise, at Pearl Harbor by the Empire of Japan on December 7, 1941. Unlike the War of 1812, the Mexican-American War, or the Spanish American War, World War II was fought to defend the territory and people of the United States and not to acquire territory. In fact, shortly after the end of World War II, the United States recognized the independence of the Philippines, which the Spanish-American War had turned into a U.S. territory. Because of Japan's surprise attack, and the devastating blow it landed on the U.S. Navy in the Pacific, Americans were terrified of an invasion of Hawaii or even California. In both places, there were large populations of loyal Japanese-American citizens. The New Deal Supreme Court, all but one of whose nine members had been appointed by President Franklin D. Roosevelt, upheld the internment of 100,000 Japanese-Americans in Internment Centers other than their houses. While this decision was formally repudiated in 2018, *see Trump v. Hawaii,* 138 S.Ct. 2392, 2423 (2018) ("*Korematsu* was gravely wrong the day it was decided, has been overruled in the court of history, and—to be clear—'has no place in law under the Constitution.' "), it stands as a testament to the constant tug of war against the rule of law.

Korematsu v. United States

323 U.S. 214 (1944)

■ MR. JUSTICE BLACK delivered the opinion of the Court.

The petitioner, an American citizen of Japanese descent, was convicted in a federal district court for remaining in San Leandro, California, a "Military Area," contrary to Civilian Exclusion Order No. 34 of the Commanding General of the Western Command, U.S. Army, which directed that after May 9, 1942, all persons of Japanese ancestry should be excluded from that area. No question was raised as to petitioner's loyalty to the United States. The Circuit Court of Appeals affirmed, and the importance of the constitutional question involved caused us to grant certiorari.

It should be noted, to begin with, that all legal restrictions which curtail the civil rights of a single racial group are immediately suspect. That is not to say that all such restrictions are unconstitutional. It is to say that courts must subject them to the most rigid scrutiny. Pressing public necessity may sometimes justify the existence of such restrictions; racial antagonism never can.

In the instant case prosecution of the petitioner was begun by information charging violation of an Act of Congress, of March 21, 1942, 56 Stat. 173, which provides that

". . . whoever shall enter, remain in, leave, or commit any act in any military area or military zone prescribed, under the authority of an Executive order of the President, by the Secretary of War, or by any military commander designated by the Secretary of War, contrary to the restrictions applicable to any such area or zone or contrary to the order of the Secretary of War or any such military commander, shall, if it appears that he knew or should have known of the existence and extent of the restrictions or order and that his act was in violation thereof, be guilty of a misdemeanor and upon conviction shall be liable to a fine of not to exceed $ 5,000 or to imprisonment for not more than one year, or both, for each offense."

Exclusion Order No. 34, which the petitioner knowingly and admittedly violated, was one of a number of military orders and proclamations, all of which were substantially based upon Executive Order No. 9066, 7 Fed. Reg. 1407. That order, issued after we were at war with Japan, declared that "the successful prosecution of the war requires every possible protection against espionage and against sabotage to national-defense material, national-defense premises, and national-defense utilities. . . ."

One of the series of orders and proclamations, a curfew order, which like the exclusion order here was promulgated pursuant to Executive Order 9066, subjected all persons of Japanese ancestry in prescribed West Coast military areas to remain in their residences from 8 p.m. to 6 a.m. As is the case with the exclusion order here, that prior curfew order was designed as a "protection against espionage and against sabotage." In *Hirabayashi v. United States*, [320 U.S. 81 (1943),] we sustained a conviction obtained for violation of the curfew order. The Hirabayashi conviction and this one thus rest on the same 1942 Congressional Act and the same basic executive and military orders, all of which orders were aimed at the twin dangers of espionage and sabotage.

The 1942 Act was attacked in the *Hirabayashi* case as an unconstitutional delegation of power; it was contended that the curfew order and other orders on which it rested were beyond the war powers of the Congress, the military authorities and of the President, as Commander in Chief of the Army; and finally that to apply the curfew order against none but citizens of Japanese ancestry amounted to a constitutionally prohibited discrimination solely on account of race. To these questions, we gave the serious consideration which their importance justified. We upheld the curfew order as an exercise of the power of the government to take steps necessary to prevent espionage and sabotage in an area threatened by Japanese attack.

In the light of the principles we announced in the *Hirabayashi* case, we are unable to conclude that it was beyond the war power of Congress and the Executive to exclude those of Japanese ancestry from the West Coast war area at the time they did. True, exclusion from the area in which one's home is located is a far greater deprivation than constant confinement to the home from 8 p.m. to 6 a.m. Nothing short of apprehension by the proper military authorities of the gravest imminent danger to the public safety can constitutionally justify either. But exclusion from a threatened area, no less than curfew, has a definite and close relationship to the prevention of espionage and sabotage. The military authorities, charged with the primary responsibility of defending our shores, concluded that curfew provided inadequate protection and ordered exclusion. They did so, as pointed out in our *Hirabayashi* opinion, in accordance with Congressional authority to the military to say who should, and who should not, remain in the threatened areas.

In this case the petitioner challenges the assumptions upon which we rested our conclusions in the *Hirabayashi* case. He also urges that by May 1942, when Order No. 34 was promulgated, all danger of Japanese invasion of the West Coast had disappeared. After careful consideration of these contentions we are compelled to reject them.

Here, as in the *Hirabayashi* case, ". . . we cannot reject as unfounded the judgment of the military authorities and of Congress that there were disloyal members of that population, whose number and strength could not be precisely and quickly ascertained. We cannot say that the war-making branches of the Government did not have ground for believing that in a critical hour such persons could not readily be isolated and separately dealt with, and constituted a menace to the national defense and safety, which demanded that prompt and adequate measures be taken to guard against it."

Like curfew, exclusion of those of Japanese origin was deemed necessary because of the presence of an unascertained number of disloyal members of the group, most of whom we have no doubt were loyal to this country. It was because we could not reject the finding of the military authorities that it was impossible to bring about an immediate segregation of the disloyal from the loyal that we sustained the validity of the curfew order as applying to the whole group. In the instant case, temporary exclusion of the entire group was rested by the military on the same ground. The judgment that exclusion of the whole group was for the same reason a military imperative answers the contention that the exclusion was in the nature of group punishment based on antagonism to those of Japanese origin. That there were members of the group who retained loyalties to Japan has been confirmed by investigations made subsequent to the exclusion. Approximately five thousand American citizens of Japanese ancestry refused to swear unqualified allegiance to the United States and to renounce allegiance to the Japanese Emperor, and several thousand evacuees requested repatriation to Japan.

We uphold the exclusion order as of the time it was made and when the petitioner violated it. In doing so, we are not unmindful of the hardships imposed by it upon a large group of American citizens. But hardships are part of war, and war is an aggregation of hardships. All citizens alike, both in and out of uniform, feel the impact of war in greater or lesser measure. Citizenship has its responsibilities as well as its privileges, and in time of war the burden is always heavier. Compulsory exclusion of large groups of citizens from their homes, except under circumstances of direst emergency and peril, is inconsistent with our basic governmental institutions. But when under conditions of modern warfare our shores are threatened by hostile forces, the power to protect must be commensurate with the threatened danger.

It is argued that on May 30, 1942, the date the petitioner was charged with remaining in the prohibited area, there were conflicting orders outstanding, forbidding him both to leave the area and to remain there. Of course, a person cannot be convicted for doing the very thing which it is a crime to fail to do. But the outstanding orders here contained no such contradictory commands.

* * *

It is said that we are dealing here with the case of imprisonment of a citizen in a concentration camp solely because of his ancestry, without evidence or inquiry concerning his loyalty and good disposition towards the United States. Our task would be simple, our duty clear, were this a case involving the imprisonment of a loyal citizen in a concentration camp because of racial prejudice. Regardless of the true nature of the assembly and relocation centers—and we deem it unjustifiable to call them concentration camps with all the ugly connotations that term implies—we are dealing specifically with nothing but an exclusion order. To cast this case into outlines of racial prejudice, without reference to the real military dangers which were presented, merely confuses the issue. Korematsu was not excluded from the Military

Area because of hostility to him or his race. He *was* excluded because we are at war with the Japanese Empire, because the properly constituted military authorities feared an invasion of our West Coast and felt constrained to take proper security measures, because they decided that the military urgency of the situation demanded that all citizens of Japanese ancestry be segregated from the West Coast temporarily, and finally, because Congress, reposing its confidence in this time of war in our military leaders—as inevitably it must—determined that they should have the power to do just this. There was evidence of disloyalty on the part of some, the military authorities considered that the need for action was great, and time was short. We cannot—by availing ourselves of the calm perspective of hindsight—now say that at that time these actions were unjustified.

Affirmed.

■ MR. JUSTICE FRANKFURTER, concurring.

* * *

The provisions of the Constitution which confer on the Congress and the President powers to enable this country to wage war are as much part of the Constitution as provisions looking to a nation at peace. And we have had recent occasion to quote approvingly the statement of former Chief Justice Hughes that the war power of the Government is "the power to wage war successfully." Therefore, the validity of action under the war power must be judged wholly in the context of war. That action is not to be stigmatized as lawless because like action in times of peace would be lawless. To talk about a military order that expresses an allowable judgment of war needs by those entrusted with the duty of conducting war as "an unconstitutional order" is to suffuse a part of the Constitution with an atmosphere of unconstitutionality. The respective spheres of action of military authorities and of judges are of course very different. But within their sphere, military authorities are no more outside the bounds of obedience to the Constitution than are judges within theirs. "The war power of the United States, like its other powers . . . is subject to applicable constitutional limitations[.]" To recognize that military orders are "reasonably expedient military precautions" in time of war and yet to deny them constitutional legitimacy makes of the Constitution an instrument for dialectic subtleties not reasonably to be attributed to the hard-headed Framers, of whom a majority had had actual participation in war. If a military order such as that under review does not transcend the means appropriate for conducting war, such action by the military is as constitutional as would be any authorized action by the Interstate Commerce Commission within the limits of the constitutional power to regulate commerce. And being an exercise of the war power explicitly granted by the Constitution for safeguarding the national life by prosecuting war effectively, I find nothing in the Constitution which denies to Congress the power to enforce such a valid military order by making its violation an offense triable in the civil courts. To find that the Constitution does not forbid the military measures now complained of does not carry with it approval of that which Congress and the Executive did. That is their business, not ours.

■ MR. JUSTICE ROBERTS, dissenting.

I dissent, because I think the indisputable facts exhibit a clear violation of Constitutional rights.

This is not a case of keeping people off the streets at night as was *Hirabayashi v. United States*, nor a case of temporary exclusion of a citizen from an area for his own safety or that of the community, nor a case of offering him an opportunity to go temporarily out of an area where his presence might cause danger to himself or to his fellows. On the contrary, it is the case of convicting a citizen as a punishment for not submitting to imprisonment in a concentration camp, based on his ancestry, and solely because of his ancestry, without evidence or inquiry concerning his loyalty and good disposition towards the United States. If this be a correct statement of the facts disclosed by this record, and facts of which we take judicial notice, I need hardly labor the conclusion that Constitutional rights have been violated.

* * *

■ MR. JUSTICE MURPHY, dissenting.

This exclusion of "all persons of Japanese ancestry, both alien and non-alien," from the Pacific Coast area on a plea of military necessity in the absence of martial law ought not to be approved. Such exclusion goes over "the very brink of constitutional power" and falls into the ugly abyss of racism.

In dealing with matters relating to the prosecution and progress of a war, we must accord great respect and consideration to the judgments of the military authorities who are on the scene and who have full knowledge of the military facts. The scope of their discretion must, as a matter of necessity and common sense, be wide. And their judgments ought not to be overruled lightly by those whose training and duties ill-equip them to deal intelligently with matters so vital to the physical security of the nation.

At the same time, however, it is essential that there be definite limits to military discretion, especially where martial law has not been declared. Individuals must not be left impoverished of their constitutional rights on a plea of military necessity that has neither substance nor support. Thus, like other claims conflicting with the asserted constitutional rights of the individual, the military claim must subject itself to the judicial process of having its reasonableness determined and its conflicts with other interests reconciled. "What are the allowable limits of military discretion, and whether or not they have been overstepped in a particular case, are judicial questions."

The judicial test of whether the Government, on a plea of military necessity, can validly deprive an individual of any of his constitutional rights is whether the deprivation is reasonably related to a public danger that is so "immediate, imminent, and impending" as not to admit of delay and not to permit the intervention of ordinary constitutional processes to alleviate the danger. Civilian Exclusion Order No. 34, banishing from a prescribed area of the Pacific Coast "all persons of Japanese ancestry, both alien and non-alien," clearly does not meet that test. Being an obvious racial discrimination, the order deprives all those within its scope of the equal protection of the laws as guaranteed by the Fifth Amendment. It further deprives these individuals of their constitutional rights to live and work where they will, to establish a home where they choose and to move about freely. In excommunicating them without benefit of hearings, this order also deprives them of all their constitutional rights to procedural due process. Yet no reasonable relation to an "immediate, imminent, and impending" public danger is evident to support this racial restriction which is one of the most sweeping and complete deprivations of constitutional rights in the history of this nation in the absence of martial law.

It must be conceded that the military and naval situation in the spring of 1942 was such as to generate a very real fear of invasion of the Pacific Coast, accompanied by fears of sabotage and espionage in that area. The military command was therefore justified in adopting all reasonable means necessary to combat these dangers. In adjudging the military action taken in light of the then apparent dangers, we must not erect too high or too meticulous standards; it is necessary only that the action have some reasonable relation to the removal of the dangers of invasion, sabotage and espionage. But the exclusion, either temporarily or permanently, of all persons with Japanese blood in their veins has no such reasonable relation. And that relation is lacking because the exclusion order necessarily must rely for its reasonableness upon the assumption that *all* persons of Japanese ancestry may have a dangerous tendency to commit sabotage and espionage and to aid our Japanese enemy in other ways. It is difficult to believe that reason, logic or experience could be marshalled in support of such an assumption.

That this forced exclusion was the result in good measure of this erroneous assumption of racial guilt rather than bona fide military necessity is evidenced by the Commanding General's Final Report on the evacuation from the Pacific Coast area. In it he refers to all individuals of Japanese descent as "subversive," as belonging to "an enemy race" whose "racial strains are undiluted," and as constituting "over 112,000 potential enemies . . . at large today" along the Pacific Coast. In support of this blanket condemnation of all persons of Japanese descent, however, no reliable evidence is cited to show that such individuals were generally disloyal, or had generally so conducted themselves in this area as to constitute a special menace to defense installations or war industries, or had otherwise by their behavior furnished reasonable ground for their exclusion as a group.

Justification for the exclusion is sought, instead, mainly upon questionable racial and sociological grounds not ordinarily within the realm of expert military judgment, supplemented by certain semi-military conclusions drawn from an unwarranted use of circumstantial evidence. Individuals of Japanese ancestry are condemned because they are said to be "a large, unassimilated, tightly knit racial group, bound to an enemy nation by strong ties of race, culture, custom and religion." They are claimed to be given to "emperor worshipping ceremonies" and to "dual citizenship." Japanese language schools and allegedly pro-Japanese organizations are cited as evidence of possible group disloyalty, together with facts as to certain persons being educated and residing at length in Japan. It is intimated that many of these individuals deliberately resided "adjacent to strategic points," thus enabling them "to carry into execution a tremendous program of sabotage on a mass scale should any considerable number of them have been inclined to do so." The need for protective custody is also asserted. The report refers without identity to "numerous incidents of violence" as well as to other admittedly unverified or cumulative incidents. From this, plus certain other events not shown to have been connected with the Japanese Americans, it is concluded that the "situation was fraught with danger to the Japanese population itself" and that the general public "was ready to take matters into its own hands." Finally, it is intimated, though not directly charged or proved, that persons of Japanese ancestry were responsible for three minor isolated shellings and bombings of the Pacific Coast area, as well as for unidentified radio transmissions and night signaling.

The main reasons relied upon by those responsible for the forced evacuation, therefore, do not prove a reasonable relation between the group characteristics of Japanese Americans and the dangers of invasion, sabotage and espionage. The reasons appear, instead, to be largely an accumulation of much of the misinformation, half-truths and insinuations that for years have been directed against Japanese Americans by people with racial and economic prejudices—the same people who have been among the foremost advocates of the evacuation. A military judgment based upon such racial and sociological considerations is not entitled to the great weight ordinarily given the judgments based upon strictly military considerations. Especially is this so when every charge relative to race, religion, culture, geographical location, and legal and economic status has been substantially discredited by independent studies made by experts in these matters.

The military necessity which is essential to the validity of the evacuation order thus resolves itself into a few intimations that certain individuals actively aided the enemy, from which it is inferred that the entire group of Japanese Americans could not be trusted to be or remain loyal to the United States. No one denies, of course, that there were some disloyal persons of Japanese descent on the Pacific Coast who did all in their power to aid their ancestral land. Similar disloyal activities have been engaged in by many persons of German, Italian and even more pioneer stock in our country. But to infer that examples of individual disloyalty prove group disloyalty and justify discriminatory action against the entire group is to deny that under our system of law individual guilt is the sole basis for deprivation of rights. Moreover, this inference, which is at the very heart of the evacuation orders, has been used in support of the abhorrent and despicable treatment of minority groups by the dictatorial tyrannies which this nation is now pledged to destroy. To give constitutional sanction to that inference in this case, however well-intentioned may have been the military command on the Pacific Coast, is to adopt one of the cruelest of the rationales used by our enemies to destroy the dignity of the individual and to encourage and open the door to discriminatory actions against other minority groups in the passions of tomorrow.

No adequate reason is given for the failure to treat these Japanese Americans on an individual basis by holding investigations and hearings to separate the loyal from the disloyal, as was done in the case of persons of German and Italian ancestry. It is asserted merely that the loyalties of this group "were unknown and time was of the essence." Yet nearly four months elapsed after Pearl Harbor before the first exclusion order was issued; nearly eight months went by until the last order was issued; and the last of these "subversive" persons was not actually removed until almost eleven months had elapsed. Leisure and deliberation seem to have been more of the essence than speed. And the fact that conditions were not such as to warrant a declaration of martial law adds strength to the belief that the factors of time and military necessity were not as urgent as they have been represented to be.

Moreover, there was no adequate proof that the Federal Bureau of Investigation and the military and naval intelligence services did not have the espionage and sabotage situation well in hand during this long period. Nor is there any denial of the fact that not one person of Japanese ancestry was accused or convicted of espionage or sabotage after Pearl Harbor while they were still free, a fact which is some evidence of the loyalty of the vast majority of these individuals and of the effectiveness of the established methods of combatting these evils. It seems incredible that under these circumstances it would have been impossible to hold loyalty hearings for the mere 112,000 persons involved—or at least for the 70,000 American citizens—especially when a large part of this number represented children and elderly men and women. Any inconvenience that may have accompanied an attempt to conform to procedural due process cannot be said to justify violations of constitutional rights of individuals.

I dissent, therefore, from this legalization of racism. Racial discrimination in any form and in any degree has no justifiable part whatever in our democratic way of life. It is unattractive in any setting but it is utterly revolting among a free people who have embraced the principles set forth in the Constitution of the United States. All residents of this nation are kin in some way by blood or culture to a foreign land. Yet they are primarily and necessarily a part of the new and distinct civilization of the United States. They must accordingly be treated at all times as the heirs of the American experiment and as entitled to all the rights and freedoms guaranteed by the Constitution.

■ MR. JUSTICE JACKSON, dissenting.

Korematsu was born on our soil, of parents born in Japan. The Constitution makes him a citizen of the United States by nativity and a citizen of California by residence. No claim is made that he is not loyal to this country. There is no suggestion that apart from the matter involved here he is not law-abiding and well disposed. Korematsu, however, has been convicted of an act not commonly a crime. It consists merely of being present in the state whereof he is a citizen, near the place where he was born, and where all his life he has lived.

Even more unusual is the series of military orders which made this conduct a crime. They forbid such a one to remain, and they also forbid him to leave. They were so drawn that the only way Korematsu could avoid violation was to give himself up to the military authority. This meant submission to custody, examination, and transportation out of the territory, to be followed by indeterminate confinement in detention camps.

A citizen's presence in the locality, however, was made a crime only if his parents were of Japanese birth. Had Korematsu been one of four—the others being, say, a German alien enemy, an Italian alien enemy, and a citizen of American-born ancestors, convicted of treason but out on parole—only Korematsu's presence would have violated the order. The difference between their innocence and his crime would result, not from anything he did, said, or thought, different than they, but only in that he was born of different racial stock.

Now, if any fundamental assumption underlies our system, it is that guilt is personal and not inheritable. Even if all of one's antecedents had been convicted of treason, the Constitution forbids its penalties to be visited upon him, for it provides that "no attainder of treason shall work corruption of blood, or forfeiture except during the life of the person attainted." But here is an attempt to make an otherwise innocent act a crime merely because this prisoner is the son of parents as to whom he had no choice, and belongs to a race from which there is no way to resign. If Congress in peace-time legislation should enact such a criminal law, I should suppose this Court would refuse to enforce it.

But the "law" which this prisoner is convicted of disregarding is not found in an act of Congress, but in a military order. Neither the Act of Congress nor the Executive Order of the President, nor both together, would afford a basis for this conviction. It rests on the orders of General DeWitt. And it is said that if the military commander had reasonable military grounds for promulgating the orders, they are constitutional and become law, and the Court is required to enforce them. There are several reasons why I cannot subscribe to this doctrine.

It would be impracticable and dangerous idealism to expect or insist that each specific military command in an area of probable operations will conform to conventional tests of constitutionality. When an area is so beset that it must be put under military control at all, the paramount consideration is that its measures be successful, rather than legal. The armed services must protect a society, not merely its Constitution. The very essence of the military job is to marshal physical force, to remove every obstacle to its effectiveness, to give it every strategic advantage. Defense measures will not, and often should not, be held within the limits that bind civil authority in peace. No court can require such a commander in such circumstances to act as a reasonable man; he may be unreasonably cautious and exacting. Perhaps he should be. But a commander in temporarily focusing the life of a community on defense is carrying out a military program; he is not making law in the sense the courts know the term. He issues orders, and they may have a certain authority as military commands, although they may be very bad as constitutional law.

But if we cannot confine military expedients by the Constitution, neither would I distort the Constitution to approve all that the military may deem expedient. That is what the Court appears to be doing, whether consciously or not. I cannot say, from any evidence before me, that the orders of General DeWitt were not reasonably expedient military precautions, nor could I say that they were. But even if they were permissible military procedures, I deny that it follows that they are constitutional. If, as the Court holds, it does follow, then we may as well say that any military order will be constitutional and have done with it.

The limitation under which courts always will labor in examining the necessity for a military order are illustrated by this case. How does the Court know that these orders have a reasonable basis in necessity? No evidence whatever on that subject has been taken by this or any other court. There is sharp controversy as to the credibility of the DeWitt report. So the Court, having no real evidence before it, has no choice but to accept General DeWitt's own unsworn, self-serving statement, untested by any cross-examination, that what he did was reasonable. And thus it will always be when courts try to look into the reasonableness of a military order.

In the very nature of things, military decisions are not susceptible of intelligent judicial appraisal. They do not pretend to rest on evidence, but are made on information that often would not be admissible and on assumptions that could not be proved. Information in support of an order could not be disclosed to courts without danger that it would reach the enemy. Neither can courts act on communications made in confidence. Hence courts can never have any real alternative to accepting the mere declaration of the authority that issued the order that it was reasonably necessary from a military viewpoint.

Much is said of the danger to liberty from the Army program for deporting and detaining these citizens of Japanese extraction. But a judicial construction of the due process clause that will sustain this order is a far more subtle blow to liberty than the promulgation of the order itself. A military order, however unconstitutional, is not apt to last longer than the military emergency. Even during that period a succeeding commander may revoke it all. But once a judicial opinion rationalizes such an order to show that it conforms to the Constitution, or rather rationalizes the Constitution to show that the Constitution sanctions such an order, the Court for all time has validated the principle of racial discrimination in criminal procedure and of transplanting American citizens. The principle then lies about like a loaded weapon ready for the hand of any authority that can bring forward a plausible claim of an urgent need. Every repetition imbeds that principle more deeply in our law and thinking and expands it to new purposes. All who observe the work of courts are familiar with what Judge Cardozo described as "the tendency of a principle to expand itself to the limit of its logic." A military commander may overstep the bounds of constitutionality, and it is an incident. But if we review and approve, that passing incident becomes the doctrine of the Constitution. There it has a generative power of its own, and all that it creates will be in its own image. Nothing better illustrates this danger than does the Court's opinion in this case.

* * *

I should hold that a civil court cannot be made to enforce an order which violates constitutional limitations even if it is a reasonable exercise of military authority. The courts can exercise only the judicial power, can apply only law, and must abide by the Constitution, or they cease to be civil courts and become instruments of military policy.

* * *

My duties as a justice as I see them do not require me to make a military judgment as to whether General DeWitt's evacuation and detention program was a reasonable military necessity. I do not suggest that the courts should have attempted to interfere with the Army in carrying out its task. But I do not think they may be asked to execute a military expedient that has no place in law under the Constitution. I would reverse the judgment and discharge the prisoner.

NOTES AND QUESTIONS

1. *Korematsu* involved the detention and imprisonment of civilian non-combatants, in time of war, on the basis of ethnicity. That is a far cry from the traditional military authority to detain enemy combatants who are demonstrated to be members of, or who are acting on behalf of, a nation or other entity with whom America is at war. Detention of captured enemy soldiers in war time as prisoners of war falls under a different heading than civilian criminal justice. May courts properly entertain challenges to detention that are brought by non-citizens captured as part of war operations? The courts have, until recently, tended to leave those types of determinations to military authorities.

An issue arose during the Civil War as to how to treat Confederate soldiers, Confederate non-combatants who were editorializing in favor of the South, and Northern citizens of the United State who were editorializing or speaking in favor of the South. President Abraham Lincoln quickly realized that he could not try such individuals in front of a Southern jury because they would all be acquitted. He thus extended an old English military practice of trying individuals in front of a military commission of several army officers without affording a jury trial. President Lincoln made widespread use of military commissions during the Civil War to try people in the South, but he did not authorize their use even against disloyal Northerners in States, which had not seceded, and where the writ of habeas corpus had not been suspended so the ordinary courts of justice were open.

Notwithstanding Lincoln's precautions, a military commission on December 10, 1864 sentenced U.S. and Indiana citizen Lambdin P. Milligan to death by hanging for offering aid and comfort to the Confederacy. Milligan asked the federal District Court in Indiana to order him to be released on *habeas corpus* on the ground a Military Commission, convened in Indianapolis, could not be used to try a citizen of Indiana and of the United States who was not a military officer and who had a right to jury trial. In *Ex Parte Milligan*, 71 U.S. 2 (1866), the Supreme Court agreed and ordered that Milligan be free, saying that military commissions cannot constitutionally be used to try civilians in areas where the federal courts are open for business and the writ of habeas corpus has not been properly suspended. This was a great victory for civil liberties, but, quite unfortunately, it was overruled during the depths of World War II.

In *Ex Parte Quirin*, 317 U.S. 1 (1942), the Supreme Court (*wrongly*, in our view) upheld the use of military commissions as vehicles for imposing punishment on "unlawful enemy combatants"—quintessentially, spies, saboteurs, persons who do not wear soldiers' uniforms and who target civilians—for violations of the laws of war. The two issues are related, but distinct. They both raise the broad question: what is the scope of the war power as applied to persons captured in war operations?

As it happens, there has been a great deal of litigation since *Ex Parte Quirin* about the question of whether and when enemy combatants in wartime can be made subject to trial by military tribunals and also on whether they can be held, at all, without access to some kind of hearing in which they can protest their innocence. A full description of the law on this subject is impossible here, so we will instead identify some of the leading cases and explain their holdings.

From 1950 until the early 2000s, the leading case on this subject had been an old chestnut named *Johnson v. Eisentrager*, 339 U.S. 763 (1950), which had held that German war criminals captured in China and imprisoned in Germany, who had never set foot in the United States, could not challenge their military imprisonment by filing a habeas corpus petition with the U.S. District Court for the District of Columbia. The D.C. District Court so held, ruling that it lacked the power to issue orders to the military officers imprisoning Eisentrager in Germany. Eisentrager appealed, and the U.S. Court of Appeals reversed the District Court. The Supreme Court divided 6 to 3 on the case. Justice Jackson's majority opinion reversed the Court of Appeals and dismissed Eisentrager's *habeas corpus* petition. Justice Jackson stressed the fact the Eisentrager was being held by the U.S. military outside of the territory of the United States, and he was a non-resident alien who had been convicted by a military commission of violating the law of war. He was thus outside of the jurisdiction of all the Article III courts, and the U.S. Bill of Rights did not apply to him at all in his prison in Germany, even if U.S. soldiers, whose power stems from the Constitution and Bill of Rights, were incarcerating him. Justice Jackson thought it unprecedented for alien prisoners of power outside the United States to be invoking the habeas corpus jurisdiction of any of the federal courts.

Justices Black, Douglas, and Burton dissented. In their view, no U.S. official, even one acting overseas or in the military during a time of war, can exercise any power not constitutionally delegated to him or her by the Constitution and not prohibited by the

Bill of Rights. Justice Black's view was that the Constitution follows the flag. Wherever the flag goes, the Constitution goes there with it. *But see The Insular Cases*, a series of Supreme Court cases from 1901–1922 holding that the U.S. right of jury trial did not apply after the Spanish-American War to jurisdictions like Puerto Rico and the Philippines, which as civil law countries had never had jury trial. *See infra* pages 1164–1171. Justice Black may well have thought that Puerto Ricans had a U.S. constitutional law right to jury trial, and he certainly thought Eisentrager could bring Bill of Rights challenges to his imprisonment by U.S. troops in Germany.

The issue of habeas corpus review of military detentions and of trials by military authorities reached the Supreme Court repeatedly during the administration of former President George W. Bush because of the War on Terror. After the 9/11 attacks on the twin World Trade Center buildings, in New York City, and on the Pentagon, Congress passed a sweeping "Authorization for the Use of Military Force (AUMF), which gave President Bush a green light to do anything that was "appropriate" i.e. "convenient" or "useful" to subduing Al Qaeda or those who had harbored or aided them in anyway. *See supra* page 504. To accomplish this, President Bush invaded and conquered both Afghanistan and Iraq; he set up a special terrorist detention center at a U.S. military base in Guantanamo Bay Cuba, which is outside of the jurisdiction of any of the ninety-two federal district courts; he detained hundreds of alleged enemy combatants in the War on Terror without giving them any status hearing in which they could plead innocence; and he instituted a policy of water-boarding VIP suspects who might have had valuable intelligence information. This later action in many peoples' minds violated a federal law, which makes torture a federal crime. Water-boarding involves repeatedly dunking someone's head under water until they feel they are drowning as their lungs fill up with water and then raising them up to see if they will talk; and, if they don't, pushing their head back under water again. This practice leaves no permanent bodily scars, and it supposedly gets everyone to talk, although whether what they say when they talk is true is highly questionable.

The U.S. Supreme Court, in a series of cases in which Justice Anthony M. Kennedy was the swing vote, repeatedly pushed back at President George W. Bush's tactics against detained enemy combatants in the War on Terror. *See, e.g., Hamdi v. Rumsfeld*, 542 U.S. 507 (2004) (holding that U.S. citizens who are detained as enemy combatants have a constitutional due process clause right to a hearing in which they can seek to prove their innocence); *Rasul v. Bush*, 542 U.S. 466 (2004) (holding that foreign nationals detained at Guantanamo Bay could, notwithstanding *Johnson v. Eisentrager*, bring *habeas corpus* petitions in the U.S. District Court for the District of Columbia challenging the conditions and legality of their confinement); *Hamdan v. Rumsfeld*, 548 U.S. 557 (2006) (holding that military commissions at Guantanamo Bay violate both the Uniform Code of Military Justice and four Geneva Conventions); and, finally, *Boumediene v. Bush*, 553 U.S. 723 (2008) (holding the Military Commissions Act of 2006 unconstitutional and inadequate).

These embarrassing setbacks in the Supreme Court hurt former President George W. Bush politically, and his successor, President Obama, was elected on a platform in which he pledged to close the prison at Guantanamo Bay, end water-boarding and other harsh forms of incarceration, and stop taking prisoners in the War on Terror and interrogating them. (Those promises may have won him a Nobel Peace Prize.) President Obama was prevented by Congress from closing the prison at Guantanamo Bay, but he did release or move to other countries most of the people who had been held there. President Obama also stopped water-boarding and all harsh interrogation techniques. And, finally, President Obama stopped taking and interrogating prisoners in the War on Terror. Instead, he stepped up Predator Drone attacks against suspected terrorist in the

Middle East. These attacks were lethal not only to those attacked, but also to anyone to whom the targets were talking when attacked. President Bush launched fifty-seven Predator Drone attacks on Pakistan, Somalia, and Yemen. President Obama launched 563 Predator Drone attacks on those same three countries during his years in office. We have no idea how many Predator Drone attacks have been launched on those three countries under President Trump because he has stopped the prior practice of reporting the attacks.

The bottom line in this story is that Justice Anthony M. Kennedy's, and the Supreme Court's, humanitarian civil rights concerns backfired. The Supreme Court made it very politically costly to take prisoners and to interrogate them, and so the executive branch, under both Presidents Obama ad Trump, has taken to simply killing alleged terrorists with a Predator Drone strike. This is not the outcome the Supreme Court was seeking, but it is a final example as to what happens when one unleashes the "Dogs of War."

I. PRESIDENTIAL PRIVILEGES AND IMMUNITIES

We may be done with the text of Article II, but we are not quite done with the caselaw under Article II. Most presidents have argued that implicit in Article II is a doctrine called executive privilege, under which presidential communications with advisors and Cabinet secretaries are absolutely privileged from discovery in judicial proceedings or in congressional oversight proceedings. Often presidents have been bullied into waiving executive privilege by Congress, but on occasion they have asserted it and have made their assertions stick. The argument that there is such a thing as executive privilege assumes that the President would be unable to exercise the powers and live up to the duties of the office without confidential advice from advisors. Similarly, presidents would claim, Supreme Court justices have an absolute judicial privilege to get confidential advice from their law clerks. Efforts by congressional oversight committees to compel Supreme Court law clerks to testify about the advice they gave to the various justices would therefore be unconstitutional.

The text of Article II is silent about whether there is such a thing as executive privilege, just as the text of Article III is silent about whether there is such a thing as judicial privilege (and Article I is equally silent about a congressional power of investigation). Article I, Section 6, however, is not silent on the question whether members of Congress enjoy a kind of legislative privilege, as we saw earlier in this course. *See supra* pages 271–272. It specifically says that members shall be "privileged from Arrest during their attendance at the Session of their respective Houses, and in going to and returning from the same" and it also says that members of Congress "shall not be questioned in any other Place" . . . "for any Speech or Debate in either House." This privilege of members of Congress has been taken to extend as well to their legislative staff.

Some have argued that the existence of a specific Speech or Debate Clause for Congress, coupled with the failure of Articles II and III to mention anything like executive or judicial privilege, means that such privileges do not exist. Others have argued that the President and the Supreme Court would be unable to function if they could not get confidential advice and that it is a mistake to read anything into the absence of an equivalent to the Speech or Debate Clause in Articles II and III. Still others have argued that any executive or judicial privilege that may exist is an implied power and is thus subject to congressional control under the Necessary and Proper Clause.

The Supreme Court recognized a constitutionally based executive privilege, with some limits, in *United States v. Nixon*, 418 U.S. 683 (1974). A special prosecutor subpoenaed White House documents as part of his criminal investigation As a matter of separation of powers, the case probably should not have been justiciable, since it was merely an internal dispute between the President and a subordinate on a matter of internal executive policy. Nonetheless, the Court—in the era before *Buckley v. Valeo* revived concern for separation of powers—held that a presidential privilege "is fundamental to the operation of Government and inextricably rooted in the separation of powers under the Constitution," *id.* at 708, but that the privilege is only "presumptive" and can be outweighed by other considerations, such as "the demonstrated, specific need for evidence in a pending criminal trial." *Id.* at 713. Ever since, courts have in principle needed to adjudicate claims of executive privilege against, for example, demands by Congress for documents or testimony from executive officials, though almost always courts defer ruling until Congress and the executive can work it out amongst themselves.

In 2020, the House of Representatives voted articles of impeachment against President Trump for his assertion of executive privilege in congressional investigations of his administration. Is that a valid ground for impeachment? Does it depend on any particular facts regarding the President's assertions of executive privilege? What facts?

Can the President be sued civilly while serving in office? In 1997, the Supreme Court said yes, allowing a civil lawsuit by Paula Jones alleging sexual harassment by President Bill Clinton while he was governor of Arkansas to proceed during President Clinton's term. *See Clinton v. Jones,* 520 U.S. 681 (1997). The Court expressed doubt that exposing the President to civil suits would interfere significantly with his or her duties:

> [I]n the more than 200-year history of the Republic, only three sitting Presidents have been subjected to suits for their private actions. If the past is any indicator, it seems unlikely that a deluge of such litigation will ever engulf the Presidency. As for the case at hand, if properly managed by the District Court, it appears to us highly unlikely to occupy any substantial amount of petitioner's time.

Id. at 702. In an era of polarization, and even "resistance" to presidents, is it reasonable to rely on the good faith of district judges to manage litigation against sitting presidents? What about actions, civil or criminal, brought by state attorneys general? Can a state prosecutor bring criminal charges against a sitting president?

[Assignment 26]

VII. ARTICLE III: THE FEDERAL COURTS' POWER OF JUDGMENT

We now move to the third of the three Articles in the Constitution that create a government of constitutionally separated and shared powers. Article III describes the judicial power of the federal courts, and it is by far the briefest and the sketchiest of the first three articles. We quote it below in full:

Section 1: The judicial Power of the United States, shall be vested in one supreme Court, and in such inferior Courts as the Congress may from time to time ordain and establish. The Judges, both of the supreme and inferior Courts, shall hold their Offices during good Behaviour, and shall, at stated Times, receive for their Services, a Compensation, which shall not be diminished during their Continuance in Office.

Section 2: The judicial Power shall extend to all Cases, in Law and Equity, arising under this Constitution, the Laws of the United States, and Treaties made, or which shall be made, under their Authority;—to all Cases affecting Ambassadors, other public Ministers and Consuls;—to all Cases of admiralty and maritime Jurisdiction;—to Controversies to which the United States shall be a Party;—to Controversies between two or more States;—between a State and Citizens of another State;—between Citizens of different States;—between Citizens of the same State claiming Lands under Grants of different States, and between a State, or the Citizens thereof, and foreign States, Citizens or Subjects.

In all Cases affecting Ambassadors, other public Ministers and Consuls, and those in which a State shall be Party, the supreme Court shall have original Jurisdiction. In all the other Cases before mentioned, the supreme Court shall have appellate Jurisdiction, both as to Law and Fact, with such Exceptions, and under such Regulations as the Congress shall make.

The Trial of all Crimes, except in Cases of Impeachment, shall be by Jury; and such Trial shall be held in the State where the said Crimes shall have been committed; but when not committed within any State, the Trial shall be at such Place or Places as the Congress may by Law have directed.

Section 3: Treason against the United States, shall consist only in levying War against them, or in adhering to their Enemies, giving them Aid and Comfort. No Person shall be convicted of Treason unless on the Testimony of two Witnesses to the same overt Act, or on Confession in open Court.

The Congress shall have Power to declare the Punishment of Treason, but no Attainder of Treason shall work Corruption of Blood, or Forfeiture except during the Life of the Person attainted.

A. THE POWER OF JUDGMENT

The Framers seem to have had a much clearer idea of what they wanted to say about the legislative and executive power than of what they wanted to say about the judicial power. The Power of the Purse and the Power of the Sword were the stuff of legends in 1787. The mere Power of Judgment was then but a gleam in the Framers' eyes. Little did they know how very powerful, indeed, this new Privy Council that they had created would become in adjudicating the constitutional rights of persons and in defining the respective roles of the One, the Few, and the Many in the new republican regime.

Article III creates one federal Supreme Court, but it punts to Congress the decision whether to create any lower or inferior federal courts. It also leaves to Congress the power to set the size of the Supreme Court: it has varied from six to ten justices at different points in our history, though for the last century and a half the number of justices has been set at nine. From the beginning, Congress has chosen to create at least some lower federal courts, even though it arguably did not have to do so. (More about that later.) The Judiciary Act of 1789 created sixteen district court judgeships, and today we have roughly 1000 lower federal court appellate and trial judges. Congress is free under Article III to change that number at any time. Thus, Congress could tomorrow abolish 900 of the 1000 lower federal court judgeships, or it could increase the total number to 10,000. Thus, the Framers left to the two political branches a significant amount of constitutional power over the structure of the federal judiciary.

Article III begins, like Article II, with a Vesting Clause: it vests "[t]he judicial Power of the United States" in "one supreme Court, and in such inferior Courts as the Congress may from time to time ordain and establish." Note that the Constitution's use of the words "ordain and establish" echoes the Preamble of the Constitution, where We the People ordain and establish the Constitution. Article I, Section 8, Clause 9 confirms that Congress has power "To constitute Tribunals inferior to the supreme Court." This is the only place in the Constitution where the document uses the word "constitute" in any form. The power to "constitute" a tribunal or to "ordain and establish" inferior federal courts is an awesome one indeed.

As you by now know, we believe the Vesting Clause of Article III is a grant of all of the judicial power of the United States to the one Supreme Court created by the Constitution "and" (not "or") to the inferior courts Congress may choose to create. The Vesting Clause of Article III might as well be worded: "The federal courts created by this Article, and by Congress pursuant to its enumerated powers, shall have the judicial power." Look through all six paragraphs of Article III and ask yourself whether there is any other clause in the Article which even arguably could empower the federal courts to act. There is none. The closest thing to a candidate is section 2, clause 1, which says that the judicial power "shall extend" to certain specified cases. The occasional scholar has suggested that this provision might be a grant of power, *see* A. Michael Froomkin, *The Imperial Presidency's New Vestments,* 88 NW. U.L. REV. 1346, 1352–55 (1994), but it is wild stretch. Section 2 defines *to what class of cases* a power *already granted extends*. Section 1 defines the *kind of institutions* that can wield that power. Thus, one should not argue about Article III (as Justice Jackson and many scholars have argued about Article II) that the Vesting Clause merely confers a title. Instead, Sections 2 and 3 of Article III define, limit, explicate, and give further content to the judicial power which is granted to the federal courts by Article III, Section 1.

What is "[t]he judicial Power of the United States" according to the Constitution? Recall that for most of English legal history, there was no "judicial Power" separate and apart from executive power, so there was no tradition of independent judicial action on which the founding generation could draw. What would a judiciary that was separate and apart from the executive actually do? There is very little in the founding era formally defining what is meant by "judicial Power," but one can fairly say that the essence of judicial power is the power (and duty) to resolve disputes within the court's jurisdiction according to governing law. *See* PHILIP

HAMBURGER, LAW AND JUDICIAL DUTY *passim* (2008). In the words of James Wilson: "The judicial authority consists in applying, according to the principles of right and justice, the constitution and laws to facts and transactions in cases, in which the manner or principles of this application are disputed by the parties interested in them." 1 THE WORKS OF JAMES WILSON 296 (Robert Green McCloskey ed., 1967). That is fine as far as it goes, but how far does it go?.

It is high time that we read in full what Alexander Hamilton and James Madison had to say about the judicial Power of Judgment and how the U.S. Constitution is enforced. You have seen large portions of these essays already, but they are two of the most famous and important essays in *The Federalist*, and it is well worthwhile to read those portions again.

1. THE FEDERALIST NO. 78 (HAMILTON)

WE PROCEED now to an examination of the judiciary department of the proposed government.

In unfolding the defects of the existing Confederation, the utility and necessity of a federal judicature have been clearly pointed out. It is the less necessary to recapitulate the considerations there urged, as the propriety of the institution in the abstract is not disputed; the only questions which have been raised being relative to the manner of constituting it, and to its extent. To these points, therefore, our observations shall be confined.

The manner of constituting it seems to embrace these several objects: 1st. The mode of appointing the judges. 2d. The tenure by which they are to hold their places. 3d. The partition of the judiciary authority between different courts, and their relations to each other.

First. As to the mode of appointing the judges; this is the same with that of appointing the officers of the Union in general, and has been so fully discussed in the two last numbers, that nothing can be said here which would not be useless repetition.

Second. As to the tenure by which the judges are to hold their places; this chiefly concerns their duration in office; the provisions for their support; the precautions for their responsibility.

According to the plan of the convention, all judges who may be appointed by the United States are to hold their offices DURING GOOD BEHAVIOR * * *. The standard of good behavior for the continuance in office of the judicial magistracy, is certainly one of the most valuable of the modern improvements in the practice of government. In a monarchy it is an excellent barrier to the despotism of the prince; in a republic it is a no less excellent barrier to the encroachments and oppressions of the representative body. And it is the best expedient which can be devised in any government, to secure a steady, upright, and impartial administration of the laws.

Whoever attentively considers the different departments of power must perceive, that, in a government in which they are separated from each other, the judiciary, from the nature of its functions, will always be the least dangerous to the political rights of the Constitution; because it will be least in a capacity to annoy or injure them. The Executive not only dispenses the honors, but holds the sword of the community. The legislature not only commands the purse, but prescribes the rules by which the duties and rights of every citizen are to be regulated. The judiciary, on the contrary, has no influence over either the sword or the purse; no direction either of the strength or of the wealth of the society; and can take no active resolution whatever. It may truly be said to have neither FORCE nor WILL, but merely judgment; and must ultimately depend upon the aid of the executive arm even for the efficacy of its judgments.

This simple view of the matter suggests several important consequences. It proves incontestably, that the judiciary is beyond comparison the weakest of the three departments of power; that it can never attack with success either of the other two; and that all possible care is requisite to enable it to defend itself against their attacks. It equally proves, that though individual oppression may now and then proceed from the courts of justice, the general liberty of the people can never be endangered from that quarter; I mean so long as the judiciary remains truly distinct from both the legislature and the Executive. For I agree, that "there is no liberty, if the power of judging be not separated from the legislative and executive powers." And it proves, in the last place, that as liberty can have nothing to fear from the judiciary alone, but would have every thing to fear from its union with either of the other departments * * *.

The complete independence of the courts of justice is peculiarly essential in a limited Constitution. By a limited Constitution, I understand one which contains certain specified exceptions to the legislative authority; such, for instance, as that it shall pass no bills of attainder, no ex-post-facto laws, and the like. Limitations of this kind can be preserved in practice no other way than through the medium of courts of justice, whose duty it must be to declare all acts contrary to the manifest tenor of the Constitution void. Without this, all the reservations of particular rights or privileges would amount to nothing.

Some perplexity respecting the rights of the courts to pronounce legislative acts void, because contrary to the Constitution, has arisen from an imagination that the doctrine would imply a superiority of the judiciary to the legislative power. It is urged that the authority which can declare the acts of another void, must necessarily be superior to the one whose acts may be declared void. As this doctrine is of great importance in all the American constitutions, a brief discussion of the ground on which it rests cannot be unacceptable.

There is no position which depends on clearer principles, than that every act of a delegated authority, contrary to the tenor of the commission under which it is exercised, is void. No legislative act, therefore, contrary to the Constitution, can be valid. To deny this, would be to affirm, that the deputy is greater than his principal; that the servant is above his master; that the representatives of the people are superior to the people themselves; that men acting by virtue of powers, may do not only what their powers do not authorize, but what they forbid.

If it be said that the legislative body are themselves the constitutional judges of their own powers, and that the construction they put upon them is conclusive upon the other departments, it may be answered, that this cannot be the natural presumption, where it is not to be collected from any particular provisions in the Constitution. It is not otherwise to be supposed, that the Constitution could intend to enable the representatives of the people to substitute their WILL to that of their constituents. It is far more rational to suppose, that the courts were designed to be an intermediate body between the people and the legislature, in order, among other things, to keep the latter within the limits assigned to their authority. The interpretation of the laws is the proper and peculiar province of the courts. A constitution is, in fact, and must be regarded by the judges, as a fundamental law. It therefore belongs to them to ascertain its meaning, as well as the meaning of any particular act proceeding from the legislative body. If there should happen to be an irreconcilable variance between the two, that which has the superior obligation and validity ought, of course, to be preferred; or, in other words, the Constitution ought to be preferred to the statute, the intention of the people to the intention of their agents.

Nor does this conclusion by any means suppose a superiority of the judicial to the legislative power. It only supposes that the power of the people is superior to both; and that where the will of the legislature, declared in its statutes, stands in opposition to that of the people, declared in the Constitution, the judges ought to be governed by the latter rather than the former. They ought to regulate their decisions by the fundamental laws, rather than by those which are not fundamental.

This exercise of judicial discretion, in determining between two contradictory laws, is exemplified in a familiar instance. It not uncommonly happens, that there are two statutes existing at one time, clashing in whole or in part with each other, and neither of them containing any repealing clause or expression. In such a case, it is the province of the courts to liquidate and fix their meaning and operation. So far as they can, by any fair construction, be reconciled to each other, reason and law conspire to dictate that this should be done; where this is impracticable, it becomes a matter of necessity to give effect to one, in exclusion of the other. The rule which has obtained in the courts for determining their relative validity is, that the last in order of time shall be preferred to the first. But this is a mere rule of construction, not derived from any positive law, but from the nature and reason of the thing. It is a rule not enjoined upon the courts by legislative provision, but adopted by themselves, as consonant to truth and propriety, for the direction of their conduct as interpreters of the law. They thought it reasonable, that between the interfering acts of an EQUAL authority, that which was the last indication of its will should have the preference.

But in regard to the interfering acts of a superior and subordinate authority, of an original and derivative power, the nature and reason of the thing indicate the converse of that rule as proper to be followed. They teach us that the prior act of a superior ought to be preferred to the subsequent act of an inferior and subordinate authority; and that accordingly, whenever a particular statute contravenes the Constitution, it will be the duty of the judicial tribunals to adhere to the latter and disregard the former.

It can be of no weight to say that the courts, on the pretense of a repugnancy, may substitute their own pleasure to the constitutional intentions of the legislature. This might as well happen in the case of two contradictory statutes; or it might as well happen in every adjudication upon any single statute. The courts must declare the sense of the law; and if they should be disposed to exercise WILL instead of JUDGMENT, the consequence would equally be the substitution of their pleasure to that of the legislative body. The observation, if it prove any thing, would prove that there ought to be no judges distinct from that body.

If, then, the courts of justice are to be considered as the bulwarks of a limited Constitution against legislative encroachments, this consideration will afford a strong argument for the permanent tenure of judicial offices, since nothing will contribute so much as this to that independent spirit in the judges which must be essential to the faithful performance of so arduous a duty.

* * *

That inflexible and uniform adherence to the rights of the Constitution, and of individuals, which we perceive to be indispensable in the courts of justice, can certainly not be expected from judges who hold their offices by a temporary commission. Periodical appointments, however regulated, or by whomsoever made, would, in some way or other, be fatal to their necessary independence. If the power of making them was committed either to the Executive or legislature, there would be danger of an improper complaisance to the branch which possessed it; if to both, there would be an unwillingness to hazard the displeasure of either; if to the people, or to persons chosen by them for the special purpose, there would be too great a disposition to consult popularity, to justify a reliance that nothing would be consulted but the Constitution and the laws.

There is yet a further and a weightier reason for the permanency of the judicial offices, which is deducible from the nature of the qualifications they require. It has been frequently remarked, with great propriety, that a voluminous code of laws is one of the inconveniences necessarily connected with the advantages of a free government. To avoid an arbitrary discretion in the courts, it is indispensable that they should be bound down by strict rules and precedents, which serve to define and point out their duty in every particular case that comes before them; and it will readily be conceived from the variety of controversies which grow out of the folly and wickedness of mankind, that the records of those precedents must unavoidably swell to a very considerable bulk, and must demand long and laborious study to acquire a competent knowledge of them. Hence it is, that there can be but few men in the society who will have sufficient skill in the laws to qualify them for the stations of judges. And making the proper deductions for the ordinary depravity of human nature, the number must be still smaller of those who unite the requisite integrity with the requisite knowledge. These considerations apprise us, that the government can have no great option between fit character; and that a temporary duration in office, which would naturally discourage such characters from quitting a lucrative line of practice to accept a seat on the bench, would have a tendency to throw the administration of justice into hands less able, and less well qualified, to conduct it with utility and dignity. In the present circumstances of this country, and in those in which it is likely to be for a long time to come, the disadvantages on this score would be greater than they may at first sight appear; but it must be confessed, that they are far inferior to those which present themselves under the other aspects of the subject.

Upon the whole, there can be no room to doubt that the convention acted wisely in copying from the models of those constitutions which have established GOOD BEHAVIOR as the tenure of their judicial offices, in point of duration; and that so far from being blamable on this account, their plan would have been inexcusably defective, if it had wanted this important feature of good government. The experience of Great Britain affords an illustrious comment on the excellence of the institution.

NOTES AND QUESTIONS

1. Alexander Hamilton makes it quite clear in *The Federalist* No. 78 that, in his opinion, the federal courts were the weakest of the three branches of the federal government, lacking either the Power of the Purse or the Power of the Sword. Americans today would likely cite as examples of the judicial power: *Brown v. Board of Education*, 347 U.S. 483 (1954), striking down as unconstitutional the *de jure* racial segregation of public schools; the one-person, one-vote cases of the 1960s, *Baker v. Carr*, 369 U.S. 186 (1962), and *Reynolds v. Sims*, 377 U.S. 533 (1964); *Loving v. Virginia*, 388 U.S. 1 (1967), striking down racial anti-miscegenation laws; *Roe v. Wade*, 410 U.S. 113 (1973), recognizing a woman's right to an abortion; *Gregg v. Georgia*, 428 U.S. 153 (1976), reinstating the death penalty after a prior decision effectively invalidated it nationwide; *INS v. Chadha*, 462 U.S. 919 (1983), striking down more than 200 federal statutory legislative vetoes; *Morrison v. Olson*, 487 U.S. 654 (1988), upholding the Independent Counsel Act; *Bush v. Gore*, 531 U.S. 98 (2000), resolving the year 2000 presidential election; *Lawrence v. Texas*, 539 U.S. 558 (2003), invalidating all laws criminalizing sodomy; *Citizens United v. FEC*, 558 U.S. 310 (2010), striking down two federal election regulation statues; *Shelby County v. Holder*, 570 U.S. 529 (2013), invalidating portions of the Voting Rights Act of 1965; *Obergefell v. Hodges*, 576 U.S. ___, 135 S.Ct. 2584 (2015), finding a federal constitutional right, applicable to the fifty States, of same-sex marriage, and countless other landmark decisions that have changed the face of the country. Was Hamilton wrong? Or are the federal courts still the weakest federal institutions, given the concomitant growth in power of Congress and the President?

2. Does Hamilton anticipate that the courts will use, or not use, any particular modalities of interpretation?

3. Hamilton in the *Federalist* No. 78 seems to think it will be primarily the Article III federal courts which will interpret and enforce the original, pre-Bill of Rights Constitution. Does the famous essay below agree about that?

2. THE FEDERALIST NO. 51 (MADISON)

TO WHAT expedient, then, shall we finally resort, for maintaining in practice the necessary partition of power among the several departments, as laid down in the Constitution? The only answer that can be given is, that as all these exterior provisions are found to be inadequate, the defect must be supplied, by so contriving the interior structure of the government as that its several constituent parts may, by their mutual relations, be the means of keeping each other in their proper places. Without presuming to undertake a full development of this important idea, I will hazard a few general observations, which may perhaps place it in a clearer light, and enable us to form a more correct judgment of the principles and structure of the government planned by the convention.

In order to lay a due foundation for that separate and distinct exercise of the different powers of government, which to a certain extent is admitted on all hands to be essential to the preservation of liberty, it is evident that each department should have a will of its own; and consequently should be so constituted that the members of each should have as little agency as possible in the appointment of the members of the others. Were this principle rigorously adhered to, it would require that all the appointments for the supreme executive, legislative, and judiciary magistracies should be drawn from the same fountain of authority, the people, through channels having no communication whatever with one another. Perhaps such a plan of constructing the several departments would be less difficult in practice than it may in contemplation appear. Some difficulties, however, and some additional expense would attend the execution of it. Some deviations, therefore, from the principle must be admitted. In the constitution of the judiciary department in particular, it might be inexpedient to insist rigorously on the principle: first, because peculiar qualifications being essential in the members, the primary consideration ought to be to select that mode of choice which best secures these qualifications; secondly, because the permanent tenure by which the appointments are held in that department, must soon destroy all sense of dependence on the authority conferring them.

It is equally evident, that the members of each department should be as little dependent as possible on those of the others, for the emoluments annexed to their offices. Were the executive magistrate, or the judges, not independent of the legislature in this particular, their independence in every other would be merely nominal. But the great security against a gradual concentration of the several powers in the same department, consists in giving to those who administer each department the necessary constitutional means and personal motives to resist encroachments of the others. The provision for defense must in this, as in all other cases, be made commensurate to the danger of attack. Ambition must be made to counteract ambition. The interest of the man must be connected with the constitutional rights of the place. It may be a reflection on human nature, that such devices should be necessary to control the abuses of government. But what is government itself, but the greatest of all reflections on human nature? If men were angels, no government would be necessary. If angels were to govern men, neither external nor internal controls on government would be necessary. In framing a government which is to be administered by men over men, the great difficulty lies in this: you must first enable the government to control the governed; and in the next place oblige it to control itself.

A dependence on the people is, no doubt, the primary control on the government; but experience has taught mankind the necessity of auxiliary precautions. This policy of supplying, by opposite and rival interests, the defect of better motives, might be traced through the whole system of human affairs, private as well as public. We see it particularly displayed in all the subordinate distributions of power, where the constant aim is to divide and arrange the several offices in such a manner as that each may be a check on the other that the private interest of every individual may be a sentinel over the public rights. These inventions of prudence cannot be less requisite in the distribution of the supreme powers of the State. But it is not possible to give to each department an equal power of self-defense. In republican government, the legislative authority necessarily predominates. The remedy for this inconveniency is to divide the legislature into different branches; and to render them, by different modes of election and different principles of action, as little connected with each other as the nature of their common functions and their common dependence on the society will admit. It may even be necessary to guard against dangerous encroachments by still further precautions. As the weight of the legislative authority requires that it should be thus divided, the weakness of the executive may require, on the other hand, that it should be fortified.

* * *

There are, moreover, two considerations particularly applicable to the federal system of America, which place that system in a very interesting point of view. First. In a single republic, all the power surrendered by the people is submitted to the administration of a single government; and the usurpations are guarded against by a division of the government into distinct and separate departments. In the compound republic of America, the power surrendered by the people is first divided between two distinct governments, and then the portion allotted to each subdivided among distinct and separate departments. Hence a double security arises to the rights of the people. The different governments will control each other, at the same time that each will be controlled by itself. Second. It is of great importance in a republic not only to guard the society against the oppression of its rulers, but to guard one part of the society against the injustice of the other part. Different interests necessarily exist in different classes of citizens. If a majority be united by a common interest, the rights of the minority will be insecure.

There are but two methods of providing against this evil: the one by creating a will in the community independent of the majority that is, of the society itself; the other, by comprehending in the society so many separate descriptions of citizens as will render an unjust combination of a majority of the whole very improbable, if not impracticable. The first method prevails in all governments possessing an hereditary or self-appointed authority. This, at best, is but a precarious security; because a power independent of the society may as well espouse the unjust views of the major, as the rightful interests of the minor party, and may possibly be turned against both parties. The second method will be exemplified in the federal republic of the United States. Whilst all authority in it will be derived from and dependent on the society, the society itself will be broken into so many parts, interests, and classes of citizens, that the rights of individuals, or of the minority, will be in little danger from interested combinations of the majority.

NOTES AND QUESTIONS

1. Isn't it striking how little attention James Madison devotes in *The Federalist* No. 51 to judicial review as being the, or even a, mechanism by which the Constitution would be self-enforcing? Most Americans today labor under what we think is the mistaken impression that the Supreme Court is the principal enforcer of the structural Constitution, the Bill of Rights, and the Reconstruction constitutional amendments. Obviously, the Supreme Court does do all of this to some degree. But, as James Madison warns earlier in *The Federalist,* men should not put too much hope in judges, who are only human beings, enforcing "a mere parchment barrier" to keep their government from running off the rails. Madison argues that the Constitution will be enforced primarily by differently constituted, independent branches of government in a federal republic, with many States, all of which have their own separation of powers, ensuring that at the federal level "ambition will be made to counteract ambition." It is this federal structure of sovereign power, divided horizontally into three branches, and vertically into two levels of government, which will produce a political marketplace where self-interest will lead government officials to follow the Constitution and to respect the people's rights.

2. In contrast, Alexander Hamilton said in *The Federalist* No. 78 that: "The complete independence of the courts of justice is peculiarly essential in a limited Constitution * * *. Limitations of this kind can be preserved in practice no other way than through the medium of courts of justice, whose duty it must be to declare all acts contrary to the manifest tenor of the Constitution void. Without this, all the reservations of

particular rights or privileges would amount to nothing." Hamilton thus looks for constitutional enforcement to the federal courts, which he rightly expects will be the aristocratic part of the government—a part he expects to favor the most. Madison says something entirely different. "Ambition counteracting ambition" is what will enforce the Constitution. The federal courts will play a role in that struggle, but they will not be the superstars. Presidents, senators, governors, and ordinary citizens perhaps playing extraordinary roles will be the stars. Has history proved Hamilton right? Have judges been the guardians of the Constitution? The course is not nearly over, so perhaps it is premature to make that judgment now. Whatever the answer proves to be, federal courts have definitely played a role that neither Hamilton nor Madison could have envisioned. To some extent, that is a result of constitutional amendments, which we will study in more detail later, that place States under constitutional restraints that would have been unthinkable in 1788. But even taking all of that into account, federal courts today are central actors in areas that make it very hard to think of them as having either Hamiltonian weakness or Madisonian lack of relevance.

3. In another essay, Hamilton suggested that judicial review was clearly necessary to rein in the *States*:

> The States, by the plan of the convention, are prohibited from doing a variety of things, some of which are incompatible with the interests of the Union, and others with the principles of good government. The imposition of duties on imported articles, and the emission of paper money, are specimens of each kind. No man of sense will believe, that such prohibitions would be scrupulously regarded, without some effectual power in the government to restrain or correct the infractions of them. This power must either be a direct negative on the State laws, or an authority in the federal courts to overrule such as might be in manifest contravention of the articles of Union. There is no third course that I can imagine. The latter appears to have been thought by the convention preferable to the former, and, I presume, will be most agreeable to the States.

The Federalist No. 80 (Hamilton). Does Madison have anything to say about that topic? Keep in mind that under the original Constitution, the state legislatures directly selected the Senate. In that scheme, would Congress be an effective guard against state encroachments on the Constitution? Does the move to popular election of the Senate change that dynamic significantly?

4. In yet another essay, Hamilton dismissed worries that the federal courts' power of judgment was too powerful because it could be misused to trench on the proper sphere of the legislature:

> It may in the last place be observed that the supposed danger of judiciary encroachments on the legislative authority, which has been upon many occasions reiterated, is in reality a phantom. Particular misconstructions and contraventions of the will of the legislature may now and then happen; but they can never be so extensive as to amount to an inconvenience, or in any sensible degree to affect the order of the political system. This may be inferred with certainty, from the general nature of the judicial power, from the objects to which it relates, from the manner in which it is exercised, from its comparative weakness, and from its total incapacity to support its usurpations by force. And the inference is greatly fortified by the consideration of the important constitutional check which the power of instituting impeachments in one part of the legislative body, and of determining upon them in the other, would give to that body upon the members of the judicial department. This is alone a complete security. There never can be danger that the judges, by a series of

> deliberate usurpations on the authority of the legislature, would hazard the united resentment of the body intrusted with it, while this body was possessed of the means of punishing their presumption, by degrading them from their stations. While this ought to remove all apprehensions on the subject, it affords, at the same time, a cogent argument for constituting the Senate a court for the trial of impeachments.

The Federalist No. 81 (Hamilton). Was Hamilton suggesting that Congress should regularly impeach judges for making what Congress regards as bad decisions? Without that kind of policing, what would Hamilton think constrains the judges to stay within the law? What would Madison think constrains the judges to stay within the law?

To explore these issues preliminarily, we present at this point two relatively recent (and, as is usually the case in this and other law school courses, heavily edited) Supreme Court cases, which were highly controversial when they were argued and which the Supreme Court decided by a 5–4 margin. Both of the cases involve constitutional clauses and doctrines that we have not yet studied, so do not focus too carefully on the underlying doctrine. What is so striking about both of these cases is that the losing side generally accepted that it had lost and followed the Supreme Court's judgments (though it is easy to overstate this effect). These cases demonstrate: 1) that the modern Supreme Court decides on 5–4 votes highly controversial and important issues; and 2) that most of the general public (even if not all of it) normally accepts the Supreme Court's judgments as the last word on the subject, even when the People may disagree with the Supreme Court. These two cases illustrate the Supreme Court's widespread legitimacy in the eyes of modern Americans and the very broad scope of its Power of Judgment. And, for whatever it is worth, the editors do not agree with each other on the proper resolution of either of these cases, notwithstanding their general agreement on methodology and modalities. Does that suggest anything about exactly how we should understand the term "Judgment" in the phrase "the power of Judgment"?

Bush v. Gore

531 U.S. 98 (2000)

■ PER CURIAM.

On December 8, 2000, the Supreme Court of Florida ordered that the Circuit Court of Leon County tabulate by hand 9,000 ballots in Miami-Dade County. It also ordered the inclusion in the certified vote totals of 215 votes identified in Palm Beach County and 168 votes identified in Miami-Dade County for Vice President Albert Gore, Jr., and Senator Joseph Lieberman, Democratic Candidates for President and Vice President. The State Supreme Court noted that petitioner [Governor] George W. Bush asserted that the net gain for Vice President Gore in Palm Beach County was 176 votes, and directed the Circuit Court to resolve that dispute on remand. The court further held that relief would require manual recounts in all Florida counties where so-called "undervotes" had not been subject to manual tabulation. The court ordered all manual recounts to begin at once. Governor Bush and Richard Cheney, Republican Candidates for the Presidency and Vice Presidency, filed an emergency application for a stay of this mandate. On December 9, we granted the application, treated the application as a petition for a writ of certiorari, and granted certiorari.

* * * On November 8, 2000, the day following the Presidential election, the Florida Division of Elections reported that petitioner Governor Bush had received 2,909,135 votes, and respondent Gore had received 2,907,351 votes, a margin of 1,784

for Governor Bush. Because Governor Bush's margin of victory was less than "one-half of a percent . . . of the votes cast," an automatic machine recount was conducted under § 102.141(4) of the Florida Election Code, the results of which showed Governor Bush still winning the race but by a diminished margin. Vice President Gore then sought manual recounts in Volusia, Palm Beach, Broward, and Miami-Dade Counties, pursuant to Florida's election protest provisions. Fla. Stat. § 102.166. A dispute arose concerning the deadline for local county canvassing boards to submit their returns to the Secretary of State (Secretary). The Secretary declined to waive the November 14 deadline imposed by statute. §§ 102.111, 102.112. The Florida Supreme Court, however, set the deadline at November 26. We granted certiorari and vacated the Florida Supreme Court's decision, finding considerable uncertainty as to the grounds on which it was based. On December 11, the Florida Supreme Court issued a decision on remand reinstating that date.

On November 26, the Florida Elections Canvassing Commission certified the results of the election and declared Governor Bush the winner of Florida's 25 electoral votes. On November 27, Vice President Gore, pursuant to Florida's contest provisions, filed a complaint in Leon County Circuit Court contesting the certification. Fla. Stat. § 102.168. He sought relief pursuant to § 102.168(3)(c), which provides that "[r]eceipt of a number of illegal votes or rejection of a number of legal votes sufficient to change or place in doubt the result of the election" shall be grounds for a contest. The Circuit Court denied relief, stating that Vice President Gore failed to meet his burden of proof. He appealed to the First District Court of Appeal, which certified the matter to the Florida Supreme Court.

Accepting jurisdiction, the Florida Supreme Court affirmed in part and reversed in part. *Gore* v. *Harris,* 772 So. 2d. 1243 (2000). The court held that the Circuit Court had been correct to reject Vice President Gore's challenge to the results certified in Nassau County and his challenge to the Palm Beach County Canvassing Board's determination that 3,300 ballots cast in that county were not, in the statutory phrase, "legal votes."

The [Florida] Supreme Court held that Vice President Gore had satisfied his burden of proof under § 102.168(3)(c) with respect to his challenge to Miami-Dade County's failure to tabulate, by manual count, 9,000 ballots on which the machines had failed to detect a vote for President ("undervotes"). Noting the closeness of the election, the court explained that "[o]n this record, there can be no question that there are legal votes within the 9,000 uncounted votes sufficient to place the results of this election in doubt." A "legal vote," as determined by the [Florida] Supreme Court, is "one in which there is a 'clear indication of the intent of the voter.' " The court therefore ordered a hand recount of the 9,000 ballots in Miami-Dade County. Observing that the contest provisions vest broad discretion in the circuit judge to "provide any relief appropriate under such circumstances," Fla. Stat. § 102.168(8), the Supreme Court further held that the Circuit Court could order "the Supervisor of Elections and the Canvassing Boards, as well as the necessary public officials, in all counties that have not conducted a manual recount or tabulation of the undervotes . . . to do so forthwith, said tabulation to take place in the individual counties where the ballots are located." *Id.* at 1262.

The [Florida] Supreme Court also determined that both Palm Beach County and Miami-Dade County, in their earlier manual recounts, had identified a net gain of 215 and 168 legal votes for Vice President Gore. Rejecting the Circuit Court's conclusion that Palm Beach County lacked the authority to include the 215 net votes submitted past the November 26 deadline, the Supreme Court explained that the deadline was not intended to exclude votes identified after that date through ongoing manual recounts. As to Miami-Dade County, the court concluded that although the 168 votes identified were the result of a partial recount, they were "legal votes [that] could change the outcome of the election." The [Florida] Supreme Court therefore directed the Circuit Court to include those totals in the certified results, subject to resolution of the actual vote total from the Miami-Dade partial recount.

The petition presents the following questions: whether the Florida Supreme Court established new standards for resolving Presidential election contests, thereby violating Art. II, § 1, cl. 2, of the United States Constitution and failing to comply with 3 U.S.C. § 5 and whether the use of standardless manual recounts violates the Equal Protection and Due Process Clauses. With respect to the equal protection question, we find a violation of the Equal Protection Clause.

* * * The individual citizen has no federal constitutional right to vote for electors for the President of the United States unless and until the state legislature chooses a statewide election as the means to implement its power to appoint members of the Electoral College. U.S. Const., Art. II, § 1. This is the source for the statement in *McPherson* v. *Blacker*, 146 U.S. 1, 35 (1892), that the state legislature's power to select the manner for appointing electors is plenary; it may, if it so chooses, select the electors itself, which indeed was the manner used by state legislatures in several States for many years after the framing of our Constitution. *Id.*, at 28–33. History has now favored the voter, and in each of the several States the citizens themselves vote for Presidential electors. When the state legislature vests the right to vote for President in its people, the right to vote as the legislature has prescribed is fundamental; and one source of its fundamental nature lies in the equal weight accorded to each vote and the equal dignity owed to each voter. The State, of course, after granting the franchise in the special context of Article II, can take back the power to appoint electors. See *id.*, at 35 ("[T]here is no doubt of the right of the legislature to resume the power at any time, for it can neither be taken away nor abdicated") (quoting S. Rep. No. 395, 43d Cong., 1st Sess. 9 (1874)).

The right to vote is protected in more than the initial allocation of the franchise. Equal protection applies as well to the manner of its exercise. Having once granted the right to vote on equal terms, the State may not, by later arbitrary and disparate treatment, value one person's vote over that of another. It must be remembered that "the right of suffrage can be denied by a debasement or dilution of the weight of a citizen's vote just as effectively as by wholly prohibiting the free exercise of the franchise." *Reynolds* v. *Sims*, 377 U.S. 533, 555 (1964).

* * *

Much of the controversy seems to revolve around ballot cards designed to be perforated by a stylus but which, either through error or deliberate omission, have not been perforated with sufficient precision for a machine to count them. In some cases a piece of the card—a chad—is hanging, say, by two corners. In other cases there is no separation at all, just an indentation.

The Florida Supreme Court has ordered that the intent of the voter be discerned from such ballots. For purposes of resolving the equal protection challenge, it is not necessary to decide whether the Florida Supreme Court had the authority under the legislative scheme for resolving election disputes to define what a legal vote is and to mandate a manual recount implementing that definition. The recount mechanisms implemented in response to the decisions of the Florida Supreme Court do not satisfy the minimum requirement for nonarbitrary treatment of voters necessary to secure the fundamental right. Florida's basic command for the count of legally cast votes is to consider the "intent of the voter." 772 So.2d at 1262. This is unobjectionable as an abstract proposition and a starting principle. The problem inheres in the absence of specific standards to ensure its equal application. The formulation of uniform rules to determine intent based on these recurring circumstances is practicable and, we conclude, necessary.

The law does not refrain from searching for the intent of the actor in a multitude of circumstances; and in some cases the general command to ascertain intent is not susceptible to much further refinement. In this instance, however, the question is not whether to believe a witness but how to interpret the marks or holes or scratches on an inanimate object, a piece of cardboard or paper which, it is said, might not have registered as a vote during the machine count. The factfinder confronts a thing, not a person. The search for intent can be confined by specific rules designed to ensure uniform treatment.

The want of those rules here has led to unequal evaluation of ballots in various respects. As seems to have been acknowledged at oral argument, the standards for accepting or rejecting contested ballots might vary not only from county to county but indeed within a single county from one recount team to another.

The record provides some examples. A monitor in Miami-Dade County testified at trial that he observed that three members of the county canvassing board applied different standards in defining a legal vote. 3 Tr. 497, 499 (Dec. 3, 2000). And testimony at trial also revealed that at least one county changed its evaluative standards during the counting process. Palm Beach County, for example, began the process with a 1990 guideline which precluded counting completely attached chads, switched to a rule that considered a vote to be legal if any light could be seen through a chad, changed back to the 1990 rule, and then abandoned any pretense of a *per se* rule, only to have a court order that the county consider dimpled chads legal. This is not a process with sufficient guarantees of equal treatment.

* * *

The recount process, in its features here described, is inconsistent with the minimum procedures necessary to protect the fundamental right of each voter in the special instance of a statewide recount under the authority of a single state judicial officer. Our consideration is limited to the present circumstances, for the problem of equal protection in election processes generally presents many complexities.

The question before the Court is not whether local entities, in the exercise of their expertise, may develop different systems for implementing elections. Instead, we are presented with a situation where a state court with the power to assure uniformity has ordered a statewide recount with minimal procedural safeguards. When a court orders a statewide remedy, there must be at least some assurance that the rudimentary requirements of equal treatment and fundamental fairness are satisfied.

* * *

Upon due consideration of the difficulties identified to this point, it is obvious that the recount cannot be conducted in compliance with the requirements of equal protection and due process without substantial additional work. It would require not only the adoption (after opportunity for argument) of adequate statewide standards for determining what is a legal vote, and practicable procedures to implement them, but also orderly judicial review of any disputed matters that might arise * * *.

The Supreme Court of Florida has said that the legislature intended the State's electors to "participat[e] fully in the federal electoral process," as provided in 3 U.S.C. § 5. That statute, in turn, requires that any controversy or contest that is designed to lead to a conclusive selection of electors be completed by December 12. That date is upon us, and there is no recount procedure in place under the State Supreme Court's order that comports with minimal constitutional standards. Because it is evident that any recount seeking to meet the December 12 date will be unconstitutional for the reasons we have discussed, we reverse the judgment of the Supreme Court of Florida ordering a recount to proceed.

Seven Justices of the Court agree that there are constitutional problems with the recount ordered by the Florida Supreme Court that demand a remedy. See post, at 134 (SOUTER, J., dissenting); *post*, at 145–46 (BREYER, J., dissenting). The only disagreement is as to the remedy. Because the Florida Supreme Court has said that the Florida Legislature intended to obtain the safe-harbor benefits of 3 U.S.C. § 5, Justice BREYER's proposed remedy—remanding to the Florida Supreme Court for its ordering of a constitutionally proper contest until December 18—contemplates action in violation of the Florida Election Code, and hence could not be part of an "appropriate" order authorized by Fla. Stat. Ann. § 102.168(8).

None are more conscious of the vital limits on judicial authority than are the Members of this Court, and none stand more in admiration of the Constitution's design to leave the selection of the President to the people, through their legislatures, and to the political sphere. When contending parties invoke the process of the courts, however, it becomes our unsought responsibility to resolve the federal and constitutional issues the judicial system has been forced to confront.

The judgment of the Supreme Court of Florida is reversed, and the case is remanded for further proceedings not inconsistent with this opinion.

* * *.

■ CHIEF JUSTICE REHNQUIST, with whom JUSTICE SCALIA and JUSTICE THOMAS join, concurring.

We join the *per curiam* opinion. We write separately because we believe there are additional grounds that require us to reverse the Florida Supreme Court's decision.

* * *

In most cases, comity and respect for federalism compel us to defer to the decisions of state courts on issues of state law. That practice reflects our understanding that the decisions of state courts are definitive pronouncements of the will of the States as sovereigns. Of course, in ordinary cases, the distribution of powers among the branches of a State's government raises no questions of federal constitutional law, subject to the requirement that the government be republican in character. See U.S. Const., Art. IV, § 4. But there are a few exceptional cases in which the Constitution imposes a duty or confers a power on a particular branch of a State's government. This is one of them. Article II, § 1, cl. 2, provides that "[e]ach State shall appoint, in such Manner as the *Legislature* thereof may direct," electors for President and Vice President. (Emphasis added.) Thus, the text of the election law itself, and not just its interpretation by the courts of the States, takes on independent significance.

* * *

* * * [T]he Florida Supreme Court's interpretation of the Florida election laws impermissibly distorted them beyond what a fair reading required, in violation of Article II.

* * *

Acting pursuant to its constitutional grant of authority, the Florida Legislature has created a detailed, if not perfectly crafted, statutory scheme that provides for appointment of Presidential electors by direct election. Fla. Stat. Ann. § 103.011 (1992). Under the statute, "[v]otes cast for the actual candidates for President and Vice President shall be counted as votes cast for the presidential electors supporting such candidates." *Ibid.* The legislature has designated the Secretary [of State] as the "chief election officer," with the responsibility to "[o]btain and maintain uniformity in the application, operation, and interpretation of the election laws." Fla. Stat. Ann. § 97.012. The state legislature has delegated to county canvassing boards the duties of administering elections. § 102.141. Those boards are responsible for providing results to the state Elections Canvassing Commission, comprising the Governor, the Secretary of State, and the Director of the Division of Elections. § 102.111.

After the election has taken place, the canvassing boards receive returns from precincts, count the votes, and in the event that a candidate was defeated by 0.5% or less, conduct a mandatory recount. Fla. Stat. § 102.141(4). The county canvassing boards must file certified election returns with the Department of State by 5 p.m. on the seventh day following the election. § 102.112(1). The Elections Canvassing Commission must then certify the results of the election. § 102.111(1).

The state legislature has also provided mechanisms both for protesting election returns and for contesting certified election results. Section 102.166 governs protests. Any protest must be filed prior to the certification of election results by the county canvassing board. § 102.166(4)(b). Once a protest has been filed, "[t]he county canvassing board may authorize a manual recount." § 102.166(4)(c). If a sample recount conducted pursuant to § 102.166(5) "indicates an error in the vote tabulation which could affect the outcome of the election," the county canvassing board is instructed to: "(a) Correct the error and recount the remaining precincts with the vote tabulation system; (b) Request the Department of State to verify the tabulation software; or (c) Manually recount all ballots," § 102.166(5). In the event a canvassing board chooses to conduct a manual recount of all ballots, § 102.166(7) prescribes procedures for such a recount.

Contests to the certification of an election, on the other hand, are controlled by § 102.168. The grounds for contesting an election include "[r]eceipt of a number of illegal votes or rejection of a number of legal votes sufficient to change or place in doubt the result of the election." § 102.168(3)(c). Any contest must be filed in the appropriate Florida circuit court, § 102.168(1), and the canvassing board or election board is the proper party defendant, § 102.168(4). Section 102.168(8) provides that "[t]he circuit judge to whom the contest is presented may fashion such orders as he or she deems necessary to ensure that each allegation in the complaint is investigated, examined, or checked, to prevent or correct any alleged wrong, and to provide any relief appropriate under such circumstances." In Presidential elections, the contest period necessarily terminates on the date set by 3 U.S.C. § 5 for concluding the State's "final determination" of election controversies.

In its first decision, *Palm Beach Canvassing Bd. v. Harris,* 772 So.2d 1220 (2000) (*Harris I*), the Florida Supreme Court extended the 7-day statutory certification deadline established by the legislature. This modification of the code, by lengthening the protest period, necessarily shortened the contest period for Presidential elections. Underlying the extension of the certification deadline and the shortchanging of the contest period was, presumably, the clear implication that certification was a matter of significance: The certified winner would enjoy presumptive validity, making a contest proceeding by the losing candidate an uphill battle. In its latest opinion, however, the court empties certification of virtually all legal consequence during the contest, and in doing so departs from the provisions enacted by the Florida Legislature.

The court determined that canvassing boards' decisions regarding whether to recount ballots past the certification deadline (even the certification deadline established by *Harris I*) are to be reviewed *de novo,* although the Election Code clearly vests discretion whether to recount in the boards, and sets strict deadlines subject to the Secretary's rejection of late tallies and monetary fines for tardiness. See Fla. Stat. Ann. § 102.112. Moreover, the Florida court held that all late vote tallies arriving during the contest period should be automatically included in the certification regardless of the certification deadline (even the certification deadline established by *Harris I*), thus virtually eliminating both the deadline and the Secretary's discretion to disregard recounts that violate it.

Moreover, the court's interpretation of "legal vote," and hence its decision to order a contest-period recount, plainly departed from the legislative scheme. Florida statutory law cannot reasonably be thought to *require* the counting of improperly marked ballots. Each Florida precinct before election day provides instructions on how properly to cast a vote, each polling place on election day contains a working model of the voting machine it uses, and each voting booth contains a sample ballot. In precincts using punchcard ballots, voters are instructed to punch out the ballot cleanly * * *.

No reasonable person would call it "an error in the vote tabulation," Fla. Stat. Ann. § 102.166(5), or a "rejection of . . . legal votes," § 102.168(3)(c), when electronic or electromechanical equipment performs precisely in the manner designed, and fails to count those ballots that are not marked in the manner that these voting instructions explicitly and prominently specify. The scheme that the Florida Supreme Court's opinion attributes to the legislature is one in which machines are *required* to be "capable of correctly counting votes," § 101.5606(4), but which nonetheless regularly produces elections in which legal votes are predictably *not* tabulated, so that in close elections manual recounts are regularly required. This is of course absurd. The Secretary, who is authorized by law to issue binding interpretations of the Election Code, §§ 97.012, 106.23, rejected this peculiar reading of the statutes. See DE 00–13 (opinion of the Division of Elections). The Florida Supreme Court, although it must defer to the Secretary's interpretations, see

Krivanek v. Take Back Tampa Political Committee, 625 So.2d 840, 844 (Fla.1993), rejected her reasonable interpretation and embraced the peculiar one. See *Palm Beach County Canvassing Bd. v. Harris,* 772 So.2d 1273 (2000) (*Harris III*).

* * * For the court to step away from this established practice, prescribed by the Secretary, the state official charged by the legislature with "responsibility to . . . [o]btain and maintain uniformity in the application, operation, and interpretation of the election laws," § 97.012(1), was to depart from the legislative scheme.

* * *

For these reasons, in addition to those given in the *per curiam* opinion, we would reverse.

■ JUSTICE STEVENS, with whom JUSTICE GINSBURG and JUSTICE BREYER join, dissenting.

The Constitution assigns to the States the primary responsibility for determining the manner of selecting the Presidential electors. See Art. II, § 1, cl. 2. When questions arise about the meaning of state laws, including election laws, it is our settled practice to accept the opinions of the highest courts of the States as providing the final answers. On rare occasions, however, either federal statutes or the Federal Constitution may require federal judicial intervention in state elections. This is not such an occasion.

The federal questions that ultimately emerged in this case are not substantial * * *.

* * *

Nor are petitioners correct in asserting that the failure of the Florida Supreme Court to specify in detail the precise manner in which the "intent of the voter," Fla. Stat. § 101.5614(5), is to be determined rises to the level of a constitutional violation. We found such a violation when individual votes within the same State were weighted unequally, see, *e.g., Reynolds* v. *Sims*, 377 U.S. 533, 568 (1964), but we have never before called into question the substantive standard by which a State determines that a vote has been legally cast * * *.

Admittedly, the use of differing substandards for determining voter intent in different counties employing similar voting systems may raise serious concerns. Those concerns are alleviated—if not eliminated—by the fact that a single impartial magistrate will ultimately adjudicate all objections arising from the recount process * * *.

* * *

In the interest of finality, however, the majority effectively orders the disenfranchisement of an unknown number of voters whose ballots reveal their intent—and are therefore legal votes under state law—but were for some reason rejected by ballot-counting machines * * *.

* * * [Nor] did the Florida Supreme Court make any substantive change in Florida electoral law. Its decisions were rooted in long-established precedent and were consistent with the relevant statutory provisions, taken as a whole. It did what courts do—it decided the case before it in light of the legislature's intent to leave no legally cast vote uncounted * * *. If we assume—as I do—that the members of that

court and the judges who would have carried out its mandate are impartial, its decision does not even raise a colorable federal question.

What must underlie petitioners' entire federal assault on the Florida election procedures is an unstated lack of confidence in the impartiality and capacity of the state judges who would make the critical decisions if the vote count were to proceed. Otherwise, their position is wholly without merit. The endorsement of that position by the majority of this Court can only lend credence to the most cynical appraisal of the work of judges throughout the land. It is confidence in the men and women who administer the judicial system that is the true backbone of the rule of law. Time will one day heal the wound to that confidence that will be inflicted by today's decision. One thing, however, is certain. Although we may never know with complete certainty the identity of the winner of this year's Presidential election, the identity of the loser is perfectly clear. It is the Nation's confidence in the judge as an impartial guardian of the rule of law. I respectfully dissent.

■ JUSTICE SOUTER, with whom JUSTICE BREYER joins, and with whom JUSTICE STEVENS and JUSTICE GINSBURG join as to all but Part III, dissenting.

* * *

* * * I am in substantial agreement with the dissenting opinions of Justice STEVENS, Justice GINSBURG, and Justice BREYER. I write separately only to say how straightforward the issues before us really are.

* * *

■ JUSTICE GINSBURG, with whom JUSTICE STEVENS joins, and with whom JUSTICE SOUTER and JUSTICE BREYER join as to Part I, dissenting.

THE CHIEF JUSTICE acknowledges that provisions of Florida's Election Code "may well admit of more than one interpretation." But instead of respecting the state high court's province to say what the State's Election Code means, THE CHIEF JUSTICE maintains that Florida's Supreme Court has veered so far from the ordinary practice of judicial review that what it did cannot properly be called judging. My colleagues have offered a reasonable construction of Florida's law. Their construction coincides with the view of one of Florida's seven Supreme Court justices. I might join THE CHIEF JUSTICE were it my commission to interpret Florida law. But disagreement with the Florida court's interpretation of its own State's law does not warrant the conclusion that the justices of that court have legislated. There is no cause here to believe that the members of Florida's high court have done less than "their mortal best to discharge their oath of office," *Sumner v. Mata,* 449 U.S. 539, 549 (1981), and no cause to upset their reasoned interpretation of Florida law.

* * *

I agree with Justice STEVENS that petitioners have not presented a substantial equal protection claim. Ideally, perfection would be the appropriate standard for judging the recount. But we live in an imperfect world, one in which thousands of votes have not been counted. I cannot agree that the recount adopted by the Florida court, flawed as it may be, would yield a result any less fair or precise than the certification that preceded that recount.

* * *

■ JUSTICE BREYER, with whom JUSTICE STEVENS and JUSTICE GINSBURG join except as to Part I-A-1, and with whom JUSTICE SOUTER joins as to Part I, dissenting.

* * *

The political implications of this case for the country are momentous. But the federal legal questions presented, with one exception, are insubstantial.

The majority raises three equal protection problems with the Florida Supreme Court's recount order: first, the failure to include overvotes in the manual recount; second, the fact that *all* ballots, rather than simply the undervotes, were recounted in some, but not all, counties; and third, the absence of a uniform, specific standard to guide the recounts. As far as the first issue is concerned, petitioners presented no evidence, to this Court or to any Florida court, that a manual recount of overvotes would identify additional legal votes. The same is true of the second, and, in addition, the majority's reasoning would seem to invalidate any state provision for a manual recount of individual counties in a statewide election.

The majority's third concern does implicate principles of fundamental fairness. The majority concludes that the Equal Protection Clause requires that a manual recount be governed not only by the uniform general standard of the "clear intent of the voter," but also by uniform subsidiary standards (for example, a uniform determination whether indented, but not perforated, "undervotes" should count). The opinion points out that the Florida Supreme Court ordered the inclusion of Broward County's undercounted "legal votes" even though those votes included ballots that were not perforated but simply "dimpled," while newly recounted ballots from other counties will likely include only votes determined to be "legal" on the basis of a stricter standard. In light of our previous remand, the Florida Supreme Court may have been reluctant to adopt a more specific standard than that provided for by the legislature for fear of exceeding its authority under Article II. However, since the use of different standards could favor one or the other of the candidates, since time was, and is, too short to permit the lower courts to iron out significant differences through ordinary judicial review, and since the relevant distinction was embodied in the order of the State's highest court, I agree that, in these very special circumstances, basic principles of fairness may well have counseled the adoption of a uniform standard to address the problem. In light of the majority's disposition, I need not decide whether, or the extent to which, as a remedial matter, the Constitution would place limits upon the content of the uniform standard.

Nonetheless, there is no justification for the majority's remedy, which is simply to reverse the lower court and halt the recount entirely. An appropriate remedy would be, instead, to remand this case with instructions that, even at this late date, would permit the Florida Supreme Court to require recounting *all* undercounted votes in Florida, including those from Broward, Volusia, Palm Beach, and Miami-Dade Counties, whether or not previously recounted prior to the end of the protest period, and to do so in accordance with a single uniform standard.

* * *

NOTES AND QUESTIONS

1. After the Supreme Court's opinion was issued in *Bush v. Gore*, Vice President Al Gore conceded defeat, and George W. Bush was sworn in as President on January 20, 2001. Gallup polls continued to show the Supreme Court as being the institution of the federal government in which the voters had the most confidence. More Republicans than Democrats temporarily said they had confidence in the Supreme Court, but with the

passage of time those partisan approval numbers returned to what they had been before *Bush v. Gore*. The Court's Power of Judgment was accepted by most Americans as a legitimate way in which to resolve a closely fought, and very partisan, presidential election. The Supreme Court may not have either the Power of the Purse or the Power of the Sword, but its Power of Judgment is formidable by any measure.

2. The doctrinal issues in this case span a range of provisions, including the Equal Protection Clause, which we have not yet addressed. Those issues involve the relationship of the federal courts to state legal institutions. That topic will loom large in the next chapter, though we will not take up the niceties of equal protection doctrine until much later.

3. One possible resolution of the case would have been to decide that it was a political question into which the federal courts should not intervene. *See* Steven G. Calabresi, *A Political Question, in* BUSH V. GORE: THE QUESTION OF LEGITIMACY (Bruce Ackerman ed., 2002). In that case, who would decide which person was properly elected President in 2000?

4. During the election controversy in 2000, the Florida Secretary of State was a Republican, while a majority of the Florida Supreme Court had been appointed by Democratic governors and a majority of the canvassers examining ballots in the four counties conducting recounts were Democrats. Is any of that relevant to federal constitutional law?

Obergefell v. Hodges

576 U.S. ___, 135 S.Ct. 2584 (2015)

■ JUSTICE KENNEDY delivered the opinion of the Court.

The Constitution promises liberty to all within its reach, a liberty that includes certain specific rights that allow persons, within a lawful realm, to define and express their identity. The petitioners in these cases seek to find that liberty by marrying someone of the same sex and having their marriages deemed lawful on the same terms and conditions as marriages between persons of the opposite sex.

These cases come from Michigan, Kentucky, Ohio, and Tennessee, States that define marriage as a union between one man and one woman. See, *e.g.*, Mich. Const., Art. I, § 25; Ky. Const. § 233A; Ohio Rev. Code Ann. § 3101.01 (Lexis 2008); Tenn. Const., Art. XI, § 18. The petitioners are 14 same-sex couples and two men whose same-sex partners are deceased. The respondents are state officials responsible for enforcing the laws in question. The petitioners claim the respondents violate the Fourteenth Amendment by denying them the right to marry or to have their marriages, lawfully performed in another State, given full recognition.

* * * Before addressing the principles and precedents that govern these cases, it is appropriate to note the history of the subject now before the Court.

From their beginning to their most recent page, the annals of human history reveal the transcendent importance of marriage. The lifelong union of a man and a woman always has promised nobility and dignity to all persons, without regard to their station in life. Marriage is sacred to those who live by their religions and offers unique fulfillment to those who find meaning in the secular realm. Its dynamic allows two people to find a life that could not be found alone, for a marriage becomes greater than just the two persons. Rising from the most basic human needs, marriage is essential to our most profound hopes and aspirations.

The centrality of marriage to the human condition makes it unsurprising that the institution has existed for millennia and across civilizations. Since the dawn of history, marriage has transformed strangers into relatives, binding families and societies together. Confucius taught that marriage lies at the foundation of government. 2 Li Chi: Book of Rites 266 (C. Chai & W. Chai eds., J. Legge transl. 1967). This wisdom was echoed centuries later and half a world away by Cicero, who wrote, "The first bond of society is marriage; next, children; and then the family." See De Officiis 57 (W. Miller transl. 1913). There are untold references to the beauty of marriage in religious and philosophical texts spanning time, cultures, and faiths, as well as in art and literature in all their forms. It is fair and necessary to say these references were based on the understanding that marriage is a union between two persons of the opposite sex.

That history is the beginning of these cases. The respondents say it should be the end as well. To them, it would demean a timeless institution if the concept and lawful status of marriage were extended to two persons of the same sex. Marriage, in their view, is by its nature a gender-differentiated union of man and woman. This view long has been held—and continues to be held—in good faith by reasonable and sincere people here and throughout the world.

The petitioners acknowledge this history but contend that these cases cannot end there. Were their intent to demean the revered idea and reality of marriage, the petitioners' claims would be of a different order. But that is neither their purpose nor their submission. To the contrary, it is the enduring importance of marriage that underlies the petitioners' contentions. This, they say, is their whole point. Far from seeking to devalue marriage, the petitioners seek it for themselves because of their respect—and need—for its privileges and responsibilities. And their immutable nature dictates that same-sex marriage is their only real path to this profound commitment.

* * *

The ancient origins of marriage confirm its centrality, but it has not stood in isolation from developments in law and society. The history of marriage is one of both continuity and change. That institution—even as confined to opposite-sex relations—has evolved over time.

For example, marriage was once viewed as an arrangement by the couple's parents based on political, religious, and financial concerns; but by the time of the Nation's founding it was understood to be a voluntary contract between a man and a woman. See N. Cott, Public Vows: A History of Marriage and the Nation 9–17 (2000); S. Coontz, Marriage, A History 15–16 (2005). As the role and status of women changed, the institution further evolved. Under the centuries-old doctrine of coverture, a married man and woman were treated by the State as a single, male-dominated legal entity. See 1 W. Blackstone, Commentaries on the Laws of England 430 (1765). As women gained legal, political, and property rights, and as society began to understand that women have their own equal dignity, the law of coverture was abandoned. See Brief for Historians of Marriage et al. as *Amici Curiae* 16–19. These and other developments in the institution of marriage over the past centuries were not mere superficial changes. Rather, they worked deep transformations in its structure, affecting aspects of marriage long viewed by many as essential.

These new insights have strengthened, not weakened, the institution of marriage. Indeed, changed understandings of marriage are characteristic of a Nation where new dimensions of freedom become apparent to new generations, often through perspectives that begin in pleas or protests and then are considered in the political sphere and the judicial process.

This dynamic can be seen in the Nation's experiences with the rights of gays and lesbians. Until the mid-20th century, same-sex intimacy long had been condemned as immoral by the state itself in most Western nations, a belief often embodied in the criminal law. For this reason, among others, many persons did not deem homosexuals to have dignity in their own distinct identity. A truthful declaration by same-sex couples of what was in their hearts had to remain unspoken. Even when a greater awareness of the humanity and integrity of homosexual persons came in the period after World War II, the argument that gays and lesbians had a just claim to dignity was in conflict with both law and widespread social conventions. Same-sex intimacy remained a crime in many States. Gays and lesbians were prohibited from most government employment, barred from military service, excluded under immigration laws, targeted by police, and burdened in their rights to associate.

For much of the 20th century, moreover, homosexuality was treated as an illness. When the American Psychiatric Association published the first Diagnostic and Statistical Manual of Mental Disorders in 1952, homosexuality was classified as a mental disorder, a position adhered to until 1973. See Position Statement on Homosexuality and Civil Rights, 1973, in 131 Am. J. Psychiatry 497 (1974). Only in more recent years have psychiatrists and others recognized that sexual orientation is both a normal expression of human sexuality and immutable. See Brief for American Psychological Association et al. as *Amici Curiae* 7–17.

In the late 20th century, following substantial cultural and political developments, same-sex couples began to lead more open and public lives and to establish families. This development was followed by a quite extensive discussion of the issue in both governmental and private sectors and by a shift in public attitudes toward greater tolerance. As a result, questions about the rights of gays and lesbians soon reached the courts, where the issue could be discussed in the formal discourse of the law.

This Court first gave detailed consideration to the legal status of homosexuals in *Bowers v. Hardwick,* 478 U.S. 186 (1986). There it upheld the constitutionality of a Georgia law deemed to criminalize certain homosexual acts. Ten years later, in *Romer v. Evans,* 517 U.S. 620 (1996), the Court invalidated an amendment to Colorado's Constitution that sought to foreclose any branch or political subdivision of the State from protecting persons against discrimination based on sexual orientation. Then, in 2003, the Court overruled *Bowers,* holding that laws making same-sex intimacy a crime "demea[n] the lives of homosexual persons." *Lawrence v. Texas,* 539 U.S. 558, 575.

Against this background, the legal question of same-sex marriage arose * * *.

The new and widespread discussion of the subject led * * * [different] States to * * * different conclusion[s] * * *.

* * *

Under the Due Process Clause of the Fourteenth Amendment, no State shall "deprive any person of life, liberty, or property, without due process of law." The fundamental liberties protected by this Clause include most of the rights enumerated in the Bill of Rights. See *Duncan* v. *Louisiana*, 391 U. S. 145, 147–149 (1968). In addition these liberties extend to certain personal choices central to individual dignity and autonomy, including intimate choices that define personal identity and beliefs. See, *e.g., Eisenstadt* v. *Baird*, 405 U. S. 438, 453 (1972); *Griswold* v. *Connecticut*, 381 U. S. 479, 484–486 (1965).

The identification and protection of fundamental rights is an enduring part of the judicial duty to interpret the Constitution. That responsibility, however, "has not been reduced to any formula." *Poe* v. *Ullman*, 367 U. S. 497, 542 (1961) (Harlan, J., dissenting). Rather, it requires courts to exercise reasoned judgment in identifying interests of the person so fundamental that the State must accord them its respect. See *ibid.* That process is guided by many of the same considerations relevant to analysis of other constitutional provisions that set forth broad principles rather than specific requirements. History and tradition guide and discipline this inquiry but do not set its outer boundaries. See *Lawrence*, *supra*, at 572. That method respects our history and learns from it without allowing the past alone to rule the present.

The nature of injustice is that we may not always see it in our own times. The generations that wrote and ratified the Bill of Rights and the Fourteenth Amendment did not presume to know the extent of freedom in all of its dimensions, and so they entrusted to future generations a charter protecting the right of all persons to enjoy liberty as we learn its meaning. When new insight reveals discord between the Constitution's central protections and a received legal stricture, a claim to liberty must be addressed.

Applying these established tenets, the Court has long held the right to marry is protected by the Constitution. In *Loving* v. *Virginia*, 388 U. S. 1, 12 (1967), which invalidated bans on interracial unions, a unanimous Court held marriage is "one of the vital personal rights essential to the orderly pursuit of happiness by free men." The Court reaffirmed that holding in *Zablocki* v. *Redhail*, 434 U. S. 374, 384 (1978), which held the right to marry was burdened by a law prohibiting fathers who were behind on child support from marrying. The Court again applied this principle in *Turner* v. *Safley*, 482 U. S. 78, 95 (1987), which held the right to marry was abridged by regulations limiting the privilege of prison inmates to marry. Over time and in other contexts, the Court has reiterated that the right to marry is fundamental under the Due Process Clause.

It cannot be denied that this Court's cases describing the right to marry presumed a relationship involving opposite-sex partners. The Court, like many institutions, has made assumptions defined by the world and time of which it is a part. This was evident in *Baker v. Nelson,* 409 U.S. 810, a one-line summary decision issued in 1972, holding the exclusion of same-sex couples from marriage did not present a substantial federal question.

Still, there are other, more instructive precedents. This Court's cases have expressed constitutional principles of broader reach. In defining the right to marry these cases have identified essential attributes of that right based in history, tradition, and other constitutional liberties inherent in this intimate bond. See, *e.g.*,

Lawrence, 539 U.S., at 574; *Turner, supra,* at 95; *Zablocki, supra,* at 384; *Loving, supra,* at 12; *Griswold, supra,* at 486. And in assessing whether the force and rationale of its cases apply to same-sex couples, the Court must respect the basic reasons why the right to marry has been long protected. See, *e.g., Eisenstadt, supra,* at 453–454; *Poe, supra,* at 542–553 (Harlan, J., dissenting).

This analysis compels the conclusion that same-sex couples may exercise the right to marry. The * * * reasons marriage is fundamental under the Constitution apply with equal force to same-sex couples.

A first premise of the Court's relevant precedents is that the right to personal choice regarding marriage is inherent in the concept of individual autonomy * * *. Like choices concerning contraception, family relationships, procreation, and childrearing, all of which are protected by the Constitution, decisions concerning marriage are among the most intimate that an individual can make * * *.

* * *

A second principle in this Court's jurisprudence is that the right to marry is fundamental because it supports a two-person union unlike any other in its importance to the committed individuals * * *. The right to marry thus dignifies couples who "wish to define themselves by their commitment to each other." *Windsor, supra,* at ___ (slip op., at 14). Marriage responds to the universal fear that a lonely person might call out only to find no one there. It offers the hope of companionship and understanding and assurance that while both still live there will be someone to care for the other.

* * *

A third basis for protecting the right to marry is that it safeguards children and families and thus draws meaning from related rights of childrearing, procreation, and education * * *.

As all parties agree, many same-sex couples provide loving and nurturing homes to their children, whether biological or adopted * * *.

Excluding same-sex couples from marriage thus conflicts with a central premise of the right to marry * * *.

* * *

Fourth and finally, this Court's cases and the Nation's traditions make clear that marriage is a keystone of our social order * * *.

* * *

There is no difference between same- and opposite-sex couples with respect to this principle. Yet by virtue of their exclusion from that institution, same-sex couples are denied the constellation of benefits that the States have linked to marriage * * *.

The limitation of marriage to opposite-sex couples may long have seemed natural and just, but its inconsistency with the central meaning of the fundamental right to marry is now manifest. With that knowledge must come the recognition that laws excluding same-sex couples from the marriage right impose stigma and injury of the kind prohibited by our basic charter.

* * *

The right to marry is fundamental as a matter of history and tradition, but rights come not from ancient sources alone. They rise, too, from a better informed understanding of how constitutional imperatives define a liberty that remains urgent in our own era. Many who deem same-sex marriage to be wrong reach that conclusion based on decent and honorable religious or philosophical premises, and neither they nor their beliefs are disparaged here. But when that sincere, personal opposition becomes enacted law and public policy, the necessary consequence is to put the imprimatur of the State itself on an exclusion that soon demeans or stigmatizes those whose own liberty is then denied. Under the Constitution, same-sex couples seek in marriage the same legal treatment as opposite-sex couples, and it would disparage their choices and diminish their personhood to deny them this right.

* * *

The dynamic of our constitutional system is that individuals need not await legislative action before asserting a fundamental right. The Nation's courts are open to injured individuals who come to them to vindicate their own direct, personal stake in our basic charter. An individual can invoke a right to constitutional protection when he or she is harmed, even if the broader public disagrees and even if the legislature refuses to act. The idea of the Constitution "was to withdraw certain subjects from the vicissitudes of political controversy, to place them beyond the reach of majorities and officials and to establish them as legal principles to be applied by the courts." *West Virginia Bd. of Ed.* v. *Barnette*, 319 U. S. 624, 638 (1943). This is why "fundamental rights may not be submitted to a vote; they depend on the outcome of no elections." *Ibid.* It is of no moment whether advocates of same-sex marriage now enjoy or lack momentum in the democratic process. The issue before the Court here is the legal question whether the Constitution protects the right of same-sex couples to marry.

* * *

Being married in one State but having that valid marriage denied in another is one of "the most perplexing and distressing complication[s]" in the law of domestic relations. *Williams* v. *North Carolina*, 317 U. S. 287, 299 (1942) (internal quotation marks omitted). Leaving the current state of affairs in place would maintain and promote instability and uncertainty. For some couples, even an ordinary drive into a neighboring State to visit family or friends risks causing severe hardship in the event of a spouse's hospitalization while across state lines. In light of the fact that many States already allow same-sex marriage—and hundreds of thousands of these marriages already have occurred—the disruption caused by the recognition bans is significant and ever-growing.

As counsel for the respondents acknowledged at argument, if States are required by the Constitution to issue marriage licenses to same-sex couples, the justifications for refusing to recognize those marriages performed elsewhere are undermined. See Tr. of Oral Arg. on Question 2, p. 44. The Court, in this decision, holds same-sex couples may exercise the fundamental right to marry in all States. It follows that the Court also must hold—and it now does hold—that there is no lawful basis for a State to refuse to recognize a lawful same-sex marriage performed in another State on the ground of its same-sex character.

No union is more profound than marriage, for it embodies the highest ideals of love, fidelity, devotion, sacrifice, and family. In forming a marital union, two people become something greater than once they were. As some of the petitioners in these cases demonstrate, marriage embodies a love that may endure even past death. It would misunderstand these men and women to say they disrespect the idea of marriage. Their plea is that they do respect it, respect it so deeply that they seek to find its fulfillment for themselves. Their hope is not to be condemned to live in loneliness, excluded from one of civilization's oldest institutions. They ask for equal dignity in the eyes of the law. The Constitution grants them that right.

The judgment of the Court of Appeals for the Sixth Circuit is reversed.

It is so ordered.

■ CHIEF JUSTICE ROBERTS, with whom JUSTICE SCALIA and JUSTICE THOMAS join, dissenting.

Petitioners make strong arguments rooted in social policy and considerations of fairness. They contend that same-sex couples should be allowed to affirm their love and commitment through marriage, just like opposite-sex couples. That position has undeniable appeal; over the past six years, voters and legislators in eleven States and the District of Columbia have revised their laws to allow marriage between two people of the same sex.

But this Court is not a legislature. Whether same-sex marriage is a good idea should be of no concern to us. Under the Constitution, judges have power to say what the law is, not what it should be. The people who ratified the Constitution authorized courts to exercise "neither force nor will but merely judgment." The Federalist No. 78, p. 465 (C. Rossiter ed. 1961) (A. Hamilton) (capitalization altered).

Although the policy arguments for extending marriage to same-sex couples may be compelling, the legal arguments for requiring such an extension are not. The fundamental right to marry does not include a right to make a State change its definition of marriage. And a State's decision to maintain the meaning of marriage that has persisted in every culture throughout human history can hardly be called irrational. In short, our Constitution does not enact any one theory of marriage. The people of a State are free to expand marriage to include same-sex couples, or to retain the historic definition.

Today, however, the Court takes the extraordinary step of ordering every State to license and recognize same-sex marriage. Many people will rejoice at this decision, and I begrudge none their celebration. But for those who believe in a government of laws, not of men, the majority's approach is deeply disheartening. Supporters of same-sex marriage have achieved considerable success persuading their fellow citizens—through the democratic process—to adopt their view. That ends today. Five lawyers have closed the debate and enacted their own vision of marriage as a matter of constitutional law. Stealing this issue from the people will for many cast a cloud over same-sex marriage, making a dramatic social change that much more difficult to accept.

The majority's decision is an act of will, not legal judgment. The right it announces has no basis in the Constitution or this Court's precedent. The majority expressly disclaims judicial "caution" and omits even a pretense of humility, openly relying on its desire to remake society according to its own "new insight" into the "nature of injustice." As a result, the Court invalidates the marriage laws of more than half the States and orders the transformation of a social institution that has formed the basis of human society for millennia, for the Kalahari Bushmen and the Han Chinese, the Carthaginians and the Aztecs. Just who do we think we are?

* * *

* * * Petitioners do not contend that their States' marriage laws violate an *enumerated* constitutional right, such as the freedom of speech protected by the First Amendment. There is, after all, no "Companionship and Understanding" or "Nobility and Dignity" Clause in the Constitution. They argue instead that the laws violate a right *implied* by the Fourteenth Amendment's requirement that "liberty" may not be deprived without "due process of law."

This Court has interpreted the Due Process Clause to include a "substantive" component that protects certain liberty interests against state deprivation "no matter what process is provided." *Reno v. Flores,* 507 U.S. 292, 302 (1993). The theory is that some liberties are "so rooted in the traditions and conscience of our people as to be ranked as fundamental," and therefore cannot be deprived without compelling justification.

Allowing unelected federal judges to select which unenumerated rights rank as "fundamental"—and to strike down state laws on the basis of that determination—raises obvious concerns about the judicial role. Our precedents have accordingly insisted that judges "exercise the utmost care" in identifying implied fundamental rights, "lest the liberty protected by the Due Process Clause be subtly transformed into the policy preferences of the Members of this Court." *Washington v. Glucksberg,* 521 U.S. 702, 720 (1997) (internal quotation marks omitted); see Kennedy, Unenumerated Rights and the Dictates of Judicial Restraint 13 (1986) (Address at Stanford) ("One can conclude that certain essential, or fundamental, rights should exist in any just society. It does not follow that each of those essential rights is one that we as judges can enforce under the written Constitution. The Due Process Clause is not a guarantee of every right that should inhere in an ideal system.")

* * *

* * *[T]o avoid * * * converting personal preferences into constitutional mandates, our modern substantive due process cases have stressed the need for "judicial self-restraint." *Collins v. Harker Heights,* 503 U.S. 115, 125 (1992). Our precedents have required that implied fundamental rights be "objectively, deeply rooted in this Nation's history and tradition," and "implicit in the concept of ordered liberty, such that neither liberty nor justice would exist if they were sacrificed." *Glucksberg,* 521 U.S., at 720–721.

* * *

* * * The elevation of the fullest individual self-realization over the constraints that society has expressed in law may or may not be attractive moral philosophy. But a Justice's commission does not confer any special moral, philosophical, or social insight sufficient to justify imposing those perceptions on fellow citizens under the pretense of "due process." There is indeed a process due the people on issues of this sort—the democratic process. Respecting that understanding requires the Court to be guided by law, not any particular school of social thought * * *. And it certainly does not enact any one concept of marriage.

The majority's understanding of due process lays out a tantalizing vision of the future for Members of this Court: If an unvarying social institution enduring over all of recorded history cannot inhibit judicial policymaking, what can? But this approach is dangerous for the rule of law. The purpose of insisting that implied fundamental rights have roots in the history and tradition of our people is to ensure that when unelected judges strike down democratically enacted laws, they do so based on something more than their own beliefs. The Court today not only overlooks our country's entire history and tradition but actively repudiates it, preferring to live only in the heady days of the here and now. I agree with the majority that the "nature of injustice is that we may not always see it in our own times." As petitioners put it, "times can blind." Tr. of Oral Arg. on Question 1, at 9, 10. But to blind yourself to history is both prideful and unwise. "The past is never dead. It's not even past." W. Faulkner, Requiem for a Nun 92 (1951).

* * *

If you are among the many Americans—of whatever sexual orientation—who favor expanding same-sex marriage, by all means celebrate today's decision. Celebrate the achievement of a desired goal. Celebrate the opportunity for a new expression of commitment to a partner. Celebrate the availability of new benefits. But do not celebrate the Constitution. It had nothing to do with it.

I respectfully dissent.

■ JUSTICE SCALIA, with whom JUSTICE THOMAS joins, dissenting.

I join THE CHIEF JUSTICE's opinion in full. I write separately to call attention to this Court's threat to American democracy.

* * *

* * * Buried beneath the mummeries and straining-to-be-memorable passages of the opinion is a candid and startling assertion: No matter *what* it was the People ratified, the Fourteenth Amendment protects those rights that the Judiciary, in its "reasoned judgment," thinks the Fourteenth Amendment ought to protect. That is so because "[t]he generations that wrote and ratified the Bill of Rights and the Fourteenth Amendment did not presume to know the extent of freedom in all of its dimensions. . . ." One would think that sentence would continue: ". . . and therefore they provided for a means by which the People could amend the Constitution," or perhaps ". . . and therefore they left the creation of additional liberties, such as the freedom to marry someone of the same sex, to the People, through the never-ending process of legislation." But no. What logically follows, in the majority's judge-empowering estimation, is: "and so they entrusted to future generations a charter protecting the right of all persons to enjoy liberty as we learn its meaning." The "we," needless to say, is the nine of us. "History and tradition guide and discipline [our] inquiry but do not set its outer boundaries." Thus, rather than focusing on *the People's* understanding of "liberty"—at the time of ratification or even today—the majority focuses on four "principles and traditions" that, *in the majority's view,* prohibit States from defining marriage as an institution consisting of one man and one woman.

This is a naked judicial claim to legislative—indeed, *super*-legislative—power; a claim fundamentally at odds with our system of government. Except as limited by a constitutional prohibition agreed to by the People, the States are free to adopt whatever laws they like, even those that offend the esteemed Justices' "reasoned judgment." A system of government that makes the People subordinate to a committee of nine unelected lawyers does not deserve to be called a democracy.

Judges are selected precisely for their skill as lawyers; whether they reflect the policy views of a particular constituency is not (or should not be) relevant. Not surprisingly then, the Federal Judiciary is hardly a cross-section of America. Take, for example, this Court, which consists of only nine men and women, all of them successful lawyers who studied at Harvard or Yale Law School. Four of the nine are natives of New York City. Eight of them grew up in east- and west-coast States. Only one hails from the vast expanse in-between. Not a single Southwesterner or even, to tell the truth, a genuine Westerner (California does not count). Not a single evangelical Christian (a group that comprises about one quarter of Americans), or even a Protestant of any denomination. The strikingly unrepresentative character of the body voting on today's social upheaval would be irrelevant if they were functioning as *judges,* answering the legal question whether the American people had ever ratified a constitutional provision that was understood to proscribe the traditional definition of marriage. But of course the Justices in today's majority are not voting on that basis; *they say they are not.* And to allow the policy question of same-sex marriage to be considered and resolved by a select, patrician, highly unrepresentative panel of nine is to violate a principle even more fundamental than no taxation without representation: no social transformation without representation.

* * *

The opinion is couched in a style that is as pretentious as it is egoistic * * *.

Hubris is sometimes defined as o'erweening pride; and pride, we know, goeth before a fall. The Judiciary is the "least dangerous" of the federal branches because it has "neither Force nor Will, but merely judgment; and must ultimately depend upon the aid of the executive arm" and the States, "even for the efficacy of its judgments." With each decision of ours that takes from the People a question properly left to them—with each decision that is unabashedly based not on law, but on the "reasoned judgment" of a bare majority of this Court—we move one step closer to being reminded of our impotence.

[*Editors' Note: The dissenting opinions of Justice Thomas and Justice Alito are omitted.*]

NOTES AND QUESTIONS

1. *Obergefell v. Hodges* redefined marriage in more than thirty States. It settled by a 5–4 vote a highly contentious social issue that had roiled American politics for at least thirty years. Yet, the result—the judgment—in *Obergefell* has been accepted by all fifty States. This case is, along with *Bush v. Gore,* an illustration of the fact that the Supreme Court's Power of Judgment is formidable indeed.

2. Note that only one Justice—Anthony M. Kennedy—was in the majority in both cases! Was he right both times? Wrong both times? Inconsistent in his methodology or modalities?

3. One of us thinks that the result in *Obergefell* is consistent with the original meaning of the Fourteenth Amendment, though for reasons very different than the ones given by the Court. *See* Steven C. Calabresi & Hannah M. Begley, *Originalism and Same Sex Marriage,* 70 U. MIAMI L. REV. 648 (2016). Another of us thinks that this position is (as Justice Scalia once said in a different context) sheer applesauce. Is that disagreement

sufficient reason to think that the Court got it wrong? How certain about constitutional meaning must the Court be in order to invalidate a law? Does it matter which level of government enacted the law?

4. We will revisit many of the doctrinal and interpretative issues raised by *Obergefell* later in the course. *See infra* pages 1533–1552.

[Assignment 27]

B. THE POLITICAL QUESTION DOCTRINE

Article III, Section 1: The judicial power of the United States, shall be vested in one Supreme Court, and in such inferior courts as the Congress may from time to time ordain and establish.

We saw in *Marbury v. Madison* that there is no judicial review clause in Article III or anywhere else in the Constitution. There is also no clause that gives the federal courts the power or the duty to interpret or defend the Constitution. The text of the U.S. Constitution differs in this respect from the text of the German or other modern constitutions that specify a Constitutional Court or Supreme Court that alone has the power of constitutional interpretation. Indeed, Article II, Section 1 ends by requiring that the President (and not the judges) swear a special oath to preserve, protect and defend the Constitution. This could be read to imply a power of presidential but not judicial review! Article III does, however, give federal judges the final power to decide cases or controversies according to law, and that grant flows directly from We the People who are sovereign. If Congress, which is not sovereign, passes a law that violates the supreme law of the Constitution, the judges must refuse to give effect to that law in any case or controversy before them. Congress may not tell federal judges how to decide a case. *See* Gary Lawson, *Controlling Precedent: Congressional Regulation of Judicial Decisionmaking,* 18 CONST. COMMENTARY 191 (2001). Nor may Congress revise a judge's decision in a case. Federal judges have the last word on the decision of cases and controversies, and they must decide them according to law, giving effect if need be to the supreme law of the Constitution over contrary actions by the legislative and executive branch.

But are there other matters as to which the text of the Constitution leaves the last word with the President, the Senate, the House of Representatives, or even the States? Do the President and executive branch officials have the last word on whether a prosecution gets started, or can a court order a prosecution (as Judge Cox tried to do, *see supra* pages 369–381)? If Congress impeaches and removes a federal judge from office for high crimes and misdemeanors, can the removed judge appeal the decision to the Supreme Court and argue that actually he or she was guilty only of "low" crimes and misdemeanors?

These issues are addressed by the so-called political question doctrine, which you have already seen at work in several cases. What general rules can be identified to help render concrete the situations where the political question doctrine applies? The answer to some degree is that we have to look historically at our practice over the last 230 years of American history and ask what questions have been thought to be judicially reviewable and what questions have been ones on which the political branches have had the last word. We know from the Constitution that the "judicial Power" was thought to be different from the "legislative Powers herein granted" and from the "executive Power" of the President. Practice shows that Congress has the last word on impeachments, the President has the last word on bringing prosecutions, and the judiciary has the last word on deciding cases in law and equity on the scope of the commerce power. Is there any rhyme and reason to this? We think so, but whether there is or not, it is a fact that the political question label traditionally pops up in some areas of constitutional law and not in others. Consider below eight categories of cases in law and equity or controversies that have often historically been thought to raise political questions. As a general rule of thumb, if a question of constitutional interpretation arises in a case in law and equity or in a controversy and it is not in one of these eight areas, it is probably judicially reviewable and probably does not raise a political question.

(1) Cases arising under the Guarantee Clause (or Republican Form of Government Clause) in Article IV, Section 4. Interpretation of this clause produced *Luther v. Borden,* which was arguably the very first political question doctrine case, and we excerpt parts of *Luther* below.

(2) Cases about whether a war has begun or ended and whether to recognize or withdraw recognition from a foreign government.

(3) Cases challenging the rules adopted by the Senate and the House to govern their own proceedings. Rules awarding committee seats disproportionately to the majority party in the House or establishing a right to filibuster in the Senate thus are political questions.

(4) Cases about the ratification of a constitutional amendment. Although there were serious objections raised to the process by which the Fourteenth Amendment was ratified, the Court deferred to the judgment by Congress and Secretary of State Seward that it had been validly ratified.

(5) Impeachment. Here the Court always defers to Congress. Since the powers to impeach and to amend the Constitution are both ways in which Congress can check and balance the Supreme Court, it would seem to violate the spirit of *The Federalist* No. 51 and its emphasis on separated powers to allow Congress's use of those two powers to be subjected to judicial review.

(6) Training procedures for national guard units. This question was raised in the wake of the Kent State shootings in 1970, and national guard training was deemed to be totally within the discretion of the executive branch and not subject to judicial review because of the political question doctrine.

(7) Cases involving the regulation of political parties.

(8) Cases involving the status of Native American tribal groups.

We have given you below two leading political question cases: *Luther v. Borden,* the first political question case; and *Rucho v. Common Cause,* the most recent political question case. Ask yourselves as you read these two cases whether under their reasoning any case in law or equity about the Guarantee Clause or about partisan districting could ever be justiciable notwithstanding the political question doctrine.

Luther v. Borden

48 U.S. (7 How.) 1 (1849)

■ MR. CHIEF JUSTICE TANEY delivered the opinion of the court.

This case has arisen out of the unfortunate political differences which agitated the people of Rhode Island in 1841 and 1842.

It is an action of trespass brought by Martin Luther, the plaintiff in error, against Luther M. Borden and others, the defendants, in the Circuit Court of the United States for the District of Rhode Island, for breaking and entering the plaintiff's house. The defendants justify upon the ground that large numbers of men were assembled in different parts of the State for the purpose of overthrowing the government by military force, and were actually levying war upon the State; that, in order to defend itself from this insurrection, the State was declared by competent authority to be under martial law; that the plaintiff was engaged in the insurrection; and that the defendants, being in the military service of the State, by command of their superior officer, broke and entered the house and searched the rooms for the plaintiff, who was supposed to be there concealed, in order to arrest him, doing as little damage as possible. The plaintiff replied, that the trespass was committed by the defendants of their own proper wrong, and without any such cause; and upon the issue joined on this replication, the parties proceeded to trial.

The evidence offered by the plaintiff and the defendants is stated at large in the record; and the questions decided by the Circuit Court, and brought up by the writ of error, are not such as commonly arise in an action of trespass. The existence and authority of the government under which the defendants acted was called in question; and the plaintiff insists, that, before the acts complained of were committed, that government had been displaced and annulled by the people of Rhode Island, and that the plaintiff was engaged in supporting the lawful authority of the State, and the defendants themselves were in arms against it.

This is a new question in this court, and certainly a very grave one; and at the time when the trespass is alleged to have been committed it had produced a general and painful excitement in the State, and threatened to end in bloodshed and civil war.

The evidence shows that the defendants, in breaking into the plaintiff's house and endeavouring to arrest him, as stated in the pleadings, acted under the authority of the government which was established in Rhode Island at the time of the Declaration of Independence, and which is usually called the charter government. For when the separation from England took place, Rhode Island did not, like the other States, adopt a new constitution, but continued the form of government established by the charter of Charles the Second in 1663; making only such alterations, by acts of the legislature, as were necessary to adapt it to their condition and rights as an independent State. It was under this form of government that Rhode Island united with the other States in the Declaration of Independence, and afterwards ratified the Constitution of the United States and became a member of this Union; and it continued to be the established and unquestioned government of the State until the difficulties took place which have given rise to this action.

In this form of government no mode of proceeding was pointed out by which amendments might be made. It authorized the legislature to prescribe the qualification of voters, and in the exercise of this power the right of suffrage was confined to freeholders, until thc adoption of the constitution of 1843.

For some years previous to the disturbances of which we are now speaking, many of the citizens became dissatisfied with the charter government, and particularly with the restriction upon the right of suffrage. Memorials were addressed to the legislature upon this subject, urging the justice and necessity of a more liberal and extended rule. But they failed to produce the desired effect. And thereupon meetings were held and associations formed by those who were in favor of a more extended right of suffrage, which finally resulted in the election of a convention to form a new constitution to be submitted to the people for their adoption or rejection. This convention was not authorized by any law of the existing government. It was elected at voluntary meetings, and by those citizens only who favored this plan of reform; those who were opposed to it, or opposed to the manner in which it was proposed to be accomplished, taking no part in the proceedings. The persons chosen as above mentioned came together and framed a constitution, by which the right of suffrage was extended to every male citizen of twenty-one years of age, who had resided in the State for one year, and in the town in which he offered to vote for six months, next preceding the election. The convention also prescribed the manner in which this constitution should be submitted to the decision of the people,—permitting every one to vote on that question who was an American citizen, twenty-one years old, and who had a permanent residence or home in the State, and directing the votes to be returned to the convention.

Upon the return of the votes, the convention declared that the constitution was adopted and ratified by a majority of the people of the State, and was the paramount law and constitution of Rhode Island. And it communicated this decision to the governor under the charter government, for the purpose of being laid before the legislature; and directed elections to be held for a governor, members of the legislature, and other officers under the new constitution. These elections accordingly took place, and the governor, lieutenant-governor, secretary of state, and senators and representatives thus appointed assembled at the city of Providence on May 3d, 1842, and immediately proceeded to organize the new government, by appointing the officers and passing the laws necessary for that purpose.

The charter government did not, however, admit the validity of these proceedings, nor acquiesce in them. On the contrary, in January, 1842, when this new constitution was communicated to the governor, and by him laid before the legislature, it passed resolutions declaring all acts done for the purpose of imposing that constitution upon the State to be an assumption of the powers of government, in violation of the rights of the existing government and of the people at large; and that it would maintain its authority and defend the legal and constitutional rights of the people.

In adopting this measure, as well as in all others taken by the charter government to assert its authority, it was supported by a large number of the citizens of the State, claiming to be a majority, who regarded the proceedings of the adverse party as unlawful and disorganizing, and maintained that, as the existing government had been established by the people of the State, no convention to frame a new constitution could be called without its sanction; and that the times and places of taking the votes, and the officers to receive them, and the qualification of voters, must be previously regulated and appointed by law.

But, notwithstanding the determination of the charter government, and of those who adhered to it, to maintain its authority, Thomas W. Dorr, who had been elected governor under the new constitution, prepared to assert the authority of that government by force, and many citizens assembled in arms to support him. The charter government thereupon passed an act declaring the State under martial law, and at the same time proceeded to call out the militia, to repel the threatened attack and to subdue those who were engaged in it. In this state of the contest, the house of the plaintiff, who was engaged in supporting the authority of the new government, was broken and entered in order to arrest him. The defendants were, at the time, in the military service of the old government, and in arms to support its authority.

It appears, also, that the charter government at its session of January, 1842, took measures to call a convention to revise the existing form of government; and after various proceedings, which it is not material to state, a new constitution was formed by a convention elected under the authority of the charter government, and afterwards adopted and ratified by the people; the times and places at which the votes were to be given, the persons who were to receive and return them, and the qualification of the voters, having all been previously authorized and provided for by law passed by the charter government. This new government went into operation in May, 1843, at which time the old government formally surrendered all its powers; and this constitution has continued ever since to be the admitted and established government of Rhode Island.

The difficulties with the government of which Mr. Dorr was the head were soon over. They had ceased before the constitution was framed by the convention elected by the authority of the charter government. For after an unsuccessful attempt made by Mr. Dorr in May, 1842, at the head of a military force, to get possession of the State arsenal at Providence, in which he was repulsed, and an assemblage of some hundreds of armed men under his command at Chepatchet in the June following, which dispersed upon the approach of the troops of the old government, no further effort was made to establish it; and until the constitution of 1843 went into operation the charter government continued to assert its authority and exercise its powers, and to enforce obedience, throughout the State, arresting and imprisoning, and punishing in its judicial tribunals, those who had appeared in arms against it.

We do not understand from the argument that the constitution under which the plaintiff acted is supposed to have been in force after the constitution of May, 1843, went into operation. The contest is confined to the year preceding. The plaintiff contends that the charter government was displaced, and ceased to have any lawful power, after the organization, in May, 1842, of the government which he supported, and although that government never was able to exercise any authority in the State, nor to command obedience to its laws or to its officers, yet he insists that it was the lawful and established government, upon the ground that it was ratified by a large majority of the male people of the State of the age of twenty-one and upwards, and also by a majority of those who were entitled to vote for general officers under the then existing laws of the State. The fact that it was so ratified was not admitted; and at the trial in the Circuit Court he offered to prove it by the production of the original ballots, and the original registers of the persons voting, verified by the oaths of the several moderators and clerks of the meetings, and by the testimony of all the persons so voting, and by the said constitution; and also offered in evidence, for the same purpose, that part of the census of the United States for the year 1840 which applies to Rhode Island; and a certificate of the secretary of state of the charter government, showing the number of votes polled by the freemen of the State for the ten years then last past.

The Circuit Court rejected this evidence, and instructed the jury that the charter government and laws under which the defendants acted were, at the time the trespass is alleged to have been committed, in full force and effect as the form of government and paramount law of the State, and constituted a justification of the acts of the defendants as set forth in their pleas.

It is this opinion of the Circuit Court that we are now called upon to review. It is set forth more at large in the exception, but is in substance as above stated; and the question presented is certainly a very serious one: For, if this court is authorized to enter upon this inquiry as proposed by the plaintiff, and it should be decided that the charter government had no legal existence during the period of time above mentioned,—if it had been annulled by the adoption of the opposing government,—then the laws passed by its legislature during that time were nullities; its taxes wrongfully collected; its salaries and compensation to its officers illegally paid; its public accounts improperly settled; and the judgments and sentences of its courts in civil and criminal cases null and void, and the officers who carried their decisions into operation answerable as trespassers, if not in some cases as criminals.

When the decision of this court might lead to such results, it becomes its duty to examine very carefully its own powers before it undertakes to exercise jurisdiction.

Certainly, the question which the plaintiff proposed to raise by the testimony he offered has not heretofore been recognized as a judicial one in any of the State courts. In forming the constitutions of the different States, after the Declaration of Independence, and in the various changes and alterations which have since been made, the political department has always determined whether the proposed constitution or amendment was ratified or not by the people of the State, and the judicial power has followed its decision. In Rhode Island, the question has been directly decided. Prosecutions were there instituted against some of the persons who had been active in the forcible opposition to the old government. And in more than one of the cases evidence was offered on the part of the defence similar to the testimony offered in the Circuit Court, and for the same purpose; that is, for the purpose of showing that the proposed constitution had been adopted by the people of Rhode Island, and had, therefore, become the established government, and consequently that the parties accused were doing nothing more than their duty in endeavouring to support it.

But the courts uniformly held that the inquiry proposed to be made belonged to the political power and not to the judicial * * *. This doctrine is clearly and forcibly stated in the opinion of the Supreme Court of the State in the trial of Thomas W. Dorr, who was the governor elected under the opposing constitution, and headed the armed force which endeavoured to maintain its authority.

Indeed, we do not see how the question could be tried and judicially decided in a State court. Judicial power presupposes an established government capable of enacting laws and enforcing their execution, and of appointing judges to expound and administer them. The acceptance of the judicial office is a recognition of the authority of the government from which it is derived. And if the authority of that government is annulled and overthrown, the power of its courts and other officers is

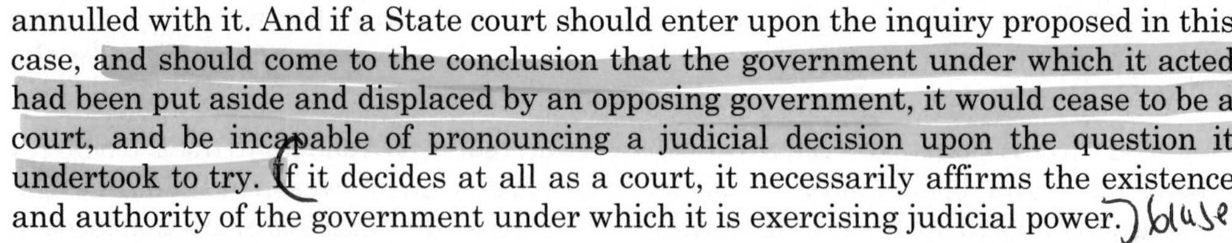

annulled with it. And if a State court should enter upon the inquiry proposed in this case, and should come to the conclusion that the government under which it acted had been put aside and displaced by an opposing government, it would cease to be a court, and be incapable of pronouncing a judicial decision upon the question it undertook to try. If it decides at all as a court, it necessarily affirms the existence and authority of the government under which it is exercising judicial power.

It is worthy of remark, however, when we are referring to the authority of State decisions, that the trial of Thomas W. Dorr took place after the constitution of 1843 went into operation. The judges who decided that case held their authority under that constitution; and it is admitted on all hands that it was adopted by the people of the State, and is the lawful and established government. It is the decision, therefore, of a State court, whose judicial authority to decide upon the constitution and laws of Rhode Island is not questioned by either party to this controversy, although the government under which it acted was framed and adopted under the sanction and laws of the charter government.

The point, then, raised here has been already decided by the courts of Rhode Island. The question relates, altogether, to the constitution and laws of that State; and the well settled rule in this court is, that the courts of the United States adopt and follow the decisions of the State courts in questions which concern merely the constitution and laws of the State.

Upon what ground could the Circuit Court of the United States which tried this case have departed from this rule, and disregarded and overruled the decisions of the courts of Rhode Island? Undoubtedly the courts of the United States have certain powers under the Constitution and laws of the United States which do not belong to the State courts. But the power of determining that a State government has been lawfully established, which the courts of the State disown and repudiate, is not one of them. Upon such a question the courts of the United States are bound to follow the decisions of the State tribunals, and must therefore regard the charter government as the lawful established government during the time of this contest.

Besides, if the Circuit Court had entered upon this inquiry, by what rule could it have determined the qualification of voters upon the adoption or rejection of the proposed constitution, unless there was some previous law of the State to guide it? It is the province of a court to expound the law, not to make it. And certainly it is no part of the judicial functions of any court of the United States to prescribe the qualification of voters in a State, giving the right to those to whom it is denied by the written and established constitution and laws of the State, or taking it away from those to whom it is given; nor has it the right to determine what political privileges the citizens of a State are entitled to, unless there is an established constitution or law to govern its decision.

And if the then existing law of Rhode Island which confined the right of suffrage to freeholders is to govern, and this question is to be tried by that rule, how could the majority have been ascertained by legal evidence, such as a court of justice might lawfully receive? The written returns of the moderators and clerks of mere voluntary meetings, verified by affidavit, certainly would not be admissible; nor their opinions or judgments as to the freehold qualification of the persons who voted. The law requires actual knowledge in the witness of the fact to which he testifies in a court of justice. How, then, could the majority of freeholders have been determined in a judicial proceeding?

The court had not the power to order a census of the freeholders to be taken; nor would the census of the United States of 1840 be any evidence of the number of freeholders in the State in 1842. Nor could the court appoint persons to examine and determine whether every person who had voted possessed the freehold qualification which the law then required. In the nature of things, the Circuit Court could not know the name and residence of every citizen, and bring him before the court to be examined. And if this were attempted, where would such an inquiry have terminated? And how long must the people of Rhode Island have waited to learn from this court under what form of government they were living during the year in controversy?

But this is not all. The question as to the majority is a question of fact. It depends upon the testimony of witnesses, and if the testimony offered by the plaintiff had been received, the defendants had the right to offer evidence to rebut it; and there might, and probably would, have been conflicting testimony as to the number of voters in the State, and as to the legal qualifications of many of the individuals who had voted. The decision would, therefore, have depended upon the relative credibility of witnesses, and the weight of testimony; and as the case before the Circuit Court was an action at common law, the question of fact, according to the seventh amendment to the Constitution of the United States, must have been tried by the jury. In one case a jury might find that the constitution which the plaintiff supported was adopted by a majority of the citizens of the State, or of the voters entitled to vote by the existing law. Another jury in another case might find otherwise. And as a verdict is not evidence in a suit between different parties, if the courts of the United States have the jurisdiction contended for by the plaintiff, the question whether the acts done under the charter government during the period in contest are valid or not must always remain unsettled and open to dispute. The authority and security of the State governments do not rest on such unstable foundations.

Moreover, the Constitution of the United States, as far as it has provided for an emergency of this kind, and authorized the general government to interfere in the domestic concerns of a State, has treated the subject as political in its nature, and placed the power in the hands of that department.

The fourth section of the fourth article of the Constitution of the United States provides that the United States shall guarantee to every State in the Union a republican form of government, and shall protect each of them against invasion; and on the application of the legislature or of the executive (when the legislature cannot be convened) against domestic violence.

Under this article of the Constitution it rests with Congress to decide what government is the established one in a State. For as the United States guarantee to each State a republican government, Congress must necessarily decide what government is established in the State before it can determine whether it is republican or not. And when the senators and representatives of a State are admitted into the councils of the Union, the authority of the government under which they are appointed, as well as its republican character, is recognized by the proper constitutional authority. And its decision is binding on every other department of the government, and could not be questioned in a judicial tribunal. It is true that the contest in this case did not last long enough to bring the matter to this issue; and as no senators or representatives were elected under the authority of the government of which Mr. Dorr was the head, Congress was not called upon to decide the controversy. Yet the right to decide is placed there, and not in the courts.

* * *

The remaining question is whether the defendants, acting under military orders issued under the authority of the government, were justified in breaking and entering the plaintiff's house. In relation to the act of the legislature declaring martial law, it is not necessary in the case before us to inquire to what extent, nor under what circumstances, that power may be exercised by a State. Unquestionably a military government, established as the permanent government of the State, would not be a republican government, and it would be the duty of Congress to overthrow it. But the law of Rhode Island evidently contemplated no such government. It was intended merely for the crisis, and to meet the peril in which the existing government was placed by the armed resistance to its authority. It was so understood and construed by the State authorities. And, unquestionably, a State may use its military power to put down an armed insurrection, too strong to be controlled by the civil authority. The power is essential to the existence of every government, essential to the preservation of order and free institutions, and is as necessary to the States of this Union as to any other government. The State itself must determine what degree of force the crisis demands. And if the government of Rhode Island deemed the armed opposition so formidable, and so ramified throughout the State, as to require the use of its military force and the declaration of martial law, we see no ground upon which this court can question its authority * * *.

* * *

* * * No one, we believe, has ever doubted the proposition, that, according to the institutions of this country, the sovereignty in every State resides in the people of the State, and that they may alter and change their form of government at their own pleasure. But whether they have changed it or not by abolishing an old government, and establishing a new one in its place, is a question to be settled by the political power. And when that power has decided, the courts are bound to take notice of its decision, and to follow it.

The judgment of the Circuit Court must therefore be affirmed.

[*Editors' Note: The dissenting opinion of Justice Woodbury, which focused on the mechanics of martial law, is omitted.*]

NOTES AND QUESTIONS

1. Did the rebels in *Luther v. Borden* do anything different than the Framers? Remember James Madison's explanation for why ratification of the Constitution was valid even though it was contrary to the rules in state constitutions. Was the Court in *Luther* wrong to duck the issue because the Constitution legally and readily answered the question before it?

2. To whom did the Court think that the decision of the validity of the Rhode Island government was committed? To Congress? To the state courts of the post-1843 Rhode Island government, whose legitimacy was accepted by everyone? On what legal basis would those bodies decide which government was legitimate? Was that basis

unavailable to the Supreme Court? Or did the Supreme Court actually decide the case in favor of the Charter government despite disclaiming authority to do so?

3. *Luther* is a fairly extreme example of a case involving the "political process" of a State—in that case involving which of two competing state governments was the real deal. In the twentieth century, additional Guarantee Clause challenges to lesser but still important aspects of state political processes arose, and until the 1960s they were consistently found to be nonjusticiable political questions. During the Progressive Era, for example, initiatives and referenda were often employed as alternative methods of state lawmaking (and state constitutional amending) as a response to the perceived corruption of the "representative" political process. But since the Constitution guarantees to each State a "Republican Form of Government," not a "Democratic Form of Government," it was (and to some of us still is) an open question whether direct democracy of that sort is consistent with constitutionally mandated republicanism. The Supreme Court in 1912, relying almost exclusively on *Luther,* determined that it was a political question. *See Pacific States Telephone & Telegraph Co. v. Oregon,* 223 U.S. 118 (1912):

> It is indeed a singular misconception of the nature and character of our constitutional system of government to suggest that the settled distinction * * * between judicial authority over justiciable controversies and legislative power as to purely political questions tends to destroy the duty of the judiciary in proper cases to enforce the Constitution. The suggestion but results from failing to distinguish between things which are widely different; that is, the legislative duty to determine the political questions involved in deciding whether a state government republican in form exists, and the judicial power and ever-present duty whenever it becomes necessary, in a controversy properly submitted, to enforce and uphold the applicable provisions of the Constitution as to each and every exercise of governmental power.
>
> How better can the broad lines which distinguish these two subjects be pointed out than by considering the character of the defense in this very case? The defendant company does not contend here that it could not have been required to pay a license tax. It does not assert that it was denied an opportunity to be heard as to the amount for which it was taxed, or that there was anything inhering in the tax or involved intrinsically in the law which violated any of its constitutional rights. If such questions had been raised, they would have been justiciable, and therefore would have required the calling into operation of judicial power. Instead, however, of doing any of these things, the attack on the statute here made is of a wholly different character. Its essentially political nature is at once made manifest by understanding that the assault which the contention here advanced makes is not on the tax as a tax, but on the state as a state. It is addressed to the framework and political character of the government by which the statute levying the tax was passed. It is the government, the political entity, which (reducing the case to its essence) is called to the bar of this court, not for the purpose of testing judicially some exercise of power, assailed on the ground that its exertion has injuriously affected the rights of an individual because of repugnancy to some constitutional limitation, but to demand of the state that it establish its right to exist as a state, republican in form.
>
> As the issues presented, in their very essence, are, and have long since by this court been, definitely determined to be political and governmental, and embraced within the scope of the powers conferred upon Congress, and not,

therefore, within the reach of judicial power, it follows that the case presented is not within our jurisdiction, and the writ of error must therefore be, and it is, dismissed for want of jurisdiction.

Id. at 149–51. If Congress thought that the referendum process was non-republican, what should Congress do about it? Is there actually anything that Congress can do about it?

4. Perhaps the most contentious "Guarantee Clause" cases have not been argued or decided as Guarantee Clause cases, no doubt because of the settled caselaw declaring such challenges nonjusticiable. Instead, they have been brought and decided under the Fourteenth Amendment's Equal Protection Clause, of which we will hear much more later. Election of members of Congress and of state legislatures is normally done by district. From the earliest days of the Nation, those districts were normally drawn based on geographical, economic, and crassly political considerations rather than population, so it was possible for there to be orders-of-magnitude differences between the number of voters in each district. Because that method of apportionment favored certain representatives, and those representatives were the ones who drew the district lines, States were often reluctant to reconsider their districting policies when new censuses showed massive changes in population. The Court initially considered the districting process a political question, *see Colegrove v. Green,* 328 U.S. 549 (1946), but changed its mind in the early 1960s, in cases that you will read later. *See infra* pages 955–962. For the past sixty years, the courts have considered it a justiciable question whether district lines depart so far from a baseline of rough (not exact) population equality that they deprive some voters of equal protection. But that does not establish *how* the district lines are to be drawn. Can representatives construct districts that have roughly equal population, but which zig and zag through the State in order to maximize the chances of grouping voters for partisan advantage? In 2019, after decades of avoiding a direct answer, the Supreme Court announced, 5–4, that no direct answer was forthcoming.

Rucho v. Common Cause

588 U.S. ___, 139 S.Ct. 2484 (2019)

■ CHIEF JUSTICE ROBERTS delivered the opinion of the Court.

Voters and other plaintiffs in North Carolina and Maryland challenged their States' congressional districting maps as unconstitutional partisan gerrymanders. The North Carolina plaintiffs complained that the State's districting plan discriminated against Democrats; the Maryland plaintiffs complained that their State's plan discriminated against Republicans. The plaintiffs alleged that the gerrymandering violated the First Amendment, the Equal Protection Clause of the Fourteenth Amendment, the Elections Clause, and Article I, § 2, of the Constitution. The District Courts in both cases ruled in favor of the plaintiffs, and the defendants appealed directly to this Court.

These cases require us to consider once again whether claims of excessive partisanship in districting are "justiciable"—that is, properly suited for resolution by the federal courts. This Court has not previously struck down a districting plan as an unconstitutional partisan gerrymander, and has struggled without success over the past several decades to discern judicially manageable standards for deciding such claims. The districting plans at issue here are highly partisan, by any measure. The question is whether the courts below appropriately exercised judicial power when they found them unconstitutional as well.

The first case involves a challenge to the congressional redistricting plan enacted by the Republican-controlled North Carolina General Assembly in 2016. The Republican legislators leading the redistricting effort instructed their mapmaker to use political data to draw a map that would produce a congressional delegation of ten Republicans and three Democrats. 318 F.Supp.3d 777, 807–808 (M.D.N.C. 2018). As one of the two Republicans chairing the redistricting committee stated, "I think electing Republicans is better than electing Democrats. So I drew this map to help foster what I think is better for the country." He further explained that the map was drawn with the aim of electing ten Republicans and three Democrats because he did "not believe it [would be] possible to draw a map with 11 Republicans and 2 Democrats." One Democratic state senator objected that entrenching the 10–3 advantage for Republicans was not "fair, reasonable, [or] balanced" because, as recently as 2012, "Democratic congressional candidates had received more votes on a statewide basis than Republican candidates." The General Assembly was not swayed by that objection and approved the 2016 Plan by a party-line vote.

In November 2016, North Carolina conducted congressional elections using the 2016 Plan, and Republican candidates won 10 of the 13 congressional districts. Id., at 810. In the 2018 elections, Republican candidates won nine congressional districts, while Democratic candidates won three. The Republican candidate narrowly prevailed in the remaining district, but the State Board of Elections called a new election after allegations of fraud.

* * *

The second case before us is *Lamone v. Benisek*. In 2011, the Maryland Legislature—dominated by Democrats—undertook to redraw the lines of that State's eight congressional districts. The Governor at the time, Democrat Martin O'Malley, led the process. He appointed a redistricting committee to help redraw the map, and asked Congressman Steny Hoyer, who has described himself as a "serial gerrymanderer," to advise the committee. 348 F.Supp.3d 493, 502 (D. Md. 2018). The Governor later testified that his aim was to "use the redistricting process to change the overall composition of Maryland's congressional delegation to 7 Democrats and 1 Republican by flipping" one district. "[A] decision was made to go for the Sixth," which had been held by a Republican for nearly two decades. To achieve the required equal population among districts, only about 10,000 residents needed to be removed from that district. The 2011 Plan accomplished that by moving roughly 360,000 voters out of the Sixth District and moving 350,000 new voters in. Overall, the Plan reduced the number of registered Republicans in the Sixth District by about 66,000 and increased the number of registered Democrats by about 24,000. The map was adopted by a party-line vote. It was used in the 2012 election and succeeded in flipping the Sixth District. A Democrat has held the seat ever since.

* * *

Chief Justice Marshall famously wrote that it is "the province and duty of the judicial department to say what the law is." *Marbury v. Madison*, 1 Cranch 137, 177 (1803). Sometimes, however, "the law is that the judicial department has no business entertaining the claim of unlawfulness—because the question is entrusted to one of the political branches or involves no judicially enforceable rights." *Vieth v. Jubelirer*, 541 U.S. 267, 277 (2004) (plurality opinion). In such a case the claim is said to present a "political question" and to be nonjusticiable—outside the courts' competence and

therefore beyond the courts' jurisdiction. *Baker v. Carr*, 369 U.S. 186, 217 (1962). Among the political question cases the Court has identified are those that lack "judicially discoverable and manageable standards for resolving [them]." *Ibid.*

* * *

Partisan gerrymandering is nothing new. Nor is frustration with it. The practice was known in the Colonies prior to Independence, and the Framers were familiar with it at the time of the drafting and ratification of the Constitution. During the very first congressional elections, George Washington and his Federalist allies accused Patrick Henry of trying to gerrymander Virginia's districts against their candidates—in particular James Madison, who ultimately prevailed over fellow future President James Monroe. Hunter, The First Gerrymander? 9 Early Am. Studies 792–794, 811 (2011). See 5 Writings of Thomas Jefferson 71 (P. Ford ed. 1895) (Letter to W. Short (Feb. 9, 1789)) ("Henry has so modelled the districts for representatives as to tack Orange [county] to counties where he himself has great influence that Madison may not be elected into the lower federal house").

In 1812, Governor of Massachusetts and future Vice President Elbridge Gerry notoriously approved congressional districts that the legislature had drawn to aid the Democratic-Republican Party. The moniker "gerrymander" was born when an outraged Federalist newspaper observed that one of the misshapen districts resembled a salamander. E. Griffith, The Rise and Development of the Gerrymander 17–19 (1907) * * *.

The Framers addressed the election of Representatives to Congress in the Elections Clause. Art. I, § 4, cl. 1. That provision assigns to state legislatures the power to prescribe the "Times, Places and Manner of holding Elections" for Members of Congress, while giving Congress the power to "make or alter" any such regulations * * *.

* * *

Congress has regularly exercised its Elections Clause power, including to address partisan gerrymandering. The Apportionment Act of 1842, which required single-member districts for the first time, specified that those districts be "composed of contiguous territory," Act of June 25, 1842, ch. 47, 5 Stat. 491, in "an attempt to forbid the practice of the gerrymander," Griffith, *supra*, at 12. Later statutes added requirements of compactness and equality of population. Act of Jan. 16, 1901, ch. 93, § 3, 31 Stat. 733; Act of Feb. 2, 1872, ch. 11, § 2, 17 Stat. 28. (Only the single member district requirement remains in place today. 2 U.S.C. § 2c.) Congress also used its Elections Clause power in 1870, enacting the first comprehensive federal statute dealing with elections as a way to enforce the Fifteenth Amendment. Force Act of 1870, ch. 114, 16 Stat. 140. Starting in the 1950s, Congress enacted a series of laws to protect the right to vote through measures such as the suspension of literacy tests and the prohibition of English-only elections. See, e.g., 52 U.S.C. § 10101 et seq.

Appellants suggest that, through the Elections Clause, the Framers set aside electoral issues such as the one before us as questions that only Congress can resolve. We do not agree. In two areas—one-person, one-vote and racial gerrymandering—our cases have held that there is a role for the courts with respect to at least some issues that could arise from a State's drawing of congressional districts. See *Wesberry v. Sanders*, 376 U.S. 1 (1964); *Shaw v. Reno*, 509 U.S. 630 (1993) (*Shaw I*).

But the history is not irrelevant. The Framers were aware of electoral districting problems and considered what to do about them. They settled on a characteristic approach, assigning the issue to the state legislatures, expressly checked and balanced by the Federal Congress * * *. At no point was there a suggestion that the federal courts had a role to play. Nor was there any indication that the Framers had ever heard of courts doing such a thing.

Courts have nevertheless been called upon to resolve a variety of questions surrounding districting * * *.

In the leading case of *Baker v. Carr*, voters in Tennessee complained that the State's districting plan for state representatives "debase[d]" their votes, because the plan was predicated on a 60-year-old census that no longer reflected the distribution of population in the State. The plaintiffs argued that votes of people in overpopulated districts held less value than those of people in less-populated districts, and that this inequality violated the Equal Protection Clause of the Fourteenth Amendment. The District Court dismissed the action on the ground that the claim was not justiciable * * *. This Court reversed. It identified various considerations relevant to determining whether a claim is a nonjusticiable political question, including whether there is "a lack of judicially discoverable and manageable standards for resolving it." 369 U.S. at 217. The Court concluded that the claim of population inequality among districts did not fall into that category, because such a claim could be decided under basic equal protection principles. *Id.*, at 226. In *Wesberry v. Sanders,* the Court extended its ruling to malapportionment of congressional districts, holding that Article I, § 2, required that "one man's vote in a congressional election is to be worth as much as another's." 376 U.S. at 8.

Another line of challenges to districting plans has focused on race. Laws that explicitly discriminate on the basis of race, as well as those that are race neutral on their face but are unexplainable on grounds other than race, are of course presumptively invalid. The Court applied those principles to electoral boundaries in *Gomillion v. Lightfoot*, concluding that a challenge to an "uncouth twenty-eight sided" municipal boundary line that excluded black voters from city elections stated a constitutional claim. 364 U.S. 339, 340 (1960). In *Wright v. Rockefeller*, 376 U.S. 52 (1964), the Court extended the reasoning of *Gomillion* to congressional districting.

Partisan gerrymandering claims have proved far more difficult to adjudicate. The basic reason is that, while it is illegal for a jurisdiction to depart from the one-person, one-vote rule, or to engage in racial discrimination in districting, "a jurisdiction may engage in constitutional political gerrymandering." *Hunt v. Cromartie*, 526 U.S. 541, 551 (1999).

To hold that legislators cannot take partisan interests into account when drawing district lines would essentially countermand the Framers' decision to entrust districting to political entities. The "central problem" is not determining whether a jurisdiction has engaged in partisan gerrymandering. It is "determining when political gerrymandering has gone too far." *Vieth*, 541 U.S. at 296 (plurality opinion).

* * *

In considering whether partisan gerrymandering claims are justiciable, we are mindful of Justice Kennedy's counsel in *Vieth*: Any standard for resolving such claims must be grounded in a "limited and precise rationale" and be "clear, manageable, and politically neutral." 541 U.S. at 306–308 (opinion concurring in judgment) * * *.

* * * If federal courts are to "inject [themselves] into the most heated partisan issues" by adjudicating partisan gerrymandering claims, they must be armed with a standard that can reliably differentiate unconstitutional from "constitutional political gerrymandering."

Partisan gerrymandering claims rest on an instinct that groups with a certain level of political support should enjoy a commensurate level of political power and influence. Explicitly or implicitly, a districting map is alleged to be unconstitutional because it makes it too difficult for one party to translate statewide support into seats in the legislature. But such a claim is based on a "norm that does not exist" in our electoral system—"statewide elections for representatives along party lines."

Partisan gerrymandering claims invariably sound in a desire for proportional representation. As Justice O'Connor put it, such claims are based on "a conviction that the greater the departure from proportionality, the more suspect an apportionment plan becomes." "Our cases, however, clearly foreclose any claim that the Constitution requires proportional representation or that legislatures in reapportioning must draw district lines to come as near as possible to allocating seats to the contending parties in proportion to what their anticipated statewide vote will be."

The Founders certainly did not think proportional representation was required. For more than 50 years after ratification of the Constitution, many States elected their congressional representatives through at-large or "general ticket" elections. Such States typically sent single-party delegations to Congress. That meant that a party could garner nearly half of the vote statewide and wind up without any seats in the congressional delegation * * *.

Unable to claim that the Constitution requires proportional representation outright, plaintiffs inevitably ask the courts to make their own political judgment about how much representation particular political parties deserve—based on the votes of their supporters—and to rearrange the challenged districts to achieve that end. But federal courts are not equipped to apportion political power as a matter of fairness, nor is there any basis for concluding that they were authorized to do so * * *.

The initial difficulty in settling on a "clear, manageable and politically neutral" test for fairness is that it is not even clear what fairness looks like in this context. There is a large measure of "unfairness" in any winner-take-all system. Fairness may mean a greater number of competitive districts. Such a claim seeks to undo packing and cracking so that supporters of the disadvantaged party have a better shot at electing their preferred candidates. But making as many districts as possible more competitive could be a recipe for disaster for the disadvantaged party. As Justice White has pointed out, "[i]f all or most of the districts are competitive . . . even a narrow statewide preference for either party would produce an overwhelming majority for the winning party in the state legislature." *Bandemer,* 478 U.S. at 130 (plurality opinion).

On the other hand, perhaps the ultimate objective of a "fairer" share of seats in the congressional delegation is most readily achieved by yielding to the gravitational pull of proportionality and engaging in cracking and packing, to ensure each party its "appropriate" share of "safe" seats. Such an approach, however, comes at the expense of competitive districts and of individuals in districts allocated to the opposing party.

Or perhaps fairness should be measured by adherence to "traditional" districting criteria, such as maintaining political subdivisions, keeping communities of interest together, and protecting incumbents. But protecting incumbents, for example, enshrines a particular partisan distribution. And the "natural political geography" of a State—such as the fact that urban electoral districts are often dominated by one political party—can itself lead to inherently packed districts * * *.

Deciding among just these different visions of fairness (you can imagine many others) poses basic questions that are political, not legal. There are no legal standards discernible in the Constitution for making such judgments, let alone limited and precise standards that are clear, manageable, and politically neutral. Any judicial decision on what is "fair" in this context would be an "unmoored determination" of the sort characteristic of a political question beyond the competence of the federal courts.

And it is only after determining how to define fairness that you can even begin to answer the determinative question: "How much is too much?" At what point does permissible partisanship become unconstitutional? If compliance with traditional districting criteria is the fairness touchstone, for example, how much deviation from those criteria is constitutionally acceptable and how should mapdrawers prioritize competing criteria? Should a court "reverse gerrymander" other parts of a State to counteract "natural" gerrymandering caused, for example, by the urban concentration of one party? If a districting plan protected half of the incumbents but redistricted the rest into head to head races, would that be constitutional? A court would have to rank the relative importance of those traditional criteria and weigh how much deviation from each to allow.

If a court instead focused on the respective number of seats in the legislature, it would have to decide the ideal number of seats for each party and determine at what point deviation from that balance went too far * * *.

Appellees contend that if we can adjudicate one-person, one-vote claims, we can also assess partisan gerrymandering claims. But the one-person, one-vote rule is relatively easy to administer as a matter of math. The same cannot be said of partisan gerrymandering claims, because the Constitution supplies no objective measure for assessing whether a districting map treats a political party fairly. It hardly follows from the principle that each person must have an equal say in the election of representatives that a person is entitled to have his political party achieve representation in some way commensurate to its share of statewide support.

* * *

Nor do our racial gerrymandering cases provide an appropriate standard for assessing partisan gerrymandering. "[N]othing in our case law compels the conclusion that racial and political gerrymanders are subject to precisely the same constitutional scrutiny. In fact, our country's long and persistent history of racial discrimination in voting—as well as our Fourteenth Amendment jurisprudence, which always has reserved the strictest scrutiny for discrimination on the basis of race—would seem to compel the opposite conclusion." *Shaw I*, 509 U.S. at 650 (citation omitted). Unlike partisan gerrymandering claims, a racial gerrymandering claim does not ask for a fair share of political power and influence, with all the justiciability conundrums that entails. It asks instead for the elimination of a racial classification. A partisan gerrymandering claim cannot ask for the elimination of partisanship.

Appellees and the dissent propose a number of "tests" for evaluating partisan gerrymandering claims, but none meets the need for a limited and precise standard that is judicially discernible and manageable. And none provides a solid grounding for judges to take the extraordinary step of reallocating power and influence between political parties.

* * *

* * * In racial gerrymandering cases, we rely on a "predominant intent" inquiry to determine whether race was, in fact, the reason particular district boundaries were drawn the way they were. If district lines were drawn for the purpose of separating racial groups, then they are subject to strict scrutiny because "race-based decisionmaking is inherently suspect." But determining that lines were drawn on the basis of partisanship does not indicate that the districting was improper. A permissible intent—securing partisan advantage—does not become constitutionally impermissible, like racial discrimination, when that permissible intent "predominates."

* * *

The plaintiffs' argument is that partisanship in districting should be regarded as simple discrimination against supporters of the opposing party on the basis of political viewpoint. Under that theory, any level of partisanship in districting would constitute an infringement of their First Amendment rights. But as the Court has explained, "[i]t would be idle . . . to contend that any political consideration taken into account in fashioning a reapportionment plan is sufficient to invalidate it." The First Amendment test simply describes the act of districting for partisan advantage. It provides no standard for determining when partisan activity goes too far.

* * *

Excessive partisanship in districting leads to results that reasonably seem unjust. But the fact that such gerrymandering is "incompatible with democratic principles" does not mean that the solution lies with the federal judiciary. We conclude that partisan gerrymandering claims present political questions beyond the reach of the federal courts. Federal judges have no license to reallocate political power between the two major political parties, with no plausible grant of authority in the Constitution, and no legal standards to limit and direct their decisions. "[J]udicial action must be governed by standard, by rule," and must be "principled, rational, and based upon reasoned distinctions" found in the Constitution or laws. *Vieth*, 541 U.S. at 278, 279 (plurality opinion). Judicial review of partisan gerrymandering does not meet those basic requirements.

* * *

What the appellees and dissent seek is an unprecedented expansion of judicial power. We have never struck down a partisan gerrymander as unconstitutional—despite various requests over the past 45 years. The expansion of judicial authority would not be into just any area of controversy, but into one of the most intensely partisan aspects of American political life. That intervention would be unlimited in scope and duration—it would recur over and over again around the country with each new round of districting, for state as well as federal representatives. Consideration of the impact of today's ruling on democratic principles cannot ignore the effect of the unelected and politically unaccountable branch of the Federal Government assuming such an extraordinary and unprecedented role.

* * *

No one can accuse this Court of having a crabbed view of the reach of its competence. But we have no commission to allocate political power and influence in the absence of a constitutional directive or legal standards to guide us in the exercise of such authority. "It is emphatically the province and duty of the judicial department to say what the law is." *Marbury v. Madison*, 1 Cranch at 177. In this rare circumstance, that means our duty is to say "this is not law."

The judgments of the United States District Court for the Middle District of North Carolina and the United States District Court for the District of Maryland are vacated, and the cases are remanded with instructions to dismiss for lack of jurisdiction.

It is so ordered.

■ JUSTICE KAGAN, with whom JUSTICE GINSBURG, JUSTICE BREYER, and JUSTICE SOTOMAYOR join, dissenting.

For the first time ever, this Court refuses to remedy a constitutional violation because it thinks the task beyond judicial capabilities.

And not just any constitutional violation. The partisan gerrymanders in these cases deprived citizens of the most fundamental of their constitutional rights: the rights to participate equally in the political process, to join with others to advance political beliefs, and to choose their political representatives. In so doing, the partisan gerrymanders here debased and dishonored our democracy, turning upside-down the core American idea that all governmental power derives from the people. These gerrymanders enabled politicians to entrench themselves in office as against voters' preferences. They promoted partisanship above respect for the popular will. They encouraged a politics of polarization and dysfunction. If left unchecked, gerrymanders like the ones here may irreparably damage our system of government.

And checking them is not beyond the courts. The majority's abdication comes just when courts across the country, including those below, have coalesced around manageable judicial standards to resolve partisan gerrymandering claims. Those standards satisfy the majority's own benchmarks. They do not require—indeed, they do not permit—courts to rely on their own ideas of electoral fairness, whether proportional representation or any other. And they limit courts to correcting only egregious gerrymanders, so judges do not become omnipresent players in the political process. But yes, the standards used here do allow—as well they should—judicial intervention in the worst-of-the-worst cases of democratic subversion, causing blatant constitutional harms. In other words, they allow courts to undo partisan gerrymanders of the kind we face today from North Carolina and Maryland. In giving such gerrymanders a pass from judicial review, the majority goes tragically wrong.

* * *

"Governments," the Declaration of Independence states, "deriv[e] their just Powers from the Consent of the Governed." * * *

Free and fair and periodic elections are the key to that vision * * *.

And partisan gerrymandering can make it meaningless. At its most extreme—as in North Carolina and Maryland—the practice amounts to "rigging elections." * * *

* * *

Partisan gerrymandering of the kind before us not only subverts democracy (as if that weren't bad enough). It violates individuals' constitutional rights as well * * *.

Partisan gerrymandering operates through vote dilution—the devaluation of one citizen's vote as compared to others. A mapmaker draws district lines to "pack" and "crack" voters likely to support the disfavored party He packs supermajorities of those voters into a relatively few districts, in numbers far greater than needed for their preferred candidates to prevail. Then he cracks the rest across many more districts, spreading them so thin that their candidates will not be able to win. Whether the person is packed or cracked, his vote carries less weight—has less consequence—than it would under a neutrally drawn (non-partisan) map. In short, the mapmaker has made some votes count for less, because they are likely to go for the other party.

That practice implicates the Fourteenth Amendment's Equal Protection Clause * * *.

And partisan gerrymandering implicates the First Amendment too * * *.

* * *

So the only way to understand the majority's opinion is as follows: In the face of grievous harm to democratic governance and flagrant infringements on individuals' rights—in the face of escalating partisan manipulation whose compatibility with this Nation's values and law no one defends—the majority declines to provide any remedy. For the first time in this Nation's history, the majority declares that it can do nothing about an acknowledged constitutional violation because it has searched high and low and cannot find a workable legal standard to apply.

The majority gives two reasons for thinking that the adjudication of partisan gerrymandering claims is beyond judicial capabilities. First and foremost, the majority says, it cannot find a neutral baseline—one not based on contestable notions of political fairness—from which to measure injury * * * And second, the majority argues that even after establishing a baseline, a court would have no way to answer "the determinative question: 'How much is too much?' " * * *.

I'll give the majority this one—and important—thing: It identifies some dangers everyone should want to avoid. Judges should not be apportioning political power based on their own vision of electoral fairness, whether proportional representation or any other. And judges should not be striking down maps left, right, and center, on the view that every smidgen of politics is a smidgen too much. Respect for state legislative processes—and restraint in the exercise of judicial authority—counsels intervention in only egregious cases.

But in throwing up its hands, the majority misses something under its nose: What it says can't be done has been done. Over the past several years, federal courts across the country—including, but not exclusively, in the decisions below—have largely converged on a standard for adjudicating partisan gerrymandering claims (striking down both Democratic and Republican districting plans in the process). And that standard does what the majority says is impossible. The standard does not use any judge-made conception of electoral fairness—either proportional representation or any other; instead, it takes as its baseline a State's own criteria of fairness, apart from partisan gain. And by requiring plaintiffs to make difficult showings relating to both purpose and effects, the standard invalidates the most extreme, but only the most extreme, partisan gerrymanders.

Start with the standard the lower courts used * * *. [B]oth courts (like others around the country) used basically the same three-part test to decide whether the plaintiffs had made out a vote dilution claim. As many legal standards do, that test has three parts: (1) intent; (2) effects; and (3) causation. First, the plaintiffs challenging a districting plan must prove that state officials' "predominant purpose" in drawing a district's lines was to "entrench [their party] in power" by diluting the votes of citizens favoring its rival. Second, the plaintiffs must establish that the lines drawn in fact have the intended effect by "substantially" diluting their votes. And third, if the plaintiffs make those showings, the State must come up with a legitimate, non-partisan justification to save its map. If you are a lawyer, you know that this test looks utterly ordinary. It is the sort of thing courts work with every day.

* * *

* * * Contrary to the majority's suggestion, the District Courts did not have to—and in fact did not—choose among competing visions of electoral fairness. That is because they did not try to compare the State's actual map to an "ideally fair" one (whether based on proportional representation or some other criterion). Instead, they looked at the difference between what the State did and what the State would have done if politicians hadn't been intent on partisan gain * * *.

* * *

The majority's "how much is too much" critique fares no better than its neutrality argument. How about the following for a first-cut answer: This much is too much. By any measure, a map that produces a greater partisan skew than any of 3,000 randomly generated maps (all with the State's political geography and districting criteria built in) reflects "too much" partisanship * * *. If the majority had done nothing else, it could have set the line here. How much is too much? At the least, any gerrymanders as bad as these.

And if the majority thought that approach too case-specific, it could have used the lower courts' general standard—focusing on "predominant" purpose and "substantial" effects—without fear of indeterminacy * * *. Those inquiries would be no harder here than in other contexts.

* * *

Of all times to abandon the Court's duty to declare the law, this was not the one. The practices challenged in these cases imperil our system of government. Part of the Court's role in that system is to defend its foundations. None is more important than free and fair elections. With respect but deep sadness, I dissent.

NOTES AND QUESTIONS

1. *Rucho* says that federal courts cannot adjudicate claims of partisan gerrymandering. State courts, legislatures of all stripes, and voters through referenda are still free to do so. What standards will those institutions use? If state courts choose

to adjudicate such claims under their own state constitutions, are they doing something improper or unjudicial?

2. Congressional elections occur by district because of an 1842 statute, not because of anything required by the Constitution. If a majority of Congress votes to repeal that 1842 statute for partisan reasons, thinking that at-large elections would improve the position of the party in power, would the dissent find that act unconstitutional? Would you?

3. Sometimes, as with impeachment, the Court concludes that matters are textually or structurally committed to some particular institution. Is that what happened in *Rucho*? Which text or structure did the work?

4. Implicit, or perhaps explicit, in *Rucho* is the notion that the "judicial Power" can only operate when it can apply objective norms in a neutral fashion. A legal doctrine that says, "courts should just do whatever is fair," would presumably fail this test and thus not be an exercise of "judicial Power." Do any other doctrines that you have encountered thus far fail this test? Is there something distinctive about a decisionmaking process, other than the title of the person employing it, that marks it out as "judicial"? How "rule-like" does a legal norm have to be before it counts as law enforceable by the "judicial Power"? *Compare* Antonin Scalia, *The Rule of Law as a Law of Rules,* 56 U. CHI. L. REV. 1175 (1989) *with* Steven G. Calabresi & Gary Lawson, *The Rule of Law as a Law of Law,* 90 NOTRE DAME L. REV. 483 (2014).

[Assignment 28]

C. THE CASE OR CONTROVERSY REQUIREMENT OF ARTICLE III, SECTION 2

Article III, Section 2: The judicial Power shall extend to all Cases, in Law and Equity, arising under this Constitution, the Laws of the United States, and Treaties made, or which shall be made, under their Authority;—to all Cases affecting Ambassadors, other public Ministers and Consuls;—to all Cases of admiralty and maritime Jurisdiction;—to Controversies to which the United States shall be a Party;—to Controversies between two or more States;—between a State and Citizens of another State;—between Citizens of different States;—between Citizens of the same State claiming Lands under Grants of different States, and between a State, or the Citizens thereof, and foreign States, Citizens or Subjects.

The first paragraph of Article III, Section 2 says that the judicial power granted by the Article III Vesting Clause "shall extend to" nine categories of "cases" or "controversies." What is a "case" or a "controversy" for purposes of this language? That is a topic that is usually dealt with in some detail in courses on Federal Courts (or Federal Jurisdiction, as the courses are sometimes called). Here we can only give a brief introduction to one of the most difficult, convoluted, and controversial of all constitutional law doctrines.

The issue came up in the early 1790s. At President Washington's request, Secretary of State Thomas Jefferson asked the justices for legal advice on dozens of questions involving international law and a U.S. treaty with France. The Court, in a letter of August 8, 1793 signed by all justices, politely but firmly declined to answer:

Sir

We have considered the *previous* Question stated in a Letter written to us by your Direction, by the Secretary of State, on the 18th of last month.

The Lines of Separation drawn by the Constitution between the three Departments of Government—their being in certain Respects checks on each other—and our being Judges of a court in the last Resort—are Considerations which afford strong arguments against the Propriety of our extrajudicially deciding the questions alluded to; especially as the Power given by the Constitution to the President of calling on the Heads of Departments for opinions, seems to have been *purposely* as well as expressly limited to *executive* Departments.

We exceedingly regret every Event that may cause Embarrassment to your administration; but we derive Consolation from the Reflection, that your Judgment will discern what is Right, and that your usual Prudence, Decision and Firmness will surmount every obstacle to the Preservation of the Rights, Peace, and Dignity of the united States. We have the Honor to be, with perfect Respect, Sir, your most obedient and most h'ble servants.

Technically, answering a request for advice from the President on foreign policy is no more forbidden to Supreme Court justices by the Constitution than is answering a request for advice from a close friend on whether and whom to marry. The Constitution forbids members of Congress, but not federal judges, from simultaneously holding executive positions; in theory, someone could serve both as a federal judge and as a Cabinet officer. But the Court's answer (and the long-standing tradition against dual service of federal judges) draws on a deeper structural point—a lack of "Propriety" in giving such an answer—that accurately reflects founding-era thinking about the judicial role. Madison's notes taken at the Philadelphia Constitutional Convention show that proposals were made to give the courts power to issue advisory opinions in matters other than concrete disputes, and they were rejected because the Framers thought the courts ought only to decide cases of a judiciary nature. A proposal to vest the veto power jointly in the President and the Supreme Court justices in what was called a Council of Revision was also rejected. The Framers felt the justices ought not to be involved in policy making or in giving advice in any way, even if the Constitution does not formally forbid it in all circumstances.

The prohibition against advisory opinions was thus understood in the "Correspondence of the Justices," as the justices' letter has come to be called, as requiring that for the judicial power to be invoked there had to be an actual dispute between adverse litigants. This requirement guarantees notice and an opportunity to be heard to adverse parties, and it has been understood as precluding collusive suits.

A second aspect of the prohibition on advisory opinions also emerged in the 1790s in *Hayburn's Case*, 2 U.S. (2 Dall.) 408 (1792) where the federal courts were confronted with a federal statute that required them to issue decisions on the amount of benefits owed under federal law to veterans of the Revolutionary War. The judges' decisions were not final and conclusive, however, but were subject to change and revision by executive branch officials. The constitutionality of this statute never reached the Supreme Court, but five of the six Supreme Court justices riding circuit ruled that the statute unconstitutionally asked them to give an advisory opinion because there was no substantial likelihood that a federal court decision would have an effect in the real world. Thus were born the two prongs of the Supreme Court's bar on federal court issuance of advisory opinions. At a bare minimum, the case or controversy requirement of Article III, Section 2, clause 1 requires that there be: (1) an actual dispute between adverse litigants on a matter within judicial cognizance and (2) a substantial likelihood that a federal court decision will have an effect in the real world.

Today, the ban on advisory opinions is operationalized through a series of so-called "justiciability" doctrines that determine who can bring lawsuits in federal court and at what point in a dispute they can bring them. In theory, these doctrines flesh out what it means for there to be a "case" or "controversy" within the meaning of the jurisdictional heads in Article III. In practice, those doctrines have taken on a life of their own, sometime connected only loosely, if at all, to the constitutional text. The three principal doctrinal categories of justiciability (apart from the political question doctrine and the ban on advisory opinions) are *standing, mootness,* and *ripeness.* The Supreme Court has built up an elaborate, and in many ways arcane, body of caselaw on these justiciability doctrines. To our knowledge, no one at present, from any perspective or modality, is satisfied with the state of the doctrine, though people disagree wildly on the source and direction of the problems and potential solutions. Nonetheless, these doctrines are vital to get one's case into federal court, and so questions about them frequently arise in both private and governmental practice. In fact, in the private practice of law, one is far more likely to run into questions about justiciability than about any other constitutional law issue, especially if one's practice includes an appreciable amount of administrative law, where these doctrines (and some even more arcane statutory and common law analogues to these doctrines) are ubiquitous. Here a few key introductory points about these doctrines:

Standing concerns who is the proper party to bring a legal challenge. This idea permeates the legal system, even though the label of "standing" is not always employed to describe it. Suppose that someone breaches a contract with your neighbor, and the neighbor chooses not to sue. You are offended at the thought of contracts being breached with impunity. Can you sue? Obviously not. It was your neighbor's contract, not yours. But you claim that worry about the breach keeps you awake at nights. You wake up screaming, in cold sweats, with visions of breaches dancing in your head. The law still will not let you sue. Not every injury gives rise to a legal action; only those kinds of injuries for which the law provides a cause of action entitle you to sue. There is no cause of action for mental anguish at a world full of contractual infidelity.

This basic idea that only *legally protected* injuries count in court obviously applies in federal courts as well as state courts: If you have no cause of action, you will lose on a motion to dismiss. It is not enough to show that there is a general "cause of action" for breach of contract. There must be a cause of action for *you* in regard to the breach of the *specific* contract that you are complaining about. Whether one calls this idea "lack of standing," because you are the wrong person to sue, or simply lack of a cause of action makes no difference. At a minimum, the "case" or "controversy" requirement of Article III constitutionalizes this basic model of adjudication requiring a showing of personal injury to a legal right.

But writing that model into Article III has other consequences. First, it may limit what Congress can do by statute. Suppose that Congress passes a law purporting to allow federal courts to hear complaints by neighbors of other people's broken contracts. Can the courts now hear those claims (again assuming that the other jurisdictional requirements are met)? If the words "case" or "controversy" in Article III have substantive content, the answer is "no." When the Constitution was ratified in 1788, the English law courts only recognized certain kinds of claims as justiciable, and those claims did not include mental anguish at the thought of broken contracts. If the "case" or "controversy" requirement *constitutionally limits* federal courts to hearing cases involving—or at least that are analogous to—the kinds of personal injuries to legal rights of the kind that were judicially cognizable before the English courts at Westminster in 1788, Congress in 2020 could not allow them to hear newfangled kinds of action with no eighteenth-century analogue. Congress cannot create a "case" or "controversy" out of thin air; only certain kinds of injuries constitutionally count.

The second consequence is that federal courts must therefore determine the minimum requirements for making a dispute a constitutional "case" or "controversy." What kinds of injuries count? Does it matter what kind of relief the court is being asked to give? Does it matter what kind of relief a court thinks it will be able to give? The short version is that courts over the last century have crystallized the standing inquiry into three questions: (1) has the plaintiff suffered an "injury in fact" of the kind that is legally protected, (2) did the defendant's conduct cause the injury proximately enough to generate a "case" or "controversy" between the parties before the court, and (3) if the court rules for the plaintiff, is there a significant likelihood that the court can issue an order that will remedy the problem? If the answer to any of these three questions is "no," the plaintiff does not have standing to sue.

The third consequence is that federal courts must decide how this model works when the plaintiff is claiming unconstitutional action by the federal government. In one sense, every unconstitutional action by the government works an "injury" of sorts to every citizen; it is a breach of the government's fiduciary duty to stay within the scope of its granted powers. Does that mean that every citizen can sue to prevent every federal constitutional violation? Or does that kind of "public law" litigation need to be analogized to the "private law" model of standing to require some kind of concrete, individualized harm to the specific plaintiff? What do those harms have to look like in constitutional cases?

Fourth, remember that *Marbury v. Madison* said that the power of judicial review is triggered by the obligation and duty of the federal courts to decide cases or controversies. The Supreme Court's standing rules, which help define what is a case or controversy, thus mark the outer boundaries of judicial review.

To explore these questions through caselaw would require far more time and space than this course can provide. The seminal decisions are the twin cases of *Massachusetts v. Mellon*, 262 U.S. 447 (1923), and *Frothingham v. Mellon*, 262 U.S. 447 (1923), involving constitutional challenges to a federal spending measure brought by a State and a taxpayer, respectively. The Court held that neither party had standing. In dismissing the taxpayer's challenge, the Court wrote:

> We have no power *per se* to review and annul acts of Congress on the ground that they are unconstitutional. That question may be considered only when

> the justification for some direct injury suffered or threatened, presenting a justiciable issue, is made to rest upon such an act. Then the power exercised is that of ascertaining and declaring the law applicable to the controversy. It amounts to little more than the negative power to disregard an unconstitutional enactment, which otherwise would stand in the way of the enforcement of a legal right. The party who invokes the power must be able to show, not only that the statute is invalid, but that he has sustained or is immediately in danger of sustaining some direct injury as the result of its enforcement, and not merely that he suffers in some indefinite way in common with people generally * * *. Looking through forms of words to the substance of their complaint, it is merely that officials of the executive department of the government are executing and will execute an act of Congress asserted to be unconstitutional; and this we are asked to prevent. To do so would be, not to decide a judicial controversy, but to assume a position of authority over plainly we do not possess.

Id. at 488–89. From that seed has grown a doctrine of almost indescribable complexity. For the some of the most interesting (if not necessarily enlightening) illustrations of the requirements of injury-in-fact, causation, and redressability, and the sharp divisions they sometimes generation in the application of those elements, see *Lujan v. Defenders of Wildlife,* 504 U.S. 555 (1992); *Friends of the Earth, Inc. v. Laidlaw Environmental Services (TOC), Inc.,* 528 U.S. 167 (2000); *Summers v. Earth Island Institute,* 555 U.S. 488 (2009). For the special problems posed by the standing of States (including the problem of who counts as the "State"), see *Massachusetts v. EPA,* 549 U.S. 497 (2007); *Hollingsworth v. Perry,* 570 U.S. 693 (2013).

The standing requirement gives rise to a second potential justiciability doctrine. Suppose that you have standing at the time you bring a lawsuit, but the injury that you complain about gets fixed. Congress, let us say, imposes what you regard as an unconstitutional tax, and you according sue, and Congress responds by repealing the tax and refunding your money. You had a justiciable claim when you filed your suit. Has it now gone away because there is longer anything for you to sue about? The *mootness doctrine* says that your suit has indeed gone away; there is no longer a live "case" or "controversy," even though there might have been one when the suit began. As an especially dramatic example: In the 1820s, the State of Georgia and the Cherokee Nation were arguing about whether the Cherokees had sovereignty over their tribal lands and thus had authority to try people for murders committed in Cherokee territory. While the two sides were litigating who could try a particular murder suspect, Georgia simply executed him, thereby "mooting" that case. (The Cherokees eventually won a pyrrhic victory in the Supreme Court, *see Worcester v. Georgia,* 31 U.S. (6 Pet.) 515 (1832), but were forced out of their lands by Congress and President Jackson three years after that legal victory and sent on the "trail of tears." *See* Gerard N. Magliocca, *Preemptive Opinions: The Secret History of* Worcester v. Georgia *and* Dred Scott, 63 U. Pitt. L. Rev. 487 (2002).) The death of a party often moots a case, though sometimes the cause of action can persist as an action of the person's estate, as in *Humphrey's Executor,* where the estate could maintain the action for back pay even after Humphrey died.

There are some important exceptions to the mootness doctrine that allow courts to hear claims that may technically be moot. First, where there are collateral consequences or secondary injuries that survive even after the primary injury has been mooted, the case can still continue. A good example is *Powell v. McCormack*. By the time the case reached the Supreme Court, Rep. Powell's claim to be seated in his session of Congress was moot because that session had ended, and he had been allowed sit in the new Congress to which he had been re-elected. But he could still sue regarding his expulsion because he had a claim for backpay and financial benefits from the time that he was denied his seat. A second exception to mootness doctrine was created when *Roe v. Wade* created a constitutional right to abortion. Plaintiff Roe was no longer pregnant when the case reached the Justices: litigating a case to the Supreme Court takes much longer than nine months. The Court said that where there are wrongs that are capable of repetition to the same plaintiff, yet that would evade review because of timing, the case should not be deemed moot. This exception has been applied in other contexts. Third, the Court has quite rightly said that where defendants voluntarily cease the conduct for which they are being sued, and yet they are free to resume that conduct at any time, the case ought not to be deemed moot. Finally, in class action litigation, a properly certified class action can continue even if the named plaintiff's claims have become moot so long as the case is not moot as to some members of the certified class. These four exceptions to mootness doctrine greatly limit that doctrine's significance.

Apart from these judicially self-imposed doctrines, the other major constraint on the ability of federal courts to hear cases comes from Congress. Remember that the Constitution does not require Congress to create any federal courts other than the Supreme Court. If Congress chooses to create lower federal courts, can Congress limit those courts to hearing only a subset of the cases and controversies identified in Article III as the objects of the "judicial Power"? The doctrinal answer has long been yes, *see Sheldon v. Sill,* 49 U.S. (8 How.) 441 (1850), though the reasoning in the case is a bit thin for a proposition of that magnitude. After all, the language of Article III seems to vest all of the "judicial Power" in all federal courts and then, of its own force, extend that judicial power to a defined set of cases and controversies. Nonetheless, Congress's power to control the jurisdiction of the lower federal courts is a staple of modern law, and anytime you want to bring your case in lower federal court, you need to find not only an applicable head of jurisdiction in Article III but also a congressional statute conferring jurisdiction on the court in which you are trying to sue.

The Constitution is a bit more specific about the jurisdiction of the Supreme Court, and in particular about which cases the Supreme Court can hear without any need to go through a lower court first:

> In all cases affecting ambassadors, other public ministers and consuls, and those in which a state shall be party, the Supreme Court shall have original jurisdiction. In all the other cases before mentioned, the Supreme Court shall have appellate jurisdiction, both as to law and fact, with such exceptions, and under such regulations as the Congress shall make.

Does the reference to "exceptions" made by Congress mean that Congress, with respect to cases within the Court's appellate rather than original jurisdiction, can eliminate some of those cases from the Court's jurisdiction altogether? And if so, can Congress combine that with a power to define and limit the jurisdiction of lower federal courts to take certain "cases" out of the power of the federal courts altogether? This kind of legislative attempt to remove cases from the federal courts altogether is generally called "jurisdiction-stripping." It is a topic whose theoretical interest and importance has largely outstripped its practical import over the years, but as a matter of both theory and practice it warrants a brief look.

Efforts to pass jurisdiction-stripping bills have been around for a very long time. In the 1820s, some congressional Democrats noisily argued that the Supreme Court should be stripped of its power to hear appeals from the highest court of a State because those members of Congress disapproved of the Marshall Court's decisions emphasizing federal power. After the Civil War, congressional Republicans became very concerned that Reconstruction might be held unconstitutional in a case that was before the Supreme Court, *Ex parte McCardle,* 74 U.S. (7 Wall.) 506 (1869). The case had already been briefed and argued, but Congress stripped the Court of jurisdiction to decide the case, even overriding a veto of President Johnson in order to do so. In a somewhat cryptic opinion, the Court gave effect to the congressional statute depriving it of power to hear the case, but only while noting that another avenue to Court review was available, so that Congress had merely closed off one avenue of jurisdiction without entirely stripping the Court of jurisdiction over the case.

Jurisdiction-stripping bills have been introduced but not passed in Congress in the modern era as well. Southern segregationist members of Congress tried to no avail to strip the federal courts of jurisdiction in school desegregation cases. Conservatives like former Senator Jesse Helms tried in the 1980s to strip the federal courts of jurisdiction to hear abortion or school prayer cases. None of these measures ever passed, in part because of serious doubts as to their constitutionality.

The proponents of a broad congressional power to strip the Supreme Court of appellate jurisdiction over a single class of cases leap to the final clause of the provision about the Supreme Court's original and appellate jurisdiction quoted above and say: "Aha. Congress has plenary power to make 'exceptions' to the Supreme Court's appellate jurisdiction. That means we can take certain cases away from the Supreme Court (while also denying jurisdiction to the lower federal courts under *Sheldon v. Sill)* and leave them to be decided in the final instance in the fifty state supreme courts, which are more likely to rule our way." Ponder this argument for a moment and consider how persuasive it is.

We think the argument for plenary congressional power over Supreme Court jurisdiction is not as persuasive as it looks at first glance. We think that the Vesting Clause of Article III itself gives the Supreme Court all of the judicial power, just as the Vesting Clause of Article II gives the President all of the executive power. See Steven G. Calabresi, *The Vesting Clauses as Power Grants*, 88 NORTHWESTERN UNIV. L. REV. 1377 (1993). Article III, Section 2 makes it clear that the Supreme Court's judicial power must "extend to" all cases arising under federal law. That plainly does not mean that the Supreme Court has to decide itself all cases arising under federal law, just as the President need not personally execute every federal law. It does mean, however, that the Supreme Court's essential role at the apex of the federal judiciary cannot be taken away, so it must have at least some opportunity to rule on those cases if it wishes to do so.

Well then, one might ask, what about the Exceptions Clause language quoted above? Clearly Congress has some power to make exceptions to the Supreme Court's appellate jurisdiction. There are multiple possible explanations for this clause. It could, for example, allow regulations governing the timing of appeals brought before the Supreme Court, but not substantive efforts to overturn the Court's caselaw on a question. More intriguingly, we think, the Clause could have been meant to give Congress the power to take cases away from the Supreme Court's appellate jurisdiction by *adding them to its original jurisdiction*, in contravention of *Marbury v. Madison*. Look again at the clauses from Article III quoted above. The Vesting Clause and the Shall Extend Clause give the Supreme Court judicial power to decide all cases arising under federal law. The Original Jurisdiction Clause gives the Supreme Court original jurisdiction over cases affecting ambassadors, other public ministers and consuls, and those to which a State is a party. But the Original Jurisdiction clause never explicitly says that Congress cannot add additional cases to the Court's original jurisdiction. Therefore, if Congress excepts, say, a flag-burning case out of the appellate jurisdiction of the Supreme Court, maybe the Vesting Clause of Article III commands that Congress add that case to the Supreme Court's original jurisdiction. And maybe if Congress fails to do that, its use of its Exceptions Clause power is an unconstitutional effort by the legislative branch to decapitate the judicial branch, which is its co-equal by virtue of the Vesting Clause of Article III. We have made this argument at great length elsewhere. *See* Steven G. Calabresi & Gary Lawson, *The Unitary Executive, Jurisdiction Stripping, and the* Hamdan *Opinions: A Textualist Response to Justice Scalia,* 107 COLUM. L. REV. 1002 (2007).

Unfortunately for us, the textual argument we just made above is foreclosed by the holding of *Marbury v. Madison* that Congress cannot add to the original jurisdiction of the Supreme Court. As a practical matter, it is obvious that the Supreme Court is not going to reconsider and overrule *Marbury v. Madison* at this late date, no matter how wrongly decided it may have been. (So you are reading a book edited by two people who think *Marbury v. Madison* was wrong? On that particular point—and several others as well, such as the ability of Congress to create justices of the peace in the District of Columbia who are neither Article III judges nor executive officials controllable by the President—most definitely yes. With regard to the more famous dictum in *Marbury* regarding judicial review, on the other hand, we think *Marbury* was dead-on right.) But except for the cryptic opinion in *Ex Parte McCardle*, the Supreme Court has never clearly ruled on the question whether Congress can use its Exceptions Clause power to take particular issues away from the Supreme Court. If confronted with such a case, our analysis suggests that Congress's Exceptions Clause power ought to be read quite narrowly. And just to be clear: We do not think that the Article III Exceptions Clause is a grant of power to Congress at all. It is a cross-reference to possible exercises of Congress's power under the Necessary and Proper Clause to make laws "necessary and proper for carrying into Execution" the federal judicial power. *See* David E. Engdahl, *Intrinsic Limits of Congress' Power Regarding the Judicial Branch*, 1999 B.Y.U. L. REV. 75, 119–32.

If Congress does not create lower federal courts, or creates lower federal courts with less than the full range of constitutionally permissible jurisdiction, cases for which there is no available federal court must be brought in state courts, which will either be authorized to hear those cases by their own state laws and constitutions or perhaps ordered to hear them by Congress using its power to "constitute Tribunals." Will the Supreme Court be able to hear those cases on appeal? The first Congress assumed that it could by authorizing review in 1789 of state court decisions

> where is drawn in question the validity of a treaty or statute of, or an authority exercised under the United States, and the decision is against

> their validity; or where is drawn in question the validity of a statute of, or an authority exercised under any State, on the ground of their being repugnant to the constitution, treaties or laws of the United States, and the decision is in favour of such their validity, or where is drawn in question the construction of any clause of the constitution, or of a treaty, or statute of, or commission held under the United States, and the decision is against the title, right, privilege or exemption specially set up or claimed by either party, under such clause of the said Constitution, treaty, statute or commission.

Act of Sept. 24, 1789, ch. XX, § 25, 1 Stat. 73, 85–86. The Court early on held this statute constitutional. *See Martin v. Hunter's Lessee,* 14 U.S. (1 Wheat.) 304 (1816); *Cohens v. Virginia,* 19 U.S. (6 Wheat.) 264 (1821). The latter case, *Cohens v. Virginia,* is especially interesting, because it was a criminal appeal. The State is always a party in a criminal case, so a criminal defendant who claims a violation of federal constitutional or statutory rights is suing against a State. The Constitution, we saw, gives the Supreme Court original, trial-court jurisdiction in cases in which "a State shall be a party." Does this specific grant of original jurisdiction foreclose giving the Supreme Court appellate jurisdiction in criminal cases that originate in state courts? The Supreme Court said no:

> The constitution gives the Supreme Court original jurisdiction in certain enumerated cases, and gives it appellate jurisdiction in all others. Among those in which jurisdiction must be exercised in the appellate form, are cases arising under the constitution and laws of the United States. These provisions of the constitution are equally obligatory, and are to be equally respected. If a State be a party, the jurisdiction of this Court is original; if the case arise under a constitution or a law, the jurisdiction is appellate. But a case to which a State is a party may arise under the constitution or a law of the United States. What rule is applicable to such a case? What, then, becomes the duty of the Court? Certainly, we think, so to construe the constitution as to give effect to both provisions, as far as it is possible to reconcile them, and not to permit their seeming repugnancy to destroy each other. We must endeavor so to construe them as to preserve the true intent and meaning of the instrument.
>
> In one description of cases, the jurisdiction of the Court is founded entirely on the character of the parties; and the nature of the controversy is not contemplated by the constitution. The character of the parties is every thing, the nature of the case nothing. In the other description of cases, the jurisdiction is founded entirely on the character of the case, and the parties are not contemplated by the constitution. In these, the nature of the case is every thing, the character of the parties nothing. When, then, the constitution declares the jurisdiction, in cases where a State shall be a party, to be original, and in all cases arising under the constitution or a law, to be appellate—the conclusion seems irresistible, that its framers designed to include in the first class those cases in which jurisdiction is given, because a State is a party; and to include in the second, those in which jurisdiction is given, because the case arises under the constitution or a law.

This reasonable construction is rendered necessary by other considerations.

That the constitution or a law of the United States, is involved in a case, and makes a part of it, may appear in the progress of a cause, in which the Courts of the Union, but for that circumstance, would have no jurisdiction, and which of consequence could not originate in the Supreme Court. In such a case, the jurisdiction can be exercised only in its appellate form. To deny its exercise in this form is to deny its existence, and would be to construe a clause, dividing the power of the Supreme Court, in such manner, as in a considerable degree to defeat the power itself. All must perceive, that this construction can be justified only where it is absolutely necessary. We do not think the article under consideration presents that necessity.

* * *

* * * It is admitted, that "affirmative words are often, in their operation, negative of other objects than those affirmed;" and that where "a negative or exclusive sense must be given to them, or they have no operation at all," they must receive that negative or exclusive sense. But where they have full operation without it; where it would destroy some of the most important objects for which the power was created; then, we think, affirmative words ought not to be construed negatively.

The constitution declares, that in cases where a State is a party, the Supreme Court shall have original jurisdiction; but does not say that its appellate jurisdiction shall not be exercised in cases where, from their nature, appellate jurisdiction is given, whether a State be or be not a party. It may be conceded, that where the case is of such a nature as to admit of its originating in the Supreme Court, it ought to originate there; but where, from its nature, it cannot originate in that Court, these words ought not to be so construed as to require it. There are many cases in which it would be found extremely difficult, and subversive of the spirit of the constitution, to maintain the construction, that appellate jurisdiction cannot be exercised where one of the parties might sue or be sued in this Court.

* * *

It is, we think, apparent, that to give this distributive clause the interpretation contended for, to give to its affirmative words a negative operation, in every possible case, would, in some instances, defeat the obvious intention of the article. Such an interpretation would not consist with those rules which, from time immemorial, have guided Courts, in their construction of instruments brought under their consideration. It must, therefore, be discarded. Every part of the article must be taken into view, and that construction adopted which will consist with its words, and promote its general intention. The Court may imply a negative from affirmative words, where the implication promotes, not where it defeats the intention.

If we apply this principle, the correctness of which we believe will not be controverted, to the distributive clause under consideration, the result, we think, would be this: the original jurisdiction of the Supreme Court, in

> cases where a State is a party, refers to those cases in which, according to the grant of power made in the preceding clause, jurisdiction might be exercised in consequence of the character of the party, and an original suit might be instituted in any of the federal Courts; not to those cases in which an original suit might not be instituted in a federal Court. Of the last description, is every case between a State and its citizens, and, perhaps, every case in which a State is enforcing its penal laws. In such cases, therefore, the Supreme Court cannot take original jurisdiction. In every other case, that is, in every case to which the judicial power extends, and in which original jurisdiction is not expressly given, that judicial power shall be exercised in the appellate, and only in the appellate form. The original jurisdiction of this Court cannot be enlarged, but its appellate jurisdiction may be exercised in every case cognizable under the third article of the constitution, in the federal Courts, in which original jurisdiction cannot be exercised; and the extent of this judicial power is to be measured, not by giving the affirmative words of the distributive clause a negative operation in every possible case, but by giving their true meaning to the words which define its extent.

19 U.S. (6 Wheat.) at 392–95, 398–99. As you go through this course, imagine how different it would be if the Supreme Court could not, for instance, review criminal convictions from state courts.

The above reasoning of the Court in *Cohens* seems in tension with the reasoning in *Marbury v. Madison* which concluded (wrongly, in our view) that Congress could not give the Supreme Court original jurisdiction in any cases other than those specifically designated for its original jurisdiction in Article III. This tension did not escape the notice of counsel for Virginia. The Court's oft-quoted response:

> It is a maxim not to be disregarded, that general expressions, in every opinion, are to be taken in connection with the case in which those expressions are used. If they go beyond the case, they may be respected, but ought not to control the judgment in a subsequent suit when the very point is presented for decision. The reason of this maxim is obvious. The question actually before the Court is investigated with care, and considered in its full extent. Other principles which may serve to illustrate it, are considered in their relation to the case decided, but their possible bearing on all other cases is seldom completely investigated.

Id. at 399–400. This has become the standard citation when courts seek to limit the effect of prior decisions (in other words, to say "oops").

CHAPTER 3

NATIONAL LEGISLATIVE POWER IN A FEDERAL SYSTEM: THE ENUMERATION OF FEDERAL POWERS AND ARTICLES IV–VII

[Assignment 29]

I. FEDERALISM AND EMPIRE

The United States of America is the world's first and most successful republican empire. It started as thirteen contiguous States located along the Atlantic seacoast. It now stretches across a continent as the third most populous and fourth largest nation in the world (and even the third largest nation if one does not include Tibet as part of China). Alaska and Hawaii are not contiguous with the rest of the country, and the United States maintains overseas possessions—colonies, if you will—in the Pacific, Atlantic, and Caribbean. In 1809, Thomas Jefferson told James Madison that he expected America to expand into "such an empire for liberty as she has never surveyed since the creation." Thomas Jefferson to the President of the United States, Apr. 27, 1809, *in* THE WRITINGS OF THOMAS JEFFERSON 275, 288 (Albert Ellery Bergh ed., 1905). Whether or not that prediction has been borne out, the United States has definitely endured and prospered, with more than enough elements of "empire" to warrant the label. The history of the world is full of the story of the rise and fall of empires, such as those of ancient China, ancient Rome, and more recently the British Empire, which was so large that the sun never set on its possessions. These empires flourished for a number of reasons, including the free trade zones they created and the legal order (e.g., *Pax Romana* or *Pax Britannica*), they brought to their citizens. But they were not democracies or republics. As the Roman Republic became the Roman Empire, the democratic inputs into Roman governance came to an end. The British Empire was partially democratic, for the citizens of England, Wales, Scotland, and Ireland could vote for Members of the House of Commons, just as the British colonies could usually elect a colonial legislature. The British colonies, however, were not represented in the House of Commons; the British House of Lords retained full legislative power until 1911; and the Monarch, and his or her colonial Royal Governors, were not historically, and are not now, popularly elected.

In the United States, by contrast, thirty-seven States have been added to the original thirteen, and they are all co-equal members of the American democratic-republican empire. The U.S. does have a few anomalous territories that are disenfranchised, such as Puerto Rico, Guam, the Virgin Islands, and the District of Columbia, but they are an exception and not the rule. When the United States defeated Germany in World Wars I and II, and Japan and Italy in World War II, and the Soviet Union and its Eastern European allies in the Cold War, it did not try to annex those vanquished enemies' territories. The U.S., instead, supported—and in the case of World War II imposed—democratic governments on the vanquished, and then it withdrew, to provide a free military defense for its former foes. Germany, Japan, and many of the countries of Eastern Europe remain, to this day, completely reliant on the United States for their military defense.

There have been many successful democracies, republican or otherwise, on a small scale: ancient Athens, the Roman Republic, the Venetian Republic, the Netherlands, England, Switzerland, and the New England colonies' town meetings. But, by and large, empires have not been democracies. One reason for this is undoubtedly that the strong army and navy needed to win and retain an empire could so easily become a threat to popular self-rule. Many thoughtful observers, in 1787, denied that it was possible to create a truly democratic empire. They believed that democracy could only flourish in small, homogeneous city-states. They feared that if the thirteen free colonies on the Atlantic seacoast of North America formed a strong central government empire, freedom and democracy would perish along the way. Most of the people who thought this way became Anti-Federalist opponents of the new Constitution of 1787. But even some supporters of the U.S. Constitution of 1787 worried about the threat a stronger national government might pose to democracy and freedom.

The Framers of the Constitution, many of whom read widely in Greek, Roman, and (then-)modern European history, thought they had found an answer to the democrats' worries about empire. The answer they came up with was *federalism*, the division of power, especially legislative power, vertically between a federal government and concurrent State governments. Federal power was further limited by the separation of powers and by bicameralism for the Congress. Federalism is America's distinctive contribution to political theory. It was such a key part of the constitutional framework that the advocates of the Constitution of 1787 became known as "Federalists." Federalism is neither purely a doctrine of nationalism nor purely a doctrine of State's rights. Thus, a Federalist in 1787 could perfectly well have thought that the federal government was too weak, while a Federalist today might think the State governments are currently too weak. Federalism defines a strategy—divide powers between different levels of government—but it does not dictate a specific division of power to implement that strategy. Federalism requires a balance—an Aristotelian Golden Mean—of federal and of State power, as well as checks and balances by each level of government on the other. A successful federation is thus a well-balanced federation, with the States and the federal government both retaining significant power. The trick is getting the right balance.

America's federal system had its origins, in part, in the federalism of the British Empire, in which thirteen chartered royal colonies were created as independent and partially self-governing entities on the North American continent, with their laws and judicial decisions open to reversal by the Privy Council (also sometimes called the Board of Trade). These thirteen British colonies were democracies with often loose ties to the British motherland. In most colonies, the King appointed a Royal Governor, and the colonists elected by popular vote a lower house of the legislature, which had the sole power to raise taxes. *See supra* pages 11–12.

By the time of American Independence in 1776, democracy (but with a constitutional monarch in England) was 169 years old in Virginia and 156 years old in the Massachusetts Bay colony. The existence of these, and the other eleven, polities as separate and distinct States was thus a given. The framers could not politically have abolished the States even if they had wanted to do so, which they did not. Thus, the American Revolution sought the independence of a group of united States. The Constitution, in turn, was designed to form "a more perfect Union" of the thirteen United States of America, each with its own State constitution and republican form of government. What would be the powers of each level of government under that Constitution? What would be the relationship between these levels of government? Which would be "sovereign," and would sovereignty be in some sense "divided," or should each government be thought of as simply a different set of "agents" of the We the Sovereign *People* of the United States, as we believe? What would be the relationship among States within this union, keeping in mind that the States differed on such fundamental issues as slavery?

These are some of the great questions of American federalism. This chapter explores how the Constitution and subsequent practice have tried to address them. They continue to this day to be among the most pressing and contested questions in constitutional law. Before diving into those questions, there are six core features of American federalism that should always be kept in mind.

First, the present U.S. federation consists of an unusually large number of States (50) as compared to other federations with fewer State-like entities, such as India (27), Brazil (27), Germany (16), Canada (10), Australia (6), and the United Kingdom (4). The numbers can make a difference. *See* Steven G. Calabresi & Nicholas Terrell, *The Number of States and the Economics of American Federalism* 63 FLORIDA L. REV. 1 to 45 (2011). Imagine a United States with four mega-States: the Northeast, the South, the Midwest, and the West. In such a world, the federal government would likely be much weaker than is the federal government today in a world with fifty States facing collective-action problems for coordinated action (and an antitrust-like constitutional prohibition against interstate compacts without congressional approval). Regional secession would surely be a more serious threat with four mega-States than is the non-existent threat of secession from individual States today. Moreover, the large number of federal sub-units in the U.S. means more competition among the States and more experimentation. We thus reap the economic benefits of both national power *and* decentralized state power.

Second, the federal government is formally one of limited and enumerated powers whereas the state governments are not. The state governments have a general "Police Power" to protect the safety, health, morality, and well-being of their citizens. The Federal government does not have a general "Police Power," although, as we will see, the world in practice is more complicated than that simple observation suggests. Much depends on how those limited and enumerated federal powers are understood, and much of this chapter addresses the twists and turns of the multiple possible understandings of the scope of federal power.

Third, federalism is baked into the political structure of the Constitution. The States are equally represented in the Senate, draw the boundary lines of the districts which elect Members of the House of Representatives, and specify the process for picking presidential electors in each State and for allocating a State's electoral votes. Constitutional amendments must be approved by three-quarters of the States.

Fourth, thirty-nine out of the fifty States choose their governors in elections that do not coincide with the national presidential election, and the party out of power in the White House often gains gubernatorial and state legislative offices. Thus,

American federalism guarantees that not too long after a presidential election, the new President will usually be faced with a majority of State governors of the opposite party. Steven G. Calabresi & James Lindgren, *The President: Lightning Rod or King?*, 115 YALE L. J. 2611 (2006). This system of checks and balances promotes government by consensus and protects against presidential dictatorship, which most other presidential regimes have suffered from.

Fifth, the expanded American empire has not gone the way of the Roman Empire by becoming less democratic than it was at the Founding. To the contrary, the country has become spectacularly more democratic and representative, as African-Americans, women, and 18 year-olds have all been guaranteed the right to vote through the Fifteenth, Nineteenth, and Twenty-Sixth Amendments. Popular election of senators, enacted in 1913 through the adoption of the Seventeenth Amendment, has also made the United States more democratic than it was in 1789 or 1870. Under the Twenty-Third Amendment, residents in the District of Columbia do not get senators or a voting member in the House, but they do get three electoral votes for the presidency. So much, then, for all those eighteenth-century political philosophers who thought that democracy could subsist only in a small Athenian city-state!

Sixth, and finally, neither the federal government nor the States are sovereign or co-sovereigns in the American political order. Instead, sovereignty is vested in a majority of We the People in three-quarters of the States. Article VII of the Constitution explicitly provides that "[t]he Ratification of the Conventions of nine States, shall be sufficient for the Establishment of this Constitution between the States so ratifying the same." Because Rhode Island did not send anyone to the Constitutional Convention, the Convention drafted a Constitution which would go into effect once nine out of twelve States—a three-quarters super-majority—had ratified the Constitution. Under Article V, amendments to the Constitution require approval from popular conventions or republican legislatures in three-quarters of the States. Sovereignty in the American polity thus lies in a majority of the people in a super-majority three-quarters of the States. They alone can make or unmake the Constitution or amend it. This "majority of We the People in a three-quarters super-majority of States" is the *grundnorm*—the basic law or ground rule of a society through which sovereignty is exercised, *see* HANS KELSEN, PURE THEORY OF LAW (2nd ed. 1960)—which underlies the U.S. Constitution.

By contrast, in the United Kingdom, sovereignty lies in the Queen-in-Parliament, which can alter the U.K.'s Constitution by a narrow majority in the House of Commons. The French Constitution of the Fifth Republic and the provision for direct election by the voters of the President of France were both enacted into law by a bare majority of French citizens voting in a national popular referendum. Such referenda are thought by the French to reflect Rousseau's idea of the *volonte generale* (or "general will of the people"). The *grundnorm* in the U.K. is thus Parliamentary sovereignty, while in France it is a simple majority of the nationwide vote in a one-off national referendum. The U.S. super-majoritarian *grundnorm* makes constitutional change much harder to achieve in the U.S. than in the U.K. or France. This enhances predictability and certainty and reduces the risk factor in investments. For an argument that the U.S. super-majoritarian process systematically lead to better results than straight-up majoritarianism, see JOHN O.

MCGINNIS & MICHAEL B. RAPPAPORT, ORIGINALISM AND THE GOOD CONSTITUTION (2013).

We can now begin to explore the mechanics of American federalism as it is reflected in the constitutional assignment of national legislative powers. We start with how these issues were handled at the Constitutional Convention.

II. DRAFTING NATIONAL POWERS

A. CATEGORICAL FEDERALISM

The first proposal for the scope of powers to be given to the new federal government came in the Virginia Resolutions, which were presented to the delegates at the start of the Convention.

The Virginia Resolutions * * *

> 6. Resolved * * *. that the National Legislature ought to be impowered to enjoy the Legislative Rights vested in Congress by the Confederation & moreover to legislate in all cases to which the separate States are incompetent: or in which the harmony of the United States may be interrupted by the exercise of individual Legislation; to negative all laws passed by the several States, contravening, in the opinion of the National Legislature the articles of Union * * *.

1 THE RECORDS OF THE FEDERAL CONVENTION 21 (Max Farrand ed., 1911). In response, the smaller States put forward a New Jersey Plan, which more sharply limited the scope of federal power.

> The New Jersey Plan * * *
>
> 2. Resd. that in addition to the powers vested in the U. States in Congress, by the present existing articles of Confederation, they be authorized to pass acts for raising a revenue, by levying a duty or duties on all goods or merchandizes of foreign growth or manufacture, imported into any part of the U. States, by Stamps on paper, vellum or parchment, and by a postage on all letters or packages passing through the general post-Office, to be applied to such federal purposes as they shall deem proper & expedient; to make rules & regulations for the collection thereof; and the same from time to time, to alter & amend in such manner as they shall think proper: to pass Acts for the regulation of trade & commerce as well with foreign nations as with each other: provided that all punishments, fines, forfeitures & penalties to be incurred for contravening such acts rules and regulations shall be adjudged by the Common law Judiciaries of the State in which any offense contrary to the true intent & meaning of such Acts rules & regulations shall have been committed or perpetrated, with liberty of commencing in the first instance all suits & prosecutions for that purpose in the superior common law Judiciary in such State, subject nevertheless, for the correction of all errors, both in law & fact in rendering Judgment, to an appeal to the Judiciary of the U. States.
>
> * * *
>
> 8. Resd. the rule for naturalization ought to be the same in every State.

Id. at 243, 245.

There were three key differences between the Virginia Resolutions and the New Jersey Plan with respect to the scope of federal legislative power. First, the Virginia Resolutions gave the federal government the power to legislate "in all cases where the separate States were incompetent," whereas the New Jersey Plan had a very limited menu of specific federal powers, confined to foreign and domestic commerce and naturalization. Second, the Virginia Resolutions gave the federal government the power to legislate in cases "in which the harmony of the United States may be interrupted by the exercise of [State] legislation." The New Jersey Plan again rejected this purposed-based account of national powers in favor of a more specific approach. And, third, the Virginia Resolutions gave the national government a veto over all State laws that contravened federal law in Congress's opinion. The New Jersey Plan instead had a version of what is now the Article VI Supremacy Clause, *id.* at 245, making courts rather than Congress the primary guardians of national prerogatives. For a careful study of the oft-neglected New Jersey Plan, see Aaron T. Knapp, *The New Jersey Plan and the Structure of the American Union,* 15 GEO. J.L. & PUB. POL'Y 615 (2017).

James Madison was especially emphatic about the need for a federal legislative veto over State laws. *See* 2 THE RECORDS OF THE FEDERAL CONVENTION 27–28 (Max Farrand ed., 1911). The Philadelphia Convention, however, was steadfast in repeatedly rejecting James Madison's idea for a national veto over State laws. *See, e.g., id.* at 28. But the Convention did initially adopt the Virginia Plan's purpose-based account of federal powers. On July 17, 1787, the Convention voted 8–2 in favor of a version of the sixth Virginia Resolution that gave Congress power

> To make laws binding on the People of the United States in all cases which may concern the common interests of the Union: and moreover to legislate in all cases for the general interests of the Union, and also in those to which the States are separately incompetent, or in which the harmony of the United States may be interrupted by the exercise of individual legislation.

Id. at 21. After a proposal from Roger Sherman of Connecticut to enumerate federal powers more specifically was voted down, *see id.* at 26, Gunning Bedford of Delaware immediately followed with another proposal along the lines of the Virginia Resolutions: Congress would be able to exercise all powers from the Articles of Confederation " '(and moreover) to legislate in all cases for the general interests of the Union, and also in those to which the States are separately incompetent,' (or in which the harmony of the U. States may be interrupted by the exercise of individual Legislation.' " *Id.* This motion carried 8–2.

The resolution represented by Bedford's motion was among the resolutions that apparently defined the mission of the five-member Committee of Detail, *see id.* at 131–32, whose job was to turn the general principles of the Convention into specific language "conformable to the Resolutions passed by the Convention." *Id.* at 106. For a valuable study of the crucial role of the Committee of Detail—an all-star gathering of Oliver Ellsworth, Nathaniel Gorham, Edmund Randolph, John Rutledge, and James Wilson—in the construction of the Constitution, see William Ewald, *The Committee of Detail,* 28 CONST. COMMENTARY 197 (2012).

The Committee of Detail charged with drafting the final text of the Constitution came up with a document listing broad but specific enumerated powers rather than granting Congress the power to legislate wherever the purposes identified in the Bedford resolution were implicated. Whether this was a flouting of the Convention's resolution, or whether enumeration was always the Convention's goal provided that it could be done effectively, is perhaps ambiguous from the available records. *See* Ewald, *supra,* at 260–69. Whatever the case, the document that was put before the public for ratification identified, in Article I, Section 8, the following powers that were "herein granted" to Congress, some of which you saw in the previous chapter:

> **[1] The Congress shall have Power To lay and collect Taxes, Duties, Imposts and Excises, to pay the Debts and provide for the common Defence and general Welfare of the United States; but all Duties, Imposts and Excises shall be uniform throughout the United States;**
>
> **[2] To borrow Money on the credit of the United States;**
>
> **[3] To regulate Commerce with foreign Nations, and among the several States, and with the Indian Tribes;**
>
> **[4] To establish an uniform Rule of Naturalization, and uniform Laws on the subject of Bankruptcies throughout the United States;**
>
> **[5] To coin Money, regulate the Value thereof, and of foreign Coin, and fix the Standard of Weights and Measures;**
>
> **[6] To provide for the Punishment of counterfeiting the Securities and current Coin of the United States;**
>
> **[7] To establish Post Offices and post Roads;**
>
> **[8] To promote the Progress of Science and useful Arts, by securing for limited Times to Authors and Inventors the exclusive Right to their respective Writings and Discoveries;**
>
> **[9] To constitute Tribunals inferior to the supreme Court;**
>
> **[10] To define and punish Piracies and Felonies committed on the high Seas, and Offences against the Law of Nations;**
>
> **[11] To declare War, grant Letters of Marque and Reprisal, and make Rules concerning Captures on Land and Water;**
>
> **[12] To raise and support Armies, but no Appropriation of Money to that Use shall be for a longer Term than two Years;**
>
> **[13] To provide and maintain a Navy;**
>
> **[14] To make Rules for the Government and Regulation of the land and naval Forces;**
>
> **[15] To provide for calling forth the Militia to execute the Laws of the Union, suppress Insurrections and repel Invasions;**
>
> **[16] To provide for organizing, arming, and disciplining, the Militia, and for governing such Part of them as may be employed in the Service of the United States, reserving to the States respectively, the Appointment of the Officers, and the Authority of training the Militia according to the discipline prescribed by Congress;**

[17] To exercise exclusive Legislation in all Cases whatsoever, over such District (not exceeding ten Miles square) as may, by Cession of particular States, and the Acceptance of Congress, become the Seat of the Government of the United States, and to exercise like Authority over all Places purchased by the Consent of the Legislature of the State in which the Same shall be, for the Erection of Forts, Magazines, Arsenals, dock-Yards, and other needful Buildings;—and

[18] To make all Laws which shall be necessary and proper for carrying into Execution the foregoing Powers, and all other Powers vested by this Constitution in the Government of the United States, or in any Department or Officer thereof.

Other portions of the Constitution enumerate additional powers of Congress. Article IV provides:

Section 1

Full Faith and Credit shall be given in each State to the public Acts, Records, and judicial Proceedings of every other State. And the Congress may by general Laws prescribe the Manner in which such Acts, Records and Proceedings shall be proved, and the Effect thereof.

*** * ***

Section 3

[1] New States may be admitted by the Congress into this Union; but no new State shall be formed or erected within the Jurisdiction of any other State; nor any State be formed by the Junction of two or more States, or Parts of States, without the Consent of the Legislatures of the States concerned as well as of the Congress.

[2] The Congress shall have Power to dispose of and make all needful Rules and Regulations respecting the Territory or other Property belonging to the United States; and nothing in this Constitution shall be so construed as to Prejudice any Claims of the United States, or of any particular State.

Article V gives a two-thirds majority in Congress power to propose constitutional amendments and a simple majority in Congress power to choose whether ratification of amendments shall occur by State legislatures or by State conventions. Article II jointly gives the treaty power to the President and a super-majority in the Senate: "[The President] shall have Power, by and with the Advice and Consent of the Senate, to make Treaties, provided two thirds of the Senators present concur."

This was the document that was ratified in 1788. What can we make of the final product's account of national legislative power?

B. NATIONAL POWERS IN CONTEXT

There are several ways to interpret the move from the broad purposive definition of federal powers in the sixth Virginia and Bedford Resolutions to the detailed enumeration of powers that we find in the enacted Constitution. One interpretation is that the Committee of Detail simply ignored its instructions to follow the purposive route, but since the document as ratified contains the Convention's actual work product, and the machinations leading up to the final product were not publicly known, the enumeration simply stands as written, whatever its origins. A second interpretation is that the final enumeration reflected a shift in thinking at the Convention away from the original Virginia Resolutions, especially once small States secured equal representation in the Senate, as the larger States, which initially expected to dominate Congress, soured on a too-broad view of national powers. A third is to think that the Convention all along favored enumeration, worried about the ability effectively to implement an enumeration strategy, and was thrilled that the Committee of Detail did the job so well. A fourth interpretation is that the Committee of Detail never wavered from the original resolutions; and the seeming enumerations of power in the Constitution are just illustrative, not exhaustive, of the broad, purposively defined federal power to solve national problems that is implicit in the document. And a fifth interpretation is that the enumerations were designed fully to implement the Virginia and Bedford Resolutions and thus must be interpreted broadly enough to allow the Congress to address any and all problems of national scope, just as if the Virginia and Bedford Resolutions had prevailed.

We will have many occasions to refer to these possible interpretations of the Constitution's enumerated powers scheme throughout the course. For the moment, however, we want to take a step back and see how those powers, whatever their correct interpretation, fit into a larger constitutional plan for a federal system that includes States as active units of government.

The federal power-granting clauses of Article I, Section 8 operate to some degree in tandem with various clauses in Article I, Section 10, which forbid the States from doing many of the things Congress is empowered to do. When read together, Sections 8 and 10 of Article I explicitly give Congress the following *exclusive* legislative powers: (1) the power to lay uniform duties, imposts, and excise taxes for the purpose of raising revenue; (2) the power to coin money, emit bills of credit, or make any thing but gold and silver coin a tender in payment of debts; (3) the power to declare war, issue letters of marquee and reprisal, keep troops or ships of war in time of peace, and to define and punish piracies and offenses against the law of nations; and (4) the power to legislate for the District of Columbia. (Note as well that Article II, Section 2 reserves the exclusive power to make treaties to the President acting with the concurrence of two-thirds of the Senate.)

Article I, Section 8 gives Congress other powers which would seem to be impliedly exclusive (though, as we will see, the case law sometimes says otherwise). These include: (1) the power to borrow money on the credit of the United States; (2) the power to adopt a uniform rule of naturalization; (3) the power to fix the standard of weights and measures; (4) the power to punish the counterfeiters of U.S. coins; (5) the power to establish post offices and post roads; (6) the power to protect copyrights and patents; (7) the power to constitute tribunals inferior to the Supreme Court; (8) the power to provide rules and regulations for the armed forces of the United States; and (9) the power to provide for the organizing, arming and disciplining of the militias. Some of these powers were exercised by the States, after 1789, for a while, including the power of naturalization. GERALD L. NEUMAN, STRANGERS TO THE

CONSTITUTION: IMMIGRANTS, BORDERS, AND FUNDAMENTAL LAW (1996). One might have thought that Congress's power to establish "uniform" bankruptcy laws was an exclusive federal power, but the Supreme Court ruled otherwise in *Sturges v. Crowninshield*, 17 U.S. 122 (1819); and States have retained some power to define and regulate intellectual property rights. Note, however, that Chief Justice Marshall and Justice Story later took a position in dissent (*Ogden v. Saunders*, 25 U.S. 213 (1827)) that suggests they thought the power to enact bankruptcy laws was exclusively federal.

Many of the additional powers of Congress suggested by Articles IV, V, and VI are also necessarily exclusive federal powers. The Supreme Court, for example, even held that the power to recover fugitive slaves was an exclusive federal power in *Prigg v. Pennsylvania*, 41 U.S. 539 (1842). That decision, as we will see, was problematic at best, but the power to admit new States into the Union, the power to govern the territories and property of the United States, the power/duty to guarantee to the States a republican form of government, and the implied power to effectuate duties imposed by Article VI certainly seem to be exclusively federal powers. And a number of constitutional amendments—the Thirteenth, Fourteenth, Fifteenth, Sixteenth, Nineteenth, Twentieth, Twenty-First, Twenty-Third, Twenty-Fourth, Twenty-Fifth, and Twenty-Sixth Amendments—give Congress power to enforce them by enacting "appropriate" legislation. The grants of power to Congress in these eleven amendments are sometimes exclusive; more often these are grants to Congress of concurrent enforcement power.

What powers then are left over from Article I, Section 8 that are held concurrently with the States? The Supreme Court has identified three powers that are at least partly concurrent: (1) Congress's power to regulate commerce, whether with foreign nations, among the several states, or with the Indian tribes; (2) Congress's power to make all laws which shall be necessary and proper for carrying into execution its other powers; and (3) Congress's power to pass income taxes. We will briefly discuss each of these "concurrent" powers in turn.

The first concurrent power is Congress's concurrent power to regulate commerce. The tricky thing here, however, is that the Supreme Court has said that sometimes the Commerce Clause power is exclusively federal, at least when state regulations and laws unreasonably burden the "commerce among the several States" or with foreign nations and Indian tribes, even though it is often concurrent. The Supreme Court tells us on a case by case basis which state regulations it thinks are unconstitutionally burdensome and which it thinks are not. *See infra* pages 692–694.

As we will soon see, discussion of the commerce power is inextricably linked with discussion of the Necessary and Proper Clause. The Necessary and Proper Clause power would seem on the face of things to be concurrent with State authority, and it usually is. But sometimes, as with the power to create federal offices, the power by its nature is exclusively federal, and other times the Supreme Court finds, as it did in *McCulloch v. Maryland*, 17 U.S. 316 (1819), and, as it has done in a slew of so-called new federal common law cases, that the Constitution of its own force preempts state laws and executive or judicial actions that are unreasonably burdensome to or discriminatory against federal powers, institutions of governance, or federal officials. *See, e.g., Boyle v. United Technologies*, 487 U.S. 500 (1988).

The third concurrent power is the power to tax incomes, which the Sixteenth Amendment gives to Congress, and which the States have long asserted for themselves. The taxing power, in general, is (with the exception of tariffs) generally a concurrent power. Thus, Congress could enact a national sales tax or a national Value-Added Tax, even though the States already have sales taxes.

The bottom line is that Article I, Section 8 creates a formidably powerful federal government whose powers have been greatly augmented by subsequent constitutional amendments and by generous interpretations (whether or not inspired by the Virginia or Bedford Resolutions) of the enumerated powers. The federal government may be one of limited and enumerated powers, but many of those powers are exclusive and many more powers have been implied. Congress cannot directly control the legislative or executive institutions or instrumentalities of state governance, since doing so is not "necessary and proper," and it cannot force a State which outlaws alcohol to legalize it. But there is not much else that is today beyond the scope of federal power under modern Supreme Court caselaw. We will take a close look shortly at precisely what that "not much else" involves.

But there is one more necessary detour before we hit the cases. We think it of vital importance that you read the most important essay on political theory ever written by an American—James Madison's Tenth Federalist Paper. If you want even to begin to understand why our democratic empire works, with the unwieldy number of fifty member States which compose it, you need to read and re-read *The Federalist* No. 10.

C. FEDERALIST NO. 10 (MADISON)

To the People of the State of New York:

AMONG the numerous advantages promised by a well constructed Union, none deserves to be more accurately developed than its tendency to break and control the violence of faction. The friend of popular governments never finds himself so much alarmed for their character and fate, as when he contemplates their propensity to this dangerous vice. He will not fail, therefore, to set a due value on any plan which, without violating the principles to which he is attached, provides a proper cure for it. The instability, injustice, and confusion introduced into the public councils, have, in truth, been the mortal diseases under which popular governments have everywhere perished; as they continue to be the favorite and fruitful topics from which the adversaries to liberty derive their most specious declamations. The valuable improvements made by the American constitutions on the popular models, both ancient and modern, cannot certainly be too much admired; but it would be an unwarrantable partiality, to contend that they have as effectually obviated the danger on this side, as was wished and expected. Complaints are everywhere heard from our most considerate and virtuous citizens, equally the friends of public and private faith, and of public and personal liberty, that our governments are too unstable, that the public good is disregarded in the conflicts of rival parties, and that measures are too often decided, not according to the rules of justice and the rights of the minor party, but by the superior force of an interested and overbearing majority. However anxiously we may wish that these complaints had no foundation, the evidence, of known facts will not permit us to deny that they are in some degree true. It will be found, indeed, on a candid review of our situation, that some of the distresses under which we labor have been erroneously charged on the operation of our governments; but it will be found, at the same time, that other causes will not alone account for many of our heaviest misfortunes; and, particularly, for that prevailing and increasing distrust of public engagements, and alarm for private rights, which are echoed from one end of the continent to the other. These must be chiefly, if not wholly, effects of the unsteadiness and injustice with which a factious spirit has tainted our public administrations.

By a faction, I understand a number of citizens, whether amounting to a majority or a minority of the whole, who are united and actuated by some common impulse of passion, or of interest, adverse to the rights of other citizens, or to the permanent and aggregate interests of the community.

There are two methods of curing the mischiefs of faction: the one, by removing its causes; the other, by controlling its effects.

There are again two methods of removing the causes of faction: the one, by destroying the liberty which is essential to its existence; the other, by giving to every citizen the same opinions, the same passions, and the same interests.

It could never be more truly said than of the first remedy, that it was worse than the disease. Liberty is to faction what air is to fire, an aliment without which it instantly expires. But it could not be less folly to abolish liberty, which is essential to political life, because it nourishes faction, than it would be to wish the annihilation of air, which is essential to animal life, because it imparts to fire its destructive agency.

The second expedient is as impracticable as the first would be unwise. As long as the reason of man continues fallible, and he is at liberty to exercise it, different opinions will be formed. As long as the connection subsists between his reason and his self-love, his opinions and his passions will have a reciprocal influence on each other; and the former will be objects to which the latter will attach themselves. The diversity in the faculties of men, from which the rights of property originate, is not less an insuperable obstacle to a uniformity of interests. The protection of these faculties is the first object of government. From the protection of different and unequal faculties of acquiring property, the possession of different degrees and kinds of property immediately results; and from the influence of these on the sentiments and views of the respective proprietors, ensues a division of the society into different interests and parties.

The latent causes of faction are thus sown in the nature of man; and we see them everywhere brought into different degrees of activity, according to the different circumstances of civil society. A zeal for different opinions concerning religion, concerning government, and many other points, as well of speculation as of practice; an attachment to different leaders ambitiously contending for pre-eminence and power; or to persons of other descriptions whose fortunes have been interesting to the human passions, have, in turn, divided mankind into parties, inflamed them with mutual animosity, and rendered them much more disposed to vex and oppress each other than to co-operate for their common good. So strong is this propensity of mankind to fall into mutual animosities, that where no substantial occasion presents itself, the most frivolous and fanciful distinctions have been sufficient to kindle their unfriendly passions and excite their most violent conflicts. But the most common and durable source of factions has been the various and unequal distribution of property.

Those who hold and those who are without property have ever formed distinct interests in society. Those who are creditors, and those who are debtors, fall under a like discrimination. A landed interest, a manufacturing interest, a mercantile interest, a moneyed interest, with many lesser interests, grow up of necessity in civilized nations, and divide them into different classes, actuated by different sentiments and views. The regulation of these various and interfering interests forms the principal task of modern legislation, and involves the spirit of party and faction in the necessary and ordinary operations of the government.

No man is allowed to be a judge in his own cause, because his interest would certainly bias his judgment, and, not improbably, corrupt his integrity. With equal, nay with greater reason, a body of men are unfit to be both judges and parties at the same time; yet what are many of the most important acts of legislation, but so many judicial determinations, not indeed concerning the rights of single persons, but concerning the rights of large bodies of citizens? And what are the different classes of legislators but advocates and parties to the causes which they determine? Is a law proposed concerning private debts? It is a question to which the creditors are parties on one side and the debtors on the other. Justice ought to hold the balance between them. Yet the parties are, and must be, themselves the judges; and the most numerous party, or, in other words, the most powerful faction must be expected to prevail. Shall domestic manufactures be encouraged, and in what degree, by restrictions on foreign manufactures? are questions which would be differently decided by the landed and the manufacturing classes, and probably by neither with a sole regard to justice and the public good. The apportionment of taxes on the various descriptions of property is an act which seems to require the most exact impartiality; yet there is, perhaps, no legislative act in which greater opportunity and temptation are given to a predominant party to trample on the rules of justice. Every shilling with which they overburden the inferior number, is a shilling saved to their own pockets.

It is in vain to say that enlightened statesmen will be able to adjust these clashing interests, and render them all subservient to the public good. Enlightened statesmen will not always be at the helm. Nor, in many cases, can such an adjustment be made at all without taking into view indirect and remote considerations, which will rarely prevail over the immediate interest which one party may find in disregarding the rights of another or the good of the whole.

The inference to which we are brought is, that the CAUSES of faction cannot be removed, and that relief is only to be sought in the means of controlling its EFFECTS.

If a faction consists of less than a majority, relief is supplied by the republican principle, which enables the majority to defeat its sinister views by regular vote. It may clog the administration, it may convulse the society; but it will be unable to execute and mask its violence under the forms of the Constitution. When a majority is included in a faction, the form of popular government, on the other hand, enables it to sacrifice to its ruling passion or interest both the public good and the rights of other citizens. To secure the public good and private rights against the danger of such a faction, and at the same time to preserve the spirit and the form of popular government, is then the great object to which our inquiries are directed. Let me add that it is the great desideratum by which this form of government can be rescued from the opprobrium under which it has so long labored, and be recommended to the esteem and adoption of mankind.

By what means is this object attainable? Evidently by one of two only. Either the existence of the same passion or interest in a majority at the same time must be prevented, or the majority, having such coexistent passion or interest, must be rendered, by their number and local situation, unable to concert and carry into effect schemes of oppression. If the impulse and the opportunity be suffered to coincide, we well know that neither moral nor religious motives can be relied on as an adequate control. They are not found to be such on the injustice and violence of individuals, and lose their efficacy in proportion to the number combined together, that is, in proportion as their efficacy becomes needful.

From this view of the subject it may be concluded that a pure democracy, by which I mean a society consisting of a small number of citizens, who assemble and administer the government in person, can admit of no cure for the mischiefs of faction. A common passion or interest will, in almost every case, be felt by a majority of the whole; a communication and concert result from the form of government itself; and there is nothing to check the inducements to sacrifice the weaker party or an obnoxious individual. Hence it is that such democracies have ever been spectacles of turbulence and contention; have ever been found incompatible with personal security or the rights of property; and have in general been as short in their lives as they have been violent in their deaths. Theoretic politicians, who have patronized this species of government, have erroneously supposed that by reducing mankind to a perfect equality in their political rights, they would, at the same time, be perfectly equalized and assimilated in their possessions, their opinions, and their passions.

A republic, by which I mean a government in which the scheme of representation takes place, opens a different prospect, and promises the cure for which we are seeking. Let us examine the points in which it varies from pure democracy, and we shall comprehend both the nature of the cure and the efficacy which it must derive from the Union.

The two great points of difference between a democracy and a republic are: first, the delegation of the government, in the latter, to a small number of citizens elected by the rest; secondly, the greater number of citizens, and greater sphere of country, over which the latter may be extended.

The effect of the first difference is, on the one hand, to refine and enlarge the public views, by passing them through the medium of a chosen body of citizens, whose wisdom may best discern the true interest of their country, and whose patriotism and love of justice will be least likely to sacrifice it to temporary or partial considerations. Under such a regulation, it may well happen that the public voice, pronounced by the representatives of the people, will be more consonant to the public good than if pronounced by the people themselves, convened for the purpose. On the other hand, the effect may be inverted. Men of factious tempers, of local prejudices, or of sinister designs, may, by intrigue, by corruption, or by other means, first obtain the suffrages, and then betray the interests, of the people. The question resulting is, whether small or extensive republics are more favorable to the election of proper guardians of the public weal; and it is clearly decided in favor of the latter by two obvious considerations:

In the first place, it is to be remarked that, however small the republic may be, the representatives must be raised to a certain number, in order to guard against the cabals of a few; and that, however large it may be, they must be limited to a certain number, in order to guard against the confusion of a multitude. Hence, the number of representatives in the two cases not being in proportion to that of the two constituents, and being proportionally greater in the small republic, it follows that, if the proportion of fit characters be not less in the large than in the small republic, the former will present a greater option, and consequently a greater probability of a fit choice.

In the next place, as each representative will be chosen by a greater number of citizens in the large than in the small republic, it will be more difficult for unworthy candidates to practice with success the vicious arts by which elections are too often carried; and the suffrages of the people being more free, will be more likely to centre in men who possess the most attractive merit and the most diffusive and established characters.

It must be confessed that in this, as in most other cases, there is a mean, on both sides of which inconveniences will be found to lie. By enlarging too much the number of electors, you render the representatives too little acquainted with all their local circumstances and lesser interests; as by reducing it too much, you render him unduly attached to these, and too little fit to comprehend and pursue great and national objects. The federal Constitution forms a happy combination in this respect; the great and aggregate interests being referred to the national, the local and particular to the State legislatures.

The other point of difference is, the greater number of citizens and extent of territory which may be brought within the compass of republican than of democratic government; and it is this circumstance principally which renders factious combinations less to be dreaded in the former than in the latter. The smaller the society, the fewer probably will be the distinct parties and interests composing it; the fewer the distinct parties and interests, the more frequently will a majority be found of the same party; and the smaller the number of individuals composing a majority, and the smaller the compass within which they are placed, the more easily will they concert and execute their plans of oppression. Extend the sphere, and you take in a greater variety of parties and interests; you make it less probable that a majority of the whole will have a common motive to invade the rights of other citizens; or if such a common motive exists, it will be more difficult for all who feel it to discover their own strength, and to act in unison with each other. Besides other impediments, it may be remarked that, where there is a consciousness of unjust or dishonorable purposes, communication is always checked by distrust in proportion to the number whose concurrence is necessary.

Hence, it clearly appears, that the same advantage which a republic has over a democracy, in controlling the effects of faction, is enjoyed by a large over a small republic,—is enjoyed by the Union over the States composing it. Does the advantage consist in the substitution of representatives whose enlightened views and virtuous sentiments render them superior to local prejudices and schemes of injustice? It will not be denied that the representation of the Union will be most likely to possess these requisite endowments. Does it consist in the greater security afforded by a greater variety of parties, against the event of any one party being able to outnumber and oppress the rest? In an equal degree does the increased variety of parties comprised within the Union, increase this security. Does it, in fine, consist in the greater obstacles opposed to the concert and accomplishment of the secret wishes of an unjust and interested majority? Here, again, the extent of the Union gives it the most palpable advantage.

The influence of factious leaders may kindle a flame within their particular States, but will be unable to spread a general conflagration through the other States. A religious sect may degenerate into a political faction in a part of the Confederacy; but the variety of sects dispersed over the entire face of it must secure the national councils against any danger from that source. A rage for paper money, for an abolition of debts, for an equal division of property, or for any other improper or wicked project, will be less apt to pervade the whole body of the Union than a particular member of it; in the same proportion as such a malady is more likely to taint a particular county or district, than an entire State.

In the extent and proper structure of the Union, therefore, we behold a republican remedy for the diseases most incident to republican government. And according to the degree of pleasure and pride we feel in being republicans, ought to be our zeal in cherishing the spirit and supporting the character of Federalists.

NOTES AND QUESTIONS

1. Is Madison right or is he overly pessimistic in saying that the causes of faction are sown in the nature of man? Are human beings inherently good, so that, as Karl Marx hypothesized, if private property were abolished, everyone would behave like angels and factions would disappear? *See* CONSTITUTION (FUNDAMENTAL LAW) OF THE UNION OF SOVIET SOCIALIST REPUBLICS Preamble (1977) (the Soviet government's "far-reaching social and economic transformations * * * put an end once and for all to exploitation of man by man, antagonisms between classes, and strife between nationalities"). *Cf.* John Lennon, *Imagine,* IMAGINE (Apple 1971) ("Imagine no possessions." "And no religion, too.") Are human beings instead so inherently prone to wage a Hobbesian war of all against all that only an absolute monarchy or dictatorship can prevent disaster? *See* THOMAS HOBBES, LEVIATHAN (1651). Or is the truth about human nature somewhere between the utopianism of Karl Marx and the despair of Thomas Hobbes? Does Madison occupy that middle ground? *See* Steven G. Calabresi & Gary Lawson, *Foreword: Two Visions of the Nature of Man,* 16 HARV. J.L. & PUB. POL'Y 1 (1993).

2. Is Madison right that permanently entrenched majorities engaged in self-dealing will be less likely in a national Congress than in a small city-state more like, say, Rhode Island? Has the federal government in fact had a better record than the States in protecting minority rights like the rights, for example, of African-Americans? What about with respect to protecting women, or Asian Americans, or Native Americans? For a classic and influential discussion of *Federalist* No. 10 that relates it to a theory of judicial review, see JOHN HART ELY, DEMOCRACY AND DISTRUST: A THEORY OF JUDICIAL REVIEW (1980). *See also* Steven G. Calabresi, Note, *A Madisonian Interpretation of the Equal Protection Clause*, 91 YALE L. J. 1403 (1982).

3. A possible counter to James Madison is that while larger, or extended, federal republics may increase the costs of assembling ruling coalitions and thus dampen the effects of factions, the centralization that comes with federations also increases the potential returns from successful coalition-building. Put bluntly, larger extended republics generally have more wealth to loot than do smaller ones. *See* ALBERTO ALESINA & ENRICO SPOLAORE, THE SIZE OF NATIONS (2003). Finding the optimal degree of centralization and localization—as well as defining what counts as "optimal"—is a

difficult task. As you read the rest of this chapter, think about how well the U.S. has done in hitting the Aristotelian golden mean in this regard.

[Assignment 30]

III. PARADIGM FEDERALISM CASES

From the heady world of speculative political theory, we now move to American caselaw and political development. We conclude this introduction to American federalism with two paradigm cases separated by 176 years. The first, *McCulloch v. Maryland,* focuses on the Necessary and Proper Clause, the last of the eighteen power-granting clauses in Article I, Section 8. The second, *United States v. Lopez,* seems at first glance to be about Congress's power to regulate interstate commerce, but on closer examination concerns essentially the same issues under the Necessary and Proper Clause addressed nearly two centuries earlier in *McCulloch.* Individually, they each rank among the most important cases in American legal history (and *McCulloch* would garner a lot of votes for the top spot on that list). Together, they frame most of the issues that will be fleshed out in the remaining materials on federalism in this casebook.

A. THE BANK OF THE UNITED STATES AND *MCCULLOCH V. MARYLAND*

One of the most important controversies over the scope of national legislative powers—a controversy sustained for more than half a century from the founding into the early 1840's—concerned the constitutionality of an institution set up by the First Congress called the Bank of the United States. The Bank was the brainchild of Alexander Hamilton, the first Secretary of the Treasury. Hamilton modelled the Bank on the Bank of England, set up in 1694, which turned England into the financial center of the world. In part for this reason, England surpassed France as the leading power in the world. Indeed, the Continental Congress under the Articles of Confederation had set up a Bank of North America in 1781 to obtain "the support which the finances of the United States would receive from the establishment of a national bank." 21 J. Continental Cong. 1187–88 (1781). It is not at all obvious where the Continental Congress thought it got the power to create a national bank.

The Bank of the United States was a federally chartered corporation, owned mostly by private stockholders, run by a board of directors partially appointed by the President and partially privately selected. It was thus a quasi-public and quasi-private corporation. The Bank had the power to receive deposits, to provide savings accounts and manage trusts, and to issue "reserve notes"—paper notes supported by deposits on reserve with the Bank. These reserve notes functioned as a form of paper currency prior to the printing of dollar-denominated bills, which did not begin in this country until the Civil War.

The creation of the Bank was a cornerstone of Secretary of the Treasury Alexander Hamilton's ambitious economic plans to transform the United States from a nation of farmers into a global commercial economy. Thomas Jefferson, James Madison, and the other leaders of the Democratic-Republican Party did not want the United States to cease to be a nation of farmers, and they were suspicious, even contemptuous, of commerce. (A career in business, producing goods consumers want to buy, was evidently unworthy of gentlemen slave owners.) The fight over the Bank was thus not only a constitutional dispute but also, in the minds of those waging it, a social one. It was a fight over what kind of nation America would become.

The First Congress chartered the Bank as a monopoly federal corporation. Congressman James Madison voted against creating the Bank because he knew that the Framers at the Philadelphia Constitutional Convention had voted against giving the federal government the power to charter corporations. Indeed, Madison himself had originally proposed giving the federal government the power "[t]o grant charters of incorporation," 2 THE RECORDS OF THE FEDERAL CONVENTION 325 (Max Farrand ed., 1911), which he later modified to the power "to grant charters of incorporation where the interest of the U.S. might require & the legislative provisions of individual States may be incompetent." *Id.* at 615. (Why does this language sound familiar?) This proposal for a federal incorporation power was rejected 8–3 in 1787. *See* id. at 615–16. The first Congress in 1791 nonetheless approved the bank by a 39–20 vote in the House, with all but one of the negative votes coming from representatives from agricultural slave states. (The precise vote in the Senate is unclear. *See* 1 ANNALS OF CONG. 1791.)

President Washington, who was aware of the controversy over the constitutionality of the Bank, asked three members of his Cabinet—Attorney General Edmund Randolph; Secretary of State Thomas Jefferson; and Treasury Secretary Alexander Hamilton—for their opinions in writing as to whether the Bank was constitutional. Randolph and Jefferson argued that the Bank was unconstitutional while Hamilton defended its constitutionality. In the end, President Washington sided with Hamilton, and he signed into law the Bill creating the Bank for a period of twenty years.

In 1811, the Bank of the United States' twenty-year charter ended, and a Jeffersonian Congress refused to recreate the Bank, in part because of doubts as to its constitutionality. In 1815, Congress changed its mind and voted to recreate a Second Bank of the United States for another twenty years because of economic problems growing out of the War of 1812. President James Madison vetoed the Second Bank bill for policy reasons only, saying that despite his own doubts about the Bank's constitutionality, he considered the constitutional issue "as being precluded in my judgment by repeated recognitions under varied circumstances of the validity of such an institution in acts of the legislative, executive, and judicial branches of the Government, accompanied by indications, in different modes, of a concurrence of the general will of the nation." 2 A COMPILATION OF THE MESSAGES AND PAPERS OF THE PRESIDENTS 1789–1897, at 555 (James D. Richardson ed., 1897). He invited Congress to pass a better bill, and within a year, another bill recreating the Bank for twenty years, until 1836, passed Congress and was signed into law by President Madison.

Several states responded to the 1816 re-creation of the Bank with opposition. The State of Maryland, in particular, whose congressional delegation had uniformly opposed the first Bank in 1791, imposed a special—and enormously large—tax on the Bank of the United States branch in Maryland, which did not apply to any other banks doing business in Maryland (since every other Maryland bank had a State-issued charter of incorporation, and the tax only applied to banks without State charters). James McCulloch, the cashier of the Baltimore branch of the Bank of the

United States, refused to pay the tax. The Maryland state courts ruled against the Bank, and Chief Justice Marshall can take it from there.

1. McCulloch v. Maryland

17 U.S. (4 Wheat.) 316 (1819)

■ CHIEF JUSTICE MARSHALL delivered the opinion of the Court.

In the case now to be determined, the defendant, a sovereign State, denies the obligation of a law enacted by the legislature of the Union, and the plaintiff, on his part, contests the validity of an act which has been passed by the legislature of that State. The constitution of our country, in its most interesting and vital parts, is to be considered; the conflicting powers of the government of the Union and of its members, as marked in that constitution, are to be discussed; and an opinion given, which may essentially influence the great operations of the government. No tribunal can approach such a question without a deep sense of its importance, and of the awful responsibility involved in its decision. But it must be decided peacefully, or remain a source of hostile legislation, perhaps, of hostility of a still more serious nature; and if it is to be so decided, by this tribunal alone can the decision be made. On the Supreme Court of the United States has the constitution of our country devolved this important duty.

The first question made in the cause is—has Congress power to incorporate a bank?

It has been truly said, that this can scarcely be considered as an open question, entirely unprejudiced by the former proceedings of the nation respecting it. The principle now contested was introduced at a very early period of our history, has been recognised by many successive legislatures, and has been acted upon by the judicial department, in cases of peculiar delicacy, as a law of undoubted obligation.

It will not be denied, that a bold and daring usurpation might be resisted, after an acquiescence still longer and more complete than this. But it is conceived that a doubtful question, one on which human reason may pause, and the human judgment be suspended, in the decision of which the great principles of liberty are not concerned, but the respective powers of those who are equally the representatives of the people, are to be adjusted; if not put at rest by the practice of the government, ought to receive a considerable impression from that practice. An exposition of the constitution, deliberately established by legislative acts, on the faith of which an immense property has been advanced, ought not to be lightly disregarded.

The power now contested was exercised by the first Congress elected under the present constitution. The bill for incorporating the bank of the United States did not steal upon an unsuspecting legislature, and pass unobserved. Its principle was completely understood, and was opposed with equal zeal and ability. After being resisted, first in the fair and open field of debate, and afterwards in the executive cabinet, with as much persevering talent as any measure has ever experienced, and being supported by arguments which convinced minds as pure and as intelligent as this country can boast, it became a law. The original act was permitted to expire; but a short experience of the embarrassments to which the refusal to revive it exposed the government, convinced those who were most prejudiced against the measure of its necessity, and induced the passage of the present law. It would require no ordinary share of intrepidity to assert that a measure adopted under these circumstances was a bold and plain usurpation to which the constitution gave no countenance.

These observations belong to the cause; but they are not made under the impression that, were the question entirely new, the law would be found irreconcilable with the constitution.

In discussing this question, the counsel for the State of Maryland have deemed it of some importance, in the construction of the Constitution, to consider that instrument not as emanating from the people, but as the act of sovereign and independent States. The powers of the general government, it has been said, are delegated by the States, who alone are truly sovereign; and must be exercised in subordination to the States, who alone possess supreme dominion.

It would be difficult to sustain this proposition. The Convention which framed the constitution was indeed elected by the State legislatures. But the instrument, when it came from their hands, was a mere proposal, without obligation or pretensions to it. It was reported to the then existing Congress of the United States, with a request that it might "be submitted to a Convention of Delegates, chosen in each State by the people thereof, under the recommendation of its Legislature, for their assent and ratification." This mode of proceeding was adopted; and by the Convention, by Congress, and by the State legislatures, the instrument was submitted to the people. They acted upon it in the only manner in which they can act safely, effectively and wisely, on such a subject, by assembling in Convention. It is true, they assembled in their several States—and where else should they have assembled? No political dreamer was ever wild enough to think of breaking down the lines which separate the States, and of compounding the American people into one common mass. Of consequence, when they act, they act in their States. But the measures they adopt do not, on that account, cease to be the measures of the people themselves, or become the measures of the State governments.

From these Conventions the constitution derives its whole authority. The government proceeds directly from the people; is "ordained and established" in the name of the people, and is declared to be ordained, "in order to form a more perfect union, establish justice, insure domestic tranquillity, and secure the blessings of liberty to themselves and to their posterity." The assent of the States, in their sovereign capacity, is implied in calling a Convention, and thus submitting that instrument to the people. But the people were at perfect liberty to accept or reject it; and their act was final. It required not the affirmance, and could not be negatived, by the State governments. The constitution, when thus adopted, was of complete obligation, and bound the State sovereignties.

It has been said, that the people had already surrendered all their powers to the State sovereignties, and had nothing more to give. But, surely, the question whether they may resume and modify the powers granted to government does not remain to be settled in this country. Much more might the legitimacy of the general government be doubted, had it been created by the States. The powers delegated to the State sovereignties were to be exercised by themselves, not by a distinct and independent sovereignty, created by themselves. To the formation of a league, such as was the confederation, the State sovereignties were certainly competent. But when, "in order to form a more perfect union," it was deemed necessary to change this alliance into an effective government, possessing great and sovereign powers and acting directly on the people, the necessity of referring it to the people, and of deriving its powers directly from them, was felt and acknowledged by all.

The government of the Union then (whatever may be the influence of this fact on the case,) is, emphatically and truly, a government of the people. In form and in substance it emanates from them. Its powers are granted by them, and are to be exercised directly on them, and for their benefit.

This government is acknowledged by all to be one of enumerated powers. The principle, that it can exercise only the powers granted to it, would seem too apparent to have required to be enforced by all those arguments which its enlightened friends, while it was depending before the people, found it necessary to urge. That principle is now universally admitted. But the question respecting the extent of the powers actually granted, is perpetually arising, and will probably continue to arise, so long as our system shall exist.

In discussing these questions, the conflicting powers of the general and State governments must be brought into view, and the supremacy of their respective laws, when they are in opposition, must be settled.

If any one proposition could command the universal assent of mankind, we might expect it would be this—that the government of the Union, though limited in its powers, is supreme within its sphere of action. This would seem to result necessarily from its nature. It is the government of all; its powers are delegated by all; it represents all, and acts for all. Though any one State may be willing to control its operations, no State is willing to allow others to control them. The nation, on those subjects on which it can act, must necessarily bind its component parts. But this question is not left to mere reason: the people have, in express terms, decided it, by saying, "this constitution, and the laws of the United States, which shall be made in pursuance thereof," "shall be the supreme law of the land," and by requiring that the members of the State legislatures, and the officers of the executive and judicial departments of the States, shall take the oath of fidelity to it.

The government of the United States, then, though limited in its powers, is supreme; and its laws, when made in pursuance of the constitution, form the supreme law of the land, "any thing in the constitution or laws of any State to the contrary notwithstanding."

Among the enumerated powers, we do not find that of establishing a bank or creating a corporation. But there is no phrase in the instrument which, like the articles of confederation, excludes incidental or implied powers; and which requires that everything granted shall be expressly and minutely described. Even the 10th amendment, which was framed for the purpose of quieting the excessive jealousies which had been excited, omits the word "expressly," and declares only that the powers "not delegated to the United States, nor prohibited to the States, are reserved to the States or to the people;" thus leaving the question, whether the particular power which may become the subject of contest has been delegated to the one government, or prohibited to the other, to depend on a fair construction of the whole instrument. The men who drew and adopted this amendment had experienced the embarrassments resulting from the insertion of this word in the articles of confederation, and probably omitted it to avoid those embarrassments. A constitution, to contain an accurate detail of all the subdivisions of which its great powers will admit, and of all the means by which they may be carried into execution, would partake of the prolixity of a legal code, and could scarcely be embraced by the human mind. It would probably never be understood by the public. Its nature, therefore, requires that only its great outlines should be marked, its important objects designated, and the minor ingredients which compose those objects be deduced from the nature of the objects themselves. That this idea was entertained by the framers of the American constitution, is not only to be inferred from the nature of the instrument, but from the language. Why else were some of the limitations found in the ninth section of the 1st article, introduced? It is also, in some degree, warranted by their having omitted to use any restrictive term which might prevent its receiving a fair and just interpretation. In considering this question, then, we must never forget that it is *a constitution* we are expounding.

Although, among the enumerated powers of government, we do not find the word "bank" or "incorporation," we find the great powers to lay and collect taxes; to borrow money; to regulate commerce; to declare and conduct a war; and to raise and support armies and navies. The sword and the purse, all the external relations, and no inconsiderable portion of the industry of the nation, are intrusted to its government. It can never be pretended that these vast powers draw after them others of inferior importance, merely because they are inferior. Such an idea can never be advanced. But it may with great reason be contended, that a government intrusted with such ample powers, on the due execution of which the happiness and prosperity of the nation so vitally depends, must also be intrusted with ample means for their execution. The power being given, it is the interest of the nation to facilitate its execution. It can never be their interest, and cannot be presumed to have been their intention, to clog and embarrass its execution by withholding the most appropriate means. Throughout this vast republic, from the St. Croix to the Gulph of Mexico, from the Atlantic to the Pacific, revenue is to be collected and expended, armies are to be marched and supported. The exigencies of the nation may require that the treasure raised in the north should be transported to the south, *that* raised in the east conveyed to the west, or that this order should be reversed. Is that construction of the constitution to be preferred which would render these operations difficult, hazardous and expensive? Can we adopt that construction (unless the words imperiously require it,) which would impute to the framers of that instrument, when granting these powers for the public good, the intention of impeding their exercise by withholding a choice of means? If, indeed, such be the mandate of the constitution, we have only to obey; but that instrument does not profess to enumerate the means by which the powers it confers may be executed; nor does it prohibit the creation of a corporation, if the existence of such a being be essential to the beneficial exercise of those powers. It is, then, the subject of fair inquiry, how far such means may be employed.

It is not denied, that the powers given to the government imply the ordinary means of execution. That, for example, of raising revenue, and applying it to national purposes, is admitted to imply the power of conveying money from place to place, as the exigencies of the nation may require, and of employing the usual means of conveyance. But it is denied that the government has its choice of means; or, that it may employ the most convenient means if, to employ them, it be necessary to erect a corporation.

On what foundation does this argument rest? On this alone: The power of creating a corporation, is one appertaining to sovereignty, and is not expressly conferred on Congress. This is true. But all legislative powers appertain to sovereignty. The original power of giving the law on any subject whatever is a sovereign power; and if the government of the Union is restrained from creating a corporation, as a means for performing its functions, on the single reason that the creation of a corporation is an act of sovereignty; if the sufficiency of this reason be acknowledged, there would be some difficulty in sustaining the authority of Congress to pass other laws for the accomplishment of the same objects.

The government which has a right to do an act, and has imposed on it the duty of performing that act, must, according to the dictates of reason, be allowed to select the means; and those who contend that it may not select any appropriate means, that one particular mode of effecting the object is excepted, take upon themselves the burden of establishing that exception.

* * * The power of creating a corporation, though appertaining to sovereignty, is not, like the power of making war, or levying taxes, or of regulating commerce, a great substantive and independent power, which cannot be implied as incidental to other powers, or used as a means of executing them. It is never the end for which other powers are exercised, but a means by which other objects are accomplished. No contributions are made to charity for the sake of an incorporation, but a corporation is created to administer the charity; no seminary of learning is instituted in order to be incorporated, but the corporate character is conferred to subserve the purposes of education. No city was ever built with the sole object of being incorporated, but is incorporated as affording the best means of being well governed. The power of creating a corporation is never used for its own sake, but for the purpose of effecting something else. No sufficient reason is, therefore, perceived why it may not pass as incidental to those powers which are expressly given, if it be a direct mode of executing them.

But the constitution of the United States has not left the right of Congress to employ the necessary means, for the execution of the powers conferred on the government, to general reasoning. To its enumeration of powers is added that of making "all laws which shall be necessary and proper, for carrying into execution the foregoing powers, and all other powers vested by this constitution, in the government of the United States or in any department thereof."

The counsel for the State of Maryland have urged various arguments, to prove that this clause, though in terms a grant of power, is not so in effect; but is really restrictive of the general right, which might otherwise be implied, of selecting means for executing the enumerated powers.

In support of this proposition, they have found it necessary to contend, that this clause was inserted for the purpose of conferring on Congress the power of making laws. That, without it, doubts might be entertained, whether Congress could exercise its powers in the form of legislation.

But could this be the object for which it was inserted? * * * Could it be necessary to say, that a legislature should exercise legislative powers, in the shape of legislation? After allowing each house to prescribe its own course of proceeding, after describing the manner in which a bill should become a law, would it have entered into the mind of a single member of the Convention, that an express power to make laws was necessary to enable the legislature to make them? That a legislature, endowed with legislative powers, can legislate, is a proposition too self-evident to have been questioned.

But the argument on which most reliance is placed, is drawn from that peculiar language of this clause. Congress is not empowered by it to make all laws, which may have relation to the powers conferred on the government, but such only as may be "*necessary and proper*" for carrying them into execution. The word "*necessary,*" is considered as controlling the whole sentence, and as limiting the right to pass laws for the execution of the granted powers, to such as are indispensable, and without which the power would be nugatory. That it excludes the choice of means, and leaves to Congress, in each case, that only which is most direct and simple.

Is it true, that this is the sense in which the word "necessary" is always used? Does it always import an absolute physical necessity, so strong, that one thing, to which another may be termed necessary, cannot exist without that other? We think it does not. If reference be had to its use, in the common affairs of the world, or in approved authors, we find that it frequently imports no more than that one thing is convenient, or useful, or essential to another. To employ the means necessary to an end, is generally understood as employing any means calculated to produce the end, and not as being confined to those single means without which the end would be entirely unattainable. Such is the character of human language, that no word conveys to the mind, in all situations, one single definite idea; and nothing is more common than to use words in a figurative sense. Almost all compositions contain words, which, taken in their rigorous sense, would convey a meaning different from that which is obviously intended. It is essential to just construction, that many words which import something excessive, should be understood in a more mitigated sense—in that sense which common usage justifies. The word "necessary" is of this description. It has not a fixed character peculiar to itself. It admits of all degrees of comparison; and is often connected with other words, which increase or diminish the impression the mind receives of the urgency it imports. A thing may be necessary, very necessary, absolutely or indispensably necessary. To no mind would the same idea be conveyed, by these several phrases. The comment on the word is well illustrated, by the passage cited at the bar, from the 10th section of the 1st article of the constitution. It is, we think, impossible to compare the sentence which prohibits a State from laying "imposts, or duties on imports or exports, except what may be *absolutely* necessary for executing its inspection laws," with that which authorizes Congress "to make all laws which shall be necessary and proper for carrying into execution" the powers of the general government, without feeling a conviction that the convention understood itself to change materially the meaning of the word "necessary," by prefixing the word "absolutely." This word, then, like others, is used in various senses; and, in its construction, the subject, the context, the intention of the person using them, are all to be taken into view.

Let this be done in the case under consideration. The subject is the execution of those great powers on which the welfare of a nation essentially depends. It must have been the intention of those who gave these powers, to insure, so far as human prudence could insure, their beneficial execution. This could not be done by confiding the choice of means to such narrow limits as not to leave it in the power of Congress to adopt any which might be appropriate, and which were conducive to the end. This provision is made in a constitution intended to endure for ages to come, and, consequently, to be adapted to the various *crises* of human affairs. To have prescribed the means by which government should, in all future time, execute its powers, would have been to change, entirely, the character of the instrument, and give it the properties of a legal code. It would have been an unwise attempt to provide, by immutable rules, for exigencies which, if foreseen at all, must have been seen dimly, and which can be best provided for as they occur. To have declared that the best means shall not be used, but those alone without which the power given would be nugatory, would have been to deprive the legislature of the capacity to avail itself of experience, to exercise its reason, and to accommodate its legislation to circumstances. If we apply this principle of construction to any of the powers of the government, we shall find it so pernicious in its operation that we shall be compelled to discard it * * *.

So, with respect to the whole penal code of the United States: whence arises the power to punish in cases not prescribed by the constitution? All admit that the government may, legitimately, punish any violation of its laws; and yet, this is not among the enumerated powers of Congress. The right to enforce the observance of law, by punishing its infraction, might be denied with the more plausibility, because it is expressly given in some cases. Congress is empowered "to provide for the punishment of counterfeiting the securities and current coin of the United States," and "to define and punish piracies and felonies committed on the high seas, and offences against the law of nations." The several powers of Congress may exist, in a very imperfect state to be sure, but they may exist and be carried into execution, although no punishment should be inflicted in cases where the right to punish is not expressly given.

Take, for example, the power "to establish post-offices and post roads." This power is executed by the single act of making the establishment. But, from this has been inferred the power and duty of carrying the mail along the post road, from one post office to another. And, from this implied power, has again been inferred the right to punish those who steal letters from the post office, or rob the mail. It may be said, with some plausibility, that the right to carry the mail, and to punish those who rob it, is not indispensably necessary to the establishment of a post office and post road. This right is indeed essential to the beneficial exercise of the power, but not indispensably necessary to its existence. So, of the punishment of the crimes of stealing or falsifying a record or process of a Court of the United States, or of perjury in such Court. To punish these offences is certainly conducive to the due administration of justice. But courts may exist, and may decide the causes brought before them, though such crimes escape punishment.

The baneful influence of this narrow construction on all the operations of the government, and the absolute impracticability of maintaining it without rendering the government incompetent to its great objects, might be illustrated by numerous examples drawn from the constitution, and from our laws. The good sense of the public has pronounced, without hesitation, that the power of punishment appertains to sovereignty, and may be exercised, whenever the sovereign has a right to act, as incidental to his constitutional powers. It is a means for carrying into execution all sovereign powers, and may be used, although not indispensably necessary. It is a right incidental to the power, and conducive to its beneficial exercise.

If this limited construction of the word "necessary" must be abandoned in order to punish, whence is derived the rule which would reinstate it, when the government would carry its powers into execution by means not vindictive in their nature? If the word "necessary" means "needful," "requisite," "essential," "conducive to," in order to let in the power of punishment for the infraction of law; why is it not equally comprehensive when required to authorize the use of means which facilitate the execution of the powers of government without the infliction of punishment?

In ascertaining the sense in which the word "necessary" is used in this clause of the constitution, we may derive some aid from that with which it is associated. Congress shall have power "to make all laws which shall be necessary and *proper* to carry into execution" the powers of the government. If the word "necessary" was used in that strict and rigorous sense for which the counsel for the State of Maryland contend, it would be an extraordinary departure from the usual course of the human mind, as exhibited in composition, to add a word, the only possible effect of which is to qualify that strict and rigorous meaning; to present to the mind the idea of some choice of means of legislation not straitened and compressed within the narrow limits for which gentlemen contend.

But the argument which most conclusively demonstrates the error of the construction contended for by the counsel for the State of Maryland, is founded on the intention of the Convention, as manifested in the whole clause. To waste time and argument in proving that, without it, Congress might carry its powers into execution, would be not much less idle than to hold a lighted taper to the sun. As little can it be required to prove, that in the absence of this clause, Congress would have some choice of means. That it might employ those which, in its judgment, would most advantageously effect the object to be accomplished. That any means adapted to the end, any means which tended directly to the execution of the constitutional powers of the government, were in themselves constitutional. This clause, as construed by the State of Maryland, would abridge, and almost annihilate this useful and necessary right of the legislature to select its means. That this could not be intended is, we should think, had it not been already controverted, too apparent for controversy.

We think so for the following reasons:

1st. The clause is placed among the powers of Congress, not among the limitations on those powers.

2nd. Its terms purport to enlarge, not to diminish, the powers vested in the government. It purports to be an additional power, not a restriction on those already granted * * *.

The result of the most careful and attentive consideration bestowed upon this clause is, that if it does not enlarge, it cannot be construed to restrain the powers of Congress, or to impair the right of the legislature to exercise its best judgment in the selection of measures to carry into execution the constitutional powers of the government. If no other motive for its insertion can be suggested, a sufficient one is found in the desire to remove all doubts respecting the right to legislate on that vast mass of incidental powers which must be involved in the constitution, if that instrument be not a splendid bauble.

We admit, as all must admit, that the powers of the government are limited, and that its limits are not to be transcended. But we think the sound construction of the constitution must allow to the national legislature that discretion, with respect to the means by which the powers it confers are to be carried into execution, which will enable that body to perform the high duties assigned to it, in the manner most beneficial to the people. Let the end be legitimate, let it be within the scope of the constitution, and all means which are appropriate, which are plainly adapted to that end, which are not prohibited, but consist with the letter and spirit of the constitution, are constitutional.

That a corporation must be considered as a means not less usual, not of higher dignity, not more requiring a particular specification than other means has been sufficiently proved. If we look to the origin of corporations, to the manner in which they have been framed in that government from which we have derived most of our legal principles and ideas, or to the uses to which they have been applied, we find no reason to suppose that a constitution, omitting, and wisely omitting, to enumerate all the means for carrying into execution the great powers vested in government, ought to have specified this. Had it been intended to grant this power as one which should be distinct and independent, to be exercised in any case whatever, it would have found a place among the enumerated powers of the government. But being considered merely as a means, to be employed only for the purpose of carrying into execution the given powers, there could be no motive for particularly mentioning it.

The propriety of this remark would seem to be generally acknowledged by the universal acquiescence in the construction which has been uniformly put on the 3rd section of the 4th article of the constitution. The power to "make all needful rules and regulations respecting the territory or other property belonging to the United States," is not more comprehensive than the power "to make all laws which shall be necessary and proper for carrying into execution" the powers of the government. Yet all admit the constitutionality of a territorial government, which is a corporate body.

If a corporation may be employed indiscriminately with other means to carry into execution the powers of the government, no particular reason can be assigned for excluding the use of a bank, if required for its fiscal operations. To use one, must be within the discretion of Congress, if it be an appropriate mode of executing the powers of government. That it is a convenient, a useful, and essential instrument in the prosecution of its fiscal operations, is not now a subject of controversy. All those who have been concerned in the administration of our finances, have concurred in representing its importance and necessity; and so strongly have they been felt, that statesmen of the first class, whose previous opinions against it had been confirmed by every circumstance which can fix the human judgment, have yielded those opinions to the exigencies of the nation. Under the confederation, Congress, justifying the measure by its necessity, transcended perhaps, its powers to obtain the advantage of a bank; and our own legislation attests the universal conviction of the utility of this measure. The time has passed away when it can be necessary to enter into any discussion in order to prove the importance of this instrument, as a means to effect the legitimate objects of the Government.

But, were its necessity less apparent, none can deny its being an appropriate measure; and if it is, the decree of its necessity, as has been very justly observed, is to be discussed in another place. Should Congress, in the execution of its powers, adopt measures which are prohibited by the constitution; or should Congress, under the pretext of executing its powers, pass laws for the accomplishment of objects not intrusted to the government; it would become the painful duty of this tribunal, should a case requiring such a decision come before it, to say that such an act was not the law of the land. But where the law is not prohibited, and is really calculated to effect any of the objects intrusted to the government, to undertake here to inquire into the decree of its necessity, would be to pass the line which circumscribes the judicial department, and to tread on legislative ground. This court disclaims all pretensions to such a power.

After this declaration, it can scarcely be necessary to say, that the existence of State banks can have no possible influence on the question. No trace is to be found in the constitution of an intention to create a dependence of the government of the Union on those of the States, for the execution of the great powers assigned to it. Its means are adequate to its ends; and on those means alone was it expected to rely for the accomplishment of its ends. To impose on it the necessity of resorting to means which it cannot control, which another government may furnish or withhold, would render its course precarious, the result of its measures uncertain, and create a dependence on other governments, which might disappoint its most important designs, and is incompatible with the language of the constitution. But were it otherwise, the choice of means implies a right to choose a national bank in preference to State banks, and Congress alone can make the election.

After the most deliberate consideration, it is the unanimous and decided opinion of this Court, that the act to incorporate the Bank of the United States is a law made in pursuance of the constitution, and is a part of the supreme law of the land.

* * *

It being the opinion of the Court, that the act incorporating the bank is constitutional; and that the power of establishing a branch in the State of Maryland might be properly exercised by the bank itself, we proceed to inquire—

2. Whether the State of Maryland may, without violating the constitution, tax that branch?

That the power of taxation is one of vital importance; that it is retained by the States; that it is not abridged by the grant of a similar power to the government of the Union; that it is to be concurrently exercised by the two Governments: are truths which have never been denied. But, such is the paramount character of the constitution, that its capacity to withdraw any subject from the action of even this power, is admitted. The States are expressly forbidden to lay any duties on imports or exports, except what may be absolutely necessary for executing their inspection laws. If the obligation of this prohibition must be conceded—if it may restrain a State from the exercise of its taxing power on imports and exports; the same paramount character would seem to restrain, as it certainly may restrain, a State from such other exercise of this power, as is in its nature incompatible with, and repugnant to, the constitutional laws of the Union. A law, absolutely repugnant to another, as entirely repeals that other as if express terms of repeal were used.

On this ground the counsel for the bank place its claim to be exempted from the power of a State to tax its operations. There is no express provision for the case, but the claim has been sustained on a principle which so entirely pervades the constitution, is so intermixed with the materials which compose it, so interwoven with its web, so blended with its texture, as to be incapable of being separated from it, without rending it into shreds.

This great principle is, that the constitution and the laws made in pursuance thereof are supreme; that they control the constitution and laws of the respective States, and cannot be controlled by them. From this, which may be almost termed an axiom, other propositions are deduced as corollaries, on the truth or error of which, and on their application to this case, the cause has been supposed to depend. These are, 1st. that a power to create implies a power to preserve. 2nd. That a power to destroy, if wielded by a different hand, is hostile to, and incompatible with these powers to create and to preserve. 3d. That, where this repugnancy exists, that authority which is supreme must control, not yield to that over which it is supreme.

These propositions, as abstract truths, would, perhaps, never be controverted. Their application to this case, however, has been denied; and, both in maintaining the affirmative and the negative, a splendor of eloquence, and strength of argument, seldom, if ever, surpassed, have been displayed.

The power of Congress to create, and of course, to continue, the bank, was the subject of the preceding part of this opinion; and is no longer to be considered as questionable.

That the power of taxing it by the States may be exercised so as to destroy it, is too obvious to be denied. But taxation is said to be an absolute power, which acknowledges no other limits than those expressly prescribed in the constitution, and like sovereign power of every other description, is intrusted to the discretion of those who use it. But the very terms of this argument admit that the sovereignty of the State, in the article of taxation itself, is subordinate to, and may be controlled by the constitution of the United States. How far it has been controlled by that instrument must be a question of construction. In making this construction, no principle not declared, can be admissible, which would defeat the legitimate operations of a supreme government. It is of the very essence of supremacy to remove all obstacles to its action within its own sphere, and so to modify every power vested in subordinate governments, as to exempt its own operations from their own influence. This effect need not be stated in terms. It is so involved in the declaration of supremacy, so necessarily implied in it, that the expression of it could not make it more certain. We must, therefore, keep it in view while construing the constitution.

The argument on the part of the State of Maryland, is, not that the States may directly resist a law of Congress, but that they may exercise their acknowledged powers upon it, and that the constitution leaves them this right in the confidence that they will not abuse it.

Before we proceed to examine this argument, and to subject it to test of the constitution, we must be permitted to bestow a few considerations on the nature and extent of this original right of taxation, which is acknowledged to remain with the States. It is admitted that the power of taxing the people and their property is essential to the very existence of government, and may be legitimately exercised on the objects to which it is applicable, to the utmost extent to which the government may chuse to carry it. The only security against the abuse of this power, is found in the structure of the government itself. In imposing a tax the legislature acts upon its constituents. This is in general a sufficient security against erroneous and oppressive taxation.

The people of a State, therefore, give to their government a right of taxing themselves and their property, and as the exigencies of government cannot be limited, they prescribe no limits to the exercise of this right, resting confidently on the interest of the legislator, and on the influence of the constituent over their representative, to guard them against its abuse. But the means employed by the government of the Union have no such security, nor is the right of a State to tax them sustained by the same theory. Those means are not given by the people of a particular State, not given by the constituents of the legislature, which claim the right to tax them, but by the people of all the States They are given by all, for the benefit of all—and upon theory, should be subjected to that government only which belongs to all.

It may be objected to this definition, that the power of taxation is not confined to the people and property of a State. It may be exercised upon every object brought within its jurisdiction.

This is true. But to what source do we trace this right? It is obvious, that it is an incident of sovereignty, and is co-extensive with that to which it is an incident. All subjects over which the sovereign power of a State extends, are objects of taxation; but those over which it does not extend, are, upon the soundest principles, exempt from taxation. This proposition may almost be pronounced self-evident.

The sovereignty of a State extends to everything which exists by its own authority, or is introduced by its permission; but does it extend to those means which are employed by Congress to carry into execution powers conferred on that body by the people of the United States? We think it demonstrable that it does not. Those powers are not given by the people of a single State. They are given by the people of the United States, to a government whose laws, made in pursuance of the constitution, are declared to be supreme. Consequently, the people of a single State cannot confer a sovereignty which will extend over them.

* * *

We find, then, on just theory, a total failure of this original right to tax the means employed by the government of the Union, for the execution of its powers. The right never existed, and the question whether it has been surrendered, cannot arise.

But, waiving this theory for the present, let us resume the inquiry, whether this power can be exercised by the respective States, consistently with a fair construction of the constitution?

That the power to tax involves the power to destroy; that the power to destroy may defeat and render useless the power to create; that there is a plain repugnance, in conferring on one government a power to control the constitutional measures of another, which other, with respect to those very measures, is declared to be supreme over that which exerts the control, are propositions not to be denied. But all inconsistencies are to be reconciled by the magic of the word CONFIDENCE. Taxation, it is said, does not necessarily and unavoidably destroy. To carry it to the excess of destruction would be an abuse, to presume which would banish that confidence which is essential to all government.

But is this a case of confidence? Would the people of any one State trust those of another with a power to control the most insignificant operations of their State government? We know they would not. Why, then, should we suppose that the people of any one State should be willing to trust those of another with a power to control the operations of a government to which they have confided their most important and most valuable interests? In the legislature of the Union alone, are all represented. The legislature of the Union alone, therefore, can be trusted by the people with the power of controlling measures which concern all, in the confidence that it will not be abused. This, then, is not a case of confidence, and we must consider it is as it really is.

If we apply the principle for which the State of Maryland contends, to the constitution generally, we shall find it capable of changing totally the character of that instrument. We shall find it capable of arresting all the measures of the government, and of prostrating it at the foot of the States. The American people have declared their constitution, and the laws made in pursuance thereof, to be supreme; but this principle would transfer the supremacy, in fact, to the States.

If the States may tax one instrument, employed by the government in the execution of its powers, they may tax any and every other instrument. They may tax the mail; they may tax the mint; they may tax patent rights; they may tax the papers of the custom-house; they may tax judicial process; they may tax all the means employed by the government to an excess which would defeat all the ends of government. This was not intended by the American people. They did not design to make their government dependent on the States.

* * *

In the course of the argument, the *Federalist* has been quoted; and the opinions expressed by the authors of that work have been justly supposed to be entitled to great respect in expounding the constitution. No tribute can be paid to them which exceeds their merit; but in applying their opinions to the cases which may arise in the progress of our government, a right to judge of their correctness must be retained; and, to understand the argument, we must examine the proposition it maintains, and the objections against which it is directed. The subject of those numbers, from which passages have been cited, is the unlimited power of taxation which is vested in the general government. The objection to this unlimited power, which the argument seeks to remove, is stated with fulness and clearness. It is, "that an indefinite power of taxation in the latter (the government of the Union) might, and probably would, in time, deprive the former (the government of the States) of the means of providing for their own necessities, and would subject them entirely to the mercy of the national ;legislature * * *."

The objections to the constitution which are noticed in these numbers, were to the undefined power of the government to tax, not to the incidental privilege of exempting its own measures from State taxation. The consequences apprehended from this undefined power were, that it would absorb all the objects of taxation, "to the exclusion and destruction of the State Governments." The arguments of the *Federalist* are intended to prove the fallacy of these apprehensions; not to prove that the government was incapable of executing any of its powers ,without exposing the means it employed to the embarrassments of State taxation. Arguments urged against these objections, and these apprehensions, are to be understood as relating to the points they mean to prove. Had the authors of those excellent essays been asked, whether they contended for that construction of the constitution which would place within the reach of the States those measures which the government might adopt for the execution of its powers; no man who has read their instructive pages, will hesitate to admit, that their answer must have been in the negative.

It has also been insisted that, as the power of taxation in the general and State governments is acknowledged to be concurrent, every argument which would sustain the right of the general government to tax banks chartered by the States, will equally sustain the right of the States to tax banks chartered by the general government.

But the two cases are not on the same reason. The people of all the States have created the general government, and have conferred upon it the general power of taxation. The people of all the States, and the States themselves, are represented in Congress, and, by their representatives, exercise this power. When they tax the chartered institutions of the States, they tax their constituents; and these taxes must be uniform. But when a State taxes the operations of the government of the United States, it acts upon institutions created, not by their own constituents, but by people over whom they claim no control. It acts upon the measures of a government created by others as well as themselves, for the benefit of others in common with themselves. The difference is that which always exists, and always must exist, between the action of the whole on a part, and the action of a part on the whole—between the laws of a government declared to be supreme, and those of a government which, when in opposition to those laws, is not supreme.

But if the full application of this argument could be admitted, it might bring into question the right of Congress to tax the State banks, and could not prove the rights of the States to tax the Bank of the United States.

The Court has bestowed on this subject its most deliberate consideration. The result is a conviction that the States have no power, by taxation or otherwise, to retard, impede, burden, or in any manner control, the operations of the constitutional laws enacted by Congress to carry into execution the powers vested in the general government. This is, we think, the unavoidable consequence of that supremacy which the constitution has declared.

We are unanimously of opinion, that the law passed by the Legislature of Maryland, imposing a tax on the Bank of the United States, is unconstitutional and void.

This opinion does not deprive the States of any resources which they originally possessed. It does not extend to a tax paid by the real property of the bank, in common with the other real property within the State, nor to a tax imposed on the interest which the citizens of Maryland may hold in this institution, in common with other property of the same description throughout the State. But this is a tax on the operations of the bank, and is, consequently, a tax on the operation of an instrument employed by the government of the Union to carry its powers into execution. Such a tax must be unconstitutional.

NOTES AND QUESTIONS

1. There is a *lot* going on in *McCulloch v. Maryland,* which is why many consider it to be the most important decision every rendered by the Supreme Court. *See* Daniel A. Farber, *The Story of* McCulloch: *Banking on National Power,* 20 CONST. COMMENTARY 679, 679 (2003–04). There were two key issues: Did Congress have the power to incorporate a bank (if it did not, then the Bank had no plausible defense against Maryland's tax) and, if so, was the Bank for some reason exempt from State taxation? In theory, one could resolve one but not the other issue in favor of the Bank. One could think that Congress had power to create the Bank but that it was properly subject to State taxation, and one could believe that federal instrumentalities are not subject to State taxation but doubt that the Bank was in fact constitutionally established as a federal instrumentality. And, of course, one could resolve both or neither issues in either direction. Chief Justice Marshall resolved both issues in the Bank's favor, and both parts of his opinions have had incalculable impact on the course of American law.

2. Marshall defends the constitutionality of the Bank and its exemption from State taxation using all the modalities of constitutional interpretation discussed in the introduction to this casebook, *see supra* pages 54–61, including arguments from: 1) text, 2) structure, 3) history and purpose, 4) practice and precedent, and 5) policy. Go back though Marshall's opinion and highlight each type of constitutional argument. (Yes, you really should do that. Trust us—it is well worth the effort.) The opinion in *McCulloch* is especially famous for the structural arguments Marshall makes. *See* CHARLES BLACK, STRUCTURE AND RELATIONSHIP IN CONSTITUTIONAL LAW (1969). Can you identify all of the structural arguments in the opinion?

3. Marshall's first argument in favor of Congress's power to incorporate the Bank was an argument from precedent. Note, however, who had previously done the deciding. In 1819, there was no prior judicial opinion on the constitutionality of the Bank. There had, however, been extensive discussions on the subject in the executive and legislative departments, on multiple occasions. The discussion in the Washington Administration pitted Alexander Hamilton against Thomas Jefferson and Edmund Randolph. Chief Justice Marshall's opinion draws heavily on Hamilton's opinion from nearly thirty years earlier, often adapting portions of Hamilton's argument almost word for word. In the end, how much weight does the opinion in *McCulloch* give to those legislative and executive precedents? How much weight should it have given them?

4. Once Marshall turned to (re-)deciding the merits of the case, he focused on the Necessary and Proper Clause as the source of congressional authority to incorporate the bank. Is there any other enumerated power that could sustain the Bank? The Bank's defenders did not point to one. As did Marshall, they rested their argument on the Necessary and Proper Clause. While this was not the Court's first opinion addressing the Necessary and Proper Clause, *see United States v. Fisher,* 6 U.S. (2 Cranch) 358 (1805), it was by far the most thorough and influential. While the opinion is best known for its discussion of the meaning of the word "necessary"—more on that in a moment—something important happened *before* Chief Justice Marshall got to that part of his opinion. Seven pages of the United States Reports were devoted to whether the power to incorporate a bank was "incidental" or was instead a "great substantive and independent power, which cannot be implied as incidental to other powers." This discussion, reproduced on pages 607–609, *supra,* mostly disappeared from jurisprudence for nearly two centuries, only to reappear, somewhat dramatically, in 2010. You will hear more about it shortly.

5. The parties, as so often happens in adversarial litigation, presented the Court with a stark choice on the meaning of the word "necessary." Maryland, echoing arguments from Thomas Jefferson from the debate in the Washington Administration, argued that a law could only be "necessary" under the Necessary and Proper Clause if it was *indispensable* to the exercise of a federal power. The United States, echoing Hamilton from the same debate, said that "necessary" could mean merely "convenient" or "useful." Marshall famously sided with the United States (and Hamilton) on that point. As between those two poles, which side has the better argument? See if your view is affected at all by "Justice Calabresi's" or "Justice Lawson's" dissenting opinions below. As it happens, there was, at the very least, a third possible understanding of "necessary" that was not advanced by either party in the case. After the opinion in *McCulloch* was issued, James Madison opined that a law was "necessary" if it had "a definite connection between means and ends" in which the law and the power executed by the law are linked "by some obvious and precise affinity." Letter from James Madison to Spencer Roane, Sept. 2, 1819, *in* THE WRITINGS OF JAMES MADISON 447, 448 (Gaillard Hunt ed., 1908). This calls for a

connection tighter than Hamilton's but looser than Jefferson's. Does that definition of "necessary" sound better than either of the definitions put forward in *McCulloch*?

6. Nobody in *McCulloch* argued that the Bank, even if "necessary," was not "proper" for executing federal powers. That is, the entire argument focused on the means-ends relationship between the Bank and some precisely enumerated federal powers, such as the power to tax or to raise armies. This reflects the quite sensible intuition that "necessary" refers to some causal connection between means and ends, with the dispute centering on how tight the causal connection must be. But then what work is done by the word "proper"? Chief Justice Marshall has little to say on that subject, other than to suggest in passing that "proper" is a looser, less restrictive term than "necessary." Does that seem right? We will have more to say about what it means for a law to be "proper" later on. *See infra* pages 806–819. Similarly, Chief Justice Marshall (and the parties) did not address what it might mean for a law to be "for carrying into Execution" federal powers; more on that later as well. *See infra* pages 841–842.

7. On the other hand, Chief Justice Marshall did spend a great deal of energy establishing that the Constitution was the work product of "We the People" rather than the States. As you know by now, we think Marshall was right on this point. Does it have any bearing at all on this case? Marshall probably did not think so. He noted that "counsel for the State of Maryland have deemed it of some importance, in the construction of the Constitution, to consider that instrument not as emanating from the people, but as the act of sovereign and independent States." And indeed, Luther Martin, who appeared on behalf of Maryland, did make such an argument at considerable length. But Martin, initially a prominent Anti-Federalist who was instrumental in securing passage of the Bill of Rights, never explained *why* he thought it was important to make that argument. Does it seem to you important to resolve that question in this case?

8. Taking as given that Congress had power to incorporate the Bank, does it follow that Maryland could not tax it? If Congress had passed a law declaring that the Bank was immune from State taxation, such a law might well be "necessary and proper for carrying into Execution" federal powers, and Maryland's anti-federal tax would then be expressly preempted by a federal statute, which the Article VI Supremacy Clause declares to be supreme over competing State law. But Congress passed no such statute. Does the Constitution itself, without any congressional action, preempt state laws that the Court deems to interfere with federal operations? The second part of the opinion in *McCulloch* says yes. Are you persuaded that Marshall is right that the Constitution preempts Maryland's discriminatory tax of its own force even in the absence of any need for Congress to pass a federal statute preempting Maryland's discriminatory tax? What else does the Constitution, of its own force, stop a State from doing, apart from the very specific "thou shalt nots" in Article I, section 10? Suppose a state court jury awards huge tort damages to a plaintiff who sues a federal military contractor for the faulty design of escape hatches in military helicopters. The Supreme Court has held that the jury award second-guessing federal military officials is null and void because it is preempted by the Constitution. *Boyle v. United Technologies*, 487 U.S. 500 (1988). May a State prosecute a sitting President for a violation of state law? Or is that prosecution preempted until the President leaves office? Does a state government violate the Supremacy Clause of Article VI of the Constitution any time it interferes with the operation of a federal instrumentality, agency, program, or policy? Does a state income tax interfere with federal operations if it applies to federal employees exactly the same way that it applies to everyone else in the State, so that federal employees should be exempt from general state taxation? The Supreme Court, by the way, for a long time said "yes" to this last question, until finally rejecting that view in 1939. *See Graves v. New York ex rel. O'Keefe,*

306 U.S. 466 (1939). Current law says that "state regulation is invalid only if it regulates the United States directly or discriminates against the Federal Government or those with whom it deals." *North Dakota v. United States,* 495 U.S. 423, 435 (1990) (plurality opinion). Do you think this rule is derivable from the Constitution, in the absence of a congressional statute?

9. There is far too much involved in *McCulloch* for even a lengthy list of "Notes and Questions" to address. Accordingly, we offer some thoughts in the form of two "dissenting opinions" from Chief Justice Marshall's opinion in *McCulloch v. Maryland*, written by each of us in turn. "Justice" Calabresi cites some federal Supreme Court cases between 1819 and 2020 in his fictional (but he thinks persuasive) dissent, but all of the issues are raised in *McCulloch*. Do either or both of us get the better of Chief Justice Marshall?

2. "JUSTICE" CALABRESI'S DISSENTING OPINION IN *MCCULLOCH V. MARYLAND*

I dissent from the Majority's conclusion that the Bank of the United States is constitutional. The Majority opinion sounds the death knell for American federalism, and it destroys the key idea that our government is one of limited and enumerated powers. Moreover, the majority's statement of the test for evaluating whether laws are consistent with the Necessary and Proper Clause misstates the meaning of the Clause in a gross way and turns it into a rubberstamp for all congressional legislation. This test single-handedly does away with the notion that the U.S. federal government is one of limited and enumerated powers.

I.

I begin, of course, with the words of the Constitution, which the Majority so badly mangles and contorts. The key issue in this case is whether the incorporation of a federal Bank of the United States "is necessary and proper" for "the carrying into Execution" of some other enumerated federal power. The word "necessary" means necessary, essential, or indispensable. It does not mean "convenient" or "useful." It also does not allow the government all implied powers "but for which" an enumerated power can be expanded or caused to flourish. Samuel Johnson's *Dictionary of the English Language*, which was by far and away the leading dictionary in use in 1787, when the Constitution was drafted, defined the meaning of "necessary" as being "indispensable." That is the original plain meaning of the constitutional text, and that ought to be the end of this case.

It is obvious that the incorporation of a Bank of the United States is not indispensable to the flourishing of the federal government. The First Bank of the United States sunsetted out of existence in 1811 because Congress for both constitutional and policy reasons chose not to renew its corporate charter. Between then and 1815, we fought and won the War of 1812—a war in which we took on and defeated the world's largest super-power, the British Empire. If we did not need the Bank of the United States to fight and win the War of 1812, then no one can plausibly argue that such a bank is "indispensable" to our national economy.

Not only is the Bank of the United States not "necessary," it is also not a "proper" exercise of federal power. The word "proper" comes from Latin roots that suggest that something is "proper" if it belongs to an institution, a person, or a level of government in a federation, or a branch of government where there is a separation of powers.

Under the U.S. Constitution, the power to charter corporations—which is a great and independent power—belongs to the States and not to the federal government. All of our major business corporations are chartered at the State level, and most of them have chosen to be chartered and incorporated in Delaware because that State has the most optimal rules for corporate law. There are no federally chartered private business corporations because Congress has no enumerated power to charter corporations. Corporate chartering in the United States is proper at the state level, but not at the federal level. For this reason alone, the 1816 Act chartering the corporate Bank of the United States is not only unnecessary; it is also "improper."

The Bank of the United States is made even less necessary and proper when we consider the fact that it has a monopoly on the federal government's banking business, which gives it a huge leg up in its competition with other private banks. Ever since Sir Edward Coke reported the *Case of the Monopolies* in England in (1602) 74 ER 1131, it has been a maxim of English and American law that monopolies run contrary to the common law and are thus inherently "improper" and can only be authorized in England by the King-in-Parliament, which is sovereign in that country. Applying Coke's reasoning to the United States, we should hold that monopolies can only be authorized by Article V amendments to the Constitution, to which a majority of the people in three quarters of the States have assented. The popularity of Coke's principle in the U.S. is reflected in many of the State constitutions today, which have clauses in them that ban giving favors to one group or class of people or that require that legislation be for the common benefit. The act incorporating the Bank of the United States is thus neither necessary nor proper. The plain meaning of the text of the Necessary and Proper Clause supports this conclusion.

Moreover, the federal powers to tax and spend to promote the general welfare, to borrow money, to regulate commerce, and to pay soldiers and sailors can all be carried out perfectly well without there being a federally chartered Bank of the United States with a monopoly on the federal government's banking business. From 1832 to 1914, the United States flourished and grew into one of the wealthiest and most powerful nations in the world without either a Bank of the United States or a Federal Reserve Board. The creation of the Bank is thus neither necessary nor proper for carrying into execution *any* of the federal government's enumerated powers. It is a project that will benefit special, corrupt financial interests, which the nation neither needs nor wants.

An examination of the structure of the Constitution reveals that the Necessary and Proper Clause should be given the restrained construction for which I contend in my dissent today. First, I agree with the Majority that the Framers of our Constitution deliberately omitted the word "expressly," which had been used in Article II of the Articles of Confederation, when they wrote the Tenth Amendment, which declares: "The powers not delegated to the United States by the Constitution, nor prohibited by it to the States, are reserved to the States respectively, or to the people." The Framers of our Constitution thus contemplated that, under our Constitution, the federal government would have implied powers, unlike the government created by the Articles of Confederation.

The Framers, however, did not want to write a blank check with respect to implied federal powers, and it is for this reason, in my opinion, that they cabined the implied federal powers with the carefully chosen words of the Necessary and Proper Clause. Implied powers exist, but they must be "indispensable and proper" for "carrying into execution" an enumerated or implied powers end, and they must be properly federal powers and not State powers. Making it illegal to steal from the mail or to perjure oneself in federal court is both indispensable to carrying out a federally enumerated power, and it is also a proper thing for the federal and not the State governments to do.

The same thing cannot be said about the federal corporate chartering of a Bank of the United States, which has a monopoly on the federal government's banking business. Such a bank is neither "indispensable" nor is it a "proper" federal function in our system of federalism, which disfavors government-granted monopolies at any level. The placement of the Necessary and Proper Clause at the end of an 18-clause long list of limited and enumerated powers, which are "herein granted" to Congress by the Vesting Clause of Article I, suggests that the meaning of the Necessary and Proper Clause must be very closely tied to the seventeen enumerated powers which precede it and which it will carry into execution.

The majority makes much of the fact that Article I, Section 10, Clause 2 limits the states to certain "absolutely necessary" laws, thus suggesting that when the framers wanted to confine power grants to indispensable situations, they knew how to do it. But, it is a mistake to draw such a far-reaching conclusion from an isolated reference to the States, which was probably made inadvertently. A fairer comparison would be to compare the Necessary and Proper Clause to the District of Columbia Clause in Article I, Section 8, Clause 17 or to the Territories Clause in Article IV, Section 3. Allow me to quote both below together, with the Necessary and Proper Clause, so the reader can properly compare them. The District of Columbia Clause gives Congress the power **"[t]o exercise exclusive Legislation in all Cases whatsoever, over [the District of Columbia],"** U.S. CONST. art. I, § 8, cl. 17, and the Territories Clause says that **"[t]he Congress shall have Power to dispose of and make all Needful Rules and Regulations respecting the Territory or other Property belonging to the United States * * *.** *Id.* art. IV, § 3, cl. 2. In contrast, the Necessary and Proper Clause says that Congress shall have power "[t]**o** make all Laws, which shall be **necessary and proper for carrying into Execution the foregoing Powers** and all other Powers vested by this Constitution in the Government of the United States, or in any Department or Officer thereof." *Id.* art. I, § 8, cl. 18.

It is obvious that any fair-minded reader who compares congressional power over the District of Columbia and the Territories, and under the Necessary and Proper Clause, must conclude from the structure of the Constitution that the Necessary and Proper Clause is a much more limited grant of power to Congress than are the powers conferred by the Territories Clause or the District of Columbia Clause, both of which give Congress all the powers of a general government within their limited geographic sphere. Congress may well be able to establish municipal corporations in the District of Columbia or in the Territories, but it cannot do so throughout the United States. I therefore contend that the structure of the rest of the Constitution bears out my conclusion that the Necessary and Proper Clause is written the way it is because, while that Clause does grant the federal government implied powers, it limits sharply what the scope of those implied powers must be.

The history of the writing of the Constitution supports my conclusion that the Bank of the United States is unconstitutional. First, James Madison's Notes of the Philadelphia Constitutional Convention reveal that a motion was made at that convention to give the new federal government the power to charter corporations, and it was defeated because Pennsylvania and New York did not want any newly chartered federal corporations to compete with the then-existing state corporations.

For this reason, Congressman James Madison argued in 1791 that the bill to incorporate a federal Bank of the United States was unconstitutional. Madison said as much in a speech on the floor of the House of Representatives. Secretary of State Thomas Jefferson was also of this view, which he expressed in writing to President George Washington urging him to veto the bill creating the Bank. Attorney General Edmund Randolph also thought the Bill creating the First Bank of the United States was unconstitutional, and he urged President Washington to veto it. Indeed, the only defender of the Bank in Washington's Cabinet was his Secretary of the Treasury, Alexander Hamilton, who was practically a monarchist, and had very unconventional views on many subjects and especially believed in unlimited federal power.

Although the Bill creating the First Bank was signed into law, the Bank was allowed to sunset out of existence in 1811 in part because many members of Congress doubted its constitutionality. The bill creating the Third Bank of the United States was vetoed in 1832 by President Andrew Jackson who also ordered his Secretary of the Treasury to withdraw all the federal money that was invested in the Bank. Jackson believed the Bank bill was unconstitutional and unwise, and he succeeded in killing the Bank until 1913, when President Woodrow Wilson recreated it as the Federal Reserve Board. Jackson said "mere precedential arguments for the constitutionality of the Bank were a dangerous source of authority." This is undoubtedly true. We had a long period of time where African-Americans were enslaved or were blatantly discriminated against because of Jim Crow laws. No one would argue we should follow that practice, and, similarly, no one should argue that we should follow the precedent of the establishment of the First Bank.

Our most recent federalism caselaw relevant to this subject is Chief Justice Roberts' opinion in *NFIB v. Sebelius*, where he correctly argues that the Necessary and Proper Clause authorizes only means to a constitutionally permissible end. A power that is such a great and important power that one ought to expect to find it on the Article I, Section 8 list as a separately enumerated power is by definition not a power that can be supported under a fair reading of the Necessary and Proper Clause. For this reason, Chief Justice Roberts held that Congress did not have the power to compel the buying of goods in commerce under the Necessary and Proper Clause. Such a power was, according to Chief Justice Roberts, such a great and independent power that it could not exist unless it was enumerated on its own.

The majority could rely on dubious Necessary and Proper Clause precedents, like *Knox v. Lee,* the case which upheld the printing of paper money after the Civil War. Suffice it to say that a lot of constitutionally dubious things came out of the Civil War for obvious reasons, one of which was federal power to print paper money. This is not a time period one should look to for guidance.

The Bank of the United State is not only unconstitutional; its creation is also a bad idea. It will give monopoly power and enormous wealth to unscrupulous individuals like Nicholas Biddle, who corruptly tried to influence federal elections, including presidential elections, in the 1830's. The government should not be in the business of running a bank, and it should not give one bank all the business which it is engaged in. The majority's decision in this case is not only unconstitutional, upending forever our constitutional system of a federal government with limited and enumerated powers. It is also an opening of the door to crony capitalism of the worst kind. The nation will rue the day this opinion was handed down.

Finally, the majority opinion disgracefully and subtly alters the test for evaluating the constitutionality of laws enacted under the Necessary and Proper Clause. The majority says: "Let the end be legitimate, let it be within the scope of the Constitution, and all means which are appropriate, which are plainly adapted to that end, which are not prohibited, but consist with the letter and spirit of the Constitution, are Constitutional." This is, with all due respect "an appropriateness test," with appropriate defined to mean "convenient" or "useful". The actual language of the Clause, in contrast, requires that laws enacted under it be "**necessary and proper for carrying into Execution**" an enumerated power.

It is the oldest lawyer's trick in the book to take some provision of a legal text, talk about the grand "purposes" it serves, and then formulate a highly permissive new "test" with which the restrictive original legal language of the original legal text is in conflict. Chief Justice Marshall buries his "new appropriateness test" in a maze of language about the importance of the Constitution and of the federal government. He thus slips by the eyes of the discerning reader a mammoth shift in federal power! Chief Justice Marshall's opinion in *McCulloch* is dishonest, misleading, and dangerously permissive.

The Maryland tax on the Bank of the United States is obviously constitutional, in my opinion, since I think the Bank itself is unconstitutional * * *.

I respectfully dissent from the majority's decision today destroying our constitutional system of a federal government that was supposed to have only limited and enumerated powers.

3. "JUSTICE" LAWSON'S DISSENTING OPINION IN *MCCULLOCH V. MARYLAND*

I agree with almost everything in Justice Calabresi's persuasive dissenting opinion. I write separately for three reasons. First, while I am in strong sympathy with his views about both the drafting history of the Constitution and the likely policy consequences of the Court's decision, I do not want to express or endorse those views formally in a judicial opinion, as I consider them irrelevant to the legal question before us. Second, while I wholeheartedly agree that the monopoly Bank is not a "proper" means for executing federal powers, no party before us has raised that issue, and I therefore would not decide it in this particular case. Third, I want to highlight some features of the Constitution, and of the Necessary and Proper Clause, that further demonstrate, in addition to the reasons expressed so well by Justice Calabresi, how the Court's opinion distorts the Constitution's text and structure.

The Majority quite properly concedes that if the power to incorporate a bank is a "great substantive and independent power," then it cannot be implied through the Necessary and Proper Clause. But the Majority does not adequately explain *how and why* that is so. Two consequences flow from that omission. First, there is some risk that the Majority's too-casual treatment of the subject will cause its discussion to vanish into a legal black hole for two centuries or so, with accompanying grave damage to constitutional law. Second, by not focusing adequately on the true import and significance of the difference between incidental powers and "great substantive and independent powers," the Majority probably gets this case wrong.

Start with something on which we can all agree: If there was no Necessary and Proper Clause, Congress would still be able to enact legislation to carry into effect its enumerated powers. But it is crucial to understand why this is so and how far that power would extend.

If you authorize someone to act on your behalf as an agent, you will never be able to anticipate every contingency that might arise in the exercise of their functions. To enumerate each and every action that the agent can take, in all circumstances, would be fruitless (not to mention very expensive on hourly billing by the lawyers drafting the documents). Fortunately, the law for centuries has understood that agency instruments are always drafted against a background set of expectations and legal rules. One important set of those legal rules concerns the scope of the powers of agents. It is settled law that, absent some indication to the contrary in a document, agents who are granted express, or *principal,* powers will normally also have implied, or *incidental,* powers that customarily accompany those express powers. This legal convention spares parties the need to try to spell out in gruesome detail each and every implementing action that agents can take. Parties can always draft around that convention if they wish by giving agents broader or fewer (or even no) incidental powers, but the baseline assumption is that grants of powers carry their incidents in their wake. An incident, according to the leading eighteenth-century legal dictionary, is "a thing necessarily depending upon, appertaining to, or following another thing that is *more worthy or principal.*" GILES JACOB, A NEW LAW DICTIONARY (10th ed. 1782) (emphasis added). Incidents must be subsidiary to, or less "worthy" than, the principal power that they accompany. For example, the power to manage a farm ordinarily includes the power to lease it, but not the power to sell it. *See* 1 MATTHEW BACON, A NEW ABRIDGEMENT OF THE LAW 235–36 (5th ed., John Exshaw ed., 1786). Leasing is an incident to management, but sale of the farm is not. *See* 3 CHARLES VINER, A GENERAL ABRIDGEMENT OF LAW AND EQUITY 538–40 (1742). The power to sell is a "great substantive and independent" power, which is as or more "worthy" than the power to manage. If the principal wants the agent to be able to sell the farm, the principal needs to say so.

The Constitution is an agency instrument of sorts. In the Constitution, its legal author, We the People, entrusts certain agents with management authority over some portion of We the People's affairs. It is not necessary here to identify exactly which kind of agency instrument—a power of attorney, a corporate charter, a trust, etc.—the Constitution most resembles, because the background rules of principal and incidental powers are invariant across the entire range of agency instruments. Given that characterization of the Constitution, it would naturally follow, in the absence of the Necessary and Proper Clause, that Congress's express grants of principal powers, primarily in Article, Section 8, carry with them incidental powers as a normal inference. That is why Congress could criminalize mail theft, create federal offices, and prescribe the form of oath for federal officials even if the Constitution did not contain an express "incidental powers" clause such as the Necessary and Proper Clause. But *only* incidental powers can be implied in this fashion. If a power is a great substantive and independent power, as worthy as the named principal powers, it *cannot* be implied as an incident, absent something in the document that expands the scope of the agent's incidental powers beyond the ordinary baseline.

The Necessary and Proper Clause is an express "incidental powers" clause. It codifies and clarifies the doctrine of incidental powers. That is its obvious function and meaning to anyone with even a casual acquaintance with eighteenth-century agency law. (The drafters of the Constitution, as it happens, were more than casually acquainted with eighteenth-century agency law. The Necessary and Proper Clause was drafted by the Committee of Detail, which consisted of four lawyers who spent their lives drafting agency instruments and a businessman who spent his life having lawyers draft them.) But instead of expanding Congress's incidental powers to infinity and beyond, as the Majority suggests, the clause as written *confines* and *limits* Congress's incidental powers. If one examines eighteenth-century agency instruments, one will find many different formulations to express how the parties to the agency agreement want the agents' incidental powers to be understood. They could, as did the Articles of Confederation, rule out *any* incidental powers. They could try to *expand* the common-law baseline of incidental powers by saying, for instance, that the agent can do anything that could reasonably be thought conducive to carrying out the agent's task. They could *codify* the common-law baselines, either by saying nothing or by using neutral language such as "any appropriate powers." Or they could try to *limit* but not eliminate the agent's incidental powers by saying—hmm, let's think about how one might word this—"*only use incidental powers that are both necessary and proper—in the conjunctive—for executing principal powers.*" That is exactly what a number of eighteenth-century agency instruments did, and it is exactly what the eighteenth-century Constitution does. It allows incidental powers, as Justice Calabresi so eloquently confirms, but it does so in a limited and cabined fashion.

Understood in this way, there is no doubt that the power to incorporate a bank is a great substantive and independent power, at least as worthy as many of the principal powers identified in the Constitution. If it existed, it would need to be enumerated. The fact that corporations are means rather than ends is irrelevant. The Necessary and Proper Clause does not authorize all possible, or even all convenient, or even all helpful, means. Selling a farm is a means to making money, not an end in itself. That does not mean that an agent charged with managing the farm gets to sell it. The Majority asks the right questions on this score, but it gets the wrong answers.

If the power to incorporate a bank is not an incidental power, then it is not within the scope of Congress's implied, or incidental (the more precise term for "implied"), powers whether or not it is necessary and proper for anything. One only asks whether a power is necessary and proper after one has *first* established that is properly an incident. The Majority gets this sequence of reasoning exactly right. It just answers the initial question incorrectly.

Even if the power to incorporate a bank is somehow seen as an incidental rather than principal power, the Constitution's express incidental powers clause requires that it be "necessary and proper for carrying into Execution" some other federal power. I have little to add to Justice Calabresi's perceptive remarks on why the Bank is not "necessary," except three things. First, I note that in the late eighteenth century, incidental powers were considered "necessary" when they were either indispensable, customary, or, in the words of the great eighteenth-century legal scholar William Blackstone, "so annexed to and so necessary to the well-being of the [principal power] * * * that they shall accompany * * * [the principal power] wherever it vests." Second, in light of this information, I would have preferred to have one of the parties offer James Madison's account of "necessary" as an alternative, rather than forcing us to choose between an extreme view of "necessary" as either strictly "indispensable" or merely "helpful." Third, if forced to choose between the two options offered by Maryland and the United States, I agree with Justice Calabresi that Maryland's view is far closer to the ordinary-language meaning of "necessary," notwithstanding the Majority's legitimate intra-textual comparison of the Necessary and Proper Clause and the Imposts Clause. The Majority repeats, in substance, Alexander Hamilton's famous observation from 1791 that "[i]t is a common mode of expression to say, that it is necessary for a government or a person to do this or that thing, when nothing more is intended or understood, than that the interests of the government or person require, or will be promoted by, the doing of this or that thing." *Final Version of an Opinion on the Constitutionality of an Act to Establish a Bank, in* 8 THE PAPERS OF ALEXANDER HAMILTON 97, 102 (Harold C. Syrett & Jacob E. Cooke eds., 1965). A "common mode of expression," he claims? I have examined every usage of the word "necessary," prior to or contemporaneous with Mr. Hamilton's comment, that appears in a rather large database of important public legal discussions, and none—literally none, as in "not one"—of those usages even remotely conforms to Mr. Hamilton's. To what should be no one's great surprise, Samuel Johnson has much the better account of the public meaning of "necessary" than does Alexander Hamilton in the heat of a political fight or, through him, the Majority.

The Majority tries to reason from first principles. There is nothing necessarily (in the ordinary-language sense of that term) wrong with such reasoning. No document contains all of the rules for its own interpretation, so one must always bring in some context from outside the document. But instead of using the context of agency law to interpret what is obviously an agency instrument, the Majority instead overlays on the Constitution a conception of governmental power that, in essence, treat the enumerations of power as suggestions or starting points rather than as definitions. The Majority sees a government capable of solving any and all national problems, where the "purposes" of the Constitution define its powers. I see a Constitution in which the granted powers, and their "necessary and proper" incidents, define the extent to and manner in which government agents can pursue the instrument's purposes. I have no doubt that many people share the Majority's normative vision of what a good constitution would say. I have no doubt that many people in 1787 hoped that they were drafting a constitution along the lines favored by the Majority. But the document that was ratified by the ninth State on June 6, 1788 simply is not the kind of constitution favored by the Majority. It does contain a provision—Article V—that allows the Majority to pursue its favored vision. But it must do so by convincing a majority of citizens in three-quarters of the States, rather than by convincing a simple majority of the Justices on this Court.

Accordingly, I also dissent.

NOTES AND QUESTIONS

1. *McCulloch v. Maryland* was hardly the end of the legal saga of the Bank of the United States. In 1832, four years before the second Bank's charter was set to expire by

its own terms, a bill re-chartering the Bank of the United States for an additional fifteen years was passed by Congress and vetoed by then-President Andrew Jackson. Jackson wrote a blistering veto message attacking the Bank as being both unconstitutional, notwithstanding the decision in *McCulloch v. Maryland,* and bad policy, largely because the bill called for the Bank to pay only $200,000 per year for the renewal of monopoly privileges worth millions of dollars. President Jackson then ordered all the federal governmental deposits to be withdrawn from the Bank of the United States and deposited in State chartered banks across the country. The public strongly supported Jackson in two elections, so his actions stuck, and the Bank of the United States ceased to exist. Here is an excerpt from Jackson's veto message.

B. PRESIDENT JACKSON'S VETO MESSAGE REGARDING THE BANK OF THE UNITED STATES

July 10, 1832

To the Senate.

The bill "to modify and continue" the act entitled "An act to incorporate the subscribers to the Bank of the United States" was presented to me on the 4th July instant. Having considered it with that solemn regard to the principles of the Constitution which the day was calculated to inspire, and come to the conclusion that it ought not to become a law, I herewith return it to the Senate, in which it originated, with my objections.

A bank of the United States is in many respects convenient for the Government and useful to the people. Entertaining this opinion, and deeply impressed with the belief that some of the powers and privileges possessed by the existing bank are unauthorized by the Constitution, subversive of the rights of the States, and dangerous to the liberties of the people, I felt it my duty at an early period of my Administration to call the attention of Congress to the practicability of organizing an institution combining all its advantages and obviating these objections. I sincerely regret that in the act before me I can perceive none of those modifications of the bank charter which are necessary, in my opinion, to make it compatible with justice, with sound policy, or with the Constitution of our country.

The present corporate body, denominated the president, directors, and company of the Bank of the United States, will have existed at the time this act is intended to take effect twenty years. It enjoys an exclusive privilege of banking under the authority of the General Government, a monopoly of its favor and support, and, as a necessary consequence, almost a monopoly of the foreign and domestic exchange. The powers, privileges, and favors bestowed upon it in the original charter, by increasing the value of the stock far above its par value, operated as a gratuity of many millions to the stockholders.

An apology may be found for the failure to guard against this result in the consideration that the effect of the original act of incorporation could not be certainly foreseen at the time of its passage. The act before me proposes another gratuity to the holders of the same stock, and in many cases to the same men, of at least seven millions more. This donation finds no apology in any uncertainty as to the effect of the act. On all hands it is conceded that its passage will increase at least so or 30 per cent more the market price of the stock, subject to the payment of the annuity of $200,000 per year secured by the act, thus adding in a moment one-fourth to its par value. It is not our own citizens only who are to receive the bounty of our Government. More than eight millions of the stock of this bank are held by foreigners. By this act the American Republic proposes virtually to make them a present of some millions of dollars. For these gratuities to foreigners and to some of our own opulent citizens the act secures no equivalent whatever. They are the certain gains of the present stockholders under the operation of this act, after making full allowance for the payment of the [$200,000] bonus.

Every monopoly and all exclusive privileges are granted at the expense of the public, which ought to receive a fair equivalent. The many millions which this act proposes to bestow on the stockholders of the existing bank must come directly or indirectly out of the earnings of the American people. It is due to them, therefore, if their Government sell monopolies and exclusive privileges, that they should at least exact for them as much as they are worth in open market. The value of the monopoly in this case may be correctly ascertained. The twenty-eight millions of stock would probably be at an advance of 50 per cent, and command in market at least $42,000,000, subject to the payment of the present bonus. The present value of the monopoly, therefore, is $17,000,000, and this the act proposes to sell for three millions, payable in fifteen annual installments of $200,000 each.

It is not conceivable how the present stockholders can have any claim to the special favor of the Government. The present corporation has enjoyed its monopoly during the period stipulated in the original contract. If we must have such a corporation, why should not the Government sell out the whole stock and thus secure to the people the full market value of the privileges granted? Why should not Congress create and sell twenty-eight millions of stock, incorporating the purchasers with all the powers and privileges secured in this act and putting the premium upon the sales into the Treasury?

But this act does not permit competition in the purchase of this monopoly. It seems to be predicated on the erroneous idea that the present stockholders have a prescriptive right not only to the favor but to the bounty of Government. It appears that more than a fourth part of the stock is held by foreigners and the residue is held by a few hundred of our own citizens, chiefly of the richest class. For their benefit does this act exclude the whole American people from competition in the purchase of this monopoly and dispose of it for many millions less than it is worth. This seems the less excusable because some of our citizens not now stockholders petitioned that the door of competition might be opened, and offered to take a charter on terms much more favorable to the Government and country.

* * * I can not perceive the justice or policy of this course. If our Government must sell monopolies, it would seem to be its duty to take nothing less than their full value, and if gratuities must be made once in fifteen or twenty years let them not be bestowed on the subjects of a foreign government nor upon a designated and favored class of men in our own country * * *.

* * *

In another of its bearings this provision is fraught with danger. Of the twenty-five directors of this bank five are chosen by the Government and twenty by the citizen stockholders. From all voice in these elections the foreign stockholders are excluded by the charter. In proportion, therefore, as the stock is transferred to foreign holders the extent of suffrage in the choice of directors is curtailed. Already is almost a third of the stock in foreign hands and not represented in elections. It is constantly passing out of the country, and this act will accelerate its departure. The entire control of the institution would necessarily fall into the hands of a few citizen stockholders, and the ease with which the object would be accomplished would be a temptation to designing men to secure that control in their own hands by monopolizing the remaining stock. There is danger that a president and directors would then be able to elect themselves from year to year, and without responsibility or control manage the whole concerns of the bank during the existence of its charter. It is easy to conceive that great evils to our country and its institutions might flow from such a concentration of power in the hands of a few men irresponsible to the people.

* * *

It is maintained by the advocates of the bank that its constitutionality in all its features ought to be considered as settled by precedent and by the decision of the Supreme Court. To this conclusion I can not assent. Mere precedent is a dangerous source of authority, and should not be regarded as deciding questions of constitutional power except where the acquiescence of the people and the States can be considered as well settled. So far from this being the case on this subject, an argument against the bank might be based on precedent. One Congress, in 1791, decided in favor of a bank; another, in 1811, decided against it. One Congress, in 1815, decided against a bank; another, in 1816, decided in its favor. Prior to the present Congress, therefore, the precedents drawn from that source were equal. If we resort to the States, the expressions of legislative, judicial, and executive opinions against the bank have been probably to those in its favor as 4 to 1. There is nothing in precedent, therefore, which, if its authority were admitted, ought to weigh in favor of the act before me.

If the opinion of the Supreme Court covered the whole ground of this act, it ought not to control the coordinate authorities of this Government. The Congress, the Executive, and the Court must each for itself be guided by its own opinion of the Constitution. Each public officer who takes an oath to support the Constitution swears that he will support it as he understands it, and not as it is understood by others. It is as much the duty of the House of Representatives, of the Senate, and of the President to decide upon the constitutionality of any bill or resolution which may be presented to them for passage or approval as it is of the supreme judges when it may be brought before them for judicial decision. The opinion of the judges has no more authority over Congress than the opinion of Congress has over the judges, and on that point the President is independent of both. The authority of the Supreme Court must not, therefore, be permitted to control the Congress or the Executive when acting in their legislative capacities, but to have only such influence as the force of their reasoning may deserve.

* * *

The principle * * * affirmed [in *McCulloch*] is that the "degree of its necessity," involving all the details of a banking institution, is a question exclusively for legislative consideration. A bank is constitutional, but it is the province of the Legislature to determine whether this or that particular power, privilege, or exemption is "necessary and proper" to enable the bank to discharge its duties to the Government, and from their decision there is no appeal to the courts of justice. Under the decision of the Supreme Court, therefore, it is the exclusive province of Congress and the President to decide whether the particular features of this act are *necessary* and *proper* in order to enable the bank to perform conveniently and efficiently the public duties assigned to it as a fiscal agent, and therefore constitutional, or *unnecessary* and *improper*, and therefore unconstitutional.

Without commenting on the general principle affirmed by the Supreme Court, let us examine the details of this act in accordance with the rule of legislative action which they have laid down. It will be found that many of the powers and privileges conferred on it can not be supposed necessary for the purpose for which it is proposed to be created, and are not, therefore, means necessary to attain the end in view, and consequently not justified by the Constitution.

The original act of incorporation, section 2I, enacts "that no other bank shall be established by any future law of the United States during the continuance of the corporation hereby created, for which the faith of the United States is hereby pledged: *Provided*, Congress may renew existing charters for banks within the District of Columbia not increasing the capital thereof, and may also establish any other bank or banks in said District with capitals not exceeding in the whole $6,000,000 if they shall deem it expedient." This provision is continued in force by the act before me fifteen years from the ad of March, 1836.

If Congress possessed the power to establish one bank, they had power to establish more than one if in their opinion two or more banks had been "necessary" to facilitate the execution of the powers delegated to them in the Constitution. If they possessed the power to establish a second bank, it was a power derived from the Constitution to be exercised from time to time, and at any time when the interests of the country or the emergencies of the Government might make it expedient. It was possessed by one Congress as well as another, and by all Congresses alike, and alike at every session. But the Congress of 1816 have taken it away from their successors for twenty years, and the Congress of 1832 proposes to abolish it for fifteen years more. It can not be *"necessary"* or *"proper"* for Congress to barter away or divest themselves of any of the powers-vested in them by the Constitution to be exercised for the public good. It is not "necessary" to the efficiency of the bank, nor is it *"proper"* in relation to themselves and their successors. They may *properly* use the discretion vested in them, but they may not limit the discretion of their successors. This restriction on themselves and grant of a monopoly to the bank is therefore unconstitutional.

In another point of view this provision is a palpable attempt to amend the Constitution by an act of legislation. The Constitution declares that "the Congress shall have power to exercise exclusive legislation in all cases whatsoever" over the District of Columbia. Its constitutional power, therefore, to establish banks in the District of Columbia and increase their capital at will is unlimited and uncontrollable by any other power than that which gave authority to the Constitution. Yet this act declares that Congress shall not increase the capital of existing banks, nor create other banks with capitals exceeding in the whole $6,000,000. The Constitution declares that Congress *shall* have power to exercise exclusive legislation over this District *"in all cases whatsoever,"* and this act declares they shall not. Which is the supreme law of the land? This provision can not be *"necessary"* or *"proper"* or *constitutional* unless the absurdity be admitted that whenever it be "necessary and proper" in the opinion of Congress they have a right to barter away one portion of the powers vested in them by the Constitution as a means of executing the rest.

On two subjects only does the Constitution recognize in Congress the power to grant exclusive privileges or monopolies. It declares that "Congress shall have power to promote the progress of science and useful arts by securing for limited times to authors and inventors the exclusive right to their respective writings and discoveries." Out of this express delegation of power have grown our laws of patents and copyrights. As the Constitution expressly delegates to Congress the power to grant exclusive privileges in these cases as the means of executing the substantive power "to promote the progress of science and useful arts," it is consistent with the fair rules of construction to conclude that such a power was not intended to be granted as a means of accomplishing any other end. On every other subject which comes within the scope of Congressional power there is an ever-living discretion in the use of proper means, which can not be restricted or abolished without an amendment of the Constitution. Every act of Congress, therefore, which attempts by grants of monopolies or sale of exclusive privileges for a limited time, or a time without limit, to restrict or extinguish its own discretion in the choice of means to execute its delegated powers is equivalent to a legislative amendment of the Constitution, and palpably unconstitutional.

* * *

It is maintained by some that the bank is a means of executing the constitutional power "to coin money and regulate the value thereof." Congress have established a mint to coin money and passed laws to regulate the value thereof. The money so coined, with its value so regulated, and such foreign coins as Congress may adopt are the only currency known to the Constitution. But if they have other power to regulate the currency, it was conferred to be exercised by themselves, and not to be transferred to a corporation. If the bank be established for that purpose, with a charter unalterable without its consent, Congress have parted with their power for a term of years, during which the Constitution is a dead letter. It is neither necessary nor proper to transfer its legislative power to such a bank, and therefore unconstitutional.

* * *

* * * A general discussion will now take place, eliciting new light and settling important principles; and a new Congress, elected in the midst of such discussion, and furnishing an equal representation of the people according to the last census, will bear to the Capitol the verdict of public opinion, and, I doubt not, bring this important question to a satisfactory result.

* * *

It is to be regretted that the rich and powerful too often bend the acts of government to their selfish purposes. Distinctions in society will always exist under every just government. Equality of talents, of education, or of wealth can not be produced by human institutions. In the full enjoyment of the gifts of Heaven and the fruits of superior industry, economy, and virtue, every man is equally entitled to protection by law; but when the laws undertake to add to these natural and just advantages artificial distinctions, to grant titles, gratuities, and exclusive privileges, to make the rich richer and the potent more powerful, the humble members of society—the farmers, mechanics, and laborers—who have neither the time nor the means of securing like favors to themselves, have a right to complain of the injustice of their Government. There are no necessary evils in government. Its evils exist only in its abuses. If it would confine itself to equal protection, and, as Heaven does its rains, shower its favors alike on the high and the low, the rich and the poor, it would be an unqualified blessing. In the act before me there seems to be a wide and unnecessary departure from these just principles.

* * *

Experience should teach us wisdom. Most of the difficulties our Government now encounters and most of the dangers which impend over our Union have sprung from an abandonment of the legitimate objects of Government by our national legislation, and the adoption of such principles as are embodied in this act. Many of our rich men have not been content with equal protection and equal benefits, but have besought us to make them richer by act of Congress. By attempting to gratify their desires we have in the results of our legislation arrayed section against section, interest against interest, and man against man, in a fearful commotion which threatens to shake the foundations of our Union. It is time to pause in our career to review our principles, and if possible revive that devoted patriotism and spirit of compromise which distinguished the sages of the Revolution and the fathers of our Union. If we can not at once, in justice to interests vested under improvident legislation, make our Government what it ought to be, we can at least take a stand against all new grants of monopolies and exclusive privileges, against any prostitution of our Government to the advancement of the few at the expense of the many, and in favor of compromise and gradual reform in our code of laws and system of political economy.

* * *

ANDREW JACKSON.

NOTES AND QUESTIONS

1. Isn't President Jackson right to oppose giving the federal Bank of the United States a monopoly on banking? Note that Nicholas Biddle, the President of the Bank did everything in his power to cause President Jackson to lose his bid for re-election in 1832. Once re-elected, President Jackson ordered his Treasury Secretary to remove the federal government's deposits from the Bank of the United States. Jackson's Treasury Secretary refused, and Jackson appointed his Attorney General Roger Taney to be his new Treasury Secretary, and future Chief Justice Taney removed the federal government's deposits from the Bank. The Senate, which was controlled by the Whig Party, censured President Jackson for this action. Nicholas Biddle, and the Bank of the United States, then deliberately caused a financial panic to induce Jackson to change his mind. Jackson barnstormed the country accusing the Bank of causing financial distress, and his Democratic Party won a majority in the Senate in the 1834 mid-term elections, after which the Senate expunged its resolution of censure of President Jackson from its official records. Don't these events prove Jackson to have been right about the dangerous power accumulated by the Bank of the United States?

2. You have now read Chief Justice Marshall's opinion in *McCulloch v. Maryland*, Professor Calabresi's and Professor Lawson's dissents from that opinion, and President Andrew Jackson's 1832 veto message denouncing the Bank as being unconstitutional. Who do you agree with and why?

3. In the 1840's, after Jackson was out of office, Congress twice voted to re-charter the Bank of the United States, and both times President John Tyler vetoed the Bank, citing Jackson's veto message. As a result, the Bank was not re-created in any form until Congress and President Woodrow Wilson set up the Federal Reserve Board in 1914. During the 82 years between President Jackson's veto of the renewal of the Bank of the United States in 1832 and the creation of the Federal Reserve Board in 1914, the U.S. economy grew by leaps and bounds, and the nation prospered greatly *without a Bank of the United States*. There perhaps were sharper boom and bust cycles during these years than there have been since 1914 (though that is debatable), but otherwise the nation flourished even without the Bank. Is any of that relevant to the constitutional questions concerning the Bank?

[Assignment 31]

C. COMMERCE, EFFECTS ON COMMERCE, AND *UNITED STATES V. LOPEZ*

Chief Justice Marshall's opinion in *McCulloch* reflected a broad view of federal power. But even Marshall could not imagine the federal government that we have today. Much of the rest of this course tracks how the federal government grew into its present form. For the moment, here is what you need to know:

One of the most important considerations leading to adoption of the Constitution was the perceived need for centralized regulation of trade, both foreign and domestic. Most notably, States pursued mercantilist and protectionist policies that made interstate commerce risky and expensive. Accordingly, Congress was given power "[t]o regulate Commerce with foreign Nations, and among the several States, and with the Indian tribes." U.S. CONST. art. I, § 8, cl. 3. This was among the least controversial provisions in the Constitution. James Madison in *The Federalist* No. 45 described the commerce power as "an addition which few oppose and from which no apprehensions are entertained."

In the twentieth century, the commerce power, along with the Necessary and Proper Clause, became the engine that drove the transformation of the federal government, especially during and after the New Deal. The provision "from which no apprehensions are entertained" became a source of power to regulate how much wheat farmers could grow, *see Wickard v. Filburn,* 317 U.S. 111 (1942); the content of intra-state labor contracts, *see United States v. Darby,* 312 U.S. 100 (1941), and insurance contracts, *see United States v. South-Eastern Underwriters Ass'n,* 322 U.S. 533 (1944); and even local street-corner loan-sharking, *see Perez v. United States,* 402 U.S. 146 (1971), and what kinds of plants people can grow in their kitchen windows. *See Gonzalez v. Raich,* 545 U.S. 1 (2005). The commerce power, rather than the seemingly more suited amendments ratified after the Civil War, was also invoked as the constitutional ground for the Civil Rights Act of 1964, on the theory that restaurants receive some of their supplies through interstate commerce and are therefore subject to federal regulation regarding who they serve. *See Katzenbach v. McClung,* 379 U.S. 294 (1964). The bottom line is that from 1937 through 1995—a fifty-eight-year period of explosive growth in the size and scope of the federal government, exactly one Supreme Court case found (in a 5–4 vote) that Congress had exceeded the scope of the Commerce and Necessary and Proper Clauses. *See National League of Cities v. Usery,* 426 U.S. 833 (1976). That decision involved federal regulation of the hours and working conditions of *State employees,* which implicated federalism and the Tenth Amendment in an especially direct way—and the decision was promptly overruled nine years later. *See Garcia v. San Antonio Metropolitan Transit Authority,* 469 U.S. 528 (1985). This sixty-year run without any judicially enforced limits on the scope of the congressional commerce power is the context leading up the next case.

United States v. Lopez

514 U.S. 549 (1995)

■ CHIEF JUSTICE REHNQUIST delivered the opinion of the Court.

In the Gun-Free School Zones Act of 1990, Congress made it a federal offense "for any individual knowingly to possess a firearm at a place that the individual knows, or has reasonable cause to believe, is a school zone." 18 U.S.C. § 922(q)(1)(A). The Act neither regulates a commercial activity nor contains a requirement that the possession be connected in any way to interstate commerce. We hold that the Act exceeds the authority of Congress "[t]o regulate Commerce . . .among the several States . . . ." U. S. Const., Art. I, § 8, cl. 3.

On March 10, 1992, respondent, who was then a 12th grade student, arrived at Edison High School in San Antonio, Texas, carrying a concealed .38-caliber handgun and five bullets. Acting upon an anonymous tip, school authorities confronted respondent, who admitted that he was carrying the weapon. He was arrested and charged under Texas law with firearm possession on school premises. The next day, the state charges were dismissed after federal agents charged respondent by complaint with violating the Gun-Free School Zones Act of 1990. 18 U.S.C. § 922(q)(1)(A).

* * * The District Court conducted a bench trial, found him guilty of violating § 922(q), and sentenced him to six months' imprisonment and two years' supervised release.

On appeal, respondent challenged his conviction based on his claim that § 922(q) exceeded Congress' power to legislate under the Commerce Clause. The Court of Appeals for the Fifth Circuit agreed and reversed respondent's conviction. It held that, in light of what it characterized as insufficient congressional findings and legislative history, "section 922(q), in the full reach of its terms, is invalid as beyond the power of Congress under the Commerce Clause." 2 F.3d 1342, 1367–1368 (1993). Because of the importance of the issue, we granted certiorari, 511 U. S. 1029 (1994), and we now affirm.

We start with first principles. The Constitution creates a Federal Government of enumerated powers. See U. S. Const., Art. I, § 8. As James Madison wrote: "The powers delegated by the proposed Constitution to the federal government are few and defined. Those which are to remain in the State governments are numerous and indefinite." The Federalist No. 45. This constitutionally mandated division of authority "was adopted by the Framers to ensure protection of our fundamental liberties." *Gregory* v. *Ashcroft*, 501 U.S. 452, 458 (1991). "Just as the separation and independence of the coordinate branches of the Federal Government serves to prevent the accumulation of excessive power in any one branch, a healthy balance of power between the States and the Federal Government will reduce the risk of tyranny and abuse from either front." *Ibid.*

The Constitution delegates to Congress the power "[t]o regulate Commerce with foreign Nations, and among the several States, and with the Indian Tribes." U. S. Const. Art. I, § 8, cl. 3. The Court, through Chief Justice Marshall, first defined the nature of Congress' commerce power in *Gibbons* v. *Ogden*, 9 Wheat. 1, 189–190 (1824):

> "Commerce, undoubtedly, is traffic, but it is something more: it is intercourse. It describes the commercial intercourse between nations, and parts of nations, in all its branches, and is regulated by prescribing rules for carrying on that intercourse."

The commerce power "is the power to regulate; that is, to prescribe the rule by which commerce is to be governed. This power, like all others vested in congress, is complete in itself, may be exercised to its utmost extent, and acknowledges no limitations, other than are prescribed in the constitution." *Id.*, at 196. The *Gibbons* Court, however, acknowledged that limitations on the commerce power are inherent in the very language of the Commerce Clause.

> "It is not intended to say that these words comprehend that commerce, which is completely internal, which is carried on between man and man in a State, or between different parts of the same State, and which does not extend to or affect other States. Such a power would be inconvenient, and is certainly unnecessary.
>
> "Comprehensive as the word 'among' is, it may very properly be restricted to that commerce which concerns more States than one. . . . The enumeration presupposes something not enumerated; and that something, if we regard the language or the subject of the sentence, must be the exclusively internal commerce of a State." *Id.*, at 194–195.

For nearly a century thereafter, the Court's Commerce Clause decisions dealt but rarely with the extent of Congress' power * * *. Under this line of precedent, the Court held that certain categories of activity such as "production," "manufacturing," and "mining" were within the province of state governments, and thus were beyond the power of Congress under the Commerce Clause.

In 1887, Congress enacted the Interstate Commerce Act and in 1890, Congress enacted the Sherman Antitrust Act. These laws ushered in a new era of federal regulation under the commerce power. When cases involving these laws first reached this Court, we imported * * * the approach that Congress could not regulate activities such as "production," "manufacturing," and "mining." See, *e.g., United States* v. *E.C. Knight Co.*, 156 U.S. 1, 12 (1895) ("Commerce succeeds to manufacture, and is not part of it"); *Carter* v. *Carter Coal Co.*, 298 U.S. 238, 304 (1936) ("Mining brings the subject matter of commerce into existence. Commerce disposes of it"). Simultaneously, however, the Court held that, where the interstate and intrastate aspects of commerce were so mingled together that full regulation of interstate commerce required incidental regulation of intrastate commerce, the Commerce Clause authorized such regulation. See, *e.g., Shreveport Rate Cases,* 234 U.S. 342 (1914).

In *A. L. A. Schechter Poultry Corp.* v. *United States*, 295 U.S. 495, 550 (1935), the Court struck down regulations that fixed the hours and wages of individuals employed by an intrastate business because the activity being regulated related to interstate commerce only indirectly. In doing so, the Court characterized the distinction between direct and indirect effects of intrastate transactions upon interstate commerce as "a fundamental one, essential to the maintenance of our constitutional system." Activities that affected interstate commerce directly were within Congress' power; activities that affected interstate commerce indirectly were beyond Congress' reach. The justification for this formal distinction was rooted in the fear that otherwise "there would be virtually no limit to the federal power and for all practical purposes we should have a completely centralized government."

Two years later, in the watershed case of *NLRB* v. *Jones & Laughlin Steel Corp.*, 301 U.S. 1 (1937), the Court upheld the National Labor Relations Act against a Commerce Clause challenge, and in the process, departed from the distinction between "direct" and "indirect" effects on interstate commerce. *Id.* at 36–38 ("The question [of the scope of Congress' power] is necessarily one of degree"). The Court held that intrastate activities that "have such a close and substantial relation to interstate commerce that their control is essential or appropriate to protect that commerce from burdens and obstructions" are within Congress' power to regulate. *Id.* at 37.

In *United States* v. *Darby*, 312 U.S. 100 (1941), the Court upheld the Fair Labor Standards Act, stating:

> "The power of Congress over interstate commerce is not confined to the regulation of commerce among the states. It extends to those activities intrastate which so affect interstate commerce or the exercise of the power of Congress over it as to make regulation of them appropriate means to the attainment of a legitimate end, the exercise of the granted power of Congress to regulate interstate commerce." *Id.*, at 118.

In *Wickard* v. *Filburn*, the Court upheld the application of amendments to the Agricultural Adjustment Act of 1938 to the production and consumption of homegrown wheat. 317 U. S., at 128–129. The *Wickard* Court explicitly rejected earlier distinctions between direct and indirect effects on interstate commerce, stating:

> "[E]ven if appellee's activity be local and though it may not be regarded as commerce, it may still, whatever its nature, be reached by Congress if it exerts a substantial economic effect on interstate commerce, and this irrespective of whether such effect is what might at some earlier time have been defined as 'direct' or 'indirect.'" *Id.*, at 125.

The *Wickard* Court emphasized that although Filburn's own contribution to the demand for wheat may have been trivial by itself, that was not "enough to remove him from the scope of federal regulation where, as here, his contribution, taken together with that of many others similarly situated, is far from trivial." *Id.* at 127–28.

Jones & Laughlin Steel, *Darby,* and *Wickard* ushered in an era of Commerce Clause jurisprudence that greatly expanded the previously defined authority of Congress under that Clause. In part, this was a recognition of the great changes that had occurred in the way business was carried on in this country. Enterprises that had once been local or at most regional in nature had become national in scope. But the doctrinal change also reflected a view that earlier Commerce Clause cases artificially had constrained the authority of Congress to regulate interstate commerce.

But even these modern-era precedents which have expanded congressional power under the Commerce Clause confirm that this power is subject to outer limits. In *Jones & Laughlin Steel*, the Court warned that the scope of the interstate commerce power "must be considered in the light of our dual system of government and may not be extended so as to embrace effects upon interstate commerce so indirect and remote that to embrace them, in view of our complex society, would effectually obliterate the distinction between what is national and what is local and create a completely centralized government." 301 U. S., at 37; see also *Darby, supra*, at 119–120 (Congress may regulate intrastate activity that has a "substantial effect" on interstate commerce); *Wickard, supra*, at 125 (Congress may regulate activity that "exerts a substantial economic effect on interstate commerce"). Since that time, the Court has heeded that warning and undertaken to decide whether a rational basis existed for concluding that a regulated activity sufficiently affected interstate commerce.

* * *

Consistent with this structure, we have identified three broad categories of activity that Congress may regulate under its commerce power. First, Congress may regulate the use of the channels of interstate commerce. See, *e.g., Darby*, 312 U. S., at 114; *Heart of Atlanta Motel, supra*, at 256 (" '[T]he authority of Congress to keep the channels of interstate commerce free from immoral and injurious uses has been frequently sustained, and is no longer open to question.' " Second, Congress is empowered to regulate and protect the instrumentalities of interstate commerce, or persons or things in interstate commerce, even though the threat may come only from intrastate activities. See, *e.g., Shreveport Rate Cases*, 234 U.S. 342 (1914). Finally, Congress' commerce authority includes the power to regulate those activities having a substantial relation to interstate commerce, *Jones & Laughlin Steel*, 301 U. S., at 37, *i.e.,* those activities that substantially affect interstate commerce.

Within this final category, admittedly, our case law has not been clear whether an activity must "affect" or "substantially affect" interstate commerce in order to be within Congress' power to regulate it under the Commerce Clause. We conclude, consistent with the great weight of our case law, that the proper test requires an analysis of whether the regulated activity "substantially affects" interstate commerce.

We now turn to consider the power of Congress, in the light of this framework, to enact § 922(q). The first two categories of authority may be quickly disposed of: § 922(q) is not a regulation of the use of the channels of interstate commerce, nor is it an attempt to prohibit the interstate transportation of a commodity through the channels of commerce; nor can § 922(q) be justified as a regulation by which Congress has sought to protect an instrumentality of interstate commerce or a thing in interstate commerce. Thus, if § 922(q) is to be sustained, it must be under the third category as a regulation of an activity that substantially affects interstate commerce.

First, we have upheld a wide variety of congressional Acts regulating intrastate economic activity where we have concluded that the activity substantially affected interstate commerce. Examples include the regulation of intrastate coal mining, intrastate extortionate credit transactions, restaurants utilizing substantial interstate supplies, inns and hotels catering to interstate guests, and production and consumption of home grown wheat. These examples are by no means exhaustive, but the pattern is clear. Where economic activity substantially affects interstate commerce, legislation regulating that activity will be sustained.

Even *Wickard*, which is perhaps the most far reaching example of Commerce Clause authority over intrastate activity, involved economic activity in a way that the possession of a gun in a school zone does not. Roscoe Filburn operated a small farm in Ohio, on which, in the year involved, he raised 23 acres of wheat. It was his practice to sow winter wheat in the fall, and after harvesting it in July to sell a portion of the crop, to feed part of it to poultry and livestock on the farm, to use some in making flour for home consumption, and to keep the remainder for seeding future crops. The Secretary of Agriculture assessed a penalty against him under the Agricultural Adjustment Act of 1938 because he harvested about 12 acres more wheat than his allotment under the Act permitted. The Act was designed to regulate the volume of wheat moving in interstate and foreign commerce in order to avoid surpluses and shortages, and concomitant fluctuation in wheat prices, which had previously obtained. The Court said, in an opinion sustaining the application of the Act to Filburn's activity:

> "One of the primary purposes of the Act in question was to increase the market price of wheat and to that end to limit the volume thereof that could affect the market. It can hardly be denied that a factor of such volume and variability as home consumed wheat would have a substantial influence on price and market conditions. This may arise because being in marketable condition such wheat overhangs the market and, if induced by rising prices, tends to flow into the market and check price increases. But if we assume that it is never marketed, it supplies a need of the man who grew it which would otherwise be reflected by purchases in the open market. Home-grown wheat in this sense competes with wheat in commerce." 317 U. S., at 128.

§ 922(q) is a criminal statute that by its terms has nothing to do with "commerce" or any sort of economic enterprise, however broadly one might define those terms. § 922(q)is not an essential part of a larger regulation of economic activity, in which the regulatory scheme could be undercut unless the intrastate activity were regulated. It cannot, therefore, be sustained under our cases upholding regulations of activities that arise out of or are connected with a commercial transaction, which viewed in the aggregate, substantially affects interstate commerce.

Second, § 922(q)contains no jurisdictional element which would ensure, through case-by-case inquiry, that the firearm possession in question affects interstate commerce. For example, in *United States* v. *Bass*, 404 U.S. 336 (1971), the Court interpreted former 18 U.S.C. § 1202(a), which made it a crime for a felon to "receiv[e], posses[s], or transpor[t] in commerce or affecting commerce . . . any firearm." 404 U. S., at 337. The Court interpreted the possession component of § 1202(a) to require an additional nexus to interstate commerce both because the statute was ambiguous and because "unless Congress conveys its purpose clearly, it will not be deemed to have significantly changed the federal-state balance." *Id.*, at 349. The *Bass* Court set aside the conviction because although the Government had demonstrated that Bass had possessed a firearm, it had failed "to show the requisite nexus with interstate commerce." *Id.*, at 347. The Court thus interpreted the statute to reserve the constitutional question whether Congress could regulate, without more, the "mere possession" of firearms. Unlike the statute in *Bass,* § 922(q) has no express jurisdictional element which might limit its reach to a discrete set of firearm possessions that additionally have an explicit connection with or effect on interstate commerce.

* * *

The Government's essential contention, *in fine,* is that we may determine here that § 922(q) is valid because possession of a firearm in a local school zone does indeed substantially affect interstate commerce. The Government argues that possession of a firearm in a school zone may result in violent crime and that violent crime can be expected to affect the functioning of the national economy in two ways. First, the costs of violent crime are substantial, and, through the mechanism of insurance, those costs are spread throughout the population. Second, violent crime reduces the willingness of individuals to travel to areas within the country that are perceived to be unsafe. Cf. *Heart of Atlanta Motel,* 379 U. S., at 253. The Government also argues that the presence of guns in schools poses a substantial threat to the educational process by threatening the learning environment. A handicapped educational process, in turn, will result in a less productive citizenry. That, in turn, would have an adverse effect on the Nation's economic well-being. As a result, the Government argues that Congress could rationally have concluded that § 922(q) substantially affects interstate commerce.

We pause to consider the implications of the Government's arguments. The Government admits, under its "costs of crime" reasoning, that Congress could regulate not only all violent crime, but all activities that might lead to violent crime, regardless of how tenuously they relate to interstate commerce. See Tr. of Oral Arg. 8–9. Similarly, under the Government's "national productivity" reasoning, Congress could regulate any activity that it found was related to the economic productivity of individual citizens: family law (including marriage, divorce, and child custody), for example. Under the theories that the Government presents in support of § 922(q), it is difficult to perceive any limitation on federal power, even in areas such as criminal law enforcement or education where States historically have been sovereign. Thus, if we were to accept the Government's arguments, we are hard pressed to posit any activity by an individual that Congress is without power to regulate.

Although JUSTICE BREYER argues that acceptance of the Government's rationales would not authorize a general federal police power, he is unable to identify any activity that the States may regulate but Congress may not. JUSTICE BREYER posits that there might be some limitations on Congress' commerce power, such as family law or certain aspects of education. These suggested limitations, when viewed in light of the dissent's expansive analysis, are devoid of substance.

* * *

For instance, if Congress can, pursuant to its Commerce Clause power, regulate activities that adversely affect the learning environment, then, *a fortiori*, it also can regulate the educational process directly. Congress could determine that a school's curriculum has a significant" effect on the extent of classroom learning. As a result, Congress could mandate a federal curriculum for local elementary and secondary schools because what is taught in local schools has a significant "effect on classroom learning," and that, in turn, has a substantial effect on interstate commerce.

* * * We do not doubt that Congress has authority under the Commerce Clause to regulate numerous commercial activities that substantially affect interstate commerce and also affect the educational process. That authority, though broad, does not include the authority to regulate each and every aspect of local schools.

Admittedly, a determination whether an intrastate activity is commercial or noncommercial may in some cases result in legal uncertainty. But, so long as Congress' authority is limited to those powers enumerated in the Constitution, and so long as those enumerated powers are interpreted as having judicially enforceable outer limits, congressional legislation under the Commerce Clause always will engender "legal uncertainty" * * *. The Constitution mandates this uncertainty by withholding from Congress a plenary police power that would authorize enactment of every type of legislation. Any possible benefit from eliminating this "legal uncertainty" would be at the expense of the Constitution's system of enumerated powers.

* * *

* * * The possession of a gun in a local school zone is in no sense an economic activity that might, through repetition elsewhere, substantially affect any sort of interstate commerce. Respondent was a local student at a local school; there is no indication that he had recently moved in interstate commerce, and there is no requirement that his possession of the firearm have any concrete tie to interstate commerce.

To uphold the Government's contentions here, we would have to pile inference upon inference in a manner that would bid fair to convert congressional authority under the Commerce Clause to a general police power of the sort retained by the States. Admittedly, some of our prior cases have taken long steps down that road, giving great deference to congressional action. The broad language in these opinions has suggested the possibility of additional expansion, but we decline here to proceed any further. To do so would require us to conclude that the Constitution's enumeration of powers does not presuppose something not enumerated, cf. *Gibbons* v. *Ogden*, *supra*, at 195, and that there never will be a distinction between what is truly national and what is truly local. This we are unwilling to do.

For the foregoing reasons the judgment of the Court of Appeals is

Affirmed.

■ JUSTICE KENNEDY, with whom JUSTICE O'CONNOR joins, concurring.

* * *

* * * *Stare decisis* operates with great force in counseling us not to call in question the essential principles now in place respecting the congressional power to regulate transactions of a commercial nature. That fundamental restraint on our power forecloses us from reverting to an understanding of commerce that would serve only an 18th-century economy, dependent then upon production and trading practices that had changed but little over the preceding centuries; it also mandates against returning to the time when congressional authority to regulate undoubted commercial activities was limited by a judicial determination that those matters had an insufficient connection to an interstate system. Congress can regulate in the commercial sphere on the assumption that we have a single market and a unified purpose to build a stable national economy.

* * * It does not follow, however, that in every instance the Court lacks the authority and responsibility to review congressional attempts to alter the federal balance * * *.

* * *

The statute now before us forecloses the States from experimenting and exercising their own judgment in an area to which States lay claim by right of history and expertise, and it does so by regulating an activity beyond the realm of commerce in the ordinary and usual sense of that term. The tendency of this statute to displace state regulation in areas of traditional state concern is evident from its territorial operation. There are over 100,000 elementary and secondary schools in the United States. Each of these now has an invisible federal zone extending 1,000 feet beyond the (often irregular) boundaries of the school property. In some communities no doubt it would be difficult to navigate without infringing on those zones. Yet throughout these areas, school officials would find their own programs for the prohibition of guns in danger of displacement by the federal authority unless the State chooses to enact a parallel rule.

* * * Absent a stronger connection or identification with commercial concerns that are central to the Commerce Clause, that interference contradicts the federal balance the Framers designed and that this Court is obliged to enforce.

For these reasons, I join in the opinion and judgment of the Court.

■ JUSTICE THOMAS, concurring.

* * * Although I join the majority, I write separately to observe that our case law has drifted far from the original understanding of the Commerce Clause. In a future case, we ought to temper our Commerce Clause jurisprudence in a manner that both makes sense of our more recent case law and is more faithful to the original understanding of that Clause.

We have said that Congress may regulate not only "Commerce . . . among the several states," U. S. Const., Art. I, § 8, cl. 3, but also anything that has a "substantial effect" on such commerce. This test, if taken to its logical extreme, would give Congress a "police power" over all aspects of American life. Unfortunately, we have never come to grips with this implication of our substantial effects formula. Although we have supposedly applied the substantial effects test for the past 60 years, we *always* have rejected readings of the Commerce Clause and the scope of federal power that would permit Congress to exercise a police power; our cases are quite clear that there are real limits to federal power. Indeed, on this crucial point, the majority and JUSTICE BREYER agree in principle: the Federal Government has nothing approaching a police power.

While the principal dissent concedes that there are limits to federal power, the sweeping nature of our current test enables the dissent to argue that Congress can regulate gun possession. But it seems to me that the power to regulate "commerce" can by no means encompass authority over mere gun possession, any more than it empowers the Federal Government to regulate marriage, littering, or cruelty to animals, throughout the 50 States. Our Constitution quite properly leaves such matters to the individual States, notwithstanding these activities' effects on interstate commerce. Any interpretation of the Commerce Clause that even suggests that Congress could regulate such matters is in need of reexamination.

In an appropriate case, I believe that we must further reconsider our "substantial effects" test with an eye toward constructing a standard that reflects the text and history of the Commerce Clause without totally rejecting our more recent Commerce Clause jurisprudence.

Today, however, I merely support the Court's conclusion with a discussion of the text, structure, and history of the Commerce Clause and an analysis of our early case law. My goal is simply to show how far we have departed from the original understanding and to demonstrate that the result we reach today is by no means "radical." * * *

At the time the original Constitution was ratified, "commerce" consisted of selling, buying, and bartering, as well as transporting for these purposes. See 1 S. Johnson, A Dictionary of the English Language 361 (4th ed. 1773) (defining commerce as "Intercour[s]e; exchange of one thing for another; interchange of any thing; trade; traffick"); N. Bailey, An Universal Etymological English Dictionary (26th ed. 1789) ("trade or traffic"); T. Sheridan, A Complete Dictionary of the English Language (6th ed. 1796) ("Exchange of one thing for another; trade, traffick"). This understanding finds support in the etymology of the word, which literally means "with merchandise." See 3 Oxford English Dictionary 552 (2d ed. 1989) (com—"with"; merci—"merchandise"). In fact, when Federalists and Anti-Federalists discussed the Commerce Clause during the ratification period, they often used trade (in its selling/bartering sense) and commerce interchangeably.

As one would expect, the term "commerce" was used in contradistinction to productive activities such as manufacturing and agriculture. Alexander Hamilton, for example, repeatedly treated commerce, agriculture, and manufacturing as three separate endeavors. See, *e.g.,* The Federalist No. 36, at 224 (referring to "agriculture, commerce, manufactures"); *id.,* No. 21, at 133 (distinguishing commerce, arts, and industry); *id.,* No. 12, at 74 (asserting that commerce and agriculture have shared interests). The same distinctions were made in the state ratification conventions.

Moreover, interjecting a modern sense of commerce into the Constitution generates significant textual and structural problems. For example, one cannot replace "commerce" with a different type of enterprise, such as manufacturing. When a manufacturer produces a car, assembly cannot take place "with a foreign nation" or "with the Indian Tribes." Parts may come from different States or other nations and hence may have been in the flow of commerce at one time, but manufacturing takes place at a discrete site. Agriculture and manufacturing involve the production of goods; commerce encompasses traffic in such articles.

* * *

The Constitution not only uses the word "commerce" in a narrower sense than our case law might suggest, it also does not support the proposition that Congress has authority over all activities that "substantially affect" interstate commerce. The Commerce Clause does not state that Congress may "regulate matters that substantially affect commerce with foreign Nations, and among the several States, and with the Indian Tribes." * * * Clearly, the Framers could have drafted a Constitution that contained a "substantially affects interstate commerce" clause had that been their objective.

In addition to its powers under the Commerce Clause, Congress has the authority to enact such laws as are "necessary and proper" to carry into execution its power to regulate commerce among the several States. U. S. Const., Art. I, § 8, cl. 18. But on this Court's understanding of congressional power under these two Clauses, many of Congress' other enumerated powers under Art. I, § 8 are wholly superfluous. After all, if Congress may regulate all matters that substantially affect commerce, there is no need for the Constitution to specify that Congress may enact bankruptcy laws, cl. 4, or coin money and fix the standard of weights and measures, cl. 5, or punish counterfeiters of United States coin and securities, cl. 6. Likewise, Congress would not need the separate authority to establish post offices and post roads, cl. 7, or to grant patents and copyrights, cl. 8, or to "punish Piracies and Felonies committed on the high Seas," cl. 10. It might not even need the power to raise and support an Army and Navy, cls. 12 and 13, for fewer people would engage in commercial shipping if they thought that a foreign power could expropriate their property with ease. Indeed, if Congress could regulate matters that substantially affect interstate commerce, there would have been no need to specify that Congress can regulate international trade and commerce with the Indians. As the Framers surely understood, these other branches of trade substantially affect interstate commerce.

Put simply, much if not all of Art. I, § 8 (including portions of the Commerce Clause itself) would be surplusage if Congress had been given authority over matters that substantially affect interstate commerce. An interpretation of cl. 3 that makes the rest of § 8 superfluous simply cannot be correct. Yet this Court's Commerce Clause jurisprudence has endorsed just such an interpretation: the power we have accorded Congress has swallowed Art. I, § 8.

Indeed, if a "substantial effects" test can be appended to the Commerce Clause, why not to every other power of the Federal Government? There is no reason for singling out the Commerce Clause for special treatment. Accordingly, Congress could regulate all matters that "substantially affect" the Army and Navy, bankruptcies, tax collection, expenditures, and so on. In that case, the Clauses of § 8 all mutually overlap, something we can assume the Founding Fathers never intended.

* * *

The exchanges during the ratification campaign reveal the relatively limited reach of the Commerce Clause and of federal power generally. The Founding Fathers confirmed that most areas of life (even many matters that would have substantial effects on commerce) would remain outside the reach of the Federal Government. Such affairs would continue to be under the exclusive control of the States.

* * *

Where the Constitution was meant to grant federal authority over an activity substantially affecting interstate commerce, the Constitution contains an enumerated power over that particular activity. Indeed, the Framers knew that many of the other enumerated powers in § 8 dealt with matters that substantially affected interstate commerce. Madison, for instance, spoke of the bankruptcy power as being "intimately connected with the regulation of commerce." The Federalist No. 42, at 287. Likewise, Hamilton urged that "[i]f we mean to be a commercial people or even to be secure on our Atlantic side, we must endeavour as soon as possible to have a navy." *Id.*, No. 24, at 157 (A. Hamilton).

In short, the Founding Fathers were well aware of what the principal dissent calls " 'economic . . . realities.' " See *post,* at 625 (BREYER, J.) (citing *North American*

Co. v. *SEC,* 327 U.S. 686, 705 (1946)). Even though the boundary between commerce and other matters may ignore "economic reality" and thus seem arbitrary or artificial to some, we must nevertheless respect a constitutional line that does not grant Congress power over all that substantially affects interstate commerce.

* * *

* * * From the time of the ratification of the Constitution to the mid-1930's, it was widely understood that the Constitution granted Congress only limited powers, notwithstanding the Commerce Clause. Moreover, there was no question that activities wholly separated from business, such as gun possession, were beyond the reach of the commerce power. If anything, the "wrong turn" was the Court's dramatic departure in the 1930's from a century and a half of precedent.

Apart from its recent vintage and its corresponding lack of any grounding in the original understanding of the Constitution, the substantial effects test suffers from the further flaw that it appears to grant Congress a police power over the Nation. When asked at oral argument if there were *any* limits to the Commerce Clause, the Government was at a loss for words. Tr. of Oral Arg. 5. Likewise, the principal dissent insists that there are limits, but it cannot muster even one example. *Post,* at 624. Indeed, the dissent implicitly concedes that its reading has no limits when it criticizes the Court for "threaten[ing] legal uncertainty in an area of law that . . . seemed reasonably well settled." The one advantage of the dissent's standard is certainty: it is certain that under its analysis everything may be regulated under the guise of the Commerce Clause.

* * *

At an appropriate juncture, I think we must modify our Commerce Clause jurisprudence. Today, it is easy enough to say that the Clause certainly does not empower Congress to ban gun possession within 1,000 feet of a school.

■ JUSTICE STEVENS, dissenting. * * *

Guns are both articles of commerce and articles that can be used to restrain commerce. Their possession is the consequence, either directly or indirectly, of commercial activity. In my judgment, Congress' power to regulate commerce in firearms includes the power to prohibit possession of guns at any location because of their potentially harmful use; it necessarily follows that Congress may also prohibit their possession in particular markets * * *. Whether or not the national interest in eliminating that market would have justified federal legislation in 1789, it surely does today.

■ JUSTICE SOUTER, dissenting.

In reviewing congressional legislation under the Commerce Clause, we defer to what is often a merely implicit congressional judgment that its regulation addresses a subject substantially affecting interstate commerce "if there is any rational basis for such a finding." If that congressional determination is within the realm of reason, "the only remaining question for judicial inquiry is whether 'the means chosen by Congress [are] reasonably adapted to the end permitted by the Constitution.' "

The practice of deferring to rationally based legislative judgments "is a paradigm of judicial restraint." *FCC v. Beach Communications, Inc.,* 508 U.S. 307, 314 (1993). In judicial review under the Commerce Clause, it reflects our respect for the institutional competence of the Congress on a subject expressly assigned to it by the Constitution and our appreciation of the legitimacy that comes from Congress's political accountability in dealing with matters open to a wide range of possible choices.

* * *

■ JUSTICE BREYER, with whom JUSTICE STEVENS, JUSTICE SOUTER, and JUSTICE GINSBURG join, dissenting.

The issue in this case is whether the Commerce Clause authorizes Congress to enact a statute that makes it a crime to possess a gun in, or near, a school. In my view, the statute falls well within the scope of the commerce power as this Court has understood that power over the last half century.

In reaching this conclusion, I apply three basic principles of Commerce Clause interpretation. First, the power to "regulate Commerce . . . among the several States," U. S. Const., Art. I, § 8, cl. 3, encompasses the power to regulate local activities insofar as they significantly affect interstate commerce. As the majority points out, the Court, in describing how much of an effect the Clause requires, sometimes has used the word "substantial" and sometimes has not. And, as the majority also recognizes in quoting Justice Cardozo, the question of degree (how *much* effect) requires an estimate of the "size" of the effect that no verbal formulation can capture with precision. I use the word "significant" because the word "substantial" implies a somewhat narrower power than recent precedent suggests. But, to speak of "substantial effect" rather than "significant effect" would make no difference in this case.

Second, in determining whether a local activity will likely have a significant effect upon interstate commerce, a court must consider, not the effect of an individual act (a single instance of gun possession), but rather the cumulative effect of all similar instances (*i.e.*, the effect of all guns possessed in or near schools). See, *e.g.*, *Wickard*, *supra*, at 127–128. * * *

Third, the Constitution requires us to judge the connection between a regulated activity and interstate commerce, not directly, but at one remove. Courts must give Congress a degree of leeway in determining the existence of a significant factual connection between the regulated activity and interstate commerce—both because the Constitution delegates the commerce power directly to Congress and because the determination requires an empirical judgment of a kind that a legislature is more likely than a court to make with accuracy. The traditional words "rational basis" capture this leeway. Thus, the specific question before us, as the Court recognizes, is not whether the "regulated activity sufficiently affected interstate commerce," but, rather, whether Congress could have had "*a rational basis*" for so concluding.

I recognize that we must judge this matter independently. "[S]imply because Congress may conclude that a particular activity substantially affects interstate commerce does not necessarily make it so." * * *

* * *

Applying these principles to the case at hand, we must ask whether Congress could have had a *rational basis* for finding a significant (or substantial) connection between gun related school violence and interstate commerce * * *. Numerous reports and studies—generated both inside and outside government—make clear that Congress could reasonably have found the empirical connection that its law, implicitly or explicitly, asserts.

For one thing, reports, hearings, and other readily available literature make clear that the problem of guns in and around schools is widespread and extremely serious * * *. And, they report that this widespread violence in schools throughout the Nation significantly interferes with the quality of education in those schools * * *. Congress could therefore have found a substantial educational problem—teachers unable to teach, students unable to learn—and concluded that guns near schools contribute substantially to the size and scope of that problem.

Having found that guns in schools significantly undermine the quality of education in our Nation's classrooms, Congress could also have found, given the effect of education upon interstate and foreign commerce, that gun-related violence in and around schools is a commercial, as well as a human, problem. Education, although far more than a matter of economics, has long been inextricably intertwined with the Nation's economy * * *.

* * *

Specifically, Congress could have found that gun-related violence near the classroom poses a serious economic threat (1) to consequently inadequately educated workers who must endure low paying jobs and (2) to communities and businesses that might (in today's "information society") otherwise gain, from a well-educated work force, an important commercial advantage, of a kind that location near a railhead or harbor provided in the past. Congress might also have found these threats to be no different in kind from other threats that this Court has found within the commerce power, such as the threat that loan sharking poses to the "funds" of "numerous localities," *Perez v. United States,* 402 U.S., at 157, and that unfair labor practices pose to instrumentalities of commerce, see *Consolidated Edison Co. v. NLRB,* 305 U.S. 197, 221–222 (1938). As I have pointed out, Congress has written that "the occurrence of violent crime in school zones" has brought about a "decline in the quality of education" that "has an adverse impact on interstate commerce and the foreign commerce of the United States." 18 U.S.C. §§ 922(q)(1)(F), (G). The violence-related facts, the educational facts, and the economic facts, taken together, make this conclusion rational. And, because under our case law, the sufficiency of the constitutionally necessary Commerce Clause link between a crime of violence and interstate commerce turns simply upon size or degree, those same facts make the statute constitutional.

* * * [A major] legal problem the Court creates comes from its apparent belief that it can reconcile its holding with earlier cases by making a critical distinction between "commercial" and noncommercial "transaction[s]." That is to say, the Court believes the Constitution would distinguish between two local activities, each of which has an identical effect upon interstate commerce, if one, but not the other, is "commercial" in nature. As a general matter, this approach fails to heed this Court's earlier warning not to turn "questions of the power of Congress" upon "formula[s]" that would give

> "controlling force to nomenclature such as 'production' and 'indirect' and foreclose consideration of the actual effects of the activity in question upon interstate commerce." *Wickard, supra,* at 120.

* * *

* * * [Another] legal problem created by the Court's holding is that it threatens legal uncertainty in an area of law that, until this case, seemed reasonably well settled. Congress has enacted many statutes (more than 100 sections of the United States Code), including criminal statutes (at least 25 sections), that use the words "affecting commerce" to define their scope, see, *e.g.,* 18 U.S.C. § 844(i) (destruction of buildings used in activity affecting interstate commerce), and other statutes that contain no jurisdictional language at all, see, *e.g.,* 18 U.S.C. § 922(*o*)(1) (possession of machineguns). Do these, or similar, statutes regulate noncommercial activities? * * * However these questions are eventually resolved, the legal uncertainty now created will restrict Congress' ability to enact criminal laws aimed at criminal behavior that, considered problem by problem rather than instance by instance, seriously threatens the economic, as well as social, well-being of Americans.

* * * Upholding this legislation would do no more than simply recognize that Congress had a "rational basis" for finding a significant connection between guns in or near schools and (through their effect on education) the interstate and foreign commerce they threaten. For these reasons, I would reverse the judgment of the Court of Appeals. Respectfully, I dissent.

NOTES AND QUESTIONS

1. The Supreme Court's decision in *Lopez* in 1995 was something of a shock to the legal community because it represented the first time since 1937 that the Supreme Court had found a congressional exercise of power to exceed the permissible scope of the Commerce Clause. *Lopez* dealt with a wholly intra-state activity that was alleged to substantially affect interstate commerce. The case makes clear that wholly *intra-state* activities must "*substantially*" affect interstate commerce before they are regulable by Congress. Justice Breyer's dissent argues that Congress need only *rationally believe* that wholly intra-state activities might "*significantly*" affect interstate commerce for them to be regulable under the Commerce Clause. Which modalities of interpretation support which position?

2. The Constitution gives Congress power "To regulate Commerce with foreign Nations, and among the several States, and with the Indian Tribes.". The text itself thus gives Congress only the power to regulate "Commerce * * * among the several States" and not wholly intra-state activities which substantially affect interstate Commerce. Could Congress regulate French or British or Native American internal commerce on the grounds that it "*substantially affects*" Commerce with foreign Nations or with the Indian Tribes? No one has ever argued as much. Is Justice Thomas right in *Lopez* that the Supreme Court went too far when it recognized a federal power under the Commerce Clause to regulate wholly intra-state activities that *substantially affect* interstate Commerce?

3. Congress, of course, also has power "[t]o make all Laws which shall be necessary and proper for carrying into Execution" its power to regulate commerce among the several States. As interpreted in *McCulloch v. Maryland*, 17 U.S. 316 (1819), this is a power "to make all laws which shall be *convenient or useful* for carrying into execution" Congress's Commerce Clause power. Isn't the law in *Lopez* convenient or useful to regulating the interstate market in guns or to promoting better learning in schools, as Justice Breyer argues in his dissent? The Necessary and Proper Clause, as reinterpreted in *McCulloch,* provides the actual foundation for the wholly-intrastate-commerce-*substantially-affecting*-interstate-commerce line of cases. Thus, *Lopez* is thus not really a Commerce Clause case at all. It is a Necessary and Proper Clause case (even though no

Justice in the case really argued it this way). Keep this in mind when we get to the Necessary and Proper Clause. Also, when you read the forthcoming Commerce Clause cases, see how much of the work is being done by the Necessary and Proper Clause instead.

4. Justice Breyer's dissent states the view of national power under the Commerce and Necessary and Proper Clauses that prevailed from 1937 to 1995. Is there anything under that view that Congress cannot do? Does Justice Breyer's approach make the enumeration of federal powers insignificant and meaningless? Could Congress under Breyer's approach pass federal marriage, family, and education laws? If so, does that make his view legally wrong?

5. Is the power to regulate "commerce" among the States a power to regulate all "intercourse" among the States? Yale Law Professor Jack Balkin so argues in JACK M. BALKIN, LIVING ORIGINALISM (2011). Professor Balkin draws on linguistic usages of "commerce" in a broad sense to conclude that the New Deal cases expanding commerce to include just about everything were right:

> In the eighteenth century * * * the word *commerce* did not have * * * narrowly economic connotations. Instead, *commerce* meant "intercourse," and it had strongly social overtones. Commerce was interaction and exchange between persons or peoples. To have commerce with someone meant to exchange things or ideas with them, converse with them, or interact with them. Thus, commerce naturally included all trade and economic activity because economic activity involved social interaction * * *. But the idea of commerce-as intercourse was broader than economics narrowly conceived * * *.

Id. at 140. There are linguistic contexts in which Professor Balkin is surely right; it is possible to use the word "commerce" to describe many kinds of, and perhaps even all, human interaction. But is that the best way to read the word *as it appears in Article I, Section 8, Clause 3 of the Constitution*? Surely not. *See* Steven G. Calabresi, *The Right to Buy Health Insurance Across State Lines: Crony Capitalism and the Supreme Court,* 81 U. CINN. L. REV. 1447, 1455–59 (2013); Robert G. Natelson & David Kopel, *Commerce in the Commerce Clause: A Response to Jack Balkin,* 109 MICH. L. REV. FIRST IMPRESSIONS 55, 56 (2010) ("There is little question that the ordinary and common meaning of 'commerce,' both in common discourse and in legal language, was mercantile trade and traditionally associated activities. The social, religious, and sexual meanings of 'commerce,' while sometimes employed, were figurative or metaphorical, derived from the mercantile meaning."). On the other hand, if one thinks—as does Professor Balkin—that the Constitution's enumerated powers must be read to instantiate the Virginia and Bedford Resolutions giving Congress power to address all national problems, a near-limitless understanding of "Commerce" is not a bad way to do it. As you read the later cases on the Commerce Clause, consider to what extent they reflect larger views of the role and significance of the Constitution's enumerations of power. In particular, note how the majority in *Lopez* began its opinion.

6. What do you make of the originalism of Justice Thomas's *Lopez* concurrence? Is it more law-like than the policy and pragmatic arguments of Justice Breyer's dissent? What about Chief Justice Rehnquist's argument that no Supreme Court precedent had ever gone as far as did *Lopez*? Which modality of constitutional argument is most persuasive?7. How do you think Chief Justice John Marshall would have approached this case? How does the reasoning of *McCulloch* track the arguments of the various opinions in *Lopez*?

7. Finally in the wake of *Lopez*, Congress repassed the Gun Free School Zones Act with a new requirement that the law applied only to possession of guns which it was proven had travelled in interstate commerce. Is this statute constitutional? We think it is not because there is no real nexus between possessing a gun within 1000 feet of a school and the interstate travel of the gun. Commerce was over once Lopez legally bought the gun. It did not resume when he brought it within 1000 feet of a school. Would the majority in *Lopez* have a problem with that law?

[Assignment 32]

IV. THE POWER TO TAX

Article I, Section 8, Clause 1: The Congress shall have Power To Lay and collect Taxes, Duties, Imposts and Excises, to pay the Debts and provide for the common Defense and general Welfare of the United States; but all Duties, Imposts and Excises shall be uniform throughout the United States; * * *

Article I, Section 9, Clause 4: No Capitation, or other direct, Tax shall be laid, unless in Proportion to the Census of Enumeration herein before directed to be taken.

Article I, Section 9, Clause 5: No Tax or Duty shall be laid on Articles exported from any State.

Amendment XVI [adopted in 1913]: The Congress shall have power to lay and collect taxes on incomes, from whatever source derived, without apportionment among the several States, and without regard to any census or enumeration.

The Continental Congress, under the Articles of Confederation, lacked the power directly to tax citizens, and so it was perpetually bankrupt. It could not pay its debts, and accordingly could not readily borrow additional funds when needed. The Framers of the U.S. Constitution addressed this problem in the very first clause of Article I, Section 8 by giving Congress the power to lay and collect taxes. Article I, Section 9 then limited the power of taxation in two very important respects. One hundred thirty-five years later, one part—but only one part—of those Article I, Section 9 limitations was swept away by the Sixteenth Amendment. Notwithstanding the breadth of the Sixteenth Amendment, many of the principles and limitations of the original constitutional scheme for federal taxation remain relevant today. Three features of that scheme bear emphasis.

First, the Taxing Clause contains the proviso that taxes may be laid and collected "to pay the Debts and provide for the common Defense and general Welfare of the United States." We saw in an earlier chapter that this proviso, and in particular its reference to the "general Welfare," is sometimes used as a source for the federal spending power, *see supra* page 291, and we will hear more about that move shortly, *see infra* pages 666–685. As a matter of original meaning, the meaning of the proviso was very clear. Founding-era theories of taxation wondered whether taxes could ever be used as regulatory measures (as the British sought to do through the tax on colonial tea) or purely for purposes of raising revenue. That could matter a lot, because if revenue was the only proper purpose of a tax, then a tariff on imports designed to subsidize domestic industries might be unlawful. The language in the

Taxing Clause clarified that taxes could be used for purposes other than pure revenue-raising. *See* Jeffrey T. Renz, *What Spending Clause? (or the President's Paramour): An Examination of the Views of Hamilton, Madison, and Story on Article I, Section 8, Clause 1 of the United States Constitution,* 33 JOHN MARSHALL L. REV. 81 (1999). As a result, the second statute passed by the First Congress in 1789 was a tariff measure that announced its purposes to be "for the support of government, for the discharge of the debts of the United States, and the encouragement and protection of manufactures." Act of July 4, 1789, 1 Stat. 24, 24.

Second, the Taxing Clause separately identifies "Taxes, Duties, Imposts and Excises." Do those labels matter? James Madison did not think so; in an 1828 letter, he wrote that "*taxes,* if standing *alone,* would certainly have included duties, imposts, & excises." Letter from James Madison to Joseph Cabell, Sept. 18, 1828, *in* 9 THE WRITINGS OF JAMES MADISON 316, 321 (Gaillard Hunt ed., 1910). Joseph Story explained what he thought the different terms meant in 1840:

> The word "duties," is often used as synonymous with taxes; but is more often used as synonymous with "customs," which are taxes levied upon goods and merchandise, which are exported or imported. In this sense, duties are equivalent to "imposts," although the latter word is often restrained to duties on goods and merchandise, which are imported from abroad. "Excises," is a word, generally used in contradistinction to "imposts," in its restricted sense; and is applied to internal or inland impositions, levied sometimes upon the consumption of a commodity, sometimes upon the retail sale of it, and sometimes upon the manufacture of it. Thus, a tax, levied upon goods imported from a foreign country, is generally called an "impost" duty and a tax, levied upon goods manufactured or sold in a country, is called an "excise" duty. The meanings of these words, therefore, often run into each other and all of them are used in the Constitution, to avoid any ambiguity, as to any one of them being used in a general sense, or in a restricted sense, which might involve endless doubts as to the true extent of the constitutional power.

JOSEPH STORY, A FAMILIAR EXPOSITION OF THE CONSTITUTION OF THE UNITED STATES § 156, at 103–04 (1840). Does that clear up everything?

Third, each component of the taxing power is subject to important limitations. The Constitution specifies that all duties, imposts, and excises—known as indirect taxes—shall be "uniform throughout the United States." Article I, Section 9 specifies that "[n]o capitation, or other direct tax, can be laid unless it is done in proportion to the census," and it flatly forbids any federal taxes, however uniform, on State exports. The Constitution thus provides different structural limitations for direct and indirect taxes: an apportionment requirement for direct taxes and a uniformity requirement for indirect taxes. The Sixteenth Amendment removes the apportionment requirement for "taxes on incomes," but any direct tax *other* than a tax on incomes is still subject to the 1788 apportionment rule. As a practical matter, direct taxes that are subject to apportionment are politically almost impossible to enact—which was the whole point of the provision (essentially in order to prevent the federal government from taxing ownership of slaves). An urgent question thus arises as to which taxes are indirect and are subject only to the rule of uniformity and which taxes are direct and must be apportioned according to the census.

The obvious, plain meaning of the phrases "direct tax" and "indirect tax" are not hard to decipher. A direct tax is a tax that falls directly on the individual being taxed. Thus, a head-tax—everyone in the country must pay $1,000—or a federal real estate tax—everyone in the country must pay a real estate tax of 1% a year of the assessed value of their real estate—are obviously direct taxes. They fall directly on the person being taxed.

An indirect tax falls on a transaction like importing goods into the United States, for which you might have to pay a tariff, or buying goods from a merchant, for which you might have to pay a sales tax or a value added tax. The only constraint on Congress's power to pass indirect taxes is that they must be uniform throughout the United States. From 1789 to 1913, Congress raised almost all its revenue through a combination of land sales and indirect taxes, mainly in the form of tariffs. Because uniform indirect taxes are politically more palatable than apportioned direct taxes, the narrower the category of direct taxes, the broader the federal government's effective power of taxation. Accordingly, founding-era proponents of a powerful national government, led by Alexander Hamilton, cooked up what was probably a feigned case called *Hylton v. United States*, 3 U.S. (3 Dall.) 171 (1796), to establish at an early date a narrow definition of "direct" taxes. Congress enacted a tax on carriages. Had Congress taxed *transactions* involving carriages, such as sales or rentals, it would obviously have been an indirect "Excise" tax subject to uniformity but not apportionment (just as there are currently federal excise taxes on things like gasoline sales and phone service). The tax, however, purported to tax the mere *ownership* of the carriages. Hylton insisted that even though he owned 125 carriages, "the chariots were kept exclusively for the Defendant's own private use, and not to let out to hire, or for the conveyance of persons for hire." *Id.* at 171–72. (Why would someone keep a fleet of 125 chariots for personal use? This is why we suspect that the case was a collusive suit.). Thus, the case, as framed by the parties, posed the question whether a tax on carriage ownership was a direct rather than indirect tax. In reality, it was obviously a direct tax, just as would be a tax on the ownership of land. Nonetheless, the Supreme Court upheld the unapportioned carriage tax as an indirect tax. (If it had not done so, *Hylton* rather than *Marbury v. Madison* would be the seminal case on judicial review!) The seriatim opinions of the Justices said, in essence, that the only "direct" taxes were head taxes and real estate taxes, in large measure because it would be very difficult to apportion any other taxes. Of course, since the whole point of the apportionment requirement was to make direct taxes difficult to enact, it seems peculiar, to say the least, to hold that taxes that are difficult to enact therefore cannot be direct. In any event, a century later, the Court decided its most famous—or, to some people, infamous—case involving the federal taxing power, which reflected a very different account of what makes a tax "direct."

A. POLLOCK V. FARMER'S LOAN AND TRUST

157 U.S. 429 (1895)

■ MR. CHIEF JUSTICE FULLER delivered the opinion of the court.

[*Editors' Note: As part of a lengthy tariff law, a Progressive-era Congress in 1894 imposed a two-percent tax "upon the gains, profits, and income received * * * by every citizen of the United States * * *, whether said gains, profits, or income be derived from any kind of property, rents, interest, dividends, or salaries, or from any* *profession, trade, employment, or vocation carried on in the United States or elsewhere, or from any other source whatever * * *." Act of Aug. 27, 1894, ch. 349, § 27, 28 Stat. 509, 553. Pollock owned stock in the Farmer's Loan and Trust, and he sued to prevent the directors of the Trust from paying tax on the Trust's income.*]

* * *

* * * [T]his bill proceeds on the ground that the defendants would be guilty of such breach of trust or duty in voluntarily making returns for the imposition of, and paying, an unconstitutional tax * * *.

* * *

The contention of the complainant is:

First. That the law in question, in imposing a tax on the income or rents of real estate, imposes a tax upon the real estate itself; and in imposing a tax on the interest or other income of bonds or other personal property held for the purposes of income or ordinarily yielding income, imposes a tax upon the personal estate itself; that such tax is a direct tax, and void because imposed without regard to the rule of apportionment; and that by reason thereof the whole law is invalidated.

* * *

The Constitution provides that representatives and direct taxes shall be apportioned among the several States according to numbers, and that no direct tax shall be laid except according to the enumeration provided for; and also that all duties, imposts, and excises shall be uniform throughout the United States * * *.

* * *

Thus, in the matter of taxation, the Constitution recognizes the two great classes of direct and indirect taxes, and lays down two rules by which their imposition must be governed, namely: The rule of apportionment as to direct taxes, and the rule of uniformity as to duties, imposts and excises.

* * *

The first question to be considered is whether a tax on the rents or income of real estate is a direct tax within the meaning of the Constitution. Ordinarily all taxes paid primarily by persons who can shift the burden upon someone else, or who are under no legal compulsion to pay them, are considered indirect taxes; but a tax upon property holders in respect of their estates, whether real or personal, or of the income yielded by such estates, and the payment of which cannot be avoided, are direct taxes. Nevertheless, it may be admitted that although this definition of direct taxes is *prima facie* correct, and to be applied in the consideration of the question before us, yet that the Constitution may bear a different meaning, and that such different meaning must be recognized. But in arriving at any conclusion upon this point, we are at liberty to refer to the historical circumstances attending the framing and adoption of the Constitution as well as the entire frame and scheme of the instrument, and the consequences naturally attendant upon the one construction or the other.

We inquire, therefore, what, at the time the Constitution was framed and adopted, were recognized as direct taxes? What did those who framed and adopted it understand the terms to designate and include?

* * *

Congress, under the articles of confederation, had no actual operative power of taxation. It could call upon the States for their respective contributions or quotas as previously determined on; but in case of the failure or omission of the States to furnish such contribution, there were no means of compulsion, as Congress had no power whatever to lay any tax upon individuals. This imperatively demanded a remedy; but the opposition to granting the power of direct taxation in addition to the substantially exclusive power of laying imposts and duties was so strong that it required the convention, in securing effective powers of taxation to the Federal government, to use the utmost care and skill to so harmonize conflicting interests that the ratification of the instrument could be obtained.

* * *

The compromise, in embracing the power of direct taxation, consisted not simply in including part of the slaves in the enumeration of population, but in providing that, as between State and State such taxation should be proportioned to representation. The establishment of the same rule for the apportionment of taxes as for regulating the proportion of representatives, observed Mr. Madison in No. 54 of the Federalist, was by no means founded on the same principle, for as to the former it had reference to the proportion of wealth, and although in respect of that it was in ordinary cases a very unfit measure, it "had too recently obtained the general sanction of America not to have found a ready preference with the convention," while the opposite interests of the States, balancing each other, would produce impartiality in enumeration. By prescribing this rule, Hamilton wrote (Federalist, No. 36) that the door was shut "to partiality or oppression," and "the abuse of this power of taxation to have been provided against with guarded circumspection;" and obviously the operation of direct taxation on every State tended to prevent resort to that mode of supply except under pressure of necessity and to promote prudence and economy in expenditure.

* * *

* * * [T]hat the difference between direct and indirect taxation was fully appreciated is supported by the congressional debates after the government was organized.

In the debates in the House of Representatives preceding the passage of the act of Congress to lay "duties upon carriages for the conveyance of persons," approved June 5, 1794 (1 Stat. 373, c. 45), Mr. Sedgwick said that "a capitation tax, and taxes on land and on property and income generally, were direct charges, as well in the immediate as ultimate sources of contribution. He had considered those, and those only, as direct taxes in their operation and effects. On the other hand, a tax imposed on a specific article of personal property, and particularly if objects of luxury, as in the case under consideration, he had never supposed had been considered a direct tax within the meaning of the Constitution."

* * *

At a subsequent day of the debate, Mr. Madison objected to the tax on carriages as "an unconstitutional tax," but Fisher Ames declared that he had satisfied himself that it was not a direct tax, as "the duty falls not on the possession but on the use." Annals 730.

Mr. Madison wrote to Jefferson on May 11, 1794: "And the tax on carriages succeeded, in spite of the Constitution, by a majority of twenty, the advocates for the principle being reinforced by the adversaries to luxuries." "Some of the motives which they decoyed to their support ought to premonish them of the danger. By breaking down the barriers of the Constitution, and giving sanction to the idea of sumptuary regulations, wealth may find a precarious defence in the shield of justice. If luxury, *as such,* is to be taxed, the greatest of all luxuries, says Paine, is a great estate. Even on the present occasion, it has been found prudent to yield to a tax on transfers of stock in the funds and in the banks." 2 Madison's Writings 14.

But Albert Gallatin, in his "Sketch of the Finances of the United States," published in November, 1796, said: "The most generally received opinion, however, is, that by direct taxes in the Constitution, those are meant which are raised on the capital or revenue of the people; by indirect, such as are raised on their expense. As that opinion is in itself rational, and conformable to the decision which has taken place on the subject of the carriage tax, and as it appears important, for the sake of preventing future controversies, which may be not more fatal to the revenue than to the tranquility of the Union, that a fixed interpretation should be generally adopted, it will not be improper to corroborate it by quoting the author from whom the idea seems to have been borrowed." He then quotes from Smith's Wealth of Nations, and continues: "The remarkable coincidence of the clause of the Constitution with this passage in using the word 'capitation' as a generic expression, including the different species of direct taxes, an acceptation of the word peculiar, it is believed, to Dr. Smith, leaves little doubt that the framers of the one had the other in view at the time, and that they, as well as he, by *direct* taxes, meant those paid *directly* from, and falling *immediately* on, the revenue; and by *indirect,* those which are paid *indirectly* out of the revenue by falling immediately upon the expense." 3 Gallatin's Writings (Adams' ed.) 74, 75.

The act provided in its first section "that there shall be levied, collected, and paid upon all carriages for the conveyance of persons, which shall be kept by or for any person for his or her own use, or to be let out to hire or for the conveyance of passengers, the several duties and rates following," and then followed a fixed yearly rate on every coach; chariot; phaeton; and coachee; every four-wheel and every two-wheel top carriage; and upon every other two-wheel carriage varying according to the vehicle.

In *Hylton v. United States,* 3 Dall. 171, decided in March, 1796, this court held the act to be constitutional, because not laying a direct tax. Chief Justice Ellsworth and Mr. Justice Cushing took no part in the decision, and Mr. Justice Wilson gave no reasons.

* * *

It will be perceived that each of the justices, while suggesting doubt whether anything but a capitation or a land tax was a direct tax within the meaning of the Constitution, distinctly avoided expressing an opinion upon that question or laying down a comprehensive definition, but confined his opinion to the case before the court.

* * * From the foregoing, it is apparent: 1. That the distinction between direct and indirect taxation was well understood by the framers of the Constitution and those who adopted it. 2. That under the state systems of taxation all taxes on real estate or personal property or the rents or income thereof were regarded as direct taxes. 3. That the rules of apportionment and of uniformity were adopted in view of

that distinction and those systems. 4. That whether the tax on carriages was direct or indirect was disputed, but the tax was sustained as a tax on the use and an excise. 5. That the original expectation was that the power of direct taxation would be exercised only in extraordinary exigencies and down to August 1894, this expectation has been realized. The act of that date was passed in a time of profound peace, and if we assume that no special exigency called for unusual legislation, and that resort to this mode of taxation is to become an ordinary and usual means of supply, that fact furnishes an additional reason for circumspection and care in disposing of the case.

* * *

As no capitation, or other direct, tax was to be laid otherwise than in proportion to the population, some other direct tax than a capitation tax (and it might well enough be argued some other tax of the same kind as a capitation tax) must be referred to, and it has always been considered that a tax upon real estate *eo nomine* or upon its owners in respect thereof is a direct tax within the meaning of the Constitution. But is there any distinction between the real estate itself or its owners in respect of it and the rents or income of the real estate coming to the owners as the natural and ordinary incident of their ownership?

If the Constitution had provided that Congress should not levy any tax upon the real estate of any citizen of any State, could it be contended that Congress could put an annual tax for five or any other number of years upon the rent or income of the real estate? And if, as the Constitution now reads, no unapportioned tax can be imposed upon real estate, can Congress without apportionment nevertheless impose taxes upon such real estate under the guise of an annual tax upon its rents or income?

* * *

The requirement of the Constitution is that no direct tax shall be laid otherwise than by apportionment—the prohibition is not against direct taxes on land, from which the implication is sought to be drawn that indirect taxes on land would be constitutional, but it is against all direct taxes—and it is admitted that a tax on real estate is a direct tax. Unless, therefore, a tax upon rents or income issuing out of lands is intrinsically so different from a tax on the land itself that it belongs to a wholly different class of taxes, such taxes must be regarded as falling within the same category as a tax on real estate *eo nomine*. The name of the tax is unimportant. The real question is, is there any basis upon which to rest the contention that real estate belongs to one of the two great classes of taxes, and the rent or income which is the incident of its ownership belongs to the other? We are unable to perceive any ground for the alleged distinction. An annual tax upon the annual value or annual user of real estate appears to us the same in substance as an annual tax on the real estate, which would be paid out of the rent or income. This law taxes the income received from land and the growth or produce of the land * * *

* * *

Nothing can be clearer than that what the Constitution intended to guard against was the exercise by the general government of the power of directly taxing persons and property within any State through a majority made up from the other States. It is true that the effect of requiring direct taxes to be apportioned among the States in proportion to their population is necessarily that the amount of taxes on the individual taxpayer in a State having the taxable subject-matter to a larger extent in proportion to its population than another State has, would be less than in such other State, but this inequality must be held to have been contemplated, and was manifestly designed to operate to restrain the exercise of the power of direct taxation to extraordinary emergencies, and to prevent an attack upon accumulated property by mere force of numbers.

It is not doubted that property owners ought to contribute in just measure to the expenses of the government. As to the States and their municipalities, this is reached largely through the imposition of direct taxes. As to the Federal government, it is attained in part through excises and indirect taxes upon luxuries and consumption generally, to which direct taxation may be added to the extent the rule of apportionment allows. And through one mode or the other, the entire wealth of the country, real and personal, may be made, as it should be, to contribute to the common defence and general welfare.

But the acceptance of the rule of apportionment was one of the compromises which made the adoption of the Constitution possible, and secured the creation of that dual form of government, so elastic and so strong, which has thus far survived in unabated vigor. If, by calling a tax indirect when it is essentially direct, the rule of protection could be frittered away, one of the great landmarks defining the boundary between the Nation and the States of which it is composed would have disappeared, and with it one of the bulwarks of private rights and private property.

We are of opinion that the law in question, so far as it levies a tax on the rents or income of real estate, is in violation of the Constitution, and is invalid.

* * *

[*Editors' Note: Justice Field's concurring opinion is omitted. Justice White, joined by Justice Harlan, dissented at great length. The key passage was:*

> *In considering whether we are to regard an income tax as "direct" or otherwise, it will, in my opinion, serve no useful purpose, at this late period of our political history, to seek to ascertain the meaning of the word "direct" in the constitution by resorting to the theoretical opinions on taxation found in the writings of some economists prior to the adoption of the constitution or since * * *. I say it will serve no useful purpose to examine these writers, because, whatever may have been the value of their opinions as to the economic sense of the word "direct," they cannot now afford any criterion for determining its meaning in the constitution, inasmuch as an authoritative and conclusive construction has been given to that term, as there used, by an interpretation adopted shortly after the formation of the constitution by the legislative department of the government, and approved by the executive; by the adoption of that interpretation from that time to the present without question, and its exemplification and enforcement in many legislative enactments, and its acceptance by the authoritative text writers on the constitution; by the sanction of that interpretation, in a decision of this court rendered shortly after the constitution was adopted; and finally by the repeated reiteration and affirmance of that interpretation, so that it has become imbedded in our jurisprudence, and therefore may be considered almost a part of the written constitution itself.*]

NOTES AND QUESTIONS

1. The opinion you just read seems obviously right to us because the income from land, which may be rented, is in essence a federal real estate tax, which is by definition a direct tax. Moreover, income taxes in general fall directly on the person whose income is taxed and not on a third-party merchant, as with a federal tariff or sales tax or value added tax, which falls on the third party merchant from whom a person buys something. Federal income taxes are thus clearly direct taxes.

2. In the wake of the issuance of this opinion holding the federal income tax unconstitutional, the Sixteenth Amendment was ratified giving Congress the power to enact income taxes. You will hear more about the Sixteenth Amendment later in the course. *See infra* pages 1731–1733. For now, it is enough to note that the Sixteenth Amendment does not abolish the line between direct and indirect taxes. It simply says that *income* taxes may be assessed according to the rule of uniformity without regard to the rule of apportionment. The direct tax rule of apportionment thus lives on and prevents Congress from enacting head taxes, federal real estate taxes, wealth taxes, or other direct taxes, with the possible exception of taxes on the possession of luxury items, which *Hylton v. United States* had upheld.

3. The next case involves when, if ever, Congress can use its power to tax to achieve a result that is forbidden by its other enumerated powers. The background to *Bailey v. Drexel Furniture Company*—sometimes called *The Child Labor Tax Case*—is that Congress had banned labor by children under the age of sixteen in the United States, and the Supreme Court had struck down this ban under the then-dominant (and soon to be overruled) reading of the Commerce and Necessary and Proper Clauses in a case called *Hammer v. Dagenhart*, 247 U.S. 251 (1918). Congress responded by enacting a steep tax on goods made with child labor, and the Supreme Court considered the constitutionality of that tax in the case below.

B. BAILEY V. DREXEL FURNITURE CO.

259 U.S. 20 (1922)

■ MR. CHIEF JUSTICE TAFT delivered the opinion of the court.

This case presents the question of the constitutional validity of the Child Labor Tax Law. The plaintiff below, the Drexel Furniture Company, is engaged in the manufacture of furniture in the Western District of North Carolina. On September 20, 1921, it received a notice from Bailey, United States Collector of Internal Revenue for the District, that it had been assessed $6,312.79 for having during the taxable year 1919 employed and permitted to work in its factory a boy under fourteen years of age, thus incurring the tax of ten percent on its net profits for that year. The Company paid the tax under protest, and after rejection of its claim for a refund, brought this suit * * *.

The Child Labor Tax Law is Title XII of an act entitled "An Act To provide revenue, and for other purposes", approved February 24, 1919, c. 18, 40 Stat. 1057, 1138. The heading of the title is "Tax on Employment of Child Labor". It begins with § 1200, and includes eight sections. Section 1200 is as follows:

"SEC. 1200. That every person * * * operating (a) any mine or quarry situated in the United States in which children under the age of sixteen years have been employed or permitted to work during any portion of the taxable year; or (b) any mill, cannery, workshop, factory, or manufacturing establishment situated in the United

States in which children under the age of fourteen years have been employed or permitted to work, or children between the ages of fourteen and sixteen have been employed or permitted to work more than eight hours in any day or more than six days in any week, or after the hour of seven o'clock post meridian, or before the hour of six o'clock ante meridian, during any portion of the taxable year, shall pay for each taxable year, in addition to all other taxes imposed by law, an excise tax equivalent to 10 percentum of the entire net profits received or accrued for such year from the sale or disposition of the product of such mine, quarry, mill, cannery, workshop, factory, or manufacturing establishment."

* * *

The law is attacked on the ground that it is a regulation of the employment of child labor in the States—an exclusively state function under the Federal Constitution and within the reservations of the Tenth Amendment. It is defended on the ground that it is a mere excise tax levied by the Congress of the United States under its broad power of taxation conferred by § 8, Article I, of the Federal Constitution. We must construe the law and interpret the intent and meaning of Congress from the language of the act. The words are to be given their ordinary meaning unless the context shows that they are differently used. Does this law impose a tax with only that incidental restraint and regulation which a tax must inevitably involve? Or does it regulate by the use of the so-called tax as a penalty? If a tax, it is clearly an excise. If it were an excise on a commodity or other thing of value we might not be permitted under previous decisions of this court to infer solely from its heavy burden that the act intends a prohibition instead of a tax. But this act is more. It provides a heavy exaction for a departure from a detailed and specified course of conduct in business * * * If an employer departs from this prescribed course of business, he is to pay to the Government one-tenth of his entire net income in the business for a full year. The amount is not to be proportioned in any degree to the extent or frequency of the departures, but is to be paid by the employer in full measure whether he employs five hundred children for a year, or employs only one for a day. Moreover, if he does not know the child is within the named age limit, he is not to pay; that is to say, it is only where he knowingly departs from the prescribed course that payment is to be exacted. Scienter is associated with penalties not with taxes. The employer's factory is to be subject to inspection at any time not only by the taxing officers of the Treasury, the Department normally charged with the collection of taxes, but also by the Secretary of Labor and his subordinates whose normal function is the advancement and protection of the welfare of the workers. In the light of these features of the act, a court must be blind not to see that the so-called tax is imposed to stop the employment of children within the age limits prescribed. Its prohibitory and regulatory effect and purpose are palpable. All others can see and understand this. How can we properly shut our minds to it?

* * *

Out of a proper respect for the acts of a coordinate branch of the Government, this court has gone far to sustain taxing acts as such, even though there has been ground for suspecting from the weight of the tax it was intended to destroy its subject. But, in the act before us, the presumption of validity cannot prevail, because the proof of the contrary is found on the very face of its provisions. Grant the validity of this law, and all that Congress would need to do, hereafter, in seeking to take over to its control anyone of the great number of subjects of public interest, jurisdiction of which the States have never parted with, and which are reserved to them by the Tenth Amendment, would be to enact a detailed measure of complete regulation of the subject and enforce it by a so-called tax upon departures from it. To give such magic to the word "tax" would be to break down all constitutional limitation of the powers of Congress and completely wipe out the sovereignty of the States.

The difference between a tax and a penalty is sometimes difficult to define and yet the consequences of the distinction in the required method of their collection often are important. Where the sovereign enacting the law has power to impose both tax and penalty the difference between revenue production and mere regulation may be immaterial, but not so when one sovereign can impose a tax only, and the power of regulation rests in another. Taxes are occasionally imposed in the discretion of the legislature on proper subjects with the primary motive of obtaining revenue from them and with the incidental motive of discouraging them by making their continuance onerous. They do not lose their character as taxes because of the incidental motive. But there comes a time in the extension of the penalizing features of the so-called tax when it loses its character as such and becomes a mere penalty with the characteristics of regulation and punishment. Such is the case in the law before us. Although Congress does not invalidate the contract of employment or expressly declare that the employment within the mentioned ages is illegal, it does exhibit its intent practically to achieve the latter result by adopting the criteria of wrongdoing and imposing its principal consequence on those who transgress its standard.

The case before us cannot be distinguished from that of *Hammer v. Dagenhart,* 247 U.S. 251. Congress there enacted a law to prohibit transportation in interstate commerce of goods made at a factory in which there was employment of children within the same ages and for the same number of hours a day and days in a week as are penalized by the act in this case. This court held the law in that case to be void * * *.

In the case at the bar, Congress in the name of a tax which on the face of the act is a penalty seeks to do the same thing, and the effort must be equally futile.

* * *

But it is pressed upon us that this court has gone so far in sustaining taxing measures the effect or tendency of which was to accomplish purposes not directly within congressional power that we are bound by authority to maintain this law.

* * *

[*Editors' Note*: *The Court discussed four prior precedents which upheld federal excise taxes—on such items as bank notes, margarine, corporate income, and opium (yes, opium was legal for quite some time)—against challenges that thee amounts of the taxes were excessive. The Court emphasized that no one argued in those cases that the objects of the taxes were beyond Congress's power to control.*]

It should be noted, too, that the court [in the first of these cases], speaking of the extent of the taxing power, used these cautionary words (p. 541):

"There are, indeed, certain virtual limitations, arising from the principles of the Constitution itself. It would undoubtedly be an abuse of the power if so exercised as to impair the separate existence and independent self-government of the States, or if exercised for ends inconsistent with the limited grants of power in the Constitution."

* * *

[In *United States v. Doremus,* 249 U.S. 86 (1919), the case involving taxes on opium,] [t]he court said that the act could not be declared invalid just because another motive than taxation, not shown on the face of the act, might have contributed to its passage. This case does not militate against the conclusion we have reached in respect of the law now before us. The court there made manifest its view that the provisions of the so-called taxing act must be naturally and reasonably adapted to the collection of the tax, and not solely to the achievement of some other purpose plainly within state power.

For the reason given, we must hold the Child Labor Tax Law invalid, and the judgment of the District Court is

Affirmed.

■ MR. JUSTICE CLARKE, dissents [without opinion].

NOTES AND QUESTIONS

1. If the Taxing Clause includes a reference to the "general Welfare" precisely in order to allow Congress to enact taxes for regulatory as well as revenue-raising purposes, *see supra* pages 291–292, why does it matter whether the tax affects activity that Congress otherwise might not be able to regulate? Recall that the first tax law enacted by Congress had as one of its purposes "the encouragement and protection of manufactures." Under pre-1930s understandings of interstate commerce, Congress had no power directly to regulate manufacturing. Was that original 1789 tariff law unconstitutional on the reasoning of *Drexel Furniture*?

2. All taxes have a regulatory as well as a revenue-raising effect. If the government taxes cigarettes or goods made with child labor, the production and consumption of those goods will go down. What infuriated Chief Justice Taft in *Drexel Furniture* is that the *whole purpose* of the tax was to get around the Supreme Court's precedent in *Hammer v. Dagenhart* and not to raise revenue. Does that make a difference? Does Congress need to announce in its tax laws what percentage of their purpose is revenue and what percentage is regulatory?

3. How much of *Drexel Furniture* survives this next case?

C. UNITED STATES V. KAHRIGER

345 U.S. 22 (1953)

■ MR. JUSTICE REED delivered the opinion of the Court.

The issue raised by this appeal is the constitutionality of the occupational tax provisions of the Revenue Act of 1951, which levy a tax on persons engaged in the business of accepting wagers, and require such persons to register with the Collector of Internal Revenue. The unconstitutionality of the tax is asserted on two grounds. First, it is said that Congress, under the pretense of exercising its power to tax has attempted to penalize illegal intrastate gambling through the regulatory features of the Act and has thus infringed the police power which is reserved to the states. Secondly, it is urged that the registration provisions of the tax violate the privilege against self-incrimination and are arbitrary and vague, contrary to the guarantees of the Fifth Amendment.

* * *

The substance of respondent's position * * * is that Congress has chosen to tax a specified business which is not within its power to regulate. The precedents are many upholding taxes similar to this wagering tax as a proper exercise of the federal taxing power * * *.

Appellee would have us say, that because there is legislative history indicating a congressional motive to suppress wagering, this tax is not a proper exercise of such taxing power. In the *License Cases* [upholding a federal tax on the sale of lottery tickets or liquor], it was admitted that the federal license "discouraged" the activities. The intent to curtail and hinder, as well as tax, was also manifest in the following cases, and in each of them the tax was upheld: [*Editors' Note: the Court listed essentially the same cases distinguished in Drexel Furniture involving bank notes, margarine, opium, and the like*] * * *.

It is conceded that a federal excise tax does not cease to be valid merely because it discourages or deters the activities taxed. Nor is the tax invalid because the revenue obtained its negligible. Appellee, however, argues that the sole purpose of the statute is to penalize only illegal gambling in the states through the guise of a tax measure. As with the above excise taxes which we have held to be valid, the instant tax has a regulatory effect. But regardless of its regulatory effect, the wagering tax produces revenue. As such it surpasses both the narcotics and firearms taxes which we have found valid.

It is axiomatic that the power of Congress to tax is extensive and sometimes falls with crushing effect on businesses deemed unessential or inimical to the public welfare, or where, as in dealings with narcotics, the collection of the tax also is difficult. As is well known, the constitutional restraints on taxing are few. * * *. The remedy for excessive taxation is in the hands of Congress, not the courts * * *.

The difficulty of saying when the power to lay uniform taxes is curtailed, because its use brings a result beyond the direct legislative power of Congress, has given rise to diverse decisions. In that area of abstract ideas, a final definition of the line between state and federal power has baffled judges and legislators.

* * * Where federal legislation has rested on other congressional powers, such as the Necessary and Proper Clause or the Commerce Clause, this Court has generally sustained the statutes, despite their effect on matters ordinarily considered state concern. When federal power to regulate is found, its exercise is a matter for Congress * * *. Without any specific differentiation between the power to tax and other federal powers, the indirect results from the exercise of the power to tax have raised more doubts * * *. [T]he *Veazie Bank* case * * * allowed a tax, however, that obliterated from circulation all state bank notes. A reason was that "the judicial cannot prescribe to the legislative departments of the government limitations upon the exercise of its acknowledged powers." * * *. It is hard to understand why the power to tax should raise more doubts because of indirect effects than other federal powers.

Penalty provisions in tax statutes added for breach of a regulation concerning activities in themselves subject only to state regulation have caused this Court to declare the enactments invalid [citing, *inter alia, Drexel Furniture*]. Unless there are provisions extraneous to any tax need, courts are without authority to limit the exercise of the taxing power. All the provisions of this excise are adapted to the collection of a valid tax.

* * *

Reversed.

■ MR. JUSTICE JACKSON, concurring.

I concur in the judgment and opinion of the Court, but with such doubt that if the minority agreed upon an opinion which did not impair legitimate use of the taxing power I probably would join it. But we deal here with important and contrasting values in our scheme of government, and it is important that neither be allowed to destroy the other.

* * *

But here is a purported tax law which requires no reports and lays no tax except on specified gamblers whose calling in most states is illegal. It requires this group to step forward and identify themselves, not because they, like others, have income, but because of its source. This is difficult to regard as a rational or good-faith revenue measure, despite the deference that is due Congress. On the contrary, it seems to be a plan to tax out of existence the professional gambler whom it has been found impossible to prosecute out of existence. Few pursuits are entitled to less consideration at our hands than professional gambling, but the plain unwelcome fact is that it continues to survive because a large and influential part of our population patronizes and protects it.

The United States has a system of taxation by confession. That a people so numerous, scattered and individualistic annually assesses itself with a tax liability, often in highly burdensome amounts, is a reassuring sign of the stability and vitality of our system of self-government. What surprised me in once trying to help administer these laws was not to discover examples of recalcitrance, fraud or self-serving mistakes in reporting, but to discover that such derelictions were so few. It will be a sad day for the revenues if the good will of the people toward their taxing system is frittered away in efforts to accomplish by taxation moral reforms that cannot be accomplished by direct legislation. But the evil that can come from this statute will probably soon make itself manifest to Congress. The evil of a judicial decision impairing the legitimate taxing power by extreme constitutional interpretations might not be transient. Even though this statute approaches the fair limits of constitutionality, I join the decision of the Court.

[*Editors' Note: Justices Black and Douglas dissented on the ground that the law violated the Fifth Amendment by compelling people to incriminate themselves.*]

■ MR. JUSTICE FRANKFURTER, dissenting.

The Court's opinion manifests a natural difficulty in reaching its conclusion. Constitutional issues are likely to arise whenever Congress draws on the taxing power not to raise revenue but to regulate conduct. This is so, of course, because of the distribution of legislative power as between the Congress and the State Legislatures in the regulation of conduct.

* * *

* * * [It] was revealed on the floor of Congress * * * that what was formally a means of raising revenue for the Federal Government was essentially an effort to check if not to stamp out professional gambling.

A nominal taxing measure must be found an inadmissible intrusion into a domain of legislation reserved for the States not merely when Congress requires that such a measure is to be enforced through a detailed scheme of administration beyond the obvious fiscal needs, as in [*Drexel* Furniture] * * *. That is one ground for holding that Congress was constitutionally disrespectful of what is reserved to the States. Another basis for deeming such a formal revenue measure inadmissible is presented by this case. In addition to the fact that Congress was concerned with activity beyond the authority of the Federal Government, the enforcing provision of this enactment is designed for the systematic confession of crimes with a view to prosecution for such crimes under State law.

* * *

I would affirm this judgment.

Mr. JUSTICE DOUGLAS, while not joining in the entire opinion, agrees with the views expressed herein that this tax is an attempt by the Congress to control conduct which the Constitution has left to the responsibility of the States.

NOTES AND QUESTIONS

1. Justices Frankfurter, Black, and Douglas dissented in this case (though Justice Black did so on Fifth Amendment rather than Taxing Clause grounds), and Justice Jackson came close to joining them. The majority offers no effective response to their concerns. Nor did the majority formally overrule *Bailey v. Drexel Furniture Co.*, though it very clearly signals its disagreement with *Drexel Furniture's* holding and analysis. If you were a lower court judge trying to apply Supreme Court precedent, how would you understand the law governing when a congressional tax is invalid as an attempt to regulate conduct otherwise outside Congress's regulatory authority?

2. For half a century after *Kahriger,* the Court said little about how to ascertain the limits, if any, on the federal taxing power. That is not surprising. When *Drexel Furniture* was decided in 1922, there were serious limits on the scope of Congress's regulatory powers under the Commerce Clause and Necessary and Proper Clause, so Congress had many occasions to try to skirt those limits through creative uses of the taxing power. As you might have gathered from *United States v. Lopez,* and as you will see more directly in short order, those limits today are minimal, so Congress does not need to use the taxing power to pursue regulatory goals that the law now allows to be pursued directly. But post-*Lopez,* to the extent that any limits on Congress's regulatory powers are reintroduced into the law, questions about the scope of the taxing power re-emerged.

3. The Court's most recent pronouncement on the scope of the federal taxing power came in a lone opinion, joined by no other justice, authored by Chief Justice Roberts in *National Federation of Independent Business v. Sebelius,* 567 U.S. 519 (2012). We have reproduced that discussion elsewhere. *See supra* pages 305–306. Because Chief Justice Roberts was the fifth vote to uphold the Obamacare individual mandate, his lone opinion has more relevance than the run-of-the-mill lone opinion. It would be wise to review that material at this juncture.

4. Much of the lengthy debate between Chief Justice Roberts and the four dissenters in *NFIB,* which we have not reproduced here, concerns statutory interpretation. Everyone agrees that Congress *could* have placed a tax on not having government-approved health insurance (subject to the considerations discussed in the next note), but they disagree about whether Congress did so. The dissenters maintained that Congress conspicuously had repeatedly avoided calling the individual mandate a "tax," instead characterizing it solely as a "penalty." Chief Justice Roberts actually agreed with the dissenters that the "most straightforward" reading of the statute was that Congress chose a regulatory penalty rather than a tax, but he thought that courts should prefer a less plausible reading in order to render the statute constitutional. This so-called "avoidance canon" has a venerable history. Does the canon cross the line between judicial and legislative powers? Is it a proper judicial function to rewrite a law in order to save it?

5. As the dissent in *NFIB* pointed out, once you decide that the individual mandate is a tax, the next question is whether it is a direct tax subject to apportionment or an indirect tax subject to a uniformity requirement. If the former, the individual mandate "tax" was prima facie unconstitutional because no effort at apportionment was even attempted. Chief Justice Roberts appears to embrace the (unlikely) idea from *Hylton v. United States* that only capitation and federal real estate taxes are direct taxes. Is that now the rule? Can one say that this discussion of the direct/indirect line was dicta because the tax in *NFIB v. Sebelius* is owed on one's income taxes, which are exempted from the direct tax/indirect tax line by the explicit words of the Sixteenth Amendment? One of us thinks so; the other is not sure. *See* Gary Lawson & David B. Kopel, *The PPACA in Wonderland,* 38 AM. J.L. & MED. 269, 279–80 (2012) ("A fee for not having a governmentally approved health insurance policy is not a tax on incomes authorized by the Sixteenth Amendment * * *. Sixteenth Amendment income is an 'undeniable accession[ ] to wealth.' * * * If you choose not to purchase congressionally designed health insurance, there is no 'accession to wealth.' You have exactly as much money as you did before; there is no 'income' to tax."). Congress could probably have solved all of these problems, at least under current spending power doctrine, by giving people a credit on their income tax for purchasing approved health insurance, but even Chief Justice Roberts could not interpret the statute to accomplish that end.

6. As of this writing in early 2020, at least one prominent presidential candidate has proposed that everyone worth more than $50,000,000 pay a 2% annual "wealth tax." Is that a direct tax that would have to be apportioned among the States or an indirect tax? *Compare* Calvin H. Johnson, *A Wealth Tax Is Constitutional,* 38 A.B.A. TAX TIMES, vol. 4 (2019), https://www.americanbar.org/groups/taxation/publications/abataxtimes_home/19aug/19aug-pp-johnson-a-wealth-tax-is-constitutional/ *with* Daniel Hemel & Rebecca Kysar, *The Big Problem with Wealth Taxes,* N.Y. TIMES, Nov. 7, 2019, https://www.nytimes.com/2019/11/07/opinion/wealth-tax-constitution.html. We think it is pretty obviously a direct tax, but the issue may come down to whether one thinks that *Pollock* is still good law.

[Assignment 33]

V. THE FEDERAL SPENDING POWER

The source and scope of, and the limits on, the federal spending power were a major subject of controversy in the Nation's early years. Alexander Hamilton suggested that "the power to raise money is plenary and indefinite; and the objects to which it may be appropriated are no less comprehensive, than the payment of the public debt and the providing for the common defense and 'general Welfare.' "

Alexander Hamilton, *Report on Manufactures*, 2 ANNALS OF CONG. 971, 1011–12 (1791). Hamilton, in other words, saw the proviso in the Taxing Clause *as a source and definition of the federal power to spend.* Congress, on Hamilton's view, can spend money for the "general Welfare" without needing to link that spending to some other enumerated federal power. Hamilton's view seemingly prevailed on perhaps the most important spending measure in the First Congress: The assumption by the federal government of the States' Revolutionary War debts. *See* Act of Aug.4, 1790, ch. 34, 1 Stat. 138. But shortly thereafter the controversy rose again.

On November 26, 1796, the city of Savannah, Georgia, was devastated by a fire. Proposed legislation calling for federal aid to rebuild the city met with constitutional objections. One representative remarked that "[t]he sufferings of the people of Savannah were doubtless very great; no one could help feeling for them. But he wished gentlemen to put their finger upon that part of the Constitution which gave that House power to afford them relief * * *. He felt for the sufferers * * * but he felt as tenderly for the Constitution; he had examined it, and it did not authorize any such grant." 6 ANNALS OF CONG. 1717 (1796) (statement of Rep. Macon). Another representative added that "every individual citizen could, if he pleased, show his individual humanity by subscribing to their relief; but it was not Constitutional for them to afford relief from the Treasury." *Id.* at 1718 (statement of Rep. Moore). The aid bill was defeated in the House by a lopsided majority.

Another major controversy concerned federal spending for roads and canals. The Constitution specifically allows Congress to "establish Post Offices and post Roads." U.S. CONST. art. I, § 8, cl. 7. Does that implicitly forbid Congress from establishing other kinds of roads or aids to travel? Presidents James Madison, James Monroe, and Andrew Jackson all objected to various measures for "internal improvements," as roads and canals were then called; and while the grounds for objection were many and varied, at least some of them were cast as direct challenges to the Hamiltonian view of the federal spending power. James Madison, for instance, vetoed one such internal improvements spending bill with the following message:

> Having considered the bill this day presented to me entitled "An act to set apart and pledge certain funds for internal improvements," and which sets apart and pledges funds "for constructing roads and canals, and improving the navigation of water courses, in order to facilitate, promote, and give security to internal commerce among the several States, and to render more easy and less expensive the means and provisions for the common defense," I am constrained by the insuperable difficulty I feel in reconciling the bill with the Constitution of the United States to return it with that objection to the House of Representatives, in which it originated.
>
> The legislative powers vested in Congress are specified and enumerated in the eighth section of the first article of the Constitution, and it does not appear that the power proposed to be exercised by the bill is among the enumerated powers, or that it falls by any just interpretation within the power to make laws necessary and proper for carrying into execution those or other powers vested by the Constitution in the Government of the United States.
>
> "The power to regulate commerce among the several States" can not include a power to construct roads and canals, and to improve the

> navigation of water courses in order to facilitate, promote, and secure such a commerce without a latitude of construction departing from the ordinary import of the terms strengthened by the known inconveniences which doubtless led to the grant of this remedial power to Congress.
>
> To refer the power in question to the clause "to provide for the common defense and general welfare" would be contrary to the established and consistent rules of interpretation, as rendering the special and careful enumeration of powers which follow the clause nugatory and improper. Such a view of the Constitution would have the effect of giving to Congress a general power of legislation instead of the defined and limited one hitherto understood to belong to them, the terms "common defense and general welfare" embracing every object and act within the purview of a legislative trust * * *.
>
> A restriction of the power "to provide for the common defense and general welfare" to cases which are to be provided for by the expenditure of money would still leave within the legislative power of Congress all the great and most important measures of Government, money being the ordinary and necessary means of carrying them into execution.

Message of James Madison to the House of Representatives, Mar. 3, 1817, 30 ANNALS OF CONG. 1060–61 (1817).

The debate was settled for modern law in favor of Hamilton by dictum in *United States v. Butler,* 297 U.S. 1 (1936), involving a challenge to the Agricultural Adjustment Act of 1933, which limited farm outputs and compensated farmers with federal subsidies. The Court invalidated the law on difficult-to-follow federalism grounds. That holding has been superseded by subsequent case law, but the Court's discussion of the federal spending power has had enduring influence:

> * * *[T]he government asserts that * * * Congress may appropriate and authorize the spending of moneys for the "general welfare"; that the phrase should be liberally construed to cover anything conducive to national welfare; that decision as to what will promote such welfare rests with Congress alone, and the courts may not review its determination; and finally that the appropriation under attack was in fact for the general welfare of the United States.
>
> The Congress is expressly empowered to lay taxes to provide for the general welfare. Funds in the Treasury as a result of taxation may be expended only through appropriation. Article 1, § 9, cl. 7. They can never accomplish the objects for which they were collected unless the power to appropriate is as broad as the power to tax. The necessary implication from the terms of the grant is that the public funds may be appropriated "to provide for the general welfare of the United States." These words cannot be meaningless, else they would not have been used. The conclusion must be that they were intended to limit and define the granted power to raise and to expend money. How shall they be construed to effectuate the intent of the instrument?
>
> Since the foundation of the nation, sharp differences of opinion have persisted as to the true interpretation of the phrase. Madison asserted it amounted to no more than a reference to the other powers enumerated in

> the subsequent clauses of the same section; that, as the United States is a government of limited and enumerated powers, the grant of power to tax and spend for the general national welfare must be confined to the enumerated legislative fields committed to the Congress. In this view the phrase is mere tautology, for taxation and appropriation are or may be necessary incidents of the exercise of any of the enumerated legislative powers. Hamilton, on the other hand, maintained the clause confers a power separate and distinct from those later enumerated, is not restricted in meaning by the grant of them, and Congress consequently has a substantive power to tax and to appropriate, limited only by the requirement that it shall be exercised to provide for the general welfare of the United States. Each contention has had the support of those whose views are entitled to weight. This court has noticed the question, but has never found it necessary to decide which is the true construction. Mr. Justice Story, in his Commentaries, espouses the Hamiltonian position. We shall not review the writings of public men and commentators or discuss the legislative practice. Study of all these leads us to conclude that the reading advocated by Mr. Justice Story is the correct one. While, therefore, the power to tax is not unlimited, its confines are set in the clause which confers it, and not in those of § 8 which bestow and define the legislative powers of the Congress. It results that the power of Congress to authorize expenditure of public moneys for public purposes is not limited by the direct grants of legislative power found in the Constitution.

297 U.S. at 64–66.

As a matter of original meaning, Hamilton, Story, and the *Butler* Court are pretty clearly wrong: The source of the federal spending power is the Necessary and Proper Clause, not the Taxing Clause, with the consequence that federal spending must be "for carrying into Execution" some specific federal power. *See* Gary Lawson, *Making a Federal Case Out of It:* Sabri v. United States *and the Constitution of Leviathan,* 2004 CATO SUP. CT. REV. 119, 134–39. As a doctrinal matter, however, the issue is firmly settled in favor of the position advanced in *Butler*. Indeed, just two years after the *Butler* decision, the Court employed its reasoning to uphold the constitutionality of Social Security:

> Congress may spend money in aid of the "general welfare." *United States v. Butler,* 297 U.S. 1, 65. There have been great statesmen in our history who have stood for other views. We will not resurrect the contest. It is now settled by decision. *United States v. Butler*, supra. The conception of the spending power advocated by Hamilton and strongly reinforced by Story has prevailed over that of Madison, which has not been lacking in adherents. Yet difficulties are left when the power is conceded. The line must still be drawn between one welfare and another, between particular and general. Where this shall be placed cannot be known through a formula in advance of the event. There is a middle ground or certainly a penumbra in which discretion is at large. The discretion, however, is not confided to the courts. The discretion belongs to Congress, unless the choice is clearly wrong, a display of arbitrary power, not an exercise of judgment * * *. Nor is the concept of the general welfare static. Needs that were narrow or

parochial a century ago may be interwoven in our day with the well-being of the Nation. What is critical or urgent changes with the times.

The purge of nation-wide calamity that began in 1929 has taught us many lessons. Not the least is the solidarity of interests that may once have seemed to be divided. Unemployment spreads from State to State, the hinterland now settled that in pioneer days gave an avenue of escape. Spreading from State to State, unemployment is an ill not particular but general, which may be checked, if Congress so determines, by the resources of the nation * * *. But the ill is all one or at least not greatly different, whether men are thrown out of work because there is no longer work to do or because the disabilities of age make them incapable of doing it. Rescue becomes necessary irrespective of the cause. The hope behind this statute is to save men and women from the rigors of the poor house as well as from the haunting fear that such a lot awaits them when journey's end is near.

* * *

The problem is plainly national in area and dimensions. Moreover, laws of the separate states cannot deal with it effectively. Congress, at least, had a basis for that belief. States and local governments are often lacking in the resources that are necessary to finance an adequate program of security for the aged * * *. Apart from the failure of resources, states and local governments are at times reluctant to increase so heavily the burden of taxation to be borne by their residents for fear of placing themselves in a position of economic disadvantage as compared with neighbors or competitors * * *. A system of old age pensions has special dangers of its own, if put in force in one state and rejected in another. The existence of such a system is a bait to the needy and dependent elsewhere, encouraging them to migrate and seek a haven of repose. Only a power that is national can serve the interests of all.

Whether wisdom or unwisdom resides in the scheme of benefits set forth in Title II, it is not for us to say. The answer to such inquiries must come from Congress, not the courts. Our concern here as often is with power, not with wisdom * * *.

Helvering v. Davis, 301 U.S. 619, 640–44 (1937).

Similar reasoning supports the vast expanse of federal spending—from Medicare to farm subsidies to support for the arts to subsidized student loans—that now constitutes the principal function of the national government. And, as *Helvering v Davis* suggests, the decision whether spending promotes the "general Welfare" has not been regarded as a fit subject for judicial review. James Madison predicted as much in his 1817 veto message, noting that adoption of the Hamiltonian view of federal spending "would have the effect of excluding the judicial authority of the United States from its participation in guarding the boundary between the legislative powers of the General and the State Governments, inasmuch as questions relating to the general welfare, being questions of policy and expediency, are unsusceptible of judicial cognizance and decision." 30 ANNALS OF CONG. 1060. Accordingly, under modern law, Congress can spend for any purpose deemed to be for the "general Welfare," and no court decision has yet second-guessed Congress's judgment about what constitutes the "general Welfare." *See* John C. Eastman, *Restoring the "General" to the General Welfare Clause,* 4 CHAPMAN L. REV. 63 (2001).

Madison's prediction of complete judicial retreat from review of federal spending, however, has not quite materialized. Courts do not try to ascertain what does or does not promote the "general Welfare," but they do constrain federal spending in another fashion. Suppose that Congress conditions receipt of a government benefit on the recipient agreeing, for example, to give up the future right to a jury trial in any subsequent criminal proceeding. Such arrangements happen every day in criminal plea bargaining, where the benefit of a lesser charge and lighter sentence is traded for a whole panoply of constitutional rights that accompany a criminal trial. Can Congress incorporate the same principles into federal spending? Could receipt of welfare, for example, be conditioned on the surrender of First Amendment or Fourth Amendment rights? (The latter exchange also happens routinely, by the way.) The old saying is that whoever pays the piper calls the tune. Does that apply to the federal government?

No one is obliged to accept federal spending when it is offered. But federal spending is so pervasive that refusal to accept is often not a realistic option, even when the spending comes with strings attached. Accordingly, over the past century, courts have devised something called the "unconstitutional conditions" doctrine as a limitation on the federal spending power: Congress cannot attach conditions to receipt of federal spending that unduly implicate protected constitutional interests of the recipient. Figuring out the contours and limits of this doctrine is a near-impossible task; "[t]he doctrine of unconstitutional conditions is notoriously complex, convoluted, and inconsistent." Louis W. Fisher, *Contracting Around the Constitution: An Anticommodificationist Perspective on Unconstitutional Conditions,* 21 U. PA. J. CONST. L. 1167, 1168 (2019). As one scholar puts it: "Unconstitutional conditions are a conundrum. On the one hand, if government can spend, why can't it place whatever conditions it wants on its spending? On the other hand, if it can place any conditions on spending, won't it be able to impose restrictions that evade much of the Constitution, including most constitutional rights? This enigma is notoriously complex, and unconstitutional conditions therefore are considered a sort of Gordian knot." Philip Hamburger, *Unconstitutional Conditions: The Irrelevance of Consent,* 98 VA. L. REV. 479 (2012). If we had a crisp, clear theory of this doctrine, we would offer it to you. Alas, we do not. See if this relatively recent case sheds any light.

A. AGENCY FOR INT'L DEVELOPMENT V. ALLIANCE FOR OPEN SOCIETY INT'L, INC.

570 U.S. 205 (2013)

■ CHIEF JUSTICE ROBERTS delivered the opinion of the Court.

The United States Leadership Against HIV/AIDS, Tuberculosis, and Malaria Act of 2003 (Leadership Act), 117 Stat. 711, as amended, 22 U.S.C. § 7601 *et seq.*, outlined a comprehensive strategy to combat the spread of HIV/AIDS around the world. As part of that strategy, Congress authorized the appropriation of billions of dollars to fund efforts by nongovernmental organizations to assist in the fight. The Act imposes two related conditions on that funding: First, no funds made available by the Act "may be used to promote or advocate the legalization or practice of prostitution or sex trafficking." § 7631(e). And second, no funds may be used by an organization "that does not have a policy explicitly opposing prostitution and sex trafficking." § 7631(f). This case concerns the second of these conditions, referred to as the Policy Requirement. The question is whether that funding condition violates a recipient's First Amendment rights.

* * *

The Department of Health and Human Services (HHS) and the United States Agency for International Development (USAID) are the federal agencies primarily responsible for overseeing implementation of the Leadership Act. To enforce the Policy Requirement, the agencies have directed that the recipient of any funding under the Act agree in the award document that it is opposed to "prostitution and sex trafficking because of the psychological and physical risks they pose for women, men, and children." 45 CFR § 89.1(b) (2012); USAID, Acquisition & Assistance Policy Directive 12–04, p. 6 (AAPD 12–04).

* * *

The Policy Requirement mandates that recipients of Leadership Act funds explicitly agree with the Government's policy to oppose prostitution and sex trafficking. It is, however, a basic First Amendment principle that "freedom of speech prohibits the government from telling people what they must say." * * * Were it enacted as a direct regulation of speech, the Policy Requirement would plainly violate the First Amendment. The question is whether the Government may nonetheless impose that requirement as a condition on the receipt of federal funds.

The Spending Clause of the Federal Constitution grants Congress the power "[t]o lay and collect Taxes, Duties, Imposts and Excises, to pay the Debts and provide for the common Defence and general Welfare of the United States." Art. I, § 8, cl. 1. The Clause provides Congress broad discretion to tax and spend for the "general Welfare," including by funding particular state or private programs or activities. That power includes the authority to impose limits on the use of such funds to ensure they are used in the manner Congress intends. *Rust v. Sullivan*, 500 U.S. 173, 195, n. 4 (1991) ("Congress' power to allocate funds for public purposes includes an ancillary power to ensure that those funds are properly applied to the prescribed use.").

As a general matter, if a party objects to a condition on the receipt of federal funding, its recourse is to decline the funds. This remains true when the objection is that a condition may affect the recipient's exercise of its First Amendment rights.

At the same time, * * * [i]n some cases, a funding condition can result in an unconstitutional burden on First Amendment rights.

The dissent thinks that can only be true when the condition is not relevant to the objectives of the program (although it has its doubts about that), or when the condition is actually coercive, in the sense of an offer that cannot be refused. Our precedents, however, are not so limited. In the present context, the relevant distinction that has emerged from our cases is between conditions that define the limits of the government spending program—those that specify the activities Congress wants to subsidize—and conditions that seek to leverage funding to regulate speech outside the contours of the program itself. The line is hardly clear, in part because the definition of a particular program can always be manipulated to subsume the challenged condition. We have held, however, that "Congress cannot recast a condition on funding as a mere definition of its program in every case, lest the First Amendment be reduced to a simple semantic exercise." *Legal Services Corporation v. Velazquez*, 531 U.S. 533, 547 (2001).

A comparison of two cases helps illustrate the distinction: In *Regan v. Taxation With Representation of Washington*, [461 U.S. 540 (1983),] the Court upheld a requirement that nonprofit organizations seeking tax-exempt status under 26 U.S.C. § 501(c)(3) not engage in substantial efforts to influence legislation. The tax-exempt status, we explained, "ha[d] much the same effect as a cash grant to the organization." 461 U.S., at 544. And by limiting § 501(c)(3) status to organizations that did not attempt to influence legislation, Congress had merely "chose[n] not to subsidize lobbying." *Ibid.* In rejecting the nonprofit's First Amendment claim, the Court highlighted * * * the fact that the condition did not prohibit that organization from lobbying Congress altogether. By returning to a "dual structure" it had used in the past—separately incorporating as a § 501(c)(3) organization and § 501(c)(4) organization—the nonprofit could continue to claim § 501(c)(3) status for its nonlobbying activities, while attempting to influence legislation in its § 501(c)(4) capacity with separate funds. Maintaining such a structure, the Court noted, was not "unduly burdensome." *Id.*, at 545, n. 6, * * *.

In *FCC v. League of Women Voters of Cal.*, by contrast, the Court struck down a condition on federal financial assistance to noncommercial broadcast television and radio stations that prohibited all editorializing, including with private funds. 468 U.S. 364, 399–401 (1984). Even a station receiving only one percent of its overall budget from the Federal Government, the Court explained, was "barred absolutely from all editorializing." *Id.*, at 400. Unlike the situation in *Regan*, the law provided no way for a station to limit its use of federal funds to noneditorializing activities, while using private funds "to make known its views on matters of public importance." 468 U.S., at 400. The prohibition thus went beyond ensuring that federal funds not be used to subsidize "public broadcasting station editorials," and instead leveraged the federal funding to regulate the stations' speech outside the scope of the program. *Id.*, at 399.

Our decision in *Rust v. Sullivan* elaborated on the approach reflected in *Regan* and *League of Women Voters*. In *Rust*, we considered Title X of the Public Health Service Act, a Spending Clause program that issued grants to nonprofit health-care organizations "to assist in the establishment and operation of voluntary family planning projects [to] offer a broad range of acceptable and effective family planning methods and services." 500 U.S., at 178. The organizations received funds from a variety of sources other than the Federal Government for a variety of purposes. The Act, however, prohibited the Title X federal funds from being "used in programs where abortion is a method of family planning." *Ibid.* To enforce this provision, HHS regulations barred Title X projects from advocating abortion as a method of family planning, and required grantees to ensure that their Title X projects were " 'physically and financially separate' " from their other projects that engaged in the prohibited activities. *Id.*, at 180–181. A group of Title X funding recipients brought suit, claiming the regulations imposed an unconstitutional condition on their First Amendment rights. We rejected their claim.

We explained that Congress can, without offending the Constitution, selectively fund certain programs to address an issue of public concern, without funding alternative ways of addressing the same problem. In Title X, Congress had defined the federal program to encourage only particular family planning methods. The challenged regulations were simply "designed to ensure that the limits of the federal program are observed," and "that public funds [are] spent for the purposes for which they were authorized." *Rust*, 500 U.S., at 193, 196.

In making this determination, the Court stressed that "Title X expressly distinguishes between a Title X *grantee* and a Title X *project*." *Id.*, at 196. The regulations governed only the scope of the grantee's Title X projects, leaving it "unfettered in its other activities." *Ibid.* "The Title X grantee can continue to . . . engage in abortion advocacy; it simply is required to conduct those activities through programs that are separate and independent from the project that receives Title X funds." *Ibid.* Because the regulations did not "prohibit[ ] the recipient from engaging in the protected conduct outside the scope of the federally funded program," they did not run afoul of the First Amendment. *Id.*, at 197.

As noted, the distinction drawn in these cases—between conditions that define the federal program and those that reach outside it—is not always self-evident * * *. Here, however, we are confident that the Policy Requirement falls on the unconstitutional side of the line.

To begin, it is important to recall that the Leadership Act has two conditions relevant here. The first—unchallenged in this litigation—prohibits Leadership Act funds from being used "to promote or advocate the legalization or practice of prostitution or sex trafficking." 22 U.S.C. § 7631 (e). The Government concedes that § 7631(e) by itself ensures that federal funds will not be used for the prohibited purposes.

The Policy Requirement therefore must be doing something more—and it is. The dissent views the Requirement as simply a selection criterion by which the Government identifies organizations "who believe in its ideas to carry them to fruition." As an initial matter, whatever purpose the Policy Requirement serves in selecting funding recipients, its effects go beyond selection. The Policy Requirement is an ongoing condition on recipients' speech and activities, a ground for terminating a grant after selection is complete. In any event, as the Government acknowledges, it is not simply seeking organizations that oppose prostitution. Rather, it explains, "Congress has expressed its purpose 'to eradicate' prostitution and sex trafficking, 22 U.S.C. § 7601(23), and it wants recipients to *adopt* a similar stance." Brief for Petitioners 32 (emphasis added). This case is not about the Government's ability to enlist the assistance of those with whom it already agrees. It is about compelling a grant recipient to adopt a particular belief as a condition of funding.

* * * A recipient cannot avow the belief dictated by the Policy Requirement when spending Leadership Act funds, and then turn around and assert a contrary belief, or claim neutrality, when participating in activities on its own time and dime. By requiring recipients to profess a specific belief, the Policy Requirement goes beyond defining the limits of the federally funded program to defining the recipient.

* * *

* * * [T]he Policy Requirement goes beyond preventing recipients from using private funds in a way that would undermine the federal program. It requires them to pledge allegiance to the Government's policy of eradicating prostitution * * *.

The Policy Requirement compels as a condition of federal funding the affirmation of a belief that by its nature cannot be confined within the scope of the

Government program. In so doing, it violates the First Amendment and cannot be sustained. The judgment of the Court of Appeals is affirmed.

It is so ordered.

■ KAGAN, J., took no part in the consideration or decision of this case.

■ JUSTICE SCALIA, with whom JUSTICE THOMAS joins, dissenting.

The * * * Policy Requirement is nothing more than a means of selecting suitable agents to implement the Government's chosen strategy to eradicate HIV/AIDS. That is perfectly permissible under the Constitution.

The First Amendment does not mandate a viewpoint-neutral government. Government must choose between rival ideas and adopt some as its own: competition over cartels, solar energy over coal, weapon development over disarmament, and so forth. Moreover, the government may enlist the assistance of those who believe in its ideas to carry them to fruition; and it need not enlist for that purpose those who oppose or do not support the ideas. That seems to me a matter of the most common common sense. For example: One of the purposes of America's foreign-aid programs is the fostering of good will towards this country. If the organization Hamas—reputed to have an efficient system for delivering welfare—were excluded from a program for the distribution of U.S. food assistance, no one could reasonably object. And that would remain true if Hamas were an organization of United States citizens entitled to the protection of the Constitution. So long as the unfunded organization remains free to engage in its activities (including anti-American propaganda) "without federal assistance," refusing to make use of its assistance for an enterprise to which it is opposed does not abridge its speech. And the same is true when the rejected organization is not affirmatively opposed to, but merely unsupportive of, the object of the federal program, which appears to be the case here. (Respondents do not promote prostitution, but neither do they wish to oppose it.) A federal program to encourage healthy eating habits need not be administered by the American Gourmet Society, which has nothing against healthy food but does not insist upon it.

The argument is that this commonsense principle will enable the government to discriminate against, and injure, points of view to which it is opposed. Of course the Constitution does not prohibit government spending that discriminates against, and injures, points of view to which the government is opposed; every government program which takes a position on a controversial issue does that. Anti-smoking programs injure cigar aficionados, programs encouraging sexual abstinence injure free-love advocates, etc. The constitutional prohibition at issue here is not a prohibition against discriminating against or injuring opposing points of view, but the First Amendment's prohibition against the coercing of speech. I am frankly dubious that a condition for eligibility to participate in a minor federal program such as this one runs afoul of that prohibition even when the condition is irrelevant to the goals of the program. Not every disadvantage is a coercion.

But that is not the issue before us here. Here the views that the Government demands an applicant forswear—or that the Government insists an applicant favor—are relevant to the program in question. The program is valid only if the Government is entitled to disfavor the opposing view (here, advocacy of or toleration of prostitution). And if the program can disfavor it, so can the selection of those who are to administer the program. There is no risk that this principle will enable the Government to discriminate arbitrarily against positions it disfavors. It would not, for example, permit the Government to exclude from bidding on defense contracts anyone who refuses to abjure prostitution. But here a central part of the Government's HIV/AIDS strategy is the suppression of prostitution, by which HIV is transmitted. It is entirely reasonable to admit to participation in the program only those who believe in that goal.

* * *

Of course the most obvious manner in which the admission to a program of an ideological opponent can frustrate the purpose of the program is by freeing up the opponent's funds for use in its ideological opposition * * *. Money is fungible. The economic reality is that when NGOs can conduct their AIDS work on the Government's dime, they can expend greater resources on policies that undercut the Leadership Act. The Government need not establish by record evidence that this will happen. To make it a valid consideration in determining participation in federal programs, it suffices that this is a real and obvious risk.

* * *

* * * There is no case of ours in which a condition that is relevant to a statute's valid purpose and that is not in itself unconstitutional (*e.g.,* a religious-affiliation condition that violates the Establishment Clause) has been held to violate the [unconstitutional conditions] doctrine. Moreover, as I suggested earlier, the contention that the condition here "coerces" respondents' speech is on its face implausible * * *. As the Court acknowledges, "[a]s a general matter, if a party objects to a condition on the receipt of federal funding, its recourse is to decline the funds," and to draw on its own coffers.

The majority cannot credibly say that this speech condition is coercive, so it does not. It pussyfoots around the lack of coercion by invalidating the Leadership Act for "*requiring* recipients to profess a specific belief" and "*demanding* that funding recipients adopt—as their own—the Government's view on an issue of public concern" (emphasis mine). But like King Cnut's commanding of the tides, here the Government's "requiring" and "demanding" have no coercive effect. In the end, and in the circumstances of this case, compell[ing] *as a condition* of federal funding the affirmation of a belief" (emphasis mine), is no compulsion at all. It is the reasonable price of admission to a limited government-spending program that each organization remains free to accept or reject. Section 7631(f) "defin[es] the recipient" only to the extent he decides that it is in his interest to be so defined.

* * *

* * * What Congress has done here—requiring an ideological commitment relevant to the Government task at hand—is approved by the Constitution itself. Americans need not support the Constitution; they may be Communists or anarchists. But "[t]he Senators and Representatives . . ., and the Members of the several State Legislatures, and all executive and judicial Officers, both of the United States and of the several States, shall be bound by Oath or Affirmation, to support [the] Constitution." U.S. Const., Art. VI, cl. 3. The Framers saw the wisdom of imposing affirmative ideological commitments prerequisite to assisting in the government's work. And so should we.

NOTES AND QUESTIONS

1. The unconstitutional conditions doctrine has application in contexts other than federal spending. States as well as the federal government cannot condition receipt of certain benefits, such as licenses to develop property, on concessions from the recipient "unless there is a 'nexus' and 'rough proportionality' between the government's demand and the effects of the proposed land use." *Koontz v. St. John's River Water Mgmt. Dist.*, 570 U.S. 595 (2013). The doctrine has special bite in the context of land use regulation, which is a setting in which local governments are especially prone to try to (for lack of a better word) extort value from landowners in return for permission to improve or develop land. *See Dolan v. City of Tigard,* 512 U.S. 374 (1994). The Court has been more forgiving of state and federal conditions on the receipt of welfare, especially conditions that involve waiver of rights to privacy and freedom from search and seizure. *See Wyman v. James,* 400 U.S. 309 (1971) (home inspections of welfare recipients by social workers do not violate the Fourth Amendment because the recipients can turn down the money); Dorothy E. Roberts, *The Only Good Poor Woman: Unconstitutional Conditions and Welfare,* 72 DENVER U.L. REV. 931 (1995).

2. "When law schools began restricting the access of military recruiters to their students because of disagreement with the Government's policy on homosexuals in the military, Congress responded by enacting the Solomon Amendment. *See* 10 U.S.C. § 983 (2000 ed. and Supp.IV). That provision specifies that if any part of an institution of higher education denies military recruiters access equal to that provided other recruiters, the entire institution would lose certain federal funds." *Rumsfeld v. Forum for Academic & Institutional Rights, Inc. ["FAIR"],* 547 U.S. 47, 51 (2006). In *FAIR,* the Supreme Court *unanimously* rejected a challenge brought by some law schools claiming that requiring equal access for military recruiters on campus as a condition to receipt of federal funds was unconstitutional:

> Some of this Court's leading First Amendment precedents have established the principle that freedom of speech prohibits the government from telling people what they must say. In *West Virginia Bd. of Ed. v. Barnette,* 319 U.S. 624, 642 (1943), we held unconstitutional a state law requiring schoolchildren to recite the Pledge of Allegiance and to salute the flag. And in *Wooley v. Maynard*, 430 U.S. 705, 717 (1977), we held unconstitutional another that required New Hampshire motorists to display the state motto—"Live Free or Die"—on their license plates.
>
> The Solomon Amendment does not require any similar expression by law schools. Nonetheless, recruiting assistance provided by the schools often includes elements of speech. For example, schools may send e-mails or post notices on bulletin boards on an employer's behalf. Law schools offering such services to other recruiters must also send e-mails and post notices on behalf of the military to comply with the Solomon Amendment. As FAIR points out, these compelled statements of fact ("The U.S. Army recruiter will meet interested students in Room 123 at 11 a.m."), like compelled statements of opinion, are subject to First Amendment scrutiny.
>
> This sort of recruiting assistance, however, is a far cry from the compelled speech in *Barnette* and *Wooley*. The Solomon Amendment, unlike the laws at issue in those cases, does not dictate the content of the speech at all, which is only "compelled" if, and to the extent, the school provides such speech for other recruiters * * *.

> * * * Compelling a law school that sends scheduling e-mails for other recruiters to send one for a military recruiter is simply not the same as forcing a student to pledge allegiance, or forcing a Jehovah's Witness to display the motto "Live Free or Die," and it trivializes the freedom protected in *Barnette* and *Wooley* to suggest that it is.

547 U.S. at 61–62.

3. Why isn't plea bargaining an unconstitutional condition? Or is it? *See* Jason Mazzone, *The Waiver Paradox,* 97 NW. U.L. REV. 801 (2003).

4. Oftentimes, the recipients of federal funds are States. Do they stand in a better, worse, or the same position as against the federal government as landowners, welfare recipients, criminal defendants, or aid organizations? Does the growth of federal spending threaten in some fundamental way the role of the States in the constitutional order? Does the Tenth Amendment, which says only that "[t]he powers not delegated to the United States by the Constitution, nor prohibited by it to the States, are reserved to the States, respectively, or to the people," U.S. CONST. amend. X, implicitly limit the kinds of conditions that the federal government can attach to State funding? In 1984, Congress ordered the Secretary of Transportation to withhold federal highway funds from States that did not adopt a legal drinking age of at least twenty-one years. The State of South Dakota claimed that this was an unconstitutional attempt by Congress to legislate a national drinking age, which it has no power to do, especially in view of the Twenty-First Amendment. The Supreme Court upheld the statute in *South Dakota v. Dole,* 483 U.S. 203 (1987):

> Our decisions have recognized that in some circumstances the financial inducement offered by Congress might be so coercive as to pass the point at which "pressure turns into compulsion." Here, however, Congress has directed only that a State desiring to establish a minimum drinking age lower than 21 lose a relatively small percentage of certain federal highway funds. Petitioner contends that the coercive nature of this program is evident from the degree of success it has achieved. We cannot conclude, however, that a conditional grant of federal money of this sort is unconstitutional simply by reason of its success in achieving the congressional objective.
>
> When we consider, for a moment, that all South Dakota would lose if she adheres to her chosen course as to a suitable minimum drinking age is 5% of the funds otherwise obtainable under specified highway grant programs, the argument as to coercion is shown to be more rhetoric than fact * * *.

Id. at 211. In 2012, for the first time, a majority of the Court found "circumstances" sufficiently "coercive" to pass constitutional limits.

B. NATIONAL FEDERATION OF INDEPENDENT BUSINESS V. SEBELIUS

567 U.S. 519 (2012)

[Editors' Note: Medicaid is a program of government-financed medical care for the poor. As with many welfare and regulatory programs, it is funded in large measure by the federal government but administered at the state level. The Patient Protection and Affordable Care Act provided that States would lose all of their federal Medicaid funding unless they expanded their Medicaid coverage to federal specifications. Some States challenged this aspect of the Act as an unconstitutionally coercive use of the spending power. The Supreme Court had never before found

conditions for States in a federal spending program to be unconstitutionally coercive. The portion of Chief Justice Roberts' opinion below ("Part IV") was joined by six other justices. Only Justices Ruth Bader Ginsburg and Sonia Sotomayor dissented from this part of the Court's holding.]

■ CHIEF JUSTICE ROBERTS announced the judgment of the Court and delivered the opinion of the Court with respect to Parts I, II, and III-C, an opinion with respect to Part IV, in which JUSTICE BREYER and JUSTICE KAGAN join, and an opinion with respect to Parts III-A, III-B, and III-D.

* * *

IV

The States also contend that the Medicaid expansion exceeds Congress's authority under the Spending Clause. They claim that Congress is coercing the States to adopt the changes it wants by threatening to withhold all of a State's Medicaid grants, unless the State accepts the new expanded funding and complies with the conditions that come with it * * *.

There is no doubt that the Act dramatically increases state obligations under Medicaid. The current Medicaid program requires States to cover only certain discrete categories of needy individuals—pregnant women, children, needy families, the blind, the elderly, and the disabled. There is no mandatory coverage for most childless adults, and the States typically do not offer any such coverage. The States also enjoy considerable flexibility with respect to the coverage levels for parents of needy families. On average States cover only those unemployed parents who make less than 37 percent of the federal poverty level, and only those employed parents who make less than 63 percent of the poverty line.

The Medicaid provisions of the Affordable Care Act, in contrast, require States to expand their Medicaid programs by 2014 to cover *all* individuals under the age of 65 with incomes below 133 percent of the federal poverty line. § 1396a(a)(10)(A)(i)(VIII). The Act also establishes a new "[e]ssential health benefits" package, which States must provide to all new Medicaid recipients—a level sufficient to satisfy a recipient's obligations under the individual mandate. §§ 1396a(k)(1), 1396u–7(b)(5), 18022(b). The Affordable Care Act provides that the Federal Government will pay 100 percent of the costs of covering these newly eligible individuals through 2016. § 1396d(y)(1). In the following years, the federal payment level gradually decreases, to a minimum of 90 percent. In light of the expansion in coverage mandated by the Act, the Federal Government estimates that its Medicaid spending will increase by approximately $100 billion per year, nearly 40 percent above current levels.

The Spending Clause grants Congress the power "to pay the Debts and provide for the . . . general Welfare of the United States." U.S. Const., Art. I, § 8, cl. 1. We have long recognized that Congress may use this power to grant federal funds to the States, and may condition such a grant upon the States' "taking certain actions that Congress could not require them to take." * * *

At the same time, our cases have recognized limits on Congress's power under the Spending Clause to secure state compliance with federal objectives * * *. Otherwise the two-government system established by the Framers would give way to a system that vests power in one central government, and individual liberty would suffer.

That insight has led this Court to * * * scrutinize Spending Clause legislation to ensure that Congress is not using financial inducements to exert a "power akin to undue influence." *Steward Machine Co. v. Davis*, 301 U. S. 548, 590 (1937). Congress may use its spending power to create incentives for States to act in accordance with federal policies. But when "pressure turns into compulsion," *ibid.*, the legislation runs contrary to our system of federalism * * *.

Permitting the Federal Government to force the States to implement a federal program would threaten the political accountability key to our federal system * * *. Spending Clause programs do not pose this danger when a State has a legitimate choice whether to accept the federal conditions in exchange for federal funds. In such a situation, state officials can fairly be held politically accountable for choosing to accept or refuse the federal offer. But when the State has no choice, the Federal Government can achieve its objectives without accountability * * *.

* * *

The States * * * argue * * * that Congress has "crossed the line distinguishing encouragement from coercion" in the way it has structured the funding: Instead of simply refusing to grant the new funds to States that will not accept the new conditions, Congress has also threatened to withhold those States' existing Medicaid funds. The States claim that this threat serves no purpose other than to force unwilling States to sign up for the dramatic expansion in health care coverage effected by the Act.

Given the nature of the threat and the programs at issue here, we must agree. We have upheld Congress's authority to condition the receipt of funds on the States' complying with restrictions on the use of those funds, because that is the means by which Congress ensures that the funds are spent according to its view of the "general Welfare." Conditions that do not here govern the use of the funds, however, cannot be justified on that basis. When, for example, such conditions take the form of threats to terminate other significant independent grants, the conditions are properly viewed as a means of pressuring the States to accept policy changes.

In *South Dakota v. Dole,* we considered a challenge to a federal law that threatened to withhold five percent of a State's federal highway funds if the State did not raise its drinking age to 21. The Court found that the condition was "directly related to one of the main purposes for which highway funds are expended—safe interstate travel." * * *

We accordingly asked whether "the financial inducement offered by Congress" was "so coercive as to pass the point at which 'pressure turns into compulsion.' " * * * We found that the inducement was not impermissibly coercive, because Congress was offering only "relatively mild encouragement to the States." * * *

In this case, the financial "inducement" Congress has chosen is much more than "relatively mild encouragement"—it is a gun to the head. Section 1396c of the Medicaid Act provides that if a State's Medicaid plan does not comply with the Act's requirements, the Secretary of Health and Human Services may declare that "further payments will not be made to the State." 42 U. S. C. § 1396c. A State that opts out of the Affordable Care Act's expansion in health care coverage thus stands to lose not merely "a relatively small percentage" of its existing Medicaid funding, but *all* of it. *Dole, supra*, at 211. Medicaid spending accounts for over 20 percent of the average State's total budget, with federal funds covering 50 to 83 percent of those costs * * *. It is easy to see how the *Dole* Court could conclude that the threatened loss of less than half of one percent of South Dakota's budget left that State with a "prerogative" to reject Congress's desired policy, "not merely in theory but in fact." 483 U.S., at 211–212. The threatened loss of over 10 percent of a State's overall budget, in contrast, is economic dragooning that leaves the States with no real option but to acquiesce in the Medicaid expansion.

JUSTICE GINSBURG claims that *Dole* is distinguishable because here "Congress has not threatened to withhold funds earmarked for any other program." But that begs the question: The States contend that the expansion is in reality a new program and that Congress is forcing them to accept it by threatening the funds for the existing Medicaid program. We cannot agree that existing Medicaid and the expansion dictated by the Affordable Care Act are all one program simply because "Congress styled" them as such. If the expansion is not properly viewed as a modification of the existing Medicaid program, Congress's decision to so title it is irrelevant.

* * *

The Medicaid expansion * * * accomplishes a shift in kind, not merely degree. The original program was designed to cover medical services for four particular categories of the needy: the disabled, the blind, the elderly, and needy families with dependent children. See 42 U. S. C. § 1396a(a)(10). Previous amendments to Medicaid eligibility merely altered and expanded the boundaries of these categories. Under the Affordable Care Act, Medicaid is transformed into a program to meet the health care needs of the entire nonelderly population with income below 133 percent of the poverty level. It is no longer a program to care for the neediest among us, but rather an element of a comprehensive national plan to provide universal health insurance coverage.

Indeed, the manner in which the expansion is structured indicates that while Congress may have styled the expansion a mere alteration of existing Medicaid, it recognized it was enlisting the States in a new health care program. Congress created a separate funding provision to cover the costs of providing services to any person made newly eligible by the expansion. While Congress pays 50 to 83 percent of the costs of covering individuals currently enrolled in Medicaid, once the expansion is fully implemented Congress will pay 90 percent of the costs for newly eligible persons. The conditions on use of the different funds are also distinct. Congress mandated that newly eligible persons receive a level of coverage that is less comprehensive than the traditional Medicaid benefit package.

* * *

The Court in *Steward Machine* did not attempt to "fix the outermost line" where persuasion gives way to coercion. 301 U.S., at 591. The Court found it "[e]nough for present purposes that wherever the line may be, this statute is within it." *Ibid.* We have no need to fix a line either. It is enough for today that wherever that line may be, this statute is surely beyond it * * *.

* * *

■ JUSTICE GINSBURG, joined by JUSTICE SOTOMAYOR, concurring in the judgment in part and dissenting in part.

* * *

Through Medicaid, Congress has offered the States an opportunity to furnish health care to the poor with the aid of federal financing. To receive federal Medicaid funds, States must provide health benefits to specified categories of needy persons, including pregnant women, children, parents, and adults with disabilities. Guaranteed eligibility varies by category: for some it is tied to the federal poverty level (incomes up to 100% or 133%); for others it depends on criteria such as eligibility for designated state or federal assistance programs. The ACA enlarges the population of needy people States must cover to include adults under age 65 with incomes up to 133% of the federal poverty level. The spending power conferred by the Constitution, the Court has never doubted, permits Congress to define the contours of programs financed with federal funds. And to expand coverage, Congress could have recalled the existing legislation, and replaced it with a new law making Medicaid as embracive of the poor as Congress chose.

The question posed by the 2010 Medicaid expansion, then, is essentially this: To cover a notably larger population, must Congress take the repeal/reenact route, or may it achieve the same result by amending existing law? The answer should be that Congress may expand by amendment the classes of needy persons entitled to Medicaid benefits. A ritualistic requirement that Congress repeal and reenact spending legislation in order to enlarge the population served by a federally funded program would advance no constitutional principle and would scarcely serve the interests of federalism. To the contrary, such a requirement would rigidify Congress' efforts to empower States by partnering with them in the implementation of federal programs.

* * *

THE CHIEF JUSTICE acknowledges that Congress may "condition the receipt of [federal] funds on the States' complying with restrictions on the use of those funds," but nevertheless concludes that the 2010 expansion is unduly coercive. His conclusion rests on three premises, each of them essential to his theory. First, the Medicaid expansion is, in THE CHIEF JUSTICE'S view, a new grant program, not an addition to the Medicaid program existing before the ACA's enactment. Congress, THE CHIEF JUSTICE maintains, has threatened States with the loss of funds from an old program in an effort to get them to adopt a new one. Second, the expansion was unforeseeable by the States when they first signed on to Medicaid. Third, the threatened loss of funding is so large that the States have no real choice but to participate in the Medicaid expansion. THE CHIEF JUSTICE therefore—*for the first time ever*—finds an exercise of Congress' spending power unconstitutionally coercive.

Medicaid, as amended by the ACA, however, is not two spending programs; it is a single program with a constant aim—to enable poor persons to receive basic health care when they need it. Given past expansions, plus express statutory warning that Congress may change the requirements participating States must meet, there can be no tenable claim that the ACA fails for lack of notice. Moreover, States have no entitlement to receive any Medicaid funds; they enjoy only the opportunity to accept funds on Congress' terms. Future Congresses are not bound by their predecessors' dispositions; they have authority to spend federal revenue as they see fit. The Federal Government, therefore, is not, as THE CHIEF JUSTICE charges, threatening States with the loss of "existing" funds from one spending program in order to induce them to opt into another program. Congress is simply requiring States to do what

States have long been required to do to receive Medicaid funding: comply with the conditions Congress prescribes for participation.

* * *

Yes, there are federalism-based limits on the use of Congress' conditional spending power. In the leading decision in this area, *South Dakota v. Dole,* 483 U.S. 203 (1987), the Court identified four criteria. The conditions placed on federal grants to States must (1) promote the "general welfare," (2) "unambiguously" inform States what is demanded of them, (3) be germane "to the federal interest in particular national projects or programs," and (4) not "induce the States to engage in activities that would themselves be unconstitutional."

The Court in *Dole* mentioned, but did not adopt, a further limitation, one hypothetically raised a half-century earlier: In "some circumstances," Congress might be prohibited from offering a "financial inducement . . . so coercive as to pass the point at which 'pressure turns into compulsion.'" Prior to today's decision, however, the Court has never ruled that the terms of any grant crossed the indistinct line between temptation and coercion.

* * *

This litigation does not present the concerns that led the Court in *Dole* even to consider the prospect of coercion * * *.

* * *

The starting premise on which THE CHIEF JUSTICE'S coercion analysis rests is that the ACA did not really "extend" Medicaid; instead, Congress created an entirely new program to coexist with the old. THE CHIEF JUSTICE calls the ACA new, but in truth, it simply reaches more of America's poor than Congress originally covered.

* * *

Congress styled and clearly viewed the Medicaid expansion as an amendment to the Medicaid Act, not as a "new" health-care program * * *.

Congress has broad authority to construct or adjust spending programs to meet its contemporary understanding of "the general Welfare." *Helvering v. Davis,* 301 U.S. 619, 640–641 (1937). Courts owe a large measure of respect to Congress' characterization of the grant programs it establishes. Even if courts were inclined to second-guess Congress' conception of the character of its legislation, how would reviewing judges divine whether an Act of Congress, purporting to amend a law, is in reality not an amendment, but a new creation? At what point does an extension become so large that it "transforms" the basic law?

* * *

Consider also that Congress could have repealed Medicaid. Thereafter, Congress could have enacted Medicaid II, a new program combining the pre-2010 coverage with the expanded coverage required by the ACA. By what right does a court stop Congress from building up without first tearing down?

* * *

When future Spending Clause challenges arrive, as they likely will in the wake of today's decision, how will litigants and judges assess whether "a State has a legitimate choice whether to accept the federal conditions in exchange for federal funds"? Are courts to measure the number of dollars the Federal Government might withhold for noncompliance? The portion of the State's budget at stake? And which State's—or States'—budget is determinative: the lead plaintiff, all challenging States (26 in this litigation, many with quite different fiscal situations), or some national median? Does it matter that Florida, unlike most States, imposes no state income tax, and therefore might be able to replace foregone federal funds with new state revenue? Or that the coercion state officials in fact fear is punishment at the ballot box for turning down a politically popular federal grant?

The coercion inquiry, therefore, appears to involve political judgments that defy judicial calculation. See *Baker v. Carr,* 369 U.S. 186, 217 (1962). Even commentators sympathetic to robust enforcement of *Dole*'s limitations have concluded that conceptions of "impermissible coercion" premised on States' perceived inability to decline federal funds "are just too amorphous to be judicially administrable." Baker & Berman, Getting Off the *Dole,* 78 Ind. L.J. 459, 521, 522, n. 307 (2003).

At bottom, my colleagues' position is that the States' reliance on federal funds limits Congress' authority to alter its spending programs. This gets things backwards: Congress, not the States, is tasked with spending federal money in service of the general welfare. And each successive Congress is empowered to appropriate funds as it sees fit. When the 110th Congress reached a conclusion about Medicaid funds that differed from its predecessors' view, it abridged no State's right to "existing," or "pre-existing," funds. For, in fact, there are no such funds. There is only money States *anticipate* receiving from future Congresses.

* * * For the foregoing reasons, I disagree that any such withholding would violate the Spending Clause. Accordingly, I would affirm the decision of the Court of Appeals for the Eleventh Circuit in this regard.

* * *

NOTES AND QUESTIONS

1. Is Justice Ginsburg right that trying to figure out when and if States have been coerced by offers of federal money is a nonjusticiable political question? One of the criteria for a political question, as was made clear in a recent opinion authored by Chief Justice Roberts, is the lack of judicially manageable standards for decision. *See supra* pages 566–576. What are the judicially manageable standards articulated by Chief Justice Roberts in *NFIB* for this inquiry?

2. On the other hand, the Court has almost surely allowed Congress to exceed its (original-meaning) constitutional spending limits by allowing Congress to spend on matters unconnected to its other enumerated powers. That expansive spending doctrine acquires additional significance after ratification of the Sixteenth Amendment, once Congress can control a much larger percentage of the national wealth than under the original Constitution with its apportionment requirement for direct taxes. The role of the States under the post-New Deal fiscal constitution is dramatically different from the original design. As with so many other issues in constitutional law, is the state coercion doctrine an instance of two wrongs making, if not a right, then at least a less-wrong-than-without-it?

3. Decoupling the federal spending power from other enumerated powers only matters if there are limits on those other enumerated powers. Congress does not need to do something indirectly, through spending or spending conditions, if it can do it directly. When Alexander Hamilton proposed his broad theory of federal spending in 1791, it was

against a backdrop of assumed limitations on the federal government's regulatory powers. When *United States v. Butler* was decided in 1935, those same assumptions were in place. *United States v. Lopez, supra* pages 636–649, illustrates that understandings of the federal government's *regulatory* power have changed dramatically in the ensuing years. It is now time to trace that crucial development, which is among the most important developments in American constitutional law.

[Assignment 34]

VI. INTERSTATE (AND INTRASTATE) COMMERCE: 1787 TO 1941

Article I, Section 8, Clause 3: The Congress shall have Power * * * To regulate Commerce with foreign Nations, and among the several States, and with the Indian Tribes;

Article I, Section 8, Clause 18: The Congress shall have Power * * * To make all Laws which shall be necessary and proper for carrying into Execution the foregoing Powers * * *

A major defect in the Articles of Confederation was the absence of a Commerce Clause allowing the Continental Congress to regulate either international or interstate commerce. An amendment to the Articles giving Congress a commerce power was submitted to the States, was supported by twelve of the thirteen States, but was vetoed by the tiny State of Rhode Island. The desire to add a Commerce Clause to the Articles of Confederation was a major cause of the calling of the Philadelphia Constitutional Convention. *See Tennessee Wine & Spirits Retailers Ass'n v. Thomas,* 139 S.Ct. 2449, 2460 (2019). That Convention, of course, ran away and wrote a whole new Constitution, but it is no surprise that, right after giving Congress the power to tax in Article I, Section 8, Clause 1, and the accompanying power to "borrow Money on the credit of the United States," U.S. CONST. art. I, § 8, cl. 2, the Philadelphia Convention also proposed the Commerce Clause of Article I, Section 8, Clause 3.

The grant to Congress of the Commerce Power was not a subject of controversy when the Constitution was ratified. As James Madison put it, the commerce power was a power "from which no apprehensions are entertained." *The Federalist* No. 45 (Madison). From 1789 to the adoption of the Interstate Commerce Act in 1887, Congress passed very few laws under its commerce power. The economic divisions among regions, and the equal division of the Senate between slave state senators and free state senators, led to congressional paralysis until well after the Civil War when it came to regulations of commerce. As a result, most Commerce Clause litigation between 1787 and 1887 involved the question whether the Commerce Clause was an exclusive federal power that of its own force invalidated State laws that interfered with interstate commerce, much as *McCulloch* held that the Constitution of its own force invalidated State taxes on federal instrumentalities. This theory, known as the Dormant Commerce Clause theory, held that the U.S. Constitution created a system of "Dual Federalism" under which federal powers were exclusively federal and state powers were exclusively state. Believers in Dual Federalism thought that only the power of taxation and the incidental powers conferred by the Necessary and Proper Clause were truly concurrent federal and state powers. On this theory, any pre-constitutional power of the States to regulate interstate commerce was surrendered to the federal government in 1788, so State laws regulating such commerce were void, whether or not Congress had chosen to exercise its own powers. More on that shortly. One other consideration that led to a relative dearth of federal regulation of commerce during this period was a narrow understanding of what "commerce" would involve. Agriculture and manufacturing, for example, were understood to be activities distinct from commerce and thus not subject to congressional regulation, which considerably reduced the plausible scope of federal lawmaking. What about navigation?

That was the subject of the first and only big Commerce Clause case between 1789 and 1887. *Gibbons v. Ogden*, 22 U.S. (9 Wheat.) 1 (1824), concerned whether a New York State monopoly on the right to run a commercial ferry boat between New York City and Elizabethtown, New Jersey could be granted by New York to one person, who assigned that monopoly to a man named Ogden. Another man, Gibbons, decided he wanted to compete with Ogden for business, and so he set up his own ferryboat charging his own fees between New York City and Elizabethtown, New Jersey. Gibbons had a federal coasting license, which appears to have authorized him to travel in interstate waters.

Ogden sued to enforce his monopoly in the New York State courts, where he won in that State's highest Court, which enjoined Gibbons from competing with Ogden. Gibbons appealed the State court decision against him to the U.S. Supreme Court, claiming the New York State monopoly violated federal power, either under the Commerce Clause itself or by virtue of the federal coasting license granted by Congress pursuant to the Commerce Clause. Chief Justice John Marshall ruled for Gibbons in the following famous opinion.

Gibbons v. Ogden

22 U.S. (9 Wheat.) 1 (1824)

■ MR. CHIEF JUSTICE MARSHALL delivered the opinion of the Court.

* * *

The words are, "Congress shall have power to regulate commerce with foreign nations, and among the several States, and with the Indian tribes."

The subject to be regulated is commerce; and our constitution being, as was aptly said at the bar, one of enumeration, and not of definition, to ascertain the extent of the power, it becomes necessary to settle the meaning of the word. The counsel for the appellee would limit it to traffic, to buying and selling, or the interchange of commodities, and do not admit that it comprehends navigation. This would restrict a general term, applicable to many objects, to one of its significations. Commerce, undoubtedly, is traffic, but it is something more: it is intercourse. It describes the commercial intercourse between nations, and parts of nations, in all its branches, and is regulated by prescribing rules for carrying on that intercourse. The mind can scarcely conceive a system for regulating commerce between nations, which shall exclude all laws concerning navigation, which shall be silent on the admission of the vessels of the one nation into the ports of the other, and be confined to prescribing rules for the conduct of individuals, in the actual employment of buying and selling, or of barter.

If commerce does not include navigation, the government of the Union has no direct power over that subject, and can make no law prescribing what shall constitute American vessels, or requiring that they shall be navigated by American seamen. Yet this power has been exercised from the commencement of the government, has been exercised with the consent of all, and has been understood by all to be a commercial regulation. All America understands, and has uniformly understood, the word "commerce," to comprehend navigation. It was so understood, and must have been so understood, when the constitution was framed. The power over commerce, including navigation, was one of the primary objects for which the people of America adopted their government, and must have been contemplated in forming it. The convention must have used the word in that sense, because all have understood it in that sense; and the attempt to restrict it comes too late.

* * *

The word used in the constitution, then, comprehends, and has been always understood to comprehend, navigation within its meaning; and a power to regulate navigation, is as expressly granted, as if that term had been added to the word "commerce."

To what commerce does this power extend? The constitution informs us, to commerce "with foreign nations, and among the several States, and with the Indian tribes."

It has, we believe, been universally admitted that these words comprehend every species of commercial intercourse between the United States and foreign nations. No sort of trade can be carried on between this country and any other to which this power does not extend. It has been truly said, that commerce, as the word is used in the constitution, is a unit, every part of which is indicated by the term.

If this be the admitted meaning of the word, in its application to foreign nations, it must carry the same meaning throughout the sentence, and remain a unit, unless there be some plain intelligible cause which alters it.

The subject to which the power is next applied, is to commerce "among the several States." The word "among" means intermingled with. A thing which is among others, is intermingled with them. Commerce among the States cannot stop at the external boundary line of each State, but may be introduced into the interior.

It is not intended to say that these words comprehend that commerce, which is completely internal, which is carried on between man and man in a State, or between different parts of the same State, and which does not extend to or affect other States. Such a power would be inconvenient, and is certainly unnecessary.

Comprehensive as the word "among" is, it may very properly be restricted to that commerce which concerns more States than one. The phrase is not one which would probably have been selected to indicate the completely interior traffic of a State, because it is not an apt phrase for that purpose; and the enumeration of the particular classes of commerce, to which the power was to be extended, would not have been made, had the intention been to extend the power to every description. The enumeration presupposes something not enumerated; and that something, if we regard the language or the subject of the sentence, must be the exclusively internal commerce of a State. The genius and character of the whole government seem to be, that its action is to be applied to all the external concerns of the nation, and to those internal concerns which affect the States generally; but not to those which are completely within a particular State, which do not affect other States, and with which it is not necessary to interfere for the purpose of executing some of the general powers of the government. The completely internal commerce of a State, then, may be considered as reserved for the State itself.

But, in regulating commerce with foreign nations, the power of Congress does not stop at the jurisdictional lines of the several States. It would be a very useless power, if it could not pass those lines. The commerce of the United States with foreign nations, is that of the whole United States. Every district has a right to participate in it. The deep streams which penetrate our country in every direction, pass through the interior of almost every State in the Union, and furnish the means of exercising this right. If Congress has the power to regulate it, that power must be exercised whenever the subject exists. If it exists within the States, if a foreign voyage may commence or terminate at a port within a State, then the power of Congress may be exercised within a State.

This principle is, if possible, still more clear, when applied to commerce "among the several States." They either join each other, in which case they are separated by a mathematical line, or they are remote from each other, in which case other States lie between them. What is commerce "among" them; and how is it to be conducted? Can a trading expedition between two adjoining States, commence and terminate outside of each? And if the trading intercourse be between two States remote from each other, must it not commence in one, terminate in the other, and probably pass through a third? Commerce among the States must, of necessity, be commerce with the States * * *.

We are now arrived at the inquiry—What is this power?

It is the power to regulate; that is, to prescribe the rule by which commerce is to be governed. This power, like all others vested in Congress, is complete in itself, may be exercised to its utmost extent, and acknowledges no limitations, other than are prescribed in the constitution. These are expressed in plain terms, and do not affect the questions which arise in this case, or which have been discussed at the bar. If, as has always been understood, the sovereignty of Congress, though limited to specified objects, is plenary as to those objects, the power over commerce with foreign nations, and among the several States, is vested in Congress as absolutely as it would be in a single government, having in its constitution the same restrictions on the exercise of the power as are found in the constitution of the United States. The wisdom and the discretion of Congress, their identity with the people, and the influence which their constituents possess at elections, are, in this, as in many other instances, as that, for example, of declaring war, the sole restraints on which they have relied, to secure them from its abuse. They are the restraints on which the people must often rely solely, in all representative governments.

The power of Congress, then, comprehends navigation, within the limits of every State in the Union; so far as that navigation may be, in any manner, connected with "commerce with foreign nations, or among the several States, or with the Indian tribes." It may, of consequence, pass the jurisdictional line of New-York, and act upon the very waters to which the prohibition now under consideration applies.

But it has been urged with great earnestness, that, although the power of Congress to regulate commerce with foreign nations, and among the several States, be co-extensive with the subject itself, and have no other limits than are prescribed in the constitution, yet the States may severally exercise the same power, within their respective jurisdictions. In support of this argument, it is said, that they possessed it as an inseparable attribute of sovereignty, before the formation of the constitution, and still retain it, except so far as they have surrendered it by that instrument; that this principle results from the nature of the government, and is secured by the tenth amendment; that an affirmative grant of power is not exclusive unless in its own nature it be such that the continued exercise of it by the former possessor is inconsistent with the grant, and that this is not of that description.

The appellant [Gibbons], conceding these postulates, except the last, contends, that full power to regulate a particular subject, implies the whole power, and leaves no residuum; that a grant of the whole is incompatible with the existence of a right in another to any part of it.

Both parties have appealed to the constitution, to legislative acts, and judicial decisions; and have drawn arguments from all these sources, to support and illustrate the propositions they respectively maintain.

* * *

In discussing the question, whether this power is still in the States, in the case under consideration, we may dismiss from it the inquiry, whether it is surrendered by the mere grant to Congress, or is retained until Congress shall exercise the power. We may dismiss that inquiry, because it has been exercised, and the regulations which Congress deemed it proper to make, are now in full operation. The sole question is, can a State regulate commerce with foreign nations and among the States, while Congress is regulating it?

* * *

It has been contended by the counsel for the appellant, that, as the word "to regulate" implies in its nature, full power over the thing to be regulated, it excludes, necessarily, the action of all others that would perform the same operation on the same thing. That regulation is designed for the entire result, applying to those parts which remain as they were, as well as to those which are altered. It produces a uniform whole, which is as much disturbed and deranged by changing what the regulating power designs to leave untouched, as that on which it has operated.

There is great force in this argument, and the Court is not satisfied that it has been refuted.

Since, however, in exercising the power of regulating their own purely internal affairs, whether of trading or police, the States may sometimes enact laws, the validity of which depends on their interfering with, and being contrary to, an act of Congress passed in pursuance of the constitution, the Court will enter upon the inquiry, whether the laws of New-York, as expounded by the highest tribunal of that State, have, in their application to this case, come into collision with an act of Congress, and deprived a citizen of a right to which that act entitles him. Should this collision exist, it will be immaterial whether those laws were passed in virtue of a concurrent power "to regulate commerce with foreign nations and among the several States," or in virtue of a power to regulate their domestic trade and police. In one case and the other, the acts of New-York must yield to the law of Congress; and the decision sustaining the privilege they confer, against a right given by a law of the Union, must be erroneous.* * *

* * *

* * *[T]he framers of our Constitution foresaw this state of things, and provided for it, by declaring the supremacy not only of itself, but of the laws made in pursuance of it. The nullity of any act, inconsistent with the Constitution, is produced by the declaration that the Constitution is the supreme law * * *. In every such case, the act of Congress, or the treaty, is supreme; and the law of the State, though enacted in the exercise of powers not controverted, must yield to it.

* * *

The first section [of the federal coasting law under which Gibbons was licensed] declares, that vessels enrolled by virtue of a previous law, and certain other vessels, enrolled as described in that act, and having a license in force, as is by the act required, "and no others, shall be deemed ships or vessels of the United States, entitled to the privileges of ships or vessels employed in the coasting trade."

This section seems to the Court to contain a positive enactment, that the vessels it describes shall be entitled to the privileges of ships or vessels employed in the coasting trade. These privileges cannot be separated from the trade, and cannot be enjoyed, unless the trade may be prosecuted. The grant of the privilege is an idle, empty form, conveying nothing, unless it convey the right to which the privilege is attached, and in the exercise of which its whole value consists. To construe these words otherwise than as entitling the ships or vessels described, to carry on the coasting trade, would be, we think, to disregard the apparent intent of the act.

* * *

But, if the license be a permit to carry on the coasting trade, the respondent denies that these boats were engaged in that trade, or that the decree under consideration has restrained them from prosecuting it. The boats of the appellant were, we are told, employed in the transportation of passengers; and this is no part of that commerce which Congress may regulate.

* * * A coasting vessel employed in the transportation of passengers, is as much a portion of the American marine, as one employed in the transportation of a cargo; and no reason is perceived why such vessel should be withdrawn from the regulating power of that government, which has been thought best fitted for the purpose generally. The provisions of the law respecting native seamen, and respecting ownership, are as applicable to vessels carrying men, as to vessels carrying manufactures; and no reason is perceived why the power over the subject should not be placed in the same hands. The argument urged at the bar, rests on the foundation, that the power of Congress does not extend to navigation, as a branch of commerce, and can only be applied to that subject incidentally and occasionally. But if that foundation be removed, we must show some plain, intelligible distinction, supported by the constitution, or by reason, for discriminating between the power of Congress over vessels employed in navigating the same seas. We can perceive no such distinction.

* * *

Powerful and ingenious minds, taking, as postulates, that the powers expressly granted to the government of the Union, are to be contracted by construction, into the narrowest possible compass, and that the original powers of the States are retained, if any possible construction will retain them, may, by a course of well digested, but refined and metaphysical reasoning, founded on these premises, explain away the constitution of our country, and leave it, a magnificent structure, indeed, to look at, but totally unfit for use. They may so entangle and perplex the understanding, as to obscure principles, which were before thought quite plain, and induce doubts where, if the mind were to pursue its own course, none would be perceived. In such a case, it is peculiarly necessary to recur to safe and fundamental principles to sustain those principles, and when sustained, to make them the tests of the arguments to be examined.

[*Editors' Note: The concurring opinion of Justice Johnson, who argued that federal power over commerce is exclusive even when it has not been exercised by Congress, is omitted.*]

NOTES AND QUESTIONS

1. Despite the case's extensive discussion (and, as usual, we have edited out much of it), this is a fairly simple case: Congress had passed a statute licensing someone to operate a ship in interstate commerce, and New York wanted to stop them from operating. If the congressional statute was valid, of course it overrode, or "pre-empted," the contrary State statute. Federal law beats state law if they are in conflict. All that is necessary to decide this case is to figure out whether Congress could validly grant an interstate shipping license. That turns on whether commercial navigation between New York and New Jersey is "Commerce * * * among the several States." Of course it is. *See* Randy E. Barnett, *The Original Meaning of the Commerce Clause,* 68 U. CHI. L. REV. 101, 125–29 (2001). Transporting people by ferry boat, for money, from one State to another is obviously interstate commerce. Case closed. As was often his wont, however Chief Justice Marshall's opinion delves into matters far beyond the facts of the case, and *Gibbons'* dicta has had far more impact than its modest holding.

2. Dicta # 1: "The power of Congress, then, comprehends navigation, *within the limits of every State in the Union, so far as that navigation may be in any manner connected"* to interstate, foreign, or Indian commerce. Does that mean that Congress can regulate matters on a wholly intrastate portion of an interstate navigable river (such as requiring the removal of obstructions or controlling the height of bridges) because that would be "in any manner connected" to interstate commerce? That is surely what Chief Justice Marshall meant. And Chief Justice Marshall was surely (at least largely) right. But he was not right because Congress would thereby be regulating "Commerce * * * among the several States." Instead, such intrastate regulations of navigation would have to be justified, under the Necessary and Proper Clause, as incidental laws "necessary and proper for carrying into Execution" the power to regulate interstate commerce. The source of the power matters. If wholly intrastate matters are literally "Commerce * * * among the several States," then, as Chief Justice Marshall further observed, "[t]his power, like all others vested in Congress, is complete in itself, may be exercised to its utmost extent, and acknowledges no limitations other than are prescribed in the Constitution," such as the rule against port preferences. But if intrastate matters are not themselves interstate commerce and can be regulated only pursuant to the Necessary and Proper Clause, those laws are subject to whatever internal constraints the Necessary and Proper Clause contains. It seems clear that Chief Justice Marshall was trying to decide, not just this case about interstate ferry traffic, but the larger controversy in the 1820s about Congress's power to make "internal improvements." The resulting confusion of the power to regulate "Commerce" and the power to pass incidental laws for executing the power to regulate "Commerce" is still with us today, as you will see.

3. Dicta #2: "The power of Congress, then, comprehends navigation * * *." Isn't this the same as dicta #1? Yes, but here the issue is not what Chief Justice Marshall said but what he did not say. He did not say that Congress's power "comprehends *commercial* navigation." *Gibbons* involved transport of passengers for hire. What if Gibbons just wanted to sail his steamboat for fun between New York and New Jersey? Could Congress tell New York that it cannot regulate steamboat traffic for leisure within its waters? How is pleasure boating possibly "Commerce * * * among the several States"? Unless one adopts an unsustainably broad conception of "Commerce" as including all human interaction, *see supra* page 650, it rather obviously is not. If Congress can override state laws on pleasure boating, it would have to be through the Necessary and Proper Clause. And again, the source of the power matters very much for determining its scope. Maybe, under some circumstances recreation navigation interferes with commercial navigation. If so, that is far from apparent on the very limited facts of *Gibbons v. Ogden*.

4. Dicta # 3: "The genius and character of the whole government seem to be that its action is to be applied to all the external concerns of the nation, *and to those internal concerns which affect the States generally*, but not to those which are completely within a particular State, which *do not affect other States*, and with which it *is not necessary* to interfere for the purpose of executing some of the general powers of the government." Suppose that a commercial transaction takes place entirely within the boundaries of one State; a person in Ohio, for example, buys wheat from his or her neighbor, or a factory in Georgia emits pollutants into the surrounding Georgia air. Can Congress regulate either of those activities? Neither activity is itself "Commerce * * * among the several States" by any plausible understanding; both activities take place entirely within one State. But both activities have some measure of *effects* on other States. The pollution in Georgia might travel to Florida or South Carolina, depending on wind patterns. The neighborly purchase of wheat has some effect, however minimal, on the overall market price for wheat and thus, like the flapping of a butterfly's wings, might affect economic conditions in Wyoming. Does that mean that Congress can regulate either or both of those intrastate activities because they might "affect" interstate commerce? Chief Justice Marshall's dicta suggests yes. Once again, he does not specifically identify the source of this supposed congressional power. If matters become "Commerce" simply by affecting other States, then the prior dicta about the unlimited character of the commerce power comes into play. Note, however, that Chief Justice Marshall adds here that federal power does not extend to matters for which "it is not necessary" to interfere with the States. That seems like an obvious reference to the Necessary and Proper Clause. So exactly when is it "necessary and proper for carrying into Execution" federal powers for Congress to regulate intrastate activity that is not itself "Commerce * * * among the several States"? *Gibbons* does not say, because it does not need to say. Later cases will have to sort this out. Chief Justice Marshall was obviously doing battlefield preparation for those looming conflicts.

5. Dicta #4: "It has been contended by the counsel for the appellant that, as the word 'to regulate' implies in its nature full power over the thing to be regulated, it excludes necessarily the action of all others that would perform the same operation on the same thing. That regulation is designed for the entire result, applying to those parts which remain as they were, as well as to those which are altered. It produces a uniform whole which is as much disturbed and deranged by changing what the regulating power designs to leave untouched as that on which it has operated. There is great force in this argument, and the Court is not satisfied that it has been refuted." Because there was a federal statute giving Gibbons the right to operate his boat, the Court did not need to decide whether the federal commerce power was *exclusive* of the power of the States. Even if both levels of government had power over commerce, Congress's exercise of that power

trumped New York's exercise. But what if there was no federal coasting license? Gibbons would still have been arguing against New York's monopoly regulation on the ground that the Constitution divested New York, and every other State, of *all power* over interstate, foreign, and Indian commerce. The Constitution, on this reasoning, created a baseline rule of free trade and exchange, subject only to national regulation. If Congress chose not to exercise its power, the State could no more change that baseline with commercial regulations than they could override positive congressional enactments. Justice Johnson thought this argument sound, and while Chief Justice Marshall did not need to adopt it, he did say that he found it persuasive. Thus was borne the theory of the "Dormant Commerce Clause," which invalidates State laws and regulations even when they are not formally pre-empted by affirmative federal action. If the Court had simply adopted the view that the commerce power was exclusively federal, application of this "Dormant Commerce Clause" doctrine would be relatively easy: If an activity was interstate, foreign, or Indian commerce, no State could regulate it—period. (Of course, given the post-New Deal understanding of "commerce," that would effectively disable States from acting on virtually any subject.) However, when the Court formally adopted the "Dormant Commerce Clause" theory half a century after *Gibbons,* it said:

> It is not necessary to the present case to go at large into the much-debated question whether the power given to Congress by the Constitution to regulate commerce among the States is exclusive. In the earlier decisions of this court it was said to have been so entirely vested in Congress that no part of it can be exercised by a State. It has, indeed, often been argued, and sometimes intimated, by the court that, so far as Congress has not legislated on the subject, the States may legislate respecting interstate commerce * * *. However this may be, the rule has been asserted with great clearness, that whenever the subjects over which a power to regulate commerce is asserted are in their nature national, or admit of one uniform system or plan of regulation, they may justly be said to be of such a nature as to require exclusive legislation by Congress.

In re State Freight Tax, 82 U.S. (15 Wall.) 232, 279–80 (1872). Over the next century, the Court, in trying to figure out how to sort out valid from invalid State commercial regulations, settled on a two-part inquiry:

> Although the criteria for determining the validity of state statutes affecting interstate commerce have been variously stated, the general rule that emerges can be phrased as follows: Where the statute regulates *even-handedly* to effectuate a legitimate local public interest, and its effects on interstate commerce are only *incidental,* it will be upheld unless the burden imposed on such commerce is clearly excessive in relation to the putative local benefits. If a legitimate local purpose is found, then the question becomes one of degree. And the extent of the burden that will be tolerated will of course depend on the nature of the local interest involved, and on whether it could be promoted as well with a lesser impact on interstate activities. Occasionally the Court has candidly undertaken a balancing approach in resolving these issues, but more frequently it has spoken in terms of 'direct' and 'indirect' effects and burdens.

Pike v. Bruce Church, Inc., 397 U.S. 137, 142 (1970) (emphasis added). Thus, State regulations cannot *discriminate* against interstate (as opposed to intrastate) commerce, and, even if neutral between in-state and out-of-state business, they cannot unduly burden commercial affairs. As the Court summarized it in 2018:

> * * * Modern precedents rest upon two primary principles that mark the boundaries of a State's authority to regulate interstate commerce. First, state

> regulations may not discriminate against interstate commerce; and second, States may not impose undue burdens on interstate commerce. State laws that discriminate against interstate commerce face "a virtually *per se* rule of invalidity." *Granholm v. Heald,* 544 U.S. 460, 476, (2005) (internal quotation marks omitted). State laws that "regulat[e] even-handedly to effectuate a legitimate local public interest . . . will be upheld unless the burden imposed on such commerce is clearly excessive in relation to the putative local benefits." *Pike v. Bruce Church, Inc.,* 397 U.S. 137 (1970).

South Dakota v. Wayfair, Inc., 138 S.Ct. 2080, 2090–91 (2018). The Court has also held, however, that Congress can by statute authorize States to enact laws that would violate the Dormant Commerce Clause doctrine in the absence of the authorizing congressional legislation. *See Prudential Insurance Co. v. Benjamin,* 328 U.S. 408 (1946). While several Justices have called for reconsideration of this doctrine, especially the part that requires courts to take a "balancing approach" to deciding whether State burdens are "clearly excessive," *see, e.g., Tyler Pipe Industries, Inc. v. Washington Dep't of Revenue,* 483 U.S. 232, 254 (1987) (Scalia, J., concurring in part and dissenting in part), the Court has recently strongly reaffirmed its commitment to the Dormant Commerce Clause doctrine. *See Tennessee Wine & Spirits Retailers Ass'n v. Thomas,* 139 S.Ct. 2449, 2459–61 (2019).

6. As we explained earlier, it seems clear that, as a matter of original meaning, most federal powers are exclusive. *See supra* pages 595–596; *see also* Steven G. Calabresi, *The Right to Buy Health Insurance Across State Lines: Crony Capitalism and the Supreme Court,* 81 U. CINN. L. REV. 1447, 1459–76 (2013). There is no obvious reason why this would not apply to the commerce power, in which case a very powerful version of the Dormant Commerce Clause doctrine is probably correct. The difficulty with this view, as we have noted, is that it means that state power shrinks as federal power expands. In 1788, the exclusive commerce power was a narrow commerce power. In 2020, an exclusive commerce power would negate almost all state authority. If there had been any hint in 1788 that the commerce power would extend as far as modern law has taken it, there is no chance that it would have been crafted as an exclusive federal power (and, indeed, there is no chance that the Constitution would have been ratified). Does that make the existing Dormant Commerce Clause doctrine, with all of its uncertainties and hard-to-fathom doctrinal twists, a tolerable second-best solution?

7. The hundred years after *Gibbons,* until the 1930s, produced a number of important decisions leading up to modern law. One of the most important was *United States v. E.C. Knight Co.*, 156 U.S. 1 (1895), in which the Supreme Court held the Sherman Antitrust Act unconstitutional as it was applied to the manufacturing of sugar in-state by the E.C. Knight Company prior to the shipment of that sugar in interstate commerce. Chief Justice Fuller distinguished between "manufacturing," which was controlled by the States, and "commerce," which was within the power of the federal government. Fuller famously said:

> Doubtless the power to control the manufacture of a given thing involves in a certain sense the control of its disposition, but this is a secondary and not the primary sense; and although the exercise of that power may result in bringing the power of commerce into play, it does not control it, and affects it only incidentally and indirectly. *Commerce succeeds to manufacture and is not a part of it.*

Id. at 253 (emphasis added). This followed naturally from a decision from seven years earlier:

No distinction is more popular to the common mind, or more clearly expressed in economic and political literature, than that between manufactures and commerce. Manufacture is transformation—the fashioning of raw materials into a change of form for use. The functions of commerce are different. The buying and selling and the transportation incidental thereto constitute commerce; and the regulation of commerce in the constitutional sense embraces the regulation at least of such transportation. The legal definition of the term, as given by this court in *County of Mobile v. Kimball*, 102 U. S. 691, 702, is as follows: "Commerce with foreign nations and among the states, strictly considered, consists in intercourse and traffic, including in these terms navigation and the transportation and transit of persons and property, as well as the purchase, sale, and exchange of commodities." If it be held that the term includes the regulation of all such manufactures as are intended to be the subject of commercial transactions in the future, it is impossible to deny that it would also include all productive industries that contemplate the same thing. The result would be that Congress would be invested, to the exclusion of the States, with the power to regulate, not only manufactures, but also agriculture, horticulture, stock raising, domestic fisheries, mining—in short, every branch of human industry.

Kidd v. Pearson, 128 U.S. 1, 20–21 (1888). Thus, the case law of that era left entirely to the States (subject to the Dormant Commerce Clause doctrine, the Fourteenth Amendment, and other constitutional limitations) such areas as 1) manufacturing, 2) farming, 3) mining, 4) most criminal law, 5) tort, contract, property, and family law, 6) education, 7) public health and safety, and 8) public morals.

8. If public morals are a state rather than federal function, does that mean that Congress cannot regulate commerce for moral purposes? Can Congress altogether ban interstate transactions in certain goods deemed immoral? These issues were raised by "An Act for the Suppression of Lottery Traffic through National and Interstate Commerce and the Postal Service, Subject to the Jurisdiction and Laws of the United States," Act of Mar. 2, 1895, ch. 191, 28 Stat. 963, which criminalized carrying or transporting lottery tickets across state lines. A 5–4 Court upheld a conviction under this statute. After finding that lottery tickets are valuable items, and thus articles of commerce when transported or carried, the Court held:

But it is said that the statute in question does not regulate the carrying of lottery tickets from State to State, but by punishing those who cause them to be so carried Congress in effect prohibits such carrying; that in respect of the carrying from one State to another of articles or things that are, in fact, or according to usage in business, the subjects of commerce, the authority given Congress was not to *prohibit*, but only to *regulate*. This view was earnestly pressed at the bar by learned counsel, and must be examined.

* * *

We have said that the carrying from State to State of lottery tickets constitutes interstate commerce, and that the regulation of such commerce is within the power of Congress under the Constitution. Are we prepared to say that a provision which is, in effect, a *prohibition* of the carriage of such articles from State to State is not a fit or appropriate mode for the *regulation* of that particular kind of commerce? If lottery traffic, *carried on through interstate commerce*, is a matter of which Congress may take cognizance and over which its power may be exerted, can it be possible that it must tolerate the traffic, and simply regulate the manner in which it may be carried on? Or may not

Congress, for the protection of the people of all the States, and under the power to regulate interstate commerce, devise such means, within the scope of the Constitution, and not prohibited by it, as will drive that traffic out of commerce among the States?

In determining whether regulation may not under some circumstances properly take the form or have the effect of prohibition, the nature of the interstate traffic which it was sought by the act of May 2d, 1895, to suppress cannot be overlooked. When enacting that statute Congress no doubt shared the views upon the subject of lotteries heretofore expressed by this court. In *Phalen v. Virginia*, 8 How. 163, after observing that the suppression of nuisances injurious to public health or morality is among the most important duties of Government, this court said: 'Experience has shown that the common forms of gambling are comparatively innocuous when placed in contrast with the widespread pestilence of lotteries" * * *.

If a State, when considering legislation for the suppression of lotteries within its own limits, may properly take into view the evils that inhere in the raising of money, in that mode, why may not Congress, invested with the power to regulate commerce among the several States, provide that such commerce shall not be polluted by the carrying of lottery tickets from one state to another? * * *

* * *

* * * If the carrying of lottery tickets from one State to another be interstate commerce, and if Congress is of opinion that an effective regulation for the suppression of lotteries, carried on through such commerce, is to make it a criminal offense to cause lottery tickets to be carried from one State to another, we know of no authority in the courts to hold that the means thus devised are not appropriate and necessary to protect the country at large against a species of interstate commerce which, although in general use and somewhat favored in both national and state legislation in the early history of the country, has grown into disrepute and has become offensive to the entire people of the nation. It is a kind of traffic which no one can be entitled to pursue as of right.

* * *

It is said, however, that if, in order to suppress lotteries carried on through interstate commerce, Congress may exclude lottery tickets from such commerce, that principle leads necessarily to the conclusion that Congress may arbitrarily exclude from commerce among the States any article, commodity, or thing, of whatever kind or nature, or however useful or valuable, which it may choose, no matter with what motive, to declare shall not be carried from one State to another. It will be time enough to consider the constitutionality of such legislation when we must do so. The present case does not require the court to declare the full extent of the power that Congress may exercise in the regulation of commerce among the States. We may, however, repeat, in this connection, what the court has heretofore said, that the power of Congress to regulate commerce among the States, although plenary, cannot be deemed arbitrary, since it is subject to such limitations or restrictions as are prescribed by the Constitution. This power, therefore, may not be exercised so as to infringe rights secured or protected by that instrument * * *.

188 U.S. at 354–56, 358, 362–63. Four justices dissented, agreeing that Congress could use its enumerated postal power to prohibit sending lottery tickets through the mail but maintaining that it could not prohibit the simple transportation of tickets in person across state lines. The Court had previously—somewhat oddly—held that the formation of a contract was not itself an act of commerce. *See Paul v. Virginia,* 75 U.S. (8 Wall.) 168 (1868). (Such an act may not be *interstate* commerce, but it is surely commerce, no?) From that premise, the dissent reasoned: "If a lottery ticket is not an article of commerce, how can it become so when placed in an envelope or box or other covering, and transported by an express company? To say that the mere carrying of an article which is not an article of commerce in and of itself nevertheless becomes such the moment it is to be transported from one state to another, is to transform a non-commercial article into a commercial one simply because it is transported. I cannot conceive that any such result can properly follow." 188 U.S. at 371 (Fuller, C.J., dissenting). The dissent also concluded, through reasoning that is frankly hard to follow, "that the right of passage of persons and property from one state to another cannot be prohibited by Congress," *id.* at 374, though Congress can absolutely forbid *foreign* traffic in both goods and persons under its power to regulate "Commerce with foreign Nations." To continue the theme of this section: It is hard to see how carrying an item across State lines as a consumer and not as part of a sales transaction is itself an act of "commerce," unless one understands "commerce" to include all human interaction. The mere transport of the item is not itself a commercial act of buying or selling, though such acts may precede or follow it. Accordingly, any power that Congress has to regulate the interstate *transport* of items comes not from the Commerce Clause but from the Necessary and Proper Clause, as an incident to the power to regulate true acts of commerce. In any event, in the wake of *Champion v. Ames*, similar decisions followed upholding federal power to regulate interstate shipment of meatpacking, *see Swift v. United States*, 196 U.S. 375 (1905) and of women for debauched purposes. *See Caminetti v. United States*, 242 U.S. 470 (1917). One thing that *Champion v. Ames* did settle was that Congress could regulate interstate commerce for moral purposes as well as for commercial/business purposes.

The limits of Congress's power were tested in a big way in 1918. Recall that, in that era, manufacturing was not considered commerce, so Congress had no direct power to regulate the process of manufacturing. Similarly, the execution of contracts was not considered commerce. The result was that Congress, in 1918, had no power to determine working conditions in factories; that was solely a state function. And if Congress could not regulate factory working conditions, it could not prohibit child labor on a nationwide basis. The solution was to prohibit the *interstate transportation* of goods produced with child labor. *See* Act of Sept. 1, 1916, ch. 432, 39 Stat. 675. Would that work when a direct prohibition on child labor would not? On the reasoning of *Champion v. Ames* and subsequent cases, it was hard to see why that would not work. But the Supreme Court, in yet another 5–4 decision in *Hammer v. Daggenhart,* 247 U.S. 251 (1918), had other ideas:

> In each of these [prior cases] * * * the use of interstate transportation was necessary to the accomplishment of harmful results. In other words, although the power over interstate transportation was to regulate, that could only be accomplished by prohibiting the use of the facilities of interstate commerce to effect the evil intended.
>
> This element is wanting in the present case. The thing intended to be accomplished by this statute is the denial of the facilities of interstate commerce to those manufacturers in the States who employ children within the prohibited ages. The act in its effect does not regulate transportation among

the States, but aims to standardize the ages at which children may be employed in mining and manufacturing within the States. The goods shipped are of themselves harmless. The act permits them to be freely shipped after thirty days from the time of their removal from the factory. When offered for shipment, and before transportation begins, the labor of their production is over, and the mere fact that they were intended for interstate commerce transportation does not make their production subject to federal control under the commerce power.

Commerce "consists of intercourse and traffic * * * and includes the transportation of persons and property, as well as the purchase, sale and exchange of commodities." The making of goods and the mining of coal are not commerce, nor does the fact that these things are to be afterwards shipped or used in interstate commerce make their production a part thereof.

Over interstate transportation, or its incidents, the regulatory power of Congress is ample, but the production of articles, intended for interstate commerce, is a matter of local regulation.

* * * If it were otherwise, all manufacture intended for interstate shipment would be brought under federal control to the practical exclusion of the authority of the States, a result certainly not contemplated by the framers of the Constitution when they vested in Congress the authority to regulate commerce among the States.

It is further contended that the authority of Congress may be exerted to control interstate commerce in the shipment of child-made goods because of the effect of the circulation of such goods in other States where the evil of this class of labor has been recognized by local legislation, and the right to thus employ child labor has been more rigorously restrained than in the State of production. In other words, that the unfair competition, thus engendered, may be controlled by closing the channels of interstate commerce to manufacturers in those States where the local laws do not meet what Congress deems to be the more just standard of other States.

There is no power vested in Congress to require the States to exercise their police power so as to prevent possible unfair competition. Many causes may cooperate to give one State, by reason of local laws or conditions, an economic advantage over others. The Commerce Clause was not intended to give to Congress a general authority to equalize such conditions. In some of the States laws have been passed fixing minimum wages for women, in others the local law regulates the hours of labor of women in various employments. Business done in such States may be at an economic disadvantage when compared with States which have no such regulations; surely, this fact does not give Congress the power to deny transportation in interstate commerce to those who carry on business where the hours of labor and the rate of compensation for women have not been fixed by a standard in use in other States and approved by Congress.

* * *

In our view the necessary effect of this act is, by means of a prohibition against the movement in interstate commerce of ordinary commercial commodities to regulate the hours of labor of children in factories and mines within the States, a purely state authority. Thus the act in a two fold sense is repugnant to the Constitution. It not only transcends the authority delegated to Congress over commerce but also exerts a power as to a purely local matter

> to which the federal authority does not extend. The far reaching result of upholding the act cannot be more plainly indicated than by pointing out that if Congress can thus regulate matters entrusted to local authority by prohibition of the movement of commodities in interstate commerce, all freedom of commerce will be at an end, and the power of the States over local matters may be eliminated, and thus our system of government be practically destroyed.

247 U.S. at 271–73, 276. Four justices dissented:

> The act does not meddle with anything belonging to the States. They may regulate their internal affairs and their domestic commerce as they like. But when they seek to send their products across the state line they are no longer within their rights. If there were no Constitution and no Congress their power to cross the line would depend upon their neighbors. Under the Constitution such commerce belongs not to the States but to Congress to regulate. It may carry out its views of public policy whatever indirect effect they may have upon the activities of the States. Instead of being encountered by a prohibitive tariff at her boundaries the State encounters the public policy of the United States which it is for Congress to express. The public policy of the United States is shaped with a view to the benefit of the nation as a whole. If, as has been the case within the memory of men still living, a State should take a different view of the propriety of sustaining a lottery from that which generally prevails, I cannot believe that the fact would require a different decision from that reached in *Champion v. Ames*. Yet in that case it would be said with quite as much force as in this that Congress was attempting to intermeddle with the State's domestic affairs. The national welfare as understood by Congress may require a different attitude within its sphere from that of some self-seeking State. It seems to me entirely constitutional for Congress to enforce its understanding by all the means at its command.

Id. at 281 (Holmes, J., dissenting). *Hammer v. Daggenhart* initiated a more than twenty-year fight over whether Congress could regulate the interstate transportation of goods made with child labor, without a minimum wage being paid, or under other working conditions deemed inappropriate by Congress. We will shortly get to the resolution of that fight, and the birth of the modern era of federal power, in *United States v. Darby*, 312 U.S. 100 (1941), but one more way station first has to be covered.

9. From *Gibbons v. Ogden* onward, it has been clear that there is a close connection between the Commerce Clause and the Necessary and Proper Clause when ascertaining the scope of congressional power. Many objects that appear to be likely candidates for congressional power, such as removing physical obstacles to interstate travel from rivers, are not themselves regulations of "Commerce * * * among the several States" but might well be laws "necessary and proper for carrying into Execution" direct exercises of the commerce power. Congress, for example, has authority under the Commerce Clause to set rates for interstate rail traffic but has no authority under that clause to set rates for wholly *intrastate* travel. Using the Commerce Clause, Congress can fix the rates for travel from Dallas, Texas to Shreveport, Louisiana, but not the rates from Dallas, Texas to anywhere else in the State of Texas. But suppose that Texas rail carriers set lower prices for shipments within Texas than for shipments from Texas to Louisiana, thereby discriminating against interstate commerce? Congress can obviously end that discrimination by ordering lower prices for the Texas-Louisiana trips, but can it do so by ordering higher prices for the Texas-Texas trips—not because Texas-Texas trips are interstate commerce (they obviously are not) but because regulating Texas-Texas trips is

"necessary and proper for carrying into Execution" the undoubted congressional power to fix rates for the Texas-Louisiana routes? In 1914, the Supreme Court said yes:

> Congress is empowered to regulate,—that is, to provide the law for the government of interstate commerce * * *. Its authority, extending to these interstate carriers as instruments of interstate commerce, necessarily embraces the right to control their operations in all matters having such a close and substantial relation to interstate traffic that the control is essential or appropriate to the security of that traffic, to the efficiency of the interstate service, and to the maintenance of conditions under which interstate commerce may be conducted upon fair terms and without molestation or hindrance. As it is competent for Congress to legislate to these ends, unquestionably it may seek their attainment by requiring that the agencies of interstate commerce shall not be used in such manner as to cripple, retard, or destroy it. The fact that carriers are instruments of intrastate commerce, as well as of interstate commerce, does not derogate from the complete and paramount authority of Congress over the latter or preclude the Federal power from being exerted to prevent the intrastate operations of such carriers from being made a means of injury to that which has been confided to Federal care. Wherever the interstate and intrastate transactions of carriers are so related that the government of the one involves the control of the other, it is Congress, and not the State, that is entitled to prescribe the final and dominant rule, for otherwise Congress would be denied the exercise of its constitutional authority and the State, and not the Nation, would be supreme within the national field.
>
> * * *
>
> * * * This is not to say that Congress possesses the authority to regulate the internal commerce of a State, as such, but that it does possess the power to foster and protect interstate commerce, and to take all measures necessary or appropriate to that end, although intrastate transactions of interstate carriers may thereby be controlled.
>
> This principle is applicable here. We find no reason to doubt that Congress is entitled to keep the highways of interstate communication open to interstate traffic upon fair and equal terms. That an unjust discrimination in the rates of a common carrier, by which one person or locality is unduly favored as against another under substantially similar conditions of traffic, constitutes an evil is undeniable; and where this evil consists in the action of an interstate carrier in unreasonably discriminating against interstate traffic over its line, the authority of Congress to prevent it is equally clear. It is immaterial, so far as the protecting power of Congress is concerned, that the discrimination arises from intrastate rates as compared with interstate rates. The use of the instrument of interstate commerce in a discriminatory manner so as to inflict injury upon that commerce, or some part thereof, furnishes abundant ground for Federal intervention. Nor can the attempted exercise of state authority alter the matter, where Congress has acted, for a State may not authorize the carrier to do that which Congress is entitled to forbid and has forbidden.
>
> * * *
>
> It is also clear that, in removing the injurious discriminations against interstate traffic arising from the relation of intrastate to interstate rates, Congress is not bound to reduce the latter below what it may deem to be a proper standard fair to the carrier and to the public. Otherwise, it could prevent

> the injury to interstate commerce only by the sacrifice of its judgment as to interstate rates. Congress is entitled to maintain its own standard as to these rates and to forbid any discriminatory action by interstate carriers which will obstruct the freedom of movement of interstate traffic over their lines in accordance with the terms it establishes.

Shreveport Rate Cases, 234 U.S. 342, 351–55 (1914). This principle, as we will see, proved to be a key engine that drove the dramatic changes in federal power that came with the New Deal.

VII. FEDERAL POWER FROM THE NEW DEAL TO THE PRESENT

In 1932, the country was in the midst of a severe economic depression. In previous eras, the federal government's response would have been to ride it out. Instead, President Herbert Hoover foolishly sought to constrict the money supply, thus creating a ruinous deflation, and he imposed the Smoot-Hawley Tariff of 1930, which raised prices for U.S. consumers while wrecking the economy of Germany to the point where Adolf Hitler came to power in that country. The public demanded strong, bold action by the federal government, but President Franklin D. Roosevelt did not understand that it was a combination of deflation and the Smoot-Hawley tariff that had wrecked the economy. President Roosevelt, drawing on decades of Progressive thought, decided that what the country need was a much bigger and more interventionist government. The question he faced was how to square such a government with the written Constitution of 1788.

We have already seen that some of the most important New Deal programs, most notably the National Industrial Recovery Act, were found unconstitutional unanimously by the Supreme Court in 1935. *See supra* pages 192–201. Other New Deal programs were also held to be unconstitutional in the early 1930s. After Franklin Roosevelt and the Democratic Party won smashing electoral victories in 1936, however, there was serious talk of "packing" the Supreme Court with additional justices in order to stop the Court from interfering with the New Deal agenda. In 1937, however, the Supreme Court upheld, by a 5–4 vote, the National Labor Relations Act, which federally guarantees rights to unionize and forbids employers from interfering with those rights when such interference was "affecting commerce." How could Congress regulate working conditions when neither manufacturing nor contracting were "Commerce * * * among the several States"? Drawing on the principles from the *Shreveport Rate Cases*, the Court held:

> * * * The congressional authority to protect interstate commerce from burdens and obstructions is not limited to transactions which can be deemed to be an essential part of a "flow" of interstate or foreign commerce. Burdens and obstructions may be due to injurious action springing from other sources. The fundamental principle is that the power to regulate commerce is the power to enact "all appropriate legislation" for its "protection or advancement"; to adopt measures "to promote its growth and insure its safety"; "to foster, protect, control, and restrain." That power is plenary and may be exerted to protect interstate commerce "no matter what the source of the dangers which threaten it." *Although activities may be intrastate in character when separately considered, if they have such a close and substantial relation to interstate commerce that their control is essential or appropriate to protect that commerce from burdens and obstructions,*

> *Congress cannot be denied the power to exercise that control*. Undoubtedly the scope of this power must be considered in the light of our dual system of government and may not be extended so as to embrace effects upon interstate commerce so indirect and remote that to embrace them, in view of our complex society, would effectually obliterate the distinction between what is national and what is local and create a completely centralized government. The question is necessarily one of degree * * *.
>
> That intrastate activities, by reason of close and intimate relation to interstate commerce, may fall within federal control is demonstrated in the case of carriers who are engaged in both interstate and intrastate transportation. There federal control has been found essential to secure the freedom of interstate traffic from interference or unjust discrimination and to promote the efficiency of the interstate service. *Shreveport Case (Houston, E. & W.T.R. Co. v. United States),* 234 U.S. 342, 351, 352. It is manifest that intrastate rates deal *primarily* with a local activity. But in rate-making they bear such a close relation to interstate rates that effective control of the one must embrace some control over the other * * *.
>
> The close and intimate effect which brings the subject within the reach of federal power may be due to activities in relation to productive industry although the industry when separately viewed is local * * *.

NLRB v. Jones & Laughlin Steel Corp., 301 U.S. 1, 36–38 (1937) (first emphasis added). That set the stage for the two landmark decisions to follow, which fixed the course for modern law. As you read these decisions, think about what roles are being played by the Commerce Clause and the Necessary and Proper Clause.

A. UNITED STATES V. DARBY

312 U.S. 100 (1941)

■ MR. JUSTICE STONE delivered the opinion of the Court.

The two principal questions raised by the record in this case are, *first*, whether Congress has constitutional power to prohibit the shipment in interstate commerce of lumber manufactured by employees whose wages are less than a prescribed minimum or whose weekly hours of labor at that wage are greater than a prescribed maximum, and, *second*, whether it has power to prohibit the employment of workmen in the production of goods "for interstate commerce" at other than prescribed wages and hours * * *.

* * *

* * * The Fair Labor Standards Act set up a comprehensive legislative scheme for preventing the shipment in interstate commerce of certain products and commodities produced in the United States under labor conditions as respects wages and hours which fail to conform to standards set up by the Act. Its purpose * * * is to exclude from interstate commerce goods produced for the commerce and to prevent their production for interstate commerce, under conditions detrimental to the maintenance of the minimum standards of living necessary for health and general well-being; and to prevent the use of interstate commerce as the means of competition in the distribution of goods so produced, and as the means of spreading

and perpetuating such substandard labor conditions among the workers of the several states * * *.

* * *

The indictment charges that appellee is engaged, in the State of Georgia, in the business of acquiring raw materials, which he manufactures into finished lumber with the intent, when manufactured, to ship it in interstate commerce to customers outside the state, and that he does in fact so ship a large part of the lumber so produced. There are numerous counts charging appellee with the shipment in interstate commerce from Georgia to points outside the state of lumber in the production of which, for interstate commerce, appellee has employed workmen at less than the prescribed minimum wage or more than the prescribed maximum hours without payment to them of any wage for overtime * * *.

* * * The district court quashed the indictment in its entirety upon the broad grounds that the Act, which it interpreted as a regulation of manufacture within the states, is unconstitutional. It declared that manufacture is not interstate commerce and that the regulation by the Fair Labor Standards Act of wages and hours of employment of those engaged in the manufacture of goods which it is intended at the time of production "may or will be" after production "sold in interstate commerce in part or in whole" is not within the congressional power to regulate interstate commerce.

The effect of the court's decision and judgment is thus to deny the power of Congress to prohibit shipment in interstate commerce of lumber produced for interstate commerce under the proscribed substandard labor conditions of wages and hours * * *.

* * *

While manufacture is not of itself interstate commerce, the shipment of manufactured goods interstate is such commerce and the prohibition of such shipment by Congress is indubitably a regulation of the commerce. The power to regulate commerce * * * extends not only to those regulations which aid, foster and protect the commerce, but embraces those which prohibit it. It is conceded that the power of Congress to prohibit transportation in interstate commerce includes noxious articles, *Lottery Case, supra;* stolen articles, kidnapped persons, and articles such as intoxicating liquor or convict made goods * * *.

But it is said that the present prohibition falls within the scope of none of these categories; that while the prohibition is nominally a regulation of the commerce its motive or purpose is regulation of wages and hours of persons engaged in manufacture, the control of which has been reserved to the states and upon which Georgia and some of the states of destination have placed no restriction * * *.

The power of Congress over interstate commerce "is complete in itself, may be exercised to its utmost extent, and acknowledges no limitations other than are prescribed in the Constitution." *Gibbons v. Ogden, supra,* 196. That power can neither be enlarged nor diminished by the exercise or non-exercise of state power. Congress, following its own conception of public policy concerning the restrictions which may appropriately be imposed on interstate commerce, is free to exclude from the commerce articles whose use in the states for which they are destined it may conceive to be injurious to the public health, morals or welfare, even though the state has not sought to regulate their use.

Such regulation is not a forbidden invasion of state power merely because either its motive or its consequence is to restrict the use of articles of commerce within the states of destination; and is not prohibited unless by other Constitutional provisions. It is no objection to the assertion of the power to regulate interstate commerce that its exercise is attended by the same incidents which attend the exercise of the police power of the states.

The motive and purpose of the present regulation are plainly to make effective the Congressional conception of public policy that interstate commerce should not be made the instrument of competition in the distribution of goods produced under substandard labor conditions, which competition is injurious to the commerce and to the states from and to which the commerce flows. The motive and purpose of a regulation of interstate commerce are matters for the legislative judgment upon the exercise of which the Constitution places no restriction and over which the courts are given no control * * *.

In the more than a century which has elapsed since the decision of *Gibbons v. Ogden,* these principles of constitutional interpretation have been so long and repeatedly recognized by this Court as applicable to the Commerce Clause, that there would be little occasion for repeating them now were it not for the decision of this Court twenty-two years ago in *Hammer v. Dagenhart,* 247 U.S. 251. In that case it was held by a bare majority of the Court over the powerful and now classic dissent of Mr. Justice Holmes setting forth the fundamental issues involved, that Congress was without power to exclude the products of child labor from interstate commerce. The reasoning and conclusion of the Court's opinion there cannot be reconciled with the conclusion which we have reached, that the power of Congress under the Commerce Clause is plenary to exclude any article from interstate commerce subject only to the specific prohibitions of the Constitution.

Hammer v. Dagenhart has not been followed. The distinction on which the decision was rested that Congressional power to prohibit interstate commerce is limited to articles which in themselves have some harmful or deleterious property—a distinction which was novel when made and unsupported by any provision of the Constitution—has long since been abandoned. The thesis of the opinion that the motive of the prohibition or its effect to control in some measure the use or production within the states of the article thus excluded from the commerce can operate to deprive the regulation of its constitutional authority has long since ceased to have force. And finally we have declared "The authority of the federal government over interstate commerce does not differ in extent or character from that retained by the states over intrastate commerce."

The conclusion is inescapable that *Hammer v. Dagenhart,* was a departure from the principles which have prevailed in the interpretation of the Commerce Clause both before and since the decision and that such vitality, as a precedent, as it then had has long since been exhausted. It should be and now is overruled.

* * *

There remains the question whether such restriction on the production of goods for commerce is a permissible exercise of the commerce power. The power of Congress over interstate commerce is not confined to the regulation of commerce among the states. It extends to those activities intrastate which so affect interstate commerce or the exercise of the power of Congress over it as to make regulation of them appropriate means to the attainment of a legitimate end, the exercise of the granted power of Congress to regulate interstate commerce. See *McCulloch v. Maryland*, 4 Wheat. 316, 421.

* * *

* * * A recent example is the National Labor Relations Act, for the regulation of employer and employee relations in industries in which strikes, induced by unfair labor practices named in the Act, tend to disturb or obstruct interstate commerce. *See National Labor Relations Board v. Jones & Laughlin Steel Corp.*, 301 U.S. 1, 38, 40. But long before the adoption of the National Labor Relations Act this Court had many times held that the power of Congress to regulate interstate commerce extends to the regulation through legislative action of activities intrastate which have a substantial effect on the commerce or the exercise of the Congressional power over it.

In such legislation Congress has sometimes left it to the courts to determine whether the intrastate activities have the prohibited effect on the commerce, as in the Sherman Act. It has sometimes left it to an administrative board or agency to determine whether the activities sought to be regulated or prohibited have such effect, as in the case of the Interstate Commerce Act, and the National Labor Relations Act, or whether they come within the statutory definition of the prohibited Act, as in the Federal Trade Commission Act. And sometimes Congress itself has said that a particular activity affects the commerce, as it did in the present Act * * *. In passing on the validity of legislation of the class last mentioned the only function of courts is to determine whether the particular activity regulated or prohibited is within the reach of the federal power.

Congress, having by the present Act adopted the policy of excluding from interstate commerce all goods produced for the commerce which do not conform to the specified labor standards, it may choose the means reasonably adapted to the attainment of the permitted end, even though they involve control of intrastate activities. Such legislation has often been sustained with respect to powers, other than the commerce power granted to the national government, when the means chosen, although not themselves within the granted power, were nevertheless deemed appropriate aids to the accomplishment of some purpose within an admitted power of the national government * * *. A familiar like exercise of power is the regulation of intrastate transactions which are so commingled with or related to interstate commerce that all must be regulated if the interstate commerce is to be effectively controlled. *Shreveport Case,* 234 U.S. 342 * * *.

* * *

The Sherman Act and the National Labor Relations Act are familiar examples of the exertion of the commerce power to prohibit or control activities wholly intrastate because of their effect on interstate commerce * * *.

The means adopted by § 15(a)(2) for the protection of interstate commerce by the suppression of the production of the condemned goods for interstate commerce is so related to the commerce and so affects it as to be within the reach of the commerce power. Congress, to attain its objective in the suppression of nationwide competition in interstate commerce by goods produced under substandard labor conditions, has made no distinction as to the volume or amount of shipments in the commerce or of production for commerce by any particular shipper or producer. It recognized that in present day industry, competition by a small part may affect the whole and that the total effect of the competition of many small producers may be great. The legislation aimed at a whole embraces all its parts.

* * *

Our conclusion is unaffected by the Tenth Amendment which provides: "The powers not delegated to the United States by the Constitution, nor prohibited by it to the States, are reserved to the States respectively, or to the people." The amendment states but a truism that all is retained which has not been surrendered. There is nothing in the history of its adoption to suggest that it was more than declaratory of the relationship between the national and state governments as it had been established by the Constitution before the amendment or that its purpose was other than to allay fears that the new national government might seek to exercise powers not granted, and that the states might not be able to exercise fully their reserved powers.

From the beginning and for many years the amendment has been construed as not depriving the national government of authority to resort to all means for the exercise of a granted power which are appropriate and plainly adapted to the permitted end. Whatever doubts may have arisen of the soundness of that conclusion, they have been put at rest by the decisions under the Sherman Act and the National Labor Relations Act which we have cited.

* * *

Reversed.

B. WICKARD V. FILBURN

317 U.S. 111 (1942)

■ MR. JUSTICE JACKSON delivered the opinion of the Court.

The appellee [Filburn, a farmer,] * * * sought to enjoin enforcement against himself of the marketing penalty imposed by the amendment of May 26, 1941, to the Agricultural Adjustment Act of 1938, upon that part of his 1941 wheat crop which was available for marketing in excess of the marketing quota established for his farm. He also sought a declaratory judgment that the wheat marketing quota provisions of the Act as amended and applicable to him were unconstitutional because not sustainable under the Commerce Clause or consistent with the Due Process Clause of the Fifth Amendment.

* * *

The appellee for many years past has owned and operated a small farm in Montgomery County, Ohio, maintaining a herd of dairy cattle, selling milk, raising poultry, and selling poultry and eggs. It has been his practice to raise a small acreage of winter wheat, sown in the Fall and harvested in the following July; to sell a portion of the crop; to feed part to poultry and livestock on the farm, some of which is sold; to use some in making flour for home consumption; and to keep the rest for the following seeding. The intended disposition of the crop here involved has not been expressly stated.

In July of 1940, pursuant to the Agricultural Adjustment Act of 1938, as then amended, there were established for the appellee's 1941 crop a wheat acreage allotment of 11.1 acres and a normal yield of 20.1 bushels of wheat an acre. He was given notice of such allotment in July of 1940, before the Fall planting of his 1941 crop of wheat, and again in July of 1941, before it was harvested. He sowed, however, 23 acres, and harvested from his 11.9 acres of excess acreage 239 bushels, which under the terms of the Act as amended on May 26, 1941, constituted farm marketing excess, subject to a penalty of 49 cents a bushel, or $117.11 in all. The appellee [Filburn] has not paid the penalty and he has not postponed or avoided it by storing the excess under regulations of the Secretary of Agriculture, or by delivering it up to the Secretary. The Committee, therefore, refused him a marketing card, which was, under the terms of Regulations promulgated by the Secretary, necessary to protect a buyer from liability to the penalty and upon its protecting lien.

The general scheme of the Agricultural Adjustment Act of 1938 as related to wheat is to control the volume moving in interstate and foreign commerce in order to avoid surpluses and shortages and the consequent abnormally low or high wheat prices and obstructions to commerce. Within prescribed limits and by prescribed standards the Secretary of Agriculture is directed to ascertain and proclaim each year a national acreage allotment for the next crop of wheat, which is then apportioned to the states and their counties, and is eventually broken up into allotments for individual farms. Loans and payments to wheat farmers are authorized in stated circumstances.

* * *

It is urged that, under the Commerce Clause of the Constitution, Article I, § 8, clause 3, Congress does not possess the power it has in this instance sought to exercise [of forbidding a farmer to grow wheat for his own consumption on his own farm]. The question would merit little consideration since our decision in *United States v. Darby,* 312 U.S. 100, sustaining the federal power to regulate production of goods for commerce, except for the fact that this Act extends federal regulation to production not intended in any part for commerce but wholly for consumption on the farm. The Act includes a definition of "market" and its derivatives, so that as related to wheat, in addition to its conventional meaning, it also means to dispose of "by feeding (in any form) to poultry or livestock which, or the products of which, are sold, bartered, or exchanged, or to be so disposed of." Hence, marketing quotas not only embrace all that may be sold without penalty but also what may be consumed on the premises. Wheat produced on excess acreage is designated as "available for marketing" as so defined, and the penalty is imposed thereon. Penalties do not depend upon whether any part of the wheat, either within or without the quota, is sold or intended to be sold. The sum of this is that the Federal Government fixes a quota including all that the farmer may harvest for sale or for his own farm needs, and declares that wheat produced on excess acreage may neither be disposed of nor used except upon payment of the penalty, or except it is stored as required by the Act or delivered to the Secretary of Agriculture.

Appellee [Filburn] says that this is a regulation of production and consumption of wheat. Such activities are, he urges, beyond the reach of Congressional power under the Commerce Clause, since they are local in character, and their effects upon interstate commerce are, at most, "indirect." In answer the Government argues that the statute regulates neither production nor consumption, but only marketing; and, in the alternative, that if the Act does go beyond the regulation of marketing, it is sustainable as a "necessary and proper" implementation of the power of Congress over interstate commerce.

The Government's concern lest the Act be held to be a regulation of production or consumption, rather than of marketing, is attributable to a few dicta and decisions of this Court which might be understood to lay it down that activities such as "production," "manufacturing," and "mining" are strictly "local" and, except in special circumstances which are not present here, cannot be regulated under the commerce power because their effects upon interstate commerce are, as matter of law, only "indirect." Even today, when this power has been held to have great latitude, there is no decision of this Court that such activities may be regulated where no part of the product is intended for interstate commerce or intermingled with the subjects thereof. We believe that a review of the course of decision under the Commerce Clause will make plain, however, that questions of the power of Congress are not to be decided by reference to any formula which would give controlling force to nomenclature such as "production" and "indirect" and foreclose consideration of the actual effects of the activity in question upon interstate commerce.

At the beginning Chief Justice Marshall described the federal commerce power with a breadth never yet exceeded. *Gibbons v. Ogden,* 9 Wheat. 1, 194–195. He made emphatic the embracing and penetrating nature of this power by warning that effective restraints on its exercise must proceed from political rather than from judicial processes. *Id.* at 197.

For nearly a century, however, decisions of this Court under the Commerce Clause dealt rarely with questions of what Congress might do in the exercise of its granted power under the Clause, and almost entirely with the permissibility of state activity which it was claimed discriminated against or burdened interstate commerce. During this period there was perhaps little occasion for the affirmative exercise of the commerce power, and the influence of the Clause on American life and law was a negative one, resulting almost wholly from its operation as a restraint upon the powers of the states. In discussion and decision, the point of reference, instead of being what was "necessary and proper" to the exercise by Congress of its granted power, was often some concept of sovereignty thought to be implicit in the status of statehood. Certain activities such as "production," "manufacturing," and "mining" were occasionally said to be within the province of state governments and beyond the power of Congress under the Commerce Clause.

It was not until 1887, with the enactment of the Interstate Commerce Act, that the interstate commerce power began to exert positive influence in American law and life. This first important federal resort to the commerce power was followed in 1890 by the Sherman Anti-Trust Act and, thereafter, mainly after 1903, by many others. These statutes ushered in new phases of adjudication, which required the Court to approach the interpretation of the Commerce Clause in the light of an actual exercise by Congress of its power thereunder.

When it first dealt with this new legislation, the Court adhered to its earlier pronouncements, and allowed but little scope to the power of Congress. *United States v. E. C. Knight Co.*, 156 U.S. 1 * * *.

Even while important opinions in this line of restrictive authority were being written, however, other cases called forth broader interpretations of the Commerce

Clause destined to supersede the earlier ones, and to bring about a return to the principles first enunciated by Chief Justice Marshall in *Gibbons v. Ogden, supra.*

Not long after the decision of *United States v. E. C. Knight Co., supra* * * *, [i]t was soon demonstrated that the effects of many kinds of intrastate activity upon interstate commerce were such as to make them a proper subject of federal regulation. In some cases sustaining the exercise of federal power over intrastate matters the term "direct" was used for the purpose of stating, rather than of reaching, a result; in others it was treated as synonymous with "substantial" or "material;" and in others it was not used at all. Of late its use has been abandoned in cases dealing with questions of federal power under the Commerce Clause.

In the *Shreveport Rate Cases*, the Court held that railroad rates of an admittedly intrastate character and fixed by authority of the state might, nevertheless, be revised by the Federal Government because of the economic effects which they had upon interstate commerce. The opinion of Mr. Justice Hughes found federal intervention constitutionally authorized because of "matters having such a close and substantial relation to interstate traffic that the control is essential or appropriate to the security of that traffic, to the efficiency of the interstate service, and to the maintenance of the conditions under which interstate commerce may be conducted upon fair terms and without molestation or hindrance." 234 U.S. at page 351.

The Court's recognition of the relevance of the economic effects in the application of the Commerce Clause * * * has made the mechanical application of legal formulas no longer feasible. Once an economic measure of the reach of the power granted to Congress in the Commerce Clause is accepted, questions of federal power cannot be decided simply by finding the activity in question to be "production," nor can consideration of its economic effects be foreclosed by calling them "indirect" * * *.

Whether the subject of the regulation in question was "production," "consumption," or "marketing" is, therefore, not material for purposes of deciding the question of federal power before us. That an activity is of local character may help in a doubtful case to determine whether Congress intended to reach it. The same consideration might help in determining whether in the absence of Congressional action it would be permissible for the state to exert its power on the subject matter, even though in so doing it to some degree affected interstate commerce. But even if appellee's activity be local and though it may not be regarded as commerce, it may still, whatever its nature, be reached by Congress if it exerts a substantial economic effect on interstate commerce, and this irrespective of whether such effect is what might at some earlier time have been defined as "direct" or "indirect."

The parties have stipulated a summary of the economics of the wheat industry * * *.

The wheat industry has been a problem industry for some years. Largely as a result of increased foreign production and import restrictions, annual exports of wheat and flour from the United States during the ten-year period ending in 1940 averaged less than 10 percent of total production, while, during the 1920's they averaged more than 25 percent. The decline in the export trade has left a large surplus in production which, in connection with an abnormally large supply of wheat and other grains in recent years, caused congestion in a number of markets; tied up railroad cars; and caused elevators in some instances to turn away grains, and railroads to institute embargoes to prevent further congestion.

Many countries, both importing and exporting, have sought to modify the impact of the world market conditions on their own economy * * *. Such plans have generally evolved towards control by the central government.

In the absence of regulation, the price of wheat in the United States would be much affected by world conditions. During 1941, producers who cooperated with the Agricultural Adjustment program received an average price on the farm of about $1.16 a bushel, as compared with the world market price of 40 cents a bushel.

* * *

The effect of consumption of home-grown wheat on interstate commerce is due to the fact that it constitutes the most variable factor in the disappearance of the wheat crop. Consumption on the farm where grown appears to vary in an amount greater than 20 percent of average production. The total amount of wheat consumed as food varies but relatively little, and use as seed is relatively constant.

The maintenance by government regulation of a price for wheat undoubtedly can be accomplished as effectively by sustaining or increasing the demand as by limiting the supply. The effect of the statute before us is to restrict the amount which may be produced for market and the extent as well to which one may forestall resort to the market by producing to meet his own needs. That appellee's own contribution to the demand for wheat may be trivial by itself is not enough to remove him from the scope of federal regulation where, as here, his contribution, taken together with that of many others similarly situated, is far from trivial. *Labor Board v. Fairblatt*, 306 U.S. 601, 606 *et seq.; United States v. Darby supra* at 123.

It is well established by decisions of this Court that the power to regulate commerce includes the power to regulate the prices at which commodities in that commerce are dealt in and practices affecting such prices. One of the primary purposes of the Act in question was to increase the market price of wheat, and to that end to limit the volume thereof that could affect the market. It can hardly be denied that a factor of such volume and variability as home-consumed wheat would have a substantial influence on price and market conditions. This may arise because being in marketable condition such wheat overhangs the market and, if induced by rising prices, tends to flow into the market and check price increases. But if we assume that it is never marketed, it supplies a need of the man who grew it which would otherwise be reflected by purchases in the open market. Home-grown wheat in this sense competes with wheat in commerce. The stimulation of commerce is a use of the regulatory function quite as definitely as prohibitions or restrictions thereon. This record leaves us in no doubt that Congress may properly have considered that wheat consumed on the farm where grown, if wholly outside the scheme of regulation, would have a substantial effect in defeating and obstructing its purpose to stimulate trade therein at increased prices.

It is said, however, that this Act, forcing some farmers into the market to buy what they could provide for themselves, is an unfair promotion of the markets and prices of specializing wheat growers. It is of the essence of regulation that it lays a restraining hand on the self-interest of the regulated and that advantages from the regulation commonly fall to others. The conflicts of economic interest between the regulated and those who advantage by it are wisely left under our system to resolution by the Congress under its more flexible and responsible legislative process. Such conflicts rarely lend themselves to judicial determination. And with the wisdom, workability, or fairness, of the plan of regulation, we have nothing to do.

* * *

Reversed.

NOTES AND QUESTIONS

1. Did *United States v. Darby* redefine "Commerce * * * among the several States," apply the Necessary and Proper Clause, or both? What does it think are the limits of either power?

2. Did *Wickard v. Filburn* redefine "Commerce * * * among the several States," apply the Necessary and Proper Clause, or both? Again, what does it think are the limits of either power?

3. Is the effect of those two cases to make the scope of Congress's power to regulate the economy a nonjusticiable political question?

4. *Wickard v. Filburn* is famous for its "aggregation test" for determining which wholly intrastate activities affect interstate commerce. What matters is not whether Filburn's own use of wheat grown for his own consumption on his own farm affects the national price of wheat. Instead, Justice Jackson holds that all the home-grown wheat in the country must be considered, and that surely would affect the price of wheat nationally and internationally in commerce. Is there any human activity—or inactivity—whose effects cannot be aggregated in this fashion to yield some kind of effect on interstate commerce? Hold that question until the next principal case.

5. Is there any way to distinguish *The Shreveport Rate Case, NLRB v. Jones & Laughlin Steel Corp.*, and *United States v. Darby* on the one hand and *Wickard v. Filburn* on the other? Is it that the regulation in the first three cases was both important and needed to reach intrastate activity to be effective, while the regulation in the latter case was just a government-sponsored anti-consumer cartel? Are those sorts of considerations, if true, constitutionally relevant? Is there any other way to distinguish *Wickard*?

6. While *Darby* and *Wickard* did not formally make enumerated-powers-based challenges to federal economic regulation nonjusticiable, it came very close to doing so in practical terms for half a century. With expansive understandings of both the Commerce Clause and the Necessary and Proper Clause in hand, Congress did not need to worry much about finding constitutional sources of power for whatever it wanted to do—and it invoked the Commerce Clause in situations where other enumerated powers made more sense. Congress, for instance, passed the Civil Rights Act of 1964 based, not on any of the Civil War Amendments, but on the Commerce and Necessary and Proper Clauses. The Civil Rights Act outlaws discrimination in employment, schools, and places of public accommodation based on race, color, religion, sex, or national origin. The Supreme Court unanimously upheld the constitutionality of the Act in two cases: *Heart of Atlanta Motel v. United States*, 379 U.S. 241 (1964) and *Katzenbach v. McClung*, 379 U.S. 294 (1964). One might think that antidiscrimination statutes would be based on Congress's power to enforce the Fourteenth Amendment, which we will address later. Those cases, however, were decided as Commerce Clause cases because the Warren Court did not want to have to overrule a longstanding precedent (which you will soon read), *The Civil Rights Cases*, 109 U.S. 3 (1883), in which the U.S. Supreme Court struck down as unconstitutional the Civil Rights Act of 1875 banning racial discrimination in places of public accommodation, on the ground that the Civil War amendments did not give Congress power to regulate

private conduct, except in the most narrow sense of banning slavery. That left the Commerce Clause and the Necessary and Proper Clause as the only available sources of congressional power. After *Darby* and *Wickard,* that was plenty.

Heart of Atlanta Motel v. United States, 379 U.S. 241 (1964), for example, involved the constitutionality of forbidding race discrimination by a wholly intrastate motel that provided accommodations to significant numbers of white people travelling in interstate commerce, but which did not provide accommodation to African-Americans travelling in interstate commerce. The Supreme Court easily upheld the federal ban on intrastate race discrimination by hotels and inns. saying that it acted as a clog on and as an impediment to interstate commerce:

> The same interest in protecting interstate commerce which led Congress to deal with segregation in interstate carriers and the white-slave traffic has prompted it to extend the exercise of its power to gambling, to criminal enterprises, to deceptive practices in the sale of products, to fraudulent security transactions, to misbranding of drugs, to wages and hours, to members of labor unions, to crop control, to discrimination against shippers, to the protection of small business from injurious price cutting, to resale price maintenance, to professional football, and to racial discrimination by owners and managers of terminal restaurants.
>
> That Congress was legislating against moral wrongs in many of these areas rendered its enactments no less valid. In framing Title II of this Act Congress was also dealing with what it considered a moral problem. But that fact does not detract from the overwhelming evidence of the disruptive effect that racial discrimination has had on commercial intercourse. It was this burden which empowered Congress to enact appropriate legislation, and, given this basis for the exercise of its power, Congress was not restricted by the fact that the particular obstruction to interstate commerce with which it was dealing was also deemed a moral and social wrong.
>
> It is said that the operation of the motel here is of a purely local character * * *. As Chief Justice Stone put it in *United States v. Darby*:
>
> > "The power of Congress over interstate commerce is not confined to the regulation of commerce among the states. It extends to those activities intrastate which so affect interstate commerce or the exercise of the power of Congress over it as to make regulation of them appropriate means to the attainment of a legitimate end, the exercise of the granted power of Congress to regulate interstate commerce. See *McCulloch v. Maryland,* 4 Wheat. 316, 421."
>
> 
>
> Thus the power of Congress to promote interstate commerce also includes the power to regulate the local incidents thereof, including local activities in both the States of origin and destination, which might have a substantial and harmful effect upon that commerce. One need only examine the evidence which we have discussed above [*Editors' Note: showing "overwhelming evidence that discrimination by hotels and motels impedes interstate travel"*] to see that Congress may—as it has—prohibit racial discrimination by motels serving travelers, however "'local" their operations may appear.

379 U.S. at 256–58.

The issue in *Katzenbach v. McClung,* 379 U.S. 294 (1964) was the application of the Civil Rights Act of 1964 to an intrastate diner called "Ollie's Barbecue." This restaurant was located eleven blocks from an interstate highway, and it imported half its food from out of state. The Supreme Court held that racial discrimination by restaurants was just as much of a clog on interstate commerce as was racial discrimination by hotels, and it relied on the reasoning in *Heart of Atlanta Motel. Katzenbach* added, however, that "[o]f course, the mere fact that Congress has said when particular activity shall be deemed to affect commerce does not preclude further examination by this Court. But where we find that the legislators, in light of the facts and testimony before them, have a *rational basis* for finding a chosen regulatory scheme necessary to the protection of commerce, our investigation is at an end." 379 U.S. at 303–04 (emphasis added). As you will discover throughout this course, a "rational basis" inquiry is very close to a sure win for the government.

From 1937 to 1995, no federal law was held unconstitutional because it exceeded the enumerated powers of Congress, with one possible, and modest, exception. In *National League of Cities v. Usery,* 426 U.S. 833 (1976), a 5–4 majority held that the wage and hour provisions of the Fair Labor Standards Act could not be applied to State government employees. The case was not formally about Congress's enumerated powers:

> Appellants in no way challenge these decisions establishing the breadth of authority granted Congress under the commerce power. Their contention, on the contrary, is that when Congress seeks to regulate directly the activities of States as public employers, it transgresses an affirmative limitation on the exercise of its power akin to other commerce power affirmative limitations contained in the Constitution. Congressional enactments which may be fully within the grant of legislative authority contained in the Commerce Clause may nonetheless be invalid because found to offend against the right to trial by jury contained in the Sixth Amendment or the Due Process Clause of the Fifth Amendment. Appellants' essential contention is that the 1974 amendments to the Act, while undoubtedly within the scope of the Commerce Clause, encounter a similar constitutional barrier because they are to be applied directly to the States and subdivisions of States as employers.

426 U.S. at 841. The claim, in other words, was that the Tenth Amendment functioned as an affirmative limitation on Congress, just as do the other provisions of the Bill of Rights. But because the Tenth Amendment simply declares that Congress only possesses whatever powers it possesses, it is possible to read *National League of Cities* as a ruling that the Commerce Clause does not affirmatively grant power to Congress to regulate the working conditions of State employees. The proper reading of *National League of Cities* is a moot point, however, as it was overruled (5–4) nine years later in *Garcia v. San Antonio Metropolitan Transit Authority,* 469 U.S. 528 (1985). *See infra* pages 1175–1176.

United States v. Lopez was thus the first case in almost fifty years to find that Congress had exceeded its enumerated powers. It was followed by *United States v. Morrison,* 529 U.S. 598 (2000), in which the Court found that Congress did not have power to regulate wholly local gender-motivated violence under either the Commerce and Necessary Proper Clauses or the Civil War amendments. (We will examine the case's discussion of the Civil War amendments later. *See infra* pages 878–884.) In *Gonzales v. Raich,* 545 U.S. 1 (2005), however, the Supreme Court upheld the federal narcotics conviction of Angel Raich for possessing six homegrown marijuana plants, which she grew after California voters passed Proposition 215 in 1996 legalizing the use of medical marijuana. Raich used the marijuana to alleviate crippling pain she was suffering from a medical condition. The possession of any amount of marijuana is a violation of the federal Controlled Substances Act. Federal prosecutors chose to prosecute Raich to prevent States like California from legalizing either the medical or the recreational use of marijuana. Raich argued that her possession of a small amount of homegrown marijuana for her own personal use did not constitute a wholly intrastate activity that substantially affected interstate commerce under *United States v. Lopez* and *United States v. Morrison*. She lost in the Supreme Court 6–3, with Justices John Paul Stevens, Antonin Scalia, Anthony Kennedy, David Souter, Ruth Bader Ginsburg, and Stephen Breyer in the majority. Three justices dissented: Chief Justice William H. Rehnquist, the author of *United States v. Lopez*; Justice Sandra Day O'Connor, a fan of federalism; and Clarence Thomas, whose *Lopez* concurrence called for reconsidering every Commerce Clause case since 1937. The majority treated the case as a reprise of *Wickard v. Filburn*, which *United States v. Lopez* had narrowed to its facts but had not overturned. The Court asked whether Congress could rationally have believed (a la *Katzenbach v. McClung*) that all the home-grown marijuana in the U.S., in the aggregate, had an effect on the black market for marijuana. The majority easily concluded the answer was "yes" and upheld Raich's conviction. Justices Scalia and Kennedy broke from the 5–4 lineup in *Lopez* to produce the 6 to 3 vote upholding Raich's conviction. (Justice Scalia later said he regretted his vote and opinion in this case.)

[Assignment 35]

All of the threads in all of these cases came to a head in 2010 when the Court upheld the constitutionality of the Patient Protection and Affordable Care Act, or "Obamacare." You have already seen two parts of this decision, dealing with the taxing and spending powers. *See supra* pages 306, 678–684. Here is the part addressing whether Congress had the enumerated power to enact the individual mandate requiring (almost) everyone to buy government-approved health insurance. Chief Justice Roberts, recall, was the fifth vote to uphold the law *solely* on the ground that he thought it could be sustained as an exercise of the taxing power. For those keeping track, the portion of Chief Justice Roberts' opinion reproduced below, after the first two paragraphs, is "Part III-A" of his opinion, meaning that it was not joined by any other justice. But if you add his opinion to that of the four dissenting justices, you get . . . what, exactly do you get?

C. NATIONAL FEDERATION OF INDEPENDENT BUSINESS V. SEBELIUS

567 U.S. 519 (2012)

■ CHIEF JUSTICE ROBERTS announced the judgment of the Court and delivered the opinion of the Court with respect to Parts I, II, and III-C, an opinion with respect to Part IV, in which JUSTICE BREYER and JUSTICE KAGAN join, and an opinion with respect to Parts III-A, III-B, and III-D.

Today we resolve constitutional challenges to * * * the individual mandate [of the Patient Protection and Affordable Care Act], which requires individuals to purchase a health insurance policy providing a minimum level of coverage * * *. We do not consider whether the Act embodies sound policies. That judgment is entrusted to the Nation's elected leaders. We ask only whether Congress has the power under the Constitution to enact the challenged provisions.

In our federal system, the National Government possesses only limited powers; the States and the people retain the remainder. Nearly two centuries ago, Chief Justice Marshall observed that "the question respecting the extent of the powers actually granted" to the Federal Government "is perpetually arising, and will probably continue to arise, as long as our system shall exist." *McCulloch v. Maryland*,

4 Wheat. 316, 405 (1819). In this case we must again determine whether the Constitution grants Congress powers it now asserts, but which many States and individuals believe it does not possess. Resolving this controversy requires us to examine both the limits of the Government's power, and our own limited role in policing those boundaries.

* * *

The Government's first argument is that the individual mandate is a valid exercise of Congress's power under the Commerce Clause and the Necessary and Proper Clause. According to the Government, the health care market is characterized by a significant cost-shifting problem. Everyone will eventually need health care at a time and to an extent they cannot predict, but if they do not have insurance, they often will not be able to pay for it. Because state and federal laws nonetheless require hospitals to provide a certain degree of care to individuals without regard to their ability to pay, see, e.g., 42 U. S. C. § 1395dd; Fla. Stat. Ann. § 395.1041, hospitals end up receiving compensation for only a portion of the services they provide. To recoup the losses, hospitals pass on the cost to insurers through higher rates, and insurers, in turn, pass on the cost to policy holders in the form of higher premiums. Congress estimated that the cost of uncompensated care raises family health insurance premiums, on average, by over $1,000 per year.

In the Affordable Care Act, Congress addressed the problem of those who cannot obtain insurance coverage because of pre-existing conditions or other health issues. It did so through the Act's "guaranteed-issue" and "community-rating" provisions. These provisions together prohibit insurance companies from denying coverage to those with such conditions or charging unhealthy individuals higher premiums than healthy individuals.

The guaranteed-issue and community-rating reforms do not, however, address the issue of healthy individuals who choose not to purchase insurance to cover potential health care needs. In fact, the reforms sharply exacerbate that problem, by providing an incentive for individuals to delay purchasing health insurance until they become sick, relying on the promise of guaranteed and affordable coverage. The reforms also threaten to impose massive new costs on insurers, who are required to accept unhealthy individuals but prohibited from charging them rates necessary to pay for their coverage. This will lead insurers to significantly increase premiums on everyone.

The individual mandate was Congress's solution to these problems. By requiring that individuals purchase health insurance, the mandate prevents cost shifting by those who would otherwise go without it. In addition, the mandate forces into the insurance risk pool more healthy individuals, whose premiums on average will be higher than their health care expenses. This allows insurers to subsidize the costs of covering the unhealthy individuals the reforms require them to accept. The Government claims that Congress has power under the Commerce and Necessary and Proper Clauses to enact this solution.

The Government contends that the individual mandate is within Congress's power because the failure to purchase insurance "has a substantial and deleterious effect on interstate commerce" by creating the cost-shifting problem. The path of our Commerce Clause decisions has not always run smooth, see *United States v. Lopez*, 514 U. S. 549–559 (1995), but it is now well established that Congress has broad authority under the Clause. We have recognized, for example, that "[t]he power of Congress over interstate commerce is not confined to the regulation of commerce among the states," but extends to activities that "have a substantial effect on interstate commerce." *United States v. Darby*, 312 U. S. 100, 118–119 (1941). Congress's power, moreover, is not limited to regulation of an activity that by itself substantially affects interstate commerce, but also extends to activities that do so only when aggregated with similar activities of others. See *Wickard*, 317 U. S., at 127–128.

Given its expansive scope, it is no surprise that Congress has employed the commerce power in a wide variety of ways to address the pressing needs of the time. But Congress has never attempted to rely on that power to compel individuals not engaged in commerce to purchase an unwanted product. Legislative novelty is not necessarily fatal; there is a first time for everything. But sometimes "the most telling indication of [a] severe constitutional problem . . . is the lack of historical precedent" for Congress's action. *Free Enterprise Fund v. Public Company Accounting Oversight Bd.*, 561 U. S. 477, 505 (2010). At the very least, we should "pause to consider the implications of the Government's arguments" when confronted with such new conceptions of federal power. *Lopez, supra*, at 564.

The Constitution grants Congress the power to "*regulate* Commerce." Art. I, § 8, cl. 3 (emphasis added). The power to *regulate* commerce presupposes the existence of commercial activity to be regulated. If the power to "regulate" something included the power to create it, many of the provisions in the Constitution would be superfluous. For example, the Constitution gives Congress the power to "coin Money," in addition to the power to "regulate the Value thereof." *Id.*, cl. 5. And it gives Congress the power to "raise and support Armies" and to "provide and maintain a Navy," in addition to the power to "make Rules for the Government and Regulation of the land and naval Forces." *Id.*, cls. 12–14. If the power to regulate the Armed Forces or the value of money included the power to bring the subject of the regulation into existence, the specific grant of such powers would have been unnecessary. The language of the Constitution reflects the natural understanding that the power to regulate assumes there is already something to be regulated.

Our precedent also reflects this understanding. As expansive as our cases construing the scope of the commerce power have been, they all have one thing in common: They uniformly describe the power as reaching "activity." It is nearly impossible to avoid the word when quoting them.

The individual mandate, however, does not regulate existing commercial activity. It instead compels individuals to *become active* in commerce by purchasing a product, on the ground that their failure to do so affects interstate commerce. Construing the Commerce Clause to permit Congress to regulate individuals precisely *because* they are doing nothing would open a new and potentially vast domain to congressional authority. Every day individuals do not do an infinite number of things. In some cases they decide not to do something; in others they simply fail to do it. Allowing Congress to justify federal regulation by pointing to the effect of inaction on commerce would bring countless decisions an individual could *potentially* make within the scope of federal regulation, and—under the Government's theory—empower Congress to make those decisions for him.

Applying the Government's logic to the familiar case of *Wickard v. Filburn* shows how far that logic would carry us from the notion of a government of limited powers. In *Wickard*, the Court famously upheld a federal penalty imposed on a farmer for growing wheat for consumption on his own farm. That amount of wheat caused the farmer to exceed his quota under a program designed to support the price of wheat by limiting supply. The Court rejected the farmer's argument that growing wheat for home consumption was beyond the reach of the commerce power. It did so on the ground that the farmer's decision to grow wheat for his own use allowed him to avoid purchasing wheat in the market. That decision, when considered in the aggregate along with similar decisions of others, would have had a substantial effect on the interstate market for wheat.

Wickard has long been regarded as "perhaps the most far reaching example of Commerce Clause authority over intrastate activity," *Lopez*, 514 U. S., at 560, but the Government's theory in this case would go much further. Under *Wickard* it is within Congress's power to regulate the market for wheat by supporting its price. But price can be supported by increasing demand as well as by decreasing supply. The aggregated decisions of some consumers not to purchase wheat have a substantial effect on the price of wheat, just as decisions not to purchase health insurance have on the price of insurance. Congress can therefore command that those not buying wheat do so, just as it argues here that it may command that those not buying health insurance do so. The farmer in *Wickard* was at least actively engaged in the production of wheat, and the Government could regulate that activity because of its effect on commerce. The Government's theory here would effectively override that limitation, by establishing that individuals may be regulated under the Commerce Clause whenever enough of them are not doing something the Government would have them do.

Indeed, the Government's logic would justify a mandatory purchase to solve almost any problem. To consider a different example in the health care market, many Americans do not eat a balanced diet. That group makes up a larger percentage of the total population than those without health insurance. The failure of that group to have a healthy diet increases health care costs, to a greater extent than the failure of the uninsured to purchase insurance. Those increased costs are borne in part by other Americans who must pay more, just as the uninsured shift costs to the insured. Congress addressed the insurance problem by ordering everyone to buy insurance. Under the Government's theory, Congress could address the diet problem by ordering everyone to buy vegetables.

People, for reasons of their own, often fail to do things that would be good for them or good for society. Those failures—joined with the similar failures of others—can readily have a substantial effect on interstate commerce. Under the Government's logic, that authorizes Congress to use its commerce power to compel citizens to act as the Government would have them act.

That is not the country the Framers of our Constitution envisioned. James Madison explained that the Commerce Clause was "an addition which few oppose and from which no apprehensions are entertained." The Federalist No. 45, at 293. While Congress's authority under the Commerce Clause has of course expanded with the growth of the national economy, our cases have "always recognized that the power to regulate commerce, though broad indeed, has limits." *Maryland v. Wirtz*, 392 U. S. 183, 196 (1968). The Government's theory would erode those limits, permitting Congress to reach beyond the natural extent of its authority, "everywhere extending the sphere of its activity and drawing all power into its impetuous vortex." The Federalist No. 48, at 309 (J. Madison). Congress already enjoys vast power to regulate much of what we do. Accepting the Government's theory would give Congress the same license to regulate what we do not do, fundamentally changing the relation between the citizen and the Federal Government.

To an economist, perhaps, there is no difference between activity and inactivity; both have measurable economic effects on commerce. But the distinction between doing something and doing nothing would not have been lost on the Framers, who were "practical statesmen," not metaphysical philosophers * * *. The Framers gave Congress the power to *regulate* commerce, not to *compel* it, and for over 200 years both our decisions and Congress's actions have reflected this understanding. There is no reason to depart from that understanding now.

The Government sees things differently. It argues that because sickness and injury are unpredictable but unavoidable, "the uninsured as a class are active in the market for health care, which they regularly seek and obtain." The individual mandate "merely regulates how individuals finance and pay for that active participation—requiring that they do so through insurance, rather than through attempted self-insurance with the back-stop of shifting costs to others."

The Government repeats the phrase "active in the market for health care" throughout its brief, but that concept has no constitutional significance. An individual who bought a car two years ago and may buy another in the future is not "active in the car market" in any pertinent sense. The phrase "active in the market" cannot obscure the fact that most of those regulated by the individual mandate are not currently engaged in any commercial activity involving health care, and that fact is fatal to the Government's effort to "regulate the uninsured as a class." Our precedents recognize Congress's power to regulate "class[es] of *activities*," *Gonzales v. Raich*, 545 U. S. 1, 17 (2005) (emphasis added), not classes of *individuals*, apart from any activity in which they are engaged.

* * *

The Government, however, claims that this does not matter. The Government regards it as sufficient to trigger Congress's authority that almost all those who are uninsured will, at some unknown point in the future, engage in a health care transaction. Asserting that "[t]here is no temporal limitation in the Commerce Clause," the Government argues that because "[e]veryone subject to this regulation is in or will be in the health care market," they can be "regulated in advance." Tr. of Oral Arg. 111 (Mar. 27, 2012).

The proposition that Congress may dictate the conduct of an individual today because of prophesied future activity finds no support in our precedent. We have said that Congress can anticipate the *effects* on commerce of an economic activity. See, e.g., *Consolidated Edison Co. v. NLRB*, 305 U. S. 197 (1938) (regulating the labor practices of utility companies); *Heart of Atlanta Motel, Inc. v. United States*, 379 U. S. 241 (1964) (prohibiting discrimination by hotel operators); *Katzenbach v. McClung*, 379 U. S. 294 (1964) (prohibiting discrimination by restaurant owners). But we have never permitted Congress to anticipate that activity itself in order to regulate individuals not currently engaged in commerce. Each one of our cases * * * involved preexisting economic activity. See, e.g., *Wickard*, 317 U. S., at 127–129 (producing wheat); *Raich*, *supra*, at 25 (growing marijuana).

Everyone will likely participate in the markets for food, clothing, transportation, shelter, or energy; that does not authorize Congress to direct them to purchase particular products in those or other markets today. The Commerce Clause is not a general license to regulate an individual from cradle to grave, simply because he will predictably engage in particular transactions. Any police power to regulate individuals as such, as opposed to their activities, remains vested in the States.

* * *

The Government next contends that Congress has the power under the Necessary and Proper Clause to enact the individual mandate because the mandate is an "integral part of a comprehensive scheme of economic regulation"—the guaranteed-issue and community-rating insurance reforms. Under this argument, it is not necessary to consider the effect that an individual's inactivity may have on interstate commerce; it is enough that Congress regulate commercial activity in a way that requires regulation of inactivity to be effective.

The power to "make all Laws which shall be necessary and proper for carrying into Execution" the powers enumerated in the Constitution, Art. I, § 8, cl. 18, vests Congress with authority to enact provisions "incidental to the [enumerated] power, and conducive to its beneficial exercise," *McCulloch*, 4 Wheat., at 418. Although the Clause gives Congress authority to "legislate on that vast mass of incidental powers which must be involved in the constitution," it does not license the exercise of any "great substantive and independent power[s]" beyond those specifically enumerated. *Id.*, at 411, 421. Instead, the Clause is " 'merely a declaration, for the removal of all uncertainty, that the means of carrying into execution those [powers] otherwise granted are included in the grant.' "

As our jurisprudence under the Necessary and Proper Clause has developed, we have been very deferential to Congress's determination that a regulation is "necessary." We have thus upheld laws that are " 'convenient, or useful' or 'conducive' to the authority's 'beneficial exercise.' " But we have also carried out our responsibility to declare unconstitutional those laws that undermine the structure of government established by the Constitution. Such laws, which are not "consist[ent] with the letter and spirit of the constitution," *McCulloch, supra*, at 421, are not "*proper* [means] for carrying into Execution" Congress's enumerated powers. Rather, they are, "in the words of The Federalist, 'merely acts of usurpation' which 'deserve to be treated as such.' " *Printz v. United States*, 521 U. S. 898, 924 (1997).

Applying these principles, the individual mandate cannot be sustained under the Necessary and Proper Clause as an essential component of the insurance reforms. Each of our prior cases upholding laws under that Clause involved exercises of authority derivative of, and in service to, a granted power. For example, we have upheld provisions permitting continued confinement of those *already in federal custody* when they could not be safely released, criminalizing bribes involving organizations *receiving* federal funds, and tolling state statutes of limitations while cases are *pending in federal court*. The individual mandate, by contrast, vests Congress with the extraordinary ability to create the necessary predicate to the exercise of an enumerated power.

This is in no way an authority that is * * * "incidental" to the exercise of the commerce power, *McCulloch, supra*, at 418. Rather, such a conception of the Necessary and Proper Clause would work a substantial expansion of federal authority. No longer would Congress be limited to regulating under the Commerce Clause those who by some pre-existing activity bring themselves within the sphere of federal regulation. Instead, Congress could reach beyond the natural limit of its authority and draw within its regulatory scope those who otherwise would be outside of it. Even if the individual mandate is "necessary" to the Act's insurance reforms, such an expansion of federal power is not a "proper" means for making those reforms effective.

The Government relies primarily on our decision in *Gonzales v. Raich*. In *Raich*, we considered "comprehensive legislation to regulate the interstate market" in marijuana. 545 U. S., at 22. Certain individuals sought an exemption from that regulation on the ground that they engaged in only intrastate possession and consumption. We denied any exemption, on the ground that marijuana is a fungible commodity, so that any marijuana could be readily diverted into the interstate market. Congress's attempt to regulate the interstate market for marijuana would therefore have been substantially undercut if it could not also regulate intrastate possession and consumption. Accordingly, we recognized that "Congress was acting well within its authority" under the Necessary and Proper Clause even though its "regulation ensnare[d] some purely intrastate activity." *Id.*, at 22 *Raich* thus did not involve the exercise of any "great substantive and independent power," *McCulloch*, supra, at 411, of the sort at issue here. Instead, it concerned only the constitutionality of "individual *applications* of a concededly valid statutory scheme." *Raich, supra*, at 23 (emphasis added).

Just as the individual mandate cannot be sustained as a law regulating the substantial effects of the failure to purchase health insurance, neither can it be upheld as a "necessary and proper" component of the insurance re-forms. The commerce power thus does not authorize the mandate. Accord, post, at 649–60 (joint opinion of SCALIA, KENNEDY, THOMAS, and ALITO, JJ., dissenting).

* * *

■ JUSTICE GINSBURG, with whom JUSTICE SOTOMAYOR joins, and with whom JUSTICE BREYER and JUSTICE KAGAN join as to Parts I, II, III, and IV, concurring in part, concurring in the judgment in part, and dissenting in part.

* * * Unlike THE CHIEF JUSTICE * * *, I would hold * * * that the Commerce Clause authorizes Congress to enact the minimum coverage provision * * *.

The provision of health care is today a concern of national dimension, just as the provision of old-age and survivors' benefits was in the 1930's. In the Social Security Act, Congress installed a federal system to provide monthly benefits to retired wage earners and, eventually, to their survivors. Beyond question, Congress could have adopted a similar scheme for health care. Congress chose, instead, to preserve a central role for private insurers and state governments. According to THE CHIEF JUSTICE, the Commerce Clause does not permit that preservation. This rigid reading of the Clause makes scant sense and is stunningly retrogressive.

Since 1937, our precedent has recognized Congress' large authority to set the Nation's course in the economic and social welfare realm. See *United States v. Darby*, 312 U. S. 100, 115 (1941) (overruling *Hammer v. Dagenhart*, 247 U. S. 251 (1918),

and recognizing that "regulations of commerce which do not infringe some constitutional prohibition are within the plenary power conferred on Congress by the Commerce Clause"); *NLRB v. Jones & Laughlin Steel Corp.*, 301 U. S. 1, 37 (1937) ("[The commerce] power is plenary and may be exerted to protect interstate commerce no matter what the source of the dangers which threaten it." (internal quotation marks omitted)). THE CHIEF JUSTICE'S crabbed reading of the Commerce Clause harks back to the era in which the Court routinely thwarted Congress' efforts to regulate the national economy in the interest of those who labor to sustain it. It is a reading that should not have staying power.

In enacting the Patient Protection and Affordable Care Act (ACA), Congress comprehensively reformed the national market for health-care products and services. By any measure, that market is immense. Collectively, Americans spent $2.5 trillion on health care in 2009, accounting for 17.6% of our Nation's economy. Within the next decade, it is anticipated, spending on health care will nearly double.

The health-care market's size is not its only distinctive feature. Unlike the market for almost any other product or service, the market for medical care is one in which all individuals inevitably participate. Virtually every person residing in the United States, sooner or later, will visit a doctor or other health-care professional. Most people will do so repeatedly.

When individuals make those visits, they face another reality of the current market for medical care: its high cost * * *.

Although every U. S. domiciliary will incur significant medical expenses during his or her lifetime, the time when care will be needed is often unpredictable. An accident, a heart attack, or a cancer diagnosis commonly occurs without warning. Inescapably, we are all at peril of needing medical care without a moment's notice.

To manage the risks associated with medical care—its high cost, its unpredictability, and its inevitability—most people in the United States obtain health insurance. Many (approximately 170 million in 2009) are insured by private insurance companies. Others, including those over 65 and certain poor and disabled persons, rely on government-funded insurance programs, notably Medicare and Medicaid. Combined, private health insurers and State and Federal Governments finance almost 85% of the medical care administered to U. S. residents.

Not all U. S. residents, however, have health insurance. In 2009, approximately 50 million people were uninsured, either by choice or, more likely, because they could not afford private insurance and did not qualify for government aid * * *. Over 60% of those without insurance visit a doctor's office or emergency room in a given year.

The large number of individuals without health insurance, Congress found, heavily burdens the national health-care market. As just noted, the cost of emergency care or treatment for a serious illness generally exceeds what an individual can afford to pay on her own. Unlike markets for most products, however, the inability to pay for care does not mean that an uninsured individual will receive no care. Federal and state law, as well as professional obligations and embedded social norms, require hospitals and physicians to provide care when it is most needed, regardless of the patient's ability to pay.

As a consequence, medical-care providers deliver significant amounts of care to the uninsured for which the providers receive no payment. In 2008, for example, hospitals, physicians, and other health-care professionals received no compensation for $43 billion worth of the $116 billion in care they administered to those without insurance.

Health-care providers do not absorb these bad debts. Instead, they raise their prices, passing along the cost of uncompensated care to those who do pay reliably: the government and private insurance companies. In response, private insurers increase their premiums, shifting the cost of the elevated bills from providers onto those who carry insurance. The net result: Those with health insurance subsidize the medical care of those without it. As economists would describe what happens, the uninsured "free ride" on those who pay for health insurance.

* * *

And it is hardly just the currently sick or injured among the uninsured who prompt elevation of the price of health care and health insurance. Insurance companies and health-care providers know that some percentage of healthy, uninsured people will suffer sickness or injury each year and will receive medical care despite their inability to pay. In anticipation of this uncompensated care, health-care companies raise their prices, and insurers their premiums. In other words, because any uninsured person may need medical care at any moment and because health-care companies must account for that risk, every uninsured person impacts the market price of medical care and medical insurance.

The failure of individuals to acquire insurance has other deleterious effects on the health-care market. Because those without insurance generally lack access to preventative care, they do not receive treatment for conditions—like hypertension and diabetes—that can be successfully and affordably treated if diagnosed early on. When sickness finally drives the uninsured to seek care, once treatable conditions have escalated into grave health problems, requiring more costly and extensive intervention. The extra time and resources providers spend serving the uninsured lessens the providers' ability to care for those who do have insurance.

States cannot resolve the problem of the uninsured on their own. Like Social Security benefits, a universal health-care system, if adopted by an individual State, would be "bait to the needy and dependent elsewhere, encouraging them to migrate and seek a haven of repose." *Helvering v. Davis*, 301 U. S. 619, 644 (1937). See also Brief for Commonwealth of Massachusetts as Amicus Curiae in No. 11–398, p. 15 (noting that, in 2009, Massachusetts' emergency rooms served thousands of uninsured, out-of-state residents). An influx of unhealthy individuals into a State with universal health care would result in increased spending on medical services. To cover the increased costs, a State would have to raise taxes, and private health-insurance companies would have to increase premiums. Higher taxes and increased insurance costs would, in turn, encourage businesses and healthy individuals to leave the State.

* * * Facing that risk, individual States are unlikely to take the initiative in addressing the problem of the uninsured, even though solving that problem is in all States' best interests. Congress' intervention was needed to overcome this collective-action impasse.

Aware that a national solution was required, Congress could have taken over the health-insurance market by establishing a tax-and-spend federal program like Social Security. Such a program, commonly referred to as a single-payer system (where the sole payer is the Federal Government), would have left little, if any, room for private enterprise or the States. Instead of going this route, Congress enacted the ACA, a solution that retains a robust role for private insurers and state governments. To make its chosen approach work, however, Congress had to use some new tools, including a requirement that most individuals obtain private health insurance coverage. As explained below, by employing these tools, Congress was able to achieve a practical, altogether reasonable, solution.

A central aim of the ACA is to reduce the number of uninsured U. S. residents. The minimum coverage provision advances this objective by giving potential recipients of health care a financial incentive to acquire insurance. Per the minimum coverage provision, an individual must either obtain insurance or pay a toll constructed as a tax penalty.

The minimum coverage provision serves a further purpose vital to Congress' plan to reduce the number of uninsured. Congress knew that encouraging individuals to purchase insurance would not suffice to solve the problem, because most of the uninsured are not uninsured by choice. Of particular concern to Congress were people who, though desperately in need of insurance, often cannot acquire it: persons who suffer from preexisting medical conditions.

Before the ACA's enactment, private insurance companies took an applicant's medical history into account when setting insurance rates or deciding whether to insure an individual. Because individuals with preexisting medical conditions cost insurance companies significantly more than those without such conditions, insurers routinely re-fused to insure these individuals, charged them substantially higher premiums, or offered only limited coverage that did not include the preexisting illness.

To ensure that individuals with medical histories have access to affordable insurance, Congress devised a three-part solution. First, Congress imposed a "guaranteed issue" requirement, which bars insurers from denying coverage to any person on account of that person's medical condition or history. Second, Congress required insurers to use "community rating" to price their insurance policies. Community rating, in effect, bars insurance companies from charging higher premiums to those with preexisting conditions.

But these two provisions, Congress comprehended, could not work effectively unless individuals were given a powerful incentive to obtain insurance.

* * *

Congress comprehended that guaranteed-issue and community-rating laws alone will not work. When insurance companies are required to insure the sick at affordable prices, individuals can wait until they become ill to buy insurance. Pretty soon, those in need of immediate medical care—*i.e.*, those who cost insurers the most—become the insurance companies' main customers. This "adverse selection" problem leaves insurers with two choices: They can either raise premiums dramatically to cover their ever-increasing costs or they can exit the market. In the seven States that tried guaranteed-issue and community-rating requirements without a minimum coverage provision, that is precisely what insurance companies did.

Massachusetts, Congress was told, cracked the adverse selection problem. By requiring most residents to obtain insurance, see Mass. Gen. Laws, ch. 111M, § 2 (West 2011), the Commonwealth ensured that insurers would not be left with only the sick as customers. As a result, federal lawmakers observed, Massachusetts succeeded where other States had failed. In coupling the minimum coverage provision with guaranteed-issue and community-rating prescriptions, Congress followed Massachusetts' lead.

In sum, Congress passed the minimum coverage provision as a key component of the ACA to address an economic and social problem that has plagued the Nation for decades: the large number of U. S. residents who are unable or unwilling to obtain health insurance. Whatever one thinks of the policy decision Congress made, it was Congress' prerogative to make it. Reviewed with appropriate deference, the minimum coverage provision, allied to the guaranteed-issue and community-rating prescriptions, should survive measurement under the Commerce and Necessary and Proper Clauses.

* * *

The Framers understood that the "general Interests of the Union" would change over time, in ways they could not anticipate. Accordingly, they recognized that the Constitution was of necessity a "great outlin[e]," not a detailed blueprint, see *McCulloch v. Maryland*, 4 Wheat. 316, 407 (1819) * * *. "Nothing . . . can be more fallacious," Alexander Hamilton emphasized, "than to infer the extent of any power, proper to be lodged in the national government, from . . . its immediate necessities. There ought to be a CAPACITY to provide for future contingencies[,] as they may happen; and as these are illimitable in their nature, it is impossible safely to limit that capacity." The Federalist No. 34, pp. 205, 206 (John Harvard Library ed. 2009). See also *McCulloch*, 4 Wheat., at 415 (The Necessary and Proper Clause is lodged "in a constitution[,] intended to endure for ages to come, and consequently, to be adapted to the various crises of human affairs.").

Consistent with the Framers' intent, we have repeatedly emphasized that Congress' authority under the Commerce Clause is dependent upon "practical" considerations, including "actual experience." *Jones & Laughlin Steel Corp.*, 301 U. S., at 41–42; see *Wickard v. Filburn*, 317 U. S. 111, 122 (1942). We afford Congress the leeway "to undertake to solve national problems directly and realistically."

Until today, this Court's pragmatic approach to judging whether Congress validly exercised its commerce power was guided by two familiar principles. First, Congress has the power to regulate economic activities "that substantially affect interstate commerce." *Gonzales v. Raich*, 545 U. S. 1, 17 (2005). This capacious power extends even to local activities that, viewed in the aggregate, have a substantial impact on interstate commerce. See *ibid*. See also *Wickard*, 317 U. S., at 125; *Jones & Laughlin Steel Corp.*, 301 U. S., at 37.

Second, we owe a large measure of respect to Congress when it frames and enacts economic and social legislation. See *Raich*, 545 U. S., at 17. When appraising such legislation, we ask only (1) whether Congress had a "rational basis" for concluding that the regulated activity substantially affects interstate commerce, and (2) whether there is a "reasonable connection between the regulatory means selected and the asserted ends." In answering these questions, we presume the statute under review is constitutional and may strike it down only on a "plain showing" that Congress acted irrationally.

Straightforward application of these principles would require the Court to hold that the minimum coverage provision is proper Commerce Clause legislation. Beyond dispute, Congress had a rational basis for concluding that the uninsured, as a class, substantially affect interstate commerce. Those without insurance consume billions of dollars of health-care products and services each year. Those goods are produced, sold, and delivered largely by national and regional companies who routinely transact business across state lines. The uninsured also cross state lines to receive care. Some have medical emergencies while away from home. Others, when sick, go to a neighboring State that provides better care for those who have not prepaid for care.

Not only do those without insurance consume a large amount of health care each year; critically, as earlier explained, their inability to pay for a significant portion of that consumption drives up market prices, foists costs on other consumers, and reduces market efficiency and stability. Given these far-reaching effects on interstate commerce, the decision to forgo insurance is hardly inconsequential or equivalent to "doing nothing," it is, instead, an economic decision Congress has the authority to address under the Commerce Clause.

The minimum coverage provision, furthermore, bears a "reasonable connection" to Congress' goal of protecting the health-care market from the disruption caused by individuals who fail to obtain insurance. By requiring those who do not carry insurance to pay a toll, the minimum coverage provision gives individuals a strong incentive to insure. This incentive, Congress had good reason to believe, would reduce the number of uninsured and, correspondingly, mitigate the adverse impact the uninsured have on the national health-care market.

Congress also acted reasonably in requiring uninsured individuals, whether sick or healthy, either to obtain insurance or to pay the specified penalty. As earlier observed, because every person is at risk of needing care at any moment, all those who lack insurance, regardless of their current health status, adversely affect the price of health care and health insurance. Moreover, an insurance-purchase requirement limited to those in need of immediate care simply could not work. Insurance companies would either charge these individuals prohibitively expensive premiums, or, if community-rating regulations were in place, close up shop.

* * * Rather than evaluating the constitutionality of the minimum coverage provision in the manner established by our precedents, THE CHIEF JUSTICE relies on a newly minted constitutional doctrine. The commerce power does not, THE CHIEF JUSTICE announces, permit Congress to "compe[l] individuals to become active in commerce by purchasing a product."

THE CHIEF JUSTICE'S novel constraint on Congress' commerce power gains no force from our precedent and for that reason alone warrants disapprobation. But even assuming, for the moment, that Congress lacks authority under the Commerce Clause to "compel individuals not engaged in commerce to purchase an unwanted product," such a limitation would be inapplicable here. Everyone will, at some point, consume health-care products and services. Thus, if THE CHIEF JUSTICE is correct that an insurance-purchase requirement can be applied only to those who "actively" consume health care, the minimum coverage provision fits the bill.

THE CHIEF JUSTICE does not dispute that all U. S. residents participate in the market for health services over the course of their lives. But, THE CHIEF JUSTICE insists, the uninsured cannot be considered active in the market for health care, because "[t]he proximity and degree of connection between the [uninsured today] and [their] subsequent commercial activity is too lacking."

This argument has multiple flaws. First, more than 60% of those without insurance visit a hospital or doctor's office each year. Nearly 90% will within five years. An uninsured's consumption of health care is thus quite proximate: It is virtually certain to occur in the next five years and more likely than not to occur this year.

Equally evident, Congress has no way of separating those uninsured individuals who will need emergency medical care today (surely their consumption of medical care is sufficiently imminent) from those who will not need medical services for years to come. No one knows when an emergency will occur, yet emergencies involving the uninsured arise daily. To capture individuals who unexpectedly will obtain medical care in the very near future, then, Congress needed to include individuals who will not go to a doctor anytime soon. Congress, our decisions instruct, has authority to cast its net that wide.

Second, it is Congress' role, not the Court's, to delineate the boundaries of the market the Legislature seeks to regulate. THE CHIEF JUSTICE defines the health-care market as including only those transactions that will occur either in the next instant or within some (unspecified) proximity to the next instant. But Congress could reasonably have viewed the market from a long-term perspective, encompassing all transactions virtually certain to occur over the next decade, not just those occurring here and now.

Third, contrary to THE CHIEF JUSTICE'S contention, our precedent does indeed support "[t]he proposition that Congress may dictate the conduct of an individual today because of prophesied future activity." In *Wickard*, the Court upheld a penalty the Federal Government imposed on a farmer who grew more wheat than he was permitted to grow under the Agricultural Adjustment Act of 1938 (AAA). 317 U. S., at 114–115. He could not be penalized, the farmer argued, as he was growing the wheat for home consumption, not for sale on the open market. The Court rejected this argument. Wheat intended for home consumption, the Court noted, "overhangs the market, and if induced by rising prices, tends to flow into the market and check price increases [intended by the AAA]." *Id.*, at 128.

Similar reasoning supported the Court's judgment in *Raich*, which upheld Congress' authority to regulate marijuana grown for personal use. 545 U. S., at 19. Home-grown marijuana substantially affects the interstate market for marijuana, we observed, for "the high demand in the interstate market will [likely] draw such marijuana into that market." *Ibid.*

Our decisions thus acknowledge Congress' authority, under the Commerce Clause, to direct the conduct of an individual today (the farmer in *Wickard*, stopped from growing excess wheat; the plaintiff in *Raich*, ordered to cease cultivating marijuana) because of a prophesied future transaction (the eventual sale of that wheat or marijuana in the interstate market). Congress' actions are even more rational in this case, where the future activity (the consumption of medical care) is certain to occur, the sole uncertainty being the time the activity will take place.

Maintaining that the uninsured are not active in the health-care market, THE CHIEF JUSTICE draws an analogy to the car market. An individual "is not 'active in the car market,'" THE CHIEF JUSTICE observes, simply because he or she may someday buy a car. The analogy is inapt. The inevitable yet unpredictable need for medical care and the guarantee that emergency care will be provided when required are conditions nonexistent in other markets. That is so of the market for cars, and of the market for broccoli as well. Although an individual *might* buy a car or a crown of broccoli one day, there is no certainty she will ever do so. And if she eventually wants a car or has a craving for broccoli, she will be obliged to pay at the counter before receiving the vehicle or nourishment. She will get no free ride or food, at the expense of another consumer forced to pay an inflated price. Upholding the minimum coverage provision on the ground that all are participants or will be participants in the health-care market would therefore carry no implication that Congress may justify under the Commerce Clause a mandate to buy other products and services.

Nor is it accurate to say that the minimum coverage provision "compel[s] individuals . . . to purchase an unwanted product," *ante*, at 18, or "suite of products," post, at 11, n. 2 (joint opinion of SCALIA, KENNEDY, THOMAS, and ALITO, JJ.).

If unwanted today, medical service secured by insurance may be desperately needed tomorrow. Virtually everyone, I reiterate, consumes health care at some point in his or her life. Health insurance is a means of paying for this care, nothing more. In requiring individuals to obtain insurance, Congress is therefore not mandating the purchase of a discrete, unwanted product. Rather, Congress is merely defining the terms on which individuals pay for an interstate good they consume: Persons subject to the mandate must now pay for medical care in advance (instead of at the point of service) and through insurance (instead of out of pocket). Establishing payment terms for goods in or affecting interstate commerce is quintessential economic regulation well within Congress' domain.

* * *

In any event, THE CHIEF JUSTICE's limitation of the commerce power to the regulation of those actively engaged in commerce finds no home in the text of the Constitution or our decisions. Article I, § 8, of the Constitution grants Congress the power "[t]o regulate Commerce . . . among the several States." Nothing in this language implies that Congress' commerce power is limited to regulating those actively engaged in commercial transactions. Indeed, as the D. C. Circuit observed, "[a]t the time the Constitution was [framed], to 'regulate' meant," among other things, "to require action." See *Seven-Sky v. Holder*, 661 F. 3d 1, 16 (2011).

* * *

Nor does our case law toe the activity versus inactivity line. In *Wickard*, for example, we upheld the penalty imposed on a farmer who grew too much wheat, even though the regulation had the effect of compelling farmers to purchase wheat in the open market. "[F]orcing some farmers into the market to buy what they could provide for themselves" was, the Court held, a valid means of regulating commerce. In another context, this Court similarly upheld Congress' authority under the commerce power to compel an "inactive" landholder to submit to an unwanted sale.

In concluding that the Commerce Clause does not permit Congress to regulate commercial "inactivity," and therefore does not allow Congress to adopt the practical solution it devised for the health-care problem, THE CHIEF JUSTICE views the Clause as a "technical legal conception," precisely what our case law tells us not to do. This Court's former endeavors to impose categorical limits on the commerce power have not fared well. In several pre-New Deal cases, the Court attempted to cabin Congress'

Commerce Clause authority by distinguishing "commerce" from activity once conceived to be noncommercial, notably, "production," "mining," and "manufacturing." The Court also sought to distinguish activities having a "direct" effect on interstate commerce, and for that reason, subject to federal regulation, from those having only an "indirect" effect, and therefore not amenable to federal control.

These line-drawing exercises were untenable, and the Court long ago abandoned them * * *.

It is not hard to show the difficulty courts (and Congress) would encounter in distinguishing statutes that regulate "activity" from those that regulate "inactivity" * * *. Take the instant litigation as an example. An individual who opts not to purchase insurance from a private insurer can be seen as actively selecting another form of insurance: self-insurance. The minimum coverage provision could therefore be described as regulating activists in the self-insurance market. *Wickard* is another example. Did the statute there at issue target activity (the growing of too much wheat) or inactivity (the farmer's failure to purchase wheat in the marketplace)? If anything, the Court's analysis suggested the latter. See 317 U. S., at 127–129.

* * *

Underlying THE CHIEF JUSTICE'S view that the Commerce Clause must be confined to the regulation of active participants in a commercial market is a fear that the commerce power would otherwise know no limits * * *. This concern is unfounded.

First, THE CHIEF JUSTICE could certainly uphold the individual mandate without giving Congress *carte blanche* to enact any and all purchase mandates. As several times noted, the unique attributes of the health-care market render everyone active in that market and give rise to a significant free-riding problem that does not occur in other markets.

Nor would the commerce power be unbridled, absent THE CHIEF JUSTICE'S "activity" limitation. Congress would remain unable to regulate noneconomic conduct that has only an attenuated effect on interstate commerce and is traditionally left to state law. See *Lopez*, 514 U. S., at 567; *Morrison*, 529 U. S., at 617–619. In *Lopez*, for example, the Court held that the Federal Government lacked power, under the Commerce Clause, to criminalize the possession of a gun in a local school zone. Possessing a gun near a school, the Court reasoned, "is in no sense an economic activity that might, through repetition elsewhere, substantially affect any sort of interstate commerce." 514 U. S., at 567; *ibid.* (noting that the Court would have "to pile inference upon inference" to conclude that gun possession has a substantial effect on commerce). Relying on similar logic, the Court concluded in *Morrison* that Congress could not regulate gender-motivated violence, which the Court deemed to have too "attenuated [an] effect upon interstate commerce." 529 U. S., at 615.

An individual's decision to self-insure, I have explained, is an economic act with the requisite connection to interstate commerce. Other choices individuals make are unlikely to fit the same or similar description. As an example of the type of regulation he fears, THE CHIEF JUSTICE cites a Government mandate to purchase green vegetables. One could call this concern "the broccoli horrible." Congress, THE CHIEF JUSTICE posits, might adopt such a mandate, reasoning that an individual's failure to eat a healthy diet, like the failure to purchase health insurance, imposes costs on others.

Consider the chain of inferences the Court would have to accept to conclude that a vegetable-purchase mandate was likely to have a substantial effect on the health-care costs borne by lithe Americans. The Court would have to believe that individuals forced to buy vegetables would then eat them (instead of throwing or giving them away), would prepare the vegetables in a healthy way (steamed or raw, not deep fried), would cut back on unhealthy foods, and would not allow other factors (such as lack of exercise or little sleep) to trump the improved diet. Such "pil[ing of] inference upon inference" is just what the Court refused to do in *Lopez* and *Morrison*.

Other provisions of the Constitution also check congressional overreaching. A mandate to purchase a particular product would be unconstitutional if, for example, the edict impermissibly abridged the freedom of speech, interfered with the free exercise of religion, or infringed on a liberty interest protected by the Due Process Clause.

Supplementing these legal restraints is a formidable check on congressional power: the democratic process. As the controversy surrounding the passage of the ACA attests, purchase mandates are likely to engender political resistance. This prospect is borne out by the behavior of state legislators. Despite their possession of unquestioned authority to impose mandates, state governments have rarely done so.

When contemplated in its extreme, almost any power looks dangerous. The commerce power, hypothetically, would enable Congress to prohibit the purchase and home production of all meat, fish, and dairy goods, effectively compelling Americans to eat only vegetables. Yet no one would offer the "hypothetical and unreal possibilit[y]" of a vegetarian state as a credible reason to deny Congress the authority ever to ban the possession and sale of goods * * *.

To bolster his argument that the minimum coverage provision is not valid Commerce Clause legislation, THE CHIEF JUSTICE emphasizes the provision's novelty * * *. For decades, the Court has declined to override legislation because of its novelty, and for good reason. As our national economy grows and changes, we have recognized, Congress must adapt to the changing "economic and financial realities." Hindering Congress' ability to do so is shortsighted; if history is any guide, today's constriction of the Commerce Clause will not endure.

* * *. When viewed as a component of the entire ACA, the provision's constitutionality becomes even plainer.

The Necessary and Proper Clause "empowers Congress to enact laws in effectuation of its [commerce] powe[r] that are not within its authority to enact in isolation." *Raich*, 545 U. S., at 39 (SCALIA, J., concurring in judgment) * * *. See also *Raich,* 545 U. S., at 24–25 (A challenged statutory provision fits within Congress' commerce authority if it is an "essential par[t] of a larger regulation of economic activity," such that, in the absence of the provision, "the regulatory scheme could be undercut." (quoting *Lopez,* 514 U. S., at 561)); *Raich*, 545 U. S., at 37 (SCALIA, J., concurring in judgment) ("Congress may regulate even noneconomic local activity if that regulation is a necessary part of a more general regulation of interstate commerce. The relevant question is simply whether the means chosen are 'reasonably adapted' to the attainment of a legitimate end under the commerce power." (citation omitted)).

Recall that one of Congress' goals in enacting the ACA was to eliminate the insurance industry's practice of charging higher prices or denying coverage to individuals with preexisting medical conditions. The commerce power allows Congress to ban this practice, a point no one disputes. See *United States v. South-Eastern Underwriters Assn.*, 322 U. S. 533–553 (1944) (Congress may regulate "the methods by which interstate insurance companies do business.").

Congress knew, however, that simply barring insurance companies from relying on an applicant's medical history would not work in practice. Without the individual mandate, Congress learned, guaranteed-issue and community-rating requirements would trigger an adverse-selection death spiral in the health-insurance market: Insurance premiums would skyrocket, the number of uninsured would increase, and insurance companies would exit the market. When complemented by an insurance mandate, on the other hand, guaranteed issue and community rating would work as intended, increasing access to insurance and reducing uncompensated care. The minimum coverage provision is thus an "essential par[t] of a larger regulation of economic activity"; without the provision, "the regulatory scheme [w]ould be undercut." *Raich*, 545 U. S., at 24–25 (internal quotation marks omitted) * * *.

Asserting that the Necessary and Proper Clause does not authorize the minimum coverage provision, THE CHIEF JUSTICE focuses on the word "proper." A mandate to purchase health insurance is not "proper" legislation, THE CHIEF JUSTICE urges, because the command "undermine[s] the structure of government established by the Constitution." If long on rhetoric, THE CHIEF JUSTICE'S argument is short on substance.

THE CHIEF JUSTICE cites only two cases in which this Court concluded that a federal statute impermissibly transgressed the Constitution's boundary between state and federal authority: *Printz v. United States*, 521 U. S. 898 (1997), and *New York v. United States*, 505 U. S. 144 (1992). The statutes at issue in both cases, however, compelled *state officials* to act on the Federal Government's behalf. "[Federal] laws conscripting state officers," the Court reasoned, "violate state sovereignty and are thus not in accord with the Constitution." *Printz*, 521 U. S., at 925, 935; *New York*, 505 U. S., at 176.

The minimum coverage provision, in contrast, acts "directly upon individuals, without employing the States as intermediaries." *New York*, 505 U. S., at 164. The provision is thus entirely consistent with the Constitution's design.

* * *

Nor does The Chief Justice pause to explain *why* the power to direct either the purchase of health insurance or, alternatively, the payment of a penalty collectible as a tax is more far-reaching than other implied powers this Court has found meet under the Necessary and Proper Clause. These powers include the power to enact criminal laws, the power to imprison, including civil imprisonment, and the power to create a national bank.

In failing to explain why the individual mandate threatens our constitutional order, THE CHIEF JUSTICE disserves future courts. How is a judge to decide, when ruling on the constitutionality of a federal statute, whether Congress employed an "independent power" or merely a "derivative' one? Whether the power used is "substantive" or just "incidental"? The instruction THE CHIEF JUSTICE, in effect, provides lower courts: You will know it when you see it.

* * *

Second, and perhaps most important, the minimum coverage provision, along with other provisions of the ACA, addresses the very sort of interstate problem that made the commerce power essential in our federal system. The crisis created by the large number of U. S. residents who lack health insurance is one of national dimension that States are "separately incompetent" to handle. Far from trampling on States' sovereignty, the ACA attempts a federal solution for the very reason that the States, acting separately, cannot meet the need. Notably, the ACA serves the general welfare of the people of the United States while retaining a prominent role for the States.

In the early 20th century, this Court regularly struck down economic regulation enacted by the peoples' representatives in both the States and the Federal Government. THE CHIEF JUSTICE'S Commerce Clause opinion, and even more so the joint dissenters' reasoning, bear a disquieting resemblance to those long-overruled decisions.

Ultimately, the Court upholds the individual mandate as a proper exercise of Congress' power to tax and spend "for the . . . general Welfare of the United States." Art. I, § 8, cl. 1. I concur in that determination, which makes THE CHIEF JUSTICE'S Commerce Clause essay all the more puzzling. Why should THE CHIEF JUSTICE strive so mightily to hem in Congress' capacity to meet the new problems arising constantly in our ever-developing modern economy? I find no satisfying response to that question in his opinion.

* * *

■ JUSTICE SCALIA, JUSTICE KENNEDY, JUSTICE THOMAS, and JUSTICE ALITO, dissenting.

* * *

* * * What is absolutely clear, affirmed by the text of the 1789 Constitution, by the Tenth Amendment ratified in 1791, and by innumerable cases of ours in the 220 years since, is that there are structural limits upon federal power—upon what it can prescribe with respect to private conduct, and upon what it can impose upon the sovereign States. Whatever may be the conceptual limits upon the Commerce Clause and upon the power to tax and spend, they cannot be such as will enable the Federal Government to regulate all private conduct and to compel the States to function as administrators of federal programs.

That clear principle carries the day here. The striking case of *Wickard v. Filburn,* 317 U.S. 111 (1942), which held that the economic activity of growing wheat, even for one's own consumption, affected commerce sufficiently that it could be regulated, always has been regarded as the *ne plus ultra* of expansive Commerce Clause jurisprudence. To go beyond that, and to say the *failure* to grow wheat (which is *not* an economic activity, or any activity at all) nonetheless affects commerce and therefore can be federally regulated, is to make mere breathing in and out the basis for federal prescription and to extend federal power to virtually all human activity.

* * *

Article I, § 8, of the Constitution gives Congress the power to "regulate Commerce . . . among the several States." The Individual Mandate in the Act commands that every "applicable individual shall for each month beginning after 2013 ensure that the individual, and any dependent of the individual who is an applicable individual, is covered under minimum essential coverage." If this provision "regulates" anything, it is the *failure* to maintain minimum essential coverage. One might argue that it regulates that failure by requiring it to be accompanied by payment of a penalty. But that failure—that abstention from commerce—is not "Commerce." To be sure, *purchasing* insurance *is* "Commerce"; but one does not regulate commerce that does not exist by compelling its existence.

* * *

In response, the Government offers two theories as to why the Individual Mandate is nevertheless constitutional. Neither theory suffices to sustain its validity.

First, the Government submits that * * * [the individual mandate] is "integral to the Affordable Care Act's insurance reforms" and "necessary to make effective the Act's core reforms." * * *

* * *

The Government presents the Individual Mandate as a unique feature of a complicated regulatory scheme governing many parties with countervailing incentives that must be carefully balanced. Congress has imposed an extensive set of regulations on the health insurance industry, and compliance with those regulations will likely cost the industry a great deal. If the industry does not respond by increasing premiums, it is not likely to survive. And if the industry does increase premiums, then there is a serious risk that its products—insurance plans—will become economically undesirable for many and prohibitively expensive for the rest.

This is not a dilemma unique to regulation of the health insurance industry. Government regulation typically imposes costs on the regulated industry—especially regulation that prohibits economic behavior in which most market participants are already engaging, such as "piecing out" the market by selling the product to different classes of people at different prices (in the present context, providing much lower insurance rates to young and healthy buyers). And many industries so regulated face the reality that, without an artificial increase in demand, they cannot continue on. When Congress is regulating these industries directly, it enjoys the broad power to enact " 'all appropriate legislation' " to " 'protec[t]' " and " 'advanc[e]' " commerce, *NLRB v. Jones & Laughlin Steel Corp.*, 301 U.S. 1, 36–37 (1937). Thus, Congress might protect the imperiled industry by prohibiting low-cost competition, or by according it preferential tax treatment, or even by granting it a direct subsidy.

Here, however, Congress has impressed into service third parties, healthy individuals who could be but are not customers of the relevant industry, to offset the undesirable consequences of the regulation. Congress' desire to force these individuals to purchase insurance is motivated by the fact that they are further removed from the market than unhealthy individuals with pre-existing conditions, because they are less likely to need extensive care in the near future. If Congress can reach out and command even those furthest removed from an interstate market to participate in the market, then the Commerce Clause becomes a font of unlimited power, or in Hamilton's words, "the hideous monster whose devouring jaws . . . spare neither sex nor age, nor high nor low, nor sacred nor profane." The Federalist No. 33, p. 202 (C. Rossiter ed. 1961).

At the outer edge of the commerce power, this Court has insisted on careful scrutiny of regulations that do not act directly on an interstate market or its participants. In *New York v. United States,* 505 U.S. 144 (1992), we held that Congress could not, in an effort to regulate the disposal of radioactive waste produced in several different industries, order the States to take title to that waste. *Id.,* at 174–177. In *Printz v. United States,* 521 U.S. 898 (1997), we held that Congress could not, in an effort to regulate the distribution of firearms in the interstate market, compel state law enforcement officials to perform background checks. *Id.,* at 933–935. In *United States v. Lopez,* 514 U.S. 549 (1995), we held that Congress could not, as a means of fostering an educated interstate labor market through the protection of schools, ban the possession of a firearm within a school zone. *Id.,* at 559–563. And in *United States v. Morrison,* 529 U.S. 598 (2000), we held that Congress could not, in an effort to ensure the full participation of women in the interstate economy, subject private individuals and companies to suit for gender-motivated violent torts. *Id.,* at 609–619. The lesson of these cases is that the Commerce Clause, even when supplemented by the Necessary and Proper Clause, is not *carte blanche* for doing whatever will help achieve the ends Congress seeks by the regulation of commerce. And the last two of these cases show that the scope of the Necessary and Proper Clause is exceeded not only when the congressional action directly violates the sovereignty of the States but also when it violates the background principle of enumerated (and hence limited) federal power.

The case upon which the Government principally relies to sustain the Individual Mandate under the Necessary and Proper Clause is *Gonzales v. Raich,* 545 U.S. 1 (2005). That case held that Congress could, in an effort to restrain the interstate market in marijuana, ban the local cultivation and possession of that drug. *Id.,* at 15–22. *Raich* is no precedent for what Congress has done here. That case's prohibition of growing (cf. *Wickard,* 317 U.S. 111), and of possession (cf. innumerable federal statutes) did not represent the expansion of the federal power to direct into a broad new field. The mandating of economic activity does, and since it is a field so limitless that it converts the Commerce Clause into a general authority to direct the economy, that mandating is not "consist[ent] with the letter and spirit of the constitution." *McCulloch v. Maryland,* 4 Wheat. 316, 421 (1819).

Moreover, *Raich* is far different from the Individual Mandate in another respect. The Court's opinion in *Raich* pointed out that the growing and possession prohibitions were the only practicable way of enabling the prohibition of interstate traffic in marijuana to be effectively enforced. Intrastate marijuana could no more be distinguished from interstate marijuana than, for example, endangered-species trophies obtained before the species was federally protected can be distinguished from trophies obtained afterwards—which made it necessary and proper to prohibit the sale of all such trophies, see *Andrus v. Allard,* 444 U.S. 51 (1979).

With the present statute, by contrast, there are many ways other than this unprecedented Individual Mandate by which the regulatory scheme's goals of reducing insurance premiums and ensuring the profitability of insurers could be achieved. For instance, those who did not purchase insurance could be subjected to a surcharge when they do enter the health insurance system. Or they could be denied a full income tax credit given to those who do purchase the insurance.

The Government was invited, at oral argument, to suggest what federal controls over private conduct (other than those explicitly prohibited by the Bill of Rights or other constitutional controls) could *not* be justified as necessary and proper for the carrying out of a general regulatory scheme. See Tr. of Oral Arg. 27–30, 43–45 (Mar.

27, 2012). It was unable to name any. As we said at the outset, whereas the precise scope of the Commerce Clause and the Necessary and Proper Clause is uncertain, the proposition that the Federal Government cannot do everything is a fundamental precept * * *.

The Government's second theory in support of the Individual Mandate is that § 5000A is valid because it is actually a "regulat[ion of] activities having a substantial relation to interstate commerce, . . . *i.e.,* . . . activities that substantially affect interstate commerce." *Id.,* at 558–559. See also *Shreveport Rate Cases, supra.* This argument takes a few different forms, but the basic idea is that § 5000A regulates "the way in which individuals finance their participation in the health-*care* market." Petitioners' Minimum Coverage Brief 33 (emphasis added). That is, the provision directs the manner in which individuals purchase health care services and related goods (directing that they be purchased through insurance) and is therefore a straightforward exercise of the commerce power.

The primary problem with this argument is that § 5000A does not apply only to persons who purchase all, or most, or even any, of the health care services or goods that the mandated insurance covers. Indeed, the main objection many have to the Mandate is that they have no intention of purchasing most or even any of such goods or services and thus no need to buy insurance for those purchases. The Government responds that the health care market involves "essentially universal participation," *id.,* at 35. The principal difficulty with this response is that it is, in the only relevant sense, not true. It is true enough that everyone consumes "health care," if the term is taken to include the purchase of a bottle of aspirin. But the health care "market" that is the object of the Individual Mandate not only includes but principally consists of goods and services that the young people primarily affected by the Mandate *do not purchase.* They are quite simply not participants in that market, and cannot be made so (and thereby subjected to regulation) by the simple device of defining participants to include all those who will, later in their lifetime, probably purchase the goods or services covered by the mandated insurance. Such a definition of market participants is unprecedented, and were it to be a premise for the exercise of national power, it would have no principled limits.

In a variation on this attempted exercise of federal power, the Government points out that Congress in this Act has purported to regulate "economic and financial decision[s] to forego health insurance coverage and [to] attempt to self-insure," since those decisions have "a substantial and deleterious effect on interstate commerce," Petitioners' Minimum Coverage Brief 34. But as the discussion above makes clear, the decision to forgo participation in an interstate market is not itself commercial activity (or indeed any activity at all) within Congress' power to regulate. It is true that, at the end of the day, it is inevitable that each American will affect commerce and become a part of it, even if not by choice. But if every person comes within the Commerce Clause power of Congress to regulate by the simple reason that he will one day engage in commerce, the idea of a limited Government power is at an end.

Wickard v. Filburn has been regarded as the most expansive assertion of the commerce power in our history. A close second is *Perez v. United States,* 402 U.S. 146 (1971), which upheld a statute criminalizing the eminently local activity of loan-sharking. Both of those cases, however, involved commercial *activity.* To go beyond that, and to say that the failure to grow wheat or the refusal to make loans affects commerce, so that growing and lending can be federally compelled, is to extend federal power to virtually everything. All of us consume food, and when we do so the Federal Government can prescribe what its quality must be and even how much we must pay. But the mere fact that we all consume food and are thus, sooner or later, participants in the "market" for food, does not empower the Government to say when and what we will buy. That is essentially what this Act seeks to do with respect to the purchase of health care. It exceeds federal power.

A few respectful responses to JUSTICE GINSBURG'S dissent on the issue of the Mandate are in order. That dissent duly recites the test of Commerce Clause power that our opinions have applied, but disregards the premise the test contains. It is true enough that Congress needs only a " 'rational basis' for concluding that the *regulated activity* substantially affects interstate commerce," *ante,* at 602 (emphasis added). But it must be *activity* affecting commerce that is regulated, and not merely the failure to engage in commerce. And one is not now purchasing the health care covered by the insurance mandate simply because one is likely to be purchasing it in the future. Our test's premise of regulated activity is not invented out of whole cloth, but rests upon the Constitution's requirement that it be commerce which is regulated. If all inactivity affecting commerce is commerce, commerce is everything. Ultimately the dissent is driven to saying that there is really no difference between action and inaction, a proposition that has never recommended itself, neither to the law nor to common sense. To say, for example, that the inaction here consists of activity in "the self-insurance market" seems to us wordplay. By parity of reasoning the failure to buy a car can be called participation in the non-private-car-transportation market. Commerce becomes everything.

The dissent claims that we "fai[l] to explain why the individual mandate threatens our constitutional order." *Ante,* at 621. But we have done so. It threatens that order because it gives such an expansive meaning to the Commerce Clause that *all* private conduct (including failure to act) becomes subject to federal control, effectively destroying the Constitution's division of governmental powers. Thus the dissent, on the theories proposed for the validity of the Mandate, would alter the accepted constitutional relation between the individual and the National Government. The dissent protests that the Necessary and Proper Clause has been held to include "the power to enact criminal laws, . . . the power to imprison, . . . and the power to create a national bank," *ibid,*. Is not the power to compel purchase of health insurance much lesser? No, not if (unlike those other dispositions) its application rests upon a theory that everything is within federal control simply because it exists.

The dissent's exposition of the wonderful things the Federal Government has achieved through exercise of its assigned powers, such as "the provision of old-age and survivors' benefits" in the Social Security Act, *ante,* at 589, is quite beside the point. The issue here is whether the Federal Government can impose the Individual Mandate through the Commerce Clause. And the relevant history is not that Congress has achieved wide and wonderful results through the proper exercise of its assigned powers in the past, but that it has never before used the Commerce Clause to compel entry into commerce. The dissent treats the Constitution as though it is an enumeration of those problems that the Federal Government can address—among which, it finds, is "the Nation's course in the economic and social welfare realm," *ibid.,* and more specifically "the problem of the uninsured," *ante,* at 595. The

Constitution is not that. It enumerates not federally soluble *problems,* but federally available *powers.* The Federal Government can address whatever problems it wants but can bring to their solution only those powers that the Constitution confers, among which is the power to regulate commerce. None of our cases say anything else. Article I contains no whatever-it-takes-to-solve-a-national-problem power.

* * *

NOTES AND QUESTIONS

1. Isn't Chief Justice Roberts right that if one can compel a person to buy health insurance, one can compel him or her to buy broccoli or a membership in a gym to work out for an hour a day? All these things might reduce current U.S. health care costs. Does Justice Ginsburg respond adequately? Is the correct answer that, yes, Congress could require those things if it felt like it? Can your state or local government require you to buy those things?

2. Five justices agreed that there is a constitutional line between activity and inactivity. Commerce Clause cases have drawn many formal lines over the years, including the lines between commerce and agriculture/mining/manufacturing, between direct and indirect effects on commerce, and between articles being shipped and articles waiting to be shipped. Justice Ginsburg's dissenting opinion correctly points out that all of those lines have been discarded. Is that a good reason not to try to draw further ones? Is the activity/inactivity line better grounded in any fashion than are those other lines?

3. It frankly seems obvious to us that inactivity is not "Commerce * * * among the several States." It was accepted by everyone in *NFIB,* however, that the insurance market *does* constitute "Commerce * * * among the several States," so that the congressional regulations of insurance in the ACA, such as requiring insurance companies to cover certain claims and forbidding them from charging higher rates to people with higher actuarial risks, were clearly constitutional. The real question, then, is whether the individual mandate was "necessary and proper for carrying into Execution" those conceded exercises of the commerce power. Is it surprising that the three opinions spend so much time on the Commerce Clause and so little on the Necessary and Proper Clause?

4. Go back to *Lopez.* How much does it say about the Necessary and Proper Clause? We will save you the trouble: Neither *Lopez* nor *United States v. Morrison* discuss the Necessary and Proper Clause at all. Both opinions are all about whether activity must be in some sense "commercial" in order to be within the scope of the commerce power. But as with the individual mandate, isn't the most obvious defense of the laws in those cases that they are incidental to conceded congressional powers, such as the power to control the interstate flow of goods and people? The Commerce Clause, after all, authorizes Congress to regulate "Commerce," not activity that is not itself "Commerce" but which substantially affects commerce. If Congress can regulate activity that substantially affects commerce, it is because such regulation is "necessary and proper for carrying into Execution" the commerce power. Court decisions from *Gibbons* onward have often elided this key point, though it occasionally rises to the fore. *See Gonzales v. Raich,* 545 U.S. 1, 33–35 (2005) (Scalia, J., concurring in the judgment). The joint dissent in *NFIB* claims that *Lopez* and *Morrison* "show that the scope of the Necessary and Proper Clause is exceeded not only when the congressional action directly violates the sovereignty of the States but also when it violates the background principle of enumerated (and hence limited) federal power." The Chief Justice appears to agree on this point. Are *Lopez* and *Morrison,* along with *NFIB,* therefore precedents on the meaning of the Necessary and Proper Clause—and for the proposition that the "substantial effects" inquiry is really

about the Necessary and Proper Clause rather than about the meaning of "Commerce * * * among the several States"?

5. With respect to the meaning of the Necessary and Proper Clause, the Chief Justice resurrected, for the first time in nearly two centuries, Chief Justice Marshall's language from *McCulloch* regarding "incidental" and "great substantive and independent" powers. Is the power to compel people to engage in commercial transactions a "great substantive and independent power" that would have to be enumerated and cannot be incidental? One of us so argued in *NFIB*. *See* Brief of Authors of *The Origins of the Necessary and Proper Clause* (Gary Lawson, Robert G. Natelson & Guy Seidman) and the Independence Institute As Amici Curiae in Support of Respondents (Minimum Coverage Provision), Dep't. of Health & Human Servs. v. Florida, No. 11–398 (U.S. Feb. 13, 2012), 2012 WL 484061. If that is correct, then one can find the individual mandate unconstitutional without overruling, or even limiting, any other cases, including *Wickard*. Justice Ginsburg worried that lower court judges (and future Supreme Courts) will not know how to apply this test, and a phalanx of academic commentators raise the same concern. *See* GARY LAWSON & GUY SEIDMAN, "A GREAT POWER OF ATTORNEY": UNDERSTANDING THE FIDUCIARY CONSTITUTION 98 (2017) (spending half a page rattling off such comments). A possible answer is that "[c]ourts, and drafters of agency instruments, had been distinguishing principals from incidents for centuries before the Constitution was ratified * * *. If the academic community wants to know how to tell a principal power from an incidental power, or at least to tell what the founding generation would have considered a principal power, it needs to look beyond the pages of the United States Reports to the background ideas of agency that give content to the necessary and proper clause." *Id.* at 99.

6. Is the power to regulate intrastate commerce when it has a substantial effect on interstate commerce a "great substantive and independent power"?

7. The excerpt from the joint dissent concludes: "Article I contains no whatever-it-takes-to-solve-a-national-problem power." If Article I was meant to incorporate the Virginia and Bedford Resolutions, that is simply not true; the purpose of those Resolutions was precisely to empower the national government to solve national problems, leaving local problems to the States. The case law that has developed over the last century is largely consistent with this national-problem-solving vision of national power—certainly more consistent than with an originalist, ordinary-language reading of the specific enumerations in Article I, Section 8. Is there a way, without overruling dozens of landmark cases on which major institutions have been built, to provide a structure for this case law that conforms it to principles of federalism better than does a "rational basis" test looking for "substantial effects" on commerce? Consider the efforts of one of us to provide a descriptive and normative structure for the caselaw regarding the vertical division of governmental power.

8. Professor Calabresi has offered a theory of federalism that synthesizes many of the themes from the preceding cases. He does not maintain that his proposed decision structure, using the "Economics of Federalism," is easy to administer, explains all of the prior cases, or achieves desirable results in all circumstances. He says only that it does those things, on balance, *better* than do either the current "substantial effects" inquiry or complete deference to Congress and the President. Can you come up with a better structure that does not require overruling more than a handful of cases? For an argument in favor of a very similar structure, see Robert D. Cooter & Neil S. Siegel, *Collective Action Federalism: A General Theory of Article I, Section 8*, 63 STAN. L. REV. 115 (2010).

D. THE ECONOMICS OF FEDERALISM

Steven G. Calabresi & Lucy D. Bickford, Federalism and Subsidiarity: Perspectives from U.S. Constitutional Law[1]

Economics teaches us some simple but fundamental truths about when government decision making is best done at the state or local level versus the national level * * *.

Restricting lawmaking to the state or provincial level in any federation has at least four obvious advantages: (1) regional variation in preferences; (2) competition for taxpayers and businesses; (3) experimentation to develop the best set of rules; and (4) lower monitoring costs.

First, tastes, preferences, and real-world conditions may often differ between territories in a large, continental-sized democracy. For example, some states like Alaska or Montana with a very low population density may prefer a higher speed limit for automobiles than a high-density state like New Jersey. If the national government decides all speed limits, the result may be too low for Alaska and too high for New Jersey. In contrast, if speed limits are decided at the state level, each state can tailor its speed limit to conform to local tastes, preferences, and real-world conditions * * *.

Second, in a federal system where states make certain decisions, the states compete for people, taxpayers, businesses, and other financial resources to the extent that property and persons are fully mobile (which is not always the case). Each state offers a different bundle of public goods, level of taxation, and package of government services. Residents weigh these bundles to decide whether to stay put or to move if another state offers a perceived superior bundle * * *. Monopoly providers are often inefficient and dismissive of consumer preferences. The same holds true for government monopoly providers of bundles of public goods * * *.

* * *

A third Economics of Federalism argument for state-level decision making is that states will continually experiment with new bundles of services to attract new taxpayers and businesses * * *. Currently, the fifty United States are experimenting with legalizing gay marriage, allowing assisted suicide, and legalizing medical marijuana use. These experiments are beneficial for the country. Experimentation and competition among the states thus support reserving decision-making power to the state level.

Finally, monitoring state officials as compared to national officials may cost less. The smaller territorial size of state legislative districts may produce greater congruence between the mores of the legislators and the people. Also, the people may more easily physically observe and question government officials in close proximity rather than many miles away. Local officials may thus avoid what has been called an "inside-the-beltway mentality." Large, multilayered bureaucracies cannot efficiently process new information—neither in government nor in the private sector—as Friedrich Hayek shows in *Law, Legislation, and Liberty* and Thomas

[1] Reprinted in: NOMOS LV: FEDERALISM AND SUBSIDIARITY 123 (James E. Fleming & Jacob T. Levy eds., 2014).

Sowell shows in *Knowledge and Decisions*. Federalism avoids overly centralized, top-down command and control mechanisms that national governments might otherwise tend to favor.

* * * [T]hese four arguments for leaving governmental decision-making power at the state or provincial level establish a presumption in favor of state over national decision making * * *.

* * * Unless one of the arguments for national power described in the following applies, a matter ought to be decided at the state or provincial level.

There are at least four arguments for allowing a national government to legislate and preempt state lawmaking power in some circumstances.

First, sometimes there are substantial economies of scale in undertaking an activity or financing a program only once rather than fifty times. Surely economies of scale may be realized as a result, for example, of one federal space program rather than fifty separate programs. There are probably economies of scale in most national defense and foreign policy activities. One danger is that rent-seeking efforts at regulatory capture may be rewarded more fully at the federal level because federal capture is more likely to yield rents in the absence of competing jurisdictions. This cost must be weighed against the benefits from economies of scale or otherwise that may be available when national governments act.

Second, national action can overcome the high costs of collective action that the states would otherwise face. It would be very time-consuming and expensive for the fifty states to act collectively on foreign policy, or defense, or national economic policy. Some states might refuse to join in policies that a majority of states representing a majority of the people endorse. Such holdout states might trigger a race to the bottom and cause the legal standard of the most permissive state to force all other states to comply, even if a majority of the nation wished otherwise. An example is no-fault divorce law; Nevada's easy divorce policies ultimately set a national standard. The states also famously raced to the bottom by allowing child labor in the first decades of the twentieth century. Federal action can stop races to the bottom and can overcome collective action problems, which is the primary justification for federal power in some circumstances.

Third, national action may be necessary if the states' activities generate serious external costs on out-of-state residents. For example, when a state pollutes the air or the water and downwind states bear the burden, the polluting state may need incentives to reduce pollution. If a state could realize the economic benefits of a factory while the costs of its pollution fell mostly on other states, the polluting state would have no incentive to clean up its act. National regulation of clean air and water is thus essential to correct for the externalities problem. Other circumstances may also necessitate national lawmaking when state action negatively affects other states.

Fourth, the national government is better at handling civil rights issues than are the states. James Madison first predicted this phenomenon in *The Federalist* No. 10, where he noted that the legislature of a large continental democracy would represent many more factions or interest groups than a small democratic city-state. Therefore, it is less likely that a permanent, oppressive majority coalition will capture the legislature of a large federation than that it might capture the legislature of a member unit of the federation. There are more interest groups vying to capture

Congress than vie to capture the Illinois legislature, so it is harder to form and hold together a permanent entrenched majority coalition. Also, discrete and insular minorities face lower organizational costs in lobbying Congress than are faced by the so-called silent majority nationwide. Part of the reason national majorities are "silent" is because it is so hard and expensive for them to organize.

As Madison predicted in *The Federalist* No. 10, the U.S. national government has in fact been much more protective of the civil rights of minority groups than the states. Congress freed the slaves, helped to end segregation, and was the first institution to protect women's equal rights in the Civil Rights Act of 1964. Federal action is thus warranted when a matter concerns fundamental civil rights. Federal action may also be needed if state laws infringe on immobile property, like real estate, or on people who may find it overly burdensome to move, like the elderly.

One difficulty is that one person's fundamental civil rights issue may be another person's instance where varying tastes and cultural preferences favor state-level decision making. There is no easy answer to this problem. In general, we must fall back on practical wisdom and common sense to try to decide whether the issue implicates fundamental civil rights or varying tastes and cultural preferences. Decision makers should approach this problem in a spirit of tolerance and of willingness to "live and let live."

* * *

In sum, there is a strong economic case for presumptively leaving power at the state level unless the presumption is trumped by evidence that (1) there are economies of scale to national action; (2) the states are suffering from a collective action problem; (3) the states are imposing negative external costs on their neighbors; or (4) there is a bona fi de fundamental civil rights issue at stake * * *.

A second conclusion is that federalism inherently calls for some balance between state and national power. Sometimes it will be a close judgment call as to whether the economic arguments for state-level or national action predominate. Federalism is neither the same thing as nationalism nor the same thing as states' rights. Federalism is inherently about the need for a balance—a golden mean—between the extremes of nationalism and of states' rights.

Third, the analysis thus far has implications for national supreme courts enforcing vague human rights guarantees in national constitutions * * *. Those courts must balance the need to protect fundamental human rights with the fact that tastes, cultural preferences, and real-world conditions may differ at the state level in the United States * * *

Finally, some American critics of constitutional federalism have suggested that the economic arguments presented earlier counsel in favor of decentralization at the grace of the national government. We disagree. The problem is that it is too easy for the national government to legislate in circumstances where it ought to defer to the states because Congress and the president are self-interested national actors. Ensuring the right balance requires a constitutional federal structure such that neither the central government nor the states are the sole judges of what gets nationalized and what is left to the states. It is a fundamental maxim of Anglo-American constitutional law that no man ought to be a judge in his own cause. The advocates of decentralization over constitutional federalism would wrongly make the national government the judge of the extent of its own powers vis-à-vis the states.

* * *

* * * From 1789 to the present, the Supreme Court has consistently read the Constitution as giving the federal government the power under the Necessary and Proper Clause "to legislate in all cases for the general interests of the Union, and also in those to which the States are separately incompetent, or in which the harmony of the United States may be interrupted by the exercise of individual legislation." The categorical listing of powers in Article I, Section 8, Clauses 1 to 17 did not prevent the Supreme Court from reading the Constitution as if it had enacted the words of the Bedford Resolution rather than a categorical enumeration of powers.

* * *

The Supreme Court famously rejected categorical federalism in favor of an Economics of Federalism approach in *The Shreveport Rate Cases*, decided in 1914. In that series of cases the Court considered whether the Interstate Commerce Commission could regulate wholly intrastate rates along interstate railway lines. Justice Charles Evans Hughes wrote that congressional power in these circumstances "necessarily embraces the right to control . . .operations in all matters having a close and substantial relation to interstate traffic, to the efficiency of interstate service, and to the maintenance of conditions under which interstate commerce may be conducted upon fair terms." The power to regulate wholly intrastate railway shipments that have "a close and substantial relation to interstate commerce" is a Bedford Resolution-type power accomplished under the guise of the Necessary and Proper Clause. Between 1895 and 1937, the Supreme Court did strike down acts of Congress to enforce categorical constitutional federalism in a series of cases * * *. In those cases the Court distinguished between commerce, which Congress could regulate, and manufacturing or agriculture, which it could not. Among these cases are *United States v. E. C. Knight Co.*; *Hammer v. Dagenhart*; *Bailey v. Drexel Furniture Co.*; *Schechter Poultry Corp. v. United States*; *Carter v. Carter Coal Co.*; and *United States v. Butler*. Though these cases are all now overruled (except for *Bailey*), they importantly foreshadow the reemergence of judicially enforced constitutional federalism in the 1995 *United States v. Lopez* decision discussed later.

During the New Deal constitutional revolution of 1937, the Supreme Court decisively rejected categorical federalism * * *, holding that all wholly intrastate commerce that substantially affects commerce among the states is regulable under the Necessary and Proper Clause. The Court held in *National Labor Relations Board v. Jones & Laughlin Steel Corp.* that the National Labor Relations Act of 1935, popularly known as the Wagner Act, was constitutional. The Wagner Act effectively governed labor law in manufacturing entities that shipped goods nationwide. Chief Justice Charles Evans Hughes found the same "close and substantial" connection between a wholly intrastate activity and interstate commerce that he had found as an associate justice in *The Shreveport Rate Cases*. *Jones & Laughlin Steel* says that labor peace is so important to commerce among the several states that Congress can regulate it as a means (under the Necessary and Proper Clause) toward promoting interstate commerce. *Jones & Laughlin Steel*, together with *McCulloch* * * * and the *Shreveport Rate Cases* [among other decisions], made it clear beyond any doubt that the federal government has power under Article I, Section 8 to solve all collective action and Economics of Federalism problems.

* * * [Thus], in a series of landmark Supreme Court opinions from the Founding era up until 1995, the Supreme Court has held that the national government may regulate all wholly intrastate activities that *substantially* affect commerce or any other federal power. This test, indeterminate on its face, invites consideration of the Economics of Federalism as a way to supply needed content * * *.

* * *

In its 1995 decision in *United States v. Lopez*, the U.S. Supreme Court held by a vote of 5 to 4 that Congress lacked power under the Commerce Clause and the Necessary and Proper Clause to criminalize bringing a gun within 1,000 feet of a school. The Court distinguished all the cases previously discussed, noting that they all involved commercial activities whereas *Lopez* involved a garden-variety state law crime. Further, more than forty states criminalized bringing guns to school, which meant there was no race to the bottom over the issue. It was also clear from the facts of the case that federal regulation would realize no economies of scale, there were no negative external effects of state law to correct, and there were no civil rights issues lurking in the case. The outcome in *Lopez* was thus entirely consistent with the Economics of Federalism. *Lopez* reiterated the doctrine of *Jones & Laughlin Steel* that Congress could only regulate wholly intrastate activities that *substantially* burdened interstate commerce, but this time it struck down a federal statute instead of upholding it.

Since *Lopez*, the Supreme Court has applied the substantial effects test twice—and reached the wrong result both times in our view. In *United States v. Morrison*, the Supreme Court wrongly struck down a civil rights measure, the Violence Against Women Act, while in *Gonzales v. Raich*, the Court wrongly upheld a federal statute that criminally punished a woman who grew six marijuana plants in her house, which was legal under California state law. The Court's holding in *Morrison* was consistent with a categorical approach but inconsistent with the Economics of Federalism. The law at issue in *Morrison* was a civil rights law, and, as we argued earlier, the federal government ought to have the power to adopt such measures. The Court's holding in *Gonzales v. Raich* was problematic because states differed in their tastes, preferences, and conditions on the medical use of marijuana and because the federal interest in regulating possession of very small amounts of homegrown marijuana by very ill people was quite small * * *.

* * *

In summary, since the 1995 decision in *United States v. Lopez*, the Supreme Court has vigorously enforced federalism limits on congressional legislative power * * *.

The Supreme Court has not, however, articulated a very useful test to evaluate whether a federal law is unconstitutional. It continues to use Chief Justice Hughes's test from *Jones & Laughlin Steel*, that Congress may regulate wholly intrastate activities only if they *substantially* affect interstate commerce. But what does the word "substantially" really mean? How do we know which wholly intrastate activities "substantially" affect interstate commerce and which do not? The Supreme Court simply never says.

* * *

* * * The Economics of Federalism approach would better resolve whether an act inherently falls within the sphere of national power or state power. The

Economics of Federalism reveals the Gun Free School Zones Act in *Lopez* was unnecessary grandstanding; the states had no race to the bottom or other problem to correct. The statute in *Morrison*, on the other hand, might have been a valid federal civil rights measure. Finally, the Controlled Substances Act, as applied in *Gonzales v. Raich*, and the federal statute in *Wickard v. Filburn*, hardly met the "substantial" effects test because homegrown marijuana or wheat has at most an indirect effect on national markets. Also, California is among eighteen states that have legalized medical marijuana in recent years. Given that more than one-third of the fifty states have spoken on the issue, it is apparent that tastes and cultural preferences vary sharply across the United States. It is thus a classic Economics of Federalism issue, which ought to be left at the state level to accommodate many viewpoints and to permit this experiment with the medical marijuana to proceed.

[Assignment 36]

VIII. FEDERAL POWER: IMMIGRATION AND EXPULSION OF ALIENS

Congress shall have Power * * *

To establish an uniform Rule of Naturalization;

To declare War, grant Letters of Marque and Reprisal, and make Rules concerning Captures on Land and Water.

From 1789 to 1882, the States exercised all power over immigration of non-citizens into the United States, GERALD L. NEUMAN, STRANGERS TO THE CONSTITUTION (1996), and non-citizens who stated an intent to become citizens had the right to vote in most state and federal elections. This situation changed in 1882 when Congress passed and President Chester Arthur signed the Chinese Exclusion Act, which prohibited the immigration to the United States of all Chinese laborers. *See* Act of May 6, 1882, ch. 126, § 1, 22 Stat. 587–59:

> Whereas, in the opinion of the Government of the United States the coming of Chinese laborers to this country endangers the good order of certain localities within the territory thereof: Therefore,
>
> *Be it enacted by the Senate and House of Representatives of the United States of America in Congress assembled*, That from and after the expiration of ninety days next after the passage of this act, and until the expiration of ten years next after the passage of this act, the coming of Chinese laborers to the United States be, and the same is hereby, suspended; and during such suspension it shall not be lawful for any Chinese laborer to come, or, having so come after the expiration of said ninety days, to remain within the United States.

This act was the first comprehensive federal immigration law—and the first law since Reconstruction to apply to only one race or ethnic group. It was followed in 1888 by a statute forbidding any person of Chinese descent who left the United States after 1882 from returning to the country. *See* Act of Oct. 1. 1888, ch. 1064, 25 Stat. 504. In 1892, Congress extended the ban on Chinese immigration for another ten years, *see* Act of May 5, 1892, ch. 60, § 1, 27 Stat. 25, and added provisions requiring any Chinese-American already present in the country to obtain a certificate of residency or face deportation, "unless he shall establish clearly * * * that by reason of accident, sickness or other unavoidable cause, he has been unable to procure his certificate * * *, and by at least one credible white witness, that he was a resident of the United States at the time of the passage of this act." *Id.* § 6, 27 Stat. at 26. Although the Constitution gives Congress the power to enact "uniform Rule[s] of Naturalization," it is silent as to whether Congress has the power to pass immigration laws. It is also silent about whether and under what circumstances Congress has the power to order the deportation of aliens who have not become citizens (or to prescribe the proper race of witnesses, though that is another matter). The following two cases from the late nineteenth century, dealing with the 1888 and 1892 acts, respectively, have, for better or worse, been the foundations of the constitutional law of immigration and deportation for the last century and a half.

A. CHAE CHAN PING V. UNITED STATES

130 U.S. 581 (1889)

■ MR. JUSTICE FIELD delivered the opinion of the court.

The appeal involves a consideration of the validity of the act of Congress of October 1, 1888, prohibiting Chinese laborers from entering the United States who had departed before its passage, having a certificate issued under the act of 1882 as amended by the act of 1884, granting them permission to return * * *.

* * *

The discovery of gold in California in 1848, as is well known, was followed by a large immigration thither from all parts of the world, attracted not only by the hope of gain from the mines, but from the great prices paid for all kinds of labor. The news of the discovery penetrated China, and laborers came from there in great numbers, a few with their own means, but by far the greater number under contract with employers, for whose benefit they worked. These laborers readily secured employment, and, as domestic servants, and in various kinds of out-door work, proved to be exceedingly useful. For some years little opposition was made to them, except when they sought to work in the mines, but, as their numbers increased, they began to engage in various mechanical pursuits and trades, and thus came in competition with our artisans and mechanics, as well as our laborers in the field.

The competition steadily increased as the laborers came in crowds on each steamer that arrived from China, or Hong Kong, an adjacent English port. They were generally industrious and frugal. Not being accompanied by families, except in rare instances, their expenses were small; and they were content with the simplest fare, such as would not suffice for our laborers and artisans. The competition between them and our people was for this reason altogether in their favor, and the consequent irritation, proportionately deep and bitter, was followed, in many cases, by open conflicts, to the great disturbance of the public peace.

The differences of race added greatly to the difficulties of the situation * * * [T]hey remained strangers in the land, residing apart by themselves, and adhering to the customs and usages of their own country. It seemed impossible for them to assimilate with our people or to make any change in their habits or modes of living. As they grew in numbers each year the people of the coast saw, or believed they saw, in the facility of immigration, and in the crowded millions of China, where population presses upon the means of subsistence, great danger that at no distant day that portion of our country would be overrun by them unless prompt action was taken to restrict their immigration. The people there accordingly petitioned earnestly for protective legislation.

* * *

* * * On the 6th of May, 1882, an act of Congress was approved * * *. Its first section declares that after ninety days from the passage of the act, and for the period of ten years from its date, the coming of Chinese laborers to the United States is suspended, and that it shall be unlawful for any such laborer to come, or, having come, to remain within the United States. The second makes it a misdemeanor, punishable by fine, to which imprisonment may be added, for the master of any vessel knowingly to bring within the United States from a foreign country, and land, any such Chinese laborer. The third provides that those two sections shall not apply to Chinese laborers who were in the United States November 17, 1880, or who shall come within ninety days after the passage of the act * * *.

The enforcement of this act with respect to laborers who were in the United States on November 17, 1880, was attended with great embarrassment, from the suspicious nature, in many instances, of the testimony offered to establish the residence of the parties, arising from the loose notions entertained by the witnesses of the obligation of an oath * * *.

* * * To prevent the possibility of the policy of excluding Chinese laborers being evaded, the act of October 1, 1888, the validity of which is the subject of consideration in this case, was passed * * *. It is as follows:

" '* * *[F]rom and after the passage of this act it shall be unlawful for any Chinese laborer who shall at any time heretofore have been, or who may now or hereafter be, a resident within the United States, and who shall have departed, or shall depart, therefrom, and shall not have returned before the passage of this act, to return to or remain the United States * * *."

[*Editors' Note*: *The statute was attacked as inconsistent with treaties between the U.S. and China dealing with immigration and emigration. The Court held, as it had in the past, that, as a matter of domestic constitutional law, treaties and statutes are of equal force, so that a later act supersedes an earlier one. Thus, a statute in violation of an earlier treaty may violate international law but is still valid as a matter of domestic law.*]

* * *

There being nothing in the treaties between China and the United States to impair the validity of the act of Congress of October 1, 1888, was it on any other ground beyond the competency of Congress to pass it? If so, it must be because it was not within the power of Congress to prohibit Chinese laborers who had at the time departed from the United States, or should subsequently depart, from returning to the United States. Those laborers are not citizens of the United States; they are aliens. That the government of the United States, through the action of the legislative department, can exclude aliens from its territory is a proposition which we do not think open to controversy. Jurisdiction over its own territory to that extent is an incident of every independent nation. It is a part of its independence. If it could not exclude aliens it would be to that extent subject to the control of another power * * *.

While under our Constitution and form of government the great mass of local matters is controlled by local authorities, the United States, in their relation to foreign countries and their subjects or citizens are one nation, invested with powers which belong to independent nations, the exercise of which can be invoked for the maintenance of its absolute independence and security throughout its entire territory. The powers to declare war, make treaties, suppress insurrection, repel invasion, regulate foreign commerce, secure republican governments to the States, and admit subjects of other nations to citizenship, are all sovereign powers, restricted in their exercise only by the Constitution itself and considerations of public policy and justice which control, more or less, the conduct of all civilized nations * * *.

The control of local matters being left to local authorities, and national matters being intrusted to the government of the Union, the problem of free institutions existing over a widely extended country, having different climates and varied interests, has been happily solved. For local interests the several States of the Union exist, but for national purposes, embracing our relations with foreign nations, we are but one people, one nation, one power.

To preserve its independence, and give security against foreign aggression and encroachment, is the highest duty of every nation, and to attain these ends nearly all other considerations are to be subordinated. It matters not in what form such aggression and encroachment come, whether from the foreign nation acting in its national character or from vast hordes of its people crowding in upon us. The government, possessing the powers which are to be exercised for protection and security, is clothed with authority to determine the occasion on which the powers shall be called forth; and its determinations, so far as the subjects affected are concerned, are necessarily conclusive upon all its departments and officers. If, therefore, the government of the United States, through its legislative department, considers the presence of foreigners of a different race in this country, who will not assimilate with us, to be dangerous to its peace and security, their exclusion is not to be stayed because at the time there are no actual hostilities with the nation of which the foreigners are subjects. The existence of war would render the necessity of the proceeding only more obvious and pressing. The same necessity, in a less pressing degree, may arise when war does not exist, and the same authority which adjudges the necessity in one case must also determine it in the other. In both cases its determination is conclusive upon the judiciary. If the government of the country of which the foreigners excluded are subjects is dissatisfied with this action it can make complaint to the executive head of our government, or resort to any other measure which, in its judgment, its interests or dignity may demand; and there lies its only remedy.

The power of the government to exclude foreigners from the country whenever, in its judgment, the public interests require such exclusion, has been asserted in repeated instances, and never denied by the executive or legislative departments * * *.

The exclusion of paupers, criminals, and persons afflicted with incurable diseases, for which statutes have been passed, is only an application of the same power to particular classes of persons, whose presence is deemed injurious or a source of danger to the country * * *.

The power of exclusion of foreigners being an incident of sovereignty belonging to the government of the United States, as a part of those sovereign powers delegated by the Constitution, the right to its exercise at any time when, in the judgment of the government, the interests of the country require it, cannot be granted away or restrained on behalf of any one * * * Whatever license, therefore, Chinese laborers may have obtained, previous to the act of October 1, 1888, to return to the United States after their departure, is held at the will of the government, revocable at any time, at its pleasure * * *.

During the argument reference was made by counsel to the alien law of June 25, 1798, and to opinions expressed at the time by men of great ability and learning against its constitutionality. 1 St. 570, c. 58. We do not attach importance to those opinions in their bearing upon this case. The act vested in the President power to order all such aliens as he should judge dangerous to the peace and safety of the United States, or should have reasonable grounds to suspect were concerned in any treasonable or secret machination against the government, to depart out of the territory of the United States within such time as should be expressed in his order. There were other provisions also distinguishing it from the act under consideration. The act was passed during a period of great political excitement, and it was attacked and defended with great zeal and ability. It is enough, however, to say that it is entirely different from the act before us, and the validity of its provisions was never brought to the test of judicial decision in the courts of the United States.

Order affirmed.

B. FONG YUE TING V. UNITED STATES

149 U.S. 698 (1893)

* * *

These were three writs of *habeas corpus*, granted by the Circuit Court of the United States for the Southern District of New York, upon petitions of Chinese laborers arrested and held by the marshal of the district for not having certificates of residence, under section 6 of the act of May 5, 1892, c. 60 * * *.

* * *

Each petition alleged that the petitioner was arrested and detained without due process of law, and that section 6 of the act of May 5, 1892, was unconstitutional and void.

* * *

■ MR. JUSTICE GRAY delivered the opinion of the court.

The general principles of public law which lie at the foundation of these cases are clearly established by previous judgments of this court, and by the authorities therein referred to.

In the recent case of *Nishimura Ekiu v. U. S.,* 142 U. S. 651, 659, the court, in sustaining the action of the executive department, putting in force an act of Congress for the exclusion of aliens, said: "It is an accepted maxim of international law, that every sovereign nation has the power, as inherent in sovereignty, and essential to self-preservation, to forbid the entrance of foreigners within its dominions, or to admit them only in such cases and upon such conditions as it may see fit to prescribe.

In the United States, this power is vested in the national government, to which the Constitution has committed the entire control of international relations, in peace as well as in war. It belongs to the political department of the government, and may be exercised either through treaties made by the President and Senate or through statutes enacted by Congress."

The same views were more fully expounded in the earlier case of *Chae Chan Ping v. U. S.,* 130 U. S. 581, in which the validity of a former act of Congress, excluding Chinese laborers from the United States, under the circumstances therein stated, was affirmed.

* * *

The right of a nation to expel or deport foreigners, who have not been naturalized, or taken any steps towards becoming citizens of the country, rests upon the same grounds, and is as absolute and unqualified, as the right to prohibit and prevent their entrance into the country.

* * *

In England, the only question that has ever been made in regard to the power to expel aliens has been whether it could be exercised by the King without the consent of Parliament. It was formerly exercised by the King, but in later times by Parliament, which passed several acts on the subject between 1793 and 1848.

Eminent English judges, sitting in the Judicial Committee of the Privy Council, have gone very far in supporting the exclusion or expulsion, by the executive authority of a colony, of aliens having no absolute right to enter its territory or to remain therein.

* * *

The right to exclude or to expel all aliens, or any class of aliens, absolutely or upon certain conditions, in war or in peace, being an inherent and inalienable right of every sovereign and independent nation, essential to its safety, its independence, and its welfare, the question now before the court is whether the manner in which congress has exercised this right in sections 6 and 7 of the act of 1892 is consistent with the constitution.

The power to exclude or to expel aliens, being a power affecting international relations, is vested in the political departments of the government, and is to be regulated by treaty or by act of Congress, and to be executed by the executive authority according to the regulations so established, except so far the judicial department has been authorized by treaty or by statute, or is required by the paramount law of the Constitution, to intervene.

* * *

The power of Congress, therefore, to expel, like the power to exclude, aliens, or any specified class of aliens, from the country, may be exercised entirely through executive officers, or Congress may call in the aid of the judiciary to ascertain any contested facts on which an alien's right to be in the country has been made by Congress to depend.

Congress, having the right, as it may see fit, to expel aliens of a particular class, or to permit them to remain, has undoubtedly the right to provide a system of registration and identification of the members of that class within the country, and to take all proper means to carry out the system which it provides.

It is no new thing for the lawmaking power, acting either through treaties made by the President and Senate, or by the more common method of acts of Congress, to submit the decision of questions, not necessarily of judicial cognizance, either to the final determination of executive officers, or to the decision of such officers in the first instance, with such opportunity for judicial review of their action as Congress may see fit to authorize or permit.

* * *

Chinese laborers, * * * like all other aliens residing in the United States for a shorter or longer time, are entitled, so long as they are permitted by the government of the United States to remain in the country, to the safeguards of the Constitution, and to the protection of the laws, in regard to their rights of person and of property, and to their civil and criminal responsibility. But they continue to be aliens, having taken no steps towards becoming citizens, and incapable of becoming such under the naturalization laws, and therefore remain subject to the power of Congress to expel them, or to order them to be removed and deported from the country, whenever in its judgment their removal is necessary or expedient for the public interest.

* * *

For the reasons stated in the earlier part of this opinion, Congress, under the power to exclude or expel aliens, might have directed any Chinese laborer found in the United States without a certificate of residence, to be removed out of the country by executive officers, without judicial trial or examination, just as it might have authorized such officers absolutely to prevent his entrance into the country * * *.

* * *

The question whether, and upon what conditions, these aliens shall be permitted to remain within the United States being one to be determined by the political departments of the government, the judicial department cannot properly express an opinion upon the wisdom, the policy, or the justice of the measures enacted by Congress in the exercise of the powers confided to it by the Constitution over this subject.

The three cases now before us do not differ from one another in any material particular.

In the first case, the petitioner had wholly neglected, failed, and refused to apply to the collector of internal revenue for a certificate of residence * * *.

In the second case, the petitioner had likewise neglected, failed, and refused to apply to the collector of internal revenue for a certificate of residence * * *.

In the third case, the petitioner had, within the year, applied to a collector of internal revenue for a certificate of residence, and had been refused it, because he produced, and could produce none but Chinese witnesses to prove the residence necessary to entitle him to a certificate * * *.

* * *

Upon careful consideration of the subject, the only conclusion which appears to us to be consistent with the principles of international law, with the Constitution and laws of the United States, and with the previous decisions of this court, is that in each of these cases the judgment of the Circuit Court, dismissing the writ of *habeas corpus*, is right, and must be affirmed.

■ MR. JUSTICE BREWER dissenting.

* * *

I rest my dissent on three propositions: First, that the persons against whom the penalties of section 6 of the act of 1892 are directed are persons lawfully residing within the United States, secondly, that as such they are within the protection of the Constitution, and secured by its guaranties against oppression and wrong, and, third, that section 6 deprives them of liberty and imposes punishment without due process of law, and in disregard of constitutional guaranties, especially those found in the Fourth, Fifth, Sixth, and Eighth Articles of the Amendments.

* * *

* * * [W]hatever rights a resident alien might have in any other nation, here he is within the express protection of the Constitution, especially in respect to those guaranties which are declared in the original amendments. It has been repeated so often as to become axiomatic, that this government is one of enumerated and delegated powers * * *.

It is said that the power here asserted is inherent in sovereignty. This doctrine of powers inherent in sovereignty is one both indefinite and dangerous. Where are the limits to such powers to be found, and by whom are they to be pronounced? Is it within legislative capacity to declare the limits? If so, then the mere assertion of an inherent power creates it, and despotism exists. May the courts establish the boundaries? Whence do they obtain the authority for this? Shall they look to the practices of other nations to ascertain the limits? The governments of other nations have elastic powers—ours is fixed and bounded by a written constitution. The expulsion of a race may be within the inherent powers of a despotism. History, before the adoption of this Constitution, was not destitute of examples of the exercise of such a power, and its framers were familiar with history, and wisely, and it seems to me, they gave to this government no general power to banish. Banishment may be resorted to as punishment for crime, but among the powers reserved to the people and not delegated to the government is that of determining whether whole classes in our midst shall, for no crime but that of their race and birthplace, be driven from our territory.

Whatever may be true as to exclusion, and as to that see *Chinese Exclusion Case*, 130 U. S. 581, I deny that there is any arbitrary and unrestrained power to banish residents, even resident aliens. What, it may be asked, is the reason for any difference? The answer is obvious. The Constitution has no extraterritorial effect, and those who have not come lawfully within our territory cannot claim any protection from its provisions. And it may be that the national government, having full control of all matters relating to other nations, has the power to build, as it were, a Chinese wall around our borders and absolutely forbid aliens to enter. But the Constitution has potency everywhere within the limits of our territory, and the powers which the national government may exercise within such limits are those, and only those, given to it by that instrument. Now, the power to remove resident aliens is, confessedly, not expressed. Even if it be among the powers implied, yet still it can be exercised only in subordination to the limitations and restrictions imposed by the Constitution * * *.

* * *

I pass, therefore, to the consideration of my third proposition: Section 6 deprives of "life, liberty, and property without due process of law." It imposes punishment without a trial, and punishment cruel and severe. It places the liberty of one individual subject to the unrestrained control of another * * *. Deportation is punishment. It involves first an arrest, a deprival of liberty, and, second, a removal from home, from family, from business, from property * * *.

* * *

But punishment implies a trial * * *. Due process requires that a man be heard before he is condemned, and both heard and condemned in the due and orderly procedure of a trial as recognized by the common law from time immemorial * * *.

* * * [Under the statute in this case], it is absolutely within the discretion of the collector to give or refuse a certificate to one who applies therefor. Nowhere is it provided what evidence shall be furnished to the collector, and nowhere is it made mandatory upon him to grant a certificate on the production of such evidence. It cannot be due process of law to impose punishment on any person for failing to have that in his possession, the possession of which he can obtain only at the arbitrary and unregulated discretion of any official. It will not do to say that the presumption is that the official will act reasonably and not arbitrarily. When the right to liberty and residence is involved, some other protection than the mere discretion of any official is required * * *.

* * *

It is true this statute is directed only against the obnoxious Chinese, but, if the power exists, who shall say it will not be exercised to-morrow against other classes and other people? If the guaranties of these amendments can be thus ignored in order to get rid of this distasteful class, what security have others that a like disregard of its provisions may not be resorted to? * * *

* * *

In view of this enactment of the highest legislative body of the foremost Christian nation, may not the thoughtful Chinese disciple of Confucius fairly ask, "Why do they send missionaries here?"

■ MR. JUSTICE FIELD, dissenting.

I also wish to say a few words upon these cases, and upon the extraordinary doctrines announced in support of the orders of the court below.

With the * * * legislation adopted by Congress to prevent the immigration of Chinese laborers into this country, resulting in the Exclusion Act of October 1, 1888, the court is familiar * * *. The validity of this act was sustained by this court * * *.

I had the honor to be the organ of the court in announcing this opinion and judgment. I still adhere to the views there expressed, in all particulars, but between legislation for the exclusion of Chinese persons—that is, to prevent them from entering the country,—and legislation for the deportation of those who have acquired a residence in the country under a treaty with China, there is a wide and essential difference. The power of the government to exclude foreigners from this country that is, to prevent them from entering it, whenever the public interests, in its judgment require such exclusion, has been repeatedly asserted by the legislative and executive departments of our government and never denied, but its power to deport from the country persons lawfully domiciled therein by its consent, and engaged in the ordinary pursuits of life, has never been asserted by the legislative or executive departments except for crime, or as an act of war, in view of existing or anticipated hostilities, unless the alien act of 1798 can be considered as recognizing that doctrine. 1 Stat. p. 570, c. 58 * * *.

The passage of * * * [the Alien Acts of 1798] produced great excitement throughout the country, and was severely denounced by many of its ablest statesmen and jurists as unconstitutional and barbarous, and among them may be mentioned the great names of Jefferson and Madison, who are throughout our country honored and revered for their lifelong devotion to principles of constitutional liberty. It was defended by its advocates as a war measure. John Adams, the President of the United States at the time, who approved the bill and against whom the responsibility for its passage was charged, states in his correspondence that the bill was intended as a measure of that character * * *.

* * *

The duration of the * * * [Alien Act] was limited to two years, and it has ever since been the subject of universal condemnation. In no other instance, until the law before us was passed, has any public man had the boldness to advocate the deportation of friendly aliens in time of peace. I repeat the statement, that in no other instance has the deportation of friendly aliens been advocated as a lawful measure by any department of our government. And it will surprise most people to learn that any such dangerous and despotic power lies in our government—a power which will authorize it to expel at pleasure, in time of peace, the whole body of friendly foreigners of any country domiciled herein by its permission, a power which can be brought into exercise whenever it may suit the pleasure of Congress, and be enforced without regard to the guaranties of the Constitution intended for the protection of the rights of all persons in their liberty and property. Is it possible that Congress can, at its pleasure, in disregard of the guaranties of the Constitution, expel at any time the Irish, German, French, and English who may have taken up their residence here on the invitation of the government, while we are at peace with the countries from which they came, simply on the ground that they have not been naturalized?

* * *

* * * There is no dispute about the power of Congress to prevent the landing of aliens in the country, the question is as to the power of Congress to deport them, without regard to the guaranties of the Constitution. The statement that in England the power to expel aliens has always been recognized and often exercised, and the only question that has ever been as to this power is whether it could be exercised by the King without the consent of Parliament, is, I think, not strictly accurate. The citations given by Mr. Choate in his brief show conclusively, it seems to me, that deportation from the realm has not been exercised in England since Magna Charta, except in punishment for crime, or as a measure in view of existing or anticipated hostilities. But even if that power were exercised by every government of Europe, it would have no bearing in these cases. It may be admitted that the power has been exercised by the various governments of Europe. Spain expelled the Moors, England, in the reign of Edward I, banished fifteen thousand Jews and Louis XIV, in 1685, by

revoking the Edict of Nantes, which gave religious liberty to Protestants in France, drove out the Huguenots. Nor does such severity of European governments belong only to the distant post. Within three years Russia has banished many thousands of Jews, and apparently intends the expulsion of the whole race—an act of barbarity which has aroused the indignation of all Christendom. Such was the feeling in this country that, friendly as our relations with Russia had always been, President Harrison felt compelled to call the attention of Congress to it in his message in 1891 as a fit subject for national remonstrance. Indeed, all the instances mentioned have been condemned for their barbarity and cruelty, and no power to perpetrate such barbarity is to be implied from the nature of our government, and certainly is not found in any delegated powers under the Constitution.

The government of the United States is one of limited and delegated powers. It takes nothing from the usages or the former action of European governments, nor does it take any power by any supposed inherent sovereignty * * *.

* * *

* * * The decision of the court and the sanction it would give to legislation depriving resident aliens of the guaranties of the Constitution fill me with apprehensions. Those guaranties are of priceless value to every one resident in the country, whether citizen or alien * * *. How far will its legislation go? The unnaturalized resident feels it to-day, but if Congress can disregard the guaranties with respect to any one domiciled in the country with its consent, it may disregard the guaranties with respect to naturalized citizens. What assurance have we that it may not declare that naturalized citizens of a particular country cannot remain in the United States after a certain day, unless they have in their possession a certificate that they are of good moral character and attached to the principles of our Constitution, which certificate they must obtain from a collector of internal revenue upon the testimony of at least one competent witness of a class or nationality to be designated by the government?

What answer could the naturalized citizen in that case make to his arrest for deportation, which cannot be urged in behalf of the Chinese laborers of to-day?

* * *

■ MR. CHIEF JUSTICE FULLER, dissenting.

I also dissent from the opinion and judgment of the court in these cases.

* * *

* * * [W]hile the general government is invested, in respect of foreign countries and their subjects or citizens, with the powers necessary to the maintenance of its absolute independence and security throughout its entire territory, it cannot, in virtue of any delegated power, or power implied therefrom, of a supposed inherent sovereignty, arbitrarily deal with persons lawfully within the peace of its dominion * * *. No euphuism can disguise the character of the act in this regard. It directs the performance of a judicial function in a particular way, and inflicts punishment without a judicial trial. It is, in effect, a legislative sentence of banishment, and, as such, absolutely void. Moreover, it contains within it the germs of the assertion of an unlimited and arbitrary power, in general, incompatible with the immutable principles of justice, inconsistent with the nature of our government, and in conflict

with the written constitution by which that government was created, and those principles secured.

NOTES AND QUESTIONS

1. Isn't the majority opinion in *Fong Yue Ting* despicable? Why are so many of the best opinions in constitutional law the dissents rather than the majority opinion? Note that unlike *Dred Scott v. Sandford*, *see infra* pages 932–953, *Fong Yue Ting* remains good law in the United States today. Resident aliens in the U.S. remain subject to expulsion through non-Article III proceedings even if they have long lived here with children and families.

2. The argument for federal power to control immigration in the first of the two cases above is surprisingly weak, isn't it? There is no limited and enumerated power that supports the immigration laws. If the country is at war, the President's "executive Power" surely includes power to control the Nation's borders, and Congress could therefore, in times of war, pass legislation "necessary and proper for carrying into Execution" that power, but in 1882 or 1892, the United States was not at war with China. Absent a war, it is very hard to see, as a matter of original meaning, from where a federal power over immigration might come. *See* Gary Lawson, *Original Foreign Affairs Federalism,* 97 B.U. L. REV. 301, 310–13 (2017).

3. On the other hand, there probably does need to be a power to expel aliens in any country, under at least some circumstances. Expulsion of aliens might be necessary and proper to winning a war or to prevent losing one. Under the original Constitution, the States had the primary power to control immigration. The nineteenth-century caselaw, however, declares immigration to be, not merely a federal, but an *exclusively* federal function. As a practical matter, the fifty States today would be unable to exercise such a power collectively. The theory of the Economics of Federalism sketched above may thus explain why U.S. power to expel aliens has been recognized as an exclusive federal power.

4. Placing the power in the federal government leaves open two crucial questions: (1) Does the power belong to Congress, the President, or both and (2) what procedures do due process of law and other rights-conferring constitutional provisions require for the exercise of that power? The majority in *Chae Chan Ping* assumes that the power that it infers must be primarily in Congress. Does the Court offer any argument for that assumption? To say that the federal government has a power—whether inherent or implied—does not say which institutions of the federal government are supposed to exercise it. Of course, in the modern era of delegation, it is not surprising that Congress has effectively transferred much of its authority to the President. *See, e.g.,* 8 U.S.C. § 1182(f) (2018) ("Whenever the President finds that the entry of any aliens or of any class of aliens into the United States would be detrimental to the interests of the United States, he may by proclamation, and for such period as he shall deem necessary, suspend the entry of all aliens or any class of aliens as immigrants or nonimmigrants, or impose on the entry of aliens any restrictions he may deem to be appropriate.") This sweeping authority allowed, inter alia, President Trump to restrict immigration from Chad, Iran, Libya, North Korea, Syria, Venezuela, and Yemen, *see* Pres. Proc. No. 9645, *Enhancing Vetting Capabilities and Processes for Detecting Attempted Entry Into the United States by Terrorists or Other Public-Safety Threats*, 82 Fed. Reg. 45161 (2017), as the Supreme Court concluded by a 5–4 vote. *See Trump v. Hawaii,* 138 S.Ct. 2392 (2018); *infra* pages 1008–1020.

5. As an illustration of the modern conception of immigration as an exclusively federal matter, consider the following case, which also addresses a subject that we have encountered before, and will encounter later in more detail, *see infra* pages 971–987: the "preemption" of state law by federal law. As you read this decision, ask to what extent the Court's preemption analysis focuses on the exercise of federal *legislative* power or federal *executive* power. Which federal institution does the Court think is the appropriate constitutional actor in the field of immigration?

C. ARIZONA V. UNITED STATES

567 U.S. 387 (2012)

■ JUSTICE KENNEDY delivered the opinion of the Court.

To address pressing issues related to the large number of aliens within its borders who do not have a lawful right to be in this country, the State of Arizona in 2010 enacted a statute called the Support Our Law Enforcement and Safe Neighborhoods Act. The law is often referred to as S.B. 1070, the version introduced in the State Senate. Its stated purpose is to "discourage and deter the unlawful entry and presence of aliens and economic activity by persons unlawfully present in the United States." The law's provisions establish an official state policy of "attrition through enforcement." The question before the Court is whether federal law pre-empts and renders invalid four separate provisions of the state law.

The United States filed this suit against Arizona, seeking to enjoin S.B. 1070 as pre-empted. Four provisions of the law are at issue here. Two create new state offenses. Section 3 makes failure to comply with federal alien-registration requirements a state misdemeanor. Section 5, in relevant part, makes it a misdemeanor for an unauthorized alien to seek or engage in work in the State; this provision is referred to as § 5(C). Two other provisions give specific arrest authority and investigative duties with respect to certain aliens to state and local law enforcement officers. Section 6 authorizes officers to arrest without a warrant a person "the officer has probable cause to believe . . . has committed any public offense that makes the person removable from the United States." Section 2(B) provides that officers who conduct a stop, detention, or arrest must in some circumstances make efforts to verify the person's immigration status with the Federal Government.

* * * This Court granted certiorari to resolve important questions concerning the interaction of state and federal power with respect to the law of immigration and alien status.

The Government of the United States has broad, undoubted power over the subject of immigration and the status of aliens. This authority rests, in part, on the National Government's constitutional power to "establish an uniform Rule of Naturalization," Art. I, § 8, cl. 4, and its inherent power as sovereign to control and conduct relations with foreign nations.

The federal power to determine immigration policy is well settled. Immigration policy can affect trade, investment, tourism, and diplomatic relations for the entire Nation, as well as the perceptions and expectations of aliens in this country who seek the full protection of its laws. See, e.g., Brief for United Mexican States as *Amici Curiae*. Perceived mistreatment of aliens in the United States may lead to harmful reciprocal treatment of American citizens abroad.

It is fundamental that foreign countries concerned about the status, safety, and security of their nationals in the United States must be able to confer and communicate on this subject with one national sovereign, not the 50 separate States. This Court has reaffirmed that "[o]ne of the most important and delicate of all international relationships . . . has to do with the protection of the just rights of a country's own nationals when those nationals are in another country." *Hines v. Davidowitz,* 312 U.S. 52, 64 (1941).

Federal governance of immigration and alien status is extensive and complex. Congress has specified categories of aliens who may not be admitted to the United States. See 8 U.S.C. § 1182. Unlawful entry and unlawful reentry into the country are federal offenses. §§ 1325, 1326. Once here, aliens are required to register with the Federal Government and to carry proof of status on their person. See §§ 1301–1306. Failure to do so is a federal misdemeanor. §§ 1304(e), 1306(a). Federal law also authorizes States to deny noncitizens a range of public benefits, § 1622; and it imposes sanctions on employers who hire unauthorized workers, § 1324a.

Congress has specified which aliens may be removed from the United States and the procedures for doing so. Aliens may be removed if they were inadmissible at the time of entry, have been convicted of certain crimes, or meet other criteria set by federal law. See § 1227. Removal is a civil, not criminal, matter. A principal feature of the removal system is the broad discretion exercised by immigration officials. Federal officials, as an initial matter, must decide whether it makes sense to pursue removal at all. If removal proceedings commence, aliens may seek asylum and other discretionary relief allowing them to remain in the country or at least to leave without formal removal. See § 1229a(c)(4); see also, e.g., §§ 1158 (asylum), 1229b (cancellation of removal), 1229c (voluntary departure).

Discretion in the enforcement of immigration law embraces immediate human concerns. Unauthorized workers trying to support their families, for example, likely pose less danger than alien smugglers or aliens who commit a serious crime. The equities of an individual case may turn on many factors, including whether the alien has children born in the United States, long ties to the community, or a record of distinguished military service. Some discretionary decisions involve policy choices that bear on this Nation's international relations. Returning an alien to his own country may be deemed inappropriate even where he has committed a removable offense or fails to meet the criteria for admission. The foreign state may be mired in civil war, complicit in political persecution, or enduring conditions that create a real risk that the alien or his family will be harmed upon return. The dynamic nature of relations with other countries requires the Executive Branch to ensure that enforcement policies are consistent with this Nation's foreign policy with respect to these and other realities.

* * *

The pervasiveness of federal regulation does not diminish the importance of immigration policy to the States. Arizona bears many of the consequences of unlawful immigration. Hundreds of thousands of deportable aliens are apprehended in Arizona each year. Unauthorized aliens who remain in the State constitute, by one estimate, almost 6% of the population. And in the State's most populous county, these aliens are reported to be responsible for a disproportionate share of serious crime.

* * *

These concerns are the background for the formal legal analysis that follows. The issue is whether, under pre-emption principles, federal law permits Arizona to implement the state-law provisions in dispute.

Federalism, central to the constitutional design, adopts the principle that both the National and State Governments have elements of sovereignty the other is bound to respect. From the existence of two sovereigns follows the possibility that laws can be in conflict or at cross-purposes. The Supremacy Clause provides a clear rule that federal law "shall be the supreme Law of the Land; and the Judges in every State shall be bound thereby, any Thing in the Constitution or Laws of any state to the Contrary notwithstanding." Art. VI, cl. 2. Under this principle, Congress has the power to pre-empt state law. See *Crosby v. National Foreign Trade Council*, 530 U.S. 363, 372 (2000); *Gibbons v. Ogden*, 9 Wheat. 1, 210–211 (1824). There is no doubt that Congress may withdraw specified powers from the States by enacting a statute containing an express preemption provision.

State law must also give way to federal law in at least two other circumstances. First, the States are precluded from regulating conduct in a field that Congress, acting within its proper authority, has determined must be regulated by its exclusive governance. The intent to displace state law altogether can be inferred from a framework of regulation "so pervasive . . . that Congress left no room for the States to supplement it" or where there is a "federal interest . . . so dominant that the federal system will be assumed to preclude enforcement of state laws on the same subject." *Rice v. Santa Fe Elevator Corp.*, 331 U.S. 218, 230 (1947)

Second, state laws are pre-empted when they conflict with federal law. This includes cases where "compliance with both federal and state regulations is a physical impossibility," *Florida Lime & Avocado Growers, Inc. v. Paul*, 373 U.S. 132, 142–143 (1963), and those instances where the challenged state law "stands as an obstacle to the accomplishment and execution of the full purposes and objectives of Congress," *Hines*, 312 U.S., at 67; see also *Crosby, supra*, at 373 ("What is a sufficient obstacle is a matter of judgment, to be informed by examining the federal statute as a whole and identifying its purpose and intended effects"). In pre-emption analysis, courts should assume that "the historic police powers of the States" are not superseded "unless that was the clear and manifest purpose of Congress." *Rice, supra*, at 230.

Section 3 of S.B. 1070 creates a new state misdemeanor. It forbids the "willful failure to complete or carry an alien registration document . . . in violation of 8 United States Code § 1304(e) or 1306(a)." In effect, § 3 adds a state-law penalty for conduct proscribed by federal law. The United States contends that this state enforcement mechanism intrudes on the field of alien registration, a field in which Congress has left no room for States to regulate.

* * *

The framework enacted by Congress leads to the conclusion * * * that the Federal Government has occupied the field of alien registration. The federal statutory directives provide a full set of standards governing alien registration, including the punishment for noncompliance * * *. Where Congress occupies an entire field, as it has in the field of alien registration, even complementary state regulation is impermissible. Field pre-emption reflects a congressional decision to foreclose any state regulation in the area, even if it is parallel to federal standards. *See Silkwood v. Kerr-McGee Corp.,* 464 U.S. 238, 249 (1984).

Federal law makes a single sovereign responsible for maintaining a comprehensive and unified system to keep track of aliens within the Nation's borders. If § 3 of the Arizona statute were valid, every State could give itself independent authority to prosecute federal registration violations, "diminish[ing] the [Federal Government]'s control over enforcement" and "detract[ing] from the 'integrated scheme of regulation' created by Congress." *Wisconsin Dept. of Industry v. Gould Inc.,* 475 U.S. 282, 288–289 (1986). Even if a State may make violation of federal law a crime in some instances, it cannot do so in a field (like the field of alien registration) that has been occupied by federal law.

Arizona contends that § 3 can survive pre-emption because the provision has the same aim as federal law and adopts its substantive standards. This argument not only ignores the basic premise of field pre-emption—that States may not enter, in any respect, an area the Federal Government has reserved for itself—but also is unpersuasive on its own terms. Permitting the State to impose its own penalties for the federal offenses here would conflict with the careful framework Congress adopted. Were § 3 to come into force, the State would have the power to bring criminal charges against individuals for violating a federal law even in circumstances where federal officials in charge of the comprehensive scheme determine that prosecution would frustrate federal policies.

There is a further intrusion upon the federal scheme. Even where federal authorities believe prosecution is appropriate, there is an inconsistency between § 3 and federal law with respect to penalties. Under federal law, the failure to carry registration papers is a misdemeanor that may be punished by a fine, imprisonment, or a term of probation. State law, by contrast, rules out probation as a possible sentence (and also eliminates the possibility of a pardon). This state framework of sanctions creates a conflict with the plan Congress put in place.

These specific conflicts between state and federal law simply underscore the reason for field pre-emption. * * *[T]he Court now concludes that, with respect to the subject of alien registration, Congress intended to preclude States from "complement[ing] the federal law, or enforc[ing] additional or auxiliary regulations." Section 3 is pre-empted by federal law.

Unlike § 3, which replicates federal statutory requirements, § 5(C) enacts a state criminal prohibition where no federal counterpart exists. The provision makes it a state misdemeanor for "an unauthorized alien to knowingly apply for work, solicit work in a public place or perform work as an employee or independent contractor" in Arizona. Violations can be punished by a $2,500 fine and incarceration for up to six months. The United States contends that the provision upsets the balance struck by the Immigration Reform and Control Act of 1986 (IRCA) and must be pre-empted as an obstacle to the federal plan of regulation and control.

When there was no comprehensive federal program regulating the employment of unauthorized aliens, this Court found that a State had authority to pass its own laws on the subject. In 1971, for example, California passed a law imposing civil penalties on the employment of aliens who were "not entitled to lawful residence in the United States if such employment would have an adverse effect on lawful resident workers." 1971 Cal. Stats. ch. 1442, § 1(a). The law was upheld against a pre-emption challenge in *De Canas v. Bica*, 424 U.S. 351 (1976). *De Canas* recognized that "States possess broad authority under their police powers to regulate the employment relationship to protect workers within the State." *Id.*, at 356. At that point, however, the Federal Government had expressed no more than "a peripheral concern with [the] employment of illegal entrants." *Id.*, at 360.

Current federal law is substantially different from the regime that prevailed when *De Canas* was decided. Congress enacted IRCA as a comprehensive framework for "combating the employment of illegal aliens." *Hoffman Plastic Compounds, Inc. v. NLRB*, 535 U.S. 137, 147 (2002). The law makes it illegal for employers to knowingly hire, recruit, refer, or continue to employ unauthorized workers. See 8 U.S.C. §§ 1324a(a)(1)(A), (a)(2). It also requires every employer to verify the employment authorization status of prospective employees. See §§ 1324a(a)(1)(B), (b); 8 CFR § 274a.2(b) (2012). These requirements are enforced through criminal penalties and an escalating series of civil penalties tied to the number of times an employer has violated the provisions. See 8 U.S.C. §§ 1324a(e)(4), (f); 8 CFR § 274a.10.

This comprehensive framework does not impose federal criminal sanctions on the employee side (i.e., penalties on aliens who seek or engage in unauthorized work). Under federal law some civil penalties are imposed instead * * *.

The legislative background of IRCA underscores the fact that Congress made a deliberate choice not to impose criminal penalties on aliens who seek, or engage in, unauthorized employment * * *.

IRCA's express pre-emption provision, which in most instances bars States from imposing penalties on employers of unauthorized aliens, is silent about whether additional penalties may be imposed against the employees themselves. See 8 U.S.C. § 1324a(h)(2). But the existence of an "express pre-emption provisio[n] does not bar the ordinary working of conflict pre-emption principles" or impose a "special burden" that would make it more difficult to establish the pre-emption of laws falling outside the clause.

The ordinary principles of pre-emption include the well-settled proposition that a state law is pre-empted where it "stands as an obstacle to the accomplishment and execution of the full purposes and objectives of Congress." *Hines*, 312 U.S., at 67. Under § 5(C) of S.B. 1070, Arizona law would interfere with the careful balance struck by Congress with respect to unauthorized employment of aliens. Although § 5(C) attempts to achieve one of the same goals as federal law—the deterrence of unlawful employment—it involves a conflict in the method of enforcement * * *. The correct instruction to draw from the text, structure, and history of IRCA is that Congress decided it would be inappropriate to impose criminal penalties on aliens who seek or engage in unauthorized employment. It follows that a state law to the contrary is an obstacle to the regulatory system Congress chose. Section 5(C) is pre-empted by federal law.

Section 6 of S.B. 1070 provides that a state officer, "without a warrant, may arrest a person if the officer has probable cause to believe . . . [the person] has committed any public offense that makes [him] removable from the United States." The United States argues that arrests authorized by this statute would be an obstacle to the removal system Congress created.

As a general rule, it is not a crime for a removable alien to remain present in the United States. If the police stop someone based on nothing more than possible removability, the usual predicate for an arrest is absent. When an alien is suspected of being removable, a federal official issues an administrative document called a "Notice to Appear." See 8 U.S.C. § 1229(a); 8 CFR § 239.1(a). The form does not authorize an arrest. Instead, it gives the alien information about the proceedings, including the time and date of the removal hearing. See 8 U.S.C. § 1229(a)(1). If an alien fails to appear, an *in absentia* order may direct removal. § 1229a(b)(5)(A).

The federal statutory structure instructs when it is appropriate to arrest an alien during the removal process * * *.

Section 6 attempts to provide state officers even greater authority to arrest aliens on the basis of possible removability than Congress has given to trained federal immigration officers * * *.

This is not the system Congress created * * *

By authorizing state officers to decide whether an alien should be detained for being removable, § 6 violates the principle that the removal process is entrusted to the discretion of the Federal Government. A decision on removability requires a determination whether it is appropriate to allow a foreign national to continue living in the United States. Decisions of this nature touch on foreign relations and must be made with one voice.

* * *

Section 2(B) of S.B. 1070 requires state officers to make a "reasonable attempt . . . to determine the immigration status" of any person they stop, detain, or arrest on some other legitimate basis if "reasonable suspicion exists that the person is an alien and is unlawfully present in the United States." The law also provides that "[a]ny person who is arrested shall have the person's immigration status determined before the person is released." The accepted way to perform these status checks is to contact ICE, which maintains a database of immigration records.

* * *

The United States argues that making status verification mandatory interferes with the federal immigration scheme. It is true that § 2(B) does not allow state officers to consider federal enforcement priorities in deciding whether to contact ICE about someone they have detained. In other words, the officers must make an inquiry even in cases where it seems unlikely that the Attorney General would have the alien removed. This might be the case, for example, when an alien is an elderly veteran with significant and longstanding ties to the community.

Congress has done nothing to suggest it is inappropriate to communicate with ICE in these situations, however. Indeed, it has encouraged the sharing of information about possible immigration violations * * *. The federal scheme thus leaves room for a policy requiring state officials to contact ICE as a routine matter.

* * *

However the law is interpreted, if § 2(B) only requires state officers to conduct a status check during the course of an authorized, lawful detention or after a detainee has been released, the provision likely would survive pre-emption—at least absent some showing that it has other consequences that are adverse to federal law and its objectives. There is no need in this case to address whether reasonable suspicion of illegal entry or another immigration crime would be a legitimate basis for prolonging a detention, or whether this too would be pre-empted by federal law.

The nature and timing of this case counsel caution in evaluating the validity of § 2(B). The Federal Government has brought suit against a sovereign State to challenge the provision even before the law has gone into effect. There is a basic uncertainty about what the law means and how it will be enforced. At this stage, without the benefit of a definitive interpretation from the state courts, it would be inappropriate to assume § 2(B) will be construed in a way that creates a conflict with federal law. As a result, the United States cannot prevail in its current challenge. This opinion does not foreclose other pre-emption and constitutional challenges to the law as interpreted and applied after it goes into effect.

* * *

The National Government has significant power to regulate immigration. With power comes responsibility, and the sound exercise of national power over immigration depends on the Nation's meeting its responsibility to base its laws on a political will informed by searching, thoughtful, rational civic discourse. Arizona may have understandable frustrations with the problems caused by illegal immigration while that process continues, but the State may not pursue policies that undermine federal law.

* * *

■ JUSTICE KAGAN took no part in the consideration or decision of this case.

■ JUSTICE SCALIA, concurring in part and dissenting in part.

The United States is an indivisible "Union of sovereign States." *Hinderlider v. La Plata River & Cherry Creek Ditch Co.*, 304 U.S. 92, 104 (1938). Today's opinion, approving virtually all of the Ninth Circuit's injunction against enforcement of the four challenged provisions of Arizona's law, deprives States of what most would consider the defining characteristic of sovereignty: the power to exclude from the sovereign's territory people who have no right to be there. Neither the Constitution itself nor even any law passed by Congress supports this result. I dissent.

As a sovereign, Arizona has the inherent power to exclude persons from its territory, subject only to those limitations expressed in the Constitution or constitutionally imposed by Congress. That power to exclude has long been recognized as inherent in sovereignty * * *.

There is no doubt that "before the adoption of the constitution of the United States" each State had the authority to "prevent [itself] from being burdened by an influx of persons." *Mayor of New York v. Miln*, 11 Pet. 102, 132–133 (1837). And the Constitution did not strip the States of that authority. To the contrary, two of the Constitution's provisions were designed to enable the States to prevent "the intrusion of obnoxious aliens through other States." Letter from James Madison to Edmund Randolph (Aug. 27, 1782), in 1 Writings of James Madison 226 (G. Hunt ed. 1900); accord, The Federalist No. 42, pp. 269–271 (C. Rossiter ed. 1961) (J. Madison). The Articles of Confederation had provided that "the free inhabitants of each of these States, paupers, vagabonds and fugitives from justice excepted, shall be entitled to all privileges and immunities of free citizens in the several States." Art. IV. This meant that an unwelcome alien could obtain all the rights of a citizen of one State simply by first becoming an *inhabitant* of another. To remedy this, the Constitution's

Privileges and Immunities Clause provided that "[t]he *Citizens* of each State shall be entitled to all Privileges and Immunities of Citizens in the several States." Art. IV, § 2, cl. 1 (emphasis added). But if one State had particularly lax citizenship standards, it might still serve as a gateway for the entry of "obnoxious aliens" into other States. This problem was solved "by authorizing the general government to establish a uniform rule of naturalization throughout the United States." The Federalist No. 42, supra, at 271; see Art. I, § 8, cl. 4. In other words, the naturalization power was given to Congress not to abrogate States' power to exclude those they did not want, but to vindicate it.

* * *

In fact, the controversy surrounding the Alien and Sedition Acts involved a debate over whether, under the Constitution, the States had *exclusive* authority to enact such immigration laws * * *.

The Kentucky and Virginia Resolutions, written in denunciation of these Acts, insisted that the power to exclude unwanted aliens rested solely in the States. Jefferson's Kentucky Resolutions insisted "that alien friends are under the jurisdiction and protection of the laws of the state wherein they are [and] that no power over them has been delegated to the United States, nor prohibited to the individual states, distinct from their power over citizens." Kentucky Resolutions of 1798, reprinted in J. Powell, Languages of Power: A Sourcebook of Early American Constitutional History 131 (1991). Madison's Virginia Resolutions likewise contended that the Alien Act purported to give the President "a power nowhere delegated to the federal government." Virginia Resolutions of 1798, in id. at 134 (emphasis omitted). Notably, moreover, the Federalist proponents of the Act defended it primarily on the ground that "[t]he removal of aliens is the usual preliminary of hostility" and could therefore be justified in exercise of the Federal Government's war powers. Massachusetts Resolutions in Reply to Virginia, in id. at 136.

* * *

One would conclude from the foregoing that after the adoption of the Constitution there was some doubt about the power of the Federal Government to control immigration, but no doubt about the power of the States to do so. Since the founding era (though not immediately), doubt about the Federal Government's power has disappeared. Indeed, primary responsibility for immigration policy has shifted from the States to the Federal Government. Congress exercised its power "[t]o establish an uniform Rule of Naturalization," Art. I, § 8, cl. 4, very early on, see An Act to establish an uniform Rule of Naturalization, ch. 3, 1 Stat. 103. But with the fleeting exception of the Alien Act, Congress did not enact any legislation regulating *immigration* for the better part of a century * * *. [I]n 1882, Congress enacted the first general immigration statute. Of course, it hardly bears mention that federal immigration law is now extensive.

I accept that as a valid exercise of federal power—not because of the Naturalization Clause (it has no necessary connection to citizenship) but because it is an inherent attribute of sovereignty no less for the United States than for the States * * *. That is why there was no need to set forth control of immigration as one of the enumerated powers of Congress * * *.

In light of the predominance of federal immigration restrictions in modern times, it is easy to lose sight of the States' traditional role in regulating immigration—and to overlook their sovereign prerogative to do so. I accept as a given that state regulation is excluded by the Constitution when (1) it has been prohibited by a valid federal law, or (2) it conflicts with federal regulation—when, for example, it admits those whom federal regulation would exclude, or excludes those whom federal regulation would admit.

Possibility (1) need not be considered here: There is no federal law prohibiting the States' sovereign power to exclude (assuming federal authority to enact such a law). The mere existence of federal action in the immigration area—and the so-called field pre-emption arising from that action, upon which the Court's opinion so heavily relies, cannot be regarded as such a prohibition. We are not talking here about a federal law prohibiting the States from regulating bubble-gum advertising, or even the construction of nuclear plants. We are talking about a federal law going to the *core* of state sovereignty: the power to exclude. Like elimination of the States' other inherent sovereign power, immunity from suit, elimination of the States' sovereign power to exclude requires that "Congress . . . unequivocally expres[s] its intent to abrogate," *Seminole Tribe of Fla. v. Florida*, 517 U.S. 44, 55 (1996). Implicit "field pre-emption" will not do.

* * * Even in its international relations, the Federal Government must live with the inconvenient fact that it is a Union of independent States, who have their own sovereign powers. This is not the first time it has found that a nuisance and a bother in the conduct of foreign policy * * *. Though it may upset foreign powers—and even when the Federal Government desperately wants to avoid upsetting foreign powers—the States have the right to protect their borders against foreign nationals, just as they have the right to execute foreign nationals for murder.

What this case comes down to, then, is whether the Arizona law conflicts with federal immigration law—whether it excludes those whom federal law would admit, or admits those whom federal law would exclude. It does not purport to do so. It applies only to aliens who neither possess a privilege to be present under federal law nor have been removed pursuant to the Federal Government's inherent authority * * *.

* * *

The brief for the Government in this case asserted that "the Executive Branch's ability to exercise discretion and set priorities is particularly important because of the need to allocate scarce enforcement resources wisely." Brief for United States 21. Of course there is no reason why the Federal Executive's need to allocate *its* scarce enforcement resources should disable Arizona from devoting *its* resources to illegal immigration in Arizona that in its view the Federal Executive has given short shrift * * *

But leave that aside. It has become clear that federal enforcement priorities—in the sense of priorities based on the need to allocate "scarce enforcement resources"—is not the problem here. After this case was argued and while it was under consideration, the Secretary of Homeland Security announced a program exempting from immigration enforcement some 1.4 million illegal immigrants under the age of 30. If an individual unlawfully present in the United States

"• came to the United States under the age of sixteen;

"• has continuously resided in the United States for at least five years . . .;

"• is currently in school, has graduated from high school, has obtained a general education development certificate, or is an honorably discharged veteran . . .;

"• has not been convicted of a [serious crime]; and

"• is not above the age of thirty,"

then U.S. immigration officials have been directed to "defe[r] action" against such individual "for a period of two years, subject to renewal." The husbanding of scarce enforcement resources can hardly be the justification for this, since the considerable administrative cost of conducting as many as 1.4 million background checks, and ruling on the biennial requests for dispensation that the nonenforcement program envisions, will necessarily be *deducted* from immigration enforcement. The President said at a news conference that the new program is "the right thing to do" in light of Congress's failure to pass the administration's proposed revision of the Immigration Act. Perhaps it is, though Arizona may not think so. But to say, as the Court does, that Arizona *contradicts federal law* by enforcing applications of the Immigration Act that the President declines to enforce boggles the mind.

The Court opinion's looming specter of inutterable horror—"[i]f § 3 of the Arizona statute were valid, every State could give itself independent authority to prosecute federal registration violations," seems to me not so horrible and even less looming. But there has come to pass, and is with us today, the specter that Arizona and the States that support it predicted: a Federal Government that does not want to enforce the immigration laws as written, and leaves the States' borders unprotected against immigrants whom those laws would exclude. So the issue is a stark one. Are the sovereign States at the mercy of the Federal Executive's refusal to enforce the Nation's immigration laws?

A good way of answering that question is to ask: Would the States conceivably have entered into the Union if the Constitution itself contained the Court's holding? Today's judgment surely fails that test * * *.

* * *

Arizona has moved to protect its sovereignty—not in contradiction of federal law, but in complete compliance with it. The laws under challenge here do not extend or revise federal immigration restrictions, but merely enforce those restrictions more effectively. If securing its territory in this fashion is not within the power of Arizona, we should cease referring to it as a sovereign State. I dissent.

■ JUSTICE THOMAS, concurring in part and dissenting in part.

I agree with Justice SCALIA that federal immigration law does not pre-empt any of the challenged provisions of S.B. 1070. I reach that conclusion, however, for the simple reason that there is no conflict between the "ordinary meanin[g]" of the relevant federal laws and that of the four provisions of Arizona law at issue here.

* * *

Despite the lack of any conflict between the ordinary meaning of the Arizona law and that of the federal laws at issue here, the Court holds that various provisions of the Arizona law are pre-empted because they "stan[d] as an obstacle to the accomplishment and execution of the full purposes and objectives of Congress." *Hines, supra*, at 67 * * *. [T]he "purposes and objectives" theory of implied pre-emption is inconsistent with the Constitution because it invites courts to engage in freewheeling speculation about congressional purpose that roams well beyond statutory text. Under the Supremacy Clause, pre-emptive effect is to be given to congressionally enacted laws, not to judicially divined legislative purposes. Thus, even assuming the existence of some tension between Arizona's law and the supposed "purposes and objectives" of Congress, I would not hold that any of the provisions of the Arizona law at issue here are pre-empted on that basis.

■ JUSTICE ALITO, concurring in part and dissenting in part.

* * *

I agree with the Court that § 2(B) is not pre-empted * * *.

I also agree with the Court that § 3 is pre-empted by virtue of our decision in *Hines v. Davidowitz*, 312 U.S. 52 (1941). Our conclusion in that case that Congress had enacted an "all-embracing system" of alien registration and that States cannot "enforce additional or auxiliary regulations," id., at 66–67, 74, forecloses Arizona's attempt here to impose additional, state-law penalties for violations of the federal registration scheme.

While I agree with the Court on §§ 2(B) and 3, I part ways on §§ 5(C) and 6. The Court's holding on § 5(C) is inconsistent with *De Canas v. Bica*, 424 U.S. 351 (1976), which held that employment regulation, even of aliens unlawfully present in the country, is an area of traditional state concern. Because state police powers are implicated here, our precedents require us to presume that federal law does not displace state law unless Congress' intent to do so is clear and manifest. I do not believe Congress has spoken with the requisite clarity to justify invalidation of § 5(C). Nor do I believe that § 6 is invalid. Like § 2(B), § 6 adds virtually nothing to the authority that Arizona law enforcement officers already exercise. And whatever little authority they have gained is consistent with federal law.

* * *

The United States' attack on § 2(B) is quite remarkable. The United States suggests that a state law may be pre-empted, not because it conflicts with a federal statute or regulation, but because it is inconsistent with a federal agency's current enforcement priorities. Those priorities, however, are not law. They are nothing more than agency policy * * *. If § 2(B) were pre-empted at the present time because it is out of sync with the Federal Government's current priorities, would it be unpre-empted at some time in the future if the agency's priorities changed?

* * *

NOTES AND QUESTIONS

1. For nearly 150 years, the Supreme Court's chief justification for the federal power over immigration has been an argument of the form, "Every respectable sovereign government can do X; the United States has a respectable sovereign government; therefore, the United States government can do X." As a matter of original meaning, this kind of argument is obviously out of bounds, if only because of the Tenth Amendment. As a matter of the Economics of Federalism, and the spirit of the Virginia and Bedford Resolutions, it looks more plausible, at least when the "X" involves matters appropriate to national solutions. Whatever its merits, this was a popular form of argument in the Supreme Court for many decades in the nineteenth and early twentieth centuries after

the North won the Civil War. See how that argument played out with respect to the next two sets of powers described below, which, along with the federal immigration power, are still with us today.

[Assignment 37]

IX. THE POWER TO PRINT PAPER MONEY

Article I, Section 8, Clause 5: The Congress shall have Power * * * To coin Money, regulate the Value thereof, and of foreign Coin, * * *

Article I, Section 10, Clause 2: No State shall * * * coin Money; Emit Bills of Credit; make any other Thing but gold and silver Coin a Tender in Payment of Debts; * * *

A major concern of the Framers was their desire to eliminate the ruinous inflation that had wrecked the value of the federal and state paper currencies of the 1780's. The Clauses in the Constitution quoted above were the result. They appear to have contemplated only the issuance of gold and silver coins. Nevertheless, during the Civil War, President Abraham Lincoln issued paper money. President Lincoln's issuance of paper money as a war measure was challenged as being unconstitutional after the Civil War had been won, and by a 4 to 3 vote the Supreme Court held it was unconstitutional in *Hepburn v. Griswold*, 75 U.S. 603 (1870). Congress and President Ulysses S. Grant responded by increasing the size of the Supreme Court from seven justices to nine. A year later the newly reconstituted Supreme Court overruled *Hepburn v. Griswold* in *Knox v. Lee*, 79 U.S. 457 (1871). Eventually, in *Julliard v. Greenman*, 110 U.S. 421 (1884), the Supreme Court upheld the constitutionality of federally printed paper money in peacetime, as well as during emergencies like the Civil War. The power has been unchallenged since that time.

At first glance, it would appear that the Supreme Court's upholding of the constitutionality of federally coined paper money is at odds with the document's original meaning, but at least one serious originalist scholar has argued that the original meaning of the Coin Money power allowed for this. *See* Robert G. Natelson, *Paper Money and the Original Understanding of the Coinage Clause*, 31 HARV. J.L. & POL'Y 1017 (2008). Professor Natelson's originalist arguments, you will see in a moment, were not the arguments relied upon by the Court in *Knox v. Lee*.

Knox v. Lee

79 U.S. (12 Wall.) 457 (1871)

■ MR. JUSTICE STRONG delivered the opinion of the court.

The controlling questions in these cases are the following: Are the acts of Congress, known as the legal tender acts, constitutional when applied to contracts made before their passage; and, secondly, are they valid as applicable to debts contracted since their enactment? * * * It would be difficult to overestimate the consequences which must follow our decision. They will affect the entire business of the country, and take hold of the possible continued existence of the government. If it be held by this court that Congress has no constitutional power, under any circumstances, or in any emergency, to make treasury notes a legal tender for the payment of all debts (a power confessedly possessed by every independent sovereignty other than the United States), the government is without those means of self-preservation which, all must admit, may, in certain contingencies, become indispensable, even if they were not when the acts of Congress now called in question were enacted. It is also clear that if we hold the acts invalid as applicable to debts incurred, or transactions which have taken place since their enactment, our decision must cause, throughout the country, great business derangement, widespread distress, and the rankest injustice * * *. Men have bought and sold, borrowed and lent, and assumed every variety of obligations contemplating that payment might be made with such notes. Indeed, legal tender treasury notes have become the universal measure of values * * *.

The consequences of which we have spoken, serious as they are, must be accepted, if there is a clear incompatibility between the Constitution and the legal tender acts. But we are unwilling to precipitate them upon the country unless such an incompatibility plainly appears * * *. It is incumbent, therefore, upon those who affirm the unconstitutionality of an act of Congress to show clearly that it is in violation of the provisions of the Constitution. It is not sufficient for them that they succeed in raising a doubt.

Nor can it be questioned that, when investigating the nature and extent of the powers conferred by the Constitution upon Congress, it is indispensable to keep in view the objects for which those powers were granted * * *. [T]he powers conferred upon Congress must be regarded as related to each other, and all means for a common end. Each is but part of a system, a constituent of one whole. No single power is the ultimate end for which the Constitution was adopted. It may, in a very proper sense, be treated as a means for the accomplishment of a subordinate object, but that object is itself a means designed for an ulterior purpose. Thus the power to levy and collect taxes, to coin money and regulate its value, to raise and support armies, or to provide for and maintain a navy, are instruments for the paramount object, which was to establish a government, sovereign within its sphere, with capability of self-preservation, thereby forming a union more perfect than that which existed under the old Confederacy.

The same may be asserted also of all the non-enumerated powers included in the authority expressly given "to make all laws which shall be necessary and proper for carrying into execution the specified powers vested in Congress, and all other powers vested by the Constitution in the government of the United States, or in any department or officer thereof." It is impossible to know what those non-enumerated powers are, and what is their nature and extent, without considering the purposes they were intended to subserve * * *. It certainly was intended to confer upon the government the power of self-preservation * * *.

And here it is to be observed it is not indispensable to the existence of any power claimed for the Federal government that it can be found specified in the words of the Constitution, or clearly and directly traceable to some one of the specified powers. Its existence may be deduced fairly from more than one of the substantive powers expressly defined, or from them all combined. It is allowable to group together any number of them and infer from them all that the power claimed has been conferred. Such a treatment of the Constitution is recognized by its own provisions. This is well illustrated in its language respecting the writ of habeas corpus. The power to suspend the privilege of that writ is not expressly given, nor can it be deduced from any one of the particularized grants of power. Yet it is provided that the privileges of the writ shall not be suspended except in certain defined contingencies. This is no express grant of power. It is a restriction. But it shows irresistibly that somewhere in the Constitution power to suspend the privilege of the writ was granted, either by some one or more of the specifications of power, or by them all combined. And, that important powers were understood by the people who adopted the Constitution to have been created by it, powers not enumerated, and not included incidentally in any one of those enumerated, is shown by the amendments. The first ten of these were suggested in the conventions of the States, and proposed at the first session of the first Congress, before any complaint was made of a disposition to assume doubtful powers * * * They tend plainly to show that, in the judgment of those who adopted the Constitution, there were powers created by it, neither expressly specified nor deducible from any one specified power, or ancillary to it alone, but which grew out of the aggregate of powers conferred upon the government, or out of the sovereignty instituted. Most of these amendments are denials of power which had not been expressly granted, and which cannot be said to have been necessary and proper for carrying into execution any other powers. Such, for example, is the prohibition of any laws respecting the establishment of religion, prohibiting the free exercise thereof, or abridging the freedom of speech or of the press.

And it is of importance to observe that Congress has often exercised, without question, powers that are not expressly given nor ancillary to any single enumerated power. Powers thus exercised are what are called by Judge Story in his Commentaries on the Constitution, resulting powers, arising from the aggregate powers of the government. He instances the right to sue and make contracts. Many others might be given. The oath required by law from officers of the government is one. So is building a capitol or a presidential mansion, and so also is the penal code * * *.

Indeed the whole history of the government and of congressional legislation has exhibited the use of a very wide discretion, even in times of peace and in the absence of any trying emergency, in the selection of the necessary and proper means to carry into effect the great objects for which the government was framed, and this discretion has generally been unquestioned, or, if questioned, sanctioned by this court * * *.

* * *

* * * Before we can hold the legal tender acts unconstitutional, we must be convinced they were not appropriate means, or means conducive to the execution of any or all of the powers of Congress, or of the government, not appropriate in any degree (for we are not judges of the degree of appropriateness), or we must hold that they were prohibited. This brings us to the inquiry whether they were, when enacted, appropriate instrumentalities for carrying into effect, or executing any of the known powers of Congress, or of any department of the government. Plainly to this inquiry, a consideration of the time when they were enacted, and of the circumstances in which the government then stood, is important. It is not to be denied that acts may be adapted to the exercise of lawful power, and appropriate to it, in seasons of exigency, which would be inappropriate at other times.

We do not propose to dilate at length upon the circumstances in which the country was placed, when Congress attempted to make treasury notes a legal tender. They are of too recent occurrence to justify enlarged description. Suffice it to say that a civil war was then raging which seriously threatened the overthrow of the government and the destruction of the Constitution itself. It demanded the equipment and support of large armies and navies, and the employment of money to an extent beyond the capacity of all ordinary sources of supply. Meanwhile the public treasury was nearly empty, and the credit of the government, if not stretched to its utmost tension, had become nearly exhausted. Moneyed institutions had advanced largely of their means, and more could not be expected of them. They had been compelled to suspend specie payments. Taxation was inadequate to pay even the interest on the debt already incurred, and it was impossible to await the income of additional taxes. The necessity was immediate and pressing. The army was unpaid. There was then due to the soldiers in the field nearly a score of millions of dollars. The requisitions from the War and Navy Departments for supplies exceeded fifty millions, and the current expenditure was over one million per day. The entire amount of coin in the country, including that in private hands, as well as that in banking institutions, was insufficient to supply the need of the government three months, had it all been poured into the treasury. Foreign credit we had none. We say nothing of the overhanging paralysis of trade, and of business generally, which threatened loss of confidence in the ability of the government to maintain its continued existence, and therewith the complete destruction of all remaining national credit.

It was at such a time and in such circumstances that Congress was called upon to devise means for maintaining the army and navy, for securing the large supplies of money needed, and, indeed, for the preservation of the government created by the Constitution. It was at such a time and in such an emergency that the legal tender acts were passed * * *.

* * * It is urged now, after the lapse of nine years, and when the emergency has passed, that treasury notes without the legal tender clause might have been issued, and that the necessities of the government might thus have been supplied * * *. But admitting it to be true, what does it prove? Nothing more than that Congress had the choice of means for a legitimate end, each appropriate, and adapted to that end, though, perhaps, in different degrees. What then? Can this court say that it ought to have adopted one rather than the other? Is it our province to decide that the means selected were beyond the constitutional power of Congress, because we may think that other means to the same ends would have been more appropriate and equally efficient? That would be to assume legislative power, and to disregard the accepted rules for construing the Constitution. The degree of the necessity for any congressional enactment, or the relative degree of its appropriateness, if it have any appropriateness, is for consideration in Congress, not here * * *.

* * *

It may be conceded that Congress is not authorized to enact laws in furtherance even of a legitimate end, merely because they are useful, or because they make the government stronger. There must be some relation between the means and the end; some adaptedness or appropriateness of the laws to carry into execution the powers created by the Constitution. But when a statute has proved effective in the execution of powers confessedly existing, it is not too much to say that it must have had some appropriateness to the execution of those powers. The rules of construction heretofore adopted, do not demand that the relationship between the means and the end shall be direct and immediate * * *.

Concluding, then, that the provision which made treasury notes a legal tender for the payment of all debts other than those expressly excepted, was not an inappropriate means for carrying into execution the legitimate powers of the government, we proceed to inquire whether it was forbidden by the letter or spirit of the Constitution. It is not claimed that any express prohibition exists, but it is insisted that the spirit of the Constitution was violated by the enactment. Here those who assert the unconstitutionality of the acts mainly rest their argument. They claim that the clause which conferred upon Congress power "to coin money, regulate the value thereof, and of foreign coin," contains an implication that nothing but that which is the subject of coinage, nothing but the precious metals can ever be declared by law to be money, or to have the uses of money. If by this is meant that because certain powers over the currency are expressly given to Congress, all other powers relating to the same subject are impliedly forbidden, we need only remark that such is not the manner in which the Constitution has always been construed. On the contrary it has been ruled that power over a particular subject may be exercised as auxiliary to an express power, though there is another express power relating to the same subject, less comprehensive. There an express power to punish a certain class of crimes (the only direct reference to criminal legislation contained in the Constitution), was not regarded as an objection to deducing authority to punish other crimes from another substantive and defined grant of power. There are other decisions to the same effect. To assert, then, that the clause enabling Congress to coin money and regulate its value tacitly implies a denial of all other power over the currency of the nation, is an attempt to introduce a new rule of construction against the solemn decisions of this court. So far from its containing a lurking prohibition, many have thought it was intended to confer upon Congress that general power over the currency which has always been an acknowledged attribute of sovereignty in every other civilized nation than our own * * *.

* * *

We do not, however, rest our assertion of the power of Congress to enact legal tender laws upon this grant. We assert only that the grant can, in no just sense, be regarded as containing an implied prohibition against their enactment, and that, if it raises any implications, they are of complete power over the currency, rather than restraining.

* * *

Nor can it be truly asserted that Congress may not, by its action, indirectly impair the obligation of contracts, if by the expression be meant rendering contracts fruitless, or partially fruitless. Directly it may, confessedly, by passing a bankrupt act, embracing past as well as future transactions. This is obliterating contracts entirely. So it may relieve parties from their apparent obligations indirectly in a multitude of ways. It may declare war, or, even in peace, pass non-intercourse acts, or direct an embargo. All such measures may, and must operate seriously upon existing contracts, and may not merely hinder, but relieve the parties to such contracts entirely from performance. It is, then, clear that the powers of Congress may be exerted, though the effect of such exertion may be in one case to annul, and in other cases to impair the obligation of contracts * * *.

* * *.

[W]ithout extending our remarks further, it will be seen that we hold the acts of Congress constitutional as applied to contracts made either before or after their passage. In so holding, we overrule so much of what was decided in *Hepburn v. Griswold*, as ruled the acts unwarranted by the Constitution so far as they apply to contracts made before their enactment. That case was decided by a divided court, and by a court having a less number of judges than the law then in existence provided this court shall have. These cases have been heard before a full court, and they have received our most careful consideration * * *. [I]t is no unprecedented thing in courts of last resort, both in this country and in England, to overrule decisions previously made. We agree this should not be done inconsiderately, but in a case of such far-reaching consequences as the present, thoroughly convinced as we are that Congress has not transgressed its powers, we regard it as our duty so to decide and to affirm both these judgments.

* * *

■ JUSTICE BRADLEY, concurring. [Omitted.]

■ THE CHIEF JUSTICE, dissenting.

* * *

A majority of the court, five of four, in the opinion which has just been read, reverses the judgment rendered by the former majority of five to three, in pursuance of an opinion formed after repeated arguments, at successive terms, and careful consideration; and declares the legal tender clause to be constitutional; that is to say, that an act of Congress making promises to pay dollars legal tender as coined dollars in payment of pre-existing debts is a means appropriate and plainly adapted to the exercise of powers expressly granted by the Constitution, and not prohibited itself by the Constitution but consistent with its letter and spirit. And this reversal, unprecedented in the history of the court, has been produced by no change in the opinions of those who concurred in the former judgment. One closed an honorable judicial career by resignation after the case had been decided, after the opinion had been read and agreed to in conference, and after the day when it would have been delivered in court, had not the delivery been postponed for a week to give time for the preparation of the dissenting opinion. The court was then full, but the vacancy caused by the resignation of Mr. Justice Grier having been subsequently filled and an additional justice having been appointed under the act increasing the number of judges to nine, which took effect on the first Monday of December, 1869, the then majority find themselves in a minority of the court, as now constituted, upon the question.

Their convictions, however, remain unchanged. We adhere to the opinion pronounced in *Hepburn* v. *Griswold*. Reflection has only wrought a firmer belief in the soundness of the constitutional doctrines maintained, and in the importance of them to the country.

* * *

The power to coin money was a power to determine the fineness, weight, and denominations of the metallic pieces by which values were to be measured; and we do not perceive how this meaning can be extended without doing violence to the very words of the Constitution by imposing on them a sense they were never intended to bear. This construction is supported by contemporaneous and all subsequent action of the legislature; by all the recorded utterances of statesmen and jurists, and the unbroken tenor of judicial opinion until a very recent period, when the excitement of the civil war led to the adoption, by many, of different views.

* * *

My brothers CLIFFORD and FIELD concur in these views, gut in consideration of the importance of the principles involved will deliver their separate opinions. My brother NELSON also dissents.

■ MR. JUSTICE CLIFFORD, dissenting:

Money, in the constitutional sense, means coins of gold and silver fabricated and stamped by authority of law as a measure of value, pursuant to the power vested in Congress by the Constitution.

Coins of copper may also be minted for small fractional circulation, as authorized by law and the usage of the government for eighty years, but it is not necessary to discuss that topic at large in this investigation.

Even the authority of Congress upon the general subject does not extend beyond the power to coin money, regulate the value thereof and of foreign coin,

* * *

■ MR. JUSTICE FIELD, dissenting.

* * *

There has been much confusion on this subject from a failure to distinguish between the adaptation of particular means to an end and the effect, or supposed effect, of those means in producing results desired by the government. The argument is stated thus: the object of borrowing is to raise funds; the annexing of the quality of legal tender to the notes of the government induces parties the more readily to loan upon them; the result desired by the government—the acquisition of funds—is thus accomplished; therefore, the annexing of the quality of legal tender is an appropriate means to the execution of the power to borrow. But it is evident that the same reasoning would justify, as appropriate means to the execution of this power, any measures which would result in obtaining the required funds. The annexing of a provision by which the notes of the government should serve as a free ticket in the public conveyances of the country, or for ingress into places of public amusement, or which would entitle the holder to a percentage out of the revenues of private corporations, or exempt his entire property, as well as the notes themselves, from State and municipal taxation, would produce a ready acceptance of the notes. But the advocate of the most liberal construction would hardly pretend that these measures, or similar measures touching the property of third parties, would be appropriate as a means to the execution of the power to borrow. Indeed, there is no invasion by government of the rights of third parties which might not thus be sanctioned upon the pretence that its allowance to the holder of the notes would lead to their ready acceptance and produce the desired loan.

* * *

The Constitution has specifically designated the means by which funds can be raised for the uses of the government, either in war or peace. These are taxation, borrowing, coining, and the sale of its public property. Congress is empowered to levy and collect taxes, duties, imposts, and excises of any extent which the public necessities may require. Its power to borrow is equally unlimited. It can convert any bullion it may possess into coin, and it can dispose of the public lands and other property of the United States or any part of such property. The designation of these means exhausts the powers of Congress on the subject of raising money. The designation of the means is a negation of all others, for the designation would be unnecessary and absurd if the use of any and all means were permissible without it. These means exclude a resort to forced loans, and to any compulsory interference with the property of third persons, except by regular taxation in one of the forms mentioned.

But this is not all. The power "to coin money" is, in my judgment, inconsistent with and repugnant to the existence of a power to make anything but coin a legal tender. To coin money is to mould metallic substances having intrinsic value into certain forms convenient for commerce, and to impress them with the stamp of the government indicating their value. Coins are pieces of metal, of definite weight and value, thus stamped by national authority. Such is the natural import of the terms "to coin money" and "coin;" and if there were any doubt that this is their meaning in the Constitution, it would be removed by the language which immediately follows the grant of the "power to coin," authorizing Congress to regulate the value of the money thus coined, and also "of foreign coin," and by the distinction made in other clauses between coin and the obligations of the General government and of the several States.

The power of regulation conferred is the power to determine the weight and purity of the several coins struck, and their consequent relation to the monetary unit which might be established by the authority of the government—a power which can be exercised with reference to the metallic coins of foreign countries, but which is incapable of execution with reference to their obligations or securities.

Then, in the clause of the Constitution immediately following, authorizing Congress "to provide for the punishment of counterfeiting the securities and current coin of the United States," a distinction between the obligations and coins of the General government is clearly made. And in the tenth section, which forbids the States to "coin money, emit bills of credit, and make anything but gold and silver coin a tender in payment of debts," a like distinction is made between coin and the obligations of the several States. The terms gold and silver as applied to the coin exclude the possibility of any other conclusion.

* * *

The position that Congress possesses some undefined power to do anything which it may deem expedient, as a resulting power from the general purposes of the government, which is advanced in the opinion of the majority, would of course settle the question under consideration without difficulty, for it would end all controversy by changing our government from one of enumerated powers to one resting in the unrestrained will of Congress.

* * *

NOTES AND QUESTIONS

1. The dissenting opinions of Chief Justice Chase, Justice Clifford, and Justice Field are very long. (Justice Nelson dissented without writing separately.) Everyone understood that this was a milestone case.

2. Is Justice Strong's opinion persuasive? Does it follow that because other Western democracies can print paper money, our federal government of limited and enumerated powers can do so as well? Doesn't invoking the Bill of Rights as suggesting unenumerated federal powers violate the literal terms of the Ninth Amendment? As we suggested above, this was one of a series of cases in this post era of rampant nationalism of inferring federal powers from perceived necessities and the general nature of governments.

3. What do the Economics of Federalism imply as to whether the federal government ought to have an exclusive power to print paper money? Is there a clear answer? If there is no *clear* answer, what should be the default?

4. Is the power to make paper money legal tender a "great substantive and independent power," so that it cannot be derived from the Necessary and Proper Clause? Can it perhaps be derived from the Necessary and Proper Clause during wartime but not peacetime? Or is it a great substantive and independent power whenever it is exercised?

5. Article I, Section 10 forbids the States from emitting Bills of Credit or making any Thing but gold and silver coin a Tender in payment of debts. Article I, Section 9 does not forbid Congress from doing either of these things. Does this imply that Congress can do these things?

6. Without regard to the Necessary and Proper Clause or arguments from the nature of sovereignty, could one find a legal tender power directly in the power to "coin Money, regulate the Value thereof, and of foreign Coin"? If other countries issue paper money, can Congress regulate its value—or can Congress only regulate the value of foreign metallic coins? If "foreign Coin" includes paper money, why wouldn't the power to "coin Money" include paper money? *See* Natelson, *supra*, at 1064–65.

7. For what propositions would you consider *The Legal Tender Cases* to be a strong precedent? For whatever this is worth, they do not get cited very often by the Supreme Court and are almost never cited for broad propositions about governmental powers.

X. THE MILITARY DRAFT

Article I, Section 8, Clause 12: Congress shall have Power * * * To raise and support Armies, but no Appropriation of Money to that Use shall be for a longer Term than two years;

Article I, Section 8, Clause 13: Congress shall have Power * * * To provide and maintain a Navy;

Article I, Section 8, Clause 14: Congress shall have Power * * * To make Rules for the Government and Regulation of the land and naval Forces;

Article I, Section 8, Clause 15: Congress shall have Power * * * To provide for calling forth the Militia to execute the Laws of the Union, suppress Insurrections and repeal Invasions.

Article I, Section 8, Clause 16: Congress shall have Power * * * To provide for organizing, arming, and disciplining, the Militia, and for governing such Part of them as may be employed in the Service of the United States, reserving to the States, respectively, the Appointment of the Officers, and the Authority of training the Militia according to the discipline prescribed by Congress.

The original Constitution assumed that the thirteen United States would have their own state militias, in which every able-bodied man could be compelled to serve The militias could be federalized in an emergency, in which case the President of the United States would be the Commander-in-Chief of the thirteen state militias—though, to maintain an element of localism, the Constitution reserved to the States "the Appointment of the Officers, and the Authority of training the Militia according to the discipline prescribed by Congress." *Id.* art. I, § 8, cl. 16. The federal government could also hire a mercenary army and navy, but no appropriation to pay the mercenaries in the army could last for longer than two years. Thus, there was established a Founding Era military system of checks and balances. There was a federal army and navy, but it was checked by the existence in each State of citizen militias (with their own officers). A federal military draft would have been inconceivable in such a world, because it was the States who had the power to draft their own citizens to serve in their respective state militias.

The Framers military system of checks and balances collapsed once the eleven Confederate state militias rebelled against the Union and fought the Union Army in the Civil War. After the War, the State militias were reorganized as being only State National Guard units and compulsory service in them came to an end. Moreover, during the Civil War, President Abraham Lincoln got Congress to enact the first-ever national draft law, although this law expired once the Civil War came to an end. Compulsory military service in the U.S. Armed Services was reintroduced during World War I. We reproduce for you below the post-World War I Supreme Court decision unanimously upholding the constitutionality of a national draft. For a powerful overview of the history, which (we think) convincingly shows the federal military draft is unconstitutional on originalist grounds, see Leon Friedman, *Conscription and the Constitution: The Original Understanding*, 67 MICH. L. REV. 1493 (1969).

A. SELECTIVE DRAFT LAW CASES

245 U.S. 366 (1918)

■ MR. CHIEF JUSTICE WHITE delivered the opinion of the court.

We are here concerned with some of the provisions of the Act of May 18, 1917, c. 15, 40 Stat. 76, entitled "An Act to authorize the President to increase temporarily the Military Establishment of the United States." The law, as its opening sentence declares, was intended to supply temporarily the increased military force which was required by the existing emergency, the war then and now flagrant. The clauses we must pass upon and those which will throw light on their significance are briefly summarized:

The act proposed to raise a national army * * * by subjecting all male citizens between the ages of twenty-one and thirty to duty in the national army for the period of the existing emergency after the proclamation of the President announcing the necessity for their service, and * * * by providing for selecting from the body so called, on the further proclamation of the President, 500,000 enlisted men, and a second body of the same number should the President in his discretion deem it necessary. To carry out its purposes the act made it the duty of those liable to the call to present themselves for registration on the proclamation of the President so as to subject themselves to the terms of the act and provided full federal means for carrying out the selective draft. It gave the President in his discretion power to create local boards to consider claims for exemption for physical disability or otherwise made by those called. The act exempted from subjection to the draft designated United States and state officials as well as those already in the military or naval service of the United States, regular or duly ordained ministers of religion and theological students under the conditions provided for, and, while relieving from military service in the strict sense the members of religious sects as enumerated whose tenets excluded the moral right to engage in war, nevertheless subjected such persons to the performance of service of a non-combatant character to be defined by the President.

The proclamation of the President calling the persons designated within the ages described in the statute was made, and the plaintiffs in error, who were in the class and under the statute were obliged to present themselves for registration and subject themselves to the law, failed to do so and were prosecuted under the statute for the penalties for which it provided. They all defended by denying that there had been conferred by the Constitution upon Congress the power to compel military service by a selective draft * * *.

The possession of authority to enact the statute must be found in the clauses of the Constitution giving Congress power "to declare war; . . . to raise and support armies, but no appropriation of money to that use shall be for a longer term than two years; . . . to make rules for the government and regulation of the land and naval forces." Article I, § 8. And of course the powers conferred by these provisions like all other powers given carry with them, as provided by the Constitution, the authority "to make all laws which shall be necessary and proper for carrying into execution the foregoing powers." Article I, § 8.

As the mind cannot conceive an army without the men to compose it, on the face of the Constitution the objection that it does not give power to provide for such men would seem to be too frivolous for further notice. It is said, however, that * * * the right to provide is not denied by calling for volunteer enlistments, but it does not and cannot include the power to exact enforced military duty by the citizen. This however but challenges the existence of all power, for a governmental power which has no sanction to it and which therefore can only be exercised provided the citizen consents to its exertion is in no substantial sense a power. It is argued, however, that although this is abstractly true, it is not concretely so because as compelled military service is repugnant to a free government and in conflict with all the great guarantees of the Constitution as to individual liberty, it must be assumed that the authority to raise armies was intended to be limited to the right to call an army into existence counting alone upon the willingness of the citizen to do his duty in time of public need, that is, in time of war. But the premise of this proposition is so devoid of foundation that it leaves not even a shadow of ground upon which to base the conclusion. Let us see if this is not at once demonstrable. It may not be doubted that the very conception of a just government and its duty to the citizen includes the reciprocal obligation of the citizen to render military service in case of need, and the right to compel it. Vattel, Law of Nations, Book III, c. 1 & 2. To do more than state the proposition is absolutely unnecessary in view of the practical illustration afforded by the almost universal legislation to that effect now in force.[1] * * *

---

1 In the argument of the Government, it is stated: "The Stateman's Year-book for 1917 cites the following governments as enforcing military service: Argentine Republic, p. 656; Austria-Hungary, p. 667; Belgium, p. 712; Brazil, p. 738; Bulgaria, p. 747; Bolivia, p. 728; Colombia, p. 790; Chile, p. 754; China, p.

In the Colonies before the separation from England there cannot be the slightest doubt that the right to enforce military service was unquestioned and that practical effect was given to the power in many cases. Indeed, the brief of the Government contains a list of Colonial acts manifesting the power and its enforcement in more than two hundred cases. And this exact situation existed also after the separation. Under the Articles of Confederation it is true Congress had no such power, as its authority was absolutely limited to making calls upon the States for the military forces needed to create and maintain the army, each State being bound for its quota as called. But it is indisputable that the States in response to the calls made upon them met the situation when they deemed it necessary by directing enforced military service on the part of the citizens. In fact the duty of the citizen to render military service and the power to compel him against his consent to do so was expressly sanctioned by the constitutions of at least nine of the States, an illustration being afforded by the following provision of the Pennsylvania constitution of 1776: "That every member of society hath a right to be protected in the enjoyment of life, liberty and property, and therefore is bound to contribute his proportion towards the expense of that protection, and yield his personal service when necessary, or an equivalent thereto." Art. 8, (Thorpe, American Charters, Constitutions and Organic Laws, vol. 5, pp. 3081, 3083).[1] * * *

When the Constitution came to be formed it may not be disputed that one of the recognized necessities for its adoption was the want of power in Congress to raise an army and the dependence upon the States for their quotas. In supplying the power it was manifestly intended to give it all and leave none to the States, since besides the delegation to Congress of authority to raise armies the Constitution prohibited the States, without the consent of Congress, from keeping troops in time of peace or engaging in war. Article I, § 10.

To argue that, as the state authority over the militia prior to the Constitution embraced every citizen, the right of Congress to raise an army should not be considered as granting authority to compel the citizen's service in the army, is but to express in a different form the denial of the right to call any citizen to the army. Nor is this met by saying that it does not exclude the right of Congress to organize an army by voluntary enlistments, that is, by the consent of the citizens, for if the proposition be true, the right of the citizen to give consent would be controlled by the

770; Denmark, p. 811; Ecuador, p. 820; France, p. 841; Greece, p. 1001; Germany, p. 914; Guatemala, p. 1009; Honduras, p. 1018; Italy, p. 1036; Japan, p. 1064; Mexico, p. 1090; Montenegro, p. 1098; Netherlands, p. 1119; Nicaragua, p. 1142; Norway, p. 1152; Peru, p. 1191; Portugal, p. 1201; Roumania, p. 1220; Russia, p. 1240; Serbia, p. 1281; Siam, p. 1288; Spain, p. 1300; Switzerland, p. 1337; Salvador, p. 1270; Turkey, p. 1353." See also the recent Canadian conscription act, entitled, "Military Service Act" of August 27, 1917, expressly providing for service abroad (printed in the Congressional Record of September 20, 1917, 55th Cong.Rec. p. 7959); the Conscription Law of the Orange Free State, Law No. 10, 1899, Military Service and Commando Law, sections 10 and 28, Laws of Orange River Colony, 1901, p. 855; of the South African Republic, "De Locale Wetten en Volksraadsbesluiten der Zuid-Afr. Republick," 1898, Law No. 20, pp. 230, 233, article 6, 28; Constitution, German Empire, April 16, 1871, Art. 57, 59, Dodd, 1 Modern Constitutions, p. 344; Gesetz, betreffend Aenderungen der Wehrpflicht, vom 11 Feb. 1888, No. 1767, Reichs-Gesetzblatt, p. 11, amended by law of July 22, 1913, No. 4264, RGBI., p. 593; Loi sur le recrutement de l'armee of 15 July, 1889 (Duvergier, vol. 89, p. 440), modified by act of 21 March, 1905 (Duvergier, vol. 105, p. 133).

[1] *See also* Constitution of Vermont, 1777, c. 1, Art. 9 (Thorpe, vol. 6, pp. 4747, 3740); New York, 1777, Art. 40 (*id.*, vol. 5, p. 2637); Massachusetts Bill of Rights, 1780, Art. 10 (*id.*, vol. 3, p. 1891); New Hampshire, 1784, pt. 1, Bill of Rights, Art. 12 (*id.*, vol. 4, p. 2455); Delaware, 1776, Art. 9 (*id.*, vol. 1, pp. 562, 564); Maryland, 1776, Art. 33 (*id.*, vol. 3, pp. 1686, 1696); Virginia, 1776, Militia (*id.*, vol. 7, p. 3817); Georgia, 1777, Art. 33, 35 (*id.*, vol. 2, pp. 777, 782).

same prohibition which would deprive Congress of the right to compel unless it can be said that although Congress had not the right to call because of state authority, the citizen had a right to obey the call and set aside state authority if he pleased to do so. And a like conclusion demonstrates the want of foundation for the contention that, although it be within the power to call the citizen into the army without his consent, the army into which he enters after the call is to be limited in some respects to services for which the militia it is assumed may only be used, since this admits the appropriateness of the call to military service in the army and the power to make it and yet destroys the purpose for which the call is authorized—the raising of armies to be under the control of the United States.

The fallacy of the argument results from confounding the constitutional provisions concerning the militia with that conferring upon Congress the power to raise armies. It treats them as one, while they are different.

* * *

And, upon this understanding of the two powers, the legislative and executive authority has been exerted from the beginning * * *. When the War of 1812 came * * *, the Government determined that the exercise of the power to organize an army by compulsory draft was necessary and Mr. Monroe, the Secretary of War, (Mr. Madison being President) in a letter to Congress recommended several plans of legislation on that subject. It suffices to say that by each of them it was proposed that the United States deal directly with the body of citizens subject to military duty and call a designated number out of the population between the ages of 18 and 45 for service in the army * * *. A bill was introduced giving effect to the plan. Opposition developed, but we need not stop to consider it because it substantially rested upon the incompatibility of compulsory military service with free government, a subject which, from what we have said, has been disposed of. Peace came before the bill was enacted.

Down to the Mexican War the legislation exactly portrayed the same condition of mind which we have previously stated. In that war, however, no draft was suggested, because the army created by the United States immediately resulting from the exercise by Congress of its power to raise armies, that organized under its direction from the militia and the volunteer commands which were furnished, proved adequate to carry the war to a successful conclusion.

So the course of legislation from that date to 1861 affords no ground for any other than the same conception of legislative power which we have already stated * * *. [T]he Act of March 3, 1863, c. 75, 12 Stat. 731, was adopted entitled "An Act for enrolling and calling out the National Forces and for other purposes." By that act which was clearly intended to directly exert upon all the citizens of the United States the national power which it had been proposed to exert in 1814 on the recommendation of the then Secretary of War, Mr. Monroe, every male citizen of the United States between the ages of twenty and forty-five was made subject by the direct action of Congress to be called by compulsory draft to service in a national army at such time and in such numbers as the President in his discretion might find necessary. In that act, as in the one of 1814, and in this one, the means by which the act was to be enforced were directly federal and the force to be raised as a result of the draft was therefore typically national as distinct from the call into active service of the militia as such. And under the power thus exerted four separate calls for draft were made by the President and enforced, that of July, 1863, of February and March, 1864, of July and December, 1864, producing a force of about a quarter of a million men. It is undoubted that the men thus raised by draft were treated as subject to direct national authority and were used either in filling the gaps occasioned by the vicissitudes of war in the ranks of the existing national forces or for the purpose of organizing such new units as were deemed to be required. It would be childish to deny the value of the added strength which was thus afforded * * *.

* * * Thus, sanctioned as is the act before us by the text of the Constitution, and by its significance as read in the light of the fundamental principles with which the subject is concerned, by the power recognized and carried into effect in many civilized countries, by the authority and practice of the colonies before the Revolution, of the States under the Confederation, and of the Government since the formation of the Constitution, the want of merit in the contentions that the act in the particulars which we have been previously called upon to consider was beyond the constitutional power of Congress is manifest * * *.

In reviewing the subject, we have hitherto considered it, as it has been argued, from the point of view of the Constitution as it stood prior to the adoption of the Fourteenth Amendment. But to avoid all misapprehension we briefly direct attention to that Amendment for the purpose of pointing out, as has been frequently done in the past, how completely it broadened the national scope of the Government under the Constitution by causing citizenship of the United States to be paramount and dominant instead of being subordinate and derivative, and therefore, operating as it does upon all the powers conferred by the Constitution, leaves no possible support for the contentions made, if their want of merit was otherwise not so clearly made manifest.

* * *

Finally, as we are unable to conceive upon what theory the exaction by government from the citizen of the performance of his supreme and noble duty of contributing to the defense of the rights and honor of the nation, as the result of a war declared by the great representative body of the people, can be said to be the imposition of involuntary servitude in violation of the prohibitions of the Thirteenth Amendment, we are constrained to the conclusion that the contention to that effect is refuted by its mere statement.

Affirmed.

NOTES AND QUESTIONS

1. You have not yet read the Fourteenth Amendment, but do you think it is plausible to say that a provision designed to imposed constitutional limits on *States* and to ensure that all persons born in the United States are American citizens (thereby overturning the infamous *Dred Scott)* decision supports a federal power of conscription? Did the Court really say that it did? Were its other arguments more persuasive? Is it a good argument for a constitutional power to draft people that a bill for a draft was produced but not passed in 1812?

2. The fact that empires like Austria-Hungary, France, Germany, Russia, and the United Kingdom (along with countries from South Africa to Montenegro) had military drafts does not seem like a good argument to find such a power in the U.S. Constitution. These imperial governments are not governments of limited and enumerated power. Nor

does the Necessary and Proper Clause seem to be a likely prospect; the power of conscription is surely a "great substantive and independent power." In the end, isn't this another case of "All respectable governments can do X . . ."?

3. On the other hand, how does one replicate the balance between the federal armed services and the state national guard units after the fiasco of the Civil War? Did the Civil War in some fashion change the constitutional allocation of military powers, so that the (conceded) state power of conscription somehow moved to the federal government?

4. From time to time, politicians talk about imposing a year or two of mandatory community service on young people. This is obviously akin to the draft. Does Congress have power under the Constitution to do this?

5. For what propositions do you think the *Selective Draft Law Cases* stand as strong precedents?

6. The Constitution specifically reserves to the States authority for training the militia "according to the discipline prescribed by Congress." Congress thus has power for "organizing, arming, and disciplining, the militia," but the actual training is seemingly left to the States. Suppose that it is peacetime, and the President orders state National Guard units to report for training in a foreign country, but the State governor does not want that State's militia training outside the United States? This was not an eighteenth- or nineteenth-century controversy; it was decided by the Supreme Court in 1990.

B. PERPICH V. DEP'T OF DEFENSE

496 U.S. 334 (1990)

■ JUSTICE STEVENS delivered the opinion of the Court.

The question presented is whether the Congress may authorize the President to order members of the National Guard to active duty for purposes of training outside the United States during peacetime without either the consent of a State Governor or the declaration of a national emergency.

A gubernatorial consent requirement that had been enacted in 1952 was partially repealed in 1986 by the "Montgomery Amendment," which provides:

> "The consent of a Governor described in subsections (b) and (d) may not be withheld (in whole or in part) with regard to active duty outside the United States, its territories, and its possessions, because of any objection to the location, purpose, type, or schedule of such active duty."

In this litigation the Governor of Minnesota and the State of Minnesota (hereinafter collectively referred to as the Governor), challenge the constitutionality of that amendment. The Governor contends that it violates the Militia Clauses of the Constitution.

In his complaint the Governor alleged that pursuant to a state statute the Minnesota National Guard is the organized militia of the State of Minnesota and that pursuant to a federal statute members of that militia "are also members of either the Minnesota unit of the Air National Guard of the United States or the Minnesota unit of the Army National Guard of the United States (hereinafter collectively referred to as the 'National Guard of the United States')." App. 5. The complaint further alleged that the Montgomery Amendment had prevented the Governor from withholding his consent to a training mission in Central America for certain members of the Minnesota National Guard in January 1987, and prayed for an injunction against the implementation of any similar orders without his consent.

* * *

* * * Over the dissent of two judges, the en banc [Eighth Circuit] court agreed with the District Court's conclusion that "Congress' army power is plenary and exclusive" and that the State's authority to train the militia did not conflict with congressional power to raise armies for the common defense and to control the training of federal reserve forces. 880 F.2d 11, 17–18 (1989).

* * *[W]e conclude that the plain language of Article I of the Constitution, read as whole, requires affirmance of the Court of Appeals' judgment [in favor of the congressional statute] * * *.

Two conflicting themes, developed at the Constitutional Convention and repeated in debates over military policy during the next century, led to a compromise in the text of the Constitution and in later statutory enactments. On the one hand, there was a widespread fear that a national standing Army posed an intolerable threat to individual liberty and to the sovereignty of the separate States, while, on the other hand, there was a recognition of the danger of relying on inadequately trained soldiers as the primary means of providing for the common defense. Thus, Congress was authorized both to raise and support a national Army and also to organize "the Militia."

In the early years of the Republic, Congress did neither. In 1792, it did pass a statute that purported to establish "an Uniform Militia throughout the United States," but its detailed command that every able-bodied male citizen between the ages of 18 and 45 be enrolled therein and equip himself with appropriate weaponry was virtually ignored for more than a century, during which time the militia proved to be a decidedly unreliable fighting force. The statute was finally repealed in 1901. It was in that year that President Theodore Roosevelt declared: "Our militia law is obsolete and worthless." The process of transforming "the National Guard of the several States" into an effective fighting force then began.

The Dick Act divided the class of able-bodied male citizens between 18 and 45 years of age into an "organized militia" to be known as the National Guard of the several States, and the remainder of which was then described as the "reserve militia," and which later statutes have termed the "unorganized militia." The statute created a table of organization for the National Guard conforming to that of the Regular Army, and provided that federal funds and Regular Army instructors should be used to train its members. It is undisputed that Congress was acting pursuant to the Militia Clauses of the Constitution in passing the Dick Act * * *. In 1908 * * *, the statute was amended to provide expressly that the Organized Militia should be available for service "either within or without the territory of the United States."

When the Army made plans to invoke that authority by using National Guard units south of the Mexican border, Attorney General Wickersham expressed the opinion that the Militia Clauses precluded such use outside the Nation's borders. In response to that opinion and to the widening conflict in Europe, in 1916 Congress decided to "federalize" the National Guard. In addition to providing for greater federal control and federal funding of the Guard, the statute required every guardsman to take a dual oath—to support the Nation as well as the States and to obey the President as well as the Governor—and authorized the President to draft members of the Guard into federal service. The statute expressly provided that the Army of the United States should include not only "the Regular Army," but also "the National Guard while in the service of the United States," and that when drafted into federal service by the President, members of the Guard so drafted should "from the date of their draft, stand discharged from the militia, and shall from said date be subject to" the rules and regulations governing the Regular Army.

During World War I, the President exercised the power to draft members of the National Guard into the Regular Army. That power, as well as the power to compel civilians to render military service, was upheld in the *Selective Draft Law Cases*, 245 U.S. 366 (1918) * * *.

The draft of the individual members of the National Guard into the Army during World War I virtually destroyed the Guard as an effective organization. The draft terminated the members' status as militiamen, and the statute did not provide for a restoration of their prewar status as members of the Guard when they were mustered out of the Army. This problem was ultimately remedied by the 1933 amendments to the 1916 Act. Those amendments created * * * the National Guard of the various States and the National Guard of the United States.

Since 1933 all persons who have enlisted in a State National Guard unit have simultaneously enlisted in the National Guard of the United States. In the latter capacity they became a part of the Enlisted Reserve Corps of the Army, but unless and until ordered to active duty in the Army, they retained their status as members of a separate State Guard unit. Under the 1933 Act, they could be ordered into active service whenever Congress declared a national emergency and authorized the use of troops in excess of those in the Regular Army * * *. Thus, under the "dual enlistment" provisions of the statute that have been in effect since 1933, a member of the Guard who is ordered to active duty in the federal service is thereby relieved of his or her status in the State Guard for the entire period of federal service.

Until 1952 the statutory authority to order National Guard units to active duty was limited to periods of national emergency. In that year, Congress broadly authorized orders to "active duty or active duty for training" without any emergency requirement, but provided that such orders could not be issued without gubernatorial consent. The National Guard units have under this plan become a sizable portion of the Nation's military forces; for example, "the Army National Guard provides 46 percent of the combat units and 28 percent of the support forces of the Total Army." Apparently gubernatorial consents to training missions were routinely obtained until 1985, when the Governor of California refused to consent to a training mission for 450 members of the California National Guard in Honduras, and the Governor of Maine shortly thereafter refused to consent to a similar mission. Those incidents led to the enactment of the Montgomery Amendment and this litigation ensued.

The Governor's attack on the Montgomery Amendment relies in part on the traditional understanding that "the Militia" can only be called forth for three limited purposes that do not encompass either foreign service or nonemergency conditions, and in part on the express language in the second Militia Clause reserving to the States "the Authority of training the Militia." The Governor does not, however, challenge the authority of Congress to create a dual enlistment program. Nor does the Governor claim that membership in a State Guard unit—or any type of state militia—creates any sort of constitutional immunity from being drafted into the Federal Armed Forces. Indeed, it would be ironic to claim such immunity when every member of the Minnesota National Guard has voluntarily enlisted, or accepted a commission as an officer, in the National Guard of the United States and thereby become a member of the Reserve Corps of the Army.

The unchallenged validity of the dual enlistment system means that the members of the National Guard of Minnesota who are ordered into federal service with the National Guard of the United States lose their status as members of the state militia during their period of active duty. If that duty is a training mission, the training is performed by the Army in which the trainee is serving, not by the militia from which the member has been temporarily disassociated. "Each member of the Army National Guard of the United States or the Air National Guard of the United States who is ordered to active duty is relieved from duty in the National Guard of his State or Territory, or of Puerto Rico or the District of Columbia, as the case may be, from the effective date of his order to active duty until he is relieved from that duty." 32 U.S.C. § 325(a).

This change in status is unremarkable in light of the traditional understanding of the militia as a part-time, nonprofessional fighting force * * *. Notwithstanding the brief periods of federal service, the members of the State Guard unit * * * now must keep three hats in their closets—a civilian hat, a state militia hat, and an army hat—only one of which is worn at any particular time. When the state militia hat is being worn, the "drilling and other exercises" * * * are performed pursuant to "the Authority of training the Militia according to the discipline prescribed by Congress," but when that hat is replaced by the federal hat, the second Militia Clause is no longer applicable.

This conclusion is unaffected by the fact that prior to 1952 Guard members were traditionally not ordered into active service in peacetime or for duty abroad. That tradition is at least partially the product of political debate and political compromise, but even if the tradition were compelled by the text of the Constitution, its constitutional aspect is related only to service by State Guard personnel who retain their state affiliation during their periods of service. There now exists a wholly different situation, in which the state affiliation is suspended in favor of an entirely federal affiliation during the period of active duty.

This view of the constitutional issue was presupposed by our decision in the *Selective Draft Law Cases*, 245 U.S. 366 (1918). Although the Governor is correct in pointing out that those cases were decided in the context of an actual war, the reasoning in our opinion was not so limited. After expressly noting that the 1916 Act had incorporated members of the National Guard into the National Army, the Court held that the Militia Clauses do not constrain the powers of Congress "to provide for the common Defence," to "raise and support Armies," to "make Rules for the Government and Regulation of the land and naval Forces," or to enact such laws as "shall be necessary and proper" for executing those powers. The Court instead held that, far from being a limitation on those powers, the Militia Clauses are—as the constitutional text plainly indicates—additional grants of power to Congress.

The first empowers Congress to call forth the militia "to execute the Laws of the Union, suppress Insurrections and repel Invasions." We may assume that Attorney General Wickersham was entirely correct in reasoning that when a National Guard unit retains its status as a state militia, Congress could not "impress" the entire unit for any other purpose. Congress did, however, authorize the President to call forth the entire membership of the Guard into federal service during World War I, even though the soldiers who fought in France were not engaged in any of the three specified purposes. Membership in the militia did not exempt them from a valid order to perform federal service, whether that service took the form of combat duty or training for such duty. The congressional power to call forth the militia may in appropriate cases supplement its broader power to raise armies and provide for the common defense and general welfare, but it does not limit those powers.

The second Militia Clause enhances federal power in three additional ways. First, it authorizes Congress to provide for "organizing, arming and disciplining the Militia." It is by congressional choice that the available pool of citizens has been formed into organized units. Over the years, Congress has exercised this power in various ways, but its current choice of a dual enlistment system is just as permissible as the 1792 choice to have the members of the militia arm themselves. Second, the Clause authorizes Congress to provide for governing such part of the militia as may be employed in the service of the United States. Surely this authority encompasses continued training while on active duty. Finally, although the appointment of officers "and the Authority of training the Militia" is reserved to the States respectively, that limitation is, in turn, limited by the words "according to the discipline prescribed by Congress." If the discipline required for effective service in the Armed Forces of a global power requires training in distant lands, or distant skies, Congress has the authority to provide it. The subordinate authority to perform the actual training prior to active duty in the federal service does not include the right to edit the discipline that Congress may prescribe for Guard members after they are ordered into federal service.

The Governor argues that this interpretation of the Militia Clauses has the practical effect of nullifying an important state power that is expressly reserved in the Constitution. We disagree. It merely recognizes the supremacy of federal power in the area of military affairs * * *.

In light of the Constitution's more general plan for providing for the common defense, the powers allowed to the States by existing statutes are significant. As has already been mentioned, several constitutional provisions commit matters of foreign policy and military affairs to the exclusive control of the National Government. This Court in *Tarble's Case*, 80 U.S. (13 Wall.) 397 (1872), had occasion to observe that the constitutional allocation of powers in this realm gave rise to a presumption that federal control over the Armed Forces was exclusive. Were it not for the Militia Clauses, it might be possible to argue on like grounds that the constitutional allocation of powers precluded the formation of organized state militia. The Militia Clauses, however, subordinate any such structural inferences to an express permission while also subjecting state militia to express federal limitations.

We thus conclude that the Montgomery Amendment is not inconsistent with the Militia Clauses * * *.

The judgment of the Court of Appeals is affirmed.

It is so ordered.

NOTES AND QUESTIONS

1. The Second Amendment says that "[a] well regulated Militia * * * [is] necessary to the security of a free State." Does the militia still exist?

2. The nineteenth-century immigration cases, the *Legal Tender Cases,* and the *Selective Draft Law Cases* all invoke inferences of congressional power from the nature of governments. Other cases from that era, roughly 1870–1920, contained similar reasoning (and perhaps *United States v. Curtiss-Wright Export Corp.,* 299 U.S. 304 (1936), *see supra* pages 473–477, is in the same family). For the Nation's first century, the federal government did not exercise a power of eminent domain—that is, a power to force a sale of private land to the government at a judicially fixed "just compensation" price—within States for post roads, forts, or any other federal purpose. States unquestionably had such powers; so if the federal government wanted land, it asked a State to exercise eminent domain to acquire the land and then bought it from the State. *See* William Baude, *Rethinking the Federal Eminent Domain Power,* 122 YALE L.J. 1738 (2013). (The federal government could exercise eminent domain power in the District of Columbia or federally owned territory, where Congress possesses the powers of a general rather than limited government.) The Supreme Court did not recognize a self-contained federal power of eminent domain until 1875. *See Kohl v. United States,* 91 U.S. 367 (1875). The Court would later locate, at least implicitly, such a power in the Necessary and Proper Clause, *see United States v. Gettysburg Electric R. Co.,* 160 U.S. 668, 679 (1896), but *Kohl* relied on the idea of inherent governmental powers:

> It has not been seriously contended during the argument that the United States government is without power to appropriate lands or other property within the States for its own uses, and to enable it to perform its proper functions. Such an authority is essential to its independent existence and perpetuity. These cannot be preserved if the obstinacy of a private person, or if any other authority, can prevent the acquisition of the means or instruments by which alone governmental functions can be performed. The powers vested by the Constitution in the general government demand for their exercise the acquisition of lands in all the States. These are needed for forts, armories, and arsenals, for navy-yards and light-houses, for custom-houses, post-offices, and court-houses, and for other public uses. If the right to acquire property for such uses may be made a barren right by the unwillingness of property-holders to sell, or by the action of a State prohibiting a sale to the Federal government, the constitutional grants of power may be rendered nugatory, and the government is dependent for its practical existence upon the will of a State, or even upon that of a private citizen. This cannot be * * *. The right is the offspring of political necessity; and it is inseparable from sovereignty, unless denied to it by its fundamental law * * *.
>
> But, if the right of eminent domain exists in the Federal government, it is a right which may be exercised within the States, so far as is necessary to the enjoyment of the powers conferred upon it by the Constitution * * *. When the power to establish post-offices and to create courts within the States was conferred upon the Federal government, included in it was authority to obtain sites for such offices and for court-houses, and to obtain them by such means as were known and appropriate. The right of eminent domain was one of those means well known when the Constitution was adopted, and employed to obtain lands for public uses. Its existence, therefore, in the grantee of that power, ought not to be questioned * * *.

> * * *
>
> It is true, this power of the Federal government has not heretofore been exercised adversely; but the non-user of a power does not disprove its existence * * *.

91 U.S. at 371–73. The same reasoning supported a federal power to enact criminal codes for Indian reservations. The Constitution gives Congress power "[t]o regulate Commerce * * * with the Indian tribes," but contains no other express power dealing with federal-Indian relations. A criminal code prohibiting, for example, murder or robbery by Indians on reservations is obviously not a regulation of commerce. The Court in 1886 inferred a general federal regulatory power over Indian affairs: "The power of the General Government over these remnants of a race once powerful, now weak and diminished in numbers, is necessary to their protection, as well as to the safety of those among whom they dwell. It must exist in that government, because it never has existed anywhere else, because the theatre of its exercise is within the geographical limits of the United States, because it has never been denied, and because it alone can enforce its laws on all the tribes." *United States v. Kagama,* 118 U.S. 375, 384–85 (1886). For a detailed study of the era of "inherent" federal powers, see (even though it is very long, it is worth it) Sarah H. Cleveland, *Powers Inherent in Sovereignty: Indians, Aliens, Territories, and the Nineteenth Century Origins of Plenary Power over Foreign Affairs,* 81 TEX. L. REV. 1 (2002).

[Assignment 38]

XI. MISCELLANEOUS CONGRESSIONAL POWERS

> **Congress shall have Power * * * To establish * * * uniform Laws on the subject of Bankruptcies throughout the United States;**
>
> **To * * * fix the Standard of Weights and Measures;**
>
> **To provide for the Punishment of counterfeiting the Securities and current Coin of the United States;**
>
> **To establish Post Offices and post Roads;**
>
> **To define and punish Piracies and Felonies committed on the high Seas, and Offenses against the Law of Nations.**

The Bankruptcy Clause, along with the Article I, section 10 Contracts Clause, was designed to protect commercial affairs by guarding against unduly pro-debtor State laws. The Bankruptcy Clause grants to Congress a pre-emptive power, while the Contracts Clause by itself purports to forbid state laws that redistribute wealth by rewriting contracts. *But see supra* pages 332–335. One might naturally assume, giving its language and the general structure of Article I, Section 8, that the bankruptcy power would be exclusive in Congress, but the Supreme Court early on held the power to be concurrent with the States. *See Sturges v. Crowninshield,* 17 U.S. (4 Wheat.) 122 (1819). That decision also confirmed that "Bankruptcies" included personal as well as commercial insolvencies. The constitutional issues that have subsequently arisen from the bankruptcy power mostly concern the status of federal bankruptcy judges rather than the bankruptcy power itself.

The Weights and Measures Clause, which had a precursor in article 9, section 4 of the Articles of Confederation, is also designed to facilitate commercial intercourse. Oddly enough, Congress has done very little with this clause; there has never been comprehensive federal legislation prescribing uniform standards of measurement. *See* David P. Currie, 2 GREEN BAG 2d 261 (1999).

The Counterfeiting Clause and the Piracies and Law of Nations Clause, along with the Article III Treason Clause, are the only provisions expressly dealing with federal crimes. The Piracies and Law of Nations Clause makes obvious sense as a jurisdictional allocation of authority, but because Congress has power under the Necessary and Proper Clause to prescribe criminal (and civil) penalties for violations of federal law, why did the Constitution need a specific Counterfeiting Clause? Perhaps it didn't. Or perhaps, because British law included counterfeiting as a kind of treason, the Counterfeiting Clause avoided any argument that the Treason Clause might disable Congress from punishing counterfeiting. *See* David F. Forte, *Counterfeiting, in* THE HERITAGE GUIDE TO THE CONSTITUTION 149 (2d ed. 2014).

We have already seen that the Postal Clause was the locus of the first extended congressional debate over subdelegation of legislative authority. *See supra* pages 183–185. For the first half-century of the Nation's history, there was also grave doubt about whether the power to "establish" post roads included the power to *create* new roads or was merely a power to *designate* existing State-created roads as postal routes. *See* Letter from Thomas Jefferson to James Madison (Mar. 6, 1796), in 3 THE FOUNDERS' CONSTITUTION 28 (Philip B. Kurland & Ralph Lerner eds., 1987) (suggesting that the postal power encompasses only the power to "select from those [roads] already made, those on which there shall be a post"); James Monroe, *Views of the President of the United States on the Subject of Internal Improvements* (1822), *in* 2 A COMPILATION OF THE MESSAGES AND PAPERS OF THE PRESIDENTS, 1787–1897, at 142, 156–59 (James D. Richardson ed., 1896) (doubting Congress's power to construct post roads). At least one U.S. Supreme Court Justice doubted Congress's power to build roads as late as 1845, *see Searight v. Stokes*, 44 U.S. (3 How.) 151, 181 (1845) (Daniel, J., dissenting) ("I believe that the authority vested in Congress by the Constitution to establish post-roads, confers no right to open new roads."), though dictum in the majority opinion in *Searight* settled the matter in favor of a power to construct new roads. That result is surely right; the power to "establish an uniform Rule for Naturalization" obviously includes the power to create a new rule, so it is hard to see why a power to "establish * * * post Roads" would not include a power to create new roads. For a thorough study of the Founding-era importance of the postal power, see Robert G. Natelson, *Founding-Era Socialism: The Original Meaning of the Constitution's Postal Clause,* 7 BR. J. AM. LEGAL STUD. 1 (2018).

XII. THE INTELLECTUAL PROPERTY CLAUSE

Congress shall have Power * * * To promote the Progress of Science and useful Arts, by securing for limited Times to Authors and Inventors the exclusive Right to their respective Writings and Discoveries

The founding generation hated monopolies. *See* Steven G. Calabresi & Larissa C. Leibowitz, *Monopolies and the Constitution: A History of Crony Capitalism,* 36 HARV. J. L. & PUB. POL'Y 983 (2013). As James Madison put it: "With regard to monopolies they are justly classified among the greatest nuisances in Government." Letter from James Madison to Thomas Jefferson (Oct. 17, 1788), *in* 14 THE PAPERS OF THOMAS JEFFERSON 21 (Julian P. Boyd ed., 1958). The one partial exception in the

Constitution was monopoly grants for intellectual property—partial because copyrights and patents could only be issued "for limited Times." The significance of that proviso regarding "limited Times" was tested in 2003.

Eldred v. Ashcroft

537 U.S. 186 (2003)

■ JUSTICE GINSBURG delivered the opinion of the Court.

This case concerns the authority the Constitution assigns to Congress to prescribe the duration of copyrights. The Copyright and Patent Clause of the Constitution, Art. I, § 8, cl. 8, provides as to copyrights: "Congress shall have Power . . . [t]o promote the Progress of Science . . . by securing [to Authors] for limited Times . . . the exclusive Right to their . . . Writings." In 1998, in the measure here under inspection, Congress enlarged the duration of copyrights by 20 years. Copyright Term Extension Act (CTEA), Pub.L. 105–298, §§ 102(b) and (d), 112 Stat. 2827–2828 (amending 17 U.S.C. §§ 302, 304). As in the case of prior extensions, principally in 1831, 1909, and 1976, Congress provided for application of the enlarged terms to existing and future copyrights alike.

Petitioners are individuals and businesses whose products or services build on copyrighted works that have gone into the public domain. They seek a determination that the CTEA fails constitutional review under both the Copyright Clause's "limited Times" prescription and the First Amendment's free speech guarantee. Under the 1976 Copyright Act, copyright protection generally lasted from the work's creation until 50 years after the author's death. Pub.L. 94–553, § 302(a), 90 Stat. 2572 (1976 Act). Under the CTEA, most copyrights now run from creation until 70 years after the author's death. 17 U.S.C. § 302(a). Petitioners do not challenge the "life-plus-70-years" timespan itself. "Whether 50 years is enough, or 70 years too much," they acknowledge, "is not a judgment meet for this Court." Brief for Petitioners 14. Congress went awry, petitioners maintain, not with respect to newly created works, but in enlarging the term for published works with existing copyrights. The "limited Tim[e]" in effect when a copyright is secured, petitioners urge, becomes the constitutional boundary, a clear line beyond the power of Congress to extend * * *.

In accord with the District Court and the Court of Appeals, we reject petitioners' challenges to the CTEA. In that 1998 legislation, as in all previous copyright term extensions, Congress placed existing and future copyrights in parity. In prescribing that alignment, we hold, Congress acted within its authority and did not transgress constitutional limitations.

We evaluate petitioners' challenge to the constitutionality of the CTEA against the backdrop of Congress' previous exercises of its authority under the Copyright Clause. The Nation's first copyright statute, enacted in 1790, provided a federal copyright term of 14 years from the date of publication, renewable for an additional 14 years if the author survived the first term. The 1790 Act's renewable 14-year term applied to existing works (*i.e.*, works already published and works created but not yet published) and future works alike. Congress expanded the federal copyright term to 42 years in 1831 (28 years from publication, renewable for an additional 14 years), and to 56 years in 1909 (28 years from publication, renewable for an additional 28 years). Both times, Congress applied the new copyright term to existing and future works; to qualify for the 1831 extension, an existing work had to be in its initial copyright term at the time the Act became effective.

In 1976, Congress altered the method for computing federal copyright terms. For works created by identified natural persons, the 1976 Act provided that federal copyright protection would run from the work's creation, not—as in the 1790, 1831, and 1909 Acts—its publication; protection would last until 50 years after the author's death * * *. For anonymous works, pseudonymous works, and works made for hire, the 1976 Act provided a term of 75 years from publication or 100 years from creation, whichever expired first.

* * *

The measure at issue here, the CTEA, installed the fourth major duration extension of federal copyrights. Retaining the general structure of the 1976 Act, the CTEA enlarges the terms of all existing and future copyrights by 20 years. For works created by identified natural persons, the term now lasts from creation until 70 years after the author's death * * *.

Paralleling the 1976 Act, the CTEA applies these new terms to all works not published by January 1, 1978. For works published before 1978 with existing copyrights as of the CTEA's effective date, the CTEA extends the term to 95 years from publication * * *.

* * *

We granted certiorari to address * * * whether the CTEA's extension of existing copyrights exceeds Congress' power under the Copyright Clause * * *.

* * * Congress has authority under the Copyright Clause to extend the terms of existing copyrights. Text, history, and precedent, we conclude, confirm that the Copyright Clause empowers Congress to prescribe "limited Times" for copyright protection and to secure the same level and duration of protection for all copyright holders, present and future.

The CTEA's baseline term of life plus 70 years, petitioners concede, qualifies as a "limited Tim[e]" as applied to future copyrights. Petitioners contend, however, that existing copyrights extended to endure for that same term are not "limited." Petitioners' argument essentially reads into the text of the Copyright Clause the command that a time prescription, once set, becomes forever "fixed" or "inalterable." The word "limited," however, does not convey a meaning so constricted. At the time of the Framing, that word meant what it means today: "confine[d] within certain bounds," "restrain[ed]," or "circumscribe[d]." S. Johnson, A Dictionary of the English Language (7th ed. 1785); see T. Sheridan, A Complete Dictionary of the English Language (6th ed. 1796) ("confine[d] within certain bounds"); Webster's Third New International Dictionary 1312 (1976) ("confined within limits"; "restricted in extent, number, or duration"). Thus understood, a timespan appropriately "limited" as applied to future copyrights does not automatically cease to be "limited" when applied to existing copyrights. And as we observe, there is no cause to suspect that a purpose to evade the "limited Times" prescription prompted Congress to adopt the CTEA.

To comprehend the scope of Congress' power under the Copyright Clause, "a page of history is worth a volume of logic." *New York Trust Co. v. Eisner*, 256 U.S. 345, 349 (Holmes, J.). History reveals an unbroken congressional practice of granting to authors of works with existing copyrights the benefit of term extensions so that all under copyright protection will be governed evenhandedly under the same regime. As earlier recounted, the First Congress accorded the protections of the Nation's first federal copyright statute to existing and future works alike. Since then, Congress has regularly applied duration extensions to both existing and future copyrights.

Because the Clause empowering Congress to confer copyrights also authorizes patents, congressional practice with respect to patents informs our inquiry. We count it significant that early Congresses extended the duration of numerous individual patents as well as copyrights * * *.

Further, although prior to the instant case this Court did not have occasion to decide whether extending the duration of existing copyrights complies with the "limited Times" prescription, the Court has found no constitutional barrier to the legislative expansion of existing patents. *McClurg v. Kingsland*, 1 How. 202 (1843), is the pathsetting precedent. The patentee in that case was unprotected under the law in force when the patent issued because he had allowed his employer briefly to practice the invention before he obtained the patent. Only upon enactment, two years later, of an exemption for such allowances did the patent become valid, retroactive to the time it issued. *McClurg* upheld retroactive application of the new law. The Court explained that the legal regime governing a particular patent "depend[s] on the law as it stood at the emanation of the patent, together with such changes as have been since made; for though they may be retrospective in their operation, that is not a sound objection to their validity." *Id.*, at 206. Neither is it a sound objection to the validity of a copyright term extension, enacted pursuant to the same constitutional grant of authority, that the enlarged term covers existing copyrights.

Congress' consistent historical practice of applying newly enacted copyright terms to future and existing copyrights reflects a judgment stated concisely by Representative Huntington at the time of the 1831 Act: "[J]ustice, policy, and equity alike forb[id]" that an "author who had sold his [work] a week ago, be placed in a worse situation than the author who should sell his work the day after the passing of [the] act." 7 Cong. Deb. 424 (1831). The CTEA follows this historical practice by keeping the duration provisions of the 1976 Act largely in place and simply adding 20 years to each of them. Guided by text, history, and precedent, we cannot agree with petitioners' submission that extending the duration of existing copyrights is categorically beyond Congress' authority under the Copyright Clause.

Satisfied that the CTEA complies with the "limited Times" prescription, we turn now to whether it is a rational exercise of the legislative authority conferred by the Copyright Clause. On that point, we defer substantially to Congress.

The CTEA reflects judgments of a kind Congress typically makes, judgments we cannot dismiss as outside the Legislature's domain. As respondent describes,, a key factor in the CTEA's passage was a 1993 European Union (EU) directive instructing EU members to establish a copyright term of life plus 70 years. EU Council Directive 93/98, Art. 1(1), p. 11; see 144 Cong. Rec. S12377–S12378 (daily ed. Oct. 12, 1998) (statement of Sen. Hatch). Consistent with the Berne Convention, the EU directed its members to deny this longer term to the works of any non-EU country whose laws did not secure the same extended term. By extending the baseline United States copyright term to life plus 70 years, Congress sought to ensure that American authors would receive the same copyright protection in Europe as their European counterparts. The CTEA may also provide greater incentive for American and other authors to create and disseminate their work in the United States.

In addition to international concerns, Congress passed the CTEA in light of demographic, economic, and technological changes, and rationally credited projections that longer terms would encourage copyright holders to invest in the restoration and public distribution of their works; see H.R.Rep. No. 105–452, p. 4 (1998) (term extension "provide[s] copyright owners generally with the incentive to restore older works and further disseminate them to the public").

In sum, we find that the CTEA is a rational enactment; we are not at liberty to second-guess congressional determinations and policy judgments of this order, however debatable or arguably unwise they may be. Accordingly, we cannot conclude that the CTEA—which continues the unbroken congressional practice of treating future and existing copyrights in parity for term extension purposes—is an impermissible exercise of Congress' power under the Copyright Clause.

* * *

Petitioners contend that even if the CTEA's 20-year term is literally a "limited Tim[e]," permitting Congress to extend existing copyrights allows it to evade the "limited Times" constraint by creating effectively perpetual copyrights through repeated extensions. We disagree.

* * * Nothing before this Court warrants construction of the CTEA's 20-year term extension as a congressional attempt to evade or override the "limited Times" constraint * * *.

Petitioners dominantly advance a series of arguments all premised on the proposition that Congress may not extend an existing copyright absent new consideration from the author. They pursue this main theme under three headings. Petitioners contend that the CTEA's extension of existing copyrights (1) overlooks the requirement of "originality," (2) fails to "promote the Progress of Science," and (3) ignores copyright's *quid pro quo*.

Petitioners' "originality" argument draws on *Feist Publications, Inc. v. Rural Telephone Service Co.*, 499 U.S. 340. In *Feist*, we observed that "[t]he *sine qua non* of copyright is originality," id., at 345, and held that copyright protection is unavailable to "a narrow category of works in which the creative spark is utterly lacking or so trivial as to be virtually nonexistent," id., at 359. Relying on *Feist*, petitioners urge that even if a work is sufficiently "original" to qualify for copyright protection in the first instance, any extension of the copyright's duration is impermissible because, once published, a work is no longer original.

Feist, however, did not touch on the duration of copyright protection. Rather, the decision addressed the core question of copyrightability, *i.e.*, the "creative spark" a work must have to be eligible for copyright protection at all. Explaining the originality requirement, *Feist* trained on the Copyright Clause words "Authors" and "Writings." *Id.*, at 346–347. The decision did not construe the "limited Times" for which a work may be protected, and the originality requirement has no bearing on that prescription.

More forcibly, petitioners contend that the CTEA's extension of existing copyrights does not "promote the Progress of Science" as contemplated by the preambular language of the Copyright Clause. Art. I, § 8, cl. 8. To sustain this objection, petitioners do not argue that the Clause's preamble is an independently enforceable limit on Congress' power. Rather, they maintain that the preambular language identifies the sole end to which Congress may legislate; accordingly, they conclude, the meaning of "limited Times" must be "determined in light of that specified end." Brief for Petitioners 19. The CTEA's extension of existing copyrights categorically fails to "promote the Progress of Science," petitioners argue, because it does not stimulate the creation of new works but merely adds value to works already created.

As petitioners point out, we have described the Copyright Clause as "both a grant of power and a limitation," *Graham v. John Deere Co. of Kansas City*, 383 U.S. 1, 5 (1966), and have said that "[t]he primary objective of copyright" is "[t]o promote the Progress of Science," *Feist*, 499 U.S., at 349. The "constitutional command," we have recognized, is that Congress, to the extent it enacts copyright laws at all, create a "system" that "promote[s] the Progress of Science." *Graham*, 383 U.S., at 6.

We have also stressed, however, that it is generally for Congress, not the courts, to decide how best to pursue the Copyright Clause's objectives. The justifications we earlier set out for Congress' enactment of the CTEA provide a rational basis for the conclusion that the CTEA "promote[s] the Progress of Science."

On the issue of copyright duration, Congress, from the start, has routinely applied new definitions or adjustments of the copyright term to both future works and existing works not yet in the public domain. Such consistent congressional practice is entitled to "very great weight, and when it is remembered that the rights thus established have not been disputed during a period of [over two] centur[ies], it is almost conclusive." *Burrow-Giles Lithographic Co. v. Sarony*, 111 U.S., at 57, 4 S.Ct. 279. Indeed, "[t]his Court has repeatedly laid down the principle that a contemporaneous legislative exposition of the Constitution when the founders of our Government and framers of our Constitution were actively participating in public affairs, acquiesced in for a long term of years, fixes the construction to be given [the Constitution's] provisions." *Myers v. United States*, 272 U.S. 52, 175 (1926). Congress' unbroken practice since the founding generation thus overwhelms petitioners' argument that the CTEA's extension of existing copyrights fails *per se* to "promote the Progress of Science."

Closely related to petitioners' preambular argument, or a variant of it, is their assertion that the Copyright Clause "imbeds a quid pro quo." Brief for Petitioners 23. They contend, in this regard, that Congress may grant to an "Autho[r]" an "exclusive Right" for a "limited Tim[e]," but only in exchange for a "Writin[g]." Congress' power to confer copyright protection, petitioners argue, is thus contingent upon an exchange: The author of an original work receives an "exclusive Right" for a "limited Tim[e]" in exchange for a dedication to the public thereafter. Extending an existing copyright without demanding additional consideration, petitioners maintain, bestows an unpaid-for benefit on copyright holders and their heirs, in violation of the *quid pro quo* requirement.

We can demur to petitioners' description of the Copyright Clause as a grant of legislative authority empowering Congress "to secure a bargain—this for that." But the legislative evolution earlier recalled demonstrates what the bargain entails. Given the consistent placement of existing copyright holders in parity with future holders, the author of a work created in the last 170 years would reasonably comprehend, as the "this" offered her, a copyright not only for the time in place when protection is gained, but also for any renewal or extension legislated during that time. Congress could rationally seek to "promote . . . Progress" by including in every copyright statute an express guarantee that authors would receive the benefit of any later legislative extension of the copyright term. Nothing in the Copyright Clause bars Congress from creating the same incentive by adopting the same position as a matter of unbroken practice.

* * *

We note, furthermore, that patents and copyrights do not entail the same exchange, and that our references to a *quid pro quo* typically appear in the patent context. This is understandable, given that immediate disclosure is not the objective of, but is *exacted from*, the patentee. It is the price paid for the exclusivity secured. For the author seeking copyright protection, in contrast, disclosure is the desired objective, not something exacted from the author in exchange for the copyright. Indeed, since the 1976 Act, copyright has run from creation, not publication.

Further distinguishing the two kinds of intellectual property, copyright gives the holder no monopoly on any knowledge. A reader of an author's writing may make full use of any fact or idea she acquires from her reading. See § 102(b). The grant of a patent, on the other hand, does prevent full use by others of the inventor's knowledge * * *.

* * *

For the several reasons stated, we find no Copyright Clause impediment to the CTEA's extension of existing copyrights.

* * *

As we read the Framers' instruction, the Copyright Clause empowers Congress to determine the intellectual property regimes that, overall, in that body's judgment, will serve the ends of the Clause. Beneath the facade of their inventive constitutional interpretation, petitioners forcefully urge that Congress pursued very bad policy in prescribing the CTEA's long terms. The wisdom of Congress' action, however, is not within our province to second-guess. Satisfied that the legislation before us remains inside the domain the Constitution assigns to the First Branch, we affirm the judgment of the Court of Appeals.

It is so ordered.

■ JUSTICE STEVENS, dissenting.

Writing for a unanimous Court in 1964, Justice Black stated that it is obvious that a State could not "extend the life of a patent beyond its expiration date," *Sears, Roebuck & Co. v. Stiffel Co.*, 376 U.S. 225, 231 (1964). As I shall explain, the reasons why a State may not extend the life of a patent apply to Congress as well. If Congress may not expand the scope of a patent monopoly, it also may not extend the life of a copyright beyond its expiration date. Accordingly, insofar as the 1998 Sonny Bono Copyright Term Extension Act, 112 Stat. 2827, purported to extend the life of unexpired copyrights, it is invalid. Because the majority's contrary conclusion rests on the mistaken premise that this Court has virtually no role in reviewing congressional grants of monopoly privileges to authors, inventors, and their successors, I respectfully dissent.

The authority to issue copyrights stems from the same Clause in the Constitution that created the patent power. It provides:

> "Congress shall have Power . . . To promote the Progress of Science and useful Arts, by securing for limited Times to Authors and Inventors the exclusive Right to their respective Writings and Discoveries." Art. I, § 8, cl. 8.

It is well settled that the Clause is "both a grant of power and a limitation" and that Congress "may not overreach the restraints imposed by the stated constitutional purpose." *Graham v. John Deere Co. of Kansas City,* 383 U.S. 1, 5–6 (1966). As we have made clear in the patent context, that purpose has two dimensions. Most obviously the grant of exclusive rights to their respective writings and discoveries is intended to encourage the creativity of "Authors and Inventors." But the requirement that those exclusive grants be for "limited Times" serves the ultimate purpose of promoting the "Progress of Science and useful Arts" by guaranteeing that those innovations will enter the public domain as soon as the period of exclusivity expires:

* * * It is that ultimate purpose that explains why a patent may not issue unless it discloses the invention in such detail that one skilled in the art may copy it. Complete disclosure as a precondition to the issuance of a patent is part of the *quid pro quo* that justifies the limited monopoly for the inventor as consideration for full and immediate access by the public when the limited time expires.

* * *

The issuance of a patent is appropriately regarded as a *quid pro quo*—the grant of a limited right for the inventor's disclosure and subsequent contribution to the public domain. It would be manifestly unfair if, after issuing a patent, the Government as a representative of the public sought to modify the bargain by shortening the term of the patent in order to accelerate public access to the invention. The fairness considerations that underlie the constitutional protections against *ex post facto* laws and laws impairing the obligation of contracts would presumably disable Congress from making such a retroactive change in the public's bargain with an inventor without providing compensation for the taking. Those same considerations should protect members of the public who make plans to exploit an invention as soon as it enters the public domain from a retroactive modification of the bargain that extends the term of the patent monopoly * * *.

Neither the purpose of encouraging new inventions nor the overriding interest in advancing progress by adding knowledge to the public domain is served by retroactively increasing the inventor's compensation for a completed invention and frustrating the legitimate expectations of members of the public who want to make use of it in a free market. Because those twin purposes provide the only avenue for congressional action under the Copyright/Patent Clause of the Constitution, any other action is manifestly unconstitutional.

We have recognized that these twin purposes of encouraging new works and adding to the public domain apply to copyrights as well as patents. Thus, with regard to copyrights on motion pictures, we have clearly identified the overriding interest in the "release to the public of the products of [the author's] creative genius." *United States v. Paramount Pictures, Inc.,* 334 U.S. 131 (1948). And, as with patents, we have emphasized that the overriding purpose of providing a reward for authors' creative activity is to motivate that activity and "to allow the public access to the products of their genius after the limited period of exclusive control has expired." *Sony Corp. of America v. Universal City Studios, Inc.*, 464 U.S. 417, 429 (1984). *Ex post facto* extensions of copyrights result in a gratuitous transfer of wealth from the public to authors, publishers, and their successors in interest. Such retroactive extensions do not even arguably serve either of the purposes of the Copyright/Patent Clause. The reasons why such extensions of the patent monopoly are unconstitutional apply to copyrights as well.

* * *

The history of retroactive extensions of existing and expired copyrights and patents, though relevant, is not conclusive of the constitutionality of the Sonny Bono Act. The fact that the Court has not previously passed upon the constitutionality of retroactive copyright extensions does not insulate the present extension from constitutional challenge.

Respondent also argues that the Act promotes the useful arts by providing incentives to restore old movies. For at least three reasons, the interest in preserving perishable copies of old copyrighted films does not justify a wholesale extension of existing copyrights. First, such restoration and preservation will not even arguably promote any new works by authors or inventors. And, of course, any original expression in the restoration and preservation of movies will receive new copyright protection. Second, however strong the justification for preserving such works may be, that justification applies equally to works whose copyrights have already expired. Yet no one seriously contends that the Copyright/Patent Clause would authorize the grant of monopoly privileges for works already in the public domain solely to encourage their restoration. Finally, even if this concern with aging movies would permit congressional protection, the remedy offered—a blanket extension of all copyrights—simply bears no relationship to the alleged harm.

* * *

The express grant of a perpetual copyright would unquestionably violate the textual requirement that the authors' exclusive rights be only "for limited Times." Whether the extraordinary length of the grants authorized by the 1998 Act are invalid because they are the functional equivalent of perpetual copyrights is a question that need not be answered in this case because the question presented by the certiorari petition merely challenges Congress' power to extend retroactively the terms of existing copyrights. Accordingly, there is no need to determine whether the deference that is normally given to congressional policy judgments may save from judicial review its decision respecting the appropriate length of the term. It is important to note, however, that a categorical rule prohibiting retroactive extensions would effectively preclude perpetual copyrights. More importantly * * *, unless the Clause is construed to embody such a categorical rule, Congress may extend existing monopoly privileges *ad infinitum* under the majority's analysis.

By failing to protect the public interest in free access to the products of inventive and artistic genius—indeed, by virtually ignoring the central purpose of the Copyright/Patent Clause—the Court has quitclaimed to Congress its principal responsibility in this area of the law. Fairly read, the Court has stated that Congress' actions under the Copyright/Patent Clause are, for all intents and purposes, judicially unreviewable * * *.

I respectfully dissent.

■ JUSTICE BREYER, dissenting.

The Constitution's Copyright Clause grants Congress the power to "*promote* the Progress of Science . . . by securing for *limited* Times to *Authors* . . . the exclusive Right to their respective Writings." Art. I, § 8, cl. 8 (emphasis added). The statute before us, the 1998 Sonny Bono Copyright Term Extension Act, extends the term of most existing copyrights to 95 years and that of many new copyrights to 70 years after the author's death. The economic effect of this 20-year extension—the longest blanket extension since the Nation's founding—is to make the copyright term not limited, but virtually perpetual. Its primary legal effect is to grant the extended term not to authors, but to their heirs, estates, or corporate successors. And most importantly, its practical effect is not to promote, but to inhibit, the progress of "Science"—by which word the Framers meant learning or knowledge, E. Walterscheid, The Nature of the Intellectual Property Clause: A Study in Historical Perspective 125–126 (2002).

The majority believes these conclusions rest upon practical judgments that at most suggest the statute is unwise, not that it is unconstitutional. Legal distinctions, however, are often matters of degree. And in this case the failings of degree are so serious that they amount to failings of constitutional kind. Although the Copyright Clause grants broad legislative power to Congress, that grant has limits. And in my view this statute falls outside them.

The "monopoly privileges" that the Copyright Clause confers "are neither unlimited nor primarily designed to provide a special private benefit." * * *

The Copyright Clause and the First Amendment seek related objectives—the creation and dissemination of information. When working in tandem, these provisions mutually reinforce each other, the first serving as an "engine of free expression," the second assuring that government throws up no obstacle to its dissemination. At the same time, a particular statute that exceeds proper Copyright Clause bounds may set Clause and Amendment at cross-purposes, thereby depriving the public of the speech-related benefits that the Founders, through both, have promised.

Consequently, I would review plausible claims that a copyright statute seriously, and unjustifiably, restricts the dissemination of speech somewhat more carefully than reference to this Court's traditional Copyright Clause jurisprudence might suggest * * *.

Thus, I would find that the statute lacks the constitutionally necessary rational support (1) if the significant benefits that it bestows are private, not public; (2) if it threatens seriously to undermine the expressive values that the Copyright Clause embodies; and (3) if it cannot find justification in any significant Clause-related objective. Where, after examination of the statute, it becomes difficult, if not impossible, even to dispute these characterizations, Congress' "choice is clearly wrong."

Because we must examine the relevant statutory effects in light of the Copyright Clause's own purposes, we should begin by reviewing the basic objectives of that Clause. The Clause authorizes a "tax on readers for the purpose of giving a bounty to writers." 56 Parl. Deb. (3d Ser.) (1841) 341, 350 (Lord Macaulay). Why? What constitutional purposes does the "bounty" serve?

The Constitution itself describes the basic Clause objective as one of "promot[ing] the Progress of Science," *i.e.*, knowledge and learning. The Clause exists not to "provide a special private benefit," *Sony, supra*, at 429, but "to stimulate artistic creativity for the general public good," *Twentieth Century Music Corp. v. Aiken*, 422 U.S. 151, 156 (1975). It does so by "motivat[ing] the creative activity of authors" through "the provision of a special reward." *Sony, supra*, at 429. The "reward" is a means, not an end. And that is why the copyright term is limited. It is limited so that its beneficiaries—the public—"will not be permanently deprived of the fruits of an artist's labors." *Stewart v. Abend*, 495 U.S. 207, 228 (1990).

* * *

Madison, like Jefferson and others in the founding generation, warned against the dangers of monopolies * * *.

* * *

For present purposes, then, we should take the following as well established: that copyright statutes must serve public, not private, ends; that they must seek "to promote the Progress" of knowledge and learning; and that they must do so both by creating incentives for authors to produce and by removing the related restrictions on dissemination after expiration of a copyright's "limited Tim[e]"—a time that (like "a *limited* monarch") is "restrain[ed]" and "circumscribe[d]," "not [left] at large," 2 S. Johnson, A Dictionary of the English Language 1151 (4th rev. ed. 1773). I would examine the statute's effects in light of these well-established constitutional purposes.

This statute, like virtually every copyright statute, imposes upon the public certain expression-related costs in the form of (1) royalties that may be higher than necessary to evoke creation of the relevant work, and (2) a requirement that one seeking to reproduce a copyrighted work must obtain the copyright holder's permission. The first of these costs translates into higher prices that will potentially restrict a work's dissemination. The second means search costs that themselves may prevent reproduction even where the author has no objection. Although these costs are, in a sense, inevitable concomitants of copyright protection, there are special reasons for thinking them especially serious here.

First, the present statute primarily benefits the holders of existing copyrights, i.e., copyrights on works already created * * *. [O]ne might conservatively estimate that 20 extra years of copyright protection will mean the transfer of several billion extra royalty dollars to holders of existing copyrights—copyrights that, together, already will have earned many billions of dollars in royalty "reward."

* * *

A second, equally important, cause for concern arises out of the fact that copyright extension imposes a "permissions" requirement—not only upon potential users of "classic" works that still retain commercial value, but also upon potential users of *any other work* still in copyright * * *.

The potential users of such works include not only movie buffs and aging jazz fans, but also historians, scholars, teachers, writers, artists, database operators, and researchers of all kinds—those who want to make the past accessible for their own use or for that of others. The permissions requirement can inhibit their ability to accomplish that task. Indeed, in an age where computer-accessible databases promise to facilitate research and learning, the permissions requirement can stand as a significant obstacle to realization of that technological hope.

The reason is that the permissions requirement can inhibit or prevent the use of old works (particularly those without commercial value): (1) because it may prove expensive to track down or to contract with the copyright holder, (2) because the holder may prove impossible to find, or (3) because the holder when found may deny permission either outright or through misinformed efforts to bargain * * *

* * *

What copyright-related benefits might justify the statute's extension of copyright protection? First, no one could reasonably conclude that copyright's traditional economic rationale applies here. The extension will not act as an economic spur encouraging authors to create new works. No potential author can reasonably believe that he has more than a tiny chance of writing a classic that will survive commercially long enough for the copyright extension to matter. After all, if, after 55 to 75 years, only 2% of all copyrights retain commercial value, the percentage surviving after 75 years or more (a typical pre-extension copyright term)—must be far smaller. And any remaining monetary incentive is diminished dramatically by the fact that the relevant royalties will not arrive until 75 years or more into the future, when, not the author, but distant heirs, or shareholders in a successor corporation, will receive them * * *. [I]t seems fair to say that, for example, a 1% likelihood of earning $100 annually for 20 years, starting 75 years into the future, is worth less than seven cents today.

What potential Shakespeare, Wharton, or Hemingway would be moved by such a sum? What monetarily motivated Melville would not realize that he could do better for his grandchildren by putting a few dollars into an interest-bearing bank account? * * *

* * *

This statute will cause serious expression-related harm. It will likely restrict traditional dissemination of copyrighted works. It will likely inhibit new forms of dissemination through the use of new technology. It threatens to interfere with efforts to preserve our Nation's historical and cultural heritage and efforts to use that heritage, say, to educate our Nation's children. It is easy to understand how the statute might benefit the private financial interests of corporations or heirs who own existing copyrights. But I cannot find any constitutionally legitimate, copyright-related way in which the statute will benefit the public. Indeed, in respect to existing works, the serious public harm and the virtually nonexistent public benefit could not be more clear.

I have set forth the analysis upon which I rest these judgments. This analysis leads inexorably to the conclusion that the statute cannot be understood rationally to advance a constitutionally legitimate interest. The statute falls outside the scope of legislative power that the Copyright Clause, read in light of the First Amendment, grants to Congress. I would hold the statute unconstitutional.

I respectfully dissent.

NOTES AND QUESTIONS

1. If Congress creates a 400-year period for copyright and a 100-year period for patents, are those periods for "limited Times"? Does the Intellectual Property Clause contain an implicit limit on the length of monopoly terms? Does that limit depend on the sorts of practical and economic considerations emphasized by Justice Breyer? Or is the proper time limit, as Justice Stevens suggests the Court has held in *Eldred*, essentially a political question?

2. What is the legal significance of the preamble to the Intellectual Property Clause, which indicates the purposes for which monopoly grants are made? Does it mean that copyrights and patents must, as a constitutional matter, affirmatively promote scientific or artistic progress? *Eldred* left that question open; for a suggestion that the answer is "yes," see Dotan Oliar, *Making Sense of the Intellectual Property Clause: Promotion of Progress as a Limitation on Congress's Intellectual Property Power,* 94 GEO. L.J. 1771 (2006). If so, does that place substantive limits on the kind of matters for which Congress can authorize monopolies? The patent statutes contain a wide range of constraints on patentability. Are those constraints constitutionally required?

3. The Court has specifically held that some element of originality is constitutionally required for copyright. *See Feist Publications, Inc. v. Rural Telephone Service Co.*, 499 U.S. 340 (1991) (alphabetizing names and phone numbers in telephone white pages is not copyrightable):

> This case concerns the interaction of two well-established propositions. The first is that facts are not copyrightable; the other, that compilations of facts generally are. Each of these propositions possesses an impeccable pedigree * * *.
>
> There is an undeniable tension between these two propositions. Many compilations consist of nothing but raw data—*i.e.,* wholly factual information not accompanied by any original written expression. On what basis may one claim a copyright in such a work? Common sense tells us that 100 uncopyrightable facts do not magically change their status when gathered together in one place. Yet copyright law seems to contemplate that compilations that consist exclusively of facts are potentially within its scope.
>
> The key to resolving the tension lies in understanding why facts are not copyrightable. The *sine qua non* of copyright is originality. To qualify for copyright protection, a work must be original to the author. Original, as the term is used in copyright, means only that the work was independently created by the author (as opposed to copied from other works), and that it possesses at least some minimal degree of creativity. To be sure, the requisite level of creativity is extremely low; even a slight amount will suffice. The vast majority of works make the grade quite easily, as they possess some creative spark, "no matter how crude, humble or obvious" it might be. Originality does not signify novelty; a work may be original even though it closely resembles other works so long as the similarity is fortuitous, not the result of copying. To illustrate, assume that two poets, each ignorant of the other, compose identical poems. Neither work is novel, yet both are original and, hence, copyrightable.
>
> Originality is a constitutional requirement * * *. In two decisions from the late 19th century—*The Trade-Mark Cases*, 100 U.S. 82 (1879); and *Burrow-Giles Lithographic Co. v. Sarony*, 111 U.S. 53 (1884)—this Court defined the crucial terms "authors" and "writings." In so doing, the Court made it unmistakably clear that these terms presuppose a degree of originality.

In *The Trade-Mark Cases*, the Court addressed the constitutional scope of "writings." For a particular work to be classified "under the head of writings of authors," the Court determined, "originality is required." The Court explained that originality requires independent creation plus a modicum of creativity * * *.

In *Burrow-Giles*, the Court distilled the same requirement from the Constitution's use of the word "authors." The Court defined "author," in a constitutional sense, to mean "he to whom anything owes its origin; originator; maker." As in *The Trade-Mark Cases*, the Court emphasized the creative component of originality * * *.

The originality requirement articulated in *The Trade-Mark Cases* and *Burrow-Giles* remains the touchstone of copyright protection today * * *.

It is this bedrock principle of copyright that mandates the law's seemingly disparate treatment of facts and factual compilations. "No one may claim originality as to facts." This is because facts do not owe their origin to an act of authorship. The distinction is one between creation and discovery: The first person to find and report a particular fact has not created the fact; he or she has merely discovered its existence * * *.

Factual compilations, on the other hand, may possess the requisite originality. The compilation author typically chooses which facts to include, in what order to place them, and how to arrange the collected data so that they may be used effectively by readers. These choices as to selection and arrangement, so long as they are made independently by the compiler and entail a minimal degree of creativity, are sufficiently original that Congress may protect such compilations through the copyright laws. Thus, even a directory that contains absolutely no protectible written expression, only facts, meets the constitutional minimum for copyright protection if it features an original selection or arrangement.

* * * Others may copy the underlying facts from the publication, but not the precise words used to present them * * *.

This inevitably means that the copyright in a factual compilation is thin. Notwithstanding a valid copyright, a subsequent compiler remains free to use the facts contained in another's publication to aid in preparing a competing work, so long as the competing work does not feature the same selection and arrangement * * *.

499 U.S. at 344–49. If this much can be derived from the language of the copyright portion of the clause, what might be derivable from the patent portion of the clause?

4. The Court in *Eldred* noted that "there is no cause to suspect that a purpose to evade the 'limited Times' prescription prompted Congress to adopt the CTEA." What kind of evidence would give rise to suspicion of such a purpose? Would such a purpose be enough to invalidate a law even if the time period in question was "limited"? Is it easier for the Court to enforce a suspicion-of-purpose test than it would be for the Court to enforce a too-long-a-time-period test?

5. Intellectual property protection is not an exclusively federal function. States are allowed to have intellectual property laws, provided that they are not preempted by national laws. Under general preemption doctrine, State laws can be preempted if they conflict with the purposes of the federal scheme even if they are not literally inconsistent

with the federal scheme. *See, e.g., Bonito Boats, Inc. v. Thunder Craft Boats, Inc.*, 489 U.S. 141 (1989).

[Assignment 39]

XIII. THE NECESSARY AND PROPER CLAUSE: APPLICATIONS

We have seen throughout this book that the Necessary and Proper Clause is a vital part of the constitutional structure for federalism (and separation of powers as well). Most of the major federalism cases in this chapter either explicitly or implicitly involve constructions of the Necessary and Proper Clause. Almost two and a half centuries after ratification of the Constitution, the clause remains one of the most hotly contested, and strangely underappreciated and under-analyzed, features of the document.

First is the question whether the Necessary and Proper Clause is a standard (if relatively restrictive) eighteenth-century "incidental powers" clause, of the sort that would be commonplace in agency instruments of the time, or is instead a mechanism for incorporating the Virginia and Bedford Resolutions and thus creating a federal government capable of solving all problems of national scope. The stakes are obviously enormous. If the first view is correct, the Necessary and Proper Clause authorizes only the enactment of "incidental" laws, foreclosing its use in support of laws involving, in the language of *McCulloch v. Maryland*, any "great substantive and independent power." If the second view is correct, constitutional inquiry should focus much less on the language of the Constitution and much more on general theories of government, such as the Economics of Federalism. The former view is surely more correct as a matter of original meaning. *See* GARY LAWSON, "A GREAT POWER OF ATTORNEY": UNDERSTANDING THE FIDUCIARY CONSTITUTION 78–103 (2017); GARY LAWSON, GEOFFREY P. MILLER, ROBERT G. NATELSON & GUY SEIDMAN, THE ORIGINS OF THE NECESSARY AND PROPER CLAUSE (2010); Robert G. Natelson, *The Agency Law Origins of the Necessary and Proper Clause,* 55 CASE WESTERN RES. L. REV. 243 (2004). The latter view is surely more correct as a description of the course of American case law and constitutional practice. *See* pretty much everything else in the book so far. As the law moves forward, how do you think the Court should balance original meaning with precedent and practice?

Once one is past that rather large question concerning the role and function of the Necessary and Proper Clause, three textual questions remain: What does it mean for a law to be "necessary," what does it mean for a law to be "proper," and what does it mean for a law to be "for carrying into Execution" other federal powers? We have already discussed at some length what it means for a law to be "necessary." *See supra* pages 619–620. Doctrine since *McCulloch* treats the word as requiring nothing more than "means-end rationality," *Sabri v. United States,* 541 U.S. 600, 605 (2004), and, as a result, *no* federal statute has ever been found unconstitutional by the Supreme Court because it was not "necessary" for executing federal powers. We will soon say something about what it means for a law to be "for carrying into Execution" other powers, *see infra* page 841, though we can reveal that no law has yet been found unconstitutional on those grounds either. That leaves the requirement that laws for implementing federal powers be "proper." What might that mean?

One possibility is that it means nothing at all. Daniel Webster argued as much in *McCulloch* on behalf of the Bank: "These words, 'necessary and proper,' in such an instrument, are probably to be considered as synonimous." 17 U.S. (4 Wheat.) at 324 (argument of Mr. Webster). One of has argued (he would like to say "conclusively demonstrated," but that seems tacky) that this is both textually and intratextually implausible. *See* Gary Lawson, *Discretion as Delegation: The "Proper" Understanding of the Nondelegation Doctrine,* 73 GEO. WASH. L. REV. 235, 249–55 (2005).

A second possibility is that "proper" means something different from "necessary," but that the former is entirely subsumed within the latter. While *McCulloch* did not directly address the meaning of "proper," Chief Justice Marshall suggested in passing that "proper" was a relatively generous term, "present[ing] to the mind the idea of some choice of means of legislation, not strained and compressed within the narrow limits for which gentlemen contend." *Id.* at 419. This is linguistically possible but also seems hard to square with the Constitution's general usage of conjoined adjectives.

A third possibility is that "necessary and proper" does not mean "necessary" and "proper," in the conjunctive, but that "necessary and proper" is itself a unitary phrase with a single meaning (the grammatical name for this literary device is "hendiadys"). *See* Samuel L. Bray, *"Necessary and Proper" and "Cruel and Unusual": Hendiadys in the Constitution,* 102 VA. L. REV. 687 (2016). This theory also runs into some intratextual difficulties—the Constitution uses conjunctive adjectives too frequently to assume that the use of them in the Necessary and Proper Clause is casual—and it poses rather than answers the problem of defining the clause's unitary meaning, if there is one.

A fourth possibility is that "proper" is a term distinct from "necessary" with a distinct meaning. If "necessary" describes a causal relationship between means and ends, what might "proper" describe? Perhaps it means "suited to the kind of entity that is doing the acting"; a "proper" law, on this understanding, "is one that is within the peculiar jurisdiction or responsibility of the relevant governmental actor." Gary Lawson & Patricia B. Granger, *The "Proper" Scope of Federal Power: A Jurisdictional Interpretation of the Sweeping Clause,* 43 DUKE L.J. 267 (1993).

A fifth possibility combines the previous two: Perhaps "necessary and proper" is a unitary phrase, but the meaning of the unitary phrase includes not just the causal means-ends relationship suggested by "necessary" alone but also something like a "jurisdictional" requirement limiting "necessary and proper" laws to those that are structurally appropriate in the overall context of the Constitution. This possibility is especially attractive if one regards the Constitution as part of the family of eighteenth-century agency, or fiduciary, legal instruments, in which case the "Necessary and Proper Clause" would rather obviously be the kind of "incidental powers" clause commonplace in those kinds of instruments. *See* LAWSON, MILLER, NATELSON & SEIDMAN, *supra*.

For more than two centuries, case law implicitly assumed without deciding that one of the first two possibilities was correct. No Supreme Court decision prior to 1997 explicitly relied on the word "proper" to do any relevant legal work, either as a term distinct from "necessary" or as part of a hendiadys whose meaning extended beyond what "necessary" would mean on its own. This is true even in cases where that would seem to have been the most natural grounding for the rulings.

Several cases are instructive. For example, the Constitution says that "[n]ew States may be admitted by the Congress into this Union." U.S. Const. art. IV, § 3, cl. 1. When Congress admitted Oklahoma as a State in 1906, the admitting statute provided that "[t]he capital of said State shall temporarily be at the city of Guthrie * * * and shall not be changed therefrom previous to anno Domini nineteen hundred and thirteen." Act of June 16, 1906, ch. 3335, 34 Stat. 267, 269. In *Coyle v. Smith*, 221 U.S. 559 (1911), the Supreme Court (with two Justices dissenting without opinion) held that Congress lacked the enumerated power to tell the State of Oklahoma—which wanted to move its capital to Oklahoma City—where its capital city had to be located. The Court said this statute violated a fundamental constitutional principle that all States entered the Union on an equal footing with the pre-existing States. Since Congress could not tell any of those States where their capital city had to be, the Equal Footing Doctrine provided that Congress could not do so as to the newly admitted State of Oklahoma. The Court never specifically identified the textual grounding for its decision, but a fairly natural rationale would have been that a law prescribing a State's capital upon admission is not "necessary and proper" for executing the Admissions Clause. The Necessary and Proper Clause, however, was not mentioned in the decision.

Eight decades later, the Supreme Court again held that certain implicit principles of federalism limited Congress's power, but again did so without precisely locating those principles in the Necessary and Proper Clause. No State wants to be a dumping ground for radioactive waste from other States. But there must be disposal sites *somewhere*. After some unsuccessful efforts to get States to agree on disposal regimes through interstate compacts, Congress in 1985 prescribed:

> If a State (or, where applicable, a compact region) in which low level radioactive waste is generated is unable to provide for the disposal of all such waste generated within such State or compact region by January 1, 1996, each State in which such waste is generated, upon the request of the generator or owner of the waste, shall take title to the waste, be obligated to take possession of the waste, and shall be liable for all damages directly or indirectly incurred by such generator or owner as a consequence of the failure of the State to take possession * * *.

Low-Level Radioactive Waste Policy Amendments Act of 1985, § 5(d)(2)(C), 99 Stat. 1842. In other words, Congress told States that they either needed to come up with some legislative solution to the waste disposal problem or assume ownership of and responsibility for the waste within their borders. In *New York v. United States,* 505 U.S. 144 (1992), the Court, by a 6–3 vote, held that Congress could not "commandeer" State legislatures in this fashion, though it relied upon the Tenth Amendment rather than the Necessary and Proper Clause (which made only a passing appearance in the Court's decision):

> Congress exercises its conferred powers subject to the limitations contained in the Constitution. Thus, for example, under the Commerce Clause Congress may regulate publishers engaged in interstate commerce, but Congress is constrained in the exercise of that power by the First Amendment. The Tenth Amendment likewise restrains the power of Congress, but this limit is not derived from the text of the Tenth Amendment itself, which, as we have discussed, is essentially a tautology. Instead, the Tenth Amendment confirms that the power of the Federal

Government is subject to limits that may, in a given instance, reserve power to the States. The Tenth Amendment thus directs us to determine, as in this case, whether an incident of state sovereignty is protected by a limitation on an Article I power.

* * *.

Most of our recent cases interpreting the Tenth Amendment have concerned the authority of Congress to subject state governments to generally applicable laws. The Court's jurisprudence in this area has traveled an unsteady path. This case presents no occasion to apply or revisit the holdings of any of these cases, as this is not a case in which Congress has subjected a State to the same legislation applicable to private parties.

This litigation instead concerns the circumstances under which Congress may use the States as implements of regulation; that is, whether Congress may direct or otherwise motivate the States to regulate in a particular field or a particular way. Our cases have established a few principles that guide our resolution of the issue.

As an initial matter, Congress may not simply "commandee[r] the legislative processes of the States by directly compelling them to enact and enforce a federal regulatory program." *Hodel* v. *Virginia Surface Mining & Reclamation Assn., Inc.*, 452 U.S. 264, 288 (1981) * * *.

* * *

* * * While Congress has substantial powers to govern the Nation directly, including in areas of intimate concern to the States, the Constitution has never been understood to confer upon Congress the ability to require the States to govern according to Congress' instructions. See *Coyle* v. *Oklahoma*, 221 U.S. 559, 565 (1911) * * *.

* * *

This is not to say that Congress lacks the ability to encourage a State to regulate in a particular way, or that Congress may not hold out incentives to the States as a method of influencing a State's policy choices. Our cases have identified a variety of methods, short of outright coercion, by which Congress may urge a State to adopt a legislative program consistent with federal interests. Two of these methods are of particular relevance here.

First, under Congress' spending power, "Congress may attach conditions on the receipt of federal funds." *South Dakota* v. *Dole*, 483 U. S., at 206 * * *.

Second, where Congress has the authority to regulate private activity under the Commerce Clause, we have recognized Congress' power to offer States the choice of regulating that activity according to federal standards or having state law pre-empted by federal regulation. *Hodel* v. *Virginia Surface Mining & Reclamation Assn., Inc.*, *supra*, at 288 * * *.

By either of these two methods, as by any other permissible method of encouraging a State to conform to federal policy choices, the residents of the State retain the ultimate decision as to whether or not the State will comply. If a State's citizens view federal policy as sufficiently contrary to local interests, they may elect to decline a federal grant. If state residents would prefer their government to devote its attention and resources to problems other than those deemed important by Congress, they may choose to have the Federal Government rather than the State bear the expense of a federally mandated regulatory program, and they may continue to supplement that program to the extent state law is not pre-empted. Where Congress encourages state regulation rather than compelling it, state governments remain responsive to the local electorate's preferences; state officials remain accountable to the people.

By contrast, where the Federal Government compels States to regulate, the accountability of both state and federal officials is diminished. If the citizens of New York, for example, do not consider that making provision for the disposal of radioactive waste is in their best interest, they may elect state officials who share their view. That view can always be pre-empted under the Supremacy Clause if is contrary to the national view, but in such a case it is the Federal Government that makes the decision in full view of the public, and it will be federal officials that suffer the consequences if the decision turns out to be detrimental or unpopular. But where the Federal Government directs the States to regulate, it may be state officials who will bear the brunt of public disapproval, while the federal officials who devised the regulatory program may remain insulated from the electoral ramifications of their decision. Accountability is thus diminished when, due to federal coercion, elected state officials cannot regulate in accordance with the views of the local electorate in matters not pre-empted by federal regulation.

* * *

The take title provision offers state governments a "choice" of either accepting ownership of waste or regulating according to the instructions of Congress. Respondents do not claim that the Constitution would authorize Congress to impose either option as a freestanding requirement. On one hand, the Constitution would not permit Congress simply to transfer radioactive waste from generators to state governments. Such a forced transfer, standing alone, would in principle be no different than a congressionally compelled subsidy from state governments to radioactive waste producers. The same is true of the provision requiring the States to become liable for the generators' damages. Standing alone, this provision would be indistinguishable from an Act of Congress directing the States to assume the liabilities of certain state residents. Either type of federal action would "commandeer" state governments into the service of federal regulatory purposes, and would for this reason be inconsistent with the Constitution's division of authority between federal and state governments. On the other hand, the second alternative held out to state governments—regulating pursuant to Congress' direction—would, standing alone, present a simple command to state governments to implement legislation enacted by Congress. As we have seen, the Constitution does not empower Congress to subject state governments to this type of instruction.

Because an instruction to state governments to take title to waste, standing alone, would be beyond the authority of Congress, and because a

> direct order to regulate, standing alone, would also be beyond the authority of Congress, it follows that Congress lacks the power to offer the States a choice between the two. Unlike the first two sets of incentives, the take title incentive does not represent the conditional exercise of any congressional power enumerated in the Constitution. In this provision, Congress has not held out the threat of exercising its spending power or its commerce power; it has instead held out the threat, should the States not regulate according to one federal instruction, of simply forcing the States to submit to another federal instruction. A choice between two unconstitutionally coercive regulatory techniques is no choice at all. Either way, "the Act commandeers the legislative processes of the States by directly compelling them to enact and enforce a federal regulatory program," *Hodel* v. *Virginia Surface Mining & Reclamation Assn., Inc., supra*, at 288, an outcome that has never been understood to lie within the authority conferred upon Congress by the Constitution.

505 U.S. at 156–57, 160–62, 166–69, 175–76. The dissenting Justices wrote that "the Court's civics lecture has a decidedly hollow ring at a time when action, rather than rhetoric, is needed to solve a national problem." *Id.* at 207 (White, J., concurring in part and dissenting in part).'

Coyle and *New York* thus describe federalism-based limits on Congress's power directly to try to control the activities of state governments but are less than clear about the textual basis for the decisions. Is the following case any clearer?

Printz v. United States

521 U.S. 898 (1997)

■ JUSTICE SCALIA delivered the opinion of the Court.

The question presented in these cases is whether certain interim provisions of the Brady Handgun Violence Prevention Act, Pub. L. 103–159, 107 Stat. 1536, commanding state and local law enforcement officers to conduct background checks on prospective handgun purchasers and to perform certain related tasks, violate the Constitution.

The Gun Control Act of 1968 (GCA), 18 U.S.C. § 921 *et seq.*, establishes a detailed federal scheme governing the distribution of firearms. It prohibits firearms dealers from transferring handguns to any person under 21, not resident in the dealer's State, or prohibited by state or local law from purchasing or possessing firearms. It also forbids possession of a firearm by, and transfer of a firearm to, convicted felons, fugitives from justice, unlawful users of controlled substances, persons adjudicated as mentally defective or committed to mental institutions, aliens unlawfully present in the United States, persons dishonorably discharged from the Armed Forces, persons who have renounced their citizenship, and persons who have been subjected to certain restraining orders or been convicted of a misdemeanor offense involving domestic violence,

In 1993, Congress amended the GCA by enacting the Brady Act. The Act requires the Attorney General to establish a national instant background-check system by November 30, 1998, and immediately puts in place certain interim provisions until that system becomes operative. Under the interim provisions, a firearms dealer who proposes to transfer a handgun must first: (1) receive from the transferee a statement (the Brady Form) containing the name, address and date of birth of the proposed transferee along with a sworn statement that the transferee is not among any of the classes of prohibited purchasers, (2) verify the identity of the transferee by examining an identification document, and (3) provide the "chief law enforcement officer" (CLEO) of the transferee's residence with notice of the contents (and a copy) of the Brady Form. With some exceptions, the dealer must then wait five business days before consummating the sale, unless the CLEO earlier notifies the dealer that he has no reason to believe the transfer would be illegal.

* * * When a CLEO receives the required notice of a proposed transfer from the firearms dealer, the CLEO must "make a reasonable effort to ascertain within 5 business days whether receipt or possession would be in violation of the law, including research in whatever State and local record keeping systems are available and in a national system designated by the Attorney General." The Act does not require the CLEO to take any particular action if he determines that a pending transaction would be unlawful; he may notify the firearms dealer to that effect, but is not required to do so * * *. Under a separate provision of the GCA, any person who "knowingly violates [the section of the GCA amended by the Brady Act] shall be fined under this title, imprisoned for no more than 1 year, or both."

Petitioners Jay Printz and Richard Mack, the CLEOs for Ravalli County, Montana, and Graham County, Arizona, respectively, filed separate actions challenging the constitutionality of the Brady Act's interim provisions. In each case, the District Court held that the provision requiring CLEOs to perform background checks was unconstitutional, but * * * [a] divided panel of the Court of Appeals for the Ninth Circuit reversed, finding none of the Brady Act's interim provisions to be unconstitutional * * *.

From the description set forth above, it is apparent that the Brady Act purports to direct state law enforcement officers to participate, albeit only temporarily, in the administration of a federally enacted regulatory scheme. Regulated firearms dealers are required to forward Brady Forms not to a federal officer or employee, but to the CLEOs, whose obligation to accept those forms is implicit in the duty imposed upon them to make "reasonable efforts" within five days to determine whether the sales reflected in the forms are lawful. While the CLEOs are subjected to no federal requirement that they prevent the sales determined to be unlawful (it is perhaps assumed that their state law duties will require prevention or apprehension), they are empowered to grant, in effect, waivers of the federally prescribed 5-day waiting period for handgun purchases by notifying the gun dealers that they have no reason to believe the transactions would be illegal.

The petitioners here object to being pressed into federal service, and contend that congressional action compelling state officers to execute federal laws is unconstitutional. Because there is no constitutional text speaking to this precise question, the answer to the CLEOs' challenge must be sought in historical understanding and practice, in the structure of the Constitution, and in the jurisprudence of this Court * * *.

Petitioners contend that compelled enlistment of state executive officers for the administration of federal programs is, until very recent years at least, unprecedented. The Government contends, to the contrary, that "the earliest

Congresses enacted statutes that required the participation of state officials in the implementation of federal laws." The Government's contention demands our careful consideration, since early congressional enactments "provid[e] 'contemporaneous and weighty evidence' of the Constitution's meaning," *Bowsher* v. *Synar,* 478 U.S. 714, 723–724 (1986) (quoting *Marsh* v. *Chambers,* 463 U.S. 783, 790 (1983)). Indeed, such "contemporaneous legislative exposition of the Constitution . . ., acquiesced in for a long term of years, fixes the construction to be given its provisions." *Myers* v. *United States,* 272 U.S. 52, 175 (1926) (citing numerous cases). Conversely if, as petitioners contend, earlier Congresses avoided use of this highly attractive power, we would have reason to believe that the power was thought not to exist.

The Government observes that statutes enacted by the first Congresses required state courts to record applications for citizenship, to transmit abstracts of citizenship applications and other naturalization records to the Secretary of State, and to register aliens seeking naturalization and issue certificates of registry. It may well be, however, that these requirements applied only in States that authorized their courts to conduct naturalization proceedings. Other statutes of that era apparently or at least arguably required state courts to perform functions unrelated to naturalization, such as resolving controversies between a captain and the crew of his ship concerning the seaworthiness of the vessel, hearing the claims of slave owners who had apprehended fugitive slaves and issuing certificates authorizing the slave's forced removal to the State from which he had fled, taking proof of the claims of Canadian refugees who had assisted the United States during the Revolutionary War, and ordering the deportation of alien enemies in times of war.

These early laws establish, at most, that the Constitution was originally understood to permit imposition of an obligation on state *judges* to enforce federal prescriptions, insofar as those prescriptions related to matters appropriate for the judicial power. That assumption was perhaps implicit in one of the provisions of the Constitution, and was explicit in another. In accord with the so-called Madisonian Compromise, Article III, § 1, established only a Supreme Court, and made the creation of lower federal courts optional with the Congress—even though it was obvious that the Supreme Court alone could not hear all federal cases throughout the United States. And the Supremacy Clause, Art. VI, cl. 2, announced that "the Laws of the United States . . . shall be the supreme Law of the Land; and the Judges in every State shall be bound thereby." It is understandable why courts should have been viewed distinctively in this regard; unlike legislatures and executives, they applied the law of other sovereigns all the time. The principle underlying so called "transitory" causes of action was that laws which operated elsewhere created obligations in justice that courts of the forum State would enforce. The Constitution itself, in the Full Faith and Credit Clause, Art. IV, § 1, generally required such enforcement with respect to obligations arising in other States.

For these reasons, we do not think the early statutes imposing obligations on state courts imply a power of Congress to impress the state executive into its service. Indeed, it can be argued that the numerousness of these statutes, contrasted with the utter lack of statutes imposing obligations on the States' executive (notwithstanding the attractiveness of that course to Congress), suggests an assumed *absence* of such power. The only early federal law the Government has brought to our attention that imposed duties on state executive officers is the Extradition Act of 1793, which required the "executive authority" of a State to cause the arrest and delivery of a fugitive from justice upon the request of the executive authority of the State from which the fugitive had fled. That was in direct implementation, however, of the Extradition Clause of the Constitution itself, see Art. IV, § 2.

Not only do the enactments of the early Congresses, as far as we are aware, contain no evidence of an assumption that the Federal Government may command the States' executive power in the absence of a particularized constitutional authorization, they contain some indication of precisely the opposite assumption. On September 23, 1789—the day before its proposal of the Bill of Rights, see 1 Annals of Congress 912–913—the First Congress enacted a law aimed at obtaining state assistance of the most rudimentary and necessary sort for the enforcement of the new Government's laws: the holding of federal prisoners in state jails at federal expense. Significantly, the law issued not a command to the States' executive, but a recommendation to their legislatures. Congress "recommended to the legislatures of the several States to pass laws, making it expressly the duty of the keepers of their gaols, to receive and safe keep therein all prisoners committed under the authority of the United States," and offered to pay 50 cents per month for each prisoner. Moreover, when Georgia refused to comply with the request, Congress's only reaction was a law authorizing the marshal in any State that failed to comply with the Recommendation of September 23, 1789, to rent a temporary jail until provision for a permanent one could be made.

In addition to early legislation, the Government also appeals to other sources we have usually regarded as indicative of the original understanding of the Constitution. It points to portions of The Federalist which reply to criticisms that Congress's power to tax will produce two sets of revenue officers—for example, "Brutus's" assertion in his letter to the New York Journal of December 13, 1787, that the Constitution "opens a door to the appointment of a swarm of revenue and excise officers to prey upon the honest and industrious part of the community, eat up their substance, and riot on the spoils of the country," reprinted in 1 Debate on the Constitution 502 (B. Bailyn ed. 1993). "Publius" responded that Congress will probably "make use of the State officers and State regulations, for collecting" federal taxes, The Federalist No. 36, p. 221 (C. Rossiter ed. 1961) (A. Hamilton) (hereinafter The Federalist), and predicted that "the eventual collection [of internal revenue] under the immediate authority of the Union, will generally be made by the officers, and according to the rules, appointed by the several States," *id.*, No. 45, at 292 (J. Madison) * * *. But none of these statements necessarily implies—what is the critical point here—that Congress could impose these responsibilities *without the consent of the States*. They appear to rest on the natural assumption that the States would consent to allowing their officials to assist the Federal Government, an assumption proved correct by the extensive mutual assistance the States and Federal Government voluntarily provided one another in the early days of the Republic, including voluntary *federal implementation of state law*.

* * *

To complete the historical record, we must note that there is not only an absence of executive commandeering statutes in the early Congresses, but there is an absence of them in our later history as well, at least until very recent years. The Government points to the Act of August 3, 1882, which enlisted state officials "to take charge of the local affairs of immigration in the ports within such State, and to provide for the support and relief of such immigrants therein landing as may fall into distress or need of public aid"; to inspect arriving immigrants and exclude any person found to be a "convict, lunatic, idiot," or indigent; and to send convicts back to their country of origin "without compensation." The statute did not, however, *mandate* those duties, but merely empowered the Secretary of the Treasury "to *enter into contracts* with such State . . . officers as *may be designated* for that purpose *by the governor* of any State." (Emphasis added.)

* * *

The Government points to a number of federal statutes enacted within the past few decades that require the participation of state or local officials in implementing federal regulatory schemes. Some of these are connected to federal funding measures, and can perhaps be more accurately described as conditions upon the grant of federal funding than as mandates to the States; others, which require only the provision of information to the Federal Government, do not involve the precise issue before us here, which is the forced participation of the States' executive in the actual administration of a federal program. We of course do not address these or other currently operative enactments that are not before us; it will be time enough to do so if and when their validity is challenged in a proper case. For deciding the issue before us here, they are of little relevance. Even assuming they represent assertion of the very same congressional power challenged here, they are of such recent vintage that they are no more probative than the statute before us of a constitutional tradition that lends meaning to the text. Their persuasive force is far outweighed by almost two centuries of apparent congressional avoidance of the practice. Compare *INS v. Chadha,* 462 U.S. 919 (1983), in which the legislative veto, though enshrined in perhaps hundreds of federal statutes, most of which were enacted in the 1970's and the earliest of which was enacted in 1932, see *id.,* at 967–975 (White, J., dissenting), was nonetheless held unconstitutional.

The constitutional practice we have examined above tends to negate the existence of the congressional power asserted here, but is not conclusive. We turn next to consideration of the structure of the Constitution, to see if we can discern among its "essential postulate[s]" a principle that controls the present cases.

It is incontestible that the Constitution established a system of "dual sovereignty." *Gregory* v. *Ashcroft,* 501 U.S. 452, 457 (1991); *Tafflin* v. *Levitt,* 493 U.S. 455, 458 (1990). Although the States surrendered many of their powers to the new Federal Government, they retained "a residuary and inviolable sovereignty," The Federalist No. 39, at 245 (J. Madison). This is reflected throughout the Constitution's text, including (to mention only a few examples) the prohibition on any involuntary reduction or combination of a State's territory, Art. IV, § 3; the Judicial Power Clause, Art. III, § 2, and the Privileges and Immunities Clause, Art. IV, § 2, which speak of the "Citizens" of the States; the amendment provision, Article V, which requires the votes of three fourths of the States to amend the Constitution; and the Guarantee Clause, Art. IV, § 4, which "presupposes the continued existence of the states and . . . those means and instrumentalities which are the creation of their sovereign and reserved rights," *Helvering* v. *Gerhardt,* 304 U.S. 405, 414–415 (1938). Residual state sovereignty was also implicit, of course, in the Constitution's conferral upon Congress of not all governmental powers, but only discrete, enumerated ones, Art. I, § 8, which implication was rendered express by the Tenth Amendment's assertion that "[t]he powers not delegated to the United States by the Constitution, nor prohibited by it to the States, are reserved to the States respectively, or to the people."

* * * [T]he Framers rejected the concept of a central government that would act upon and through the States, and instead designed a system in which the State and Federal Governments would exercise concurrent authority over the people—who were, in Hamilton's words, "the only proper objects of government," The Federalist No. 15, at 109. We have set forth the historical record in more detail elsewhere, see *New York* v. *United States,* 505 U. S., at 161–166, and need not repeat it here. It suffices to repeat the conclusion: "The Framers explicitly chose a Constitution that confers upon Congress the power to regulate individuals, not States." *Id.,* at 166. The great innovation of this design was that "our citizens would have two political capacities, one state and one federal, each protected from incursion by the other"—"a legal system unprecedented in form and design, establishing two orders of government, each with its own direct relationship, its own privity, its own set of mutual rights and obligations to the people who sustain it and are governed by it." *U.S. Term Limits, Inc.* v. *Thornton,* 514 U.S. 779, 838 (1995) (KENNEDY, J., concurring). The Constitution thus contemplates that a State's government will represent and remain accountable to its own citizens. As Madison expressed it: "[T]he local or municipal authorities form distinct and independent portions of the supremacy, no more subject, within their respective spheres, to the general authority than the general authority is subject to them, within its own sphere." The Federalist No. 39, at 245.

This separation of the two spheres is one of the Constitution's structural protections of liberty * * *. To quote Madison once again:

> "In the compound republic of America, the power surrendered by the people is first divided between two distinct governments, and then the portion allotted to each subdivided among distinct and separate departments. Hence a double security arises to the rights of the people. The different governments will control each other, at the same time that each will be controlled by itself." The Federalist No. 51, at 323.

The power of the Federal Government would be augmented immeasurably if it were able to impress into its service—and at no cost to itself—the police officers of the 50 States.

We have thus far discussed the effect that federal control of state officers would have upon the first element of the "double security" alluded to by Madison: the division of power between State and Federal Governments. It would also have an effect upon the second element: the separation and equilibration of powers between the three branches of the Federal Government itself. The Constitution does not leave to speculation who is to administer the laws enacted by Congress; the President, it says, "shall take Care that the Laws be faithfully executed," Art. II, § 3, personally and through officers whom he appoints (save for such inferior officers as Congress may authorize to be appointed by the "Courts of Law" or by "the Heads of Departments" who are themselves presidential appointees), Art. II, § 2. The Brady Act effectively transfers this responsibility to thousands of CLEOs in the 50 States, who are left to implement the program without meaningful Presidential control (if indeed meaningful Presidential control is possible without the power to appoint and remove). The insistence of the Framers upon unity in the Federal Executive—to insure both vigor and accountability—is well known. See The Federalist No. 70 (A. Hamilton); 2 Documentary History of the Ratification of the Constitution 495 (M. Jensen ed. 1976) (statement of James Wilson); see also Calabresi & Prakash, The President's Power to Execute the Laws, 104 Yale L. J. 541 (1994). That unity would be shattered, and the power of the President would be subject to reduction, if Congress could act as effectively without the President as with him, by simply requiring state officers to execute its laws.

The dissent of course resorts to the last, best hope of those who defend ultra vires congressional action, the Necessary and Proper Clause. It reasons that the power to regulate the sale of handguns under the Commerce Clause, coupled with the power to "make all Laws which shall be necessary and proper for carrying into Execution the foregoing Powers," Art. I, § 8, conclusively establishes the Brady Act's constitutional validity, because the Tenth Amendment imposes no limitations on the exercise of *delegated* powers but merely prohibits the exercise of powers "*not* delegated to the United States." What destroys the dissent's Necessary and Proper Clause argument, however, is not the Tenth Amendment but the Necessary and Proper Clause itself. When a "La[w] . . . for carrying into Execution" the Commerce Clause violates the principle of state sovereignty reflected in the various constitutional provisions we mentioned earlier, it is not a "La[w] . . . *proper* for carrying into Execution the Commerce Clause," and is thus, in the words of The Federalist, "merely [an] ac[t] of usurpation" which "deserve[s] to be treated as such." The Federalist No. 33, at 204 (A. Hamilton). See Lawson & Granger, The "Proper" Scope of Federal Power: A Jurisdictional Interpretation of the Sweeping Clause, 43 Duke L. J. 267, 297–326, 330–333 (1993). We in fact answered the dissent's Necessary and Proper Clause argument in *New York*: "[E]ven where Congress has the authority under the Constitution to pass laws requiring or prohibiting certain acts, it lacks the power directly to compel the States to require or prohibit those acts. . . . [T]he Commerce Clause, for example, authorizes Congress to regulate interstate commerce directly; it does not authorize Congress to regulate state governments' regulation of interstate commerce." 505 U. S., at 166.

* * *

Finally, and most conclusively in the present litigation, we turn to the prior jurisprudence of this Court. Federal commandeering of state governments is such a novel phenomenon that this Court's first experience with it did not occur until the 1970's, when the Environmental Protection Agency promulgated regulations requiring States to prescribe auto emissions testing, monitoring and retrofit programs, and to designate preferential bus and carpool lanes. The Courts of Appeals for the Fourth and Ninth Circuits invalidated the regulations on statutory grounds in order to avoid what they perceived to be grave constitutional issues, see *Maryland* v. *EPA,* 530 F. 2d 215, 226 (CA4 1975); *Brown* v. *EPA,* 521 F. 2d 827, 838–842 (CA9 1975); and the District of Columbia Circuit invalidated the regulations on both constitutional and statutory grounds, see *District of Columbia* v. *Train,* 521 F. 2d 971, 994 (CADC 1975). After we granted certiorari to review the statutory and constitutional validity of the regulations, the Government declined even to defend them, and instead rescinded some and conceded the invalidity of those that remained, leading us to vacate the opinions below and remand for consideration of mootness. *EPA* v. *Brown,* 431 U.S. 99 (1977).

Although we had no occasion to pass upon the subject in *Brown,* later opinions of ours have made clear that the Federal Government may not compel the States to implement, by legislation or executive action, federal regulatory programs. In *Hodel* v. *Virginia Surface Mining & Reclamation Assn., Inc.,* 452 U.S. 264 (1981), and *FERC* v. *Mississippi,* 456 U.S. 742 (1982), we sustained statutes against constitutional challenge only after assuring ourselves that they did not require the States to enforce federal law * * *. We warned that "this Court never has sanctioned explicitly a federal command to the States to promulgate and enforce laws and regulations.".

When we were at last confronted squarely with a federal statute that unambiguously required the States to enact or administer a federal regulatory program, our decision should have come as no surprise. At issue in *New York* v. *United States,* 505 U.S. 144 (1992), were the so called "take title" provisions of the Low-Level Radioactive Waste Policy Amendments Act of 1985, which required States either to enact legislation providing for the disposal of radioactive waste generated within their borders, or to take title to, and possession of the waste—effectively requiring the States either to legislate pursuant to Congress's directions, or to implement an administrative solution. We concluded that Congress could constitutionally require the States to do neither. "The Federal Government," we held, "may not compel the States to enact or administer a federal regulatory program." *Id.,* at 188.

The Government contends that *New York* is distinguishable on the following ground: Unlike the "take title" provisions invalidated there, the background-check provision of the Brady Act does not require state legislative or executive officials to make policy, but instead issues a final directive to state CLEOs. It is permissible, the Government asserts, for Congress to command state or local officials to assist in the implementation of federal law so long as "Congress itself devises a clear legislative solution that regulates private conduct" and requires state or local officers to provide only "limited, non-policymaking help in enforcing that law." "[T]he constitutional line is crossed only when Congress compels the States to make law in their sovereign capacities."

The Government's distinction between "making" law and merely "enforcing" it, between "policymaking" and mere "implementation," is an interesting one * * * Executive action that has utterly no policymaking component is rare, particularly at an executive level as high as a jurisdiction's chief law enforcement officer. Is it really true that there is no policymaking involved in deciding, for example, what "reasonable efforts" shall be expended to conduct a background check? It may well satisfy the Act for a CLEO to direct that (a) no background checks will be conducted that divert personnel time from pending felony investigations, and (b) no background check will be permitted to consume more than one half hour of an officer's time. But nothing in the Act *requires* a CLEO to be so parsimonious; diverting at least *some* felony-investigation time, and permitting at least *some* background checks beyond one-half hour would certainly not be *un*reasonable. Is this decision whether to devote maximum "reasonable efforts" or minimum "reasonable efforts" not preeminently a matter of policy? It is quite impossible, in short, to draw the Government's proposed line at "no policymaking," and we would have to fall back upon a line of "not too much policymaking." How much is too much is not likely to be answered precisely; and an imprecise barrier against federal intrusion upon state authority is not likely to be an effective one.

Even assuming, moreover, that the Brady Act leaves no "policymaking" discretion with the States, we fail to see how that improves rather than worsens the intrusion upon state sovereignty. Preservation of the States as independent and autonomous political entities is arguably less undermined by requiring them to make policy in certain fields than (as Judge Sneed aptly described it over two decades ago) by "reduc[ing] [them] to puppets of a ventriloquist Congress," *Brown* v. *EPA,* 521 F. 2d, at 839 * * *. It is no more compatible with this independence and autonomy that their officers be "dragooned" (as Judge Fernandez put it in his dissent below, 66 F. 3d, at 1035) into administering federal law, than it would be compatible with the independence and autonomy of the United States that its officers be impressed into service for the execution of state laws.

The Government purports to find support for its proffered distinction of *New York* in our decisions in *Testa* v. *Katt,* 330 U.S. 386 (1947) * * *. *Testa* stands for the proposition that state courts cannot refuse to apply federal law—a conclusion mandated by the terms of the Supremacy Clause ("the Judges in every State shall be bound [by federal law]") * * *. [T]hat says nothing about whether state executive officers must administer federal law * * *.

The Government also maintains that requiring state officers to perform discrete, ministerial tasks specified by Congress does not violate the principle of *New York* because it does not diminish the accountability of state or federal officials. This argument fails even on its own terms. By forcing state governments to absorb the financial burden of implementing a federal regulatory program, Members of Congress can take credit for "solving" problems without having to ask their constituents to pay for the solutions with higher federal taxes. And even when the States are not forced to absorb the costs of implementing a federal program, they are still put in the position of taking the blame for its burdensomeness and for its defects. Under the present law, for example, it will be the CLEO and not some federal official who stands between the gun purchaser and immediate possession of his gun. And it will likely be the CLEO, not some federal official, who will be blamed for any error (even one in the designated federal database) that causes a purchaser to be mistakenly rejected.

* * *

Finally, the Government puts forward a cluster of arguments that can be grouped under the heading: "The Brady Act serves very important purposes, is most efficiently administered by CLEOs during the interim period, and places a minimal and only temporary burden upon state officers." There is considerable disagreement over the extent of the burden, but we need not pause over that detail. Assuming *all* the mentioned factors were true, they might be relevant if we were evaluating whether the incidental application to the States of a federal law of general applicability excessively interfered with the functioning of state governments. But where, as here, it is the whole *object* of the law to direct the functioning of the state executive, and hence to compromise the structural framework of dual sovereignty, such a "balancing" analysis is inappropriate. It is the very *principle* of separate state sovereignty that such a law offends, and no comparative assessment of the various interests can overcome that fundamental defect * * *.

* * *

We held in *New York* that Congress cannot compel the States to enact or enforce a federal regulatory program. Today we hold that Congress cannot circumvent that prohibition by conscripting the State's officers directly. The Federal Government may neither issue directives requiring the States to address particular problems, nor command the States' officers, or those of their political subdivisions, to administer or enforce a federal regulatory program. It matters not whether policymaking is involved, and no case-by-case weighing of the burdens or benefits is necessary; such commands are fundamentally incompatible with our constitutional system of dual sovereignty. Accordingly, the judgment of the Court of Appeals for the Ninth Circuit is reversed.

It is so ordered.

[*Editors' Note: Concurring opinions from Justice O'Connor and Justice Thomas and a dissenting opinion from Justice Souter are omitted.*]

■ JUSTICE STEVENS, with whom JUSTICE SOUTER, JUSTICE GINSBURG, and JUSTICE BREYER join, dissenting.

When Congress exercises the powers delegated to it by the Constitution, it may impose affirmative obligations on executive and judicial officers of state and local governments as well as ordinary citizens. This conclusion is firmly supported by the text of the Constitution, the early history of the Nation, decisions of this Court, and a correct understanding of the basic structure of the Federal Government.

These cases do not implicate the more difficult questions associated with congressional coercion of state legislatures addressed in *New York v. United States,* 505 U.S. 144 (1992). Nor need we consider the wisdom of relying on local officials rather than federal agents to carry out aspects of a federal program, or even the question whether such officials may be required to perform a federal function on a permanent basis. The question is whether Congress, acting on behalf of the people of the entire Nation, may require local law enforcement officers to perform certain duties during the interim needed for the development of a federal gun control program. It is remarkably similar to the question, heavily debated by the Framers of the Constitution, whether Congress could require state agents to collect federal taxes. Or the question whether Congress could impress state judges into federal service to entertain and decide cases that they would prefer to ignore.

* * *

Article I, § 8, grants Congress the power to regulate commerce among the States * * *. Moreover, the additional grant of authority in that section of the Constitution "[t]o make all Laws which shall be necessary and proper for carrying into Execution the foregoing Powers" is surely adequate to support the temporary enlistment of local police officers in the process of identifying persons who should not be entrusted with the possession of handguns. In short, the affirmative delegation of power in Article I provides ample authority for the congressional enactment.

* * *

* * * [T]he majority's opinion consists almost entirely of arguments *against* the substantial evidence weighing in opposition to its view; the Court's ruling is strikingly lacking in affirmative support. Absent even a modicum of textual foundation for its judicially crafted constitutional rule, there should be a

presumption that if the Framers had actually intended such a rule, at least one of them would have mentioned it.

The Court's "structural" arguments are not sufficient to rebut that presumption. The fact that the Framers intended to preserve the sovereignty of the several States simply does not speak to the question whether individual state employees may be required to perform federal obligations, such as registering young adults for the draft, 40 Stat. 80–81, creating state emergency response commissions designed to manage the release of hazardous substances, 42 U.S.C. §§ 11001, 11003, collecting and reporting data on underground storage tanks that may pose an environmental hazard, § 6991a, and reporting traffic fatalities, 23 U.S.C. § 402(a), and missing children, 42 U.S.C. § 5779(a), to a federal agency.

As we explained in *Garcia v. San Antonio Metropolitan Transit Authority,* 469 U.S. 528 (1985): "[T]he principal means chosen by the Framers to ensure the role of the States in the federal system lies in the structure of the Federal Government itself. It is no novelty to observe that the composition of the Federal Government was designed in large part to protect the States from overreaching by Congress." *Id.,* at 550–551. Given the fact that the Members of Congress are elected by the people of the several States, with each State receiving an equivalent number of Senators in order to ensure that even the smallest States have a powerful voice in the Legislature, it is quite unrealistic to assume that they will ignore the sovereignty concerns of their constituents. It is far more reasonable to presume that their decisions to impose modest burdens on state officials from time to time reflect a considered judgment that the people in each of the States will benefit therefrom.

* * *

Far more important than the concerns that the Court musters in support of its new rule is the fact that the Framers entrusted Congress with the task of creating a working structure of intergovernmental relationships around the framework that the Constitution authorized. Neither explicitly nor implicitly did the Framers issue any command that forbids Congress from imposing federal duties on private citizens or on local officials. As a general matter, Congress has followed the sound policy of authorizing federal agencies and federal agents to administer federal programs. That general practice, however, does not negate the existence of power to rely on state officials in occasional situations in which such reliance is in the national interest. Rather, the occasional exceptions confirm the wisdom of Justice Holmes' reminder that "the machinery of government would not work if it were not allowed a little play in its joints." *Bain Peanut Co. of Tex. v. Pinson,* 282 U.S. 499, 501 (1931).

■ JUSTICE BREYER, with whom JUSTICE STEVENS joins, dissenting.

I would add to the reasons JUSTICE STEVENS sets forth the fact that the United States is not the only nation that seeks to reconcile the practical need for a central authority with the democratic virtues of more local control. At least some other countries, facing the same basic problem, have found that local control is better maintained through application of a principle that is the direct opposite of the principle the majority derives from the silence of our Constitution. The federal systems of Switzerland, Germany, and the European Union, for example, all provide that constituent states, not federal bureaucracies, will themselves implement many of the laws, rules, regulations, or decrees enacted by the central "federal" body. Lenaerts, Constitutionalism and the Many Faces of Federalism, 38 Am. J. Comp. L.

205, 237 (1990); D. Currie, The Constitution of the Federal Republic of Germany 66, 84 (1994); Mackenzie-Stuart, Foreword, Comparative Constitutional Federalism: Europe and America ix (M. Tushnet ed.1990); Kimber, A Comparison of Environmental Federalism in the United States and the European Union, 54 Md. L.Rev. 1658, 1675–1677 (1995). They do so in part because they believe that such a system interferes less, not more, with the independent authority of the "state," member nation, or other subsidiary government, and helps to safeguard individual liberty as well.

Of course, we are interpreting our own Constitution, not those of other nations, and there may be relevant political and structural differences between their systems and our own. But their experience may nonetheless cast an empirical light on the consequences of different solutions to a common legal problem—in this case the problem of reconciling central authority with the need to preserve the liberty-enhancing autonomy of a smaller constituent governmental entity. And that experience here offers empirical confirmation of the implied answer to a question JUSTICE STEVENS asks: Why, or how, would what the majority sees as a constitutional alternative—the creation of a new federal gun-law bureaucracy, or the expansion of an existing federal bureaucracy—better promote either state sovereignty or individual liberty?

As comparative experience suggests, there is no need to interpret the Constitution as containing an absolute principle—forbidding the assignment of virtually any federal duty to any state official * * *.

* * * [T]he Constitution itself is silent on the matter. Precedent supports the Government's position here. And the fact that there is not more precedent—that direct federal assignment of duties to state officers is not common—likely reflects, not a widely shared belief that any such assignment is incompatible with basic principles of federalism, but rather a widely shared practice of assigning such duties in other ways. Thus, there is neither need nor reason to find in the Constitution an absolute principle, the inflexibility of which poses a surprising and technical obstacle to the enactment of a law that Congress believed necessary to solve an important national problem.

For these reasons and those set forth in JUSTICE STEVENS' opinion, I join his dissent.

NOTES AND QUESTIONS

1. Justice Scalia's opinion in *Printz* is the first majority holding as to the meaning of the word "proper" in the Necessary and Proper Clause. The second came two years later in *Alden v. Maine,* 527 U.S. 706 (1999), which held (5–4) that Congress could not use its Article I powers to override State sovereign immunity and subject States without their consent to private damages actions, in either state or federal court, for violating federal labor laws:

> Nor can we conclude that the specific Article I powers delegated to Congress necessarily include, by virtue of the Necessary and Proper Clause or otherwise, the incidental authority to subject the States to private suits as a means of achieving objectives otherwise within the scope of the enumerated powers * * *. As we have recognized in an analogous context:

"When a 'La[w] . . . for carrying into Execution' the Commerce Clause violates the principle of state sovereignty reflected in the various constitutional provisions . . . it is not a 'La[w] . . . *proper* for carrying into Execution the Commerce Clause,' and is thus, in the words of The Federalist, 'merely [an] ac[t] of usurpation' which 'deserve[s] to be treated as such.' " *Printz, supra,* at 923–924 (quoting The Federalist No. 33, at 204) (ellipses and alterations in *Printz*).

527 U.S. at 732–33. The third holding came in Chief Justice Roberts' discussion in *NFIB v. Sebelius* of why it was improper for Congress to compel people to buy a product—in that case health insurance. *See supra* pages 719–720. *NFIB* was the first time that the word "proper" was given constitutional significance outside the context of direct regulation of States. All three decisions were 5–4 on the point.

2. Professor Saikrishna Prakash has argued that, while he thinks *New York v. United States* is correct in holding that Congress cannot commandeer State legislatures, which he views as being co-sovereign with the national government, he thinks Congress can commander state executive and judicial officials, which are simply the magistrature. See Saikrishna Bangalore Prakash, *Field Office Federalism*, 79 VA. L. REV. 1957 (1993). We think that this is half-right. Congress can indeed "commandeer" State judicial officials. The Supreme Court so held in *Testa v. Katt,* 330 U.S. 386 (1947). Congress passed a World War II price control act which provided that buyers who thought they were overcharged could sue "in any court of competent jurisdiction," and specifically said that federal courts would have jurisdiction "concurrently with State * * * courts." Emergency Price Control Act of 1942, § 205(c) & (e), 56 Stat. 23, 33–34. The Rhode Island courts concluded that the statute was "penal" in nature, and they determined as a matter of State law that they could not entertain claims under penal laws of any jurisdiction other than Rhode Island. The Supreme Court reversed:

> For the purposes of this case, we assume, without deciding, that § 205(e) is a penal statute in the "public international," "private international," or any other sense. So far as the question of whether the Rhode Island courts properly declined to try this action, it makes no difference into which of these categories the Rhode Island court chose to place the statute which Congress has passed. For we cannot accept the basic premise on which the Rhode Island Supreme Court held that it has no more obligation to enforce a valid penal law of the United States than it has to enforce a penal law of another state or a foreign country. Such a broad assumption flies in the face of the fact that the States of the Union constitute a nation. It disregards the purpose and effect of Article VI, § 2 of the Constitution * * *.
>
> It cannot be assumed, the supremacy clause considered, that the responsibilities of a state to enforce the laws of a sister state are identical with its responsibilities to enforce federal laws * * *.
>
> * * *
>
> So here, the fact that Rhode Island has an established policy against enforcement by its courts of statutes of other states and the United States which it deems penal, cannot be accepted as a "valid excuse." * * *
>
> * * *
>
> It is conceded that this same type of claim arising under Rhode Island law would be enforced by that State's courts * * *. Thus the Rhode Island courts have jurisdiction adequate and appropriate under established local law to

> adjudicate this action. Under these circumstances the State courts are not free to refuse enforcement of petitioners' claim * * *.

330 U.S. at 389, 392, 394. We think this is correct, but for somewhat different reasons than were given by the Court. The answer does not lie in the Article IV, section 2 Supremacy Clause but in the Article I Tribunals Clause, which allows Congress to "constitute Tribunals inferior to the Supreme Court." U.S. CONST. art I, § 8, cl. 9. As we have earlier suggested, *see supra* page 289, this explicitly allows Congress to "commandeer" state courts into the federal judicial hierarchy. This express power with respect to state judicial officials is strong evidence that Congress cannot similarly "commandeer" state legislative or executive officials:

> * * * There is no comparable constitutional provision authorizing Congress to "constitute Executives inferior to the President" or to "constitute Legislatures inferior to Congress." It would do considerable violence to the constitutional structure, and therefore be improper under the Sweeping Clause, for Congress to try to do with state executive and legislative officials what the Constitution carefully permits Congress to do with state judicial officials.
>
> Professor Saikrishna Prakash has argued that commandeering of state legislatures is constitutionally forbidden but commandeering of state executive and judicial institutions is permissible. His argument is based on the historical and conceptual linkages between executive and judicial officers, and his starting point is correct: the eighteenth-century conceptual line between executive and judicial officers was thin at best. The Constitution, however, does unambiguously try to distinguish executive from judicial institutions [in the three Vesting Clauses], and by making specific provision for the "commandeering" of state judicial but not executive institutions, it rules out Professor Prakash's abstract argument, however theoretically appealing it might be.

Gary Lawson, *A Truism with Attitude: The Tenth Amendment in Constitutional Context,* 83 NOTRE DAME L. REV. 469, 497–98 (2008).

3. What else might not be a "proper" means for executing federal power? Is the word "proper" a textual hook for principles of separation of powers? Does it render the Bill of Rights mostly superfluous? *See* Gary Lawson, *The Bill of Rights as an Exclamation Point,* 33 RICHMOND L. REV. 511, 513–16 (1999). Does it incorporate principles of State sovereign immunity, as *Alden v. Maine* suggests?

4. In *McCulloch,* Chief Justice Marshall said that the Necessary and Proper Clause does not authorize laws that are contrary to the "spirit" of the Constitution. Is that just another way of saying that laws that violate key rights or structural principles are not "proper"?

5. If the federal spending power really comes from the Necessary and Proper Clause rather than from the Taxing Clause, *see supra* pages 291–292, what might make a federal spending law not "proper"?

[Assignment 40]

XIV. THE TREATY POWER

Article II, Section 2, Clause 2: [The President shall have Power, by and with the advice and consent of the Senate, to make Treaties, provided that two thirds of the Senators present concur;

Article VI, Clause 2: This Constitution, and the Laws of the United States which shall be made in Pursuance thereof; and all Treaties made, or which shall be made, under the Authority of the United States, shall be the supreme Law of the Land; and the Judges in every State shall be bound thereby, any Thing in the Constitutions or Laws of any state to the contrary notwithstanding.

Most federal legislative powers appear in Article I, Section 8. Some important legislative powers, however, appear in Articles IV and V and in various constitutional amendments; we explore those powers shortly. One power that is hard to classify but which shares at least some features of the legislative power is the power to make treaties. In England, and uniformly among commentators who would have been familiar to an eighteenth-century audience, the treaty-making power was an executive power. *See* Saikrishna B. Prakash & Michael D. Ramsey, *The Executive Power over Foreign Affairs,* 111 YALE L.J. 231, 269–75 (2001). The English monarch made and unmade treaties. The U.S. Constitution reflects this understanding by locating the Treaty Clause in the middle of Article II rather than in Article I (or Article IV). In the absence of a Treaty Clause, the grant of the "executive Power" would surely have given the President the exclusive right to make treaties.

The U.S. Constitution, however, takes a slightly different tack. It denies altogether any treaty-making power in the States, *see* U.S. CONST. art. I, § 10, cl. 1 ("No State shall enter into any Treaty"), and then divides the (federal) treaty-making power between the President and the Senate. Treaties thus are not legislation, because they do not involve the approval of the House. But treaties are supreme law just as much as is legislation, by the plain terms of the Supremacy Clause. Does that mean that the President and Senate function as an alternative lawmaking body to Congress? Are there things that the President and Senate can do by treaty that Congress cannot do by law? These are vital questions, because the careful structural provisions for lawmaking outlined in Article I, Section 7 do not apply to treaties. Depending on the composition of the House and Senate, at any given moment in time it might be either easier or harder to enact legislation (majorities in both Houses of Congress) than to ratify a treaty (presidential negotiation plus a two-thirds majority in the Senate). For example, when Texas was considered for admission to the Union, the first proposed route was by treaty, but the Senate failed to ratify the treaty (and indeed voted it down by a substantial margin the first time around). When it became clear, in a subsequent Congress, that majorities in both Houses were going to be easier to assemble than a two-thirds Senate majority, with Northern senators justifiably wary about admitting yet another slave State, statehood supporters switched from treaty to annexation, requiring only ordinary legislation. *See* GARY LAWSON & GUY SEIDMAN, THE CONSTITUTION OF EMPIRE: TERRITORIAL EXPANSION AND AMERICAN LEGAL HISTORY 92 (2004). One could easily imagine circumstances in which the political calculation would point towards the Senate rather than the Congress as a whole. So it is very important to know what treaties can and cannot do.

Treaties can obviously do at least one thing that ordinary legislation cannot: Treaties create obligations under international law:

> Suppose that the United States and France want to enter into an agreement providing for reciprocal duty-free entry of perfumes. Congress can pass a law exempting French perfumes from all American duties. But if Congress later changes that law, the French government would have no legal recourse. The French government could change its own domestic law, make diplomatic hay, begin a trade war, or even throw legality to the wind and begin a shooting war, but the American action would not violate any legal norm. If, however, the arrangement is embodied in a treaty, then subsequent legislation contrary to the terms of the treaty would violate international law. Congress could still pass legislation in violation of the treaty that would be fully effective as a matter of domestic law—the treaty does not constitutionally disable Congress. But a treaty that "locks in" an international agreement raises the cost of such legislation by whatever amount a violation of international law is considered or expected to entail. Similarly, a treaty, and only a treaty, can secure an internationally binding agreement from a foreign sovereign.

Gary Lawson & Guy Seidman, *The Jeffersonian Treaty Clause,* 2006 U. ILL. L. REV. 1, 12–13. The big question is whether treaties can do things *domestically* that ordinary legislation cannot. Suppose that a particular subject is conceded to be beyond the legislative powers of Congress. Can the President and Senate nonetheless regulate that subject via a treaty (or perhaps a succession of treaties with different countries)? Even if Article I does not embody the Virginia and Bedford Resolutions, do they come into the Constitution through the back door of Article II?

This issue was starkly posed in 1920. Under then-existing understandings of Congress's Article I powers, which have since been overruled, Congress could not directly regulate migratory birds within the United States. Could the President and Senate nonetheless agree to a treaty that regulated migratory birds? And if they did make such a treaty, would Congress then be able to pass legislation "necessary and proper for carrying into Execution" the treaty that Congress could not pass using just its own Article I powers? In other words, can the President and Senate expand the legislative authority of Congress by means of a treaty? Consider the answer provided in the Supreme Court's leading Treaty Clause decision. The case is remarkably short for a landmark decision, and we reproduce it with only minor wordsmithing edits.

A. MISSOURI V. HOLLAND

252 U.S. 416 (1920)

■ MR. JUSTICE HOLMES delivered the opinion of the court.

This is a bill in equity brought by the State of Missouri to prevent a game warden of the United States from attempting to enforce the Migratory Bird Treaty Act of July 3, 1918, c. 128, 40 Stat. 755, and the regulations made by the Secretary of Agriculture in pursuance of the same. The ground of the bill is that the statute is an unconstitutional interference with the rights reserved to the States by the Tenth

Amendment, and that the acts of the defendant done and threatened under that authority invade the sovereign right of the State and contravene its will manifested in statutes. The State also alleges a pecuniary interest, as owner of the wild birds within its borders and otherwise, admitted by the Government to be sufficient, but it is enough that the bill is a reasonable and proper means to assert the alleged quasi sovereign rights of a State. A motion to dismiss was sustained by the District Court on the ground that the act of Congress is constitutional. The State appeals.

On December 8, 1916, a treaty between the United States and Great Britain was proclaimed by the President. It recited that many species of birds in their annual migrations traversed certain parts of the United States and of Canada, that they were of great value as a source of food and in destroying insects injurious to vegetation, but were in danger of extermination through lack of adequate protection. It therefore provided for specified close seasons and protection in other forms, and agreed that the two powers would take or propose to their law-making bodies the necessary measures for carrying the treaty out. 39 Stat. 1702. The above mentioned Act of July 3, 1918, entitled an act to give effect to the convention, prohibited the killing, capturing or selling any of the migratory birds included in the terms of the treaty except as permitted by regulations compatible with those terms, to be made by the Secretary of Agriculture. Regulations were proclaimed on July 31, and October 25, 1918. 40 Stat. 1812; 1863. It is unnecessary to go into any details because, as we have said, the question raised is the general one whether the treaty and statute are void as an interference with the rights reserved to the States.

To answer this question it is not enough to refer to the Tenth Amendment, reserving the powers not delegated to the United States, because by Article II, § 2, the power to make treaties is delegated expressly, and by Article VI treaties made under the authority of the United States, along with the Constitution and laws of the United States made in pursuance thereof, are declared the supreme law of the land. If the treaty is valid there can be no dispute about the validity of the statute under Article I, § 8, as a necessary and proper means to execute the powers of the Government. The language of the Constitution as to the supremacy of treaties being general, the question before us is narrowed to an inquiry into the ground upon which the present supposed exception is placed.

It is said that a treaty cannot be valid if it infringes the Constitution, that there are limits, therefore, to the treaty-making power, and that one such limit is that what an act of Congress could not do unaided, in derogation of the powers reserved to the States, a treaty cannot do. An earlier act of Congress that attempted by itself and not in pursuance of a treaty to regulate the killing of migratory birds within the States had been held bad in the District Court. *United States v. Shauver*, 214 Fed. 154. *United States v. McCullagh*, 221 Fed. 288. Those decisions were supported by arguments that migratory birds were owned by the States in their sovereign capacity for the benefit of their people, and that under cases like *Geer v. Connecticut,* 161 U.S. 519, this control was one that Congress had no power to displace. The same argument is supposed to apply now with equal force.

Whether the two cases cited were decided rightly or not they cannot be accepted as a test of the treaty power. Acts of Congress are the supreme law of the land only when made in pursuance of the Constitution, while treaties are declared to be so when made under the authority of the United States. It is open to question whether the authority of the United States means more than the formal acts prescribed to make the convention. We do not mean to imply that there are no qualifications to the treaty-making power; but they must be ascertained in a different way. It is obvious that there may be matters of the sharpest exigency for the national well being that an act of Congress could not deal with, but that a treaty followed by such an act could, and it is not lightly to be assumed that, in matters requiring national action, "a power which must belong to and somewhere reside in every civilized government" is not to be found. *Andrews v Andrews,* 188 U.S. 14, 33. What was said in that case with regard to the powers of the States applies with equal force to the powers of the nation in cases where the States individually are incompetent to act. We are not yet discussing the particular case before us but only are considering the validity of the test proposed. With regard to that we may add that when we are dealing with words that also are a constituent act, like the Constitution of the United States, we must realize that they have called into life a being the development of which could not have been foreseen completely by the most gifted of its begetters. It was enough for them to realize or to hope that they had created an organism; it has taken a century and has cost their successors much sweat and blood to prove that they created a nation. The case before us must be considered in the light of our whole experience and not merely in that of what was said a hundred years ago. The treaty in question does not contravene any prohibitory words to be found in the Constitution. The only question is whether it is forbidden by some invisible radiation from the general terms of the Tenth Amendment. We must consider what this country has become in deciding what that Amendment has reserved.

The State as we have intimated founds its claim of exclusive authority upon an assertion of title to migratory birds, an assertion that is embodied in statute. No doubt it is true that, as between a State and its inhabitants the State may regulate the killing and sale of such birds, but it does not follow that its authority is exclusive of paramount powers. To put the claim of the State upon title is to lean upon a slender reed. Wild birds are not in the possession of anyone, and possession is the beginning of ownership. The whole foundation of the State's rights is the presence within their jurisdiction of birds that yesterday had not arrived, tomorrow may be in another State, and, in a week, a thousand miles away. If we are to be accurate we cannot put the case of the State upon higher ground than that the treaty deals with creatures that for the moment are within the state borders, that it must be carried out by officers of the United States within the same territory, and that but for the treaty the State would be free to regulate this subject itself.

As most of the laws of the United States are carried out within the States and as many of them deal with matters which in the silence of such laws the State might regulate, such general grounds are not enough to support Missouri's claim. Valid treaties of course "are as binding within the territorial limits of the States as they are elsewhere throughout the dominion of the United States." No doubt the great body of private relations usually fall within the control of the State, but a treaty may override its power. We do not have to invoke the later developments of constitutional law for this proposition; it was recognized * * * early * * * with regard to statutes of limitation, and even earlier, as to confiscation. It was assumed by Chief Justice Marshall with regard to the escheat of land to the State in * * * [1817 and in three subsequent cases]. So as to a limited jurisdiction of foreign consuls within a State. Further illustration seems unnecessary, and it only remains to consider the application of established rules to the present case.

Here, a national interest of very nearly the first magnitude is involved. It can be protected only by national action in concert with that of another power. The subject-matter is only transitorily within the State, and has no permanent habitat therein. But for the treaty and the statute there soon might be no birds for any powers to deal with. We see nothing in the Constitution that compels the Government to sit by while a food supply is cut off and the protectors of our forests and our crops are destroyed. It is not sufficient to rely upon the States. The reliance is vain, and were it otherwise, the question is whether the United States is forbidden to act. We are of opinion that the treaty and statute must be upheld.

Decree affirmed.

■ MR. JUSTICE VAN DEVANTER and MR. JUSTICE PITNEY dissent.

NOTES AND QUESTIONS

1. *Holland* is perhaps *the* classic expression of the notion of a "living" Constitution—complete with an organic metaphor. The case was decided in 1920, during the era of "inherent" national powers that included the *Selective Draft Law Cases* from two years earlier. Is this case another example of "every respectable government can do X . . .?"

2. One question in *Holland* is whether the treaty itself was valid. Why wouldn't it be? It was negotiated by the President and approved by the required two-thirds of the Senate. What else does the Treaty Clause require for a valid treaty? Procedurally, it requires nothing else. Substantively, the question is whether there are any subjects that cannot be regulated by treaty. To be sure, if there are any subjects that are categorically out of bounds, migratory animals do not seem like a promising candidate: English kings and queens had signed treaties concerning fishing and hunting rights between 1066 and 1776. But the federal courts had already ruled in 1920 that Congress could not regulate migratory birds under the Commerce Clause. Whatever the scope of the English treaty power might have been in 1788, did the U.S. Constitution give the federal government a narrower treaty power than was possessed by all other respectable governments, such that matters left beyond the legislative power of Congress are also beyond the treaty power of the President and Senate? There are at least two powers beyond Congress's legislative powers that no one has ever thought were beyond the scope of the treaty power: ending a war and ceding U.S. territory to another country. Those matters, of course, are utterly beyond the power of any individual States and thus could never be among those powers "reserved" to States mentioned in the Tenth Amendment. Migratory birds, though, are another matter altogether. With respect to powers exercisable by States, is the scope of the Treaty Clause limited by the scope of the Constitution's other enumerated powers? Thomas Jefferson thought so. In a parliamentary manual that he wrote while President of the Senate (i.e., Vice President), he wrote:

> By the Constitution of the United States, this department of legislation is confided to two branches only of the ordinary legislature; the President originating, and Senate having a negative. To what subjects this power extends, has not been defined in detail by the constitution; nor are we entirely agreed among ourselves. 1. It is admitted that it must concern the foreign nation party to the contract, or it would be a mere nullity, res inter alios acta. 2. By the general power to make treaties, the constitution must have intended to comprehend only those subjects which are usually regulated by treaty, and cannot be otherwise regulated. 3. *It must have meant to except out of these the rights reserved to the states; for surely the President and Senate cannot do by*

> *treaty what the whole government is interdicted from doing in any way*. 4. And also to except those subjects of legislation in which it gave a participation to the House of Representatives. This last exception is denied by some, on the ground that it would leave very little matter for the treaty power to work on. The less the better, say others.

Thomas Jefferson, *A Manual of Parliamentary Practice: For the Use of the Senate of the United States, in* JEFFERSON'S PARLIAMENTARY WRITINGS 353, 420–21 (Charles T. Cullen ed., 1988) (emphasis added). In later correspondence, Jefferson clarified:

> If [the Treaty Clause] has bounds they can be no others than the definitions of the powers which that instrument gives. It specifies & delineates the operations permitted to the federal government, and gives all the powers necessary to carry these into execution. Whatever of these enumerated objects is proper for a law, Congress may make the law; whatever is proper to be executed by way of a treaty, the President & Senate may enter into the treaty; whatever is to be done by a judicial sentence, the judges may pass the sentence.

Letter from Thomas Jefferson to Wilson Cary Nicholas (Sept. 7, 1803), *in* 8 THE WRITINGS OF THOMAS JEFFERSON 241 n.1 (Paul L. Ford ed., 1897). For Jefferson, in other words, "[t]he treaty power * * * is a vehicle for implementing otherwise-granted national powers in the international arena. It may be used to carry into effect national powers found in the Constitution, but it cannot function as a free-standing power, divorced from the exercise of some other enumerated power. In this respect, the Treaty Clause is analogous to the Sweeping Clause of Article I: the Sweeping Clause permits Congress to implement otherwise-granted national powers domestically, while the treaty power permits the President and Senate to implement otherwise-granted national powers internationally by entering into agreements with foreign sovereigns." Lawson & Seidman, *The Jeffersonian Treaty Clause, supra,* at 15–16. Jefferson, as it happens, was notoriously hostile to treaties; and his views, whatever their merits as a matter of original meaning, never prevailed. Instead, the Treaty Clause has generally always been seen—and certainly has been seen since *Missouri v. Holland*—as "an independent grant of power to the federal government to enter into treaties that enact rules that Congress might not otherwise have been able to enact." Gerald L. Neuman, *The Nationalization of Civil Liberties,* 99 COLUM. L. REV. 1630, 1646–47 (1999). No treaty has even been found invalid because it regulated subjects outside the scope of the Treaty Clause.

3. A second question is whether a valid treaty gives Congress legislative powers that it otherwise would not have. This was really the key question in *Holland.* Congress had passed a statute pursuant to the treaty that it could not have passed without it. *Holland* devotes exactly one sentence to that question: "If the treaty is valid, there can be no dispute about the validity of the statute under Article I, § 8, as a necessary and proper means to execute the powers of the Government." Is it really that simple? We will explore this question shortly.

4. A third question is whether treaties are "self-executing," in that they create law of their own force without any need for congressional implementation, or whether treaties become effective as domestic law only when Congress implements them. A debate over this question consumed 303 pages of a law review in 1999. *See* John C. Yoo, *Globalism and the Constitution: Treaties, Non-Self-Execution, and the Original Understanding,* 99 COLUM. L. REV. 1955, 1958 (1999); Martin S. Flaherty, *History Right?: Historical Scholarship, Original Understanding, and Treaties As "Supreme Law of the Land,"* 99 COLUM. L. REV. 2095 (1999); Carlos Manual Vazquez, *Laughing At Treaties,* 99 COLUM. L. REV. 2154 (1999); John C. Yoo, *Treaties and Public Lawmaking: A Textual and*

Structural Defense of Non-Self-Execution, 99 Colum. L. Rev. 2218 (1999). Doctrine says that treaties sometimes are self-executing and sometimes are not:

> This Court has long recognized the distinction between treaties that automatically have effect as domestic law, and those that—while they constitute international law commitments—do not by themselves function as binding federal law. The distinction was well explained by Chief Justice Marshall's opinion in *Foster v. Neilson,* 2 Pet. 253, 315 (1829), *overruled on other grounds, United States v. Percheman,* 7 Pet. 51 (1833), which held that a treaty is "equivalent to an act of the legislature," and hence self-executing, when it "operates of itself without the aid of any legislative provision." When, in contrast, "[treaty] stipulations are not self-executing they can only be enforced pursuant to legislation to carry them into effect." *Whitney v. Robertson,* 124 U.S. 190, 194 (1888). In sum, while treaties "may comprise international commitments . . . they are not domestic law unless Congress has either enacted implementing statutes or the treaty itself conveys an intention that it be 'self-executing' and is ratified on these terms." *Igartua-De La Rosa v. United States,* 417 F.3d 145, 150 (C.A.1 2005) (en banc) (Boudin, C. J.).

Medellin v. Texas, 552 U.S. 491, 504–05 (2008). In *Medellin,* the Justices split 5–4 on whether a provision in the Vienna Convention on Consular Relations was self-executing and thus, under the Supremacy Clause, obliged state courts to obey judgments of the International Court of Justice issued pursuant to that treaty. The justices disagreed, among other things, about whether it is reasonable to expect treaties to contain explicit language indicating that they are or are not intended to be self-executing. *See id.* at 514–17) (defending the majority's focus on treaty language in finding no intention to make the Vienna Convention self-executing against the dissent's "grab bag of no less than seven reasons" why this particular provision was self-executing).

5. A fourth question, not presented by *Holland,* is whether substantive constitutional constraints on legislation, such as the First Amendment, Fifth Amendment, or Sixth Amendment, also apply to treaties. That question is not nearly as trivial as it might at first sound. The Supreme Court addressed it in *Reid v. Covert,* 354 U.S. 1 (1957), but could not produce a majority opinion. The case involved whether the spouse of a serviceperson who was not herself in the military but who allegedly committed a crime on an overseas military base (two spouses were separately accused of killing their active service husbands on military bases in England and Japan) could be tried in the military justice system, without the full panoply of Fifth and Sixth Amendment trial rights, rather than in the U.S. civilian courts. Four justices categorically said no:

> The United States is entirely a creature of the Constitution. Its power and authority have no other source. It can only act in accordance with all the limitations imposed by the Constitution. When the Government reaches out to punish a citizen who is abroad, the shield which the Bill of Rights and other parts of the Constitution provide to protect his life and liberty should not be stripped away just because he happens to be in another land.
>
> * * *
>
> While it has been suggested that only those constitutional rights which are "fundamental" protect Americans abroad, * * * we can find no warrant, in logic or otherwise, for picking and choosing among the remarkable collection of "Thou shalt nots" which were explicitly fastened on all departments and agencies of the Federal Government by the Constitution and its Amendments. Moreover, in view of our heritage and the history of the adoption of the

Constitution and the Bill of Rights, it seems peculiarly anomalous to say that trial before a civilian judge and by an independent jury picked from the common citizenry is not a fundamental right * * *.

* * *

At the time of Mrs. Covert's alleged offense, an executive agreement was in effect between the United States and Great Britain which permitted United States' military courts to exercise exclusive jurisdiction over offenses committed in Great Britain by American servicemen or their dependents * * *. The obvious and decisive answer to this, of course, is that no agreement with a foreign nation can confer power on the Congress, or on any other branch of Government, which is free from the restraints of the Constitution.

* * *

There is nothing in *Missouri v. Holland,* 252 U.S. 416, which is contrary to the position taken here. There, the Court carefully noted that the treaty involved was not inconsistent with any specific provision of the Constitution. The Court was concerned with the Tenth Amendment, which reserves to the States or the people all power not delegated to the National Government. To the extent that the United States can validly make treaties, the people and the States have delegated their power to the National Government, and the Tenth Amendment is no barrier.

* * *

* * * Ours is a government of divided authority on the assumption that in division there is not only strength but freedom from tyranny. And, under our Constitution, courts of law alone are given power to try civilians for their offenses against the United States. The philosophy expressed by Lord Coke, speaking long ago from a wealth of experience, is still timely:

"God send me never to live under the Law of Conveniency or Discretion. Shall the Souldier and Justice Sit on one Bench, the Trumpet will not let the Cryer speak in Westminster-Hall."

Two concurrences on narrower ground sustained the judgment.

6. *Reid v. Covert* involved an executive agreement, *see supra* page 492, and not a treaty. The six justices in the combined majority made no distinction between executive agreements and treaties. If there are substantive or subject-matter constitutional limits on what can be done through executive agreements, those limits surely apply as well to treaties.

7. Presumably, the President and Senate could not make a treaty that required the United States to have a government censor for all news stories, confiscate all handguns, or deprive some States of their equal representation in the Senate. Could a treaty require a State to move its capital city? Compel a State's executive officials to enforce federal law? If the answer to all of these questions is "no," how can a treaty regulate migratory birds if Congress otherwise could not do so? If treaties are subject to constitutional limitations, what does that really mean? Which constitutional limitations count and which do not?

8. We noted earlier that *Missouri v. Holland* assumed without argument that if there was a valid treaty, Congress could enact legislation to implement it. *Reid v. Covert* operates on the same assumption; it simply finds substantive constraints on the implementing laws. The question what it means to "carry[ ] into Execution" the treaty power, however, is not necessarily as simple as *Holland* made it sound. The issue came

up, but was not resolved, in 2014, in a case that technically involves only statutory interpretation but which has important constitutional implications.

B. BOND V. UNITED STATES

572 U.S. 844 (2014)

■ CHIEF JUSTICE ROBERTS delivered the opinion of the Court.

The horrors of chemical warfare were vividly captured by John Singer Sargent in his 1919 painting Gassed. The nearly life-sized work depicts two lines of soldiers, blinded by mustard gas, clinging single file to orderlies guiding them to an improvised aid station. There they would receive little treatment and no relief; many suffered for weeks only to have the gas claim their lives. The soldiers were shown staggering through piles of comrades too seriously burned to even join the procession.

The painting reflects the devastation that Sargent witnessed in the aftermath of the Second Battle of Arras during World War I. That battle and others like it led to an overwhelming consensus in the international community that toxic chemicals should never again be used as weapons against human beings. Today that objective is reflected in the international Convention on Chemical Weapons, which has been ratified or acceded to by 190 countries. The United States, pursuant to the Federal Government's constitutionally enumerated power to make treaties, ratified the treaty in 1997. To fulfill the United States' obligations under the Convention, Congress enacted the Chemical Weapons Convention Implementation Act of 1998. The Act makes it a federal crime for a person to use or possess any chemical weapon, and it punishes violators with severe penalties. It is a statute that, like the Convention it implements, deals with crimes of deadly seriousness.

The question presented by this case is whether the Implementation Act also reaches a purely local crime: an amateur attempt by a jilted wife to injure her husband's lover, which ended up causing only a minor thumb burn readily treated by rinsing with water. Because our constitutional structure leaves local criminal activity primarily to the States, we have generally declined to read federal law as intruding on that responsibility, unless Congress has clearly indicated that the law should have such reach. The Chemical Weapons Convention Implementation Act contains no such clear indication, and we accordingly conclude that it does not cover the unremarkable local offense at issue here.

In 1997, the President of the United States, upon the advice and consent of the Senate, ratified the Convention on the Prohibition of the Development, Production, Stockpiling, and Use of Chemical Weapons and on Their Destruction * * *.

* * *

The Convention provides:

"(1) Each State Party to this Convention undertakes never under any circumstances:

"(a) To develop, produce, otherwise acquire, stockpile or retain chemical weapons, or transfer, directly or indirectly, chemical weapons to anyone;

"(b) To use chemical weapons;

"(c) To engage in any military preparations to use chemical weapons;

> "(d) To assist, encourage or induce, in any way, anyone to engage in any activity prohibited to a State Party under this Convention."

"Chemical Weapons" are defined in relevant part as "[t]oxic chemicals and their precursors, except where intended for purposes not prohibited under this Convention, as long as the types and quantities are consistent with such purposes." "Toxic Chemical," in turn, is defined as "Any chemical which through its chemical action on life processes can cause death, temporary incapacitation or permanent harm to humans or animals. This includes all such chemicals, regardless of their origin or of their method of production, and regardless of whether they are produced in facilities, in munitions or elsewhere." "Purposes Not Prohibited Under this Convention" means "[i]ndustrial, agricultural, research, medical, pharmaceutical or other peaceful purposes" and other specific purposes not at issue here.

Although the Convention is a binding international agreement, it is "not self-executing." W. Krutzsch & R. Trapp, A Commentary on the Chemical Weapons Convention 109 (1994). That is, the Convention creates obligations only for State Parties and "does not by itself give rise to domestically enforceable federal law" absent "implementing legislation passed by Congress." *Medellín v. Texas*, 552 U.S. 491, 505, n. 2 (2008). It instead provides that "[e]ach State Party shall, in accordance with its constitutional processes, adopt the necessary measures to implement its obligations under this Convention." "In particular," each State Party shall "[p]rohibit natural and legal persons anywhere . . . under its jurisdiction . . . from undertaking any activity prohibited to a State Party under this Convention, including enacting penal legislation with respect to such activity."

Congress gave the Convention domestic effect in 1998 when it passed the Chemical Weapons Convention Implementation Act. See 112 Stat. 2681–856. The Act closely tracks the text of the treaty: It forbids any person knowingly "to develop, produce, otherwise acquire, transfer directly or indirectly, receive, stockpile, retain, own, possess, or use, or threaten to use, any chemical weapon." 18 U.S.C. § 229(a)(1). It defines "chemical weapon" in relevant part as "[a] toxic chemical and its precursors, except where intended for a purpose not prohibited under this chapter as long as the type and quantity is consistent with such a purpose." § 229F(1)(A). "Toxic chemical," in turn, is defined in general as "any chemical which through its chemical action on life processes can cause death, temporary incapacitation or permanent harm to humans or animals. The term includes all such chemicals, regardless of their origin or of their method of production, and regardless of whether they are produced in facilities, in munitions or elsewhere." § 229F(8)(A). Finally, "purposes not prohibited by this chapter" is defined as "[a]ny peaceful purpose related to an industrial, agricultural, research, medical, or pharmaceutical activity or other activity," and other specific purposes. § 229F(7). A person who violates section 229 may be subject to severe punishment: imprisonment "for any term of years," or if a victim's death results, the death penalty or imprisonment "for life." § 229A (a).

Petitioner Carol Anne Bond is a microbiologist from Lansdale, Pennsylvania. In 2006, Bond's closest friend, Myrlinda Haynes, announced that she was pregnant. When Bond discovered that her husband was the child's father, she sought revenge against Haynes. Bond stole a quantity of 10-chloro-10H-phenoxarsine (an arsenic-based compound) from her employer, a chemical manufacturer. She also ordered a vial of potassium dichromate (a chemical commonly used in printing photographs or cleaning laboratory equipment) on Amazon.com. Both chemicals are toxic to humans and, in high enough doses, potentially lethal. It is undisputed, however, that Bond did not intend to kill Haynes. She instead hoped that Haynes would touch the chemicals and develop an uncomfortable rash.

Between November 2006 and June 2007, Bond went to Haynes's home on at least 24 occasions and spread the chemicals on her car door, mailbox, and door knob. These attempted assaults were almost entirely unsuccessful. The chemicals that Bond used are easy to see, and Haynes was able to avoid them all but once. On that occasion, Haynes suffered a minor chemical burn on her thumb, which she treated by rinsing with water. Haynes repeatedly called the local police to report the suspicious substances, but they took no action. When Haynes found powder on her mailbox, she called the police again, who told her to call the post office. Haynes did so, and postal inspectors placed surveillance cameras around her home. The cameras caught Bond opening Haynes's mailbox, stealing an envelope, and stuffing potassium dichromate inside the muffler of Haynes's car.

Federal prosecutors naturally charged Bond with two counts of mail theft, in violation of 18 U.S.C. § 1708. More surprising, they also charged her with two counts of possessing and using a chemical weapon, in violation of section 229(a). Bond moved to dismiss the chemical weapon counts on the ground that section 229 exceeded Congress's enumerated powers and invaded powers reserved to the States by the Tenth Amendment. The District Court denied Bond's motion. She then entered a conditional guilty plea that reserved her right to appeal. The District Court sentenced Bond to six years in federal prison plus five years of supervised release, and ordered her to pay a $2,000 fine and $9,902.79 in restitution.

Bond appealed, raising a Tenth Amendment challenge to her conviction * * *.

* * * She also argued that section 229 does not reach her conduct because the statute's exception for the use of chemicals for "peaceful purposes" should be understood in contradistinction to the "warlike" activities that the Convention was primarily designed to prohibit * * *.

The Third Circuit * * * rejected Bond's constitutional challenge to her conviction, holding that section 229 was "necessary and proper to carry the Convention into effect." *Id.*, at 162. The Court of Appeals relied on this Court's opinion in *Missouri v. Holland*, 252 U.S. 416 (1920), which stated that "[i]f the treaty is valid there can be no dispute about the validity of the statute" that implements it "as a necessary and proper means to execute the powers of the Government," *id.*, at 432.

* * *

In our federal system, the National Government possesses only limited powers; the States and the people retain the remainder. The States have broad authority to enact legislation for the public good—what we have often called a "police power." *United States v. Lopez*, 514 U.S. 549, 567 (1995). The Federal Government, by contrast, has no such authority and "can exercise only the powers granted to it," *McCulloch v. Maryland*, 4 Wheat. 316, 405 (1819), including the power to make "all Laws which shall be necessary and proper for carrying into Execution" the enumerated powers, U.S. Const., Art. I, § 8, cl. 18. For nearly two centuries it has been "clear" that, lacking a police power, "Congress cannot punish felonies generally." *Cohens v. Virginia*, 6 Wheat. 264, 428 (1821). A criminal act committed wholly within a State "cannot be made an offence against the United States, unless it have some relation to the execution of a power of Congress, or to some matter within the jurisdiction of the United States." *United States v. Fox,* 95 U.S. 670, 672 (1878).

The Government frequently defends federal criminal legislation on the ground that the legislation is authorized pursuant to Congress's power to regulate interstate commerce. In this case, however, the Court of Appeals held that the Government had explicitly disavowed that argument before the District Court. 681 F.3d, at 151, n. 1. As a result, in this Court the parties have devoted significant effort to arguing whether section 229, as applied to Bond's offense, is a necessary and proper means of executing the National Government's power to make treaties. U.S. Const., Art. II, § 2, cl. 2. Bond argues that the lower court's reading of *Missouri v. Holland* would remove all limits on federal authority, so long as the Federal Government ratifies a treaty first. She insists that to effectively afford the Government a police power whenever it implements a treaty would be contrary to the Framers' careful decision to divide power between the States and the National Government as a means of preserving liberty. To the extent that *Holland* authorizes such usurpation of traditional state authority, Bond says, it must be either limited or overruled.

The Government replies that this Court has never held that a statute implementing a valid treaty exceeds Congress's enumerated powers. To do so here, the Government says, would contravene another deliberate choice of the Framers: to avoid placing subject matter limitations on the National Government's power to make treaties. And it might also undermine confidence in the United States as an international treaty partner.

Notwithstanding this debate, it is "a well-established principle governing the prudent exercise of this Court's jurisdiction that normally the Court will not decide a constitutional question if there is some other ground upon which to dispose of the case." Bond argues that section 229 does not cover her conduct. So we consider that argument first.

Section 229 exists to implement the Convention, so we begin with that international agreement * * *.There is no reason to think the sovereign nations that ratified the Convention were interested in anything like Bond's common law assault.

Even if the treaty does reach that far, nothing prevents Congress from implementing the Convention in the same manner it legislates with respect to innumerable other matters—observing the Constitution's division of responsibility between sovereigns and leaving the prosecution of purely local crimes to the States. The Convention, after all, is agnostic between enforcement at the state versus federal level: It provides that "[e]ach State Party shall, in accordance with its constitutional processes, adopt the necessary measures to implement its obligations under this Convention."

Fortunately, we have no need to interpret the scope of the Convention in this case. Bond was prosecuted under section 229, and the statute—unlike the Convention—must be read consistent with principles of federalism inherent in our constitutional structure.

In the Government's view, the conclusion that Bond "knowingly" "use[d]" a "chemical weapon" in violation of section 229(a) is simple: The chemicals that Bond placed on Haynes's home and car are "toxic chemical[s]" as defined by the statute, and Bond's attempt to assault Haynes was not a "peaceful purpose." §§ 229F(1), (8),

(7). The problem with this interpretation is that it would "dramatically intrude[ ] upon traditional state criminal jurisdiction," and we avoid reading statutes to have such reach in the absence of a clear indication that they do. *United States v. Bass*, 404 U.S. 336, 350 (1971).

Part of a fair reading of statutory text is recognizing that "Congress legislates against the backdrop" of certain unexpressed presumptions * * *. For example, we presume that a criminal statute derived from the common law carries with it the requirement of a culpable mental state—even if no such limitation appears in the text—unless it is clear that the Legislature intended to impose strict liability. To take another example, we presume, absent a clear statement from Congress, that federal statutes do not apply outside the United States. So even though section 229, read on its face, would cover a chemical weapons crime if committed by a U.S. citizen in Australia, we would not apply the statute to such conduct absent a plain statement from Congress. The notion that some things "go without saying" applies to legislation just as it does to everyday life.

Among the background principles of construction that our cases have recognized are those grounded in the relationship between the Federal Government and the States under our Constitution. It has long been settled, for example, that we presume federal statutes do not abrogate state sovereign immunity, *Atascadero State Hospital v. Scanlon*, 473 U.S. 234, 243 (1985), impose obligations on the States pursuant to section 5 of the Fourteenth Amendment, *Pennhurst State School and Hospital v. Halderman*, 451 U.S. 1, 16–17 (1981), or preempt state law, *Rice v. Santa Fe Elevator Corp.*, 331 U.S. 218, 230 (1947).

Closely related to these is the well-established principle that " 'it is incumbent upon the federal courts to be certain of Congress' intent before finding that federal law overrides' " the "usual constitutional balance of federal and state powers." *Gregory v. Ashcroft*, 501 U.S. 452, 460 (1991) * * *.

* * *

* * * [P]recedents [applying this canon of construction] make clear that it is appropriate to refer to basic principles of federalism embodied in the Constitution to resolve ambiguity in a federal statute. In this case, the ambiguity derives from the improbably broad reach of the key statutory definition given the term—"chemical weapon"—being defined; the deeply serious consequences of adopting such a boundless reading; and the lack of any apparent need to do so in light of the context from which the statute arose—a treaty about chemical warfare and terrorism. We conclude that, in this curious case, we can insist on a clear indication that Congress meant to reach purely local crimes, before interpreting the statute's expansive language in a way that intrudes on the police power of the States.

We do not find any such clear indication in section 229. "Chemical weapon" is the key term that defines the statute's reach, and it is defined extremely broadly. But that general definition does not constitute a clear statement that Congress meant the statute to reach local criminal conduct.

In fact, a fair reading of section 229 suggests that it does not have as expansive a scope as might at first appear. To begin, as a matter of natural meaning, an educated user of English would not describe Bond's crime as involving a "chemical weapon." Saying that a person "used a chemical weapon" conveys a very different idea than saying the person "used a chemical in a way that caused some harm." The natural meaning of "chemical weapon" takes account of both the particular chemicals that the defendant used and the circumstances in which she used them.

When used in the manner here, the chemicals in this case are not of the sort that an ordinary person would associate with instruments of chemical warfare * * *. [N]o speaker in natural parlance would describe Bond's feud-driven act of spreading irritating chemicals on Haynes's door knob and mailbox as "combat." Nor do the other circumstances of Bond's offense—an act of revenge born of romantic jealousy, meant to cause discomfort, that produced nothing more than a minor thumb burn—suggest that a chemical weapon was deployed in Norristown, Pennsylvania. Potassium dichromate and 10-chloro-10H-phenoxarsine might be chemical weapons if used, say, to poison a city's water supply. But Bond's crime is worlds apart from such hypotheticals, and covering it would give the statute a reach exceeding the ordinary meaning of the words Congress wrote.

* * *

The Government's reading of section 229 would " 'alter sensitive federal-state relationships,' " convert an astonishing amount of "traditionally local criminal conduct" into "a matter for federal enforcement," and "involve a substantial extension of federal police resources." *Bass*, 404 U.S., at 349–350 * * *. But the background principle that Congress does not normally intrude upon the police power of the States is critically important. In light of that principle, we are reluctant to conclude that Congress meant to punish Bond's crime with a federal prosecution for a chemical weapons attack.

* * *

In sum, the global need to prevent chemical warfare does not require the Federal Government to reach into the kitchen cupboard, or to treat a local assault with a chemical irritant as the deployment of a chemical weapon. There is no reason to suppose that Congress—in implementing the Convention on Chemical Weapons—thought otherwise.

* * *

The judgment of the Court of Appeals is reversed, and the case is remanded for further proceedings consistent with this opinion.

It is so ordered.

■ JUSTICE SCALIA, with whom JUSTICE THOMAS joins, and with whom JUSTICE ALITO joins as to Part I, concurring in the judgment.

Somewhere in Norristown, Pennsylvania, a husband's paramour suffered a minor thumb burn at the hands of a betrayed wife. The United States Congress—"every where extending the sphere of its activity, and drawing all power into its impetuous vortex"—has made a federal case out of it. What are we to do?

It is the responsibility of "the legislature, not the Court, . . . to define a crime, and ordain its punishment." And it is "emphatically the province and duty of the judicial department to say what the law [including the Constitution] is." *Marbury v. Madison*, 1 Cranch 137, 177 (1803) (same). Today, the Court shirks its job and performs Congress's. As sweeping and unsettling as the Chemical Weapons Convention Implementation Act of 1998 may be, it is clear beyond doubt that it covers what Bond did; and we have no authority to amend it. So we are forced to decide—there is no way around it—whether the Act's application to what Bond did was constitutional.

I would hold that it was not, and for that reason would reverse the judgment of the Court of Appeals for the Third Circuit.

I. The Statutory Question

The meaning of the Act is plain * * *.

Applying those provisions to this case is hardly complicated. Bond possessed and used "chemical[s] which through [their] chemical action on life processes can cause death, temporary incapacitation or permanent harm." Thus, she possessed "toxic chemicals." And, because they were not possessed or used only for a "purpose not prohibited," § 229F(1)(A), they were "chemical weapons." Ergo, Bond violated the Act. End of statutory analysis, I would have thought.

The Court does not think the interpretive exercise so simple. But that is only because its result-driven antitextualism befogs what is evident.

The Court's account of the clear-statement rule reads like a really good lawyer's brief for the wrong side, relying on cases that are *so close* to being on point that someone eager to reach the favored outcome might swallow them * * *.

* * *

* * * Just ponder what the Court says: "[The Act's] ambiguity *derives* from the improbably broad reach of the key statutory definition . . . the deeply serious consequences of adopting such a boundless reading; and the lack of any apparent need to do so. . . ." *Ibid.* (emphasis added). Imagine what future courts can do with that judge-empowering principle: Whatever has improbably broad, deeply serious, and apparently unnecessary consequences . . . is *ambiguous*!

* * *

But even text clear on its face, the Court suggests, must be read against the backdrop of established interpretive presumptions. Thus, we presume "that a criminal statute derived from the common law carries with it the requirement of a culpable mental state—even if no such limitation appears in the text." And we presume that "federal statutes do not apply outside the United States." Both of those are, indeed, established interpretive presumptions that are (1) based upon realistic assessments of congressional intent, and (2) well known to Congress—thus furthering rather than subverting genuine legislative intent. To apply these presumptions, then, is not to rewrite clear text; it is to interpret words fairly, in light of their statutory context. But there is nothing either (1) realistic or (2) well known about the presumption the Court shoves down the throat of a resisting statute today. Who in the world would have thought that a definition is inoperative if it contradicts ordinary meaning? When this statute was enacted, there was not yet a "*Bond* presumption" to that effect—though presumably Congress will have to take account of the *Bond* presumption in the future, perhaps by adding at the end of all its definitions that depart from ordinary connotation "and we really mean it."

* * *

II. The Constitutional Question

Since the Act is clear, the *real* question this case presents is whether the Act is constitutional as applied to petitioner. An unreasoned and citation-less sentence from our opinion in *Missouri v. Holland*, 252 U.S. 416 (1920), purported to furnish the answer: "If the treaty is valid"—and no one argues that the Convention is not—"there can be no dispute about the validity of the statute under Article I, § 8, as a necessary and proper means to execute the powers of the Government." *Id.*, at 432. Petitioner and her *amici* press us to consider whether there is anything to this *ipse dixit*. The Constitution's text and structure show that there is not.

Under Article I, § 8, cl. 18, Congress has the power "[t]o make all Laws which shall be necessary and proper for carrying into Execution the foregoing Powers and all other Powers vested by this Constitution in the Government of the United States, or in any Department or Officer thereof." One such "other Powe[r]" appears in Article II, § 2, cl. 2: "[The President] shall have Power, by and with the Advice and Consent of the Senate, to make Treaties, provided two thirds of the Senators present concur." Read together, the two Clauses empower Congress to pass laws "necessary and proper for carrying into Execution . . . [the] Power . . . to make Treaties."

It is obvious what the Clauses, read together, do *not* say. They do not authorize Congress to enact laws for carrying into execution "Treaties," even treaties that do not execute themselves, such as the Chemical Weapons Convention. Surely it makes sense, the Government contends, that Congress would have the power to carry out the obligations to which the President and the Senate have committed the Nation. The power to "carry into Execution" the "Power . . . to make Treaties," it insists, *has* to mean the power to execute the treaties themselves.

That argument, which makes no pretense of resting on text, unsurprisingly misconstrues it. Start with the phrase "to make Treaties." A treaty is a contract with a foreign nation *made*, the Constitution states, by the President with the concurrence of "two thirds of the Senators present." That is true of self-executing and non-self-executing treaties alike; the Constitution does not distinguish between the two. So, because the President and the Senate can enter into a non-self-executing compact with a foreign nation but can never by themselves (without the House) give that compact domestic effect through legislation, the power of the President and the Senate "to make" a Treaty cannot possibly mean to "enter into a compact with a foreign nation and then give that compact domestic legal effect." We have said in another context that a right "to make contracts" (a treaty, of course, is a contract) does not "extend . . . to conduct . . . *after* the contract relation has been established. . . . Such *postformation* conduct does not involve the right to make a contract, but rather implicates the *performance* of established contract obligations." *Patterson v. McLean Credit Union*, 491 U.S. 164, 177 (1989) (emphasis added). Upon the President's agreement and the Senate's ratification, a treaty—no matter what kind—has been *made* and is not susceptible of any more making.

How might Congress have helped "carr[y]" the power to make the treaty—here, the Chemical Weapons Convention—"into Execution"? In any number of ways. It could have appropriated money for hiring treaty negotiators, empowered the Department of State to appoint those negotiators, formed a commission to study the benefits and risks of entering into the agreement, or paid for a bevy of spies to monitor the treaty-related deliberations of other potential signatories. See G. Lawson & G. Seidman, The Constitution of Empire: Territorial Expansion and American Legal History 63 (2004). The Necessary and Proper Clause interacts similarly with other Article II powers: "[W]ith respect to the executive branch, the Clause would allow Congress to institute an agency to help the President wisely employ his pardoning power. . . . Most important, the Clause allows Congress to establish officers to assist the President in exercising his 'executive Power.'" Calabresi & Prakash, The President's Power to Execute the Laws, 104 Yale L.J. 541, 591 (1994).

But a power to help the President *make* treaties is not a power to *implement* treaties already made. See generally Rosenkranz, Executing the Treaty Power, 118 Harv. L. Rev. 1867 (2005). Once a treaty has been made, Congress's power to do what is "necessary and proper" to assist the making of treaties drops out of the picture. To legislate compliance with the United States' treaty obligations, Congress must rely upon its independent (though quite robust) Article I, § 8, powers.

"[T]he Constitutio[n] confer[s] upon Congress . . . not all governmental powers, but only discrete, enumerated ones." *Printz v. United States*, 521 U.S. 898, 919 (1997). And, of course, "enumeration presupposes something not enumerated." *Gibbons v. Ogden*, 9 Wheat. 1, 195 (1824).

But in *Holland*, the proponents of unlimited congressional power found a loophole: "By negotiating a treaty and obtaining the requisite consent of the Senate, the President . . . may endow Congress with a source of legislative authority independent of the powers enumerated in Article I." L. Tribe, American Constitutional Law § 4–4, pp. 645–646 (3d ed. 2000). Though *Holland's* change to the Constitution's text appears minor (the power to carry into execution the *power to make treaties* becomes the power to carry into execution *treaties*), the change to its structure is seismic.

To see why vast expansion of congressional power is not just a remote possibility, consider two features of the modern practice of treaty making. In our Nation's early history, and extending through the time when *Holland* was written, treaties were typically bilateral, and addressed only a small range of topics relating to the obligations of each state to the other, and to citizens of the other—military neutrality, for example, or military alliance, or guarantee of most-favored-nation trade treatment. See Bradley, The Treaty Power and American Federalism, 97 Mich. L. Rev. 390, 396 (1998). But beginning in the last half of the last century, many treaties were "detailed multilateral instruments negotiated and drafted at international conferences," *ibid.*, and they sought to regulate states' treatment of their own citizens, or even "the activities of individuals and private entities," A. Chayes & A. Chayes, The New Sovereignty: Compliance with International Regulatory Agreements 14 (1995). "[O]ften vague and open-ended," such treaties "touch on almost every aspect of domestic civil, political, and cultural life." Bradley & Goldsmith, Treaties, Human Rights, and Conditional Consent, 149 U. Pa. L. Rev. 399, 400 (2000).

Consider also that, at least according to some scholars, the Treaty Clause comes with no implied subject-matter limitations. See, e.g., L. Henkin, Foreign Affairs and the United States Constitution 191, 197 (2d ed. 1996); but see Bradley, *supra*, at 433–439. on this view, "[t]he Tenth Amendment . . . does not limit the power to make treaties or other agreements," Restatement (Third) of Foreign Relations Law of the United States § 302, Comment d, p. 154 (1986), and the treaty power can be used to regulate matters of strictly domestic concern, see *id.*, at Comment c, p. 153.

If that is true, then the possibilities of what the Federal Government may accomplish, with the right treaty in hand, are endless and hardly farfetched. It could begin, as some scholars have suggested, with abrogation of this Court's constitutional rulings. For example, the holding that a statute prohibiting the carrying of firearms near schools went beyond Congress's enumerated powers, *United States v. Lopez*, 514 U.S. 549, 551 (1995), could be reversed by negotiating a treaty with Latvia providing that neither sovereign would permit the carrying of guns near schools. Similarly, Congress could reenact the invalidated part of the Violence Against Women Act of 1994 that provided a civil remedy for victims of gender-motivated violence, just so long as there were a treaty on point—and some authors think there already is, see MacKinnon, The Supreme Court, 1999 Term, Comment, 114 Harv. L. Rev. 135, 167 (2000).

But reversing some of this Court's decisions is the least of the problem. Imagine the United States' entry into an Antipolygamy Convention, which called for—and Congress enacted—legislation providing that, when a spouse of a man with more than one wife dies intestate, the surviving husband may inherit no part of the estate. Constitutional? The Federalist answers with a rhetorical question: "Suppose by some forced constructions of its authority (which indeed cannot easily be imagined) the Federal Legislature should attempt to vary the law of descent in any State; would it not be evident that . . . it had exceeded its jurisdiction and infringed upon that of the State?" The Federalist No. 33, at 206 (A. Hamilton). Yet given the Antipolygamy Convention, *Holland* would uphold it. Or imagine that, to execute a treaty, Congress enacted a statute prohibiting state inheritance taxes on real property. Constitutional? Of course not. Again, The Federalist: "Suppose . . . [Congress] should undertake to abrogate a land tax imposed by the authority of a State, would it not be equally evident that this was an invasion of that concurrent jurisdiction in respect to this species of tax which its constitution plainly supposes to exist in the State governments?" No. 33, at 206. *Holland* would uphold it. As these examples show, *Holland* places Congress only one treaty away from acquiring a general police power.

The Necessary and Proper Clause cannot bear such weight. As Chief Justice Marshall said regarding it, no "great substantive and independent power" can be "implied as incidental to other powers, or used as a means of executing them." *McCulloch v. Maryland*, 4 Wheat. 316, 411 (1819); see Baude, Rethinking the Federal Eminent Domain Power, 122 Yale L.J. 1738, 1749–1755 (2013). No law that flattens the principle of state sovereignty, whether or not "necessary," can be said to be "proper." As an old, well-known treatise put it, "it would not be a proper or constitutional exercise of the treaty-making power to provide that Congress should have a general legislative authority over a subject which has not been given it by the Constitution." 1 W. Willoughby, The Constitutional Law of the United States § 216, p. 504 (1910).

We would not give the Government's support of the *Holland* principle the time of day were we confronted with "treaty-implementing" legislation that abrogated the freedom of speech or some other constitutionally protected individual right. We proved just that in *Reid v. Covert*, 354 U.S. 1 (1957), which held that commitments made in treaties with Great Britain and Japan would not permit civilian wives of American servicemen stationed in those countries to be tried for murder by court-martial. The plurality opinion said that "no agreement with a foreign nation can confer power on the Congress, or on any other branch of Government, which is free from the restraints of the Constitution." *Id.*, at 16.

To be sure, the *Reid* plurality purported to distinguish the *ipse dixit* of *Holland* with its own unsupported *ipse dixit*. "[T]he people and the States," it said, "have delegated [the treaty] power to the National Government [so] the Tenth Amendment is no barrier." 354 U.S., at 18. The opinion does not say why (and there is no reason why) only the Tenth Amendment, and not the other nine, has been "delegated" away by the treaty power. The distinction between provisions protecting individual liberty, on the one hand, and "structural" provisions, on the other, cannot be the explanation, since structure in general—and especially the structure of limited federal powers—is *designed* to protect individual liberty * * *.

The Government raises a functionalist objection: If the Constitution does not limit a *self-executing treaty* to the subject matter delineated in Article I, § 8, then it makes no sense to impose that limitation upon a statute implementing a *non-self-executing treaty*. See Tr. of Oral Arg. 32–33. The premise of the objection (that the power to make self-executing treaties is limitless) is, to say the least, arguable. But even if it is correct, refusing to extend that proposition to non-self-executing treaties makes a great deal of sense. Suppose, for example, that the self-aggrandizing Federal Government wishes to take over the law of intestacy. If the President and the Senate find in some foreign state a ready accomplice, they have two options. First, they can enter into a treaty with "stipulations" specific enough that they "require no legislation to make them operative," *Whitney v. Robertson*, 124 U.S. 190, 194 (1888), which would mean in this example something like a comprehensive probate code. But for that to succeed, the President and a supermajority of the Senate would need to reach agreement on all the details—which, when once embodied in the treaty, could not be altered or superseded by ordinary legislation. The second option—far the better one—is for Congress to gain lasting and flexible control over the law of intestacy by means of a non-self-executing treaty. "[Implementing] legislation is as much subject to modification and repeal by Congress as legislation upon any other subject." *Ibid.* And to make such a treaty, the President and Senate would need to agree only that they desire power over the law of intestacy.

* * *

We have here a supposedly "narrow" opinion which, in order to be "narrow," sets forth interpretive principles never before imagined that will bedevil our jurisprudence (and proliferate litigation) for years to come. The immediate product of these interpretive novelties is a statute that should be the envy of every lawmaker bent on trapping the unwary with vague and uncertain criminal prohibitions. All this to leave in place an ill-considered *ipse dixit* that enables the fundamental constitutional principle of limited federal powers to be set aside by the President and Senate's exercise of the treaty power. We should not have shirked our duty and distorted the law to preserve that assertion; we should have welcomed and eagerly grasped the opportunity—nay, the obligation—to consider and repudiate it.

■ JUSTICE THOMAS, with whom JUSTICE SCALIA joins, and with whom JUSTICE ALITO joins as to Parts I, II, and III, concurring in the judgment.

By its clear terms, the statute at issue in this case regulates local criminal conduct that is subject to the powers reserved to the States. That aggrandizement of federal power cannot be justified as a "necessary and proper" means of implementing a treaty addressing similar subject matter. To the contrary, reading the Necessary and Proper Clause to expand Congress' power upon the ratification of every new treaty defies an indisputable first principle of our constitutional order: " '[T]he Constitution created a Federal Government of limited powers.' " *New York v. United States*, 505 U.S. 144, 155 (1992). I accordingly join JUSTICE SCALIA'S opinion in full.

I write separately to suggest that the Treaty Power is itself a limited federal power * * *.

* * * [T]o interpret the Treaty Power as extending to every conceivable domestic subject matter—even matters without any nexus to foreign relations—would destroy the basic constitutional distinction between domestic and foreign powers. It would also lodge in the Federal Government the potential for "a 'police power' over all aspects of American life." * * *

I doubt the Treaty Power creates such a gaping loophole in our constitutional structure. Although the parties have not challenged the constitutionality of the particular treaty at issue here, in an appropriate case I believe the Court should address the scope of the Treaty Power as it was originally understood. Today, it is enough to highlight some of the structural and historical evidence suggesting that the Treaty Power can be used to arrange intercourse with other nations, but not to regulate purely domestic affairs.

The Treaty Power was not drafted on a blank slate. To the contrary, centuries of experience—reflected in treatises, dictionaries, and actual practice—shaped the contours of that power.

Early treatises discussed a wide variety of treaties that nevertheless shared a common thread: All of them governed genuinely international matters such as war, peace, and trade between nations.

Founding-era dictionaries reflect a similar understanding * * *.

Treaty practice under the Articles of Confederation was also consistent with the understanding that treaties govern matters of international intercourse * * *.

* * * Preconstitutional practice therefore reflects the use of the treaty-making power only for matters of international intercourse; that practice provides no support for using treaties to regulate purely domestic affairs.

Debates preceding the ratification of the proposed Constitution confirm the limited scope of the powers possessed by the Federal Government generally; the Treaty Power was no exception. The Framers understood that most regulatory matters were to be left to the States * * *. Consistent with that general understanding of limited federal power, evidence from the ratification campaign suggests that the Treaty Power was limited and, in particular, confined to matters of intercourse with other nations.

* * *

It did not escape the attention of the Framers that the Treaty Power was drafted without explicitly enumerated limits on what sorts of treaties are permissible. The Articles of Confederation had, for example, explicitly restricted certain categories of treaties. See Art. IX ("[N]o treaty of commerce shall be made whereby the legislative power of the respective States shall be restrained from imposing such imposts and duties on foreigners, as their own people are subjected to, or from prohibiting the exportation or importation of any species of goods or commodities whatsoever"). The Constitution omitted those restrictions.

That decision was not a grant of unlimited power, but rather a grant of flexibility; the Federal Government needed the ability to respond to unforeseeable varieties of intercourse with other nations. James Madison, for example, did "not think it possible to enumerate all the cases in which such external regulations would be necessary." 3 Elliot's Debates 514; *see also id.*, at 363 (E. Randolph) ("The various contingencies which may form the object of treaties, are, in the nature of things, incapable of definition"). But Madison nevertheless recognized that any exercise of the Treaty Power "must be consistent with the object of the delegation," which is "the regulation of intercourse with foreign nations." *Id.*, at 514. That understanding of the Treaty Power did not permit the President and the Senate to exercise domestic authority commensurate with their substantial power over external affairs.

The understanding that treaties are limited to, in Madison's words, "the regulation of intercourse with foreign nations," endured in the years after the Constitution was ratified.

* * *

The postratification theory and practice of treaty-making accordingly confirms the understanding that treaties by their nature relate to intercourse with other nations (including their people and property), rather than to purely domestic affairs.

The original understanding that the Treaty Power was limited to international intercourse has been well represented in this Court's precedents * * *.

* * *

Whatever its other defects, *Missouri v. Holland*, 252 U.S. 416 (1920), is consistent with that view. There, the Court addressed the constitutionality of a treaty that regulated the capture of birds that migrated between Canada and the United States. Convention with Great Britain for the Protection of Migratory Birds, Aug. 16, 1916, 39 Stat. 1702, T.S. No. 628. Although the Court upheld a statute implementing that treaty based on an improperly broad view of the Necessary and Proper Clause, *Holland* did not conclude that the Treaty Power itself was unlimited. To the contrary, the holding in *Holland* is consistent with the understanding that treaties are limited to matters of international intercourse. The Court observed that the treaty at issue addressed *migratory* birds that were "only transitorily within the State and ha[d] no permanent habitat therein." *Id.*, at 435; see also id., at 434 ("[T]he treaty deals with creatures that [only] for the moment are within the state borders"). As such, the birds were naturally a matter of international intercourse because they were creatures in international transit.

At least until recently, the original understanding that the Treaty Power is limited was widely shared outside the Court as well * * *. Only in the latter part of the past century have treaties challenged that prevailing conception by addressing "matters that in the past countries would have addressed wholly domestically" and "purport[ing] to regulate the relationship between nations and their own citizens * * *.

* * *

In an appropriate case, I would draw a line that respects the original understanding of the Treaty Power. I acknowledge that the distinction between matters of international intercourse and matters of purely domestic regulation may not be obvious in all cases. But this Court has long recognized that the Treaty Power is limited, and hypothetical difficulties in line-drawing are no reason to ignore a constitutional limit on federal power.

The parties in this case have not addressed the proper scope of the Treaty Power or the validity of the treaty here. The preservation of limits on the Treaty Power is nevertheless a matter of fundamental constitutional importance, and the Court ought to address the scope of the Treaty Power when that issue is presented. Given the increasing frequency with which treaties have begun to test the limits of the Treaty Power, that chance will come soon enough.

■ JUSTICE ALITO, concurring in the judgment. [Omitted].

NOTES AND QUESTIONS

1. Textually, Justice Scalia seems right at first glance. The Necessary and Proper Clause authorizes laws "for carrying into Execution the foregoing *Powers,* and all other *Powers* vested by this Constitution." The clause does not seem to authorize laws for carrying into execution the *objects of exercise* of those powers rather than the powers themselves. *See* Nicholas Quinn Rosenkranz, *Executing the Treaty Power,* 118 HARV. L. REV. 1867 (2005). Thus, if Justice Scalia is correct, any treaty that is not self-executing can only be implemented, once the treaty is finalized, if Congress can pass the needed laws using some enumerated powers other than the Necessary and Proper Clause. But there is nothing that limits such an understanding of the Necessary and Proper Clause to implementation of the treaty power. If Justice Scalia is correct in *Bond,* does it mean that Congress cannot use the Necessary and Proper Clause to, for example, regulate intrastate commerce as a means for making its regulation of interstate commerce—the objects of exercise of the commerce power—more effective? That it can authorize spending laws, administrative personnel to enforce the laws, penalties for violation of laws, and the like, and that is all? The case law, as you have seen, clearly says otherwise; it allows Congress to pass at least some laws that make the exercises of its enumerated powers more effective. Does that foreclose Justice Scalia's position in the context of "carrying into Execution" the President and Senate's power under the Treaty Clause?

2. But, to take it one step further, don't even laws providing for spending, administrative personnel, and civil and criminal penalties also "carry[ ] into Execution" the objects of exercise of powers rather than the literal powers themselves? Actually, as a textual matter, those laws "carry[ ] into Execution" *the executive power*. Once statutes are enacted, the President has the "executive Power" to put them into effect. Spending, personnel, and penalty laws thus carry into effect that presidential enforcement power (and the accompanying judicial power of adjudication), not the literal congressional power to enact the statutes. The "executive Power" includes the power to execute treaties as well as statutes (though the duty in the Take Care Clause does not, by its terms, apply to treaties), so, on this reasoning, Congress can authorize spending, personnel, and penalty laws for carrying treaties into execution in the same way that it can authorize such laws for statutes. Since *Bond* involved a penalty statute, would this argument validate the statute in that case?

3. Perhaps, however, Justice Scalia was focusing on the wrong question. The Necessary and Proper Clause is an incidental-powers clause. Isn't the real question therefore what is incidental to the treaty power? If Congress, in implementing a treaty, tried to exercise a "great substantive and independent power," it would exceed its powers. (And if the President and Senate negotiate and enact a treaty that purports to require Congress to exercise a "great substantive and independent power," they will have exceeded their authority.) Passing penalty statutes is not such a forbidden power, but

regulating subjects outside the enumerated powers of Congress, such as local crimes, most certainly is. How would that play out in *Bond,* in which the penalties were for purely local intrastate crimes? Was Justice Scalia right for the wrong reasons?

4. Re-read *Holland*—it will not take very long. Justice Holmes writes about the Treaty Clause in the spirit of the Virginia and Bedford Resolutions: Some institution of the national government *must* have power to solve all national problems, so the Treaty Clause *must* authorize all manner of treaties that affect the national interest and Congress *must* have the power to make those agreements fully effective. Is the debate in *Bond* (and *Holland)* therefore yet another iteration of the basic question whether the Constitution's purposes define its powers or its powers define its purposes?

5. Justice Thomas suggests that treaties must pertain to "international" matters. What does that mean? Justice Thomas's target is clearly "human rights" treaties that purport to require signatory nations to conduct their domestic internal affairs in certain ways. Does the eighteenth-century understanding of a "treaty" really contain this limitation on subject matter? An alternative path to a similar result comes from Thomas Jefferson's view of treaties as means to implement in the international arena other enumerated powers. On this view, treaties can only carry into effect other governmental powers, such as the powers of war and peace or the power to regulate foreign commerce, *see* Gary Lawson & Guy Seidman, *The Jeffersonian Treaty Clause,* 2006 U. ILL. L. REV. 1; and the Treaty Clause is thus analogous to the Necessary and Proper Clause, in that its exercise depends on its link to some other power. No justice has yet advanced this Jeffersonian position.

6. If justices who lean towards originalism have doubts about *Holland,* and if the number of justices who lean towards originalism on the Court continues to increase, is *Holland* a candidate for overruling?

7. Has *Holland* already been overruled? At least two prominent scholars, who are strong defenders of *Holland,* think that *Bond* overruled it sub silentio by not treating the validity of the treaty, which everyone conceded, as sufficient to insulate the statute implementing the treaty from federalism-based attacks. *See* Michael J. Glennon & Robert D. Sloane, *The Sad, Quiet Death of* Missouri v. Holland: *How* Bond *Hobbled the Treaty Power,* 41 YALE J. INT'L L. 51 (2016).

[Assignment 41]

XV. POWER TO ENFORCE THE RECONSTRUCTION AMENDMENTS

Amend. XIII, Section 2: Congress shall have power to enforce this article [which bans slavery] by appropriate legislation.

Amend. XIV, Section 5: The Congress shall have power to enforce, by appropriate legislation, the provisions of this article [which forbid States from abridging the privileges or immunities of citizens, denying any person the equal protection of the laws, or depriving any person of life, liberty, or property without due process of law].

Amend. XV, Section 2: Congress shall have power to enforce this article [which forbids discrimination in voting on account of race, color, or previous condition of servitude] by appropriate legislation.

There are some important congressional powers in Articles IV and V of the Constitution of 1788, and we will get to those powers shortly. But on the heels of discussion of the Necessary and Proper Clause and the Treaty Clause—two provisions that are in their nature implementational of other governmental powers—it seems appropriate to consider some congressional powers that were added to the Constitution in the 1860s and 1870s and that share this implementational character. They are among the most important powers in the Constitution of 2020, and they require some background.

The original Constitution contains very few direct restrictions on the States. That had to change after the Civil War.

Most obviously, slavery had to be formally abolished. This was accomplished in 1865 through the Thirteenth Amendment: "**Neither slavery nor involuntary servitude, except as punishment for a crime whereof the party shall have been duly convicted, shall exist within the United States, or any place subject to their jurisdiction.**" U.S. CONST. amend. XIII, § 1.

But that was only a first step. It was not enough to abolish slavery if the rebel States had laws saying that only white people could own property, make contracts, work in any occupations other than manual labor, testify in court, or exercise the other ordinary rights of civil society; or if the State's law enforcement machinery would not enforce laws evenhandedly. Accordingly, in 1868, the Fourteenth Amendment added:

> **All persons born or naturalized in the United States and subject to the jurisdiction thereof, are citizens of the United States and of the State wherein they reside. No State shall make or enforce any law which shall abridge the privileges or immunities of citizens of the United States; nor shall any State deprive any person of life, liberty, or property, without due process of law; nor deny to any person within its jurisdiction the equal protection of the laws.**

Id. amend. XIV, § 1. We will explore the meaning of this provision in a subsequent chapter.

Finally, the subject of voter qualifications had been traditionally left to the States; under the Constitution, the congressional electorate is defined as the electorate for the most numerous branch of the State legislature. *See id.* art. I, § 2, cl. 1. The rebel States were obviously not going to let freed slaves vote. The Fourteenth Amendment initially addressed this by leaving voter qualifications entirely to the States but reducing a State's representation in Congress and the electoral college to the extent that "the right to vote * * * is denied to any of the male inhabitants of such State, being twenty-one years of age, and citizens of the United States * * *." *Id.* amend. XIV, § 2. States could thus discriminate on the basis of race in voting rights, but they would pay in price in lost representation in the national government. Two years later, when it became clear that the Fourteenth Amendment solution was inadequate, the Fifteenth Amendment flatly declared: **"The right of citizens of the United States to vote shall not be denied or abridged by the United States or by any State on account of race, color, or previous condition of servitude."** *Id.* amend. XV, § 1.

How would the principles of these amendments be translated into concrete action? Congress during this time was engaged in the massive project of Reconstruction, in which governmental and social institutions needed to be re-crafted to mitigate the effects of generations of slavery. It was natural that Congress would assume the key role in enforcing the provisions of the Reconstruction Amendments. Accordingly, each of the Thirteenth, Fourteenth, and Fifteenth Amendments concluded with a provision specifically giving Congress a new enumerated power to enforce those provisions:

> **Congress shall have power to enforce this article by appropriate legislation.** *Id.* amend. XIII, § 2.
>
> **The Congress shall have power to enforce, by appropriate legislation, the provisions of this article.** *Id.* amend. XIV, § 5.
>
> **The Congress shall have power to enforce this article by appropriate legislation.** *Id.* amend. XV, § 2.

The key phrase in each provision is "appropriate legislation."

Of course, it is impossible to determine the scope of "appropriate legislation" without knowing for what it is appropriate. The enforcement provisions of the Reconstruction Amendments are *enforcement* provisions, so to know the scope of Congress's power, one must have some idea what the substantive terms of the Reconstruction Amendments forbid. That large topic merits, and receives, its own chapter in this book. For present purposes, the following will have to do:

The three Reconstruction constitutional amendments were, in essence, a new Constitution because they so sweepingly repudiated original constitutional provisions. The Thirteenth Amendment abolished slavery or indentured servitude, whether state-sponsored or private, throughout the United States. As we will soon see, it is not as obvious as one might think what counts as "slavery." The Fourteenth Amendment, we believe, abolished all systems of caste in the United States—and possibly created a presumption of liberty that could only be overcome by the States when they justly prescribed laws enacted for the general good of the whole people. This is, to say the very least, not an uncontroversial summary of Section 1 of the Fourteenth Amendment, and you may come to a very different view of the meaning of that provision when you encounter materials on it later (indeed, one of us has doubts about the "presumption of liberty" part), but we will take it as a working hypothesis for the moment. The Fifteenth Amendment is more straightforward: It bans racial discrimination in all federal and state elections.

All three Reconstruction Amendments are enforceable by citizens brining litigation in court—they are "self-executing," in the lingo of the Treaty Clause—but they are all also enforceable by Congress when it enacts "appropriate" legislation to enforce them. The language of the Reconstruction Amendment enforcement provisions is different from the language of the Necessary and Proper Clause. That difference was deliberate.

The text of the Thirteenth Amendment, including the "appropriate legislation" language in Section 2, originated in 1864 with the Senate Committee on the Judiciary. *See* CONG. GLOBE, 38th Cong., 1st Sess. 1313 (1864). Senator Charles Sumner proposed importing "necessary and proper" language into the Thirteenth Amendment, *see id.* at 1482–83, 1487–88, but these proposals went nowhere. In the House, by contrast, John Bingham's original draft of the Fourteenth Amendment directly tracked the language of the Necessary and Proper Clause, *see* CONG. GLOBE, 39th Cong., 1st Sess. 1034 (1866), but the Joint Committee on Reconstruction's subsequent draft, which ultimately became the Fourteenth Amendment, instead substituted the phrase "appropriate legislation." *See id.* at 2286 (statement of Representative Stevens). The term "appropriate" was clearly drawn from Chief Justice Marshall's opinion in *McCulloch v. Maryland.* In the 1866 debates on the Civil Rights Act, Representative Wilson copiously cited *McCulloch* as an authoritative exposition of the meaning of Section 2 of the Thirteenth Amendment. *See* CONG. GLOBE, 39th Cong., 1st Sess. 1118 (1866). In subsequent debates on civil rights legislation, Senator Thurman flatly said of Section 5 of the Fourteenth Amendment: "What is meant by this term 'appropriate legislation?' We know where the term comes from. We know it comes from an opinion of Chief Justice Marshall, and was applied by him simply to the old provision of the Constitution that Congress has power to make all laws necessary and proper for carrying into effect the foregoing powers." CONG. GLOBE, 41st Cong., 2d Sess. 602 (1870); *see also id.* at 3663 (statement of Senator Thurman similarly tracing the origin of Section 2 of the Fifteenth Amendment). Representative Shellabarger and Willard also identified Section 5 of the Fourteenth Amendment with the Necessary and Proper Clause. *See* CONG. GLOBE, 42d Cong., 1st Sess.app. 71 (1871) (statement of Representatives Shellabarger); *id.* at 189 (statement of Representative Willard). But when the Reconstruction Congress talked about the Necessary and Proper Clause, it was talking about the Necessary and Proper Clause *as they understood it to have been construed in McCulloch. v. Maryland,* not as it might have been originally understood in 1788 (or even necessarily as it was *actually* construed in *McCulloch*). For the Reconstruction Congress, the bare word "appropriate" (with no accompanying requirement that enforcement laws be "proper") called to mind the sweeping Hamiltonian account of the Necessary and Proper Clause, so that any enforcement legislation that was merely "convenient" or "useful" under the Hamiltonian interpretation of Chief Justice John Marshall's opinion in *McCulloch v. Maryland* was authorized by the Reconstruction Amendments. That makes a great deal of sense; the kinds of federalism restrictions on Congress that were part of the common background in 1788 were wholly unsuited to the circumstances of 1865–1870 and were very unlikely to be in the forefront of the minds of a Reconstruction Congress. Thus, while we think the test in *McCulloch* is too lenient with respect to the Necessary and Proper Clause, where the Supreme Court should insist that federal laws be tightly connected to, and proper for carrying into execution, a federal power, we think that that federal laws enforcing the three Reconstruction Amendments need only be "convenient" or "useful" to enforcing those Amendments. As you will see, case law does not reflect our view of the Reconstruction Amendments any more than it (yet?) reflects our view of the Necessary and Proper Clause.

We reproduce below five major U.S. Supreme Court decisions below on the scope of the enforcement provisions of the Reconstruction Amendments, four of them striking down as unconstitutional a major congressional civil rights statute. While, as we have noted, it is impossible to assess the scope of the enforcement provisions without knowing what they are enforcing, we think there is enough in these cases to let you make up your own minds about whether the Court has correctly understood the power given to Congress after the Civil War. As you may have guessed, we are skeptical. We begin in 1883.

A. THE CIVIL RIGHTS CASES

109 U.S. 3 (1883)

These cases are all founded on the first and second sections of the Act of Congress, known as the Civil Rights Act, passed March 1, 1875, entitled "An Act to protect all citizens in their civil and legal rights." 18 St. 335. Two of the cases, those against Stanley and Nichols, were indictments for denying to persons of color the accommodations and privileges of an inn or hotel; two of them, those against Ryan and Singleton, were, one on information, the other an indictment, for denying to individuals the privileges and accommodations of a theatre, the information against Ryan being for refusing a colored person a seat in the dress circle of Maguire's theatre in San Francisco; and the indictment against Singleton was for denying to another person, whose color is not stated, the full enjoyment of the accommodations of the theatre known as the Grand Opera House in New York, "said denial not being made for any reasons by law applicable to citizens of every race and color, and regardless of any previous condition of servitude." * * *.

■ MR. JUSTICE BRADLEY delivered the opinion of the court.

It is obvious that the primary and important question in all the cases is the constitutionality of the law: for if the law is unconstitutional none of the prosecutions can stand.

The [relevant] sections of the law * * * provide as follows:

"SEC. 1. That all persons within the jurisdiction of the United States shall be entitled to the full and equal enjoyment of the accommodations, advantages, facilities, and privileges of inns, public conveyances on land or water, theatres, and other places of public amusement; subject only to the conditions and limitations established by law, and applicable alike to citizens of every race and color, regardless of any previous condition of servitude.

"SEC. 2. That any person who shall violate the foregoing section * * * shall for every such offence forfeit and pay the sum of five hundred dollars to the person aggrieved thereby, to be recovered in an action of debt, with full costs; and shall also, for every such offence, be deemed guilty of a misdemeanor, and, upon conviction thereof, shall be fined not less than five hundred nor more than one thousand dollars, or shall be imprisoned not less than thirty days nor more than one year * * *."

Are these sections constitutional? The first section, which is the principal one, cannot be fairly understood without attending to the last clause, which qualifies the preceding part.

The essence of the law is, not to declare broadly that all persons shall be entitled to the full and equal enjoyment of the accommodations, advantages, facilities, and privileges of inns, public conveyances, and theatres; but that such enjoyment shall not be subject to any conditions applicable only to citizens of a particular race or color, or who had been in a previous condition of servitude. In other words, it is the purpose of the law to declare that, in the enjoyment of the accommodations and privileges of inns, public conveyances, theatres, and other places of public amusement, no distinction shall be made between citizens of different race or color, or between those who have, and those who have not, been slaves * * *.

Has Congress constitutional power to make such a law? Of course, no one will contend that the power to pass it was contained in the Constitution before the adoption of the last three amendments. The power is sought, first, in the Fourteenth Amendment, and the views and arguments of distinguished Senators, advanced whilst the law was under consideration, claiming authority to pass it by virtue of that amendment, are the principal arguments adduced in favor of the power. We have carefully considered those arguments, as was due to the eminent ability of those who put them forward, and have felt, in all its force, the weight of authority which always invests a law that Congress deems itself competent to pass. But the responsibility of an independent judgment is now thrown upon this court; and we are bound to exercise it according to the best lights we have.

The first section of the Fourteenth Amendment (which is the one relied on), after declaring who shall be citizens of the United States, and of the several States, is prohibitory in its character, and prohibitory upon the States. It declares that:

"No State shall make or enforce any law which shall abridge the privileges or immunities of citizens of the United States; nor shall any State deprive any person of life, liberty, or property without due process of law; nor deny to any person within its jurisdiction the equal protection of the laws."

It is State action of a particular character that is prohibited. Individual invasion of individual rights is not the subject-matter of the amendment. It has a deeper and broader scope. It nullifies and makes void all State legislation, and State action of every kind, which impairs the privileges and immunities of citizens of the United States, or which injures them in life, liberty or property without due process of law, or which denies to any of them the equal protection of the laws. It not only does this, but, in order that the national will, thus declared, may not be a mere *brutum fulmen,* the last section of the amendment invests Congress with power to enforce it by appropriate legislation. To enforce what? To enforce the prohibition. To adopt appropriate legislation for correcting the effects of such prohibited State laws and State acts, and thus to render them effectually null, void, and innocuous. This is the legislative power conferred upon Congress, and this is the whole of it. It does not invest Congress with power to legislate upon subjects which are within the domain of State legislation; but to provide modes of relief against State legislation, or State action, of the kind referred to. It does not authorize Congress to create a code of municipal law for the regulation of private rights; but to provide modes of redress against the operation of State laws, and the action of State officers executive or judicial, when these are subversive of the fundamental rights specified in the amendment. Positive rights and privileges are undoubtedly secured by the Fourteenth Amendment; but they are secured by way of prohibition against State laws and State proceedings affecting those rights and privileges, and by power given to Congress to legislate for the purpose of carrying such prohibition into effect; and such legislation must necessarily be predicated upon such supposed State laws or State proceedings, and be directed to the correction of their operation and effect. A quite full discussion of this aspect of the amendment may be found in *U.S. v. Cruikshank,* 92 U. S. 542; *Virginia v. Rives*, 100 U. S. 313, and I, 100 U.S. 339.

* * *

* * *[U]ntil some State law has been passed, or some State action through its officers or agents has been taken, adverse to the rights of citizens sought to be

protected by the Fourteenth Amendment, no legislation of the United States under said amendment, nor any proceeding under such legislation, can be called into activity: for the prohibitions of the amendment are against State laws and acts done under State authority. Of course, legislation may, and should, be provided in advance to meet the exigency when it arises; but it should be adapted to the mischief and wrong which the amendment was intended to provide against; and that is, State laws, or State action of some kind, adverse to the rights of the citizen secured by the amendment. Such legislation cannot properly cover the whole domain of rights appertaining to life, liberty and property, defining them and providing for their vindication. That would be to establish a code of municipal law regulative of all private rights between man and man in society. It would be to make Congress take the place of the State legislatures and to supersede them * * * In fine, the legislation which Congress is authorized to adopt in this behalf is not general legislation upon the rights of the citizen, but corrective legislation, that is, such as may be necessary and proper for counteracting such laws as the States may adopt or enforce, and which, by the amendment, they are prohibited from making or enforcing * * *,

An inspection of the law shows that it makes no reference whatever to any supposed or apprehended violation of the Fourteenth Amendment on the part of the States. It is not predicated on any such view. It proceeds *ex directo* to declare that certain acts committed by individuals shall be deemed offences, and shall be prosecuted and punished by proceedings in the courts of the United States. It does not profess to be corrective of any constitutional wrong committed by the States; it does not make its operation to depend upon any such wrong committed. It applies equally to cases arising in States which have the justest laws respecting the personal rights of citizens, and whose authorities are ever ready to enforce such laws, as to those which arise in States that may have violated the prohibition of the amendment. In other words, it steps into the domain of local jurisprudence, and lays down rules for the conduct of individuals in society towards each other, and imposes sanctions for the enforcement of those rules, without referring in any manner to any supposed action of the State or its authorities.

If this legislation is appropriate for enforcing the prohibitions of the amendment, it is difficult to see where it is to stop. Why may not Congress, with equal show of authority, enact a code of laws for the enforcement and vindication of all rights of life, liberty, and property? * * * The assumption is certainly unsound. It is repugnant to the Tenth Amendment of the Constitution, which declares that powers not delegated to the United States by the Constitution, nor prohibited by it to the States, are reserved to the States respectively or to the people.

* * * [T]he fourth section of the act now under consideration has been held by this court to be constitutional. That section declares "that no citizen, possessing all other qualifications which are or may be prescribed by law, shall be disqualified for service as grand or petit juror in any court of the United States, or of any State, on account of race, color, or previous condition of servitude * * *." In *Ex parte Virginia*, 100 U. S. 339, it was held that an indictment against a State officer under this section for excluding persons of color from the jury list is sustainable. But a moment's attention to its terms will show that the section is entirely corrective in its character. Disqualifications for service on juries are only created by the law * * *. In the Virginia case, the State, through its officer, enforced a rule of disqualification which the law was intended to abrogate and counteract. Whether the statute book of the

State actually laid down any such rule of disqualification or not, the State, through its officer, enforced such a rule; and it is against such State action, through its officers and agents, that the last clause of the section is directed. This aspect of the law was deemed sufficient to divest it of any unconstitutional character, and makes it differ widely from the first and second sections of the same act which we are now considering.

These sections, in the objectionable features before referred to, are different also from the law ordinarily called the "Civil Rights Bill," * * * declaring that all persons within the jurisdiction of the United States shall have the same right in every State and Territory to make and enforce contracts, to sue, be parties, give evidence, and to the full and equal benefit of all laws and proceedings for the security of persons and property as is enjoyed by white citizens * * *. This law is clearly corrective in its character, intended to counteract and furnish redress against State laws and proceedings, and customs having the force of law, which sanction the wrongful acts specified * * *.

In this connection, it is proper to state that civil rights, such as are guaranteed by the Constitution against State aggression, cannot be impaired by the wrongful acts of individuals, unsupported by State authority in the shape of laws, customs, or judicial or executive proceedings. The wrongful act of an individual, unsupported by any such authority, is simply a private wrong, or a crime of that individual; an invasion of the rights of the injured party, it is true, whether they affect his person, his property, or his reputation; but if not sanctioned in some way by the State, or not done under State authority, his rights remain in full force, and may presumably be vindicated by resort to the laws of the State for redress. An individual cannot deprive a man of his right to vote, to hold property, to buy and to sell, to sue in the courts, or to be a witness or a juror; he may, by force or fraud, interfere with the enjoyment of the right in a particular case; he may commit an assault against the person, or commit murder, or use ruffian violence at the polls, or slander the good name of a fellow citizen; but, unless protected in these wrongful acts by some shield of State law or State authority, he cannot destroy or injure the right; he will only render himself amenable to satisfaction or punishment; and amenable therefor to the laws of the State where the wrongful acts are committed * * *. Th[e] abrogation and denial of rights, for which the States alone were or could be responsible, was the great seminal and fundamental wrong which was intended to be remedied. And the remedy to be provided must necessarily be predicated upon that wrong. It must assume that in the cases provided for, the evil or wrong actually committed rests upon some State law or State authority for its excuse and perpetration.

Of course, these remarks do not apply to those cases in which Congress is clothed with direct and plenary powers of legislation over the whole subject, accompanied with an express or implied denial of such power to the States, as in the regulation of commerce with foreign nations, among the several States, and with the Indian tribes, the coining of money, the establishment of post offices and post roads, the declaring of war, etc. In these cases Congress has power to pass laws for regulating the subjects specified in every detail, and the conduct and transactions of individuals in respect thereof. But where a subject is not submitted to the general legislative power of Congress, but is only submitted thereto for the purpose of rendering effective some prohibition against particular State legislation or State action in reference to that subject, the power given is limited by its object, and any legislation by Congress in the matter must necessarily be corrective in its character, adapted to counteract and redress the operation of such prohibited State laws or proceedings of State officers.

* * * [I]t is clear that the law in question cannot be sustained by any grant of legislative power made to Congress by the Fourteenth Amendment * * *. The law in question, without any reference to adverse State legislation on the subject, declares that all persons shall be entitled to equal accommodations and privileges of inns, public conveyances, and places of public amusement, and imposes a penalty upon any individual who shall deny to any citizen such equal accommodations and privileges. This is not corrective legislation; it is primary and direct; it takes immediate and absolute possession of the subject of the right of admission to inns, public conveyances, and places of amusement. It supersedes and displaces State legislation on the same subject, or only allows it permissive force. It ignores such legislation, and assumes that the matter is one that belongs to the domain of national regulation. Whether it would not have been a more effective protection of the rights of citizens to have clothed Congress with plenary power over the whole subject is not now the question. What we have to decide is whether such plenary power has been conferred upon Congress by the Fourteenth Amendment; and, in our judgment, it has not.

* * *

We have * * * discussed the validity of the law in reference to cases arising in the States only; and not in reference to cases arising in the Territories or the District of Columbia, which are subject to the plenary legislation of Congress in every branch of municipal regulation. Whether the law would be a valid one as applied to the Territories and the District is not a question for consideration in the cases before us: they all being cases arising within the limits of States. And whether Congress, in the exercise of its power to regulate commerce amongst the several States, might or might not pass a law regulating rights in public conveyances passing from one State to another, is also a question which is not now before us, as the sections in question are not conceived in any such view.

But the power of Congress to adopt direct and primary, as distinguished from corrective legislation, on the subject in hand, is sought, in the second place, from the Thirteenth Amendment, which abolishes slavery * * *.

This amendment, as well as the Fourteenth, is undoubtedly self-executing without any ancillary legislation, so far as its terms are applicable to any existing state of circumstances. By its own unaided force and effect it abolished slavery, and established universal freedom. Still, legislation may be necessary and proper to meet all the various cases and circumstances to be affected by it, and to prescribe proper modes of redress for its violation in letter or spirit. And such legislation may be primary and direct in its character; for the amendment is not a mere prohibition of State laws establishing or upholding slavery, but an absolute declaration that slavery or involuntary servitude shall not exist in any part of the United States.

It is true, that slavery cannot exist without law, any more than property in lands and goods can exist without law: and, therefore, the Thirteenth Amendment may be regarded as nullifying all State laws which establish or uphold slavery. But it has a reflex character also, establishing and decreeing universal civil and political freedom throughout the United States; and it is assumed, that the power vested in Congress to enforce the article by appropriate legislation, clothes Congress with power to pass all laws necessary and proper for abolishing all badges and incidents of slavery in the United States: and upon this assumption it is claimed, that this is sufficient authority for declaring by law that all persons shall have equal accommodations and privileges in all inns, public conveyances, and places of amusement; the argument being, that the denial of such equal accommodations and privileges is, in itself, a subjection to a species of servitude within the meaning of the amendment. Conceding the major proposition to be true, that Congress has a right to enact all necessary and proper laws for the obliteration and prevention of slavery with all its badges and incidents, is the minor proposition also true, that the denial to any person of admission to the accommodations and privileges of an inn, a public conveyance, or a theatre, does subject that person to any form of servitude, or tend to fasten upon him any badge of slavery? If it does not, then power to pass the law is not found in the Thirteenth Amendment.

* * * Should any such servitudes be imposed by a state law, there can be no doubt that the law would be repugnant to the Fourteenth, no less than to the Thirteenth Amendment; nor any greater doubt that Congress has adequate power to forbid any such servitude from being exacted.

But is there any similarity between such servitudes and a denial by the owner of an inn, a public conveyance, or a theatre, of its accommodations and privileges to an individual, even though the denial be founded on the race or color of that individual? Where does any slavery or servitude, or badge of either, arise from such an act of denial? Whether it might not be a denial of a right which, if sanctioned by the state law, would be obnoxious to the prohibitions of the Fourteenth Amendment, is another question. But what has it to do with the question of slavery?

* * *

The long existence of African slavery in this country gave us very distinct notions of what it was, and what were its necessary incidents. Compulsory service of the slave for the benefit of the master, restraint of his movements except by the master's will, disability to hold property, to make contracts, to have a standing in court, to be a witness against a white person, and such like burdens and incapacities, were the inseparable incidents of the institution * * *. Congress, as we have seen, by the Civil Rights Bill of 1866, passed in view of the Thirteenth Amendment, before the Fourteenth was adopted, undertook to wipe out these burdens and disabilities, the necessary incidents of slavery; constituting its substance and visible form; and to secure to all citizens of every race and color, and without regard to previous servitude, those fundamental rights which are the essence of civil freedom, namely, the same right to make and enforce contracts, to sue, be parties, give evidence, and to inherit, purchase, lease, sell and convey property as is enjoyed by white citizens. Whether this legislation was fully authorized by the Thirteenth Amendment alone, without the support which it afterward received from the Fourteenth Amendment, after the adoption of which it was re-enacted with some additions, it is not necessary to inquire. It is referred to for the purpose of showing that, at that time (in 1866) Congress did not assume, under the authority given by the Thirteenth Amendment, to adjust what may be called the social rights of men and races in the community; but only to declare and vindicate those fundamental rights which appertain to the essence of citizenship, and the enjoyment or deprivation of which constitutes the essential distinction between freedom and slavery.

* * *

The only question under the present head, therefore, is, whether the refusal to any persons of the accommodations of an inn, or a public conveyance, or a place of public amusement, by an individual, and without any sanction or support from any State law or regulation, does inflict upon such persons any manner of servitude, or form of slavery, as those terms are understood in this country? Many wrongs may be obnoxious to the prohibitions of the Fourteenth Amendment which are not, in any just sense, incidents or elements of slavery. Such, for example, would be the taking of private property without due process of law; or allowing persons who have committed certain crimes (horse stealing, for example) to be seized and hung by the *posse comitatus* without regular trial; or denying to any person, or class of persons, the right to pursue any peaceful avocations allowed to others. What is called class legislation would belong to this category, and would be obnoxious to the prohibitions of the Fourteenth Amendment, but would not necessarily be so to the Thirteenth, when not involving the idea of any subjection of one man to another. The Thirteenth Amendment has respect, not to distinctions of race or class or color, but to slavery. The Fourteenth Amendment extends its protection to races and classes, and prohibits any State legislation which has the effect of denying to any race or class, or to any individual, the equal protection of the laws.

Now, conceding for the sake of the argument, that the admission to an inn, a public conveyance, or a place of public amusement, on equal terms with all other citizens, is the right of every man and all classes of men, is it any more than one of those rights which the states by the Fourteenth Amendment are forbidden to deny to any person? And is the Constitution violated until the denial of the right has some State sanction or authority? Can the act of a mere individual, the owner of the inn, the public conveyance or place of amusement, refusing the accommodation, be justly regarded as imposing any badge of slavery or servitude upon the applicant, or only as inflicting an ordinary civil injury, properly cognizable by the laws of the State, and presumably subject to redress by those laws until the contrary appears?

After giving to these questions all the consideration which their importance demands, we are forced to the conclusion that such an act of refusal has nothing to do with slavery or involuntary servitude, and that if it is violative of any right of the party, his redress is to be sought under the laws of the State; or if those laws are adverse to his rights and do not protect him, his remedy will be found in the corrective legislation which Congress has adopted, or may adopt, for counteracting the effect of State laws, or State action, prohibited by the Fourteenth Amendment. It would be running the slavery argument into the ground to make it apply to every act of discrimination which a person may see fit to make as to the guests he will entertain, or as to the people he will take into his coach or cab or car, or admit to his concert or theatre, or deal with in other matters of intercourse or business. Innkeepers and public carriers, by the laws of all the States, so far as we are aware, are bound, to the extent of their facilities, to furnish proper accommodation to all unobjectionable persons who in good faith apply for them. If the laws themselves make any unjust discrimination amenable to the prohibitions of the Fourteenth Amendment, Congress has full power to afford a remedy under that amendment and in accordance with it.

When a man has emerged from slavery, and, by the aid of beneficent legislation has shaken off the inseparable concomitants of that state, there must be some stage in the progress of his elevation when he takes the rank of a mere citizen, and ceases to be the special favorite of the laws, and when his rights as a citizen, or a man, are to be protected in the ordinary modes by which other men's rights are protected. There were thousands of free colored people in this country before the abolition of slavery, enjoying all the essential rights of life, liberty and property the same as white citizens; yet no one, at that time, thought that it was any invasion of his personal status as a freeman because he was not admitted to all the privileges enjoyed by white citizens, or because he was subjected to discriminations in the enjoyment of accommodations in inns, public conveyances and places of amusement * * *.

On the whole, we are of opinion that no countenance of authority for the passage of the law in question can be found in either the Thirteenth or Fourteenth Amendment of the Constitution; and no other ground of authority for its passage being suggested, it must necessarily be declared void, at least so far as its operation in the several States is concerned.

* * *

■ MR. JUSTICE HARLAN, dissenting.

The opinion in these cases proceeds, it seems to me, upon grounds entirely too narrow and artificial. I cannot resist the conclusion that the substance and spirit of the recent amendments of the Constitution have been sacrificed by a subtle and ingenious verbal criticism. "It is not the words of the law but the internal sense of it that makes the law: the letter of the law is the body; the sense and reason of the law is the soul." Constitutional provisions, adopted in the interest of liberty and for the purpose of securing, through national legislation, if need be, rights inhering in a state of freedom and belonging to American citizenship, have been so construed as to defeat the ends the people desired to accomplish, which they attempted to accomplish, and which they supposed they had accomplished by changes in their fundamental law. By this I do not mean that the determination of these cases should have been materially controlled by considerations of mere expediency or policy. I mean only, in this form, to express an earnest conviction that the court has departed from the familiar rule requiring, in the interpretation of constitutional provisions, that full effect be given to the intent with which they were adopted.

The purpose of the first section of the act of Congress of March 1, 1875, was to prevent *race* discrimination * * *. It does not assume to define the general conditions and limitations under which inns, public conveyances, and places of public amusement may be conducted, but only declares that such conditions and limitations, whatever they may be, shall not be applied so as to work discrimination solely because of race, color, or previous condition of servitude * * *

* * *

The court adjudges, I think erroneously, that Congress is without power, under either the Thirteenth or Fourteenth Amendment, to establish such regulations, and that the first and second sections of the statute are, in all their parts, unconstitutional and void.

* * *

The Thirteenth Amendment, it is conceded, did something more than to prohibit slavery as an *institution,* resting upon distinctions of race, and upheld by positive law. My brethren admit that it established and decreed universal *civil freedom* throughout the United States. But did the freedom thus established involve nothing more than exemption from actual slavery? Was nothing more intended than to forbid one man from owning another as property? Was it the purpose of the nation simply to destroy the institution, and then remit the race, theretofore held in bondage, to the several States for such protection, in their civil rights, necessarily growing out of freedom, as those States, in their discretion, might choose to provide? Were the States against whose protest the institution was destroyed, to be left free, so far as national interference was concerned, to make or allow discriminations against that race, as such, in the enjoyment of those fundamental rights which by universal concession, inhere in a state of freedom? Had the Thirteenth Amendment stopped with the sweeping declaration, in its first section, against the existence of slavery and involuntary servitude, except for crime, Congress would have had the power, by implication, according to the doctrines of *Prigg v. Commonwealth of Pennsylvania,* repeated in *Strauder v. West Virginia,* to protect the freedom established, and consequently, to secure the enjoyment of such civil rights as were fundamental in freedom. That it can exert its authority to that extent is made clear, and was intended to be made clear, by the express grant of power contained in the second section of the Amendment.

That there are burdens and disabilities which constitute badges of slavery and servitude, and that the power to enforce by appropriate legislation the Thirteenth Amendment may be exerted by legislation of a direct and primary character, for the eradication, not simply of the institution, but of its badges and incidents, are propositions which ought to be deemed indisputable. They lie at the foundation of the Civil Rights Act of 1866. Whether that act was authorized by the Thirteenth Amendment alone, without the support which it subsequently received from the Fourteenth Amendment, after the adoption of which it was re-enacted with some additions, my brethren do not consider it necessary to inquire. But I submit, with all respect to them, that its constitutionality is conclusively shown by their opinion. * * *. I do not contend that the Thirteenth Amendment invests Congress with authority, by legislation, to define and regulate the entire body of the civil rights which citizens enjoy, or may enjoy, in the several States. But I hold that, since slavery, as the court has repeatedly declared, *Slaughterhouse Cases,* 16 Wall. 36; *Strauder West Virginia,* 100 U.S. 303, was the moving or principal cause of the adoption of that amendment, and since that institution rested wholly upon the inferiority, as a race, of those held in bondage, their freedom necessarily involved immunity from, and protection against, all discrimination against them, because of their race, in respect of such civil rights as belong to freemen of other races. Congress, therefore, under its express power to enforce that amendment by appropriate legislation, may enact laws to protect that people against the deprivation, *because of their race,* of any civil rights granted to other freemen in the same State; and such legislation may be of a direct and primary character, operating upon States, their officers and agents, and also, upon, at least such individuals and corporations as exercise public functions and wield power and authority under the State.

* * *

What has been said is sufficient to show that the power of Congress under the Thirteenth Amendment is not necessarily restricted to legislation against slavery as an institution upheld by positive law, but may be exerted to the extent, at least, of protecting the liberated race against discrimination in respect of legal rights belonging to freemen, where such discrimination is based upon race.

It remains now to inquire what are the legal rights of colored persons in respect of the accommodations, privileges and facilities of public conveyances, inns, and places of public amusement?

First, as to public conveyances on land and water * * * In *Olcott v. Supervisor,* 16 Wall. 678, it was ruled that railroads are public highways, established by authority of the State for the public use; that they are none the less public highways, because controlled and owned by private corporations; that it is a part of the function of government to make and maintain highways for the convenience of the public; that no matter who is the agent, or what is the agency, the function performed is *that of the State;* that, although the owners may be private companies, they may be compelled to permit the public to use these works in the manner in which they can be used * * *.

* * *

Such being the relations these corporations hold to the public, it would seem that the right of a colored person to use an improved public highway, upon the terms accorded to freemen of other races, is as fundamental, in the state of freedom established in this country, as are any of the rights which my brethren concede to be so far fundamental as to be deemed the essence of civil freedom * * *. The Thirteenth Amendment alone obliterated the race line, so far as all rights fundamental in a state of freedom are concerned.

Second, as to inns. The same general observations which have been made as to railroads are applicable to inns. The word "inn" has a technical legal signification. It means, in the act of 1875, just what it meant at common law. A mere private boarding-house is not an inn, nor is its keeper subject to the responsibilities, or entitled to the privileges of a common innkeeper. "To constitute one an innkeeper, within the legal force of that term, he must keep a house of entertainment or lodging for all travelers or wayfarers who might choose to accept the same, being of good character or conduct." Redfield on Carriers, etc., § 575. Says Judge Story:

> "An innkeeper may be defined to be the keeper of a common inn for the lodging and entertainment of travelers and passengers, their horses and attendants. An innkeeper is bound to take in all travelers and wayfaring persons, and to entertain them, if he can accommodate them, for a reasonable compensation; and he must guard their goods with proper diligence. . . . If an innkeeper improperly refuses to receive or provide for a guest, he is liable to be indicted therefor. . . . They (carriers of passengers) are no more at liberty to refuse a passenger, if they have sufficient room and accommodations, than an innkeeper is to refuse suitable room and accommodations to a guest." Story on Bailments §§ 475–6.

* * *

These authorities are sufficient to show that a keeper of an inn is in the exercise of a quasi public employment. The law gives him special privileges and he is charged with certain duties and responsibilities to the public. The public nature of his employment forbids him from discriminating against any person asking admission as a guest on account of the race or color of that person.

Third. As to places of public amusement. It may be argued that the managers of such places have no duties to perform with which the public are, in any legal sense, concerned, or with which the public have any right to interfere; and, that the exclusion of a black man from a place of public amusement on account of his race, or the denial to him on that ground of equal accommodations at such places, violates no legal right for the vindication of which he may invoke the aid of the courts. My answer is that places of public amusement, within the meaning of the act of 1875, are such as are established and maintained under direct license of the law. The authority to establish and maintain them comes from the public. The colored race is a part of that public. The local government granting the license represents them as well as all other races within its jurisdiction. A license from the public to establish a place of public amusement, imports, in law, equality of right, at such places, among all the members of that public. This must be so unless it be—which I deny—that the common municipal government of all the people may, in the exertion of its powers, conferred for the benefit of all, discriminate or authorize discrimination against a particular race, solely because of its former condition of servitude.

* * *

Congress has not, in these matters, entered the domain of State control and supervision. It does not, as I have said, assume to prescribe the general conditions and limitations under which inns, public conveyances, and places of public amusement, shall be conducted or managed. It simply declares, in effect, that since the nation has established universal freedom in this country, for all time, there shall be no discrimination, based merely upon race or color, in respect of the accommodations and advantages of public conveyances, inns, and places of public amusement.

I am of the opinion that such discrimination practised by corporations and individuals in the exercise of their public or quasi-public functions is a badge of servitude the imposition of which Congress may prevent under its power, by appropriate legislation, to enforce the Thirteenth Amendment; and, consequently, without reference to its enlarged power under the Fourteenth Amendment, the act of March 1, 1875, is not, in my judgment, repugnant to the Constitution.

It remains now to consider these cases with reference to the power Congress has possessed since the adoption of the Fourteenth Amendment. Much that has been said as to the power of Congress under the Thirteenth Amendment is applicable to this branch of the discussion, and will not be repeated.

* * * [B]etween the adoption of the Thirteenth Amendment and the proposal by Congress of the Fourteenth Amendment, on June 16, 1866, the statute books of several of the States, as we have seen, had become loaded down with enactments which, under the guise of Apprentice, Vagrant, and Contract regulations, sought to keep the colored race in a condition, practically, of servitude * * *. To meet this new peril to the black race, that the purposes of the nation might not be doubted or defeated, and by way of further enlargement of the power of Congress, the Fourteenth Amendment was proposed for adoption.

* * *

But when, under what circumstances, and to what extent, may Congress, by means of legislation, exert its power to enforce the provisions of this amendment? The theory of the opinion of the majority of the court—the foundation upon which their reasoning seems to rest—is that the general government cannot, in advance of hostile State laws or hostile State proceedings, actively interfere for the protection of any of the rights, privileges, and immunities secured by the Fourteenth Amendment. It is said that such rights, privileges, and immunities are secured by way of *prohibition* against State laws and State proceedings affecting such rights and privileges, and by power given to Congress to legislate for the purpose of carrying *such prohibition* into effect; also, that congressional legislation must necessarily be predicated upon such supposed State laws or State proceedings, and be directed to the correction of their operation and effect.

* * *

The assumption that this amendment consists wholly of prohibitions upon State laws and State proceedings in hostility to its provisions, is unauthorized by its language. The first clause of the first section—"All persons born or naturalized in the United States, and subject to the jurisdiction thereof, are citizens of the United States, and of the State wherein they reside"—is of a distinctly affirmative character. In its application to the colored race, previously liberated, it created and granted, as well citizenship of the United States, as citizenship of the State in which they respectively resided. It introduced all of that race, whose ancestors had been imported and sold as slaves, at once, into the political community known as the "People of the United States." They became, instantly, citizens of the United States *and* of their respective States. Further, they were brought, by this supreme act of the nation within the direct operation of that provision of the Constitution which declares that "the citizens of each State shall be entitled to all privileges and immunities of citizens in the several States." Art. 4, § 2.

The citizenship thus acquired, by that race, in virtue of an affirmative grant from the nation, may be protected, not alone by the judicial branch of the government, but by congressional legislation of a primary direct character; this, because the power of Congress is not restricted to the enforcement of prohibitions upon State laws or State action. It is, in terms distinct and positive, to enforce "the *provisions of this article*" of amendment; not simply those of a prohibitive character, but the provisions—*all* of the provisions—affirmative and prohibitive, of the amendment. It is, therefore, a grave misconception to suppose that the fifth section of the amendment has reference exclusively to express prohibitions upon State laws or State action. If any right was created by that amendment, the grant of power through appropriate legislation, to enforce its provisions, authorizes Congress, by means of legislation, operating throughout the entire Union, to guard, secure, and protect that right.

It is, therefore, an essential inquiry what, if any, right, privilege or immunity was given, by the nation, to colored persons, when they were made citizens of the State in which they reside? Did the constitutional grant of State citizenship to that race, of its own force, invest them with any rights, privileges and immunities whatever? * * * To this it may be answered, generally, upon the authority of the adjudged cases, that they are those which are fundamental in citizenship in a free republican government, such as are "common to the citizens in the latter States under their constitutions and laws by virtue of their being citizens." * * *

* * *

But what was secured to colored citizens of the United States—as between them and their respective States—by the national grant to them of State citizenship? With what rights, privileges, or immunities did this grant invest them? There is one, if there be no other—exemption from race discrimination in respect of any civil right belonging to citizens of the white race in the same State. That, surely, is their constitutional privilege when within the jurisdiction of other States. And such must be their constitutional right, in their own State, unless the recent amendments be splendid baubles, thrown out to delude those who deserved fair and generous treatment at the hands of the nation. Citizenship in this country necessarily imports at least equality of civil rights among citizens of every race in the same State. It is fundamental in American citizenship that, in respect of such rights, there shall be no discrimination by the State, or its officers, or by individuals or corporations exercising public functions or authority, against any citizen because of his race or previous condition of servitude * * *

* * *

If, then, exemption from discrimination, in respect of civil rights, is a new constitutional right, secured by the grant of State citizenship to colored citizens of the United States—and I do not see how this can now be questioned—why may not the nation, by means of its own legislation of a primary direct character, guard, protect, and enforce that right? It is a right and privilege which the nation conferred. It did not come from the States in which those colored citizens reside. It has been the established doctrine of this court during all its history, accepted as essential to the national supremacy, that Congress, in the absence of a positive delegation of power to the State legislatures, may, by its own legislation, enforce and protect any right derived from or created by the national Constitution * * *.

This court has always given a broad and liberal construction to the Constitution, so as to enable Congress, by legislation, to enforce rights secured by that instrument. The legislation which Congress may enact, in execution of its power to enforce the provisions of this amendment, is such as may be appropriate to protect the right granted. The word appropriate was undoubtedly used with reference to its meaning, as established by repeated decisions of this court. Under given circumstances, that which the court characterizes as corrective legislation might be deemed by Congress appropriate and entirely sufficient. Under other circumstances primary direct legislation may be required. But it is for Congress, not the judiciary, to say that legislation is appropriate—that is—best adapted to the end to be attained. The judiciary may not, with safety to our institutions, enter the domain of legislative discretion, and dictate the means which Congress shall employ in the exercise of its granted powers * * *.

* * *

This construction does not in any degree intrench upon the just rights of the States in the control of their domestic affairs. It simply recognizes the enlarged powers conferred by the recent amendments upon the general government. In the view which I take of those amendments, the States possess the same authority which they have always had to define and regulate the civil rights which their own people, in virtue of State citizenship, may enjoy within their respective limits; except that its exercise is now subject to the expressly granted power of Congress, by legislation, to enforce the provisions of such amendments—a power which necessarily carries with it authority, by national legislation, to protect and secure the privileges and immunities which are created by or are derived from those amendments. That exemption of citizens from discrimination based on race or color, in respect of civil rights, is one of those privileges or immunities, can no longer be deemed an open question in this court.

* * *

In every material sense applicable to the practical enforcement of the Fourteenth Amendment, railroad corporations, keepers of inns, and managers of places of public amusement are agents or instrumentalities of the State, because they are charged with duties to the public, and are amenable, in respect of their duties and functions, to governmental regulation. It seems to me that, within the principle settled in *Ex parte Virginia,* a denial by these instrumentalities of the State, to the citizen, because of his race, of that equality of civil rights secured to him by law, is a denial by the State within the meaning of the Fourteenth Amendment * * *.

* * * I agree that government has nothing to do with social, as distinguished from technically legal, rights of individuals. No government ever has brought, or ever can bring, its people into social intercourse against their wishes. Whether one person will permit or maintain social relations with another is a matter with which government has no concern. I agree that if one citizen chooses not to hold social intercourse with another, he is not and cannot be made amenable to the law for his conduct in that regard; for even upon grounds of race no legal right of a citizen is violated by the refusal of others to maintain merely social relations with him. What I affirm is that no State, nor the officers of any State, nor any corporation or individual wielding power under State authority for the public benefit or the public convenience, can, consistently either with the freedom established by the fundamental law, or with that equality of civil rights which now belongs to every citizen, discriminate against freemen or citizens, in those rights, because of their race, or because they once labored under disabilities of slavery imposed upon them as a race. The rights which Congress, by the act of 1875, endeavored to secure and protect are legal, not social rights. The right, for instance, of a colored citizen to use the accommodations of a public highway, upon the same terms as are permitted to white citizens, is no more a social right than his right, under the law, to use the public streets of a city, or a town, or a turnpike road, or a public market, or a post office, or his right to sit in a public building with others, of whatever race, for the purpose of hearing the political questions of the day discussed * * *.

* * *

My brethren say, that when a man has emerged from slavery, and by the aid of beneficent legislation has shaken off the inseparable concomitants of that state, there must be some stage in the progress of his elevation when he takes the rank of a mere citizen, and ceases to be the special favorite of the laws, and when his rights as a citizen, or a man, are to be protected in the ordinary modes by which other men's rights are protected. It is, I submit, scarcely just to say that the colored race has been the special favorite of the laws * * *. The one underlying purpose of congressional legislation has been to enable the black race to take the rank of mere citizens * * *. At every step, in this direction, the nation has been confronted with class tyranny, which a contemporary English historian says is, of all tyrannies, the most intolerable, "for it is ubiquitous in its operation, and weighs, perhaps, most heavily on those whose obscurity or distance would withdraw them from the notice of a single despot." To-day it is the colored race which is denied, by corporations and individuals wielding public authority, rights fundamental in their freedom and citizenship. At some future time, it may be that some other race will fall under the ban of race discrimination. If the constitutional amendments be enforced according to the intent with which, as I conceive, they were adopted, there cannot be, in this republic, any class of human beings in practical subjection to another class with power in the latter to dole out to the former just such privileges as they may choose to grant * * *.

For the reasons stated, I feel constrained to withhold my assent to the opinion of the court.

NOTES AND QUESTIONS

1. Notice how the majority opinion characterizes the power to enact "appropriate" legislation under Section 2 of the Thirteenth Amendment and Section 5 of the Fourteenth Amendment: "the legislation which Congress is authorized to adopt in this behalf is * * * corrective legislation; that is, such as may be *necessary and proper* for counteracting such laws as the States may adopt or enforce" (emphasis added). Do the Reconstruction Amendments say that congressional laws under them must be "necessary and proper," which is a relatively restrictive formulation for an incidental powers clause? Is it obvious—or even plausible—that the scope of Congress's implementational power under the Reconstruction Amendments is exactly the same as its power under the Necessary and Proper Clause?

2. Would Justice Harlan have been on stronger grounds relying on the Ancient Constitution? Remember that under the Ancient Constitution colonial Americans believed they had many enumerated and unenumerated rights of Englishmen. Once the Thirteenth Amendment abolished slavery, free African-Americans had all those rights under the Ancient Constitution too. Could those rights plausibly include the kinds of rights protected by the 1875 Civil Rights Act? The majority doubts it, on the ground that the Civil Rights Act tried to reach *private* conduct rather than action by *state governments*. In other contexts, Justice Harlan might well have agreed with the majority—if, for example, the 1875 statute had, like the modern Civil Rights Act of 1964, regulated employment. But the rights involved in *The Civil Rights Cases* lay in a twilight zone between what today we would call public and private rights, for two key reasons. First, many of the services covered by the statute were provided by corporations, and Justice Harlan treats corporations as arms of the State. Corporations plainly are not arms of the State today, and in most cases they were not arms of the State when Justice Harlan wrote his opinion in 1883 either, but Justice Harlan's account was at least partially accurate when he received his legal education in the 1850s. Corporations were originally quasi-public instrumentalities of the government, and every corporation needed specific legislative authorization to operate. The modern conception of a corporation as a wholly private business, organized under general incorporation laws that do not require specific legislative approval for each entity, did not emerge in more than a handful of States until, ironically enough, roughly the period between Justice Harlan's legal education and his opinion in *The Civil Rights Cases*. *See* Susan Pace Hamill, *From Special Privilege to General Utility: A Continuation of Willard Hurst's Study of Corporations,* 49 AM. U.L. REV. 81, 100–07 (1999). (Justice Harlan's home state of Kentucky passed its general incorporation statute in 1870.) Justice Harlan in 1883 was factually wrong to view all corporations essentially as state actors, but his position had

centuries of history behind it—and it would have been mostly correct just two or three decades earlier. Second, and more fundamentally, the 1875 Civil Rights Act was not an all-encompassing antidiscrimination act. It was targeted specifically at (1) public conveyances, (2) inns and other public accommodations, and (3) places of public entertainment. At least the first two of these categories had long histories of being treated as public or quasi-public entities, as Justice Harlan correctly documented. Innkeepers and common carriers had common-law duties to serve all customers equally and fairly, and those duties were very much on the minds of the drafters of the 1875 Civil Rights Act; the background common-law (or "Ancient-Constitution") rights of travelers to fair service shaped—and even determined—the coverage of the statute. *See* A.K. Sandoval-Strausz, *Travelers, Strangers, and Jim Crow: Law, Public Accommodations, and Civil Rights in America,* 23 L. & HIST. REV. 53 (2005). Places of public entertainment were the closest analogues to innkeepers and common carriers. The Civil Rights Act of 1875 was thus structured to cover precisely those activities engaged in by nominally private actors that traditionally had been understood to be "public" in character. The majority's worry that upholding the statute would constitute Congress as a general government capable of regulating all affairs or interactions simply passes over the long-established distinction between the covered classes of "public" business and ordinary "private" commercial enterprises.

3. What about those ordinary "private" enterprises that did not fall under the Ancient-Constitution protections for travelers? Justice Harlan had a second reason for thinking that the Civil Rights Act of 1875 was constitutional that potentially swept much more broadly than his "public actors" rationale: Congress could use Section 2 of the Thirteenth Amendment to eliminate the "badges and incidents" of slavery. Unlike the Fourteenth Amendment, the Thirteenth Amendment operates directly on private parties; it is the only provision of the Constitution with this effect. Congress's enforcement powers under the Thirteenth Amendment thus unambiguously give it authority to regulate private parties and not simply State actors—provided that Congress is enforcing the ban against slavery. How far does that ban against slavery extend? Does it authorize elimination only of the formal institution of slavery, or could "appropriate" legislation to abolish slavery seek to root out lingering *effects* of slavery, such as social and economic patterns of racial discrimination? Does Section 2 of the Thirteenth Amendment extend far enough to reach the world of commerce, so that Congress could pass general statutes against race discrimination in fields such as employment, housing, and commercial contracting? Far enough to reach even noncommercial social interaction? Justice Harlan did not need to address these questions in 1883, because he was only invoking the Thirteenth Amendment in support of a federal public accommodations law, and for the reasons given in the previous note, that was a relatively easy case for him. Nearly a century later, however, the Court took on some of the broader questions.

B. JONES V. ALFRED H. MAYER CO.

392 U.S. 409 (1968)

■ MR. JUSTICE STEWART delivered the opinion of the Court.

In this case we are called upon to determine the scope and constitutionality of an Act of Congress, 42 U.S.C. § 1982, which provides that:

> "All citizens of the United States shall have the same right, in every State and Territory, as is enjoyed by white citizens thereof to inherit, purchase, lease, sell, hold, and convey real and personal property."

On September 2, 1965, the petitioners filed a complaint in the District Court for the Eastern District of Missouri, alleging that the respondents had refused to sell them a home in the Paddock Woods community of St. Louis County for the sole reason that petitioner Joseph Lee Jones is a Negro. Relying in part upon § 1982, the petitioners sought injunctive and other relief. The District Court sustained the respondents' motion to dismiss the complaint, and the Court of Appeals for the Eighth Circuit affirmed, concluding that § 1982 applies only to state action and does not reach private refusals to sell. We granted certiorari to consider the questions thus presented. For the reasons that follow, we reverse the judgment of the Court of Appeals. We hold that § 1982 bars *all* racial discrimination, private as well as public, in the sale or rental of property, and that the statute, thus construed, is a valid exercise of the power of Congress to enforce the Thirteenth Amendment.

* * *

We begin with the language of the statute itself. In plain and unambiguous terms, § 1982 grants to all citizens, without regard to race or color, "the same right" to purchase and lease property "as is enjoyed by white citizens." As the Court of Appeals in this case evidently recognized, that right can be impaired as effectively by "those who place property on the market" as by the State itself. For, even if the State and its agents lend no support to those who wish to exclude persons from their communities on racial grounds, the fact remains that, whenever property "is placed on the market for whites only, whites have a right denied to Negroes." So long as a Negro citizen who wants to buy or rent a home can be turned away simply because he is not white, he cannot be said to enjoy "the *same* right * * * as is enjoyed by white citizens * * * to * * * purchase (and) lease * * * real and personal property." 42 U.S.C. § 1982. (Emphasis added.)

On its face, therefore, § 1982 appears to prohibit *all* discrimination against Negroes in the sale or rental of property—discrimination by private owners as well as discrimination by public authorities * * *. Stressing what they consider to be the revolutionary implications of so literal a reading of § 1982, the respondents argue that Congress cannot possibly have intended any such result. Our examination of the relevant history, however, persuades us that Congress meant exactly what it said.

In its original form, 42 U.S.C. § 1982 was part of § 1 of the Civil Rights Act of 1866. That section was cast in sweeping terms:

> "*Be it enacted by the Senate and House of Representatives of the United States of America in Congress assembled*, That all persons born in the United States and not subject to any foreign power, * * * are hereby declared to be citizens of the United States; and such citizens, of every race and color, without regard to any previous condition of slavery or involuntary servitude, * * * shall have the same right, in every State and Territory in the United States, to make and enforce contracts, to sue, be parties, and give evidence, to inherit, purchase, lease, sell, hold, and convey real and personal property, and to full and equal benefit of all laws and proceedings for the security of person and property, as is enjoyed by white citizens, and shall be subject to like punishment, pains, and penalties, and to none other, any law, statute, ordinance, regulation, or custom, to the contrary notwithstanding."

* * * To the Congress that passed the Civil Rights Act of 1866, it was clear that the right to do these things might be infringed not only by "State or local law" but also by "custom, or prejudice." Thus, when Congress provided in § 1 of the Civil Rights Act that the right to purchase and lease property was to be enjoyed equally throughout the United States by Negro and white citizens alike, it plainly meant to secure that right against interference from any source whatever, whether governmental or private.

* * *

In attempting to demonstrate the contrary, the respondents rely heavily upon the fact that the Congress which approved the 1866 statute wished to eradicate the recently enacted Black Codes * * *. The respondents suggest that the only evil Congress sought to eliminate was that of racially discriminatory laws in the former Confederate States. But the Civil Rights Act was drafted to apply throughout the country, and its language was far broader than would have been necessary to strike down discriminatory statutes.

That broad language, we are asked to believe, was a mere slip of the legislative pen. We disagree. For the same Congress that wanted to do away with the Black Codes *also* had before it an imposing body of evidence pointing to the mistreatment of Negroes by private individuals and unofficial groups, mistreatment unrelated to any hostile state legislation. "Accounts in newspapers North and South, Freedmen's Bureau and other official documents, private reports and correspondence were all adduced" to show that "private outrage and atrocity" were "daily inflicted on freedmen * * *." The congressional debates are replete with references to private injustices against Negroes—references to white employers who refused to pay their Negro workers, white planters who agreed among themselves not to hire freed slaves without the permission of their former masters, white citizens who assaulted Negroes or who combined to drive them out of their communities.

Indeed, one of the most comprehensive studies then before Congress stressed the prevalence of private hostility toward Negroes and the need to protect them from the resulting persecution and discrimination. The report noted the existence of laws virtually prohibiting Negroes from owning or renting property in certain towns, but described such laws as "mere isolated cases," representing "the local outcroppings of a spirit * * * found to prevail everywhere"—a spirit expressed, for example, by lawless acts of brutality directed against Negroes who traveled to areas where they were not wanted. The report concluded that, even if anti-Negro legislation were "repealed in all the States lately in rebellion," equal treatment for the Negro would not yet be secured.

In this setting, it would have been strange indeed if Congress had viewed its task as encompassing merely the nullification of racist laws in the former rebel States * * *.

* * *

* * * [W]hen the House passed the Civil Rights Act on March 13, 1866, it did so on the same assumption that had prevailed in the Senate: It too believed that it was approving a comprehensive statute forbidding all racial discrimination affecting the basic civil rights enumerated in the Act.

President Andrew Johnson vetoed the Act on March 27, and in the brief congressional debate that followed, his supporters characterized its reach in all-embracing terms. One stressed the fact that § 1 would confer "the right * * * to purchase * * * real estate * * * without any qualification and without any restriction whatever * * *." Another predicted, as a corollary, that the Act would preclude preferential treatment for white persons in the rental of hotel rooms and in the sale of church pews. Those observations elicited no reply. On April 6 the Senate, and on April 9 the House, overrode the President's veto by the requisite majorities, and the Civil Rights Act of 1866 became law.

In light of the concerns that led Congress to adopt it and the contents of the debates that preceded its passage, it is clear that the Act was designed to do just what its terms suggest: to prohibit all racial discrimination, whether or not under color of law, with respect to the rights enumerated therein—including the right to purchase or lease property.

Nor was the scope of the 1866 Act altered when it was re-enacted in 1870, some two years after the ratification of the Fourteenth Amendment. It is quite true that some members of Congress supported the Fourteenth Amendment "in order to eliminate doubt as to the constitutional validity of the Civil Rights Act as applied to the States." *Hurd v. Hodge*, 334 U.S. 24, 32–33. But it certainly does not follow that the adoption of the Fourteenth Amendment or the subsequent readoption of the Civil Rights Act were meant somehow to *limit* its application to state action. The legislative history furnishes not the slightest factual basis for any such speculation, and the conditions prevailing in 1870 make it highly implausible. For by that time most, if not all, of the former Confederate States, then under the control of "reconstructed" legislatures, had formally repudiated racial discrimination, and the focus of congressional concern had clearly shifted from hostile statutes to the activities of groups like the Ku Klux Klan, operating wholly outside the law.

* * *

The remaining question is whether Congress has power under the Constitution to do what § 1982 purports to do: to prohibit all racial discrimination, private and public, in the sale and rental of property. Our starting point is the Thirteenth Amendment, for it was pursuant to that constitutional provision that Congress originally enacted what is now § 1982 * * *.

As its text reveals, the Thirteenth Amendment "is not a mere prohibition of state laws establishing or upholding slavery, but an absolute declaration that slavery or involuntary servitude shall not exist in any part of the United States." *Civil Rights Cases*, 109 U.S. 3, 20. It has never been doubted, therefore, "that the power vested in Congress to enforce the article by appropriate legislation," *ibid.*, includes the power to enact laws "direct and primary, operating upon the acts of individuals, whether sanctioned by state legislation or not." *Id.*, at 23

Thus, the fact that § 1982 operates upon the unofficial acts of private individuals, whether or not sanctioned by state law, presents no constitutional problem. If Congress has power under the Thirteenth Amendment to eradicate conditions that prevent Negroes from buying and renting property because of their race or color, then no federal statute calculated to achieve that objective can be thought to exceed the constitutional power of Congress simply because it reaches beyond state action to regulate the conduct of private individuals. The constitutional question in this case, therefore, comes to this: Does the authority of Congress to enforce the Thirteenth Amendment "by appropriate legislation" include the power to eliminate all racial barriers to the acquisition of real and personal property? We think the answer to that question is plainly yes.

* * *

Those who opposed passage of the Civil Rights Act of 1866 argued in effect that the Thirteenth Amendment merely authorized Congress to dissolve the legal bond by which the Negro slave was held to his master. Yet many had earlier opposed the Thirteenth Amendment on the very ground that it would give Congress virtually unlimited power to enact laws for the protection of Negroes in every State. And the majority leaders in Congress—who were, after all, the authors of the Thirteenth Amendment—had no doubt that its Enabling Clause contemplated the sort of positive legislation that was embodied in the 1866 Civil Rights Act. Their chief spokesman, Senator Trumbull of Illinois, the Chairman of the Judiciary Committee, had brought the Thirteenth Amendment to the floor of the Senate in 1864. In defending the constitutionality of the 1866 Act, he argued that, if the narrower construction of the Enabling Clause were correct, then

> "the trumpet of freedom that we have been blowing throughout the land has given an 'uncertain sound,' and the promised freedom is a delusion. Such was not the intention of Congress, which proposed the constitutional amendment, nor is such the fair meaning of the amendment itself . . . . I have no doubt that under this provision . . . we may destroy all these discriminations in civil rights against the black man; and if we cannot, our constitutional amendment amounts to nothing. It was for that purpose that the second clause of that amendment was adopted, which says that Congress shall have authority, by appropriate legislation, to carry into effect the article prohibiting slavery. Who is to decide what that appropriate legislation is to be? The Congress of the United States; and it is for Congress to adopt such appropriate legislation as it may think proper, so that it be a means to accomplish the end."

Surely Senator Trumbull was right. Surely Congress has the power under the Thirteenth Amendment rationally to determine what are the badges and the incidents of slavery, and the authority to translate that determination into effective legislation. Nor can we say that the determination Congress has made is an irrational one. For this Court recognized long ago that, whatever else they may have encompassed, the badges and incidents of slavery—its "burdens and disabilities"—included restraints upon "those fundamental rights which are the essence of civil freedom, namely, the same right * * * to inherit, purchase, lease, sell and convey property, as is enjoyed by white citizens." *Civil Rights Cases*, 109 U.S. 3, 22. Just as the Black Codes, enacted after the Civil War to restrict the free exercise of those rights, were substitutes for the slave system, so the exclusion of Negroes from white communities became a substitute for the Black Codes. And when racial discrimination herds men into ghettos and makes their ability to buy property turn on the color of their skin, then it too is a relic of slavery.

* * * At the very least, the freedom that Congress is empowered to secure under the Thirteenth Amendment includes the freedom to buy whatever a white man can buy, the right to live wherever a white man can live. If Congress cannot say that being a free man means at least this much, then the Thirteenth Amendment made a promise the Nation cannot keep.

Representative Wilson of Iowa was the floor manager in the House for the Civil Rights Act of 1866. In urging that Congress had ample authority to pass the pending bill, he recalled the celebrated words of Chief Justice Marshall in *McCulloch v. State of Maryland*, 4 Wheat. 316, 421:

> "Let the end by legitimate, let it be within the scope of the constitution, and all means which are appropriate, which are plainly adapted to that end, which are not prohibited, but consist with the letter and spirit of the constitution, are constitutional."

"The end is legitimate," the Congressman said, "because it is defined by the Constitution itself. The end is the maintenance of freedom . . . . A man who enjoys the civil rights mentioned in this bill cannot be reduced to slavery. . . . This settles the appropriateness of this measure, and that settles its constitutionality."

We agree. The judgment is reversed.

Reversed.

■ MR. JUSTICE DOUGLAS, concurring. [Omitted.]

■ MR. JUSTICE HARLAN, whom MR. JUSTICE WHITE joins, dissenting.

The decision in this case appears to me to be most ill-considered and ill-advised.

* * *

* * * I believe that the Court's construction of § 1982 as applying to purely private action is almost surely wrong, and at the least is open to serious doubt. The issues of the constitutionality of § 1982 * * * also presents formidable difficulties. Moreover, the political processes of our own era have, since the date of oral argument in this case, given birth to a civil rights statute embodying "fair housing" provisions * * *. It seems to me that this latter factor so diminishes the public importance of this case that by far the wisest course would be for this Court to refrain from decision and to dismiss the writ as improvidently granted.

* * *

Like the Court, I began analysis of § 1982 by examining its language * * *.

The Court finds it "plain and unambiguous that this language forbids purely private as well as state-authorized discrimination. With all respect, I do not find it so. For me, there is an inherent ambiguity in the term "right," as used in § 1982. The "right" referred to may either be a right to equal status under the law, in which case the statute operates only against state-sanctioned discrimination, or it may be an "absolute" right enforceable against private individuals. To me, the words of the statute, taken alone, suggest the former interpretation, not the latter.

* * *

The Court rests its opinion chiefly upon the legislative history of the Civil Rights Act of 1866 * * *. [T]hose debates do not, as the Court would have it, overwhelmingly support the result reached by the Court, and in fact that a contrary conclusion may equally well be drawn * * *.

* * *

* * * [T]he Senate debates contain many explicit statements by the bill's own author, to whom the Senate naturally looked for an explanation of its terms, indicating that the bill would prohibit only state-sanctioned discrimination.

* * *

The House debates are even fuller of statements indicating that the civil rights bill was intended to reach only state-endorsed discrimination * * *.

* * *

In sum, the most which can be said with assurance about the intended impact of the 1866 Civil Rights Act upon purely private discrimination is that the Act probably was envisioned by most members of Congress as prohibiting official, community-sanctioned discrimination in the South, engaged in pursuant to local "customs" which in the recent time of slavery probably were embodied in laws or regulations. Acts done under the color of such "customs" were, of course, said by the Court in the *Civil Rights Cases*, 109 U.S. 3, to constitute "state action" prohibited by the Fourteenth Amendment. *See id.*, at 16, 17, 21. Adoption of a "state action" construction of the Civil Rights Act would therefore have the additional merit of bringing its interpretation into line with that of the Fourteenth Amendment, which this Court has consistently held to reach only "state action." This seems especially desirable in light of the wide agreement that a major purpose of the Fourteenth Amendment, at least in the minds of its congressional proponents, was to assure that the rights conferred by the then recently enacted Civil Rights Act could not be taken away by a subsequent Congress.

* * * In holding that the Thirteenth Amendment is sufficient constitutional authority for § 1982 as interpreted, the Court also decides a question of great importance. Even contemporary supporters of the aims of the 1866 Civil Rights Act doubted that those goals could constitutionally be achieved under the Thirteenth Amendment, and this Court has twice expressed similar doubts. *See Hodges v. United States*, 203 U.S. 1, 16–18; *Corrigan v. Buckley*, 271 U.S. 323, 330. Thus, it is plain that the course of decision followed by the Court today entails the resolution of important and difficult issues.

The only apparent way of deciding this case without reaching those issues would be to hold that the petitioners are entitled to relief on the alternative ground advanced by them: that the respondents' conduct amounted to "state action" forbidden by the Fourteenth Amendment. However, that route is not without formidable obstacles of its own, for the opinion of the Court of Appeals makes it clear that this case differs substantially from any "state action" case previously decided by this Court.

The fact that a case is "hard" does not, of course, relieve a judge of his duty to decide it. Since, the Court did vote to hear this case, I normally would consider myself obligated to decide whether the petitioners are entitled to relief on either of the grounds on which they rely. After mature reflection, however, I have concluded that this is one of those rare instances in which an event which occurs after the hearing of argument so diminishes a case's public significance, when viewed in light of the difficulty of the questions presented, as to justify this Court in dismissing the writ as improvidently granted.

The occurrence to which I refer is the recent enactment of the Civil Rights Act of 1968, Pub.L. 90–284, 82 Stat. 73. Title VIII of that Act contains comprehensive "fair housing" provisions, which by the terms of § 803 will become applicable on January 1, 1969, to persons who, like the petitioners, attempt to buy houses from developers. Under those provisions, such persons will be entitled to injunctive relief and damages from developers who refuse to sell to them on account of race or color, unless the parties are able to resolve their dispute by other means. Thus, the type of relief which the petitioners seek will be available within seven months' time under the terms of a presumptively constitutional Act of Congress. In these circumstances, it seems obvious that the case has lost most of its public importance, and I believe that it would be much the wiser course for this Court to refrain from deciding it * * *. The political process now having taken hold again in this very field, I am at a loss to understand why the Court should have deemed it appropriate or, in the circumstances of this case, necessary to proceed with such precipitate and insecure strides.

* * *

For these reasons, I would dismiss the writ of certiorari as improvidently granted.

NOTES AND QUESTIONS

1. The second Justice Harlan, who dissented in *Jones v. Alfred Mayer,* was the grandson of the first Justice Harlan, who dissented in *The Civil Rights Cases*. How do you think the first Justice Harlan would have decided *Jones v. Alfred Mayer*?

2. Four years before *Jones v. Alfred Mayer,* Congress enacted the Civil Rights Act of 1964, which contained broad prohibitions on discrimination in public accommodations and employment. The public accommodations provisions of the statute swept much more broadly than the common-law definition, including essentially all restaurants. The statute was upheld as constitutional under the Commerce Clause and the Necessary and Proper Clause. *See supra* pages 711–713. The Thirteenth Amendment reasoning of *Jones v. Alfred Mayer,* and possibly of the first Justice Harlan, might well have sustained the 1964 Act if it had been limited to racial discrimination. But the Civil Rights Act of 1964 prohibits discrimination on the basis of "race, color, *religion, sex, or national origin.*" 42 U.S.C. § 2000e(2)(A)(1) (2018) (emphasis added). The Thirteenth Amendment can potentially support laws against racial discrimination but not against sex- or religion-based discrimination. If those wider laws are going to rely on the Reconstruction Amendments, they have to be based on Section 5 of the Fourteenth Amendment. As we will explain in a subsequent chapter, we think it is quite clear that the Fourteenth Amendment prohibits at least some forms of sex- and religion-based discrimination, as the caselaw holds, but that leaves the difficult question whether Section 5 of the Fourteenth Amendment, rather than Section 2 of the Thirteenth Amendment, can reach private discrimination that does not have the "state-action" character of public accommodations. Those concerns about the reach of Section 5 led Congress and the Supreme Court in 1964 to rely on the Commerce Clause and the Necessary and Proper Clause rather than on Section 5. The Court in *Jones v. Alfred Mayer* said only: "Because we have concluded that the discrimination alleged in the petitioners' complaint violated a federal statute that Congress had the power to enact under the Thirteenth Amendment, we find it unnecessary to decide whether that discrimination also violated the Equal Protection Clause of the Fourteenth Amendment." 392 U.S. at 413 n.5.

3. *Jones v. Alfred Mayer* addressed a provision of the 1866 Civil Rights Act, now codified at 42 U.S.C. § 1982, which deals with real property. Another section of the 1866 Civil Rights Act deals with a range of legal capacities, including the right to make contracts: "All persons within the jurisdiction of the United States shall have the same right in every State and Territory to make and enforce contracts, to sue, be parties, give evidence, and to the full and equal benefit of all laws and proceedings for the security of

persons and property as is enjoyed by white citizens * * *." 42 U.S.C. § 1981 (2018). In *Runyon v. McRary,* 427 U.S. 160 (1976), the Court held that Section 1981, as with Section 1982, prohibits private racial discrimination in contracting, including employment. As with *Jones v Alfred Mayer,* the Court located the constitutional authority for such a law in Section 2 of the Thirteenth Amendment. *See* 427 U.S. at 179 ("Section 1981, as applied to the conduct at issue here, constitutes an exercise of federal legislative power under § 2 of the Thirteenth Amendment"). More than a decade later, the Court declined to overrule *Runyon's* interpretation of the statute as reaching private conduct—five justices on the ground of stare decisis and four justices on the ground that *Runyon* was correct. *See Patterson v. McLean Credit Union,* 491 U.S. 164 (1989). The constitutionality of applying Section 1981 to reach private conduct was not contested in *Patterson.*

4. Much of the time, the line between state and private actors is not at issue because activity is directly and obviously the product of state action. In those cases, the main issue is normally whether the state action violates the "self-executing" substantive terms of the Fourteenth Amendment. We will examine many such cases in a subsequent chapter. What happens, however, if Congress passes statutes pursuant to Section 5 of the Fourteenth Amendment that construe the substantive terms of the amendment differently from court decisions? Can Congress "enforce" its own vision of the Fourteenth Amendment or must it accept the Court's? This crucial question was addressed (to say "resolved" would, of course, beg the question) by the Court in 1997.

[Assignment 42]

C. CITY OF BOERNE V. FLORES

521 U.S. 507 (1997)

■ JUSTICE KENNEDY delivered the opinion of the Court.

A decision by local zoning authorities to deny a church a building permit was challenged under the Religious Freedom Restoration Act of 1993 (RFRA). The case calls into question the authority of Congress to enact RFRA. We conclude the statute exceeds Congress' power.

Situated on a hill in the city of Boerne, Texas, some 28 miles northwest of San Antonio, is St. Peter Catholic Church. Built in 1923, the church's structure replicates the mission style of the region's earlier history. The church seats about 230 worshippers, a number too small for its growing parish. Some 40 to 60 parishioners cannot be accommodated at some Sunday masses. In order to meet the needs of the congregation the Archbishop of San Antonio gave permission to the parish to plan alterations to enlarge the building.

A few months later, the Boerne City Council passed an ordinance authorizing the city's Historic Landmark Commission to prepare a preservation plan with proposed historic landmarks and districts. Under the ordinance, the Commission must preapprove construction affecting historic landmarks or buildings in a historic district.

Soon afterwards, the Archbishop applied for a building permit so construction to enlarge the church could proceed. City authorities, relying on the ordinance and the designation of a historic district (which, they argued, included the church), denied the application. The Archbishop brought this suit challenging the permit denial in the United States District Court for the Western District of Texas. 877 F. Supp. 355 (1995).

The complaint contained various claims, but to this point the litigation has centered on RFRA and the question of its constitutionality. The Archbishop relied upon RFRA as one basis for relief from the refusal to issue the permit. The District Court concluded that by enacting RFRA Congress exceeded the scope of its enforcement power under § 5 of the Fourteenth Amendment. The court certified its order for interlocutory appeal and the Fifth Circuit reversed, finding RFRA to be constitutional. 73 F.3d 1352 (1996). We granted certiorari and now reverse.

Congress enacted RFRA in direct response to the Court's decision in *Employment Div., Dept. of Human Resources of Ore. v. Smith*, 494 U.S. 872 (1990). There we considered a [First Amendment] Free Exercise Clause claim brought by members of the Native American Church who were denied unemployment benefits when they lost their jobs because they had used peyote. Their practice was to ingest peyote for sacramental purposes, and they challenged an Oregon statute of general applicability which made use of the drug criminal. In evaluating the claim, we declined to apply the balancing test set forth in *Sherbert v. Verner*, 374 U.S. 398 (1963), under which we would have asked whether Oregon's prohibition substantially burdened a religious practice and, if it did, whether the burden was justified by a compelling government interest. We stated:

> "[G]overnment's ability to enforce generally applicable prohibitions of socially harmful conduct . . . cannot depend on measuring the effects of a governmental action on a religious objector's spiritual development. To make an individual's obligation to obey such a law contingent upon the law's coincidence with his religious beliefs, except where the State's interest is 'compelling' . . . contradicts both constitutional tradition and common sense." 494 U.S., at 885 (internal quotation marks and citation omitted).
>
> * * *

* * * *Smith* held that neutral, generally applicable laws may be applied to religious practices even when not supported by a compelling governmental interest.

Four Members of the Court disagreed. They argued the law placed a substantial burden on the Native American Church members so that it could be upheld only if the law served a compelling state interest and was narrowly tailored to achieve that end * * *.

These points of constitutional interpretation were debated by Members of Congress in hearings and floor debates. Many criticized the Court's reasoning, and this disagreement resulted in the passage of RFRA. Congress announced:

> "(1) [T]he framers of the Constitution, recognizing free exercise of religion as an unalienable right, secured its protection in the First Amendment to the Constitution;
>
> "(2) laws 'neutral' toward religion may burden religious exercise as surely as laws intended to interfere with religious exercise;
>
> "(3) governments should not substantially burden religious exercise without compelling justification;
>
> "(4) in Employment Division v. Smith, 494 U.S. 872 (1990), the Supreme Court virtually eliminated the requirement that the government justify burdens on religious exercise imposed by laws neutral toward religion; and

"(5) the compelling interest test as set forth in prior Federal court rulings is a workable test for striking sensible balances between religious liberty and competing prior governmental interests." 42 U.S.C. § 2000bb(a).

The Act's stated purposes are:

"(1) to restore the compelling interest test as set forth in Sherbert v. Verner, 374 U.S. 398 (1963) and Wisconsin v. Yoder, 406 U.S. 205 (1972) and to guarantee its application in all cases where free exercise of religion is substantially burdened; and

"(2) to provide a claim or defense to persons whose religious exercise is substantially burdened by government." § 2000bb(b).

RFRA prohibits "[g]overnment" from "substantially burden[ing]" a person's exercise of religion even if the burden results from a rule of general applicability unless the government can demonstrate the burden "(1) is in furtherance of a compelling governmental interest; and (2) is the least restrictive means of furthering that compelling governmental interest." The Act's mandate applies to any "branch, department, agency, instrumentality, and official (or other person acting under color of law) of the United States," as well as to any "State, or . . . subdivision of a State" * * *.

* * *

Congress relied on its Fourteenth Amendment enforcement power in enacting the most far-reaching and substantial of RFRA's provisions, those which impose its requirements on the States * * *.

The parties disagree over whether RFRA is a proper exercise of Congress' § 5 power "to enforce" by "appropriate legislation" the constitutional guarantee that no State shall deprive any person of "life, liberty, or property, without due process of law" nor deny any person "equal protection of the laws."

In defense of the Act, respondent the Archbishop contends, with support from the United States as *amicus*, that RFRA is permissible enforcement legislation. Congress, it is said, is only protecting by legislation one of the liberties guaranteed by the Fourteenth Amendment's Due Process Clause, the free exercise of religion, beyond what is necessary under *Smith*. It is said the congressional decision to dispense with proof of deliberate or overt discrimination and instead concentrate on a law's effects accords with the settled understanding that § 5 includes the power to enact legislation designed to prevent, as well as remedy, constitutional violations. It is further contended that Congress' § 5 power is not limited to remedial or preventive legislation.

All must acknowledge that § 5 is "a positive grant of legislative power" to Congress, *Katzenbach v. Morgan*, 384 U.S. 641, 651 (1966) * * *. Legislation which deters or remedies constitutional violations can fall within the sweep of Congress' enforcement power even if in the process it prohibits conduct which is not itself unconstitutional and intrudes into "legislative spheres of autonomy previously reserved to the States." *Fitzpatrick v. Bitzer*, 427 U.S. 445, 455 (1976). For example, the Court upheld a suspension of literacy tests and similar voting requirements under Congress' parallel power to enforce the provisions of the Fifteenth Amendment, see U.S. Const., Amdt. 15, § 2, as a measure to combat racial discrimination in voting, *South Carolina v. Katzenbach,* 383 U.S. 301, 308 (1966), despite the facial constitutionality of the tests * * *.

* * *

Congress' power under § 5, however, extends only to "enforc[ing]" the provisions of the Fourteenth Amendment * * *. The design of the Amendment and the text of § 5 are inconsistent with the suggestion that Congress has the power to decree the substance of the Fourteenth Amendment's restrictions on the States. Legislation which alters the meaning of the Free Exercise Clause cannot be said to be enforcing the Clause. Congress does not enforce a constitutional right by changing what the right is. It has been given the power "to enforce," not the power to determine what constitutes a constitutional violation. Were it not so, what Congress would be enforcing would no longer be, in any meaningful sense, the "provisions of [the Fourteenth Amendment]."

While the line between measures that remedy or prevent unconstitutional actions and measures that make a substantive change in the governing law is not easy to discern, and Congress must have wide latitude in determining where it lies, the distinction exists and must be observed. There must be a congruence and proportionality between the injury to be prevented or remedied and the means adopted to that end. Lacking such a connection, legislation may become substantive in operation and effect. History and our case law support drawing the distinction, one apparent from the text of the Amendment.

* * *

Any suggestion that Congress has a substantive, non-remedial power under the Fourteenth Amendment is not supported by our case law. In *Oregon v. Mitchell,* [400 U.S. 112 (1970)], a majority of the Court concluded Congress had exceeded its enforcement powers by enacting legislation lowering the minimum age of voters from 21 to 18 in state and local elections. The five Members of the Court who reached this conclusion explained that the legislation intruded into an area reserved by the Constitution to the States. Four of these five were explicit in rejecting the position that § 5 endowed Congress with the power to establish the meaning of constitutional provisions. Justice Black's rejection of this position might be inferred from his disagreement with Congress' interpretation of the Equal Protection Clause.

There is language in our opinion in *Katzenbach v. Morgan*, 384 U.S. 641 (1966), which could be interpreted as acknowledging a power in Congress to enact legislation that expands the rights contained in § 1 of the Fourteenth Amendment. This is not a necessary interpretation, however, or even the best one. In *Morgan*, the Court considered the constitutionality of § 4(e) of the Voting Rights Act of 1965, which provided that no person who had successfully completed the sixth primary grade in a public school in, or a private school accredited by, the Commonwealth of Puerto Rico in which the language of instruction was other than English could be denied the right to vote because of an inability to read or write English. New York's Constitution, on the other hand, required voters to be able to read and write English. The Court provided two related rationales for its conclusion that § 4(e) could "be viewed as a measure to secure for the Puerto Rican community residing in New York nondiscriminatory treatment by government." Under the first rationale, Congress could prohibit New York from denying the right to vote to large segments of its Puerto Rican community, in order to give Puerto Ricans "enhanced political power" that would be "helpful in gaining nondiscriminatory treatment in public services for the entire Puerto Rican community." Section 4(e) thus could be justified as a remedial measure to deal with "discrimination in governmental services." The second rationale, an alternative holding, did not address discrimination in the provision of public services but "discrimination in establishing voter qualifications." The Court perceived a factual basis on which Congress could have concluded that New York's literacy requirement "constituted an invidious discrimination in violation of the Equal Protection Clause." Both rationales for upholding § 4 (e) rested on unconstitutional discrimination by New York and Congress' reasonable attempt to combat it. As Justice Stewart explained in *Oregon v. Mitchell, supra,* at 296, interpreting *Morgan* to give Congress the power to interpret the Constitution "would require an enormous extension of that decision's rationale."

If Congress could define its own powers by altering the Fourteenth Amendment's meaning, no longer would the Constitution be "superior paramount law, unchangeable by ordinary means." It would be "on a level with ordinary legislative acts, and, like other acts, . . . alterable when the legislature shall please to alter it." *Marbury v. Madison*, 1 Cranch, at 177. Under this approach, it is difficult to conceive of a principle that would limit congressional power. Shifting legislative majorities could change the Constitution and effectively circumvent the difficult and detailed amendment process contained in Article V.

We now turn to consider whether RFRA can be considered enforcement legislation under § 5 of the Fourteenth Amendment.

Respondent contends that RFRA is a proper exercise of Congress' remedial or preventive power. The Act, it is said, is a reasonable means of protecting the free exercise of religion as defined by *Smith*. It prevents and remedies laws which are enacted with the unconstitutional object of targeting religious beliefs and practices. See *Church of the Lukumi Babalu Aye, Inc. v. Hialeah*, 508 U.S. 520, 533 (1993) ("[A] law targeting religious beliefs as such is never permissible"). To avoid the difficulty of proving such violations, it is said, Congress can simply invalidate any law which imposes a substantial burden on a religious practice unless it is justified by a compelling interest and is the least restrictive means of accomplishing that interest. If Congress can prohibit laws with discriminatory effects in order to prevent racial discrimination in violation of the Equal Protection Clause, then it can do the same, respondent argues, to promote religious liberty.

While preventive rules are sometimes appropriate remedial measures, there must be a congruence between the means used and the ends to be achieved. The appropriateness of remedial measures must be considered in light of the evil presented. Strong measures appropriate to address one harm may be an unwarranted response to another, lesser one.

A comparison between RFRA and the Voting Rights Act is instructive. In contrast to the record which confronted Congress and the Judiciary in the voting rights cases, RFRA's legislative record lacks examples of modern instances of generally applicable laws passed because of religious bigotry. The history of persecution in this country detailed in the hearings mentions no episodes occurring in the past 40 years * * *. Rather, the emphasis of the hearings was on laws of general applicability which place incidental burdens on religion * * *. Congress' concern was with the incidental burdens imposed, not the object or purpose of the legislation * * *

Regardless of the state of the legislative record, RFRA cannot be considered remedial, preventive legislation, if those terms are to have any meaning. RFRA is so out of proportion to a supposed remedial or preventive object that it cannot be understood as responsive to, or designed to prevent, unconstitutional behavior. It appears, instead, to attempt a substantive change in constitutional protections. Preventive measures prohibiting certain types of laws may be appropriate when there is reason to believe that many of the laws affected by the congressional enactment have a significant likelihood of being unconstitutional * * *.

RFRA is not so confined. Sweeping coverage ensures its intrusion at every level of government, displacing laws and prohibiting official actions of almost every description and regardless of subject matter. RFRA's restrictions apply to every agency and official of the Federal, State, and local Governments. RFRA applies to all federal and state law, statutory or otherwise, whether adopted before or after its enactment. RFRA has no termination date or termination mechanism. Any law is subject to challenge at any time by any individual who alleges a substantial burden on his or her free exercise of religion.

* * *

The stringent test RFRA demands of state laws reflects a lack of proportionality or congruence between the means adopted and the legitimate end to be achieved. If an objector can show a substantial burden on his free exercise, the State must demonstrate a compelling governmental interest and show that the law is the least restrictive means of furthering its interest * * *. Requiring a State to demonstrate a compelling interest and show that it has adopted the least restrictive means of achieving that interest is the most demanding test known to constitutional law * * *. Laws valid under *Smith* would fall under RFRA without regard to whether they had the object of stifling or punishing free exercise. We make these observations not to reargue the position of the majority in *Smith* but to illustrate the substantive alteration of its holding attempted by RFRA * * *.

The substantial costs RFRA exacts, both in practical terms of imposing a heavy litigation burden on the States and in terms of curtailing their traditional general regulatory power, far exceed any pattern or practice of unconstitutional conduct under the Free Exercise Clause as interpreted in *Smith*. Simply put, RFRA is not designed to identify and counteract state laws likely to be unconstitutional because of their treatment of religion. In most cases, the state laws to which RFRA applies are not ones which will have been motivated by religious bigotry * * *. When the exercise of religion has been burdened in an incidental way by a law of general application, it does not follow that the persons affected have been burdened any more than other citizens, let alone burdened because of their religious beliefs. In addition, the Act imposes in every case a least restrictive means requirement—a requirement that was not used in the pre-*Smith* jurisprudence RFRA purported to codify—which also indicates that the legislation is broader than is appropriate if the goal is to prevent and remedy constitutional violations.

When Congress acts within its sphere of power and responsibilities, it has not just the right but the duty to make its own informed judgment on the meaning and force of the Constitution. This has been clear from the early days of the Republic

* * *. Were it otherwise, we would not afford Congress the presumption of validity its enactments now enjoy.

Our national experience teaches that the Constitution is preserved best when each part of the government respects both the Constitution and the proper actions and determinations of the other branches. When the Court has interpreted the Constitution, it has acted within the province of the Judicial Branch, which embraces the duty to say what the law is. *Marbury v. Madison*, 1 Cranch, at 177. When the political branches of the Government act against the background of a judicial interpretation of the Constitution already issued, it must be understood that in later cases and controversies the Court will treat its precedents with the respect due them under settled principles, including *stare decisis*, and contrary expectations must be disappointed. RFRA was designed to control cases and controversies, such as the one before us; but as the provisions of the federal statute here invoked are beyond congressional authority, it is this Court's precedent, not RFRA, which must control.

* * * The judgment of the Court of Appeals sustaining the Act's constitutionality is reversed.

■ JUSTICE STEVENS, concurring. [Omitted.]

■ JUSTICE SCALIA, with whom JUSTICE STEVENS joins, concurring in part. [Omitted.]

■ JUSTICE O'CONNOR, with whom JUSTICE BREYER joins except as to the first paragraph of Part I, dissenting.

* * *

I

I agree with much of the reasoning set forth in Part III-A of the Court's opinion. Indeed, if I agreed with the Court's standard in *Smith,* I would join the opinion. As the Court's careful and thorough historical analysis shows, Congress lacks the "power to decree the *substance* of the Fourteenth Amendment's restrictions on the States." Rather, its power under § 5 of the Fourteenth Amendment extends only to *enforcing* the Amendment's provisions. In short, Congress lacks the ability independently to define or expand the scope of constitutional rights by statute. Accordingly, whether Congress has exceeded its § 5 powers turns on whether there is a "congruence and proportionality between the injury to be prevented or remedied and the means adopted to that end." This recognition does not, of course, in any way diminish Congress' obligation to draw its own conclusions regarding the Constitution's meaning. Congress, no less than this Court, is called upon to consider the requirements of the Constitution and to act in accordance with its dictates. But when it enacts legislation in furtherance of its delegated powers, Congress must make its judgments consistent with this Court's exposition of the Constitution and with the limits placed on its legislative authority by provisions such as the Fourteenth Amendment.

The Court's analysis of whether RFRA is a constitutional exercise of Congress' § 5 power, set forth in Part III-B of its opinion, is premised on the assumption that *Smith* correctly interprets the Free Exercise Clause. This is an assumption that I do not accept. I continue to believe that *Smith* adopted an improper standard for deciding free exercise claims * * *

* * *

■ JUSTICE SOUTER, dissenting. [Omitted.]

■ JUSTICE BREYER, dissenting.

I agree with JUSTICE O'CONNOR that the Court should direct the parties to brief the question whether *Employment Div., Dept. of Human Resources of Oregon v. Smith,* 494 U.S. 872 (1990), was correctly decided, and set this case for reargument. I do not, however, find it necessary to consider the question whether, assuming *Smith* is correct, § 5 of the Fourteenth Amendment would authorize Congress to enact the legislation before us. Thus, while I agree with some of the views expressed in the first paragraph of Part I of JUSTICE O'Connor's dissent, I do not necessarily agree with all of them * * *.

NOTES AND QUESTIONS

1. *Employment Division v. Smith* was one of the most controversial Supreme Court decisions of recent times, and much of the energy of the justices in *City of Boerne* was devoted to re-arguing the merits of that case. No justice objected to Justice Kennedy's account of Congress's power under Section 5 (though Justice Breyer did not join it). Does that seem strange? Does Justice Kennedy's "congruence and proportionality" test for judging the constitutionality of Congress's Section 5 power sound like a Hamiltonian account of "convenient" or "useful" legislation? Would a Hamiltonian account second-guess Congress's judgment about how best to police hard-to-detect discrimination? Remember that the guiding doctrinal test for "fit" under the Necessary and Proper Clause is "rational basis," which is generally code for "the government wins." Given both the text and history of the Reconstruction Amendments, can it possibly make sense to read Section 5 *more strictly* than one reads the Necessary and Proper Clause? Isn't the reverse obviously more sensible? Or are we missing something important?

2. The big question in *City of Boerne* is whether Congress is allowed to disagree with the Supreme Court. The Court frames the issue as whether Congress can change the meaning of the Constitution. Put that way, of course Congress cannot change the meaning of the Constitution. If something does not actually violate the Constitution, Congress cannot pretend that it does—no more than Congress can pretend that something does not violate the Constitution when it actually does. But is that really the best way to frame this case? The disagreement on the Supreme Court in the 5 to 4 ruling in *Employment Division v. Smith*, 494 U.S. 872 (1990), was over whether laws which did not on their face discriminate on the basis of race, but which did disparately impact a religious group, violated the Free Exercise Clause of the First Amendment as incorporated and applied to the States by the Fourteenth Amendment. This is, at its core, a question about how you prove discrimination on the basis of religion: 1) by looking for whether a law is discriminatory on its face; 2) by looking for discriminatory intent; and/or 3) by looking for a disparate impact on religious groups that does not serve a compelling governmental purpose as evidence of discriminatory intent. Doesn't legislation about the modes of proof sound like "appropriate" legislation, at least on Hamiltonian grounds, regardless of how one views the content of the underlying constitutional norm?

3. Justice Kennedy's opinion simply does not believe that there is enough religious discrimination (as opposed, say, to racial discrimination) in legislatures to justify a law as broadly framed as RFRA. If Section 5 really contained a "congruence and proportionality" requirement, this kind of inquiry would perhaps be (for lack of a better word) appropriate for the Court. Perhaps the Court should be asking these kinds of questions under the Necessary and Proper Clause. Are those really Section-5-type questions?

4. The "congruence and proportionality" inquiry has been applied in a substantial number of subsequent cases. The Court has found, usually in closely divided votes, that Congress does not have power under Section 5 to override state sovereign immunity in patent infringement cases, *see Florida Prepaid Postsecondary Educ. Expense Bd. v. College Savings Bank,* 527 U.S. 627 (1999); in suits by government employees for age discrimination, *see Kimel v. Florida Bd. Of Regents,* 528 U.S. 62 (2000), or for generalized handicap discrimination. *See Board of Trustees of the Univ. of Alabama v. Garrett,* 531 U.S. 356 (2001). Laws that survived the Court's "congruence and proportionality" review include the Family and Medical Leave Act, aimed at gender discrimination, *see Nevada Dep't of Human Resources v. Hibbs,* 538 U.S. 721 (2003)—well, at least *sometimes, see Coleman v. Court of Appeals of Maryland,* 566 U.S. 30 (2012) (Section 5 *does not* authorize Congress to override state sovereign immunity in claims for medical leave for self-care as opposed to medical leave for family care, which *Hibbs* approved under Section 5)—and the Americans with Disabilities Act *specifically with reference to the provision of and access to State services, see Tennessee v. Lane,* 541 U.S. 509 (2004), but not with reference to *generalized* handicap discrimination, which *Board of Trustees v. Garrett* held could not be sustained under Section 5. If this short description of the cases under the "congruence and proportionality" test has you scratching your head, you are not alone. In *Coleman v. Court of Appeals of Maryland,* Justice Scalia wrote:

> The plurality's opinion seems to me a faithful application of our "congruence and proportionality" jurisprudence. So does the opinion of the dissent. That is because the varying outcomes we have arrived at under the "congruence and proportionality" test make no sense. Which in turn is because that flabby test is "a standing invitation to judicial arbitrariness and policy-driven decisionmaking," *Tennessee v. Lane,* 541 U.S. 509, 557–558 (2004) (SCALIA, J., dissenting). Moreover, in the process of applying (or seeming to apply) the test, we must scour the legislative record in search of evidence that supports the congressional action. This grading of Congress's homework is a task we are ill suited to perform and ill advised to undertake.
>
> I adhere to my view that we should instead adopt an approach that is properly tied to the text of § 5, which grants Congress the power "to *enforce,* by appropriate legislation," the other provisions of the Fourteenth Amendment. (Emphasis added.) As I have explained in greater detail elsewhere, see *Lane, supra,* at 558–560, outside of the context of racial discrimination (which is different for *stare decisis* reasons), I would limit Congress's § 5 power to the regulation of conduct that *itself* violates the Fourteenth Amendment. Failing to grant state employees leave for the purpose of self-care—or any other purpose, for that matter—does not come close.

566 U.S. at 44–45 (Scalia, J., concurring in the judgment). Does Justice Scalia's approach, which forbids Congress from enacting prophylactic legislation for anything other than race discrimination, answer the question to what extent Section 5 gives Congress's power to establish the methods of proof of a constitutional violation? Do you agree with his answer?

5. What happens when the "congruence and proportionality" inquiry runs into the state action problem, in which Congress tries to regulate what seems to be private conduct?

D. UNITED STATES V. MORRISON

529 U.S. 598 (2000)

■ CHIEF JUSTICE REHNQUIST delivered the opinion of the Court.

In these cases we consider the constitutionality of 42 U.S.C. § 13981 [The Violence Against Women Act], which provides a federal civil remedy for the victims of gender-motivated violence. The United States Court of Appeals for the Fourth Circuit, sitting en banc, struck down § 13981 because it concluded that Congress lacked constitutional authority to enact the section's civil remedy. Believing that these cases are controlled by our decisions in *United States v. Lopez*, 514 U.S. 549 (1995), *United States v. Harris*, 106 U.S. 629 (1883), and the *Civil Rights Cases*, 109 U.S. 3 (1883), we affirm.

Petitioner Christy Brzonkala enrolled at Virginia Polytechnic Institute (Virginia Tech) in the fall of 1994. In September of that year, Brzonkala met respondents Antonio Morrison and James Crawford, who were both students at Virginia Tech and members of its varsity football team. Brzonkala alleges that, within 30 minutes of meeting Morrison and Crawford, they assaulted and repeatedly raped her. After the attack, Morrison allegedly told Brzonkala, "You better not have any . . . diseases." Complaint ¶ 22. In the months following the rape, Morrison also allegedly announced in the dormitory's dining room that he "like[d] to get girls drunk and . . . ." Id., ¶ 31. The omitted portions, quoted verbatim in the briefs on file with this Court, consist of boasting, debased remarks about what Morrison would do to women, vulgar remarks that cannot fail to shock and offend.

Brzonkala alleges that this attack caused her to become severely emotionally disturbed and depressed. She sought assistance from a university psychiatrist, who prescribed antidepressant medication. Shortly after the rape Brzonkala stopped attending classes and withdrew from the university.

In early 1995, Brzonkala filed a complaint against respondents under Virginia Tech's Sexual Assault Policy. During the school-conducted hearing on her complaint, Morrison admitted having sexual contact with her despite the fact that she had twice told him "no." After the hearing, Virginia Tech's Judicial Committee found insufficient evidence to punish Crawford, but found Morrison guilty of sexual assault and sentenced him to immediate suspension for two semesters.

Virginia Tech's dean of students upheld the judicial committee's sentence. However, in July 1995, Virginia Tech informed Brzonkala that Morrison intended to initiate a court challenge to his conviction under the Sexual Assault Policy. University officials told her that a second hearing would be necessary to remedy the school's error in prosecuting her complaint under that policy, which had not been widely circulated to students. The university therefore conducted a second hearing under its Abusive Conduct Policy, which was in force prior to the dissemination of the Sexual Assault Policy. Following this second hearing the Judicial Committee again found Morrison guilty and sentenced him to an identical 2-semester suspension. This time, however, the description of Morrison's offense was, without explanation, changed from "sexual assault" to "using abusive language."

Morrison appealed his second conviction through the university's administrative system. On August 21, 1995, Virginia Tech's senior vice president and provost set aside Morrison's punishment. She concluded that it was " 'excessive when compared with other cases where there has been a finding of violation of the Abusive Conduct Policy,'" 132 F.3d 950, 955 (CA4 1997). Virginia Tech did not inform Brzonkala of this decision. After learning from a newspaper that Morrison would be returning to Virginia Tech for the fall 1995 semester, she dropped out of the university.

In December 1995, Brzonkala sued Morrison, Crawford, and Virginia Tech in the United States District Court for the Western District of Virginia. Her complaint alleged that Morrison's and Crawford's attack violated § 13981 and that Virginia Tech's handling of her complaint violated Title IX of the Education Amendments of 1972. Morrison and Crawford moved to dismiss this complaint on the grounds that it failed to state a claim and that § 13981's civil remedy is unconstitutional. The United States, petitioner in No. 99–5, intervened to defend § 13981's constitutionality.

The District Court * * * held that Brzonkala's complaint stated a claim against Morrison and Crawford under § 13981, but dismissed the complaint because it concluded that Congress lacked authority to enact the section under either the Commerce Clause or § 5 of the Fourteenth Amendment.

A divided panel of the Court of Appeals reversed the District Court * * *. The full Court of Appeals vacated the panel's opinion and reheard the case en banc. The en banc court * * * by a divided vote affirmed the District Court's conclusion that Congress lacked constitutional authority to enact § 13981's civil remedy * * *.

Section 13981was part of the Violence Against Women Act of 1994. It states that "[a]ll persons within the United States shall have the right to be free from crimes of violence motivated by gender." To enforce that right, subsection (c) declares:

> "A person (including a person who acts under color of any statute, ordinance, regulation, custom, or usage of any State) who commits a crime of violence motivated by gender and thus deprives another of the right declared in subsection (b) of this section shall be liable to the party injured, in an action for the recovery of compensatory and punitive damages, injunctive and declaratory relief, and such other relief as a court may deem appropriate."

Section 13981 defines a "crim[e] of violence motivated by gender" as "a crime of violence committed because of gender or on the basis of gender, and due, at least in part, to an animus based on the victim's gender." * * *

* * *

Every law enacted by Congress must be based on one or more of its powers enumerated in the Constitution * * *. Congress explicitly identified the sources of federal authority on which it relied in enacting § 13981. It said that a "Federal civil rights cause of action" is established "[p]ursuant to the affirmative power of Congress . . . under section 5 of the Fourteenth Amendment to the Constitution, as well as under section 8 of Article I of the Constitution." 42 U.S.C. § 13981(a) * * *.

* * *

Because we conclude that the Commerce Clause does not provide Congress with authority to enact § 13981, we address petitioners' alternative argument that the section's civil remedy should be upheld as an exercise of Congress' remedial power under § 5 of the Fourteenth Amendment * * *.

The principles governing an analysis of congressional legislation under § 5 are well settled * * *. [S]everal limitations inherent in § 5's text and constitutional context have been recognized since the Fourteenth Amendment was adopted.

Petitioners' § 5 argument is founded on an assertion that there is pervasive bias in various state justice systems against victims of gender-motivated violence. This assertion is supported by a voluminous congressional record. Specifically, Congress received evidence that many participants in state justice systems are perpetuating an array of erroneous stereotypes and assumptions. Congress concluded that these discriminatory stereotypes often result in insufficient investigation and prosecution of gender-motivated crime, inappropriate focus on the behavior and credibility of the victims of that crime, and unacceptably lenient punishments for those who are actually convicted of gender-motivated violence. Petitioners contend that this bias denies victims of gender-motivated violence the equal protection of the laws and that Congress therefore acted appropriately in enacting a private civil remedy against the perpetrators of gender-motivated violence to both remedy the States' bias and deter future instances of discrimination in the state courts.

As our cases have established, state-sponsored gender discrimination violates equal protection unless it " 'serves "important governmental objectives and . . . the discriminatory means employed" are "substantially related to the achievement of those objectives." ' " *United States v. Virginia*, 518 U.S. 515, 533 (1996). However, the language and purpose of the Fourteenth Amendment place certain limitations on the manner in which Congress may attack discriminatory conduct. These limitations are necessary to prevent the Fourteenth Amendment from obliterating the Framers' carefully crafted balance of power between the States and the National Government. Foremost among these limitations is the time-honored principle that the Fourteenth Amendment, by its very terms, prohibits only state action. "[T]he principle has become firmly embedded in our constitutional law that the action inhibited by the first section of the Fourteenth Amendment is only such action as may fairly be said to be that of the States. That Amendment erects no shield against merely private conduct, however discriminatory or wrongful." *Shelley v. Kraemer*, 334 U.S. 1, 13, and n. 12 (1948).

Shortly after the Fourteenth Amendment was adopted, we decided two cases interpreting the Amendment's provisions, *United States v. Harris*, 106 U.S. 629 (1883), and the *Civil Rights Cases*, 109 U.S. 3 (1883). In *Harris*, the Court considered a challenge to § 2 of the Civil Rights Act of 1871. That section sought to punish "private persons" for "conspiring to deprive any one of the equal protection of the laws enacted by the State." 106 U.S., at 639. We concluded that this law exceeded Congress' § 5 power because the law was "directed exclusively against the action of private persons, without reference to the laws of the State, or their administration by her officers." * * *

We reached a similar conclusion in the *Civil Rights Cases*. In those consolidated cases, we held that the public accommodation provisions of the Civil Rights Act of 1875, which applied to purely private conduct, were beyond the scope of the § 5 enforcement power.

The force of the doctrine of *stare decisis* behind these decisions stems not only from the length of time they have been on the books, but also from the insight attributable to the Members of the Court at that time. Every Member had been appointed by President Lincoln, Grant, Hayes, Garfield, or Arthur—and each of their judicial appointees obviously had intimate knowledge and familiarity with the events surrounding the adoption of the Fourteenth Amendment.

Petitioners contend that two more recent decisions have in effect overruled this longstanding limitation on Congress' § 5 authority. They rely on *United States v. Guest*, 383 U.S. 745 (1966), for the proposition that the rule laid down in the *Civil Rights Cases* is no longer good law. In *Guest*, * * * [t]hree Members of the Court, in a separate opinion by Justice Brennan, expressed the view that the *Civil Rights Cases* were wrongly decided * * *. Three other Members of the Court, who joined the opinion of the Court, joined a separate opinion by Justice Clark which in two or three sentences stated the conclusion that Congress could "punis[h] all conspiracies—with or without state action—that interfere with Fourteenth Amendment rights."

* * *

To accept petitioners' argument * * *, one must add to the three Justices joining Justice Brennan's reasoned explanation for his belief that the *Civil Rights Cases* were wrongly decided, the three Justices joining Justice Clark's opinion who gave no explanation whatever for their similar view. This is simply not the way that reasoned constitutional adjudication proceeds. We accordingly have no hesitation in saying that it would take more than the naked dicta contained in Justice Clark's opinion, when added to Justice Brennan's opinion, to cast any doubt upon the enduring vitality of the *Civil Rights Cases* and *Harris*.

* * * We believe that the description of the § 5 power contained in the *Civil Rights Cases* is correct:

> "But where a subject has not submitted to the general legislative power of Congress, but is only submitted thereto for the purpose of rendering effective some prohibition against particular [s]tate legislation or [s]tate action in reference to that subject, the power given is limited by its object, and any legislation by Congress in the matter must necessarily be corrective in its character, adapted to counteract and redress the operation of such prohibited state laws or proceedings of [s]tate officers." 109 U.S., at 18.

Petitioners alternatively argue that, unlike the situation in the *Civil Rights Cases*, here there has been gender-based disparate treatment by state authorities, whereas in those cases there was no indication of such state action. There is abundant evidence, however, to show that the Congresses that enacted the Civil Rights Acts of 1871 and 1875 had a purpose similar to that of Congress in enacting § 13981: There were state laws on the books bespeaking equality of treatment, but in the administration of these laws there was discrimination against newly freed slaves * * *.

But even if that distinction were valid, we do not believe it would save § 13981's civil remedy. For the remedy is simply not "corrective in its character, adapted to counteract and redress the operation of such prohibited [s]tate laws or proceedings of [s]tate officers." *Civil Rights Cases*, 109 U.S., at 18. Or, as we have phrased it in more recent cases, prophylactic legislation under § 5 must have a " 'congruence and proportionality between the injury to be prevented or remedied and the means adopted to that end." *Florida Prepaid Postsecondary Ed. Expense Bd. v. College Savings Bank*, 527 U.S. 627, 639 (1999). Section 13981 is not aimed at proscribing discrimination by officials which the Fourteenth Amendment might not itself proscribe; it is directed not at any State or state actor, but at individuals who have committed criminal acts motivated by gender bias.

In the present cases, for example, § 13981 visits no consequence whatever on any Virginia public official involved in investigating or prosecuting Brzonkala's assault. The section is, therefore, unlike any of the § 5 remedies that we have previously upheld * * *.

* * *

For these reasons, we conclude that Congress' power under § 5 does not extend to the enactment of § 13981.

Petitioner Brzonkala's complaint alleges that she was the victim of a brutal assault. But Congress' effort in § 13981 to provide a federal civil remedy can be sustained neither under the Commerce Clause nor under § 5 of the Fourteenth Amendment. If the allegations here are true, no civilized system of justice could fail to provide her a remedy for the conduct of respondent Morrison. But under our federal system that remedy must be provided by the Commonwealth of Virginia, and not by the United States. The judgment of the Court of Appeals is

Affirmed.

■ JUSTICE THOMAS, concurring. [Omitted.]

■ JUSTICE SOUTER, with whom JUSTICE STEVENS, JUSTICE GINSBURG, and JUSTICE BREYER join, dissenting. [Omitted, as it focuses solely on Congress's commerce power.]

■ JUSTICE BREYER, with whom JUSTICE STEVENS joins, and with whom JUSTICE SOUTER and JUSTICE GINSBURG join as to Part I-A, dissenting.

* * *

II

Given my conclusion on the Commerce Clause question, I need not consider Congress' authority under § 5 of the Fourteenth Amendment. Nonetheless, I doubt the Court's reasoning rejecting that source of authority. The Court points out that in *United States v. Harris,* 106 U.S. 629 (1883), and the *Civil Rights Cases,* 109 U.S. 3, 3 S.Ct. 18 (1883), the Court held that § 5 does not authorize Congress to use the Fourteenth Amendment as a source of power to remedy the conduct of *private persons.* That is certainly so. The Federal Government's argument, however, is that Congress used § 5 to remedy the actions of *state actors,* namely, those States which, through discriminatory design or the discriminatory conduct of their officials, failed to provide adequate (or any) state remedies for women injured by gender-motivated violence—a failure that the States, and Congress, documented in depth.

Neither *Harris* nor the *Civil Rights Cases* considered this kind of claim. The Court in *Harris* specifically said that it treated the federal laws in question as "directed *exclusively* against the action of private persons, without reference to the laws of the State or their administration by her officers." 106 U.S., at 640 (emphasis added).

The Court responds directly to the relevant "state actor" claim by finding that the present law lacks " 'congruence and proportionality' " to the state discrimination that it purports to remedy. *City of Boerne v. Flores,* 521 U.S. 507, 526 (1997). That is because the law, unlike federal laws prohibiting literacy tests for voting, imposing voting rights requirements, or punishing state officials who intentionally discriminated in jury selection, is not "directed . . . at any State or state actor."

But why can Congress not provide a remedy against private actors? Those private actors, of course, did not themselves violate the Constitution. But this Court has held that Congress at least sometimes can enact remedial "[l]egislation . . . [that] prohibits conduct which is not itself unconstitutional." The statutory remedy does not in any sense purport to "determine what constitutes a constitutional violation." It intrudes little upon either States or private parties. It may lead state actors to improve their own remedial systems, primarily through example. It restricts private actors only by imposing liability for private conduct that is, in the main, already forbidden by state law. Why is the remedy "disproportionate"? And given the relation between remedy and violation—the creation of a federal remedy to substitute for constitutionally inadequate state remedies—where is the lack of "congruence"?

The majority adds that Congress found that the problem of inadequacy of state remedies "does not exist in all States, or even most States." But Congress had before it the task force reports of at least 21 States documenting constitutional violations. And it made its own findings about pervasive gender-based stereotypes hampering many state legal systems, sometimes unconstitutionally so. The record nowhere reveals a congressional finding that the problem "does not exist" elsewhere. Why can Congress not take the evidence before it as evidence of a national problem? This Court has not previously held that Congress must document the existence of a problem in every State prior to proposing a national solution. And the deference this Court gives to Congress' chosen remedy under § 5 suggests that any such requirement would be inappropriate.

Despite my doubts about the majority's § 5 reasoning, I need not, and do not, answer the § 5 question, which I would leave for more thorough analysis if necessary on another occasion. Rather, in my view, the Commerce Clause provides an adequate basis for the statute before us. And I would uphold its constitutionality as the "necessary and proper" exercise of legislative power granted to Congress by that Clause.

NOTES AND QUESTIONS

1. A state system in which public officials fail to enforce certain laws on the basis of caste-like considerations, such as sex, is a paradigmatic violation of the Fourteenth Amendment which says that no State may "deny to any person within its jurisdiction the equal protection of the laws." The relevant state action in these circumstances is *inaction*—the refusal of state executive or judicial officials to enforce laws evenhandedly. That kind of state-action-by-inaction is precisely what the Equal Protection Clause of the Fourteenth Amendment targeted. If the allegations in Brzonkala's complaint are true, she was denied the equal protection of the laws; and if the reports presented to Congress were accurate, equal protection violations of this kind were (and no doubt are) pervasive. Does that mean that the Court was wrong in *Morrison*? The Violence Against Women Act provided a remedy against the perpetrators of the underlying crime, not the state officials who did nothing about it. Did the perpetrators violate the Constitution? (Remember that this is sex discrimination, which does not come within the purview of the Thirteenth Amendment.) What kind of statute would Congress need to draft in order to target the Constitution-offending state officials rather than the lawless-but-not-necessarily-

Constitution-offending private actors? Would any such statute provide a practical remedy for someone like Brzonkala?

2. Can Congress use Section 5 essentially to take over or replace a State's executive arm or judicial system if Congress thinks that the State is not fulfilling its constitutional obligations? Is that what the Violence Against Women Act did? It is precisely what Reconstruction did. Does Section 5 of the Fourteenth Amendment authorize Reconstruction-like federal actions? Does it do so, but only under the circumstances of the aftermath of a civil war? Not at all? If Section 5 does not authorize congressional action on that scale, what constitutional provisions might authorize it? Or was Reconstruction unconstitutional? Hold those last two questions for a short while; we will get back to them soon enough.

3. The vast majority of *Morrison* was devoted to the commerce power, with four justices calling for reconsideration of the Court's post-*Lopez* jurisprudence and a return to the deferential practices of 1937–1995. Notice that Justice Breyer—joined in this part of his dissent only by Justice Stevens—expresses doubts about the majority's holding regarding Section 5 but reserves ultimate judgment on the scope of Section 5 for another day. Is the Court's apparent consensus about the scope of Section 5 surprising? Should the state-action holding of *The Civil Rights Cases* be overruled—not just for common carriers and public accommodations but for all activities?

4. We have not yet addressed the enforcement provision for the Fifteenth Amendment, which forbids racial discrimination in voting. This provision has been a fertile source of litigation for decades; many of the precedents relied on in the cases that you have seen thus far were actually cases involving Section 2 of the Fifteenth Amendment. A full treatment of the modern constitutional law of voting would require a separate course. Consider the following controversial and (as is typical in this area of the law) sharply divided decision, which found unconstitutional one of the most prominent modern federal civil rights statutes.

E. SHELBY COUNTY V. HOLDER

570 U.S. 529 (2013)

■ CHIEF JUSTICE ROBERTS delivered the opinion of the Court.

The Voting Rights Act of 1965 employed extraordinary measures to address an extraordinary problem. Section 5 of the Act required States to obtain federal permission before enacting any law related to voting—a drastic departure from basic principles of federalism. And § 4 of the Act applied that requirement only to some States—an equally dramatic departure from the principle that all States enjoy equal sovereignty. This was strong medicine, but Congress determined it was needed to address entrenched racial discrimination in voting, "an insidious and pervasive evil which had been perpetuated in certain parts of our country through unremitting and ingenious defiance of the Constitution." *South Carolina* v. *Katzenbach*, 383 U. S. 301, 309 (1966). As we explained in upholding the law, "exceptional conditions can justify legislative measures not otherwise appropriate." *Id.*, at 334. Reflecting the unprecedented nature of these measures, they were scheduled to expire after five years. See Voting Rights Act of 1965, § 4(a), 79Stat. 438.

Nearly 50 years later, they are still in effect; indeed, they have been made more stringent, and are now scheduled to last until 2031. There is no denying, however, that the conditions that originally justified these measures no longer characterize voting in the covered jurisdictions. By 2009, "the racial gap in voter registration and

turnout [was] lower in the States originally covered by § 5 than it [was] nationwide." *Northwest Austin Municipal Util. Dist. No. One* v. *Holder*, 557 U. S. 193, 203–204 (2009). Since that time, Census Bureau data indicate that African-American voter turnout has come to exceed white voter turnout in five of the six States originally covered by § 5, with a gap in the sixth State of less than one half of one percent.

At the same time, voting discrimination still exists; no one doubts that. The question is whether the Act's extraordinary measures, including its disparate treatment of the States, continue to satisfy constitutional requirements. As we put it a short time ago, "the Act imposes current burdens and must be justified by current needs." *Northwest Austin*, 557 U. S., at 203. 

The Fifteenth Amendment was ratified in 1870, in the wake of the Civil War. It provides that "[t]he right of citizens of the United States to vote shall not be denied or abridged by the United States or by any State on account of race, color, or previous condition of servitude," and it gives Congress the "power to enforce this article by appropriate legislation."

"The first century of congressional enforcement of the Amendment, however, can only be regarded as a failure." In the 1890s, Alabama, Georgia, Louisiana, Mississippi, North Carolina, South Carolina, and Virginia began to enact literacy tests for voter registration and to employ other methods designed to prevent African-Americans from voting. *Katzenbach*, 383 U. S., at 310. Congress passed statutes outlawing some of these practices and facilitating litigation against them, but litigation remained slow and expensive, and the States came up with new ways to discriminate as soon as existing ones were struck down. Voter registration of African-Americans barely improved.

Inspired to action by the civil rights movement, Congress responded in 1965 with the Voting Rights Act. Section 2 was enacted to forbid, in all 50 States, any "standard, practice, or procedure . . . imposed or applied . . . to deny or abridge the right of any citizen of the United States to vote on account of race or color." 79 Stat. 437. The current version forbids any "standard, practice, or procedure" that "results in a denial or abridgement of the right of any citizen of the United States to vote on account of race or color." 42 U. S. C. § 1973(a). Both the Federal Government and individuals have sued to enforce § 2, see, *e.g., Johnson* v. *De Grandy*, 512 U. S. 997 (1994), and injunctive relief is available in appropriate cases to block voting laws from going into effect, see 42 U. S. C. § 1973j(d). Section 2 is permanent, applies nationwide, and is not at issue in this case.

Other sections targeted only some parts of the country. At the time of the Act's passage, these "covered" jurisdictions were those States or political subdivisions that had maintained a test or device as a prerequisite to voting as of November 1, 1964, and had less than 50 percent voter registration or turnout in the 1964 Presidential election. Such tests or devices included literacy and knowledge tests, good moral character requirements, the need for vouchers from registered voters, and the like. A covered jurisdiction could "bail out" of coverage if it had not used a test or device in the preceding five years "for the purpose or with the effect of denying or abridging the right to vote on account of race or color." In 1965, the covered States included Alabama, Georgia, Louisiana, Mississippi, South Carolina, and Virginia. The additional covered subdivisions included 39 counties in North Carolina and one in Arizona.

In those jurisdictions, § 4 of the Act banned all such tests or devices. Section 5 provided that no change in voting procedures could take effect until it was approved by federal authorities in Washington, D. C.—either the Attorney General or a court of three judges. A jurisdiction could obtain such "preclearance" only by proving that the change had neither "the purpose [nor] the effect of denying or abridging the right to vote on account of race or color."

Sections 4 and 5 were intended to be temporary; they were set to expire after five years. In *South Carolina* v. *Katzenbach*, we upheld the 1965 Act against constitutional challenge, explaining that it was justified to address "voting discrimination where it persists on a pervasive scale." 383 U. S., at 308.

In 1970, Congress reauthorized the Act for another five years, and extended the coverage formula in § 4(b) to jurisdictions that had a voting test and less than 50 percent voter registration or turnout as of 1968. That swept in several counties in California, New Hampshire, and New York. Congress also extended the ban in § 4(a) on tests and devices nationwide.

In 1975, Congress reauthorized the Act for seven more years, and extended its coverage to jurisdictions that had a voting test and less than 50 percent voter registration or turnout as of 1972. Congress also amended the definition of "test or device" to include the practice of providing English-only voting materials in places where over five percent of voting-age citizens spoke a single language other than English. As a result of these amendments, the States of Alaska, Arizona, and Texas, as well as several counties in California, Florida, Michigan, New York, North Carolina, and South Dakota, became covered jurisdictions. Congress correspondingly amended § 2 and § 5 to forbid voting discrimination on the basis of membership in a language minority group, in addition to discrimination on the basis of race or color. Finally, Congress made the nationwide ban on tests and devices permanent.

In 1982, Congress reauthorized the Act for 25 years, but did not alter its coverage formula. See Voting Rights Act Amendments, Congress did, however, amend the bailout provisions, allowing political subdivisions of covered jurisdictions to bail out. Among other prerequisites for bailout, jurisdictions and their subdivisions must not have used a forbidden test or device, failed to receive preclearance, or lost a § 2 suit, in the ten years prior to seeking bailout.

We upheld each of these reauthorizations against constitutional challenge. See *Georgia* v. *United States*, 411 U. S. 526 (1973); *City of Rome* v. *United States*, 446 U. S. 156 (1980); *Lopez* v. *Monterey County*, 525 U. S. 266 (1999).

In 2006, Congress again reauthorized the Voting Rights Act for 25 years, again without change to its coverage formula. Congress also amended § 5 to prohibit more conduct than before. Section 5 now forbids voting changes with "any discriminatory purpose" as well as voting changes that diminish the ability of citizens, on account of race, color, or language minority status, "to elect their preferred candidates of choice." 42 U. S. C. §§ 1973c(b)–(d).

Shortly after this reauthorization, a Texas utility district brought suit, seeking to bail out from the Act's coverage and, in the alternative, challenging the Act's constitutionality. See *Northwest Austin*, 557 U. S., at 200–201. A three-judge District Court explained that only a State or political subdivision was eligible to seek bailout under the statute, and concluded that the utility district was not a political subdivision, a term that encompassed only "counties, parishes, and voter-registering subunits."

We reversed * * *. Concluding that "underlying constitutional concerns," among other things, "compel[led] a broader reading of the bailout provision," we construed the statute to allow the utility district to seek bailout. *Northwest Austin*, 557 U. S., at 207. In doing so we expressed serious doubts about the Act's continued constitutionality.

We explained that § 5 "imposes substantial federalism costs" and "differentiates between the States, despite our historic tradition that all the States enjoy equal sovereignty." *Id.*, at 202, 203. We also noted that "[t]hings have changed in the South. Voter turnout and registration rates now approach parity. Blatantly discriminatory evasions of federal decrees are rare. And minority candidates hold office at unprecedented levels." *Id.*, at 202. Finally, we questioned whether the problems that § 5 meant to address were still "concentrated in the jurisdictions singled out for preclearance." *Id.*, at 203.

Eight Members of the Court subscribed to these views, and the remaining Member would have held the Act unconstitutional. Ultimately, however, the Court's construction of the bailout provision left the constitutional issues for another day.

Shelby County is located in Alabama, a covered jurisdiction. It has not sought bailout, as the Attorney General has recently objected to voting changes proposed from within the county. Instead, in 2010, the county sued the Attorney General in Federal District Court in Washington, D. C., seeking a declaratory judgment that § 4(b) and § 5 of the Voting Rights Act are facially unconstitutional, as well as a permanent injunction against their enforcement. The District Court ruled against the county and upheld the Act. 811 F. Supp. 2d 424, 508 (2011). The court found that the evidence before Congress in 2006 was sufficient to justify reauthorizing § 5 and continuing the § 4(b) coverage formula.

The Court of Appeals for the D. C. Circuit affirmed * * *.

* * *

Judge Williams dissented * * *. Judge Williams would have held the coverage formula of § 4(b) "irrational" and unconstitutional. *Id.*, at 885.

* * *

In *Northwest Austin*, we stated that "the Act imposes current burdens and must be justified by current needs." 557 U. S., at 203. And we concluded that "a departure from the fundamental principle of equal sovereignty requires a showing that a statute's disparate geographic coverage is sufficiently related to the problem that it targets." *Ibid.* These basic principles guide our review of the question before us.

* * *

Outside the strictures of the Supremacy Clause, States retain broad autonomy in structuring their governments and pursuing legislative objectives. Indeed, the Constitution provides that all powers not specifically granted to the Federal Government are reserved to the States or citizens. Amdt. 10. This "allocation of powers in our federal system preserves the integrity, dignity, and residual sovereignty of the States." *Bond* v. *United States*, 564 U. S. 211, 221 (2011). But the federal balance "is not just an end in itself: Rather, federalism secures to citizens the liberties that derive from the diffusion of sovereign power." *Ibid.*

More specifically, " 'the Framers of the Constitution intended the States to keep for themselves, as provided in the Tenth Amendment, the power to regulate elections.' " *Gregory* v. *Ashcroft*, 501 U. S. 452, 461–462 (1991) (quoting *Sugarman* v. *Dougall*, 413 U. S. 634, 647 (1973)). Of course, the Federal Government retains significant control over federal elections. For instance, the Constitution authorizes Congress to establish the time and manner for electing Senators and Representatives. Art. I, § 4, cl. 1. But States have "broad powers to determine the conditions under which the right of suffrage may be exercised." *Carrington* v. *Rash*, 380 U. S. 89, 91 (1965). And "[e]ach State has the power to prescribe the qualifications of its officers and the manner in which they shall be chosen." *Boyd* v. *Nebraska ex rel. Thayer*, 143 U. S. 135, 161 (1892). Drawing lines for congressional districts is likewise "primarily the duty and responsibility of the State." *Perry* v. *Perez*, 565 U. S. 388, 392 (2012) (*per curiam*).

Not only do States retain sovereignty under the Constitution, there is also a "fundamental principle of *equal* sovereignty" among the States. *Northwest Austin*, *supra*, at 203. Over a hundred years ago, this Court explained that our Nation "was and is a union of States, equal in power, dignity and authority." *Coyle* v. *Smith*, 221 U. S. 559, 567 (1911) * * *. [A]s we made clear in *Northwest Austin*, the fundamental principle of equal sovereignty remains highly pertinent in assessing subsequent disparate treatment of States. 557 U. S., at 203.

The Voting Rights Act sharply departs from these basic principles. It suspends "*all* changes to state election law—however innocuous—until they have been precleared by federal authorities in Washington, D. C." *Id.*, at 202. States must beseech the Federal Government for permission to implement laws that they would otherwise have the right to enact and execute on their own, subject of course to any injunction in a § 2 action. The Attorney General has 60 days to object to a preclearance request, longer if he requests more information. See 28 CFR §§ 51.9, 51.37. If a State seeks preclearance from a three-judge court, the process can take years.

And despite the tradition of equal sovereignty, the Act applies to only nine States (and several additional counties). While one State waits months or years and expends funds to implement a validly enacted law, its neighbor can typically put the same law into effect immediately, through the normal legislative process * * *.

All this explains why, when we first upheld the Act in 1966, we described it as "stringent" and "potent." *Katzenbach,* 383 U. S., at 308, 315, 337. We recognized that it "may have been an uncommon exercise of congressional power," but concluded that "legislative measures not otherwise appropriate" could be justified by "exceptional conditions." *Id.,* at 334. We have since noted that the Act "authorizes federal intrusion into sensitive areas of state and local policymaking," *Lopez*, 525 U. S., at 282, and represents an "extraordinary departure from the traditional course of relations between the States and the Federal Government," *Presley* v. *Etowah County Comm'n*, 502 U. S. 491, 500–501 (1992). As we reiterated in *Northwest Austin*, the Act constitutes "extraordinary legislation otherwise unfamiliar to our federal system." 557 U. S., at 211.

In 1966, we found these departures from the basic features of our system of government justified. The "blight of racial discrimination in voting" had "infected the electoral process in parts of our country for nearly a century." *Katzenbach*, 383 U. S., at 308. Several States had enacted a variety of requirements and tests "specifically designed to prevent" African-Americans from voting. *Id.*, at 310. Case-by-case litigation had proved inadequate to prevent such racial discrimination in voting, in part because States "merely switched to discriminatory devices not covered by the federal decrees," "enacted difficult new tests," or simply "defied and evaded court orders." *Id.*, at 314. Shortly before enactment of the Voting Rights Act, only 19.4 percent of African-Americans of voting age were registered to vote in Alabama, only 31.8 percent in Louisiana, and only 6.4 percent in Mississippi. *Id.*, at 313. Those figures were roughly 50 percentage points or more below the figures for whites. *Ibid.*

In short, we concluded that "[u]nder the compulsion of these unique circumstances, Congress responded in a permissibly decisive manner." *Id.*, at 334, 335. We also noted then and have emphasized since that this extraordinary legislation was intended to be temporary, set to expire after five years. *Id.*, at 333; *Northwest Austin*, *supra*, at 199.

At the time, the coverage formula—the means of linking the exercise of the unprecedented authority with the problem that warranted it—made sense. We found that "Congress chose to limit its attention to the geographic areas where immediate action seemed necessary." *Katzenbach*, 383 U. S., at 328. The areas where Congress found "evidence of actual voting discrimination" shared two characteristics: "the use of tests and devices for voter registration, and a voting rate in the 1964 presidential election at least 12 points below the national average." *Id.*, at 330. We explained that "[t]ests and devices are relevant to voting discrimination because of their long history as a tool for perpetrating the evil; a low voting rate is pertinent for the obvious reason that widespread disenfranchisement must inevitably affect the number of actual voters." *Ibid.* We therefore concluded that "the coverage formula [was] rational in both practice and theory." *Ibid.* It accurately reflected those jurisdictions uniquely characterized by voting discrimination "on a pervasive scale," linking coverage to the devices used to effectuate discrimination and to the resulting disenfranchisement. *Id.*, at 308. The formula ensured that the "stringent remedies [were] aimed at areas where voting discrimination ha[d] been most flagrant." *Id.*, at 315.

Nearly 50 years later, things have changed dramatically. Shelby County contends that the preclearance requirement, even without regard to its disparate coverage, is now unconstitutional. Its arguments have a good deal of force. In the covered jurisdictions, "[v]oter turnout and registration rates now approach parity. Blatantly discriminatory evasions of federal decrees are rare. And minority candidates hold office at unprecedented levels." *Northwest Austin*, 557 U. S., at 202. The tests and devices that blocked access to the ballot have been forbidden nationwide for over 40 years. See § 6, 84 Stat. 315; § 102, 89 Stat. 400.

* * *

Yet the Act has not eased the restrictions in § 5 or narrowed the scope of the coverage formula in § 4(b) along the way. Those extraordinary and unprecedented features were reauthorized—as if nothing had changed. In fact, the Act's unusual remedies have grown even stronger * * *.

* * *

Respondents do not deny that there have been improvements on the ground, but argue that much of this can be attributed to the deterrent effect of § 5, which dissuades covered jurisdictions from engaging in discrimination that they would resume should § 5 be struck down. Under this theory, however, § 5 would be effectively immune from scrutiny; no matter how "clean" the record of covered jurisdictions, the argument could always be made that it was deterrence that accounted for the good behavior.

The provisions of § 5 apply only to those jurisdictions singled out by § 4. We now consider whether that coverage formula is constitutional in light of current conditions.

When upholding the constitutionality of the coverage formula in 1966, we concluded that it was "rational in both practice and theory." *Katzenbach*, 383 U. S., at 330. The formula looked to cause (discriminatory tests) and effect (low voter registration and turnout), and tailored the remedy (preclearance) to those jurisdictions exhibiting both.

* * *

Coverage today is based on decades-old data and eradicated practices. The formula captures States by reference to literacy tests and low voter registration and turnout in the 1960s and early 1970s. But such tests have been banned nationwide for over 40 years. And voter registration and turnout numbers in the covered States have risen dramatically in the years since. Racial disparity in those numbers was compelling evidence justifying the preclearance remedy and the coverage formula. See, *e.g., Katzenbach, supra*, at 313, 329–330. There is no longer such a disparity.

In 1965, the States could be divided into two groups: those with a recent history of voting tests and low voter registration and turnout, and those without those characteristics. Congress based its coverage formula on that distinction. Today the Nation is no longer divided along those lines, yet the Voting Rights Act continues to treat it as if it were.

* * *

The Government falls back to the argument that because the formula was relevant in 1965, its continued use is permissible so long as any discrimination remains in the States Congress identified back then—regardless of how that discrimination compares to discrimination in States unburdened by coverage. Brief for Federal Respondent 49–50 * * *.

But history did not end in 1965. By the time the Act was reauthorized in 2006, there had been 40 more years of it. In assessing the "current need[ ]" for a preclearance system that treats States differently from one another today, that history cannot be ignored. During that time, largely because of the Voting Rights Act, voting tests were abolished, disparities in voter registration and turnout due to race were erased, and African-Americans attained political office in record numbers. And yet the coverage formula that Congress reauthorized in 2006 ignores these developments, keeping the focus on decades-old data relevant to decades-old problems, rather than current data reflecting current needs.

* * *

In defending the coverage formula, the Government, the intervenors, and the dissent also rely heavily on data from the record that they claim justify disparate coverage * * *. Regardless of how to look at the record, however, no one can fairly say that it shows anything approaching the "pervasive," "flagrant," "widespread," and "rampant" discrimination that faced Congress in 1965, and that clearly distinguished the covered jurisdictions from the rest of the Nation at that time.

But a more fundamental problem remains: Congress did not use the record it compiled to shape a coverage formula grounded in current conditions. It instead reenacted a formula based on 40-year-old facts having no logical relation to the present day. The dissent relies on "second-generation barriers," which are not impediments to the casting of ballots, but rather electoral arrangements that affect the weight of minority votes. That does not cure the problem. Viewing the preclearance requirements as targeting such efforts simply highlights the irrationality of continued reliance on the § 4 coverage formula, which is based on voting tests and access to the ballot, not vote dilution. We cannot pretend that we are reviewing an updated statute, or try our hand at updating the statute ourselves, based on the new record compiled by Congress. Contrary to the dissent's contention, we are not ignoring the record; we are simply recognizing that it played no role in shaping the statutory formula before us today.

The dissent also turns to the record to argue that, in light of voting discrimination in Shelby County, the county cannot complain about the provisions that subject it to preclearance. But that is like saying that a driver pulled over pursuant to a policy of stopping all redheads cannot complain about that policy, if it turns out his license has expired. Shelby County's claim is that the coverage formula here is unconstitutional in all its applications, because of how it selects the jurisdictions subjected to preclearance. The county was selected based on that formula, and may challenge it in court.

* * *

The dissent treats the Act as if it were just like any other piece of legislation, but this Court has made clear from the beginning that the Voting Rights Act is far from ordinary * * *.

* * *

There is no valid reason to insulate the coverage formula from review merely because it was previously enacted 40 years ago. If Congress had started from scratch in 2006, it plainly could not have enacted the present coverage formula. It would have been irrational for Congress to distinguish between States in such a fundamental way based on 40-year-old data, when today's statistics tell an entirely different story. And it would have been irrational to base coverage on the use of voting tests 40 years ago, when such tests have been illegal since that time. But that is exactly what Congress has done.

* * *

Our decision in no way affects the permanent, nationwide ban on racial discrimination in voting found in § 2. We issue no holding on § 5 itself, only on the coverage formula. Congress may draft another formula based on current conditions. Such a formula is an initial prerequisite to a determination that exceptional conditions still exist justifying such an "extraordinary departure from the traditional course of relations between the States and the Federal Government." *Presley*, 502 U. S., at 500–501. Our country has changed, and while any racial discrimination in voting is too much, Congress must ensure that the legislation it passes to remedy that problem speaks to current conditions.

The judgment of the Court of Appeals is reversed.

It is so ordered.

■ JUSTICE THOMAS, concurring.

I join the Court's opinion in full but write separately to explain that I would find § 5 of the Voting Rights Act unconstitutional as well. The Court's opinion sets forth the reasons.

* * *

* * * By leaving the inevitable conclusion unstated, the Court needlessly prolongs the demise of that provision. For the reasons stated in the Court's opinion, I would find § 5 unconstitutional.

■ JUSTICE GINSBURG, with whom JUSTICE BREYER, JUSTICE SOTOMAYOR, and JUSTICE KAGAN join, dissenting.

In the Court's view, the very success of § 5 of the Voting Rights Act demands its dormancy. Congress was of another mind. Recognizing that large progress has been made, Congress determined, based on a voluminous record, that the scourge of discrimination was not yet extirpated. The question this case presents is who decides whether, as currently operative, § 5 remains justifiable, this Court, or a Congress charged with the obligation to enforce the post-Civil War Amendments "by appropriate legislation." * * *

"[V]oting discrimination still exists; no one doubts that." But the Court today terminates the remedy that proved to be best suited to block that discrimination. The Voting Rights Act of 1965 (VRA) has worked to combat voting discrimination where other remedies had been tried and failed. Particularly effective is the VRA's requirement of federal preclearance for all changes to voting laws in the regions of the country with the most aggravated records of rank discrimination against minority voting rights.

* * *

Although the VRA wrought dramatic changes in the realization of minority voting rights, the Act, to date, surely has not eliminated all vestiges of discrimination against the exercise of the franchise by minority citizens. Jurisdictions covered by the preclearance requirement continued to submit, in large numbers, proposed changes to voting laws that the Attorney General declined to approve, auguring that barriers to minority voting would quickly resurface were the preclearance remedy eliminated. Congress also found that as "registration and voting of minority citizens increas[ed], other measures may be resorted to which would dilute increasing minority voting strength." Efforts to reduce the impact of minority votes, in contrast to direct attempts to block access to the ballot, are aptly described as "second-generation barriers" to minority voting.

Second-generation barriers come in various forms. One of the blockages is racial gerrymandering, the redrawing of legislative districts in an "effort to segregate the races for purposes of voting." Another is adoption of a system of at-large voting in lieu of district-by-district voting in a city with a sizable black minority. By switching to at-large voting, the overall majority could control the election of each city council member, effectively eliminating the potency of the minority's votes. A similar effect could be achieved if the city engaged in discriminatory annexation by incorporating majority-white areas into city limits, thereby decreasing the effect of VRA-occasioned increases in black voting. Whatever the device employed, this Court has long recognized that vote dilution, when adopted with a discriminatory purpose, cuts down the right to vote as certainly as denial of access to the ballot.

In response to evidence of these substituted barriers, Congress reauthorized the VRA for five years in 1970, for seven years in 1975, and for 25 years in 1982. Each time, this Court upheld the reauthorization as a valid exercise of congressional power. As the 1982 reauthorization approached its 2007 expiration date, Congress again considered whether the VRA's preclearance mechanism remained an appropriate response to the problem of voting discrimination in covered jurisdictions.

Congress did not take this task lightly. Quite the opposite * * *.

In the long course of the legislative process, Congress "amassed a sizable record." The House and Senate Judiciary Committees held 21 hearings, heard from scores of witnesses, received a number of investigative reports and other written documentation of continuing discrimination in covered jurisdictions. In all, the legislative record Congress compiled filled more than 15,000 pages. The compilation presents countless "examples of flagrant racial discrimination" since the last reauthorization; Congress also brought to light systematic evidence that "intentional racial discrimination in voting remains so serious and widespread in covered jurisdictions that section 5 preclearance is still needed."

After considering the full legislative record, Congress made the following findings: The VRA has directly caused significant progress in eliminating first-generation barriers to ballot access, leading to a marked increase in minority voter registration and turnout and the number of minority elected officials. But despite this progress, "second generation barriers constructed to prevent minority voters from fully participating in the electoral process" continued to exist, as well as racially polarized voting in the covered jurisdictions, which increased the political vulnerability of racial and language minorities in those jurisdictions. Extensive "[e]vidence of continued discrimination," Congress concluded, "clearly show[ed] the continued need for Federal oversight" in covered jurisdictions. The overall record demonstrated to the federal lawmakers that, "without the continuation of the Voting Rights Act of 1965 protections, racial and language minority citizens will be deprived of the opportunity to exercise their right to vote, or will have their votes diluted, undermining the significant gains made by minorities in the last 40 years."

Based on these findings, Congress reauthorized preclearance for another 25 years, while also undertaking to reconsider the extension after 15 years to ensure that the provision was still necessary and effective. The question before the Court is whether Congress had the authority under the Constitution to act as it did.

In answering this question, the Court does not write on a clean slate. It is well established that Congress' judgment regarding exercise of its power to enforce the Fourteenth and Fifteenth Amendments warrants substantial deference. The VRA addresses the combination of race discrimination and the right to vote, which is "preservative of all rights." *Yick Wo* v. *Hopkins*, 118 U. S. 356, 370 (1886). When confronting the most constitutionally invidious form of discrimination, and the most fundamental right in our democratic system, Congress' power to act is at its height.

The basis for this deference is firmly rooted in both constitutional text and precedent. The Fifteenth Amendment, which targets precisely and only racial discrimination in voting rights, states that, in this domain, "Congress shall have power to enforce this article by appropriate legislation." In choosing this language, the Amendment's framers invoked Chief Justice Marshall's formulation of the scope of Congress' powers under the Necessary and Proper Clause:

> "Let the end be legitimate, let it be within the scope of the constitution, and *all means which are appropriate, which are plainly adapted to that end*, which are not prohibited, but consist with the letter and spirit of the constitution, are constitutional." *McCulloch* v. *Maryland*, 4 Wheat. 316, 421 (1819) (emphasis added).

It cannot tenably be maintained that the VRA, an Act of Congress adopted to shield the right to vote from racial discrimination, is inconsistent with the letter or spirit of the Fifteenth Amendment, or any provision of the Constitution read in light of the Civil War Amendments. Nowhere in today's opinion, or in *Northwest Austin*, is there clear recognition of the transformative effect the Fifteenth Amendment aimed to achieve * * *.

* * * [W]hen Congress acts to enforce the right to vote free from racial discrimination, we ask not whether Congress has chosen the means most wise, but whether Congress has rationally selected means appropriate to a legitimate end. "It is not for us to review the congressional resolution of [the need for its chosen remedy]. It is enough that we be able to perceive a basis upon which the Congress might resolve the conflict as it did." *Katzenbach* v. *Morgan*, 384 U. S. 641, 653 (1966).

* * *

* * * [L]egislation reauthorizing an existing statute is especially likely to satisfy the minimal requirements of the rational-basis test * * *.

* * *

* * * [A] reviewing court should expect the record supporting reauthorization to be less stark than the record originally made. Demand for a record of violations equivalent to the one earlier made would expose Congress to a catch-22. If the statute was working, there would be less evidence of discrimination, so opponents might argue that Congress should not be allowed to renew the statute. In contrast, if the statute was not working, there would be plenty of evidence of discrimination, but scant reason to renew a failed regulatory regime.

This is not to suggest that congressional power in this area is limitless. It is this Court's responsibility to ensure that Congress has used appropriate means. The question meet for judicial review is whether the chosen means are "adapted to carry out the objects the amendments have in view." The Court's role, then, is not to substitute its judgment for that of Congress, but to determine whether the legislative record sufficed to show that "Congress could rationally have determined that [its chosen] provisions were appropriate methods."

* * *

There is no question * * * that the covered jurisdictions have a unique history of problems with racial discrimination in voting. Consideration of this long history, still in living memory, was altogether appropriate. The Court criticizes Congress for failing to recognize that "history did not end in 1965." But the Court ignores that "what's past is prologue." W. Shakespeare, The Tempest, act 2, sc. 1. And "[t]hose who cannot remember the past are condemned to repeat it." 1 G. Santayana, The

Life of Reason 284 (1905). Congress was especially mindful of the need to reinforce the gains already made and to prevent backsliding.

Of particular importance, even after 40 years and thousands of discriminatory changes blocked by preclearance, conditions in the covered jurisdictions demonstrated that the formula was still justified by "current needs." *Northwest Austin*, 557 U. S., at 203.

Congress learned of these conditions through a report, known as the Katz study * * *. The study's findings * * * indicated that racial discrimination in voting remains "concentrated in the jurisdictions singled out for preclearance." *Northwest Austin*, 557 U. S., at 203.

* * * From these findings—ignored by the Court—Congress reasonably concluded that the coverage formula continues to identify the jurisdictions of greatest concern.

The evidence before Congress, furthermore, indicated that voting in the covered jurisdictions was more racially polarized than elsewhere in the country. While racially polarized voting alone does not signal a constitutional violation, it is a factor that increases the vulnerability of racial minorities to discriminatory changes in voting law. The reason is twofold. First, racial polarization means that racial minorities are at risk of being systematically outvoted and having their interests underrepresented in legislatures. Second, "when political preferences fall along racial lines, the natural inclinations of incumbents and ruling parties to entrench themselves have predictable racial effects. Under circumstances of severe racial polarization, efforts to gain political advantage translate into race-specific disadvantages."

* * *

The case for retaining a coverage formula that met needs on the ground was therefore solid. Congress might have been charged with rigidity had it afforded covered jurisdictions no way out or ignored jurisdictions that needed superintendence. Congress, however, responded to this concern. Critical components of the congressional design are the statutory provisions allowing jurisdictions to "bail out" of preclearance, and for court-ordered "bail ins." See *Northwest Austin*, 557 U. S., at 199. The VRA permits a jurisdiction to bail out by showing that it has complied with the Act for ten years, and has engaged in efforts to eliminate intimidation and harassment of voters. It also authorizes a court to subject a noncovered jurisdiction to federal preclearance upon finding that violations of the Fourteenth and Fifteenth Amendments have occurred there.

* * *

This experience exposes the inaccuracy of the Court's portrayal of the Act as static, unchanged since 1965. Congress designed the VRA to be a dynamic statute, capable of adjusting to changing conditions. True, many covered jurisdictions have not been able to bail out due to recent acts of noncompliance with the VRA, but that truth reinforces the congressional judgment that these jurisdictions were rightfully subject to preclearance, and ought to remain under that regime.

Congress approached the 2006 reauthorization of the VRA with great care and seriousness. The same cannot be said of the Court's opinion today. The Court makes no genuine attempt to engage with the massive legislative record that Congress assembled. Instead, it relies on increases in voter registration and turnout as if that were the whole story. Without even identifying a standard of review, the Court dismissively brushes off arguments based on "data from the record," and declines to enter the "debat[e about] what [the] record shows." One would expect more from an opinion striking at the heart of the Nation's signal piece of civil-rights legislation.

* * *

The Court stops any application of § 5 by holding that § 4(b)'s coverage formula is unconstitutional. It pins this result, in large measure, to "the fundamental principle of equal sovereignty." In *Katzenbach*, however, the Court held, in no uncertain terms, that the principle "*applies only to the terms upon which States are admitted to the Union*, and not to the remedies for local evils which have subsequently appeared." 383 U. S., at 328–329 (emphasis added).

* * *

Today's unprecedented extension of the equal sovereignty principle outside its proper domain—the admission of new States—is capable of much mischief. Federal statutes that treat States disparately are hardly novelties. See, *e.g.,* 28 U. S. C. § 3704 (no State may operate or permit a sports-related gambling scheme, unless that State conducted such a scheme "at any time during the period beginning January 1, 1976, and ending August 31, 1990"); 26 U. S. C. § 142(*l*) (Environmental Protection Agency required to locate green building project in a State meeting specified population criteria); 42 U. S. C. § 3796bb (at least 50 percent of rural drug enforcement assistance funding must be allocated to States with "a population density of fifty-two or fewer persons per square mile or a State in which the largest county has fewer than one hundred and fifty thousand people, based on the decennial census of 1990 through fiscal year 1997"); §§ 13925, 13971 (similar population criteria for funding to combat rural domestic violence); § 10136 (specifying rules applicable to Nevada's Yucca Mountain nuclear waste site, and providing that "[n]o State, other than the State of Nevada, may receive financial assistance under this subsection after December 22, 1987"). Do such provisions remain safe given the Court's expansion of equal sovereignty's sway?

* * *

The Court has time and again declined to upset legislation of this genre unless there was no or almost no evidence of unconstitutional action by States. See, *e.g., City of Boerne* v. *Flores*, 521 U. S. 507, 530 (1997) (legislative record "mention[ed] no episodes [of the kind the legislation aimed to check] occurring in the past 40 years"). No such claim can be made about the congressional record for the 2006 VRA reauthorization. Given a record replete with examples of denial or abridgment of a paramount federal right, the Court should have left the matter where it belongs: in Congress' bailiwick.

* * *

Consider once again the components of the record before Congress in 2006. The coverage provision identified a known list of places with an undisputed history of serious problems with racial discrimination in voting. Recent evidence relating to Alabama and its counties was there for all to see. Multiple Supreme Court decisions had upheld the coverage provision, most recently in 1999. There was extensive evidence that, due to the preclearance mechanism, conditions in the covered jurisdictions had notably improved. And there was evidence that preclearance was still having a substantial real-world effect, having stopped hundreds of discriminatory voting changes in the covered jurisdictions since the last reauthorization. In addition, there was evidence that racial polarization in voting was higher in covered jurisdictions than elsewhere, increasing the vulnerability of minority citizens in those jurisdictions. And countless witnesses, reports, and case studies documented continuing problems with voting discrimination in those jurisdictions. In light of this record, Congress had more than a reasonable basis to conclude that the existing coverage formula was not out of sync with conditions on the ground in covered areas. And certainly Shelby County was no candidate for release through the mechanism Congress provided.

* * *

Beyond question, the VRA is no ordinary legislation. It is extraordinary because Congress embarked on a mission long delayed and of extraordinary importance: to realize the purpose and promise of the Fifteenth Amendment. For a half century, a concerted effort has been made to end racial discrimination in voting. Thanks to the VRA, progress once the subject of a dream has been achieved and continues to be made.

* * *

For the reasons stated, I would affirm the judgment of the Court of Appeals.

NOTES AND QUESTIONS

1. The dissent claims that the majority does not set forth a standard of review (the dissent suggests a "rational basis" test). Is that a correct account of the majority opinion? What standard of review does the majority apply in this case? Has it imported the "congruence and proportionality" inquiry from Section 5? Is that a plausible interpretation of Section 2 of the Fifteenth Amendment? More on that below.

2. Is the majority worried that Congress has treated States *badly,* that it has treated States *differently,* or both? On the latter front: Chief Justice Roberts is right that an underlying structural premise of the Constitution, and indeed of the New States Admissions Clause, is that all the States are completely equal to one another. New States admitted to the Union have exactly the same status—such as a right to two Senators—as did all the pre-existing States on the date a new State was added. This so-called "equal footing doctrine" has generated much litigation, mostly involving newly admitted state ownership of land under navigable waters. *See, e.g., PPL Montana, LLC v. Montana,* 565 U.S. 576 (2012). (Keep in mind that, apart from the original thirteen States, the few—such as Vermont, Maine and West Virginia—formed out of those original States, and the annexed States of Hawaii and Texas, all of the States came from land that was once under federal ownership. Those States automatically enter the Union at a substantial disadvantage, because the federal government is going to own much of their land—it owns, for example, 99 percent of the land in Alaska. The equal footing doctrine at least gives the new States the same authority over navigable waters as was possessed by the original States.) Does the equal footing doctrine mean that every congressional law must impact every State equally? Obviously not; the Constitution is very clear about those matters for which it requires uniformity among States, such as indirect taxes and port regulations. The equal footing doctrine guarantees state equality in legal capacities, not substantive state equality. Is there any reason to think that congressional legislation under the Reconstruction Amendments(!) must treat all States the same? Section 2 of the Fourteenth Amendment explicitly treated States differently by denying representation

in the House and electoral college to States that discriminated on the basis of race in voting rights. Did the Reconstruction Amendments thereby amend, in 1870, any pre-existing "equal footing doctrine"?

3. On the other hand, even under a deferential rational basis test, Congress must have *some* reason for passing laws that apply to some States but not others, especially when those laws deprive States of the right to establish their own political processes. Is past history a sufficient reason to apply the Voting Rights Act to some States but not others? Does the Fifteenth Amendment give Congress power essentially to tell States that supported slavery, tried to secede from the Union, fought a Civil War, and maintained a system of Jim Crow segregation for decades afterwards that they might just have to suck it up for a while longer? If so, for how much longer? Is it relevant that the coverage formula of Section 4 included many jurisdictions that were not part of the 1861 Confederacy?

4. With respect to treating States badly rather than unequally: Under a rational basis test, isn't Justice Ginsburg pretty obviously right in this case, because the congressional legislation is not actually irrational—it is just a very imperfect leaky bucket? It will likely stop some race discrimination in voting, and that is all that "rational" legislation under Section 2 of the Fifteenth Amendment must do. On a more stringent standard of review, however, the majority's position starts to look stronger, because the remedial regime in the Voting Rights Act is poorly tailored, both substantively and geographically, to the underlying constitutional violations. If, as Congress thinks, States have devised new and innovative ways to discriminate, wouldn't one think that a new and innovative law targeting those new and innovative devices would be in order? A forty-year-old coverage formula is very unlikely to meet a "congruence and proportionality" test when we are talking about telling States how to structure their political institutions. Does *Shelby County* therefore hold that "congruence and proportionality" applies to Section 2 of the Fifteenth Amendment? If so, it overruled *Katzenbach v. Morgan* without saying so—and *Katzenbach v. Morgan* is perhaps the central case in modern voting rights law. If the majority is not applying a congruence and proportionality test, what is it doing?

[Assignment 43]

XVI. ARTICLE IV: SECTIONS 1 AND 2

A. THE FULL FAITH AND CREDIT CLAUSE

Article IV, Section 1: Full Faith and Credit shall be given in each State to the public Acts, Records, and judicial Proceedings of every other State; And the Congress may by general Laws prescribe the Manner in which such Acts, Records, and Proceedings shall be proved, and the Effect thereof.

The Full Faith and Credit Clause contains two separate provisions. The first copies an almost identical provision in the Articles of Confederation and deals with the obligations each State owes to other States in the Union. States must recognize out-of-state "public Acts, Records, and judicial Proceedings." The second part of the clause gives Congress an enumerated power to define how judgments and acts of State A are going to be proved in State B (after all, a party claiming to have a judgment from State A might just be making it up) and also, importantly, to prescribe "the Effect thereof." The *recognition* of the act and the *effect* of the act are, both textually and conceptually, two different things. Once you, as a legal actor in State A, have recognized an act, record, or judgment from State B as valid, what do you have to do with that act? What if Congress passes no statutes on the subject? What obligation does State A have towards State B's judgments and laws simply by virtue of the Full Faith and Credit Clause itself?

Modern law, drawing on some remarks from Justice Story in an 1833 treatise, says that the Constitution itself requires States to give effect to the judgments and laws of other States. There is some reason to think that this misunderstands the Clause's original meaning, which only requires States to *acknowledge* other States' laws and judgments while leaving it to Congress to determine whether and when States must give *effect* to out-of-state laws and judgments, *see* David E. Engdahl, *The Classic Rule of Faith and Credit,* 118 YALE L.J. 1584 (2009); Ralph U. Whitten, *Full Faith and Credit for Dummies,* 38 CREIGHTON L. REV. 465 (2008), but the doctrine has been settled to the contrary for a long time.

With this understanding, it is easy enough to see what it means to give full faith and credit to "judicial proceedings" of other States: judgments entered by courts in State A must be enforceable in the courts of State B without need for re-litigation of the claims. But what does it mean to give full faith and credit to the "Acts" of another State? If State A and State B both have laws on a subject, and those laws differ in some important respect, does State A fail to give "Full Faith and Credit" to the acts of State B if State A applies its own law to a citizen of State B who happens to be in State A? That seems extraordinary—surely the Constitution does not let people carry the laws of their States with them as they travel.to other States. On the other hand, if a statute in State B invalidates a transaction, can a party travel to State A, re-litigate the matter, and have the transaction validated there? The Full Faith and Credit Clause, as construed by the courts to prescribe the effects of out-of-state law, thus constitutionalizes to some extent the problem of "choice of law." Choice of law is a sub-specialty, complete with its own law school course (often called "Conflicts of Laws"), and we do not presume to say much about it here. But a recent trilogy of Supreme Court decisions—all involving the same parties and the same transaction—illustrates how complex these issues can become and summarizes much of the current constitutional law on the subject. We present below the first of these cases; we will get to the two sequels shortly.

B. FRANCHISE TAX BOARD OF CALIFORNIA V. HYATT

538 U.S. 488 (2003)

■ JUSTICE O'CONNOR delivered the opinion of the Court.

We granted certiorari to resolve whether the Nevada Supreme Court's refusal to extend full faith and credit to California's statute immunizing its tax collection agency from suit violates Article IV, § 1, of the Constitution. We conclude it does not, and we therefore affirm the judgment of the Nevada Supreme Court.

Respondent Gilbert P. Hyatt (hereinafter respondent) filed a "part-year" resident income tax return in California for 1991. In the return, respondent represented that as of October 1, 1991, he had ceased to be a California resident and had become a resident of Nevada. In 1993, petitioner California Franchise Tax Board (CFTB) commenced an audit to determine whether respondent had underpaid state income taxes. The audit focused on respondent's claim that he had changed residency shortly before receiving substantial licensing fees for certain patented inventions related to computer technology.

At the conclusion of its audit, CFTB determined that respondent was a California resident until April 3, 1992, and accordingly issued notices of proposed assessments for income taxes for 1991 and 1992 and imposed substantial civil fraud penalties. Respondent protested the proposed assessments and penalties in California through CFTB's administrative process.

On January 6, 1998, with the administrative protest ongoing in California, respondent filed a lawsuit against CFTB in Nevada in Clark County District Court. Respondent alleges that CFTB directed "numerous and continuous contacts . . . at Nevada" and committed several torts during the course of the audit, including invasion of privacy, outrageous conduct, abuse of process, fraud, and negligent misrepresentation. Respondent seeks punitive and compensatory damages * * *.

* * * CFTB argued that the District Court lacked subject matter jurisdiction because principles of sovereign immunity, full faith and credit, choice of law, comity, and administrative exhaustion all required that the District Court apply California law, under which:

> "Neither a public entity nor a public employee is liable for an injury caused by:
>
> "(a) Instituting any judicial or administrative proceeding or action for or incidental to the assessment or collection of a tax [or]
>
> "(b) An act or omission in the interpretation or application of any law relating to a tax." Cal. Govt.Code Ann. § 860.2 (West 1995).

The District Court denied CFTB's motion * * *.

* * * [T]he Nevada Supreme Court * * * held that the District Court "should have declined to exercise its jurisdiction over the underlying negligence claim under comity principles" but that the intentional tort claims could proceed to trial.

The Nevada Supreme Court noted that both Nevada and California have generally waived their sovereign immunity from suit in state court and "have extended the waivers to their state agencies or public employees except when state statutes expressly provide immunity." Whereas Nevada has not conferred immunity on its state agencies for intentional torts committed within the course and scope of employment, the court acknowledged that "California has expressly provided [CFTB] with complete immunity." To determine which State's law should apply, the court applied principles of comity.

Though the Nevada Supreme Court recognized the doctrine of comity as "an accommodation policy, under which the courts of one state voluntarily give effect to the laws and judicial decisions of another state out of deference and respect, to promote harmonious interstate relations," the court also recognized its duty to determine whether the application of California law "would contravene Nevada's policies or interests," giving "due regard to the duties, obligations, rights and convenience of Nevada's citizens." * * * With respect to the intentional torts * * *, the court held that "affording [CFTB] statutory immunity . . . does contravene Nevada's policies and interests in this case." Because Nevada "does not allow its agencies to claim immunity for discretionary acts taken in bad faith, or for intentional torts committed in the course and scope of employment," the court held that "Nevada's interest in protecting its citizens from injurious intentional torts and bad faith acts committed by sister states' government employees" should be accorded greater weight "than California's policy favoring complete immunity for its taxation agency."

We granted certiorari to resolve whether Article IV, § 1, of the Constitution requires Nevada to give full faith and credit to California's statute providing its tax agency with immunity from suit, and we now affirm.

The Constitution's Full Faith and Credit Clause provides: "Full Faith and Credit shall be given in each State to the public Acts, Records, and judicial Proceedings of every other State. And the Congress may by general Laws prescribe the Manner in which such Acts, Records and Proceedings shall be proved, and the Effect thereof." Art. IV, § 1. As we have explained, "[o]ur precedent differentiates the credit owed to laws (legislative measures and common law) and to judgments." *Baker v. General Motors Corp.*, 522 U.S. 222, 232 (1998). Whereas the full faith and credit command "is exacting" with respect to "[a] final judgment . . . rendered by a court with adjudicatory authority over the subject matter and persons governed by the judgment," *id.*, at 233, it is less demanding with respect to choice of laws. We have held that the Full Faith and Credit Clause does not compel " 'a state to substitute the statutes of other states for its own statutes dealing with a subject matter concerning which it is competent to legislate.' "

The State of Nevada is undoubtedly "competent to legislate" with respect to the subject matter of the alleged intentional torts here, which, it is claimed, have injured one of its citizens within its borders. " '[F]or a State's substantive law to be selected in a constitutionally permissible manner, that State must have a significant contact or significant aggregation of contacts, creating state interests, such that choice of its law is neither arbitrary nor fundamentally unfair.' " *Phillips Petroleum Co. v. Shutts*, 472 U.S. 797, 818 (1985). Such contacts are manifest in this case: the plaintiff claims to have suffered injury in Nevada while a resident there; and it is undisputed that at least some of the conduct alleged to be tortious occurred in Nevada.

CFTB does not contend otherwise. Instead, CFTB urges this Court to adopt a "new rule" mandating that a state court extend full faith and credit to a sister State's statutorily recaptured sovereign immunity from suit when a refusal to do so would "interfer[e] with a State's capacity to fulfill its own sovereign responsibilities." Brief for Petitioner 13.

We have, in the past, appraised and balanced state interests when invoking the Full Faith and Credit Clause to resolve conflicts between overlapping laws of coordinate States. See *Bradford Elec. Light Co. v. Clapper*, 286 U.S. 145 (1932) (holding that the Constitution required a federal court sitting in New Hampshire to apply a Vermont workers' compensation statute in a tort suit brought by the administrator of a Vermont worker killed in New Hampshire). This balancing approach quickly proved unsatisfactory. As Justice Robert H. Jackson, recounting these cases, aptly observed, "it [is] difficult to point to any field in which the Court has more completely demonstrated or more candidly confessed the lack of guiding standards of a legal character than in trying to determine what choice of law is required by the Constitution." Full Faith and Credit—The Lawyer's Clause of the Constitution, 45 Colum. L. Rev. 1, 16 (1945).

In light of this experience, we abandoned the balancing-of-interests approach to conflicts of law under the Full Faith and Credit Clause. We have recognized, instead, that "it is frequently the case under the Full Faith and Credit Clause that a court can lawfully apply either the law of one State or the contrary law of another." *Sun Oil Co. v. Wortman*, [486 U.S. 717, 727 (1988)]. We thus have held that a State need not "substitute the statutes of other states for its own statutes dealing with a subject matter concerning which it is competent to legislate." Acknowledging this shift, CFTB contends that this case demonstrates the need for a new rule under the Full Faith and Credit Clause that will protect "core sovereignty" interests as expressed in state statutes delineating the contours of the State's immunity from suit. Brief for Petitioner 13.

We disagree. We have confronted the question whether the Full Faith and Credit Clause requires a forum State to recognize a sister State's legislatively recaptured immunity once before. In *Nevada v. Hall*, 440 U.S. 410 (1979), an employee of the University of Nevada was involved in an automobile accident with California residents, who filed suit in California and named Nevada as a defendant. The California courts refused to apply a Nevada statute that capped damages in tort suits against the State on the ground that "to surrender jurisdiction or to limit respondents' recovery to the $25,000 maximum of the Nevada statute would be obnoxious to its statutorily based policies of jurisdiction over nonresident motorists and full recovery." *Id.*, at 424.

We affirmed, holding, first, that the Constitution does not confer sovereign immunity on States in the courts of sister States. Petitioner does not ask us to reexamine that ruling, and we therefore decline the invitation of petitioner's *amici* States, see Brief for State of Florida et al. as *Amici Curiae* 2, to do so.

The question presented here instead implicates *Hall*'s second holding: that the Full Faith and Credit Clause did not require California to apply Nevada's sovereign immunity statutes where such application would violate California's own legitimate public policy. The Court observed in a footnote:

> "California's exercise of jurisdiction in this case poses no substantial threat to our constitutional system of cooperative federalism. Suits involving traffic accidents occurring outside of Nevada could hardly interfere with Nevada's capacity to fulfill its own sovereign responsibilities. We have no occasion, in this case, to consider whether different state policies, either of California or of Nevada, might require a different analysis or a different result." Id., at 424, n. 24.

CFTB asserts that an analysis of this lawsuit's effects should lead to a different result: that the Full Faith and Credit Clause requires Nevada to apply California's immunity statute to avoid interference with California's "sovereign responsibility" of enforcing its income tax laws.

Our past experience with appraising and balancing state interests under the Full Faith and Credit Clause counsels against adopting CFTB's proposed new rule. Having recognized, in *Hall,* that a suit against a State in a sister State's court "necessarily implicates the power and authority" of both sovereigns, 440 U.S., at 416, the question of which sovereign interest should be deemed more weighty is not one that can be easily answered. Yet petitioner's rule would elevate California's sovereignty interests above those of Nevada, were we to deem this lawsuit an interference with California's "core sovereign responsibilities." We rejected as "unsound in principle and unworkable in practice" a rule of state immunity from federal regulation under the Tenth Amendment that turned on whether a particular state government function was "integral" or "traditional." *Garcia v. San Antonio Metropolitan Transit Authority*, 469 U.S. 528, 546–547 (1985). CFTB has convinced us of neither the relative soundness nor the relative practicality of adopting a similar distinction here.

Even were we inclined to embark on a course of balancing States' competing sovereign interests to resolve conflicts of laws under the Full Faith and Credit Clause, this case would not present the occasion to do so. There is no principled distinction between Nevada's interests in tort claims arising out of its university employee's automobile accident, at issue in *Hall*, and California's interests in the tort claims here arising out of its tax collection agency's residency audit. To be sure, the power to promulgate and enforce income tax laws is an essential attribute of sovereignty. But the university employee's educational mission in *Hall* might also be so described.

If we were to compare the degree to which the allegedly tortious acts here and in *Hall* are related to a core sovereign function, we would be left to ponder the relationship between an automobile accident and educating, on one hand, and the intrusions alleged here and collecting taxes, on the other. We discern no constitutionally significant distinction between these relationships. To the extent CFTB complains of the burdens and expense of out-of-state litigation, and the diversion of state resources away from the performance of important state functions, those burdens do not distinguish this case from any other out-of-state lawsuit against California or one of its agencies.

States' sovereignty interests are not foreign to the full faith and credit command. But we are not presented here with a case in which a State has exhibited a "policy of hostility to the public Acts" of a sister State. The Nevada Supreme Court sensitively applied principles of comity with a healthy regard for California's sovereign status, relying on the contours of Nevada's own sovereign immunity from suit as a benchmark for its analysis.

* * *

The judgment of the Nevada Supreme Court is affirmed.

It is so ordered.

NOTES AND QUESTIONS

1. This case was one chapter of a lengthy saga. The parties returned to the Supreme Court thirteen years later, in 2016, where Justice Breyer picks up the story:

> On remand, the case went to trial. A jury found in Hyatt's favor and awarded him close to $500 million in damages (both compensatory and punitive) and fees (including attorney's fees). California appealed. It argued that the trial court had not properly followed the Nevada Supreme Court's earlier decision. California explained that in a similar suit against similar Nevada officials, Nevada statutory law would limit damages to $50,000, and it argued that the Constitution's Full Faith and Credit Clause required Nevada to limit damages similarly here.
>
> The Nevada Supreme Court accepted the premise that Nevada statutes would impose a $50,000 limit in a similar suit against its own officials. But the

court rejected California's conclusion. Instead, while setting aside much of the damages award, it nonetheless affirmed $1 million of the award (earmarked as compensation for fraud), and it remanded for a retrial on the question of damages for intentional infliction of emotional distress. In doing so, it stated that "damages awarded on remand . . . are not subject to any statutory cap." The Nevada Supreme Court explained its holding by stating that California's efforts to control the actions of its own agencies were inadequate as applied to Nevada's own citizens. Hence, Nevada's "policy interest in providing adequate redress to Nevada's citizens [wa]s paramount to providing [California] a statutory cap on damages under comity."

California petitioned for certiorari. We agreed to decide two questions. First, whether to overrule [*Nevada v.*] *Hall.* And, second, if we did not do so, whether the Constitution permits Nevada to award Hyatt damages against a California state agency that are greater than those that Nevada would award in a similar suit against its own state agencies.

In light of our 4-to-4 [split on whether to overrule *Nevada v. Hall,* which said that States are not constitutionally entitled to sovereign immunity against suit in the courts of other States] * * *, we must consider the second question: Whether the Constitution permits Nevada to award damages against California agencies under Nevada law that are greater than it could award against Nevada agencies in similar circumstances. We conclude that it does not. The Nevada Supreme Court has ignored both Nevada's typical rules of immunity and California's immunity-related statutes (insofar as California's statutes would prohibit a monetary recovery that is greater in amount than the maximum recovery that Nevada law would permit in similar circumstances). Instead, it has applied a special rule of law that evinces a " 'policy of hostility' " toward California. Doing so violates the Constitution's requirement that "Full Faith and Credit shall be given in each State to the public Acts, Records and judicial Proceedings of every other State." Art. IV, § 1.

The Court's precedents strongly support this conclusion. A statute is a "public Act" within the meaning of the Full Faith and Credit Clause. We have said that the Clause "does not require a State to substitute for its own statute, applicable to persons and events within it, the statute of another State reflecting a conflicting and opposed policy." But when affirming a State's decision to decline to apply another State's statute on this ground, we have consistently emphasized that the State had "not adopt[ed] any policy of hostility to the public Acts" of that other State.

* * *

The Nevada decision before us embodies a critical departure from its earlier approach. Nevada has not applied the principles of Nevada law ordinarily applicable to suits against Nevada's own agencies. Rather, it has applied a special rule of law applicable only in lawsuits against its sister States, such as California. With respect to damages awards greater than $50,000, the ordinary principles of Nevada law do not "conflic[t]" with California law, for both laws would grant immunity. Similarly, in respect to such amounts, the "polic[ies]" underlying California law and Nevada's usual approach are not "opposed"; they are consistent.

But that is not so in respect to Nevada's special rule. That rule, allowing damages awards greater than $50,000, is not only "opposed" to California law,

> it is also inconsistent with the general principles of Nevada immunity law. The Nevada Supreme Court explained its departure from those general principles by describing California's system of controlling its own agencies as failing to provide "adequate" recourse to Nevada's citizens * * *. Such an explanation, which amounts to little more than a conclusory statement disparaging California's own legislative, judicial, and administrative controls, cannot justify the application of a special and discriminatory rule. Rather, viewed through a full faith and credit lens, a State that disregards its own ordinary legal principles on this ground is hostile to another State. A constitutional rule that would permit this kind of discriminatory hostility is likely to cause chaotic interference by some States into the internal, legislative affairs of others * * *. In our view, Nevada's rule lacks the "healthy regard for California's sovereign status" that was the hallmark of its earlier decision, and it reflects a constitutionally impermissible " 'policy of hostility to the public Acts' of a sister State."
>
> In so holding we need not, and do not, intend to return to a complex "balancing-of-interests approach to conflicts of law under the Full Faith and Credit Clause." Long ago this Court's efforts to apply that kind of analysis led to results that seemed to differ depending, for example, upon whether the case involved commercial law, a shareholders' action, insurance claims, or workman's compensation statutes. We have since abandoned that approach, and we continue to recognize that a State need not " 'substitute the statutes of other states for its own statutes dealing with a subject matter concerning which it is competent to legislate.' " But here, we can safely conclude that, in devising a special—and hostile—rule for California, Nevada has not "sensitively applied principles of comity with a healthy regard for California's sovereign status."

Franchise Tax Board of California v. Hyatt, 136 S.Ct. 1277, 1280–83 (2016). Chief Justice Roberts and Justice Thomas did not think that Nevada had violated the Constitution:

> In this case, the Nevada Supreme Court applied Nevada rather than California immunity law in order to uphold the "state's policy interest in providing adequate redress to Nevada citizens." This Court has long recognized that "[f]ew matters could be deemed more appropriately the concern of the state in which the injury occurs or more completely within its power" than "the bodily safety and economic protection" of people injured within its borders * * *.
>
> The majority, however, does not regard that policy interest as sufficient justification for denying the Board immunity. Despite this Court's decision to get out of the business of "appraising and balancing state interests under the Full Faith and Credit Clause," *Franchise Tax Bd.,* 538 U.S., at 498, the majority concludes that Nevada cannot *really* have a state policy to protect its citizens from the kinds of torts alleged here, because the State capped its own liability at $50,000 in similar situations. But that fails to credit the Nevada Supreme Court's explanation for why a damages cap for Nevada state agencies is fully consistent with the State's policy of protecting its citizens.
>
> According to the Nevada Supreme Court, Nevada law treats its own agencies differently from the agencies of other States because Nevada agencies are "subject to legislative control, administrative oversight, and public accountability" in Nevada. 130 Nev., at ___, 335 P.3d, at 147 The same is not true of other litigants, such as the Board, who operate "outside such controls." *Ibid.* (internal quotation marks omitted). The majority may think that Nevada is being unfair, but it cannot be said that the State failed to articulate a

> sufficient policy explanation for its decision to apply a damages cap to Nevada state agencies, but not to the agencies of other States.

Id. at 1286–87 (Roberts, C.J., dissenting). But even that was not the end of the story. These cases involved an agency of the California State government being sued in Nevada courts without its consent. The Supreme Court, in *Nevada v. Hall* in 1979, had permitted such suits. The Court in *Franchise Tax II* split 4–4 on whether to overrule *Hall*. Three years later, in 2019, *Hall* was overruled (5–4), and the saga came to an end. *See Franchise Tax Board of California v. Hyatt,* 139 S.Ct. 1485 (2019). The suit was dismissed. Accordingly, State agencies can no longer be sued in the courts of other States without their consent, but the underlying full-faith-and-credit issues regarding choice of law remain unresolved.

2. *Franchise Tax* illustrates the difficulty of determining when, if ever, States are required to apply the laws of other States. None of those problems arises, of course, if Congress rather than the Court determines when and how State laws must be given effect within other States.

3. Do States really have to give effect to judicial judgments in other States even if those judgments reflect policy views anathema to the State? The short answer is "yes," which is why "quickie" Nevada divorces had to be recognized everywhere even when most States had far more restrictive divorce laws. *See Williams v. State of North Carolina,* 317 U.S. 287 (1942); *Sherrer v. Sherrer,* 334 U.S. 343 (1948). At one point in the debate over gay marriage, Hawaii was expected to try to take advantage of this doctrine by specifying that same-sex marriages recognized in that State would all be codified in a judicial judgment, which would then force every State to recognize those Hawaii marriages under the Full Faith and Credit Clause. Had this come to pass, courts might have had to decide whether marriages, which are non-adversarial proceedings, really count as "judicial Proceedings" under the Full Faith and Credit Clause just because a State says that they do. But Congress, with President Bill Clinton's signature, responded in 1996 with the Defense of Marriage Act ("DOMA"), part of which defined marriage as the union of one man and one woman for federal purposes and another part of which relieved States of any obligation to credit the judgments or legislative acts of other States purporting to validate same-sex marriages. In *United States v. Windsor,* 570 U.S. 744 (2013), the Supreme Court invalidated the federal-law portion of DOMA. The full-faith-and-credit portion of the statute was hotly debated by academics for two decades but was rendered moot by *Obergefell v. Hodges,* 135 S.Ct. 2584 (2015). *See supra* pages 546–555.

C. THE PRIVILEGES AND IMMUNITIES CLAUSE

Article IV, Section 2, Clause 1: The Citizens of each State shall be entitled to all Privileges and Immunities of Citizens in the several States.

The Privileges or Immunities Clause of Article IV, Section 2 descends from the following Clause in Article IV of the Articles of Confederation:

> The better to secure and perpetuate mutual friendship and intercourse among the people of the different States in this Union, the free inhabitants of each of these States, paupers, vagabonds, and fugitives from justice excepted, shall be entitled to all privileges and immunities of free citizens in the several States; and the people of each State shall free ingress and regress to and from any other State, and shall enjoy therein all the privileges of trade and commerce, subject to the same duties, impositions,

> and restrictions as the inhabitants thereof respectively, provided that such restrictions shall not extend so far as to prevent the removal of property imported into any State, to any other State, of which the owner is an inhabitant; provided also that no imposition, duties or restriction shall be laid by any State, on the property of the United States, or either of them.

Several things are noteworthy here. First, under the Articles of Confederation, all free inhabitants of the thirteen original states, including, of course, free African-Americans, were entitled as of right "to all privilege and immunities of free citizens in the several States. Does this mean that free African-Americans were recognized as being U.S. citizens when the Constitution was proposed and ratified between 1787 and 1791? What is the significance of the fact that free African-Americans voted for delegates to the state conventions which ratified the U.S. Constitution in five of the thirteen original states?

Second, the Privileges and Immunities Clause of Article IV has been construed to mean that persons from State B enjoyed in State A exactly the same civil rights as were enjoyed by citizens of State A. Examples of such civil rights, which out-of-state citizens were guaranteed under the Privileges or Immunities Clause, include: 1) State A's common law rights of torts, contracts, property, inheritance, and family law; 2) civil rights which State A gave to its own citizens in state statutes, such as state anti-discrimination laws; and 3) civil rights which State A gave to its own citizens in its state constitution, such as the right to freedom of expression, freedom of religion, or to own a gun. *See Saenz v. Roe,* 526 U.S. 489, 501–02 (1999):

> Thus, by virtue of a person's state citizenship, a citizen of one State who travels in other States, intending to return home at the end of his journey, is entitled to enjoy the "Privileges and Immunities of Citizens in the several States" that he visits. This provision removes "from the citizens of each State the disabilities of alienage in the other States." *Paul v. Virginia*, 8 Wall. 168, 180 (1868). It provides important protections for nonresidents who enter a State whether to obtain employment, *Hicklin v. Orbeck*, 437 U.S. 518 (1978), to procure medical services, *Doe v. Bolton*, 410 U.S. 179, 200 (1973), or even to engage in commercial shrimp fishing, *Toomer v. Witsell*, 334 U.S. 385 (1948). Those protections are not "absolute," but the Clause "does bar discrimination against citizens of other States where there is no substantial reason for the discrimination beyond the mere fact that they are citizens of other States." *Id.*, at 396. There may be a substantial reason for requiring the nonresident to pay more than the resident for a hunting license, see *Baldwin v. Fish and Game Comm'n of Mont.,* 436 U.S. 371, 390–391 (1978), or to enroll in the state university, see *Vlandis v. Kline*, 412 U.S. 441, 445 (1973), but our cases have not identified any acceptable reason for qualifying the protection afforded by the Clause for "the 'citizen of State A who ventures into State B' to settle there and establish a home." As a matter of original meaning, at least some of these results are questionable (notice that the clause speaks of "Privileges and Immunities" rather than "Rights" as the objects of equality), but the doctrine has long settled on a broad construction.

The purpose of the Privileges and Immunities Clause of Article IV, Section 2 was to help knit the thirteen states into one nation by forbidding the States from discriminating against out-of-state citizens. There were, however, two categories of rights that a State gives to its citizens which are not "Privileges and Immunities" and which a State does not need to, and does not in practice accord to, out-of-state citizens. The first category is *political rights* as opposed to *civil rights*. Political rights included: 1) the right to vote in State or municipal elections, 2) the right to run for state or municipal office, 3) the right to serve as a juror in a state trail, and 4) the right to serve in a State militia or national guard units. Citizens of State B do not enjoy equal *political rights* with citizens of State A. If they want to obtain those rights, they have to change their State citizenship, which they can do. The second category involves State proprietary rights. Citizens of State A are not categorically obligated to share State property equally with out-of-State citizens. This is why today the University of Virginia School of Law, for example, can charge higher tuition to out-of-state students than it charges to in-state students. *But see* Robert G. Natelson, *The Original Meaning of the Privileges and Immunities Clause,* 43 GA. L. REV. 1117 (2009) (suggesting that differential tuition for in-state and out-of-state students probably violates the original meaning of the Privileges and Immunities Clause). Early cases suggested that States might have an absolute right to discriminate against out-of-staters in the use and distribution of State-owned resources, *see McCready v. Virginia,* 94 U.S. (4 Otto) 391, 395 (1876) ("we think we may safely hold that the citizens of one State are not invested by this clause of the Constitution with any interest in the common property of the citizens of another State"), but modern cases are more equivocal:

> We do not agree that the fact that a State owns a resource, of itself, completely removes a law concerning that resource from the prohibitions of the Clause. Although some courts, including the court below, have read *McCready* as creating an "exception" to the Privileges and Immunities Clause, we have just recently confirmed that "[i]n more recent years . . . the Court has recognized that the States' interest in regulating and controlling those things they claim to 'own' . . . is by no means absolute." *Baldwin v. Montana Fish and Game Comm'n,* 436 U.S., at 385. Rather than placing a statute completely beyond the Clause, a State's ownership of the property with which the statute is concerned is a factor—although often the crucial factor—to be considered in evaluating whether the statute's discrimination against noncitizens violates the Clause.

Hicklin v. Orbeck, 437 U.S. 518, 528–29 (1978).

Very early in our constitutional history, an enormously consequential case arose under the Privileges and Immunities Clause, which was decided by Supreme Court Justice Bushrod Washington riding circuit as a lower court judge. In that case, *Corfield v. Coryell*, 6 Fed. Cas. 546 (No. 3,230) (C.C.E.D. Pa. 1825), Mr. Corfield, a citizen of Delaware, challenged the validity of a New Jersey statute which prohibited out-of-staters from raking for oysters, clams, or shells in New Jersey waters. Justice Washington ruled for the State of New Jersey and against Corfield, holding that the oyster beds in question were *state property* and that Mr. Corfield was thus not being deprived of any of his civil or fundamental rights by New Jersey in violation of Article IV, Section 2. This holding seems unexceptionable, but along the way Justice Washington made the following observations:

> The inquiry is, what are the privileges and immunities of citizens in the several states? We feel no hesitation in confining these expressions to those privileges and immunities which are, in their nature, fundamental;

> which belong, of right, to the citizens of all free governments; and which have, at all times, been enjoyed by the citizens of the several states which compose this Union, from the time of their becoming free, independent, and sovereign. What these fundamental principles are, it would perhaps be more tedious than difficult to enumerate. They may, however, be all comprehended under the following general heads: Protection by the government; the enjoyment of life and liberty, with the right to acquire and possess property of every kind, and to pursue and obtain happiness and safety; subject nevertheless to such restraints as the government may justly prescribe for the general good of the whole.
>
> The right of a citizen of one state to pass through, or to reside in any other state, for purposes of trade, agriculture, professional pursuits, or otherwise; to claim the benefit of the writ of habeas corpus; to institute and maintain actions of any kind in the courts of the state; to take, hold and dispose of property, either real or personal; and an exemption from higher taxes or impositions that are paid by the other citizens of the state; may be mentioned as some of the particular privileges and immunities of citizens, which are clearly embraced by the general description of privileges deemed to be fundamental: * * * These, and many others which might be mentioned, are, strictly speaking, privileges and immunities, and the enjoyment of them by the citizens of each state, in every other state, was manifestly calculated (to use the expressions of the preamble of the corresponding provision in the old articles of confederation) "the better to secure and perpetuate mutual friendship and intercourse among the people of the different states of the Union."

Obviously, this was all dictum, because the case concerned only rights of access to natural resources. But, as we will see later, the dictum has assumed far more significance than the holding.

Part—but only a part—of the significance of *Corfield* concerns the modern Court's notion that the Privileges and Immunities Clause protects "fundamental" but not "non-fundamental" rights. Consider, for example, the following (relatively) modern Supreme Court Privileges and Immunities Clause case involving the practice of law.

D. SUPREME COURT OF NEW HAMPSHIRE V. PIPER

470 U.S. 274 (1985)

■ JUSTICE POWELL delivered the opinion of the Court.

The Rules of the Supreme Court of New Hampshire limit bar admission to state residents. We here consider whether this restriction violates the Privileges and Immunities Clause of the United States Constitution, Art. IV, § 2.

Kathryn Piper lives in Lower Waterford, Vermont, about 400 yards from the New Hampshire border. In 1979, she applied to take the February 1980 New Hampshire bar examination. Piper submitted with her application a statement of intent to become a New Hampshire resident. Following an investigation, the Board of Bar Examiners found that Piper was of good moral character and met the other requirements for admission. She was allowed to take, and passed, the examination.

Piper was informed by the Board that she would have to establish a home address in New Hampshire prior to being sworn in.

On May 7, 1980, Piper requested from the Clerk of the New Hampshire Supreme Court a dispensation from the residency requirement. Although she had a "possible job" with a lawyer in Littleton, New Hampshire, Piper stated that becoming a resident of New Hampshire would be inconvenient. Her house in Vermont was secured by a mortgage with a favorable interest rate, and she and her husband recently had become parents. According to Piper, these "problems peculiar to [her] situation . . . warrant[ed] that an exception be made."

On May 13, 1980, the Clerk informed Piper that her request had been denied. She then formally petitioned the New Hampshire Supreme Court for permission to become a member of the bar * * *. The Supreme Court denied Piper's formal request on December 31, 1980.

On March 22, 1982, Piper filed this action in the United States District Court for the District of New Hampshire * * *. She alleged that Rule 42 of the New Hampshire Supreme Court, that excludes nonresidents from the bar, violates the Privileges and Immunities Clause of Art. IV, § 2, of the United States Constitution.

[Editors' Note: Piper won in federal district court, and the judgment survived review in an evenly divided en banc First Circuit Court of Appeals.]

* * *

Article IV, § 2, of the Constitution provides that the "Citizens of each State shall be entitled to all Privileges and Immunities of Citizens in the several States." This Clause was intended to "fuse into one Nation a collection of independent, sovereign States." *Toomer v. Witsell*, 334 U.S. 385, 395 (1948). Recognizing this purpose, we have held that it is "[o]nly with respect to those 'privileges' and 'immunities' bearing on the vitality of the Nation as a single entity" that a State must accord residents and nonresidents equal treatment. *Baldwin v. Montana Fish & Game Comm'n*, [436 U.S. 371, 383 (1978). In *Baldwin*, for example, we concluded that a State may charge a nonresident more than it charges a resident for the same elk-hunting license. Because elk hunting is "recreation," rather than a "means of a livelihood," we found that the right to a hunting license was not "fundamental" to the promotion of interstate harmony. 436 U.S. at 388.

Derived, like the Commerce Clause, from the fourth of the Articles of Confederation, the Privileges and Immunities Clause was intended to create a national economic union. It is therefore not surprising that this Court repeatedly has found that one of the privileges which the Clause guarantees to citizens of State A is that of doing business in State B on terms of substantial equality with the citizens of that State. In *Ward v. Maryland*, 12 Wall. 418 (1871), the Court invalidated a statute under which nonresidents were required to pay $300 per year for a license to trade in goods not manufactured in Maryland, while resident traders paid a fee varying from $12 to $150. Similarly, in *Toomer, supra*, the Court held that nonresident fishermen could not be required to pay a license fee of $2,500 for each shrimp boat owned when residents were charged only $25 per boat. Finally, in *Hicklin v. Orbeck*, 437 U.S. 518 (1978), we found violative of the Privileges and Immunities Clause a statute containing a resident hiring preference for all employment related to the development of the State's oil and gas resources.

There is nothing in *Ward, Toomer*, or *Hicklin* suggesting that the practice of law should not be viewed as a "privilege" under Art. IV, § 2. Like the occupations considered in our earlier cases, the practice of law is important to the national economy. As the Court noted in *Goldfarb v. Virginia State Bar*, 421 U.S. 773, 788 (1975), the "activities of lawyers play an important part in commercial intercourse."

The lawyer's role in the national economy is not the only reason that the opportunity to practice law should be considered a "fundamental right." We believe that the legal profession has a noncommercial role and duty that reinforce the view that the practice of law falls within the ambit of the Privileges and Immunities Clause. Out-of-state lawyers may—and often do—represent persons who raise unpopular federal claims. In some cases, representation by nonresident counsel may be the only means available for the vindication of federal rights. The lawyer who champions unpopular causes surely is as important to the "maintenance or well-being of the Union," *Baldwin*, 436 U.S. at 388, as was the shrimp fisherman in *Toomer* or the pipeline worker in *Hicklin*.

Appellant asserts that the Privileges and Immunities Clause should be held inapplicable to the practice of law because a lawyer's activities are "bound up with the exercise of judicial power and the administration of justice." Its contention is based on the premise that the lawyer is an "officer of the court," who "exercises state power on a daily basis." Appellant concludes that, if the State cannot exclude nonresidents from the bar, its ability to function as a sovereign political body will be threatened.

Lawyers do enjoy a "broad monopoly . . . to do things other citizens may not lawfully do." We do not believe, however, that the practice of law involves an "exercise of state power" justifying New Hampshire's residency requirement * * *.

* * * [A] lawyer is not an "officer" of the State in any political sense, [so] there is no reason for New Hampshire to exclude from its bar nonresidents. We therefore conclude that the right to practice law is protected by the Privileges and Immunities Clause.

The conclusion that Rule 42 deprives nonresidents of a protected privilege does not end our inquiry. The Court has stated that "[l]ike many other constitutional provisions, the privileges and immunities clause is not an absolute." *Toomer v. Witsell,* 334 U.S., at 396; see *United Building & Construction Trades Council v. Mayor & Council of Camden,* 465 U.S. 208, 222 (1984). The Clause does not preclude discrimination against nonresidents where (i) there is a substantial reason for the difference in treatment; and (ii) the discrimination practiced against nonresidents bears a substantial relationship to the State's objective. *Ibid.* In deciding whether the discrimination bears a close or substantial relationship to the State's objective, the Court has considered the availability of less restrictive means.

The Supreme Court of New Hampshire offers several justifications for its refusal to admit nonresidents to the bar. It asserts that nonresident members would be less likely (i) to become, and remain, familiar with local rules and procedures; (ii) to behave ethically; (iii) to be available for court proceedings; and (iv) to do *pro bono* and other volunteer work in the State. We find that none of these reasons meets the test of "substantiality," and that the means chosen do not bear the necessary relationship to the State's objectives.

* * *

We conclude that New Hampshire's bar residency requirement violates the Privileges and Immunities Clause of Art. IV, § 2, of the United States Constitution. The nonresident's interest in practicing law is a "privilege" protected by the Clause. Although the lawyer is "an officer of the court," he does not hold a position that can be entrusted only to a "full-fledged member of the political community." A State may discriminate against nonresidents only where its reasons are "substantial," and the difference in treatment bears a close or substantial relation to those reasons. No such showing has been made in this case. Accordingly, we affirm the judgment of the Court of Appeals.

It is so ordered.

■ JUSTICE WHITE, concurring in the result. [Omitted.]

■ JUSTICE REHNQUIST, dissenting.

Today the Court holds that New Hampshire cannot decide that a New Hampshire lawyer should live in New Hampshire. This may not be surprising to those who view law as just another form of business frequently practiced across state lines by interchangeable actors; the Privileges and Immunities Clause of Art. IV, § 2, has long been held to apply to States' attempts to discriminate against nonresidents who seek to ply their trade interstate. The decision will be surprising to many, however, because it so clearly disregards the fact that the practice of law is—almost by definition—fundamentally different from those other occupations that are practiced across state lines without significant deviation from State to State. The fact that each State is free, in a large number of areas, to establish *independently* of the other States its own laws for the governance of its citizens, is a fundamental precept of our Constitution that, I submit, is of equal stature with the need for the States to form a cohesive union. What is at issue here is New Hampshire's right to decide that those people who in many ways will intimately deal with New Hampshire's self-governance should reside within that State.

* * *

NOTES AND QUESTIONS

1. The Privileges and Immunities Clause played a major role in an important New York State Court of Appeals case heard right before the Civil War called *Lemmon v. the People of New York*, 20 N.Y. 562 (1860). The State of New York freed its last slave in 1817. New York eventually amended its State law to provide that any enslaved person brought into New York, except for fugitives from slavery, were to be freed upon their arrival in New York waters, as *Somerset v. Stewart* had provided in England in 1772 as a matter of common law. *See supra* page 10. Jonathan Lemmon and his wife Juliet were residents of Virginia who had decided to move with their eight slaves, a husband and wife and their six children, to Texas. For some reason, the fastest way to do this involved taking a boat to New York City and then catching a steamer from New York to Houston, Texas. Upon the Lemmon's arrival in New York, an abolitionist filed a writ of habeas corpus with the New York state courts demanding that the Lemmon's slaves, who were not fugitives, be set free. The highest court in New York ruled to free the Lemmons' slaves The Lemmon's objected, saying they had a *civil right* under the Privileges and Immunities Clause to travel interstate for recreational purposes with their slaves. The New York Court of Appeals (correctly) held that the Lemmons, as citizens of Virginia, had while they were in New York State exactly the same, and only the same, *civil rights* as were held by New York citizens. Since New York citizens could not own a slave for

even a second in New York, neither could the Lemmons. Nor were the slaves *fugitives* who New York had to return, because the Lemmons brought them voluntarily to New York. Finally, there was no interference with interstate commerce or the Dormant Commerce Clause because the Lemmons were traveling recreationally and were not engaged in interstate travel for purposes of buying and selling. Northern abolitionists were worried in 1860 that *Lemmon v. the People of New York*, 20 N.Y. 562 (1860) would be appealed to Chief Justice Roger B. Taney's pro-slave-power Supreme Court, which would reverse the New York Court of Appeals and hold that slave owners had a federal constitutional right to travel wherever they wanted the Union with their slaves, thus nationalizing slavery. The case never reached the Supreme Court because the Civil War intervened.

2. Can Virginia pass a Freedom of Information Act that gives its own citizens, but not non-citizens, a right to access public records? A unanimous Supreme Court said yes in *McBurney v. Young*, 569 U.S. 221 (2013). The plaintiff claimed, inter alia, that his occupation was obtaining public records for clients and that Virginia's law systematically advantaged in-state citizens in that calling. The Court did not agree: "The challenged provision of the state FOIA does not violate the Privileges and Immunities Clause simply because it has the incidental effect of preventing citizens of other States from making a profit by trading on information contained in state records. While the Clause forbids a State from intentionally giving its own citizens a competitive advantage in business or employment, the Clause does not require that a State tailor its every action to avoid any incidental effect on out-of-state tradesmen." *Id.* at 228–29.

E. RETURN OF FUGITIVES

Article IV, Section 2, Clause 2: A Person charged in any State with Treason, Felony, or other Crime, who shall flee from Justice, and be found in another State, shall on Demand of the executive Authority of the State from which he fled, be delivered up, to be removed to the State having Jurisdiction of the Crime.

Article IV, Section 2, Clause 3: No Person held to Service or Labour in one State, under the Laws thereof, escaping into another, shall, in Consequence of any Law or Regulation therein, be discharged from such Service or Labour, but shall be delivered up on Claim of the Party to whom such Service or Labour may be due.

Article IV contains two clauses that involve escapees from one State into another. The first of those clauses, the Extradition Clause, is very much alive and vibrant. The second of those clauses, the Fugitive Slave Clause, is mercifully relegated to history by the Thirteenth Amendment. But before the Civil War, the Fugitive Slave Clause played an important, and tragic, role in American constitutional history.

The Fugitive Slave Clause was deemed necessary, indeed essential, by the Southern States at the Philadelphia Constitutional Convention because Lord Chief Justice Mansfield of the English Court of King's Bench had held in 1772 that all slaves who arrive in a country where there is not positive statutory law authorizing slavery are automatically free because slavery is "so odious, that nothing can support it but positive law." *Somerset v. Stewart*, (1772) 98 ER 499. *See supra* page 10. To be sure, the rule in *Somerset* conspicuously did not apply to British colonies that had positive law permitting slavery, but once the former colonies became nation-states of their own, they inherited the common law of England, which included the principles of *Somerset v. Stewart*. Under *Somerset v. Stewart*, fugitive slaves would be legally free once they reached free state territory, with no positive law in place to support the "odious" institution of slavery. The South could not live with that conclusion. The Articles of Confederation addressed the issue indirectly by providing that States could regulate trade and commerce in their boundaries, "provided that such restrictions shall not extend so far as to prevent the removal of property imported into any State, to any other State, of which the owner is an inhabitant." ARTICLES OF CONFEDERATION § 4, cl. 1. Was that enough to overrule *Somerset*? The Southern States took no chances at the Convention and demanded, and were very reluctantly given, the Fugitive Slave Clause.

Note that the Fugitive Slave Clause declares a duty to return fugitive slaves "on Claim of the Party to whom such Service or Labour may be due," but the clause does not—unlike the Article IV Full Faith and Credit Clause before it and the provisions in Article IV, Section 3 that follow it—on its face empower either Congress or the state governments to enforce it. Which level of government could enforce it, and through what institutions and means? Also, what due process of law was to be given to an alleged fugitive slave to be able to show that he or she was really legally free? Whichever entities enforced the Fugitive Slave Clause would presumably be able to determine these procedural and evidentiary matters. Was enforcement of the clause left to state courts and legislatures in free States?

Congress passed several acts for the recovery of fugitive slaves, most notably in 1793 and 1850. *See* Act of Feb. 12, 1793, ch. VII, 1 Stat. 302; Act of Sept. 18, 1850, ch. LX, 9 Stat. 462. Was it empowered to do so? Consider the following infamous case. Margaret Morgan, once a slave, had been allowed by her former owner to move to Pennsylvania in 1832, where she married a free African-American man. Morgan's former owner never formally manumitted her, and his heirs hired Edward Prigg, a professional slave catcher, to kidnap her and bring her back to Maryland, a slave State, for sale with her children at 4 AM on the night of April 1, 1837—five years after she had been allowed to move to Pennsylvania. Prigg was criminally prosecuted under Pennsylvania law and claimed that the prosecution was unconstitutional.

1. PRIGG V. PENNSYLVANIA

41 U.S. (16 Pet.) 539 (1842)

■ MR. JUSTICE STORY delivered the opinion of the court.

This is a writ of error to the Supreme Court of Pennsylvania * * * for the purpose of revising the judgment of that Court, in a case involving the construction of the Constitution and laws of the United States.

The facts are briefly these: The plaintiff in error [Prigg] was indicted * * * [by the State of Pennsylvania], for having, with force and violence, taken and carried away from that county, to the state of Maryland, a certain negro woman, named Margaret Morgan, with a design and intention of selling and disposing of, and keeping her as a slave or servant for life, contrary to a statute of Pennsylvania, passed on the 26th of March, 1826. That statute * * * provides, that if any person or persons shall * * *, by force and violence take and carry away * * * any negro or mulatto from any part of that commonwealth, with a design and intention of selling and disposing of * * *, as a slave or servant for life, or for any term whatsoever; every such person or persons, his or their aiders or abettors, shall, on conviction thereof, be deemed guilty of felony * * *.

* * *

* * * [Prigg] * * * was [found] guilty of the offence charged in the indictment * * *.

* * *

* * * The counsel for * * * [Prigg] have contended, that the statute of Pennsylvania is unconstitutional; first, because Congress has the exclusive power of legislation upon the subject-matter, under the Constitution of the United States, and under the act of the 12th of February 1793, ch. 51, (7), which was passed in pursuance thereof; secondly, that if this power is not exclusive in Congress, still the concurrent power of the state legislatures is suspended by the actual exercise of the power by Congress; and thirdly, that if not suspended, still the statute of Pennsylvania, in all its provisions applicable to this case, is in direct collision with the act of Congress, and therefore, is unconstitutional and void. The counsel for Pennsylvania maintain the negative of all those points.

Few questions which have ever come before this Court involve more delicate and important considerations; and few upon which the public at large may be presumed to feel a more profound and pervading interest. We have accordingly given them our most deliberate examination; and it has become my duty to state the result to which we have arrived, and the reasoning by which it is supported.

* * *

* * * Historically, it is well known, that the object of this [Fugitive Slave] clause was to secure to the citizens of the slaveholding states the complete right and title of ownership in their slaves, as property, in every state in the Union into which they might escape from the state where they were held in servitude. The full recognition of this right and title was indispensable to the security of this species of property in all the slaveholding states; and, indeed, was so vital to the preservation of their domestic interests and institutions, that it cannot be doubted, that it constituted a fundamental article, without the adoption of which the Union could not have been formed. Its true design was to guard against the doctrines and principles prevalent in the non-slaveholding states, by preventing them from intermeddling with, or obstructing, or abolishing the rights of the owners of slaves.

By the general law of nations, no nation is bound to recognise the state of slavery, as to foreign slaves found within its territorial dominions, when it is in opposition to its own policy and institutions * * *. This was fully recognized in Somerset's Case, which was decided before the American revolution. It is manifest from this consideration, that if the Constitution had not contained this clause, every non-slaveholding state in the Union would have been at liberty to have declared free all runaway slaves coming within its limits, and to have given them entire immunity and protection against the claims of their masters * * *.

How, then, are we to interpret the language of the clause? The true answer is, in such a manner as, consistently with the words, shall fully and completely effectuate the whole objects of it. If by one mode of interpretation the right must become shadowy and unsubstantial, and without any remedial power adequate to the end; and by another mode it will attain its just end and secure its manifest purpose; it would seem, upon principles of reasoning, absolutely irresistible, that the latter ought to prevail. No Court of justice can be authorized so to construe any clause of the Constitution as to defeat its obvious ends, when another construction, equally accordant with the words and sense thereof, will enforce and protect them.

The clause manifestly contemplates the existence of a positive, unqualified right on the part of the owner of the slave, which no state law or regulation can in any way qualify, regulate, control or restrain. The slave is not to be discharged from service or labour, in consequence of any state law or regulation. Now, certainly, without indulging in any nicety of criticism upon words, it may fairly and reasonably be said, that any state law or state regulation, which interrupts, limits, delays or postpones the right of the owner to the immediate possession of the slave, and the immediate command of his service and labour, operates, pro tanto, a discharge of the slave therefrom. The question can never be, how much the slave is discharged from; but whether he is discharged from any, by the natural or necessary operation of state laws or state regulations. The question is not one of quantity or degree, but of withholding, or controlling the incidents of a positive and absolute right.

* * * [T]he owner must, therefore, have the right to seize and repossess the slave, which the local laws of his own state confer upon him as property; and we all know that this right of seizure and recaption is universally acknowledged in all the slaveholding states * * *. Upon this ground we have not the slightest hesitation in holding, that, under and in virtue of the Constitution, the owner of a slave is clothed with entire authority, in every state in the Union, to seize and recapture his slave, whenever he can do it without any breach of the peace or any illega[l] violence. In this sense, and to this extent this clause of the Constitution may properly be said to execute itself; and to require no aid from legislation, state or national.

But the clause of the Constitution does not stop here; nor indeed, consistently with its professed objects, could it do so. Many cases must arise in which, if the remedy of the owner were confined to the mere right of seizure and recaption, he would be utterly without any adequate redress. He may not be able to lay his hands upon the slave. He may not be able to enforce his rights against persons who either secrete or conceal, or withhold the slave. He may be restricted by local legislation as to the mode of proofs of his ownership; as to the Courts in which he shall sue, and as to the actions which he may bring; or the process he may use to compel the delivery of the slave. Nay, the local legislation may be utterly inadequate to furnish the appropriate redress, by authorizing no process in rem, or no specific mode of repossessing the slave, leaving the owner, at best, not that right which the Constitution designed to secure—a specific delivery and repossession of the slave, but a mere remedy in damages; and that perhaps against persons utterly insolvent or worthless. The state legislation may be entirely silent on the whole subject, and its ordinary remedial process framed with different views and objects; and this may be innocently as well as designedly done, since every state is perfectly competent, and has the exclusive right to prescribe the remedies in its own judicial tribunals, to limit the time as well as the mode of redress, and to deny jurisdiction over cases, which its own policy and its own institutions either prohibit or discountenance.

If, therefore, the clause of the Constitution had stopped at the mere recognition of the right, without providing or contemplating any means by which it might be established and enforced, in cases where it did not execute itself, it is plain, that it would have been, in a great variety of cases, a delusive and empty annunciation * * *.

And this leads us to the consideration of the other part of the clause, which implies at once a guarantee and duty. It says, "but he (the slave) shall be delivered up on claim of the party to whom such service or labour may be due." Now, we think it exceedingly difficult, if not impracticable, to read this language and not to feel that it contemplated some further remedial redress than that which might be administered at the hands of the owner himself. A claim is to be made. * * * The slave is to be delivered up on the claim. By whom to be delivered up? In what mode to be delivered up? How, if a refusal takes place, is the right of delivery to be enforced? Upon what proofs? What shall be the evidence of a rightful recaption or delivery? * * *

These, and many other questions, will readily occur upon the slightest attention to the clause; and it is obvious that they can receive but one satisfactory answer. They require the aid of legislation to protect the right, to enforce the delivery, and to secure the subsequent possession of the slave. If, indeed, the Constitution guaranties the right, and if it requires the delivery upon the claim of the owner, (as cannot well be doubted,) the natural inference certainly is, that the national government is clothed with the appropriate authority and functions to enforce it. The fundamental principle applicable to all cases of this sort, would seem to be, that where the end is required, the means are given; and where the duty is enjoined, the ability to perform it is contemplated to exist on the part of the functionaries to whom it is intrusted. The clause is found in the national Constitution, and not in that of any state. It does not point out any state functionaries, or any state action to carry its provisions into effect. The states cannot, therefore, be compelled to enforce them; and it might well be deemed an unconstitutional exercise of the power of interpretation, to insist that the states are bound to provide means to carry into effect the duties of the national government, nowhere delegated or intrusted to them by the Constitution. On the contrary, the natural, if not the necessary conclusion is, that the national government, in the absence of all positive provisions to the contrary, is bound, through its own proper departments, legislative; judicial, or executive, as the case may require, to carry into effect all the rights and duties imposed upon it by the Constitution * * *.

It is plain, then, that where a claim is made by the owner, out of possession, for the delivery of a slave, it must be made, if at all, against some other person; and inasmuch as the right is a right of property capable of being recognised and asserted by proceedings before a Court of justice, between parties adverse to each other, it constitutes, in the strictest sense, a controversy between the parties, and a case "arising under the Constitution" of the United States; within the express delegation of judicial power given by that instrument. Congress, then, may call that power into activity for the very purpose of giving effect to that right; and if so, then it may prescribe the mode and extent in which it shall be applied, and how, and under what circumstances the proceedings shall afford a complete protection and guarantee to the right.

Congress has taken this very view of the power and duty of the national government. As early as the year 1791, the attention of Congress was drawn to it, (as we shall hereafter more fully see,) in consequence of some practical difficulties arising under the other clause, respecting fugitives from justice escaping into other states. The result of their deliberations was the passage of the act of the 12th of February 1793, ch. 51, (7), which * * * provide[s], that when a person held to labour or service in any of the United States, shall escape into any other of the states or territories, the person to whom such labour or service may be due, his agent or attorney, is hereby empowered to seize or arrest such fugitive from labour, and take him or her before any judge of the Circuit or District Courts of the United States, residing or being within the state, or before any magistrate of a county, city or town corporate, wherein such seizure or arrest shall be made; and upon proof to the satisfaction of such judge or magistrate, either by oral evidence or affidavit, &c., that the person * * * owe service or labour to the person claiming him or her, it shall be the duty of such judge or magistrate, to give a certificate thereof to such claimant, his agent or attorney, which shall be sufficient warrant for removing the said fugitive from labour, to the state or territory from which he or she fled * * *.

In a general sense, this act may be truly said to cover the whole ground of the Constitution * * * because it points out fully all the modes of attaining those objects, which Congress, in their discretion, have as yet deemed expedient or proper to meet the exigencies of the Constitution. If this be so, then it would seem, upon just principles of construction, that the legislation of Congress, if constitutional, must supersede all state legislation upon the same subject; and by necessary implication prohibit it. For if Congress have a constitutional power to regulate a particular subject, and they do actually regulate it in a given manner, and in a certain form, it cannot be, that the state legislatures have a right to interfere; and, as it were, by way of complement to the legislation of Congress, to prescribe additional regulations, and what they may deem auxiliary provisions for the same purpose. In such a case, the legislation of Congress, in what it does prescribe, manifestly indicates that it does not intend that there shall be any farther legislation to act upon the subject-matter. Its silence as to what it does not do, is as expressive of what its intention is as the direct provisions made by it * * *.

But it has been argued, that the act of Congress is unconstitutional, because it does not fall within the scope of any of the enumerated powers of legislation confided to that body; and therefore, it is void. Stripped of its artificial and technical structure, the argument comes to this, that although rights are exclusively secured by, or duties are exclusively imposed upon the national government, yet, unless the power to enforce these rights, or to execute these duties, can be found among the express powers of legislation enumerated in the Constitution, they remain without any means of giving them effect by any act of Congress; and they must operate solely proprio vigore, however defective may be their operation; nay, even although, in a practical sense, they may become a nullity from the want of a proper remedy to enforce them, or to provide against their violation. If this be the true interpretation of the Constitution, it must, in a great measure, fail to attain many of its avowed and positive objects as a security of rights, and a recognition of duties. Such a limited construction of the Constitution has never yet been adopted as correct, either in theory or practice. No one has ever supposed, that Congress could, constitutionally, by its legislation, exercise powers, or enact laws beyond the powers delegated to it by the Constitution; but it has, on various occasions, exercised powers which were necessary and proper as means to carry into effect rights expressly given, and duties expressly enjoined thereby. The end being required, it has been deemed a just and necessary implication, that the means to accomplish it are given also; or, in other words, that the power flows as a necessary means to accomplish the end.

* * *

The very act of 1793, now under consideration, affords the most conclusive proof that Congress has acted upon a very different rule of interpretation, and has supposed that the right as well as the duty of legislation on the subject of fugitives from justice, and fugitive slaves was within the scope of the constitutional authority conferred on the national legislature * * *.

* * *

But we do not wish to rest our present opinion upon the ground either of contemporaneous exposition, or long acquiescence, or even practical action; neither do we mean to admit the question to be of a doubtful nature, and therefore as properly calling for the aid of such considerations. On the contrary, our judgment would be the same if the question were entirely new, and the act of Congress were of recent enactment. We hold the act to be clearly constitutional in all its leading provisions, and, indeed, with the exception of that part which confers authority upon state magistrates, to be free from reasonable doubt and difficulty upon the grounds already stated. As to the authority so conferred upon state magistrates, while a difference of opinion has existed, and may exist still on the point, in different states, whether state magistrates are bound to act under it; none is entertained by this Court that state magistrates may, if they choose, exercise that authority, unless prohibited by state legislation.

The remaining question is, whether the power of legislation upon this subject is exclusive in the national government, or concurrent in the states, until it is exercised by Congress. In our opinion, it is exclusive * * *

* * * Before the adoption of the Constitution, no state had any power whatsoever over the subject, except within its own territorial limits, and could not bind the sovereignty or the legislation of other states. Whenever the right was acknowledged or the duty enforced, in any state, it was as a matter of comity and favour, and not as a matter of strict moral, political, or international obligation or duty. Under the Constitution it is recognised as an absolute, positive, right and duty, pervading the whole Union with an equal and supreme force, uncontrolled and uncontrollable by state sovereignty or state legislation. It is therefore, in a just sense a new and positive right, independent of comity, confined to no territorial limits, and bounded by no state institutions or policy. The natural inference deducible from this consideration certainly is, in the absence of any positive delegation of power to the state legislatures, that it belongs to the legislative department of the national government, to which it owes its origin and establishment * * *.

In the next place, the nature of the provision and the objects to be attained by it, require that it should be controlled by one and the same will, and act uniformly by the same system of regulations throughout the Union * * *.

It is scarcely conceivable, that the slaveholding states would have been satisfied with leaving to the legislation of the non-slaveholding states, a power of regulation, in the absence of that of Congress, which would or might practically amount to a power to destroy the rights of the owner. If the argument, therefore, of a concurrent power in the states to act upon the subject-matter in the absence of legislation by Congress, be well founded; then, if Congress had never acted at all; or if the act of

Congress should be repealed without providing a substitute, there would be a resulting authority in each of the states to regulate the whole subject at its pleasure; and to dole out its own remedial justice, or withhold it at its pleasure and according to its own views of policy and expediency. Surely such a state of things never could have been intended, under such a solemn guarantee of right and duty. On the other hand, construe the right of legislation as exclusive in Congress, and every evil and every danger vanishes. The right and the duty are then co-extensive and uniform in remedy and operation throughout the whole Union. The owner has the same security, and the same remedial justice, and the same exemption from state regulation and control, through however many states he may pass with his fugitive slave in his possession, in transitu to his own domicile * * *.

* * * We entertain no doubt whatsoever, that the states, in virtue of their general police power, possesses full jurisdiction to arrest and restrain runaway slaves, and remove them from their borders, and otherwise to secure themselves against their depredations and evil example, as they certainly may do in cases of idlers, vagabonds, and paupers. The rights of the owners of fugitive slaves are in no just sense interfered with, or regulated by such a course; and in many cases, the operations of this police power, although designed generally for other purposes, for protection, safety, and peace of the state, may essentially promote and aid the interests of the owners. But such regulations can never be permitted to interfere with or to obstruct the just rights of the owner to reclaim his slave, derived from the Constitution of the United States; or with the remedies prescribed by Congress to aid and enforce the same.

Upon these grounds, we are of opinion that the act of Pennsylvania upon which this indictment is unfounded, is unconstitutional and void * * *.

■ MR. CHIEF JUSTICE TANEY. [*Editors' Note: Omitted. Chief Justice Taney agreed with most of the majority opinion but disagreed that all state laws on the subject were preempted. He thought that States had power, and a duty, to protect slaveowners in the recovery of slaves but no power to hinder them.*]

[*Editors' Note: Separate opinions of Justices Baldwin, Thompson, Wayne, and Daniel are all omitted.*]

■ MR. JUSTICE M'LEAN.

* * *

I come now to a most delicate and important inquiry in this case, and that is, whether the claimant of a fugitive from labour may seize and remove him by force out of the state in which he may be found, in defiance of its laws. I refer not to laws which are in conflict with the Constitution, or the act of 1793. Such state laws, I have already said, are void. But I have reference to those laws which regulate the police of the state, maintain the peace of its citizens, and preserve its territory and jurisdiction from acts of violence.

* * *

Both the Constitution and the act of 1793, require the fugitive from labour to be delivered up on claim being made, by the party, or his agent, to whom the service is due. Not that a suit should be regularly instituted. The proceeding authorized by the law is summary and informal. The fugitive is seized by the claimant, and taken before a judge or magistrate within the state, and on proof, parol or written, that he owes labour to the claimant, it is made the duty of the judge or magistrate to give the certificate, which authorizes the removal of the fugitive to the state from whence he absconded.

* * *

* * * In my judgment, there is not the least foundation in the act for the right asserted in the argument to take the fugitive by force and remove him out of the state.

Such a proceeding can receive no sanction under the act, for it is in express violation of it. The claimant having seized the fugitive, is required by the act to take him before a federal judge within the state, or a state magistrate within the county, city or town corporate, within which the seizure was made. Now, can there be any pretence that after the seizure under the statute, the claimant may disregard the other express provision of it, by taking the fugitive, without claim, out of the state * * *.

* * *

In a state where slavery is allowed, every coloured person is presumed to be a slave; and on the same principle, in a non-slaveholding state, every person is presumed to be free without regard to colour. On this principle, the states, both slaveholding and non-slaveholding, legislate. The latter may prohibit, as Pennsylvania has done, under a certain penalty, the forcible removal of a coloured person out of the state. Is such law in conflict with the act of 1793?

The act of 1793 authorizes a forcible seizure of the slave by the master, not to take him out of the state, but to take him before some judicial officer within it. The act of Pennsylvania punishes a forcible removal of a coloured person out of the state. Now, here is no conflict between the law of the state and the law of Congress. The execution of neither law can, by any just interpretation, in my opinion, interfere with the execution of the other. The laws in this respect stand in harmony with each other.

* * *

No conflict can arise between the act of Congress and this state law; the conflict can only arise between the forcible acts of the master and the law of the state. The master exhibits no proof of right to the services of the slave, but seizes him and is about to remove him by force. I speak only of the force exerted on the slave. The law of the state presumes him to be free, and prohibits his removal. Now, which shall give way, the master or the state? The law of the state does, in no case, discharge, in the language of the Constitution, the slave from the service of his master.

It is a most important police regulation. And if the master violate it, is he not amenable? The offence consists in the abduction of a person of colour. And this is attempted to be justified upon the simple ground that the slave is property. That a slave is property must be admitted. The state law is not violated by the seizure of the slave by the master, for this is authorized by the act of Congress; but by removing him out of the state by force, and without proof of right, which the act does not authorize. Now, is not this an act which a state may prohibit? The presumption in a non-slaveholding state is against the right of the master, and in favor of the freedom of the person he claims. This presumption may be rebutted, but until it is rebutted by the proof required in the act of 1793, and also, in my judgment, by the Constitution, must not the law of the state be respected and obeyed?

* * *

The presumption of the state that the coloured person is free may be erroneous in fact; and if so, there can be no difficulty in proving it. But may not the assertion of the master be erroneous also; and if so, how is his act of force to be remedied? The coloured person is taken, and forcibly conveyed beyond the jurisdiction of the state. This force, not being authorized by the act of Congress nor by the Constitution, may be prohibited by the state * * *.

* * *

NOTES AND QUESTIONS

1. Does the Necessary and Proper Clause grant Congress an implied power to effectuate the constitutionally sanctioned end of recovering fugitive slaves? Keep in mind that the Necessary and Proper Clause grants power to carry into effect "Powers vested by this Constitution." What vested power did the Court in *Prigg* think Congress was carrying into effect? Did the Court in *Prigg* rely on the Necessary and Proper Clause at all? Where did it think the congressional power to enforce the Fugitive Slave Clause came from? Was the Court reasoning from purposes to powers rather than from powers to purposes? Was it drawing on the Bedford and Virginia Resolutions to infer a power to solve "national" problems?

2. Assuming such a congressional power, why was the Pennsylvania law preempted? Because States are entirely disabled from acting with respect to fugitive slaves? A number of justices wrote separately to express the view that States are wholly capable of legislating to *help* slaveowners; if the "power" inferred from the Fugitive Slave Clause is truly exclusive, presumably this would not be possible. Does the majority really think the power is exclusive? Or is it conducting a preemption analysis?

3. If this is simply a preemption case, isn't Justice McLean correct that the free States have a legitimate interest in preserving the peace to legislate against self-help repossession of slaves? The Fugitive Slave Act of 1793, after all, did not say that slaveowners could grab anyone they wished and leave the State. They needed to adjudicate their claims before a magistrate to prove that they person they seized was actually a slave. The conduct forbidden by Pennsylvania was not at all authorized by the Fugitive Slave Act. So how could Pennsylvania's law be preempted?

4. Do the free States have a duty under the original Constitution to assist slaveowners in recovering their fugitive slaves, as Chief Justice Taney says? Is that what the Fugitive Slave Clause says?

5. Joseph Story was raised in Massachusetts and was generally considered anti-slavery. It is reported that he thought of his decision in *Prigg* as a "triumph of freedom." *See* Leslie Friedman Goldstein, *A "Triumph of Freedom" After All?* Prigg v, Pennsylvania *Re-examined*, 29 L. & HIST. REV. 763 (2011). How is that perception even thinkable? One possible answer is that by holding the power to deal with fugitive slaves to be exclusively in Congress, the decision in *Prigg* effectively gutted the protections for slaveowners. There simply were not enough federal magistrates to make the procedures in the Fugitive Slave Act effective, *see id.* at 782, and nothing in *Prigg* required States to have their own officials enforce federal law. Whether or not this is an accurate account of the real effects of and motivations behind *Prigg,* the Southern States were not enamored of the decision. They insisted on a new fugitive slave act to provide more federal magistrates and fewer rights and procedural safeguards to those who were alleged to be fugitive slaves, and they got their wish in 1850. The new fugitive slave law was proclaimed (without discussion)

constitutional by the Court on the eve of the Civil War. *See Abelman v. Booth,* 62 U.S. (21 How.) 506, 526 (1859). As the old saying goes, that decision was reversed a few years later by Justice Grant and Justice Sherman.

6. While the Fugitive Slave Clause is now effectively moot, the immediately preceding Extradition Clause is still vibrant and important. A similar provision was in the Articles of Confederation, *see* ARTICLES OF CONFEDERATION § 4, cl. 2, and it is a natural provision for a confederal system. The clause specifies that the triggering event for the duty to return escaped fugitives is a "Demand of the executive Authority of the State from which he fled." But suppose that the State in which the fugitive is located doubts whether the person is really a fugitive? Do they have to take the word of the "executive Authority" of the requesting State? Can federal courts order a State to turn over a person just on the say-so of a governor? And what if the State which receives the request does not approve of the policies of the requesting State? Does it have to defer to the requesting State no matter what?

2. PUERTO RICO V. BRANSTAD

483 U.S. 219 (1987)

■ JUSTICE MARSHALL delivered the opinion of the Court.

This case requires that we reconsider the holding of *Kentucky v. Dennison,* 24 How. 66 (1861), that federal courts have no power to order the Governor of a State to fulfill the State's obligation under the Extradition Clause of the Constitution, Art. IV, § 2, to deliver up fugitives from justice.

On January 25, 1981, respondent Ronald Calder, then a civilian air traffic controller employed by the Federal Aviation Administration in San Juan, Puerto Rico, struck two people with his automobile. One of the victims, Antonio de Jesus Gonzalez, was injured; his wife, Army Villalba, was killed. Villalba was eight months pregnant; her unborn child did not survive. The incident occurred in the parking lot of a grocery store in Aguadilla, Puerto Rico, after what was apparently an altercation between Calder and de Jesus Gonzalez. According to two sworn statements taken by police, one from de Jesus Gonzalez and one from a witness to the incident, after striking the couple Calder backed his car two or three times over the prostrate body of Villalba.

* * * On February 4, 1981, Calder was arraigned before a District Court of the Commonwealth of Puerto Rico, charged with first-degree murder and attempted murder. Calder failed to appear at a preliminary hearing on March 4, 1981 * * *. Despite representations by counsel that Calder would appear at a preliminary hearing on April 13, 1981, he did not do so. At that time Calder was declared a fugitive from justice * * *. The Puerto Rican police, having reason to believe that Calder had left Puerto Rico and returned to his family's home in Iowa, notified local authorities in Iowa that Calder was a fugitive wanted in Puerto Rico on murder charges. On April 24, 1981, Calder surrendered to local authorities in Polk County, Iowa, posted the $20,000 bond set by an Iowa Magistrate, and was released.

On May 15, 1981, the Governor of Puerto Rico submitted to the Governor of Iowa a request for Calder's extradition * * *. Counsel for Calder requested that the Governor of Iowa hold an extradition hearing, which was conducted by the Governor's counsel on June 17, 1981. This hearing was only partially transcribed, but the record does show that one of Calder's counsel was permitted to testify to his belief that "a white American man . . . could not receive a fair trial in the Commonwealth of Puerto Rico," while Calder himself testified to his understanding that "on numerous occasions" witnesses in Puerto Rican courts had been "bought."

After the extradition hearing in Iowa, discussions between and among Calder's counsel, the Governors of Iowa and Puerto Rico, and the prosecutorial authorities in Puerto Rico were held, apparently with a view to negotiating a reduction of the charges lodged against Calder. These discussions were unavailing, and on December 28, 1981, Iowa's Governor, Robert Ray, formally notified the Governor of Puerto Rico that in the absence of a "change to a more realistic charge," the request for extradition was denied. A subsequent extradition request made to Governor Ray's successor in office, respondent Terry Branstad, was also denied.

On February 15, 1984, petitioner Commonwealth of Puerto Rico filed a complaint in the United States District Court for the Southern District of Iowa against respondents Governor Branstad and the State of Iowa, seeking a declaration that failure to deliver Calder upon presentation of proper extradition papers violated the Extradition Clause and the Extradition Act, 18 U.S.C. § 3182 (Act). The complaint further requested the issuance of a writ of mandamus directing respondent Branstad to perform the "ministerial duty" of extradition. Respondents stipulated before the District Court that the extradition papers fully complied with the requirements of the Act. The District Court dismissed the complaint, agreeing with respondents that this Court's holding *in Kentucky v. Dennison*, 24 How. 66, 16 L.Ed. 717 (1861), absolutely barred any attempt to invoke federal judicial authority to compel compliance with the Clause or the Act. The Court of Appeals "[r]eluctantly" affirmed. We granted certiorari to consider whether the propositions concerning the limitation of federal judicial power stated in *Kentucky v. Dennison* in 1861 retain their validity today. We reverse.

Kentucky v. Dennison was an action brought under this Court's original jurisdiction to compel by writ of mandamus the extradition of a fugitive felon. The grand jury of Woodford County, Kentucky, returned an indictment in October 1859 charging Willis Lago, a "free man of color," with the crime of assisting the escape of a slave. The defendant was a resident of Ohio, and papers requesting his extradition were served upon William Dennison, the Governor of that State. Dennison secured an opinion from Ohio's Attorney General, who took the view that the Extradition Clause covered only those acts which were crimes under the law of the asylum State, or which were "regarded as *malum in se* by the general judgment and conscience of civilized nations." *Id.*, at 69. On this basis Dennison refused extradition, and Kentucky brought its mandamus action in this Court.

The case was heard in February 1861, and decided on March 14. On that date secession was a fact, and civil war a threatening possibility. The Representatives of the States of the Deep South had withdrawn from the Congress. Justice Campbell was reputedly engaged in mediation efforts between the seceding States and the Lincoln administration, but his resignation from the Court and departure from Washington were imminent; he resigned on April 30, 1861. It was in these circumstances, with the practical power of the Federal Government at its lowest ebb since the adoption of the Constitution, that Chief Justice Taney delivered the opinion of the Court.

The Court firmly rejected the position taken by Dennison and the Governors of other free States that the Extradition Clause required only the delivery of fugitives charged with acts which would be criminal by the law of the asylum State. "Under such a vague and indefinite construction," the Court said, "the article would not be a bond of peace and union, but a constant source of controversy and irritating discussion." 24 How., at 102. Interpreting for the first time the language of the Clause, the Court looked to the fundamental role of the right to request extradition in binding the individual States into a nation:

> "Looking, therefore, to the words of the Constitution—to the obvious policy and necessity of this provision to preserve harmony between States, and order and law within their respective borders . . .—the conclusion is irresistible, that this compact engrafted in the Constitution included, and was intended to include, every offence made punishable by the law of the State in which it was committed, and that it gives the right to the Executive authority of the State to demand the fugitive from the Executive authority of the State in which he is found; that the right given to 'demand' implies that it is an absolute right; and it follows that there must be a correlative obligation to deliver, without any reference to the character of the crime charged, or to the policy or laws of the State to which the fugitive has fled." *Id.*, at 103.

The Court then turned to the Extradition Act of 1793, 1 Stat. 302. In the procedures for the regulation of extradition established by that Act, the Court found the same absolute right to demand and correlative obligation to deliver. As to the Governor of the asylum State under the Act, the Court determined that "[t]he duty which he is to perform is . . . merely ministerial—that is, to cause the party to be arrested, and delivered to the agent or authority of the State where the crime was committed." 24 How., at 106. But the Court concluded that "the words 'it shall be the duty' were not used as mandatory and compulsory, but as declaratory of the moral duty" created by the Constitution. *Id.*, at 107. Such a construction was necessary, in the Court's view, to avoid constitutional infirmity * * *.

Thus, for over 125 years, *Kentucky v. Dennison* has stood for two propositions: first, that the Extradition Clause creates a mandatory duty to deliver up fugitives upon proper demand; and second, that the federal courts have no authority under the Constitution to compel performance of this ministerial duty of delivery. As to the first of these conclusions, the passage of time has revealed no occasion for doubt * * *. We reaffirm the conclusion that the commands of the Extradition Clause are mandatory, and afford no discretion to the executive officers or courts of the asylum State.

The second, and dispositive, holding of *Kentucky v. Dennison* rests upon a foundation with which time and the currents of constitutional change have dealt much less favorably. If it seemed clear to the Court in 1861, facing the looming shadow of a Civil War, that "the Federal Government, under the Constitution, has no power to impose on a State officer, as such, any duty whatever, and compel him to perform it," 24 How., at 107, basic constitutional principles now point as clearly the other way. Within 15 years of the decision in *Dennison* it was said that "when a plain official duty, requiring no exercise of discretion, is to be performed, and performance is refused, any person who will sustain personal injury by such refusal may have a *mandamus* to compel its performance," and it was no objection that such an order might be sought in the federal courts against a state officer. *Board of Liquidation v. McComb*, 92 U.S. 531, 541 (1876). It has long been a settled principle that federal courts may enjoin unconstitutional action by state officials. See *Ex parte Young*, 209 U.S. 123, 155–156 (1908). It would be superfluous to restate all the occasions on which this Court has imposed upon state officials a duty to obey the requirements of the Constitution, or compelled the performance of such duties; it may suffice to refer to *Brown v. Board of Education*, 349 U.S. 294 (1955), and *Cooper v. Aaron*, 358 U.S. 1 (1958). The fundamental premise of the holding in *Dennison*—"that the States and the Federal Government in all circumstances must be viewed as coequal sovereigns—is not representative of the law today." *FERC v. Mississippi*, 456 U.S. 742, 761 (1982).

Yet, with respect to extradition, the law has remained as it was more than a century ago. Considered *de novo*, there is no justification for distinguishing the duty to deliver fugitives from the many other species of constitutional duty enforceable in the federal courts. Indeed the nature of the obligation here is such as to avoid many of the problems with which federal courts must cope in other circumstances. That this is a ministerial duty precludes conflict with essentially discretionary elements of state governance, and eliminates the need for continuing federal supervision of state functions. The explicit and long-settled nature of the command, contained in a constitutional provision and a statute substantially unchanged for 200 years, eliminates the possibility that state officers will be subjected to inconsistent direction. Because the duty is directly imposed upon the States by the Constitution itself, there can be no need to weigh the performance of the federal obligation against the powers reserved to the States under the Tenth Amendment.

* * *

Respondents further contend that even if the holding in *Kentucky v. Dennison* cannot withstand contemporary scrutiny, petitioner would not profit from its demise because Puerto Rico is not a State, and has no right to demand rendition of fugitives under the Extradition Clause. It is true that the words of the Clause apply only to "States," and we have never held that the Commonwealth of Puerto Rico is entitled to all the benefits conferred upon the States under the Constitution. We need not decide today what applicability the Extradition Clause may have to the Commonwealth of Puerto Rico, however, for the Extradition Act clearly applies * * *. Since the Act applies to Puerto Rico, the Commonwealth may invoke the power of federal courts to enforce against state officers rights created by federal statutes, including equitable relief to compel performance of federal statutory duties. Accordingly, Puerto Rico may predicate its mandamus action on the Act, without regard to the direct applicability of the Extradition Clause.

Kentucky v. Dennison is the product of another time. The conception of the relation between the States and the Federal Government there announced is fundamentally incompatible with more than a century of constitutional development. Yet this decision has stood while the world of which it was a part has passed away. We conclude that it may stand no longer. The decision of the Court of Appeals is

Reversed.

■ JUSTICE O'CONNOR, with whom JUSTICE POWELL joins, concurring in part and concurring in the judgment.

* * * Because the Court ultimately resolves this case under the Extradition Act, 18 U.S.C. § 3182, I do not find * * * its statements concerning the Extradition Clause of the Constitution, necessary to the decision of this case. Accordingly, I do not subscribe to that part of the Court's opinion.

■ JUSTICE SCALIA, concurring in part and concurring in the judgment.

I concur in the result, and in the portions of the Court's opinion applying 18 U.S.C. § 3182 and overruling *Kentucky v. Dennison*, 24 How. 66 (1861), insofar as it interpreted the predecessor of that statute. I note that no party before us has asserted the lack of power of Congress to require extradition from a State to a Territory.

NOTES AND QUESTIONS

1. *Kentucky v. Dennison* involved the federal courts' power to issue orders to state governors. As the Court points out, any doubts about that power had been long settled before 1987, and *Kentucky v. Dennison* was simply a Civil War-era anomaly. No one in 1987 really defended it.

2. The Extradition Clause presents the same problem of congressional power as did the Fugitive Slave Clause. The Extradition Clause imposes a duty on States but does not seem to grant any power to Congress. Nor, as Justice Scalia suggested in his separate opinion, would any implied power from the Extradition Clause seem to extend to demands for extradition to federal territories, since a territorial demand does not come from "the executive Authority of the State." Nonetheless, both Congress's power to enact extradition legislation and its ability to authorize territorial executives to demand extradition from States is effectively unchallenged today.

3. The Iowa governors in *Branstad* were second-guessing the law enforcement decisions of Puerto Rico. Can they do that? Clearly not. The Extradition Clause, and the federal statute enforcing it, requires only a demand from the proper executive authority and nothing more. In 1998, courts in New Mexico refused to permit extradition of an alleged fugitive from Ohio, who claimed that Ohio was going to violate his due process rights and harm him physically. A unanimous Supreme Court, in a *per curiam* opinion, reversed:

> In *Michigan v. Doran*, 439 U.S. 282 (1978), we said:
>
> "Once the Governor has granted extradition, a court considering release on habeas corpus can do no more than decide (a) whether the extradition documents on their face are in order; (b) whether the petitioner has been charged with a crime in the demanding state; (c) whether the petitioner is the person named in the request for extradition; and (d) whether the petitioner is a fugitive. These are historic facts readily verifiable." *Id.*, at 289, 99 S.Ct., at 535.
>
> The Supreme Court of New Mexico agreed that the first three requirements had been met, but decided that respondent was not a "fugitive" from justice; in the words of the Supreme Court of New Mexico, he was a "refugee from injustice." That court held that respondent fled Ohio because of fear that his parole would be revoked without due process, and that he would be thereafter returned to prison where he faced the threat of bodily injury. This "duress" negated his status as a fugitive under Article IV.
>
> * * *

> We accept, of course, the determination of the Supreme Court of New Mexico that respondent's testimony was credible, but this is simply not the kind of issue that may be tried in the asylum State. In case after case we have held that claims relating to what actually happened in the demanding State, the law of the demanding State, and what may be expected to happen in the demanding State when the fugitive returns are issues that must be tried in the courts of that State, and not in those of the asylum State * * *.
>
> There are practical reasons as well as legal reasons which support this result * * *. The burden on a demanding State of producing witnesses and records in the asylum State to counter allegations such as those of respondent's in this case would be substantial, indeed.

New Mexico, ex rel. Ortiz v. Reed, 524 U.S. 151, 152–54 (1998).

4. Nor does the federal statute leave much for the asylum State's executive arm to decide or choose:

> Whenever the executive authority of any State or Territory demands any person as a fugitive from justice, of the executive authority of any State, District, or Territory to which such person has fled, and produces a copy of an indictment found or an affidavit made before a magistrate of any State or Territory, charging the person demanded with having committed treason, felony, or other crime, certified as authentic by the governor or chief magistrate of the State or Territory from whence the person so charged has fled, the executive authority of the State, District, or Territory to which such person has fled shall cause him to be arrested and secured, and notify the executive authority making such demand, or the agent of such authority appointed to receive the fugitive, and shall cause the fugitive to be delivered to such agent when he shall appear. If no such agent appears within thirty days from the time of the arrest, the prisoner may be discharged.

18 U.S.C. § 3812 (2018). Does this statute unconstitutionally commandeer state executive officials? *See supra* pages 802–817.

[Assignment 44]

XVII. ARTICLE IV: SECTION 3

A. THE NEW STATES ADMISSIONS CLAUSE

> **Article IV, Section 3, Clause 1: New States may be admitted by the Congress into this Union; but no new State shall be formed or erected within the Jurisdiction of any other State, nor any State be formed by the Junction of two or more States, without the Consent of the Legislatures of the States concerned, as well as of the Congress.**

The United States entered the Constitutional Convention owning a great deal of land—namely, the Northwest Territory that had been ceded by Connecticut, Massachusetts, New York, and Virginia. The Continental Congress in July 1787 adopted the Northwest Ordinance to govern that territory. *See* Ordinance of 1787: The Northwest Territorial Government, *reprinted in* 1 U.S.C. at LV (2012). As early as 1780, Congress had promised that the Northwest Territory would eventually become new States. *See* Robert S. Hill, *Federalism, Republicanism, and the*

Northwest Ordinance, 18 PUBLIUS 41, 43 (1988). The Northwest Ordinance formalized this promise by stipulating that "there shall be formed, in said territory, not less than three nor more than five States." Northwest Ordinance, § 14, art. 5. This promise was made binding on the post-constitutional United States government through the Article VI Engagements Clause, *see infra* page 969. The Articles of Confederation had even provided for automatic admission for Canada into the Union, ARTICLES OF CONFEDERATION § 11, and many founding-era figures thought of Cuba as a prime statehood candidate. Everyone understood in 1788—long before the Louisiana Purchase—that there would be new States. The only question was how they were going to be admitted.

The Admissions Clause makes it clear that new States may be admitted by Congress. We have already seen that States enter on the same terms and with the same legal capacities as the original thirteen states had. *See supra* pages 897–898. As we saw in *Shelby County v. Holder* above, the scope of that equality of the States rule remains a subject of contention.

Several States have been created out of other States in American history. Maine was originally part of Massachusetts, but in 1819, Massachusetts consented to Maine's separation into a separate State, and Maine was admitted by Congress in 1820. *See* Act of Mar. 3, 1820, ch. XIX, 3 Stat. 544 (1820). Kentucky and Vermont entered by similar routes, with the respective consent of Virginia and New York. The admission of West Virginia was more eventful. After Virginia voted to secede from the Union, the loyalist members of the Virginia state legislature fled to West Virginia, where they held a meeting. As the legislature of loyalist Virginia, they granted the western portion of that State permission to form the new loyalist State of West Virginia. The voters of West Virginia then elected a loyalist legislature, which agreed to the creation of the new State. The process was legal in form, although arguably contrary to the spirit of the Admissions Clause. For a full and entertaining discussion, see Vasan Kesavan & Michael Stokes Paulsen, *Is West Virginia Unconstitutional?*, 90 CALIF. L. REV. 291 (2002).

The other major issue concerning admission of a new State involved Texas in 1845. Texas, styling itself an independent nation after militarily defeating Mexico, sought admission in 1844 via treaty. For a variety of legal and political reasons, the treaty was voted down in the United States Senate. Supporters of admission then turned to annexation by ordinary legislation, on the theory that majorities in both the House and Senate were going to be easier to achieve than a two-thirds majority in the Senate. Texas was annexed by Congress, *see* Act of Mar. 1, 1845, J. Res. No. 8, 5 Stat. 797 (1845), and subsequently admitted. It was generally accepted by 1845 that the United States could acquire new territory by treaty, but many people at that time—including the Senate Committee on Foreign Relations—doubted whether the United States could simply annex a foreign country by statute. *See* GARY LAWSON & GUY SEIDMAN, THE CONSTITUTION OF EMPIRE: TERRITORIAL EXPANSION & AMERICAN LEGAL HISTORY 92 (2004); Mark A. Graber, *Settling the West: The Annexation of Texas, the Louisiana Purchase, and* Bush v. Gore, *in* THE LOUISIANA PURCHASE AND AMERICAN EXPANSION, 1803–1898, at 83, 86–94 (Sanford Levinson & Bartholomew H. Sparrow eds., 2005). A few people today still maintain that the "Republic of Texas" was never legally annexed and remains an independent nation. Is the following argument in favor of the legality of admission by annexation at all persuasive?

(Hawaii was also admitted by annexation, so if the argument is not persuasive, Hawaii is also at risk!)

> Suppose, for instance, that North Carolina or Georgia wants to cede land to the United States * * *. By what mechanism does the United States acquire title to the ceded land? The answer is simple: by legislation, which is exactly how the United States accepted cessions from North Carolina and Georgia in 1790 and 1802 * * *. The treaty power has nothing to do with this kind of transaction, which does not involve any foreign sovereigns.
>
> Now suppose that the United States wants to accept a cession of land from a foreign sovereign like Spain. If Congress passed (and the President signed) ordinary legislation authorizing the annexation of Spanish territory, that legislation would be fully effective as a matter of domestic law * * *. The only problem would be securing compliance from Spain and recognition of Spain's obligation from the international community. Congressional legislation could not bind Spain. In order to validate the transaction on an international level * * *, a treaty would be necessary. But * * * the treaty would be necessary in order to bind Spain * * * to deliver the property, not in order to authorize the United States as a matter of domestic law to receive it.
>
> For exactly the same reasons, the annexation of Texas by statute was entirely constitutional * * *. In the case of annexation of an entire foreign sovereign, no treaty is necessary if the foreign sovereign accedes to the acquisition, because the foreign sovereign ceases to exist upon annexation and there is accordingly nothing for the treaty to operate upon. There is literally no one left against whom to enforce it * * *. Indeed, the interesting question is not whether a treaty was *required* for the annexation of Texas, but whether it would have been *effective* for the annexation of Texas.

LAWSON & SEIDMAN, *supra,* at 92–94.

B. THE TERRITORIES CLAUSE

Article IV, Section 3, Clause 2: The Congress shall have Power to dispose of and make all needful Rules and Regulations respecting the Territory or other Property belonging to the United States; and nothing in this Constitution shall be so construed as to Prejudice any Claims of the United States, or of any particular State.

When the Articles of Confederation were adopted in 1781, the United States had already received large cessions of land from New York, and more cessions were on the way. The Articles of Confederation contained no provision authorizing Congress to govern the territory (though an early draft written by John Dickinson would have done so), *see* Denis P. Duffey, *The Northwest Ordinance as a Constitutional Document*, 95 COLUM. L. REV. 929, 940 n.77 (1995), but no one at the time seemed to worry much about that, and Congress passed the Northwest Ordinance without any objections regarding lack of power. The Constitution, by contrast, expressly gives Congress power to govern federally owned territory and to manage all other "Property belonging to the United States." The clause does not distinguish territory from other property; what is true for territory is true as well for paper clips and aircraft carriers. The clause is often called the "Territories Clause," or sometimes the "Property Clause," but it is really the "Territories and other Property Clause."

This simple observation about the equivalence between territory and other property defeats the claim, strangely prevalent in the founding era, that the United States had no power to acquire and govern new territory after 1788. Thomas Jefferson most famously expressed these doubts in connection with the Louisiana Purchase—which President Jefferson executed notwithstanding his doubts. The doubts were needless: The United States can acquire and govern new land just as readily as it can acquire and govern new office supplies. For an extended argument to this effect, see GARY LAWSON & GUY SEIDMAN, THE CONSTITUTION OF EMPIRE: TERRITORIAL EXPANSION AND AMERICAN LEGAL HISTORY 21–85 (2004).

The power of territorial (and proprietary) governance is fundamentally different from Congress's other enumerated powers. The Territories (and Other Property) Clause gives Congress essentially the same powers over federal territory that States possess within their jurisdiction. In other words, the enumerated power to enact "needful Rules and Regulations" establishes Congress as a general governing authority over federal territories, capable of enacting criminal codes, rules of tort and contract, marriage and divorce law, and anything else within federal territory that a State can do within its own boundaries. *See Late Corp. of the Church of Jesus Christ of Latter-Day Saints v. United States,* 136 U.S. 1, 42 (1890) (Congress has "general and plenary" power over federal territories); *National Bank v. County of Yankton,* 101 U.S. 129, 133 (1880) ("full and complete authority"). Does that mean that there are literally no constitutional limits on what Congress can do within territories?

This question is quite possibly the most important question in American legal history. On more than one occasion, the scope of congressional power over territories has been *the* central issue in American legal and political life. The Louisiana Purchase and its aftermath is only the mildest of examples; for that particular story, see Gary Lawson & Guy Seidman, *The First "Incorporation" Debate, in* THE LOUISIANA PURCHASE AND AMERICAN EXPANSION, 1803–1898, at 19 (Sanford Levinson & Bartholomew H. Sparrow eds., 2005). Early questions concerned whether the Constitution's general separation of powers clauses and principles applied to territorial legislation. Surely, for instance, Congress cannot avoid the Article I, Section 7 presentment requirement when it is legislating for territories. Can it avoid the Appointments Clause by, for example, allowing territorial inhabitants to elect their governors? As it happens, the legislative answer until 1947 was "no." Territorial governors and other executive officials were appointed in conformance with the Appointments Clause until a 1947 statute allowed an elected governor in Puerto Rico. Other statutes followed, such as a 1968 act providing for an elected governor of Guam, and the constitutionality of that arrangement for elected territorial executives has not (yet) been challenged in court. *See* LAWSON & SEIDMAN, *supra,* at 129–38. On the other hand, Congress from an early date allowed territorial inhabitants to elect their own legislatures, even though the practice seems to raise questions under both the Appointments Clause and the subdelegation doctrine. *See id.* at 124–29; Gary Lawson, *The Return of the King: The Unsavory Origins of Administrative Law,* 93 TEX. L. REV. 1521, 1540–41 (2015) (modifying some views in the previously cited work). A number of subdelegation challenges to territorial legislatures have been roundly rejected by the courts over the years. *See, e.g., Cincinnati Soap Co. v. United States,* 301 U.S. 308, 323 (1937).

What about territorial courts? Do they need to conform to the tenure and salary requirements of Article III?

After some fits and starts in the Nation's first few decades, some of which strongly suggested that the answer was "yes," *see* LAWSON & SEIDMAN, *supra*, at 140–46, the Supreme Court gave a resounding "no" in *American Insurance Co. v. 356 Bales of Cotton*, 26 U.S. (1 Pet.) 511 (1828), in which it upheld the validity of territorial courts exercising, among other things, admiralty jurisdiction without the tenure and salary guarantees of Article III. As a matter of policy, it is easy to see why Congress would not want to create life-tenured local judges in territories that might become States (and then want their own judges) within a short time. But that is not a reason to ignore the dictates of Article III, and *American Ins. Co.* is among the most widely criticized Supreme Court decisions across virtually all relevant spectrums. *See* LAWSON & SEIDMAN, *supra,* at 146–50. Nonetheless, it remains a cornerstone of constitutional jurisprudence and one of the key precedents for "non-Article III" federal courts. *See supra* page 173.

When Congress legislates for the territories, does it have to obey individual rights provisions, such as the Article I, Section 9 prohibitions and the various "thou shalt nots" in the Bill of Rights? Hold that thought for the moment; the doctrinal answer is much trickier than you probably think.

But in whatever way those questions about individual rights and separation of powers are ultimately answered, the one constant seems to be Congress's broad power as a general government over federal territory. If a State can criminalize murder, so can Congress in federal territories. If a State can charter a bank, so can Congress in federal territories. If a State can ban slavery within its borders, so can Congress in federal territories—as the Congress in fact did in the Northwest Ordinance of 1787, which eventually led to creation of the (free) States of Ohio, Indiana, Illinois, Michigan, Wisconsin, and Minnesota. Under Article IV, Section 3, Clause 2 of the U.S. Constitution, Congress had even greater, or at least more explicit, power to ban slavery in the territories than it had had under the Articles of Confederation. There could thus be no question about Congress's power to ban slavery in federally owned territories. Congress exercised this power in the Missouri Compromise of 1820, which led to the admission of Missouri as a slave State, Maine as a free State, and the banning of slavery in all federal territories north of 36 degrees 30 parallel. This Compromise was accepted as being constitutional by every president and congress from 1820 until 1857—a period of thirty-seven years. Thomas Jefferson, James Madison, John Adams and many others of the Founding generation were alive in 1820 when the Missouri Compromise was agreed to. No one *ever* suggested that the Missouri Compromise was unconstitutional.

No one, that is, until the Supreme Court decided *Dred Scott v. Sandford,* 60 U.S. (19 How.) 393 (1857). Both of us have excoriated this decision in print elsewhere, so we don't think we are committing an editorial faux pas by announcing that we regard this monstrosity as, if not the worst and most intellectually dishonest opinion ever produced by the Supreme Court, then at least a serious contender for that title. You are, of course, in this as in all things, free to disagree with us once the issues are explained and addressed. But we don't think that many of you will. Not all Supreme Court decisions deserve their reputations. We think this one does. You need to know a few things before plunging into the case.

First, the background rule of law in the United States, going back to the great English case of *Somerset v. Stewart*, 98 ER 499 (1772), was that slavery was so odious and so contrary to both natural law and the common law of England that it could only exist where the positive law of a state or nation explicitly provided for slavery. As a result, Somerset, a slave brought voluntarily to London, became automatically free under the common law as soon as the ship that was carrying him reached English waters. Because of the *Somerset* case, the South insisted that a fugitive slave clause be included in the U.S. Constitution, since otherwise fugitive slaves would be free as soon as they escaped to a free State. The Fugitive Slave Clause was added, but it was always understood that if a slave owner voluntarily took his slave with him into a free State or territory, that slave became free as soon as he or she set foot on free soil.

Second, one of the consequences of the Louisiana Purchase of 1803 and the Mexican-American War of 1846–48 was that the U.S. acquired a lot of western territory, out of which were carved many new States. This set off a competition between slave owners and abolitionists over which of the new States would be slave States and which would be free States. Some Northern abolitionists, like then-Congressman Abraham Lincoln, voted against the Declaration of War in the Mexican-American War because they did not want any new Southern territories admitted into the Union that might become slave States. Southerners, in turn, dreamed of admitting Cuba or other Caribbean islands into the Union as new slave States. The status of the new western territories was a huge irritant in North-South relations by the 1850's.

Third, the background facts of the *Dred Scott* case are as follows: Dred Scott was born a slave in Virginia in 1795. He was sold to a U.S. Army surgeon, Dr. John Emerson, in St. Louis, Missouri—a slave State. Dr. Emerson took Dred Scott with him to Fort Armstrong in Illinois, a free State. Under the rule of *Somerset's Case,* Dred Scott, who was not a fugitive slave, should have become free as soon as he entered the State of Illinois. In 1851, however, the Supreme Court, in an opinion by Chief Justice Taney, held—without offering anything by way of argument—that when a slave is sent voluntarily by the owner to a free State and then returns to the slave State, the slave State's law determines the person's status. *See Strader v. Graham,* 51 U.S. (10 How.) 82, 93–94 (1851).

In 1836, Dr. Emerson moved with Dred Scott to an area of federal territory in what is now Minnesota, in which slavery had been banned under the Missouri Compromise. While there, Scott married Harriet Robinson in a civil ceremony conducted by a justice of the peace. The ceremony would have been unnecessary if Scott were a slave, since slave marriages were not recognized by law. Again under *Somerset's Case,* that presence in federal territory should have freed Scott. And the then-forthcoming rule in *Strader v. Graham* would not apply, because even if the Court correctly ruled that Ohio law could not trump Kentucky law (the two States involved in *Strader*), federal law most certainly could trump Missouri, law in Scott's case. But we continue.

In 1837, the army ordered Dr. Emerson to move to a military base near St. Louis, Missouri, and Dred Scott and his wife voluntarily accompanied Dr. Emerson back to Missouri. Scott had a daughter, Eliza, who was born on a steamboat on the Mississippi River in a part of the river where slavery was banned by federal law. Dr. Emerson married Eliza Sanford in 1838. After he died in 1843, his widow treated

Dred Scott as a slave. Dred Scott sued in 1846 in the Missouri state courts for a declaration that he was a free man as a result of *Somerset's Case*, federal law, and Dred Scott's sojourn in Illinois and in the Minnesota Territory. Missouri State law at the time Scott sued showed that he had an open-and-shut case that he was actually a free man. The Missouri Supreme Court had so ruled in more than ten other cases similar to Dred Scott's, and Scott won in the Missouri lower courts. The Missouri State Supreme Court, however, overruled decades of precedent and held that Dred Scott was still a slave, at least in part because of the darkening clouds of impending Civil War, which the state Supreme Court cited. *See Scott v. Emerson,* 15 Mo. 576 (1851). Scott became the property at this point of Eliza Sanford's brother, John Stanford, who was a citizen of New York state.

Having lost in the Missouri courts, in 1853, Dred Scott sued John Stanford in federal district court, seeking a declaration he was a free man. The basis for federal court jurisdiction was diversity of citizenship. John Stanford was a citizen of New York State. Dred Scott was, if free, a citizen of Missouri. Federal law allowed citizens of different states to sue each other in federal district court, so Scott sued Stanford. At trial in 1854, the U.S. District Judge for Missouri ordered the jury to rely on Missouri law in determining whether Scott was free. This, of course, led to a holding that Dred Scott was a slave because the Missouri Supreme Court had so ruled in Dred Scott's prior state court case. Scott appealed to the U.S. Supreme Court for his freedom, and for unknown reasons the case was captioned *Dred Scott v. Sanford*, misspelling the defendants' last name.

You are now ready to read *Dred Scott v. Sanford*. Be warned that the case in its unedited form consumes 240 pages of the United States Reports, and there are multiple opinions by various justices. It is actually quite difficult to determine which propositions commanded a majority of the Court. In particular, it is doubtful whether Chief Justice Taney's views on whether Scott could be a "citizen"—a position explicitly repudiated by the Fourteenth Amendment a decade later—were joined by more than a plurality of the Court. For present purposes, pay special attention to the question of Congress's power over slavery in federal territory.

Dred Scott v. Sandford

60 U.S. (19 How.) 393 (1857)

■ MR. CHIEF JUSTICE TANEY delivered the opinion of the Court.

* * *

There are two leading questions presented by the record:

1. Had the Circuit Court of the United States jurisdiction to hear and determine the case between these parties? And

2. If it had jurisdiction, is the judgment it has given erroneous or not?

* * * [Dred Scott] brought this action in the Circuit Court of the United States for that district, to assert the title of himself and his family to freedom.

* * *

The defendant pleaded in abatement to the jurisdiction of the court, that the plaintiff was not a citizen of the State of Missouri, as alleged in his declaration, being a negro of African descent, whose ancestors were of pure African blood, and who were brought into this country and sold as slaves.

* * *

The question is simply this: can a negro whose ancestors were imported into this country, and sold as slaves, become a member of the political community formed and brought into existence by the Constitution of the United States, and as such become entitled to all the rights, and privileges, and immunities, guarantied by that instrument to the citizen, one of which rights is the privilege of suing in a court of the United States in the cases specified in the Constitution?

It will be observed, that the plea applies to that class of persons only whose ancestors were negroes of the African race, and imported into this country, and sold and held as slaves. The only matter in issue before the court, therefore, is, whether the descendants of such slaves, when they shall be emancipated, or who are born of parents who had become free before their birth, are citizens of a State, in the sense in which the word citizen is used in the Constitution of the United States. And this being the only matter in dispute on the pleadings, the court must be understood as speaking in this opinion of that class only, that is, of those persons who are the descendants of Africans who were imported into this country, and sold as slaves.

* * *

The words "people of the United States" and "citizens" are synonymous terms * * *. They both describe the political body who, according to our republican institutions, form the sovereignty, and who hold the power and conduct the Government through their representatives. They are what we familiarly call the "sovereign people," and every citizen is one of this people, and a constituent member of this sovereignty. The question before us is, whether the class of persons described in the plea in abatement compose a portion of this people, and are constituent members of this sovereignty? We think they are not, and that they are not included, and were not intended to be included, under the word "citizens" in the Constitution, and can therefore claim none of the rights and privileges which that instrument provides for and secures to citizens of the United States. On the contrary, they were at that time considered as a subordinate and inferior class of beings, who had been subjugated by the dominant race, and, whether emancipated or not, yet remained subject to their authority, and had no rights or privileges but such as those who held the power and the Government might choose to grant them.

* * *

In discussing this question, we must not confound the rights of citizenship which a State may confer within its own limits, and the rights of citizenship as a member of the Union. It does not by any means follow, because he has all the rights and privileges of a citizen of a State, that he must be a citizen of the United States. He may have all of the rights and privileges of the citizen of a State, and yet not be entitled to the rights and privileges of a citizen in any other State. For, previous to the adoption of the Constitution of the United States, every State had the undoubted right to confer on whomsoever it pleased the character of citizen, and to endow him with all its rights. But this character of course was confined to the boundaries of the State, and gave him no rights or privileges in other States beyond those secured to him by the laws of nations and the comity of States. Nor have the several States surrendered the power of conferring these rights and privileges by adopting the

Constitution of the United States. Each State may still confer them upon an alien, or anyone it thinks proper, or upon any class or description of persons; yet he would not be a citizen in the sense in which that word is used in the Constitution of the United States, nor entitled to sue as such in one of its courts, nor to the privileges and immunities of a citizen in the other States. The rights which he would acquire would be restricted to the State which gave them. The Constitution has conferred on Congress the right to establish an uniform rule of naturalization, and this right is evidently exclusive, and has always been held by this court to be so. Consequently, no State, since the adoption of the Constitution, can by naturalizing an alien invest him with the rights and privileges secured to a citizen of a State under the Federal Government, although, so far as the State alone was concerned, he would undoubtedly be entitled to the rights of a citizen, and clothed with all the rights and immunities which the Constitution and laws of the State attached to that character.

It is very clear, therefore, that no State can, by any act or law of its own, passed since the adoption of the Constitution, introduce a new member into the political community created by the Constitution of the United States. It cannot make him a member of this community by making him a member of its own. And for the same reason it cannot introduce any person, or description of persons, who were not intended to be embraced in this new political family, which the Constitution brought into existence, but were intended to be excluded from it.

The question then arises, whether the provisions of the Constitution, in relation to the personal rights and privileges to which the citizen of a State should be entitled, embraced the negro African race, at that time in this country, or who might afterwards be imported, who had then or should afterwards be made free in any State; and to put it in the power of a single State to make him a citizen of the United States, and endue him with the full rights of citizenship in every other State without their consent? Does the Constitution of the United States act upon him whenever he shall be made free under the laws of a State, and raised there to the rank of a citizen, and immediately clothe him with all the privileges of a citizen in every other State, and in its own courts?

The court think the affirmative of these propositions cannot be maintained. And if it cannot, the plaintiff in error could not be a citizen of the State of Missouri, within the meaning of the Constitution of the United States, and, consequently, was not entitled to sue in its courts.

It is true, every person, and every class and description of persons, who were at the time of the adoption of the Constitution recognised as citizens in the several States, became also citizens of this new political body; but none other; it was formed by them, and for them and their posterity, but for no one else. And the personal rights and privileges guarantied to citizens of this new sovereignty were intended to embrace those only who were then members of the several State communities, or who should afterwards by birthright or otherwise become members, according to the provisions of the Constitution and the principles on which it was founded * * *.

It becomes necessary, therefore, to determine who were citizens of the several States when the Constitution was adopted. And in order to do this, we must recur to the Governments and institutions of the thirteen colonies, when they separated from Great Britain and formed new sovereignties, and took their places in the family of independent nations * * *.

In the opinion of the court, the legislation and histories of the times, and the language used in the Declaration of Independence, show, that neither the class of persons who had been imported as slaves, nor their descendants, whether they had become free or not, were then acknowledged as a part of the people, nor intended to be included in the general words used in that memorable instrument.

It is difficult at this day to realize the state of public opinion in relation to that unfortunate race, which prevailed in the civilized and enlightened portions of the world at the time of the Declaration of Independence, and when the Constitution of the United States was framed and adopted. But the public history of every European nation displays it in a manner too plain to be mistaken.

They had for more than a century before been regarded as beings of an inferior order, and altogether unfit to associate with the white race, either in social or political relations; and so far inferior, that they had no rights which the white man was bound to respect; and that the negro might justly and lawfully be reduced to slavery for his benefit. He was bought and sold, and treated as an ordinary article of merchandise and traffic, whenever a profit could be made by it. This opinion was at that time fixed and universal in the civilized portion of the white race. It was regarded as an axiom in morals as well as in politics, which no one thought of disputing or supposed to be open to dispute; and men in every grade and position in society daily and habitually acted upon it in their private pursuits, as well as in matters of public concern, without doubting for a moment the correctness of this opinion.

And in no nation was this opinion more firmly fixed or more uniformly acted upon than by the English Government and English people. They not only seized them on the coast of Africa, and sold them or held them in slavery for their own use; but they took them as ordinary articles of merchandise to every country where they could make a profit on them, and were far more extensively engaged in this commerce than any other nation in the world.

The opinion thus entertained and acted upon in England was naturally impressed upon the colonies they founded on this side of the Atlantic. And, accordingly, a negro of the African race was regarded by them as an article of property, and held, and bought and sold as such, in every one of the thirteen colonies which united in the Declaration of Independence, and afterwards formed the Constitution of the United States. The slaves were more or less numerous in the different colonies, as slave labor was found more or less profitable. But no one seems to have doubted the correctness of the prevailing opinion of the time.

The legislation of the different colonies furnishes positive and indisputable proof of this fact.

* * *

The language of the Declaration of Independence is equally conclusive:

* * *

> * * * "We hold these truths to be self-evident: that all men are created equal; that they are endowed by their Creator with certain unalienable rights; that among them is life, liberty, and the pursuit of happiness; that to secure these rights, Governments are instituted, deriving their just powers from the consent of the governed."

The general words above quoted would seem to embrace the whole human family, and if they were used in a similar instrument at this day would be so understood. But it is too clear for dispute, that the enslaved African race were not intended to be included, and formed no part of the people who framed and adopted this declaration; for if the language, as understood in that day, would embrace them, the conduct of the distinguished men who framed the Declaration of Independence would have been utterly and flagrantly inconsistent with the principles they asserted; and instead of the sympathy of mankind, to which they so confidently appealed, they would have deserved and received universal rebuke and reprobation.

Yet the men who framed this declaration were great men—high in literary acquirements—high in their sense of honor, and incapable of asserting principles inconsistent with those on which they were acting. They perfectly understood the meaning of the language they used, and how it would be understood by others; and they knew that it would not in any part of the civilized world be supposed to embrace the negro race, which, by common consent, had been excluded from civilized Governments and the family of nations, and doomed to slavery * * *.

* * *

* * * [T]here are two clauses in the Constitution which point directly and specifically to the negro race as a separate class of persons, and show clearly that they were not regarded as a portion of the people or citizens of the Government then formed.

One of these clauses reserves to each of the thirteen States the right to import slaves until the year 1808 if it thinks proper * * *. And by the other provision the States pledge themselves to each other to maintain the right of property of the master, by delivering up to him any slave who may have escaped from his service, and be found within their respective territories. By the first above-mentioned clause, therefore, the right to purchase and hold this property is directly sanctioned and authorized for twenty years by the people who framed the Constitution. And by the second, they pledge themselves to maintain and uphold the right of the master in the manner specified, as long as the Government they then formed should endure. And these two provisions show, conclusively, that neither the description of persons therein referred to, nor their descendants, were embraced in any of the other provisions of the Constitution; for certainly these two clauses were not intended to confer on them or their posterity the blessings of liberty, or any of the personal rights so carefully provided for the citizen.

No one of that race had ever migrated to the United States voluntarily; all of them had been brought here as articles of merchandise. The number that had been emancipated at that time were but few in comparison with those held in slavery; and they were identified in the public mind with the race to which they belonged, and regarded as a part of the slave population rather than the free. It is obvious that they were not even in the minds of the framers of the Constitution when they were conferring special rights and privileges upon the citizens of a State in every other part of the Union.

* * *

* * * The right of naturalization was * * * confided to the Federal Government. And this power granted to Congress to establish an uniform rule of *naturalization* is, by the well-understood meaning of the word, confined to persons born in a foreign

country, under a foreign Government. It is not a power to raise to the rank of a citizen any one born in the United States, who, from birth or parentage, by the laws of the country, belongs to an inferior and subordinate class. And when we find the States guarding themselves from the indiscreet or improper admission by other States of emigrants from other countries, by giving the power exclusively to Congress, we cannot fail to see that they could never have left with the States a much more important power—that is, the power of transforming into citizens a numerous class of persons, who in that character would be much more dangerous to the peace and safety of a large portion of the Union, than the few foreigners one of the States might improperly naturalize * * *. And no law of a State, therefore, passed since the Constitution was adopted, can give any right of citizenship outside of its own territory.

* * *

And upon a full and careful consideration of the subject, the court is of opinion, that, upon the facts stated in the plea in abatement, Dred Scott was not a citizen of Missouri within the meaning of the Constitution of the United States, and not entitled as such to sue in its courts; and consequently that the Circuit Court had no jurisdiction of the case * * *.

We are aware that doubts are entertained by some of the members of the court * * * [as to whether we lack jurisdiction over this case, so we go on to show that even under the facts Dred Scott alleges, he was not in fact made a free man by his sojourn in the free State of Illinois and in the Minnesota Territory.]

* * *

It is true that the result either way, by dismissal or by a judgment for the defendant, makes very little, if any, difference in a pecuniary or personal point of view to either party. But the fact that the result would be very nearly the same to the parties in either form of judgment, would not justify this court in sanctioning an error in the judgment which is patent on the record, and which, if sanctioned, might be drawn into precedent, and lead to serious mischief and injustice in some future suit.

We proceed, therefore, to inquire whether the facts relied on by the plaintiff entitled him to his freedom.

* * *

In considering this part of the controversy, two questions arise: 1. Was he, together with his family, free in Missouri by reason of the stay in the territory of the United States hereinbefore mentioned? And 2. If they were not, is Scott himself free by reason of his removal to Rock Island, in the State of Illinois, as stated in the above admissions?

We proceed to examine the first question.

The act of Congress upon which the plaintiff relies, declares that slavery and involuntary servitude, except as a punishment for crime, shall be forever prohibited in all that part of the territory ceded by France, under the name of Louisiana, which lies north of thirty-six degrees thirty minutes north latitude, and not included within the limits of Missouri. And the difficulty which meets us at the threshold of this part of the inquiry is whether Congress was authorized to pass this law under any of the powers granted to it by the Constitution; for if the authority is not given by that instrument, it is the duty of this court to declare it void and inoperative, and incapable of conferring freedom upon anyone who is held as a slave under the laws of anyone of the States.

* * * [Dred Scott's counsel] has laid much stress upon that article in the Constitution which confers on Congress the power "to dispose of and make all needful rules and regulations respecting the territory or other property belonging to the United States;" but, in the judgment of the court, that provision has no bearing on the present controversy, and the power there given, whatever it may be, is confined, and was intended to be confined, to the territory which at that time belonged to, or was claimed by, the United States, and was within their boundaries as settled by the treaty with Great Britain, and can have no influence upon a territory afterwards acquired from a foreign Government. It was a special provision for a known and particular territory, and to meet a present emergency, and nothing more.

* * *

* * * It was intended * * * to transfer to the new Government the property then held in common by the States, and to give to that Government power to apply it to the objects for which it had been destined by mutual agreement among the States before their league was dissolved. It applied only to the property which the States held in common at that time, and has no reference whatever to any territory or other property which the new sovereignty might afterwards itself acquire.

* * *

The words "needful rules and regulations" would seem, also, to have been cautiously used for some definite object. They are not the words usually employed by statesmen, when they mean to give the powers of sovereignty, or to establish a Government, or to authorize its establishment. Thus, in the law to renew and keep alive the Ordinance of 1787, and to reestablish the Government, the title of the law is: "An act to provide for the government of the territory northwest of the river Ohio." And in the Constitution, when granting the power to legislate over the territory that may be selected for the seat of Government independently of a State, it does not say Congress shall have power "to make all needful rules and regulations respecting the territory," but it declares that "Congress shall have power to exercise exclusive legislation in all cases whatsoever over such District (not exceeding ten miles square) as may, by cession of particular States and the acceptance of Congress, become the seat of the Government of the United States."

* * *

Whether, therefore, we take the particular clause in question, by itself, or in connection with the other provisions of the Constitution, we think it clear, that it applies only to the particular territory of which we have spoken, and cannot, by any just rule of interpretation, be extended to territory which the new Government might afterwards obtain from a foreign nation. Consequently, the power which Congress may have lawfully exercised in this Territory, while it remained under a Territorial Government, and which may have been sanctioned by judicial decision, can furnish no justification and no argument to support a similar exercise of power over territory afterwards acquired by the Federal Government. We put aside, therefore, any argument, drawn from precedents, showing the extent of the power which the General Government exercised over slavery in this Territory, as altogether inapplicable to the case before us.

* * *

This brings us to examine by what provision of the Constitution the present Federal Government, under its delegated and restricted powers, is authorized to acquire territory outside of the original limits of the United States, and what powers it may exercise therein over the person or property of a citizen of the United States, while it remains a Territory and until it shall be admitted as one of the States of the Union.

There is certainly no power given by the Constitution to the Federal Government to establish or maintain colonies bordering on the United States or at a distance, to be ruled and governed at its own pleasure; nor to enlarge its territorial limits in any way, except by the admission of new States. That power is plainly given; and if a new State is admitted, it needs no further legislation by Congress, because the Constitution itself defines the relative rights and powers, and duties of the State, and the citizens of the State, and the Federal Government. But no power is given to acquire a Territory to be held and governed permanently in that character.

* * *

We do not mean, however, to question the power of Congress in this respect. The power to expand the territory of the United States by the admission of new States is plainly given; and, in the construction of this power by all the departments of the Government, it has been held to authorize the acquisition of territory, not fit for admission at the time, but to be admitted as soon as its population and situation would entitle it to admission. It is acquired to become a State, and not to be held as a colony and governed by Congress with absolute authority * * *. [A]s there is no express regulation in the Constitution defining the power which the General Government may exercise over the person or property of a citizen in a Territory thus acquired, the court must necessarily look to the provisions and principles of the Constitution, and its distribution of powers, for the rules and principles by which its decision must be governed.

Taking this rule to guide us, it may be safely assumed that citizens of the United States who migrate to a Territory belonging to the people of the United States, cannot be ruled as mere colonists, dependent upon the will of the General Government, and to be governed by any laws it may think proper to impose * * *.

* * *

* * * The power to acquire necessarily carries with it the power to preserve and apply to the purposes for which it was acquired * * *. [S]ome form of civil authority would be absolutely necessary to organize and preserve civilized society, and prepare it to become a State; and what is the best form must always depend on the condition of the Territory at the time, and the choice of the mode must depend upon the exercise of a discretionary power by Congress * * *.

But the power of Congress over the person or property of a citizen can never be a mere discretionary power under our Constitution and form of Government. The powers of the Government and the rights and privileges of the citizen are regulated and plainly defined by the Constitution itself. And when the Territory becomes a part of the United States, the Federal Government enters into possession in the character impressed upon it by those who created it. It enters upon it with its powers over the citizen strictly defined, and limited by the Constitution, from which it derives its own existence and by virtue of which alone it continues to exist and act as a Government and sovereignty. It has no power of any kind beyond it; and it cannot, when it enters a Territory of the United States, put off its character, and assume discretionary or despotic powers which the Constitution has denied to it * * *.

A reference to a few of the provisions of the Constitution will illustrate this proposition.

For example, no one, we presume, will contend that Congress can make any law in a Territory respecting the establishment of religion, or the free exercise thereof, or abridging the freedom of speech or of the press, or the right of the people of the Territory peaceably to assemble, and to petition the Government for the redress of grievances.

Nor can Congress deny to the people the right to keep and bear arms, nor the right to trial by jury, nor compel anyone to be a witness against himself in a criminal proceeding.

These powers, and others in relation to rights of person, which it is not necessary here to enumerate, are, in express and positive terms, denied to the General Government; and the rights of private property have been guarded with equal care. Thus the rights of property are united with the rights of person, and placed on the same ground by the fifth amendment to the Constitution, which provides that no person shall be deprived of life, liberty, and property, without due process of law. And an act of Congress which deprives a citizen of the United States of his liberty or property, merely because he came himself or brought his property into a particular Territory of the United States, and who had committed no offence against the laws, could hardly be dignified with the name of due process of law.

* * *

Now, as we have already said in an earlier part of this opinion, upon a different point, the right of property in a slave is distinctly and expressly affirmed in the Constitution * * *.

Upon these considerations, it is the opinion of the court that the act of Congress which prohibited a citizen from holding and owning property of this kind in the territory of the United States north of the line therein mentioned, is not warranted by the Constitution, and is therefore void; and that neither Dred Scott himself, nor any of his family, were made free by being carried into this territory; even if they had been carried there by the owner, with the intention of becoming a permanent resident.

We have so far examined the case, as it stands under the Constitution of the United States, and the powers thereby delegated to the Federal Government.

But there is another point in the case which depends on State power and State law. And it is contended, on the part of the plaintiff, that he is made free by being taken to Rock Island, in the State of Illinois, independently of his residence in the territory of the United States; and being so made free, he was not again reduced to a state of slavery by being brought back to Missouri.

Our notice of this part of the case will be very brief; for the principle on which it depends was decided in this court, upon much consideration, in the case of Strader et al. *v.* Graham * * *.

* * *

Upon the whole, therefore, it is the judgment of this court, that it appears by the record before us that the plaintiff in error is not a citizen of Missouri, in the sense in which that word is used in the Constitution; and that the Circuit Court of the United States, for that reason, had no jurisdiction in the case, and could give no judgment in it. Its judgment for the defendant must, consequently, be reversed, and a mandate issued directing the suit to be dismissed for want of jurisdiction.

[The concurring opinions of JUSTICES WAYNE, GRIER, DANIEL; CAMPBELL, CATRON, and NELSON are omitted.]

■ MR. JUSTICE MCLEAN, dissenting.

* * *

We need not refer to the mercenary spirit which introduced the infamous traffic in slaves, to show the degradation of negro slavery in our country. This system was imposed upon our colonial settlements by the mother country, and it is due to truth to say that the commercial colonies and States were chiefly engaged in the traffic. But we know as a historical fact, that James Madison, that great and good man, a leading member in the Federal Convention, was solicitous to guard the language of that instrument so as not to convey the idea that there could be property in man.

I prefer the lights of Madison, Hamilton, and Jay, as a means of construing the Constitution in all its bearings, rather than to look behind that period, into a traffic which is now declared to be piracy, and punished with death by Christian nations. I do not like to draw the sources of our domestic relations from so dark a ground. Our independence was a great epoch in the history of freedom; and while I admit the Government was not made expecially for the colored race, yet many of them were citizens of the New England States, and exercised, the rights of suffrage when the Constitution was adopted, and it was not doubted by any intelligent person that its tendencies would greatly ameliorate their condition.

Many of the States, on the adoption of the Constitution, or shortly afterward, took measures to abolish slavery within their respective jurisdictions; and it is a well-known fact that a belief was cherished by the leading men, South as well as North, that the institution of slavery would gradually decline, until it would become extinct. The increased value of slave labor, in the culture of cotton and sugar, prevented the realization of this expectation. Like all other communities and States, the South were influenced by what they considered to be their own interests.

But if we are to turn our attention to the dark ages of the world, why confine our view to colored slavery? On the same principles, white men were made slaves. All slavery has its origin in power, and is against right.

The power of Congress to establish Territorial Governments, and to prohibit the introduction of slavery therein, is the next point to be considered.

* * *

If the [Territories Clause] * * * were before us now for consideration for the first time, under the facts stated, I could not hesitate to say there was adequate legislative power given in it. The power to make all needful rules and regulations is a power to legislate. This no one will controvert, as Congress cannot make "rules and regulations," except by legislation * * *.

* * *

The judicial mind of this country, State and Federal, has agreed on no subject, within its legitimate action, with equal unanimity, as on the power of Congress to establish Territorial Governments. No court, State or Federal, no judge or statesman, is known to have had any doubts on this question for nearly sixty years after the power was exercised. Such Governments have been established from the sources of the Ohio to the Gulf of Mexico, extending to the Lakes on the north and the Pacific Ocean on the west, and from the lines of Georgia to Texas.

Great interests have grown up under the Territorial laws over a country more than five times greater in extent than the original thirteen States; and these interests, corporate or otherwise, have been cherished and consolidated by a benign policy, without any one supposing the law-making power had united with the Judiciary, under the universal sanction of the whole country, to usurp a jurisdiction which did not belong to them. Such a discovery at this late date is more extraordinary than anything which has occurred in the judicial history of this or any other country * * *.

* * *

If the great and fundamental principles of our Government are never to be settled, there can be no lasting prosperity. The Constitution will become a floating waif on the billows of popular excitement.

* * *

If Congress may establish a Territorial Government in the exercise of its discretion, it is a clear principle that a court cannot control that discretion. This being the case, I do not see on what ground the act is held to be void. It did not purport to forfeit property, or take it for public purposes. It only prohibited slavery; in doing which, it followed the ordinance of 1787.

I will now consider the fourth head, which is: 'The effect of taking slaves into a State or Territory, and so holding them, where slavery is prohibited.'

* * *

Now, if a slave abscond, he may be reclaimed; but if he accompany his master into a State or Territory where slavery is prohibited, such slave cannot be said to have left the service of his master where his services were legalized. And if slavery be limited to the range of the territorial laws, how can the slave be coerced to serve in a State or Territory, not only without the authority of law, but against its express provisions? What gives the master the right to control the will of his slave? The local law, which exists in some form. But where there is no such law, can the master control the will of the slave by force? Where no slavery exists, the presumption, without regard to color, is in favor of freedom. Under such a jurisdiction, may the colored man be levied on as the property of his master by a creditor? On the decease of the master, does the slave descend to his heirs as property? Can the master sell him? Any one or all of these acts may be done to the slave, where he is legally held to service. But where the law does not confer this power, it cannot be exercised.

* * *

A slave is brought to England from one of its islands, where slavery was introduced and maintained by the mother country. Although there is no law prohibiting slavery in England, yet there is no law authorizing it; and, for near a century, its courts have declared that the slave there is free from the coercion of the master * * *.

* * * Does not this show that property in a human being does not arise from nature or from the common law, but, in the language of this court, 'it is a mere municipal regulation, founded upon and limited to the range of the territorial laws?' This decision is not a mere argument, but it is the end of the law, in regard to the extent of slavery. Until it shall be overturned, it is not a point for argument; it is obligatory on myself and my brethren, and on all judicial tribunals over which this court exercises an appellate power.

* * *

In this case, a majority of the court have said that a slave may be taken by his master into a Territory of the United States, the same as a horse, or any other kind of property. It is true, this was said by the court, as also many other things, which are of no authority. Nothing that has been said by them, which has not a direct bearing on the jurisdiction of the court, against which they decided, can be considered as authority. I shall certainly not regard it as such. The question of jurisdiction, being before the court, was decided by them authoritatively, but nothing beyond that question. A slave is not a mere chattel. He bears the impress of his Maker, and is amenable to the laws of God and man; and he is destined to an endless existence.

* * *

■ MR. JUSTICE CURTIS dissenting.

I dissent from the opinion pronounced by the Chief Justice, and from the judgment which the majority of the court think it proper to render in this case * * *.

* * *

* * * [T]he question is, whether any person of African descent, whose ancestors were sold as slaves in the United States, can be a citizen of the United States. If any such person can be a citizen, this plaintiff has the right to the judgment of the court that he is so; for no cause is shown by the plea why he is not so, except his descent and the slavery of his ancestors.

The first section of the second article of the Constitution uses the language, "a citizen of the United States at the time of the adoption of the Constitution." One mode of approaching this question is, to inquire who were citizens of the United States at the time of the adoption of the Constitution.

Citizens of the United States at the time of the adoption of the Constitution can have been no other than citizens of the United States under the Confederation. By the Articles of Confederation, a Government was organized, the style whereof was, "The United States of America." This Government was in existence when the Constitution was framed and proposed for adoption, and was to be superseded by the new Government of the United States of America, organized under the Constitution. When, therefore, the Constitution speaks of citizenship of the United States, existing at the time of the adoption of the Constitution, it must necessarily refer to citizenship under the Government which existed prior to and at the time of such adoption.

Without going into any question concerning the powers of the Confederation to govern the territory of the United States out of the limits of the States, and consequently to sustain the relation of Government and citizen in respect to the inhabitants of such territory, it may safely be said that the citizens of the several States were citizens of the United States under the Confederation.

That Government was simply a confederacy of the several States, possessing a few defined powers over subjects of general concern, each State retaining every power, jurisdiction, and right, not expressly delegated to the United States in Congress assembled. And no power was thus delegated to the Government of the Confederation, to act on any question of citizenship, or to make any rules in respect thereto. The whole matter was left to stand upon the action of the several States, and to the natural consequence of such action, that the citizens of each State should be citizens of that Confederacy into which that State had entered, the style whereof was, "The United States of America."

To determine whether any free persons, descended from Africans held in slavery, were citizens of the United States under the Confederation, and consequently at the time of the adoption of the Constitution of the United States, it is only necessary to know whether any such persons were citizens of either of the States under the Confederation, at the time of the adoption of the Constitution.

Of this there can be no doubt. At the time of the ratification of the Articles of Confederation, all free native-born inhabitants of the States of New Hampshire, Massachusetts, New York, New Jersey, and North Carolina, though descended from African slaves, were not only citizens of those States, but such of them as had the other necessary qualifications possessed the franchise of electors, on equal terms with other citizens.

* * *

The fourth of the fundamental articles of the Confederation was as follows: "The free inhabitants of each of these States, paupers, vagabonds, and fugitives from justice, excepted, shall be entitled to all the privileges and immunities of free citizens in the several States."

The fact that free persons of color were citizens of some of the several States, and the consequence, that this fourth article of the Confederation would have the effect to confer on such persons the privileges and immunities of general citizenship, were not only known to those who framed and adopted those articles, but the evidence is decisive that the fourth article was intended to have that effect, and that more restricted language, which would have excluded such persons, was deliberately and purposely rejected.

On the 25th of June, 1778, the Articles of Confederation being under consideration by the Congress, the delegates from South Carolina moved to amend this fourth article by inserting after the word "free," and before the word "inhabitants," the word "white," so that the privileges and immunities of general citizenship would be secured only to white persons. Two States voted for the amendment, eight States against it, and the vote of one State was divided. The language of the article stood unchanged, and both by its terms of inclusion, "free inhabitants," and the strong implication from its terms of exclusion, "paupers, vagabonds, and fugitives from justice," who alone were excepted, it is clear, that under the Confederation, and at the time of the adoption of the Constitution, free colored persons of African descent might be, and, by reason of their citizenship in certain States, were entitled to the privileges and immunities of general citizenship of the United States.

Did the Constitution of the United States deprive them or their descendants of citizenship?

That Constitution was ordained and established by the people of the United States, through the action, in each State, or those persons who were qualified by its laws to act thereon, in behalf of themselves and all other citizens of that State. In some of the States, as we have seen, colored persons were among those qualified by law to act on this subject. These colored persons were not only included in the body of "the people of the United States," by whom the Constitution was ordained and established, but in at least five of the States they had the power to act, and doubtless did act, by their suffrages, upon the question of its adoption. It would be strange, if we were to find in that instrument anything which deprived of their citizenship any part of the people of the United States who were among those by whom it was established.

I can find nothing in the Constitution which, *proprio vigore,* deprives of their citizenship any class of persons who were citizens of the United States at the time of its adoption, or who should be native-born citizens of any State after its adoption; nor any power enabling Congress to disfranchise persons born on the soil of any State, and entitled to citizenship of such State by its Constitution and laws. And my opinion is that, under the Constitution of the United States, every free person born on the soil of a State, who is a citizen of that State by force of its Constitution or laws, is also a citizen of the United States.

* * *

The first section of the second article of the Constitution uses the language, "a natural-born citizen." It thus assumes that citizenship may be acquired by birth. Undoubtedly, this language of the Constitution was used in reference to that principle of public law, well understood in this country at the time of the adoption of the Constitution, which referred citizenship to the place of birth * * *.

The Constitution having recognized the rule that persons born within the several States are citizens of the United States, one of four things must be true:

First. That the Constitution itself has described what native-born persons shall or shall not be citizens of the United States; or,

Second. That it has empowered Congress to do so; or,

Third. That all free persons, born within the several States, are citizens of the United States; or,

Fourth. That it is left to each State to determine what free persons, born within its limits, shall be citizens of such State, and *thereby* be citizens of the United States.

* * *

That the Constitution itself has defined citizenship of the United States by declaring what persons born within the several States shall or shall not be citizens of the United States, will not be pretended. It contains no such declaration * * *.

Has it empowered Congress to enact what free persons, born within the several States, shall or shall not be citizens of the United States?

* * *

It is a substantive power, distinct in its nature from all others; capable of affecting not only the relations of the States to the General Government, but of controlling the political condition of the people of the United States. Certainly we ought to find this power granted by the Constitution, at least by some necessary inference, before we can say it does not remain to the States or the people. I proceed therefore to examine all the provisions of the Constitution which may have some bearing on this subject.

Among the powers expressly granted to Congress is "the power to establish a uniform rule of naturalization." It is not doubted that this is a power to prescribe a rule for the removal of the disabilities consequent on foreign birth. To hold that it extends further than this, would do violence to the meaning of the term naturalization * * *.

It appears, then that the only power expressly granted to Congress to legislate concerning citizenship, is confined to the removal of the disabilities of foreign birth.

* * *

Laying aside, then, the case of aliens, concerning which the Constitution of the United States has provided, and confining our view to free persons born within the several States, we find that the Constitution has recognized the general principle of public law, that allegiance and citizenship depend on the place of birth; that it has not attempted practically to apply this principle by designating the particular classes of persons who should or should not come under it; that when we turn to the Constitution for an answer to the question, what free persons, born within the several States, are citizens of the United States, the only answer we can receive from any of its express provisions is, the citizens of the several States are to enjoy the privileges and immunities of citizens in every State, and their franchise as electors under the Constitution depends on their citizenship in the several States. Add to this, that the Constitution was ordained by the citizens of the several States; that they were "the people of the United States," for whom and whose posterity the Government was declared in the preamble of the Constitution to be made; that each of them was "a citizen of the United States at the time of the adoption of the Constitution," within the meaning of those words in that instrument; that by them the Government was to be and was in fact organized; and that no power is conferred on the Government of the Union to discriminate between them, or to disfranchise any of them—the necessary conclusion is, that those persons born within the several States, who, by force of their respective Constitutions and laws, are citizens of the State, are thereby citizens of the United States.

* * *

It has been often asserted that the Constitution was made exclusively by and for the white race. It has already been shown that in five of the thirteen original States, colored persons then possessed the elective franchise, and were among those by whom the Constitution was ordained and established. If so, it is not true, in point of fact, that the Constitution was made exclusively by the white race. And that it was made exclusively for the white race is, in my opinion, not only an assumption not warranted by anything in the Constitution, but contradicted by its opening declaration, that it was ordained and established by the people of the United States, for themselves and their posterity. And as free colored persons were then citizens of at least five States, and so in every sense part of the people of the United States, they were among those for whom and whose posterity the Constitution was ordained and established.

* * *

I dissent, therefore, from that part of the opinion of the majority of the court, in which it is held that a person of African descent cannot be a citizen of the United States; and I regret I must go further, and dissent both from what I deem their assumption of authority to examine the constitutionality of the act of Congress commonly called the Missouri compromise act, and the grounds and conclusions announced in their opinion.

* * *

The residence of the plaintiff in the State of Illinois, and the residence of himself and his wife in the territory acquired from France lying north of latitude thirty-six degrees thirty minutes and north of the State of Missouri, are each relied on by the plaintiff in error. As the residence in the territory affects the plaintiff's wife and children as well as himself, I must inquire what was its effect.

The general question may be stated to be, whether the plaintiff's *status,* as a slave, was so changed by his residence within that territory, that he was not a slave in the State of Missouri at the time this action was brought.

* * *

* * * By the eighth section of the Act of March 6, 1820 (3 Stat. at Large 548,) it was enacted that, within this Territory [of Wisconsin], "slavery and involuntary servitude, otherwise than in the punishment of crimes, whereof the parties shall have been duly convicted, shall be, and is hereby, forever prohibited * * *."

* * *

It thus appears that, by these acts of Congress * * * it was positively enacted that slavery and involuntary servitude * * * should not exist there. It is not simply that slavery is not recognised and cannot be aided by the municipal law. It is recognised for the purpose of being absolutely prohibited, and declared incapable of existing within the Territory, save in the instance of a fugitive slave.

* * * I must conclude, therefore, that it was the will of Congress that the state of involuntary servitude of a slave, coming into the Territory with his master, should cease to exist * * *

* * *

I have thus far assumed, merely for the purpose of the argument, that the laws of the United States, respecting slavery in this Territory, were constitutionally enacted by Congress. It remains to inquire whether they are constitutional and binding laws.

* * *

Keeping these facts in view, it may confidently be asserted that there is very strong reason to believe, before we examine the Constitution itself, that the necessity for a competent grant of power to hold, dispose of, and govern territory, ceded and expected to be ceded, could not have escaped the attention of those who framed or adopted the Constitution; and that if it did not escape their attention, it could not fail to be adequately provided for.

* * *

It is said that * * * [the Territories Clause] has no application to any territory save that then belonging to the United States * * *. [W]hen the Constitution was framed, a confident expectation was entertained, which was speedily realized, that North Carolina and Georgia would cede their claims to that great territory which lay west of those States. No doubt has been suggested that the first clause of this same article, which enabled Congress to admit new States, refers to and includes new States to be formed out of this territory, expected to be thereafter ceded by North Carolina and Georgia, as well as new States to be formed out of territory northwest of the Ohio, which then had been ceded by Virginia. It must have been seen, therefore, that the same necessity would exist for an authority to dispose of and make all needful regulations respecting this territory, when ceded, as existed for a like authority respecting territory which had been ceded.

No reason has been suggested why any reluctance should have been felt, by the framers of the Constitution, to apply this provision to all the territory which might belong to the United States, or why any distinction should have been made, founded on the accidental circumstance of the dates of the cessions; a circumstance in no way material as respects the necessity for rules and regulations, or the propriety of conferring on the Congress power to make them. And if we look at the course of the debates in the Convention on this article, we shall find that the then unceded lands, so far from having been left out of view in adopting this article, constituted, in the minds of members, a subject of even paramount importance.

* * *

There was to be established by the Constitution a frame of government, under which the people of the United States and their posterity were to continue indefinitely. To take one of its provisions, the language of which is broad enough to extend throughout the existence of the Government, and embrace all territory belonging to the United States throughout all time, and the purposes and objects of which apply to all territory of the United States, and narrow it down to territory belonging to the United States when the Constitution was framed, while at the same time it is admitted that the Constitution contemplated and authorized the acquisition, from time to time, of other and foreign territory, seems to me to be an interpretation as inconsistent with the nature and purposes of the instrument, as it is with its language, and I can have no hesitation in rejecting it.

* * *

It has been urged that the words "rules and regulations" are not appropriate terms in which to convey authority to make laws for the government of the territory.

But it must be remembered that this is a grant of power to the Congress—that it is therefore necessarily a grant of power to legislate—and, certainly, rules and regulations respecting a particular subject, made by the legislative power of a country, can be nothing but laws * * *.

* * *

If, then, this clause does contain a power to legislate respecting the territory, what are the limits of that power?

To this I answer, that, in common with all the other legislative powers of Congress, it finds limits in the express prohibitions on Congress not to do certain things; that, in the exercise of the legislative power, Congress cannot pass an ex post facto law or bill of attainder; and so in respect to each of the other prohibitions contained in the Constitution.

Besides this, the rules and regulations must be needful. But undoubtedly the question whether a particular rule or regulation be needful, must be finally determined by Congress itself. Whether a law be needful, is a legislative or political, not a judicial, question. Whatever Congress deems needful is so, under the grant of power.

* * *

The subject-matter is the territory of the United States out of the limits of every State, and consequently under the exclusive power of the people of the United States * * *. It will not be questioned that, when the Constitution of the United States was framed and adopted, the allowance and the prohibition of negro slavery were recognized subjects of municipal legislation; every State had in some measure acted thereon; and the only legislative act concerning the territory—the ordinance of 1787, which had then so recently been passed—contained a prohibition of slavery. The purpose and object of the clause being to enable Congress to provide a body of municipal law for the government of the settlers, the allowance or the prohibition of slavery comes within the known and recognized scope of that purpose and object.

There is nothing in the context which qualifies the grant of power * * *. No other clause of the Constitution has been referred to at the bar, or has been seen by me, which imposes any restriction or makes any exception concerning the power of Congress to allow or prohibit slavery in the territory belonging to the United States.

* * *

If it can be shown, by anything in the Constitution itself, that when it confers on Congress the power to make *all* needful rules and regulations respecting the territory belonging to the United States, the exclusion or the allowance of slavery was excepted; or if anything in the history of this provision tends to show that such an exception was intended by those who framed and adopted the Constitution to be introduced into it, I hold it to be my duty carefully to consider, and to allow just weight to such considerations in interpreting the positive text of the Constitution. But where the Constitution has said *all* needful rules and regulations, I must find something more than theoretical reasoning to induce me to say it did not mean all.

* * *

I confess myself unable to perceive any difference whatever between my own opinion of the general extent of the power of Congress and the opinion of the majority of the court, save that I consider it derivable from the express language of the Constitution, while they hold it to be silently implied from the power to acquire territory. Looking at the power of Congress over the Territories as of the extent just described, what positive prohibition exists in the Constitution, which restrained Congress from enacting a law in 1820 to prohibit slavery north of thirty-six degrees thirty minutes north latitude?

The only one suggested is that clause in the fifth article of the amendments of the Constitution which declares that no person shall be deprived of his life, liberty, or property, without due process of law. I will now proceed to examine the question, whether this clause is entitled to the effect thus attributed to it. It is necessary, first, to have a clear view of the nature and incidents of that particular species of property which is now in question.

Slavery, being contrary to natural right, is created only by municipal law. This is not only plain in itself, and agreed by all writers on the subject, but is inferable from the Constitution and has been explicitly declared by this court * * *.

* * *

Is it conceivable that the Constitution has conferred the right on every citizen to become a resident on the territory of the United States with his slaves, and there to hold them as such, but has neither made nor provided for any municipal regulations which are essential to the existence of slavery?

Is it not more rational to conclude that they who framed and adopted the Constitution were aware that persons held to service under the laws of a State are property only to the extent and under the conditions fixed by those laws; that they must cease to be available as property, when their owners voluntarily place them permanently within another jurisdiction, where no municipal laws on the subject of slavery exist; and that, being aware of these principles, and having said nothing to interfere with or displace them, or to compel Congress to legislate in any particular manner on the subject, and having empowered Congress to make all needful rules and regulations respecting the territory of the United States, it was their intention to leave to the discretion of Congress what regulations, if any, should be made concerning slavery therein? * * *

* * *

Nor, in my judgment, will the position that a prohibition to bring slaves into a Territory deprives anyone of his property without due process of law, bear examination.

It must be remembered that this restriction on the legislative power is not peculiar to the Constitution of the United States; it was borrowed from *Magna Charta*; was brought to America by our ancestors, as part of their inherited liberties, and has existed in all the States, usually in the very words of the great charter. It existed in every political community in America in 1787, when the ordinance prohibiting slavery north and west of the Ohio was passed.

And if a prohibition of slavery in a Territory in 1820 violated this principle of *Magna Charta*, the Ordinance of 1787 also violated it, and what power had, I do not say the Congress of the Confederation alone, but the Legislature of Virginia, of the Legislature of any or all the States of the Confederacy, to consent to such a violation? The people of the States had conferred no such power. I think I may at least say, if the Congress did then violate *Magna Charta* by the ordinance, no one discovered that violation. Besides, if the prohibition upon all persons, citizens as well as others, to bring slaves into a Territory, and a declaration that if brought they shall be free, deprives citizens of their property without due process of law, what shall we say of the legislation of many of the slaveholding States which have enacted the same prohibition? As early as October, 1778, a law was passed in Virginia that thereafter no slave should be imported into that Commonwealth by sea or by land, and that every slave who should be imported should become free * * *. I am not aware that such laws, though they exist in many States, were ever supposed to be in conflict with the principle of *Magna Charta* incorporated into the State Constitutions * * *.

* * *

For these reasons, I am of opinion that so much of the several acts of Congress as prohibited slavery and involuntary servitude within that part of the Territory of Wisconsin lying north of thirty-six degrees thirty minutes north latitude and west of the river Mississippi, were constitutional and valid laws.

* * *

In my opinion, the judgment of the Circuit Court should be reversed, and the cause remanded for a new trial.

NOTES AND QUESTIONS

1. Where to start? President-elect James Buchanan, quite improperly, urged Chief Justice Taney to decide the *Dred Scott* case as broadly as possible so as to forever end agitation over the matter of slavery. The 7–2 opinion was issued in March of 1857, and it set off a political firestorm. The Supreme Court had held both that: 1) free African Americans could never be U.S. citizens, and thus the Supreme Court lacked jurisdiction over Dred Scott's case; and 2) Dred Scott could not have become free by virtue of his sojourn and marriage in the Minnesota Territory, because Congress lacked the power to outlaw slavery in any of the federal territories, and the thirty-seven-year-old Missouri Compromise was therefore unconstitutional! This last ruling, in a case in which the Court had just announced that it had no jurisdiction, is a breathtaking use of dicta to upset thirty-seven years of practice by countless presidents, senators, congressmen, and territorial governors. Along the way, Chief Justice Taney had declared that the political platform of the newly emerging Republican Party, which wanted to ban slavery in all the territories, was unconstitutional. It is fair to say that this attempted exercise of judicial "statesmanship" did not end agitation over the matter of slavery. The immediate effect of Chief Justice Taney's opinion was to infuriate the North and galvanize the Republican Party. The Republican Party won the 1858 midterm elections and then elected Abraham Lincoln as President in 1860 on a platform of banning slavery in all the federal territories. Lincoln's election, in turn, led to southern secession. In a very real sense then, *Dred Scott v. Sandford* was the proximate cause of the Civil War.

2. On the question whether free African-Americans can ever become citizens of the United States: What do the facts that under the Articles of Confederation "all free inhabitants" were citizens and that in five out of thirteen States free African-Americans voted for the state conventions ratifying the Constitution mean for Chief Justice Taney's argument? When Chief Justice Taney said that the Constitution was clearly not meant for all free inhabitants, was he speaking for the country or only for the part of the country with which Taney (from Maryland, a slave State) was most familiar?

3. Chief Justice Taney claims that it was hard in 1857 to recollect how racially biased the Framers of the Constitution were in the 1770s and 1780s. Consider again what Confederate Vice President Alexander Stephens said in his infamous Corner-Stone speech comparing the United States and Confederate constitutions. *See supra* page 76. It bears reading again. Chief Justice Taney is obviously right that there are several provisions in the Constitution that are infused with racism. Do those provisions somehow radiate their energy into the rest of the document? Can you derive from the Slave Trade Clause and the Fugitive Slave Clause a more general principle that forever excludes all African-Americans and their descendants, whether or not free, from the political community? What modalities of interpretation would generate that conclusion?

4. Chief Justice Taney's argument that the Territories Clause of Article IV does not apply to any federal territory other than the Northwest Territory is bizarre. Taney was a smart lawyer. Why would he make such an obviously silly argument? Is it because Congress had abolished slavery in the Northwest Territory, and he needed to get rid of that precedent somehow? Does it actually help his argument at all? If the Territories Clause does not give Congress power to govern after-acquired territory (or other property?), then what gives Congress the power to govern it? If you are going to infer a power to govern from the power to acquire, why would that inferred power to govern be any different from the power expressed in the Territories Clause? Why would it be narrower rather than broader or the same? And why would any such inferred power be in Congress rather than in the President? Exactly what power to govern territory does Chief Justice Taney think that Congress possesses?

5. What do you think of Taney's statement that depriving a slave owner of his slave property when he enters into a free territory violates the Due Process Clause of the Fifth Amendment? If a State legalized possession of anthrax, would Congress have to allow people to bring their anthrax into federal territories or else violate the Due Process Clause? Drawing on Article 39 of Magna Carta from eight centuries ago, the Due Process Clause had long been understood to mean that "No person could be deprived of life, liberty or property except by the law of the land or by a jury of their peers." *See infra* page 1109. Here, slave owners who brought their slave property into free federal territories were deprived of property by the law of the land as expressed in an act of Congress. Chief Justice Taney's Due Process Clause argument in *Dred Scott v. Sandford* is widely regarded as the first use of so-called "substantive due process," of which we will hear much more later.

6. "Hard cases sometimes make bad law. In *Dred Scott,* an easy case made terrible law." LAWSON & SEIDMAN, *supra,* at 201.Why did the Supreme Court rule as erroneously as it did in such an easy case by a 7–2 margin? A possible answer is that the Three-Fifths Clause had given the South enough additional presidential electors so that they had a lock on the presidency from 1789 to 1860. Of the thirty-six Supreme Court Justices appointed between 1789 and 1860, thirty-two were appointed by slave owners or supporters of slavery. Is the problem with *Dred Scott* that the Supreme Court made policy instead of finding law or that it just made bad policy?

[Assignment 45]

XVIII. THE GUARANTEE CLAUSE

> **Article IV, Section 4: The United States shall guarantee to every State in this Union a Republican Form of Government, and shall protect each of them against Invasion; and on Application of the Legislature, or of the Executive (when the Legislature cannot be convened) against domestic Violence.**

The last provision in Article IV is framed as a duty on the federal government: To ensure the survival of republican institutions in the States. Does the clause grant any power? Notice that the Guarantee Clause is addressed to the "United States" rather than to Congress, the President, the federal courts, or any other specific person or institution. If the Guarantee Clause grants power, to whom does it grant it?

We have already seen one instance in which the Guarantee Clause at least arguably was treated as a source of federal power: the post-Civil War Reconstruction.

See supra pages 138–141. We have also seen a case in which the Supreme Court seemed to treat the meaning of the Guarantee Clause as non-justiciable. *See supra* pages 558–564. While that reading of *Luther v. Borden* is not inevitable, *see* Tara Leigh Grove, *The Lost History of the Political Question Doctrine,* 90 N.Y.U. L. REV. 1908, 1924–29 (2015), it has been widely enough accepted to lead to a dearth of caselaw on the Guarantee Clause. Scholarship on the clause is more plentiful, though it is too diverse for easy summary. For a good start, see Ryan C. Williams, *The "Guarantee" Clause,* 132 HARV. L. REV. 602 (2018).

It is possible, however, that some cases that formally apply other provisions and doctrines are actually grounded, at least partly, in the Guarantee Clause. Consider, for example, a modern "equal protection" case, which transformed American politics. The issue was the failure of the States in many instances to redraw their congressional and state legislative district lines every ten years after the census. As a result, some districts quite literally had ten times as many people living in them as did others. Public interest litigators challenged this malapportionment as being a violation of the Fourteenth Amendment's Privileges or Immunities Clause. In *Colegrove v. Green*, 328 U.S. 549 (1946), the Supreme Court ruled (4–3) that the issue of drawing electoral district lines is inherently a political question that is not justiciable in court. Justice Frankfurter, who authored the majority opinion, argued that political change had to come from the political process itself, even though incumbent politicians have no desire ever to change the district lines that got them elected to legislative office.

In *Baker v. Carr*, 369 U.S. 186 (1962), below, the Supreme Court considered a challenge to Tennessee legislative districts where the districts lines in 1963 had not been changed since 1901. One rural county in Tennessee, as a result, had one representative for 2,340 voters, while another district had eight representatives for 312,000 voters. Basically, rural areas were over-represented while cities and suburbs were grossly unrepresented. The case is about standing and justiciability, but think carefully about precisely what injury is being claimed and what constitutional norms are being violated.

Baker v. Carr

369 U.S. 186 (1962)

■ MR. JUSTICE BRENNAN delivered the opinion of the Court.

This civil action was brought under 42 U.S.C. §§ 1983 and 1988 to redress the alleged deprivation of federal constitutional rights. The complaint, alleging that, by means of a 1901 statute of Tennessee apportioning the members of the General Assembly among the State's 95 counties, "these plaintiffs and others similarly situated, are denied the equal protection of the laws accorded them by the Fourteenth Amendment to the Constitution of the United States by virtue of the debasement of their votes," was dismissed by a three-judge court * * * in the Middle District of Tennessee. The court held that it lacked jurisdiction of the subject matter and also that no claim was stated upon which relief could be granted * * *. We hold that the dismissal was error, and remand the cause to the District Court for trial and further proceedings consistent with this opinion.

The General Assembly of Tennessee consists of the Senate, with 33 members, and the House of Representatives, with 99 members * * *.

* * * Tennessee's standard for allocating legislative representation among her counties is the total number of qualified voters resident in the respective counties, subject only to minor qualifications. Decennial reapportionment in compliance with the constitutional scheme was effected by the General Assembly each decade from 1871 to 1901 * * *. In 1901, the General Assembly * * * passed the Apportionment Act here in controversy. In the more than 60 years since that action, all proposals in both Houses of the General Assembly for reapportionment have failed to pass.

Between 1901 and 1961, Tennessee has experienced substantial growth and redistribution of her population. In 1901, the population was 2,020,616, of whom 487,380 were eligible to vote. The 1960 Federal Census reports the State's population at 3,567,089, of whom 2,092,891 are eligible to vote. The relative standings of the counties in terms of qualified voters have changed significantly. It is primarily the continued application of the 1901 Apportionment Act to this shifted and enlarged voting population which gives rise to the present controversy.

* * * It is * * * alleged that "because of the population changes since 1900, and the failure of the Legislature to reapportion itself since 1901," the 1901 statute became "unconstitutional and obsolete." Appellants also argue that, because of the composition of the legislature effected by the 1901 Apportionment Act, redress in the form of a state constitutional amendment to change the entire mechanism for reapportioning, or any other change short of that, is difficult or impossible. The complaint concludes that "these plaintiffs and others similarly situated, are denied the equal protection of the laws accorded them by the Fourteenth Amendment to the Constitution of the United States by virtue of the debasement of their votes." * * *

* * * [W]e hold today only (a) that the court possessed jurisdiction of the subject matter; (b) that a justiciable cause of action is stated upon which appellants would be entitled to appropriate relief; and (c) because appellees raise the issue before this Court, that the appellants have standing to challenge the Tennessee apportionment statutes. Beyond noting that we have no cause at this stage to doubt the District Court will be able to fashion relief if violations of constitutional rights are found, it is improper now to consider what remedy would be most appropriate if appellants prevail at the trial.

* * *

The complaint was filed by residents of Davidson, Hamilton, Knox, Montgomery, and Shelby Counties. Each is a person allegedly qualified to vote for members of the General Assembly representing his county * * *.

We hold that the appellants do have standing to maintain this suit. Our decisions plainly support this conclusion. Many of the cases have assumed, rather than articulated, the premise in deciding the merits of similar claims. And *Colegrove v. Green, supra,* squarely held that voters who allege facts showing disadvantage to themselves as individuals have standing to sue * * *.

* * * Their constitutional claim is, in substance, that the 1901 statute constitutes arbitrary and capricious state action, offensive to the Fourteenth Amendment in its irrational disregard of the standard of apportionment prescribed by the State's Constitution or of any standard, effecting a gross disproportion of representation to voting population. The injury which appellants assert is that this classification disfavors the voters in the counties in which they reside, placing them in a position of constitutionally unjustifiable inequality *vis-a-vis* voters in

irrationally favored counties. A citizen's right to a vote free of arbitrary impairment by state action has been judicially recognized as a right secured by the Constitution, when such impairment resulted from dilution by a false tally or by a refusal to count votes from arbitrarily selected precincts or by a stuffing of the ballot box.

* * *

In holding that the subject matter of this suit was not justiciable, the District Court relied on *Colegrove v. Green* * * *. We hold that this challenge to an apportionment presents no nonjusticiable "political question." The cited cases do not hold the contrary.

Of course, the mere fact that the suit seeks protection of a political right does not mean it presents a political question. Such an objection "is little more than a play upon words." *Nixon v. Herndon,* 273 U.S. 536, 540. Rather, it is argued that apportionment cases, whatever the actual wording of the complaint, can involve no federal constitutional right except one resting on the guaranty of a republican form of government, and that complaints based on that clause have been held to present political questions which are nonjusticiable.

We hold that the claim pleaded here neither rests upon nor implicates the Guaranty Clause, and that its justiciability is therefore not foreclosed by our decisions of cases involving that clause * * *.

* * *

We come, finally, to the ultimate inquiry whether our precedents as to what constitutes a nonjusticiable "political question" bring the case before us under the umbrella of that doctrine. A natural beginning is to note whether any of the common characteristics which we have been able to identify and label descriptively are present. We find none: the question here is the consistency of state action with the Federal Constitution. We have no question decided, or to be decided, by a political branch of government coequal with this Court. Nor do we risk embarrassment of our government abroad, or grave disturbance at home if we take issue with Tennessee as to the constitutionality of her action here challenged. Nor need the appellants, in order to succeed in this action, ask the Court to enter upon policy determinations for which judicially manageable standards are lacking. Judicial standards under the Equal Protection Clause are well developed and familiar, and it has been open to courts since the enactment of the Fourteenth Amendment to determine, if on the particular facts they must, that a discrimination reflects *no* policy, but simply arbitrary and capricious action.

This case does, in one sense, involve the allocation of political power within a State, and the appellants might conceivably have added a claim under the Guaranty Clause. Of course, as we have seen, any reliance on that clause would be futile. But because any reliance on the Guaranty Clause could not have succeeded it does not follow that appellants may not be heard on the equal protection claim which in fact they tender. True, it must be clear that the Fourteenth Amendment claim is not so enmeshed with those political question elements which render Guaranty Clause claims nonjusticiable as actually to present a political question itself. But we have found that not to be the case here.

* * *

We conclude then that the nonjusticiability of claims resting on the Guaranty Clause which arises from their embodiment of questions that were thought "political," can have no bearing upon the justiciability of the equal protection claim presented in this case. Finally, we emphasize that it is the involvement in Guaranty Clause claims of the elements thought to define "political questions," and no other feature, which could render them nonjusticiable. Specifically, we have said that such claims are not held nonjusticiable because they touch matters of state governmental organization * * *.

* * *

We conclude that the complaint's allegations of a denial of equal protection present a justiciable constitutional cause of action upon which appellants are entitled to a trial and a decision. The right asserted is within the reach of judicial protection under the Fourteenth Amendment.

The judgment of the District Court is reversed, and the cause is remanded for further proceedings consistent with this opinion.

Reversed and remanded.

[Concurring opinions of JUSTICES DOUGLAS, CLARK, and STEWART are omitted.]

■ MR. JUSTICE FRANKFURTER, with whom MR. JUSTICE HARLAN joins, dissenting.

The Court today reverses a uniform course of decision established by a dozen cases, including one by which the very claim now sustained was unanimously rejected only five years ago. The impressive body of rulings thus cast aside reflected the equally uniform course of our political history regarding the relationship between population and legislative representation—a wholly different matter from denial of the franchise to individuals because of race, color, religion or sex. Such a massive repudiation of the experience of our whole past in asserting destructively novel judicial power demands a detailed analysis of the role of this Court in our constitutional scheme. Disregard of inherent limits in the effective exercise of the Court's 'judicial Power' not only presages the futility of judicial intervention in the essentially political conflict of forces by which the relation between population and representation has time out of mind been and now is determined. It may well impair the Court's position as the ultimate organ of 'the supreme Law of the Land' in that vast range of legal problems, often strongly entangled in popular feeling, on which this Court must pronounce. The Court's authority—possessed of neither the purse nor the sword—ultimately rests on sustained public confidence in its moral sanction. Such feeling must be nourished by the Court's complete detachment, in fact and in appearance, from political entanglements and by abstention from injecting itself into the clash of political forces in political settlements.

* * *

Manifestly, the Equal Protection Clause supplies no clearer guide for judicial examination of apportionment methods than would the Guarantee Clause itself. Apportionment, by its character, is a subject of extraordinary complexity, involving—even after the fundamental theoretical issues concerning what is to be represented in a representative legislature have been fought out or compromised—considerations of geography, demography, electoral convenience, economic and social cohesions or divergencies among particular local groups, communications, the practical effects of political institutions like the lobby and the city machine, ancient traditions and ties of settled usage, respect for proven incumbents of long experience and senior status, mathematical mechanics, censuses compiling relevant data, and a host of others. Legislative responses throughout the country to the reapportionment demands of the 1960 Census have glaringly confirmed that these are not factors that lend themselves to evaluations of a nature that are the staple of judicial determinations or for which judges are equipped to adjudicate by legal training or experience or native wit. And this is the more so true because in every strand of this complicated, intricate web of values meet the contending forces of partisan politics. The practical significance of apportionment is that the next election results may differ because of it. Apportionment battles are overwhelmingly party or intra-party contests. It will add a virulent source of friction and tension in federal-state relations to embroil the federal judiciary in them.

* * *

■ Dissenting opinion of MR. JUSTICE HARLAN, whom MR. JUSTICE FRANKFURTER joins.

* * *

In short, there is nothing in the Federal Constitution to prevent a State, acting not irrationally, from choosing any electoral legislative structure it thinks best suited to the interests, temper, and customs of its people * * *. A State's choice to distribute electoral strength among geographical units, rather than according to a census of population, is certainly no less a rational decision of policy than would be its choice to levy a tax on property rather than a tax on income. Both are legislative judgments entitled to equal respect from this Court.

* * *

NOTES AND QUESTIONS

1. In subsequent cases, the Supreme Court announced what it characterized as a "one person, one vote" rule, which required that all state legislative districts and congressional districts (by way of Article I, Section 2, which has been held to embody the same representational principles as the Fourteenth Amendment) be as nearly equal in population as possible. *See, e.g., Gray v. Sanders,* 372 U.S. 368, 381 (1963): "The conception of political equality from the Declaration of Independence, to Lincoln's Gettysburg Address, to the Fifteenth, Seventeenth, and Nineteenth Amendments can mean only one thing—one person, one vote." This is certainly stirring rhetoric, but the only way to assure that kind of vote-equality in a jurisdiction is to abolish all districts and have elections at large, which no one suggests is constitutionally required. Shortly after *Gray,* the Court acknowledged that "[m]athematical exactness or precision is hardly a workable constitutional requirement." *Reynolds v. Sims,* 377 U.S. 533, 577 (1964). Accordingly, the actual rule, as applied, requires a *rough* equality of population among districts, with much litigation over the permissible magnitudes and rationales for deviations. The Court has rejected a "safe harbor" rule for population deviations that are less than one percent, *see Karcher v. Daggett,* 462 U.S. 725 (1983), though the Court in more recent years has become a bit more tolerant of districting considerations other than population:

> Article I, § 2, of the United States Constitution requires that Members of the House of Representatives "be apportioned among the several States . . .

according to their respective Numbers" and "chosen every second Year by the People of the several States." In *Wesberry v. Sanders*, 376 U.S. 1 (1964), we held that these commands require that "as nearly as is practicable one man's vote in a congressional election is to be worth as much as another's." *Id.*, at 7–8. We have since explained that the "as nearly as is practicable" standard does not require that congressional districts be drawn with "precise mathematical equality," but instead that the State justify population differences between districts that could have been avoided by "a good-faith effort to achieve absolute equality." *Karcher, supra*, at 730.

Karcher set out a two-prong test to determine whether a State's congressional redistricting plan meets this standard. First, the parties challenging the plan bear the burden of proving the existence of population differences that "could practicably be avoided." 462 U.S., at 734. If they do so, the burden shifts to the State to "show with some specificity" that the population differences "were necessary to achieve some legitimate state objective." *Id.*, at 741, 740. This burden is a "flexible" one, which "depend[s] on the size of the deviations, the importance of the State's interests, the consistency with which the plan as a whole reflects those interests, and the availability of alternatives that might substantially vindicate those interests yet approximate population equality more closely." *Id.*, at 741. As we recently reaffirmed, redistricting "ordinarily involves criteria and standards that have been weighed and evaluated by the elected branches in the exercise of their political judgment." *Perry v. Perez*, 565 U.S. 388, 393 (2012) (per curiam). "[W]e are willing to defer to [such] state legislative policies, so long as they are consistent with constitutional norms, even if they require small differences in the population of congressional districts." *Karcher, supra*, at 740.

In this case, plaintiffs claim that West Virginia's redistricting plan, adopted following the 2010 decennial United States census, violates Article I, § 2, of the United States Constitution * * *.

* * *

S.B. 1008 [the redistricting statute] * * * has a population variance of 0.79%, the second highest variance of the plans the legislature considered. That is, the population difference between the largest and smallest districts in S.B. 1008 equals 0.79% of the population of the average district.

* * *

Given the State's concession that it could achieve smaller population variations, the remaining question under *Karcher* is whether the State can demonstrate that "the population deviations in its plan were necessary to achieve some legitimate state objective." 462 U.S., at 740. Considering, as *Karcher* instructs, "the size of the deviations, the importance of the State's interests, the consistency with which the plan as a whole reflects those interests, and the availability of alternatives that might substantially vindicate those interests," *id.*, at 741, it is clear that West Virginia has carried its burden.

* * *

* * * [O]ur cases leave little doubt that avoiding contests between incumbents and not splitting political subdivisions are valid, neutral state districting policies. The majority [of the three-judge district court that rejected the West Virginia plan] cited no precedent for requiring legislative findings on

> the "discrete, numerically precise portion" of the variance attributable to each factor, and we are aware of none.
>
> * * *
>
> * * * The desire to minimize population shifts between districts is clearly a valid, neutral state policy. S.B. 1008 achieves significantly lower population shifts than the alternative plans—more than four times lower than the closest alternative, and more than 25 times lower than others.
>
> * * * [H]ere, given the small "size of the deviations," as balanced against "the importance of the State's interests, the consistency with which the plan as a whole reflects those interests," and the lack of available "alternatives that might substantially vindicate those interests yet approximate population equality more closely," *Karcher, supra,* at 741, S.B. 1008 is justified by the State's legitimate objectives.

Tennant v. Jefferson County Comm'n, 567 U.S. 758, 759–65 (2012) (per curiam). Notwithstanding the nontrivial problems of translating the "one person, one vote" concept into the practicalities of districting, the concept is enormously popular and is firmly a part of American legal culture. Read the text below of Sections 1 and 2 of the Fourteenth Amendment:

> Section 1: All persons born or naturalized in the United States, and subject to the jurisdiction thereof, are citizens of the United States and of the state wherein they reside. No state shall make or enforce any law which shall abridge the privileges or immunities of citizens of the United States; nor shall any state deprive any person of life, liberty, or property, without due process of law; nor deny to any person within its jurisdiction the equal protection of the laws.
>
> Section 2. Representatives shall be apportioned among the several states according to their respective numbers, counting the whole number of persons in each state, excluding Indians not taxed. But when the right to vote at any election for the choice of electors for President and Vice President of the United States, Representatives in Congress, the executive and judicial officers of a state, or the members of the legislature thereof, is denied to any of the male inhabitants of such state, being twenty-one years of age, and citizens of the United States, or in any way abridged, except for participation in rebellion, or other crime, the basis of representation therein shall be reduced in the proportion which the number of such male citizens shall bear to the whole number of male citizens twenty-one years of age in such state.

It is abundantly clear that Section 1 of the Amendment creates equality of civil rights while Section 2 addresses equality of political rights, such as the right to vote. The fact that the Equal Protection Clause of Section 1 did not apply to voting rights is further proved by the fact that the Reconstruction Framers thought the Fifteenth Amendment was necessary to secure to African-American men the right to vote. It is thus as clear as day that the Equal Protection Clause cannot support the outcome in *Baker v. Carr*. That does not mean, however, that *Baker v. Carr* was wrong to find something constitutionally suspect about self-perpetuating political corruption that effectively disenfranchises much of the electorate. Perhaps the best way of understanding *Baker v. Carr* is to conclude that it *sub silentio* overruled *Colegrove v. Green* and announced a "one person, one vote" principle under the Guarantee Clause, notwithstanding the Court's repeated insistence that the Guarantee Clause played no role in its decision. And because the Guarantee Clause is addressed to the "United States" as an undifferentiated whole rather than to Congress or the President, the federal courts are bound to enforce the Guarantee Clause in appropriate cases. We think *Baker v. Carr* was correctly decided as a disguised Guarantee Clause case but not as an Equal Protection Clause case. What do you think? Given the express statements in *Baker* that the Court was not invoking the Guarantee Clause, if we made this argument in a brief, would it run afoul of Fed. R. Civ. Proc. 11?

2. Many States allow lawmaking, including constitutional amendments, by popular referendum. Are such direct-democracy measures consistent with "a Republican form of Government"? The Supreme Court found such a claim nonjusticiable more than a century ago. *See Pacific States Telephone & Telegraph Co. v. State of Oregon,* 223 U.S. 118 (1912). Is it still nonjusticiable after *Baker v. Carr*? For an intriguing defense of lawmaking by referendum as consistent with republicanism, see Robert G. Natelson, *A Republic, Not a Democracy? Initiative, Referendum, and the Constitution's Guarantee Clause,* 80 TEX. L. REV. 807 (2002).

XIX. ARTICLE V

> **The Congress, whenever two thirds of both Houses shall deem it necessary, shall propose Amendments to this Constitution, or, on the Application of the Legislatures of two thirds of the several States, shall call a Convention for proposing Amendments, which, in either Case, shall be valid to all Intents and Purposes, as Part of this Constitution, when ratified by the Legislatures of three fourths of the several States, or by Conventions in three fourths thereof, as the one or the other Mode of Ratification may be proposed by the Congress; Provided that no Amendment which may be made prior to the Year One thousand eight hundred and eight shall in any Manner affect the first and fourth Clauses in the Ninth Section of the first Article; and that no State, without its consent, shall be deprived of its equal Suffrage in the Senate.**

Article V of the Constitution sets forth the rules for amending the Constitution and the *grundnorm, see supra* page 590, that sovereignty under the Constitution rests with a majority of the people in three-quarters of the States. Questions under this provision have not often reached the courts, though Article V has been the subject of much commentary in the academy and in the political departments. *See, e.g.,* Aziz Z. Huq, *The Function of Article V,* 162 U. PA. L. REV. 1165 (2014); Michael Stokes Paulsen, *A General Theory of Article V: The Constitutional Lessons of the Twenty-seventh Amendment,* 103 YALE L.J. 677 (1993); Michael B. Rappaport, *The Constitutionality of a Limited Convention: An Originalist Analysis,* 28 CONST. COMMENTARY 53 (2012). Early in the twentieth century, the Court did decide that a State could not allow its electorate by referendum to serve as the State's ratifying agent, because Article V requires ratification by "the Legislatures" of the States, *see Hawke v. Smith,* 253 U.S. 221 (1920); and it also concluded that State legislature were capable of ratifying constitutional amendments even if their own State constitutions denied them that authority, because the power of ratification comes from the federal Constitution. *See Leser v. Garnett,* 258 U.S. 130 (1922). One important question that has arisen is whether the Supreme Court can adjudicate cases or controversies involving the legality of the approval or disapproval of a constitutional amendment. Consider the following opinion on that point:

Coleman v. Miller

307 U.S. 433 (1939)

■ Opinion of the Court by MR. CHIEF JUSTICE HUGHES * * *.

In June, 1924, the Congress proposed an amendment to the Constitution, known as the Child Labor Amendment. In January, 1925, the Legislature of Kansas adopted a resolution rejecting the proposed amendment * * *. In January, 1937, a resolution known as "Senate Concurrent Resolution No. 3" was introduced in the Senate of Kansas ratifying the proposed amendment. There were forty senators. When the resolution came up for consideration, twenty senators voted in favor of its adoption and twenty voted against it. The Lieutenant Governor, the presiding officer of the Senate, then cast his vote in favor of the resolution. The resolution was later adopted by the House of Representatives on the vote of a majority of its members.

This original proceeding in mandamus was then brought in the Supreme Court of Kansas by twenty-one members of the Senate, including the twenty senators who had voted against the resolution, and three members of the House of Representatives, to compel the Secretary of the Senate to erase an endorsement on the resolution to the effect that it had been adopted by the Senate and to endorse thereon the words "was not passed", and to restrain the officers of the Senate and House of Representatives from signing the resolution and the Secretary of State of Kansas from authenticating it and delivering it to the Governor. The petition challenged the right of the Lieutenant Governor to cast the deciding vote in the Senate. The petition also set forth the prior rejection of the proposed amendment and alleged that in the period from June, 1924, to March, 1927, the amendment had been rejected by both houses of the legislatures of twenty-six States, and had been ratified in only five States, and that by reason of that rejection and the failure of ratification within a reasonable time the proposed amendment had lost its vitality.

* * *

* * * Petitioners contend * * * the Lieutenant Governor was not a part of the "legislature" so that under Article V of the Federal Constitution, he could be permitted to have a deciding vote on the ratification of the proposed amendment, when the senate was equally divided.

Whether this contention presents a justiciable controversy, or a question which is political in its nature and hence not justiciable, is a question upon which the Court is equally divided and therefore the Court expresses no opinion upon that point.

* * *

* * * The state court adopted the view expressed by text-writers that a state legislature which has rejected an amendment proposed by the Congress may later ratify. The argument in support of that view is that Article V says nothing of rejection but speaks only of ratification and provides that a proposed amendment shall be valid as part of the Constitution when ratified by three-fourths of the States; that the power to ratify is thus conferred upon the State by the Constitution and, as a ratifying power, persists despite a previous rejection. The opposing view proceeds on an assumption that if ratification by "Conventions" were prescribed by the Congress, a convention could not reject and, having adjourned *sine die*, be reassembled and ratify. It is also premised, in accordance with views expressed by text-writers, that ratification if once given cannot afterwards be rescinded and the amendment

rejected, and it is urged that the same effect in the exhaustion of the State's power to act should be ascribed to rejection; that a State can act "but once, either by convention or through its legislature".

Historic instances are cited * * *.

* * * [In connection with the Fourteenth Amendment,] the political departments of the Government dealt with the effect both of previous rejection and of attempted withdrawal and determined that both were ineffectual in the presence of an actual ratification * * *. This decision by the political departments of the Government as to the validity of the adoption of the Fourteenth Amendment has been accepted.

We think that in accordance with this historic precedent the question of the efficacy of ratifications by state legislatures, in the light of previous rejection or attempted withdrawal, should be regarded as a political question pertaining to the political departments, with the ultimate authority in the Congress in the exercise of its control over the promulgation of the adoption of the amendment.

* * *

* * * The more serious question is whether the proposal by the Congress of the Amendment had lost its vitality through lapse of time and hence it could not be ratified by the Kansas legislature in 1937. The argument of petitioners stresses the fact that nearly thirteen years elapsed between the proposal in 1924 and the ratification in question. It is said that when the amendment was proposed there was a definitely adverse popular sentiment and that at the end of 1925 there had been rejection by both houses of the legislatures of sixteen States and ratification by only four States, and that it was not until about 1933 that an aggressive campaign was started in favor of the amendment. In reply, it is urged that Congress did not fix a limit of time for ratification and that an unreasonably long time had not elapsed since the submission; that the conditions which gave rise to the amendment had not been eliminated; that the prevalence of child labor, the diversity of state laws and the disparity in their administration, with the resulting competitive inequalities, continued to exist. Reference is also made to the fact that a number of the States have treated the amendment as still pending and that in the proceedings of the national government there have been indications of the same view. It is said that there were fourteen ratifications in 1933, four in 1935, one in 1936, and three in 1937.

We have held that the Congress in proposing an amendment may fix a reasonable time for ratification. *Dillon v. Gloss*, 256 U.S. 368. There we sustained the action of the Congress in providing in the proposed Eighteenth Amendment that it should be inoperative unless ratified within seven years. No limitation of time for ratification is provided in the instant case either in the proposed amendment or in the resolution of submission. But petitioners contend that, in the absence of a limitation by the Congress, the Court can and should decide what is a reasonable period within which ratification may be had. We are unable to agree with that contention.

It is true that in *Dillon v. Gloss, supra*, the Court said that nothing was found in Article V which suggested that an amendment once proposed was to be open to ratification for all time, or that ratification in some States might be separated from that in others by many years and yet be effective; that there was a strong suggestion to the contrary in that proposal and ratification were but succeeding steps in a single endeavor; that as amendments were deemed to be prompted by necessity, they should be considered and disposed of presently; and that there is a fair implication that ratification must be sufficiently contemporaneous in the required number of States to reflect the will of the people in all sections at relatively the same period; and hence that ratification must be within some reasonable time after the proposal. These considerations were cogent reasons for the decision in *Dillon v. Gloss,* that the Congress had the power to fix a reasonable time for ratification. But it does not follow that, whenever Congress has not exercised that power, the Court should take upon itself the responsibility of deciding what constitutes a reasonable time and determine accordingly the validity of ratifications. That question was not involved in *Dillon v. Gloss* and, in accordance with familiar principle, what was there said must be read in the light of the point decided.

Where are to be found the criteria for such a judicial determination? None are to be found in Constitution or statute. In their endeavor to answer this question petitioners' counsel have suggested that at least two years should be allowed; that six years would not seem to be unreasonably long; that seven years had been used by the Congress as a reasonable period; that one year, six months and thirteen days was the average time used in passing upon amendments which have been ratified since the first ten amendments; that three years, six months and twenty-five days has been the longest time used in ratifying. To this list of variables, counsel add that "the nature and extent of publicity and the activity of the public and of the legislatures of the several States in relation to any particular proposal should be taken into consideration". That statement is pertinent, but there are additional matters to be examined and weighed. When a proposed amendment springs from a conception of economic needs, it would be necessary, in determining whether a reasonable time had elapsed since its submission, to consider the economic conditions prevailing in the country, whether these had so far changed since the submission as to make the proposal no longer responsive to the conception which inspired it or whether conditions were such as to intensify the feeling of need and the appropriateness of the proposed remedial action. In short, the question of a reasonable time in many cases would involve, as in this case it does involve, an appraisal of a great variety of relevant conditions, political, social and economic, which can hardly be said to be within the appropriate range of evidence receivable in a court of justice and as to which it would be an extravagant extension of judicial authority to assert judicial notice as the basis of deciding a controversy with respect to the validity of an amendment actually ratified. On the other hand, these conditions are appropriate for the consideration of the political departments of the Government. The questions they involve are essentially political and not justiciable. They can be decided by the Congress with the full knowledge and appreciation ascribed to the national legislature of the political, social and economic conditions which have prevailed during the period since the submission of the amendment.

* * *

It would unduly lengthen this opinion to attempt to review our decisions as to the class of questions deemed to be political and not justiciable * * *.

For the reasons we have stated, which we think to be as compelling as those which underlay the cited decisions, we think that the Congress in controlling the promulgation of the adoption of a constitutional amendment has the final determination of the question whether by lapse of time its proposal of the amendment had lost its vitality prior to the required ratifications. The state officials should not be restrained from certifying to the Secretary of State the adoption by the legislature of Kansas of the resolution of ratification.

As we find no reason for disturbing the decision of the Supreme Court of Kansas in denying the mandamus sought by petitioners, its judgment is affirmed but upon the grounds stated in this opinion.

■ Concurring opinion by MR. JUSTICE BLACK, in which MR. JUSTICE ROBERTS, MR. JUSTICE FRANKFURTER, and MR. JUSTICE DOUGLAS join.

Although * * * we believe this cause should be dismissed, the ruling of the Court just announced removes from the case the question of petitioners' standing to sue. Under the compulsion of that ruling * * * [we] have participated in the discussion of other questions considered by the Court and we concur in the result reached, but for somewhat different reasons.

The Constitution grants Congress exclusive power to control submission of constitutional amendments. Final determination by Congress that ratification by three-fourths of the States has taken place "is conclusive upon the courts." * * * Proclamation under authority of Congress that an amendment has been ratified will carry with it a solemn assurance by the Congress that ratification has taken place as the Constitution commands. Upon this assurance a proclaimed amendment must be accepted as a part of the Constitution, leaving to the judiciary its traditional authority of interpretation. To the extent that the Court's opinion in the present case even impliedly assumes a power to make judicial interpretation of the exclusive constitutional authority of Congress over submission and ratification of amendments, we are unable to agree.

The state court below assumed jurisdiction to determine whether the proper procedure is being followed between submission and final adoption. However, it is apparent that judicial review of or pronouncements upon a supposed limitation of a "reasonable time" within which Congress may accept ratification; as to whether duly authorized state officials have proceeded properly in ratifying or voting for ratification; or whether a State may reverse its action once taken upon a proposed amendment; and kindred questions, are all consistent only with an ultimate control over the amending process in the courts. And this must inevitably embarrass the course of amendment by subjecting to judicial interference matters that we believe were intrusted by the Constitution solely to the political branch of government.

The Court here treats the amending process of the Constitution in some respects as subject to judicial construction, in others as subject to the final authority of the Congress. There is no disapproval of the conclusion arrived at in *Dillon v. Gloss*, that the Constitution impliedly requires that a properly submitted amendment must die unless ratified within a "reasonable time." Nor does the Court now disapprove its prior assumption of power to make such a pronouncement. And it is not made clear that only Congress has constitutional power to determine if there is any such implication in Article V of the Constitution. On the other hand, the Court's opinion declares that Congress has the exclusive power to decide the "political questions" of whether a State whose legislature has once acted upon a proposed amendment may subsequently reverse its position, and whether, in the circumstances of such a case as this, an amendment is dead because an "unreasonable" time has elapsed. No such division between the political and judicial branches of the government is made by

Article V which grants power over the amending of the Constitution to Congress alone. Undivided control of that process has been given by the Article exclusively and completely to Congress. The process itself is 'political' in its entirety, from submission until an amendment becomes part of the Constitution, and is not subject to judicial guidance, control or interference at any point.

Since Congress has sole and complete control over the amending process, subject to no judicial review, the views of any court upon this process cannot be binding upon Congress, and insofar as *Dillon v. Gloss* attempts judicially to impose a limitation upon the right of Congress to determine final adoption of an amendment, it should be disapproved * * *.

* * *

[Dissenting opinions of JUSTICE FRANKFURTER and JUSTICE BUTLER are omitted.]

NOTES AND QUESTIONS

1. Are questions concerning the ratification of constitutional amendments inherently political questions, which the federal courts cannot address? Constitutional amendments, like impeachment proceedings, are one of the two ways in which the political process can check and balance the federal courts. Four constitutional amendments were passed explicitly to overturn Supreme Court decisions: 1) the Eleventh Amendment, which overturns *Chisholm v. Georgia*, 2 U.S. 419 (1793); 2) the Fourteenth Amendment, which overrules *Dred Scott v. Sandford*, 60 U.S. 393 (1857); 3) the Sixteenth Amendment, which overrules *Pollock v. Farmers' Loan and Trust Co.*, 157 U.S. 429 (1895); and the Twenty-Sixth Amendment, which overrules *Oregon v. Mitchell*, 400 U.S. 112 (1970). Does that counsel for or against (or neither for nor against) judicial review of the amendment process?

2. Some constitutional amendments were ratified in dubious ways. For example, the Fourteenth Amendment was ratified by three-quarters of the States only because Congress refused to allow the eleven Confederate States to have their senators or congressmen seated unless those States ratified the Fourteenth Amendment. *See* John Harrison, *The Lawfulness of the Reconstruction Amendments,* 68 U. CHI. L. REV. 375 (2001). The Sixteenth Amendment was declared valid by Congress even though the precise texts "ratified" by the various States were not identical. The courts consider all of these matters to be political questions.

3. *Coleman* involved, at least in part, a timing question: If Congress does not put a time limit on ratification, can the courts imply one? *Coleman* says no. What if the time between ratifications is 200 years? That is precisely the situation with the Twenty-Seventh Amendment, which provides that "[n]o law, varying the compensation for the services of the Senators and Representatives, shall take effect, until an election of Representatives shall have intervened." The Twenty-Seventh Amendment was proposed by James Madison as one of twelve amendments in 1789, the first ten of which were quickly ratified and became the federal Bill of Rights. The Twenty-Seventh Amendment languished in the States, with no deadline attached to it for approval, where it lay largely forgotten until 1982, when Gregory Watson, a sophomore at the University of Texas at Austin, discovered it. He launched a successful nationwide campaign, which resulted in three-quarters of the States ratifying the Amendment on May 5, 1992. Ratification thus extended over a record-breaking period of 202 years, seven months, and ten days! On May 18, 1992, Don W. Wilson, the archivist of the United States, certified that ratification

had been completed. Some members of Congress then protested against this assertion of authority, and, on May 20, 1992, both Houses of Congress passed a concurrent resolution declaring that the amendment had been validly ratified. The vote in the Senate was 99 to 0 and the vote in the House of Representatives was 414 to 3. Those who argued against the validity of ratification claimed that the purpose of Article V was to ensure that there was a contemporaneous consensus of two-thirds of both Houses of Congress and of three-quarters of the States that a constitutional amendment was warranted. What do you think? Is ratification over a period of more than 202 years legitimate, particularly in light of the changes that have occurred since 1789, such as African-Americans and women acquiring the right to vote? On the other hand, the Twenty-Seventh Amendment contained no time limit, and all the literal requirements of Article V were met. It was ratified by two-thirds of both Houses of Congress in 1789 and by three-quarters of the States by 1992. A textualist or formalist would say this is all that is required. Doesn't the congressional concurrent resolution accepting the validity of the ratification process settle the matter? For an elegant discussion of these issues, see Michael Stokes Paulsen, *A General Theory of Article V: The Constitutional Lessons of the Twenty-Seventh Amendment*, 103 YALE L.J. 677 (1993).

4. Article V declares that no State can be deprived of its equal suffrage in the Senate without its consent. Thus, an alteration of the rule that each State has two and only two senators could be made only by unanimous consent of all fifty States. Article V does not, however, say that an amendment deleting the unanimous consent requirement for equal state suffrage requires the unanimous consent of the States. Could one use the text of Article V in a manner contrary to the purpose of Article V to delete the unanimity requirement for constitutional amendments altering the equal suffrage of the States in the U.S. Senate? It seems to us that one could do that. The literal text of Article V allows for it. The challengers in *Leser v. Barnett* tried to argue that the Nineteenth Amendment, which guaranteed women the right to vote, "is that so great an addition to the electorate, if made without the state's consent, destroys its autonomy as a political body." 258 U.S. at 136. The Court pointed out that the same could be said of the Fifteenth Amendment and quickly brushed aside the suggestion. Similar arguments, as it happens, were made (and dismissed) against the Louisiana Purchase, on the theory that anything that changes the country so dramatically needs the unanimous approval of the States. *See* GARY LAWSON & GUY SEIDMAN, THE CONSTITUTION OF EMPIRE: TERRITORIAL EXPANSION AND AMERICAN LEGAL HISTORY 75–77 (2004). Are there aspects of the Constitution that are implicitly unamendable through the Article V process? *See* Jeffrey Rosen, *Was the Flag Burning Amendment Unconstitutional?*, 100 YALE L.J. 1073 (1990). Or does any such notion violate the basic rule that We the People in three-quarters of the States are sovereign?

5. In some foreign countries, especially Germany, India, and Brazil, the constitutions of those countries declare that some constitutional provisions are unamendable. Case-law has thus grown up in Germany, India, and Brazil as to what constitutional amendments are constitutional. What do you think of this idea?

6. In Germany, in particular, the Bill of Rights of the German Basic Law, as the Constitution of Germany is called, is unamendable because of the horrific experience Germany went through with Nazism. Unamendability of the Bill of rights makes perfect sense in this context. In India, constitutional amendments can often by adopted by a majority vote of both houses of parliament so it is too easy to amend the Constitution of India. The Supreme Court of India has j pushed back by declaring that constitutional amendments that alter the Basic Structure of the Constitution of India are unconstitutional. This approach makes a measure of sense in the context of India. The

unamendability of almost all of the Constitution of Brazil has been a disaster because it has prevented that country from getting rid of proportional representation, which has given it thirty parties in the lower house of the legislature, and it has prevented it from amending its right to health care so that it does not benefit the wealthy. What do you think about there being unamendable portions of Constitutions? Is this desirable or not?

[Assignment 46]

XX. ARTICLE VI

> **All Debts contracted and Engagements entered into, before the Adoption of this Constitution, shall be as valid against the United States under this Constitution, as under the Confederation.**
>
> **This Constitution, and the Laws of the United States which shall be made in Pursuance thereof; and all Treaties made, or which shall be made, under the Authority of the United States, shall be the supreme Law of the Land; and the Judges in every State shall be bound thereby, any Thing in the Constitution or Laws of any State to the contrary notwithstanding.**
>
> **The Senators and Representatives before mentioned, and the Members of the several State Legislatures, and all executive and judicial Officers, both of the United States and of the several States, shall be bound by Oath or Affirmation, to support this Constitution; but no religious Test shall ever be required as a Qualification to any Office or public Trust under the United States.**

Article VI (almost) completes the Constitution with three provisions: The Engagements Clause, the Supremacy Clause, and the Oath Clause. You have already seen the Supremacy Clause at work in several contexts, and we will return to it in a moment. But the other two clauses deserve a brief mention.

The Engagements Clause is in the Constitution for a single purpose: To assure that Revolutionary War debts incurred by the United States were honored. As a matter of international law, rules of state succession would determine whether the new government was liable for the debts of the old. (The matter of state succession is very much a live issue today, as new countries and governments emerge at a rapid pace. *See* Robert D. Sloane, *The Policies of State Succession: Harmonizing Self-Determination and Global Order in the Twenty-First Century,* 30 FORDHAM INT'L L.J. 1288 (2007) (reviewing TAI-HENG CHENG, STATE SUCCESSION AND COMMERCIAL OBLIGATIONS (2006).) The Engagements Clause was a strong statement that the United States intended to honor those obligations post-Constitution as a matter of domestic law—to domestic as well as to foreign creditors. But while the clause was targeted at the continued validity of War debts, its language was broad enough to include other "Engagements" as well. Treaties are the most obvious "Engagements" whose validity would continue through the change in governmental form. Less obvious, perhaps, is the Northwest Ordinance, which contained specific promises that the Northwest Territory would become a certain number of States once population levels were reached. That "Engagement[ ]" remained binding on the United States, which made good on that "Engagement[ ]" by admitting Ohio, Indiana, Illinois, Michigan, and Wisconsin.

The Oath Clause both requires an oath for *all* government officials, state and federal, and also rules out religious tests for federal (but not state) offices. The Constitution prescribes the precise form of the oath for the President in Article II, but the Oath Clause merely requires an oath for everyone else without specifying its form. Nor does the clause grant any power to Congress. Nonetheless, it is obviously "necessary and proper for carrying into Execution" all other federal powers for Congress to prescribe the form of an oath for federal officials. Indeed, literally the first statute ever passed by the very first Congress was "[a]n Act to regulate the Time and Manner of administering certain Oaths." Act of June 1, 1789, ch. I, 1 Stat. 23. Unfortunately, Congress took it upon itself in this statute to prescribe the form of oath for *state* as well as federal officials. *See id.* § 3. Unless those state officials are acting pursuant to federal law, as in ratifying constitutional amendments, there is no plausible source of congressional power for this portion of the statute. States need to prescribe (adequate) oaths on their own. This obvious lack of power was pointed out in the First Congress, but it did not seem to bother very many people, and Congress enacted the law anyway, without anyone offering a serious response to the constitutional challenge. *See* Gary Lawson, *The Constitution's Congress,* 89 B.U. L. REV. 399, 403–06 (2009). Thus, the first statute enacted by the first Congress was rather blatantly unconstitutional.

The prohibition on religious tests for office obviously has in the mind the English Test Acts from a century earlier. *See supra* page 8. Under modern Establishment Clause jurisprudence, the prohibition is now essentially superfluous. *See* Gerard V. Bradley, *The No Religious Test Clause and the Constitution of Religious Liberty: A Machine That Has Gone of Itself,* 37 CASE WESTERN RES. L. REV. 674 (1987).

The second paragraph of Article VI contains a sweeping Supremacy Clause, which makes federal statutes, treaties, and the Constitution supreme over State constitutions and laws. By its terms, the Supremacy Clause addresses only five categories of legal entities: the federal Constitution, federal statutes and treaties, and state constitutions and laws. It says nothing about the relative place in a legal hierarchy of administrative regulations (state or federal), judicial decisions (state or federal), general law, international law, natural law, or any other possible source of law. If the Supremacy Clause was the sole source of a hierarchy of legal norms, it would be woefully inadequate.

The Supremacy Clause has no such grand ambitions. It deals specifically with the conflict-of-laws situations that are most likely to arise and cause trouble: State courts ignoring federal law. The clause does not answer all, or even most, questions about conflicts of laws. It does not even say that the Constitution is supreme over federal statutes and treaties; as far as the text of the Supremacy Clause is concerned, they are all equal. The main conflict-of-laws rules come from outside the Supremacy Clause. *See* Gary Lawson, *Rebel without a Clause: The Irrelevance of Article VI to Constitutional Supremacy,* 110 MICH. L. REV. FIRST IMPRESSIONS 33 (2011). Constitutional supremacy over all competing sources of law, for example, comes from the kinds of inferences from text and structure relied upon by Chief Justice Marshall in *Marbury v. Madison,* with the Supremacy Clause playing only a minor supporting role. One can perhaps use similar structural reasoning to infer a rule that places federal statutes over federal treaties, *see* Vasan Kesavan, *The Three Tiers of Federal Law,* 100 NW. U.L. REV. 1479 (2006), although current law applies a "last in time" rule for those conflicts. But none of that comes from the Supremacy Clause.

Historically, however, the Supremacy Clause has come to be seen as a powerful font of conflicts-of-laws rules, including rules that go beyond its text. We have already seen some of those effects, in the form of preemption law. *See, e.g., supra* pages 755–765. Under the mantle of preemption, the Supreme Court has identified two contexts in which federal law trumps state law: First, when federal and state law expressly conflict or where federal law states that it preempts State law; and second, when the federal government has so occupied a field of legislation that all State law touching on that field is preempted. Can preemption happen when a state law in some sense "frustrates the purpose" of a federal law? What if the federal "law" is an administrative policy or regulation rather than a congressional statute?

A. GEIER V. AMERICAN HONDA MOTOR CO., INC.

529 U.S. 861 (2000)

■ JUSTICE BREYER delivered the opinion of the Court.

This case focuses on the 1984 version of a Federal Motor Vehicle Safety Standard promulgated by the Department of Transportation under the authority of the National Traffic and Motor Vehicle Safety Act of 1966, 80 Stat. 718, 15 U.S.C. § 1381 *et seq.* (1988 ed.). The standard, FMVSS 208, required auto manufacturers to equip some but not all of their 1987 vehicles with passive restraints. We ask whether the Act pre-empts a state common-law tort action in which the plaintiff claims that the defendant auto manufacturer, who was in compliance with the standard, should nonetheless have equipped a 1987 automobile with airbags. We conclude that the Act, taken together with FMVSS 208, pre-empts the lawsuit.

In 1992, petitioner Alexis Geier, driving a 1987 Honda Accord, collided with a tree and was seriously injured. The car was equipped with manual shoulder and lap belts which Geier had buckled up at the time. The car was not equipped with airbags or other passive restraint devices.

Geier and her parents, also petitioners, sued the car's manufacturer, American Honda Motor Company, Inc., and its affiliates (hereinafter American Honda), under District of Columbia tort law. They claimed, among other things, that American Honda had designed its car negligently and defectively because it lacked a driver's side airbag. The District Court dismissed the lawsuit. The court noted that FMVSS 208 gave car manufacturers a choice as to whether to install airbags. And the court concluded that petitioners' lawsuit, because it sought to establish a different safety standard—*i.e.*, an airbag requirement—was expressly pre-empted by a provision of the Act which pre-empts "any safety standard" that is not identical to a federal safety standard applicable to the same aspect of performance, 15 U.S.C. § 1392(d) (1988 ed.). (We, like the courts below and the parties, refer to the pre-1994 version of the statute throughout the opinion; it has been recodified at 49 U.S.C. § 30101 *et seq.*)

The Court of Appeals agreed with the District Court's conclusion but on somewhat different reasoning. It had doubts, given the existence of the Act's "saving" clause, 15 U.S.C. § 1397(k) (1988 ed.), that petitioners' lawsuit involved the potential creation of the kind of "safety standard" to which the Safety Act's express pre-emption provision refers. But it declined to resolve that question because it found that petitioners' state-law tort claims posed an obstacle to the accomplishment of FMVSS 208's objectives. For that reason, it found that those claims conflicted with FMVSS 208, and that, under ordinary pre-emption principles, the Act consequently pre-empted the lawsuit. The Court of Appeals thus affirmed the District Court's dismissal. 166 F.3d 1236, 1238–1243 (C.A.D.C.1999).

Several state courts have held to the contrary * * *. All of the Federal Circuit Courts that have considered the question, however, have found pre-emption * * *. We now hold that this kind of "no airbag" lawsuit conflicts with the objectives of FMVSS 208, a standard authorized by the Act, and is therefore pre-empted by the Act.

In reaching our conclusion, we consider three subsidiary questions. First, does the Act's express pre-emption provision pre-empt this lawsuit? We think not. Second, do ordinary pre-emption principles nonetheless apply? We hold that they do. Third, does this lawsuit actually conflict with FMVSS 208, hence with the Act itself? We hold that it does.

We first ask whether the Safety Act's express pre-emption provision pre-empts this tort action. The provision reads as follows:

> "Whenever a Federal motor vehicle safety standard established under this subchapter is in effect, no State or political subdivision of a State shall have any authority either to establish, or to continue in effect, with respect to any motor vehicle or item of motor vehicle equipment[,] any safety standard applicable to the same aspect of performance of such vehicle or item of equipment which is not identical to the Federal standard." 15 U.S.C. § 1392(d) (1988 ed.).
>
> * * *

* * * [But] the Act contains * * * a "saving" clause, [which] says that "[c]ompliance with" a federal safety standard "does not exempt any person from any liability under common law." 15 U.S.C. § 1397(k) (1988 ed.). The saving clause assumes that there are some significant number of common-law liability cases to save * * *. Without the saving clause, a broad reading of the express pre-emption provision arguably might pre-empt those actions * * *. On that broad reading of the pre-emption clause little, if any, potential "liability at common law" would remain. And few, if any, state tort actions would remain for the saving clause to save. We have found no convincing indication that Congress wanted to pre-empt, not only state statutes and regulations, but also common-law tort actions, in such circumstances. Hence the broad reading cannot be correct. The language of the pre-emption provision permits a narrow reading that excludes common-law actions. Given the presence of the saving clause, we conclude that the pre-emption clause must be so read.

We have just said that the saving clause *at least* removes tort actions from the scope of the express pre-emption clause. Does it do more? In particular, does it foreclose or limit the operation of ordinary pre-emption principles insofar as those principles instruct us to read statutes as pre-empting state laws (including common-law rules) that "actually conflict" with the statute or federal standards promulgated thereunder? * * *

* * * We * * * conclude that the saving clause (like the express pre-emption provision) does *not* bar the ordinary working of conflict pre-emption principles.

Nothing in the language of the saving clause suggests an intent to save state-law tort actions that conflict with federal regulations * * *.

Moreover, this Court has repeatedly "decline[d] to give broad effect to saving clauses where doing so would upset the careful regulatory scheme established by federal law." We find this concern applicable in the present case. And we conclude that the saving clause foresees—it does not foreclose—the possibility that a federal safety standard will pre-empt a state common-law tort action with which it conflicts * * *.

Neither do we believe that the pre-emption provision, the saving provision, or both together, create some kind of "special burden" beyond that inherent in ordinary pre-emption principles—which "special burden" would specially disfavor pre-emption here * * *.

* * *

Why, in any event, would Congress not have wanted ordinary pre-emption principles to apply where an actual conflict with a federal objective is at stake? * * * To the extent that such an interpretation of the saving provision reads into a particular federal law toleration of a conflict that those principles would otherwise forbid, it permits that law to defeat its own objectives, or potentially, as the Court has put it before, to " 'destroy itself.' " We do not claim that Congress lacks the constitutional power to write a statute that mandates such a complex type of state/federal relationship. But there is no reason to believe Congress has done so here.

* * *

The basic question, then, is whether a common-law "no airbag" action like the one before us actually conflicts with FMVSS 208. We hold that it does.

In petitioners' and the dissent's view, FMVSS 208 sets a minimum airbag standard. As far as FMVSS 208 is concerned, the more airbags, and the sooner, the better. But that was not the Secretary's view. The Department of Transportation's (DOT's) comments, which accompanied the promulgation of FMVSS 208, make clear that the standard deliberately provided the manufacturer with a range of choices among different passive restraint devices. Those choices would bring about a mix of different devices introduced gradually over time; and FMVSS 208 would thereby lower costs, overcome technical safety problems, encourage technological development, and win widespread consumer acceptance—all of which would promote FMVSS 208's safety objectives. See generally 49 Fed.Reg. 28962 (1984).

* * *

The 1984 FMVSS 208 standard * * * deliberately sought a *gradual* phase-in of passive restraints. It required the manufacturers to equip only 10% of their car fleet manufactured after September 1, 1986, with passive restraints. It then increased the percentage in three annual stages, up to 100% of the new car fleet for cars manufactured after September 1, 1989. And it explained that the phased-in requirement would allow more time for manufacturers to develop airbags or other, better, safer passive restraint systems. It would help develop information about the comparative effectiveness of different systems, would lead to a mix in which airbags and other nonseatbelt passive restraint systems played a more prominent role than would otherwise result, and would promote public acceptance.

* * *

Finally, FMVSS 208's passive restraint requirement was conditional. DOT believed that ordinary manual lap and shoulder belts would produce about the same amount of safety as passive restraints, and at significantly lower costs—*if only auto occupants would buckle up*. Thus, FMVSS 208 provided for rescission of its passive restraint requirement if, by September 1, 1989, two-thirds of the States had laws in place that, like those of many other nations, required auto occupants to buckle up (and which met other requirements specified in the standard). The Secretary wrote that "coverage of a large percentage of the American people by seatbelt laws that are enforced would largely negate the incremental increase in safety to be expected from an automatic protection requirement." In the end, two-thirds of the States did not enact mandatory buckle-up laws, and the passive restraint requirement remained in effect.

In sum, as DOT now tells us through the Solicitor General, the 1984 version of FMVSS 208 "embodies the Secretary's policy judgment that safety would best be promoted if manufacturers installed *alternative* protection systems in their fleets rather than one particular system in every car." Brief for United States as *Amicus Curiae* 25; see 49 Fed.Reg. 28997 (1984). Petitioners' tort suit claims that the manufacturers of the 1987 Honda Accord "had a duty to design, manufacture, distribute and sell a motor vehicle with an effective and safe passive restraint system, including, but not limited to, airbags." App. 3 (Complaint, ¶ 11).

In effect, petitioners' tort action depends upon its claim that manufacturers had a duty to install an airbag when they manufactured the 1987 Honda Accord. Such a state law—*i.e.*, a rule of state tort law imposing such a duty—by its terms would have required manufacturers of all similar cars to install airbags rather than other passive restraint systems, such as automatic belts or passive interiors. It thereby would have presented an obstacle to the variety and mix of devices that the federal regulation sought. It would have required all manufacturers to have installed airbags in respect to the entire District-of-Columbia-related portion of their 1987 new car fleet, even though FMVSS 208 at that time required only that 10% of a manufacturer's nationwide fleet be equipped with any passive restraint device at all. It thereby also would have stood as an obstacle to the gradual passive restraint phase-in that the federal regulation deliberately imposed. In addition, it could have made less likely the adoption of a state mandatory buckle-up law. Because the rule of law for which petitioners contend would have stood "as an obstacle to the accomplishment and execution of" the important means-related federal objectives that we have just discussed, it is pre-empted.

* * *

One final point: We place some weight upon DOT's interpretation of FMVSS 208's objectives and its conclusion, as set forth in the Government's brief, that a tort suit such as this one would " 'stan[d] as an obstacle to the accomplishment and execution' " of those objectives. Brief for United States as *Amicus Curiae* 25–26 (quoting *Hines, supra*, at 67). Congress has delegated to DOT authority to implement the statute; the subject matter is technical; and the relevant history and background are complex and extensive. The agency is likely to have a thorough understanding of its own regulation and its objectives and is "uniquely qualified" to comprehend the likely impact of state requirements * * *.

* * *

Regardless, the language of FMVSS 208 and the contemporaneous 1984 DOT explanation is clear enough—even without giving DOT's own view special weight.

FMVSS 208 sought a gradually developing mix of alternative passive restraint devices for safety-related reasons. The rule of state tort law for which petitioners argue would stand as an "obstacle" to the accomplishment of that objective. And the statute foresees the application of ordinary principles of pre-emption in cases of actual conflict. Hence, the tort action is pre-empted.

The judgment of the Court of Appeals is affirmed.

It is so ordered.

■ JUSTICE STEVENS, with whom JUSTICE SOUTER, JUSTICE THOMAS, and JUSTICE GINSBURG join, dissenting.

Airbag technology has been available to automobile manufacturers for over 30 years. There is now general agreement on the proposition "that, to be safe, a car must have an airbag." Indeed, current federal law imposes that requirement on all automobile manufacturers. See 49 U.S.C. § 30127; 49 C.F.R. § 571.208, S4.1.5.3 (1998). The question raised by petitioners' common-law tort action is whether that proposition was sufficiently obvious when Honda's 1987 Accord was manufactured to make the failure to install such a safety feature actionable under theories of negligence or defective design. The Court holds that an interim regulation motivated by the Secretary of Transportation's desire to foster gradual development of a variety of passive restraint devices deprives state courts of jurisdiction to answer that question. I respectfully dissent from that holding, and especially from the Court's unprecedented extension of the doctrine of pre-emption. As a preface to an explanation of my understanding of the statute and the regulation, these preliminary observations seem appropriate.

"This is a case about federalism," *Coleman v. Thompson*, 501 U.S. 722, 726 (1991), that is, about respect for "the constitutional role of the States as sovereign entities." *Alden v. Maine*, 527 U.S. 706, 713 (1999). It raises important questions concerning the way in which the Federal Government may exercise its undoubted power to oust state courts of their traditional jurisdiction over common-law tort actions. The rule the Court enforces today was not enacted by Congress and is not to be found in the text of any Executive Order or regulation. It has a unique origin: It is the product of the Court's interpretation of the final commentary accompanying an interim administrative regulation and the history of airbag regulation generally. Like many other judge-made rules, its contours are not precisely defined. I believe, however, that it is fair to state that if it had been expressly adopted by the Secretary of Transportation, it would have read as follows:

> "No state court shall entertain a common-law tort action based on a claim that an automobile was negligently or defectively designed because it was not equipped with an airbag;
>
> "Provided, however, that this rule shall not apply to cars manufactured before September 1, 1986, or after such time as the Secretary may require the installation of airbags in all new cars; and
>
> "Provided further, that this rule shall not preclude a claim by a driver who was not wearing her seatbelt that an automobile was negligently or defectively designed because it was not equipped with any passive restraint whatsoever, or a claim that an automobile with particular design features was negligently or defectively designed because it was equipped with one type of passive restraint instead of another."

Perhaps such a rule would be a wise component of a legislative reform of our tort system. I express no opinion about that possibility. It is, however, quite clear to me that Congress neither enacted any such rule itself nor authorized the Secretary of Transportation to do so. It is equally clear to me that the objectives that the Secretary intended to achieve through the adoption of Federal Motor Vehicle Safety Standard 208 would not be frustrated one whit by allowing state courts to determine whether in 1987 the lifesaving advantages of airbags had become sufficiently obvious that their omission might constitute a design defect in some new cars * * *.

* * *

When a state statute, administrative rule, or common-law cause of action conflicts with a federal statute, it is axiomatic that the state law is without effect. U.S. Const., Art. VI, cl. 2. On the other hand, it is equally clear that the Supremacy Clause does not give unelected federal judges *carte blanche* to use federal law as a means of imposing their own ideas of tort reform on the States. Because of the role of States as separate sovereigns in our federal system, we have long presumed that state laws—particularly those, such as the provision of tort remedies to compensate for personal injuries, that are within the scope of the States' historic police powers—are not to be pre-empted by a federal statute unless it is the clear and manifest purpose of Congress to do so.

When a federal statute contains an express pre-emption provision, "the task of statutory construction must in the first instance focus on the plain wording of [that provision], which necessarily contains the best evidence of Congress' pre-emptive intent." *CSX Transp., Inc. v. Easterwood*, 507 U.S. 658, 664 (1993). The Safety Act contains both an express pre-emption provision, 15 U.S.C. § 1392(d), and a saving clause that expressly preserves common-law claims, § 1397(k) * * *.

The latter states:

> "Compliance with any Federal motor vehicle safety standard issued under this subchapter does not exempt any person from any liability under common law."

* * *

Given the cumulative force of the fact that § 1392(d) does not expressly pre-empt common-law claims and the fact that § 1397(k) was obviously intended to limit the pre-emptive effect of the Secretary's safety standards, it is quite wrong for the Court to assume that a possible implicit conflict with the purposes to be achieved by such a standard should have the same pre-emptive effect " 'as an obstacle to the accomplishment and execution of the full purposes and objectives of Congress.' " Properly construed, the Safety Act imposes a special burden on a party relying on an arguable, implicit conflict with a temporary regulatory policy—rather than a conflict with congressional policy or with the text of any regulation—to demonstrate that a common-law claim has been pre-empted.

Even though the Safety Act does not expressly pre-empt common-law claims, Honda contends that Standard 208—of its own force—implicitly pre-empts the claims in this case.

> "We have recognized that a federal statute implicitly overrides state law either when the scope of a statute indicates that Congress intended federal law to occupy a field exclusively, *English v. General Elec. Co.*, 496

> U.S. 72, 78–79 (1990), or when state law is in actual conflict with federal law. We have found implied conflict pre-emption where it is 'impossible for a private party to comply with both state and federal requirements,' *id.*, at 79, or where state law 'stands as an obstacle to the accomplishment and execution of the full purposes and objectives of Congress.' *Hines v. Davidowitz,* 312 U.S. 52, 67 (1941)." *Freightliner Corp. v. Myrick*, 514 U.S. 280, 287 (1995).

In addition, we have concluded that regulations "intended to pre-empt state law" that are promulgated by an agency acting nonarbitrarily and within its congressionally delegated authority may also have pre-emptive force. *Fidelity Fed. Sav. & Loan Assn. v. De la Cuesta*, 458 U.S. 141, 153–154 (1982). In this case, Honda relies on the last of the implied pre-emption principles stated in *Freightliner*, arguing that the imposition of common-law liability for failure to install an airbag would frustrate the purposes and objectives of Standard 208.

Both the text of the statute and the text of the standard provide persuasive reasons for rejecting this argument. The saving clause of the Safety Act arguably denies the Secretary the authority to promulgate standards that would pre-empt common-law remedies. Moreover, the text of Standard 208 says nothing about pre-emption, and I am not persuaded that Honda has overcome our traditional presumption that it lacks any implicit pre-emptive effect.

Honda argues, and the Court now agrees, that the risk of liability presented by common-law claims that vehicles without airbags are negligently and defectively designed would frustrate the policy decision that the Secretary made in promulgating Standard 208. This decision, in their view, was that safety—including a desire to encourage "public acceptance of the airbag technology and experimentation with better passive restraint systems"—would best be promoted through gradual implementation of a passive restraint requirement making airbags only one of a variety of systems that a manufacturer could install in order to comply, rather than through a requirement mandating the use of one particular system in every vehicle * * *.

There are at least three flaws in this argument that provide sufficient grounds for rejecting it. First, the entire argument is based on an unrealistic factual predicate. Whatever the risk of liability on a no-airbag claim may have been prior to the promulgation of the 1984 version of Standard 208, that risk did not lead any manufacturer to install airbags in even a substantial portion of its cars. If there had been a realistic likelihood that the risk of tort liability would have that consequence, there would have been no need for Standard 208 * * *.

Second, even if the manufacturers' assessment of their risk of liability ultimately proved to be wrong, the purposes of Standard 208 would not be frustrated. In light of the inevitable time interval between the eventual filing of a tort action alleging that the failure to install an airbag is a design defect and the possible resolution of such a claim against a manufacturer, as well as the additional interval between such a resolution (if any) and manufacturers' "compliance with the state-law duty in question," by modifying their designs to avoid such liability in the future, it is obvious that the phase-in period would have ended long before its purposes could have been frustrated by the specter of tort liability. Thus, even without pre-emption, the public would have been given the time that the Secretary deemed necessary to gradually adjust to the increasing use of airbag technology and allay their unfounded concerns about it * * *.

Third, despite its acknowledgment that the saving clause "preserves those actions that seek to establish greater safety than the minimum safety achieved by a federal regulation intended to provide a floor," the Court completely ignores the important fact that by definition all of the standards established under the Safety Act—like the British regulations that governed the number and capacity of lifeboats aboard the *Titanic*—impose minimum, rather than fixed or maximum, requirements * * *. Moreover, even if variety and gradualism had been independently important to the Secretary, there is nothing in the standard, the accompanying commentary, or the history of airbag regulation to support the notion that the Secretary intended to advance those purposes at all costs, without regard to the detrimental consequences that pre-emption of tort liability could have for the achievement of her avowed purpose of reducing vehicular injuries.

* * *

For these reasons, it is evident that Honda has not crossed the high threshold established by our decisions regarding pre-emption of state laws that allegedly frustrate federal purposes: it has not demonstrated that allowing a common-law no-airbag claim to go forward would impose an obligation on manufacturers that directly and irreconcilably contradicts any primary objective that the Secretary set forth with clarity in Standard 208. Furthermore, it is important to note that the text of Standard 208 (which the Court does not even bother to quote in its opinion), unlike the regulation we reviewed in *Fidelity Fed. Sav. & Loan Assn. v. de la Cuesta*, 458 U.S., at 158, does not contain any expression of an intent to displace state law. Given our repeated emphasis on the importance of the presumption against pre-emption, this silence lends additional support to the conclusion that the continuation of whatever common-law liability may exist in a case like this poses no danger of frustrating any of the Secretary's primary purposes in promulgating Standard 208.

* * *

Our presumption against pre-emption is rooted in the concept of federalism. It recognizes that when Congress legislates "in a field which the States have traditionally occupied . . . [,] we start with the assumption that the historic police powers of the States were not to be superseded by the Federal Act unless that was the clear and manifest purpose of Congress." *Rice v. Santa Fe Elevator Corp.*, 331 U.S., at 230. The signal virtues of this presumption are its placement of the power of pre-emption squarely in the hands of Congress, which is far more suited than the Judiciary to strike the appropriate state/federal balance (particularly in areas of traditional state regulation), and its requirement that Congress speak clearly when exercising that power. In this way, the structural safeguards inherent in the normal operation of the legislative process operate to defend state interests from undue infringement. In addition, the presumption serves as a limiting principle that prevents federal judges from running amok with our potentially boundless (and perhaps inadequately considered) doctrine of implied conflict pre-emption based on frustration of purposes—i.e., that state law is pre-empted if it "stands as an obstacle to the accomplishment and execution of the full purposes and objectives of Congress." *Hines v. Davidowitz*, 312 U.S. 52, 67 (1941).

While the presumption is important in assessing the pre-emptive reach of federal statutes, it becomes crucial when the pre-emptive effect of an administrative regulation is at issue. Unlike Congress, administrative agencies are clearly not designed to represent the interests of States, yet with relative ease they can promulgate comprehensive and detailed regulations that have broad pre-emption ramifications for state law. We have addressed the heightened federalism and nondelegation concerns that agency pre-emption raises by using the presumption to build a procedural bridge across the political accountability gap between States and administrative agencies. Thus, even in cases where implied regulatory pre-emption is at issue, we generally "expect an administrative regulation to declare any intention to pre-empt state law with some specificity." *California Coastal Comm'n v. Granite Rock Co.*, 480 U.S. 572, 583 (1987) * * *.

When the presumption and its underpinnings are properly understood, it is plain that Honda has not overcome the presumption in this case. Neither Standard 208 nor its accompanying commentary includes the slightest specific indication of an intent to pre-empt common-law no-airbag suits * * *.

Furthermore, the Court identifies no case in which we have upheld a regulatory claim of frustration-of-purposes implied conflict pre-emption based on nothing more than an *ex post* administrative litigating position and inferences from regulatory history and final commentary. The latter two sources are even more malleable than legislative history. Thus, when snippets from them are combined with the Court's broad conception of a doctrine of frustration-of-purposes pre-emption untempered by the presumption, a vast, undefined area of state law becomes vulnerable to pre-emption by any related federal law or regulation. In my view, however, "preemption analysis is, or at least should be, a matter of precise statutory [or regulatory] construction rather than an exercise in free-form judicial policymaking." 1 L. Tribe, American Constitutional Law § 6–28, p. 1177 (3d ed.2000).

* * *

Because neither the text of the statute nor the text of the regulation contains any indication of an intent to pre-empt petitioners' cause of action, and because I cannot agree with the Court's unprecedented use of inferences from regulatory history and commentary as a basis for implied pre-emption, I am convinced that Honda has not overcome the presumption against pre-emption in this case. I therefore respectfully dissent.

NOTES AND QUESTIONS

1. Should administrative agencies be able to preempt state laws? States as political entities are represented in Congress, but they are not represented in the National Highway Traffic Safety Administration, which is run by a few presidential appointees and a large career staff. The Supremacy Clause does not mention administrative regulations. Why do state courts have to prefer those regulations to their own state constitutions?

2. If federal agencies are going to have some measure of preemptive authority, should it be coextensive with the authority of Congress? Should courts demand more clarity, and perhaps a stronger showing of conflict, before finding that administrative regulations preempt state law?

3. Justice Stevens points out that the majority never cites the precise text of the agency regulation that supposedly had preemptive effect. Was the state tort suit in this case inconsistent with the agency's *regulation* or with the agency's *policy goals*? If the latter, what in the Constitution allows preemption by executive policy goals? Review in this respect *Arizona v. United States, supra* pages 755–765, which raises some of the same issues.

4. The number of federal administrative regulations dwarfs the number of federal statutes. Preemption by administrative rule is a much more consequential matter than is preemption by congressional statute.

5. Justice Stevens' dissent is correct that preemption is fundamentally about federalism. It is thus a fitting topic with which to close this chapter. Also fitting, in some sense, is the 3–3–3 split in the Court's most recent (as of 2020) preemption decision:

B. VIRGINIA URANIUM, INC. V. WARREN

587 U.S. ___, 139 S.Ct. 1894 (2019)

■ JUSTICE GORSUCH announced the judgment of the Court and delivered an opinion, in which JUSTICE THOMAS and JUSTICE KAVANAUGH join.

Virginia Uranium insists that the federal Atomic Energy Act preempts a state law banning uranium mining, but we do not see it. True, the AEA gives the Nuclear Regulatory Commission significant authority over the milling, transfer, use, and disposal of uranium, as well as the construction and operation of nuclear power plants. But Congress conspicuously chose to leave untouched the States' historic authority over the regulation of mining activities on private lands within their borders. Nor do we see anything to suggest that the enforcement of Virginia's law would frustrate the AEA's purposes and objectives. And we are hardly free to extend a federal statute to a sphere Congress was well aware of but chose to leave alone. In this, as in any field of statutory interpretation, it is our duty to respect not only what Congress wrote but, as importantly, what it didn't write.

Virginia Uranium thought its plan was pretty straightforward. First, the company wanted to use conventional mining techniques to extract raw uranium ore from a site near Coles Hill, Virginia. Next, it intended to mill that ore into a usable form. Typically performed at the mine site, milling involves grinding the ore into sand-sized grains and then exposing it to a chemical solution that leaches out pure uranium. Once dried, the resulting mixture forms a solid "yellowcake," which the company planned to sell to enrichment facilities that produce fuel for nuclear reactors. Finally, because the leaching process does not remove all of the uranium from the ore, the company expected to store the leftover "tailings" near the mine to reduce the chances of contaminating the air or water.

But putting the plan into action didn't prove so simple. Pursuant to the AEA, ch. 724, 60 Stat. 755, 42 U.S.C. § 2011 et seq., the NRC regulates milling and tailing storage activities nationwide, and it has issued an array of rules on these subjects. None of those, though, proved the real problem for Virginia Uranium. The company hit a roadblock even before it could get to the point where the NRC's rules kick in: State law flatly prohibits uranium mining in Virginia.

To overcome that obstacle, Virginia Uranium filed this lawsuit. The company alleged that, under the Constitution's Supremacy Clause, the AEA preempts state uranium mining laws like Virginia's and ensconces the NRC as the lone regulator in the field. And because the NRC's regulations say nothing about uranium mining, the company continued, it remains free to mine as it will in Virginia or elsewhere.

Both the district court and a divided panel of the Fourth Circuit rejected the company's argument. The courts acknowledged that the AEA affords the NRC considerable authority over the nuclear fuel life cycle. But both courts found missing from the AEA any hint that Congress sought to strip States of their traditional power to regulate mining on private lands within their borders. Given the significance of the question presented, we granted review.

The Supremacy Clause supplies a rule of priority. It provides that the "Constitution, and the Laws of the United States which shall be made in Pursuance thereof," are "the supreme Law of the Land . . . any Thing in the Constitution or Laws of any state to the Contrary notwithstanding." Art. VI, cl. 2. This Court has sometimes used different labels to describe the different ways in which federal statutes may displace state laws—speaking, for example, of express, field, and conflict preemption. But these categories "are not rigidly distinct." *Crosby v. National Foreign Trade Council*, 530 U. S. 363, 372, n. 6 (2000). And at least one feature unites them: Invoking some brooding federal interest or appealing to a judicial policy preference should never be enough to win preemption of a state law; a litigant must point specifically to "a constitutional text or a federal statute" that does the displacing or conflicts with state law. *Puerto Rico Dept. of Consumer Affairs v. ISLA Petroleum Corp.*, 485 U. S. 495, 503 (1988); see also 3 J. Story, Commentaries on the Constitution of the United States § 1831, p. 694 (1st ed. 1833) ("the supremacy of the laws is attached to those only, which are made in pursuance of the constitution").

Before us, Virginia Uranium contends that the AEA (and only the AEA) unseats state uranium mining regulations and that it does so under the doctrines of both field and conflict preemption. We examine these arguments about the AEA's preemptive effect much as we would any other about statutory meaning, looking to the text and context of the law in question and guided by the traditional tools of statutory interpretation. Here, no more than in any statutory interpretation dispute, is it enough for any party or court to rest on a supposition (or wish) that "it must be in there somewhere."

We begin with the company's claim that the text and structure of the AEA reserve the regulation of uranium mining for the purpose of addressing nuclear safety concerns to the NRC alone—and almost immediately problems emerge. Unlike many federal statutes, the AEA contains no provision preempting state law in so many words. Even more pointedly, the statute grants the NRC extensive and sometimes exclusive authority to regulate nearly every aspect of the nuclear fuel life cycle *except* mining. Companies like Virginia Uranium must abide the NRC's rules and regulations if they wish to handle enriched uranium, to mill uranium ore or store tailings, or to build or run a nuclear power plant. See 42 U.S.C. §§ 2111(a), 2113(a), 2073. But when it comes to mining, the statute speaks very differently, expressly stating that the NRC's regulatory powers arise only "*after* [uranium's] removal from its place of deposit in nature." § 2092 (emphasis added). As the government itself has conceded, this means that "uranium mining" lies "outside the NRC's jurisdiction," Brief for United States as *Amicus Curiae* 14, and the agency's grip takes hold only "at the mill, rather than at the mine," *In re Hydro Resources, Inc.*, 63 N. R. C. 510, 512 (2006).

What the text states, context confirms. After announcing a general rule that mining regulation lies outside the NRC's jurisdiction, the AEA carves out a notably narrow exception. On *federal* lands, the statute says, the NRC may regulate uranium mining. § 2097. And if the federal government wants to control mining of uranium on *private* land, the AEA tells the NRC exactly what to do: It may purchase or seize the land by eminent domain and *make* it federal land. § 2096. Congress thus has spoken directly to the question of uranium mining on private land, and every bit of what it's said indicates that state authority remains untouched.

* * *

If the AEA doesn't occupy the field of radiation safety in uranium mining, Virginia Uranium suggests the statute still displaces state law through what's sometimes called conflict preemption. In particular, the company suggests, Virginia's mining law stands as an impermissible "obstacle to the accomplishment and execution of the full purposes and objectives of Congress." *Hines v. Davidowitz*, 312 U. S. 52, 67 (1941). On Virginia Uranium's account, Congress sought to capture the benefits of developing nuclear power while mitigating its safety and environmental costs. And, the company contends, Virginia's moratorium disrupts the delicate "balance" Congress sought to achieve between these benefits and costs. Maybe the text of the AEA doesn't touch on mining in so many words, but its authority to regulate later stages of the nuclear fuel life cycle would be effectively undermined if mining laws like Virginia's were allowed.

A sound preemption analysis cannot be as simplistic as that. No more than in field preemption can the Supremacy Clause be deployed here to elevate abstract and unenacted legislative desires above state law; only federal laws "made in pursuance of" the Constitution, through its prescribed processes of bicameralism and presentment, are entitled to preemptive effect. Art. VI, cl. 2. So any "[e]vidence of pre-emptive purpose," whether express or implied, must therefore be "sought in the text and structure of the statute at issue." *CSX Transp., Inc. v. Easterwood*, 507 U. S. 658, 664 (1993).

Sound and well-documented reasons underlie this rule too * * *. Trying to discern what motivates legislators individually and collectively invites speculation and risks overlooking the reality that individual Members of Congress often pursue multiple and competing purposes, many of which are compromised to secure a law's passage and few of which are fully realized in the final product. Hefty inferences may be required, as well, when trying to estimate whether Congress would have wanted to prohibit States from pursuing regulations that may happen to touch, in various degrees and different ways, on unenacted federal purposes and objectives. Worse yet, in piling inference upon inference about hidden legislative wishes we risk displacing the legislative compromises actually reflected in the statutory text—compromises that sometimes may seem irrational to an outsider coming to the statute cold, but whose genius lies in having won the broad support our Constitution demands of any new law. In disregarding these legislative compromises, we may only wind up displacing perfectly legitimate state laws on the strength of "purposes" that only we can see, that may seem perfectly logical to us, but that lack the democratic provenance the Constitution demands before a federal law may be declared supreme.

So it may be that Congress meant the AEA to promote the development of nuclear power. It may be that Congress meant the AEA to balance that goal against various safety concerns. But it also may be that Members of Congress held many other disparate or conflicting goals in mind when they voted to enact and amend the AEA, and many different views on exactly how to manage the competing costs and benefits. If polled, they might have reached very different assessments, as well, about the consistency of Virginia's law with their own purposes and objectives. The only thing a court can be sure of is what can be found in the law itself. And every indication in the law before us suggests that Congress elected to leave mining regulation on private land to the States and grant the NRC regulatory authority only *after* uranium is removed from the earth. That compromise may not be the only permissible or even the most rationally attractive one, but it is surely both permissible and rational to think that Congress might have chosen to regulate the more novel aspects of nuclear power while leaving to States their traditional function of regulating mining activities on private lands within their boundaries.

As an alternative to proceeding down the purposes-and-objectives branch of conflict preemption, Virginia Uranium might have pursued another. Our cases have held that we can sometimes infer a congressional intent to displace a state law that makes compliance with a federal statute impossible. But Virginia Uranium hasn't pursued an argument along any of these lines, and understandably so. Not only *can* Virginia Uranium comply with both state and federal laws; it is also unclear whether laws like Virginia's might have a meaningful impact on the development of nuclear power in this country. Some estimate that the United States currently imports over 90 percent of the uranium used in this country. Domestic uranium mines currently exist on federal lands as well and are thus beyond the reach of state authorities. And if the federal government concludes that development of the Coles Hill deposit or any other like it is crucial, it may always purchase the site (or seize it through eminent domain) under the powers Congress has supplied. 42 U.S.C. § 2096. All this may be done without even amending the AEA, itself another course which Congress is always free to pursue—but which this Court should never be tempted into pursuing on its own.

The judgment of the court of appeals is

Affirmed.

■ JUSTICE GINSBURG, with whom JUSTICE SOTOMAYOR and JUSTICE KAGAN join, concurring in the judgment.

Soon after discovery of a large deposit of uranium ore in Virginia in the late 1970s, the Commonwealth banned uranium mining. Petitioners (collectively, Virginia Uranium) now seek to mine that deposit. They challenge the Commonwealth's uranium mining ban as preempted by the Atomic Energy Act (AEA or Act), 42 U.S.C. § 2011 *et seq.*, either because the ban intrudes on the federally occupied field of nuclear safety, or because it obstructs realization of federal purposes and objectives.

I reach the same bottom-line judgment as does Justice GORSUCH: The Commonwealth's mining ban is not preempted. And I agree with much contained in Justice GORSUCH's opinion. But his discussion of the perils of inquiring into legislative motive sweeps well beyond the confines of this case, and therefore seems to me inappropriate in an opinion speaking for the Court, rather than for individual members of the Court. Further, Virginia Uranium's obstacle preemption arguments fail under existing doctrine, so there is little reason to question, as Justice GORSUCH does, whether that doctrine should be retained. For these reasons, I join the Court's judgment, and separately state how I would resolve the instant controversy.

* * *

This Court has delineated three circumstances in which state law must yield to federal law. First, and most obvious, federal law operates exclusively when Congress expressly preempts state law. Second, state law can play no part when "Congress has legislated comprehensively to occupy an entire field of regulation, leaving no room for the States to supplement federal law." Third, state law is rendered inoperative when it "actually conflicts with federal law," as when a private party cannot "comply with both state and federal requirements," or when state law "creates an unacceptable 'obstacle to the accomplishment and execution of the full purposes and objectives of Congress.'" Whatever the category of preemption asserted, "the purpose of Congress is the ultimate touchstone" in determining whether federal law preempts state law. Virginia Uranium invokes both field and obstacle preemption; I address each in turn.

Virginia Uranium's primary contention is that Congress has occupied the field of nuclear safety regulation, preempting state laws enacted because of concerns about the radiation safety of federally regulated activities * * *. The Commonwealth Defendants would exclude from federal foreclosure state laws directed to activities not regulated by the NRC. The Commonwealth Defendants have the better reading of the statute.

The Commonwealth has forbidden only conventional uranium mining on private land, an activity all agree is not federally regulated * * *. And if Congress did not provide for regulation of private conventional mining, it is hard to see how or why state law on the subject would be preempted, whatever the reason for the law's enactment.

* * *

Nor is the Commonwealth's mining ban preempted as an "unacceptable obstacle to the accomplishment and execution of the full purposes and objectives of Congress." Together, Virginia Uranium and the United States identify four ways in which the mining ban supposedly conflicts with federal purposes and objectives. None carry the day.

First, Virginia Uranium contends that the mining ban conflicts with the "delicate balance" federal law has struck between promoting nuclear power and ensuring public safety. Brief for Petitioners 55–56; see Brief for United States as *Amicus Curiae* 31–33. But the Federal Government does not regulate the radiological safety of conventional uranium mining on private land, so federal law struck *no* balance in this area.

Second, Virginia Uranium contends that the mining ban "*prohibit[s]* the achievement of one of Congress['] 'primary purpose[s]': 'the promotion of nuclear power.'" Brief for Petitioners 56 * * *.

Virginia Uranium warns of dire consequences if all 50 States enact bans similar to the Commonwealth's. Brief for Petitioners 56–57. But, as the Court of Appeals explained, numerous domestic uranium recovery facilities are federally regulated (either because they sit on federal land or use unconventional mining techniques) and are "thus beyond the reach of any state bans"; and the AEA authorizes the

Federal Government to develop uranium deposits on public lands and to acquire private deposits. 848 F. 3d at 599; see 42 U.S.C. §§ 2096–2097. Federal purposes and objectives do not require judicial supplementation of the AEA's express provisions for maintaining the uranium supply.

* * *

Third, Virginia Uranium argues that § 2021 provides the sole means for States to regulate radiological safety hazards resulting from milling and tailings storage, and that Virginia has effectively regulated milling and tailings storage without obtaining authority to do so through an adequate § 2021 agreement. As explained, Virginia has not regulated the radiological safety of tailings storage; it has prohibited only an antecedent activity subject to exclusive state authority.

Finally, the United States contends that Virginia's mining ban frustrates federal purposes and objectives by "prevent[ing] the occurrence of" activities that Congress intended the Federal Government to regulate. But federal regulation of certain activities does not mean that States must authorize activities antecedent to those federally regulated. For example, federal regulation of nuclear powerplants does not demand that States allow the construction of such powerplants in the first place.

For the reasons stated, I concur in the Court's judgment affirming the judgment of the Court of Appeals.

■ CHIEF JUSTICE ROBERTS, with whom JUSTICE BREYER and JUSTICE ALITO join, dissenting.

Although one party will be happy with the result of today's decision, both will be puzzled by its reasoning. That's because the lead opinion sets out to defeat an argument that no one made, reaching a conclusion with which no one disagrees. Specifically, the opinion devotes its analysis to whether the field of uranium mining safety is preempted under the Atomic Energy Act, ultimately concluding that it is not. But no party disputes that. Rather, the question we agreed to address is whether a State can purport to regulate a field that is *not* preempted (uranium mining safety) as an indirect means of regulating other fields that *are* preempted (safety concerns about uranium milling and tailings). And on that question, our precedent is clear: The AEA prohibits state laws that have the purpose and effect of regulating preempted fields.

As relevant here, processing uranium ore involves three steps: mining, milling, and storing "tailings." *Mining* is the extracting of uranium ore from the ground; *milling* is the process of turning the substance into a usable form; and *tailings* are the leftover radioactive waste that must be safely stored.

There is no dispute over which of these fields the AEA reserves to the exclusive jurisdiction of the Nuclear Regulatory Commission. The parties agree that the field of uranium *mining* safety is not preempted. And it is undisputed that radiological safety concerns about *milling* and *tailings* are preempted fields * * *.

Despite all this, the lead opinion insists that petitioners (hereafter the company) press an entirely different argument. "Before us, Virginia Uranium contends that the AEA (and only the AEA) unseats state uranium mining regulations," but "almost immediately problems emerge." Problems do immediately emerge in the opinion, but they are of its own making. The company does not argue that the AEA reserves the field of uranium *mining* safety. After attributing this failing argument to the company, the lead opinion then proceeds to explain why the argument must, in fact, fail.

Turning to the question presented, however, the company's theory of the case is fairly straightforward. The property at issue here contains the largest known uranium deposit in the country and one of the largest in the world. Shortly after its discovery, Virginia enacted a complete ban on uranium mining. According to the company, the ban was not motivated by concerns about mining safety. Instead, it was motivated by Virginia's desire to ban the more hazardous steps that come after mining—uranium milling and the storage of radioactive tailings—due to the Commonwealth's disagreement with the NRC over how to safely regulate those activities. And, crucially, Virginia has yet to put forward any other rationale to support the ban. Thus, the question before us is whether, consistent with the AEA and our precedents, the Commonwealth may purport to regulate a non-preempted field (mining safety) with the purpose and effect of indirectly regulating a preempted field (milling and tailings). That should have made for an easy case.

Under our AEA precedents, a state law is preempted not only when it "conflicts with federal law," but also when its *purpose* is to regulate within a preempted field. *Pacific Gas & Elec. Co. v. State Energy Resources Conservation and Development Comm'n*, 461 U. S. 190, 212–213 (1983). Because "the Federal Government has occupied the entire field of nuclear safety concerns," a state law that is "grounded in [such] safety concerns falls squarely within the prohibited field." *Ibid*. For example, even though a State may generally regulate its roads, it may not shut down all of the roads to a nuclear power plant simply because it disagrees with the NRC's nuclear safety regulations. Here, because Virginia has not even disputed that its uranium mining ban was "grounded in" its "nuclear safety concerns" about uranium milling and tailings, the company's preemption claim should not have been dismissed.

* * *

The central argument from my colleagues appears to be that the AEA authorizes a purpose inquiry only when a State "targets" or "seek[s] to regulate" an activity that is also regulated by the federal statute. And because the Virginia statute *seeks* to regulate mining, the AEA "does not authorize any judicial inquiry into state legislative purpose in this case." But it is conceded that the mining ban was adopted because of radiological safety concerns about milling and tailings. That is why Virginia argues, as it must, that its mining ban would not be preempted even if it expressly stated that it was enacted due to the Commonwealth's disagreement with the NRC's nuclear safety regulations. Tr. of Oral Arg. 33. If such a statute does not "target" or "seek to regulate" a preempted field, what would?

States may try to regulate one activity by exercising their authority over another * * *.

The AEA's purpose inquiry is most useful precisely when the challenged state law does *not* purport to regulate a preempted field. If a State disagrees with the AEA's nuclear safety regulations, and thus wants to block nuclear development within its borders, it has myriad ways to do so through its broad police powers. Under the rule adopted by the lead opinion and the concurrence, so long as the State is not boneheaded enough to express its real purpose in the statute, the State will have free rein to subvert Congress's judgment on nuclear safety.

A State could, for instance, restrict the ability of a county to provide a nuclear facility with municipal services like law enforcement, fire protection, and garbage collection. If it wanted to target investors, a State could eliminate limited liability for the stockholders of companies that operate nuclear facilities. Although these examples may seem farfetched, they have already happened * * *.

* * *

* * * The lead opinion finds this purpose-based approach discomfiting, citing the "well-known conceptual and practical" difficulties about inquiring into legislative motive. The statute and our precedent plainly require such an approach here, however, and the difficulty of the task does not permit us to choose an easier way. I respectfully dissent.

XXI. ARTICLE VII

> **The Ratification of the Conventions of nine States, shall be sufficient for the Establishment of this Constitution between the States so ratifying the Same.**

As we have already discussed, Article VII reflects the fact that only twelve States sent delegates to the Philadelphia Constitutional Convention in 1787. Rhode Island sent no delegate. According to the three-quarters-of-the-States rule for making national constitutional law, Article VII required that nine of the twelve States represented at Philadelphia—three quarters—would be sufficient for the Constitution to go into effect. This reflects the U.S. *grundnorm* that sovereignty rests with a majority of the people in three-quarters of the states.

Three features of Article VII bear mention. One we have already discussed: Article VII overrode contrary provisions in a good many state constitutions, but the ratification process was nonetheless accepted even by the most vocal Antifederalists. *See supra* page 42. Second, Article VII dovetails with the Preamble, including the use in both provisions of terms with the root "establish." As Professor Akhil Reed Amar has elegantly stated it:

> The Preamble said that Americans would "establish this Constitution"; Article VII said *how* we would "Establish[ ] this Constitution." The Preamble said this deed would be done by "the People"; Article VII clarified that the people would act via specially elected "Conventions." The Preamble invoked the people of "the United States"; Article VII defined what that phrase meant both before and after the act of constitution.

AKHIL REED AMAR, AMERICA'S CONSTITUTION: A BIOGRAPHY 29 (2005). Third, the Constitution was "Establish[ed]" for nine States on June 6, 1788, when New Hampshire became the decisive vote for ratification. That does not necessarily mean that *all* of the Constitution became effective immediately. It could not have done so, because at least some provisions require a Congress, a President, and/or a Chief Justice of the Supreme Court, or perhaps all three (in the case of a presidential impeachment). Provisions requiring those institutions to be in place—and they were not fully in place until the Spring of 1789—could not be fully "Establish[ed]," in the sense of being legally operational, until some later date. The legal framework, however, was fixed at that time, so the Constitution's effectiveness would develop in stages as institutions came into being. Were any of the Constitution's provisions, such as the Article I, Section 10 prohibitions on various state actions, immediately effective on June 6, 1788? One of us thinks so. *See* Gary Lawson & Guy Seidman, *When Did the Constitution Become Law?*, 77 NOTRE DAME L. REV. 1 (2001). He also thinks that at least some portions of the Articles of Confederation remained in force for at least some time after ratification of the Constitution. *See* Gary Lawson & Guy Seidman, *The First "Establishment" Clause: Article VII and the Post-Constitutional Confederation,* 78 NOTRE DAME L. REV. 83 (2002). Does any of this matter? It actually might. The effective date of the Constitution matters if, for example, States made treaties or issued paper money after June 6, 1788 but before the spring of 1789. This happened on more than one occasion, and it reached the Supreme Court once. *See Owings v. Speed,* 18 U.S. (5 Wheat.) 420 (1820). The case held that a Virginia statute enacted on December 2, 1788 could not violate the Contracts Clause of Article I, Section 10, because the Constitution did not take effect until March 4, 1789, when Congress first assembled. (The President was sworn in on April 30,1789.) If the Constitution took effect in stages, and the first stage gave immediate legal effect to "self-executing" provisions such as those parts of Article I, Section 10 that do not call for congressional action, *Owings* may have been wrongly decided—as may have been some modern cases involving post-ratification state treaties with Indian tribes that would be invalid under Article I, Section 10. *See, e.g., Oneida Indian Nation v. New York,* 520 F. Supp. 1278 (N.D.N.Y. 1981), *aff'd in part & rev'd in part,* 691 F.2d 1070 (2d Cir. 1982), *on remand,* 649 F. Supp. 420 (N.D.N.Y. 1986), *aff'd,* 860 F.2d 1145 (2d. Cir. 1988).

This is why we love Constitutional Law.

CHAPTER 4

THE BILL OF RIGHTS

[Assignment 47]

The supporters of ratification of the Constitution would never have succeeded in the large and critical States of Massachusetts, Virginia, or New York without solemnly promising that they would add a Bill of Rights to the federal Constitution. Once the first Congress was convened, it drew on a draft from Representative James Madison and proposed twelve amendments to the Constitution, which passed Congress by the required two thirds majority. The last ten of these amendments were ratified by three quarters of the States by December 15, 1791, and those first ten amendments to the Constitution eventually became known as the Bill of Rights. We say "eventually," because the term "the Bill of Rights" was not commonly used to describe the first ten amendments until the twentieth century. *See* Michael J. Douma, *How the First Ten Amendments Became the Bill of Rights,* 15 GEO. J.L. & PUB. POL'Y 593 (2017); Gerard N. Magliocca, *The Bill of Rights as a Term of Art,* 92 NOTRE DAME L. REV. 231 (2016). That linguistic development might prove important in the next chapter, so keep it in mind. Of the two proposed amendments that were not immediately ratified, the second, now known as the Twenty-Seventh Amendment, was eventually ratified in 1992. *See supra* pages 271, 967.

Madison proposed interlineating the amendments into Article I, Section 9, among the limits on the powers of Congress, but this approach was rejected, and the amendments were all listed in numerical order after the text of the original Constitution. This latter approach makes sense. While the First Amendment refers only to "Congress," many of the amendments obviously affect executive and judicial power as much or more than they affect legislative power. Moreover, every new amendment amends not only the Constitution of 1788, but also the prior amendments to the Constitution. The long-established later-in-time rule of interpretation states that a text that is legally enacted trumps all texts enacted previously to the extent they are inconsistent. On the other hand, Article V says that amendments, once ratified, "shall be valid to all Intents and Purposes, as Part of *this* Constitution." U.S. CONST. art. V (emphasis added). By referring to "this" Constitution—meaning the Constitution of 1788—does Article V override the later-in-time rule and put all constitutional provisions, whenever enacted, on the same interpretative footing? *See* Gary Lawson & Guy Seidman, *Originalism as a Legal Enterprise,* 23 CONST. COMMENTARY 47, 73–76 (2006) (suggesting this possibility). Or is that the kind of too-clever-by-half argument that gives lawyers a bad name? Whatever the proper answer may be, later amendments clearly sometimes require us to reinterpret previously enacted amendments—so that, for example, the ratification of the Fifteenth and Nineteenth Amendments prohibiting discrimination in voting on the basis of race and sex, respectively, may require us to think differently about the Sixth and Seventh Amendment rights to jury trial than would have been the case in 1791.

The Federalists almost uniformly opposed a Bill of Rights in 1787 and 1788, for reasons famously expressed by Alexander Hamilton: A Bill of Rights was unnecessary because the national government had no enumerated power to violate cherished rights, and a Bill of Rights was dangerous because it might give rise to inferences of power that were never granted. *See* THE FEDERALIST No. 84 (Hamilton). A simple thought experiment can test the Federalists' claims:

> Suppose that on December 14, 1791, Congress passed a statute forbidding the publication of any pamphlets that were deemed by a government censorship board to be unduly critical of Congress. In order to enforce the statute and effectively ferret out offending material, courts were authorized to issue to Treasury Department agents general warrants to seize and search shipments of goods without particularized cause or identification. Finally, the statute specified that charges brought under the statute, including charges implicating the death penalty, shall be by information rather than indictment * * *.

Gary Lawson, *A Truism with Attitude: The Tenth Amendment in Constitutional Context*, 83 NOTRE DAME L. REV. 469, 475 (2008). This statute flagrantly violates at least three provisions of the Bill of Rights (and possibly more, depending on how one counts), but on December 14, 1791, there was no Bill of Rights. Ratification was still one day away. The Federalists would nonetheless insist that the law was unconstitutional because Congress's enumerated powers did not authorize those provisions. Whether it was because such laws would not be "proper for carrying into Execution" federal powers; or would violate background fiduciary norms; or would run up against limitations built into the definitions of the legislative, executive, and judicial powers, the Federalists all agreed that basic rights were protected even before December 15, 1791. On Federalist premises, the Bill of Rights is primarily just an "exclamation point" that highlights rights protections already baked into the Constitution of 1788. *See id.* at 476–91; Gary Lawson, *Take the Fifth . . . Please! The Original Insignificance of the Fifth Amendment's Due Process of Law Clause*, 2017 B.Y.U. L. REV. 611.

The Anti-Federalists were dubious enough of these claims to insist on a Bill of Rights, and the Federalists obliged. Does that mean that the Constitution really did allow the federal government to violate all of these rights for the Nation's first two-and-a-half years? How many laws that would have been constitutional on December 14, 1791 suddenly became unconstitutional on December 15, 1791?

One important point to keep in mind is that the restrictions on governmental actions in the Bill of Rights, as enacted in 1791, apply *only* to institutions of the federal government. One of the "default" interpretative rules for the Constitution is that it applies only to the federal government unless it says otherwise—which is why, for example, the Article II Vesting Clause does not give the U.S. President the "executive Power" of each of the fifty States. *Barron v. Baltimore* so held in 1833, as you saw earlier. *See supra* pages 52–54. Nonetheless, the overwhelming majority of the caselaw interpreting the Bill of Rights has concerned action by *State* governments rather than the federal government. In the next chapter, we will explore the process by which this transformation in the effect of the Bill of Rights took place. The short answer is that, beginning in the late nineteenth century and then accelerating in the middle of the twentieth century, primarily in the 1960s, the Supreme Court began systematically "incorporating" most—though, as we will see, not quite all—of the provisions of the Bill of Rights against the States through the Fourteenth Amendment. (Through which clause of the Fourteenth Amendment remains a matter of controversy.) Once that move was made, it would have been possible in theory to apply the Bill of Rights provisions differently to the State and federal governments. Indeed, in many instances there are good, and even overwhelming, reasons to do so. But the post-incorporation courts have never shown any enthusiasm for differential application of the Bill of Rights to state and federal actors, so cases applying, for example, the Takings Clause of the Fifth Amendment to the federal government are treated as binding precedents for review of State action as well, and vice versa.

For a variety of reasons too involved to explore here, we think this indiscriminate mixing of federal and state action is a legal and conceptual mistake (even though it has often generated tolerably accurate results). Accordingly, in this chapter we look only at cases that apply the Bill of Rights to federal action, leaving the cases involving state (and local) governments for the next chapter. For the reasons given above, this division is somewhat artificial doctrinally, as the "federal" cases cannot fully be understood without reference to the "State" precedents and vice versa. The cases that you read will amply demonstrate that basic fact. But because the Bill of Rights was designed with the federal government in mind, we think its provisions are best studied in two stages: first, in the context to which those provisions' original meaning was directed and then, second and subsequently, in the "translated" context of state (and local) governmental action in the aftermath of the post-Civil War Reconstruction Amendments. Accordingly, this chapter merely sketches the broad outlines—the "big picture"—of the Bill of Rights; we provide additional depth on many of the provisions in the next chapter.

Most of the provisions of the Bill of Rights have origins in earlier documents, such as the English Bill of Rights of 1689, *see supra* pages 8–9, and the state constitutions of 1776–1791. Others responded to specific historical concerns; the Third Amendment's prohibition on quartering of soldiers in peacetime, for example, is in direct reaction to the old English monarchical practice of "billeting." *See supra* page 7. Still others respond to timeless problems of government overreaching, and the key interpretative question is often how to adapt ancient principles to novel circumstances. Once again, a full treatment of the subject requires a delicate blend of history and interpretative theory, and we plan here to provide relatively little of either.

One final thing to keep in mind before we begin: The caselaw under many of the Bill of Rights provisions is massive. Entire courses are often devoted to subparts of the Bill of Rights—courses on the First Amendment (and often separate courses on freedom of speech and freedom of religion), the Fifth Amendment's Due Process of Law Clause, or Constitutional Criminal Procedure (the Fourth, Fifth, Sixth, and Eighth Amendments). Even this and the succeeding chapter combined only touch the surface. We will try to give you a basic doctrinal grounding, but in law, as in so much else, the devil is in the details, and we make no pretense of providing much in the way of details.

I. THE FIRST AMENDMENT

The Bill of Rights begins famously with the First Amendment, which protects: 1) religious liberty; 2) freedom of expression; and 3) the right to petition the government for the redress of grievances. As we will see in the next chapter, courts have further interpolated a right of association from those listed rights. We will begin, as the Bill of Rights does, with the cornerstone right of religious freedom.

A. FREEDOM OF RELIGION

Congress shall make no law respecting an establishment of religion, or prohibiting the free exercise thereof;

The central importance of freedom of religion in Western thought begins with the fact that two of the seminal influences on Western thinking were both martyred because of their speech about matters of religion. Socrates was executed by the democratic government of Athens in 399 B.C. for allegedly causing Athenian youth not to be believe in the Greek gods. Socrates' execution led to the writings of his disciples Plato and Aristotle—and thereby to most of Western philosophy. Jesus of Nazareth, in turn, was executed by the Romans in approximately 33 A.D., and his execution led the Apostles and his disciples to found Christianity, which has been the major Western religious tradition for almost 2,000 years.

Religious persecution was constant for centuries in England, the country from which most of the American colonists came. King Henry II had St. Thomas Becket, the Archbishop of Canterbury, murdered in 1170 A.D. The Pope canonized St. Thomas, and, as the *Canterbury Tales* by Chaucer illustrate, English pilgrims regularly visited his burial site until the 1530s, when King Henry VIII dug up St. Thomas's bones and had them burned, with the ashes spread to all corners of the kingdom to stop the pilgrimages. England had been a deeply Catholic country until King Henry VIII decided to split with Rome in 1534 so he could divorce his first wife, Catherine of Aragon, and marry Ann Boleyn. Henry VIII instituted a Protestant Church of England, of which he was the head, and he took on the title of "Defender of the Faith." All English monarchs down to the present day have retained this title, and they appoint the Archbishop of Canterbury, who is the head of the Church of England (whose offshoot in the United States is called the Episcopal Church).

England also expelled all of its Jewish citizens during the reign of King Edward I circa 1200 A.D., since the King wanted to seize their property. Jews were not allowed back into England until the 1650s under the rule of Oliver Cromwell. Englishmen were fascinated by Shakespeare's portrayal of Shylock in his play *The Merchant of Venice* because there were no Jews in England during Shakespeare's lifetime.

Religious warfare and struggle wreaked havoc on England from Henry VIII's death up until the Glorious Revolution of 1688. England was Catholic under Queen Mary, who persecuted Protestants; it was Protestant under Queen Elizabeth and James I; and then there was constant struggle between Episcopalians, Puritans, and Catholics from the 1620's until the Glorious Revolution of 1688, which overthrew James II, the last Catholic King of England. The important points of this history for American constitutional law are twofold. First, the New England colonies were settled by Puritan dissidents from the Church of England who fled to the New World seeking religious freedom for themselves (though not necessarily for others). Second, the Framers of the American Constitution were desperate to constitutionalize religious freedom and toleration so that the religious warfare which England—and to a lesser extent the American colonies—experienced would not wreak havoc in the United States. The original Constitution, for example, preempted any controversy over Test Acts, whether directed at Catholics or anyone else, through the Oath Clause. *See supra* page 970.

As we noted above, the Puritans came to the United States freely to practice their own religion, but that did not translate into tolerance for the dissenting views of others. The first American colony to experiment with religious freedom was Rhode Island, which was founded by Roger Williams, who rejected the established congregational church in Massachusetts. Rhode Island was granted a colonial Charter in 1663 by King Charles II, which established religious freedom in that colony. The Rhode Island Charter said, among other things (with the archaic spelling modernized), that:

> [B]ecause some of the people and inhabitants of the * * * [Rhode Island colony] cannot, in their private opinions, conform to the public exercise of religion, according to the liturgy, forms and ceremonies of the Church of England, or take or subscribe the oaths and articles made and established in that behalf; and for that the same, by reason of the remoted distances of these places, will (as we hope) be no breach of the unity and uniformity established in this nation Have therefore thought fit, and do hereby publish, grant, ordain and declare that our royal will and pleasure is, that no person within the said colony, at any time hereafter, shall be in any wise molested, punished, disquieted, or called in question, for any differences in opinion in matters of religion, and do not actually disturb the civil peace of our said colony; but that all and every person and persons may, from time to time, and at all times hereafter, freely and fully have and enjoy his and their own judgments and consciences, in matters of religious concernments, throughout the tract of land hereafter mentioned, they behaving themselves peaceably and quietly, and not using this liberty to licentiousness and profaneness, nor to the civil injury or outward disturbance of others; any law, statute, or clause therein contained, or to be contained, usage or custom of this realm, to the contrary hereof, in any wise, notwithstanding.

Rhode Island opened its doors to Baptists, Quakers, Anabaptists, Episcopalians, and one of the two first Jewish settlements in the thirteen North American colonies. Meanwhile, the neighboring Massachusetts Bay theocracy executed witches and Quakers and sent all religious dissidents fleeing south to Rhode Island. Puritan New England, with the exception of Rhode Island, was just as hostile to religious freedom as old England had been.

Happily, in most of the other colonies, there was more religious toleration than was present in Puritan Massachusetts or New Haven. In the New York colony, many religious groups flourished together in toleration, including members of the Dutch Reformed Church, Lutherans, Episcopalians, Quakers, and Jews. The same thing happened in Pennsylvania, which was a proprietary colony of the famous Quaker, William Penn, for whom the colony was named. The same religious diversity existed in Delaware, which was at times under William Penn's control. Lord Baltimore, who founded the Maryland colony, was an English Roman Catholic. He tolerated Catholicism and all forms of religious freedom in Maryland. Virginia, the Carolinas, and Georgia were all Episcopalian, but they were not as hostile to other faiths as were members of the Church of England in the seventeenth century. The net result was that, by the time of American independence in 1776, the United States was a religiously diverse nation, albeit still mainly a nation of Protestants. Thirteen States out of fourteen (Vermont having been admitted on March 4, 1791) protected the free exercise of religion in 1791 when the Bill of Rights was ratified. Steven G. Calabresi, Sarah E. Agudo, and Kathryn L. Dore, *State Bills of Rights in 1787 and 1791: What Individual Rights are Really Deeply Rooted in American History and Tradition?*, 85 SO. CAL. L. REV. 1451, 1472–1473 (2012). In 1868, when the Fourteenth Amendment was ratified, all thirty-seven States protected the free exercise of religion in their State constitutions, and all fifty States protect that right in their constitutions today. Steven Gow Calabresi, James Lindgren, Hannah M. Begley, Kathryn L. Dore & Sarah E. Agudo, *Individual Rights Under State Constitutions in 2018: What Rights are Deeply Rooted in a Modern Day Consensus of the States*, 94 NOTRE DAME L. REV. 49, 62 (2018). The right to the free exercise of religion is thus very deeply rooted in American history, tradition, and a consensus of the States in 2020.

One of the first reasons for the ban on a federal establishment of religion was thus a reassurance to all the very different religious groups in the United States that there would be no national religious establishment in the U.S., as there had been in England. The established congregational churches of New England faced no threat from the established Episcopal churches of the southern colonies. There would be no national faith. Americans decentralized religion, and as a result we got a lot more of it! One recent scholar has written that 95% of Americans believe in God as compared to 49% of U.K. nationals. EDWARD J. EBERLE, CHURCH AND STATE IN WESTERN SOCIETY: ESTABLISHED CHURCH, COOPERATION, AND SEPARATION (2011).

Several key documents post-dating the Rhode Island Charter represent important milestones in the emergence of the American understanding of religious liberty. One is James Madison's *Memorial and Remonstrance Against Religious Assessments* of June 20, 1785, in response to a proposal in the Virginia legislature for a state-wide tax for the support of all Christian denominations: "That for the support of Christian teachers, per centum on the amount, or in the pound on the sum payable for tax on the property within this Commonwealth, is hereby assessed, and shall be paid by every person chargeable with the said tax at the time the same shall become due." The money was to be distributed to all Christian sects for "provision for a Minister or Teacher of the Gospel of their denomination, or the providing places of divine worship, and to none other use whatsoever," but with a special exception for Quakers and Mennonites, who could use the money "in a manner which they shall think best calculated to promote their particular mode of worship."

1. A MEMORIAL AND REMONSTRANCE AGAINST RELIGIOUS ASSESSMENTS

To the Honorable the General Assembly of the Commonwealth of Virginia
A Memorial and Remonstrance

We the subscribers, citizens of the said Commonwealth, having taken into serious consideration, a Bill printed by order of the last Session of General Assembly, entitled "A Bill establishing a provision for Teachers of the Christian Religion," and conceiving that the same if finally armed with the sanctions of a law, will be a dangerous abuse of power, are bound as faithful members of a free State to remonstrate against it, and to declare the reasons by which we are determined. We remonstrate against the said Bill,

1. Because we hold it for a fundamental and undeniable truth, "that Religion or the duty which we owe to our Creator and the manner of discharging it, can be directed only by reason and conviction, not by force or violence." The Religion then of every man must be left to the conviction and conscience of every man; and it is the right of every man to exercise it as these may dictate. This right is in its nature an unalienable right. It is unalienable, because the opinions of men, depending only on the evidence contemplated by their own minds cannot follow the dictates of other men: It is unalienable also, because what is here a right towards men, is a duty towards the Creator. It is the duty of every man to render to the Creator such homage and such only as he believes to be acceptable to him. This duty is precedent, both in order of time and in degree of obligation, to the claims of Civil Society. Before any man can be considered as a member of Civil Society, he must be considered as a subject of the Governour of the Universe: And if a member of Civil Society, who enters into any subordinate Association, must always do it with a reservation of his duty to the General Authority; much more must every man who becomes a member of any particular Civil Society, do it with a saving of his allegiance to the Universal Sovereign. We maintain therefore that in matters of Religion, no mans right is abridged by the institution of Civil Society and that Religion is wholly exempt from its cognizance. True it is, that no other rule exists, by which any question which may divide a Society, can be ultimately determined, but the will of the majority; but it is also true that the majority may trespass on the rights of the minority.

2. Because if Religion be exempt from the authority of the Society at large, still less can it be subject to that of the Legislative Body. The latter are but the creatures and vicegerents of the former. Their jurisdiction is both derivative and limited: it is limited with regard to the co-ordinate departments, more necessarily is it limited with regard to the constituents. The preservation of a free Government requires not merely, that the metes and bounds which separate each department of power be invariably maintained; but more especially that neither of them be suffered to overleap the great Barrier which defends the rights of the people. The Rulers who are guilty of such an encroachment, exceed the commission from which they derive their authority, and are Tyrants. The People who submit to it are governed by laws made neither by themselves nor by an authority derived from them, and are slaves.

3. Because it is proper to take alarm at the first experiment on our liberties. We hold this prudent jealousy to be the first duty of Citizens, and one of the noblest characteristics of the late Revolution. The free men of America did not wait till usurped power had strengthened itself by exercise, and entangled the question in precedents. They saw all the consequences in the principle, and they avoided the consequences by denying the principle. We revere this lesson too much soon to forget it. Who does not see that the same authority which can establish Christianity, in exclusion of all other Religions, may establish with the same ease any particular sect of Christians, in exclusion of all other Sects? that the same authority which can force a citizen to contribute three pence only of his property for the support of any one establishment, may force him to conform to any other establishment in all cases whatsoever?

4. Because the Bill violates that equality which ought to be the basis of every law, and which is more indispensible, in proportion as the validity or expediency of any law is more liable to be impeached * * *. As the Bill violates equality by subjecting some to peculiar burdens, so it violates the same principle, by granting to

others peculiar exemptions. Are the Quakers and Menonists the only sects who think a compulsive support of their Religions unnecessary and unwarrantable? * * *

5. Because the Bill implies either that the Civil Magistrate is a competent Judge of Religious Truth; or that he may employ Religion as an engine of Civil policy. The first is an arrogant pretension falsified by the contradictory opinions of Rulers in all ages, and throughout the world: the second an unhallowed perversion of the means of salvation.

6. Because the establishment proposed by the Bill is not requisite for the support of the Christian Religion. To say that it is, is a contradiction to the Christian Religion itself, for every page of it disavows a dependence on the powers of this world * * *.

7. Because experience witnesseth that ecclesiastical establishments, instead of maintaining the purity and efficacy of Religion, have had a contrary operation. During almost fifteen centuries has the legal establishment of Christianity been on trial. What have been its fruits? More or less in all places, pride and indolence in the Clergy, ignorance and servility in the laity, in both, superstition, bigotry and persecution. Enquire of the Teachers of Christianity for the ages in which it appeared in its greatest lustre; those of every sect, point to the ages prior to its incorporation with Civil policy. Propose a restoration of this primitive State in which its Teachers depended on the voluntary rewards of their flocks, many of them predict its downfall. On which Side ought their testimony to have greatest weight, when for or when against their interest?

8. Because the establishment in question is not necessary for the support of Civil Government * * *. What influence in fact have ecclesiastical establishments had on Civil Society? In some instances they have been seen to erect a spiritual tyranny on the ruins of the Civil authority; in many instances they have been seen upholding the thrones of political tyranny: in no instance have they been seen the guardians of the liberties of the people. Rulers who wished to subvert the public liberty, may have found an established Clergy convenient auxiliaries. A just Government instituted to secure & perpetuate it needs them not. Such a Government will be best supported by protecting every Citizen in the enjoyment of his Religion with the same equal hand which protects his person and his property; by neither invading the equal rights of any Sect, nor suffering any Sect to invade those of another.

* * *

11. Because it will destroy that moderation and harmony which the forbearance of our laws to intermeddle with Religion has produced among its several sects. Torrents of blood have been spilt in the old world, by vain attempts of the secular arm, to extinguish Religious discord, by proscribing all difference in Religious opinion. Time has at length revealed the true remedy. Every relaxation of narrow and rigorous policy, wherever it has been tried, has been found to assuage the disease. The American Theatre has exhibited proofs that equal and compleat liberty, if it does not wholly eradicate it, sufficiently destroys its malignant influence on the health and prosperity of the State. If with the salutary effects of this system under our own eyes, we begin to contract the bounds of Religious freedom, we know no name that will too severely reproach our folly. At least let warning be taken at the first fruits of the threatened innovation. The very appearance of the Bill has transformed

"that Christian forbearance, love and charity," which of late mutually prevailed, into animosities and jealousies, which may not soon be appeased. What mischiefs may not be dreaded, should this enemy to the public quiet be armed with the force of a law?

* * *

15. Because finally, "the equal right of every citizen to the free exercise of his Religion according to the dictates of conscience" is held by the same tenure with all our other rights. If we recur to its origin, it is equally the gift of nature; if we weigh its importance, it cannot be less dear to us; if we consult the "Declaration of those rights which pertain to the good people of Virginia, as the basis and foundation of Government," it is enumerated with equal solemnity, or rather studied emphasis. Either then, we must say, that the Will of the Legislature is the only measure of their authority; and that in the plenitude of this authority, they may sweep away all our fundamental rights; or, that they are bound to leave this particular right untouched and sacred: Either we must say, that they may controul the freedom of the press, may abolish the Trial by Jury, may swallow up the Executive and Judiciary Powers of the State; nay that they may despoil us of our very right of suffrage, and erect themselves into an independent and hereditary Assembly or, we must say, that they have no authority to enact into law the Bill under consideration. We the Subscribers say, that the General Assembly of this Commonwealth have no such authority: And that no effort may be omitted on our part against so dangerous an usurpation, we oppose to it, this remonstrance; earnestly praying, as we are in duty bound, that the Supreme Lawgiver of the Universe, by illuminating those to whom it is addressed, may on the one hand, turn their Councils from every act which would affront his holy prerogative, or violate the trust committed to them: and on the other, guide them into every measure which may be worthy of his [blessing, may re]dound to their own praise, and may establish more firmly the liberties, the prosperity and the happiness of the Commonwealth.

NOTES AND QUESTIONS

1. Note the theological nature of the arguments in Madison's first paragraph. It may be helpful to know that the leading opponents of the bill were the Virginia Baptists—the most fervent evangelical sect in the Commonwealth. They opposed the bill, not because it "advanced" religion, but because it invaded a province reserved to the authority of God.

2. The Memorial and Remonstrance is commonly employed (it has been cited in more than three dozen Supreme Court cases) in support of the disestablishment of religion. But note its implications for the free exercise of religion. If duties to the Creator are "precedent, both in order of time and in degree of obligation, to the claims of Civil Society," what does that say about the rights of free exercise of one's religion?

3. In addition to arguments directly from religious freedom, the document also invokes constitutionalism and what today we might call "equal protection" principles. The arguments prevailed. The law did not pass, and Madison the next year introduced a bill, drafted years earlier by Thomas Jefferson, that broadly protected religious liberty. That bill passed; it included a declaration that "to compel a man to furnish contributions of money for the propagation of opinions which he disbelieves is sinful and tyrannical; that even the forcing him to support this or that teacher of his own religious persuasion is depriving him of the comfortable liberty of giving his contributions to the particular

pastor, whose morals he would make his pattern, and whose powers he feels most persuasive to righteousness." http://www.virginiamemory.com/docs/ReligiousFree.pdf.

4. In 1790, President George Washington visited a Jewish synagogue in Newport, Rhode Island. In response to a welcoming letter from the congregation, President Washington wrote:

> The citizens of the United States of America have a right to applaud themselves for having given to mankind examples of an enlarged and liberal policy—a policy worthy of imitation. All possess alike liberty of conscience and immunities of citizenship. It is now no more that toleration is spoken of as if it were the indulgence of one class of people that another enjoyed the exercise of their inherent natural rights, for, happily, the Government of the United States, which gives to bigotry no sanction, to persecution no assistance, requires only that they who live under its protection should demean themselves as good citizens in giving it on all occasions their effectual support.
>
> * * * May the children of the stock of Abraham who dwell in this land continue to merit and enjoy the good will of the other inhabitants—while every one shall sit in safety under his own vine and fig tree and there shall be none to make him afraid. May the father of all mercies scatter light, and not darkness, upon our paths, and make us all in our several vocations useful here, and in His own due time and way everlastingly happy.

https://founders.archives.gov/documents/Washington/05-06-02-0135.

5. As this historical introduction makes clear, religious liberty is very deeply rooted in American history and tradition. There are two textual prongs to the protection of religious liberty in the First Amendment: A prohibition on government establishment of religion and a protected sphere for the free exercise of religion. Together, they pose a common question: To what extent does religious freedom serve as a shield against otherwise valid federal regulation? Consider the following landmark—and unanimous—decision that brings both prongs into play.

2. HOSANNA-TABOR EVANGELICAL LUTHERAN CHURCH & SCHOOL V. EQUAL EMPLOYMENT OPPORTUNITY COMMISSION

565 U.S. 171 (2012)

■ CHIEF JUSTICE ROBERTS delivered the opinion of the Court.

Certain employment discrimination laws authorize employees who have been wrongfully terminated to sue their employers for reinstatement and damages. The question presented is whether the Establishment and Free Exercise Clauses of the First Amendment bar such an action when the employer is a religious group and the employee is one of the group's ministers.

Petitioner Hosanna-Tabor Evangelical Lutheran Church and School is a member congregation of the Lutheran Church-Missouri Synod, the second largest Lutheran denomination in America. Hosanna-Tabor operated a small school in Redford, Michigan, offering a "Christ-centered education" to students in kindergarten through eighth grade.

The Synod classifies teachers into two categories: "called" and "lay." "Called" teachers are regarded as having been called to their vocation by God through a congregation. To be eligible to receive a call from a congregation, a teacher must satisfy certain academic requirements. One way of doing so is by completing a "colloquy" program at a Lutheran college or university. The program requires candidates to take eight courses of theological study, obtain the endorsement of their local Synod district, and pass an oral examination by a faculty committee. A teacher who meets these requirements may be called by a congregation. Once called, a teacher receives the formal title "Minister of Religion, Commissioned." A commissioned minister serves for an open-ended term; at Hosanna-Tabor, a call could be rescinded only for cause and by a supermajority vote of the congregation.

"Lay" or "contract" teachers, by contrast, are not required to be trained by the Synod or even to be Lutheran. At Hosanna-Tabor, they were appointed by the school board, without a vote of the congregation, to one-year renewable terms. Although teachers at the school generally performed the same duties regardless of whether they were lay or called, lay teachers were hired only when called teachers were unavailable.

Respondent Cheryl Perich was first employed by Hosanna-Tabor as a lay teacher in 1999. After Perich completed her colloquy later that school year, Hosanna-Tabor asked her to become a called teacher. Perich accepted the call and received a "diploma of vocation" designating her a commissioned minister.

Perich taught kindergarten during her first four years at Hosanna-Tabor and fourth grade during the 2003–2004 school year. She taught math, language arts, social studies, science, gym, art, and music. She also taught a religion class four days a week, led the students in prayer and devotional exercises each day, and attended a weekly school-wide chapel service. Perich led the chapel service herself about twice a year.

Perich became ill in June 2004 with what was eventually diagnosed as narcolepsy. Symptoms included sudden and deep sleeps from which she could not be roused. Because of her illness, Perich began the 2004–2005 school year on disability leave. On January 27, 2005, however, Perich notified the school principal, Stacey Hoeft, that she would be able to report to work the following month. Hoeft responded that the school had already contracted with a lay teacher to fill Perich's position for the remainder of the school year. Hoeft also expressed concern that Perich was not yet ready to return to the classroom.

On January 30, Hosanna-Tabor held a meeting of its congregation at which school administrators stated that Perich was unlikely to be physically capable of returning to work that school year or the next. The congregation voted to offer Perich a "peaceful release" from her call, whereby the congregation would pay a portion of her health insurance premiums in exchange for her resignation as a called teacher. Perich refused to resign and produced a note from her doctor stating that she would be able to return to work on February 22. The school board urged Perich to reconsider, informing her that the school no longer had a position for her, but Perich stood by her decision not to resign.

On the morning of February 22—the first day she was medically cleared to return to work—Perich presented herself at the school. Hoeft asked her to leave but she would not do so until she obtained written documentation that she had reported to work. Later that afternoon, Hoeft called Perich at home and told her that she would likely be fired. Perich responded that she had spoken with an attorney and intended to assert her legal rights.

Following a school board meeting that evening, board chairman Scott Salo sent Perich a letter stating that Hosanna-Tabor was reviewing the process for rescinding her call in light of her "regrettable" actions. Salo subsequently followed up with a letter advising Perich that the congregation would consider whether to rescind her call at its next meeting. As grounds for termination, the letter cited Perich's "insubordination and disruptive behavior" on February 22, as well as the damage she had done to her "working relationship" with the school by "threatening to take legal action." The congregation voted to rescind Perich's call on April 10, and Hosanna-Tabor sent her a letter of termination the next day.

Perich filed a charge with the Equal Employment Opportunity Commission, alleging that her employment had been terminated in violation of the Americans with Disabilities Act, 104 Stat. 327, 42 U. S. C. § 12101 *et seq.* (1990). The ADA prohibits an employer from discriminating against a qualified individual on the basis of disability. It also prohibits an employer from retaliating "against any individual because such individual has opposed any act or practice made unlawful by [the ADA] or because such individual made a charge, testified, assisted, or participated in any manner in an investigation, proceeding, or hearing under [the ADA]."

The EEOC brought suit against Hosanna-Tabor, alleging that Perich had been fired in retaliation for threatening to file an ADA lawsuit. Perich intervened in the litigation, claiming unlawful retaliation under both the ADA and the Michigan Persons with Disabilities Civil Rights Act. The EEOC and Perich sought Perich's reinstatement to her former position (or front pay in lieu thereof), along with back pay, compensatory and punitive damages, attorney's fees, and other injunctive relief.

Hosanna-Tabor moved for summary judgment. Invoking what is known as the "ministerial exception," the Church argued that the suit was barred by the First Amendment because the claims at issue concerned the employment relationship between a religious institution and one of its ministers. According to the Church, Perich was a minister, and she had been fired for a religious reason—namely, that her threat to sue the Church violated the Synod's belief that Christians should resolve their disputes internally.

The District Court agreed that the suit was barred by the ministerial exception and granted summary judgment in Hosanna-Tabor's favor * * *.

The Court of Appeals for the Sixth Circuit vacated and remanded, directing the District Court to proceed to the merits of Perich's retaliation claims. The Court of Appeals recognized the existence of a ministerial exception barring certain employment discrimination claims against religious institutions—an exception "rooted in the First Amendment's guarantees of religious freedom." 597 F. 3d 769, 777 (2010). The court concluded, however, that Perich did not qualify as a "minister" under the exception, noting in particular that her duties as a called teacher were identical to her duties as a lay teacher. *Id.*, at 778–781. Judge White concurred. She viewed the question whether Perich qualified as a minister to be closer than did the majority, but agreed that the "fact that the duties of the contract teachers are the same as the duties of the called teachers is telling."

We granted certiorari.

The First Amendment provides, in part, that "Congress shall make no law respecting an establishment of religion, or prohibiting the free exercise thereof." We have said that these two Clauses "often exert conflicting pressures," *Cutter* v.

Wilkinson, 544 U. S. 709, 719 (2005), and that there can be "internal tension . . . between the Establishment Clause and the Free Exercise Clause," *Tilton* v. *Richardson*, 403 U. S. 672, 677 (1971) (plurality opinion). Not so here. Both Religion Clauses bar the government from interfering with the decision of a religious group to fire one of its ministers.

Controversy between church and state over religious offices is hardly new. In 1215, the issue was addressed in the very first clause of Magna Carta. There, King John agreed that "the English church shall be free, and shall have its rights undiminished and its liberties unimpaired." The King in particular accepted the "freedom of elections," a right "thought to be of the greatest necessity and importance to the English church." J. Holt, Magna Carta App. IV, p. 317, cl. 1 (1965).

That freedom in many cases may have been more theoretical than real. See, *e.g.*, W. Warren, Henry II 312 (1973) (recounting the writ sent by Henry II to the electors of a bishopric in Winchester, stating: "I order you to hold a free election, but forbid you to elect anyone but Richard my clerk"). In any event, it did not survive the reign of Henry VIII, even in theory. The Act of Supremacy of 1534, 26 Hen. 8, ch. 1, made the English monarch the supreme head of the Church, and the Act in Restraint of Annates, 25 Hen. 8, ch. 20, passed that same year, gave him the authority to appoint the Church's high officials. Various Acts of Uniformity, enacted subsequently, tightened further the government's grip on the exercise of religion. The Uniformity Act of 1662, for instance, limited service as a minister to those who formally assented to prescribed tenets and pledged to follow the mode of worship set forth in the Book of Common Prayer. Any minister who refused to make that pledge was "deprived of all his Spiritual Promotions." Act of Uniformity, 1662, 14 Car. 2, ch. 4.

Seeking to escape the control of the national church, the Puritans fled to New England, where they hoped to elect their own ministers and establish their own modes of worship. William Penn, the Quaker proprietor of what would eventually become Pennsylvania and Delaware, also sought independence from the Church of England. The charter creating the province of Pennsylvania contained no clause establishing a religion.

Colonists in the South, in contrast, brought the Church of England with them. But even they sometimes chafed at the control exercised by the Crown and its representatives over religious offices. In Virginia, for example, the law vested the governor with the power to induct ministers presented to him by parish vestries, 2 Hening's Statutes at Large 46 (1642), but the vestries often refused to make such presentations and instead chose ministers on their own. Controversies over the selection of ministers also arose in other Colonies with Anglican establishments, including North Carolina. There, the royal governor insisted that the right of presentation lay with the Bishop of London, but the colonial assembly enacted laws placing that right in the vestries. Authorities in England intervened, repealing those laws as inconsistent with the rights of the Crown.

It was against this background that the First Amendment was adopted. Familiar with life under the established Church of England, the founding generation sought to foreclose the possibility of a national church. See 1 Annals of Cong. 730–731 (1789) (noting that the Establishment Clause addressed the fear that "one sect might obtain a pre-eminence, or two combine together, and establish a religion to which they would compel others to conform"). By forbidding the "establishment of religion" and guaranteeing the "free exercise thereof," the Religion Clauses ensured that the new Federal Government—unlike the English Crown—would have no role in filling ecclesiastical offices. The Establishment Clause prevents the Government from appointing ministers, and the Free Exercise Clause prevents it from interfering with the freedom of religious groups to select their own.

This understanding of the Religion Clauses was reflected in two events involving James Madison, " 'the leading architect of the religion clauses of the First Amendment.' " *Arizona Christian School Tuition Organization* v. *Winn*, 563 U. S. 125, 141 (2011) (quoting *Flast* v. *Cohen*, 392 U. S. 83, 103 (1968)). The first occurred in 1806, when John Carroll, the first Catholic bishop in the United States, solicited the Executive's opinion on who should be appointed to direct the affairs of the Catholic Church in the territory newly acquired by the Louisiana Purchase. After consulting with President Jefferson, then-Secretary of State Madison responded that the selection of church "functionaries" was an "entirely ecclesiastical" matter left to the Church's own judgment. Letter from James Madison to Bishop Carroll (Nov. 20, 1806), reprinted in 20 Records of the American Catholic Historical Society 63 (1909). The "scrupulous policy of the Constitution in guarding against a political interference with religious affairs," Madison explained, prevented the Government from rendering an opinion on the "selection of ecclesiastical individuals." *Id.,* at 63–64.

The second episode occurred in 1811, when Madison was President. Congress had passed a bill incorporating the Protestant Episcopal Church in the town of Alexandria in what was then the District of Columbia. Madison vetoed the bill, on the ground that it "exceeds the rightful authority to which Governments are limited, by the essential distinction between civil and religious functions, and violates, in particular, the article of the Constitution of the United States, which declares, that 'Congress shall make no law respecting a religious establishment.' " 22 Annals of Cong. 982–983 (1811). Madison explained:

> "The bill enacts into, and establishes by law, sundry rules and proceedings relative purely to the organization and polity of the church incorporated, *and comprehending even the election and removal of the Minister of the same*; so that no change could be made therein by the particular society, or by the general church of which it is a member, and whose authority it recognises." *Id.,* at 983 (emphasis added).

Given this understanding of the Religion Clauses—and the absence of government employment regulation generally—it was some time before questions about government interference with a church's ability to select its own ministers came before the courts. This Court touched upon the issue indirectly, however, in the context of disputes over church property. Our decisions in that area confirm that it is impermissible for the government to contradict a church's determination of who can act as its ministers.

In *Watson* v. *Jones*, 13 Wall. 679 (1872), the Court considered a dispute between antislavery and proslavery factions over who controlled the property of the Walnut Street Presbyterian Church in Louisville, Kentucky. The General Assembly of the Presbyterian Church had recognized the antislavery faction, and this Court—applying not the Constitution but a "broad and sound view of the relations of church and state under our system of laws"—declined to question that determination. *Id.,* at 727. We explained that "whenever the questions of discipline, or of faith, or ecclesiastical rule, custom, or law have been decided by the highest of [the] church judicatories to which the matter has been carried, the legal tribunals must accept such decisions as final, and as binding on them." *Ibid.* As we would put it later, our opinion in *Watson* "radiates . . . a spirit of freedom for religious organizations, an independence from secular control or manipulation—in short, power to decide for themselves, free from state interference, matters of church government as well as those of faith and doctrine." *Kedroff* v. *Saint Nicholas Cathedral of Russian Orthodox Church in North America*, 344 U. S. 94, 116 (1952).

* * *

Until today, we have not had occasion to consider whether this freedom of a religious organization to select its ministers is implicated by a suit alleging discrimination in employment. The Courts of Appeals, in contrast, have had extensive experience with this issue. Since the passage of Title VII of the Civil Rights Act of 1964, 42 U. S. C. § 2000e *et seq.*, and other employment discrimination laws, the Courts of Appeals have uniformly recognized the existence of a "ministerial exception," grounded in the First Amendment, that precludes application of such legislation to claims concerning the employment relationship between a religious institution and its ministers.

We agree that there is such a ministerial exception. The members of a religious group put their faith in the hands of their ministers. Requiring a church to accept or retain an unwanted minister, or punishing a church for failing to do so, intrudes upon more than a mere employment decision. Such action interferes with the internal governance of the church, depriving the church of control over the selection of those who will personify its beliefs. By imposing an unwanted minister, the state infringes the Free Exercise Clause, which protects a religious group's right to shape its own faith and mission through its appointments. According the state the power to determine which individuals will minister to the faithful also violates the Establishment Clause, which prohibits government involvement in such ecclesiastical decisions.

The EEOC and Perich acknowledge that employment discrimination laws would be unconstitutional as applied to religious groups in certain circumstances. They grant, for example, that it would violate the First Amendment for courts to apply such laws to compel the ordination of women by the Catholic Church or by an Orthodox Jewish seminary. Brief for Federal Respondent 31; Brief for Respondent Perich 35–36. According to the EEOC and Perich, religious organizations could successfully defend against employment discrimination claims in those circumstances by invoking the constitutional right to freedom of association—a right "implicit" in the First Amendment. *Roberts* v. *United States Jaycees*, 468 U. S. 609, 622 (1984). The EEOC and Perich thus see no need—and no basis—for a special rule for ministers grounded in the Religion Clauses themselves.

We find this position untenable. The right to freedom of association is a right enjoyed by religious and secular groups alike. It follows under the EEOC's and Perich's view that the First Amendment analysis should be the same, whether the association in question is the Lutheran Church, a labor union, or a social club. That result is hard to square with the text of the First Amendment itself, which gives special solicitude to the rights of religious organizations. We cannot accept the remarkable view that the Religion Clauses have nothing to say about a religious organization's freedom to select its own ministers.

The EEOC and Perich also contend that our decision in *Employment Div., Dept. of Human Resources of Ore.* v. *Smith*, 494 U. S. 872 (1990), precludes recognition of a ministerial exception. In *Smith*, two members of the Native American Church were denied state unemployment benefits after it was determined that they had been fired from their jobs for ingesting peyote, a crime under Oregon law. We held that this did not violate the Free Exercise Clause, even though the peyote had been ingested for sacramental purposes, because the "right of free exercise does not relieve an individual of the obligation to comply with a valid and neutral law of general applicability on the ground that the law proscribes (or prescribes) conduct that his religion prescribes (or proscribes)." *Id.,* at 879 (internal quotation marks omitted).

It is true that the ADA's prohibition on retaliation, like Oregon's prohibition on peyote use, is a valid and neutral law of general applicability. But a church's selection of its ministers is unlike an individual's ingestion of peyote. *Smith* involved government regulation of only outward physical acts. The present case, in contrast, concerns government interference with an internal church decision that affects the faith and mission of the church itself. See *id.,* at 877 (distinguishing the government's regulation of "physical acts" from its "lend[ing] its power to one or the other side in controversies over religious authority or dogma"). The contention that *Smith* forecloses recognition of a ministerial exception rooted in the Religion Clauses has no merit.

Having concluded that there is a ministerial exception grounded in the Religion Clauses of the First Amendment, we consider whether the exception applies in this case. We hold that it does.

Every Court of Appeals to have considered the question has concluded that the ministerial exception is not limited to the head of a religious congregation, and we agree. We are reluctant, however, to adopt a rigid formula for deciding when an employee qualifies as a minister. It is enough for us to conclude, in this our first case involving the ministerial exception, that the exception covers Perich, given all the circumstances of her employment.

To begin with, Hosanna-Tabor held Perich out as a minister, with a role distinct from that of most of its members. When Hosanna-Tabor extended her a call, it issued her a "diploma of vocation" according her the title "Minister of Religion, Commissioned." She was tasked with performing that office "according to the Word of God and the confessional standards of the Evangelical Lutheran Church as drawn from the Sacred Scriptures." The congregation prayed that God "bless [her] ministrations to the glory of His holy name, [and] the building of His church." In a supplement to the diploma, the congregation undertook to periodically review Perich's "skills of ministry" and "ministerial responsibilities," and to provide for her "continuing education as a professional person in the ministry of the Gospel."

Perich's title as a minister reflected a significant degree of religious training followed by a formal process of commissioning. To be eligible to become a commissioned minister, Perich had to complete eight college-level courses in subjects including biblical interpretation, church doctrine, and the ministry of the Lutheran teacher. She also had to obtain the endorsement of her local Synod district by submitting a petition that contained her academic transcripts, letters of recommendation, personal statement, and written answers to various ministry-related questions. Finally, she had to pass an oral examination by a faculty committee at a Lutheran college. It took Perich six years to fulfill these requirements. And when she eventually did, she was commissioned as a minister only upon election by the congregation, which recognized God's call to her to teach. At that point, her call could be rescinded only upon a supermajority vote of the congregation—a protection designed to allow her to "preach the Word of God boldly."

Perich held herself out as a minister of the Church by accepting the formal call to religious service, according to its terms. She did so in other ways as well. For example, she claimed a special housing allowance on her taxes that was available only to employees earning their compensation " 'in the exercise of the ministry.' " In a form she submitted to the Synod following her termination, Perich again indicated that she regarded herself as a minister at Hosanna-Tabor, stating: "I feel that God is leading me to serve in the teaching ministry . . . . I am anxious to be in the teaching ministry again soon.

Perich's job duties reflected a role in conveying the Church's message and carrying out its mission. Hosanna-Tabor expressly charged her with "lead[ing] others toward Christian maturity" and "teach[ing] faithfully the Word of God, the Sacred Scriptures, in its truth and purity and as set forth in all the symbolical books of the Evangelical Lutheran Church." * * * As a source of religious instruction, Perich performed an important role in transmitting the Lutheran faith to the next generation.

In light of these considerations—the formal title given Perich by the Church, the substance reflected in that title, her own use of that title, and the important religious functions she performed for the Church—we conclude that Perich was a minister covered by the ministerial exception.

In reaching a contrary conclusion, the Court of Appeals committed three errors. First, the Sixth Circuit failed to see any relevance in the fact that Perich was a commissioned minister. Although such a title, by itself, does not automatically ensure coverage, the fact that an employee has been ordained or commissioned as a minister is surely relevant, as is the fact that significant religious training and a recognized religious mission underlie the description of the employee's position. It was wrong for the Court of Appeals * * * to say that an employee's title does not matter.

Second, the Sixth Circuit gave too much weight to the fact that lay teachers at the school performed the same religious duties as Perich. We express no view on whether someone with Perich's duties would be covered by the ministerial exception in the absence of the other considerations we have discussed. But though relevant, it cannot be dispositive that others not formally recognized as ministers by the church perform the same functions—particularly when, as here, they did so only because commissioned ministers were unavailable.

Third, the Sixth Circuit placed too much emphasis on Perich's performance of secular duties. It is true that her religious duties consumed only 45 minutes of each workday, and that the rest of her day was devoted to teaching secular subjects. The EEOC regards that as conclusive, contending that any ministerial exception "should be limited to those employees who perform exclusively religious functions." Brief for Federal Respondent 51. We cannot accept that view. Indeed, we are unsure whether any such employees exist. The heads of congregations themselves often have a mix of duties, including secular ones such as helping to manage the congregation's finances, supervising purely secular personnel, and overseeing the upkeep of facilities.

Although the Sixth Circuit did not adopt the extreme position pressed here by the EEOC, it did regard the relative amount of time Perich spent performing religious functions as largely determinative. The issue before us, however, is not one that can be resolved by a stopwatch. The amount of time an employee spends on particular activities is relevant in assessing that employee's status, but that factor cannot be considered in isolation, without regard to the nature of the religious functions performed and the other considerations discussed above.

Because Perich was a minister within the meaning of the exception, the First Amendment requires dismissal of this employment discrimination suit against her religious employer. The EEOC and Perich originally sought an order reinstating Perich to her former position as a called teacher. By requiring the Church to accept a minister it did not want, such an order would have plainly violated the Church's freedom under the Religion Clauses to select its own ministers.

* * *

The EEOC and Perich suggest that Hosanna-Tabor's asserted religious reason for firing Perich—that she violated the Synod's commitment to internal dispute resolution—was pretextual. That suggestion misses the point of the ministerial exception. The purpose of the exception is not to safeguard a church's decision to fire a minister only when it is made for a religious reason. The exception instead ensures that the authority to select and control who will minister to the faithful—a matter "strictly ecclesiastical," *Kedroff*, 344 U. S., at 119—is the church's alone.

The EEOC and Perich foresee a parade of horribles that will follow our recognition of a ministerial exception to employment discrimination suits. According to the EEOC and Perich, such an exception could protect religious organizations from liability for retaliating against employees for reporting criminal misconduct or for testifying before a grand jury or in a criminal trial. What is more, the EEOC contends, the logic of the exception would confer on religious employers "unfettered discretion" to violate employment laws by, for example, hiring children or aliens not authorized to work in the United States. Brief for Federal Respondent 29.

Hosanna-Tabor responds that the ministerial exception would not in any way bar criminal prosecutions for interfering with law enforcement investigations or other proceedings. Nor, according to the Church, would the exception bar government enforcement of general laws restricting eligibility for employment, because the exception applies only to suits by or on behalf of ministers themselves. Hosanna-Tabor also notes that the ministerial exception has been around in the lower courts for 40 years, see *McClure* v. *Salvation Army*, 460 F. 2d 553, 558 (CA5 1972), and has not given rise to the dire consequences predicted by the EEOC and Perich.

The case before us is an employment discrimination suit brought on behalf of a minister, challenging her church's decision to fire her. Today we hold only that the ministerial exception bars such a suit. We express no view on whether the exception bars other types of suits, including actions by employees alleging breach of contract or tortious conduct by their religious employers. There will be time enough to address the applicability of the exception to other circumstances if and when they arise.

The interest of society in the enforcement of employment discrimination statutes is undoubtedly important. But so too is the interest of religious groups in choosing who will preach their beliefs, teach their faith, and carry out their mission. When a minister who has been fired sues her church alleging that her termination was discriminatory, the First Amendment has struck the balance for us. The church must be free to choose those who will guide it on its way.

The judgment of the Court of Appeals for the Sixth Circuit is reversed.

It is so ordered.

[Concurring opinions of JUSTICE THOMAS and JUSTICE ALITO are omitted.]

NOTES AND QUESTIONS

1. As Chief Justice Roberts quite rightly notes, the *Hosanna-Tabor* case implicates both the Establishment Clause and the Free Exercise Clause of the First Amendment. The Establishment Clause is implicated because one of the purposes of that Clause, according to James Madison, was to prevent the government from having the power to hire or pay ministers, priests, rabbis, or imams. The Free Exercise clause is implicated because professing one's faith as a minister is, for some people, a core way in which they engage in "the free *exercise*" of their religion, and exercise of religion is certainly involved in selecting those who will serve as ministers, lead religious services, or conduct religious education, Note that the Free Exercise Clause protects more than simply freedom of "conscience" or "belief". It protects taking actions, so long as they do not actually hurt another person, by which a person *exercises* his beliefs. This suggests that if a facially neutral law disparately impacts the exercise of religion by, for example, forbidding the ingestion of an hallucinogen during a Native American religious ritual, that law is unconstitutional because its forbids the free exercise of religion. You will see in the next chapter that the Supreme Court has held to the contrary. *See Employment Div., Dep't of Human Resources of Oregon v. Smith*, 494 U.S. 872 (1990); *infra* pages 1629–1631. You have already seen that Congress responded to that decision by passing the Religious Freedom Restoration Act ("RFRA"). *See supra* pages 869–876. While the Court has held RFRA unconstitutional as applied to States, RFRA is enforceable against the federal government, because Congress can create extra-constitutional obligations for federal institutions even if it cannot impose them on States. Thus, as a statutory matter, the federal government cannot (currently) apply facially neutral laws in a fashion that burdens religion unless the government can show that such application of the law serves a compelling interest and is the least restrictive means of serving that interest. The federal government thus could not use the Controlled Substances Act to forbid a sect with approximately 130 adherents from using a sacramental tea that contains hallucinogens that fall within the scope of the statute. *See Gonzalez v. O Centro Espirita Beneficente Uniao,* 546 U.S. 418 (2006). Similar action by a State would presumably be constitutional under *Smith*.

2. Speaking of *Smith,* the majority in *Hosanna-Tabor* tries to distinguish *Smith*. Does it succeed? The Americans with Disabilities Act is a facially neutral statute that burdens religion when it is applied to force a church school to hire or retain a minister/teacher. Is the State interest in preventing peyote use in *Smith* more compelling, or more narrowly tailored, than the federal interest in preventing disability discrimination in *Hosanna-Tabor?* One could limit *Hosanna-Tabor* to its facts and say it is just about a

"ministerial exception," which has long existed in the employment anti-discrimination context. Or one could limit *Employment Division v. Smith* to its facts and make *Hosanna-Tabor* the new rule. What rule would that be? When you come to *Smith* in the next chapter, these questions will arise anew.

3. If the Court was worried about involving the federal government, and the judiciary in particular, in the affairs of religious organizations, does the majority's decision solve that problem? Under the Court's approach, don't judges have to conduct fact-intensive inquiries into precisely what functions people performed and how those functions fit into a particular religion? In *Hosanna-Tabor,* the plaintiff identified herself as a religious figure, but what if she hadn't done so? Would there have to be a trial about what she did and how religiously important it was? Justice Thomas wrote a concurrence which proposed that "the Religion Clauses require civil courts to apply the ministerial exception and to defer to a religious organization's good-faith understanding of who qualifies as its minister." 565 U.S. at 196 (Thomas, J., concurring). Does that solve the problem? Is it a better approach than the majority's?

4. No one thinks that Congress passed the Americans with Disabilities Act *intending* to harm any particular religious group (or to harm religion in general). History suggests that such motives are not unthinkable. Are such motives alone enough to invalidate governmental action? How would such motives ever be proven? How certain must a court be that government actors are motivated by religious animus before finding action unconstitutional?

3. TRUMP V. HAWAII

585 U.S. ___, 138 S. Ct. 2392 (2018)

■ CHIEF JUSTICE ROBERTS delivered the opinion of the Court.

Under the Immigration and Nationality Act, foreign nationals seeking entry into the United States undergo a vetting process to ensure that they satisfy the numerous requirements for admission. The Act also vests the President with authority to restrict the entry of aliens whenever he finds that their entry "would be detrimental to the interests of the United States." 8 U.S.C. § 1182(f). Relying on that delegation, the President concluded that it was necessary to impose entry restrictions on nationals of countries that do not share adequate information for an informed entry determination, or that otherwise present national security risks. Presidential Proclamation No. 9645, 82 Fed. Reg. 45161 (2017) (Proclamation). The plaintiffs in this litigation, respondents here, challenged the application of those entry restrictions to certain aliens abroad. We now decide whether * * * the entry policy violates the Establishment Clause of the First Amendment.

Shortly after taking office, President Trump signed Executive Order No. 13769, Protecting the Nation From Foreign Terrorist Entry Into the United States. 82 Fed. Reg. 8977 (2017) (EO–1). EO–1 directed the Secretary of Homeland Security to conduct a review to examine the adequacy of information provided by foreign governments about their nationals seeking to enter the United States. § 3(a). Pending that review, the order suspended for 90 days the entry of foreign nationals from seven countries—Iran, Iraq, Libya, Somalia, Sudan, Syria, and Yemen—that had been previously identified by Congress or prior administrations as posing heightened terrorism risks. § 3(c). The District Court for the Western District of Washington entered a temporary restraining order blocking the entry restrictions, and the Court of Appeals for the Ninth Circuit denied the Government's request to stay that order. *Washington v. Trump*, 847 F.3d 1151 (2017) (*per curiam*).

In response, the President revoked EO–1, replacing it with Executive Order No. 13780, which again directed a worldwide review. 82 Fed. Reg. 13209 (2017) (EO–2). Citing investigative burdens on agencies and the need to diminish the risk that dangerous individuals would enter without adequate vetting, EO–2 also temporarily restricted the entry (with case-by-case waivers) of foreign nationals from six of the countries covered by EO–1: Iran, Libya, Somalia, Sudan, Syria, and Yemen. §§ 2(c), 3(a). The order explained that those countries had been selected because each "is a state sponsor of terrorism, has been significantly compromised by terrorist organizations, or contains active conflict zones." § 1(d). The entry restriction was to stay in effect for 90 days, pending completion of the worldwide review.

These interim measures were immediately challenged in court * * *. The temporary restrictions in EO–2 expired before this Court took any action, and we vacated the lower court decisions as moot.

On September 24, 2017, after completion of the worldwide review, the President issued the Proclamation before us—Proclamation No. 9645, Enhancing Vetting Capabilities and Processes for Detecting Attempted Entry Into the United States by Terrorists or Other Public-Safety Threats. 82 Fed. Reg. 45161. The Proclamation (as its title indicates) sought to improve vetting procedures by identifying ongoing deficiencies in the information needed to assess whether nationals of particular countries present "public safety threats." § 1(a). To further that purpose, the Proclamation placed entry restrictions on the nationals of eight foreign states whose systems for managing and sharing information about their nationals the President deemed inadequate.

The Proclamation described how foreign states were selected for inclusion based on the review undertaken pursuant to EO–2. As part of that review, the Department of Homeland Security (DHS), in consultation with the State Department and several intelligence agencies, developed a "baseline" for the information required from foreign governments to confirm the identity of individuals seeking entry into the United States, and to determine whether those individuals pose a security threat. § 1(c). The baseline included three components. The first, "identity-management information," focused on whether a foreign government ensures the integrity of travel documents by issuing electronic passports, reporting lost or stolen passports, and making available additional identity-related information. Second, the agencies considered the extent to which the country discloses information on criminal history and suspected terrorist links, provides travel document exemplars, and facilitates the U.S. Government's receipt of information about airline passengers and crews traveling to the United States. Finally, the agencies weighed various indicators of national security risk, including whether the foreign state is a known or potential terrorist safe haven and whether it regularly declines to receive returning nationals following final orders of removal from the United States.

DHS collected and evaluated data regarding all foreign governments. § 1(d). It identified 16 countries as having deficient information-sharing practices and presenting national security concerns, and another 31 countries as "at risk" of similarly failing to meet the baseline. § 1(e). The State Department then undertook diplomatic efforts over a 50-day period to encourage all foreign governments to improve their practices. § 1(f). As a result of that effort, numerous countries provided DHS with travel document exemplars and agreed to share information on known or suspected terrorists.

Following the 50-day period, the Acting Secretary of Homeland Security concluded that eight countries—Chad, Iran, Iraq, Libya, North Korea, Syria, Venezuela, and Yemen—remained deficient in terms of their risk profile and willingness to provide requested information. The Acting Secretary recommended that the President impose entry restrictions on certain nationals from all of those countries except Iraq. §§ 1(g), (h). She also concluded that although Somalia generally satisfied the information-sharing component of the baseline standards, its "identity-management deficiencies" and "significant terrorist presence" presented special circumstances justifying additional limitations. She therefore recommended entry limitations for certain nationals of that country. § 1(i). As for Iraq, the Acting Secretary found that entry limitations on its nationals were not warranted given the close cooperative relationship between the U.S. and Iraqi Governments and Iraq's commitment to combating ISIS. § 1(g).

After consulting with multiple Cabinet members and other officials, the President adopted the Acting Secretary's recommendations and issued the Proclamation. Invoking his authority under 8 U.S.C. §§ 1182(f) and 1185(a), the President determined that certain entry restrictions were necessary to "prevent the entry of those foreign nationals about whom the United States Government lacks sufficient information"; "elicit improved identity-management and information-sharing protocols and practices from foreign governments"; and otherwise "advance [the] foreign policy, national security, and counterterrorism objectives" of the United States. Proclamation § 1(h). The President explained that these restrictions would be the "most likely to encourage cooperation" while "protect[ing] the United States until such time as improvements occur." *Ibid.*

* * *

The Proclamation exempts lawful permanent residents and foreign nationals who have been granted asylum. § 3(b). It also provides for case-by-case waivers when a foreign national demonstrates undue hardship, and that his entry is in the national interest and would not pose a threat to public safety. § 3(c)(i); see also § 3(c)(iv) (listing examples of when a waiver might be appropriate, such as if the foreign national seeks to reside with a close family member, obtain urgent medical care, or pursue significant business obligations). The Proclamation further directs DHS to assess on a continuing basis whether entry restrictions should be modified or continued, and to report to the President every 180 days. § 4. Upon completion of the first such review period, the President, on the recommendation of the Secretary of Homeland Security, determined that Chad had sufficiently improved its practices, and he accordingly lifted restrictions on its nationals. Presidential Proclamation No. 9723, 83 Fed. Reg. 15937 (2018).

Plaintiffs in this case are the State of Hawaii, three individuals (Dr. Ismail Elshikh, John Doe # 1, and John Doe # 2), and the Muslim Association of Hawaii. The State operates the University of Hawaii system, which recruits students and faculty from the designated countries. The three individual plaintiffs are U.S. citizens or lawful permanent residents who have relatives from Iran, Syria, and

Yemen applying for immigrant or nonimmigrant visas. The Association is a nonprofit organization that operates a mosque in Hawaii.

Plaintiffs * * * claimed that the Proclamation violates the Establishment Clause of the First Amendment, because it was motivated not by concerns pertaining to national security but by animus toward Islam.

* * *

The First Amendment provides, in part, that "Congress shall make no law respecting an establishment of religion, or prohibiting the free exercise thereof." Our cases recognize that "[t]he clearest command of the Establishment Clause is that one religious denomination cannot be officially preferred over another." *Larson v. Valente*, 456 U.S. 228, 244 (1982). Plaintiffs believe that the Proclamation violates this prohibition by singling out Muslims for disfavored treatment. The entry suspension, they contend, operates as a "religious gerrymander," in part because most of the countries covered by the Proclamation have Muslim-majority populations. And in their view, deviations from the information-sharing baseline criteria suggest that the results of the multi-agency review were "foreordained." Relying on Establishment Clause precedents concerning laws and policies applied domestically, plaintiffs allege that the primary purpose of the Proclamation was religious animus and that the President's stated concerns about vetting protocols and national security were but pretexts for discriminating against Muslims.

At the heart of plaintiffs' case is a series of statements by the President and his advisers casting doubt on the official objective of the Proclamation. For example, while a candidate on the campaign trail, the President published a "Statement on Preventing Muslim Immigration" that called for a "total and complete shutdown of Muslims entering the United States until our country's representatives can figure out what is going on." App. 158. That statement remained on his campaign website until May 2017. Then-candidate Trump also stated that "Islam hates us" and asserted that the United States was "having problems with Muslims coming into the country." *Id.*, at 120–121, 159. Shortly after being elected, when asked whether violence in Europe had affected his plans to "ban Muslim immigration," the President replied, "You know my plans. All along, I've been proven to be right." *Id.*, at 123.

One week after his inauguration, the President issued EO–1. In a television interview, one of the President's campaign advisers explained that when the President "first announced it, he said, 'Muslim ban.' He called me up. He said, 'Put a commission together. Show me the right way to do it legally.' " *Id.*, at 125. The adviser said he assembled a group of Members of Congress and lawyers that "focused on, instead of religion, danger. . . . [The order] is based on places where there [is] substantial evidence that people are sending terrorists into our country." *Id.*, at 229.

Plaintiffs also note that after issuing EO–2 to replace EO–1, the President expressed regret that his prior order had been "watered down" and called for a "much tougher version" of his "Travel Ban." Shortly before the release of the Proclamation, he stated that the "travel ban . . . should be far larger, tougher, and more specific," but "stupidly that would not be politically correct." *Id.*, at 132–133. More recently, on November 29, 2017, the President retweeted links to three anti-Muslim propaganda videos. In response to questions about those videos, the President's deputy press secretary denied that the President thinks Muslims are a threat to the United States, explaining that "the President has been talking about these security issues for years now, from the campaign trail to the White House" and "has addressed these issues with the travel order that he issued earlier this year and the companion proclamation." *IRAP v. Trump*, 883 F.3d 233, 267 (C.A.4 2018).

The President of the United States possesses an extraordinary power to speak to his fellow citizens and on their behalf. Our Presidents have frequently used that power to espouse the principles of religious freedom and tolerance on which this Nation was founded. In 1790 George Washington reassured the Hebrew Congregation of Newport, Rhode Island that "happily the Government of the United States . . . gives to bigotry no sanction, to persecution no assistance [and] requires only that they who live under its protection should demean themselves as good citizens." 6 Papers of George Washington 285 (D. Twohig ed. 1996). President Eisenhower, at the opening of the Islamic Center of Washington, similarly pledged to a Muslim audience that "America would fight with her whole strength for your right to have here your own church," declaring that "[t]his concept is indeed a part of America." Public Papers of the Presidents, Dwight D. Eisenhower, June 28, 1957, p. 509 (1957). And just days after the attacks of September 11, 2001, President George W. Bush returned to the same Islamic Center to implore his fellow Americans—Muslims and non-Muslims alike—to remember during their time of grief that "[t]he face of terror is not the true faith of Islam," and that America is "a great country because we share the same values of respect and dignity and human worth." Public Papers of the Presidents, George W. Bush, Vol. 2, Sept. 17, 2001, p. 1121 (2001). Yet it cannot be denied that the Federal Government and the Presidents who have carried its laws into effect have—from the Nation's earliest days—performed unevenly in living up to those inspiring words.

Plaintiffs argue that this President's words strike at fundamental standards of respect and tolerance, in violation of our constitutional tradition. But the issue before us is not whether to denounce the statements. It is instead the significance of those statements in reviewing a Presidential directive, neutral on its face, addressing a matter within the core of executive responsibility. In doing so, we must consider not only the statements of a particular President, but also the authority of the Presidency itself.

The case before us differs in numerous respects from the conventional Establishment Clause claim. Unlike the typical suit involving religious displays or school prayer, plaintiffs seek to invalidate a national security directive regulating the entry of aliens abroad. Their claim accordingly raises a number of delicate issues regarding the scope of the constitutional right and the manner of proof. The Proclamation, moreover, is facially neutral toward religion. Plaintiffs therefore ask the Court to probe the sincerity of the stated justifications for the policy by reference to extrinsic statements—many of which were made before the President took the oath of office. These various aspects of plaintiffs' challenge inform our standard of review.

For more than a century, this Court has recognized that the admission and exclusion of foreign nationals is a "fundamental sovereign attribute exercised by the Government's political departments largely immune from judicial control." *Fiallo v. Bell*, 430 U.S. 787, 792 (1977). Because decisions in these matters may implicate "relations with foreign powers," or involve "classifications defined in the light of changing political and economic circumstances," such judgments "are frequently of a character more appropriate to either the Legislature or the Executive." *Mathews v. Diaz*, 426 U.S. 67, 81 (1976).

Nonetheless, although foreign nationals seeking admission have no constitutional right to entry, this Court has engaged in a circumscribed judicial inquiry when the denial of a visa allegedly burdens the constitutional rights of a U.S. citizen. In *Kleindienst v. Mandel*, [408 U.S. 753 (1972),] the Attorney General denied admission to a Belgian journalist and self-described "revolutionary Marxist," Ernest Mandel, who had been invited to speak at a conference at Stanford University. The professors who wished to hear Mandel speak challenged that decision under the First Amendment, and we acknowledged that their constitutional "right to receive information" was implicated. But we limited our review to whether the Executive gave a "facially legitimate and bona fide" reason for its action. Given the authority of the political branches over admission, we held that "when the Executive exercises this [delegated] power negatively on the basis of a facially legitimate and bona fide reason, the courts will neither look behind the exercise of that discretion, nor test it by balancing its justification" against the asserted constitutional interests of U.S. citizens.

The principal dissent suggests that *Mandel* has no bearing on this case, but our opinions have reaffirmed and applied its deferential standard of review across different contexts and constitutional claims * * *.

* * *

Given the standard of review, it should come as no surprise that the Court hardly ever strikes down a policy as illegitimate under rational basis scrutiny. On the few occasions where we have done so, a common thread has been that the laws at issue lack any purpose other than a "bare . . . desire to harm a politically unpopular group." *Department of Agriculture v. Moreno*, 413 U.S. 528 (1973) * * *.

The Proclamation does not fit this pattern. It cannot be said that it is impossible to "discern a relationship to legitimate state interests" or that the policy is "inexplicable by anything but animus." Indeed, the dissent can only attempt to argue otherwise by refusing to apply anything resembling rational basis review. But because there is persuasive evidence that the entry suspension has a legitimate grounding in national security concerns, quite apart from any religious hostility, we must accept that independent justification.

The Proclamation is expressly premised on legitimate purposes: preventing entry of nationals who cannot be adequately vetted and inducing other nations to improve their practices. The text says nothing about religion. Plaintiffs and the dissent nonetheless emphasize that five of the seven nations currently included in the Proclamation have Muslim-majority populations. Yet that fact alone does not support an inference of religious hostility, given that the policy covers just 8% of the world's Muslim population and is limited to countries that were previously designated by Congress or prior administrations as posing national security risks. See 8 U.S.C. § 1187(a)(12)(A) (identifying Syria and state sponsors of terrorism such as Iran as "countr[ies] or area[s] of concern" for purposes of administering the Visa Waiver Program); Dept. of Homeland Security, DHS Announces Further Travel Restrictions for the Visa Waiver Program (Feb. 18, 2016) (designating Libya, Somalia, and Yemen as additional countries of concern); see also *Rajah*, 544 F.3d, at

433, n. 3 (describing how nonimmigrant aliens from Iran, Libya, Somalia, Syria, and Yemen were covered by the National Security Entry-Exit Registration System).

The Proclamation, moreover, reflects the results of a worldwide review process undertaken by multiple Cabinet officials and their agencies. Plaintiffs seek to discredit the findings of the review, pointing to deviations from the review's baseline criteria resulting in the inclusion of Somalia and omission of Iraq. But as the Proclamation explains, in each case the determinations were justified by the distinct conditions in each country. Although Somalia generally satisfies the information-sharing component of the baseline criteria, it "stands apart . . . in the degree to which [it] lacks command and control of its territory." Proclamation § 2(h)(i). As for Iraq, the Secretary of Homeland Security determined that entry restrictions were not warranted in light of the close cooperative relationship between the U.S. and Iraqi Governments and the country's key role in combating terrorism in the region. § 1(g). It is, in any event, difficult to see how exempting one of the largest predominantly Muslim countries in the region from coverage under the Proclamation can be cited as evidence of animus toward Muslims.

The dissent likewise doubts the thoroughness of the multi-agency review because a recent Freedom of Information Act request shows that the final DHS report "was a mere 17 pages." Yet a simple page count offers little insight into the actual substance of the final report, much less predecisional materials underlying it. See 5 U.S.C. § 552(b)(5) (exempting deliberative materials from FOIA disclosure).

More fundamentally, plaintiffs and the dissent challenge the entry suspension based on their perception of its effectiveness and wisdom. They suggest that the policy is overbroad and does little to serve national security interests. But we cannot substitute our own assessment for the Executive's predictive judgments on such matters * * *. While we of course "do not defer to the Government's reading of the First Amendment," the Executive's evaluation of the underlying facts is entitled to appropriate weight, particularly in the context of litigation involving "sensitive and weighty interests of national security and foreign affairs." *Humanitarian Law Project*, 561 U.S., at 33–34.

Three additional features of the entry policy support the Government's claim of a legitimate national security interest. First, since the President introduced entry restrictions in January 2017, three Muslim-majority countries—Iraq, Sudan, and Chad—have been removed from the list of covered countries. The Proclamation emphasizes that its "conditional restrictions" will remain in force only so long as necessary to "address" the identified "inadequacies and risks," Proclamation Preamble, and § 1(h), and establishes an ongoing process to engage covered nations and assess every 180 days whether the entry restrictions should be terminated, §§ 4(a), (b). In fact, in announcing the termination of restrictions on nationals of Chad, the President also described Libya's ongoing engagement with the State Department and the steps Libya is taking "to improve its practices." Proclamation No. 9723, 83 Fed. Reg. 15939.

Second, for those countries that remain subject to entry restrictions, the Proclamation includes significant exceptions for various categories of foreign nationals. The policy permits nationals from nearly every covered country to travel to the United States on a variety of nonimmigrant visas. See, e.g., §§ 2(b)–(c), (g), (h) (permitting student and exchange visitors from Iran, while restricting only business and tourist nonimmigrant entry for nationals of Libya and Yemen, and imposing no restrictions on nonimmigrant entry for Somali nationals). These carveouts for nonimmigrant visas are substantial: Over the last three fiscal years—before the Proclamation was in effect—the majority of visas issued to nationals from the covered countries were nonimmigrant visas. The Proclamation also exempts permanent residents and individuals who have been granted asylum. §§ 3(b)(i), (vi).

Third, the Proclamation creates a waiver program open to all covered foreign nationals seeking entry as immigrants or nonimmigrants * * *.

Finally, the dissent invokes *Korematsu v. United States*, 323 U.S. 214 (1944). Whatever rhetorical advantage the dissent may see in doing so, *Korematsu* has nothing to do with this case. The forcible relocation of U.S. citizens to concentration camps, solely and explicitly on the basis of race, is objectively unlawful and outside the scope of Presidential authority. But it is wholly inapt to liken that morally repugnant order to a facially neutral policy denying certain foreign nationals the privilege of admission. The entry suspension is an act that is well within executive authority and could have been taken by any other President—the only question is evaluating the actions of this particular President in promulgating an otherwise valid Proclamation.

The dissent's reference to *Korematsu*, however, affords this Court the opportunity to make express what is already obvious: *Korematsu* was gravely wrong the day it was decided, has been overruled in the court of history, and—to be clear—"has no place in law under the Constitution." 323 U.S., at 248 (Jackson, J., dissenting).

* * *

Under these circumstances, the Government has set forth a sufficient national security justification to survive rational basis review. We express no view on the soundness of the policy. We simply hold today that plaintiffs have not demonstrated a likelihood of success on the merits of their constitutional claim.

* * *

■ JUSTICE KENNEDY, concurring. [Omitted.]

■ THOMAS, J., concurring. [Omitted.]

■ JUSTICE BREYER, with whom JUSTICE KAGAN joins, dissenting.

The question before us is whether Proclamation No. 9645 is lawful. If its promulgation or content was significantly affected by religious animus against Muslims, it would violate the relevant statute or the First Amendment itself. If, however, its sole *ratio decidendi* was one of national security, then it would be unlikely to violate either the statute or the Constitution. Which is it? Members of the Court principally disagree about the answer to this question, *i.e.*, about whether or the extent to which religious animus played a significant role in the Proclamation's promulgation or content.

In my view, the Proclamation's elaborate system of exemptions and waivers can and should help us answer this question. That system provides for case-by-case consideration of persons who may qualify for visas despite the Proclamation's general ban. Those persons include lawful permanent residents, asylum seekers, refugees, students, children, and numerous others. There are likely many such persons, perhaps in the thousands * * *.

On the one hand, if the Government is applying the exemption and waiver provisions as written, then its argument for the Proclamation's lawfulness is strengthened * * *.

* * *

On the other hand, if the Government is *not* applying the system of exemptions and waivers that the Proclamation contains, then its argument for the Proclamation's lawfulness becomes significantly weaker * * *.

* * *

Unfortunately there is evidence that supports the second possibility, *i.e.*, that the Government is not applying the Proclamation as written. The Proclamation provides that the Secretary of State and the Secretary of Homeland Security "shall coordinate to adopt guidance" for consular officers to follow when deciding whether to grant a waiver. § 3(c)(ii). Yet, to my knowledge, no guidance has issued. The only potentially relevant document I have found consists of a set of State Department answers to certain Frequently Asked Questions, but this document simply restates the Proclamation in plain language for visa applicants. It does not provide guidance for consular officers as to how they are to exercise their discretion. See Dept. of State, FAQs on the Presidential Proclamation, https://travel.state.gov/content/travel/en/us-visas/visa-information-resources/presidential-proclamation-archive/2017-12-04-Presidential-Proclamation.html (all Internet materials as last visited June 25, 2018).

An examination of publicly available statistics also provides cause for concern. The State Department reported that during the Proclamation's first month, two waivers were approved out of 6,555 eligible applicants. Letter from M. Waters, Assistant Secretary Legislative Affairs, to Sen. Van Hollen (Feb. 22, 2018). In its reply brief, the Government claims that number increased from 2 to 430 during the first four months of implementation. Reply Brief 17. That number, 430, however, when compared with the number of pre-Proclamation visitors, accounts for a miniscule percentage of those likely eligible for visas, in such categories as persons requiring medical treatment, academic visitors, students, family members, and others belonging to groups that, when considered as a group (rather than case by case), would not seem to pose security threats.

* * *

Anecdotal evidence further heightens these concerns * * *.

* * *

Declarations, anecdotal evidence, facts, and numbers taken from *amicus briefs* are not judicial factfindings. The Government has not had an opportunity to respond, and a court has not had an opportunity to decide. But, given the importance of the decision in this case, the need for assurance that the Proclamation does not rest upon a "Muslim ban," and the assistance in deciding the issue that answers to the "exemption and waiver" questions may provide, I would send this case back to the District Court for further proceedings. And, I would leave the injunction in effect while the matter is litigated. Regardless, the Court's decision today leaves the District Court free to explore these issues on remand.

If this Court must decide the question without this further litigation, I would, on balance, find the evidence of antireligious bias, including statements on a website taken down only after the President issued the two executive orders preceding the

Proclamation, along with the other statements also set forth in Justice SOTOMAYOR's opinion, a sufficient basis to set the Proclamation aside. And for these reasons, I respectfully dissent.

■ JUSTICE SOTOMAYOR, with whom JUSTICE GINSBURG joins, dissenting.

The United States of America is a Nation built upon the promise of religious liberty. Our Founders honored that core promise by embedding the principle of religious neutrality in the First Amendment. The Court's decision today fails to safeguard that fundamental principle. It leaves undisturbed a policy first advertised openly and unequivocally as a "total and complete shutdown of Muslims entering the United States" because the policy now masquerades behind a facade of national-security concerns. But this repackaging does little to cleanse Presidential Proclamation No. 9645 of the appearance of discrimination that the President's words have created. Based on the evidence in the record, a reasonable observer would conclude that the Proclamation was motivated by anti-Muslim animus. That alone suffices to show that plaintiffs are likely to succeed on the merits of their Establishment Clause claim. The majority holds otherwise by ignoring the facts, misconstruing our legal precedent, and turning a blind eye to the pain and suffering the Proclamation inflicts upon countless families and individuals, many of whom are United States citizens. Because that troubling result runs contrary to the Constitution and our precedent, I dissent.

* * *

"When the government acts with the ostensible and predominant purpose" of disfavoring a particular religion, "it violates that central Establishment Clause value of official religious neutrality, there being no neutrality when the government's ostensible object is to take sides." *McCreary County v. American Civil Liberties Union of Ky.*, 545 U.S. 844, 860 (2005). To determine whether plaintiffs have proved an Establishment Clause violation, the Court asks whether a reasonable observer would view the government action as enacted for the purpose of disfavoring a religion. *See id.*, at 862, 866.

* * *

Although the majority briefly recounts a few of the statements and background events that form the basis of plaintiffs' constitutional challenge, that highly abridged account does not tell even half of the story. See Brief for The Roderick & Solange MacArthur Justice Center as *Amicus Curiae* 5–31 (outlining President Trump's public statements expressing animus toward Islam). The full record paints a far more harrowing picture, from which a reasonable observer would readily conclude that the Proclamation was motivated by hostility and animus toward the Muslim faith.

During his Presidential campaign, then-candidate Donald Trump pledged that, if elected, he would ban Muslims from entering the United States. Specifically, on December 7, 2015, he issued a formal statement "calling for a total and complete shutdown of Muslims entering the United States." App. 119 * * *.

On December 8, 2015, Trump justified his proposal during a television interview by noting that President Franklin D. Roosevelt "did the same thing" with respect to the internment of Japanese Americans during World War II. In January 2016, during a Republican primary debate, Trump was asked whether he wanted to "rethink [his] position" on "banning Muslims from entering the country." He answered, "No." A month later, at a rally in South Carolina, Trump told an apocryphal story about United States General John J. Pershing killing a large group of Muslim insurgents in the Philippines with bullets dipped in pigs' blood in the early 1900's. In March 2016, he expressed his belief that "Islam hates us. . . . [W]e can't allow people coming into this country who have this hatred of the United States . . . [a]nd of people that are not Muslim." That same month, Trump asserted that "[w]e're having problems with the Muslims, and we're having problems with Muslims coming into the country." He therefore called for surveillance of mosques in the United States, blaming terrorist attacks on Muslims' lack of "assimilation" and their commitment to "sharia law." A day later, he opined that Muslims "do not respect us at all" and "don't respect a lot of the things that are happening throughout not only our country, but they don't respect other things."

As Trump's presidential campaign progressed, he began to describe his policy proposal in slightly different terms. In June 2016, for instance, he characterized the policy proposal as a suspension of immigration from countries "where there's a proven history of terrorism." He also described the proposal as rooted in the need to stop "importing radical Islamic terrorism to the West through a failed immigration system." Asked in July 2016 whether he was "pull[ing] back from" his pledged Muslim ban, Trump responded, "I actually don't think it's a rollback. In fact, you could say it's an expansion." He then explained that he used different terminology because "[p]eople were so upset when [he] used the word Muslim."

A month before the 2016 election, Trump reiterated that his proposed "Muslim ban" had "morphed into a[n] extreme vetting from certain areas of the world." Then, on December 21, 2016, President-elect Trump was asked whether he would "rethink" his previous "plans to create a Muslim registry or ban Muslim immigration." He replied: "You know my plans. All along, I've proven to be right."

* * *

As the majority correctly notes, "the issue before us is not whether to denounce" these offensive statements. Rather, the dispositive and narrow question here is whether a reasonable observer, presented with all "openly available data," the text and "historical context" of the Proclamation, and the "specific sequence of events" leading to it, would conclude that the primary purpose of the Proclamation is to disfavor Islam and its adherents by excluding them from the country. *See McCreary*, 545 U.S., at 862–863. The answer is unquestionably yes.

Taking all the relevant evidence together, a reasonable observer would conclude that the Proclamation was driven primarily by anti-Muslim animus, rather than by the Government's asserted national-security justifications. Even before being sworn into office, then-candidate Trump stated that "Islam hates us," warned that "[w]e're having problems with the Muslims, and we're having problems with Muslims coming into the country," promised to enact a "total and complete shutdown of Muslims entering the United States," and instructed one of his advisers to find a "lega[l]" way to enact a Muslim ban. The President continued to make similar statements well after his inauguration, as detailed above.

Moreover, despite several opportunities to do so, President Trump has never disavowed any of his prior statements about Islam. Instead, he has continued to make remarks that a reasonable observer would view as an unrelenting attack on the Muslim religion and its followers. Given President Trump's failure to correct the reasonable perception of his apparent hostility toward the Islamic faith, it is unsurprising that the President's lawyers have, at every step in the lower courts, failed in their attempts to launder the Proclamation of its discriminatory taint * * *.

Ultimately, what began as a policy explicitly "calling for a total and complete shutdown of Muslims entering the United States" has since morphed into a "Proclamation" putatively based on national-security concerns. But this new window dressing cannot conceal an unassailable fact: the words of the President and his advisers create the strong perception that the Proclamation is contaminated by impermissible discriminatory animus against Islam and its followers.

Rather than defend the President's problematic statements, the Government urges this Court to set them aside and defer to the President on issues related to immigration and national security. The majority accepts that invitation and incorrectly applies a watered-down legal standard in an effort to short circuit plaintiffs' Establishment Clause claim.

* * *

But even under rational-basis review, the Proclamation must fall. That is so because the Proclamation is " 'divorced from any factual context from which we could discern a relationship to legitimate state interests,' and 'its sheer breadth [is] so discontinuous with the reasons offered for it' " that the policy is " 'inexplicable by anything but animus.' " * * *

* * *

The majority first emphasizes that the Proclamation "says nothing about religion." Even so, the Proclamation, just like its predecessors, overwhelmingly targets Muslim-majority nations. Given the record here, including all the President's statements linking the Proclamation to his apparent hostility toward Muslims, it is of no moment that the Proclamation also includes minor restrictions on two non-Muslim majority countries, North Korea and Venezuela, or that the Government has removed a few Muslim-majority countries from the list of covered countries since EO–1 was issued. Consideration of the entire record supports the conclusion that the inclusion of North Korea and Venezuela, and the removal of other countries, simply reflect subtle efforts to start "talking territory instead of Muslim," precisely so the Executive Branch could evade criticism or legal consequences for the Proclamation's otherwise clear targeting of Muslims * * *

The majority next contends that the Proclamation "reflects the results of a worldwide review process undertaken by multiple Cabinet officials." * * *

* * * [T]he worldwide review does little to break the clear connection between the Proclamation and the President's anti-Muslim statements. For "[n]o matter how many officials affix their names to it, the Proclamation rests on a rotten foundation." Brief for Constitutional Law Scholars as *Amici Curiae* 7 (filed Apr. 2, 2018). The President campaigned on a promise to implement a "total and complete shutdown of Muslims" entering the country, translated that campaign promise into a concrete policy, and made several statements linking that policy (in its various forms) to anti-Muslim animus.

* * *

The First Amendment stands as a bulwark against official religious prejudice and embodies our Nation's deep commitment to religious plurality and tolerance * * *. Instead of vindicating those principles, today's decision tosses them aside. In holding that the First Amendment gives way to an executive policy that a reasonable observer would view as motivated by animus against Muslims, the majority opinion upends this Court's precedent, repeats tragic mistakes of the past, and denies countless individuals the fundamental right of religious liberty.

* * *

Today's holding is all the more troubling given the stark parallels between the reasoning of this case and that of *Korematsu v. United States*, 323 U.S. 214 (1944) * * *. As here, the Government invoked an ill-defined national-security threat to justify an exclusionary policy of sweeping proportion. As here, the exclusion order was rooted in dangerous stereotypes about, *inter alia*, a particular group's supposed inability to assimilate and desire to harm the United States * * *. And as here, there was strong evidence that impermissible hostility and animus motivated the Government's policy.

* * *

Our Constitution demands, and our country deserves, a Judiciary willing to hold the coordinate branches to account when they defy our most sacred legal commitments. Because the Court's decision today has failed in that respect, with profound regret, I dissent.

NOTES AND QUESTIONS

1. If the order in *Trump v. Hawaii* does truly discriminate on the basis of religion, it violates at least the Establishment Clause, and possibly the Free Exercise Clause (though there may be an issue with giving constitutional weight to free exercise rights of persons who are not yet admitted to the country). *See* Steven G. Calabresi & Abe Salander, *Religion and the Equal Protection Clause: Why the Constitution Requires School Vouchers*, 65 FLA. L. REV. 909–1087 (2013) (arguing for strict scrutiny of classifications on the basis of religion). Does the order truly discriminate on the basis of religion? Is that a legal question or a factual question? If it is a factual question, how would courts find the relevant facts? Is it relevant what kind of order President Trump may have wanted (either as President Trump or Candidate Trump), or is it only relevant what kind of order he ended up with?

2. Justice Breyer focuses on the post-Order application of the waiver provisions. Is that analysis relevant to the validity of the Order itself or only to the validity of specific actions taken under it? Be warned that this question is much bigger than it sounds. If your instructor is bolder than your editors, you might now hear something, if you have not heard it already, about "facial" vs. "as-applied" challenges to governmental action. *See* Michael C. Dorf, *Facial Challenges to State and Federal Statutes*, 46 STAN. L. REV. 235 (1994); Richard H. Fallon, Jr., *As-Applied and Facial Challenges and Third-Party Standing*, 113 HARV. L. REV. 1321 (2000).

[Assignment 48]

B. FREEDOM OF SPEECH AND OF THE PRESS

Congress shall make no law * * * abridging the freedom of speech, or of the press

The First Amendment says Congress shall pass no law "abridging the freedom of speech, or of the press." The Supreme Court has held that this clause protects freedom of expression in all contexts including: in letters, in diaries, in broadcasting, in exchanges over the internet, and through expressive conduct like flag burning. The Court has read this clause in light of its underlying purposes in our democratic government, and it has not read the clause in a literal or wooden way.

The history of freedom of expression, like the history of freedom of religion, starts in Western thought with the execution of Socrates for expressing his beliefs in 399 B.C. and of Jesus for preaching the Gospel in 36 A.D. [T]he two men became the leading martyrs of Western thought, which in turn became progressively more committed to the value of freedom of expression.

Freedom of expression, and of religion, were greatly facilitated by the development of the printing press in 1439 A.D. One of the first texts printed, of course, was the Bible, and soon enough translations of the Bible into vernacular languages became commonplace. This in turn helped to start the Protestant Reformation in 1517, when Martin Luther posted ninety-five theses on a church door in Wittenberg, Germany. Freedom of expression in the form of Bibles in the vernacular caused a revolution, which shook the whole Western world.

One element of that revolution was the printing by Nicolaus Copernicus in 1514 of a theory that the earth revolved around the sun, which was picked up and publicized by Galileo Galilei, who told friends in 1597 that Copernicus was right and that the ancient Greeks were wrong. Galileo was eventually prosecuted by the Roman Inquisition, at the urging of the Pope and of Cardinal Bellarmine, for teaching and printing books that took the Copernican view. Galileo was sentenced to life imprisonment for his expression of his beliefs; and the wrongness and injustice of this censorship helped to cause John Milton to write *Areopagitica: A Speech of Mr. John Milton for the Liberty of Unlicensed Printing to the Parliament of England* in 1644. In this tract, Milton denounced the censorship of Galileo, and he begged the Protestant English Parliament, unsuccessfully, not to pass a law requiring licensing of books. Milton argued for freedom of expression because everyone learns in a marketplace of ideas, because virtue compelled is not virtue, and because government officials cannot be trusted to decide what speech is good and true as opposed to being false and evil. *See* JOHN MILTON, AREOPAGITICA (General Books 2009) (1644). (For a version of *Areopagitica* with the spelling modernized, see VINCENT BLASI, IDEAS OF THE FIRST AMENDMENT 52–89 (2005). For an excerpt from this work, which with considerable reluctance we elected not to include here, see STEVEN GOW CALABRESI, BRADLEY G. SILVERMAN & JOSHUA BRAVER, THE U.S. CONSTITUTION AND COMPARATIVE CONSTITUTIONAL LAW 965–72 (2016).) Notwithstanding Milton's pleas, the Licensing Act of 1662 imposed prepublication censorship of works deemed by the government to be "heretical, seditious, schismatical, or offensive," 14 Car. II, c.33, and strictly regulated the printing industry.

Milton's ideas eventually triumphed, at least partially, in England in the 1690s; the Licensing Act was allowed to lapse in 1695. *See* Philip Hamburger, *The Development of the Law of Seditious Libel and the Control of the Press*, 37 Stan. L. Rev. 661, 714–25 (1985). While all laws licensing books, *i.e.* imposing prior restraints to publication, were repealed, post-publication prosecutions for seditious libel continued for some time. Nonetheless, William Blackstone in the mid-eighteenth century described freedom from prior restraints as being at the core of the common law in his famous *Commentaries on the Laws of England*.

Americans took Milton and Blackstone's teaching to heart, but they developed an even broader view of freedom of expression in the eighteenth century. In the 1730s, a New York printer named John Peter Zenger was tried for seditious libel of the Governor of New York. Seditious libel involved statements tending to call into disrepute a government official, and the truer the statements were, the greater the damage to the public peace, and so the greater was the penalty. A New York jury simply refused to convict Zenger, and this was widely accepted as an American expansion of freedom of expression rights to include protection of so-called seditious libels. *See* Albert W. Alschuler & Andrew P. Deiss, *A Brief History of Criminal Jury in the United States,* 61 U. CHI. L. REV. 867, 871–74 (1994). Thomas Jefferson and James Madison were very strongly of the view that sedition laws and seditious libel actions in court violated the First Amendment.

Americans were also greatly influenced in their ideas about the fundamental importance of freedom of expression by the publication in 1755 of two letters by Thomas Gordon published under the pseudonym Cato. Gordon wrote that: "Without freedom of thought, there can be no such thing as wisdom; and no such thing as publick liberty, without freedom of speech." Cato strongly defends freedom of speech as being essential both for democracy to function and for liberty to exist. The founding fathers of the U.S. Constitution and Bill of Rights were all steeped in Thomas Gordon's ideas on the subject; in the founding era, *Cato's Letters* by Gordon and John Trenchard "ranked with the treatises of Locke as the most authoritative statement of the nature of political liberty and above Locke as an exposition of the social sources of the threats it faced." BERNARD BAILYN, THE IDEOLOGICAL ORIGINS OF THE AMERICAN REVOLUTION 36 (1967).

Please read the excerpts from the John Peter Zenger trial, Blackstone, and two Letters of Cato below to get an idea of the American belief at the Founding with respect to freedom of the press and of speech. We also provide an excerpt from John Stuart Mill's *On Liberty,* published in 1859, to provide context for attitudes in the mid-nineteenth century, when the Fourteenth Amendment was ratified. As you will see in the next chapter, the Fourteenth Amendment has been held to incorporate free speech principles against the state governments.

1. THE TRIAL OF JOHN PETER ZENGER

DOUGLAS W. KMIEC & STEPHEN B. PRESSER, THE AMERICAN CONSTITUTIONAL ORDER: HISTORY, CASES, AND PHILOSOPHY 958–59 (1998):[1]

In England, until the late eighteenth century, even true criticism of the government was not permitted, pursuant to the doctrine of seditious libel. Under traditional English common law seditious libel doctrine, one could be criminally punished for the publication of any information, true or false, which tended to turn the sentiments of the people against the government * * *. In colonial America the doctrine of seditious libel came under fire early on, most notably in the trial of John Peter Zenger, a New York printer, who was prosecuted for seditious libel in the 1730's for comments critical of the New York Governor (then a Crown appointee). There was no doubt that under the English common law of seditious libel Zenger was

---

[1] Reprinted from Kmiec & Presser, The American Constitutional Order: Cases, History and Philosophy with permission. Copyright 1998 Matthew Bender & Company, Inc., a LexisNexis company. All rights reserved.

guilty of [the crime of seditious] libel whether what he published was true or not. 'The greater the truth, the greater the libel,' was the English common law maxim * * *.

Zenger's lawyer, a hoary barrister from Philadelphia, one Andrew Hamilton, argued to the jury that whatever the law was in England, in America citizens needed more freedom to criticize their governors, who were not, after all, members of the royal family, but just their representatives in the colonies. Hamilton was not permitted to prove the truth of Zenger's allegations, since the common law rule was that truth was no defense to a charge of seditious libel. In a famous and elegant move, Hamilton then argued to the jury that they should take the fact he was not permitted to prove truth as a strong argument for the truth of what Zenger had published. Remarkably, Hamilton was not censured by the court. What Hamilton argued—that truth ought to be a defense—was clearly not then the law, but he did manage to get the jury to acquit Zenger, even though, under the law as it then was, he should have been convicted. Can you understand what is meant by the term 'Philadelphia lawyer'? From that time to this the Zenger trial has been taken to stand for the proposition that freedom of the press is one of the most important features of American law.

2. WILLIAM BLACKSTONE ON THE LIBERTY OF THE PRESS

4 COMMENTARIES ON THE LAWS OF ENGLAND *151–53 (first published 1756)

In this, and the other instances which we have lately considered, where blasphemous, immoral, treasonable, schismatical, seditious, or scandalous libels are punished by the English law, some with a greater, others with a lesser degree of severity; the liberty of the press, properly understood, is by no means infringed or violated. The liberty of the press is indeed essential to the nature of a free state: but this consists in laying no previous restraints upon publications, and not in freedom from censure for criminal matter when published. Every freeman has an undoubted right to lay what sentiments he pleases before the public: to forbid this, is to destroy the freedom of the press: but if he publishes what is improper, mischievous, or illegal, he must take the consequence of his own temerity. To subject the press to the restrictive power of a licenser, as was formerly done, both before and since the revolution, is to subject all freedom of sentiment to the prejudices of one man, and make him the arbitrary and infallible judge of (as the law does at present) any dangerous or offensive writings, which, when published, shall on a fair and impartial trial be adjudged of a pernicious tendency, is necessary for the preservation of peace and good order, of government and religion, the only solid foundations of civil liberty. Thus the will of individuals is still left free; the abuse only of that free will is the object of legal punishment. Neither is any restraint hereby laid upon freedom of thought or enquiry: liberty of private sentiments is still left; the disseminating, or making public, of bad sentiments, destructive of the ends of society, is the crime which society corrects. A man (says a fine writer on this subject) may be allowed to keep poisons in his closet, but not publicly to vend them as cordials. And to this we may add, that the only plausible argument heretofore used for restraining the just freedom of the press 'that it was necessary to prevent the daily abuse of it,' will entirely lose its force, when it is shewn (by a seasonable exertion of the laws) that the press cannot be abused to any bad purpose, without incurring a suitable punishment: whereas it never can be used to any good one, when under the control of an inspector. So true will it be found, that to censure the licentiousness, is to maintain the liberty of the press.

3. CATO'S LETTER NO. 15, "OF FREEDOM OF SPEECH: THAT THE SAME IS INSEPARABLE FROM PUBLICK LIBERTY"

(Thomas Gordon, Feb. 4, 1720)

SIR,

Without freedom of thought, there can be no such thing as wisdom; and no such thing as publick liberty, without freedom of speech: Which is the right of every man, as far as by it he does not hurt and control the right of another; and this is the only check which it ought to suffer, the only bounds which it ought to know. * * * This sacred privilege is so essential to free government, that the security of property; and the freedom of speech, always go together; and in those wretched countries where a man can not call his tongue his own, he can scarce call any thing else his own. Whoever would overthrow the liberty of the nation, must begin by subduing the freedom of speech; a thing terrible to publick traitors.

This secret was so well known to the court of King Charles I that his wicked ministry procured a proclamation to forbid the people to talk of Parliaments, which those traitors had laid aside. To assert the undoubted right of the subject, and defend his Majesty's legal prerogative, was called disaffection, and punished as sedition. Nay, people were forbid to talk of religion in their families: For the priests had combined with the ministers to cook up tyranny, and suppress truth and the law. While the late King James, when Duke of York, went avowedly to mass; men were fined, imprisoned, and undone, for saying that he was a papist: And, that King Charles II might live more securely a papist, there was an act of Parliament made, declaring it treason to say that he was one.

That men ought to speak well of their governors, is true, while their governors deserve to be well spoken of; but to do publick mischief, without hearing of it, is only the prerogative and felicity of tyranny: A free people will be shewing that they are so, by their freedom of speech. * * * The administration of government is nothing else, but the attendance of the trustees of the people upon the interest and affairs of the people. And as it is the part and business of the people, for whose sake alone all publick matters are, or ought to be, transacted, to see whether they be well or ill transacted; so it is the interest, and ought to be the ambition, of all honest magistrates, to have their deeds openly examined, and publickly scanned: Only the wicked governors of men dread what is said of them * * *.

Freedom of speech is the great bulwark of liberty; they prosper and die together: And it is the terror of traitors and oppressors, and a barrier against them. It produces excellent writers, and encourages men of fine genius. Tacitus tells us, that the Roman commonwealth bred great and numerous authors, who writ with equal boldness and eloquence: But when it was enslaved, those great wits were no more * * *. The minds of men, terrified by unjust power, degenerated into all the vileness and methods of servitude: Abject sycophancy and blind submission grew the only means of preferment, and indeed of safety; men durst not open their mouths, but to flatter * * *.

All ministers, therefore, who were oppressors, or intended to be oppressors, have been loud in their complaints against freedom of speech, and the licence of the press;

and always restrained, or endeavoured to restrain, both. In consequence of this, they have brow-beaten writers, punished them violently, and against law, and burnt their works. By all which they shewed how much truth alarmed them, and how much they were at enmity with truth * * *. * * * The best princes have ever encouraged and promoted freedom of speech; they knew that upright measures would defend themselves, and that all upright men would defend them * * *.

4. CATO'S LETTER NO. 38, "THE RIGHT AND CAPACITY OF THE PEOPLE TO JUDGE OF GOVERNMENT"

(Thomas Gordon, July 22, 1721)

Of all the sciences that I know in the world, that of government concerns us most, and is the easiest to be known, and yet is the least understood. Most of those who manage it would make the lower world believe that there is I know not what difficulty and mystery in it, far above vulgar understandings; which proceeding of theirs is direct craft and imposture: Every ploughman knows a good government from a bad one, from the effects of it: he knows whether the fruits of his labour be his own, and whether he enjoy them in peace and security: And if he do not know the principles of government, it is for want of thinking and enquiry, for they lie open to common sense; but people are generally taught not to think of them at all, or to think wrong of them.

What is government, but a trust committed by all, or the most, to one, or a few, who are to attend upon the affairs of all, that every one may, with the more security, attend upon his own? A great and honourable trust; but too seldom honourably executed; those who possess it having it often more at heart to increase their power, than to make it useful; and to be terrible, rather than beneficent. It is therefore a trust, which ought to be bounded with many and strong restraints, because power renders men wanton, insolent to others, and fond of themselves * * *.

But some have said, It is not the business of private man to meddle with government. A bold, false, and dishonest saying; and whoever says it, either knows not what he says, or cares not, or slavishly speaks the sense of others. It is a cant now almost forgot in England, and which never prevailed but when liberty and the constitution were attacked, and never can prevail but upon the like occasion * * *. Publick truths ought never to be kept secrets; and they who do it, are guilty of a solecism, and a contradiction: Every man ought to know what it concerns all to know. Now, nothing upon earth is of a more universal nature than government; and every private man upon earth has a concern in it, because in it is concerned, and nearly and immediately concerned, his virtue, his property, and the security of his person * * *.

Such is the difference between one government and another, and of such important concernment is the nature and administration of government to a people. And to say that private men have nothing to do with government, is to say that private men have nothing to do with their own happiness and misery. What is the publick, but the collective body of private men, as every private man is a member of the publick? And as the whole ought to be concerned for the preservation of every private individual, it is the duty of every individual to be concerned for the whole, in which himself is included * * *.

For myself, who have thought pretty much of these matters, I am of opinion, that a whole nation are like to be as much attached to themselves, as one man or a few men are like to be, who may by many means be detached from the interest of a nation. It is certain that one man, and several men, may be bribed into an interest opposite to that of the publick; but it is as certain that a whole country can never find an equivalent for itself, and consequently a whole country can never be bribed. It is the eternal interest of every nation, that their government should be good; but they who direct it frequently reason a contrary way and find their own account in plunder and oppression; and while the publick voice is pretended to be declared, by one or a few, for vile and private ends, the publick know nothing of what is done, till they feel the terrible effects of it.

By the Bill of Rights, and the Act of Settlement, at the Revolution; a right is asserted to the people applying to the King and to the Parliament, by petition and address, for a redress of publick grievances and mismanagements, when such there are, of which they are left to judge; and the difference between free and enslaved countries lies principally here, that in the former, their magistrates must consult the voice and interest of the people; but in the latter, the private will, interest, and pleasure of the governors, are the sole end and motives of their administration.

5. JOHN STUART MILL, ON LIBERTY, CHAPTER TWO, *OF THE LIBERTY OF THOUGHT AND DISCUSSION*

(1859)

* * * If all mankind minus one, were of one opinion, and only one person were of the contrary opinion, mankind would be no more justified in silencing that one person, than he, if he had the power, would be justified in silencing mankind. Were an opinion a personal possession of no value except to the owner; if to be obstructed in the enjoyment of it were simply a private injury, it would make some difference whether the injury was inflicted only on a few persons or on many. But the peculiar evil of silencing the expression of an opinion is, that it is robbing the human race; posterity as well as the existing generation; those who dissent from the opinion, still more than those who hold it. If the opinion is right, they are deprived of the opportunity of exchanging error for truth: if wrong, they lose, what is almost as great a benefit, the clearer perception and livelier impression of truth, produced by its collision with error * * *.

First: the opinion which it is attempted to suppress by authority may possibly be true. Those who desire to suppress it, of course deny its truth; but they are not infallible * * *. All silencing of discussion is an assumption of infallibility. Its condemnation may be allowed to rest on this common argument, not the worse for being common * * *.

There is the greatest difference between presuming an opinion to be true, because, with every opportunity for contesting it, it has not been refuted, and assuming its truth for the purpose of not permitting its refutation. Complete liberty of contradicting and disproving our opinion, is the very condition which justifies us in assuming its truth for purposes of action; and on no other terms can a being with human faculties have any rational assurance of being right * * *.

Mankind can hardly be too often reminded, that there was once a man named Socrates, between whom and the legal authorities and public opinion of his time, there took place a memorable collision. Born in an age and country abounding in individual greatness, this man has been handed down to us by those who best knew both him and the age, as the most virtuous man in it; while *we* know him as the head and prototype of all subsequent teachers of virtue, the source equally of the lofty inspiration of Plato and the judicious utilitarianism of Aristotle, "*i maëstri di color che sanno,*" the two headsprings of ethical as of all other philosophy. This acknowledged master of all the eminent thinkers who have since lived—whose fame, still growing after more than two thousand years, all but outweighs the whole remainder of the names which make his native city illustrious—was put to death by his countrymen, after a judicial conviction, for impiety and immorality. Impiety, in denying the gods recognised by the State; indeed his accuser asserted (see the *Apologia)* that he believed in no gods at all. Immorality, in being, by his doctrines and instructions, a "corrupter of youth." Of these charges the tribunal, there is every ground for believing, honestly found him guilty, and condemned the man who probably of all then born had deserved best of mankind, to be put to death as a criminal * * *.

It still remains to speak of one of the principal causes which make diversity of opinion advantageous, and will continue to do so until mankind shall have entered a stage of intellectual advancement which at present seems at an incalculable distance. We have hitherto considered only two possibilities: that the received opinion may be false, and some other opinion, consequently, true; or that, the received opinion being true, a conflict with the opposite error is essential to a clear apprehension and deep feeling of its truth. But there is a commoner case than either of these; when the conflicting doctrines, instead of being one true and the other false, share the truth between them; and the nonconforming opinion is needed to supply the remainder of the truth, of which the received doctrine embodies only a part. Popular opinions, on subjects not palpable to sense, are often true, but seldom or never the whole truth * * *.

NOTES AND QUESTIONS

1. There are four common arguments in favor of protecting freedom of expression:

First, freedom of expression is essential to making democracy work. One cannot have elections or hold government officers accountable for what they do without protecting freedom of expression.

Second, as Milton and Mill argued, a free market in ideas is essential for science, progress, human happiness, and the pursuit of truth.

Third, freedom of expression is for some people, like novelists and playwrights, the way in which they freely develop their personalities and their identities. Banning freedom of expression would crush these people's lives.

Fourth, and finally, Milton made the point that government officials could never be expert enough or honest enough or of high enough character to censor freedom of expression sensibly. The best way to respond to freedom of expression that you think is wrong is by expressing what you think is right instead. Don't ban speech you dislike; respond to it effectively.

2. The protection of freedom of expression is deeply rooted in American constitutional law. Ten States out of twelve which wrote new state constitutions after 1776 protected freedom of the press in 1791 when the Bill of Rights was ratified. Seventy-

eight percent of the American people lived in those States. Steven G. Calabresi, Sarah E. Agudo, and Kathryn L. Dore, *State Bills of Rights in 1787 and 1791: What Individual Rights are Really Deeply Rooted in American History and Tradition?*, 85 SO. CAL. L. REV. 1451, 1478 (2012). Freedom of the press was also protected in all thirty-seven state constitutions in 1868, when the Fourteenth Amendment was ratified, and it is protected in all fifty state constitutions today. Steven G. Calabresi, et al., *Individual Rights Under State Constitutions in 2018: What Rights are Deeply Rooted in a Modern-Day Consensus of the States?*, 94 NOTRE DAME L. REV. 49, 73, 75 (2018). There is no question that the right to freedom of expression is deeply rooted in American history and tradition, and it remains a cornerstone constitutional right today.

3. The Constitution of 1788, of course, contained no specific protection for freedom of speech. But the Constitution of 1788 contained very few specific protections. It relied on the lack of enumerated powers. As Alexander Hamilton argued in *The Federalist*:

> I go further, and affirm that bills of rights, in the sense and to the extent in which they are contended for, are not only unnecessary in the proposed Constitution, but would even be dangerous. They would contain various exceptions to powers not granted; and, on this very account, would afford a colorable pretext to claim more than were granted. For why declare that things shall not be done which there is no power to do? Why, for instance, should it be said that the liberty of the press shall not be restrained, when no power is given by which restrictions may be imposed?

THE FEDERALIST No. 84 (Hamilton). A parade of Federalists echoed Hamilton's claim that the Constitution gave the national government no power over speech and the press. As Hugh Williamson put it, "examine the Plan [of the Constitution], and you will find that the liberty of the press and the laws of Mahomet are equally affected by it." Hugh Williamson, *Remarks on the New Plan of Government* (1788), *reprinted in* 1 BERNARD SCHWARTZ, THE BILL OF RIGHTS: A DOCUMENTARY HISTORY 550, 551 (1971). Similar comments came from James Wilson, *see* 2 DEBATES IN THE SEVERAL STATE CONVENTIONS ON THE ADOPTION OF THE FEDERAL CONSTITUTION 449 (Jonathan Elliot ed., 2d ed. 1836) ("ELLIOT'S DEBATES") ("it is very true, sir, that this Constitution says nothing with regard to that subject [of the press], nor was it necessary; because it will be found that there is given to the general government no power whatsoever concerning it; and no law, in pursuance of the Constitution, can possibly be enacted to destroy that liberty"); Edmund Randolph, *see* 3 ELLIOT'S DEBATES, at 203 ("Go through these powers, examine every one, and tell me if the most exalted genius can prove that the liberty of the press is in danger."); Charles Cotesworth Pinckney, *see* 4 ELLIOT'S DEBATES, at 315 ("The general government has no powers but what are expressly granted to it; it therefore has no power to take away the liberty of the press."); Roger Sherman, *see A Citizen of New Haven*, Conn. Courant, Jan. 7, 1788, *reprinted in* 3 DOCUMENTARY HISTORY OF THE RATIFICATION OF THE CONSTITUTION 525 (Merrill Jensen ed., 1978) ("The liberty of the press can be in no danger, because that is not put under the direction of the new government."); Oliver Ellsworth, *see Landholder VI*, Conn. Courant, Dec. 10, 1787, *reprinted in* 14 DOCUMENTARY HISTORY OF THE RATIFICATION OF THE CONSTITUTION 401 (John P. Kaminski & Gaspare J. Saladino eds., 1983) ("There is no declaration of any kind to preserve the liberty of the press, & c. Nor is liberty of conscience, or of matrimony, or of burial of the dead; it is enough that congress have no power to prohibit either"), and a host of others.

4. Imagine the surprise of those who relied on these representations from the Constitution's advocates a decade later. In 1798, Alexander Hamilton, as the leader of the Federalist Party, was deeply upset about criticisms being made by then-Vice

President Thomas Jefferson, James Madison, and their allies with respect to Federalist President John Adams. As a result, the Hamiltonians, who controlled Congress and the presidency, adopted:

> The Sedition Act of 1798: FIFTH CONGRESS OF THE UNITED STATES:
> At the Second Session, Begun and help at the city of Philadelphia,
> in the state of Pennsylvania, on Monday, the thirteenth of November,
> one thousand seven hundred and ninety-seven.
>
> An Act in Addition to the Act, Entitled "An Act for the Punishment
> of Certain Crimes Against the United States."
>
> * * *
>
> SEC. 2. And be it farther enacted, That if any person shall write, print, utter or publish, or shall cause or procure to be written, printed, uttered or published, or shall knowingly and willingly assist or aid in writing, printing, uttering or publishing any false, scandalous and malicious writing or writings against the government of the United States, or either house of the Congress of the United States, or the President of the United States, with intent to defame the said government, or either house of the said Congress, or the said President, or to bring them, or either of them, into contempt or disrepute; or to excite against them, or either or any of them, the hatred of the good people of the United States, or to stir up sedition within the United States, or to excite any unlawful combinations therein, for opposing or resisting any law of the United States, or any act of the President of the United States, done in pursuance of any such law, or of the powers in him vested by the constitution of the United States, or to resist, oppose, or defeat any such law or act, or to aid, encourage or abet any hostile designs of any foreign nation against United States, their people or government, then such person, being thereof convicted before any court of the United States having jurisdiction thereof, shall be punished by a fine not exceeding two thousand dollars, and by imprisonment not exceeding two years.

Comically, this Act, which passed both Houses of Congress and was signed into law by President John Adams, made it illegal to criticize Adams or Congress, but not Vice President Thomas Jefferson! Moreover, the Act expired by its own terms on March 3, 1801, in case Jefferson should win the presidency in the election of 1800, which he did. While the Act was in force, events like the following happened:

6. UNITED STATES V. LYON

15 F. Cas. 1183 (D. Vt. 1798)

[This was an indictment, under the act of July 14, 1798, against Matthew Lyon, for the publication of a seditious libel.]

The indictment which was found on October 5, 1798, contained three counts, the first of which, after averring the intent to be "to stir up sedition, and to bring the president and the government of the United States into contempt," laid the following libelous matter: "As to the executive, when I shall see the efforts of that power bent on the promotion of the comfort, the happiness, and accommodation of the people, that executive shall have my zealous and uniformed support: but whenever I shall, on the part of the executive, see every consideration of the public welfare swallowed up in a continual grasp for power, in an unbounded thirst for ridiculous pomp, foolish adulation, and selfish avarice; when I shall behold men of real merit daily turned out of office, for no other cause but independency of sentiment; when I shall see men of firmness, merit, years, abilities, and experience, discarded in their applications for office, for fear they possess that independence, and men of meanness preferred for the ease with which they take up and advocate opinions, the consequences of which they know but little of—when I shall see the sacred name of religion employed as a state engine to make mankind hate and persecute one another, I shall not be their humble advocate."

The second count consisted of having maliciously, & c., and with intent, & c., published a letter, said to be a letter from a diplomatic character in France, containing two paragraphs in the words following: "The misunderstanding between the two governments (France and the United States), has become extremely alarming; confidence is completely destroyed, mistrusts, jealousy, and a disposition to a wrong attribution of motives, are so apparent, as to require the utmost caution in every word and action that are to come from your executive. I mean, if your object is to avoid hostilities. Had this truth been understood with you before the recall of Monroe, before the coming and second coming of Pinckney; had it guided the pens that wrote the bullying speech of your president, and stupid answer of your senate, at the opening of congress in November last, I should probably had no occasion to address you this letter.—But when we found him borrowing the language of Edmund Burke, and telling the world that although he should succeed in treating with the French, there was no dependence to be placed on any of their engagements, that their religion and morality were at an end, that they would turn pirates and plunderers, and it would be necessary to be perpetually armed against them, though you were at peace: we wondered that the answer of both houses had not been an order to send him to a mad house. Instead of this the senate have echoed the speech with more servility than ever George III. experienced from either House of Parliament."

The third count was for assisting, counseling, aiding, and abetting the publication of the same.

* * *

The district attorney having opened the case, produced a letter from the defendant, dated Philadelphia, July 7, 1798, and post marked on the same day, which was printed in Vermont on July 23. The authorship of the letter and the fact of publication were admitted by the defendant. It was further proved that the defendant had several times read at public meetings in Vermont the letter (known at the time as the "Barlow" letter) from which the libellous matter in the second count was taken. Several witnesses were called to show that the defendant, both in public and in private, had extensively used the letter for political purposes, and in doing so had frequently made use of language highly disrespectful to the administration * * *.

The prosecution having closed its case, the defendant stated his defence to consist in three points: First, that the court had no jurisdiction of the offence, the act of congress being unconstitutional and void, if not so generally, at least, as to writings composed before its passage; second, that the publication was innocent; and third, that the contents were true.

On the first two points he offered no testimony, but on the third he proposed to call Judge PATERSON, the presiding judge, and Judge SMITH.

Judge PATERSON being then on the bench, was then asked by the defendant, whether he had not frequently "dined with the president, and observed his ridiculous pomp and parade?" Judge PATERSON replied that he had sometimes, though rarely, dined with the president, but that he had never seen any pomp or parade; he had seen, on the contrary, a great deal of plainness and simplicity. The defendant then asked whether he (the judge) had not seen at the president's more pomp and servants there, than at the tavern at Rutland? To this no answer was given. No other witness was called.

* * *

At about eight o'clock in the evening of the same day, after about an hour's absence, the jury returned with a verdict of guilty.

* * *

NOTES AND QUESTIONS

1. "Lyon" was Matthew Lyon, who at the time of the trial in 1798 was a Member of Congress from Vermont. He was fined and sentenced to four months' imprisonment. While in prison, he was re-elected to Congress.

2. In another case involving the Sedition Act of 1798, a scandal-mongering journalist, James Callender, was prosecuted and convicted for saying that:

> "The reign of Mr. Adams has been one continuous tempest of malignant passion. As President, he has never opened his lips, or lifted his pen without threatening and scolding; the grand object of his administration has been to exasperate the rage of contending parties, to calumniate and destroy every man who differs from his opinions. Mr. Adams has labored, and with melancholy success, to break up the bonds of social affection, and under the ruins of confidence and friendship, to extinguish the only gleam of happiness that glimmers through the dark and despicable farce of life."

United States v. Callender, 25 Fed. Cas. 239 (1800). Calendar was fined $200 and sentenced to prison time. The Sedition Act passed and was upheld by the federal courts because in 1798 only one party, the Federalist Party, had controlled the White House, the Senate, and the House of Representatives, as well as all federal judicial appointments, continuously for nine years. Having lost in federal court, Thomas Jefferson and James Madison got the Virginia and Kentucky legislatures to protest officially that the Sedition Act of 1798 was unconstitutional. *See supra* pages 124–125. The Election of 1800 was fought in part on the constitutionality of the Sedition Act of 1798, and Thomas Jefferson won at the polls. The American people enforced the First Amendment and made it clear that Sedition Acts were unconstitutional and un-American. President Jefferson pardoned everyone convicted under the Sedition Act, and he directed that the one on-going Sedition Act prosecution, which he had inherited from President Adams, be stopped. Congress appropriated money to repay all fines assessed under the Act. The long-term legacy of the Sedition Act controversy was a robust and vigorous First Amendment.

3. In *New York Times v. Sullivan*, 376 U.S. 254 (1964), the Supreme Court officially in *dicta* embraced the view that the Sedition Act had always been unconstitutional. In the ensuing years after *Sullivan*, the Supreme Court has often taken a vigorous stance in favor of free speech and free expression. (Its record prior to the emergence of the Warren Court in the 1960s was much different. The Court upheld World War I sedition act prosecutions, *see supra* page 511, and in during the Cold War upheld

a statute banning the Communist Party. *See Dennis v. United States,* 341 U.S. 494 (1951). As an illustration of the later twentieth-century approach to federal speech restrictions, consider one of the Court's most famous First Amendment cases, *New York Times v. United States,* 403 U.S. 713 (1971). The background is as follows: In the late 1960s, the United States Department of Defense prepared a report chronicling the history of U.S. involvement in Southeast Asia. The mammoth, classified document, known popularly as "The Pentagon Papers," contained information embarrassing to several presidential administrations. A former military analyst, Daniel Ellsberg, leaked the material to the *New York Times* and the *Washington Post.* After considering the matter for several months, the *Times* decided to publish portions of the Pentagon Papers. The United States sued to stop publication, and the government secured from one lower court an injunction against further publication, and the case went to the Supreme Court. We have edited out nothing from the Court's per curiam opinion except a few citations:

> We granted certiorari in these cases in which the United States seeks to enjoin the New York Times and the Washington Post from publishing the contents of a classified study entitled "History of U.S. Decision-Making Process on Viet Nam Policy."
>
> "Any system of prior restraints of expression comes to this Court bearing a heavy presumption against its constitutional validity." *Bantam Books, Inc. v. Sullivan,* 372 U.S. 58, 70 (1963); *see also Near v. Minnesota,* 283 U.S. 697 (1931). The Government "thus carries a heavy burden of showing justification for the imposition of such a restraint." *Organization for a Better Austin v. Keefe,* 402 U.S. 415, 419 (1971). The District Court for the Southern District of New York, in the *New York Times* case, and the District Court for the District of Columbia and the Court of Appeals for the District of Columbia Circuit, in the *Washington Post* case, held that the Government had not met that burden. We agree.
>
> The judgment of the Court of Appeals for the District of Columbia Circuit is therefore affirmed. The order of the Court of Appeals for the Second Circuit is reversed, and the case is remanded with directions to enter a judgment affirming the judgment of the District Court for the Southern District of New York. The stays entered June 25, 1971, by the Court are vacated. The judgments shall issue forthwith.

Id. at 714. This "per curiam" consensus immediately collapsed into six concurring opinions and two dissenting opinions, with the final vote being 6–3. The opinions ranged from full-throated opposition to any prior restraints, *see id.* at 714 (Black, J., concurring), to balancing that strongly favored free expression, *see id.* at 727 (Stewart, J., concurring), to concerns that the case was decided too quickly, before all relevant facts were known. *See id.* at 752 (Harlan, J., dissenting). What kinds of facts might be relevant here? What if the information concerned ship or troop movements during World War II? The location of Trident submarines today? We saw above that the Anglo-American idea of freedom of the press rejects any prior restraints on publication even of classified material. In this case, the Supreme Court upholds that principle with vigor. Would it have upheld it with such vigor if the Vietnam War had not been so unpopular in 1971?

4. The First Amendment protects "the freedom of speech." Does it matter what kind of speech we are talking about? The Pentagon Papers contained speech involving the operations of government, which are the core of anything that the First Amendment might involve. Does the protection for speech vary as you move from that core of "political" speech towards the periphery? If the *New York Times* was printing misogynistic pornography, would prior restraints (or after-the-fact punishment) be just as much an

abridgment of free speech as a prior restraint on information about government activity? We will say a bit more about these questions in the next chapter. For the moment, consider the implications of government speech restrictions. A lengthy 1930 tariff act prohibited importation of any "obscene book, pamphlet, paper, writing, advertisement, circular, print, picture, drawing, or other representation, figure, or image on or of paper or other material, or any cast, instrument, or other article which is obscene or immoral." Act of June 17, 1930, ch. 497, § 305(a), 46 Stat. 590, 688. The following case ensued, involving a federal action for forfeiture under the statute of imported copies of James Joyce's novel *Ulysses*.

7. UNITED STATES V. ONE BOOK CALLED "ULYSSES"

5 F. Supp. 182 (S.D.N.Y. 1933)

* * *

II. I have read "Ulysses" once in its entirety and I have read those passages of which the government particularly complains several times. In fact, for many weeks, my spare time has been devoted to the consideration of the decision which my duty would require me to make in this matter.

"Ulysses" is not an easy book to read or to understand. But there has been much written about it, and in order properly to approach the consideration of it it is advisable to read a number of other books which have now become its satellites. The study of "Ulysses" is, therefore, a heavy task.

III. The reputation of "Ulysses" in the literary world, however, warranted my taking such time as was necessary to enable me to satisfy myself as to the intent with which the book was written, for, of course, in any case where a book is claimed to be obscene it must first be determined, whether the intent with which it was written was what is called, according to the usual phrase, pornographic, that is, written for the purpose of exploiting obscenity.

If the conclusion is that the book is pornographic, that is the end of the inquiry and forfeiture must follow.

But in "Ulysses," in spite of its unusual frankness, I do not detect anywhere the leer of the sensualist. I hold, therefore, that it is not pornographic.

IV. In writing 'Ulysses,' Joyce sought to make a serious experiment in a new, if not wholly novel, literary genre. He takes persons of the lower middle class living in Dublin in 1904 and seeks, not only to describe what they did on a certain day early in June of that year as they went about the city bent on their usual occupation, but also to tell what many of them thought about the while.

Joyce has attempted—it seems to me, with astonishing success—to show how the screen of consciousness with its ever-shifting kaleidoscopic impressions carries, as it were on a plastic palimpsest, not only what is in the focus of each man's observation of the actual things about him, but also in a penumbral zone residua of past impressions, some recent and some drawn up by association from the domain of the subconscious. He shows how each of these impressions affect the life and behavior of the character which he is describing.

What he seeks to get is not unlike the result of a double or, if that is possible, a multiple exposure on a cinema film, which would give a clear foreground with a background visible but somewhat blurred and out of focus in varying degrees.

To convey by words an effect which obviously lends itself more appropriately to a graphic technique, accounts, it seems to me, for much of the obscurity which meets a reader of "Ulysses." And it also explains another aspect of the book, which I have further to consider, namely, Joyce's sincerity and his honest effort to show exactly how the minds of his characters operate.

If Joyce did not attempt to be honest in developing the technique which he has adopted in "Ulysses," the result would be psychologically misleading and thus unfaithful to his chosen technique. Such an attitude would be artistically inexcusable.

It is because Joyce has been loyal to his technique and has not funked its necessary implications, but has honestly attempted to tell fully what his characters think about, that he has been the subject of so many attacks and that his purpose has been so often misunderstood and misrepresented. For his attempt sincerely and honestly to realize his objective has required him incidentally to use certain words which are generally considered dirty words and has led at times to what many think is a too poignant preoccupation with sex in the thoughts of his characters.

The words which are criticized as dirty are old Saxon words known to almost all men and, I venture, to many women, and are such words as would be naturally and habitually used, I believe, by the types of folk whose life, physical and mental, Joyce is seeking to describe. In respect of the recurrent emergence of the theme of sex in the minds of his characters, it must always be remembered that his locale was Celtic and his season spring.

Whether or not one enjoys such a technique as Joyce uses is a matter of taste on which disagreement or argument is futile, but to subject that technique to the standards of some other technique seems to me to be little short of absurd.

Accordingly, I hold that "Ulysses" is a sincere and honest book, and I think that the criticisms of it are entirely disposed of by its rationale.

V. Furthermore, "Ulysses" is an amazing tour de force when one considers the success which has been in the main achieved with such a difficult objective as Joyce set for himself. As I have stated, "Ulysses" is not an easy book to read. It is brilliant and dull, intelligible and obscure, by turns. In many places it seems to me to be disgusting, but although it contains, as I have mentioned above, many words usually considered dirty, I have not found anything that I consider to be dirt for dirt's sake. Each word of the book contributes like a bit of mosaic to the detail of the picture which Joyce is seeking to construct for his readers.

If one does not wish to associate with such folk as Joyce describes, that is one's own choice. In order to avoid indirect contact with them one may not wish to read "Ulysses"; that is quite understandable. But when such a great artist in words, as Joyce undoubtedly is, seeks to draw a true picture of the lower middle class in a European city, ought it to be impossible for the American public legally to see that picture?

To answer this question it is not sufficient merely to find, as I have found above, that Joyce did not write "Ulysses" with what is commonly called pornographic intent, I must endeavor to apply a more objective standard to his book in order to determine its effect in the result, irrespective of the intent with which it was written.

VI. The statute under which the libel is filed only denounces, in so far as we are here concerned, the importation into the United States from any foreign country of "any obscene book." It does not marshal against books the spectrum of condemnatory adjectives found, commonly, in laws dealing with matters of this kind. I am, therefore, only required to determine whether "Ulysses" is obscene within the legal definition of that word.

The meaning of the word "obscene" as legally defined by the courts is: Tending to stir the sex impulses or to lead to sexually impure and lustful thoughts.

Whether a particular book would tend to excite such impulses and thoughts must be tested by the court's opinion as to its effect on a person with average sex instincts—what the French would call *l'homme moyen sensuel*—who plays, in this branch of legal inquiry, the same role of hypothetical reagent as does the "reasonable man" in the law of torts and "the man learned in the art" on questions of invention in patent law.

The risk involved in the use of such a reagent arises from the inherent tendency of the trier of facts, however fair he may intend to be, to make his reagent too much subservient to his own idiosyncrasies. Here, I have attempted to avoid this, if possible, and to make my reagent herein more objective than he might otherwise be, by adopting the following course:

After I had made my decision in regard to the aspect of "Ulysses," now under consideration, I checked my impressions with two friends of mine who in my opinion answered to the above-stated requirement for my reagent.

These literary assessors—as I might properly describe them—were called on separately, and neither knew that I was consulting the other. They are men whose opinion on literature and life I value most highly. They had both read "Ulysses," and, of course, were wholly unconnected with this cause.

Without letting either of my assessors know what my decision was, I gave to each of them the legal definition of obscene and asked each whether in his opinion "Ulysses" was obscene within that definition.

I was interested to find that they both agreed with my opinion: That reading "Ulysses" in its entirety, as a book must be read on such a test as this, did not tend to excite sexual impulses or lustful thoughts, but that its net effect on them was only that of a somewhat tragic and very powerful commentary on the inner lives of men and women.

It is only with the normal person that the law is concerned. Such a test as I have described, therefore, is the only proper test of obscenity in the case of a book like "Ulysses" which is a sincere and serious attempt to devise a new literary method for the observation and description of mankind.

I am quite aware that owing to some of its scenes "Ulysses" is a rather strong draught to ask some sensitive, though normal, persons to take. But my considered opinion, after long reflection, if that, whilst in many places the effect of "Ulysses" on the reader undoubtedly is somewhat emetic, nowhere does it tend to be an aphrodisiac.

"Ulysses" may, therefore, be admitted into the United States.

NOTES AND QUESTIONS

1. Do these seem like the kinds of questions that judges should be asking and answering? That prosecutors should be asking and answering? Would your answer be different if the statute said "offensive" rather than "obscene"?

2. The U.S. Attorney for the Southern District of New York appealed the District Court's decision to the U.S. Court of Appeals for the Second Circuit, where the case was heard by a three-judge panel that included Judges Learned Hand, Augustus N. Hand, and Chief Judge Martin Manton. By a two to one vote, the Second Circuit upheld the District Court's ruling, over the dissent of Chief Judge Manton. *See* 72 F.2d 705 (2d Cir. 1934).

3. *United States v. One Book called "Ulysses"* is a cringing illustration of how the criminal law enforcement process can go badly awry when allegedly lewd and lascivious expression is subject to prosecution. This problem is illustrated in other constitutional democracies as well. LADY CHATTERLEY'S LOVER was banned in India and in Japan by censors who thought the famous novel was lewd, lascivious, and pornographic.

4. The U.S. Supreme Court addressed the question of obscenity in 1973 in *Miller v. California*, 413 U.S. 15 (1973), which raised the question of whether materials mailed to individuals who had not requested them were "obscene," and thus unprotected by the First Amendment, or pornographic, and thus protected by the First Amendment. The Supreme Court held:

> The basic guidelines for the trier of fact must be: (a) whether "the average person, applying contemporary community standards" would find that the work, taken as a whole, appeals to the prurient interest, (b) whether the work depicts or describes, in a patently offensive way, sexual conduct specifically defined by the applicable state law; and (c) whether the work, taken as a whole, lacks serious literary, artistic, political, or scientific value * * *.
>
> We emphasize that it is not our function to propose regulatory schemes for the States. That must await their concrete legislative efforts * * *.
>
> * * *
>
> Under a National Constitution, fundamental First Amendment limitations on the powers of the States do not vary from community to community, but this does not mean that there are, or should or can be, fixed, uniform national standards of precisely what appeals to the "prurient interest" or is "patently offensive." These are essentially questions of fact, and our Nation is simply too big and too diverse for this Court to reasonably expect that such standards could be articulated for all 50 States in a single formulation, even assuming the prerequisite consensus exists * * *.

Id. at 24–25, 30.

5. Consider now a case that involves the kind of political speech that is at the core of the First Amendment.

8. CITIZENS UNITED V. FEDERAL ELECTION COMMISSION

558 U.S. 310 (2010)

■ JUSTICE KENNEDY delivered the opinion of the Court.

Federal law prohibits corporations and unions from using their general treasury funds to make independent expenditures for speech defined as an "electioneering communication" or for speech expressly advocating the election or defeat of a candidate. 2 U.S.C. § 441b. Limits on electioneering communications were upheld in *McConnell v. Federal Election Comm'n,* 540 U.S. 93, 203–209 (2003). The holding of *McConnell* rested to a large extent on an earlier case, *Austin v. Michigan Chamber of Commerce,* 494 U.S. 652 (1990). *Austin* had held that political speech may be banned based on the speaker's corporate identity.

In this case we are asked to reconsider *Austin* and, in effect, *McConnell.* It has been noted that "*Austin* was a significant departure from ancient First Amendment principles," *Federal Election Comm'n v. Wisconsin Right to Life, Inc.,* 551 U.S. 449, 490 (2007) *(WRTL)* (SCALIA, J., concurring in part and concurring in judgment). We agree with that conclusion and hold that *stare decisis* does not compel the continued acceptance of *Austin.* The Government may regulate corporate political speech through disclaimer and disclosure requirements, but it may not suppress that speech altogether. We turn to the case now before us.

Citizens United is a nonprofit corporation * * *.

Citizens United has an annual budget of about $12 million. Most of its funds are from donations by individuals; but, in addition, it accepts a small portion of its funds from for-profit corporations.

In January 2008, Citizens United released a film entitled *Hillary: The Movie.* We refer to the film as *Hillary.* It is a 90-minute documentary about then-Senator Hillary Clinton, who was a candidate in the Democratic Party's 2008 Presidential primary elections. *Hillary* mentions Senator Clinton by name and depicts interviews with political commentators and other persons, most of them quite critical of Senator Clinton. *Hillary* was released in theaters and on DVD, but Citizens United wanted to increase distribution by making it available through video-on-demand.

* * *

To implement the proposal, Citizens United was prepared to pay for the video-on-demand; and to promote the film, it produced two 10-second ads and one 30-second ad for *Hillary.* Each ad includes a short (and, in our view, pejorative) statement about Senator Clinton, followed by the name of the movie and the movie's Web site address. Citizens United desired to promote the video-on-demand offering by running advertisements on broadcast and cable television.

Before the Bipartisan Campaign Reform Act of 2002 (BCRA), federal law prohibited—and still does prohibit—corporations and unions from using general treasury funds to make direct contributions to candidates or independent expenditures that expressly advocate the election or defeat of a candidate, through any form of media, in connection with certain qualified federal elections. BCRA § 203 amended § 441b to prohibit any "electioneering communication" as well. An electioneering communication is defined as "any broadcast, cable, or satellite communication" that "refers to a clearly identified candidate for Federal office" and is made within 30 days of a primary or 60 days of a general election * * * Corporations and unions are barred from using their general treasury funds for express advocacy or electioneering communications. They may establish, however, a "separate segregated fund" (known as a political action committee, or PAC) for these purposes. The moneys received by the segregated fund are limited to donations from stockholders and employees of the corporation or, in the case of unions, members of the union.

Citizens United wanted to make *Hillary* available through video-on-demand within 30 days of the 2008 primary elections. It feared, however, that both the film and the ads would be covered by § 441b's ban on corporate-funded independent expenditures, thus subjecting the corporation to civil and criminal penalties under § 437g. In December 2007, Citizens United sought declaratory and injunctive relief against the FEC. It argued that (1) § 441b is unconstitutional as applied to *Hillary;* and (2) BCRA's disclaimer and disclosure requirements, BCRA §§ 201 and 311, are unconstitutional as applied to *Hillary* and to the three ads for the movie.

* * *

The First Amendment provides that "Congress shall make no law . . . abridging the freedom of speech." Laws enacted to control or suppress speech may operate at different points in the speech process. The following are just a few examples of restrictions that have been attempted at different stages of the speech process—all laws found to be invalid: restrictions requiring a permit at the outset, *Watchtower Bible & Tract Soc. of N.Y., Inc. v. Village of Stratton,* 536 U.S. 150, 153 (2002); imposing a burden by impounding proceeds on receipts or royalties, *Simon & Schuster, Inc. v. Members of N.Y. State Crime Victims Bd.,* 502 U.S. 105, 108, 123 (1991); seeking to exact a cost after the speech occurs, *New York Times Co. v. Sullivan,* 376 U.S., at 267; and subjecting the speaker to criminal penalties, *Brandenburg v. Ohio,* 395 U.S. 444, 445 (1969) *(per curiam).*

The law before us is an outright ban, backed by criminal sanctions. Section 441b makes it a felony for all corporations—including nonprofit advocacy corporations—either to expressly advocate the election or defeat of candidates or to broadcast electioneering communications within 30 days of a primary election and 60 days of a general election. Thus, the following acts would all be felonies under § 441b: The Sierra Club runs an ad, within the crucial phase of 60 days before the general election, that exhorts the public to disapprove of a Congressman who favors logging in national forests; the National Rifle Association publishes a book urging the public to vote for the challenger because the incumbent U.S. Senator supports a handgun ban; and the American Civil Liberties Union creates a Web site telling the public to vote for a Presidential candidate in light of that candidate's defense of free speech. These prohibitions are classic examples of censorship.

* * *

Speech is an essential mechanism of democracy, for it is the means to hold officials accountable to the people. The right of citizens to inquire, to hear, to speak, and to use information to reach consensus is a precondition to enlightened self-government and a necessary means to protect it. The First Amendment " 'has its fullest and most urgent application' to speech uttered during a campaign for political office."

For these reasons, political speech must prevail against laws that would suppress it, whether by design or inadvertence. Laws that burden political speech are "subject to strict scrutiny," which requires the Government to prove that the restriction "furthers a compelling interest and is narrowly tailored to achieve that interest." * * *

Premised on mistrust of governmental power, the First Amendment stands against attempts to disfavor certain subjects or viewpoints. See, *e.g., United States v. Playboy Entertainment Group, Inc.,* 529 U.S. 803, 813 (2000) (striking down content-based restriction). Prohibited, too, are restrictions distinguishing among different speakers, allowing speech by some but not others. See *First Nat. Bank of Boston v. Bellotti,* 435 U.S. 765, 784 (1978). As instruments to censor, these categories are interrelated: Speech restrictions based on the identity of the speaker are all too often simply a means to control content.

Quite apart from the purpose or effect of regulating content, moreover, the Government may commit a constitutional wrong when by law it identifies certain preferred speakers. By taking the right to speak from some and giving it to others, the Government deprives the disadvantaged person or class of the right to use speech to strive to establish worth, standing, and respect for the speaker's voice. The Government may not by these means deprive the public of the right and privilege to determine for itself what speech and speakers are worthy of consideration. The First Amendment protects speech and speaker, and the ideas that flow from each.

The Court has upheld a narrow class of speech restrictions that operate to the disadvantage of certain persons, but these rulings were based on an interest in allowing governmental entities to perform their functions. See, *e.g., Bethel School Dist. No. 403 v. Fraser,* 478 U.S. 675, 683 (1986) (protecting the "function of public school education"); *Jones v. North Carolina Prisoners' Labor Union, Inc.,* 433 U.S. 119, 129 (1977) (furthering "the legitimate penological objectives of the corrections system" (internal quotation marks omitted)); *Parker v. Levy,* 417 U.S. 733, 759 (1974) (ensuring "the capacity of the Government to discharge its [military] responsibilities" (internal quotation marks omitted)); *Civil Service Comm'n v. Letter Carriers,* 413 U.S. 548, 557 (1973) ("[F]ederal service should depend upon meritorious performance rather than political service"). The corporate independent expenditures at issue in this case, however, would not interfere with governmental functions, so these cases are inapposite. These precedents stand only for the proposition that there are certain governmental functions that cannot operate without some restrictions on particular kinds of speech. By contrast, it is inherent in the nature of the political process that voters must be free to obtain information from diverse sources in order to determine how to cast their votes. At least before *Austin,* the Court had not allowed the exclusion of a class of speakers from the general public dialogue.

We find no basis for the proposition that, in the context of political speech, the Government may impose restrictions on certain disfavored speakers. Both history and logic lead us to this conclusion.

* * *

The Court is * * * confronted with conflicting lines of precedent: a pre-*Austin* line that forbids restrictions on political speech based on the speaker's corporate identity and a post-*Austin* line that permits them * * *

* * *

There is simply no support for the view that the First Amendment, as originally understood, would permit the suppression of political speech by media corporations. The Framers may not have anticipated modern business and media corporations. Yet television networks and major newspapers owned by media corporations have become the most important means of mass communication in modern times. The First Amendment was certainly not understood to condone the suppression of political speech in society's most salient media * * *. The great debates between the Federalists and the Anti-Federalists over our founding document were published and expressed in the most important means of mass communication of that era—newspapers owned by individuals. At the founding, speech was open, comprehensive, and vital to society's definition of itself; there were no limits on the sources of speech and knowledge * * *.

Austin interferes with the "open marketplace" of ideas protected by the First Amendment. It permits the Government to ban the political speech of millions of associations of citizens * * *.

The censorship we now confront is vast in its reach. The Government has "muffle[d] the voices that best represent the most significant segments of the economy." *McConnell, supra,* at 257–258 (opinion of SCALIA, J.) * * *. Factions will necessarily form in our Republic, but the remedy of "destroying the liberty" of some factions is "worse than the disease." The Federalist No. 10, p. 130 (B. Wright ed.1961) (J. Madison). Factions should be checked by permitting them all to speak and by entrusting the people to judge what is true and what is false.

* * *

* * * [T]he Government falls back on the argument that corporate political speech can be banned in order to prevent corruption or its appearance. In *Buckley* [*v. Valeo,* 424 U.S. 1 (1976)], the Court found this interest "sufficiently important" to allow limits on contributions but did not extend that reasoning to expenditure limits. 424 U.S., at 25. When *Buckley* examined an expenditure ban, it found "that the governmental interest in preventing corruption and the appearance of corruption [was] inadequate to justify [the ban] on independent expenditures." *Id.,* at 45.

* * *

When *Buckley* identified a sufficiently important governmental interest in preventing corruption or the appearance of corruption, that interest was limited to *quid pro quo* corruption. The fact that speakers may have influence over or access to elected officials does not mean that these officials are corrupt * * *.

* * *

Austin is overruled, so it provides no basis for allowing the Government to limit corporate independent expenditures. As the Government appears to concede, overruling *Austin* "effectively invalidate[s] not only BCRA Section 203, but also 2 U.S.C. 441b's prohibition on the use of corporate treasury funds for express advocacy." Section 441b's restrictions on corporate independent expenditures are therefore invalid and cannot be applied to *Hillary*.

Given our conclusion we are further required to overrule the part of *McConnell* that upheld BCRA § 203's extension of § 441b's restrictions on corporate independent expenditures. The *McConnell* Court relied on the antidistortion interest recognized in *Austin* to uphold a greater restriction on speech than the restriction upheld in *Austin,* and we have found this interest unconvincing and insufficient. This part of *McConnell* is now overruled.

* * *

The judgment of the District Court is reversed with respect to the constitutionality of 2 U.S.C. § 441b's restrictions on corporate independent expenditures. The judgment is affirmed with respect to BCRA's disclaimer and disclosure requirements. The case is remanded for further proceedings consistent with this opinion.

■ CHIEF JUSTICE ROBERTS, with whom JUSTICE ALITO joins, concurring. [Omitted.]

■ JUSTICE SCALIA, with whom JUSTICE ALITO joins, and with whom JUSTICE THOMAS joins in part, concurring.

* * *

* * * The [First] Amendment is written in terms of "speech," not speakers. Its text offers no foothold for excluding any category of speaker, from single individuals to partnerships of individuals, to unincorporated associations of individuals, to incorporated associations of individuals—and the dissent offers no evidence about the original meaning of the text to support any such exclusion. We are therefore simply left with the question whether the speech at issue in this case is "speech" covered by the First Amendment. No one says otherwise. A documentary film critical of a potential Presidential candidate is core political speech, and its nature as such does not change simply because it was funded by a corporation. Nor does the character of that funding produce any reduction whatever in the "inherent worth of the speech" and "its capacity for informing the public," *First Nat. Bank of Boston v. Bellotti,* 435 U.S. 765, 777 (1978). Indeed, to exclude or impede corporate speech is to muzzle the principal agents of the modern free economy. We should celebrate rather than condemn the addition of this speech to the public debate.

■ JUSTICE STEVENS, with whom JUSTICE GINSBURG, JUSTICE BREYER, and JUSTICE SOTOMAYOR join, concurring in part and dissenting in part.

* * *

The basic premise underlying the Court's ruling is its iteration, and constant reiteration, of the proposition that the First Amendment bars regulatory distinctions based on a speaker's identity, including its "identity" as a corporation. While that glittering generality has rhetorical appeal, it is not a correct statement of the law. Nor does it tell us when a corporation may engage in electioneering that some of its shareholders oppose. It does not even resolve the specific question whether Citizens United may be required to finance some of its messages with the money in its PAC. The conceit that corporations must be treated identically to natural persons in the political sphere is not only inaccurate but also inadequate to justify the Court's disposition of this case.

In the context of election to public office, the distinction between corporate and human speakers is significant. Although they make enormous contributions to our society, corporations are not actually members of it. They cannot vote or run for office. Because they may be managed and controlled by nonresidents, their interests may conflict in fundamental respects with the interests of eligible voters. The financial resources, legal structure, and instrumental orientation of corporations raise legitimate concerns about their role in the electoral process. Our lawmakers have a compelling constitutional basis, if not also a democratic duty, to take measures designed to guard against the potentially deleterious effects of corporate spending in local and national races.

* * *

"Our jurisprudence over the past 216 years has rejected an absolutist interpretation" of the First Amendment. The First Amendment provides that "Congress shall make no law . . . abridging the freedom of speech, or of the press."

Apart perhaps from measures designed to protect the press, that text might seem to permit no distinctions of any kind. Yet in a variety of contexts, we have held that speech can be regulated differentially on account of the speaker's identity, when identity is understood in categorical or institutional terms. The Government routinely places special restrictions on the speech rights of students, prisoners, members of the Armed Forces, foreigners, and its own employees. When such restrictions are justified by a legitimate governmental interest, they do not necessarily raise constitutional problems * * *.

* * * It is fair to say that our First Amendment doctrine has "frowned on" certain identity-based distinctions, particularly those that may reflect invidious discrimination or preferential treatment of a politically powerful group. But it is simply incorrect to suggest that we have prohibited all legislative distinctions based on identity or content. Not even close.

* * *

On numerous occasions we have recognized Congress' legitimate interest in preventing the money that is spent on elections from exerting an " 'undue influence on an officeholder's judgment' " and from creating " 'the appearance of such influence,' " beyond the sphere of *quid pro quo* relationships * * *.

* * *

■ JUSTICE THOMAS, concurring in part and dissenting in part. [Omitted.]

NOTES AND QUESTIONS

1. As is often true in this book, considerations of space prevent us from giving fair treatment to any of the opinions in this case, which collectively consume 175 pages of the United States Reports. Suffice it to say that the dissenters in this case focus on the fact that the speech limited is by corporations. *The New York Times, The Washington Post, Fox News, CNN,* and *MSNBC* are all also corporations, and, if corporate speech by *Citizens United* can be regulated, so too can corporate speech by every major news organization in the United States! It is quite possible, as it happens, that the founding generation would have agreed with the dissent, because eighteenth-century corporations, in an era nearly a century before general incorporation laws, were arms of the government. *See supra* pages 860–861. A more interesting question, given the economic and legal structure of modern corporations, might be how the founding generation would have viewed political speech by, for example, partnerships.

2. Under current doctrine, the government can limit speech if it has a "compelling" reason for doing so. Was there a compelling reason for forbidding Citizens United from showing or advertising its movie within thirty days of an election? What might that reason be? We have had to leave out *extensive* discussion of that question by the majority and dissenting justices.

3. Everyone agrees that, at least on some occasions, the identity of the speaker matters for First Amendment purposes—as the dissent points out, just think of students or prisoners. What considerations make the speaker's identity relevant? Do those considerations apply to Citizens United and organizations like it?

C. THE RIGHT TO PETITION

Congress shall make no law * * * abridging * * * the right of the people peaceably to assemble, and to petition the Government for a redress of grievances.

The Petition Clause—or perhaps the Assembly and Petition Clause—is the First Amendment's poor relation. There is extensive caselaw and commentary on the Religion and Speech Clauses, but very little on petitioning and assembly.

The right to petition the government has a long history. A millennium ago, it was a vital tool of communication between rulers and ruled. *See* Gary Lawson & Guy Seidman, *Downsizing the Right to Petition,* 93 NW. U.L. REV. 739, 743–47 (1999). As legislatures waxed and monarchs waned, one could imagine the principle of representation replacing petitioning, but instead petitioning expanded from monarchs to legislatures, both in England and later in colonial America. *See id.* at 747–50. By the late seventeenth century, the right to petition without fear of retribution was important enough to be included in the 1689 Bill of Rights: "it is the right of the subjects to petition the king, and all commitments and prosecutions for such petitioning are illegal." A century later, on the eve of the revolution, five colonies expressly protected the right to petition. *See* Julie M. Spanbauer, *The First Amendment Right to Petition Government for a Redress of Grievances: Cut from a Different Cloth,* HASTINGS CONST. L.Q. 15, 28 (1993). It is no surprise that the right was included in the Bill of Rights.

On its face, the Petition Clause assures only that citizens will have a mechanism for communicating grievances to the government. The clause says nothing about what, if anything, the government will do in response to petitions. Does the First Amendment guarantee you a response from the government when you send in a petition?

As is often the case, the answer depends on what one means by "the government." If one is petitioning a court for a redress of grievances by filing a lawsuit within the court's jurisdiction, of course one is entitled to a response (even if the response is "case dismissed," followed by Rule 11 sanctions). That result stems, not from the Petition Clause, but from the grant of the "judicial Power." The right to a response—even a negative or dismissive one—from the courts to a lawsuit existed in 1789, before the Petition Clause was ratified. As with most of the Bill of Rights, the Petition Clause is largely declaratory of pre-existing rights. If the petition is sent to the President, there is no obligation that the President respond to you. What about Congress? Does Congress have to respond to petitions? *Compare* James E. Pfander, *Sovereign Immunity and the Right to Petition: Toward a First Amendment Right to Pursue Judicial Claims Against the Government,* 91 Nw. U.L. Rev. 899, 905 n.22 (1997) ("As a matter of history, most scholars agree that the right to petition includes a right to some sort of considered response") *with* Lawson & Seidman, *supra,* at 759 ("The Constitution * * * provides no support for the claim that Congress must consider and respond to petitions. On the contrary, it contains overwhelming evidence against such a claim."). Could Congress use its power to make its own rules to *forbid* itself from responding to petitions?

The last question is not hypothetical. In the 1830s, Congress was inundated with abolitionist petitions urging it to do all within its power to end slavery. Under pressure from southern members, the House in 1840 adopted what has come to be called the "gag rule," which was a resolution stating "[t]hat no petition, memorial, resolution, or other paper praying the abolition of slavery in the District of Columbia, or any State or Territory, or the slave trade between the States or Territories of the United States in which it now exists, shall be received by this House, or entertained in any way whatever." 26 CONG. GLOBE 150 (1840). Did this "gag rule" violate the Petition Clause? Even if Congress does not have an obligation to respond to petitions, does it at least have an obligation to receive and consider them? Whatever the answer, Congress clearly cannot prevent people from sending in petitions; that would be a direct violation of the Petition Clause.

What if a petition contains libelous matter? Does the Petition Clause shield the *content* of petitions from any kind of legal scrutiny? The Supreme Court has said "no." *See McDonald v. Smith,* 472 U.S. 479 (1985) (statements are not privileged against libel actions simply because they are in a letter to the President).

The "right of the people peaceably to assemble" has received even less attention than has the right to petition. The clause specifies no particular purpose to which assembly must be directed in order to receive constitutional protection, so presumably assembly is protected for political, religious, and social purposes alike. Does that mean that governments cannot require licenses for parades or demonstrations on government property? That antidiscrimination laws compelling associations violate the Constitution? As is true of many Bill of Rights provisions, most of the caselaw in this area has involved state and local governments. *See, e.g., Boy Scouts of America v. Dale,* 530 U.S. 640 (2000); *Roberts v. United States Jaycees,* 468 U.S. 609 (1984).

[Assignment 49]

II. THE SECOND AMENDMENT

A well regulated Militia, being necessary to the security of a free State, the right of the people to keep and bear Arms, shall not be infringed.

The right to keep and bear arms is deeply rooted in American history and tradition. It first appears as a right of all Protestant Englishmen to keep and bear arms in the English Bill of Rights of 1689. When the U.S. Constitution was ratified in 1791, four states—Massachusetts, North Carolina, New York, Pennsylvania, and Vermont—had explicit constitutional clauses recognizing this right. Moreover, Pennsylvania and Vermont explicitly recognized the right to keep and bear arms for one's own defense and not merely as a part of the militia. Forty-four percent of the population in 1791 lived in these States. Steven G. Calabresi, Sarah E. Agudo, and Kathryn L. Dore, *States Bills of Rights in 1787 and 1791: What Individual Rights are Really Deeply Rooted in American History and Tradition?,* 85 SO. CAL. L. REV. 1451, 1485–1487.

This, however, does not fully capture the Founding era commitment to the right to self-defense. Seven States in 1791 had "Lockean" clauses in their state constitutions, which in many instances protected a person's presumptive right to defend themselves with firearms. Thus, the Massachusetts Constitution of 1780 said (and still says) in Article I that:

> All men are born free and equal, and have certain natural, essential, and unalienable rights; among which may be reckoned the right of enjoying *and defending* their lives and liberties; that of acquiring, possessing, *and protecting property*; in fine, that of seeking and obtaining their safety and happiness.

MASS. CONST. OF 1780 art. I (emphasis added). Over time, the American people made it very clear that the right to keep and bear arms in self-defense is a fundamental liberty. In 1868, twenty-two state constitutions had keep-and-bear-arms clauses and 61% of the public lived in those states. Steven Gow Calabresi, et al., *Individual Rights Under State Constitutions in 2018: What Rights are Deeply Rooted in a Modern-Day Consensus of the States?*, 94 NOTRE DAME L. REV. 83 (2018). Twelve States in 1868 explicitly protected an individual's right to bear arms for his own defense. *Id.* Twenty-four States had "Lockean" Clauses like Article I of the Massachusetts Constitution of 1780, which recognized a right to defend life and liberty and to protect property.

Forty-four States in 2018, in which 74.2% of the U.S. population currently lives, have keep-and-bear-arms clauses and, of these, at least thirty-three Sates protect the right to keep and bear arms as an individual right. *Id.*, at 80. This does not even include the thirty-nine States today with "Lockean" Clauses, some of which protect the right to defend life and liberty and to protect property. It follows that the right to keep and bear arms for one's own defense is deeply rooted in American history, tradition, and in a modern-day consensus of the fifty state constitutions. Does that necessarily mean that the Second Amendment guarantees the right to keep and bear weapons for self-defense? The leading Supreme Court decision on this question—a relatively rare question of first impression in the twenty-first century—is reproduced below:

District of Columbia v. Heller

554 U.S. 570 (2008)

■ JUSTICE SCALIA delivered the opinion of the Court.

We consider whether a District of Columbia prohibition on the possession of usable handguns in the home violates the Second Amendment to the Constitution.

The District of Columbia generally prohibits the possession of handguns. It is a crime to carry an unregistered firearm, and the registration of handguns is prohibited. Wholly apart from that prohibition, no person may carry a handgun without a license, but the chief of police may issue licenses for 1-year periods. District of Columbia law also requires residents to keep their lawfully owned firearms, such as registered long guns, "unloaded and dissembled or bound by a trigger lock or similar device" unless they are located in a place of business or are being used for lawful recreational activities.

Respondent Dick Heller is a D. C. special police officer authorized to carry a handgun while on duty at the Thurgood Marshall Judiciary Building. He applied for a registration certificate for a handgun that he wished to keep at home, but the District refused. He thereafter filed a lawsuit in the Federal District Court for the District of Columbia seeking, on Second Amendment grounds, to enjoin the city from enforcing the bar on the registration of handguns, the licensing requirement insofar as it prohibits the carrying of a firearm in the home without a license, and the trigger-lock requirement insofar as it prohibits the use of "functional firearms within the home." * * *

* * *

The Second Amendment provides: "A well regulated Militia, being necessary to the security of a free State, the right of the people to keep and bear Arms, shall not be infringed." In interpreting this text, we are guided by the principle that "[t]he Constitution was written to be understood by the voters; its words and phrases were used in their normal and ordinary as distinguished from technical meaning." *United States* v. *Sprague*, 282 U. S. 716, 731 (1931). Normal meaning may of course include an idiomatic meaning, but it excludes secret or technical meanings that would not have been known to ordinary citizens in the founding generation.

The two sides in this case have set out very different interpretations of the Amendment. Petitioners and today's dissenting Justices believe that it protects only the right to possess and carry a firearm in connection with militia service. See Brief for Petitioners 11–12; *post*, at 636–37 (STEVENS, J., dissenting). Respondent argues that it protects an individual right to possess a firearm unconnected with service in a militia, and to use that arm for traditionally lawful purposes, such as self-defense within the home. See Brief for Respondent 2–4.

The Second Amendment is naturally divided into two parts: its prefatory clause and its operative clause. The former does not limit the latter grammatically, but rather announces a purpose. The Amendment could be rephrased, "Because a well regulated Militia is necessary to the security of a free State, the right of the people to keep and bear Arms shall not be infringed." See J. Tiffany, A Treatise on Government and Constitutional Law § 585, p. 394 (1867); Brief for Professors of Linguistics and English as *Amici Curiae* 3 (hereinafter Linguists' Brief). Although this structure of the Second Amendment is unique in our Constitution, other legal documents of the founding era, particularly individual-rights provisions of state constitutions, commonly included a prefatory statement of purpose. See generally Volokh, The Commonplace Second Amendment, 73 N. Y. U. L. Rev. 793, 814–821 (1998).

Logic demands that there be a link between the stated purpose and the command. The Second Amendment would be nonsensical if it read, "A well regulated Militia, being necessary to the security of a free State, the right of the people to petition for redress of grievances shall not be infringed." That requirement of logical connection may cause a prefatory clause to resolve an ambiguity in the operative clause * * *. But apart from that clarifying function, a prefatory clause does not limit or expand the scope of the operative clause * * *. Therefore, while we will begin our textual analysis with the operative clause, we will return to the prefatory clause to ensure that our reading of the operative clause is consistent with the announced purpose.

1. **Operative Clause.**

a. **"Right of the People."** The first salient feature of the operative clause is that it codifies a "right of the people." The unamended Constitution and the Bill of Rights use the phrase "right of the people" two other times, in the First Amendment's Assembly-and-Petition Clause and in the Fourth Amendment's Search-and-Seizure Clause. The Ninth Amendment uses very similar terminology ("The enumeration in the Constitution, of certain rights, shall not be construed to deny or disparage others retained by the people"). All three of these instances unambiguously refer to individual rights, not "collective" rights, or rights that may be exercised only through participation in some corporate body.

Three provisions of the Constitution refer to "the people" in a context other than "rights"—the famous preamble ("We the people"), § 2 of Article I (providing that "the people" will choose members of the House), and the Tenth Amendment (providing that those powers not given the Federal Government remain with "the States" or "the people"). Those provisions arguably refer to "the people" acting collectively—but they deal with the exercise or reservation of powers, not rights. Nowhere else in the Constitution does a "right" attributed to "the people" refer to anything other than an individual right.

What is more, in all six other provisions of the Constitution that mention "the people," the term unambiguously refers to all members of the political community, not an unspecified subset. As we said in *United States* v. *Verdugo-Urquidez*, 494 U. S. 259, 265 (1990):

> " '[T]he people' seems to have been a term of art employed in select parts of the Constitution. . . . [Its uses] sugges[t] that 'the people' protected by the Fourth Amendment, and by the First and Second Amendments, and to whom rights and powers are reserved in the Ninth and Tenth Amendments, refers to a class of persons who are part of a national community or who have otherwise developed sufficient connection with this country to be considered part of that community."

This contrasts markedly with the phrase "the militia" in the prefatory clause. As we will describe below, the "militia" in colonial America consisted of a subset of "the people"—those who were male, able bodied, and within a certain age range. Reading the Second Amendment as protecting only the right to "keep and bear Arms" in an organized militia therefore fits poorly with the operative clause's description of the holder of that right as "the people."

We start therefore with a strong presumption that the Second Amendment right is exercised individually and belongs to all Americans.

b. **"Keep and bear Arms."** We move now from the holder of the right—"the people"—to the substance of the right: "to keep and bear Arms."

Before addressing the verbs "keep" and "bear," we interpret their object: "Arms." The 18th-century meaning is no different from the meaning today. The 1773 edition of Samuel Johnson's dictionary defined "arms" as "weapons of offence, or armour of defence." 1 Dictionary of the English Language 106 (4th ed.) (hereinafter Johnson). Timothy Cunningham's important 1771 legal dictionary defined "arms" as "any thing that a man wears for his defence, or takes into his hands, or useth in wrath to cast at or strike another." 1 A New and Complete Law Dictionary (1771); see also N. Webster, American Dictionary of the English Language (1828) (reprinted 1989) (hereinafter Webster) (similar).

The term was applied, then as now, to weapons that were not specifically designed for military use and were not employed in a military capacity * * *.

Some have made the argument, bordering on the frivolous, that only those arms in existence in the 18th century are protected by the Second Amendment. We do not interpret constitutional rights that way. Just as the First Amendment protects modern forms of communications, *e.g.*, *Reno* v. *American Civil Liberties Union*, 521 U. S. 844, 849 (1997), and the Fourth Amendment applies to modern forms of search, *e.g.*, *Kyllo* v. *United States*, 533 U. S. 27, 35–36 (2001), the Second Amendment extends, prima facie, to all instruments that constitute bearable arms, even those that were not in existence at the time of the founding.

We turn to the phrases "keep arms" and "bear arms." Johnson defined "keep" as, most relevantly, "[t]o retain; not to lose," and "[t]o have in custody." Johnson 1095. Webster defined it as "[t]o hold; to retain in one's power or possession." No party has apprised us of an idiomatic meaning of "keep Arms." Thus, the most natural reading of "keep Arms" in the Second Amendment is to "have weapons."

* * *

At the time of the founding, as now, to "bear" meant to "carry." See Johnson 161; Webster; T. Sheridan, A Complete Dictionary of the English Language (1796); 2 Oxford English Dictionary 20 (2d ed. 1989) (hereinafter Oxford). When used with "arms," however, the term has a meaning that refers to carrying for a particular purpose—confrontation * * *. Although the phrase implies that the carrying of the weapon is for the purpose of "offensive or defensive action," it in no way connotes participation in a structured military organization.

From our review of founding-era sources, we conclude that this natural meaning was also the meaning that "bear arms" had in the 18th century. In numerous instances, "bear arms" was unambiguously used to refer to the carrying of weapons outside of an organized militia. The most prominent examples are those most relevant to the Second Amendment: Nine state constitutional provisions written in the 18th century or the first two decades of the 19th, which enshrined a right of citizens to "bear arms in defense of themselves and the state" or "bear arms in defense of himself and the state." It is clear from those formulations that "bear arms" did not refer only to carrying a weapon in an organized military unit. Justice James Wilson interpreted the Pennsylvania Constitution's arms-bearing right, for example, as a recognition of the natural right of defense "of one's person or house"—what he called the law of "self preservation." 2 Collected Works of James Wilson 1142, and n. x (K. Hall & M. Hall eds. 2007) (citing Pa. Const., Art. IX, § 21 (1790)). That was also the interpretation of those state constitutional provisions adopted by pre-Civil War state courts. These provisions demonstrate—again, in the most analogous linguistic context—that "bear arms" was not limited to the carrying of arms in a militia.

The phrase "bear Arms" also had at the time of the founding an idiomatic meaning that was significantly different from its natural meaning: "to serve as a soldier, do military service, fight" or "to wage war." See Linguists' Brief 18; *post*, at 146 (STEVENS, J., dissenting). But it *unequivocally* bore that idiomatic meaning only when followed by the preposition "against," which was in turn followed by the target of the hostilities. See 2 Oxford 21. (That is how, for example, our Declaration of Independence ¶ 28, used the phrase: "He has constrained our fellow Citizens taken Captive on the high Seas to bear Arms against their Country . . . .") * * *.

In any event, the meaning of "bear arms" that petitioners and JUSTICE STEVENS propose is *not even* the (sometimes) idiomatic meaning. Rather, they manufacture a hybrid definition, whereby "bear arms" connotes the actual carrying of arms (and therefore is not really an idiom) but only in the service of an organized militia. No dictionary has ever adopted that definition, and we have been apprised of no source that indicates that it carried that meaning at the time of the founding. But it is easy to see why petitioners and the dissent are driven to the hybrid definition. Giving "bear Arms" its idiomatic meaning would cause the protected right to consist of the right to be a soldier or to wage war—an absurdity that no commentator has ever endorsed. See L. Levy, Origins of the Bill of Rights 135 (1999). Worse still, the phrase "keep and bear Arms" would be incoherent. The word "Arms" would have two different meanings at once: "weapons" (as the object of "keep") and (as the object of "bear") one-half of an idiom. It would be rather like saying "He filled and kicked the bucket" to mean "He filled the bucket and died." Grotesque.

Petitioners justify their limitation of "bear arms" to the military context by pointing out the unremarkable fact that it was often used in that context—the same mistake they made with respect to "keep arms." It is especially unremarkable that the phrase was often used in a military context in the federal legal sources (such as records of congressional debate) that have been the focus of petitioners' inquiry. Those sources would have had little occasion to use it *except* in discussions about the standing army and the militia. And the phrases used primarily in those military discussions include not only "bear arms" but also "carry arms," "possess arms," and "have arms"—though no one thinks that those *other* phrases also had special military meanings * * *.

* * *

c. **Meaning of the Operative Clause**. Putting all of these textual elements together, we find that they guarantee the individual right to possess and carry weapons in case of confrontation. This meaning is strongly confirmed by the historical background of the Second Amendment. We look to this because it has always been widely understood that the Second Amendment, like the First and Fourth Amendments, codified a *pre-existing* right. The very text of the Second Amendment implicitly recognizes the pre-existence of the right and declares only that it "shall not be infringed." * * *

Between the Restoration and the Glorious Revolution, the Stuart Kings Charles II and James II succeeded in using select militias loyal to them to suppress political dissidents, in part by disarming their opponents. See J. Malcolm, To Keep and Bear Arms 31–53 (1994) (hereinafter Malcolm); L. Schwoerer, The Declaration of Rights, 1689, p. 76 (1981). Under the auspices of the 1671 Game Act, for example, the Catholic James II had ordered general disarmaments of regions home to his Protestant enemies. See Malcolm 103–106. These experiences caused Englishmen to be extremely wary of concentrated military forces run by the state and to be jealous of their arms. They accordingly obtained an assurance from William and Mary, in the Declaration of Right (which was codified as the English Bill of Rights), that Protestants would never be disarmed: "That the Subjects which are Protestants, may have Arms for their Defence suitable to their Conditions, and as allowed by law." 1 W. & M., c. 2, § 7, in 3 Eng. Stat. at Large 441 (1689). This right has long been understood to be the predecessor to our Second Amendment. See E. Dumbauld, The Bill of Rights and What It Means Today 51 (1957); W. Rawle, A View of the Constitution of the United States of America 122 (1825) (hereinafter Rawle). It was clearly an individual right, having nothing whatever to do with service in a militia * * *.

* * *

And, of course, what the Stuarts had tried to do to their political enemies, George III had tried to do to the colonists. In the tumultuous decades of the 1760's and 1770's, the Crown began to disarm the inhabitants of the most rebellious areas. That provoked polemical reactions by Americans invoking their rights as Englishmen to keep arms. A New York article of April 1769 said that "[i]t is a natural right which the people have reserved to themselves, confirmed by the Bill of Rights, to keep arms for their own defence." A Journal of the Times: Mar. 17, New York Journal, Supp. 1, Apr. 13, 1769, in Boston Under Military Rule 79 (O. Dickerson ed. 1936); see also, *e.g.*, Shippen, Boston Gazette, Jan. 30, 1769, in 1 The Writings of Samuel Adams 299 (H. Cushing ed. 1968). They understood the right to enable individuals to defend themselves. As the most important early American edition of Blackstone's Commentaries (by the law professor and former Antifederalist St. George Tucker) made clear in the notes to the description of the arms right, Americans understood the "right of self-preservation" as permitting a citizen to "repe[l] force by force" when "the intervention of society in his behalf, may be too late to prevent an injury." 1 Blackstone's Commentaries 145–146, n. 42 (1803) (hereinafter Tucker's Blackstone). See also W. Duer, Outlines of the Constitutional Jurisprudence of the United States 31–32 (1833).

There seems to us no doubt, on the basis of both text and history, that the Second Amendment conferred an individual right to keep and bear arms. Of course the right was not unlimited, just as the First Amendment's right of free speech was not. Thus, we do not read the Second Amendment to protect the right of citizens to carry arms for *any sort* of confrontation, just as we do not read the First Amendment to protect the right of citizens to speak for *any purpose*. Before turning to limitations upon the individual right, however, we must determine whether the prefatory clause of the Second Amendment comports with our interpretation of the operative clause.

2. **Prefatory Clause.**

The prefatory clause reads: "A well regulated Militia, being necessary to the security of a free State . . . ."

a. **"Well-Regulated Militia."** In *United States* v. *Miller*, 307 U. S. 174, 179 (1939), we explained that "the Militia comprised all males physically capable of acting in concert for the common defense." That definition comports with founding-era sources.

Petitioners take a seemingly narrower view of the militia, stating that "[m]ilitias are the state- and congressionally-regulated military forces described in the Militia Clauses (art. I, § 8, cls. 15–16)." Brief for Petitioners 12. Although we agree with petitioners' interpretive assumption that "militia" means the same thing in Article I and the Second Amendment, we believe that petitioners identify the wrong thing, namely, the organized militia. Unlike armies and navies, which Congress is given the power to create ("to raise . . . Armies"; "to provide . . . a Navy," Art. I, § 8, cls. 12–13), the militia is assumed by Article I already to be *in existence*. Congress is given the power to "provide for calling forth the militia," § 8, cl. 15; and the power not to create, but to "organiz[e]" it—and not to organize "a" militia, which is what one would expect if the militia were to be a federal creation, but to organize "the" militia, connoting a body already in existence, *ibid.*, cl. 16. This is fully consistent with the ordinary definition of the militia as all able-bodied men. From that pool, Congress has plenary power to organize the units that will make up an effective fighting force * * *.

Finally, the adjective "well-regulated" implies nothing more than the imposition of proper discipline and training. See Johnson 1619 ("Regulate": "To adjust by rule or method"); Rawle 121–122; cf. Va. Declaration of Rights § 13 (1776), in 7 Thorpe 3812, 3814 (referring to "a well-regulated militia, composed of the body of the people, trained to arms").

b. **"Security of a Free State."** The phrase "security of a free State" meant "security of a free polity," not security of each of the several States as the dissent below argued * * *. It is true that the term "State" elsewhere in the Constitution refers to individual States, but the phrase "security of a free State" and close variations seem to have been terms of art in 18th-century political discourse, meaning a " 'free country' " or free polity * * *.

There are many reasons why the militia was thought to be "necessary to the security of a free State." First, of course, it is useful in repelling invasions and suppressing insurrections. Second, it renders large standing armies unnecessary—an argument that Alexander Hamilton made in favor of federal control over the militia. Third, when the able-bodied men of a nation are trained in arms and organized, they are better able to resist tyranny.

3. **Relationship between Prefatory Clause and Operative Clause**

We reach the question, then: Does the preface fit with an operative clause that creates an individual right to keep and bear arms? It fits perfectly, once one knows the history that the founding generation knew and that we have described above. That history showed that the way tyrants had eliminated a militia consisting of all the able-bodied men was not by banning the militia but simply by taking away the people's arms, enabling a select militia or standing army to suppress political opponents. This is what had occurred in England that prompted codification of the right to have arms in the English Bill of Rights.

* * *

It is therefore entirely sensible that the Second Amendment's prefatory clause announces the purpose for which the right was codified: to prevent elimination of the militia. The prefatory clause does not suggest that preserving the militia was the only reason Americans valued the ancient right; most undoubtedly thought it even more important for self-defense and hunting. But the threat that the new Federal Government would destroy the citizens' militia by taking away their arms was the reason that right—unlike some other English rights—was codified in a written Constitution * * *.

* * *

Our interpretation is confirmed by analogous arms-bearing rights in state constitutions that preceded and immediately followed adoption of the Second Amendment * * *.

* * *

The historical narrative that petitioners must endorse would thus treat the Federal Second Amendment as an odd outlier, protecting a right unknown in state constitutions or at English common law, based on little more than an overreading of the prefatory clause.

* * *

* * * [V]irtually all interpreters of the Second Amendment in the century after its enactment interpreted the Amendment as we do.

* * *

We conclude that nothing in our precedents forecloses our adoption of the original understanding of the Second Amendment. It should be unsurprising that such a significant matter has been for so long judicially unresolved. For most of our history, the Bill of Rights was not thought applicable to the States, and the Federal Government did not significantly regulate the possession of firearms by law-abiding citizens. Other provisions of the Bill of Rights have similarly remained unilluminated for lengthy periods. This Court first held a law to violate the First Amendment's guarantee of freedom of speech in 1931, almost 150 years after the Amendment was ratified * * *.

Like most rights, the right secured by the Second Amendment is not unlimited. From Blackstone through the 19th-century cases, commentators and courts routinely explained that the right was not a right to keep and carry any weapon whatsoever in any manner whatsoever and for whatever purpose. For example, the majority of the 19th-century courts to consider the question held that prohibitions on carrying concealed weapons were lawful under the Second Amendment or state analogues. Although we do not undertake an exhaustive historical analysis today of the full scope of the Second Amendment, nothing in our opinion should be taken to cast doubt on longstanding prohibitions on the possession of firearms by felons and the mentally ill, or laws forbidding the carrying of firearms in sensitive places such as schools and government buildings, or laws imposing conditions and qualifications on the commercial sale of arms.

We also recognize another important limitation on the right to keep and carry arms [to] * * * the sorts of weapons * * * "in common use at the time." We think that limitation is fairly supported by the historical tradition of prohibiting the carrying of "dangerous and unusual weapons."

It may be objected that if weapons that are most useful in military service—M-16 rifles and the like—may be banned, then the Second Amendment right is completely detached from the prefatory clause. But as we have said, the conception of the militia at the time of the Second Amendment's ratification was the body of all citizens capable of military service, who would bring the sorts of lawful weapons that they possessed at home to militia duty. It may well be true today that a militia, to be as effective as militias in the 18th century, would require sophisticated arms that are highly unusual in society at large. Indeed, it may be true that no amount of small arms could be useful against modern-day bombers and tanks. But the fact that modern developments have limited the degree of fit between the prefatory clause and the protected right cannot change our interpretation of the right.

We turn finally to the law at issue here. As we have said, the law totally bans handgun possession in the home. It also requires that any lawful firearm in the home be disassembled or bound by a trigger lock at all times, rendering it inoperable.

As the quotations earlier in this opinion demonstrate, the inherent right of self-defense has been central to the Second Amendment right. The handgun ban amounts to a prohibition of an entire class of "arms" that is overwhelmingly chosen by American society for that lawful purpose. The prohibition extends, moreover, to the home, where the need for defense of self, family, and property is most acute. Under any of the standards of scrutiny that we have applied to enumerated constitutional rights, banning from the home "the most preferred firearm in the nation to 'keep' and use for protection of one's home and family," 478 F. 3d, at 400, would fail constitutional muster.

* * *

It is no answer to say, as petitioners do, that it is permissible to ban the possession of handguns so long as the possession of other firearms (*i.e.*, long guns) is allowed. It is enough to note, as we have observed, that the American people have considered the handgun to be the quintessential self-defense weapon. There are many reasons that a citizen may prefer a handgun for home defense: It is easier to store in a location that is readily accessible in an emergency; it cannot easily be redirected or wrestled away by an attacker; it is easier to use for those without the upper-body strength to lift and aim a long gun; it can be pointed at a burglar with one hand while the other hand dials the police. Whatever the reason, handguns are the most popular weapon chosen by Americans for self-defense in the home, and a complete prohibition of their use is invalid.

We must also address the District's requirement (as applied to respondent's handgun) that firearms in the home be rendered and kept inoperable at all times. This makes it impossible for citizens to use them for the core lawful purpose of self-defense and is hence unconstitutional * * *.

* * *

JUSTICE BREYER * * * proposes * * * a judge-empowering "interest-balancing inquiry" that "asks whether the statute burdens a protected interest in a way or to an extent that is out of proportion to the statute's salutary effects upon other important governmental interests." After an exhaustive discussion of the arguments for and against gun control, JUSTICE BREYER arrives at his interest-balanced answer: Because handgun violence is a problem, because the law is limited to an urban area, and because there were somewhat similar restrictions in the founding period (a false proposition that we have already discussed), the interest-balancing inquiry results in the constitutionality of the handgun ban. QED.

We know of no other enumerated constitutional right whose core protection has been subjected to a freestanding "interest-balancing" approach. The very enumeration of the right takes out of the hands of government—even the Third Branch of Government—the power to decide on a case-by-case basis whether the right is *really worth* insisting upon. A constitutional guarantee subject to future judges' assessments of its usefulness is no constitutional guarantee at all * * *.

* * *

In sum, we hold that the District's ban on handgun possession in the home violates the Second Amendment, as does its prohibition against rendering any lawful firearm in the home operable for the purpose of immediate self-defense. Assuming that Heller is not disqualified from the exercise of Second Amendment rights, the District must permit him to register his handgun and must issue him a license to carry it in the home.

We are aware of the problem of handgun violence in this country, and we take seriously the concerns raised by the many *amici* who believe that prohibition of handgun ownership is a solution. The Constitution leaves the District of Columbia a variety of tools for combating that problem, including some measures regulating handguns. But the enshrinement of constitutional rights necessarily takes certain policy choices off the table. These include the absolute prohibition of handguns held and used for self-defense in the home. Undoubtedly some think that the Second Amendment is outmoded in a society where our standing army is the pride of our Nation, where well-trained police forces provide personal security, and where gun violence is a serious problem. That is perhaps debatable, but what is not debatable is that it is not the role of this Court to pronounce the Second Amendment extinct.

We affirm the judgment of the Court of Appeals.

It is so ordered.

■ JUSTICE STEVENS, with whom JUSTICE SOUTER, JUSTICE GINSBURG, and JUSTICE BREYER join, dissenting.

The question presented by this case is not whether the Second Amendment protects a "collective right" or an "individual right." Surely it protects a right that can be enforced by individuals. But a conclusion that the Second Amendment protects an individual right does not tell us anything about the scope of that right.

Guns are used to hunt, for self-defense, to commit crimes, for sporting activities, and to perform military duties. The Second Amendment plainly does not protect the right to use a gun to rob a bank; it is equally clear that it *does* encompass the right to use weapons for certain military purposes. Whether it also protects the right to possess and use guns for nonmilitary purposes like hunting and personal self-defense is the question presented by this case. The text of the Amendment, its history, and our decision in *United States* v. *Miller*, 307 U. S. 174 (1939), provide a clear answer to that question.

The Second Amendment was adopted to protect the right of the people of each of the several States to maintain a well-regulated militia. It was a response to concerns raised during the ratification of the Constitution that the power of Congress to disarm the state militias and create a national standing army posed an intolerable threat to the sovereignty of the several States. Neither the text of the Amendment nor the arguments advanced by its proponents evidenced the slightest interest in limiting any legislature's authority to regulate private civilian uses of firearms. Specifically, there is no indication that the Framers of the Amendment intended to enshrine the common-law right of self-defense in the Constitution.

* * *

The text of the Second Amendment is brief. It provides: "A well regulated Militia, being necessary to the security of a free State, the right of the people to keep and bear Arms, shall not be infringed."

Three portions of that text merit special focus: the introductory language defining the Amendment's purpose, the class of persons encompassed within its reach, and the unitary nature of the right that it protects.

"A well regulated Militia, being necessary to the security of a free State"

The preamble to the Second Amendment makes three important points. It identifies the preservation of the militia as the Amendment's purpose; it explains that the militia is necessary to the security of a free State; and it recognizes that the militia must be "well regulated." In all three respects it is comparable to provisions in several State Declarations of Rights that were adopted roughly contemporaneously with the Declaration of Independence. Those state provisions highlight the importance members of the founding generation attached to the maintenance of state militias; they also underscore the profound fear shared by many in that era of the dangers posed by standing armies. While the need for state militias has not been a matter of significant public interest for almost two centuries, that fact should not obscure the contemporary concerns that animated the Framers.

* * *

The preamble thus both sets forth the object of the Amendment and informs the meaning of the remainder of its text * * *.

The Court today tries to denigrate the importance of this clause of the Amendment by beginning its analysis with the Amendment's operative provision and returning to the preamble merely "to ensure that our reading of the operative clause is consistent with the announced purpose." That is not how this Court ordinarily reads such texts, and it is not how the preamble would have been viewed at the time the Amendment was adopted. While the Court makes the novel suggestion that it need only find some "logical connection" between the preamble and the operative provision, it does acknowledge that a prefatory clause may resolve an ambiguity in the text. Without identifying any language in the text that even mentions civilian uses of firearms, the Court proceeds to "find" its preferred reading in what is at best an ambiguous text, and then concludes that its reading is not foreclosed by the preamble. Perhaps the Court's approach to the text is acceptable advocacy, but it is surely an unusual approach for judges to follow.

"The right of the people"

The centerpiece of the Court's textual argument is its insistence that the words "the people" as used in the Second Amendment must have the same meaning, and protect the same class of individuals, as when they are used in the First and Fourth Amendments. According to the Court, in all three provisions—as well as the Constitution's preamble, section 2 of Article I, and the Tenth Amendment—"the term unambiguously refers to all members of the political community, not an unspecified subset." But the Court *itself* reads the Second Amendment to protect a "subset" significantly narrower than the class of persons protected by the First and Fourth Amendments; when it finally drills down on the substantive meaning of the Second Amendment, the Court limits the protected class to "law-abiding, responsible citizens." But the class of persons protected by the First and Fourth Amendments is *not* so limited; for even felons (and presumably irresponsible citizens as well) may invoke the protections of those constitutional provisions. The Court offers no way to harmonize its conflicting pronouncements.

The Court also overlooks the significance of the way the Framers used the phrase "the people" in these constitutional provisions. In the First Amendment, no words define the class of individuals entitled to speak, to publish, or to worship; in that Amendment it is only the right peaceably to assemble, and to petition the Government for a redress of grievances, that is described as a right of "the people." These rights contemplate collective action. While the right peaceably to assemble protects the individual rights of those persons participating in the assembly, its concern is with action engaged in by members of a group, rather than any single individual. Likewise, although the act of petitioning the Government is a right that can be exercised by individuals, it is primarily collective in nature. For if they are to be effective, petitions must involve groups of individuals acting in concert.

Similarly, the words "the people" in the Second Amendment refer back to the object announced in the Amendment's preamble. They remind us that it is the collective action of individuals having a duty to serve in the militia that the text directly protects and, perhaps more importantly, that the ultimate purpose of the Amendment was to protect the States' share of the divided sovereignty created by the Constitution.

* * *

"[T]o keep and bear Arms"

Although the Court's discussion of these words treats them as two "phrases"—as if they read "to keep" and "to bear"—they describe a unitary right: to possess arms if needed for military purposes and to use them in conjunction with military activities.

* * *

The term "bear arms" is a familiar idiom; when used unadorned by any additional words, its meaning is "to serve as a soldier, do military service, fight." 1 Oxford English Dictionary 634 (2d ed. 1989). It is derived from the Latin *arma ferre,* which, translated literally, means "to bear *[ferre]* war equipment *[arma]*." Brief for Professors of Linguistics and English as *Amici Curiae* 19 * * *.

The Court argues that a "qualifying phrase that contradicts the word or phrase it modifies is unknown this side of the looking glass." *Ante,* at 15. But this fundamentally fails to grasp the point. The stand-alone phrase "bear arms" most naturally conveys a military meaning *unless* the addition of a qualifying phrase signals that a different meaning is intended. When, as in this case, there is no such qualifier, the most natural meaning is the military one; and, in the absence of any qualifier, it is all the more appropriate to look to the preamble to confirm the natural meaning of the text * * *.

* * *

When each word in the text is given full effect, the Amendment is most naturally read to secure to the people a right to use and possess arms in conjunction with service in a well-regulated militia. So far as appears, no more than that was contemplated by its drafters or is encompassed within its terms. Even if the meaning of the text were genuinely susceptible to more than one interpretation, the burden would remain on those advocating a departure from the purpose identified in the preamble and from settled law to come forward with persuasive new arguments or evidence. The textual analysis offered by respondent and embraced by the Court falls far short of sustaining that heavy burden * * *.

* * *

The history of the adoption of the Amendment thus describes an overriding concern about the potential threat to state sovereignty that a federal standing army would pose, and a desire to protect the States' militias as the means by which to guard against that danger. But state militias could not effectively check the prospect of a federal standing army so long as Congress retained the power to disarm them, and so a guarantee against such disarmament was needed * * *. The evidence plainly refutes the claim that the Amendment was motivated by the Framers' fears that Congress might act to regulate any civilian uses of weapons * * *.

* * *

The Court may well be correct that the English Bill of Rights protected the right of *some* English subjects to use *some* arms for personal self-defense free from restrictions by the Crown (but not Parliament). But that right—adopted in a different historical and political context and framed in markedly different language—tells us little about the meaning of the Second Amendment.

* * *

The Court concludes its opinion by declaring that it is not the proper role of this Court to change the meaning of rights "enshrine[d]" in the Constitution. But the right the Court announces was not "enshrined" in the Second Amendment by the Framers; it is the product of today's law-changing decision. The majority's exegesis has utterly failed to establish that as a matter of text or history, "the right of law-abiding, responsible citizens to use arms in defense of hearth and home" is "elevate[d] above all other interests" by the Second Amendment.

Until today, it has been understood that legislatures may regulate the civilian use and misuse of firearms so long as they do not interfere with the preservation of a well-regulated militia. The Court's announcement of a new constitutional right to own and use firearms for private purposes upsets that settled understanding, but leaves for future cases the formidable task of defining the scope of permissible regulations * * *.

* * *

■ JUSTICE BREYER, with whom JUSTICE STEVENS, JUSTICE SOUTER, and JUSTICE GINSBURG join, dissenting.

We must decide whether a District of Columbia law that prohibits the possession of handguns in the home violates the Second Amendment. The majority, relying upon its view that the Second Amendment seeks to protect a right of personal self-defense, holds that this law violates that Amendment. In my view, it does not.

The majority's conclusion is wrong for two independent reasons. The first reason is that set forth by Justice Stevens—namely that the Second Amendment protects militia-related, not self-defense-related, interests. These two interests are sometimes intertwined. To assure 18th-century citizens that they could keep arms for militia purposes would necessarily have allowed them to keep arms that they could have used for self-defense as well. But self-defense alone, detached from any militia-related objective, is not the Amendment's concern.

The second independent reason is that the protection the Amendment provides is not absolute. The Amendment permits government to regulate the interests that it serves. Thus, irrespective of what those interests are—whether they do or do not include an independent interest in self-defense—the majority's view cannot be correct unless it can show that the District's regulation is unreasonable or inappropriate in Second Amendment terms. This the majority cannot do.

* * * In this opinion I shall focus upon the second reason. I shall show that the District's law is consistent with the Second Amendment even if that Amendment is interpreted as protecting a wholly separate interest in individual self-defense. That is so because the District's regulation, which focuses upon the presence of handguns

in high-crime urban areas, represents a permissible legislative response to a serious, indeed life-threatening, problem.

* * *

* * * [C]olonial history itself offers important examples of the kinds of gun regulation that citizens would then have thought compatible with the "right to keep and bear arms," whether embodied in Federal or State Constitutions, or the background common law. And those examples include substantial regulation of firearms in urban areas, including regulations that imposed obstacles to the use of firearms for the protection of the home.

* * *

* * * The majority is wrong when it says that the District's law is unconstitutional "[u]nder any of the standards of scrutiny that we have applied to enumerated constitutional rights." How could that be? It certainly would not be unconstitutional under, for example, a "rational-basis" standard, which requires a court to uphold regulation so long as it bears a "rational relationship" to a "legitimate governmental purpose." *Heller v. Doe,* 509 U.S. 312, 320 (1993). The law at issue here, which in part seeks to prevent gun-related accidents, at least bears a "rational relationship" to that "legitimate" life-saving objective * * *.

* * *

* * * [A]doption of a true strict-scrutiny standard for evaluating gun regulations would be impossible. That is because almost every gun-control regulation will seek to advance (as the one here does) a "primary concern of every government—a concern for the safety and indeed the lives of its citizens." The Court has deemed that interest, as well as "the Government's general interest in preventing crime," to be "compelling," and the Court has in a wide variety of constitutional contexts found such public-safety concerns sufficiently forceful to justify restrictions on individual liberties. Thus, any attempt *in theory* to apply strict scrutiny to gun regulations will *in practice* turn into an interest-balancing inquiry, with the interests protected by the Second Amendment on one side and the governmental public-safety concerns on the other, the only question being whether the regulation at issue impermissibly burdens the former in the course of advancing the latter.

I would simply adopt such an interest-balancing inquiry explicitly. The fact that important interests lie on both sides of the constitutional equation suggests that review of gun-control regulation is not a context in which a court should effectively presume either constitutionality (as in rational-basis review) or unconstitutionality (as in strict scrutiny). Rather, "where a law significantly implicates competing constitutionally protected interests in complex ways," the Court generally asks whether the statute burdens a protected interest in a way or to an extent that is out of proportion to the statute's salutary effects upon other important governmental interests * * *.

In applying this kind of standard the Court normally defers to a legislature's empirical judgment in matters where a legislature is likely to have greater expertise and greater institutional factfinding capacity * * *.

* * *

The upshot is a set of studies and counterstudies that, at most, could leave a judge uncertain about the proper policy conclusion. But from respondent's perspective any such uncertainty is not good enough. That is because legislators, not judges, have primary responsibility for drawing policy conclusions from empirical fact. And, given that constitutional allocation of decisionmaking responsibility, the empirical evidence presented here is sufficient to allow a judge to reach a firm *legal* conclusion.

* * *

* * * Given the purposes for which the Framers enacted the Second Amendment, how should it be applied to modern-day circumstances that they could not have anticipated? Assume, for argument's sake, that the Framers did intend the Amendment to offer a degree of self-defense protection. Does that mean that the Framers also intended to guarantee a right to possess a loaded gun near swimming pools, parks, and playgrounds? That they would not have cared about the children who might pick up a loaded gun on their parents' bedside table? That they (who certainly showed concern for the risk of fire, see *supra,* at 684–86) would have lacked concern for the risk of accidental deaths or suicides that readily accessible loaded handguns in urban areas might bring? Unless we believe that they intended future generations to ignore such matters, answering questions such as the questions in this case requires judgment—judicial judgment exercised within a framework for constitutional analysis that guides that judgment and which makes its exercise transparent. One cannot answer those questions by combining inconclusive historical research with judicial *ipse dixit.*

* * *

For these reasons, I conclude that the District's measure is a proportionate, not a disproportionate, response to the compelling concerns that led the District to adopt it. And, for these reasons as well as the independently sufficient reasons set forth by JUSTICE STEVENS, I would find the District's measure consistent with the Second Amendment's demands.

With respect, I dissent.

NOTES AND QUESTIONS

1. Both Justice Scalia's majority opinion and Justice Stevens' dissent are originalist, textual opinions, but they reach opposite outcomes. Which opinion are you persuaded by, and why? Or do you prefer Justice Breyer's pragmatic balancing?

2. For us, the most compelling fact about the text is that it talks about "[t]he right of the people," which seems to us to pre-exist government. This is the same sense in which the right of the people is asserted in the Preamble ("We the People"), and in the First and Fourth Amendments. It is a Lockean "natural" right. The state Bills of Rights from 1776 to 1791 were almost always called "Declarations of Rights" and not "Bills of Rights" because they were conceived as being liquidations of natural law Lockean rights, and not exercises in positive lawmaking. The federal reference to a "Bill of Rights" has to be understood in this vein.

3. What is the relevant "right" of the people? To use a gun in self-defense, to be sure, but self-defense against whom and what? Home burglars? Or does the Second Amendment have a deeper meaning and purpose? Everyone agrees that the founding generation was afraid of standing armies. An armed citizenry was a bulwark against a tyrannical federal government, as an armed citizenry was a bulwark against British tyranny. Keep in mind that the Battle of Lexington and Concord was precipitated by

British troops marching to an armory to seize colonial weapons and ammunition. When the Second Amendment says that a well regulated militia is "essential to a free society," is it thinking about the American Revolution? And if the Second Amendment is really about the militia as a check on the national government, does that say anything about the kinds of weapons that the Second Amendment covers? Must citizens have access to the same kinds of weapons that are available to the government's standing army? Does the Second Amendment therefore protect the right to own machine guns, aircraft carriers, and nuclear missiles? What does the majority say about that, and why? Machine guns and other automatic weapons have been illegal since 1934. Does *Heller* call that law into question?

4. Justice Breyer's policy argument that the carrying of guns can be regulated in some fashion is obviously right, as the majority concedes. He is also right that the key question is the standard of review: rational basis, strict scrutiny, or something in between. (You will hear more about those "tiers of scrutiny" in the next chapter.) If courts defer to the empirical judgments of legislatures, does that effectively turn Justice Breyer's standard of review into rational basis review? How deferential must a court be to uphold a regulation that prevents a licensed special police officer from owning a handgun at home for his self-protection?

5. Interestingly, the right to own a firearm for self-defense purposes has, if anything, become much more popular over time. Today, as mentioned above, thirty-three States expressly protect the right to own a gun as an individual and not only as a collective right. Approximately half of all American households own at least one gun. Does that establish the individual right to own a gun as being a fundamental right for Americans today? Fundamental rights, you will soon see, are generally protected by "strict scrutiny," and under strict scrutiny, the D.C. handgun ban stood no chance.

6. The Third Amendment protects the people from having soldiers quartered in their homes. This reflects again the Framers' fear of standing armies and the privacy interests protected by the Fourth Amendment, as well as being a specific response to the billeting of soldiers complained about in the Petition of Right a century and a half before the Constitution.

[Assignment 50]

III. THE FOURTH AMENDMENT

> **The right of the people to be secure in their persons, houses, papers, and effects, against unreasonable searches and seizures, shall not be violated, and no warrants shall issue, but upon probable cause, supported by oath or affirmation, and particularly describing the place to be searched, and the persons or things to be seized.**

The Fourth Amendment was shaped in part by the British practice of issuing "writs of assistance," which helped customs officials search for smuggled goods by serving as general search warrants that eliminated a need to get a specific warrant to search for a specific item. Warrants were important, because a government official who conducted an intrusive search pursuant to a valid warrant could not be sued in tort, while an official who conducted an illegal search would be treated as an ordinary trespasser or converter. (The notion of "qualified immunity" for government officials was a twentieth-century development.) *See* AKHIL REED AMAR, THE BILL OF RIGHTS: CREATION AND RECONSTRUCTION 68–71 (1998). General writs of assistance played a major role in the tensions in the 1760s and 1770s that led to the Revolutionary War. Famously, in 1761, sixty-three Boston merchants represented by James Otis sued British customs officials, claiming that the British were violating the rights of Englishman, as Sir Edward Coke had described them in his writings on the Ancient Constitution. Otis's arguments greatly impressed the young John Adams, and they were eventually memorialized by Otis in a pamphlet. Parliament affirmed the legality of writs of assistance in the Townsend Acts in 1767, but most colonial courts refused to issue such writs. The Fourth Amendment's particularity requirement as to the item or items being search for is a direct result of the colonial controversy over writs of assistance. Here is Otis's argument against them:

A. AGAINST WRITS OF ASSISTANCE BY JAMES OTIS

February 24, 1761

MAY it please your Honors: I was desired by one of the court to look into the books, and consider the question now before them concerning Writs of Assistance. I have accordingly considered it, and now appear not only in obedience to your order, but likewise in behalf of the inhabitants of this town, who have presented another petition, and out of regard to the liberties of the subject. And I take this opportunity to declare that whether under a fee or not (for in such a cause as this I despise a fee) I will to my dying day oppose, with all the powers and faculties God has given me, all such instruments of slavery on the one hand and villainy on the other as this Writ of Assistance is.

It appears to me the worst instrument of arbitrary power, the most destructive of English liberty and the fundamental principles of law, that ever was found in an English law-book. I must therefore beg your Honors' patience and attention to the whole range of an argument that may perhaps appear uncommon in many things, as well as to points of learning that are more remote and unusual, that the whole tendency of my design may the more easily be perceived, the conclusions better descend, and the force of them be better felt. I shall not think much of my pains in this cause, as I engaged in it from principle.

I was solicited to argue this cause as Advocate-General; and, because I would not, I have been charged with desertion from my office. To this charge I can give a very sufficient answer. I renounced that office and I argue this cause from the same principle; and I argue it with the greater pleasure, as it is in favor of British liberty, at a time when we hear the greatest monarch upon earth declaring from his throne that he glories in the name of Briton and that the privileges of his people are dearer to him than the most valuable prerogatives of his crown; and as it is in opposition to a kind of power, the exercise of which in former periods of history cost one king of England his head and another his throne * * *.

* * * Your Honors will find in the old books concerning the office of a justice of the peace precedents of general warrants to search suspected houses. But in more modern books you will find only special warrants to search such and such houses, specially named, in which the complainant has before sworn that he suspects his goods are concealed; and will find it adjudged that special warrants only are legal. In the same manner I rely on it, that the writ prayed for in this petition, being general, is illegal. It is a power that places the liberty of every man in the hands of every petty officer. I say I admit that special Writs of Assistance, to search special

places, may be granted to certain persons on oath; but I deny that the writ now prayed for can be granted, for I beg leave to make some observations on the writ itself, before I proceed to other Acts of Parliament.

In the first place, the writ is universal, being directed "to all and singular justices, sheriffs, constables, and all other officers and subjects"; so that, in short, it is directed to every subject in the King's dominions. Every one with this writ may be a tyrant; if this commission be legal, a tyrant in a legal manner, also, may control, imprison, or murder any one within the realm. In the next place, it is perpetual; there is no return. A man is accountable to no person for his doings. Every man may reign secure in his petty tyranny, and spread terror and desolation around him, until the trump of the Archangel shall excite different emotions in his soul. In the third place, a person with this writ, in the daytime, may enter all houses, shops, etc., at will, and command all to assist him. Fourthly, by this writ not only deputies, etc., but even their menial servants, are allowed to lord it over us. What is this but to have the curse of Canaan with a witness on us: to be the servants of servants, the most despicable of God's creation?

Now, one of the most essential branches of English liberty is the freedom of one's house. A man's house is his castle; and whilst he is quiet, he is as well guarded as a prince in his castle. This writ, if it should be declared legal, would totally annihilate this privilege. Custom-house officers may enter our houses when they please; we are commanded to permit their entry. Their menial servants may enter, may break locks, bars, and everything in their way; and whether they break through malice or revenge, no man, no court can inquire. Bare suspicion without oath is sufficient.

This wanton exercise of this power is not a chimerical suggestion of a heated brain. I will mention some facts. Mr. Pew had one of these writs, and, when Mr. Ware succeeded him, he endorsed this writ over to Mr. Ware; so that these writs are negotiable from one officer to another; and so your Honors have no opportunity of judging the persons to whom this vast power is delegated. Another instance is this: Mr. Justice Walley had called this same Mr. Ware before him, by a constable, to answer for a breach of the Sabbath-day Acts, or that of profane swearing. As soon as he had finished, Mr. Ware asked him if he had done. He replied, "Yes." "Well then," said Mr. Ware, "I will show you a little of my power. I command you to permit me to search your house for uncustomed goods"—and went on to search the house from the garret to the cellar; and then served the constable in the same manner!

But to show another absurdity in this writ: if it should be established, I insist upon it every person, by the 14th Charles Second, has this power as well as the custom-house officers. The words are: "It shall be lawful for any person or persons authorized," etc. What a scene does this open! Every man prompted by revenge, ill-humor, or wantonness to inspect the inside of his neighbor's house, may get a Writ of Assistance. Others will ask it from self-defence; one arbitrary exertion will provoke another, until society be involved in tumult and in blood.

[*Editors' Note: The remainder of the speech exists only in the following summary by John Adams:*]

A dissertation on the rights of man in a state of nature. He asserted that every man, merely natural, was an independent sovereign, subject to no law but the law written on his heart and revealed to him by his Maker, in the constitution of his nature and the inspiration of his understanding and his conscience. His right to his life, his liberty, no created being could rightfully contest. Nor was his right to his property less incontestable. The club that he had snapped from a tree, for a staff or for defense, was his own. His bow and arrow were his own; if by a pebble he had killed a partridge or a squirrel, it was his own. No creature, man or beast, had a right to take it from him. If he had taken an eel or a smelt or a sculpin, it was his property. In short, he sported upon this topic with so much wit and humor, and at the same time with so much indisputable truth and reason, that he was not less entertaining than instructive.

He asserted that these rights were inherent and inalienable * * *. These principles and these rights were wrought into the English constitution as fundamental laws. And under this head he went back to the old Saxon laws and to Magna Carta and the fifty confirmations of it in Parliament and the executions ordained against the violators of it and the national vengeance which had been taken on them from time to time, down to the Jameses and Charleses, and to the position of rights and the Bill of Rights and the revolution.

He asserted that the security of these rights to life, liberty, and property had been the object of all those struggles against arbitrary power, temporal and spiritual, civil and political, military and ecclesiastical, in every age. He asserted that our ancestors, as British subjects, and we their descendants, as British subjects, were entitled to all those rights by the British constitution as well as by the law of nature and our provincial character as much as any inhabitant of London or Bristol or any part of England, and were not to be cheated out of them by any phantom of "virtual representation" or any other fiction of law or politics or any monkish trick of deceit and hypocrisy.

* * *

NOTES AND QUESTIONS

1. Eight States out of twelve that wrote new state constitutions between 1776 and 1791, comprising 68% of the total U.S. population, included Fourth Amendment analogues that banned general warrants. Steven G. Calabresi, Sarah E. Agudo, and Kathryn L. Dore, *State Bills of Rights in 1787 and 1791: What Individual Rights are Really Deeply Rooted in American History and Tradition?*, 85 SO. CAL. L. REV. 1491–1492 (2012). By 1868, the year the Fourteenth Amendment was ratified, an Article V consensus of thirty-six out of thirty-seven state constitutions recognized this right. Today, all fifty state constitutions have Fourth Amendment analogues. Steven Gow Calabresi, et al., *Individual Rights Under State Constitutions in 2018: What Rights are Deeply rooted in a modern-Day consensus of the States?*, 94 NOTRE DAME L. REV. 86–87 (2018). The right, which James Otis spoke out about is very deeply rooted both in American history and tradition and in the contemporary practice of the States.

2. Notwithstanding the historical importance of the controversies over writs of assistance, the Declaration of Independence does not mention them as a cause of revolution. And, as Akhil Amar rightly points out, the Fourth Amendment does not mention writs of assistance; it refers instead to "Warrants." *See* AMAR, *supra,* at 66 n.*. The most relevant antecedent for the Fourth Amendment therefore might be *Wilkes v. Wood,* 98 Eng. Rep. 489 (1763), decided two years after the writs of assistance case argued by Otis. A publication vigorously criticized King George III's handling of the end of the Seven Years' War. Suspecting that Wilkes, a member of Parliament, was the likely author, the Secretary of State secured a general warrant to search and seize Wilkes's

papers. Wood and others showed up pursuant to that warrant and took Wilkes's papers, breaking open drawers in the process. Wilkes sued, claiming that general warrants were unlawful and could not authorize the search. Lord Chief Justice Pratt said of such warrants:

> [T]he present case chiefly turned upon the general question, whether a Secretary of State has the power to force persons houses, break open their locks, seize their papers, &c. upon a bare suspicion of a libel by a general warrant, without name of the person charged. A strange question, to be agitated in these days, when the constitution is so well fixed, when we have a prince upon the throne, whose virtues are so great and amiable, and whose regard for the subject is such, that he must frown upon every incroachment upon their liberty * * *. No legal authority, in the present case, to justify the action. No precedents, no legal determinations, not an Act of Parliament itself, is sufficient to warrant any proceeding contrary to the spirit of the constitution.

Id. at 490. The jury awarded Wilkes 1,000 pounds in damages. The case was widely known and celebrated in America; it was a case "whose plot and cast of characters were familiar to every schoolboy in America, and whose lessons the Fourth Amendment was undeniably designed to embody." Akhil Reed Amar, *Fourth Amendment First Principles,* 107 HARV. L. REV. 757, 772 (1994). *See also Entick v. Carrington,* 19 Howell's State Trials 1029 (1765).

3. In the founding era, the key to Fourth Amendment protection was the jury, which could award damages against the offending government officials if the searches were illegal. A warrant, however, issued by a judge, insulated the government official from suit. Hence, the Fourth Amendment enforced privacy rights by placing *limitations* on the government's ability to get warrants. In modern times, with the rise of official immunity doctrines, the threat of damages actions has lost much of its force. Whether for that reason or for other reasons, courts have shifted focus so that the *reasonableness* of a search now depends primarily on *whether or not the government got a warrant before searching*. Ironically, the judicial warrants that the founding generation found so threatening are today seen as the principle protection secured by the Fourth Amendment. With that in mind, you can now see the seminal case for modern Fourth Amendment Law.

B. KATZ V. UNITED STATES

389 U.S. 347 (1967)

■ MR. JUSTICE STEWART delivered the opinion of the Court.

The petitioner was convicted in the District Court for the Southern District of California under an eight-count indictment charging him with transmitting wagering information by telephone from Los Angeles to Miami and Boston, in violation of a federal statute. At trial, the Government was permitted, over the petitioner's objection, to introduce evidence of the petitioner's end of telephone conversations, overheard by FBI agents who had attached an electronic listening and recording device to the outside of the public telephone booth from which he had placed his calls. In affirming his conviction, the Court of Appeals rejected the contention that the recordings had been obtained in violation of the Fourth Amendment, because "[t]here was no physical entrance into the area occupied by [the petitioner]." We granted certiorari in order to consider the constitutional questions thus presented.

The petitioner has phrased those questions as follows:

"A. Whether a public telephone booth is a constitutionally protected area so that evidence obtained by attaching an electronic listening recording device to the top of such a booth is obtained in violation of the right to privacy of the user of the booth. *[Aged Editors' Note: Public telephone booths were glass-enclosed entities in which one made telephone calls prior to the invention of cell phones. One could expect to be seen but not overheard while in a telephone booth (though Clark Kent somehow thought that he could surreptitiously change to Superman in them).]*

"B. Whether physical penetration of a constitutionally protected area is necessary before a search and seizure can be said to be violative of the Fourth Amendment to the United States Constitution."

We decline to adopt this formulation of the issues. In the first place, the correct solution of Fourth Amendment problems is not necessarily promoted by incantation of the phrase "constitutionally protected area." Secondly, the Fourth Amendment cannot be translated into a general constitutional "right to privacy." That Amendment protects individual privacy against certain kinds of governmental intrusion, but its protections go further, and often have nothing to do with privacy at all. Other provisions of the Constitution protect personal privacy from other forms of governmental invasion. But the protection of a person's *general* right to privacy—his right to be let alone by other people—is, like the protection of his property and of his very life, left largely to the law of the individual States.

Because of the misleading way the issues have been formulated, the parties have attached great significance to the characterization of the telephone booth from which the petitioner placed his calls. The petitioner has strenuously argued that the booth was a "constitutionally protected area." The Government has maintained with equal vigor that it was not. But this effort to decide whether or not a given "area," viewed in the abstract, is "constitutionally protected" deflects attention from the problem presented by this case. For the Fourth Amendment protects people, not places. What a person knowingly exposes to the public, even in his own home or office, is not a subject of Fourth Amendment protection. *See Lewis v. United States,* 385 U.S. 206, 210; *United States v. Lee,* 274 U.S. 559, 563. But what he seeks to preserve as private, even in an area accessible to the public, may be constitutionally protected. *See Rios v. United States,* 364 U.S. 253; *Ex parte Jackson,* 96 U.S. 727, 733.

The Government stresses the fact that the telephone booth from which the petitioner made his calls was constructed partly of glass, so that he was as visible after he entered it as he would have been if he had remained outside. But what he sought to exclude when he entered the booth was not the intruding eye—it was the uninvited ear. He did not shed his right to do so simply because he made his calls from a place where he might be seen. No less than an individual in a business office, in a friend's apartment, or in a taxicab, a person in a telephone booth may rely upon the protection of the Fourth Amendment. One who occupies it, shuts the door behind him, and pays the toll that permits him to place a call is surely entitled to assume that the words he utters into the mouthpiece will not be broadcast to the world. To read the Constitution more narrowly is to ignore the vital role that the public telephone has come to play in private communication.

The Government contends, however, that the activities of its agents in this case should not be tested by Fourth Amendment requirements, for the surveillance technique they employed involved no physical penetration of the telephone booth from which the petitioner placed his calls. It is true that the absence of such penetration was at one time thought to foreclose further Fourth Amendment inquiry, *Olmstead v. United States,* 277 U.S. 438, 457, 464, 466; *Goldman v. United States,* 316 U.S. 129, 134–136, for that Amendment was thought to limit only searches and seizures of tangible property. But "[t]he premise that property interests control the right of the Government to search and seize has been discredited." *Warden v. Hayden,* 387 U.S. 294, 304. Thus, although a closely divided Court supposed in *Olmstead* that surveillance without any trespass and without the seizure of any material object fell outside the ambit of the Constitution, we have since departed from the narrow view on which that decision rested. Indeed, we have expressly held that the Fourth Amendment governs not only the seizure of tangible items, but extends as well to the recording of oral statements, overheard without any "technical trespass under . . . local property law." *Silverman v. United States,* 365 U.S. 505, 511. Once this much is acknowledged, and once it is recognized that the Fourth Amendment protects people—and not simply "areas"—against unreasonable searches and seizures, it becomes clear that the reach of that Amendment cannot turn upon the presence or absence of a physical intrusion into any given enclosure.

We conclude that the underpinnings of *Olmstead* and *Goldman* have been so eroded by our subsequent decisions that the "trespass" doctrine there enunciated can no longer be regarded as controlling. The Government's activities in electronically listening to and recording the petitioner's words violated the privacy upon which he justifiably relied while using the telephone booth, and thus constituted a "search and seizure" within the meaning of the Fourth Amendment. The fact that the electronic device employed to achieve that end did not happen to penetrate the wall of the booth can have no constitutional significance.

The question remaining for decision, then, is whether the search and seizure conducted in this case complied with constitutional standards. In that regard, the Government's position is that its agents acted in an entirely defensible manner: they did not begin their electronic surveillance until investigation of the petitioner's activities had established a strong probability that he was using the telephone in question to transmit gambling information to persons in other States, in violation of federal law. Moreover, the surveillance was limited, both in scope and in duration, to the specific purpose of establishing the contents of the petitioner's unlawful telephonic communications. The agents confined their surveillance to the brief periods during which he used the telephone booth, and they took great care to overhear only the conversations of the petitioner himself.

Accepting this account of the Government's actions as accurate, it is clear that this surveillance was so narrowly circumscribed that a duly authorized magistrate, properly notified of the need for such investigation, specifically informed of the basis on which it was to proceed, and clearly apprised of the precise intrusion it would entail, could constitutionally have authorized, with appropriate safeguards, the very limited search and seizure that the Government asserts, in fact, took place * * *.

* * * Yet the inescapable fact is that this restraint was imposed by the agents themselves, not by a judicial officer. They were not required, before commencing the search, to present their estimate of probable cause for detached scrutiny by a neutral

magistrate. They were not compelled, during the conduct of the search itself, to observe precise limits established in advance by a specific court order. Nor were they directed, after the search had been completed, to notify the authorizing magistrate in detail of all that had been seized. In the absence of such safeguards, this Court has never sustained a search upon the sole ground that officers reasonably expected to find evidence of a particular crime and voluntarily confined their activities to the least intrusive means consistent with that end. Searches conducted without warrants have been held unlawful "notwithstanding facts unquestionably showing probable cause," *Agnello v. United States,* 269 U.S. 20, 33, for the Constitution requires "that the deliberate, impartial judgment of a judicial officer . . . be interposed between the citizen and the police. . . ." *Wong Sun v. United States,* 371 U.S. 471, 481–482. "Over and again, this Court has emphasized that the mandate of the [Fourth] Amendment requires adherence to judicial processes," *United States v. Jeffers,* 342 U.S. 48, 51, and that searches conducted outside the judicial process, without prior approval by judge or magistrate, are *per se* unreasonable under the Fourth Amendment—subject only to a few specifically established and well-delineated exceptions.

It is difficult to imagine how any of those exceptions could ever apply to the sort of search and seizure involved in this case. Even electronic surveillance substantially contemporaneous with an individual's arrest could hardly be deemed an "incident" of that arrest. Nor could the use of electronic surveillance without prior authorization be justified on grounds of "hot pursuit." And, of course, the very nature of electronic surveillance precludes its use pursuant to the suspect's consent.

The Government does not question these basic principles. Rather, it urges the creation of a new exception to cover this case. It argues that surveillance of a telephone booth should be exempted from the usual requirement of advance authorization by a magistrate upon a showing of probable cause. We cannot agree. Omission of such authorization

> "bypasses the safeguards provided by an objective predetermination of probable cause, and substitutes instead the far less reliable procedure of an after-the-event justification for the . . . search, too likely to be subtly influenced by the familiar shortcomings of hindsight judgment." *Beck v. Ohio,* 379 U.S. 89, 96.

And bypassing a neutral predetermination of the *scope* of a search leaves individuals secure from Fourth Amendment violations "only in the discretion of the police." *Id.* at 97.

These considerations do not vanish when the search in question is transferred from the setting of a home, an office, or a hotel room to that of a telephone booth. Wherever a man may be, he is entitled to know that he will remain free from unreasonable searches and seizures. The government agents here ignored "the procedure of antecedent justification . . . that is central to the Fourth Amendment," a procedure that we hold to be a constitutional precondition of the kind of electronic surveillance involved in this case. Because the surveillance here failed to meet that condition, and because it led to the petitioner's conviction, the judgment must be reversed.

It is so ordered.

[Concurring opinions by JUSTICES DOUGLAS and WHITE are omitted.]

■ MR. JUSTICE HARLAN, concurring.

* * *

As the Court's opinion states, "the Fourth Amendment protects people, not places." The question, however, is what protection it affords to those people. Generally, as here, the answer to that question requires reference to a "place." My understanding of the rule that has emerged from prior decisions is that there is a twofold requirement, first that a person have exhibited an actual (subjective) expectation of privacy and, second, that the expectation be one that society is prepared to recognize as "reasonable." Thus a man's home is, for most purposes, a place where he expects privacy, but objects, activities, or statements that he exposes to the "plain view" of outsiders are not "protected" because no intention to keep them to himself has been exhibited. On the other hand, conversations in the open would not be protected against being overheard, for the expectation of privacy under the circumstances would be unreasonable.

The critical fact in this case is that "(o)ne who occupies it, (a telephone booth) shuts the door behind him, and pays the toll that permits him to place a call is surely entitled to assume" that his conversation is not being intercepted. The point is not that the booth is "accessible to the public" at other times, but that it is a temporarily private place whose momentary occupants' expectations of freedom from intrusion are recognized as reasonable.

* * * [R]easonable expectations of privacy may be defeated by electronic as well as physical invasion.

Finally, I do not read the Court's opinion to declare that no interception of a conversation one-half of which occurs in a public telephone booth can be reasonable in the absence of a warrant. As elsewhere under the Fourth Amendment, warrants are the general rule, to which the legitimate needs of law enforcement may demand specific exceptions. It will be time enough to consider any such exceptions when an appropriate occasion presents itself, and I agree with the Court that this is not one.

■ MR. JUSTICE BLACK, dissenting.

If I could agree with the Court that eavesdropping carried on by electronic means (equivalent to wiretapping) constitutes a "search" or "seizure," I would be happy to join the Court's opinion * * *.

My basic objection is twofold: (1) I do not believe that the words of the Amendment will bear the meaning given them by today's decision, and (2) I do not believe that it is the proper role of this Court to rewrite the Amendment in order "to bring it into harmony with the times" and thus reach a result that many people believe to be desirable.

* * * The first clause [of the Fourth Amendment] protects "persons, houses, papers, and effects, against unreasonable searches and seizures * * *." These words connote the idea of tangible things with size, form, and weight, things capable of being searched, seized, or both. The second clause of the Amendment still further establishes its Framers' purpose to limit its protection to tangible things by providing that no warrants shall issue but those "particularly describing the place to be searched, and the persons or things to be seized." A conversation overheard by eavesdropping, whether by plain snooping or wiretapping, is not tangible and, under the normally accepted meanings of the words, can neither be searched nor seized. In

addition the language of the second clause indicates that the Amendment refers not only to something tangible so it can be seized but to something already in existence so it can be described. Yet the Court's interpretation would have the Amendment apply to overhearing future conversations which by their very nature are nonexistent until they take place. How can one "describe" a future conversation, and, if one cannot, how can a magistrate issue a warrant to eavesdrop one in the future? It is argued that information showing what is expected to be said is sufficient to limit the boundaries of what later can be admitted into evidence; but does such general information really meet the specific language of the Amendment which says 'particularly describing'? Rather than using language in a completely artificial way, I must conclude that the Fourth Amendment simply does not apply to eavesdropping.

* * *

NOTES AND QUESTIONS

1. *Katz v. United States* involved the question of how to apply an old text, the Fourth Amendment, to new facts which implicate that text. In this case, the new facts are the ability of the FBI or the police to wiretap telephone calls. The Supreme Court's first reaction, in *Olmstead v. United States*, 277 U.S. 438 (1928), was to hold that wiretapping telephones was not literally a seizure under the First Amendment, nor did it invade a defendants house or office, so it must be constitutional. In *Katz*, the Supreme Court overruled *Olmstead* because it recognized that the new technology that allowed for telephone calls created a new kind of property or zone in which individual privacy could manifest itself. Just as it would be wrong to read the First Amendment's protection of freedom of the press as protecting only printing press and not broadcasting, television, movies, and the internet, so too would it be wrong to read the Fourth Amendment as not applying to searches conducted by wiretapping telephone calls instead of breaking into houses. Or are we wrong and is Justice Black right? Does the answer depend on something as esoteric as the philosophy of language? *See* Gary Lawson, *Reflections of an Empirical Reader (or: Could Fleming Be Right This Time?)*, 96 B.U. L. REV. 1457 (2016). Judge Robert H. Bork wrote in THE TEMPTING OF AMERICA: THE POLITICAL SEDUCTION OF THE LAW (1990): "The world changes in which unchanging values find their application." He argues judges can and should take account of those changes. Is Judge Bork right?

2. Notice how the Court in *Katz* places emphasis on the need for "neutral" judicial approval of searches before they are considered reasonable under the Fourth Amendment. This is the linchpin of modern Fourth Amendment law: Searches conducted without warrants are presumptively "unreasonable." That is pretty obviously not the amendment's original meaning, but no one today is calling for significant changes in that aspect of doctrine.

3. Justice Harlan's concurrence, as you will soon see, has been remarkably influential. It spoke of reasonable expectations of privacy—that is, subjective expectations that society regards as reasonable. This phrase became the standard account of the *Katz* inquiry. Justice Harlan, by the way, cited no authority in support of his formulation.

4. Technology continues to advance, creating new forms of communication and new methods of detection. The old days of government agents entering a house, breaking drawers, and stuffing papers into a sack (which is what happened to Wilkes in England in 1763) are by no means gone, but they are supplemented by wiretaps, helicopter overflights, satellite surveillance, heat sensors, and the like. The Court continues to wrestle with these issues, including the problem of determining when a search can be

reasonable without a warrant. In the case that you are about to read, "the Government has conceded noncompliance with the warrant and has argued only that a warrant was not required." *United States v. Jones,* 565 U.S. 400 (2012).

C. UNITED STATES V. JONES

565 U.S. 400 (2012)

■ JUSTICE SCALIA delivered the opinion of the Court.

We decide whether the attachment of a Global-Positioning-System (GPS) tracking device to an individual's vehicle, and subsequent use of that device to monitor the vehicle's movements on public streets, constitutes a search or seizure within the meaning of the Fourth Amendment.

In 2004 respondent Antoine Jones, owner and operator of a nightclub in the District of Columbia, came under suspicion of trafficking in narcotics and was made the target of an investigation by a joint Federal Bureau of Investigation and Metropolitan Police Department task force. Officers employed various investigative techniques, including visual surveillance of the nightclub, installation of a camera focused on the front door of the club, and a pen register and wiretap covering Jones's cellular phone.

Based in part on information gathered from these sources, in 2005 the Government applied to the United States District Court for the District of Columbia for a warrant authorizing the use of an electronic tracking device on the Jeep Grand Cherokee registered to Jones's wife. A warrant issued, authorizing installation of the device in the District of Columbia and within 10 days.

On the 11th day, and not in the District of Columbia but in Maryland, agents installed a GPS tracking device on the undercarriage of the Jeep while it was parked in a public parking lot. Over the next 28 days, the Government used the device to track the vehicle's movements, and once had to replace the device's battery when the vehicle was parked in a different public lot in Maryland. By means of signals from multiple satellites, the device established the vehicle's location within 50 to 100 feet, and communicated that location by cellular phone to a Government computer. It relayed more than 2,000 pages of data over the 4-week period.

The Government ultimately obtained a multiple-count indictment charging Jones and several alleged co-conspirators with, as relevant here, conspiracy to distribute and possess with intent to distribute five kilograms or more of cocaine and 50 grams or more of cocaine base * * *. Before trial, Jones filed a motion to suppress evidence obtained through the GPS device. The District Court granted the motion only in part, suppressing the data obtained while the vehicle was parked in the garage adjoining Jones's residence. 451 F. Supp. 2d 71, 88 (2006). It held the remaining data admissible, because " '[a] person traveling in an automobile on public thoroughfares has no reasonable expectation of privacy in his movements from one place to another.' " *Ibid.* (quoting *United States* v. *Knotts*, 460 U. S. 276, 281 (1983)). Jones's trial in October 2006 produced a hung jury on the conspiracy count.

In March 2007, a grand jury returned another indictment, charging Jones and others with the same conspiracy. The Government introduced at trial the same GPS-derived locational data admitted in the first trial, which connected Jones to the alleged conspirators' stash house that contained $850,000 in cash, 97 kilograms of cocaine, and 1 kilogram of cocaine base. The jury returned a guilty verdict, and the District Court sentenced Jones to life imprisonment.

The United States Court of Appeals for the District of Columbia Circuit reversed the conviction because of admission of the evidence obtained by warrantless use of the GPS device which, it said, violated the Fourth Amendment. *United States* v. *Maynard*, 615 F. 3d 544 (2010). The D. C. Circuit denied the Government's petition for rehearing en banc, with four judges dissenting. 625 F. 3d 766 (2010). We granted certiorari, 564 U. S. 1036 (2011).

The Fourth Amendment provides in relevant part that "[t]he right of the people to be secure in their persons, houses, papers, and effects, against unreasonable searches and seizures, shall not be violated." It is beyond dispute that a vehicle is an "effect" as that term is used in the Amendment. *United States* v. *Chadwick*, 433 U. S. 1, 12 (1977). We hold that the Government's installation of a GPS device on a target's vehicle, and its use of that device to monitor the vehicle's movements, constitutes a "search."

It is important to be clear about what occurred in this case: The Government physically occupied private property for the purpose of obtaining information. We have no doubt that such a physical intrusion would have been considered a "search" within the meaning of the Fourth Amendment when it was adopted. *Entick* v. *Carrington*, 95 Eng. Rep. 807 (C. P. 1765), is a "case we have described as a 'monument of English freedom' 'undoubtedly familiar' to 'every American statesman' at the time the Constitution was adopted, and considered to be 'the true and ultimate expression of constitutional law' " with regard to search and seizure. *Brower* v. *County of Inyo*, 489 U. S. 593, 596 (1989) (quoting *Boyd* v. *United States*, 116 U. S. 616, 626 (1886)). In that case, Lord Camden expressed in plain terms the significance of property rights in search-and-seizure analysis:

> "[O]ur law holds the property of every man so sacred, that no man can set his foot upon his neighbour's close without his leave; if he does he is a trespasser, though he does no damage at all; if he will tread upon his neighbour's ground, he must justify it by law." *Entick, supra,* at 817.

The text of the Fourth Amendment reflects its close connection to property, since otherwise it would have referred simply to "the right of the people to be secure against unreasonable searches and seizures"; the phrase "in their persons, houses, papers, and effects" would have been superfluous.

Consistent with this understanding, our Fourth Amendment jurisprudence was tied to common-law trespass, at least until the latter half of the 20th century. Thus, in *Olmstead* v. *United States*, 277 U. S. 438 (1928), we held that wiretaps attached to telephone wires on the public streets did not constitute a Fourth Amendment search because "[t]here was no entry of the houses or offices of the defendants," *id.*, at 464.

Our later cases, of course, have deviated from that exclusively property-based approach. In *Katz* v. *United States*, 389 U. S. 347, 351 (1967), we said that "the Fourth Amendment protects people, not places," and found a violation in attachment of an eavesdropping device to a public telephone booth. Our later cases have applied the analysis of Justice Harlan's concurrence in that case, which said that a violation occurs when government officers violate a person's "reasonable expectation of privacy," *id.*, at 360.

The Government contends that the Harlan standard shows that no search occurred here, since Jones had no "reasonable expectation of privacy" in the area of the Jeep accessed by Government agents (its underbody) and in the locations of the Jeep on the public roads, which were visible to all. But we need not address the Government's contentions, because Jones's Fourth Amendment rights do not rise or fall with the *Katz* formulation. At bottom, we must "assur[e] preservation of that degree of privacy against government that existed when the Fourth Amendment was adopted." *Kyllo, supra*, at 34. As explained, for most of our history the Fourth Amendment was understood to embody a particular concern for government trespass upon the areas ("persons, houses, papers, and effects") it enumerates. *Katz* did not repudiate that understanding. Less than two years later the Court upheld defendants' contention that the Government could not introduce against them conversations between *other* people obtained by warrantless placement of electronic surveillance devices in their homes. The opinion rejected the dissent's contention that there was no Fourth Amendment violation "unless the conversational privacy of the homeowner himself is invaded." *Alderman* v. *United States*, 394 U. S. 165, 176 (1969). "[W]e [do not] believe that *Katz*, by holding that the Fourth Amendment protects persons and their private conversations, was intended to withdraw any of the protection which the Amendment extends to the home . . . ." *Id.*, at 180.

* * *

The concurrence begins by accusing us of applying "18th-century tort law." That is a distortion. What we apply is an 18th-century guarantee against unreasonable searches, which we believe must provide *at a minimum* the degree of protection it afforded when it was adopted. The concurrence does not share that belief. It would apply *exclusively* *Katz*'s reasonable-expectation-of-privacy test, even when that eliminates rights that previously existed.

The concurrence faults our approach for "present[ing] particularly vexing problems" in cases that do not involve physical contact, such as those that involve the transmission of electronic signals. *Post*, at 426. We entirely fail to understand that point. For unlike the concurrence, which would make *Katz* the *exclusive* test, we do not make trespass the exclusive test. Situations involving merely the transmission of electronic signals without trespass would *remain* subject to *Katz* analysis.

* * *

* * * The concurrence posits that "relatively short-term monitoring of a person's movements on public streets" is okay, but that "the use of longer term GPS monitoring in investigations *of most offenses*" is no good. *Post*, at 430 (emphasis added) * * *. There is no precedent for the proposition that whether a search has occurred depends on the nature of the crime being investigated. And even accepting that novelty, it remains unexplained why a 4-week investigation is "surely" too long and why a drug-trafficking conspiracy involving substantial amounts of cash and narcotics is not an "extraordinary offens[e]" which may permit longer observation. What of a 2-day monitoring of a suspected purveyor of stolen electronics? Or of a 6-month monitoring of a suspected terrorist? * * *

The Government argues in the alternative that even if the attachment and use of the device was a search, it was reasonable—and thus lawful—under the Fourth Amendment because "officers had reasonable suspicion, and indeed probable cause, to believe that [Jones] was a leader in a large-scale cocaine distribution conspiracy." Brief for United States 50–51. We have no occasion to consider this argument. The Government did not raise it below, and the D. C. Circuit therefore did not address it. We consider the argument forfeited.

The judgment of the Court of Appeals for the D. C. Circuit is affirmed.

It is so ordered.

■ JUSTICE SOTOMAYOR, concurring.

I join the Court's opinion because I agree that a search within the meaning of the Fourth Amendment occurs, at a minimum, "[w]here, as here, the Government obtains information by physically intruding on a constitutionally protected area." * * *

Of course, the Fourth Amendment is not concerned only with trespassory intrusions on property. See, *e.g., Kyllo* v. *United States*, 533 U. S. 27–33 (2001). Rather, even in the absence of a trespass, "a Fourth Amendment search occurs when the government violates a subjective expectation of privacy that society recognizes as reasonable." *Id.*, at 33; see also *Smith* v. *Maryland*, 442 U. S. 735–741 (1979); *Katz* v. *United States*, 389 U. S. 347, 361 (1967) (Harlan, J., concurring). In *Katz*, this Court enlarged its then-prevailing focus on property rights by announcing that the reach of the Fourth Amendment does not "turn upon the presence or absence of a physical intrusion." *Id.*, at 353. As the majority's opinion makes clear, however, *Katz*'s reasonable-expectation-of-privacy test augmented, but did not displace or diminish, the common-law trespassory test that preceded it * * *. JUSTICE ALITO's approach, which discounts altogether the constitutional relevance of the Government's physical intrusion on Jones' Jeep, erodes that longstanding protection for privacy expectations inherent in items of property that people possess or control * * *.

Nonetheless, as JUSTICE ALITO notes, physical intrusion is now unnecessary to many forms of surveillance. With increasing regularity, the Government will be capable of duplicating the monitoring undertaken in this case by enlisting factory- or owner-installed vehicle tracking devices or GPS-enabled smartphones. In cases of electronic or other novel modes of surveillance that do not depend upon a physical invasion on property, the majority opinion's trespassory test may provide little guidance. But "[s]ituations involving merely the transmission of electronic signals without trespass would *remain* subject to *Katz* analysis." As JUSTICE ALITO incisively observes, the same technological advances that have made possible nontrespassory surveillance techniques will also affect the *Katz* test by shaping the evolution of societal privacy expectations. Under that rubric, I agree with JUSTICE ALITO that, at the very least, "longer term GPS monitoring in investigations of most offenses impinges on expectations of privacy."

In cases involving even short-term monitoring, some unique attributes of GPS surveillance relevant to the *Katz* analysis will require particular attention. GPS monitoring generates a precise, comprehensive record of a person's public movements that reflects a wealth of detail about her familial, political, professional, religious, and sexual associations. The Government can store such records and efficiently mine them for information years into the future. And because GPS monitoring is cheap in comparison to conventional surveillance techniques and, by design, proceeds surreptitiously, it evades the ordinary checks that constrain abusive law enforcement practices: "limited police resources and community hostility." *Illinois* v. *Lidster*, 540 U. S. 419, 426 (2004).

Awareness that the Government may be watching chills associational and expressive freedoms. And the Government's unrestrained power to assemble data that reveal private aspects of identity is susceptible to abuse. The net result is that GPS monitoring—by making available at a relatively low cost such a substantial quantum of intimate information about any person whom the Government, in its unfettered discretion, chooses to track—may "alter the relationship between citizen and government in a way that is inimical to democratic society." *United States* v. *Cuevas-Perez*, 640 F. 3d 272, 285 (CA7 2011) (Flaum, J., concurring).

I would take these attributes of GPS monitoring into account when considering the existence of a reasonable societal expectation of privacy in the sum of one's public movements. I would ask whether people reasonably expect that their movements will be recorded and aggregated in a manner that enables the Government to ascertain, more or less at will, their political and religious beliefs, sexual habits, and so on. I do not regard as dispositive the fact that the Government might obtain the fruits of GPS monitoring through lawful conventional surveillance techniques. I would also consider the appropriateness of entrusting to the Executive, in the absence of any oversight from a coordinate branch, a tool so amenable to misuse, especially in light of the Fourth Amendment's goal to curb arbitrary exercises of police power to and prevent "a too permeating police surveillance," *United States* v. *Di Re*, 332 U. S. 581, 595 (1948).

More fundamentally, it may be necessary to reconsider the premise that an individual has no reasonable expectation of privacy in information voluntarily disclosed to third parties. *E.g., Smith*, 442 U. S., at 742; *United States* v. *Miller*, 425 U. S. 435, 443 (1976). This approach is ill suited to the digital age, in which people reveal a great deal of information about themselves to third parties in the course of carrying out mundane tasks * * *.

Resolution of these difficult questions in this case is unnecessary, however, because the Government's physical intrusion on Jones' Jeep supplies a narrower basis for decision. I therefore join the majority's opinion.

■ JUSTICE ALITO, with whom JUSTICE GINSBURG, JUSTICE BREYER, and JUSTICE KAGAN join, concurring in the judgment.

This case requires us to apply the Fourth Amendment's prohibition of unreasonable searches and seizures to a 21st-century surveillance technique, the use of a Global Positioning System (GPS) device to monitor a vehicle's movements for an extended period of time. Ironically, the Court has chosen to decide this case based on 18th-century tort law * * *.

This holding, in my judgment, is unwise. It strains the language of the Fourth Amendment; it has little if any support in current Fourth Amendment case law; and it is highly artificial.

I would analyze the question presented in this case by asking whether respondent's reasonable expectations of privacy were violated by the long-term monitoring of the movements of the vehicle he drove.

The Fourth Amendment prohibits "unreasonable searches and seizures," and the Court makes very little effort to explain how the attachment or use of the GPS device fits within these terms. The Court does not contend that there was a seizure. A seizure of property occurs when there is "some meaningful interference with an individual's possessory interests in that property," *United States* v. *Jacobsen,* 466 U. S. 109, 113 (1984), and here there was none. Indeed, the success of the surveillance technique that the officers employed was dependent on the fact that the GPS did not interfere in any way with the operation of the vehicle, for if any such interference had been detected, the device might have been discovered.

The Court does claim that the installation and use of the GPS constituted a search, but this conclusion is dependent on the questionable proposition that these two procedures cannot be separated for purposes of Fourth Amendment analysis. If these two procedures are analyzed separately, it is not at all clear from the Court's opinion why either should be regarded as a search. It is clear that the attachment of the GPS device was not itself a search; if the device had not functioned or if the officers had not used it, no information would have been obtained. And the Court does not contend that the use of the device constituted a search either. On the contrary, the Court accepts the holding in *United States* v. *Knotts*, 460 U. S. 276 (1983), that the use of a surreptitiously planted electronic device to monitor a vehicle's movements on public roads did not amount to a search.

* * *

The Court's reasoning in this case is very similar to that in the Court's early decisions involving wiretapping and electronic eavesdropping, namely, that a technical trespass followed by the gathering of evidence constitutes a search. In the early electronic surveillance cases, the Court concluded that a Fourth Amendment search occurred when private conversations were monitored as a result of an "unauthorized physical penetration into the premises occupied" by the defendant. *Silverman* v. *United States*, 365 U. S. 505, 509 (1961). In *Silverman*, police officers listened to conversations in an attached home by inserting a "spike mike" through the wall that this house shared with the vacant house next door. *Id.,* at 506. This procedure was held to be a search because the mike made contact with a heating duct on the other side of the wall and thus "usurp[ed] . . . an integral part of the premises." *Id.,* at 511.

By contrast, in cases in which there was no trespass, it was held that there was no search. Thus, in *Olmstead* v. *United States*, 277 U. S. 438 (1928), the Court found that the Fourth Amendment did not apply because "[t]he taps from house lines were made in the streets near the houses." *Id.*, at 457. Similarly, the Court concluded that no search occurred in *Goldman* v. *United States*, 316 U. S. 129, 135 (1942), where a "detectaphone" was placed on the outer wall of defendant's office for the purpose of overhearing conversations held within the room.

This trespass-based rule was repeatedly criticized * * *.

Katz v. *United States*, 389 U. S. 347 (1967), finally did away with the old approach, holding that a trespass was not required for a Fourth Amendment violation * * *. What mattered, the Court now held, was whether the conduct at issue "violated the privacy upon which [the defendant] justifiably relied while using the telephone booth." *Katz, supra*, at 353.

Under this approach, as the Court later put it when addressing the relevance of a technical trespass, "an actual trespass is neither necessary *nor sufficient* to establish a constitutional violation." *United States* v. *Karo,* 468 U. S. 705, 713 (1984) (emphasis added) * * *.

* * *

I will briefly note four [problems with the Court's approach in this case] * * *. First, the Court's reasoning largely disregards what is really important (the *use* of a GPS for the purpose of long-term tracking) and instead attaches great significance to something that most would view as relatively minor (attaching to the bottom of a car a small, light object that does not interfere in any way with the car's operation) * * *. [I]f long-term monitoring can be accomplished without committing a technical trespass—suppose, for example, that the Federal Government required or persuaded auto manufacturers to include a GPS tracking device in every car—the Court's theory would provide no protection.

Second, the Court's approach leads to incongruous results. If the police attach a GPS device to a car and use the device to follow the car for even a brief time, under the Court's theory, the Fourth Amendment applies. But if the police follow the same car for a much longer period using unmarked cars and aerial assistance, this tracking is not subject to any Fourth Amendment constraints.

* * *

Third, under the Court's theory, the coverage of the Fourth Amendment may vary from State to State. If the events at issue here had occurred in a community-property State, or a State that has adopted the Uniform Marital Property Act, respondent would likely be an owner of the vehicle, and it would not matter whether the GPS was installed before or after his wife turned over the keys. In non-community-property States, on the other hand, the registration of the vehicle in the name of respondent's wife would generally be regarded as presumptive evidence that she was the sole owner.

Fourth, the Court's reliance on the law of trespass will present particularly vexing problems in cases involving surveillance that is carried out by making electronic, as opposed to physical, contact with the item to be tracked. For example, suppose that the officers in the present case had followed respondent by surreptitiously activating a stolen vehicle detection system that came with the car when it was purchased. Would the sending of a radio signal to activate this system constitute a trespass to chattels? Trespass to chattels has traditionally required a physical touching of the property. In recent years, courts have wrestled with the application of this old tort in cases involving unwanted electronic contact with computer systems, and some have held that even the transmission of electrons that occurs when a communication is sent from one computer to another is enough. See, *e.g., CompuServe, Inc.* v. *Cyber Promotions, Inc.* 962 F. Supp. 1015, 1021 (SD Ohio 1997); *Thrifty-Tel, Inc.* v. *Bezenek*, 46 Cal. App. 4th 1559, 1566, n. 6 (1996). But may such decisions be followed in applying the Court's trespass theory? Assuming that what matters under the Court's theory is the law of trespass as it existed at the time of the adoption of the Fourth Amendment, do these recent decisions represent a change in the law or simply the application of the old tort to new situations?

The *Katz* expectation-of-privacy test avoids the problems and complications noted above, but it is not without its own difficulties. It involves a degree of circularity, and judges are apt to confuse their own expectations of privacy with those of the hypothetical reasonable person to which the *Katz* test looks. In addition, the

Katz test rests on the assumption that this hypothetical reasonable person has a well-developed and stable set of privacy expectations. But technology can change those expectations. Dramatic technological change may lead to periods in which popular expectations are in flux and may ultimately produce significant changes in popular attitudes. New technology may provide increased convenience or security at the expense of privacy, and many people may find the tradeoff worthwhile. And even if the public does not welcome the diminution of privacy that new technology entails, they may eventually reconcile themselves to this development as inevitable.

On the other hand, concern about new intrusions on privacy may spur the enactment of legislation to protect against these intrusions. This is what ultimately happened with respect to wiretapping. After *Katz*, Congress did not leave it to the courts to develop a body of Fourth Amendment case law governing that complex subject. Instead, Congress promptly enacted a comprehensive statute, see 18 U. S. C. §§ 2510–2522 (2006 ed. and Supp. IV), and since that time, the regulation of wiretapping has been governed primarily by statute and not by case law. In an ironic sense, although *Katz* overruled *Olmstead*, Chief Justice Taft's suggestion in the latter case that the regulation of wiretapping was a matter better left for Congress, see 277 U. S., at 465–466, has been borne out.

Recent years have seen the emergence of many new devices that permit the monitoring of a person's movements. In some locales, closed-circuit television video monitoring is becoming ubiquitous. On toll roads, automatic toll collection systems create a precise record of the movements of motorists who choose to make use of that convenience. Many motorists purchase cars that are equipped with devices that permit a central station to ascertain the car's location at any time so that roadside assistance may be provided if needed and the car may be found if it is stolen.

Perhaps most significant, cell phones and other wireless devices now permit wireless carriers to track and record the location of users * * *. The availability and use of these and other new devices will continue to shape the average person's expectations about the privacy of his or her daily movements.

In the pre-computer age, the greatest protections of privacy were neither constitutional nor statutory, but practical. Traditional surveillance for any extended period of time was difficult and costly and therefore rarely undertaken. The surveillance at issue in this case—constant monitoring of the location of a vehicle for four weeks—would have required a large team of agents, multiple vehicles, and perhaps aerial assistance. Only an investigation of unusual importance could have justified such an expenditure of law enforcement resources. Devices like the one used in the present case, however, make long-term monitoring relatively easy and cheap * * *.

To date, however, Congress and most States have not enacted statutes regulating the use of GPS tracking technology for law enforcement purposes. The best that we can do in this case is to apply existing Fourth Amendment doctrine and to ask whether the use of GPS tracking in a particular case involved a degree of intrusion that a reasonable person would not have anticipated.

Under this approach, relatively short-term monitoring of a person's movements on public streets accords with expectations of privacy that our society has recognized as reasonable. But the use of longer term GPS monitoring in investigations of most offenses impinges on expectations of privacy. For such offenses, society's expectation has been that law enforcement agents and others would not—and indeed, in the main, simply could not—secretly monitor and catalogue every single movement of an individual's car for a very long period. In this case, for four weeks, law enforcement agents tracked every movement that respondent made in the vehicle he was driving. We need not identify with precision the point at which the tracking of this vehicle became a search, for the line was surely crossed before the 4-week mark. Other cases may present more difficult questions. But where uncertainty exists with respect to whether a certain period of GPS surveillance is long enough to constitute a Fourth Amendment search, the police may always seek a warrant. We also need not consider whether prolonged GPS monitoring in the context of investigations involving extraordinary offenses would similarly intrude on a constitutionally protected sphere of privacy. In such cases, long-term tracking might have been mounted using previously available techniques.

For these reasons, I conclude that the lengthy monitoring that occurred in this case constituted a search under the Fourth Amendment. I therefore agree with the majority that the decision of the Court of Appeals must be affirmed.

NOTES AND QUESTIONS

1. All of the opinions above explain valid reasons for thinking that the attaching of GPS devices by the police to private cars is an unconstitutional search. First, there is a trespass on a property right, however, minor. Second, there is a general warrant for information as to all of the defendant's travel with the hope that something suspicious will turn up. Third, there is an invasion of reasonably-expected privacy because people do not expect to be generally followed around wherever they go by the police, unless they have done something specific to trigger a search. Is it a strength or weakness of Fourth Amendment doctrine if vastly different methodologies lead to similar results?

2. *Jones* left open how to deal with government attempts to acquire cell-phone data from communications carriers. That problem not only involves yet another instance of applying the Fourth Amendment to new technology but also raises the problem that government searches of cell-phone carrier records are not obviously searches of the *customers'* persons or effects. As more and more information about people ends up in the possession of third parties, how does the Fourth Amendment respond? In 2018, the Supreme Court divided, along multiple lines, on this crucial question. In so doing, at least some justices suggested some very broad changes in doctrine.

D. CARPENTER V. UNITED STATES

585 U.S. ___, 138 S.Ct. 2206 (2018)

■ CHIEF JUSTICE ROBERTS delivered the opinion of the Court.

This case presents the question whether the Government conducts a search under the Fourth Amendment when it accesses historical cell phone records that provide a comprehensive chronicle of the user's past movements.

There are 396 million cell phone service accounts in the United States—for a Nation of 326 million people. Cell phones perform their wide and growing variety of functions by connecting to a set of radio antennas called "cell sites." Although cell sites are usually mounted on a tower, they can also be found on light posts, flagpoles, church steeples, or the sides of buildings. Cell sites typically have several directional antennas that divide the covered area into sectors.

Cell phones continuously scan their environment looking for the best signal, which generally comes from the closest cell site. Most modern devices, such as smartphones, tap into the wireless network several times a minute whenever their signal is on, even if the owner is not using one of the phone's features. Each time the phone connects to a cell site, it generates a time-stamped record known as cell-site location information (CSLI). The precision of this information depends on the size of the geographic area covered by the cell site. The greater the concentration of cell sites, the smaller the coverage area. As data usage from cell phones has increased, wireless carriers have installed more cell sites to handle the traffic. That has led to increasingly compact coverage areas, especially in urban areas.

Wireless carriers collect and store CSLI for their own business purposes, including finding weak spots in their network and applying "roaming" charges when another carrier routes data through their cell sites. In addition, wireless carriers often sell aggregated location records to data brokers, without individual identifying information of the sort at issue here. While carriers have long retained CSLI for the start and end of incoming calls, in recent years phone companies have also collected location information from the transmission of text messages and routine data connections. Accordingly, modern cell phones generate increasingly vast amounts of increasingly precise CSLI.

In 2011, police officers arrested four men suspected of robbing a series of Radio Shack and (ironically enough) T-Mobile stores in Detroit. One of the men confessed that, over the previous four months, the group (along with a rotating cast of getaway drivers and lookouts) had robbed nine different stores in Michigan and Ohio. The suspect identified 15 accomplices who had participated in the heists and gave the FBI some of their cell phone numbers; the FBI then reviewed his call records to identify additional numbers that he had called around the time of the robberies.

Based on that information, the prosecutors applied for court orders under the Stored Communications Act to obtain cell phone records for petitioner Timothy Carpenter and several other suspects. That statute, as amended in 1994, permits the Government to compel the disclosure of certain telecommunications records when it "offers specific and articulable facts showing that there are reasonable grounds to believe" that the records sought "are relevant and material to an ongoing criminal investigation." 18 U.S.C. § 2703(d). Federal Magistrate Judges issued two orders directing Carpenter's wireless carriers—MetroPCS and Sprint—to disclose "cell/site sector [information] for [Carpenter's] telephone[ ] at call origination and at call termination for incoming and outgoing calls" during the four-month period when the string of robberies occurred * * *. Altogether the Government obtained 12,898 location points cataloging Carpenter's movements—an average of 101 data points per day.

Carpenter was charged with six counts of robbery and an additional six counts of carrying a firearm during a federal crime of violence. Prior to trial, Carpenter moved to suppress the cell-site data provided by the wireless carriers. He argued that the Government's seizure of the records violated the Fourth Amendment because they had been obtained without a warrant supported by probable cause. The District Court denied the motion.

At trial, seven of Carpenter's confederates pegged him as the leader of the operation. In addition, FBI agent Christopher Hess offered expert testimony about the cell-site data. Hess explained that each time a cell phone taps into the wireless network, the carrier logs a time-stamped record of the cell site and particular sector that were used. With this information, Hess produced maps that placed Carpenter's phone near four of the charged robberies. In the Government's view, the location records clinched the case: They confirmed that Carpenter was "right where the . . . robbery was at the exact time of the robbery." App. 131 (closing argument). Carpenter was convicted on all but one of the firearm counts and sentenced to more than 100 years in prison.

The Court of Appeals for the Sixth Circuit affirmed. The court held that Carpenter lacked a reasonable expectation of privacy in the location information collected by the FBI because he had shared that information with his wireless carriers. Given that cell phone users voluntarily convey cell-site data to their carriers as "a means of establishing communication," the court concluded that the resulting business records are not entitled to Fourth Amendment protection.

* * *

The Fourth Amendment protects "[t]he right of the people to be secure in their persons, houses, papers, and effects, against unreasonable searches and seizures." The "basic purpose of this Amendment," our cases have recognized, "is to safeguard the privacy and security of individuals against arbitrary invasions by governmental officials." *Camara v. Municipal Court of City and County of San Francisco*, 387 U.S. 523, 528 (1967). The Founding generation crafted the Fourth Amendment as a "response to the reviled 'general warrants' and 'writs of assistance' of the colonial era, which allowed British officers to rummage through homes in an unrestrained search for evidence of criminal activity." *Riley v. California*, 573 U.S. ___, ___ (2014). In fact, as John Adams recalled, the patriot James Otis's 1761 speech condemning writs of assistance was "the first act of opposition to the arbitrary claims of Great Britain" and helped spark the Revolution itself.

For much of our history, Fourth Amendment search doctrine was "tied to common-law trespass" and focused on whether the Government "obtains information by physically intruding on a constitutionally protected area." *United States v. Jones*, 565 U.S. 400, 405, 406, n. 3 (2012). More recently, the Court has recognized that "property rights are not the sole measure of Fourth Amendment violations." In *Katz v. United States*, 389 U.S. 347, 351 (1967), we established that "the Fourth Amendment protects people, not places," and expanded our conception of the Amendment to protect certain expectations of privacy as well * * *.

Although no single rubric definitively resolves which expectations of privacy are entitled to protection, the analysis is informed by historical understandings "of what was deemed an unreasonable search and seizure when [the Fourth Amendment] was adopted." *Carroll v. United States*, 267 U.S. 132, 149 (1925). On this score, our cases have recognized some basic guideposts. First, that the Amendment seeks to secure "the privacies of life" against "arbitrary power." Second, and relatedly, that a central aim of the Framers was "to place obstacles in the way of a too permeating police surveillance."

We have kept this attention to Founding-era understandings in mind when applying the Fourth Amendment to innovations in surveillance tools. As technology has enhanced the Government's capacity to encroach upon areas normally guarded from inquisitive eyes, this Court has sought to "assure[ ] preservation of that degree of privacy against government that existed when the Fourth Amendment was adopted." *Kyllo v. United States*, 533 U.S. 27, 34 (2001). For that reason, we rejected in *Kyllo* a "mechanical interpretation" of the Fourth Amendment and held that use of a thermal imager to detect heat radiating from the side of the defendant's home was a search. *Id.*, at 35. Because any other conclusion would leave homeowners "at the mercy of advancing technology," we determined that the Government—absent a warrant—could not capitalize on such new sense-enhancing technology to explore what was happening within the home. Ibid.

* * *

The case before us involves the Government's acquisition of wireless carrier cell-site records revealing the location of Carpenter's cell phone whenever it made or received calls. This sort of digital data—personal location information maintained by a third party—does not fit neatly under existing precedents. Instead, requests for cell-site records lie at the intersection of two lines of cases, both of which inform our understanding of the privacy interests at stake.

The first set of cases addresses a person's expectation of privacy in his physical location and movements. In *United States v. Knotts*, 460 U.S. 276 (1983), we considered the Government's use of a "beeper" to aid in tracking a vehicle through traffic. Police officers in that case planted a beeper in a container of chloroform before it was purchased by one of Knotts's co-conspirators. The officers (with intermittent aerial assistance) then followed the automobile carrying the container from Minneapolis to Knotts's cabin in Wisconsin, relying on the beeper's signal to help keep the vehicle in view. The Court concluded that the "augment[ed]" visual surveillance did not constitute a search because "[a] person traveling in an automobile on public thoroughfares has no reasonable expectation of privacy in his movements from one place to another." *Id.*, at 281, 282. Since the movements of the vehicle and its final destination had been "voluntarily conveyed to anyone who wanted to look," Knotts could not assert a privacy interest in the information obtained. *Id.*, at 281.

* * *

Three decades later, the Court considered more sophisticated surveillance of the sort envisioned in *Knotts* and found that different principles did indeed apply. In *United States v. Jones*, FBI agents installed a GPS tracking device on Jones's vehicle and remotely monitored the vehicle's movements for 28 days. The Court decided the case based on the Government's physical trespass of the vehicle. At the same time, five Justices agreed that related privacy concerns would be raised by, for example, "surreptitiously activating a stolen vehicle detection system" in Jones's car to track Jones himself, or conducting GPS tracking of his cell phone. *Id.*, at 426, 428 (ALITO, J., concurring in judgment); *id.*, at 415 (SOTOMAYOR, J., concurring). Since GPS monitoring of a vehicle tracks "every movement" a person makes in that vehicle, the concurring Justices concluded that "longer term GPS monitoring in investigations of most offenses impinges on expectations of privacy"—regardless whether those movements were disclosed to the public at large.

In a second set of decisions, the Court has drawn a line between what a person keeps to himself and what he shares with others. We have previously held that "a person has no legitimate expectation of privacy in information he voluntarily turns over to third parties." That remains true "even if the information is revealed on the assumption that it will be used only for a limited purpose." *United States v. Miller*, 425 U.S. 435, 443 (1976). As a result, the Government is typically free to obtain such information from the recipient without triggering Fourth Amendment protections.

This third-party doctrine largely traces its roots to *Miller*. While investigating Miller for tax evasion, the Government subpoenaed his banks, seeking several months of canceled checks, deposit slips, and monthly statements. The Court rejected a Fourth Amendment challenge to the records collection. For one, Miller could "assert neither ownership nor possession" of the documents; they were "business records of the banks." *Id.*, at 440. For another, the nature of those records confirmed Miller's limited expectation of privacy, because the checks were "not confidential communications but negotiable instruments to be used in commercial transactions," and the bank statements contained information "exposed to [bank] employees in the ordinary course of business." *Id.*, at 442. The Court thus concluded that Miller had "take[n] the risk, in revealing his affairs to another, that the information [would] be conveyed by that person to the Government." *Id.*, at 443.

* * *

We decline to extend * * * *Miller* to cover these novel circumstances. Given the unique nature of cell phone location records, the fact that the information is held by a third party does not by itself overcome the user's claim to Fourth Amendment protection. Whether the Government employs its own surveillance technology as in *Jones* or leverages the technology of a wireless carrier, we hold that an individual maintains a legitimate expectation of privacy in the record of his physical movements as captured through CSLI. The location information obtained from Carpenter's wireless carriers was the product of a search.

A person does not surrender all Fourth Amendment protection by venturing into the public sphere * * *. Prior to the digital age, law enforcement might have pursued a suspect for a brief stretch, but doing so "for any extended period of time was difficult and costly and therefore rarely undertaken." For that reason, "society's expectation has been that law enforcement agents and others would not—and indeed, in the main, simply could not—secretly monitor and catalogue every single movement of an individual's car for a very long period."

Allowing government access to cell-site records contravenes that expectation. Although such records are generated for commercial purposes, that distinction does not negate Carpenter's anticipation of privacy in his physical location. Mapping a cell phone's location over the course of 127 days provides an all-encompassing record of the holder's whereabouts. As with GPS information, the time-stamped data provides an intimate window into a person's life * * *. And like GPS monitoring, cell phone tracking is remarkably easy, cheap, and efficient compared to traditional investigative tools. With just the click of a button, the Government can access each carrier's deep repository of historical location information at practically no expense.

* * * Accordingly, when the Government tracks the location of a cell phone it achieves near perfect surveillance, as if it had attached an ankle monitor to the phone's user.

* * *

The Government and Justice KENNEDY contend, however, that the collection of CSLI should be permitted because the data is less precise than GPS information. Not to worry, they maintain, because the location records did "not on their own suffice to place [Carpenter] at the crime scene"; they placed him within a wedge-shaped sector ranging from one-eighth to four square miles. Brief for United States 24. Yet the Court has already rejected the proposition that "inference insulates a search." *Kyllo,* 533 U.S., at 36. From the 127 days of location data it received, the Government could, in combination with other information, deduce a detailed log of Carpenter's movements, including when he was at the site of the robberies. And the Government thought the CSLI accurate enough to highlight it during the closing argument of his trial.

* * *

Accordingly, when the Government accessed CSLI from the wireless carriers, it invaded Carpenter's reasonable expectation of privacy in the whole of his physical movements.

The Government's primary contention to the contrary is that the third-party doctrine governs this case. In its view, cell-site records are fair game because they are "business records" created and maintained by the wireless carriers. The Government (along with Justice KENNEDY) recognizes that this case features new technology, but asserts that the legal question nonetheless turns on a garden-variety request for information from a third-party witness.

The Government's position fails to contend with the seismic shifts in digital technology that made possible the tracking of not only Carpenter's location but also everyone else's, not for a short period but for years and years. Sprint Corporation and its competitors are not your typical witnesses. Unlike the nosy neighbor who keeps an eye on comings and goings, they are ever alert, and their memory is nearly infallible * * *.The Government thus is not asking for a straightforward application of the third-party doctrine, but instead a significant extension of it to a distinct category of information.

* * *

* * * Cell phone location information is not truly "shared" as one normally understands the term. In the first place, cell phones and the services they provide are "such a pervasive and insistent part of daily life" that carrying one is indispensable to participation in modern society. *Riley*, 573 U.S., at ___. Second, a cell phone logs a cell-site record by dint of its operation, without any affirmative act on the part of the user beyond powering up. Virtually any activity on the phone generates CSLI, including incoming calls, texts, or e-mails and countless other data connections that a phone automatically makes when checking for news, weather, or social media updates. Apart from disconnecting the phone from the network, there is no way to avoid leaving behind a trail of location data. As a result, in no meaningful sense does the user voluntarily "assume[ ] the risk" of turning over a comprehensive dossier of his physical movements.

We therefore decline to extend * * * *Miller* to the collection of CSLI. Given the unique nature of cell phone location information, the fact that the Government obtained the information from a third party does not overcome Carpenter's claim to Fourth Amendment protection. The Government's acquisition of the cell-site records was a search within the meaning of the Fourth Amendment.

Our decision today is a narrow one. We do not express a view on matters not before us: real-time CSLI or "tower dumps" (a download of information on all the devices that connected to a particular cell site during a particular interval). We do not * * * call into question conventional surveillance techniques and tools, such as security cameras. Nor do we address other business records that might incidentally reveal location information. Further, our opinion does not consider other collection techniques involving foreign affairs or national security. As Justice Frankfurter noted when considering new innovations in airplanes and radios, the Court must tread carefully in such cases, to ensure that we do not "embarrass the future." *Northwest Airlines, Inc. v. Minnesota*, 322 U.S. 292, 300 (1944).

Having found that the acquisition of Carpenter's CSLI was a search, we also conclude that the Government must generally obtain a warrant supported by probable cause before acquiring such records. Although the "ultimate measure of the constitutionality of a governmental search is 'reasonableness,' " our cases establish that warrantless searches are typically unreasonable where "a search is undertaken by law enforcement officials to discover evidence of criminal wrongdoing." *Vernonia School Dist. 47J v. Acton*, 515 U.S. 646, 652–653 (1995). Thus, "[i]n the absence of a warrant, a search is reasonable only if it falls within a specific exception to the warrant requirement." *Riley*, 573 U.S., at ___.

The Government acquired the cell-site records pursuant to a court order issued under the Stored Communications Act, which required the Government to show "reasonable grounds" for believing that the records were "relevant and material to an ongoing investigation." 18 U.S.C. § 2703(d). That showing falls well short of the probable cause required for a warrant. The Court usually requires "some quantum of individualized suspicion" before a search or seizure may take place. Under the standard in the Stored Communications Act, however, law enforcement need only show that the cell-site evidence might be pertinent to an ongoing investigation—a "gigantic" departure from the probable cause rule, as the Government explained below. Consequently, an order issued under Section 2703(d) of the Act is not a permissible mechanism for accessing historical cell-site records. Before compelling a wireless carrier to turn over a subscriber's CSLI, the Government's obligation is a familiar one—get a warrant.

* * *

Further, even though the Government will generally need a warrant to access CSLI, case-specific exceptions may support a warrantless search of an individual's cell-site records under certain circumstances * * *.

As a result, if law enforcement is confronted with an urgent situation, such fact-specific threats will likely justify the warrantless collection of CSLI. Lower courts, for instance, have approved warrantless searches related to bomb threats, active shootings, and child abductions. Our decision today does not call into doubt warrantless access to CSLI in such circumstances. While police must get a warrant when collecting CSLI to assist in the mine-run criminal investigation, the rule we set forth does not limit their ability to respond to an ongoing emergency.

* * *

We decline to grant the state unrestricted access to a wireless carrier's database of physical location information. In light of the deeply revealing nature of CSLI, its depth, breadth, and comprehensive reach, and the inescapable and automatic nature of its collection, the fact that such information is gathered by a third party does not make it any less deserving of Fourth Amendment protection. The Government's acquisition of the cell-site records here was a search under that Amendment.

The judgment of the Court of Appeals is reversed, and the case is remanded for further proceedings consistent with this opinion.

It is so ordered.

■ JUSTICE KENNEDY, with whom JUSTICE THOMAS and JUSTICE ALITO join, dissenting.

This case involves new technology, but the Court's stark departure from relevant Fourth Amendment precedents and principles is, in my submission, unnecessary and incorrect, requiring this respectful dissent.

The new rule the Court seems to formulate puts needed, reasonable, accepted, lawful, and congressionally authorized criminal investigations at serious risk in serious cases, often when law enforcement seeks to prevent the threat of violent crimes. And it places undue restrictions on the lawful and necessary enforcement powers exercised not only by the Federal Government, but also by law enforcement in every State and locality throughout the Nation. Adherence to this Court's longstanding precedents and analytic framework would have been the proper and prudent way to resolve this case.

The Court has twice held that individuals have no Fourth Amendment interests in business records which are possessed, owned, and controlled by a third party. *United States v. Miller*, 425 U.S. 435 (1976); *Smith v. Maryland*, 442 U.S. 735 (1979). This is true even when the records contain personal and sensitive information. So when the Government uses a subpoena to obtain, for example, bank records, telephone records, and credit card statements from the businesses that create and keep these records, the Government does not engage in a search of the business's customers within the meaning of the Fourth Amendment.

In this case petitioner challenges the Government's right to use compulsory process to obtain a now-common kind of business record: cell-site records held by cell phone service providers. The Government acquired the records through an investigative process enacted by Congress. Upon approval by a neutral magistrate, and based on the Government's duty to show reasonable necessity, it authorizes the disclosure of records and information that are under the control and ownership of the cell phone service provider, not its customer. Petitioner acknowledges that the Government may obtain a wide variety of business records using compulsory process, and he does not ask the Court to revisit its precedents. Yet he argues that, under those same precedents, the Government searched his records when it used court-approved compulsory process to obtain the cell-site information at issue here.

Cell-site records, however, are no different from the many other kinds of business records the Government has a lawful right to obtain by compulsory process. Customers like petitioner do not own, possess, control, or use the records, and for that reason have no reasonable expectation that they cannot be disclosed pursuant to lawful compulsory process.

The Court today disagrees. It holds for the first time that by using compulsory process to obtain records of a business entity, the Government has not just engaged in an impermissible action, but has conducted a search of the business's customer. The Court further concludes that the search in this case was unreasonable and the Government needed to get a warrant to obtain more than six days of cell-site records.

In concluding that the Government engaged in a search, the Court unhinges Fourth Amendment doctrine from the property-based concepts that have long grounded the analytic framework that pertains in these cases. In doing so it draws an unprincipled and unworkable line between cell-site records on the one hand and financial and telephonic records on the other. According to today's majority opinion, the Government can acquire a record of every credit card purchase and phone call a person makes over months or years without upsetting a legitimate expectation of privacy. But, in the Court's view, the Government crosses a constitutional line when it obtains a court's approval to issue a subpoena for more than six days of cell-site records in order to determine whether a person was within several hundred city blocks of a crime scene. That distinction is illogical and will frustrate principled application of the Fourth Amendment in many routine yet vital law enforcement operations.

It is true that the Cyber Age has vast potential both to expand and restrict individual freedoms in dimensions not contemplated in earlier times. For the reasons that follow, however, there is simply no basis here for concluding that the Government interfered with information that the cell phone customer, either from a legal or commonsense standpoint, should have thought the law would deem owned or controlled by him.

* * *

Here the only question necessary to decide is whether the Government searched anything of Carpenter's when it used compulsory process to obtain cell-site records from Carpenter's cell phone service providers * * *.

Miller and *Smith* hold that individuals lack any protected Fourth Amendment interests in records that are possessed, owned, and controlled only by a third party. In *Miller* federal law enforcement officers obtained four months of the defendant's banking records. And in *Smith* state police obtained records of the phone numbers dialed from the defendant's home phone. The Court held in both cases that the officers did not search anything belonging to the defendants within the meaning of the Fourth Amendment. The defendants could "assert neither ownership nor possession" of the records because the records were created, owned, and controlled by the companies. And the defendants had no reasonable expectation of privacy in information they "voluntarily conveyed to the [companies] and exposed to their employees in the ordinary course of business." Rather, the defendants "assumed the risk that the information would be divulged to police."

Miller and *Smith* have been criticized as being based on too narrow a view of reasonable expectations of privacy * * *. Those criticisms, however, are unwarranted. The principle established in *Miller* and *Smith* is correct for two reasons, the first relating to a defendant's attenuated interest in property owned by another, and the second relating to the safeguards inherent in the use of compulsory process.

* * *

Miller and *Smith* * * * rest upon the commonsense principle that the absence of property law analogues can be dispositive of privacy expectations. The defendants in those cases could expect that the third-party businesses could use the records the companies collected, stored, and classified as their own for any number of business and commercial purposes. The businesses were not bailees or custodians of the records, with a duty to hold the records for the defendants' use. The defendants could make no argument that the records were their own papers or effects. The records were the business entities' records, plain and simple. The defendants had no reason to believe the records were owned or controlled by them and so could not assert a reasonable expectation of privacy in the records.

The second principle supporting *Miller* and *Smith* is the longstanding rule that the Government may use compulsory process to compel persons to disclose documents and other evidence within their possession and control. See *United States v. Nixon*, 418 U.S. 683, 709 (1974) (it is an "ancient proposition of law" that "the public has a right to every man's evidence" (internal quotation marks and alterations omitted)). A subpoena is different from a warrant in its force and intrusive power. While a warrant allows the Government to enter and seize and make the examination itself, a subpoena simply requires the person to whom it is directed to make the disclosure. A subpoena, moreover, provides the recipient the "opportunity to present objections" before complying, which further mitigates the intrusion.

For those reasons this Court has held that a subpoena for records, although a "constructive" search subject to Fourth Amendment constraints, need not comply with the procedures applicable to warrants—even when challenged by the person to whom the records belong. Rather, a subpoena complies with the Fourth Amendment's reasonableness requirement so long as it is " 'sufficiently limited in scope, relevant in purpose, and specific in directive so that compliance will not be unreasonably burdensome.' " *Donovan v. Lone Steer, Inc.*, 464 U.S. 408, 415 (1984). Persons with no meaningful interests in the records sought by a subpoena, like the defendants in *Miller* and *Smith*, have no rights to object to the records' disclosure—much less to assert that the Government must obtain a warrant to compel disclosure of the records.

* * *

Carpenter does not question these traditional investigative practices. And he does not ask the Court to reconsider *Miller* and *Smith*. Carpenter argues only that, under *Miller* and *Smith*, the Government may not use compulsory process to acquire cell-site records from cell phone service providers.

There is no merit in this argument. Cell-site records, like all the examples just discussed, are created, kept, classified, owned, and controlled by cell phone service providers, which aggregate and sell this information to third parties. As in *Miller*, Carpenter can "assert neither ownership nor possession" of the records and has no control over them. 425 U.S., at 440.

* * *

Because Carpenter lacks a requisite connection to the cell-site records, he also may not claim a reasonable expectation of privacy in them. He could expect that a third party—the cell phone service provider—could use the information it collected, stored, and classified as its own for a variety of business and commercial purposes.

All this is not to say that *Miller* and *Smith* are without limits. *Miller* and *Smith* may not apply when the Government obtains the modern-day equivalents of an individual's own "papers" or "effects," even when those papers or effects are held by a third party. See *Ex parte Jackson*, 96 U.S. 727, 733 (1878) (letters held by mail carrier); *United States v. Warshak*, 631 F.3d 266, 283–288 (C.A.6 2010) (e-mails held by Internet service provider). As already discussed, however, this case does not involve property or a bailment of that sort. Here the Government's acquisition of cell-site records falls within the heartland of *Miller* and *Smith*.

* * *

The Court errs at the outset by attempting to sidestep *Miller* and *Smith*. The Court frames this case as following instead from *United States v. Knotts*, 460 U.S. 276 (1983), and *United States v. Jones*, 565 U.S. 400 (2012). Those cases, the Court suggests, establish that "individuals have a reasonable expectation of privacy in the whole of their physical movements."

Knotts held just the opposite: "A person traveling in an automobile on public thoroughfares has no reasonable expectation of privacy in his movements from one place to another." 460 U.S., at 281 * * *.

* * *

The Court's reliance on *Jones* fares no better. In *Jones* the Government installed a GPS tracking device on the defendant's automobile. The Court held the Government searched the automobile because it "physically occupied private property [of the defendant] for the purpose of obtaining information." 565 U.S., at 404. So in Jones it was "not necessary to inquire about the target's expectation of privacy in his vehicle's movements."

* * *

* * * [T]he Court errs, in my submission, when it concludes that cell-site records implicate greater privacy interests—and thus deserve greater Fourth Amendment protection—than financial records and telephone records.

Indeed, the opposite is true. A person's movements are not particularly private * * *. Today expectations of privacy in one's location are, if anything, even less reasonable than when the Court decided *Knotts* over 30 years ago. Millions of Americans choose to share their location on a daily basis, whether by using a variety of location-based services on their phones, or by sharing their location with friends and the public at large via social media.

* * *

By contrast, financial records and telephone records do " 'revea[l] . . . personal affairs, opinions, habits and associations.' " What persons purchase and to whom they talk might disclose how much money they make; the political and religious organizations to which they donate; whether they have visited a psychiatrist, plastic surgeon, abortion clinic, or AIDS treatment center; whether they go to gay bars or straight ones; and who are their closest friends and family members. The troves of intimate information the Government can and does obtain using financial records and telephone records dwarfs what can be gathered from cell-site records.

* * *

Technological changes involving cell phones have complex effects on crime and law enforcement. Cell phones make crimes easier to coordinate and conceal, while also providing the Government with new investigative tools that may have the potential to upset traditional privacy expectations. How those competing effects balance against each other, and how property norms and expectations of privacy form around new technology, often will be difficult to determine during periods of rapid technological change. In those instances, and where the governing legal standard is one of reasonableness, it is wise to defer to legislative judgments like the one embodied in § 2703(d) of the Stored Communications Act * * *.

* * *

■ JUSTICE THOMAS, dissenting.

This case should not turn on "whether" a search occurred. It should turn, instead, on *whose* property was searched. The Fourth Amendment guarantees individuals the right to be secure from unreasonable searches of "*their* persons, houses, papers, and effects." (Emphasis added.) In other words, "*each* person has the right to be secure against unreasonable searches . . . in his *own* person, house, papers, and effects." *Minnesota v. Carter*, 525 U.S. 83, 92 (1998) (Scalia, J., concurring). By obtaining the cell-site records of MetroPCS and Sprint, the Government did not search Carpenter's property. He did not create the records, he does not maintain them, he cannot control them, and he cannot destroy them. Neither the terms of his contracts nor any provision of law makes the records his. The records belong to MetroPCS and Sprint.

* * *

The more fundamental problem with the Court's opinion, however, is its use of the "reasonable expectation of privacy" test, which was first articulated by Justice Harlan in *Katz v. United States*, 389 U.S. 347, 360–361 (1967) (concurring opinion). The *Katz* test has no basis in the text or history of the Fourth Amendment. And, it invites courts to make judgments about policy, not law. Until we confront the problems with this test, *Katz* will continue to distort Fourth Amendment jurisprudence. I respectfully dissent.

* * *

* * * The Fourth Amendment, as relevant here, protects "[t]he right of the people to be secure in their persons, houses, papers, and effects, against unreasonable searches." By defining "search" to mean "any violation of a reasonable expectation of privacy," the *Katz* test misconstrues virtually every one of these words.

* * *

At the founding, "search" did not mean a violation of someone's reasonable expectation of privacy. The word was probably not a term of art, as it does not appear in legal dictionaries from the era. And its ordinary meaning was the same as it is today: " '[t]o look over or through for the purpose of finding something; to explore; to examine by inspection; as, to *search* the house for a book; to *search* the wood for a thief.' " *Kyllo v. United States*, 533 U.S. 27, 32, n. 1 (2001) (quoting N. Webster, An American Dictionary of the English Language 66 (1828) (reprint 6th ed. 1989)); accord, 2 S. Johnson, A Dictionary of the English Language (5th ed. 1773) ("Inquiry by looking into every suspected place"); N. Bailey, An Universal Etymological English Dictionary (22d ed. 1770) ("a seeking after, a looking for, & c."); 2 J. Ash, The New and Complete Dictionary of the English Language (2d ed. 1795) ("An enquiry, an examination, the act of seeking, an enquiry by looking into every suspected place; a quest; a pursuit"); T. Sheridan, A Complete Dictionary of the English Language (6th ed. 1796) (similar). The word "search" was not associated with "reasonable expectation of privacy" until Justice Harlan coined that phrase in 1967. The phrase "expectation(s) of privacy" does not appear in the pre-*Katz* federal or state case reporters, the papers of prominent Founders, early congressional documents and debates, collections of early American English texts, or early American newspapers.

The *Katz* test strays even further from the text by focusing on the concept of "privacy." The word "privacy" does not appear in the Fourth Amendment (or anywhere else in the Constitution for that matter) * * *.

* * *

In shifting the focus of the Fourth Amendment from property to privacy, the *Katz* test also reads the words "persons, houses, papers, and effects" out of the text * * *. The Founders decided to protect the people from unreasonable searches and seizures of four specific things—persons, houses, papers, and effects * * *.

This limiting language was important to the founders. Madison's first draft of the Fourth Amendment used a different phrase: "their persons, their houses, their papers, and their *other property*." 1 Annals of Cong. 452 (1789) (emphasis added). In one of the few changes made to Madison's draft, the House Committee of Eleven changed "other property" to "effects." See House Committee of Eleven Report (July 28, 1789), in N. Cogan, The Complete Bill of Rights 334 (2d ed. 2015). This change might have narrowed the Fourth Amendment by clarifying that it does not protect real property (other than houses). Or the change might have broadened the Fourth Amendment by clarifying that it protects commercial goods, not just personal possessions. Or it might have done both. Whatever its ultimate effect, the change reveals that the Founders understood the phrase "persons, houses, papers, and effects" to be an important measure of the Fourth Amendment's overall scope. The *Katz* test, however, displaces and renders that phrase entirely "superfluous."

* * *

* * * Although the *Katz* test is phrased in descriptive terms about society's views, this Court treats it like a normative question—whether a particular practice *should* be considered a search under the Fourth Amendment. Justice Harlan thought this was the best way to understand his test. And a normative understanding is the only way to make sense of this Court's precedents, which bear the hallmarks of subjective policymaking instead of neutral legal decisionmaking. "[T]he only thing the past three decades have established about the *Katz* test" is that society's expectations of privacy "bear an uncanny resemblance to those expectations of privacy that this Court considers reasonable." Yet, "[t]hough we know ourselves to be eminently reasonable, self-awareness of eminent reasonableness is not really a substitute for democratic election." *Sosa v. Alvarez-Machain*, 542 U.S. 692, 750 (2004) (Scalia, J., concurring in part and concurring in judgment).

* * *

Because the *Katz* test is a failed experiment, this Court is dutybound to reconsider it. Until it does, I agree with my dissenting colleagues' reading of our precedents. Accordingly, I respectfully dissent.

■ JUSTICE ALITO, with whom JUSTICE THOMAS joins, dissenting. [Omitted.]

■ JUSTICE GORSUCH, dissenting.

In the late 1960s this Court suggested for the first time that a search triggering the Fourth Amendment occurs when the government violates an "expectation of privacy" that "society is prepared to recognize as 'reasonable.'" *Katz v. United States*, 389 U.S. 347, 361 (1967) (Harlan, J., concurring). Then, in a pair of decisions in the

1970s applying the *Katz* test, the Court held that a "reasonable expectation of privacy" *doesn't* attach to information shared with "third parties." See *Smith v. Maryland*, 442 U.S. 735, 743–744 (1979); *United States v. Miller*, 425 U.S. 435, 443 (1976). By these steps, the Court came to conclude, the Constitution does nothing to limit investigators from searching records you've entrusted to your bank, accountant, and maybe even your doctor.

What's left of the Fourth Amendment? Today we use the Internet to do most everything. Smartphones make it easy to keep a calendar, correspond with friends, make calls, conduct banking, and even watch the game. Countless Internet companies maintain records about us and, increasingly, *for* us. Even our most private documents—those that, in other eras, we would have locked safely in a desk drawer or destroyed—now reside on third party servers. *Smith* and *Miller* teach that the police can review all of this material, on the theory that no one reasonably expects any of it will be kept private. But no one believes that, if they ever did.

What to do? It seems to me we could respond in at least three ways. The first is to ignore the problem, maintain *Smith* and *Miller*, and live with the consequences. If the confluence of these decisions and modern technology means our Fourth Amendment rights are reduced to nearly nothing, so be it. The second choice is to set *Smith* and *Miller* aside and try again using the *Katz* "reasonable expectation of privacy" jurisprudence that produced them. The third is to look for answers elsewhere.

Start with the first option. *Smith* held that the government's use of a pen register to record the numbers people dial on their phones doesn't infringe a reasonable expectation of privacy because that information is freely disclosed to the third party phone company. 442 U.S., at 743–744. *Miller* held that a bank account holder enjoys no reasonable expectation of privacy in the bank's records of his account activity * * *. Those cases announced a categorical rule: Once you disclose information to third parties, you forfeit any reasonable expectation of privacy you might have had in it * * *.

* * * But that result strikes most lawyers and judges today—me included—as pretty unlikely * * *. People often *do* reasonably expect that information they entrust to third parties, especially information subject to confidentiality agreements, will be kept private. Meanwhile, if the third party doctrine is supposed to represent a normative assessment of when a person should expect privacy, the notion that the answer might be "never" seems a pretty unattractive societal prescription.

What, then, is the explanation for our third party doctrine? The truth is, the Court has never offered a persuasive justification * * *.

* * *

There's a second option. What if we dropped *Smith* and *Miller*'s third party doctrine and retreated to the root *Katz* question whether there is a "reasonable expectation of privacy" in data held by third parties? Rather than solve the problem with the third party doctrine, I worry this option only risks returning us to its source: After all, it was *Katz* that produced *Smith* and *Miller* in the first place.

Katz's problems start with the text and original understanding of the Fourth Amendment, as JUSTICE THOMAS thoughtfully explains today * * *.

* * *

In the end, our lower court colleagues are left with two amorphous balancing tests, a series of weighty and incommensurable principles to consider in them, and a few illustrative examples that seem little more than the product of judicial intuition. In the Court's defense, though, we have arrived at this strange place not because the Court has misunderstood *Katz*. Far from it. We have arrived here because this is where *Katz* inevitably leads.

There is another way. From the founding until the 1960s, the right to assert a Fourth Amendment claim didn't depend on your ability to appeal to a judge's personal sensibilities about the "reasonableness" of your expectations or privacy. It was tied to the law. The Fourth Amendment protects "the right of the people to be secure in their persons, houses, papers and effects, against unreasonable searches and seizures." True to those words and their original understanding, the traditional approach asked if a house, paper or effect was *yours* under law. No more was needed to trigger the Fourth Amendment. Though now often lost in *Katz*'s shadow, this traditional understanding persists. *Katz* only "supplements, rather than displaces the traditional property-based understanding of the Fourth Amendment."

* * *

Given the prominence *Katz* has claimed in our doctrine, American courts are pretty rusty at applying the traditional approach to the Fourth Amendment. We know that if a house, paper, or effect is yours, you have a Fourth Amendment interest in its protection. But what kind of legal interest is sufficient to make something *yours*? And what source of law determines that? Current positive law? The common law at 1791, extended by analogy to modern times? Both? Much work is needed to revitalize this area and answer these questions. I do not begin to claim all the answers today, but (unlike with *Katz*) at least I have a pretty good idea what the questions are. And it seems to me a few things can be said.

First, the fact that a third party has access to or possession of your papers and effects does not necessarily eliminate your interest in them. Ever hand a private document to a friend to be returned? Toss your keys to a valet at a restaurant? Ask your neighbor to look after your dog while you travel? You would not expect the friend to share the document with others; the valet to lend your car to his buddy; or the neighbor to put Fido up for adoption. Entrusting your stuff to others is a *bailment*. A bailment is the "delivery of personal property by one person (the *bailor*) to another (the *bailee*) who holds the property for a certain purpose." Black's Law Dictionary 169 (10th ed. 2014). A bailee normally owes a legal duty to keep the item safe, according to the terms of the parties' contract if they have one, and according to the "implication[s] from their conduct" if they don't. 8 C.J. S., Bailments § 36, pp. 468–469 (2017) * * *. This approach is quite different from *Smith* and *Miller*'s (counter)-intuitive approach to reasonable expectations of privacy; where those cases extinguish Fourth Amendment interests once records are given to a third party, property law may preserve them.

* * *

These ancient principles may help us address modern data cases too. Just because you entrust your data—in some cases, your modern-day papers and effects—to a third party may not mean you lose any Fourth Amendment interest in its contents. Whatever may be left of *Smith* and *Miller*, few doubt that e-mail should be treated much like the traditional mail it has largely supplanted—as a bailment in which the owner retains a vital and protected legal interest * * *.

Second, I doubt that complete ownership or exclusive control of property is always a necessary condition to the assertion of a Fourth Amendment right. Where houses are concerned, for example, individuals can enjoy Fourth Amendment protection without fee simple title * * *. That is why tenants and resident family members—though they have no legal title—have standing to complain about searches of the houses in which they live.

Another point seems equally true: just because you *have* to entrust a third party with your data doesn't necessarily mean you should lose all Fourth Amendment protections in it. Not infrequently one person comes into possession of someone else's property without the owner's consent. Think of the finder of lost goods or the policeman who impounds a car. The law recognizes that the goods and the car still belong to their true owners, for "where a person comes into lawful possession of the personal property of another, even though there is no formal agreement between the property's owner and its possessor, the possessor will become a constructive bailee when justice so requires." *Christensen v. Hoover*, 643 P.2d 525, 529 (Colo.1982) (en banc); Laidlaw, Principles of Bailment, 16 Cornell L.Q. 286 (1931). At least some of this Court's decisions have already suggested that use of technology is functionally compelled by the demands of modern life, and in that way the fact that we store data with third parties may amount to a sort of involuntary bailment too.

Third, positive law may help provide detailed guidance on evolving technologies without resort to judicial intuition. State (or sometimes federal) law often creates rights in both tangible and intangible things * * *.

Fourth, while positive law may help establish a person's Fourth Amendment interest there may be some circumstances where positive law cannot be used to defeat it * * *. Legislatures cannot pass laws declaring your house or papers to be your property except to the extent the police wish to search them without cause * * *.

Fifth, this constitutional floor may, in some instances, bar efforts to circumvent the Fourth Amendment's protection through the use of subpoenas * * *.

* * *

Our case offers a cautionary example. It seems to me entirely possible a person's cell-site data could qualify as *his* papers or effects under existing law. Yes, the telephone carrier holds the information. But 47 U.S.C. § 222 designates a customer's cell-site location information as "customer proprietary network information" (CPNI), § 222(h)(1)(A), and gives customers certain rights to control use of and access to CPNI about themselves. The statute generally forbids a carrier to "use, disclose, or permit access to individually identifiable" CPNI without the customer's consent, except as needed to provide the customer's telecommunications services. § 222(c)(1). It also requires the carrier to disclose CPNI "upon affirmative written request by the customer, to any person designated by the customer." § 222(c)(2). Congress even afforded customers a private cause of action for damages against carriers who violate the Act's terms. § 207. Plainly, customers have substantial legal interests in this information, including at least some right to include, exclude, and control its use. Those interests might even rise to the level of a property right.

The problem is that we do not know anything more. Before the district court and court of appeals, Mr. Carpenter pursued only a *Katz* "reasonable expectations" argument. He did not invoke the law of property or any analogies to the common law, either there or in his petition for certiorari. Even in his merits brief before this Court, Mr. Carpenter's discussion of his positive law rights in cell-site data was cursory. He offered no analysis, for example, of what rights state law might provide him in addition to those supplied by § 222. In these circumstances, I cannot help but conclude—reluctantly—that Mr. Carpenter forfeited perhaps his most promising line of argument.

* * *

NOTES AND QUESTIONS

1. Two justices—the two most committed to a jurisprudence of original meaning—have now called for *Katz* to be overruled, or at least substantially revised. Do you agree?

2. Justice Alito's dissent, which we omitted, concerned primarily whether the Fourth Amendment applies to subpoenas, which are a standard way in which the government collects information from party about another. Why wouldn't the Fourth Amendment apply to a search via a subpoena just as much as it applies to any other kind of search? Or does the prior judicial approval of the subpoena cure all problems?

3. Which do you think offers more secure protection against government overreaching: Tying the Fourth Amendment to property concepts or having judges determine one's reasonable expectations of privacy? Or should both concepts be employed?

4. The usual remedy for a Fourth Amendment violation is to preclude illegally seized evidence from being introduced against a defendant. In 1763 (and 1791), the remedy was a tort suit against the offending government officials, with the illegality of the search stripping away any legal authorization that they could try to claim. The U.S. Supreme Court adopted the exclusionary rule in *Weeks v. United States,* 232 U.S. 383 (1914), a case in which Weeks' house and papers were searched and seized without a search warrant or his permission. The Supreme Court held that the federal courts would exclude such evidence from consideration because the federal courts could not condone or be part of such constitutional violations. The Supreme Court did not initially apply the exclusionary rule against the States, see *Wolf v. Colorado,* 338 U.S. 25 (1949), but eventually reversed itself in *Mapp v. Ohio,* 367 U.S. 643 (1961). The Supreme Court cut back sharply on the exclusionary rule in *United States v. Leon,* 468 U.S. 897 (1984) where it created a good faith exception to the rule. For a thorough treatment, see TRACEY MACLIN, THE SUPREME COURT AND THE FOURTH AMENDMENT'S EXCLUSIONARY RULE (2012). The argument against the exclusionary rule is that if an individual does something illegal and then the police violate the Constitution in exposing the wrongdoing; you have two wrongdoers, both of whom should be punished. Supporters of the exclusionary rule think that a tort system of enforcing Fourth and Fifth Amendment rights would never work. It is not even clear that our tort system works well for product liability, so why expand it into a new area, and the knowledge that the courts will exclude illegally obtained evidence gives the police an incentive to follow the Constitution. Justice Clarence Thomas is the only current member of the Supreme Court to call for overruling the exclusionary rule, though a significant number of scholars continue to oppose the rule. *See, e.g.,* Akhil Reed Amar, *Fourth Amendment First Principles,* 107 HARV. L. REV. 757, 785–801 (1994). If one were to discard the exclusionary rule, one would also need to reform "qualified immunity" doctrine, which shields government officials from personal liability unless they have violated "clearly established" norms, *see Harlow v. Fitzgerald,* 457 U.S. 800 (1982). *See* Amar, *supra,* at 812–14.

[Assignment 51]

IV. THE FIFTH AMENDMENT

> **No person shall be held to answer for a capital, or otherwise infamous crime, unless on a presentment or indictment of a grand jury, except in cases arising in the land or naval forces, or in the militia, when in actual service in time of war or public danger; nor shall any person be subject for the same offense to be twice put in jeopardy of life or limb; nor shall be compelled in any criminal case to be a witness against himself, nor be deprived of life, liberty, or property, without due process of law; nor shall private property be taken for public use, without just compensation.**

The Fifth Amendment recognizes the existence of five different rights: 1) the right to be indicted by a grand jury in cases of civilian criminal justice; 2) the right against double jeopardy; 3) the right against self-incrimination; 4) the right not to be deprived of life, liberty, or property without due process of law; and 5) the right not to have property taken except for a public use or with just compensation being paid. In this chapter, we present cases on double jeopardy, due process of law, and takings. We only briefly mention the other two rights protected by the Fifth Amendment, not because they are unimportant but simply for lack of space and time.

The right not to be indicted except by a grand jury has been discussed already in this casebook, in *United States v. Cox,* 342 F. 2d 167 (5th Cir. 1965). *See supra* pages 369–381. Grand juries were intended to be a protection for the citizen against being indicted by a prosecutor alone, and the mere decision of a grand jury that it wants to indict someone is not binding on the prosecutor, as *United States v. Cox* holds. As we noted earlier, however, grand juries in this day and age are not much of an impediment to a prosecutor who wants to indict. *See supra* page 368. Indeed, because grand juries have sweeping investigatory powers, there is reason to think that they are more beneficial to prosecutors than to defendants. *See* Andrew D. Leipold, *Why Grand Juries Do Not (AND Cannot) Protect the Accused,* 80 CORNELL L. REV. 260 (1995). Evidence collected in grand jury proceedings is generally kept secret. *See* Fed. R. Crim. Proc. 6(e). This has been illustrated recently by the Justice Department's determination to keep the grand jury information developed by Robert Mueller in his criminal investigation of President Trump strictly secret. The right against self-incrimination developed at common law to protect individuals who were tortured by the King to confess by holding that statements incriminating oneself were inadmissible in court. The right against self-incrimination exists only in common law countries and not in the civil law countries of Continental Europe, Asia, and Latin America. In civil law countries, the criminal defendant is always called as the first witness at trial, and conclusions may be drawn from his or her failure to answer questions. Since the bench in civil law countries simultaneously convicts and sentences criminal defendants, such defendants face a powerful incentive to testify at trial. The origins of the privilege against self-incrimination in English law can be found in R.H. HELMHOLZ, CHARLES M. GRAY, JOHN H. LANGBEIN, EBEN MOGLEN, HENRY E. SMITH, & ALBERT W. ALSCHULER, THE PRIVILEGE AGAINST SELF-INCRIMINATION: ITS ORIGINS AND DEVELOPMENT (1997). For a masterful account of the origins in the United States of the privilege against self-incrimination, see JOHN H. LANGBEIN, THE ORIGINS OF ADVERSARY CRIMINAL TRIAL (2005). For a riveting account of how differently criminal trials are conducted when the defendant always speaks and conclusions are drawn from his or her silence and changing stories, see Renee Lettow Lerner, *The Intersection of Two Systems: An American on Trial for an American Murder in the French Cour d'Assises*, 2001 U. ILL. L. REV. 791.

The most important U.S. self-incrimination case is *Miranda v. Arizona*, 384 U.S. 436 (1966), which is actually a Fourteenth Amendment case incorporating the Fifth Amendment to apply against the States. In this case, the Warren Court held that the police must issue a standard warning to all defendants upon their arrest advising them of their right to remain silent and of the fact that anything they say or do may be held against them when they are prosecuted. (When you take a course in Evidence, you will learn why the police can testify about what criminal defendants said even though it seems like hearsay.) Congress attempted to overrule *Miranda v. Arizona* by statute in federal criminal trials, but in *United States v. Dickerson,* 530 U.S. 428 (2000), the Supreme Court held the federal statute overruling *Miranda* unconstitutional on Fifth Amendment grounds.

The Double Jeopardy Clause "protects against successive prosecutions for the same offense after acquittal or conviction and against multiple criminal punishments for the same offense." *Monge v. California,* 524 U.S. 721 (1998). The prohibition against double jeopardy is deeply rooted in American law: "All state constitutions drafted prior to Bill of Rights contained a double jeopardy provision." G. Robert Blakey, *Double Jeopardy, in* THE HERITAGE GUIDE TO THE CONSTITUTION 435 (rev. 2d ed. 2014). Question can arise about what constitutes punishment—do civil fines count?—and exactly when one is put in "jeopardy," but the biggest questions under the clause have concerned what counts as an "offence." Suppose Congress defines two separate crimes—for example, "counterfeiting of federal documents" and "counterfeiting of passports." The proof of the first constitutes conclusive proof of the second as well. Can the government try you for the first crime, lose, and then take another shot under the second "crime"? Generally speaking, the answer is no. *See Blockburger v. United States,* 284 U.S. 299, 304 (1932) ("where the same act or transaction constitutes a violation of two distinct statutory provisions, the test to be applied to determine whether there are two offenses or only one, is whether each provision requires proof of a fact which the other does not"). A more profound question is how to handle double jeopardy in a federal system. Suppose that both the State and federal governments have jurisdiction over a matter, and each government criminalizes the same conduct. Does prosecution by one government foreclose prosecution by the other? The Supreme Court took up that question in 2019.

A. DOUBLE JEOPARDY

Gamble v. United States

587 U.S. ___, 139 S.Ct. 1960 (2019)

■ JUSTICE ALITO delivered the opinion of the Court.

We consider in this case whether to overrule a longstanding interpretation of the Double Jeopardy Clause of the Fifth Amendment. That Clause provides that no person may be "twice put in jeopardy" "for the same offence." Our double jeopardy case law is complex, but at its core, the Clause means that those acquitted or convicted of a particular "offence" cannot be tried a second time for the same "offence." But what does the Clause mean by an "offence"?

We have long held that a crime under one sovereign's laws is not "the same offence" as a crime under the laws of another sovereign. Under this "dual-sovereignty" doctrine, a State may prosecute a defendant under state law even if the Federal Government has prosecuted him for the same conduct under a federal statute.

Or the reverse may happen, as it did here. Terance Gamble, convicted by Alabama for possessing a firearm as a felon, now faces prosecution by the United States under its own felon-in-possession law. Attacking this second prosecution on double jeopardy grounds, Gamble asks us to overrule the dual-sovereignty doctrine. He contends that it departs from the founding-era understanding of the right enshrined by the Double Jeopardy Clause. But the historical evidence assembled by Gamble is feeble; pointing the other way are the Clause's text, other historical evidence, and 170 years of precedent. Today we affirm that precedent, and with it the decision below.

In November 2015, a local police officer in Mobile, Alabama, pulled Gamble over for a damaged headlight. Smelling marijuana, the officer searched Gamble's car, where he found a loaded 9-mm handgun. Since Gamble had been convicted of second-degree robbery, his possession of the handgun violated an Alabama law providing that no one convicted of "a crime of violence" "shall own a firearm or have one in his or her possession." After Gamble pleaded guilty to this state offense, federal prosecutors indicted him for the same instance of possession under a federal law—one forbidding those convicted of "a crime punishable by imprisonment for a term exceeding one year . . . to ship or transport in interstate or foreign commerce, or possess in or affecting commerce, any firearm or ammunition."

Gamble moved to dismiss on one ground: The federal indictment was for "the same offence" as the one at issue in his state conviction and thus exposed him to double jeopardy. But because this Court has long held that two offenses "are *not* the 'same offence' " for double jeopardy purposes if "prosecuted by different sovereigns," *Heath v. Alabama*, 474 U.S. 82, 92 (1985), the District Court denied Gamble's motion to dismiss * * * [and] the Eleventh Circuit affirmed, citing the dual-sovereignty doctrine * * * We granted certiorari to determine whether to overturn that doctrine.

* * *

We start with the text of the Fifth Amendment. Although the dual-sovereignty rule is often dubbed an "exception" to the double jeopardy right, it is not an exception at all. On the contrary, it follows from the text that defines that right in the first place. "[T]he language of the Clause . . . protects individuals from being twice put in jeopardy 'for the same *offence*,' not for the same *conduct* or *actions*," *Grady v. Corbin*, 495 U.S. 508, 529 (1990), as Justice Scalia wrote in a soon-vindicated dissent, see *United States v. Dixon*, 509 U.S. 688 (1993) (overruling *Grady*). And the term " '[o]ffence' was commonly understood in 1791 to mean 'transgression,' that is, 'the Violation or Breaking of a Law.' " *Grady*, 495 U. S., at 529 (Scalia, J., dissenting) (quoting Dictionarium Britannicum (Bailey ed. 1730)). See also 2 R. Burn & J. Burn, A New Law Dictionary 167 (1792) ("OFFENCE, is an act committed against law, or omitted where the law requires it"). As originally understood, then, an "offence" is defined by a law, and each law is defined by a sovereign. So where there are two sovereigns, there are two laws, and two "offences."

Faced with this reading, Gamble falls back on an episode from the Double Jeopardy Clause's drafting history. The first Congress, working on an earlier draft that would have banned " 'more than one trial or one punishment for the same offence,' " voted down a proposal to add " 'by any law of the United States.' " 1 Annals of Cong. 753 (1789). In rejecting this addition, Gamble surmises, Congress must have intended to bar successive prosecutions regardless of the sovereign bringing the charge.

Even if that inference were justified—something that the Government disputes—it would count for little. The private intent behind a drafter's rejection of one version of a text is shoddy evidence of the public meaning of an altogether different text.

* * *

We see no reason to abandon the sovereign-specific reading of the phrase "same offence," from which the dual-sovereignty rule immediately follows.

Our cases reflect the same reading. A close look at them reveals how fidelity to the Double Jeopardy Clause's text does more than honor the formal difference between two distinct criminal codes. It honors the substantive differences between the interests that two sovereigns can have in punishing the same act.

* * * *Fox v. Ohio*, 5 How. 410 (1847), involved an Ohio prosecution for the passing of counterfeit coins. The defendant argued that since Congress can punish counterfeiting, the States must be barred from doing so, or else a person could face two trials for the same offense, contrary to the Fifth Amendment. We rejected the defendant's premise that under the Double Jeopardy Clause "offences falling within the competency of different authorities to restrain or punish them would not properly be subjected to the consequences which those authorities might ordain and affix to their perpetration." *Id.*, at 435. Indeed, we observed, the nature of the crime or its effects on "public safety" might well "deman[d]" separate prosecutions. *Ibid.* Generalizing from this point, we declared in a second case that "the same act might, as to its character and tendencies, and the consequences it involved, constitute an offence against both the State and Federal governments, and might draw to its commission the penalties denounced by either, as appropriate to its character in reference to each." *United States v. Marigold*, 9 How. 560, 569 (1850).

A third antebellum case, *Moore v. Illinois*, 14 How. 13, expanded on this concern for the different interests of separate sovereigns, after tracing it to the text in the manner set forth above. Recalling that the Fifth Amendment prohibits double jeopardy not "for the same ac[t]" but "for the same offence," and that "[a]n offence, in its legal signification, means the transgression of a law," *id.*, at 19, we drew the now-familiar inference: A single act "may be an offence or transgression of the laws of" two sovereigns, and hence punishable by both, *id.*, at 20. Then we gave color to this abstract principle—and to the diverse interests it might vindicate—with an example. An assault on a United States marshal, we said, would offend against the Nation and a State: the first by "hindering" the "execution of legal process," and the second by "breach[ing]" the "peace of the State." *Ibid.* That duality of harm explains how "one act" could constitute "two offences, for each of which [the offender] is justly punishable." *Ibid.*

* * *

We cemented that foundation 70 years after the last of those antebellum cases, in a decision upholding a federal prosecution that followed one by a State. See *United States v. Lanza*, 260 U.S. 377, 382 (1922) ("[A]n act denounced as a crime by both national and state sovereignties is an offense against the peace and dignity of both and may be punished by each"). And for decades more, we applied our precedent without qualm or quibble * * *.

We briefly address two objections to this analysis.

First, the dissents contend that our dual-sovereignty rule errs in treating the Federal and State *Governments* as two separate sovereigns when in fact sovereignty belongs to the people. See *post*, at 3 (opinion of GINSBURG, J.); *post*, at 7 (opinion of GORSUCH, J.). This argument is based on a non sequitur. Yes, our Constitution rests on the principle that the people are sovereign, but that does not mean that they have conferred all the attributes of sovereignty on a single government. Instead, the people, by adopting the Constitution, " 'split the atom of sovereignty.' " *Alden v. Maine*, 527 U.S. 706, 751 (1999) * * *.

It is true that the Republic is " 'ONE WHOLE.' " But there is a difference between the whole and a single part * * *. The United States is a *federal* republic; it is not, contrary to JUSTICE GORSUCH's suggestion, *post*, at 10–11, a unitary state like the United Kingdom.

Gamble and the dissents lodge a second objection to this line of reasoning. They suggest that because the division of federal and state power was meant to promote liberty, it cannot support a rule that exposes Gamble to a second sentence. This argument fundamentally misunderstands the governmental structure established by our Constitution. Our federal system advances individual liberty in many ways. Among other things, it limits the powers of the Federal Government and protects certain basic liberties from infringement. But because the powers of the Federal Government and the States often overlap, allowing both to regulate often results in two layers of regulation. Taxation is an example that comes immediately to mind. It is also not at all uncommon for the Federal Government to permit activities that a State chooses to forbid or heavily restrict—for example, gambling and the sale of alcohol. And a State may choose to legalize an activity that federal law prohibits, such as the sale of marijuana. So while our system of federalism is fundamental to the protection of liberty, it does not always maximize individual liberty at the expense of other interests. And it is thus quite extraordinary to say that the venerable dual-sovereignty doctrine represents a " 'desecrat[ion]' " of federalism. *Post*, at 9 (opinion of GORSUCH, J.).

Gamble claims that our precedent contradicts the common-law rights that the Double Jeopardy Clause was originally understood to engraft onto the Constitution—rights stemming from the "common-law pleas of *auterfoits acquit* [former acquittal] and auterfoits convict [former conviction]." *Grady*, 495 U. S., at 530 (Scalia, J., dissenting) * * *. Gamble argues that those who ratified the Fifth Amendment understood these common-law principles (which the Amendment constitutionalized) to bar a domestic prosecution following one by a foreign nation. For support, he appeals to early English and American cases and treatises. We have highlighted one hurdle to Gamble's reading: the sovereign-specific original meaning of "offence." But the doctrine of *stare decisis* is another obstacle.

Stare decisis "promotes the evenhanded, predictable, and consistent development of legal principles, fosters reliance on judicial decisions, and contributes to the actual and perceived integrity of the judicial process." *Payne v. Tennessee*, 501 U.S. 808, 827 (1991). Of course, it is also important to be right, especially on constitutional matters, where Congress cannot override our errors by ordinary legislation. But even in constitutional cases, a departure from precedent "demands special justification." This means that something more than "ambiguous historical evidence" is required before we will "flatly overrule a number of major decisions of this Court." And the strength of the case for adhering to such decisions grows in proportion to their "antiquity." Here, as noted, Gamble's historical arguments must overcome *numerous* "major decisions of this Court" spanning *170 years*. In light of these factors, Gamble's historical evidence must, at a minimum, be better than middling.

And it is not. The English cases are a muddle. Treatises offer spotty support. And early state and federal cases are by turns equivocal and downright harmful to Gamble's position. All told, this evidence does not establish that those who ratified the Fifth Amendment took it to bar successive prosecutions under different sovereigns' laws—much less do so with enough force to break a chain of precedent linking dozens of cases over 170 years.

Gamble's core claim is that early English cases reflect an established common-law rule barring domestic prosecution following a prosecution for the same act under a different sovereign's laws. But from the very dawn of the common law in medieval England until the adoption of the Fifth Amendment in 1791, there is not one reported decision barring a prosecution based on a prior trial under foreign law. We repeat: Gamble has not cited and we have not found a single pre-Fifth Amendment case in which a foreign acquittal or conviction barred a second trial in a British or American court * * *.

* * *

* * * [T]he premises of the dual-sovereignty doctrine have survived incorporation intact. Incorporation meant that the States were now required to abide by this Court's interpretation of the Double Jeopardy Clause. But that interpretation has long included the dual-sovereignty doctrine, and there is no logical reason why incorporation should change it. After all, the doctrine rests on the fact that only same-sovereign successive prosecutions are prosecutions for the "same offense"—and that is just as true after incorporation as before.

* * *

The judgment of the Court of Appeals for the Eleventh Circuit is affirmed.

It is so ordered.

■ JUSTICE THOMAS, concurring.

I agree that the historical record does not bear out my initial skepticism of the dual-sovereignty doctrine * * *.

I write separately to address the proper role of the doctrine of *stare decisis*. In my view, the Court's typical formulation of the *stare decisis* standard does not comport with our judicial duty under Article III because it elevates demonstrably erroneous decisions—meaning decisions outside the realm of permissible interpretation—over the text of the Constitution and other duly enacted federal law.

* * *

The Court currently views *stare decisis* as a " 'principle of policy' " that balances several factors to decide whether the scales tip in favor of overruling precedent. Among these factors are the "workability" of the standard, "the antiquity of the precedent, the reliance interests at stake, and of course whether the decision was well reasoned." The influence of this last factor tends to ebb and flow with the Court's desire to achieve a particular end, and the Court may cite additional, ad hoc factors to reinforce the result it chooses. But the shared theme is the need for a "special reason over and above the belief that a prior case was wrongly decided" to overrule a precedent. *Planned Parenthood of Southeastern Pa. v. Casey*, 505 U. S. 833, 864 (1992). The Court has advanced this view of *stare decisis* on the ground that "it promotes the evenhanded, predictable, and consistent development of legal principles" and "contributes to the actual and perceived integrity of the judicial process."

This approach to *stare decisis* might have made sense in a common-law legal system in which courts systematically developed the law through judicial decisions apart from written law. But our federal system is different. The Constitution tasks the political branches—not the Judiciary—with systematically developing the laws that govern our society. The Court's role, by contrast, is to exercise the "judicial Power," faithfully interpreting the Constitution and the laws enacted by those branches. Art. III, § 1.

A proper understanding of *stare decisis* in our constitutional structure requires a proper understanding of the nature of the "judicial Power" vested in the federal courts. That "Power" is—as Chief Justice Marshall put it—the power "to say what the law is" in the context of a particular "case" or "controversy" before the court. *Marbury v. Madison*, 1 Cranch 137, 177 (1803); Art. III, § 2. Phrased differently, the "judicial Power" "is fundamentally the power to decide cases in accordance with law." Lawson, The Constitutional Case Against Precedent, 17 Harv. J. L.& Pub. Pol'y 23, 26 (1994) (Lawson). It refers to the duty to exercise "judicial discretion" as distinct from "arbitrary discretion." The Federalist No. 78, at 468, 471

* * *

* * * "[J]udicial discretion" requires the "liquidat[ion]"or "ascertain[ment]" of the meaning of the law. *Id.*, at 467–468; see *id.*, No. 37. At the time of the founding, "to liquidate" meant "to make clear or plain"; "to render un-ambiguous; to settle (differences, disputes)." Nelson, *Stare Decisis* and Demonstrably Erroneous Precedents. Therefore, judicial discretion is not the power to "alter" the law; it is the duty to correctly "expound" it. Letter from J. Madison to N. Trist (Dec. 1831), in 9 The Writings of James Madison 477 (G. Hunt ed. 1910) (Writings of Madison).

This understanding of the judicial power had long been accepted at the time of the founding. But the federalist structure of the constitutional plan had significant implications for the exercise of that power by the newly created Federal Judiciary. Whereas the common-law courts of England discerned and defined many legal principles in the first instance, the Constitution charged federal courts primarily with applying a limited body of written laws articulating those legal principles. This shift profoundly affects the application of *stare decisis* today.

Stare decisis has its pedigree in the unwritten common law of England * * *.

"[C]ommon law doctrines, as articulated by judges, were seen as principles that had been discovered rather than new laws that were being made." 3–4 G. White, The Marshall Court and Cultural Change, 1815–35, History of the Supreme Court of the United States 129 (1988). "It was the application of the dictates of natural justice, and of cultivated reason, to particular cases." 1 J. Kent, Commentaries on American Law 439 (1826) (Kent). The common law therefore rested on "unarticulated social processes to mobilize and coordinate knowledge" gained primarily through "the social experience of the many," rather than the "specifically articulated *reason* of the few." T. Sowell, A Conflict of Visions: Ideological Origins of Political Struggles 49, 42 (1987). In other words, the common law was based in the collective, systematic development of the law through reason. See *id.*, at 49–55.

Importantly, however, the common law did not view precedent as unyielding when it was "most evidently contrary to reason" or "divine law." Blackstone 69–70. The founding generation recognized that a "judge may *mistake* the law." *Id.*, at 71; see also 1 Kent 444 ("Even a series of decisions are not always conclusive evidence of what is law"). And according to Blackstone, judges *should* disregard precedent that articulates a rule incorrectly when necessary "to vindicate the old [rule] from misrepresentation." Blackstone 70; see also 1 Kent 443 ("If . . . any solemnly adjudged case can be shown to be founded in error, it is no doubt the right and the duty of the judges who have a similar case before them, to correct the error") * * *.

* * *

Federal courts today look to different sources of law when exercising the judicial power than did the common-law courts of England * * *. We operate in a system of written law in which courts need not—and generally cannot—articulate the law in the first instance. The Constitution, federal statutes, and treaties *are* the law, and the systematic development of the law is accomplished democratically. Our judicial task is modest: We interpret and apply written law to the facts of particular cases.

Underlying this legal system is the key premise that words, including written laws, are capable of objective, ascertainable meaning. As I have previously explained, "[m]y vision of the process of judging is unabashedly based on the proposition that there are right and wrong answers to legal questions." Thomas, Judging, 45 U. Kan. L. Rev. 1, 5 (1996). Accordingly, judicial decisions may incorrectly interpret the law, and when they do, subsequent courts must confront the question when to depart from them.

* * *

When faced with a demonstrably erroneous precedent, my rule is simple: We should not follow it. This view of *stare decisis* follows directly from the Constitution's supremacy over other sources of law—including our own precedents. That the Constitution outranks other sources of law is inherent in its nature. See A. Amar, America's Constitution 5 (2005) (explaining that the Constitution is a constitutive document); Kesavan, The Three Tiers of Federal Law, 100 NW.U. L. Rev. 1479, 1499, n. 99 (2006) (arguing that "[i]t is unnecessary for the Constitution to specify that it is superior to other law because it is higher law made by We the People—and the only such law") * * *. And the Court has long recognized the supremacy of the Constitution with respect to executive action and "legislative act[s] repugnant to" it. *Marbury*, 1 Cranch at 177; *Youngstown Sheet & Tube Co. v. Sawyer*, 343 U.S. 579, 587–589 (1952).

The same goes for judicial precedent. The "judicial Power" must be understood in light of "the Constitution's status as the supreme legal document" over "lesser sources of law." Lawson, 29–30. This status necessarily limits "the power of a court to give legal effect to prior judicial decisions" that articulate demonstrably erroneous interpretations of the Constitution because those prior decisions cannot take precedence over the Constitution itself. *Ibid.* Put differently, because the Constitution is supreme over other sources of law, it requires us to privilege its text over our own precedents when the two are in conflict. I am aware of no legitimate reason why a court may privilege a demonstrably erroneous interpretation of the Constitution over the Constitution itself.

* * *

For the reasons explained above, the Court's multifactor approach to *stare decisis* invites conflict with its constitutional duty. Whatever benefits may be seen to inhere in that approach—*e.g.*, "stability" in the law, preservation of reliance interests, or judicial "humility," they cannot overcome that fundamental flaw.

In any event, these oft-cited benefits are frequently illusory. The Court's multifactor balancing test for invoking *stare decisis* has resulted in policy-driven, "arbitrary discretion." The inquiry attempts to quantify the unquantifiable and, by frequently sweeping in subjective factors, provides a ready means of justifying whatever result five Members of the Court seek to achieve * * *.

* * *

Our judicial duty to interpret the law requires adherence to the original meaning of the text. For that reason, we should not invoke *stare decisis* to uphold precedents that are demonstrably erroneous. Because petitioner and the dissenting opinions have not shown that the Court's dual-sovereignty doctrine is incorrect, much less demonstrably erroneous, I concur in the majority's opinion.

■ JUSTICE GINSBURG, dissenting.

* * *

* * * Instead of "fritter[ing] away [Gamble's] libert[y] upon a metaphysical subtlety, two sovereignties," Grant, The *Lanza* Rule of Successive Prosecutions, 32 Colum. L. Rev. 1309, 1331 (1932), I would hold that the Double Jeopardy Clause bars "successive prosecutions [for the same offense] by parts of the whole USA."

* * *

In *United States v. Lanza*, 260 U. S. 377 (1922), this Court held that "an act denounced as a crime by both national and state sovereignties is an offense against the peace and dignity of both and may be punished by each." *Id.*, at 382. Decades later, a sharply divided Court reaffirmed this separate-sovereigns doctrine. I would not cling to those ill-advised decisions.

Justification for the separate-sovereigns doctrine centers on the word "offence": An "offence," the argument runs, is the violation of a sovereign's law, the United States and each State are separate sovereigns, ergo successive state and federal prosecutions do not place a defendant in "jeopardy . . . for the same offence."

This "compact syllogism" is fatally flawed. The United States and its constituent States, unlike foreign nations, are "kindred systems," "parts of ONE WHOLE." The Federalist No. 82, p. 493 (C. Rossiter ed. 1961) (A. Hamilton). They compose one people, bound by an overriding Federal Constitution. Within that "WHOLE," the Federal and State Governments should be disabled from accomplishing together "what neither government [could] do alone—prosecute an ordinary citizen twice for the same offence." Amar & Marcus, Double Jeopardy Law After Rodney King, 95 Colum. L. Rev. 1, 2 (1995).

The notion that the Federal Government and the States are separate sovereigns overlooks a basic tenet of our federal system. The doctrine treats *governments* as sovereign, with state power to prosecute carried over from years predating the Constitution. In the system established by the Federal Constitution, however, "ultimate sovereignty" resides in the *governed*. Insofar as a crime offends the "peace and dignity" of a sovereign, that "sovereign" is the people, the "original fountain of all legitimate authority." States may be separate, but their populations are part of the people composing the United States.

* * *

The separate-sovereigns doctrine * * * has been subject to relentless criticism by members of the bench, bar, and academy. Nevertheless, the Court reaffirms the doctrine, thereby diminishing the individual rights shielded by the Double Jeopardy Clause. Different parts of the "WHOLE" United States should not be positioned to prosecute a defendant a second time for the same offense. I would reverse Gamble's federal conviction.

■ JUSTICE GORSUCH, dissenting.

A free society does not allow its government to try the same individual for the same crime until it's happy with the result. Unfortunately, the Court today endorses a colossal exception to this ancient rule against double jeopardy. My colleagues say that the federal government and each State are "separate sovereigns" entitled to try the same person for the same crime. So if all the might of one "sovereign" cannot succeed against the presumptively free individual, another may insist on the chance to try again. And if both manage to succeed, so much the better; they can add one punishment on top of the other. But this "separate sovereigns exception" to the bar against double jeopardy finds no meaningful support in the text of the Constitution, its original public meaning, structure, or history. Instead, the Constitution promises all Americans that they will never suffer double jeopardy. I would enforce that guarantee.

"Fear and abhorrence of governmental power to try people twice for the same conduct is one of the oldest ideas found in western civilization." Throughout history, people have worried about the vast disparity of power between governments and individuals, the capacity of the state to bring charges repeatedly until it wins the result it wants, and what little would be left of human liberty if that power remained unchecked. To address the problem, the law in ancient Athens held that "[a] man could not be tried twice for the same offense." The Roman Republic and Empire incorporated a form of double jeopardy protection in their laws. The Old Testament and later church teachings endorsed the bar against double jeopardy too. And from the earliest days of the common law, courts recognized that to "punish a man twice over for one offence" would be deeply unjust.

The rule against double jeopardy was firmly entrenched in both the American colonies and England at the time of our Revolution. And the Fifth Amendment, which prohibits placing a defendant "twice . . . in jeopardy of life or limb" for "the same offence" sought to carry the traditional common law rule into our Constitution * * *.

Given all this, it might seem that Mr. Gamble should win this case handily * * *. Most any ordinary speaker of English would say that Mr. Gamble was tried twice for "the same offence," precisely what the Fifth Amendment prohibits. Tellingly, no one before us doubts that if either the federal government or Alabama had prosecuted Mr. Gamble twice on these facts and in this manner, it surely would have violated the Constitution.

So how does the government manage to evade the Fifth Amendment's seemingly plain command? On the government's account, the fact that federal and state authorities split up the prosecutions makes all the difference. Though the Double Jeopardy Clause doesn't say anything about allowing "separate sovereigns" to do sequentially what neither may do separately, the government assures us the Fifth Amendment's phrase "same offence" does this work. Adopting the government's argument, the Court supplies the following syllogism: "[A]n 'offence' is defined by a law, and each law is defined by a sovereign. So where there are two sovereigns, there are two laws, and two 'offences.' "

But the major premise of this argument—that "where there are two laws there are 'two offenses' "—is mistaken. We know that the Constitution is not so easily evaded and that two statutes *can* punish the same offense. The framers understood the term "offence" to mean a "transgression." And they understood that the same transgression might be punished by two pieces of positive law * * *. So if two laws demand proof of the same facts to secure a conviction, they constitute a single offense under our Constitution and a second trial is forbidden. And by everyone's admission, that is exactly what we have here: The statute under which the federal government proceeded required it to prove no facts beyond those Alabama needed to prove under state law to win its conviction; the two prosecutions *were* for the same offense.

That leaves the government and the Court to rest on the fact that distinct governmental entities, federal and state, enacted these identical laws. This, we are told, is enough to transform what everyone agrees would otherwise be the same offense into two different offenses. But where is *that* distinction to be found in the Constitution's text or original public understanding? We know that the framers didn't conceive of the term "same offence" in some technical way as referring only to the same statute. And if double jeopardy prevents *one* government from prosecuting a defendant multiple times for the same offense under the banner of separate statutory labels, on what account can it make a difference when *many* governments collectively seek to do the same thing?

The government identifies no evidence suggesting that the framers understood the term "same offence" to bear such a lawyerly sovereign-specific meaning. Meanwhile, Blackstone's Commentaries explained how "Roman law," "Athens," "the Jewish republic," and "English Law" addressed the singular "offence of homicide," and how the Roman, Gothic, and ancient Saxon law approached the singular "offence of arson." Other treatises of the period contain similar taxonomies of "offences" that are not sovereign-specific. Members of the Continental Congress, too, used the word "offence" in this same way. In 1786, a congressional committee endorsed federal control over import duties because otherwise "thirteen separate authorities" might "ordain various penalties for the same offence." In 1778, the Continental Congress passed a resolution declaring that a person should not be tried in state court "for the same offense, for which he had previous thereto been tried by a Court Martial." And in 1785, the Continental Congress considered an ordinance declaring that a defendant could "plead a formal Acquital on a Trial" in a maritime court "for the same supposed Offences, in a similar Court in one of the other United States." In all of these examples, early legislators—including many of the same people who would vote to add the Fifth Amendment to the Bill of Rights just a few years later—recognized that transgressions of state and federal law could constitute the "same offence."

* * *

Without meaningful support in the text of the Double Jeopardy Clause, the government insists that the separate sovereigns exception is at least compelled by the structure of our Constitution. On its view, adopted by the Court today, allowing the federal and state governments to punish the same defendant for the same conduct "honors the substantive differences between the interests that two sovereigns can have" in our federal system.

But this argument errs from the outset. The Court seems to assume that sovereignty in this country belongs to the state and federal governments, much as it once belonged to the King of England. But as Chief Justice Marshall explained, "[t]he government of the Union . . . is emphatically, and truly, a government of the people," and all sovereignty "emanates from them" * * *. Under our Constitution, the federal and state governments are but two expressions of a single and sovereign people.

* * *

From its mistaken premise, the Court continues to the flawed conclusion that the federal and state governments can successively prosecute the same person for the same offense. This turns the point of our federal experiment on its head. When the "ONE WHOLE" people of the United States assigned different aspects of their sovereign power to the federal and state governments, they sought not to *multiply* governmental power but to *limit* it * * *. Yet today's Court invokes federalism not to protect individual liberty but to threaten it, allowing two governments to achieve together an objective denied to each * * *.

If the Constitution's text and structure do not supply persuasive support for the government's position, what about a more thorough exploration of the common law from which the Fifth Amendment was drawn?

By 1791 when the Fifth Amendment was adopted, an array of common law authorities suggested that a prosecution in *any* court, so long as the court had jurisdiction over the offense, was enough to bar future re-prosecution in another court. Blackstone, for example, reported that an acquittal "before any court having competent jurisdiction of the offence" could be pleaded "in bar of any subsequent accusation for the same crime." * * * Another treatise by William Hawkins likewise considered it "settled" as early as 1716"[t]hat an Acquittal *in any Court whatsoever*, which has a Jurisdiction of the Cause, is as good a Bar of any subsequent Prosecution for the same Crime."

* * * Henry Bathurst's 1761 treatise on evidence taught that "a final Determination in a Court having competent Jurisdiction is conclusive in all Courts of concurrent Jurisdiction." Nor was this merely a rule about the competency of evidence, as the next sentence reveals: "If *A.* having killed a Person in *Spain* was

there prosecuted, tried, and acquitted, and afterwards was indicted here [in England], he might plead the Acquittal in *Spain* in Bar." Francis Buller's 1772 treatise repeated the same rule, articulating it the same way. And to illustrate their point, both treatises cited the 1678 English case of *King* v. *Hutchinson* * * *. All agreed that it barred the retrial in England of a defendant previously tried for murder in Spain or Portugal.

When they envisioned the relationship between the national government and the States under the new Constitution, the framers sometimes referenced by way of comparison the relationship between Wales, Scotland, and England. And prosecutions in one of these places pretty plainly barred subsequent prosecutions for the same offense in the others. So, for example, treatises explained that "an Acquittal of Murder at a Grand Sessions in *Wales*, may be pleaded to an Indictment for the same Murder in *England*. For the Rule is, That a Man's Life shall not be brought into Danger for the same Offence more than once." Indeed, when an English county indicted a defendant "for a murder committed . . . in Wales," it was barred from proceeding when the court learned that the defendant had already been tried and acquitted "of the same offence" in Wales.

* * *

In the end, then, it's hard to see how anyone consulting the common law in 1791 could have avoided this conclusion: While the issue may not have arisen often, the great weight of authority indicated that successive prosecutions by different sovereigns—even sovereigns as foreign to each other as England and Portugal—were out of bounds. And anyone familiar with the American federal system likely would have thought the rule applied with even greater force to successive prosecutions by the United States and a constituent State, given that both governments derive their sovereignty from the American people.

* * *

With the text, principles of federalism, and history now arrayed against it, the government is left to suggest that we should retain the separate sovereigns exception under the doctrine of *stare decisis* * * *.

Stare decisis has many virtues, but when it comes to enforcing the Constitution this Court must take (and always has taken) special care in the doctrine's application * * *.

* * * In deciding whether one of our cases should be retained or overruled, this Court has traditionally considered "the quality of the decision's reasoning; its consistency with related decisions; legal developments since the decision; and reliance on the decision." Each of these factors, I believe, suggests we should reject the separate sovereigns exception.

* * *

It matters, too, that these cases [upholding the separate sovereignties doctrine] "were decided by the narrowest of margins, over spirited dissents challenging the basic underpinnings of those decisions." In *Moore* [*v. Illinois,* 55 U.S. (14 How.) 13 (1952)], Justice McLean wrote that although "the Federal and State Governments emanate from different sovereignties," they "operate upon the same people, and should have the same end in view." He "deeply regret[ted] that our government should be an exception to a great principle of action, sanctioned by humanity and justice." *Bartkus* [*v. People of the State of Ill.,* 359 U.S. 121 (1959)] and *Abbate* [*v. United States,* 359 U.S. 187 (1959)], cases decided in the 1950s that more clearly approved the separate sovereigns exception, were decided only by 5-to-4 and 6-to-3 margins, and Justice Black's eloquent dissents in those cases have triggered an avalanche of persuasive academic support.

* * *

* * * In the era when the separate sovereigns exception first emerged, the federal criminal code was new, thin, modest, and restrained. Today, it can make none of those of boasts. Some suggest that "the federal government has [now] duplicated virtually every major state crime." Others estimate that the U.S. Code contains more than 4,500 criminal statutes, not even counting the hundreds of thousands of federal regulations that can trigger criminal penalties. Still others suggest that " '[t]here is no one in the United States over the age of 18 who cannot be indicted for some federal crime.' " If long ago the Court could have thought "the benignant spirit" of prosecutors rather than unwavering enforcement of the Constitution sufficient protection against the threat of double prosecutions, it's unclear how we still might.

* * *

Enforcing the Constitution always bears its costs. But when the people adopted the Constitution and its Bill of Rights, they thought the liberties promised there worth the costs. It is not for this Court to reassess this judgment to make the prosecutor's job easier. Nor is there any doubt that the benefits the framers saw in prohibiting double prosecutions remain real, and maybe more vital than ever, today. When governments may unleash all their might in multiple prosecutions against an individual, exhausting themselves only when those who hold the reins of power are content with the result, it is "the poor and the weak," and the unpopular and controversial, who suffer first—and there is nothing to stop them from being the last. The separate sovereigns exception was wrong when it was invented, and it remains wrong today.

I respectfully dissent.

NOTES AND QUESTIONS

1. What do you think of the four different opinions reproduced above? Is it possible to resolve this case without resolving deep questions about the nature of sovereignty? Is it clear what any of the justices in this case mean by "sovereignty"? Are they all talking about different things?

2. The Framers created a system of "Dual Federalism" in which most powers were not congruent but were mostly exclusive. *See supra* pages 595–597. Under this system, dual jeopardy would almost never happen. Almost any law one violated was either in the federal or in the state sphere of prosecution, and that almost always meant "state," as the number of federal crimes was very small. (Indeed, do yourself a favor and read the first federal criminal statute, which provided the *entirety* of the federal criminal code in 1790. *See* Act of Apr. 30, 1790, ch. IX, 1 Stat. 112. It will not take you more than a few minutes—which is precisely the point.) Today, however, there are countless crimes, like bringing a gun that has traveled in interstate commerce within 1000 feet of a school, which are both federal and state crimes. The stakes for double jeopardy are much larger than anyone in 1791 could have imagined. Is that relevant for ascertaining the meaning of the Double Jeopardy Clause?

3. Is the huge growth in federal criminal law a reason to reconsider the Court's numerous precedents upholding the separate sovereigns doctrine? How strong do the reasons for reconsidering a doctrine have to be? At this stage of the course, with a fair amount of doctrine in mind, what do you think of Justice Thomas's all-out assault on precedent? For the extended argument on which Justice Thomas's position is founded, see Gary Lawson, *The Constitutional Case Against Precedent,* 17 HARV. J.L. & PUB. POL'Y 23 (1994); Gary Lawson, *Mostly Unconstitutional: The Case Against Precedent Revisited,* 5 AVE MARIA L. REV. 1 (2007). Compare Steven G. Calabresi, *The Tradition of the Written Constitution: Text, Precedent, and Burke,* 57 ALA. L. REV. 635 (2006); Steven G. Calabresi, *Text vs. Precedent in Constitutional Law,* 31 HARV. J.L. & PUB. POL'Y 947 (2008).

B. DUE PROCESS CLAUSE OF THE FIFTH AMENDMENT

> **No person shall be * * * deprived of life, liberty or property without due process of law;**

One could conduct—and one sometimes encounters in law school—entire courses on the meaning of the Due Process of Law Clause of the Fifth Amendment and its counterpart in the Fourteenth Amendment, which we will discuss in the next chapter. In some respects, American constitutional history has largely been the history of the Due Process of Law Clauses. Both clauses have been the vehicles for doctrinal moves that would have startled the Framers of the Bill of Rights and the Reconstruction Amendments. In these materials, we can provide only the briefest introduction to the development of Fifth Amendment due process of law doctrine. Fourteenth Amendment due process of law doctrine, as we shall later see, has complications all its own.

Article 39 of the 1215 Magna Carta famously provided that "[n]o free man shall be taken or imprisoned or disseised or outlawed or exiled or in any way ruined, nor will we go or send against him, except by the lawful judgment of his peers or by the law of the land." The reissuance of the Great Charter in 1225 similarly provided:

> No Freeman shall be taken or imprisoned, or be disseised of his Freehold, or Liberties, or free Customs, or be outlawed, or exiled, or any other wise destroyed; nor will We not pass upon him, nor condemn him, but by lawful judgment of his Peers, or by the Law of the Land. We will sell to no man, we will not deny or defer to any man either Justice or Right.

As Joseph Story explained in 1833, the Due Process of Law Clause was an expression of the ideas from half a millennium beforehand:

> The [Due Process of Law Clause of the Fifth amendment] is but an enlargement of the language of magna charta, "*nee super eum thymus, nee super eum mittimas, nisi per legale judicium parium suorum, vel per legume terrae,*" neither will we pass upon him, or condemn him, but by the lawful judgment of his peers, or by the law of the land. Lord Coke says, that these latter words, *per legume terrae* (by the law of the land,) mean by due process of law, that is, without due presentment or indictment, and being brought in answer thereto by due process of the common law. So that this clause in effect affirms the right of trial according to the process and proceedings of the common law.

JOSEPH STORY, COMMENTARIES ON THE CONSTITUTION § 1783 (1833). What does this really mean?

> Although there is some risk of anachronism in applying a term such as "separation of powers" to Magna Carta, Article 39 of the charter, in either of its original thirteenth-century forms, can fairly be described as a kind of separation-of-powers provision, in that it denied the King the ability to act in the absence of law from another source when such action would result in loss of property, imprisonment, or other criminal punishment imposed on the King's subjects. More abstractly: according to Magna Carta, executive enforcement action resulting in loss of life, liberty, or property can take place only pursuant to general norms of conduct ("the law of the land" or after determination by an institution other than the executive ("the lawful judgment of his peers").

Gary Lawson, *Take the Fifth . . . Please!: The Original Insignificance of the Fifth Amendment's Due Process of Law Clause,* 2017 B.Y.U. L. REV. 611, 620–21. This notion that executive and judicial (because courts were arms of the executive until just a few years before the Constitution) deprivations of certain protected interests can take place only pursuant to established law is sometimes called the "principle of legality." There is no doubt that the Due Process of Law Clause was, at a minimum, designed to express that basic idea. The real question is whether it does anything more.

In addressing that question, it is important to keep in mind that the principle of legality was part of the Constitution of 1788. The Due Process of Law Clause, as with most of the Bill of Rights provisions, emphasized but did not create the set of rights that existed even before December 15, 1791. Executive and judicial actors could not deprive people of life, liberty, or property without pre-existing law in 1788, 1789, 1790, and the portion of 1791 until the middle of December, simply because the "executive Power" and the "judicial Power" included no such ability. Thus:

> The principle of legality flows naturally from these [constitutional] allocations of power. There must be law for the executive to execute. There must be law for the judiciary to construe and apply. That law can come from statutes or from the general law, but law there must be. Execution, construal, or application without law simply lies beyond the enumerated scope of executive and judicial power whenever that execution, construal, or application deprives subjects of rights. One does not need a due process of law clause to generate this principle of legality. It follows from—or, rather, is baked into—the nature of the powers granted to executive and judicial agents by the Constitution.

Id. at 625. What else might be baked into the executive and judicial powers?

Without going into too much detail, the "judicial Power" requires certain procedural forms for its exercise. Those forms were not specified in the Constitution of 1788 because there was no need: Everyone in 1788 knew what proper exercise of the "judicial Power" looked like. For example, the Judiciary Act of 1789, which set up the federal court system, contained much detail about the jurisdiction of the various federal courts that it established but said very little about the manner in which courts would decide cases. It assumed that everyone understood the forms of judicial action. Federal courts were authorized to issue writs "agreeable to the principles and usages of law." An Act to establish the Judicial Courts of the United States, ch. 20, § 14, 1 Stat. 73, 82. Courts could demand the production of evidence "by the ordinary rules of processes in chancery." *Id.* § 15, 1 Stat. at 82. The forms of proof and evidence were to be "as of actions at common law." *Id.* § 30, 1 Stat. at 88.

Proper exercises of judicial power also required such things as notice to the parties. In 1830, in *Hollingsworth v. Barbour*, 29 U.S. (4 Pet.) 466 (1830), the Supreme Court adopted the reasoning of a Kentucky circuit court:

> [B]y the general law of the land, no court is authorised to render a judgment or decree against any one or his estate; until after due notice by service of process to appear and defend. This principle is dictated by natural justice; and is only to be departed from in cases expressly warranted by law, and excepted out of the general rule.

Id. at 472. Neither *Hollingsworth* nor any other early cases applying a notice requirement relied on the Fifth Amendment's Due Process of Law Clause. They just assumed that a notice requirement was part and parcel of the "judicial Power." In sum, there are certain traditional procedural forms that collectively make up exercises of "judicial Power."

Another crucial aspect of due process of law in the context of judging is the idea—part of the Ancient Constitution—that no person should be a judge in their own cause. Lord Coke famously applied this idea in *Dr. Bonham's Case* (1610) 77 Eng. Rep. 646; 8 Co. Rep. 113b, and it represents the broader notion that due process of law requires an impartial decisionmaker. Suppose, for instance, that the mayor of a town is paid entirely out of fines imposed by the mayor for violations of local ordinances. If the mayor imposes no fines, the mayor does not get paid. If you were tried and fined by this person, would you have a legitimate due process of law claim? *See Tumey v. Ohio*, 273 U.S. 510 (1927) (answering "yes"). What if a state Board of Optometry, which regulates the profession and consists entirely of solo practitioners, determines that working for a corporation (such as Pearle Vision Center) is "unprofessional conduct" that warrants revoking the license of all optometrists who are not solo practitioners. Is this a due process of law violation because the decisionmaker is financially interested in the outcome? *See Gibson v. Berryhill*, 411 U.S. 564 (1973) (answering "yes). Is it a due process of law violation that lawyers grade bar exams and thereby determine how many competitors the lawyers will face in the market? The Fugitive Slave Act of 1850 provided for federal commissioners to determine whether persons brought before them were or were not in fact escaped slaves. The commissioners received ten dollars for each case in which they ruled that the person was a slave and five dollars for each case in which they ruled that the person was free. *See* Act of Sept. 18, 1850, ch. LX, § 8, 9 Stat. 462, 464. Was that due process of law? Suppose that the House impeaches the Vice President. The Vice President, by constitutional command, is the president of the Senate. *See* U.S. CONST. art. I, § 3, cl. 4. Does the Vice President get to preside over his or her own impeachment trial, or would that also violate due process of law? *See* AKHIL REED AMAR, AMERICA'S UNWRITTEN CONSTITUTION: THE PRECEDENTS AND PRINCIPLES WE LIVE BY 3–19 (2012).

Figuring out what "due process of law" meant in the founding era in the context of executive actors is a bit more complicated. There were well understood procedural forms for judicial action. The Constitution spells out in detail in Article I, Section 7 the appropriate procedural forms for legislative actions. But there was no eighteenth-century body of law prescribing procedures for executive action. So how would one know when and whether executive actors were following constitutionally appropriate procedures?

Because much of due process doctrine today concerns precisely the answer to that last question, it will surprise many modern observers to learn that the founding generation would have considered the question baffling and misguided. Due process of law simply could not occur without judicial action. Executive actors, as a matter of original meaning, have *no* unilateral authority to deprive people of life, liberty, or property, no matter how extensive or impressive the procedures employed for that deprivation may be. That is the point of the principle of legality, as it has existed since Magna Carta. As applied to executive action, "due process of law" is a *substantive* rather than *procedural* principle. "It concerns what the 'executive Power' can do, not how or by what procedures it can do it." Lawson, *supra,* at 626. And the executive power can do quite a bit, because a great deal of executive action does not deprive citizens of life, liberty, or property. Those actions may be important and necessary steps in a process that ultimately leads to such deprivations, and the executive can take those steps, but the executive cannot impose the deprivations unilaterally. The President cannot put someone in jail or execute them without a judicial trial. Enforcement agents cannot seize your property without a judicial trial. Or so the Constitution, as originally understood, prescribes.

Having told that story, we can now tell you that modern law does not remotely follow it. Not even close. The modern law of due process of law under the Fifth Amendment largely concerns what procedures executive agents—primarily administrative agencies—must follow in order validly to deprive people of liberty or property. (No one thinks that executive agents can unilaterally implement the death penalty outside the context of military justice.) The origins and mechanics of that body of law are best left to courses in Administrative Law, but a short version of the story is appropriate here.

Part of the reason for the shift in focus of modern law from executive *legality* to executive *procedures* concerns changes in the scope of interests deemed protected by due process of law. In the founding era, the phrase "life, liberty, or property" meant more or less what it says, but not necessarily in the way that one would expect. "Life" was a relatively capacious concept, including not only physical existence but also bodily integrity and reputation. "Liberty" was a relatively narrow concept, meaning only freedom of movement or lack of physical restraint. "Property" was more ambiguous than one might think, but it likely included those items considered "property" by general law. *See* Paul J. Larkin, Jr., *The Original Understanding of "Property" in the Constitution*, 100 MARQUETTE L. REV. 1 (2016). The phrase "life, liberty, and property" *did not* include prospective expectations of benefits from the government, such as continued government employment, renewal of a government license, or the future receipt of benefits (though benefits already received counted as property). That changed in the 1950s and 1960s, for reasons too involved to address here. Suffice it to say that modern law recognizes as "liberty" or "property" a much wider range of interests, including prospective receipt of certain (but not all) government benefits, than would have been imaginable in 1791. *See* GARY LAWSON, FEDERAL ADMINISTRATIVE LAW 891–963 (8th ed. 2019). To apply a strict principle of legality to this expanded range of protected interests would be impossible. A second reason is the introduction of a Due Process of Law Clause into the Fourteenth Amendment. A principle-of-legality interpretation of the Fourteenth Amendment's

Due Process of Law Clause would make little sense, because the Constitution does not impose a federal-like separation of powers regime on States. Rather than develop two distinct bodies of due process of law doctrine for state and federal actors, the courts developed a unified body of law, and they chose procedural robustness over the principle of legality as the guiding norm. Third, there were some doctrinal twists that fostered this understanding.

The most important was a mid-nineteenth-century case called *Murray's Lessee v Hoboken Land & Improvement Co.*, 59 U.S. (18 How.) 272 (1856). In those days, tax collectors really were tax collectors. Government agents physically collected money. They then had to turn the money over to the Treasury, and officials in the Treasury Department would audit their accounts to make sure that the tax collectors were not pocketing the proceeds. Well, one customs collector in the Port of New York named Samuel Swartout walked away with more than one million dollars. Or so the government auditors concluded—there was no federal court determination of Swartout's liability. The government did not think that it needed any prior judicial action either to determine liability or to levy (seize) property owned by Swartout to settle his debt, because there was a statute which provided:

> [I]f any collector of the revenue, receiver of public money, or other officer who shall have received the public money before it is paid into the treasury of the United States, shall fail to render his account, or pay over the same in the manner, or within the time required by law, it shall be the duty of the first comptroller of the treasury to cause to be stated the account of such collector, receiver of public money, or other officer, exhibiting truly the amount due to the United States, and certify the same to the agent of the treasury, who is hereby authorized and required to issue a warrant of distress against such delinquent officer and his sureties, directed to the marshal of the district in which such delinquent officer and his surety or sureties shall reside * * *; therein specifying the amount with which such delinquent is chargeable, and the sums, if any, which have been paid. And the marshal authorized to execute such warrant, shall, by himself or by his deputy, proceed to levy and collect the sum remaining due, by distress and sale of the goods and chattels of such delinquent officer; having given ten days' previous notice of such intended sale * * *; and if the goods and chattels be not sufficient to satisfy the said warrant, the same may be levied upon the person of such officer, who may be committed to prison, there to remain until discharged by due course of law * * *. And the amount due by any such officer as aforesaid, shall be, and the same is hereby declared to be, a lien upon the lands, tenements, and hereditaments of such officer and his sureties, from the date of a levy in pursuance of the warrant of distress issued against him or them * * *. And for want of goods and chattels of such officer, or his surety or sureties, sufficient to satisfy any warrant of distress issued pursuant to the provisions of this act, the land, tenements, and hereditaments of such officer * * * may and shall be sold by the marshal of such district or his deputy; and * * * shall give a valid title against all persons claiming under such delinquent officer, or his surety or sureties.

Act of May 15, 1820, ch. 107, § 2, 3 Stat. 592, 592–93. This law not only gave the executive unilateral authority to determine liability and seize property; it allowed the executive to put people in prison without a prior judicial determination. *See Ex parte Randolph,* 20 Fed. Cas. 242 (C.C.D. Va. 1833) (habeas action by a naval purser imprisoned under this statute). There was provision in the statute for judicial review, § 4, 3 Stat. at 595, but such review *would not* affect any lien that was placed on the tax collector's property by the executive. The government sold off some of Swartout's property pursuant to one of those liens, and the purchaser from the government and a purchaser at a state common-law foreclosure fought over title. The government purchaser would win if, but only if, the sale pursuant to the above statute was lawful. The Supreme Court held that it was lawful:

> No objection has been taken to the warrant on account of any defect or irregularity in the proceedings which preceded its issue * * * Its validity is denied by the plaintiffs, upon the ground that so much of the act of congress as authorized it is in conflict with the constitution of the United States.
>
> * * *
>
> It must be admitted that, if the auditing of this account, and the ascertainment of its balance, and the issuing of this process, was an exercise of the judicial power of the United States, the proceeding was void; for the officers who performed these acts could exercise no part of that judicial power. They neither constituted a court of the United States, nor were they, or either of them, so connected with any such court as to perform even any of the ministerial duties which arise out of judicial proceedings.
>
> The question, whether these acts were an exercise of the judicial power of the United States, can best be considered under another inquiry, raised by the further objection of the plaintiff, that the effect of the proceedings authorized by the act in question is to deprive the party, against whom the warrant issues, of his liberty and property, "without due process of law"; and, therefore, is in conflict with the fifth article of the amendments of the constitution.
>
> Taking these two objections together, they raise the questions, whether, under the constitution of the United States, a collector of the customs, from whom a balance of account has been found to be due by accounting officers of the treasury, designated for that purpose by law, can be deprived of his liberty, or property, in order to enforce payment of that balance, without the exercise of the judicial power of the United States, and yet by due process of law, within the meaning of those terms in the constitution; and if so, then, secondly, whether the warrant in question was such due process of law?
>
> The words, "due process of law," were undoubtedly intended to convey the same meaning as the words, "by the law of the land," in *Magna Charta.* Lord Coke, in his commentary on those words, (2 Inst. 50,) says they mean due process of law. The constitutions which had been adopted by the several States before the formation of the federal constitution, following the language of the great charter more closely, generally contained the words, "but by the judgment of his peers, or the law of the land." The ordinance of congress of July 13, 1787, for the government of the territory of the United States northwest of the River Ohio, used the same words.
>
> The constitution of the United States, as adopted, contained the provision, that "the trial of all crimes, except in cases of impeachment, shall

be by jury." When the fifth article of amendment containing the words now in question was made, the trial by jury in criminal cases had thus already been provided for. By the sixth and seventh articles of amendment, further special provisions were separately made for that mode of trial in civil and criminal cases. To have followed, as in the state constitutions, and in the ordinance of 1787, the words of *Magna Charta*, and declared that no person shall be deprived of his life, liberty, or property but by the judgment of his peers or the law of the land, would have been in part superfluous and inappropriate. To have taken the clause, "law of the land," without its immediate context, might possibly have given rise to doubts, which would be effectually dispelled by using those words which the great commentator on *Magna Charta* [*Editors' Note: the "great commentator" was Sir Edward Coke*] had declared to be the true meaning of the phrase, "law of the land," in that instrument, and which were undoubtedly then received as their true meaning.

That the warrant now in question is legal process, is not denied. It was issued in conformity with an act of Congress. But is it "due process of law?" The constitution contains no description of those processes which it was intended to allow or forbid. It does not even declare what principles are to be applied to ascertain whether it be due process. It is manifest that it was not left to the legislative power to enact any process which might be devised. The article is a restraint on the legislative as well as on the executive and judicial powers of the government, and cannot be so construed as to leave congress free to make any process "due process of law," by its mere will. To what principles, then, are we to resort to ascertain whether this process, enacted by congress, is due process? To this the answer must be twofold. We must examine the constitution itself, to see whether this process be in conflict with any of its provisions. If not found to be so, we must look to those settled usages and modes of proceeding existing in the common and statute law of England, before the emigration of our ancestors, and which are shown not to have been unsuited to their civil and political condition by having been acted on by them after the settlement of this country. We apprehend there has been no period, since the establishment of the English monarchy, when there has not been, by the law of the land, a summary method for the recovery of debts due to the crown, and especially those due from receivers of the revenues. It is difficult, at this day, to trace with precision all the proceedings had for these purposes in the earliest ages of the common law. That they were summary and severe, and had been used for purposes of oppression, is inferable from the fact that one chapter of *Magna Charta* treats of their restraint * * *.

* * *

It is certain that this diversity in "the law of the land" between public defaulters and ordinary debtors was understood in this country, and entered into the legislation of the colonies and provinces, and more especially of the States, after the declaration of independence and before the formation of the constitution of the United States. Not only was the process of distress in nearly or quite universal use for the collection of taxes, but what was generally termed a warrant of distress, running against the

> body, goods, and chattels of defaulting receivers of public money, was issued to some public officer, to whom was committed the power to ascertain the amount of the default, and by such warrant proceed to collect it * * *.
>
> Tested by the common and statute law of England prior to the emigration of our ancestors, and by the laws of many of the States at the time of the adoption of this amendment, the proceedings authorized by the act of 1820 cannot be denied to be due process of law, when applied to the ascertainment and recovery of balances due to the government from a collector of customs * * *.

59 U.S. (18 How.) at 275–80.

There is a great deal in this passage (and even more in the parts of the opinion that we have not reproduced, including some seminal comments on the propriety and limits of federal adjudication by non-Article III bodies). First, there is a clear declaration that the Fifth Amendment Due Process of Law Clause should be understood in light of Magna Carta and the tradition of the Ancient Constitution that arose under it, since the Court was relying on the understanding of Magna Carta held by Edward Coke. Second, the Court stated that the Due Process of Law Clause binds the legislature—not because it imposes procedural (or generalized substantive) constraints on the legislature but because it limits the legislature's ability to modify traditional procedural forms for judicial and executive action. Third, it upholds the validity of the statute authorizing executive determination of liability, but it does so *only* in the context of tax collectors. That result can be justified by either or both of two lines of reasoning. For one thing, there was a long history of both British and colonial governments using summary (non-judicial) procedures to monitor tax collectors. If the Due Process of Law Clause simply incorporates traditional understandings of procedural fairness, few things were more traditional than internal executive monitoring of tax collectors. Notice that the Court mentions the "diversity in 'the law of the land' between public defaulters and ordinary debtors," meaning that this kind of summary procedure would never do for "ordinary debtors." A related but alternative explanation for the result is that that perhaps tax collectors waive their procedural constitutional rights when they accept the job; the idea of waiver of constitutional rights was well settled by 1856. *See Bank of Colom. v. Okely*, 17 U.S. (4 Wheat.) 235, 243–44 (1819). The first of these reasons directs attention away from the principle of legality and focuses instead on "those settled usages and modes of proceeding existing in the common and statute law of England"—in other words, procedural adequacy. That reason had come to represent the settled reading of *Murray's Lessee*, making the case the foundation of what is often called the law of "procedural due process." The year after *Murray's Lessee,* of course, the Court introduced the branch of doctrine known as "substantive due process" by declaring in *Dred Scott* that a federal law prohibiting slave ownership in federal territory "could hardly be dignified with the name of due process of law."

We will say more about substantive due process later in this chapter, in connection with the Ninth Amendment, and in the next chapter. For now, we have a bit more to say about procedural due process.

The threshold question for matters of both substantive and procedural due process is whether the government is depriving you of life, liberty, or property. If the answer is "no," the Due Process of Law Clause is the wrong place to look for protection. Sometimes that is an easy question to answer: If the government is trying to put you in jail, it is trying to deprive you of "liberty." If the government is taking your money or your land, it is depriving you of "property." If it is firing you from a government job or denying you a license or benefits, things get much trickier, and the answer depends largely on how the government has chosen to write the statutes or regulations that define the job, license, or benefit in question. *See* GARY LAWSON, FEDERAL ADMINISTRATIVE LAW 906–63 (8th ed. 2019). If the interest that you claim does not fit easily into these categories, things can get even trickier. *See, e.g., Kerry v. Din,* 575 U.S. 86 (2015) (splitting 3–2–4 over the due process of law claim brought by a citizen whose non-citizen spouse was denied entry into the United States). This topic is often covered in depth in courses in Administrative Law.

Once you have determined that the federal government is depriving you of something that falls within the broad modern understanding of "life, liberty, or property," to what procedures are you entitled before that deprivation occurs? The answer depends on which institution of the federal government is doing the depriving. If the deprivation comes from the legislature, the only procedures to which you are entitled are the procedures for valid legislation under Article I, Section 7; the Due Process of Law Clause imposes no additional procedural requirements on Congress, which does not need to give you notice or allow you to present evidence before it passes laws. If the deprivation comes from a court, you are entitled to all of the traditional procedures that are baked into the "judicial Power," including notice, an opportunity to be heard, and an impartial decisionmaker. What if the deprivation results from executive action, such as adjudication by an administrative agency? As an empirical matter, the overwhelming bulk of actual deprivations occur through executive rather than legislative or judicial action, so the answer to this question is very important. With the proviso that the details are best left to courses in Administrative Law: If the executive acts through rulemaking, the Constitution imposes essentially no procedural requirements, though statutes often impose requirements as or more extensive than the Constitution would require. If the executive acts through adjudication—particularized, case-by-case determinations—then the Constitution requires a range of procedures depending on a number of factors:

> * * * " '[D]ue process,' unlike some legal rules, is not a technical conception with a fixed content unrelated to time, place and circumstances." *Cafeteria Workers v. McElroy*, 367 U.S. 886, 895 (1961). "(D)ue process is flexible and calls for such procedural protections as the particular situation demands." *Morrissey v. Brewer*, 408 U.S. 471, 481 (1972). Accordingly, resolution of the issue whether the administrative procedures provided here are constitutionally sufficient requires analysis of the governmental and private interests that are affected. More precisely, our prior decisions indicate that identification of the specific dictates of due process generally requires consideration of three distinct factors: First, the private interest that will be affected by the official action; second, the risk of an erroneous deprivation of such interest through the procedures used, and the probable value, if any, of additional or substitute procedural safeguards; and finally, the Government's interest, including the function involved and the fiscal and administrative burdens that the additional or substitute procedural requirement would entail.

Mathews v. Eldridge, 424 U.S. 319, 334–35 (1976). While the decision in *Mathews v. Eldridge* emphatically *did not* intend to set forth a rigid and exclusive three-part "test" for procedural adequacy, subsequent cases have morphed this simple description of past caselaw into a mantra that now governs virtually all cases involving the procedural adequacy of executive adjudicative deprivations. *See* GARY LAWSON, FEDERAL ADMINISTRATIVE LAW 978–80 (8th ed. 2019).

[Assignment 52]

C. THE TAKINGS CLAUSE OF THE FIFTH AMENDMENT

nor shall private property be taken for public use, without just compensation.

The Takings Clause of the Fifth Amendment was added at James Madison's initiative, with no State having asked for it. It appears almost hidden in the Fifth Amendment, with unrelated procedural rights to help it slip through unnoticed, which it did. Nonetheless, it should be noted that six out of twelve States that wrote new constitutions between 1776 and 1791 had Takings Clauses in them. Moreover, forty-nine state constitutions have such clauses today. Steven Gow Calabresi, et. al., *Individual Rights Under State Constitutions in 2018: What Rights are Deeply Rooted in a Modern-Day Consensus of the States*, 94 NOTRE DAME L. REV. 49, 103–104 (2018).

The federal Takings Clause imposes two limits on government power. First, a taking has to be for a public use and not merely to transfer the property of A to B. Second, when the government confiscates property, it has to pay just compensation.

The Takings Clause, of course, only applies to takings. If there is no taking of private property, the clause has no work to do. The most obvious form of a taking is an exercise of the power of eminent domain, in which the government forces an owner to sell their property to the government for "just compensation" as determined in a judicial proceeding. In these cases, no question arises about whether private property has been "taken": the only question is how much the government will have to pay. (As an aside: The Constitution contains no explicit enumerated power of eminent domain in the federal government. For the Nation's first century, the federal government did not exercise any such power outside of federal territory; it if wanted land within a State, it asked the State to take the property and then sell it to the federal government. *See* William Baude, *Rethinking the Federal Eminent Domain Power,* 122 YALE L.J. 1738 (2013). A federal eminent domain power was not acknowledged by the courts until 1876. *See Kohl v. United States,* 91 U.S. 367 (1876).)

Can the government take property without exercising an eminent domain power? Suppose that the government simply occupies your property without formally condemning it and forcing a sale? That certainly seems like a taking, doesn't it? But if property can be "taken" other than through eminent domain, where, if at all, does that stop? Suppose now that the government does not itself occupy your land but engineers a dam that floods your property. You still own the formal title to the land, but you can no longer use it for any purpose other than as a lake bed. Is that a taking? The Supreme Court decided at a fairly early time, in a case involving a Wisconsin constitutional provision substantively identical to the Fifth Amendment's Takings Clause, that the answer is yes:

The argument of the defendant is that there is no *taking* of the land within the meaning of the constitutional provision, and that the damage is a consequential result of such use of a navigable stream as the government had a right to for the improvement of its navigation.

It would be a very curious and unsatisfactory result, if in construing a provision of constitutional law, always understood to have been adopted for protection and security to the rights of the individual as against the government, and which has received the commendation of jurists, statesmen, and commentators as placing the just principles of the common law on that subject beyond the power of ordinary legislation to change or control them, it shall be held that if the government refrains from the absolute conversion of real property to the uses of the public it can destroy its value entirely, can inflict irreparable and permanent injury to any extent, can, in effect, subject it to total destruction without making any compensation, because, in the narrowest sense of that word, it is not *taken* for the public use. Such a construction would pervert the constitutional provision into a restriction upon the rights of the citizen, as those rights stood at the common law, instead of the government, and make it an authority for invasion of private right under the pretext of the public good, which had no warrant in the laws or practices of our ancestors.

* * *

We are not unaware of the numerous cases in the State courts in which the doctrine has been successfully invoked that for a consequential injury to the property of the individual arising from the prosecution of improvements of roads, streets, rivers, and other highways, for the public good, there is no redress; and we do not deny that the principle is a sound one, in its proper application, to many injuries to property so originating. And when, in the exercise of our duties here, we shall be called upon to construe other State constitutions, we shall not be unmindful of the weight due to the decisions of the courts of those States. But we are of opinion that the decisions referred to have gone to the uttermost limit of sound judicial construction in favor of this principle, and, in some cases, beyond it, and that it remains true that where real estate is actually invaded by superinduced additions of water, earth, sand, or other material, or by having any artificial structure placed on it, so as to effectually destroy or impair its usefulness, it is a taking, within the meaning of the Constitution, and that this proposition is not in conflict with the weight of judicial authority in this country, and certainly not with sound principle. Beyond this we do not go, and this case calls us to go no further.

Pumpelly v. Green Bay Co., 80 U.S. (13 Wall.) 166, 177–78, 180–81.

From that modest beginning has grown a doctrine of staggering complexity and uncertainty. For if loss of the use of (but not the title to) land through governmental *flooding* is a taking, what about loss of the use of (but not the title to) property as a result of governmental *regulations*? From the standpoint of the property owner, the effect is the same. And in the 150 years since *Pumpelly,* courts have wrestled with the problem of ascertaining when government regulations of property go "too far," *Pennsylvania Coal Co. v. Mahon,* 260 U.S. 393, 415 (1922), and "will be recognized as a taking." *Id.* The vast majority of the cases applying this "regulatory takings" doctrine, as it has come to be known, involve state or local regulations evaluated under the Fourteenth Amendment. In 1978, the Court summarized the inquiry for determining when regulations constitute takings:

> The question of what constitutes a "taking" for purposes of the Fifth Amendment has proved to be a problem of considerable difficulty. While this Court has recognized that the "Fifth Amendment's guarantee . . . [is] designed to bar Government from forcing some people alone to bear public burdens which, in all fairness and justice, should be borne by the public as a whole," *Armstrong v. United States*, 364 U.S. 40, 49 (1960), this Court, quite simply, has been unable to develop any "set formula" for determining when "justice and fairness" require that economic injuries caused by public action be compensated by the government, rather than remain disproportionately concentrated on a few persons * * *.
>
> In engaging in these essentially ad hoc, factual inquiries, the Court's decisions have identified several factors that have particular significance. The economic impact of the regulation on the claimant and, particularly, the extent to which the regulation has interfered with distinct investment-backed expectations are, of course, relevant considerations. So, too, is the character of the governmental action. A "taking" may more readily be found when the interference with property can be characterized as a physical invasion by government, than when interference arises from some public program adjusting the benefits and burdens of economic life to promote the common good.

Penn Central Transportation Co. v. City of New York, 438 U.S. 104, 123–24 (1978). As with *Mathews v Eldridge* in due process law, the Court obviously had no intention of setting out these considerations as an exclusive "test," but the formulation (perhaps predictably) became a mantra in fairly short order. *See* Gary Lawson, Katharine Ferguson & Guillermo Montero, *"Oh Lord, Please Don't Let Me Be Misunderstood!": Rediscovering the* Mathews v. Eldridge *and* Penn Central *Frameworks,* 81 NOTRE DAME L. REV. 1, 34 (2005) ("By 1987, however, for no reason that is readily apparent, the Court appears to have begun treating the *Penn Central* formulation as an outcome-determinative test even in circumstances in which a single factor is not dispositive. That is largely where we have stood ever since and where we stand today."). Property owners seldom win when the *Penn Central* "test" is applied.

Sometimes it is difficult to tell whether the government is actually occupying property, which everyone agrees is always a taking, or whether it is regulating property, which sometimes is and sometimes is not a taking. The case below is an important one involving federal regulation.

1. HORNE V. U.S. DEPARTMENT OF AGRICULTURE

576 U.S. ___, 135 S.Ct. 2419 (2015)

■ CHIEF JUSTICE ROBERTS delivered the opinion of the Court.

Under the United States Department of Agriculture's California Raisin Marketing Order, a percentage of a grower's crop must be physically set aside in certain years for the account of the Government, free of charge. The Government then sells, allocates, or otherwise disposes of the raisins in ways it determines are best suited to maintaining an orderly market. The question is whether the Takings Clause of the Fifth Amendment bars the Government from imposing such a demand on the growers without just compensation.

The Agricultural Marketing Agreement Act of 1937 authorizes the Secretary of Agriculture to promulgate "marketing orders" to help maintain stable markets for particular agricultural products. The marketing order for raisins requires growers in certain years to give a percentage of their crop to the Government, free of charge. The required allocation is determined by the Raisin Administrative Committee, a Government entity composed largely of growers and others in the raisin business appointed by the Secretary of Agriculture. In 2002–2003, this Committee ordered raisin growers to turn over 47 percent of their crop. In 2003–2004, 30 percent.

Growers generally ship their raisins to a raisin "handler," who physically separates the raisins due the Government (called "reserve raisins"), pays the growers only for the remainder ("free-tonnage raisins"), and packs and sells the free-tonnage raisins. The Raisin Committee acquires title to the reserve raisins that have been set aside, and decides how to dispose of them in its discretion. It sells them in noncompetitive markets, for example to exporters, federal agencies, or foreign governments; donates them to charitable causes; releases them to growers who agree to reduce their raisin production; or disposes of them by "any other means" consistent with the purposes of the raisin program. 7 CFR § 989.67(b)(5) (2015). Proceeds from Committee sales are principally used to subsidize handlers who sell raisins for export (not including the Hornes, who are not raisin exporters). Raisin growers retain an interest in any net proceeds from sales the Raisin Committee makes, after deductions for the export subsidies and the Committee's administrative expenses. In the years at issue in this case, those proceeds were less than the cost of producing the crop one year, and nothing at all the next.

The Hornes—Marvin Horne, Laura Horne, and their family—are both raisin growers and handlers. They "handled" not only their own raisins but also those produced by other growers, paying those growers in full for all of their raisins, not just the free-tonnage portion. In 2002, the Hornes refused to set aside any raisins for the Government, believing they were not legally bound to do so. The Government sent trucks to the Hornes' facility at eight o'clock one morning to pick up the raisins, but the Hornes refused entry. The Government then assessed against the Hornes a fine equal to the market value of the missing raisins—some $480,000—as well as an additional civil penalty of just over $200,000 for disobeying the order to turn them over.

When the Government sought to collect the fine, the Hornes turned to the courts, arguing that the reserve requirement was an unconstitutional taking of their property under the Fifth Amendment. Their case eventually made it to this Court when the Government argued that the lower courts had no jurisdiction to consider the Hornes' constitutional defense to the fine. *Horne v. Department of Agriculture*, 569 U.S. ___, (2013) (*Horne I*). We rejected the Government's argument and sent the case back to the Court of Appeals so it could address the Hornes' contention on the merits.

On remand, the Ninth Circuit agreed with the Hornes that the validity of the fine rose or fell with the constitutionality of the reserve requirement. 750 F.3d 1128,

1137 (2014). The court then considered whether that requirement was a physical appropriation of property, giving rise to a *per se* taking, or a restriction on a raisin grower's use of his property, properly analyzed under the more flexible and forgiving standard for a regulatory taking. The court rejected the Hornes' argument that the reserve requirement was a *per se* taking, reasoning that "the Takings Clause affords less protection to personal than to real property," and concluding that the Hornes "are not completely divested of their property rights," because growers retain an interest in the proceeds from any sale of reserve raisins by the Raisin Committee. *Id.*, at 1139.

The court instead viewed the reserve requirement as a use restriction, similar to a government condition on the grant of a land use permit. See *Dolan v. City of Tigard*, 512 U.S. 374 (1994); *Nollan v. California Coastal Comm'n*, 483 U.S. 825 (1987). As in such permit cases, the Court of Appeals explained, the Government here imposed a condition (the reserve requirement) in exchange for a Government benefit (an orderly raisin market). And just as a landowner was free to avoid the government condition by forgoing a permit, so too the Hornes could avoid the reserve requirement by "planting different crops." 750 F.3d, at 1143. Under that analysis, the court found that the reserve requirement was a proportional response to the Government's interest in ensuring an orderly raisin market, and not a taking under the Fifth Amendment.

We granted certiorari.

The petition for certiorari poses three questions, which we answer in turn.

The first question presented asks "Whether the government's 'categorical duty' under the Fifth Amendment to pay just compensation when it 'physically takes possession of an interest in property,' *Arkansas Game & Fish Comm'n v. United States*, ___ U.S. ___ (2012), applies only to real property and not to personal property." The answer is no.

There is no dispute that the "classic taking [is one] in which the government directly appropriates private property for its own use." *Tahoe-Sierra Preservation Council, Inc. v. Tahoe Regional Planning Agency*, 535 U.S. 302, 324 (2002). Nor is there any dispute that, in the case of real property, such an appropriation is a per se taking that requires just compensation. See *Loretto v. Teleprompter Manhattan CATV Corp.*, 458 U.S. 419, 426–435 (1982).

Nothing in the text or history of the Takings Clause, or our precedents, suggests that the rule is any different when it comes to appropriation of personal property. The Government has a categorical duty to pay just compensation when it takes your car, just as when it takes your home.

The Takings Clause provides: "[N]or shall private property be taken for public use, without just compensation." U.S. Const., Amdt. 5. It protects "private property" without any distinction between different types. The principle reflected in the Clause goes back at least 800 years to Magna Carta, which specifically protected agricultural crops from uncompensated takings. Clause 28 of that charter forbade any "constable or other bailiff" from taking "corn or other provisions from any one without immediately tendering money therefor, unless he can have postponement thereof by permission of the seller." Cl. 28 (1215), in W. McKechnie, Magna Carta, A Commentary on the Great Charter of King John 329 (2d ed. 1914).

The colonists brought the principles of Magna Carta with them to the New World, including that charter's protection against uncompensated takings of personal property. In 1641, for example, Massachusetts adopted its Body of Liberties, prohibiting "mans Cattel or goods of what kinde soever" from being "pressed or taken for any publique use or service, unlesse it be by warrant grounded upon some act of the generall Court, nor without such reasonable prices and hire as the ordinarie rates of the Countrie do afford." Massachusetts Body of Liberties ¶ 8, in R. Perry, Sources of Our Liberties 149 (1978). Virginia allowed the seizure of surplus "live stock, or beef, pork, or bacon" for the military, but only upon "paying or tendering to the owner the price so estimated by the appraisers." 1777 Va. Acts ch. XII. And South Carolina authorized the seizure of "necessaries" for public use, but provided that "said articles so seized shall be paid for agreeable to the prices such and the like articles sold for on the ninth day of October last." 1779 S.C. Acts § 4.

Given that background, it is not surprising that early Americans bridled at appropriations of their personal property during the Revolutionary War, at the hands of both sides. John Jay, for example, complained to the New York Legislature about military impressment by the Continental Army of "Horses, Teems, and Carriages," and voiced his fear that such action by the "little Officers" of the Quartermasters Department might extend to "Blankets, Shoes, and many other articles." A Hint to the Legislature of the State of New York (1778), in John Jay, The Making of a Revolutionary 461–463 (R. Morris ed. 1975). The legislature took the "hint," passing a law that, among other things, provided for compensation for the impressment of horses and carriages. 1778 N.Y. Laws ch. 29. According to the author of the first treatise on the Constitution, St. George Tucker, the Takings Clause was "probably" adopted in response to "the arbitrary and oppressive mode of obtaining supplies for the army, and other public uses, by impressment, as was too frequently practised during the revolutionary war, without any compensation whatever." 1 Blackstone's Commentaries, Editor's App. 305–306 (1803).

Nothing in this history suggests that personal property was any less protected against physical appropriation than real property * * *.

* * *

The reserve requirement imposed by the Raisin Committee is a clear physical taking. Actual raisins are transferred from the growers to the Government. Title to the raisins passes to the Raisin Committee. The Committee's raisins must be physically segregated from free-tonnage raisins. 7 CFR § 989.66(b)(2). Reserve raisins are sometimes left on the premises of handlers, but they are held "for the account" of the Government. § 989.66(a). The Committee disposes of what become its raisins as it wishes, to promote the purposes of the raisin marketing order.

* * * The Government's formal demand that the Hornes turn over a percentage of their raisin crop without charge, for the Government's control and use, is "of such a unique character that it is a taking without regard to other factors that a court might ordinarily examine."

The Government thinks it "strange" and the dissent "baffling" that the Hornes object to the reserve requirement, when they nonetheless concede that "the government may prohibit the sale of raisins without effecting a per se taking." Brief for Respondent 35. But that distinction flows naturally from the settled difference in our takings jurisprudence between appropriation and regulation. A physical taking of raisins and a regulatory limit on production may have the same economic impact on a grower. The Constitution, however, is concerned with means as well as ends. The Government has broad powers, but the means it uses to achieve its ends must be "consist[ent] with the letter and spirit of the constitution." *McCulloch v. Maryland*, 4 Wheat. 316, 421 (1819) * * *.

The second question presented asks "Whether the government may avoid the categorical duty to pay just compensation for a physical taking of property by reserving to the property owner a contingent interest in a portion of the value of the property, set at the government's discretion." The answer is no.

The Government and dissent argue that raisins are fungible goods whose only value is in the revenue from their sale. According to the Government, the raisin marketing order leaves that interest with the raisin growers: After selling reserve raisins and deducting expenses and subsidies for exporters, the Raisin Committee returns any net proceeds to the growers. The Government contends that because growers are entitled to these net proceeds, they retain the most important property interest in the reserve raisins, so there is no taking in the first place. The dissent agrees, arguing that this possible future revenue means there has been no taking * * *.

But when there has been a physical appropriation, "we do not ask . . . whether it deprives the owner of all economically valuable use" of the item taken. *Tahoe-Sierra Preservation Council*, 535 U.S., at 323; see *id.*, at 322 ("When the government physically takes possession of an interest in property for some public purpose, it has a categorical duty to compensate the former owner, regardless of whether the interest that is taken constitutes an entire parcel or merely a part thereof." For example, in *Loretto*, we held that the installation of a cable box on a small corner of Loretto's rooftop was a *per se* taking, even though she could of course still sell and economically benefit from the property. 458 U.S., at 430, 436. The fact that the growers retain a contingent interest of indeterminate value does not mean there has been no physical taking, particularly since the value of the interest depends on the discretion of the taker, and may be worthless, as it was for one of the two years at issue here.

The dissent points to *Andrus v. Allard*, 444 U.S. 51 (1979), noting that the Court found no taking in that case, even though the owners' artifacts could not be sold at all. The dissent suggests that the Hornes should be happy, because they might at least get something from what had been their raisins. But *Allard* is a very different case. As the dissent recognizes, the owners in that case retained the rights to possess, donate, and devise their property. In finding no taking, the Court emphasized that the Government did not "compel the surrender of the artifacts, and there [was] no physical invasion or restraint upon them." 444 U.S., at 65–66. Here of course the raisin program requires physical surrender of the raisins and transfer of title, and the growers lose any right to control their disposition.

* * *

The third question presented asks "Whether a governmental mandate to relinquish specific, identifiable property as a 'condition' on permission to engage in commerce effects a per se taking." The answer, at least in this case, is yes.

The Government contends that the reserve requirement is not a taking because raisin growers voluntarily choose to participate in the raisin market. According to the Government, if raisin growers don't like it, they can "plant different crops," or "sell their raisin-variety grapes as table grapes or for use in juice or wine." Brief for Respondent 32.

"Let them sell wine" is probably not much more comforting to the raisin growers than similar retorts have been to others throughout history. In any event, the Government is wrong as a matter of law. In *Loretto*, we rejected the argument that the New York law was not a taking because a landlord could avoid the requirement by ceasing to be a landlord. We held instead that "a landlord's ability to rent his property may not be conditioned on his forfeiting the right to compensation for a physical occupation." 458 U.S., at 439, n. 17. As the Court explained, the contrary argument "proves too much":

> "For example, it would allow the government to require a landlord to devote a substantial portion of his building to vending and washing machines, with all profits to be retained by the owners of these services and with no compensation for the deprivation of space. It would even allow the government to requisition a certain number of apartments as permanent government offices." *Ibid.*

As the Court concluded, property rights "cannot be so easily manipulated." *Ibid.*

The Government and dissent rely heavily on *Ruckelshaus v. Monsanto Co.*, 467 U.S. 986 (1984). There we held that the Environmental Protection Agency could require companies manufacturing pesticides, fungicides, and rodenticides to disclose health, safety, and environmental information about their products as a condition to receiving a permit to sell those products. While such information included trade secrets in which pesticide manufacturers had a property interest, those manufacturers were not subjected to a taking because they received a "valuable Government benefit" in exchange—a license to sell dangerous chemicals. *Id.*, at 1007; see *Nollan,* 483 U.S., at 834, n. 2 (discussing *Monsanto*).

The taking here cannot reasonably be characterized as part of a similar voluntary exchange. In one of the years at issue here, the Government insisted that the Hornes turn over 47 percent of their raisin crop, in exchange for the "benefit" of being allowed to sell the remaining 53 percent. The next year, the toll was 30 percent. We have already rejected the idea that *Monsanto* may be extended by regarding basic and familiar uses of property as a "Government benefit" on the same order as a permit to sell hazardous chemicals. See *Nollan*, 483 U.S., at 834, n. 2 (distinguishing *Monsanto* on the ground that "the right to build on one's own property—even though its exercise can be subjected to legitimate permitting requirements—cannot remotely be described as a 'governmental benefit' "). Selling produce in interstate commerce, although certainly subject to reasonable government regulation, is similarly not a special governmental benefit that the Government may hold hostage, to be ransomed by the waiver of constitutional protection. Raisins are not dangerous pesticides; they are a healthy snack. A case about conditioning the sale of hazardous substances on disclosure of health, safety, and environmental information related to those hazards is hardly on point.

* * *

Finally, the Government briefly argues that if we conclude that the reserve requirement effects a taking, we should remand for the Court of Appeals to calculate "what compensation would have been due if petitioners had complied with the reserve requirement." Brief for Respondent 55. The Government contends that the calculation must consider what the value of the reserve raisins would have been without the price support program, as well as "other benefits . . . from the regulatory program, such as higher consumer demand for raisins spurred by enforcement of quality standards and promotional activities." *Id.*, at 55–56. Indeed, according to the Government, the Hornes would "likely" have a net gain under this theory.

The best defense may be a good offense, but the Government cites no support for its hypothetical-based approach, or its notion that general regulatory activity such as enforcement of quality standards can constitute just compensation for a specific physical taking. Instead, our cases have set forth a clear and administrable rule for just compensation: "The Court has repeatedly held that just compensation normally is to be measured by 'the market value of the property at the time of the taking.'" *United States v. 50 Acres of Land*, 469 U.S. 24, 29 (1984) (quoting *Olson v. United States*, 292 U.S. 246, 255 (1934)).

JUSTICE BREYER is concerned that applying this rule in this case will affect provisions concerning whether a condemning authority may deduct special benefits—such as new access to a waterway or highway, or filling in of swampland—from the amount of compensation it seeks to pay a landowner suffering a partial taking. He need not be. Cases of that sort can raise complicated questions involving the exercise of the eminent domain power, but they do not create a generally applicable exception to the usual compensation rule, based on asserted regulatory benefits of the sort at issue here. Nothing in the cases JUSTICE BREYER labels "*Bauman* and its progeny" suggests otherwise, which may be why the Solicitor General does not cite them.

In any event, this litigation presents no occasion to consider the broader issues discussed by JUSTICE BREYER. The Government has already calculated the amount of just compensation in this case, when it fined the Hornes the fair market value of the raisins: $483,843.53. The Government cannot now disavow that valuation, and does not suggest that the marketing order affords the Hornes compensation in that amount. There is accordingly no need for a remand; the Hornes should simply be relieved of the obligation to pay the fine and associated civil penalty they were assessed when they resisted the Government's effort to take their raisins. This case, in litigation for more than a decade, has gone on long enough.

The judgment of the United States Court of Appeals for the Ninth Circuit is reversed.

It is so ordered.

■ JUSTICE THOMAS, concurring.

I join the Court's opinion in full. I write separately to offer an additional observation concerning JUSTICE BREYER's argument that we should remand the case. The Takings Clause prohibits the government from taking private property except "for public use," even when it offers "just compensation." U.S. Const., Amdt. 5. That requirement, as originally understood, imposes a meaningful constraint on the power of the state—"the government may take property only if it actually uses or gives the public a legal right to use the property." *Kelo v. New London*, 545 U.S. 469, 521 (2005) (THOMAS, J., dissenting). It is far from clear that the Raisin Administrative Committee's conduct meets that standard. It takes the raisins of citizens and, among other things, gives them away or sells them to exporters, foreign importers, and foreign governments. 7 CFR § 989.67(b) (2015). To the extent that the Committee is not taking the raisins "for public use," having the Court of Appeals calculate "just compensation" in this case would be a fruitless exercise.

■ JUSTICE BREYER, with whom JUSTICE GINSBURG and JUSTICE KAGAN join, concurring in part and dissenting in part.

I agree with Parts I and II of the Court's opinion. However, I cannot agree with the Court's rejection, in Part III, of the Government's final argument. The Government contends that we should remand the case for a determination of whether any compensation would have been due if the Hornes had complied with the California Raisin Marketing Order's reserve requirement. In my view, a remand for such a determination is necessary.

The question of just compensation was not presented in the Hornes' petition for certiorari. It was barely touched on in the briefs. And the courts below did not decide it. At the same time, the case law that I have found indicates that the Government may well be right: The marketing order may afford just compensation for the takings of raisins that it imposes. If that is correct, then the reserve requirement does not violate the Takings Clause.

* * *

On the record before us, the Hornes have not established that the Government, through the raisin reserve program, takes raisins *without just compensation*. When the Government takes as reserve raisins a percentage of the annual crop, the raisin owners retain the remaining, free-tonnage, raisins. The reserve requirement is intended, at least in part, to enhance the price that free-tonnage raisins will fetch on the open market. And any such enhancement matters. This Court's precedents indicate that, when calculating the just compensation that the Fifth Amendment requires, a court should deduct from the value of the taken (reserve) raisins any enhancement caused by the taking to the value of the remaining (free-tonnage) raisins.

More than a century ago, in *Bauman v. Ross*, 167 U.S. 548 (1897), this Court established an exception to the rule that "just compensation normally is to be measured by 'the market value of the property at the time of the taking.' " *United States v. 50 Acres of Land*, 469 U.S. 24, 29 (1984). We considered in *Bauman* how to calculate just compensation when the Government takes only a portion of a parcel of property:

> "[W]hen part only of a parcel of land is taken for a highway, the value of that part is not the sole measure of the compensation or damages to be paid to the owner; but the incidental injury or benefit to the part not taken is also to be considered. When the part not taken is left in such shape or condition, as to be in itself of less value than before, the owner is entitled to additional damages on that account. When, on the other hand, the part which he retains is specially and directly increased in value by the public improvement, the damages to the whole parcel by the appropriation of part of it are lessened." 167 U.S., at 574.

"The Constitution of the United States," the Court stated, "contains no express prohibition against considering benefits in estimating the just compensation to be paid for private property taken for the public use." *Id.*, at 584.

The Court has consistently applied this method for calculating just compensation: It sets off from the value of the portion that was taken the value of any benefits conferred upon the remaining portion of the property.

* * *

If we apply *Bauman* and its progeny to the marketing order's reserve requirement, "the benefit [to the free-tonnage raisins] may be set off against the value of the [reserve raisins] taken." The value of the raisins taken might exceed the value of the benefit conferred. In that case, the reserve requirement effects a taking without just compensation, and the Hornes' decision not to comply with the requirement was justified. On the other hand, the benefit might equal or exceed the value of the raisins taken. In that case, the California Raisin Marketing Order does not effect a taking without just compensation. And even the Hornes agree that if the reserve requirement does not effect a taking without just compensation, then they cannot use the Takings Clause to excuse their failure to comply with the marketing order—or to justify their refusal to pay the fine and penalty imposed based on that failure.

The majority believes the *Bauman* line of cases most likely does not apply here. It says that those cases do "not create a generally applicable exception to the usual compensation rule, based on asserted regulatory benefits of the sort at issue here." But it is unclear to me what distinguishes this case from those.

* * *

Ultimately, the majority rejects the Government's request for a remand because it believes that the Government "does not suggest that the marketing order affords the Hornes compensation" in the amount of the fine that the Government assessed. In my view, however, the relevant precedent indicates that the Takings Clause requires compensation in an amount equal to the value of the reserve raisins adjusted to account for the benefits received. And the Government does, indeed, suggest that the marketing order affords just compensation. Further, the Hornes have not demonstrated the contrary. Before granting judgment in favor of the Hornes, a court should address the issue in light of all of the relevant facts and law.

* * *

Given the precedents, the parties should provide full briefing on this question. I would remand the case, permitting the lower courts to consider argument on the question of just compensation.

For these reasons, while joining Parts I and II of the Court's opinion, I respectfully dissent from Part III.

■ JUSTICE SOTOMAYOR, dissenting.

The Hornes claim, and the Court agrees, that the Raisin Marketing Order, 7 CFR pt. 989 (2015) (hereinafter Order), effects a *per se* taking under our decision in *Loretto v. Teleprompter Manhattan CATV Corp.*, 458 U.S. 419 (1982). But *Loretto* sets a high bar for such claims: It requires that each and every property right be destroyed by governmental action before that action can be said to have effected a *per se* taking. Because the Order does not deprive the Hornes of all of their property rights, it does not effect a *per se* taking. I respectfully dissent from the Court's contrary holding.

Our Takings Clause jurisprudence has generally eschewed "magic formula[s]" and has "recognized few invariable rules." Most takings cases therefore proceed under the fact-specific balancing test set out in *Penn Central Transp. Co. v. New York City*, 438 U.S. 104 (1978). The Hornes have not made any argument under *Penn Central*. In order to prevail, they therefore must fit their claim into one of the three narrow categories in which we have assessed takings claims more categorically.

In the "special context of land-use exactions," we have held that "government demands that a landowner dedicate an easement allowing public access to her property as a condition of obtaining a development permit" constitute takings unless the government demonstrates a nexus and rough proportionality between its demand and the impact of the proposed development. We have also held that a regulation that deprives a property owner of "*all* economically beneficial us[e]" of his or her land is a *per se* taking. *Lucas v. South Carolina Coastal Council*, 505 U.S. 1003, 1019 (1992) (emphasis in original). The Hornes have not relied on either of these rules in this Court.

Finally—and this is the argument the Hornes do rely on—we have held that the government effects a *per se* taking when it requires a property owner to suffer a "permanent physical occupation" of his or her property. *Loretto*, 458 U.S., at 426. In my view, however, *Loretto*—when properly understood—does not encompass the circumstances of this case because it only applies where all property rights have been destroyed by governmental action. Where some property right is retained by the owner, no *per se* taking under *Loretto* has occurred.

This strict rule is apparent from the reasoning in *Loretto* itself. We explained that "[p]roperty rights in a physical thing have been described as the rights 'to possess, use and dispose of it.' " A "permanent physical occupation" of property occurs, we said, when governmental action "destroys *each* of these rights." When, as we held in *Loretto*, each of these rights is destroyed, the government has not simply "take[n] a single 'strand' from the 'bundle' of property rights"; it has "chop[ped] through the bundle" entirely. In the narrow circumstance in which a property owner has suffered this "most serious form of invasion of [his or her] property interests," a taking can be said to have occurred without any further showing on the property owner's part.

By contrast, in the mine run of cases where governmental action impacts property rights in ways that do not chop through the bundle entirely, we have declined to apply *per se* rules and have instead opted for the more nuanced *Penn Central* test * * *.

* * * Simply put, the retention of even one property right that is not destroyed is sufficient to defeat a claim of a *per se* taking under Loretto.

* * *

The Hornes, however, retain at least one meaningful property interest in the reserve raisins: the right to receive some money for their disposition * * *.

Granted, this equitable distribution may represent less income than what some or all of the reserve raisins could fetch if sold in an unregulated market. In some years, it may even turn out (and has turned out) to represent no net income. But whether and when that occurs turns on market forces for which the Government cannot be blamed and to which all commodities—indeed, all property—are subject * * *.

* * *

The fact that at least one property right is not destroyed by the Order is alone sufficient to hold that this case does not fall within the narrow confines of *Loretto*. But such a holding is also consistent with another line of cases that, when viewed together, teach that the government may require certain property rights to be given up as a condition of entry into a regulated market without effecting a *per se* taking.

* * *

* * * [I]n *Ruckelshaus v. Monsanto Co.*, 467 U.S. 986, we held that no taking occurred when a provision of the Federal Insecticide, Fungicide, and Rodenticide Act required companies that wished to sell certain pesticides to first submit sensitive data and trade secrets to the Environmental Protection Agency as part of a registration process. Even though the EPA was permitted to publicly disclose some of that submitted data—which would have had the effect of revealing trade secrets, thus substantially diminishing or perhaps even eliminating their value—we reasoned that * * * the disclosure requirement was the price Monsanto had to pay for " 'the advantage of living and doing business in a civilized community.' " We offered nary a suggestion that the law at issue could be considered a *per se* taking, and instead recognized that "a voluntary submission of data by an applicant" in exchange for the ability to participate in a regulated market "can hardly be called a taking." 467 U.S., at 1007.

Finally, in *Yee v. Escondido*, 503 U.S. 519 (1992), we addressed a mobile-home park rent-control ordinance that set rents at below-market rates. We held the ordinance did not effect a taking under *Loretto*, even when it was considered in conjunction with other state laws regarding eviction that effectively permitted tenants to remain at will, because it only regulated the terms of market participation. See 503 U.S., at 527–529.

Understood together, these cases demonstrate that the Government may condition the ability to offer goods in the market on the giving-up of certain property interests without effecting a *per se* taking. The Order is a similar regulation. It has no effect whatsoever on raisins that the Hornes grow for their own use. But insofar as the Hornes wish to sell some raisins in a market regulated by the Government and at a price supported by governmental intervention, the Order requires that they give up the right to sell a portion of those raisins at that price and instead accept disposal of them at a lower price. Given that we have held that the Government may impose a price on the privilege of engaging in a particular business without effecting a taking—which is all that the Order does—it follows that the Order at the very least does not run afoul of our *per se* takings jurisprudence. Under a different takings test, one might reach a different conclusion. But the Hornes have advanced only this narrow per se takings claim, and that claim fails.

* * *

The Hornes and the Court both concede that a cap on the quantity of raisins that the Hornes can sell would not be a *per se* taking. The Court's focus on the physical nature of the intrusion also suggests that merely arranging for the sale of the reserve raisins would not be a *per se* taking. The rub for the Court must therefore be not that the Government is doing these things, but that it is accomplishing them by the altogether understandable requirement that the reserve raisins be physically set aside. I know of no principle, however, providing that if the Government achieves a permissible regulatory end by asking regulated individuals or entities to physically move the property subject to the regulation, it has committed a *per se* taking rather than a potential regulatory taking * * *.

* * *

Because a straightforward application of our precedents reveals that the Hornes have not suffered a *per se* taking, I would affirm the judgment of the Ninth Circuit. The Court reaches a contrary conclusion only by expanding our *per se* takings doctrine in a manner that is as unwarranted as it is vague. I respectfully dissent.

NOTES AND QUESTIONS

1. Under *Horne,* if the government in *Wickard v. Filburn, see supra* pages 706–711, had seized part of Filburn's wheat, or had ordered him to set some aside physically, it would be a taking of his property. Instead, the government ordered Filburn not to grow the wheat in the first place. Is there really a difference between those two orders? Does *Horne* undermine *Wickard v. Filburn* through the back door? Or does the formal line between regulation of property and occupation of property make sense?

2. The Eagle Protection Act makes it unlawful to "take, possess, sell, purchase, barter, offer to sell, purchase or barter, transport, export or import, at any time or in any manner, any bald eagle commonly known as the American eagle, or any golden eagle, alive or dead, or any part, nest, or egg thereof of the foregoing eagles." 16 U.S.C. § 668(a) (2018). If you owned any eagle feathers or other eagle parts before the Act took effect in 1940, you could still possess and transport them, but you could not sell them. Does the Act so restrict your rights with respect to your pre-1940 eagle feathers that it constitutes a taking? A unanimous Supreme Court, applying the *Penn Central* inquiry, said no:

> The regulations challenged here do not compel the surrender of the artifacts, and there is no physical invasion or restraint upon them. Rather, a significant restriction has been imposed on one means of disposing of the artifacts. But the denial of one traditional property right does not always amount to a taking. At least where an owner possesses a full "bundle" of property rights, the destruction of one "strand" of the bundle is not a taking, because the aggregate must be viewed in its entirety. In this case, it is crucial that appellees retain the rights to possess and transport their property, and to donate or devise the protected birds.
>
> It is, to be sure, undeniable that the regulations here prevent the most profitable use of appellees' property. Again, however, that is not dispositive. When we review regulation, a reduction in the value of property is not necessarily equated with a taking. In the instant case, it is not clear that appellees will be unable to derive economic benefit from the artifacts; for example, they might exhibit the artifacts for an admissions charge. At any rate, loss of future profits—unaccompanied by any physical property restriction—provides a slender reed upon which to rest a takings claim. Prediction of profitability is essentially a matter of reasoned speculation that courts are not especially competent to perform. Further, perhaps because of its very uncertainty, the interest in anticipated gains has traditionally been viewed as less compelling than other property-related interests.
>
> * * *
>
> It is true that appellees must bear the costs of these regulations. But, within limits, that is a burden borne to secure "the advantage of living and

> doing business in a civilized community." *Pennsylvania Coal Co. v. Mahon, supra*, 260 U.S., at 422 (Brandeis, J., dissenting). We hold that the simple prohibition of the sale of lawfully acquired property in this case does not effect a taking in violation of the Fifth Amendment.

Andrus v. Allard, 444 U.S. 51, 65–68 (1979). In 1983, Congress, concerned about allotted Indian lands passing by will to multiple claimants and creating tiny and hard-to-administer fractional shares in land, passed a statute saying that holders of such low-value land could not pass their interests by will: "No undivided fractional interest in any tract of trust or restricted land within a tribe's reservation or otherwise subjected to a tribe's jurisdiction shall descedent [sic] by intestacy or devise but shall escheat to that tribe if such interest represents 2 per centum or less of the total acreage in such tract and has earned to its owner less than $100 in the preceding year before it is due to escheat." Indian Land Consolidation Act of 1983, Pub. L. No. 97–459, § 207, 96 Stat. 2519. The statute was challenged as a taking of the right to pass property by will. The Court, again applying *Penn Central,* agreed that it was a taking:

> There is no question that the relative economic impact of § 207 upon the owners of these property rights can be substantial. Section 207 provides for the escheat of small undivided property interests that are unproductive during the year preceding the owner's death. Even if we accept the Government's assertion that the income generated by such parcels may be properly thought of as *de minimis*, their value may not be * * *. Of course, the whole of appellees' decedents' property interests were not taken by § 207. Appellees' decedents retained full beneficial use of the property during their lifetimes as well as the right to convey it inter vivos. There is no question, however, that the right to pass on valuable property to one's heirs is itself a valuable right * * *.
>
> The extent to which any of appellees' decedents had "investment-backed expectations" in passing on the property is dubious * * *. None of the appellees here can point to any specific investment-backed expectations beyond the fact that their ancestors agreed to accept allotment only after ceding to the United States large parts of the original Great Sioux Reservation.
>
> Also weighing weakly in favor of the statute is the fact that there is something of an "average reciprocity of advantage," *Pennsylvania Coal Co. v. Mahon*, 260 U.S. 393, 415 (1922), to the extent that owners of escheatable interests maintain a nexus to the Tribe * * *.
>
> If we were to stop our analysis at this point, we might well find § 207 constitutional. But the character of the Government regulation here is extraordinary * * *. In one form or another, the right to pass on property—to one's family in particular—has been part of the Anglo-American legal system since feudal times. The fact that it may be possible for the owners of these interests to effectively control disposition upon death through complex inter vivos transactions such as revocable trusts is simply not an adequate substitute for the rights taken, given the nature of the property * * *

Hodel v. Irving, 481 U.S. 704, 714–16 (1987). Did the owners of eagle feathers in *Andrus v. Allard* lose less of their "bundle of rights" than did the landowners in *Hodel*? Three concurring Justices wrote: "I join the opinion of the Court. I write separately to note that in my view the present statute, insofar as concerns the balance between rights taken and rights left untouched, is indistinguishable from the statute that was at issue in *Andrus v. Allard*, 444 U.S. 51 (1979). Because that comparison is determinative of whether there has been a taking, in finding a taking today our decision effectively limits *Allard* to its facts." *Id.* at 719 (Scalia, J., concurring). Three other concurring Justices responded: "I find nothing in today's opinion that would limit *Andrus v. Allard*, 444 U.S. 51 (1979), to its facts. Indeed, largely for reasons discussed by the Court of Appeals, I am of the view that the unique negotiations giving rise to the property rights and expectations at issue here make this case the unusual one. Accordingly, I join the opinion of the Court." *Id.* at 718 (Brennan, J., concurring). How did the majority opinion handle the matter? Its full, unedited discussion was: "But cf. *Andrus v. Allard*, 444 U.S. 51 (1979) (upholding abrogation of the right to sell endangered eagles' parts as necessary to environmental protection regulatory scheme)." *Id.* at 717.

V. THE SIXTH AMENDMENT

In all criminal prosecutions, the accused shall enjoy the right to a speedy and public trial, by an impartial jury of the state and district wherein the crime shall have been committed, which district shall have been previously ascertained by law, and to be informed of the nature and cause of the accusation; to be confronted with the witnesses against him; to have compulsory process for obtaining witnesses in his favor, and to have the assistance of counsel for his defense.

The Sixth Amendment codifies many important rights at criminal trial, including the right to counsel and the right to confront the witnesses against you. We will return to this subject when we consider how this amendment applies to the States through the Fourteenth Amendment. *See infra* pages 1687–1703.

VI. THE SEVENTH AMENDMENT

In suits at common law, where the value in controversy shall exceed twenty dollars, the right of trial by jury shall be preserved, and no fact tried by a jury, shall be otherwise reexamined in any court of the United States, than according to the rules of the common law.

The Seventh Amendment codifies the right to civil jury trial, which was a major demand of the Anti-Federalists. The right is a very important one that would seem on its face to apply to suits in which the government is a party. The Supreme Court has thus far refused to incorporate the Seventh Amendment through the Fourteenth Amendment, so it is one of a handful of Bill of Rights provisions that do not apply against the States. This is quite astonishing as a legal matter, because all twelve States which wrote new constitutions between 1776 and 1791 included a right to civil jury trial in their state constitutions. Steven G. Calabresi, Sarah E. Agudo, and Kathryn L. Dore, *State Bills of Rights in 1787 and 1791: What Individual Rights are Really Deeply Rooted in American History and Tradition?,* 85 SO. CAL. L. REV. 1451, 1511–1512 (2012). Forty-nine out of fifty States today seem to protect the right to civil jury trial, and thirty-six States do so explicitly. Thirty-six States out of thirty-seven explicitly protected the right to civil jury trial in 1868 when the Fourteenth Amendment was ratified. Steven Gow Calabresi, et. al., *Individual Rights Under State Constitutions in 2018: What Rights are Deeply Rooted in a Modern-Day Consensus of the States*?, 94 NOTRE DAME L. REV. 49, 113–115 (2018).

Not every federal civil dispute is subject to the Seventh Amendment. First, suits at common law involving less than twenty dollars do not require a jury. Does that mean "twenty dollars" in modern, nominal money, or does it refer to a specific quantity of gold? *See* Lawrence B. Solum, *Surprising Originalism: The Regula Lecture,* 9 CONLAWNOW 235, 243–45 (2018). Second, because the amendment only applies to "suits at common law," it presumably does not apply to suits in equity or admiralty. Some very tricky questions arise in the modern world, in which the distinction between law and equity is not as sharp as it was in 1791 and in which Congress creates causes of action unknown to the founding generation. We leave those complexities to courses in Civil Procedure. Perhaps most importantly, the vast majority of federal adjudication do not take place in court. They take place before administrative agencies. Those administrative adjudications can involve enormous sums of money, including millions of dollars in fines and penalties. Does the Seventh Amendment guarantee a right to jury trial in those cases? Given the history of jury trial, one might think that these are precisely the cases in which the jury is most important, as a bulwark of liberty against government overreaching. The Supreme Court disagrees, as you are about to see.

Atlas Roofing Co. v. OSHA

430 U.S. 442 (1977)

■ JUSTICE WHITE delivered the opinion of the Court.

The issue in these cases is whether, consistent with the Seventh Amendment, Congress may create a new cause of action in the Government for civil penalties enforceable in an administrative agency where there is no jury trial.

After extensive investigation, Congress concluded, in 1970, that work-related deaths and injuries had become a "drastic" national problem. Finding the existing state statutory remedies as well as state common-law actions for negligence and wrongful death to be inadequate to protect the employee population from death and injury due to unsafe working conditions, Congress enacted the Occupational Safety and Health Act of 1970 (OSHA or Act). The Act created a new statutory duty to avoid maintaining unsafe or unhealthy working conditions, and empowers the Secretary of Labor to promulgate health and safety standards. Two new remedies were provided—permitting the Federal Government, proceeding before an administrative agency, (1) to obtain abatement orders requiring employers to correct unsafe working conditions and (2) to impose civil penalties on any employer maintaining any unsafe working condition. Each remedy exists whether or not an employee is actually injured or killed as a result of the condition, and existing state statutory and common-law remedies for actual injury and death remain unaffected.

* * *

If the employer wishes to contest the penalty or the abatement order, * * * [a]n evidentiary hearing is then held before an administrative law judge of the Occupational Safety and Health Review Commission. The Commission consists of three members, appointed for six-year terms, each of whom is qualified "by reason of training, education or experience" to adjudicate contested citations and assess penalties. At this hearing the burden is on the Secretary to establish the elements of the alleged violation and the propriety of his proposed abatement order and proposed penalty; and the [administrative law] judge is empowered to affirm, modify, or vacate any or all of these items, giving due consideration in his penalty assessment to "the size of the business of the employer . . ., the gravity of the violation, the good faith of the employer, and the history of previous violations." The [administrative law] judge's decision becomes the Commission's final and appealable order unless within 30 days a Commissioner directs that it be reviewed by the full Commission.

If review is granted, the Commission's subsequent order directing abatement and the payment of any assessed penalty becomes final unless the employer timely petitions for judicial review in the appropriate court of appeals. The Secretary similarly may seek review of Commission orders, but, in either case, "(t)he findings of the Commission with respect to questions of fact, if supported by substantial evidence on the record considered as a whole, shall be conclusive." If the employer fails to pay the assessed penalty, the Secretary may commence a collection action in a federal district court in which neither the fact of the violation nor the propriety of the penalty assessed may be retried. Thus, the penalty may be collected without the employer's ever being entitled to a jury determination of the facts constituting the violation.

* * *

The Seventh Amendment provides that "(i)n Suits at common law, where the value in controversy shall exceed twenty dollars, the right of trial by jury shall be preserved * * *." The phrase "Suits at common law" has been construed to refer to cases tried prior to the adoption of the Seventh Amendment in courts of law in which jury trial was customary as distinguished from courts of equity or admiralty in which jury trial was not. Petitioners claim that a suit in a federal court by the Government for civil penalties for violation of a statute is a suit for a money judgment which is classically a suit at common law, and that the defendant therefore has a Seventh Amendment right to a jury determination of all issues of fact. Petitioners then claim that to permit Congress to assign the function of adjudicating the Government's rights to civil penalties for violation of the statute to a different forum—an administrative agency in which no jury is available—would be to permit Congress to deprive a defendant of his Seventh Amendment jury right. We disagree. At least in cases in which "public rights" are being litigated—*e.g.*, cases in which the Government sues in its sovereign capacity to enforce public rights created by statutes within the power of Congress to enact—the Seventh Amendment does not prohibit Congress from assigning the factfinding function and initial adjudication to an administrative forum with which the jury would be incompatible.

Congress has often created new statutory obligations, provided for civil penalties for their violation, and committed exclusively to an administrative agency the function of deciding whether a violation has in fact occurred. These statutory schemes have been sustained by this Court, albeit often without express reference to the Seventh Amendment. Thus taxes may constitutionally be assessed and collected together with penalties, with the relevant facts in some instances being adjudicated only by an administrative agency * * *. Congress has entrusted to an administrative agency the task of adjudicating violations of the customs and immigration laws and assessing penalties based thereon.

* * *

* * * [W]hen Congress creates new statutory "public rights," it may assign their adjudication to an administrative agency with which a jury trial would be

incompatible, without violating the Seventh Amendment's injunction that jury trial is to be "preserved" in "suits at common law." Congress is not required by the Seventh Amendment to choke the already crowded federal courts with new types of litigation or prevented from committing some new types of litigation to administrative agencies with special competence in the relevant field. This is the case even if the Seventh Amendment would have required a jury where the adjudication of those rights is assigned instead to a federal court of law instead of an administrative agency * * *.

* * *

[Petitioners assert] * * * that the right to jury trial was never intended to depend on the identity of the forum to which Congress has chosen to submit a dispute; otherwise, it is said, Congress could utterly destroy the right to a jury trial by always providing for administrative rather than judicial resolution of the vast range of cases that now arise in the courts. The argument is well put, but it overstates the holdings of our prior cases and is in any event unpersuasive. Our prior cases support administrative factfinding in only those situations involving "public rights," *e. g.*, where the Government is involved in its sovereign capacity under an otherwise valid statute creating enforceable public rights. Wholly private tort, contract, and property cases, as well as a vast range of other cases as well are not at all implicated.

* * * [I]t is apparent from the history of jury trial in civil matters that factfinding, which is the essential function of the jury in civil cases, was never the exclusive province of the jury under either the English or American legal systems at the time of the adoption of the Seventh Amendment; and the question whether a fact would be found by a jury turned to a considerable degree on the nature of the forum in which a litigant found himself. Critical factfinding was performed without juries in suits in equity, and there were no juries in admiralty; nor were there juries in the military justice system. The jury was the factfinding mode in most suits in the common-law courts, but it was not exclusively so: Condemnation was a suit at common law but constitutionally could be tried without a jury * * *.

The Seventh Amendment was declaratory of the existing law, for it required only that jury trial in suits at common law was to be "preserved." It thus did not purport to require a jury trial where none was required before. Moreover, it did not seek to change the factfinding mode in equity or admiralty or to freeze equity jurisdiction as it existed in 1789, preventing it from developing new remedies where those available in courts of law were inadequate * * *.

The point is that the Seventh Amendment was never intended to establish the jury as the exclusive mechanism for factfinding in civil cases. It took the existing legal order as it found it, and there is little or no basis for concluding that the Amendment should now be interpreted to provide an impenetrable barrier to administrative factfinding under otherwise valid federal regulatory statutes. We cannot conclude that the Amendment rendered Congress powerless—when it concluded that remedies available in courts of law were inadequate to cope with a problem within Congress' power to regulate—to create new public rights and remedies by statute and commit their enforcement, if it chose, to a tribunal other than a court of law—such as an administrative agency—in which facts are not found by juries * * *

* * * The Seventh Amendment is no bar to the creation of new rights or to their enforcement outside the regular courts of law.

NOTES AND QUESTIONS

1. If King George III had done what Congress did in the Occupational Safety and Health Act, would complaints about it have shown up in the Declaration of Independence?

2. Do you think lay people should play a role in the adjudication of Administrative Law cases?

3. *Atlas Roofing* was limited to some extent in *Tull v. United States,* 481 U.S. 412 (1987), which held that government actions to collect civil penalties were suits at common law and had to be tried before juries. Oddly enough, however, the Court said that the jury only had to decide on liability; a jury was not required to fix the amount of a civil penalty once liability was found. Administrative cases that do not involve civil penalties are still governed wholly by *Atlas Roofing*. For an argument that *Tull* extends a bit farther than the cases have thus far recognized, see Matthew T. Martens & Troy A. Paredes, *The Scope of the Jury Trial Right in SEC Enforcement Actions,* 71 N.Y.U. ANN. SURVEY AM. L. 147 (2018).

VII. THE EIGHTH AMENDMENT

Excessive bail shall not be required, nor excessive fines imposed, nor cruel and unusual punishments inflicted.

The Eighth Amendment's ban on punishments encompasses, in our view, a proportionality requirement that dates back to Magna Carta. Certainly, the Framers of the U.S. Constitution, who so greatly admired the penal reform writings of Cesare Beccaria, believed in the idea that punishments must be proportionate to the crimes for which they are imposed. The ban on *excessive* bail and on *excessive* fines captures this idea. In our view, the ban on cruel and unusual punishments, under the canon of *noscitur a sociis*—a clause takes its meaning from the company it keeps—ought to be construed as including a proportionality requirement. This principle emerged in *Weems v. United States,* 217 U.S. 349 (1910), a case involving review of a judgment of the Philippine Islands supreme court when that country was a U.S. federal territory. The relevant legal text was a provision in the federally prescribed Philippine Bill of Rights "prohibiting the infliction of cruel and unusual punishment, [which] was taken from the Constitution of the United States, and must have the same meaning * * *." *Id.* at 367. A Coast Guard disbursing officer was convicted of making a false entry and was sentenced to fifteen years in prison (which included hard labor and wrist and ankle chains) plus "accessories," which included lifetime surveillance. The Court found this sentence a violation of the "cruel and unusual punishment" clause, over the dissents of Justices White and Harlan. The idea of proportionality saw its modern elaboration in the next case, which (as happens more than occasionally in constitutional law) produced no majority opinion.

Trop v. Dulles

356 U.S. 86 (1958)

■ MR. CHIEF JUSTICE WARREN announced the judgment of the Court and delivered an opinion, in which MR. JUSTICE BLACK, MR. JUSTICE DOUGLAS, and MR. JUSTICE WHITTAKER join.

The petitioner in this case, a native-born American, is declared to have lost his United States citizenship and become stateless by reason of his conviction by court-martial for wartime desertion * * *. [T]he issue before us is whether this forfeiture of citizenship comports with the Constitution.

The facts are not in dispute. In 1944, petitioner was a private in the United States Army, serving in French Morocco. On May 22, he escaped from a stockade at Casablanca, where he had been confined following a previous breach of discipline. The next day petitioner and a companion were walking along a road towards Rabat, in the general direction back to Casablanca, when an Army truck approached and stopped. A witness testified that petitioner boarded the truck willingly and that no words were spoken. In Rabat petitioner was turned over to military police. Thus, ended petitioner's "desertion." He had been gone less than a day, and had willingly surrendered to an officer on an Army vehicle while he was walking back towards his base. He testified that at the time he and his companion were picked up by the Army truck, "we had decided to return to the stockade. The going was tough. We had no money to speak of, and at the time we were on foot and we were getting cold and hungry." A general court-martial convicted petitioner of desertion and sentenced him to three years at hard labor, forfeiture of all pay and allowances and a dishonorable discharge.

In 1952, petitioner applied for a passport. His application was denied on the ground that under the provisions of Section 401(g) of the Nationality Act of 1940, as amended. he had lost his citizenship by reason of his conviction and dishonorable discharge for wartime desertion. In 1955 petitioner commenced this action in the District Court, seeking a declaratory judgment that he is a citizen. The Government's motion for summary judgment was granted, and the Court of Appeals for the Second Circuit affirmed, Chief Judge Clark dissenting. 239 F.2d 527. We granted certiorari.

Section 401(g), the statute that decrees the forfeiture of this petitioner's citizenship, is based directly on a Civil War statute, which provided that a deserter would lose his "rights of citizenship." The meaning of this phrase was not clear. When the 1940 codification and revision of the nationality laws was prepared, the Civil War statute was amended to make it certain that what a convicted deserter would lose was nationality itself. In 1944 the statute was further amended to provide that a convicted deserter would lose his citizenship only if he was dismissed from the service or dishonorably discharged. At the same time it was provided that citizenship could be regained if the deserter was restored to active duty in wartime with the permission of the military authorities.

* * *

The constitutional question posed by Section 401(g) would appear to be whether or not denationalization may be inflicted as a punishment, even assuming that citizenship may be divested pursuant to some governmental power * * *.

* * *

* * * If it is assumed that the power of Congress extends to divestment of citizenship, the problem still remains as to this statute whether denationalization is a cruel and unusual punishment within the meaning of the Eighth Amendment. Since wartime desertion is punishable by death, there can be no argument that the penalty of denationalization is excessive in relation to the gravity of the crime. The question is whether this penalty subjects the individual to a fate forbidden by the principle of civilized treatment guaranteed by the Eighth Amendment.

At the outset, let us put to one side the death penalty as an index of the constitutional limit on punishment. Whatever the arguments may be against capital punishment, both on moral grounds and in terms of accomplishing the purposes of punishment—and they are forceful—the death penalty has been employed throughout our history, and, in a day when it is still widely accepted, it cannot be said to violate the constitutional concept of cruelty. But it is equally plain that the existence of the death penalty is not a license to the Government to devise any punishment short of death within the limit of its imagination.

The exact scope of the constitutional phrase "cruel and unusual" has not been detailed by this Court. But the basic policy reflected in these words is firmly established in the Anglo-American tradition of criminal justice. The phrase in our Constitution was taken directly from the English Declaration of Rights of 1688, and the principle it represents can be traced back to the Magna Carta. The basic concept underlying the Eighth Amendment is nothing less than the dignity of man. While the State has the power to punish, the Amendment stands to assure that this power be exercised within the limits of civilized standards. Fines, imprisonment and even execution may be imposed depending upon the enormity of the crime, but any technique outside the bounds of these traditional penalties is constitutionally suspect. This Court has had little occasion to give precise content to the Eighth Amendment, and, in an enlightened democracy such as ours, this is not surprising. But when the Court was confronted with a punishment of 12 years in irons at hard and painful labor imposed for the crime of falsifying public records, it did not hesitate to declare that the penalty was cruel in its excessiveness and unusual in its character. *Weems v. United States*, 217 U.S. 349. The Court recognized in that case that the words of the Amendment are not precise, * and that their scope is not static. The Amendment must draw its meaning from the evolving standards of decency that mark the progress of a maturing society.

We believe, as did Chief Judge Clark in the court below, that use of denationalization as a punishment is barred by the Eighth Amendment. There may be involved no physical mistreatment, no primitive torture. There is instead the total destruction of the individual's status in organized society. It is a form of punishment more primitive than torture, for it destroys for the individual the political existence that was centuries in the development. The punishment strips the citizen of his status in the national and international political community. His very existence is at the sufferance of the country in which he happens to find himself. While any one country may accord him some rights and presumably as long as he remained in this country he would enjoy the limited rights of an alien, no country need do so because he is stateless. Furthermore, his enjoyment of even the limited rights of an alien might be subject to termination at any time by reason of deportation. In short, the expatriate has lost the right to have rights.

This punishment is offensive to cardinal principles for which the Constitution stands. It subjects the individual to a fate of ever-increasing fear and distress. He knows not what discriminations may be established against him, what proscriptions may be directed against him, and when and for what cause his existence in his native land may be terminated. He may be subject to banishment, a fate universally decried by civilized people. He is stateless, a condition deplored in the international community of democracies. It is no answer to suggest that all the disastrous consequences of this fate may not be brought to bear on a stateless person. The threat makes the punishment obnoxious.

The civilized nations of the world are in virtual unanimity that statelessness is not to be imposed as punishment for crime * * *. The United Nations' survey of the nationality laws of 84 nations of the world reveals that only two countries, the Philippines and Turkey, impose denationalization as a penalty for desertion. In this country, the Eighth Amendment forbids this to be done.

* * *.

The provisions of the Constitution are not time-worn adages or hollow shibboleths. They are vital, living principles that authorize and limit governmental powers in our Nation. They are the rules of government. When the constitutionality of an Act of Congress is challenged in this Court, we must apply those rules. If we do not, the words of the Constitution become little more than good advice.

* * *

The judgment of the Court of Appeals for the Second Circuit is reversed, and the cause is remanded to the District Court for appropriate proceedings.

Reversed and remanded.

■ MR. JUSTICE BLACK, whom MR. JUSTICE DOUGLAS joins, concurring. [Omitted.]

■ MR. JUSTICE BRENNAN, concurring. [Omitted.]

■ MR. JUSTICE FRANKFURTER, whom MR. JUSTICE BURTON, MR. JUSTICE CLARK and MR. JUSTICE HARLAN join, dissenting.

* * *

Petitioner contends that loss of citizenship is an unconstitutionally disproportionate "punishment" for desertion and that it constitutes "cruel and unusual punishment" within the scope of the Eighth Amendment. Loss of citizenship entails undoubtedly severe—and in particular situations even tragic—consequences. Divestment of citizenship by the Government has been characterized, in the context of denaturalization, as "more serious than a taking of one's property, or the imposition of a fine or other penalty." However, like denaturalization, expatriation under the Nationality Act of 1940 is not "punishment" in any valid constitutional sense * * *. The process of denationalization * * * was related to the authority of Congress, pursuant to its constitutional powers, to regulate conduct free from restrictions that pertain to legislation in the field technically described as criminal justice. Since there are legislative ends within the scope of Congress' war power that are wholly consistent with a "non-penal" purpose to regulate the military forces, and since there is nothing on the face of this legislation or in its history to indicate that Congress had a contrary purpose, there is no warrant for this Court's labeling the disability imposed by § 401(g) as a "punishment."

Even assuming, *arguendo,* that § 401(g) can be said to impose "punishment," to insist that denationalization is "cruel and unusual" punishment is to stretch that concept beyond the breaking point. It seems scarcely arguable that loss of citizenship is within the Eighth Amendment's prohibition because disproportionate to an offense that is capital and has been so from the first year of Independence. Art. 58, *supra;* § 6, Art. 1, Articles of War of 1776, 5 J. Cont. Cong. (Ford ed.1906) 792. Is constitutional dialectic so empty of reason that it can be seriously urged that loss of citizenship is a fate worse than death? The seriousness of abandoning one's country when it is in the grip of mortal conflict precludes denial to Congress of the power to terminate citizenship here, unless that power is to be denied to Congress under any circumstance.

Many civilized nations impose loss of citizenship for indulgence in designated prohibited activities. See generally Laws Concerning Nationality, U.N. Doc. No. ST/LEG/SER.B/4 (1954) * * *. In this country, desertion has been punishable by loss of at least the "rights of citizenship" since 1865. The Court today reaffirms its decisions (*Mackenzie v. Hare*, 239 U.S. 299; *Savorgnan v. United States*, 338 U.S. 491) sustaining the power of Congress to denationalize citizens who had no desire or intention to give up their citizenship. If loss of citizenship may constitutionally be made the consequence of such conduct as marrying a foreigner, and thus certainly not "cruel and unusual," it seems more than incongruous that such loss should be thought "cruel and unusual" when it is the consequence of conduct that is also a crime. In short, denationalization, when attached to the offense of wartime desertion, cannot justifiably be deemed so at variance with enlightened concepts of "humane justice," see *Weems v. United States*, 217 U.S. 349, 78, as to be beyond the power of Congress, because constituting a "cruel and unusual" punishment within the meaning of the Eighth Amendment.

Nor has Congress fallen afoul of that prohibition because a person's post-denationalization status has elements of unpredictability. Presumably a denationalized person becomes an alien *vis-à-vis* the United States. The very substantial rights and privileges that the alien in this country enjoys under the federal and state constitutions puts him in a very different condition from that of an outlaw in fifteenth-century England * * *. The multitudinous decisions of this Court protective of the rights of aliens bear weighty testimony. And the assumption that brutal treatment is the inevitable lot of denationalized persons found in other countries is a slender basis on which to strike down an Act of Congress otherwise amply sustainable.

* * *

NOTES AND QUESTIONS

1. If the idea of proportionality seems fuzzy, does Chief Justice Warren make things better or worse by suggesting that the Eighth Amendment "must draw its meaning from the evolving standards of decency that mark the progress of a maturing society"? Even if one thinks that adding rights to the Constitution is a good idea, constitutional "growth" or "evolution" can often lead to eliminating rights that were in the Constitution rather than adding to the rights that were already there. Isn't it enough to say that the Eighth Amendment includes a proportionality requirement and that that requirement was violated here? Or is it impossible to say that a proportionality requirement was

violated here? Or are we (and Chief Justice Warren) just flat wrong to think that the Constitution requires punishments to be proportional to the crime?

2. Justice Brennan's concurrence, which we omitted, argues that Congress lacks the enumerated power under the various war powers and the Necessary and Proper Clause to impose banishment as a punishment for Trop's crime. Is that a better way to address this case than invoking the Eighth Amendment? Or is Congress's power to "make Rules for the Government and Regulation of the land and naval Forces" essentially unlimited? Could Congress impose the death penalty for failing to salute a superior officer?

[Assignment 53]

VIII. THE NINTH AMENDMENT

> **The enumeration in the Constitution, of certain rights, shall not be construed to deny or disparage others retained by the people.**

The Ninth Amendment is simultaneously the simplest and most enigmatic of the Bill of Rights provisions. Both textually and historically, its purpose is clear. The Federalists insisted that a Bill of Rights was (1) unnecessary, because the scheme of enumerated powers did not give the national government the power to violate cherished rights, and (2) dangerous, because listing some rights that the federal government had no power to violate might either suggest that the list was exclusive or, even more threateningly, undermine the scheme of enumerated powers by encouraging an inference that the federal government *really did,* absent the Bill of Rights, have the power to violate rights to speech, press, assembly, and so forth. The Ninth Amendment responds directly to those concerns by *forbidding an inference* that by listing some rights in the Bill of Rights, the Constitution meant to suggest that others do not exist or are less important. The target of the Ninth Amendment is a false *construal.* It forbids a particular line of argument. *See* Ryan C. Williams, *The Ninth Amendment as a Rule of Construction,* 111 COLUM. L. REV. 498 (2011). (The Court nonetheless made precisely the forbidden argument—in flagrant contradiction to the most uncontroversial and obvious meaning of the Ninth Amendment—in *The Legal Tender Cases,* 79 U.S. (12 Wall.) 457, 534–35 (1871). *See supra* pages 766–773.)

So where does one go from there? We know from reading the Ninth Amendment that the specific listing of a right in the Bill of Rights is not really all that special an event. Other rights "retained by the people" are just as real and just as important as the ones that got listed. How would one ascertain the content of those other equally important rights "retained by the people"? At this point, consensus breaks down.

One school of thought argues that "the other rights retained by the people are defined residually from the powers granted to the national government." Thomas B. McAffee, *The Original Meaning of the Ninth Amendment,* 90 COLUM. L. REV. 1215, 1221 (1990). This view sees the Ninth Amendment solely as a restatement of the principle of enumerated powers; if the national government is truly exercising an enumerated power, then by definition it cannot violate the Ninth Amendment. *See United Public Workers v. Mitchell,* 330 U.S. 75, 96 (1947) ("when objection is made that the exercise of a federal power infringes upon rights reserved by the Ninth and Tenth Amendments, the inquiry must be directed toward the granted power under which the action of the Union was taken. If granted power is found, necessarily the objection of invasion of those rights, reserved by the Ninth and Tenth Amendments, must fail.")

A second school of thought counters that the Ninth Amendment refers to rights which "are to be defined independently of, and may serve to limit the scope of, powers granted to the national government by the Constitution." McAffee, *supra*, at 1222. As explained by one of its proponents, who calls this view the "power-constraint" position, in opposition to the "rights-powers" position described above:

> Constitutional rights can be conceived as power-constraints that regulate the exercise of power by Congress and the executive branch by constraining either their choice of means or their choice of ends * * *. [I]n contrast with the rights-powers conception, the power-constraint conception contemplates a potential conflict between constitutional rights and enumerated powers.
>
> Under this conception, it is possible that means chosen to pursue a constitutionally permissible end might infringe on a constitutional right. Suppose, for example, that in pursuit of its enumerated power to "lay and collect Taxes" * * *, Congress infringed on the enumerated rights of free speech and assembly. If so, Congress would not have violated the Tenth Amendment for it was acting within its delegated powers. But it may have violated the First Amendment * * *.
>
> * * *
>
> * * * [T]he rights-powers conception becomes a dubious interpretation of the Ninth Amendment. For such an interpretation implies that a fundamentally different conception of constitutional rights applies to the "retained" rights of the Ninth Amendment than applies to the enumerated rights.

Randy E. Barnett, *Introduction: James Madison's Ninth Amendment, in* THE RIGHTS RETAINED BY THE PEOPLE 1, 14–15, 18 (Randy E. Barnett ed., 1989). On this view, the Ninth Amendment is a potential font of individual rights just as legally binding as the individual rights found in the first eight amendments. Supporters of this position splinter badly over how to determine the content of the unenumerated rights that federal actors might violate when executing their enumerated powers. *Compare* RANDY E. BARNETT, RESTORING THE LOST CONSTITUTION: THE PRESUMPTION OF LIBERTY (2004), *with* DANIEL A. FARBER, RETAINED BY THE PEOPLE: THE "SILENT" NINTH AMENDMENT AND THE CONSTITUTIONAL RIGHTS AMERICANS DON'T KNOW THEY HAVE (2007).

A third position agrees that the simple rights-powers conception is inadequate but believes that the rights "retained" under the Ninth Amendment include (perhaps in addition to the individual rights mentioned above) the rights of the *States* and the people as a collective. On this reading, the amendment protects state governments against federal overreaching by forbidding overbroad interpretations of federal powers and thereby protects the rights of majorities in the States to self-governance. *See* KURT T. LASH, THE LOST HISTORY OF THE NINTH AMENDMENT (2009).

A fourth position essentially declares the Ninth Amendment uninterpretable. At his (unsuccessful) confirmation hearing to the Supreme Court in 1987, Judge Robert Bork famously said, in response to a question about the Ninth Amendment: "I do not think you can use the ninth amendment unless you know something of what it means. For example, if you had an amendment that says 'Congress shall make no' and then there is an ink blot and you cannot read the rest of it and that is the only copy you have, I do not think the court can make up what might be under the ink blot if you cannot read it." Nomination of Robert H. Bork to be Associate Justice of the Supreme Court of the United States: Hearing Before the Sen. Comm. on the Judiciary, 100th Cong. 249 (1989).

As a matter of doctrine, some variant of either the first or fourth view appear to have prevailed. The Supreme Court has never invalidated a federal statute or federal executive action on the express ground that it violated the Ninth Amendment. On the other hand, there are some doctrines that are hard to explain without reference to some conception of unenumerated rights, stemming either from the Ninth Amendment or elsewhere. (Where elsewhere? We will get to that.) Think about race and sex discrimination. As we will see in detail in the next chapter, the Fourteenth Amendment creates a powerful antidiscrimination principle that applies to state governmental actors. There is no equivalent express provision in the Constitution for the federal government. Indeed, because there are several express provisions dealing specifically with *religious* discrimination, *see* U.S. CONST. art. VI, cl. 3; Amend. I, it would seem plausible to infer that no wider antidiscrimination principle applies to federal action. Later amendments forbid discrimination based on race, sex, and age specifically with respect to *voting, see id.* Amends. XV, XIX, XXVI, but the terms of those amendments extend no farther than the right to vote. Does that mean that the Constitution does not generally bar the federal government from discriminating on the basis of race or sex?

As you will see in the next chapter, in 1954 the Supreme Court held that the Fourteenth Amendment forbids States from discriminating on the basis of race in the provision of public education. *See Brown v. Board of Education,* 347 U.S. 483 (1954). In 1971, the Court held that sex discrimination by States was subject to a significant measure of judicial scrutiny. *See Reed v. Reed,* 404 U.S. 71 (1971). Even if these were (as we think they were, though you may ultimately disagree) easy cases under the original meaning of the Fourteenth Amendment, how, if at all, do the antidiscrimination principles that underlie them apply to equivalent federal action, given that the Fourteenth Amendment does not apply to the federal government? After you read the next two cases, we will offer some thoughts on that question, which you may or may not find persuasive but that we hope will prompt reflection on some of the most important issues in constitutional law. Neither of the cases to follow mentions the Ninth Amendment. Does that amendment nonetheless underlie them?

A. BOLLING V. SHARPE

347 U.S. 497 (1954)

■ MR. CHIEF JUSTICE WARREN delivered the opinion of the Court.

This case challenges the validity of segregation in the public schools of the District of Columbia. The petitioners, minors of the Negro race, allege that such segregation deprives them of due process of law under the Fifth Amendment. They were refused admission to a public school attended by white children solely because of their race. They sought the aid of the District Court for the District of Columbia in obtaining admission. That court dismissed their complaint. The Court granted a writ of certiorari before judgment in the Court of Appeals because of the importance of the constitutional question presented.

We have this day [in *Brown v. Board of Education*] held that the Equal Protection Clause of the Fourteenth Amendment prohibits the states from maintaining racially segregated public schools. The legal problem in the District of Columbia is somewhat different, however. The Fifth Amendment, which is applicable in the District of Columbia, does not contain an equal protection clause as does the Fourteenth Amendment, which applies only to the states. But the concepts of equal protection and due process, both stemming from our American ideal of fairness, are not mutually exclusive. The "equal protection of the laws" is a more explicit safeguard of prohibited unfairness than "due process of law," and, therefore, we do not imply that the two are always interchangeable phrases. But, as this Court has recognized, discrimination may be so unjustifiable as to be violative of due process.

Classifications based solely upon race must be scrutinized with particular care, since they are contrary to our traditions and hence constitutionally suspect. As long ago as 1896, this Court declared the principle "that the Constitution of the United States, in its present form, forbids, so far as civil and political rights are concerned, discrimination by the General Government, or by the States, against any citizen because of his race." And in *Buchanan v. Warley,* 245 U.S. 60, the Court held that a statute which limited the right of a property owner to convey his property to a person of another race was, as an unreasonable discrimination, a denial of due process of law.

Although the Court has not assumed to define "liberty" with any great precision, that term is not confined to mere freedom from bodily restraint. Liberty under law extends to the full range of conduct which the individual is free to pursue, and it cannot be restricted except for a proper governmental objective. Segregation in public education is not reasonably related to any proper governmental objective, and thus it imposes on Negro children of the District of Columbia a burden that constitutes an arbitrary deprivation of their liberty in violation of the Due Process Clause.

In view of our decision that the Constitution prohibits the states from maintaining racially segregated public schools, it would be unthinkable that the same Constitution would impose a lesser duty on the Federal Government. We hold that racial segregation in the public schools of the District of Columbia is a denial of the due process of law guaranteed by the Fifth Amendment to the Constitution.

For the reasons set out in *Brown v. Board of Education,* this case will be restored to the docket for reargument on Questions 4 and 5 previously propounded by the Court.

It is so ordered.

B. FRONTIERO V. RICHARDSON

411 U.S. 677 (1973)

■ MR. JUSTICE BRENNAN announced the judgment of the Court and an opinion in which MR. JUSTICE DOUGLAS, MR. JUSTICE WHITE, and MR. JUSTICE MARSHALL join.

The question before us concerns the right of a female member of the uniformed services to claim her spouse as a "dependent" for the purposes of obtaining increased quarters allowances and medical and dental benefits under 37 U.S.C. §§ 401 403, and 10 U.S.C. §§ 1072 1076, on an equal footing with male members. Under these statutes, a serviceman may claim his wife as a "dependent" without regard to whether she is in fact dependent upon him for any part of her support. A servicewoman, on the other hand, may not claim her husband as a "dependent" under these programs unless he is in fact dependent upon her for over one-half of his support. Thus, the question for decision is whether this difference in treatment constitutes an unconstitutional discrimination against servicewomen in violation of the Due Process Clause of the Fifth Amendment. A three-judge District Court for the Middle District of Alabama, one judge dissenting, rejected this contention and sustained the constitutionality of the provisions of the statutes making this distinction. 341 F. Supp. 201 (1972). We noted probable jurisdiction. We reverse.

I

In an effort to attract career personnel through reenlistment, Congress established * * * a scheme for the provision of fringe benefits to members of the uniformed services on a competitive basis with business and industry. Thus, under 37 U.S.C. § 403 a member of the uniformed services with dependents is entitled to an increased "basic allowance for quarters" and, under 10 U.S.C. § 1076, a member's dependents are provided comprehensive medical and dental care.

Appellant Sharron Frontiero, a lieutenant in the United States Air Force, sought increased quarters allowances, and housing and medical benefits for her husband, appellant Joseph Frontiero, on the ground that he was her "dependent." Although such benefits would automatically have been granted with respect to the wife of a male member of the uniformed services, appellant's application was denied because she failed to demonstrate that her husband was dependent on her for more than one-half of his support. Appellants then commenced this suit, contending that, by making this distinction, the statutes unreasonably discriminate on the basis of sex in violation of the Due Process Clause of the Fifth Amendment.[5] In essence, appellants asserted that the discriminatory impact of the statutes is twofold: first, as a procedural matter, a female member is required to demonstrate her spouse's dependency, while no such burden is imposed upon male members; and, second, as a substantive matter, a male member who does not provide more than one-half of his wife's support receives benefits, while a similarly situated female member is denied such benefits. Appellants therefore sought a permanent injunction against the continued enforcement of these statutes and an order directing the appellees to provide Lieutenant Frontiero with the same housing and medical benefits that a similarly situated male member would receive.

Although the legislative history of these statutes sheds virtually no light on the purposes underlying the differential treatment accorded male and female members, a majority of the three-judge District Court surmised that Congress might reasonably have concluded that, since the husband in our society is generally the "breadwinner" in the family—and the wife typically the "dependent" partner—"it would be more economical to require married female members claiming husbands to prove actual dependency than to extend the presumption of dependency to such members." 341 F. Supp. at 207. Indeed, given the fact that approximately 99% of all

---

5 "(W)hile the Fifth Amendment contains no equal protection clause, it does forbid discrimination that is 'so unjustifiable as to be violative of due process." *Schneider v. Rusk*, 377 U.S. 163, 168 (1964); see *Shapiro v. Thompson*, 394 U.S. 618, 641–642 (1969); *Bolling v. Sharpe*, 347 U.S. 497 (1954).

members of the uniformed services are male, the District Court speculated that such differential treatment might conceivably lead to a "considerable saving of administrative expense and manpower." *Ibid.*

II

At the outset, appellants contend that classifications based upon sex, like classifications based upon race, alienage, and national origin, are inherently suspect, and must therefore be subjected to close judicial scrutiny. We agree, and, indeed, find at least implicit support for such an approach in our unanimous decision only last Term in *Reed v. Reed*, 404 U.S. 71 (1971).

In *Reed*, the Court considered the constitutionality of an Idaho statute providing that, when two individuals are otherwise equally entitled to appointment as administrator of an estate, the male applicant must be preferred to the female. Appellant, the mother of the deceased, and appellee, the father, filed competing petitions for appointment as administrator of their son's estate. Since the parties, as parents of the deceased, were members of the same entitlement class, the statutory preference was invoked and the father's petition was therefore granted. Appellant claimed that this statute, by giving a mandatory preference to males over females without regard to their individual qualifications, violated the Equal Protection Clause of the Fourteenth Amendment.

The Court noted that the Idaho statute "provides that different treatment be accorded to the applicants on the basis of their sex; it thus establishes a classification subject to scrutiny under the Equal Protection Clause." 404 U.S. at 75. Under "traditional" equal protection analysis, a legislative classification must be sustained unless it is "patently arbitrary" and bears no rational relationship to a legitimate governmental interest.

In an effort to meet this standard, appellee contended that the statutory scheme was a reasonable measure designed to reduce the workload on probate courts by eliminating one class of contests. Moreover, appellee argued that the mandatory preference for male applicants was in itself reasonable, since "men [are] as a rule more conversant with business affairs than . . . women." Indeed, appellee maintained that "it is a matter of common knowledge that women still are not engaged in politics, the professions, business or industry to the extent that men are." And the Idaho Supreme Court, in upholding the constitutionality of this statute, suggested that the Idaho Legislature might reasonably have "concluded that in general men are better qualified to act as an administrator than are women."

Despite these contentions, however, the Court held the statutory preference for male applicants unconstitutional. In reaching this result, the Court implicitly rejected appellee's apparently rational explanation of the statutory scheme, and concluded that, by ignoring the individual qualifications of particular applicants, the challenged statute provided "dissimilar treatment for men and women who are . . . similarly situated." 404 U.S. at 77. The Court therefore held that, even though the State's interest in achieving administrative efficiency "is not without some legitimacy," "[t]o give a mandatory preference to members of either sex over members of the other merely to accomplish the elimination of hearings on the merits is to make the very kind of arbitrary legislative choice forbidden by the [Constitution]. . . ." *Id.* at 76. This departure from "traditional" rational basis analysis with respect to sex-based classifications is clearly justified.

There can be no doubt that our Nation has had a long and unfortunate history of sex discrimination. Traditionally, such discrimination was rationalized by an attitude of "romantic paternalism" which, in practical effect, put women, not on a pedestal, but in a cage. Indeed, this paternalistic attitude became so firmly rooted in our national consciousness that, 100 years ago, a distinguished Member of this Court was able to proclaim:

> "Man is, or should be, woman's protector and defender. The natural and proper timidity and delicacy which belongs to the female sex evidently unfits it for many of the occupations of civil life. The constitution of the family organization, which is founded in the divine ordinance, as well as in the nature of things, indicates the domestic sphere as that which properly belongs to the domain and functions of womanhood. The harmony, not to say identity, of interests and views which belong, or should belong, to the family institution is repugnant to the idea of a woman adopting a distinct and independent career from that of her husband. . . .
>
> ". . . The paramount destiny and mission of woman are to fulfil the noble and benign offices of wife and mother. This is the law of the Creator." *Bradwell v. State*, 16 Wall. 130, 141 (1873) (Bradley, J., concurring).

As a result of notions such as these, our statute books gradually became laden with gross, stereotyped distinctions between the sexes and, indeed, throughout much of the 19th century the position of women in our society was, in many respects, comparable to that of blacks under the pre-Civil War slave codes. Neither slaves nor women could hold office, serve on juries, or bring suit in their own names, and married women traditionally were denied the legal capacity to hold or convey property or to serve as legal guardians of their own children. See generally L. Kanowitz, Women and the Law: The Unfinished Revolution 5–6 (1969); G. Myrdal, An American Dilemma 1073 (20th anniversary ed.1962). And although blacks were guaranteed the right to vote in 1870, women were denied even that right—which is itself "preservative of other basic civil and political rights"—until adoption of the Nineteenth Amendment half a century later.

It is true, of course, that the position of women in America has improved markedly in recent decades. Nevertheless, it can hardly be doubted that, in part because of the high visibility of the sex characteristic, women still face pervasive, although at times more subtle, discrimination in our educational institutions, in the job market and, perhaps most conspicuously, in the political arena.

Moreover, since sex, like race and national origin, is an immutable characteristic determined solely by the accident of birth, the imposition of special disabilities upon the members of a particular sex because of their sex would seem to violate "the basic concept of our system that legal burdens should bear some relationship to individual responsibility. . . ." *Weber v. Aetna Casualty & Surety Co.*, 406 U.S. 164, 175 (1972). And what differentiates sex from such nonsuspect statuses as intelligence or physical disability, and aligns it with the recognized suspect criteria, is that the sex characteristic frequently bears no relation to ability to perform or contribute to society. As a result, statutory distinctions between the sexes often have the effect of invidiously relegating the entire class of females to inferior legal status without regard to the actual capabilities of its individual members.

We might also note that, over the past decade, Congress has itself manifested an increasing sensitivity to sex-based classifications. In Tit. VII of the Civil Rights Act of 1964, for example, Congress expressly declared that no employer, labor union, or other organization subject to the provisions of the Act shall discriminate against any individual on the basis of "race, color, religion, sex, or national origin." Similarly, the Equal Pay Act of 1963 provides that no employer covered by the Act "shall discriminate . . . between employees on the basis of sex." And § 1 of the Equal Rights Amendment, passed by Congress on March 22, 1972, and submitted to the legislatures of the States for ratification, declares that "[e]quality of rights under the law shall not be denied or abridged by the United States or by any State on account of sex." Thus, Congress itself has concluded that classifications based upon sex are inherently invidious, and this conclusion of a coequal branch of Government is not without significance to the question presently under consideration.

With these considerations in mind, we can only conclude that classifications based upon sex, like classifications based upon race, alienage, or national origin, are inherently suspect, and must therefore be subjected to strict judicial scrutiny. Applying the analysis mandated by that stricter standard of review, it is clear that the statutory scheme now before us is constitutionally invalid.

III

The sole basis of the classification established in the challenged statutes is the sex of the individuals involved. Thus, under 37 U.S.C. §§ 401, 403, and 10 U.S.C. §§ 1072, 1076, a female member of the uniformed services seeking to obtain housing and medical benefits for her spouse must prove his dependency in fact, whereas no such burden is imposed upon male members. In addition, the statutes operate so as to deny benefits to a female member, such as appellant Sharron Frontiero, who provides less than one-half of her spouse's support, while at the same time granting such benefits to a male member who likewise provides less than one-half of his spouse's support. Thus, to this extent, at least, it may fairly be said that these statutes command "dissimilar treatment for men and women who are . . . similarly situated." *Reed v. Reed*, 404 U.S. at 77.

Moreover, the Government concedes that the differential treatment accorded men and women under these statutes serves no purpose other than mere "administrative convenience." In essence, the Government maintains that, as an empirical matter, wives in our society frequently are dependent upon their husbands, while husbands rarely are dependent upon their wives. Thus, the Government argues that Congress might reasonably have concluded that it would be both cheaper and easier simply conclusively to presume that wives of male members are financially dependent upon their husbands, while burdening female members with the task of establishing dependency in fact.

The Government offers no concrete evidence, however, tending to support its view that such differential treatment in fact saves the Government any money. In order to satisfy the demands of strict judicial scrutiny, the Government must demonstrate, for example, that it is actually cheaper to grant increased benefits with respect to *all* male members, than it is to determine which male members are in fact entitled to such benefits, and to grant increased benefits only to those members whose wives actually meet the dependency requirement. Here, however, there is substantial evidence that, if put to the test, many of the wives of male members would fail to qualify for benefits. And in light of the fact that the dependency determination with respect to the husbands of female members is presently made solely on the basis of affidavits, rather than through the more costly hearing process, the Government's explanation of the statutory scheme is, to say the least, questionable.

In any case, our prior decisions make clear that, although efficacious administration of governmental programs is not without some importance, "the Constitution recognizes higher values than speed and efficiency." *Stanley v. Illinois*, 405 U.S. 645, 656 (1972). And when we enter the realm of "strict judicial scrutiny," there can be no doubt that "administrative convenience" is not a shibboleth, the mere recitation of which dictates constitutionality. On the contrary, any statutory scheme which draws a sharp line between the sexes, *solely* for the purpose of achieving administrative convenience, necessarily commands "dissimilar treatment for men and women who are . . . similarly situated," and therefore involves the "very kind of arbitrary legislative choice forbidden by the [Constitution]. . . ." *Reed v. Reed*, 404 U.S. at 77, 76. We therefore conclude that, by according differential treatment to male and female members of the uniformed services for the sole purpose of achieving administrative convenience, the challenged statutes violate the Due Process Clause of the Fifth Amendment insofar as they require a female member to prove the dependency of her husband.

Reversed.

■ MR. JUSTICE STEWART concurs in the judgment, agreeing that the statutes before us work an invidious discrimination in violation of the Constitution. *Reed v. Reed*, 404 U.S. 71.

■ MR. JUSTICE REHNQUIST dissents for the reasons stated by Judge Rives in his opinion for the District Court, *Frontiero v. Laird*, 341 F. Supp. 201 (1972).

■ MR. JUSTICE POWELL, with whom THE CHIEF JUSTICE and MR. JUSTICE BLACKMUN join, concurring in the judgment.

I agree that the challenged statutes constitute an unconstitutional discrimination against servicewomen in violation of the Due Process Clause of the Fifth Amendment, but I cannot join the opinion of MR. JUSTICE BRENNAN, which would hold that all classifications based upon sex, "like classifications based upon race, alienage, and national origin," are "inherently suspect and must therefore be subjected to close judicial scrutiny." It is unnecessary for the Court in this case to characterize sex as a suspect classification, with all of the far-reaching implications of such a holding. *Reed v. Reed*, 404 U.S. 71 (1971), which abundantly supports our decision today, did not add sex to the narrowly limited group of classifications which are inherently suspect. In my view, we can and should decide this case on the authority of *Reed* and reserve for the future any expansion of its rationale.

There is another, and I find compelling, reason for deferring a general categorizing of sex classifications as invoking the strictest test of judicial scrutiny. The Equal Rights Amendment, which if adopted will resolve the substance of this precise question, has been approved by the Congress and submitted for ratification by the States. If this Amendment is duly adopted, it will represent the will of the people accomplished in the manner prescribed by the Constitution. By acting prematurely and unnecessarily, as I view it, the Court has assumed a decisional responsibility at the very time when state legislatures, functioning within the traditional democratic process, are debating the proposed Amendment. It seems to me that this reaching out to pre-empt by judicial action a major political decision which is currently in process of resolution does not reflect appropriate respect for duly prescribed legislative processes.

There are times when this Court, under our system, cannot avoid a constitutional decision on issues which normally should be resolved by the elected representatives of the people. But democratic institutions are weakened, and confidence in the restraint of the Court is impaired, when we appear unnecessarily to decide sensitive issues of broad social and political importance at the very time they are under consideration within the prescribed constitutional processes.

NOTES AND QUESTIONS

1. The Equal Rights Amendment mentioned in the opinions in *Frontiero v. Richardson* was never enacted, because it failed to receive the necessary votes for ratification.

2. *Bolling* and *Frontiero* both say that the basis for an antidiscrimination norm against the federal government is the Due Process of Law Clause of the Fifth Amendment. Based on what you saw earlier in this chapter, is that a correct interpretation of the Due Process of Law Clause? Is it even a remotely plausible interpretation of the Due Process of Law Clause? If it is not even remotely plausible, does that mean that *Bolling* and *Frontiero* were wrong?

3. The justices in *Bolling* and *Frontiero* shared the instinct that there just *has* to be some kind of constitutional bar against discrimination by the federal government. If there is no express text, those cases reason, the Due Process of Law Clause will just have to do. For whatever it is worth, we think their instinct was exactly correct, but, as with Belloc's team in *Raiders of the Lost Ark*, "They're digging in the wrong place!" There are at least four potential sites that the Court in *Bolling* and *Frontiero* overlooked.

4. One is the Fifteenth and Nineteenth Amendments. Those amendments prohibit the federal government, as well as the state governments, from discriminating on the basis of race and sex in voting rights (and the Twenty-Sixth Amendment to some extent does the same for age). Voting rights include *all* forms of voting—including voting in legislatures (the right to run for and hold political office), on courts (the right to serve as judges), and on juries (the right to be included on juries). In short, the right to vote represents a basket of *political* rights; the Fifteenth and Nineteenth Amendments in substance guarantee that political equality will not be denied on the basis of race or sex. (As we will later see, Section 1 of the Fourteenth Amendment conspicuously did not address issues of political equality.) But "political rights exist at the apex of a rights hierarchy." Steven G. Calabresi & Julia T. Rickert, *Originalism and Sex Discrimination,* 90 TEX. L. REV. 1, 76 (2011). One can have civil rights without political rights, but the reverse makes no sense. "The idea that women would be able to vote but would still in some respects be second-class citizens is an implausible synthesis of the constitutional text * * * with the constitutional text of the Nineteenth Amendment." *Id.* at 10. While a general civil-rights antidiscrimination norm, such as the norm in Section 1 of the Fourteenth Amendment, does not assure equality in political rights, once one has obtained equality of political rights, equality of civil rights necessarily follows. For an extended argument to this effect in the context of the Fourteenth Amendment, which could readily be extended to the federal government as well, see *id.*

5. A second digging site breaks ground from the premise that the Constitution is a kind of fiduciary instrument. *See supra* pages 82–83. Federal officials, on this understanding, are agents who hold their positions subject to the background rules of agency law that would be applied to all fiduciaries in the late eighteenth century. One clearly settled fiduciary principle concerned agents who serve multiple principals. This could happen in many settings: the administrator of a trust might have to allocate assets between multiple claimants and/or holders of present and future interests, the holder of a power of appointment under a will might have to deal with competing beneficiaries, and a factor might represent more than one merchant. If the agency instrument did not specifically address how the agent was supposed to deal with multiple principals, the default rule of agency law was to treat each of the multiple principals *fairly*. That did not necessarily mean that each principal had to be treated *equally*; an agent dividing an estate among multiple beneficiaries, for example, "must divide it amongst them equally, *unless a good reason can be given for doing otherwise*." *Astry v. Astry,* 24 Eng. Rep. 124, 124 (1706) (emphasis added). Fair treatment starts with a presumption of equality, but the faithful agent can deviate from that baseline if, but only if, there are good reasons for it. Pre-founding British public law extended the same obligation to government officials, who had to exercise their discretion reasonably when their actions would differentially affect people. *See, e.g., Rooke's Case,* 5 Co. Rep. 99b, 77 Eng. Rep. 209 (1598); *Keighley's Case,* 10 Co. Rep. 139a, 77 Eng. Rep. 1136 (1609). If the Constitution is really a fiduciary instrument, it follows readily that federal officials must exercise their discretion reasonably, discriminating among "We the People" only when there is good reason to do so. *See* Gary Lawson, Robert G. Natelson & Guy Seidman, *The Fiduciary Foundations of Federal Equal Protection,* 94 B.U. L. REV. 415 (2014).

6. A third source is the Necessary and Proper Clause. Recall that the founding generation was confident that the unamended Constitution gave the federal government no power to violate the rights later protected by the Bill of Rights. *See supra* pages 989–990. That belief is correct if Congress simply has no power to authorize the use of means that would violate those rights, such as general warrants to enforce the tax laws, criminal trials without juries to enforce commerce regulations, and so forth. On Federalist premises, such laws would not be "necessary and proper," and most emphatically not "proper," "for carrying into Execution" federal powers. On this understanding, the "rights-powers" and "power-constraint" positions merge. The enumerated powers, even without the Bill of Rights, do not authorize the national government to violate individual rights because the Necessary and Proper Clause does not authorize their violation. *See* Gary Lawson & Patricia B. Granger, *The "Proper" Scope of Federal Power: A Jurisdictional Interpretation of the Sweeping Clause,* 43 DUKE L.J. 267, 326–330 (1993). And the right to reasonable and fair treatment, as was seen in the previous note, was a fairly obvious background right of the people in 1788, violation of which would not be "proper." Professor Calabresi agrees with Lawson and Granger's analysis in this law review article.

7. A fourth source for a federal antidiscrimination principle is, of course, the Ninth Amendment, which supplements rather than supplants any of the other three possible sources. One might determine that a right to fair (perhaps meaning presumptively equal) treatment is among the rights "retained by the people" that deserve constitutional protection against the federal government just as surely as do the rights enumerated in the first eight amendments. Any of the previous three lines of reasoning would lead to this conclusion.

8. All of these four routes can generate the principles reflected in *Bolling* and *Frontiero,* though they have different implications for other cases (and possibly for *Bolling* on its facts). An argument from the Fifteenth and Nineteenth Amendments is

limited to discrimination based on race or sex, with an argument against age discrimination grounded in the Twenty-Sixth Amendment possibly waiting in the wings. An argument from the Necessary and Proper Clause only applies to instances in which the Necessary and Proper Clause is needed to authorize the relevant government action. There are many contexts, including most notably the governance of the District of Columbia at issue in *Bolling,* in which Congress does not need to employ the Necessary and Proper Clause, so it is not at all clear that an argument grounded in the Necessary and Proper Clause yields the result in *Bolling* (though it would forbid federal race discrimination in many other contexts). The broadest argument is the argument from fiduciary duties, under which prohibitions on race and sex discrimination are simply special cases of a more general requirement that *all* citizens be treated fairly by the government, with differential treatment justified if, but only if, there are good reasons for it. What count as good reasons will differ with the context and with the grounds for discrimination. Might there, for instance, be more circumstances in which good reasons can be given for sex discrimination than for race discrimination? In the next chapter, you will see that modern law, under the Fourteenth Amendment and the Due Process of Law Clause of the Fifth Amendment, has had to deal with precisely that question. Indeed, the questions that arise under a fiduciary-based understanding of nondiscrimination turn out to be remarkably—or, rather, unremarkably—similar to the questions that have arisen under modern antidiscrimination doctrine grounded in other sources. *See* Lawson, Natelson & Seidman, *supra,* at 444–45. In particular, does the constitutional norm against racial discrimination—from whatever source—flatly forbid affirmative action? Or can there sometimes be "good reasons" for the government to discriminate on the basis of race? We will take up that question in more detail in the next chapter, but for the moment consider the leading case addressing it in the context of federal affirmative action.

C. ADARAND CONSTRUCTORS, INC. V. PENA

515 U.S. 200 (1995)

■ JUSTICE O'CONNOR announced the judgment of the Court and delivered an opinion with respect to Parts I, II, III-A, III-B, III-D, and IV, which is for the Court except insofar as it might be inconsistent with the views expressed in JUSTICE SCALIA's concurrence, and an opinion with respect to Part III-C in which JUSTICE KENNEDY joins.

Petitioner Adarand Constructors, Inc., claims that the Federal Government's practice of giving general contractors on Government projects a financial incentive to hire subcontractors controlled by "socially and economically disadvantaged individuals," and in particular, the Government's use of race-based presumptions in identifying such individuals, violates the equal protection component of the Fifth Amendment's Due Process Clause. The Court of Appeals rejected Adarand's claim. We conclude, however, that courts should analyze cases of this kind under a different standard of review than the one the Court of Appeals applied. We therefore vacate the Court of Appeals' judgment and remand the case for further proceedings.

I

In 1989, the Central Federal Lands Highway Division (CFLHD), which is part of the United States Department of Transportation (DOT), awarded the prime contract for a highway construction project in Colorado to Mountain Gravel & Construction Company. Mountain Gravel then solicited bids from subcontractors for the guardrail portion of the contract. Adarand, a Colorado-based highway construction company specializing in guardrail work, submitted the low bid. Gonzales Construction Company also submitted a bid.

The prime contract's terms provide that Mountain Gravel would receive additional compensation if it hired subcontractors certified as small businesses controlled by "socially and economically disadvantaged individuals." Gonzales is certified as such a business; Adarand is not. Mountain Gravel awarded the subcontract to Gonzales, despite Adarand's low bid, and Mountain Gravel's Chief Estimator has submitted an affidavit stating that Mountain Gravel would have accepted Adarand's bid, had it not been for the additional payment it received by hiring Gonzales instead. Federal law requires that a subcontracting clause similar to the one used here must appear in most federal agency contracts, and it also requires the clause to state that "[t]he contractor shall presume that socially and economically disadvantaged individuals include Black Americans, Hispanic Americans, Native Americans, Asian Pacific Americans, and other minorities, or any other individual found to be disadvantaged by the [Small Business] Administration pursuant to section 8(a) of the Small Business Act." 15 U.S.C. §§ 637(d)(2), (3). Adarand claims that the presumption set forth in that statute discriminates on the basis of race in violation of the Federal Government's Fifth Amendment obligation not to deny anyone equal protection of the laws.

* * *

* * * The District Court granted the Government's motion for summary judgment. The Court of Appeals for the Tenth Circuit affirmed. 16 F.3d 1537 (1994). It understood our decision in *Fullilove v. Klutznick*, 448 U.S. 448 (1980), to have adopted "a lenient standard, resembling intermediate scrutiny, in assessing" the constitutionality of federal race-based action. 16 F.3d, at 1544. Applying that "lenient standard," as further developed in *Metro Broadcasting, Inc. v. FCC*, 497 U.S. 547 (1990), the Court of Appeals upheld the use of subcontractor compensation clauses. 16 F.3d, at 1547. We granted certiorari.

II

* * *

* * * Because the evidence in this case indicates that the CFLHD is likely to let contracts involving guardrail work that contain a subcontractor compensation clause at least once per year in Colorado, that Adarand is very likely to bid on each such contract, and that Adarand often must compete for such contracts against small disadvantaged businesses, we are satisfied that Adarand has standing to bring this lawsuit.

III

Respondents urge that "[t]he Subcontracting Compensation Clause program is . . . a program based on *disadvantage*, not on race," and thus that it is subject only to "the most relaxed judicial scrutiny." Brief for Respondents 26. To the extent that the statutes and regulations involved in this case are race neutral, we agree. Respondents concede, however, that "the race-based rebuttable presumption used in some certification determinations under the Subcontracting Compensation Clause" is subject to some heightened level of scrutiny. *Id.*, at 27. The parties disagree as to what that level should be. (We note, incidentally, that this case concerns only classifications based explicitly on race, and presents none of the additional difficulties posed by laws that, although facially race neutral, result in racially disproportionate impact and are motivated by a racially discriminatory purpose. See generally *Arlington Heights v. Metropolitan Housing Development Corp.,* 429 U.S. 252 (1977); Washington v. Davis, 426 U.S. 229 (1976).)

Adarand's claim arises under the Fifth Amendment to the Constitution, which provides that "No person shall . . . be deprived of life, liberty, or property, without due process of law." Although this Court has always understood that Clause to provide some measure of protection against *arbitrary* treatment by the Federal Government, it is not as explicit a guarantee of *equal* treatment as the Fourteenth Amendment, which provides that "No *State* shall . . . deny to any person within its jurisdiction the equal protection of the laws" (emphasis added). Our cases have accorded varying degrees of significance to the difference in the language of those two Clauses. We think it necessary to revisit the issue here.

A

Through the 1940's, this Court had routinely taken the view in non-race-related cases that, "[u]nlike the Fourteenth Amendment, the Fifth contains no equal protection clause and it provides no guaranty against discriminatory legislation by Congress." *Detroit Bank v. United States*, 317 U.S. 329, 337 (1943). When the Court first faced a Fifth Amendment equal protection challenge to a federal racial classification, it adopted a similar approach, with most unfortunate results. In *Hirabayashi v. United States*, 320 U.S. 81 (1943), the Court considered a curfew applicable only to persons of Japanese ancestry. The Court observed—correctly—that "[d]istinctions between citizens solely because of their ancestry are by their very nature odious to a free people whose institutions are founded upon the doctrine of equality," and that "racial discriminations are in most circumstances irrelevant and therefore prohibited." *Id.*, at 100. But it also cited *Detroit Bank* for the proposition that the Fifth Amendment "restrains only such discriminatory legislation by Congress as amounts to a denial of due process," 320 U.S., at 100, and upheld the curfew because "circumstances within the knowledge of those charged with the responsibility for maintaining the national defense afforded a rational basis for the decision which they made." *Id.*, at 102.

Eighteen months later, the Court again approved wartime measures directed at persons of Japanese ancestry. *Korematsu v. United States*, 323 U.S. 214 (1944), concerned an order that completely excluded such persons from particular areas. The Court did not address the view, expressed in cases like *Hirabayashi* and *Detroit Bank*, that the Federal Government's obligation to provide equal protection differs significantly from that of the States. Instead, it began by noting that "all legal restrictions which curtail the civil rights of a single racial group are immediately suspect . . . [and] courts must subject them to the most rigid scrutiny." 323 U.S., at 216. That promising dictum might be read to undermine the view that the Federal Government is under a lesser obligation to avoid injurious racial classifications than are the States. But in spite of the "most rigid scrutiny" standard it had just set forth, the Court then inexplicably relied on "the principles we announced in the *Hirabayashi* case" to conclude that, although "exclusion from the area in which one's home is located is a far greater deprivation than constant confinement to the home from 8 p.m. to 6 a.m.," *id.*, at 218, the racially discriminatory order was nonetheless within the Federal Government's power.

In *Bolling v. Sharpe*, 347 U.S. 497 (1954), the Court for the first time explicitly questioned the existence of any difference between the obligations of the Federal Government and the States to avoid racial classifications. *Bolling* did note that "[t]he 'equal protection of the laws' is a more explicit safeguard of prohibited unfairness than 'due process of law,' " *id.*, at 499. But *Bolling* then concluded that, "[i]n view of [the] decision that the Constitution prohibits the states from maintaining racially segregated public schools, it would be unthinkable that the same Constitution would impose a lesser duty on the Federal Government." *Id.*, at 500.

Bolling's facts concerned school desegregation, but its reasoning was not so limited * * *.

Later cases in contexts other than school desegregation did not distinguish between the duties of the States and the Federal Government to avoid racial classifications * * *.

* * *

[Those] [c]ases * * * continued to treat the equal protection obligations imposed by the Fifth and the Fourteenth Amendments as indistinguishable; one commentator observed that "[i]n case after case, fifth amendment equal protection problems are discussed on the assumption that fourteenth amendment precedents are controlling." Karst, The Fifth Amendment's Guarantee of Equal Protection, 55 N.C.L.Rev. 541, 554 (1977) * * *.

B

Most of the cases discussed above involved classifications burdening groups that have suffered discrimination in our society. In 1978, the Court confronted the question whether race-based governmental action designed to *benefit* such groups should also be subject to "the most rigid scrutiny." *Regents of Univ. of Cal. v. Bakke*, 438 U.S. 265, involved an equal protection challenge to a state-run medical school's practice of reserving a number of spaces in its entering class for minority students. The petitioners argued that "strict scrutiny" should apply only to "classifications that disadvantage 'discrete and insular minorities.' " *Id.*, at 287–288 (opinion of Powell, J.) (citing *United States v. Carolene Products Co.*, 304 U.S. 144, 152, n. 4 (1938)). *Bakke* did not produce an opinion for the Court, but Justice Powell's opinion announcing the Court's judgment rejected the argument. In a passage joined by Justice White, Justice Powell wrote that "[t]he guarantee of equal protection cannot mean one thing when applied to one individual and something else when applied to a person of another color." 438 U.S., at 289–290. He concluded that "[r]acial and ethnic distinctions of any sort are inherently suspect and thus call for the most exacting judicial examination." *Id.*, at 291. On the other hand, four Justices in *Bakke* would have applied a less stringent standard of review to racial classifications "designed to further remedial purposes," see *id.*, at 359 (Brennan, White, Marshall, and Blackmun, JJ., concurring in judgment in part and dissenting in part). And four Justices thought the case should be decided on statutory grounds.

Two years after *Bakke*, the Court faced another challenge to remedial race-based action, this time involving action undertaken by the Federal Government. In *Fullilove v. Klutznick*, 448 U.S. 448 (1980), the Court upheld Congress' inclusion of a 10% set-aside for minority-owned businesses in the Public Works Employment Act of 1977. As in *Bakke*, there was no opinion for the Court. Chief Justice Burger, in an opinion joined by Justices White and Powell, observed that "[a]ny preference based on racial or ethnic criteria must necessarily receive a most searching examination to make sure that it does not conflict with constitutional guarantees." 448 U.S., at 491. That opinion, however, "d[id] not adopt, either expressly or implicitly, the formulas of analysis articulated in such cases as [*Bakke*]." *Id.*, at 492. It employed instead a two-part test which asked, first, "whether the *objectives* of th[e] legislation are within the power of Congress," and second, "whether the limited use of racial and ethnic criteria, in the context presented, is a constitutionally permissible *means* for achieving the congressional objectives." *Id.*, at 473. It then upheld the program under that test, adding at the end of the opinion that the program also "would survive judicial review under either 'test' articulated in the several *Bakke* opinions." *Id.*, at 492. Justice Powell wrote separately to express his view that the plurality opinion had essentially applied "strict scrutiny" as described in his *Bakke* opinion * * *. Justice Stewart (joined by then-JUSTICE REHNQUIST) dissented, arguing that the Constitution required the Federal Government to meet the same strict standard as the States when enacting racial classifications, *id.*, at 523, and n. 1, and that the program before the Court failed that standard. JUSTICE STEVENS also dissented, arguing that "[r]acial classifications are simply too pernicious to permit any but the most exact connection between justification and classification," *id.*, at 537, and that the program before the Court could not be characterized "as a 'narrowly tailored' remedial measure." *Id.*, at 541. Justice Marshall (joined by Justices Brennan and Blackmun) concurred in the judgment, reiterating the view of four Justices in *Bakke* that any race-based governmental action designed to "remed[y] the present effects of past racial discrimination" should be upheld if it was "substantially related" to the achievement of an "important governmental objective"—i.e., such action should be subjected only to what we now call "intermediate scrutiny." 448 U.S., at 518–519.

* * *

The Court's failure to produce a majority opinion in *Bakke*, *Fullilove*, and *Wygant* [*v. Jackson Bd. of Ed.*, 476 U.S. 267 (1986),] left unresolved the proper analysis for remedial race-based governmental action.

The Court resolved the issue, at least in part, in 1989. *Richmond v. J.A. Croson Co.*, 488 U.S. 469 (1989), concerned a city's determination that 30% of its contracting work should go to minority-owned businesses. A majority of the Court in *Croson* held that "the standard of review under the Equal Protection Clause is not dependent on the race of those burdened or benefited by a particular classification," and that the single standard of review for racial classifications should be "strict scrutiny." *Id.*, at 493–494 (opinion of O'CONNOR, J., joined by REHNQUIST, C.J., and WHITE and KENNEDY, JJ.); *id.*, at 520 (SCALIA, J., concurring in judgment) ("I agree . . . with JUSTICE O'CONNOR's conclusion that strict scrutiny must be applied to all governmental classification by race"). As to the classification before the Court, the plurality agreed that "a state or local subdivision . . . has the authority to eradicate the effects of private discrimination within its own legislative jurisdiction," *id.*, at 491–492, but the Court thought that the city had not acted with "a 'strong basis in evidence for its conclusion that remedial action was necessary,'" *id.*, at 500 * * *.

With *Croson*, the Court finally agreed that the Fourteenth Amendment requires strict scrutiny of all race-based action by state and local governments. But *Croson* of course had no occasion to declare what standard of review the Fifth Amendment requires for such action taken by the Federal Government * * *. Thus, some uncertainty persisted with respect to the standard of review for federal racial classifications.

Despite lingering uncertainty in the details, however, the Court's cases through *Croson* had established three general propositions with respect to governmental racial classifications. First, skepticism: " 'Any preference based on racial or ethnic criteria must necessarily receive a most searching examination.' " Second, consistency: "[T]he standard of review under the Equal Protection Clause is not dependent on the race of those burdened or benefited by a particular classification." And third, congruence: "Equal protection analysis in the Fifth Amendment area is the same as that under the Fourteenth Amendment." Taken together, these three propositions lead to the conclusion that any person, of whatever race, has the right to demand that any governmental actor subject to the Constitution justify any racial classification subjecting that person to unequal treatment under the strictest judicial scrutiny * * *.

A year later, however, the Court took a surprising turn. *Metro Broadcasting, Inc. v. FCC*, involved a Fifth Amendment challenge to two race-based policies of the Federal Communications Commission (FCC). In *Metro Broadcasting*, the Court repudiated the long-held notion that "it would be unthinkable that the same Constitution would impose a lesser duty on the Federal Government" than it does on a State to afford equal protection of the laws, *Bolling, supra*, at 500. It did so by holding that "benign" federal racial classifications need only satisfy intermediate scrutiny, even though *Croson* had recently concluded that such classifications enacted by a State must satisfy strict scrutiny. "[B]enign" federal racial classifications, the Court said, "—even if those measures are not 'remedial' in the sense of being designed to compensate victims of past governmental or societal discrimination—are constitutionally permissible to the extent that they serve *important* governmental objectives within the power of Congress and are *substantially related* to achievement of those objectives." *Metro Broadcasting*, 497 U.S., at 564–565 (emphasis added). The Court did not explain how to tell whether a racial classification should be deemed "benign," other than to express "confiden[ce] that an 'examination of the legislative scheme and its history' will separate benign measures from other types of racial classifications." *Id.*, at 564, n. 12.

* * *

* * * *Metro Broadcasting* squarely rejected one of the three propositions established by the Court's earlier equal protection cases, namely, congruence between the standards applicable to federal and state racial classifications, and in so doing also undermined the other two—skepticism of all racial classifications and consistency of treatment irrespective of the race of the burdened or benefited group. Under *Metro Broadcasting*, certain racial classifications ("benign" ones enacted by the Federal Government) should be treated less skeptically than others; and the race of the benefited group is critical to the determination of which standard of review to apply. *Metro Broadcasting* was thus a significant departure from much of what had come before it.

The three propositions undermined by *Metro Broadcasting* all derive from the basic principle that the Fifth and Fourteenth Amendments to the Constitution protect *persons*, not *groups*. It follows from that principle that all governmental action based on race—a *group* classification long recognized as "in most circumstances irrelevant and therefore prohibited" * * *—should be subjected to detailed judicial inquiry to ensure that the *personal* right to equal protection of the laws has not been infringed * * *. In other words, such classifications are constitutional only if they are narrowly tailored measures that further compelling governmental interests. To the extent that *Metro Broadcasting* is inconsistent with that holding, it is overruled.

* * *

C

"Although adherence to precedent is not rigidly required in constitutional cases, any departure from the doctrine of stare decisis demands special justification." *Arizona v. Rumsey*, 467 U.S. 203, 212 (1984) * * *.

As we have explained, *Metro Broadcasting* undermined important principles of this Court's equal protection jurisprudence, established in a line of cases stretching back over 50 years * * *.

* * *

* * * *Metro Broadcasting*'s untenable distinction between state and federal racial classifications lacks support in our precedent, and undermines the fundamental principle of equal protection as a personal right. In this case, as between that principle and "its later misapplications," the principle must prevail.

D

Our action today makes explicit what Justice Powell thought implicit in the *Fullilove* lead opinion: Federal racial classifications, like those of a State, must serve a compelling governmental interest, and must be narrowly tailored to further that interest. Of course, it follows that to the extent (if any) that *Fullilove* held federal racial classifications to be subject to a less rigorous standard, it is no longer controlling * * *.

* * *

Finally, we wish to dispel the notion that strict scrutiny is "strict in theory, but fatal in fact." *Fullilove, supra,* at 519 (Marshall, J., concurring in judgment). The unhappy persistence of both the practice and the lingering effects of racial discrimination against minority groups in this country is an unfortunate reality, and government is not disqualified from acting in response to it * * *. When race-based action is necessary to further a compelling interest, such action is within constitutional constraints if it satisfies the "narrow tailoring" test this Court has set out in previous cases.

IV

Because our decision today alters the playing field in some important respects, we think it best to remand the case to the lower courts for further consideration in light of the principles we have announced * * *.

* * *

Accordingly, the judgment of the Court of Appeals is vacated, and the case is remanded for further proceedings consistent with this opinion.

It is so ordered.

■ JUSTICE SCALIA, concurring in part and concurring in the judgment.

I join the opinion of the Court, except Part III-C, and except insofar as it may be inconsistent with the following: In my view, government can never have a "compelling interest" in discriminating on the basis of race in order to "make up" for past racial discrimination in the opposite direction. Individuals who have been wronged by unlawful racial discrimination should be made whole; but under our Constitution there can be no such thing as either a creditor or a debtor race. That concept is alien to the Constitution's focus upon the individual. To pursue the concept of racial entitlement—even for the most admirable and benign of purposes—is to reinforce and preserve for future mischief the way of thinking that produced race slavery, race privilege and race hatred. In the eyes of government, we are just one race here. It is American.

It is unlikely, if not impossible, that the challenged program would survive under this understanding of strict scrutiny, but I am content to leave that to be decided on remand.

■ JUSTICE THOMAS, concurring in part and concurring in the judgment.

I agree with the majority's conclusion that strict scrutiny applies to *all* government classifications based on race. I write separately, however, to express my disagreement with the premise underlying JUSTICE STEVENS' and JUSTICE GINSBURG's dissents: that there is a racial paternalism exception to the principle of equal protection. I believe that there is a "moral [and] constitutional equivalence" between laws designed to subjugate a race and those that distribute benefits on the basis of race in order to foster some current notion of equality. Government cannot make us equal; it can only recognize, respect, and protect us as equal before the law.

That these programs may have been motivated, in part, by good intentions cannot provide refuge from the principle that under our Constitution, the government may not make distinctions on the basis of race. As far as the Constitution is concerned, it is irrelevant whether a government's racial classifications are drawn by those who wish to oppress a race or by those who have a sincere desire to help those thought to be disadvantaged. There can be no doubt that the paternalism that appears to lie at the heart of this program is at war with the principle of inherent equality that underlies and infuses our Constitution. See Declaration of Independence ("We hold these truths to be self-evident, that all men are created equal, that they are endowed by their Creator with certain unalienable Rights, that among these are Life, Liberty, and the pursuit of Happiness").

These programs not only raise grave constitutional questions, they also undermine the moral basis of the equal protection principle. Purchased at the price of immeasurable human suffering, the equal protection principle reflects our Nation's understanding that such classifications ultimately have a destructive impact on the individual and our society * * *. [T]here can be no doubt that racial paternalism and its unintended consequences can be as poisonous and pernicious as any other form of discrimination. So-called "benign" discrimination teaches many that because of chronic and apparently immutable handicaps, minorities cannot compete with them without their patronizing indulgence. Inevitably, such programs engender attitudes of superiority or, alternatively, provoke resentment among those who believe that they have been wronged by the government's use of race. These programs stamp minorities with a badge of inferiority and may cause them to develop dependencies or to adopt an attitude that they are "entitled" to preferences * * *.

In my mind, government-sponsored racial discrimination based on benign prejudice is just as noxious as discrimination inspired by malicious prejudice. In each instance, it is racial discrimination, plain and simple.

■ JUSTICE STEVENS, with whom JUSTICE GINSBURG joins, dissenting.

Instead of deciding this case in accordance with controlling precedent, the Court today delivers a disconcerting lecture about the evils of governmental racial classifications. For its text the Court has selected three propositions, represented by the bywords "skepticism," "consistency," and "congruence." I shall comment on each of these propositions, then add a few words about *stare decisis*, and finally explain why I believe this Court has a duty to affirm the judgment of the Court of Appeals.

The Court's concept of skepticism is, at least in principle, a good statement of law and of common sense. Undoubtedly, a court should be wary of a governmental decision that relies upon a racial classification * * *. But, as the opinions in *Fullilove* demonstrate, substantial agreement on the standard to be applied in deciding difficult cases does not necessarily lead to agreement on how those cases actually should or will be resolved. In my judgment, because uniform standards are often anything but uniform, we should evaluate the Court's comments on "consistency," "congruence," and *stare decisis* with the same type of skepticism that the Court advocates for the underlying issue.

The Court's concept of "consistency" assumes that there is no significant difference between a decision by the majority to impose a special burden on the members of a minority race and a decision by the majority to provide a benefit to certain members of that minority notwithstanding its incidental burden on some members of the majority. In my opinion that assumption is untenable. There is no moral or constitutional equivalence between a policy that is designed to perpetuate a caste system and one that seeks to eradicate racial subordination. Invidious discrimination is an engine of oppression, subjugating a disfavored group to enhance or maintain the power of the majority. Remedial race-based preferences reflect the opposite impulse: a desire to foster equality in society * * *.

* * *

The consistency that the Court espouses would disregard the difference between a "No Trespassing" sign and a welcome mat. It would treat a Dixiecrat Senator's decision to vote against Thurgood Marshall's confirmation in order to keep African-Americans off the Supreme Court as on a par with President Johnson's evaluation of his nominee's race as a positive factor * * *.

* * *

As a matter of constitutional and democratic principle, a decision by representatives of the majority to discriminate against the members of a minority race is fundamentally different from those same representatives' decision to impose incidental costs on the majority of their constituents in order to provide a benefit to a disadvantaged minority * * *.

The Court's concept of "congruence" assumes that there is no significant difference between a decision by the Congress of the United States to adopt an affirmative-action program and such a decision by a State or a municipality. In my opinion that assumption is untenable. It ignores important practical and legal differences between federal and state or local decisionmakers.

* * *

* * * [F]ederal affirmative-action programs represent the will of our entire Nation's elected representatives, whereas a state or local program may have an impact on nonresident entities who played no part in the decision to enact it. Thus, in the state or local context, individuals who were unable to vote for the local representatives who enacted a race-conscious program may nonetheless feel the effects of that program. * * *.

* * *

* * * [I]t is one thing to say (as no one seems to dispute) that the Fifth Amendment encompasses a general guarantee of equal protection as broad as that contained within the Fourteenth Amendment. It is another thing entirely to say that Congress' institutional competence and constitutional authority entitles it to no greater deference when it enacts a program designed to foster equality than the deference due a state legislature. The latter is an extraordinary proposition; and, as the foregoing discussion demonstrates, our precedents have rejected it explicitly and repeatedly.

* * * The Fourteenth Amendment directly empowers Congress at the same time it expressly limits the States. This is no accident. It represents our Nation's consensus, achieved after hard experience throughout our sorry history of race relations, that the Federal Government must be the primary defender of racial minorities against the States, some of which may be inclined to oppress such minorities. A rule of "congruence" that ignores a purposeful "incongruity" so fundamental to our system of government is unacceptable.

In my judgment, the Court's novel doctrine of "congruence" is seriously misguided. Congressional deliberations about a matter as important as affirmative action should be accorded far greater deference than those of a State or municipality.

* * *

■ JUSTICE SOUTER, with whom JUSTICE GINSBURG and JUSTICE BREYER join, dissenting.

* * *

* * * *[S]tare decisis* compels the application of *Fullilove*. Although *Fullilove* did not reflect doctrinal consistency, its several opinions produced a result on shared grounds that petitioner does not attack: that discrimination in the construction industry had been subject to government acquiescence, with effects that remain and that may be addressed by some preferential treatment falling within the congressional power under § 5 of the Fourteenth Amendment. Once *Fullilove* is applied * * *, it follows that the statutes in question here (which are substantially better tailored to the harm being remedied than the statute endorsed in *Fullilove*) pass muster under Fifth Amendment due process and Fourteenth Amendment equal protection.

* * *

When the extirpation of lingering discriminatory effects is thought to require a catch-up mechanism, like the racially preferential inducement under the statutes considered here, the result may be that some members of the historically favored race are hurt by that remedial mechanism, however innocent they may be of any personal responsibility for any discriminatory conduct. When this price is considered reasonable, it is in part because it is a price to be paid only temporarily; if the justification for the preference is eliminating the effects of a past practice, the assumption is that the effects will themselves recede into the past, becoming attenuated and finally disappearing. Thus, Justice Powell wrote in his concurring opinion in *Fullilove* that the "temporary nature of this remedy ensures that a race-conscious program will not last longer than the discriminatory effects it is designed to eliminate." 448 U.S., at 513.

Surely the transition from the *Fullilove* plurality view (in which Justice Powell joined) to today's strict scrutiny (which will presumably be applied as Justice Powell employed it) does not signal a change in the standard by which the burden of a remedial racial preference is to be judged as reasonable or not at any given time. If in the District Court Adarand had chosen to press a challenge to the reasonableness of the burden of these statutes, more than a decade after *Fullilove* had examined such a burden, I doubt that the claim would have fared any differently from the way it will now be treated on remand from this Court.

■ JUSTICE GINSBURG, with whom JUSTICE BREYER joins, dissenting.

For the reasons stated by JUSTICE SOUTER, and in view of the attention the political branches are currently giving the matter of affirmative action, I see no compelling cause for the intervention the Court has made in this case. I further agree with JUSTICE STEVENS that, in this area, large deference is owed by the Judiciary to "Congress' institutional competence and constitutional authority to overcome historic racial subjugation." I write separately to underscore not the differences the several opinions in this case display, but the considerable field of agreement—the common understandings and concerns—revealed in opinions that together speak for a majority of the Court.

* * *

The divisions in this difficult case should not obscure the Court's recognition of the persistence of racial inequality and a majority's acknowledgment of Congress' authority to act affirmatively, not only to end discrimination, but also to counteract discrimination's lingering effects. Those effects, reflective of a system of racial caste only recently ended, are evident in our workplaces, markets, and neighborhoods. Job applicants with identical resumés, qualifications, and interview styles still experience different receptions, depending on their race. White and African-American consumers still encounter different deals. People of color looking for housing still face discriminatory treatment by landlords, real estate agents, and mortgage lenders. Minority entrepreneurs sometimes fail to gain contracts though they are the low bidders, and they are sometimes refused work even after winning contracts. Bias both conscious and unconscious, reflecting traditional and unexamined habits of thought, keeps up barriers that must come down if equal opportunity and nondiscrimination are ever genuinely to become this country's law and practice.

Given this history and its practical consequences, Congress surely can conclude that a carefully designed affirmative action program may help to realize, finally, the "equal protection of the laws" the Fourteenth Amendment has promised since 1868.

The lead opinion uses one term, "strict scrutiny," to describe the standard of judicial review for all governmental classifications by race. But that opinion's elaboration strongly suggests that the strict standard announced is indeed "fatal" for classifications burdening groups that have suffered discrimination in our society. That seems to me, and, I believe, to the Court, the enduring lesson one should draw from *Korematsu v. United States*, 323 U.S. 214 (1944) * * *. A *Korematsu*-type classification, as I read the opinions in this case, will never again survive scrutiny: Such a classification, history and precedent instruct, properly ranks as prohibited.

* * *

While I would not disturb the programs challenged in this case, and would leave their improvement to the political branches, I see today's decision as one that allows our precedent to evolve, still to be informed by and responsive to changing conditions.

[Assignment 54]

D. THE BILL OF RIGHTS IN FEDERAL TERRITORIES

Bolling v. Sharpe involved congressional legislation for the District of Columbia, enacted pursuant to Congress's power "to exercise exclusive Legislation in all Cases whatsoever," U.S. CONST., art. I, § 8, cl. 17, over the District. Congress similarly has power to "make all needful Rules and Regulations respecting the Territory or other Property belonging to the United States." *Id.* art. IV, § 3, cl. 2. When Congress uses those powers, is it bound by the Constitution?

It sounds like a strange question. In many ways, it is a strange question. Surely Congress cannot enact legislation for the District of Columbia or federal territories without using the procedures for lawmaking enumerated in Article I, Section 7, so of course the Constitution applies to territorial legislation. But does all of the Constitution apply? The enumerations of powers in Article I, Section 8 do not limit Congress when it legislates for territories or the District, because the enumerations of power for governance of those areas are self-contained grants of general governmental power, as full as the power of States over their own jurisdictions. But what about structural provisions? Does the Appointments Clause apply to territorial governors, for example? The law is actually very unclear about this. And what of the Bill of Rights? Can Congress enact laws abridging rights of speech or religion in federal territories that it could not enact as a general matter? Do jury trial rights apply in federal territories?

The Court in *Dred Scott* assumed that the Bill of Rights, or at least the Fifth Amendment Due Process of Law Clause, applied to federal territory—and that might be the only thing in Chief Justice Taney's *Dred Scott* opinion that makes any sense. No Justice in *Dred Scott* contested the basic proposition that the Bill of Rights applies to territories. Why *wouldn't* the Bill of Rights apply to federal territories? It is almost impossible to imagine a reason why it wouldn't. *See* GARY LAWSON & GUY SEIDMAN, THE CONSTITUTION OF EMPIRE: TERRITORIAL EXPANSION AND AMERICAN LEGAL HISTORY 191–94 (2004).

For more than a century after the founding, no one imagined any such reasons. The Spanish-American War changed all of that. As a result of that war, the United States emerged in 1898 possessing, as federally governed territory, Puerto Rico, Guam, and the Philippine Islands. (The United States also occupied Cuba for a time, but it was understood that Cuba would soon emerge as an independent nation, which it did in 1902.) Those islands were noncontiguous with the continental United States, had no common law tradition, in the case of the Philippines were halfway around the world, and—most saliently—were populated primarily by people of color. Did the Constitution require Congress to govern those distant, alien territories the same way that it governed the Northwest Territory and the land from the Louisiana Purchase? Would those societies need to use jury trials, even though juries were unknown to the civil law that had governed them for centuries?

The issue first came up indirectly, through the provision of the Constitution requiring that all tariffs on imports "shall be uniform throughout the United States." U.S. CONST. art. I, § 8, cl 1. The Constitution flatly forbids any tariffs on imports from States, *see id.* art. I, § 9, cl. 5, so if territories such as Puerto Rico are part of "the United States," the only tariff level that can be uniform is zero. In other words, if the limitations in the Taxing Clause apply to territories, Congress cannot impose any tariffs on exports of goods from those territories to anywhere else in the United States. But when the United States took possession of Puerto Rico, Congress passed a statute imposing a modest (fifteen percent of the regular rate) tariff on goods imported into the continental United States from Puerto Rico. *See* Foraker Act, ch. 191, § 3, 31 Stat. 77, 77 (1900). Some exporters sued, claiming that no tariffs could be imposed on goods imported from Puerto Rico. In a series of cases that have come to be known collectively as "the Insular Tariff Cases," the Supreme Court upheld the tariffs. It also upheld tariffs on goods imported into Puerto Rico from the States. *See Dooley v. United States,* 183 U.S. 151 (1901). The reasoning in these cases was, to say the least, obscure. The leading case, *Downes v. Bidwell,* 182 U.S. 244 (1901), produced no majority rationale for the holding. The opinions were often long and meandering, and while the specific issues at stake were tariffs, it was obvious to everyone that lurking behind the scenes was the application of the Bill of Rights. After all, if the Taxing Clause applies to Puerto Rico, it is hard to imagine why the Sixth Amendment would not apply as well. On the other hand, if the Taxing Clause did not apply, then there was precedent for picking and choosing in some fashion which parts of the Constitution applied and which did not.

What would the justices consider so awful about applying the Bill of Rights to territories? The questions posed above about overlaying Anglo-American common law institutions and values onto civil law systems populated by people of color were precisely the questions openly raised in the Insular Tariff Cases. The issues were best (or, rather, worst) put by Justice Henry Brown in *Downes v. Bidwell,* whose plurality opinion explained:

> A false step at this time might be fatal to the development of what Chief Justice Marshall called the American empire. Choice in some cases, the natural gravitation of small bodies towards large ones in others, the result of a successful war in still others, may bring about conditions which would render the annexation of distant possessions desirable. If those possessions are inhabited by alien races, differing from us in religion, customs, laws, methods of taxation and modes of thought, the administration of government and justice, according to Anglo-Saxon principles, may for a time be impossible; and the question at once arises whether large concessions ought not to be made for a time, that, ultimately, our own theories may be carried out, and the blessings of a free government under the Constitution extended to them. We decline to hold that there is anything in the Constitution to forbid such action.

> We are therefore of opinion that the island of Porto Rico is a territory appurtenant and belonging to the United States, but not a part of the United States within the revenue clauses of the Constitution; that the Foraker act is constitutional, so far as it imposes duties upon imports from such island, and that the plaintiff cannot recover back the duties exacted in this case.

182 U.S. at 286–87. Similar sentiments emerged in subsequent cases that expressly raised the issue of the Bill of Rights, most notably the right to jury trial:

> In every case where Congress undertakes to legislate in the exercise of the power conferred by the Constitution, the question may arise as to how far the exercise of the power is limited by the "prohibitions" of that instrument. The limitations which are to be applied in any given case involving territorial government must depend upon the relation of the particular territory to the United States, concerning which Congress is exercising the power conferred by the Constitution. That the United States may have territory which is not incorporated into the United States as a body politic, we think was recognized by the framers of the Constitution in enacting the article already considered, giving power over the territories, and is sanctioned by the opinions of the justices concurring in the judgment in *Downes v. Bidwell*.
>
> Until Congress shall see fit to incorporate territory ceded by treaty into the United States, we regard it as settled by that decision that the territory is to be governed under the power existing in Congress to make laws for such territories, and subject to such constitutional restrictions upon the powers of that body as are applicable to the situation.
>
> For this case, the practical question is, must Congress, in establishing a system for trial of crimes and offenses committed in the Philippine Islands, carry to their people by proper affirmative legislation a system of trial by jury?
>
> If the treaty-making power could incorporate territory into the United States without Congressional action, it is apparent that the treaty with Spain, ceding the Philippines to the United States [30 Stat. at L. 1759], carefully refrained from so doing; for it is expressly provided that (article IX: "The civil rights and political status of the native inhabitants of the territories hereby ceded to the United States shall be determined by the Congress." In this language it is clear that it was the intention of the framers of the treaty to reserve to Congress, so far as it could be constitutionally done, a free hand in dealing with these newly-acquired possessions.
>
> The legislation upon the subject shows that * * * Congress hitherto refrained from incorporating the Philippines into the United States * * *.
>
> * * *
>
> It was said in the *Mankichi* case [190 U. S. 197], that when the territory [of Hawaii] had not been incorporated into the United States these requirements were not limitations upon the power of Congress in providing a government for territory in execution of the powers conferred upon Congress.

In the same case Mr. Justice Brown, in the course of his opinion, said:

"We would even go farther, and say that most, if not all, the privileges and immunities contained in the bill of rights of the Constitution were intended to apply from the moment of annexation; but we place our decision of this case upon the ground that the two rights alleged to be violated in this case [right to trial by jury and presentment by grand jury] are not fundamental in their nature, but concern merely a method of procedure which sixty years of practice had shown to be suited to the conditions of the islands, and well calculated to conserve the rights of their citizens to their lives, their property, and their well being."

As we have had occasion to see in the case of *Kepner v. United States*, [195 U. S. 100] the President, in his instructions to the Philippine Commission, while impressing the necessity of carrying into the new government the guaranties of the Bill of Rights securing those safeguards to life and liberty which are deemed essential to our government, was careful to reserve the right to trial by jury, which was doubtless due to the fact that the civilized portion of the islands had a system of jurisprudence founded upon the civil law, and the uncivilized parts of the archipelago were wholly unfitted to exercise the right of trial by jury * * *.

* * *

If the right to trial by jury were a fundamental right which goes wherever the jurisdiction of the United States extends, or if Congress, in framing laws for outlying territory belonging to the United States, was obliged to establish that system by affirmative legislation, it would follow that, no matter what the needs or capacities of the people, trial by jury, and in no other way, must be forthwith established, although the result may be to work injustice and provoke disturbance rather than to aid the orderly administration of justice. If the United States, impelled by its duty or advantage, shall acquire territory peopled by savages, and of which it may dispose or not hold for ultimate admission to statehood, if this doctrine is sound, it must establish there the trial by jury. To state such a proposition demonstrates the impossibility of carrying it into practice. Again, if the United States shall acquire by treaty the cession of territory having an established system of jurisprudence, where jury trials are unknown, but a method of fair and orderly trial prevails under an acceptable and long-established code, the preference of the people must be disregarded, their established customs ignored, and they themselves coerced to accept, in advance of incorporation into the United States, a system of trial unknown to them and unsuited to their needs. We do not think it was intended, in giving power to Congress to make regulations for the territories, to hamper its exercise with this condition.

We conclude that the power to govern territory, implied in the right to acquire it, and given to Congress in the Constitution in Article IV, § 3, to whatever other limitations it may be subject, the extent of which must be decided as questions arise, does not require that body to enact for ceded territory, not made a part of the United States by Congressional action, a system of laws which shall include the right of trial by jury, and that the

Constitution does not, without legislation and of its own force, carry such right to territory so situated.

Dorr v. United States, 195 U.S. 138, 142–45, 148–49 (1904). Does that mean that Congress did not have to provide for jury trial in the Northwest Territory or the Louisiana Purchase property when it was acquired?

It does not mean that, said the Court. That is because the prior acquisitions before the Spanish-American War were of territory that was "incorporated" into the United States, and for "incorporated" territories, all of the Bill of Rights apply of their own force, regardless of the wishes of Congress. For "unincorporated" territories, however, only those rights which are "fundamental" apply of their own force. For "non-fundamental" rights in "unincorporated" territories, it is up to Congress to decide whether to apply them.

Confused about what it means for a territory to be "unincorporated" or for a right to be "non-fundamental"—especially when rights to jury trial are in that "non-fundamental" category? See if the explanation in the following case, which summarizes two decades of case law on the subject, makes things clearer or foggier.

Balzac v. Porto Rico

258 U.S. 298 (1922)

■ MR. CHIEF JUSTICE TAFT delivered the opinion of the Court.

These are two prosecutions for criminal libel, brought against the same defendant, Jesus M. Balzac, on informations filed in the District Court for Arecibo, Porto Rico, by the District Attorney for that District. Balzac was the editor of a daily paper published in Arecibo, known as :El Baluarte," and the articles upon which the charges of libel were based were published on April 16 and April 23, 1918, respectively. In each case the defendant demanded a jury. The code of criminal procedure of Porto Rico grants a jury trial in cases of felony, but not in misdemeanors. The defendant, nevertheless, contended that he was entitled to a jury in such a case, under the Sixth Amendment to the Constitution, and that the language of the alleged libels was only fair comment, and their publication was protected by the First Amendment. His contentions were overruled; he was tried by the court and was convicted in both cases and sentenced to five months' imprisonment in the district jail in the first, and to four months in the second, and to the payment of the costs in each. The defendant appealed to the Supreme Court of Porto Rico. That court affirmed both judgments.

* * *

We have now to inquire whether that part of the Sixth Amendment to the Constitution, which requires that in all criminal prosecutions, the accused shall enjoy the right to a speedy and public trial, by an impartial jury of the State and district wherein the crime shall have been committed, which district shall have been previously ascertained by law, applies to Porto Rico. Another provision on the subject is in Article III of the Constitution providing that the trial of all crimes, except in cases of impeachment, shall be by jury * * *. The Seventh Amendment of the Constitution provides that in suits at common law, when the value in controversy shall exceed twenty dollars, the right of trial by jury shall be preserved. It is well settled that these provisions for jury trial in criminal and civil cases apply to the

Territories of the United States. But it is just as clearly settled that they do not apply to territory belonging to the United States which has not been incorporated into the Union. *Hawaii v. Mankichi*, 190 U. S. 197; *Dorr v. United States*, 195 U. S. 138, 145. It was further settled in *Downes v. Bidwell*, 182 U. S. 244, and confirmed by *Dorr v. United States*, 195 U. S. 138, that neither the Philippines nor Porto Rico was territory which had been incorporated in the Union or become a part of the United States, as distinguished from merely belonging to it; and that the acts giving temporary governments to the Philippines, 32 Stat. 691, and to Porto Rico, 31 Stat. 77, had no such effect. The *Insular Cases* revealed much diversity of opinion in this court as to the constitutional status of the territory acquired by the Treaty of Paris ending the Spanish War, but the *Dorr Case* shows that the opinion of Mr. Justice White of the majority, in *Downes v. Bidwell*, has become the settled law of the court. The conclusion of this court in the *Dorr Case* was as follows:

"We conclude that the power to govern territory, implied in the right to acquire it, and given to Congress in the Constitution in Article IV, § 3, to whatever other limitations it may be subject, the extent of which must be decided as questions arise, does not require that body to enact for ceded territory, not made part of the United States by Congressional action, a system of laws which shall include the right of trial by jury, and that the Constitution does not, without legislation and of its own force, carry such right to territory so situated."

The question before us, therefore, is: Has Congress, since the Foraker Act of April 12, 1900, c. 191 (31 Stat. 77) enacted legislation incorporating Porto Rico into the Union? Counsel for the plaintiff in error give, in their brief, an extended list of acts, to which we shall refer later, which they urge as indicating a purpose to make the Island a part of the United States, but they chiefly rely on the Organic Act of Porto Rico of March 2, 1917, c. 195, 39 Stat. 951, known as the Jones Act.

The act is entitled "An Act To provide a civil government for Porto Rico and for other purposes." It does not indicate by its title that it has a purpose to incorporate the Island into the Union. It does not contain any clause which declares such purpose or effect. While this is not conclusive, it strongly tends to show that Congress did not have such an intention. Few questions have been the subject of such discussion and dispute in our country as the status of our territory acquired from Spain in 1899. The division between the political parties in respect to it, the diversity of the views of the members of this court in regard to its constitutional aspects, and the constant recurrence of the subject in the Houses of Congress, fixed the attention of all on the future relation of this acquired territory to the United States. Had Congress intended to take the important step of changing the treaty status of Porto Rico by incorporating it into the Union, it is reasonable to suppose that it would have done so by the plain declaration, and would not have left it to mere inference. Before the question became acute at the close of the Spanish War, the distinction between acquisition and incorporation was not regarded as important, or at least it was not fully understood and had not aroused great controversy. Before that, the purpose of Congress might well be a matter of mere inference from various legislative acts; but in these latter days, incorporation is not to be assumed without express declaration, or an implication so strong as to exclude any other view.

Again, the second section of the act is called a "Bill of Rights", and included therein is substantially every one of the guaranties of the Federal Constitution, except those relating to indictment by a grand jury in the case of infamous crimes and the right of trial by jury in civil and criminal cases. If it was intended to incorporate Porto Rico into the Union by this act, which would *ex proprio vigore* make applicable the whole Bill of Rights of the Constitution to the Island, why was it thought necessary to create for it a Bill of Rights and carefully exclude trial by jury? In the very forefront of the act is this substitute for incorporation and application of the Bill of Rights of the Constitution. This seems to us a conclusive argument against the contention of counsel for the plaintiff in error.

The section of the Jones Act which counsel press on us is § 5. This in effect declares that all persons who under the Foraker Act were made citizens of Porto Rico and certain other residents shall become citizens of the United States, unless they prefer not to become such, in which case they are to declare such preference within six months, and thereafter they lose certain political rights under the new government. In the same section the United States District Court is given power separately to naturalize individuals of some other classes of residents * * *. Unaffected by the considerations already suggested, perhaps the declaration of § 5 would furnish ground for an inference such as counsel for plaintiff in error contend, but under the circumstances we find it entirely consistent with non-incorporation. When Porto Ricans passed from under the government of Spain, they lost the protection of that government as subjects of the King of Spain, a title by which they had been known for centuries. They had a right to expect, in passing under the dominion of the United States, a status entitling them to the protection of their new sovereign. In theory and in law, they had it as citizens of Porto Rico, but it was an anomalous status, or seemed to be so in view of the fact that those who owed and rendered allegiance to the other great world powers were given the same designation and status as those living in their respective home countries so far as protection against foreign injustice went. It became a yearning of the Porto Ricans to be American citizens, therefore, and this act gave them the boon. What additional rights did it give them? It enabled them to move into the continental United States and becoming residents of any State there to enjoy every right of any other citizen of the United States, civil, social and political. A citizen of the Philippines must be naturalized before he can settle and vote in this country. Act of June 29, 1906, c. 3592, § 30, 34 Stat. 606. Not so the Porto Rican under the Organic Act of 1917.

In Porto Rico, however, the Porto Rican can not insist upon the right of trial by jury, except as his own representatives in his legislature shall confer it on him. The citizen of the United States living in Porto Rico cannot there enjoy a right of trial by jury under the Federal Constitution, any more than the Porto Rican. It is locality that is determinative of the application of the Constitution, in such matters as judicial procedure, and not the status of the people who live in it.

It is true that, in the absence of other and countervailing evidence, a law of Congress or a provision in a treaty acquiring territory, declaring an intention to confer political and civil rights on the inhabitants of the new lands as American citizens, may be properly interpreted to mean an incorporation of it into the Union, as in the case of Louisiana and Alaska. This was one of the chief grounds upon which this court placed its conclusion that Alaska had been incorporated in the Union, in *Rasmussen v. United States*, 197 U. S. 516. But Alaska was a very different case from that of Porto Rico. It was an enormous territory, very sparsely settled and offering opportunity for immigration and settlement by American citizens. It was on the American continent and within easy reach of the then United States. It involved none of the difficulties which incorporation of the Philippines and Porto Rico presents, and one of them is in the very matter of trial by jury. This court refers to the difficulties in *Dorr v. United States* * * *.

The jury system needs citizens trained to the exercise of the responsibilities of jurors. In common-law countries centuries of tradition have prepared a conception of the impartial attitude jurors must assume. The jury system postulates a conscious duty of participation in the machinery of justice which it is hard for people not brought up in fundamentally popular government at once to acquire. One of its greatest benefits is in the security it gives the people that they, as jurors, actual or possible, being part of the judicial system of the country can prevent its arbitrary use or abuse. Congress has thought that a people like the Filipinos or the Porto Ricans, trained to a complete judicial system which knows no juries, living in compact and ancient communities, with definitely formed customs and political conceptions, should be permitted themselves to determine how far they wish to adopt this institution of Anglo-Saxon origin, and when. Hence the care with which * * * the United States has been liberal in granting to the Islands acquired by the Treaty of Paris most of the American constitutional guaranties, but has been sedulous to avoid forcing a jury system on a Spanish and civil-law country until it desired it. We cannot find any intention to depart from this policy in making Porto Ricans American citizens, explained as this is by the desire to put them as individuals on an exact equality with citizens from the American homeland, to secure them more certain protection against the world, and to give them an opportunity, should they desire, to move into the United States proper and there without naturalization to enjoy all political and other rights.

We need not dwell on another consideration which requires us not lightly to infer, from acts thus easily explained on other grounds, an intention to incorporate in the Union these distant ocean communities of a different origin and language from those of our continental people. Incorporation has always been a step, and an important one, leading to statehood. Without, in the slightest degree, intimating an opinion as to the wisdom of such a policy, for that is not our province, it is reasonable to assume that when such a step is taken it will be begun and taken by Congress deliberately and with a clear declaration of purpose, and not left a matter of mere inference or construction.

* * *

The judgments of the Supreme Court of Porto Rico are

Affirmed.

■ MR. JUSTICE HOLMES concurs in the result.

NOTES AND QUESTIONS

1. The notion of "incorporating" territory into the United States comes from the Louisiana Purchase Treaty, which included a provision stating:

> The inhabitants of the ceded territory shall be incorporated into the Union of the United States, and admitted as soon as possible, according to the principles of the Federal Constitution, to the enjoyment of the rights, advantages and immunities of citizens of the United States; and in the meantime they shall be maintained and protected in the free enjoyment of their liberty, property, and the religion which they profess.

Treaty Between the United States of America and the French Republic, Apr. 30, 1803, Art. III, 8 Stat. 200, 202. A close reading of the debates concerning that treaty demonstrates that "most contemporary observers had no clue what Article III meant by the phrase 'incorporated into the Union of the United States.' The vast majority of participants in the congressional debates concerning the implementation of the treaty simply proceeded without ever defining the term 'incorporated.' " Gary Lawson & Guy Seidman, *The First "Incorporation" Debate, in* THE LOUISIANA PURCHASE AND AMERICAN EXPANSION, 1803–1898, at 19, 34 (Sanford Levinson & Bartholomew H. Sparrow eds., 2005). Representative James Elliot crisply remarked that Article III's language about incorporating territory was "of a novel, singular, and curious nature." 8 ANNALS OF CONG. 450 (1803). Justice Edward White nonetheless employed the idea of "incorporation"—without providing a definition—in a lengthy concurring opinion in *Downes v. Bidwell,* which also introduced a distinction between constitutional provisions being "operative" and "applicable." *See* 182 U.S. at 289 (White, J., concurring). According to Justice White (and two other justices who joined him), the Constitution is everywhere "operative," but not all of its provisions are everywhere "applicable." All provisions are "applicable" to "incorporated" territory, but only "fundamental" provisions are "applicable" to unincorporated territory. This is precisely the view that ultimately prevailed, as *Balzac* illustrates. As for what Justice White meant by "incorporated" territory, Justice Harlan in dissent, echoing Representative Elliot from a century beforehand, observed: "I am constrained to say that this idea of 'incorporation' has some occult meaning which my mind does not apprehend. It is enveloped in some mystery which I am unable to unravel." *Id.* at 391 (Harlan, J., dissenting).

2. Subsequent cases have understood "incorporation" of territory as an explicit or implicit promise of ultimately statehood. *See Boumediene v. Bush,* 553 U.S. 723, 757 (2008) ("the Constitution applies in full in incorporated Territories surely destined for statehood but only in part in unincorporated Territories"); *United States v. Verdugo-Urquidez,* 494 U.S. 259, 268 (1990) (describing unincorporated territories as possessions "not clearly destined for statehood"). Of course, no promise of statehood post-Constitution is binding, as the President and Senate by treaty cannot force the House to admit a new State. (The Engagements Clause of Article VI obligated Congress to fulfill the promises of statehood in the Northwest Ordinance, but that clause has no application to after-acquired territory.) Nonetheless, it may be possible to make educated guesses about the likely futures of various territories. No one doubted that the territory from the Louisiana Purchase would eventually become States—though it took more than a century to complete the process. Alaska in 1867 was perhaps a close call for future statehood at the time, though no one who objected to the purchase (and there were plenty) did so on the grounds that Alaska was unsuited for potential future statehood. The Philippine Islands, by contrast, were widely seen in 1898 and thereafter as an unlikely candidate for future statehood. Former Vice-President Adlai E. Stevenson said in an 1899 speech entitled "The Democratic Party":

> As precedents for the proposed policy of expansion we are referred by its advocates to the Louisiana purchase and to the vast area added to our Republic by the treaty of Guadalupe Hidalgo. Neither the purchase from France in 1803 nor the cession by Mexico half a century ago furnish a precedent for the policy now proposed to be inaugurated * * *.
>
> * * * The territory thus acquired was the fit abode for men of our own race. Either at the period of annexation or soon thereafter it passed under the rule of the Anglo-Saxon. who had carried with him our language and our laws. It was territory contiguous to our own, and acquired with the intention at the

> proper time—when population and conditions would justify—of carving it into States * * *.
>
> Are we to be told that history is but repeating itself, and that the contemplated annexation or absorption of the Philippine Archipelago finds precedent in the historic events I have mentioned? The answer is found in the bare statement of facts. The acquired territory is contiguous; the Philippine islands, 8,000 miles distant. The former adapted to the residence, comfort, and happiness of our own people; the latter the fit abode for the half-civilized and degraded races, its only occupants amid poverty and wretchedness for centuries * * *.
>
> * * *
>
> * * * The instances already cited, of the Louisiana purchase and that by treaty from Mexico, are well established precedents. In these cases, however, it was never questioned that, with suitable boundaries and division and under proper regulations, the entire territory would ultimately attain to statehood.
>
> The question recurs, What form of government do the expansionists propose for the Philippine Islands? Are the Territorial or colonial governments which Congress may possibly establish to be only preliminary to the creation of sovereign States to be admitted into the Federal Union? * * * In view of the degraded character of the population, their total unfitness for self-government, the proposition is monstrous. Its consummation would be a. crime against civilization.

32 Cong. Rec. 1538 (1899). Vice President Stevenson was hardly alone in his sentiments. *But see* 32 Cong. Rec. 327 (1898) (statement by Sen. Teller) ("Nobody wants to make Cuba or Porto Rico or the Philippines States of the Union . . . . And yet, in the course of time, if they shall become fitted, they may become States and admitted to the Union.") Guam was an even unlikelier candidate for statehood, which carries with it two senators and three electoral votes. Ironically, of course, the key cases in the saga of the Insular Tariff Cases and their aftermath involved Puerto Rico. If the United States ever gains a fifty-first State, Puerto Rico is probably the most likely prospect. Does the application of basic constitutional provisions, such as the right to jury trial, depend on judicial guesses about the likely suitability of territory for ultimate (perhaps a century down the road) statehood? The *Insular Tariff Cases* say "yes." For an extended argument that the United States simply has no power to acquire territory that is not at least a plausible candidate for statehood (and thus "incorporated" under this definition), see GARY LAWSON & GUY SEIDMAN, THE CONSTITUTION OF EMPIRE: TERRITORIAL EXPANSION AND AMERICAN LEGAL HISTORY 21–118 (2004).

3. The plurality opinion in *Reid v. Covert,* 354 U.S. 1 (1957), *see supra* pages 826–827, called for limiting the *Insular Tariff Cases* to their narrow facts. *See id.* at 14 ("it is our judgment that neither the cases nor their reasoning should be given any further expansion"). Four justices echoed those thoughts in 1979. *See Torres v. Puerto Rico,* 442 U.S. 465, 475–76 (1979) (Brennan, J., concurring in the judgment). The *Insular Tariff Cases* have been subject to a withering torrent of academic criticism from as diverse a group of scholars as have ever agreed on anything; "to the best of our knowledge and research, no current scholar, from any methodological perspective, defends *The Insular Cases.*" Gary Lawson & Robert D. Sloane, *The Constitutionality of Decolonization by Associated Statehood: Puerto Rico's Legal Status Reconsidered,* 50 B.C. L. REV. 1123, 1146 (2009). Nonetheless, as recently as 2008, the Supreme Court said that the Insular Tariff

Cases "inform[ ] our analysis in the present matter." *Boumediene,* 553 U.S. at 759. As of early 2020, they still stand as precedents. For exactly what do they stand as precedents?

4. Are persons born in American territories, such as American Samoa, automatically American citizens by virtue of Section 1 of the Fourteenth Amendment, which provides that "[a]ll persons born or naturalized *in the United States* and subject to the jurisdiction thereof, are citizens of the United States"? U.S. CONST. Amend. XIV, § 1 (emphasis added). Or do the *Insular Tariff Cases* establish that unincorporated territories are not "in the United States" for this purpose? At least one federal district court has held that the *Insular Tariff Cases* do not control construction of the Fourteenth Amendment, so that persons born in American Samoa receive birthright citizenship. *See Fitisemanu v. United States,* 2019 WL 6766502 (D. Utah 2019).

IX. THE TENTH AMENDMENT

> **The powers not delegated to the United States by the Constitution, nor prohibited by it to the States, are reserved to the States respectively, or to the people.**

In 1941, the Supreme Court dismissed the Tenth Amendment as "but a truism." *United States v. Darby*, 312 U.S. 100, 124 (1941). There is a sense in which this characterization is correct. The Tenth Amendment tells us that all which has not been delegated is retained, but it tells us nothing of the scope of what has been delegated. No law that was constitutional on December 14, 1791 suddenly became unconstitutional on December 15, 1791 as a result of ratification of the Tenth Amendment. But the Tenth Amendment is an important truism. The Tenth Amendment is a reminder that the principle of enumerated federal powers is basic to the Constitution. It clarifies that the States and the people pre-exist the Constitution, enter the Constitution with certain powers, and exit the Constitution with at least some of those powers intact. The Tenth Amendment thus pairs with the Ninth Amendment as a statement about constitutional structure; indeed, an early draft of the Bill of Rights combined what are now the Ninth and Tenth Amendments into a single provision:

> The exceptions here or elsewhere in the constitution, made in favor of particular rights, shall not be construed as to diminish the just importance of other rights retained by the people, or as to enlarge the powers delegated by the constitution; but either as actual limitations of such powers, or as inserted merely for greater caution.

1 ANNALS OF CONG. 452 (1789).

Is that enough to generate a body of law that can be called "Tenth Amendment doctrine"? Before answering, consider a similar question about the First Amendment. If the Federalists were right (and we think they were right), Congress had no power to suppress speech, religion, or assembly rights even before December 15, 1791. The First Amendment clarified those rights, but it did not create them. Every "First Amendment" case could, in theory, be decided without reference to the First Amendment just be applying the principle of enumerated powers—as, indeed, all Due Process of Law cases were actually decided prior to 1856. Nonetheless, there are some benefits, as well as some risks, in channeling those decisions through the First Amendment instead, just as there are benefits and risks in doing so with the Tenth Amendment:

> The obvious benefits are the increased likelihood that constitutional principles will be respected and the minimization of conflict in areas where the costs of conflict are potentially high. The corresponding risk is that the clarifying or amplifying provisions will take on a life of their own that is not connected to their original meaning or function. There is a good argument that those risks have been realized with many provisions of the Bill of Rights. It is, for example, doubtful that the set of laws affecting speech that would not be "necessary and proper for carrying into Execution" federal power maps precisely onto the set of laws invalidated under modern First Amendment doctrine. Because doctrine regarding speech has developed under the rubric of the First Amendment rather than (as the Federalists would have preferred) as a search for enumerated federal powers, the contours of that doctrine are no doubt quite different than those that would have resulted from a different analytical framework.
>
> The Tenth Amendment offers the same benefits and risks. There is value in clarifying the limited scope of federal power and the residual role of the states, but there is also a risk that expressing those principles in a distinct clause will give rise to doctrinal developments that might be far removed from the original constitutional principles that were sought to be clarified or amplified by the Tenth Amendment. Has this in fact happened, or has Tenth Amendment doctrine more or less accurately reflected the constitutional world created by the pre-December 15, 1791, Constitution?

Gary Lawson, *A Truism with Attitude: The Tenth Amendment in Constitutional Context,* 83 NOTRE DAME L. REV. 469, 495 (2008). That last question is posed by the line of cases that has developed over the past half-century explicitly invoking the Tenth Amendment. Many of the "federalism" cases in the previous chapter involved this question at least implicitly, but only since 1976 has the Court developed caselaw that can fairly be described as "Tenth Amendment doctrine." It began in *National League of Cities v. Usery,* 426 U.S. 833 (1976), which held, in a 5–4 decision, that Congress could not constitutionally apply the Fair Labor Standards Act, which requires overtime pay for workers who work more than forty hours per week, to state governments. The case was something of a shock to the legal community, as it was the first time since 1937 that a law had been found to exceed Congress's powers on federalism grounds—just as *Buckley v. Valeo,* 424 U.S. 1, *see supra* pages 385–390, was the first time since 1937 that a congressional statute was found unconstitutional on separation of powers grounds. But while *Buckley* has led to decades of vibrant caselaw on separation of powers, *National League of Cities* lasted only nine years, after which it was overruled, in another 5–4 decision, in *Garcia v. San Antonio Metropolitan Transit Authority,* 469 U.S. 528 (1985). *Garcia* decried the ability of courts to discern what kinds of state functions were fundamental, or "traditional," enough to merit special constitutional protection, and it famously argued that state sovereignty was protected through the role of the States in the political process rather than through judicially enforced constitutional limitations on congressional power: "the Framers chose to rely on a federal system in which special restraints on federal power over the States inhered principally in the workings of the National Government itself, rather than in discrete limitations in the objects of federal authority. State sovereign interests, then, are more properly protected by procedural safeguards inherent in the structure of the federal system then by judicially created limitations on federal power." 469 U.S. at 551.

If the majority in *Garcia* hoped to render federalism issues effectively nonjusticiable, its effort, as with *National League of Cities,* lasted less than a decade. But instead of the emergence of a robust "Tenth Amendment" doctrine, the Court instead turned to the Eleventh Amendment the Commerce Clause, and the Necessary and Proper Clause. On the latter front, you have seen that 1995 brought *Lopez, see supra* pages 636–649, and 1997 brought *Printz, see supra* pages 806–817. To the extent that the Tenth Amendment was standing in for more direct limitations on federal power, the rediscovery by the Court of enumerated powers rendered reliance on the Tenth Amendment unnecessary. As for the Eleventh Amendment, although *Garcia* was never formally overruled, state sovereign immunity was redefined in two cases that made it impossible for state employees denied Fair Labor Standards Act benefits to sue in either federal or state court. *Seminole Tribe v. Florida,* 517 U.S. 44 (1996) (can't sue in federal court); *Alden v. Maine,* 527 U.S. 706 (1999) (can't sue in state court). *Garcia* was rendered essentially a dead letter.

Six years after *Garcia,* in 1991, the Supreme Court held in *Gregory v. Ashcroft,* 501 U.S. 452 (1991), that the federal Age Discrimination in Employment Act did not invalidate a Missouri state constitutional provision imposing a mandatory 70-year retirement age for certain state court judges. While the case involved statutory interpretation (plus an equal protection of the laws challenge), the case had constitutional overtones, suggesting that federalism was far from nonjusticiable. The Court explained both the benefits of federalism and how it constrains the process of statutory interpretation:

> The Constitution created a Federal Government of limited powers. "The powers not delegated to the United States by the Constitution, nor prohibited by it to the States, are reserved to the States respectively, or to the people." U.S. Const., Amdt. 10. The States thus retain substantial sovereign authority under our constitutional system * * *.
>
> This federalist structure of joint sovereigns preserves to the people numerous advantages. It assures a decentralized government that will be more sensitive to the diverse needs of a heterogenous society; it increases opportunity for citizen involvement in democratic processes; it allows for more innovation and experimentation in government; and it makes government more responsive by putting the States in competition for a mobile citizenry. See generally McConnell, Federalism: Evaluating the Founders' Design, 54 U.Chi.L.Rev. 1484, 1491–1511 (1987).
>
> Perhaps the principal benefit of the federalist system is a check on abuses of government power. "The 'constitutionally mandated balance of power' between the States and the Federal Government was adopted by the Framers to ensure the protection of 'our fundamental liberties.'" *Atascadero State Hospital v. Scanlon,* 473 U.S. 234, 242 (1985), quoting *Garcia v. San Antonio Metropolitan Transit Authority,* 469 U.S. 528, 572 (1985) (Powell, J., dissenting). Just as the separation and independence of the coordinate branches of the Federal Government serve to prevent the accumulation of excessive power in any one branch, a healthy balance of

power between the States and the Federal Government will reduce the risk of tyranny and abuse from either front * * *.

* * * These twin powers will act as mutual restraints only if both are credible. In the tension between federal and state power lies the promise of liberty.

The Federal Government holds a decided advantage in this delicate balance: the Supremacy Clause. U.S. Const., Art. VI, cl. 2. As long as it is acting within the powers granted it under the Constitution, Congress may impose its will on the States. Congress may legislate in areas traditionally regulated by the States. This is an extraordinary power in a federalist system. It is a power that we must assume Congress does not exercise lightly.

The present case concerns a state constitutional provision through which the people of Missouri establish a qualification for those who sit as their judges. This provision goes beyond an area traditionally regulated by the States; it is a decision of the most fundamental sort for a sovereign entity. Through the structure of its government, and the character of those who exercise government authority, a State defines itself as a sovereign * * *.

Congressional interference with this decision of the people of Missouri, defining their constitutional officers, would upset the usual constitutional balance of federal and state powers. For this reason, "it is incumbent upon the federal courts to be certain of Congress' intent before finding that federal law overrides" this balance. *Atascadero, supra*, 473 U.S., at 243, 105 S.Ct., at 3147. We explained recently:

> "[I]f Congress intends to alter the 'usual constitutional balance between the States and the Federal Government,' it must make its intention to do so 'unmistakably clear in the language of the statute.' *Atascadero State Hospital v. Scanlon*, 473 U.S. 234, 242 (1985); see also *Pennhurst State School and Hospital v. Halderman*, 465 U.S. 89, 99 (1984) * * *. Congress should make its intention 'clear and manifest' if it intends to pre-empt the historic powers of the States, *Rice v. Santa Fe Elevator Corp.*, 331 U.S. 218, 230 (1947).... 'In traditionally sensitive areas, such as legislation affecting the federal balance, the requirement of clear statement assures that the legislature has in fact faced, and intended to bring into issue, the critical matters involved in the judicial decision.' *United States v. Bass*, 404 U.S. 336, 349 (1971)." *Will v. Michigan Dept. of State Police*, 491 U.S. 58, 65 (1989).

This plain statement rule is nothing more than an acknowledgment that the States retain substantial sovereign powers under our constitutional scheme, powers with which Congress does not readily interfere.

501 U.S. at 457–61. The "plain statement" rule of *Gregory* is a sub-constitutional rule of great important. It follows the *Pennhurst* decision from 1984 that articulated a similar rule for federal spending conditions on state and local governments, but extends that rule to, in effect, any statutes that affect the States as governmental institutions.

Thus, federalism on the Court is alive and well notwithstanding *Garcia*. Whether it is actually the federalism prescribed by the Constitution is, of course, another matter altogether. From everything that you have seen in this chapter, what do you think are the constitutional limits, if any, on Congress when it regulates "States as States"?

X. THE ELEVENTH AMENDMENT

The judicial power of the United States shall not be construed to extend to any suit in law or equity, commenced or prosecuted against one of the United States by citizens of another state, or by citizens or subjects of any foreign state.

The Eleventh and Twelfth Amendments are not part of the Bill of Rights, but they do represent the Founding generation's understanding of the Constitution. The Eleventh Amendment was enacted in shock, horror, and surprise after the Supreme Court's decision in *Chisholm v. Georgia*, 2 U.S. 419 (1793). In that case, the Court had held that an out-of-state creditor could sue the State of Georgia for money damages, notwithstanding the time-immemorial rule of English law that actions for money damages against the government did not lie in the Court of King's Bench, the Court of Exchequer, the Court of Common Pleas, the Admiralty Courts, or the Court of Chancery. Instead, such petitions had to be filed as private bills in Parliament and be voted on by that body. In that respect, they were just like actions of impeachment.

The Eleventh Amendment restored the English status quo as to diversity of citizenship suits, but not as to cases in law or equity arising under federal law. In *Hans v. Louisiana,* 134 U.S. 1 (1890), the Supreme Court said the same rule of non-justiciability applied in cases arising under the Constitution, the laws, or the treaties of the United States. Technically, the wording of the Eleventh Amendment does not cover such cases, but the prevailing understanding in 1787 was that a petition for money damages was not a suit in law, equity, or admiralty that could be brought in federal court. From 1789 to the 1850's, Congress had voted private bills to award money to petitioners who were owed it by the federal government. Eventually, the Court of Claims was set up as an Article I court to hear such claims with Congress's permission. *Hans v. Louisiana* remains good law today, and it was affirmed in *Seminole Tribe v. Florida,* 517 U.S. 44 (1996), and in *Alden v. Maine,* 527 U.S. 706 (1999).The substantial, complex, and highly controverted body of modern caselaw under the Eleventh Amendment is generally dealt with in courses in Federal Courts (sometimes called Federal Jurisdiction).

XI. THE TWELFTH AMENDMENT

The electors shall meet in their respective states and vote by ballot for President and Vice-President, one of whom, at least, shall not be an inhabitant of the same state with themselves; they shall name in their ballots the person voted for as President, and in distinct ballots the person voted for as Vice-President, and they shall make distinct lists of all persons voted for as President, and of all persons voted for as Vice-President, and of the number of votes for each, which lists they shall sign and certify, and transmit sealed to the seat of the government of the United States, directed

to the President of the Senate;—The President of the Senate shall, in the presence of the Senate and House of Representatives, open all the certificates and the votes shall then be counted;—the person having the greatest number of votes for President, shall be the President, if such number be a majority of the whole number of electors appointed; and if no person have such majority, then from the persons having the highest numbers not exceeding three on the list of those voted for as President, the House of Representatives shall choose immediately, by ballot, the President. But in choosing the President, the votes shall be taken by states, the representation from each state having one vote; a quorum for this purpose shall consist of a member or members from two-thirds of the states, and a majority of all the states shall be necessary to a choice. And if the House of Representatives shall not choose a President whenever the right of choice shall devolve upon them, before the fourth day of March next following, then the Vice-President shall act as President, as in the case of the death or other constitutional disability of the President. The person having the greatest number of votes as Vice-President, shall be the Vice-President, if such number be a majority of the whole number of electors appointed, and if no person have a majority, then from the two highest numbers on the list, the Senate shall choose the Vice-President; a quorum for the purpose shall consist of two-thirds of the whole number of Senators, and a majority of the whole number shall be necessary to a choice. But no person constitutionally ineligible to the office of President shall be eligible to that of Vice-President of the United States.

The Framers originally provided in Article II of the Constitution that the President would be the person getting the most votes in the Electoral College, so long as he or she won a majority, and the Vice President would be the person would had gotten the second most votes in the Electoral College. This led to a lot of Northern/ Southern tickets like George Washington of Virginia and John Adams of Massachusetts. The system proved disastrous, however, when President John Adams' chief political rival, Thomas Jefferson, turned out to be his Vice President; and then when Jefferson was almost denied the presidency because his vice presidential running mate, the unscrupulous Aaron Burr, fought Jefferson for the presidency in the Election of 1800, which had to be decided by the House of Representatives.

Determined never to have such problems again, Jefferson and his allies added the Twelfth Amendment to the Constitution, guaranteeing that the people would vote separately for presidential/vice presidential tickets. This confirmed the existence of a two-party system in the U.S., which persists to the present day. For a fascinating discussion of the history of the Twelfth Amendment, see BRUCE ACKERMAN, THE FAILURE OF THE FOUNDING FATHERS: JEFFERSON, MARSHALL, AND THE RISE OF PRESIDENTIAL DEMOCRACY (2005).

CHAPTER 5

THE RECONSTRUCTION AMENDMENTS

[Assignment 55]

For all the wonders of the original Constitution and the Bill of Rights, the United States of America prior to the Civil War (and even prior to 1920) was not truly a republic. The United States federal government under the original Constitution was, in large measure, a slave owner's oligarchy with pseudo-democratic institutions that were controlled by the Southern Slave Power. *See* LEONARD L. RICHARDS, THE SLAVE POWER: THE FREE NORTH AND SOUTHERN DOMINATION 1780–1860 (2000). As we have pointed out on several occasions, the Constitution awarded Southern voters a House of Representatives and an Electoral College in which slaves counted as three-fifths of a person even though they could not vote. This slavery bonus allowed the South to win the election of 1800 between John Adams and Thomas Jefferson even though a majority of the free inhabitants of the United States voted for Adams. *See* GARY WILLS, THE NEGRO PRESIDENT: JEFFERSON AND THE SLAVE POWER (2003). We suspect that some of the other close presidential elections "won" by the Jeffersonians and the Jacksonians between 1800 and 1860 were won by pro-slavery candidates because of the three fifths bonus. Of the first fifteen presidents prior to Abraham Lincoln, ten (Washington, Jefferson, Madison, Monroe, Jackson, Van Buren, Harrison, Polk, Taylor, and Tyler) owned slaves themselves; three (Fillmore, Pierce, and Buchanan) were Northerners committed to preserving slavery; and only two (the Adamses) personally opposed slavery, and they were forced to serve with ardent Southern supporters of slavery as their Vice President, like John Calhoun in John Quincy Adam's case. To be sure, President George Washington freed his own slaves upon his death and the death of his wife Martha, hoping to set a precedent for the nation, but for seven decades, slave interests could feel comfortable about their representation in the federal executive department. The thirteen slave-owners and "doughfaces" (as Northern politicians pliable enough to support slavery were known) appointed thirty-two out of thirty-six Supreme Court justices between 1790 and 1860; the two Adamses appointed only four.

The Three-Fifths Clause gave Southern slave-owners close to a lock on the presidency until Abraham Lincoln's election in 1860. It was the shock of losing their 71-year old lock on the presidency—and on Supreme Court nominations—that led to Southern secession.

The bloodshed of the Civil War changed the country, and it also changed the Constitution—in a fashion dramatic enough so that the period from 1865–1870 that yielded the Thirteenth, Fourteenth, and Fifteenth Amendments can justifiably be called a Second Founding. *See* ERIC FONER, THE SECOND FOUNDING: HOW THE CIVIL WAR AND RECONSTRUCTION REMADE THE CONSTITUTION (2019). The Thirteenth Amendment, ratified in 1865, declared the abolition of public or private slavery. The Fourteenth Amendment, ratified in 1868, protected civil rights (in a fashion that we will explore throughout this chapter). The Fifteenth Amendment, ratified in 1870, abolished race discrimination in voting. Congress was given sweeping power to enforce these amendments by all "appropriate" means. *See supra* pages 842–898.

The most obvious target of these amendments was state-sponsored race discrimination, but only the Fifteenth Amendment actually speaks of race. The Thirteenth Amendment and Section 1 of the Fourteenth Amendment are framed in more general terms. How general? What exactly do these amendments forbid?

As is often true, the answers that we think are correct as a matter of original meaning and the answers provided by the case law—today, in the 1870s, and in between—do not always match up well. Nor do the editors always agree between themselves on all of the fine points of original meaning in this context. Nor is there a consensus among judges or scholars, even judges or scholars who share a general methodological commitment to original meaning, about some very basic elements of the meaning of these amendments. Throw in judges and scholars who bring to bear different modalities of interpretation and you get perhaps the most difficult—both doctrinally and theoretically—branch of constitutional law.

Yet another word of caution: The Reconstruction Amendments have provided more than a few scholars with enough material for lifetimes of study, and we can only introduce here what we consider the major themes in the development of the amendments and the practices that emerged under—and, quite often, despite—them. But since the three Reconstruction Amendments literally reconstructed the Constitution while Congress was reconstructing the South, it is worth a good deal of time and effort to try to understand what they are about.

The story of the Reconstruction Amendments is, obviously, primarily the story of slavery and its aftermath. We will get to that story shortly. But there is a less obvious, but critically important, backdrop to the post-Civil War amendments that is often overlooked—most notably, as you will soon enough see, by the Supreme Court in some of its earliest decisions (mis?)interpreting the scope of the Reconstruction Amendments. Perhaps the reason why the Thirteenth and Fourteenth Amendments did not specifically make reference to race is that they had broader aims in mind.

I. THE AVERSION PRIOR TO 1860 TO MONOPOLIES AND TO CLASS LEGISLATION

In short order, we will describe the abolitionist movement and the growth of moral opposition to slavery. Even before the denunciation of slavery itself, however, Anglo-American constitutionalists committed themselves to a policy of opposing monopolies, special governmental privileges, and class-based emoluments or immunities. This background led them to characterize Southern slave owners as having a *monopoly* on the labor of their slaves, which was inherently illegitimate—a violation of the Ancient Constitution—even aside from the more pressing human rights concerns with the slavery. (The discussion that follows grows out of Steven G. Calabresi and Larissa C. Leibowitz, *Monopolies and the Constitution: A History of Crony Capitalism,* 36 HARV. J.L. & PUB. POL'Y 982, 989–994 (2013).)

According to Sir Edward Coke in 1644 (as printed in a 1797 edition), "A monopoly is an institution, or allowance by the King by his grant, commission, or otherwise to any person or persons, bodies politick or corporate, of or for the sole buying, selling, making, working, or using of any thing, whereby any person or persons, bodies politick or corporate, are sought to be restrained of any freedome or liberty that they had before, or hindred in their lawful trade." EDWARD COKE, THIRD PART OF THE INSTITUTES OF THE LAWS OF ENGLAND 181 (1797). Such monopolies were void at common law. So said *Darcy v. Allen*, [1603] 77 Eng. Rep. 1260 (QB), also referred to as *The Case of Monopolies*. In this case, Coke reported a decision under which a royal grant of a monopoly over the production and sale of playing cards was struck down as a violation of the common law and of the rights of Englishmen under the Ancient Constitution. Coke reported (whether accurately or not is subject to some question) that the judge had found:

> All trades, as well mechanical and others, which prevent idleness * * * and exercise men and youth in labour, for the maintenance of themselves and their families, and for the increase of their substance, to serve the Queen when occasion shall require, are profitable for the commonwealth, and therefore grant to the plaintiff to have the sole making of them is against the common law, and the benefit and liberty of the subject.
>
> * * * The sole trade of any mechanical artifice, or any other monopoly, is not only a damage and prejudice to those who exercise the same trade, but also to all other subjects, for the end of all these monopolies is for the private gain of the patentees; and although provisions and cautions are added to moderate them, yet * * * it is mere folly to think that there is any measure in mischief or wickedness; and, therefore, there are three inseparable incidents to every monopoly against the commonwealth, 1. That the price of the same commodity will be raised, for he who has the sole selling of any commodity, may and will make the price as he pleases * * *. The 2d incident to a monopoly is, that after the monopoly granted, the commodity is not so good and merchantable as it was before: for the patentee having the sole trade, regards only his private benefit, and not the common wealth. 3. It tends to the impoverishment of divers artificers and others, who before, by the labour of their hands in their art or trade, had maintained themselves and their families, who will now of necessity be constrained to live in idleness and beggary.

77 Eng. Rep. at 1263. Whether or not Coke's account of the case was accurate is irrelevant for our purposes, as founding-era Americans relied on Coke's views. *See* Calabresi & Leibowitz, *supra,* at 995–96, 1005–07. In any event, Lord Chief Justice Coke took matters into his own hands and, in *The Case of the Tailors, &c. of Ipswich* [1614] 77 Eng. Rep. 1218 (K.B.), struck down a guild set up by King James I under a royal charter. Eventually, in The Statute of Monopolies in 1624, Parliament outlawed royally granted monopolies except for the chartering of corporations and the granting of patents for inventions. Parliament, which could change the common law by statute, retained the right itself to issue monopolies.

In the colonies, the Massachusetts 1641 Body of Liberties declared (as its ninth liberty): "No monopolies shall be granted or allowed amongst us, but of such new Inventions that are profitable to the Countrie, and that for a short time." Connecticut passed a ban on monopolies in 1672. William Penn in 1687, commenting on the Magna Carta, wrote (or at least reprinted) that "Generally all monopolies are against this Great Charter because they are against the liberty and freedom of the subject, and against the law of the land." THE EXCELLENT PRIVILEDGE OF LIBERTY AND PROPERTY 56 (Philobiblon Club edition, 1897).

This deep distaste for monopoly persisted into the founding era. Indeed, "England's continued practice of issuing monopolies was a direct cause of the American Revolution. England enacted an extensive set of laws granting English merchants monopolies in colonial trade for a variety of markets—from manufactured goods to all kinds of raw materials. Black markets arose in the colonies as a response to England's mercantilist trade policy." Calabresi & Leibowitz, *supra,* at 1007. A classic example was the monopoly on tea given to the British East India Company, which led to the Boston Tea Party. The Stamp Act was also attacked for creating a monopoly on stamp paper. In all, "the efforts of the English government, backed by English merchants and manufacturers, to deny to the Americans the right to compete in foreign markets and to secure the benefits of foreign competition was one of the most potent causes of the American Revolution." Franklin D. Jones, *Historical Development of the Law of Business Competition,* 36 YALE L.J. 42, 52 (1926). The "spirit of monopoly," *id.*, so contrary to Coke's Ancient Constitution, was antithetical to the emerging American nation.

Monopoly was not simply an economic matter. It represented a kind of governmental favoritism—a special benefit granted to some but not others. It represented an idea of class, or "caste," legislation that favored some people at the direct expense of others. A majority of the States that wrote new constitutions between 1776 and 1791 had state constitutional clauses that dealt specifically with the issue of monopolies or more generally with private legislation that benefitted particular people and did not promote the common good. Two States, Maryland and North Carolina, expressly prohibited the granting of monopolies in their state constitutions. Other States, such as Massachusetts, New Hampshire, Pennsylvania, and Virginia (and the territory of Vermont) had "common benefit" clauses decrying private or class legislation. The Massachusetts provision (which is still active) was typical:

> No man, or corporation or association of men, have any other title to obtain advantages, or particular and exclusive privileges, distinct from those of the community, than what arises from the consideration of services rendered to the public; and this title being in nature neither hereditary, nor transmissible to children, or descendants, or relations by blood, the idea of a man born a magistrates, a lawgiver, or judge, is absurd and unnatural.
>
> Government is instituted for the common good, for the protection, safety, prosperity, and happiness of the people, and not for the profit, honor, or private interest of any one man, family, or class of men; therefore the people alone have an incontestable, unalienable, and indefeasible right to institute government, and to reform, alter, or totally change the same when their protection, safety, prosperity, and happiness require it.

MASS. CONST. OF 1780, Part the First, arts. VI-VII.

In view of the widespread opposition to monopoly or other forms of governmental favoritism, it is thus not surprising that the failure of the U.S. Constitution to contain either a common benefit clause or an anti-monopoly clause in 1787 drew a strong reaction. Six States—Massachusetts, New Hampshire, New York, North Carolina, Rhode Island, and Virginia—proposed anti-monopoly amendments to the

Constitution. *See* Calabresi & Leibowitz, *supra*, at 1013–14. In addition, Thomas Jefferson wrote to James Madison, urging that a bill of rights include a "restriction against monopolies." Letter from Thomas Jefferson to James Madison (Dec. 20, 1787), *in* 12 THE PAPERS OF THOMAS JEFFERSON 438, 440 (Julian P. Boyd ed., 1966). Madison resisted, because he thought that a ban might sweep in patents and copyrights, which he favored. But as a general matter he agreed that "[w]ith regard to Monopolies, they are justly classed among the greatest nuisances in Government." Letter from James Madison to Thomas Jefferson (Oct. 17, 1788), *in* 1 BERNARD SCHWARTZ, THE BILL OF RIGHTS: DOCUMENTARY HISTORY 614, 617–18 (1971). The Constitution specifically includes a clause authorizing patents and copyrights. *See supra* pages 787–788. Apart from that context, it is doubtful whether most Americans in 1788 would have thought a law conferring a monopoly was either "necessary" or "proper" for carrying into execution a federal power. *See, e.g., An Impartial Citizen V*, Petersburg Va. Gazette, Feb. 28, 1788, *in* 8 DOCUMENTARY HISTORY OF THE RATIFICATION OF THE CONSTITUTION 428, 431 (John P. Kaminski & Gaspare J. Saladino eds., 1988) ("In this case, the laws which Congress can make, for carrying into execution the conceded powers, must not only be necessary, but proper—So that if those powers cannot be executed without the aid of a law, *granting commercial monopolies*, inflicting unusual punishments, creating new crimes, or commanding any unconstitutional act; yet, as such a law would be manifestly not proper, it would not be warranted by this clause, without absolutely departing from the usual acceptation of words") (emphasis added).

Nineteenth-century Jacksonians were also strongly opposed to monopoly. You have already seen Andrew Jackson's veto message for the renewal of the Bank of the United States' corporate charter, which was dripping with anti-monopoly venom. *See supra* pages 629–634. An important opinion by the Jacksonian Chief Justice Roger Taney showed similar sentiments. In *Charles River Bridge v. Warren Bridge*, 36 U.S. (11 Pet.) 420 (1837), the Taney Court considered whether the Charles River Bridge's grant of an exclusive monopoly to build a bridge connecting Cambridge, Massachusetts to Boston until 1862 was a contract which could not be revoked under the Contracts Clause. Chief Justice Taney, held that exclusive corporate charters should be construed as grudgingly as possible because monopolies were contrary to the genius of the common law: "it would present a singular spectacle, if, while the courts in England are restraining, within the strictest limits, the spirit of monopoly, and exclusive privileges in nature of monopolies, and confining corporations to the privileges plainly given to them in their charter; the courts of this country should be found enlarging these privileges by implication; and construing a statute more unfavorably to the public, and to the rights of community, than would be done in a like case in an English court of justice." *Id.* at 545–46.

The opposition to monopoly was the wedge of a broader opposition to special laws or privileges providing favors to some at the expense of others. President Jackson's and Chief Justice Taney's opposition to monopoly led many States to amend their constitutions to restrict the States' ability to grant special privileges or to pass class legislation during the period leading up to the Civil War. Class legislation was understood to mean any legislation that singles out groups, individuals, or classes of people and grants them privileges or imposes on them burdens that are not shared by the rest of society. The Jacksonian aversion to class legislation is broader than an aversion to "caste," a term that refers only to hereditary class traits which may be immutable (such as race or other physical features) or which are theoretically mutable but practically immutable because of social attitudes. A widely mentioned example of a "caste" system in the nineteenth century was the Hindu Caste system, in which some people are born Brahmins and others are born Untouchables. This aversion during the Jacksonian period to class legislation is well documented by Melissa Saunders, *Equal Protection, Class Legislation, and Colorblindness*, 96 MICH. L. REV. 245, 252–62 (1997). Examples abound. *See, e.g., Lewis v. Webb,* 3 Me. 326, 336 (1825) ("On principle then it can never be within the bounds of legitimate legislation, to enact a special law, or pass a resolve dispensing with the general law, in a particular case, and granting a privilege and indulgence to one man, by way of exemption from the operation and effect of such general law, leaving all other persons under its operation."); *Budd v. State,* 22 Tenn. 483, 491 (1842) ("[T]he law of the land is a rule alike embracing, and equally affecting, all persons in general * * * [in] like state and circumstances. A partial law, on the contrary, embraces only a portion of those persons who exist in the same State, and are surrounded by like circumstances. If peculiar felonies * * * were held to be 'law of the land,' it would be difficult to say for what object that clause was inserted in the Bill of Rights.").

By the 1840s and 1850s, opposition to special and partial laws was so widespread among Jacksonian Democrats that even their Abolitionist opponents began to borrow the Jacksonian idea. Abolitionists argued—quite rightly—that the "Slave Power" had seized the government and was using it to create an oligarchy that oppressed African-Americans. During the debates in Congress in the years before the Reconstruction constitutional amendments, the following striking statements appear:

> Democracy and slavery are directly antagonistic. Democracy is opposed to caste, slavery creates it; Democracy is opposed to special privileges; slavery is but the privilege specially enjoyed by one class—to use another as brute beasts and take their labor without wages * * *. [S]lavery is but the extreme of class legislation . . . . [S]lavery is nothing more than the privilege some have of living out of others * * *.

CONG. GLOBE, 32nd Cong., 1st Sess. App. 713 (1852) (statement of Rep. Townsend).

> As a moral being, as a man, I hate slavery in the States of this Union as I hate serfdom in Russia—which by the way is about to be abolished in that Empire, while we are quarrelling over the extension of slavery in this—just as I hate caste in India; just as I hate oppression everywhere.

CONG. GLOBE, 36th Cong., 2d Sess. App. 120 (1861) (statement of Rep. Farnsworth).

Indeed, as Professor Saunders explained, by the mid-1850s "thousands of these heirs of the Jacksonian political tradition left the Democratic Party for the Republican Party, driven by the belief that the former was 'no longer the champion of popular rights that it had been in Jackson's day' but had become 'the tool of a slave holding oligarchy.' " Saunders, *supra,* at 266.

Thus, by the time of the Civil War, an important segment of the population, which may have had little sympathy for the moral plight of enslaved African-Americans but which had rejected the idea of monopoly at the time the Constitution was written and which had come to reject the idea of class legislation early in its history, viewed the enslavement of African-Americans as a monopolization of their labor and the worst form of class legislation. Other segments of the population, of course, focused on the moral horror of slavery, and to them we now turn.

II. THE ABOLITIONIST MOVEMENT

A fundamental principle of the Enlightenment was that all men were created equal, as Thomas Jefferson claimed in the Declaration of Independence, and that the European feudalism under which some men were born kings, others were born nobles, and most were born commoners was both unjust and contrary to natural law. It took little effort to realize that if European feudalism was contrary to natural law, along with the Hindu caste system, then the enslavement of Africans by Europeans must be fundamentally wrong as well.

By the time of the Constitution, slavery did not exist in England and was contrary to the common law and to the natural rights and freedoms of Englishmen. As we mentioned at the start of this casebook, *see supra* page 10, the Chief Justice of England, Lord Mansfield, ruled in 1772 in *Somerset v. Stewart*, 98 Eng. Rep. 499 (K.B. 1771), that a slave brought by an Englishmen from Virginia to London on a trip that was planned to end with the slave, Somerset, being sold in Jamaica, resulted in the former slave's freedom, because the Court of King's Bench ruled that slavery was illegal under the common law and in England. Indeed, the Court said that slavery was so odious and so contrary to natural law that nothing but specifically enacted positive law statutes could suffer to allow it to exist.

The first nineteen or so African slaves were brought to Jamestown, Virginia in 1619. The settlers treated them as indentured servants and freed them, like indentured white Europeans, after a term of years. In 1641, Massachusetts by statute recognized the legality of slavery, and it was also legally recognized in Virginia in the 1640s. Only 5,649 slaves were brought to the American colonies prior to 1676, but the numbers rose sharply after that time. Approximately, 473,000 Africans were ultimately brought as slaves to the area that became the United States. The South had much larger numbers of slaves than did the Northern colonies, but it was the merchants of New England who brought the kidnapped African slaves to the American south to be sold as part of the so-called triangle trade. All parts of the United States were thus complicit with the enslavement of Africans in the United States.

When *Somerset v. Stewart* was decided in 1772, it applied to the thirteen North American colonies, but since all thirteen colonies had legalized slavery by statute, the ruling had no effect in the United States. Shortly thereafter some small movement towards abolitionism began to appear in the colonies.

In 1774, when the American colonists adopted the Articles of Association pledging to boycott British goods in response to King George III's closing of the port of Boston, the Second Article was quite striking. It said that:

> *2.* We will neither import nor purchase, any slave imported after the first day of December next; after which time, we will wholly discontinue the slave trade, and will neither be concerned in it ourselves, nor will we hire our vessels, nor sell our commodities or manufactures to those who are concerned in it.

Thomas Jefferson even made an attempt in drafting the Declaration of Independence to blame the British monarchy for North American slavery, but this language did not appear in the final draft. Many Americans realized the hypocrisy of their fighting for liberty from Britain while denying liberty to African slaves. Abolitionist groups were formed in New England, New York, and in Pennsylvania in the period between 1776 and 1796. As a result of their efforts, the territory of Vermont abolished slavery in 1777; and Massachusetts abolished it in 1783, holding it to be a violation of the "Born Free and Equal clause" of the Massachusetts Constitution. All the other New England States began abolishing slavery in the 1780s, including New Hampshire in 1783 and Connecticut and Rhode Island in 1784. Pennsylvania took the same step in 1780. These abolitions did not free existing slaves immediately, but they forbade the introduction of new slaves and hastened the abolition of those still held in slavery. New York in 1799 and New Jersey in 1804 abolished slavery. And, most important of all, the Continental Congress, in passing the Northwest Ordinance of 1787, abolished slavery in the vast Northwest Territories that became the free States of Ohio, Indiana, Illinois, Michigan, Wisconsin, and part of Minnesota, though a precursor of the Fugitive Slave Clause prevented the territory from becoming a haven for escaped slaves. Article VI of the Northwest Ordinance provided that:

> There shall be neither slavery nor involuntary servitude in the said territory, otherwise than in the punishment of crimes, whereof the party shall have been duly convicted. *Provided always,* That any person escaping into the same, from whom service or labor is lawfully claimed in any one of the original States, such fugitive may be lawfully reclaimed and conveyed to the person claiming his or her labor or service as aforesaid * * *.

The federal Constitution of 1788 was two-faced on the subject of slavery. On the one hand, it did not authorize slavery or even use the word "slave"; and on the other hand, it gave the South a three-fifths bonus in seats in the House of Representatives and in the Electoral College and contained a Fugitive Slave Clause.

There was a major effort made to condemn slavery in 1790. A group of Quakers from Pennsylvania, Rhode Island, New Jersey and other States petitioned Congress to do whatever it could legally do to discourage slavery. At the same time, a secular abolitionist group in Pennsylvania, with Benjamin Franklin, as its president, did its best to encourage Congress to act against slavery. Finally, in New York, Alexander Hamilton and John Jay formed an abolitionist group. Congress did not act immediately, but in 1794, Congress did pass a federal law, which was signed by President Washington, forbidding American citizens from engaging in the American slave trade. In 1808, at the earliest date possible under the Constitution, Congress outlawed the international slave trade. Unfortunately, the development of the cotton gin made slavery economically viable in the Southern States where cotton was grown, and so the movement toward abolition at the time of the Framing did not end slavery.

The acquisition of the Louisiana Purchase, during Thomas Jefferson's presidency, raised a new and highly divisive question related to slavery, which was whether the new States formed out of the vast acquired territory would be free States or slave States. This matter became a constitutional crisis when Missouri sought to join the Union in 1820 as a new slave State. A compromise was reached, whereby Maine was carved out of Massachusetts to be a new free State, with Missouri being admitted as a new slave State, thus maintaining the existing balance in the Senate.

It was also agreed that all federal territory north of Missouri's Southern border would be free territory while all federal territory south of Missouri's Southern border would be slave territory. This compromise, of course, pleased no one, but it held the Union together until it was struck down as unconstitutional in *Dred Scott* in 1857.

The Abolitionist Movement grew by leaps and bounds in the 1830s. An early and persistent leader was the Massachusetts-born journalist and political commentator, William Lloyd Garrison, who founded the most important abolitionist newspaper, *The Liberator*, in 1831. He continued to publish it until slavery was abolished by constitutional amendment after the Civil War. Garrison was in favor of women's suffrage and equal civil rights as well as abolition of slavery by any means possible. On July 4, 1854, Garrison publicly burned a copy of the Constitution before a large audience, condemning it as "A Covenant with Death, an Agreement with Hell." Garrison's most important contribution to the cause of abolition came with his discovery, and decision to make famous, a former slave, Frederick Douglass, who wrote an autobiography of his years as a slave. Garrison said the following about slavery in the book's preface:

> So profoundly ignorant of the nature of slavery are many persons, that they are stubbornly incredulous whenever they read or listen to any recital of the cruelties which are daily inflicted on its victims. They do not deny that the slaves are held as property; but that terrible fact seems to convey to their minds no idea of injustice, exposure to outrage, or savage barbarity. Tell them of cruel scourgings, of mutilations and brandings, of scenes of pollution and blood, of the banishment of all light and knowledge, and they affect to be greatly indignant at such enormous exaggerations, such wholesale misstatements, such abominable libels on the character of the southern planters! As if all these direful outrages were not the natural results of slavery! As if it were less cruel to reduce a human being to the condition of a thing, than to give him a severe flagellation, or to deprive him of necessary food and clothing! As if whips, chains, thumb-screws, paddles, bloodhounds, overseers, drivers, patrols, were not all indispensable to keep the slaves down, and to give protection to their ruthless oppressors! As if, when the marriage institution is abolished, concubinage, adultery, and incest, must not necessarily abound; when all the rights of humanity are annihilated, any barrier remains to protect the victim from the fury of the spoiler; when absolute power is assumed over life and liberty, it will not be wielded with destructive sway!
>
> Skeptics of this character abound in society. In some few instances, their incredulity arises from a want of reflection; but, generally, it indicates a hatred of the light, a desire to shield slavery from the assaults of its foes, a contempt of the colored race, whether bond or free. Such will try to discredit the shocking tales of slaveholding cruelty which are recorded in this truthful Narrative; but they will labor in vain. Mr. DOUGLAS has frankly disclosed the place of his birth, the names of those who claimed ownership in his body and soul, and the names also of those who committed the crimes which he has alleged against them. His statements, therefore, may easily be disproved, if they are untrue.
>
> In the course of his Narrative, he relates two instances of murderous cruelty,—in one of which a planter deliberately shot a slave belonging to a

neighboring plantation, who had unintentionally gotten within his lordly domain in quest of fish; and in the other, an overseer blew out the brains of a slave who had fled to a stream of water to escape a bloody scourging * * *. Let it never be forgotten, that no slaveholder or overseer can be convicted of any outrage perpetrated on the person of a slave, however diabolical it may be, on the testimony of colored witnesses, whether bond or free. By the slave code, they are adjudged to be as incompetent to testify against a white man, as though they were indeed a part of the brute creation. Hence, there is no legal protection in fact, whatever there may be in form, for the slave population; and any amount of cruelty may be inflicted on them with impunity.

* * *

A slaveholder's profession of Christianity is a palpable imposture. He is a felon of the highest grade. He is a man-stealer. It is of no importance what you put in the other scale. Reader! are you with the man-stealers in sympathy and purpose, or on the side of their down-trodden victims? If with the former, then are you the foe of God and man. If with the latter, what are you prepared to do and dare in their behalf? Be faithful, be vigilant, be untiring in your efforts to break every yoke, and let the oppressed go free. Come what may—cost what it may—inscribe on the banner which you unfurl to the breeze, as your religious and political motto—"NO COMPROMISE WITH SLAVERY! NO UNION WITH SLAVEHOLDERS!" WM. LLOYD GARRISON. BOSTON, May 1, 1845.

Garrison broke off ties with Frederick Douglass, the most important abolitionist in the country, because Douglass was not ready to dissolve the United States as a Union because of the Three-Fifths Clause and the Fugitive Slave Clause. Douglass countered that disunion would slow down the elimination of slavery in North America rather than speeding it up. Nor was Douglass convinced that the Constitution was fundamentally evil, as Garrison maintained. Consider the following speech by Douglass, delivered in Glasgow, Scotland, responding to Garrison's call for disunion and withdrawal from the political process.

"The Constitution of the United States: Is it Pro-Slavery or Anti-Slavery?"

By Frederick Douglass,
March 26, 1860

* * * [F]irst let me state what is not the question. It is not whether slavery existed in the United States at the time of the adoption of the Constitution; it is not whether slaveholders took part in the framing of the Constitution; it is not whether those slaveholders, in their hearts, intended to secure certain advantages in that instrument for slavery; it is not whether the American Government has been wielded during seventy-two years in favour of the propagation and permanence of slavery; it is not whether a pro-slavery interpretation has been put upon the Constitution by the American Courts—all these points may be true or they may be false, they may be accepted or they may be rejected, without in any wise affecting the real question in debate. The real and exact question between myself and the class of persons represented by the speech at the City Hall may be fairly stated thus:—1st, Does the

United States Constitution guarantee to any class or description of people in that country the right to enslave, or hold as property, any other class or description of people in that country? 2nd, Is the dissolution of the union between the slave and free States required by fidelity to the slaves, or by the just demands of conscience? Or, in other words, is the refusal to exercise the elective franchise, and to hold office in America, the surest, wisest, and best way to abolish slavery in America?

To these questions the Garrisonians say Yes. They hold the Constitution to be a slaveholding instrument, and will not cast a vote or hold office, and denounce all who vote or hold office, no matter how faithfully such persons labour to promote the abolition of slavery. I, on the other hand, deny that the Constitution guarantees the right to hold property in man, and believe that the way to abolish slavery in America is to vote such men into power as well use their powers for the abolition of slavery. This is the issue plainly stated, and you shall judge between us. Before we examine into the disposition, tendency, and character of the Constitution, I think we had better ascertain what the Constitution itself is.

Before looking for what it means, let us see what it is. Here, too, there is much dust to be cleared away. What, then, is the Constitution? I will tell you. It is not even like the British Constitution, which is made up of enactments of Parliament, decisions of Courts, and the established usages of the Government. The American Constitution is a written instrument full and complete in itself. No Court in America, no Congress, no President, can add a single word thereto, or take a single word thereto. It is a great national enactment done by the people, and can only be altered, amended, or added to by the people. I am careful to make this statement here; in America it would not be necessary. It would not be necessary here if my assailant had shown the same desire to be set before you the simple truth, which he manifested to make out a good case for himself and friends.

Again, it should be borne in mind that the mere text, and only the text, and not any commentaries or creeds written by those who wished to give the text a meaning apart from its plain reading, was adopted as the Constitution of the United States. It should also be borne in mind that the intentions of those who framed the Constitution, be they good or bad, for slavery or against slavery, are so respected so far, and so far only, as we find those intentions plainly stated in the Constitution. It would be the wildest of absurdities, and lead to endless confusion and mischiefs, if, instead of looking to the written paper itself, for its meaning, it were attempted to make us search it out, in the secret motives, and dishonest intentions, of some of the men who took part in writing it. It was what they said that was adopted by the people, not what they were ashamed or afraid to say, and really omitted to say. Bear in mind, also, and the fact is an important one, that the framers of the Constitution sat with doors closed, and that this was done purposely, that nothing but the result of their labours should be seen, and that that result should be judged of by the people free from any of the bias shown in the debates. It should also be borne in mind, and the fact is still more important, that the debates in the convention that framed the Constitution, and by means of which a pro-slavery interpretation is now attempted to be forced upon that instrument, were not published till more than a quarter of a century after the presentation and the adoption of the Constitution.

These debates were purposely kept out of view, in order that the people should adopt, not the secret motives or unexpressed intentions of any body, but the simple text of the paper itself. Those debates form no part of the original agreement. I repeat, the paper itself, and only the paper itself, with its own plainly written purposes, is the Constitution. It must stand or fall, flourish or fade, on its own individual and self-declared character and objects. Again, where would be the advantage of a written Constitution, if, instead of seeking its meaning in its words, we had to seek them in the secret intentions of individuals who may have had something to do with writing the paper? What will the people of America a hundred years hence care about the intentions of the scriveners who wrote the Constitution? These men are already gone from us, and in the course of nature were expected to go from us. They were for a generation, but the Constitution is for ages. Whatever we may owe to them, we certainly owe it to ourselves, and to mankind, and to God, to maintain the truth of our own language, and to allow no villainy, not even the villainy of holding men as slaves—which Wesley says is the sum of all villainies—to shelter itself under a fair-seeming and virtuous language. We owe it to ourselves to compel the devil to wear his own garments, and to make wicked laws speak out their wicked intentions.

Common sense, and common justice, and sound rules of interpretation all drive us to the words of the law for the meaning of the law. The practice of the Government is dwelt upon with much fervour and eloquence as conclusive as to the slaveholding character of the Constitution. This is really the strong point and the only strong point, made in the speech in the City Hall. But good as this argument is, it is not conclusive. A wise man has said that few people have been found better than their laws, but many have been found worse. To this last rule America is no exception. Her laws are one thing, her practice is another thing. We read that the Jews made void the law by their tradition, that Moses permitted men to put away their wives because of the hardness of their hearts, but that this was not so at the beginning. While good laws will always be found where good practice prevails, the reverse does not always hold true. Far from it. The very opposite is often the case. What then? Shall we condemn the righteous law because wicked men twist it to the support of wickedness? Is that the way to deal with good and evil? Shall we blot out all distinction between them, and hand over to slavery all that slavery may claim on the score of long practice? Such is the course commended to us in the City Hall speech. After all, the fact that men go out of the Constitution to prove it pro-slavery, whether that going out is to the practice of the Government, or to the secret intentions of the writers of the paper, the fact that they do go out is very significant. It is a powerful argument on my side. It is an admission that the thing for which they are looking is not to be found where only it ought to be found, and that is in the Constitution itself. If it is not there, it is nothing to the purpose, be it wheresoever else it may be. But I shall have no more to say on this point hereafter.

The very eloquent lecturer at the City Hall doubtless felt some embarrassment from the fact that he had literally to *give* the Constitution a pro-slavery interpretation; because upon its face it of itself conveys no such meaning, but a very opposite meaning. He thus sums up what he calls the slaveholding provisions of the Constitution. I quote his own words:—"Article 1, section 9, provides for the continuance of the African slave trade for the 20 years, after the adoption of the Constitution. Art. 4, section 2, provides for the recovery from the other States of fugitive slaves. Art. 1, section 2, gives the slave States a representation of the three-fifths of all the slave population; and Art. 1, section 8, requires the President to use the military, naval, ordnance, and militia resources of the entire country for the suppression of slave insurrection, in the same manner as he would employ them to repel invasion." Now any man reading this statement, or hearing it made with such a show of exactness, would unquestionably suppose that he speaker or writer had given the plain written text of the Constitution itself.

I can hardly believe that [he] intended to make any such impression. It would be a scandalous imputation to say he did. Any yet what are we to make of it? How can we regard it? How can he be screened from the charge of having perpetrated a deliberate and point-blank misrepresentation? That individual has seen fit to place himself before the public as my opponent, and yet I would gladly find some excuse for him. I do not wish to think as badly of him as this trick of his would naturally lead me to think. Why did he not read the Constitution? Why did he read that which was not the Constitution? He pretended to be giving chapter and verse, section and clause, paragraph and provision. The words of the Constitution were before him. Why then did he not give you the plain words of the Constitution? Oh, sir, I fear that the gentleman knows too well why he did not. It so happens that no such words as "African slave trade," no such words as "slave insurrections," are anywhere used in that instrument. These are the words of that orator, and not the words of the Constitution of the United States.

Now you shall see a slight difference between my manner of treating this subject and what which my opponent has seen fit, for reasons satisfactory to himself, to pursue. What he withheld, that I will spread before you: what he suppressed, I will bring to light: and what he passed over in silence, I will proclaim: that you may have the whole case before you, and not be left to depend upon either his, or upon my inferences or testimony. Here then are several provisions of the Constitution to which reference has been made.

I read them word for word just as they stand in the paper, called the United States Constitution, Art. I, sec. 2. "Representatives and direct taxes shall be apportioned among the several States which may be included in this Union, according to their respective numbers, which shall be determined by adding to the whole number of free persons, including those bound to service for a term years, and excluding Indians not taxed, three-fifths of all other persons; Art. I, sec. 9. The migration or importation of such persons as any of the States now existing shall think fit to admit, shall not be prohibited by the Congress prior to the year one thousand eight hundred and eight, but a tax or duty may be imposed on such importation, not exceeding tend dollars for each person; Art. 4, sec. 2. No person held to service or labour in one State, under the laws thereof, escaping into another shall, in consequence of any law or regulation therein, be discharged from service or labour; but shall be delivered up on claim of the party to whom such service or labour may be due; Art. I, sec. 8. To provide for calling for the militia to execute the laws of the Union, suppress insurrections, and repel invasions." Here then, are those provisions of the Constitution, which the most extravagant defenders of slavery can claim to guarantee a right of property in man.

These are the provisions which have been pressed into the service of the human fleshmongers of America. Let us look at them just as they stand, one by one. Let us grant, for the sake of the argument, that the first of these provisions, referring to the basis of representation and taxation, does refer to slaves. We are not compelled to make that admission, for it might fairly apply to aliens—persons living in the country, but not naturalized. But giving the provisions the very worse construction, what does it amount to? I answer—It is a downright disability laid upon the slaveholding States; one which deprives those States of two-fifths of their natural basis of representation. A black man in a free State is worth just two-fifths more than a black man in a slave State, as a basis of political power under the Constitution. Therefore, instead of encouraging slavery, the Constitution encourages freedom by giving an increase of "two-fifths" of political power to free over slave States. So much for the three-fifths clause; taking it at is worst, it still leans to freedom, not slavery; for, be it remembered that the Constitution nowhere forbids a coloured man to vote.

I come to the next, that which it is said guaranteed the continuance of the African slave trade for twenty years. I will also take that for just what my opponent alleges it to have been, although the Constitution does not warrant any such conclusion. But, to be liberal, let us suppose it did, and what follows? Why, this—that this part of the Constitution, so far as the slave trade is concerned, became a dead letter more than 50 years ago, and now binds no man's conscience for the continuance of any slave trade whatsoever. Mr. Thompson is just 52 years too late in dissolving the Union on account of this clause. He might as well dissolve the British Government, because Queen Elizabeth granted to Sir John Hawkins to import Africans into the West Indies 300 years ago! But there is still more to be said about this abolition of the slave trade. Men, at that time, both in England and in America, looked upon the slave trade as the life of slavery. The abolition of the slave trade was supposed to be the certain death of slavery. Cut off the stream, and the pond will dry up, was the common notion at the time.

Wilberforce and Clarkson, clear-sighted as they were, took this view; and the American statesmen, in providing for the abolition of the slave trade, thought they were providing for the abolition of the slavery. This view is quite consistent with the history of the times. All regarded slavery as an expiring and doomed system, destined to speedily disappear from the country. But, again, it should be remembered that this very provision, if made to refer to the African slave trade at all, makes the Constitution anti-slavery rather than for slavery; for it says to the slave States, the price you will have to pay for coming into the American Union is, that the slave trade, which you would carry on indefinitely out of the Union, shall be put an end to in twenty years if you come into the Union. Secondly, if it does apply, it expired by its own limitation more than fifty years ago. Thirdly, it is anti-slavery, because it looked to the abolition of slavery rather than to its perpetuity. Fourthly, it showed that the intentions of the framers of the Constitution were good, not bad.

I think this is quite enough for this point. I go to the "slave insurrection" clause, though, in truth, there is no such clause. The one which is called so has nothing whatever to do with slaves or slaveholders any more than your laws for suppression of popular outbreaks has to do with making slaves of you and your children. It is only a law for suppression of riots or insurrections. But I will be generous here, as well as elsewhere, and grant that it applies to slave insurrections. Let us suppose that an anti-slavery man is President of the United States (and the day that shall see this the case is not distant) and this very power of suppressing slave insurrections would put an end to slavery. The right to put down an insurrection carries with it the right to determine the means by which it shall be put down. If it should turn out that slavery is a source of insurrection, that there is no security from insurrection while slavery lasts, why, the Constitution would be best obeyed by putting an end to slavery, and an anti-slavery Congress would do the very same thing.

Thus, you see, the so-called slave-holding provisions of the American Constitution, which a little while ago looked so formidable, are, after all, no defence or guarantee for slavery whatever. But there is one other provision. This is called the "Fugitive Slave Provision." It is called so by those who wish to make it subserve the interest of slavery in America, and the same by those who wish to uphold the views of a party in this country. It is put thus in the speech at the City Hall:—"Let us go back to 1787, and enter Liberty Hall, Philadelphia, where sat in convention the illustrious men who framed the Constitution—with George Washington in the chair. On the 27th of September, Mr. Butler and Mr. Pinckney, two delegates from the State of South Carolina, moved that the Constitution should require that fugitive slaves and servants should be delivered up like criminals, and after a discussion on the subject, the clause, as it stands in the Constitution, was adopted. After this, in the conventions held in the several States to ratify the Constitution, the same meaning was attached to the words. For example, Mr. Madison (afterwards President), when recommending the Constitution to his constituents, told them that the clause would secure them their property in slaves." I must ask you to look well to this statement. Upon its face, it would seem a full and fair statement of the history of the transaction it professes to describe and yet I declare unto you, knowing as I do the facts in the case, my utter amazement at the downright untruth conveyed under the fair seeming words now quoted. The man who could make such a statement may have all the craftiness of a lawyer, but who can accord to him the candour of an honest debater? What could more completely destroy all confidence in his statements? Mark you, the orator had not allowed his audience to hear read the provision of the Constitution to which he referred. He merely characterized it as one to "deliver up fugitive slaves and servants like criminals," and tells you that this was done "after discussion." But he took good care not to tell you what was the nature of that discussion. He have would have spoiled the whole effect of his statement had he told you the whole truth.

Now, what are the facts connected with this provision of the Constitution? You shall have them. It seems to take two men to tell the truth. It is quite true that Mr. Butler and Mr. Pinckney introduced a provision expressly with a view to the recapture of fugitive slaves: it is quite true also that there was some discussion on the subject—and just here the truth shall come out. These illustrious kidnappers were told promptly in that discussion that no such idea as property in man should be admitted into the Constitution. The speaker in question might have told you, and he would have told you but the simple truth, if he had told you that he proposition of Mr. Butler and Mr. Pinckney—which he leads you to infer was adopted by the convention that from the Constitution—was, in fact, promptly and indignantly rejected by that convention. He might have told you, had it suited his purpose to do so, that the words employed in the first draft of the fugitive slave clause were such as applied to the condition of slaves, and expressly declared that persons held to "servitude" should be given up; but that the word "servitude" was struck from the provision, for the very reason that it applied to slaves. He might have told you that the same Mr. Madison declared that the word was struck out because the convention would not consent that the idea of property in men should be admitted into the Constitution. The fact that Mr. Madison can be cited on both sides of this question is another evidence of the folly and absurdity of making the secret intentions of the framers the criterion by which the Constitution is to be construed. But it may be asked—if this clause does not apply to slaves, to whom does it apply?

I answer, that when adopted, it applies to a very large class of persons—namely, redemptioners—persons who had come to America from Holland, from Ireland, and other quarters of the globe—like the Coolies to the West Indies—and had, for a consideration duly paid, become bound to "serve and labour" for the parties two whom their service and labour was due. It applies to indentured apprentices and others who have become bound for a consideration, under contract duly made, to serve and labour, to such persons this provision applies, and only to such persons. The plain reading of this provision shows that it applies, and that it can only properly and legally apply, to persons "bound to service." Its object plainly is, to secure the fulfillment of contracts for "service and labour." It applies to indentured apprentices, and any other persons from whom service and labour may be due.

The legal condition of the slave puts him beyond the operation of this provision. He is not described in it. He is a simple article of property. He does not owe and cannot owe service. He cannot even make a contract. It is impossible for him to do so. He can no more make such a contract than a horse or an ox can make one. This provision, then, only respects persons who owe service, and they only can owe service who can receive an equivalent and make a bargain. The slave cannot do that, and is therefore exempted from the operation of this fugitive provision.

In all matters where laws are taught to be made the means of oppression, cruelty, and wickedness, I am for strict construction. I will concede nothing. It must be shown that it is so nominated in the bond. The pound of flesh, but not one drop of blood. The very nature of law is opposed to all such wickedness, and makes it difficult to accomplish such objects under the forms of law. Law is not merely an arbitrary enactment with regard to justice, reason, or humanity. Blackstone defines it to be a rule prescribed by the supreme power of the State commanding what is right and forbidding what is wrong. The speaker at the City Hall laid down some rules of legal interpretation. These rules send us to the history of the law for its meaning. I have no objection to such a course in ordinary cases of doubt. But where human liberty and justice are at stake, the case falls under an entirely different class of rules. There must be something more than history—something more than tradition. The Supreme Court of the United States lays down this rule, and it meets the case exactly—"Where rights are infringed—where the fundamental principles of the law are overthrown—where the general system of the law is departed from, the legislative intention must be expressed with irresistible clearness." The same court says that the language of the law must be construed strictly in favour of justice and liberty. Again, there is another rule of law. It is—Where a law is susceptible of two meanings, the one making it accomplish an innocent purpose, and the other making it accomplish a wicked purpose, we must in all cases adopt that which makes it accomplish an innocent purpose. Again, the details of a law are to be interpreted in the light of the declared objects sought by the law. I set these rules down against those employed at the City Hall. To me they seem just and rational.

I only ask you to look at the American Constitution in the light of them, and you will see with me that no man is guaranteed a right of property in man, under the provisions of that instrument. If there are two ideas more distinct in their character and essence than another, those ideas are "persons" and "property," "men" and "things." Now, when it is proposed to transform persons into "property" and men into beasts of burden, I demand that the law that completes such a purpose shall be expressed with irresistible clearness. The thing must not be left to inference, but must be done in plain English. I know how this view of the subject is treated by the class represented at the City Hall. They are in the habit of treating the Negro as an exception to general rules. When their own liberty is in question they will avail themselves of all rules of law which protect and defend their freedom; but when the black man's rights are in question they concede everything, admit everything for slavery, and put liberty to the proof. They reserve the common law usage, and presume the Negro a slave unless he can prove himself free.

I, on the other hand, presume him free unless he is proved to be otherwise. Let us look at the objects for which the Constitution was framed and adopted, and see if slavery is one of them. Here are its own objects as set forth by itself:—"We, the people of these United States, in order to form a more perfect union, establish justice, ensure domestic tranquility, provide for the common defense, promote the general welfare, and secure the blessings of liberty to ourselves and our posterity, do ordain and establish this Constitution of the United States of America." The objects here set forth are six in number: union, defence, welfare, tranquility, justice, and liberty. These are all good objects, and slavery, so far from being among them, is a foe of them all.

But it has been said that Negroes are not included within the benefits sought under this declaration. This is said by the slaveholders in America—it is said by the City Hall orator—but it is not said by the Constitution itself. Its language is "we the people;" not we the white people, not even we the citizens, not we the privileged class, not we the high, not we the low, but we the people; not we the horses, sheep, and swine, and wheel-barrows, but we the people, we the human inhabitants; and, if Negroes are people, they are included in the benefits for which the Constitution of America was ordained and established. But how dare any man who pretends to be a friend to the Negro thus gratuitously concede away what the Negro has a right to claim under the Constitution? Why should such friends invent new arguments to increase the hopelessness of his bondage?

This, I undertake to say, as the conclusion of the whole matter, that the constitutionality of slavery can be made out only by disregarding the plain and common-sense reading of the Constitution itself; by discrediting and casting away as worthless the most beneficent rules of legal interpretation; by ruling the Negro outside of these beneficent rules; by claiming that the Constitution does not mean what it says, and that it says what it does not mean; by disregarding the written Constitution, and interpreting it in the light of a secret understanding. It is in this mean, contemptible, and underhand method that the American Constitution is pressed into the service of slavery. They go everywhere else for proof that the Constitution declares that no person shall be deprived of life, liberty, or property without due process of law; it secures to every man the right of trial by jury, the privilege of the writ of habeas corpus—the great writ that put an end to slavery and slave-hunting in England—and it secures to every State a republican form of government. Anyone of these provisions in the hands of abolition statesmen, and backed up by a right moral sentiment, would put an end to slavery in America. The Constitution forbids the passing of a bill of attainder: that is, a law entailing upon the child the disabilities and hardships imposed upon the parent.

Every slave law in America might be repealed on this very ground. The slave is made a slave because his mother is a slave. But to all this it is said that the practice of the American people is against my view. I admit it. They have given the Constitution a slaveholding interpretation. I admit it. Thy have committed innumerable wrongs against the Negro in the name of the Constitution. Yes, I admit it all; and I go with him who goes farthest in denouncing these wrongs. But it does not follow that the Constitution is in favour of these wrongs because the slaveholders have given it that interpretation. To be consistent in his logic, the City Hall speaker must follow the example of some of his brothers in America—he must not only fling away the Constitution, but the Bible. The Bible must follow the Constitution, for that, too, has been interpreted for slavery by American divines. Nay, more, he must not stop with the Constitution of America, but make war with the British Constitution, for, if I mistake not, the gentleman is opposed to the union of Church and State. In America he called himself a Republican. Yet he does not go for breaking down the British Constitution, although you have a Queen on the throne, and bishops in the House of Lords.

My argument against the dissolution of the American Union is this: It would place the slave system more exclusively under the control of the slaveholding States, and withdraw it from the power in the Northern States which is opposed to slavery. Slavery is essentially barbarous in its character. It, above all things else, dreads the presence of an advanced civilisation. It flourishes best where it meets no reproving frowns, and hears no condemning voices. While in the Union it will meet with both. Its hope of life, in the last resort, is to get out of the Union. I am, therefore, for drawing the bond of the Union more completely under the power of the Free States. What they most dread, that I most desire. I have much confidence in the instincts of the slaveholders. They see that the Constitution will afford slavery no protection when it shall cease to be administered by slaveholders. They see, moreover, that if there is once a will in the people of America to abolish slavery, this is no word, no syllable in the Constitution to forbid that result.

They see that the Constitution has not saved slavery in Rhode Island, in Connecticut, in New York, or Pennsylvania; that the Slave States have only added three to their original number. There were twelve Slave States at the beginning of the Government: there are fifteen now. They dissolution of the Union would not give the North a single advantage over slavery, but would take from it many. Within the Union we have a firm basis of opposition to slavery. It is opposed to all the great objects of the Constitution. The dissolution of the Union is not only an unwise but a cowardly measure—15 millions running away from three hundred and fifty thousand slaveholders.

Mr. Garrison and his friends tell us that while in the Union we are responsible for slavery. He and they sing out "No Union with slaveholders," and refuse to vote. I admit our responsibility for slavery while in the Union but I deny that going out of the Union would free us from that responsibility. There now clearly is no freedom from responsibility for slavery to any American citizen short to the abolition of slavery. The American people have gone quite too far in this slaveholding business now to sum up their whole business of slavery by singing out the cant phrase, "No union with slaveholders." To desert the family hearth may place the recreant husband out of the presence of his starving children, but this does not free him from responsibility. If a man were on board of a pirate ship, and in company with others had robbed and plundered, his whole duty would not be performed simply by taking the longboat and singing out, "No union with pirates." His duty would be to restore the stolen property. The American people in the Northern States have helped to enslave the black people. Their duty will not have been done till they give them back their plundered rights.

Reference was made at the City Hall to my having once held other opinions, and very different opinions to those I have now expressed. An old speech of mine delivered fourteen years ago was read to show—I know not what. Perhaps it was to show that I am not infallible. If so, I have to say in defence, that I never pretended to be. Although I cannot accuse myself of being remarkably unstable, I do not pretend that I have never altered my opinion both in respect to men and things. Indeed, I have been very much modified both in feeling and opinion within the last fourteen years. When I escaped from slavery, and was introduced to the Garrisonians, I adopted very many of their opinions, and defended them just as long as I deemed them true. I was young, had read but little, and naturally took some things on trust. Subsequent experience and reading have led me to examine for myself. This had brought me to other conclusions. When I was a child, I thought and spoke as a child.

But the question is not as to what were my opinions fourteen years ago, but what they are now. If I am right now, it really does not matter what I was fourteen years ago. My position now is one of reform, not of revolution. I would act for the abolition of slavery through the Government—not over its ruins. If slaveholders have ruled the American Government for the last fifty years, let the anti-slavery men rule the nation for the next fifty years. If the South has made the Constitution bend to the purposes of slavery, let the North now make that instrument bend to the cause of freedom and justice. If 350,000 slaveholders have, by devoting their energies to that single end, been able to make slavery the vital and animating spirit of the American Confederacy for the last 72 years, now let the freemen of the North, who have the power in their own hands, and who can make the American Government just what they think fit, resolve to blot out for ever the foul and haggard crime, which is the blight and mildew, the curse and the disgrace of the whole United States.

[Assignment 56]

III. THE THIRTEENTH, FOURTEENTH, AND FIFTEENTH AMENDMENTS

President Abraham Lincoln's Emancipation Proclamation of January 1, 1863 freed 3 million of the 4 million slaves then in the United States. The Emancipation Proclamation devastated the South. Slaves fled the plantations and headed north. African-American men joined the Union Army in huge numbers and fought bravely and valiantly to end slavery and crush the Southern rebellion; by the end of the Civil War, twenty percent of the soldiers in the Union army were African-Americans. And the United Kingdom and France found themselves unable to exchange ambassadors with the Confederacy once the Civil War became a conflict about ending slavery as well as keeping the Union together.

After key military victories in September 1864, Abraham Lincoln was re-elected to a second term as President. In January 1865, President Lincoln lobbied and cajoled the House of Representatives into joining the Senate and passing the

Thirteenth Amendment to the Constitution. President Lincoln was assassinated before the Amendment was ratified, but by then its eventual ratification on December 6, 1865 had become a foregone conclusion.

The text of the Thirteenth Amendment reads as follows:

> **Section 1.**
>
> **Neither slavery nor involuntary servitude, except as a punishment for crime whereof the party shall have been duly convicted, shall exist within the United States, or any place subject to their jurisdiction.**
>
> **Section 2.**
>
> **Congress shall have power to enforce this article by appropriate legislation.**

After losing the Battle of Richmond, Virginia, in which General Ulysses S. Grant conquered the Confederate capital city, General Robert E. Lee retreated westward hoping to join the one remaining Confederate army of Tennessee commanded by General Joseph E. Johnston. Grant's army pursued Lee rapidly, cornered him, and defeated his army on April 9, 1865. Cut off from retreat and surrounded by vastly larger forces, General Lee signed a surrender document in General Ulysses S. Grant's presence on the afternoon of April 9th in the parlor of a private home. The long and bloody War of the Rebellion, as Abraham Lincoln called the Civil War, was finally over. The North had won a complete and unqualified victory.

Five days after the war was won, President Abraham Lincoln was assassinated on April 14, 1865 while attending a play at Ford's Theater in Washington, D.C. His assassin, John Wilkes Booth, was a Confederate terrorist who was captured and executed along with his co-conspirators. Five weeks earlier, President Lincoln had delivered his second inaugural address, which concluded with the words: "With malice toward none, with charity for all, with firmness in the right as God gives us to see the right, let us strive on to finish the work we are in, to bind up the nation's wounds, to care for him who shall have borne the battle and for his widow and his orphan, to do all which may achieve and cherish a just and lasting peace among ourselves and with all nations." Lincoln's assassination deprived the nation of a President who respected the civil rights of African-Americans but who wanted to show charity toward the conquered South. Sadly, Lincoln's Vice President and successor, Andrew Johnson, was a pro-North Democrat from Tennessee who was a racist, a drunkard, and politically tone deaf. The Union was held together from Lincoln's assassination until March 4, 1869, by General-in-Chief Ulysses S. Grant who supported Congress's desire to reconstruct the South over Johnson's opposition to Reconstruction.

President Johnson followed Lincoln's policy of charity toward the former rebels, and only Jefferson Davis, the former President of the Confederacy, was punished, and he received only a two-year prison sentence. Johnson also pardoned thousands of Confederates who were guilty of treason and other crimes. In May 1865, President Johnson allowed the Southern States to elect new governments to govern themselves. The Southern States immediately took two actions that infuriated the North. First, they elected high former Confederate government officials, like Alexander Stephens—the Vice President of the Confederacy—to seats in Congress and in their newly reconstituted state governments. And, second, they passed legislation, called the Black Codes, which reduced the newly freed African-American slaves to second-class citizens with almost no legal rights.

The Black Codes greatly restricted the ability of free African-Americans in the South to own property, conduct business or make contracts, to buy and lease land, and to be free in public spaces. The central feature of the Black Codes were strict vagrancy laws, which made it a crime not to have a job. The only jobs that were available involved signing a one-year contract to work for minimal wages picking cotton on a plantation. Violation of such a contract, or failure to have a job, was made a crime that would relegate the free African-American to working on a prison chain gang. The Black Codes were an abomination, which almost completely denied to free African-Americans basic common law rights and civil rights. They were an obvious attempt to maintain the social conditions of slave society without the formal law of slavery.

A. THE CIVIL RIGHTS ACT OF 1866

The North was outraged about these developments throughout the South. When Congress met in December 1865, it refused to seat the representatives and senators from the eleven formerly Confederate States, and it announced that a program of Reconstruction was needed under the Guarantee of a Republican Form of Government Clause of Article IV, section 4. In the North's view, and in Congress's view, once slavery had been ended by the Thirteenth Amendment, the former slaves became American citizens like all other American citizens, with equal civil rights. Public sentiment in the North about the Black Codes was well captured in an editorial in the *Chicago Tribune* in January 1866, which explained that the Black Codes were a repugnant, oligarchic form of class legislation contrary to American values:

> We have seen, through bitter experience, the evils of class legislation as practiced by the States, in the form of slave and black codes. * * *. And if the several States can practice class legislation, as between whites and blacks * * * they can also create class distinctions in the future between native and adopted citizens, between rich and poor, or between any other divisions of society. The most effectual way to reach to the root of this matter, is to amend the Constitution so as to forbid class legislation entirely by prohibiting the enactment of laws creating or recognizing any political distinctions because of class, race, or color between the inhabitants of any State or Territory, and providing that all classes shall possess the same civil rights and immunities, and be liable to the same penalties, and giving Congress the power to carry the clause into effect * * *. [W]e believe that we might as well level the evil of caste at one blow, as to fight it by driplets and sections, through another long course of years.

Editorial, *Class Legislation*, CHI. TRIB., Jan. 12, 1866.

With public sentiment in this state of alarm in the North, Congress went to work on writing and passing a statute—the Civil Rights Act of 1866—which recognized the equal civil rights of citizens of all races. That Act read as follows (bolded emphasis added):

> *An Act to protect all Persons in the United States in their Civil Rights, and furnish the Means of their Vindication.*

> *Be it enacted by the Senate and House of Representatives of the United States of America in Congress assembled*, **That all persons born in the United States** and not subject to any foreign power, excluding Indians not taxed, **are hereby declared to be citizens of the United States; and such citizens, of every race and color,** without regard to any previous condition of slavery or involuntary servitude, except as a punishment for crime whereof the party shall have been duly convicted, **shall have the same right,** in every State and Territory in the United States, to make and enforce contracts, to sue, be parties, and give evidence, to inherit, purchase, lease, sell, hold, and convey real and personal property, and to full and equal benefit of all laws and proceedings for the security of person and property, **as is enjoyed by white citizens,** and shall be subject to like punishment, pains, and penalties, and to none other, any law, statute, ordinance, regulation, or custom, to the contrary notwithstanding.

Act of Apr. 9, 1866, ch. XXXI, § 1, 14 Stat. 27. The Civil Rights Act of 1866 was exclusively enforceable in federal and not state court, and violations were punishable by up to one year in prison or a fine of up to $1,000. There are seven key points about the Civil Rights Act of 1866—which remains in the United States Code today in only a slightly modified form, *see* 42 U.S.C. §§ 1981–1982 (2018)—of which you should take note.

First, the 1866 Act overruled *Dred Scott v. Sandford* by providing that "all persons born in the United States" are "hereby declared to be citizens of the United States."

Second, the 1866 Act extends equality of all the traditional common law rights, such as the right to make contracts and to own property and to testify in court, by explicitly forbidding race discrimination as to those enumerated common law rights.

Third, by providing for the "full and equal benefit of all laws and proceedings for the security of person and property," the 1866 Act gives African-Americans the right to the same proceedings for the security of person and property "as is enjoyed by white citizens," which meant that Southern police departments, fire departments, prosecutors, and judges were legally obligated to protect the freed African-Americans from private violence by, for example, the Ku Klux Klan. According to then-contemporary dictionaries, the words "same," "full," and "equal" in 1866 had their ordinary meanings; they meant exactly what they seem to mean. *See* Steven G. Calabresi & Andrea Matthews, *Originalism and Loving v. Virginia*, 2012 B.Y.U. L. REV. 1393. The Civil Rights Act of 1866 really did outlaw race discrimination as to all common law rights.

Fourth, the statute was expressly tied to race. The baseline rights were those of "white citizens." If the common law made distinctions among "white citizens," those same distinctions could be applied across the board. The statute forbids distinctions among white citizens and others.

Fifth, while the statute outlaws race discrimination in the provision of common law rights, it does not tell the States what their common law has to be. Instead, it says that "citizens of every race and color" shall have the same common law rights "as are enjoyed by white citizens." Note that the Act does not say that "citizens of every race and color" shall have the same state statutory or constitutional rights "as are enjoyed by white citizens." In this respect, the Civil Rights Act of 1866 is narrower than the Fourteenth Amendment, which does extend racial equality to all state common law, statutory, and constitutional rights.

Sixth, the language of the statute reeks of the distaste for partial or special legislation that dominated the legal scene for decades beforehand. To anticipate some forthcoming language, the statute overrode common law doctrines that created privileges or immunities for some people and then denied them to others based on race.

Seventh, the Civil Rights Act of 1866 was enacted pursuant to Congress's Section 2 power to enforce the Thirteenth Amendment's ban on slavery. In Congress's view, one could be either a citizen with civil rights or a slave, but not some in-between person who had no civil rights but was not a slave. To the Congress of 1866, abolishing slavery meant more than doing away with a formal legal institution. It meant securing basic rights of legal capacity. It thus seemed entirely proper to Congress to enact the Civil Rights Act of 1866 under Section 2 of the Thirteenth Amendment.

President Andrew Johnson of Tennessee disagreed with Congress about the scope of federal authority under the Thirteenth Amendment. He vetoed the bill, arguing that the power to prohibit slavery did not include a power to protect civil rights.

President Andrew Johnson's Veto of the Civil Rights Act of 1866

WASHINGTON, D.C., March 27, 1866.

To the Senate of the United States:

I regret that the bill, which has passed both Houses of Congress, entitled "An act to protect all persons in the United States in their civil rights and furnish the means of their vindication," contains provisions which I can not approve consistently with my sense of duty to the whole people and my obligations to the Constitution of the United States. I am therefore constrained to return it to the Senate, the House in which it originated, with my objections to its becoming a law.

By the first section of the bill all persons born in the United States and not subject to any foreign power, excluding Indians not taxed, are declared to be citizens of the United States * * *. It does not purport to give these classes of persons any status as citizens of States, except that which may result from their status as citizens of the United States. The power to confer the right of State citizenship is just as exclusively with the several States as the power to confer the right of Federal citizenship is with Congress. The right of Federal citizenship thus to be conferred on the several excepted races before mentioned is now for the first time proposed to be given by law. If, as is claimed by many, all persons who are native born already are, by virtue of the Constitution, citizens of the United States, the passage of the pending bill can not be necessary to make them such. If, on the other hand, such persons are not citizens, as may be assumed from the proposed legislation to make them such, the grave question presents itself whether, when eleven of the thirty-six States are unrepresented in Congress at the present time, it is sound policy to make our entire colored population and all other excepted classes citizens of the United States. Four millions of them have just emerged from slavery into freedom * * *. It may also be asked whether it is necessary that they should be declared citizens in order that they may be secured in the enjoyment of the civil rights proposed to be conferred by the bill.

Those rights are, by Federal as well as State laws, secured to all domiciled aliens and foreigners, even before the completion of the process of naturalization; and it may safely be assumed that the same enactments are sufficient to give like protection and benefits to those for whom this bill provides special legislation. Besides, the policy of the Government from its origin to the present time seems to have been that persons who are strangers to and unfamiliar with our institutions and our laws should pass through a certain probation, at the end of which, before attaining the coveted prize, they must give evidence of their fitness to receive and to exercise the rights of citizens as contemplated by the Constitution of the United States. The bill in effect proposes a discrimination against large numbers of intelligent, worthy, and patriotic foreigners, and in favor of the negro, to whom, after long years of bondage, the avenues to freedom and intelligence have just now been suddenly opened * * *.

The first section of the bill also contains an enumeration of the rights to be enjoyed by these classes so made citizens "in every State and Territory in the United States." These rights are "to make and enforce contracts; to sue, be parties, and give evidence; to inherit, purchase, lease, sell, hold, and convey real and personal property," and to have "full and equal benefit of all laws and proceedings for the security of person and property as is enjoyed by white citizens." So, too, they are made subject to the same punishment, pains, and penalties in common with white citizens, and to none other. Thus a perfect equality of the white and colored races is attempted to be fixed by Federal law in every State of the Union over the vast field of State jurisdiction covered by these enumerated rights. In no one of these can any State ever exercise any power of discrimination between the different races * * *.

Hitherto every subject embraced in the enumeration of rights contained in this bill has been considered as exclusively belonging to the States. They all relate to the internal police and economy of the respective States. They are matters which in each State concern the domestic condition of its people, varying in each according to its own peculiar circumstances and the safety and well-being of its own citizens. I do not mean to say that upon all these subjects there are not Federal restraints—as, for instance, in the State power of legislation over contracts there is a Federal limitation that no State shall pass a law impairing the obligations of contracts; and, as to crimes, that no State shall pass an ex post facto law; and, as to money, that no State shall make anything but gold and silver a legal tender; but where can we find a Federal prohibition against the power of any State to discriminate, as do most of them, between aliens and citizens, between artificial persons, called corporations, and natural persons, in the right to hold real estate? If it be granted that Congress can repeal all State laws discriminating between whites and blacks in the subjects covered by this bill, why, it may be asked, may not Congress repeal in the same way all State laws discriminating between the two races on the subjects of suffrage and office? If Congress can declare by law who shall hold lands, who shall testify, who shall have capacity to make a contract in a State, then Congress can by law also declare who, without regard to color or race, shall have the right to sit as a juror or as a judge, to hold any office, and, finally, to vote "in every State and Territory of the United States." As respects the Territories, they come within the power of Congress, for as to them the lawmaking power is the Federal power; but as to the States no similar provision exists vesting in Congress the power "to make rules and regulations" for them.

The object of the second section of the bill is to afford discriminating protection to colored persons in the full enjoyment of all the rights secured to them by the preceding section * * *.This provision of the bill seems to be unnecessary, as adequate judicial remedies could be adopted to secure the desired end without invading the immunities of legislators, always important to be preserved in the interest of public liberty; without assailing the independence of the judiciary, always essential to the preservation of individual rights; and without impairing the efficiency of ministerial officers, always necessary for the maintenance of public peace and order. The remedy proposed by this section seems to be in this respect not only anomalous, but unconstitutional; for the Constitution guarantees nothing with certainty if it does not insure to the several States the right of making and executing laws in regard to all matters arising within their jurisdiction, subject only to the restriction that in cases of conflict with the Constitution and constitutional laws of the United States the latter should be held to be the supreme law of the land * * *.

In all our history, in all our experience as people living under Federal and State law, no such system as that contemplated by the details of this bill has ever before been proposed or adopted. They establish for the security of the colored race safeguards which go infinitely beyond any that the General Government has ever provided for the white race. In fact, the distinction of race and color is by the bill made to operate in favor of the colored and against the white race. They interfere with the municipal legislation of the States, with the relations existing exclusively between a State and its citizens, or between inhabitants of the same State—an absorption and assumption of power by the General Government which, if acquiesced in, must sap and destroy our federative system of limited powers and break down the barriers which preserve the rights of the States. It is another step, or rather stride, toward centralization and the concentration of all legislative powers in the National Government. The tendency of the bill must be to resuscitate the spirit of rebellion and to arrest the progress of those influences which are more closely drawing around the States the bonds of union and peace * * *.

ANDREW JOHNSON.

NOTES AND QUESTIONS

1. Congress passed the Civil Rights Act of 1866 into law over President Johnson's veto. This marked the first time in American history that an important law was adopted by overriding a presidential veto.

2. Senator Charles Sumner explained how the Civil Rights Act of 1866 enforced the Thirteenth Amendment in the following terms:

> You have, sir, decreed that colored persons shall enjoy the same civil rights as white persons; in other words, that, with regard to civil rights, there shall be no Oligarchy, Aristocracy, Caste, or Monopoly, but that all shall be equal before the law without distinction of color. And this great decree you have made as "appropriate legislation" under the Constitutional Amendment "to enforce" the abolition of slavery.

CONG. GLOBE, 39th Cong., 1st Sess. 684 (1866).

3. Consider the following speech from Rep. William Lawrence, given two days before Congress overrode President Johnson's veto of the Civil Rights Act of 1866:

> * * * I will again perform the proudest act of my political life in voting to make this bill the law of the land.
>
> It is scarcely less to the people of this country than Magna Charta was to the people of England.
>
> It declares who are citizens.
>
> It does not affect any political right, as that of suffrage, the right to sit on juries, hold office, &c. This is leaves to the states to be determined by each for itself. It does not confer any civil right, but so far as there is any power in the States to limit, enlarge, or declare civil rights, all these are left to the States.
>
> But it does provide as to certain enumerated civil rights every citizen "shall have the same right in every State and Territory." That is whatever of certain civil rights may be enjoyed by any shall be shared by all citizens in each State, and in the Territories, and these are:
>
> 1. To make and enforce contracts.
>
> 2. To sue, to be sued, and to be parties.
>
> 3. To give evidence.
>
> 4. To inherit, purchase, lease, sell, hold, and convey real and personal property.
>
> 5. To be entitled to full and equal benefit of all laws and proceedings for the security of person and property.
>
> * * *
>
> There is * * * a national citizenship. And citizenship implies certain rights which are to be protected, and imposes the duty of allegiance and obedience to the laws * * *.
>
> It has never been deemed necessary to enact in any constitution or law that citizens should have the right to life or liberty or the right to acquire property. Those rights are recognized by the Constitution as existing anterior to and independently of all laws and all constitutions.
>
> Without further authority I may assume, then, that there are certain absolute rights which pertain to every citizen * * *. [N]ot only are these rights inherent and indestructible, but the means whereby they may be possessed and enjoyed are equally so.
>
> We learn from Coke that—
>
> "Where the law granted anything to anyone that also is granted without which the thing itself cannot be." *Oath before the Justices,* 12 *Co.* 130, *Heard v. Pierce,* 8 *Cush.* 338–345.
>
> In law the incident always adheres to and accompanies the princip[al].
>
> It is idle to say that a citizen shall have the right to life, yet to deny him the right to labor, whereby alone he can live. It is a mockery to say that a citizen may have a right to live, and yet deny him the right to make a contract to secure the privileges and rewards of labor. It is worse than mockery to say that men may be clothed by the national authority with the character of citizens, yet may be stripped by State authority of the means by which citizens may exist.

* * *

It is barbarous, inhuman, infamous, to turn over four million liberated slaves, always loyal to the Government, to the fury of their rebel masters, who deny them the benefit of all laws for the protection of their civil rights * * *.

* * *

Congress has the incidental power to enforce and protect the equal enjoyment in the States of civil rights which are inherent in national citizenship.

CONG. GLOBE, 39th Cong, 1st Sess. 1832–35 (1866).

4. Numerous newspaper articles and editorials in 1866—enough to fill up twenty-five pages of a law review article, *see* Steven G. Calabresi & Andrea Matthews, *Originalism and* Loving v. Virginia, 2012 B.Y.U. L. REV. 1393, 1437–63—further illustrated the public understanding of the Civil Rights Act of 1866. The columns, both pro and con, show that "the interpretation of the Act as conferring the same common law civil rights on all citizens without regard to race was broadly accepted across the country. *Id.* at 1437. Consider, for example, the following article from *The New York Tribune* on February 5, 1867:

> Mr. Trumbull's two bills—to enlarge the powers of the Freedmen's Bureau, and to protect all the American People in their natural civil rights—are notoriously demanded by and adapted to our existing state of facts. If the laws and usages of the Southern States were just and equal, they would be superfluous. They are needed simply because at the South a Black man, solely because he is Black, is denied the common rights of human beings—is treated as having no rights that Whites are bound to respect. The laws of the South, and still more the dominant opinion and spirit of the South, treat the Blacks as brutes rather than men. All this will pass away; but meantime, a good many of the humbler race will be starved or lashed to death, unless Congress shall protect them. This, and nothing more, is what Mr. Trumbull's bills aim to do—what they seem admirably calculated to do; and Congress is not merely justified in passing them—it could not fail to do so without a gross and cruel violation of public faith.

The *Chicago Tribune* celebrated the passage of the Civil Rights Act of 1866 over President Andrew Johnson's veto, saying on April 8, 1866:

> The Southern Legislature can[not] now enact that a colored man shall not own real or personal property, shall not work at any mechanical trade, shall not learn to read, shall not have a house, shall not leave his employer's premises without a pass, shall be subject to corporal punishment at the hands of his "master" or any other of those oppressive and mischievous laws by which the Southern Legislatures have already attempted to re-enslave the three millions which Abraham Lincoln and our Union armies made free. Every member of a Legislature who votes for a law, and every judge or officer who enforces one which operates any differently on a black man than it does upon a white, is liable to a fine of one thousand dollars and a term of imprisonment. Colored men born in this country are henceforth citizens of the United States and their respective states and are to be so regarded.
>
> The achievement of this great triumph sent a thrill of satisfaction and relief throughout the hearts of the entire loyal people. We breathed freer, on learning that at last the law-making power, the supreme legislature of the

country has asserted its own rights, and vindicated the cause of liberty, and that an effectual check is at least imposed on the President, who has all the arbitrary disposition of a Napoleon without his capacity to respond to the progressive instincts of the people.

There is no reasonable doubt as what the reasonable public understanding was of the Civil Rights Act of 1866. It banned race discrimination as to all common law rights throughout the United States.

B. THE DRAFTING OF THE FOURTEENTH AMENDMENT

Congress was concerned after President Johnson's veto of the Civil Rights Act of 1866 that the Supreme Court might strike the Act down as being unconstitutional. Moreover, members of Congress were equally concerned that some future Democratic Congress dominated by Southerners might repeal the Civil Rights Act of 1866. Finally, Congress wanted to apply its anti-discrimination command not only to state common law rights, but also to state statutory and constitutional law rights, *i.e.*, to all civil rights, known as privileges or immunities, of both state and federal citizenship. As a result, Congress set about drafting what became the Fourteenth Amendment to the Constitution.

The task of drafting a new amendment was turned over to The Joint Committee on Reconstruction, which was established by Congress on December 13, 1865 to determine what the seceded Southern States needed to do before they could regain their membership in Congress. This Committee both drafted the Fourteenth Amendment and established a rule that no formerly Confederate State would be allowed to seat delegates in the Senate or the House of Representatives unless that State ratified the Fourteenth Amendment. Representative Thaddeus Stevens of Pennsylvania and Senator William P. Fessenden of Maine served as co-chairmen. The committee had nine members from the House of Representatives and six from the Senate. Members of the Joint Committee who played an especially important role included, in addition to the co-chairmen, Senators Jacob Howard and Reverdy Johnson and Representatives John Bingham, Roscoe Conkling, and George Boutwell. The Joint Committee produced a report that was signed by twelve of the Committee's fifteen members, and Senator Howard gave an especially long and detailed speech on the floor of the Senate explaining the meaning of the new Fourteenth Amendment. Thaddeus Stevens, the House Co-Chair of the Joint Committee on Reconstruction, and Representative John Bingham served together on a subcommittee in January 1866, which proposed two amendments that failed: one giving Congress the unqualified power to secure equal rights, privileges, and protections for all citizens; the other explicitly annulling all racially discriminatory laws.

The Joint Committee's first full proposal to both Houses of Congress would have denied all representation in Congress to any State that denied its citizens the right to vote. This proposal passed the House but was defeated in the Senate. The Committee then proposed an amendment with the following language: "The Congress shall have power to make all laws which shall be necessary and proper to secure to the citizens of each State all privileges and immunities of citizens in the several States, and to all persons in the several States equal protection in the rights of life, liberty, and property." This proposal was rejected by the House of Representatives. It shows, however, the early interest in protecting all civil rights, called privileges and immunities of state citizenship, borrowing that language from Article IV, Section 2 of the original Constitution and from Article IV of the Articles of Confederation. The House rejected this proposal because it merely empowered Congress to protect civil rights. The Reconstruction Congress wanted more than just the power to pass the Civil Rights Act of 1866. It wanted to write the Act or something even broader into the text of the Constitution itself. It wanted the federal courts as well as Congress to be empowered to enforce civil rights, thus providing a double security.

The Joint Committee then in April 1866 submitted a draft of what eventually grew into the Fourteenth Amendment. The Joint Committee draft read as follows:

> Section 1. No discrimination shall be made by any state, nor by the United States, as to the civil rights of persons because of race, color, or previous condition of servitude.
>
> Section 2. From and after the fourth day of July, in the year one thousand eight hundred and seventy-six, no discrimination shall be made by any state, nor by the United States, as to the enjoyment by classes of persons of the right of suffrage, because of race, color, or previous condition of servitude.
>
> Section 3. Until the fourth day of July, one thousand eight hundred and seventy-six, no class of persons, as to the right of any of whom to suffrage discrimination shall be made by any state, shall be included in the basis of representation.

BENJ. B. KENDRICK, THE JOURNAL OF THE JOINT COMMITTEE OF FIFTEEN ON RECONSTRUCTION 83–84 (1914).

"This version obviously differed from the Fourteenth Amendment as we know it today in important ways. Most obviously, it was confined to prohibiting only race discrimination. The narrow scope of this proposed race discrimination version of the Fourteenth Amendment caused the draft to be rejected both by members of Congress * * * who wanted to prohibit all forms of caste and by members * * * who wanted to protect the rights of white Unionists in the South and to refer to race obliquely." Steven G. Calabresi & Julia T. Rickert, *Originalism and Sex Discrimination*, 90 TEX. L. REV. 1, 32 (2011). A new version of Section 1 was then introduced by Thaddeus Stevens on April 30, 1866, and it dropped the words "race" and "color." Its meaning was explained in most detail by Senator Howard (emphasis added):

> The last two clauses of the first section of the amendment disable a State from depriving not merely a citizen of the United States, but any person, whoever he may be of life, liberty, or property without due process of law, or from denying him the equal protection of the laws of the State. *This abolishes all class legislation in the States and does away with the injustice of subjecting one caste of persons to a code not applicable to another.*

CONG. GLOBE, 39th Cong., 1st Sess. 2766 (1866). Senator Elliot explained the meaning of the revised Section 1 in similar terms:

> I support the first sections because the doctrine it declares is right, and if, under the Constitution as it now stands, Congress has not the power to prohibit * * * State legislation discriminating against classes of citizens or

> depriving persons of life, liberty, or property without due process of law, or denying to any persons within the State the equal protection of the laws, then, in my judgment, such power should distinctly be conferred.

This understanding of Section 1 as banning all class legislation was discussed at length, but it was not contested. Suggestions that Section 1 protected only black people were explicitly rejected. Those who opposed the Amendment did not dispute the idea that it prohibited class legislation; they simply were unabashedly in favor of class legislation.

C. THE FINAL TEXT OF THE FOURTEENTH AMENDMENT

It is time now to examine the final language of the Fourteenth Amendment as it was transmitted to the States on June 18, 1866. The Amendment contains five sections, and it is necessary to parse all of them carefully to understand the Fourteenth Amendment's original public meaning. One overarching point that might be made is that the meaning of the Fourteenth Amendment to the members of the Joint Committee on Reconstruction, which shaped it, is peculiarly important because the eleven formerly Confederate States were obliged by the Joint Committee on Reconstruction to ratify the Amendment *as the Joint Committee understood it* as a condition for resuming representation in the House and Senate. The congressional legislative history is thus much more indicative of original public meaning of the Fourteenth Amendment than would be the case with the legislative history of the twenty-six other constitutional amendments. That being said, let us now proceed through the five sections of the Fourteenth Amendment.

Section 1.

> **All persons born or naturalized in the United States, and subject to the jurisdiction thereof, are citizens of the United States and of the state wherein they reside. No state shall make or enforce any law which shall abridge the privileges or immunities of citizens of the United States; nor shall any state deprive any person of life, liberty, or property, without due process of law; nor deny to any person within its jurisdiction the equal protection of the laws.**

The first sentence of the Fourteenth amendment overturns *Dred Scott v. Sandford* by providing for birthright national citizenship (and residence-based state citizenship) in the United States. This sentence is called "The Citizenship Clause." It provides for one of the most liberal citizenship rules of any constitutional democracy in existence today, and Congress has power to enforce these citizenship guarantees if it so chooses. In addition, Justice Harlan argued in his dissent in the *Civil Rights Cases* that the Citizenship Clause confers birthright *equality* on all American citizens, who are all born equal to one another. *See supra* pages 853–860. There can be no preferred classes or castes of citizens under the Citizenship Clause, according to Justice Harlan's dissent.

The second sentence of Section 1 says: "No state shall make or enforce any law which shall abridge the privileges or immunities of citizens of the United States." This makes it doubly clear that the States cannot override the Citizenship Clause's guarantee of equal citizenship by creating favored castes or classes of people. The phrase "privileges or immunities" is a synonym for civil rights and is borrowed from the Privileges and Immunities Clause of Article IV, Section 2 and from the Privileges and Immunities Clause of Article IV of the Articles of Confederation. That latter provision extended equal privileges and immunities of citizenship to "all free inhabitants" of the thirteen States. The words clearly hearken back to the idea of banning special or class legislation. Whatever privileges or immunities exist for some citizens must exist in the same way and to the same degree for all citizens, without favoritism. The sentence is addressed to all institutions of the state governments, whether legislative, executive, or judicial, as it forbids States either to "make" (enact by legislation) or "enforce" (carry into effect through executive or judicial action) special or partial laws. This is an enormously powerful clause, but its scope is limited to civil rights rather than political rights. The analogous Article IV Clause, from 1788, forbids the States from discriminating against out-of-state citizens as to civil rights but not as to political rights like the right to vote or to serve on a jury, and it is clear that "privileges or immunities" as used in Section 1 is similarly limited. Notice that the clause does not merely forbid States to "deny" privileges or immunities but says that States shall not "abridge" them. This is a much broader term than "deny." *Webster's Dictionary* in 1828 defined "abridge" as "2. To lessen; to diminish; as to abridge labor; to abridge power or rights * * *." The "same" rights but in lesser amounts do not satisfy Section 1. Hence, the Black Codes "abridged" the privilege or immunities of African-Americans by lessening them from those enjoyed by white Americans. As a matter of original meaning, this is why the Privileges or Immunities Clause is at the heart of the Fourteenth Amendment.

The second sentence of Section 1 also says in its second clause that: "No State shall * * * deprive any person of life, liberty, or property, without due process of law." This is actually the toughest portion of the Fourteenth Amendment to decipher as a matter of original meaning. It is quite clear what the equivalent phrase means in the Fifth Amendment with respect to the federal government: it establishes that executive and judicial deprivations of rights can take place only in accordance with pre-existing law and must follow traditional procedural forms for such action (and Congress is limited in its ability to alter those procedural forms). In the Fifth Amendment, "due process of law" is essentially a restatement and codification of the Constitution's separations and enumerations of power. *See* Nathan S. Chapman & Michael W. McConnell, *Due Process as Separation of Powers,* 121 YALE L.J. 1672 (2012); Gary Lawson, *Take the Fifth . . . Please! The Original Insignificance of the Fifth Amendment's Due Process of Law Clause,* 2017 B.Y.U. L. REV. 611. By the time we get to 1868, however, it is much less clear that the term "due process of law" had this, or any other specific, meaning. The separation-and-enumeration meaning of the Fifth Amendment makes no sense in the context of state governments, which are not governments of enumerated powers and which do not need to conform to the Constitution's unique scheme for a separation of powers. As a matter of doctrine rather than original meaning, as you will see in the rest of this chapter, the Fourteenth Amendment's Due Process of Law Clause has become the Supreme Court's chosen vehicle for a wide range of legal doctrines, some of which are grounded in the principle of legality represented by the Fifth Amendment, some of which are better placed elsewhere in the Fourteenth Amendment, and some of which are hard to place anywhere in the Constitution. It has also become a font of procedural requirements for executive action, which modern courts have read as well into the Fifth Amendment. The details of this doctrine of "procedural due process," as it is often called, are generally left to courses in Administrative Law. *See* GARY LAWSON, FEDERAL ADMINISTRATIVE LAW 875–1002 (8th ed. 2019).

The third and final clause in the second sentence of Section1 of the Fourteenth Amendment provides: "No State shall * * * deny to any person within its jurisdiction the equal protection of the laws." The noun in this clause is "protection," and "equal" is only an adjective. The modern Supreme Court has read this clause as the main limit on state legislatures in passing discriminatory laws, though the Framers of the Fourteenth Amendment thought that that role should be played by the Privileges or Immunities Clause, which directly addresses the "making" of laws. The Equal Protection Clause, in contrast, does not address the "making" of laws, but instead it discusses the "protection" afforded to persons of facially neutral laws that are already on the books—like state laws against murder and assault and rape.

What then is the original function of the "equal *protection* clause"? Its purpose was to ensure that freed African-Americans in the South, or Northerners in the South, got the "same protection" against private violence that white Southerners got from their police departments, fire departments, prosecutors, and state judges as to neutrally-worded laws that were already enacted. The Equal Protection Clause was meant to convey the right in the Civil Rights Act of 1866 that "citizens of every race and color [shall receive the] * * * full and equal benefit of all laws and proceedings for the security of person and property, *as is enjoyed by white citizens*, and shall be subject to like punishment, pains, and penalties, and to none other, any law, statute, ordinance, regulation, or custom, to the contrary notwithstanding." Importantly, this is a positive entitlement to governmental or state action. It is not a negative liberty against government, as is most of the Constitution, but it is instead an affirmative right to be protected by the criminal law, tort law, and other bodies of law protective of rights. States most emphatically can violate the Equal Protection Clause by sitting by and doing nothing when the Equal Protection Clause compels them to act.

Section 2 of the Fourteenth Amendment is now essentially moot, but in 1868 it was very important. It provides (with emphasis added):

> **Representatives shall be apportioned among the several states according to their respective numbers, counting the whole number of persons in each state, excluding Indians not taxed. But when the right to vote at any election for the choice of electors for President and Vice President of the United States, Representatives in Congress, the executive and judicial officers of a state, or the members of the legislature thereof, is denied to any of the *male* inhabitants of such state, being twenty-one years of age, and citizens of the United States, or in any way abridged, except for participation in rebellion, or other crime, the basis of representation therein shall be reduced in the proportion which the number of such *male* citizens shall bear to the whole number of *male* citizens twenty-one years of age in such state.**

Section 2 penalizes a State for not giving voting rights to, for example, its African-American men of voting age by taking away seats in the House of Representatives and votes in the Electoral College in proportion to the degree of discrimination. The ratification of the Fifteenth Amendment in 1870, which flatly forbids States—and the federal government—from discriminating by race with respect to voting, rendered this clause pointless in practice (though in theory there could still be non-race-based discrimination that might implicate this provision).

Section 2 infuriated the leaders of the Womens' Suffrage movement, who had been staunch allies of the Abolitionists, because it inserted the word "male" into the Constitution in the only three places where it remains today. (We read the male pronouns in the Constitution today as being generic rather than sex-specific, although it is not clear that they were always so read prior to the enactment of the Nineteenth Amendment giving women the right to vote. The use of the word "male" in the Fourteenth Amendment, by contrast, is sex-specific as to voting rights.) Section 2 also makes it clear that Section 1 of the Fourteenth Amendment is only about civil rights and not about the political right to vote. By the same token, Section 1 is not at all sex-specific.

Section 3 of the Fourteenth Amendment provides as follows:

> **No person shall be a Senator or Representative in Congress, or elector of President and Vice President, or hold any office, civil or military, under the United States, or under any state, who, having previously taken an oath, as a member of Congress, or as an officer of the United States, or as a member of any state legislature, or as an executive or judicial officer of any state, to support the Constitution of the United States, shall have engaged in insurrection or rebellion against the same, or given aid or comfort to the enemies thereof. But Congress may by a vote of two-thirds of each House, remove such disability.**

This provision—which one scholar says "was the most controversial of the sections of the Fourteenth Amendment," Paul Moreno, *Disqualification for Rebellion, in* THE HERITAGE GUIDE TO THE CONSTITUTION 518 (2d ed. 2014)—was a response to public fury in the North over, for example, the election of Alexander Stephens, the Vice President of the Confederacy, to a seat in the House of Representatives only months after the Civil War's end. Congress ended up by a two-thirds vote allowing most former rebel traitors to serve in public office, especially after the end of Reconstruction in 1877.

Section 4 of the Fourteenth Amendment provides as follows:

> **The validity of the public debt of the United States, authorized by law, including debts incurred for payment of pensions and bounties for services in suppressing insurrection or rebellion, shall not be questioned. But neither the United States nor any state shall assume or pay any debt or obligation incurred in aid of insurrection or rebellion against the United States, or any claim for the loss or emancipation of any slave; but all such debts, obligations and claims shall be held illegal and void.**

This provision was uncontroversial, since the Union's war debts would obviously be paid and the rebel States' war debts would obviously not be paid. Nor was there by this time any question of paying slave owners just compensation for the loss of their slaves. The Civil War had settled all of that.

Finally, and very importantly, Section 5 of the Fourteenth amendment says that: "t]he Congress shall have power to enforce, by appropriate legislation, the provisions of this article." We have elsewhere explored the meaning of, and caselaw under, this provision at some length. *See supra* pages 842–898. At some point, you should briefly review that material before plunging much further into this chapter.

D. RATIFICATION

Once the Fourteenth Amendment was submitted to the States for ratification on June 18, 1866, there was a wild political campaign both for and against the amendment during the midterm elections of 1866. President Andrew Johnson had broken with the moderate wing of the Republican Party in Congress when he vetoed the Civil Rights Act of 1866. Johnson was a Democrat from Tennessee who was a racist. But he was the only Southern Senator to support the Union during the Civil War, so when it looked like President Lincoln might lose his bid for re-election, Lincoln added Johnson to his unity ticket as a running mate, replacing his first Vice President, Hannibal Hamlin of Maine. President Johnson decided to go all out in opposing ratification. He launched a "Swing Around the Circle" speaking tour, which included speeches in Chicago, St. Louis, Indianapolis, and Columbus, where he made a complete fool of himself. He nationalized the mid-term elections, which resulted in a landslide victory for the Republican Party and, indirectly, complete public support for the ratification of the Fourteenth Amendment. The Republicans increased their two-thirds majority in Congress and made plans to make Reconstruction much tougher on the South.

The public understanding of the Fourteenth Amendment was both reflected and shaped by the debates mentioned above. Two prominent statements appear below:

Report to the U.S. Senate by Senator Jacob Howard

who presented the Joint Committee's Amendment to the Senate on May 23, 1866

One result of [the joint committee's] investigations has been the joint resolutions for the amendment of the Constitution of the United States now under consideration * * *. The first section of the amendment they have submitted for the consideration of the two houses relates to the privileges and immunities of citizens of the several States, and to the rights and privileges of all persons, whether citizens or others, under the laws of the United States * * *.

It will be observed that this is a general prohibition on the States, as such, from abridging the privileges and immunities of the citizens of the United States. That is its first clause, and I regard it as very important * * *. The first clause of this section relates to the privileges and immunities of citizens of the United States * * *. It is not, perhaps, very easy to define with accuracy what is meant by the expression, "citizen of the United States," although that expression appears twice in the Constitution * * *. A citizen of the United States is held by the courts to be a person who was born within the limits of the United States and was subject to their laws. Before the adoption of the Constitution of the United States, the citizens of each States were, in a qualified sense at least, aliens to one another * * *. With a view to * * * put the citizens of the several States on an equality with each other as to all fundamental rights, a clause was introduced into the Constitution declaring that "the citizens of each State shall be entitled to all privileges and immunities of citizens in the several States."

The effect of this clause was to constitutionalize *ipso facto* the citizens of each one of the original States citizens of the United States * * *. They are, by constitutional right, entitled to these privileges and immunities, and may assert this right and these privileges and immunities, and ask for their enforcement whenever they go within the limits of the several States of the Union.

It would be a curious question to solve what are the privileges and immunities of citizens of each of the States in the several States * * *. I am not aware that the Supreme Court have ever undertaken to define either the nature or extent of the privileges and immunities thus guarantied * * *. But we may gather some intimation of what probably will be the opinion of the judiciary by referring to [*Corfield v. Coryell, see supra* pages 908–909, which Senator Howard quotes at length] * * *.

* * * To these privileges and immunities, whatever they may be—for they are not and cannot be fully defined in their entire extent and precise nature—to these should be added the personal rights guarantied and secured by the first eight amendments of the Constitution: such as the freedom of speech and of the press; the right of the people to peaceably assemble and petition for redress of grievances, a right appertaining to each and all the people; the right to keep and bear arms; the right to be exempted from the quartering of soldiers in a house without the consent of the owner; the right to be exempt from unreasonable searches and seizures;, and from any search or seizure except by virtue of a warrant issued upon a formal oath or affidavit; the right of an accused person to be informed of the nature of the accusations against him, and his right to be tried by an impartial jury of the vicinage; and also the right to be secure against excessive bail and against cruel and unusual punishments.

Now, sir, here is a mass of privileges, immunities, and rights, some of them secured by the second section of the fourth article of the Constitution, which I have recited, some by the first eight amendments of the Constitution; and it is a fact well worthy of attention that the course of decision of our courts and the present settled doctrine is, that all these immunities, privileges, rights, thus guaranteed by the Constitution * * * do not operate in the slightest degree as a restraint or prohibition upon State legislation * * *.

* * * The great object of the first section of * * * [the Fourteenth Amendment] is, therefore, to restrain the power of the States and compel them at all times to respect these great fundamental guarantees.

Speaker of the House of Representatives, Schuyler Colfax on the Fourteenth Amendment

Speech in Indianapolis, Indiana, August 7, 1866, reprinted in Cincinnati Commercial Speeches of the Campaign of 1866: In the States of Ohio, Indiana, and Kentucky 14 (1866)

The first section of this constitutional amendment * * * is going to be the gem of the Constitution * * *. I will tell you why I love it. It is because it is the Declaration of Independence placed immutably and forever in our Constitution. What does the Declaration of Independence say?—that baptismal vow that our fathers took upon their lips when this Republic of ours was born into the family of nations. It says that all men are created equal, and are endowed by their Creator with certain inalienable rights, among which are life, liberty, and the pursuit of happiness; *and that to secure these rights governments were instituted among men*. That is the paramount object of government, to secure the right of all men to equality before the law. So said our fathers at the beginning of the Revolution. So say their sons today, in this Constitutional Amendment. It declares that every person—every man, every woman, every child, born under our flag, or naturalized under our laws, shall have a birthright in this land of ours. High or low, rich or humble, learned or unlearned, distinguished or obscure, white or black, born in a palatial residence or born in the humblest cabin in the land, this great Government says "the *aegis* of protection is over you; you can look up to this flag and your country, and say they are yours * * *.

But they shudderingly say, on the other side, 'This is going to protect a n***** as a citizen. Who is it that most needs protection from the law in this land? It is not the rich man; it is not the man of great intellect; it is not the influential man; but it is the weak and obscure man; it is the down-trodden, the degraded and the oppressed; and the glory of a free land is that it will stretch out its arm and protect the obscurest man under its flag * * *.

E. THE FIFTEENTH AMENDMENT

Once Ulysses S. Grant assumed the presidency, he pushed very hard for a constitutional amendment allowing African-American men to vote. After all, at the end of the war, twenty percent of the Union Army consisted of African-American soldiers, and it was offensive for those who fought to save the Union to be disenfranchised on account of their race. In 1870, the Fifteenth Amendment was adopted, giving African-American men equal political rights with white men. (Voting rights for women would take another half-century.) The Fifteenth Amendment provides:

> **Section 1: The right of citizens of the United States to vote shall not be denied or abridged by the United States or by any state on account of race, color, or previous condition of servitude.**
>
> **Section 2: The Congress shall have power to enforce this article by appropriate legislation.**

[Assignment 57]

IV. THE EARLY EVISCERATION OF THE CIVIL RIGHTS ACT OF 1866 AND OF THE FOURTEENTH AMENDMENT

If one tried in 1870 to discern the original meaning of the Reconstruction Amendments, one would at the very least see (1) a prohibition of slavery and all of its incidents and badges, (2) a broad grant of national citizenship with all of its incidents, including equal civil rights for all social castes or classes of people, that go along with federal and state citizenship, (3) a flat prohibition on race discrimination in voting rights, (4) protection of all civil rights against partial or special state enactment or enforcement of laws that make those state common law, statutory, or constitutional rights differentially available to different classes of persons, (5) guarantees against state discriminatory enforcement of all laws providing for protection of rights against either state or private interference, and (6) very broad congressional power to enforce all of these principles by "appropriate," *i.e.* reasonable, legislation. One conceivably could find even more in these provisions. Perhaps one could read the Due Process of Law Clause as a prohibition on state action that is arbitrary, even if it is not describable as discriminatory. Perhaps one could think, as Senator Howard thought, that Section 1 of the Fourteenth Amendment effectively overruled *Barron v. Baltimore* and made the first eight amendments applicable to the States, so that the "privileges or immunities" that States cannot abridge involve more than just state common law rights. One thing is certain: You would know in 1870 that the U.S. constitutional order had been dramatically changed. You would know that the relationship of the States to the federal government had been fundamentally altered. You would know that the role of the federal government in policing discrimination had been extraordinarily enhanced.

To someone who knows all—or even many—of these things in 1870, the next few decades of Supreme Court decisions borders on being incomprehensible. To put it bluntly (and at the risk of violating principles of editorial neutrality): The Supreme Court in the 1870s eviscerated the Thirteenth and Fourteenth Amendments by reading them so narrowly that they did not accomplish almost any of the things they were supposed to accomplish. The effects of some of those decisions are still with us today, and they have profoundly shaped (or, in some cases, mis-shaped) the development of 150 years of Supreme Court doctrine. To understand the caselaw that we now have, you need to understand the caselaw that the early Supreme Court invented—and, more importantly, the aspects of the originally intended meaning of the Reconstruction Amendments which the Supreme Court nipped in the bud and has never respected. Obviously, decisions can be overruled, but once doctrine has moved as far down certain paths as Fourteenth Amendment doctrine has travelled, undoing the past is not as simple as it might sound. Keep these cases in mind when we get to modern law. Try to see how current law is molded—sometimes openly, sometimes subtly—by decisions made just a few years after the Civil War.

The first case involves interpretation of a provision of the Civil Rights Act of 1866, whose constitutionality was not subject to question after ratification of the Fourteenth Amendment, giving federal courts jurisdiction over "all causes, civil and criminal, affecting persons who are denied, or cannot enforce in the courts or judicial tribunals of the State, or locality, where they may be, any of the rights secured to them by the first section of the act." Consider as you read the case whether the Fourteenth Amendment itself might have been relevant to its proper disposition. Why did the majority not even mention the Fourteenth Amendment? Was the Thirteenth Amendment implicated?

A. BLYEW V. UNITED STATES

80 U.S. (13 Wall.) 581 (1871)

* * *

* * * [T]wo persons, Blyew and Kennard, were indicted October 7th, 1868, in the [federal] Circuit Court for the District of Kentucky, for the murder, on the 29th of August preceding, within that district, of a colored woman named Lucy Armstrong. The indictment contained three counts, all of them charging the murder in the usual form of indictments for that offence, and with sufficient certainty. But, in order to show jurisdiction in the Circuit Court of the United States, an averment was made in the first court that the said Lucy Armstrong was a citizen of the United States, having been born therein, and not subject to any foreign power; that she was of the African race, and was above the age of seventy-five years; that Blyew and Kennard (the persons indicted) were white persons, each of them at the time of the alleged killing and murder above the age of eighteen years; that the said killing and murder,

done and committed, as averred, were seen and witnessed by one Richard Foster, and one Laura Foster, citizens of the United States, having been born therein and not subject to any foreign power, both of the African race; and that the said Lucy Armstrong, Richard Foster, and Laura Foster were then and there denied the right to testify against the said Blyew and Kennard, or either of them, concerning the said killing and murder, in the courts and judicial tribunals of the State of Kentucky, solely on account of their race and color. The second and third counts contained substantially the same averments.

* * * [A] verdict of guilty having been returned, a motion was made in arrest of judgment, which the court also overruled. The ground alleged for this motion was, that "the facts stated in the indictment did not constitute a public offence within the jurisdiction of the court."

There were thus three questions presented by the record:

First. Whether the Circuit Court had jurisdiction of the offence charged in the indictment?

Second. Whether the court erred in sustaining the demurrer to the defendants' special plea?

Third. Whether the evidence to which the defendants objected should have been received?

Of course, if the first question was resolved in the negative, any resolution of the remaining ones became unnecessary.

* * *

The murder for which the defendants were convicted, and as they now sought to show illegally, had been one of peculiar atrocity. A number of witnesses testified that on a summer evening of 1868 (August 29th), towards eleven o'clock, at the cabin of a colored man named Jack Foster, there were found the dead bodies of the said Jack, of Sallie Foster, his wife, and of Lucy Armstrong, for the murder of whom Blyew and Kennard stood convicted; this person, a blind woman, over ninety years old, and the mother of Mrs. Foster; all persons of color; their bodies yet warm. Lucy Armstrong was wounded in the head; her head cut open as with a broad-axe. Jack Foster and Sallie, his wife, were cut in several places, almost to pieces. Richard Foster, a son of Jack, who was in his seventeenth year, was found about two hundred yards from the house of his father, at the house of a Mr. Nichols, whither he had crawled from the house of his father, mortally wounded by an instrument corresponding to one used in the killing of Lucy Armstrong, Jack and Sallie Foster. He died two days afterwards from the effects of his wounds aforesaid, having made a dying declaration tending to fix the crime on Blyew and Kennard. Two young children, girls, one aged ten years and the other thirteen (this last, the Laura Foster above mentioned), asleep in a trundle-bed, escaped, and the latter was a witness on the trial.

Evidence was produced on the part of the United States, that a short time previous to the murder, Kennard was heard to declare, in presence of Blyew, "that he (Kennard) thought there would soon be another war about the n*****s; that when it did come he intended to go to killing n*****s, and he was not sure that he would not begin his work of killing them before the war should actually commence."

Such a case, and the withdrawal of it from the State courts, naturally excited great interest throughout the State of Kentucky, and by a joint resolution of the General Assembly of that State, passed at its adjourned session in 1869, the governor of the State was directed to cause the commonwealth above mentioned to be represented in this court. Being brought here the case was very fully and interestingly argued; the point to which counsel here addressed themselves chiefly being the one already stated as the first one presented by the record, the point of the jurisdiction of the Circuit Court.

* * *

■ MR. JUSTICE STRONG delivered the opinion of the court.

Addressing ourselves to the first of the questions presented by the record—the question of jurisdiction—it may be remarked that clearly the Circuit Court had no jurisdiction of the crime of murder committed within the district of Kentucky, unless it was conferred by the third section of the [Civil Rights] act of Congress of April 9th, 1866 [giving federal courts jurisdiction "of all causes, civil and criminal, affecting persons who are denied, or cannot enforce in the courts or judicial tribunals of the State, or locality, where they may be, any of the rights secured to them by the first section of the act"].

It must be admitted that the crimes and offences of which the District Courts are, by this section, given exclusive jurisdiction, are only those which are against the provisions of the act, or those enumerated in the second and sixth sections * * *. They are described as causes "affecting persons who are denied, or cannot enforce in the courts of judicial tribunals of the State, or locality, where they may be, any of the rights secured to them by the first section of the act."

Was, then, the prosecution, or indictment, against these defendants a cause affecting any such person or persons? If it was, then by the provisions of the act it was within the jurisdiction of the court, and if it was not, that court had no jurisdiction.

It was, the record shows, an indictment for the murder of Lucy Armstrong, a citizen of the United States of the African race, and it contained an averment that other citizens of the United States of the same race, witnessed the alleged murder. It contained also an averment that those other persons, namely, Richard Foster and Laura Foster, as well as the deceased Lucy Armstrong, were, on account of their race and color, denied the right to testify against the defendants, or either of them, of and concerning the killing and murder, in the courts and judicial tribunals of the State of Kentucky.

We are thus brought to the question whether a criminal prosecution for a public offence is a cause "affecting," within the meaning of the act of Congress, persons who may be called to testify therein. Obviously the only parties to such a cause are the government and the persons indicted. They alone can be reached by any judgment that may be pronounced. No judgment can either enlarge or diminish the personal, relative, or property rights of any others than those who are parties. It is true there are some cases which may affect the rights of property of persons who are not parties to the record. Such cases, however, are all of a civil nature, and none of them even touch rights of person. But an indictment prosecuted by the government against an alleged criminal, is a cause in which none but the parties can have any concern, except what is common to all the members of the community. Those who may possibly be witnesses, either for the prosecution or for the defence, are no more affected by it than is every other person, for any one may be called as a witness. It will not be thought that Congress intended to give to the District and Circuit Courts jurisdiction over all causes both civil and criminal. They have expressly confined it to causes affecting certain persons. And yet, if all those who may be called as witnesses in a case, and who may be alleged to be important witnesses, were intended to be described in the class of persons affected by it, and if the jurisdiction of the Federal courts can be invoke by the assertion that there are persons who may be witnesses, but who, because of their race or color, are incompetent to testify in the courts of the State, there is no cause either civil or criminal of which those courts may not at the option of either party take jurisdiction. The statute of Kentucky which was in existence when this indictment was found, and which denied the right of Richard Foster and Laura Foster to testify in the courts of the State, enacted as follows: "that a slave, negro, or Indian shall be a competent witness in the case of the commonwealth for or against a slave, negro, or Indian, or in a civil case to which only negroes or Indians are parties, but in no other case.: It will be observed that this statute prohibits the testimony of colored persons either for or against a white person in any civil or criminal cause to which he may be a party. If, therefore, they are persons affected by the cause, whenever they might be witnesses were they competent to testify, it follows that in any suit between white citizens, jurisdiction might be taken by the Federal courts whenever it was alleged that a citizen of the African race was or might be an important witness. And such an allegation might always be made. So in all criminal prosecutions against white persons a similar allegation would call into existence the like jurisdiction. We cannot think that such was the purpose of Congress in the statute of April 9th, 1866. It would seem rather to have been to afford protection to persons of the colored race by giving to the Federal courts jurisdiction of cases, the decision of which might injuriously affect them either in their personal, relative, or property rights, whenever they are denied in the State courts any of the rights mentioned and assured to them in the first section of the act.

Nor can it be said that such a construction allows little or no effect to the enactment. On the contrary, it concedes to it a far-reaching purpose. That purpose was to guard all the declared rights of colored persons, in all civil actions to which they may be parties in interest, by giving to the District and Circuit Courts of the United States jurisdiction of such actions whenever in the State courts any right enjoyed by white citizens is denied them. And in criminal prosecutions against them, it extends a like protection. We cannot be expected to be ignorant of the condition of things which existed when the statute was enacted, or of the evils which it was intended to remedy. It is well known that in many of the States, laws existed which subjected colored men convicted of criminal offences to punishments different from and often severer than those which were inflicted upon white persons convicted of similar offences. The modes of trial were also different, and the right of trial by jury was sometimes denied them. It is also well known that in many quarters prejudices existed against the colored race, which naturally affected the administration of justice in the State courts, and operated harshly when one of the race was a party accused. These were evils doubtless which the act of Congress had in view, and which it intended to remove. And so far as it reaches, it extends to both races the same rights, and the same means of vindicating them.

In view of these considerations we are of opinion that the case now before us is not within the provisions of the act of April 9th, 1866, and that the Circuit Court had not jurisdiction of the crime of murder committed in the district of Kentucky, merely because two persons who witnessed the murder were citizens of the African race, and for that reason incompetent by the law of Kentucky to testify in the courts of that State. They are not persons affected by the cause.

We need hardly add that the jurisdiction of the Circuit Court is not sustained by the fact averred in the indictment that Lucy Armstrong, the person murdered, was a citizen of the African race, and for that reason denied the right to testify in the Kentucky courts. In no sense can she be said to be affected by the cause. Manifestly the act refers to persons in existence. She was the victim of the frightful outrage which gave rise to the cause, but she is beyond being affected by the cause itself.

* * *

It is unnecessary, therefore, to consider the other questions presented by the record.

JUDGEMENT REVERSED.

■ THE CHIEF JUSTICE was not present at the argument, and took no part in the judgment.

■ MR. JUSTICE BRADLEY, with whom concurred MR. JUSTICE SWAYNE, dissenting.

I dissent from the opinion of the court in this case for the following reasons:

The civil rights bill (passed April 9th, 1866, and under which the indictment in this case was found and prosecuted) was primarily intended to carry out, in all its length and breadth, and to all its legitimate consequences, the then recent constitutional amendment abolishing slavery in the United States, and to place persons of African descent on an equality of rights and privileges with other citizens of the United States. To do this effectually it was not only necessary to declare this equality and impose penalties for its violation, but, as far as practicable, to counteract those unjust and discriminating laws of some of the States by which persons of African descent were subjected to punishments of peculiar harshness and ignominy, and deprived of rights and privileges enjoyed by white citizens.

This general scope and object of the act will often furnish us a clue to its just construction. It may be remarked, however, that the terms of the act are broad enough to embrace other persons as well as those of African descent, but that is a point not now in question in this case.

The first section declares that all persons born in the United States, not subject to a foreign power, and not including untaxed Indians, are citizens of the United States, and that such citizens, of every race and color, without regard to previous condition of slavery, shall have the same right, in every State and Territory in the United States, to make and enforce contracts; to sue, be parties, and give evidence; to inherit, purchase, lease, sell, hold, and convey real and personal property, and to the full and equal benefit of all laws and proceedings for the security of person and property, as is enjoyed by white citizens, and shall be subject to like punishment, pains, and penalties, and to none other, any law or custom to the contrary notwithstanding.

This is the fundamental section of the act. All that follows is intended to secure and vindicate, to the objects of it, the rights herein declared, and to establish the requisite machinery for that end.

This section is in direct conflict with those State laws which forbade a free colored person to remove to or pass through the State, from having firearms, from exercising the functions of a minister of the gospel, and from keeping a house of entertainment; laws which prohibited all colored persons from being taught to read and write, from holding or conveying property, and from being witnesses in any case where a white person was concerned; and laws which subjected them to cruel and ignominious punishments not imposed upon white persons, such as to be sold as vagrants, to be tied to the whipping-post, &c., &c. All these, and all other discriminations, were intended to be abolished and done away with.

The second section makes it a misdemeanor, punishable by fine or imprisonment, for any person, under color of any law or custom, to deprive any inhabitant of a State or Territory of any right secured by the act, or to subject him to different punishment or penalties on account of his having been a slave, or by reason of his color or race, than is prescribed for the punishment of white persons.

The third section proceeds to confer upon the District Courts of the United States, exclusive of the State courts, jurisdiction to try these offences, and then follows the clause under which the indictment in the present case was found, declaring that the said District Courts shall also have cognizance, concurrently with the Circuit Courts of the United States, "of all causes, civil and criminal, affecting persons who are denied, or cannot enforce in the courts or judicial tribunals of the State, or locality where they may be, any of the rights secured to them by the first section," with right of removal of causes from State courts, &c. It is evident that the provisions of the second section, making it a criminal offence to deprive a person of his rights, or to subject him to a discriminating punishment, would fail to reach a great number of cases which the broad and liberal provisions of the first section were intended to cover and protect. The clause in question is intended to reach these cases, or, at least, a large class of them. It provides a remedy where the State refuses to give one; where the mischief consists in inaction or refusal to act, or refusal to give requisite relief; whereas the second section provides for actual, positive invasion of rights. Thus, if the State should refuse to allow a freedman to sue in its courts, thereby denying him judicial relief, or should fail to provide laws for the punishment of white persons guilty of criminal acts against his person or property, thereby denying him judicial redress, there can be no doubt that the case would come within the scope of the clause under consideration. Suppose that, in any State, assault and battery, mayhem—nay, murder itself, could be perpetrated upon a colored man with impunity, no law being provided for punishing the offender, would not that be a case of denial of rights to the colored population of that State? Would not the clause of the civil rights bill now under consideration give jurisdiction to the United States courts in such a case? Yet, if an indictment should be found in one of those courts against the offender, the technical parties to the record would only be the United States as plaintiff and the criminal as defendant. Nevertheless could it be said, with any truth or justice, that this would not be a cause affecting persons denied the rights secured to them by the first section of the law?

The case before us is just as clearly within the scope of the law as such a case would be. I do not put it upon the ground that the witnesses of the murder, or some of them, are colored persons, disqualified by the laws of Kentucky to testify, but on the ground that the cause is one affecting the person murdered, as well as the whole class of persons to which she belonged. Had the case been simple assault and battery, the injured party would have been deprived of a right, enjoyed by every white citizen, of entering a complaint before a magistrate, or the grand jury, and of appearing as a witness on the trial of the offender. I say "right," for it is a right, an inestimable right, that of invoking the penalties of the law upon those who criminally or feloniously attack our persons or our property. Civil society has deprived us of the natural right of avenging ourselves, but it has preserved to us, all the more jealously, the right of bringing the offender to justice. By the common law of England the injured party was the actual prosecutor of criminal offences, although the proceeding was in the king's name; but in felonies, which involved a forfeiture to the crown of the criminal's property, it was also the duty of the crown officers to superintend the prosecution. And, although in this country it is almost the universal practice to appoint public and official prosecutors in criminal cases, yet it is the right of the injured party, and a duty he owes to society, to furnish what aid he can in bringing the offender to justice; and an important part of that right and duty consists in giving evidence against him.

To deprive a whole class of the community of this right, to refuse their evidence and their sworn complaints, is to brand them with a badge of slavery; is to expose them to wanton insults and fiendish assaults; is to leave their lives, their families, and their property unprotected by law. It gives unrestricted license and impunity to vindictive outlaws and felons to rush upon these helpless people and kill and slay them at will, as was done in this case. To say that actions or prosecutions intended for the redress of such outrages are not "causes affecting the persons" who are the victims of them, is to take, it seems to me, a view of the law too narrow, too technical, and too forgetful of the liberal objects it had in view. If, in such a raid as I have supposed, a colored person is merely wounded or maimed, but is still capable of making complaint, and on appearing to do so, has the doors of justice shut in his face on the ground that he is a colored person, and cannot testify against a white citizen, it seems to me almost a stultification of the law to say that the case is not within its scope. Let us read it once more: "The District Courts shall, concurrently with the Circuit Courts, have cognizance of all causes, civil and criminal, affecting persons who are denied or cannot enforce in the courts or judicial tribunals of the State or locality where they may be, any of the rights secured to them by the first section of this act."

If the case above supposed is within the act (as it assuredly must be), does it cease to be so when the violence offered is so great as to deprive the victim of life? Such a construction would be a premium on murder. If mere violence offered to a colored person (who, by the law of Kentucky, was denied the privilege of complaint), gives the United States court jurisdiction, when such violence is short of being fatal, that jurisdiction cannot cease when death is the result. The reason for its existence is stronger than before. If it would have been a cause affecting him when living, it will be a cause affecting him though dead * * *.

* * *

I have considered the case irrespective of the fact that the witnesses of the transaction were all colored people who, at the time this indictment was found, were denied the right to testify against white persons in Kentucky. I have placed it on the sole ground, that prosecutions for crimes committed against colored persons, are causes which, in the sense of the civil rights bill, most seriously affect them; and that in Kentucky they were denied the privilege of being witnesses in these causes. I do not mean to be understood as saying that every cause in which a colored person may be called as a witness, for that reason belongs to the cognizance of the United States courts. In ordinary cases of a civil character, the party calling such a person as a witness is the person affected. Such party, be he black or white, may except to the rejection of his witness, and bring the case to this court by writ of error from the State court of last resort under the 25th section of the Judiciary Act. A defendant in a criminal prosecution may do the same thing where a bill of exceptions is allowed in criminal cases.

To conclude, I have no doubt of the power of Congress to pass the law now under consideration. Slavery, when it existed, extended its influence in every direction, depressing and disfranchising the slave and his race in every possible way. Hence, in order to give full effect to the National will in abolishing slavery, it was necessary in some way to counteract these various disabilities and the effects flowing from them. Merely striking off the fetters of the slave, without removing the incidents and consequences of slavery, would hardly have been a boon to the colored race. Hence, also, the amendment abolishing slavery was supplemented by a clause giving Congress power to enforce it by appropriate legislation. No law was necessary to abolish slavery; the amendment did that. The power to enforce the amendment by appropriate legislation must be a power to do away with the incidents and consequences of slavery, and to instate the freedmen in the full enjoyment of that civil liberty and equality which the abolition of slavery meant.

In my opinion the judgment of the Circuit Court should be affirmed.

NOTES AND QUESTIONS

1. The Kentucky law forbidding African-Americans from testifying against white persons was obviously unlawful, on multiple grounds. It flatly violated the Civil Rights Act of 1866, it likely violated the Thirteenth Amendment, and it probably violated the Citizenship Clause, the Privileges or Immunities Clause, and the Equal Protection Clause of the Fourteenth Amendment. But who could bring that claim, and how? The persons most directly denied rights under this law, on the facts of *Blyew,* were the prospective witnesses. If they were not also parties to the case, how would they have standing to sue? And if they did have standing, it would perhaps entitle them to bring a damages action against the state officials who denied them the right to testify, but that would not affect the prosecution of the criminals in this case. Victims of crimes could certainly be disadvantaged by not having witnesses testify to the crimes, but victims are not parties to criminal prosecutions; a crime victim cannot appeal if the government bungles the prosecution. Neither Kentucky nor the defendants in this case had any interest in challenging the exclusion of African-American witnesses in state court. So how would the constitutional prohibition against the Kentucky witness law get enforced? As a matter of statutory interpretation, isn't it blindingly obvious that this is precisely the kind of circumstance that the federal jurisdictional law in *Blyew* was designed to handle? If a fair trial cannot be had in state court because of discriminatory state laws or practices, the federal forum is made available. One suspects that with the Kentucky State Legislature and Governor being "up in arms" over this federal prosecution, the Supreme Court simply wilted under political pressure and construed away the statute.

2. If you think (as we think is pretty clear) that the statute covers this case, the next logical question, which the majority in *Blyew* did not need to reach, is whether the jurisdictional statute is constitutional. That is not a trivial question. It is one thing to create a federal cause of action against state officials who deprive people of rights, such as the right to testify in court. No one doubts that Congress has power to create that cause of action. The more difficult question is whether Congress has power to set up an alternative system of justice when state systems fail. *Blyew* did not involve a federal cause of action, either by a prospective witness or by a crime victim, against an offending state official. It was a federal murder prosecution for a local crime. What gives Congress the authority to, in essence, take over the State of Kentucky's law enforcement machinery (the federal court, after all, was adjudicating the case under Kentucky's murder statute, as there is no general federal murder statute that applies outside of federally owned territory)? Justice Bradley, in dissenting from the majority's (mis)construction of the statute, knew that he had to take on that constitutional question. His answer is that Section 2 of the Thirteenth Amendment authorized the prosecution—not because of a denial of the rights of the witnesses but because of a denial of the rights of the crime victims. If a State makes it difficult to prosecute perpetrators when the victim is African-American, the State has obviously violated the Constitution. Most obviously, it has violated the Equal Protection Clause of the Fourteenth Amendment, and Congress can enforce that norm pursuant to its broad Section 5 powers. *But* the Fourteenth Amendment applies only to action by the *State*. Does the *State's* failure to live up to its constitutional duty to protect the lives of its African-American citizens as it does with its white citizens authorize the federal government to act directly against *private citizens* in place of the state government as well as against the offending state officials? It could be argued that Blyew and Kennard, for all their brutality, did not violate the Fourteenth Amendment; they were private actors. That is why Justice Bradley turned to the Thirteenth Amendment, which reaches private as well as governmental conduct. Justice Bradley's (implicit) claim is that the Thirteenth Amendment does, in fact, authorize Congress to place a State's legal system in a kind of receivership and substitute its own form of protection when the alternative is to leave in place a system that perpetuates badges and incidents of slavery. Is he right about that? If he is not right about that, then what does it mean to be a freed African-American in Kentucky if whites can kill you in the presence of your family and your family cannot testify in state court because state law does not allow African-Americans to testify in court against whites? If Justice Bradley is right, can Congress also use the Thirteenth Amendment to have federal courts adjudicate state-law actions in tort, contract, and property if the state legal system is, in Congress's judgment, systematically biased? If that kind of power seems extraordinary, isn't that what Reconstruction was all about?

3. Professor Calabresi thinks that Blyew and Kennard did directly violate the Fourteenth Amendment's Citizenship Clause by denying their African-American victims their right of birthright citizenship. He also thinks that state inaction in the context of these facts is a plain violation of the Equal Protection Clause, so that Congress could and did, by enacting the Civil Rights Act of 1866, authorize federal courts to step into the shoes of Kentucky state officials by using a federal court to prosecute Blyew and Kennard for a criminal violation of the civil rights of their murder victims and by enforcing Kentucky's murder laws against Blyew and Kennard. Professor Lawson finds Professor Calabresi's construction of the word "citizens," which purports to confer rights against private parties simply by virtue of citizenship, extravagant. He is more open to the idea that a complete failure of state legal process allows Congress essentially to "shadow" the state legal system with federal law enforcement machinery. He is less sure that such an event is a "plain" violation of the Fourteenth Amendment rather than a possible or

plausible one, depending on the facts in particular jurisdictions. These intramural disagreements about the scope of the Reconstruction Amendments will show up again. What do you think at this point? Keep in mind, before you commit to anything, that we are just getting started; there is much more to come.

4. For a detailed analysis of the facts and issues in *Blyew,* see Robert D. Goldstein, Blyew: *Variations on a Jurisdictional Theme,* 41 STAN. L. REV. 469 (1989).

5. To pursue a theme from Note 3: If Section 2 of the Thirteenth Amendment authorizes federal takeovers of state legal systems, does Section 5 of the Fourteenth Amendment do so as well? Under what factual circumstances? Who determines whether those facts exist?

6. If one of the prospective witnesses in *Blyew* wanted to sue to vindicate their rights, exactly who would they sue?

7. Perhaps the most important case in the 1870s about the Reconstruction Amendments did not involve race. It did, however, involve the provision of the Fourteenth Amendment that was designed as the clause's central instrument against racial and other forms of discrimination. Few decisions have had doctrinal consequences as massive as the case that you are about to read.

B. THE SLAUGHTER-HOUSE CASES

83 U.S. (16 Wall.) 36 (1873)

■ MR. JUSTICE MILLER delivered the opinion of the court.

These cases are brought here by writs of error to the Supreme Court of the State of Louisiana. They arise out of the efforts of the butchers of New Orleans to resist the Crescent City Live-Stock Landing and Slaughter-House Company in the exercise of certain powers conferred by the charter which created it, and which was granted by the legislature of that State.

The cases * * * were all decided by the Supreme Court of Louisiana in favor of the Slaughter-House Company, as we shall hereafter call it for the sake of brevity, and these writs are brought to reverse those decisions.

* * *

The statute thus assailed as unconstitutional was passed March 8th, 1869, and is entitled "An act to protect the health of the city of New Orleans, to locate the stock-landings and slaughter-houses, and to incorporate the Crescent City Live-Stock Landing and Slaughter-House Company."

The first section forbids the landing or slaughtering of animals whose flesh is intended for food, within the city of New Orleans and other parishes and boundaries named and defined, or the keeping or establishing any slaughter-houses or *abattoirs* within those limits except by the corporation thereby created, which is also limited to certain places afterwards mentioned. Suitable penalties are enacted for violations of this prohibition.

The second section designates the corporators, gives the name to the corporation, and confers on it the usual corporate powers.

The third and fourth sections authorize the company to establish and erect within certain territorial limits, therein defined, one or more stock-yards, stock-landings, and slaughter-houses, and imposes upon it the duty of erecting, on or before the first day of June, 1869, one grand slaughter-house of sufficient capacity for slaughtering five hundred animals per day.

It declares that the company, after it shall have prepared all the necessary buildings, yards, and other conveniences for that purpose, shall have the sole and exclusive privilege of conducting and carrying on the live-stock landing and slaughter-house business within the limits and privilege granted by the act, and that all such animals shall be landed at the stock-landings and slaughtered at the slaughter-houses of the company, and nowhere else. Penalties are enacted for infractions of this provision, and prices fixed for the maximum charges of the company for each steamboat and for each animal landed.

Section five orders the closing up of all other stock-landings and slaughter-houses after the first day of June, in the parishes of Orleans, Jefferson, and St. Bernard * * *.

These are the principal features of the statute, and are all that have any bearing upon the questions to be decided by us.

This statute is denounced not only as creating a monopoly and conferring odious and exclusive privileges upon a small number of persons at the expense of the great body of the community of New Orleans, but it is asserted that it deprives a large and meritorious class of citizens—the whole of the butchers of the city—of the right to exercise their trade, the business to which they have been trained and on which they depend for the support of themselves and their families, and that the unrestricted exercise of the business of butchering is necessary to the daily subsistence of the population of the city.

* * *

The wisdom of the monopoly granted by the legislature may be open to question, but it is difficult to see a justification for the assertion that the butchers are deprived of the right to labor in their occupation, or the people of their daily service in preparing food, or how this statute, with the duties and guards imposed upon the company, can be said to destroy the business of the butcher, or seriously interfere with its pursuit.

The power here exercised by the legislature of Louisiana is, in its essential nature, one which has been, up to the present period in the constitutional history of this country, always conceded to belong to the States, however it may *now* be questioned in some of its details.

"Unwholesome trades, slaughterhouses, operations offensive to the senses, the deposit of powder, the application of steam power to propel cars, the building with combustible materials, and the burial of the dead, may all," says Chancellor Kent, "be interdicted by law, in the midst of dense masses of population, on the general and rational principle that every person ought so to use his property as not to injure his neighbors, and that private interests must be made subservient to the general interests of the community." This is called the police power * * *.

This power is, and must be from its very nature, incapable of any very exact definition or limitation. Upon it depends the security of social order, the life and health of the citizen, the comfort of an existence in a thickly populated community, the enjoyment of private and social life, and the beneficial use of property. "It extends,' says another eminent judge, 'to the protection of the lives, limbs, health, comfort, and quiet of all persons, and the protection of all property within the State; . . . and persons and property are subject to all kinds of restraints and burdens in order to secure the general comfort, health, and prosperity of the State. Of the perfect right of the legislature to do this no question ever was, or, upon acknowledged general principles, ever can be made, so far as natural persons are concerned."

The regulation of the place and manner of conducting the slaughtering of animals, and the business of butchering within a city, and the inspection of the animals to be killed for meat, and of the meat afterwards, are among the most necessary and frequent exercises of this power. It is not, therefore, needed that we should seek for a comprehensive definition, but rather look for the proper source of its exercise.

* * *

It cannot be denied that the statute under consideration is aptly framed to remove from the more densely populated part of the city the noxious slaughterhouses, and large and offensive collections of animals necessarily incident to the slaughtering business of a large city, and to locate them where the convenience, health, and comfort of the people require they shall be located. And it must be conceded that the means adopted by the act for this purpose are appropriate, are stringent, and effectual. But it is said that, in creating a corporation for this purpose, and conferring upon it exclusive privileges—privileges which it is said constitute a monopoly—the legislature has exceeded its power * * *.

* * *

The proposition is therefore reduced to these terms: can any exclusive privileges be granted to any of its citizens, or to a corporation, by the legislature of a State?

The eminent and learned counsel who has twice argued the negative of this question has displayed a research into the history of monopolies in England and the European continent only equalled by the eloquence with which they are denounced.

But it is to be observed that all such references are to monopolies established by the monarch in derogation of the rights of his subjects, or arise out of transactions in which the people were unrepresented, and their interests uncared for. The great *Case of Monopolies,* reported by Coke and so fully stated in the brief, was undoubtedly a contest of the commons against the monarch. The decision is based upon the ground that it was against common law, and the argument was aimed at the unlawful assumption of power by the crown, for whoever doubted the authority of Parliament to change or modify the common law? The discussion in the House of Commons cited from Macaulay clearly establishes that the contest was between the crown and the people represented in Parliament.

But we think it may be safely affirmed, that the Parliament of Great Britain, representing the people in their legislative functions, and the legislative bodies of this country, have from time immemorial to the present day, continued to grant to persons and corporations exclusive privileges—privileges denied to other citizens—privileges which come within any just definition of the word monopoly, as much as those now under consideration; and that the power to do this has never been questioned or denied. Nor can it be truthfully denied, that some of the most useful and beneficial enterprises set on foot for the general good, have been made successful by means of these exclusive rights, and could only have been conducted to success in that way.

It may, therefore, be considered as established that the authority of the legislature of Louisiana to pass the present statute is ample unless some restraint in the exercise of that power be found in the constitution of that State or in the amendments to the Constitution of the United States, adopted since the date of the decisions we have already cited.

* * *

The plaintiffs in error, accepting this issue, allege that the statute is a violation of the Constitution of the United States in these several particulars:

* * *

That it abridges the privileges and immunities of citizens of the United States;

That it denies to the plaintiffs the equal protection of the laws; and,

That it deprives them of their property without due process of law, contrary to the provisions of the first section of the fourteenth article of amendment.

This court is thus called upon for the first time to give construction to these articles.

We do not conceal from ourselves the great responsibility which this duty devolves upon us. No questions so far-reaching and pervading in their consequences, so profoundly interesting to the people of this country, and so important in their bearing upon the relations of the United States, of the several States to each other, and to the citizens of the States and of the United States, have been before this court during the official life of any of its present members * * *.

* * *

The most cursory glance at * * * [the Reconstruction Amendments] discloses a unity of purpose, when taken in connection with the history of the times, which cannot fail to have an important bearing on any question of doubt concerning their true meaning. Nor can such doubts, when any reasonably exist, be safely and rationally solved without a reference to that history, for in it is found the occasion and the necessity for recurring again to the great source of power in this country, the people of the States, for additional guarantees of human rights, additional powers to the Federal government; additional restraints upon those of the States. Fortunately, that history is fresh within the memory of us all, and its leading features, as they bear upon the matter before us, free from doubt.

The institution of African slavery, as it existed in about half the States of the Union, and the contests pervading the public mind for many years between those who desired its curtailment and ultimate extinction and those who desired additional safeguards for its security and perpetuation, culminated in the effort, on the part of most of the States in which slavery existed, to separate from the Federal government and to resist its authority. This constituted the war of the rebellion, and whatever auxiliary causes may have contributed to bring about this war, undoubtedly the overshadowing and efficient cause was African slavery.

In that struggle, slavery, as a legalized social relation, perished. It perished as a necessity of the bitterness and force of the conflict. When the armies of freedom found themselves upon the soil of slavery, they could do nothing less than free the poor victims whose enforced servitude was the foundation of the quarrel. And when hard-pressed in the contest, these men (for they proved themselves men in that terrible crisis) offered their services and were accepted by thousands to aid in suppressing the unlawful rebellion, slavery was at an end wherever the Federal government succeeded in that purpose. The proclamation of President Lincoln expressed an accomplished fact as to a large portion of the insurrectionary districts, when he declared slavery abolished in them all. But the war being over, those who had succeeded in reestablishing the authority of the Federal government were not content to permit this great act of emancipation to rest on the actual results of the contest or the proclamation of the Executive, both of which might have been questioned in after times, and they determined to place this main and most valuable result in the Constitution of the restored Union as one of its fundamental articles. Hence, the thirteenth article of amendment of that instrument. Its two short sections seem hardly to admit of construction, so vigorous is their expression and so appropriate to the purpose we have indicated.

* * *

The process of restoring to their proper relations with the Federal government and with the other States those which had sided with the rebellion * * *, developed the fact that, notwithstanding the formal recognition by those States of the abolition of slavery, the condition of the slave race would, without further protection of the Federal government, be almost as bad as it was before. Among the first acts of legislation adopted by several of the States in the legislative bodies which claimed to be in their normal relations with the Federal government were laws which imposed upon the colored race onerous disabilities and burdens and curtailed their rights in the pursuit of life, liberty, and property to such an extent that their freedom was of little value, while they had lost the protection which they had received from their former owners from motives both of interest and humanity.

They were in some States forbidden to appear in the towns in any other character than menial servants. They were required to reside on and cultivate the soil without the right to purchase or own it. They were excluded from many occupations of gain, and were not permitted to give testimony in the courts in any case where a white man was a party. It was said that their lives were at the mercy of bad men, either because the laws for their protection were insufficient or were not enforced.

These circumstances, whatever of falsehood or misconception may have been mingled with their presentation, forced upon the statesmen who had conducted the Federal government in safety through the crisis of the rebellion, and who supposed that, by the thirteenth article of amendment, they had secured the result of their labors, the conviction that something more was necessary in the way of constitutional protection to the unfortunate race who had suffered so much. They accordingly passed through Congress the proposition for the fourteenth amendment, and they declined to treat as restored to their full participation in the government of the Union the States which had been in insurrection, until they ratified that article by a formal vote of their legislative bodies.

* * *

We repeat, then, in the light of this recapitulation of events, almost too recent to be called history, but which are familiar to us all; and on the most casual examination of the language of these amendments, no one can fail to be impressed with the one pervading purpose found in them all, lying at the foundation of each, and without which none of them would have been even suggested; we mean the freedom of the slave race, the security and firm establishment of that freedom, and the protection of the newly made freeman and citizen from the oppressions of those who had formerly exercised unlimited dominion over him. It is true that only the fifteenth amendment, in terms, mentions the negro by speaking of his color and his slavery. But it is just as true that each of the other articles was addressed to the grievances of that race, and designed to remedy them as the fifteenth.

We do not say that no one else but the negro can share in this protection. Both the language and spirit of these articles are to have their fair and just weight in any question of construction. Undoubtedly while negro slavery alone was in the mind of the Congress which proposed the thirteenth article, it forbids any other kind of slavery, now or hereafter. If Mexican peonage or the Chinese coolie labor system shall develop slavery of the Mexican of Chinese race within our territory, this amendment may safely be trusted to make it void. And so, if other rights are assailed by the States which properly and necessarily fall within the protection of these articles, that protection will apply, though the party interested may not be of African descent. But what we do say, and what we wish to be understood, is that, in any fair and just construction of any section or phrase of these amendments, it is necessary to look to the purpose which we have said was the pervading spirit of them all, the evil which they were designed to remedy, and the process of continued addition to the Constitution, until that purpose was supposed to be accomplished as far as constitutional law can accomplish it.

The first section of the fourteenth article to which our attention is more specially invited opens with a definition of citizenship—not only citizenship of the United States, but citizenship of the States. No such definition was previously found in the Constitution, nor had any attempt been made to define it by act of Congress * * *.

To * * * establish clear and comprehensive definition of citizenship which should declare what should constitute citizenship of the United States and also citizenship of a State, the first clause of the first section was framed.

"All persons born or naturalized in the United States, and subject to the jurisdiction thereof, are citizens of the United States and of the State wherein they reside."

The first observation we have to make on this clause is, that it puts at rest both the questions which we stated to have been the subject of differences of opinion. It declares that persons may be citizens of the United States without regard to their citizenship of a particular State, and it overturns the Dred Scott decision by making *all persons* born within the United States and subject to its jurisdiction citizens of the United States. That its main purpose was to establish the citizenship of the negro can admit of no doubt. The phrase, "subject to its jurisdiction" was intended to exclude from its operation children of ministers, consuls, and citizens or subjects of foreign States born within the United States.

The next observation is more important in view of the arguments of counsel in the present case. It is, that the distinction between citizenship of the United States and citizenship of a State is clearly recognized and established. Not only may a man be a citizen of the United States without being a citizen of a State, but an important element is necessary to convert the former into the latter. He must reside within the

State to make him a citizen of it, but it is only necessary that he should be born or naturalized in the United States to be a citizen of the Union.

It is quite clear, then, that there is a citizenship of the United States, and a citizenship of a State, which are distinct from each other, and which depend upon different characteristics or circumstances in the individual.

We think this distinction and its explicit recognition in this amendment of great weight in this argument, because the next paragraph of this same section, which is the one mainly relied on by the plaintiffs in error, speaks only of privileges and immunities of citizens of the United States, and does not speak of those of citizens of the several States. The argument, however, in favor of the plaintiffs rests wholly on the assumption that the citizenship is the same, and the privileges and immunities guaranteed by the clause are the same.

The language is, "No State shall make or enforce any law which shall abridge the privileges or immunities of citizens of *the United States*." It is a little remarkable, if this clause was intended as a protection to the citizen of a State against the legislative power of his own State, that the word citizen of the State should be left out when it is so carefully used, and used in contradistinction to citizens of the United States in the very sentence which precedes it. It is too clear for argument that the change in phraseology was adopted understandingly and, with a purpose.

Of the privileges and immunities of the citizen of the United States, and of the privileges and immunities of the citizen of the State, and what they respectively are, we will presently consider; but we wish to state here that it is only the former which are placed by this clause under the protection of the Federal Constitution, and that the latter, whatever they may be, are not intended to have any additional protection by this paragraph of the amendment.

* * *

Fortunately, we are not without judicial construction of this [the Privileges and Immunities] clause of [Article IV, Section 2 of] the Constitution. The first and the leading case on the subject is that of *Corfield v. Coryell,* decided by Mr. Justice Washington in the Circuit Court for the District of Pennsylvania in 1823.

"The inquiry," he says, "is what are the privileges and immunities of citizens of the several States? We feel no hesitation in confining these expressions to those privileges and immunities which are *fundamental*; which belong of right to the citizens of all free governments, and which have at all times been enjoyed by citizens of the several States which compose this Union, from the time of their becoming free, independent, and sovereign. What these fundamental principles are it would be more tedious than difficult to enumerate. They may all, however, be comprehended under the following general heads: protection by the government, with the right to acquire and possess property of every kind and to pursue and obtain happiness and safety, subject, nevertheless, to such restraints as the government may prescribe for the general good of the whole."

* * * The description, when taken to include others not named, but which are of the same general character, embraces nearly every civil right for the establishment and protection of which organized government is instituted. They are, in the language of Judge Washington, those rights which are fundamental. Throughout his opinion, they are spoken of as rights belonging to the individual as a citizen of a State. They are so spoken of in the constitutional provision which he was construing.

And they have always been held to be the class of rights which the State governments were created to establish and secure.

* * *

The * * * [Article IV Privileges and Immunities Clause] did not create those rights, which it called privileges and immunities of citizens of the States. It threw around them in that clause no security for the citizen of the State in which they were claimed or exercised. Nor did it profess to control the power of the State governments over the rights of its own citizens.

Its sole purpose was to declare to the several States that, whatever those rights, as you grant or establish them to your own citizens, or as you limit or qualify or impose restrictions on their exercise, the same, neither more nor less, shall be the measure of the rights of citizens of other States within your jurisdiction.

* * * [The] entire domain of the privileges and immunities of citizens of the States, as above defined, lay within the constitutional and legislative power of the States, and without that of the Federal government. Was it the purpose of the fourteenth amendment, by the simple declaration that no State should make or enforce any law which shall abridge the privileges and immunities of *citizens of the United States*, to transfer the security and protection of all the civil rights which we have mentioned, from the States to the Federal government? And where it is declared that Congress shall have the power to enforce that article, was it intended to bring within the power of Congress the entire domain of civil rights heretofore belonging exclusively to the States?

All this and more must follow, if the proposition of the plaintiffs in error be sound. For not only are these rights subject to the control of Congress whenever in its discretion any of them are supposed to be abridged by State legislation, but that body may also pass laws in advance, limiting and restricting the exercise of legislative power by the States, in their most ordinary and usual functions, as in its judgment it may think proper on all such subjects. And still further, such a construction followed by the reversal of the judgments of the Supreme Court of Louisiana in these cases, would constitute this court a perpetual censor upon all legislation of the States, on the civil rights of their own citizens, with authority to nullify such as it did not approve as consistent with those rights, as they existed at the time of the adoption of this amendment. The argument we admit is not always the most conclusive which is drawn from the consequences urged against the adoption of a particular construction of an instrument. But when, as in the case before us, these consequences are so serious, so far-reaching and pervading, so great a departure from the structure and spirit of our institutions; when the effect is to fetter and degrade the State governments by subjecting them to the control of Congress in the exercise of powers heretofore universally conceded to them of the most ordinary and fundamental character; when in fact it radically changes the whole theory of the relations of the State and Federal governments to each other and of both these governments to the people; the argument has a force that is irresistible, in the absence of language which expresses such a purpose too clearly to admit of doubt.

We are convinced that no such results were intended by the Congress which proposed these amendments, nor by the legislatures of the States which ratified them.

Having shown that the privileges and immunities relied on in the argument are those which belong to citizens of the States as such, and that they are left to the State governments for security and protection, and not by this article placed under the special care of the Federal government, we may hold ourselves excused from defining the privileges and immunities of citizens of the United States which no State can abridge, until some case involving those privileges may make it necessary to do so.

But lest it should be said that no such privileges and immunities are to be found if those we have been considering are excluded, we venture to suggest some which owe their existence to the Federal government, its National character, its Constitution, or its laws.

One of these is well described in the case of *Crandall v. Nevada*. It is said to be the right of the citizen of this great country, protected by implied guarantees of its Constitution, "to come to the seat of government to assert any claim he may have upon that government, to transact any business he may have with it, to seek its protection, to share its offices, to engage in administering its functions. He has the right of free access to its seaports, through which operations of foreign commerce are conducted, to the sub-treasuries, land offices, and courts of justice in the several States." * * *

Another privilege of a citizen of the United States is to demand the care and protection of the Federal government over his life, liberty, and property when on the high seas or within the jurisdiction of a foreign government. Of this there can be no doubt, nor that the right depends upon his character as a citizen of the United States. The right to peaceably assemble and petition for redress of grievances, the privilege of the writ of *habeas corpus*, are rights of the citizen guaranteed by the Federal Constitution. The right to use the navigable waters of the United States, however they may penetrate the territory of the several States, all rights secured to our citizens by treaties with foreign nations, are dependent upon citizenship of the United States, and not citizenship of a State. One of these privileges is conferred by the very article under consideration. It is that a citizen of the United States can, of his own volition, become a citizen of any State of the Union by a *bona fide* residence therein, with the same rights as other citizens of that State. To these may be added the rights secured by the thirteenth and fifteenth articles of amendment, and by the other clause of the fourteenth, next to be considered.

But it is useless to pursue this branch of the inquiry, since we are of opinion that the rights claimed by these plaintiffs in error, if they have any existence, are not privileges and immunities of citizens of the United States within the meaning of the clause of the fourteenth amendment under consideration.

* * *

The argument has not been much pressed in these cases that the defendant's charter deprives the plaintiffs of their property without due process of law, or that it denies to them the equal protection of the law. The first of these paragraphs has been in the Constitution since the adoption of the fifth amendment, as a restraint upon the Federal power. It is also to be found in some form of expression in the constitutions of nearly all the States as a restraint upon the power of the States. This law, then, has practically been the same as it now is during the existence of the government, except so far as the present amendment may place the restraining power over the States in this matter in the hands of the Federal government.

We are not without judicial interpretation, therefore, both State and National, of the meaning of this clause. And it is sufficient to say that under no construction of that provision that we have ever seen, or any that we deem admissible, can the restraint imposed by the State of Louisiana upon the exercise of their trade by the butchers of New Orleans be held to be a deprivation of property within the meaning of that provision.

"Nor shall any State deny to any person within its jurisdiction the equal protection of the laws."

In the light of the history of these amendments, and the pervading purpose of them, which we have already discussed, it is not difficult to give a meaning to this clause. The existence of laws in the States where the newly emancipated negroes resided, which discriminated with gross injustice and hardship against them as a class, was the evil to be remedied by this clause, and by it such laws are forbidden.

If, however, the States did not conform their laws to its requirements, then by the fifth section of the article of amendment Congress was authorized to enforce it by suitable legislation. We doubt very much whether any action of a State not directed by way of discrimination against the negroes as a class, or on account of their race, will ever be held to come within the purview of this provision. It is so clearly a provision for that race and that emergency that a strong case would be necessary for its application to any other. But as it is a State that is to be dealt with, and not alone the validity of its laws, we may safely leave that matter until Congress shall have exercised its power, or some case of State oppression, by denial of equal justice in its courts, shall have claimed a decision at our hands. We find no such case in the one before us, and do not deem it necessary to go over the argument again, as it may have relation to this particular clause of the amendment.

* * *

The judgments of the Supreme Court of Louisiana in these cases are

AFFIRMED.

■ MR. JUSTICE FIELD, dissenting.

I am unable to agree with the majority of the court in these cases, and will proceed to state the reasons of my dissent from their judgment.

* * *

The plaintiffs in error deny the validity of the act in question, so far as it confers the special and exclusive privileges mentioned * * *.

* * *

No one will deny the abstract justice which lies in the position of the plaintiffs in error; and I shall endeavor to show that the position has some support in the fundamental law of the country.

It is contended in justification for the act in question that it was adopted in the interest of the city, to promote its cleanliness and protect its health, and was the legitimate exercise of what is termed the police power of the State. That power undoubtedly extends to all regulations affecting the health, good order, morals, peace, and safety of society, and is exercised on a great variety of subjects, and in almost numberless ways. All sorts of restrictions and burdens are imposed under it, and when these are not in conflict with any constitutional prohibitions or fundamental principles, they cannot be successfully assailed in a judicial tribunal. With this power of the State and its legitimate exercise I shall not differ from the majority of the court. But under the pretence of prescribing a police regulation the State cannot be permitted to encroach upon any of the just rights of the citizen, which the Constitution intended to secure against abridgment.

In the law in question there are only two provisions which can properly be called police regulations—the one which requires the landing and slaughtering of animals below the city of New Orleans, and the other which requires the inspection of the animals before they are slaughtered. When these requirements are complied with, the sanitary purposes of the act are accomplished. In all other particulars the act is a mere grant to a corporation created by it of special and exclusive privileges by which the health of the city is in no way promoted * * *.

It is also sought to justify the act in question on the same principle that exclusive grants for ferries, bridges, and turnpikes are sanctioned. But it can find no support there. Those grants are of franchises of a public character appertaining to the government. Their use usually requires the exercise of the sovereign right of eminent domain * * *.

Nor is there any analogy between this act of Louisiana and the legislation which confers upon the inventor of a new and useful improvement an exclusive right to make and sell to others his invention. The government in this way only secures to the inventor the temporary enjoyment of that which, without him, would not have existed. It thus only recognizes in the inventor a temporary property in the product of his own brain.

The act of Louisiana presents the naked case, unaccompanied by any public considerations, where a right to pursue a lawful and necessary calling, previously enjoyed by every citizen, and in connection with which a thousand persons were daily employed, is taken away and vested exclusively for twenty-five years, for an extensive district and a large population, in a single corporation, or its exercise is for that period restricted to the establishments of the corporation, and there allowed only upon onerous conditions.

If exclusive privileges of this character can be granted to a corporation of seventeen persons, they may, in the discretion of the legislature, be equally granted to single individual. If they may be granted for twenty-five years, they may be equally granted for a century, and in perpetuity * * *. Indeed, upon the theory on which the exclusive privileges granted by the act in question are sustained, there is no monopoly, in the most odious form, which may not be upheld.

The question presented is, therefore, one of the gravest importance, not merely to the parties here, but to the whole country. It is nothing less than the question whether the recent amendments to the Federal Constitution protect the citizens of the United States against the deprivation of their common rights by State legislation. In my judgment, the fourteenth amendment does afford such protection, and was so intended by the Congress which framed and the States which adopted it.

* * *

But if the exclusive privileges conferred upon the Louisiana corporation can be sustained, it is not perceived why exclusive privileges for the construction and keeping of ovens, machines, grindstones, wine-presses, and for all the numerous trades and pursuits for the prosecution of which buildings are required, may not be equally bestowed upon other corporations or private individuals, and for periods of indefinite duration.

* * * The provisions of the fourteenth amendment * * * cover, in my judgment, the case before us, and inhibit any legislation which confers special and exclusive privileges like these under consideration. The amendment was adopted to obviate objections which had been raised and pressed with great force to the validity of the Civil Rights Act, and to place the common rights of American citizens under the protection of the National government * * *.

* * *

The amendment does not attempt to confer any new privileges or immunities upon citizens, or to enumerate or define those already existing. It assumes that there are such privileges and immunities which belong of right to citizens as such, and ordains that they shall not be abridged by State legislation. If this inhibition has no reference to privileges and immunities of this character, but only refers, as held by the majority of the court in their opinion, to such privileges and immunities as were before its adoption specially designated in the Constitution or necessarily implied as belonging to citizens of the United States, it was a vain and idle enactment, which accomplished nothing, and most unnecessarily excited Congress and the people on its passage. With privileges and immunities thus designated or implied no State could ever have interfered by its laws, and no new constitutional provision was required to inhibit such interference. The supremacy of the Constitution and the laws of the United States always controlled any State legislation of that character. But if the amendment refers to the natural and inalienable rights which belong to all citizens, the inhibition has a profound significance and consequence.

What, then, are the privileges and immunities which are secured against abridgment by State legislation?

In the first section of the Civil Rights Act, Congress has given its interpretation to these terms, or at least has stated some of the rights which, in its judgment, these terms include; it has there declared that they include the right "to make and enforce contracts, to sue, be parties and give evidence, to inherit, purchase, lease, sell, hold, and convey real and personal property, and to full and equal benefit of all laws and proceedings for the security of person and property." That act, it is true, was passed before the fourteenth amendment, but the amendment was adopted, as I have already said, to obviate objections to the act, or, speaking more accurately, I should say, to obviate objections to legislation of a similar character, extending the protection of the National government over the common rights of all citizens of the United States. Accordingly, after its ratification, Congress re-enacted the act under the belief that whatever doubts may have previously existed of its validity, they were removed by the amendment.

The terms, privileges and immunities, are not new in the amendment; they were in the Constitution before the amendment was adopted. They are found in the second section of the fourth article, which declares that "the citizens of each State shall be entitled to all privileges and immunities of citizens in the several States," and they have been the subject of frequent consideration in judicial decisions [such as Justice Washington's discussion in *Corfield v. Coryell*] * * *. This appears to me to be a sound construction of the clause in question. The privileges and immunities designated are those *which of right belong to the citizens of all free governments*. Clearly among these must be placed the right to pursue a lawful employment in a lawful manner, without other restraint than such as equally affects all persons * * *.

* * *

What the [Article IV, Section 2] clause in question did for the protection of the citizens of one State against hostile and discriminating legislation of other States, the fourteenth amendment does for the protection of every citizen of the United States against hostile and discriminating legislation against him in favor of others, whether they reside in the same or in different States. If under the fourth article of the Constitution equality of privileges and immunities is secured between citizens of different States, under the fourteenth amendment, the same equality is secured between citizens of the United States.

It will not be pretended that under the fourth article of the Constitution any State could create a monopoly in any known trade or manufacture in favor of her own citizens, or any portion of them, which would exclude an equal participation in the trade or manufacture monopolized by citizens of other States. She could not confer, for example, upon any of her citizens the sole right to manufacture shoes, or boots, or silk, or the sole right to sell those articles in the State so as to exclude non-resident citizens from engaging in a similar manufacture or sale. The non-resident citizens could claim equality of privilege under the provisions of the fourth article with the citizens of the State exercising the monopoly as well as with others, and thus, as respects them, the monopoly would cease. If this were not so it would be in the power of the State to exclude at any time the citizens of other States from participation in particular branches of commerce or trade, and extend the exclusion from time to time so as effectually to prevent any traffic with them.

Now, what the clause in question does for the protection of citizens of one State against the creation of monopolies in favor of citizens of other States, the fourteenth amendment does for the protection of every citizen of the United States against the creation of any monopoly whatever. The privileges and immunities of citizens of the United States, of every one of them, is secured against abridgment in any form by any State. The fourteenth amendment places them under the guardianship of the National authority. All monopolies in any known trade or manufacture are an invasion of these privileges, for they encroach upon the liberty of citizens to acquire property and pursue happiness, and were held void at common law in the great *Case of Monopolies,* decided during the reign of Queen Elizabeth.

A monopoly is defined "to be an institution or allowance from the sovereign power of the State by grant, commission, or otherwise, to any person or corporation, for the sole buying, selling, making, working, or using of anything, whereby any person or persons, bodies politic or corporate, are sought to be restrained of any freedom or liberty they had before, or hindered in their lawful trade." All such grants relating to any known trade or manufacture have been held by all the judges of England, whenever they have come up for consideration, to be void at common law as destroying the freedom of trade, discouraging labor and industry, restraining persons from getting an honest livelihood, and putting it into the power of the grantees to enhance the price of commodities * * *.

* * *

The common law of England is the basis of the jurisprudence of the United States * * *.

* * * [T]he fourteenth amendment secures the like protection to all citizens in that State against any abridgment of their common rights, as in other States. That amendment was intended to give practical effect to the declaration of 1776 of inalienable rights, rights which are the gift of the Creator, which the law does not confer, but only recognizes. If the trader in London could plead that he was a free citizen of that city against the enforcement to his injury of monopolies, surely under the fourteenth amendment every citizen of the United States should be able to plead his citizenship of the republic as a protection against any similar invasion of his privileges and immunities.

* * *

In all these [reported] cases there is a recognition of the equality of right among citizens in the pursuit of the ordinary avocations of life, and a declaration that all grants of exclusive privileges, in contravention of this equality, are against common right, and void.

This equality of right, with exemption from all disparaging and partial enactments, in the lawful pursuits of life, throughout the whole country, is the distinguishing privilege of citizens of the United States. To them, everywhere, all pursuits, all professions, all avocations are open without other restrictions than such as are imposed equally upon all others of the same age, sex, and condition. The State may prescribe such regulations for every pursuit and calling of life as will promote the public health, secure the good order and advance the general prosperity of society, but, when once prescribed, the pursuit or calling must be free to be followed by every citizen who is within the conditions designated, and will conform to the regulations. This is the fundamental idea upon which our institutions rest, and, unless adhered to in the legislation of the country our government will be a republic only in name * * *.

I am authorized by the CHIEF JUSTICE, MR. JUSTICE SWAYNE, and MR. JUSTICE BRADLEY to state that they concur with me in this dissenting opinion.

■ MR. JUSTICE BRADLEY, also dissenting.

* * *

It is contended that this [monopoly] * * * abridges the privileges and immunities of citizens of the United States, especially of the plaintiffs in error, who were particularly affected thereby; and whether it does so or not is the simple question in this case. And the solution of this question depends upon the solution of two other questions, to wit:

First. Is it one of the rights and privileges of a citizen of the United States to pursue such civil employment as he may choose to adopt, subject to such reasonable regulations as may be prescribed by law?

Secondly. Is a monopoly, or exclusive right, given to one person to the exclusion of all others, to keep slaughterhouses, in a district of nearly twelve hundred square miles, for the supply of meat for a large city, a reasonable regulation of that employment which the legislature has a right to impose?

The first of these questions is one of vast importance, and lies at the very foundations of our government. The question is now settled by the fourteenth amendment itself, that citizenship of the United States is the primary citizenship in this country; and that State citizenship is secondary and derivative, depending upon citizenship of the United States and the citizen's place of residence. The States have not now, if they ever had, any power to restrict their citizenship to any classes or persons * * * If a man be denied full equality before the law, he is denied one of the essential rights of citizenship as a citizen of the United States.

Every citizen, then, being primarily a citizen of the United States, and, secondarily, a citizen of the State where he resides, what, in general, are the privileges and immunities of a citizen of the United States? Is the right, liberty, or privilege of choosing any lawful employment one of them?

If a State legislature should pass a law prohibiting the inhabitants of a particular township, county, or city, from tanning leather or making shoes, would such a law violate any privileges or immunities of those inhabitants as citizens of the United States, or only their privileges and immunities as citizens of that particular State? Or if a State legislature should pass a law of caste, making all trades and professions, or certain enumerated trades and professions, hereditary, so that no one could follow any such trades or professions except that which was pursued by his father, would such a law violate the privileges and immunities of the people of that State as citizens of the United States, or only as citizens of the State? Would they have no redress but to appeal to the courts of that particular State?

This seems to me to be the essential question before us for consideration. And, in my judgment, the right of any citizen to follow whatever lawful employment he chooses to adopt (submitting himself to all lawful regulations) is one of his most valuable rights, and one which the legislature of a State cannot invade, whether restrained by its own constitution or not.

* * *

The people of this country brought with them to its shores the rights of Englishmen; the rights which had been wrested from English sovereigns at various periods of the nation's history * * *.

* * *

* * * It was not necessary to say in words that the citizens of the United States should have and exercise all the privileges of citizens; the privilege of buying, selling, and enjoying property; the privilege of engaging in any lawful employment for a livelihood; the privilege of resorting to the laws for redress of injuries, and the like. Their very citizenship conferred these privileges, if they did not possess them before * * *.

II. The next question to be determined in this case is: Is a monopoly or exclusive right, given to one person, or corporation, to the exclusion of all others, to keep slaughterhouses in a district of nearly twelve hundred square miles, for the supply of meat for a great city, a reasonable regulation of that employment which the legislature has a right to impose?

The keeping of a slaughter-house is part of, and incidental to, the trade of a butcher—one of the ordinary occupations of human life. To compel a butcher, or rather all the butchers of a large city and an extensive district, to slaughter their cattle in another person's slaughter-house and pay him a toll therefor, is such a restriction upon the trade as materially to interfere with its prosecution. It is onerous, unreasonable, arbitrary, and unjust. It has none of the qualities of a police regulation * * *. It is one of those arbitrary and unjust laws made in the interest of a few scheming individuals, by which some of the Southern States have, within the past few years, been so deplorably oppressed and impoverished. It seems to me strange that it can be viewed in any other light.

The granting of monopolies, or exclusive privileges to individuals or corporations, is an invasion of the right of others to choose a lawful calling, and an infringement of personal liberty. It was so felt by the English nation as far back as the reigns of Elizabeth and James. A fierce struggle for the suppression of such monopolies, and for abolishing the prerogative of creating them, was made, and was successful * * *.

* * *

The amendment also prohibits any State from depriving any person (citizen or otherwise) of life, liberty, or property, without due process of law.

In my view, a law which prohibits a large class of citizens from adopting a lawful employment, or from following a lawful employment previously adopted, does deprive them of liberty as well as property, without due process of law. Their right of choice is a portion of their liberty; their occupation is their property. Such a law also deprives those citizens of the equal protection of the laws, contrary to the last clause of the section.

* * *

It is futile to argue that none but persons of the African race are intended to be benefited by this amendment. They may have been the primary cause of the amendment, but its language is general, embracing all citizens, and I think it was purposely so expressed.

The mischief to be remedied was not merely slavery and its incidents and consequences; but that spirit of insubordination and disloyalty to the National government which had troubled the country for so many years in some of the States, and that intolerance of free speech and free discussion which often rendered life and property insecure, and led to much unequal legislation. The amendment was an attempt to give voice to the strong National yearning for that time and that condition of things, in which American citizenship should be a sure guaranty of safety, and in which every citizen of the United States might stand erect on every portion of its soil, in the full enjoyment of every right and privilege belonging to a freeman, without fear of violence or molestation.

But great fears are expressed that this construction of the amendment will lead to enactments by Congress interfering with the internal affairs of the States * * *.

* * * The great question is, What is the true construction of the amendment? When once we find that, we shall find the means of giving it effect. The argument from inconvenience ought not to have a very controlling influence in questions of this sort. The National will and National interest are of far greater importance.

* * *

■ MR. JUSTICE SWAYNE, dissenting.

* * *

* * * A more flagrant and indefensible invasion of the rights of many for the benefit of a few has not occurred in the legislative history of the country * * *.

These amendments are all consequences of the late civil war. The prejudices and apprehension as to the central government which prevailed when the Constitution was adopted were dispelled by the light of experience * * *. By the Constitution, as it stood before the war, ample protection was given against oppression by the Union, but little was given against wrong and oppression by the States. That want was intended to be supplied by this amendment. Against the former this court has been called upon more than once to interpose. Authority of the same amplitude was intended to be conferred as to the latter. But this arm of our jurisdiction is, in these cases, stricken down by the judgment just given. Nowhere, than in this court, ought the will of the nation, as thus expressed, to be more liberally construed or more cordially executed. This determination of the majority seems to me to lie far in the other direction.

I earnestly hope that the consequences to follow may prove less serious and far-reaching than the minority fear they will be.

NOTES AND QUESTIONS

1. Is it even remotely plausible that the Congress and the country went through the process of drafting and enacting the Fourteenth Amendment in order to protect, against discriminatory state action, the minimal rights of national citizenship identified by the majority (such as the right to travel to the Nation's capitol) that existed even before the Fourteenth Amendment was ratified? Isn't Justice Field right that state laws interfering with those narrow pre-existing rights would be preempted even without the Fourteenth Amendment?

2. The majority worried that reading the Privileges or Immunities Clause to guarantee all Americans equality in basic civil rights "radically changes the whole theory of the relations of the State and Federal governments to each other and of both these governments to the people." Is that a good reason to read the Fourteenth Amendment's Privileges or Immunities Clause narrowly?

3. The language and history of the Privileges or Immunities Clause, as we have seen, appears to be well designed to enforce a broad ban against partial or special legislation, especially monopolies. If the Louisiana slaughterhouse monopoly does not come within this clause, it is hard to imagine what kind of special legislation will do so. And, indeed, in the century and a half since the *Slaughter-House Cases,* no state statute has been found by the Supreme Court to violate the Privileges or Immunities Clause. For all practical purposes, the Privileges or Immunities Clause was read out of the Constitution in 1873 (though a few justices, as we will later see, have shown some interest in reviving it, *see infra* pages 1585–1602, 1609). This is devastating news because the Framers of the Fourteenth Amendment thought the Privileges or Immunities Clause was the most important clause in the Amendment.

4. Everyone in 1868, friend and foe alike of the Fourteenth Amendment, agreed that, at the very least, the Fourteenth Amendment was designed to provide unshakeable constitutional support for the Civil Rights Act of 1866 and similar statutes. "Any theory of the Fourteenth Amendment must therefore explain how it validates the Civil Rights Act." John Harrison, *Reconstructing the Privileges or Immunities Clause,* 101 YALE L.J. 1385, 1390 (1992). The Civil Rights Act did not concern itself with the narrow kinds of "rights of national citizenship" discussed by the *Slaughter-House* majority. It concerned common law rights of contract, property, and tort. If the Privileges or Immunities Clause simply does not protect those rights at all, it does not protect them against racially discriminatory abridgments either. But then, according to the majority, what part of the

Fourteenth Amendment protects common law rights against racially discriminatory abridgements? Did the country fail in 1868 to accomplish the single most obvious goal that the Fourteenth Amendment set out to accomplish? Or do other parts of the Fourteenth Amendment do at least some of the work that the Fourteenth Amendment's framers anticipated would be performed by the Privileges or Immunities Clause? As you will see in the rest of this chapter, the Equal Protection Clause and the Due Process of Law Clause have been pressed into service to achieve results that everyone knows must be correct under the Fourteenth Amendment but for which the *Slaughter-House Cases* have removed the most direct textual path. Justice Swayne's assessment of the likely consequences of the majority's decision has been amply vindicated.

5. If the majority is wrong, and the Privileges or Immunities Clause gives *all American citizens* the privileges or immunities of *state citizenship,* what would that mean in practice? Would every State need to have exactly the same laws of contract, tort, and property? Would Congress under Section 5 be authorized to adopt a uniform body of general law? Or is the effect of the Privileges or Immunities Clause, as construed by the dissenting justices (and us) more limited? The key is to understand what it means to "abridge" a privilege or immunity of citizenship. For the seminal argument that the core of the Privileges or Immunities Clause is an *antidiscrimination* principle that allows States to have any common law rules they wish, provided that those rules apply equally to all, see Harrison, *supra*. But then what does it mean to say that laws must apply equally to all? Infants are citizens. Are rules declaring infants legally incapable of contracting thereby unconstitutional? Had the *Slaughter-House Cases* come out the other way, the last century and a half of caselaw would have needed to wrestle with the question of what kinds of classifications and discriminations the Privileges or Immunities Clause forbids and permits. Because the Fourteenth Amendment obviously imposes *some kind* of equality norm on the States, the decision in the *Slaughter-House Cases* has not avoided the need for those questions; it has just forced them into the unpromising language of the Equal Protection Clause and the Due Process of Law Clause, as you will see in the rest of this chapter. The questions will always be there.

6. If you care to know what we think (and you absolutely do not need to care to know what we think): Professor Calabresi believes that the Privileges or Immunities Clause enacts a rule against class legislation and systems of caste.

> Caste, as Senator Charles Sumner—one of the Amendment's Framers—explained in 1869, was once confined to describing the famously stratified social system of India but had by "natural extension" come to mean "any separate and fixed order of society." When one group "claim[s] hereditary rank and privilege" and another is "doomed to hereditary degradation and disability," you have a caste system. From the time of the Jacksonians on, Americans had been opposed to monopolies, systems of class, and special hereditary privileges, immunities, and emoluments. Section One of the Fourteenth Amendment constitutionalized America's rejection of systems of class- or caste-based laws.

Steven G. Calabresi & Julia T. Rickert, *Originalism and Sex Discrimination,* 90 TEX. L. REV. 1, 17–19 (2011) (footnotes omitted). For Professor Calabresi, the chief interpretative question—and the subject of a whole series of his law review articles—is what kinds of classifications count as class- or caste-based. Race, certainly, but sex? (He says yes. *See id.*) Sexual orientation? (He says yes. *See* Steven G. Calabresi & Hannah M. Begley, *Originalism and Same-Sex Marriage,* 70 U. MIAMI L. REV. 648 (2016).) Professor Lawson, for his part, has spent much less time thinking about the Reconstruction Amendments and has never gone into print with a general theory of them. He agrees with the basic premise that the Privileges or Immunities Clause forbids partial or special legislation, but he might frame the inquiry in agency-law terms. Perhaps the Fourteenth Amendment imposes on States essentially the same fiduciary obligations of impartiality towards multiple principals—its (and all American) citizens—that the federal government always had towards them. In that case, the rule of the Fourteenth Amendment would be one of *fair treatment* rather than strictly *equal treatment.* Equal treatment of all citizens is the baseline, but departures can be justified by good reasons. Thus, Professor Calabresi thinks that the Fourteenth Amendment instructs us to ask questions about class and caste, while Professor Lawson suspects (without a lot of confidence) that it instructs us to ask questions about fiduciary obligation. Both approaches converge over a large range, but there is a nontrivial set of cases for which the different approaches yield very different results.

7. The two above views reflect only a sliver of the spectrum of views about the original meaning of the Privileges or Immunities Clause. Another view is that the Privileges or Immunities Clause protects only rights enumerated in the Constitution, including the Bill of Rights. *See* KURT T. LASH, THE FOURTEENTH AMENDMENT AND THE PRIVILEGES OR IMMUNITIES OF AMERICAN CITIZENSHIP (2014). For a response, which promises a forthcoming future account of the clause that will extend it further than just explicitly enumerated rights, see Randy E. Barnett & Evan D. Bernick, *The Privileges or Immunities Clause, Abridged: A Critique of Kurt Lash on the Fourteenth Amendment,* 95 NOTRE DAME L. REV. 499 (2019). Add in non-originalist perspectives and one has a cornucopia of options from which to choose. Few questions in constitutional law generate such a range of responses, and few questions in constitutional law are as important, as the meaning of the Privileges or Immunities Clause.

8. As you read the rest of the cases in this chapter, think about how they might have come out differently, or been written differently, if the *Slaughter-House* dissenters had prevailed.

9. Senator Howard's speech presenting the Fourteenth Amendment to the Senate identified as "privileges or immunities" the rights guaranteed by the Bill of Rights. Under the majority opinion in the *Slaughter-House Cases*, one's rights under the federal Bill of Rights are presumably core" Privileges or Immunities" of national citizenship! Certainly, if the right to travel to the seat of government is a privilege or immunity of federal citizenship, then so too is the right to assemble and petition for the redress of grievances or to keep and bear arms. If so, the States cannot make or enforce any law which abridges the federal Bill of Rights or which abridges the unenumerated but implicit federal right to travel to the seat of government in Washington, D.C.

10. Is one function of the Fourteenth Amendment therefore to make the Bill of Rights provisions applicable to the States? We will soon see how that question has shaped much of constitutional law over the last century, but first consider the answer given in the 1870s in the next case. The context is the pervasive private violence experienced by African-Americans in the south, as you saw in *Blyew*.

C. UNITED STATES V. CRUIKSHANK

92 U.S. (2 Otto) 542 (1876)

■ MR. CHIEF JUSTICE WAITE delivered the opinion of the court.

[*Editors' Note: This federal criminal prosecution arose from a massacre at Colfax, Louisiana on Easter Sunday, 1873. An armed white militia attacked an almost entirely unarmed group of African-American freedmen who had gathered at a courthouse to prevent it from being taken over. The dispute arose because of a hotly contested 1872 Louisiana gubernatorial election. Estimates were that between 100 and 280 African-Americans and three white people were killed—many of them after they had surrendered. The Justice Department brought federal criminal law charges under the Enforcement Act of 1870, quoted below, against several white members of the mob that committed the Colfax, Massacre. That Act was passed by Congress to allow President Ulysses S. Grant to enforce African-American voting rights under the Fifteenth Amendment. Federal criminal charges included hindering the freedmen's First Amendment right to assemble freely and their Second Amendment right to keep and bear arms.*]

This case comes here with a certificate by the judges of the Circuit Court for the District of Louisiana that they were divided in opinion upon a question which occurred at the hearing. It presents for our consideration an indictment containing sixteen counts, divided into two series of eight counts each, based upon sect. 6 of the Enforcement Act of May 31, 1870. That section is as follows:—

"That if two or more persons shall band or conspire together, or go in disguise upon the public highway, or upon the premises of another, with intent to violate any provision of this act, or to injure, oppress, threaten, or intimidate any citizen, with intent to prevent or hinder his free exercise and enjoyment of any right or privilege granted or secured to him by the constitution or laws of the United States, or because of his having exercised the same, such persons shall be held guilty of felony, and, on conviction thereof, shall be fined or imprisoned, or both, at the discretion of the court,—the fine not to exceed $5,000, and the imprisonment not to exceed ten years; and shall, moreover, be thereafter ineligible to, and disabled from holding, any office or place of honor, profit, or trust created by the constitution or laws of the United States." 16 Stat. 141.

The question certified arose upon a motion in arrest of judgment after a verdict of guilty generally upon the whole sixteen counts, and is stated to be, whether "the said sixteen counts of said indictment are severally good and sufficient in law, and contain charges of criminal matter indictable under the laws of the United States."

The general charge in the first eight counts is that of "banding," and in the second eight, that of "conspiring" together to injure, oppress, threaten, and intimidate Levi Nelson and Alexander Tillman, citizens of the United States, of African descent and persons of color, with the intent thereby to hinder and prevent them in their free exercise and enjoyment of rights and privileges "granted and secured" to them "in common with all other good citizens of the United States by the constitution and laws of the United States."

The offences provided for by the statute in question do not consist in the mere "banding" or "conspiring" of two or more persons together, but in their banding or conspiring with the intent, or for any of the purposes, specified. To bring this case under the operation of the statute, therefore, it must appear that the right, the enjoyment of which the conspirators intended to hinder or prevent, was one granted or secured by the constitution or laws of the United States. If it does not so appear, the criminal matter charged has not been made indictable by any act of Congress.

* * *Experience made the fact known to the people of the United States that they required a national government for national purposes * * *.

The government thus established and defined is to some extent a government of the States in their political capacity. It is also, for certain purposes, a government of the people. Its powers are limited in number, but not in degree. Within the scope of its powers, as enumerated and defined, it is supreme and above the States; but beyond, it has no existence. It was erected for special purposes, and endowed with all the powers necessary for its own preservation and the accomplishment of the ends its people had in view. It can neither grant nor secure to its citizens any right or privilege not expressly or by implication placed under its jurisdiction.

The people of the United States resident within any State are subject to two governments: one State, and the other National; but there need be no conflict between the two. The powers which one possesses, the other does not. They are established for different purposes, and have separate jurisdictions. Together they make one whole, and furnish the people of the United States with a complete government, ample for the protection of all their rights at home and abroad * * *.

The government of the United States is one of delegated powers alone. Its authority is defined and limited by the Constitution. All powers not granted to it by that instrument are reserved to the States or the people. No rights can be acquired under the constitution or laws of the United States, except such as the government of the United States has the authority to grant or secure. All that cannot be so granted or secured are left under the protection of the States.

We now proceed to an examination of the indictment, to ascertain whether the several rights, which it is alleged the defendants intended to interfere with, are such as had been in law and in fact granted or secured by the constitution or laws of the United States.

The first and ninth counts state the intent of the defendants to have been to hinder and prevent the citizens named in the free exercise and enjoyment of their "lawful right and privilege to peaceably assemble together with each other and with other citizens of the United States for a peaceful and lawful purpose." The right of the people peaceably to assemble for lawful purposes existed long before the adoption of the Constitution of the United States * * *. It was not, therefore, a right granted to the people by the Constitution. The government of the United States when established found it in existence, with the obligation on the part of the States to afford it protection. As no direct power over it was granted to Congress, it remains * * * subject to State jurisdiction. Only such existing rights were committed by the people to the protection of Congress as came within the general scope of the authority granted to the national government.

The first amendment to the Constitution prohibits Congress from abridging "the right of the people to assemble and to petition the government for a redress of grievances." This, like the other amendments proposed and adopted at the same time, was not intended to limit the powers of the State governments in respect to their own citizens, but to operate upon the National government alone. *Barron v. The City of Baltimore*, 7 Pet. 250 * * *.

The particular amendment now under consideration assumes the existence of the right of the people to assemble for lawful purposes, and protects it against encroachment by Congress. The right was not created by the amendment; neither was its continuance guaranteed, except as against congressional interference. For their protection in its enjoyment, therefore, the people must look to the States. The power for that purpose was originally placed there, and it has never been surrendered to the United States.

The right of the people peaceably to assemble for the purpose of petitioning Congress for a redress of grievances, or for anything else connected with the powers or the duties of the national government, is an attribute of national citizenship, and, as such, under the protection of, and guaranteed by, the United States. The very idea of a government, republican in form, implies a right on the part of its citizens to meet peaceably for consultation in respect to public affairs and to petition for a redress of grievances. If it had been alleged in these counts that the object of the defendants was to prevent a meeting for such a purpose, the case would have been within the statute, and within the scope of the sovereignty of the United States. Such, however, is not the case. The offence, as stated in the indictment, will be made out, if it be shown that the object of the conspiracy was to prevent a meeting for any lawful purpose whatever.

The second and tenth counts are equally defective. The right there specified is that of "bearing arms for a lawful purpose." This is not a right granted by the Constitution. Neither is it in any manner dependent upon that instrument for its existence. The second amendment declares that it shall not be infringed; but this, as has been seen, means no more than that it shall not be infringed by Congress. This is one of the amendments that has no other effect than to restrict the powers of the national government, leaving the people to look for their protection against any violation by their fellow-citizens of the rights it recognizes, to what is called, in *The City of New York v. Miln*, 11 Pet. 139, the "powers which relate to merely municipal legislation, or what was, perhaps, more properly called internal police," "not surrendered or restrained" by the Constitution of the United States.

The third and eleventh counts are even more objectionable. They charge the intent to have been to deprive the citizens named, they being in Louisiana, "of their respective several lives and liberty of person without due process of law." This is nothing else than alleging a conspiracy to falsely imprison or murder citizens of the United States, being within the territorial jurisdiction of the State of Louisiana. The rights of life and personal liberty are natural rights of man. "To secure these rights," says the Declaration of Independence, "governments are instituted among men, deriving their just powers from the consent of the governed." The very highest duty of the States, when they entered into the Union under the Constitution, was to protect all persons within their boundaries in the enjoyment of these "unalienable rights with which they were endowed by their Creator." Sovereignty, for this purpose, rests alone with the States. It is no more the duty or within the power of the United States to punish for a conspiracy to falsely imprison or murder within a State, than it would be to punish for false imprisonment or murder itself.

The fourteenth amendment prohibits a State from depriving any person of life, liberty, or property, without due process of law; but this adds nothing to the rights of one citizen as against another. It simply furnishes an additional guaranty against any encroachment by the States upon the fundamental rights which belong to every citizen as a member of society. As was said by Mr. Justice Johnson, in *Bank of Columbia v. Okely*, 4 Wheat. 244, it secures "the individual from the arbitrary exercise of the powers of government, unrestrained by the established principles of private rights and distributive justice." These counts in the indictment do not call for the exercise of any of the powers conferred by this provision in the amendment.

* * *

The fourteenth amendment prohibits a State from denying to any person within its jurisdiction the equal protection of the laws; but this provision does not, any more than the one which precedes it, and which we have just considered, add anything to the rights which one citizen has under the Constitution against another. The equality of the rights of citizens is a principle of republicanism. Every republican government is in duty bound to protect all its citizens in the enjoyment of this principle, if within its power. That duty was originally assumed by the States; and it still remains there. The only obligation resting upon the United States is to see that the States do not deny the right. This the amendment guarantees, but no more. The power of the national government is limited to the enforcement of this guaranty.

No question arises under the Civil Rights Act of April 9, 1866 (14 Stat. 27), which is intended for the protection of citizens of the United States in the enjoyment of certain rights, without discrimination on account of race, color, or previous condition of servitude, because, as has already been stated, it is nowhere alleged in these counts that the wrong contemplated against the rights of these citizens was on account of their race or color.

* * *

The order of the Circuit Court arresting the judgment upon the verdict is, therefore, affirmed; and the cause remanded, with instructions to discharge the defendants.

■ MR. JUSTICE CLIFFORD, dissenting. [Omitted.] [*Editors' Note: Justice Clifford did not actually dissent. He agreed that the case should be dismissed but disagreed with the majority's reasoning. He thought that the indictment was so vague that it violated the Sixth Amendment.*]

NOTES AND QUESTIONS

1. Why did "[n]o question arise[ ] under the Civil Rights Act"? If you were a government prosecutor, would you allege a violation of the Civil Rights Act on these facts? If such an allegation were made and proven, would that bring into play Section 2 of the Thirteenth Amendment to validate the prosecution?

2. As in *Blyew*, the problem in *Cruikshank* is that the direct actors being prosecuted were private citizens, not state governmental actors. Even if the Bill of Rights constitutes a font of "privileges or immunities" made applicable to the States by the Fourteenth Amendment, it arguably does not impose obligations on private citizens. If you steal your neighbor's gun, you have committed theft, but you have not violated the Second Amendment or the Fifth Amendment's Takings Clause (unless you are doing so under the authority of the State). Does that mean that *Cruikshank* was right? That Congress cannot reach the kind of private violence on open display in *Cruikshank* (absent an allegation that "the object of the defendants was to prevent" the victims from "meet[ing] peaceably for consultation in respect to public affairs and to petition for a redress of grievances")? Think about what kinds of rights Congress has the power to enforce under the Fourteenth Amendment. One is the right to birthright equal citizenship conferred by the Citizenship Clause. Cannot (Professor Calabresi asks) Congress legislate to protect a class of citizens whose lives and liberties are endangered because they are being denied their equal birthright citizenship? (Professor Lawson doubts whether citizenship can carry this much legal baggage.) Another relevant clause is the right of every person to equal *protection* of the laws. States violate the Constitution, not simply by making or enforcing laws which abridge privileges or immunities or depriving people

of rights without due process of law, but also by *failing* to enforce laws in an evenhanded fashion. If state legal processes are inadequate to mete out justice evenhandedly in cases of private violence because of neglect, could it be "appropriate" legislation for Congress to provide a federal cause of action to substitute for the absent state equal protection of the laws? Note that this goes beyond the jurisdictional statute in *Blyew,* in which federal courts simply applied already-existing state criminal laws. Here one is talking about Congress providing a distinct federal cause of action separate and apart from any state laws that the States inadequately enforce. Can Congress do that under Section 5 of the Fourteenth Amendment? *See* DAVID P. CURRIE, THE CONSTITUTION IN THE SUPREME COURT: THE FIRST HUNDRED YEARS 1789–1888, at 397 (1985):

> A strong argument can be made, on the basis of the origins of the equal protection clause, that private lynching was among the evils that Congress was meant to have power to forbid. Although none of the prohibitory clauses of the amendment speaks directly to private action, the equal protection clause seems to impose upon the states a unique duty to take affirmative action to protect black persons from private attack * * *. Thus a state that systematically failed to prosecute those who committed offenses against blacks would itself violate the equal protection clause * * *. [A] strong argument could be made that in such circumstances a federal prohibition of the private activity itself would be an appropriate means of remedying the state's failure to afford equal protection.

Would the criminal indictment in such a case need to allege (and the case need to prove), as part of the basis for federal jurisdiction, that the state legal process was inadequate? *See* Pamela Brandwein, *A Judicial Abandonment of Blacks? Rethinking the "State Action" Cases of the Waite Court,* 41 L. & SOC. REV. 343 (2007). Is the problem in *Cruikshank* a bona fide lack of congressional power, poor prosecutorial choices and bad drafting of an indictment, a racist judiciary, or any or all of the above?

3. What about the argument that the white racists in this case violated the Citizenship Clause of the Fourteenth Amendment by depriving African-Americans of their birthright equal citizenship with white Americans? There is no state action requirement in the Citizenship Clause. Justice Harlan relied upon that Clause in his powerful dissent in *The Civil Rights Cases*, 109 U.S. 3 (1883), which is discussed *supra.* Professor Calabresi agrees with Justice Harlan's dissent that the Citizenship Clause confers birthright equality on all classes and castes of citizens, with no state action limitation. Professor Lawson is highly dubious that the concept of citizenship, by itself, yields a large enough package of rights—enforceable against fellow citizens as a matter of constitutional law—to generate the doctrinal results anticipated by Justice Harlan and Professor Calabresi. What do you think? Are we both wrong?

4. *Cruikshank* is sometimes read as denying that the Bill of Rights was incorporated against the States through the Fourteenth Amendment. Does it say that?

5. In 1878, the Court finally found a state statute unconstitutional—this time a state statute *forbidding* race discrimination. Yes, that is exactly what happened.

D. HALL V. DECUIR

95 U.S. (5 Otto) 485 (1878)

By the thirteenth article of the Constitution of Louisiana it is provided that "all persons shall enjoy equal rights and privileges upon any conveyance of a public character." By an act of the General Assembly, entitled "An Act to enforce the thirteenth article of the Constitution of this State, and to regulate the licenses mentioned in said thirteenth article," approved Feb. 23, 1869, it was enacted as follows:—

"SECTION 1. All persons engaged within this State, in the business of common carriers of passengers, shall have the right to refuse to admit any person to their railroad cars, street cars, steamboats, or other water-crafts, stage-coaches, omnibuses, or other vehicles, or to expel any person therefrom after admission, when such person shall, on demand, refuse or neglect to pay the customary fare, or when such person shall be of infamous character, or shall be guilty, after admission to the conveyance of the carrier, of gross, vulgar, or disorderly conduct, or who shall commit any act tending to injure the business of the carrier, prescribed for the management of his business, after such rules and regulations shall have been made known: *Provided*, said rules and regulations make no discrimination on account of race or color * * *."

* * *

■ MR. CHIEF JUSTICE WAITE delivered the opinion of the court.

For the purposes of this case, we must treat the act of Louisiana of Feb. 23, 1869, as requiring those engaged in inter-state commerce to give all persons travelling in that State, upon the public conveyances employed in such business, equal rights and privileges in all parts of the conveyance, without distinction or discrimination on account of race or color. Such was the construction given to that act in the courts below, and it is conclusive upon us as the construction of a State law by the State courts * * *.

There can be no doubt but that exclusive power has been conferred upon Congress in respect to the regulation of commerce among the several States. The difficulty has never been as to the existence of this power, but as to what is to be deemed an encroachment upon it * * *. The line which separates the powers of the States from this exclusive power of Congress is not always distinctly marked, and oftentimes it is not easy to determine on which side a particular case belongs. Judges not unfrequently differ in their reasons for a decision in which they concur. Under such circumstances it would be a useless task to undertake to fix an arbitrary rule by which the line must in all cases be located. It is far better to leave a matter of such delicacy to be settled in each case upon a view of the particular rights involved.

But we think it may safely be said that State legislation which seeks to impose a direct burden upon inter-state commerce, or to interfere directly with its freedom, does encroach upon the exclusive power of Congress. The statute now under consideration, in our opinion, occupies that position. It does not act upon the business through the local instruments to be employed after coming within the State, but directly upon the business as it comes into the State from without or goes out from within. While it purports only to control the carrier when engaged within the State, it must necessarily influence his conduct to some extent in the management of his business throughout his entire voyage. His disposition of passengers taken up and put down within the State, or taken up within to be carried without, cannot but affect in a greater or less degree those taken up without and brought within, and sometimes those taken up and put down without. A passenger in the cabin set apart for the use of whites without the State must, when the boat comes within, share the accommodations of that cabin with such colored persons as may come on board afterwards, if the law is enforced.

It was to meet just such a case that the commercial clause in the Constitution was adopted. The river Mississippi passes through or along the borders of ten different States, and its tributaries reach many more. The commerce upon these waters is immense, and its regulation clearly a matter of national concern. If each State was at liberty to regulate the conduct of carriers while within its jurisdiction, the confusion likely to follow could not but be productive of great inconvenience and unnecessary hardship * * *. No carrier of passengers can conduct his business with satisfaction to himself, or comfort to those employing him, if on one side of a State line his passengers, both white and colored, must be permitted to occupy the same cabin, and on the other be kept separate. Uniformity in the regulations by which he is to be governed from one end to the other of his route is a necessity in his business, and to secure it Congress, which is untrammelled by State lines, has been invested with the exclusive legislative power of determining what such regulations shall be. If this statute can be enforced against those engaged in inter-state commerce, it may be as well against those engaged in foreign; and the master of a ship clearing from New Orleans for Liverpool, having passengers on board, would be compelled to carry all, white and colored, in the same cabin during his passage down the river, or be subject to an action for damages, "exemplary as well as actual," by anyone who felt himself aggrieved because he had been excluded on account of his color.

This power of regulation may be exercised without legislation as well as with it. By refraining from action, Congress, in effect, adopts as its own regulations those which the common law or the civil law, where that prevails, has provided for the government of such business, and those which the States, in the regulation of their domestic concerns, have established affecting commerce, but not regulating it within the meaning of the Constitution. In fact, congressional legislation is only necessary to cure defects in existing laws, as they are discovered, and to adapt such laws to new developments of trade. As was said by Mr. Justice Field, speaking for the court in *Welton v. The State of Missouri*, 91 U. S. 282, "inaction by Congress . . . is equivalent to a declaration that inter-state commerce shall remain free and untrammelled." Applying that principle to the circumstances of this case, congressional inaction left Benson at liberty to adopt such reasonable rules and regulations for the disposition of passengers upon his boat, while pursuing her voyage within Louisiana or without, as seemed to him most for the interest of all concerned. The statute under which this suit is brought, as construed by the State court, seeks to take away from him that power so long as he is within Louisiana; and while recognizing to the fullest extent the principle which sustains a statute, unless its unconstitutionality is clearly established, we think this statute, to the extent that it requires those engaged in the transportation of passengers among the States to carry colored passengers in Louisiana in the same cabin with whites, is unconstitutional and void. If the public good requires such legislation, it must come from Congress and not from the States.

We confine our decision to the statute in its effect upon foreign and inter-state commerce, expressing no opinion as to its validity in any other respect.

Judgment will be reversed and the cause remanded, with instructions to reverse the judgment of the District Court, and direct such further proceedings in conformity with this opinion as may appear to be necessary; and it is

So ordered.

■ MR. JUSTICE CLIFFORD concurred in the judgment, and delivered the following opinion: [Omitted.]

NOTES AND QUESTIONS

1. Some of the facts of *DeCuir* are set out in Justice Clifford's concurrence, which we have omitted. Here is the gist:

> Sufficient appears to show that the plaintiff is a person of color, and that the defendant is the master and owner of the steamer, which is a packet vessel duly enrolled and licensed for the coasting trade, and that the vessel was engaged in carrying passengers and cargo between the port of New Orleans in the State of Louisiana and the port of Vicksburg in the State of Mississippi; that the steamer has two cabins for the accommodation of passengers, conveniently arranged one above the other; that the upper is assigned to white persons and that the lower is assigned to persons of color, both being constructed with state-rooms, cabin, and a hall used as a dining-room where meals are furnished; that the plaintiff, being at the time in New Orleans and desiring to visit her plantation in another parish of the same State, went on board the steamer to secure her passage to the proper landing near her plantation; that the clerk of the steamer, to whom she applied for a passage in the upper cabin, having previously informed her agent that he could not give her a passage in that cabin, refused her request, telling her at the same time that he would give her a passage in the lower cabin; that the plaintiff declined to accept a berth in the lower cabin, and that she passed the night during which she remained on board sitting in a chair in what is known as the recess back of the upper cabin.
>
> * * *
>
> Proof of a decisive character is exhibited that the plaintiff applied for a berth in the upper cabin, which was refused, and that she declined to accept one in the lower cabin, which by the rules and regulations of the steamer is assigned for persons of color. Based upon these undisputed facts, the charge of the declaration is that the plaintiff was denied the equal rights and privileges guaranteed and secured to all persons by the State Constitution and the aforesaid act of the State legislature. Superadded to that is also the charge that such equal rights and privileges were denied to her on account of her race and color, for which she claims actual and exemplary damages in the sum of $75,000.

95 U.S. (5 Otto) at 492–93.

2. Three years before *DeCuir,* Congress had passed the Civil Rights Act of 1875, providing that "all persons within the jurisdiction of the United States shall be entitled to the full and equal enjoyment of * * * public conveyances on land or water." The Supreme Court had not yet in 1878 found this statute unconstitutional (though it would do so five years later). Did the Louisiana statute do anything that the Civil Rights Act of 1875 did not? Then again, if the commerce power is truly exclusively federal, does it matter what the Louisiana statute did or did not do?

3. If Louisiana imposed safety standards for boilers on steamships, would that also violate the Dormant Commerce Clause?

[Assignment 58]

V. RECONSTRUCTION AND COLOR-BLINDNESS

To place the rest of the cases from this era in context, a brief discussion of the history of Reconstruction is necessary. From 1865 to 1877—a period of twelve years—Ulysses S. Grant was the most prominent and powerful man in the country. When President Johnson asked Grant if he and the U.S. Army would seat Southern congressional delegations, over the objections of the Northern Republicans, General Grant said "no," he would protect the Congress as it had existed during the Civil War. *See* JEAN EDWARD SMITH, GRANT (2002). President Johnson's request that General Grant seat the Southern delegations to Congress elected in 1865, and General Grant's refusal to do so, and his decision to protect militarily the Congress as it was composed during the Civil War, amounted to a mild *coup d'etat.* From December 1865, Andrew Johnson was President in name, and had the veto power, but he was not the most powerful man in the land. That title belonged to General Ulysses S. Grant who served as Commander in Chief of the Union Army until his own election as President officially gave him that title.

After President Johnson campaigned against Reconstruction in the mid-term elections of 1866, Grant and the Republicans won a huge triumph, and then road a powerful wave into presidential terms in 1868 and 1872. During this twelve-year period of time, from 1865 to 1877, the Thirteenth, Fourteenth, and Fifteenth Amendment were ratified; many civil rights laws were passed; and, by 1875, Congress outlawed separate-but-equal rules in public places of accommodation. Congress almost banned public school segregation at this time. *See* Michael W. McConnell, *Originalism and the Desegregation Decisions,* 81 Va. L. Rev. 947 (1995). It failed only because a two-thirds vote could not then be mustered up in the House of Representatives on a procedural motion to allow the bill to reach the floor during that session of Congress. Two Southern state supreme courts even held there was a constitutional right to racial intermarriage in the 1870s, as we shall see below.

Nevertheless, there was a lot of racism in the U.S., both South and North, during Reconstruction. Congress, during Reconstruction, ran segregated public schools in the District of Columbia, and many of the people who voted for the Civil Rights Act of 1866 and the Fourteenth Amendment said that they did not think the Act or the Amendment created a right to racial intermarriage or to desegregated public schools.

Nonetheless, President Grant did achieve a lot during his twelve years in power. In 1874, however, the Democrats won a majority in the House of Representatives. Their main demand was the immediate removal of Northern troops from their army bases in the occupied States of the former Confederacy. President Grant would not budge on this, but congressional Republicans gave in to the Democrats' demand in order to place Republican Rutherford B. Hayes in the White House after the razor-thin, very close presidential election of 1876 had to be decided by the House of Representatives. Once President Hayes took office, he acted boldly on behalf of the cause of civil rights. He appointed John Marshall Harlan, the elder, to the U.S. Supreme Court; you will hear from Justice Harlan shortly. And, by 1880, Hayes had created a situation where James A. Garfield another Republican former Union war general was elected President with the full intention of sending U.S. soldiers back into the South in 1881.

Tragically, President Garfield was assassinated by a disappointed and delusional office seeker six months into his first term, and his Vice President, Chester A. Arthur was a corrupt opponent of civil rights. From that moment on, the cause of Reconstruction was spent. Finally, a Democrat—Grover Cleveland of New York—won a majority of the popular vote in the next three presidential elections 1884, 1888, and 1892. From President Garfield's assassination on, opponents of Reconstruction and advocates of Jim Crow enacted into law more and more statutes that discriminated on the basis of race. The pace sped up mightily after *The Civil Rights Cases, see supra* pages 846–860, came down.

The Supreme Court during this time, as we just saw, gave many of the provisions of the Reconstruction Amendments a narrow—and in some cases absurdly narrow—reading. Other cases, however, were quite broad in their sweep. And, as we will see, some state courts went so far as to find bans on interracial marriage unconstitutional—a full century before the U.S. Supreme Court reached that conclusion in 1967. See if you can reconcile the cases below with decisions such as *Blyew, Cruikshank,* and *Slaughter-House.* We start, however, with a case involving the straightforward interpretation of a federal statute. The statute's principle is of fundamental importance, and one should not take for granted that the Court gave it full effect.

A. RAILROAD COMPANY V. BROWN

84 U.S. (17 Wall.) 445 (1873)

* * *

* * * Catharine Brown, a colored woman, on the 8th of February, 1868, anterior to the adoption of the fourteenth and fifteenth amendments to the Constitution, bought a ticket to come from Alexandria to Washington. The ticket was issued in the name of "the Washington, Georgetown, and Alexandria Railroad Company;" as were, indeed, all the tickets at each end of the route. No tickets were distinguished as for white persons or colored persons, nor for any particular sort or class of cars. All were exactly alike.

When the woman went to take her place in the cars there were standing there two cars, alike comfortable; the one, however, set apart for colored persons, and the other "for white ladies, and gentlemen accompanying them;" the regulation having been that in going down from Washington to Alexandria, the first should be occupied by the former, and the last by the latter; and that in coming back the use should be simply reversed. When about to get into one of the cars, a servant of the persons managing the road, stationed near the cars to direct passengers, told the woman not to get into the car into which she was about to enter, but to get into the one before it; that he had been instructed by persons in charge of the road not to permit colored persons to ride in the car in which she was getting, but to have them go in the other. The woman, however, persisted in going into the car appropriated for white ladies, and the man put her out with force, and as she alleged, some insult. She then got into the car into which she had been directed to get—the one assigned to colored people—was carried safely into Washington and got out there.

Hereupon she sued the *Washington, Alexandria, and Georgetown Railroad Company* in the Supreme Court of the District.

* * *

* * * [A] verdict having been given in $1500 for the plaintiff and judgment entered on it, the company brought the case here * * *.

■ MR. JUSTICE DAVIS delivered the opinion of the court.

* * *

The third and last assignment of error asserts the right of the company to make the regulation separating the colored from the white passengers.

If the defendant in error had the right to retain the seat she had first taken, it is conceded the verdict of the jury should not be disturbed.

It appears that the Washington and Alexandria Railroad Company, in 1863, was desirous of extending its road from the south side of the Potomac near to the Baltimore and Ohio depot, in Washington, and Congressional aid was asked to enable it to do so. The authority to make the extension was granted, and the streets designated across which the road should pass. This grant was accompanied with several provisions, among the number was one that no person shall be excluded from the cars on account of color. In 1866, the plaintiff in error, which had succeeded to the chartered rights of the previous company, obtained from Congress an amendment to the former act, so as to change the route of the extension, and for other purposes. The latter act leaves all the provisions of the former act in full force, and the present company, therefore, is obliged to observe in the running of its road all the requirements imposed by Congress in its previous legislation on the subject. This leads us to consider what Congress meant in directing that no person should be excluded from the cars of the company on account of color.

The plaintiff in error contends that it has literally obeyed the direction, because it has never excluded this class of persons from the cars, but on the contrary, has always provided accommodations for them.

This is an ingenious attempt to evade a compliance with the obvious meaning of the requirement. It is true the words taken literally might bear the interpretation put upon them by the plaintiff in error, but evidently Congress did not use them in any such limited sense. There was no occasion in legislating for a railroad corporation to annex a condition to a grant of power, that the company should allow colored persons to ride in its cars. This right had never been refused, nor could there have been in the mind of any one an apprehension that such a state of things would ever occur, for self-interest would clearly induce the carrier—south as well as north—to transport, if paid for it, all persons, whether white or black, who should desire transportation. It was the discrimination in the use of the cars on account of color, where slavery obtained, which was the subject of discussion at the time, and not the fact that the colored race could not ride in the cars at all. Congress, in the belief that this discrimination was unjust, acted. It told this company, in substance, that it could extend its road within the District as desired, but that this discrimination must cease, and the colored and white race, in the use of the cars, be placed on an equality. This condition it had the right to impose, and in the temper of Congress at the time, it is manifest the grant could not have been made without it. It was the privilege of the company to reject it, but to do this, it must reject the whole legislation with which it was connected. It cannot accept a part and repudiate the rest. Having, therefore, constructed its road as it was authorized to do, and in this way greatly added to the value of its property, it will be held to a faithful compliance with all the terms accompanying the grant by which it was enabled to secure this pecuniary advantage.

In our opinion there is no error in the record, and the judgment below must be

AFFIRMED.

NOTES AND QUESTIONS

1. To anticipate some language to come shortly, the congressional statute in this case was understood to require equality of treatment of customers. Separate cars were not equal, even if they were of comparable quality. It is critical to note that the U.S. Supreme Court understood that point in *Railroad Co. v. Brown* decided in 1873, but it had forgotten the point by 1896 when it upheld the concept of separate, but equal railway cars in *Plessy v. Ferguson*. *See infra* pages 1284–1294.

2. Note the Court's statement that: "This is an ingenious attempt to evade a compliance with the obvious meaning of [the words that] no person shall be excluded from the cars of the railroad on account of color." This phrase sums up, in a nutshell, the entire period of Jim Crow segregation: It was an ingenious attempt to evade a compliance with the obvious meaning of the Reconstruction Amendments.

3. Sometimes those attempts at evasion were far from ingenious; they were blatant and obvious. And sometimes the Supreme Court said so.

B. STRAUDER V. WEST VIRGINIA

100 U.S. 303 (1880)

■ MR. JUSTICE STRONG delivered the opinion of the court.

The plaintiff in error, a colored man, was indicted for murder in the Circuit Court of Ohio County in West Virginia, on the 20th of October, 1874, and, upon trial, was convicted and sentenced * * *. [I]t is now, in substance, averred that, at the trial in the State court, the defendant (now plaintiff in error) was denied rights to which he was entitled under the Constitution and laws of the United States.

In the Circuit Court of the State, before the trial of the indictment was commenced, the defendant presented his petition, verified by his oath, praying for a removal of the cause into the Circuit Court of the United States, assigning, as ground for the removal, that, "by virtue of the laws of the State of West Virginia, no colored man was eligible to be a member of the grand jury or to serve on a petit jury in the State; that white men are so eligible, and that, by reason of his being a colored man and having been a slave, he had reason to believe, and did believe, he could not have the full and equal benefit of all laws and proceedings in the State of West Virginia for the security of his person as is enjoyed by white citizens, and that he had less chance of enforcing in the courts of the State his rights on the prosecution, as a citizen of the United States, and that the probabilities of a denial of them to him as such citizen on every trial which might take place on the indictment in the courts of the State were much more enhanced than if he was a white man." This petition was denied by the State court, and the cause was forced to trial.

* * *

The law of the State to which reference was made in the petition for removal and in the several motions was enacted on the 12th of March, 1873 (Acts of 18778, p. 102), and it is as follows: "All white male persons who are twenty-one year of age and who are citizens of this State shall be liable to serve as jurors, except as herein provided." The persons excepted are State officials.

In this court, several errors have been assigned, and the controlling question underlying them all are, first, whether, by the Constitution and laws of the United States, every citizen of the United States has a right to a trial of an indictment against him by a jury selected and impaneled without discrimination against his race or color, because of race or color; and, second, if he has such a right, and is denied its enjoyment by the State in which he is indicted, may he cause the case to be removed into the Circuit Court of the United States?

It is to be observed that the first of these questions is not whether a colored man, when an indictment has been preferred against him, has a right to a grand or a petit jury composed in whole or in part of persons of his own race or color, but it is whether, in the composition or selection of juror by whom he is to be indicted or tried, all persons of his race or color may be excluded by law solely because of their race or color, so that by no possibility can any colored man sit upon the jury.

The questions are important, for they demand a construction of the recent amendment of the Constitution. If the defendant has a right to have a jury selected for the trial of his case without discrimination against all persons of his race or color, because of their race or color, the right, if not created, is protected by those amendments and the legislation of Congress under them. The Fourteenth Amendment ordains that "all persons born or naturalized in the United States and subject to the jurisdiction thereof are citizens of the United States and of the State wherein they reside. No State shall make or enforce any laws which shall abridge the privilege or immunities of citizens of the United States, nor shall any State deprive any person of life, liberty, or property without due process of law, nor deny to any person within its jurisdiction the equal protection of the laws."

This is one of a series of constitutional provisions having a common purpose; namely, securing to a race recently emancipated, a race that, through many generations had been held in slavery, all the civil rights that the superior race enjoy. The true spirit and meaning of the amendments, as we said in the *Slaughter-house Cases,* 16 Wall. 36, cannot be understood without keeping in view the history of the times when they were adopted, and the general objects they plainly sought to accomplish. At the time when they were incorporated into the Constitution, it required little knowledge of human nature to anticipate that those who had long been regarded as an inferior and subject race would, when suddenly raised to the rank of citizenship, be looked upon with jealousy and positive dislike, and that State laws might be enacted or enforced to perpetuate the distinctions that had before existed. Discriminations against them had been habitual. It was well known that, in some States laws making such discrimination then existed, and others might well be expected. The colored race, as a race, was abject and ignorant, and in that condition was unfitted to command the respect of those who had superior intelligence. Their training had left them mere children, and as such they needed the protection which a wise government extends to those who are unable to protect themselves. They especially needed protection against unfriendly action in the States where they were resident. It was in view of these considerations the Fourteenth Amendment was framed and adopted. It was designed to assure to the colored race the enjoyment of all the civil rights that under the law are enjoyed by white persons, and to give to that race the protection of the general government in that enjoyment, whenever it should be denied by the States. It not only gave citizenship and the privileges of citizenship to persons of color, but it denied to any State the power to withhold from them the equal protection of the laws, and authorized Congress to enforce its provisions by appropriate legislation * * *.

If this is the spirit and meaning of the amendment, whether it means more or not, it is to be construed liberally, to carry out the purposes of its framers. It ordains that no State shall make or enforce any laws which shall abridge the privileges or immunities of citizens of the United States (evidently referring to the newly made citizens, who, being citizens of the United States, are declared to be also citizens of the State in which they reside). It ordains that no State shall deprive any person of life, liberty, or property without due process of law, or deny to any person within its jurisdiction the equal protection of the laws. What is this but declaring that the law in the States shall be the same for the black as for the white; that all persons, whether colored or white, shall stand equal before the laws of the States, and, in regard to the colored race, for whose protection the amendment was primarily designed, that no discrimination shall be made against them by law because of their color? The words of the amendment, it is true, are prohibitory, but they contain a necessary implication of a positive immunity, or right, most valuable to the colored race—the right to exemption from unfriendly legislation against them distinctively as colored,—exemption from legal discriminations, implying inferiority in civil society, lessening the security of their enjoyment of the rights which others enjoy, and discriminations which are steps towards reducing them to the condition of a subject race.

That the West Virginia statute respecting juries—the statute that controlled the selection of the grand and petit jury in the case of the plaintiff in error—is such a discrimination ought not to be doubted. Nor would it be if the persons excluded by it were white men. If in those States where the colored people constitute a majority of the entire population a law should be enacted excluding all white men from jury service, thus denying to them the privilege of participating fully with the blacks in the administration of justice, we apprehend no one would be heard to claim that it would not be a denial to white men of the equal protection of the laws. Nor if a law should be passed excluding all naturalized Celtic Irishmen, would there be any doubt of its inconsistency with the spirit of the amendment. The very fact that colored people are singled out and expressly denied by a statute all right to participate in the administration of the law, as jurors, because of their color, though they are citizens, and may be in other respects fully qualified, is practically a brand upon them affixed by the law, an assertion of their inferiority, and a stimulant to that race prejudice which is an impediment to securing to individuals of the race that equal justice which the law aims to secure to all others.

The right to a trial by jury is guaranteed to every citizen of West Virginia by the Constitution of that State, and the constitution of juries is a very essential part of the protection such a mode of trial is intended to secure. The very idea of a jury is a body of men composed of the peers or equals of the person whose rights it is selected or summoned to determine; that is, of his neighbors, fellows, associates, persons having the same legal status in society as that which he holds. Blackstone, in his Commentaries, says, "The right of trial by jury, or the country, is a trial by the peers of every Englishman, and is the grand bulwark of his liberties, and is secured to him by the Great Charter." It is also guarded by statutory enactments intended to make impossible what Mr. Bentham called "packing juries." It is well known that prejudices often exist against particular classes in the community, which sway the judgment of jurors, and which therefore operate in some cases to deny to persons of those classes the full enjoyment of that protection which others enjoy. Prejudice in a local community is held to be a reason for a change of venue. The framers of the constitutional amendment must have known full well the existence of such prejudice and its likelihood to continue against the manumitted slaves and their race, and that knowledge was doubtless a motive that led to the amendment * * *.

In view of these considerations, it is hard to see why the statute of West Virginia should not be regarded as discriminating against a colored man when he is put upon trial for an alleged criminal offence against the State. It is not easy to comprehend how it can be said that while every white man is entitled to a trial by a jury selected from persons of his own race or color, or, rather, selected without discrimination against his color, and a negro is not, the latter is equally protected by the law with the former. Is not protection of life and liberty against race or color prejudice a right, a legal right, under the constitutional amendment? And how can it be maintained that compelling a colored man to submit to a trial for his life by a jury drawn from a panel from which the State has expressly excluded every man of his race, because of color alone, however well qualified in other respects, is not a denial to him of equal legal protection?

We do not say that within the limits from which it is not excluded by the amendment a State may not prescribe the qualifications of its jurors, and in so doing make discriminations. It may confine the selection to males, to freeholders, to citizens, to persons within certain ages, or to persons having educational qualifications. We do not believe the Fourteenth Amendment was ever intended to prohibit this. Looking at its history, it is clear it had no such purpose. Its aim was against discrimination because of race or color. As we have said more than once, its design was to protect an emancipated race, and to strike down all possible legal discriminations against those who belong to it. To quote further from 16 Wall., *supra:* "In giving construction to any of these article [amendments], it is necessary to keep the main purpose steadily in view." "It is so clearly a provision for that race and that emergency that a strong case would be necessary for its application to any other." We are not now called upon to affirm or deny that it had other purposes.

* * *.

Concluding, therefore, that the statute of West Virginia, discriminating in the selection of jurors, as it does, against negroes because of their color, amounts to a denial of the equal protection of the laws to a colored man when he is put upon trial for an alleged offence against the State, it remains only to be considered whether the power of Congress to enforce the provisions of the Fourteenth Amendment by appropriate legislation is sufficient to justify the enactment of sect. 641 of the Revised Statutes.

A right or an immunity, whether created by the Constitution or only guaranteed by it, even without any express delegation of power, may be protected by Congress * * *. And one very efficient and appropriate mode of extending such protection and securing to a party the enjoyment of the right or immunity, is a law providing for the removal of his case from a State court, in which the right is denied by the State law, into a Federal court, where it will be upheld. This is an ordinary mode of protecting rights and immunities conferred by the Federal Constitution and laws. Sect. 641 is such a provision * * *.

* * * This act puts in the form of a statute what had been substantially ordained by the constitutional amendment. It was a step towards enforcing the constitutional provisions. Sect. 641 was an advanced step, fully warranted, we think, by the fifth section of the Fourteenth Amendment.

* * *

The judgment of the Supreme Court of West Virginia will be reversed, and the case remitted with instructions to reverse the judgment of the Circuit Court of Ohio county, and it is

So ordered.

[*Editors' Note: Justices Field and Clifford both dissented for the same reasons they dissented in the case below, which you are about to read.*]

NOTES AND QUESTIONS

1. Note that Justice Strong reads the Equal Protection Clause as protecting more than just the rights of African-Americans to be tried by a jury from which their race has been excluded He also reads it as conferring on white Americans and Celtic Irishmen the right to be tried by a jury from which their peers have been excluded. This makes it clear that the ban on discrimination in the Fourteenth Amendment bans not only discrimination against African-Americans but discrimination against all classes of people on the basis of race or nationality (understanding that, in the nineteenth century, many nationalities, and even some religions, were widely perceived as distinct races). What does the opinion say about discrimination on bases other than race or nationality? Does it say that the Section 1 of the Fourteenth Amendment is exclusively limited to race discrimination? Did the *Slaughter-House Cases* say that? Section 2 of the Amendment expressly protects only the political rights of "male" citizens and not of women. Does the explicit mention of the word "male" in Section 2 imply anything by the absence of such a word in Section 1, which grants equal civil rights?

2. Justice Strong reads Congress's power under Section 5 of the Fourteenth Amendment broadly to allow African-Americans to remove to federal court any state criminal case in which they are being discriminated against because of their race. Unlike in *Blyew* or *Cruikshank,* here the plaintiff was complaining about governmental action; there was no issue in *Strauder* about State versus private action.

3. The Court seems to say that the statute in question was a denial of equal protection of the laws. But it was a *statute,* not executive or judicial action, that discriminated on the basis of race. Putting the *Slaughter-House Cases* aside, as a matter of original meaning should this case have been decided under the Privileges or Immunities Clause, which deals with the "mak[ing]" of laws? *See* CURRIE, *supra,* at 383 ("One may quibble over whether as an original matter the clause applicable to *Strauder* was that guaranteeing equal protection or that securing privileges and immunities"). Or does the Equal Protection Clause cover the making as well as the enforcing of statutes? Once the *Slaughter-House Cases* are decided, do you *have* to interpret the Equal Protection Clause to include the making of statutes even if, as an original matter, one thinks it a mistake? Do two wrongs make a right?

4. Would a right not be tried by a jury pool that excludes a certain race count as a "privilege or immunity" of citizenship? Would the rights of prospective jurors to be included in the jury pool count as a "privilege or immunity" of citizenship? Or is *Strauder* truly a "core" equal protection case because it concerns the State's failure to provide a fair

judicial process, just as it would be a "core" equal protection case if the State's prosecutors were systematically biased?

C. EX PARTE VIRGINIA

100 U.S. 339 (1879)

■ MR. JUSTICE STRONG delivered the opinion of the court.

The petitioner, J. D. Coles, was arrested, and he is now held in custody under an indictment found against him in the District Court of the United States for the Western District of Virginia. The indictment alleged that he, being a judge of the county court of Pittsylvania County of that State, and an officer charged by law with the selection of jurors to serve in the circuit and county courts of said county in the year 1878, did then and there exclude and fail to select as grand and petit jurors certain citizens of said county of Pittsylvania, of African race and black color, said citizens possessing all other qualifications prescribed by law, and being by him excluded from the jury lists made out by him as such judge, on account of their race, color, and previous condition of servitude, and for no other reason, against the peace and dignity of the United States, and against the form of the statute of the United States in such case made and provided.

* * *[H]e avers that the District Court had and has no jurisdiction of the matters charged against him in said indictment; that they constitute no offence punishable in said District Court; and that the finding of said indictment, and his consequent arrest and imprisonment, are unwarranted by the Constitution of the United States, or by any law made in pursuance thereof, and are in violation of his rights and of the rights of the State of Virginia, whose judicial officer he is.

A similar petition has been presented by the State of Virginia, praying for a *habeas corpus* and for the discharge of the said Coles * * *.

* * *

The indictment and bench-warrant, in virtue of which the petitioner Coles has been arrested and is held in custody, have their justification,—if any they have,—in the act of Congress of March 1, 1875, sect. 4. 18 Stat., part 3, 336. That section enacts that "no citizen, possessing all other qualifications which are or may be prescribed by law shall be disqualified for service as grand or petit juror in any court of the United States, or of any State, on account of race, color, or previous condition of servitude; and any officer or other person charged with any duty in the selection or summoning of jurors who shall exclude or fail to summon any citizen for the cause aforesaid shall, on conviction thereof, be deemed guilty of a misdemeanor, and be fined not more than $5,000." The defendant has been indicted for the misdemeanor described in this act, and it is not denied that he is now properly held in custody to answer the indictment, if the act of Congress was warranted by the Constitution. The whole merits of the case are involved in the question, whether the act was thus warranted.

The provisions of the Constitution that relate to this subject are found in the Thirteenth and Fourteenth Amendments * * *.

One great purpose of these amendments was to raise the colored race from that condition of inferiority and servitude in which most of them had previously stood, into perfect equality of civil rights with all other persons within the jurisdiction of the States. They were intended to take away all possibility of oppression by law because of race or color. They were intended to be, what they really are, limitations of the power of the States and enlargements of the power of Congress. They are to some extent declaratory of rights, and though in form prohibitions, they imply immunities, such as may be protected by congressional legislation. We had occasion in the *Slaughter-House Cases* (16 Wall. 27) to express our opinion of their spirit and purpose, and to some extent of their meaning. We have again been called to consider them in *Tennessee v. Davis* (supra, p. 257) and *Strauder v. West Virginia, supra*, p. 303. In this latter case we held that the Fourteenth Amendment secures, among other civil rights, to colored men, when charged with criminal offences against a State, an impartial jury trial, by jurors indifferently selected or chosen without discrimination against such jurors because of their color. We held that immunity from any such discrimination is one of the equal rights of all persons, and that any withholding it by a State is a denial of the equal protection of the laws, within the meaning of the amendment. We held that such an equal right to an impartial jury trial, and such an immunity from unfriendly discrimination, are placed by the amendment under the protection of the general government and guaranteed by it. We held, further, that this protection and this guarantee, as the fifth section of the amendment expressly ordains, may be enforced by Congress by means of appropriate legislation.

All of the amendments derive much of their force from this latter provision. It is not said the *judicial power* of the general government shall extend to enforcing the prohibitions and to protecting the rights and immunities guaranteed. It is not said that branch of the government shall be authorized to declare void any action of a State in violation of the prohibitions. It is the power of Congress which has been enlarged. Congress is authorized to *enforce* the prohibitions by appropriate legislation. Some legislation is contemplated to make the amendments fully effective. Whatever legislation is appropriate, that is, adapted to carry out the objects the amendments have in view, whatever tends to enforce submission to the prohibitions they contain, and to secure to all persons the enjoyment of perfect equality of civil rights and the equal protection of the laws against State denial or invasion, if not prohibited, is brought within the domain of congressional power.

Nor does it make any difference that such legislation is restrictive of what the State might have done before the constitutional amendment was adopted. The prohibitions of the Fourteenth Amendment are directed to the States, and they are to a degree restrictions of State power. It is these which Congress is empowered to enforce, and to enforce against State action, however put forth, whether that action be executive, legislative, or judicial. Such enforcement is no invasion of State sovereignty. No law can be, which the people of the States have, by the Constitution of the United States, empowered Congress to enact * * *.

* * * The argument in support of the petition for a *habeas corpus* ignores entirely the power conferred upon Congress by the Fourteenth Amendment. Were it not for the fifth section of that amendment, there might be room for argument that the first section is only declaratory of the moral duty of the State * * *. But the Constitution now expressly gives authority for congressional interference and compulsion in the cases embraced within the Fourteenth Amendment. It is but a limited authority, true, extending only to a single class of cases; but within its limits it is complete * * *.

We do not perceive how holding an office under a State, and claiming to act for the State, can relieve the holder from obligation to obey the Constitution of the United States, or take away the power of Congress to punish his disobedience.

It was insisted during the argument on behalf of the petitioner that Congress cannot punish a State judge for his official acts; and it was assumed that Judge Cole, in selecting the jury as he did, was performing a judicial act. This assumption cannot be admitted. Whether the act done by him was judicial or not is to be determined by its character, and not by the character of the agent. Whether he was a county judge or not is of no importance. The duty of selecting jurors might as well have been committed to a private person as to one holding the office of a judge. It often is given to county commissioners, or supervisors, or assessors. In former times, the selection was made by the sheriff. In such cases, it surely is not a judicial act, in any such sense as is contended for here * * *.

But if the selection of jurors could be considered in any case a judicial act, can the act charged against the petitioner be considered such when he acted outside of his authority and in direct violation of the spirit of the State statute? That statute gave him no authority, when selecting jurors, from whom a panel might be drawn for a circuit court, to exclude all colored men merely because they were colored. Such an exclusion was not left within the limits of his discretion. It is idle, therefore, to say that the act of Congress is unconstitutional because it inflicts penalties upon State judges for their judicial action. It does no such thing.

Upon the whole, as we are of opinion that the act of Congress upon which the indictment against the petitioner was founded is constitutional, and that he is correctly held to answer it, and as, therefore, no object would be secured by issuing a writ of *habeas corpus*, the petitions are

Denied.

■ MR. JUSTICE FIELD, with whom concurred MR. JUSTICE CLIFFORD, dissenting.

I dissent from the judgment of the court in this case, and from the reasons by which it is supported; and I will state the grounds of my dissent.

* * *

The petitioner, J. D. Coles, is the judge of the county court of the county of Pittsylvania, in Virginia, and has held that office for some years. It is not pretended that, in the discharge of his judicial duties, he has ever selected as jurors persons who were not qualified to serve in that character, or who were not of sound judgment, or who were not free from legal exception. It is not even suggested in argument that he has not at all times faithfully obeyed the law of the State; yet he has been indicted in the District Court of the United States for the Western District of Virginia for having, on some undesignated day in the year 1878, excluded and failed to select as grand and petit jurors citizens of the county, on account of race, color, and previous condition of servitude. The indictment does not state who those citizens were, or set forth any particulars of the offence, but charges it in the general words of a definition. The District Court, nevertheless, issued a bench-warrant, upon which the judge was arrested, and, refusing to give bail, he is held in custody to answer the indictment. He therefore petitions for a *certiorari* to that court to send up the record of its proceedings for our examination, and for a writ of *habeas corpus*, alleging that its action was without jurisdiction, and that his imprisonment thereunder is unlawful; and he prays to be released therefrom.

The Commonwealth of Virginia has also presented a similar petition, declaring that she is injured by being deprived of the services of her judicial officer, by his unlawful arrest and imprisonment.

If the District Court had no jurisdiction, as alleged, of the matters charged against the county judge, if they constitute no public offence for which he could be held, his arrest and imprisonment upon process issued upon the indictment were unlawful, and his petition should be granted.

* * *

* * * [T]he fourth section of the act of 1875, so far as it applies to the selection of jurors in the State courts, is unconstitutional and void. Previous to the late amendments, it would not have been contended, by any one familiar with the Constitution, that Congress was vested with any power to exercise supervision over the conduct of State officers in the discharge of their duties under the laws of the State, and prescribe a punishment for disregarding its directions. It would have been conceded that the selection of jurors was a subject exclusively for regulation by the States[,] that it was for them to determine who should act as jurors in their courts, from what class they should be taken, and what qualifications they should possess; and that their officers in carrying out the laws in this respect were responsible only to them. The States could have abolished jury trials altogether, and required all controversies to be submitted to the courts without their intervention. The Sixth and Seventh Amendments, in which jury trials are mentioned, apply only to the Federal courts, as has been repeatedly adjudged.

The government created by the Constitution was not designed for the regulation of matters of purely local concern. The States required no aid from any external authority to manage their domestic affairs. They were fully competent to provide for the due administration of justice between their own citizens in their own courts; and they needed no directions in that matter from any other government, any more than they needed directions as to their highways and schools, their hospitals and charitable institutions, their public libraries, or the magistrates they should appoint for their towns and counties. It was only for matters which concerned all the States, and which could not be managed by them in their independent capacity, or managed only with great difficulty and embarrassment, that a general and common government was desired * * *.

* * *

Nothing, in my judgment, could have a greater tendency to destroy the independence and autonomy of the States; reduce them to a humiliating and degrading dependence upon the central government; engender constant irritation; and destroy that domestic tranquillity which it was one of the objects of the Constitution to insure,—than the doctrine asserted in this case, that Congress can exercise coercive authority over judicial officers of the States in the discharge of their duties under State laws. It will be only another step in the same direction towards consolidation, when it assumes to exercise similar coercive authority over governors and legislators of the States.

* * *

The Thirteenth and Fourteenth Amendments are relied upon, as already stated, to support the legislation in question * * *.

The history of the amendments is fresh in the recollection of all of us. They grew out of the late civil war and the events which followed it. They were primarily designed to give freedom to persons of the African race, prevent their future enslavement, make them citizens, prevent discriminating State legislation against their rights as freemen, and secure to them the ballot. The generality of the language used necessarily extends some of their provisions to all persons of every race and color; but in construing the amendments and giving effect to them, the occasion of their adoption and the purposes they were designed to attain should be always borne in mind. Nor should it be forgotten that they are additions to the previous amendments, and are to be construed in connection with them and the original Constitution as one instrument. They do not, in terms, contravene or repeal any thing which previously existed in the Constitution and those amendments. Aside from the extinction of slavery, and the declaration of citizenship, their provisions are merely prohibitory upon the States and there is nothing in their language or purpose which indicates that they are to be construed or enforced in any way different from that adopted with reference to previous restraints upon the States. The provision authorizing Congress to enforce them by appropriate legislation does not enlarge their scope, nor confer any authority which would not have existed independently of it * * *. The Constitution, as already stated, contemplates the existence and independence of the States in all their reserved powers * * *. Legislation could not, therefore, be appropriate which, under pretence of prohibiting a State from doing certain things, should tend to destroy it, or any of its essential attributes * * *.

I cannot think I am mistaken in saying that a change so radical in the relation between the Federal and State authorities, as would justify legislation interfering with the independent action of the different departments of the State governments, in all matters over which the States retain jurisdiction, was never contemplated by the recent amendments. The people in adopting them did not suppose they were altering the fundamental theory of their dual system of governments * * *.

* * *

The fourth clause in the first section of the [fourteenth] amendment declares that no State shall "deny to any person within its jurisdiction the equal protection of the laws." Upon this clause the counsel of the district judge chiefly rely to sustain the validity of the legislation in question. But the universality of the protection secured necessarily renders their position untenable. All persons within the jurisdiction of the State, whether permanent residents or temporary sojourners, whether old or young, male or female, are to be equally protected. Yet no one will contend that equal protection to women, to children, to the aged, to aliens, can only be secured by allowing persons of the class to which they belong to act as jurors in cases affecting their interests. The equality of protection intended does not require that all persons shall be permitted to participate in the government of the State and the administration of its laws, to hold its offices, or be clothed with any public trusts. As already said, the universality of the protection assured repels any such conclusion.

The equality of the protection secured extends only to civil rights as distinguished from those which are political, or arise from the form of the government and its mode of administration. And yet the reach and influence of the amendment are immense. It opens the courts of the country to every one, on the same terms, for the security of his person and property, the prevention and redress of wrongs, and the enforcement of contracts; it assures to every one the same rules of evidence and modes of procedure; it allows no impediments to the acquisition of property and the pursuit of happiness, to which all are not subjected; it suffers no other or greater burdens or charges to be laid upon one than such as are equally borne by others; and in the administration of criminal justice it permits no different or greater punishment to be imposed upon one than such as is prescribed to all for like offences. It secures to all persons their civil rights upon the same terms; but it leaves political rights, or such as arise from the form of government and its administration, as they stood previous to its adoption. It has no more reference to them than it has to social rights and duties, which do not rest upon any positive law, though they are more potential in controlling the intercourse of individuals. In the consideration of questions growing out of these amendments much confusion has arisen from a failure to distinguish between the civil and the political rights of citizens. Civil rights are absolute and personal. Political rights, on the other hand, are conditioned and dependent upon the discretion of the elective or appointing power, whether that be the people acting through the ballot, or one of the departments of their government. The civil rights of the individual are never to be withheld, and may be always judicially enforced. The political rights which he may enjoy, such as holding office and discharging a public trust, are qualified because their possession depends on his fitness, to be adjudged by those whom society has clothed with the elective authority. The Thirteenth and Fourteenth Amendments were designed to secure the civil rights of all persons, of every race, color, and condition; but they left to the States to determine to whom the possession of political powers should be intrusted. This is manifest from the fact that when it was desired to confer political power upon the newly made citizens of the States, as was done by inhibiting the denial to them of the suffrage on account of race, color, or previous condition of servitude, a new amendment was required.

* * *

The position that in cases where the rights of colored persons are concerned, justice will not be done to them unless they have a mixed jury, is founded upon the notion that in such cases white persons will not be fair and honest jurors. If this position be correct, there ought not to be any white persons on the jury where the interests of colored persons only are involved. That jury would not be an honest or fair one, of which any of its members should be governed in his judgment by other considerations than the law and the evidence; and that decision would hardly be considered just which should be reached by a sort of compromise, in which the prejudices of one race were set off against the prejudices of the other. To be consistent, those who hold this notion should contend that in cases affecting members of the colored race only, the juries should be composed entirely of colored persons, and that the presiding judge should be of the same race. To this result the doctrine asserted by the District Court logically leads * * *.

If these views as to the purport and meaning of the Thirteenth and Fourteenth Amendments to the Constitution be correct, there is no warrant for the act of Congress under which the indictment in this case was found, and the arrest and imprisonment of the petitioner were unlawful, and his release should be ordered.

* * *

NOTES AND QUESTIONS

1. Justices Field and Clifford, who dissented, were the only two Democrats on the Supreme Court at a time when the Democrats were advocates of states' rights. Field was appointed by President Lincoln, while Clifford had been appointed by President James Buchanan to replace Justice Curtis after he resigned from the Supreme Court because of its decision in the *Dred Scott Case*. Justices Field and Clifford seem not to have understood at all how very sharply the federal-state balance of power had been shifted toward national power as a result of the Reconstruction Amendments. They were truly relics of an older and bygone past.

2. On the other hand, Justice Field was also a very smart lawyer. He is correct that Section 1 of the Fourteenth Amendment deals with civil rights and not political rights. But perhaps because he did not grasp the seismic nature of the Reconstruction Amendments, he stopped too soon at that simple observation. At least four paths—branching in quite different directions—potentially lead to the conclusion that race discrimination in jury service is unconstitutional. First, one might see such discrimination as a badge or incident of slavery forbidden by the Thirteenth Amendment. This rationale would forbid race discrimination in jury service and support the indictment in *Ex parte Virginia*, but it would not forbid discrimination based on sex, age, or other considerations. Second, because the first sentence of the Fourteenth Amendment confers national citizenship on all Americans, the right to serve on a jury—one of the central institutions of Anglo-American jurisprudence—could be seen as an incident of citizenship. (The same rationale would also support the conclusion, which to Justice Field was unthinkable, that all citizens have a right to seek and serve in political office.) As Justice Field pointed out, however, infants are citizens, so an argument from citizenship surely cuts too broadly to be plausible—at least without a worked-out conception of citizenship behind it that the Court has never produced. Third, as in *Strauder,* one can focus on the equal protection of the laws *for litigants*. The relevant right would not necessarily be the right of a person to serve in a jury pool but rather the right to be tried through a nondiscriminatory jury pool, to help secure the decidedly civil right to equal protection of the laws. A statute assuring the nondiscriminatory nature of the jury pool would seem fairly clearly to be "appropriate legislation" to secure that civil right. Such an argument would be as broad (or narrow) as the Equal Protection Clause turns out to be and thus could invalidate restrictions other than those based on race. As Justice Field points out, this argument makes certain assumptions about how jurors are likely to behave. Could Justice Field, in the immediate aftermath of the Civil War, seriously have thought either that those assumptions were unjustified or that the Reconstruction Congress might not have made them? Finally, the Fifteenth Amendment forbids discriminating against United States citizens with respect to their right "to vote." To vote on what? The Amendment does not say. From the context, it is obvious that the Amendment is talking at least about the political right to vote in elections. But isn't the right to vote on a jury also a political right—and, indeed, a political right of the highest and most venerable order? *See* AKHIL REED AMAR, THE BILL OF RIGHTS: CREATION AND RECONSTRUCTION 273–74 (1998). Isn't the Fifteenth Amendment, helping secure the Ancient Constitution's fundamental role of the jury in civil and political life, the most straightforward path to both *Strauder* and *Ex parte Virginia*?

3. Does the majority in *Ex parte Virginia* say that judges have no power to enforce the Reconstruction Amendments until and unless Congress has acted? Do the enforcement clauses say that? Would the Reconstruction Amendments—or any other part of the Constitution—need to say that judges can enforce them? Obviously, that dictum has not stuck.

4. The majority argues that the function of jury selection is not necessarily "judicial." What does that matter? Why would "judicial" acts be beyond the reach of the Reconstruction Amendments (and Congress's power to enforce them) any more than legislative or executive acts? For whatever this is worth, in 1871 the Court—meaning essentially the same Court that decided *Ex parte Virginia*—crafted a broad immunity from civil liability for all judges performing judicial functions, even when they performed those functions maliciously or corruptly. *See Bradley v. Fisher,* 80 U.S. (13 Wall.) 375 (1871). The opinion in *Bradley v. Fisher* was authored by Justice Field (though Justice Clifford was one of the two dissenters in that case). If the majority in *Ex parte Virginia* agreed with Justice Field (and the State of Virginia) that the judge had performed a judicial function, would it have decided the case differently?

D. INTERRACIAL MARRIAGE AS A CONSTITUTIONAL RIGHT

At one time or another, more than forty States had formal bans on interracial marriages. *See* Cyrus E. Phillips IV, *Miscegenation: The Courts and the Constitution*, 8 WM. & MARY L. REV. 133, 133 (1966). Many of those bans persisted into the 1960s, until the Supreme Court found them unconstitutional in *Loving v. Virginia,* 388 U.S. 1 (1967), which we discuss later. *See infra* pages 1327–1331. In the 1870s, however, a number of state courts concluded that bans on interracial marriages—so-called anti-miscegenation acts—were inconsistent with both the Constitution and the Civil Rights Act of 1866. One state court disagreed—and its views somehow became the received wisdom in federal court for nearly a century. Consider the following three cases and decide which ones best grasp the meaning—original or otherwise—of the Reconstruction Amendments and statutes.

Burns v. State

48 Ala. 195 (1872)

■ B. F. SAFFOLD, J.

The appellant was convicted and fined under an indictment, charging him as a justice of the peace, with solemnizing the rites of matrimony between a white person and a negro, contrary to the provisions of sections 3602, 3603 of the Revised Code. It is contended for him that these statutes are superseded by an act of congress, passed April 9, 1866, "to protect all persons in the United States in their civil rights, and furnish the means for their vindication;" and also, that they are in violation of both the State and Federal constitutions.

The first section of the act is in the following words: "All persons born in the United States, and not subject to any foreign power, excluding Indians not taxed, are hereby declared to be citizens of the United States; and such citizens of every race and color, without regard to any previous condition of slavery or involuntary servitude, except as a punishment for crime, whereof the party shall have been duly convicted, shall have the same right in every State and territory in the United States, to make and enforce contracts, to sue, be parties, and give evidence, to inherit, purchase, lease, sell, hold and convey real and personal property, and to full and equal benefit of all laws and proceedings for the security of person and property, as is enjoyed by white citizens, and shall be subject to like punishment, pains and penalties, and to none other, any law, statute, ordinance, regulation or custom to the contrary, notwithstanding." The second section imposes punishment on any person who, under color of any law, statute, &c., subjects or causes to be subjected, any inhabitant of any State or territory to the deprivation of any right secured or protected by the act.

In *Ellis v. The State,* (42 Ala. 525,) it was held that there is no conflict between this act and the sections of the Revised Code referred to. Marriage is a civil contract, and in that character alone is dealt with by the municipal law. The same right to make a contract as is enjoyed by white citizens, means the right to make any contract which a white citizen may make. The law intended to destroy the distinctions of race and color in respect to the rights secured by it. It did not aim to create merely an equality of the races in reference to each other. If so, laws prohibiting the races from suing each other, giving evidence for or against, or dealing with one another, would be permissible. The very excess to which such a construction would lead is conclusive against it.

It is self-evident that an inhabitant of a country, proscribed by its laws, approaches equality with the more favored population in proportion as the proscription is removed. The supreme court of the United States, in the *Dred Scott* case, (19 How. 393,) decided that a free negro, of the African race, whose ancestors were brought to this country and sold as slaves, was not a "citizen" within the meaning of the constitution of the United States. In proof of this, for the constitution did not so declare at that time, Chief Justice Taney, with much stress, referred to the laws of many of the States, prohibiting marriage between such persons and the white population. It can not be supposed that this discrimination was otherwise than against the negro, on account of his servile condition, because no State would be so unwise as to impose disabilities in so important a matter as marriage on its most favored citizens, without consideration of their advantage. Dred Scott was not allowed to sue a citizen because he was not himself a citizen. One of the rights conferred by citizenship, therefore, is that of suing any other citizen. The civil rights bill now confers this right upon the negro in express terms, as also the right to make and enforce contracts, amongst which is that of marriage with any citizen capable of entering into that relation.

It is no argument against this conclusion that many citizens are debarred from rights and privileges allowed to others, as is the case with married women and children. The power to regulate society is interwoven with the duty to preserve it. But on account of the abuse to which this power is subject, communities, as they increase in knowledge of the science of government, find it necessary to limit and restrain it by provisions of their fundamental law. Whether congress, at the time it passed the civil rights bill, had authority to do so or not, which is gravely questioned in the Dred Scott case, there can be no doubt that its cardinal principle is now declared by the 14th amendment to the Federal constitution * * *. The spirit and express declaration of this section are, that no person shall be disfranchised, in any respect whatever, without fault on his part, except for his own good, reasonably apparent, and that the persons who acquire citizenship under it shall not be distinguished from the former citizens for any of the causes, or on any of the grounds, which previously characterized their want of citizenship. The second section of article 1 of our State constitution, is to the same effect. The indictment fails to charge any offense, and the facts set forth in it show that no prosecution can be sustained against the defendant.

The judgment is reversed, and an order will be made in this court to discharge the accused.

Bonds v. Foster

36 Tex. 68 (1872)

■ WALKER, J.

This case was submitted to his honor the district judge, on the law and the facts, and his judgment is appealed from to this court.

A. H. Foster many years ago resided in the State of Louisiana, and, among other slaves, was the owner of one Leah, whom he made either his wife or his concubine. The question here presented is, was Leah the wife of Foster, and are her children the offspring of his loins?

By the laws of Louisiana in force at the time Foster resided there, he could not have made Leah his lawful wife; but we learn, from the statement of facts, that he took the woman and several children of hers to the State of Ohio, and established them in a home in the city of Cincinnati, where he provided them with the necessaries of life; he also emancipated the woman and her children. They remained in the city of Cincinnati four years, Foster spending a portion of each year with them, and, according to the testimony of Fields Foster, the eldest son, he spent his nights and frequently took his meals with the family. After the expiration of four years, Foster brought this family away from Cincinnati, and with them removed to the State of Texas.

By the laws of Ohio, the woman having been emancipated, the parties may have been legally married, or their conduct may have been such as to raise a legal presumption of a marriage; and if so, their coming to the State of Texas, where the law prohibited marriage between the white and black races, did not, *per se*, operate a dissolution of the marriage, although, at the time, none of the marital rights of the parties could have been enforced by the laws of Texas.

But the parties continued to live together, habiting themselves as man and wife, until after the law prohibiting such a marriage had been abrogated by the 14th Amendment to the Constitution of the United States. A marriage might then be presumed in the State of Texas upon the same state of facts, which would raise a similar presumption in Indiana or Ohio.

After Foster came to the State of Texas, bringing Leah and her children with him, Leah became the mother of several other children by Foster, two of whom are the minors named in the petition. The District Court adjudged the parties to be man and wife, from the evidence adduced upon the trial, and Leah, as the widow, entitled to a homestead. It is contended on the part of appellants, that the evidence did not warrant this finding.

The evidence, no doubt, has its weak points and its strong ones. That Foster himself regarded this woman and her family in the light of a wife and children, cannot be doubted; perhaps the strongest evidence to prove a marriage relation is furnished by his will. He not only devises his property mainly to this woman and children, but he provides by a clause (often found in the testaments of jealous husbands) that if Leah shall marry, she is to forfeit all her right and interest in his estate. We confess it is somewhat difficult to account for this inhibition of a second marriage in any case, but it would be still more difficult to find a reason for this kind of embargo upon marital commerce in the will of one who had not been the husband of her upon whom he intends to place the fate of Jephtha's daughter. But the learned judge who has decided this case was much more competent to give due weight and consideration to the evidence than any ordinary jury would have been, and we certainly should not disturb their verdict if they had found the facts as the court found them.

* * * The judgment of the District Court is affirmed.

Affirmed.

NOTES AND QUESTIONS

1. According to the court in *Foster,* any anti-miscegenation laws "had been abrogated by the 14th Amendment." According to the Alabama court in *Burns,* marriage is a kind of contract—in which case its similar conclusion follows naturally from both the Fourteenth Amendment and the Civil Rights Act of 1866. Restrictions on contractual capacity are precisely the kinds of discriminations that the statute and Constitution were designed to forbid. A law forbidding people of different races from forming commercial partnerships or owning stock in the same corporations would obviously be unconstitutional. If a white person has the contractual capacity to marry a white person, all citizens must have the same contractual capacity. Isn't that precisely what the Civil Rights Act of 1866 says and that the Fourteenth Amendment constitutionalizes? Aren't these easy cases? Of course, many people involved in the drafting and ratification process of the Reconstruction-era statutes and amendments may not have intended to forbid anti-miscegenation acts. Under what modalities of interpretation are those historical intentions controlling? Under what modalities are they relevant? *See* Steven G. Calabresi & Andrew Matthews, *Originalism and* Loving v. Virginia, 2012 B.Y.U. L. REV. 1393 (arguing at length in favor of reliance on original public *meaning* rather than concrete historical *intentions*).

2. Two Southern courts thus concluded, rather easily and with no fanfare, that anti-miscegenation acts did not survive the Fourteenth Amendment (and were invalid as of 1866 if the Thirteenth Amendment was enough to sustain the Civil Rights Act). Consider the following opinion by a Northern court in 1871.

State v. Gibson

36 Ind. 389 (1871)

It appears of record in this cause, that appellee was charged by indictment in the court below with having unlawfully and knowingly married, in the county and State aforesaid, one Jennie Williams, a white woman of this State, he then and there having one-eighth part or more of negro blood.

The indictment was, upon the motion of the appellee, quashed, and the State, by her prosecuting attorney, excepted and prosecutes this appeal to obtain a reversal of the judgment.

The indictment was based upon the forty-seventh section of the act defining felonies, which reads as follows:

> "Section 47. No person having one-eighth part or more of negro blood shall be permitted to marry any white woman of this State, nor shall any

> white man be permitted to marry any negro woman, or any woman having one-eighth part or more of negro blood, and every person who shall knowingly marry in violation of the provisions of this section, shall, upon conviction thereof, be imprisoned in the State's prison not less than one, nor more than ten years, and be fined not less than one thousand nor more than five thousand dollars." 2 G. & H. 452.

The sole question which is presented for our consideration and decision is as to the correctness of the ruling of the court in quashing the indictment. It seems to be conceded by the appellee, that the indictment, under our code of criminal procedure, is good, in substance and matter of form, if the section of our statute above quoted is still in force; but it is earnestly maintained that all the laws of our State prohibiting the intermarriage of negroes and white persons were abrogated by the ratification of the fourteenth amendment of the constitution of the United States, and the passage of the civil rights bill. The position assumed by the attorney of the appellee is stated in these words:

> "The appellee contends that all the laws of this State prohibiting the marrying of blacks and whites are abrogated by the fourteenth amendment to the constitution of the United States, and the law of Congress passed in pursuance to that amendment, which, in express terms, confers upon colored people the power of making contracts.
>
> Marriage, by the laws of Indiana, being only a civil contract, 1 G. & H. 428, sec. 1, it follows that the marriage specified in this indictment was lawful; and hence the judgment of the court is correct."

The only question presented for the decision of this court is, whether the position assumed by the appellee is correct. The magnitude and importance of the question involved cannot be overestimated, and we have given it our best and most thoughtful consideration. We approach its investigation, profoundly impressed with the weight of responsibility that our oath to support the Constitution of the United States and of the State of Indiana has imposed upon us.

* * *

This [Fourteenth] amendment contains four separate and distinct propositions: first, it confers the right of citizenship upon all persons born or naturalized in the United States, and who are subject to the jurisdiction thereof; second, it declares that no state shall make or enforce any law which shall abridge the privileges or immunities of citizens of the United States; third, it prohibits any state from depriving any citizen of life, liberty, or property, without due process of law; fourth, it provides that no state shall deny to any person within its jurisdiction the equal protection of the law.

* * *

The learned attorney for the appellee has not informed us, in his brief, which one of the clauses of the said section has had the effect to abrogate our laws prohibiting the intermarriage of persons of the white and black races. It certainly cannot be the first, for the only object and effect of that clause was to confer the right of citizenship upon certain classes of persons who had not been theretofore citizens, and among these classes were persons of the African race.

Nor can the second clause be construed to have that effect. The purpose of this clause was to secure to the newly created citizens the same privileges and immunities which had theretofore been enjoyed by the former citizens of the United States. It is quite probable that this clause had reference to the political rights and privileges of the persons who had by the first clause been made citizens of the United States and of the state wherein they resided. The purpose of the third clause was to protect the persons referred to and embraced in the first clause, in life, liberty, and property. The plain and manifest intention was to make all the citizens of the United States equal before the law in all the states of the Union. The fourth clause seems to have been added in the abundance of caution, for it provides in express terms what was the fair, logical, and just implication from what had preceded it, and that was, that the persons made citizens by the amendment should be protected by the laws in the same manner, and to the same extent, that white citizens were protected.

The fourteenth amendment contains no new grant of power from the people, who are the inherent possessors of all power, to the federal government. It did not enlarge the powers of the federal government, nor diminish those of the states. The inhibitions against the states doing certain things have no force or effect. They do not prohibit the states from doing any act that they could have done without them * * *. Nor has the ratification of this amendment in any manner or to any extent impaired, weakened, or taken away any of the reserved rights of the states, as they had existed and been fully recognized by every department of the national government from its creation. This amendment conferred citizenship upon persons of the African race, but we will hereafter inquire and decide whether citizenship conferred on them the right to intermarry with persons of the white race.

But it is urged that the civil rights bill has abrogated the section of our statute which renders it a felony for a negro to marry a white woman of this State, or for a white man to marry a negro woman. It is claimed that the first section of the said act which confers upon persons of the African race the right to make and enforce contracts has made it lawful for negroes, in all of the states, to make and enter into contracts of marriage with persons of the white race. The argument is, that under our laws marriage is a civil contract, and as negroes are authorized to make contracts, that, therefore, they can make any kind of contracts, notwithstanding the contract may be in violation of the laws of an independent and sovereign state. Waiving for the present the power of Congress to pass a law authorizing any class of persons to make and enforce contracts in a state, we proceed to examine the first section of the civil rights bill, and to determine whether the position assumed by the appellee is sustained thereby. In our opinion it is wholly untenable, and that this is demonstrated by the plain, express, and undoubted language of the said section.

* * *

* * * The only force and effect of this section was to confer upon persons of the African race the same civil rights, privileges, and immunities as had been enjoyed by persons of the white race.

It, therefore, becomes necessary for us to inquire whether Congress possesses the power, under the federal constitution, to pass a law regulating and controlling the institution of marriage in the several states of this union * * *.

* * *

Both the states and the United States existed before the constitution. The people, through that instrument, established a more perfect union by substituting a national government, acting, with ample power, directly upon the citizens, instead of the confederate government, which acted with powers greatly restricted, only upon the states. But in many articles of the constitution the necessary existence of the states, and within their proper spheres the independent authority of the states, is distinctly recognized. To them nearly the whole charge of interior regulation is committed or left; to them, and to the people, all powers not expressly delegated to the national government are reserved * * *.

* * *

True, the national government is our government, and we will not anticipate an attempt by it at our destruction as a state, but, as the Chief Justice remarked in discussing this very question in *M'Culloch v. Maryland*, 'this is not a case of confidence.

* * *

There can be no doubt that Congress possesses the power to determine who may, or may not, make contracts, and prescribe the manner of their enforcement, in the District of Columbia, and in all other places where the federal government has exclusive jurisdiction; but we deny the power and authority of Congress to determine who shall make contracts or the manner of enforcing them in the several states. Nor is there any doubt that Congress may provide for the punishment of those who violate the laws of Congress; but we utterly deny the power of Congress to regulate, control, or in any manner to interfere with the states in determining what shall constitute crimes against the laws of the state, or the manner or extent of the punishment of persons charged and convicted with the violation of the criminal laws of a sovereign state. In this State marriage is treated as a civil contract, but it is more than a mere civil contract. It is a public institution established by God himself, is recognized in all Christian and civilized nations, and is essential to the peace, happiness, and well-being of society. In fact, society could not exist without the institution of marriage, for upon it all the social and domestic relations are based. The right, in the states, to regulate and control, to guard, protect, and preserve this God-given, civilizing, and Christianizing institution is of inestimable importance, and cannot be surrendered, nor can the states suffer or permit any interference therewith. If the federal government can determine who may marry in a state, there is no limit to its power. It can legislate upon all subjects connected with, or growing out of this relation. It can determine the rights, duties, and obligations of husband and wife, parent and child, guardian and ward. It may pass laws regulating the granting of divorces. It may assume, exercise, and absorb all the powers of a local and domestic character. This would result in the destruction of the states. The federal government cannot exist without the states, but the states could exist without the federal government, as they did before its creation. There is no necessity for the destruction of either. The authority of the federal government begins where the authority of the state ceases. The state government controls all matters of a local and domestic character. The federal government regulates matters between the states and with foreign governments. There is, and can be no conflict between the state and federal governments, if each will act within the sphere assigned to each. The necessity for states and local self-government is shown by the character of our people. The customs, habits. and thoughts of the people in one state differ widely from those of the people in another state, and this results in different laws.

The laws of this state provide that males of the age of seventeen, and females of the age of fourteen years, not within the prohibited degrees of consanguinity, are capable of entering into the contract of marriage. The statute provides that the following marriages are void: when one of the parties is a white person, and the other possessed of one-eighth or more of negro blood; and when either party is insane or idiotic, at the time of the marriage. Under the police power possessed by the states, they undoubtedly have the power to pass such laws. The people of this State have declared that they are opposed to the intermixture of races and all amalgamation. If the people of other states desire to permit a corruption of blood, and a mixture of races, they have the power to adopt such a policy. When the legislature of the State shall declare such policy by positive enactment, we will enforce it, but until thus required we shall not give such policy our sanction.

* * *

* * * It is quite clear to us, that neither the fourteenth amendment nor the civil rights bill has impaired or abrogated the laws of this State on the subject of marriage of whites and negroes. The court erred in quashing the indictment.

The judgment is reversed, and the cause is remanded, with directions to the court below to overrule the motion to quash the indictment, and to place the appellee upon his trial for the crime charged in said indictment.

NOTES AND QUESTIONS

1. According to the court in *Gibson:* "The fourteenth amendment contains no new grant of power from the people, who are the inherent possessors of all power, to the federal government. It did not enlarge the powers of the federal government, nor diminish those of the states." As editors, we generally try to keep our pontificating to a minimum, but !!!!!????? This was not the ranting of a crackpot pamphleteer. This was the decision of a state supreme court in 1871. The decision never mentions Section 5 of the Fourteenth Amendment (we edited the opinion heavily but did not omit any discussion of Section 5). The court essentially pronounced the Fourteenth Amendment, and the entire process of Reconstruction, a nullity.

2. It may or may not surprise you to learn that *Gibson* soon became a leading case. In 1877, a Texas appeals court relied on *Gibson* (and drew on much of its language, sometimes with and sometimes without attribution) to uphold application of the 1858 Texas anti-miscegenation statute. *See Frasher v. State,* 3 Tex.App. 263 (Ct. App. 1877). According to the court of appeals, "Mr. Buskirk, Justice of the Supreme Court of Indiana, has so ably discussed the question, in an opinion delivered by him, that at the expense of being tedious we will copy a portion of what he has said, fully indorsing the same." *Id.* at 274. What about *Bonds v. Foster,* a decision of the Texas Supreme Court? It was not cited. In the same year, the Alabama Supreme Court overruled *Burns* and upheld the State's miscegenation act, citing the "able and emphatic opinion" in *Gibson. See Green v. State,* 58 Ala. 190, 195 (1877). You will see *Gibson* cited again shortly.

3. What changed between 1871 and 1877? That is a matter for historians, which we are not, but the easy answer is that in 1874 the Democrats won a majority in Congress, in 1876 the Republicans bargained away Reconstruction to get the presidency in a contested election in the House, in 1873 the Supreme Court had obliterated the Privileges

or Immunities Clause in the *Slaughter-House Cases,* and people assumed that the tide had turned decisively away from civil rights. They assumed correctly, as we will now see.

[Assignment 59]

VI. RACE DISCRIMINATION DURING THE JIM CROW ERA: 1881–1954

As we explained above, Reconstruction died on September 19, 1881 when President James A. Garfield died from an assassin's bullet. As we just saw above with the state anti-miscegenation cases, any momentum in favor of racial equality was already dissolving by the end of the 1870s. The Supreme Court's narrow interpretations of the Reconstruction Amendments, and sometimes inexplicable interpretations of statutes, surely egged on racists all over the country to experiment with new forms of race discrimination under the separate but equal label. In addition to *Blyew, see supra* pages 1217–1224, which narrowly interpreted a jurisdictional provision for federal enforcement of civil rights, the Court in *United States v. Reese,* 92 U.S. (2 Otto) 214 (1876), *broadly* construed a federal statute designed to enforce the Fifteenth Amendment right to vote—only to find the statute unconstitutional because of the broad construction:

> This case * * * presents an indictment containing four counts, under sects. 3 and 4 of the act of May 31, 1870 (16 Stat. 140), against two of the inspectors of a municipal election in the State of Kentucky, for refusing to receive and count at such election the vote of William Garner, a citizen of the United States of African descent * * *.
>
> * * *
>
> * * * [T]he principal question * * * is, whether the act under which the indictment is found can be made effective for the punishment of inspectors of elections who refuse to receive and count the votes of citizens of the United States, having all the qualifications of voters, because of their race, color, or previous condition of servitude.
>
> * * *
>
> Looking, then, to this statute, we find that its first section provides that all citizens of the United States, who are or shall be otherwise qualified by law to vote at any election, &c., shall be entitled and allowed to vote thereat, without distinction of race, color, or previous condition of servitude, any constitution, &c., of the State to the contrary notwithstanding * * *.
>
> The second section provides for the punishment of any officer charged with the duty of furnishing to citizens an opportunity to perform any act, which, by the constitution or laws of any State, is made a prerequisite or qualification of voting, who shall omit to give all citizens of the United States the same and equal opportunity to perform such prerequisite, and become qualified on account of the race, color, or previous condition of servitude, of the applicant * * *.
>
> The third section is to the effect, that, whenever by or under the constitution or laws of any State, &c., any act is or shall be required to be done by any citizen as a prerequisite to qualify or entitle him to vote, the

offer of such citizen to perform the act required to be done "as aforesaid" shall, if it fail to be carried into execution by reason of the wrongful act or omission "aforesaid" of the person or officer charged with the duty of receiving or permitting such performance, or offer to perform, or acting thereon, be deemed and held as a performance in law of such act; and the person so offering and failing as aforesaid, and being otherwise qualified, shall be entitled to vote in the same manner, and to the same extent, as if he had, in fact, performed such act; and any judge, inspector, or other officer of election, whose duty it is to receive, count, &c., or give effect to, the vote of any such citizen, who shall wrongfully refuse or omit to receive, count, & c., the vote of such citizen * * * shall, for every such offence, forfeit and pay, &c.

The fourth section provides for the punishment of any person who shall, by force, bribery, threats, intimidation, or other unlawful means, hinder, delay, &c., or shall combine with others to hinder, delay, prevent, or obstruct, any citizen from doing any act required to be done to qualify him to vote, or from voting, at any election.

The second count in the indictment is based upon the fourth section of this act, and the fourth upon the third section.

* * *

The Fifteenth Amendment does not confer the right of suffrage upon any one. It prevents the States, or the United States, however, from giving preference, in this particular, to one citizen of the United States over another on account of race, color, or previous condition of servitude * * *. It follows that the amendment has invested the citizens of the United States with a new constitutional right which is within the protecting power of Congress * * *.

This leads us to inquire whether the act now under consideration is "appropriate legislation" for that purpose. The power of Congress to legislate at all upon the subject of voting at State elections rests upon this amendment * * *.

The third section does not in express terms limit the offence of an inspector of elections, for which the punishment is provided, to a wrongful discrimination on account of race, &c. This is conceded; but it is urged, that when this section is construed with those which precede it, and to which, as is claimed, it refers, it is so limited. The argument is, that the only wrongful act, on the part of the officer whose duty it is to receive or permit the requisite qualification, which can dispense with actual qualification under the State laws, and substitute the prescribed affidavit therefor, is that mentioned and prohibited in sect. 2,—to wit, discrimination on account of race, &c.; and that, consequently, sect. 3 is confined in its operation to the same wrongful discrimination.

This is a penal statute, and must be construed strictly * * *.

* * * The law ought not to be in such a condition that the elector may act upon one idea of its meaning, and the inspector upon another.

> The elector, under the provisions of the statute, is only required to state in his affidavit that he has been wrongfully prevented by the officer from qualifying. There are no words of limitation in this part of the section. In a case like this, if an affidavit is in the language of the statute, it ought to be sufficient both for the voter and the inspector. Laws which prohibit the doing of things, and provide a punishment for their violation, should have no double meaning. A citizen should not unnecessarily be placed where, by an honest error in the construction of a penal statute, he may be subjected to a prosecution for a false oath; and an inspector of elections should not be put in jeopardy because he, with equal honesty, entertains an opposite opinion * * *.
>
> But when we go beyond the third section, and read the fourth, we find there no words of limitation, or reference even, that can be construed as manifesting any intention to confine its provisions to the terms of the Fifteenth Amendment. That section has for its object the punishment of all persons, who, by force, bribery, &c., hinder, delay, &c., any person from qualifying or voting. In view of all these facts, we feel compelled to say, that, in our opinion, the language of the third and fourth sections does not confine their operation to unlawful discriminations on account of race, &c. If Congress had the power to provide generally for the punishment of those who unlawfully interfere to prevent the exercise of the elective franchise without regard to such discrimination, the language of these sections would be broad enough for that purpose.
>
> * * *
>
> We must, therefore, decide that Congress has not as yet provided by "appropriate legislation" for the punishment of the offence charged in the indictment; and that the Circuit Court properly sustained the demurrers, and gave judgment for the defendants.

Id. at 215–20, 222. The Court construed the statutes so broadly that they were unconstitutional, as Congress has no general power to regulate state voting procedures in state elections where there is no constitutional violation by the State. Was there any serious doubt at all that each of the provisions of the statute dealt with race discrimination? Did it matter that the allegations in *Reese* were of racial discrimination, which everyone agreed Congress had power to prohibit?

The 1880s marked the real beginning of the post-Reconstruction era. We have already seen one major case from that decade—the *Civil Rights Cases, see supra* pages 846–860, in which the Court in 1883 invalidated the public accommodations provisions in the Civil Rights Act of 1875. Another case in 1883 defined discrimination in a fashion that today seems bizarre, and that is contrary to the approach taken by the Supreme Court in *Railway Commission v. Brown* in 1873.

A. PACE V. ALABAMA

106 U.S. (16 Otto) 583 (1883)

Section 4184 of the Code of Alabama provides that "if any man and woman live together in adultery or fornication, each of them must, on the first conviction of the offense, be fined not less than $100, and may also be imprisoned in the county jail or sentenced to hard labor for the county for not more than six months. On the second conviction for the offense, with the same person, the offender must be fined not less than $300, and may be imprisoned in the county jail, or sentenced to hard labor for the county, for not more than 12 months; and for a third or any subsequent conviction with the same person, must be imprisoned in the penitentiary or sentenced to hard labor for the county for two years."

Section 4189 of the same Code declares that "if any white person and any negro, or the descendant of any negro to the third generation, inclusive, though one ancestor of each generation was a white person, intermarry or live in adultery or fornication with each other, each of them must, on conviction, be imprisoned in the penitentiary or sentenced to hard labor for the county for not less than two nor more than seven years."

In November, 1881, the plaintiff in error, Tony Pace, a negro man, and Mary J. Cox, a white woman, were indicted under section 4189, in a circuit court of Alabama, for living together in a state of adultery or fornication, and were tried, convicted, and sentenced, each to two years' imprisonment in the State penitentiary. On appeal to the Supreme Court of the State the judgment was affirmed, and he brought the case here on writ of error, insisting that the act under which he was indicted and convicted is in conflict with the concluding clause of the first section of the Fourteenth Amendment of the Constitution, which declares that no State shall "deny to any person the equal protection of the laws."

■ FIELD, J. The counsel of the plaintiff in error compares sections 4184 and 4189 of the Code of Alabama, and assuming that the latter relates to the same offense as the former, and prescribes a greater punishment for it, because one of the parties is a negro, or of negro descent, claims that a discrimination is made against the colored person in the punishment designated, which conflicts with the clause of the Fourteenth Amendment prohibiting a State from denying to any person within its jurisdiction the equal protection of the laws.

The counsel is undoubtedly correct in his view of the purpose of the clause of the amendment in question, that it was to prevent hostile and discriminating State legislation against any person or class of persons. Equality of protection under the laws implies not only accessibility by each one, whatever his race, on the same terms with others to the courts of the country for the security of his person and property, but that in the administration of criminal justice he shall not be subjected, for the same offense, to any greater or different punishment * * *.

The defect in the argument of counsel consists in his assumption that any discrimination is made by the laws of Alabama in the punishment provided for the offense for which the plaintiff in error was indicted when committed by a person of the African race and when committed by a white person. The two sections of the Code cited are entirely consistent. The one prescribes, generally, a punishment for an offense committed between persons of different sexes; the other prescribes a punishment for an offense which can only be committed where the two sexes are of different races. There is in neither section any discrimination against either race. Section 4184 equally includes the offense when the persons of the two sexes are both white and when they are both black. Section 4189 applies the same punishment to both offenders, the white and the black. Indeed, the offense against which this latter section is aimed cannot be committed without involving the persons of both races in the same punishment. Whatever discrimination is made in the punishment prescribed in the two sections is directed against the offense designated and not against the person of any particular color or race. The punishment of each offending person, whether white or black, is the same.

Judgment affirmed.

NOTES AND QUESTIONS

1. The opinion in *Pace*, from which we have edited out only the Court's quotation of the Civil Rights Act, was unanimous, including Justice John Marshall Harlan the elder. Justice Field is trivially right that members of each race are treated equally by the Alabama statute in the punishment of interracial sex. But that is like saying that members of each race are equally disadvantaged if a State bans interracial business partnerships. Is this decision a product of the *Slaughter-House Cases*? If one focuses only on "equal protection," as that term would have been understood in the 1880s, the Court's position is not absurd. The real discrimination came from the law's distinction between single-race and multi-racial associations, and as a matter of original meaning that is the province of the Privileges or Immunities Clause rather than the Equal Protection Clause. Having closed off one avenue of constitutional protection in *Slaughter-House*, was the Court obliged to open another in its stead by taking a mare capacious view of the Equal Protection Clause?

2. If the parties had expressed their relationship in contractual form, wouldn't it be obvious that the Civil Rights Act of 1866 was violated? Does it matter that it was a personal relationship rather than a business contract?

3. Is it fair to say that the Supreme Court's definition of discrimination in *Pace* amounts to "equal but separate"?

4. The *Civil Rights Cases,* recall, involved nondiscrimination in public accommodations and common carriers. For reasons discussed earlier, *see supra* pages 860–861, those were the strongest cases for finding federal power to reach nominally private conduct under the Fourteenth Amendment. What about straight-up private violence? Murder, assault, battery, kidnapping, and rape are all *state* crimes. The federal criminal code circa 1880 was quite thin. In the aftermath of the Civil War, was it realistic to expect state law enforcement and judicial machinery fairly to apply those laws to acts of violence against African-Americans? Could Congress step in with its own criminal code? Did it need to use Section 5 of the Fourteenth Amendment, or was Section 2 of the Thirteenth Amendment enough? These questions came up yet again in the next case, which continues to get cited in the modern era. The case involved a classic lynch mob, and prosecutions were brought under Section 5519 of the Revised Statutes of the United States, which declared:

> If two or more persons in any state or territory conspire or go in disguise upon the highway or on the premises of another for the purpose of depriving, either directly or indirectly, any person or class of persons of the equal protection of the laws, or of equal privileges or immunities under the laws, or for the purpose of preventing or hindering the constituted authorities of any state or territory from giving or securing to all persons within such state or territory the equal protection of the laws, each of said persons shall be punished by a fine of not less than $500 nor more than $5,000, or by imprisonment, with or without hard labor, not less than six months nor more than six years, or by both such fine and imprisonment.

Act of Apr. 20, 1871, ch. XXII, § 2. The statute was popularly known as the "Ku Klux Klan Act," and it was aimed at precisely the conduct in the following case, in which a group of twenty men (including a sheriff, the named defendant Harris) removed four men from a Tennessee jail, beat them, and killed one of them.

B. UNITED STATES V. HARRIS

106 U.S. (16 Otto) 629 (1883)

■ MR. JUSTICE WOODS delivered the opinion of the court * * *.

* * *

The demurrer filed to the indictment in this case questions the power of congress to pass the law under which the indictment was found. It is, therefore, necessary to search the constitution to ascertain whether or not the power is conferred.

* * *

It is * * * strenuously insisted that the legislation under consideration finds its warrant in the first and fifth sections of the Fourteenth Amendment. The first section declares. "all persons born or naturalized in the United States, and subject to the jurisdiction thereof, are citizens of the United States and of the state wherein they reside. No state shall make or enforce any law which shall abridge the privileges or immunities of citizens of the United States, nor shall any state deprive any person of life, liberty, or property without due process of law, nor deny to any person within its jurisdiction the equal protection of the laws."

The fifth section declares "the congress shall have power to enforce by appropriate legislation the provisions of this amendment."

* * *

The purpose and effect of the two sections of the Fourteenth Amendment above quoted were clearly defined by Mr. Justice Bradley in the case of *U. S. v. Cruikshank*, 1 Woods, 316, as follows: "It is a guaranty of protection against the acts of the State government itself. It is a guaranty against the exertion of arbitrary and tyrannical power on the part of the government and legislature of the State, not a guaranty against the commission of individual offenses; and the power of Congress, whether express or implied, to legislate for the enforcement of such a guaranty, does not extend to the passage of laws for the suppression of crime within the states. The enforcement of the guaranty does not require or authorize congress to perform "the duty that the guaranty itself supposes it to be the duty of the State to perform, and which it requires the State to perform."

When the case of *U. S. v. Cruikshank* came to this court the same view was taken here. The Chief Justice, delivering the opinion of the court in that case, said: "The Fourteenth Amendment prohibits a State from depriving any person of life, liberty, or property without due process of law, or from denying to any person the equal protection of the laws; but this provision does not add anything to the rights of one citizen as against another. It simply furnishes an additional guaranty against any encroachment by the States upon the fundamental rights which belong to every citizen as a member of society. The duty of protecting all its citizens in the enjoyment of an equality of rights was originally assumed by the States, and it remains there. The only obligation resting upon the United States is to see that the States do not deny the right. This the amendment guaranties, and no more. The power of the national government is limited to this guaranty." 92 U. S. 542.

So, in *Virginia v. Rives*, 100 U. S. 313, it was declared by this court, speaking through Mr. Justice Strong, that "these provisions of the fourteenth amendment have reference to state action exclusively, and not to any action of private individuals."

These authorities show conclusively that the legislation under consideration finds no warrant for its enactment in the Fourteenth Amendment.

The language of the amendment does not leave this subject in doubt. When the State has been guilty of no violation of its provisions; when it has not made or enforced any law abridging the privileges or immunities of citizens of the United States; when no one of its departments has deprived any person of life, liberty, or property without due process of law, or denied to any person within its jurisdiction the equal protection of the laws; when, on the contrary, the laws of the State, as enacted by its legislative, and construed by its judicial, and administered by its executive departments, recognize and protect the rights of all persons, the amendment imposes no duty and confers no power upon Congress.

Section 5519 of the Revised Statutes is not limited to take effect only in case the State shall abridge the privileges or immunities of citizens of the United States, or deprive any person of life, liberty, or property without due process of law, or deny to any person the equal protection of the laws. It applies, no matter how well the State may have performed its duty. Under it private persons are liable to punishment for conspiring to deprive any one of the equal protection of the laws enacted by the State.

In the indictment in this case, for instance, which would be a good indictment under the law if the law itself were valid, there is no intimation that the state of Tennessee has passed any law or done any act forbidden by the Fourteenth Amendment. On the contrary, the *gravamen* of the charge against the accused is that they conspired to deprive certain citizens of the United States and of the State of Tennessee of the equal protection accorded them by the laws of Tennessee.

As, therefore, the section of the law under consideration is directed exclusively against the action of private persons, without reference to the laws of the States, or their administration by the officers of the State, we are clear in the opinion that it is not warranted by any clause in the Fourteenth Amendment to the Constitution.

We are next to consider whether the Thirteenth Amendment to the Constitution furnishes authority for the enactment of the law under review * * *.

* * *

* * * We are of opinion that it does not. Our conclusion is based on the fact that the provisions of that section are broader than the Thirteenth Amendment would justify. Under that section it would be an offense for two or more white persons to conspire, etc., for the purpose of depriving another white person of the equal protection of the laws. It would be an offense for two or more colored persons, enfranchised slaves, to conspire with the same purpose against a white citizen or against another colored citizen who had never been a slave. Even if the amendment is held to be directed against the action of private individuals, as well as against the action of the States and United States, the law under consideration covers cases both within and without the provisions of the amendment. It covers any conspiracy

between two free white men against another free white man to deprive the latter of any right accorded him by the laws of the State or of the United States. A law under which two or more free white private citizens could be punished for conspiring or going in disguise for the purpose of depriving another free white citizen of a right accorded by the law of the State to all classes of persons,—as, for instance, the right to make a contract, bring a suit, or give evidence,—clearly cannot be authorized by the amendment which simply prohibits slavery and involuntary servitude.

Those provisions of the law, which are broader than is warranted by the article of the Constitution by which they are supposed to be authorized, cannot be sustained.

* * *

There is another view which strengthens this conclusion. If Congress has constitutional authority under the Thirteenth Amendment to punish conspiracy between two persons to do an unlawful act, it can punish the act itself, whether done by one or more persons.

A private person cannot make constitutions or laws, nor can he with authority construe them, nor can he administer or execute them. The only way, therefore, in which one private person can deprive another of the equal protection of the laws is by the commission of some offense against the laws which protect the rights of persons, as by theft, burglary, arson, libel, assault, or murder. If, therefore, we hold that section 5519 is warranted by the Thirteenth Amendment, we should by virtue of that amendment, accord to Congress the power to punish every crime by which the right of any person to life, property, or reputation is invaded. Thus, under a provision of the Constitution which simply abolished slavery and involuntary servitude, we should, with few exceptions, invest Congress with power over the whole catalogue of crimes. A construction of the amendment which leads to such a result is clearly unsound.

* * *

We have, therefore, been unable to find any constitutional authority for the enactment of section 5519 of the Revised Statutes. The decisions of this court above referred to leave no constitutional ground for the act to stand on.

The point in reference to which the judges of the circuit court were divided in opinion must, therefore, be decided against the *constitutionality of the law*.

■ MR. JUSTICE HARLAN dissented on the question of jurisdiction. He expressed no opinion on the merits.

NOTES AND QUESTIONS

1. There are two senses in which a case can be considered "hard." One—the sense in the old maxim that "hard cases make bad law"—uses "hard" to describe circumstances in which the legally correct result leads to unfortunate, or even unacceptable, practical consequences The other sense uses "hard" to describe circumstances in which it is difficult to discern the legally correct result. Is *Harris* hard in either of those senses? Is it easy in the second sense because it is just obviously wrong? Is it easy in the second sense (and therefore hard in the first) because it is obviously right? Hard in the second sense? If you figure out your views on those questions, there is a good chance that you will have figured out your views on the overall meaning of the Reconstruction Amendments.

2. The majority is right that Rev. Stat. § 5519—a version of which is still on the books, *see* 42 U.S.C. § 1985(3) (2018)—had no geographical limitation and no limitation to racially motivated violence. Did it need either of those things in order to be valid? It also does not require any prior showing that the State in which the crime took place was failing to provide constitutionally adequate protection. Did it need that showing in order to be valid? Or did the Reconstruction Amendments really give Congress general power to construct a criminal code to supplement, or supplant, whatever the States provide whenever Congress thinks it "appropriate"? *See* Jack M. Balkin, *The Reconstruction Power,* 85 N.Y.U. L. REV. 1801, 1801–02 (2010):

> When it enforces the Reconstruction Amendments, Congress is not limited to remedying or preventing state violations of rights. It has long been recognized that Congress may reach private conduct through its Thirteenth Amendment powers to eradicate the badges and incidents of slavery. But Congress also has the power to enforce the Fourteenth Amendment's Citizenship Clause—a guarantee of equal citizenship that, like the Thirteenth Amendment, contains no state action requirement. The Citizenship Clause, designed to secure equality of citizenship for freedmen, gives Congress the corresponding power to protect the badges and incidents of citizenship. Congress may therefore ban discriminatory private conduct that it reasonably believes will contribute to or produce second-class citizenship.
>
> In addition to having powers to enforce the Citizenship Clause, Congress also may reach private action to prevent interference with federal constitutional rights. Along with its powers to enforce the Guarantee Clause, Congress may therefore reach private violence designed to deter political participation, terrorize political opponents, or undermine representative government.

Would the "Reconstruction power" described by Professor Balkin validate Rev. Stat. § 5519 as it was written? *See id.* at 1849–56.

3. The Supreme Court in *Harris* does not cite either *Strauder v. West Virginia* or *Ex parte Virginia*. Should it have done so? For what propositions?

4. One thing, at least, is clear: In the wake of the *Harris* opinion, private violence against African-Americans because of their race inevitably increased. The case made it much harder for the federal government to suppress violence by the Ku Klux Klan, the organization at which the statute was specifically directed.

5. The Supreme Court in *United States v. Morrison,* 529 U.S. 598 (2000), cited *United States v. Harris* as still being good law today. Is *Harris* so clearly wrong that citation to it by the modern Court is offensive? For whatever it is worth, one of the editors thinks so. The other disagrees, thinking that *Harris* is a hard case. Everyone, on the other hand, agrees on the next case. As with *Dred Scott,* this case richly deserves its reputation.

C. PLESSY V. FERGUSON

163 U.S. 537 (1896)

■ MR. JUSTICE BROWN, after stating the case, delivered the opinion of the court.

This case turns upon the constitutionality of an act of the General Assembly of the State of Louisiana, passed in 1890, providing for separate railway carriages for the white and colored races. Acts 1890, No. 111, p. 152.

The first section of the statute enacts "that all railway companies carrying passengers in their coaches in this State shall provide equal but separate accommodations for the white, and colored races, by providing two or more passenger coaches for each passenger train, or by dividing the passenger coaches by a partition so as to secure separate accommodations: *Provided,* That this section shall not be construed to apply to street railroads. No person or persons, shall be admitted to occupy seats in coaches, other than, the ones, assigned, to them on account of the race they belong to."

By the second section, it was enacted "that the officers of such passenger trains shall have power and are hereby required to assign each passenger to the coach or compartment used for the race to which such passenger belongs; any passenger insisting on going into a coach or compartment to which by race he does not belong, shall be liable to a fine of twenty-five dollars, or in lieu thereof to imprisonment for a period of not more than twenty days in the parish prison, and any officer of any railroad insisting on assigning a passenger to a coach or compartment other than the one set aside for the race to which said passenger belongs, shall be liable to a fine of twenty-five dollars, or in lieu thereof to imprisonment for a period of not more than twenty days in the parish prison; and should any passenger refuse to occupy the coach or compartment to which he or she is assigned by the officer of such railway, said officer shall have power to refuse to carry such passenger on his train, and for such refusal neither he nor the railway company which he represents shall be liable for damages in any of the courts of this State."

The third section provides penalties for the refusal or neglect of the officers, directors, conductors, and employees of railway companies to comply with the act, with a proviso that "nothing in this act shall be construed as applying to nurses attending children of the other race." The fourth section is immaterial.

The information filed in the criminal District Court charged in substance that Plessy, being a passenger between two stations within the State of Louisiana, was assigned by officers of the company to the coach used for the race to which he belonged, but he insisted upon going into a coach used by the race to which he did not belong. Neither in the information nor plea was his particular race or color averred.

The petition for the writ of prohibition averred that petitioner was seven-eighths Caucasian and one eighth African blood; that the mixture of colored blood was not discernible in him, and that he was entitled to every right, privilege and immunity secured to citizens of the United States of the white race; and that, upon such theory, he took possession of a vacant seat in a coach where passengers of the white race were accommodated, and was ordered by the conductor to vacate said coach and take a seat in another assigned to persons of the colored race, and, having refused to comply with such demand he was forcibly ejected with the aid of a police officer, and imprisoned in the parish jail to answer a charge of having violated the above act.

The constitutionality of this act is attacked upon the ground that it conflicts both with the Thirteenth Amendment of the Constitution, abolishing slavery, and the Fourteenth Amendment, which prohibits certain restrictive legislation on the part of the States.

1. That it does not conflict with the Thirteenth Amendment, which abolished slavery and involuntary servitude, except as a punishment for crime, is too clear for

argument. Slavery implies involuntary servitude—a state of bondage; the ownership of mankind as a chattel, or at least the control of the labor and services of one man for the benefit of another, and the absence of a legal right to the disposal of his own person, property and services * * *.

So, too, in the *Civil Rights cases,* 109 U.S. 3, 24, it was said that the act of a mere individual, the owner of an inn, a public conveyance or place of amusement, refusing accommodations to colored people cannot be justly regarded as imposing any badge of slavery or servitude upon the applicant, but only as involving an ordinary civil injury, properly cognizable by the laws of the State and presumably subject to redress by those laws until the contrary appears * * *.

A statute which implies merely a legal distinction between the white and colored races—a distinction which is founded in the color of the two races, and which must always exist so long as white men are distinguished from the other race by color—has no tendency to destroy the legal equality of the two races, or reestablish a state of involuntary servitude. Indeed, we do not understand that the Thirteenth Amendment is strenuously relied upon by the plaintiff in error in this connection.

2. By the Fourteenth Amendment, all persons born or naturalized in the United States and subject to the jurisdiction thereof are made citizens of the United States and of the State wherein they reside; and the States are forbidden from making or enforcing any law which shall abridge the privileges or immunities of citizens of the United States, or shall deprive any person of life, liberty, or property without due process of law, or deny to any person within their jurisdiction the equal protection of the laws.

The proper construction of this amendment was first called to the attention of this court in the *Slaughter-house cases,* 16 Wall. 36, which involved, however, not a question of race, but one of exclusive privileges. The case did not call for any expression of opinion as to the exact rights it was intended to secure to the colored race, but it was said generally that its main purpose was to establish the citizenship of the negro; to give definitions of citizenship of the United States and of the States, and to protect from the hostile legislation of the States the privileges and immunities of citizens of the United States, as distinguished from those of citizens of the States.

The object of the amendment was undoubtedly to enforce the absolute equality of the two races before the law, but in the nature of things it could not have been intended to abolish distinctions based upon color, or to enforce social, as distinguished from political, equality, or a commingling of the two races upon terms unsatisfactory to either. Laws permitting, and even requiring, their separation in places where they are liable to be brought into contact do not necessarily imply the inferiority of either race to the other, and have been generally, if not universally, recognized as within the competency of the state legislatures in the exercise of their police power. The most common instance of this is connected with the establishment of separate schools for white and colored children, which has been held to be a valid exercise of the legislative power even by courts of States where the political rights of the colored race have been longest and most earnestly enforced.

* * *

Laws forbidding the intermarriage of the two races may be said in a technical sense to interfere with the freedom of contract, and yet have been universally recognized as within the police power of the State. *State v. Gibson,* 36 Indiana 389.

The distinction between laws interfering with the political equality of the negro and those requiring the separation of the two races in schools, theatres and railway carriages has been frequently drawn by this court. Thus, in *Strauder v. West Virginia,* 100 U.S. 303, it was held that a law of West Virginia limiting to white male persons, 21 years of age and citizens of the State, the right to sit upon juries, was a discrimination which implied a legal inferiority in civil society, which lessened the security of the right of the colored race, and was a step toward reducing them to a condition of servility. Indeed, the right of a colored man that, in the selection of jurors to pass upon his life, liberty and property, there shall be no exclusion of his race, and no discrimination against them because of color, has been asserted in a number of cases. *Virginia v. Rives,* 100 U.S. 313; *Neal v. Delaware,* 103 U.S. 370; *Bush v. Kentucky,* 107 U.S. 110; *Gibson v. Mississippi,* 162 U.S. 565. So, where the laws of a particular locality or the charter of a particular railway corporation has provided that no person shall be excluded from the cars on account of color, we have held that this meant that persons of color should travel in the same car as white ones, and that the enactment was not satisfied by the company's providing cars assigned exclusively to people of color, though they were as good as those which they assigned exclusively to white persons. *Railroad Company v. Brown,* 17 Wall. 445.

Upon the other hand, where a statute of Louisiana required those engaged in the transportation of passengers among the States to give to all persons traveling within that State, upon vessels employed in that business, equal rights and privileges in all parts of the vessel, without distinction on account of race or color, and subjected to an action for damages the owner of such a vessel, who excluded colored passengers on account of their color from the cabin set aside by him for the use of whites, it was held to be, so far as it applied to interstate commerce, unconstitutional and void. *Hall v. De Cuir,* 95 U.S. 48. The court in this case, however, expressly disclaimed that it had anything whatever to do with the statute as a regulation of internal commerce, or affecting anything else than commerce among the States.

* * *

Much nearer, and, indeed, almost directly in point is the case of the *Louisville, New Orleans &c. Railway v. Mississippi,* 133 U.S. 587, wherein the railway company was indicted for a violation of a statute of Mississippi, enacting that all railroads carrying passengers should provide equal but separate accommodations for the white and colored races by providing two or more passenger cars for each passenger train, or by dividing the passenger cars by a partition, so as to secure separate accommodations. The case was presented in a different aspect from the one under consideration, inasmuch as it was an indictment against the railway company for failing to provide the separate accommodations, but the question considered was the constitutionality of the law. In that case, the Supreme Court of Mississippi, 66 Mississippi 662, had held that the statute applied solely to commerce within the State, and that, being the construction of the state statute by its highest court, was accepted as conclusive. "If it be a matter," said the court, p. 591, respecting commerce wholly within a State, and not interfering with commerce between the States, then obviously there is no violation of the commerce clause of the Federal Constitution * * *. No question arises under this section as to the power of the State to separate in different compartments interstate passengers, or affect, in any manner, the privileges and rights of such passengers. All that we can consider is whether the

State has the power to require that railroad trains within her limits shall have separate accommodations for the two races; that affecting only commerce within the State is no invasion of the power given to Congress by the commerce clause."

A like course of reasoning applies to the case under consideration, since the Supreme Court of Louisiana in the case of the *State ex rel. Abbott v. Hicks, Judge, et al.,* 44 La.Ann. 770, held that the statute in question did not apply to interstate passengers, but was confined in its application to passengers traveling exclusively within the borders of the State. The case was decided largely upon the authority of *Railway Co. v. State,* 66 Mississippi 662, and affirmed by this court in 133 U.S. 587. In the present case, no question of interference with interstate commerce can possibly arise, since the East Louisiana Railway appears to have been purely a local line, with both its termini within the State of Louisiana * * *.

While we think the enforced separation of the races, as applied to the internal commerce of the State, neither abridges the privileges or immunities of the colored man, deprives him of his property without due process of law, nor denies him the equal protection of the laws, within the meaning of the Fourteenth Amendment, we are not prepared to say that the conductor, in assigning passengers to the coaches according to their race, does not act at his peril, or that the provision of the second section of the act, that denies to the passenger compensation in damages for a refusal to receive him into the coach in which he properly belongs, is a valid exercise of the legislative power. Indeed, we understand it to be conceded by the State's Attorney, that such part of the act as exempts from liability the railway company and its officers is unconstitutional. The power to assign to a particular coach obviously implies the power to determine to which race the passenger belongs, as well as the power to determine who, under the laws of the particular State, is to be deemed a white, and who a colored person. This question, though indicated in the brief of the plaintiff in error, does not properly arise upon the record in this case, since the only issue made is as to the unconstitutionality of the act so far as it requires the railway to provide separate accommodations, and the conductor to assign passengers according to their race.

It is claimed by the plaintiff in error that, in any mixed community, the reputation of belonging to the dominant race, in this instance the white race, is *property,* in the same sense that a right of action, or of inheritance, is property. Conceding this to be so, for the purposes of this case, we are unable to see how this statute deprives him of, or in any way affects his right to, such property. If he be a white man and assigned to a colored coach, he may have his action for damages against the company for being deprived of his so-called property. Upon the other hand, if he be a colored man and be so assigned, he has been deprived of no property, since he is not lawfully entitled to the reputation of being a white man.

In this connection, it is also suggested by the learned counsel for the plaintiff in error that the same argument that will justify the state legislature in requiring railways to provide separate accommodations for the two races will also authorize them to require separate cars to be provided for people whose hair is of a certain color, or who are aliens, or who belong to certain nationalities, or to enact laws requiring colored people to walk upon one side of the street and white people upon the other, or requiring white men's houses to be painted white, and colored men's black, or their vehicles or business signs to be of different colors, upon the theory that one side of the street is as good as the other, or that a house or vehicle of one color is as good as one of another color. The reply to all this is that every exercise of the police power must be reasonable, and extend only to such laws as are enacted in good faith for the promotion for the public good, and not for the annoyance or oppression of a particular class. Thus, in *Yick Wo v. Hopkins,* 118 U.S. 356, it was held by this court that a municipal ordinance of the city of San Francisco to regulate the carrying on of public laundries within the limits of the municipality, violated the provisions of the Constitution of the United States, if it conferred upon the municipal authorities arbitrary power, at their own will, and without regard to discretion, in the legal sense of the term, to give or withhold consent as to persons or places, without regard to the competency of the persons applying, or the propriety of the places selected for the carrying on of the business. It was held to be a covert attempt on the part of the municipality to make an arbitrary and unjust discrimination against the Chinese race. While this was the case of a municipal ordinance, a like principle has been held to apply to acts of a state legislature passed in the exercise of the police power.

So far, then, as a conflict with the Fourteenth Amendment is concerned, the case reduces itself to the question whether the statute of Louisiana is a reasonable regulation, and with respect to this there must necessarily be a large discretion on the part of the legislature. In determining the question of reasonableness it is at liberty to act with reference to the established usages, customs, and traditions of the people, and with a view to the promotion of their comfort and the preservation of the public peace and good order. Gauged by this standard, we cannot say that a law which authorizes or even requires the separation of the two races in public conveyances is unreasonable, or more obnoxious to the Fourteenth Amendment than the acts of Congress requiring separate schools for colored children in the District of Columbia, the constitutionality of which does not seem to have been questioned, or the corresponding acts of state legislatures.

We consider the underlying fallacy of the plaintiff's argument to consist in the assumption that the enforced separation of the two races stamps the colored race with a badge of inferiority. If this be so, it is not by reason of anything found in the act, but solely because the colored race chooses to put that construction upon it. The argument necessarily assumes that if, as has been more than once the case, and is not unlikely to be so again, the colored race should become the dominant power in the state legislature, and should enact a law in precisely similar terms, it would thereby relegate the white race to an inferior position. We imagine that the white race, at least, would not acquiesce in this assumption. The argument also assumes that social prejudices may be overcome by legislation, and that equal rights cannot be secured to the negro except by an enforced commingling of the two races. We cannot accept this proposition. If the two races are to meet upon terms of social equality, it must be the result of natural affinities, a mutual appreciation of each other's merits, and a voluntary consent of individuals * * *. Legislation is powerless to eradicate racial instincts or to abolish distinctions based upon physical differences, and the attempt to do so can only result in accentuating the difficulties of the present situation. If the civil and political rights of both races be equal one cannot be inferior to the other civilly or politically. If one race be inferior to the other socially, the Constitution of the United States cannot put them upon the same plane.

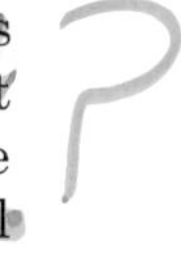

It is true that the question of the proportion of colored blood necessary to constitute a colored person, as distinguished from a white person, is one upon which there is a difference of opinion in the different States, some holding that any visible admixture of black blood stamps the person as belonging to the colored race (*State v. Chaver,* 5 Jones [N.C.] 1, p. 11); others that it depends upon the preponderance of blood (*Gray v. State,* 4 Ohio 354; *Monroe v. Collins,* 17 Ohio St. 665); and still others that the predominance of white blood must only be in the proportion of three fourths. (*People v. Dean,* 4 Michigan 406; *Jones v. Commonwealth,* 80 Virginia 538). But these are questions to be determined under the laws of each State and are not properly put in issue in this case. Under the allegations of his petition it may undoubtedly become a question of importance whether, under the laws of Louisiana, the petitioner belongs to the white or colored race.

The judgment of the court below is, therefore,

Affirmed.

■ MR. JUSTICE BREWER did not hear the argument or participate in the decision of this case.

■ MR. JUSTICE HARLAN, dissenting.

By the Louisiana statute, the validity of which is here involved, all railway companies (other than street railroad companies) carrying passengers in that State are required to have separate but equal accommodations for white and colored persons, "by providing two or more passenger coaches for each passenger train, *or* by dividing the passenger coaches by a *partition* so as to secure separate accommodations." * * *

Only "nurses attending children of the other race" are excepted from the operation of the statute. No exception is made of colored attendants traveling with adults. A white man is not permitted to have his colored servant with him in the same coach, even if his condition of health requires the constant, personal assistance of such servant. If a colored maid insists upon riding in the same coach with a white woman whom she has been employed to serve, and who may need her personal attention while traveling, she is subject to be fined or imprisoned for such an exhibition of zeal in the discharge of duty.

While there may be in Louisiana persons of different races who are not citizens of the United States, the words in the act, "white and colored races," necessarily include all citizens of the United States of both races residing in that State. So that we have before us a state enactment that compels, under penalties, the separation of the two races in railroad passenger coaches, and makes it a crime for a citizen of either race to enter a coach that has been assigned to citizens of the other race.

Thus, the State regulates the use of a public highway by citizens of the United States solely upon the basis of race.

However apparent the injustice of such legislation may be, we have only to consider whether it is consistent with the Constitution of the United States.

That a railroad is a public highway, and that the corporation which owns or operates it is in the exercise of public functions, is not, at this day, to be disputed. Mr. Justice Nelson, speaking for this court in *New Jersey Steam Navigation Co. v. Merchants' Bank,* 6 How. 344, 382, said that a common carrier was in the exercise "of a sort of public office, and has public duties to perform, from which he should not be permitted to exonerate himself without the assent of the parties concerned." * * * So, in *Township of Pine Grove v. Talcott,* 19 Wall. 666, 676: "Though the corporation [a railroad company] was private, its work was public, as much so as if it were to be constructed by the State." * * *

In respect of civil rights common to all citizens, the Constitution of the United States does not, I think, permit any public authority to know the race of those entitled to be protected in the enjoyment of such rights. Every true man has pride of race, and under appropriate circumstances when the rights of others, his equals before the law, are not to be affected, it is his privilege to express such pride and to take such action based upon it as to him seems proper. But I deny that any legislative body or judicial tribunal may have regard to the race of citizens when the civil rights of those citizens are involved. Indeed, such legislation, as that here in question, is inconsistent not only with that equality of rights which pertains to citizenship, National and State, but with the personal liberty enjoyed by everyone within the United States.

The Thirteenth Amendment does not permit the withholding or the deprivation of any right necessarily inhering in freedom. It not only struck down the institution of slavery as previously existing in the United States, but it prevents the imposition of any burdens or disabilities that constitute badges of slavery or servitude. It decreed universal civil freedom in this country. This court has so adjudged. But that amendment having been found inadequate to the protection of the rights of those who had been in slavery, it was followed by the Fourteenth Amendment, which added greatly to the dignity and glory of American citizenship, and to the security of personal liberty * * *. These two amendments, if enforced according to their true intent and meaning, will protect all the civil rights that pertain to freedom and citizenship * * *.

These notable additions to the fundamental law were welcomed by the friends of liberty throughout the world. They removed the race line from our governmental systems * * *.* * *

It was said in argument that the statute of Louisiana does not discriminate against either race, but prescribes a rule applicable alike to white and colored citizens. But this argument does not meet the difficulty. Everyone knows that the statute in question had its origin in the purpose, not so much to exclude white persons from railroad cars occupied by blacks, as to exclude colored people from coaches occupied by or assigned to white persons. Railroad corporations of Louisiana did not make discrimination among whites in the matter of accommodation for travelers. The thing to accomplish was, under the guise of giving equal accommodation for whites and blacks, to compel the latter to keep to themselves while traveling in railroad passenger coaches. No one would be so wanting in candor as to assert the contrary. The fundamental objection, therefore, to the statute is that it interferes with the personal freedom of citizens. "Personal liberty," it has been well said, "consists in the power of locomotion, of changing situation, or removing one's person to whatsoever places one's own inclination may direct, without imprisonment or restraint unless by due course of law." 1 Bl.Com. *134. If a white man and a black man choose to occupy the same public conveyance on a public highway, it is their right to do so, and no government, proceeding alone on grounds of race, can prevent it without infringing the personal liberty of each.

It is one thing for railroad carriers to furnish, or to be required by law to furnish, equal accommodations for all whom they are under a legal duty to carry. It is quite another thing for government to forbid citizens of the white and black races from traveling in the same public conveyance, and to punish officers of railroad companies for permitting persons of the two races to occupy the same passenger coach. If a State can prescribe, as a rule of civil conduct, that whites and blacks shall not travel as passengers in the same railroad coach, why may it not so regulate the use of the streets of its cities and towns as to compel white citizens to keep on one side of a street and black citizens to keep on the other? Why may it not, upon like grounds, punish whites and blacks who ride together in streetcars or in open vehicles on a public road or street? Why may it not require sheriffs to assign whites to one side of a court-room and blacks to the other? And why may it not also prohibit the commingling of the two races in the galleries of legislative halls or in public assemblages convened for the consideration of the political questions of the day? Further, if this statute of Louisiana is consistent with the personal liberty of citizens, why may not the State require the separation in railroad coaches of native and naturalized citizens of the United States, or of Protestants and Roman Catholics?

The answer given at the argument to these questions was that regulations of the kind they suggest would be unreasonable, and could not, therefore, stand before the law. Is it meant that the determination of questions of legislative power depends upon the inquiry whether the statute whose validity is questioned is, in the judgment of the courts, a reasonable one, taking all the circumstances into consideration? A statute may be unreasonable merely because a sound public policy forbade its enactment. But I do not understand that the courts have anything to do with the policy or expediency of legislation. A statute may be valid, and yet, upon grounds of public policy, may well be characterized as unreasonable * * *. There is a dangerous tendency in these latter days to enlarge the functions of the courts by means of judicial interference with the will of the people as expressed by the legislature * * *. [I]f the particular statute in question is valid, although the courts, looking at the public interests, may conceive the statute to be both unreasonable and impolitic. If the power exists to enact a statute, that ends the matter so far as the courts are concerned. The adjudged cases in which statutes have been held to be void, because unreasonable, are those in which the means employed by the legislature were not at all germane to the end to which the legislature was competent.

The white race deems itself to be the dominant race in this country. And so it is, in prestige, in achievements, in education, in wealth and in power. So, I doubt not, it will continue to be for all time, if it remains true to its great heritage and holds fast to the principles of constitutional liberty. But in view of the Constitution, in the eye of the law, there is in this country no superior, dominant, ruling class of citizens. There is no caste here. Our Constitution is color-blind, and neither knows nor tolerates classes among citizens. In respect of civil rights, all citizens are equal before the law. The humblest is the peer of the most powerful. The law regards man as man, and takes no account of his surroundings or of his color when his civil rights as guaranteed by the supreme law of the land are involved. It is therefore to be regretted that this high tribunal, the final expositor of the fundamental law of the land, has reached the conclusion that it is competent for a State to regulate the enjoyment by citizens of their civil rights solely upon the basis of race.

In my opinion, the judgment this day rendered will, in time, prove to be quite as pernicious as the decision made by this tribunal in the *Dred Scott Case* * * *.

The present decision, it may well be apprehended, will not only stimulate aggressions, more or less brutal and irritating, upon the admitted rights of colored citizens, but will encourage the belief that it is possible, by means of state enactments, to defeat the beneficent purposes which the people of the United States had in view when they adopted the recent amendments of the Constitution, by one of which the blacks of this country were made citizens of the United States and of the States in which they respectively reside, and whose privileges and immunities, as citizens, the States are forbidden to abridge. Sixty millions of whites are in no danger from the presence here of eight millions of blacks. The destinies of the two races in this country, are indissolubly linked together, and the interests of both require that the common government of all shall not permit the seeds of race hate to be planted under the sanction of law. What can more certainly arouse race hate, what more certainly create and perpetuate a feeling of distrust between these races, than state enactments, which, in fact, proceed on the ground that colored citizens are so inferior and degraded that they cannot be allowed to sit in public coaches occupied by white citizens. That, as all will admit, is the real meaning of such legislation as was enacted in Louisiana.

* * * This question is not met by the suggestion that social equality cannot exist between the white and black races in this country. That argument, if it can be properly regarded as one, is scarcely worthy of consideration; for social equality no more exists between two races when traveling in a passenger coach or a public highway than when members of the same races sit by each other in a street car or in the jury box, or stand or sit with each other in a political assembly, or when they use in common the street of a city or town, or when they are in the same room for the purpose of having their names placed on the registry of voters, or when they approach the ballot box in order to exercise the high privilege of voting.

There is a race so different from our own that we do not permit those belonging to it to become citizens of the United States. Persons belonging to it are, with few exceptions, absolutely excluded from our country. I allude to the Chinese race. But, by the statute in question, a Chinaman can ride in the same passenger coach with white citizens of the United States, while citizens of the black race in Louisiana, many of whom, perhaps, risked their lives for the preservation of the Union, who are entitled, by law, to participate in the political control of the State and nation, who are not excluded, by law or by reason of their race, from public stations of any kind, and who have all the legal rights that belong to white citizens, are yet declared to be criminals, liable to imprisonment, if they ride in a public coach occupied by citizens of the white race. It is scarcely just to say that a colored citizen should not object to occupying a public coach assigned to his own race. He does not object, nor, perhaps, would he object to separate coaches for his race if his rights under the law were recognized. But he does object, and ought never to cease objecting to the proposition, that citizens of the white and black race can be adjudged criminals because they sit, or claim the right to sit, in the same public coach on a public highway.

The arbitrary separation of citizens on the basis of race, while they are on a public highway is a badge of servitude wholly inconsistent with the civil freedom and the equality before the law established by the Constitution. It cannot be justified upon any legal grounds.

If evils will result from the commingling of the two races upon public highways established for the benefit of all, they will be infinitely less than those that will surely come from state legislation regulating the enjoyment of civil rights upon the basis of race. We boast of the freedom enjoyed by our people above all other peoples. But it is difficult to reconcile that boast with a state of the law which, practically, puts the brand of servitude and degradation upon a large class of our fellow-citizens, our equals before the law. The thin disguise of "equal" accommodations for passengers in railroad coaches will not mislead anyone, nor atone for the wrong this day done.

* * * May it not now be reasonably expected that astute men of the dominant race, who affect to be disturbed at the possibility that the integrity of the white race may be corrupted, or that its supremacy will be imperiled, by contact on public highways with black people, will endeavor to procure statutes requiring white and black jurors to be separated in the jury box by a "partition," and that, upon retiring from the courtroom to consult as to their verdict, such partition, if it be a moveable one, shall be taken to their consultation room, and set up in such way as to prevent black jurors from coming too close to their brother jurors of the white race. If the "partition" used in the courtroom happens to be stationary, provision could be made for screens with openings through which jurors of the two races could confer as to their verdict without coming into personal contact with each other. I cannot see but that, according to the principles this day announced, such state legislation, although conceived in hostility to, and enacted for the purpose of humiliating, citizens of the United States of a particular race, would be held to be consistent with the Constitution.

* * *

For the reasons stated, I am constrained to withhold my assent from the opinion and judgment of the majority.

NOTES AND QUESTIONS

1. The Louisiana statute in this case clearly violated both the Civil Rights Act of 1866 and Section 1 of the Fourteenth Amendment. Citizens of every race and color simply did not have "the same right" * * * "to make and enforce contracts" * * * as "is enjoyed by white citizens." Certain products—tickets to enter certain railroad cars—were available for some people but not others. This was a not a result of market forces—it was a *statute* denying certain people the legal *capacity* to enter into contracts because of their race. It is hard to conceive of a clearer violation of the Fourteenth Amendment. The Supreme Court in *Railroad Co. v. Brown*, *supra*, had no difficulty in seeing that "separate but equal" was not "equal." Why do you think the Court in *Plessy*, a quarter century later, failed to make this connection?

2. There was no "state action" problem in this case—the Louisiana legislature had acted—but did the statute also violate the Thirteenth Amendment? Are separate transportation facilities a badge or incident of slavery? Did it also violate the Fourteenth Amendment's Citizenship Clause?

3. The majority did find one part of the statute unconstitutional: The part that immunized railroad employees from lawsuits by *whites* who were wrongly identified as *colored*. That immunity, said the Court, went too far.

4. Does the Court adequately distinguish *DeCuir, see supra* pages 1249–1252? Recall in that case a Louisiana statute (from an earlier era) *forbidding* discrimination in the assignment of steamship cabins was held to violate the dormant commerce clause. The argument in *Plessy* is that the rail line operates entirely within the State. Is the

Court conceding that the law would be unconstitutional—on Commerce Clause rather than Fourteenth Amendment grounds—if it applied to interstate lines?

5. The Court invokes examples of statutes providing for segregated schools. Had any Supreme Court case before 1897 adjudicated that question? Notice also the citation to *State v. Gibson* for the proposition that "[l]aws forbidding the intermarriage of the two races may be said in a technical sense to interfere with the freedom of contract, and yet have been universally recognized as within the police power of the State." Do you think the justices in *Plessy* carefully read *Gibson*? Did they think it well reasoned? Does something coming within the police power of the States mean that it cannot be touched by the Fourteenth Amendment?

6. Consider Justice John Marshall Harlan's now-famous dissent. He understands and explains to the Supreme Court that the Fourteenth Amendment abolished systems of castes and does not permit the government to know the race of its citizens when it acts. Hold this question for later: Does Justice Harlan's dissent say that the Constitution requires the government to be colorblind when it acts?

7. Once again, is this a case where the shadow of the *Slaughter-House Cases* still looms large? If *Plessy* was a case argued and decided under the original meaning of the Privileges or Immunities Clause, it is hard to see how anyone could get it wrong. It is much harder, however, to describe the problem with the Louisiana statute in terms of due process of law or equal protection of the laws.

8. In response to the parade of horribles of state laws discriminating on all kinds of foolish or offensive grounds, the Court says that all state regulations have to be reasonable. Where does the Court get that idea from? Does it say? Assuming that regulations must be reasonable, what makes this regulation based on skin color reasonable and regulations based on, for example, hair color unreasonable? The Court's main answer is that segregated rail cars are not much different from segregated schools. Granted. What makes racially segregated schools reasonable? Why would highly educated judges, three decades after the Civil War and the Reconstruction Amendments, think that racial segregation was reasonable?

9. As it happens, those three decades after the Civil War were very eventful intellectually as well as socially and legally—and not always in good ways. In some respects, one of the worst things to happen to the law in the late nineteenth and early twentieth centuries was scientific progress, which is something that is very easy to admire and even easier to misunderstand and misapply. Perhaps the biggest and most tragic victim of this combination of admiration and misapplication was Charles Darwin. Darwin put forward (or, perhaps more accurately, popularized) a theory of biological evolution. The combination of this idea with the historicism and scientism that characterized the Progressive era was a recipe for finding a newfound "scientific" basis for racism and social distinctions. (This idea has come to be called "Social Darwinism," though that term was not commonly employed until after the 1940s, when Richard Hofstadter published his influential 1944 book *Social Darwinism in American Thought*. *See* Thomas C. Leonard, *Origins of the Myth of Social Darwinism: The Ambiguous Legacy of Richard Hofstadter's* Social Darwinism in American Thought, 71 J. ECON. BEHAV. & ORG. 37, 39–40 (2009).)

Abraham Lincoln began the Gettysburg Address by hearkening back to the Enlightenment view, reflected in the Declaration of Independence and in numerous "born free and equal" clauses in founding-era state constitutions, that all men are created equal. The Framers of the Fourteenth Amendment clearly shared Lincoln's egalitarian views.

By the end of the nineteenth century, that consensus ideal, still dominant when the Reconstruction Amendments were ratified, *see* Steven G. Calabresi & Gary Lawson, *The Depravity of the 1930s and the Modern Administrative State,* 94 NOTRE DAME L. REV. 821, 845–49 (2018), was dissolving among much of the intelligentsia. The emerging view—shared by educated people from Theodore Roosevelt to Woodrow Wilson to Margaret Sanger—was that there were feeble-minded individuals *and races* who should not be allowed to breed and have children (and certainly should not be allowed to pollute the gene pool by interbreeding with their "betters"). Anti-miscegenation statutes were only the opening wedge.

A majority of the States in the early twentieth century passed eugenics laws providing for compulsory sterilization of "feeble-minded" individual Americans. By 1933, twenty-seven States had sterilization laws. *See* VICTORIA F. NOURSE, IN RECKLESS HANDS: *SKINNER V. OKLAHOMA* AND THE NEAR TRIUMPH OF AMERICAN EUGENICS 20 (2008). Governor Woodrow Wilson of New Jersey signed that State's eugenics bill into law. By 1935, only a dozen States did not have eugenics laws in force or pending. *See id.* at 20–22. The Supreme Court upheld these laws as constitutional in a dreadful opinion by Justice Oliver Wendell Holmes in *Buck v. Bell,* 274 U.S. 200 (1927), *see infra* pages 1435–1436, which contained the infamous comment: "The principle that sustains compulsory vaccination is broad enough to cover cutting the Fallopian tubes. Three generations of imbeciles are enough." *Id.* at 207. More than 60,000 (and quite possibly more, as records were not always kept) American citizens were compulsorily sterilized as a result. This "scientific racism" had an influence, including (and even especially) within the Progressive movement, *see* THOMAS C. LEONARD, ILLIBERAL REFORMERS: RACE, EUGENICS & AMERICAN ECONOMICS IN THE PROGRESSIVE ERA 117 (2016), that is hard to grasp in this day and age. As Victoria Nourse aptly put it:

> It was not only the openly racist Aryan-lovers who wrote of the "iron law of inequality" and touted racist aristocracy. Eugenic pioneers such as Charles Davenport had written that all men were "*bound* by their protoplasmic makeup and *unequal* in their powers and responsibilities." Geneticists like Harvard's Edward M. East wrote that equality was a fraud: the "cult of *égalité* . . . is a pose." Henry Fairfield Osborn, the president of the American Museum of Natural History, publicly derided the claim that all men were created equal as "political sophistry." The eugenics popularizer Albert Wiggam insisted that men were "irremediably and ineradicably *unequal*." The zoologist S.J. Holmes summed it all up: "If there is any one thing which has been thrown absolutely out of court by the advances of biology and psychology, it is the dogma of the natural equality of man."

NOURSE, *supra,* at 83. Among the admirers of this American development was the German National Socialist Workers Party—a.k.a., the "Nazis"—in the 1930s. In 1933, one of the first things Adolf Hitler's Nazi Party did when it came to power in Germany was to pass an American-style eugenics law because, as one Nazi put it, "The Americans are beating us at our own game." The German Reich's eugenics law resulted from "a sustained engagement with America's eugenics movement," JAMES Q. WHITMAN, HITLER'S AMERICAN MODEL: THE UNITED STATES AND THE MAKING OF NAZI RACE LAW 8 (2017), and the "Nazis even looked to the United States as a 'model.' " *Id.* (quoting STEFAN KÜHL, THE NAZI CONNECTION: EUGENICS, AMERICAN RACISM, AND GERMAN NATIONAL SOCIALISM, at xii (1994)); *see also* HARRY BRUINIUS, BETTER FOR ALL THE WORLD: THE SECRET HISTORY OF FORCED STERILIZATION AND AMERICA'S QUEST FOR RACIAL PURITY 283–86 (2006) (describing American influence on German eugenics); EDWIN BLACK, WAR AGAINST THE WEAK: EUGENICS AND AMERICA'S CAMPAIGN TO CREATE A MASTER RACE (2003).

While these ideas about genetics and race crested in the 1930s, by 1896 it was not surprising to see highly educated people convinced that race-mixing was socially and *scientifically* wrong. Social Darwinism, which was embraced by Oliver Wendell Holmes, Theodore Roosevelt, Woodrow Wilson, the presidents of Yale and Harvard, and the heads of all the major American charitable foundations, came to an end only as a result of the Holocaust. People were so horrified by the murder of six million Jews to eliminate their bad genes from the gene pool that they went back to the Founders and Abraham Lincoln and adopted a Universal Declaration of Human Rights at the U.N. in 1948, Article I of which says: "All human beings are born free and equal in dignity and rights. They are endowed with reason and conscience and should act towards one another in a spirit of brotherhood." *See infra* pages 1313–1314. But for more than half a century, that insight was lost among far too many "proper" people.

10. Racism was thus on everyone's mind when *Plessy v. Ferguson* was decided, which explains in part the holding of the case (and Justice Harlan's derogatory reference to Chinese-Americans in his dissent). European and American colonialism, in, for example, the Spanish-American War, also had its roots in Social Darwinism.

11. Once *Plessy* accepts racial classification as "reasonable," it has to deal with the tricky question whether someone like Plessy, who was seven-eighths white and one-eighth black, was an African-American for purposes of rail car assignment. The Supreme Court said it would defer to the States to have differing rules from State to State as to who was an African-American and who was not. These American race laws, determining the "purity" of one's blood line, were all of great interest to Adolf Hitler and his Nazis. *See* WHITMAN, *supra*.

12. And, of course, once "separate but equal" was accepted as "reasonable" for rail cars, the question arose what other privileges or immunities of citizenship could be parceled out separately but "equally." Statutes requiring segregated schools were common—in many cases by virtue of state constitutional provisions mandating such segregated schools. Those provisions generally went unchallenged. In *Cummings v. Board of Education,* 175 U.S. 528 (1899), the Court rejected a challenge by plaintiffs to a public school board's discretionary decision to fund an all-white, all-male high school, but the case did not resolve any broad questions of the permissibility of school segregation. According to Justice Harlan's unanimous opinion:

> It was said at the argument that the vice in the common-school system of Georgia was the requirement that the white and colored children of the state be educated in separate schools. But we need not consider that question in this case. No such issue was made in the pleadings. Indeed, the plaintiffs distinctly state that they have no objection to the tax in question so far as levied for the support of primary, intermediate, and grammar schools, in the management of which the rule as to the separation of races is enforced.

Id. at 543–44. *See also id.* at 544–45 ("We are not permitted by the evidence in the record to regard that decision as having been made with any desire or purpose on the part of the board to discriminate against any of the colored school children of the county on account of their race * * *. [I]f it appeared that the board's refusal to maintain such a school was in fact an abuse of its discretion and in hostility to the colored population because of their race, different questions might have arisen in the state court.").

13. A case with more impact was *Berea College v. Kentucky,* 211 U.S. 45 (1908), which involved a Kentucky statute forbidding *private* colleges from holding integrated classes(!): "it shall be unlawful for any person, corporation, or association of persons to maintain or operate any college, school, or institution where persons of the white and

negro races are both received as pupils for instruction * * *." Ky. Acts 1904, ch. 85, § 1. The Court declined to say whether the statute was valid as applied in all circumstances, but it held—with no analysis at all under the Fourteenth Amendment—that the State's power over corporations (Berea College was a corporation) was plenary. It was evidently considered too obvious for discussion that state-mandated segregated schools, in matters subject to state control, was obviously constitutional. Justice Harlan was the lone dissenter. He thought the statute as written applied to corporate and non-corporate entities alike and thus had to be judged in all of its applications, which made it invalid. But pay close attention to the grounds on which Justice Harlan thought the statute invalid:

> The capacity to impart instruction to others is given by the Almighty for beneficent purposes and its use may not be forbidden or interfered with by Government—certainly not, unless such instruction is, in its nature, harmful to the public morals or imperils the public safety. The right to impart instruction, harmless in itself or beneficial to those who receive it, is a substantial right of property—especially, where the services are rendered for compensation. But even if such right be not strictly a property right, it is, beyond question, part of one's liberty as guaranteed against hostile state action by the Constitution of the United States. This court has more than once said that the liberty guaranteed by the 14th Amendment embraces "the right of the citizen to be free in the enjoyment of all his faculties," and "to be free to use them in all lawful ways." If pupils, of whatever race—certainly, if they be citizens—choose with the consent of their parents or voluntarily to sit together in a private institution of learning while receiving instruction which is not in its nature harmful or dangerous to the public, no government, whether Federal or state, can legally forbid their coming together, or being together temporarily, for such an innocent purpose. If the Commonwealth of Kentucky can make it a crime to teach white and colored children together at the same time, in a private institution of learning, it is difficult to perceive why it may not forbid the assembling of white and colored children in the same Sabbath-school, for the purpose of being instructed in the Word of God, although such teaching may be done under the authority of the church to which the school is attached as well as with the consent of the parents of the children. So, if the state court be right, white and colored children may even be forbidden to sit together in a house of worship or at a communion table in the same Christian church. In the cases supposed there would be the same association of white and colored persons as would occur when pupils of the two races sit together in a private institution of learning for the purpose of receiving instruction in purely secular matters. Will it be said that the cases supposed and the case here in hand are different in that no government, in this country, can lay unholy hands on the religious faith of the people? The answer to this suggestion is that in the eye of the law, the right to enjoy one's religious belief, unmolested by any human power, is no more sacred nor more fully or distinctly recognized than is the right to impart and receive instruction not harmful to the public. The denial of either right would be an infringement of the liberty inherent in the freedom secured by the fundamental law. Again, if the views of the highest court of Kentucky be sound, that commonwealth may, without infringing the Constitution of the United States, forbid the association in the same private school of pupils of the Anglo-Saxon and Latin races respectively, or pupils of the Christian and Jewish faiths, respectively. Have we become so inoculated with prejudice of race that an American government, professedly based on the principles of freedom, and

> charged with the protection of all citizens alike, can make distinctions between such citizens in the matter of their voluntary meeting for innocent purposes simply because of their respective races?

211 U.S. at 67–69. Is the real problem with the Kentucky statute that it deprives (non-corporate) persons of liberty or property without due process of law? And Justice Harlan made very clear that "what I have said has no reference to regulations prescribed for *public* schools, established at the pleasure of the state and maintained at the public expense. No such question is here presented and it need not be now discussed. My observations have reference to the case before the court, and only to the provision of the statute making it a crime for any person to impart harmless instruction to white and colored pupils together, at the same time, in the same *private* institution of learning." *Id.* at 69 (emphasis added).

14. "Separate but equal" was not the only doctrine of this era of major consequence. The Fifteenth Amendment, prohibiting racial discrimination in voting, was evaded in countless ways, most notably the devices that gave rise to the still-utilized verb "grandfathered," referring to statutory provisions that automatically register to vote anyone whose grandfather was registered (you can see how that would work to Southern white people's advantage while burdening Southern African-Americans circa 1900). These grandfather voting registration laws imposed onerous voter registration restrictions on those whose grandfathers had not been registered to vote. The Supreme Court took up a variation on such a device in 1903.

[Assignment 60]

D. GILES V. HARRIS

189 U.S. 475 (1903)

■ MR. JUSTICE HOLMES delivered the opinion of the court:

This is a bill in equity brought by a colored man, on behalf of himself "and on behalf of more than five thousand negroes, citizens of the county of Montgomery, Alabama, similarly situated and circumstanced as himself," against the board of registrars of that county. The prayer of the bill is in substance that the defendants may be required to enroll upon the voting lists the name of the plaintiff and of all other qualified members of his race who applied for registration before August 1, 1902, and were refused, and that certain sections of the Constitution of Alabama, may be declared contrary to the Fourteenth and Fifteenth Amendments of the Constitution of the United States, and void.

The allegations of the bill may be summed up as follows. The plaintiff is subject to none of the disqualifications set forth in the constitution of Alabama and is entitled to vote—entitled, as the bill plainly means, under the constitution as it is. He applied in March, 1902, for registration as a voter, and was refused arbitrarily on the ground of his color, together with large numbers of other duly qualified negroes, while all white men were registered. The same thing was done all over the state. Under § 187 of article 8 of the Alabama constitution persons registered before January 1, 1903, remain electors for life unless they become disqualified by certain crimes, etc., while after that date severer tests come into play which would exclude, perhaps, a large part of the black race. Therefore, by the refusal, the plaintiff and the other negroes excluded were deprived not only of their vote at an election which has taken place since the bill was filed, but of the permanent advantage incident to registration before 1903. The white men generally are registered for good under the easy test and the black men are likely to be kept out in the future as in the past. This refusal to register the blacks was part of a general scheme to disfranchise them, to which the defendants and the State itself, according to the bill, were parties. The defendants accepted their office for the purpose of carrying out the scheme. The part taken by the State, that is, by the white population which framed the constitution, consisted in shaping that instrument so as to give opportunity and effect to the wholesale fraud which has been practised.

The bill sets forth the material sections of the state Constitution * * * [B]y § 180, before 1903 the following male citizens of the State, who are citizens of the United States, were entitled to register, viz.: First. All who had served honorably in the enumerated wars of the United States, including those on either side in the "war between the states.'" Second. All lawful descendants of persons who served honorably in the enumerated wars or in the war of the Revolution. Third. "All persons who are of good character and who understand the duties and obligations of citizenship under a republican form of government." As we have said, according to the allegations of the bill this part of the constitution, as practically administered and as intended to be administered, let in all whites and kept out a large part, if not all, of the blacks, and those who were let in retained their right to vote after 1903, when tests which might be too severe for many of the whites as well as the blacks went into effect. By § 181, after January 1, 1903, only the following persons are entitled to register: First. Those who can read and write any article of the Constitution of the United States in the English language, and who either are physically unable to work or have been regularly engaged in some lawful business for the greater part of the last twelve months, and those who are unable to read and write solely because physically disabled. Second. Owners or husbands of owners of forty acres of land in the State, upon which they reside, and owners or husbands of owners of real or personal estate in the State assessed for taxation at three hundred dollars or more, if the taxes have been paid, unless under contest * * *.

* * *

It seems to us impossible to grant the equitable relief which is asked * * *.

The difficulties which we cannot overcome are two, and the first is this: The plaintiff alleges that the whole registration scheme of the Alabama constitution is a fraud upon the Constitution of the United States, and asks us to declare it void. But of course he could not maintain a bill for a mere declaration in the air. He does not try to do so, but asks to be registered as a party qualified under the void instrument. If then we accept the conclusion which it is the chief purpose of the bill to maintain, how can we make the court a party to the unlawful scheme by accepting it and adding another voter to its fraudulent lists? If a white man came here on the same general allegations, admitting his sympathy with the plan, but alleging some special prejudice that had kept him off the list, we hardly should think it necessary to meet him with a reasoned answer. But the relief cannot be varied because we think that in the future the particular plaintiff is likely to try to overthrow the scheme. If we accept the plaintiff's allegations for the purposes of his case, he cannot complain. We must accept or reject them. It is impossible simply to shut our eyes, put the plaintiff on the lists, be they honest or fraudulent, and leave the determination of the fundamental question for the future. If we have an opinion that the bill is right on its face, or if we are undecided, we are not at liberty to assume it to be wrong for the purposes of decision. It seems to us that unless we are prepared to say that it is wrong, that all its principal allegations are immaterial, and that the registration plan of the Alabama constitution is valid, we cannot order the plaintiff's name to be registered. It is not an answer to say that if all the blacks who are qualified according to the letter of the instrument were registered, the fraud would be cured. In the first place, there is no probability that any way now is open by which more than a few could be registered, but if all could be the difficulty would not be overcome. If the sections of the constitution concerning registration were illegal in their inception, it would be a new doctrine in constitutional law that the original invalidity could be cured by an administration which defeated their intent. We express no opinion as to the alleged fact of their unconstitutionality beyond saying that we are not willing to assume that they are valid, in the face of the allegations and main object of the bill, for the purpose of granting the relief which it was necessary to pray in order that that object should be secured.

The other difficulty is of a different sort, and strikingly reinforces the argument that equity cannot undertake now, any more than it has in the past, to enforce political rights * * *. In determining whether a court of equity can take jurisdiction, one of the first questions is what it can do to enforce any order that it may make. This is alleged to be the conspiracy of a State, although the State is not and could not be made a party to the bill. *Hans v. Louisiana*, 134 U. S. 1, (1890). The Circuit Court has no constitutional power to control its action by any direct means. And if we leave the State out of consideration, the court has as little practical power to deal with the people of the State in a body. The bill imports that the great mass of the white population intends to keep the blacks from voting. To meet such an intent something more than ordering the plaintiff's name to be inscribed upon the lists of 1902 will be needed. If the conspiracy and the intent exist, a name on a piece of paper will not defeat them. Unless we are prepared to supervise the voting in that State by officers of the court, it seems to us that all that the plaintiff could get from equity would be an empty form. Apart from damages to the individual, relief from a great political wrong, if done, as alleged, by the people of a State and the State itself, must be given by them or by the legislative and political department of the government of the United States.

Decree affirmed.

■ MR. JUSTICE BREWER dissenting:

I am unable to concur in either the opinion or judgment in this case. The single question is whether the Circuit Court of the United States had jurisdiction. Accepting the statement of facts in the opinion of the majority as sufficiently full, it appears that the plaintiff was entitled to a place on the permanent registry and was denied it by the defendants, the board of registrars in the county in which he lived. No one was allowed to vote who was not registered. He desired to vote at the coming election for representative in Congress. He was deprived of that right by the action of the defendants * * *.

* * *

* * * That many others were similarly treated does not destroy his rights or deprive him of relief in the courts. That such relief will be given has been again and again affirmed in both national and state courts.

■ MR. JUSTICE BROWN also dissents.

■ MR. JUSTICE HARLAN, dissenting. [Omitted. *Editors' Note: Justice Harlan thought the only question properly before the Court concerned the meaning of a jurisdictional statute. He added at the end: "As these are my views as to the jurisdiction of this court, upon this record, I will not formulate and discuss my views upon the merits of this case. But to avoid misapprehension, I may add that my conviction is that * * * the plaintiff is entitled to relief in respect of his right to be registered as a voter. I agree with Mr. Justice Brewer that it is competent for the courts to give relief in such cases as this."*]

NOTES AND QUESTIONS

1. The Alabama state constitutional provisions in question in *Giles v. Harris* were obviously designed to make it harder for African-Americans to register to vote than it was for white Americans. They were a plain and obvious violation of the Fifteenth Amendment, which bans state laws "abridging," *i.e.*. "shortening" or "lessening," the right to vote on account of "race, color, or previous condition of servitude." Does the majority ever say otherwise? Or does the majority say that the constitutional violation is so massive that federal courts have no power to grant relief? Does that make any sense? If the plaintiffs' claim was overbroad, what would the Court have wanted them to claim in order to seek relief?

2. Would the Court really have been participating in a fraud by ordering the State to register the plaintiffs? Is the Court participating in a fraud—on its own analysis—by doing nothing?

3. If the Court simply declared the entire voting scheme an unconstitutional fraud, what would happen then? Would the prior voting scheme still be in effect because it had never been superseded? Would the federal executive provide the necessary means to enforce any orders issued by the courts? Did that concern underlie the Court's comment that "relief from a great political wrong, if done, as alleged, by the people of a state and the state itself, must be given by them or by the legislative and political department of the government of the United States"? Is that a sufficient reason for a court not to act? At one point in the opinion (which we did not reproduce above), the Court observed: "On these assumptions we are not prepared to say that an action at law could not be maintained on the facts alleged in the bill." 189 U.S. at 485–86. In an action at law, a court has no discretion to withhold a remedy if it rules for the plaintiff. In equity, however, a court has such power. *See* Steven G. Calabresi & Gary Lawson, *Equity and Hierarchy: Reflections on the Harris Execution,* 102 YALE L. J. 255 (1992). If *Giles* was really just a case about remedial discretion, did the Court apply that discretion reasonably? If Giles wanted to sue for damages, who would Giles sue?

4. For a detailed analysis of *Giles* and its often underappreciated significance, see Richard H. Pildes, *Democracy, Anti-Democracy, and the Canon,* 17 CONST. COMMENTARY 295 (2000).

5. In 1915, the Court faced a literal "grandfather" clause in Oklahoma, and it easily found it unconstitutional (in the first case in which the National Association for the Advancement of Colored People, or NAACP, filed a brief in the Court). *See Guinn v. United States,* 238 U.S. 347 (1915). The Court did not cite *Giles*. How were those cases different? A quarter century later, the Court addressed that question in a follow-up case to *Guinn,* in which the Oklahoma "state legislature responded to the ruling [in *Guinn*] by 'grandfathering' the grandfather clause." Michael J. Klarman, *Race and the Court in the Progressive Era,* 51 VAND. L. REV. 881, 921 (1998).

E. LANE V. WILSON

307 U.S. 268 (1939)

■ MR. JUSTICE FRANKFURTER delivered the opinion of the Court.

The case is here on *certiorari* to review the judgment of the Circuit Court of Appeals for the Tenth Circuit affirming that of the United States District Court for the Eastern District of Oklahoma, entered upon a directed verdict in favor of the defendants. The action was one for $5,000 damages brought under Section 1979 of the Revised Statutes (8 U.S.C. § 43) by a colored citizen claiming discriminatory treatment resulting from electoral legislation of Oklahoma, in violation of the Fifteenth Amendment. *Certiorari* was granted because of the importance of the question and an asserted conflict with the decision in *Guinn v. United States,* 238 U.S. 347.

The constitution under which Oklahoma was admitted into the Union regulated the suffrage by Article III, whereby its "qualified electors" were to be "citizens of the State * * * who are over the age of twenty-one years" with disqualifications in the case of felons, paupers and lunatics. Soon after its admission the suffrage provisions of the Oklahoma Constitution were radically amended by the addition of a literacy test from which white voters were in effect relieved through the operation of a "grandfather clause." The clause was stricken down by this Court as violative of the prohibition against discrimination "on account of race, color, or previous condition of servitude" of the Fifteenth Amendment. This outlawry occurred on June 21, 1915. In the meantime the Oklahoma general election of 1914 had been based on the offending "grandfather clause." After the invalidation of that clause a special session of the Oklahoma legislature enacted a new scheme for registration as a prerequisite to voting. Oklahoma Laws of 1916, Act of February 26, 1916, c. 24. Section 4 of this statute (now Section 5654, Oklahoma Statutes 1931, 26 Okl.St.Ann. § 74) was obviously directed towards the consequences of the decision in *Guinn v. United States, supra.* Those who had voted in the general election of 1914, automatically remained qualified voters. The new registration requirements affected only others. These had to apply for registration between April 30, 1916 and May 11, 1916, if qualified at that time, with an extension to June 30, 1916, given only to those "absent from the county * * * during such period of time, or * * * prevented by sickness or unavoidable misfortune from registering * * * within such time." The crux of the present controversy is the validity of this registration scheme, with its dividing line between white citizens who had voted under the "grandfather clause" immunity prior to *Guinn v. United States, supra,* and citizens who were outside it, and the not more than 12 days as the normal period of registration for the theretofore proscribed class.

The petitioner, a colored citizen of Oklahoma, who was the plaintiff below and will hereafter be referred to as such, sued three county election officials for declining to register him on October 17, 1934. He was qualified for registration in 1916 but did not then get on the registration list. The evidence is in conflict whether he presented himself in that year for registration and, if so, under what circumstances registration was denied him. The fact is that plaintiff did not get on the register in 1916. Under the terms of the statute he thereby permanently lost the right to register and hence the right to vote. The central claim of plaintiff is that of the unconstitutionality of Section 5654. The defendants joined issue on this claim and further insisted that if there had been illegality in a denial of the plaintiff's right to registration, his proper recourse was to the courts of Oklahoma. The District Court took the case from the jury and its action was affirmed by the Circuit Court of Appeals. It found no proof of discrimination against negroes in the administration of Section 5654 and denied that the legislation was in conflict with the Fifteenth Amendment.

The defendants * * * say that on the plaintiff's own assumption of its invalidity, there is no Oklahoma statute under which he could register and therefore no right to registration has been denied * * *.

The first objection derives from a misapplication of *Giles v. Harris*, 189 U.S. 475. In that case a bill in equity was brought by a colored man on behalf of himself "and on behalf of more than five thousand negroes, citizens of the county of Montgomery, Alabama, similarly situated" which in effect asked the federal court "to supervise the voting in that State by officers of the court." What this Court called a "new and extraordinary situation" was found "strikingly" to reinforce "the argument that equity cannot undertake now, any more than it has in the past, to enforce political rights." See 189 U.S., at page 487. Apart from this traditional restriction upon the exercise of equitable jurisdiction there was another difficulty in *Giles v. Harris*. The plaintiff there was in effect asking for specific performance of his right under Alabama electoral legislation. This presupposed the validity of the legislation under which he was claiming. But the whole theory of his bill was the invalidity of this legislation. Naturally enough, this Court took his claim at its face value and found no legislation on the basis of which specific performance could be decreed.

This case is very different from *Giles v. Harris*—the difference having been explicitly foreshadowed by *Giles v. Harris* itself. In that case this Court declared "we are not prepared to say that an action at law could not be maintained on the facts alleged in the bill." 189 U.S. at 485. That is precisely the basis of the present action, brought under the following "appropriate legislation" of Congress to enforce the Fifteenth Amendment:

"Every person who, under color of any statute, * * * of any State * * * subjects, or causes to be subjected, any citizen of the United States * * * within the jurisdiction thereof to the deprivation of any rights, privileges, or immunities secured by the Constitution and laws, shall be liable to the party injured in an action at law * * *."

* * *

We therefore cannot avoid passing on the merits of plaintiff's constitutional claims. The reach of the Fifteenth Amendment against contrivances by a state to thwart equality in the enjoyment of the right to vote by citizens of the United States regardless of race or color, has been amply expounded by prior decisions. The Amendment nullifies sophisticated as well as simple-minded modes of discrimination. It hits onerous procedural requirements which effectively handicap exercise of the franchise by the colored race although the abstract right to vote may remain unrestricted as to race. When in *Guinn v. United States, supra*, the Oklahoma "grandfather clause" was found violative of the Fifteenth Amendment, Oklahoma was confronted with the serious task of devising a new registration system consonant with her own political ideas but also consistent with the Federal Constitution. We are compelled to conclude, however reluctantly, that the legislation of 1916 partakes too much of the infirmity of the "grandfather clause" to be able to survive.

Section 5652 of the Oklahoma statutes makes registration a prerequisite to voting. By Sections 5654 and 5659 all citizens who were qualified to vote in 1916 but had not voted in 1914 were required to register, save in the exceptional circumstances, between April 30 and May 11, 1916, and in default of such registration were perpetually disenfranchised. Exemption from this onerous provision was enjoyed by all who had registered in 1914. But this registration was held under the statute which was condemned in the *Guinn* case. Unfair discrimination was thus retained by automatically granting voting privileges for life to the white citizens whom the constitutional "grandfather clause" had sheltered while subjecting colored citizens to a new burden. The practical effect of the 1916 legislation was to accord to the members of the negro race who had been discriminated against in the outlawed registration system of 1914, not more than 12 days within which to reassert constitutional rights which this Court found in the *Guinn* case to have been improperly taken from them. We believe that the opportunity thus given negro voters to free themselves from the effects of discrimination to which they should never have been subjected was too cabined and confined. The restrictions imposed must be judged with reference to those for whom they were designed. It must be remembered that we are dealing with a body of citizens lacking the habits and traditions of political independence and otherwise living in circumstances which do not encourage initiative and enterprise. To be sure, in exceptional cases a supplemental period was available. But the narrow basis of the supplemental registration, the very brief normal period of relief for the persons and purposes in question, the practical difficulties, of which the record in this case gives glimpses, inevitable in the administration of such strict registration provisions, leave no escape from the conclusion that the means chosen as substitutes for the invalidated "grandfather clause" were themselves invalid under the Fifteenth Amendment. They operated unfairly against the very class on whose behalf the protection of the Constitution was here successfully invoked.

The judgment of the Circuit Court of Appeals must, therefore, be reversed and the cause remanded to the District Court for further proceedings in accordance with this opinion.

Reversed and remanded.

■ MR. JUSTICE MCREYNOLDS and MR. JUSTICE BUTLER think that the court below reached the right conclusion and that its judgment should be affirmed.

■ MR. JUSTICE DOUGLAS took no part in the consideration or disposition of this case.

NOTES AND QUESTIONS

1. The period from 1903 (*Giles*) to 1939 (*Wilson*) covers one-and-a-half to two generations. What happened with voting rights during that time? *See* Michael J. Klarman, *Race and the Court in the Progressive Era,* 51 VAND. L. REV. 881, 919–21 (1998):

> In terms of practical consequences, moreover, the grandfather clause cases were truly trivial. First, Oklahoma was the only southern state that used a grandfather clause as a permanent feature of its suffrage scheme. Thus the Court in *Guinn* was only suppressing an outlier, not challenging a prevalent southern practice. As one Richmond newspaper cooly observed after the ruling, the South's grandfather clauses already had accomplished their purpose and were no longer necessary.

> Second * * *, the Court in *Guinn* found the grandfather clause to be a surrogate racial classification on its face and thus avoided any inquiry into legislative motive. In light of southern ingenuity and intransigence, the judicial battle against Jim Crow had little chance of success until courts became willing either to undertake motive inquiries or to shift the constitutional focus from purpose to effect. *Guinn* reflected no movement at all in this direction. Third and relatedly, the Court explicitly noted that a literacy test divorced from the grandfather clause posed no constitutional difficulty. Yet, this conclusion gave away the ballgame. Several southern states already had discovered that a literacy test without a grandfather clause could be used successfully to disfranchise blacks. Thus a New Orleans newspaper correctly observed that the Court's ruling would enfranchise no blacks and was "not of the slightest political importance in the South." So long as the literacy test was subject to discretionary enforcement by voter registrars committed to preserving white supremacy, illiterate whites would gain registration while literate blacks would not. As late as the 1940s and 1950s, Alabama registrars were finding black PhDs from Tuskegee to be illiterate. This problem could be solved only at the level of the system where discretion inhered—a lesson eventually learned by Congress and applied with extraordinary effectiveness in the 1965 Voting Rights Act. Further, *Guinn* had no bearing on the numerous alternative disfranchisement techniques employed by southern states—poll taxes, white primaries, complex registration requirements, or criminal exclusions designed to catch blacks but not whites.

2. A series of cases and statutes, plus a constitutional amendment, eventually addressed most of the devices mentioned by Professor Klarman, but it took decades. A live issue today is the extent to which "criminal exclusions designed to catch blacks but not whites" continues to affect voting rights.

3. We have heard little from the Thirteenth Amendment in the story thus far. That amendment, by its terms, does not ban only "slavery." It also bans "involuntary servitude." How much broader than "slavery" does that latter term extend? An important decision from 1911 addresses that question.

F. BAILEY V. ALABAMA

219 U.S. 219 (1911)

■ MR. JUSTICE HUGHES delivered the opinion of the court:

This is a writ of error to review a judgment of the Supreme Court of the State of Alabama, affirming a judgment of conviction in the Montgomery City Court. The statute, upon which the conviction was based, is assailed as in violation of the Fourteenth Amendment of the Constitution of the United States upon the ground that it deprived the plaintiff in error of his liberty without due process of law and denied him the equal protection of the laws, and also of the Thirteenth Amendment and of the act of Congress providing for the enforcement of that Amendment, in that the effect of the statute is to enforce involuntary servitude by compelling personal service in liquidation of a debt.

The statute in question is § 4730 of the Code of Alabama of 1896, as amended in 1903 and 1907. The section of the Code as it stood before the amendments provided that any person who with intent to injure or defraud his employer entered into a written contract for service and thereby obtained from his employer money or other personal property, and with like intent and without just cause, and without refunding the money or paying for the property refused to perform the service, should be punished as if he had stolen it. In 1903 (Gen. Acts Ala. 1903, p. 345) the section was amended so as to make the refusal or failure to perform the service, or to refund the money, or pay for the property, without just cause, *prima facie* evidence of the intent to injure or defraud. This amendment was [further] enlarged by that of 1907. Gen. Acts. (Ala.) 1907, p. 636 * * *.

There is also a rule of evidence enforced by the courts of Alabama which must be regarded as having the same effect as if read into the statute itself, that the accused, for the purpose of rebutting the statutory presumption, shall not be allowed to testify "as to his uncommunicated motives, purpose, or intention."

Bailey, the plaintiff in error, was committed for detention on the charge of obtaining fifteen dollars under a contract in writing with intent to injure or defraud his employer. He sued out a writ of *habeas corpus* challenging the validity of the statute. His discharge was refused, and the Supreme Court of the State [of Alabama] affirmed the order, holding the statute to be constitutional * * *.

* * *

* * * Upon the trial the following facts appeared: On December 26, 1907, Bailey entered into a written contract with the Riverside Company, which provided:

> "That I Lonzo Bailey for and in consideration of the sum of Fifteen Dollars in money, this day in hand paid to me by said The Riverside Co., the receipt whereof, I do hereby acknowledge, I, the said Lonzo Bailey do hereby consent, contract, and agree to work and labor for the said Riverside Co. as a farm hand on their Scott's Bend Place in Montgomery County, Alabama, from the 30 day of December, 1907, to the 30 day of December, 1908, at and for the sum of 12.00 per month.
>
> "And the said Lonzo Bailey agrees to render respectful and faithful service to the said The Riverside Co., and to perform diligently and actively all work pertaining to such employment, in accordance with the instructions of the said The Riverside Co. or ag't.
>
> "And the said The Riverside Co. in consideration of the agreement above mentioned of the said Lonzo Bailey, hereby employs the said Lonzo Bailey as such farm hand for the time above set out, and agrees to pay the said Lonzo Bailey the sum of $10.75 per month."

The manager of the employing company testified that at the time of entering into this contract there were present only the witness and Bailey and that the latter then obtained from the company the sum of fifteen dollars; that Bailey worked under the contract throughout the month of January and for three or four days in February, 1908, and then, "without just cause, and without refunding the money, ceased to work for said Riverside Company, and has not since that time performed any service for said company in accordance with or under said contract, and has refused and failed to perform any further service thereunder, and has, without just cause, refused and failed to refund said fifteen dollars." He also testified, in response to a question from the attorney for the defendant, and against the objection of the State, that Bailey was a negro. No other evidence was introduced.

* * *

The jury found the accused guilty, fixed the damages sustained by the injured party at fifteen dollars, and assessed a fine of thirty dollars. Thereupon Bailey was sentenced by the court to pay the fine of thirty dollars and the costs, and in default thereof to hard labor "for twenty days in lieu of said fine, and one hundred and sixteen days on account of said costs."

On appeal to the Supreme Court of the State [of Alabama], the constitutionality of the statute was again upheld and the judgment affirmed.

We at once dismiss from consideration the fact that the plaintiff in error is a black man. While the action of a State through its officers charged with the administration of a law, fair in appearance, may be of such a character as to constitute a denial of the equal protection of the laws (*Yick Wo v. Hopkins*, 118 U. S. 356, 373), such a conclusion is here neither required nor justified. The statute, on its face, makes no racial discrimination, and the record fails to show its existence in fact. No question of a sectional character is presented, and we may view the legislation in the same manner as if it had been enacted in New York or in Idaho. Opportunities for coercion and oppression, in varying circumstances, exist in all parts of the Union, and the citizens of all the States are interested in the maintenance of the constitutional guaranties, the consideration of which is here involved.

Prior to the amendment of the year 1903, enlarged in 1907, the statute did not make the mere breach of the contract, under which the employee had obtained from his employer money which was not refunded or property which was not paid for, a crime. The essential ingredient of the offense was the intent of the accused to injure or defraud. To justify conviction, it was necessary that this intent should be established by competent evidence, aided only by such inferences as might logically be derived from the facts proved, and should not be the subject of mere surmise or arbitrary assumption.

* * *

We pass then to the consideration of the amendment, through the operation of which under the charge of the trial court this conviction was obtained * * *.By this amendment it was provided, in substance, that the refusal or failure to perform the service contracted for, or to refund the money obtained, without just cause, should be *prima facie* evidence of the intent to injure or defraud.

* * *

While in considering the natural operation and effect of the statute, as amended, we are not limited to the particular facts of the case at the bar, they present an illuminating illustration. We may briefly restate them. Bailey made a contract to work for a year at $12 a month. He received $15, and he was to work this out, being entitled monthly only to $10.75 of his wages. No one was present when he made the contract but himself and the manager of the employing company. There is not a particle of evidence of any circumstance indicating that he made the contract or received the money with any intent to injure or defraud his employer. On the contrary, he actually worked for upwards of a month. His motive in leaving does not appear, the only showing being that it was without legal excuse and that he did not repay the money received. For this he is sentenced to a fine of $30 and to imprisonment at hard labor, in default of the payment of the fine and costs for 136 days. Was not the case the same in effect as if the statute had made it a criminal act to leave the service without just cause and without liquidating the debt? To say that he has been found guilty of an intent to injure or defraud his employer, and not merely for breaking his contract and not paying his debt, is a distinction without a difference to Bailey.

* * *

We cannot escape the conclusion that, although the statute in terms is to punish fraud, still its natural and inevitable effect is to expose to conviction for crime those who simply fail or refuse to perform contracts for personal service in liquidation of a debt, and judging its purpose by its effect, that it seeks in this way to provide the means of compulsion through which performance of such service may be secured. The question is whether such a statute is constitutional.

This court has frequently recognized the general power of every legislature to prescribe the evidence which shall be received, and the effect of that evidence in the courts of its own government. In the exercise of this power numerous statutes have been enacted providing that proof of one fact shall be *prima facie* evidence of the main fact in issue; and where the inference is not purely arbitrary and there is a rational relation between the two facts, and the accused is not deprived of a proper opportunity to submit all the facts bearing upon the issue, it has been held that such statutes do not violate the requirements of due process of law.

* * *

* * * But where the conduct or fact, the existence of which is made the basis of the statutory presumption, itself falls within the scope of a provision of the Federal Constitution, a further question arises. It is apparent that a constitutional prohibition cannot be transgressed indirectly by the creation of a statutory presumption any more than it can be violated by direct enactment. The power to create presumptions is not a means of escape from constitutional restrictions. And the State may not in this way interfere with matters withdrawn from its authority by the Federal Constitution or subject an accused to conviction for conduct which it is powerless to proscribe.

In the present case it is urged that the statute as amended, through the operation of the presumption for which it provides, violates the Thirteenth Amendment of the Constitution of the United States and the act of Congress passed for its enforcement.

The Thirteenth Amendment provides:

> "SECTION 1. Neither slavery nor involuntary servitude, except as a punishment for crime whereof the party shall have been duly convicted, shall exist within the United States, or any place subject to their jurisdiction.
>
> "SECTION 2. Congress shall have power to enforce this article by appropriate legislation."

Pursuant to the authority thus conferred, Congress passed the act of March 2, 1867, chap. 187, 14 Stat. at L. 546, the provisions of which are now found in §§ 1990 and 5526 of the Revised Statutes (U. S. Comp. Stat. 1901, pp. 1266, 3715), as follows:

> "SEC. 1990. The holding of any person to service or labor under the system known as peonage is abolished and forever prohibited in the Territory of New Mexico, or in any other Territory or State of the United States; and all acts, laws, resolutions, orders, regulations, or usages of the

> Territory of New Mexico, or of any other Territory or State, which have heretofore established, maintained, or enforced, or by virtue of which any attempt shall hereafter be made to establish, maintain, or enforce, directly or indirectly, the voluntary or involuntary service or labor of any persons as peons, in liquidation of any debt or obligation, or otherwise, are declared null and void."
>
> "SEC. 5526. Every person who holds, arrests, returns, or causes to be held, arrested, or returned, or in any manner aids in the arrest or return, of any person to a condition of peonage, shall be punished by a fine of not less than one thousand nor more than five thousand dollars, or by imprisonment not less than one year nor more than five years, or by both."

The language of the Thirteenth Amendment was not new. It reproduced the historic words of the ordinance of 1787 for the government of the Northwest Territory and gave them unrestricted application within the United States and all places subject to their jurisdiction. While the immediate concern was with African slavery, the Amendment was not limited to that. It was a charter of universal civil freedom for all persons, of whatever race, color, or estate, under the flag.

The words involuntary servitude have a "larger meaning than slavery." "It was very well understood that, in the form of apprenticeship for long terms, as it had been practised in the West India Islands, on the abolition of slavery by the English government, or by reducing the slaves to the condition of serfs attached to the plantation, the purpose of the article might have been evaded, if only the word slavery had been used." *Slaughter-House Cases*, 16 Wall. p. 69. The plain intention was to abolish slavery of whatever name and form and all its badges and incidents; to render impossible any state of bondage; to make labor free, by prohibiting that control by which the personal service of one man is disposed of or coerced for another's benefit, which is the essence of involuntary servitude.

While the Amendment was self-executing, so far as its terms were applicable to any existing condition, Congress was authorized to secure its complete enforcement by appropriate legislation * * *.

The act of March 2, 1867 (Rev. Stat. §§ 1990 and 5526, *supra*), was a valid exercise of this express authority. It declared that all laws of any State, by virtue of which any attempt should be made "to establish, maintain, or enforce, directly or indirectly, the voluntary or involuntary service or labor of any person as peons, in liquidation of any debt or obligation, or otherwise," should be null and void.

Peonage is a term descriptive of a condition which has existed in Spanish America, and especially in Mexico. The essence of the thing is compulsory service in payment of a debt. A peon is one who is compelled to work for his creditor until his debt is paid. And in this explicit and comprehensive enactment, Congress was not concerned with mere names or manner of description, or with a particular place or section of the country. It was concerned with a fact, wherever it might exist; with a condition, however named and wherever it might be established, maintained or enforced.

The fact that the debtor contracted to perform the labor which is sought to be compelled does not withdraw the attempted enforcement from the condemnation of the statute. The full intent of the constitutional provision could be defeated with obvious facility if, through the guise of contracts under which advances had been made, debtors could be held to compulsory service. It is the compulsion of the service that the statute inhibits, for when that occurs, the condition of servitude is created, which would be not less involuntary because of the original agreement to work out the indebtedness. The contract exposes the debtor to liability for the loss due to the breach, but not to enforced labor * * *.

The act of Congress, nullifying all state laws by which it should be attempted to enforce the "service or labor of any persons as peons, in liquidation of any debt or obligation, or otherwise," necessarily embraces all legislation which seeks to compel the service or labor by making it a crime to refuse or fail to perform it. Such laws would furnish the readiest means of compulsion. The Thirteenth Amendment prohibits involuntary servitude except as punishment for crime. But the exception, allowing full latitude for the enforcement of penal laws, does not destroy the prohibition. It does not permit slavery or involuntary servitude to be established or maintained through the operation of the criminal law by making it a crime to refuse to submit to the one or to render the service which would constitute the other. The State may impose involuntary servitude as a punishment for crime, but it may not compel one man to labor for another in payment of a debt, by punishing him as a criminal if he does not perform the service or pay the debt.

If the statute in this case had authorized the employing company to seize the debtor, and hold him to the service until he paid the fifteen dollars, or had furnished the equivalent in labor, its invalidity would not be questioned. It would be equally clear that the State could not authorize its constabulary to prevent the servant from escaping and to force him to work out his debt. But the State could not avail itself of the sanction of the criminal law to supply the compulsion any more than it could use or authorize the use of physical force * * *.

What the State may not do directly it may not do indirectly. If it cannot punish the servant as a criminal for the mere failure or refusal to serve without paying his debt, it is not permitted to accomplish the same result by creating a statutory presumption which upon proof of no other fact exposes him to conviction and punishment * * *.

In this view it is unnecessary to consider the contentions which have been made under the Fourteenth Amendment. As the case was given to the jury under instructions which authorized a verdict in accordance with the statutory presumption, and the opposing instructions requested by the accused were refused, the judgment must be reversed.

Reversed and cause remanded for further proceedings not inconsistent with this opinion.

■ MR. JUSTICE HOLMES, with whom concurred MR. JUSTICE LURTON, dissenting:

We all agree that this case is to be considered and decided in the same way as if it arose in Idaho or New York. Neither public document nor evidence discloses a law which by its administration is made something different from what it appears on its face, and therefore the fact that in Alabama it mainly concerns the blacks does not matter. *Yick Wo v. Hopkins*, 118 U. S. 356, does not apply. I shall begin then by assuming for the moment what I think is not true and shall try to show not to be true, that this statute punishes the mere refusal to labor according to contract as a crime, and shall inquire whether there would be anything contrary to the Thirteenth Amendment or the statute if it did, supposing it to have been enacted in the State of

New York. I cannot believe it. The Thirteenth Amendment does not outlaw contracts for labor. That would be at least as great a misfortune for the laborer as for the man that employed him. For it certainly would affect the terms of the bargain unfavorably for the laboring man if it were understood that the employer could do nothing in case the laborer saw fit to break his word. But any legal liability for breach of a contract is a disagreeable consequence which tends to make the contractor do as he said he would. Liability to an action for damages has that tendency as well a fine. If the mere imposition of such consequences as tend to make a man keep to his promise is the creation of peonage when the contract happens to be for labor, I do not see why the allowance of a civil action is not, as well as an indictment ending in fine. Peonage is service to a private master at which a man is kept by bodily compulsion against his will. But the creation of the ordinary legal motives for right conduct does not produce it. Breach of a legal contract without excuse is wrong conduct, even if the contract is for labor, and if a State adds to civil liability a criminal liability to fine, it simply intensifies the legal motive for doing right, it does not make the laborer a slave.

But if a fine may be imposed, imprisonment may be imposed in case of a failure to pay it. Nor does it matter if labor is added to the imprisonment. Imprisonment with hard labor is not stricken from the statute books. On the contrary, involuntary servitude as a punishment for crime is excepted from the prohibition of the Thirteenth Amendment in so many words. Also the power of the States to make breach of contract a crime is not done away with by the abolition of slavery. But if breach of contract may be made a crime at all, it may be made a crime with all the consequences usually attached to crime * * *.

* * * [T]he statute is in general terms and applies to a departure at any time without excuse or repayment, but that does no harm except on a tacit assumption that this law is not administered as it would be in New York, and that juries will act with prejudice against the laboring man. For *prima facie* evidence is only evidence, and as such may be held by the jury insufficient to make out guilt * * *.

* * *

To sum up, I think that obtaining money by fraud may be made a crime as well as murder or theft; that a false representation, expressed or implied, at the time of making a contract of labor that one intends to perform it and thereby obtaining an advance, may be declared a case of fraudulently obtaining money as well as any other; that if made a crime it may be punished like any other crime; and that an unjustified departure from the promised service without repayment may be declared a sufficient case to go to the jury for their judgment; all without in any way infringing the Thirteenth Amendment or the statutes of the United States.

NOTES AND QUESTIONS

1. At first glance, this seems like a very odd case in which to invoke the Thirteenth Amendment. The Alabama statute was an evidentiary rule creating a presumption of fraud from breach of contract and then forbidding testimonial evidence by the defendant of the reasons for the breach. How could that possibly be "involuntary servitude" forbidden by the Thirteenth Amendment? Can't States create criminal penalties for fraud? And can't States create their own rules of evidence about how fraud can be proven? In the abstract, the answers to those questions are obviously "yes," and in the abstract Justice Holmes' dissent makes a great deal of sense. The problem, of course, as Justice Holmes' dissent recognizes but passes over, is the "tacit assumption that this law is not

administered as it would be in New York, and that juries will act with prejudice against the laboring man." If you believe that the process of civil justice under this statute is going to be administered by adherents to Jim Crow, the Alabama statute gives juries, and therefore employers, near total power over employees to force them to keep working, even when the conditions of employment are not materially different than slavery. (Since juries are drawn from voter registration rolls, one could expect all-white juries during this time period.) The employee, remember, is not even allowed to testify as to the reasons for breaking the contract (mistreatment, and even violent mistreatment, by the employer?), so those reasons never enter the record. Leaving employment by itself authorizes the (Jim Crow) jury to find criminal fraud. Combine this scheme with vagrancy laws, and you have something that does indeed start to look much like a system of forced labor. But to see anything resembling a constitutional violation requires looking through form to substance. Absent the assumption of a dysfunctional state legal system, it is hard to imagine the Court finding a constitutional violation here. Was the Court being dishonest in not saying so? Are you at all surprised that the Court was willing to look through the form of the scheme to its substance?

2. Would the Alabama scheme be constitutional without the evidentiary rules creating a presumption of fraud and forbidding testimony by the employee? If your answer is "no," does that mean that no State can impose criminal penalties for fraud in connection with employment contracts? Or is it just that Alabama in 1911 could not do so?

3. You learn in first-year Contracts that personal service contracts are not specifically enforceable. *See* 81A C.J.S. § 72. Is that common law rule mandated by the Thirteenth Amendment?

[Assignment 61]

VII. RACE DISCRIMINATION DURING THE MODERN ERA

The Social Darwinism that had sustained Jim Crow segregation was dealt a crippling blow by the discovery of the Holocaust and by the end of the European colonial empires after 1945. In 1948, the U.S. Ambassador to the United Nations, Eleanor Roosevelt, led the world in adopting the Universal Declaration of Human Rights. MARY ANN GLENDON, A WORLD MADE NEW: ELEANOR ROOSEVELT AND THE UNIVERSAL DECLARATION OF HUMAN RIGHTS (2002). Articles I and II of the Universal Declaration read as follows:

> **Article 1:** All human beings are born free and equal in dignity and rights. They are endowed with reason and conscience and should act towards one another in a spirit of brotherhood.
>
> **Article 2:** Everyone is entitled to all the rights and freedoms set forth in this Declaration, without distinction of any kind, such as race, colour, sex, language, religion, political or other opinion, national or social origin, property, birth or other status. Furthermore, no distinction shall be made on the basis of the political, jurisdictional or international status of the country or territory to which a person belongs, whether it be independent, trust, non-self-governing or under any other limitation of sovereignty.

By leading the world in denouncing race discrimination at the United Nations, Eleanor Roosevelt implicitly committed the United States to getting rid of Jim Crow racial segregation. President Harry S. Truman signaled his support for this goal in 1948 by desegregating the U.S. armed forces.

The post-World War II period also saw intense competition between the United States and the former Soviet Union for the allegiance of the newly emerged post-colonial nations like India, which formed a part of the so-called Third World. Since the people of the Third World were generally people of color, Jim Crow segregation was a huge foreign policy embarrassment for the U.S. in its new global fight against the Soviet Union. The fact that ambassadors to the U.S. from Third World countries could not travel in the American South due to racially segregated hotels and restaurants was a huge problem for the national government.

In the meantime, the legal campaign by the Legal Defense Fund of the National Association for the Advancement of Colored People was winning important cases in the Supreme Court. In *Sweatt v. Painter*, 339 U.S. 629 (1950), the Supreme Court held that Texas had acted unconstitutionally in denying an African-American man admission to its law school. This helped set the stage for the Supreme Court's landmark decision below eliminating racial segregation altogether in all U.S. public schools. *Brown v. Board of Education* is rightly regarded as one of the greatest triumphs of judicial review. It is one of the most important Supreme Court decisions of all time. And yet, the opinion in the case is widely regarded as being a disappointment—inferior to Justice Harlan's dissent in *Plessy v. Ferguson* more than half a century earlier. Read *Brown* now yourself and see what you think.

A. BROWN V. BOARD OF EDUCATION

347 U.S. 483 (1954)

■ MR. CHIEF JUSTICE WARREN delivered the opinion of the Court.

These cases come to us from the States of Kansas, South Carolina, Virginia, and Delaware. They are premised on different facts and different local conditions, but a common legal question justifies their consideration together in this consolidated opinion.

In each of the cases, minors of the Negro race, through their legal representatives, seek the aid of the courts in obtaining admission to the public schools of their community on a nonsegregated basis. In each instance, they had been denied admission to schools attended by white children under laws requiring or permitting segregation according to race. This segregation was alleged to deprive the plaintiffs of the equal protection of the laws under the Fourteenth Amendment. In each of the cases other than the Delaware case, a three-judge federal district court denied relief to the plaintiffs on the so-called "separate but equal" doctrine announced by this Court in *Plessy v. Ferguson,* 163 U.S. 537. Under that doctrine, equality of treatment is accorded when the races are provided substantially equal facilities, even though these facilities be separate. In the Delaware case, the Supreme Court of Delaware adhered to that doctrine, but ordered that the plaintiffs be admitted to the white schools because of their superiority to the Negro schools.

The plaintiffs contend that segregated public schools are not "equal" and cannot be made "equal," and that hence they are deprived of the equal protection of the laws. Because of the obvious importance of the question presented, the Court took jurisdiction. Argument was heard in the 1952 Term, and reargument was heard this Term on certain questions propounded by the Court.

Reargument was largely devoted to the circumstances surrounding the adoption of the Fourteenth Amendment in 1868. It covered exhaustively consideration of the Amendment in Congress, ratification by the states, then-existing practices in racial segregation, and the views of proponents and opponents of the Amendment. This discussion and our own investigation convince us that, although these sources cast some light, it is not enough to resolve the problem with which we are faced. At best, they are inconclusive. The most avid proponents of the post-War Amendments undoubtedly intended them to remove all legal distinctions among "all persons born or naturalized in the United States." Their opponents, just as certainly, were antagonistic to both the letter and the spirit of the Amendments and wished them to have the most limited effect. What others in Congress and the state legislatures had in mind cannot be determined with any degree of certainty.

An additional reason for the inconclusive nature of the Amendment's history with respect to segregated schools is the status of public education at that time. In the South, the movement toward free common schools, supported by general taxation, had not yet taken hold. Education of white children was largely in the hands of private groups. Education of Negroes was almost nonexistent, and practically all of the race were illiterate. In fact, any education of Negroes was forbidden by law in some states. Today, in contrast, many Negroes have achieved outstanding success in the arts and sciences, as well as in the business and professional world. It is true that public school education at the time of the Amendment had advanced further in the North, but the effect of the Amendment on Northern States was generally ignored in the congressional debates. Even in the North, the conditions of public education did not approximate those existing today. The curriculum was usually rudimentary; ungraded schools were common in rural areas; the school term was but three months a year in many states; and compulsory school attendance was virtually unknown. As a consequence, it is not surprising that there should be so little in the history of the Fourteenth Amendment relating to its intended effect on public education.

In the first cases in this Court construing the Fourteenth Amendment, decided shortly after its adoption, the Court interpreted it as proscribing all state-imposed discriminations against the Negro race. The doctrine of "separate but equal" did not make its appearance in this Court until 1896 in the case of *Plessy v. Ferguson, supra,* involving not education but transportation. American courts have since labored with the doctrine for over half a century. In this Court, there have been six cases involving the "separate but equal" doctrine in the field of public education. In *Cumming v. County Board of Education,* 175 U.S. 528, and *Gong Lum v. Rice,* 275 U.S. 78, the validity of the doctrine itself was not challenged. In more recent cases, all on the graduate school level, inequality was found in that specific benefits enjoyed by white students were denied to Negro students of the same educational qualifications. *Missouri ex rel. Gaines v. Canada,* 305 U.S. 337; *Sipuel v. Oklahoma,* 332 U.S. 631; *Sweatt v. Painter,* 339 U.S. 629; *McLaurin v. Oklahoma State Regents,* 339 U.S. 637. In none of these cases was it necessary to re-examine the doctrine to grant relief to the Negro plaintiff. And in *Sweatt v. Painter, supra,* the Court expressly reserved decision on the question whether *Plessy v. Ferguson* should be held inapplicable to public education.

In the instant cases, that question is directly presented. Here, unlike *Sweatt v. Painter,* there are findings below that the Negro and white schools involved have been equalized, or are being equalized, with respect to buildings, curricula, qualifications and salaries of teachers, and other "tangible" factors. Our decision, therefore, cannot turn on merely a comparison of these tangible factors in the Negro and white schools involved in each of the cases. We must look instead to the effect of segregation itself on public education.

In approaching this problem, we cannot turn the clock back to 1868, when the Amendment was adopted, or even to 1896, when *Plessy v. Ferguson* was written. We must consider public education in the light of its full development and its present place in American life throughout the Nation. Only in this way can it be determined if segregation in public schools deprives these plaintiffs of the equal protection of the laws.

Today, education is perhaps the most important function of state and local governments. Compulsory school attendance laws and the great expenditures for education both demonstrate our recognition of the importance of education to our democratic society. It is required in the performance of our most basic public responsibilities, even service in the armed forces. It is the very foundation of good citizenship. Today it is a principal instrument in awakening the child to cultural values, in preparing him for later professional training, and in helping him to adjust normally to his environment. In these days, it is doubtful that any child may reasonably be expected to succeed in life if he is denied the opportunity of an education. Such an opportunity, where the state has undertaken to provide it, is a right which must be made available to all on equal terms.

We come then to the question presented: Does segregation of children in public schools solely on the basis of race, even though the physical facilities and other "tangible" factors may be equal, deprive the children of the minority group of equal educational opportunities? We believe that it does.

In *Sweatt v. Painter, supra,* in finding that a segregated law school for Negroes could not provide them equal educational opportunities, this Court relied in large part on "those qualities which are incapable of objective measurement but which make for greatness in a law school." In *McLaurin v. Oklahoma State Regents, supra,* the Court, in requiring that a Negro admitted to a white graduate school be treated like all other students, again resorted to intangible considerations: ". . . his ability to study, to engage in discussions and exchange views with other students, and, in general, to learn his profession." Such considerations apply with added force to children in grade and high schools. To separate them from others of similar age and qualifications solely because of their race generates a feeling of inferiority as to their status in the community that may affect their hearts and minds in a way unlikely ever to be undone. The effect of this separation on their educational opportunities was well stated by a finding in the Kansas case by a court which nevertheless felt compelled to rule against the Negro plaintiffs:

> "Segregation of white and colored children in public schools has a detrimental effect upon the colored children. The impact is greater when it has the sanction of the law; for the policy of separating the races is usually interpreted as denoting the inferiority of the negro group. A sense of inferiority affects the motivation of a child to learn. Segregation with the sanction of law, therefore, has a tendency to [retard] the educational and

mental development of negro children and to deprive them of some of the benefits they would receive in a racial[ly] integrated school system."

Whatever may have been the extent of psychological knowledge at the time of *Plessy v. Ferguson,* this finding is amply supported by modern authority.[11] Any language in *Plessy v. Ferguson* contrary to this finding is rejected.

We conclude that, in the field of public education, the doctrine of "separate but equal" has no place. Separate educational facilities are inherently unequal. Therefore, we hold that the plaintiffs and others similarly situated for whom the actions have been brought are, by reason of the segregation complained of, deprived of the equal protection of the laws guaranteed by the Fourteenth Amendment. This disposition makes unnecessary any discussion whether such segregation also violates the Due Process Clause of the Fourteenth Amendment.[12]

Because these are class actions, because of the wide applicability of this decision, and because of the great variety of local conditions, the formulation of decrees in these cases presents problems of considerable complexity. On reargument, the consideration of appropriate relief was necessarily subordinated to the primary question—the constitutionality of segregation in public education. We have now announced that such segregation is a denial of the equal protection of the laws. In order that we may have the full assistance of the parties in formulating decrees, the cases will be restored to the docket, and the parties are requested to present further argument on Questions 4 and 5 previously propounded by the Court for the reargument this Term. The Attorney General of the United States is again invited to participate. The Attorneys General of the states requiring or permitting segregation in public education will also be permitted to appear as *amici curiae* upon request to do so by September 15, 1954, and submission of briefs by October 1, 1954.

It is so ordered.

NOTES AND QUESTIONS

1. The opinion in *Brown v. Board of Education* relies on sociological doll studies, quoted in footnote 11, to prove that racial segregation stigmatizes African-American school children. This suggests that if new sociological evidence emerged "proving" that racial segregation benefitted or did not harm African-Americans, Jim Crow might again become constitutional. Is that the correct basis for constitutional decisionmaking? Was *Plessy* therefore correct in 1896, because all the "best" social scientific minds at the time "knew" that racial separation was inevitable and desirable? Does the meaning of the Constitution depend on the findings of academic social scientists (which social scientists? from which academies?) at any given moment?

2. As you know by now, we are not fans of discerning constitutional meaning by reference to citations to social scientists. We discern constitutional meaning by ascertaining the public meaning of texts, and social scientists are valuable contributors

[11] K. B. Clark, Effect of Prejudice and Discrimination on Personality Development (Midcentury White House Conference on Children and Youth, 1950); Witmer and Kotinsky, Personality in the Making (1952), c. VI; Deutscher and Chein, The Psychological Effects of Enforced Segregation: A Survey of Social Science Opinion, 26 J.Psychol. 259 (1948); Chein, What are the Psychological Effects of Segregation Under Conditions of Equal Facilities?, 3 Int. J. Opinion and Attitude Res. 229 (1949); Brameld, Educational Costs, in Discrimination and National Welfare (MacIver, ed., 1949), 44–48; Frazier, The Negro in the United States (1949), 674–681. And see generally Myrdal, An American Dilemma (1944).

[12] See *Bolling v. Sharpe,* 347 U.S. 497, concerning the Due Process Clause of the Fifth Amendment.

to that enterprise only to the extent that their findings bear on that public meaning (as might well be true at times of the work of some historians, linguists, legal scholars, and the like). For what modalities of interpretation would the Court's reasoning in *Brown* be relevant? What modalities of interpretation was the Court in *Brown* employing?

3. As a matter of original public meaning, *Brown* is an easy case: racial segregation in public schools always violated the Fourteenth Amendment from 1868 on. Steven G. Calabresi and Michael W. Perl, *Originalism and* Brown v. Board of Education, 2014 MICH. STATE L. REV. 429; Michael W. McConnell, *Originalism and the Desegregation Decisions,* 81 VA. L. REV. 947 (1995). The fact that the Fourteenth Amendment creates birthright equality and bans a racial caste system is self-evident from our discussion above of the drafting and ratification of the Fourteenth Amendment. (We will say a bit more on that subject below). What did the majority in *Brown* say about reliance on original public meaning?

4. The majority did make a brief reference to the history of the adoption of the Fourteenth Amendment, finding it "inconclusive"? Why would the majority say that the historical evidence is ambiguous, devote no attention at all to original public meaning, and resolve this case instead based on sociological doll studies? There are at least five answers to this question.

First, the majority, as a public relations matter, did not want to say that the South's Jim Crow laws, which had been in place from the 1880s to 1954, had always been unconstitutional. The majority thought that was too confrontational and would generate more of a backlash in the South. So, instead, the majority came up with the argument that the meaning of the Constitution had *evolved* to ban segregated schools. Was that more likely to secure acceptance of the decision than a simple declaration that the unitary, unchanging meaning of the Constitution commanded, and had always commanded, the result?

Second, the majority, in 1954, did not want to say that all Southern Jim Crow laws were unconstitutional, including bans on racial intermarriage, so the Court produced a very narrow opinion that just dealt with segregation in public schools. This was designed to mute Southern opposition to what the Court had done. Note the opinion does not even overrule *Plessy v. Ferguson*. It simply says that language in that case, which might support segregation in public schools in 1954, was now disapproved. Since the anti-caste meaning of the Fourteenth Amendment pretty obviously invalidated anti-miscegenation laws, *see supra* pages 1268–1271, reliance on that meaning in 1954 might indeed have led to immediate challenges to those laws. Were the justices therefore behaving like wise statesman to write the opinion as they did?

Third, the opinion in *Brown* was unanimous in order to make it harder for the South to oppose it. But to get unanimity Chief Justice Warren had to bring on board Justice Stanley Reed of Kentucky, a racist (he refused to attend a Court Christmas party if African-American employees were allowed to come), and Justice Felix Frankfurter, an extreme advocate of judicial restraint. The only way Chief Justice Warren could get their votes was by distinguishing rather than overruling *Plessy v. Ferguson* and by writing a narrow opinion tied only to public schools. Was Chief Justice Warren right to opt for unanimity in *Brown*, or should he have written a bolder opinion from which Frankfurter and Reed might have dissented? Note that *Brown v. Board of Education* was highly controversial even written as it was. President Dwight D. Eisenhower is said to have privately disapproved of it. Should justices ever write opinions to attract votes rather than to give what they think is the right answer?

Fourth, the Supreme Court in 1954 simply was not a textualist, originalist, or formalist Court—much less so than is the Court in 2020. No one on the Court at that time could give a sophisticated account of original meaning even if they were inclined to do so. Notice that the Court's only paragraph on "original meaning" simply made reference to the specific thoughts or comments of supporters or opponents of the Fourteenth Amendment—many of whom in 1868 no doubt believed that the Fourteenth Amendment would not require integrated public schools. This kind of specific-intent-based "legislative history" is often only minimally relevant to original meaning, but Justice Frankfurter and his law clerk—and later very influential law professor—Alexander Bickel thought it was very important. This, too, contributed to the weak opinion in *Brown v. Board of Education*.

Fifth, and finally, the *Slaughter-House Cases* reached forward eight decades to skew the discussion. As a matter of original meaning, the relevant question for *Brown* is whether the right to a public school education was among the "privileges or immunities" of citizenship protected in 1868. If it was, then state-mandated segregation obviously abridged that privilege or immunity—as the Supreme Court implicitly recognized in the "other" *Brown* case, *Railroad Co. v. Brown,* in 1873. *See supra* pages 1254–1256. As it happens, thirty of the thirty-seven States in 1868—an Article V three-quarters majority—had clauses in their state constitutions guaranteeing all their citizens a free public school education. Three other States arguably recognized this right as well. *See* Calabresi & Perl, *supra*, at 450–57. Of these thirty-three state constitutions, none required racially segregated public schools and only one permitted them. Two state constitutions in 1868—South Carolina's and Louisiana's—explicitly required racially *integrated* public schools. These "Free Public School Education Clauses," making it a duty of the States, in thirty States or more, to provide a free public school education in 1868, means that these children had an individual fundamental right that was a "privilege[ ] or immunit[y]" of their state citizenship to such an education. Out-of-staters resident for a year in a neighboring State could have sent their children to a State's public schools pursuant to the Privileges and Immunities Clause of Article IV. Therefore, the Privileges or Immunities Clause of the Fourteenth Amendment did protect this right. (For a discussion of state statutes and caselaw on school segregation and how they do not undermine this conclusion, *see* Calabresi & Perl at 490–548.) This straightforward argument, however, was not available after 1873, because public education was obviously not a right *distinctively of national citizenship* rather than state citizenship, and the *Slaughter-House Cases* limited the Privileges or Immunities Clause to the former only. Explaining why segregated public schools deny "equal protection of the laws" or "due process of law" is much harder than explaining how they abridge the privileges or immunities of citizens.

5. Sadly, and ironically, by 1954, when *Brown v. Board of Education* was decided, fifteen state constitutions out of 48 explicitly *required* racial segregation in public schools, whereas not a single State had required this in 1868. Thus, by 1954, there was no longer an Article V three-quarters-of-the-States consensus that race discrimination in public schools was unconstitutional *even though there had been such an understanding in 1868 when the Fourteenth Amendment was ratified*. If one is looking for what constitutes "privileges or immunities" under the Fourteenth Amendment rather than for what social scientists think about doll studies, *Brown v. Board of Education* is better supported by looking at the original public meaning of the Fourteenth Amendment than by looking at evolution in the amendment's meaning over time.

6. Many critics of *Brown* argued that since public schools were *de facto* segregated in much of the country in 1868, including in the District of Columbia run by the federal

government, the original meaning of the Fourteenth Amendment could not have included a public school desegregation command. But the Fourteenth Amendment was a *transformative amendment*, which was meant to change existing social practices and not to codify them. One might as well argue that the Fourteenth Amendment did not overrule the Black Codes because they were in existence when the amendment passed Congress. Or do legal enactments cover only the specific practices that the lawmakers have in mind at the moment of their enactment rather than the practices encompassed by their actual public meaning?

7. Columbia Law School Professor Herbert Wechsler criticized the opinion in *Brown v. Board of Education* for failing to state a neutral principle—like no race discrimination—which would give guidance to lower courts in other cases. There is much to this criticism: Asking courts to make fact-based judgments about effects based on judicial assessments of social science data is not much of a neutral principle. We have already seen that the justices felt they had to write *Brown v. Board* narrowly for political reasons. The justices—or at least a clear majority of them—obviously had in mind a no-race-discrimination rule, which became clear when they struck down segregation summarily in several contexts which had nothing to do with public schools. They felt, quite reasonably in Professor Calabresi's view, that the Supreme Court ought to proceed one case at a time as a matter of judicial restraint. There is an inherent tension faced by court opinion writers between, on the one hand, saying no more than you must in order to decide the case before the Court and, on the other hand, stating a rule which the Court applies and which will cover future cases. The latter practice is most consistent with the rule of law, *see* Tara Leigh Grove, *The Structural Case for Vertical Maximalism*, 95 CORNELL L. REV. 1 (2009), but in controversial cases it may have to be abandoned for a one-case-at-a-time approach. *See* CASS SUNSTEIN, ONE CASE AT A TIME: JUDICIAL MINIMALISM ON THE SUPREME COURT (2001). Professor Lawson is fine with all of this in the abstract but thinks that each of the one cases at a time must still be decided on the basis of generalizable legal principles, and he is skeptical that principles of reasoning that make excellent sense in common law adjudication can be extended to cases of textual interpretation. Professor Calabresi agrees with Professor Lawson to some extent. But this subject would be the topic of several class sessions in a course on Jurisprudence or Philosophy of Law.

8. *Brown v. Board of Education* was foreshadowed to some extent by the Supreme Court's opinion in *Shelley v. Kraemer*, 334 U.S. 1 (1948), which held that racially restrictive covenants, whereby property owners promised not to sell their property to "people of the Negro or Mongolian Race," were unconstitutional. The only state action in that circumstance was the action of state courts in enforcing the covenants; the State was not involved in crafting the covenants' content. Once the Civil Rights Act of 1866 was held to apply to private conduct by virtue of Section 2 of the Thirteenth Amendment, these practices in connection with the sale or lease of real property were clearly unlawful, but that holding in *Jones v. Alfred Mayer, see supra* pages 861–868, and the contemporaneous enactment of the Fair Housing Act of 1968 were still twenty years away in 1948. Relying on the *Civil Rights Cases*, the Court in *Shelley* concluded that the covenants, standing alone and enforced only through voluntary action by the property owners, were not unlawful, but that *enforcement* of the covenants by the state courts violated the Fourteenth Amendment. That particular line of reasoning has found no traction in subsequent decisions; *Shelley's* account of state action has been treated as a one-off "purple cow." (You might, at some point in your lifetime, perhaps see a purple cow. You will surely never see more than one.) Was the Court in *Shelley* surreptitiously concluding that racially restrict covenants are badges and incidents of slavery, as Justice John Marshall Harlan explained in his lone dissent in the *Civil Rights Cases, see supra*

pages 853–860? If it had so held openly, could it have then said in *Brown* that racial segregation in schools is also a badge or incident of slavery? Would that alone have invalidated school segregation (in private as well as public education), or are badges and incidents of slavery only unlawful if and when Congress passes "appropriate" legislation outlawing them? A simpler explanation for *Shelley* is that there *really was* discriminatory state action by the state courts. You learn in your first-year Property class that restraints on alienation of fee simple interests in land are generally void. The courts in Missouri (where the events in *Shelley* took place) did not overturn that rule, but instead essentially carved out an exception for race-based restraints on alienation. Thus, the state courts were not neutrally enforcing private contracts but were enforcing them on a racially selective basis, at least with respect to covenants dealing with fee simples. *See* Laurence H. Tribe, *The Curvature of Constitutional Space: What Lawyers Can Learn from Modern Physics,* 103 HARV. L. REV. 1, 25–26 (1989). The Court in *Shelley* never expressly said any of this.

9. GERALD ROSENBERG, THE HOLLOW HOPE: CAN COURTS BRING ABOUT SOCIAL CHANGE? (1991), famously argues that the federal courts are utterly powerless to bring about social change. Rosenberg notes that Jim Crow really died ten years after the opinion in *Brown* when Congress passed the Civil Rights Act of 1964 and the Voting Rights Act of 1965. Rosenberg may undervalue the role the opinion in *Brown* had in: 1) motivating bus and restaurant boycotts and demonstrations throughout the South; 2) the fact that those demonstrations were put down violently and with water cannons by racist Southern police officers; 3) the fact that Northern public opinion was outraged by television coverage of this police violence; and that 4) the net result was that the North demanded and got adopted the Civil Rights Act of 1964 and the Voting Rights Act of 1965. Obviously, the opinion in *Brown* did not end in a day practices of seventy years' duration, but *Brown* led the country in that direction. How fast it would lead was the specific subject of a sequel to *Brown* in 1955.

B. BROWN V. BOARD OF EDUCATION II

349 U.S. 294 (1955)

■ MR. CHIEF JUSTICE WARREN delivered the opinion of the Court.

These cases were decided on May 17, 1954. The opinions of that date, declaring the fundamental principle that racial discrimination in public education is unconstitutional, are incorporated herein by reference. All provisions of federal, state, or local law requiring or permitting such discrimination must yield to this principle. There remains for consideration the manner in which relief is to be accorded.

Because these cases arose under different local conditions and their disposition will involve a variety of local problems, we requested further argument on the question of relief. In view of the nationwide importance of the decision, we invited the Attorney General of the United States and the Attorneys General of all states requiring or permitting racial discrimination in public education to present their views on that question. The parties, the United States, and the States of Florida, North Carolina, Arkansas, Oklahoma, Maryland, and Texas filed briefs and participated in the oral argument.

These presentations were informative and helpful to the Court in its consideration of the complexities arising from the transition to a system of public education freed of racial discrimination. The presentations also demonstrated that substantial steps to eliminate racial discrimination in public schools have already been taken, not only in some of the communities in which these cases arose, but in some of the states appearing as *amici curiae,* and in other states as well. Substantial progress has been made in the District of Columbia and in the communities in Kansas and Delaware involved in this litigation. The defendants in the cases coming to us from South Carolina and Virginia are awaiting the decision of this Court concerning relief.

Full implementation of these constitutional principles may require solution of varied local school problems. School authorities have the primary responsibility for elucidating, assessing, and solving these problems; courts will have to consider whether the action of school authorities constitutes good faith implementation of the governing constitutional principles. Because of their proximity to local conditions and the possible need for further hearings, the courts which originally heard these cases can best perform this judicial appraisal. Accordingly, we believe it appropriate to remand the cases to those courts.

In fashioning and effectuating the decrees, the courts will be guided by equitable principles. Traditionally, equity has been characterized by a practical flexibility in shaping its remedies and by a facility for adjusting and reconciling public and private needs. These cases call for the exercise of these traditional attributes of equity power. At stake is the personal interest of the plaintiffs in admission to public schools as soon as practicable on a nondiscriminatory basis. To effectuate this interest may call for elimination of a variety of obstacles in making the transition to school systems operated in accordance with the constitutional principles set forth in our May 17, 1954, decision. Courts of equity may properly take into account the public interest in the elimination of such obstacles in a systematic and effective manner. But it should go without saying that the vitality of these constitutional principles cannot be allowed to yield simply because of disagreement with them.

While giving weight to these public and private considerations, the courts will require that the defendants make a prompt and reasonable start toward full compliance with our May 17, 1954, ruling. Once such a start has been made, the courts may find that additional time is necessary to carry out the ruling in an effective manner. The burden rests upon the defendants to establish that such time is necessary in the public interest and is consistent with good faith compliance at the earliest practicable date. To that end, the courts may consider problems related to administration, arising from the physical condition of the school plant, the school transportation system, personnel, revision of school districts and attendance areas into compact units to achieve a system of determining admission to the public schools on a nonracial basis, and revision of local laws and regulations which may be necessary in solving the foregoing problems. They will also consider the adequacy of any plans the defendants may propose to meet these problems and to effectuate a transition to a racially nondiscriminatory school system. During this period of transition, the courts will retain jurisdiction of these cases.

The judgments below, except that, in the Delaware case, are accordingly reversed, and the cases are remanded to the District Courts to take such proceedings and enter such orders and decrees consistent with this opinion as are necessary and proper to admit to public schools on a racially nondiscriminatory basis with all deliberate speed the parties to these cases. The judgment in the Delaware case—ordering the immediate admission of the plaintiffs to schools previously attended only by white children—is affirmed on the basis of the principles stated in our May 17, 1954, opinion, but the case is remanded to the Supreme Court of Delaware for such further proceedings as that Court may deem necessary in light of this opinion.

It is so ordered.

NOTES AND QUESTIONS

1. In its last paragraph, the Court famously said that school desegregation must take place "with all deliberate speed." Do you have any idea what that phrase means? What do you think lower courts or state officials would have taken it to mean in 1955? In fact, *Brown II*'s "all deliberate speed" formula led to a lot of foot-dragging by segregated public schools in complying with *Brown I*. Even the individual plaintiffs who brought the cases consolidated in *Brown I* did not end up getting admitted to the public schools right away. Was this another concession to Justices Reed and Frankfurter? Was unanimity important enough to justify it?

2. Unanimity reached a new level in 1958 in *Cooper v. Aaron,* 358 U.S. 1 (1958). Right after *Brown,* the Little Rock, Arkansas school district announced a plan gradually to desegregate its schools by 1963—a period of nearly ten years. The lower federal courts upheld that plan as consistent with *Brown I* and *Brown II*, and no appeal to the Supreme Court was taken. When, at the initial stage of this plan, nine African-American children showed up to attend a previously segregated high school in 1957, the Governor of Arkansas, Orval Faubus, ordered state national guard troops to prevent the African-American students from entering the school. After some legal maneuverings, President Eisenhower eventually called in the American military to enforce the desegregation plan, and for two months U.S. soldiers were present at the school to prevent obstruction from Arkansas authorities. Federalized national guard units—under Eisenhower's command—remained for the rest of the school year to assure compliance with desegregation. Here is what happened next:

> * * * On February 20, 1958, the School Board and the Superintendent of Schools filed a petition in the District Court seeking a postponement of their program for desegregation. Their position in essence was that because of extreme public hostility, which they stated had been engendered largely by the official attitudes and actions of the Governor and the Legislature, the maintenance of a sound educational program at Central High School, with the Negro students in attendance, would be impossible. The Board therefore proposed that the Negro students already admitted to the school be withdrawn and sent to segregated schools, and that all further steps to carry out the Board's desegregation program be postponed for a period later suggested by the Board to be two and one-half years.
>
> After a hearing the District Court granted the relief requested by the Board. Among other things the court found that the past year at Central High School had been attended by conditions of "chaos, bedlam and turmoil"; that there were "repeated incidents of more or less serious violence directed against the Negro students and their property"; that there was "tension and unrest among the school administrators, the class-room teachers, the pupils, and the latters' parents, which inevitably had an adverse effect upon the educational program"; that a school official was threatened with violence; that a "serious financial burden" had been cast on the School District; that the education of the students had suffered "and under existing conditions will continue to suffer"; that the Board would continue to need "military assistance or its equivalent";

that the local police department would not be able "to detail enough men to afford the necessary protection"; and that the situation was "intolerable."

* * * The Court of Appeals * * * reversed the District Court * * *.

In affirming the judgment of the Court of Appeals which reversed the District Court we have accepted without reservation the position of the School Board, the Superintendent of Schools, and their counsel that they displayed entire good faith in the conduct of these proceedings and in dealing with the unfortunate and distressing sequence of events which has been outlined. We likewise have accepted the findings of the District Court as to the conditions at Central High School during the 1957–1958 school year, and also the findings that the educational progress of all the students, white and colored, of that school has suffered and will continue to suffer if the conditions which prevailed last year are permitted to continue.

The significance of these findings, however, is to be considered in light of the fact, indisputably revealed by the record before us, that the conditions they depict are directly traceable to the actions of legislators and executive officials of the State of Arkansas, taken in their official capacities, which reflect their own determination to resist this Court's decision in the *Brown* case and which have brought about violent resistance to that decision in Arkansas. In its petition for certiorari filed in this Court, the School Board itself describes the situation in this language: 'The legislative, executive, and judicial departments of the state government opposed the desegregation of Little Rock schools by enacting laws, calling out troops, making statements villifying federal law and federal courts, and failing to utilize state law enforcement agencies and judicial processes to maintain public peace.'

One may well sympathize with the position of the Board in the face of the frustrating conditions which have confronted it, but, regardless of the Board's good faith, the actions of the other state agencies responsible for those conditions compel us to reject the Board's legal position * * *.

The constitutional rights of respondents are not to be sacrificed or yielded to the violence and disorder which have followed upon the actions of the Governor and Legislature * * *. Thus law and order are not here to be preserved by depriving the Negro children of their constitutional rights. The record before us clearly establishes that the growth of the Board's difficulties to a magnitude beyond its unaided power to control is the product of state action. Those difficulties, as counsel for the Board forthrightly conceded on the oral argument in this Court, can also be brought under control by state action.

The controlling legal principles are plain. The command of the Fourteenth Amendment is that no "State" shall deny to any person within its jurisdiction the equal protection of the laws * * *. Thus the prohibitions of the Fourteenth Amendment extend to all action of the State denying equal protection of the laws; whatever the agency of the State taking the action or whatever the guise in which it is taken. In short, the constitutional rights of children not to be discriminated against in school admission on grounds of race or color declared by this Court in the *Brown* case can neither be nullified openly and directly by state legislators or state executive or judicial officers, nor nullified indirectly by them through evasive schemes for segregation whether attempted "ingeniously or ingenuously."

What has been said, in the light of the facts developed, is enough to dispose of the case. However, we should answer the premise of the actions of the Governor and Legislature that they are not bound by our holding in the *Brown* case. It is necessary only to recall some basic constitutional propositions which are settled doctrine.

Article VI of the Constitution makes the Constitution the "supreme Law of the Land." In 1803, Chief Justice Marshall, speaking for a unanimous Court, referring to the Constitution as "the fundamental and paramount law of the nation," declared in the notable case of *Marbury v. Madison*, 1 Cranch 137, 177, that "It is emphatically the province and duty of the judicial department to say what the law is." This decision declared the basic principle that the federal judiciary is supreme in the exposition of the law of the Constitution, and that principle has ever since been respected by this Court and the Country as a permanent and indispensable feature of our constitutional system. It follows that the interpretation of the Fourteenth Amendment enunciated by this Court in the *Brown* case is the supreme law of the land, and Art. VI of the Constitution makes it of binding effect on the States "any Thing in the Constitution or Laws of any State to the Contrary notwithstanding." Every state legislator and executive and judicial officer is solemnly committed by oath taken pursuant to Art. VI, ¶ 3 "to support this Constitution." * * *

* * *.

It is, of course, quite true that the responsibility for public education is primarily the concern of the States, but it is equally true that such responsibilities, like all other state activity, must be exercised consistently with federal constitutional requirements as they apply to state action. The Constitution created a government dedicated to equal justice under law. The Fourteenth Amendment embodied and emphasized that ideal. State support of segregated schools through any arrangement, management, funds, or property cannot be squared with the Amendment's command that no State shall deny to any person within its jurisdiction the equal protection of the laws. The right of a student not to be segregated on racial grounds in schools so maintained is indeed so fundamental and pervasive that it is embraced in the concept of due process of law. *Bolling v. Sharpe*, 347 U.S. 497. The basic decision in *Brown* was unanimously reached by this Court only after the case had been briefed and twice argued and the issues had been given the most serious consideration. Since the first *Brown* opinion three new Justices have come to the Court. They are at one with the Justices still on the Court who participated in that basic decision as to its correctness, and that decision is now unanimously reaffirmed. The principles announced in that decision and the obedience of the States to them, according to the command of the Constitution, are indispensable for the protection of the freedoms guaranteed by our fundamental charter for all of us. Our constitutional ideal of equal justice under law is thus made a living truth.

358 U.S. at 12–20. In an unprecedented—and to this day never repeated—step, all nine justices jointly signed and issued the opinion in *Cooper*. In the face of open resistance, the Court believed that something more than just a unanimous opinion was needed. The Court also believed that it needed to assert supreme authority to interpret the Constitution and that its views are equivalent to the Constitution itself, even for purposes of the Supremacy Clause. Was that assertion necessary to the decision in *Cooper*? Is it correct? The next day, Justice Frankfurter issued a separate concurring opinion. It did not disagree with anything in the main opinion. Indeed, it emphasized "[t]he duty to

abstain from resistance to 'the supreme Law of the Land,' U.S.Const., Art. VI, ¶ 2, as declared by *the organ of our Government for ascertaining it* * * *." 358 U.S. at 24 (Frankfurter, J. concurring). Is the Court "the" organ for ascertaining constitutional meaning? Was the problem in *Cooper* that state officials challenged the Court, that they challenged the Court by defying a specific order in a specific case, or that they challenged the Court in a case in which the Court was right and the state officials were wrong?

C. FROM *BROWN V. BOARD OF EDUCATION* TO *LOVING V. VIRGINIA*

In the thirteen years between 1954 and 1967, the Supreme Court expanded its holding in *Brown v. Board of Education* from being a ban on segregated schools into being a ban on all forms of racial discrimination. One important step was taken in *Browder v. Gayle,* 352 U.S. 903 (1956), where the Supreme Court summarily upheld a district court ruling that the Montgomery, Alabama ordinance requiring segregation on buses was unconstitutional. The entire per curiam opinion read: "The motion to affirm is granted and the judgment is affirmed. *Brown v. Board of Education,* 347 U.S. 483; *Mayor and City Council of Baltimore v. Dawson,* 350 U.S. 877; *Holmes v. City of Atlanta,* 350 U.S. 879." The *Dawson* case, in turn, had summarily affirmed a lower court ruling that segregated public swimming pools and bath houses were unconstitutional, *see Dawson v. Mayor & City Council of Baltimore City,* 220 F.2d 386 (4th Cir. 1955); and *Holmes* had summarily remanded a case involving segregated public parks and golf courses, *see Holmes v. City of Atlanta,* 223 F.2d 93 (5th Cir. 1955), "with directions to enter a decree for petitioners in conformity with *Mayor & City Council of Baltimore City v. Dawson,* 350 U.S. 877." It was clear that *Brown* meant that all forms of public segregation were unlawful.

The Court, however, was not prepared in the 1950s to acknowledge the full implications of these doctrinal developments. In 1955, the courts of Virginia upheld the State's anti-miscegenation law (citing, among other things, *State v. Gibson.*) *See Naim v. Naim,* 197 Va. 80 (1955). As we saw in the earlier post-Reconstruction cases, *see supra* pages 1268–1271, it is impossible to uphold such statutes under any plausible understanding of the Reconstruction Amendments and the Civil Rights Act of 1866, and the Court that decided *Brown* had to be aware of this fact in some fashion. On appeal from the Virginia decision, here is the entirety of the Supreme Court's per curiam opinion in *Naim v. Naim,* 350 U.S. 891 (1955): "The inadequacy of the record as to the relationship of the parties to the Commonwealth of Virginia at the time of the marriage in North Carolina and upon their return to Virginia, and the failure of the parties to bring here all questions relevant to the disposition of the case, prevents the constitutional issue of the validity of the Virginia statute on miscegenation tendered here being considered 'in clean cut and concrete form, unclouded' by such problems. *Rescue Army v. Municipal Court,* 331 U.S. 549, 584. The judgment is vacated and the case remanded to the Supreme Court of Appeals in order that the case may be returned to the Circuit Court of the City of Portsmouth for action not inconsistent with this opinion." In other words, the Court ducked the issue on technical grounds. On remand, the Virginia courts found nothing new to add or consider. *See Naim v. Naim,* 197 Va. 734 (1956). The Supreme Court's final word in the case was: "The motion to recall the mandate and to set the case down for oral argument upon the merits, or, in the alternative, to recall and amend the mandate is denied. The decision of the Supreme Court of Appeals of Virginia of January 18,

1956, 197 Va. 734, 90 S.E.2d 849, in response to our order of November 14, 1955, 350 U.S. 891, leaves the case devoid of a properly presented federal question." *Naim v. Naim,* 350 U.S. 985 (1956). The Court was not yet ready in the mid-1950s to tackle the constitutionality of interracial marriage bans because the issue stirred such strong emotions in the South.

A decade later the justices were ready. One important event in the interim was a speech by Dr. Martin Luther King, Jr., a key leader of the political and social movement for equal rights for African-Americans. On August 28, 1963, Dr. King gave a speech in front of the Lincoln Memorial in Washington, D.C. to more than 250,000 civil rights supporters. Just as Abraham Lincoln had recalled the Declaration of Independence in his momentous Gettysburg Address in 1863, so too did Dr. King hearken back to the centrality of that document in his speech given 100 years later. Dr. King noted that in standing in front of the Lincoln Memorial, he was standing in the symbolic shadow of the man who had freed three million of the four million slaves in the United States. He described the demonstration before him as the most important in American history. Dr. King, observed, however, that 100 years after President Lincoln has signed the Emancipation Proclamation, African-Americans were still not free but were crippled by a system of Jim Crown discrimination. He then spoke the following immortal words: "I say to you today, my friends, [that] I still have a dream. It is a dream deeply rooted in the American dream. I have a dream that one day this nation will rise up, [and] live out the true meaning of its creed: 'We hold these truths to be self-evident, that all men are created equal.'" Dr. King's speech helped induce Congress to pass the Civil Rights Act of 1964, the Voting Rights Act of 1965, and the Fair Housing Act of 1968, which collectively struck at the key elements of Jim Crow segregation. By 1967, the U.S. Supreme Court finally concluded it had enough political support to issue the following momentous opinion striking down as unconstitutional state laws banning interracial marriage.

D. LOVING V. VIRGINIA

388 U.S. 1 (1967)

■ MR. CHIEF JUSTICE WARREN delivered the opinion of the Court.

This case presents a constitutional question never addressed by this Court: whether a statutory scheme adopted by the State of Virginia to prevent marriages between persons solely on the basis of racial classifications violates the Equal Protection and Due Process Clauses of the Fourteenth Amendment. For reasons which seem to us to reflect the central meaning of those constitutional commands, we conclude that these statutes cannot stand consistently with the Fourteenth Amendment.

In June, 1958, two residents of Virginia, Mildred Jeter, a Negro woman, and Richard Loving, a white man, were married in the District of Columbia pursuant to its laws. Shortly after their marriage, the Lovings returned to Virginia and established their marital abode in Caroline County. At the October Term, 1958, of the Circuit Court of Caroline County, a grand jury issued an indictment charging the Lovings with violating Virginia's ban on interracial marriages. On January 6, 1959, the Lovings pleaded guilty to the charge, and were sentenced to one year in jail; however, the trial judge suspended the sentence for a period of 25 years on the condition that the Lovings leave the State and not return to Virginia together for 25 years. He stated in an opinion that:

> "Almighty God created the races white, black, yellow, malay and red, and he placed them on separate continents. And, but for the interference with his arrangement, there would be no cause for such marriage. The fact that he separated the races shows that he did not intend for the races to mix."

After their convictions, the Lovings took up residence in the District of Columbia. On November 6, 1963, they filed a motion in the state trial court to vacate the judgment and set aside the sentence on the ground that the statutes which they had violated were repugnant to the Fourteenth Amendment * * *.

The [Virginia] Supreme Court of Appeals upheld the constitutionality of the anti-miscegenation statutes and, after modifying the sentence, affirmed the convictions * * *. The Lovings appealed this decision * * *.

The two statutes under which appellants were convicted and sentenced are part of a comprehensive statutory scheme aimed at prohibiting and punishing interracial marriages. The Lovings were convicted of violating § 258 of the Virginia Code:

> "*Leaving State to evade law.*—If any white person and colored person shall go out of this State, for the purpose of being married, and with the intention of returning, and be married out of it, and afterwards return to and reside in it, cohabiting as man and wife, they shall be punished as provided in § 20–59, and the marriage shall be governed by the same law as if it had been solemnized in this State. The fact of their cohabitation here as man and wife shall be evidence of their marriage."

Section 259, which defines the penalty for miscegenation, provides:

> "*Punishment for marriage.*—If any white person intermarry with a colored person, or any colored person intermarry with a white person, he shall be guilty of a felony and shall be punished by confinement in the penitentiary for not less than one nor more than five years."

Other central provisions in the Virginia statutory scheme are § 20–57, which automatically voids all marriages between "a white person and a colored person" without any judicial proceeding, and §§ 20–54 and 1–14 which, respectively, define "white persons" and "colored persons and Indians" for purposes of the statutory prohibitions.[4] The Lovings have never disputed in the course of this litigation that

---

[4] Section 20–54 of the Virginia Code provides:

> 'Intermarriage prohibited; meaning of term 'white persons.'—It shall hereafter be unlawful for any white person in this State to marry any save a white person, or a person with no other admixture of blood than white and American Indian. For the purpose of this chapter, the term 'white person' shall apply only to such person as has no trace whatever of any blood other than Caucasian; but persons who have one-sixteenth or less of the blood of the American Indian and have no other non-Caucasic blood shall be deemed to be white persons * * *.' Va.Code Ann. § 20–54 (1960 Repl.Vol.).

The exception for persons with less than one-sixteenth 'of the blood of the American Indian' is apparently accounted for, in the words of a tract issued by the Registrar of the State Bureau of Vital Statistics, by 'the desire of all to recognize as an integral and honored part of the white race the descendants of John Rolfe and Pocahontas * * *.' Plecker, The New Family and Race Improvement, 17 Va.Health Bull., Extra No. 12, at 25–26 (New Family Series No. 5, 1925), cited in Wadlington, The Loving Case; Virginia's Anti-Miscegenation Statute in Historical Perspective, 52 Va.L.Rev. 1189, 1202, n. 93 (1966).

Section 1–14 of the Virginia Code provides:

Mrs. Loving is a "colored person" or that Mr. Loving is a "white person" within the meanings given those terms by the Virginia statutes.

Virginia is now one of 16 States which prohibit and punish marriages on the basis of racial classifications. Penalties for miscegenation arose as an incident to slavery and have been common in Virginia since the colonial period. The present statutory scheme dates from the adoption of the Racial Integrity Act of 1924, passed during the period of extreme nativism which followed the end of the First World War. The central features of this Act, and current Virginia law, are the absolute prohibition of a "white person" marrying other than another "white person," a prohibition against issuing marriage licenses until the issuing official is satisfied that the applicants' statements as to their race are correct, certificates of "racial composition" to be kept by both local and state registrars, and the carrying forward of earlier prohibitions against racial intermarriage.

In upholding the constitutionality of these provisions in the decision below, the Supreme Court of Appeals of Virginia referred to its 1955 decision in *Naim v. Naim,* 197 Va. 80, 87 S.E.2d 749, as stating the reasons supporting the validity of these laws. In *Naim,* the state court concluded that the State's legitimate purposes were "to preserve the racial integrity of its citizens," and to prevent "the corruption of blood," "a mongrel breed of citizens," and "the obliteration of racial pride," obviously an endorsement of the doctrine of White Supremacy. *Id.* at 90, 87 S.E.2d at 756. The court also reasoned that marriage has traditionally been subject to state regulation without federal intervention, and, consequently, the regulation of marriage should be left to exclusive state control by the Tenth Amendment.

While the state court is no doubt correct in asserting that marriage is a social relation subject to the State's police power, the State does not contend in its argument before this Court that its powers to regulate marriage are unlimited notwithstanding the commands of the Fourteenth Amendment. Nor could it do so in light of *Meyer v. Nebraska,* 262 U.S. 390 (1923), and *Skinner v. Oklahoma,* 316 U.S. 535 (1942). Instead, the State argues that the meaning of the Equal Protection Clause, as illuminated by the statements of the Framers, is only that state penal laws containing an interracial element as part of the definition of the offense must apply equally to whites and Negroes in the sense that members of each race are punished to the same degree. Thus, the State contends that, because its miscegenation statutes punish equally both the white and the Negro participants in an interracial marriage, these statutes, despite their reliance on racial classifications, do not constitute an invidious discrimination based upon race. The second argument advanced by the State assumes the validity of its equal application theory. The argument is that, if the Equal Protection Clause does not outlaw miscegenation statutes because of their reliance on racial classifications, the question of constitutionality would thus become whether there was any rational basis for a State to treat interracial marriages differently from other marriages. On this question, the State argues, the scientific evidence is substantially in doubt and,

Colored persons and Indians defined.—Every person in whom there is ascertainable any Negro blood shall be deemed and taken to be a colored person, and every person not a colored person having one fourth or more of American Indian blood shall be deemed an American Indian; except that members of Indian tribes existing in this Commonwealth having one fourth or more of Indian blood and less than one sixteenth of Negro blood shall be deemed tribal Indians.' Va.Code Ann. § 1–14 (1960 Repl.Vol.).

consequently, this Court should defer to the wisdom of the state legislature in adopting its policy of discouraging interracial marriages.

Because we reject the notion that the mere "equal application" of a statute containing racial classifications is enough to remove the classifications from the Fourteenth Amendment's proscription of all invidious racial discriminations, we do not accept the State's contention that these statutes should be upheld if there is any possible basis for concluding that they serve a rational purpose. The mere fact of equal application does not mean that our analysis of these statutes should follow the approach we have taken in cases involving no racial discrimination where the Equal Protection Clause has been arrayed against a statute discriminating between the kinds of advertising which may be displayed on trucks in New York City, *Railway Express Agency, Inc. v. New York,* 336 U.S. 106 (1949), or an exemption in Ohio's *ad valorem* tax for merchandise owned by a nonresident in a storage warehouse, *Allied Stores of Ohio, Inc. v. Bowers,* 358 U.S. 522 (1959). In these cases, involving distinctions not drawn according to race, the Court has merely asked whether there is any rational foundation for the discriminations, and has deferred to the wisdom of the state legislatures. In the case at bar, however, we deal with statutes containing racial classifications, and the fact of equal application does not immunize the statute from the very heavy burden of justification which the Fourteenth Amendment has traditionally required of state statutes drawn according to race.

The State argues that statements in the Thirty-ninth Congress about the time of the passage of the Fourteenth Amendment indicate that the Framers did not intend the Amendment to make unconstitutional state miscegenation laws. Many of the statements alluded to by the State concern the debates over the Freedmen's Bureau Bill, which President Johnson vetoed, and the Civil Rights Act of 1866, 14 Stat. 27, enacted over his veto. While these statements have some relevance to the intention of Congress in submitting the Fourteenth Amendment, it must be understood that they pertained to the passage of specific statutes, and not to the broader, organic purpose of a constitutional amendment. As for the various statements directly concerning the Fourteenth Amendment, we have said in connection with a related problem that, although these historical sources "cast some light" they are not sufficient to resolve the problem; "[a]t best, they are inconclusive. The most avid proponents of the post-War Amendments undoubtedly intended them to remove all legal distinctions among 'all persons born or naturalized in the United States.' Their opponents, just as certainly, were antagonistic to both the letter and the spirit of the Amendments, and wished them to have the most limited effect." *Brown v. Board of Education,* 347 U.S. 483, 489 (1954). *See also Strauder v. West Virginia,* 100 U.S. 303, 310 (1880). We have rejected the proposition that the debates in the Thirty-ninth Congress or in the state legislatures which ratified the Fourteenth Amendment supported the theory advanced by the State, that the requirement of equal protection of the laws is satisfied by penal laws defining offenses based on racial classifications so long as white and Negro participants in the offense were similarly punished. *McLaughlin v. Florida,* 379 U.S. 184 (1964).

The State finds support for its "equal application" theory in the decision of the Court in *Pace v. Alabama,* 106 U.S. 583 (1883). In that case, the Court upheld a conviction under an Alabama statute forbidding adultery or fornication between a white person and a Negro which imposed a greater penalty than that of a statute proscribing similar conduct by members of the same race. The Court reasoned that the statute could not be said to discriminate against Negroes because the punishment for each participant in the offense was the same. However, as recently as the 1964 Term, in rejecting the reasoning of that case, we stated "*Pace* represents a limited view of the Equal Protection Clause which has not withstood analysis in the subsequent decisions of this Court." *McLaughlin v. Florida, supra,* at 188. As we there demonstrated, the Equal Protection Clause requires the consideration of whether the classifications drawn by any statute constitute an arbitrary and invidious discrimination. The clear and central purpose of the Fourteenth Amendment was to eliminate all official state sources of invidious racial discrimination in the States. *Slaughter-House Cases,* 16 Wall. 36, 71 (1873); *Strauder v. West Virginia,* 100 U.S. 303, 307–308 (1880); *Ex parte Virginia,* 100 U.S. 339, 334–335 (1880).

There can be no question but that Virginia's miscegenation statutes rest solely upon distinctions drawn according to race. The statutes proscribe generally accepted conduct if engaged in by members of different races. Over the years, this Court has consistently repudiated "[d]istinctions between citizens solely because of their ancestry" as being "odious to a free people whose institutions are founded upon the doctrine of equality." *Hirabayashi v. United States,* 320 U.S. 81, 100 (1943). At the very least, the Equal Protection Clause demands that racial classifications, especially suspect in criminal statutes, be subjected to the "most rigid scrutiny," *Korematsu v. United States,* 323 U.S. 214, 216 (1944), and, if they are ever to be upheld, they must be shown to be necessary to the accomplishment of some permissible state objective, independent of the racial discrimination which it was the object of the Fourteenth Amendment to eliminate * * *.

There is patently no legitimate overriding purpose independent of invidious racial discrimination which justifies this classification. The fact that Virginia prohibits only interracial marriages involving white persons demonstrates that the racial classifications must stand on their own justification, as measures designed to maintain White Supremacy. We have consistently denied the constitutionality of measures which restrict the rights of citizens on account of race. There can be no doubt that restricting the freedom to marry solely because of racial classifications violates the central meaning of the Equal Protection Clause.

These statutes also deprive the Lovings of liberty without due process of law in violation of the Due Process Clause of the Fourteenth Amendment. The freedom to marry has long been recognized as one of the vital personal rights essential to the orderly pursuit of happiness by free men.

Marriage is one of the "basic civil rights of man," fundamental to our very existence and survival. *Skinner v. Oklahoma,* 316 U.S. 535, 541 (1942). *See also Maynard v. Hill,* 125 U.S. 190 (1888). To deny this fundamental freedom on so unsupportable a basis as the racial classifications embodied in these statutes, classifications so directly subversive of the principle of equality at the heart of the Fourteenth Amendment, is surely to deprive all the State's citizens of liberty without due process of law. The Fourteenth Amendment requires that the freedom of choice to marry not be restricted by invidious racial discriminations. Under our Constitution, the freedom to marry, or not marry, a person of another race resides with the individual, and cannot be infringed by the State.

These convictions must be reversed. *It is so ordered.*

NOTES AND QUESTIONS

1. As you know by now, we think *Loving* is an easy case under the original understanding of the Reconstruction Amendments and the Civil Rights Act of 1866. *See* Steven G. Calabresi & Andrea Matthews, *Originalism and Loving v. Virginia*, 2012 B.Y.U. L. REV. 1393. As we saw, two Southern state supreme courts struck down anti-miscegenation laws in the early 1870s under the Civil Rights Act of 1866 and the Fourteenth Amendment. Those cases were the tip of a large iceberg. "[B]y 1873, within five years of the [Fourteenth] Amendment's ratification, racial-endogamy laws either did not exist or were not in force, in both a clear majority of states and a super-majority of the states that had ratified the Amendment. The absence of enforced racial-endogamy largely resulted from the conclusion of Republican officials—including almost *every* Republican judge to face the question before *Slaughter-House* was decided in 1873—that the Amendment and/or the Civil Rights Act precluded the making or enforcing of such laws." David R. Upham, *Interracial Marriage and the Original Understanding of the Privileges or Immunities Clause*, 42 HASTINGS CONST. L.Q. 213, 259–60 (2015). But the most obvious vehicle for that conclusion is the Privileges or Immunities Clause, and the *Slaughter-House Cases* in 1873 removed that foundation. Note that the Court in *Loving* relies on both the Equal Protection Clause and the Due Process of Law Clause but makes no mention of the Privileges or Immunities Clause. Why do you think the Court has consistently been so reluctant to revisit the *Slaughter-House Cases*, when they are so clearly the main obstacle to a jurisprudence of the Fourteenth Amendment based on original meaning?

2. The Court says that there is "no legitimate overriding purpose independent of invidious racial discrimination which justifies this classification." What if someone thought that there was such a "legitimate overriding purpose"? Are racial classifications constitutionally fine as long as there is a "legitimate overriding purpose" for them? What might count as such a purpose? We are going to revisit those vital questions, which lie at the heart of much modern law, shortly.

3. Another vital question concerns how one ascertains whether a law or practice is discriminatory. Part of that question is substantive: Does every difference in treatment constitute discrimination or do only a subclass of differences count? We will get to that part of the question in due course. A second part of the question is (at least on a first take) evidentiary: Once you know what makes a law or practice discriminatory, how would you ever prove that a particular law or practice meets those criteria? Often, as in *Brown* and *Loving*, the text of a law itself will be nakedly discriminatory by any plausible understanding of that term, and once the appropriate legal standard is applied, there are no further problems of proof to address. Sometimes, however, a statute or practice will be facially neutral as to race but will have an obvious disparate and negative effect on African-Americans. A classic example of such a statute was *Guinn v. United States*, 238 U.S. 347 (1915), *see supra* page 1302, where some "grandfather clause" exceptions to the State's literacy test were permitted. Since few African-Americans in Oklahoma in 1915 could prove that their grandfathers had been eligible to vote, the net effect was that the facially neutral voting law had a huge negative disparate impact. An example of an enforcement practice that predictably would result in a disparate impact was the Alabama system of employment fraud litigation described in *Bailey v. Alabama*, 219 U.S. 219 (1911), *see supra* pages 1306–1312. The laws on their face made no mention of race, but everyone knew how they would work in application. In both cases, the Supreme Court found constitutional violations by looking through the form of the state action. How deeply does one look? And exactly what is one looking for?

Consider an analogous problem under Title VII of the Civil Rights Act of 1964, which, among other things, says:

> It shall be an unlawful employment practice for an employer—
>
> (1) to fail or refuse to hire or to discharge any individual, or otherwise to *discriminate* against any individual with respect to his compensation, terms, conditions, or privileges of employment, *because of* such individual's race, color, religion, sex, or national origin; or
>
> (2) to limit, segregate, or classify his employees or applicants for employment in any way which would deprive or tend to deprive any individual of employment opportunities or otherwise adversely affect his status as an employee, *because of* such individual's race, color, religion, sex, or national origin.

42 U.S.C. § 2000e–2(a) (2018) (emphasis added). What does it mean to "discriminate" or "segregate" "because of" the forbidden grounds for action? The most obvious meaning is that action takes place "because of" a forbidden ground when the forbidden ground is the *reason* for the action. On this understanding, a claim under the statute must allege and prove that the employer *intended* to discriminate against or segregate employees. The employer's state of mind becomes an essential element of the cause of action. This is known as a *disparate treatment* cause of action. Courts have developed evidentiary mechanisms to allow disparate treatment claims to proceed to discovery and trial, *see Young v. United Parcel Service,* 575 U.S. 206, 212–13 (2015), but those devices must lead to a conclusion of *intentional* discrimination or the plaintiff loses. To be sure, the effects of a practice (for example, a requirement that employees be at least 6' 5" tall will systematically exclude more women than men) could certainly be introduced as *evidence* of the state of mind required by a disparate treatment cause of action, but the ultimate issue in the case is still the employer's intentions. Can the effects of a practice themselves ever constitute unlawful discrimination, rather than, as under a disparate treatment claim, evidence of discrimination?

The Supreme Court said yes in 1971, in *Griggs v. Duke Power Co.*, 401 U.S. 424 (1971), a case involving tests administered by an employer that generated results more favorable to white applicants than to African-American applicants, thus giving rise to a second distinct theory of Title VII liability called *disparate impact* discrimination. Under this model, the employer's state of mind is irrelevant. The plaintiff need not prove discriminatory intent; the disparate, or differential, impact of a practice itself constitutes a violation of the statute. Importantly, however, not every disparate impact is unlawful. Rather, disparate impacts are unlawful if, but only if, they are not warranted by business necessity. Decades of statutes, regulations, and case law have discussed what counts as a prohibited disparate impact (you need, for example, a statistically significant number of events in order to have a plausible claim for disparate impact) and what counts as business necessity justifying a disparate impact. In a disparate treatment case, by contrast, the employer's claims of business necessity are irrelevant; if the requisite state of mind to discriminate is proven, the law is not interested in the motives or reasons behind that state of mind (with a very narrow exception for so-called "bona fide occupational qualifications" based on sex, which has almost no applications in the modern world). Courses in Employment Discrimination Law cover these issues in depth.

The scheme of liability under Title VII, with separate tracks for intentional and unintentional discrimination, is the product of a specific statutory scheme, and it therefore may apply as well to other statutory schemes that largely copy the language and structure of Title VII, such as the Fair Housing Act of 1968. *See Texas Dep't of*

Housing & Community Affairs v. Inclusive Community Project, Inc., 135 S.Ct. 2507 (2015). What about the Reconstruction Amendments? Do they require proof of discriminatory intent in order to show a violation?

The Framers of the Reconstruction Amendments might have found this question odd. In early cases like *Railroad Co. v. Brown* and *Strauder v. West Virginia,* the Supreme Court did not focus on intent. Citizens of every race and color either had the same rights as are enjoyed by white citizens or they did not have them. Privileges or immunities were either *abridged* on account of race or they were not abridged. Indeed, in the case of statutes, it is hard to see how one would determine whether a statute had a discriminatory intent (unless, as with anti-miscegenation statutes, they announced the intent on the face of the law). Do you need to engage in fact-finding about the mental states of a majority of the legislature? If not, does that mean that some kind of disparate impact liability applies to the Reconstruction Amendments? If so, what kind? Is there some analogue to the "business necessity" defense under Title VII? These difficult and important questions arose in 1976, in a case involving Reconstruction-Amendment principles applied to the District of Columbia through the Fifth Amendment Due Process of Law Clause. The Supreme Court's answer, which remains good law under both the Fifth and Fourteenth Amendments, probably pleases no one.

E. WASHINGTON V. DAVIS

426 U.S. 229 (1976)

■ MR. JUSTICE WHITE delivered the opinion of the Court.

This case involves the validity of a qualifying test administered to applicants for positions as police officers in the District of Columbia Metropolitan Police Department. The test was sustained by the District Court but invalidated by the Court of Appeals. We are in agreement with the District Court and hence reverse the judgment of the Court of Appeals.

This action began on April 10, 1970, when two Negro police officers filed suit against the then Commissioner of the District of Columbia, the Chief of the District's Metropolitan Police Department, and the Commissioners of the United States Civil Service Commission. An amended complaint, filed December 10, alleged that the promotion policies of the Department * * * and * * * the Department's recruiting procedures discriminated on the basis of race against black applicants by a series of practices including, but not limited to, a written personnel test which excluded a disproportionately high number of Negro applicants. These practices were asserted to violate respondents' rights "under the due process clause of the Fifth Amendment to the United States Constitution * * *

According to the findings and conclusions of the District Court, to be accepted by the Department and to enter an intensive 17-week training program, the police recruit was required to satisfy certain physical and character standards, to be a high school graduate or its equivalent, and to receive a grade of at least 40 out of 80 on "Test 21," which is "an examination that is used generally throughout the federal service," which "was developed by the Civil Service Commission, not the Police Department," and which was "designed to test verbal ability, vocabulary, reading and comprehension."

The validity of Test 21 was the sole issue before the court on the motions for summary judgment. The District Court noted that there was no claim of "an intentional discrimination or purposeful discriminatory acts" but only a claim that Test 21 bore no relationship to job performance and "has a highly discriminatory impact in screening out black candidates." Respondents' evidence, the District Court said, warranted three conclusions: "(a) The number of black police officers, while substantial, is not proportionate to the population mix of the city. (b) A higher percentage of blacks fail the Test than whites. (c) The Test has not been validated to establish its reliability for measuring subsequent job performance." This showing was deemed sufficient to shift the burden of proof to the defendants in the action, petitioners here; but the court nevertheless concluded that on the undisputed facts respondents were not entitled to relief * * * The District Court rejected the assertion that Test 21 was culturally slanted to favor whites and was "satisfied that the undisputable facts prove the test to be reasonably and directly related to the requirements of the police recruit training program and that it is neither so designed nor operates (Sic) to discriminate against otherwise qualified blacks" * * * The District Court ultimately concluded that "(t)he proof is wholly lacking that a police officer qualifies on the color of his skin rather than ability" and that the Department "should not be required on this showing to lower standards or to abandon efforts to achieve excellence."

Having lost * * * in the District Court, respondents brought the case to the Court of Appeals claiming that their summary judgment motion, which rested on purely constitutional grounds, should have been granted. The tendered constitutional issue was whether the use of Test 21 invidiously discriminated against Negroes and hence denied them due process of law contrary to the commands of the Fifth Amendment. The Court of Appeals, addressing that issue, announced that it would be guided by *Griggs v. Duke Power Co.*, 401 U.S. 424, (1971), a case involving the interpretation and application of Title VII of the Civil Rights Act of 1964, and held that the statutory standards elucidated in that case were to govern the due process question tendered in this one. The court went on to declare that lack of discriminatory intent in designing and administering Test 21 was irrelevant; the critical fact was rather that a far greater proportion of blacks four times as many failed the test than did whites. This disproportionate impact, standing alone and without regard to whether it indicated a discriminatory purpose, was held sufficient to establish a constitutional violation, absent proof by petitioners that the test was an adequate measure of job performance in addition to being an indicator of probable success in the training program, a burden which the court ruled petitioners had failed to discharge. That the Department had made substantial efforts to recruit blacks was held beside the point and the fact that the racial distribution of recent hirings and of the Department itself might be roughly equivalent to the racial makeup of the surrounding community, broadly conceived, was put aside as a "comparison (not) material to this appeal." The Court of Appeals, over a dissent, accordingly reversed the judgment of the District Court and directed that respondents' motion for partial summary judgment be granted. We granted the petition for certiorari * * *.

Because the Court of Appeals erroneously applied the legal standards applicable to Title VII cases in resolving the constitutional issue before it, we reverse its judgment in respondents' favor. Although the petition for certiorari did not present this ground for reversal, our Rule 40(1)(d)(2) provides that we "may notice a plain error not presented"; and this is an appropriate occasion to invoke the Rule.

As the Court of Appeals understood Title VII, employees or applicants proceeding under it need not concern themselves with the employer's possibly discriminatory purpose but instead may focus solely on the racially differential impact of the challenged hiring or promotion practices. This is not the constitutional rule. We have never held that the constitutional standard for adjudicating claims of invidious racial discrimination is identical to the standards applicable under Title VII, and we decline to do so today.

The central purpose of the Equal Protection Clause of the Fourteenth Amendment is the prevention of official conduct discriminating on the basis of race. It is also true that the Due Process Clause of the Fifth Amendment contains an equal protection component prohibiting the United States from invidiously discriminating between individuals or groups. *Bolling v. Sharpe*, 347 U.S. 497 (1954). But our cases have not embraced the proposition that a law or other official act, without regard to whether it reflects a racially discriminatory purpose, is unconstitutional solely because it has a racially disproportionate impact.

Almost 100 years ago, *Strauder v. West Virginia*, 100 U.S. 303 (1880), established that the exclusion of Negroes from grand and petit juries in criminal proceedings violated the Equal Protection Clause, but the fact that a particular jury or a series of juries does not statistically reflect the racial composition of the community does not in itself make out an invidious discrimination forbidden by the Clause. "A purpose to discriminate must be present which may be proven by systematic exclusion of eligible jurymen of the proscribed race or by unequal application of the law to such an extent as to show intentional discrimination." *Akins v. Texas*, 325 U.S. 398, 403–404 (1945) * * *.

* * *

The school desegregation cases have also adhered to the basic equal protection principle that the invidious quality of a law claimed to be racially discriminatory must ultimately be traced to a racially discriminatory purpose. That there are both predominantly black and predominantly white schools in a community is not alone violative of the Equal Protection Clause. The essential element of *de jure* segregation is "a current condition of segregation resulting from intentional state action. *Keyes v. School Dist. No. 1*, 413 U.S. 189, 205 (1973). The differentiating factor between *de jure* segregation and so-called *de facto* segregation . . . is *purpose* or *intent* to segregate." The Court has also recently rejected allegations of racial discrimination based solely on the statistically disproportionate racial impact of various provisions of the Social Security Act because "(t)he acceptance of appellants' constitutional theory would render suspect each difference in treatment among the grant classes, however lacking in racial motivation and however otherwise rational the treatment might be." *Jefferson v. Hackney*, 406 U.S. 535, 548, 92 S.Ct. 1724, 1732, 32 L.Ed.2d 285, 297 (1972).

This is not to say that the necessary discriminatory racial purpose must be express or appear on the face of the statute, or that a law's disproportionate impact is irrelevant in cases involving Constitution-based claims of racial discrimination. A statute, otherwise neutral on its face, must not be applied so as invidiously to discriminate on the basis of race. *Yick Wo v. Hopkins*, 118 U.S. 356 (1886). It is also clear from the cases dealing with racial discrimination in the selection of juries that the systematic exclusion of Negroes is itself such an "unequal application of the law

. . . as to show intentional discrimination." *Akins v. Texas*. A prima facie case of discriminatory purpose may be proved as well by the absence of Negroes on a particular jury combined with the failure of the jury commissioners to be informed of eligible Negro jurors in a community, *Hill v. Texas*, 316 U.S. 400, 404 (1942), or with racially non-neutral selection procedures. With a prima facie case made out, "the burden of proof shifts to the State to rebut the presumption of unconstitutional action by showing that permissible racially neutral selection criteria and procedures have produced the monochromatic result."

Necessarily, an invidious discriminatory purpose may often be inferred from the totality of the relevant facts, including the fact, if it is true, that the law bears more heavily on one race than another. It is also not infrequently true that the discriminatory impact in the jury cases for example, the total or seriously disproportionate exclusion of Negroes from jury venires may for all practical purposes demonstrate unconstitutionality because in various circumstances the discrimination is very difficult to explain on nonracial grounds. Nevertheless, we have not held that a law, neutral on its face and serving ends otherwise within the power of government to pursue, is invalid under the Equal Protection Clause simply because it may affect a greater proportion of one race than of another. Disproportionate impact is not irrelevant, but it is not the sole touchstone of an invidious racial discrimination forbidden by the Constitution. Standing alone, it does not trigger the rule, *McLaughlin v. Florida*, 379 U.S. 184, 85 (1964), that racial classifications are to be subjected to the strictest scrutiny and are justifiable only by the weightiest of considerations.

* * *

* * * [V]arious Courts of Appeals have held in several contexts, including public employment, that the substantially disproportionate racial impact of a statute or official practice standing alone and without regard to discriminatory purpose, suffices to prove racial discrimination violating the Equal Protection Clause absent some justification going substantially beyond what would be necessary to validate most other legislative classifications. The cases impressively demonstrate that there is another side to the issue; but, with all due respect, to the extent that those cases rested on or expressed the view that proof of discriminatory racial purpose is unnecessary in making out an equal protection violation, we are in disagreement.

As an initial matter, we have difficulty understanding how a law establishing a racially neutral qualification for employment is nevertheless racially discriminatory and denies "any person . . . equal protection of the laws" simply because a greater proportion of Negroes fail to qualify than members of other racial or ethnic groups. Had respondents, along with all others who had failed Test 21, whether white or black, brought an action claiming that the test denied each of them equal protection of the laws as compared with those who had passed with high enough scores to qualify them as police recruits, it is most unlikely that their challenge would have been sustained. Test 21, which is administered generally to prospective Government employees, concededly seeks to ascertain whether those who take it have acquired a particular level of verbal skill; and it is untenable that the Constitution prevents the Government from seeking modestly to upgrade the communicative abilities of its employees rather than to be satisfied with some lower level of competence, particularly where the job requires special ability to communicate orally and in writing. Respondents, as Negroes, could no more successfully claim that the test denied them equal protection than could white applicants who also failed. The conclusion would not be different in the face of proof that more Negroes than whites had been disqualified by Test 21. That other Negroes also failed to score well would, alone, not demonstrate that respondents individually were being denied equal protection of the laws by the application of an otherwise valid qualifying test being administered to prospective police recruits.

Nor on the facts of the case before us would the disproportionate impact of Test 21 warrant the conclusion that it is a purposeful device to discriminate against Negroes and hence an infringement of the constitutional rights of respondents as well as other black applicants. As we have said, the test is neutral on its face and rationally may be said to serve a purpose the Government is constitutionally empowered to pursue. Even agreeing with the District Court that the differential racial effect of Test 21 called for further inquiry, we think the District Court correctly held that the affirmative efforts of the Metropolitan Police Department to recruit black officers, the changing racial composition of the recruit classes and of the force in general, and the relationship of the test to the training program negated any inference that the Department discriminated on the basis of race or that "a police officer qualifies on the color of his skin rather than ability."

Under Title VII, Congress provided that when hiring and promotion practices disqualifying substantially disproportionate numbers of blacks are challenged, discriminatory purpose need not be proved, and that it is an insufficient response to demonstrate some rational basis for the challenged practices. It is necessary, in addition, that they be "validated" in terms of job performance * * *. However this process proceeds, it involves a more probing judicial review of, and less deference to, the seemingly reasonable acts of administrators and executives than is appropriate under the Constitution where special racial impact, without discriminatory purpose, is claimed. We are not disposed to adopt this more rigorous standard for the purposes of applying the Fifth and the Fourteenth Amendments in cases such as this.

A rule that a statute designed to serve neutral ends is nevertheless invalid, absent compelling justification, if in practice it benefits or burdens one race more than another would be far-reaching and would raise serious questions about, and perhaps invalidate, a whole range of tax, welfare, public service, regulatory, and licensing statutes that may be more burdensome to the poor and to the average black than to the more affluent white.

Given that rule, such consequences would perhaps be likely to follow. However, in our view, extension of the rule beyond those areas where it is already applicable by reason of statute, such as in the field of public employment, should await legislative prescription.

As we have indicated, it was error to direct summary judgment for respondents based on the Fifth Amendment.

We also hold that the Court of Appeals should have affirmed the judgment of the District Court granting the motions for summary judgment filed by petitioners and the federal parties * * *.

* * *

* * * Based on the evidence before him, the District Judge concluded that Test 21 was directly related to the requirements of the police training program and that a positive relationship between the test and training-course performance was

sufficient to validate the former, wholly aside from its possible relationship to actual performance as a police officer * * *.

The District Court's accompanying conclusion that Test 21 was in fact directly related to the requirements of the police training program was supported by a validation study, as well as by other evidence of record; and we are not convinced that this conclusion was erroneous.

* * *

The judgment of the Court of Appeals accordingly is reversed.

So ordered.

■ MR. JUSTICE STEVENS, concurring.

While I agree with the Court's disposition of this case, I add these comments on the constitutional issue * * *.

The requirement of purposeful discrimination is a common thread running through the cases * * *. These cases include criminal convictions which were set aside because blacks were excluded from the grand jury, a reapportionment case in which political boundaries were obviously influenced to some extent by racial considerations, a school desegregation case, and a case involving the unequal administration of an ordinance purporting to prohibit the operation of laundries in frame buildings. Although it may be proper to use the same language to describe the constitutional claim in each of these contexts, the burden of proving a prima facie case may well involve differing evidentiary considerations. The extent of deference that one pays to the trial court's determination of the factual issue, and indeed, the extent to which one characterizes the intent issue as a question of fact or a question of law, will vary in different contexts.

Frequently the most probative evidence of intent will be objective evidence of what actually happened rather than evidence describing the subjective state of mind of the actor. For normally the actor is presumed to have intended the natural consequences of his deeds. This is particularly true in the case of governmental action which is frequently the product of compromise, of collective decisionmaking, and of mixed motivation. It is unrealistic, on the one hand, to require the victim of alleged discrimination to uncover the actual subjective intent of the decisionmaker or, conversely, to invalidate otherwise legitimate action simply because an improper motive affected the deliberation of a participant in the decisional process. A law conscripting clerics should not be invalidated because an atheist voted for it.

My point in making this observation is to suggest that the line between discriminatory purpose and discriminatory impact is not nearly as bright, and perhaps not quite as critical, as the reader of the Court's opinion might assume. I agree, of course, that a constitutional issue does not arise every time some disproportionate impact is shown. On the other hand, when the disproportion is as dramatic as in *Gomillion v. Lightfoot,* 364 U.S. 339, or *Yick Wo v. Hopkins*, 118 U.S. 356 (1886), it really does not matter whether the standard is phrased in terms of purpose or effect. Therefore, although I accept the statement of the general rule in the Court's opinion, I am not yet prepared to indicate how that standard should be applied in the many cases which have formulated the governing standard in different language.

* * *

■ MR. JUSTICE BRENNAN, with whom MR. JUSTICE MARSHALL joins, dissenting. [Omitted. *Editors' Note: Justice Brennan's dissent addressed the statutory standards for test validation under Title VII and concluded that Test 21 did not meet those standards. The dissent did not directly engage the broader constitutional questions.*]

NOTES AND QUESTIONS

1. Everyone agrees that disparate impact can be used as *evidence* of discriminatory intent. And everyone agrees that, in some cases, the effect is so palpable that any inference other than an inference of discriminatory intent would be unreasonable, so that nothing further needs to be shown. For example, in *Yick Wo. v. Hopkins*, 118 U.S. 356 (1886), San Francisco had passed an ordinance making it illegal to operate a laundry in a wooden building without getting a special permit. At the time, 95% of the city's laundries were operated in wooden buildings and two-thirds were owned by Chinese immigrants. Justice Matthews wrote a unanimous opinion holding that the facially neutral law had been administered in a racially discriminatory way that violated the Equal Protection Clause. Does this call into question the test of *Washington v. Davis* that discriminatory intent must be proved before race discrimination can be found, or is *Yick Wo* a case in which the discriminatory intent was obvious? Did the intent/effects distinction not arise much before modern times because the discriminatory intent behind state schemes was typically so obvious that it did not need to be formally found? Was Justice Stevens right that the difference between disparate treatment and disparate impact is smaller than it looks at first glance?

2. The rule of *Washington v. Davis* has much of its bite with respect to claims of implicit bias or unconscious discrimination. To the extent that those phenomena generate disparate impacts, an explicitly intent-based liability scheme makes it almost impossible to prove a constitutional violation.

3. As we shall see below, *see infra* pages 1672–1677, the U.S. Supreme Court in *Buchanan v. Warley,* 245 U.S. 60 (1917), unanimously struck down a Louisville, Kentucky ordinance that prohibited the sale of real estate to African-Americans in white majority neighborhoods and vice versa as violating the Lochnerian right to freedom of contract. In 1926, however, in *Village of Euclid, Ohio v. Amber Realty Co.,* 272 U.S. 365 (1926), the Supreme court upheld the constitutionality of the new practice of facially neutral residential zoning laws. The Village of Euclid imposed three classes of the height to which new buildings could be built and four classes of acreage which any subdivided lot must meet. Ambler Realty sued, claiming their property had been taken without just compensation because it was now worth much less than when they bought the 68 acres in the Village of Euclid. The Supreme Court famously upheld the novel use of facially neutral residential zoning, distinguishing *Buchanan v. Warley* on the ground that that case had involved facial discrimination on the basis of race. At the time *Euclid* was decided, residential zoning was very rare, and many thought it was unconstitutional. Today, virtually every suburb and city has zoning ordinances in place that make it prohibitively expensive for African-Americans, who are on average poorer than white Americans, to own land in the suburbs and send their children to good suburban schools. Residential zoning leads to race discrimination in housing, which leads to race discrimination in local public schools. If this outcome is consistent with *Washington v. Davis*, then should that case be overruled?

4. If *Washington v. Davis* was overruled, what would take its place? What would a Fourteenth-Amendment rule of disparate impact look like? Recall that under Title VII, disparate impacts are unlawful *only* if they are not justified by business necessity.

Similarly, when the Court extended disparate impact liability to the Fair Housing Act of 1968 in *Texas Dep't of Housing & Community Affairs v. Inclusive Community Project, Inc.*, 135 S.Ct. 2507 (2015), Justice Kennedy's majority opinion spent most of its considerable length explaining why plaintiffs were almost sure to lose in almost every case because not every disparate impact from housing regulations or practices is unlawful. As noted above, Congress, federal agencies, and courts have spent almost half a century trying to craft standards for sorting out justifiable from unjustifiable disparity-producing employment practices, and the results have not yielded much by way of certainty or predictability. The "safe" response by an employer is to make sure that the numbers work out right so that practices do not have to be defended in court or before an administrative agency. If disparate impact liability was extended to the Fourteenth Amendment, would government agencies have to make sure that the numbers work out right in everything that they do? Would that be a bad thing? Would it be a constitutional thing if, in order to make the numbers work out right, the government agencies had to give express consideration to the kinds of grounds for decision that the Fourteenth Amendment seems to forbid? Or does the Fourteenth Amendment only forbid grounds for decision that work *against* historically disadvantaged groups while permitting (or even requiring) race-conscious (and sex-conscious, and sexual-orientation-conscious, and religion-conscious) decisionmaking when it benefits historically disadvantaged groups? These huge—and hugely contentious—questions are the next topic.

[Assignment 62]

VIII. AFFIRMATIVE ACTION AND RACE DISCRIMINATION

Since the Nixon Administration, both public and private institutions in the United States have broadly employed race-based affirmative action for African-Americans and Latinos and sex-based affirmative action for women. This is the classic context for raising the question, noted above, whether race or sex classifications can be made constitutionally when they *benefit* rather than harm an historically oppressed group. This question divides originalists as much as it divides the country (and, as we will soon see, divides the Court).

The originalist argument in favor of the constitutionality of affirmative action stresses that the Fourteenth Amendment banned systems of caste. No one looking at American affirmative action today would say that African-Americans and women are being relegated to a higher caste than white men. Modern day affirmative action is remedial and does not create a caste system. With respect to the federal government, a fiduciary principle requires *fair* treatment, not strictly *equal* treatment by an agent of multiple principals. Favoritism is not always unfair; it depends on the context. And if the import of the Fourteenth Amendment is to extend that fiduciary obligation to state actors, the same rationale might justify even race- or sex-based favoritism if, all things considered, it is fair in a given context.

The originalist argument against the constitutionality of affirmative action stresses that the Fourteenth Amendment was based on the Civil Rights Act of 1866, which gave citizens of every race and color "the same rights as are enjoyed by white citizens." Not more rights and not less rights, but the same rights. Moreover, the Privileges or Immunities and Equal Protection Clauses apply to all citizens and persons and not merely to African-Americans, Latinos, or women. White men enjoy the same rights under these clauses as do all other citizens or persons. Finally, affirmative action could be seen as being a form of class legislation forbidden by the

Constitution—a law that, as you will, unconstitutionally works corruption of the blood.

How do you expect other modalities of interpretation to handle affirmative action? See if the next principal case meets your expectation.

The Supreme Court cautiously gave a green light to limited affirmative action in *Regents of the University of California v. Bakke*, 438 U.S. 265 (1978). You have already seen something of the evolution of the practice in *Adarand Constructors v. Pena,* 515 U.S. 200 (1995). *See supra* pages 1153–1164. The Court continues to wrestle with affirmative action in higher education, with results that (at least as of 2020) allow some measure of race-consciousness in college and university admissions, but only as one piece of a wider effort at diversity. *See Fisher v. Univ. of Texas,* 136 S.Ct. 2198 (2016).

With respect to primary and secondary education, matters are not much clearer. *Brown* swept aside state-sponsored segregation. Did that foreclose all race-consciousness in school placement? What if residential housing patterns—some of which might be the result of government policies, as we will explore later, *see infra*—lead inexorably to many, or even most, schools being predominantly single-race—something that is often called "de facto" (or practical) segregation rather than "de jure" (or formally commanded by law) segregation? Or what if a district court enforcing *Brown* determines that the best remedy for segregation—whether de facto or de jure—is to assign children, based on their race, to schools that are possibly quite distant from their homes in order to provide racially integrated school settings? The students might have to spend several hours per day on busses. Does the Constitution require, or permit, that practice? In the face of dilatory local (non)action more than a decade after *Brown,* from the late 1960s through the 1970s, the federal courts experimented with forced bussing of children to non-local schools to foster racial integration of public schools. This was upheld as a permissible remedy by the Court in *Swann v. Charlotte-Mecklenburg Bd. of Educ.,* 402 U.S. 1 (1971). Bussing, however, generated a huge social backlash, and by the 1990s its heyday was over.

Those cases concerned bussing that was ordered by courts as a remedy for governmental discrimination. What if a local government decides to combat de facto segregation by making race an explicit consideration in school assignment decisions, with the stated goal of producing more racially integrated schools? Recall that we asked whether Justice Harlan's dissent in *Plessy* commanded unconditional color-blindness. *See supra* pages 1672–1684. That is precisely the question posed in the following blockbuster case from 2007, in which Justice Kennedy—who is no longer on the Court—was the swing vote. As is often true, we have had to edit the case considerably, but we have tried to maintain a sense of both the substance *and the tone* of the various opinions. This is obviously a subject that implicates strongly held beliefs among the justices, as it does among many people.

Parents Involved in Community Schools v. Seattle School Dist. No. 1

551 U.S. 701 (2007)

■ CHIEF JUSTICE ROBERTS announced the judgment of the Court, and delivered the opinion of the Court with respect to Parts I, II, III-A, and III-C, and an opinion with respect to Parts III-B and IV, in which JUSTICE SCALIA, JUSTICE THOMAS, and JUSTICE ALITO join.

The school districts in these cases voluntarily adopted student assignment plans that rely upon race to determine which public schools certain children may attend. The Seattle school district classifies children as white or nonwhite; the Jefferson County school district as black or "other." In Seattle, this racial classification is used to allocate slots in oversubscribed high schools. In Jefferson County, it is used to make certain elementary school assignments and to rule on transfer requests. In each case, the school district relies upon an individual student's race in assigning that student to a particular school, so that the racial balance at the school falls within a predetermined range based on the racial composition of the school district as a whole. Parents of students denied assignment to particular schools under these plans solely because of their race brought suit, contending that allocating children to different public schools on the basis of race violated the Fourteenth Amendment guarantee of equal protection. The Courts of Appeals below upheld the plans. We granted certiorari, and now reverse.

I

Both cases present the same underlying legal question—whether a public school that had not operated legally segregated schools or has been found to be unitary may choose to classify students by race and rely upon that classification in making school assignments. Although we examine the plans under the same legal framework, the specifics of the two plans, and the circumstances surrounding their adoption, are in some respects quite different.

A

Seattle School District No. 1 operates 10 regular public high schools. In 1998, it adopted the plan at issue in this case for assigning students to these schools. The plan allows incoming ninth graders to choose from among any of the district's high schools, ranking however many schools they wish in order of preference.

Some schools are more popular than others. If too many students list the same school as their first choice, the district employs a series of "tiebreakers" to determine who will fill the open slots at the oversubscribed school. The first tiebreaker selects for admission students who have a sibling currently enrolled in the chosen school. The next tiebreaker depends upon the racial composition of the particular school and the race of the individual student. In the district's public schools approximately 41 percent of enrolled students are white; the remaining 59 percent, comprising all other racial groups, are classified by Seattle for assignment purposes as nonwhite. If an oversubscribed school is not within 10 percentage points of the district's overall white/nonwhite racial balance, it is what the district calls "integration positive," and the district employs a tiebreaker that selects for assignment students whose race "will serve to bring the school into balance." If it is still necessary to select students for the school after using the racial tiebreaker, the next tiebreaker is the geographic proximity of the school to the student's residence.

Seattle has never operated segregated schools—legally separate schools for students of different races—nor has it ever been subject to court-ordered desegregation. It nonetheless employs the racial tiebreaker in an attempt to address the effects of racially identifiable housing patterns on school assignments. Most white students live in the northern part of Seattle, most students of other racial backgrounds in the southern part. Four of Seattle's high schools are located in the north—Ballard, Nathan Hale, Ingraham, and Roosevelt—and five in the south—Rainier Beach, Cleveland, West Seattle, Chief Sealth, and Franklin. One school—Garfield—is more or less in the center of Seattle.

For the 2000–2001 school year, five of these schools were oversubscribed—Ballard, Nathan Hale, Roosevelt, Garfield, and Franklin—so much so that 82 percent of incoming ninth graders ranked one of these schools as their first choice. Three of the oversubscribed schools were "integration positive" because the school's white enrollment the previous school year was greater than 51 percent—Ballard, Nathan Hale, and Roosevelt. Thus, more nonwhite students (107, 27, and 82, respectively) who selected one of these three schools as a top choice received placement at the school than would have been the case had race not been considered, and proximity been the next tiebreaker. Franklin was "integration positive" because its nonwhite enrollment the previous school year was greater than 69 percent; 89 more white students were assigned to Franklin by operation of the racial tiebreaker in the 2000–2001 school year than otherwise would have been. Garfield was the only oversubscribed school whose composition during the 1999–2000 school year was within the racial guidelines, although in previous years Garfield's enrollment had been predominantly nonwhite, and the racial tiebreaker had been used to give preference to white students.

Petitioner Parents Involved in Community Schools (Parents Involved) is a nonprofit corporation comprising the parents of children who have been or may be denied assignment to their chosen high school in the district because of their race. The concerns of Parents Involved are illustrated by Jill Kurfirst, who sought to enroll her ninth-grade son, Andy Meeks, in Ballard High School's special Biotechnology Career Academy. Andy suffered from attention deficit hyperactivity disorder and dyslexia, but had made good progress with hands-on instruction, and his mother and middle school teachers thought that the smaller biotechnology program held the most promise for his continued success. Andy was accepted into this selective program but, because of the racial tiebreaker, was denied assignment to Ballard High School. Parents Involved commenced this suit in the Western District of Washington, alleging that Seattle's use of race in assignments violated the Equal Protection Clause of the Fourteenth Amendment * * *.

* * *

B

Jefferson County Public Schools operates the public school system in metropolitan Louisville, Kentucky. In 1973 a federal court found that Jefferson County had maintained a segregated school system, and in 1975 the District Court entered a desegregation decree. Jefferson County operated under this decree until 2000, when the District Court dissolved the decree after finding that the district had achieved unitary status by eliminating "[t]o the greatest extent practicable" the vestiges of its prior policy of segregation.

In 2001, after the decree had been dissolved, Jefferson County adopted the voluntary student assignment plan at issue in this case. Approximately 34 percent of the district's 97,000 students are black; most of the remaining 66 percent are white. The plan requires all nonmagnet schools to maintain a minimum black enrollment of 15 percent, and a maximum black enrollment of 50 percent.

At the elementary school level, based on his or her address, each student is designated a "resides" school to which students within a specific geographic area are assigned; elementary resides schools are "grouped into clusters in order to facilitate integration." The district assigns students to nonmagnet schools in one of two ways: Parents of kindergartners, first graders, and students new to the district may submit an application indicating a first and second choice among the schools within their cluster; students who do not submit such an application are assigned within the cluster by the district. "Decisions to assign students to schools within each cluster are based on available space within the schools and the racial guidelines in the District's current student assignment plan." If a school has reached the "extremes of the racial guidelines," a student whose race would contribute to the school's racial imbalance will not be assigned there. After assignment, students at all grade levels are permitted to apply to transfer between nonmagnet schools in the district. Transfers may be requested for any number of reasons, and may be denied because of lack of available space or on the basis of the racial guidelines.

When petitioner Crystal Meredith moved into the school district in August 2002, she sought to enroll her son, Joshua McDonald, in kindergarten for the 2002–2003 school year. His resides school was only a mile from his new home, but it had no available space—assignments had been made in May, and the class was full. Jefferson County assigned Joshua to another elementary school in his cluster, Young Elementary. This school was 10 miles from home, and Meredith sought to transfer Joshua to a school in a different cluster, Bloom Elementary, which—like his resides school—was only a mile from home. Space was available at Bloom, and intercluster transfers are allowed, but Joshua's transfer was nonetheless denied because, in the words of Jefferson County, "[t]he transfer would have an adverse effect on desegregation compliance" of Young.

Meredith brought suit in the Western District of Kentucky, alleging violations of the Equal Protection Clause of the Fourteenth Amendment * * *.

II

* * *

III

A

It is well established that when the government distributes burdens or benefits on the basis of individual racial classifications, that action is reviewed under strict scrutiny. *Johnson v. California*, 543 U.S. 499, 505–506 (2005); *Grutter v. Bollinger*, 539 U.S. 306, 326 (2003); *Adarand, supra*, at 224. As the Court recently reaffirmed, " 'racial classifications are simply too pernicious to permit any but the most exact connection between justification and classification.' " *Gratz v. Bollinger*, 539 U.S. 244, 270 (2003). In order to satisfy this searching standard of review, the school districts must demonstrate that the use of individual racial classifications in the assignment plans here under review is "narrowly tailored" to achieve a "compelling" government interest. *Adarand, supra*, at 227.

Without attempting in these cases to set forth all the interests a school district might assert, it suffices to note that our prior cases, in evaluating the use of racial classifications in the school context, have recognized two interests that qualify as compelling. The first is the compelling interest of remedying the effects of past intentional discrimination. See *Freeman v. Pitts*, 503 U.S. 467, 494 (1992). Yet the

Seattle public schools have not shown that they were ever segregated by law, and were not subject to court-ordered desegregation decrees. The Jefferson County public schools were previously segregated by law and were subject to a desegregation decree entered in 1975. In 2000, the District Court that entered that decree dissolved it, finding that Jefferson County had "eliminated the vestiges associated with the former policy of segregation and its pernicious effects," and thus had achieved "unitary" status. Jefferson County accordingly does not rely upon an interest in remedying the effects of past intentional discrimination in defending its present use of race in assigning students.

Nor could it. We have emphasized that the harm being remedied by mandatory desegregation plans is the harm that is traceable to segregation, and that "the Constitution is not violated by racial imbalance in the schools, without more." *Milliken v. Bradley*, 433 U.S. 267, 280, n. 14 (1977). Once Jefferson County achieved unitary status, it had remedied the constitutional wrong that allowed race-based assignments. Any continued use of race must be justified on some other basis.

The second government interest we have recognized as compelling for purposes of strict scrutiny is the interest in diversity in higher education upheld in *Grutter*, 539 U.S., at 328. The specific interest found compelling in *Grutter* was student body diversity "in the context of higher education." *Ibid.* The diversity interest was not focused on race alone but encompassed "all factors that may contribute to student body diversity." *Id.,* at 337. We described the various types of diversity that the law school sought:

> "[The law school's] policy makes clear there are many possible bases for diversity admissions, and provides examples of admittees who have lived or traveled widely abroad, are fluent in several languages, have overcome personal adversity and family hardship, have exceptional records of extensive community service, and have had successful careers in other fields." *Id.*, at 338, 123 S.Ct. 2325 (brackets and internal quotation marks omitted) * * *.

The entire gist of the analysis in *Grutter* was that the admissions program at issue there focused on each applicant as an individual, and not simply as a member of a particular racial group. The classification of applicants by race upheld in *Grutter* was only as part of a "highly individualized, holistic review," 539 U.S., at 337. As the Court explained, "[t]he importance of this individualized consideration in the context of a race-conscious admissions program is paramount." *Ibid.* The point of the narrow tailoring analysis in which the *Grutter* Court engaged was to ensure that the use of racial classifications was indeed part of a broader assessment of diversity, and not simply an effort to achieve racial balance, which the Court explained would be "patently unconstitutional." *Id.*, at 330.

In the present cases, by contrast, race is not considered as part of a broader effort to achieve "exposure to widely diverse people, cultures, ideas, and viewpoints," *ibid.*; race, for some students, is determinative standing alone. The districts argue that other factors, such as student preferences, affect assignment decisions under their plans, but under each plan when race comes into play, it is decisive by itself. It is not simply one factor weighed with others in reaching a decision, as in *Grutter*; it is *the* factor * * *.

Even when it comes to race, the plans here employ only a limited notion of diversity, viewing race exclusively in white/nonwhite terms in Seattle and black/"other" terms in Jefferson County * * *. But under the Seattle plan, a school with 50 percent Asian-American students and 50 percent white students but no African-American, Native-American, or Latino students would qualify as balanced, while a school with 30 percent Asian-American, 25 percent African-American, 25 percent Latino, and 20 percent white students would not. It is hard to understand how a plan that could allow these results can be viewed as being concerned with achieving enrollment that is " 'broadly diverse,' " *Grutter, supra*, at 329.

* * *

B

Perhaps recognizing that reliance on *Grutter* cannot sustain their plans, both school districts assert additional interests, distinct from the interest upheld in *Grutter*, to justify their race-based assignments. In briefing and argument before this Court, Seattle contends that its use of race helps to reduce racial concentration in schools and to ensure that racially concentrated housing patterns do not prevent nonwhite students from having access to the most desirable schools. Jefferson County has articulated a similar goal, phrasing its interest in terms of educating its students "in a racially integrated environment." Each school district argues that educational and broader socialization benefits flow from a racially diverse learning environment, and each contends that because the diversity they seek is racial diversity—not the broader diversity at issue in *Grutter*—it makes sense to promote that interest directly by relying on race alone.

The parties and their *amici* dispute whether racial diversity in schools in fact has a marked impact on test scores and other objective yardsticks or achieves intangible socialization benefits. The debate is not one we need to resolve, however, because it is clear that the racial classifications employed by the districts are not narrowly tailored to the goal of achieving the educational and social benefits asserted to flow from racial diversity. In design and operation, the plans are directed only to racial balance, pure and simple, an objective this Court has repeatedly condemned as illegitimate.

The plans are tied to each district's specific racial demographics, rather than to any pedagogic concept of the level of diversity needed to obtain the asserted educational benefits * * *.

The districts offer no evidence that the level of racial diversity necessary to achieve the asserted educational benefits happens to coincide with the racial demographics of the respective school districts—or rather the white/nonwhite or black/"other" balance of the districts, since that is the only diversity addressed by the plans. Indeed, in its brief Seattle simply assumes that the educational benefits track the racial breakdown of the district. See Brief for Respondents in No. 05–908, at 36 ("For Seattle, 'racial balance' is clearly not an end in itself but rather a measure of the extent to which the educational goals the plan was designed to foster are likely to be achieved"). When asked for "a range of percentage that would be diverse," however, Seattle's expert said it was important to have "sufficient numbers so as to avoid students feeling any kind of specter of exceptionality." The district did not attempt to defend the proposition that anything outside its range posed the "specter of exceptionality." Nor did it demonstrate in any way how the educational and social benefits of racial diversity or avoidance of racial isolation are more likely to be achieved at a school that is 50 percent white and 50 percent Asian-American, which would qualify as diverse under Seattle's plan, than at a school that is 30 percent Asian-American, 25 percent African-American, 25 percent Latino, and 20 percent white, which under Seattle's definition would be racially concentrated.

* * * The Jefferson County plan * * * is based on a goal of replicating at each school "an African-American enrollment equivalent to the average district-wide African-American enrollment." Joshua McDonald's requested transfer was denied because his race was listed as "other" rather than black, and allowing the transfer would have had an adverse effect on the racial guideline compliance of Young Elementary, the school he sought to leave. At the time, however, Young Elementary was 46.8 percent black. The transfer might have had an adverse effect on the effort to approach districtwide racial proportionality at Young, but it had nothing to do with preventing either the black or "other" group from becoming "small" or "isolated" at Young.

* * *

This working backward to achieve a particular type of racial balance, rather than working forward from some demonstration of the level of diversity that provides the purported benefits, is a fatal flaw under our existing precedent. We have many times over reaffirmed that "[r]acial balance is not to be achieved for its own sake." *Freeman*, 503 U.S., at 494 * * *.

Accepting racial balancing as a compelling state interest would justify the imposition of racial proportionality throughout American society, contrary to our repeated recognition that "[a]t the heart of the Constitution's guarantee of equal protection lies the simple command that the Government must treat citizens as individuals, not as simply components of a racial, religious, sexual or national class." *Miller v. Johnson,* 515 U.S. 900, 911 (1995). Allowing racial balancing as a compelling end in itself would "effectively assur[e] that race will always be relevant in American life, and that the 'ultimate goal' of 'eliminating entirely from governmental decisionmaking such irrelevant factors as a human being's race' will never be achieved." * * *

* * *

* * *[I]n Seattle the plans are defended as necessary to address the consequences of racially identifiable housing patterns. The sweep of the mandate claimed by the district is contrary to our rulings that remedying past societal discrimination does not justify race-conscious government action. See, e.g., *Shaw v. Hunt*, 517 U.S. 899, 909–910 (1996) ("[A]n effort to alleviate the effects of societal discrimination is not a compelling interest").

The principle that racial balancing is not permitted is one of substance, not semantics. Racial balancing is not transformed from "patently unconstitutional" to a compelling state interest simply by relabeling it "racial diversity." While the school districts use various verbal formulations to describe the interest they seek to promote—racial diversity, avoidance of racial isolation, racial integration—they offer no definition of the interest that suggests it differs from racial balance.

* * *

* * * To the extent the objective is sufficient diversity so that students see fellow students as individuals rather than solely as members of a racial group, using means that treat students solely as members of a racial group is fundamentally at cross-purposes with that end.

C

* * *

The districts have also failed to show that they considered methods other than explicit racial classifications to achieve their stated goals. Narrow tailoring requires "serious, good faith consideration of workable race-neutral alternatives," *Grutter, supra*, at 339, and yet in Seattle several alternative assignment plans—many of which would not have used express racial classifications—were rejected with little or no consideration. Jefferson County has failed to present any evidence that it considered alternatives, even though the district already claims that its goals are achieved primarily through means other than the racial classifications.

IV

JUSTICE BREYER's dissent takes a different approach to these cases, one that fails to ground the result it would reach in law. Instead, it selectively relies on inapplicable precedent and even dicta while dismissing contrary holdings, alters and misapplies our well-established legal framework for assessing equal protection challenges to express racial classifications, and greatly exaggerates the consequences of today's decision.

To begin with, JUSTICE BREYER seeks to justify the plans at issue under our precedents recognizing the compelling interest in remedying past intentional discrimination. Not even the school districts go this far, and for good reason. The distinction between segregation by state action and racial imbalance caused by other factors has been central to our jurisprudence in this area for generations. The dissent elides this distinction between *de jure* and *de facto* segregation, casually intimates that Seattle's school attendance patterns reflect illegal segregation, and fails to credit the judicial determination—under the most rigorous standard—that Jefferson County had eliminated the vestiges of prior segregation. The dissent thus alters in fundamental ways not only the facts presented here but the established law.

* * *

At the same time it relies on inapplicable desegregation cases, misstatements of admitted dicta, and other noncontrolling pronouncements, JUSTICE BREYER's dissent candidly dismisses the significance of this Court's repeated *holdings* that all racial classifications must be reviewed under strict scrutiny, arguing that a different standard of review should be applied because the districts use race for beneficent rather than malicious purposes.

This Court has recently reiterated, however, that " '*all* racial classifications [imposed by government] . . . must be analyzed by a reviewing court under strict scrutiny.' " *Johnson*, 543 U.S., at 505 (quoting *Adarand*, 515 U.S., at 227; emphasis added by *Johnson* Court). JUSTICE BREYER nonetheless relies on the good intentions and motives of the school districts, stating that he has found "no case that . . . repudiated this constitutional asymmetry between that which seeks to *exclude* and that which seeks to *include* members of minority races." We have found many * * *.

This argument that different rules should govern racial classifications designed to include rather than exclude is not new; it has been repeatedly pressed in the past and has been repeatedly rejected.

* * * Accepting JUSTICE BREYER's approach would "do no more than move us from 'separate but equal' to 'unequal but benign.' " *Metro Broadcasting, supra*, at 638 (KENNEDY, J., dissenting).

* * *

* * * Simply because the school districts may seek a worthy goal does not mean they are free to discriminate on the basis of race to achieve it, or that their racial classifications should be subject to less exacting scrutiny.

* * *

* * * In *Brown v. Board of Education*, 347 U.S. 483 (1954) (*Brown I*), we held that segregation deprived black children of equal educational opportunities regardless of whether school facilities and other tangible factors were equal, because government classification and separation on grounds of race themselves denoted inferiority. It was not the inequality of the facilities but the fact of legally separating children on the basis of race on which the Court relied to find a constitutional violation in 1954. The next Term, we accordingly stated that "full compliance" with *Brown I* required school districts "to achieve a system of determining admission to the public schools on a *nonracial* basis." *Brown II*, 349 U.S., at 300–301 (emphasis added).

The parties and their *amici* debate which side is more faithful to the heritage of *Brown*, but the position of the plaintiffs in *Brown* was spelled out in their brief and could not have been clearer: "[T]he Fourteenth Amendment prevents states from according differential treatment to American children on the basis of their color or race." Brief for Appellants in Nos. 1, 2, and 4 and for Respondents in No. 10 on Reargument in *Brown I*, O.T.1953, p. 15 (Summary of Argument). What do the racial classifications at issue here do, if not accord differential treatment on the basis of race? * * *

Before *Brown*, schoolchildren were told where they could and could not go to school based on the color of their skin. The school districts in these cases have not carried the heavy burden of demonstrating that we should allow this once again—even for very different reasons. For schools that never segregated on the basis of race, such as Seattle, or that have removed the vestiges of past segregation, such as Jefferson County, the way "to achieve a system of determining admission to the public schools on a nonracial basis," *Brown II, supra*, at 300–301, is to stop assigning students on a racial basis. The way to stop discrimination on the basis of race is to stop discriminating on the basis of race.

The judgments of the Courts of Appeals for the Sixth and Ninth Circuits are reversed, and the cases are remanded for further proceedings.

It is so ordered.

■ JUSTICE THOMAS, concurring.

Today, the Court holds that state entities may not experiment with race-based means to achieve ends they deem socially desirable. I wholly concur in THE CHIEF JUSTICE's opinion. I write separately to address several of the contentions in JUSTICE BREYER's dissent * * *. Disfavoring a colorblind interpretation of the Constitution, the dissent would give school boards a free hand to make decisions on the basis of race—an approach reminiscent of that advocated by the segregationists in *Brown v. Board of Education*, 347 U.S. 483 (1954). This approach is just as wrong today as it was a half century ago. The Constitution and our cases require us to be much more demanding before permitting local school boards to make decisions based on race.

* * *

Racial imbalance is the failure of a school district's individual schools to match or approximate the demographic makeup of the student population at large. Racial imbalance is not segregation. Although presently observed racial imbalance might result from past *de jure* segregation, racial imbalance can also result from any number of innocent private decisions, including voluntary housing choices. Because racial imbalance is not inevitably linked to unconstitutional segregation, it is not unconstitutional in and of itself.

Although there is arguably a danger of racial imbalance in schools in Seattle and Louisville, there is no danger of resegregation. No one contends that Seattle has established or that Louisville has reestablished a dual school system that separates students on the basis of race * * *. To raise the specter of resegregation to defend these programs is to ignore the meaning of the word and the nature of the cases before us.

* * *

Despite the dissent's repeated intimation of a remedial purpose, neither of the programs in question qualifies as a permissible race-based remedial measure. Thus, the programs are subject to the general rule that government race-based decisionmaking is unconstitutional.

* * *

* * * The dissent asserts that racially balanced schools improve educational outcomes for black children. In support, the dissent unquestioningly cites certain social science research to support propositions that are hotly disputed among social scientists. In reality, it is far from apparent that coerced racial mixing has any educational benefits, much less that integration is necessary to black achievement.

Scholars have differing opinions as to whether educational benefits arise from racial balancing. Some have concluded that black students receive genuine educational benefits. See, *e.g.*, Crain & Mahard, Desegregation and Black Achievement: A Review of the Research, 42 Law & Contemp. Prob. 17, 48 (Summer 1978). Others have been more circumspect. See, e.g., Henderson, Greenberg, Schneider, Uribe, & Verdugo, High-Quality Schooling for African American Students, in Beyond Desegregation 162, 166 (M. Shujaa ed. 1996) ("Perhaps desegregation does not have a single effect, positive or negative, on the academic achievement of African American students, but rather some strategies help, some hurt, and still others make no difference whatsoever. It is clear to us that focusing simply on demographic issues detracts from focusing on improving schools"). And some have concluded that there are no demonstrable educational benefits. See, *e.g.*, Armor & Rossell, Desegregation and Resegregation in the Public Schools, in Beyond the Color Line: New Perspectives on Race and Ethnicity in America 219, 239, 251 (A. Thernstrom & S. Thernstrom eds.2002).

The *amicus* briefs in the cases before us mirror this divergence of opinion. Supporting the school boards, one *amicus* has assured us that "both early desegregation research and recent statistical and econometric analyses . . . indicate that there are positive effects on minority student achievement scores arising from diverse school settings." Brief for American Educational Research Association 10. Another brief claims that "school desegregation has a modest positive impact on the achievement of African-American students." App. to Brief for 553 Social Scientists as *Amici Curiae* 13–14 (footnote omitted). Yet neither of those briefs contains specific details like the magnitude of the claimed positive effects or the precise demographic mix at which those positive effects begin to be realized. Indeed, the social scientists' brief rather cautiously claims the existence of any benefit at all, describing the "positive impact" as "modest," *id.*, at 13, acknowledging that "there appears to be little or no effect on math scores," *id.*, at 14, and admitting that the "underlying reasons for these gains in achievement are not entirely clear," *id.*, at 15.11

Other *amici* dispute these findings. One *amicus* reports that "[i]n study after study, racial composition of a student body, when isolated, proves to be an insignificant determinant of student achievement." Brief for Dr. John Murphy et al. in No. 05–908, p. 8; see also *id.*, at 9 ("[T]here is no evidence that diversity in the K–12 classroom positively affects student achievement"). Another amicus surveys several social science studies and concludes that "a fair and comprehensive analysis of the research shows that there is no clear and consistent evidence of [educational] benefits." Brief for David J. Armor et al. 29.

* * *

Given this tenuous relationship between forced racial mixing and improved educational results for black children, the dissent cannot plausibly maintain that an educational element supports the integration interest, let alone makes it compelling.

* * *

Most of the dissent's criticisms of today's result can be traced to its rejection of the colorblind Constitution. The dissent attempts to marginalize the notion of a colorblind Constitution by consigning it to me and Members of today's plurality. But I am quite comfortable in the company I keep. My view of the Constitution is Justice Harlan's view in *Plessy*: "Our Constitution is color-blind, and neither knows nor tolerates classes among citizens." *Plessy v. Ferguson*, 163 U.S. 537, 559 (1896) (dissenting opinion). And my view was the rallying cry for the lawyers who litigated *Brown*. See, e.g., Brief for Appellants in Nos. 1, 2, and 4, and for Respondents in No. 10 on Reargument in *Brown v. Board of Education*, O.T.1953, p. 65 ("That the Constitution is color blind is our dedicated belief"); Brief for Appellants in *Brown v. Board of Education*, O.T.1952, No. 8, p. 5 ("The Fourteenth Amendment precludes a state from imposing distinctions or classifications based upon race and color alone").

The dissent appears to pin its interpretation of the Equal Protection Clause to current societal practice and expectations, deference to local officials, likely practical consequences, and reliance on previous statements from this and other courts. Such a view was ascendant in this Court's jurisprudence for several decades. It first appeared in *Plessy*, where the Court asked whether a state law providing for segregated railway cars was "a reasonable regulation." 163 U.S., at 550. The Court deferred to local authorities in making its determination, noting that in inquiring into reasonableness "there must necessarily be a large discretion on the part of the legislature." *Ibid.* The Court likewise paid heed to societal practices, local expectations, and practical consequences by looking to "the established usages, customs and traditions of the people, and with a view to the promotion of their comfort, and the preservation of the public peace and good order." *Ibid.* Guided by these principles, the Court concluded: "[W]e cannot say that a law which authorizes or even requires the separation of the two races in public conveyances is unreasonable, or more obnoxious to the Fourteenth Amendment than the acts of Congress requiring separate schools for colored children in the District of Columbia." *Id.*, at 550–551.

The segregationists in *Brown* embraced the arguments the Court endorsed in *Plessy*. Though *Brown* decisively rejected those arguments, today's dissent replicates them to a distressing extent. Thus, the dissent argues that "[e]ach plan embodies the results of local experience and community consultation." Similarly, the segregationists made repeated appeals to societal practice and expectation. See, e.g., Brief for Appellees on Reargument in *Briggs v. Elliott*, O.T.1953, No. 2, p. 76 ("[A] State has power to establish a school system which is capable of efficient administration, taking into account local problems and conditions"). The dissent argues that "weight [must be given] to a local school board's knowledge, expertise, and concerns," and with equal vigor, the segregationists argued for deference to local authorities. See, e.g., Brief for Kansas on Reargument in *Brown v. Board of Education*, O.T.1953, No. 1, p. 14 ("We advocate only a concept of constitutional law that permits determinations of state and local policy to be made on state and local levels. We defend only the validity of the statute that enables the Topeka Board of Education to determine its own course"). The dissent argues that today's decision "threatens to substitute for present calm a disruptive round of race-related litigation" and claims that today's decision "risks serious harm to the law and for the Nation." The segregationists also relied upon the likely practical consequences of ending the state-imposed system of racial separation. See, e.g., Brief for Appellees on Reargument in *Davis v. County School Board*, O.T.1953, No. 4, p. 37 ("Yet a holding that school segregation by race violates the Constitution will result in upheaval in all of those places not now subject to Federal judicial scrutiny. This Court has made many decisions of widespread effect; none would affect more people more directly in more fundamental interests and, in fact, cause more chaos in local government than a reversal of the decision in this case"). And foreshadowing today's dissent, the segregationists most heavily relied upon judicial precedent. See, e.g., Brief for Appellees on Reargument in *Briggs v. Elliott*, O.T.1953, No. 2, at 59 ("[I]t would be difficult indeed to find a case so favored by precedent as is the case for South Carolina here").

The similarities between the dissent's arguments and the segregationists' arguments do not stop there. Like the dissent, the segregationists repeatedly cautioned the Court to consider practicalities and not to embrace too theoretical a view of the Fourteenth Amendment. And just as the dissent argues that the need for these programs will lessen over time, the segregationists claimed that reliance on segregation was lessening and might eventually end.

What was wrong in 1954 cannot be right today. Whatever else the Court's rejection of the segregationists' arguments in *Brown* might have established, it certainly made clear that state and local governments cannot take from the Constitution a right to make decisions on the basis of race by adverse possession.

The fact that state and local governments had been discriminating on the basis of race for a long time was irrelevant to the *Brown* Court. The fact that racial discrimination was preferable to the relevant communities was irrelevant to the *Brown* Court. And the fact that the state and local governments had relied on statements in this Court's opinions was irrelevant to the *Brown* Court. The same principles guide today's decision. None of the considerations trumpeted by the dissent is relevant to the constitutionality of the school boards' race-based plans because no contextual detail—or collection of contextual details—can "provide refuge from the principle that under our Constitution, the government may not make distinctions on the basis of race." *Adarand,* 515 U.S., at 240 (THOMAS, J., concurring in part and concurring in judgment).

In place of the colorblind Constitution, the dissent would permit measures to keep the races together and proscribe measures to keep the races apart. Although no such distinction is apparent in the Fourteenth Amendment, the dissent would constitutionalize today's faddish social theories that embrace that distinction. The Constitution is not that malleable. Even if current social theories favor classroom racial engineering as necessary to "solve the problems at hand," the Constitution enshrines principles independent of social theories.

* * *

■ JUSTICE KENNEDY, concurring in part and concurring in the judgment.

The Nation's schools strive to teach that our strength comes from people of different races, creeds, and cultures uniting in commitment to the freedom of all. In these cases two school districts in different parts of the country seek to teach that principle by having classrooms that reflect the racial makeup of the surrounding community. That the school districts consider these plans to be necessary should remind us our highest aspirations are yet unfulfilled. But the solutions mandated by these school districts must themselves be lawful. To make race matter now so that it might not matter later may entrench the very prejudices we seek to overcome. In my view the state-mandated racial classifications at issue, official labels proclaiming the race of all persons in a broad class of citizens—elementary school students in one case, high school students in another—are unconstitutional as the cases now come to us.

* * *

* * * I do not join Parts III-B and IV. Diversity, depending on its meaning and definition, is a compelling educational goal a school district may pursue.

* * * The government bears the burden of justifying its use of individual racial classifications. As part of that burden it must establish, in detail, how decisions based on an individual student's race are made in a challenged governmental program. The Jefferson County Board of Education fails to meet this threshold mandate.

* * *

As for the Seattle case, the school district has gone further in describing the methods and criteria used to determine assignment decisions on the basis of individual racial classifications. The district, nevertheless, has failed to make an adequate showing in at least one respect. It has failed to explain why, in a district composed of a diversity of races, with fewer than half of the students classified as "white," it has employed the crude racial categories of "white" and "non-white" as the basis for its assignment decisions.

* * * As the district fails to account for the classification system it has chosen, despite what appears to be its ill fit, Seattle has not shown its plan to be narrowly tailored to achieve its own ends; and thus it fails to pass strict scrutiny.

Our Nation from the inception has sought to preserve and expand the promise of liberty and equality on which it was founded. Today we enjoy a society that is remarkable in its openness and opportunity. Yet our tradition is to go beyond present achievements, however significant, and to recognize and confront the flaws and injustices that remain. This is especially true when we seek assurance that opportunity is not denied on account of race. The enduring hope is that race should not matter; the reality is that too often it does.

This is by way of preface to my respectful submission that parts of the opinion by THE CHIEF JUSTICE imply an all-too-unyielding insistence that race cannot be a factor in instances when, in my view, it may be taken into account. The plurality opinion is too dismissive of the legitimate interest government has in ensuring all people have equal opportunity regardless of their race. The plurality's postulate that "[t]he way to stop discrimination on the basis of race is to stop discriminating on the basis of race," is not sufficient to decide these cases. Fifty years of experience since *Brown v. Board of Education*, 347 U.S. 483 (1954), should teach us that the problem before us defies so easy a solution. School districts can seek to reach *Brown's* objective of equal educational opportunity. The plurality opinion is at least open to the interpretation that the Constitution requires school districts to ignore the problem of *de facto* resegregation in schooling. I cannot endorse that conclusion. To the extent the plurality opinion suggests the Constitution mandates that state and local school authorities must accept the status quo of racial isolation in schools, it is, in my view, profoundly mistaken.

The statement by Justice Harlan that "[o]ur Constitution is color-blind" was most certainly justified in the context of his dissent in *Plessy v. Ferguson*, 163 U.S. 537, 559 (1896). The Court's decision in that case was a grievous error it took far too long to overrule. *Plessy*, of course, concerned official classification by race applicable to all persons who sought to use railway carriages. And, as an aspiration, Justice Harlan's axiom must command our assent. In the real world, it is regrettable to say, it cannot be a universal constitutional principle.

* * *

Each respondent has asserted that its assignment of individual students by race is permissible because there is no other way to avoid racial isolation in the school districts. Yet, as explained, each has failed to provide the support necessary for that proposition. And individual racial classifications employed in this manner may be considered legitimate only if they are a last resort to achieve a compelling interest.

* * *

The dissent rests on the assumptions that these sweeping race-based classifications of persons are permitted by existing precedents; that its confident endorsement of race categories for each child in a large segment of the community presents no danger to individual freedom in other, prospective realms of governmental regulation; and that the racial classifications used here cause no hurt or anger of the type the Constitution prevents. Each of these premises is, in my respectful view, incorrect.

* * *

This Nation has a moral and ethical obligation to fulfill its historic commitment to creating an integrated society that ensures equal opportunity for all of its children. A compelling interest exists in avoiding racial isolation, an interest that a school district, in its discretion and expertise, may choose to pursue. Likewise, a district may consider it a compelling interest to achieve a diverse student population. Race may be one component of that diversity, but other demographic factors, plus special talents and needs, should also be considered. What the government is not permitted to do, absent a showing of necessity not made here, is to classify every student on the basis of race and to assign each of them to schools based on that classification. Crude measures of this sort threaten to reduce children to racial chits valued and traded according to one school's supply and another's demand.

That statement, to be sure, invites this response: A sense of stigma may already become the fate of those separated out by circumstances beyond their immediate control. But to this the replication must be: Even so, measures other than differential treatment based on racial typing of individuals first must be exhausted.

The decision today should not prevent school districts from continuing the important work of bringing together students of different racial, ethnic, and economic backgrounds. Due to a variety of factors—some influenced by government, some not—neighborhoods in our communities do not reflect the diversity of our Nation as a whole. Those entrusted with directing our public schools can bring to bear the creativity of experts, parents, administrators, and other concerned citizens to find a way to achieve the compelling interests they face without resorting to widespread governmental allocation of benefits and burdens on the basis of racial classifications.

With this explanation I concur in the judgment of the Court.

■ JUSTICE STEVENS, dissenting.

While I join JUSTICE BREYER's eloquent and unanswerable dissent in its entirety, it is appropriate to add these words.

There is a cruel irony in THE CHIEF JUSTICE's reliance on our decision in *Brown v. Board of Education*, 349 U.S. 294 (1955). The first sentence in the concluding paragraph of his opinion states: "Before *Brown*, schoolchildren were told where they could and could not go to school based on the color of their skin." This sentence reminds me of Anatole France's observation: "[T]he majestic equality of the la[w], . . . forbid[s] rich and poor alike to sleep under the bridges, to beg in the streets, and to steal their bread." THE CHIEF JUSTICE fails to note that it was only black schoolchildren who were so ordered; indeed, the history books do not tell stories of white children struggling to attend black schools * * *.

■ JUSTICE BREYER, with whom JUSTICE STEVENS, JUSTICE SOUTER, and JUSTICE GINSBURG join, dissenting.

These cases consider the longstanding efforts of two local school boards to integrate their public schools. The school board plans before us resemble many others adopted in the last 50 years by primary and secondary schools throughout the Nation. All of those plans represent local efforts to bring about the kind of racially integrated education that *Brown v. Board of Education*, 347 U.S. 483 (1954), long ago promised—efforts that this Court has repeatedly required, permitted, and encouraged local authorities to undertake. This Court has recognized that the public interests at stake in such cases are "compelling." We have approved of "narrowly tailored" plans that are no less race conscious than the plans before us. And we have understood that the Constitution *permits* local communities to adopt desegregation plans even where it does not *require* them to do so.

The plurality pays inadequate attention to this law, to past opinions' rationales, their language, and the contexts in which they arise. As a result, it reverses course and reaches the wrong conclusion. In doing so, it distorts precedent, it misapplies the relevant constitutional principles, it announces legal rules that will obstruct efforts by state and local governments to deal effectively with the growing resegregation of public schools, it threatens to substitute for present calm a disruptive round of race-related litigation, and it undermines *Brown's* promise of integrated primary and secondary education that local communities have sought to make a reality. This cannot be justified in the name of the Equal Protection Clause.

* * *

I * * * highlight three important features of these cases. First, the school districts' plans serve "compelling interests" and are "narrowly tailored" on any reasonable definition of those terms. Second, the distinction between *de jure* segregation (caused by school systems) and *de facto* segregation (caused, *e.g.*, by housing patterns or generalized societal discrimination) is meaningless in the present context, thereby dooming the plurality's endeavor to find support for its views in that distinction. Third, real-world efforts to substitute racially diverse for racially segregated schools (however caused) are complex, to the point where the Constitution cannot plausibly be interpreted to rule out categorically all local efforts to use means that are "conscious" of the race of individuals.

In both Seattle and Louisville, the local school districts began with schools that were highly segregated in fact. In both cities, plaintiffs filed lawsuits claiming unconstitutional segregation. In Louisville, a Federal District Court found that school segregation reflected pre-*Brown* state laws separating the races. In Seattle, the plaintiffs alleged that school segregation unconstitutionally reflected not only generalized societal discrimination and residential housing patterns, but also *school board policies and actions* that had helped to create, maintain, and aggravate racial segregation. In Louisville, a federal court entered a remedial decree. In Seattle, the parties settled after the school district pledged to undertake a desegregation plan. In both cities, the school boards adopted plans designed to achieve integration by bringing about more racially diverse schools. In each city, the school board modified its plan several times in light of, for example, hostility to busing, the threat of resegregation, and the desirability of introducing greater student choice. And in each city, the school boards' plans have evolved over time in ways that progressively *diminish* the plans' use of explicit race-conscious criteria.

* * *

Both districts sought greater racial integration for educational and democratic, as well as for remedial, reasons. Both sought to achieve these objectives while preserving their commitment to other educational goals, *e.g.*, district-wide commitment to high quality public schools, increased pupil assignment to neighborhood schools, diminished use of busing, greater student choice, reduced risk of white flight, and so forth. Consequently, the present plans expand student choice; they limit the burdens (including busing) that earlier plans had imposed upon students and their families; and they use race-conscious criteria in limited and gradually diminishing ways. In particular, they use race-conscious criteria only to mark the outer bounds of broad population-related ranges.

* * *

* * * The [school] boards work in communities where demographic patterns change, where they must meet traditional learning goals, where they must attract and retain effective teachers, where they should (and will) take account of parents' views and maintain *their* commitment to public school education, where they must adapt to court intervention, where they must encourage voluntary student and parent action—where they will find that their own good faith, their knowledge, and their understanding of local circumstances are always necessary but often insufficient to solve the problems at hand.

These facts and circumstances help explain why in this context, as to means, the law often leaves legislatures, city councils, school boards, and voters with a broad range of choice, thereby giving "different communities" the opportunity to "try different solutions to common problems and gravitate toward those that prove most successful or seem to them best to suit their individual needs."

* * *

A longstanding and unbroken line of legal authority tells us that the Equal Protection Clause permits local school boards to use race-conscious criteria to achieve positive race-related goals, even when the Constitution does not compel it * * *.

* * *

Courts are not alone in accepting as constitutionally valid the legal principle * * * that the government may voluntarily adopt race-conscious measures to improve conditions of race even when it is not under a constitutional obligation to do so. That principle has been accepted by every branch of government and is rooted in the history of the Equal Protection Clause itself. Thus, Congress has enacted numerous race-conscious statutes that illustrate that principle or rely upon its validity. See, *e.g.*, No Child Left Behind Act of 2001, 20 U.S.C. § 6311(b)(2)(C)(v) (2000 ed., Supp. IV); § 1067 *et seq.* (authorizing aid to minority institutions). In fact, without being exhaustive, I have counted 51 federal statutes that use racial classifications. I have counted well over 100 state statutes that similarly employ racial classifications. Presidential administrations for the past half century have used and supported various race-conscious measures. See, *e.g.*, Exec. Order No. 10925, 26 Fed.Reg.1977 (1961) (President Kennedy); Exec. Order No. 11246, 30 Fed.Reg. 12319 (1965) (President Johnson); Sugrue, Breaking Through: The Troubled Origins of Affirmative Action in the Workplace, in Color Lines: Affirmative Action, Immigration, and Civil Rights Options for America 31 (J. Skrentny ed.2001) (describing President Nixon's lobbying for affirmative action plans, *e.g.*, the Philadelphia Plan); White, Affirmative Action's Alamo: Gerald Ford Returns to Fight Once More for Michigan, Time, Aug. 23, 1999, p. 48 (reporting on President Ford's support for affirmative action); Schuck, Affirmative Action: Past, Present, and Future, 20 Yale L. & Pol'y Rev. 1, 50 (2002) (describing President Carter's support for affirmation action). And during the same time, hundreds of local school districts have adopted student assignment plans that use race-conscious criteria.

That [principle] * * * is predicated upon a well-established legal view of the Fourteenth Amendment. That view understands the basic objective of those who wrote the Equal Protection Clause as forbidding practices that lead to racial exclusion. The Amendment sought to bring into American society as full members those whom the Nation had previously held in slavery.

There is reason to believe that those who drafted an Amendment with this basic purpose in mind would have understood the legal and practical difference between the use of race-conscious criteria in defiance of that purpose, namely to keep the races apart, and the use of race-conscious criteria to further that purpose, namely to bring the races together. Although the Constitution almost always forbids the former, it is significantly more lenient in respect to the latter.

* * * I can find no case in which this Court has followed JUSTICE THOMAS's "color-blind" approach. And I have found no case that otherwise repudiated this constitutional asymmetry between that which seeks to *exclude* and that which seeks to *include* members of minority races.

* * *

* * * [A]s *Grutter* specified, "[c]ontext matters when reviewing race-based governmental action under the Equal Protection Clause." 539 U.S., at 327. And contexts differ dramatically one from the other. Governmental use of race-based criteria can arise in the context of, for example, census forms, research expenditures for diseases, assignments of police officers patrolling predominantly minority-race neighborhoods, efforts to desegregate racially segregated schools, policies that favor minorities when distributing goods or services in short supply, actions that create majority-minority electoral districts, peremptory strikes that remove potential jurors on the basis of race, and others. Given the significant differences among these contexts, it would be surprising if the law required an identically strict legal test for evaluating the constitutionality of race-based criteria as to each of them.

Here, the context is one in which school districts seek to advance or to maintain racial integration in primary and secondary schools. It is a context * * * where history has required special administrative remedies. And it is a context in which the school boards' plans simply set race-conscious limits at the outer boundaries of a broad range.

This context is *not* a context that involves the use of race to decide who will receive goods or services that are normally distributed on the basis of merit and which are in short supply. It is not one in which race-conscious limits stigmatize or exclude; the limits at issue do not pit the races against each other or otherwise significantly exacerbate racial tensions. They do not impose burdens unfairly upon members of one race alone but instead seek benefits for members of all races alike. The context here is one of racial limits that seek, not to keep the races apart, but to bring them together.

* * *

If one examines the context more specifically, one finds that the districts' plans reflect efforts to overcome a history of segregation, embody the results of broad experience and community consultation, seek to expand student choice while reducing the need for mandatory busing, and use race-conscious criteria in highly limited ways that diminish the use of race compared to preceding integration efforts * * *. In a word, the school plans under review do not involve the kind of race-based harm that has led this Court, in other contexts, to find the use of race-conscious criteria unconstitutional.

* * *

In my view, this contextual approach to scrutiny is altogether fitting. I believe that the law requires application here of a standard of review that is not "strict" in the traditional sense of that word, although it does require the careful review I have just described * * *.

* * *

The principal interest advanced in these cases to justify the use of race-based criteria goes by various names. Sometimes a court refers to it as an interest in achieving racial "diversity." Other times a court, like the plurality here, refers to it as an interest in racial "balancing." I have used more general terms to signify that interest, describing it, for example, as an interest in promoting or preserving greater racial "integration" of public schools. By this term, I mean the school districts' interest in eliminating school-by-school racial isolation and increasing the degree to which racial mixture characterizes each of the district's schools and each individual student's public school experience.

Regardless of its name, however, the interest at stake possesses three essential elements. First, there is a historical and remedial element: an interest in setting right the consequences of prior conditions of segregation. This refers back to a time when public schools were highly segregated, often as a result of legal or administrative policies that facilitated racial segregation in public schools. It is an interest in continuing to combat the remnants of segregation caused in whole or in part by these school-related policies, which have often affected not only schools, but also housing patterns, employment practices, economic conditions, and social attitudes. It is an interest in maintaining hard-won gains. And it has its roots in preventing what gradually may become the *de facto* resegregation of America's public schools.

Second, there is an educational element: an interest in overcoming the adverse educational effects produced by and associated with highly segregated schools. Studies suggest that children taken from those schools and placed in integrated settings often show positive academic gains. See, *e.g.*, Powell, Living and Learning: Linking Housing and Education, in Pursuit of a Dream Deferred: Linking Housing and Education Policy 15, 35 (J. Powell, G. Kearney, & V. Kay eds.2001) (hereinafter Powell); Hallinan, Diversity Effects on Student Outcomes: Social Science Evidence, 59 Ohio St. L.J. 733, 741–742 (1998) (hereinafter Hallinan).

Other studies reach different conclusions. But the evidence supporting an educational interest in racially integrated schools is well established and strong enough to permit a democratically elected school board reasonably to determine that this interest is a compelling one.

Research suggests, for example, that black children from segregated educational environments significantly increase their achievement levels once they are placed in a more integrated setting * * *.

One commentator, reviewing dozens of studies of the educational benefits of desegregated schooling, found that the studies have provided "remarkably consistent" results, showing that: (1) black students' educational achievement is improved in integrated schools as compared to racially isolated schools, (2) black students' educational achievement is improved in integrated classes, and (3) the earlier that black students are removed from racial isolation, the better their educational outcomes. See Hallinan 741–742. Multiple studies also indicate that black alumni of integrated schools are more likely to move into occupations traditionally closed to African-Americans, and to earn more money in those fields. See, *e.g.*, Schofield, Review of Research on School Desegregation's Impact on Elementary and Secondary School Students, in Handbook of Research on Multicultural Education 597, 606–607 (J. Banks & C. Banks eds.1995). Cf. W. Bowen & D. Bok, The Shape of the River 118 (1998) (hereinafter Bowen & Bok).

Third, there is a democratic element: an interest in producing an educational environment that reflects the "pluralistic society" in which our children will live. It is an interest in helping our children learn to work and play together with children of different racial backgrounds. It is an interest in teaching children to engage in the kind of cooperation among Americans of all races that is necessary to make a land of 300 million people one Nation.

Again, data support this insight. See, *e.g.*, Hallinan 745; Quillian & Campbell, Beyond Black and White: The Present and Future of Multiracial Friendship Segregation, 68 Am. Sociological Rev. 540, 541 (2003) (hereinafter Quillian & Campbell); Dawkins & Braddock, The Continuing Significance of Desegregation: School Racial Composition and African American Inclusion in American Society, 63 J. Negro Educ. 394, 401–403 (1994) (hereinafter Dawkins & Braddock); Wells & Crain, Perpetuation Theory and the Long-Term Effects of School Desegregation, 64 Rev. Educ. Research 531, 550 (1994) (hereinafter Wells & Crain).

There are again studies that offer contrary conclusions. See, *e.g.*, Schofield, School Desegregation and Intergroup Relations: A Review of the Literature, in 17 Review of Research in Education 335, 356 (G. Grant ed.1991). Again, however, the evidence supporting a democratic interest in racially integrated schools is firmly established and sufficiently strong to permit a school board to determine, as this Court has itself often found, that this interest is compelling.

* * *

The opinions cited by the plurality to justify its reliance upon the *de jure/de facto* distinction only address what remedial measures a school district may be constitutionally *required* to undertake. As to what is *permitted*, nothing in our equal protection law suggests that a State may right only those wrongs that it committed. No case of this Court has ever relied upon the *de jure/de facto* distinction in order to limit what a school district is voluntarily allowed to do. That is what is at issue here * * *.

* * *

The school boards' widespread consultation, their experimentation with numerous other plans, indeed, the 40-year history that Part I sets forth, make clear that plans that are less explicitly race-based are unlikely to achieve the boards' "compelling" objectives. The history of each school system reveals highly segregated schools, followed by remedial plans that involved forced busing, followed by efforts to attract or retain students through the use of plans that abandoned busing and replaced it with greater student choice. Both cities once tried to achieve more integrated schools by relying solely upon measures such as redrawn district boundaries, new school building construction, and unrestricted voluntary transfers. In neither city did these prior attempts prove sufficient to achieve the city's integration goals.

Moreover, giving some degree of weight to a local school board's knowledge, expertise, and concerns in these particular matters is not inconsistent with rigorous judicial scrutiny. It simply recognizes that judges are not well suited to act as school administrators * * *.

* * *

The Founders meant the Constitution as a practical document that would transmit its basic values to future generations through principles that remained workable over time. Hence it is important to consider the potential consequences of the plurality's approach, as measured against the Constitution's objectives. To do so provides further reason to believe that the plurality's approach is legally unsound.

* * *

* * * *[D]e facto* resegregation is on the rise. It is reasonable to conclude that such resegregation can create serious educational, social, and civic problems. Given the conditions in which school boards work to set policy, they may need all of the means presently at their disposal to combat those problems. Yet the plurality would deprive them of at least one tool that some districts now consider vital—the limited use of broad race-conscious student population ranges.

* * *

Indeed, the consequences of the approach the Court takes today are serious. Yesterday, the plans under review were lawful. Today, they are not. Yesterday, the citizens of this Nation could look for guidance to this Court's unanimous pronouncements concerning desegregation. Today, they cannot. Yesterday, school boards had available to them a full range of means to combat segregated schools. Today, they do not.

* * *

And what of respect for democratic local decisionmaking by States and school boards? * * *

And what of law's concern to diminish and peacefully settle conflict among the Nation's people? * * *

And what of the long history and moral vision that the Fourteenth Amendment itself embodies? The plurality cites in support those who argued in *Brown* against segregation, and JUSTICE THOMAS likens the approach that I have taken to that of segregation's defenders. But segregation policies did not simply tell schoolchildren "where they could and could not go to school based on the color of their skin," they perpetuated a caste system rooted in the institutions of slavery and 80 years of legalized subordination. The lesson of history is not that efforts to continue racial segregation are constitutionally indistinguishable from efforts to achieve racial integration. Indeed, it is a cruel distortion of history to compare Topeka, Kansas, in the 1950's to Louisville and Seattle in the modern day—to equate the plight of Linda Brown (who was ordered to attend a Jim Crow school) to the circumstances of Joshua McDonald (whose request to transfer to a school closer to home was initially declined). This is not to deny that there is a cost in applying "a state-mandated racial label." But that cost does not approach, in degree or in kind, the terrible harms of slavery, the resulting caste system, and 80 years of legal racial segregation.

Finally, what of the hope and promise of *Brown*? For much of this Nation's history, the races remained divided. It was not long ago that people of different races drank from separate fountains, rode on separate buses, and studied in separate schools. In this Court's finest hour, *Brown v. Board of Education* challenged this history and helped to change it. For *Brown* held out a promise. It was a promise embodied in three Amendments designed to make citizens of slaves. It was the promise of true racial equality—not as a matter of fine words on paper, but as a matter of everyday life in the Nation's cities and schools. It was about the nature of a democracy that must work for all Americans. It sought one law, one Nation, one people, not simply as a matter of legal principle but in terms of how we actually live.

Not everyone welcomed this Court's decision in *Brown*. Three years after that decision was handed down, the Governor of Arkansas ordered state militia to block the doors of a white schoolhouse so that black children could not enter. The President of the United States dispatched the 101st Airborne Division to Little Rock, Arkansas, and federal troops were needed to enforce a desegregation decree. See *Cooper v. Aaron*, 358 U.S. 1 (1958). Today, almost 50 years later, attitudes toward race in this Nation have changed dramatically. Many parents, white and black alike, want their children to attend schools with children of different races. Indeed, the very school districts that once spurned integration now strive for it. The long history of their efforts reveals the complexities and difficulties they have faced. And in light of those challenges, they have asked us not to take from their hands the instruments they have used to rid their schools of racial segregation, instruments that they believe are needed to overcome the problems of cities divided by race and poverty. The plurality would decline their modest request.

The plurality is wrong to do so. The last half century has witnessed great strides toward racial equality, but we have not yet realized the promise of *Brown*. To invalidate the plans under review is to threaten the promise of *Brown*. The plurality's position, I fear, would break that promise. This is a decision that the Court and the Nation will come to regret.

I must dissent.

NOTES AND QUESTIONS

1. When Justice Thomas calls for government to be colorblind, does he really mean it? Consider the facts in *Johnson v. California*, 543 U.S. 499 (2005):

> The California Department of Corrections (CDC) has an unwritten policy of racially segregating prisoners in double cells in reception centers for up to 60 days each time they enter a new correctional facility * * *.
>
> CDC institutions house all new male inmates and all male inmates transferred from other state facilities in reception centers for up to 60 days upon their arrival. During that time, prison officials evaluate the inmates to determine their ultimate placement. Double-cell assignments in the reception centers are based on a number of factors, predominantly race. In fact, the CDC has admitted that the chances of an inmate being assigned a cellmate of another race are " '[p]retty close' " to zero percent. App. to Pet. for Cert. 3a. The CDC further subdivides prisoners within each racial group. Thus, Japanese-

> Americans are housed separately from Chinese-Americans, and northern California Hispanics are separated from southern California Hispanics.
>
> The CDC's asserted rationale for this practice is that it is necessary to prevent violence caused by racial gangs. It cites numerous incidents of racial violence in CDC facilities and identifies five major prison gangs in the State: Mexican Mafia, Nuestra Familia, Black Guerilla Family, Aryan Brotherhood, and Nazi Low Riders. The CDC also notes that prison-gang culture is violent and murderous. An associate warden testified that if race were not considered in making initial housing assignments, she is certain there would be racial conflict in the cells and in the yard. Other prison officials also expressed their belief that violence and conflict would result if prisoners were not segregated. The CDC claims that it must therefore segregate all inmates while it determines whether they pose a danger to others.
>
> With the exception of the double cells in reception areas, the rest of the state prison facilities—dining areas, yards, and cells—are fully integrated. After the initial 60-day period, prisoners are allowed to choose their own cellmates. The CDC usually grants inmate requests to be housed together, unless there are security reasons for denying them.

543 U.S. at 502–03. Is that racial classification permissible? The Court held that the practice must be subject to strict scrutiny, rather than the rational basis standard normally applied to prison regulations, and it remanded for consideration of the case under that standard. Justice Thomas dissented:

> The Constitution has always demanded less within the prison walls. Time and again, even when faced with constitutional rights no less "fundamental" than the right to be free from state-sponsored racial discrimination, we have deferred to the reasonable judgments of officials experienced in running this Nation's prisons. There is good reason for such deference in this case. California oversees roughly 160,000 inmates in prisons that have been a breeding ground for some of the most violent prison gangs in America—all of them organized along racial lines. In that atmosphere, California racially segregates a portion of its inmates, in a part of its prisons, for brief periods of up to 60 days, until the State can arrange permanent housing. The majority is concerned with sparing inmates the indignity and stigma of racial discrimination. California is concerned with their safety and saving their lives. I respectfully dissent.

Id. at 524 (Thomas, J., dissenting). Is that inconsistent with his position in *Parents Involved*?

2. Strict scrutiny, as applied in this case and in *Adarand*, is not the same thing as colorblindness. Under strict scrutiny, the government can take race into account in decisionmaking if there is no other feasible way to achieve a compelling governmental goal; the standard phrase is "narrowly tailored measures that further compelling governmental interests." *Adarand*, 515 U.S. at 227. Did the justices in *Parents Involved* disagree about what counts as a compelling interest, whether the school district measures were narrowly tailored, whether strict scrutiny was the appropriate standard of review, or all three? Given that standard of review, is it at all surprising that the Court often decides affirmative action cases by sharply divided votes—and often with no majority opinion?

3. Every single opinion in *Parents Involved* tries to claim the legacy of *Brown v. Board of Education*. Does any of them succeed? Is there such a thing as "the" legacy of *Brown*, or is it wholly in the eye of the beholder?

[Assignment 63]

IX. SEX AND GENDER DISCRIMINATION

We saw in the Introduction the critical importance of the Declaration of Independence and its statement that all men are created equal and have certain inherent and inalienable rights. President Abraham Lincoln reiterated the importance of the Declaration of Independence when he said in the Gettysburg Address:

> Four score and seven years ago our fathers brought forth on this continent, a new nation, conceived in Liberty, and dedicated to the proposition that all men are created equal.
>
> Now we are engaged in a great civil war, testing whether that nation, or any nation so conceived and so dedicated, can long endure.

When the Declaration spoke of "men" and Lincoln spoke of "fathers," were those generic terms, or were the promises of liberty that they conveyed genuinely sex-specific? That question was raised in the following remarkable document, issued more than a decade before President Lincoln's address, which once again shows the centrality of the Declaration of Independence to American constitutional law.

In 1848, a historic assembly of women gathered in Seneca Falls, New York, the home of Elizabeth Cady Stanton. Stanton organized the Seneca Falls Convention with Lucretia Mott, who, like her, had been excluded from the World Anti-Slavery Convention in London eight years earlier. Together, they wrote and published in 1848, the historic document below. These two advocates of women's suffrage were close allies of Frederick Douglass, William Lloyd Garrison, and the other advocates of the abolition of slavery. Douglass attended the Seneca Falls Convention. We reproduce this document here because it is highly relevant to the next Privileges or Immunities Clause case.

A. THE SENECA FALLS DECLARATION OF SENTIMENTS

By Elizabeth Cady Stanton and Lucretia Mott

When, in the course of human events, it becomes necessary for one portion of the family of man to assume among the people of the earth a position different from that which they have hitherto occupied, but one to which the laws of nature and of nature's God entitle them, a decent respect to the opinions of mankind requires that they should declare the causes that impel them to such a course.

We hold these truths to be self-evident; that all men and women are created equal; that they are endowed by their Creator with certain inalienable rights; that among these are life, liberty, and the pursuit of happiness; that to secure these rights governments are instituted, deriving their just powers from the consent of the governed. Whenever any form of government becomes destructive of these ends, it is the right of those who suffer from it to refuse allegiance to it, and to insist upon the institution of a new government, laying its foundation on such principles, and organizing its powers in such form, as to them shall seem most likely to effect their safety and happiness. Prudence, indeed, will dictate that governments long established should not be changed for light and transient causes; and, accordingly, all experience hath shown that mankind are more disposed to suffer, while evils are sufferable, than to right themselves by abolishing the forms to which they were accustomed. But when a long train of abuses and usurpations, pursuing invariably the same object, evinces a design to reduce them under absolute despotism, it is their duty to throw off such government, and to provide new guards for their future security. Such has been the patient sufferance of the women under this government, and such is now the necessity which constrains them to demand the equal station to which they are entitled.

The history of mankind is a history of repeated injuries and usurpations on the part of man toward woman, having in direct object the establishment of an absolute tyranny over her. To prove this, let facts be submitted to a candid world.

He has never permitted her to exercise her inalienable right to the elective franchise.

He has compelled her to submit to laws, in the formation of which she had no voice.

He has withheld from her rights which are given to the most ignorant and degraded men—both natives and foreigners.

Having deprived her of this first right as a citizen, the elective franchise, thereby leaving her without representation in the halls of legislation, he has oppressed her on all sides.

He has made her, if married, in the eye of the law, civilly dead.

He has taken from her all right in property, even to the wages she earns.

He has made her morally, an irresponsible being, as she can commit many crimes with impunity, provided they be done in the presence of her husband. In the covenant of marriage, she is compelled to promise obedience to her husband, he becoming, to all intents and purposes, her master—the law giving him power to deprive her of her liberty, and to administer chastisement.

He has so framed the laws of divorce, as to what shall be the proper causes of divorce, in case of separation, to whom the guardianship of the children shall be given; as to be wholly regardless of the happiness of the women—the law, in all cases, going upon a false supposition of the supremacy of man, and giving all power into his hands.

After depriving her of all rights as a married woman, if single and the owner of property, he has taxed her to support a government which recognizes her only when her property can be made profitable to it.

He has monopolized nearly all the profitable employments, and from those she is permitted to follow, she receives but a scanty remuneration.

He closes against her all the avenues to wealth and distinction, which he considers most honorable to himself. As a teacher of theology, medicine, or law, she is not known.

He has denied her the facilities for obtaining a thorough education—all colleges being closed against her.

He allows her in church, as well as State, but a subordinate position, claiming Apostolic authority for her exclusion from the ministry, and, with some exceptions, from any public participation in the affairs of the Church.

He has created a false public sentiment by giving to the world a different code of morals for men and women, by which moral delinquencies which exclude women from society, are not only tolerated but deemed of little account in man.

He has usurped the prerogative of Jehovah himself, claiming it as his right to assign for her a sphere of action, when that belongs to her conscience and her God.

He has endeavored, in every way that he could to destroy her confidence in her own powers, to lessen her self-respect, and to make her willing to lead a dependent and abject life.

Now, in view of this entire disfranchisement of one-half the people of this country, their social and religious degradation,—in view of the unjust laws above mentioned, and because women do feel themselves aggrieved, oppressed, and fraudulently deprived of their most sacred rights, we insist that they have immediate admission to all the rights and privileges which belong to them as citizens of these United States.

In entering upon the great work before us, we anticipate no small amount of misconception, misrepresentation, and ridicule; but we shall use every instrumentality within our power to effect our object. We shall employ agents, circulate tracts, petition the State and national Legislatures, and endeavor to enlist the pulpit and the press in our behalf. We hope this Convention will be followed by a series of Conventions, embracing every part of the country.

Firmly relying upon the final triumph of the Right and the True, we do this day affix our signatures to this declaration.

NOTES AND QUESTIONS

1. This historic document explains some of the many ways in which women were legally oppressed until they first got the right to vote in 1920 and then, in modern times, received a greater equality of rights with men. On women's voting rights, *see infra* pages 1379–1380, 1736–1739.

2. Ever since the Enlightenment, leading political theorists had begun to argue that women ought to have the same rights as men. In 1791, Olympe de Gouges wrote a document entitled: "Declaration of the Rights of Women and of the Female Citizen," which meticulously paralleled the "Declaration of the Rights of Man and of the Citizen" written by the Marquis de Lafayette in 1789 and which drew on the original American state Declarations of Rights. Olympe de Gouges was one of only three women executed during the reign of terror in revolutionary France.

B. WOMEN AND THE FOURTEENTH AMENDMENT (1868)

From the 1830s through the 1860s, the abolitionists and the advocates of women's rights had supported one another. This alliance persisted but was put under much strain when the Fourteenth Amendment was proposed and adopted. The Framers of the Fourteenth Amendment wanted to accomplish two inconsistent goals. First, they wanted to protect the civil rights of African-Americans and of women. Second, they wanted to penalize States which denied African-American men the right to vote, but they were not ready yet to give women the right to vote. This history is well documented in Nina Morais, *Sex Discrimination and the Fourteenth Amendment: Lost History*, 97 YALE L. J. 1153 (1988); Sandra Rierson, *Race and*

Gender Discrimination: A Historical Case for Equal Treatment Under the Fourteenth Amendment, 1 DUKE J. OF GENDER LAW & POL'Y 89 (1994).

To accomplish these twin goals the Framers of the Fourteenth Amendment wrote Section 1 of the amendment to apply to all persons—white and black, male and female—who were born or naturalized in the United States. All these persons—white and black, male and female—were citizens of the United States and the State wherein they resided, and they were entitled to "the privileges or immunities of citizens of the United States." U.S. citizens and non-citizens—white and black, male and female—were in addition persons protected by the Due Process of Law and Equal Protection Clauses. But Section 2 of the Fourteenth Amendment conspicuously used the word "male" with respect to voting rights. Please read again closely the text of Sections 1 and 2 (our emphasis added) and note how the word "male" appears in Section 2 but not in Section 1:

> Section 1. All persons born or naturalized in the United States, and subject to the jurisdiction thereof, are citizens of the United States and of the state wherein they reside. No state shall make or enforce any law which shall abridge the privileges or immunities of citizens of the United States; nor shall any state deprive any person of life, liberty, or property, without due process of law; nor deny to any person within its jurisdiction the equal protection of the laws.
>
> Section 2. Representatives shall be apportioned among the several states according to their respective numbers, counting the whole number of persons in each state, excluding Indians not taxed. But when the right to vote at any election for the choice of electors for President and Vice President of the United States, Representatives in Congress, the executive and judicial officers of a state, or the members of the legislature thereof, is denied to any of the *male* inhabitants of such state, being twenty-one years of age, and citizens of the United States, or in any way abridged, except for participation in rebellion, or other crime, the basis of representation therein shall be reduced in the proportion which the number of such male citizens shall bear to the whole number of *male* citizens twenty-one years of age in such state.

It is crystal clear that the Framers of the Fourteenth Amendment knew how to give civil rights to every adult citizen. It is crystal clear that they were not granting voting rights to women. As Nina Morais says:

> * * * By January of 1866, more than 10,000 supporters of women's rights had written to their Congressmen to protest the Fourteenth Amendment's second section * * *. This paper deluge was then followed by 'interviews with Congressmen, begging them to heed the petitions which were pouring in . . . .'
>
> * * * Petitions protesting the Amendment's second section were presented on the floor of Congress at least five times in January and February of 1866. On one occasion, debate over the petitions was interrupted by so much applause from the "large number of persons" in the galleries and the representatives on the floor that the Speaker of the House had to reprimand both groups for their lack of decorum.

> * * * It is true that the framers had little respect for the suffragists' arguments and that black rights remained uppermost in their minds.
>
> But if suffragist petitions jammed congressional mailboxes and noisy women overflowed the galleries, it is difficult to argue, as many do, that the framers hadn't given much thought to the demands of other politically disadvantaged groups * * *.
>
> * * * In 1866, many members of Congress perceived a great gulf between civil rights, like the right to personal security or ownership of property, and political rights, like the right to vote [or serve on a jury or be a member of a State militia] * * *. When all the framers' comments on women are read together, they suggest that women's rights, short of suffrage, were thought to be within the reach of the Fourteenth Amendment."

Morais, *supra* at 1156–58.

C. BRADWELL V. ILLINOIS

83 U.S. (16 Wall.) 130 (1873)

IN error to the Supreme Court of the State of Illinois.

Mrs. Myra Bradwell, residing in the State of Illinois, made application to the judges of the Supreme Court of that State for a license to practice law. She accompanied her petition with the usual certificate from an inferior court of her good character, and that on due examination she had been found to possess the requisite qualifications. Pending this application she also filed an affidavit, to the effect "that she was born in the State of Vermont; that she was (had been) a citizen of that State; that she is now a citizen of the United States, and has been for many years past a resident of the city of Chicago, in the State of Illinois." And with this affidavit she also filed a paper asserting that, under the foregoing facts, she was entitled to the license prayed for by virtue of the second section of the fourth article of the Constitution of the United States, and of the fourteenth article of amendment of that instrument.

* * *

On Mrs. Bradwell's application first coming before the court, the license was refused, and it was stated as a sufficient reason that under the decisions of the Supreme Court of Illinois, the applicant—"as a married woman would be bound neither by her express contracts nor by those implied contracts which it is the policy of the law to create between attorney and client." After the announcement of this decision, Mrs. Bradwell, admitting that she was a married woman—though she expressed her belief that such fact did not appear in the record—filed a printed argument in which her right to admission, notwithstanding that fact, was earnestly and ably maintained. The court thereupon gave an opinion in writing. Extracts are here given:

> "Our statute provides that no person shall be permitted to practice as an attorney or counsellor at law without having previously obtained a license for that purpose from two of the justices of the Supreme Court * * *. [I]t is left to our discretion to establish the rules by which admission to this office shall be determined. But this discretion is not an arbitrary one * * *.

> [We] should not admit any persons or class of persons who are not intended by the legislature to be admitted, even though their exclusion is not expressly required by the statute.
>
> * * *
>
> "It is to be remembered that at the time this statute was enacted we had, by express provision, adopted the common law of England * * *.
>
> "It is to be also remembered that female attorneys at law were unknown in England, and a proposition that a woman should enter the courts of Westminster Hall in that capacity, or as a barrister, would have created hardly less astonishment than one that she should ascend the bench of bishops, or be elected to a seat in the House of Commons.
>
> "It is to be further remembered, that when our act was passed, that school of reform which claims for women participation in the making and administering of the laws had not then arisen, or, if here and there a writer had advanced such theories, they were regarded rather as abstract speculations than as an actual basis for action.
>
> "That God designed the sexes to occupy different spheres of action, and that it belonged to men to make, apply, and execute the laws, was regarded as an almost axiomatic truth.
>
> "In view of these facts, we are certainly warranted in saying that when the legislature gave to this court the power of granting licenses to practice law, it was with not the slightest expectation that this privilege would be extended to women."

The court having thus denied the application, Mrs. Bradwell brought the case here * * *.

■ MR. JUSTICE MILLER delivered the opinion of the court.

* * *

* * * [C]ounsel for the plaintiff in this court truly says that there are certain privileges and immunities which belong to a citizen of the United States as such; otherwise it would be nonsense for the fourteenth amendment to prohibit a State from abridging them, and he proceeds to argue that admission to the bar of a State of a person who possesses the requisite learning and character is one of those which a State may not deny.

In this latter proposition we are not able to concur with counsel. We agree with him that there are privileges and immunities belonging to citizens of the United States, in that relation and character, and that it is these and these alone which a State is forbidden to abridge. But the right to admission to practice in the courts of a State is not one of them. This right in no sense depends on citizenship of the United States. It has not, as far as we know, ever been made in any State, or in any case, to depend on citizenship at all. Certainly many prominent and distinguished lawyers have been admitted to practice, both in the State and Federal courts, who were not citizens of the United States or of any State. But, on whatever basis this right may be placed, so far as it can have any relation to citizenship at all, it would seem that, as to the courts of a State, it would relate to citizenship of the State, and as to Federal courts, it would relate to citizenship of the United States.

The opinion just delivered in the *Slaughter-House Cases* renders elaborate argument in the present case unnecessary; for, unless we are wholly and radically mistaken in the principles on which those cases are decided, the right to control and regulate the granting of license to practice law in the courts of a State is one of those powers which are not transferred for its protection to the Federal government, and its exercise is in no manner governed or controlled by citizenship of the United States in the party seeking such license.

It is unnecessary to repeat the argument on which the judgment in those cases is founded. It is sufficient to say they are conclusive of the present case.

JUDGMENT AFFIRMED.

■ MR. JUSTICE BRADLEY:

I concur in the judgment of the court in this case, by which the judgment of the Supreme Court of Illinois is affirmed, but not for the reasons specified in the opinion just read.

The claim of the plaintiff, who is a married woman, to be admitted to practice as an attorney and counsellor-at-law, is based upon the supposed right of every person, man or woman, to engage in any lawful employment for a livelihood * * *.

The claim that, under the fourteenth amendment of the Constitution, which declares that no State shall make or enforce any law which shall abridge the privileges and immunities of citizens of the United States, the statute law of Illinois, or the common law prevailing in that State, can no longer be set up as a barrier against the right of females to pursue any lawful employment for a livelihood (the practice of law included), assumes that it is one of the privileges and immunities of women as citizens to engage in any and every profession, occupation, or employment in civil life.

It certainly cannot be affirmed, as an historical fact, that this has ever been established as one of the fundamental privileges and immunities of the sex. On the contrary, the civil law, as well as nature herself, has always recognized a wide difference in the respective spheres and destinies of man and woman. Man is, or should be, woman's protector and defender. The natural and proper timidity and delicacy which belongs to the female sex evidently unfits it for many of the occupations of civil life. The constitution of the family organization, which is founded in the divine ordinance, as well as in the nature of things, indicates the domestic sphere as that which properly belongs to the domain and functions of womanhood. The harmony, not to say identity, of interest and views which belong, or should belong, to the family institution is repugnant to the idea of a woman adopting a distinct and independent career from that of her husband. So firmly fixed was this sentiment in the founders of the common law that it became a maxim of that system of jurisprudence that a woman had no legal existence separate from her husband, who was regarded as her head and representative in the social state; and, notwithstanding some recent modifications of this civil status, many of the special rules of law flowing from and dependent upon this cardinal principle still exist in full force in most States. One of these is, that a married woman is incapable, without her husband's consent, of making contracts which shall be binding on her or him. This very incapacity was one circumstance which the Supreme Court of Illinois deemed important in rendering a married woman incompetent fully to perform the duties and trusts that belong to the office of an attorney and counsellor.

It is true that many women are unmarried and not affected by any of the duties, complications, and incapacities arising out of the married state, but these are exceptions to the general rule. The paramount destiny and mission of woman are to fulfil the noble and benign offices of wife and mother. This is the law of the Creator. And the rules of civil society must be adapted to the general constitution of things, and cannot be based upon exceptional cases.

The humane movements of modern society, which have for their object the multiplication of avenues for woman's advancement, and of occupations adapted to her condition and sex, have my heartiest concurrence. But I am not prepared to say that it is one of her fundamental rights and privileges to be admitted into every office and position, including those which require highly special qualifications and demanding special responsibilities. In the nature of things it is not every citizen of every age, sex, and condition that is qualified for every calling and position. It is the prerogative of the legislator to prescribe regulations founded on nature, reason, and experience for the due admission of qualified persons to professions and callings demanding special skill and confidence. This fairly belongs to the police power of the State; and, in my opinion, in view of the peculiar characteristics, destiny, and mission of woman, it is within the province of the legislature to ordain what offices, positions, and callings shall be filled and discharged by men, and shall receive the benefit of those energies and responsibilities, and that decision and firmness which are presumed to predominate in the sterner sex.

For these reasons I think that the laws of Illinois now complained of are not obnoxious to the charge of abridging any of the privileges and immunities of citizens of the United States.

■ MR. JUSTICE SWAYNE and MR. JUSTICE FIELD concurred in the foregoing opinion of MR. JUSTICE BRADLEY.

■ THE CHIEF JUSTICE dissented from the judgment of the court, and from all the opinions.

NOTES AND QUESTIONS

1. Justice Bradley's concurring opinion—joined by two other justices—has, for obvious reasons, become (in)famous. But the case was decided by the majority, not by the concurrence. Do you see why we keep harping on the significance of the *Slaughter-House Cases*? The right to practice law in a particular State is obviously not a privilege or immunity of distinctively "national" citizenship, as that concept was narrowly defined in the *Slaughter-House Cases*. Almost nothing that a State wasn't already forbidden to abridge before ratification of the Fourteenth Amendment meets that criterion. But if the Privileges or Immunities Clause is given its natural meaning rather than the *Slaughter-House* meaning, *Bradwell* becomes a very different case. The right to choose and pursue a profession is clearly a civil right that is at the heart of what the Fourteenth Amendment was seeking to protect. The only remaining question would be whether the Illinois law "abridge[s]" that right, and the answer is obviously yes—*provided* that one understands Section 1 of the Fourteenth Amendment to address forms of discrimination other than the racial discrimination addressed by the Civil Rights Act of 1866. That also has an easy answer: The amendment's broad and general language refers to "citizens" without qualification and, unlike the Civil Rights Acts of 1866 and the subsequent Fifteenth Amendment, contains no explicit reference to race. So, does that mean that Myra

Bradwell easily wins if the *Slaughter-House Cases* are decided differently? As we explain below, she wins, but not quite as easily as all that. Stay tuned.

2. Justices Bradley, Swayne, and Field dissented in the *Slaughter-House Cases,* maintaining that everyone has a fundamental right to pursue their own occupation free of class legislation or monopolies. Unless they were prepared to abandon that position in favor of precedent after losing in the *Slaughter-House Cases,* they had to address Ms. Bradwell's claim head-on. And address it they did. You read for yourself how they addressed it. This opinion came a quarter century after the Seneca Falls Declaration of Sentiments of 1848. Old ideas often die hard.

3. The Chief Justice was the lone dissenter, and he did not write an opinion. Chief Justice Chase was dying when this case was handed down, but had he lived, he might well have taken Myra Bradwell's side with some force. He was a very progressive man for his time.

4. We said that if the *Slaughter-House Cases* had come out differently, Ms. Bradwell would have won, but not necessarily in a straightforward fashion. Why is that? Suppose that Illinois required that one reach the age of majority—let us say eighteen—before becoming a lawyer. A ten-year-old applies for a license and (let us assume) meets all criteria other than the age requirement. Is the age requirement invalid, because the ten-year-old is a citizen whose privileges or immunities were abridged? Virtually every law classifies and discriminates in some fashion. That is what laws do. If every classification is an abridgement of a privilege or immunity, virtually all laws are unconstitutional. There is no plausible account of the meaning—original or otherwise—of the Fourteenth Amendment under which this makes any sense. So what kinds of laws does the Privileges or Immunities Clause actually forbid States from making or enforcing? You have already seen many indications of Professor Calabresi's views: The Fourteenth Amendment prohibits classifications that are or resemble caste or class legislation or that create special privileges or monopolies. Discrimination against ten-year-olds in the practice of law is not caste- or class-like in the same way as discrimination because of race. There can be hard cases regarding what kinds of classifications have this forbidden caste- or class-like character, but there are plenty of easy cases as well. Race is an easy case. Sex is also an easy case, for some of the same reasons of history that race is an easy case, and any doubts about the application of that principle in 1868 vanished in 1920 with ratification of the Nineteenth Amendment. *See* Steven G. Calabresi & Julia T. Rickert, *Originalism and Sex Discrimination,* 90 TEX. L. REV. 1 (2011). Professor Lawson, for his part, is not a student of the Fourteenth Amendment and is therefore reluctant to say much. He finds a lot that seems right in Professor Calabresi's analysis (though he is not persuaded that the Nineteenth Amendment retroactively changes the Fourteenth Amendment), but he approaches the subject a bit differently. If the essence of the Privileges or Immunities Clause is to force States to act like fiduciaries to their citizenry with respect to civil rights, the answers will be found in pre-1868 agency law dealing with multiple principals. In those settings, agents could treat multiple beneficiaries unequally if they had, and could articulate to courts, good reasons for so doing. He thus does not see any escape from the need to ask whether a particular classification is supported by good reasons that warrant departure from a baseline presumption of equality. Race-based classifications will almost never meet that standard. Sex-based classifications might meet it in a few more cases, but not many. Age-based restrictions generally have stronger justifications. That's it? Application of common sense and nothing more elaborate than that? That's all Professor Lawson has to offer right now. As you read the rest of the cases in this chapter, see if the

Supreme Court has come up with anything better. Does Professor Calabresi's focus on caste and class privilege lead to a more structured analysis?

5. There was one other nineteenth-century case which you should know about concerning the rights of women. In *Minor v. Happersett*, 88 U.S. (21 Wall.) 162 (1875), the Supreme Court turned down a Fourteenth Amendment claim brought by several women seeking the right to vote in state and federal elections. The decision is worth reading even after the Nineteenth Amendment makes it a relic because 1) the Court took the argument very seriously—far more seriously than it took Myra Bradwell's claim; 2) the case was argued and decided under the Privileges or Immunities Clause but, unlike almost every other case, was not summarily disposed of by reference to the *Slaughter-House Cases*; and 3) the decision contains an important discussion about the post-Civil War understanding of citizenship.

Minor v. Happersett

88 U.S. (21 Wall.) 162 (1875)

■ THE CHIEF JUSTICE delivered the opinion of the court.

The question is presented in this case, whether, since the adoption of the fourteenth amendment, a woman, who is a citizen of the United States and of the State of Missouri, is a voter in that State, notwithstanding the provision of the constitution and laws of the State, which confine the right of suffrage to men alone. We might, perhaps, decide the case upon other grounds, but this question is fairly made * * *.

It is contended that the provisions of the constitution and laws of the State of Missouri which confine the right of suffrage and registration therefor to men, are in violation of the Constitution of the United States, and therefore void. The argument is, that as a woman, born or naturalized in the United States and subject to the jurisdiction thereof, is a citizen of the United States and of the State in which she resides, she has the right of suffrage as one of the privileges and immunities of her citizenship, which the State cannot by its laws or constitution abridge.

There is no doubt that women may be citizens. They are persons, and by the fourteenth amendment "all persons born or naturalized in the United States and subject to the jurisdiction thereof" are expressly declared to be "citizens of the United States and of the State wherein they reside." But, in our opinion, it did not need this amendment to give them that position. Before its adoption the Constitution of the United States did not in terms prescribe who should be citizens of the United States or of the several States, yet there were necessarily such citizens without such provision. There cannot be a nation without a people. The very idea of a political community, such as a nation is, implies an association of persons for the promotion of their general welfare * * *.

* * *

To determine, then, who were citizens of the United States before the adoption of the amendment it is necessary to ascertain what persons originally associated themselves together to form the nation, and what were afterwards admitted to membership.

Looking at the Constitution itself we find that it was ordained and established by "the people of the United States," and then going further back, we find that these were the people of the several States that had before dissolved the political bands which connected them with Great Britain, and assumed a separate and equal station among the powers of the earth * * *.

Whoever, then, was one of the people of either of these States when the Constitution of the United States was adopted, became *ipso facto* a citizen—a member of the nation created by its adoption. He was one of the persons associating together to form the nation, and was, consequently, one of its original citizens. As to this there has never been a doubt. Disputes have arisen as to whether or not certain persons or certain classes of persons were part of the people at the time, but never as to their citizenship if they were.

Additions might always be made to the citizenship of the United States in two ways: first, by birth, and second, by naturalization. This is apparent from the Constitution itself, for it provides that "no person except a natural-born citizen, or a citizen of the United States at the time of the adoption of the Constitution, shall be eligible to the office of President," and that Congress shall have power "to establish a uniform rule of naturalization." Thus new citizens may be born or they may be created by naturalization.

The Constitution does not, in words, say who shall be natural-born citizens. Resort must be had elsewhere to ascertain that. At common-law, with the nomenclature of which the framers of the Constitution were familiar, it was never doubted that all children born in a country of parents who were its citizens became themselves, upon their birth, citizens also. These were natives, or natural-born citizens, as distinguished from aliens or foreigners. Some authorities go further and include as citizens children born within the jurisdiction without reference to the citizenship of their parents. As to this class there have been doubts, but never as to the first. For the purposes of this case it is not necessary to solve these doubts. It is sufficient for everything we have now to consider that all children born of citizen parents within the jurisdiction are themselves citizens. The words "all children" are certainly as comprehensive, when used in this connection, as "all persons," and if females are included in the last they must be in the first. That they are included in the last is not denied. In fact the whole argument of the plaintiffs proceeds upon that idea.

* * *

As early as 1804 it was enacted by Congress that when any alien who had declared his intention to become a citizen in the manner provided by law died before he was actually naturalized, his widow and children should be considered as citizens of the United States, and entitled to all rights and privileges as such upon taking the necessary oath; and in 1855 it was further provided that any woman who might lawfully be naturalized under the existing laws, married, or who should be married to a citizen of the United States, should be deemed and taken to be a citizen.

From this it is apparent that from the commencement of the legislation upon this subject alien women and alien minors could be made citizens by naturalization, and we think it will not be contended that this would have been done if it had not been supposed that native women and native minors were already citizens by birth.

But if more is necessary to show that women have always been considered as citizens the same as men, abundant proof is to be found in the legislative and judicial history of the country. Thus, by the Constitution, the judicial power of the United

States is made to extend to controversies between citizens of different States. Under this it has been uniformly held that the citizenship necessary to give the courts of the United States jurisdiction of a cause must be affirmatively shown on the record. Its existence as a fact may be put in issue and tried. If found not to exist the case must be dismissed. Notwithstanding this the records of the courts are full of cases in which the jurisdiction depends upon the citizenship of women, and not one can be found, we think, in which objection was made on that account. Certainly none can be found in which it has been held that women could not sue or be sued in the courts of the United States. Again, at the time of the adoption of the Constitution, in many of the States (and in some probably now) aliens could not inherit or transmit inheritance. There are a multitude of cases to be found in which the question has been presented whether a woman was or was not an alien, and as such capable or incapable of inheritance, but in no one has it been insisted that she was not a citizen because she was a woman. On the contrary, her right to citizenship has been in all cases assumed. The only question has been whether, in the particular case under consideration, she had availed herself of the right.

* * *

Other proof of like character might be found, but certainly more cannot be necessary to establish the fact that sex has never been made one of the elements of citizenship in the United States. In this respect men have never had an advantage over women. The same laws precisely apply to both. The fourteenth amendment did not affect the citizenship of women any more than it did of men. In this particular, therefore, the rights of Mrs. Minor do not depend upon the amendment. She has always been a citizen from her birth, and entitled to all the privileges and immunities of citizenship. The amendment prohibited the State, of which she is a citizen, from abridging any of her privileges and immunities as a citizen of the United States; but it did not confer citizenship on her. That she had before its adoption.

If the right of suffrage is one of the necessary privileges of a citizen of the United States, then the constitution and laws of Missouri confining it to men are in violation of the Constitution of the United States, as amended, and consequently void. The direct question is, therefore, presented whether all citizens are necessarily voters.

The Constitution does not define the privileges and immunities of citizens. For that definition we must look elsewhere. In this case we need not determine what they are, but only whether suffrage is necessarily one of them.

It certainly is nowhere made so in express terms. The United States has no voters in the States of its own creation. The elective officers of the United States are all elected directly or indirectly by State voters. The members of the House of Representatives are to be chosen by the people of the States, and the electors in each State must have the qualifications requisite for electors of the most numerous branch of the State legislature. Senators are to be chosen by the legislatures of the States, and necessarily the members of the legislature required to make the choice are elected by the voters of the State. Each State must appoint in such manner, as the legislature thereof may direct, the electors to elect the President and Vice-President * * *.

The amendment did not add to the privileges and immunities of a citizen. It simply furnished an additional guaranty for the protection of such as he already had. No new voters were necessarily made by it. Indirectly it may have had that effect, because it may have increased the number of citizens entitled to suffrage under the constitution and laws of the States, but it operates for this purpose, if at all, through the States and the State laws, and not directly upon the citizen.

It is clear, therefore, we think, that the Constitution has not added the right of suffrage to the privileges and immunities of citizenship as they existed at the time it was adopted. This makes it proper to inquire whether suffrage was coextensive with the citizenship of the States at the time of its adoption. If it was, then it may with force be argued that suffrage was one of the rights which belonged to citizenship, and in the enjoyment of which every citizen must be protected. But if it was not, the contrary may with propriety be assumed.

When the Federal Constitution was adopted, all the States, with the exception of Rhode Island and Connecticut, had constitutions of their own. These two continued to act under their charters from the Crown. Upon an examination of those constitutions we find that in no State were all citizens permitted to vote. Each State determined for itself who should have that power * * *.

In this condition of the law in respect to suffrage in the several States it cannot for a moment be doubted that if it had been intended to make all citizens of the United States voters, the framers of the Constitution would not have left it to implication. So important a change in the condition of citizenship as it actually existed, if intended, would have been expressly declared.

But if further proof is necessary to show that no such change was intended, it can easily be found both in and out of the Constitution. By Article 4, section 2, it is provided that "the citizens of each State shall be entitled to all the privileges and immunities of citizens in the several States." If suffrage is necessarily a part of citizenship, then the citizens of each State must be entitled to vote in the several States precisely as their citizens are. This is more than asserting that they may change their residence and become citizens of the State and thus be voters. It goes to the extent of insisting that while retaining their original citizenship they may vote in any State. This, we think, has never been claimed. And again, by the very terms of the amendment we have been considering (the fourteenth), "Representatives shall be apportioned among the several States according to their respective numbers, counting the whole number of persons in each State, excluding Indians not taxed. But when the right to vote at any election for the choice of electors for President and Vice-President of the United States, representatives in Congress, the executive and judicial officers of a State, or the members of the legislature thereof, is denied to any of the male inhabitants of such State, being twenty-one years of age and citizens of the United States, or in any way abridged, except for participation in the rebellion, or other crimes, the basis of representation therein shall be reduced in the proportion which the number of such male citizens shall bear to the whole number of male citizens twenty-one years of age in such State." Why this, if it was not in the power of the legislature to deny the right of suffrage to some male inhabitants? And if suffrage was necessarily one of the absolute rights of citizenship, why confine the operation of the limitation to male inhabitants? Women and children are, as we have seen, "persons." They are counted in the enumeration upon which the apportionment is to be made, but if they were necessarily voters because of their citizenship unless clearly excluded, why inflict the penalty for the exclusion of males alone? Clearly, no such form of words would have been selected to express the idea here indicated if suffrage was the absolute right of all citizens.

And still again, after the adoption of the fourteenth amendment, it was deemed necessary to adopt a fifteenth, as follows: "The right of citizens of the United States to vote shall not be denied or abridged by the United States, or by any State, on account of race, color, or previous condition of servitude." The fourteenth amendment had already provided that no State should make or enforce any law which should abridge the privileges or immunities of citizens of the United States. If suffrage was one of these privileges or immunities, why amend the Constitution to prevent its being denied on account of race, &c.? Nothing is more evident than that the greater must include the less, and if all were already protected why go through with the form of amending the Constitution to protect a part?

* * *

But we have already sufficiently considered the proof found upon the inside of the Constitution. That upon the outside is equally effective.

The Constitution was submitted to the States for adoption in 1787, and was ratified by nine States in 1788, and finally by the thirteen original States in 1790. Vermont was the first new State admitted to the Union, and it came in under a constitution which conferred the right of suffrage only upon men of the full age of twenty-one years, having resided in the State for the space of one whole year next before the election, and who were of quiet and peaceable behavior. This was in 1791. The next year, 1792, Kentucky followed with a constitution confining the right of suffrage to free male citizens of the age of twenty-one years who had resided in the State two years or in the county in which they offered to vote one year next before the election. Then followed Tennessee, in 1796, with voters of freemen of the age of twenty-one years and upwards, possessing a freehold in the county wherein they may vote, and being inhabitants of the State or freemen being inhabitants of any one county in the State six months immediately preceding the day of election. But we need not particularize further. No new State has ever been admitted to the Union which has conferred the right of suffrage upon women, and this has never been considered a valid objection to her admission. On the contrary, as is claimed in the argument, the right of suffrage was withdrawn from women as early as 1807 in the State of New Jersey, without any attempt to obtain the interference of the United States to prevent it. Since then the governments of the insurgent States have been reorganized under a requirement that before their representatives could be admitted to seats in Congress they must have adopted new constitutions, republican in form. In no one of these constitutions was suffrage conferred upon women, and yet the States have all been restored to their original position as States in the Union.

Besides this, citizenship has not in all cases been made a condition precedent to the enjoyment of the right of suffrage. Thus, in Missouri, persons of foreign birth, who have declared their intention to become citizens of the United States, may under certain circumstances vote. The same provision is to be found in the constitutions of Alabama, Arkansas, Florida, Georgia, Indiana, Kansas, Minnesota, and Texas.

Certainly, if the courts can consider any question settled, this is one. For nearly ninety years the people have acted upon the idea that the Constitution, when it conferred citizenship, did not necessarily confer the right of suffrage. If uniform practice long continued can settle the construction of so important an instrument as the Constitution of the United States confessedly is, most certainly it has been done here. Our province is to decide what the law is, not to declare what it should be.

We have given this case the careful consideration its importance demands. If the law is wrong, it ought to be changed; but the power for that is not with us. The arguments addressed to us bearing upon such a view of the subject may perhaps be sufficient to induce those having the power, to make the alteration, but they ought not to be permitted to influence our judgment in determining the present rights of the parties now litigating before us. No argument as to woman's need of suffrage can be considered. We can only act upon her rights as they exist. It is not for us to look at the hardship of withholding. Our duty is at an end if we find it is within the power of a State to withhold.

Being unanimously of the opinion that the Constitution of the United States does not confer the right of suffrage upon any one, and that the constitutions and laws of the several States which commit that important trust to men alone are not necessarily void, we

AFFIRM THE JUDGMENT.

NOTES AND QUESTIONS

1. If you think that the decision in *Happersett* was wrong in 1875, what was the Court's mistake? How would you have written the opinion?

2. In the wake of their loss in *Minor v. Happersett,* the women's suffrage movement began a nationwide campaign to get the right to vote, first in some of the several States, and, ultimately, by constitutional amendment nationwide. Several Western frontier states had too many men and not enough women, and they began to offer women the right to vote as an inducement to encourage women to move out west. Elizabeth Cady Stanton and Susan B. Anthony founded the National Woman Suffrage Campaign (NWSC) in 1869 to lobby the States to give women the right to vote. Another group of women organized the American Woman Suffrage Association (AWSA) also to lobby to get States to amend their constitutions to allow women to vote. In 1869, the Wyoming Territory was organized with a woman's suffrage provision for territorial elections. In 1890, Wyoming was admitted to the Union as a State with a woman's suffrage guarantee in its state constitution. In 1893, Colorado adopted woman's suffrage, and, in 1896, Utah and Idaho adopted woman's suffrage. In 1910, Washington State adopted woman's suffrage, followed in 1911 by woman's suffrage in California. In 1912, Theodore Roosevelt' Bull Moose Party endorsed woman's suffrage, and Oregon, Kansas, and Arizona adopted woman's suffrage. In 1914, Nevada and Montana adopted woman's suffrage, making this the policy of all of the Western States.

Two critical events occurred in 1916 that led to the adoption of the Nineteenth Amendment. First, a radical Quaker activist name Alice Paul formed the National Woman's Party with the sole goal of achieving an amendment to the U.S. Constitution granting women the right to vote. Alice Paul was impatient with the successors to Susan B. Anthony and Elizabeth Cady Stanton, who were dead by 1916. She wanted national women's suffrage NOW! Alice Paul led a brilliant public relations campaign in which she and her cohorts got themselves arrested, went on a hunger strike in prison, and got themselves force-fed, to the disgust of many male Americans. The sensationalist press covered Alice Paul's every move. As a Quaker, she studiously avoided violence, but in every non-violent way she simply refused to accept the status quo. She set a standard for massive, non-violent public resistance, which was later followed by Mahatma Gandhi in India, by Dr. Martin Luther King, Jr. in the U.S., and by President Nelson Mandela in Africa. She was truly a pioneer and, more than any other woman, Alice Paul caused the Nineteenth Amendment to be adopted.

Second, and also in 1916, Jeanette Rankin of Montana became the first woman to be elected to the House of Representatives. Woodrow Wilson's platform in the 1916 presidential election adopted woman's suffrage. Woman's suffrage then triumphed in New York in 1917; and, in 1918, in Michigan, South Dakota, and Oklahoma. Rep. Jeanette Rankin's constitutional amendment giving women the right to vote passed the House of Representative in 1918 and the Senate in 1919. On August 26, 1920, three quarters of the States ratified the Nineteenth Amendment to the Constitution. The U.S. became the first independent nation to give women the right to vote—the Dominion of Australia within the British Empire having preceded it. The United Kingdom gave women the right to vote in 1928, and German, France, Japan, Italy and most other countries in the world gave women the right to vote only after 1945.

3. One question that arose once women had the political right to vote in the United States was whether the passage of the Nineteenth Amendment meant women henceforth had equal civil rights to men under the Fourteenth Amendment. The Framers of the Fourteenth Amendment always had said that political rights, such as the right to vote, were at the apex of the pyramid of rights, and they could not have imagined a world in which a class of people had equal political rights but not equal civil rights. It would be nonsensical to allow women to run for and to vote for president, senator, congressman, or governor, but not to have equal rights to own property or to make contracts with men. For this reason, says Professor Calabresi, the Nineteenth Amendment transformed the meaning of the Fourteenth Amendment to give women equal civil rights to men. This argument is developed in Steven G. Calabresi & Julia T. Rickert, *Originalism and Sex Discrimination*, 90 TEX. L. REV. 1 (2011).

4. While Professor Lawson has some doubts about the foregoing argument (he is not convinced that amendments can retroactively change the meaning of other provisions without saying so expressly), the Supreme Court essentially adopted such an argument in *Adkins v. Children's Hospital*, 261 U.S. 525 (1923)—a case in which the pre-New Deal Supreme Court struck down a minimum wage law applicable only to women as a violation of liberty of contract, which was at that time recognized as an element of due process of law under *Lochner v. New York*, 198 U.S. 45 (1905). Conservative Republican Justice George Sutherland wrote in *Adkins*:

> the ancient inequality of the sexes, otherwise than physical, as suggested in the *Muller* case (p. 421) has continued "with diminishing intensity." In view of the great—not to say revolutionary—changes which have taken place since that utterance, in the contractual, political and civil status of women, culminating in the Nineteenth Amendment, it is not unreasonable to say that these differences have now come almost, if not quite, to the vanishing point. In this aspect of the matter, while the physical differences must be recognized in appropriate cases, and legislation fixing hours or conditions of work may properly take them into account, we cannot accept the doctrine that women of mature age, *sui juris,* require or may be subjected to restrictions upon their liberty of contract which could not lawfully be imposed in the case of men under similar circumstances. To do so would be to ignore all the implications to be drawn from the present day trend of legislation, as well as that of common thought and usage, by which woman is accorded emancipation from the old doctrine that she must be given special protection or be subjected to special restraint in her contractual and civil relationships. In passing, it may be noted that the instant statute applies in the case of a woman employer contracting with a woman employee as it does when the former is a man.

Justice Sutherland's opinion was joined by Justices McKenna, Van Devanter, McReynolds, and Butler. Justice Oliver Wendell Holmes, however, quipped in dissent:

> It will need more than the Nineteenth Amendment to convince me that there are no differences between men and women, or that legislation cannot take those differences into account. I should not hesitate to take them into account if I thought it necessary to sustain this act.

Justice Brandeis did not participate in the case.

From 1923 until 1937, Supreme Court caselaw held that the Nineteenth Amendment had affected the way in which the Supreme Court should read the Fourteenth Amendment, which now protected women's civil rights just as it protected the civil rights of men. Unfortunately for women, the New Deal labor union bosses were determined to keep women from competing with men in the workplace. Accordingly, Washington State passed a minimum wage law for women only, and the Supreme Court upheld it by a 5 to 4 vote in *West Coast Hotel Co. v. Parrish*, 300 U.S. 379 (1937). *See infra* pages 1449–1457. The case was part of the so-called "switch-in-time that saved nine" by which the Supreme Court abandoned its *Lochner*-era jurisprudence, *see infra* pages 1426–1434, to enshrine the "rational basis" test for all state social and economic legislation which did not affect discrete and insular minorities—a group which did not include women. *West Cost Hotel Co. v. Parrish* overruled *Adkins v. Children's Hospital*, with Justices Sutherland, Van Devanter, McReynolds, and Butler—the pre-New Deal holdovers—in dissent. The Justices who gave sex discriminatory laws only "rational basis" scrutiny, which essentially guarantees their constitutional survival, were Chief Justice Hughes and Justices Brandeis, Stone, Roberts, and Cardozo. As a result, from 1937 to 1971, sex classifications were given only rational basis scrutiny by the Supreme Court. You can see the consequences of that development in the next two cases from the Vinson Court and the Warren Court.

D. GOESAERT V. CLEARY

335 U.S. 464 (1948)

■ MR. JUSTICE FRANKFURTER delivered the opinion of the Court.

As part of the Michigan system for controlling the sale of liquor, bartenders are required to be licensed in all cities having a population of 50,000, or more, but no female may be so licensed unless she be "the wife or daughter of the male owner" of a licensed liquor establishment * * *. The claim, denied below, one judge dissenting, and renewed here, is that Michigan cannot forbid females generally from being barmaids and at the same time make an exception in favor of the wives and daughters of the owners of liquor establishments. Beguiling as the subject is, it need not detain us long. To ask whether or not the Equal Protection of the Laws Clause of the Fourteenth Amendment barred Michigan from making the classification the State has made between wives and daughters of owners of liquor places and wives and daughters of non-owners, is one of those rare instances where to state the question is in effect to answer it.

We are, to be sure, dealing with a historic calling. We meet the alewife, sprightly and ribald, in Shakespeare, but centuries before him she played a role in the social life of England. See, e.g., Jusserand, English Wayfaring Life, 133, 134, 136–37 (1889). The Fourteenth Amendment did not tear history up by the roots, and the regulation of the liquor traffic is one of the oldest and most untrammeled of legislative powers. Michigan could, beyond question, forbid all women from working behind a bar. This is so despite the vast changes in the social and legal position of women. The fact that women may now have achieved the virtues that men have long claimed as their prerogatives and now indulge in vices that men have long practiced, does not preclude the States from drawing a sharp line between the sexes, certainly, in such matters as the regulation of the liquor traffic. The Constitution does not require legislatures to reflect sociological insight, or shifting social standards, any more than it requires them to keep abreast of the latest scientific standards.

While Michigan may deny to all women opportunities for bartending, Michigan cannot play favorites among women without rhyme or reasons. The Constitution in enjoining the equal protection of the laws upon States precludes irrational discrimination as between persons or groups of persons in the incidence of a law. But the Constitution does not require situations "which are different in fact or opinion to be treated in law as though they were the same." *Tigner v. State of Texas*, 310 U.S. 141. Since bartending by women may, in the allowable legislative judgment, give rise to moral and social problems against which it may devise preventive measures, the legislature need not go to the full length of prohibition if it believes that as to a defined group of females other factors are operating which either eliminate or reduce the moral and social problems otherwise calling for prohibition. Michigan evidently believes that the oversight assured through ownership of a bar by a barmaid's husband or father minimizes hazards that may confront a barmaid without such protecting oversight. This Court is certainly not in a position to gainsay such belief by the Michigan legislature. If it is entertainable, as we think it is, Michigan has not violated its duty to afford equal protection of its laws. We cannot cross-examine either actually or argumentatively the mind of Michigan legislators nor question their motives. Since the line they have drawn is not without a basis in reason, we cannot give ear to the suggestion that the real impulse behind this legislation was an unchivalrous desire of male bartenders to try to monopolize the calling.

It would be an idle parade of familiar learning to review the multitudinous cases in which the constitutional assurance of the equal protection of the laws has been applied. The generalities on this subject are not in dispute; their application turns peculiarly on the particular circumstances of a case. Thus, it would be a sterile inquiry to consider whether this case is nearer to the nepotic pilotage law of Louisiana, sustained in *Kotch v. River Port Pilot Commissioners*, than it is to the Oklahoma sterilization law, which fell in *Skinner v. State of Oklahoma*. Suffice it to say that "A statute is not invalid under the Constitution because it might have gone farther than it did, or because it may not succeed in bringing about the result that it tends to produce."

Nor is it unconstitutional for Michigan to withdraw from women the occupation of bartending because it allows women to serve as waitresses where liquor is dispensed. The District Court has sufficiently indicated the reasons that may have influenced the legislature in allowing women to be waitresses in a liquor establishment over which a man's ownership provides control. Nothing need be added to what was said below as to the other grounds on which the Michigan law was assailed.

Judgment affirmed.

■ MR. JUSTICE RUTLEDGE, with whom MR. JUSTICE DOUGLAS and MR. JUSTICE MURPHY join, dissenting.

While the equal protection clause does not require a legislature to achieve "abstract symmetry" or to classify with "mathematical nicety," that clause does require law-markers to refrain from invidious distinctions of the sort drawn by the statute challenged in this case.

The statute arbitrarily discriminates between male and female owners of liquor establishments. A male owner, although he himself is always absent from his bar, may employ his wife and daughter as barmaids. A female owner may neither work as a barmaid herself nor employ her daughter in that position, even if a man is always present in the establishment to keep order. This inevitable result of the classification belies the assumption that the statute was motivated by a legislative solicitude for the moral and physical well-being of women who, but for the law, would be employed as barmaids. Since there could be no other conceivable justification for such discrimination against women owners of liquor establishments, the statute should be held invalid as a denial of equal protection.

E. HOYT V. FLORIDA

368 U.S. 57 (1961)

■ MR. JUSTICE HARLAN delivered the opinion of the Court.

Appellant, a woman, has been convicted in Hillsborough County, Florida, of second-degree murder of her husband. On this appeal * * * from the Florida Supreme Court's affirmance of the judgment of conviction, we noted probable jurisdiction to consider appellant's claim that her trial before an all-male jury violated rights assured by the Fourteenth Amendment. The claim is that such jury was the product of a state jury statute which works an unconstitutional exclusion of women from jury service.

The jury law primarily in question is Fla. Stat., 1959, § 40.01(1). This Act, which requires that grand and petit jurors be taken from "male and female" citizens of the State possessed of certain qualifications, contains the following proviso:

> "provided, however, that the name of no female person shall be taken for jury service unless said person has registered with the clerk of the circuit court her desire to be placed on the jury list."

Showing that, since the enactment of the statute, only a minimal number of women have so registered, appellant challenges the constitutionality of the statute both on its face and as applied in this case. For reasons now to follow we decide that both contentions must be rejected.

At the core of appellant's argument is the claim that the nature of the crime of which she was convicted peculiarly demanded the inclusion of persons of her own sex on the jury. She was charged with killing her husband by assaulting him with a baseball bat. An information was filed against her under Fla. Stat., 1959, § 782.04, which punishes as murder in the second degree "any act imminently dangerous to another, and evincing a depraved mind regardless of human life, although without any premeditated design to effect the death of any particular individual. . . ." As described by the Florida Supreme Court, the affair occurred in the context of a marital upheaval involving, among other things, the suspected infidelity of appellant's husband, and culminating in the husband's final rejection of his wife's efforts at reconciliation. It is claimed, in substance, that women jurors would have been more understanding or compassionate than men in assessing the quality of appellant's act and her defense of "temporary insanity." No claim is made that the jury as constituted was otherwise afflicted by any elements of supposed unfairness.

Of course, these premises misconceive the scope of the right to an impartially selected jury assured by the Fourteenth Amendment. That right does not entitle one accused of crime to a jury tailored to the circumstances of the particular case, whether relating to the sex or other condition of the defendant, or to the nature of the charges to be tried. It requires only that the jury be indiscriminately drawn from among those eligible in the community for jury service, untrammelled by any arbitrary and systematic exclusions. The result of this appeal must therefore depend on whether such an exclusion of women from jury service has been shown.

We address ourselves first to appellant's challenge to the statute on its face.

Several observations should initially be made. We, of course, recognize that the Fourteenth Amendment reaches not only arbitrary class exclusions from jury service based on race or color, but also all other exclusions which "single out" any class of persons "for different treatment not based on some reasonable classification." *Hernandez v. Texas,* 347 U.S. 475, 478. We need not, however, accept appellant's invitation to canvass in this case the continuing validity of this Court's dictum in *Strauder v. West Virginia,* 100 U.S. 303, 310, to the effect that a State may constitutionally "confine" jury duty "to males." This constitutional proposition has gone unquestioned for more than eighty years in the decisions of the Court, and had been reflected, until 1957, in congressional policy respecting jury service in the federal courts themselves. Even were it to be assumed that this question is still open to debate, the present case tenders narrower issues.

Manifestly, Florida's § 40.01(1) does not purport to exclude women from state jury service. Rather, the statute "gives to women the privilege to serve, but does not impose service as a duty." It accords women an absolute exemption from jury service unless they expressly waive that privilege. This is not to say, however, that what in form may be only an exemption of a particular class of persons can in no circumstances be regarded as an exclusion of that class. Where, as here, an exemption of a class in the community is asserted to be in substance an exclusionary device, the relevant inquiry is whether the exemption itself is based on some reasonable classification and whether the manner in which it is exercisable rests on some rational foundation.

In the selection of jurors Florida has differentiated between men and women in two respects. It has given women an absolute exemption from jury duty based solely on their sex, no similar exemption obtaining as to men. And it has provided for its effectuation in a manner less onerous than that governing exemptions exercisable by men: women are not to be put on the jury list unless they have voluntarily registered for such service; men, on the other hand, even if entitled to an exemption, are to be included on the list unless they have filed a written claim of exemption as provided by law.

In neither respect can we conclude that Florida's statute is not "based on some reasonable classification," and that it is thus infected with unconstitutionality. Despite the enlightened emancipation of women from the restrictions and protections of bygone years, and their entry into many parts of community life formerly considered to be reserved to men, woman is still regarded as the center of home and family life. We cannot say that it is constitutionally impermissible for a State, acting in pursuit of the general welfare, to conclude that a woman should be relieved from the civic duty of jury service unless she herself determines that such service is consistent with her own special responsibilities.

Florida is not alone in so concluding. Women are now eligible for jury service in all but three States of the Union. Of the forty-seven States where women are eligible, seventeen besides Florida, as well as the District of Columbia, have accorded women an absolute exemption based solely on their sex, exercisable in one form or another. In two of these States, as in Florida, the exemption is automatic, unless a woman volunteers for such service. It is true, of course, that Florida could have limited the exemption, as some other States have done, only to women who have family responsibilities. But we cannot regard it as irrational for a state legislature to consider preferable a broad exemption, whether born of the State's historic public policy or of a determination that it would not be administratively feasible to decide in each individual instance whether the family responsibilities of a prospective female juror were serious enough to warrant an exemption.

Likewise we cannot say that Florida could not reasonably conclude that full effectuation of this exemption made it desirable to relieve women of the necessity of affirmatively claiming it, while at the same time requiring of men an assertion of the exemptions available to them. Moreover, from the standpoint of its own administrative concerns the State might well consider that it was "impractical to compel large numbers of women, who have an absolute exemption, to come to the clerk's office for examination since they so generally assert their exemption."

Appellant argues that whatever may have been the design of this Florida enactment, the statute, in practical operation, results in an exclusion of women from jury service, because women, like men, can be expected to be available for jury service only under compulsion. In this connection she points out that, by 1957, when this trial took place, only some 220 women out of approximately 46,000 registered female voters in Hillsborough County—constituting about 40 percent of the total voting population of that county—had volunteered for jury duty since the limitation of jury service to males was removed by § 40.01(1) in 1949.

This argument, however, is surely beside the point. Given the reasonableness of the classification involved in § 40.01(1), the relative paucity of women jurors does not carry the constitutional consequence appellant would have it bear. "Circumstances or chance may well dictate that no persons in a certain class will serve on a particular jury or during some particular period."

We cannot hold this statute, as written, offensive to the Fourteenth Amendment.

Appellant's attack on the statute as applied in this case fares no better.

* * *

This case in no way resembles those involving race or color in which the circumstances shown were found by this Court to compel a conclusion of purposeful discriminatory exclusions from jury service. There is present here neither the unfortunate atmosphere of ethnic or racial prejudices which underlay the situations depicted in those cases nor the long course of discriminatory administrative practice which the statistical showing in each of them evinced.

In the circumstances here depicted, it indeed "taxes our credulity" to attribute to these administrative officials a deliberate design to exclude the very class whose eligibility for jury service the state legislature, after many years of contrary policy, had declared only a few years before. It is sufficiently evident from the record that the presence on the jury list of no more than ten or twelve women in the earlier years, and the failure to add in 1957 more women to those already on the list, are attributable not to any discriminatory motive, but to a purpose to put on the list only those women who might be expected to be qualified for service if actually called. Nor is there the slightest suggestion that the list was the product of any plan to place on it only women of a particular economic or other community or organizational group.

Finally, the disproportion of women to men on the list independently carries no constitutional significance. In the administration of the jury laws, proportional class representation is not a constitutionally required factor.

Finding no substantial evidence whatever in this record that Florida has arbitrarily undertaken to exclude women from jury service, a showing which it was incumbent on appellant to make, we must sustain the judgment of the Supreme Court of Florida.

Affirmed.

■ THE CHIEF JUSTICE, MR. JUSTICE BLACK and MR. JUSTICE DOUGLAS, concurring.

We cannot say from this record that Florida is not making a good faith effort to have women perform jury duty without discrimination on the ground of sex. Hence, we concur in the result, for the reasons set forth in Part II of the Court's opinion.

NOTES AND QUESTIONS

1. Could either of these cases come out the way they did if *Adkins v. Children's Hospital* had not been overruled? It was not until 1975 in *Taylor v. Louisiana*, 419 U.S. 522 (1975), that *Hoyt* was overruled. The Supreme Court in *Taylor* held that women could not constitutionally be excluded from a venire or jury pool. The vote on the Supreme Court that women had an equal right to men to serve on juries was eight to one, with only Justice William H. Rehnquist in dissent.

2. If the right to vote in the Nineteenth Amendment includes the right to vote on juries, *Taylor* was at least half a century late. Did women have the (unrecognized) right to serve on juries in 1868? Is the relevant right the right of women to serve on a jury or the right of the defendant to have women serve? The litigant in *Hoyt* was not a disappointed would-be juror; it was the criminal defendant who wanted women on the jury. Is the assumption that women on juries will think differently from men sexist? Is the assumption that women on juries will not think differently from men sexist? What kind of jury pool, or jury, does the Constitution guarantee to criminal defendants?

3. In 1994, in *J.E.B. v. T.B.*, 511 U.S. 127 (1994), the Supreme Court further recognized the fundamental importance of women serving on juries by holding that the making of peremptory challenges on the basis of sex was unconstitutional. This 1994 case affirmed that sex discrimination in jury selection was as objectionable as was race discrimination. Race discrimination in the making of peremptory challenges is unconstitutional under *Batson v. Kentucky*, 476 U.S. 79 (1986).

4. The 1964 Civil Rights Act, which outlawed race discrimination in employment, also outlawed sex discrimination in employment. Alice Paul had lobbied for this change

for many years. She was a good friend of Rep. Howard W. Smith, the Chair of the House Rules Committee. Smith got the Civil Rights Act of 1964 amended so that it would ban sex discrimination as well as race discrimination. The early heady days just after ratification of the Nineteenth Amendment, expressed in Justice Sutherland's opinion in *Adkins v. Children's Hospital*, returned, and as the next case shows, Supreme Court doctrine began to change to its current form.

[Assignment 64]

F. REED V. REED

404 U.S. 71 (1971)

■ MR. CHIEF JUSTICE BURGER delivered the opinion of the Court.

Richard Lynn Reed, a minor, died intestate in Ada County, Idaho, on March 29, 1967. His adoptive parents, who had separated sometime prior to his death, are the parties to this appeal. Approximately seven months after Richard's death, his mother, appellant Sally Reed, filed a petition in the Probate Court of Ada County, seeking appointment as administratrix of her son's estate. Prior to the date set for a hearing on the mother's petition, appellee Cecil Reed, the father of the decedent, filed a competing petition seeking to have himself appointed administrator of the son's estate. The probate court held a joint hearing on the two petitions and thereafter ordered that letters of administration be issued to appellee Cecil Reed upon his taking the oath and filing the bond required by law. The court treated §§ 15–312 and 15–314 of the Idaho Code as the controlling statutes, and read those sections as compelling a preference for Cecil Reed because he was a male.

Section 15–312 designates the persons who are entitled to administer the estate of one who dies intestate. In making these designations, that section lists 11 classes of persons who are so entitled, and provides, in substance, that the order in which those classes are listed in the section shall be determinative of the relative rights of competing applicants for letters of administration. One of the 11 classes so enumerated is "[t]he father or mother" of the person dying intestate. Under this section, then, appellant and appellee, being members of the same entitlement class, would seem to have been equally entitled to administer their son's estate. Section 1314 provides, however, that

> "[o]f several persons claiming and equally entitled [under § 1312] to administer, males must be preferred to females, and relatives of the whole to those of the half blood."

In issuing its order, the probate court implicitly recognized the equality of entitlement of the two applicants under § 15–312, and noted that neither of the applicants was under any legal disability; the court ruled, however, that appellee, being a male, was to be preferred to the female appellant "by reason of Section 15–314 of the Idaho Code." In stating this conclusion, the probate judge gave no indication that he had attempted to determine the relative capabilities of the competing applicants to perform the functions incident to the administration of an estate. It seems clear the probate judge considered himself bound by statute to give preference to the male candidate over the female, each being otherwise "equally entitled."

* * *

* * * Having examined the record and considered the briefs and oral arguments of the parties, we have concluded that the arbitrary preference established in favor of males by § 15–314 of the Idaho Code cannot stand in the face of the Fourteenth Amendment's command that no State deny the equal protection of the laws to any person within its jurisdiction.

Idaho does not, of course, deny letters of administration to women altogether. Indeed, under § 15–312, a woman whose spouse dies intestate has a preference over a son, father, brother, or any other male relative of the decedent. Moreover, we can judicially notice that, in this country, presumably due to the greater longevity of women, a large proportion of estates, both intestate and under wills of decedents, are administered by surviving widows.

Section 15–314 is restricted in its operation to those situations where competing applications for letters of administration have been filed by both male and female members of the same entitlement class established by § 15–312. In such situations, § 15–314 provides that different treatment be accorded to the applicants on the basis of their sex; it thus establishes a classification subject to scrutiny under the Equal Protection Clause.

In applying that clause, this Court has consistently recognized that the Fourteenth Amendment does not deny to States the power to treat different classes of persons in different ways. *Barbier v. Connolly,* 113 U.S. 27 (1885); *Lindsley v. Natural Carbonic Gas Co.,* 220 U.S. 61 (1911); *Railway Express Agency v. New York,* 336 U.S. 106 (1949); *McDonald v. Board of Election Commissioners,* 394 U.S. 802 (1969). The Equal Protection Clause of that amendment does, however, deny to States the power to legislate that different treatment be accorded to persons placed by a statute into different classes on the basis of criteria wholly unrelated to the objective of that statute. A classification "must be reasonable, not arbitrary, and must rest upon some ground of difference having a fair and substantial relation to  the object of the legislation, so that all persons similarly circumstanced shall be treated alike." *Royster Guano Co. v. Virginia,* 253 U.S. 412, 415 (1920). The question presented by this case, then, is whether a difference in the sex of competing applicants for letters of administration bears a rational relationship to a state objective that is sought to be advanced by the operation of §§ 15–312 and 15–314.

In upholding the latter section, the Idaho Supreme Court concluded that its objective was to eliminate one area of controversy when two or more persons, equally entitled under § 15–312, seek letters of administration, and thereby present the probate court "with the issue of which one should be named." The court also concluded that, where such persons are not of the same sex, the elimination of females from consideration "is neither an illogical nor arbitrary method devised by the legislature to resolve an issue that would otherwise require a hearing as to the relative merits . . . of the two or more petitioning relatives. . . ." 93 Idaho, at 514, 465 P.2d at 638.

Clearly the objective of reducing the workload on probate courts by eliminating one class of contests is not without some legitimacy. The crucial question, however, is whether § 15–314 advances that objective in a manner consistent with the command of the Equal Protection Clause. We hold that it does not. To give a mandatory preference to members of either sex over members of the other, merely to accomplish the elimination of hearings on the merits, is to make the very kind of arbitrary legislative choice forbidden by the Equal Protection Clause of the Fourteenth Amendment; and whatever may be said as to the positive values of avoiding intra-family controversy, the choice in this context may not lawfully be mandated solely on the basis of sex.

We note finally that, if § 15–314 is viewed merely as a modifying appendage to § 15–312 and as aimed at the same objective, its constitutionality is not thereby saved. The objective of § 15–312 clearly is to establish degrees of entitlement of various classes of persons in accordance with their varying degrees and kinds of relationship to the intestate. Regardless of their sex, persons within any one of the enumerated classes of that section are similarly situated with respect to that objective. By providing dissimilar treatment for men and women who are thus similarly situated, the challenged section violates the Equal Protection Clause.

The judgment of the Idaho Supreme Court is reversed, and the case remanded for further proceedings not inconsistent with this opinion.

Reversed and remanded.

NOTES AND QUESTIONS

1. The significance of this case is not necessarily apparent just from reading it. The Court purported to apply a "rational basis" test, which we have seen above was the governing standard from the New Deal onward. But "rational basis" is almost always a code phrase for "the law stands." As one commentator describes it:

> Under the familiar "rational basis" test—which is the default standard for equal protection and substantive due process claims—courts insist on little more than a plausible connection between legislative means and ends. The government need not produce any evidence to support a classification. And it does not matter if all available evidence suggests the legislature was mistaken. A statute may be upheld based on *any* conceivable basis, including one that the legislature never considered.

Maria Ponomarenko, *Administrative Rationality Review,* 104 VA. L. REV. 1399, 1400–01 (2018). The fact that the law in this case did not stand suggests that the Court was shifting its approach to sex discrimination to some kind of inquiry stricter than it would apply, for example, to state licensing rules for opticians. Indeed, the Supreme Court's invalidation of sex discrimination using the rational basis test in *Reed v. Reed* led to a subsequent victory for women's rights in *Frontiero v. Richardson,* 411 U.S. 677 (1973), *see supra* pages 1145–1151, a case in which the Supreme Court forbade sex discrimination by the U.S. military in handing out employment benefits. *Frontiero* left in doubt whether sex discrimination was subject to strict scrutiny, like race discrimination, or to some kind of "middle level," or "intermediate," scrutiny that asked for a strong connection to some important government interest (which is less demanding than insisting that classifications be narrowly tailored to a compelling government interest). It was clear at that point, however, that "rational basis" was no longer the law.

2. In *Craig v. Boren,* 429 U.S. 190 (1976), the Court struck down a sex discriminatory law as to the sale of nonintoxicating beer to those between the ages of 18 and 21, using an intermediate scrutiny test. *Craig v. Boren* was litigated by future Supreme Court Justice Ruth Bader Ginsburg, and she chose this case because it was one in which young men were being discriminated against. Justice Ginsburg thought the then all-male Supreme Court would identify more with the victims. Right or wrong, she won the case!

3. In 1973, the Supreme Court found that women have a constitutional right to have an abortion in *Roe v. Wade*, 410 U.S. 113 (1973). That case was decided under the individual rights doctrine of substantive due process, so we will discuss it at length below. *See infra* pages 1473–1488. Before she joined the Court, Justice Ginsburg suggested that the case might have been better argued and decided as a sex-based equal protection case. *See* Ruth Bader Ginsburg, *Some Thoughts on Autonomy and Equality in Relation to* Roe v. Wade, 63 N.C. L. REV. 375 (1985). When we come to *Roe* later, you can judge for yourself whether she was right.

4. An Equal Rights Amendment, written in 1923 by suffragette Alice Paul, was approved by Congress in 1972. It read: "Equality of rights under the law shall not be denied or abridged by the United States or by any state on account of sex." If the Fourteenth Amendment already bars sex discrimination—which was not at all clear in 1923 or 1972 but is clear in 2020—the amendment is superfluous. The ERA has been ratified by legislatures in thirty-seven States (one short of the necessary three-quarters majority), though some of those States subsequently rescinded their ratifications and others conditioned ratification on passage within a specified time frame that was not met.

5. In *Rostker v. Goldberg*, 453 U.S. 57 (1981), the Supreme Court upheld the constitutionality of a law passed during the Jimmy Carter presidency requiring that men, but not women, register for the military draft when they reach the age of 18. The Court upheld this sex discriminatory statute because of its usual deference toward the military concerning all things. Would that decision come out the same way today after the following case, which remains the leading case on sex discrimination and the Constitution?

G. UNITED STATES V. VIRGINIA

518 U.S. 515 (1996)

■ JUSTICE GINSBURG delivered the opinion of the Court.

Virginia's public institutions of higher learning include an incomparable military college, Virginia Military Institute (VMI). The United States maintains that the Constitution's equal protection guarantee precludes Virginia from reserving exclusively to men the unique educational opportunities VMI affords. We agree.

Founded in 1839, VMI is today the sole single sex school among Virginia's 15 public institutions of higher learning. VMI's distinctive mission is to produce "citizen soldiers," men prepared for leadership in civilian life and in military service. VMI pursues this mission through pervasive training of a kind not available anywhere else in Virginia. Assigning prime place to character development, VMI uses an "adversative method" modeled on English public schools and once characteristic of military instruction. VMI constantly endeavors to instill physical and mental discipline in its cadets and impart to them a strong moral code. The school's graduates leave VMI with heightened comprehension of their capacity to deal with duress and stress, and a large sense of accomplishment for completing the hazardous course.

VMI has notably succeeded in its mission to produce leaders; among its alumni are military generals, Members of Congress, and business executives. The school's alumni overwhelmingly perceive that their VMI training helped them to realize their personal goals. VMI's endowment reflects the loyalty of its graduates; VMI has the largest per student endowment of all undergraduate institutions in the Nation.

Neither the goal of producing citizen-soldiers nor VMI's implementing methodology is inherently unsuitable to women. And the school's impressive record in producing leaders has made admission desirable to some women. Nevertheless, Virginia has elected to preserve exclusively for men the advantages and opportunities a VMI education affords.

From its establishment in 1839 as one of the Nation's first state military colleges, VMI has remained financially supported by Virginia and "subject to the control of the [Virginia] General Assembly," Va. Code Ann. § 23–92 (1993) * * *.

* * *

VMI produces its "citizen-soldiers" through "an adversative, or doubting, model of education" which features "[p]hysical rigor, mental stress, absolute equality of treatment, absence of privacy, minute regulation of behavior, and indoctrination in desirable values." As one Commandant of Cadets described it, the adversative method " 'dissects the young student,' " and makes him aware of his " 'limits and capabilities,' " so that he knows " 'how far he can go with his anger, . . . how much he can take under stress, . . . exactly what he can do when he is physically exhausted.' "

VMI cadets live in spartan barracks where surveillance is constant and privacy nonexistent; they wear uniforms, eat together in the mess hall, and regularly participate in drills. Entering students are incessantly exposed to the rat line, "an extreme form of the adversative model," comparable in intensity to Marine Corps boot camp. Tormenting and punishing, the rat line bonds new cadets to their fellow sufferers and, when they have completed the 7 month experience, to their former tormentors.

* * *

VMI attracts some applicants because of its reputation as an extraordinarily challenging military school, and "because its alumni are exceptionally close to the school." "[W]omen have no opportunity anywhere to gain the benefits of [the system of education at VMI]."

In 1990, prompted by a complaint filed with the Attorney General by a female high school student seeking admission to VMI, the United States sued the Commonwealth of Virginia and VMI, alleging that VMI's exclusively male admission policy violated the Equal Protection Clause of the Fourteenth Amendment. Trial of the action consumed six days and involved an array of expert witnesses on each side.

In the two years preceding the lawsuit, the District Court noted, VMI had received inquiries from 347 women, but had responded to none of them. "[S]ome women, at least," the court said, "would want to attend the school if they had the opportunity." The court further recognized that, with recruitment, VMI could "achieve at least 10% female enrollment"—"a sufficient 'critical mass' to provide the female cadets with a positive educational experience." And it was also established that "some women are capable of all of the individual activities required of VMI cadets." In addition, experts agreed that if VMI admitted women, "the VMI ROTC experience would become a better training program from the perspective of the armed forces, because it would provide training in dealing with a mixed gender army."

The District Court ruled in favor of VMI, however, and rejected the equal protection challenge pressed by the United States. That court correctly recognized that *Mississippi Univ. for Women v. Hogan*, 458 U.S. 718(1982), was the closest guide. There, this Court underscored that a party seeking to uphold government action based on sex must establish an "exceedingly persuasive justification" for the classification. *Mississippi Univ. for Women*, 458 U. S., at 724. To succeed, the defender of the challenged action must show "at least that the classification serves important governmental objectives and that the discriminatory means employed are substantially related to the achievement of those objectives." *Ibid.*

The District Court reasoned that education in "a single gender environment, be it male or female," yields substantial benefits * * *.

"Women are [indeed] denied a unique educational opportunity that is available only at VMI," the District Court acknowledged. But "[VMI's] single sex status would be lost, and some aspects of the [school's] distinctive method would be altered" if women were admitted: "Allowance for personal privacy would have to be made," "[p]hysical education requirements would have to be altered, at least for the women," the adversative environment could not survive unmodified. Thus, "sufficient constitutional justification" had been shown, the District Court held, "for continuing [VMI's] single sex policy."

The Court of Appeals for the Fourth Circuit disagreed and vacated the District Court's judgment. The appellate court held: "The Commonwealth of Virginia has not. . . advanced any state policy by which it can justify its determination, under an announced policy of diversity, to afford VMI's unique type of program to men and not to women."

* * *

The parties agreed that "*some* women can meet the physical standards now imposed on men," and the court was satisfied that "neither the goal of producing citizen soldiers nor VMI's implementing methodology is inherently unsuitable to women.". The Court of Appeals, however, accepted the District Court's finding that "at least these three aspects of VMI's program—physical training, the absence of privacy, and the adversative approach—would be materially affected by coeducation." Remanding the case, the appeals court assigned to Virginia, in the first instance, responsibility for selecting a remedial course. The court suggested these options for the Commonwealth: Admit women to VMI; establish parallel institutions or programs; or abandon state support, leaving VMI free to pursue its policies as a private institution. In May 1993, this Court denied certiorari.

In response to the Fourth Circuit's ruling, Virginia proposed a parallel program for women: Virginia Women's Institute for Leadership (VWIL). The 4-year, state sponsored undergraduate program would be located at Mary Baldwin College, a private liberal arts school for women, and would be open, initially, to about 25 to 30 students. Although VWIL would share VMI's mission—to produce "citizen-soldiers"—the VWIL program would differ, as does Mary Baldwin College, from VMI in academic offerings, methods of education, and financial resources.

The average combined SAT score of entrants at Mary Baldwin is about 100 points lower than the score for VMI freshmen. Mary Baldwin's faculty holds "significantly fewer Ph.D.'s than the faculty at VMI," and receives significantly lower salaries. While VMI offers degrees in liberal arts, the sciences, and engineering, Mary Baldwin, at the time of trial, offered only bachelor of arts degrees * * *.

Experts in educating women at the college level composed the Task Force charged with designing the VWIL program; Task Force members were drawn from Mary Baldwin's own faculty and staff. Training its attention on methods of instruction appropriate for "most women," the Task Force determined that a military model would be "wholly inappropriate" for VWIL.

VWIL students would participate in ROTC programs and a newly established, "largely ceremonial" Virginia Corps of Cadets, but the VWIL House would not have a military format, and VWIL would not require its students to eat meals together or to wear uniforms during the school day. In lieu of VMI's adversative method, the VWIL Task Force favored "a cooperative method which reinforces self esteem" * * *.

Virginia represented that it will provide equal financial support for in-state VWIL students and VMI cadets * * *.

Virginia returned to the District Court seeking approval of its proposed remedial plan, and the court decided the plan met the requirements of the Equal Protection Clause * * *.

A divided Court of Appeals affirmed the District Court's judgment * * *. Respect for the "legislative will," the court reasoned, meant that the judiciary should take a "cautious approach," inquiring into the "legitima[cy]" of the governmental objective and refusing approval for any purpose revealed to be "pernicious."

"[P]roviding the option of a single gender college education may be considered a legitimate and important aspect of a public system of higher education," the appeals court observed; that objective, the court added, is "not pernicious." Moreover, the court continued, the adversative method vital to a VMI education "has never been tolerated in a sexually heterogeneous environment." The method itself "was not designed to exclude women," the court noted, but women could not be accommodated in the VMI program, the court believed, for female participation in VMI's adversative training "would destroy . . . any sense of decency that still permeates the relationship between the sexes."

Having determined, deferentially, the legitimacy of Virginia's purpose, the court considered the question of means. Exclusion of "men at Mary Baldwin College and women at VMI," the court said, was essential to Virginia's purpose, for without such exclusion, the Commonwealth could not "accomplish [its] objective of providing single gender education."

* * *

Senior Circuit Judge Phillips dissented.

Judge Phillips suggested that the Commonwealth would satisfy the Constitution's equal protection requirement if it "simultaneously opened single-gender undergraduate institutions having substantially comparable curricular and extra-curricular programs, funding, physical plant, administration and support services, and faculty and library resources." But he thought it evident that the proposed VWIL program, in comparison to VMI, fell "far short . . . from providing substantially equal tangible and intangible educational benefits to men and women."

The Fourth Circuit denied rehearing en banc, Circuit Judge Motz, joined by Circuit Judges Hall, Murnaghan, and Michael, filed a dissenting opinion * * *.

The cross petitions in this case present two ultimate issues. First, does Virginia's exclusion of women from the educational opportunities provided by VMI—

extraordinary opportunities for military training and civilian leadership development—deny to women "capable of all of the individual activities required of VMI cadets" the equal protection of the laws guaranteed by the Fourteenth Amendment? Second, if VMI's "unique" situation—as Virginia's sole single-sex public institution of higher education—offends the Constitution's equal protection principle, what is the remedial requirement?

We note, once again, the core instruction of this Court's pathmarking decisions in *J. E. B. v. Alabama ex rel. T. B.*, 511 U.S. 127, 136–137, and n. 6 (1994), and *Mississippi Univ. for Women*, 458 U. S., at 724: Parties who seek to defend gender based government action must demonstrate an "exceedingly persuasive justification" for that action.

Today's skeptical scrutiny of official action denying rights or opportunities based on sex responds to volumes of history. As a plurality of this Court acknowledged a generation ago, "our Nation has had a long and unfortunate history of sex discrimination." *Frontiero v. Richardson*, 411 U.S. 677, 684 (1973). Through a century plus three decades and more of that history, women did not count among voters composing "We the People"; not until 1920 did women gain a constitutional right to the franchise. And for a half century thereafter, it remained the prevailing doctrine that government, both federal and state, could withhold from women opportunities accorded men so long as any "basis in reason" could be conceived for the discrimination. See, e.g., *Goesaert v. Cleary*, 335 U.S. 464, 467 (1948).

In 1971, for the first time in our Nation's history, this Court ruled in favor of a woman who complained that her State had denied her the equal protection of its laws. *Reed v. Reed*, 404 U.S. 71, 73. Since *Reed*, the Court has repeatedly recognized that neither federal nor state government acts compatibly with the equal protection principle when a law or official policy denies to women, simply because they are women, full citizenship stature—equal opportunity to aspire, achieve, participate in and contribute to society based on their individual talents and capacities. See, e.g., *Kirchberg v. Feenstra*, 450 U.S. 455, 462–463 (1981) (affirming invalidity of Louisiana law that made husband "head and master" of property jointly owned with his wife, giving him unilateral right to dispose of such property without his wife's consent); *Stanton v. Stanton*, 421 U.S. 7 (1975) (invalidating Utah requirement that parents support boys until age 21, girls only until age 18).

Without equating gender classifications, for all purposes, to classifications based on race or national origin, the Court, in post-*Reed* decisions, has carefully inspected official action that closes a door or denies opportunity to women (or to men). To summarize the Court's current directions for cases of official classification based on gender: Focusing on the differential treatment or denial of opportunity for which relief is sought, the reviewing court must determine whether the proffered justification is "exceedingly persuasive." The burden of justification is demanding and it rests entirely on the State. The State must show "at least that the [challenged] classification serves 'important governmental objectives and that the discriminatory means employed' are 'substantially related to the achievement of those objectives.' " The justification must be genuine, not hypothesized or invented *post hoc* in response to litigation. And it must not rely on overbroad generalizations about the different talents, capacities, or preferences of males and females.

The heightened review standard our precedent establishes does not make sex a proscribed classification. Supposed "inherent differences" are no longer accepted as a ground for race or national origin classifications. See *Loving v. Virginia*, 388 U.S. 1 (1967). Physical differences between men and women, however, are enduring: "[T]he two sexes are not fungible; a community made up exclusively of one [sex] is different from a community composed of both." *Ballard v. United States*, 329 U.S. 187, 193 (1946).

"Inherent differences" between men and women, we have come to appreciate, remain cause for celebration, but not for denigration of the members of either sex or for artificial constraints on an individual's opportunity. Sex classifications may be used to compensate women "for particular economic disabilities [they have] suffered," *Califano v. Webster*, 430 U.S. 313, 320 (1977) (per curiam), to "promot[e] equal employment opportunity," see *California Federal Sav. & Loan Assn. v. Guerra*, 479 U.S. 272, 289 (1987), to advance full development of the talent and capacities of our Nation's people. But such classifications may not be used, as they once were, see *Goesaert*, 335 U. S., at 467, to create or perpetuate the legal, social, and economic inferiority of women.

Measuring the record in this case against the review standard just described, we conclude that Virginia has shown no "exceedingly persuasive justification" for excluding all women from the citizen-soldier training afforded by VMI. We therefore affirm the Fourth Circuit's initial judgment, which held that Virginia had violated the Fourteenth Amendment's Equal Protection Clause. Because the remedy proffered by Virginia—the Mary Baldwin VWIL program—does not cure the constitutional violation, *i.e.*, it does not provide equal opportunity, we reverse the Fourth Circuit's final judgment in this case.

* * *

Single-sex education affords pedagogical benefits to at least some students, Virginia emphasizes, and that reality is uncontested in this litigation. Similarly, it is not disputed that diversity among public educational institutions can serve the public good. But Virginia has not shown that VMI was established, or has been maintained, with a view to diversifying, by its categorical exclusion of women, educational opportunities within the Commonwealth. In cases of this genre, our precedent instructs that "benign" justifications proffered in defense of categorical exclusions will not be accepted automatically; a tenable justification must describe actual state purposes, not rationalizations for actions in fact differently grounded.

* * *

Neither recent nor distant history bears out Virginia's alleged pursuit of diversity through single-sex educational options * * *.

* * *

* * * [W]e find no persuasive evidence in this record that VMI's male-only admission policy "is in furtherance of a state policy of 'diversity.'" No such policy, the Fourth Circuit observed, can be discerned from the movement of all other public colleges and universities in Virginia away from single-sex education * * *.

Virginia next argues that VMI's adversative method of training provides educational benefits that cannot be made available, unmodified, to women. Alterations to accommodate women would necessarily be "radical," so "drastic,"

Virginia asserts, as to transform, indeed "destroy," VMI's program. Neither sex would be favored by the transformation, Virginia maintains: Men would be deprived of the unique opportunity currently available to them; women would not gain that opportunity because their participation would "eliminat[e] the very aspects of [the] program that distinguish [VMI] from . . . other institutions of higher education in Virginia."

The District Court forecast from expert witness testimony, and the Court of Appeals accepted, that coeducation would materially affect "at least these three aspects of VMI's program—physical training, the absence of privacy, and the adversative approach." And it is uncontested that women's admission would require accommodations, primarily in arranging housing assignments and physical training programs for female cadets. It is also undisputed, however, that "the VMI methodology could be used to educate women." The District Court even allowed that some women may prefer it to the methodology a women's college might pursue * * *. The parties, furthermore, agree that "*some* women can meet the physical standards [VMI] now impose[s] on men." In sum, as the Court of Appeals stated, "neither the goal of producing citizen soldiers," VMI's *raison d'être*, "nor VMI's implementing methodology is inherently unsuitable to women."

In support of its initial judgment for Virginia, a judgment rejecting all equal protection objections presented by the United States, the District Court made "findings" on "gender-based developmental differences." These "findings" restate the opinions of Virginia's expert witnesses, opinions about typically male or typically female "tendencies." For example, "[m]ales tend to need an atmosphere of adversativeness," while "[f]emales tend to thrive in a cooperative atmosphere." "I'm not saying that some women don't do well under [the] adversative model," VMI's expert on educational institutions testified, "undoubtedly there are some [women] who do"; but educational experiences must be designed "around the rule," this expert maintained, and not "around the exception."

The United States does not challenge any expert witness estimation on average capacities or preferences of men and women. Instead, the United States emphasizes that time and again since this Court's turning point decision in *Reed v. Reed*, we have cautioned reviewing courts to take a "hard look" at generalizations or "tendencies" of the kind pressed by Virginia, and relied upon by the District Court. State actors controlling gates to opportunity, we have instructed, may not exclude qualified individuals based on "fixed notions concerning the roles and abilities of males and females."

It may be assumed, for purposes of this decision, that most women would not choose VMI's adversative method. As Fourth Circuit Judge Motz observed, however, in her dissent from the Court of Appeals' denial of rehearing en banc, it is also probable that "many men would not want to be educated in such an environment." (On that point, even our dissenting colleague might agree.) Education, to be sure, is not a "one size fits all" business. The issue, however, is not whether "women—or men—should be forced to attend VMI"; rather, the question is whether the Commonwealth can constitutionally deny to women who have the will and capacity, the training and attendant opportunities that VMI uniquely affords.

The notion that admission of women would downgrade VMI's stature, destroy the adversative system and, with it, even the school, is a judgment hardly proved, a prediction hardly different from other "self fulfilling prophec[ies]" once routinely used to deny rights or opportunities. When women first sought admission to the bar and access to legal education, concerns of the same order were expressed * * *.

* * *

Medical faculties similarly resisted men and women as partners in the study of medicine. More recently, women seeking careers in policing encountered resistance based on fears that their presence would "undermine male solidarity," deprive male partners of adequate assistance, and lead to sexual misconduct. Field studies did not confirm these fears.

Women's successful entry into the federal military academies, and their participation in the Nation's military forces, indicate that Virginia's fears for the future of VMI may not be solidly grounded. The Commonwealth's justification for excluding all women from "citizen-soldier" training for which some are qualified, in any event, cannot rank as "exceedingly persuasive," as we have explained and applied that standard.

* * *

In the second phase of the litigation, Virginia presented its remedial plan—maintain VMI as a male only college and create VWIL as a separate program for women * * *. [T]he Court of Appeals concluded that Virginia had arranged for men and women opportunities "sufficiently comparable" to survive equal protection evaluation. The United States challenges this "remedial" ruling as pervasively misguided.

A remedial decree, this Court has said, must closely fit the constitutional violation; it must be shaped to place persons unconstitutionally denied an opportunity or advantage in "the position they would have occupied in the absence of [discrimination]." See *Milliken v. Bradley*, 433 U.S. 267, 280 (1977). The constitutional violation in this case is the categorical exclusion of women from an extraordinary educational opportunity afforded men * * *.

Virginia chose not to eliminate, but to leave untouched, VMI's exclusionary policy. For women only, however, Virginia proposed a separate program, different in kind from VMI and unequal in tangible and intangible facilities * * *.

VWIL affords women no opportunity to experience the rigorous military training for which VMI is famed. Instead, the VWIL program "deemphasize[s]" military education, and uses a "cooperative method" of education "which reinforces self esteem."

* * * VWIL students * * * do not experience the "barracks" life "crucial to the VMI experience," the spartan living arrangements designed to foster an "egalitarian ethic." * * *

* * * Kept away from the pressures, hazards, and psychological bonding characteristic of VMI's adversative training, VWIL students will not know the "feeling of tremendous accomplishment" commonly experienced by VMI's successful cadets.

Virginia maintains that these methodological differences are "justified pedagogically," based on "important differences between men and women in learning and developmental needs," "psychological and sociological differences" Virginia describes as "real" and "not stereotypes." * * *

As earlier stated, generalizations about "the way women are," estimates of what is appropriate for *most women*, no longer justify denying opportunity to women whose talent and capacity place them outside the average description. Notably, Virginia never asserted that VMI's method of education suits *most men* * * *.

* * *

In myriad respects other than military training, VWIL does not qualify as VMI's equal. VWIL's student body, faculty, course offerings, and facilities hardly match VMI's. Nor can the VWIL graduate anticipate the benefits associated with VMI's 157-year history, the school's prestige, and its influential alumni network.

* * *

The VWIL student does not graduate with the advantage of a VMI degree * * *.

Virginia, in sum, while maintaining VMI for men only, has failed to provide any "comparable single-gender women's institution." Instead, the Commonwealth has created a VWIL program fairly appraised as a "pale shadow" of VMI in terms of the range of curricular choices and faculty stature, funding, prestige, alumni support and influence.

Virginia's VWIL solution is reminiscent of the remedy Texas proposed 50 years ago, in response to a state trial court's 1946 ruling that, given the equal protection guarantee, African Americans could not be denied a legal education at a state facility. See *Sweatt v. Painter*, 339 U.S. 629 (1950). Reluctant to admit African-Americans to its flagship University of Texas Law School, the State set up a separate school for Herman Sweatt and other black law students. As originally opened, the new school had no independent faculty or library, and it lacked accreditation. Nevertheless, the state trial and appellate courts were satisfied that the new school offered Sweatt opportunities for the study of law "substantially equivalent to those offered by the State to white students at the University of Texas."

Before this Court considered the case, the new school had gained "a faculty of five full time professors; a student body of 23; a library of some 16,500 volumes serviced by a full time staff; a practice court and legal aid association; and one alumnus who ha[d] become a member of the Texas Bar." This Court contrasted resources at the new school with those at the school from which Sweatt had been excluded. The University of Texas Law School had a full-time faculty of 16, a student body of 850, a library containing over 65,000 volumes, scholarship funds, a law review, and moot court facilities.

More important than the tangible features, the Court emphasized, are "those qualities which are incapable of objective measurement but which make for greatness" in a school, including "reputation of the faculty, experience of the administration, position and influence of the alumni, standing in the community, traditions and prestige." Facing the marked differences reported in the *Sweatt* opinion, the Court unanimously ruled that Texas had not shown "substantial equality in the [separate] educational opportunities" the State offered. Accordingly, the Court held, the Equal Protection Clause required Texas to admit African Americans to the University of Texas Law School. In line with *Sweatt*, we rule here that Virginia has not shown substantial equality in the separate educational opportunities the State supports at VWIL and VMI.

* * *

The Fourth Circuit plainly erred in exposing Virginia's VWIL plan to a deferential analysis, for "all gender-based classifications today" warrant "heightened scrutiny." Valuable as VWIL may prove for students who seek the program offered, Virginia's remedy affords no cure at all for the opportunities and advantages withheld from women who want a VMI education and can make the grade * * *.

* * *

A prime part of the history of our Constitution, historian Richard Morris recounted, is the story of the extension of constitutional rights and protections to people once ignored or excluded. VMI's story continued as our comprehension of "We the People" expanded. There is no reason to believe that the admission of women capable of all the activities required of VMI cadets would destroy the Institute rather than enhance its capacity to serve the "more perfect Union."

* * * [T]he case is remanded for further proceedings consistent with this opinion.

It is so ordered.

■ JUSTICE THOMAS took no part in the consideration or decision of this case.

■ CHIEF JUSTICE REHNQUIST, concurring in the judgment.

* * *

While terms like "important governmental objective" and "substantially related" are hardly models of precision, they have more content and specificity than does the phrase "exceedingly persuasive justification." That phrase is best confined, as it was first used, as an observation on the difficulty of meeting the applicable test, not as a formulation of the test itself. To avoid introducing potential confusion, I would have adhered more closely to our traditional, "firmly established" standard that a gender-based classification "must bear a close and substantial relationship to important governmental objectives."

* * *

■ SCALIA, J., dissenting.

* * *

Much of the Court's opinion is devoted to deprecating the closed-mindedness of our forebears with regard to women's education, and even with regard to the treatment of women in areas that have nothing to do with education. Closed-minded they were—as every age is, including our own, with regard to matters it cannot guess, because it simply does not consider them debatable. The virtue of a democratic system with a First Amendment is that it readily enables the people, over time, to be persuaded that what they took for granted is not so, and to change their laws accordingly. That system is destroyed if the smug assurances of each age are removed from the democratic process and written into the Constitution. So to counterbalance the Court's criticism of our ancestors, let me say a word in their praise: They left us free to change. The same cannot be said of this most illiberal Court, which has embarked on a course of inscribing one after another of the current preferences of the society (and in some cases only the counter-majoritarian preferences of the society's law-trained elite) into our Basic Law. Today it enshrines the notion that no substantial educational value is to be served by an all-men's military academy—so that the decision by the people of Virginia to maintain such an institution denies equal protection to women who cannot attend that institution but can attend others.

Since it is entirely clear that the Constitution of the United States—the old one—takes no sides in this educational debate, I dissent.

I shall devote most of my analysis to evaluating the Court's opinion on the basis of our current equal protection jurisprudence, which regards this Court as free to evaluate everything under the sun by applying one of three tests: "rational basis" scrutiny, intermediate scrutiny, or strict scrutiny * * *.

I have no problem with a system of abstract tests such as rational basis, intermediate, and strict scrutiny (though I think we can do better than applying strict scrutiny and intermediate scrutiny whenever we feel like it). Such formulas are essential to evaluating whether the new restrictions that a changing society constantly imposes upon private conduct comport with that "equal protection" our society has always accorded in the past. But in my view the function of this Court is to *preserve* our society's values regarding (among other things) equal protection, not to *revise* them; to prevent backsliding from the degree of restriction the Constitution imposed upon democratic government, not to prescribe, on our own authority, progressively higher degrees. For that reason it is my view that, whatever abstract tests we may choose to devise, they cannot supersede—and indeed ought to be crafted *so as to reflect*—those constant and unbroken national traditions that embody the people's understanding of ambiguous constitutional texts. More specifically, it is my view that "when a practice not expressly prohibited by the text of the Bill of Rights bears the endorsement of a long tradition of open, widespread, and unchallenged use that dates back to the beginning of the Republic, we have no proper basis for striking it down." *Rutan v. Republican Party of Ill.,* 497 U.S. 62, 95 (1990) (SCALIA, J., dissenting). The same applies, *mutatis mutandis,* to a practice asserted to be in violation of the post-Civil War Fourteenth Amendment.

The all-male constitution of VMI comes squarely within such a governing tradition * * *. In other words, the tradition of having government-funded military schools for men is as well rooted in the traditions of this country as the tradition of sending only men into military combat. The people may decide to change the one tradition, like the other, through democratic processes; but the assertion that either tradition has been unconstitutional through the centuries is not law, but politics-smuggled-into-law.

And the same applies, more broadly, to single-sex education in general * * *. From grade school through high school, college, and graduate and professional training, much of the Nation's population during much of our history has been educated in sexually segregated classrooms." These traditions may of course be changed by the democratic decisions of the people, as they largely have been.

Today, however, change is forced upon Virginia, and reversion to single-sex education is prohibited nationwide, not by democratic processes but by order of this Court. Even while bemoaning the sorry, bygone days of "fixed notions" concerning women's education, the Court favors current notions so fixedly that it is willing to write them into the Constitution of the United States by application of custom-built "tests." This is not the interpretation of a Constitution, but the creation of one.

* * *

NOTES AND QUESTIONS

1. This is a long way to travel from the "rational basis" (non-)scrutiny of 1937–71! The Court does not formally adopt for sex-based classifications the "strict scrutiny" applicable to race discrimination. Has it done so in fact? Justice Scalia thought so, *see* 518 U.S. at 571 (Scalia, J., dissenting). At a minimum, the *VMI* decision raises the level of scrutiny in sex discrimination cases from intermediate level scrutiny to "skeptical scrutiny" whereby a challenged sex discrimination must meet "an exceedingly persuasive burden of justification." If this does not necessarily mean the same thing as strict scrutiny, it is pretty close. We doubt, for example, that *Rostker v. Goldberg*, the case upholding male-only draft registration, would come out the same way today if the *VMI* standard was applied.

2. The majority devotes a lot of space—most of which we edited out—to showing that the opportunities provided to women by Virginia at Mary Baldwin were not in fact equivalent to the opportunities provided to men at VMI. The implication is that there would have been no constitutional violation if the facilities were in fact equivalent. Does this mean that for sex discrimination in education, the constitutional rule is "separate but equal"? Separate is fine as long as it is truly equal? Is there anything wrong with that? Justice Scalia's dissent maintains that the inevitable consequence of the majority opinion is that single-sex education is per se unconstitutional. Does that seem right? Is there anything wrong with that?

3. The majority says: "Sex classifications may be used to compensate women 'for particular economic disabilities [they have] suffered,' to 'promot[e] equal employment opportunity,' to advance full development of the talent and capacities of our Nation's people. But such classifications may not be used, as they once were, to create or perpetuate the legal, social, and economic inferiority of women." Does this mean that affirmative action for women is easier to justify constitutionally than affirmative action for African-Americans, which is subject to strict scrutiny as a race-based classification? Does that make sense? If it does not make sense, where does the error lie?

4. Under the *VMI* case, we presume that a woman who wanted to play on the Ohio State college football team would have a constitutional right to do so if she could meet the physical tests used for men to become members of the football team.

5. Do public schools—at any educational level, whether higher, secondary, or primary—need to have unisex locker rooms and showers? If not, why not? What would be an "exceedingly persuasive justification" for not having them? Or are separate facilities all right so long as they are equal?

6. Justice Scalia says that the Fourteenth Amendment cannot invalidate practices that are as traditionally established as single-sex military academies. What modalities of interpretation does that view draw upon? He also warns that today's obvious truths may turn out to be tomorrow's foolishness. Is that a serious risk? Does it have any relevance for constitutional interpretation?

7. One key factor in the *VMI* case coming out the way it did is that Congress had co-educated the federal military academies at West Point and Annapolis in the 1970s and no harm whatsoever had come of this. By the time the *VMI* case reached the Supreme Court, VMI and an all-male military school called The Citadel, in South Carolina, were the only two all-male military academies in the United States. Forty-eight States had no all-male military academies, and the federal military academies had long been co-ed. This made it easy for the Supreme Court to dismiss VMI as an odd exception to the co-educational norm.

8. In the wake of the *VMI* case, it is hard to imagine sex distinctions that would be constitutional. *But see* note 5?

[Assignment 65]

X. OTHER FORBIDDEN FORMS OF DISCRIMINATION

Obviously, there are many types of class discrimination that raise Equal Protection Clause problems. An effort to cover all of them is impossible in this casebook, so we have picked three particularly interesting cases to excerpt in this assignment. Some other important cases you should be aware of, which we have not excerpted here, include *City of Cleburne v. Cleburne Living Center, Inc.*, 473 U.S. 432 (1985), in which the Supreme Court struck down a City's effort to require a special permit for building a facility to house people who were intellectually impaired. The Supreme Court struck down the City ordinance, saying it was irrational and that the intellectually disabled were a quasi-suspect or suspect class. Another important equal protection case is *Graham v. Richardson*, 403 U.S. 365 (1971), a case in which the Supreme Court held that the States, although not the federal government, cannot discriminate against legal aliens because they are a suspect class. The Supreme Court in *Eisenstadt v. Baird*, 405 U.S. 438 (1972), held that it was a violation of the Equal Protection Clause to make contraceptives available to married couples but not to unmarried couples. And in modern times, perhaps the most noteworthy cases have involved discrimination based on sexual orientation. Those cases—and there are several key ones—involve important elements of equal protection analysis and could easily be included at this point, but we think they are better addressed under substantive due process, so we present them later in this chapter. *See infra* pages 1533–1552. These four instances just mentioned, as well as the three cases excerpted below, give you a sense of the range of issues beyond race and sex, discrimination that the Supreme Court has invalidated under the Equal Protection Clause. Professor Calabresi thinks that all three of the invalidations below are correct invocations of either the Privileges or Immunities Clause or the Equal Protection Clause to bar class legislation. Professor Lawson joins Professor Calabresi in the first case, concurs in the result (with some hesitation) in the second, and vigorously dissents in the third. Read them and decide what you think.

A. SKINNER V. OKLAHOMA

316 U.S. 535 (1942)

■ MR. JUSTICE DOUGLAS delivered the opinion of the Court.

This case touches a sensitive and important area of human rights. Oklahoma deprives certain individuals of a right which is basic to the perpetuation of a race—the right to have offspring. Oklahoma has decreed the enforcement of its law against petitioner, overruling his claim that it violated the Fourteenth Amendment. Because that decision raised grave and substantial constitutional questions, we granted the petition for certiorari.

The statute involved is Oklahoma's Habitual Criminal Sterilization Act. Okla.Stat.Ann. Tit. 57, §§ 171, *et seq.;* L.1935, pp. 94 *et seq.* That Act defines an "habitual criminal" as a person who, having been convicted two or more times for crimes "amounting to felonies involving moral turpitude," either in an Oklahoma court or in a court of any other State, is thereafter convicted of such a felony in Oklahoma and is sentenced to a term of imprisonment in an Oklahoma penal institution. § 173. Machinery is provided for the institution by the Attorney General of a proceeding against such a person in the Oklahoma courts for a judgment that such person shall be rendered sexually sterile. §§ 176, 177. Notice, an opportunity to be heard, and the right to a jury trial are provided. §§ 177–181. The issues triable in such a proceeding are narrow and confined. If the court or jury finds that the defendant is an "habitual criminal" and that he "may be rendered sexually sterile without detriment to his or her general health," then the court "shall render judgment to the effect that said defendant be rendered sexually sterile" (§ 182) by the operation of vasectomy in case of a male, and of salpingectomy in case of a female. § 174. Only one other provision of the Act is material here, and that is § 195, which provides that "offenses arising out of the violation of the prohibitory laws, revenue acts, embezzlement, or political offenses, shall not come or be considered within the terms of this Act."

Petitioner was convicted in 1926 of the crime of stealing chickens, and was sentenced to the Oklahoma State Reformatory. In 1929 he was convicted of the crime of robbery with firearms and was sentenced to the reformatory. In 1934, he was convicted again of robbery with firearms, and was sentenced to the penitentiary. He was confined there in 1935 when the Act was passed. In 1936 the Attorney General instituted proceedings against him. Petitioner in his answer challenged the Act as unconstitutional by reason of the Fourteenth Amendment. A jury trial was had. The court instructed the jury that the crimes of which petitioner had been convicted were felonies involving moral turpitude, and that the only question for the jury was whether the operation of vasectomy could be performed on petitioner without detriment to his general health. The jury found that it could be. A judgment directing that the operation of vasectomy be performed on petitioner was affirmed by the Supreme Court of Oklahoma by a five-to-four decision.

Several objections to the constitutionality of the Act have been pressed upon us. It is urged that the Act cannot be sustained as an exercise of the police power, in view of the state of scientific authorities respecting inheritability of criminal traits. It is argued that due process is lacking because, under this Act, unlike the Act upheld in *Buck v. Bell,* 274 U.S. 200, the defendant is given no opportunity to be heard on the issue as to whether he is the probable potential parent of socially undesirable offspring. It is also suggested that the Act is penal in character and that the sterilization provided for is cruel and unusual punishment and violative of the Fourteenth Amendment. We pass those points without intimating an opinion on them, for there is a feature of the Act which clearly condemns it. That is its failure to meet the requirements of the equal protection clause of the Fourteenth Amendment.

We do not stop to point out all of the inequalities in this Act. A few examples will suffice. In Oklahoma, grand larceny is a felony. Okla. Stats. Ann. Tit. 21, §§ 1705, 5. Larceny is grand larceny when the property taken exceeds $20 in value. *Id.,* § 1704. Embezzlement is punishable "in the manner prescribed for feloniously stealing property of the value of that embezzled." *Id.,* § 1462. Hence, he who embezzles property worth more than $20 is guilty of a felony. A clerk who appropriates over $20 from his employer's till (*id.* § 1456) and a stranger who steals the same amount are thus both guilty of felonies. If the latter repeats his act and is convicted three times, he may be sterilized. But the clerk is not subject to the pains and penalties of the Act no matter how large his embezzlements nor how frequent his convictions. A person who enters a chicken coop and steals chickens commits a felony (*id.*, § 1719), and he may be sterilized if he is thrice convicted. If, however, he is a bailee of the property and fraudulently appropriates it, he is an embezzler. *Id.*, § 1455. Hence, no matter how habitual his proclivities for embezzlement are, and no matter how often his conviction, he may not be sterilized. Thus, the nature of the two crimes is intrinsically the same, and they are punishable in the same manner * * *.

It was stated in *Buck v. Bell, supra,* that the claim that state legislation violates the equal protection clause of the Fourteenth Amendment is "the usual last resort of constitutional arguments." 274 U.S. p. 208. Under our constitutional system the States, in determining the reach and scope of particular legislation need not provide "abstract symmetry." *Patsone v. Pennsylvania,* 232 U.S. 138, 144. They may mark and set apart the classes and types of problems according to the needs and as dictated or suggested by experience. It was in that connection that Mr. Justice Holmes, speaking for the Court in *Bain Peanut Co. v. Pinson,* 282 U.S. 499, 501, stated, "We must remember that the machinery of government would not work if it were not allowed a little play in its joints" * * *. Thus, if we had here only a question as to a State's classification of crimes, such as embezzlement or larceny, no substantial federal question would be raised * * *.

But the instant legislation runs afoul of the equal protection clause, though we give Oklahoma that large deference which the rule of the foregoing cases requires. We are dealing here with legislation which involves one of the basic civil rights of man. Marriage and procreation are fundamental to the very existence and survival of the race. The power to sterilize, if exercised, may have subtle, far-reaching and devastating effects. In evil or reckless hands, it can cause races or types which are inimical to the dominant group to wither and disappear. There is no redemption for the individual whom the law touches. Any experiment which the State conducts is to his irreparable injury. He is forever deprived of a basic liberty. We mention these matters not to reexamine the scope of the police power of the States. We advert to them merely in emphasis of our view that strict scrutiny of the classification which a State makes in a sterilization law is essential, lest unwittingly, or otherwise, invidious discriminations are made against groups or types of individuals in violation of the constitutional guaranty of just and equal laws * * *.

Oklahoma makes no attempt to say that he who commits larceny by trespass or trick or fraud has biologically inheritable traits which he who commits embezzlement lacks * * *. In terms of fines and imprisonment, the crimes of larceny and embezzlement rate the same under the Oklahoma code. Only when it comes to sterilization are the pains and penalties of the law different. The equal protection clause would indeed be a formula of empty words if such conspicuously artificial lines could be drawn. In *Buck v. Bell, supra,* the Virginia statute was upheld though it applied only to feeble-minded persons in institutions of the State. But it was pointed out that "so far as the operations enable those who otherwise must be kept confined to be returned to the world, and thus open the asylum to others, the equality aimed at will be more nearly reached." 274 U.S. p. 208. Here there is no such saving feature. Embezzlers are forever free. Those who steal or take in other ways are not. If such a classification were permitted, the technical common law concept of a "trespass" (Bishop, Criminal Law, 9th ed., vol. 1, §§ 566, 567) based on distinctions which are "very largely dependent upon history for explanation" (Holmes, The Common Law, p. 73) could readily become a rule of human genetics.

* * *

Reversed.

■ MR. CHIEF JUSTICE STONE concurring.

I concur in the result, but I am not persuaded that we are aided in reaching it by recourse to the equal protection clause.

If Oklahoma may resort generally to the sterilization of criminals on the assumption that their propensities are transmissible to future generations by inheritance, I seriously doubt that the equal protection clause requires it to apply the measure to all criminals in the first instance, or to none.

* * * And so I think the real question we have to consider is not one of equal protection, but whether the wholesale condemnation of a class to such an invasion of personal liberty, without opportunity to any individual to show that his is not the type of case which would justify resort to it, satisfies the demands of due process.

* * *

* * * Science has found and the law has recognized that there are certain types of mental deficiency associated with delinquency which are inheritable * * *. [W]hile the state may protect itself from the demonstrably inheritable tendencies of the individual which are injurious to society, the most elementary notions of due process would seem to require it to take appropriate steps to safeguard the liberty of the individual by affording him, before he is condemned to an irreparable injury in his person, some opportunity to show that he is without such inheritable tendencies * * *.

■ MR. JUSTICE JACKSON, concurring.

I join the CHIEF JUSTICE in holding that the hearings provided are too limited in the context of the present Act to afford due process of law. I also agree with the opinion of Mr. JUSTICE DOUGLAS that the scheme of classification set forth in the Act denies equal protection of the law. I disagree with the opinion of each in so far as it rejects or minimizes the grounds taken by the other.

* * *

There are limits to the extent to which a legislatively represented majority may conduct biological experiments at the expense of the dignity and personality and natural powers of a minority-even those who have been guilty of what the majority define as crimes. But this Act falls down before reaching this problem, which I mention only to avoid the implication that such a question may not exist because not discussed. On it I would also reserve judgment.

NOTES AND QUESTIONS

1. We will revisit some of the questions raised by this case when we discuss *Buck v. Bell, infra.*

2. If the Equal Protection Clause is concerned about the permissibility of classifications, what was the classification at issue here? Larcenists versus embezzlers? Surely, one might think, different categories of criminals are not castes or classes within the meaning of the Fourteenth Amendment. Or are they? Look carefully at the

exemptions in this statute, consider the social (and other) classes who the Oklahoma legislature surely believed were most likely to commit the exempted and non-exempted crimes, and now think about what would happen if those judgments were expressly included in the text of the law. To a reasonable observer in 1942, this statute fairly reeks of distinctions based on socio-economic class, and probably of race as well. Does that mean that socio-economic distinctions are class- or caste-like under the Fourteenth Amendment?

3. What standard of review did the Court apply? Strict scrutiny? Rational basis? Is this one of the few instances in which a State failed a rational basis test? Or, as Chief Justice Stone suggested, is this really not an equal protection case at all but a "fundamental rights" case in another guise? Keep in mind that in 1942, the Eighth Amendment did not apply to the States, so Skinner could not argue that sterilization for chicken-stealing was disproportionate punishment.

4. Note by Professor Lawson: Chief Justice Stone took as given that "[s]cience has found and the law has recognized that there are certain types of mental deficiency associated with delinquency which are inheritable." How many propositions for which the "science" today seems settled will be viewed 50 or 100 years from now with bemusement—or moral horror? When, if ever, should courts try to base constitutional decisionmaking on "science"? Does the Constitution ever call for it? Does the Fourteenth Amendment ever call for it?

B. TRIMBLE V. GORDON

430 U.S. 762 (1977)

■ MR. JUSTICE POWELL delivered the opinion of the Court.

At issue in this case is the constitutionality of § 12 of the Illinois Probate Act, which allows illegitimate children to inherit by intestate succession only from their mothers. Under Illinois law, legitimate children are allowed to inherit by intestate succession from both their mothers and their fathers.

Appellant Deta Mona Trimble is the illegitimate daughter of appellant Jessie Trimble and Sherman Gordon. Trimble and Gordon lived in Chicago with Deta Mona from 1970 until Gordon died in 1974, the victim of a homicide. On January 2, 1973, the Circuit Court of Cook County, Ill., had entered a paternity order finding Gordon to be the father of Deta Mona and ordering him to pay $15 per week for her support. Gordon thereafter supported Deta Mona in accordance with the paternity order and openly acknowledged her as his child. He died intestate at the age of 28, leaving an estate consisting only of a 1974 Plymouth automobile worth approximately $2,500.

Shortly after Gordon's death, Trimble, as the mother and next friend of Deta Mona, filed a petition for letters of administration, determination of heirship, and declaratory relief in the Probate Division of the Circuit Court of Cook County, Ill. That court entered an order determining heirship, identifying as the only heirs of Gordon his father, Joseph Gordon, his mother, Ethel King, and his brother, two sisters, and a half brother. All of these individuals are appellees in this appeal, but only appellee King has filed a brief.

The Circuit Court excluded Deta Mona on the authority of the negative implications of § 12 of the Illinois Probate Act, which provides in relevant part:

> "An illegitimate child is heir of his mother and of any maternal ancestor, and of any person from whom his mother might have inherited, if

> living; and the lawful issue of an illegitimate person shall represent such person and take, by descent, any estate which the parent would have taken, if living. A child who was illegitimate whose parents inter-marry and who is acknowledged by the father as the father's child is legitimate."

If Deta Mona had been a legitimate child, she would have inherited her father's entire estate under Illinois law. In rejecting Deta Mona's claim of heirship, the court sustained the constitutionality of § 12.

* * * On June 2, 1975, the Illinois Supreme Court handed down its opinion in *In re Estate of Karas*, 61 Ill.2d 40, 329 N.E.2d 234 (1975), sustaining § 12 against all constitutional challenges, * * *.

We noted probable jurisdiction to consider the arguments that § 12 violates the Equal Protection Clause of the Fourteenth Amendment by invidiously discriminating on the basis of illegitimacy and sex. We now reverse. As we conclude that the statutory discrimination against illegitimate children is unconstitutional, we do not reach the sex discrimination argument.

In *Karas*, the Illinois Supreme Court rejected the equal protection challenge to the discrimination against illegitimate children on the explicit authority of *Labine v. Vincent*, 401 U.S. 532 (1971). The court found that § 12 is supported by the state interests in encouraging family relationships and in establishing an accurate and efficient method of disposing of property at death. The court also found the Illinois law unobjectionable because no "insurmountable barrier" prevented illegitimate children from sharing in the estates of their fathers. By leaving a will, Sherman Gordon could have assured Deta Mona a share of his estate.

Appellees endorse the reasoning of the Illinois Supreme Court and suggest additional justifications for the statute. In weighing the constitutional sufficiency of these justifications, we are guided by our previous decisions involving equal protection challenges to laws discriminating on the basis of illegitimacy.[11] "[T]his Court requires, at a minimum, that a statutory classification bear some rational relationship to a legitimate state purpose." *Weber v. Aetna Casualty & Surety Co.*, 406 U.S. 164, 172 (1972). In this context, the standard just stated is a minimum; the Court sometimes requires more. "Though the latitude given state economic and social regulation is necessarily broad, when state statutory classifications approach sensitive and fundamental personal rights, this Court exercises a stricter scrutiny . . . ." *Ibid.*

Appellants urge us to hold that classifications based on illegitimacy are "suspect," so that any justifications must survive "strict scrutiny." We considered and rejected a similar argument last Term in *Mathews v. Lucas*, 427 U.S. 495 (1976). As we recognized in *Lucas*, illegitimacy is analogous in many respects to the personal characteristics that have been held to be suspect when used as the basis of statutory

---

11 This case represents the 12th time since 1968 that we have considered the constitutionality of alleged discrimination on the basis of illegitimacy. The previous decisions are as follows: Mathews v. Lucas, 427 U.S. 495 (1976); Beaty v. Weinberger, 478 F.2d 300 (CA5 1973), summarily aff'd, 418 U.S. 901 (1974); Jimenez v. Weinberger, 417 U.S. 628 (1974); New Jersey Welfare Rights Organization v. Cahill, 411 U.S. 619 (1973); Griffin v. Richardson, 346 F.Supp. 1226 (Md.), summarily aff'd, 409 U.S. 1069 (1972); Davis v. Richardson, 342 F.Supp. 588 (Conn.), summarily aff'd, 409 U.S. 1069 (1972); Gomez v. Perez, 409 U.S. 535 (1973); Weber v. Aetna Casualty & Surety Co., 406 U.S. 164 (1972); Labine v. Vincent, 401 U.S. 532 (1971); Glona v. American Guarantee & Liability Ins. Co., 391 U.S. 73 (1968); Levy v. Louisiana, 391 U.S. 68 (1968).

differentiations. *Id.* at 505. We nevertheless concluded that the analogy was not sufficient to require "our most exacting scrutiny." *Id.* at 506. Despite the conclusion that classifications based on illegitimacy fall in a "realm of less than strictest scrutiny," Lucas also establishes that the scrutiny "is not a toothless one," *id.* at 510, a proposition clearly demonstrated by our previous decisions in this area.

The Illinois Supreme Court prefaced its discussion of the state interests served by § 12 with a general discussion of the purpose of the statute. Quoting from its earlier opinions, the court concluded that the statute was enacted to ameliorate the harsh common law rule under which an illegitimate child was *filius nullius* and incapable of inheriting from anyone. Although § 12 did not bring illegitimate children into parity with legitimate children, it did improve their position, thus partially achieving the asserted objective. The sufficiency of the justifications advanced for the remaining discrimination against illegitimate children must be considered in light of this motivating purpose.

The Illinois Supreme Court relied in part on the State's purported interest in "the promotion of [legitimate] family relationships." 61 Ill.2d at 48, 329 N.E.2d at 238. Although the court noted that this justification had been accepted in *Labine*, the opinion contains only the most perfunctory analysis. This inattention may not have been an oversight, for § 12 bears only the most attenuated relationship to the asserted goal.

In a case like this, the Equal Protection Clause requires more than the mere incantation of a proper state purpose. No one disputes the appropriateness of Illinois' concern with the family unit, perhaps the most fundamental social institution of our society. The flaw in the analysis lies elsewhere. As we said in *Lucas*, the constitutionality of this law "depends upon the character of the discrimination and its relation to legitimate legislative aims." 427 U.S. at 504. The court below did not address the relation between § 12 and the promotion of legitimate family relationships, thus leaving the constitutional analysis incomplete. The same observation can be made about this Court's decision in *Labine*, but that case does not stand alone. In subsequent decisions, we have expressly considered and rejected the argument that a State may attempt to influence the actions of men and women by imposing sanctions on the children born of their illegitimate relationships.

In *Weber*, we examined a Louisiana workmen's compensation law which discriminated against one class of illegitimate children. Without questioning Louisiana's interest in protecting legitimate family relationships, we rejected the argument that "persons will shun illicit relations because the offspring may not one day reap the benefits of workmen's compensation." 406 U.S. at 173. Although *Weber* distinguished *Labine* on other grounds, the reasons for rejecting this justification are equally applicable here:

> "The status of illegitimacy has expressed through the ages society's condemnation of irresponsible liaisons beyond the bonds of marriage. But visiting this condemnation on the head of an infant is illogical and unjust. Moreover, imposing disabilities on the illegitimate child is contrary to the basic concept of our system that legal burdens should bear some relationship to individual responsibility or wrongdoing. Obviously, no child is responsible for his birth, and penalizing the illegitimate child is an ineffectual—as well as an unjust—way of deterring the parent."

406 U.S. at 175. The parents have the ability to conform their conduct to societal norms, but their illegitimate children can affect neither their parents' conduct nor their own status.

The Illinois Supreme Court relied on *Labine* for another and more substantial justification: the State's interest in "establish[ing] a method of property disposition." 61 Ill.2d at 48, 329 N.E.2d at 238. Here, the court's analysis is more complete. Focusing specifically on the difficulty of proving paternity and the related danger of spurious claims, the court concluded that this interest explained and justified the asymmetrical statutory discrimination against the illegitimate children of intestate men. The more favorable treatment of illegitimate children claiming from their mothers' estates was justified because "proof of a lineal relationship is more readily ascertainable when dealing with maternal ancestors." Alluding to the possibilities of abuse, the court rejected a case-by-case approach to claims based on alleged paternity.

The more serious problems of proving paternity might justify a more demanding standard for illegitimate children claiming under their fathers' estates than that required either for illegitimate children claiming under their mothers' estates or for legitimate children generally. We think, however, that the Illinois Supreme Court gave inadequate consideration to the relation between § 12 and the State's proper objective of assuring accuracy and efficiency in the disposition of property at death. The court failed to consider the possibility of a middle ground between the extremes of complete exclusion and case-by-case determination of paternity. For at least some significant categories of illegitimate children of intestate men, inheritance rights can be recognized without jeopardizing the orderly settlement of estates or the dependability of titles to property passing under intestacy laws. Because it excludes those categories of illegitimate children unnecessarily, § 12 is constitutionally flawed.

* * *

* * * Difficulties of proving paternity in some situations do not justify the total statutory disinheritance of illegitimate children whose fathers die intestate. The facts of this case graphically illustrate the constitutional defect of § 12. Sherman Gordon was found to be the father of Deta Mona in a state-court paternity action prior to his death. On the strength of that finding, he was ordered to contribute to the support of his child. That adjudication should be equally sufficient to establish Deta Mona's right to claim a child's share of Gordon's estate, for the State's interest in the accurate and efficient disposition of property at death would not be compromised in any way by allowing her claim in these circumstances. The reach of the statute extends well beyond the asserted purposes.

The Illinois Supreme Court also noted that the decedents whose estates were involved in the consolidated appeals could have left substantial parts of their estates to their illegitimate children by writing a will * * *.

* * *

By focusing on the steps that an intestate might have taken to assure some inheritance for his illegitimate children, the analysis loses sight of the essential question: the constitutionality of discrimination against illegitimates in a state intestate succession law. If the decedent had written a will devising property to his illegitimate child, the case no longer would involve intestate succession law at all.

Similarly, if the decedent had legitimated the child by marrying the child's mother or by complying with the requirements of some other method of legitimation, the case no longer would involve discrimination against illegitimates. Hard questions cannot be avoided by a hypothetical reshuffling of the facts. If Sherman Gordon had devised his estate to Deta Mona, this case would not be here. Similarly, in *Reed v. Reed*, 404 U.S. 71 (1971), if the decedent had left a will naming an executor, the problem of the statutory preference for male administrators of estates of intestates would not have been presented. The opinion in *Reed* gives no indication that this available alternative had any constitutional significance. We think it has none in this case.

Finally, appellees urge us to affirm the decision below on the theory that the Illinois Probate Act, including § 12, mirrors the presumed intentions of the citizens of the State regarding the disposition of their property at death * * *. Our own examination of § 12 convinces us that the statutory provisions at issue were shaped by forces other than the desire of the legislature to mirror the intentions of the citizens of the State with respect to their illegitimate children.

* * *

For the reasons stated above, we conclude that § 12 of the Illinois Probate Act * * * cannot be squared with the command of the Equal Protection Clause of the Fourteenth Amendment. Accordingly, we reverse the judgment of the Illinois Supreme Court and remand the case for further proceedings not inconsistent with this opinion.

So ordered.

■ THE CHIEF JUSTICE, MR. JUSTICE STEWART, MR. JUSTICE BLACKMUN, and MR. JUSTICE REHNQUIST dissent. Like the Supreme Court of Illinois, they find this case constitutionally indistinguishable from *Labine v. Vincent*, 401 U.S. 532 (1971). They would, therefore, affirm the judgment.

■ MR. JUSTICE REHNQUIST, dissenting.

The Fourteenth Amendment's prohibition against "any State . . . deny[ing] to any person . . . the equal protection of the laws" is undoubtedly one of the majestic generalities of the Constitution. If, during the period of more than a century since its adoption, this Court had developed a consistent body of doctrine which could reasonably be said to expound the intent of those who drafted and adopted that Clause of the Amendment, there would be no cause for judicial complaint, however unwise or incapable of effective administration one might find those intentions. If, on the other hand, recognizing that those who drafted and adopted this language had rather imprecise notions about what it meant, the Court had evolved a body of doctrine which both was consistent and served some arguably useful purpose, there would likewise be little cause for great dissatisfaction with the existing state of the law.

Unfortunately, more than a century of decisions under this Clause of the Fourteenth Amendment have produced neither of these results * * *. Except in the area of the law in which the Framers obviously meant it to apply—classifications based on race or on national origin, the first cousin of race—the Court's decisions can fairly be described as an endless tinkering with legislative judgments, a series of conclusions unsupported by any central guiding principle.

* * *

Following the Civil War, Congress propounded and the States ratified the so-called "Civil War Amendments"—the Thirteenth, Fourteenth, and Fifteenth Amendments, which, together with post-Civil War legislation, sharply altered the balance of power between the Federal and State Governments. See *Mitchum v. Foster*, 407 U.S. 225, 238–242 (1972) * * *.

This was strong medicine, and intended to be such. But * * * the Civil War Amendments did not make this Court into a council of revision, and they did not confer upon this Court any authority to nullify state laws which were merely felt to be inimical to the Court's notion of the public interest.

That much is common ground, at least at the conscious level. But, in providing the Court with the duty of enforcing such generalities as the Equal Protection Clause, the Framers of the Civil War Amendments placed it in the position of Adam in the Garden of Eden. As members of a tripartite institution of government which is responsible to no constituency, and which is held back only by its own sense of self-restraint, see *United States v. Butler*, 297 U.S. 1, 79 (1936) (Stone, J., dissenting), we are constantly subjected to the human temptation to hold that any law containing a number of imperfections denies equal protection simply because those who drafted it could have made it a fairer or a better law. The Court's opinion in the instant case is no better and no worse than the long series of cases in this line, a line which unfortunately proclaims that the Court has indeed succumbed to the temptation implicit in the Amendment.

The Equal Protection Clause is itself a classic paradox, and makes sense only in the context of a recently fought Civil War. It creates a requirement of equal treatment to be applied to the process of legislation—legislation whose very purpose is to draw lines in such a way that different people are treated differently. The problem presented is one of sorting the legislative distinctions which are acceptable from those which involve invidiously unequal treatment.

All constitutional provisions for protection of individuals involve difficult questions of line drawing. But most others have implicit within them an understandable value judgment that certain types of conduct have a favored place and are to be protected to a greater or lesser degree. Obvious examples are free speech, freedom from unreasonable search and seizure, and the right to a fair trial. The remaining judicial task in applying those guarantees is to determine whether, on given facts, the constitutional value judgment embodied in such a provision has been offended in a particular case.

In the case of equality and equal protection, the constitutional principal—the thing to be protected to a greater or lesser degree—is not even identifiable from within the four corners of the Constitution. For equal protection does not mean that all persons must be treated alike. Rather, its general principle is that persons similarly situated should be treated similarly. But that statement of the rule does little to determine whether or not a question of equality is even involved in a given case. For the crux of the problem is *whether persons are similarly situated* for purposes of the state action in issue. Nothing in the words of the Fourteenth Amendment specifically addresses this question in any way.

The essential problem of the Equal Protection Clause is therefore the one of determining where the courts are to look for guidance in defining "equal," as that word is used in the Fourteenth Amendment. Since the Amendment grew out of the

Civil War and the freeing of the slaves, the core prohibition was early held to be aimed at the protection of blacks. See *Strauder v. West Virginia*, 100 U.S. 303 (1880); Bickel, *The Original Understanding and the Segregation Decision*, 69 HARV. L. REV. 1 (1955). If race was an invalid sorting tool where blacks were concerned, it followed logically that it should not be valid where other races were concerned, either. See *Yick Wo v. Hopkins*, 118 U.S. 356 (1886). A logical, though not inexorable, next step was the extension of the protection to prohibit classifications resting on national origin. See *Oyama v. California*, 332 U.S. 633 (1948).

The presumptive invalidity of all of these classifications has made decisions involving them, for the most part, relatively easy. But when the Court has been required to adjudicate equal protection claims not based on race or national origin, it has faced a much more difficult task. In cases involving alienage, for example, it has concluded that such classifications are "suspect" because, though not necessarily involving race or national origin, they are enough like the latter to warrant similar treatment. See *Graham v. Richardson*, 403 U.S. 365 (1971); *Sugarman v. Dougall*, 413 U.S. 634 (1973); *In re Griffiths*, 413 U.S. 717 (1973). While there may be individual disagreement as to how such classes are to be singled out and as to whether specific classes are sufficiently close to the core area of race and national origin to warrant such treatment, one cannot say that the inquiry is not germane to the meaning of the Clause.

Illegitimacy, which is involved in this case, has never been held by the Court to be a "suspect classification." Nonetheless, in several opinions of the Court, statements are found which suggest that, although illegitimates are not members of a "suspect class," laws which treat them differently from those born in wedlock will receive a more far-reaching scrutiny under the Equal Protection Clause than will other laws regulating economic and social conditions. The Court's opinion today contains language to that effect. In one sense, this language is a source of consolation, since it suggests that parts of the Court's analysis used in this case will not be carried over to traditional "rational basis" or "minimum scrutiny" cases. At the same time, though, it is a source of confusion, since the unanswered question remains as to the precise sort of scrutiny to which classifications based on illegitimacy will be subject.

The appropriate "scrutiny," in the eyes of the Court, appears to involve some analysis of the relation of the "purpose" of the legislature to the "means" by which it chooses to carry out that purpose. The Court's opinion abounds in language of this sort * * *.

* * * I do not see how it can be doubted that the purpose (in the ordinary sense of that word) of the Illinois Legislature in enacting § 12 of the Illinois Probate Act was to make the language contained in that section a part of the Illinois law. I presume even the Court will concede that this purpose was accomplished. It was this particular language which the Illinois Legislature, by the required vote of both of its houses and the signature of the Governor, enacted into law. The use of the word "purpose" in today's opinion actually expands the normal meaning of the word into something more like motive. Indeed, the Court says that the law "must be considered in light of this motivating purpose." The question of what "motivated" the various individual legislators to vote for this particular section of the Probate Act, and the Governor of Illinois to sign it, is an extremely complex and difficult one to answer even if it were relevant to the constitutional question * * *.

* * *

* * * Even assuming that a court has properly accomplished the difficult task of identifying the "purpose" which a statute seeks to serve, it then sits in judgment to consider the so-called "fit" between that "purpose" and the statutory means adopted to achieve it. In most cases, and all but invariably if the Court insists on singling out a unitary "purpose," the "fit" will involve a greater or lesser degree of imperfection. Then the Court asks itself: how much "imperfection" between means and ends is permissible? In making this judgment, it must throw into the judicial hopper the whole range of factors which were first thrown into the legislative hopper. What alternatives were reasonably available? What reasons are there for the legislature to accomplish this "purpose" in the way it did? What obstacles stood in the way of other solutions?

The fundamental flaw, to me, in this approach is that there is absolutely nothing to be inferred from the fact that we hold judicial commissions that would enable us to answer any one of these questions better than the legislators to whose initial decision they were committed. Without any antecedent constitutional mandate, we have created on the premises of the Equal Protection Clause a school for legislators, whereby opinions of this Court are written to instruct them in a better understanding of how to accomplish their ordinary legislative tasks.

* * *

Here the Illinois Legislature was dealing with a problem of intestate succession of illegitimates from their fathers, which, as the Court concedes, frequently presents difficult problems of proof. The provisions of Illinois Probate Act § 12, as most recently amended, alleviate some of the difficulties which previously stood in the way of such succession. The fact that the Act in question does not alleviate all of the difficulties, or that it might have gone further than it did, is to me wholly irrelevant under the Equal Protection Clause. The circumstances which justify the distinction between illegitimates and legitimates contained in § 12 are apparent with no great exercise of imagination; they are stated in the opinion of the Court, though they are there rejected as constitutionally insufficient. Since Illinois' distinction is not mindless and patently irrational, I would affirm the judgment of the Supreme Court of Illinois.

NOTES AND QUESTIONS

1. The resolution of this case seems straightforward: 1) The Fourteenth Amendment creates birth equality of all citizens of the United States. 2) Differential treatment of illegitimate children violates that guarantee of birth equality. 3) It is also class legislation that creates shame and imposes elements of caste on illegitimate children, who themselves have done nothing wrong. Therefore, 4) the majority is right to strike down illegitimacy as a basis for classification on Equal Protection Clause grounds. In the end, we both think this reasoning is ultimately correct, but Professor Lawson thinks that the path is not quite as straight as Professor Calabresi believes it is. The following notes explore the reasons for this modest disagreement.

2. The Court does not apply the "rational basis" test to this classification; if it did, the State would surely win. Instead, it applies what is often called "intermediate scrutiny," which until the 1996 decision in *VMI, see supra* pages 1390–1400, was best known for being the standard of review in constitutional sex discrimination cases. What

features of illegitimacy place it in this category of stricter scrutiny? Is it because legitimacy and illegitimacy are immutable and unchosen aspects of a person? Because illegitimacy was for a long time a source of social stigma and hostility? Because an objectively true moral theory would deem the distinction between legitimacy and illegitimacy irrelevant? All or some of the above? Something else entirely? As Justice Rehnquist pointed out, the Supreme Court has never really explained—before or after 1977—how or why it makes judgments about which kinds of classifications require which kinds of scrutiny. Professor Lawson, unlike Professor Calabresi, has spent relatively little of his professional life studying the Fourteenth Amendment. He is persuaded that the Fourteenth Amendment bans class or caste-like legislation. Outside of core areas like race or sex, however, he is not entirely certain what combination of factors marks out permissible classifications from impermissible shadows of caste. Based on what he knows, he thinks that the judgment in *Trimble* seems right, but he does not find it easy to explain why that result seems right.

3. Justice Rehnquist would use "rational basis" review for everything except race (and perhaps national origin), on the theory that anything else overly tempts the Court to read its own policy views into the Constitution. That is pretty obviously, we both think, an indefensible reading of the Constitution. Does that make it an indefensible theory of adjudication? Should the meaning of the Constitution be the only relevant consideration in constitutional decisionmaking? What if the constitutional questions are hard? How much time and effort should the Court spend deciding cases? Does the Court need doctrinal rules of thumb as a concession to the shortness of life? And if one is crafting doctrinal rules of thumb, is it wrong to consider the likely skews that different rules of thumb will generate? Do your own answers to these questions depend on whether you think you are more likely to agree with the Court's policy views than with the policy views of either state or national legislators? All of these fundamental jurisprudential questions, and more, are posed by the seemingly simple question of how Illinois has to craft its statutes for intestate succession. This is another reason why Professor Lawson is not supremely confident about his assessment of this case.

4. At the time when Justice Rehnquist was appointed to the Supreme Court, many liberals like Alexander Bickel and Guido Calabresi, Professor Calabresi's uncle, were happy and excited about the idea of having one very bright conservative on the Burger Court. (Without speaking ill of the dead, we can safely say that Chief Justice Warren Burger was not widely viewed as a towering intellect.) Professor Calabresi's grandfather, Massimo Calabresi, who was a cardiologist, was at first puzzled by this reaction. After listening more, Massimo Calabresi said: "Yes, now I see why you are excited. It is the same way I feel when I look under the microscope at an entirely new and deadly virus."

C. PLYLER V. DOE

457 U.S. 202 (1982)

■ JUSTICE BRENNAN delivered the opinion of the Court.

The question presented by these cases is whether, consistent with the Equal Protection Clause of the Fourteenth Amendment, Texas may deny to undocumented school-age children the free public education that it provides to children who are citizens of the United States or legally admitted aliens.

Since the late 19th century, the United States has restricted immigration into this country. Unsanctioned entry into the United States is a crime, 8 U.S.C. § 1325 and those who have entered unlawfully are subject to deportation, 8 U.S.C. §§ 1251

1252 (1976 ed. and Supp. IV). But despite the existence of these legal restrictions, a substantial number of persons have succeeded in unlawfully entering the United States, and now live within various States, including the State of Texas.

In May, 1975, the Texas Legislature revised its education laws to withhold from local school districts any state funds for the education of children who were not "legally admitted" into the United States. The 1975 revision also authorized local school districts to deny enrollment in their public schools to children not "legally admitted" to the country. Tex. Educ.Code Ann. § 21.031 (Vernon Supp.1981). These cases involve constitutional challenges to those provisions.

* * *

The Fourteenth Amendment provides that "[n]o State shall . . . deprive any person of life, liberty, or property, without due process of law; nor deny to *any person within its jurisdiction* the equal protection of the laws." (Emphasis added.) Appellants argue at the outset that undocumented aliens, because of their immigration status, are not "persons within the jurisdiction" of the State of Texas, and that they therefore have no right to the equal protection of Texas law. We reject this argument. Whatever his status under the immigration laws, an alien is surely a "person" in any ordinary sense of that term. Aliens, even aliens whose presence in this country is unlawful, have long been recognized as "persons" guaranteed due process of law by the Fifth and Fourteenth Amendments. Indeed, we have clearly held that the Fifth Amendment protects aliens whose presence in this country is unlawful from invidious discrimination by the Federal Government. *Mathews v. Diaz*, 426 U.S. 67, 77 (1976).

Appellants seek to distinguish our prior cases, emphasizing that the Equal Protection Clause directs a State to afford its protection to persons *within its jurisdiction*, while the Due Process Clauses of the Fifth and Fourteenth Amendments contain no such assertedly limiting phrase * * *. We have never suggested that the class of persons who might avail themselves of the equal protection guarantee is less than coextensive with that entitled to due process. To the contrary, we have recognized that both provisions were fashioned to protect an identical class of persons, and to reach every exercise of state authority.

* * *

There is simply no support for appellants' suggestion that "due process" is somehow of greater stature than "equal protection," and therefore available to a larger class of persons. To the contrary, each aspect of the Fourteenth Amendment reflects an elementary limitation on state power. To permit a State to employ the phrase "within its jurisdiction" in order to identify subclasses of persons whom it would define as beyond its jurisdiction, thereby relieving itself of the obligation to assure that its laws are designed and applied equally to those persons, would undermine the principal purpose for which the Equal Protection Clause was incorporated in the Fourteenth Amendment. The Equal Protection Clause was intended to work nothing less than the abolition of all caste-based and invidious class-based legislation. That objective is fundamentally at odds with the power the State asserts here to classify persons subject to its laws as nonetheless excepted from its protection.

Although the congressional debate concerning § 1 of the Fourteenth Amendment was limited, that debate clearly confirms the understanding that the phrase "within its jurisdiction" was intended in a broad sense to offer the guarantee of equal protection to all within a State's boundaries, and to all upon whom the State would impose the obligations of its laws. Indeed, it appears from those debates that Congress, by using the phrase "person within its jurisdiction," sought expressly to ensure that the equal protection of the laws was provided to the alien population. Representative Bingham reported to the House the draft resolution of the Joint Committee of Fifteen on Reconstruction (H.R. 63) that was to become the Fourteenth Amendment. Cong.Globe, 39th Cong., 1st Sess., 1033 (1866). Two days later, Bingham posed the following question in support of the resolution:

> "Is it not essential to the unity of the people that the citizens of each State shall be entitled to all the privileges and immunities of citizens in the several States? Is it not essential to the unity of the Government and the unity of the people that all persons, *whether citizens or strangers, within this land,* shall have equal protection in every State in this Union in the rights of life and liberty and property?" *Id.* at 1090.

Senator Howard, also a member of the Joint Committee of Fifteen, and the floor manager of the Amendment in the Senate, was no less explicit about the broad objectives of the Amendment, and the intention to make its provisions applicable to all who "may happen to be" within the jurisdiction of a State:

> "The last two clauses of the first section of the amendment disable a State from depriving not merely a citizen of the United States, but *any person, whoever he may be,* of life, liberty, or property without due process of law, or from denying to him the equal protection of the laws of the State. This abolishes all class legislation in the States and does away with the injustice of subjecting one caste of persons to a code not applicable to another. . . . It will, if adopted by the States, forever disable every one of them from passing laws trenching upon those fundamental rights and privileges which pertain to citizens of the United States, *and to all person who may happen to be within their jurisdiction.*" *Id.* at 2766 (emphasis added).

Use of the phrase "within its jurisdiction" thus does not detract from, but rather confirms, the understanding that the protection of the Fourteenth Amendment extends to anyone, citizen or stranger, who *is* subject to the laws of a State, and reaches into every corner of a State's territory. That a person's initial entry into a State, or into the United States, was unlawful, and that he may for that reason be expelled, cannot negate the simple fact of his presence within the State's territorial perimeter. Given such presence, he is subject to the full range of obligations imposed by the State's civil and criminal laws. And until he leaves the jurisdiction—either voluntarily, or involuntarily in accordance with the Constitution and laws of the United States—he is entitled to the equal protection of the laws that a State may choose to establish.

Our conclusion that the illegal aliens who are plaintiffs in these cases may claim the benefit of the Fourteenth Amendment's guarantee of equal protection only begins the inquiry. The more difficult question is whether the Equal Protection Clause has been violated by the refusal of the State of Texas to reimburse local school boards for the education of children who cannot demonstrate that their presence within the

United States is lawful, or by the imposition by those school boards of the burden of tuition on those children. It is to this question that we now turn.

The Equal Protection Clause directs that "all persons similarly circumstanced shall be treated alike." *F. S. Royster Guano Co. v. Virginia*, 253 U.S. 412, 415 (1920). But so too, "[t]he Constitution does not require things which are different in fact or opinion to be treated in law as though they were the same." *Tigner v. Texas*, 310 U.S. 141, 147 (1940). The initial discretion to determine what is "different" and what is "the same" resides in the legislatures of the States. A legislature must have substantial latitude to establish classifications that roughly approximate the nature of the problem perceived, that accommodate competing concerns both public and private, and that account for limitations on the practical ability of the State to remedy every ill. In applying the Equal Protection Clause to most forms of state action, we thus seek only the assurance that the classification at issue bears some fair relationship to a legitimate public purpose.

But we would not be faithful to our obligations under the Fourteenth Amendment if we applied so deferential a standard to every classification. The Equal Protection Clause was intended as a restriction on state legislative action inconsistent with elemental constitutional premises. Thus, we have treated as presumptively invidious those classifications that disadvantage a "suspect class,"[14] or that impinge upon the exercise of a "fundamental right." With respect to such classifications, it is appropriate to enforce the mandate of equal protection by requiring the State to demonstrate that its classification has been precisely tailored to serve a compelling governmental interest. In addition, we have recognized that certain forms of legislative classification, while not facially invidious, nonetheless give rise to recurring constitutional difficulties; in these limited circumstances we have sought the assurance that the classification reflects a reasoned judgment consistent with the ideal of equal protection by inquiring whether it may fairly be viewed as furthering a substantial interest of the State.[16] We turn to a consideration of the standard appropriate for the evaluation of § 21.031.

Sheer incapability or lax enforcement of the laws barring entry into this country, coupled with the failure to establish an effective bar to the employment of undocumented aliens, has resulted in the creation of a substantial "shadow population" of illegal migrants—numbering in the millions—within our borders. This

---

14 Several formulations might explain our treatment of certain classifications as "suspect." Some classifications are more likely than others to reflect deep-seated prejudice rather than legislative rationality in pursuit of some legitimate objective. Legislation predicated on such prejudice is easily recognized as incompatible with the constitutional understanding that each person is to be judged individually and is entitled to equal justice under the law. Classifications treated as suspect tend to be irrelevant to any proper legislative goal. See *McLaughlin v. Florida*, 379 U.S. 184, 192 (1964); *Hirabayashi v. United States*, 320 U.S. 81, 100 (1943). Finally, certain groups, indeed largely the same groups, have historically been "relegated to such a position of political powerlessness as to command extraordinary protection from the majoritarian political process." *San Antonio Independent School Dist. v. Rodriguez*, 411 U.S. 1, 28 (1973); *Graham v. Richardson*, 403 U.S. 365, 372 (1971); see *United States v. Carolene Products Co.*, 304 U.S. 144, 152–153, n. 4 (1938). The experience of our Nation has shown that prejudice may manifest itself in the treatment of some groups. Our response to that experience is reflected in the Equal Protection Clause of the Fourteenth Amendment. Legislation imposing special disabilities upon groups disfavored by virtue of circumstances beyond their control suggests the kind of "class or caste" treatment that the Fourteenth Amendment was designed to abolish.

16 This technique of "intermediate" scrutiny permits us to evaluate the rationality of the legislative judgment with reference to well-settled constitutional principles * * *. Only when concerns sufficiently absolute and enduring can be clearly ascertained from the Constitution and our cases do we employ this standard to aid us in determining the rationality of the legislative choice.

situation raises the specter of a permanent caste of undocumented resident aliens, encouraged by some to remain here as a source of cheap labor, but nevertheless denied the benefits that our society makes available to citizens and lawful residents. The existence of such an underclass presents most difficult problems for a Nation that prides itself on adherence to principles of equality under law.

The children who are plaintiffs in these cases are special members of this underclass. Persuasive arguments support the view that a State may withhold its beneficence from those whose very presence within the United States is the product of their own unlawful conduct. These arguments do not apply with the same force to classifications imposing disabilities on the minor *children* of such illegal entrants. At the least, those who elect to enter our territory by stealth and in violation of our law should be prepared to bear the consequences, including, but not limited to, deportation. But the children of those illegal entrants are not comparably situated. Their "parents have the ability to conform their conduct to societal norms," and presumably the ability to remove themselves from the State's jurisdiction; but the children who are plaintiffs in these cases "can affect neither their parents' conduct nor their own status." *Trimble v. Gordon*, 430 U.S. 762, 770 (1977). Even if the State found it expedient to control the conduct of adults by acting against their children, legislation directing the onus of a parent's misconduct against his children does not comport with fundamental conceptions of justice * * *.

Of course, undocumented status is not irrelevant to any proper legislative goal. Nor is undocumented status an absolutely immutable characteristic, since it is the product of conscious, indeed unlawful, action. But § 21.031 is directed against children, and imposes its discriminatory burden on the basis of a legal characteristic over which children can have little control. It is thus difficult to conceive of a rational justification for penalizing these children for their presence within the United States. Yet that appears to be precisely the effect of § 21.031.

Public education is not a "right" granted to individuals by the Constitution. *San Antonio Independent School Dist. v. Rodriguez*, 411 U.S. 1, 35 (1973). But neither is it merely some governmental "benefit" indistinguishable from other forms of social welfare legislation. Both the importance of education in maintaining our basic institutions, and the lasting impact of its deprivation on the life of the child, mark the distinction. The "American people have always regarded education and [the] acquisition of knowledge as matters of supreme importance." *Meyer v. Nebraska*, 262 U.S. 390, 400 (1923). We have recognized "the public schools as a most vital civic institution for the preservation of a democratic system of government," *Abington School District v. Schempp*, 374 U.S. 203, 230 (1963) (BRENNAN, J., concurring), and as the primary vehicle for transmitting "the values on which our society rests." *Ambach v. Norwick*, 441 U.S. 68, 76 (1979) * * *.

In addition, education provides the basic tools by which individuals might lead economically productive lives to the benefit of us all. In sum, education has a fundamental role in maintaining the fabric of our society. We cannot ignore the significant social costs borne by our Nation when select groups are denied the means to absorb the values and skills upon which our social order rests.

In addition to the pivotal role of education in sustaining our political and cultural heritage, denial of education to some isolated group of children poses an affront to one of the goals of the Equal Protection Clause: the abolition of governmental barriers presenting unreasonable obstacles to advancement on the basis of individual merit. Paradoxically, by depriving the children of any disfavored group of an education, we foreclose the means by which that group might raise the level of esteem in which it is held by the majority * * *. Illiteracy is an enduring disability. The inability to read and write will handicap the individual deprived of a basic education each and every day of his life. The inestimable toll of that deprivation on the social, economic, intellectual, and psychological well-being of the individual, and the obstacle it poses to individual achievement, make it most difficult to reconcile the cost or the principle of a status-based denial of basic education with the framework of equality embodied in the Equal Protection Clause * * *.

These well-settled principles allow us to determine the proper level of deference to be afforded § 21.031. Undocumented aliens cannot be treated as a suspect class because their presence in this country in violation of federal law is not a "constitutional irrelevancy." Nor is education a fundamental right; a State need not justify by compelling necessity every variation in the manner in which education is provided to its population. But more is involved in these cases than the abstract question whether § 21.031 discriminates against a suspect class, or whether education is a fundamental right. Section 21.031 imposes a lifetime hardship on a discrete class of children not accountable for their disabling status. The stigma of illiteracy will mark them for the rest of their lives. By denying these children a basic education, we deny them the ability to live within the structure of our civic institutions, and foreclose any realistic possibility that they will contribute in even the smallest way to the progress of our Nation. In determining the rationality of § 21. 031, we may appropriately take into account its costs to the Nation and to the innocent children who are its victims. In light of these countervailing costs, the discrimination contained in § 21.031 can hardly be considered rational unless it furthers some substantial goal of the State.

It is the State's principal argument, and apparently the view of the dissenting Justices, that the undocumented status of these children *vel non* establishes a sufficient rational basis for denying them benefits that a State might choose to afford other residents * * *. But we are unable to find in the congressional immigration scheme any statement of policy that might weigh significantly in arriving at an equal protection balance concerning the State's authority to deprive these children of an education.

* * *.

We are reluctant to impute to Congress the intention to withhold from these children, for so long as they are present in this country through no fault of their own, access to a basic education. In other contexts, undocumented status, coupled with some articulable federal policy, might enhance state authority with respect to the treatment of undocumented aliens. But in the area of special constitutional sensitivity presented by these cases, and in the absence of any contrary indication fairly discernible in the present legislative record, we perceive no national policy that supports the State in denying these children an elementary education * * *.

Appellants argue that the classification at issue furthers an interest in the "preservation of the state's limited resources for the education of its lawful residents." Of course, a concern for the preservation of resources standing alone can hardly justify the classification used in allocating those resources * * *.

First, appellants appear to suggest that the State may seek to protect itself from an influx of illegal immigrants. While a State might have an interest in mitigating the potentially harsh economic effects of sudden shifts in population, § 21.031 hardly offers an effective method of dealing with an urgent demographic or economic problem. There is no evidence in the record suggesting that illegal entrants impose any significant burden on the State's economy. To the contrary, the available evidence suggests that illegal aliens underutilize public services, while contributing their labor to the local economy and tax money to the state fisc. The dominant incentive for illegal entry into the State of Texas is the availability of employment; few if any illegal immigrants come to this country, or presumably to the State of Texas, in order to avail themselves of a free education. Thus, even making the doubtful assumption that the net impact of illegal aliens on the economy of the State is negative, we think it clear that "[c]harging tuition to undocumented children constitutes a ludicrously ineffectual attempt to stem the tide of illegal immigration," at least when compared with the alternative of prohibiting the employment of illegal aliens.

Second * * *, appellants suggest that undocumented children are appropriately singled out for exclusion because of the special burdens they impose on the State's ability to provide high-quality public education. But the record in no way supports the claim that exclusion of undocumented children is likely to improve the overall quality of education in the State * * *

Finally, appellants suggest that undocumented children are appropriately singled out because their unlawful presence within the United States renders them less likely than other children to remain within the boundaries of the State, and to put their education to productive social or political use within the State. Even assuming that such an interest is legitimate, it is an interest that is most difficult to quantify * * *. It is difficult to understand precisely what the State hopes to achieve by promoting the creation and perpetuation of a subclass of illiterates within our boundaries, surely adding to the problems and costs of unemployment, welfare, and crime. It is thus clear that whatever savings might be achieved by denying these children an education, they are wholly insubstantial in light of the costs involved to these children, the State, and the Nation.

If the State is to deny a discrete group of innocent children the free public education that it offers to other children residing within its borders, that denial must be justified by a showing that it furthers some substantial state interest. No such showing was made here. Accordingly, the judgment of the Court of Appeals in each of these cases is

Affirmed

■ JUSTICE MARSHALL, concurring. [Omitted.]

■ JUSTICE BLACKMUN, concurring. [Omitted.]

■ JUSTICE POWELL, concurring.

* * *

Although the analogy is not perfect, our holding today does find support in decisions of this Court with respect to the status of illegitimates * * *.

* * *

■ CHIEF JUSTICE BURGER, with whom JUSTICE WHITE, JUSTICE REHNQUIST, and JUSTICE O'CONNOR join, dissenting.

Were it our business to set the Nation's social policy, I would agree without hesitation that it is senseless for an enlightened society to deprive any children—including illegal aliens—of an elementary education * * *. However, the Constitution does not constitute us as "Platonic Guardians" nor does it vest in this Court the authority to strike down laws because they do not meet our standards of desirable social policy, "wisdom," or "common sense." We trespass on the assigned function of the political branches under our structure of limited and separated powers when we assume a policymaking role as the Court does today.

* * *

I have no quarrel with the conclusion that the Equal Protection Clause of the Fourteenth Amendment *applies* to aliens who, after their illegal entry into this country, are indeed physically "within the jurisdiction" of a state. However, as the Court concedes, this "only begins the inquiry." The Equal Protection Clause does not mandate identical treatment of different categories of persons.

The dispositive issue in these cases, simply put, is whether, for purposes of allocating its finite resources, a state has a legitimate reason to differentiate between persons who are lawfully within the state and those who are unlawfully there. The distinction the State of Texas has drawn—based not only upon its own legitimate interests but on classifications established by the Federal Government in its immigration laws and policies—is not unconstitutional.

The Court acknowledges that, except in those cases when state classifications disadvantage a "suspect class" or impinge upon a "fundamental right," the Equal Protection Clause permits a state "substantial latitude" in distinguishing between different groups of persons. Moreover, the Court expressly—and correctly—rejects any suggestion that illegal aliens are a suspect class or that education is a fundamental right. Yet by patching together bits and pieces of what might be termed quasi-suspect-class and quasi-fundamental-rights analysis, the Court spins out a theory custom-tailored to the facts of these cases.

In the end, we are told little more than that the level of scrutiny employed to strike down the Texas law applies only when illegal alien children are deprived of a public education. If ever a court was guilty of an unabashedly result-oriented approach, this case is a prime example.

The Court first suggests that these illegal alien children, although not a suspect class, are entitled to special solicitude under the Equal Protection Clause because they lack "control" over or "responsibility" for their unlawful entry into this country * * *. However, the Equal Protection Clause does not preclude legislators from classifying among persons on the basis of factors and characteristics over which individuals may be said to lack "control." Indeed, in some circumstances persons generally, and children in particular, may have little control over or responsibility for such things as their ill health, need for public assistance, or place of residence. Yet a state legislature is not barred from considering, for example, relevant differences between the mentally healthy and the mentally ill, or between the residents of different counties, simply because these may be factors unrelated to individual choice or to any "wrongdoing." The Equal Protection Clause protects against arbitrary and irrational classifications, and against invidious discrimination stemming from prejudice and hostility; it is not an all-encompassing "equalizer" designed to eradicate every distinction for which persons are not "responsible."

The Court does not presume to suggest that appellees' purported lack of culpability for their illegal status prevents them from being deported or otherwise "penalized" under federal law. Yet would deportation be any less a "penalty" than denial of privileges provided to legal residents? Illegality of presence in the United States does not—and need not—depend on some amorphous concept of "guilt" or "innocence" concerning an alien's entry. Similarly, a state's use of federal immigration status as a basis for legislative classification is not necessarily rendered suspect for its failure to take such factors into account.

The Court's analogy to cases involving discrimination against illegitimate children is grossly misleading. The State has not thrust any disabilities upon appellees due to their "status of birth." Rather, appellees' status is predicated upon the circumstances of their concededly illegal presence in this country * * *.

The second strand of the Court's analysis rests on the premise that, although public education is not a constitutionally guaranteed right, "neither is it merely some governmental 'benefit' indistinguishable from other forms of social welfare legislation." Whatever meaning or relevance this opaque observation might have in some other context, it simply has no bearing on the issues at hand. Indeed, it is never made clear what the Court's opinion means on this score.

* * * [T]he Court points to no meaningful way to distinguish between education and other governmental benefits in this context. Is the Court suggesting that education is more "fundamental" than food, shelter, or medical care?

* * *

Once it is conceded—as the Court does—that illegal aliens are not a suspect class, and that education is not a fundamental right, our inquiry should focus on and be limited to whether the legislative classification at issue bears a rational relationship to a legitimate state purpose.

* * *

Without laboring what will undoubtedly seem obvious to many, it simply is not "irrational" for a state to conclude that it does not have the same responsibility to provide benefits for persons whose very presence in the state and this country is illegal as it does to provide for persons lawfully present * * *.

* * *

Denying a free education to illegal alien children is not a choice I would make were I a legislator. Apart from compassionate considerations, the long-range costs of excluding any children from the public schools may well outweigh the costs of educating them. But that is not the issue; the fact that there are sound *policy* arguments against the Texas Legislature's choice does not render that choice an unconstitutional one.

* * *

NOTES AND QUESTIONS

1. Professor Calabresi has written an article defending the result (though not necessarily the reasoning) in *Plyler v. Doe*. *See* Steven G. Calabresi and Lena M. Barsky,

An Originalist Defense of Plyler v. Doe 2017 B.Y.U. L. Rev. 225. He reasons that laws burdening the children of illegal aliens are unconstitutional since all "persons" are entitled to the equal protection of the laws. The Reconstruction Congress that passed the Fourteenth Amendment deliberately used the word "person" in the Equal Protection Clause, as well as in the Due Process Clause, to make it clear that while only citizens are entitled to privileges or immunities, all persons, including aliens, are entitled to protection under the Equal Protection and Due Process Clauses. The majority opinion in *Plyler v. Doe* is thus correct under the original understanding of the Equal Protection Clause. Professor Lawson agrees with all of this except for the conclusion—and the missing premise that generates it. The provision *vel non* of public education, he believes, is governed by the Privileges or Immunities Clause, not the Equal Protection Clause. The former applies only to citizens. This case did not involve citizens. Case dismissed. The recognition by state constitutions in 1868 of the right to a public education amply shows that it is a privilege or immunity of citizenship. *See supra* page 1319. It does not establish that failure to provide equivalent educational opportunities for citizens and non-citizens violates the Equal Protection Clause (or anything else in the Constitution), though failure to prosecute crimes against aliens—whether in the country legally or otherwise—is unconstitutional.

2. Professor Calabresi notes in response that John Harrison, *Reconstructing the Privileges or Immunities Clause*, 101 YALE L. J. 1385 (1992) argues that aliens were protected in 1868 by their equal protection right to state police and fire protection and to protection by local prosecutors, state judges, and state juries. If all of these rights of aliens were protected under the Equal Protection Clause, then access to state public schools was as well.

3. This intramural squabble, of course, is not what the justices in *Plyler* argued about. What did they argue about? What standard of review did the majority say that it was applying? What standard of review did the majority actually apply? Was it effectively strict scrutiny? Look carefully at how the majority responded to the alleged state interests put forward by Texas. What level of scrutiny/deference does that response represent? If it really was strict scrutiny in fact, what is the (unstated) suspect class or fundamental right that underlies the decision? Or was Chief Justice Burger right that the majority just didn't like the Texas policy?

4. Both the majority and Justice Powell analogize the children in this case to the illegitimate children in *Trimble v. Gordon*. Is that a sound analogy? Are there any material differences?

5. Did reading these cases help you at all understand how or why the Court applies various levels of scrutiny in different cases?

6. An issue lurking, but unaddressed, in *Plyler* is whether children born to aliens who are in the country illegally are U.S. citizens by virtue of the Fourteenth Amendment's Citizenship Clause, which says: "All persons *born* or naturalized in the United States *and subject to the jurisdiction thereof*, are citizens of the United States and of the State wherein they reside" (emphasis added). Such persons are unquestionably "within * * * [the] jurisdiction" of a State for purposes of the Equal Protection Clause; no Justice in *Plyler* questioned that basic point. Does the phrase "within its jurisdiction" in the Equal Protection Clause mean exactly the same thing as "subject to the jurisdiction thereof" in the Citizenship Clause? *Compare United States v. Wong Kim Ark,* 169 U.S. 649 (1898) *with Elk v. Wilkins,* 112 U.S. 94 (1884). If they mean different things, what does "subject to the jurisdiction thereof" mean? Professor Calabresi believes the phrase "and subject to the jurisdiction thereof" in Section 1 of the Fourteenth Amendment is given meaning by the phrase in Section 2 of the Fourteenth Amendment "excluding

Indians not taxed." He therefore believes that everyone born in the United States who is not the child of a foreign diplomat or of an Indian not taxed is a "citizen of the United States and of the State wherein they reside."

[Assignment 66]

XI. THE RISE AND FALL(?) OF SUBSTANTIVE DUE PROCESS

We saw above that the Privileges or Immunities Clause was originally the main anti-discrimination command in the Fourteenth Amendment. It was meant to forbid the making or enforcing of laws abridging, on account of race or caste, an American citizens' privileges or immunities of both federal and state citizenship. The Equal Protection Clause was meant to guarantee that local police and fire departments and state prosecutors would *protect* all classes of citizens equally in maintaining the peace. Because the *Slaughter-House Cases* eviscerated the Privileges or Immunities Clause, the Equal Protection Clause came to be seen as the main anti-discrimination command, which everyone knew was in Section 1 of the Fourteenth Amendment somewhere.

A similar phenomenon occurred with the "protect fundamental individual rights" command of Section 1 of the Fourteenth Amendment. This command was also (we think, though others strongly disagree) supposed to be protected by the Privileges or Immunities Clause; the *Slaughter-House Cases* made that impossible as well. You can *abridge* rights by class, which is why the Fifteenth Amendment forbids abridging voting rights on the basis of race and the Nineteenth Amendment forbids abridging rights on account of sex, but you can also *abridge* rights one person at a time, which is why the First Amendment bans laws that abridge the right to freedom of speech or of the press.

The clause that the Supreme Court seized on to protect individual rights and liberties in lieu of the Privileges or Immunities Clause was the Due Process of Law Clause of the Fourteenth Amendment. We have already seen that this clause, as with its Fifth Amendment predecessor, descends from Article 39 of Magna Charta, which essentially came to mean "no person may be deprived of life, liberty, or property except by a jury of his peers or by the law of the land." The Clause was originally a protection against arbitrary or capricious deprivations by the King's sheriffs or his judges. The clause did not protect against an Act of the King in parliament, which was in Britain the law of the land. Since the King in Parliament is sovereign under the British constitution, obviously no judge could strike down an act of the sovereign. In the United States, however, neither Congress nor the state legislatures are sovereign: We the People are sovereign instead. Accordingly, it became possible for courts to strike down arbitrary or capricious state laws as well as arbitrary and capricious executive and judicial acts. The question was how a court determines which laws are arbitrary and capricious and which are not without the judges injecting their own values into the decision. The Supreme Court amusingly decided to undertake this project by relying on the very same dicta in *Corfield v. Coryell*, which the Framers of the Fourteenth Amendment had said informed the meaning of the now defunct Privileges or Immunities Clause of the Fourteenth Amendment. *Corfield v. Coryell* was an Article IV Privileges and Immunities case, which defined which rights were privileges and immunities that the States could not deny to out-of-staters within their jurisdiction.

Corfield v. Coryell, "probably the most famous constitutional decision not issued by the Supreme Court," Gerard N. Magliocca, *Rediscovering* Corfield v. Coryell, 95 NOTRE DAME L. REV. 701, 701 (2019), was written by Justice Bushrod Washington, George Washington's nephew, while he was riding circuit. The issue was whether the raking of oysters from a seabed by out-of-staters was a protected privilege and immunity to which the out-of-staters were entitled, which would give them the same right to harvest shellfish possessed by in-state residents. The answer in that case was "no," because state property is not covered by the Privileges and Immunities Clause of Article IV (though Justice Washington appears to have changed his mind before reaching that final outcome, *see* Magliocca, *supra,* at 718–19). That clause protects out-of-staters' civil rights in another State, but not their political rights or their access to state property. In the process of answering this case, Justice Washington opined on the meaning of the Article IV Privileges and Immunities Clause in a passage cited over and over again by members of the Reconstruction Congress when they were discussing what individual rights Section 1 of the Fourteenth Amendment would protect. You have seen that passage several times, and you are about to see it again:

> The inquiry is, what are the privileges and immunities of citizens in the several states. We feel no hesitation in confining these expressions to those privileges and immunities which are, in their nature fundamental; which belong of right, to the citizens of all free governments; and which have, at all times, been enjoyed by the citizens of the states which compose this Union, from the time of their becoming free, independent, and sovereign. What these fundamental principles are, it would perhaps be more tedious than difficult to enumerate. They may, however, be all comprehended under the following general heads: *Protection by the government; the enjoyment of life and liberty; with the right to acquire and possess property of every kind, and pursue and obtain happiness and safety; subject nevertheless to such restraints as the government may justly prescribe for the general good of the whole [people].*

The italicized language quoted above is, in part, a bad copy of the "Born Free and Equal Clauses," which appeared in seven state constitutions in 1791, in twenty-four state constitutions in 1868 when the Fourteenth Amendment was ratified, and in thirty-seven state constitutions in 2018. A classic Born Free and Equal Clause was Article I of the Massachusetts Constitution of 1780, which read: "All men are born free and equal, and have certain natural, essential, and unalienable rights; among which may be reckoned the right of enjoying and defending their lives and liberties; that of acquiring, possessing, and protecting property; in fine, that of seeking and obtaining their safety and happiness."

It is quite possible that Justice Washington meant very little by this dictum, perhaps intending it to refer only to a requirement that common-law civil rights be afforded to all American citizens within the State on a non-discriminatory basis. *See* Magliocca, *supra,* at 712, 718–20. For purposes of the Fourteenth Amendment, however, what matters is not what Justice Washington intended but what reasonable actors in 1868 would have believed. A good many real-world actors at that time believed that Justice Washington's dictum protected certain rights against even non-discriminatory abridgments. If that is (as we think) the best account of what a hypothetical *reasonable* interpreter would have concluded, then, all things considered, in 1868: Putting this all together, the fundamental rights which are protected by Section 1 of the Fourteenth Amendment include: 1) the right to enjoy and defend life and liberty; 2) the right to acquire, possess, and protect property; and 3) the right to seek and obtain safety and happiness. These rights can be trumped, however, and are often trumped, by the States' police power because they are "subject nevertheless to such restraints as the government may justly prescribe for the general good of the whole [people]." *See* Randy E. Barnett, *Three Keys to the Original Meaning of the Privileges or Immunities Clause,* 43 HARV. J.L. & PUB. POL'Y 1 (2020).

In a nutshell, to the extent that the meaning of the Fourteenth Amendment is driven by *Corfield,* the amendment creates a weak presumption of liberty with respect to basic rights like those enjoyed by Englishmen under the common law, but the presumption is defeasible by just laws enacted for the general good of the whole people. *Cf.* RANDY E. BARNETT, RESTORING THE LOST CONSTITUTION: THE PRESUMPTION OF LIBERTY (2004) (defending a somewhat more robust presumption than is described here). Another way to put it might be that state governments must act like fiduciaries, exercising an appropriate duty of care in their law-making and law-applying functions—as one of us thinks that federal officials have had to do since 1788. *See* Gary Lawson & Guy Seidman, *By Any Other Name: Rational Basis Inquiry and the Federal Government's Fiduciary Duty of Care,* 69 FLA. L. REV. 1385 (2018). If, upon the demise of the Privileges or Immunities Clause, the Court was going to substitute the Due Process of Law Clause in its place as a guardian of fundamental rights, a weak presumption of this sort would have been a plausible second-best solution. The government's burden would be to show non-arbitrary, public-oriented reasons for its actions.

As you may know or have guessed, the law has developed in quite a different direction from what we have just described. The modern doctrine defies easy summary; the best way to learn the law is to plunge in and read the cases, with a keen eye on their historical evolution. Something else to watch is how due process and equal protection ideas often converge. It is sometimes difficult to predict whether a case is best argued, or will ultimately be decided, on due process or equal protection grounds. Litigants often argue both, and courts are not always clear on which doctrinal lines they are invoking in their decisions. Some of the cases presented below could easily have been included in the materials on equal protection, and vice versa.

With those cautions in mind, we start with one of the Supreme Court's most famous, though by no means first, major public forays into protecting fundamental rights using the Due Process of Law Clause. This case is notorious. Should it be?

A. LOCHNER V. NEW YORK

198 U.S. 45 (1905)

■ MR. JUSTICE PECKHAM * * * delivered the opinion of the court.

The indictment, it will be seen, charges that the plaintiff in error violated the one hundred and tenth section of article 8, chapter 415, of the Laws of 1897, known as the labor law of the State of New York, in that he wrongfully and unlawfully required and permitted an employee working for him to work more than sixty hours in one week * * *.

The statute necessarily interferes with the right of contract between the employer and employés, concerning the number of hours in which the latter may labor in the bakery of the employer. The general right to make a contract in relation to his business is part of the liberty of the individual protected by the Fourteenth Amendment of the Federal Constitution. *Allgeyer v. Louisiana*, 165 U.S. 578. Under that provision no State can deprive any person of life, liberty or property without due process of law. The right to purchase or to sell labor is part of the liberty protected by this amendment, unless there are circumstances which exclude the right. There are, however, certain powers, existing in the sovereignty of each State in the Union, somewhat vaguely termed police powers, the exact description and limitation of which have not been attempted by the courts. Those powers, broadly stated and without, at present, any attempt at a more specific limitation, relate to the safety, health, morals and general welfare of the public. Both property and liberty are held on such reasonable conditions as may be imposed by the governing power of the State in the exercise of those powers, and with such conditions the Fourteenth Amendment was not designed to interfere.

The State, therefore, has power to prevent the individual from making certain kinds of contracts, and in regard to them the Federal Constitution offers no protection. If the contract be one which the State, in the legitimate exercise of its police power, has the right to prohibit, it is not prevented from prohibiting it by the Fourteenth Amendment. Contracts in violation of a statute, either of the Federal or state government, or a contract to let one's property for immoral purposes, or to do any other unlawful act, could obtain no protection from the Federal Constitution, as coming under the liberty of person or of free contract. Therefore, when the State, by its legislature, in the assumed exercise of its police powers, has passed an act which seriously limits the right to labor or the right of contract in regard to their means of livelihood between persons who are *sui juris* (both employer and employé), it becomes of great importance to determine which shall prevail—the right of the individual to labor for such time as he may choose, or the right of the State to prevent the individual from laboring or from entering into any contract to labor, beyond a certain time prescribed by the State.

This court has recognized the existence and upheld the exercise of the police powers of the States in many cases which might fairly be considered as border ones, and it has, in the course of its determination of questions regarding the asserted invalidity of such statutes, on the ground of their violation of the rights secured by the Federal Constitution, been guided by rules of a very liberal nature, the application of which has resulted, in numerous instances, in upholding the validity of state statutes thus assailed. Among the later cases where the state law has been upheld by this court is that of *Holden v. Hardy*, 169 U.S. 366. A provision in the act of the legislature of Utah was there under consideration, the act limiting the employment of workmen in all underground mines or workings, to eight hours per day, "except in cases of emergency, where life or property is in imminent danger." It also limited the hours of labor in smelting and other institutions for the reduction or refining of ores or metals to eight hours per day, except in like cases of emergency. The act was held to be a valid exercise of the police powers of the State. A review of many of the cases on the subject, decided by this and other courts, is given in the opinion. It was held that the kind of employment, mining, smelting, etc., and the character of the employés in such kinds of labor, were such as to make it reasonable and proper for the State to interfere to prevent the employees from being constrained by the rules laid down by the proprietors in regard to labor * * *.

It will be observed that, even with regard to that class of labor, the Utah statute provided for cases of emergency wherein the provisions of the statute would not apply. The statute now before this court has no emergency clause in it, and, if the statute is valid, there are no circumstances and no emergencies under which the slightest violation of the provisions of the act would be innocent. There is nothing in *Holden v. Hardy* which covers the case now before us * * *.

The latest case decided by this court, involving the police power, is that of *Jacobson v. Massachusetts*, decided at this term and reported in 197 U.S. 11. It related to compulsory vaccination, and the law was held valid as a proper exercise of the police powers with reference to the public health. It was stated in the opinion that it was a case "of an adult who, for aught that appears, was himself in perfect health and a fit subject for vaccination, and yet, while remaining in the community, refused to obey the statute and the regulation adopted in execution of its provisions for the protection of the public health and the public safety, confessedly endangered by the presence of a dangerous disease." That case is also far from covering the one now before the court.

Petit v. Minnesota, 177 U.S. 164, was upheld as a proper exercise of the police power relating to the observance of Sunday, and the case held that the legislature had the right to declare that, as matter of law, keeping barber shops open on Sunday was not a work of necessity or charity.

It must, of course, be conceded that there is a limit to the valid exercise of the police power by the State. There is no dispute concerning this general proposition. Otherwise the Fourteenth Amendment would have no efficacy and the legislatures of the States would have unbounded power, and it would be enough to say that any piece of legislation was enacted to conserve the morals, the health or the safety of the people; such legislation would be valid, no matter how absolutely without foundation the claim might be. The claim of the police power would be a mere pretext—become another and delusive name for the supreme sovereignty of the State to be exercised free from constitutional restraint. This is not contended for. In every case that comes before this court, therefore, where legislation of this character is concerned and where the protection of the Federal Constitution is sought, the question necessarily arises: Is this a fair, reasonable and appropriate exercise of the police power of the State, or is it an unreasonable, unnecessary and arbitrary interference with the right of the individual to his personal liberty or to enter into those contracts in relation to labor which may seem to him appropriate or necessary for the support of himself and his family? Of course the liberty of contract relating to labor includes both parties to it. The one has as much right to purchase as the other to sell labor.

This is not a question of substituting the judgment of the court for that of the legislature. If the act be within the power of the State, it is valid, although the judgment of the court might be totally opposed to the enactment of such a law. But the question would still remain. Is it within the police power of the State?, and that question must be answered by the court.

The question whether this act is valid as a labor law, pure and simple, may be dismissed in a few words. There is no reasonable ground for interfering with the liberty of person or the right of free contract, by determining the hours of labor in the occupation of a baker. There is no contention that bakers as a class are not equal in intelligence and capacity to men in other trades or manual occupations, or that they are able to assert their rights and care for themselves without the protecting arm of the State, interfering with their independence of judgment and of action. They are in no sense wards of the State. Viewed in the light of a purely labor law, with no reference whatever to the question of health, we think that a law like the one before us involves neither the safety, the morals nor the welfare of the public, and that the interest of the public is not in the slightest degree affected by such an act. The law must be upheld, if at all, as a law pertaining to the health of the individual engaged in the occupation of a baker. It does not affect any other portion of the public than those who are engaged in that occupation. Clean and wholesome bread does not depend upon whether the baker works but ten hours per day or only sixty hours a week. The limitation of the hours of labor does not come within the police power on that ground.

It is a question of which of two powers or rights shall prevail—the power of the State to legislate or the right of the individual to liberty of person and freedom of contract. The mere assertion that the subject relates though but in a remote degree to the public health does not necessarily render the enactment valid. The act must have a more direct relation, as a means to an end, and the end itself must be appropriate and legitimate, before an act can be held to be valid which interferes with the general right of an individual to be free in his person and in his power to contract in relation to his own labor.

* * *

We think the limit of the police power has been reached and passed in this case. There is, in our judgment, no reasonable foundation for holding this to be necessary or appropriate as a health law to safeguard the public health or the health of the individuals who are following the trade of a baker. If this statute be valid, and if, therefore, a proper case is made out in which to deny the right of an individual, *sui juris*, as employer or employé, to make contracts for the labor of the latter under the protection of the provisions of the Federal Constitution, there would seem to be no length to which legislation of this nature might not go * * *.

* * * It is unfortunately true that labor, even in any department, may possibly carry with it the seeds of unhealthiness. But are we all, on that account, at the mercy of legislative majorities? A printer, a tinsmith, a locksmith, a carpenter, a cabinetmaker, a dry goods clerk, a bank's, a lawyer's or a physician's clerk, or a clerk in almost any kind of business, would all come under the power of the legislature, on this assumption. No trade, no occupation, no mode of earning one's living, could escape this all-pervading power, and the acts of the legislature in limiting the hours of labor in all employments would be valid, although such limitation might seriously cripple the ability of the laborer to support himself and his family. In our large cities there are many buildings into which the sun penetrates for but a short time in each day, and these buildings are occupied by people carrying on the business of bankers, brokers, lawyers, real estate, and many other kinds of business, aided by many clerks, messengers, and other employés. Upon the assumption of the validity of this act under review, it is not possible to say that an act prohibiting lawyers' or bank clerks, or others from contracting to labor for their employers more than eight hours a day, would be invalid. It might be said that it is unhealthy to work more than that

number of hours in an apartment lighted by artificial light during the working hours of the day; that the occupation of the bank clerk, the lawyer's clerk, the real estate clerk, or the broker's clerk in such offices is therefore unhealthy, and the legislature in its paternal wisdom must, therefore, have the right to legislate on the subject of and to limit the hours for such labor, and if it exercises that power and its validity be questioned, it is sufficient to say it has reference to the public health, it has reference to the health of the employés condemned to labor day after day in buildings where the sun never shines; it is a health law, and therefore it is valid, and cannot be questioned by the courts.

* * * The act is not, within any fair meaning of the term, a health law, but is an illegal interference with the rights of individuals, both employers and employés, to make contracts regarding labor upon such terms as they may think best, or which they may agree upon with the other parties to such contracts. Statutes of the nature of that under review, limiting the hours in which grown and intelligent men may labor to earn their living, are mere meddlesome interferences with the rights of the individual, and they are not saved from condemnation by the claim that they are passed in the exercise of the police power and upon the subject of the health of the individual whose rights are interfered with, unless there be some fair ground, reasonable in and of itself, to say that there is material danger to the public health or to the health of the employés if the hours of labor are not curtailed. If this be not clearly the case the individuals, whose rights are thus made the subject of legislative interference, are under the protection of the Federal Constitution regarding their liberty of contract as well as of person, and the legislature of the State has no power to limit their right as proposed in this statute. All that it could properly do has been done by it with regard to the conduct of bakeries, as provided for in the other sections of the act above set forth. These several sections provide for the inspection of the premises where the bakery is carried on, with regard to furnishing proper wash-rooms and water-closets, apart from the bake-room, also with regard to providing proper drainage, plumbing and painting; the sections, in addition, provide for the height of the ceiling, the cementing or tiling of floors, where necessary in the opinion of the factory inspector, and for other things of that nature, alterations are also provided for and are to be made where necessary in the opinion of the inspector, in order to comply with the provisions of the statute. These various sections may be wise and valid regulations, and they certainly go to the full extent of providing for the cleanliness and the healthiness, so far as possible, of the quarters in which bakeries are to be conducted. Adding to all these requirements a prohibition to enter into any contract of labor in a bakery for more than a certain number of hours a week, is, in our judgment, so wholly beside the matter of a proper, reasonable and fair provision, as to run counter to that liberty of person and of free contract provided for in the Federal Constitution.

* * *

This interference on the part of the legislatures of the several States with the ordinary trades and occupations of the people seems to be on the increase * * *.

* * *

It is impossible for us to shut our eyes to the fact that many of the laws of this character, while passed under what is claimed to be the police power for the purpose of protecting the public health or welfare, are, in reality, passed from other motives.

We are justified in saying so when, from the character of the law and the subject upon which it legislates, it is apparent that the public health or welfare bears but the most remote relation to the law. The purpose of a statute must be determined from the natural and legal effect of the language employed; and whether it is or is not repugnant to the Constitution of the United States must be determined from the natural effect of such statutes when put into operation, and not from their proclaimed purpose. The court looks beyond the mere letter of the law in such cases.

It is manifest to us that the limitation of the hours of labor as provided for in this section of the statute under which the indictment was found, and the plaintiff in error convicted, has no such direct relation to and no such substantial effect upon the health of the employé, as to justify us in regarding the section as really a health law. It seems to us that the real object and purpose were simply to regulate the hours of labor between the master and his employés (all being men, *sui juris*) in a private business, not dangerous in any degree to morals or in any real and substantial degree to the health of the employés. Under such circumstances the freedom of master and employé to contract with each other in relation to their employment, and in defining the same, cannot be prohibited or interfered with, without violating the Federal Constitution.

The judgment of the Court of Appeals of New York as well as that of the Supreme Court and of the County Court of Oneida County must be reversed and the case remanded to the County Court for further proceedings not inconsistent with this opinion.

Reversed.

■ MR. JUSTICE HOLMES dissenting.

I regret sincerely that I am unable to agree with the judgment in this case, and that I think it my duty to express my dissent.

This case is decided upon an economic theory which a large part of the country does not entertain. If it were a question whether I agreed with that theory, I should desire to study it further and long before making up my mind. But I do not conceive that to be my duty, because I strongly believe that my agreement or disagreement has nothing to do with the right of a majority to embody their opinions in law. It is settled by various decisions of this court that state constitutions and state laws may regulate life in many ways which we as legislators might think as injudicious or if you like as tyrannical, as this, and which equally with this interfere with the liberty to contract. Sunday laws and usury laws are ancient examples. A more modern one is the prohibition of lotteries. The liberty of the citizen to do as he likes so long as he does not interfere with the liberty of others to do the same, which has been a shibboleth for some well-known writers, is interfered with by school laws, by the Post Office, by every state or municipal institution which takes his money for purposes thought desirable, whether he likes it or not. The Fourteenth Amendment does not enact Mr. Herbert Spencer's Social Statics. The other day we sustained the Massachusetts vaccination law. *Jacobson v. Massachusetts*, 197 U.S. 11. United States and state statutes and decisions cutting down the liberty to contract by way of combination are familiar to this court. *Northern Securities Co. v. United States*, 193 U.S. 197. Two years ago, we upheld the prohibition of sales of stock on margins or for future delivery in the constitution of California. *Otis v. Parker*, 187 U.S. 606. The decision sustaining an eight hour law for miners is still recent. *Holden v. Hardy*,

169 U.S. 366. Some of these laws embody convictions or prejudices which judges are likely to share. Some may not. But a constitution is not intended to embody a particular economic theory, whether of paternalism and the organic relation of the citizen to the State or of *laissez faire*. It is made for people of fundamentally differing views, and the accident of our finding certain opinions natural and familiar or novel and even shocking ought not to conclude our judgment upon the question whether statutes embodying them conflict with the Constitution of the United States.

General propositions do not decide concrete cases. The decision will depend on a judgment or intuition more subtle than any articulate major premise. But I think that the proposition just stated, if it is accepted, will carry us far toward the end. Every opinion tends to become a law. I think that the word liberty in the Fourteenth Amendment is perverted when it is held to prevent the natural outcome of a dominant opinion, unless it can be said that a rational and fair man necessarily would admit that the statute proposed would infringe fundamental principles as they have been understood by the traditions of our people and our law. It does not need research to show that no such sweeping condemnation can be passed upon the statute before us. A reasonable man might think it a proper measure on the score of health. Men whom I certainly could not pronounce unreasonable would uphold it as a first instalment of a general regulation of the hours of work. Whether in the latter aspect it would be open to the charge of inequality I think it unnecessary to discuss.

■ MR. JUSTICE HARLAN, with whom MR. JUSTICE WHITE and MR. JUSTICE DAY concurred, dissenting.

While this court has not attempted to mark the precise boundaries of what is called the police power of the State, the existence of the power has been uniformly recognized, both by the Federal and state courts.

All the cases agree that this power extends at least to the protection of the lives, the health, and the safety of the public against the injurious exercise by any citizen of his own rights.

* * *

Granting then that there is a liberty of contract which cannot be violated even under the sanction of direct legislative enactment, but assuming, as according to settled law we may assume, that such liberty of contract is subject to such regulations as the State may reasonably prescribe for the common good and the well-being of society, what are the conditions under which the judiciary may declare such regulations to be in excess of legislative authority and void? Upon this point there is no room for dispute, for, the rule is universal that a legislative enactment, Federal or state, is never to be disregarded or held invalid unless it be, beyond question, plainly and palpably in excess of legislative power * * *. If there be doubt as to the validity of the statute, that doubt must therefore be resolved in favor of its validity, and the courts must keep their hands off, leaving the legislature to meet the responsibility for unwise legislation. If the end which the legislature seeks to accomplish be one to which its power extends, and if the means employed to that end, although not the wisest or best, are yet not plainly and palpably unauthorized by law, then the court cannot interfere. In other words, when the validity of a statute is questioned, the burden of proof, so to speak, is upon those who assert it to be unconstitutional.

* * *

It is plain that this statute was enacted in order to protect the physical well-being of those who work in bakery and confectionery establishments. It may be that the statute had its origin, in part, in the belief that employers and employés in such establishments were not upon an equal footing, and that the necessities of the latter often compelled them to submit to such exactions as unduly taxed their strength. Be this as it may, the statute must be taken as expressing the belief of the people of New York that, as a general rule, and in the case of the average man, labor in excess of sixty hours during a week in such establishments may endanger the health of those who thus labor. Whether or not this be wise legislation it is not the province of the court to inquire. Under our systems of government the courts are not concerned with the wisdom or policy of legislation. So that in determining the question of power to interfere with liberty of contract, the court may inquire whether the means devised by the State are germane to an end which may be lawfully accomplished and have a real or substantial relation to the protection of health, as involved in the daily work of the persons, male and female, engaged in bakery and confectionery establishments. But when this inquiry is entered upon I find it impossible, in view of common experience, to say that there is here no real or substantial relation between the means employed by the State and the end sought to be accomplished by its legislation. Nor can I say that the statute has no appropriate or direct connection with that protection to health which each State owes to her citizens, or that it is not promotive of the health of the employés in question, or that the regulation prescribed by the State is utterly unreasonable and extravagant or wholly arbitrary * * *.

* * *

I take leave to say that the New York statute, in the particulars here involved, cannot be held to be in conflict with the Fourteenth Amendment without enlarging the scope of the Amendment far beyond its original purpose and without bringing under the supervision of this court matters which have been supposed to belong exclusively to the legislative departments of the several States when exerting their conceded power to guard the health and safety of their citizens by such regulations as they in their wisdom deem best * * *.

* * *

NOTES AND QUESTIONS

1. Is *Lochner* really a free-swinging paean to liberty of contract? The Court explains that it has upheld numerous laws dealing with workplaces, health, and the like, and that would uphold this law if it was persuaded that it was a health law. The majority simply does not believe that the State has shown enough of an impact on health to justify the law. The next time around, the State might have a better showing and win. The Court may well have been wrong on the facts of this case, but was it really enacting into law Mr. Herbert Spencer's *Social Statics*?

2. There is no doubt that the rights to work and to contract are among the "privileges or immunities" protected by the Fourteenth Amendment. The real question in *Lochner*, as a matter of original meaning, is whether they were abridged by the New York maximum-hours law. Was this an instance in which a background right was validly impaired by a just law enacted for the general good? More to the point: How closely is a court supposed to look at the operation and/or motives of the law in order to make that assessment. As with so many issues in the law, the key question is the level of judicial scrutiny and the degree of deference afforded the government. Put in those terms, we

both think that the majority in *Lochner* was probably wrong, but the case is not the slam dunk that much history has portrayed. Suppose, for a moment, that there was convincing evidence that the maximum-hours law was enacted, not out of any concern for the health of bakers, but as class legislation to shut down Mom-and-Pop immigrant bakeries that were undercutting the prices of larger (and largely unionized) bakeshops. In that circumstance, the law would clearly be unconstitutional as monopolistic class legislation. As it happens, at least one scholar who has studied the case in depth believes that this is precisely what the law was about. *See* DAVID E. BERNSTEIN, REHABILITATING LOCHNER: DEFENDING INDIVIDUAL RIGHTS AGAINST PROGRESSIVE REFORM (2012). The problem is that, while this argument about the law's unsavory purposes makes a backhanded appearance near the end of the majority opinion, there is nothing in the opinion (and therefore likely nothing in the record) to establish this account of the law with any reasonable certainty. Absent that showing, one is left to assess the law on its face, and if all that the Fourteenth Amendment requires is a modest presumption of liberty, it is not irrational to see the law as a health law. Under anything resembling "rational basis" review—even a "rational basis" review with some measure of bite—it is hard to say that this is not a plausible health law. And that ends the case. Liberty to make and enforce at least some contracts is clearly a privilege or immunity but contracts that offend against the moral order, like contracts to engage in prostitution, to gamble, or to fight a duel, can clearly be banned via just laws enacted for the general good of the whole people. The New York law regulating the number of hours a week a baker could work was a new-fangled law in 1905, but that of course does not mean it is unconstitutional. Absent a showing that powerful baking interests and unions were trying to drive Mom-and-Pop immigrant bakers out of business, the law seems like a perfectly plausible exercise of the police power. This is especially the case because the Court had held in *Holden v. Hardy*, 169 U.S. 366 (1898), that eight-hour per day limits on coal mining were a justifiable use of the police power. Three years after *Lochner*, the Court held in *Muller v. Oregon*, 208 U.S. 412 (1908), that it was constitutional to allot women fewer work hours per day than men. Obviously, the Supreme Court was on thin ice once it said eight-hour a day limits for miners were constitutional but sixty-hour work weeks for bakers were unconstitutional, but shorter work weeks for women were constitutional. These numbers of work hours were clearly not coming from the Constitution but reflected the justices' own assessments as to what was "reasonable.".

3. Justice John Marshal Harlan the Elder's dissent urges a minimal "rational basis" review. Is that because he does not see the right to contract as fundamental? (The Framers of the Fourteenth Amendment would surely take issue with him about that.) Or is it because he thinks that *all* laws should be examined under "rational basis" review unless they involve racial classifications, as in *Plessy*? What level of review did the majority actually apply? Did the majority apply the right standard of review and misapply it, or did the majority apply the wrong standard of review? Or did the majority get it exactly right and we and Harlan have it wrong?

4. Justice Oliver Wendell Holmes' dissent is the most famous of his career, and it is one of the most forthright assertions of thorough-going Thayerian judicial restraint. (Thayer published his famous article only twelve years before *Lochner*.) Does his opinion sound like any modern opinions that you have read thus far? Consider where Thayerian judicial restraint leads Holmes in the following case. We have not edited the opinion in any fashion.

B. BUCK V. BELL

274 U.S. 200 (1927)

■ MR. JUSTICE HOLMES delivered the opinion of the Court.

This is a writ of error to review a judgment of the Supreme Court of Appeals of the State of Virginia, affirming a judgment of the Circuit Court of Amherst County by which the defendant in error, the superintendent of the State Colony for Epileptics and Feeble Minded, was ordered to perform the operation of salpingectomy upon Carrie Buck, the plaintiff in error, for the purpose of making her sterile. 143 Va. 310. The case comes here upon the contention that the statute authorizing the judgment is void under the Fourteenth Amendment as denying to the plaintiff in error due process of law and the equal protection of the laws.

Carrie Buck is a feeble minded white woman who was committed to the State Colony above mentioned in due form. She is the daughter of a feeble minded mother in the same institution, and the mother of an illegitimate feeble minded child. She was eighteen years old at the time of the trial of her case in the Circuit Court, in the latter part of 1924. An Act of Virginia, approved March 20, 1924, recites that the health of the patient and the welfare of society may be promoted in certain cases by the sterilization of mental defectives, under careful safeguard, &c.; that the sterilization may be effected in males by vasectomy and in females by salpingectomy, without serious pain or substantial danger to life; that the Commonwealth is supporting in various institutions many defective persons who if now discharged would become a menace but if incapable of procreating might be discharged with safety and become self-supporting with benefit to themselves and to society; and that experience has shown that heredity plays an important part in the transmission of insanity, imbecility, &c. The statute then enacts that whenever the superintendent of certain institutions including the above named State Colony shall be of opinion that it is for the best interests of the patients and of society that an inmate under his care should be sexually sterilized, he may have the operation performed upon any patient afflicted with hereditary forms of insanity, imbecility, &c., on complying with the very careful provisions by which the act protects the patients from possible abuse.

The superintendent first presents a petition to the special board of directors of his hospital or colony, stating the facts and the grounds for his opinion, verified by affidavit. Notice of the petition and of the time and place of the hearing in the institution is to be served upon the inmate, and also upon his guardian, and if there is no guardian, the superintendent is to apply to the Circuit Court of the County to appoint one. If the inmate is a minor notice also is to be given to his parents if any with a copy of the petition. The board is to see to it that the inmate may attend the hearings if desired by him or his guardian. The evidence is all to be reduced to writing, and after the board has made its order for or against the operation, the superintendent, or the inmate, or his guardian, may appeal to the Circuit Court of the County. The Circuit Court may consider the record of the board and the evidence before it and such other admissible evidence as may be offered, and may affirm, revise, or reverse the order of the board and enter such order as it deems just. Finally any party may apply to the Supreme Court of Appeals, which, if it grants the appeal, is to hear the case upon the record of the trial in the Circuit Court and may enter such order as it thinks the Circuit Court should have entered. There can be no doubt that so far as procedure is concerned the rights of the patient are most carefully considered, and as every step in this case was taken in scrupulous compliance with the statute and after months of observation, there is no doubt that in that respect the plaintiff in error has had due process of law.

The attack is not upon the procedure but upon the substantive law. It seems to be contended that in no circumstances could such an order be justified. It certainly is contended that the order cannot be justified upon the existing grounds. The judgment finds the facts that have been recited, and that Carrie Buck "is the probable potential parent of socially inadequate offspring, likewise afflicted, that she may be sexually sterilized without detriment to her general health and that her welfare and that of society will be promoted by her sterilization," and thereupon makes the order. In view of the general declarations of the legislature and the specific findings of the Court, obviously we cannot say as matter of law that the grounds do not exist, and, if they exist they justify the result. We have seen more than once that the public welfare may call upon the best citizens for their lives. It would be strange if it could not call upon those who already sap the strength of the State for these lesser sacrifices, often not felt to be such by those concerned, in order to prevent our being swamped with incompetence. It is better for all the world if, instead of waiting to execute degenerate offspring for crime, or to let them starve for their imbecility, society can prevent those who are manifestly unfit from continuing their kind. The principle that sustains compulsory vaccination is broad enough to cover cutting the Fallopian tubes. *Jacobson v. Massachusetts*, 197 U.S. 11. Three generations of imbeciles are enough.

But, it is said, however it might be if this reasoning were applied generally, it fails when it is confined to the small number who are in the institutions named and is not applied to the multitudes outside. It is the usual last resort of constitutional arguments to point out shortcomings of this sort. But the answer is that the law does all that is needed when it does all that it can, indicates a policy, applies it to all within the lines, and seeks to bring within the lines all similarly situated so far and so fast as its means allow. Of course, so far as the operations enable those who otherwise must be kept confined to be returned to the world, and thus open the asylum to others, the equality aimed at will be more nearly reached.

Judgment affirmed.

■ MR. JUSTICE BUTLER dissents.

NOTES AND QUESTIONS

1. *Buck v. Bell* represents the fruition of the American eugenics movement, which was started by Sir Francis Galton, Charles Darwin's half-cousin. Galton produced more than 340 "scholarly" papers on how intelligence is hereditary, and he argued that society should affirmatively act to improve the human species by sterilizing those who are "feeble-minded" while ensuring that persons of higher intelligence have as many children as is possible. As we discussed earlier, *see supra* pages 1295–1297, much of the resulting flood of eugenics scholarship—produced by leading academics from all of the country's leading "elite" institutions—focused explicitly on race, emphasizing the urgent need to keep gene pools pure from contamination both from "inferior" races and from "inferior" individuals like Carrie Buck. (The idea of a "race" at that time extended far more broadly than does the modern use of that term. Aryans, Irish, Italians, and Jews, among numerous others, were all considered "races." *See* VICTORIA NOURSE, IN RECKLESS HANDS: *SKINNER V. OKLAHOMA* AND THE NEAR-TRIUMPH OF AMERICAN EUGENICS 35–36, 170 (2008).

Indeed, there were fine-grained theories of race that, for example, broke down Jews into discrete categories based on countries of origin. *See* EDWIN BLACK, WAR AGAINST THE WEAK: EUGENICS AND AMERICA'S CAMPAIGN TO CREATE A MASTER RACE 190 (2003).) Galton's support for eugenics and racism swept the Western world during the period between 1877 and 1945 to a degree that is almost inconceivable in the present day. The President of Harvard was a eugenicist, the Ford and Rockefeller Foundations advocated eugenics, and more than thirty States adopted compulsory sterilization laws. Theodore Roosevelt was a eugenics enthusiast, *see* BLACK, *supra,* at 46, 99, as was Margaret Sanger, *see id.* at 127–44. Woodrow Wilson signed a New Jersey eugenics bill into law while he was the governor of that State. "Indeed, the Virginia eugenics sterilization law upheld in Buck was based on a model statute drafted by the Harriman and Carnegie funded Eugenics Record Office." Edward J. Larson, *Putting* Buck v. Bell *in Scientific and Historical Context: A Response to Victoria Nourse,* 39 PEPPERDINE L. REV. 119, 123 (2011). Justice Oliver Wendell Holmes and the near-unanimous Court majority was just parroting the scientifically evolved Constitution of 1927 when deciding *Buck v. Bell.* More than 60,000 Americans were compulsorily sterilized before a combination of *Skinner v. Oklahoma, see supra* pages 1402–1405, and the horror of Nazism and the Holocaust—which explicitly modeled its eugenics program on the American example—put American eugenicists out of business (though without formally overruling *Buck v. Bell*).

2. Eugenics was not confined to the United States and Nazi Germany, though those two countries were the leading proponents of governmental pursuit of biological purity. Finally, in 1948, after the Holocaust, the world woke up as from a bad dream, and the United Nations adopted the Universal Declaration of Human Rights. Intellectuals gave up their fascination with eugenics enough to proclaim again, in Article I of the Universal Declaration of Human Rights, that "All Human Being are born Free and Equal in Dignity and Rights"—as the American Declaration of Independence had realized more than a century and a half earlier. As Justice Scalia once said, societies do not always progress, sometimes they rot instead.

3. What about *Buck v. Bell* as a strictly legal matter? By any criteria, the right to procreate is fundamental, making it both a privilege or immunity of citizenship and an interest in life, liberty, or property protected by due process of law. Is there any non-explicitly-race-based enactment that is more clearly class- or caste-based than the sterilization statutes upheld in *Buck v. Bell*? The only question is whether compulsory sterilization based on governmental judgments of intellectual or social inferiority is a valid exercise of the police power for the general good. The Court in *Buck* thought so, relying on the "settled" scientific studies of the time. Do you think that the meaning of the Constitution changes with the latest research emanating from university academics? Is the strength of data that a legislature can rely upon to set maximum hours laws for bakers the same as the strength of data that should be required to sterilize someone? Are there certain rights so basic that no amount of data can justify their abridgment?

4. The lone dissenter in *Buck v. Bell* was Pierce Butler. He was also the lone Catholic on the Supreme Court in 1927. He did not write an opinion, so we do not know to what extent his vote was based on a religious belief that life and procreation are sacred gifts from God. "Holmes attributed the unexplained dissent by Butler to the dissenter's Roman Catholic beliefs." Larson, *supra*, at 125. If Justice Butler did evaluate the Virginia law in *Buck v. Bell* in light of his religious beliefs, is that problematic? More problematic than the majority's reliance on studies by academic biologists and sociologists? If you are going to decide that some rights are more basic than others and thus require more careful judicial scrutiny, on what grounds would you make that judgment? On what grounds is it legally permissible to make that judgment?

[Assignment 67]

There are many rights that people can plausibly claim are unconstitutionally abridged by government action. Once the Court settled on the Due Process of Law Clause rather than the Privileges or Immunities Clause as the vehicle for channeling those claims, it had to decide what counts as "life, liberty, or property" and when deprivations are without "due process of law." The 1868 meaning of those phrases as they appeared in the Fourteenth Amendment was spectacularly unsuited to the task of replicating or replacing the search for abridgements of privileges or immunities. But having set on that path, the Court needed to pave it. The following two cases are crucial—and still vital—landmarks in that development of "substantive due process."

C. MEYER V. NEBRASKA

262 U.S. 390 (1923)

■ MR. JUSTICE MCREYNOLDS delivered the opinion of the Court.

Plaintiff in error was tried and convicted in the District Court for Hamilton County, Nebraska, under an information which charged that, on May 25, 1920, while an instructor in Zion Parochial School, he unlawfully taught the subject of reading in the German language to Raymond Parpart, a child of ten years, who had not attained and successfully passed the eighth grade. The information is based upon "An act relating to the teaching of foreign languages in the State of Nebraska," approved April 9, 1919, which follows [Laws 1919, c. 249.]:

"Section 1. No person, individually or as a teacher, shall, in any private, denominational, parochial or public school, teach any subject to any person in any language other than the English language.

"Sec. 2. Languages, other than the English language, may be taught as languages only after a pupil shall have attained and successfully passed the eighth grade as evidenced by a certificate of graduation issued by the county superintendent of the county in which the child resides.

"Sec. 3. Any person who violates any of the provisions of this act shall be deemed guilty of a misdemeanor and upon conviction, shall be subject to a fine of not less than twenty-five dollars ($25), nor more than one hundred dollars ($100) or be confined in the county jail for any period not exceeding thirty days for each offense.

"Sec. 4. Whereas, an emergency exists, this act shall be in force from and after its passage and approval."

The Supreme Court of the State affirmed the judgment of conviction. 107 Neb. 657. It declared the offense charged and established was "the direct and intentional teaching of the German language as a distinct subject to a child who had not passed the eighth grade," in the parochial school maintained by Zion Evangelical Lutheran Congregation, a collection of Biblical stories being used therefor. And it held that the statute forbidding this did not conflict with the Fourteenth Amendment, but was a valid exercise of the police power. The following excerpts from the opinion sufficiently indicate the reasons advanced to support the conclusion.

"The salutary purpose of the statute is clear. The legislature had seen the baneful effects of permitting foreigners, who had taken residence in this country, to rear and educate their children in the language of their native land. The result of that condition was found to be inimical to our own safety. To allow the children of foreigners, who had emigrated here, to be taught from early childhood the language of the country of their parents was to rear them with that language as their mother tongue. It was to educate them so that they must always think in that language, and, as a consequence, naturally inculcate in them the ideas and sentiments foreign to the best interests of this country. The statute, therefore, was intended not only to require that the education of all children be conducted in the English language, but that, until they had grown into that language and until it had become a part of them, they should not in the schools be taught any other language. The obvious purpose of this statute was that the English language should be and become the mother tongue of all children reared in this state. The enactment of such a statute comes reasonably within the police power of the state. *Pohl v. State*, 132 N.E. (Ohio) 20; *State v. Bartels*, 181 N.W. (Ia.) 508.

"It is suggested that the law is an unwarranted restriction, in that it applies to all citizens of the state and arbitrarily interferes with the rights of citizens who are not of foreign ancestry, and prevents them, without reason, from having their children taught foreign languages in school. That argument is not well taken, for it assumes that every citizen finds himself restrained by the statute. The hours which a child is able to devote to study in the confinement of school are limited. It must have ample time for exercise or play. Its daily capacity for learning is comparatively small. A selection of subjects for its education, therefore, from among the many that might be taught, is obviously necessary. The legislature no doubt had in mind the practical operation of the law. The law affects few citizens, except those of foreign lineage. Other citizens, in their selection of studies, except perhaps in rare instances, have never deemed it of importance to teach their children foreign languages before such children have reached the eighth grade. In the legislative mind, the salutary effect of the statute no doubt outweighed the restriction upon the citizens generally, which, it appears, was a restriction of no real consequence."

The problem for our determination is whether the statute as construed and applied unreasonably infringes the liberty guaranteed to the plaintiff in error by the Fourteenth Amendment. "No State shall . . . deprive any person of life, liberty, or property, without due process of law."

While this Court has not attempted to define with exactness the liberty thus guaranteed, the term has received much consideration and some of the included things have been definitely stated. Without doubt, it denotes not merely freedom from bodily restraint but also the right of the individual to contract, to engage in any of the common occupations of life, to acquire useful knowledge, to marry, establish a home and bring up children, to worship God according to the dictates of his own conscience, and generally to enjoy those privileges long recognized at common law as essential to the orderly pursuit of happiness by free men. The established doctrine is that this liberty may not be interfered with, under the guise of protecting the public interest, by legislative action which is arbitrary or without reasonable relation to some purpose within the competency of the State to effect. Determination by the legislature of what constitutes proper exercise of police power is not final or conclusive but is subject to supervision by the courts.

The American people have always regarded education and acquisition of knowledge as matters of supreme importance which should be diligently promoted. The Ordinance of 1787 declares, "Religion, morality, and knowledge being necessary to good government and the happiness of mankind, schools and the means of education shall forever be encouraged." Corresponding to the right of control, it is the natural duty of the parent to give his children education suitable to their station in life; and nearly all the States, including Nebraska, enforce this obligation by compulsory laws.

Practically, education of the young is only possible in schools conducted by especially qualified persons who devote themselves thereto. The calling always has been regarded as useful and honorable, essential, indeed, to the public welfare. Mere knowledge of the German language cannot reasonably be regarded as harmful. Heretofore it has been commonly looked upon as helpful and desirable. Plaintiff in error taught this language in school as part of his occupation. His right thus to teach and the right of parents to engage him so to instruct their children, we think, are within the liberty of the Amendment.

The challenged statute forbids the teaching in school of any subject except in English; also the teaching of any other language until the pupil has attained and successfully passed the eighth grade, which is not usually accomplished before the age of twelve. The Supreme Court of the State has held that "the so-called ancient or dead languages" are not "within the spirit or the purpose of the act." *Nebraska District of Evangelical Lutheran Synod v. McKelvie*, 187 N.W. 927. Latin, Greek, Hebrew are not proscribed; but German, French, Spanish, Italian and every other alien speech are within the ban. Evidently the legislature has attempted materially to interfere with the calling of modern language teachers, with the opportunities of pupils to acquire knowledge, and with the power of parents to control the education of their own.

It is said the purpose of the legislation was to promote civic development by inhibiting training and education of the immature in foreign tongues and ideals before they could learn English and acquire American ideals; and "that the English language should be and become the mother tongue of all children reared in this State." It is also affirmed that the foreign born population is very large, that certain communities commonly use foreign words, follow foreign leaders, move in a foreign atmosphere, and that the children are thereby hindered from becoming citizens of the most useful type and the public safety is imperiled.

That the State may do much, go very far, indeed, in order to improve the quality of its citizens, physically, mentally and morally, is clear; but the individual has certain fundamental rights which must be respected. The protection of the Constitution extends to all, to those who speak other languages as well as to those born with English on the tongue. Perhaps it would be highly advantageous if all had ready understanding of our ordinary speech, but this cannot be coerced by methods which conflict with the Constitution—a desirable end cannot be promoted by prohibited means.

For the welfare of his Ideal Commonwealth, Plato suggested a law which should provide: "That the wives of our guardians are to be common, and their children are to be common, and no parent is to know his own child, nor any child his parent. . . . The proper officers will take the offspring of the good parents to the pen or fold, and there they will deposit them with certain nurses who dwell in a separate quarter; but the offspring of the inferior, or of the better when they chance to be deformed, will be put away in some mysterious, unknown place, as they should be." In order to submerge the individual. and develop ideal citizens, Sparta assembled the males at seven into barracks and intrusted their subsequent education and training to official guardians. Although such measures have been deliberately approved by men of great genius, their ideas touching the relation between individual and State were wholly different from those upon which our institutions rest; and it hardly will be affirmed that any legislature could impose such restrictions upon the people of a State without doing violence to both letter and spirit of the Constitution.

The desire of the Legislature to foster a homogeneous people with American ideals prepared readily to understand current discussions of civic matters is easy to appreciate. Unfortunate experiences during the late war and aversion toward every characteristic of truculent adversaries were certainly enough to quicken that aspiration. But the means adopted, we think, exceed the limitations upon the power of the State and conflict with rights assured to plaintiff in error. The interference is plain enough and no adequate reason therefor in time of peace and domestic tranquility has been shown.

The power of the State to compel attendance at some school and to make reasonable regulations for all schools, including a requirement that they shall give instructions in English, is not questioned. Nor has challenge been made of the State's power to prescribe a curriculum for institutions which it supports. Those matters are not within the present controversy. Our concern is with the prohibition approved by the Supreme Court. *Adams v. Tanner, supra,* p. 594, pointed out that mere abuse incident to an occupation ordinarily useful is not enough to justify its abolition, although regulation may be entirely proper. No emergency has arisen which renders knowledge by a child of some language other than English so clearly harmful as to justify its inhibition with the consequent infringement of rights long freely enjoyed. We are constrained to conclude that the statute as applied is arbitrary and without reasonable relation to any end within the competency of the State.

As the statute undertakes to interfere only with teaching which involves a modern language, leaving complete freedom as to other matters, there seems no adequate foundation for the suggestion that the purpose was to protect the child's health by limiting his mental activities. It is well known that proficiency in a foreign language seldom comes to one not instructed at an early age, and experience shows that this is not injurious to the health, morals or understanding of the ordinary child.

The judgment of the court below must be reversed, and the cause remanded for further proceedings not inconsistent with this opinion.

Reversed

■ MR. JUSTICE HOLMES and MR. JUSTICE SUTHERLAND, dissent. [*Editors' Note: The dissenting opinion below was issued in* Bartels v. State of Iowa, *262 U.S. 404 (1923), decided the same day as* Meyer *without further analysis.*]

We all agree, I take it, that it is desirable that all the citizens of the United States should speak a common tongue, and therefore that the end aimed at by the statute is a lawful and proper one. The only question is whether the means adopted deprive teachers of the liberty secured to them by the Fourteenth Amendment. It is with hesitation and unwillingness that I differ from my brethren with regard to a law like this but I cannot bring my mind to believe that in some circumstances, and circumstances existing it is said in Nebraska, the statute might not be regarded as a reasonable or even necessary method of reaching the desired result. The part of the act with which we are concerned deals with the teaching of young children. Youth is the time when familiarity with a language is established and if there are sections in the State where a child would hear only Polish or French or German spoken at home I am not prepared to say that it is unreasonable to provide that in his early years he shall hear and speak only English at school. But if it is reasonable it is not an undue restriction of the liberty either of teacher or scholar. No one would doubt that a teacher might be forbidden to teach many things, and the only criterion of his liberty under the Constitution that I can think of is "whether, considering the end in view, the statute passes the bounds of reason and assumes the character of a merely arbitrary fiat." I think I appreciate the objection to the law but it appears to me to present a question upon which men reasonably might differ and therefore I am unable to say that the Constitution of the United States prevents the experiment being tried.

* * *

D. PIERCE V. SOCIETY OF SISTERS

268 U.S. 510 (1925)

■ MR. JUSTICE MCREYNOLDS delivered the opinion of the Court.

These appeals are from decrees, based upon undenied allegations, which granted preliminary orders restraining appellants from threatening or attempting to enforce the Compulsory Education Act adopted November 7, 1922, under the initiative provision of her Constitution by the voters of Oregon. They present the same points of law; there are no controverted questions of fact. Rights said to be guaranteed by the federal Constitution were specially set up, and appropriate prayers asked for their protection.

The challenged Act, effective September 1, 1926, requires every parent, guardian or other person having control or charge or custody of a child between eight and sixteen years to send him "to a public school for the period of time a public school shall be held during the current year" in the district where the child resides; and failure so to do is declared a misdemeanor. There are exemptions—not specially important here—for children who are not normal, or who have completed the eighth grade, or whose parents or private teachers reside at considerable distances from any public school, or who hold special permits from the County Superintendent. The manifest purpose is to compel general attendance at public schools by normal children, between eight and sixteen, who have not completed the eighth grade. And without doubt enforcement of the statute would seriously impair, perhaps destroy, the profitable features of appellees' business and greatly diminish the value of their property.

Appellee, the Society of Sisters, is an Oregon corporation, organized in 1880, with power to care for orphans, educate and instruct the youth, establish and maintain academies or schools, and acquire necessary real and personal property. It has long devoted its property and effort to the secular and religious education and care of children, and has acquired the valuable good will of many parents and guardians. It conducts interdependent primary and high schools and junior colleges, and maintains orphanages for the custody and control of children between eight and sixteen. In its primary schools many children between those ages are taught the subjects usually pursued in Oregon public schools during the first eight years.

Systematic religious instruction and moral training according to the tenets of the Roman Catholic Church are also regularly provided. All courses of study, both temporal and religious, contemplate continuity of training under appellee's charge; the primary schools are essential to the system and the most profitable. It owns valuable buildings, especially constructed and equipped for school purposes. The business is remunerative—the annual income from primary schools exceeds thirty thousand dollars—and the successful conduct of this requires long time contracts with teachers and parents. The Compulsory Education Act of 1922 has already caused the withdrawal from its schools of children who would otherwise continue, and their income has steadily declined. The appellants, public officers, have proclaimed their purpose strictly to enforce the statute.

After setting out the above facts, the Society's bill alleges that the enactment conflicts with the right of parents to choose schools where their children will receive appropriate mental and religious training, the right of the child to influence the parents' choice of a school, the right of schools and teachers therein to engage in a useful business or profession, and is accordingly repugnant to the Constitution and void. And, further, that, unless enforcement of the measure is enjoined the corporation's business and property will suffer irreparable injury.

Appellee, Hill Military Academy, is a private corporation organized in 1908 under the laws of Oregon, engaged in owning, operating and conducting for profit an elementary, college preparatory and military training school for boys between the ages of five and twenty-one years. The average attendance is one hundred, and the annual fees received for each student amount to some eight hundred dollars * * *. [T]he courses of study conform to the requirements of the State Board of Education. Military instruction and training are also given, under the supervision of an Army officer. It owns considerable real and personal property, some useful only for school purposes. The business and incident good will are very valuable. In order to conduct its affairs long time contracts must be made for supplies, equipment, teachers and pupils. Appellants, law officers of the State and County, have publicly announced that the Act of November 7, 1922, is valid and have declared their intention to enforce it. By reason of the statute and threat of enforcement appellee's business is being destroyed and its property depreciated; parents and guardians are refusing to make contracts for the future instruction of their sons, and some are being withdrawn.

The Academy's bill states the foregoing facts and then alleges that the challenged Act contravenes the corporation's rights guaranteed by the Fourteenth Amendment and that unless appellants are restrained from proclaiming its validity and threatening to enforce it irreparable injury will result. The prayer is for an appropriate injunction.

No answer was interposed in either cause * * *. The court ruled that the Fourteenth Amendment guaranteed appellees against the deprivation of their property without due process of law consequent upon the unlawful interference by appellants with the free choice of patrons, present and prospective. It declared the right to conduct schools was property and that parents and guardians, as a part of their liberty, might direct the education of children by selecting reputable teachers and places. Also, that these schools were not unfit or harmful to the public, and that enforcement of the challenged statute would unlawfully deprive them of patronage and thereby destroy appellees' business and property. Finally, that the threats to enforce the Act would continue to cause irreparable injury; and the suits were not premature.

No question is raised concerning the power of the State reasonably to regulate all schools, to inspect, supervise and examine them, their teachers and pupils; to require that all children of proper age attend some school, that teachers shall be of good moral character and patriotic disposition, that certain studies plainly essential to good citizenship must be taught, and that nothing be taught which is manifestly inimical to the public welfare.

The inevitable practical result of enforcing the Act under consideration would be destruction of appellees' primary schools, and perhaps all other private primary schools for normal children within the State of Oregon. These parties are engaged in a kind of undertaking not inherently harmful, but long regarded as useful and meritorious. Certainly there is nothing in the present records to indicate that they have failed to discharge their obligations to patrons, students or the State. And there are no peculiar circumstances or present emergencies which demand extraordinary measures relative to primary education.

Under the doctrine of *Meyer v. Nebraska*, 262 U.S. 390, we think it entirely plain that the Act of 1922 unreasonably interferes with the liberty of parents and guardians to direct the upbringing and education of children under their control As often heretofore pointed out, rights guaranteed by the Constitution may not be abridged by legislation which has no reasonable relation to some purpose within the competency of the State. The fundamental theory of liberty upon which all governments in this Union repose excludes any general power of the State to standardize its children by forcing them to accept instruction from public teachers only. The child is not the mere creature of the State; those who nurture him and direct his destiny have the right, coupled with the high duty, to recognize and prepare him for additional obligations.

* * *

Generally it is entirely true, as urged by counsel, that no person in any business has such an interest in possible customers as to enable him to restrain exercise of proper power of the State upon the ground that he will be deprived of patronage. But the injunctions here sought are not against the exercise of any *proper* power. Plaintiffs asked protection against arbitrary, unreasonable, and unlawful interference with their patrons and the consequent destruction of their business and property * * *.

* * *

The decrees below are affirmed.

NOTES AND QUESTIONS

1. In both *Meyer* and *Pierce,* the plaintiffs were the educational institutions and the teachers. What was their protected right? Liberty, property, or both? What was the parents' right? Why could the schools assert the parents' rights? And did anyone mention the rights of the children?

2. The Court speaks the language of reasonableness. This is before the cases that you are about to read. In 1923, reasonableness did not mean the modern "rational basis" test, though Justice Holmes urged consistently application of that minimalist inquiry.

Nor did reasonableness mean strict scrutiny, as most laws actually survived judicial review in this era. What did reasonableness actually mean? What are the courts looking for in these cases? The failure of the courts clearly to articulate the nature of their inquiry probably had something to do with the developments noted below.

3. Professor Calabresi believes that the standard of reasonableness in all of these pre-New Deal substantive due process cases comes from the Supreme Court's adherence to Justice Bushrod Washington's test in *Corfield v. Coryell*, which was supposed to inform the meaning of the Privileges or Immunities Clause but which came to inform the meaning of the Fourteenth Amendment's Due Process of Law Clause. As Justice Washington wrote:

> The inquiry is, what are the privileges and immunities of citizens in the several states? We feel no hesitation in confining these expressions to those privileges and immunities which are, in their nature, fundamental; which belong, of right, to the citizens of all free governments; and which have, at all times, been enjoyed by the citizens of the several states which compose this Union, from the time of their becoming free, independent, and sovereign. What these fundamental principles are, it would perhaps be more tedious than difficult to enumerate. They may, however, be all comprehended under the following general heads: Protection by the government; the enjoyment of life and liberty, with the right to acquire and possess property of every kind, and to pursue and obtain happiness and safety; subject nevertheless to such restraints as the government may justly prescribe for the general good of the whole.

Justice Washington's language on "[p]rotection by the government; the enjoyment of life and liberty, with the right to acquire and possess property of every kind, and to pursue and obtain happiness and safety" was a bad paraphrase of the Born Free and Equal Clauses, which said: "All men are born free and equal, and have certain natural, essential, and unalienable rights; among which may be reckoned the right of enjoying and defending their lives and liberties; that of acquiring, possessing, and protecting property; in fine, that of seeking and obtaining their safety and happiness." Those are the rights or liberties which all citizens presumptively enjoy. They may be defeated, however, by the state police power, which makes all rights "subject nevertheless to such restraints as the government may justly prescribe for the general good of the whole" people. What that leaves us with is a presumption of liberty, which may be defeated by "reasonable" laws, *i.e.* 1) laws that are just; and 2) laws that are enacted for the general good of the whole people and which are not mere special interest legislation. (Professor Lawson gets to a vaguely similar place through application of fiduciary theory.)

4. It seems fairly obvious that the laws in these cases were driven by religious and nationalist bigotry. Was that their problem? Is that a problem of "due process of law"? If that was really the problem, should the Court have said so?

5. The statement in *Meyer* regarding the range of interests represented by "liberty" is oft-quoted even today. In 1791, liberty meant merely freedom from physical restraint. The *Meyer* Court makes very clear that this is *not* the narrow meaning that the word will be given in the Fourteenth Amendment. The list of interests given in *Meyer* is a reasonable approximation of what would constitute "privileges or immunities" circa 1868. Is the Court in these cases re-creating the lost Privileges or Immunities Clause through reinterpretation of the Due Process of Law Clause? Under the Privileges or Immunities Clause, the rights of both the teachers and the parents (and the children) are about as fundamental as they get. Did the States have good enough reasons to abridge those rights to satisfy the Constitution? What if the States had well-credentialed academic theorists of education testifying on their behalf?

6. Could a State simply outlaw private schools and home schooling and require all children to go to public schools? If the answer is yes, does that greater power include the lesser powers exercised in *Meyer* and *Pierce*?

7. *Meyer* and *Pierce* represent the high water mark of "substantive due process" before the New Deal. The next two cases, while leaving *Meyer* and *Pierce* as good law on their facts, totally undercut the methodological foundations of both cases and the half-century of doctrine on which they were built. We start with a later case (1955) which deals with both due process and law and equal protection, and which has proved influential in the development of both bodies of doctrine, and we follow with the 1937 case normally credited with turning the tide towards Justice Holmes' minimalist view of judicial review of most state legislation.

E. WILLIAMSON V. LEE OPTICAL CO.

348 U.S. 483 (1955)

■ MR. JUSTICE DOUGLAS delivered the opinion of the Court.

This suit was instituted in the District Court to have an Oklahoma law declared unconstitutional and to enjoin state officials from enforcing it * * *.

The District Court held unconstitutional portions of three sections of the Act. First, it held invalid under the Due Process Clause of the Fourteenth Amendment the portions of § 2 which make it unlawful for any person not a licensed optometrist or ophthalmologist to fit lenses to a face or to duplicate or replace into frames lenses or other optical appliances, except upon written prescriptive authority of an Oklahoma licensed ophthalmologist or optometrist.

An ophthalmologist is a duly licensed physician who specializes in the care of the eyes. An optometrist examines eyes for refractive error, recognizes (but does not treat) diseases of the eye, and fills prescriptions for eyeglasses. The optician is an artisan qualified to grind lenses, fill prescriptions, and fit frames.

The effect of § 2 is to forbid the optician from fitting or duplicating lenses without a prescription from an ophthalmologist or optometrist. In practical effect, it means that no optician can fit old glasses into new frames or supply a lens, whether it be a new lens or one to duplicate a lost or broken lens, without a prescription. The District Court conceded that it was in the competence of the police power of a State to regulate the examination of the eyes. But it rebelled at the notion that a State could require a prescription from an optometrist or ophthalmologist "to take old lenses and place them in new frames and then fit the completed spectacles to the *face* of the eyeglass wearer." It held that such a requirement was not "reasonably and rationally related to the health and welfare of the people." The court found that through mechanical devices and ordinary skills the optician could take a broken lens or a fragment thereof, measure its power, and reduce it to prescriptive terms * * *. It was, accordingly, the opinion of the court that this provision of the law violated the Due Process Clause by arbitrarily interfering with the optician's right to do business.

We think the due process question is answered in principle by *Roschen v. Ward*, 279 U.S. 337, which upheld a New York statute making it unlawful to sell eyeglasses at retail in any store, unless a duly licensed physician or optometrist were in charge and in personal attendance. The Court said, "* * * wherever the requirements of the act stop, there can be no doubt that the presence and superintendence of the specialist tend to diminish an evil." *Id.*, 279 U.S. at page 339.

The Oklahoma law may exact a needless, wasteful requirement in many cases. But it is for the legislature, not the courts, to balance the advantages and disadvantages of the new requirement. It appears that in many cases the optician can easily supply the new frames or new lenses without reference to the old written prescription. It also appears that many written prescriptions contain no directive data in regard to fitting spectacles to the face. But in some cases the directions contained in the prescription are essential, if the glasses are to be fitted so as to correct the particular defects of vision or alleviate the eye condition. The legislature might have concluded that the frequency of occasions when a prescription is necessary was sufficient to justify this regulation of the fitting of eyeglasses. Likewise, when it is necessary to duplicate a lens, a written prescription may or may not be necessary. But the legislature might have concluded that one was needed often enough to require one in every case. Or the legislature may have concluded that eye examinations were so critical, not only for correction of vision but also for detection of latent ailments or diseases, that every change in frames and every duplication of a lens should be accompanied by a prescription from a medical expert. To be sure, the present law does not require a new examination of the eyes every time the frames are changed or the lenses duplicated. For if the old prescription is on file with the optician, he can go ahead and make the new fitting or duplicate the lenses. But the law need not be in every respect logically consistent with its aims to be constitutional. It is enough that there is an evil at hand for correction, and that it might be thought that the particular legislative measure was a rational way to correct it.

The day is gone when this Court uses the Due Process Clause of the Fourteenth Amendment to strike down state laws, regulatory of business and industrial conditions, because they may be unwise, improvident, or out of harmony with a particular school of thought. We emphasize again what Chief Justice Waite said in *Munn v. State of Illinois*, 94 U.S. 113, 134, "For protection against abuses by legislatures the people must resort to the polls, not to the courts."

Secondly, the District Court held that it violated the Equal Protection Clause of the Fourteenth Amendment to subject opticians to this regulatory system and to exempt, as § 3 of the Act does, all sellers of ready-to-wear glasses. The problem of legislative classification is a perennial one, admitting of no doctrinaire definition. Evils in the same field may be of different dimensions and proportions, requiring different remedies. Or so the legislature may think. Or the reform may take one step at a time, addressing itself to the phase of the problem which seems most acute to the legislative mind. The legislature may select one phase of one field and apply a remedy there, neglecting the others. The prohibition of the Equal Protection Clause goes no further than the invidious discrimination. We cannot say that that point has been reached here. For all this record shows, the ready-to-wear branch of this business may not loom large in Oklahoma or may present problems of regulation distinct from the other branch.

Third, the District Court held unconstitutional, as violative of the Due Process Clause of the Fourteenth Amendment, that portion of § 3 which makes it unlawful "to solicit the sale of * * * frames, mountings * * * or any other optical appliances." * * * [R]egulation of the advertising of eyeglass frames was said to intrude "into a mercantile field only casually related to the visual care of the public" and restrict "an activity which in no way can detrimentally affect the people."

An eyeglass frame, considered in isolation, is only a piece of merchandise. But an eyeglass frame is not used in isolation, as Judge Murrah said in dissent below; it is used with lenses; and lenses, pertaining as they do to the human eye, enter the field of health. Therefore, the legislature might conclude that to regulate one effectively it would have to regulate the other. Or it might conclude that both the sellers of frames and the sellers of lenses were in a business where advertising should be limited or even abolished in the public interest. The advertiser of frames may be using his ads to bring in customers who will buy lenses. If the advertisement of lenses is to be abolished or controlled, the advertising of frames must come under the same restraints; or so the legislature might think. We see no constitutional reason why a State may not treat all who deal with the human eye as members of a profession was should use no merchandising methods for obtaining customers.

Fourth, the District Court held unconstitutional, as violative of the Due Process Clause of the Fourteenth Amendment, the provision of § 4 of the Oklahoma Act which reads as follows:

> "No person, firm, or corporation engaged in the business of retailing merchandise to the general public shall rent space, sublease departments, or otherwise permit any person purporting to do eye examination or visual care to occupy space in such retail store."

It seems to us that this regulation is on the same constitutional footing as the denial to corporations of the right to practice dentistry. It is an attempt to free the profession, to as great an extent as possible, from all taints of commercialism. It certainly might be easy for an optometrist with space in a retail store to be merely a front for the retail establishment. In any case, the opportunity for that nexus may be too great for safety, if the eye doctor is allowed inside the retail store. Moreover, it may be deemed important to effective regulation that the eye doctor be restricted to geographical locations that reduce the temptations of commercialism. Geographical location may be an important consideration in a legislative program which aims to raise the treatment of the human eye to a strictly professional level. We cannot say that the regulation has no rational relation to that objective and therefore is beyond constitutional bounds.

* * *

Affirmed in part and reversed in part.

■ MR. JUSTICE HARLAN took no part in the consideration or decision of this case.

NOTES AND QUESTIONS

1. This was obviously monopolistic class legislation, of the kind directly anticipated and targeted by the Privileges or Immunities Clause. The State has a constitutionally permissible interest in, for example, requiring people to have their eyes tested every five years when they renew their drivers' licenses. But this interest is not triggered every time someone breaks a pair of glasses that he or she bought the day before and wants new ones made. It takes little imagination to think of the interest groups favored by this law. In 1905, or 1923, there is no chance that the Court would have viewed this as a "health measure" sufficiently related to a public good to allow it to stand. The district court decision faithfully applied the law as it stood after *Lochner, Meyer,* and

Pierce. Nonetheless, no one was surprised by the Supreme Court's unanimous reversal of the district court in this case. What changed?

2. You will see the answer in the next case. The New Deal not only changed the nature and scope of the federal government, and the federal courts' willingness to police that government's boundaries and structure. It also changed the federal courts' view of the Fourteenth Amendment as a constraint on action by States, at least when that action involved anything fairly describable as "economic." In those numerous cases, the Thayerian restraint advocated by Justice Holmes became—and still remains today—the driving doctrinal principle. Down to the present day in 2020, a significant number of the justices of the Supreme Court are *terrified* of being said to have engaged in "*Lochner-izing*" (yes, it has become an accepted verb in legal discourse). Of course, Supreme Court justices *should* worry about striking down constitutional laws, but shouldn't they worry just as much about wrongly upholding unconstitutional laws? The Framers of the Fourteenth Amendment anticipated that state legislatures would sometimes pass monopolistic or class legislation.

3. How would the *Williamson* Court have decided *Dr. Bonham's Case*, or *the Case of the Monopolies*, or *Somerset v. Stewart*? If the Ancient Constitution, as reflected in the Fourteenth Amendment, provides even a modest presumption of liberty, it is hard to see how the legislation in this case overcomes it. Or are we just plain wrong about that?

4. *Williamson* was a natural outgrowth of doctrinal developments from the precedent two decades. One of the most important was the following 5–4 ruling from 1937, sometimes described as being "the switch in time that saved nine" (referring to President Franklin D. Roosevelt's proposal to increase the size of the Supreme Court to fifteen Justices if the Court continued to interfere with economic regulation). The conventional wisdom as of 2020 is that this case was correctly decided, but we beg to disagree! Read for yourself the great "triumph of 1937," which remains one of the cornerstones of modern constitutional doctrine, and see what you think.

F. WEST COAST HOTEL V. PARRISH

300 U.S. 379 (1937)

■ MR. CHIEF JUSTICE HUGHES delivered the opinion of the Court.

This case presents the question of the constitutional validity of the minimum wage law of the State of Washington.

The Act, entitled "Minimum Wages for Women," authorizes the fixing of minimum wages for women and minors. Laws of 1913 (Washington) chap. 174; Remington's Rev.Stat. (1932), § 7623 *et seq*. It provides:

"SECTION 1. The welfare of the State of Washington demands that women and minors be protected from conditions of labor which have a pernicious effect on their health and morals. The State of Washington, therefore, exercising herein its police and sovereign power declares that inadequate wages and unsanitary conditions of labor exert such pernicious effect.

"SEC. 2. It shall be unlawful to employ women or minors in any industry or occupation within the State of Washington under conditions of labor detrimental to their health or morals; and it shall be unlawful to employ women workers in any industry within the State of Washington at wages which are not adequate for their maintenance.

"SEC. 3. There is hereby created a commission to be known as the 'Industrial Welfare Commission' for the State of Washington, to establish such standards of wages and conditions of labor for women and minors employed within the State of Washington, as shall be held hereunder to be reasonable and not detrimental to health and morals, and which shall be sufficient for the decent maintenance of women".

Further provisions required the Commission to ascertain the wages and conditions of labor of women and minors within the State. Public hearings were to be held. If, after investigation, the Commission found that, in any occupation, trade or industry the wages paid to women were "inadequate to supply them necessary cost of living and to maintain the workers in health," the Commission was empowered to call a conference of representatives of employers and employees together with disinterested persons representing the public. The conference was to recommend to the Commission, on its request, an estimate of a minimum wage adequate for the purpose above stated, and, on the approval of such a recommendation it became the duty of the Commission to issue an obligatory order fixing minimum wages. Any such order might be reopened and the question reconsidered with the aid of the former conference or a new one. Special licenses were authorized for the employment of women who were "physically defective or crippled by age or otherwise," and also for apprentices, at less than the prescribed minimum wage.

* * *

The appellant conducts a hotel. The appellee Elsie Parrish was employed as a chambermaid and (with her husband) brought this suit to recover the difference between the wages paid her and the minimum wage fixed pursuant to the state law. The minimum wage was $14.50 per week of 48 hours. The appellant challenged the act as repugnant to the due process clause of the Fourteenth Amendment of the Constitution of the United States. The Supreme Court of the State, reversing the trial court, sustained the statute and directed judgment for the plaintiffs. The case is here on appeal.

The appellant relies upon the decision of this Court in *Adkins v. Children's Hospital,* 261 U.S. 525, which held invalid the District of Columbia Minimum Wage Act, which was attacked under the due process clause of the Fifth Amendment. On the argument at bar, counsel for the appellees attempted to distinguish the *Adkins* case upon the ground that the appellee was employed in a hotel and that the business of an innkeeper was affected with a public interest. That effort at distinction is obviously futile, as it appears that in one of the cases ruled by the *Adkins* opinion the employee was a woman employed as an elevator operator in a hotel.

* * *

* * * The Supreme Court of Washington has upheld the minimum wage statute of that State. It has decided that the statute is a reasonable exercise of the police power of the State. In reaching that conclusion the state court has invoked principles long established by this Court in the application of the Fourteenth Amendment. The state court has refused to regard the decision in the *Adkins* case as determinative and has pointed to our decisions both before and since that case as justifying its position. We are of the opinion that this ruling of the state court demands on our part a reexamination of the *Adkins* case. The importance of the question, in which many States having similar laws are concerned, the close division by which the decision in

the *Adkins* case was reached, and the economic conditions which have supervened, and in the light of which the reasonableness of the exercise of the protective power of the State must be considered, make it not only appropriate, but we think imperative, that in deciding the present case the subject should receive fresh consideration.

* * *

The * * * violation alleged by those attacking minimum wage regulation for women is deprivation of freedom of contract. What is this freedom? The Constitution does not speak of freedom of contract. It speaks of liberty and prohibits the deprivation of liberty without due process of law. In prohibiting that deprivation the Constitution does not recognize an absolute and uncontrollable liberty. Liberty in each of its phases has its history and connotation. But the liberty safeguarded is liberty in a social organization which requires the protection of law against the evils which menace the health, safety, morals and welfare of the people. Liberty under the Constitution is thus necessarily subject to the restraints of due process, and regulation which is reasonable in relation to its subject and is adopted in the interests of the community is due process.

This essential limitation of liberty in general governs freedom of contract in particular * * *.

This power under the Constitution to restrict freedom of contract has had many illustrations. That it may be exercised in the public interest with respect to contracts between employer and employee is undeniable. Thus statutes have been sustained limiting employment in underground mines and smelters to eight hours a day; in requiring redemption in cash of store orders or other evidences of indebtedness issued in the payment of wages; in forbidding the payment of seamen's wages in advance; in making it unlawful to contract to pay miners employed at quantity rates upon the basis of screened coal instead of the weight of the coal as originally produced in the mine; in prohibiting contracts limiting liability for injuries to employees; in limiting hours of work of employees in manufacturing establishments, and in maintaining workmen's compensation laws. In dealing with the relation of employer and employed, the legislature has necessarily a wide field of discretion in order that there may be suitable protection of health and safety, and that peace and good order may be promoted through regulations designed to insure wholesome conditions of work and freedom from oppression.

* * *

It is manifest that this established principle is peculiarly applicable in relation to the employment of women in whose protection the State has a special interest. That phase of the subject received elaborate consideration in *Muller v. Oregon* (1908), 208 U.S. 412, where the constitutional authority of the State to limit the working hours of women was sustained. We emphasized the consideration that "woman's physical structure and the performance of maternal functions place her at a disadvantage in the struggle for subsistence" and that her physical well being "becomes an object of public interest and care in order to preserve the strength and vigor of the race." We emphasized the need of protecting women against oppression despite her possession of contractual rights. We said that "though limitations upon personal and contractual rights may be removed by legislation, there is that in her disposition and habits of life which will operate against a full assertion of those rights. She will still be where some legislation to protect her seems necessary to secure a real equality of right." Hence she was "properly placed in a class by herself, and legislation designed for her protection may be sustained even when like legislation is not necessary for men and could not be sustained." We concluded that the limitations which the statute there in question "placed upon her contractual powers, upon her right to agree with her employer as to the time she shall labor" were "not imposed solely for her benefit, but also largely for the benefit of all." Again, in *Quong Wing v. Kirkendall,* 223 U.S. 59, 63, in referring to a differentiation with respect to the employment of women, we said that the Fourteenth Amendment did not interfere with state power by creating a "fictitious equality." We referred to recognized classifications on the basis of sex with regard to hours of work and in other matters, and we observed that the particular points at which that difference shall be enforced by legislation were largely in the power of the State * * *.

This array of precedents and the principles they applied were thought by the dissenting Justices in the *Adkins* case to demand that the minimum wage statute be sustained * * *.

* * *

* * * The statement of Mr. Justice Holmes in the *Adkins* case is pertinent: "This statute does not compel anybody to pay anything. It simply forbids employment at rates below those fixed as the minimum requirement of health and right living. It is safe to assume that women will not be employed at even the lowest wages allowed unless they earn them, or unless the employer's business can sustain the burden. In short the law in its character and operation is like hundreds of so-called police laws that have been upheld." 261 U.S. p. 570. And Chief Justice Taft forcibly pointed out the consideration which is basic in a statute of this character: "Legislatures which adopt a requirement of maximum hours or minimum wages may be presumed to believe that when sweating employers are prevented from paying unduly low wages by positive law they will continue their business, abating that part of their profits, which were wrung from the necessities of their employees, and will concede the better terms required by the law; and that while in individual cases hardship may result, the restriction will enure to the benefit of the general class of employees in whose interest the law is passed, and so to that of the community at large." *Id.,* p. 563.

We think that the views thus expressed are sound and that the decision in the *Adkins* case was a departure from the true application of the principles governing the regulation by the State of the relation of employer and employed. Those principles have been reenforced by our subsequent decisions * * *. In *Nebbia v. New York,* 291 U.S. 502, dealing with the New York statute providing for minimum prices for milk, the general subject of the regulation of the use of private property and of the making of private contracts received an exhaustive examination and we again declared that if such laws "have a reasonable relation to a proper legislative purpose, and are neither arbitrary nor discriminatory, the requirements of due process are satisfied"; That "with the wisdom of the policy adopted, with the adequacy or practicability of the law enacted to forward it, the courts are both incompetent and unauthorized to deal"; that "times without number we have said that the legislature is primarily the judge of the necessity of such an enactment, that every possible presumption is in favor of its validity, and that though the court may hold views inconsistent with the wisdom of the law, it may not be annulled unless palpably in excess of legislative power." *Id.* pp. 537, 538.

With full recognition of the earnestness and vigor which characterize the prevailing opinion in the *Adkins* case, we find it impossible to reconcile that ruling with these well-considered declarations. What can be closer to the public interest than the health of women and their protection from unscrupulous and overreaching employers? And if the protection of women is a legitimate end of the exercise of state power, how can it be said that the requirement of the payment of a minimum wage fairly fixed in order to meet the very necessities of existence is not an admissible means to that end? The legislature of the State was clearly entitled to consider the situation of women in employment, the fact that they are in the class receiving the least pay, that their bargaining power is relatively weak, and that they are the ready victims of those who would take advantage of their necessitous circumstances. The legislature was entitled to adopt measures to reduce the evils of the "sweating system," the exploiting of workers at wages so low as to be insufficient to meet the bare cost of living, thus making their very helplessness the occasion of a most injurious competition. The legislature had the right to consider that its minimum wage requirements would be an important aid in carrying out its policy of protection. The adoption of similar requirements by many States evidences a deepseated conviction both as to the presence of the evil and as to the means adapted to check it. Legislative response to that conviction cannot be regarded as arbitrary or capricious, and that is all we have to decide. Even if the wisdom of the policy be regarded as debatable and its effects uncertain, still the legislature is entitled to its judgment.

There is an additional and compelling consideration which recent economic experience has brought into a strong light. The exploitation of a class of workers who are in an unequal position with respect to bargaining power and are thus relatively defenceless against the denial of a living wage is not only detrimental to their health and well being but casts a direct burden for their support upon the community. What these workers lose in wages the taxpayers are called upon to pay. The bare cost of living must be met. We may take judicial notice of the unparalleled demands for relief which arose during the recent period of depression and still continue to an alarming extent despite the degree of economic recovery which has been achieved. It is unnecessary to cite official statistics to establish what is of common knowledge through the length and breadth of the land. While in the instant case no factual brief has been presented, there is no reason to doubt that the State of Washington has encountered the same social problem that is present elsewhere. The community is not bound to provide what is in effect a subsidy for unconscionable employers. The community may direct its law-making power to correct the abuse which springs from their selfish disregard of the public interest. The argument that the legislation in question constitutes an arbitrary discrimination, because it does not extend to men, is unavailing. This Court has frequently held that the legislative authority, acting within its proper field, is not bound to extend its regulation to all cases which it might possibly reach. The legislature "is free to recognize degrees of harm and it may confine its restrictions to those classes of cases where the need is deemed to be clearest." If the law presumably hits the evil where it is most felt, it is not to be overthrown because there are other instances to which it might have been applied * * *.

Our conclusion is that the case of *Adkins v. Children's Hospital, supra,* should be, and it is, overruled. The judgment of the Supreme Court of the State of Washington is

Affirmed.

■ MR. JUSTICE SUTHERLAND.

■ MR. JUSTICE VAN DEVANTER, MR. JUSTICE MCREYNOLDS, MR. JUSTICE BUTLER and I think the judgment of the court below should be reversed.

The principles and authorities relied upon to sustain the judgment, were considered in *Adkins v. Children's Hospital,* 261 U.S. 525, and *Morehead v. New York ex rel. Tipaldo,* 298 U.S. 587; and their lack of application to cases like the one in hand was pointed out. A sufficient answer to all that is now said will be found in the opinions of the court in those cases. Nevertheless, in the circumstances, it seems well to restate our reasons and conclusions.

* * *

It is urged that the question involved should now receive fresh consideration, among other reasons, because of "the economic conditions which have supervened"; but the meaning of the Constitution does not change with the ebb and flow of economic events. We frequently are told in more general words that the Constitution must be construed in the light of the present. If by that it is meant that the Constitution is made up of living words that apply to every new condition which they include, the statement is quite true. But to say, if that be intended, that the words of the Constitution mean today what they did not mean when written—that is, that they do not apply to a situation now to which they would have applied then—is to rob that instrument of the essential element which continues it in force as the people have made it until they, and not their official agents, have made it otherwise.

* * *

If the Constitution, intelligently and reasonably construed in the light of these principles, stands in the way of desirable legislation, the blame must rest upon that instrument, and not upon the court for enforcing it according to its terms. The remedy in that situation—and the only true remedy—is to amend the Constitution * * *.

* * *

Coming, then, to a consideration of the Washington statute, it first is to be observed that it is in every substantial respect identical with the statute involved in the *Adkins* case. Such vices as existed in the latter are present in the former. And if the *Adkins* case was properly decided, as we who join in this opinion think it was, it necessarily follows that the Washington statute is invalid.

* * *

That the clause of the Fourteenth Amendment which forbids a state to deprive any person of life, liberty or property without due process of law includes freedom of contract is so well settled as to be no longer open to question. Nor reasonably can it be disputed that contracts of employment of labor are included in the rule * * *.

In the *Adkins* case we * * * said that while there was no such thing as absolute freedom of contract, but that it was subject to a great variety of restraints, nevertheless, freedom of contract was the general rule, and restraint the exception * * *.

We further pointed out four distinct classes of cases in which this court from time to time had upheld statutory interferences with the liberty of contract. They were, in brief, (1) statutes fixing rates and charges to be exacted by businesses impressed with a public interest; (2) statutes relating to contracts for the performance of public work; (3) statutes prescribing the character, methods and time for payment of wages, and (4) statutes fixing hours of labor. It is the last class that has been most relied upon as affording support for minimum-wage legislation; and much of the opinion in the *Adkins* case (261 U.S. 547–553) is devoted to pointing out the essential distinction between fixing hours of labor and fixing wages. What is there said need not be repeated. It is enough for present purposes to say that statutes of the former class deal with an incident of the employment having no necessary effect upon wages. The parties are left free to contract about wages, and thereby equalize such additional burdens as may be imposed upon the employer as a result of the restrictions as to hours by an adjustment in respect of the amount of wages. This court, wherever the question is adverted to, has been careful to disclaim any purpose to uphold such legislation as fixing wages, and has recognized an essential difference between the two.

We then pointed out that minimum-wage legislation such as that here involved does not deal with any business charged with a public interest, or with public work, or with a temporary emergency, or with the character, methods or periods of wage payments, or with hours of labor, or with the protection of persons under legal disability, or with the prevention of fraud. It is, simply and exclusively, a law fixing wages for adult women who are legally as capable of contracting for themselves as men, and cannot be sustained unless upon principles apart from those involved in cases already decided by the court.

Two cases were involved in the *Adkins* decision. In one of them, it appeared that a woman 21 years of age, who brought the suit, was employed as an elevator operator at a fixed salary. Her services were satisfactory, and she was anxious to retain her position, and her employer, while willing to retain her, was obliged to dispense with her services on account of the penalties prescribed by the act. The wages received by her were the best she was able to obtain for any work she was capable of performing; and the enforcement of the order deprived her, as she alleged, not only of that employment, but left her unable to secure any position at which she could make a living with as good physical and moral surroundings and as good wages as she was receiving and was willing to take. The Washington statute, of course, admits of the same situation and result, and, for aught that appears to the contrary, the situation in the present case may have been the same as that just described. Certainly, to the extent that the statute applies to such cases, it cannot be justified as a reasonable restraint upon the freedom of contract. On the contrary, it is essentially arbitrary.

* * *

The Washington statute, like the one for the District of Columbia, fixes minimum wages for adult women. Adult men and their employers are left free to bargain as they please, and it is a significant and an important fact that all state statutes to which our attention has been called are of like character. The common-law rules restricting the power of women to make contracts have, under our system, long since practically disappeared. Women today stand upon a legal and political equality with men. There is no longer any reason why they should be put in different classes in respect of their legal right to make contracts; nor should they be denied, in effect, the right to compete with men for work paying lower wages which men may be willing to accept. And it is an arbitrary exercise of the legislative power to do so. In the *Tipaldo* case, 298 U.S. 587, 615, it appeared that the New York legislature had passed two minimum-wage measures—one dealing with women alone, the other with both men and women. The act which included men was vetoed by the governor. The other, applying to women alone, was approved. The "factual background" in respect of both measures was substantially the same. In pointing out the arbitrary discrimination which resulted (pp. 615–617) we said:

"These legislative declarations, in form of findings or recitals of fact, serve well to illustrate why any measure that deprives employers and adult women of freedom to agree upon wages, leaving employers and men employees free so to do, is necessarily arbitrary. Much, if not all, that in them is said in justification of the regulations that the Act imposes in respect of women's wages applies with equal force in support of the same regulation of men's wages. While men are left free to fix their wages by agreement with employers, it would be fanciful to suppose that the regulation of women's wages would be useful to prevent or lessen the evils listed in the first section of the Act. Men in need of work are as likely as women to accept the low wages offered by unscrupulous employers. Men in greater number than women support themselves and dependents and because of need, will work for whatever wages they can get and that without regard to the value of the service and even though the pay is less than minima prescribed in accordance with this Act. It is plain that, under circumstances such as those portrayed in the 'Factual background' prescribing of minimum wages for women alone would unreasonably restrain them in competition with men and tend arbitrarily to deprive them of employment and a fair chance to find work."

An appeal to the principle that the legislature is free to recognize degrees of harm and confine its restrictions accordingly, is but to beg the question, which is—since the contractual rights of men and women are the same, does the legislation here involved, by restricting only the rights of women to make contracts as to wages, create an arbitrary discrimination? We think it does. Difference of sex affords no reasonable ground for making a restriction applicable to the wage contracts of all working women from which like contracts of all working men are left free. Certainly a suggestion that the bargaining ability of the average woman is not equal to that of the average man would lack substance. The ability to make a fair bargain, as everyone knows, does not depend upon sex.

* * *

Finally, it may be said that a statute absolutely fixing wages in the various industries at definite sums and forbidding employers and employees from contracting for any other than those designated, would probably not be thought to be constitutional. It is hard to see why the power to fix minimum wages does not connote a like power in respect of maximum wages. And yet, if both powers be exercised in such a way that the minimum and the maximum so nearly approach each other as to become substantially the same, the right to make any contract in respect of wages will have been completely abrogated.

A more complete discussion may be found in the *Adkins* and *Tipaldo* cases cited *supra*.

NOTES AND QUESTIONS

1. Recall that from the decision in *Adkins v. Children's Hospital,* 261 U.S. 525 (1923) sex discrimination was subject to heightened scrutiny in Fourteenth Amendment cases. But, from the decision above in *West Coast Hotel v. Parrish*, until 1971, sex discrimination under the Equal Protection Clause was evaluated under a highly deferential "rational basis" test. Under that rational basis test the Supreme Court upheld a law excluding most women from being bartenders and it upheld an all-male jury verdict against a woman accused of killing her husband.

2. Today, with sex discrimination subject to something closer to strict scrutiny than to rational basis review, the sex-specific character of the law—it sets minimum wages for women but not for men—would be front and center. Women are portrayed in *West Coast Hotel* as being uniquely vulnerable, and other sex-based stereotypes are put forward. This would never survive "skeptical scrutiny" as "an exceedingly persuasive justification" under *United States v. Virginia* (the *VMI* case). Or would some justices sustain the law because they would consider it a law, in the language of *VMI,* to "compensate women 'for particular economic disabilities [they have] suffered,' to 'promot[e] equal employment opportunity,' to advance full development of the talent and capacities of our Nation's people"? Is that a correct understanding of the law? How would a court answer that question?

3. By 1937, inquiry under the Fourteenth Amendment Due Process of Law Clause involved a search for permissible legislative abridgements of common law or fundamental rights—and the right to contract qualifies easily under either heading of rights. The real battle in *West Coast Hotel* was about the intensity of judicial scrutiny of such laws. The majority went with Justice Holmes' all-but-categorical deference to legislative and administrative judgments. The dissenters wanted to retain the mid-level review characteristic of the pre-New Deal cases. What kinds of questions would that mid-level review ask in a case like this? Questions about the likely motives of the legislature? Questions about the likely effects of the law on different classes of people?

4. Minimum wage laws in general tend to benefit higher-wage workers at the expense of lower-wage workers. (Why? Because the real minimum wage is zero, meaning no job at all, if the statutory minimum wage is higher than the current productivity of some workers. Fewer workers means less competition—in the short term and especially in the long term—for those still in the workforce, most of whom earn considerably more than the statutory minimum wage.) Does that make all minimum wage laws unconstitutional? Surely not. The Fourteenth Amendment does not require all legislation to benefit all persons equally, nor does it require legislatures to reason with perfect accuracy about economics or any other subject. It prohibits class legislation, monopolies, and undue abridgements of common law and fundamental rights. The question is how strong and articulate the legislative rationale for the law must be. Specifying what that means in practice is somewhere between hard and spectacularly hard. Is that a good reason to adopt Holmes-style judicial restraint, as the Court has essentially done with respect to economic matters since *West Coast Hotel*?

5. One year after *West Coast Hotel,* the Court strongly reaffirmed that when legislative decisions are challenged as violations of due process of law, "by their very nature such inquiries, where the legislative judgment is drawn in question, must be restricted to the issue whether any state of facts either known or which could reasonably

be assumed affords support for it." *United States v. Carolene Products Co.,* 304 U.S. 144, 154 (1938). Justice Holmes surely smiled at that. Would the laws in *Meyer* and *Pierce* survive review under that standard? What about grandfather clauses for voting rights? Was the Court setting out a general standard of review applicable in all contexts, or was it singling out what might be called "economic" legislation (leaving to another day the task of distinguishing what makes something "economic" or "non-economic"—which is no easy feat)? A hint of, or perhaps a framework for, an answer appeared in *Carolene Products* in perhaps the most famous footnote ever to appear in the United States Reports:

> There may be narrower scope for operation of the presumption of constitutionality when legislation appears on its face to be within a specific prohibition of the Constitution, such as those of the first ten amendments, which are deemed equally specific when held to be embraced within the Fourteenth. See *Stromberg v. California*, 283 U.S. 359, 369–370; *Lovell v. Griffin*, 303 U.S. 444, 452.
>
> It is unnecessary to consider now whether legislation which restricts those political processes which can ordinarily be expected to bring about repeal of undesirable legislation, is to be subjected to more exacting judicial scrutiny under the general prohibitions of the Fourteenth Amendment than are most other types of legislation. On restrictions upon the right to vote, see *Nixon v. Herndon,* 273 U.S. 536; *Nixon v. Condon,* 286 U.S. 73; on restraints upon the dissemination of information, see *Near v. Minnesota ex rel. Olson*, 283 U.S. 697, 713–714, 718–720, 722; *Grosjean v. American Press Co.*, 297 U.S. 233; *Lovell v. Griffin, supra*; on interferences with political organizations, see *Stromberg v. California, supra*, 283 U.S. 359, 369; *Fiske v. Kansas*, 274 U.S. 380; *Whitney v. California*, 274 U.S. 357, 373–378; *Herndon v. Lowry*, 301 U.S. 242; and see Holmes, J., in *Gitlow v. New York,* 268 U.S. 652, 673; as to prohibition of peaceable assembly, see *De Jonge v. Oregon*, 299 U.S. 353, 365.
>
> Nor need we enquire whether similar considerations enter into the review of statutes directed at particular religious, *Pierce v. Society of Sisters*, 268 U.S. 510, or national, *Meyer v. Nebraska*, 262 U.S. 390; *Bartels v. Iowa,* 262 U.S. 404; *Farrington v. Tokushige,* 273 U.S. 284, or racial minorities. *Nixon v. Herndon, supra; Nixon v. Condon, supra;* whether prejudice against discrete and insular minorities may be a special condition, which tends seriously to curtail the operation of those political processes ordinarily to be relied upon to protect minorities, and which may call for a correspondingly more searching judicial inquiry.

304 U.S. at 152 n.4. From this seed has grown a veritable rain forest. It is time to explore it.

[Assignment 68]

Someone reading *West Coast Hotel Co. v. Parrish* and *Williamson v. Lee Optical* circa the early 1960s would reasonably think that substantive due process was effectively dead and buried. For nearly three decades from 1937 onward, that was largely true. Substantive due process, however, was born again, in a novel guise, in the following famous case from 1965. Please read all six of the opinions in this case with great care, because they all merit close attention.

G. GRISWOLD V. CONNECTICUT

381 U.S. 479 (1965)

■ MR. JUSTICE DOUGLAS delivered the opinion of the Court.

Appellant Griswold is Executive Director of the Planned Parenthood League of Connecticut. Appellant Buxton is a licensed physician and a professor at the Yale Medical School who served as Medical Director for the League at its Center in New Haven—a center open and operating from November 1 to November 10, 1961, when appellants were arrested.

They gave information, instruction, and medical advice to *married persons* as to the means of preventing conception. They examined the wife and prescribed the best contraceptive device or material for her use. Fees were usually charged, although some couples were serviced free.

The statutes whose constitutionality is involved in this appeal are §§ 53–32 and 54–196 of the General Statutes of Connecticut (1958 rev.). The former provides:

> "Any person who uses any drug, medicinal article or instrument for the purpose of preventing conception shall be fined not less than fifty dollars or imprisoned not less than sixty days nor more than one year or be both fined and imprisoned."

Section 54–196 provides:

> "Any person who assists, abets, counsels, causes, hires or commands another to commit any offense may be prosecuted and punished as if he were the principal offender."

The appellants were found guilty as accessories and fined $100 each, against the claim that the accessory statute as so applied violated the Fourteenth Amendment. The Appellate Division of the Circuit Court affirmed. The Supreme Court of Errors affirmed that judgment * * *.

* * *

Coming to the merits, we are met with a wide range of questions that implicate the Due Process Clause of the Fourteenth Amendment. Overtones of some arguments suggest that *Lochner v. New York,* 198 U.S. 45, should be our guide. But we decline that invitation as we did in *West Coast Hotel Co. v. Parrish* [and] *Williamson v. Lee Optical Co.,* 348 U.S. 483. We do not sit as a super-legislature to determine the wisdom, need, and propriety of laws that touch economic problems, business affairs, or social conditions. This law, however, operates directly on an intimate relation of husband and wife and their physician's role in one aspect of that relation.

The association of people is not mentioned in the Constitution nor in the Bill of Rights. The right to educate a child in a school of the parents' choice—whether public or private or parochial—is also not mentioned. Nor is the right to study any particular subject or any foreign language. Yet the First Amendment has been construed to include certain of those rights.

By *Pierce v. Society of Sisters, supra,* the right to educate one's children as one chooses is made applicable to the States by the force of the First and Fourteenth Amendments. By *Meyer v. Nebraska, supra,* the same dignity is given the right to study the German language in a private school. In other words, the State may not, consistently with the spirit of the First Amendment, contract the spectrum of available knowledge. The right of freedom of speech and press includes not only the right to utter or to print, but the right to distribute, the right to receive, the right to read (*Martin v. Struthers,* 319 U.S. 141, 143) and freedom of inquiry, freedom of thought, and freedom to teach (*see Wiemann v. Updegraff,* 344 U.S. 183, 195)—indeed, the freedom of the entire university community. *Sweezy v. New Hampshire,* 354 U.S. 234, 249–250, 261–263; *Barenblatt v. United States,* 360 U.S. 109, 112; *Baggett v. Bullitt,* 377 U.S. 360, 369. Without those peripheral rights, the specific rights would be less secure. And so we reaffirm the principle of the *Pierce* and the *Meyer* cases.

In *NAACP v. Alabama,* 357 U.S. 449, 462 we protected the "freedom to associate and privacy in one's associations," noting that freedom of association was a peripheral First Amendment right. Disclosure of membership lists of a constitutionally valid association, we held, was invalid "as entailing the likelihood of a substantial restraint upon the exercise by petitioner's members of their right to freedom of association." *Ibid.* In other words, the First Amendment has a penumbra where privacy is protected from governmental intrusion. In like context, we have protected forms of "association" that are not political in the customary sense, but pertain to the social, legal, and economic benefit of the members. *NAACP v. Button,* 371 U.S. 415, 430–431. In *Schware v. Board of Bar Examiners,* 353 U.S. 232, we held it not permissible to bar a lawyer from practice, because he had once been a member of the Communist Party. The man's "association with that Party" was not shown to be "anything more than a political faith in a political party" (*id.* at 244) and was not action of a kind proving bad moral character. *Id.* at 245–246.

* * *

The foregoing cases suggest that specific guarantees in the Bill of Rights have penumbras, formed by emanations from those guarantees that help give them life and substance. *See Poe v. Ullman,* 367 U.S. 497, 516–522 (dissenting opinion). Various guarantees create zones of privacy. The right of association contained in the penumbra of the First Amendment is one, as we have seen. The Third Amendment in its prohibition against the quartering of soldiers "in any house" in time of peace without the consent of the owner is another facet of that privacy. The Fourth Amendment explicitly affirms the "right of the people to be secure in their persons, houses, papers, and effects, against unreasonable searches and seizures." The Fifth Amendment in its Self-Incrimination Clause enables the citizen to create a zone of privacy which government may not force him to surrender to his detriment. The Ninth Amendment provides: "The enumeration in the Constitution, of certain rights, shall not be construed to deny or disparage others retained by the people."

The Fourth and Fifth Amendments were described in *Boyd v. United States,* 116 U.S. 616, 630, as protection against all governmental invasions "of the sanctity of a man's home and the privacies of life." We recently referred in *Mapp v. Ohio,* 367 U.S. 643, 656, to the Fourth Amendment as creating a "right to privacy, no less important than any other right carefully an particularly reserved to the people." *See* Beaney, The Constitutional Right to Privacy, 1962 Sup.Ct.Rev. 212; Griswold, The Right to be Let Alone, 55 Nw.U.L.Rev. 216 (1960).

We have had many controversies over these penumbral rights of "privacy and repose." These cases bear witness that the right of privacy which presses for recognition here is a legitimate one.

The present case, then, concerns a relationship lying within the zone of privacy created by several fundamental constitutional guarantees. And it concerns a law which, in forbidding the *use* of contraceptives rather than regulating their manufacture or sale, seeks to achieve its goals by means having a maximum destructive impact upon that relationship. Such a law cannot stand in light of the familiar principle, so often applied by this Court, that a "governmental purpose to control or prevent activities constitutionally subject to state regulation may not be achieved by means which sweep unnecessarily broadly and thereby invade the area of protected freedoms." *NAACP v. Alabama*, 377 U.S. 288, 307. Would we allow the police to search the sacred precincts of marital bedrooms for telltale signs of the use of contraceptives? The very idea is repulsive to the notions of privacy surrounding the marriage relationship.

We deal with a right of privacy older than the Bill of Rights—older than our political parties, older than our school system. Marriage is a coming together for better or for worse, hopefully enduring, and intimate to the degree of being sacred. It is an association that promotes a way of life, not causes; a harmony in living, not political faiths; a bilateral loyalty, not commercial or social projects. Yet it is an association for as noble a purpose as any involved in our prior decisions.

Reversed.

■ MR. JUSTICE GOLDBERG, whom THE CHIEF JUSTICE and MR. JUSTICE BRENNAN join, concurring.

I agree with the Court that Connecticut's birth-control law unconstitutionally intrudes upon the right of marital privacy, and I join in its opinion and judgment. Although I have not accepted the view that "due process" as used in the Fourteenth Amendment incorporates all of the first eight Amendments * * *, I do agree that the concept of liberty protects those personal rights that are fundamental, and is not confined to the specific terms of the Bill of Rights. My conclusion that the concept of liberty is not so restricted and that it embraces the right of marital privacy though that right is not mentioned explicitly in the Constitution is supported both by numerous decisions of this Court, referred to in the Court's opinion, and by the language and history of the Ninth Amendment. In reaching the conclusion that the right of marital privacy is protected, as being within the protected penumbra of specific guarantees of the Bill of Rights, the Court refers to the Ninth Amendment. I add these words to emphasize the relevance of that Amendment to the Court's holding.

The Court stated many years ago that the Due Process Clause protects those liberties that are "so rooted in the traditions and conscience of our people as to be ranked as fundamental." *Snyder v. Massachusetts,* 291 U.S. 7, 105 * * *.

This Court, in a series of decisions, has held that the Fourteenth Amendment absorbs and applies to the States those specifics of the first eight amendments which express fundamental personal rights. The language and history of the Ninth Amendment reveal that the Framers of the Constitution believed that there are additional fundamental rights, protected from governmental infringement, which exist alongside those fundamental rights specifically mentioned in the first eight constitutional amendments.

The Ninth Amendment reads, "The enumeration in the Constitution, of certain rights, shall not be construed to deny or disparage others retained by the people." The Amendment is almost entirely the work of James Madison. It was introduced in Congress by him and passed the House and Senate with little or no debate and virtually no change in language. It was proffered to quiet expressed fears that a bill of specifically enumerated rights could not be sufficiently broad to cover all essential rights and that the specific mention of certain rights would be interpreted as a denial that others were protected.

In presenting the proposed Amendment, Madison said:

> "It has been objected also against a bill of rights, that, by enumerating particular exceptions to the grant of power, it would disparage those rights which were not placed in that enumeration; and it might follow by implication, that those rights which were not singled out, were intended to be assigned into the hands of the General Government, and were consequently insecure. This is one of the most plausible arguments I have ever heard urged against the admission of a bill of rights into this system; but I conceive, that it may be guarded against. I have attempted it, as gentlemen may see by turning to the last clause of the fourth resolution [the Ninth Amendment]." I Annals of Congress 439 (Gales and Seaton ed. 1834).

* * *. These statements * * * make clear that the Framers did not intend that the first eight amendments be construed to exhaust the basic and fundamental rights which the Constitution guaranteed to the people.

While this Court has had little occasion to interpret the Ninth Amendment, "[i]t cannot be presumed that any clause in the constitution is intended to be without effect." *Marbury v. Madison,* 1 Cranch 137, 174. In interpreting the Constitution, "real effect should be given to all the words it uses." *Myers v. United States,* 272 U.S. 52, 151. The Ninth Amendment to the Constitution may be regarded by some as a recent discovery and may be forgotten by others, but since 1791 it has been a basic part of the Constitution which we are sworn to uphold. To hold that a right so basic and fundamental and so deep-rooted in our society as the right of privacy in marriage may be infringed because that right is not guaranteed in so many words by the first eight amendments to the Constitution is to ignore the Ninth Amendment and to give it no effect whatsoever. Moreover, a judicial construction that this fundamental right is not protected by the Constitution because it is not mentioned in explicit terms by one of the first eight amendments or elsewhere in the Constitution would violate the Ninth Amendment, which specifically states that "[t]he enumeration in the Constitution, of certain rights, shall not be *construed* to deny or disparage others retained by the people." (Emphasis added.)

* * * I do not mean to imply that the Ninth Amendment is applied against the States by the Fourteenth. Nor do I mean to state that the Ninth Amendment constitutes an independent source of rights protected from infringement by either the States or the Federal Government. Rather, the Ninth Amendment shows a belief of the Constitution's authors that fundamental rights exist that are not expressly enumerated in the first eight amendments and an intent that the list of rights

included there not be deemed exhaustive. As any student of this Court's opinions knows, this Court has held, often unanimously, that the Fifth and Fourteenth Amendments protect certain fundamental personal liberties from abridgment by the Federal Government or the States. *See, e.g., Bolling v. Sharpe,* 347 U.S. 497; *Aptheker v. Secretary of State,* 378 U.S. 500; *Kent v. Dulles,* 357 U.S. 116, *Cantwell v. Connecticut,* 310 U.S. 296; *NAACP v. Alabama,* 357 U.S. 449; *Gideon v. Wainwright,* 372 U.S. 335; *New York Times Co. v. Sullivan,* 376 U.S. 254. The Ninth Amendment simply shows the intent of the Constitution's authors that other fundamental personal rights should not be denied such protection or disparaged in any other way simply because they are not specifically listed in the first eight constitutional amendments. I do not see how this broadens the authority of the Court; rather it serves to support what this Court has been doing in protecting fundamental rights.

Nor am I turning somersaults with history in arguing that the Ninth Amendment is relevant in a case dealing with a *State's* infringement of a fundamental right. While the Ninth Amendment—and indeed the entire Bill of Rights—originally concerned restrictions upon *federal* power, the subsequently enacted Fourteenth Amendment prohibits the States as well from abridging fundamental personal liberties. And, the Ninth Amendment, in indicating that not all such liberties are specifically mentioned in the first eight amendments, is surely relevant in showing the existence of other fundamental personal rights, now protected from state, as well as federal, infringement. In sum, the Ninth Amendment simply lends strong support to the view that the "liberty" protected by the Fifth and Fourteenth Amendments from infringement by the Federal Government or the States is not restricted to rights specifically mentioned in the first eight amendments. *Cf. United Public Workers v. Mitchell,* 330 U.S. 75, 94–95.

In determining which rights are fundamental, judges are not left at large to decide cases in light of their personal and private notions. Rather, they must look to the "traditions and [collective] conscience of our people" to determine whether a principle is "so rooted [there] . . . as to be ranked as fundamental." *Snyder v. Massachusetts,* 291 U.S. 97, 105. The inquiry is whether a right involved "is of such a character that it cannot be denied without violating those 'fundamental principles of liberty and justice which lie at the base of all our civil and political institutions.' . . ." *Powell v. Alabama,* 287 U.S. 45, 67. "Liberty" also "gains content from the emanations of . . . specific [constitutional] guarantees," and "from experience with the requirements of a free society." *Poe v. Ullman,* 367 U.S. 497, 517 (dissenting opinion of Mr. JUSTICE DOUGLAS).

I agree fully with the Court that, applying these tests, the right of privacy is a fundamental personal right, emanating "from the totality of the constitutional scheme under which we live." *Id.* at 521 * * *.

The Connecticut statutes here involved deal with a particularly important and sensitive area of privacy—that of the marital relation and the marital home. This Court recognized in *Meyer v. Nebraska, supra,* that the right "to marry, establish a home and bring up children" was an essential part of the liberty guaranteed by the Fourteenth Amendment. 262 U.S. at 399. In *Pierce v. Society of Sisters,* 268 U.S. 510, the Court held unconstitutional an Oregon Act which forbade parents from sending their children to private schools because such an act "unreasonably interferes with the liberty of parents and guardians to direct the upbringing and education of children under their control." 268 U.S. at 534–535. As this Court said in *Prince v. Massachusetts,* 321 U.S. 158, at 166, the *Meyer* and *Pierce* decisions "have respected the private realm of family life which the state cannot enter."

* * *

The entire fabric of the Constitution and the purposes that clearly underlie its specific guarantees demonstrate that the rights to marital privacy and to marry and raise a family are of similar order and magnitude as the fundamental rights specifically protected.

Although the Constitution does not speak in so many words of the right of privacy in marriage, I cannot believe that it offers these fundamental rights no protection. The fact that no particular provision of the Constitution explicitly forbids the State from disrupting the traditional relation of the family—a relation as old and as fundamental as our entire civilization—surely does not show that the Government was meant to have the power to do so. Rather, as the Ninth Amendment expressly recognizes, there are fundamental personal rights such as this one, which are protected from abridgment by the Government though not specifically mentioned in the Constitution.

* * *

The logic of the dissents would sanction federal or state legislation that seems to me even more plainly unconstitutional than the statute before us. Surely the Government, absent a showing of a compelling subordinating state interest, could not decree that all husbands and wives must be sterilized after two children have been born to them. Yet by their reasoning such an invasion of marital privacy would not be subject to constitutional challenge because, while it might be "silly," no provision of the Constitution specifically prevents the Government from curtailing the marital right to bear children and raise a family. While it may shock some of my Brethren that the Court today holds that the Constitution protects the right of marital privacy, in my view it is far more shocking to believe that the personal liberty guaranteed by the Constitution does not include protection against such totalitarian limitation of family size, which is at complete variance with our constitutional concepts. Yet, if upon a showing of a slender basis of rationality, a law outlawing voluntary birth control by married persons is valid, then, by the same reasoning, a law requiring compulsory birth control also would seem to be valid. In my view, however, both types of law would unjustifiably intrude upon rights of marital privacy which are constitutionally protected.

In a long series of cases this Court has held that, where fundamental personal liberties are involved, they may not be abridged by the States simply on a showing that a regulatory statute has some rational relationship to the effectuation of a proper state purpose. "Where there is a significant encroachment upon personal liberty, the State may prevail only upon showing a subordinating interest which is compelling," *Bates v. Little Rock,* 361 U.S. 516, 524. The law must be shown "necessary, and not merely rationally related, to the accomplishment of a permissible state policy." *McLaughlin v. Florida,* 379 U.S. 184, 196.

Although the Connecticut birth-control law obviously encroaches upon a fundamental personal liberty, the State does not show that the law serves any "subordinating [state] interest which is compelling," or that it is "necessary . . . to the accomplishment of a permissible state policy." The State, at most, argues that there is some rational relation between this statute and what is admittedly a legitimate subject of state concern—the discouraging of extra-marital relations. It says that preventing the use of birth-control devices by married persons helps prevent the indulgence by some in such extramarital relations. The rationality of this justification is dubious * * *. But, in any event, it is clear that the state interest in safeguarding marital fidelity can be served by a more discriminately tailored statute, which does not, like the present one, sweep unnecessarily broadly, reaching far beyond the evil sought to be dealt with and intruding upon the privacy of all married couples * * *.

* * *

In sum, I believe that the right of privacy in the marital relation is fundamental and basic—a personal right "retained by the people" within the meaning of the Ninth Amendment. Connecticut cannot constitutionally abridge this fundamental right, which is protected by the Fourteenth Amendment from infringement by the States. I agree with the Court that petitioners' convictions must therefore be reversed.

■ MR. JUSTICE HARLAN, concurring in the judgment.

I fully agree with the judgment of reversal, but find myself unable to join the Court's opinion * * *.

* * *

In my view, the proper constitutional inquiry in this case is whether this Connecticut statute infringes the Due Process Clause of the Fourteenth Amendment because the enactment violates basic values "implicit in the concept of ordered liberty," *Palko v. Connecticut,* 302 U.S. 319, 325. For reasons stated at length in my dissenting opinion in *Poe v. Ullman, supra,* I believe that it does. While the relevant inquiry may be aided by resort to one or more of the provisions of the Bill of Rights, it is not dependent on them or any of their radiations. The Due Process Clause of the Fourteenth Amendment stands, in my opinion, on its own bottom.

* * *

■ MR. JUSTICE WHITE, concurring in the judgment.

In my view, this Connecticut law, as applied to married couples, deprives them of "liberty" without due process of law, as that concept is used in the Fourteenth Amendment. I therefore concur in the judgment of the Court reversing these convictions under Connecticut's aiding and abetting statute.

It would be unduly repetitious, and belaboring the obvious, to expound on the impact of this statute on the liberty guaranteed by the Fourteenth Amendment against arbitrary or capricious denials or on the nature of this liberty. Suffice it to say that this is not the first time this Court has had occasion to articulate that the liberty entitled to protection under the Fourteenth Amendment includes the right "to marry, establish a home and bring up children," *Meyer v. Nebraska,* 262 U.S. 390, 399, and "the liberty . . . to direct the upbringing and education of children," *Pierce v. Society of Sisters,* 268 U.S. 510, 534–535, and that these are among "the basic civil rights of man." *Skinner v. Oklahoma,* 316 U.S. 535, 541. These decisions affirm that there is a "realm of family life which the state cannot enter" without substantial justification. *Prince v. Massachusetts,* 321 U.S. 158, 166. Surely the right invoked in this case, to be free of regulation of the intimacies of the marriage relationship, "come[s] to this Court with a momentum for respect lacking when appeal is made to liberties which derive merely from shifting economic arrangements." *Kovacs v. Cooper,* 336 U.S. 77, 95 (opinion of Frankfurter, J.).

The Connecticut anti-contraceptive statute deals rather substantially with this relationship. For it forbids all married persons the right to use birth-control devices, regardless of whether their use is dictated by considerations of family planning, health, or indeed even of life itself * * *. In my view, a statute with these effects bears a substantial burden of justification when attacked under the Fourteenth Amendment.

An examination of the justification offered, however, cannot be avoided by saying that the Connecticut anti-use statute invades a protected area of privacy and association or that it demeans the marriage relationship. The nature of the right invaded is pertinent, to be sure, for statutes regulating sensitive areas of liberty do, under the cases of this Court, require "strict scrutiny," *Skinner v. Oklahoma,* 316 U.S. 535, 541, and "must be viewed in the light of less drastic means for achieving the same basic purpose." *Shelton v. Tucker,* 364 U.S. 479, 488. "Where there is a significant encroachment upon personal liberty, the State may prevail only upon showing a subordinating interest which is compelling." *Bates v. Little Rock,* 361 U.S. 516, 524. But such statutes, if reasonably necessary for the effectuation of a legitimate and substantial state interest, and not arbitrary or capricious in application, are not invalid under the Due Process Clause.

As I read the opinions of the Connecticut courts and the argument of Connecticut in this Court, the State claims but one justification for its anti-use statute. There is no serious contention that Connecticut thinks the use of artificial or external methods of contraception immoral or unwise in itself, or that the anti-use statute is founded upon any policy of promoting population expansion. Rather, the statute is said to serve the State's policy against all forms of promiscuous or illicit sexual relationships, be they premarital or extramarital, concededly a permissible and legitimate legislative goal.

Without taking issue with the premise that the fear of conception operates as a deterrent to such relationships in addition to the criminal proscriptions Connecticut has against such conduct, I wholly fail to see how the ban on the use of contraceptives by married couples in any way reinforces the State's ban on illicit sexual relationships. Connecticut does not bar the importation or possession of contraceptive devices; they are not considered contraband material under state law, and their availability in that State is not seriously disputed. The only way Connecticut seeks to limit or control the availability of such devices is through its general aiding and abetting statute whose operation in this context has been quite obviously ineffective and whose most serious use has been against birth-control clinics rendering advice to married, rather than unmarried, persons * * *.

In these circumstances one is rather hard pressed to explain how the ban on use by married persons in any way prevents use of such devices by persons engaging in illicit sexual relations and thereby contributes to the State's policy against such relationships. Neither the state courts nor the State before the bar of this Court has tendered such an explanation * * *. At most the broad ban is of marginal utility to the declared objective. A statute limiting its prohibition on use to persons engaging in the prohibited relationship would serve the end posited by Connecticut in the same way, and with the same effectiveness or ineffectiveness, as the broad anti-use statute under attack in this case. I find nothing in this record justifying the sweeping scope of this statute, with its telling effect on the freedoms of married persons, and therefore conclude that it deprives such persons of liberty without due process of law.

■ MR. JUSTICE BLACK, with whom MR. JUSTICE STEWART joins, dissenting.

I agree with my Brother STEWART's dissenting opinion. And like him I do not to any extent whatever base my view that this Connecticut law is constitutional on a belief that the law is wise or that its policy is a good one * * *. There is no single one of the graphic and eloquent strictures and criticisms fired at the policy of this Connecticut law either by the Court's opinion or by those of my concurring Brethren to which I cannot subscribe—except their conclusion that the evil qualities they see in the law make it unconstitutional.

* * *

The Court talks about a constitutional "right of privacy" as though there is some constitutional provision or provisions forbidding any law ever to be passed which might abridge the "privacy" of individuals. But there is not. There are, of course, guarantees in certain specific constitutional provisions which are designed in part to protect privacy at certain times and places with respect to certain activities. Such, for example, is the Fourth Amendment's guarantee against "unreasonable searches and seizures." But I think it belittles that Amendment to talk about it as though it protects nothing but "privacy." To treat it that way is to give it a niggardly interpretation, not the kind of liberal reading I think any Bill of Rights provision should be given. The average man would very likely not have his feelings soothed any more by having his property seized openly than by having it seized privately and by stealth. He simply wants his property left alone. And a person can be just as much, if not more, irritated, annoyed and injured by an unceremonious public arrest by a policeman as he is by a seizure in the privacy of his office or home.

One of the most effective ways of diluting or expanding a constitutionally guaranteed right is to substitute for the crucial word or words of a constitutional guarantee another word or words, more or less flexible and more or less restricted in meaning. This fact is well illustrated by the use of the term "right of privacy" as a comprehensive substitute for the Fourth Amendment's guarantee against "unreasonable searches and seizures." "Privacy" is a broad, abstract and ambiguous concept which can easily be shrunken in meaning but which can also, on the other hand, easily be interpreted as a constitutional ban against many things other than searches and seizures. I have expressed the view many times that First Amendment freedoms, for example, have suffered from a failure of the courts to stick to the simple language of the First Amendment in construing it, instead of invoking multitudes of words substituted for those the Framers used. For these reasons I get nowhere in this case by talk about a constitutional "right of privacy" as an emanation from one or more constitutional provisions. I like my privacy as well as the next one, but I am nevertheless compelled to admit that government has a right to invade it unless prohibited by some specific constitutional provision. For these reasons I cannot agree with the Court's judgment and the reasons it gives for holding this Connecticut law unconstitutional.

* * * I think that if properly construed neither the Due Process Clause nor the Ninth Amendment, nor both together, could under any circumstances be a proper basis for invalidating the Connecticut law. I discuss the due process and Ninth

Amendment arguments together because on analysis they turn out to be the same thing—merely using different words to claim for this Court and the federal judiciary power to invalidate any legislative act which the judges find irrational, unreasonable or offensive.

The due process argument which my Brothers HARLAN and WHITE adopt here is based, as their opinions indicate, on the premise that this Court is vested with power to invalidate all state laws that it considers to be arbitrary, capricious, unreasonable, or oppressive, or on this Court's belief that a particular state law under scrutiny has no "rational or justifying" purpose, or is offensive to a "sense of fairness and justice." If these formulas based on "natural justice," or others which mean the same thing, are to prevail, they require judges to determine what is or is not constitutional on the basis of their own appraisal of what laws are unwise or unnecessary. The power to make such decisions is of course that of a legislative body. Surely it has to be admitted that no provision of the Constitution specifically gives such blanket power to courts to exercise such a supervisory veto over the wisdom and value of legislative policies and to hold unconstitutional those laws which they believe unwise or dangerous. I readily admit that no legislative body, state or national, should pass laws that can justly be given any of the invidious labels invoked as constitutional excuses to strike down state laws. But perhaps it is not too much to say that no legislative body ever does pass laws without believing that they will accomplish a sane, rational, wise and justifiable purpose. While I completely subscribe to the holding of *Marbury v. Madison,* 1 Cranch 137, and subsequent cases, that our Court has constitutional power to strike down statutes, state or federal, that violate commands of the Federal Constitution, I do not believe that we are granted power by the Due Process Clause or any other constitutional provision or provisions to measure constitutionality by our belief that legislation is arbitrary, capricious or unreasonable, or accomplishes no justifiable purpose, or is offensive to our own notions of "civilized standards of conduct." Such an appraisal of the wisdom of legislation is an attribute of the power to make laws, not of the power to interpret them * * *.

Of the cases on which my Brothers WHITE and GOLDBERG rely so heavily, undoubtedly the reasoning of two of them supports their result here—as would that of a number of others which they do not bother to name, *e.g., Lochner v. New York,* 198 U.S. 45, *Coppage v. Kansas,* 236 U.S. 1, *Jay Burns Baking Co. v. Bryan,* 264 U.S. 504, and *Adkins v. Children's Hospital,* 261 U.S. 525. The two they do cite and quote from, *Meyer v. Nebraska,* 262 U.S. 390, and *Pierce v. Society of Sisters,* 268 U.S. 510, were both decided in opinions by Mr. Justice McReynolds which elaborated the same natural law due process philosophy found in *Lochner v. New York, supra,* one of the cases on which he relied in *Meyer,* along with such other long-discredited opinions as, *e.g., Adams v. Tanner,* 244 U.S. 590, and *Adkins v. Children's Hospital, supra* * * *. Without expressing an opinion as to whether either of those cases reached a correct result in light of our later decisions applying the First Amendment to the States through the Fourteenth, I merely point out that the reasoning stated in *Meyer* and *Pierce* was the same natural law due process philosophy which many later opinions repudiated, and which I cannot accept * * *. Brothers WHITE and GOLDBERG now apparently would start from this requirement that laws be narrowly drafted so as not to curtail free speech and assembly, and extend it limitlessly to require States to justify any law restricting "liberty" as my Brethren define "liberty."

This would mean at the very least, I suppose, that every state criminal statute—since it must inevitably curtail "liberty" to some extent—would be suspect; and would have to be justified to this Court.

My Brother GOLDBERG has adopted the recent discovery that the Ninth Amendment as well as the Due Process Clause can be used by this Court as authority to strike down all state legislation which this Court thinks violates "fundamental principles of liberty and justice," or is contrary to the "traditions and [collective] conscience of our people." He also states, without proof satisfactory to me, that, in making decisions on this basis judges will not consider "their personal and private notions." One may ask how they can avoid considering them. Our Court certainly has no machinery with which to take a Gallup Poll. And the scientific miracles of this age have not yet produced a gadget which the Court can use to determine what traditions are rooted in the "[collective] conscience of our people." * * * If any broad, unlimited power to hold laws unconstitutional because they offend what this Court conceives to be the "[collective] conscience of our people" is vested in this Court by the Ninth Amendment, the Fourteenth Amendment, or any other provision of the Constitution, it was not given by the Framers, but rather has been bestowed on the Court by the Court. This fact is perhaps responsible for the peculiar phenomenon that for a period of a century and a half no serious suggestion was ever made that the Ninth Amendment, enacted to protect state powers against federal invasion, could be used as a weapon of federal power to prevent state legislatures from passing laws they consider appropriate to govern local affairs. Use of any such broad, unbounded judicial authority would make of this Court's members a day-to-day constitutional convention.

* * *

I realize that many good and able men have eloquently spoken and written, sometimes in rhapsodical strains, about the duty of this Court to keep the Constitution in tune with the times. The idea is that the Constitution must be changed from time to time and that this Court is charged with a duty to make those changes. For myself, I must with all deference reject that philosophy. The Constitution makers knew the need for change and provided for it. Amendments suggested by the people's elected representatives can be submitted to the people or their selected agents for ratification. That method of change was good for our Fathers, and, being somewhat old-fashioned I must add it is good enough for me. And so, I cannot rely on the Due Process Clause or the Ninth Amendment or any mysterious and uncertain natural law concept as a reason for striking down this state law. The Due Process Clause with an "arbitrary and capricious" or "shocking to the conscience" formula was liberally used by this Court to strike down economic legislation in the early decades of this century, threatening, many people thought, the tranquility and stability of the Nation. *See, e.g., Lochner v. New York,* 198 U.S. 45. That formula, based on subjective considerations of "natural justice," is no less dangerous when used to enforce this Court's views about personal rights than those about economic rights. I had thought that we had laid that formula, as a means for striking down state legislation, to rest once and for all in cases like *West Coast Hotel Co. v. Parrish,* 300 U.S. 379; *Olsen v. Nebraska ex rel. Western Reference & Bond Assn.,* 313 U.S. 236, and many other opinions. *See also Lochner v. New York,* 198 U.S. 45, 74 (Holmes, J., dissenting).

* * *

* * * The late Judge Learned Hand, after emphasizing his view that judges should not use the due process formula suggested in the concurring opinions today or any other formula like it to invalidate legislation offensive to their "personal preferences," made the statement, with which I fully agree, that:

> "For myself, it would be most irksome to be ruled by a bevy of Platonic Guardians, even if I knew how to choose them, which I assuredly do not."

So far as I am concerned, Connecticut's law as applied here is not forbidden by any provision of the Federal Constitution as that Constitution was written, and I would therefore affirm.

■ MR. JUSTICE STEWART, whom MR. JUSTICE BLACK joins, dissenting.

Since 1879, Connecticut has had on its books a law which forbids the use of contraceptives by anyone. I think this is an uncommonly silly law. As a practical matter, the law is obviously unenforceable, except in the oblique context of the present case. As a philosophical matter, I believe the use of contraceptives in the relationship of marriage should be left to personal and private choice, based upon each individual's moral, ethical, and religious beliefs. As a matter of social policy, I think professional counsel about methods of birth control should be available to all, so that each individual's choice can be meaningfully made. But we are not asked in this case to say whether we think this law is unwise, or even asinine. We are asked to hold that it violates the United States Constitution. And that I cannot do.

In the course of its opinion the Court refers to no less than six Amendments to the Constitution: the First, the Third, the Fourth, the Fifth, the Ninth, and the Fourteenth. But the Court does not say which of these Amendments, if any, it thinks is infringed by this Connecticut law.

We are told that the Due Process Clause of the Fourteenth Amendment is not, as such, the "guide" in this case. With that much I agree. There is no claim that this law, duly enacted by the Connecticut Legislature, is unconstitutionally vague. There is no claim that the appellants were denied any of the elements of procedural due process at their trial, so as to make their convictions constitutionally invalid. And, as the Court says, the day has long passed since the Due Process Clause was regarded as a proper instrument for determining "the wisdom, need, and propriety" of state laws. *Compare Lochner v. New York,* 198 U.S. 45, *with Ferguson v. Skrupa,* 372 U.S. 726 * * *.

As to the First, Third, Fourth, and Fifth Amendments, I can find nothing in any of them to invalidate this Connecticut law, even assuming that all those Amendments are fully applicable against the States * * *.

The Court also quotes the Ninth Amendment, and my Brother GOLDBERG'S concurring opinion relies heavily upon it. But to say that the Ninth Amendment has anything to do with this case is to turn somersaults with history. The Ninth Amendment, like its companion the Tenth, which this Court held "states but a truism that all is retained which has not been surrendered," *United States v. Darby,* 312 U.S. 100, 124, was framed by James Madison and adopted by the States simply to make clear that the adoption of the Bill of Rights did not alter the plan that the *Federal* Government was to be a government of express and limited powers, and that all rights and powers not delegated to it were retained by the people and the individual States. Until today no member of this Court has ever suggested that the Ninth Amendment meant anything else, and the idea that a federal court could ever use the Ninth Amendment to annul a law passed by the elected representatives of the people of the State of Connecticut would have caused James Madison no little wonder.

What provision of the Constitution, then, does make this state law invalid? The Court says it is the right of privacy "created by several fundamental constitutional guarantees." With all deference, I can find no such general right of privacy in the Bill of Rights, in any other part of the Constitution, or in any case ever before decided by this Court.

At the oral argument in this case we were told that the Connecticut law does not "conform to current community standards." But it is not the function of this Court to decide cases on the basis of community standards. We are here to decide cases "agreeably to the Constitution and laws of the United States." It is the essence of judicial duty to subordinate our own personal views, our own ideas of what legislation is wise and what is not. If, as I should surely hope, the law before us does not reflect he standards of the people of Connecticut, the people of Connecticut can freely exercise their true Ninth and Tenth Amendment rights to persuade their elected representatives to repeal it. That is the constitutional way to take this law off the books.

NOTES AND QUESTIONS

1. When six out of the nine justices all write opinions in a case, it is a fair indication that the Supreme Court does not know what it is doing. We think that all six of the opinions you just read are wrong, and only two of them are even posing the right questions. Did you find any of the opinions persuasive?

2. Start with the opinion of the Court. Does the majority opinion ever actually say that the Connecticut statute violates the Fourteenth Amendment? That is a rhetorical question: It does not. If it did, Justice Douglas would have to explain why the methodology of the *Williamson v. Lee Optical Co.* opinion, which he wrote, either led to a different result in this case or did not apply to this case. Either move is certainly possible to make, but whether Justice Douglas could have written something on those points that four other justices would sign is another matter. Instead of relying on the Fourteenth Amendment, the majority opinion derives a "right of privacy" from various other provisions of the Constitution that, in some fashion, protect aspects of privacy. Is that a sensible methodology? There are some provisions of the Constitution that treat African-Americans as less than full citizens in some specific respects (the Three-Fifths Clause and the Fugitive Slave Clause). Does that generate a broad principle that mandates treating African-Americans as less than full citizens across the board? Someone tried that line of reasoning in 1857, and it does not improve with age. As Freud might say, sometimes a set of provisions that share some common themes is just a set of provisions that share some common themes.

3. The majority claimed that "specific guarantees in the Bill of Rights have penumbras, formed by emanations from those guarantees that help give them life and substance." Two questions: 1) Do you have the foggiest notion what this verbiage means? 2) Why is anyone talking about penumbras from emanations in the Bill of Rights when this is a state law challenged under the Fourteenth Amendment? Does the majority ever explain, even in cursory fashion, how its analysis relates to the Fourteenth Amendment?

4. The separate opinions do not fare much better. Justice Goldberg's concurrence has become somewhat legendary because it supposedly, for the first time in the Court's

history, expressly relied on the Ninth Amendment. Did it really do so? Read the opinion carefully. If you excised every reference to the Ninth Amendment in Justice Goldberg's opinion, would it be substantively any different? Does Justice Goldberg actually say anything about the Ninth Amendment that is remotely controversial or that advances the ball in this case?

5. Justices Hugo Black and Potter Stewart wrote impassioned dissents in favor of judicial restraint. Justice Black would be absolutely correct if the only rights protected by the Fourteenth Amendment are those enumerated in the Bill of Rights, and Justice Stewart would be correct if the Fourteenth Amendment placed no substantive restraints on States. As we will see shortly, there is a good case that the rights protected by the Fourteenth Amendment *include,* in some form and to some degree, the rights in the Bill of Rights, but it is tough to come up with a plausible account of the Fourteenth Amendment in which its *only* function is to make the principles of the Bill of Rights apply to States. (Would that interpretation constitutionally validate the Civil Rights Act of 1866?) To be fair, if the only alternatives to Justice Black's position were the majority's penumbral emanations or Justice Goldberg's je-ne-sais-quoi, much could be said for throwing up one's hands and looking for textually enumerated rights. And Justice Stewart would be right if one read only the original meaning of the Equal Protection Clause and Due Process of Law Clauses, while leaving intact the obliteration of the Privileges or Immunities Clause wrought by the *Slaughter-House Cases.* But is it faithful to the Fourteenth Amendment to eliminate its central provision and then read the rest of the amendment as though nothing had happened? There is a simple alternative at hand to Justice Black's despairing deference that does not involve any legal acrobatics: One can apply the Fourteenth Amendment.

6. Enter Justices Harlan and White. Their concurring opinions at least treat the case as being about the Fourteenth Amendment rather than about the Bill of Rights or the penumbral emanations therefrom, so they are at least asking the right questions. Justice Harlan finds in the Fourteenth Amendment those values "implicit in the concept of ordered liberty," which he explored more fully in his earlier dissent in *Poe v. Ullman,* 367 U.S. 497 (1961), in which he sets forth an historical way for applying *Corfield v. Coryell* which is quite compelling. But isn't the real question whether Connecticut was abridging a privilege or immunity of state or national citizenship (which the Court can then, if it wishes, re-describe as "liberty" or "property" under its post-*Slaughter-House* account of due process of law)? Values implicit in the concept of ordered liberty might well represent a subset of those privileges or immunities, but it surely does not suffice as a definition. That leaves Justice White, who we think comes closest to getting it right. There is a unique and important private right at stake here that obviously comes within the compass of any plausible account of the Fourteenth Amendment. The question is whether the State unconstitutionally abridges that right through reasonable regulations for the public good. As Justice White points out, the rationale advanced by the State—using a contraception ban to discourage extra-marital sex—makes no sense as applied to married persons (and close to no sense as applied to anyone else). Under even a moderately serious standard of review, the statute falls. Justice White's opinion would have been much stronger had it tried to anchor its analysis in the (acknowledged or unacknowledged) Privileges or Immunities Clause, and it needed to explain better how and why (and whether) this case is different from cases like *Lochner,* but his opinion at least looks like an effort to decide this case in accordance with something actually traceable to the Constitution.

7. The more interesting question is how Justice White's approach would have worked if the State had made different arguments. Do you think that the State of

Connecticut actually wanted to win this case? It had not applied its "uncommonly silly" law in almost a century. Is it remotely plausible that the rationale behind the law, when it was enacted, was the rationale put forward by the State's counsel? What if the State had instead said, "It is the policy of this State that more live humans are better than fewer live humans, so no contraception in this State is allowed"? In that circumstance, the mismatch between the statute and the claimed goals, which Justice White's opinion clearly identifies on the facts of *Griswold*, would vanish. Would such a law, justified in that fashion, violate the Fourteenth Amendment? What more would Justice White need to say in order to address that question? Is it at all conceivable that the statute in *Griswold,* if properly defended by the State, might actually be constitutional?

8. Suppose that the State instead passed a law limiting all persons to no more than one offspring, on the rationale that overpopulation is a global crisis that threatens the very existence of humanity. Would that be unconstitutional? Why and how?

[Assignment 69]

XII. THE CONSTITUTIONAL RIGHT TO AN ABORTION

The opinions in *Griswold* were all cast in terms of *marital* privacy. In a cursory opinion in *Eisenstadt v. Baird*, 405 U.S. 438 (1972), the Court extended the right to buy and use contraceptives to unmarried couples on the equal protection rationale that there is no meaningful difference between married and unmarried couples that a State can take into account in this context. In language that will loom large in the next case, the Court observed: "If the right of privacy means anything, it is the right of the individual, married or single, to be free from unwarranted governmental intrusion into matters so fundamentally affecting a person as the decision whether to bear or beget a child." *Id.* at 453.

A. ROE V. WADE

410 U.S. 113 (1973)

■ MR. JUSTICE BLACKMUN delivered the opinion of the Court.

This Texas federal appeal and its Georgia companion, *Doe v. Bolton,* present constitutional challenges to state criminal abortion legislation. The Texas statutes under attack here are typical of those that have been in effect in many States for approximately a century. The Georgia statutes, in contrast, have a modern cast and are a legislative product that, to an extent at least, obviously reflects the influences of recent attitudinal change, of advancing medical knowledge and techniques, and of new thinking about an old issue.

We forthwith acknowledge our awareness of the sensitive and emotional nature of the abortion controversy, of the vigorous opposing views, even among physicians, and of the deep and seemingly absolute convictions that the subject inspires. One's philosophy, one's experiences, one's exposure to the raw edges of human existence, one's religious training, one's attitudes toward life and family and their values, and the moral standards one establishes and seeks to observe, are all likely to influence and to color one's thinking and conclusions about abortion.

In addition, population growth, pollution, poverty, and racial overtones tend to complicate and not to simplify the problem.

Our task, of course, is to resolve the issue by constitutional measurement, free of emotion and of predilection. We seek earnestly to do this, and, because we do, we have inquired into, and in this opinion place some emphasis upon, medical and medical-legal history and what that history reveals about man's attitudes toward the abortion procedure over the centuries. We bear in mind, too, Mr. Justice Holmes' admonition in his now-vindicated dissent in *Lochner v. New York,* 198 U.S. 45, 76 (1905):

> "[The Constitution] is made for people of fundamentally differing views, and the accident of our finding certain opinions natural and familiar or novel and even shocking ought not to conclude our judgment upon the question whether statutes embodying them conflict with the Constitution of the United States."

The Texas statutes that concern us here * * * make it a crime to "procure an abortion," as therein defined, or to attempt one, except with respect to "an abortion procured or attempted by medical advice for the purpose of saving the life of the mother." Similar statutes are in existence in a majority of the States.

* * *

Jane Roe,[4] a single woman who was residing in Dallas County, Texas, instituted this federal action in March 1970 against the District Attorney of the county. She sought a declaratory judgment that the Texas criminal abortion statutes were unconstitutional on their face, and an injunction restraining the defendant from enforcing the statutes.

Roe alleged that she was unmarried and pregnant; that she wished to terminate her pregnancy by an abortion "performed by a competent, licensed physician, under safe, clinical conditions"; that she was unable to get a "legal" abortion in Texas because her life did not appear to be threatened by the continuation of her pregnancy; and that she could not afford to travel to another jurisdiction in order to secure a legal abortion under safe conditions. She claimed that the Texas statutes were unconstitutionally vague and that they abridged her right of personal privacy, protected by the First, Fourth, Fifth, Ninth, and Fourteenth Amendments. By an amendment to her complaint, Roe purported to sue "on behalf of herself and all other women" similarly situated.

* * *.

* * *

[T]he District Court held that the "fundamental right of single women and married persons to choose whether to have children is protected by the Ninth Amendment, through the Fourteenth Amendment," and that the Texas criminal abortion statutes were void on their face because they were both unconstitutionally vague and constituted an overbroad infringement of the plaintiffs' Ninth Amendment rights * * *.

* * *

The principal thrust of appellant's attack on the Texas statutes is that they improperly invade a right, said to be possessed by the pregnant woman, to choose to

---

[4] The name is a pseudonym. [*Editors' Note: "Jane Roe's" real name was Norma McCorvey. Two decades after* Roe v. Wade, *Ms. McCorvey became a staunch pro-life activist.*]

terminate her pregnancy. Appellant would discover this right in the concept of personal "liberty" embodied in the Fourteenth Amendment's Due Process Clause; or in personal, marital, familial, and sexual privacy said to be protected by the Bill of Rights or its penumbras, see *Griswold v. Connecticut,* 381 U.S. 479 (1965); *Eisenstadt v. Baird,* 405 U.S. 438 (1972); *id.* at 460 (WHITE, J., concurring in result); or among those rights reserved to the people by the Ninth Amendment, *Griswold v. Connecticut,* 381 U.S. at 486 (Goldberg, J., concurring). Before addressing this claim, we feel it desirable briefly to survey, in several aspects, the history of abortion, for such insight as that history may afford us, and then to examine the state purposes and interests behind the criminal abortion laws.

It perhaps is not generally appreciated that the restrictive criminal abortion laws in effect in a majority of States today are of relatively recent vintage. Those laws, generally proscribing abortion or its attempt at any time during pregnancy except when necessary to preserve the pregnant woman's life, are not of ancient or even of common law origin. Instead, they derive from statutory changes effected, for the most part, in the latter half of the 19th century.

* * *

[*Editors' Note: Justice Blackmun describes, with copious footnotes, attitudes toward abortion in ancient Persia, Greece, and Rome; and he discusses at some length the origins and meaning of the Hippocratic Oath, by which doctors must swear they will not perform abortions.*]

3. *The common law.* It is undisputed that at common law, abortion performed *before* "quickening"—the first recognizable movement of the fetus *in utero,* appearing usually from the 16th to the 18th week of pregnancy—was not an indictable offense. The absence of a common law crime for pre-quickening abortion appears to have developed from a confluence of earlier philosophical, theological, and civil and canon law concepts of when life begins. These disciplines variously approached the question in terms of the point at which the embryo or fetus became "formed" or recognizably human, or in terms of when a "person" came into being, that is, infused with a "soul" or "animated." A loose consensus evolved in early English law that these events occurred at some point between conception and live birth. This was "mediate animation." Although Christian theology and the canon law came to fix the point of animation at 40 days for a male and 80 days for a female, a view that persisted until the 19th century, there was otherwise little agreement about the precise time of formation or animation. There was agreement, however, that, prior to this point, the fetus was to be regarded as part of the mother, and its destruction, therefore, was not homicide. Due to continued uncertainty about the precise time when animation occurred, to the lack of any empirical basis for the 40–80-day view, and perhaps to Aquinas' definition of movement as one of the two first principles of life, Bracton focused upon quickening as the critical point. The significance of quickening was echoed by later common law scholars and found its way into the received common law in this country.

Whether abortion of a *quick* fetus was a felony at common law, or even a lesser crime, is still disputed. Bracton, writing early in the 13th century, thought it homicide. But the later and predominant view, following the great common-law scholars, has been that it was, at most, a lesser offense. In a frequently cited passage, Coke took the position that abortion of a woman "quick with childe" is "a great misprision, and no murder." Blackstone followed, saying that while abortion after quickening had once been considered manslaughter (though not murder), "modern law" took a less severe view. A recent review of the common-law precedents argues, however, that those precedents contradict Coke and that even post-quickening abortion was never established as a common-law crime. This is of some importance because while most American courts ruled, in holding or dictum, that abortion of an unquickened fetus was not criminal under their received common law, others followed Coke in stating that abortion of a quick fetus was a "misprision," a term they translated to mean "misdemeanor." That their reliance on Coke on this aspect of the law was uncritical and, apparently in all the reported cases, dictum (due probably to the paucity of common-law prosecutions for post-quickening abortion), makes it now appear doubtful that abortion was ever firmly established as a common-law crime even with respect to the destruction of a quick fetus.

* * *

5. *The American law.* In this country, the law in effect in all but a few States until mid-19th century was the pre-existing English common law * * *. By 1840, when Texas had received the common law, only eight American States had statutes dealing with abortion. It was not until after the War Between the States that legislation began generally to replace the common law. Most of these initial statutes dealt severely with abortion after quickening but were lenient with it before quickening. Most punished attempts equally with completed abortions. While many statutes included the exception for an abortion thought by one or more physicians to be necessary to save the mother's life, that provision soon disappeared and the typical law required that the procedure actually be necessary for that purpose.

Gradually, in the middle and late 19th century the quickening distinction disappeared from the statutory law of most States and the degree of the offense and the penalties were increased. By the end of the 1950's, a large majority of the jurisdictions banned abortion, however and whenever performed, unless done to save or preserve the life of the mother * * *. In the past several years, however, a trend toward liberalization of abortion statutes has resulted in adoption, by about one-third of the States, of less stringent laws * * *.

It is thus apparent that at common law, at the time of the adoption of our Constitution, and throughout the major portion of the 19th century, abortion was viewed with less disfavor than under most American statutes currently in effect. Phrasing it another way, a woman enjoyed a substantially broader right to terminate a pregnancy than she does in most States today. At least with respect to the early stage of pregnancy, and very possibly without such a limitation, the opportunity to make this choice was present in this country well into the 19th century. Even later, the law continued for some time to treat less punitively an abortion procured in early pregnancy.

* * *

[*Editors' Note: Justice Blackmun next summarized at great length the views of the American Medical Association, the American Public Health Association, and the American Bar Association on whether abortions should be criminally punished.*]

Three reasons have been advanced to explain historically the enactment of criminal abortion laws in the 19th century and to justify their continued existence.

It has been argued occasionally that these laws were the product of a Victorian social concern to discourage illicit sexual conduct. Texas, however, does not advance this justification in the present case, and it appears that no court or commentator has taken the argument seriously. The appellants and *amici* contend, moreover, that this is not a proper state purpose at all and suggest that, if it were, the Texas statutes are overbroad in protecting it since the law fails to distinguish between married and unwed mothers.

A second reason is concerned with abortion as a medical procedure. When most criminal abortion laws were first enacted, the procedure was a hazardous one for the woman. This was particularly true prior to the development of antisepsis. Antiseptic techniques, of course, were based on discoveries by Lister, Pasteur, and others first announced in 1867, but were not generally accepted and employed until about the turn of the century. Abortion mortality was high. Even after 1900, and perhaps until as late as the development of antibiotics in the 1940's, standard modern techniques such as dilation and curettage were not nearly so safe as they are today. Thus, it has been argued that a State's real concern in enacting a criminal abortion law was to protect the pregnant woman, that is, to restrain her from submitting to a procedure that placed her life in serious jeopardy.

Modern medical techniques have altered this situation. Appellants and various *amici* refer to medical data indicating that abortion in early pregnancy, that is, prior to the end of the first trimester, although not without its risk, is now relatively safe. Mortality rates for women undergoing early abortions, where the procedure is legal, appear to be as low as or lower than the rates for normal childbirth. Consequently, any interest of the State in protecting the woman from an inherently hazardous procedure, except when it would be equally dangerous for her to forgo it, has largely disappeared. Of course, important state interests in the areas of health and medical standards do remain. The State has a legitimate interest in seeing to it that abortion, like any other medical procedure, is performed under circumstances that insure maximum safety for the patient. This interest obviously extends at least to the performing physician and his staff, to the facilities involved, to the availability of after-care, and to adequate provision for any complication or emergency that might arise. The prevalence of high mortality rates at illegal "abortion mills" strengthens, rather than weakens, the State's interest in regulating the conditions under which abortions are performed. Moreover, the risk to the woman increases as her pregnancy continues. Thus, the State retains a definite interest in protecting the woman's own health and safety when an abortion is proposed at a late stage of pregnancy.

The third reason is the State's interest—some phrase it in terms of duty—in protecting prenatal life. Some of the argument for this justification rests on the theory that a new human life is present from the moment of conception. The State's interest and general obligation to protect life then extends, it is argued, to prenatal life. Only when the life of the pregnant mother herself is at stake, balanced against the life she carries within her, should the interest of the embryo or fetus not prevail. Logically, of course, a legitimate state interest in this area need not stand or fall on acceptance of the belief that life begins at conception or at some other point prior to live birth. In assessing the State's interest, recognition may be given to the less rigid claim that as long as at least *potential* life is involved, the State may assert interests beyond the protection of the pregnant woman alone.

It is with these interests, and the weight to be attached to them, that this case is concerned.

The Constitution does not explicitly mention any right of privacy. In a line of decisions, however, going back perhaps as far as *Union Pacific R. Co. v. Botsford,* 141 U.S. 250, 251 (1891), the Court has recognized that a right of personal privacy, or a guarantee of certain areas or zones of privacy, does exist under the Constitution. In varying contexts, the Court or individual Justices have, indeed, found at least the roots of that right in the First Amendment, in the Fourth and Fifth Amendments, in the penumbras of the Bill of Rights, *Griswold v. Connecticut,* 381 U.S. at 484–485; in the Ninth Amendment, *id.* at 486 (Goldberg, J., concurring); or in the concept of liberty guaranteed by the first section of the Fourteenth Amendment, see *Meyer v. Nebraska,* 262 U.S. 390, 399 (1923). These decisions make it clear that only personal rights that can be deemed "fundamental" or "implicit in the concept of ordered liberty," *Palko v. Connecticut,* 302 U.S. 319, 325 (1937), are included in this guarantee of personal privacy. They also make it clear that the right has some extension to activities relating to marriage, *Loving v. Virginia,* 388 U.S. 1, 12 (1967); procreation, *Skinner v. Oklahoma,* 316 U.S. 535, 541–542 (1942); contraception, *Eisenstadt v. Baird,* 405 U.S. at 453–454; *id.* at 460, 463–465 (WHITE, J., concurring in result); family relationships, *Prince v. Massachusetts,* 321 U.S. 158, 166 (1944); and childrearing and education, *Pierce v. Society of Sisters,* 268 U.S. 510, 535 (1925), *Meyer v. Nebraska, supra.*

This right of privacy, whether it be founded in the Fourteenth Amendment's concept of personal liberty and restrictions upon state action, as we feel it is, or, as the District Court determined, in the Ninth Amendment's reservation of rights to the people, is broad enough to encompass a woman's decision whether or not to terminate her pregnancy. The detriment that the State would impose upon the pregnant woman by denying this choice altogether is apparent. Specific and direct harm medically diagnosable even in early pregnancy may be involved. Maternity, or additional offspring, may force upon the woman a distressful life and future. Psychological harm may be imminent. Mental and physical health may be taxed by childcare. There is also the distress, for all concerned, associated with the unwanted child, and there is the problem of bringing a child into a family already unable, psychologically and otherwise, to care for it. In other cases, as in this one, the additional difficulties and continuing stigma of unwed motherhood may be involved. All these are factors the woman and her responsible physician necessarily will consider in consultation.

On the basis of elements such as these, appellant and some *amici* argue that the woman's right is absolute and that she is entitled to terminate her pregnancy at whatever time, in whatever way, and for whatever reason she alone chooses. With this we do not agree. Appellant's arguments that Texas either has no valid interest at all in regulating the abortion decision, or no interest strong enough to support any limitation upon the woman's sole determination, are unpersuasive. The Court's decisions recognizing a right of privacy also acknowledge that some state regulation in areas protected by that right is appropriate. As noted above, a State may properly assert important interests in safeguarding health, in maintaining medical standards, and in protecting potential life. At some point in pregnancy, these respective interests become sufficiently compelling to sustain regulation of the factors that govern the abortion decision. The privacy right involved, therefore, cannot be said to be absolute. In fact, it is not clear to us that the claim asserted by some *amici* that one has an unlimited right to do with one's body as one pleases bears a close relationship to the right of privacy previously articulated in the Court's decisions. The Court has refused to recognize an unlimited right of this kind in the past. *Jacobson v. Massachusetts,* 197 U.S. 11 (1905) (vaccination); *Buck v. Bell,* 274 U.S. 200 (1927) (sterilization).

We, therefore, conclude that the right of personal privacy includes the abortion decision, but that this right is not unqualified and must be considered against important state interests in regulation.

* * *

The District Court held that the appellee failed to meet his burden of demonstrating that the Texas statute's infringement upon Roe's rights was necessary to support a compelling state interest, and that, although the appellee presented "several compelling justifications for state presence in the area of abortions," the statutes outstripped these justifications and swept "far beyond any areas of compelling state interest." Appellant and appellee both contest that holding. Appellant, as has been indicated, claims an absolute right that bars any state imposition of criminal penalties in the area. Appellee argues that the State's determination to recognize and protect prenatal life from and after conception constitutes a compelling state interest. As noted above, we do not agree fully with either formulation.

The appellee and certain *amici* argue that the fetus is a "person" within the language and meaning of the Fourteenth Amendment. In support of this, they outline at length and in detail the well-known facts of fetal development. If this suggestion of personhood is established, the appellant's case, of course, collapses, for the fetus' right to life would then be guaranteed specifically by the Amendment. The appellant conceded as much on reargument. On the other hand, the appellee conceded on reargument that no case could be cited that holds that a fetus is a person within the meaning of the Fourteenth Amendment.

The Constitution does not define "person" in so many words. Section 1 of the Fourteenth Amendment contains three references to "person." The first, in defining "citizens," speaks of "persons born or naturalized in the United States." The word also appears both in the Due Process Clause and in the Equal Protection Clause. "Person" is used in other places in the Constitution: in the listing of qualifications for Representatives and Senators, Art. I, § 2, cl. 2, and § 3, cl. 3; in the Apportionment Clause, Art. I, § 2, cl. 3; in the Migration and Importation provision, Art. I, § 9, cl. 1; in the Emolument Clause, Art. I, § 9, cl. 8; in the Electors provisions, Art. II, § 1, cl. 2, and the superseded cl. 3; in the provision outlining qualifications for the office of President, Art. II, § 1, cl. 5; in the Extradition provisions, Art. IV, § 2, cl. 2, and the superseded Fugitive Slave Clause 3; and in the Fifth, Twelfth, and Twenty-second Amendments, as well as in §§ 2 and 3 of the Fourteenth Amendment. But in nearly all these instances, the use of the word is such that it has application only postnatally. None indicates, with any assurance, that it has any possible pre-natal application.

All this, together with our observation, *supra,* that throughout the major portion of the 19th century prevailing legal abortion practices were far freer than they are

today, persuades us that the word "person," as used in the Fourteenth Amendment, does not include the unborn * * *.

This conclusion, however, does not of itself fully answer the contentions raised by Texas, and we pass on to other considerations.

The pregnant woman cannot be isolated in her privacy. She carries an embryo and, later, a fetus, if one accepts the medical definitions of the developing young in the human uterus. The situation therefore is inherently different from marital intimacy, or bedroom possession of obscene material, or marriage, or procreation, or education, with which *Eisenstadt* and *Griswold, Stanley, Loving, Skinner*, and *Pierce* and *Meyer* were respectively concerned. As we have intimated above, it is reasonable and appropriate for a State to decide that at some point in time another interest, that of health of the mother or that of potential human life, becomes significantly involved. The woman's privacy is no longer sole and any right of privacy she possesses must be measured accordingly.

Texas urges that, apart from the Fourteenth Amendment, life begins at conception and is present throughout pregnancy, and that, therefore, the State has a compelling interest in protecting that life from and after conception. We need not resolve the difficult question of when life begins. When those trained in the respective disciplines of medicine, philosophy, and theology are unable to arrive at any consensus, the judiciary, at this point in the development of man's knowledge, is not in a position to speculate as to the answer.

It should be sufficient to note briefly the wide divergence of thinking on this most sensitive and difficult question. There has always been strong support for the view that life does not begin until live birth. This was the belief of the Stoics. It appears to be the predominant, though not the unanimous, attitude of the Jewish faith. It may be taken to represent also the position of a large segment of the Protestant community, insofar as that can be ascertained; organized groups that have taken a formal position on the abortion issue have generally regarded abortion as a matter for the conscience of the individual and her family. As we have noted, the common law found greater significance in quickening. Physician and their scientific colleagues have regarded that event with less interest and have tended to focus either upon conception, upon live birth, or upon the interim point at which the fetus becomes "viable," that is, potentially able to live outside the mother's womb, albeit with artificial aid. Viability is usually placed at about seven months (28 weeks) but may occur earlier, even at 24 weeks. The Aristotelian theory of "mediate animation," that held sway throughout the Middle Ages and the Renaissance in Europe, continued to be official Roman Catholic dogma until the 19th century, despite opposition to this "ensoulment" theory from those in the Church who would recognize the existence of life from the moment of conception. The latter is now, of course, the official belief of the Catholic Church. As one brief *amicus* discloses, this is a view strongly held by many non-Catholics as well, and by many physicians. Substantial problems for precise definition of this view are posed, however, by new embryological data that purport to indicate that conception is a "process" over time, rather than an event, and by new medical techniques such as menstrual extraction, the "morning-after" pill, implantation of embryos, artificial insemination, and even artificial wombs.

In areas other than criminal abortion, the law has been reluctant to endorse any theory that life, as we recognize it, begins before live birth or to accord legal rights to the unborn except in narrowly defined situations and except when the rights are contingent upon live birth. For example, the traditional rule of tort law denied recovery for prenatal injuries even though the child was born alive. That rule has been changed in almost every jurisdiction. In most States, recovery is said to be permitted only if the fetus was viable, or at least quick, when the injuries were sustained, though few courts have squarely so held. In a recent development, generally opposed by the commentators, some States permit the parents of a stillborn child to maintain an action for wrongful death because of prenatal injuries. Such an action, however, would appear to be one to vindicate the parents' interest and is thus consistent with the view that the fetus, at most, represents only the potentiality of life. Similarly, unborn children have been recognized as acquiring rights or interests by way of inheritance or other devolution of property, and have been represented by guardians *ad litem*. Perfection of the interests involved, again, has generally been contingent upon live birth. In short, the unborn have never been recognized in the law as persons in the whole sense.

In view of all this, we do not agree that, by adopting one theory of life, Texas may override the rights of the pregnant woman that are at stake. We repeat, however, that the State does have an important and legitimate interest in preserving and protecting the health of the pregnant woman, whether she be a resident of the State or a nonresident who seeks medical consultation and treatment there, and that it has still *another* important and legitimate interest in protecting the potentiality of human life. These interests are separate and distinct. Each grows in substantiality as the woman approaches term and, at a point during pregnancy, each becomes "compelling."

With respect to the State's important and legitimate interest in the health of the mother, the "compelling" point, in the light of present medical knowledge, is at approximately the end of the first trimester. This is so because of the now-established medical fact * * * that until the end of the first trimester mortality in abortion may be less than mortality in normal childbirth. It follows that, from and after this point, a State may regulate the abortion procedure to the extent that the regulation reasonably relates to the preservation and protection of maternal health. Examples of permissible state regulation in this area are requirements as to the qualifications of the person who is to perform the abortion; as to the licensure of that person; as to the facility in which the procedure is to be performed, that is, whether it must be a hospital or may be a clinic or some other place of less-than-hospital status; as to the licensing of the facility; and the like.

This means, on the other hand, that, for the period of pregnancy prior to this "compelling" point, the attending physician, in consultation with his patient, is free to determine, without regulation by the State, that, in his medical judgment, the patient's pregnancy should be terminated. If that decision is reached, the judgment may be effectuated by an abortion free of interference by the State.

With respect to the State's important and legitimate interest in potential life, the "compelling" point is at viability. This is so because the fetus then presumably has the capability of meaningful life outside the mother's womb. State regulation protective of fetal life after viability thus has both logical and biological justifications. If the State is interested in protecting fetal life after viability, it may go so far as to proscribe abortion during that period, except when it is necessary to preserve the life or health of the mother.

Measured against these standards, Art. 1196 of the Texas Penal Code, in restricting legal abortions to those "procured or attempted by medical advice for the purpose of saving the life of the mother," sweeps too broadly. The statute makes no distinction between abortions performed early in pregnancy and those performed later, and it limits to a single reason, "saving" the mother's life, the legal justification for the procedure. The statute, therefore, cannot survive the constitutional attack made upon it here.

This conclusion makes it unnecessary for us to consider the additional challenge to the Texas statute asserted on grounds of vagueness.

To summarize and to repeat:

1. A state criminal abortion statute of the current Texas type, that excepts from criminality only a *life-saving* procedure on behalf of the mother, without regard to pregnancy stage and without recognition of the other interests involved, is violative of the Due Process Clause of the Fourteenth Amendment.

(a) For the stage prior to approximately the end of the first trimester, the abortion decision and its effectuation must be left to the medical judgment of the pregnant woman's attending physician.

(b) For the stage subsequent to approximately the end of the first trimester, the State, in promoting its interest in the health of the mother, may, if it chooses, regulate the abortion procedure in ways that are reasonably related to maternal health.

(c) For the stage subsequent to viability, the State in promoting its interest in the potentiality of human life may, if it chooses, regulate, and even proscribe, abortion except where it is necessary, in appropriate medical judgment, for the preservation of the life or health of the mother.

2. The State may define the term "physician," as it has been employed in the preceding paragraphs of this Part XI of this opinion, to mean only a physician currently licensed by the State, and may proscribe any abortion by a person who is not a physician as so defined.

* * *

This holding, we feel, is consistent with the relative weights of the respective interests involved, with the lessons and examples of medical and legal history, with the lenity of the common law, and with the demands of the profound problems of the present day. The decision leaves the State free to place increasing restrictions on abortion as the period of pregnancy lengthens, so long as those restrictions are tailored to the recognized state interests. The decision vindicates the right of the physician to administer medical treatment according to his professional judgment up to the points where important state interests provide compelling justifications for intervention. Up to those points, the abortion decision in all its aspects is inherently, and primarily, a medical decision, and basic responsibility for it must rest with the physician. If an individual practitioner abuses the privilege of exercising proper medical judgment, the usual remedies, judicial and intra-professional, are available.

* * *

■ MR. JUSTICE STEWART, concurring.

In 1963, this Court, in *Ferguson v. Skrupa,* 372 U.S. 726, purported to sound the death knell for the doctrine of substantive due process, a doctrine under which many state laws had in the past been held to violate the Fourteenth Amendment. As Mr. Justice Black's opinion for the Court in *Skrupa* put it: "We have returned to the original constitutional proposition that courts do not substitute their social and economic beliefs for the judgment of legislative bodies, who are elected to pass laws." *Id.* at 730.

Barely two years later, in *Griswold v. Connecticut,* 381 U.S. 479, the Court held a Connecticut birth control law unconstitutional. In view of what had been so recently said in *Skrupa,* the Court's opinion in *Griswold* understandably did its best to avoid reliance on the Due Process Clause of the Fourteenth Amendment as the ground for decision. Yet, the Connecticut law did not violate any provision of the Bill of Rights, nor any other specific provision of the Constitution. So it was clear to me then, and it is equally clear to me now, that the *Griswold* decision can be rationally understood only as a holding that the Connecticut statute substantively invaded the "liberty" that is protected by the Due Process Clause of the Fourteenth Amendment. As so understood, *Griswold* stands as one in a long line of pre-*Skrupa* cases decided under the doctrine of substantive due process, and I now accept it as such.

* * *

Several decisions of this Court make clear that freedom of personal choice in matters of marriage and family life is one of the liberties protected by the Due Process Clause of the Fourteenth Amendment * * *. "Certainly the interests of a woman in giving of her physical and emotional self during pregnancy and the interests that will be affected throughout her life by the birth and raising of a child are of a far greater degree of significance and personal intimacy than the right to send a child to private school protected in Pierce v. Society of Sisters, 268 U.S. 510 (1925), or the right to teach a foreign language protected in Meyer v. Nebraska, 262 U.S. 390 (1923)." *Abele v. Markel,* 351 F.Supp. 224, 227 (Conn. 1972).

Clearly, therefore, the Court today is correct in holding that the right asserted by Jane Roe is embraced within the personal liberty protected by the Due Process Clause of the Fourteenth Amendment.

It is evident that the Texas abortion statute infringes that right directly. Indeed, it is difficult to imagine a more complete abridgment of a constitutional freedom than that worked by the inflexible criminal statute now in force in Texas. The question then becomes whether the state interests advanced to justify this abridgment can survive the "particularly careful scrutiny" that the Fourteenth Amendment here requires.

The asserted state interests are protection of the health and safety of the pregnant woman, and protection of the potential future human life within her. These are legitimate objectives, amply sufficient to permit a State to regulate abortions as it does other surgical procedures, and perhaps sufficient to permit a State to regulate abortions more stringently, or even to prohibit them in the late stages of pregnancy. But such legislation is not before us, and I think the Court today has thoroughly demonstrated that these state interests cannot constitutionally support the broad abridgment of personal liberty worked by the existing Texas law. Accordingly, I join the Court's opinion holding that that law is invalid under the Due Process Clause of the Fourteenth Amendment.

[*Editors' Note: Chief Justice Burger's concurrence and Justice White's dissent appear in* Doe v. Bolton, *410 U.S. 179 (1973), but apply to* Roe *as well.*]

■ MR. CHIEF JUSTICE BURGER, concurring.

I agree that, under the Fourteenth Amendment to the Constitution, the abortion statutes of Georgia and Texas impermissibly limit the performance of abortions necessary to protect the health of pregnant women, using the term health in its broadest medical context. I am somewhat troubled that the Court has taken notice of various scientific and medical data in reaching its conclusion; however, I do not believe that the Court has exceeded the scope of judicial notice accepted in other contexts.

* * *

* * * I do not read the Court's holdings today as having the sweeping consequences attributed to them by the dissenting Justices; the dissenting views discount the reality that the vast majority of physicians observe the standards of their profession, and act only on the basis of carefully deliberated medical judgments relating to life and health. Plainly, the Court today rejects any claim that the Constitution requires abortions on demand.

■ MR. JUSTICE WHITE, with whom MR. JUSTICE REHNQUIST joins, dissenting.

At the heart of the controversy in these cases are those recurring pregnancies that pose no danger whatsoever to the life or health of the mother but are, nevertheless, unwanted for any one or more of a variety of reasons—convenience, family planning, economics, dislike of children, the embarrassment of illegitimacy, etc. The common claim before us is that for any one of such reasons, or for no reason at all, and without asserting or claiming any threat to life or health, any woman is entitled to an abortion at her request if she is able to find a medical advisor willing to undertake the procedure.

The Court for the most part sustains this position: During the period prior to the time the fetus becomes viable, the Constitution of the United States values the convenience, whim, or caprice of the putative mother more than the life or potential life of the fetus; the Constitution, therefore, guarantees the right to an abortion as against any state law or policy seeking to protect the fetus from an abortion not prompted by more compelling reasons of the mother.

With all due respect, I dissent. I find nothing in the language or history of the Constitution to support the Court's judgment. The Court simply fashions and announces a new constitutional right for pregnant mothers and, with scarcely any reason or authority for its action, invests that right with sufficient substance to override most existing state abortion statutes. The upshot is that the people and the legislatures of the 50 States are constitutionally disentitled to weigh the relative importance of the continued existence and development of the fetus, on the one hand, against a spectrum of possible impacts on the mother, on the other hand. As an exercise of raw judicial power, the Court perhaps has authority to do what it does today; but in my view its judgment is an improvident and extravagant exercise of the power of judicial review that the Constitution extends to this Court.

The Court apparently values the convenience of the pregnant mother more than the continued existence and development of the life or potential life that she carries. Whether or not I might agree with that marshaling of values, I can in no event join the Court's judgment because I find no constitutional warrant for imposing such an order of priorities on the people and legislatures of the States * * *.

* * *

■ MR. JUSTICE REHNQUIST, dissenting.

* * *

* * * I have difficulty in concluding, as the Court does, that the right of "privacy" is involved in this case. Texas, by the statute here challenged, bars the performance of a medical abortion by a licensed physician on a plaintiff such as Roe. A transaction resulting in an operation such as this is not "private" in the ordinary usage of that word. Nor is the "privacy" that the Court finds here even a distant relative of the freedom from searches and seizures protected by the Fourth Amendment to the Constitution, which the Court has referred to as embodying a right to privacy. *Katz v. United States,* 389 U.S. 347 (1967).

If the Court means by the term "privacy" no more than that the claim of a person to be free from unwanted state regulation of consensual transactions may be a form of "liberty" protected by the Fourteenth Amendment, there is no doubt that similar claims have been upheld in our earlier decisions on the basis of that liberty * * *. But that liberty is not guaranteed absolutely against deprivation, only against deprivation without due process of law. The test traditionally applied in the area of social and economic legislation is whether or not a law such as that challenged has a rational relation to a valid state objective. *Williamson v. Lee Optical Co.,* 348 U.S. 483, 491 (1955). The Due Process Clause of the Fourteenth Amendment undoubtedly does place a limit, albeit a broad one, on legislative power to enact laws such as this. If the Texas statute were to prohibit an abortion even where the mother's life is in jeopardy, I have little doubt that such a statute would lack a rational relation to a valid state objective under the test stated in *Williamson, supra.* But the Court's sweeping invalidation of any restrictions on abortion during the first trimester is impossible to justify under that standard, and the conscious weighing of competing factors that the Court's opinion apparently substitutes for the established test is far more appropriate to a legislative judgment than to a judicial one.

The Court eschews the history of the Fourteenth Amendment in its reliance on the "compelling state interest" test. But the Court adds a new wrinkle to this test by transposing it from the legal considerations associated with the Equal Protection Clause of the Fourteenth Amendment to this case arising under the Due Process Clause of the Fourteenth Amendment. Unless I misapprehend the consequences of this transplanting of the "compelling state interest test," the Court's opinion will accomplish the seemingly impossible feat of leaving this area of the law more confused than it found it.

While the Court's opinion quotes from the dissent of Mr. Justice Holmes in *Lochner v. New York,* 198 U.S. 45, 74 (1905), the result it reaches is more closely attuned to the majority opinion of Mr. Justice Peckham in that case. As in *Lochner* and similar cases applying substantive due process standards to economic and social welfare legislation, the adoption of the compelling state interest standard will inevitably require this Court to examine the legislative policies and pass on the wisdom of these policies in the very process of deciding whether a particular state interest put forward may or may not be "compelling." The decision here to break pregnancy into three distinct terms and to outline the permissible restrictions the State may impose in each one, for example, partakes more of judicial legislation than it does of a determination of the intent of the drafters of the Fourteenth Amendment.

* * *

To reach its result, the Court necessarily has had to find within the scope of the Fourteenth Amendment a right that was apparently completely unknown to the drafters of the Amendment * * *. [T]he Texas statute struck down today was, as the majority notes, first enacted in 1857 and "has remained substantially unchanged to the present time."

There apparently was no question concerning the validity of this provision or of any of the other state statutes when the Fourteenth Amendment was adopted. The only conclusion possible from this history is that the drafters did not intend to have the Fourteenth Amendment withdraw from the States the power to legislate with respect to this matter.

* * *

For all of the foregoing reasons, I respectfully dissent.

NOTES AND QUESTIONS

1. Justice Blackmun's opinion in *Roe v. Wade* set off a firestorm of criticism—and a counter-firestorm of support—that continues unabated right down to the present day in 2020, nearly fifty years later. Sometimes, as we saw in Chapter 2, *see supra* pages 536–556, judicial decisions have the practical effect of settling matters even on hotly contested subjects. *Roe* has not had that effect. As you will see in the ensuing materials (and as you surely know from living in the world), debate about abortion, as a matter of both policy and constitutional law, does not take *Roe* as a given. That is surely in part a function of the issue involved, but is it also a function of the Court's performance in *Roe*? Several features of that performance might be relevant.

2. First, the decision in *Roe* held unconstitutional the abortion laws of all fifty States rather than merely striking down an outlier law, as in *Griswold v. Connecticut*. Second, the Court relied on the right to privacy articulated in *Griswold* to protect a medical procedure that occurs in a public clinic or a public hospital. There are many ways to characterize the woman's right at issue in *Roe*—some of which, as it happens, fit very naturally into either the Privileges or Immunities Clause or the Due Process of Law Clause—but a right to privacy seems like a very odd choice. Third, the Court wrote a very detailed opinion laying out the rights of the mother and unborn child in all phases of pregnancy. The end result looked very "legislative," in the same way *Lochner* looked legislative when it struck down a sixty-hour work week for bakers after the Court had already upheld in *Holden v. Hardy* the constitutionality of an eight-hour day requirement for coal miners. And, fourth, the Court said nothing at all about the text and history of Section 1 of the Fourteenth Amendment, which it was supposed to be enforcing. The Court said more about Greek history and the views of the American Bar Association than it did about the Fourteenth Amendment.

3. Even many who agree, and agree strongly, with the result in *Roe* have long had concerns about its reasoning. Justice Ruth Bader Ginsburg criticized *Roe v. Wade* in her confirmation hearing for trying to do too much, all at once, in one case. There were many

narrower avenues the Court could have taken to reach the outcome it reached in *Roe v. Wade*. For example, Professor John Hart Ely noted that the Texas abortion law at issue in *Roe* was passed in the nineteenth century when women could not vote or run for office and that the law heavily and uniquely burdened women. JOHN HART ELY, DEMOCRACY AND DISTRUST: A THEORY OF JUDICIAL REVIEW (1980). Ely proposed striking down all pre-1920 abortion laws, enacted before women had the right to vote. This would have produced the same outcome as *Roe* without nationalizing the law of abortion and forbidding new, more moderate laws regulating abortion. Would it also void all laws uniquely burdening children because children cannot vote? Then-Judge Ginsburg in 1985 suggested that *Roe* might have been better argued and decided on equal protection grounds. *See supra* page 1390. An entire book is devoted to alternative accounts that various scholars believe would provide a stronger grounding for *Roe*. *See* WHAT *ROE V. WADE* SHOULD HAVE SAID: THE NATION'S TOP LEGAL EXPERTS REWRITE AMERICA'S MOST CONTROVERSIAL DECISION (Jack Balkin ed., 2007).

4. No one seriously doubts that abortion statutes implicate constitutionally real rights. Bodily integrity was squarely within the eighteenth-century meaning of "life" (yes, "life," not "liberty," *see supra* pages 1112–1113) under the Fifth Amendment Due Process of Law Clause, and there is no reason to think that the nineteenth-century Fourteenth Amendment Due Process of Law Clause is any narrower (and some reasons to think it broader). If substantive due process is accepted as doctrine—and even Justice Stewart was willing to concede the point in 1973—the Due Process of Law Clause bears on this case. There are multiple ways in which to characterize a woman's right to decisional and bodily integrity as "privileges or immunities" if one thinks (as we do) that the Privileges or Immunities Clause is the most relevant provision of the Fourteenth Amendment here. That is not the issue.

5. A modern day version of the Massachusetts Born Free and Equal Clause would read: "All women identifying themselves as women are born free and equal, and have certain natural, essential, and unalienable rights; among which may be reckoned the right of enjoying and defending their lives and liberties; that of acquiring, possessing, and protecting property; in fine, that of seeking and obtaining their safety and happiness." Can you "enjoy and defend life and liberty" and "seek and obtain safety and happiness" if you are pregnant with a baby you do not want to raise or put up for adoption? What if your life as a woman is at risk because of your pregnancy? Should abortion be available at all stages of pregnancy when a pregnant woman's life is at risk? The state's police power makes your constitutional rights "subject nevertheless to such restraints as the government may justly prescribe for the general good of the whole" people. Is requiring a women to bear an unwanted pregnancy a "just" law enacted "for the general good of the whole" people? How would a court try to answer that question?

6. Does life begin at fourteen days after conception when implantation of the fertilized egg occurs in the uterine wall? Most fertilized eggs do not implant and start a pregnancy. Would this mean that stem cell research on fertilized eggs, the use of the "morning after pill", and the use of intra-uterine devices ("IUD's") that stop implantation are all perfectly fine? At the other end of the spectrum, fetuses, which in 1973 were only viable during the third trimester of pregnancy, are now viable after twenty-three weeks of pregnancy. Does that mean right-to-life statutes can go into effect now after twenty-three weeks of pregnancy?

7. Are anti-abortion laws a form of "indentured servitude", which is outlawed by the Thirteenth Amendment, along with slavery? Indentured servants typically took money from patrons, who paid their travel expenses to get to the U.S. and then sought to get out of the typically seven-year labor contracts, which they signed in order to get their

travel money. If you have a constitutional right not to be an indentured servant, can the government force you to bear an unwanted pregnancy? What if the unwanted pregnancy is cause by rape?

8. Is the fetus a "person" entitled to equal protection and due process of law? (It is hard to argue that a fetus is a citizen until it is "born.") After surveying the breadth of disagreement about the meaning and definition of life, the Court says: "we do not agree that, by adopting one theory of life, Texas may override the rights of the pregnant woman that are at stake." Is the Court saying that Texas has made a factually (or philosophically, or theologically) wrong judgment about the nature of life? Is the Court saying that the Constitution defines life (and therefore personhood) in a specific way? In what way? From where does the Court get that constitutional definition? Is it possible to decide *Roe* without deciding whether a fetus is a person? Are you satisfied that the Court dealt with the issue adequately? *See* Michael Stokes Paulsen, *The Plausibility of Personhood,* 74 OHIO ST. L.J. 13 (2013). The second issue, once one recognizes that a women's rights are at stake in these cases, is to determine whether there is a valid public purpose justifying the abridgement of those rights. That is obviously tied in some respect to the resolution of the first issue. But suppose that one does not think that a fetus is a constitutional person in early stages (or perhaps in any stages?) of pregnancy. Can the State still defend the fetus as a living being even though not a constitutional person—in other words, as a potential person? How does the Court address that question? How do the dissents address that question? Are you satisfied with the treatment of this basic issue in any of the opinions?

9. If you think that *Roe* was wrong, do either of the dissenting opinions satisfy you? Do they identify what you think are the most serious problems with *Roe?*

10. The majority opinion spends an *enormous* amount of time, space, and energy on a medico-historical survey of thought on abortion, across more than two millennia. On what modalities of interpretation is that discussion relevant?

11. Assume for the moment that abortion is an issue that uniquely affects women more than men. Should a state or the federal government hold a referendum (if it were constitutional to do so) in which only women could vote on what abortion laws are legitimate? Note that pollsters report that the demographic group that is most enthusiastically in favor of abortion rights is men between the ages of 18 and 30.

12. At the time *Roe v. Wade* was decided in 1973, all Western constitutional democracies were legalizing abortion to some degree, although none went nearly as far as *Roe v. Wade. See* MARY ANN GLENDON, ABORTION AND DIVORCE IN WESTERN LAW: AMERICAN FAILURES, EUROPEAN CHALLENGES (1989). In 1975, both the French and the West German national legislatures passed national laws legalizing abortion during, but only during, the first trimester of pregnancy. The French courts accepted this new law passively, but the German Constitutional Court took a much dimmer view of the development, as the opinions excerpted below indicate.

B. GERMAN ABORTION I OPINION

39 BVerfGE 1 (1975) 17

■ The Federal Constitutional Court—FIRST SENATE PRESIDENT OF THE COURT DR. BENDA, presiding, and JUSTICES RITTERSPACH, DR. HAAGER, RUPP VON BRUNNECK, DR. BOHMER, DR. FALLER, DR. BROX, DR. 1974, recognizes as law by this opinion:

HOLDING

I. Section 218a of the Penal Code in the version of the Fifth Statute to Reform the Penal Law (5 PLRS) of June 18, 1974, (Federal Law Reporter I, p. 1297) is incompatible with Article 2, Paragraph 2, Sentence 1, in conjunction with Article 1, Paragraph 1, of the Basic Law and is null insofar as it excepts the interruption of pregnancy from criminal liability when no reasons are present which, in the sense of the reasons for this decision, have validity in the ordering of values of the Basic Law * * *.

Opinion of the Court:

* * * The question of the legal treatment of the interruption of pregnancy has been discussed publicly for decades from various points of view. In fact, this phenomenon of social life raises manifold problems of a biological, especially human-genetic, anthropological, medical, psychological, social, social-political, and not least of an ethical and moral-theological nature, which touch upon the fundamental questions of human existence. It is the task of the legislature to evaluate the many sided and often opposing arguments which develop from these various ways of viewing the question, to supplement them through considerations which are specifically legal and political as well as through the practical experiences of the life of the law, and, on this basis, to arrive at a decision as to the manner in which the legal order should respond to this social process. The statutory regulation in the Fifth Statute to Reform the Penal Law which was decided upon after extraordinarily comprehensive preparatory work can be examined by the Constitutional Court only from the view-point of whether it is compatible with the Basic Law, which is the highest valid law in the Federal Republic. The gravity and the seriousness of the constitutional question posed becomes clear, if it is considered that what is involved here is the protection of human life, one of the central values of every legal order. The decision regarding the standards and limits of legislative freedom of decision demands a total view of the constitutional norms and the hierarchy of values contained therein.

Article 2, Paragraph 2, Sentence 1, of the Basic Law also protects the life developing itself in the womb of the mother as an intrinsic legal value. The express incorporation into the Basic Law of the self-evident right to life—in contrast to the Weimar Constitution—may be explained principally as a reaction to the "destruction of life unworthy of life," to the "final solution" and "liquidations," which were carried out by the National Socialistic Regime as measures of state. Article 2, Paragraph 2, Sentence 1, of the Basic Law, just as it contains the abolition of the death penalty in Article 102, includes "a declaration of the fundamental worth of human life and of a concept of the state which stands, in emphatic contrast to the philosophies of a political regime to which the individual life meant little and which therefore practiced limitless abuse with its presumed right over life and death of the citizen" (Decisions of the Federal Constitutional Court, 18, 112 117).

In construing Article 2, Paragraph 2, Sentence 1, of the Basic Law, one should begin with its language: "Everyone has a right to life . . ." Life, in the sense of historical existence of a human individual, exists according to definite biological-physiological knowledge, in any case, from the 14th day after conception ([implantation], individuation) (cf. on this point the statements of Hinrichsen before the Special Committee for the Penal Law, Sixth Election Period, 74th Session,

Stenographic Reports, p. 2142 ff.). The process of development which has begun at that point is a continuing process with no sharp demarcation and does not allow a precise division of the various steps of development of the human life. The process does not end even with birth; the phenomena of consciousness which are specific to the human personality, for example, appear for the first time a rather long time after birth. Therefore, the protection of Article 2, Paragraph 2, Sentence 1, of the Basic Law cannot be limited either to the "completed" human being after birth or to the child about to be born which is independently capable of living. The right to life is guaranteed to everyone who "lives"; no distinction can be made here between various stages of the life developing itself before birth, or between unborn and born life. "Everyone" in the sense of Article 2, Paragraph 2, Sentence 1, of the Basic Law is "every one living;" expressed in another way: every life possessing human individuality; "everyone" also includes the yet unborn human being.

This extensive interpretation corresponds to the principle established in the opinions of the Federal Constitutional Court, "according to which, in doubtful cases, that interpretation is to be selected which develops to the highest degree the judicial effectiveness of the fundamental legal norm" (Decisions of the Federal Constitutional Court. 32, 54 71; 6, 55 72) * * *. The duty of the state to protect every human life may therefore be directly deduced from Article 2, Paragraph 2, Sentence 1, of the Basic Law. In addition to that, the duty also results from the explicit provision of Article 1, Paragraph 1, Sentence 2, of the Basic Law since developing life participates in the protection which Article 1, Paragraph 1, of the Basic Law guarantees to human dignity. Where human life exists, human dignity is present to it; it is not decisive that the bearer of this dignity himself be conscious of it and know personally how to preserve it. The potential faculties present in the human being from the beginning suffice to establish human dignity * * *.

The duty of the state to protect is comprehensive. It forbids not only—self-evidently—direct state attacks on the life developing itself but also requires the state to take a position protecting and promoting this life, that is to say, it must, above all, preserve it even against illegal attacks by others * * *. Human life represents, within the order of the Basic Law, an ultimate value, the particulars of which need not be established; it is the living foundation of human dignity and the prerequisite for all other fundamental rights.

The obligation of the state to take the life developing itself under protection exists, as a matter of principle, even against the mother * * *. A compromise which guarantees the protection of the life of the one about to be born and permits the pregnant woman the freedom of abortion is not possible since the interruption of pregnancy always means the destruction of the unborn life * * *.

From this point, the fundamental attitude of the legal order which is required by the constitution with regard to the interruption of pregnancy becomes clear: the legal order may not make the woman's right to self-determination the sole guide-line of its rulemaking. The state must proceed, as a matter of principle, from a duty to carry the pregnancy to term and therefore to view, as a matter of principle, its interruption as an injustice. The condemnation of abortion must be clearly expressed in the legal order * * *. The question of the extent to which the state is obligated under the constitution to employ, even for the protection of unborn life, the penal law, the sharpest weapon standing at its disposal, cannot be answered by the simplified posing of the question whether the state must punish certain acts * * *.

The task of penal law from the beginning has been to protect the elementary values of community life. That the life of every individual human being is among the most important legal values has been established above. The interruption of pregnancy irrevocably destroys an existing human life. Abortion is an act of killing * * *.

The regulation encountered in the Fifth Statute to Reform the Penal Law at times is defended with the argument that in other democratic countries of the Western World in recent times the penal provisions regulating the interruption of pregnancy have been "liberalized" or "modernized" in a similar or an even more extensive fashion; this would be, as the argument goes, an indication that the new regulation corresponds, in any case, to the general development of theories in this area and is not inconsistent with fundamental socio-ethical and legal principles * * *. These considerations cannot influence the decision to be made here. Disregarding the fact that all of these foreign laws in their respective countries are sharply controverted, the legal standards, which are applicable there for the acts of the legislature are essentially different from those of the Federal Republic of Germany.

Underlying the Basic Law are principles for the structuring of the state that may be understood only in light of the historical experience and the spiritual-moral confrontation with the previous system of National Socialism. In opposition to the omnipotence of the totalitarian state which claimed for itself limitless dominion over all areas of social life and which, in the prosecution of its goals of state, consideration for the life of the individual fundamentally meant nothing, the Basic Law of the Federal Republic of Germany has erected an order bound together by values which places the individual human being and his dignity at the focal point of all of its ordinances * * *.

On the basis of these considerations, § 218a of the Penal Code in the version of the Fifth Statute to Reform the Penal Law is inconsistent with Article 2, Paragraph 2, Sentence 1, in conjunction with Article 1, Paragraph 1, of the Basic Law to the extent that it excepts interruption of pregnancy from punishability if no reasons are present which, according to the present opinion, have standing under the ordering of values of the Basic Law.

■ Dissenting Opinion of JUSTICE RUPP VON BRUNNECK and JUSTICE DR. SIMON.

The life of each individual human being is self-evidently a central value of the legal order. It is uncontested that the constitutional duty to protect this life also includes its preliminary stages before birth. The debates in Parliament and before the Federal Constitutional Court dealt not with the whether but rather only the how of this protection. This decision is a matter of legislative responsibility. Under no circumstances can the duty of the state to prescribe punishment for abortion in every stage of pregnancy be derived from the constitution. The legislature should be able to determine the regulations for counseling and the term solution as well as for the indications solution * * *.

The authority of the Federal Constitutional Court to annul the decisions of the legislature demands sparing use, if an imbalance between the constitutional organs is to be avoided. The requirement of judicial self-restraint, which is designated as the "elixer of life" of the jurisprudence of the Federal Constitutional Court, is especially valid when involved is not a defense from overreaching by state power but rather the making, via constitutional judicial control, of provisions for the positive structuring of the social order for the legislature which is directly legitimitized by the people. The Federal Constitutional Court must not succumb to the temptation to take over for itself the function of a controlling organ and shall not in the long run endanger the authority to judicially review constitutionality.

The test proposed in this proceeding departs from the basis of classical judicial control. The fundamental legal norms standing in the central part of our constitution guarantee as rights of defense to the citizen in relation to the state a sphere of unrestricted structuring of one's life based on personal responsibility. The classical function of the Federal Constitutional Court lies in defending against injuries to this sphere of freedom from excessive infringement by the state power. On the scale of possible infringements by the state, penal provisions are foremost: they demand of a citizen a definite behavior and subdue him in the case of a violation with grievious restrictions of freedom or with financial burdens. Judicial control of the constitutionality of such provisions therefore means a determination whether the encroachment resulting either from the enactment or application of penal provisions into protected spheres of freedom is allowable; whether, therefore, the state, generally or to the extent provided, may punish.

In the present constitutional dispute, the inverse question is presented for the first time for examination, namely whether the state must punish, whether the abolition of punishment for the interruption of pregnancy in the first three months of pregnancy is compatible with fundamental rights. It is obvious, however, that the disregard of punishment is the opposite of state encroachment * * *.

Our strongest reservation is directed to the fact that for the first time in opinions of the Constitutional Court an objective value decision should function as a duty of the legislature to enact penal norms, therefore to postulate the strongest conceivable encroachment into the sphere of freedom of the citizen. This inverts the function of the fundamental rights into its contrary * * *.

Even if one, contrary to our position, agrees with the majority that a constitutional duty to punish is conceivable, no constitutional violation can be charged to the legislature. Although it is not necessary to go into every detail, the majority reasoning encounters the following objections * * *.

The immediately impressive statements about the undisputed high rank of the protection of life neglect the uniqueness of the interruption of pregnancy in relation to other dangers of human life. Involved here is not the academic question of whether it is proper to employ the power of the state to protect against murderers and killers, who can be deterred in no other way. In the European legal history, which has been influenced by the Church, a distinction has been constantly made between born and unborn life * * *.

According to the view of the undersigned Madame Justice, the refusal of the pregnant woman to permit the child en ventre sa mere to become a human being is something essentially different from the killing of independently existing life, not only according to the natural sensitivities of the woman but also legally * * *.

In the solution chosen the legislature was within its authority to proceed on the assumption that, in view of the failure of the penal sanction, the suitable means toward a remedy are to be sought in the social and community realm and that involved is, on the one hand, facilitating the bearing of the child to term by the mother through preventive psychological, social, and social-political promotional measures and strengthening her willingness to this end; and, on the other hand, decreasing the number of unwanted pregnancies through better information about the possibilities for preventing conception * * *.

That the decision of the German legislature for the regulation of terms and counseling neither arises from a fundamental attitude which is to be morally or legally condemned nor proceeds from apparently false premises in the determination of the circumstances of life is confirmed by identical or similar provisions for reform in numerous foreign states * * *.

On the whole therefore, in our opinion, the legislature was not prevented by the constitution from dispensing with a penal sanction which, according to its unrefuted view, was largely ineffective, inadequate, and even harmful. Its attempt to remedy through socially adequate means the manifestly developing inability of state and society in the present conditions to serve the protection of life may be imperfect; it corresponds, however, more to the spirit of the Basic Law than the demand for punishment and condemnation.

NOTES AND QUESTIONS

1. The German abortion decision reproduced above seems to be the mirror opposite of the U.S. Supreme Court's opinion in *Roe v. Wade*. The U.S. Supreme Court found a constitutional right on the part of women to have an abortion in the first two trimesters of pregnancy, while the German Constitutional Court found a fetal right to life, which it ordered the government to protect with criminal laws, including during the first trimester of pregnancy. What explains the divergence in the two courts' opinions? Is the U.S. opinion a reflection of Lockean individualism and libertarianism, while the German opinion expresses a Kantian, anti-Nazi value placed on all potential human life? Note that the German opinion above claims that life begins fourteen days after conception, when implantation occurs. It thus poses no obstacle to: fetal stem cell research, the use of the morning-after pill, or the use of IUDs, which prevent pregnancy by preventing implantation.

2. The German opinion is highly unusual, as the dissent points out, because it orders the legislature to criminalize conduct. Is this an appropriate function for constitutional courts engaged in judicial review? Can you think of a context where the U.S. Supreme Court has ever criminalized conduct? Ought the U.S. Supreme Court ever do this? The traditional American view of constitutional law is that individuals have a negative entitlement to be free of governmental oppression, not a license that commands the government to criminalize and oppress. Suppose, however, that one thinks that a fetus is a "person" for purposes of the Equal Protection Clause. Would a State's failure to provide that "person" with the protection of the laws be unconstitutional class-based (in)action based on age? Could a State constitutionally announce that it will not prosecute anyone for murder if the victim is younger than ten or older than seventy?

3. Could Congress under its Section 5 power to enforce the Fourteenth Amendment overturn *Roe v. Wade* by passing a federal law defining fetuses as being persons? Would that effectively replace *Roe* with the German abortion decision requiring equal protection of the laws for "persons" of all ages?

4. Both the U.S. and the German opinions contain a lot of dicta specifying the contents of abortion legislation. *Roe v. Wade* lays out a trimester framework for regulation of abortion, which goes well beyond the facts of the case at hand, while the German Constitutional Court practically drafts a criminal law that it orders the

legislature to adopt. Are both these opinions textbook examples of judicial activism, because they are so specific and try to settle so much at once rather than merely deciding the case at hand? Or is either or both decision an example of wise judicial statesmanship in the face of obvious legislative failure?

[Assignment 70]

C. DEVELOPMENTS IN U.S. ABORTION LAW SINCE 1973

As we mentioned at the start of this assignment, *Roe v. Wade* led to a long and bitter fight over abortion law that continues unabated in 2020. Throughout President Ronald Reagan's two terms as President and during the presidency of his successor, President George H.W. Bush, the Solicitor General of the United States asked the Supreme Court on five separate occasions, without success, to overturn *Roe v. Wade.*

These efforts came to a climax in *Planned Parenthood of Southeastern Pennsylvania v. Casey*, 505 U.S. 833 (1992). The replacement of Justice Thurgood Marshall with Justice Clarence Thomas put in place a Supreme Court that seemed to have seven potential votes to overturn *Roe v. Wade*: Chief Justice Rehnquist and Justice Byron White, both of whom had dissented in *Roe v. Wade*, joined by Justices Sandra Day O'Connor, Antonin Scalia, Anthony Kennedy, David Souter, and Clarence Thomas. In 1982, with amendments in 1988 and 1989, the State of Pennsylvania had passed a modern law imposing three relatively modest restraints on the *Roe v. Wade* abortion right: 1) a required two-day waiting period before an abortion could be had; 2) a requirement that minors seeking an abortion obtain either the permission of their parents or of a judge; and 3) a requirement that male spouses consent to their wives or partner's decisions to have an abortion. The Solicitor General, on behalf of President Bush., asked the Supreme Court to overrule *Roe v. Wade* and to uphold the Pennsylvania law in its entirety.

Here is how the United States Reports describes the result in the case:

> O'CONNOR, KENNEDY, and SOUTER, JJ., announced the judgment of the Court and delivered the opinion of the Court with respect to Parts I, II, III, V-A, V-C, and VI, in which BLACKMUN and STEVENS, JJ., joined, an opinion with respect to Part V-E, in which STEVENS, J., joined, and an opinion with respect to Parts IV, V-B, and V-D. STEVENS, J., filed an opinion concurring in part and dissenting in part. BLACKMUN, J., filed an opinion concurring in part, concurring in the judgment in part, and dissenting in part. REHNQUIST, C.J., filed an opinion concurring in the judgment in part and dissenting in part, in which WHITE, SCALIA, and THOMAS, JJ., joined. SCALIA, J., filed an opinion concurring in the judgment in part and dissenting in part, in which REHNQUIST, C.J., and WHITE and THOMAS, JJ., joined.

There was no majority opinion. In an unprecedented move, the plurality opinion was jointly issued by three justices. As you will see in a moment, the plurality retained *Roe* in form as a matter of precedent but restructured its framework for evaluating abortion regulations in significant ways. Justices Blackmun and Stevens would have retained the *Roe* framework in its entirely. The opinions are long; we present only select portions below.

D. PLANNED PARENTHOOD OF SOUTHEASTERN PENNSYLVANIA V. CASEY

505 U.S. 833 (1992)

■ JUSTICE O'CONNOR, JUSTICE KENNEDY, and JUSTICE SOUTER announced the judgment of the Court * * *

I

Liberty finds no refuge in a jurisprudence of doubt. Yet 19 years after our holding that the Constitution protects a woman's right to terminate her pregnancy in its early stages, *Roe v. Wade,* 410 U.S. 113 (1973), that definition of liberty is still questioned. Joining the respondents as *amicus curiae,* the United States, as it has done in five other cases in the last decade, again asks us to overrule *Roe.*

* * *

After considering the fundamental constitutional questions resolved by *Roe,* principles of institutional integrity, and the rule of *stare decisis,* we are led to conclude this: the essential holding of *Roe v. Wade* should be retained and once again reaffirmed.

It must be stated at the outset and with clarity that *Roe*'s essential holding, the holding we reaffirm, has three parts. First is a recognition of the right of the woman to choose to have an abortion before viability and to obtain it without undue interference from the State. Before viability, the State's interests are not strong enough to support a prohibition of abortion or the imposition of a substantial obstacle to the woman's effective right to elect the procedure. Second is a confirmation of the State's power to restrict abortions after fetal viability, if the law contains exceptions for pregnancies which endanger the woman's life or health. And third is the principle that the State has legitimate interests from the outset of the pregnancy in protecting the health of the woman and the life of the fetus that may become a child. These principles do not contradict one another; and we adhere to each.

II

Constitutional protection of the woman's decision to terminate her pregnancy derives from the Due Process Clause of the Fourteenth Amendment. It declares that no State shall "deprive any person of life, liberty, or property, without due process of law." The controlling word in the cases before us is "liberty." Although a literal reading of the Clause might suggest that it governs only the procedures by which a State may deprive persons of liberty, for at least 105 years, since *Mugler v. Kansas,* 123 U.S. 623, 660–661 (1887), the Clause has been understood to contain a substantive component as well * * *. "[T]he guaranties of due process, though having their roots in Magna Carta's *'per legem terrae'* and considered as procedural safeguards 'against executive usurpation and tyranny,' have in this country 'become bulwarks also against arbitrary legislation.' " *Poe v. Ullman,* 367 U.S. 497, 541 (1961) (Harlan, J., dissenting from dismissal on jurisdictional grounds)

* * *

Neither the Bill of Rights nor the specific practices of States at the time of the adoption of the Fourteenth Amendment marks the outer limits of the substantive sphere of liberty which the Fourteenth Amendment protects. See U.S. Const., Amdt. 9. As the second Justice Harlan recognized:

> "[T]he full scope of the liberty guaranteed by the Due Process Clause cannot be found in or limited by the precise terms of the specific guarantees elsewhere provided in the Constitution. This 'liberty' is not a series of isolated points pricked out in terms of the taking of property; the freedom of speech, press, and religion; the right to keep and bear arms; the freedom from unreasonable searches and seizures; and so on. It is a rational continuum which, broadly speaking, includes a freedom from all substantial arbitrary impositions and purposeless restraints, . . . and which also recognizes, what a reasonable and sensitive judgment must, that certain interests require particularly careful scrutiny of the state needs asserted to justify their abridgment." *Poe v. Ullman, supra,* 367 U.S., at 543 (opinion dissenting from dismissal on jurisdictional grounds).
>
> * * *

The inescapable fact is that adjudication of substantive due process claims may call upon the Court in interpreting the Constitution to exercise that same capacity which by tradition courts always have exercised: reasoned judgment. Its boundaries are not susceptible of expression as a simple rule. That does not mean we are free to invalidate state policy choices with which we disagree; yet neither does it permit us to shrink from the duties of our office * * *.

Men and women of good conscience can disagree, and we suppose some always shall disagree, about the profound moral and spiritual implications of terminating a pregnancy, even in its earliest stage. Some of us as individuals find abortion offensive to our most basic principles of morality, but that cannot control our decision. Our obligation is to define the liberty of all, not to mandate our own moral code. The underlying constitutional issue is whether the State can resolve these philosophic questions in such a definitive way that a woman lacks all choice in the matter, except perhaps in those rare circumstances in which the pregnancy is itself a danger to her own life or health, or is the result of rape or incest.

It is conventional constitutional doctrine that where reasonable people disagree the government can adopt one position or the other. See, *e.g., Ferguson v. Skrupa,* 372 U.S. 726 (1963); *Williamson v. Lee Optical of Okla., Inc.,* 348 U.S. 483 (1955). That theorem, however, assumes a state of affairs in which the choice does not intrude upon a protected liberty * * *.

Our law affords constitutional protection to personal decisions relating to marriage, procreation, contraception, family relationships, child rearing, and education * * *. These matters, involving the most intimate and personal choices a person may make in a lifetime, choices central to personal dignity and autonomy, are central to the liberty protected by the Fourteenth Amendment. At the heart of liberty is the right to define one's own concept of existence, of meaning, of the universe, and of the mystery of human life. Beliefs about these matters could not define the attributes of personhood were they formed under compulsion of the State.

These considerations begin our analysis of the woman's interest in terminating her pregnancy but cannot end it, for this reason: though the abortion decision may originate within the zone of conscience and belief, it is more than a philosophic exercise. Abortion is a unique act. It is an act fraught with consequences for others: for the woman who must live with the implications of her decision; for the persons who perform and assist in the procedure; for the spouse, family, and society which must confront the knowledge that these procedures exist, procedures some deem nothing short of an act of violence against innocent human life; and, depending on one's beliefs, for the life or potential life that is aborted. Though abortion is conduct, it does not follow that the State is entitled to proscribe it in all instances. That is because the liberty of the woman is at stake in a sense unique to the human condition and so unique to the law. The mother who carries a child to full term is subject to anxieties, to physical constraints, to pain that only she must bear. That these sacrifices have from the beginning of the human race been endured by woman with a pride that ennobles her in the eyes of others and gives to the infant a bond of love cannot alone be grounds for the State to insist she make the sacrifice. Her suffering is too intimate and personal for the State to insist, without more, upon its own vision of the woman's role, however dominant that vision has been in the course of our history and our culture. The destiny of the woman must be shaped to a large extent on her own conception of her spiritual imperatives and her place in society.

* * *

While we appreciate the weight of the arguments made on behalf of the State in the cases before us, arguments which in their ultimate formulation conclude that *Roe* should be overruled, the reservations any of us may have in reaffirming the central holding of *Roe* are outweighed by the explication of individual liberty we have given combined with the force of *stare decisis*. We turn now to that doctrine.

III

A

* * *

[*Editors' Note: Demands of space require us to edit out almost all of the joint opinion's lengthy discussion of stare decisis.*]

The sum of the precedential enquiry to this point shows *Roe*'s underpinnings unweakened in any way affecting its central holding. While it has engendered disapproval, it has not been unworkable. An entire generation has come of age free to assume *Roe*'s concept of liberty in defining the capacity of women to act in society, and to make reproductive decisions; no erosion of principle going to liberty or personal autonomy has left *Roe*'s central holding a doctrinal remnant; *Roe* portends no developments at odds with other precedent for the analysis of personal liberty; and no changes of fact have rendered viability more or less appropriate as the point at which the balance of interests tips. Within the bounds of normal *stare decisis* analysis, then, and subject to the considerations on which it customarily turns, the stronger argument is for affirming *Roe*'s central holding, with whatever degree of personal reluctance any of us may have, not for overruling it.

In a less significant case, *stare decisis* analysis could, and would, stop at the point we have reached. But the sustained and widespread debate *Roe* has provoked calls for some comparison between that case and others of comparable dimension that have responded to national controversies and taken on the impress of the controversies addressed. Only two such decisional lines from the past century present themselves for examination, and in each instance the result reached by the Court accorded with the principles we apply today.

The first example is that line of cases identified with *Lochner v. New York,* 198 U.S. 45 (1905), which imposed substantive limitations on legislation limiting economic autonomy in favor of health and welfare regulation, adopting, in Justice Holmes's view, the theory of laissez-faire. The *Lochner* decisions were exemplified by *Adkins v. Children's Hospital of District of Columbia,* 261 U.S. 525 (1923), in which this Court held it to be an infringement of constitutionally protected liberty of contract to require the employers of adult women to satisfy minimum wage standards. Fourteen years later, *West Coast Hotel Co. v. Parrish,* 300 U.S. 379 (1937), signaled the demise of *Lochner* by overruling *Adkins*. In the meantime, the Depression had come and, with it, the lesson that seemed unmistakable to most people by 1937, that the interpretation of contractual freedom protected in *Adkins* rested on fundamentally false factual assumptions about the capacity of a relatively unregulated market to satisfy minimal levels of human welfare. See *West Coast Hotel Co., supra,* at 399 * * *.

The second comparison that 20th century history invites is with the cases employing the separate-but-equal rule for applying the Fourteenth Amendment's equal protection guarantee * * *.

The Court in *Brown* [observed] * * * that whatever may have been the understanding in *Plessy*'s time of the power of segregation to stigmatize those who were segregated with a "badge of inferiority," it was clear by 1954 that legally sanctioned segregation had just such an effect, to the point that racially separate public educational facilities were deemed inherently unequal. 347 U.S., at 494–495. Society's understanding of the facts upon which a constitutional ruling was sought in 1954 was thus fundamentally different from the basis claimed for the decision in 1896. While we think *Plessy* was wrong the day it was decided, we must also recognize that the *Plessy* Court's explanation for its decision was so clearly at odds with the facts apparent to the Court in 1954 that the decision to reexamine *Plessy* was on this ground alone not only justified but required.

West Coast Hotel and *Brown* each rested on facts, or an understanding of facts, changed from those which furnished the claimed justifications for the earlier constitutional resolutions. Each case was comprehensible as the Court's response to facts that the country could understand, or had come to understand already, but which the Court of an earlier day, as its own declarations disclosed, had not been able to perceive. As the decisions were thus comprehensible they were also defensible, not merely as the victories of one doctrinal school over another by dint of numbers (victories though they were), but as applications of constitutional principle to facts as they had not been seen by the Court before. In constitutional adjudication as elsewhere in life, changed circumstances may impose new obligations, and the thoughtful part of the Nation could accept each decision to overrule a prior case as a response to the Court's constitutional duty.

Because the cases before us present no such occasion it could be seen as no such response. Because neither the factual underpinnings of *Roe*'s central holding nor our understanding of it has changed (and because no other indication of weakened precedent has been shown), the Court could not pretend to be reexamining the prior law with any justification beyond a present doctrinal disposition to come out differently from the Court of 1973. To overrule prior law for no other reason than that would run counter to the view repeated in our cases, that a decision to overrule should rest on some special reason over and above the belief that a prior case was wrongly decided.

* * * Our analysis would not be complete, however, without explaining why overruling *Roe*'s central holding would not only reach an unjustifiable result under principles of *stare decisis,* but would seriously weaken the Court's capacity to exercise the judicial power and to function as the Supreme Court of a Nation dedicated to the rule of law. To understand why this would be so it is necessary to understand the source of this Court's authority, the conditions necessary for its preservation, and its relationship to the country's understanding of itself as a constitutional Republic.

* * *[T]he Court cannot buy support for its decisions by spending money and, except to a minor degree, it cannot independently coerce obedience to its decrees. The Court's power lies, rather, in its legitimacy, a product of substance and perception that shows itself in the people's acceptance of the Judiciary as fit to determine what the Nation's law means and to declare what it demands.

* * * Thus, the Court's legitimacy depends on making legally principled decisions under circumstances in which their principled character is sufficiently plausible to be accepted by the Nation.

* * *

* * * Where, in the performance of its judicial duties, the Court decides a case in such a way as to resolve the sort of intensely divisive controversy reflected in *Roe* and those rare, comparable cases, its decision has a dimension that the resolution of the normal case does not carry. It is the dimension present whenever the Court's interpretation of the Constitution calls the contending sides of a national controversy to end their national division by accepting a common mandate rooted in the Constitution.

The Court is not asked to do this very often, having thus addressed the Nation only twice in our lifetime, in the decisions of *Brown* and *Roe.* But when the Court does act in this way, its decision requires an equally rare precedential force to counter the inevitable efforts to overturn it and to thwart its implementation * * *.

* * *

It is true that diminished legitimacy may be restored, but only slowly * * *. Like the character of an individual, the legitimacy of the Court must be earned over time. So, indeed, must be the character of a Nation of people who aspire to live according to the rule of law. Their belief in themselves as such a people is not readily separable from their understanding of the Court invested with the authority to decide their constitutional cases and speak before all others for their constitutional ideals. If the Court's legitimacy should be undermined, then, so would the country be in its very ability to see itself through its constitutional ideals. The Court's concern with legitimacy is not for the sake of the Court, but for the sake of the Nation to which it is responsible.

The Court's duty in the present cases is clear. In 1973, it confronted the already-divisive issue of governmental power to limit personal choice to undergo abortion, for which it provided a new resolution based on the due process guaranteed by the Fourteenth Amendment. Whether or not a new social consensus is developing on that issue, its divisiveness is no less today than in 1973, and pressure to overrule the decision, like pressure to retain it, has grown only more intense. A decision to overrule *Roe*'s essential holding under the existing circumstances would address error, if error there was, at the cost of both profound and unnecessary damage to the

Court's legitimacy, and to the Nation's commitment to the rule of law. It is therefore imperative to adhere to the essence of *Roe*'s original decision, and we do so today.

IV

From what we have said so far it follows that it is a constitutional liberty of the woman to have some freedom to terminate her pregnancy. We conclude that the basic decision in *Roe* was based on a constitutional analysis which we cannot now repudiate. The woman's liberty is not so unlimited, however, that from the outset the State cannot show its concern for the life of the unborn, and at a later point in fetal development the State's interest in life has sufficient force so that the right of the woman to terminate the pregnancy can be restricted.

That brings us, of course, to the point where much criticism has been directed at *Roe,* a criticism that always inheres when the Court draws a specific rule from what in the Constitution is but a general standard. We conclude, however, that the urgent claims of the woman to retain the ultimate control over her destiny and her body, claims implicit in the meaning of liberty, require us to perform that function. Liberty must not be extinguished for want of a line that is clear. And it falls to us to give some real substance to the woman's liberty to determine whether to carry her pregnancy to full term.

We conclude the line should be drawn at viability, so that before that time the woman has a right to choose to terminate her pregnancy. We adhere to this principle for two reasons. First, as we have said, is the doctrine of *stare decisis* * * *.

The second reason is that the concept of viability, as we noted in *Roe,* is the time at which there is a realistic possibility of maintaining and nourishing a life outside the womb, so that the independent existence of the second life can in reason and all fairness be the object of state protection that now overrides the rights of the woman * * *.

The woman's right to terminate her pregnancy before viability is the most central principle of *Roe v. Wade.* It is a rule of law and a component of liberty we cannot renounce.

On the other side of the equation is the interest of the State in the protection of potential life * * *.

* * * [I]t must be remembered that *Roe v. Wade* speaks with clarity in establishing not only the woman's liberty but also the State's "important and legitimate interest in potential life." *Roe, supra,* at 163. That portion of the decision in *Roe* has been given too little acknowledgment and implementation by the Court in its subsequent cases * * *.

Roe established a trimester framework to govern abortion regulations * * *.

The trimester framework no doubt was erected to ensure that the woman's right to choose not become so subordinate to the State's interest in promoting fetal life that her choice exists in theory but not in fact. We do not agree, however, that the trimester approach is necessary to accomplish this objective. A framework of this rigidity was unnecessary and in its later interpretation sometimes contradicted the State's permissible exercise of its powers.

Though the woman has a right to choose to terminate or continue her pregnancy before viability, it does not at all follow that the State is prohibited from taking steps to ensure that this choice is thoughtful and informed * * *. It follows that States are free to enact laws to provide a reasonable framework for a woman to make a decision that has such profound and lasting meaning. This, too, we find consistent with *Roe*'s central premises, and indeed the inevitable consequence of our holding that the State has an interest in protecting the life of the unborn.

We reject the trimester framework, which we do not consider to be part of the essential holding of *Roe*. Measures aimed at ensuring that a woman's choice contemplates the consequences for the fetus do not necessarily interfere with the right recognized in *Roe,* although those measures have been found to be inconsistent with the rigid trimester framework announced in that case. A logical reading of the central holding in *Roe* itself, and a necessary reconciliation of the liberty of the woman and the interest of the State in promoting prenatal life, require, in our view, that we abandon the trimester framework as a rigid prohibition on all previability regulation aimed at the protection of fetal life. The trimester framework suffers from these basic flaws: in its formulation it misconceives the nature of the pregnant woman's interest; and in practice it undervalues the State's interest in potential life, as recognized in *Roe*.

As our jurisprudence relating to all liberties save perhaps abortion has recognized, not every law which makes a right more difficult to exercise is, *ipso facto,* an infringement of that right * * *.

* * * Numerous forms of state regulation might have the incidental effect of increasing the cost or decreasing the availability of medical care, whether for abortion or any other medical procedure. The fact that a law which serves a valid purpose, one not designed to strike at the right itself, has the incidental effect of making it more difficult or more expensive to procure an abortion cannot be enough to invalidate it. Only where state regulation imposes an undue burden on a woman's ability to make this decision does the power of the State reach into the heart of the liberty protected by the Due Process Clause.

* * *

* * * Because we set forth a standard of general application to which we intend to adhere, it is important to clarify what is meant by an undue burden.

A finding of an undue burden is a shorthand for the conclusion that a state regulation has the purpose or effect of placing a substantial obstacle in the path of a woman seeking an abortion of a nonviable fetus. A statute with this purpose is invalid because the means chosen by the State to further the interest in potential life must be calculated to inform the woman's free choice, not hinder it. And a statute which, while furthering the interest in potential life or some other valid state interest, has the effect of placing a substantial obstacle in the path of a woman's choice cannot be considered a permissible means of serving its legitimate ends * * *.

* * *

* * * We give this summary:

(a) To protect the central right recognized by *Roe v. Wade* while at the same time accommodating the State's profound interest in potential life, we will employ the undue burden analysis as explained in this opinion. An undue burden exists, and therefore a provision of law is invalid, if its purpose or effect is to place a substantial obstacle in the path of a woman seeking an abortion before the fetus attains viability.

(b) We reject the rigid trimester framework of *Roe v. Wade.* To promote the State's profound interest in potential life, throughout pregnancy the State may take measures to ensure that the woman's choice is informed, and measures designed to advance this interest will not be invalidated as long as their purpose is to persuade the woman to choose childbirth over abortion. These measures must not be an undue burden on the right.

(c) As with any medical procedure, the State may enact regulations to further the health or safety of a woman seeking an abortion. Unnecessary health regulations that have the purpose or effect of presenting a substantial obstacle to a woman seeking an abortion impose an undue burden on the right.

(d) Our adoption of the undue burden analysis does not disturb the central holding of *Roe v. Wade,* and we reaffirm that holding. Regardless of whether exceptions are made for particular circumstances, a State may not prohibit any woman from making the ultimate decision to terminate her pregnancy before viability.

(e) We also reaffirm *Roe*'s holding that "subsequent to viability, the State in promoting its interest in the potentiality of human life may, if it chooses, regulate, and even proscribe, abortion except where it is necessary, in appropriate medical judgment, for the preservation of the life or health of the mother." *Roe v. Wade,* 410 U.S., at 164–165.

* * *

[*Editors' Note: The plurality opinion upheld the statute's informed consent features, record-keeping requirements, waiting periods, and parental consent provisions but invalidated as an "undue burden" the spousal consent provisions.*]

Our Constitution is a covenant running from the first generation of Americans to us and then to future generations. It is a coherent succession. Each generation must learn anew that the Constitution's written terms embody ideas and aspirations that must survive more ages than one. We accept our responsibility not to retreat from interpreting the full meaning of the covenant in light of all of our precedents. We invoke it once again to define the freedom guaranteed by the Constitution's own promise, the promise of liberty.

The judgment in No. 91–902 is affirmed. The judgment in No. 91–744 is affirmed in part and reversed in part, and the case is remanded for proceedings consistent with this opinion, including consideration of the question of severability.

■ JUSTICE STEVENS, concurring in part and dissenting in part. [Omitted.]

■ JUSTICE BLACKMUN, concurring in part, concurring in the judgment in part, and dissenting in part.

Three years ago, in *Webster v. Reproductive Health Services,* 492 U.S. 490 (1989), four Members of this Court appeared poised to "cas[t] into darkness the hopes and visions of every woman in this country" who had come to believe that the Constitution guaranteed her the right to reproductive choice. *Id.,* at 557 (BLACKMUN, J., dissenting). All that remained between the promise of *Roe* and the darkness of the plurality was a single, flickering flame. Decisions since *Webster* gave little reason to hope that this flame would cast much light. But now, just when so many expected the darkness to fall, the flame has grown bright.

I do not underestimate the significance of today's joint opinion. Yet I remain steadfast in my belief that the right to reproductive choice is entitled to the full protection afforded by this Court before *Webster*. And I fear for the darkness as four Justices anxiously await the single vote necessary to extinguish the light.

* * *

■ CHIEF JUSTICE REHNQUIST, with whom JUSTICE WHITE, JUSTICE SCALIA, and JUSTICE THOMAS join, concurring in the judgment in part and dissenting in part.

* * *

In *Roe v. Wade,* the Court recognized a "guarantee of personal privacy" which "is broad enough to encompass a woman's decision whether or not to terminate her pregnancy." We are now of the view that, in terming this right fundamental, the Court in *Roe* read the earlier opinions upon which it based its decision much too broadly. Unlike marriage, procreation, and contraception, abortion "involves the purposeful termination of a potential life." *Harris v. McRae,* 448 U.S. 297, 325 (1980) * * *.

Nor do the historical traditions of the American people support the view that the right to terminate one's pregnancy is "fundamental." The common law which we inherited from England made abortion after "quickening" an offense. At the time of the adoption of the Fourteenth Amendment, statutory prohibitions or restrictions on abortion were commonplace; in 1868, at least 28 of the then-37 States and 8 Territories had statutes banning or limiting abortion. J. Mohr, Abortion in America 200 (1978). By the turn of the century virtually every State had a law prohibiting or restricting abortion on its books. By the middle of the present century, a liberalization trend had set in. But 21 of the restrictive abortion laws in effect in 1868 were still in effect in 1973 when *Roe* was decided, and an overwhelming majority of the States prohibited abortion unless necessary to preserve the life or health of the mother. On this record, it can scarcely be said that any deeply rooted tradition of relatively unrestricted abortion in our history supported the classification of the right to abortion as "fundamental" under the Due Process Clause of the Fourteenth Amendment.

We think, therefore, both in view of this history and of our decided cases dealing with substantive liberty under the Due Process Clause, that the Court was mistaken in *Roe* when it classified a woman's decision to terminate her pregnancy as a "fundamental right" that could be abridged only in a manner which withstood "strict scrutiny." * * *

* * *

■ JUSTICE SCALIA, with whom the CHIEF JUSTICE, JUSTICE WHITE, and JUSTICE THOMAS join, concurring in the judgment in part and dissenting in part.

* * * The States may, if they wish, permit abortion on demand, but the Constitution does not *require* them to do so. The permissibility of abortion, and the limitations upon it, are to be resolved like most important questions in our democracy: by citizens trying to persuade one another and then voting. As the Court acknowledges, "where reasonable people disagree the government can adopt one position or the other." The Court is correct in adding the qualification that this "assumes a state of affairs in which the choice does not intrude upon a protected liberty,"—but the crucial part of that qualification is the penultimate word. A State's

choice between two positions on which reasonable people can disagree is constitutional even when (as is often the case) it intrudes upon a "liberty" in the absolute sense. Laws against bigamy, for example—with which entire societies of reasonable people disagree—intrude upon men and women's liberty to marry and live with one another. But bigamy happens not to be a liberty specially "protected" by the Constitution.

That is, quite simply, the issue in this case: not whether the power of a woman to abort her unborn child is a "liberty" in the absolute sense; or even whether it is a liberty of great importance to many women. Of course it is both. The issue is whether it is a liberty protected by the Constitution of the United States. I am sure it is not. I reach that conclusion not because of anything so exalted as my views concerning the "concept of existence, of meaning, of the universe, and of the mystery of human life." Rather, I reach it for the same reason I reach the conclusion that bigamy is not constitutionally protected—because of two simple facts: (1) the Constitution says absolutely nothing about it, and (2) the longstanding traditions of American society have permitted it to be legally proscribed.

* * *

Beyond that brief summary of the essence of my position, I will not swell the United States Reports with repetition of what I have said before; and applying the rational basis test, I would uphold the Pennsylvania statute in its entirety. I must, however, respond to a few of the more outrageous arguments in today's opinion, which it is beyond human nature to leave unanswered. I shall discuss each of them under a quotation from the Court's opinion to which they pertain.

"The inescapable fact is that adjudication of substantive due process claims may call upon the Court in interpreting the Constitution to exercise that same capacity which by tradition courts always have exercised: reasoned judgment."

Assuming that the question before us is to be resolved at such a level of philosophical abstraction, in such isolation from the traditions of American society, as by simply applying "reasoned judgment," I do not see how that could possibly have produced the answer the Court arrived at in *Roe* v. *Wade*, 410 U.S. 113 (1973). Today's opinion describes the methodology of *Roe*, quite accurately, as weighing against the woman's interest the State's " 'important and legitimate interest in protecting the potentiality of human life.' " But "reasoned judgment" does not begin by begging the question, as *Roe* and subsequent cases unquestionably did by assuming that what the State is protecting is the mere "potentiality of human life. The whole argument of abortion opponents is that what the Court calls the fetus and what others call the unborn child *is a human life*. Thus, whatever answer *Roe* came up with after conducting its "balancing" is bound to be wrong, unless it is correct that the human fetus is in some critical sense merely potentially human. There is of course no way to determine that as a legal matter; it is in fact a value judgment. Some societies have considered newborn children not yet human, or the incompetent elderly no longer so.

* * *

The emptiness of the "reasoned judgment" that produced *Roe* is displayed in plain view by the fact that, after more than 19 years of effort by some of the brightest (and most determined) legal minds in the country, after more than 10 cases upholding abortion rights in this Court, and after dozens upon dozens of *amicus* briefs submitted in this and other cases, the best the Court can do to explain how it is that the word "liberty" *must* be thought to include the right to destroy human fetuses is to rattle off a collection of adjectives that simply decorate a value judgment and conceal a political choice * * *. It is not reasoned judgment that supports the Court's decision; only personal predilection * * *.

"Liberty finds no refuge in a jurisprudence of doubt."

One might have feared to encounter this august and sonorous phrase in an opinion defending the real *Roe* v. *Wade*, rather than the revised version fabricated today by the authors of the joint opinion. The shortcomings of *Roe* did not include lack of clarity: Virtually all regulation of abortion before the third trimester was invalid. But to come across this phrase in the joint opinion—which calls upon federal district judges to apply an "undue burden" standard as doubtful in application as it is unprincipled in origin—is really more than one should have to bear.

* * *

The joint opinion explains that a state regulation imposes an "undue burden" if it "has the purpose or effect of placing a substantial obstacle in the path of a woman seeking an abortion of a nonviable fetus." An obstacle is "substantial," we are told, if it is "calculated[,] [not] to inform the woman's free choice, [but to] hinder it." This latter statement cannot possibly mean what it says. *Any* regulation of abortion that is intended to advance what the joint opinion concedes is the State's "substantial" interest in protecting unborn life will be "calculated [to] hinder" a decision to have an abortion. It thus seems more accurate to say that the joint opinion would uphold abortion regulations only if they do not *unduly* hinder the woman's decision. That, of course, brings us right back to square one: Defining an "undue burden" as an "undue hindrance" (or a "substantial obstacle") hardly "clarifies" the test. Consciously or not, the joint opinion's verbal shell game will conceal raw judicial policy choices concerning what is "appropriate" abortion legislation.

* * *

To the extent I can discern *any* meaningful content in the "undue burden" standard as applied in the joint opinion, it appears to be that a State may not regulate abortion in such a way as to reduce significantly its incidence * * *. Thus, despite flowery rhetoric about the State's "substantial" and "profound" interest in "potential human life," and criticism of *Roe* for undervaluing that interest, the joint opinion permits the State to pursue that interest only so long as it is not too successful * * *. Reason finds no refuge in this jurisprudence of confusion.

"While we appreciate the weight of the arguments . . . that *Roe* should be overruled, the reservations any of us may have in reaffirming the central holding of *Roe* are outweighed by the explication of individual liberty we have given combined with the force of *stare decisis*."

The Court's reliance upon *stare decisis* can best be described as contrived. It insists upon the necessity of adhering not to all of *Roe*, but only to what it calls the "central holding." It seems to me that *stare decisis* ought to be applied even to the doctrine of *stare decisis*, and I confess never to have heard of this new, keep-what-you-want-and-throw-away-the-rest version. I wonder whether, as applied to *Marbury* v. *Madison*, 1 Cranch 137 (1803), for example, the new version of *stare decisis* would be satisfied if we allowed courts to review the constitutionality of only those statutes that (like the one in *Marbury*) pertain to the jurisdiction of the courts.

* * *

"Where, in the performance of its judicial duties, the Court decides a case in such a way as to resolve the sort of intensely divisive controversy reflected in *Roe* . . ., its decision has a dimension that the resolution of the normal case does not carry. It is the dimension present whenever the Court's interpretation of the Constitution calls the contending sides of a national controversy to end their national division by accepting a common mandate rooted in the Constitution."

The Court's description of the place of *Roe* in the social history of the United States is unrecognizable. Not only did *Roe* not, as the Court suggests, *resolve* the deeply divisive issue of abortion; it did more than anything else to nourish it, by elevating it to the national level where it is infinitely more difficult to resolve. National politics were not plagued by abortion protests, national abortion lobbying, or abortion marches on Congress before *Roe* v. *Wade* was decided. Profound disagreement existed among our citizens over the issue—as it does over other issues, such as the death penalty—but that disagreement was being worked out at the state level. As with many other issues, the division of sentiment within each State was not as closely balanced as it was among the population of the Nation as a whole, meaning not only that more people would be satisfied with the results of state-by-state resolution, but also that those results would be more stable. Pre-*Roe*, moreover, political compromise was possible.

Roe's mandate for abortion on demand destroyed the compromises of the past, rendered compromise impossible for the future, and required the entire issue to be resolved uniformly, at the national level. At the same time, *Roe* created a vast new class of abortion consumers and abortion proponents by eliminating the moral opprobrium that had attached to the act. ("If the Constitution *guarantees* abortion, how can it be bad?"—not an accurate line of thought, but a natural one.) Many favor all of those developments, and it is not for me to say that they are wrong. But to portray *Roe* as the statesmanlike "settlement" of a divisive issue, a jurisprudential Peace of Westphalia that is worth preserving, is nothing less than Orwellian. *Roe* fanned into life an issue that has inflamed our national politics in general, and has obscured with its smoke the selection of Justices to this Court in particular, ever since. And by keeping us in the abortion umpiring business, it is the perpetuation of that disruption, rather than of any *Pax Roeana*, that the Court's new majority decrees.

"[T]o overrule under fire . . . would subvert the Court's legitimacy . . . .

"To all those who will be . . . tested by following, the Court implicitly undertakes to remain steadfast . . . . The promise of constancy, once given, binds its maker for as long as the power to stand by the decision survives and . . . the commitment [is not] obsolete. . . .

"[The American people's] belief in themselves as . . . a people [who aspire to live according to the rule of law] is not readily separable from their understanding of the Court invested with the authority to decide their constitutional cases and speak before all others for their constitutional ideals. If the Court's legitimacy should be undermined, then,

so would the country be in its very ability to see itself through its constitutional ideals."

The Imperial Judiciary lives. It is instructive to compare this Nietzschean vision of us unelected, life tenured judges—leading a Volk who will be "tested by following," and whose very "belief in themselves" is mystically bound up in their "understanding" of a Court that "speak[s] before all others for their constitutional ideals"—with the somewhat more modest role envisioned for these lawyers by the Founders.

> "The judiciary . . . has . . . no direction either of the strength or of the wealth of the society, and can take no active resolution whatever. It may truly be said to have neither Force nor Will but merely judgment . . . ." The Federalist No. 78, pp. 393–394 (G. Wills ed. 1982).

Or, again, to compare this ecstasy of a Supreme Court in which there is, especially on controversial matters, no shadow of change or hint of alteration ("There is a limit to the amount of error that can plausibly be imputed to prior courts," *ante*, at 24), with the more democratic views of a more humble man:

> "[T]he candid citizen must confess that if the policy of the Government upon vital questions affecting the whole people is to be irrevocably fixed by decisions of the Supreme Court, . . . the people will have ceased to be their own rulers, having to that extent practically resigned their Government into the hands of that eminent tribunal." A. Lincoln, First Inaugural Address (Mar. 4, 1861), reprinted in Inaugural Addresses of the Presidents of the United States, S. Doc. No. 101–10, p. 139 (1989).
>
> * * *

I cannot agree with, indeed I am appalled by, the Court's suggestion that the decision whether to stand by an erroneous constitutional decision must be strongly influenced—*against* overruling, no less—by the substantial and continuing public opposition the decision has generated * * *.

* * * It is a bad enough idea, even in the head of someone like me, who believes that the text of the Constitution, and our traditions, say what they say and there is no fiddling with them. But when it is in the mind of a Court that believes the Constitution has an evolving meaning, that the Ninth Amendment's reference to "othe[r]" rights is not a disclaimer, but a charter for action, and that the function of this Court is to "speak before all others for [the people's] constitutional ideals" unrestrained by meaningful text or tradition—then the notion that the Court must adhere to a decision for as long as the decision faces "great opposition" and the Court is "under fire" acquires a character of almost czarist arrogance. We are offended by these marchers who descend upon us, every year on the anniversary of *Roe*, to protest our saying that the Constitution requires what our society has never thought the Constitution requires. These people who refuse to be "tested by following" must be taught a lesson. We have no Cossacks, but at least we can stubbornly refuse to abandon an erroneous opinion that we might otherwise change—to show how little they intimidate us.

Of course, as the CHIEF JUSTICE points out, we have been subjected to what the Court calls "political pressure" by *both* sides of this issue. Maybe today's decision *not* to overrule *Roe* will be seen as buckling to pressure from *that* direction. Instead of engaging in the hopeless task of predicting public perception—a job not for lawyers but for political campaign managers—the Justices should do what is *legally* right by asking two questions: (1) Was *Roe* correctly decided? (2) Has *Roe* succeeded in producing a settled body of law? If the answer to both questions is no, *Roe* should undoubtedly be overruled.

* * *

What makes all this relevant to the bothersome application of "political pressure" against the Court are the twin facts that the American people love democracy and the American people are not fools. As long as this Court thought (and the people thought) that we Justices were doing essentially lawyers' work up here—reading text and discerning our society's traditional understanding of that text—the public pretty much left us alone. Texts and traditions are facts to study, not convictions to demonstrate about. But if in reality * * * our pronouncement of constitutional law rests primarily on value judgments, then a free and intelligent people's attitude towards us can be expected to be (*ought* to be) quite different. The people know that their value judgments are quite as good as those taught in any law school—maybe better. If, indeed, the "liberties" protected by the Constitution are, as the Court says, undefined and unbounded, then the people *should* demonstrate, to protest that we do not implement *their* values instead of *ours* * * *.

* * *

We should get out of this area, where we have no right to be, and where we do neither ourselves nor the country any good by remaining.

NOTES AND QUESTIONS

1. Contrary to Justice Scalia's wishes, the Court has remained in the area, though with only episodic additional appearances. Since the opinion in *Casey*, the Supreme Court has decided only three other major abortion cases: *Stenberg v. Carhart,* 530 U.S. 914 (2000) (striking down, 5–4, a Nebraska law banning partial birth abortions, a case in which Justice Kennedy vigorously dissents); *Gonzales v. Carhart*, 550 U.S. 124 (2007) (upholding, 5–4, a federal ban on partial birth abortions, with Justice Kennedy writing the majority opinion and with Justice Alito having replaced Justice O'Connor); *Whole Women's Health v. Hellerstedt*, 579 U.S. ___, 136 S.Ct. 2292 (2016) (holding, 5–4, that States cannot so thoroughly regulate abortion providers that they put them out of existence). The Court added a case to its 2019 Term docket from Louisiana that raises again the *Whole Women's Health v. Hellerstedt* issue. *See June Medical Services, L.L.C. v. Gee,* 905 F.3d 787 (5th Cir. 2018), *cert. granted,* 140 S.Ct. 35 (2019).

2. Before we leave the topic of abortion, consider Justice Clarence Thomas's concurrence—which is in essence a dissent from a denial of certiorari—in the following case.

Box v. Planned Parenthood of Indiana and Kentucky, Inc.

587 U.S. ___, 139 S.Ct. 1780 (2019)

■ PER CURIAM.

Indiana's petition for certiorari argues that the Court of Appeals for the Seventh Circuit incorrectly invalidated two new provisions of Indiana law: the first relating to the disposition of fetal remains by abortion providers; and the second barring the knowing provision of sex-, race-, or disability-selective abortions by abortion providers. We reverse the judgment of the Seventh Circuit with respect to the first question presented, and we deny the petition with respect to the second question presented.

The first challenged provision altered the manner in which abortion providers may dispose of fetal remains. Among other changes, it excluded fetal remains from the definition of infectious and pathological waste, thereby preventing incineration of fetal remains along with surgical byproducts. It also authorized simultaneous cremation of fetal remains, which Indiana does not generally allow for human remains. The law did not affect a woman's right under existing law "to determine the final disposition of the aborted fetus."

Respondents have never argued that Indiana's law creates an undue burden on a woman's right to obtain an abortion. Respondents have instead litigated this case on the assumption that the law does not implicate a fundamental right and is therefore subject only to ordinary rational basis review. See *Planned Parenthood of Indiana and Kentucky, Inc. v. Commissioner of Indiana State Dept. of Health*, 888 F. 3d 300, 307 (C.A.7 2018). To survive under that standard, a state law need only be "rationally related to legitimate government interests." *Washington v. Glucksberg*, 521 U. S. 702, 728 (1997).

The Seventh Circuit found Indiana's disposition law invalid even under this deferential test. It first held that Indiana's stated interest in "the 'humane and dignified disposal of human remains' " was "not . . . legitimate." It went on to hold that even if Indiana's stated interest were legitimate, "it [could not] identify a rational relationship" between that interest and "the law as written," because the law preserves a woman's right to dispose of fetal remains however she wishes and allows for simultaneous cremation.

We now reverse that determination. This Court has already acknowledged that a State has a "legitimate interest in proper disposal of fetal remains." *Akron v. Akron Center for Reproductive Health, Inc.*, 462 U. S. 416, 452, n. 45 (1983). The Seventh Circuit clearly erred in failing to recognize that interest as a permissible basis for Indiana's disposition law. See *Armour v. Indianapolis*, 566 U. S. 673, 685 (2012) (on rational basis review, "the burden is on the one attacking the legislative arrangement to negative every conceivable basis which might support it"). The only remaining question, then, is whether Indiana's law is rationally related to the State's interest in proper disposal of fetal remains. We conclude that it is, even if it is not perfectly tailored to that end. See *ibid.* (the State need not have drawn "the perfect line," as long as "the line actually drawn [is] a rational" one). We therefore uphold Indiana's law under rational basis review.

We reiterate that, in challenging this provision, respondents have never argued that Indiana's law imposes an undue burden on a woman's right to obtain an abortion. This case, as litigated, therefore does not implicate our cases applying the undue burden test to abortion regulations. Other courts have analyzed challenges to similar disposition laws under the undue burden standard. Our opinion expresses no view on the merits of those challenges.

Our opinion likewise expresses no view on the merits of the second question presented, *i.e.*, whether Indiana may prohibit the knowing provision of sex-, race-, and disability-selective abortions by abortion providers. Only the Seventh Circuit has thus far addressed this kind of law. We follow our ordinary practice of denying petitions insofar as they raise legal issues that have not been considered by additional Courts of Appeals. See this Court's Rule 10.

* * *

In sum, we grant certiorari with respect to the first question presented in the petition and reverse the judgment of the Court of Appeals with respect to that question. We deny certiorari with respect to the second question presented.

It is so ordered.

■ JUSTICE SOTOMAYOR would deny the petition for a writ of certiorari as to both questions presented.

■ JUSTICE THOMAS, concurring.

Indiana law prohibits abortion providers from treating the bodies of aborted children as "infectious waste" and incinerating them alongside used needles, laboratory-animal carcasses, and surgical byproducts. A panel of the Seventh Circuit held that this fetal-remains law was irrational, and thus unconstitutional, under the doctrine of "substantive due process." That decision was manifestly inconsistent with our precedent, as the Court holds. I would have thought it could go without saying that nothing in the Constitution or any decision of this Court prevents a State from requiring abortion facilities to provide for the respectful treatment of human remains.

I write separately to address the other aspect of Indiana law at issue here—the "Sex Selective and Disability Abortion Ban." This statute makes it illegal for an abortion provider to perform an abortion in Indiana when the provider knows that the mother is seeking the abortion solely because of the child's race, sex, diagnosis of Down syndrome, disability, or related characteristics. [S]ee § 16–34–4–1(b) (excluding "lethal fetal anomal[ies]" from the definition of disability). The law requires that the mother be advised of this restriction and given information about financial assistance and adoption alternatives, but it imposes liability only on the provider. Each of the immutable characteristics protected by this law can be known relatively early in a pregnancy, and the law prevents them from becoming the sole criterion for deciding whether the child will live or die. Put differently, this law and other laws like it promote a State's compelling interest in preventing abortion from becoming a tool of modern-day eugenics.

The use of abortion to achieve eugenic goals is not merely hypothetical. The foundations for legalizing abortion in America were laid during the early 20th-century birth-control movement. That movement developed alongside the American eugenics movement. And significantly, Planned Parenthood founder Margaret Sanger recognized the eugenic potential of her cause. She emphasized and embraced the notion that birth control "opens the way to the eugenist." Sanger, Birth Control and Racial Betterment, Birth Control Rev., Feb. 1919, p. 12 (Racial Betterment). As a means of reducing the "ever increasing, unceasingly spawning class of human beings who never should have been born at all," Sanger argued that "Birth Control . . . is really the greatest and most truly eugenic method" of "human generation." M. Sanger, Pivot of Civilization 187, 189 (1922) (Pivot of Civilization). In her view, birth control had been "accepted by the most clear thinking and far seeing of the Eugenists themselves as the most constructive and necessary of the means to racial health." *Id.*, at 189.

It is true that Sanger was not referring to abortion when she made these statements, at least not directly. She recognized a moral difference between "contraceptives" and other, more "extreme" ways for "women to limit their families," such as "the horrors of abortion and infanticide." M. Sanger, Woman and the New Race 25, 5 (1920) (Woman and the New Race). But Sanger's arguments about the eugenic value of birth control in securing "the elimination of the unfit," Racial Betterment 11, apply with even greater force to abortion, making it significantly more effective as a tool of eugenics. Whereas Sanger believed that birth control could prevent "unfit" people from reproducing, abortion can prevent them from being born in the first place. Many eugenicists therefore supported legalizing abortion, and abortion advocates—including future Planned Parenthood President Alan Guttmacher—endorsed the use of abortion for eugenic reasons. Technological advances have only heightened the eugenic potential for abortion, as abortion can now be used to eliminate children with unwanted characteristics, such as a particular sex or disability.

Given the potential for abortion to become a tool of eugenic manipulation, the Court will soon need to confront the constitutionality of laws like Indiana's. But because further percolation may assist our review of this issue of first impression, I join the Court in declining to take up the issue now.

The term "eugenics" was coined in 1883 by Francis Galton, a British statistician and half-cousin of Charles Darwin. Galton described eugenics as "the science of improving stock" through "all influences that tend in however remote a degree to give to the more suitable races or strains of blood a better chance of prevailing speedily over the less suit-able than they otherwise would have." F. Galton, Inquiries Into Human Faculty and Its Development 25, n. 1 (1883) * * *. As a social theory, eugenics is rooted in social Darwinism—*i.e.*, the application of the "survival of the fittest" principle to human society. Galton argued that by promoting reproduction between people with desirable qualities and inhibiting reproduction of the unfit, man could improve society by "do[ing] providently, quickly, and kindly" "[w]hat Nature does blindly, slowly, and ruthlessly." F. Galton, Eugenics: Its Definition, Scope and Aims, in Essays in Eugenics 42 (1909).

By the 1920s, eugenics had become a "full-fledged intellectual craze" in the United States, particularly among progressives, professionals, and intellectual elites. Leaders in the eugenics movement held prominent positions at Harvard, Stanford, and Yale, among other schools, and eugenics was taught at 376 universities and colleges * * *.

Many eugenicists believed that the distinction between the fit and the unfit could be drawn along racial lines, a distinction they justified by pointing to anecdotal and statistical evidence of disparities between the races. Galton, for example, purported to show as a scientific matter that "the average intellectual standard of the negro race is some two grades below" that of the Anglo-Saxon, and that "the number among the negroes of those whom we should call half-witted men, is very large." Hereditary Genius 338–339 * * *.

Building on similar assumptions, eugenicist Lothrop Stoddard argued that the "prodigious birth-rate" of the nonwhite races was bringing the world to a racial tipping point * * *. Allowing the white race to be overtaken by inferior races, according to Stoddard, would be a tragedy of historic proportions * * *.

Eugenic arguments like these helped precipitate the Immigration Act of 1924, which significantly reduced immigration from outside of Western and Northern Europe. The perceived superiority of the white race also led to calls for race consciousness in marital and reproductive decisions, including through anti-miscegenation laws. Applied Eugenics 296 ("We hold that it is to the interests of the United States . . . to prevent further Negro-white amalgamation").

Although race was relevant, eugenicists did not define a person's "fitness" exclusively by race. A typical list of dysgenic individuals would also include some combination of the "feeble-minded," "insane," "criminalistic," "deformed," "crippled," "epileptic," "inebriate," "diseased," "blind," "deaf," and "dependent (including orphans and paupers)." Immigration policy was insufficient to address these "danger[s] from within so eugenicists turned to other solutions. Many States adopted laws prohibiting marriages between certain feebleminded, epileptic, or other "unfit" individuals, but forced sterilization emerged as the preferred solution for many classes of dysgenic individuals. Indiana enacted the first eugenic sterilization law in 1907, and a number of other States followed suit.

This Court threw its prestige behind the eugenics movement in its 1927 decision upholding the constitutionality of Virginia's forced-sterilization law, *Buck* v. *Bell*, 274 U. S. 200 * * *.

The Court's decision gave the eugenics movement added legitimacy and considerable momentum; by 1931, 28 of the Nation's 48 States had adopted eugenic sterilization laws * * *.

* * *

This case highlights the fact that abortion is an act rife with the potential for eugenic manipulation * * *. As explained below, a growing body of evidence suggests that eugenic goals are already being realized through abortion.

* * *

* * * Support for abortion can * * * be found throughout the literature on eugenics.

Abortion advocates were sometimes candid about abortion's eugenic possibilities. In 1959, for example, Guttmacher explicitly endorsed eugenic reasons for abortion. A. Guttmacher, Babies by Choice or by Chance 186–188 (1959). He explained that "the quality of the parents must be taken into account," including "[f]eeble-mindedness," and believed that "it should be permissible to abort any pregnancy . . . in which there is a strong probability of an abnormal or malformed infant." *Id.*, at 198. He added that the question whether to allow abortion must be "separated from emotional, moral and religious concepts" and "must have as its focus normal, healthy infants born into homes peopled with parents who have healthy bodies and minds." *Id.*, at 221. Similarly, legal scholar Glanville Williams wrote that he was open to the possibility of eugenic infanticide, at least in some situations, explaining that "an eugenic killing by a mother, exactly paralleled by the bitch that kills her mis-shapen puppies, cannot confidently be pronounced im-moral." G. Williams, Sanctity of Life and the Criminal Law 20 (1957). The Court cited Williams' book for a different proposition in *Roe* v. *Wade*, 410 U. S. 113, 130, n. 9 (1973).

* * *

* * * Whatever else might be said about *Casey*, it did not decide whether the Constitution requires States to allow eugenic abortions. It addressed the constitutionality of only "five provisions of the Pennsylvania Abortion Control Act of 1982" that were said to burden the supposed constitutional right to an abortion. *Casey*, *supra*, at 844. None of those provisions prohibited abortions based solely on race, sex, or disability. In fact, the very first paragraph of the respondents' brief in *Casey* made it clear to the Court that Pennsylvania's prohibition on sex-selective abortions was "not [being] challenged," Brief for Respondents in *Planned Parenthood of Southeastern Pa.* v. *Casey*, O. T. 1991, Nos. 91–744, 91–902, p. 4. In light of the Court's denial of certiorari today, the constitutionality of other laws like Indiana's thus remains an open question.

The Court's decision to allow further percolation should not be interpreted as agreement with the decisions below. Enshrining a constitutional right to an abortion based solely on the race, sex, or disability of an unborn child, as Planned Parenthood advocates, would constitutionalize the views of the 20th-century eugenics movement. In other contexts, the Court has been zealous in vindicating the rights of people even potentially subjected to race, sex, and disability discrimination.

Although the Court declines to wade into these issues today, we cannot avoid them forever. Having created the constitutional right to an abortion, this Court is duty bound to address its scope. In that regard, it is easy to understand why the District Court and the Seventh Circuit looked to *Casey* to resolve a question it did not address. Where else could they turn? The Constitution itself is silent on abortion.

With these observations, I join the opinion of the Court.

NOTES AND QUESTIONS

1. Is Justice Thomas right to equate abortion and eugenics? Even if he is wrong about that, is he right that a state legislature could believe that he is right and constitutionally limit the reasons for abortions? We edited out a lengthy discussion from Justice Thomas claiming that, both historically and in practice, abortion disparately affects African-Americans. Is abortion in twenty-first century America a modern form of eugenics?

[Assignment 71]

XIII. OTHER MODERN SUBSTANTIVE DUE PROCESS HOLDINGS

The Supreme Court has revisited the doctrine of substantive due process at least four times in the last twenty years outside of the context of abortion. Consider first the holding of the fascinating case below, which badly split the Rehnquist Court (along somewhat unusual alignments), producing no majority opinion.

A. TROXEL V. GRANVILLE

530 U.S. 57 (2000)

■ JUSTICE O'CONNOR announced the judgment of the Court and delivered an opinion, in which THE CHIEF JUSTICE, JUSTICE GINSBURG, and JUSTICE BREYER join.

Section 26.10.160(3) of the Revised Code of Washington permits "[a]ny person" to petition a superior court for visitation rights "at any time," and authorizes that court to grant such visitation rights whenever "visitation may serve the best interest of the child." Petitioners Jenifer and Gary Troxel petitioned a Washington Superior Court for the right to visit their grandchildren, Isabelle and Natalie Troxel. Respondent Tommie Granville, the mother of Isabelle and Natalie, opposed the petition. The case ultimately reached the Washington Supreme Court, which held that § 26.10.160(3) unconstitutionally interferes with the fundamental right of parents to rear their children.

Tommie Granville and Brad Troxel shared a relationship that ended in June 1991. The two never married, but they had two daughters, Isabelle and Natalie. Jenifer and Gary Troxel are Brad's parents, and thus the paternal grandparents of Isabelle and Natalie. After Tommie and Brad separated in 1991, Brad lived with his parents and regularly brought his daughters to his parents' home for weekend visitation. Brad committed suicide in May 1993. Although the Troxels at first continued to see Isabelle and Natalie on a regular basis after their son's death, Tommie Granville informed the Troxels in October 1993 that she wished to limit their visitation with her daughters to one short visit per month.

In December 1993, the Troxels commenced the present action by filing, in the Washington Superior Court for Skagit County, a petition to obtain visitation rights with Isabelle and Natalie. The Troxels filed their petition under two Washington statutes, Wash. Rev. Code §§ 26.09.240 and 26.10.160(3) (1994). Only the latter statute is at issue in this case. Section 26.10.160(3) provides: "Any person may petition the court for visitation rights at any time including, but not limited to, custody proceedings. The court may order visitation rights for any person when visitation may serve the best interest of the child whether or not there has been any change of circumstances." At trial, the Troxels requested two weekends of overnight visitation per month and two weeks of visitation each summer. Granville did not oppose visitation altogether, but instead asked the court to order one day of visitation per month with no overnight stay. In 1995, the Superior Court issued an oral ruling and entered a visitation decree ordering visitation one weekend per month, one week during the summer, and four hours on both of the petitioning grandparents' birthdays.

Granville appealed, during which time she married Kelly Wynn. Before addressing the merits of Granville's appeal, the Washington Court of Appeals remanded the case to the Superior Court for entry of written findings of fact and conclusions of law. On remand, the Superior Court found that visitation was in Isabelle and Natalie's best interests:

> "The Petitioners [the Troxels] are part of a large, central, loving family, all located in this area, and the Petitioners can provide opportunities for the children in the areas of cousins and music.
>
> ". . . The court took into consideration all factors regarding the best interest of the children and considered all the testimony before it. The children would be benefitted from spending quality time with the Petitioners, provided that that time is balanced with time with the childrens' *[sic]* nuclear family. The court finds that the childrens' *[sic]* best interests are served by spending time with their mother and stepfather's other six children." App. 70a.

Approximately nine months after the Superior Court entered its order on remand, Granville's husband formally adopted Isabelle and Natalie.

The Washington Court of Appeals reversed the lower court's visitation order and dismissed the Troxels' petition for visitation, holding that nonparents lack standing to seek visitation under § 26.10.160(3) unless a custody action is pending. In the Court of Appeals' view, that limitation on nonparental visitation actions was "consistent with the constitutional restrictions on state interference with parents' fundamental liberty interest in the care, custody, and management of their children." Having resolved the case on the statutory ground, however, the Court of Appeals did not expressly pass on Granville's constitutional challenge to the visitation statute.

The Washington Supreme Court granted the Troxels' petition for review and, after consolidating their case with two other visitation cases, affirmed. The court disagreed with the Court of Appeals' decision on the statutory issue and * * * rested its decision on the Federal Constitution, holding that § 26.10.160(3) unconstitutionally infringes on the fundamental right of parents to rear their children * * *. The Washington Supreme Court held that "[p]arents have a right to limit visitation of their children with third persons," and that between parents and judges, "the parents should be the ones to choose whether to expose their children to certain people or ideas." Four justices dissented from the Washington Supreme Court's holding on the constitutionality of the statute.

We granted certiorari and now affirm the judgment.

The demographic changes of the past century make it difficult to speak of an average American family. The composition of families varies greatly from household to household. While many children may have two married parents and grandparents who visit regularly, many other children are raised in single-parent households. In 1996, children living with only one parent accounted for 28 percent of all children under age 18 in the United States. Understandably, in these single-parent households, persons outside the nuclear family are called upon with increasing frequency to assist in the everyday tasks of child rearing. In many cases, grandparents play an important role. For example, in 1998, approximately 4 million children—or 5.6 percent of all children under age 18—lived in the household of their grandparents.

The nationwide enactment of nonparental visitation statutes is assuredly due, in some part, to the States' recognition of these changing realities of the American family. Because grandparents and other relatives undertake duties of a parental nature in many households, States have sought to ensure the welfare of the children therein by protecting the relationships those children form with such third parties * * *.The extension of statutory rights in this area to persons other than a child's parents, however, comes with an obvious cost. For example, the State's recognition of an independent third-party interest in a child can place a substantial burden on the traditional parent-child relationship * * *.

The Fourteenth Amendment provides that no State shall "deprive any person of life, liberty, or property, without due process of law." We have long recognized that the Amendment's Due Process Clause, like its Fifth Amendment counterpart, "guarantees more than fair process." *Washington* v. *Glucksberg,* 521 U.S. 702, 719 (1997). The Clause also includes a substantive component that "provides heightened protection against government interference with certain fundamental rights and liberty interests." *Id.*, at 720.

The liberty interest at issue in this case—the interest of parents in the care, custody, and control of their children—is perhaps the oldest of the fundamental liberty interests recognized by this Court. More than 75 years ago, in *Meyer* v. *Nebraska,* 262 U.S. 390, 399, 401 (1923), we held that the "liberty" protected by the Due Process Clause includes the right of parents to "establish a home and bring up children" and "to control the education of their own." Two years later, in *Pierce* v. *Society of Sisters,* 268 U.S. 510, 534–535 (1925), we again held that the "liberty of parents and guardians" includes the right "to direct the upbringing and education of children under their control." * * *

In subsequent cases also, we have recognized the fundamental right of parents to make decisions concerning the care, custody, and control of their children * * *. In light of this extensive precedent, it cannot now be doubted that the Due Process Clause of the Fourteenth Amendment protects the fundamental right of parents to make decisions concerning the care, custody, and control of their children.

Section 26.10.160(3), as applied to Granville and her family in this case, unconstitutionally infringes on that fundamental parental right. The Washington nonparental visitation statute is breathtakingly broad. According to the statute's text, "*[a]ny person* may petition the court for visitation rights *at any time*," and the court may grant such visitation rights whenever "visitation may serve *the best interest of the child*." § 26.10.160(3) (emphases added). That language effectively permits any third party seeking visitation to subject any decision by a parent concerning visitation of the parent's children to state-court review. Once the visitation petition has been filed in court and the matter is placed before a judge, a parent's decision that visitation would not be in the child's best interest is accorded no deference. Section 26.10.160(3) contains no requirement that a court accord the parent's decision any presumption of validity or any weight whatsoever. Instead, the Washington statute places the best-interest determination solely in the hands of the judge. Should the judge disagree with the parent's estimation of the child's best interests, the judge's view necessarily prevails. Thus, in practical effect, in the State of Washington a court can disregard and overturn *any* decision by a fit custodial parent concerning visitation whenever a third party affected by the decision files a visitation petition, based solely on the judge's determination of the child's best interests. The Washington Supreme Court had the opportunity to give § 26.10.160(3) a narrower reading, but it declined to do so.

Turning to the facts of this case, the record reveals that the Superior Court's order was based on precisely the type of mere disagreement we have just described and nothing more. The Superior Court's order was not founded on any special factors that might justify the State's interference with Granville's fundamental right to make decisions concerning the rearing of her two daughters. To be sure, this case involves a visitation petition filed by grandparents soon after the death of their son—the father of Isabelle and Natalie—but the combination of several factors here compels our conclusion that § 26.10.160(3), as applied, exceeded the bounds of the Due Process Clause.

First, the Troxels did not allege, and no court has found, that Granville was an unfit parent. That aspect of the case is important, for there is a presumption that fit parents act in the best interests of their children * * *.

* * *

* * * [I]t appears that the Superior Court applied exactly the opposite presumption. In reciting its oral ruling after the conclusion of closing arguments, the Superior Court judge explained:

> "The burden is to show that it is in the best interest of the children to have some visitation and some quality time with their grandparents. I think in most situations a commonsensical approach [is that] it is normally in the best interest of the children to spend quality time with the grandparent, unless the grandparent, *[sic]* there are some issues or problems involved wherein the grandparents, their lifestyles are going to impact adversely upon the children. That certainly isn't the case here from what I can tell." Verbatim Report of Proceedings in *In re Troxel*, No. 93–3–00650–7 (Wash. Super. Ct., Dec. 14, 19, 1994), p. 213 (hereinafter Verbatim Report).

The judge's comments suggest that he presumed the grandparents' request should be granted unless the children would be "impact[ed] adversely." In effect, the judge placed on Granville, the fit custodial parent, the burden of *disproving* that visitation would be in the best interest of her daughters. The judge reiterated moments later: "I think [visitation with the Troxels] would be in the best interest of the children and I haven't been shown it is not in [the] best interest of the children." *Id.*, at 214.

The decisional framework employed by the Superior Court directly contravened the traditional presumption that a fit parent will act in the best interest of his or her child. In that respect, the court's presumption failed to provide any protection for Granville's fundamental constitutional right to make decisions concerning the rearing of her own daughters * * *. [I]f a fit parent's decision of the kind at issue here becomes subject to judicial review, the court must accord at least some special weight to the parent's own determination.

Finally, we note that there is no allegation that Granville ever sought to cut off visitation entirely * * *.

Considered together with the Superior Court's reasons for awarding visitation to the Troxels, the combination of these factors demonstrates that the visitation order in this case was an unconstitutional infringement on Granville's fundamental right to make decisions concerning the care, custody, and control of her two daughters. The Washington Superior Court failed to accord the determination of Granville, a fit custodial parent, any material weight. In fact, the Superior Court made only two formal findings in support of its visitation order. First, the Troxels "are part of a large, central, loving family, all located in this area, and the [Troxels] can provide opportunities for the children in the areas of cousins and music.". Second, "[t]he children would be benefitted from spending quality time with the [Troxels], provided that that time is balanced with time with the childrens' *[sic]* nuclear family." These slender findings * * * show that this case involves nothing more than a simple disagreement between the Washington Superior Court and Granville concerning her children's best interests * * *. As we have explained, the Due Process Clause does not permit a State to infringe on the fundamental right of parents to make childrearing decisions simply because a state judge believes a "better" decision could be made. Neither the Washington nonparental visitation statute generally—which places no limits on either the persons who may petition for visitation or the circumstances in which such a petition may be granted—nor the Superior Court in this specific case required anything more. Accordingly, we hold that § 26.10.160(3), as applied in this case, is unconstitutional.

Because we rest our decision on the sweeping breadth of § 26.10.160(3) and the application of that broad, unlimited power in this case, we do not consider the primary constitutional question passed on by the Washington Supreme Court—whether the Due Process Clause requires all nonparental visitation statutes to include a showing of harm or potential harm to the child as a condition precedent to granting visitation * * *

* * *

* * * We therefore hold that the application of § 26.10.160(3) to Granville and her family violated her due process right to make decisions concerning the care, custody, and control of her daughters.

Accordingly, the judgment of the Washington Supreme Court is affirmed.

It is so ordered.

■ JUSTICE SOUTER, concurring in the judgment. [Omitted.]

■ JUSTICE THOMAS, concurring in the judgment.

I write separately to note that neither party has argued that our substantive due process cases were wrongly decided and that the original understanding of the Due Process Clause precludes judicial enforcement of unenumerated rights under that constitutional provision. As a result, I express no view on the merits of this matter, and I understand the plurality as well to leave the resolution of that issue for another day.

Consequently, I agree with the plurality that this Court's recognition of a fundamental right of parents to direct the upbringing of their children resolves this case. Our decision in *Pierce* v. *Society of Sisters,* 268 U.S. 510 (1925), holds that parents have a fundamental constitutional right to rear their children, including the right to determine who shall educate and socialize them. The opinions of the plurality, JUSTICE KENNEDY, and JUSTICE SOUTER recognize such a right, but curiously none of them articulates the appropriate standard of review. I would apply strict scrutiny to infringements of fundamental rights. Here, the State of Washington lacks even a legitimate governmental interest—to say nothing of a compelling one—in second-guessing a fit parent's decision regarding visitation with third parties. On this basis, I would affirm the judgment below.

■ JUSTICE STEVENS, dissenting.

* * *

But presumptions notwithstanding, we should recognize that there may be circumstances in which a child has a stronger interest at stake than mere protection from serious harm caused by the termination of visitation by a "person" other than a parent. The almost infinite variety of family relationships that pervade our ever-changing society strongly counsel against the creation by this Court of a constitutional rule that treats a biological parent's liberty interest in the care and supervision of her child as an isolated right that may be exercised arbitrarily. It is indisputably the business of the States, rather than a federal court employing a national standard, to assess in the first instance the relative importance of the conflicting interests that give rise to disputes such as this. Far from guaranteeing that parents' interests will be trammeled in the sweep of cases arising under the statute, the Washington law merely gives an individual—with whom a child may have an established relationship—the procedural right to ask the State to act as arbiter, through the entirely well-known best-interests standard, between the parent's protected interests and the child's. It seems clear to me that the Due Process Clause of the Fourteenth Amendment leaves room for States to consider the impact on a child of possibly arbitrary parental decisions that neither serve nor are motivated by the best interests of the child.

* * *

■ JUSTICE SCALIA, dissenting.

In my view, a right of parents to direct the upbringing of their children is among the "unalienable Rights" with which the Declaration of Independence proclaims "all Men . . . are endowed by their Creator." And in my view that right is also among the "othe[r] [rights] retained by the people" which the Ninth Amendment says the Constitution's enumeration of rights "shall not be construed to deny or disparage." The Declaration of Independence, however, is not a legal prescription conferring powers upon the courts; and the Constitution's refusal to "deny or disparage" other rights is far removed from affirming any one of them, and even farther removed from authorizing judges to identify what they might be, and to enforce the judges' list against laws duly enacted by the people. Consequently, while I would think it entirely compatible with the commitment to representative democracy set forth in the founding documents to argue, in legislative chambers or in electoral campaigns, that the State has *no power* to interfere with parents' authority over the rearing of their children, I do not believe that the power which the Constitution confers upon me *as a judge* entitles me to deny legal effect to laws that (in my view) infringe upon what is (in my view) that unenumerated right.

Only three holdings of this Court rest in whole or in part upon a substantive constitutional right of parents to direct the upbringing of their children—two of them from an era rich in substantive due process holdings that have since been repudiated. See *Meyer* v. *Nebraska,* 262 U.S. 390, 399, 401 (1923); *Pierce* v. *Society of Sisters,* 268 U.S. 510, 534–535 (1925); *Wisconsin* v. *Yoder,* 406 U.S. 205, 232–233 (1972). Cf. *West Coast Hotel Co.* v. *Parrish*, 300 U.S. 379 (1937) (overruling *Adkins* v. *Children's Hospital of D. C.*, 261 U.S. 525 (1923)). The sheer diversity of today's opinions persuades me that the theory of unenumerated parental rights underlying these three cases has small claim to *stare decisis* protection. A legal principle that can be thought to produce such diverse outcomes in the relatively simple case before us here is not a legal principle that has induced substantial reliance. While I would not now overrule those earlier cases (that has not been urged), neither would I extend the theory upon which they rested to this new context.

Judicial vindication of "parental rights" under a Constitution that does not even mention them requires (as JUSTICE KENNEDY's opinion rightly points out) not only a judicially crafted definition of parents, but also—unless, as no one believes, the parental rights are to be absolute—judicially approved assessments of "harm to the child" and judicially defined gradations of other persons (grandparents, extended family, adoptive family in an adoption later found to be invalid, long-term guardians, etc.) who may have some claim against the wishes of the parents. If we embrace this unenumerated right, I think it obvious—whether we affirm or reverse the judgment here, or remand as JUSTICE STEVENS or JUSTICE KENNEDY would do—that we will be ushering in a new regime of judicially prescribed, and federally prescribed, family law. I have no reason to believe that federal judges will be better at this than state legislatures; and state legislatures have the great advantages of doing harm in a more circumscribed area, of being able to correct their mistakes in a flash, and of being removable by the people.

For these reasons, I would reverse the judgment below.

■ JUSTICE KENNEDY, dissenting. [Omitted.]

NOTES AND QUESTIONS

1. As you know by now, we think that *Meyer* and *Pierce* were correct to recognize a fundamental parental right (a "privilege or immunity") to raise their children. Does that solve this case—or just start it? If a parent is abusive towards the child, no one questions that the State can—and must—take action on behalf of the child. In custody proceedings, the government by necessity makes decisions that supervene the rights of at least some (and quite possibly both) of the parents. The question is how far that state power runs (or, as Professor Calabresi and Justice Bushrod Washington are both fond of framing it, what constitutes a just law enacted for the general good of the whole people). In some respects, this seems like an easy case: If the Washington statute really does allow judges to determine that *any* person can have visitation with children, it is hard to see how that law could survive even rational basis review. (As Justice Thomas correctly points out, he is the only justice in this case to address the standard of review. Why do you think that rather crucial issue escaped everyone's attention?) On the other hand, one of Professor Lawson's colleagues emphatically believes (and has confirmed in conversation that she believes this) that all children have a right to the best upbringing possible, so that if parents are not making the optimal decisions for their children, the State has a right and duty to intervene and place them elsewhere. Formally, this case was a dispute between parents and grandparents. Was the Court in this case talking about the correct people's rights? How many parties' rights need to be weighed in a case like this? Are all of these crucial—and eternal—questions of family law and structure in the hands of the courts under the Fourteenth Amendment? Are courts likely to make good decisions? What if a court decides that parents are teaching their children inappropriate sex roles? Would a court be justified in ordering visitation by more progressive thinkers to counter the influence of the parents? What if the question is reversed?

2. Justice Scalia concedes in his critique of substantive due process that the right of parents to control the upbringing of their children is among the "unalienable Rights * * * among which are Life, Liberty, and the Pursuit of Happiness" covered by the Declaration of Independence. As you know by now, *Corfield v. Coryell*, the historical key precedent for understanding Section 1 of the Fourteenth Amendment, essentially bakes the Declaration of Independence—or at least a good chunk of it—into the core meaning of the Fourteenth Amendment. Consider for the umpteenth time in the book the key excerpt from *Corfield v. Coryell*:

> The inquiry is, what are the privileges and immunities of citizens in the several states? We feel no hesitation in confining these expressions to those privileges and immunities which are, in their nature, fundamental; which belong, of right, to the citizens of all free governments; and which have, at all times, been

> enjoyed by the citizens of the several states which compose this Union, from the time of their becoming free, independent, and sovereign. What these fundamental principles are, it would perhaps be more tedious than difficult to enumerate. They may, however, be all comprehended under the following general heads: Protection by the government; the enjoyment of life and liberty, with the right to acquire and possess property of every kind, and to pursue and obtain happiness and safety; subject nevertheless to such restraints as the government may justly prescribe for the general good of the whole.

Isn't this just a garbled version of the Declaration of Independence? Justice Scalia loses even under his own rules. Why do you think that Justice Scalia, supposedly an originalist, was so uninterested in the original meaning of the Fourteenth Amendment? For our speculations on this matter, see Steven G. Calabresi & Gary Lawson, *The Rule of Law as a Law of Law,* 90 NOTRE DAME L. REV. 483 (2015).

B. WASHINGTON V. GLUCKSBERG

521 U.S. 702 (1997)

■ CHIEF JUSTICE REHNQUIST delivered the opinion of the Court.

The question presented in this case is whether Washington's prohibition against "caus[ing]" or "aid[ing]" a suicide offends the Fourteenth Amendment to the United States Constitution. We hold that it does not.

It has always been a crime to assist a suicide in the State of Washington. In 1854, Washington's first Territorial Legislature outlawed "assisting another in the commission of self-murder." Today, Washington law provides: "A person is guilty of promoting a suicide attempt when he knowingly causes or aids another person to attempt suicide." Wash. Rev. Code 9A.36.060(1) (1994). "Promoting a suicide attempt" is a felony, punishable by up to five years' imprisonment and up to a $10,000 fine. §§ 9A.36.060(2) and 9A.20.021(1)(c). At the same time, Washington's Natural Death Act, enacted in 1979, states that the "withholding or withdrawal of life-sustaining treatment" at a patient's direction "shall not, for any purpose, constitute a suicide." Wash. Rev. Code § 70.122.070(1).

Petitioners in this case are the State of Washington and its Attorney General. Respondents Harold Glucksberg, M. D., Abigail Halperin, M. D., Thomas A. Preston, M. D., and Peter Shalit, M. D., are physicians who practice in Washington. These doctors occasionally treat terminally ill, suffering patients, and declare that they would assist these patients in ending their lives if not for Washington's assisted-suicide ban. In January 1994, respondents, along with three gravely ill, pseudonymous plaintiffs who have since died and Compassion in Dying, a nonprofit organization that counsels people considering physician-assisted suicide, sued in the United States District Court, seeking a declaration that Wash Rev. Code 9A.36.060(1) (1994) is, on its face, unconstitutional.

The plaintiffs asserted "the existence of a liberty interest protected by the Fourteenth Amendment which extends to a personal choice by a mentally competent, terminally ill adult to commit physician-assisted suicide." Relying primarily on *Planned Parenthood* v. *Casey*, 505 U.S. 833 (1992), and *Cruzan* v. *Director, Missouri Dept. of Health*, 497 U.S. 261 (1990), the District Court agreed, and concluded that Washington's assisted-suicide ban is unconstitutional because it "places an undue burden on the exercise of [that] constitutionally protected liberty interest." * * *

A panel of the Court of Appeals for the Ninth Circuit reversed, emphasizing that "[i]n the two hundred and five years of our existence no constitutional right to aid in killing oneself has ever been asserted and upheld by a court of final jurisdiction." The Ninth Circuit reheard the case en banc, reversed the panel's decision, and affirmed the District Court * * *. We granted certiorari, and now reverse. * * *

We begin, as we do in all due process cases, by examining our Nation's history, legal traditions, and practices. In almost every State—indeed, in almost every western democracy—it is a crime to assist a suicide. The States' assisted-suicide bans are not innovations. Rather, they are longstanding expressions of the States' commitment to the protection and preservation of all human life. Indeed, opposition to and condemnation of suicide—and, therefore, of assisting suicide—are consistent and enduring themes of our philosophical, legal, and cultural heritages.

More specifically, for over 700 years, the Anglo-American common-law tradition has punished or otherwise disapproved of both suicide and assisting suicide. In the 13th century, Henry de Bracton, one of the first legal treatise writers, observed that "[j]ust as a man may commit felony by slaying another so may he do so by slaying himself." 2 Bracton on Laws and Customs of England 423 (f. 150) (G. Woodbine ed., S. Thorne transl., 1968) * * *. Centuries later, Sir William Blackstone, whose Commentaries on the Laws of England not only provided a definitive summary of the common law but was also a primary legal authority for 18th- and 19th-century American lawyers, referred to suicide as "self-murder" * * *. 4 W. Blackstone, Commentaries *189. Blackstone emphasized that "the law has . . . ranked [suicide] among the highest crimes," *ibid*, although, anticipating later developments, he conceded that the harsh and shameful punishments imposed for suicide "borde[r] a little upon severity." *Id.*, at *190.

For the most part, the early American colonies adopted the common-law approach * * *.

* * *

That suicide remained a grievous, though nonfelonious, wrong is confirmed by the fact that colonial and early state legislatures and courts did not retreat from prohibiting assisting suicide. Swift, in his early 19th-century treatise on the laws of Connecticut, stated that "[i]f one counsels another to commit suicide, and the other by reason of the advice kills himself, the advisor is guilty of murder as principal." 2 Z. Swift, A Digest of the Laws of the State of Connecticut 270 (1823). This was the well-established common-law view, see *In re Joseph G.*, 34 Cal. 3d 429, 434–435, 667 P. 2d 1176, 1179 (1983); *Commonwealth* v. *Mink*, 123 Mass. 422, 428 (1877) (" 'Now if the murder of one's self is felony, the accessory is equally guilty as if he had aided and abetted in the murder' ") (quoting Chief Justice Parker's charge to the jury in *Commonwealth* v. *Bowen*, 13 Mass. 356 (1816)), as was the similar principle that the consent of a homicide victim is "wholly immaterial to the guilt of the person who cause[d] [his death]," 3 J. Stephen, A History of the Criminal Law of England 16 (1883); see 1 F. Wharton, Criminal Law §§ 451–452 (9th ed. 1885); *Martin* v. *Commonwealth*, 184 Va. 1009, 1018–1019, 37 S. E. 2d 43, 47 (1946) (" 'The right to life and to personal security is not only sacred in the estimation of the common law, but it is inalienable' "). And the prohibitions against assisting suicide never contained exceptions for those who were near death. Rather, "[t]he life of those to whom life ha[d] become a burden—of those who [were] hopelessly diseased or fatally wounded—nay, even the lives of criminals condemned to death, [were] under the protection of law, equally as the lives of those who [were] in the full tide of life's enjoyment, and anxious to continue to live." *Blackburn* v. *State*, 23 Ohio St. 146, 163 (1872).

The earliest American statute explicitly to outlaw assisting suicide was enacted in New York in 1828, and many of the new States and Territories followed New York's example * * *. In this century, the Model Penal Code also prohibited "aiding" suicide, prompting many States to enact or revise their assisted-suicide bans * * *.

* * *

The Washington statute at issue in this case, Wash. Rev. Code § 9A.36.060 (1994), was enacted in 1975 as part of a revision of that State's criminal code. Four years later, Washington passed its Natural Death Act, which specifically stated that the "withholding or withdrawal of life-sustaining treatment . . . shall not, for any purpose, constitute a suicide" and that "[n]othing in this chapter shall be construed to condone, authorize, or approve mercy killing . . . ." Natural Death Act, 1979 Wash. Laws, ch. 112, §§ 8(1), p. 11 (codified at Wash. Rev. Code §§ 70.122.070(1), 70.122.100 (1994)). In 1991, Washington voters rejected a ballot initiative which, had it passed, would have permitted a form of physician-assisted suicide. Washington then added a provision to the Natural Death Act expressly excluding physician assisted suicide. 1992 Wash. Laws, ch. 98, § 10; Wash. Rev. Code § 70.122.100 (1994).

California voters rejected an assisted-suicide initiative similar to Washington's in 1993. On the other hand, in 1994, voters in Oregon enacted, also through ballot initiative, that State's "Death With Dignity Act," which legalized physician-assisted suicide for competent, terminally ill adults. Since the Oregon vote, many proposals to legalize assisted-suicide have been and continue to be introduced in the States' legislatures, but none has been enacted * * *.

Thus, the States are currently engaged in serious, thoughtful examinations of physician-assisted suicide and other similar issues * * *.

Attitudes toward suicide itself have changed since Bracton, but our laws have consistently condemned, and continue to prohibit, assisting suicide. Despite changes in medical technology and notwithstanding an increased emphasis on the importance of end-of-life decisionmaking, we have not retreated from this prohibition. Against this backdrop of history, tradition, and practice, we now turn to respondents' constitutional claim.

The Due Process Clause guarantees more than fair process, and the "liberty" it protects includes more than the absence of physical restraint. *Collins* v. *Harker Heights*, 503 U.S. 115, 125 (1992) (Due Process Clause "protects individual liberty against 'certain government actions regardless of the fairness of the procedures used to implement them' "). The Clause also provides heightened protection against government interference with certain fundamental rights and liberty interests. In a long line of cases, we have held that, in addition to the specific freedoms protected by the Bill of Rights, the "liberty" specially protected by the Due Process Clause includes the rights to marry, *Loving* v. *Virginia*, 388 U.S. 1 (1967); to have children, *Skinner* v. *Oklahoma ex rel. Williamson*, 316 U.S. 535 (1942); to direct the education and upbringing of one's children, *Meyer* v. *Nebraska*, 262 U.S. 390 (1923); *Pierce* v. *Society of Sisters*, 268 U.S. 510 (1925); to marital privacy, *Griswold* v. *Connecticut*, 381 U.S. 479 (1965); to use contraception, *ibid*; *Eisenstadt* v. *Baird*, 405 U.S. 438

(1972); to bodily integrity, *Rochin* v. *California*, 342 U.S. 165 (1952), and to abortion, *Casey*, *supra*. We have also assumed, and strongly suggested, that the Due Process Clause protects the traditional right to refuse unwanted lifesaving medical treatment. *Cruzan*, 497 U. S., at 278–279.

But we "ha[ve] always been reluctant to expand the concept of substantive due process because guideposts for responsible decisionmaking in this unchartered area are scarce and open-ended." *Collins*, 503 U. S., at 125. By extending constitutional protection to an asserted right or liberty interest, we, to a great extent, place the matter outside the arena of public debate and legislative action. We must therefore "exercise the utmost care whenever we are asked to break new ground in this field," *ibid*, lest the liberty protected by the Due Process Clause be subtly transformed into the policy preferences of the Members of this Court.

Our established method of substantive-due-process analysis has two primary features: First, we have regularly observed that the Due Process Clause specially protects those fundamental rights and liberties which are, objectively, "deeply rooted in this Nation's history and tradition" and "implicit in the concept of ordered liberty," such that "neither liberty nor justice would exist if they were sacrificed," *Palko* v. *Connecticut*, 302 U.S. 319, 325, 326 (1937). Second, we have required in substantive-due-process cases a "careful description" of the asserted fundamental liberty interest. Our Nation's history, legal traditions, and practices thus provide the crucial "guideposts for responsible decisionmaking," *Collins*, *supra*, at 125, that direct and restrain our exposition of the Due Process Clause. As we stated recently * * *, the Fourteenth Amendment "forbids the government to infringe . . . 'fundamental' liberty interests *at all*, no matter what process is provided, unless the infringement is narrowly tailored to serve a compelling state interest." 507 U. S., at 302.

JUSTICE SOUTER, relying on Justice Harlan's dissenting opinion in *Poe* v. *Ullman*, would largely abandon this restrained methodology, and instead ask "whether [Washington's] statute sets up one of those 'arbitrary impositions' or 'purposeless restraints' at odds with the Due Process Clause of the Fourteenth Amendment," *post*, at 752 (quoting *Poe*, 367 U.S. 497, 543 (1961) (Harlan, J., dissenting)). In our view, however, the development of this Court's substantive-due-process jurisprudence has been a process whereby the outlines of the "liberty" specially protected by the Fourteenth Amendment—never fully clarified, to be sure, and perhaps not capable of being fully clarified—have at least been carefully refined by concrete examples involving fundamental rights found to be deeply rooted in our legal tradition. This approach tends to rein in the subjective elements that are necessarily present in due process judicial review. In addition, by establishing a threshold requirement—that a challenged state action implicate a fundamental right—before requiring more than a reasonable relation to a legitimate state interest to justify the action, it avoids the need for complex balancing of competing interests in every case.

Turning to the claim at issue here, the Court of Appeals stated that "[p]roperly analyzed, the first issue to be resolved is whether there is a liberty interest in determining the time and manner of one's death," or, in other words, "[i]s there a right to die?" Similarly, respondents assert a "liberty to choose how to die" and a right to "control of one's final days," Brief for Respondents 7, and describe the asserted liberty as "the right to choose a humane, dignified death," *id.*, at 15, and "the liberty to shape death," *id.*, at 18. As noted above, we have a tradition of carefully formulating the interest at stake in substantive-due-process cases * * *. The Washington statute at issue in this case prohibits "aid[ing] another person to attempt suicide," Wash. Rev. Code § 9A.36.060(1) (1994), and, thus, the question before us is whether the "liberty" specially protected by the Due Process Clause includes a right to commit suicide which itself includes a right to assistance in doing so.

We now inquire whether this asserted right has any place in our Nation's traditions. Here, as discussed *supra* at 710–719, we are confronted with a consistent and almost universal tradition that has long rejected the asserted right, and continues explicitly to reject it today, even for terminally ill, mentally competent adults. To hold for respondents, we would have to reverse centuries of legal doctrine and practice, and strike down the considered policy choice of almost every State. See *Jackman* v. *Rosenbaum Co.*, 260 U.S. 22, 31 (1922) ("If a thing has been practiced for two hundred years by common consent, it will need a strong case for the Fourteenth Amendment to affect it").

Respondents contend, however, that the liberty interest they assert *is* consistent with this Court's substantive-due-process line of cases, if not with this Nation's history and practice. Pointing to *Casey* and *Cruzan*, respondents read our jurisprudence in this area as reflecting a general tradition of "self-sovereignty," Brief of Respondents 12, and as teaching that the "liberty" protected by the Due Process Clause includes "basic and intimate exercises of personal autonomy," *id.*, at 10; see *Casey*, 505 U. S., at 847 ("It is a promise of the Constitution that there is a realm of personal liberty which the government may not enter"). According to respondents, our liberty jurisprudence, and the broad, individualistic principles it reflects, protects the "liberty of competent, terminally ill adults to make end-of-life decisions free of undue government interference." Brief for Respondents 10. The question presented in this case, however, is whether the protections of the Due Process Clause include a right to commit suicide with another's assistance. With this "careful description" of respondents' claim in mind, we turn to *Casey* and *Cruzan*.

In *Cruzan*, we considered whether Nancy Beth Cruzan, who had been severely injured in an automobile accident and was in a persistive vegetative state, "ha[d] a right under the United States Constitution which would require the hospital to withdraw life-sustaining treatment" at her parents' request. *Cruzan*, 497 U. S., at 269. We began with the observation that "[a]t common law, even the touching of one person by another without consent and without legal justification was a battery." *Ibid.* We then discussed the related rule that "informed consent is generally required for medical treatment." *Ibid.* After reviewing a long line of relevant state cases, we concluded that "the common-law doctrine of informed consent is viewed as generally encompassing the right of a competent individual to refuse medical treatment." *Id.*, at 277. Next, we reviewed our own cases on the subject, and stated that "[t]he principle that a competent person has a constitutionally protected liberty interest in refusing unwanted medical treatment may be inferred from our prior decisions." *Id.*, at 278. Therefore, "for purposes of [that] case, we assume[d] that the United States Constitution would grant a competent person a constitutionally protected right to refuse lifesaving hydration and nutrition." *Id.*, at 279; see *id.*, at 287 (O'CONNOR, J., concurring). We concluded that, notwithstanding this right, the Constitution permitted Missouri to require clear and convincing evidence of an incompetent patient's wishes concerning the withdrawal of life-sustaining treatment. *Id.*, at 280–281.

Respondents contend that in *Cruzan* we "acknowledged that competent, dying persons have the right to direct the removal of life-sustaining medical treatment and thus hasten death," Brief for Respondents 23, and that "the constitutional principle behind recognizing the patient's liberty to direct the withdrawal of artificial life support applies at least as strongly to the choice to hasten impending death by consuming lethal medication," *id.*, at 26. Similarly, the Court of Appeals concluded that "*Cruzan*, by recognizing a liberty interest that includes the refusal of artificial provision of life-sustaining food and water, necessarily recognize[d] a liberty interest in hastening one's own death." 79 F. 3d, at 816.

The right assumed in *Cruzan*, however, was not simply deduced from abstract concepts of personal autonomy. Given the common-law rule that forced medication was a battery, and the long legal tradition protecting the decision to refuse unwanted medical treatment, our assumption was entirely consistent with this Nation's history and constitutional traditions. The decision to commit suicide with the assistance of another may be just as personal and profound as the decision to refuse unwanted medical treatment, but it has never enjoyed similar legal protection * * *.

Respondents also rely on *Casey* * * *.

The Court of Appeals, like the District Court, found *Casey* " 'highly instructive' " and " 'almost prescriptive' " for determining " 'what liberty interest may inhere in a terminally ill person's choice to commit suicide' ":

> "Like the decision of whether or not to have an abortion, the decision how and when to die is one of 'the most intimate and personal choices a person may make in a lifetime,' a choice 'central to personal dignity and autonomy.' " 79 F. 3d, at 813–814.

Similarly, respondents emphasize the statement in *Casey* that:

> "At the heart of liberty is the right to define one's own concept of existence, of meaning, of the universe, and of the mystery of human life. Beliefs about these matters could not define the attributes of personhood were they formed under compulsion of the State." *Casey*, 505 U. S., at 851.

Brief for Respondents 12. By choosing this language, the Court's opinion in *Casey* described, in a general way and in light of our prior cases, those personal activities and decisions that this Court has identified as so deeply rooted in our history and traditions, or so fundamental to our concept of constitutionally ordered liberty, that they are protected by the Fourteenth Amendment * * *.That many of the rights and liberties protected by the Due Process Clause sound in personal autonomy does not warrant the sweeping conclusion that any and all important, intimate, and personal decisions are so protected, *San Antonio Independent School Dist.* v. *Rodriguez*, 411 U.S. 1, 33–35 (1973), and *Casey* did not suggest otherwise.

The history of the law's treatment of assisted suicide in this country has been and continues to be one of the rejection of nearly all efforts to permit it. That being the case, our decisions lead us to conclude that the asserted "right" to assistance in committing suicide is not a fundamental liberty interest protected by the Due Process Clause. The Constitution also requires, however, that Washington's assisted suicide ban be rationally related to legitimate government interests. This requirement is unquestionably met here. As the court below recognized, Washington's assisted suicide ban implicates a number of state interests.

First, Washington has an "unqualified interest in the preservation of human life." *Cruzan*, 497 U. S., at 282. The State's prohibition on assisted suicide, like all homicide laws, both reflects and advances its commitment to this interest * * *.

* * *

Those who attempt suicide—terminally ill or not—often suffer from depression or other mental disorders * * *. Thus, legal physician-assisted suicide could make it more difficult for the State to protect depressed or mentally ill persons, or those who are suffering from untreated pain, from suicidal impulses.

The State also has an interest in protecting the integrity and ethics of the medical profession * * *. And physician-assisted suicide could, it is argued, undermine the trust that is essential to the doctor-patient relationship by blurring the time-honored line between healing and harming.

Next, the State has an interest in protecting vulnerable groups—including the poor, the elderly, and disabled persons—from abuse, neglect, and mistakes. The Court of Appeals dismissed the State's concern that disadvantaged persons might be pressured into physician-assisted suicide as "ludicrous on its face." 79 F. 3d, at 825. We have recognized, however, the real risk of subtle coercion and undue influence in end-of-life situations. *Cruzan*, 497 U. S., at 281 * * *. If physician assisted suicide were permitted, many might resort to it to spare their families the substantial financial burden of end-of-life health care costs.

The State's interest here goes beyond protecting the vulnerable from coercion; it extends to protecting disabled and terminally ill people from prejudice, negative and inaccurate stereotypes, and "societal indifference." 49 F. 3d, at 592. The State's assisted-suicide ban reflects and reinforces its policy that the lives of terminally ill, disabled, and elderly people must be no less valued than the lives of the young and healthy, and that a seriously disabled person's suicidal impulses should be interpreted and treated the same way as anyone else's.

Finally, the State may fear that permitting assisted suicide will start it down the path to voluntary and perhaps even involuntary euthanasia * * *.

* * *

We need not weigh exactingly the relative strengths of these various interests. They are unquestionably important and legitimate, and Washington's ban on assisted suicide is at least reasonably related to their promotion and protection. We therefore hold that Wash. Rev. Code § 9A.36.060(1) (1994) does not violate the Fourteenth Amendment, either on its face or "as applied to competent, terminally ill adults who wish to hasten their deaths by obtaining medication prescribed by their doctors."

Throughout the Nation, Americans are engaged in an earnest and profound debate about the morality, legality, and practicality of physician-assisted suicide. Our holding permits this debate to continue, as it should in a democratic society. The decision of the en banc Court of Appeals is reversed, and the case is remanded for further proceedings consistent with this opinion.

It is so ordered.

■ JUSTICE O'CONNOR, concurring.*

Death will be different for each of us. For many, the last days will be spent in physical pain and perhaps the despair that accompanies physical deterioration and a loss of control of basic bodily and mental functions. Some will seek medication to alleviate that pain and other symptoms.

The Court frames the issue in this case as whether the Due Process Clause of the Constitution protects a "right to commit suicide which itself includes a right to assistance in doing so," and concludes that our Nation's history, legal traditions, and practices do not support the existence of such a right. I join the Court's opinions because I agree that there is no generalized right to "commit suicide." But respondents urge us to address the narrower question whether a mentally competent person who is experiencing great suffering has a constitutionally cognizable interest in controlling the circumstances of his or her imminent death. I see no need to reach that question in the context of the facial challenges to the New York and Washington laws at issue here * * *. In this light, even assuming that we would recognize such an interest, I agree that the State's interests in protecting those who are not truly competent or facing imminent death, or those whose decisions to hasten death would not truly be voluntary, are sufficiently weighty to justify a prohibition against physician assisted suicide.

* * *

* * * The difficulty in defining terminal illness and the risk that a dying patient's request for assistance in ending his or her life might not be truly voluntary justifies the prohibitions on assisted suicide we uphold here.

■ JUSTICE SOUTER, concurring in the judgment.

* * *

When the physicians claim that the Washington law deprives them of a right falling within the scope of liberty that the Fourteenth Amendment guarantees against denial without due process of law, they are not claiming some sort of procedural defect in the process through which the statute has been enacted or is administered. Their claim, rather, is that the State has no substantively adequate justification for barring the assistance sought by the patient and sought to be offered by the physician. Thus, we are dealing with a claim to one of those rights sometimes described as rights of substantive due process and sometimes as unenumerated rights, in view of the breadth and indeterminacy of the "due process" serving as the claim's textual basis. The doctors accordingly arouse the skepticism of those who find the Due Process Clause an unduly vague or oxymoronic warrant for judicial review of substantive state law, just as they also invoke two centuries of American constitutional practice in recognizing unenumerated, substantive limits on governmental action. Although this practice has neither rested on any single textual basis nor expressed a consistent theory (or, before *Poe v. Ullman,* a much articulated one), a brief overview of its history is instructive on two counts. The persistence of substantive due process in our cases points to the legitimacy of the modern justification for such judicial review found in Justice Harlan's dissent in *Poe,* on

* Justice Ginsburg concurs in the Court's judgments substantially for the reasons stated in this opinion. Justice Breyer joins this opinion except insofar as it joins the opinions of the Court.

which I will dwell further on, while the acknowledged failures of some of these cases point with caution to the difficulty raised by the present claim.

* * *

After the ratification of the Fourteenth Amendment, with its guarantee of due process protection against the States, interpretation of the words "liberty" and "property" as used in Due Process Clauses became a sustained enterprise, with the Court generally describing the due process criterion in converse terms of reasonableness or arbitrariness * * *.

The theory became serious, however, beginning with *Allgeyer v. Louisiana,* 165 U.S. 578 (1897), where the Court invalidated a Louisiana statute for excessive interference with Fourteenth Amendment liberty to contract, *id.,* at 588–593, and offered a substantive interpretation of "liberty," that in the aftermath of the so-called *Lochner* Era has been scaled back in some respects, but expanded in others, and never repudiated in principle. The Court said that Fourteenth Amendment liberty includes "the right of the citizen to be free in the enjoyment of all his faculties; to be free to use them in all lawful ways; to live and work where he will; to earn his livelihood by any lawful calling; to pursue any livelihood or avocation; and for that purpose to enter into all contracts which may be proper, necessary and essential to his carrying out to a successful conclusion the purposes above mentioned." *Id.,* at 589. "[W]e do not intend to hold that in no such case can the State exercise its police power," the Court added, but "[w]hen and how far such power may be legitimately exercised with regard to these subjects must be left for determination to each case as it arises." *Id.,* at 590.

* * * *Allgeyer* was succeeded within a decade by *Lochner v. New York,* 198 U.S. 45 (1905), and the era to which that case gave its name, famous now for striking down as arbitrary various sorts of economic regulations that post-New Deal courts have uniformly thought constitutionally sound * * *. [W]hile the cases in the *Lochner* line routinely invoked a correct standard of constitutional arbitrariness review, they harbored the spirit of *Dred Scott* in their absolutist implementation of the standard they espoused.

Even before the deviant economic due process cases had been repudiated, however, the more durable precursors of modern substantive due process were reaffirming this Court's obligation to conduct arbitrariness review, beginning with *Meyer v. Nebraska,* 262 U.S. 390 (1923). Without referring to any specific guarantee of the Bill of Rights, the Court invoked precedents from the *Slaughter-House Cases* through *Adkins* to declare that the Fourteenth Amendment protected "the right of the individual to contract, to engage in any of the common occupations of life, to acquire useful knowledge, to marry, establish a home and bring up children, to worship God according to the dictates of his own conscience, and generally to enjoy those privileges long recognized at common law as essential to the orderly pursuit of happiness by free men." 262 U.S., at 399. The Court then held that the same Fourteenth Amendment liberty included a teacher's right to teach and the rights of parents to direct their children's education without unreasonable interference by the States, *id.,* at 400, with the result that Nebraska's prohibition on the teaching of foreign languages in the lower grades was "arbitrary and without reasonable relation to any end within the competency of the State," *id.,* at 403.

After *Meyer* and *Pierce,* two further opinions took the major steps that lead to the modern law. The first was not even in a due process case but one about equal protection, *Skinner v. Oklahoma ex rel. Williamson,* 316 U.S. 535 (1942), where the Court emphasized the "fundamental" nature of individual choice about procreation and so foreshadowed not only the later prominence of procreation as a subject of liberty protection, but the corresponding standard of "strict scrutiny," in this Court's Fourteenth Amendment law. See *id.,* at 541. *Skinner,* that is, added decisions regarding procreation to the list of liberties recognized in *Meyer* and *Pierce* and loosely suggested, as a gloss on their standard of arbitrariness, a judicial obligation to scrutinize any impingement on such an important interest with heightened care * * *.

The second major opinion leading to the modern doctrine was Justice Harlan's *Poe* dissent just cited, the conclusion of which was adopted in *Griswold v. Connecticut,* 381 U.S. 479 (1965), and the authority of which was acknowledged in *Planned Parenthood of Southeastern Pa. v. Casey,* 505 U.S. 833 (1992). The dissent is important for three things that point to our responsibilities today. The first is Justice Harlan's respect for the tradition of substantive due process review itself, and his acknowledgment of the Judiciary's obligation to carry it on * * *. Like many judges who preceded him and many who followed, he found it impossible to construe the text of due process without recognizing substantive, and not merely procedural, limitations * * *.

Following the first point of the *Poe* dissent, on the necessity to engage in the sort of examination we conduct today, the dissent's second and third implicitly address those cases, already noted, that are now condemned with virtual unanimity as disastrous mistakes of substantive due process review. The second of the dissent's lessons is a reminder that the business of such review is not the identification of extratextual absolutes but scrutiny of a legislative resolution (perhaps unconscious) of clashing principles, each quite possibly worthy in and of itself, but each to be weighed within the history of our values as a people. It is a comparison of the relative strengths of opposing claims that informs the judicial task, not a deduction from some first premise. Thus informed, judicial review still has no warrant to substitute one reasonable resolution of the contending positions for another, but authority to supplant the balance already struck between the contenders only when it falls outside the realm of the reasonable * * *.

My understanding of unenumerated rights in the wake of the *Poe* dissent and subsequent cases avoids the absolutist failing of many older cases without embracing the opposite pole of equating reasonableness with past practice described at a very specific level. That understanding begins with a concept of "ordered liberty," comprising a continuum of rights to be free from "arbitrary impositions and purposeless restraints," *Poe,* 367 U.S., at 543 (Harlan, J., dissenting) * * *.

After the *Poe* dissent, as before it, this enforceable concept of liberty would bar statutory impositions even at relatively trivial levels when governmental restraints are undeniably irrational as unsupported by any imaginable rationale. Such instances are suitably rare. The claims of arbitrariness that mark almost all instances of unenumerated substantive rights are * * * interests in liberty sufficiently important to be judged "fundamental." In the face of an interest this powerful a State may not rest on threshold rationality or a presumption of constitutionality, but may prevail only on the ground of an interest sufficiently compelling to place within the realm of the reasonable a refusal to recognize the individual right asserted. *Poe, supra,* at 548 (Harlan, J., dissenting).

This approach calls for a court to assess the relative "weights" or dignities of the contending interests, and to this extent the judicial method is familiar to the common law. Common-law method is subject, however, to two important constraints in the hands of a court engaged in substantive due process review. First, such a court is bound to confine the values that it recognizes to those truly deserving constitutional stature, either to those expressed in constitutional text, or those exemplified by "the traditions from which [the Nation] developed," or revealed by contrast with "the traditions from which it broke." *Poe,* 367 U.S., at 542 (Harlan, J., dissenting) * * *.

The second constraint, again, simply reflects the fact that constitutional review, not judicial lawmaking, is a court's business here. The weighing or valuing of contending interests in this sphere is only the first step, forming the basis for determining whether the statute in question falls inside or outside the zone of what is reasonable in the way it resolves the conflict between the interests of state and individual. It is no justification for judicial intervention merely to identify a reasonable resolution of contending values that differs from the terms of the legislation under review. It is only when the legislation's justifying principle, critically valued, is so far from being commensurate with the individual interest as to be arbitrarily or pointlessly applied that the statute must give way * * *.

The *Poe* dissent thus reminds us of the nature of review for reasonableness or arbitrariness and the limitations entailed by it. But the opinion cautions against the repetition of past error in another way as well, more by its example than by any particular statement of constitutional method: it reminds us that the process of substantive review by reasoned judgment, *Poe,* 367 U.S., at 542–544, is one of close criticism going to the details of the opposing interests and to their relationships with the historically recognized principles that lend them weight or value.

* * *

[*Editors' Note: Thirteen pages later . . .*]

In my judgment, the importance of the individual interest here, as within that class of "certain interests" demanding careful scrutiny of the State's contrary claim, see *Poe, supra,* at 543, cannot be gainsaid. Whether that interest might in some circumstances, or at some time, be seen as "fundamental" to the degree entitled to prevail is not, however, a conclusion that I need draw here, for I am satisfied that the State's interests described in the following section are sufficiently serious to defeat the present claim that its law is arbitrary or purposeless.

[*Editors' Note: Seven pages later . . .*]

* * *

While I do not decide for all time that respondents' claim should not be recognized, I acknowledge the legislative institutional competence as the better one to deal with that claim at this time.

■ JUSTICE STEVENS, concurring in the judgments. [Omitted.]

■ JUSTICE GINSBURG, concurring in the judgments.

I concur in the Court's judgments in these cases substantially for the reasons stated by Justice O'CONNOR in her concurring opinion.

■ JUSTICE BREYER, concurring in the judgments. [Omitted.]

NOTES AND QUESTIONS

1. One of the reasons why substantive due process is and has been so controversial is that it interjects the Court into virtually every difficult question of social policy, from parenting to end-of-life (and beginning-of-life) decisions. Is this the Court's fault, or does the Constitution really command that it address these issues? A judge, who is a friend of Professor Calabresi joked that as a matter of truth in advertising, the Supreme Court should be renamed "The Supreme Court of Sex, Race, and Abortion!"

2. Chief Justice Rehnquist's majority opinion in *Washington v. Glucksberg* is a masterful neo-Thayerian attempt to confine substantive due process, or its equivalent under the Privileges or Immunities Clause, involving anything more than rational basis review to rights that are deeply rooted in history and tradition. Based on what you have seen thus far, does the majority fairly characterize the Court's prior decisions? Does it fairly characterize the language from the joint opinion in *Casey*? Does it fairly characterize the inquiry called for by *Corfield v. Coryell*? The operative language says that privileges or immunities "may, however, be all comprehended under the following general heads: Protection by the government; the enjoyment of life and liberty, with the right to acquire and possess property of every kind, and to pursue and obtain happiness and safety; subject nevertheless to such restraints as the government may justly prescribe for the general good of the whole" people." This test could be argued to confine judges to rights that are deeply rooted in history and tradition. But, the right that is without a doubt the most deeply rooted in American history and tradition is the idea that "All human beings are born free and equal and have certain natural and inalienable rights among which are the rights to enjoy and defend life and liberty, to acquire possess and protect property, in fine to pursue happiness and safety." The death knell for Chief Justice Rehnquist's and Justice Scalia's "deeply rooted in history and tradition test" is that the right that qualifies most readily calls for looking to natural law (or, perhaps more legalistically phrased, to the Ancient Constitution)! These rights are "subject nevertheless to such just laws as may be generally prescribed for the good of the whole" people, but that only means that the police power can be exercised reasonably, as Justice Peckham said in *Lochner v. New York,* not that it is triggered by a mere rational basis for lawmaking.

3. Justice O'Connor's concurrence, joined by Justice Ginsburg and (sort of by) Justice Breyer, holds that all agree that in Washington State pain killing medication like morphine, which can hasten the time of death by suppressing breathing, is legally available in Washington States. Thus, Justice O'Connor only provides the fifth vote in *Glucksberg* subject to the caveat that, while assisted suicide is not a legal right, there is a legal right to pain killing medication even if that medication hastens the time of death.

4. Justice Souter surveys the entire history of substantive due process and presents his own take on the subject. We have edited out more than we have left in. According to Justice Souter, how are judges to weigh and evaluate the various interests at stake in substantive due process cases? What, in his account, makes a government regulation reasonable? A standard objection to substantive due process is that it sets up judges as super-legislatures, engaged in policy judgments rather than ascertainment of legal meaning. Will Justice Souter's discussion set at ease the minds of those who hold this objection?

5. Is the right to help someone commit suicide a privilege or immunity of citizenship? Is the right to have someone help you kill yourself a privilege or immunity of citizenship?

[Assignment 72]

XIV. SEXUAL ORIENTATION DISCRIMINATION

As recently as 1960, all fifty States had laws criminalizing sexual relationships among same-sex couples, be they gay men or lesbian women. Homosexuality was classified as a mental disorder, and gays and lesbians faced persecution in every way imaginable. The rise of feminism in the 1960s began to cause people to see that sexuality was not a binary phenomenon of male men and female women but was instead a spectrum. The translation of those ideas into constitutional law that regards sexuality as a classification calling for more than perfunctory "rational basis" review was slow but real, as you will see in the following cases. We begin with an old substantive due process case and then follow with two later opinions that have more of an equal protection rationale. The line between equal protection cases and substantive due process cases is particularly hard to draw clearly in this context; the Court applies essentially the same tiers and principles of review under both lines of doctrine.

A. BOWERS V. HARDWICK

478 U.S. 186 (1986)

■ JUSTICE WHITE delivered the opinion of the Court.

In August, 1982, respondent Hardwick (hereafter respondent) was charged with violating the Georgia statute criminalizing sodomy by committing that act with another adult male in the bedroom of respondent's home. After a preliminary hearing, the District Attorney decided not to present the matter to the grand jury unless further evidence developed.

Respondent then brought suit in the Federal District Court, challenging the constitutionality of the statute insofar as it criminalized consensual sodomy. He asserted that he was a practicing homosexual, that the Georgia sodomy statute, as administered by the defendants, placed him in imminent danger of arrest, and that the statute for several reasons violates the Federal Constitution. The District Court granted the defendants' motion to dismiss for failure to state a claim, relying on *Doe v. Commonwealth's Attorney for the City of Richmond,* 403 F. Supp. 1199 (ED Va.1975), which this Court summarily affirmed, 425 U.S. 901 (1976).

A divided panel of the Court of Appeals for the Eleventh Circuit reversed * * *. Relying on our decisions in *Griswold v. Connecticut,* 381 U.S. 479 (1965); *Eisenstadt v. Baird,* 405 U.S. 438 (1972); *Stanley v. Georgia,* 394 U.S. 557 (1969); and *Roe v. Wade,* 410 U.S. 113 (1973), the court went on to hold that the Georgia statute violated respondent's fundamental rights because his homosexual activity is a private and intimate association that is beyond the reach of state regulation by reason of the Ninth Amendment and the Due Process Clause of the Fourteenth Amendment * * *.

Because other Courts of Appeals have arrived at judgments contrary to that of the Eleventh Circuit in this case, we granted the Attorney General's petition for certiorari questioning the holding that the sodomy statute violates the fundamental rights of homosexuals. We agree with petitioner that the Court of Appeals erred, and hence reverse its judgment.

This case does not require a judgment on whether laws against sodomy between consenting adults in general, or between homosexuals in particular, are wise or desirable. It raises no question about the right or propriety of state legislative decisions to repeal their laws that criminalize homosexual sodomy, or of state-court decisions invalidating those laws on state constitutional grounds. The issue presented is whether the Federal Constitution confers a fundamental right upon homosexuals to engage in sodomy and hence invalidates the laws of the many States that still make such conduct illegal and have done so for a very long time. The case also calls for some judgment about the limits of the Court's role in carrying out its constitutional mandate.

We first register our disagreement with the Court of Appeals and with respondent that the Court's prior cases have construed the Constitution to confer a right of privacy that extends to homosexual sodomy and, for all intents and purposes have decided this case. The reach of this line of cases was sketched in *Carey v. Population Services International,* 431 U.S. 678, 685 (1977). *Pierce v. Society of Sisters,* 268 U.S. 510 (1925), and *Meyer v. Nebraska,* 262 U.S. 390 (1923), were described as dealing with childrearing and education; *Prince v. Massachusetts,* 321 U.S. 158 (1944), with family relationships; *Skinner v. Oklahoma ex rel. Williamson,* 316 U.S. 535 (1942), with procreation; *Loving v. Virginia,* 388 U.S. 1 (1967), with marriage; *Griswold v. Connecticut, supra,* and *Eisenstadt v. Baird, supra,* with contraception; and *Roe v. Wade,* 410 U.S. 113 (1973), with abortion. The latter three cases were interpreted as construing the Due Process Clause of the Fourteenth Amendment to confer a fundamental individual right to decide whether or not to beget or bear a child.

* * * [N]one of the rights announced in those cases bears any resemblance to the claimed constitutional right of homosexuals to engage in acts of sodomy that is asserted in this case. No connection between family, marriage, or procreation on the one hand and homosexual activity on the other has been demonstrated, either by the Court of Appeals or by respondent. Moreover, any claim that these cases nevertheless stand for the proposition that any kind of private sexual conduct between consenting adults is constitutionally insulated from state proscription is unsupportable * * *.

Precedent aside, however, respondent would have us announce, as the Court of Appeals did, a fundamental right to engage in homosexual sodomy. This we are quite unwilling to do. It is true that despite the language of the Due Process Clauses of the Fifth and Fourteenth Amendments, which appears to focus only on the processes by which life, liberty, or property is taken, the cases are legion in which those Clauses have been interpreted to have substantive content, subsuming rights that to a great extent are immune from federal or state regulation or proscription. Among such cases are those recognizing rights that have little or no textual support in the constitutional language. *Meyer, Prince,* and *Pierce* fall in this category, as do the privacy cases from *Griswold* to *Carey.*

Striving to assure itself and the public that announcing rights not readily identifiable in the Constitution's text involves much more than the imposition of the Justices' own choice of values on the States and the Federal Government, the Court has sought to identify the nature of the rights qualifying for heightened judicial protection. In *Palko v. Connecticut,* 302 U.S. 319, 325, 326 (1937), it was said that this category includes those fundamental liberties that are "implicit in the concept of ordered liberty," such that "neither liberty nor justice would exist if [they] were sacrificed." A different description of fundamental liberties appeared in *Moore v. East Cleveland,* 431 U.S. 494, 503 (1977) (opinion of POWELL, J.), where they are characterized as those liberties that are "deeply rooted in this Nation's history and tradition." *Id.* at 503 (POWELL, J.).

It is obvious to us that neither of these formulations would extend a fundamental right to homosexuals to engage in acts of consensual sodomy. Proscriptions against that conduct have ancient roots. Sodomy was a criminal offense at common law, and was forbidden by the laws of the original 13 States when they ratified the Bill of Rights. In 1868, when the Fourteenth Amendment was ratified, all but 5 of the 37 States in the Union had criminal sodomy laws. In fact, until 1961, all 50 States outlawed sodomy, and today, 24 States and the District of Columbia continue to provide criminal penalties for sodomy performed in private and between consenting adults. Against this background, to claim that a right to engage in such conduct is "deeply rooted in this Nation's history and tradition" or "implicit in the concept of ordered liberty" is, at best, facetious.

Nor are we inclined to take a more expansive view of our authority to discover new fundamental rights imbedded in the Due Process Clause. The Court is most vulnerable and comes nearest to illegitimacy when it deals with judge-made constitutional law having little or no cognizable roots in the language or design of the Constitution. That this is so was painfully demonstrated by the face-off between the Executive and the Court in the 1930's, which resulted in the repudiation of much of the substantive gloss that the Court had placed on the Due Process Clauses of the Fifth and Fourteenth Amendments. There should be, therefore, great resistance to expand the substantive reach of those Clauses, particularly if it requires redefining the category of rights deemed to be fundamental. Otherwise, the Judiciary necessarily takes to itself further authority to govern the country without express constitutional authority. The claimed right pressed on us today falls far short of overcoming this resistance.

Respondent, however, asserts that the result should be different where the homosexual conduct occurs in the privacy of the home. He relies on *Stanley v. Georgia,* 394 U.S. 557 (1969), where the Court held that the First Amendment prevents conviction for possessing and reading obscene material in the privacy of one's home: "If the First Amendment means anything, it means that a State has no business telling a man, sitting alone in his house, what books he may read or what films he may watch." *Id.* at 565.

Stanley did protect conduct that would not have been protected outside the home, and it partially prevented the enforcement of state obscenity laws; but the decision was firmly grounded in the First Amendment. The right pressed upon us here has no similar support in the text of the Constitution, and it does not qualify for recognition under the prevailing principles for construing the Fourteenth Amendment. Its limits are also difficult to discern. Plainly enough, otherwise illegal conduct is not always immunized whenever it occurs in the home. Victimless crimes, such as the possession and use of illegal drugs, do not escape the law where they are committed at home. *Stanley* itself recognized that its holding offered no protection for the possession in the home of drugs, firearms, or stolen goods. *Id.* at 568, n. 11. And if respondent's submission is limited to the voluntary sexual conduct between consenting adults, it would be difficult, except by fiat, to limit the claimed right to homosexual conduct while leaving exposed to prosecution adultery, incest, and other sexual crimes even though they are committed in the home. We are unwilling to start down that road.

Even if the conduct at issue here is not a fundamental right, respondent asserts that there must be a rational basis for the law and that there is none in this case other than the presumed belief of a majority of the electorate in Georgia that homosexual sodomy is immoral and unacceptable. This is said to be an inadequate rationale to support the law. The law, however, is constantly based on notions of morality, and if all laws representing essentially moral choices are to be invalidated under the Due Process Clause, the courts will be very busy indeed. Even respondent makes no such claim, but insists that majority sentiments about the morality of homosexuality should be declared inadequate. We do not agree, and are unpersuaded that the sodomy laws of some 25 States should be invalidated on this basis.[8]

Accordingly, the judgment of the Court of Appeals is

Reversed.

■ CHIEF JUSTICE BURGER, concurring. [Omitted.]

■ JUSTICE POWELL, concurring. [Omitted.]

■ JUSTICE BLACKMUN, with whom JUSTICE BRENNAN, JUSTICE MARSHALL, and JUSTICE STEVENS join, dissenting.

This case is no more about "a fundamental right to engage in homosexual sodomy," as the Court purports to declare, than *Stanley v. Georgia,* 394 U.S. 557 (1969), was about a fundamental right to watch obscene movies, or *Katz v. United States,* 389 U.S. 347 (1967), was about a fundamental right to place interstate bets from a telephone booth. Rather, this case is about "the most comprehensive of rights and the right most valued by civilized men," namely, "the right to be let alone." *Olmstead v. United States,* 277 U.S. 438, 478 (1928) (Brandeis, J., dissenting).

The statute at issue denies individuals the right to decide for themselves whether to engage in particular forms of private, consensual sexual activity. The Court concludes that * * * "the laws of . . . many States . . . still make such conduct illegal and have done so for a very long time." But the fact that the moral judgments expressed by statutes * * * may be " 'natural and familiar . . . ought not to conclude our judgment upon the question whether statutes embodying them conflict with the Constitution of the United States.' " *Roe v. Wade,* 410 U.S. 113, 117 (1973), quoting *Lochner v. New York,* 198 U.S. 45, 76 (1905) (Holmes, J., dissenting). Like Justice Holmes, I believe that "[i]t is revolting to have no better reason for a rule of law than that so it was laid down in the time of Henry IV. It is still more revolting if the grounds upon which it was laid down have vanished long since, and the rule simply persists from blind imitation of the past." Holmes, The Path of the Law, 10 Harv.L.Rev. 457, 469 (1897). I believe we must analyze Hardwick's claim in the light of the values that underlie the constitutional right to privacy. If that right means anything, it means that, before Georgia can prosecute its citizens for making choices

---

[8] Respondent does not defend the judgment below based on the Ninth Amendment, the Equal Protection Clause, or the Eighth Amendment.

about the most intimate aspects of their lives, it must do more than assert that the choice they have made is an " 'abominable crime not fit to be named among Christians.' " *Herring v. State,* 119 Ga. 709, 721, 46 S.E. 876, 882 (1904).

* * *

The Court concludes today that none of our prior cases dealing with various decisions that individuals are entitled to make free of governmental interference "bears any resemblance to the claimed constitutional right of homosexuals to engage in acts of sodomy that is asserted in this case." While it is true that these cases may be characterized by their connection to protection of the family, the Court's conclusion that they extend no further than this boundary ignores the warning in *Moore v. East Cleveland,* 431 U.S. 494, 501 (1977) (plurality opinion), against "clos[ing] our eyes to the basic reasons why certain rights associated with the family have been accorded shelter under the Fourteenth Amendment's Due Process Clause." We protect those rights not because they contribute, in some direct and material way, to the general public welfare, but because they form so central a part of an individual's life * * *. And so we protect the decision whether to marry precisely because marriage "is an association that promotes a way of life, not causes; a harmony in living, not political faiths; a bilateral loyalty, not commercial or social projects." *Griswold v. Connecticut,* 381 U.S., at 486. We protect the decision whether to have a child because parenthood alters so dramatically an individual's self-definition, not because of demographic considerations or the Bible's command to be fruitful and multiply. And we protect the family because it contributes so powerfully to the happiness of individuals, not because of a preference for stereotypical households * * *.

Only the most willful blindness could obscure the fact that sexual intimacy is "a sensitive, key relationship of human existence, central to family life, community welfare, and the development of human personality." The fact that individuals define themselves in a significant way through their intimate sexual relationships with others suggests, in a Nation as diverse as ours, that there may be many "right" ways of conducting those relationships, and that much of the richness of a relationship will come from the freedom an individual has to *choose* the form and nature of these intensely personal bonds.

* * *

■ JUSTICE STEVENS, with whom JUSTICE BRENNAN and JUSTICE MARSHALL join, dissenting. [Omitted.]

NOTES AND QUESTIONS

1. In 1986, the most promising line of authority for Hardwick and others likely was the "substantive due process" line of cases rather than the Court's equal protection jurisprudence. The law had only recently subjected something as basic as sex discrimination to more than rational basis scrutiny, and the Court had not articulated any clear methodology for determining what kinds of classifications would receive rigorous scrutiny in the future. At the very least, reliance on substantive due process instead was a plausible litigation strategy at that time.

2. Under a caste- or class-based equal protection analysis, this seems like an easy case. The law in question establishes caste and treats people who do not conform to heteronormative sexual mores as second-class citizens, even though they pose no harm

to others or to society. Under a fiduciary analysis, the justifications for unequal treatment based on sexual preference are, to say the least, not apparent. Nobody on the Court in 1986 appeared to have much interest in either of those approaches to the Fourteenth Amendment.

3. As a matter of original meaning, Professor Calabresi maintains that laws that regulate sexuality interfere with people's liberty and their ability to obtain safety and happiness. They are not laws that are justly prescribed for the general good of the whole people. Professor Lawson would very much like for this to be true as a legal matter (as a hard-core libertarian, he thinks it is true as a philosophical matter), but he is not convinced that "morals legislation," as it is known, is categorically outside the police power under the Constitution. He will be very happy if Professor Calabresi turns out to be right, but he does not see it.

4. What modalities of interpretation did the majority employ? What modalities did the dissenting opinion employ? What modalities did nobody employ? Why do you think those absent modalities made no appearance?

5. The five justices in the majority in this case fail to discuss a European Court of Human Rights opinion in *Dudgeon v. United Kingdom* [1981] E.C.H.R., which struck down a U.K. anti-sodomy law in Northern Ireland as a violation of Article 8 of the European Convention on Human Rights, which says that "Everyone has the right to respect for his private and family life, his home and his correspondence." This decision is highly relevant to the question of whether so-called sodomy laws set up a caste or were a form of class legislation. It is sometimes difficult to identify forms of caste and of class legislation. Could consulting the decisions of other constitutional courts in other democratic systems be helpful and useful in this task? What about the decisions of constitutional courts in non-democratic systems?

6. The majority in *Bowers* did not discuss equal protection. If it had, there is no reason to think that it would have applied anything other than rational basis review. Ordinarily, rational basis review is simply another term for "the government wins." One of the rare exceptions to that rule was *Romer v. Evans,* 517 U.S. 620 (1996). After some of the biggest cities and counties in Colorado adopted antidiscrimination ordinances that included sexual preference as a protected category, Colorado voters amended the state constitution by referendum to say:

> No Protected Status Based on Homosexual, Lesbian, or Bisexual Orientation. Neither the State of Colorado, through any of its branches or departments, nor any of its agencies, political subdivisions, municipalities or school districts, shall enact, adopt or enforce any statute, regulation, ordinance or policy whereby homosexual, lesbian or bisexual orientation, conduct, practices or relationships shall constitute or otherwise be the basis of or entitle any person or class of persons to have or claim any minority status, quota preferences, protected status or claim of discrimination. This Section of the Constitution shall be in all respects self executing.

The measure was challenged on constitutional grounds. In an opinion by Justice Kennedy, the Court found the measure unconstitutional because it lacked even a rational basis:

> The Fourteenth Amendment's promise that no person shall be denied the equal protection of the laws must coexist with the practical necessity that most legislation classifies for one purpose or another, with resulting disadvantage to various groups or persons. We have attempted to reconcile the principle with the reality by stating that, if a law neither burdens a fundamental right nor

targets a suspect class, we will uphold the legislative classification so long as it bears a rational relation to some legitimate end.

Amendment 2 fails, indeed defies, even this conventional inquiry. First, the amendment has the peculiar property of imposing a broad and undifferentiated disability on a single named group, an exceptional and, as we shall explain, invalid form of legislation. Second, its sheer breadth is so discontinuous with the reasons offered for it that the amendment seems inexplicable by anything but animus toward the class that it affects; it lacks a rational relationship to legitimate state interests.

Taking the first point, even in the ordinary equal protection case calling for the most deferential of standards, we insist on knowing the relation between the classification adopted and the object to be attained. The search for the link between classification and objective gives substance to the Equal Protection Clause * * *. By requiring that the classification bear a rational relationship to an independent and legitimate legislative end, we ensure that classifications are not drawn for the purpose of disadvantaging the group burdened by the law. * * *

Amendment 2 confounds this normal process of judicial review. It is at once too narrow and too broad. It identifies persons by a single trait and then denies them protection across the board. The resulting disqualification of a class of persons from the right to seek specific protection from the law is unprecedented in our jurisprudence. The absence of precedent for Amendment 2 is itself instructive; "[d]iscriminations of an unusual character especially suggest careful consideration to determine whether they are obnoxious to the constitutional provision."

It is not within our constitutional tradition to enact laws of this sort. Central both to the idea of the rule of law and to our own Constitution's guarantee of equal protection is the principle that government and each of its parts remain open on impartial terms to all who seek its assistance. " 'Equal protection of the laws is not achieved through indiscriminate imposition of inequalities.' " *Sweatt* v. *Painter*, 339 U.S. 629, 635 (1950) (quoting *Shelley* v. *Kraemer*, 334 U.S. 1, 22 (1948)). Respect for this principle explains why laws singling out a certain class of citizens for disfavored legal status or general hardships are rare. A law declaring that in general it shall be more difficult for one group of citizens than for all others to seek aid from the government is itself a denial of equal protection of the laws in the most literal sense * * *.

* * *

A second and related point is that laws of the kind now before us raise the inevitable inference that the disadvantage imposed is born of animosity toward the class of persons affected * * *. Even laws enacted for broad and ambitious purposes often can be explained by reference to legitimate public policies which justify the incidental disadvantages they impose on certain persons. Amendment 2, however, in making a general announcement that gays and lesbians shall not have any particular protections from the law, inflicts on them immediate, continuing, and real injuries that outrun and belie any legitimate justifications that may be claimed for it. We conclude that, in addition to the far-reaching deficiencies of Amendment 2 that we have noted, the principles it offends, in another sense, are conventional and venerable; a law must bear a

> rational relationship to a legitimate governmental purpose, and Amendment 2 does not.
>
> * * *
>
> We must conclude that Amendment 2 classifies homosexuals not to further a proper legislative end but to make them unequal to everyone else. This Colorado cannot do. A State cannot so deem a class of persons a stranger to its laws. Amendment 2 violates the Equal Protection Clause, and the judgment of the Supreme Court of Colorado is affirmed.

517 U.S. at 631–36. Justice Scalia wrote a lengthy dissent, which we cannot reproduce here, which began and ended as follows:

> The Court has mistaken a Kulturkampf for a fit of spite. The constitutional amendment before us here is not the manifestation of a " 'bare . . . desire to harm' " homosexuals but is rather a modest attempt by seemingly tolerant Coloradans to preserve traditional sexual mores against the efforts of a politically powerful minority to revise those mores through use of the laws. That objective, and the means chosen to achieve it, are not only unimpeachable under any constitutional doctrine hitherto pronounced (hence the opinion's heavy reliance upon principles of righteousness rather than judicial holdings); they have been specifically approved by the Congress of the United States and by this Court.
>
> * * *
>
> When the Court takes sides in the culture wars, it tends to be with the knights rather than the villeins—and more specifically with the Templars, reflecting the views and values of the lawyer class from which the Court's Members are drawn. How that class feels about homosexuality will be evident to anyone who wishes to interview job applicants at virtually any of the Nation's law schools. The interviewer may refuse to offer a job because the applicant is a Republican; because he is an adulterer; because he went to the wrong prep school or belongs to the wrong country club; because he eats snails; because he is a womanizer; because she wears real-animal fur; or even because he hates the Chicago Cubs. But if the interviewer should wish not to be an associate or partner of an applicant because he disapproves of the applicant's homosexuality, *then* he will have violated the pledge which the Association of American Law Schools requires all its member schools to exact from job interviewers: "assurance of the employer's willingness" to hire homosexuals. Bylaws of the Association of American Law Schools, Inc. § 6–4(b); Executive Committee Regulations of the Association of American Law Schools § 6.19, in 1995 Handbook, Association of American Law Schools. This law-school view of what "prejudices" must be stamped out may be contrasted with the more plebeian attitudes that apparently still prevail in the United States Congress, which has been unresponsive to repeated attempts to extend to homosexuals the protections of federal civil rights laws, see, *e.g.*, Employment Non-Discrimination Act of 1994, S. 2238, 103d Cong., 2d Sess. (1994); Civil Rights Amendments of 1975, H.R. 5452, 94th Cong., 1st Sess. (1975), and which took the pains to exclude them specifically from the Americans with Disabilities Act of 1990, see 42 U.S.C. § 12211(a) (1988 ed., Supp. V).
>
> Today's opinion has no foundation in American constitutional law, and barely pretends to. The people of Colorado have adopted an entirely reasonable provision which does not even disfavor homosexuals in any substantive sense,

> but merely denies them preferential treatment. Amendment 2 is designed to prevent piecemeal deterioration of the sexual morality favored by a majority of Coloradans, and is not only an appropriate means to that legitimate end, but a means that Americans have employed before. Striking it down is an act, not of judicial judgment, but of political will. I dissent.

517 U.S. at 636, 652–53 (Scalia, J., dissenting). It seemed to many people as though the majority was employing a standard of review much more rigorous than garden-variety rational basis review. While the majority conspicuously did not say that sexual orientation was a specially protected class under equal protection or that the practice of homosexuality was a fundamental right, the analysis in *Romer* was more consistent with either of those positions than with their opposites. It was not surprising to many observers when the next case came down in 2003.

B. LAWRENCE V. TEXAS

539 U.S. 558 (2003)

■ JUSTICE KENNEDY delivered the opinion of the Court.

Liberty protects the person from unwarranted government intrusions into a dwelling or other private places. In our tradition the State is not omnipresent in the home. And there are other spheres of our lives and existence, outside the home, where the State should not be a dominant presence. Freedom extends beyond spatial bounds. Liberty presumes an autonomy of self that includes freedom of thought, belief, expression, and certain intimate conduct. The instant case involves liberty of the person both in its spatial and more transcendent dimensions.

The question before the Court is the validity of a Texas statute making it a crime for two persons of the same sex to engage in certain intimate sexual conduct.

In Houston, Texas, officers of the Harris County Police Department were dispatched to a private residence in response to a reported weapons disturbance. They entered an apartment where one of the petitioners, John Geddes Lawrence, resided. The right of the police to enter does not seem to have been questioned. The officers observed Lawrence and another man, Tyron Garner, engaging in a sexual act. The two petitioners were arrested, held in custody overnight, and charged and convicted before a Justice of the Peace.

The complaints described their crime as "deviate sexual intercourse, namely anal sex, with a member of the same sex (man)." The applicable state law is Tex. Penal Code Ann. § 21.06(a) (2003). It provides: "A person commits an offense if he engages in deviate sexual intercourse with another individual of the same sex." The statute defines "[d]eviate sexual intercourse" as follows:

> "(A) any contact between any part of the genitals of one person and the mouth or anus of another person; or
>
> "(B) the penetration of the genitals or the anus of another person with an object." § 21.01(1).

The petitioners exercised their right to a trial *de novo* in Harris County Criminal Court. They challenged the statute as a violation of the Equal Protection Clause of the Fourteenth Amendment and of a like provision of the Texas Constitution. Tex. Const., Art. 1, § 3a. Those contentions were rejected. The petitioners, having entered a plea of *nolo contendere*, were each fined $200 and assessed court costs of $141.25.

The Court of Appeals for the Texas Fourteenth District considered the petitioners' federal constitutional arguments under both the Equal Protection and Due Process Clauses of the Fourteenth Amendment. After hearing the case en banc the court, in a divided opinion, rejected the constitutional arguments and affirmed the convictions. The majority opinion indicates that the Court of Appeals considered our decision in *Bowers* v. *Hardwick,* 478 U.S. 186 (1986), to be controlling on the federal due process aspect of the case. *Bowers* then being authoritative, this was proper.

We granted certiorari to consider three questions:

> 1. Whether Petitioners' criminal convictions under the Texas "Homosexual Conduct" law—which criminalizes sexual intimacy by same-sex couples, but not identical behavior by different-sex couples—violate the Fourteenth Amendment guarantee of equal protection of laws?
>
> 2. Whether Petitioners' criminal convictions for adult consensual sexual intimacy in the home violate their vital interests in liberty and privacy protected by the Due Process Clause of the Fourteenth Amendment?
>
> 3. Whether *Bowers* v. *Hardwick*, 478 U.S. 186 (1986), should be overruled? Pet. for Cert. i.

The petitioners were adults at the time of the alleged offense. Their conduct was in private and consensual.

We conclude the case should be resolved by determining whether the petitioners were free as adults to engage in the private conduct in the exercise of their liberty under the Due Process Clause of the Fourteenth Amendment to the Constitution. For this inquiry we deem it necessary to reconsider the Court's holding in *Bowers*.

There are broad statements of the substantive reach of liberty under the Due Process Clause in earlier cases, including *Pierce* v. *Society of Sisters,* 268 U.S. 510 (1925), and *Meyer* v. *Nebraska,* 262 U.S. 390 (1923); but the most pertinent beginning point is our decision in *Griswold* v. *Connecticut,* 381 U.S. 479 (1965).

In *Griswold* the Court invalidated a state law prohibiting the use of drugs or devices of contraception and counseling or aiding and abetting the use of contraceptives. The Court described the protected interest as a right to privacy and placed emphasis on the marriage relation and the protected space of the marital bedroom.

After *Griswold* it was established that the right to make certain decisions regarding sexual conduct extends beyond the marital relationship. In *Eisenstadt* v. *Baird,* 405 U.S. 438 (1972), the Court invalidated a law prohibiting the distribution of contraceptives to unmarried persons * * *.

The opinions in *Griswold* and *Eisenstadt* were part of the background for the decision in *Roe* v. *Wade,* 410 U.S. 113 (1973). As is well known, the case involved a challenge to the Texas law prohibiting abortions, but the laws of other States were affected as well. Although the Court held the woman's rights were not absolute, her right to elect an abortion did have real and substantial protection as an exercise of her liberty under the Due Process Clause. The Court cited cases that protect spatial freedom and cases that go well beyond it. *Roe* recognized the right of a woman to make certain fundamental decisions affecting her destiny and confirmed once more that the protection of liberty under the Due Process Clause has a substantive dimension of fundamental significance in defining the rights of the person.

* * * This was the state of the law with respect to some of the most relevant cases when the Court considered *Bowers* v. *Hardwick*.

* * *

The Court began its substantive discussion in *Bowers* as follows: "The issue presented is whether the Federal Constitution confers a fundamental right upon homosexuals to engage in sodomy and hence invalidates the laws of the many States that still make such conduct illegal and have done so for a very long time." *Id.,* at 190. That statement, we now conclude, discloses the Court's own failure to appreciate the extent of the liberty at stake. To say that the issue in *Bowers* was simply the right to engage in certain sexual conduct demeans the claim the individual put forward, just as it would demean a married couple were it to be said marriage is simply about the right to have sexual intercourse. The laws involved in *Bowers* and here are, to be sure, statutes that purport to do no more than prohibit a particular sexual act. Their penalties and purposes, though, have more far-reaching consequences, touching upon the most private human conduct, sexual behavior, and in the most private of places, the home. The statutes do seek to control a personal relationship that, whether or not entitled to formal recognition in the law, is within the liberty of persons to choose without being punished as criminals.

This, as a general rule, should counsel against attempts by the State, or a court, to define the meaning of the relationship or to set its boundaries absent injury to a person or abuse of an institution the law protects. It suffices for us to acknowledge that adults may choose to enter upon this relationship in the confines of their homes and their own private lives and still retain their dignity as free persons. When sexuality finds overt expression in intimate conduct with another person, the conduct can be but one element in a personal bond that is more enduring. The liberty protected by the Constitution allows homosexual persons the right to make this choice.

* * *

At the outset it should be noted that there is no longstanding history in this country of laws directed at homosexual conduct as a distinct matter * * *. [E]arly American sodomy laws were not directed at homosexuals as such but instead sought to prohibit nonprocreative sexual activity more generally. This does not suggest approval of homosexual conduct. It does tend to show that this particular form of conduct was not thought of as a separate category from like conduct between heterosexual persons.

* * *

It was not until the 1970's that any State singled out same-sex relations for criminal prosecution, and only nine States have done so * * *.

In summary, the historical grounds relied upon in *Bowers* are more complex than the majority opinion and the concurring opinion by Chief Justice Burger indicate. Their historical premises are not without doubt and, at the very least, are overstated.

It must be acknowledged, of course, that the Court in *Bowers* was making the broader point that for centuries there have been powerful voices to condemn homosexual conduct as immoral. The condemnation has been shaped by religious beliefs, conceptions of right and acceptable behavior, and respect for the traditional family. For many persons these are not trivial concerns but profound and deep convictions accepted as ethical and moral principles to which they aspire and which thus determine the course of their lives. These considerations do not answer the question before us, however. The issue is whether the majority may use the power of the State to enforce these views on the whole society through operation of the criminal law. "Our obligation is to define the liberty of all, not to mandate our own moral code." *Planned Parenthood of Southeastern Pa.* v. *Casey,* 505 U.S. 833, 850 (1992).

* * *

* * *[A]lmost five years before *Bowers* was decided the European Court of Human Rights considered a case with parallels to *Bowers* and to today's case. An adult male resident in Northern Ireland alleged he was a practicing homosexual who desired to engage in consensual homosexual conduct. The laws of Northern Ireland forbade him that right. He alleged that he had been questioned, his home had been searched, and he feared criminal prosecution. The court held that the laws proscribing the conduct were invalid under the European Convention on Human Rights. *Dudgeon* v. *United Kingdom,* 45 Eur. Ct. H. R. (1981) ¶ 52. Authoritative in all countries that are members of the Council of Europe (21 nations then, 45 nations now), the decision is at odds with the premise in *Bowers* that the claim put forward was insubstantial in our Western civilization.

In our own constitutional system the deficiencies in *Bowers* became even more apparent in the years following its announcement. The 25 States with laws prohibiting the relevant conduct referenced in the *Bowers* decision are reduced now to 13, of which 4 enforce their laws only against homosexual conduct. In those States where sodomy is still proscribed, whether for same-sex or heterosexual conduct, there is a pattern of nonenforcement with respect to consenting adults acting in private. The State of Texas admitted in 1994 that as of that date it had not prosecuted anyone under those circumstances.

Two principal cases decided after *Bowers* cast its holding into even more doubt. In *Planned Parenthood of Southeastern Pa.* v. *Casey,* 505 U.S. 833 (1992), the Court reaffirmed the substantive force of the liberty protected by the Due Process Clause * * *. Persons in a homosexual relationship may seek autonomy for these purposes, just as heterosexual persons do. The decision in *Bowers* would deny them this right.

The second post-*Bowers* case of principal relevance is *Romer* v. *Evans,* 517 U.S. 620 (1996). There the Court struck down class-based legislation directed at homosexuals as a violation of the Equal Protection Clause. *Romer* invalidated an amendment to Colorado's Constitution which named as a solitary class persons who were homosexuals, lesbians, or bisexual either by "orientation, conduct, practices or relationships," *id.,* at 624, and deprived them of protection under state antidiscrimination laws. We concluded that the provision was "born of animosity toward the class of persons affected" and further that it had no rational relation to a legitimate governmental purpose. *Id.,* at 634.

As an alternative argument in this case, counsel for the petitioners and some *amici* contend that *Romer* provides the basis for declaring the Texas statute invalid under the Equal Protection Clause. That is a tenable argument, but we conclude the instant case requires us to address whether *Bowers* itself has continuing validity. Were we to hold the statute invalid under the Equal Protection Clause some might question whether a prohibition would be valid if drawn differently, say, to prohibit the conduct both between same-sex and different-sex participants.

* * *

The foundations of *Bowers* have sustained serious erosion from our recent decisions in *Casey* and *Romer*. When our precedent has been thus weakened, criticism from other sources is of greater significance. In the United States criticism of *Bowers* has been substantial and continuing, disapproving of its reasoning in all respects, not just as to its historical assumptions. See, *e.g.*, C. Fried, Order and Law: Arguing the Reagan Revolution—A Firsthand Account 81–84 (1991); R. Posner, Sex and Reason 341–350 (1992). The courts of five different States have declined to follow it in interpreting provisions in their own state constitutions parallel to the Due Process Clause of the Fourteenth Amendment, see *Jegley* v. *Picado*, 349 Ark. 600, 80 S. W. 3d 332 (2002); *Powell* v. *State*, 270 Ga. 327, 510 S. E. 2d 18, 24 (1998); *Gryczan* v. *State*, 283 Mont. 433, 942 P.2d 112 (1997); *Campbell* v. *Sundquist*, 926 S. W. 2d 250 (Tenn. App. 1996); *Commonwealth* v. *Wasson*, 842 S. W. 2d 487 (Ky. 1992).

To the extent *Bowers* relied on values we share with a wider civilization, it should be noted that the reasoning and holding in *Bowers* have been rejected elsewhere. The European Court of Human Rights has followed not *Bowers* but its own decision in *Dudgeon* v. *United Kingdom*. See *P. G. & J. H.* v. *United Kingdom*, App. No. 00044787/98, ¶ 56 (Eur. Ct. H. R., Sept. 25, 2001); *Modinos* v. *Cyprus*, 259 Eur. Ct. H. R. (1993); *Norris* v. *Ireland*, 142 Eur. Ct. H. R. (1988). Other nations, too, have taken action consistent with an affirmation of the protected right of homosexual adults to engage in intimate, consensual conduct. The right the petitioners seek in this case has been accepted as an integral part of human freedom in many other countries. There has been no showing that in this country the governmental interest in circumscribing personal choice is somehow more legitimate or urgent.

The doctrine of *stare decisis* is essential to the respect accorded to the judgments of the Court and to the stability of the law. It is not, however, an inexorable command * * *.

The rationale of *Bowers* does not withstand careful analysis * * *.

Bowers was not correct when it was decided, and it is not correct today. It ought not to remain binding precedent. *Bowers* v. *Hardwick* should be and now is overruled.

The present case does not involve minors. It does not involve persons who might be injured or coerced or who are situated in relationships where consent might not easily be refused. It does not involve public conduct or prostitution. It does not involve whether the government must give formal recognition to any relationship that homosexual persons seek to enter. The case does involve two adults who, with full and mutual consent from each other, engaged in sexual practices common to a homosexual lifestyle. The petitioners are entitled to respect for their private lives. The State cannot demean their existence or control their destiny by making their private sexual conduct a crime. Their right to liberty under the Due Process Clause gives them the full right to engage in their conduct without intervention of the government. "It is a promise of the Constitution that there is a realm of personal liberty which the government may not enter." *Casey*, *supra*, at 847. The Texas statute furthers no legitimate state interest which can justify its intrusion into the personal and private life of the individual.

Had those who drew and ratified the Due Process Clauses of the Fifth Amendment or the Fourteenth Amendment known the components of liberty in its manifold possibilities, they might have been more specific. They did not presume to have this insight. They knew times can blind us to certain truths and later generations can see that laws once thought necessary and proper in fact serve only to oppress. As the Constitution endures, persons in every generation can invoke its principles in their own search for greater freedom.

The judgment of the Court of Appeals for the Texas Fourteenth District is reversed, and the case is remanded for further proceedings not inconsistent with this opinion.

It is so ordered.

■ JUSTICE O'CONNOR, concurring in the judgment.

The Court today overrules *Bowers v. Hardwick,* 478 U.S. 186 (1986). I joined *Bowers,* and do not join the Court in overruling it. Nevertheless, I agree with the Court that Texas' statute banning same-sex sodomy is unconstitutional. Rather than relying on the substantive component of the Fourteenth Amendment's Due Process Clause, as the Court does, I base my conclusion on the Fourteenth Amendment's Equal Protection Clause.

* * *

This case raises a different issue than *Bowers:* whether, under the Equal Protection Clause, moral disapproval is a legitimate state interest to justify by itself a statute that bans homosexual sodomy, but not heterosexual sodomy. It is not. Moral disapproval of this group, like a bare desire to harm the group, is an interest that is insufficient to satisfy rational basis review under the Equal Protection Clause. See, *e.g., Department of Agriculture v. Moreno,* 413 U.S., at 534; *Romer v. Evans,* 517 U.S., at 634–635. Indeed, we have never held that moral disapproval, without any other asserted state interest, is a sufficient rationale under the Equal Protection Clause to justify a law that discriminates among groups of persons.

* * *

■ JUSTICE SCALIA, with whom THE CHIEF JUSTICE and JUSTICE THOMAS join, dissenting.

"Liberty finds no refuge in a jurisprudence of doubt." *Planned Parenthood of Southeastern Pa.* v. *Casey*, 505 U.S. 833, 844 (1992). That was the Court's sententious response, barely more than a decade ago, to those seeking to overrule *Roe* v. *Wade*, 410 U.S. 113 (1973). The Court's response today, to those who have engaged in a 17-year crusade to overrule *Bowers* v. *Hardwick*, 478 U.S. 186 (1986), is very different. The need for stability and certainty presents no barrier.

Most of the rest of today's opinion has no relevance to its actual holding—that the Texas statute "furthers no legitimate state interest which can justify" its application to petitioners under rational-basis review. Though there is discussion of "fundamental proposition[s]" and "fundamental decisions," nowhere does the Court's opinion declare that homosexual sodomy is a "fundamental right" under the Due Process Clause; nor does it subject the Texas law to the standard of review that would be appropriate (strict scrutiny) if homosexual sodomy *were* a "fundamental right."

Thus, while overruling the *outcome* of *Bowers*, the Court leaves strangely untouched its central legal conclusion: "[R]espondent would have us announce . . . a fundamental right to engage in homosexual sodomy. This we are quite unwilling to do." 478 U.S., at 191. Instead the Court simply describes petitioners' conduct as "an exercise of their liberty"—which it undoubtedly is—and proceeds to apply an unheard-of form of rational-basis review that will have far-reaching implications beyond this case.

I begin with the Court's surprising readiness to reconsider a decision rendered a mere 17 years ago in *Bowers* v. *Hardwick*. I do not myself believe in rigid adherence to *stare decisis* in constitutional cases; but I do believe that we should be consistent rather than manipulative in invoking the doctrine. Today's opinions in support of reversal do not bother to distinguish—or indeed, even bother to mention—the paean to *stare decisis* coauthored by three Members of today's majority in *Planned Parenthood* v. *Casey*. There, when *stare decisis* meant preservation of judicially invented abortion rights, the widespread criticism of *Roe* was strong reason to *reaffirm* it * * * Today, however, the widespread opposition to *Bowers*, a decision resolving an issue as "intensely divisive" as the issue in *Roe*, is offered as a reason in favor of *overruling* it * * *.

* * *

* * * Countless judicial decisions and legislative enactments have relied on the ancient proposition that a governing majority's belief that certain sexual behavior is "immoral and unacceptable" constitutes a rational basis for regulation. See, *e.g.*, *Williams* v. *Pryor*, 240 F.3d 944, 949 (CA11 2001) (citing *Bowers* in upholding Alabama's prohibition on the sale of sex toys on the ground that "[t]he crafting and safeguarding of public morality . . . indisputably is a legitimate government interest under rational basis scrutiny"); *Milner* v. *Apfel*, 148 F.3d 812, 814 (CA7 1998) (citing *Bowers* for the proposition that "[l]egislatures are permitted to legislate with regard to morality . . . rather than confined to preventing demonstrable harms"); *Holmes* v. *California Army National Guard* 124 F.3d 1126, 1136 (CA9 1997) (relying on *Bowers* in upholding the federal statute and regulations banning from military service those who engage in homosexual conduct); *Owens* v. *State*, 352 Md. 663, 683, 724 A. 2d 43, 53 (1999) (relying on *Bowers* in holding that "a person has no constitutional right to engage in sexual intercourse, at least outside of marriage"); *Sherman* v. *Henry*, 928 S. W. 2d 464, 469–473 (Tex. 1996) (relying on *Bowers* in rejecting a claimed constitutional right to commit adultery). We ourselves relied extensively on *Bowers* when we concluded, in *Barnes* v. *Glen Theatre, Inc.*, 501 U.S. 560, 569 (1991), that Indiana's public indecency statute furthered "a substantial government interest in protecting order and morality," *ibid.*, (plurality opinion); see also *id.*, at 575 (SCALIA, J., concurring in judgment). State laws against bigamy, same-sex marriage, adult incest, prostitution, masturbation, adultery, fornication, bestiality, and obscenity are likewise sustainable only in light of *Bowers*' validation of laws based on moral choices. Every single one of these laws is called into question by today's decision; the Court makes no effort to cabin the scope of its decision to exclude them from its holding. See *ante*, at 572 (noting "an emerging awareness that liberty gives substantial protection to adult persons in deciding how to conduct their private lives *in matters pertaining to sex*" (emphasis added)). The impossibility of distinguishing homosexuality from other traditional "morals" offenses is precisely why *Bowers* rejected the rational-basis challenge. "The law," it said, "is constantly based on

notions of morality, and if all laws representing essentially moral choices are to be invalidated under the Due Process Clause, the courts will be very busy indeed." 478 U.S., at 196.

What a massive disruption of the current social order, therefore, the overruling of *Bowers* entails * * *.

* * *

Having decided that it need not adhere to *stare decisis*, the Court still must establish that *Bowers* was wrongly decided and that the Texas statute, as applied to petitioners, is unconstitutional.

Texas Penal Code Ann. § 21.06(a) (2003) undoubtedly imposes constraints on liberty. So do laws prohibiting prostitution, recreational use of heroin, and, for that matter, working more than 60 hours per week in a bakery. But there is no right to "liberty" under the Due Process Clause, though today's opinion repeatedly makes that claim. *Ante*, at 567 ("The liberty protected by the Constitution allows homosexual persons the right to make this choice"); *ante*, at 574 (" 'These matters . . . are central to the liberty protected by the Fourteenth Amendment' "); *ante*, at 578 ("Their right to liberty under the Due Process Clause gives them the full right to engage in their conduct without intervention of the government"). The Fourteenth Amendment *expressly allows* States to deprive their citizens of "liberty," *so long as "due process of law" is provided* * * *.

Our opinions applying the doctrine known as "substantive due process" hold that the Due Process Clause prohibits States from infringing *fundamental* liberty interests, unless the infringement is narrowly tailored to serve a compelling state interest. *Washington* v. *Glucksberg*, 521 U.S., at 721. We have held repeatedly, in cases the Court today does not overrule, that *only* fundamental rights qualify for this so-called "heightened scrutiny" protection—that is, rights which are " 'deeply rooted in this Nation's history and tradition,' " *ibid*. See *Reno* v. *Flores*, 507 U.S. 292, 303 (1993) (fundamental liberty interests must be "so rooted in the traditions and conscience of our people as to be ranked as fundamental." All other liberty interests may be abridged or abrogated pursuant to a validly enacted state law if that law is rationally related to a legitimate state interest.

Bowers held, first, that criminal prohibitions of homosexual sodomy are not subject to heightened scrutiny because they do not implicate a "fundamental right" under the Due Process Clause * * *.

The Court today does not overrule this holding. Not once does it describe homosexual sodomy as a "fundamental right" or a "fundamental liberty interest," nor does it subject the Texas statute to strict scrutiny. Instead, having failed to establish that the right to homosexual sodomy is " 'deeply rooted in this Nation's history and tradition,' " the Court concludes that the application of Texas's statute to petitioners' conduct fails the rational-basis test, and overrules *Bowers*' holding to the contrary, see *id.*, at 196. "The Texas statute furthers no legitimate state interest which can justify its intrusion into the personal and private life of the individual." *Ante*, at 578.

* * *

I turn now to the ground on which the Court squarely rests its holding: the contention that there is no rational basis for the law here under attack. This proposition is so out of accord with our jurisprudence—indeed, with the jurisprudence of *any* society we know—that it requires little discussion.

The Texas statute undeniably seeks to further the belief of its citizens that certain forms of sexual behavior are "immoral and unacceptable," *Bowers*, *supra*, at 196—the same interest furthered by criminal laws against fornication, bigamy, adultery, adult incest, bestiality, and obscenity. *Bowers* held that this *was* a legitimate state interest. The Court today reaches the opposite conclusion. The Texas statute, it says, "furthers *no legitimate state interest* which can justify its intrusion into the personal and private life of the individual," *ante*, at 578 (emphasis added). The Court embraces instead JUSTICE STEVENS' declaration in his *Bowers* dissent, that "the fact that the governing majority in a State has traditionally viewed a particular practice as immoral is not a sufficient reason for upholding a law prohibiting the practice." This effectively decrees the end of all morals legislation. If, as the Court asserts, the promotion of majoritarian sexual morality is not even a *legitimate* state interest, none of the above-mentioned laws can survive rational-basis review.

* * *

Today's opinion is the product of a Court, which is the product of a law-profession culture, that has largely signed on to the so-called homosexual agenda, by which I mean the agenda promoted by some homosexual activists directed at eliminating the moral opprobrium that has traditionally attached to homosexual conduct. I noted in an earlier opinion the fact that the American Association of Law Schools (to which any reputable law school *must* seek to belong) excludes from membership any school that refuses to ban from its job-interview facilities a law firm (no matter how small) that does not wish to hire as a prospective partner a person who openly engages in homosexual conduct. See *Romer*, *supra*, at 653.

One of the most revealing statements in today's opinion is the Court's grim warning that the criminalization of homosexual conduct is "an invitation to subject homosexual persons to discrimination both in the public and in the private spheres." It is clear from this that the Court has taken sides in the culture war, departing from its role of assuring, as neutral observer, that the democratic rules of engagement are observed. Many Americans do not want persons who openly engage in homosexual conduct as partners in their business, as scoutmasters for their children, as teachers in their children's schools, or as boarders in their home. They view this as protecting themselves and their families from a lifestyle that they believe to be immoral and destructive. The Court views it as "discrimination" which it is the function of our judgments to deter. So imbued is the Court with the law profession's anti-anti-homosexual culture, that it is seemingly unaware that the attitudes of that culture are not obviously "mainstream"; that in most States what the Court calls "discrimination" against those who engage in homosexual acts is perfectly legal; that proposals to ban such "discrimination" under Title VII have repeatedly been rejected by Congress, see Employment Non-Discrimination Act of 1994, S. 2238, 103d Cong., 2d Sess. (1994); Civil Rights Amendments, H. R. 5452, 94th Cong., 1st Sess. (1975); that in some cases such "discrimination" is *mandated* by federal statute, see 10 U.S.C. § 654(b)(1) (mandating discharge from the armed forces of any service member who engages in or intends to engage in homosexual acts); and that in some cases such "discrimination" is a constitutional right, see *Boy Scouts of America* v. *Dale*, 530 U.S. 640 (2000).

Let me be clear that I have nothing against homosexuals, or any other group, promoting their agenda through normal democratic means. Social perceptions of sexual and other morality change over time, and every group has the right to persuade its fellow citizens that its view of such matters is the best. That homosexuals have achieved some success in that enterprise is attested to by the fact that Texas is one of the few remaining States that criminalize private, consensual homosexual acts. But persuading one's fellow citizens is one thing, and imposing one's views in absence of democratic majority will is something else. I would no more *require* a State to criminalize homosexual acts—or, for that matter, display *any* moral disapprobation of them—than I would *forbid* it to do so. What Texas has chosen to do is well within the range of traditional democratic action, and its hand should not be stayed through the invention of a brand-new "constitutional right" by a Court that is impatient of democratic change. It is indeed true that "later generations can see that laws once thought necessary and proper in fact serve only to oppress," and when that happens, later generations can repeal those laws. But it is the premise of our system that those judgments are to be made by the people, and not imposed by a governing caste that knows best.

One of the benefits of leaving regulation of this matter to the people rather than to the courts is that the people, unlike judges, need not carry things to their logical conclusion. The people may feel that their disapprobation of homosexual conduct is strong enough to disallow homosexual marriage, but not strong enough to criminalize private homosexual acts—and may legislate accordingly. The Court today pretends that it possesses a similar freedom of action, so that that we need not fear judicial imposition of homosexual marriage, as has recently occurred in Canada (in a decision that the Canadian Government has chosen not to appeal). See *Halpern* v. *Toronto*, 2003 WL 34950 (Ontario Ct. App.); Cohen, Dozens in Canada Follow Gay Couple's Lead, Washington Post, June 12, 2003, p. A25. At the end of its opinion—after having laid waste the foundations of our rational-basis jurisprudence—the Court says that the present case "does not involve whether the government must give formal recognition to any relationship that homosexual persons seek to enter." Do not believe it. More illuminating than this bald, unreasoned disclaimer is the progression of thought displayed by an earlier passage in the Court's opinion, which notes the constitutional protections afforded to "personal decisions relating to *marriage*, procreation, contraception, family relationships, child rearing, and education," and then declares that "[p]ersons in a homosexual relationship may seek autonomy for these purposes, just as heterosexual persons do." (emphasis added). Today's opinion dismantles the structure of constitutional law that has permitted a distinction to be made between heterosexual and homosexual unions, insofar as formal recognition in marriage is concerned. If moral disapprobation of homosexual conduct is "no legitimate state interest" for purposes of proscribing that conduct; and if, as the Court coos (casting aside all pretense of neutrality), "[w]hen sexuality finds overt expression in intimate conduct with another person, the conduct can be but one element in a personal bond that is more enduring," what justification could there possibly be for denying the benefits of marriage to homosexual couples exercising "[t]he liberty protected by the Constitution"? Surely not the encouragement of procreation, since the sterile and the elderly are allowed to marry. This case "does not involve" the issue of homosexual marriage only if one entertains the belief that principle and logic have nothing to do with the decisions of this Court. Many will hope that, as the Court comfortingly assures us, this is so.

The matters appropriate for this Court's resolution are only three: Texas's prohibition of sodomy neither infringes a "fundamental right" (which the Court does not dispute), nor is unsupported by a rational relation to what the Constitution considers a legitimate state interest, nor denies the equal protection of the laws. I dissent.

■ JUSTICE THOMAS, dissenting.

I join Justice Scalia's dissenting opinion. I write separately to note that the law before the Court today "is . . . uncommonly silly." *Griswold* v. *Connecticut*, 381 U.S. 479, 527 (1965) (Stewart, J., dissenting). If I were a member of the Texas Legislature, I would vote to repeal it. Punishing someone for expressing his sexual preference through noncommercial consensual conduct with another adult does not appear to be a worthy way to expend valuable law enforcement resources.

Notwithstanding this, I recognize that as a Member of this Court I am not empowered to help petitioners and others similarly situated. My duty, rather, is to "decide cases 'agreeably to the Constitution and laws of the United States.'" *Id.*, at 530. And, just like Justice Stewart, I "can find [neither in the Bill of Rights nor any other part of the Constitution a] general right of privacy," *ibid.*, or as the Court terms it today, the "liberty of the person both in its spatial and more transcendent dimensions."

NOTES AND QUESTIONS

1. You have already seen the next case in this sequence: In *Obergefell v. Hodges,* 135 S.Ct. 2584 (2015), Justice Scalia's prediction in *Lawrence* was realized, as the Court held that any States that recognized marriage—which means all of them—could not deny that status to same-sex couples. *See supra* pages 546–555. Was that an equal protection holding, a substantive due process of law holding, or does it not matter what label to use, given the development of modern doctrine? We have left out most of Justice O'Connor's concurrence in *Lawrence;* she thought there was a material difference between equal protection and substantive due process analysis.

2. Are these cases a triumphant model of substantive due process at its best, or are they simply judicial policymaking in accordance with the preferences of a distinct social class? Justices Scalia and Thomas object to the entire enterprise of substantive due process. Justice Scalia, unlike Justice Thomas, also had no interest in reviving the original meaning of the Privileges or Immunities Clause, as we will see shortly. *See infra* pages 1584–1585. What presents the bigger danger: Emptying the Fourteenth Amendment of much of its meaning and thereby risking legislative and executive overreach or leaving it to judges to police the boundaries of permissible (or required) social policy and thereby risking judicial overreach? Does your answer depend on which presidents you think will be appointing judges over the next few years?

3. How would a case like *Lawrence* be decided under the Privileges or Immunities Clause? There is no doubt at all that sexual choices are central to, in the ubiquitous language of *Corfield v. Coryell,* "the enjoyment of life and liberty" and the ability "to pursue and obtain happiness." This language, as we have repeatedly seen, tracks the Declaration of Independence, which is a cornerstone upon which the Constitution rests, and of the Born Free and Equal Clauses that gave concrete expression to the Declaration's ideals even before the U.S. Constitution. At a minimum, laws like those in *Lawrence* implicate the weak presumption of liberty that is part of the Ancient Constitution. The remaining questions are the same questions that arise in all of these

cases: How strong a justification does the government need to provide when it abridges privileges or immunities, and what kinds of justifications count as legitimate? (And before you conclude too quickly that moral disapproval of conduct can never count as a legitimate justification, consider whether anything *but* moral disapproval lies beneath *any* law, including laws against murder.) As you can see from the foregoing materials, there is nothing even close to a consensus on the modern Court about how to answer either of those questions. For whatever it is worth, your editors, who share a great many methodological commitments, do not wholly agree on how to answer those questions. Professor Calabresi believes that original meaning supports *Lawrence* and *Obergefell*, while Professor Lawson is pretty sure that they are wrong as a matter of original meaning. So at least one of us is mistaken. Professor Lawson would much prefer that it be he who is mistaken, but he doesn't think it is.

[Assignment 73]

XV. THE FIRST CASES THAT INCORPORATED THE BILL OF RIGHTS

The first case in this book was *Barron v. City of Baltimore,* 32 U.S. (7 Pet.) 243 (1833), in which the Court held that the 1791 Bill of Rights limited only the federal government, not the States. *See supra* pages 52–54. Notwithstanding the general language of all of the provisions in the Bill of Rights except the First Amendment, which makes specific reference to "Congress," those amendments are subject to the background rule of interpretation—clear from the Constitution's text, structure, and history—that the Constitution refers only to federal institutions unless it expressly says otherwise. *Barron's* careful legal analysis is very hard to refute. Thus, one might think, at least until 1868, there was no case to be made that the federal Bill of Rights applied to actions of state governments.

One might indeed think that, but a nontrivial number of important people before 1868 thought otherwise. In an era without broad channels of communication, even some lawyers were surely unaware of *Barron*; and if one only looks quickly at the Constitution without reading *Barron*, the generality of the language of the Second through Eighth Amendments stands out, especially in contrast with the decidedly non-general language of the First Amendment. It is very easy to conclude on a casual reading that most of the Bill of Rights applies to the States. Moreover, some prominent antebellum legal actors, including judges, were fully aware of *Barron* but thought it was wrongly decided (and some of them told the Supreme Court that they thought *Barron* was wrongly decided). Akhil Amar elegantly recounts the views of these "*Barron* contrarians" in his magisterial book on the Bill of Rights, from which we have both learned much. *See* AKHIL REED AMAR, THE BILL OF RIGHTS: CREATION AND RECONSTRUCTION 145–62 (1998).

Could both sides in that debate possibly have been right? Chief Justice Marshall's textual and structural analysis in *Barron* was sound, so in a literal sense the 1791 Bill of Rights did not create operative legal norms limiting state governments comparable to the Contracts Clause and other Article I, Section 10 provisions. But, by the same token, it is not at all clear the extent to which the Bill of Rights created operative legal norms limiting the *federal* government. The key word is "created." What did the Bill of Rights actually do? Did it create rights or just highlight them? Could the federal government really restrict freedom of the press, issue general warrants, take property without just compensation, and deprive people of life without due process of law for the entire period between June 6, 1788 and December 15, 1791? The Federalists did not think so. Perhaps, then, the Bill of Rights was, as many of its various state predecessors were labeled, a *declaration* of rights that merely clarified (or emphasized, or "liquidated") what was already true. *See* Gary Lawson, *The Bill of Rights as an Exclamation Point,* 33 RICHMOND L. REV. 511 (1999). Perhaps the various rights identified in the Bill of Rights—and the other rights retained by the people—were part of America's Ancient Constitution. And if they were part of the Ancient Constitution, perhaps *no* government could violate them, at least not without specific authorization to do so under Lockean natural law, which had many fans in 1791. Textual articulation of those rights would not be necessary to establish their existence. Perhaps they just existed, as the Ancient Constitutional Rights of Americans—growing out of the Rights of Englishmen but altered to the circumstances of the new country (which, for instance, meant more free speech rights than may have been true in England, *see supra* pages 1022–1026). Perhaps, perhaps, perhaps.

Most legal actors before the Civil War did not believe that the Bill of Rights bound the States. The "*Barron* contrarians," of whatever stripe, were a minority. But their voice is part of the context of the drafting and ratification of the Fourteenth Amendment. One obvious purpose of the Fourteenth Amendment was to provide constitutional grounding for the Civil Rights Act of 1866 and its protection of common law rights against discriminatory state action. Could another purpose—or, at the very least, consequence—of the Fourteenth Amendment be to validate the position of the "*Barron* contrarians" by establishing (or, if one was a contrarian, clarifying) that the Bill of Rights limits state governments as well as federal actors? Or, framed otherwise, were the rights referenced in the Bill of Rights themselves common law rights because part of the American Ancient Constitution? Recall that when Senator Jacob Howard presented the Fourteenth Amendment to his colleagues, he said:

> It would be a curious question to solve what are the privileges and immunities of citizens of each of the States in the several States * * *. But we may gather some intimation of what probably will be the opinion of the judiciary by referring to [*Corfield v. Coryell*] * * *.
>
> * * * To these privileges and immunities, whatever they may be—for they are not and cannot be fully defined in their entire extent and precise nature—to these should be added the personal rights guarantied and secured by the first eight amendments of the Constitution: such as the freedom of speech and of the press; the right of the people to peaceably assemble and petition for redress of grievances, a right appertaining to each and all the people; the right to keep and bear arms; the right to be exempted from the quartering of soldiers in a house without the consent of the owner; the right to be exempt from unreasonable searches and seizures;, and from any search or seizure except by virtue of a warrant issued upon a formal oath or affidavit; the right of an accused person to be informed of the nature of the accusations against him, and his right to be tried by an impartial jury of the vicinage; and also the right to be secure against excessive bail and against cruel and unusual punishments.
>
> Now, sir, here is a mass of privileges, immunities, and rights * * *.

> * * * The great object of the first section of * * * [the Fourteenth Amendment] is, therefore, to restrain the power of the States and compel them at all times to respect these great fundamental guarantees.

So does that settle it? The provisions in the Bill of Rights—or at least the first nine amendments, as the Tenth Amendments is aimed largely at preserving State authority—are among the "privileges or immunities" of federal citizenship that the Fourteenth Amendment requires the States to respect?

Alas, things are seldom that simple. The history of the Fourteenth Amendment is generally too messy to yield simple answers to interesting questions. The level of legal sophistication of the various actors involved in the amendment's drafting and ratification was uneven. Even direct references to "the Bill of Rights" in the legislative history have to be viewed cautiously, because the phrase "the Bill of Rights" was not commonly used to refer to the Constitution's first eight amendments until long after the Fourteenth Amendment was ratified. *See supra* page 989. Furthermore, even if one concludes that the Fourteenth Amendment has something to do with the Bill of Rights, there are several possible "somethings" from which to choose. Without intending this list to be exclusive, one might think:

> 1. Senator Howard was wrong; the content of the Fourteenth Amendment can be ascertained entirely without reference to the Bill of Rights, and it protects only common law rights.
>
> 2. Senator Howard was right. At least part of the content of the Fourteenth Amendment is determined by the Bill of Rights.
>
> 3. Senator Howard was righter than he knew. The *entire* content of the Fourteenth Amendment is determined by the Bill of Rights.
>
> 4. Senator Howard was partly right. The content of the Fourteenth Amendment includes some of the provisions in the Bill of Rights, but not all of them.
>
> 5. Senator Howard was right in a sorta-kinda way. The Fourteenth Amendment does not literally make the Bill of Rights applicable to the States, but the *principles* behind the Bill of Rights provisions are part of the content of the Fourteenth Amendment. Those principles might apply differently to States than they do to the Federal government, so to say that the Bill of Rights "applies" to the States is to speak metaphorically.

To give away the ending: Modern law has settled on (4), though the list of provisions of the Bill of Rights that have not yet been deemed applicable to the States is small and shrinking. Judges and scholars, as you will shortly see, have vigorously defended—and many to this day still vigorously defend—(1) and (2). Option (3) shows up from time to time but is seldom an expressly defended position. And we think the right answer is some variant of (5)—which of course therefore has attracted virtually no support from the courts.

A second issue, related to the question of the extent to which the Fourteenth Amendment's meaning draws on the Bill of Rights, is *which clause(s)* of the Fourteenth Amendment does whatever work there is to be done. As you will see, modern law has embraced option (4) above via the Due Process of Law Clause. We think, with Senator Howard and with an ever-growing body of scholars, that the key provision is the Privileges or Immunities Clause. You will see that issue discussed in the cases to follow.

Unfortunately, in the space and time available, we cannot give you enough information to allow you to make your own fully informed judgment about the relationship between the Fourteenth Amendment and the Bill of Rights. That requires at least a separate course, and quite possibly a lifetime of study. But the main themes that we have described show up in the two principal cases to follow, and we can at least provide a snapshot of the answers given by current doctrine (which we grudgingly concede might even be more interesting to students than our view of the right answer).

The relationship between the Fourteenth Amendment and the Bill of Rights came up episodically in the first eight decades after ratification. The most important development was, as is true with almost anything regarding the Fourteenth Amendment, the *Slaughter-House Cases,* 83 U.S. (16 Wall.) 36 (1873). *See supra* pages 1226–1242. The Supreme Court there limited the "privileges or immunities" mentioned in Section 1 of the Fourteenth Amendment to privileges or immunities of distinctively *national* citizenship, such as the right to travel to the seat of government in Washington, D.C. An obvious question is why the Court did not include as rights of national citizenship the express constitutional rights of citizens against the federal government. Since the Court did not discuss the matter, and it was not squarely presented by the *Slaughter-House Cases* which involved class legislation and the common law rule against monopolies, we will never know for sure. But one possibility is that, even if the *Slaughter-House Cases* had identified the Bill of Rights provisions as "privileges or immunities" of national citizenship, it would only have prevented States from interfering with citizens' ability to *exercise those rights against the federal government,* just as the Court said that States could not interfere with the exercise of other rights of national citizenship, such as traveling to the District of Columbia. The *Slaughter-House* Court's limitation of the Privileges or Immunities Clause to the rights of national *citizenship* rather than the rights of national *citizens* thus effectively foreclosed using the clause as the vehicle for finding either the provisions or the principles of the Bill of Rights applicable to the States. Because the Privileges or Immunities Clause is, as Senator Howard recognized, the obvious vehicle in the Fourteenth Amendment for "incorporating" (as we say) the Bill of Rights against the States, *see* AMAR, *supra,* at 163–74, the *Slaughter-House Cases* once again shaped the trajectory of American constitutional law.

Accordingly, when the Court first applied a Bill of Rights provision to the States, it did so via the Due Process of Law Clause rather than the Privileges or Immunities Clause. Early decisions under the Fourteenth Amendment Due Process of Law Clause confined it to ensuring fair procedures and enforcing a modest separation-of-powers rule on States, such that legislatures could not directly work deprivations of property without court proceedings. *See Davidson v. City of New Orleans,* 96 U.S. (6 Otto) 97 (1877). In *Chicago, Burlington and Quincy Railroad Co. v. Chicago,* 166 U.S. 226 (1897), the Supreme Court extended that rule to require just compensation for any legislatively prescribed takings *as an element of due process of law*:

> * * * The legislature may prescribe a form of procedure to be observed in the taking of private property for public use, but it is not due process of law if provision be not made for compensation. Notice to the owner to appear in some judicial tribunal and show cause why his property shall not

> be taken for public use without compensation would be a mockery of justice. Due process of law, as applied to judicial proceedings instituted for the taking of private property for public use means, therefore, such process as recognizes the right of the owner to be compensated if his property be wrested from him and transferred to the public. The mere form of the proceeding instituted against the owner, even if he be admitted to defend, cannot convert the process used into due process of law, if the necessary result be to deprive him of his property without compensation.

Id. at 236–37. In form, this was an application of the then-vibrant doctrine of substantive due process. In substance, it "incorporated" the just compensation requirement of the Fifth Amendment into the notion of due process of law. What else might be a necessary element of this conception of "due process of law"?

For quite a while, the answer was "nothing else." [I]n *Twining v. New Jersey*, 211 U.S. 78, 99 (1908), the Court rejected, on the authority of the *Slaughter-House Cases,* a claim that the privilege against self-incrimination enshrined in the Fifth Amendment applied to the States as a "privilege or immunity" of citizenship. *See id.* at 93–99. The Court added, however, that "it is possible that some of the personal rights safeguarded by the first eight Amendments against national action may also be safeguarded against state action, because a denial of them would be a denial of due process of law. *Chicago, B. & Q. R. Co. v. Chicago*, 166 U. S. 226. If this is so, it is not because those rights are enumerated in the first eight Amendments, but because they are of such a nature that they are included in the conception of due process of law." 211 U.S. at 99. In other words, the Court would ask "whether the exemption from self-incrimination is of such a nature that it must be included in the conception of due process. Is it a fundamental principle of liberty and justice which inheres in the very idea of free government and is the inalienable right of a citizen of such a government? If it is, and if it is of a nature that pertains to process of law, this court has declared it to be essential to due process of law." *Id.* at 106. The Court concluded that the right against self-incrimination was not of this character: "[I]t would be going far to rate it as an immutable principle of justice which is the inalienable possession of every citizen of a free government. Salutary as the principle may seem to the great majority, it cannot be ranked with the right to hearing before condemnation, the immunity from arbitrary power not acting by general laws, and the inviolability of private property. The wisdom of the exemption has never been universally assented to since the days of Bentham, many doubt it to-day, and it is best defended not as an unchangeable principle of universal justice, but as a law proved by experience to be expedient." *Id.* at 113. In other words, the right against self-incrimination was not considered part of the Ancient Constitution. On the other hand, the right to receive compensation was property is taken for public use—the "inviolability of private property"—had this fundamental character. Thus evolved the practice of selectively applying certain but not all principles in the Bill of Rights to the States via the notion of due process of law.

What about the First Amendment's free speech principles? Are they fundamental enough to be part of the Ancient Constitution substantively protected by "due process of law"? In 1925, the Supreme Court said yes: "For present purposes we may and do assume that freedom of speech and of the press—which are protected by the First Amendment from abridgment by Congress—are among the fundamental personal rights and 'liberties' protected by the due process clause of the Fourteenth

Amendment from impairment by the States." *Gitlow v. People of the State of New York,* 268 U.S. 652, 666 (1925). The right to assembly followed twelve years later:

> Freedom of speech and of the press are fundamental rights which are safeguarded by the due process clause of the Fourteenth Amendment of the Federal Constitution. The right of peaceable assembly is a right cognate to those of free speech and free press and is equally fundamental * * *. The First Amendment of the Federal Constitution expressly guarantees that right against abridgment by Congress. But explicit mention there does not argue exclusion elsewhere. For the right is one that cannot be denied without violating those fundamental principles of liberty and justice which lie at the base of all civil and political institutions—principles which the Fourteenth Amendment embodies in the general terms of its due process clause.

De Jong v. Oregon, 299 U.S. 353, 364 (1937). The same year, in *Palko v. Connecticut*, 302 U.S. 319 (1937), Justice Benjamin Cardozo refused to incorporate the Fifth Amendment's protection against double jeopardy against the States, saying that only rights that were "implicit in ordered liberty" ought to be incorporated:

> We have said that in appellant's view the Fourteenth Amendment is to be taken as embodying the prohibitions of the Fifth. His thesis is even broader. Whatever would be a violation of the original bill of rights (Amendments I to VIII) if done by the federal government is now equally unlawful by force of the Fourteenth Amendment if done by a state. There is no such general rule.
>
> The Fifth Amendment provides, among other things, that no person shall be held to answer for a capital or otherwise infamous crime unless on presentment or indictment of a grand jury. This court has held that, in prosecutions by a state, presentment or indictment by a grand jury may give way to informations at the instance of a public officer. The Fifth Amendment provides also that no person shall be compelled in any criminal case to be a witness against himself. This court has said that, in prosecutions by a state, the exemption will fail if the state elects to end it The Sixth Amendment calls for a jury trial in criminal cases and the Seventh for a jury trial in civil cases at common law where the value in controversy shall exceed twenty dollars. This court has ruled that consistently with those amendments trial by jury may be modified by a state or abolished altogether * * *.
>
> On the other hand, the due process clause of the Fourteenth Amendment may make it unlawful for a state to abridge by its statutes the freedom of speech which the First Amendment safeguards against encroachment by the Congress, or the like freedom of the press, or the free exercise of religion, or the right of peaceable assembly, without which speech would be unduly trammeled. In these and other situations immunities that are valid as against the federal government by force of the specific pledges of particular amendments have been found to be implicit in the concept of ordered liberty, and thus, through the Fourteenth Amendment, become valid as against the states.

> The line of division may seem to be wavering and broken if there is a hasty catalogue of the cases on the one side and the other. Reflection and analysis will induce a different view. There emerges the perception of a rationalizing principle which gives to discrete instances a proper order and coherence. The right to trial by jury and the immunity from prosecution except as the result of an indictment may have value and importance. Even so, they are not of the very essence of a scheme of ordered liberty. To abolish them is not to violate a "principle of justice so rooted in the traditions and conscience of our people as to be ranked as fundamental." Few would be so narrow or provincial as to maintain that a fair and enlightened system of justice would be impossible without them. What is true of jury trials and indictments is true also, as the cases show, of the immunity from compulsory self-incrimination. This too might be lost, and justice still be done. Indeed, today as in the past there are students of our penal system who look upon the immunity as a mischief rather than a benefit, and who would limit its scope, or destroy it altogether * * *. The exclusion of these immunities and privileges from the privileges and immunities protected against the action of the states has not been arbitrary or casual. It has been dictated by a study and appreciation of the meaning, the essential implications, of liberty itself.
>
> * * *
>
> Our survey of the cases serves, we think, to justify the statement that the dividing line between them, if not unfaltering throughout its course, has been true for the most part to a unifying principle. On which side of the line the case made out by the appellant has appropriate location must be the next inquiry and the final one. Is that kind of double jeopardy to which the statute has subjected him a hardship so acute and shocking that our policy will not endure it? Does it violate those "fundamental principles of liberty and justice which lie at the base of all our civil and political institutions"? The answer surely must be "no."

302 U.S. at 323–27.

One year after Justice Cardozo's famous opinion in *Palko v. Connecticut,* the Supreme Court declared in *United States v. Carolene Products*, 304 U.S. 144 (1938), that all rights under the Fourteenth Amendment, economic or social, would get only rational basis review, except possibly for those rights mentioned in the now-famous footnote four of the *Carolene Products* decision. That footnote, which you have seen already, *see supra* page 1458, read in relevant part:

> There may be narrower scope for operation of the presumption of constitutionality when legislation appears on its face to be within a specific prohibition of the Constitution, such as those of the first ten amendments, which are deemed equally specific when held to be embraced within the Fourteenth.
>
> It is unnecessary to consider now whether legislation which restricts those political processes which can ordinarily be expected to bring about repeal of undesirable legislation, is to be subjected to more exacting judicial scrutiny under the general prohibitions of the Fourteenth Amendment than are most other types of legislation * * *.

> Nor need we inquire whether similar considerations enter into the review of statutes directed at particular religious, . . . or national, . . . or racial minorities: whether prejudice against discrete and insular minorities may be a special condition, which tends seriously to curtail the operation of those political processes ordinarily to be relied upon to protect minorities, and which may call for a correspondingly more searching judicial inquiry.

Id. at 154 n.4.

The Supreme Court returned to the incorporation question two years later in *Cantwell v. Connecticut,* 310 U.S. 296 (1940), where the Supreme Court incorporated the Free Exercise Clause of the First Amendment to apply against the States, again by using substantive due process. Then, seven years later, in *Everson v. Board of Education,* 330 U.S. 1 (1947), the Supreme Court for the first time incorporated the Establishment Clause to apply against the States.

1947 proved to be a watershed year for the incorporation doctrine when a public debate appeared between New Deal Justices Hugo Black and Felix Frankfurter over whether *Twining v. New Jersey* should be overruled. Perhaps ironically, neither justice's position has prevailed, though Justice Black would surely be more satisfied with modern law, which incorporates every part of the Bill of Rights except for the Third Amendment, the Fifth Amendment right to a grand jury indictment; and the Seventh Amendment's right to civil jury trial. One other exception to the full incorporation of the Bill of Rights is before the Supreme Court in the spring of 2020: whether the Fourteenth Amendment requires criminal convictions to be by unanimous vote of a jury. *See Ramos v. Louisiana,* 139 S.Ct. 1318 (2019). The Court has previously held that, although the criminal right of jury trial is incorporated by the Fourteenth Amendment against the States, the States can satisfy that requirement by using six-member juries even though the federal government must use traditional twelve-member juries. *See Apodaca v. Oregon,* 406 U.S. 404 (1972).

Adamson v. California

332 U.S. 46 (1947)

■ MR. JUSTICE REED delivered the opinion of the Court.

The appellant, Adamson, a citizen of the United States, was convicted, without recommendation for mercy, by a jury in a Superior Court of the State of California of murder in the first degree. After considering the same objections to the conviction that are pressed here, the sentence of death was affirmed by the Supreme Court of the state * * *.The provisions of California law which were challenged in the state proceedings as invalid under the Fourteenth Amendment to the Federal Constitution * * * permit the failure of a defendant to explain or to deny evidence against him to be commented upon by court and by counsel, and to be considered by court and jury. The defendant did not testify. As the trial court gave its instructions and the District Attorney argued the case in accordance with the constitutional and statutory provisions just referred to, we have for decision the question of their constitutionality in these circumstances under the limitations of § 1 of the Fourteenth Amendment.

The appellant was charged in the information with former convictions for burglary, larceny and robbery and pursuant to § 1025, California Penal Code, answered that he had suffered the previous convictions. This answer barred allusion to these charges of convictions on the trial.[5] Under California's interpretation of § 1025 of the Penal Code and § 2051 of the Code of Civil Procedure, however, if the defendant, after answering affirmatively charges alleging prior convictions, takes the witness stand to deny or explain away other evidence that has been introduced "the commission of these crimes could have been revealed to the jury on cross-examination to impeach his testimony." *People v. Adamson,* 27 Cal.2d 478, 494, 165 P.2d 3, 11; *People v. Braun,* 14 Cal.2d 1, 6, 92 P.2d 402, 405. This forces an accused who is a repeated offender to choose between the risk of having his prior offenses disclosed to the jury or of having it draw harmful inferences from uncontradicted evidence that can only be denied or explained by the defendant.

In the first place, appellant urges that the provision of the Fifth Amendment that no person "shall be compelled in any criminal case to be a witness against himself" is a fundamental national privilege or immunity protected against state abridgment by the Fourteenth Amendment or a privilege or immunity secured, through the Fourteenth Amendment, against deprivation by state action because it is a personal right, enumerated in the federal Bill of Rights.

Secondly, appellant relies upon the due process of law clause of the Fourteenth Amendment * * * (a) because comment on failure to testify is permitted, (b) because appellant was forced to forego testimony in person because of danger of disclosure of his past convictions through cross-examination, and (c) because the presumption of innocence was infringed by the shifting of the burden of proof to appellant in permitting comment on his failure to testify.

We shall assume, but without any intention thereby of ruling upon the issue, that permission by law to the court, counsel and jury to comment upon and consider the failure of defendant "to explain or to deny by his testimony any evidence or facts in the case against him" would infringe defendant's privilege against self-incrimination under the Fifth Amendment if this were a trial in a court of the United States under a similar law. Such an assumption does not determine appellant's rights under the Fourteenth Amendment. It is settled law that the clause of the Fifth Amendment, protecting a person against being compelled to be a witness against himself, is not made effective by the Fourteenth Amendment as a protection against state action on the ground that freedom from testimonial compulsion is a right of national citizenship, or because it is a personal privilege or immunity secured by the Federal Constitution as one of the rights of man that are listed in the Bill of Rights.

The reasoning that leads to those conclusions starts with the unquestioned premise that the Bill of Rights, when adopted, was for the protection of the individual against the federal government and its provisions were inapplicable to similar actions done by the states. *Barron v. Baltimore,* 7 Peters 243; *Feldman v. United States,* 322 U.S. 487, 490. With the adoption of the Fourteenth Amendment, it was suggested that the dual citizenship recognized by its first sentence secured for citizens federal protection for their elemental privileges and immunities of state citizenship. The *Slaughter-House Cases* decided, contrary to the suggestion, that these rights, as privileges and immunities of state citizenship, remained under the sole protection of the state governments * * *. The power to free defendants in state

[5] Penal Code of California, § 1025: "* * * In case the defendant pleads not guilty, and answers that he has suffered the previous conviction, the charge of the previous conviction must not be read to the jury, nor alluded to on the trial."

trials from self-incrimination was specifically determined to be beyond the scope of the privileges and immunities clause of the Fourteenth Amendment in *Twining v. New Jersey,* 211 U.S. 78, 91–98 * * *. The *Twining* case likewise disposed of the contention that freedom from testimonial compulsion, being specifically granted by the Bill of Rights, is a federal privilege or immunity that is protected by the Fourteenth Amendment against state invasion. This Court held that the inclusion in the Bill of Rights of this protection against the power of the national government did not make the privilege a federal privilege or immunity secured to citizens by the Constitution against state action * * *. We reaffirm the conclusion of the *Twining* and *Palko* cases that protection against self-incrimination is not a privilege or immunity of national citizenship.

Appellant secondly contends that if the privilege against self-incrimination is not a right protected by the privileges and immunities clause of the Fourteenth Amendment against state action, this privilege, to its full scope under the Fifth Amendment, inheres in the right to a fair trial. A right to a fair trial is a right admittedly protected by the due process clause of the Fourteenth Amendment. Therefore, appellant argues, the due process clause of the Fourteenth Amendment protects his privilege against self-incrimination. The due process clause of the Fourteenth Amendment, however, does not draw all the rights of the federal Bill of Rights under its protection. That contention was made and rejected in *Palko v. Connecticut,* 302 U.S. 319, 323 * * *.

Specifically, the due process clause does not protect, by virtue of its mere existence, the accused's freedom from giving testimony by compulsion in state trials that is secured to him against federal interference by the Fifth Amendment. *Twining v. New Jersey,* 211 U.S. 78, 99–114; *Palko v. Connecticut, supra,* p. 323 * * *.

* * *

* * * The purpose of due process is not to protect an accused against a proper conviction but against an unfair conviction. When evidence is before a jury that threatens conviction, it does not seem unfair to require him to choose between leaving the adverse evidence unexplained and subjecting himself to impeachment through disclosure of former crimes. Indeed, this is a dilemma with which any defendant may be faced. If facts adverse to the defendant are proven by the prosecution, there may be no way to explain them favorably to the accused except by a witness who may be vulnerable to impeachment on cross-examination. The defendant must then decide whether or not to use such a witness. The fact that the witness may also be the defendant makes the choice more difficult but a denial of due process does not emerge from the circumstances.

There is no basis in the California law for appellant's objection on due process or other grounds that the statutory authorization to comment on the failure to explain or deny adverse testimony shifts the burden of proof or the duty to go forward with the evidence. Failure of the accused to testify is not an admission of the truth of the adverse evidence. Instructions told the jury that the burden of proof remained upon the state and the presumption of innocence with the accused. Comment on failure to deny proven facts does not, in California, tend to supply any missing element of proof of guilt. It only directs attention to the strength of the evidence for the prosecution or to the weakness of that for the defense * * *.

* * *

We find no other error that gives ground for our intervention in California's administration of criminal justice.

Affirmed.

■ MR. JUSTICE FRANKFURTER, concurring.

Less than ten years ago, Mr. Justice Cardozo announced as settled constitutional law that while the Fifth Amendment, "which is not directed to the states, but solely to the federal government," provides that no person shall be compelled in any criminal case to be a witness against himself, the process of law assured by the Fourteenth Amendment does not require such immunity from self-crimination * * * The matter no longer called for discussion; a reference to *Twining v. New Jersey,* 211 U.S. 78, decided thirty years before the *Palko* case, sufficed.

Decisions of this Court do not have equal intrinsic authority. The *Twining* case shows the judicial process at its best—comprehensive briefs and powerful arguments on both sides, followed by long deliberation, resulting in an opinion by Mr. Justice Moody which at once gained and has ever since retained recognition as one of the outstanding opinions in the history of the Court. After enjoying unquestioned prestige for forty years, the *Twining* case should not now be diluted, even unwittingly, either in its judicial philosophy or in its particulars. As the surest way of keeping the *Twining* case intact, I would affirm this case on its authority.

* * *

This [case] does not create an issue different from that settled in the *Twining* case. Only a technical rule of law would exclude from consideration that which is relevant, as a matter of fair reasoning, to the solution of a problem. Sensible and just-minded men, in important affairs of life, deem it significant that a man remains silent when confronted with serious and responsible evidence against himself which it is within his power to contradict. The notion that to allow jurors to do that which sensible and right-minded men do every day violates the "immutable principles of justice" as conceived by a civilized society is to trivialize the importance of "due process." * * *

For historical reasons, a limited immunity from the common duty to testify was written into the Federal Bill of Rights, and I am prepared to agree that, as part of that immunity, comment on the failure of an accused to take the witness stand is forbidden in federal prosecutions * * *. But to suggest that such a limitation can be drawn out of "due process" in its protection of ultimate decency in a civilized society is to suggest that the Due Process Clause fastened fetters of unreason upon the States. (This opinion is concerned solely with a discussion of the Due Process Clause of the Fourteenth Amendment. I put to one side the Privileges or Immunities Clause of that Amendment. For the mischievous uses to which that clause would lend itself if its scope were not confined to that given it by all but one of the decisions beginning with the *Slaughter-House Cases,* 16 Wall. 36, *see* the deviation in *Colgate v. Harvey,* 296 U.S. 404, overruled by *Madden v. Kentucky,* 309 U.S. 83.)

Between the incorporation of the Fourteenth Amendment into the Constitution and the beginning of the present membership of the Court—a period of seventy years—the scope of that Amendment was passed upon by forty-three judges. Of all these judges, only one, who may respectfully be called an eccentric exception, ever indicated the belief that the Fourteenth Amendment was a shorthand summary of the first eight Amendments theretofore limiting only the Federal Government, and that due process incorporated those eight Amendments as restrictions upon the powers of the States. Among these judges were not only those who would have to be included among the greatest in the history of the Court, but—it is especially relevant to note—they included those whose services in the cause of human rights and the spirit of freedom are the most conspicuous in our history. It is not invidious to single out Miller, Davis, Bradley, Waite, Matthews, Gray, Fuller, Holmes, Brandeis, Stone and Cardozo (to speak only of the dead) as judges who were alert in safeguarding and promoting the interests of liberty and human dignity through law. But they were also judges mindful of the relation of our federal system to a progressively democratic society and therefore duly regardful of the scope of authority that was left to the States even after the Civil War. And so they did not find that the Fourteenth Amendment, concerned as it was with matters fundamental to the pursuit of justice, fastened upon the States procedural arrangements which, in the language of Mr. Justice Cardozo, only those who are "narrow or provincial" would deem essential to "a fair and enlightened system of justice." *Palko v. Connecticut,* 302 U.S. 319, 325. To suggest that it is inconsistent with a truly free society to begin prosecutions without an indictment, to try petty civil cases without the paraphernalia of a common law jury, to take into consideration that one who has full opportunity to make a defense remains silent is, in de Tocqueville's phrase, to confound the familiar with the necessary.

The short answer to the suggestion that the provision of the Fourteenth Amendment, which ordains "nor shall any State deprive any person of life, liberty, or property, without due process of law," was a way of saying that every State must thereafter initiate prosecutions through indictment by a grand jury, must have a trial by a jury of twelve in criminal cases, and must have trial by such a jury in common law suits where the amount in controversy exceeds twenty dollars, is that it is a strange way of saying it. It would be extraordinarily strange for a Constitution to convey such specific commands in such a roundabout and inexplicit way. After all, an amendment to the Constitution should be read in a " 'sense most obvious to the common understanding at the time of its adoption.' . . . For it was for public adoption that it was proposed." Those reading the English language with the meaning which it ordinarily conveys, those conversant with the political and legal history of the concept of due process, those sensitive to the relations of the States to the central government as well as the relation of some of the provisions of the Bill of Rights to the process of justice, would hardly recognize the Fourteenth Amendment as a cover for the various explicit provisions of the first eight Amendments. Some of these are enduring reflections of experience with human nature, while some express the restricted views of Eighteenth-Century England regarding the best methods for the ascertainment of facts. The notion that the Fourteenth Amendment was a covert way of imposing upon the States all the rules which it seemed important to Eighteenth Century statesmen to write into the Federal Amendments, was rejected by judges who were themselves witnesses of the process by which the Fourteenth Amendment became part of the Constitution. Arguments that may now be adduced to prove that the first eight Amendments were concealed within the historic phrasing of the Fourteenth Amendment were not unknown at the time of its adoption. A surer estimate of their bearing was possible for judges at the time than distorting distance is likely to vouchsafe. Any evidence of design or purpose not contemporaneously known could hardly have influenced those who ratified the Amendment. Remarks of a particular proponent of the Amendment, no matter how influential, are not to be deemed part of the Amendment. What was submitted for ratification was his proposal, not his speech. Thus, at the time of the ratification of the Fourteenth Amendment the constitutions of nearly half of the ratifying States did not have the rigorous requirements of the Fifth Amendment for instituting criminal proceedings through a grand jury. It could hardly have occurred to these States that by ratifying the Amendment they uprooted their established methods for prosecuting crime and fastened upon themselves a new prosecutorial system.

Indeed, the suggestion that the Fourteenth Amendment incorporates the first eight Amendments as such is not unambiguously urged. Even the boldest innovator would shrink from suggesting to more than half the States that they may no longer initiate prosecutions without indictment by grand jury, or that thereafter all the States of the Union must furnish a jury of twelve for every case involving a claim above twenty dollars. There is suggested merely a selective incorporation of the first eight Amendments into the Fourteenth Amendment. Some are in and some are out, but we are left in the dark as to which are in and which are out. Nor are we given the calculus for determining which go in and which stay out. If the basis of selection is merely that those provisions of the first eight Amendments are incorporated which commend themselves to individual justices as indispensable to the dignity and happiness of a free man, we are thrown back to a merely subjective test. The protection against unreasonable search and seizure might have primacy for one judge, while trial by a jury of twelve for every claim above twenty dollars might appear to another as an ultimate need in a free society. In the history of thought "natural law" has a much longer and much better founded meaning and justification than such subjective selection of the first eight Amendments for incorporation into the Fourteenth. If all that is meant is that due process contains within itself certain minimal standards which are "of the very essence of a scheme of ordered liberty," *Palko v. Connecticut,* 302 U.S. 319, 325, putting upon this Court the duty of applying these standards from time to time, then we have merely arrived at the insight which our predecessors long ago expressed. We are called upon to apply to the difficult issues of our own day the wisdom afforded by the great opinions in this field, such as those in *Davidson v. New Orleans,* 96 U.S. 97; *Missouri v. Lewis,* 101 U.S. 22; *Hurtado v. California,* 110 U.S. 516; *Holden v. Hardy,* 169 U.S. 366; *Twining v. New Jersey,* 211 U.S. 78, and *Palko v. Connecticut,* 302 U.S. 319. This guidance bids us to be duly mindful of the heritage of the past, with its great lessons of how liberties are won and how they are lost. As judges charged with the delicate task of subjecting the government of a continent to the Rule of Law, we must be particularly mindful that it is "a *constitution* we are expounding," so that it should not be imprisoned in what are merely legal forms even though they have the sanction of the Eighteenth Century.

* * * It ought not to require argument to reject the notion that due process of law meant one thing in the Fifth Amendment and another in the Fourteenth. The Fifth Amendment specifically prohibits prosecution of an "infamous crime" except upon indictment; it forbids double jeopardy; it bars compelling a person to be a witness against himself in any criminal case; it precludes deprivation of "life, liberty, or property, without due process of law. . . ." Are Madison and his contemporaries in the framing of the Bill of Rights to be charged with writing into it a meaningless clause? To consider "due process of law" as merely a shorthand statement of other specific clauses in the same amendment is to attribute to the authors and proponents

of this Amendment ignorance of, or indifference to, a historic conception which was one of the great instruments in the arsenal of constitutional freedom which the Bill of Rights was to protect and strengthen.

A construction which gives to due process no independent function but turns it into a summary of the specific provisions of the Bill of Rights would, as has been noted, tear up by the roots much of the fabric of law in the several States, and would deprive the States of opportunity for reforms in legal process designed for extending the area of freedom. It would assume that no other abuses would reveal themselves in the course of time than those which had become manifest in 1791. Such a view not only disregards the historic meaning of "due process." It leads inevitably to a warped construction of specific provisions of the Bill of Rights to bring within their scope conduct clearly condemned by due process but not easily fitting into the pigeon-holes of the specific provisions. It seems pretty late in the day to suggest that a phrase so laden with historic meaning should be given an improvised content consisting of some but not all of the provisions of the first eight Amendments, selected on an undefined basis, with improvisation of content for the provisions so selected.

And so, when, as in a case like the present, a conviction in a State court is here for review under a claim that a right protected by the Due Process Clause of the Fourteenth Amendment has been denied, the issue is not whether an infraction of one of the specific provisions of the first eight Amendments is disclosed by the record. The relevant question is whether the criminal proceedings which resulted in conviction deprived the accused of the due process of law to which the United States Constitution entitled him. Judicial review of that guaranty of the Fourteenth Amendment inescapably imposes upon this Court an exercise of judgment upon the whole course of the proceedings in order to ascertain whether they offend those canons of decency and fairness which express the notions of justice of English-speaking peoples even toward those charged with the most heinous offenses. These standards of justice are not authoritatively formulated anywhere as though they were prescriptions in a pharmacopoeia. But neither does the application of the Due Process Clause imply that judges are wholly at large. The judicial judgment in applying the Due Process Clause must move within the limits of accepted notions of justice and is not to be based upon the idiosyncrasies of a merely personal judgment. The fact that judges among themselves may differ whether in a particular case a trial offends accepted notions of justice is not disproof that general, rather than idiosyncratic, standards are applied. An important safeguard against such merely individual judgment is an alert deference to the judgment of the State court under review.

■ MR. JUSTICE MURPHY, with whom MR. JUSTICE RUTLEDGE concurs, dissenting.

While in substantial agreement with the views of Mr. Justice BLACK, I have one reservation and one addition to make.

I agree that the specific guarantees of the Bill of Rights should be carried over intact into the first section of the Fourteenth Amendment. But I am not prepared to say that the latter is entirely and necessarily limited by the Bill of Rights. Occasions may arise where a proceeding falls so far short of conforming to fundamental standards of procedure as to warrant constitutional condemnation in terms of a lack of due process despite the absence of a specific provision in the Bill of Rights.

That point, however, need not be pursued here inasmuch as the Fifth Amendment is explicit in its provision that no person shall be compelled in any criminal case to be a witness against himself. That provision, as MR. JUSTICE BLACK demonstrates, is a constitutent part of the Fourteenth Amendment.

* * *

■ MR. JUSTICE BLACK, dissenting.

* * *

This decision reasserts a constitutional theory spelled out in *Twining v. New Jersey,* 211 U.S. 78, that this Court is endowed by the Constitution with boundless power under "natural law" periodically to expand and contract constitutional standards to conform to the Court's conception of what at a particular time constitutes "civilized decency" and "fundamental liberty and justice." Invoking this *Twining* rule, the Court concludes that although comment upon testimony in a federal court would violate the Fifth Amendment, identical comment in a state court does not violate today's fashion in civilized decency and fundamentals and is therefore not prohibited by the Federal Constitution as amended.

The *Twining* case was the first, as it is the only decision of this Court which has squarely held that states were free, notwithstanding the Fifth and Fourteenth Amendments, to extort evidence from one accused of crime. I agree that, if *Twining* be reaffirmed, the result reached might appropriately follow. But I would not reaffirm the *Twining* decision. I think that decision and the "natural law" theory of the Constitution upon which it relies degrade the constitutional safeguards of the Bill of Rights and simultaneously appropriate for this Court a broad power which we are not authorized by the Constitution to exercise. Furthermore, the *Twining* decision rested on previous cases and broad hypotheses which have been undercut by intervening decisions of this Court. My reasons for believing that the *Twining* decision should not be revitalized can best be understood by reference to the constitutional, judicial, and general history that preceded and followed the case. That reference must be abbreviated far more than is justified but for the necessary limitations of opinion-writing.

The first 10 amendments were proposed and adopted largely because of fear that Government might unduly interfere with prized individual liberties * * *.

But these limitations were not expressly imposed upon state court action. In 1833, *Barron v. Baltimore, supra,* was decided by this Court. It specifically held inapplicable to the states that provision of the Fifth Amendment which declares: "nor shall private property be taken for public use, without just compensation." In deciding the particular point raised, the Court there said that it could not hold that the first eight amendments applied to the states. This was the controlling constitutional rule when the Fourteenth Amendment was proposed in 1866.

My study of the historical events that culminated in the Fourteenth Amendment, and the expressions of those who sponsored and favored, as well as those who opposed its submission and passage, persuades me that one of the chief objects that the provisions of the Amendment's first section, separately and as a whole, were intended to accomplish was to make the Bill of Rights, applicable to the states. With full knowledge of the import of the *Barron* decision, the framers and backers of the Fourteenth Amendment proclaimed its purpose to be to overturn the constitutional rule that case had announced. This historical purpose has never received full consideration or exposition in any opinion of this Court interpreting the Amendment.

* * *

Investigation of the cases relied upon in *Twining v. New Jersey* * * * reveals [that] [n]either the briefs nor opinions in any of these cases, except *Maxwell v. Dow,* 176 U.S. 581, make reference to the legislative and contemporary history for the purpose of demonstrating that those who conceived, shaped, and brought about the adoption of the Fourteenth Amendment intended it to nullify this Court's decision in *Barron v. Baltimore, supra,* and thereby to make the Bill of Rights applicable to the States. In *Maxwell v. Dow, supra,* the issue turned on whether the Bill of Rights guarantee of a jury trial was, by the Fourteenth Amendment, extended to trials in state courts. In that case counsel for appellant did cite from the speech of Senator Howard which so emphatically stated the understanding of the framers of the Amendment—the Committee on Reconstruction for which he spoke—that the Bill of Rights was to be made applicable to the states by the Amendment's first section. The Court's opinion in *Maxwell v. Dow, supra,* 601, acknowledged that counsel had "cited from the speech of one of the Senators," but indicated that it was not advised what other speeches were made in the Senate or in the House. The Court considered, moreover, that "What individual Senators or Representatives may have urged in debate, in regard to the meaning to be given to a proposed constitutional amendment, or bill or resolution, does not furnish a firm ground for its proper construction, nor is it important as explanatory of the grounds upon which the members voted in adopting it." *Id.* at 601–602.

In the *Twining* case itself * * *, the Court declined, and again today declines, to appraise the relevant historical evidence of the intended scope of the first section of the Amendment. Instead it relied upon previous cases, none of which had analyzed the evidence showing that one purpose of those who framed, advocated, and adopted the Amendment had been to make the Bill of Rights applicable to the States. None of the cases relied upon by the Court today made such an analysis.

For this reason, I am attaching to this dissent an appendix which contains a résumé, by no means complete, of the Amendment's history. In my judgment, that history conclusively demonstrates that the language of the first section of the Fourteenth Amendment, taken as a whole, was thought by those responsible for its submission to the people, and by those who opposed its submission, sufficiently explicit to guarantee that thereafter no state could deprive its citizens of the privileges and protections of the Bill of Rights. Whether this Court ever will, or whether it now should, in the light of past decisions, give full effect to what the Amendment was intended to accomplish is not necessarily essential to a decision here. However that may be, our prior decisions, including *Twining,* do not prevent our carrying out that purpose, at least to the extent of making applicable to the states, not a mere part, as the Court has, but the full protection of the Fifth Amendment's provision against compelling evidence from an accused to convict him of crime. And I further contend that the "natural law" formula which the Court uses to reach its conclusion in this case should be abandoned as an incongruous excrescence on our Constitution. I believe that formula to be itself a violation of our Constitution, in that it subtly conveys to courts, at the expense of legislatures, ultimate power over public policies in fields where no specific provision of the Constitution limits legislative power. And my belief seems to be in accord with the views expressed by this Court, at least for the first two decades after the Fourteenth Amendment was adopted.

In 1872, four years after the Amendment was adopted, the *Slaughter-House* cases came to this Court. 16 Wall. 36 * * *. The majority of the Court emphatically declined the invitation of counsel to hold that the Fourteenth Amendment subjected all state regulatory legislation to continuous censorship by this Court in order for it to determine whether it collided with this Court's opinion of "natural" right and justice. In effect, the *Slaughter-House* cases rejected the very natural justice formula the Court today embraces. The Court did not meet the question of whether the safeguards of the Bill of Rights were protected against state invasion by the Fourteenth Amendment. And it specifically did not say as the Court now does, that particular provisions of the Bill of Rights could be breached by states in part, but not breached in other respects, according to this Court's notions of "civilized standards," "canons of decency," and "fundamental justice."

Later, but prior to the *Twining* case, this Court decided that the following were not "privileges or immunities" of national citizenship so as to make them immune against state invasion: the Eighth Amendment's prohibition against cruel and unusual punishment, *In re Kemmler,* 136 U.S. 436; the Seventh Amendment's guarantee of a jury trial in civil cases, *Walker v. Sauvinet,* 92 U.S. 90; the Second Amendment's "right of the people to keep and bear Arms . . .," *Presser v. Illinois,* 116 U.S. 252; the Fifth and Sixth Amendments' requirements for indictment in capital or other infamous crimes, and for trial by jury in criminal prosecutions, *Maxwell v. Dow,* 176 U.S. 581. While it can be argued that these cases implied that no one of the provisions of the Bill of Rights was made applicable to the states as attributes of national citizenship, no one of them expressly so decided * * *.

After the *Slaughter-House* decision, the Court also said that states could, despite the "due process" clause of the Fourteenth Amendment, take private property without just compensation, *Davidson v. New Orleans,* 96 U.S. 97, 105; *Pumpelly v. Green Bay Co.,* 13 Wall. 166, 176–177; abridge the freedom of assembly guaranteed by the First Amendment, *United States v. Cruikshank,* 92 U.S. 542; *see also Prudential Ins. Co. v. Cheek,* 259 U.S. 530, 543; *Patterson v. Colorado,* 205 U.S. 454; *cf. Gitlow v. New York,* 268 U.S. 652, 666 (freedom of speech); prosecute for crime by information, rather than indictment, *Hurtado v. People of California,* 110 U.S. 516; regulate the price for storage of grain in warehouses and elevators, *Munn v. Illinois,* 94 U.S. 113. But this Court also held in a number of cases that colored people must, because of the Fourteenth Amendment, be accorded equal protection of the laws. *See, e.g., Strauder v. West Virginia,* 100 U.S. 303; *cf. Virginia v. Rives,* 100 U.S. 313; *see also Yick Wo v. Hopkins,* 118 U.S. 356.

Thus, up to and for some years after 1873, when *Munn v. Illinois, supra,* was decided, this Court steadfastly declined to invalidate states' legislative regulation of property rights or business practices under the Fourteenth Amendment unless there were racial discrimination involved in the state law challenged. The first significant breach in this policy came in 1889, in *Chicago, M. & St. P. R. Co. v. Minnesota,* 134 U.S. 418. A state's railroad rate regulatory statute was there stricken as violative of the due process clause of the Fourteenth Amendment. This was accomplished by reference to a due process formula which did not necessarily operate so as to protect the Bill of Rights' personal liberty safeguards, but which gave a new and hitherto undiscovered scope for the Court's use of the due process clause to protect property rights under natural law concepts. And in 1896, in *Chicago, B. & Q. R. Co. v. Chicago*, 166 U.S. 226, this Court, in effect, overruled *Davidson v. New Orleans, supra,* by holding, under the new due process-natural law formula, that the Fourteenth Amendment forbade a state from taking private property for public use without payment of just compensation.

Following the pattern of the new doctrine formalized in the foregoing decisions, the Court in 1896 applied the due process clause to strike down a state statute which had forbidden certain types of contracts. *Allgeyer v. Louisiana,* 165 U.S. 578. In doing so, it substantially adopted the rejected argument of counsel in the *Slaughter-House* cases that the Fourteenth Amendment guarantees the liberty of all persons under "natural law" to engage in their chosen business or vocation * * *. And in 1905, three years before the *Twining* case, *Lochner v. New York,* 198 U.S. 45, followed the argument used in *Allgeyer* to hold that the due process clause was violated by a state statute which limited the employment of bakery workers to sixty hours per week and ten hours per day.

The foregoing constitutional doctrine, judicially created and adopted by expanding the previously accepted meaning of "due process," marked a complete departure from the *Slaughter-House* philosophy of judicial tolerance of state regulation of business activities. Conversely, the new formula contracted the effectiveness of the Fourteenth Amendment as a protection from state infringement of individual liberties enumerated in the Bill of Rights. Thus, the Court's second-thought interpretation of the Amendment was an about-face from the *Slaughter-House* interpretation and represented a failure to carry out the avowed purpose of the Amendment's sponsors. This reversal is dramatized by the fact that the *Hurtado* case, which had rejected the due process clause as an instrument for preserving Bill of Rights liberties and privileges, was cited as authority for expanding the scope of that clause so as to permit this Court to invalidate all state regulatory legislation it believed to be contrary to "fundamental" principles.

The *Twining* decision, rejecting the compelled testimony clause of the Fifth Amendment, and indeed rejecting all the Bill of Rights, is the end product of one phase of this philosophy. At the same time, that decision consolidated the power of the Court assumed in past cases by laying broader foundations for the Court to invalidate state and even federal regulatory legislation. For the *Twining* decision, giving separate consideration to "due process" and "privileges or immunities," went all the way to say that the "privileges or immunities" clause of the Fourteenth Amendment "did not forbid the States to abridge the personal rights enumerated in the first eight Amendments. . . ." *Twining v. New Jersey, supra,* 99. And in order to be certain, so far as possible, to leave this Court wholly free to reject all the Bill of Rights as specific restraints upon state action, the decision declared that even if this Court should decide that the due process clause forbids the states to infringe personal liberties guaranteed by the Bill of Rights, it would do so, not "because those rights are enumerated in the first eight Amendments, but because they are of such a nature that they are included in the conception of due process of law." *Ibid.*

* * * [U]nder the *Twining* formula, * * * "what is due process of law depends on circumstances." *Moyer v. Peabody,* 212 U.S. 78, 84. Thus the power of legislatures became what this Court would declare it to be at a particular time independently of the specific guarantees of the Bill of Rights such as the right to freedom of speech, religion and assembly, the right to just compensation for property taken for a public

purpose, the right to jury trial or the right to be secure against unreasonable searches and seizures. Neither the contraction of the Bill of Rights safeguards nor the invalidation of regulatory laws by this Court's appraisal of "circumstances" would readily be classified as the most satisfactory contribution of this Court to the nation * * *.

Later decisions of this Court have completely undermined that phase of the *Twining* doctrine which broadly precluded reliance on the Bill of Rights to determine what is and what is not a "fundamental" right. Later cases have also made the *Hurtado* case an inadequate support for this phase of the *Twining* formula. For despite *Hurtado* and *Twining,* this Court has now held that the Fourteenth Amendment protects from state invasion the following "fundamental" rights safeguarded by the Bill of Rights: right to counsel in criminal cases, *Powell v. Alabama,* 287 U.S. 45, 67, limiting the *Hurtado* case; see also *Betts v. Brady,* 316 U.S. 455, and *De Meerleer v. Michigan,* 329 U.S. 663; freedom of assembly, *De Jonge v. Oregon,* 299 U.S. 353, 364; at the very least, certain types of cruel and unusual punishment and former jeopardy, *State of Louisiana ex rel. Francis v. Resweber,* 329 U.S. 459; the right of an accused in a criminal case to be informed of the charge against him, *see Snyder v. Massachusetts,* 291 U.S. 97, 105; the right to receive just compensation on account of taking private property for public use, *Chicago, B. & Q. R. Co. v. Chicago,* 166 U.S. 226. And the Court has now through the Fourteenth Amendment literally and emphatically applied the First Amendment to the States in its very terms. *Everson v. Board of Education,* 330 U.S. 1; *Board of Education v. Barnette,* 319 U.S. 624, 639; *Bridges v. California,* 314 U.S. 252, 268.

* * * In the *Twining* case fundamental liberties were things apart from the Bill of Rights. Now it appears that at least some of the provisions of the Bill of Rights in their very terms satisfy the Court as sound and meaningful expressions of fundamental liberty. If the Fifth Amendment's protection against self-incrimination be such an expression of fundamental liberty, I ask, and have not found a satisfactory answer, why the Court today should consider that it should be "absorbed" in part, but not in full? Nothing in the *Palko* opinion requires that, when the Court decides that a Bill of Rights' provision is to be applied to the States, it is to be applied piecemeal. Nothing in the *Palko* opinion recommends that the Court apply part of an amendment's established meaning and discard that part which does not suit the current style of fundamentals.

* * *

I cannot consider the Bill of Rights to be an outworn 18th Century "strait jacket," as the *Twining* opinion did. Its provisions may be thought outdated abstractions by some. And it is true that they were designed to meet ancient evils. But they are the same kind of human evils that have emerged from century to century wherever excessive power is sought by the few at the expense of the many. In my judgment the people of no nation can lose their liberty so long as a Bill of Rights like ours survives and its basic purposes are conscientiously interpreted, enforced and respected so as to afford continuous protection against old, as well as new, devices and practices which might thwart those purposes. I fear to see the consequences of the Court's practice of substituting its own concepts of decency and fundamental justice for the language of the Bill of Rights as its point of departure in interpreting and enforcing that Bill of Rights. If the choice must be between the selective process of the *Palko* decision, applying some of the Bill of Rights to the

States, or the *Twining* rule applying none of them, I would choose the *Palko* selective process. But rather than accept either of these choices, I would follow what I believe was the original purpose of the Fourteenth Amendment—to extend to all the people of the nation the complete protection of the Bill of Rights. To hold that this Court can determine what, if any, provisions of the Bill of Rights will be enforced, and, if so, to what degree, is to frustrate the great design of a written Constitution.

Conceding the possibility that this Court is now wise enough to improve on the Bill of Rights by substituting natural law concepts for the Bill of Rights, I think the possibility is entirely too speculative to agree to take that course. I would therefore hold in this case that the full protection of the Fifth Amendment's proscription against compelled testimony must be afforded by California. This I would do because of reliance upon the original purpose of the Fourteenth Amendment.

* * *

■ MR. JUSTICE DOUGLAS joins in this opinion.

[Assignment 74]

XVI. THE MODERN DEBATE ON INCORPORATING THE BILL OF RIGHTS

The *Palko* strategy of selective incorporation of specific Bill of Rights provisions has prevailed, though the number of non-incorporated provisions is so small that only Justice Black would likely notice the difference. In the 1960s in particular, the Court systematically incorporated almost all of the parts of the Bill of Rights dealing with criminal procedure. That move not only revolutionalized criminal law; it revolutionalized the workload of the federal courts and the Supreme Court in particular. A substantial percentage of the Supreme Court's docket these days involves review of state criminal convictions under provisions of the Bill of Rights that were not applied to the States until very recently. That process was a ratchet: Bill of Rights provisions just kept getting added to the "incorporated" list. Indeed, for more than half a century, many thought the debate was over and that Justice Black had won in all but name—until the Court split 5–4 on whether to incorporate against the States the Second Amendment's individual right to keep and bear arms identified as such in the 5–4 opinion in *District of Columbia v. Heller*, 554 U.S. 570 (2008). *See supra* pages 1045–1059. The decision features passionately argued opinions by five different justices—all taking distinctive approaches to the incorporation debate. The case is too long for us to present all five opinions, but enjoy what we have included; it is, in the famous words of Judge Robert Bork, an intellectual feast.

McDonald v. City of Chicago

561 U.S. 742 (2010)

■ JUSTICE ALITO announced the judgment of the Court and delivered the opinion of the Court with respect to Parts I, II-A, II-B, II-D, III-A, and III-B, in which THE CHIEF JUSTICE, JUSTICE SCALIA, JUSTICE KENNEDY, and JUSTICE THOMAS join, and an opinion with respect to Parts II-C, IV, and V, in which THE CHIEF JUSTICE, JUSTICE SCALIA, and JUSTICE KENNEDY join.

Two years ago, in *District of Columbia* v. *Heller*, 554 U. S. 570 (2008), we held that the Second Amendment protects the right to keep and bear arms for the purpose of self-defense, and we struck down a District of Columbia law that banned the possession of handguns in the home. The city of Chicago (Chicago or City) and the village of Oak Park, a Chicago suburb, have laws that are similar to the District of Columbia's, but Chicago and Oak Park argue that their laws are constitutional because the Second Amendment has no application to the States. We have previously held that most of the provisions of the Bill of Rights apply with full force to both the Federal Government and the States. Applying the standard that is well established in our case law, we hold that the Second Amendment right is fully applicable to the States.

I

Otis McDonald, Adam Orlov, Colleen Lawson, and David Lawson (Chicago petitioners) are Chicago residents who would like to keep handguns in their homes for self-defense but are prohibited from doing so by Chicago's firearms laws. A City ordinance provides that "[n]o person shall . . . possess . . . any firearm unless such person is the holder of a valid registration certificate for such firearm." Chicago, Ill., Municipal Code § 8–20–040(a) (2009). The Code then prohibits registration of most handguns, thus effectively banning handgun possession by almost all private citizens who reside in the City. § 8–20–050(c). Like Chicago, Oak Park makes it "unlawful for any person to possess . . . any firearm," a term that includes "pistols, revolvers, guns and small arms . . . commonly known as handguns." Oak Park, Ill., Municipal Code §§ 27–2–1 (2007), 27–1–1 (2009).

Chicago enacted its handgun ban to protect its residents "from the loss of property and injury or death from firearms." See Chicago, Ill., Journal of Proceedings of the City Council, p. 10049 (Mar. 19, 1982). The Chicago petitioners and their *amici*, however, argue that the handgun ban has left them vulnerable to criminals. Chicago Police Department statistics, we are told, reveal that the City's handgun murder rate has actually increased since the ban was enacted and that Chicago residents now face one of the highest murder rates in the country and rates of other violent crimes that exceed the average in comparable cities.

Several of the Chicago petitioners have been the targets of threats and violence * * *. [They] own handguns that they store outside of the city limits, but they would like to keep their handguns in their homes for protection.

After our decision in *Heller*, the Chicago petitioners and two groups filed suit against the City in the United States District Court for the Northern District of Illinois. They sought a declaration that the handgun ban and several related Chicago ordinances violate the Second and Fourteenth Amendments to the United States Constitution. Another action challenging the Oak Park law was filed in the same District Court by the National Rifle Association (NRA) and two Oak Park residents. In addition, the NRA and others filed a third action challenging the Chicago ordinances. All three cases were assigned to the same District Judge.

The District Court rejected plaintiffs' argument that the Chicago and Oak Park laws are unconstitutional. The court noted that the Seventh Circuit had "squarely upheld the constitutionality of a ban on handguns a quarter century ago," and that *Heller* had explicitly refrained from "opin[ing] on the subject of incorporation vel non of the Second Amendment." The court observed that a district judge has a "duty to follow established precedent in the Court of Appeals to which he or she is beholden, even though the logic of morc recent caselaw may point in a different direction."

The Seventh Circuit affirmed, relying on three 19th-century cases—*United States* v. *Cruikshank*, 92 U. S. 542 (1876), *Presser* v. *Illinois*, 116 U. S. 252 (1886), and *Miller* v. *Texas*, 153 U. S. 535 (1894)—that were decided in the wake of this Court's interpretation of the Privileges or Immunities Clause of the Fourteenth Amendment in the *Slaughter-House Cases,* 16 Wall. 36 (1873). The Seventh Circuit described the rationale of those cases as "defunct" and recognized that they did not consider the question whether the Fourteenth Amendment's Due Process Clause incorporates the Second Amendment right to keep and bear arms. *NRA, Inc.* v. *Chicago*, 567 F. 3d 856, 857, 858 (2009). Nevertheless, the Seventh Circuit observed that it was obligated to follow Supreme Court precedents that have "direct application," and it declined to predict how the Second Amendment would fare under this Court's modern "selective incorporation" approach. *Id.,* at 857–858.

We granted certiorari.

II

A

Petitioners argue that the Chicago and Oak Park laws violate the right to keep and bear arms for two reasons. Petitioners' primary submission is that this right is among the "privileges or immunities of citizens of the United States" and that the narrow interpretation of the Privileges or Immunities Clause adopted in the *Slaughter-House Cases*, *supra*, should now be rejected. As a secondary argument, petitioners contend that the Fourteenth Amendment's Due Process Clause "incorporates" the Second Amendment right.

Chicago and Oak Park (municipal respondents) maintain that a right set out in the Bill of Rights applies to the States only if that right is an indispensable attribute of *any* " 'civilized' " legal system. Brief for Municipal Respondents 9. If it is possible to imagine a civilized country that does not recognize the right, the municipal respondents tell us, then that right is not protected by due process. *Ibid.* And since there are civilized countries that ban or strictly regulate the private possession of handguns, the municipal respondents maintain that due process does not preclude such measures. *Id.*, at 21–23. In light of the parties' far-reaching arguments, we begin by recounting this Court's analysis over the years of the relationship between the provisions of the Bill of Rights and the States.

B

The Bill of Rights, including the Second Amendment, originally applied only to the Federal Government. In *Barron ex rel. Tiernan* v. *Mayor of Baltimore*, 7 Pet. 243 (1833), the Court, in an opinion by Chief Justice Marshall, explained that this question was "of great importance" but "not of much difficulty." *Id.*, at 247. In less than four pages, the Court firmly rejected the proposition that the first eight Amendments operate as limitations on the States, holding that they apply only to the Federal Government.

The constitutional Amendments adopted in the aftermath of the Civil War fundamentally altered our country's federal system. The provision at issue in this case, § 1 of the Fourteenth Amendment, provides, among other things, that a State may not abridge "the privileges or immunities of citizens of the United States" or deprive "any person of life, liberty, or property, without due process of law."

Four years after the adoption of the Fourteenth Amendment, this Court was asked to interpret the Amendment's reference to "the privileges or immunities of citizens of the United States." The *Slaughter-House Cases, supra,* involved challenges to a Louisiana law permitting the creation of a state-sanctioned monopoly on the butchering of animals within the city of New Orleans. Justice Samuel Miller's opinion for the Court concluded that the Privileges or Immunities Clause protects only those rights "which owe their existence to the Federal government, its National character, its Constitution, or its laws." *Id.*, at 79. The Court held that other fundamental rights—rights that predated the creation of the Federal Government and that "the State governments were created to establish and secure"—were not protected by the Clause. *Id.*, at 76.

* * *

Finding no constitutional protection against state intrusion of the kind envisioned by the Louisiana statute, the Court upheld the statute * * *.

Today, many legal scholars dispute the correctness of the narrow *Slaughter-House* interpretation. See, *e.g.*, *Saenz* v. *Roe*, 526 U. S. 489, n. 1, 527 (1999) (THOMAS, J., dissenting) (scholars of the Fourteenth Amendment agree "that the Clause does not mean what the Court said it meant in 1873"); Amar, Substance and Method in the Year 2000, 28 Pepperdine L. Rev. 601, 631, n. 178 (2001) ("Virtually no serious modern scholar—left, right, and center—thinks that this [interpretation] is a plausible reading of the Amendment"); Brief for Constitutional Law Professors as *Amici Curiae* 33 (claiming an "overwhelming consensus among leading constitutional scholars" that the opinion is "egregiously wrong").

Three years after the decision in the *Slaughter-House Cases,* the Court decided *Cruikshank,* the first of the three 19th-century cases on which the Seventh Circuit relied. 92 U. S. 542. In that case, the Court reviewed convictions stemming from the infamous Colfax Massacre in Louisiana on Easter Sunday 1873. Dozens of blacks, many unarmed, were slaughtered by a rival band of armed white men. Cruikshank himself allegedly marched unarmed African-American prisoners through the streets and then had them summarily executed. Ninety-seven men were indicted for participating in the massacre, but only nine went to trial. Six of the nine were acquitted of all charges; the remaining three were acquitted of murder but convicted under the Enforcement Act of 1870, 16 Stat. 140, for banding and conspiring together to deprive their victims of various constitutional rights, including the right to bear arms.

The Court reversed all of the convictions, including those relating to the deprivation of the victims' right to bear arms. The Court wrote that the right of bearing arms for a lawful purpose "is not a right granted by the Constitution" and is not "in any manner dependent upon that instrument for its existence." "The second amendment," the Court continued, "declares that it shall not be infringed; but this . . . means no more than that it shall not be infringed by Congress." "Our later decisions in *Presser* v. *Illinois,* 116 U. S. 252, 265 (1886), and *Miller* v. *Texas,* 153 U. S. 535, 538 (1894), reaffirmed that the Second Amendment applies only to the Federal Government." *Heller*, 554 U. S., at 620, n. 23.

C

As previously noted, the Seventh Circuit concluded that *Cruikshank*, *Presser*, and *Miller* doomed petitioners' claims at the Court of Appeals level. Petitioners argue, however, that we should overrule those decisions and hold that the right to keep and bear arms is one of the "privileges or immunities of citizens of the United States." In petitioners' view, the Privileges or Immunities Clause protects all of the rights set out in the Bill of Rights, as well as some others, see Brief for Petitioners 10, 14, 15–21, but petitioners are unable to identify the Clause's full scope, Tr. of Oral Arg. 5–6, 8–11. Nor is there any consensus on that question among the scholars who agree that the *Slaughter-House Cases'* interpretation is flawed.

We see no need to reconsider that interpretation here. For many decades, the question of the rights protected by the Fourteenth Amendment against state infringement has been analyzed under the Due Process Clause of that Amendment and not under the Privileges or Immunities Clause. We therefore decline to disturb the *Slaughter-House* holding.

At the same time, however, this Court's decisions in *Cruikshank*, *Presser*, and *Miller* do not preclude us from considering whether the Due Process Clause of the Fourteenth Amendment makes the Second Amendment right binding on the States. None of those cases "engage[d] in the sort of Fourteenth Amendment inquiry required by our later cases." As explained more fully below, *Cruikshank*, *Presser*, and *Miller* all preceded the era in which the Court began the process of "selective incorporation" under the Due Process Clause, and we have never previously addressed the question whether the right to keep and bear arms applies to the States under that theory.

* * *

D

1

In the late 19th century, the Court began to consider whether the Due Process Clause prohibits the States from infringing rights set out in the Bill of Rights. See *Hurtado* v. *California*, 110 U. S. 516 (1884) (due process does not require grand jury indictment); *Chicago, B. & Q. R. Co.* v. *Chicago*, 166 U. S. 226 (1897) (due process prohibits States from taking of private property for public use without just compensation). Five features of the approach taken during the ensuing era should be noted.

First, the Court viewed the due process question as entirely separate from the question whether a right was a privilege or immunity of national citizenship. See *Twining* v. *New Jersey*, 211 U. S. 78, 99 (1908).

Second, the Court explained that the only rights protected against state infringement by the Due Process Clause were those rights "of such a nature that they are included in the conception of due process of law." *Ibid* * * *.

The Court used different formulations in describing the boundaries of due process. For example, in *Twining*, the Court referred to "immutable principles of justice which inhere in the very idea of free government which no member of the Union may disregard." 211 U. S., at 102. In *Snyder* v. *Massachusetts*, 291 U. S. 97, 105 (1934), the Court spoke of rights that are "so rooted in the traditions and conscience of our people as to be ranked as fundamental." And in *Palko*, the Court famously said that due process protects those rights that are "the very essence of a scheme of ordered liberty" and essential to "a fair and enlightened system of justice." 302 U. S., at 325.

Third, in some cases decided during this era the Court "can be seen as having asked, when inquiring into whether some particular procedural safeguard was required of a State, if a civilized system could be imagined that would not accord the particular protection." *Duncan* v. *Louisiana*, 391 U. S. 145, n. 14 (1968). Thus, in holding that due process prohibits a State from taking private property without just compensation, the Court described the right as "a principle of natural equity, recognized by all temperate and civilized governments, from a deep and universal sense of its justice." *Chicago, B. & Q. R. Co., supra,* at 238. Similarly, the Court found that due process did not provide a right against compelled incrimination in part because this right "has no place in the jurisprudence of civilized and free countries outside the domain of the common law." *Twining, supra,* at 113.

Fourth, the Court during this era was not hesitant to hold that a right set out in the Bill of Rights failed to meet the test for inclusion within the protection of the Due Process Clause. The Court found that some such rights qualified. See, *e.g.*, *Gitlow* v. *New York*, 268 U. S. 652, 666 (1925) (freedom of speech and press); *Near* v. *Minnesota ex rel. Olson*, 283 U. S. 697 (1931) (same); *Powell, supra* (assistance of counsel in capital cases); *De Jonge, supra* (freedom of assembly); *Cantwell* v. *Connecticut*, 310 U. S. 296 (1940) (free exercise of religion). But others did not. See, *e.g.*, *Hurtado, supra* (grand jury indictment requirement); *Twining, supra* (privilege against self-incrimination).

Finally, even when a right set out in the Bill of Rights was held to fall within the conception of due process, the protection or remedies afforded against state infringement sometimes differed from the protection or remedies provided against abridgment by the Federal Government. To give one example, in *Betts* the Court held that, although the Sixth Amendment required the appointment of counsel in all federal criminal cases in which the defendant was unable to retain an attorney, the Due Process Clause required appointment of counsel in state criminal proceedings only where "want of counsel in [the] particular case . . . result[ed] in a conviction lacking in . . . fundamental fairness." 316 U. S., at 473. Similarly, in *Wolf* v. *Colorado*, 338 U. S. 25 (1949), the Court held that the "core of the Fourth Amendment" was implicit in the concept of ordered liberty and thus "enforceable against the States through the Due Process Clause" but that the exclusionary rule, which applied in federal cases, did not apply to the States. *Id.*, at 27–28, 33.

2

An alternative theory regarding the relationship between the Bill of Rights and § 1 of the Fourteenth Amendment was championed by Justice Black. This theory held that § 1 of the Fourteenth Amendment totally incorporated all of the provisions of the Bill of Rights. See, *e.g.*, *Adamson, supra*, at 71–72 (Black, J., dissenting). As Justice Black noted, the chief congressional proponents of the Fourteenth Amendment espoused the view that the Amendment made the Bill of Rights applicable to the States and, in so doing, overruled this Court's decision in *Barron*. Nonetheless, the Court never has embraced Justice Black's "total incorporation" theory.

3

While Justice Black's theory was never adopted, the Court eventually moved in that direction by initiating what has been called a process of "selective incorporation," *i.e.*, the Court began to hold that the Due Process Clause fully incorporates particular rights contained in the first eight Amendments.

The decisions during this time abandoned three of the previously noted characteristics of the earlier period. The Court made it clear that the governing standard is not whether *any* "civilized system [can] be imagined that would not accord the particular protection." Instead, the Court inquired whether a particular Bill of Rights guarantee is fundamental to *our* scheme of ordered liberty and system of justice.

The Court also shed any reluctance to hold that rights guaranteed by the Bill of Rights met the requirements for protection under the Due Process Clause. The Court eventually incorporated almost all of the provisions of the Bill of Rights. Only a handful of the Bill of Rights protections remain unincorporated.

Finally, the Court abandoned "the notion that the Fourteenth Amendment applies to the States only a watered-down, subjective version of the individual guarantees of the Bill of Rights," stating that it would be "incongruous" to apply different standards "depending on whether the claim was asserted in a state or federal court." *Malloy*, 378 U. S., at 10–11. Instead, the Court decisively held that incorporated Bill of Rights protections "are all to be enforced against the States under the Fourteenth Amendment according to the same standards that protect those personal rights against federal encroachment." *Id.*, at 10.[14]

Employing this approach, the Court overruled earlier decisions in which it had held that particular Bill of Rights guarantees or remedies did not apply to the States. See, *e.g.*, *Mapp*, *supra* (overruling in part *Wolf*, 338 U. S. 25); *Gideon*, 372 U. S. 335 (overruling *Betts*, 316 U. S. 455); *Malloy*, *supra* (overruling *Adamson*, 332 U. S. 46, and *Twining*, 211 U. S. 78); *Benton*, *supra*, at 794 (overruling *Palko*, 302 U. S. 319).

III

With this framework in mind, we now turn directly to the question whether the Second Amendment right to keep and bear arms is incorporated in the concept of due process. In answering that question, as just explained, we must decide whether the right to keep and bear arms is fundamental to *our* scheme of ordered liberty, *Duncan,* 391 U. S., at 149, or as we have said in a related context, whether this right is "deeply rooted in this Nation's history and tradition," *Washington* v. *Glucksberg,* 521 U. S. 702, 721 (1997).

A

Our decision in *Heller* points unmistakably to the answer. Self-defense is a basic right, recognized by many legal systems from ancient times to the present day, and in *Heller,* we held that individual self-defense is "the *central component*" of the Second Amendment right. Explaining that "the need for defense of self, family, and

---

[14] There is one exception to this general rule. The Court has held that although the Sixth Amendment right to trial by jury requires a unanimous jury verdict in federal criminal trials, it does not require a unanimous jury verdict in state criminal trials. See *Apodaca v. Oregon,* 406 U.S. 404 (1972); see also *Johnson v. Louisiana,* 406 U.S. 356 (1972) (holding that the Due Process Clause does not require unanimous jury verdicts in state criminal trials). But that ruling was the result of an unusual division among the Justices, not an endorsement of the two-track approach to incorporation * * *.

property is most acute" in the home, we found that this right applies to handguns because they are "the most preferred firearm in the nation to 'keep' and use for protection of one's home and family," Thus, we concluded, citizens must be permitted "to use [handguns] for the core lawful purpose of self-defense."

Heller makes it clear that this right is "deeply rooted in this Nation's history and tradition." * * * [B]y 1765, Blackstone was able to assert that the right to keep and bear arms was "one of the fundamental rights of Englishmen."

Blackstone's assessment was shared by the American colonists. As we noted in *Heller*, King George III's attempt to disarm the colonists in the 1760's and 1770's "provoked polemical reactions by Americans invoking their rights as Englishmen to keep arms."

The right to keep and bear arms was considered no less fundamental by those who drafted and ratified the Bill of Rights * * *. This is surely powerful evidence that the right was regarded as fundamental in the sense relevant here.

* * *

B

1

By the 1850's, the perceived threat that had prompted the inclusion of the Second Amendment in the Bill of Rights—the fear that the National Government would disarm the universal militia—had largely faded as a popular concern, but the right to keep and bear arms was highly valued for purposes of self-defense. And when attempts were made to disarm "Free-Soilers" in "Bloody Kansas," Senator Charles Sumner, who later played a leading role in the adoption of the Fourteenth Amendment, proclaimed that "[n]ever was [the rifle] more needed in just self-defense than now in Kansas." The Crime Against Kansas: The Apologies for the Crime: The True Remedy, Speech of Hon. Charles Sumner in the Senate of the United States 64–65 (1856). Indeed, the 1856 Republican Party Platform protested that in Kansas the constitutional rights of the people had been "fraudulently and violently taken from them" and the "right of the people to keep and bear arms" had been "infringed." National Party Platforms 1840–1972, p. 27 (5th ed. 1973).

After the Civil War, many of the over 180,000 African-Americans who served in the Union Army returned to the States of the old Confederacy, where systematic efforts were made to disarm them and other blacks. See E. Foner, Reconstruction: America's Unfinished Revolution 1863–1877, p. 8 (1988) (hereinafter Foner). The laws of some States formally prohibited African-Americans from possessing firearms * * *.

Throughout the South, armed parties, often consisting of ex-Confederate soldiers serving in the state militias, forcibly took firearms from newly freed slaves. In the first session of the 39th Congress, Senator Wilson told his colleagues * * *: "There is one unbroken chain of testimony from all people that are loyal to this country, that the greatest outrages are perpetrated by armed men who go up and down the country searching houses, disarming people, committing outrages of every kind and description." 39th Cong. Globe 915 (1866).

Union Army commanders took steps to secure the right of all citizens to keep and bear arms, but the 39th Congress concluded that legislative action was necessary. Its efforts to safeguard the right to keep and bear arms demonstrate that the right was still recognized to be fundamental.

The most explicit evidence of Congress' aim appears in § 14 of the Freedmen's Bureau Act of 1866, which provided that "the right . . . to have full and equal benefit of all laws and proceedings concerning personal liberty, personal security, and the acquisition, enjoyment, and disposition of estate, real and personal, *including the constitutional right to bear arms*, shall be secured to and enjoyed by all the citizens . . . without respect to race or color, or previous condition of slavery." 14 Stat. 176–177 (emphasis added). Section 14 thus explicitly guaranteed that "all the citizens," black and white, would have "the constitutional right to bear arms."

The Civil Rights Act of 1866, 14 Stat. 27, which was considered at the same time as the Freedmen's Bureau Act, similarly sought to protect the right of all citizens to keep and bear arms * * *. See also Amar, Bill of Rights 264–265 (noting that one of the "core purposes of the Civil Rights Act of 1866 and of the Fourteenth Amendment was to redress the grievances" of freedmen who had been stripped of their arms and to "affirm the full and equal right of every citizen to self-defense").

Congress, however, ultimately deemed these legislative remedies insufficient. Southern resistance, Presidential vetoes, and this Court's pre-Civil-War precedent persuaded Congress that a constitutional amendment was necessary to provide full protection for the rights of blacks. Today, it is generally accepted that the Fourteenth Amendment was understood to provide a constitutional basis for protecting the rights set out in the Civil Rights Act of 1866. See *General Building Contractors Assn., Inc.* v. *Pennsylvania*, 458 U. S. 375, 389 (1982); see also Amar, Bill of Rights 187; Calabresi, Two Cheers for Professor Balkin's Originalism, 103 Nw. U. L. Rev. 663, 669–670 (2009).

* * *

Evidence from the period immediately following the ratification of the Fourteenth Amendment only confirms that the right to keep and bear arms was considered fundamental. In an 1868 speech addressing the disarmament of freedmen, Representative Stevens emphasized the necessity of the right: "Disarm a community and you rob them of the means of defending life. Take away their weapons of defense and you take away the inalienable right of defending liberty." "The fourteenth amendment, now so happily adopted, settles the whole question." Cong. Globe, 40th Cong., 2d Sess., 1967. And in debating the Civil Rights Act of 1871, Congress routinely referred to the right to keep and bear arms and decried the continued disarmament of blacks in the South. See Halbrook, Freedmen 120–131. Finally, legal commentators from the period emphasized the fundamental nature of the right. See, *e.g.*, T. Farrar, Manual of the Constitution of the United States of America § 118, p. 145 (1867) (reprint 1993); J. Pomeroy, An Introduction to the Constitutional Law of the United States § 239, pp. 152–153 (3d ed. 1875).

The right to keep and bear arms was also widely protected by state constitutions at the time when the Fourteenth Amendment was ratified. In 1868, 22 of the 37 States in the Union had state constitutional provisions explicitly protecting the right to keep and bear arms. See Calabresi & Agudo, Individual Rights Under State Constitutions when the Fourteenth Amendment was Ratified in 1868: What Rights Are Deeply Rooted in American History and Tradition? 87 Texas L. Rev. 7, 50

(2008).[26] Quite a few of these state constitutional guarantees, moreover, explicitly protected the right to keep and bear arms as an individual right to self-defense. What is more, state constitutions adopted during the Reconstruction era by former Confederate States included a right to keep and bear arms. See, *e.g.*, Ark. Const., Art. I, § 5 (1868); Miss. Const., Art. I, § 15 (1868); Tex. Const., Art. I, § 13 (1869). A clear majority of the States in 1868, therefore, recognized the right to keep and bear arms as being among the foundational rights necessary to our system of Government.

In sum, it is clear that the Framers and ratifiers of the Fourteenth Amendment counted the right to keep and bear arms among those fundamental rights necessary to our system of ordered liberty.

2

Despite all this evidence, municipal respondents contend that Congress, in the years immediately following the Civil War, merely sought to outlaw "discriminatory measures taken against freedmen, which it addressed by adopting a non-discrimination principle" and that even an outright ban on the possession of firearms was regarded as acceptable, "so long as it was not done in a discriminatory manner." Brief for Municipal Respondents 7. They argue that Members of Congress overwhelmingly viewed § 1 of the Fourteenth Amendment "as an antidiscrimination rule," and they cite statements to the effect that the section would outlaw discriminatory measures. *Id.*, at 64. This argument is implausible.

First, while § 1 of the Fourteenth Amendment contains "an antidiscrimination rule," namely, the Equal Protection Clause, municipal respondents can hardly mean that § 1 does no more than prohibit discrimination. If that were so, then the First Amendment, as applied to the States, would not prohibit nondiscriminatory abridgments of the rights to freedom of speech or freedom of religion; the Fourth Amendment, as applied to the States, would not prohibit all unreasonable searches and seizures but only discriminatory searches and seizures—and so on. We assume that this is not municipal respondents' view, so what they must mean is that the Second Amendment should be singled out for special—and specially unfavorable—treatment. We reject that suggestion.

Second, municipal respondents' argument ignores the clear terms of the Freedmen's Bureau Act of 1866, which acknowledged the existence of the right to bear arms * * *. It would have been nonsensical for Congress to guarantee the full and equal benefit of a constitutional right that does not exist.

Third, if the 39th Congress had outlawed only those laws that discriminate on the basis of race or previous condition of servitude, African-Americans in the South would likely have remained vulnerable to attack by many of their worst abusers: the state militia and state peace officers. In the years immediately following the Civil War, a law banning the possession of guns by all private citizens would have been nondiscriminatory only in the formal sense. Any such law—like the Chicago and Oak Park ordinances challenged here—presumably would have permitted the possession of guns by those acting under the authority of the State and would thus have left firearms in the hands of the militia and local peace officers. And as the Report of the

---

[26] More generally worded provisions in the constitutions of seven other States may also have encompassed a right to bear arms. See Calabresi & Agudo, 87 Texas L.Rev., at 52.

Joint Committee on Reconstruction revealed, those groups were widely involved in harassing blacks in the South.

Fourth, municipal respondents' purely antidiscrimination theory of the Fourteenth Amendment disregards the plight of whites in the South who opposed the Black Codes. If the 39th Congress and the ratifying public had simply prohibited racial discrimination with respect to the bearing of arms, opponents of the Black Codes would have been left without the means of self-defense—as had abolitionists in Kansas in the 1850's.

Fifth, the 39th Congress' response to proposals to disband and disarm the Southern militias is instructive. Despite recognizing and deploring the abuses of these militias, the 39th Congress balked at a proposal to disarm them. Disarmament, it was argued, would violate the members' right to bear arms, and it was ultimately decided to disband the militias but not to disarm their members. See Act of Mar. 2, 1867, § 6, 14 Stat. 485, 487; Halbrook, Freedmen 68–69; Cramer 858–861. It cannot be doubted that the right to bear arms was regarded as a substantive guarantee, not a prohibition that could be ignored so long as the States legislated in an evenhanded manner.

IV

Municipal respondents' remaining arguments are at war with our central holding in *Heller*: that the Second Amendment protects a personal right to keep and bear arms for lawful purposes, most notably for self-defense within the home. Municipal respondents, in effect, ask us to treat the right recognized in *Heller* as a second-class right, subject to an entirely different body of rules than the other Bill of Rights guarantees that we have held to be incorporated into the Due Process Clause.

Municipal respondents' main argument is nothing less than a plea to disregard 50 years of incorporation precedent and return (presumably for this case only) to a bygone era. Municipal respondents submit that the Due Process Clause protects only those rights " 'recognized by all temperate and civilized governments, from a deep and universal sense of [their] justice.' " Brief for Municipal Respondents 9 (quoting *Chicago, B. & Q. R. Co.*, 166 U. S., at 238). According to municipal respondents, if it is possible to imagine *any* civilized legal system that does not recognize a particular right, then the Due Process Clause does not make that right binding on the States. Brief for Municipal Respondents 9. Therefore, the municipal respondents continue, because such countries as England, Canada, Australia, Japan, Denmark, Finland, Luxembourg, and New Zealand either ban or severely limit handgun ownership, it must follow that no right to possess such weapons is protected by the Fourteenth Amendment. *Id.*, at 21–23.

This line of argument is, of course, inconsistent with the long-established standard we apply in incorporation cases. And the present-day implications of municipal respondents' argument are stunning. For example, many of the rights that our Bill of Rights provides for persons accused of criminal offenses are virtually unique to this country. If *our* understanding of the right to a jury trial, the right against self-incrimination, and the right to counsel were necessary attributes of *any* civilized country, it would follow that the United States is the only civilized Nation in the world.

Municipal respondents attempt to salvage their position by suggesting that their argument applies only to substantive as opposed to procedural rights. Brief for

Municipal Respondents 10, n. 3. But even in this trimmed form, municipal respondents' argument flies in the face of more than a half-century of precedent. For example, in *Everson* v. *Board of Ed. of Ewing*, 330 U. S. 1, 8 (1947), the Court held that the Fourteenth Amendment incorporates the Establishment Clause of the First Amendment. Yet several of the countries that municipal respondents recognize as civilized have established state churches. If we were to adopt municipal respondents' theory, all of this Court's Establishment Clause precedents involving actions taken by state and local governments would go by the boards.

Municipal respondents maintain that the Second Amendment differs from all of the other provisions of the Bill of Rights because it concerns the right to possess a deadly implement and thus has implications for public safety. Brief for Municipal Respondents 11. And they note that there is intense disagreement on the question whether the private possession of guns in the home increases or decreases gun deaths and injuries. *Id*, at 11, 13–17.

The right to keep and bear arms, however, is not the only constitutional right that has controversial public safety implications. All of the constitutional provisions that impose restrictions on law enforcement and on the prosecution of crimes fall into the same category * * *. Municipal respondents cite no case in which we have refrained from holding that a provision of the Bill of Rights is binding on the States on the ground that the right at issue has disputed public safety implications.

We likewise reject municipal respondents' argument that we should depart from our established incorporation methodology on the ground that making the Second Amendment binding on the States and their subdivisions is inconsistent with principles of federalism and will stifle experimentation. Municipal respondents point out—quite correctly—that conditions and problems differ from locality to locality and that citizens in different jurisdictions have divergent views on the issue of gun control. Municipal respondents therefore urge us to allow state and local governments to enact any gun control law that they deem to be reasonable, including a complete ban on the possession of handguns in the home for self-defense. Brief for Municipal Respondents 18–20, 23.

There is nothing new in the argument that, in order to respect federalism and allow useful state experimentation, a federal constitutional right should not be fully binding on the States. This argument was made repeatedly and eloquently by Members of this Court who rejected the concept of incorporation and urged retention of the two-track approach to incorporation * * *.

Time and again, however, those pleas failed. Unless we turn back the clock or adopt a special incorporation test applicable only to the Second Amendment, municipal respondents' argument must be rejected. Under our precedents, if a Bill of Rights guarantee is fundamental from an American perspective, then, unless *stare decisis* counsels otherwise, that guarantee is fully binding on the States and thus *limits* (but by no means eliminates) their ability to devise solutions to social problems that suit local needs and values * * *.

* * *

As evidence that the Fourteenth Amendment has not historically been understood to restrict the authority of the States to regulate firearms, municipal respondents and supporting *amici* cite a variety of state and local firearms laws that courts have upheld. But what is most striking about their research is the paucity of precedent sustaining bans comparable to those at issue here and in *Heller*. Municipal respondents cite precisely one case (from the late 20th century) in which such a ban was sustained. See Brief for Municipal Respondents 26–27 (citing *Kalodimos* v. *Morton Grove*, 103 Ill. 2d 483, 470 N. E. 2d 266 (1984). It is important to keep in mind that *Heller*, while striking down a law that prohibited the possession of handguns in the home, recognized that the right to keep and bear arms is not "a right to keep and carry any weapon whatsoever in any manner whatsoever and for whatever purpose." 554 U. S., at 626. We made it clear in *Heller* that our holding did not cast doubt on such longstanding regulatory measures as "prohibitions on the possession of firearms by felons and the mentally ill," "laws forbidding the carrying of firearms in sensitive places such as schools and government buildings, or laws imposing conditions and qualifications on the commercial sale of arms." *Id.*, at 626–627. We repeat those assurances here. Despite municipal respondents' doomsday proclamations, incorporation does not imperil every law regulating firearms.

* * *

V

A

We turn, finally, to the two dissenting opinions * * *. JUSTICE STEVENS would " 'ground the prohibitions against state action squarely on due process, without intermediate reliance on any of the first eight Amendments.' " * * *.

As we have explained, the Court, for the past half-century, has moved away from the two-track approach. If we were now to accept JUSTICE STEVENS' theory across the board, decades of decisions would be undermined. We assume that this is not what is proposed. What is urged instead, it appears, is that this theory be revived solely for the individual right that *Heller* recognized, over vigorous dissents.

The relationship between the Bill of Rights' guarantees and the States must be governed by a single, neutral principle. It is far too late to exhume what Justice Brennan, writing for the Court 46 years ago, derided as "the notion that the Fourteenth Amendment applies to the States only a watered-down, subjective version of the individual guarantees of the Bill of Rights." *Malloy*, *supra*, at 10–11.

B

JUSTICE BREYER's dissent makes several points to which we briefly respond. To begin, while there is certainly room for disagreement about *Heller*'s analysis of the history of the right to keep and bear arms, nothing written since *Heller* persuades us to reopen the question there decided. Few other questions of original meaning have been as thoroughly explored.

JUSTICE BREYER's conclusion that the Fourteenth Amendment does not incorporate the right to keep and bear arms appears to rest primarily on four factors: First, "there is no popular consensus" that the right is fundamental; second, the right does not protect minorities or persons neglected by those holding political power; third, incorporation of the Second Amendment right would "amount to a significant incursion on a traditional and important area of state concern, altering the constitutional relationship between the States and the Federal Government" and preventing local variations; and fourth, determining the scope of the Second Amendment right in cases involving state and local laws will force judges to answer difficult empirical questions regarding matters that are outside their area of expertise. Even if we believed that these factors were relevant to the incorporation inquiry, none of these factors undermines the case for incorporation of the right to keep and bear arms for self-defense.

First, we have never held that a provision of the Bill of Rights applies to the States only if there is a "popular consensus" that the right is fundamental, and we see no basis for such a rule. But in this case, as it turns out, there is evidence of such a consensus. An *amicus* brief submitted by 58 Members of the Senate and 251 Members of the House of Representatives urges us to hold that the right to keep and bear arms is fundamental. See Brief for Senator Kay Bailey Hutchison et al. as *Amici Curiae* 4. Another brief submitted by 38 States takes the same position. Brief for State of Texas et al. as *Amici Curiae* 6.

Second, petitioners and many others who live in high-crime areas dispute the proposition that the Second Amendment right does not protect minorities and those lacking political clout * * *. *Amici* supporting incorporation of the right to keep and bear arms contend that the right is especially important for women and members of other groups that may be especially vulnerable to violent crime. If, as petitioners believe, their safety and the safety of other law-abiding members of the community would be enhanced by the possession of handguns in the home for self-defense, then the Second Amendment right protects the rights of minorities and other residents of high-crime areas whose needs are not being met by elected public officials.

Third, JUSTICE BREYER is correct that incorporation of the Second Amendment right will to some extent limit the legislative freedom of the States * * *. This conclusion is no more remarkable with respect to the Second Amendment than it is with respect to all the other limitations on state power found in the Constitution.

Finally, JUSTICE BREYER is incorrect that incorporation will require judges to assess the costs and benefits of firearms restrictions and thus to make difficult empirical judgments in an area in which they lack expertise. As we have noted, while his opinion in *Heller* recommended an interest-balancing test, the Court specifically rejected that suggestion * * *.

In *Heller*, we held that the Second Amendment protects the right to possess a handgun in the home for the purpose of self-defense. Unless considerations of *stare decisis* counsel otherwise, a provision of the Bill of Rights that protects a right that is fundamental from an American perspective applies equally to the Federal Government and the States. We therefore hold that the Due Process Clause of the Fourteenth Amendment incorporates the Second Amendment right recognized in *Heller*. The judgment of the Court of Appeals is reversed, and the case is remanded for further proceedings.

It is so ordered.

■ JUSTICE SCALIA, concurring.

I join the Court's opinion. Despite my misgivings about substantive due process as an original matter, I have acquiesced in the Court's incorporation of certain guarantees in the Bill of Rights "because it is both long established and narrowly limited." *Albright v. Oliver,* 510 U.S. 266, 275 (1994) (SCALIA, J., concurring). This case does not require me to reconsider that view, since straightforward application of settled doctrine suffices to decide it.

I write separately only to respond to some aspects of JUSTICE STEVENS' dissent * * *.

After stressing the substantive dimension of what he has renamed the "liberty clause," JUSTICE STEVENS proceeds to urge readoption of the theory of incorporation articulated in *Palko v. Connecticut,* 302 U.S. 319, 325 (1937). But in fact he does not favor application of that theory at all. For whether *Palko* requires only that "a fair and enlightened system of justice would be impossible without" the right sought to be incorporated, 302 U.S., at 325, or requires in addition that the right be rooted in the "traditions and conscience of our people," *ibid.*, many of the rights JUSTICE STEVENS thinks are incorporated could not past muster under either test: abortion, *post,* at 864 (citing *Planned Parenthood of Southeastern Pa. v. Casey,* 505 U.S. 833, 847 (1992)); homosexual sodomy, *post,* at 873 (citing *Lawrence v. Texas,* 539 U.S. 558, 572 (2003)); the right to have excluded from criminal trials evidence obtained in violation of the Fourth Amendment, *post,* at 875 (citing *Mapp v. Ohio,* 367 U.S. 643, 650, 655–657 (1961)); and the right to teach one's children foreign languages, *post,* at 864 (citing *Meyer v. Nebraska,* 262 U.S. 390, 399–403 (1923)), among others.

That JUSTICE STEVENS is not applying any version of *Palko* is clear from comparing, on the one hand, the rights he believes *are* covered, with, on the other hand, his conclusion that the right to keep and bear arms is *not* covered. Rights that pass his test include not just those "relating to marriage, procreation, contraception, family relationships, and child rearing and education," but also rights against "[g]overnment action that shocks the conscience, pointlessly infringes settled expectations, trespasses into sensitive private realms or life choices without adequate justification, [or] perpetrates gross injustice." *Post,* at 879. Not *all* such rights are in, however, since only "*some* fundamental aspects of personhood, dignity, and the like" are protected, *post,* at 880 (emphasis added). Exactly what is covered is not clear. But whatever else is in, he *knows* that the right to keep and bear arms is out, despite its being as "deeply rooted in this Nation's history and tradition." I can find no other explanation for such certitude except that JUSTICE STEVENS, despite his forswearing of "personal and private notions," *post,* at 878 (internal quotation marks omitted), deeply believes it should be out.

* * *

* * * [T]he Court's approach intrudes less upon the democratic process because the rights it acknowledges are those established by a constitutional history formed by democratic decisions; and the rights it fails to acknowledge are left to be democratically adopted or rejected by the people, with the assurance that their decision is not subject to judicial revision. JUSTICE STEVENS' approach, on the other hand, deprives the people of that power, since whatever the Constitution and laws may say, the list of protected rights will be whatever courts wish it to be. After all, he notes, the people have been wrong before, and courts may conclude they are wrong in the future. Justice STEVENS abhors a system in which "majorities or powerful interest groups always get their way," but replaces it with a system in which unelected and life-tenured judges always get their way * * *.

■ JUSTICE THOMAS, concurring in part and concurring in the judgment.

I agree with the Court that the Fourteenth Amendment makes the right to keep and bear arms set forth in the Second Amendment "fully applicable to the States." I write separately because I believe there is a more straightforward path to this conclusion, one that is more faithful to the Fourteenth Amendment's text and history.

Applying what is now a well-settled test, the plurality opinion concludes that the right to keep and bear arms applies to the States through the Fourteenth Amendment's Due Process Clause because it is "fundamental" to the American "scheme of ordered liberty" and " 'deeply rooted in this Nation's history and tradition.' " I agree with that description of the right. But I cannot agree that it is enforceable against the States through a Clause that speaks only to "process." Instead, the right to keep and bear arms is a privilege of American citizenship that applies to the States through the Fourteenth Amendment's Privileges or Immunities Clause.

I

In *District of Columbia* v. *Heller*, 554 U. S. 570 (2008), this Court held that the Second Amendment protects an individual right to keep and bear arms for the purpose of self-defense, striking down a District of Columbia ordinance that banned the possession of handguns in the home. The question in this case is whether the Constitution protects that right against abridgment by the States.

As the Court explains, if this case were litigated before the Fourteenth Amendment's adoption in 1868, the answer to that question would be simple. In *Barron ex rel. Tiernan* v. *Mayor of Baltimore*, 7 Pet. 243 (1833), this Court held that the Bill of Rights applied only to the Federal Government * * *.

Nearly three decades after *Barron*, the Nation was splintered by a civil war fought principally over the question of slavery. As was evident to many throughout our Nation's early history, slavery, and the measures designed to protect it, were irreconcilable with the principles of equality, government by consent, and inalienable rights proclaimed by the Declaration of Independence and embedded in our constitutional structure. See, *e.g.*, 3 Records of the Federal Convention of 1787, p. 212 (M. Farrand ed. 1911) (remarks of Luther Martin) ("[S]lavery is inconsistent with the genius of republicanism, and has a tendency to destroy those principles on which it is supported, as it lessens the sense of the equal rights of mankind" (emphasis deleted)); A. Lincoln, Speech at Peoria, Ill. (Oct. 16, 1854), reprinted in 2 The Collected Works of Abraham Lincoln 266 (R. Basler ed. 1953) ("[N]o man is good enough to govern another man, *without that other's consent*. I say this is the leading principle—the sheet anchor of American republicanism. . . . Now the relation of masters and slaves is, *pro tanto*, a total violation of this principle").

After the war, a series of constitutional amendments were adopted to repair the Nation from the damage slavery had caused. The provision at issue here, § 1 of the Fourteenth Amendment, significantly altered our system of government. The first sentence of that section provides that "[a]ll persons born or naturalized in the United States and subject to the jurisdiction thereof, are citizens of the United States and of the State wherein they reside." This unambiguously overruled this Court's contrary holding in *Dred Scott* v. *Sandford*, 19 How. 393 (1857), that the Constitution did not recognize black Americans as citizens of the United States or their own State.

The meaning of § 1's next sentence has divided this Court for many years. That sentence begins with the command that "[n]o State shall make or enforce any law which shall abridge the privileges or immunities of citizens of the United States." On its face, this appears to grant the persons just made United States citizens a certain collection of rights—*i.e.*, privileges or immunities—attributable to that status.

This Court's precedents accept that point, but define the relevant collection of rights quite narrowly. In the *Slaughter-House Cases*, 16 Wall. 36 (1873), decided just five years after the Fourteenth Amendment's adoption, the Court interpreted this text, now known as the Privileges or Immunities Clause, for the first time. In a closely divided decision, the Court drew a sharp distinction between the privileges and immunities of state citizenship and those of federal citizenship, and held that the Privileges or Immunities Clause protected only the latter category of rights from state abridgment. The Court defined that category to include only those rights "which owe their existence to the Federal government, its National character, its Constitution, or its laws." This arguably left open the possibility that certain individual rights enumerated in the Constitution could be considered privileges or immunities of federal citizenship. See *ibid.* (listing "[t]he right to peaceably assemble" and "the privilege of the writ of *habeas corpus*" as rights potentially protected by the Privileges or Immunities Clause). But the Court soon rejected that proposition, interpreting the Privileges or Immunities Clause even more narrowly in its later cases.

Chief among those cases is *United States* v. *Cruikshank*, 92 U. S. 542 (1876). There, the Court held that members of a white militia who had brutally murdered as many as 165 black Louisianians congregating outside a courthouse had not deprived the victims of their privileges as American citizens to peaceably assemble or to keep and bear arms. According to the Court, the right to peaceably assemble codified in the First Amendment was not a privilege of United States citizenship because "[t]he right . . . existed long *before* the adoption of the Constitution." 92 U. S., at 551 (emphasis added). Similarly, the Court held that the right to keep and bear arms was not a privilege of United States citizenship because it was not "in any manner dependent upon that instrument for its existence." *Id.*, at 553. In other words, the reason the Framers codified the right to bear arms in the Second Amendment—its nature as an inalienable right that pre-existed the Constitution's adoption—was the very reason citizens could not enforce it against States through the Fourteenth.

That circular reasoning effectively has been the Court's last word on the Privileges or Immunities Clause. In the intervening years, the Court has held that the Clause prevents state abridgment of only a handful of rights, such as the right to travel, see *Saenz* v. *Roe*, 526 U. S. 489, 503 (1999), that are not readily described as essential to liberty.

As a consequence of this Court's marginalization of the Clause, litigants seeking federal protection of fundamental rights turned to the remainder of § 1 in search of an alternative fount of such rights. They found one in a most curious place—that section's command that every State guarantee "due process" to any person before depriving him of "life, liberty, or property." At first, litigants argued that this Due Process Clause "incorporated" certain procedural rights codified in the Bill of Rights against the States. The Court generally rejected those claims, however, on the theory that the rights in question were not sufficiently "fundamental" to warrant such treatment. See, *e.g.*, *Hurtado* v. *California*, 110 U. S. 516 (1884) (grand jury indictment requirement); *Maxwell* v. *Dow*, 176 U. S. 581 (1900) (12-person jury requirement); *Twining* v. *New Jersey*, 211 U. S. 78 (1908) (privilege against self-incrimination).

That changed with time. The Court came to conclude that certain Bill of Rights guarantees *were* sufficiently fundamental to fall within § 1's guarantee of "due process." These included not only procedural protections listed in the first eight Amendments, see, *e.g.*, *Benton* v. *Maryland*, 395 U. S. 784 (1969) (protection against double jeopardy), but substantive rights as well, see, *e.g.*, *Gitlow* v. *New York*, 268 U. S. 652, 666 (1925) (right to free speech); *Near* v. *Minnesota ex rel. Olson*, 283 U. S. 697, 707 (1931) (same). In the process of incorporating these rights against the States, the Court often applied them differently against the States than against the Federal Government on the theory that only those "fundamental" aspects of the right required Due Process Clause protection. See, *e.g.*, *Betts* v. *Brady*, 316 U. S. 455, 473 (1942) (holding that the Sixth Amendment required the appointment of counsel in all federal criminal cases in which the defendant was unable to retain an attorney, but that the Due Process Clause required appointment of counsel in state criminal cases only where "want of counsel . . . result[ed] in a conviction lacking in . . . fundamental fairness"). In more recent years, this Court has "abandoned the notion" that the guarantees in the Bill of Rights apply differently when incorporated against the States than they do when applied to the Federal Government. But our cases continue to adhere to the view that a right is incorporated through the Due Process Clause only if it is sufficiently "fundamental"—a term the Court has long struggled to define.

While this Court has at times concluded that a right gains "fundamental" status only if it is essential to the American "scheme of ordered liberty" or " 'deeply rooted in this Nation's history and tradition,' " the Court has just as often held that a right warrants Due Process Clause protection if it satisfies a far less measurable range of criteria, see *Lawrence* v. *Texas*, 539 U. S. 558, 562 (2003) (concluding that the Due Process Clause protects "liberty of the person both in its spatial and in its more transcendent dimensions"). Using the latter approach, the Court has determined that the Due Process Clause applies rights against the States that are not mentioned in the Constitution at all, even without seriously arguing that the Clause was originally understood to protect such rights. See, *e.g.*, *Lochner* v. *New York*, 198 U. S. 45 (1905); *Roe* v. *Wade*, 410 U. S. 113 (1973); *Lawrence*, *supra*.

All of this is a legal fiction. The notion that a constitutional provision that guarantees only "process" before a person is deprived of life, liberty, or property could define the substance of those rights strains credulity for even the most casual user of words. Moreover, this fiction is a particularly dangerous one. The one theme that links the Court's substantive due process precedents together is their lack of a guiding principle to distinguish "fundamental" rights that warrant protection from nonfundamental rights that do not. Today's decision illustrates the point. Replaying a debate that has endured from the inception of the Court's substantive due process jurisprudence, the dissents laud the "flexibility" in this Court's substantive due process doctrine, while the plurality makes yet another effort to impose principled restraints on its exercise. But neither side argues that the meaning they attribute to the Due Process Clause was consistent with public understanding at the time of its ratification.

To be sure, the plurality's effort to cabin the exercise of judicial discretion under the Due Process Clause by focusing its inquiry on those rights deeply rooted in

American history and tradition invites less opportunity for abuse than the alternatives. See *post*, at 918 (BREYER, J., dissenting) (arguing that rights should be incorporated against the States through the Due Process Clause if they are "well-suited to the carrying out of . . . constitutional promises"); *post*, at 878 (STEVENS, J., dissenting) (warning that there is no "all-purpose, top-down, totalizing theory of 'liberty' " protected by the Due Process Clause). But any serious argument over the scope of the Due Process Clause must acknowledge that neither its text nor its history suggests that it protects the many substantive rights this Court's cases now claim it does.

I cannot accept a theory of constitutional interpretation that rests on such tenuous footing. This Court's substantive due process framework fails to account for both the text of the Fourteenth Amendment and the history that led to its adoption, filling that gap with a jurisprudence devoid of a guiding principle. I believe the original meaning of the Fourteenth Amendment offers a superior alternative, and that a return to that meaning would allow this Court to enforce the rights the Fourteenth Amendment is designed to protect with greater clarity and predictability than the substantive due process framework has so far managed.

* * *

II

"It cannot be presumed that any clause in the constitution is intended to be without effect." *Marbury* v. *Madison*, 1 Cranch 137, 174 (1803) (Marshall, C. J.). Because the Court's Privileges or Immunities Clause precedents have presumed just that, I set them aside for the moment and begin with the text.

The Privileges or Immunities Clause of the Fourteenth Amendment declares that "[n]o State . . . shall abridge the privileges or immunities of citizens of the United States." In interpreting this language, it is important to recall that constitutional provisions are " 'written to be understood by the voters.' " *Heller*, 554 U. S., at 576 (quoting *United States* v. *Sprague*, 282 U. S. 716, 731 (1931)). Thus, the objective of this inquiry is to discern what "ordinary citizens" at the time of ratification would have understood the Privileges or Immunities Clause to mean.

A

1

At the time of Reconstruction, the terms "privileges" and "immunities" had an established meaning as synonyms for "rights." The two words, standing alone or paired together, were used interchangeably with the words "rights," "liberties," and "freedoms," and had been since the time of Blackstone. See 1 W. Blackstone, Commentaries *129 (describing the "rights and liberties" of Englishmen as "private immunities" and "civil privileges"). A number of antebellum judicial decisions used the terms in this manner. See, *e.g.*, *Magill* v. *Brown*, 16 F. Cas. 408, 428 (No. 8,952) (CC ED Pa. 1833) (Baldwin, J.) ("The words 'privileges and immunities' relate to the rights of persons, place or property; a privilege is a peculiar right, a private law, conceded to particular persons or places"). In addition, dictionary definitions confirm that the public shared this understanding. See, *e.g.*, N. Webster, An American Dictionary of the English Language 1039 (C. Goodrich & N. Porter rev. 1865) (defining "privilege" as "a right or immunity not enjoyed by others or by all" and listing among its synonyms the words "immunity," "franchise," "right," and "liberty"); *id.*, at 661 (defining "immunity" as "[f]reedom from an obligation" or "particular privilege"); *id.*, at 1140 (defining "right" as "[p]rivilege or immunity granted by authority").

The fact that a particular interest was designated as a "privilege" or "immunity," rather than a "right," "liberty," or "freedom," revealed little about its substance * * *.

2

The group of rights-bearers to whom the Privileges or Immunities Clause applies is, of course, "citizens." By the time of Reconstruction, it had long been established that both the States and the Federal Government existed to preserve their citizens' inalienable rights, and that these rights were considered "privileges" or "immunities" of citizenship.

This tradition begins with our country's English roots. Parliament declared the basic liberties of English citizens in a series of documents ranging from the Magna Carta to the Petition of Right and the English Bill of Rights. See 1 B. Schwartz, The Bill of Rights: A Documentary History 8–16, 19–21, 41–46 (1971) (hereinafter Schwartz). These fundamental rights, according to the English tradition, belonged to all people but became legally enforceable only when recognized in legal texts, including acts of Parliament and the decisions of common-law judges. These rights included many that later would be set forth in our Federal Bill of Rights, such as the right to petition for redress of grievances, the right to a jury trial, and the right of "Protestants" to "have arms for their defence." English Bill of Rights (1689), reprinted in 1 Schwartz 41, 43.

As English subjects, the colonists considered themselves to be vested with the same fundamental rights as other Englishmen. They consistently claimed the rights of English citizenship in their founding documents, repeatedly referring to these rights as "privileges" and "immunities." For example, a Maryland law provided that

> "[A]ll the Inhabitants of this Province being Christians (Slaves excepted) Shall have and enjoy all such *rights liberties immunities priviledges and free customs* within this Province as any naturall born subject of England hath or ought to have or enjoy in the Realm of England . . . ." Md. Act for the Liberties of the People (1639), in *id.*, at 68 (emphasis added).

As tensions between England and the Colonies increased, the colonists adopted protest resolutions reasserting their claim to the inalienable rights of Englishmen. Again, they used the terms "privileges" and "immunities" to describe these rights. As the Massachusetts Resolves declared:

> "*Resolved*, That there are certain essential Rights of the *British* Constitution of Government, which are founded in the Law of God and Nature, and are the common Rights of Mankind—Therefore
>
> . . . .
>
> "*Resolved,* That no Man can justly take the Property of another without his Consent: And that upon this *original* Principle the Right of Representation . . . is evidently founded.
>
> *Resolved*, That this *inherent* Right, together with all other, essential *Rights, Liberties, Privileges and Immunities* of the People of *Great Britain,* have been fully confirmed to them by *Magna Charta.*" The Massachusetts Resolves (Oct. 29, 1765), reprinted in Prologue to Revolution: Sources and

Documents on the Stamp Act Crisis, 1764–1766, p. 56 (E. Morgan ed. 1959) (some emphasis added).

In keeping with this practice, the First Continental Congress declared in 1774 that the King had wrongfully denied the colonists "the rights, liberties, and immunities of free and natural-born subjects . . . within the realm of England." 1 Journals of the Continental Congress 1774–1789, p. 68 (1904) * * *.

After declaring their independence, the newly formed States replaced their colonial charters with constitutions and state bills of rights, almost all of which guaranteed the same fundamental rights that the former colonists previously had claimed by virtue of their English heritage.

Several years later, the Founders amended the Constitution to expressly protect many of the same fundamental rights against interference by the Federal Government. Consistent with their English heritage, the founding generation generally did not consider many of the rights identified in these amendments as new entitlements, but as inalienable rights of all men, given legal effect by their codification in the Constitution's text. The Court's subsequent decision in *Barron*, however, made plain that the codification of these rights in the Bill made them legally enforceable only against the Federal Government, not the States. See 7 Pet., at 247.

3

Even though the Bill of Rights did not apply to the States, other provisions of the Constitution did limit state interference with individual rights. Article IV, § 2, cl. 1 provides that "[t]he Citizens of each State shall be entitled to all Privileges and Immunities of Citizens in the several States." The text of this provision resembles the Privileges or Immunities Clause, and it can be assumed that the public's understanding of the latter was informed by its understanding of the former.

Article IV, § 2 was derived from a similar clause in the Articles of Confederation, and reflects the dual citizenship the Constitution provided to all Americans after replacing that "league" of separate sovereign States. By virtue of a person's citizenship in a particular State, he was guaranteed whatever rights and liberties that State's constitution and laws made available. Article IV, § 2 vested citizens of each State with an additional right: the assurance that they would be afforded the "privileges and immunities" of citizenship in any of the several States in the Union to which they might travel.

What were the "Privileges and Immunities of Citizens in the several States"? That question was answered perhaps most famously by Justice Bushrod Washington sitting as Circuit Justice in *Corfield* v. *Coryell*, 6 F. Cas. 546, 551–552 (No. 3,230) (CC ED Pa. 1825) * * *. In his view, Article IV, § 2 did not guarantee equal access to all public benefits a State might choose to make available to its citizens. See *id.,* at 552. Instead, it applied only to those rights "which are, in their nature, *fundamental*; which belong, of right, to the citizens of all free governments." *Id*, at 551 (emphasis added) * * *.

When describing those "fundamental" rights, Justice Washington thought it "would perhaps be more tedious than difficult to enumerate" them all, but suggested that they could "be all comprehended under" a broad list of "general heads," such as "[p]rotection by the government," "the enjoyment of life and liberty, with the right to acquire and possess property of every kind," "the benefit of the writ of habeas corpus," and the right of access to "the courts of the state," among others. *Corfield*, *supra*, at 551–552.

Notably, Justice Washington did not indicate whether Article IV, § 2 *required* States to recognize these fundamental rights in their own citizens and thus in sojourning citizens alike, or whether the Clause simply prohibited the States from discriminating against sojourning citizens with respect to whatever fundamental rights state law happened to recognize. On this question, the weight of legal authorities at the time of Reconstruction indicated that Article IV, § 2 prohibited States from discriminating against sojourning citizens when recognizing fundamental rights, but did not require States to recognize those rights and did not prescribe their content. The highest courts of several States adopted this view. This Court adopted the same conclusion in a unanimous opinion just one year after the Fourteenth Amendment was ratified. See *Paul* v. *Virginia*, 8 Wall. 168, 180 (1869).

The text examined so far demonstrates three points about the meaning of the Privileges or Immunities Clause in § 1. First, "privileges" and "immunities" were synonyms for "rights." Second, both the States and the Federal Government had long recognized the inalienable rights of their citizens. Third, Article IV, § 2 of the Constitution protected traveling citizens against state discrimination with respect to the fundamental rights of state citizenship.

Two questions still remain, both provoked by the textual similarity between § 1's Privileges or Immunities Clause and Article IV, § 2. The first involves the nature of the rights at stake: Are the privileges or immunities of "citizens of the United States" recognized by § 1 the same as the privileges and immunities of "Citizens in the several States" to which Article IV, § 2 refers? The second involves the restriction imposed on the States: Does § 1, like Article IV, § 2, prohibit only discrimination with respect to certain rights *if* the State chooses to recognize them, or does it require States to recognize those rights? I address each question in turn.

B

I start with the nature of the rights that § 1's Privileges or Immunities Clause protects. Section 1 overruled *Dred Scott*'s holding that blacks were not citizens of either the United States or their own State and, thus, did not enjoy "the privileges and immunities of citizens" embodied in the Constitution. 19 How., at 417. The Court in *Dred Scott* did not distinguish between privileges and immunities of citizens of the United States and citizens in the several States, instead referring to the rights of citizens generally. It did, however, give examples of what the rights of citizens were—the constitutionally enumerated rights of "the full liberty of speech" and the right "to keep and carry arms." *Ibid.*

Section 1 protects the rights of citizens "of the United States" specifically. The evidence overwhelmingly demonstrates that the privileges and immunities of such citizens included individual rights enumerated in the Constitution, including the right to keep and bear arms.

1

Nineteenth-century treaties through which the United States acquired territory from other sovereigns routinely promised inhabitants of the newly acquired territories that they would enjoy all of the "rights," "privileges," and "immunities" of United States citizens. See, *e.g.*, Treaty of Amity, Settlement, and Limits, Art. 6, Feb. 22, 1819, 8 Stat. 256–258, T. S. No. 327 (entered into force Feb. 19, 1821) (cession of

Florida) ("The inhabitants of the territories which his Catholic Majesty cedes to the United States, by this Treaty, shall be incorporated in the Union of the United States, as soon as may be consistent with the principles of the Federal Constitution, and admitted to the enjoyment of *all the privileges, rights, and immunities, of the citizens of the United States*" (emphasis added)).

Commentators of the time explained that the rights and immunities of "citizens of the United States" recognized in these treaties "undoubtedly mean[t] those privileges that are common to all citizens of this republic." Marcus, An Examination of the Expediency and Constitutionality of Prohibiting Slavery in the State of Missouri 17 (1819). It is therefore altogether unsurprising that several of these treaties identify liberties enumerated in the Constitution as privileges and immunities common to all United States citizens.

For example, the Louisiana Cession Act of 1803, which codified a treaty between the United States and France culminating in the Louisiana Purchase, provided that

> "The inhabitants of the ceded territory shall be incorporated in the Union of the United States, and admitted as soon as possible, according to the principles of the Federal constitution, to the enjoyments of *all the rights, advantages and immunities of citizens of the United States;* and in the mean time they shall be maintained and protected in *the free enjoyment of their liberty, property and the religion which they profess.*" Treaty Between the United States of America and the French Republic, Art. III, Apr. 30, 1803, 8 Stat. 202, T. S. No. 86 (emphasis added).

The Louisiana Cession Act reveals even more about the privileges and immunities of United States citizenship because it provoked an extensive public debate on the meaning of that term. In 1820, when the Missouri Territory (which the United States acquired through the Cession Act) sought to enter the Union as a new State, a debate ensued over whether to prohibit slavery within Missouri as a condition of its admission. Some Congressmen argued that prohibiting slavery in Missouri would deprive its inhabitants of the "privileges and immunities" they had been promised by the Cession Act. See, *e.g.*, 35 Annals of Cong. 1083 (1855) (remarks of Kentucky Rep. Hardin). But those who opposed slavery in Missouri argued that the right to hold slaves was merely a matter of state property law, not one of the privileges and immunities of United States citizenship guaranteed by the Act.

Daniel Webster was among the leading proponents of the antislavery position. In his "Memorial to Congress," Webster argued that "[t]he rights, advantages and immunities here spoken of [in the Cession Act] must . . . be such as are recognized or communicated by the Constitution of the United States," not the "rights, advantages and immunities, derived exclusively from the *State* governments . . . ." D. Webster, A Memorial to the Congress of the United States on the Subject of Restraining the Increase of Slavery in New States to be Admitted into the Union 15 (Dec. 15, 1819) (emphasis added). "The obvious meaning" of the Act, in Webster's view, was that "*the rights derived under the federal Constitution* shall be enjoyed by the inhabitants of [the territory]." *Id.*, at 15–16 (emphasis added). In other words, Webster articulated a distinction between the rights of United States citizenship and the rights of state citizenship, and argued that the former included those rights "recognized or communicated by the Constitution." Since the right to hold slaves was not mentioned in the Constitution, it was not a right of federal citizenship.

Webster and his allies ultimately lost the debate over slavery in Missouri, and the territory was admitted as a slave State as part of the now-famous Missouri Compromise. Missouri Enabling Act of March 6, 1820, ch. 22, § 8, 3 Stat. 548. But their arguments continued to inform public understanding of the privileges and immunities of United States citizenship. In 1854, Webster's Memorial was republished in a pamphlet discussing the Nation's next major debate on slavery—the proposed repeal of the Missouri Compromise through the Kansas-Nebraska Act, see The Nebraska Question: Comprising Speeches in the United States Senate: Together with the History of the Missouri Compromise 9–12 (1854). It was published again in 1857 in a collection of famous American speeches. See The Political Text-Book, or Encyclopedia: Containing Everything Necessary for the Reference of the Politicians and Statesmen of the United States 601–604 (M. Cluskey ed. 1857); see also Lash, 98 Geo. L. J., at 1294–1296 (describing Webster's arguments and their influence).

2

Evidence from the political branches in the years leading to the Fourteenth Amendment's adoption demonstrates broad public understanding that the privileges and immunities of United States citizenship included rights set forth in the Constitution, just as Webster and his allies had argued. In 1868, President Andrew Johnson issued a proclamation granting amnesty to former Confederates, guaranteeing "to all and to every person who directly or indirectly participated in the late insurrection or rebellion, a full pardon and amnesty for the offence of treason . . . with restoration of *all rights, privileges, and immunities under the Constitution* and the laws which have been made in pursuance thereof." 15 Stat. 712.

Records from the 39th Congress further support this understanding.

a

After the Civil War, Congress established the Joint Committee on Reconstruction to investigate circumstances in the Southern States and to determine whether, and on what conditions, those States should be readmitted to the Union. That Committee would ultimately recommend the adoption of the Fourteenth Amendment, justifying its recommendation by submitting a report to Congress that extensively catalogued the abuses of civil rights in the former slave States and argued that "adequate security for future peace and safety . . . can only be found in such changes of the organic law as shall determine the civil rights and privileges of all citizens in all parts of the republic." See Report of the Joint Committee on Reconstruction, S. Rep. No. 112, 39th Cong., 1st Sess., p. 15 (1866); H. R. Rep. No. 30, 39th Cong., 1st Sess., p. XXI (1866).

As the Court notes, the Committee's Report "was widely reprinted in the press and distributed by members of the 39th Congress to their constituents." B. Kendrick, Journal of the Joint Committee of Fifteen on Reconstruction 264–265 (1914) (noting that 150,000 copies of the Report were printed and that it was widely distributed as a campaign document in the election of 1866). In addition, newspaper coverage suggests that the wider public was aware of the Committee's work even before the Report was issued * * *.

b

Statements made by Members of Congress leading up to, and during, the debates on the Fourteenth Amendment point in the same direction. The record of these debates has been combed before. See *Adamson* v. *California*, 332 U. S. 46, 92–110 (1947) (appendix to dissenting opinion of Black, J.) (concluding that the debates support the conclusion that § 1 was understood to incorporate the Bill of Rights against the States); *ante*, at 14, n. 9, 26–27, n. 23, (opinion of the Court) (counting the debates among other evidence that § 1 applies the Second Amendment against the States). Before considering that record here, it is important to clarify its relevance. When interpreting constitutional text, the goal is to discern the most likely public understanding of a particular provision at the time it was adopted. Statements by legislators can assist in this process to the extent they demonstrate the manner in which the public used or understood a particular word or phrase. They can further assist to the extent there is evidence that these statements were disseminated to the public. In other words, this evidence is useful not because it demonstrates what the draftsmen of the text may have been thinking, but only insofar as it illuminates what the public understood the words chosen by the draftsmen to mean.

(1)

* * *

(2)

When read against this backdrop, the civil rights legislation adopted by the 39th Congress in 1866 further supports this view. Between passing the Thirteenth Amendment—which outlawed slavery alone—and the Fourteenth Amendment, Congress passed two significant pieces of legislation. The first was the Civil Rights Act of 1866, which provided that "all persons born in the United States" were "citizens of the United States" and that "such citizens, of every race and color, . . . shall have the same right" to, among other things, "full and equal benefit of all laws and proceedings for the security of person and property, as is enjoyed by white citizens." Ch. 31, § 1, 14 Stat. 27.

Both proponents and opponents of this Act described it as providing the "privileges" of citizenship to freedmen, and defined those privileges to include constitutional rights, such as the right to keep and bear arms. See 39th Cong. Globe 474 (remarks of Sen. Trumbull) (stating that the "the late slaveholding States" had enacted laws "depriving persons of African descent of privileges which are essential to freemen," including "prohibit[ing] any negro or mulatto from having fire-arms" and stating that "[t]he purpose of the bill under consideration is to destroy all these discriminations"); *id.*, at 1266–1267 (remarks of Rep. Raymond) (opposing the Act, but recognizing that to "[m]ake a colored man a citizen of the United States" would guarantee to him, *inter alia*, "a defined *status* . . . a right to defend himself and his wife and children; a right to bear arms").

Three months later, Congress passed the Freedmen's Bureau Act, which also entitled all citizens to the "full and equal benefit of all laws and proceedings concerning personal liberty" and "personal security." Act of July 16, 1866, ch. 200, § 14, 14 Stat. 176. The Act stated expressly that the rights of personal liberty and security protected by the Act "includ[ed] the constitutional right to bear arms." *Ibid.*

(3)

There is much else in the legislative record. Many statements by Members of Congress corroborate the view that the Privileges or Immunities Clause enforced constitutionally enumerated rights against the States. See Curtis 112 (collecting examples). I am not aware of any statement that directly refutes that proposition. That said, the record of the debates—like most legislative history—is less than crystal clear. In particular, much ambiguity derives from the fact that at least several Members described § 1 as protecting the privileges and immunities of citizens "in the several States," harkening back to Article IV, § 2. These statements can be read to support the view that the Privileges or Immunities Clause protects some or all the fundamental rights of "citizens" described in *Corfield*. They can also be read to support the view that the Privileges or Immunities Clause, like Article IV, § 2, prohibits only state discrimination with respect to those rights it covers, but does not deprive States of the power to deny those rights to all citizens equally.

I examine the rest of the historical record with this understanding. But for purposes of discerning what the public most likely thought the Privileges or Immunities Clause to mean, it is significant that the most widely publicized statements by the legislators who voted on § 1—Bingham, Howard, and even Hale—point unambiguously toward the conclusion that the Privileges or Immunities Clause enforces at least those fundamental rights enumerated in the Constitution against the States, including the Second Amendment right to keep and bear arms.

3

Interpretations of the Fourteenth Amendment in the period immediately following its ratification help to establish the public understanding of the text at the time of its adoption.

* * *

This evidence plainly shows that the ratifying public understood the Privileges or Immunities Clause to protect constitutionally enumerated rights, including the right to keep and bear arms. As the Court demonstrates, there can be no doubt that § 1 was understood to enforce the Second Amendment against the States. In my view, this is because the right to keep and bear arms was understood to be a privilege of American citizenship guaranteed by the Privileges or Immunities Clause.

C

The next question is whether the Privileges or Immunities Clause merely prohibits States from discriminating among citizens if they recognize the Second Amendment's right to keep and bear arms, or whether the Clause requires States to recognize the right. The municipal respondents, Chicago and Oak Park, argue for the former interpretation. They contend that the Second Amendment, as applied to the States through the Fourteenth, authorizes a State to impose an outright ban on handgun possession such as the ones at issue here so long as a State applies it to all citizens equally. The Court explains why this antidiscrimination-only reading of § 1 as a whole is "implausible." *Ante*, at 31 (citing Brief for Municipal Respondents 64). I agree, but because I think it is the Privileges or Immunities Clause that applies this right to the States, I must explain why this Clause in particular protects against more than just state discrimination, and in fact establishes a minimum baseline of rights for all American citizens.

1

I begin, again, with the text. The Privileges or Immunities Clause opens with the command that "*No State shall*" abridge the privileges or immunities of citizens of the United States. Amdt. 14, § 1 (emphasis added). The very same phrase opens

Article I, § 10 of the Constitution, which prohibits the States from "pass[ing] any Bill of Attainder" or "ex post facto Law," among other things. Article I, § 10 is one of the few constitutional provisions that limits state authority. In *Barron*, when Chief Justice Marshall interpreted the Bill of Rights as lacking "plain and intelligible language" restricting state power to infringe upon individual liberties, he pointed to Article I, § 10 as an example of text that would have accomplished that task. 7 Pet., at 250. Indeed, Chief Justice Marshall would later describe Article I, § 10 as "a bill of rights for the people of each state." *Fletcher* v. *Peck*, 6 Cranch 87, 138 (1810). Thus, the fact that the Privileges or Immunities Clause uses the command "[n]o State shall"—which Article IV, § 2 does not—strongly suggests that the former imposes a greater restriction on state power than the latter.

This interpretation is strengthened when one considers that the Privileges or Immunities Clause uses the verb "abridge," rather than "discriminate," to describe the limit it imposes on state authority. The Webster's dictionary in use at the time of Reconstruction defines the word "abridge" to mean "[t]o deprive; to cut off; . . . as, to *abridge* one of his rights." Webster, An American Dictionary of the English Language, at 6. The Clause is thus best understood to impose a limitation on state power to infringe upon pre-existing substantive rights. It raises no indication that the Framers of the Clause used the word "abridge" to prohibit only discrimination.

This most natural textual reading is underscored by a well-publicized revision to the Fourteenth Amendment that the Reconstruction Congress rejected. After several Southern States refused to ratify the Amendment, President Johnson met with their Governors to draft a compromise. N. Y. Times, Feb. 5, 1867, p. 5. Their proposal eliminated Congress' power to enforce the Amendment (granted in § 5), and replaced the Privileges or Immunities Clause in § 1 with the following:

> "All persons born or naturalized in the United States, and subject to the jurisdiction thereof, are citizens of the United States, and of the States in which they reside, and the Citizens of each State shall be entitled to all *the privileges and immunities of citizens in the several States*." Draft reprinted in 1 Documentary History of Reconstruction 240 (W. Fleming ed. 1950) (hereinafter Fleming).

Significantly, this proposal removed the "[n]o State shall" directive and the verb "abridge" from § 1, and also changed the class of rights to be protected from those belonging to "citizens of the United States" to those of the "citizens in the several States." This phrasing is materially indistinguishable from Article IV, § 2, which generally was understood as an antidiscrimination provision alone. The proposal thus strongly indicates that at least the President of the United States and several Southern Governors thought that the Privileges or Immunities Clause, which they unsuccessfully tried to revise, prohibited more than just state-sponsored discrimination.

2

The argument that the Privileges or Immunities Clause prohibits no more than discrimination often is followed by a claim that public discussion of the Clause, and of § 1 generally, was not extensive. Because of this, the argument goes, § 1 must not have been understood to accomplish such a significant task as subjecting States to federal enforcement of a minimum baseline of rights. That argument overlooks critical aspects of the Nation's history that underscored the need for, and wide agreement upon, federal enforcement of constitutionally enumerated rights against the States, including the right to keep and bear arms.

* * *

b

In the contentious years leading up to the Civil War, those who sought to retain the institution of slavery found that to do so, it was necessary to eliminate more and more of the basic liberties of slaves, free blacks, and white abolitionists. Congressman Tobias Plants explained that slaveholders "could not hold [slaves] safely where dissent was permitted," so they decided that "all dissent must be suppressed by the strong hand of power." 39th Cong. Globe 1013. The measures they used were ruthless, repressed virtually every right recognized in the Constitution, and demonstrated that preventing only discriminatory state firearms restrictions would have been a hollow assurance for liberty. Public reaction indicates that the American people understood this point.

The overarching goal of pro-slavery forces was to repress the spread of abolitionist thought and the concomitant risk of a slave rebellion. Indeed, it is difficult to overstate the extent to which fear of a slave uprising gripped slaveholders and dictated the acts of Southern legislatures. Slaves and free blacks represented a substantial percentage of the population and posed a severe threat to Southern order if they were not kept in their place. According to the 1860 Census, slaves represented one quarter or more of the population in 11 of the 15 slave States, nearly half the population in Alabama, Florida, Georgia, and Louisiana, and *more* than 50% of the population in Mississippi and South Carolina. Statistics of the United States (Including Mortality, Property, &c.,) in 1860, The Eighth Census 336–350 (1866).

* * *

The fear generated by these and other rebellions led Southern legislatures to take particularly vicious aim at the rights of free blacks and slaves to speak or to keep and bear arms for their defense. Teaching slaves to read (even the Bible) was a criminal offense punished severely in some States. See K. Stampp, The Peculiar Institution: Slavery in the Ante-bellum South 208, 211 (1956). Virginia made it a crime for a member of an "abolition" society to enter the State and argue "that the owners of slaves have no property in the same, or advocate or advise the abolition of slavery." 1835–1836 Va. Acts ch. 66, p. 44. Other States prohibited the circulation of literature denying a master's right to property in his slaves and passed laws requiring postmasters to inspect the mails in search of such material. C. Eaton, The Freedom-of-Thought Struggle in the Old South 118–143, 199–200 (1964).

Many legislatures amended their laws prohibiting slaves from carrying firearms to apply the prohibition to free blacks as well. See, *e.g.*, Act of Dec. 23, 1833, § 7, 1833 Ga. Acts pp. 226, 228 (declaring that "it shall not be lawful for any free person of colour in this state, to own, use, or carry fire arms of any description whatever"); H. Aptheker, Nat Turner's Slave Rebellion 74–76, 83–94 (1966) (discussing similar Maryland and Virginia statutes); see also Act of Mar. 15, 1852, ch. 206, 1852 Miss. Laws p. 328 (repealing laws allowing free blacks to obtain firearms licenses); Act of Jan. 31, 1831, 1831 Fla. Acts p. 30 (same). Florida made it the "duty" of white citizen "patrol[s] to search negro houses or other suspected places, for fire arms." Act of Feb. 17, 1833, ch. 671, 1833 Fla. Acts pp. 26, 30. If they found any firearms, the patrols were to take the offending slave or free black "to the nearest justice of the peace," whereupon he would be "severely punished" by "whipping on the bare back, not exceeding thirty-nine lashes," unless he could give a "plain and satisfactory" explanation of how he came to possess the gun. *Ibid.*

Southern blacks were not alone in facing threats to their personal liberty and security during the antebellum era. Mob violence in many Northern cities presented dangers as well. Cottrol & Diamond, The Second Amendment: Toward an Afro-Americanist Reconsideration, 80 Geo. L. J. 309, 340 (1991) (hereinafter Cottrol) (recounting a July 1834 mob attack against "churches, homes, and businesses of white abolitionists and blacks" in New York that involved "upwards of twenty thousand people and required the intervention of the militia to suppress"); *ibid.* (noting an uprising in Boston nine years later in which a confrontation between a group of white sailors and four blacks led "a mob of several hundred whites " to "attac[k] and severely beat every black they could find").

c

After the Civil War, Southern anxiety about an uprising among the newly freed slaves peaked. As Representative Thaddeus Stevens is reported to have said, "[w]hen it was first proposed to free the slaves, and arm the blacks, did not half the nation tremble? The prim conservatives, the snobs, and the male waiting-maids in Congress, were in hysterics." K. Stampp, The Era of Reconstruction, 1865–1877, p. 104 (1965) (hereinafter Era of Reconstruction).

As the Court explains, this fear led to "systematic efforts" in the "old Confederacy" to disarm the more than 180,000 freedmen who had served in the Union Army, as well as other free blacks. Some States formally prohibited blacks from possessing firearms. Others enacted legislation prohibiting blacks from carrying firearms without a license, a restriction not imposed on whites. Additionally, "[t]hroughout the South, armed parties, often consisting of ex-Confederate soldiers serving in the state militias, forcibly took firearms from newly freed slaves."

As the Court makes crystal clear, if the Fourteenth Amendment "had outlawed only those laws that discriminate on the basis of race or previous condition of servitude, African-Americans in the South would likely have remained vulnerable to attack by many of their worst abusers: the state militia and state peace officers." *Ante,* at 779. In the years following the Civil War, a law banning firearm possession outright "would have been nondiscriminatory only in the formal sense," for it would have "left firearms in the hands of the militia and local peace officers." *Ibid.*

Evidence suggests that the public understood this at the time the Fourteenth Amendment was ratified. The publicly circulated Report of the Joint Committee on Reconstruction extensively detailed these abuses, and statements by citizens indicate that they looked to the Committee to provide a federal solution to this problem, see, *e.g.*, 39th Cong. Globe 337 (remarks of Rep. Sumner) (introducing "a memorial from the colored citizens of the State of South Carolina" asking for, *inter alia*, "constitutional protection in keeping arms, in holding public assemblies, and in complete liberty of speech and of the press").

One way in which the Federal Government responded was to issue military orders countermanding Southern arms legislation. See, *e.g.*, Jan. 17, 1866, order from Major General D. E. Sickles, reprinted in E. McPherson, The Political History of the United States of America During the Period of Reconstruction 37 (1871) ("The constitutional rights of all loyal and well-disposed inhabitants to bear arms will not be infringed"). The significance of these steps was not lost on those they were designed to protect. After one such order was issued, The Christian Recorder, published by the African Methodist Episcopal Church, published the following editorial:

> " 'We have several times alluded to the fact that the Constitution of the United States, guaranties to every citizen the right to keep and bear arms. . . . All men, without the distinction of color, have the right to keep arms to defend their homes, families, or themselves.'
>
> "We are glad to learn that [the] Commissioner for this State . . . has given freedmen to understand that they have as good a right to keep fire arms as any other citizens. The Constitution of the United States is the supreme law of the land, and we will be governed by that at present." Right to Bear Arms, Christian Recorder (Phila.), Feb. 24, 1866, pp. 29–30.
>
> * * *

Section 1 guaranteed the rights of citizenship in the United States and in the several States without regard to race. But it was understood that liberty would be assured little protection if § 1 left each State to decide which privileges or immunities of United States citizenship it would protect. As Frederick Douglass explained before § 1's adoption, "the Legislatures of the South can take from him the right to keep and bear arms, as they can—they would not allow a negro to walk with a cane where I came from, they would not allow five of them to assemble together." In What New Skin Will the Old Snake Come Forth? An Address Delivered in New York, New York, May 10, 1865, reprinted in 4 The Frederick Douglass Papers 79, 83–84 (J. Blassingame & J. McKivigan eds., 1991) (footnote omitted). "Notwithstanding the provision in the Constitution of the United States, that the right to keep and bear arms shall not be abridged," Douglass explained that "the black man has never had the right either to keep or bear arms." *Id.*, at 84. Absent a constitutional amendment to enforce that right against the States, he insisted that "the work of the Abolitionists [wa]s not finished." *Ibid.*

This history confirms what the text of the Privileges or Immunities Clause most naturally suggests: Consistent with its command that "[n]o State shall . . . abridge" the rights of United States citizens, the Clause establishes a minimum baseline of federal rights, and the constitutional right to keep and bear arms plainly was among them.

III

My conclusion is contrary to this Court's precedents, which hold that the Second Amendment right to keep and bear arms is not a privilege of United States citizenship. See *Cruikshank*, 92 U. S., at 548–549, 551–553. I must, therefore, consider whether *stare decisis* requires retention of those precedents. As mentioned at the outset, my inquiry is limited to the right at issue here. Thus, I do not endeavor to decide in this case whether, or to what extent, the Privileges or Immunities Clause applies any other rights enumerated in the Constitution against the States. Nor do I suggest that the *stare decisis* considerations surrounding the application of the right to keep and bear arms against the States would be the same as those surrounding another right protected by the Privileges or Immunities Clause. I consider *stare decisis* only as it applies to the question presented here.

* * *

* * * I reject *Slaughter-House* * * *. insofar as it precludes any overlap between the privileges and immunities of state and federal citizenship. I next proceed to the *stare decisis* considerations surrounding the precedent that expressly controls the question presented here.

B

Three years after *Slaughter-House*, the Court in *Cruikshank* squarely held that the right to keep and bear arms was not a privilege of American citizenship, thereby overturning the convictions of militia members responsible for the brutal Colfax Massacre. *Cruikshank* is not a precedent entitled to any respect. The flaws in its interpretation of the Privileges or Immunities Clause are made evident by the preceding evidence of its original meaning, and I would reject the holding on that basis alone. But, the consequences of *Cruikshank* warrant mention as well.

Cruikshank's holding that blacks could look only to state governments for protection of their right to keep and bear arms enabled private forces, often with the assistance of local governments, to subjugate the newly freed slaves and their descendants through a wave of private violence designed to drive blacks from the voting booth and force them into peonage, an effective return to slavery. Without federal enforcement of the inalienable right to keep and bear arms, these militias and mobs were tragically successful in waging a campaign of terror against the very people the Fourteenth Amendment had just made citizens.

Take, for example, the Hamburg Massacre of 1876. There, a white citizen militia sought out and murdered a troop of black militiamen for no other reason than that they had dared to conduct a celebratory Fourth of July parade through their mostly black town. The white militia commander, "Pitchfork" Ben Tillman, later described this massacre with pride: "[T]he leading white men of Edgefield" had decided "to seize the first opportunity that the negroes might offer them to provoke a riot and teach the negroes a lesson by having the whites demonstrate their superiority by killing as many of them as was justifiable." S. Kantrowitz, Ben Tillman & the Reconstruction of White Supremacy 67 (2000) (ellipsis, brackets, and internal quotation marks omitted). None of the perpetrators of the Hamburg murders was ever brought to justice.[22]

Organized terrorism like that perpetuated by Tillman and his cohorts proliferated in the absence of federal enforcement of constitutional rights. Militias such as the Ku Klux Klan, the Knights of the White Camellia, the White Brotherhood, the Pale Faces, and the '76 Association spread terror among blacks and white Republicans by breaking up Republican meetings, threatening political leaders, and whipping black militiamen. Era of Reconstruction, 199–200; Curtis 156. These groups raped, murdered, lynched, and robbed as a means of intimidating, and instilling pervasive fear in, those whom they despised. A. Trelease, White Terror: The Ku Klux Klan Conspiracy and Southern Reconstruction 28–46 (1995).

Although Congress enacted legislation to suppress these activities, Klan tactics remained a constant presence in the lives of Southern blacks for decades. Between 1882 and 1968, there were at least 3,446 reported lynchings of blacks in the South.

[22] Tillman went on to a long career as South Carolina's Governor and, later, United States Senator * * *.

Cottrol 351–352. They were tortured and killed for a wide array of alleged crimes, without even the slightest hint of due process. Emmit Till, for example, was killed in 1955 for allegedly whistling at a white woman. S. Whitfield, A Death in the Delta: The Story of Emmett Till 15–31 (1988). The fates of other targets of mob violence were equally depraved. See, *e.g.*, Lynched Negro and Wife Were First Mutilated, Vicksburg (Miss.) Evening Post, Feb. 8, 1904, reprinted in R. Ginzburg, 100 Years of Lynchings 63 (1988); Negro Shot Dead for Kissing His White Girlfriend, Chi. Defender, Feb. 31, 1915, in *id.*, at 95 (reporting incident in Florida); La. Negro Is Burned Alive Screaming "I Didn't Do It," Cleveland Gazette, Dec. 13, 1914, in *id.*, at 93 (reporting incident in Louisiana).

The use of firearms for self-defense was often the only way black citizens could protect themselves from mob violence. As Eli Cooper, one target of such violence, is said to have explained, "[t]he 'Negro has been run over for fifty years, but it must stop now, and pistols and shotguns are the only weapons to stop a mob.' " Church Burnings Follow Negro Agitator's Lynching, Chicago Defender, Sept. 6, 1919, in *id.*, at 124. Sometimes, as in Cooper's case, self-defense did not succeed. He was dragged from his home by a mob and killed as his wife looked on. *Ibid.* But at other times, the use of firearms allowed targets of mob violence to survive. One man recalled the night during his childhood when his father stood armed at a jail until morning to ward off lynchers. See Cottrol, 354. The experience left him with a sense, "not 'of powerlessness, but of the "possibilities of salvation" ' " that came from standing up to intimidation. *Ibid.*

In my view, the record makes plain that the Framers of the Privileges or Immunities Clause and the ratifying-era public understood—just as the Framers of the Second Amendment did—that the right to keep and bear arms was essential to the preservation of liberty. The record makes equally plain that they deemed this right necessary to include in the minimum baseline of federal rights that the Privileges or Immunities Clause established in the wake of the War over slavery. There is nothing about *Cruikshank*'s contrary holding that warrants its retention.

I agree with the Court that the Second Amendment is fully applicable to the States. I do so because the right to keep and bear arms is guaranteed by the Fourteenth Amendment as a privilege of American citizenship.

■ JUSTICE STEVENS dissenting.

* * *

I agree with the plurality's refusal to accept petitioners' primary submission. Their briefs marshal an impressive amount of historical evidence for their argument that the Court interpreted the Privileges or Immunities Clause too narrowly in the *Slaughter-House Cases,* 16 Wall. 36 (1873). But the original meaning of the Clause is not as clear as they suggest[2]—and not nearly as clear as it would need to be to dislodge 137 years of precedent * * *.

[2] Cf., *e.g.,* Currie, The Reconstruction Congress, 75 U. Chi. L.Rev. 383, 406 (2008) (finding "some support in the legislative history for no fewer than four interpretations" of the Privileges or Immunities Clause, two of which contradict petitioners' submission); Green, The Original Sense of the (Equal) Protection Clause: Subsequent Interpretation and Application, 19 Geo. Mason U. Civ. Rights L.J. 219, 255–277 (2009) (providing evidence that the Clause was originally conceived of as an antidiscrimination measure, guaranteeing equal rights for black citizens); Rosenthal, The New Originalism Meets the Fourteenth Amendment: Original Public Meaning and the Problem of Incorporation, 18 J. Contemp. Legal Issues 361 (2009) (detailing reasons to doubt that the Clause was originally understood to apply the Bill

I further agree with the plurality that there are weighty arguments supporting petitioners' second submission, insofar as it concerns the possession of firearms for lawful self-defense in the home. But these arguments are less compelling than the plurality suggests; they are much less compelling when applied outside the home; and their validity does not depend on the Court's holding in *Heller*. For that holding sheds no light on the meaning of the Due Process Clause of the Fourteenth Amendment. Our decisions construing that Clause to render various procedural guarantees in the Bill of Rights enforceable against the States likewise tell us little about the meaning of the word "liberty" in the Clause or about the scope of its protection of nonprocedural rights.

This is a substantive due process case.

* * *

* * * [S]ubstantive due process analysis generally requires us to consider the term "liberty" in the Fourteenth Amendment, and that this inquiry may be informed by, but does not depend upon, the content of the Bill of Rights. How should a court go about the analysis, then? Our precedents have established, not an exact methodology, but rather a framework for decisionmaking. In this respect, too, the Court's narrative fails to capture the continuity and flexibility in our doctrine.

The basic inquiry was described by Justice Cardozo more than 70 years ago. When confronted with a substantive due process claim, we must ask whether the allegedly unlawful practice violates values "implicit in the concept of ordered liberty." *Palko v. Connecticut,* 302 U.S. 319 (1937). If the practice in question lacks any "oppressive and arbitrary" character, if judicial enforcement of the asserted right would not materially contribute to "a fair and enlightened system of justice," then the claim is unsuitable for substantive due process protection. Implicit in Justice Cardozo's test is a recognition that the postulates of liberty have a universal character. Liberty claims that are inseparable from the customs that prevail in a certain region, the idiosyncratic expectations of a certain group, or the personal preferences of their champions, may be valid claims in some sense; but they are not of constitutional stature. Whether conceptualized as a "rational continuum" of legal precepts, *Poe,* 367 U.S., at 543 (Harlan, J., dissenting), or a seamless web of moral commitments, the rights embraced by the liberty clause transcend the local and the particular.

Justice Cardozo's test undeniably requires judges to apply their own reasoned judgment, but that does not mean it involves an exercise in abstract philosophy. In addition to other constraints * * *, historical and empirical data of various kinds ground the analysis. Textual commitments laid down elsewhere in the Constitution, judicial precedents, English common law, legislative and social facts, scientific and professional developments, practices of other civilized societies, and, above all else, the " 'traditions and conscience of our people,' " *Palko,* 302 U.S., at 325, are critical

of Rights to the States); Hamburger, Privileges or Immunities, 105 Nw. U.L.Rev. 61 (2011) (arguing that the Clause was meant to ensure freed slaves were afforded "the Privileges and Immunities" specified in Article IV, § 2, cl. 1, of the Constitution). Although he urges its elevation in our doctrine, Justice THOMAS has acknowledged that, in seeking to ascertain the original meaning of the Privileges or Immunities Clause, "[l]egal scholars agree on little beyond the conclusion that the Clause does not mean what the Court said it meant in 1873." *Saenz v. Roe,* 526 U.S. 489, 522, n. 1 (1999) (dissenting opinion); accord, *ante,* at 758 (plurality opinion).

variables. They can provide evidence about which rights really are vital to ordered liberty, as well as a spur to judicial action.

* * *

The question in this case, then, is not whether the Second Amendment right to keep and bear arms (whatever that right's precise contours) applies to the States because the Amendment has been incorporated into the Fourteenth Amendment. It has not been. The question, rather, is whether the particular right asserted by petitioners applies to the States because of the Fourteenth Amendment itself, standing on its own bottom. And to answer that question, we need to determine, first, the nature of the right that has been asserted and, second, whether that right is an aspect of Fourteenth Amendment "liberty." Even accepting the Court's holding in *Heller,* it remains entirely possible that the right to keep and bear arms identified in that opinion is not judicially enforceable against the States, or that only part of the right is so enforceable. It is likewise possible for the Court to find in this case that some part of the *Heller* right applies to the States, and then to find in later cases that other parts of the right also apply, or apply on different terms.

* * *

While I agree with the Court that our substantive due process cases offer a principled basis for holding that petitioners have a constitutional right to possess a usable firearm in the home, I am ultimately persuaded that a better reading of our case law supports the city of Chicago. I would not foreclose the possibility that a particular plaintiff—say, an elderly widow who lives in a dangerous neighborhood and does not have the strength to operate a long gun—may have a cognizable liberty interest in possessing a handgun. But I cannot accept petitioners' broader submission * * *.

* * *

Hence, in evaluating an asserted right to be free from particular gun-control regulations, liberty is on both sides of the equation. Guns may be useful for self-defense, as well as for hunting and sport, but they also have a unique potential to facilitate death and destruction and thereby to destabilize ordered liberty. *Your* interest in keeping and bearing a certain firearm may diminish *my* interest in being and feeling safe from armed violence. And while granting you the right to own a handgun might make you safer on any given day—assuming the handgun's marginal contribution to self-defense outweighs its marginal contribution to the risk of accident, suicide, and criminal mischief—it may make you and the community you live in less safe overall, owing to the increased number of handguns in circulation. It is at least reasonable for a democratically elected legislature to take such concerns into account in considering what sorts of regulations would best serve the public welfare.

* * *

■ JUSTICE BREYER, with whom JUSTICE GINSBURG and JUSTICE SOTOMAYOR join, dissenting.

In my view, JUSTICE STEVENS has demonstrated that the Fourteenth Amendment's guarantee of "substantive due process" does not include a general right to keep and bear firearms for purposes of private self-defense. As he argues, the Framers did not write the Second Amendment with this objective in view. Unlike other forms of substantive liberty, the carrying of arms for that purpose often puts others' lives at risk. And the use of arms for private self-defense does not warrant federal constitutional protection from state regulation.

The Court, however, does not expressly rest its opinion upon "substantive due process" concerns. Rather, it directs its attention to this Court's "incorporation" precedents and asks whether the Second Amendment right to private self-defense is "fundamental" so that it applies to the States through the Fourteenth Amendment.

I shall therefore separately consider the question of "incorporation." I can find nothing in the Second Amendment's text, history, or underlying rationale that could warrant characterizing it as "fundamental" insofar as it seeks to protect the keeping and bearing of arms for private self-defense purposes. Nor can I find any justification for interpreting the Constitution as transferring ultimate regulatory authority over the private uses of firearms from democratically elected legislatures to courts or from the States to the Federal Government. I therefore conclude that the Fourteenth Amendment does not "incorporate" the Second Amendment's right "to keep and bear Arms." And I consequently dissent.

* * * Two years ago, in *District of Columbia* v. *Heller*, 554 U. S. 570 (2008), the Court rejected the pre-existing judicial consensus that the Second Amendment was primarily concerned with the need to maintain a "well regulated Militia." * * *

The Court based its conclusions almost exclusively upon its reading of history. But the relevant history in *Heller* was far from clear: Four dissenting Justices disagreed with the majority's historical analysis. And subsequent scholarly writing reveals why disputed history provides treacherous ground on which to build decisions written by judges who are not expert at history.

* * *

My aim in referring to this history is to illustrate the reefs and shoals that lie in wait for those nonexpert judges who place virtually determinative weight upon historical considerations. In my own view, the Court should not look to history alone but to other factors as well—above all, in cases where the history is so unclear that the experts themselves strongly disagree. It should, for example, consider the basic values that underlie a constitutional provision and their contemporary significance. And it should examine as well the relevant consequences and practical justifications that might, or might not, warrant removing an important question from the democratic decisionmaking process.

In my view, taking *Heller* as a given, the Fourteenth Amendment does not incorporate the Second Amendment right to keep and bear arms for purposes of private self-defense. Under this Court's precedents, to incorporate the private self-defense right the majority must show that the right is, *e.g.*, "fundamental to the American scheme of justice," *Duncan* v. *Louisiana*, 391 U. S. 145, 149 (1968). And this it fails to do.

The majority here, like that in *Heller,* relies almost exclusively upon history to make the necessary showing. But to do so for incorporation purposes is both wrong and dangerous. As JUSTICE STEVENS points out, our society has historically made mistakes—for example, when considering certain 18th- and 19th-century property rights to be fundamental. And in the incorporation context, as elsewhere, history often is unclear about the answers.

Accordingly, this Court, in considering an incorporation question, has never stated that the historical status of a right is the only relevant consideration * * *.

I thus think it proper, above all where history provides no clear answer, to look to other factors in considering whether a right is sufficiently "fundamental" to remove it from the political process in every State. I would include among those factors the nature of the right; any contemporary disagreement about whether the right is fundamental; the extent to which incorporation will further other, perhaps more basic, constitutional aims; and the extent to which incorporation will advance or hinder the Constitution's structural aims, including its division of powers among different governmental institutions (and the people as well). Is incorporation needed, for example, to further the Constitution's effort to ensure that the government treats each individual with equal respect? Will it help maintain the democratic form of government that the Constitution foresees? In a word, will incorporation prove consistent, or inconsistent, with the Constitution's efforts to create governmental institutions well suited to the carrying out of its constitutional promises?

* * *

[A]s *Heller* concedes, the private self-defense right that the Court would incorporate has nothing to do with "the *reason*" the Framers "codified" the right to keep and bear arms "in a written Constitution." 554 U. S., at 599 (emphasis added). *Heller* immediately adds that the self-defense right was nonetheless "the *central component* of the right." *Ibid.* In my view, this is the historical equivalent of a claim that water runs uphill. But, taking it as valid, the Framers' basic *reasons* for including language in the Constitution would nonetheless seem more pertinent (in deciding about the contemporary *importance* of a right) than the particular *scope* 17th- or 18th-century listeners would have then assigned to the words they used. And examination of the Framers' motivation tells us they did not think the private armed self-defense right was of paramount importance.

Further, there is no popular consensus that the private self-defense right described in *Heller* is fundamental * * *. [E]very State regulates firearms extensively, and public opinion is sharply divided on the appropriate level of regulation. Much of this disagreement rests upon empirical considerations. One side believes the right essential to protect the lives of those attacked in the home; the other side believes it essential to regulate the right in order to protect the lives of others attacked with guns. It seems unlikely that definitive evidence will develop one way or the other. And the appropriate level of firearm regulation has thus long been, and continues to be, a hotly contested matter of political debate.

Moreover, there is no reason here to believe that incorporation of the private self-defense right will further any other or broader constitutional objective. We are aware of no argument that gun-control regulations target or are passed with the purpose of targeting "discrete and insular minorities." *Carolene Products Co., supra*, at 153, n. 4. Nor will incorporation help to assure equal respect for individuals. Unlike the First Amendment's rights of free speech, free press, assembly, and petition, the private self-defense right does not comprise a necessary part of the democratic process that the Constitution seeks to establish. See, *e.g., Whitney* v. *California*, 274 U. S. 357, 377 (1927) (Brandeis, J., concurring). Unlike the First Amendment's religious protections, the Fourth Amendment's protection against unreasonable searches and seizures, the Fifth and Sixth Amendment s' insistence upon fair criminal procedure, and the Eighth Amendment's protection against cruel and unusual punishments, the private self-defense right does not significantly seek to protect individuals who might otherwise suffer unfair or inhumane treatment at the hands of a majority. Unlike the protections offered by many of these same Amendments, it does not involve matters as to which judges possess a comparative expertise, by virtue of their close familiarity with the justice system and its operation. And, unlike the Fifth Amendment's insistence on just compensation, it does not involve a matter where a majority might unfairly seize for itself property belonging to a minority.

Finally, incorporation of the right *will* work a significant disruption in the constitutional allocation of decisionmaking authority, thereby interfering with the Constitution's ability to further its objectives.

First, on any reasonable accounting, the incorporation of the right recognized in *Heller* would amount to a significant incursion on a traditional and important area of state concern, altering the constitutional relationship between the States and the Federal Government * * *.

Second, determining the constitutionality of a particular state gun law requires finding answers to complex empirically based questions of a kind that legislatures are better able than courts to make. And it may require this kind of analysis in virtually every case.

Government regulation of the right to bear arms normally embodies a judgment that the regulation will help save lives. The determination whether a gun regulation is constitutional would thus almost always require the weighing of the constitutional right to bear arms against the "primary concern of every government—a concern for the safety and indeed the lives of its citizens." *United States* v. *Salerno*, 481 U. S. 739, 755 (1987) * * *.

Given the competing interests, courts will have to try to answer empirical questions of a particularly difficult kind. Suppose, for example, that after a gun regulation's adoption the murder rate went up. Without the gun regulation would the murder rate have risen even faster? How is this conclusion affected by the local recession which has left numerous people unemployed? What about budget cuts that led to a downsizing of the police force? How effective was that police force to begin with? And did the regulation simply take guns from those who use them for lawful purposes without affecting their possession by criminals?

* * *

[T]here is no institutional need to send judges off on this "mission-almost-impossible." Legislators are able to "amass the stuff of actual experience and cull conclusions from it." *United States* v. *Gainey*, 380 U. S. 63, 67 (1965). They are far better suited than judges to uncover facts and to understand their relevance. And legislators, unlike Article III judges, can be held democratically responsible for their empirically based and value-laden conclusions. We have thus repeatedly affirmed our preference for "legislative not judicial solutions" to this kind of problem, see, *e.g., Patsy* v. *Board of Regents of Fla.*, 457 U. S. 496, 513 (1982), just as we have repeatedly affirmed the Constitution's preference for democratic solutions legislated by those whom the people elect.

* * *

Third, the ability of States to reflect local preferences and conditions—both key virtues of federalism—here has particular importance. The incidence of gun ownership varies substantially as between crowded cities and uncongested rural communities, as well as among the different geographic regions of the country. Thus, approximately 60% of adults who live in the relatively sparsely populated Western States of Alaska, Montana, and Wyoming report that their household keeps a gun, while fewer than 15% of adults in the densely populated Eastern States of Rhode Island, New Jersey, and Massachusetts say the same.

The nature of gun violence also varies as between rural communities and cities. Urban centers face significantly greater levels of firearm crime and homicide, while rural communities have proportionately greater problems with nonhomicide gun deaths, such as suicides and accidents. And idiosyncratic local factors can lead to two cities finding themselves in dramatically different circumstances: For example, in 2008, the murder rate was 40 times higher in New Orleans than it was in Lincoln, Nebraska.

It is thus unsurprising that States and local communities have historically differed about the need for gun regulation as well as about its proper level * * *.

Fourth, although incorporation of any right removes decisions from the democratic process, the incorporation of this particular right does so without strong offsetting justification—as the example of Oak Park's handgun ban helps to show. See Oak Park, Ill., Municipal Code, § 27–2–1 (1995). Oak Park decided to ban handguns in 1983, after a local attorney was shot to death with a handgun that his assailant had smuggled into a courtroom in a blanket. A citizens committee spent months gathering information about handguns. It secured 6,000 signatures from community residents in support of a ban. And the village board enacted a ban into law.

Subsequently, at the urging of ban opponents the Board held a community referendum on the matter. The citizens committee argued strongly in favor of the ban. It pointed out that most guns owned in Oak Park were handguns and that handguns were misused more often than citizens used them in self-defense. The ban opponents argued just as strongly to the contrary. The public decided to keep the ban by a vote of 8,031 to 6,368. And since that time, Oak Park now tells us, crime has decreased and the community has seen no accidental handgun deaths.

Given the empirical and local value-laden nature of the questions that lie at the heart of the issue, why, in a Nation whose Constitution foresees democratic decisionmaking, is it so *fundamental* a matter as to require taking that power from the people? What is it here that the people did not know? What is it that a judge knows better?

* * *

In sum, the Framers did not write the Second Amendment in order to protect a private right of armed self-defense. There has been, and is, no consensus that the right is, or was, "fundamental." No broader constitutional interest or principle supports legal treatment of that right as fundamental. To the contrary, broader constitutional concerns of an institutional nature argue strongly against that treatment.

Moreover, nothing in 18th-, 19th-, 20th-, or 21st-century history shows a consensus that the right to private armed self-defense, as described in *Heller*, is "deeply rooted in this Nation's history or tradition" or is otherwise "fundamental." Indeed, incorporating the right recognized in *Heller* may change the law in many of the 50 States. Read in the majority's favor, the historical evidence is at most ambiguous. And, in the absence of any other support for its conclusion, ambiguous history cannot show that the Fourteenth Amendment incorporates a private right of self-defense against the States.

With respect, I dissent.

NOTES AND QUESTIONS

1. In *Timbs v. Indiana*, 586 U.S. ___, 139 S.Ct. 682 (2019), the Supreme Court unanimously voted to incorporate the Excessive Fines Clause of the Eighth Amendment against the States. Justice Ginsburg's opinion resolved the matter in nine brief paragraphs. Why (we ask with dripping sarcasm) do you think so many justices thought that *McDonald* posed a weaker case for incorporation under the Court's precedents? Does *McDonald* prove that the Court is a political rather than a legal body? Or is that only true, if it is actually ever true, in a few "hot button" cases?

2. Justice Thomas concurred in the judgment in *Timbs,* on the ground that freedom from excessive fines was a privilege or immunity and thus is applicable to the States via the Privileges or Immunities Clause. *See* 139 S.Ct. at 691 (Thomas, J., concurring in the judgment). Justice Gorsuch, facing his first incorporation case, wrote:

> The majority faithfully applies our precedent and, based on a wealth of historical evidence, concludes that the Fourteenth Amendment incorporates the Eighth Amendment's Excessive Fines Clause against the States. I agree with that conclusion. As an original matter, I acknowledge, the appropriate vehicle for incorporation may well be the Fourteenth Amendment's Privileges or Immunities Clause, rather than, as this Court has long assumed, the Due Process Clause. See, *e.g.*, *McDonald* v. *Chicago*, 561 U.S. 742, 805–858 (2010) (THOMAS, J., concurring in part and concurring in judgment) (documenting evidence that the "privileges or immunities of citizens of the United States" include, at minimum, the individual rights enumerated in the Bill of Rights); Wildenthal, Nationalizing the Bill of Rights: Revisiting the Original Understanding of the Fourteenth Amendment in 1866–67, 68 Ohio St. L.J. 1509 (2007); A. Amar, The Bill of Rights: Creation and Reconstruction 163–214 (1998); M. Curtis, No State Shall Abridge: The Fourteenth Amendment and the Bill of Rights (1986). But nothing in this case turns on that question, and, regardless of the precise vehicle, there can be no serious doubt that the Fourteenth Amendment requires the States to respect the freedom from excessive fines enshrined in the Eighth Amendment.

Is it premature to say that two justices might be willing to reconsider the *Slaughter-House Cases*?

3. So aren't we going to pepper you with (leading) questions about *McDonald?* We don't think it is necessary. The opinions, in light of the history of incorporation that we have presented, raise all of the questions for us. It will not surprise anyone to learn that we think Justice Thomas is right, but whatever view you ultimately find persuasive will probably find a thoughtful and articulate defense somewhere in the battery of *McDonald* opinions.

[Assignment 75]

XVII. FIRST AMENDMENT PRINCIPLES AND THE STATES

First Amendment:

Congress shall make no law respecting an establishment of religion, or prohibiting the free exercise thereof; or abridging the freedom of speech, or of the press; or the right of the people peaceably to assemble, and to petition the Government for a redress of grievances.

Fourteenth Amendment, Section 1:

All persons born or naturalized in the United States, and subject to the jurisdiction thereof, are citizens of the United States and of the state wherein they reside. No state shall make or enforce any law which shall abridge the privileges or immunities of citizens of the United States; nor shall any state deprive any person of life, liberty, or property, without due process of law; nor deny to any person within its jurisdiction the equal protection of the laws.

Now that we have established that (most of) the federal Bill of Rights is in some fashion incorporated against the States—we think, with Justice Thomas, through the Privileges or Immunities Clause of the Fourteenth Amendment, while the majority of the Court thinks through the Due Process of Law Clause—we want to explore briefly *how* the incorporated Bill of Rights provisions have been applied to the States. For the most part, the Court has staunchly resisted the idea that the various provisions might have different meanings when applied to the States or the federal government. Due process of law for state actors and federal actors is the same. The requirements of the Fifth Amendment Takings Clause apply to state regulations the same way they apply to federal regulations. The Sixth Amendment Confrontation Clause requires the same evidentiary rules for state and federal prosecutions. The one area in which there has been significant differential application of Bill of Rights provisions concerns the mechanics of the criminal jury, and by the time this book sees print, it is quite possible that those differences will also be gone, as that precise question is before the Court in the October 2019 term. Justice Black's vision of a Bill of Rights fully and uniformly applying to all American governmental actors is very close to a doctrinal reality.

As a matter of original meaning, this development was not at all inevitable. First, if one believes that the Fourteenth Amendment incorporates, not the literal texts, but the underlying principles of the (declaratory?) Bill of Rights, those principles might have different application (1) depending on the level of government involved and (2) in 1868 than in 1791. Second, even if one thinks that incorporation involves direct application of the literal texts of the Bill of Rights against the States, does that mean application of the understanding of those Bill of Rights provisions when they were enacted against the federal government in 1791 or when they were "enacted" against the States in 1868? The seventy-seven years from 1791 to 1868 were legally eventful years, and it is not obvious that public understandings of the various rights were the same at both points in time. Indeed, there is good reason to think that the incorporated Bill of Rights that applies against the States is a more libertarian document, when interpreted in light of the original meaning that its clauses had in 1868, than was the original Bill of Rights from 1791. AKHIL REED AMAR, THE BILL OF RIGHTS: CREATION AND RECONSTRUCTION (1998), argues (we think persuasively) that public opinion was more libertarian in 1868 than it was in 1791, when elite opinion was more communitarian and republican.) Here we would simply note that John Stuarts Mills' famous book *On Liberty* was published in 1859 and dominated intellectual discourse in the 1860s. Moreover, as a purely textual matter, the Privileges or Immunities Clause forbids state action that "abridge[s]" privileges or immunities. Could that prohibition be broader than at least some of the prohibitions in the 1791 Bill of Rights? If the Privileges or Immunities Clause is the proper home for the incorporation doctrine, the verb "abridge" might prove very important in assessing the extent to which States can regulate the protected privileges or immunities.

In this assignment, we will examine cases involving the incorporated rights to the free exercise of religion, the freedom of speech, and the freedom of the press that give occasion to consider this hypothesis about possibly different meanings of rights at different times and made applicable through different clauses. We start with the Religion Clauses.

A. FREEDOM OF RELIGION AND THE STATES

In 1791, the Free Exercise of Religion Clause applied only to (federal) laws that *prohibited*, *i.e.* criminalized, the free exercise of religion. The Privileges or Immunities Clause of the 1868 Fourteenth Amendment, if it incorporated the Bill of Rights, applied to all laws that *abridged* the free exercise of religion. The difference in verbs is significant. A denial of welfare payments to those who fail to observe the Sabbath on a Sunday is not a *prohibition*, or criminalization, of the free exercise of religion, but it is an *abridgement* of the right to free exercise. *See Sherbert v. Verner*, 374 U.S. 398 (1963). The Fourteenth Amendment, which substitutes "abridge" for "prohibit," is thus potentially more libertarian with respect to free exercise of religion than is the First Amendment.

The same phenomenon could be at work with respect to freedoms of speech and of the press. By 1868, John Stuart Mill had prominently argued in *On Liberty* (1859) that the freedom of speech and of the press needed to protect all speech or publications that were valuable in the marketplace of ideas, not merely narrowly defined political speech. *See supra* pages 1026–1027. As Justice Oliver Wendell Holmes puts the Millian idea of freedom of speech and of the press in his seminal dissent in *Abrams v. United States,* 250 U.S. 616 (1919), from the Court's affirmance of convictions for seditious libel:

> Persecution for the expression of opinions seems to me perfectly logical. If you have no doubt of your premises or your power and want a certain result with all your heart you naturally express your wishes in law and sweep away all opposition * * *. But when men have realized that time has upset many fighting faiths, they may come to believe even more than they believe the very foundations of their own conduct that the ultimate good desired is better reached by free trade in ideas—that best test of truth is the power of the thought to get itself accepted in the competition of the market, and that truth is the only ground upon which their wishes safely can be carried out. That at any rate is the theory of our Constitution.

Id. at 630 (Holmes, J., dissenting).

Consider the following three Millian freedom of religion and freedom of speech and of the press cases whose arguments may well have been stronger when levelled against States, after 1868, than they would have been if directed against the federal government, in 1791.

1. WEST VIRGINIA STATE BOARD OF EDUCATION V. BARNETTE

319 U.S. 624 (1943)

■ MR. JUSTICE JACKSON delivered the opinion of the Court.

Following the decision by this Court on June 3, 1940, in *Minersville School District v. Gobitis,* 310 U.S. 586, the West Virginia legislature amended its statutes to require all schools therein to conduct courses of instruction in history, civics, and in the Constitutions of the United States and of the State "for the purpose of teaching, fostering and perpetuating the ideals, principles and spirit of Americanism, and increasing the knowledge of the organization and machinery of the government." Appellant Board of Education was directed, with advice of the State Superintendent of Schools, to "prescribe the courses of study covering these subjects" for public schools. The Act made it the duty of private, parochial and denominational schools to prescribe courses of study "similar to those required for the public schools."

The Board of Education on January 9, 1942, adopted a resolution containing recitals taken largely from the Court's *Gobitis* opinion and ordering that the salute to the flag become "a regular part of the program of activities in the public schools," that all teachers and pupils "shall be required to participate in the salute honoring the Nation represented by the Flag; provided, however, that refusal to salute the Flag be regarded as an act of insubordination, and shall be dealt with accordingly."

The resolution originally required the "commonly accepted salute to the Flag," which it defined. Objections to the salute as "being too much like Hitler's" were raised * * *. Some modification appears to have been made in deference to these objections, but no concession was made to Jehovah's Witnesses.[4] What is now required is the "stiff-arm" salute, the saluter to keep the right hand raised with palm turned up while the following is repeated: "I pledge allegiance to the Flag of the United States of America and to the Republic for which it stands; one Nation, indivisible, with liberty and justice for all."

Failure to conform is "insubordination" dealt with by expulsion. Readmission is denied by statute until compliance. Meanwhile, the expelled child is "unlawfully absent," and may be proceeded against as a delinquent. His parents or guardians are liable to prosecution, and if convicted are subject to fine not exceeding $50 and Jail term not exceeding thirty days.

Appellees, citizens of the United States and of West Virginia, brought suit in the United States District Court for themselves and others similarly situated asking its

---

[4] They have offered in lieu of participating in the flag salute ceremony "periodically and publicly" to give the following pledge:

"I have pledged my unqualified allegiance and devotion to Jehovah, the Almighty God, and to His Kingdom, for which Jesus commands all Christians to pray.

"I respect the flag of the United States and acknowledge it as a symbol of freedom and justice to all.

"I pledge allegiance and obedience to all the laws of the United States that are consistent with God's law, as set forth in the Bible."

injunction to restrain enforcement of these laws and regulations against Jehovah's Witnesses. The Witnesses are an unincorporated body teaching that the obligation imposed by law of God is superior to that of laws enacted by temporal government. Their religious beliefs include a literal version of Exodus, Chapter 20, verses 4 and 5, which says: "Thou shalt not make unto thee any graven image, or any likeness of anything that is in heaven above, or that is in the earth beneath, or that is in the water under the earth; thou shalt not bow down thyself to them nor serve them." They consider that the flag is an "image" within this command. For this reason, they refuse to salute it.

Children of this faith have been expelled from school and are threatened with exclusion for no other cause. Officials threaten to send them to reformatories maintained for criminally inclined juveniles. Parents of such children have been prosecuted and are threatened with prosecutions for causing delinquency.

The Board of Education moved to dismiss the complaint setting forth these facts and alleging that the law and regulations are an unconstitutional denial of religious freedom, and of freedom of speech, and are invalid under the "due process" and "equal protection" clauses of the Fourteenth Amendment to the Federal Constitution. The cause was submitted on the pleadings to a District Court of three judges. It restrained enforcement as to the plaintiffs and those of that class. The Board of Education brought the case here by direct appeal.

This case calls upon us to reconsider a precedent decision, as the Court, throughout its history, often has been required to do. Before turning to the *Gobitis* case, however, it is desirable to notice certain characteristics by which this controversy is distinguished.

The freedom asserted by these appellees does not bring them into collision with rights asserted by any other individual. It is such conflicts which most frequently require intervention of the State to determine where the rights of one end and those of another begin. But the refusal of these persons to participate in the ceremony does not interfere with or deny rights of others to do so. Nor is there any question in this case that their behavior is peaceable and orderly. The sole conflict is between authority and rights of the individual. The State asserts power to condition access to public education on making a prescribed sign and profession and at the same time to coerce attendance by punishing both parent and child. The latter stand on a right of self-determination in matters that touch individual opinion and personal attitude.

As the present CHIEF JUSTICE said in dissent in the *Gobitis* case, the State may "require teaching by instruction and study of all in our history and in the structure and organization of our government, including the guaranties of civil liberty, which tend to inspire patriotism and love of country." 310 U.S. at 604. Here, however, we are dealing with a compulsion of students to declare a belief. They are not merely made acquainted with the flag salute so that they may be informed as to what it is or even what it means. The issue here is whether this slow and easily neglected route to aroused loyalties constitutionally may be short-cut by substituting a compulsory salute and slogan. This issue is not prejudiced by the Court's previous holding that where a State, without compelling attendance, extends college facilities to pupils who voluntarily enroll, it may prescribe military training as part of the course without offense to the Constitution. It was held that those who take advantage of its opportunities may not on ground of conscience refuse compliance with such conditions. *Hamilton v. Regents,* 293 U.S. 245. In the present case attendance is not optional. That case is also to be distinguished from the present one because, independently of college privileges or requirements, the State has power to raise militia and impose the duties of service therein upon its citizens.

There is no doubt that, in connection with the pledges, the flag salute is a form of utterance. Symbolism is a primitive but effective way of communicating ideas. The use of an emblem or flag to symbolize some system, idea, institution, or personality, is a short cut from mind to mind. Causes and nations, political parties, lodges and ecclesiastical groups seek to knit the loyalty of their followings to a flag or banner, a color or design. The State announces rank, function, and authority through crowns and maces, uniforms and black robes; the church speaks through the Cross, the Crucifix, the altar and shrine, and clerical raiment. Symbols of State often convey political ideas just as religious symbols come to convey theological ones. Associated with many of these symbols are appropriate gestures of acceptance or respect: a salute, a bowed or bared head, a bended knee. A person gets from a symbol the meaning he puts into it, and what is one man's comfort and inspiration is another's jest and scorn.

Over a decade ago, Chief Justice Hughes led this Court in holding that the display of a red flag as a symbol of opposition by peaceful and legal means to organized government was protected by the free speech guaranties of the Constitution. *Stromberg v. California,* 283 U.S. 359. Here it is the State that employs a flag as a symbol of adherence to government as presently organized. It requires the individual to communicate by word and sign his acceptance of the political ideas it thus bespeaks. Objection to this form of communication when coerced is an old one, well known to the framers of the Bill of Rights.

It is also to be noted that the compulsory flag salute and pledge requires affirmation of a belief and an attitude of mind. It is not clear whether the regulation contemplates that pupils forego any contrary convictions of their own and become unwilling converts to the prescribed ceremony or whether it will be acceptable if they simulate assent by words without belief and by a gesture barren of meaning. It is now a commonplace that censorship or suppression of expression of opinion is tolerated by our Constitution only when the expression presents a clear and present danger of action of a kind the State is empowered to prevent and punish. It would seem that involuntary affirmation could be commanded only on even more immediate and urgent grounds than silence. But here the power of compulsion is invoked without any allegation that remaining passive during a flag salute ritual creates a clear and present danger that would justify an effort even to muffle expression. To sustain the compulsory flag salute we are required to say that a Bill of Rights which guards the individual's right to speak his own mind, left it open to public authorities to compel him to utter what is not in his mind.

Whether the First Amendment to the Constitution will permit officials to order observance of ritual of this nature does not depend upon whether as a voluntary exercise we would think it to be good, bad or merely innocuous. Any credo of nationalism is likely to include what some disapprove or to omit what others think essential, and to give off different overtones as it takes on different accents or interpretations. If official power exists to coerce acceptance of any patriotic creed, what it shall contain cannot be decided by courts, but must be largely discretionary with the ordaining authority, whose power to prescribe would no doubt include power to amend. Hence validity of the asserted power to force an American citizen publicly to profess any statement of belief, or to engage in any ceremony of assent to one, presents questions of power that must be considered independently of any idea we may have as to the utility of the ceremony in question.

Nor does the issue as we see it turn on one's possession of particular religious views or the sincerity with which they are held. While religion supplies appellees' motive for enduring the discomforts of making the issue in this case, many citizens who do not share these religious views hold such a compulsory rite to infringe constitutional liberty of the individual. It is not necessary to inquire whether non-conformist beliefs will exempt from the duty to salute unless we first find power to make the salute a legal duty.

The *Gobitis* decision, however, *assumed,* as did the argument in that case and in this, that power exists in the State to impose the flag salute discipline upon school children in general. The Court only examined and rejected a claim based on religious beliefs of immunity from an unquestioned general rule. The question which underlies the flag salute controversy is whether such a ceremony so touching matters of opinion and political attitude may be imposed upon the individual by official authority under powers committed to any political organization under our Constitution. We examine rather than assume existence of this power, and, against this broader definition of issues in this case, reexamine specific grounds assigned for the *Gobitis* decision.

1. It was said that the flag-salute controversy confronted the Court with "the problem which Lincoln cast in memorable dilemma: 'Must a government of necessity be too *strong* for the liberties of its people, or too *weak* to maintain its own existence?' " and that the answer must be in favor of strength. *Minersville School District v. Gobitis, supra,* at 596.

We think these issues may be examined free of pressure or restraint growing out of such considerations.

It may be doubted whether Mr. Lincoln would have thought that the strength of government to maintain itself would be impressively vindicated by our confirming power of the State to expel a handful of children from school. Such oversimplification, so handy in political debate, often lacks the precision necessary to postulates of judicial reasoning. If validly applied to this problem, the utterance cited would resolve every issue of power in favor of those in authority and would require us to override every liberty thought to weaken or delay execution of their policies.

Government of limited power need not be anemic government. Assurance that rights are secure tends to diminish fear and jealousy of strong government, and, by making us feel safe to live under it makes for its better support. Without promise of a limiting Bill of Rights it is doubtful if our Constitution could have mustered enough strength to enable its ratification. To enforce those rights today is not to choose weak government over strong government. It is only to adhere as a means of strength to individual freedom of mind in preference to officially disciplined uniformity for which history indicates a disappointing and disastrous end.

The subject now before us exemplifies this principle. Free public education, if faithful to the ideal of secular instruction and political neutrality, will not be partisan or enemy of any class, creed, party, or faction. If it is to impose any ideological discipline, however, each party or denomination must seek to control, or, failing that, to weaken the influence of the educational system. Observance of the limitations of the Constitution will not weaken government in the field appropriate for its exercise.

2. It was also considered in the *Gobitis* case that functions of educational officers in States, counties and school districts were such that to interfere with their authority "would in effect make us the school board for the country." *Id.* at 598.

The Fourteenth Amendment, as now applied to the States, protects the citizen against the State itself and all of its creatures—Boards of Education not excepted. These have, of course, important, delicate, and highly discretionary functions, but none that they may not perform within the limits of the Bill of Rights. That they are educating the young for citizenship is reason for scrupulous protection of Constitutional freedoms of the individual, if we are not to strangle the free mind at its source and teach youth to discount important principles of our government as mere platitudes.

Such Boards are numerous and their territorial jurisdiction often small. But small and local authority may feel less sense of responsibility to the Constitution, and agencies of publicity may be less vigilant in calling it to account. The action of Congress in making flag observance voluntary and respecting the conscience of the objector in a matter so vital as raising the Army contrasts sharply with these local regulations in matters relatively trivial to the welfare of the nation. There are village tyrants as well as village Hampdens, but none who acts under color of law is beyond reach of the Constitution.

3. The *Gobitis* opinion reasoned that this is a field "where courts possess no marked, and certainly no controlling, competence," that it is committed to the legislatures as well as the courts to guard cherished liberties and that it is constitutionally appropriate to "fight out the wise use of legislative authority in the forum of public opinion and before legislative assemblies rather than to transfer such a contest to the judicial arena," since all the "effective means of inducing political changes are left free." *Id.* at 597–598, 600.

The very purpose of a Bill of Rights was to withdraw certain subjects from the vicissitudes of political controversy, to place them beyond the reach of majorities and officials and to establish them as legal principles to be applied by the courts. One's right to life, liberty, and property, to free speech, a free press, freedom of worship and assembly, and other fundamental rights may not be submitted to vote; they depend on the outcome of no elections.

In weighing arguments of the parties it is important to distinguish between the due process clause of the Fourteenth Amendment as an instrument for transmitting the principles of the First Amendment and those cases in which it is applied for its own sake. The test of legislation which collides with the Fourteenth Amendment, because it also collides with the principles of the First, is much more definite than the test when only the Fourteenth is involved. Much of the vagueness of the due process clause disappears when the specific prohibitions of the First become its standard. The right of a State to regulate, for example, a public utility may well include, so far as the due process test is concerned, power to impose all of the restrictions which a legislature may have a "rational basis" for adopting. But freedoms of speech and of press, of assembly, and of worship may not be infringed on such slender grounds. They are susceptible of restriction only to prevent grave and immediate danger to interests which the State may lawfully protect. It is important to note that while it is the Fourteenth Amendment which bears directly upon the State it is the more specific limiting principles of the First Amendment that finally govern this case.

Nor does our duty to apply the Bill of Rights to assertions of official authority depend upon our possession of marked competence in the field where the invasion of rights occurs. True, the task of translating the majestic generalities of the Bill of Rights, conceived as part of the pattern of liberal government in the eighteenth century, into concrete restraints on officials dealing with the problems of the twentieth century, is one to disturb self-confidence. These principles grew in soil which also produced a philosophy that the individual was the center of society, that his liberty was attainable through mere absence of governmental restraints, and that government should be entrusted with few controls and only the mildest supervision over men's affairs. We must transplant these rights to a soil in which the *laissez-faire* concept or principle of non-interference has withered at least as to economic affairs, and social advancements are increasingly sought through closer integration of society and through expanded and strengthened governmental controls. These changed conditions often deprive precedents of reliability and cast us more than we would choose upon our own judgment. But we act in these matters not by authority of our competence but by force of our commissions. We cannot, because of modest estimates of our competence in such specialties as public education, withhold the judgment that history authenticates as the function of this Court when liberty is infringed.

4. Lastly, and this is the very heart of the *Gobitis* opinion, it reasons that "National unity is the basis of national security," that the authorities have "the right to select appropriate means for its attainment," and hence reaches the conclusion that such compulsory measures toward "national unity" are constitutional. *Id.* at 595. Upon the verity of this assumption depends our answer in this case.

National unity as an end which officials may foster by persuasion and example is not in question. The problem is whether under our Constitution compulsion as here employed is a permissible means for its achievement.

Struggles to coerce uniformity of sentiment in support of some end thought essential to their time and country have been waged by many good as well as by evil men. Nationalism is a relatively recent phenomenon but at other times and places the ends have been racial or territorial security, support of a dynasty or regime, and particular plans for saving souls. As first and moderate methods to attain unity have failed, those bent on its accomplishment must resort to an ever-increasing severity. As governmental pressure toward unity becomes greater, so strife becomes more bitter as to whose unity it shall be. Probably no deeper division of our people could proceed from any provocation than from finding it necessary to choose what doctrine and whose program public educational officials shall compel youth to unite in embracing. Ultimate futility of such attempts to compel coherence is the lesson of every such effort from the Roman drive to stamp out Christianity as a disturber of its pagan unity, the Inquisition, as a means to religious and dynastic unity, the Siberian exiles as a means to Russian unity, down to the fast failing efforts of our present totalitarian enemies. Those who begin coercive elimination of dissent soon find themselves exterminating dissenters. Compulsory unification of opinion achieves only the unanimity of the graveyard.

It seems trite but necessary to say that the First Amendment to our Constitution was designed to avoid these ends by avoiding these beginnings. There is no mysticism in the American concept of the State or of the nature or origin of its authority. We set up government by consent of the governed, and the Bill of Rights denies those in power any legal opportunity to coerce that consent. Authority here is to be controlled by public opinion, not public opinion by authority.

The case is made difficult not because the principles of its decision are obscure but because the flag involved is our own. Nevertheless, we apply the limitations of the Constitution with no fear that freedom to be intellectually and spiritually diverse or even contrary will disintegrate the social organization. To believe that patriotism will not flourish if patriotic ceremonies are voluntary and spontaneous instead of a compulsory routine is to make an unflattering estimate of the appeal of our institutions to free minds. We can have intellectual individualism and the rich cultural diversities that we owe to exceptional minds only at the price of occasional eccentricity and abnormal attitudes. When they are so harmless to others or to the State as those we deal with here, the price is not too great. But freedom to differ is not limited to things that do not matter much. That would be a mere shadow of freedom. The test of its substance is the right to differ as to things that touch the heart of the existing order.

If there is any fixed star in our constitutional constellation, it is that no official, high or petty, can prescribe what shall be orthodox in politics, nationalism, religion, or other matters of opinion or force citizens to confess by word or act their faith therein. If there are any circumstances which permit an exception, they do not now occur to us.

We think the action of the local authorities in compelling the flag salute and pledge transcends constitutional limitations on their power and invades the sphere of intellect and spirit which it is the purpose of the First Amendment to our Constitution to reserve from all official control.

The decision of this Court in *Minersville School District v. Gobitis,* and the holdings of those few *per curiam* decisions which preceded and foreshadowed it are overruled, and the judgment enjoining enforcement of the West Virginia Regulation is

Affirmed.

■ MR. JUSTICE ROBERTS and MR. JUSTICE REED adhere to the views expressed by the Court in *Minersville School District v. Gobitis*, 310 U.S. 586, and are of the opinion that the judgment below should be reversed.

■ MR. JUSTICE BLACK and MR. JUSTICE DOUGLAS, concurring. [Omitted.]

■ MR. JUSTICE MURPHY, concurring. [Omitted.]

■ MR. JUSTICE FRANKFURTER, dissenting.

One who belongs to the most vilified and persecuted minority in history is not likely to be insensible to the freedoms guaranteed by our Constitution. Were my purely personal attitude relevant I should whole-heartedly associate myself with the general libertarian views in the Court's opinion, representing as they do the thought and action of a lifetime. But as judges we are neither Jew nor Gentile, neither Catholic nor agnostic. We owe equal attachment to the Constitution and are equally bound by our judicial obligations whether we derive our citizenship from the earliest or the latest immigrants to these shores. As a member of this Court I am not justified in writing my private notions of policy into the Constitution, no matter how deeply I may cherish them or how mischievous I may deem their disregard. They duty of a judge who must decide which of two claims before the Court shall prevail, that of a State to enact and enforce laws within its general competence or that of an individual to refuse obedience because of the demands of his conscience, is not that of the ordinary person. It can never be emphasized too much that one's own opinion about the wisdom or evil of a law should be excluded altogether when one is doing one's duty on the bench. The only opinion of our own even looking in that direction that is material is our opinion whether legislators could in reason have enacted such a law. In the light of all the circumstances, including the history of this question in this Court, it would require more daring than I possess to deny that reasonable legislators could have taken the action which is before us for review. Most unwillingly, therefore, I must differ from my brethren with regard to legislation like this. I cannot bring my mind to believe that the "liberty" secured by the Due Process Clause gives this Court authority to deny to the State of West Virginia the attainment of that which we all recognize as a legitimate legislative end, namely, the promotion of good citizenship, by employment of the means here chosen.

* * *

NOTES AND QUESTIONS

1. This landmark opinion has elements of both free exercise of religion and freedom of speech, as those terms were originally understood in 1868 when the Fourteenth Amendment was adopted, though the Court goes out of its way to avoid resting the decision solely on the deeply held religious beliefs of the Jehovah's Witnesses. Note that Justice Jackson explicitly invokes John Stuart Mills' harm principle from *On Liberty,* saying that no one else in society will be harmed if a few Jehovah's Witness children do not say the words of the flag salute. Think about what conception of "harm" underlies those comments.

2. *Barnette* was decided in 1943 as the first free exercise and free speech case since incorporation, except for *Minersville School District v. Gobitis*, 310 U.S. 586 (1940), which *Barnette* declined to follow. It was also decided in the midst of World War II. Twenty years earlier, the wartime posture of the case might well have cut in the other direction; the Supreme Court during World War I was hardly a bastion of free speech. *See supra* pages 511–512. But by 1943, the spectre of Nazism highlighted the importance of American constitutional principles; *Barnette,* along with *Skinner v. Oklahoma*, 316 U.S. 535 (1942), *see supra* pages 1402–1405, was a powerful statement of those principles. The Supreme Court's willingness to protect the Jehovah's Witnesses, even during the war, was a marked contrast with Australia's High Court, which upheld the drafting of Jehovah's Witnesses during that war, contrary to the religion clause in the Australian constitution. Ultimately, *Barnette* became the cornerstone of the Fourteenth Amendment both as to the free exercise of religion and as to the freedom of speech. All of the modern Fourteenth Amendment religion and speech caselaw flows out of *Barnette.*

3. *Barnette* goes well beyond a conception of the First Amendment as protecting only political speech that is necessary for the running of democratic government *See* ALEXANDER MEIKLEJOHN, FREE SPEECH AND ITS RELATION TO SELF GOVERNMENT (1948) (arguing that political speech needs absolute protection but non-political speech does not) It not only protects the free marketplace of political ideas but also the right of any individual freely to develop their personality through expression. See *The Basic Law of*

the Federal Republic of Germany, Article II: "Every person shall have the right to free development of his personality insofar as he does not violate the rights of others or offend against the constitutional order or the moral law." It is a very Millian and libertarian opinion. It establishes the core principle that the government cannot compel one to speak—a concept that was further developed in *Wooley v. Maynard*, 430 U.S. 705 (1977), where the U.S. Supreme Court struck down a New Hampshire law that compelled a person to display the state's motto "Live Free, or Die" on his car's license plate—a message that he disagreed with and did not want to be compelled to speak.

4. Note especially Justice Jackson's statement: "If there is any fixed star in our constitutional constellation, it is that no official, high or petty, can prescribe what shall be orthodox in politics, nationalism, religion, or other matters of opinion, or force citizens to confess by word or act their faith therein. If there are any circumstances which permit an exception, they do not now occur to us." This is a sentiment that likely would have found more acceptance in 1868 than in the more communitarian world of 1791 when the First Amendment was ratified. *See* AKHIL REED AMAR, THE BILL OF RIGHTS: CREATION AND RECONSTRUCTION 239 (1998) ("By the 1860s libertarianism had displaced federalism and majoritarianism as the dominant, unifying theme of the First Amendment's freedoms").

5. If a public school made its students recite a diversity and inclusion statement, would that be unconstitutional? How about an anti-bullying statement?

2. WISCONSIN V. YODER

406 U.S. 205 (1972)

■ MR. CHIEF JUSTICE BURGER delivered the opinion of the Court.

On petition of the State of Wisconsin, we granted the writ of certiorari in this case to review a decision of the Wisconsin Supreme Court holding that respondents' convictions of violating the State's compulsory school-attendance law were invalid under the Free Exercise Clause of the First Amendment to the United States Constitution made applicable to the States by the Fourteenth Amendment. For the reasons hereafter stated we affirm the judgment of the Supreme Court of Wisconsin.

Respondents Jonas Yoder and Wallace Miller are members of the Old Order Amish religion, and respondent Adin Yutzy is a member of the Conservative Amish Mennonite Church. They and their families are residents of Green County, Wisconsin. Wisconsin's compulsory school-attendance law required them to cause their children to attend public or private school until reaching age 16 but the respondents declined to send their children, ages 14 and 15, to public school after they completed the eighth grade. The children were not enrolled in any private school, or within any recognized exception to the compulsory-attendance law, and they are conceded to be subject to the Wisconsin statute.

On complaint of the school district administrator for the public schools, respondents were charged, tried, and convicted of violating the compulsory-attendance law in Green County Court and were fined the sum of $5 each. Respondents defended on the ground that the application of the compulsory attendance law violated their rights under the First and Fourteenth Amendments. The trial testimony showed that respondents believed, in accordance with the tenets of Old Order Amish communities generally, that their children's attendance at high school, public or private, was contrary to the Amish religion and way of life. They believed that by sending their children to high school, they would not only expose themselves to the danger of the censure of the church community, but, as found by the county court, also endanger their own salvation and that of their children. The State stipulated that respondents' religious beliefs were sincere.

In support of their position, respondents presented as expert witnesses scholars on religion and education whose testimony is uncontradicted. They expressed their opinions on the relationship of the Amish belief concerning school attendance to the more general tenets of their religion, and described the impact that compulsory high school attendance could have on the continued survival of Amish communities as they exist in the United States today. The history of the Amish sect was given in some detail, beginning with the Swiss Anabaptists of the 16th century who rejected institutionalized churches and sought to return to the early, simple, Christian life de-emphasizing material success, rejecting the competitive spirit, and seeking to insulate themselves from the modern world. As a result of their common heritage, Old Order Amish communities today are characterized by a fundamental belief that salvation requires life in a church community separate and apart from the world and worldly influence. This concept of life aloof from the world and its values is central to their faith.

* * *

Amish objection to formal education beyond the eighth grade is firmly grounded in these central religious concepts. They object to the high school, and higher education generally, because the values they teach are in marked variance with Amish values and the Amish way of life; they view secondary school education as an impermissible exposure of their children to a "worldly" influence in conflict with their beliefs. The high school tends to emphasize intellectual and scientific accomplishments, self-distinction, competitiveness, worldly success, and social life with other students. Amish society emphasizes informal learning-through-doing; a life of "goodness," rather than a life of intellect; wisdom, rather than technical knowledge; community welfare, rather than competition; and separation from, rather than integration with, contemporary worldly society.

* * * In short, high school attendance with teachers who are not of the Amish faith—and may even be hostile to it—interposes a serious barrier to the integration of the Amish child into the Amish religious community. Dr. John Hostetler, one of the experts on Amish society, testified that the modern high school is not equipped, in curriculum or social environment, to impart the values promoted by Amish society.

The Amish do not object to elementary education through the first eight grades as a general proposition because they agree that their children must have basic skills in the "three R's" in order to read the Bible, to be good farmers and citizens, and to be able to deal with non-Amish people when necessary in the course of daily affairs. They view such a basic education as acceptable because it does not significantly expose their children to worldly values or interfere with their development in the Amish community during the crucial adolescent period. While Amish accept compulsory elementary education generally, wherever possible they have established their own elementary schools in many respects like the small local schools of the past. In the Amish belief higher learning tends to develop values they reject as influences that alienate man from God.

On the basis of such considerations, Dr. Hostetler testified that compulsory high school attendance could not only result in great psychological harm to Amish children, because of the conflicts it would produce, but would also, in his opinion, ultimately result in the destruction of the Old Order Amish church community as it exists in the United States today. The testimony of Dr. Donald A. Erickson, an expert witness on education, also showed that the Amish succeed in preparing their high school age children to be productive members of the Amish community. He described their system of learning through doing the skills directly relevant to their adult roles in the Amish community as "ideal" and perhaps superior to ordinary high school education. The evidence also showed that the Amish have an excellent record as law-abiding and generally self-sufficient members of society.

Although the trial court in its careful findings determined that the Wisconsin compulsory school-attendance law "does interfere with the freedom of the Defendants to act in accordance with their sincere religious belief" it also concluded that the requirement of high school attendance until age 16 was a "reasonable and constitutional" exercise of governmental power, and therefore denied the motion to dismiss the charges. The Wisconsin Circuit Court affirmed the convictions. The Wisconsin Supreme Court, however, sustained respondents' claim under the Free Exercise Clause of the First Amendment and reversed the convictions. A majority of the court was of the opinion that the State had failed to make an adequate showing that its interest in "establishing and maintaining an educational system overrides the defendants' right to the free exercise of their religion."

There is no doubt as to the power of a State, having a high responsibility for education of its citizens, to impose reasonable regulations for the control and duration of basic education. *See, e.g., Pierce v. Society of Sisters,* 268 U.S. 510, 534 (1925). Providing public schools ranks at the very apex of the function of a State. Yet even this paramount responsibility was, in *Pierce,* made to yield to the right of parents to provide an equivalent education in a privately operated system. There the Court held that Oregon's statute compelling attendance in a public school from age eight to age 16 unreasonably interfered with the interest of parents in directing the rearing of their offspring, including their education in church-operated schools. As that case suggests, the values of parental direction of the religious upbringing and education of their children in their early and formative years have a high place in our society. Thus, a State's interest in universal education, however highly we rank it, is not totally free from a balancing process when it impinges on fundamental rights and interests, such as those specifically protected by the Free Exercise Clause of the First Amendment, and the traditional interest of parents with respect to the religious upbringing of their children so long as they, in the words of *Pierce,* "prepare [them] for additional obligations." 268 U.S. at 535.

It follows that in order for Wisconsin to compel school attendance beyond the eighth grade against a claim that such attendance interferes with the practice of a legitimate religious belief, it must appear either that the State does not deny the free exercise of religious belief by its requirement, or that there is a state interest of sufficient magnitude to override the interest claiming protection under the Free Exercise Clause * * *.

* * *

We come then to the quality of the claims of the respondents concerning the alleged encroachment of Wisconsin's compulsory school-attendance statute on their rights and the rights of their children to the free exercise of the religious beliefs they and their forebears have adhered to for almost three centuries. In evaluating those claims we must be careful to determine whether the Amish religious faith and their mode of life are, as they claim, inseparable and interdependent. A way of life, however virtuous and admirable, may not be interposed as a barrier to reasonable state regulation of education if it is based on purely secular considerations; to have the protection of the Religion Clauses, the claims must be rooted in religious belief. Although a determination of what is a "religious" belief or practice entitled to constitutional protection may present a most delicate question, the very concept of ordered liberty precludes allowing every person to make his own standards on matters of conduct in which society as a whole has important interests. Thus, if the Amish asserted their claims because of their subjective evaluation and rejection of the contemporary secular values accepted by the majority, much as Thoreau rejected the social values of his time and isolated himself at Walden Pond, their claims would not rest on a religious basis. Thoreau's choice was philosophical and personal rather than religious, and such belief does not rise to the demands of the Religion Clauses.

Giving no weight to such secular considerations, however, we see that the record in this case abundantly supports the claim that the traditional way of life of the Amish is not merely a matter of personal preference, but one of deep religious conviction, shared by an organized group, and intimately related to daily living. That the Old Order Amish daily life and religious practice stem from their faith is shown by the fact that it is in response to their literal interpretation of the Biblical injunction from the Epistle of Paul to the Romans, "be not conformed to this world. . . ." This command is fundamental to the Amish faith. Moreover, for the Old Order Amish, religion is not simply a matter of theocratic belief. As the expert witnesses explained, the Old Order Amish religion pervades and determines virtually their entire way of life, regulating it with the detail of the Talmudic diet through the strictly enforced rules of the church community.

* * *

As the society around the Amish has become more populous, urban, industrialized, and complex, particularly in this century, government regulation of human affairs has correspondingly become more detailed and pervasive. The Amish mode of life has thus come into conflict increasingly with requirements of contemporary society exerting a hydraulic insistence on conformity to majoritarian standards. So long as compulsory education laws were confined to eight grades of elementary basic education imparted in a nearby rural schoolhouse, with a large proportion of students of the Amish faith, the Old Order Amish had little basis to fear that school attendance would expose their children to the worldly influence they reject. But modern compulsory secondary education in rural areas is now largely carried on in a consolidated school, often remote from the student's home and alien to his daily home life. As the record so strongly shows, the values and programs of the modern secondary school are in sharp conflict with the fundamental mode of life mandated by the Amish religion; modern laws requiring compulsory secondary education have accordingly engendered great concern and conflict. The conclusion is inescapable that secondary schooling, by exposing Amish children to worldly influences in terms of attitudes, goals, and values contrary to beliefs, and by substantially interfering with the religious development of the Amish child and his integration into the way of life of the Amish faith community at the crucial adolescent stage of development, contravenes the basic religious tenets and practice of the Amish faith, both as to the parent and the child.

The impact of the compulsory-attendance law on respondents' practice of the Amish religion is not only severe, but inescapable, for the Wisconsin law affirmatively compels them, under threat of criminal sanction, to perform acts undeniably at odds with fundamental tenets of their religious beliefs * * *.

In sum, the unchallenged testimony of acknowledged experts in education and religious history, almost 300 years of consistent practice, and strong evidence of a sustained faith pervading and regulating respondents' entire mode of life support the claim that enforcement of the State's requirement of compulsory formal education after the eighth grade would gravely endanger if not destroy the free exercise of respondents' religious beliefs.

Neither the findings of the trial court nor the Amish claims as to the nature of their faith are challenged in this Court by the State of Wisconsin. Its position is that the State's interest in universal compulsory formal secondary education to age 16 is so great that it is paramount to the undisputed claims of respondents that their mode of preparing their youth for Amish life, after the traditional elementary education, is an essential part of their religious belief and practice. Nor does the State undertake to meet the claim that the Amish mode of life and education is inseparable from and a part of the basic tenets of their religion—indeed, as much a part of their religious belief and practices as baptism, the confessional, or a sabbath may be for others.

Wisconsin concedes that under the Religion Clauses religious beliefs are absolutely free from the State's control, but it argues that "actions," even though religiously grounded, are outside the protection of the First Amendment. But our decisions have rejected the idea that religiously grounded conduct is always outside the protection of the Free Exercise Clause. It is true that activities of individuals, even when religiously based, are often subject to regulation by the States in the exercise of their undoubted power to promote the health, safety, and general welfare, or the Federal Government in the exercise of its delegated powers. But to agree that religiously grounded conduct must often be subject to the broad police power of the State is not to deny that there are areas of conduct protected by the Free Exercise Clause of the First Amendment and thus beyond the power of the State to control, even under regulations of general applicability. This case, therefore, does not become easier because respondents were convicted for their "actions" in refusing to send their children to the public high school; in this context belief and action cannot be neatly confined in logic-tight compartments.

Nor can this case be disposed of on the grounds that Wisconsin's requirement for school attendance to age 16 applies uniformly to all citizens of the State and does not, on its face, discriminate against religions or a particular religion, or that it is motivated by legitimate secular concerns. A regulation neutral on its face may, in its application, nonetheless offend the constitutional requirement for governmental neutrality if it unduly burdens the free exercise of religion. *Sherbert v. Verner, supra; cf. Walz v. Tax Commission,* 397 U.S. 664 (1970). The Court must not ignore the danger that an exception from a general obligation of citizenship on religious grounds may run afoul of the Establishment Clause, but that danger cannot be allowed to prevent any exception, no matter how vital it may be to the protection of values promoted by the right of free exercise * * *.

We turn, then, to the State's broader contention that its interest in its system of compulsory education is so compelling that even the established religious practices of the Amish must give way. Where fundamental claims of religious freedom are at stake, however, we cannot accept such a sweeping claim; despite its admitted validity in the generality of cases, we must searchingly examine the interests that the State seeks to promote by its requirement for compulsory education to age 16, and the impediment to those objectives that would flow from recognizing the claimed Amish exemption.

The State advances two primary arguments in support of its system of compulsory education. It notes, as Thomas Jefferson pointed out early in our history, that some degree of education is necessary to prepare citizens to participate effectively and intelligently in our open political system if we are to preserve freedom and independence. Further, education prepares individuals to be self-reliant and self-sufficient participants in society. We accept these propositions.

However, the evidence adduced by the Amish in this case is persuasively to the effect that an additional one or two years of formal high school for Amish children in place of their long-established program of informal vocational education would do little to serve those interests. Respondents' experts testified at trial, without challenge, that the value of all education must be assessed in terms of its capacity to prepare the child for life. It is one thing to say that compulsory education for a year or two beyond the eighth grade may be necessary when its goal is the preparation of the child for life in modern society as the majority live, but it is quite another if the goal of education be viewed as the preparation of the child for life in the separated agrarian community that is the keystone of the Amish faith.

The State attacks respondents' position as one fostering "ignorance" from which the child must be protected by the State. No one can question the State's duty to protect children from ignorance but this argument does not square with the facts disclosed in the record. Whatever their idiosyncrasies as seen by the majority, this record strongly shows that the Amish community has been a highly successful social unit within our society, even if apart from the conventional "mainstream." Its members are productive and very law-abiding members of society; they reject public welfare in any of its usual modern forms. The Congress itself recognized their self-sufficiency by authorizing exemption of such groups as the Amish from the obligation to pay social security taxes.

It is neither fair nor correct to suggest that the Amish are opposed to education beyond the eighth grade level. What this record shows is that they are opposed to conventional formal education of the type provided by a certified high school because it comes at the child's crucial adolescent period of religious development. Dr. Donald Erickson, for example, testified that their system of learning-by-doing was an "ideal system" of education in terms of preparing Amish children for life as adults in the Amish community * * *.

We must not forget that in the Middle Ages important values of the civilization of the Western World were preserved by members of religious orders who isolated themselves from all worldly influences against great obstacles. There can be no assumption that today's majority is "right," and the Amish and others like them are "wrong." A way of life that is odd or even erratic but interferes with no rights or interests of others is not to be condemned because it is different.

The State, however, supports its interest in providing an additional one or two years of compulsory high school education to Amish children because of the possibility that some such children will choose to leave the Amish community, and that, if this occurs they will be ill-equipped for life. The State argues that if Amish children leave their church they should not be in the position of making their way in the world without the education available in the one or two additional years the State requires. However, on this record, that argument is highly speculative. There is no specific evidence of the loss of Amish adherents by attrition, nor is there any showing that, upon leaving the Amish community Amish children, with their practical agricultural training and habits of industry and self-reliance, would become burdens on society because of educational shortcomings. Indeed, this argument of the State appears to rest primarily on the State's mistaken assumption, already noted, that the Amish do not provide any education for their children beyond the eighth grade, but allow them to grow in "ignorance." To the contrary, not only do the Amish accept the necessity for formal schooling through the eighth grade level, but continue to provide what has been characterized by the undisputed testimony of expert educators as an "ideal" vocational education for their children in the adolescent years.

There is nothing in this record to suggest that the Amish qualities of reliability, self-reliance, and dedication to work would fail to find ready markets in today's society. Absent some contrary evidence supporting the State's position, we are unwilling to assume that persons possessing such valuable vocational skills and habits are doomed to become burdens on society should they determine to leave the Amish faith, nor is there any basis in the record to warrant a finding that an additional one or two years of formal school education beyond the eighth grade would serve to eliminate any such problem that might exist.

* * * When Thomas Jefferson emphasized the need for education as a bulwark of a free people against tyranny, there is nothing to indicate he had in mind compulsory education through any fixed age beyond a basic education. Indeed, the Amish communities singularly parallel and reflect many of the virtues of Jefferson's ideal of the "sturdy yeoman" who would form the basis of what he considered as the ideal of a democratic society. Even their idiosyncratic separateness exemplifies the diversity we profess to admire and encourage.

The requirement for compulsory education beyond the eighth grade is a relatively recent development in our history. Less than 60 years ago, the educational requirements of almost all of the States were satisfied by completion of the elementary grades, at least where the child was regularly and lawfully employed. The independence and successful social functioning of the Amish community for a period approaching almost three centuries and more than 200 years in this country are strong evidence that there is at best a speculative gain, in terms of meeting the duties of citizenship, from an additional one or two years of compulsory formal education. Against this background, it would require a more particularized showing from the State on this point to justify the severe interference with religious freedom such additional compulsory attendance would entail.

* * *

* * * The dissent argues that a child who expresses a desire to attend public high school in conflict with the wishes of his parents should not be prevented from doing

so. There is no reason for the Court to consider that point since it is not an issue in the case. The children are not parties to this litigation. The State has at no point tried this case on the theory that respondents were preventing their children from attending school against their expressed desires, and indeed the record is to the contrary * * *.

Our holding in no way determines the proper resolution of possible competing interests of parents, children, and the State in an appropriate state court proceeding in which the power of the State is asserted on the theory that Amish parents are preventing their minor children from attending high school despite their expressed desires to the contrary. Recognition of the claim of the State in such a proceeding would, of course, call into question traditional concepts of parental control over the religious upbringing and education of their minor children recognized in this Court's past decisions. It is clear that such an intrusion by a State into family decisions in the area of religious training would give rise to grave questions of religious freedom comparable to those raised here and those presented in *Pierce v. Society of Sisters,* 268 U.S. 510 (1925). On this record we neither reach nor decide those issues.

* * *

* * *[T]he Court's holding in *Pierce* stands as a charter of the rights of parents to direct the religious upbringing of their children. And, when the interests of parenthood are combined with a free exercise claim of the nature revealed by this record, more than merely a "reasonable relation to some purpose within the competency of the State" is required to sustain the validity of the State's requirement under the First Amendment * * *.

* * *

For the reasons stated we hold, with the Supreme Court of Wisconsin, that the First and Fourteenth Amendments prevent the State from compelling respondents to cause their children to attend formal high school to age 16 * * *.

* * *

Nothing we hold is intended to undermine the general applicability of the State's compulsory school-attendance statutes or to limit the power of the State to promulgate reasonable standards that, while not impairing the free exercise of religion, provide for continuing agricultural vocational education under parental and church guidance by the Old Order Amish or others similarly situated. The States have had a long history of amicable and effective relationships with church-sponsored schools, and there is no basis for assuming that, in this related context, reasonable standards cannot be established concerning the content of the continuing vocational education of Amish children under parental guidance, provided always that state regulations are not inconsistent with what we have said in this opinion.

Affirmed.

■ MR. JUSTICE POWELL and MR. JUSTICE REHNQUIST took no part in the consideration or decision of this case.

■ MR. JUSTICE STEWART, with whom MR. JUSTICE BRENNAN joins, concurring.

* * *

* * * [T]his record simply does not present the interesting and important issue discussed in * * * the dissenting opinion of Mr. JUSTICE DOUGLAS. With this observation, I join the opinion and the judgment of the Court.

■ MR. JUSTICE WHITE, with whom MR. JUSTICE BRENNAN and MR. JUSTICE STEWART join, concurring.

* * *

This would be a very different case for me if respondents' claim were that their religion forbade their children from attending any school at any time and from complying in any way with the educational standards set by the State * * *.

* * *

* * * I join the Court because the sincerity of the Amish religious policy here is uncontested, because the potentially adverse impact of the state requirement is great, and because the State's valid interest in education has already been largely satisfied by the eight years the children have already spent in school.

■ MR. JUSTICE DOUGLAS dissenting in part.

I agree with the Court that the religious scruples of the Amish are opposed to the education of their children beyond the grade schools, yet I disagree with the Court's conclusion that the matter is within the dispensation of parents alone. The Court's analysis assumes that the only interests at stake in the case are those of the Amish parents on the one hand and those of the State on the other. The difficulty with this approach is that, despite the Court's claim, the parents are seeking to vindicate not only their own free exercise claims, but also those of their high-school-age children.

It is argued that the right of the Amish children to religious freedom is not presented by the facts of the case, as the issue before the Court involves only the Amish parents' religious freedom to defy a state criminal statute imposing upon them an affirmative duty to cause their children to attend high school.

* * *

* * * [N]o analysis of religious-liberty claims can take place in a vacuum. If the parents in this case are allowed a religious exemption, the inevitable effect is to impose the parents' notions of religious duty upon their children. Where the child is mature enough to express potentially conflicting desires, it would be an invasion of the child's rights to permit such an imposition without canvassing his views * * *. And if an Amish child desires to attend high school, and is mature enough to have that desire respected, the State may well be able to override the parents' religiously motivated objections.

Religion is an individual experience. It is not necessary, nor even appropriate, for every Amish child to express his views on the subject in a prosecution of a single adult. Crucial, however, are the views of the child whose parent is the subject of the suit. Frieda Yoder has in fact, testified that her own religious views are opposed to high-school education. I therefore join the judgment of the Court as to respondent Jonas Yoder. But Frieda Yoder's views may not be those of Vernon Yutzy or Barbara Miller. I must dissent, therefore, as to respondents Adin Yutzy and Wallace Miller as their motion to dismiss also raised the question of their children's religious liberty.

* * *

On this important and vital matter of education, I think the children should be entitled to be heard. While the parents, absent dissent, normally speak for the entire family, the education of the child is a matter on which the child will often have decided views. He may want to be a pianist or an astronaut or an oceanographer. To do so he will have to break from the Amish tradition.

* * *

The views of the two children in question were not canvassed by the Wisconsin courts. The matter should be explicitly reserved so that new hearings can be held on remand of the case.

* * *

NOTES AND QUESTIONS

1. What do you think of *Yoder*? We both think it got matters exactly right. Obviously, both parents and society have an interest in the speech children hear and in how they are educated, and once children are old enough (how old is old enough?), their views also count. As a matter of ascertaining the "privileges or immunities" of the parents, who were facing criminal prosecutions, a core freedom of Western civilization, and certainly of the American Ancient Constitution, is supporting and deferring to parents in raising children well, subject to some limits. This case obviously builds on and elaborates on the religious freedom recognized in *Barnette* as well as *Pierce v. Society of Sisters* and *Meyer v. Nebraska.*

2. Both we and the Court say, "subject to some limits." What are those limits, and why weren't they exceeded in this case? Suppose that a particular religion calls for all girls to undergo female circumcision, such that preventing that practice would, as a factual matter, prevent the full exercise of that religion. Do States have to carve out exceptions from their usual criminal laws in order to accommodate that practice? What about polygamy? If a religion genuinely believes that polygamy is part of its necessary practice, does the State have to recognize plural marriages within that religion? In the nineteenth century, in a case involving the First Amendment rather than the Fourteenth Amendment, the Court held that Congress could outlaw polygamy in the then-federal territory of Utah. *See United States v. Reynolds,* 98 U.S. (6 Otto) 145 (1878). Justice Douglas, in his dissenting opinion in *Yoder,* claimed (approvingly): "What we do today, at least in this respect, opens the way to give organized religion a broader base than it has ever enjoyed, and it even promises that in time *Reynolds* will be overruled." 406 U.S. at 247. Is he right? Would that be a good thing? What about exemptions from antidiscrimination laws on the ground that certain religions think that racial separation is divinely commanded?

3. Many of these issues—as well as the continued vitality of *Yoder*—arose in *Employment Division, Dep't of Human Resources of Oregon v. Smith,* 494 U.S. 872 (1990), a case that split the Court on the reasoning 5–4 (though the result was 6–3), and that Congress (unsuccessfully, according to the Supreme Court) tried to overrule through the Religious Freedom Restoration Act. *See supra* pages 869–876. Two members of the Native American Church were fired from their jobs because they used peyote, an illegal hallucinogenic drug which they claimed was essential to a sacramental ceremony within their religion. They were denied unemployment benefits under a statute that disallowed benefits for work-related "misconduct," which everyone agreed normally included illegal drug use. The direct question was whether the government must, at least sometimes,

carve out exemptions from otherwise general laws in order to accommodate religious beliefs. A majority of the Supreme Court, in an opinion by Justice Scalia, said no:

> * * * We have never held that an individual's religious beliefs excuse him from compliance with an otherwise valid law prohibiting conduct that the State is free to regulate. On the contrary, the record of more than a century of our free exercise jurisprudence contradicts that proposition. As described succinctly by Justice Frankfurter in *Minersville School Dist. Bd. of Ed. v. Gobitis,* 310 U.S. 586, 594–595 (1940): "Conscientious scruples have not, in the course of the long struggle for religious toleration, relieved the individual from obedience to a general law not aimed at the promotion or restriction of religious beliefs. The mere possession of religious convictions which contradict the relevant concerns of a political society does not relieve the citizen from the discharge of political responsibilities (footnote omitted)." We first had occasion to assert that principle in *Reynolds v. United States,* 98 U.S. 145 (1878), where we rejected the claim that criminal laws against polygamy could not be constitutionally applied to those whose religion commanded the practice. "Laws," we said, "are made for the government of actions, and while they cannot interfere with mere religious belief and opinions, they may with practices. . . . Can a man excuse his practices to the contrary because of his religious belief? To permit this would be to make the professed doctrines of religious belief superior to the law of the land, and in effect to permit every citizen to become a law unto himself." *Id.,* at 166–167.
>
> * * * In *Prince v. Massachusetts,* 321 U.S. 158 (1944), we held that a mother could be prosecuted under the child labor laws for using her children to dispense literature in the streets, her religious motivation notwithstanding * * *. In *Braunfeld v. Brown,* 366 U.S. 599 (1961) (plurality opinion), we upheld Sunday-closing laws against the claim that they burdened the religious practices of persons whose religions compelled them to refrain from work on other days. In *Gillette v. United States,* 401 U.S. 437, 461 (1971), we sustained the military Selective Service System against the claim that it violated free exercise by conscripting persons who opposed a particular war on religious grounds.
>
> * * *
>
> The only decisions in which we have held that the First Amendment bars application of a neutral, generally applicable law to religiously motivated action have involved not the Free Exercise Clause alone, but the Free Exercise Clause in conjunction with other constitutional protections, such as freedom of speech and of the press, see *Cantwell v. Connecticut,* 310 U.S., at 304–307 (invalidating a licensing system for religious and charitable solicitations under which the administrator had discretion to deny a license to any cause he deemed nonreligious); *Murdock v. Pennsylvania,* 319 U.S. 105 (1943) (invalidating a flat tax on solicitation as applied to the dissemination of religious ideas); *Follett v. McCormick,* 321 U.S. 573 (1944) (same), or the right of parents, acknowledged in *Pierce v. Society of Sisters,* 268 U.S. 510 (1925), to direct the education of their children, see *Wisconsin v. Yoder,* 406 U.S. 205 (1972) (invalidating compulsory school-attendance laws as applied to Amish parents who refused on religious grounds to send their children to school) * * *.
>
> The present case does not present such a hybrid situation, but a free exercise claim unconnected with any communicative activity or parental right. Respondents urge us to hold, quite simply, that when otherwise prohibitable

> conduct is accompanied by religious convictions, not only the convictions but the conduct itself must be free from governmental regulation. We have never held that, and decline to do so now. There being no contention that Oregon's drug law represents an attempt to regulate religious beliefs, the communication of religious beliefs, or the raising of one's children in those beliefs, the rule to which we have adhered ever since *Reynolds* plainly controls.

494 U.S. at 878–81. The Court accordingly declined to require States to show a "compelling" governmental interest for applying general laws to those who religion would be burdened by application of the laws. Three justices dissented, relying heavily on *Yoder*. *Smith* remains one of the Court's most controversial cases involving the religion clauses. *Compare* Michael W. McConnell, *The Origins and Historical Understanding of Free Exercise of Religion,* 103 HARV. L. REV. 1409 (1990) (defending the need for exemptions), *with* Philip A. Hamburger, *A Constitutional Right of Religious Exemption: An Historical Perspective,* 60 GEO. WASH. L. REV. 915 (1992) (criticizing that view).

4. The Court in *Employment Division* says that *Yoder* is a case of (our phrase) "religion-plus," involving some element beyond simply a claim that free exercise of religion has been burdened by a neutral law. What was the "plus" in *Yoder*? The *Employment Division* Court also said that there was "no contention that Oregon's drug law represents an attempt to regulate religious beliefs." How would one ever know if a seemingly neutral law was imposed for the purposes of regulating religious beliefs. Legislatures have been very creative over the years in crafting neutral-sounding ways to discriminate on the basis of race. What reason is there to doubt that they might be equally creative when it comes to religion?

5. The Court in *Yoder* recognizes a possible tension between accommodating religious through exceptions and "establish[ing]" religion through the same means. If a legislature (or a court) crafts exceptions from general laws to avoid burdening some religious practices, does it thereby "establish[ ]" those practices? The First Amendment says that "Congress shall make no law respecting an establishment of religion." Few clauses have a clearer original meaning: Congress could neither establish a national church, along the lines of the Church of England, *nor prevent States from establishing official state churches*. The clause does not say that Congress shall not establish religion; it says that Congress shall make no law *respecting* the establishment of religion—either pro or con. How does that principle incorporate against the States? That is actually a difficult question as a matter of 1868 original meaning. *See* AMAR, *supra,* at 249–54. Doctrinally, the incorporation of some kind of anti-establishment principle against States has been settled since 1947. *See Everson v. Board of Educ. of Ewing Township,* 330 U.S. 1 (1947). The impact of that doctrine became clear in 1962 when the Court held that States could not require public school teachers to read a prayer before class. *See Engel v. Vitale,* 370 U.S. 421 (1962). *See also School Dist. of Abington Twshp. v. Schempp,* 374 U.S. 203 (1963) (extending *Engel* to Bible reading). In 1971, the Court summarized its law to that point as follows:

> In the absence of precisely stated constitutional prohibitions, we must draw lines with reference to the three main evils against which the Establishment Clause was intended to afford protection: "sponsorship, financial support, and active involvement of the sovereign in religious activity." *Walz v. Tax Commission*, 397 U.S. 664, 668 (1970).
>
> Every analysis in this area must begin with consideration of the cumulative criteria developed by the Court over many years. Three such tests may be gleaned from our cases. First, the statute must have a secular legislative purpose; second, its principal or primary effect must be one that

neither advances nor inhibits religion; finally, the statute must not foster "an excessive government entanglement with religion."

* * *

Our prior holdings do not call for total separation between church and state; total separation is not possible in an absolute sense. Some relationship between government and religious organizations is inevitable * * *. Judicial caveats against entanglement must recognize that the line of separation, far from being a "wall," is a blurred, indistinct, and variable barrier depending on all the circumstances of a particular relationship.

This is not to suggest, however, that we are to engage in a legalistic minuet in which precise rules and forms must govern. A true minuet is a matter of pure form and style, the observance of which is itself the substantive end. Here we examine the form of the relationship for the light that it casts on the substance.

In order to determine whether the government entanglement with religion is excessive, we must examine the character and purposes of the institutions that are benefited, the nature of the aid that the State provides, and the resulting relationship between the government and the religious authority.

Lemon v. Kurtzman, 403 U.S. 602, 612–13, 614–15 (1971). For half a century, courts, legislators, and scholars have wrestled with the meaning of this cryptic discussion and how it might apply to everything from municipal holiday displays to student-initiated high-school graduation prayers. Fortunately for us, the subject is so difficult, and the doctrine cuts across so many fact-specific complexities, that it is normally left to specialized courses. In this introduction, we present only a single case. We feel a bit less guilty than we otherwise might because the case generated seven (7) opinions, so it reflects at least a significant part of the debate as of 2020.

[Assignment 76]

3. AMERICAN LEGION V. AMERICAN HUMANIST ASS'N

588 U.S. ___, 139 S.Ct. 2067 (2019)

■ JUSTICE ALITO announced the judgment of the Court and delivered the opinion of the Court with respect to Parts I, II-B, II-C, III, and IV, and an opinion with respect to Parts II-A and II-D, in which THE CHIEF JUSTICE, JUSTICE BREYER, and JUSTICE KAVANAUGH join.

Since 1925, the Bladensburg Peace Cross (Cross) has stood as a tribute to 49 area soldiers who gave their lives in the First World War. Eighty-nine years after the dedication of the Cross, respondents filed this lawsuit, claiming that they are offended by the sight of the memorial on public land and that its presence there and the expenditure of public funds to maintain it violate the Establishment Clause of the First Amendment. To remedy this violation, they asked a federal court to order the relocation or demolition of the Cross or at least the removal of its arms. The Court of Appeals for the Fourth Circuit agreed that the memorial is unconstitutional and remanded for a determination of the proper remedy. We now reverse.

Although the cross has long been a preeminent Christian symbol, its use in the Bladensburg memorial has a special significance. After the First World War, the picture of row after row of plain white crosses marking the overseas graves of soldiers who had lost their lives in that horrible conflict was emblazoned on the minds of

Americans at home, and the adoption of the cross as the Bladensburg memorial must be viewed in that historical context. For nearly a century, the Bladensburg Cross has expressed the community's grief at the loss of the young men who perished, its thanks for their sacrifice, and its dedication to the ideals for which they fought. It has become a prominent community landmark, and its removal or radical alteration at this date would be seen by many not as a neutral act but as the manifestation of "a hostility toward religion that has no place in our Establishment Clause traditions." *Van Orden v. Perry*, 545 U.S. 677, 704 (2005) (BREYER, J., concurring in judgment). And contrary to respondents' intimations, there is no evidence of discriminatory intent in the selection of the design of the memorial or the decision of a Maryland commission to maintain it. The Religion Clauses of the Constitution aim to foster a society in which people of all beliefs can live together harmoniously, and the presence of the Bladensburg Cross on the land where it has stood for so many years is fully consistent with that aim.

The cross came into widespread use as a symbol of Christianity by the fourth century, and it retains that meaning today. But there are many contexts in which the symbol has also taken on a secular meaning. Indeed, there are instances in which its message is now almost entirely secular.

A cross appears as part of many registered trademarks held by businesses and secular organizations, including Blue Cross Blue Shield, the Bayer Group, and some Johnson & Johnson products. Many of these marks relate to health care, and it is likely that the association of the cross with healing had a religious origin. But the current use of these marks is indisputably secular.

* * *

The image used in the Bladensburg memorial—a plain Latin cross—also took on new meaning after World War I * * *. [T]he image of a simple white cross "developed into a 'central symbol' " of the conflict * * *. Perhaps most famously, John McCrae's poem, In Flanders Fields, began with these memorable lines:

> "In Flanders fields the poppies blow
>
> Between the crosses, row on row."

In Flanders Fields and Other Poems 3 (G. P. Putnam's Sons ed. 1919) * * *. The image of "the crosses, row on row," stuck in people's minds, and even today for those who view World War I cemeteries in Europe, the image is arresting.

* * *

Recognition of the cross's symbolism extended to local communities across the country. In late 1918, residents of Prince George's County, Maryland, formed a committee for the purpose of erecting a memorial for the county's fallen soldiers. Among the committee's members were the mothers of 10 deceased soldiers. The committee decided that the memorial should be a cross and hired sculptor and architect John Joseph Earley to design it. Although we do not know precisely why the committee chose the cross, it is unsurprising that the committee—and many others commemorating World War I—adopted a symbol so widely associated with that wrenching event.

After selecting the design, the committee turned to the task of financing the project. The committee held fundraising events in the community and invited donations, no matter the size * * *.

* * *

* * * By 1922, however, the committee had run out of funds, and progress on the Cross had stalled. The local post of the American Legion took over the project, and the monument was finished in 1925.

The completed monument is a 32-foot tall Latin cross that sits on a large pedestal. The American Legion's emblem is displayed at its center, and the words "Valor," "Endurance," "Courage," and "Devotion" are inscribed at its base, one on each of the four faces. The pedestal also features a 9- by 2.5-foot bronze plaque explaining that the monument is "Dedicated to the heroes of Prince George's County, Maryland who lost their lives in the Great War for the liberty of the world." (capitalization omitted). The plaque lists the names of 49 local men, both Black and White, who died in the war. It identifies the dates of American involvement, and quotes President Woodrow Wilson's request for a declaration of war: "The right is more precious than peace. We shall fight for the things we have always carried nearest our hearts. To such a task we dedicate our lives."

* * *

Since its dedication, the Cross has served as the site of patriotic events honoring veterans, including gatherings on Veterans Day, Memorial Day, and Independence Day * * *.

As the area around the Cross developed, the monument came to be at the center of a busy intersection. In 1961, the Maryland-National Capital Park and Planning Commission (Commission) acquired the Cross and the land on which it sits in order to preserve the monument and address traffic-safety concerns. The American Legion reserved the right to continue using the memorial to host a variety of ceremonies, including events in memory of departed veterans. Over the next five decades, the Commission spent approximately $117,000 to maintain and preserve the monument. In 2008, it budgeted an additional $100,000 for renovations and repairs to the Cross.

In 2012, nearly 90 years after the Cross was dedicated and more than 50 years after the Commission acquired it, the American Humanist Association (AHA) lodged a complaint with the Commission. The complaint alleged that the Cross's presence on public land and the Commission's maintenance of the memorial violate the Establishment Clause of the First Amendment. The AHA, along with three residents of Washington, D. C., and Maryland, also sued the Commission in the District Court for the District of Maryland, making the same claim. The AHA sought declaratory and injunctive relief requiring "removal or demolition of the Cross, or removal of the arms from the Cross to form a non-religious slab or obelisk." The American Legion intervened to defend the Cross.

The District Court granted summary judgment for the Commission and the American Legion. The Cross, the District Court held, satisfies both the three-pronged test announced in *Lemon v. Kurtzman*, 403 U. S. 602 (1971), and the analysis applied by JUSTICE BREYER in upholding the Ten Commandments monument at issue in *Van Orden v. Perry*, 545 U.S. 677. Under the *Lemon* test, a court must ask whether a challenged government action (1) has a secular purpose; (2) has a "principal or primary effect" that "neither advances nor inhibits religion"; and (3) does not foster "an excessive government entanglement with religion," 403 U. S., at 612–613. Applying that test, the District Court determined that the Commission had secular purposes for acquiring and maintaining the Cross—namely, to commemorate World

War I and to ensure traffic safety. The court also found that a reasonable observer aware of the Cross's history, setting, and secular elements "would not view the Monument as having the effect of impermissibly endorsing religion." 147 F.Supp.3d 373, 387 (D.Md. 2015). Nor, according to the court, did the Commission's maintenance of the memorial create the kind of "continued and repeated government involvement with religion" that would constitute an excessive entanglement. *Ibid.* Finally, in light of the factors that informed its analysis of *Lemon*'s "effects" prong, the court concluded that the Cross is constitutional under JUSTICE BREYER's approach in *Van Orden*. 147 F.Supp.3d at 388–390.

A divided panel of the Court of Appeals for the Fourth Circuit reversed. The majority relied primarily on the *Lemon* test but also took cognizance of JUSTICE BREYER's *Van Orden* concurrence. While recognizing that the Commission acted for a secular purpose, the court held that the Bladensburg Cross failed *Lemon*'s "effects" prong because a reasonable observer would view the Commission's ownership and maintenance of the monument as an endorsement of Christianity. The court emphasized the cross's "inherent religious meaning" as the " 'preeminent symbol of Christianity.' " 874 F.3d at 206–207. Although conceding that the monument had several "secular elements," the court asserted that they were "overshadow[ed]" by the Cross's size and Christian connection—especially because the Cross's location and condition would make it difficult for "passers-by" to "read" or otherwise "examine" the plaque and American Legion emblem. The court rejected as "too simplistic" an argument defending the Cross's constitutionality on the basis of its 90-year history, suggesting that "[p]erhaps the longer a violation persists, the greater the affront to those offended." *Id.*, at 208. In the alternative, the court concluded, the Commission had become excessively entangled with religion by keeping a display that "aggrandizes the Latin cross" and by spending more than *de minimis* public funds to maintain it. *Id.*, at 211–212.

Chief Judge Gregory dissented in relevant part, contending that the majority misapplied the "effects" test by failing to give adequate consideration to the Cross's "physical setting, history, and usage." *Id.*, at 218. He also disputed the majority's excessive-entanglement analysis, noting that the Commission's maintenance of the Cross was not the kind of "comprehensive, discriminating, and continuing state surveillance" of religion that *Lemon* was concerned to rule out. 874 F.3d at 221.

The Fourth Circuit denied rehearing en banc over dissents by Chief Judge Gregory, Judge Wilkinson, and Judge Niemeyer. 891 F.3d 117 (2018). The Commission and the American Legion each petitioned for certiorari. We granted the petitions and consolidated them for argument.

The Establishment Clause of the First Amendment provides that "Congress shall make no law respecting an establishment of religion." While the concept of a formally established church is straightforward, pinning down the meaning of a "law respecting an establishment of religion" has proved to be a vexing problem. Prior to the Court's decision in *Everson v. Board of Ed. of Ewing*, 330 U.S. 1 (1947), the Establishment Clause was applied only to the Federal Government, and few cases involving this provision came before the Court. After *Everson* recognized the incorporation of the Clause, however, the Court faced a steady stream of difficult and controversial Establishment Clause issues, ranging from Bible reading and prayer in the public schools, *Engel v. Vitale*, 370 U.S. 421 (1962); *School Dist. of Abington Township v. Schempp*, 374 U.S. 203 (1963), to Sunday closing laws, *McGowan v.*

Maryland, 366 U.S. 420 (1961), to state subsidies for church-related schools or the parents of students attending those schools, *Board of Ed. of Central School Dist. No. 1 v. Allen*, 392 U.S. 236 (1968); *Everson, supra*. After grappling with such cases for more than 20 years, *Lemon* ambitiously attempted to distill from the Court's existing case law a test that would bring order and predictability to Establishment Clause decisionmaking. That test, as noted, called on courts to examine the purposes and effects of a challenged government action, as well as any entanglement with religion that it might entail. *Lemon*, 403 U. S., at 612–613. The Court later elaborated that the "effect[s]" of a challenged action should be assessed by asking whether a "reasonable observer" would conclude that the action constituted an "endorsement" of religion. *County of Allegheny v. American Civil Liberties Union, Greater Pittsburgh Chapter*, 492 U.S. 573, 592 (1989); *id.* at 630 (O'Connor, J., concurring in part and concurring in the judgment).

If the *Lemon* Court thought that its test would provide a framework for all future Establishment Clause decisions, its expectation has not been met. In many cases, this Court has either expressly declined to apply the test or has simply ignored it.

This pattern is a testament to the *Lemon* test's shortcomings. As Establishment Clause cases involving a great array of laws and practices came to the Court, it became more and more apparent that the *Lemon* test could not resolve them. It could not "explain the Establishment Clause's tolerance, for example, of the prayers that open legislative meetings, . . . certain references to, and invocations of, the Deity in the public words of public officials; the public references to God on coins, decrees, and buildings; or the attention paid to the religious objectives of certain holidays, including Thanksgiving." *Van Orden, supra*, at 699 (opinion of BREYER, J.). The test has been harshly criticized by Members of this Court, lamented by lower court judges, and questioned by a diverse roster of scholars.

For at least four reasons, the *Lemon* test presents particularly daunting problems in cases, including the one now before us, that involve the use, for ceremonial, celebratory, or commemorative purposes, of words or symbols with religious associations. Together, these considerations counsel against efforts to evaluate such cases under *Lemon* and toward application of a presumption of constitutionality for longstanding monuments, symbols, and practices.

First, these cases often concern monuments, symbols, or practices that were first established long ago, and in such cases, identifying their original purpose or purposes may be especially difficult. In *Salazar v. Buono*, 559 U.S. 700 (2010), for example, we dealt with a cross that a small group of World War I veterans had put up at a remote spot in the Mojave Desert more than seven decades earlier * * *.

* * * The truth is that 70 years after the fact, there was no way to be certain about the motivations of the men who were responsible for the creation of the monument. And this is often the case with old monuments, symbols, and practices. Yet it would be inappropriate for courts to compel their removal or termination based on supposition.

Second, as time goes by, the purposes associated with an established monument, symbol, or practice often multiply. Take the example of Ten Commandments monuments, the subject we addressed in *Van Orden*, 545 U.S. 677, and *McCreary County v. American Civil Liberties Union of Ky.*, 545 U.S. 844 (2005). For believing

Jews and Christians, the Ten Commandments are the word of God handed down to Moses on Mount Sinai, but the image of the Ten Commandments has also been used to convey other meanings. They have historical significance as one of the foundations of our legal system, and for largely that reason, they are depicted in the marble frieze in our courtroom and in other prominent public buildings in our Nation's capital. In *Van Orden* and *McCreary*, no Member of the Court thought that these depictions are unconstitutional.

* * *

The existence of multiple purposes is not exclusive to longstanding monuments, symbols, or practices, but this phenomenon is more likely to occur in such cases. Even if the original purpose of a monument was infused with religion, the passage of time may obscure that sentiment. As our society becomes more and more religiously diverse, a community may preserve such monuments, symbols, and practices for the sake of their historical significance or their place in a common cultural heritage.

Third, just as the purpose for maintaining a monument, symbol, or practice may evolve, "[t]he 'message' conveyed . . . may change over time." Consider, for example, the message of the Statue of Liberty, which began as a monument to the solidarity and friendship between France and the United States and only decades later came to be seen "as a beacon welcoming immigrants to a land of freedom."

With sufficient time, religiously expressive monuments, symbols, and practices can become embedded features of a community's landscape and identity. The community may come to value them without necessarily embracing their religious roots * * *.

In the same way, consider the many cities and towns across the United States that bear religious names. Religion undoubtedly motivated those who named Bethlehem, Pennsylvania; Las Cruces, New Mexico; Providence, Rhode Island; Corpus Christi, Texas; Nephi, Utah, and the countless other places in our country with names that are rooted in religion. Yet few would argue that this history requires that these names be erased from the map. Or take a motto like Arizona's, "*Ditat Deus*" ("God enriches"), which was adopted in 1864, or a flag like Maryland's, which has included two crosses since 1904. Familiarity itself can become a reason for preservation.

Fourth, when time's passage imbues a religiously expressive monument, symbol, or practice with this kind of familiarity and historical significance, removing it may no longer appear neutral, especially to the local community for which it has taken on particular meaning. A government that roams the land, tearing down monuments with religious symbolism and scrubbing away any reference to the divine will strike many as aggressively hostile to religion. Militantly secular regimes have carried out such projects in the past, and for those with a knowledge of history, the image of monuments being taken down will be evocative, disturbing, and divisive.

These four considerations show that retaining established, religiously expressive monuments, symbols, and practices is quite different from erecting or adopting new ones. The passage of time gives rise to a strong presumption of constitutionality.

The role of the cross in World War I memorials is illustrative of each of the four preceding considerations * * *. The solemn image of endless rows of white crosses became inextricably linked with and symbolic of the ultimate price paid by 116,000 soldiers. And this relationship between the cross and the war undoubtedly influenced the design of the many war memorials that sprang up across the Nation.

This is not to say that the cross's association with the war was the sole or dominant motivation for the inclusion of the symbol in every World War I memorial that features it. But today, it is all but impossible to tell whether that was so. The passage of time means that testimony from those actually involved in the decisionmaking process is generally unavailable, and attempting to uncover their motivations invites rampant speculation. And no matter what the original purposes for the erection of a monument, a community may wish to preserve it for very different reasons, such as the historic preservation and traffic-safety concerns the Commission has pressed here.

* * *

Even the AHA recognizes that there are instances in which a war memorial in the form of a cross is unobjectionable. The AHA is not offended by the sight of the Argonne Cross or the Canadian Cross of Sacrifice, both Latin crosses commemorating World War I that rest on public grounds in Arlington National Cemetery. The difference, according to the AHA, is that their location in a cemetery gives them a closer association with individual gravestones and interred soldiers.

But a memorial's placement in a cemetery is not necessary to create such a connection. The parents and other relatives of many of the war dead lacked the means to travel to Europe to visit their graves, and the bodies of approximately 4,400 American soldiers were either never found or never identified. Thus, for many grieving relatives and friends, memorials took the place of gravestones * * *.

Similar reasoning applies to other memorials and monuments honoring important figures in our Nation's history. When faith was important to the person whose life is commemorated, it is natural to include a symbolic reference to faith in the design of the memorial. For example, many memorials for Dr. Martin Luther King, Jr., make reference to his faith. Take the Martin Luther King, Jr. Civil Rights Memorial Park in Seattle, which contains a sculpture in three segments representing "both the Christian Trinity and the union of the family." In Atlanta, the Ebenezer Baptist Church sits on the grounds of the Martin Luther King, Jr. National Historical Park. National Statuary Hall in the Capitol honors a variety of religious figures: for example, Mother Joseph Pariseau kneeling in prayer; Po'Pay, a Pueblo religious leader with symbols of the Pueblo religion; Brigham Young, president of the Church of Jesus Christ of Latter-day Saints; and Father Eusebio Kino with a crucifix around his neck and his hand raised in blessing. These monuments honor men and women who have played an important role in the history of our country, and where religious symbols are included in the monuments, their presence acknowledges the centrality of faith to those whose lives are commemorated.

Finally, as World War I monuments have endured through the years and become a familiar part of the physical and cultural landscape, requiring their removal would not be viewed by many as a neutral act * * *. [A] campaign to obliterate items with religious associations may evidence hostility to religion even if those religious associations are no longer in the forefront.

For example, few would say that the State of California is attempting to convey a religious message by retaining the names given to many of the State's cities by their original Spanish settlers—San Diego, Los Angeles, Santa Barbara, San Jose,

San Francisco, etc. But it would be something else entirely if the State undertook to change all those names. Much the same is true about monuments to soldiers who sacrificed their lives for this country more than a century ago.

While the *Lemon* Court ambitiously attempted to find a grand unified theory of the Establishment Clause, in later cases, we have taken a more modest approach that focuses on the particular issue at hand and looks to history for guidance. Our cases involving prayer before a legislative session are an example.

In *Marsh v. Chambers*, 463 U.S. 783 (1983), the Court upheld the Nebraska Legislature's practice of beginning each session with a prayer by an official chaplain, and in so holding, the Court conspicuously ignored *Lemon* and did not respond to Justice Brennan's argument in dissent that the legislature's practice could not satisfy the *Lemon* test. Instead, the Court found it highly persuasive that Congress for more than 200 years had opened its sessions with a prayer and that many state legislatures had followed suit. We took a similar approach more recently in *Town of Greece*, 572 U.S. at 577.

We reached these results even though it was clear, as stressed by the *Marsh* dissent, that prayer is by definition religious. As the Court put it in *Town of Greece*: "*Marsh* * * * teaches instead that the Establishment Clause must be interpreted 'by reference to historical practices and understandings' " and that the decision of the First Congress to "provid[e] for the appointment of chaplains only days after approving language for the First Amendment demonstrates that the Framers considered legislative prayer a benign acknowledgment of religion's role in society."

The prevalence of this philosophy at the time of the founding is reflected in other prominent actions taken by the First Congress. It requested—and President Washington proclaimed—a national day of prayer, see 1 J. Richardson, Messages and Papers of the Presidents, 1789–1897, p. 64 (1897) (President Washington's Thanksgiving Proclamation), and it reenacted the Northwest Territory Ordinance, which provided that "[r]eligion, morality, and knowledge, being necessary to good government and the happiness of mankind, schools and the means of education shall forever be encouraged," 1 Stat. 52, n. (a). President Washington echoed this sentiment in his Farewell Address, calling religion and morality "indispensable supports" to "political prosperity." Farewell Address (1796), in 35 The Writings of George Washington 229 (J. Fitzpatrick ed. 1940). See also P. Hamburger, Separation of Church and State 66 (2002). The First Congress looked to these "supports" when it chose to begin its sessions with a prayer. This practice was designed to solemnize congressional meetings, unifying those in attendance as they pursued a common goal of good governance.

To achieve that purpose, legislative prayer needed to be inclusive rather than divisive, and that required a determined effort even in a society that was much more religiously homogeneous than ours today * * *.

Over time, the members of the clergy invited to offer prayers at the opening of a session grew more and more diverse. For example, an 1856 study of Senate and House Chaplains since 1789 tallied 22 Methodists, 20 Presbyterians, 19 Episcopalians, 13 Baptists, 4 Congregationalists, 2 Roman Catholics, and 3 that were characterized as "miscellaneous." Four years later, Rabbi Morris Raphall became the first rabbi to open Congress. Since then, Congress has welcomed guest chaplains from a variety of faiths, including Islam, Hinduism, Buddhism, and Native American religions.

* * *

The practice begun by the First Congress stands out as an example of respect and tolerance for differing views, an honest endeavor to achieve inclusivity and nondiscrimination, and a recognition of the important role that religion plays in the lives of many Americans. Where categories of monuments, symbols, and practices with a longstanding history follow in that tradition, they are likewise constitutional. Applying these principles, we conclude that the Bladensburg Cross does not violate the Establishment Clause.

As we have explained, the Bladensburg Cross carries special significance in commemorating World War I. Due in large part to the image of the simple wooden crosses that originally marked the graves of American soldiers killed in the war, the cross became a symbol of their sacrifice, and the design of the Bladensburg Cross must be understood in light of that background. That the cross originated as a Christian symbol and retains that meaning in many contexts does not change the fact that the symbol took on an added secular meaning when used in World War I memorials.

Not only did the Bladensburg Cross begin with this meaning, but with the passage of time, it has acquired historical importance. It reminds the people of Bladensburg and surrounding areas of the deeds of their predecessors and of the sacrifices they made in a war fought in the name of democracy. As long as it is retained in its original place and form, it speaks as well of the community that erected the monument nearly a century ago and has maintained it ever since. The memorial represents what the relatives, friends, and neighbors of the fallen soldiers felt at the time and how they chose to express their sentiments. And the monument has acquired additional layers of historical meaning in subsequent years. The Cross now stands among memorials to veterans of later wars. It has become part of the community.

The monument would not serve that role if its design had deliberately disrespected area soldiers who perished in World War I. More than 3,500 Jewish soldiers gave their lives for the United States in that conflict, and some have wondered whether the names of any Jewish soldiers from the area were deliberately left off the list on the memorial or whether the names of any Jewish soldiers were included on the Cross against the wishes of their families. There is no evidence that either thing was done, and we do know that one of the local American Legion leaders responsible for the Cross's construction was a Jewish veteran.

The AHA's brief strains to connect the Bladensburg Cross and even the American Legion with anti-Semitism and the Ku Klux Klan, see Brief for Respondents 5–7, but the AHA's disparaging intimations have no evidentiary support. And when the events surrounding the erection of the Cross are viewed in historical context, a very different picture may perhaps be discerned. The monument was dedicated on July 12, 1925, during a period when the country was experiencing heightened racial and religious animosity. Membership in the Ku Klux Klan, which preached hatred of Blacks, Catholics, and Jews, was at its height. On August 8, 1925, just two weeks after the dedication of the Bladensburg Cross and less than 10 miles away, some 30,000 robed Klansmen marched down Pennsylvania Avenue in the

Nation's Capital. But the Bladensburg Cross memorial included the names of both Black and White soldiers who had given their lives in the war; and despite the fact that Catholics and Baptists at that time were not exactly in the habit of participating together in ecumenical services, the ceremony dedicating the Cross began with an invocation by a Catholic priest and ended with a benediction by a Baptist pastor. We can never know for certain what was in the minds of those responsible for the memorial, but in light of what we know about this ceremony, we can perhaps make out a picture of a community that, at least for the moment, was united by grief and patriotism and rose above the divisions of the day.

Finally, it is surely relevant that the monument commemorates the death of particular individuals. It is natural and appropriate for those seeking to honor the deceased to invoke the symbols that signify what death meant for those who are memorialized. In some circumstances, the exclusion of any such recognition would make a memorial incomplete. This well explains why Holocaust memorials invariably include Stars of David or other symbols of Judaism. It explains why a new memorial to Native American veterans in Washington, D. C., will portray a steel circle to represent " 'the hole in the sky where the creator lives.' " And this is why the memorial for soldiers from the Bladensburg community features the cross—the same symbol that marks the graves of so many of their comrades near the battlefields where they fell.

The cross is undoubtedly a Christian symbol, but that fact should not blind us to everything else that the Bladensburg Cross has come to represent. For some, that monument is a symbolic resting place for ancestors who never returned home. For others, it is a place for the community to gather and honor all veterans and their sacrifices for our Nation. For others still, it is a historical landmark. For many of these people, destroying or defacing the Cross that has stood undisturbed for nearly a century would not be neutral and would not further the ideals of respect and tolerance embodied in the First Amendment. For all these reasons, the Cross does not offend the Constitution.

We reverse the judgment of the Court of Appeals for the Fourth Circuit and remand the cases for further proceedings.

It is so ordered.

■ JUSTICE BREYER, with whom JUSTICE KAGAN joins, concurring.

I have long maintained that there is no single formula for resolving Establishment Clause challenges. The Court must instead consider each case in light of the basic purposes that the Religion Clauses were meant to serve: assuring religious liberty and tolerance for all, avoiding religiously based social conflict, and maintaining that separation of church and state that allows each to flourish in its "separate spher[e]."

I agree with the Court that allowing the State of Maryland to display and maintain the Peace Cross poses no threat to those ends. The Court's opinion eloquently explains why that is so: The Latin cross is uniquely associated with the fallen soldiers of World War I; the organizers of the Peace Cross acted with the undeniably secular motive of commemorating local soldiers; no evidence suggests that they sought to disparage or exclude any religious group; the secular values inscribed on the Cross and its place among other memorials strengthen its message of patriotism and commemoration; and, finally, the Cross has stood on the same land for 94 years, generating no controversy in the community until this lawsuit was filed. Nothing in the record suggests that the lack of public outcry "was due to a climate of intimidation." In light of all these circumstances, the Peace Cross cannot reasonably be understood as "a government effort to favor a particular religious sect" or to "promote religion over nonreligion." And, as the Court explains, ordering its removal or alteration at this late date would signal "a hostility toward religion that has no place in our Establishment Clause traditions."

The case would be different, in my view, if there were evidence that the organizers had "deliberately disrespected" members of minority faiths or if the Cross had been erected only recently, rather than in the aftermath of World War I. But those are not the circumstances presented to us here, and I see no reason to order *this* cross torn down simply because *other* crosses would raise constitutional concerns.

Nor do I understand the Court's opinion today to adopt a "history and tradition test" that would permit any newly constructed religious memorial on public land. The Court appropriately "looks to history for guidance," but it upholds the constitutionality of the Peace Cross only after considering its particular historical context and its long-held place in the community. A newer memorial, erected under different circumstances, would not necessarily be permissible under this approach.

* * *

■ JUSTICE KAVANAUGH, concurring.

I join the Court's eloquent and persuasive opinion in full. I write separately to emphasize two points.

Consistent with the Court's case law, the Court today applies a history and tradition test in examining and upholding the constitutionality of the Bladensburg Cross. See *Marsh v. Chambers*, 463 U.S. 783, 787–792, 795 (1983); *Van Orden v. Perry*, 545 U.S. 677, 686–690 (2005) (plurality opinion); *Town of Greece v. Galloway*, 572 U.S. 565, 575–578 (2014).

As this case again demonstrates, this Court no longer applies the old test articulated in *Lemon v. Kurtzman*, 403 U. S. 602 (1971) * * *. If *Lemon* guided this Court's understanding of the Establishment Clause, then many of the Court's Establishment Clause cases over the last 48 years would have been decided differently * * *.

* * *

* * * [E]ach category of Establishment Clause cases has its own principles based on history, tradition, and precedent. And the cases together lead to an overarching set of principles: If the challenged government practice is not coercive *and* if it (i) is rooted in history and tradition; or (ii) treats religious people, organizations, speech, or activity equally to comparable secular people, organizations, speech, or activity; or (iii) represents a permissible legislative accommodation or exemption from a generally applicable law, then there ordinarily is no Establishment Clause violation.

The practice of displaying religious memorials, particularly religious war memorials, on public land is not coercive and is rooted in history and tradition. The Bladensburg Cross does not violate the Establishment Clause.

* * * I fully understand the deeply religious nature of the cross. It would demean both believers and nonbelievers to say that the cross is not religious, or not all that

religious. A case like this is difficult because it represents a clash of genuine and important interests. Applying our precedents, we uphold the constitutionality of the cross. In doing so, it is appropriate to also restate this bedrock constitutional principle: All citizens are equally American, no matter what religion they are, or if they have no religion at all.

The conclusion that the cross does not violate the Establishment Clause does not necessarily mean that those who object to it have no other recourse. The Court's ruling *allows* the State to maintain the cross on public land. The Court's ruling does not *require* the State to maintain the cross on public land. The Maryland Legislature could enact new laws requiring removal of the cross or transfer of the land. The Maryland Governor or other state or local executive officers may have authority to do so under current Maryland law. And if not, the legislature could enact new laws to authorize such executive action. The Maryland Constitution, as interpreted by the Maryland Court of Appeals, may speak to this question. And if not, the people of Maryland can amend the State Constitution.

Those alternative avenues of relief illustrate a fundamental feature of our constitutional structure: This Court is not the *only* guardian of individual rights in America. This Court fiercely protects the individual rights secured by the U. S. Constitution. See, *e.g., West Virginia Bd. of Ed. v. Barnette*, 319 U.S. 624 (1943); *Wisconsin v. Yoder*, 406 U.S. 205 (1972). But the Constitution sets a floor for the protection of individual rights. The constitutional floor is sturdy and often high, but it is a floor. Other federal, state, and local government entities generally possess authority to safeguard individual rights above and beyond the rights secured by the U. S. Constitution. See generally J. Sutton, 51 Imperfect Solutions (2018); Brennan, State Constitutions and the Protection of Individual Rights, 90 Harv. L. Rev. 489 (1977).

■ JUSTICE KAGAN, concurring in part.

I fully agree with the Court's reasons for allowing the Bladensburg Peace Cross to remain as it is, and so join Parts I, II-B, II-C, III, and IV of its opinion, as well as JUSTICE BREYER's concurrence. Although I agree that rigid application of the *Lemon* test does not solve every Establishment Clause problem, I think that test's focus on purposes and effects is crucial in evaluating government action in this sphere—as this very suit shows. I therefore do not join Part II-A. I do not join Part II-D out of perhaps an excess of caution. Although I too "look[ ] to history for guidance," I prefer at least for now to do so case-by-case, rather than to sign on to any broader statements about history's role in Establishment Clause analysis. But I find much to admire in this section of the opinion—particularly, its emphasis on whether longstanding monuments, symbols, and practices reflect "respect and tolerance for differing views, an honest endeavor to achieve inclusivity and nondiscrimination, and a recognition of the important role that religion plays in the lives of many Americans." Here, as elsewhere, the opinion shows sensitivity to and respect for this Nation's pluralism, and the values of neutrality and inclusion that the First Amendment demands.

■ JUSTICE THOMAS, concurring in the judgment.

The Establishment Clause states that "Congress shall make no law respecting an establishment of religion." U. S. Const., Amdt. 1. The text and history of this Clause suggest that it should not be incorporated against the States. Even if the

Clause expresses an individual right enforceable against the States, it is limited by its text to "law[s]" enacted by a legislature, so it is unclear whether the Bladensburg Cross would implicate any incorporated right. And even if it did, this religious display does not involve the type of actual legal coercion that was a hallmark of historical establishments of religion. Therefore, the Cross is clearly constitutional.

As I have explained elsewhere, the Establishment Clause resists incorporation against the States. *Town of Greece v. Galloway*, 572 U.S. 565, 604–607 (2014) (opinion concurring in part and concurring in judgment). In *Everson v. Board of Ed. of Ewing*, 330 U.S. 1, 15 (1947), the Court "casually" incorporated the Clause with a declaration that because the Free Exercise Clause had been incorporated, " '[t]here is every reason to give the same application and broad interpretation to the "establishment of religion" clause.' " *Town of Greece*, 572 U.S. at 607, n. 1 (opinion of THOMAS, J.). The Court apparently did not consider that an incorporated Establishment Clause would prohibit exactly what the text of the Clause seeks to protect: state establishments of religion.

The Court's "inattention" to the significant question of incorporation "might be explained, although not excused, by the rise of popular conceptions about 'separation of church and state' as an 'American' constitutional right." *Id.*, at 608, n. 1. But an ahistorical generalization is no substitute for careful constitutional analysis. We should consider whether any longstanding right of citizenship restrains the States in the establishment context. See generally *McDonald v. Chicago*, 561 U.S. 742, 805–858, and n. 20 (2010) (THOMAS, J., concurring in part and concurring in judgment).

Further confounding the incorporation question is the fact that the First Amendment by its terms applies only to "law[s]" enacted by "Congress." Obviously, a memorial is not a law. And respondents have not identified any specific law they challenge as unconstitutional, either on its face or as applied. Thus, respondents could prevail on their establishment claim only if the prohibition embodied in the Establishment Clause was understood to be an individual right of citizenship that applied to more than just "law[s]" "ma[de]" by "Congress."

Even if the Clause applied to state and local governments in some fashion, "[t]he mere presence of the monument along [respondents'] path involves no coercion and thus does not violate the Establishment Clause." *Van Orden*, 545 U.S. at 694 (opinion of THOMAS, J.) * * *. In an action claiming an unconstitutional establishment of religion, the plaintiff must demonstrate that he was actually coerced by government conduct that shares the characteristics of an establishment as understood at the founding.

Here, respondents briefly suggest that the government's spending their tax dollars on maintaining the Bladensburg Cross represents coercion, but they have not demonstrated that maintaining a religious display on public property shares any of the historical characteristics of an establishment of religion. The local commission has not attempted to control religious doctrine or personnel, compel religious observance, single out a particular religious denomination for exclusive state subsidization, or punish dissenting worship. Instead, the commission has done something that the founding generation, as well as the generation that ratified the Fourteenth Amendment, would have found commonplace: displaying a religious symbol on government property. Lacking any characteristics of "the coercive state establishments that existed at the founding," the Bladensburg Cross is constitutional.

The Bladensburg Cross is constitutional even though the cross has religious significance as a central symbol of Christianity. Respondents' primary contention is that this characteristic of the Cross makes it "sectarian"—a word used in respondents' brief more than 40 times. Putting aside the fact that Christianity is not a "sect," religious displays or speech need not be limited to that which a "judge considers to be nonsectarian." As the Court has explained, "[a]n insistence on nonsectarian" religious speech is inconsistent with our Nation's history and traditions. *Id.*, at 578–580. Moreover, requiring that religious expressions be nonsectarian would force the courts "to act as supervisors and censors of religious speech." * * *

As to the long-discredited test set forth in *Lemon v. Kurtzman*, 403 U.S. 602, 612–613 (1971), and reiterated in *County of Allegheny v. American Civil Liberties Union, Greater Pittsburgh Chapter*, 492 U.S. 573, 592–594 (1989), the plurality rightly rejects its relevance to claims, like this one, involving "religious references or imagery in public monuments, symbols, mottos, displays, and ceremonies." I agree with that aspect of its opinion. I would take the logical next step and overrule the *Lemon* test in all contexts. First, that test has no basis in the original meaning of the Constitution. Second, "since its inception," it has "been manipulated to fit whatever result the Court aimed to achieve." Third, it continues to cause enormous confusion in the States and the lower courts. In recent decades, the Court has tellingly refused to apply *Lemon* in the very cases where it purports to be most useful. The obvious explanation is that *Lemon* does not provide a sound basis for judging Establishment Clause claims. However, the court below "s[aw] fit to apply *Lemon*." 874 F.3d 195, 205 (C.A.4 2017). It is our job to say what the law is, and because the *Lemon* test is not good law, we ought to say so.

* * *

Regrettably, I cannot join the Court's opinion because it does not adequately clarify the appropriate standard for Establishment Clause cases. Therefore, I concur only in the judgment.

■ JUSTICE GORSUCH, with whom JUSTICE THOMAS joins, concurring in the judgment.

The American Humanist Association wants a federal court to order the destruction of a 94-year-old war memorial because its members are offended. Today, the Court explains that the plaintiffs are not entitled to demand the destruction of longstanding monuments, and I find much of its opinion compelling. In my judgment, however, it follows from the Court's analysis that suits like this one should be dismissed for lack of standing. Accordingly, while I concur in the judgment to reverse and remand the court of appeals' decision, I would do so with additional instructions to dismiss the case.

The Association claims that its members "regularly" come into "unwelcome direct contact" with a World War I memorial cross in Bladensburg, Maryland "while driving in the area." 874 F.3d 195, 203 (C.A.4 2017). And this, the Association suggests, is enough to allow it to insist on a federal judicial decree ordering the memorial's removal. Maybe, the Association concedes, others who are less offended lack standing to sue. Maybe others still who are equally affected but who come into contact with the memorial too infrequently lack standing as well. See Tr. of Oral Arg. 48–49. But, the Association assures us, its members are offended enough—and with sufficient frequency—that they may sue.

This "offended observer" theory of standing has no basis in law. Federal courts may decide only those cases and controversies that the Constitution and Congress have authorized them to hear. And to establish standing to sue consistent with the Constitution, a plaintiff must show: (1) injury-in-fact, (2) causation, and (3) redressability. The injury-in-fact test requires a plaintiff to prove "an invasion of a legally protected interest which is (a) concrete and particularized . . . and (b) actual or imminent, not conjectural or hypothetical." *Lujan v. Defenders of Wildlife*, 504 U.S. 555, 560 (1992).

Unsurprisingly, this Court has already rejected the notion that offense alone qualifies as a "concrete and particularized" injury sufficient to confer standing * * *.

* * *

Offended observer standing cannot be squared with this Court's longstanding teachings about the limits of Article III. Not even today's dissent seriously attempts to defend it. So at this point you might wonder: How *did* the lower courts in this case indulge the plaintiffs' "offended observer" theory of standing? And why have other lower courts done similarly in other cases?

The truth is, the fault lies here. Lower courts invented offended observer standing for Establishment Clause cases in the 1970s in response to this Court's decision in *Lemon v. Kurtzman*, 403 U.S. 602 (1971). *Lemon* held that whether governmental action violates the Establishment Clause depends on its (1) purpose, (2) effect, and (3) potential to " 'excessive[ly] . . . entangl[e]' " church and state, *id.*, at 613, a standard this Court came to understand as prohibiting the government from doing anything that a " 'reasonable observer' " might perceive as "endorsing" religion. And lower courts reasoned that, if the Establishment Clause forbids anything a reasonable observer would view as an endorsement of religion, then such an observer must be able to sue. *Moore v. Bryant*, 853 F.3d 245, 250 (C.A.5 2017). Here alone, lower courts concluded, though never with this Court's approval, an observer's offense must "suffice to make an Establishment Clause claim justiciable." *Suhre v. Haywood Cty.*, 131 F.3d 1083, 1086 (C.A.4 1997).

As today's plurality rightly indicates in Part II-A, however, *Lemon* was a misadventure * * *.

* * *

With *Lemon* now shelved, little excuse will remain for the anomaly of offended observer standing, and the gaping hole it tore in standing doctrine in the courts of appeals should now begin to close * * *.

* * *

In a large and diverse country, offense can be easily found. Really, most every governmental action probably offends *somebody*. No doubt, too, that offense can be sincere, sometimes well taken, even wise. But recourse for disagreement and offense does not lie in federal litigation. Instead, in a society that holds among its most cherished ambitions mutual respect, tolerance, self-rule, and democratic responsibility, an "offended viewer" may "avert his eyes," *Erznoznik v. Jacksonville*, 422 U.S. 205, 212 (1975), or pursue a political solution. Today's decision represents a welcome step toward restoring this Court's recognition of these truths, and I respectfully concur in the judgment.

■ JUSTICE GINSBURG, with whom JUSTICE SOTOMAYOR joins, dissenting.

An immense Latin cross stands on a traffic island at the center of a busy three-way intersection in Bladensburg, Maryland. "[M]onumental, clear, and bold" by day, the cross looms even larger illuminated against the night-time sky. Known as the Peace Cross, the monument was erected by private citizens in 1925 to honor local soldiers who lost their lives in World War I. "[T]he town's most prominent symbol" was rededicated in 1985 and is now said to honor "the sacrifices made [in] all wars" by "all veterans." Both the Peace Cross and the traffic island are owned and maintained by the Maryland-National Capital Park and Planning Commission (Commission), an agency of the State of Maryland.

Decades ago, this Court recognized that the Establishment Clause of the First Amendment to the Constitution demands governmental neutrality among religious faiths, and between religion and nonreligion. See *Everson v. Board of Ed. of Ewing*, 330 U.S. 1, 15 (1947). Numerous times since, the Court has reaffirmed the Constitution's commitment to neutrality. Today the Court erodes that neutrality commitment, diminishing precedent designed to preserve individual liberty and civic harmony in favor of a "presumption of constitutionality for longstanding monuments, symbols, and practices."

The Latin cross is the foremost symbol of the Christian faith, embodying the "central theological claim of Christianity: that the son of God died on the cross, that he rose from the dead, and that his death and resurrection offer the possibility of eternal life." Brief for Baptist Joint Committee for Religious Liberty et al. as *Amici Curiae* 7. Precisely because the cross symbolizes these sectarian beliefs, it is a common marker for the graves of Christian soldiers. For the same reason, using the cross as a war memorial does not transform it into a secular symbol, as the Courts of Appeals have uniformly recognized. Just as a Star of David is not suitable to honor Christians who died serving their country, so a cross is not suitable to honor those of other faiths who died defending their nation. Soldiers of all faiths "are united by their love of country, but they are not united by the cross." Brief for Jewish War Veterans of the United States of America, Inc., as *Amicus Curiae* 3.

By maintaining the Peace Cross on a public highway, the Commission elevates Christianity over other faiths, and religion over nonreligion * * *.

* * * [T]he fledgling Republic ratified the Establishment Clause, in the words of Thomas Jefferson, to "buil[d] a wall of separation between church and state." Draft Reply to the Danbury Baptist Association, in 36 Papers of Thomas Jefferson 254, 255 (B. Oberg ed. 2009).

* * *

The Establishment Clause essentially instructs: "[T]he government may not favor one religion over another, or religion over irreligion." * * *

In cases challenging the government's display of a religious symbol, the Court has tested fidelity to the principle of neutrality by asking whether the display has the "effect of 'endorsing' religion." *County of Allegheny*, 492 U.S. at 592. The display fails this requirement if it objectively "convey[s] a message that religion or a particular religious belief is favored or preferred." *Id.*, at 593. To make that determination, a court must consider "the pertinent facts and circumstances surrounding the symbol and its placement."

As I see it, when a cross is displayed on public property, the government may be presumed to endorse its religious content. The venue is surely associated with the State; the symbol and its meaning are just as surely associated exclusively with Christianity * * *.

A presumption of endorsement, of course, may be overcome. A display does not run afoul of the neutrality principle if its "setting . . . plausibly indicates" that the government has not sought "either to adopt [a] religious message or to urge its acceptance by others." *Van Orden*, 545 U.S. at 737 (Souter, J., dissenting). The "typical museum setting," for example, "though not neutralizing the religious content of a religious painting, negates any message of endorsement of that content." *Lynch v. Donnelly*, 465 U.S. 668, 692 (1984) (O'Connor, J., concurring). Similarly, when a public school history teacher discusses the Protestant Reformation, the setting makes clear that the teacher's purpose is to educate, not to proselytize. The Peace Cross, however, is not of that genre.

"For nearly two millennia," the Latin cross has been the "defining symbol" of Christianity, R. Jensen, The Cross: History, Art, and Controversy ix (2017), evoking the foundational claims of that faith * * *. Christians wear crosses, not as an ecumenical symbol, but to proclaim their adherence to Christianity.

An exclusively Christian symbol, the Latin cross is not emblematic of any other faith. The principal symbol of Christianity around the world should not loom over public thoroughfares, suggesting official recognition of that religion's paramountcy.

The Commission urges in defense of its monument that the Latin cross "is not merely a reaffirmation of Christian beliefs"; rather, "when used in the context of a war memorial," the cross becomes "a universal symbol of the sacrifices of those who fought and died." Brief for Petitioner Maryland-National Capital Park and Planning Commission 34–35 (Brief for Planning Commission).

The Commission's "[a]ttempts to secularize what is unquestionably a sacred [symbol] defy credibility and disserve people of faith." *Van Orden*, 545 U.S. at 717 (Stevens, J., dissenting). The asserted commemorative meaning of the cross rests on—and is inseparable from—its Christian meaning * * *.

* * *

Every Court of Appeals to confront the question has held that "[m]aking a . . . Latin cross a war memorial does not make the cross secular," it "makes the war memorial sectarian."

The Peace Cross is no exception. That was evident from the start. At the dedication ceremony, the keynote speaker analogized the sacrifice of the honored soldiers to that of Jesus Christ, calling the Peace Cross "symbolic of Calvary," where Jesus was crucified. Local reporters variously described the monument as "[a] mammoth cross, a likeness of the Cross of Calvary, as described in the Bible," "a monster [C]alvary cross," and "a huge sacrifice cross." The character of the monument has not changed with the passage of time.

The Commission nonetheless urges that the Latin cross is a "well-established" secular symbol commemorating, in particular, "military valor and sacrifice [in] World War I." Brief for Planning Commission 21. Calling up images of United States cemeteries overseas showing row upon row of cross-shaped gravemarkers, the Commission overlooks this reality: The cross was never perceived as an appropriate headstone or memorial for Jewish soldiers and others who did not adhere to Christianity.

* * *

Far more crosses than Stars of David, as one would expect, line the grounds of American cemeteries overseas, for Jews composed only 3% of the United States population in 1917. Jews accounted for nearly 6% of U. S. forces in World War I (in numbers, 250,000), and 3,500 Jewish soldiers died in that war. Even in Flanders Field, with its " 'crosses, row on row,' " "Stars of David mark the graves of [eight American soldiers] of Jewish faith," American Battle Monuments Commission, Flanders Field American Cemetery and Memorial Visitor Booklet 11.14.

* * *

* * * In sum, "[t]here is simply 'no evidence . . . that the cross has been widely embraced by'—or even applied to—'non-Christians as a secular symbol of death' or of sacrifice in military service" in World War I or otherwise. *Trunk v. San Diego*, 629 F.3d 1099, 1116 (C.A.9 2011).

Holding the Commission's display of the Peace Cross unconstitutional would not, as the Commission fears, "inevitably require the destruction of other cross-shaped memorials throughout the country." Brief for Planning Commission 52. When a religious symbol appears in a public cemetery—on a headstone, or as the headstone itself, or perhaps integrated into a larger memorial—the setting counters the inference that the government seeks "either to adopt the religious message or to urge its acceptance by others." In a cemetery, the "privately selected religious symbols on individual graves are best understood as the private speech of each veteran." Laycock, Government-Sponsored Religious Displays: Transparent Rationalizations and Expedient Post-Modernism, 61 Case W. Res. L. Rev. 1211, 1242 (2011) * * *. They do not suggest governmental endorsement of those faith and beliefs.

Recognizing that a Latin cross does not belong on a public highway or building does not mean the monument must be "torn down." * * * In some instances, the violation may be cured by relocating the monument to private land or by transferring ownership of the land and monument to a private party.

In 1790, President Washington visited Newport, Rhode Island, "a longtime bastion of religious liberty and the home of one of the first communities of American Jews." *Town of Greece v. Galloway*, 572 U.S. 565, 636 (2014) (KAGAN, J., dissenting). In a letter thanking the congregation for its warm welcome, Washington praised "[t]he citizens of the United States of America" for "giv[ing] to mankind . . . a policy worthy of imitation": "All possess alike liberty of conscience and immunities of citizenship." Letter to Newport Hebrew Congregation (Aug. 18, 1790), in 6 Papers of George Washington 284, 285 (D. Twohig ed. 1996). As Washington and his contemporaries were aware, "some of them from bitter personal experience," *Engel*, 370 U.S. at 429, religion is "too personal, too sacred, too holy, to permit its 'unhallowed perversion' by a civil magistrate," *id.*, at 432 * * *. "If the aim of the Establishment Clause is genuinely to uncouple government from church," the Clause does "not permit . . . a display of th[e] character" of Bladensburg's Peace Cross. *Capitol Square Review and Advisory Bd. v. Pinette*, 515 U.S. 753, 817 (1995) (GINSBURG, J., dissenting).

NOTES AND QUESTIONS

1. In his search for original meaning, Justice Thomas overlooked something very important when he said that the Establishment Clause of the First Amendment does not apply to the States because the States retained a right to have established churches after 1791. By 1868, when the Fourteenth Amendment was ratified, twenty-seven States out of thirty-seven, a two-thirds majority, had no-establishment-of-religion clauses that had been added to their state bills of rights. If one asks what privilege or immunity of state citizenship state citizens have in this area, the answer would have been that a consensus of the States in 1868 had adopted no-establishment-of-religion clauses in 1868. That is not quite the three-quarters majority of States needed for a constitutional amendment. Is 27/37 enough to make freedom from establishment of religion a privilege or immunity of citizens as of 1868 (even if it might not have been in 1791)?

[Assignment 77]

B. FREE EXPRESSION AND THE STATES

We turn now to two key Fourteenth Amendment freedom of speech and of the press cases, both of which are quite libertarian—surely more libertarian than would have been comparable decisions in 1791. Do they go too far, just right, or not far enough?

1. NEW YORK TIMES V. SULLIVAN

376 U.S. 254 (1964)

■ MR. JUSTICE BRENNAN delivered the opinion of the Court.

We are required in this case to determine for the first time the extent to which the constitutional protections for speech and press limit a State's power to award damages in a libel action brought by a public official against critics of his official conduct.

Respondent L. B. Sullivan is one of the three elected Commissioners of the City of Montgomery, Alabama. He testified that he was "Commissioner of Public Affairs, and the duties are supervision of the Police Department, Fire Department, Department of Cemetery and Department of Scales." He brought this civil libel action against the four individual petitioners, who are Negroes and Alabama clergymen, and against petitioner the New York Times Company, a New York corporation which publishes the New York Times, a daily newspaper. A jury in the Circuit Court of Montgomery County awarded him damages of $500,000, the full amount claimed, against all the petitioners, and the Supreme Court of Alabama affirmed. 273 Ala. 656, 144 So.2d 25.

Respondent's complaint alleged that he had been libeled by statements in a full-page advertisement that was carried in the New York Times on March 29, 1960. Entitled "Heed Their Rising Voices," the advertisement began by stating that "As the whole world knows by now, thousands of Southern Negro students are engaged in widespread non-violent demonstrations in positive affirmation of the right to live in human dignity as guaranteed by the U.S. Constitution and the Bill of Rights." It went on to charge that "in their efforts to uphold these guarantees, they are being met by an unprecedented wave of terror by those who would deny and negate that document which the whole world looks upon as setting the pattern for modern freedom. . . ." Succeeding paragraphs purported to illustrate the "wave of terror" by describing certain alleged events. The text concluded with an appeal for funds for three purposes: support of the student movement, "the struggle for the right-to-vote," and the legal defense of Dr. Martin Luther King, Jr., leader of the movement, against a perjury indictment then pending in Montgomery.

The text appeared over the names of 64 persons, many widely known for their activities in public affairs, religion, trade unions, and the performing arts. Below these names, and under a line reading "We in the south who are struggling daily for dignity and freedom warmly endorse this appeal," appeared the names of the four individual petitioners and of 16 other persons, all but two of whom were identified as clergymen in various Southern cities. The advertisement was signed at the bottom of the page by the "Committee to Defend Martin Luther King and the Struggle for Freedom in the South," and the officers of the Committee were listed.

Of the 10 paragraphs of text in the advertisement, the third and a portion of the sixth were the basis of respondent's claim of libel. They read as follows:

Third paragraph:

> "In Montgomery, Alabama, after students sang 'My Country, 'Tis of Thee' on the State Capitol steps, their leaders were expelled from school, and truckloads of police armed with shotguns and tear-gas ringed the Alabama State College Campus. When the entire student body protested to state authorities by refusing to reregister, their dining hall was padlocked in an attempt to starve them into submission."

Sixth paragraph:

> "Again and again the Southern violators have answered Dr. King's peaceful protests with intimidation and violence. They have bombed his home, almost killing his wife and child. They have assaulted his person. They have arrested him seven times—for 'speeding,' 'loitering' and similar 'offenses.' And now they have charged him with 'perjury'—a *felony* under which they could imprison him for *ten years*. . . ."

Although neither of these statements mentions respondent by name, he contended that the word "police" in the third paragraph referred to him as the Montgomery Commissioner who supervised the Police Department, so that he was being accused of "ringing" the campus with police. He further claimed that the paragraph would be read as imputing to the police, and hence to him, the padlocking of the dining hall in order to starve the students into submission. As to the sixth paragraph, he contended that since arrests are ordinarily made by the police, the statement "They have arrested [Dr. King] seven times" would be read as referring to him; he further contended that the "They" who did the arresting would be equated with the "They" who committed the other described acts and with the "Southern violators." Thus, he argued, the paragraph would be read as accusing the Montgomery police, and hence him, of answering Dr. King's protests with "intimidation and violence," bombing his home, assaulting his person, and charging him with perjury. Respondent and six other Montgomery residents testified that they read some or all of the statements as referring to him in his capacity as Commissioner.

It is uncontroverted that some of the statements contained in the two paragraphs were not accurate descriptions of events which occurred in Montgomery.

Although Negro students staged a demonstration on the State Capitol steps, they sang the National Anthem and not "My Country, 'Tis of Thee." Although nine students were expelled by the State Board of Education, this was not for leading the demonstration at the Capitol, but for demanding service at a lunch counter in the Montgomery County Courthouse on another day. Not the entire student body, but most of it, had protested the expulsion, not by refusing to register, but by boycotting classes on a single day; virtually all the students did register for the ensuing semester. The campus dining hall was not padlocked on any occasion, and the only students who may have been barred from eating there were the few who had neither signed a preregistration application nor requested temporary meal tickets. Although the police were deployed near the campus in large numbers on three occasions, they did not at any time "ring" the campus, and they were not called to the campus in connection with the demonstration on the State Capitol steps, as the third paragraph implied. Dr. King had not been arrested seven times, but only four; and although he claimed to have been assaulted some years earlier in connection with his arrest for loitering outside a courtroom, one of the officers who made the arrest denied that there was such an assault.

On the premise that the charges in the sixth paragraph could be read as referring to him, respondent was allowed to prove that he had not participated in the events described. Although Dr. King's home had in fact been bombed twice when his wife and child were there, both of these occasions antedated respondent's tenure as Commissioner, and the police were not only not implicated in the bombings, but had made every effort to apprehend those who were. Three of Dr. King's four arrests took place before respondent became Commissioner. Although Dr. King had in fact been indicted (he was subsequently acquitted) on two counts of perjury, each of which carried a possible five-year sentence, respondent had nothing to do with procuring the indictment.

Respondent made no effort to prove that he suffered actual pecuniary loss as a result of the alleged libel. One of his witnesses, a former employer, testified that if he had believed the statements, he doubted whether he "would want to be associated with anybody who would be a party to such things that are stated in that ad," and that he would not re-employ respondent if he believed "that he allowed the Police Department to do the things that the paper say he did." But neither this witness nor any of the others testified that he had actually believed the statements in their supposed reference to respondent.

The cost of the advertisement was approximately $4800, and it was published by the Times upon an order from a New York advertising agency acting for the signatory Committee * * *. Each of the individual petitioners testified that he had not authorized the use of his name, and that he had been unaware of its use until receipt of respondent's demand for a retraction. The manager of the Advertising Acceptability Department testified that he had approved the advertisement for publication because he knew nothing to cause him to believe that anything in it was false, and because it bore the endorsement of "a number of people who are well known and whose reputation" he "had no reason to question." Neither he nor anyone else at the Times made an effort to confirm the accuracy of the advertisement, either by checking it against recent Times news stories relating to some of the described events or by any other means.

* * *

The trial judge submitted the case to the jury under instructions that the statements in the advertisement were "libelous per se" and were not privileged, so that petitioners might be held liable if the jury found that they had published the advertisement and that the statements were made "of and concerning" respondent. The jury was instructed that, because the statements were libelous *per se,* "the law . . . implies legal injury from the bare fact of publication itself," "falsity and malice are presumed," "general damages need not be alleged or proved but are presumed," and "punitive damages may be awarded by the jury even though the amount of actual damages is neither found nor shown." An award of punitive damages—as distinguished from "general" damages, which are compensatory in nature—apparently requires proof of actual malice under Alabama law, and the judge charged that "mere negligence or carelessness is not evidence of actual malice or malice in fact, and does not justify an award of exemplary or punitive damages." He refused to charge, however, that the jury must be "convinced" of malice, in the sense of "actual intent" to harm or "gross negligence and recklessness," to make such an award, and he also refused to require that a verdict for respondent differentiate between compensatory and punitive damages. The judge rejected petitioners' contention that his rulings abridged the freedoms of speech and of the press that are guaranteed by the First and Fourteenth Amendments.

In affirming the judgment, the Supreme Court of Alabama sustained the trial judge's rulings and instructions in all respects. 273 Ala. 656, 144 So.2d 25 * * *.

Because of the importance of the constitutional issues involved, we granted the separate petitions for certiorari of the individual petitioners and of the Times. We reverse the judgment. We hold that the rule of law applied by the Alabama courts is constitutionally deficient for failure to provide the safeguards for freedom of speech and of the press that are required by the First and Fourteenth Amendments in a libel action brought by a public official against critics of his official conduct. We further hold that under the proper safeguards the evidence presented in this case is constitutionally insufficient to support the judgment for respondent.

* * * Although this is a civil lawsuit between private parties, the Alabama courts have applied a state rule of law which petitioners claim to impose invalid restrictions on their constitutional freedoms of speech and press. It matters not that that law has been applied in a civil action and that it is common law only, though supplemented by statute. The test is not the form in which state power has been applied but, whatever the form, whether such power has, in fact, been exercised.

* * *

The question before us is whether this [Alabama] rule of liability, as applied to an action brought by a public official against critics of his official conduct, abridges the freedom of speech and of the press that is guaranteed by the First and Fourteenth Amendments.

Respondent relies heavily, as did the Alabama courts, on statements of this Court to the effect that the Constitution does not protect libelous publications. Those statements do not foreclose our inquiry here. None of the cases sustained the use of libel laws to impose sanctions upon expression critical of the official conduct of public officials * * *. In deciding the question now, we are compelled by neither precedent nor policy to give any more weight to the epithet "libel" than we have to other "mere labels" of state law. Like insurrection, contempt, advocacy of unlawful acts, breach of the peace, obscenity, solicitation of legal business, and the various other formulae for the repression of expression that have been challenged in this Court, libel can claim no talismanic immunity from constitutional limitations. It must be measured by standards that satisfy the First Amendment.

The general proposition that freedom of expression upon public questions is secured by the First Amendment has long been settled by our decisions. The constitutional safeguard, we have said, "was fashioned to assure unfettered interchange of ideas for the bringing about of political and social changes desired by the people." *Roth v. United States,* 354 U.S. 476, 484 * * *.The First Amendment, said Judge Learned Hand, "presupposes that right conclusions are more likely to be gathered out of a multitude of tongues, than through any kind of authoritative selection. To many, this is, and always will be, folly, but we have staked upon it our all." *United States v. Associated Press,* 52 F.Supp. 362, 372 (D.C.S.D.N.Y.1943). Mr. Justice Brandeis, in his concurring opinion in *Whitney v. California,* 274 U.S. 357, 375–376, gave the principle its classic formulation:

> "Those who won our independence believed . . . that public discussion is a political duty; and that this should be a fundamental principle of the American government. They recognized the risks to which all human institutions are subject. But they knew that order cannot be secured merely through fear of punishment for its infraction; that it is hazardous to discourage thought, hope and imagination; that fear breeds repression; that repression breeds hate; that hate menaces stable government; that the path of safety lies in the opportunity to discuss freely supposed grievances and proposed remedies; and that the fitting remedy for evil counsels is good ones. Believing in the power of reason as applied through public discussion, they eschewed silence coerced by law—the argument of force in its worst form. Recognizing the occasional tyrannies of governing majorities, they amended the Constitution so that free speech and assembly should be guaranteed."

Thus we consider this case against the background of a profound national commitment to the principle that debate on public issues should be uninhibited, robust, and wide-open, and that it may well include vehement, caustic, and sometimes unpleasantly sharp attacks on government and public officials. The present advertisement, as an expression of grievance and protest on one of the major public issues of our time, would seem clearly to qualify for the constitutional protection. The question is whether it forfeits that protection by the falsity of some of its factual statements and by its alleged defamation of respondent.

Authoritative interpretations of the First Amendment guarantees have consistently refused to recognize an exception for any test of truth—whether administered by judges, juries, or administrative officials—and especially one that puts the burden of proving truth on the speaker. The constitutional protection does not turn upon "the truth, popularity, or social utility of the ideas and beliefs which are offered." *NAACP v. Button,* 371 U.S. 415, 445. As Madison said, "Some degree of abuse is inseparable from the proper use of every thing, and in no instance is this more true than in that of the press." 4 Elliot's Debates on the Federal Constitution (1876), p. 571 * * *. That erroneous statement is inevitable in free debate, and that it must be protected if the freedoms of expression are to have the "breathing space" that they "need . . . to survive," *NAACP v. Button,* 371 U.S. 415, 433, was also recognized by the Court of Appeals for the District of Columbia Circuit in *Sweeney v. Patterson,* 76 U.S. App. D.C. 23, 24, 128 F.2d 457, 458 (1942), cert. denied, 317 U.S. 678. Judge Edgerton spoke for a unanimous court which affirmed the dismissal of a Congressman's libel suit based upon a newspaper article charging him with anti-Semitism in opposing a judicial appointment. He said:

> "Cases which impose liability for erroneous reports of the political conduct of officials reflect the obsolete doctrine that the governed must not criticize their governors. . . . The interest of the public here outweighs the interest of appellant or any other individual. The protection of the public requires not merely discussion, but information. Political conduct and views which some respectable people approve, and others condemn, are constantly imputed to Congressmen. Errors of fact, particularly in regard to a man's mental states and processes, are inevitable. . . . Whatever is added to the field of libel is taken from the field of free debate."

Injury to official reputation affords no more warrant for repressing speech that would otherwise be free than does factual error. Where judicial officers are involved, this Court has held that concern for the dignity and reputation of the courts does not justify the punishment as criminal contempt of criticism of the judge or his decision. *Bridges v. California,* 314 U.S. 252. This is true even though the utterance contains "half-truths" and "misinformation." *Pennekamp v. Florida,* 328 U.S. 331, 342, 343, n. 5, 345. Such repression can be justified, if at all, only by a clear and present danger of the obstruction of justice. *See also Craig v. Harney,* 331 U.S. 367; *Wood v. Georgia,* 370 U.S. 375. If judges are to be treated as "men of fortitude, able to thrive in a hardy climate," *Craig v. Harney, supra,* 331 U.S. at 376, surely the same must be true of other government officials, such as elected city commissioners. Criticism of their official conduct does not lose its constitutional protection merely because it is effective criticism and hence diminishes their official reputations.

If neither factual error nor defamatory content suffices to remove the constitutional shield from criticism of official conduct, the combination of the two elements is no less inadequate. This is the lesson to be drawn from the great controversy over the Sedition Act of 1798, 1 Stat. 596, which first crystallized a national awareness of the central meaning of the First Amendment. That statute made it a crime, punishable by a $5,000 fine and five years in prison, "if any person shall write, print, utter or publish . . . any false, scandalous and malicious writing or writings against the government of the United States, or either house of the Congress . . . or the President . . . with intent to defame . . . or to bring them, or either of them, into contempt or disrepute; or to excite against them, or either or any of them, the hatred of the good people of the United States." The Act allowed the defendant the defense of truth, and provided that the jury were to be judges both of the law and the facts. Despite these qualifications, the Act was vigorously condemned as unconstitutional in an attack joined in by Jefferson and Madison. In the famous Virginia Resolutions of 1798, the General Assembly of Virginia resolved that it

> "doth particularly protest against the palpable and alarming infractions of the Constitution, in the two late cases of the 'Alien and Sedition Acts,' passed at the last session of Congress. . . . [The Sedition Act] exercises . . . a power not delegated by the Constitution, but, on the contrary, expressly and positively forbidden by one of the amendments thereto—a power which, more than any other, ought to produce universal alarm, because it is leveled

> against the right of freely examining public characters and measures, and of free communication among the people thereon, which has ever been justly deemed the only effectual guardian of every other right." 4 Elliot's Debates, *supra,* pp. 553–554.

Madison prepared the Report in support of the protest. His premise was that the Constitution created a form of government under which "The people, not the government, possess the absolute sovereignty." The structure of the government dispersed power in reflection of the people's distrust of concentrated power, and of power itself at all levels. This form of government was "altogether different" from the British form, under which the Crown was sovereign and the people were subjects. "Is it not natural and necessary, under such different circumstances," he asked, "that a different degree of freedom in the use of the press should be contemplated?" *Id.,* pp. 569–570. Earlier, in a debate in the House of Representatives, Madison had said: "If we advert to the nature of Republican Government, we shall find that the censorial power is in the people over the Government, and not in the Government over the people." 4 Annals of Congress, p. 934 (1794). Of the exercise of that power by the press, his Report said: "In every state, probably, in the Union, the press has exerted a freedom in canvassing the merits and measures of public men, of every description, which has not been confined to the strict limits of the common law. On this footing the freedom of the press has stood; on this foundation it yet stands. . . ." 4 Elliot's Debates, *supra,* p. 570. The right of free public discussion of the stewardship of public officials was thus, in Madison's view, a fundamental principle of the American form of government.

Although the Sedition Act was never tested in this Court, the attack upon its validity has carried the day in the court of history. Fines levied in its prosecution were repaid by Act of Congress on the ground that it was unconstitutional. See, e.g., Act of July 4, 1840, c. 45, 6 Stat. 802, accompanied by H.R. Rep. No. 86, 26th Cong., 1st Sess. (1840). Calhoun, reporting to the Senate on February 4, 1836, assumed that its invalidity was a matter "which no one now doubts." Report with Senate bill No. 122, 24th Cong., 1st Sess., p. 3. Jefferson, as President, pardoned those who had been convicted and sentenced under the Act and remitted their fines, stating: "I discharged every person under punishment or prosecution under the sedition law, because I considered, and now consider, that law to be a nullity, as absolute and as palpable as if Congress had ordered us to fall down and worship a golden image." Letter to Mrs. Adams, July 22, 1804, 4 Jefferson's Works (Washington ed.), pp. 555, 556 * * *. These views reflect a broad consensus that the Act, because of the restraint it imposed upon criticism of government and public officials, was inconsistent with the First Amendment.

There is no force in respondent's argument that the constitutional limitations implicit in the history of the Sedition Act apply only to Congress, and not to the States. It is true that the First Amendment was originally addressed only to action by the Federal Government, and that Jefferson, for one, while denying the power of Congress "to controul the freedom of the press," recognized such a power in the States. See the 1804 Letter to Abigail Adams quoted in *Dennis v. United States,* 341 U.S. 494, 522, n. 4 (concurring opinion). But this distinction was eliminated with the adoption of the Fourteenth Amendment and the application to the States of the First Amendment's restrictions. See, *e.g., Gitlow v. New York,* 268 U.S. 652, 666.

What a State may not constitutionally bring about by means of a criminal statute is likewise beyond the reach of its civil law of libel. The fear of damage awards under a rule such as that invoked by the Alabama courts here may be markedly more inhibiting than the fear of prosecution under a criminal statute. See *City of Chicago v. Tribune Co.,* 307 Ill. 595, 607, 139 N.E. 86, 90 (1923). Alabama, for example, has a criminal libel law * * *. Alabama Code, Tit. 14, § 350. Presumably a person charged with violation of this statute enjoys ordinary criminal-law safeguards such as the requirements of an indictment and of proof beyond a reasonable doubt. These safeguards are not available to the defendant in a civil action. The judgment awarded in this case—without the need for any proof of actual pecuniary loss—was one thousand times greater than the maximum fine provided by the Alabama criminal statute, and one hundred times greater than that provided by the Sedition Act. And since there is no double-jeopardy limitation applicable to civil lawsuits, this is not the only judgment that may be awarded against petitioners for the same publication. Whether or not a newspaper can survive a succession of such judgments, the pall of fear and timidity imposed upon those who would give voice to public criticism is an atmosphere in which the First Amendment freedoms cannot survive. Plainly the Alabama law of civil libel is a form of regulation that creates hazards to protected freedoms markedly greater than those that attend reliance upon the criminal law.

The state rule of law is not saved by its allowance of the defense of truth. A defense for erroneous statements honestly made is no less essential here than was the requirement of proof of guilty knowledge which, in *Smith v. California,* 361 U.S. 147, we held indispensable to a valid conviction of a bookseller for possessing obscene writings for sale. We said:

> "For, if the bookseller is criminally liable without knowledge of the contents, . . . he will tend to restrict the books he sells to those he has inspected; and thus the State will have imposed a restriction upon the distribution of constitutionally protected as well as obscene literature. . . . And the bookseller's burden would become the public's burden, for by restricting him the public's access to reading matter would be restricted. . . . [H]is timidity in the face of his absolute criminal liability, thus would tend to restrict the public's access to forms of the printed word which the State could not constitutionally suppress directly. The bookseller's self-censorship, compelled by the State, would be a censorship affecting the whole public, hardly less virulent for being privately administered. Through it, the distribution of all books, both obscene and not obscene, would be impeded." (361 U.S. 147, 153–154.)

A rule compelling the critic of official conduct to guarantee the truth of all his factual assertions—and to do so on pain of libel judgments virtually unlimited in amount—leads to a comparable "self-censorship." Allowance of the defense of truth, with the burden of proving it on the defendant, does not mean that only false speech will be deterred * * *. Under such a rule, would-be critics of official conduct may be deterred from voicing their criticism, even though it is believed to be true and even though it is in fact true, because of doubt whether it can be proved in court or fear of the expense of having to do so. They tend to make only statements which "steer far wider of the unlawful zone." *Speiser v. Randall, supra,* 357 U.S. at 526. The rule thus dampens the vigor and limits the variety of public debate. It is inconsistent with the First and Fourteenth Amendments.

The constitutional guarantees require, we think, a federal rule that prohibits a public official from recovering damages for a defamatory falsehood relating to his official conduct unless he proves that the statement was made with "actual malice"—that is, with knowledge that it was false or with reckless disregard of whether it was false or not * * *.

Such a privilege for criticism of official conduct is appropriately analogous to the protection accorded a public official when he is sued for libel by a private citizen. In *Barr v. Matteo,* 360 U.S. 564, 575, this Court held the utterance of a federal official to be absolutely privileged if made "within the outer perimeter" of his duties * * *. It would give public servants an unjustified preference over the public they serve, if critics of official conduct did not have a fair equivalent of the immunity granted to the officials themselves.

We conclude that such a privilege is required by the First and Fourteenth Amendments.

We hold today that the Constitution delimits a State's power to award damages for libel in actions brought by public officials against critics of their official conduct. Since this is such an action, the rule requiring proof of actual malice is applicable. While Alabama law apparently requires proof of actual malice for an award of punitive damages, where general damages are concerned malice is "presumed." Such a presumption is inconsistent with the federal rule. "The power to create presumptions is not a means of escape from constitutional restrictions," *Bailey v. Alabama,* 219 U.S. 219, 239 * * *. Since the trial judge did not instruct the jury to differentiate between general and punitive damages, it may be that the verdict was wholly an award of one or the other. But it is impossible to know, in view of the general verdict returned. Because of this uncertainty, the judgment must be reversed and the case remanded.

Since respondent may seek a new trial, we deem that considerations of effective judicial administration require us to review the evidence in the present record to determine whether it could constitutionally support a judgment for respondent * * *. We must "make an independent examination of the whole record," *Edwards v. South Carolina,* 372 U.S. 229, 235, so as to assure ourselves that the judgment does not constitute a forbidden intrusion on the field of free expression.

Applying these standards, we consider that the proof presented to show actual malice lacks the convincing clarity which the constitutional standard demands, and hence that it would not constitutionally sustain the judgment for respondent under the proper rule of law. The case of the individual petitioners requires little discussion. Even assuming that they could constitutionally be found to have authorized the use of their names on the advertisement, there was no evidence whatever that they were aware of any erroneous statements or were in any way reckless in that regard. The judgment against them is thus without constitutional support.

As to the Times, we similarly conclude that the facts do not support a finding of actual malice. The statement by the Times' Secretary that, apart from the padlocking allegation, he thought the advertisement was "substantially correct," affords no constitutional warrant for the Alabama Supreme Court's conclusion that it was a "cavalier ignoring of the falsity of the advertisement [from which] the jury could not have but been impressed with the bad faith of The Times, and its maliciousness inferable therefrom." The statement does not indicate malice at the time of the publication; even if the advertisement was not "substantially correct"—although respondent's own proofs tend to show that it was—that opinion was at least a reasonable one, and there was no evidence to impeach the witness' good faith in holding it * * *.

Finally, there is evidence that the Times published the advertisement without checking its accuracy against the news stories in the Times' own files. The mere presence of the stories in the files does not, of course, establish that the Times "knew" the advertisement was false, since the state of mind required for actual malice would have to be brought home to the persons in the Times' organization having responsibility for the publication of the advertisement. With respect to the failure of those persons to make the check, the record shows that they relied upon their knowledge of the good reputation of many of those whose names were listed as sponsors of the advertisement, and upon the letter from A. Philip Randolph, known to them as a responsible individual, certifying that the use of the names was authorized. There was testimony that the persons handling the advertisement saw nothing in it that would render it unacceptable under the Times' policy of rejecting advertisements containing "attacks of a personal character"; their failure to reject it on this ground was not unreasonable. We think the evidence against the Times supports, at most, a finding of negligence in failing to discover the misstatements, and is constitutionally insufficient to show the recklessness that is required for a finding of actual malice.

We also think the evidence was constitutionally defective in another respect: it was incapable of supporting the jury's finding that the allegedly libelous statements were made "of and concerning" respondent * * *. There was no reference to respondent in the advertisement, either by name or official position * * *. This reliance on the bare fact of respondent's official position was made explicit by the Supreme Court of Alabama. That court, in holding that the trial court "did not err in overruling the demurrer [of the Times] in the aspect that the libelous matter was not of and concerning the [plaintiff,]" based its ruling on the proposition that:

> "We think it common knowledge that the average person knows that municipal agents, such as police and firemen, and others, are under the control and direction of the city governing body, and more particularly under the direction and control of a single commissioner. In measuring the performance or deficiencies of such groups, praise or criticism is usually attached to the official in complete control of the body."

This proposition has disquieting implications for criticism of governmental conduct. For good reason, "no court of last resort in this country has ever held, or even suggested, that prosecutions for libel on government have any place in the American system of jurisprudence." The present proposition would sidestep this obstacle by transmuting criticism of government, however impersonal it may seem on its face, into personal criticism, and hence potential libel, of the officials of whom the government is composed. There is no legal alchemy by which a State may thus create the cause of action that would otherwise be denied for a publication which, as respondent himself said of the advertisement, "reflects not only on me but on the other Commissioners and the community." Raising as it does the possibility that a good faith critic of government will be penalized for his criticism, the proposition relied on by the Alabama courts strikes at the very center of the constitutionally protected area of free expression. We hold that such a proposition may not constitutionally be utilized to establish that an otherwise impersonal attack on governmental operations was a libel of an official responsible for those operations. Since it was relied on exclusively here, and there was no other evidence to connect the statements with respondent, the evidence was constitutionally insufficient to support a finding that the statements referred to respondent.

The judgment of the Supreme Court of Alabama is reversed, and the case is remanded to that court for further proceedings not inconsistent with this opinion.

Reversed and remanded.

■ MR. JUSTICE BLACK, with whom MR. JUSTICE DOUGLAS joins, concurring.

I concur in reversing this half-million-dollar judgment against the New York Times Company and the four individual defendants * * *. I base my vote to reverse on the belief that the First and Fourteenth Amendments not merely "delimit" a State's power to award damages to "public officials against critics of their official conduct" but completely prohibit a State from exercising such a power. The Court goes on to hold that a State can subject such critics to damages if "actual malice" can be proved against them. "Malice," even as defined by the Court, is an elusive, abstract concept, hard to prove and hard to disprove. The requirement that malice be proved provides at best an evanescent protection for the right critically to discuss public affairs and certainly does not measure up to the sturdy safeguard embodied in the First Amendment. Unlike the Court, therefore, I vote to reverse exclusively on the ground that the Times and the individual defendants had an absolute, unconditional constitutional right to publish in the Times advertisement their criticisms of the Montgomery agencies and officials. I do not base my vote to reverse on any failure to prove that these individual defendants signed the advertisement or that their criticism of the Police Department was aimed at the plaintiff Sullivan, who was then the Montgomery City Commissioner having supervision of the city's police; for present purposes I assume these things were proved. Nor is my reason for reversal the size of the half-million-dollar judgment, large as it is. If Alabama has constitutional power to use its civil libel law to impose damages on the press for criticizing the way public officials perform or fail to perform their duties, I know of no provision in the Federal Constitution which either expressly or impliedly bars the State from fixing the amount of damages.

The half-million-dollar verdict does give dramatic proof, however, that state libel laws threaten the very existence of an American press virile enough to publish unpopular views on public affairs and bold enough to criticize the conduct of public officials * * *. There is no reason to believe that there are not more such huge verdicts lurking just around the corner for the Times or any other newspaper or broadcaster which might dare to criticize public officials. In fact, briefs before us show that in Alabama there are now pending eleven libel suits by local and state officials against the Times seeking $5,600,000, and five such suits against the Columbia Broadcasting System seeking $1,700,000. Moreover, this technique for harassing and punishing a free press—now that it has been shown to be possible—is by no means limited to cases with racial overtones; it can be used in other fields where public feelings may make local as well as out-of-state newspapers easy prey for libel verdict seekers.

In my opinion, the Federal Constitution has dealt with this deadly danger to the press in the only way possible without leaving the free press open to destruction—by granting the press an absolute immunity for criticism of the way public officials do their public duty. Stopgap measures like those the Court adopts are in my judgment not enough. This record certainly does not indicate that any different verdict would have been rendered here whatever the Court had charged the jury about "malice," "truth," "good motives," "justifiable ends," or any other legal formulas which in theory would protect the press. Nor does the record indicate that any of these legalistic words would have caused the courts below to set aside or to reduce the half-million-dollar verdict in any amount.

I agree with the Court that the Fourteenth Amendment made the First applicable to the States. This means to me that since the adoption of the Fourteenth Amendment a State has no more power than the Federal Government to use a civil libel law or any other law to impose damages for merely discussing public affairs and criticizing public officials. The power of the United States to do that is, in my judgment, precisely nil. Such was the general view held when the First Amendment was adopted and ever since * * *.

* * *An unconditional right to say what one pleases about public affairs is what I consider to be the minimum guarantee of the First Amendment.

I regret that the Court has stopped short of this holding indispensable to preserve our free press from destruction.

■ MR. JUSTICE GOLDBERG, with whom MR. JUSTICE DOUGLAS joins (concurring in the result).

* * *

In my view, the First and Fourteenth Amendments to the Constitution afford to the citizen and to the press an absolute, unconditional privilege to criticize official conduct despite the harm which may flow from excesses and abuses * * *.

* * *

NOTES AND QUESTIONS

1. The rule of *New York Times v. Sullivan* applies not just to public officials but to any public figures. The strict "actual malice" standard set forth in *Sullivan* makes libel actions by public figures almost impossible to win—which was the point. And three justices thought it should be literally impossible for government officials to win. *Sullivan* has stood as one of the cornerstones of modern free speech jurisprudence for more than half a century. There is no reason to think it is in any danger, but it is intriguing to read Justice Clarence Thomas's recently issued criticism of *Sullivan*, which we reproduce below as a kind of dissent from the opinions you just read:

2. MCKEE V. WILLIAM H. COSBY, JR.

586 U. S. ___, 139 S.Ct. 675 (2019)

The petition for a writ of certiorari is denied.

■ JUSTICE THOMAS, concurring in the denial of certiorari.

In December 2014, petitioner Kathrine McKee publicly accused actor and comedian Bill Cosby of forcibly raping her some 40 years earlier. McKee contends that Cosby's attorney responded on his behalf by writing and leaking a defamatory letter. According to McKee, the letter deliberately distorts her personal background to "damage her reputation for truthfulness and honesty, and further to embarrass, harass, humiliate, intimidate, and shame" her. She alleges that excerpts of the letter were disseminated via the Internet and published by news outlets around the world.

McKee filed suit in federal court for defamation under state law, but her case was dismissed. Applying *New York Times Co. v. Sullivan*, 376 U. S. 254 (1964), and its progeny, the Court of Appeals concluded that, by disclosing her accusation to a reporter, McKee had " 'thrust' herself to the 'forefront' " of the public controversy over "sexual assault allegations implicating Cosby" and was therefore a "limited-purpose public figure." 874 F. 3d 54, 61–62 (CA1 2017) (citing *Gertz v. Robert Welch, Inc.*, 418 U. S. 323, 345 (1974)). Under this Court's First Amendment precedents, public figures are barred from recovering damages for defamation unless they can show that the statement at issue was made with " 'actual malice'—that is, with knowledge that it was false or with reckless disregard of whether it was false or not." Like many plaintiffs subject to this "almost impossible" standard, McKee was unable to make that showing.

McKee asks us to review her classification as a limited-purpose public figure. I agree with the Court's decision not to take up that factbound question. I write to explain why, in an appropriate case, we should reconsider the precedents that require courts to ask it in the first place.

New York Times and the Court's decisions extending it were policy-driven decisions masquerading as constitutional law. Instead of simply applying the First Amendment as it was understood by the people who ratified it, the Court fashioned its own " 'federal rule[s]' " by balancing the "competing values at stake in defamation suits." *Gertz, supra*, at 334, 348 (quoting *New York Times, supra*, at 279).

We should not continue to reflexively apply this policy-driven approach to the Constitution. Instead, we should carefully examine the original meaning of the First and Fourteenth Amendments. If the Constitution does not require public figures to satisfy an actual-malice standard in state-law defamation suits, then neither should we.

From the founding of the Nation until 1964, the law of defamation was "almost exclusively the business of state courts and legislatures." *Gertz, supra*, at 369–370 (White, J., dissenting). But beginning with *New York Times*, the Court "federalized major aspects of libel law by declaring unconstitutional in important respects the prevailing defamation law in all or most of the 50 States." *Gertz, supra*, at 370. These decisions made little effort to ground their holdings in the original meaning of the Constitution.

* * *

* * * The Court [in *Sullivan*] took it upon itself "to define the proper accommodation between" two competing interests—"the law of defamation and the freedoms of speech and press protected by the First Amendment." *Gertz*, 418 U. S., at 325 * * *. Although the Court held that its newly minted actual-malice rule was "required by the First and Fourteenth Amendments," it made no attempt to base that rule on the original under-standing of those provisions.

New York Times was "the first major step in what proved to be a seemingly irreversible process of constitutionalizing the entire law of libel and slander." *Dun & Bradstreet*, 472 U. S., at 766 (White, J., concurring in judgment). The Court promptly expanded the actual-malice rule to all defamed " 'public figures,' " *Curtis Publishing*

Co. v. Butts, 388 U. S. 130, 134 (1967), which it defined to include private persons who "thrust themselves to the forefront of particular public controversies in order to influence the resolution of the issues involved," *Gertz, supra*, at 345. The Court also extended the actual-malice rule to criminal libel prosecutions, *Garrison v. Louisiana*, 379 U. S. 64 (1964), and even restricted the situations in which private figures could recover for defamation against media defendants, *Gertz, supra*, at 347, 349; *Philadelphia Newspapers, Inc. v. Hepps*, 475 U. S. 767 (1986).

None of these decisions made a sustained effort to ground their holdings in the Constitution's original meaning. As the Court itself acknowledged, "the rule enunciated in the *New York Times* case" is "largely a judge-made rule of law," the "content" of which is "given meaning through the evolutionary process of common-law adjudication." *Bose Corp. v. Consumers Union of United States, Inc.,* 466 U. S. 485, 501–502 (1984). Only Justice White grappled with the historical record, and he concluded that "there are wholly insufficient grounds for scuttling the libel laws of the States in such wholesale fashion, to say nothing of deprecating the reputation interest of ordinary citizens and rendering them powerless to protect themselves." *Gertz, supra*, at 370 (dissenting opinion).

The constitutional libel rules adopted by this Court in New York Times and its progeny broke sharply from the common law of libel, and there are sound reasons to question whether the First and Fourteenth Amendments displaced this body of common law.

The common law of libel at the time the First and Fourteenth Amendments were ratified did not require public figures to satisfy any kind of heightened liability standard as a condition of recovering damages. Typically, a defamed individual needed only to prove "a false written publication that subjected him to hatred, contempt, or ridicule." *Dun & Bradstreet, supra*, at 765 (White, J., concurring in judgment) * * *.

* * *

Far from increasing a public figure's burden in a defamation action, the common law deemed libels against public figures to be, if anything, *more* serious and injurious than ordinary libels. See 3 Blackstone *124 ("Words also tending to scandalize a magistrate, or person in a public trust, are reputed more highly injurious than when spoken of a private man"); 4 id., at *150 (defining libels as "malicious defamations of any person, *and especially a magistrate*, made public by either printing, writing, signs, or pictures, in order to provoke him to wrath, or expose him to public hatred, contempt, and ridicule" (emphasis added)). Libel of a public official was deemed an offense " 'most dangerous to the people, and deserv[ing of] punishment, because the people may be deceived and reject the best citizens to their great injury, and it may be to the loss of their liberties.' " Newell 533 (quoting *Commonwealth v. Clap*, 4 Mass. 163, 169–170 (1808)); accord, *White v. Nicholls*, 3 How. 266, 290 (1845).

The common law did afford defendants a privilege to comment on public questions and matters of public interest. This privilege extended to the "public conduct of a public man," which was a "matter of public interest" that could "be discussed with the fullest freedom" and "made the subject of hostile criticism." Under this privilege, "criticism may reasonably be applied to a public man in a public capacity which might not be applied to a private individual." And the privilege extended to the man's character " 'so far as it may respect his fitness and qualifications for the office,' " which was in the interest of the people to know.

But the purposes underlying this privilege also defined its limits. Thus, the privilege applied only when the facts stated were true. And the privilege did not afford the publisher an opportunity to defame the officer's private character * * *.

These common-law protections for the "core private righ[t]" of a person's " 'uninterrupted enjoyment of . . . his reputation' " formed the backdrop against which the First and Fourteenth Amendments were ratified. Nelson, Adjudication in the Political Branches, 107 Colum. L. Rev. 559, 567 (2007) (quoting 1 Blackstone *129). Before our decision in *New York Times* * * *, [t]he Court consistently listed libel among the "well-defined and narrowly limited classes of speech, the prevention and punishment of which have never been thought to raise any Constitutional problem." *Chaplinsky v. New Hampshire*, 315 U. S. 568, 571–572 (1942); see, *e.g., Beauharnais, supra*, at 254–256, and nn. 4–5, 266 (libelous utterances are "not . . . within the area of constitutionally protected speech"); *Near v. Minnesota ex rel. Olson*, 283 U. S. 697, 715 (1931) ("[T]he common law rules that subject the libeler to responsibility for the public offense, as well as for the private injury, are not abolished by the protection extended in our constitutions").

New York Times marked a fundamental change in the relationship between the First Amendment and state libel law. Although the Court did not repudiate its earlier statements that libel is constitutionally unprotected, it nevertheless was unable to "accept the generality of this historic view." *Gertz*, 418 U.S., at 386, 94 S.Ct. 2997 (White, J., dissenting). The Court instead observed that it had never upheld the use of libel law "to impose sanctions upon expression critical of the official conduct of public officials." *New York Times*, 376 U.S., at 268, 84 S.Ct. 710. In the Court's view, it was "writing upon a clean slate," *id.*, at 299, 84 S.Ct. 710 (Goldberg, J., concurring in result), and thus free to work a "substantial abridgement" of the common law of libel based on its balancing of competing interests, *Gertz, supra*, at 343, 94 S.Ct. 2997 (majority opinion).

There are sound reasons to question whether either the First or Fourteenth Amendment, as originally understood, encompasses an actual-malice standard for public figures or otherwise displaces vast swaths of state defamation law.

The First Amendment provides that "Congress shall make no law . . . abridging the freedom of speech, or of the press." Justice White's dissenting opinion in *Gertz* provides a helpful starting point in interpreting these terms. Justice White had joined the majority opinion in *New York Times*. But after canvassing historical practice under similar state constitutions, treatises, scholarly commentary, the ratification debates, and our precedent, he concluded that"[s]cant, if any, evidence exists that the First Amendment was intended to abolish the common law of libel, at least to the extent of depriving ordinary citizens of meaningful redress against their defamers." *Gertz,* 418 U. S., at 381 * * *.

Historical practice further suggests that protections for free speech and a free press—whether embodied in state constitutions, the First Amendment, or the Fourteenth Amendment—did not abrogate the common law of libel. See generally Chase, Criticism of Public Officers and Candidates for Office, 23 Am. L. Rev. 346 (1889) (surveying American defamation decisions). Public officers and public figures continued to be able to bring civil libel suits for unprivileged statements without showing proof of actual malice as a condition for liability. The States continued to criminalize libel, including of public figures. As of 1952, "every American jurisdiction . . . punish[ed] libels directed at individuals." And "Congresses, during the period while [the Fourteenth] Amendment was being considered or was but freshly adopted, approved Constitutions of 'Reconstructed' States that expressly mentioned state libel laws, and also approved similar Constitutions for States erected out of the federal domain." Criticism of the public actions of public figures remained privileged, allowing latitude for public discourse and disagreement on matters of public concern.

As against this body of historical evidence, *New York Times* pointed only to opposition surrounding the Sedition Act of 1798, which prohibited "any false, scandalous and malicious writing" against "the government of the United States, or either house of the Congress . . ., or the President." § 2, 1 Stat. 596; see *New York Times*, 376 U. S., at 273–277. Most prominently, the opinion discusses a report written by James Madison in support of the Virginia Resolutions of 1798, which protested the Act. The opinion highlights Madison's view that the press in every State had " 'exerted a freedom in canvassing the merits and measures of public men, of every description, which has not been confined to the strict limits of the common law.' " It also emphasizes Madison's point that " '[s]ome degree of abuse is inseparable from the proper use of every thing; and in no instance is this more true than in that of the press.' " 376 U. S., at 271 (quoting 4 Elliot's Debates). After discussing other opposition to the Act, the Court concluded that "the attack upon its validity has carried the day in the court of history." 376 U. S., at 276.

The Court gleaned from this evidence a "broad consensus" that the First Amendment protects "criticism of government and public officials." *Id.*, at 276. And the Court further inferred that because the Act allowed truth to be offered as a defense and applied to defamatory statements, a libel law prohibiting only false defamation could still fail. First Amendment scrutiny. *Id.*, at 273–274. But constitutional opposition to the Sedition Act—a federal law directly criminalizing criticism of the Government—does not necessarily support a constitutional actual-malice rule in all civil libel actions brought by public figures. Madison did not contend that the Constitution abrogated the common law applicable to these private actions. Instead, he seemed to contemplate that "those who administer [the Federal Government]" retain "a remedy, for their injured reputations, under the same laws, and in the same tribunals, which protect their lives, their liberties, and their properties." 4 Elliot's Debates 573. Moreover, a central assumption of Madison's view was the historical absence of a national common law "pervading and operating through" each colony "as one society." *Id.*, at 561. Yet the Court elevated just such a rule to constitutional status in *New York Times*.

It is certainly true that defamation law did not remain static after the founding. For example, many States acted "by judicial decision, statute or constitution" during the early 19th century to allow truth or good motives to serve as a defense to a libel prosecution. *Beauharnais, supra*, at 254–255, and n. 4. Eventually, changing views led to the "virtual disappearance" of criminal libel prosecutions involving individuals. But these changes appear to have reflected changing policy judgments, not a sense that existing law violated the original meaning of the First or Fourteenth Amendment.

In short, there appears to be little historical evidence suggesting that the *New York Times* actual-malice rule flows from the original understanding of the First or Fourteenth Amendment.

Like Justice White, I assume that *New York Times* and our other constitutional decisions displacing state defamation law have been popular in some circles, "but this is not the road to salvation for a court of law." *Gertz*, 418 U. S., at 370 (dissenting opinion). We did not begin meddling in this area until 1964, nearly 175 years after the First Amendment was ratified. The States are perfectly capable of striking an acceptable balance between encouraging robust public discourse and providing a meaningful remedy for reputational harm. We should reconsider our jurisprudence in this area.

NOTES AND QUESTIONS

1. Justice Thomas is right that the Supreme Court has not grounded its freedom of expression caselaw in the original understanding of the Framers of either the First or the Fourteenth Amendments. This does not necessarily mean, however, that that cannot be done. Justice Thomas's opinion above makes much of the fact that the First and Fourteenth Amendments were not construed to limit libel and slander actions until 1964, 173 years after the ratification of the First Amendment. However, libel and slander actions arise only under state law, and one of the first Fourteenth Amendment freedom of expression case to strike down a state law was *West Virginia State Board of Education v. Barnette,* 319 U.S. 624 (1943). The First Amendment was not even incorporated to apply against the States until *Gitlow v. United States*, 268 U.S. 652 (1925). *New York Times v. Sullivan* was decided in 1964—a mere 21 years after *Barnette*. This is not a striking gap of time.

2. English common law in 1791 surely supported the right of public officials to bring libel actions. The American colonists, however, had a more robust understanding of freedom of the press than did Blackstone. *See supra* pages 1022–1026. This is why Thomas Jefferson and James Madison, when they argued that the Sedition Act of 1798 violated the First Amendment in the famous Virginia and Kentucky Resolutions, would have been outliers in England but not necessarily in the United States. Jefferson, as President, pardoned everyone convicted under the Sedition Act; stopped the one pending prosecution under the Sedition Act, which he inherited from President Adams; and persuaded Congress to appropriate funds to repay the Sedition Act fines, which had been wrongly assessed. All of this history, of course, would have been known to everyone in 1868.

3. We have edited out most of the voluminous citations in Justice Thomas's opinion, but relatively few of them relate directly to public understandings in 1868—merely a decade after publication of Mill's *On Liberty*. On Justice Thomas's premises, isn't that the most relevant time period?

4. Libel involves speech that generates actual harms—to reputations, which the law has long recognized as a legally protected interest. What other kinds of speech can generate harms? What kinds of harms justify restrictions on speech? This, too, is a topic generally dealt with in specialized courses, but at least one case bears mention here.

3. BRANDENBURG V. OHIO

395 U.S. 444 (1969)

■ PER CURIAM.

The appellant, a leader of a Ku Klux Klan group, was convicted under the Ohio Criminal Syndicalism statute for "advocat[ing] . . . the duty, necessity, or propriety of crime, sabotage, violence, or unlawful methods of terrorism as a means of accomplishing industrial or political reform" and for "voluntarily assembl[ing] with any society, group, or assemblage of persons formed to teach or advocate the doctrines of criminal syndicalism." Ohio Rev. Code Ann. § 2923.13. He was fined $1,000 and sentenced to one to 10 years' imprisonment. The appellant challenged the constitutionality of the criminal syndicalism statute under the First and Fourteenth Amendments to the United States Constitution, but the intermediate appellate court of Ohio affirmed his conviction without opinion. The Supreme Court of Ohio dismissed his appeal, *sua sponte,* "for the reason that no substantial constitutional question exists herein." It did not file an opinion or explain its conclusions. Appeal was taken to this Court, and we noted probable jurisdiction. We reverse.

The record shows that a man, identified at trial as the appellant, telephoned an announcer-reporter on the staff of a Cincinnati television station and invited him to come to a Ku Klux Klan "rally" to be held at a farm in Hamilton County. With the cooperation of the organizers, the reporter and a cameraman attended the meeting and filmed the events. Portions of the films were later broadcast on the local station and on a national network.

The prosecution's case rested on the films and on testimony identifying the appellant as the person who communicated with the reporter and who spoke at the rally. The State also introduced into evidence several articles appearing in the film, including a pistol, a rifle, a shotgun, ammunition, a Bible, and a red hood worn by the speaker in the films.

One film showed 12 hooded figures, some of whom carried firearms. They were gathered around a large wooden cross, which they burned. No one was present other than the participants and the newsmen who made the film. Most of the words uttered during the scene were incomprehensible when the film was projected, but scattered phrases could be understood that were derogatory of Negroes and, in one instance, of Jews. Another scene on the same film showed the appellant, in Klan regalia, making a speech. The speech, in full, was as follows:

> "This is an organizers' meeting. We have had quite a few members here today which are—we have hundreds, hundreds of members throughout the State of Ohio. I can quote from a newspaper clipping from the Columbus, Ohio Dispatch, five weeks ago Sunday morning. The Klan has more members in the State of Ohio than does any other organization. We're not a revengent organization, but if our President, our Congress, our Supreme Court, continues to suppress the white, Caucasian race, it's possible that there might have to be some revengeance taken.
>
> "We are marching on Congress July the Fourth, four hundred thousand strong. From there we are dividing into two groups, one group to march on St. Augustine, Florida, the other group to march into Mississippi. Thank you."

The second film showed six hooded figures one of whom, later identified as the appellant, repeated a speech very similar to that recorded on the first film. The reference to the possibility of "revengeance" was omitted, and one sentence was added: "Personally, I believe the n*****r should be returned to Africa, the Jew returned to Israel." Though some of the figures in the films carried weapons, the speaker did not.

The Ohio Criminal Syndicalism Statute was enacted in 1919. From 1917 to 1920, identical or quite similar laws were adopted by 20 States and two territories. In 1927, this Court sustained the constitutionality of California's Criminal Syndicalism Act, Cal.Penal Code §§ 11400–11402, the text of which is quite similar to that of the laws of Ohio. *Whitney v. California,* 274 U.S. 357 (1927). The Court upheld the statute on the ground that, without more, "advocating" violent means to effect political and economic change involves such danger to the security of the State that the State may outlaw it. But *Whitney* has been thoroughly discredited by later decisions. *See Dennis v. United States,* 341 U.S. 494, at 507 (1951). These later decisions have fashioned the principle that the constitutional guarantees of free speech and free press do not permit a State to forbid or proscribe advocacy of the use of force or of law violation except where such advocacy is directed to inciting or producing imminent lawless action and is likely to incite or produce such action. As we said in *Noto v. United States,* 367 U.S. 290, 297–298 (1961), "the mere abstract teaching . . . of the moral propriety or even moral necessity for a resort to force and violence, is not the same as preparing a group for violent action and steeling it to such action." A statute which fails to draw this distinction impermissibly intrudes upon the freedoms guaranteed by the First and Fourteenth Amendments. It sweeps within its condemnation speech which our Constitution has immunized from governmental control.

Measured by this test, Ohio's Criminal Syndicalism Act cannot be sustained. The Act punishes persons who "advocate or teach the duty, necessity, or propriety" of violence "as a means of accomplishing industrial or political reform"; or who publish or circulate or display any book or paper containing such advocacy; or who "justify" the commission of violent acts "with intent to exemplify, spread or advocate the propriety of the doctrines of criminal syndicalism"; or who "voluntarily assemble" with a group formed "to teach or advocate the doctrines of criminal syndicalism." Neither the indictment nor the trial judge's instructions to the jury in any way refined the statute's bald definition of the crime in terms of mere advocacy not distinguished from incitement to imminent lawless action.

Accordingly, we are here confronted with a statute which, by its own words and as applied, purports to punish mere advocacy and to forbid, on pain of criminal punishment, assembly with others merely to advocate the described type of action. Such a statute falls within the condemnation of the First and Fourteenth Amendments. The contrary teaching of *Whitney v. California, supra,* cannot be supported, and that decision is therefore overruled.

Reversed

■ MR. JUSTICE BLACK, concurring.

I agree with the views expressed by Mr. JUSTICE DOUGLAS in his concurring opinion in this case that the "clear and present danger" doctrine should have no place in the interpretation of the First Amendment. I join the Court's opinion, which, as I understand it, simply cites *Dennis v. United States,* 341 U.S. 494 (1951), but does not indicate any agreement on the Court's part with the "clear and present danger" doctrine on which *Dennis* purported to rely.

■ MR. JUSTICE DOUGLAS, concurring.

While I join the opinion of the Court, I desire to enter a *caveat.*

The "clear and present danger" test was adumbrated by Mr. Justice Holmes in a case arising during World War I—a war "declared" by the Congress, not by the Chief Executive. The case was *Schenck v. United States,* 249 U.S. 47, 52, where the defendant was charged with attempts to cause insubordination in the military and obstruction of enlistment. The pamphlets that were distributed urged resistance to the draft, denounced conscription, and impugned the motives of those backing the war effort. The First Amendment was tendered as a defense. Mr. Justice Holmes, in rejecting that defense, said:

> "The question in every case is whether the words used are used in such circumstances and are of such a nature as to create a clear and present danger that they will bring about the substantive evils that Congress has a right to prevent. It is a question of proximity and degree."

Frohwerk v. United States, 249 U.S. 204, also authored by Mr. Justice Holmes, involved prosecution and punishment for publication of articles very critical of the war effort in World War I. *Schenck* was referred to as a conviction for obstructing security "by words of persuasion." *Id.* at 206. And the conviction in *Frohwerk* was sustained because "the circulation of the paper was in quarters where a little breath would be enough to kindle a flame." *Id.* at 209.

Debs v. United States, 249 U.S. 211, was the third of the trilogy of the 1918 Term. Debs was convicted of speaking in opposition to the war where his "opposition was so expressed that its natural and intended effect would be to obstruct recruiting." *Id.* at 215.

> "If that was intended, and if, in all the circumstances, that would be its probable effect, it would not be protected by reason of its being part of a general program and expressions of a general and conscientious belief." *Ibid.*

In the 1919 Term, the Court applied the *Schenck* doctrine to affirm the convictions of other dissidents in World War I. *Abrams v. United States,* 250 U.S. 616, was one instance. Mr. Justice Holmes, with whom Mr. Justice Brandeis concurred, dissented. While adhering to *Schenck,* he did not think that on the facts a case for overriding the First Amendment had been made out * * *.

Another instance was *Schaefer v. United States,* 251 U.S. 466, in which Mr. Justice Brandeis, joined by Mr. Justice Holmes, dissented. A third was *Pierce v. United States,* 252 U.S. 239, in which, again, Mr. Justice Brandeis, joined by Mr. Justice Holmes, dissented.

Those, then, were the World War I cases that put the gloss of "clear and present danger" on the First Amendment. Whether the war power—the greatest leveler of them all—is adequate to sustain that doctrine is debatable. The dissents in *Abrams, Schaefer,* and *Pierce* show how easily "clear and present danger" is manipulated to crush what Brandeis called "[t]he fundamental right of free men to strive for better conditions through new legislation and new institutions" by argument and discourse

(*Pierce v. United States, supra,* at 273) even in time of war. Though I doubt if the "clear and present danger" test is congenial to the First Amendment in time of a declared war, I am certain it is not reconcilable with the First Amendment in days of peace.

* * *

When one reads the opinions closely and sees when and how the "clear and present danger" test has been applied, great misgivings are aroused. First, the threats were often loud but always puny and made serious only by judges so wedded to the *status quo* that critical analysis made them nervous. Second, the test was so twisted and perverted in *Dennis* as to make the trial of those teachers of Marxism an all-out political trial which was part and parcel of the cold war that has eroded substantial parts of the First Amendment.

Action is often a method of expression, and within the protection of the First Amendment.

Suppose one tears up his own copy of the Constitution in eloquent protest to a decision of this Court. May he be indicted?

Suppose one rips his own Bible to shreds to celebrate his departure from one "faith" and his embrace of atheism. May he be indicted?

Last Term, the Court held in *United States v. O'Brien,* 391 U.S. 367, 382, that a registrant under Selective Service who burned his draft card in protest of the war in Vietnam could be prosecuted. The First Amendment was tendered as a defense and rejected, the Court saying:

> "The issuance of certificates indicating the registration and eligibility classification of individuals is a legitimate and substantial administrative aid in the functioning of this system. And legislation to insure the continuing availability of issued certificates serves a legitimate and substantial purpose in the system's administration." 391 U.S. at 377–378.

But O'Brien was not prosecuted for not having his draft card available when asked for by a federal agent. He was indicted, tried, and convicted for burning the card. And this Court's affirmance of that conviction was not, with all respect, consistent with the First Amendment.

The act of praying often involves body posture and movement as well as utterances. It is nonetheless protected by the Free Exercise Clause. Picketing, as we have said on numerous occasions, is "free speech plus." That means that it can be regulated when it comes to the "plus" or "action" side of the protest. It can be regulated as to the number of pickets and the place and hours, because traffic and other community problems would otherwise suffer.

But none of these considerations is implicated in the symbolic protest of the Vietnam war in the burning of a draft card.

One's beliefs have long been thought to be sanctuaries which government could not invade. *Barenblatt* is one example of the ease with which that sanctuary can be violated. The lines drawn by the Court between the criminal act of being an "active" Communist and the innocent act of being a nominal or inactive Communist mark the difference only between deep and abiding belief and casual or uncertain belief. But I think that all matters of belief are beyond the reach of subpoenas or the probings of investigators. That is why the invasions of privacy made by investigating committees were notoriously unconstitutional. That is the deep-seated fault in the infamous loyalty security hearings which, since 1947 when President Truman launched them, have processed 20,000,000 men and women. Those hearings were primarily concerned with one's thoughts, ideas, beliefs, and convictions. They were the most blatant violations of the First Amendment we have ever known.

The line between what is permissible and not subject to control and what may be made impermissible and subject to regulation is the line between ideas and overt acts.

The example usually given by those who would punish speech is the case of one who falsely shouts fire in a crowded theatre.

This is, however, a classic case where speech is brigaded with action. They are indeed inseparable and a prosecution can be launched for the overt acts actually caused. Apart from rare instances of that kind, speech is, I think, immune from prosecution * * *. The quality of advocacy turns on the depth of the conviction; and government has no power to invade that sanctuary of belief and conscience.

NOTES AND QUESTIONS

1. Is it possible that the Supreme Court is more "activist" in enforcing the Bill of Rights against the States than against Congress because the Court is less afraid of the States than it is of Congress? Whatever the explanation, there is no question but that the incorporated Bill of Rights under the Fourteenth Amendment is, in practice, more libertarian than was the original Bill of Rights.

2. One could fill a textbook with nothing but cases applying freedom of speech, freedom of the press, and freedom of religion cases to state action under the Fourteenth Amendment. Consider these materials nothing more than an invitation to future exploration.

[Assignment 78]

XVIII. THE DUE PROCESS AND TAKINGS CLAUSES

Amendment V:

No person shall be * * * deprived of life, liberty, or property, without due process of law; nor shall private property be taken for public use, without just compensation.

Amendment XIV, Section 1:

No state shall make or enforce any law which shall abridge the privileges or immunities of citizens of the United States; nor shall any state deprive any person of life, liberty, or property, without due process of law; nor deny to any person within its jurisdiction the equal protection of the laws.

We have already seen the most important Supreme Court case involving the right to keep and bear arms. *See McDonald v. City of Chicago,* 561 U.S. 742 (2010), *supra* pages 1571–1609. Due to space constraints, we cannot explore application of the principles in the Fourth Amendment, *see, e.g., Mapp v. Ohio,* 367 U.S. 643 (1961) (applying the exclusionary rule to all state criminal proceedings) or the Fifth Amendment right against self-incrimination, *see, e.g., Miranda v. Arizona,* 384 U.S.

436 (1966) (prescribing the warning a policeman must give all criminal suspects). These and other topics are often covered in advanced courses in Constitutional Criminal Procedure. Nor can we explore the complex topic of how the Fifth Amendment guarantee against takings of private property for public use without just compensation applies to state and local governments. As you saw, the Takings Clause was the first Bill of Rights provision whose principles were made an element of due process of law, *see supra,* and the burgeoning case law over the past century defies easy description. (For an entrée into that difficult world, see DAVID A. DANA & THOMAS W. MERRILL, PROPERTY: TAKINGS (2002).) In these materials, we explore some cases that are not generally considered canonical "takings" cases. Two of them, however, are crucial parts of a story to which we have alluded earlier, *see supra* page 1340, regarding the development of housing patterns in the United States, especially in urban and suburban areas. The third raises a very large topic that often goes by the heading "unconstitutional conditions." The cases all involve land use, and we thus group them—a bit unconventionally—under the "takings clause" rubric.

A. BUCHANAN V. WARLEY

245 U.S. 60 (1917)

■ MR. JUSTICE DAY delivered the opinion of the court.

Buchanan, plaintiff in error, brought an action in the Chancery Branch of Jefferson Circuit Court of Kentucky for the specific performance of a contract for the sale of certain real estate situated in the City of Louisville at the corner of 37th Street and Pflanz Avenue. The offer in writing to purchase the property contained a proviso:

"It is understood that I am purchasing the above property for the purpose of having erected thereon a house which I propose to make my residence, and it is a distinct part of this agreement that I shall not be required to accept a deed to the above property or to pay for said property unless I have the right under the laws of the State of Kentucky and the City of Louisville to occupy said property as a residence." This offer was accepted by the plaintiff.

To the action for specific performance the defendant by way of answer set up the condition above set forth, that he is a colored person, and that on the block of which the lot in controversy is a part, there are ten residences, eight of which at the time of the making of the contract were occupied by white people, and only two (those nearest the lot in question) were occupied by colored people, and that under and by virtue of the ordinance of the City of Louisville, approved May 11, 1914, he would not be allowed to occupy the lot as a place of residence.

In reply to this answer the plaintiff set up, among other things, that the ordinance was in conflict with the Fourteenth Amendment to the Constitution of the United States, and hence no defense to the action for specific performance of the contract.

In the court of original jurisdiction in Kentucky, and in the Court of Appeals of that State, the case was made to turn upon the constitutional validity of the ordinance. The Court of Appeals of Kentucky, 165 Kentucky 559, held the ordinance valid and of itself a complete defense to the action.

The title of the ordinance is: "An ordinance to prevent conflict and ill feeling between the white and colored races in the City of Louisville, and to preserve the public peace and promote the general welfare by making reasonable provisions requiring, as far as practicable, the use of separate blocks for residences, places of abode and places of assembly by white and colored people respectively."

By the first section of the ordinance it is made unlawful for any colored person to move into and occupy as a residence, place of abode, or to establish and maintain as a place of public assembly any house upon any block upon which a greater number of houses are occupied as residences, places of abode, or places of public assembly by white people than are occupied as residences, places of abode, or places of public assembly by colored people.

Section 2 provides that it shall be unlawful for any white person to move into and occupy as a residence, place of abode, or to establish and maintain as a place of public assembly any house upon any block upon which a greater number of houses are occupied as residences, places of abode or places of public assembly by colored people than are occupied as residences, places of abode or places of public assembly by white people.

Section 4 provides that nothing in the ordinance shall affect the location of residences, places of abode or places of assembly made previous to its approval; that nothing contained therein shall be construed so as to prevent the occupancy of residences, places of abode or places of assembly by white or colored servants or employees of occupants of such residences, places of abode or places of public assembly on the block on which they are so employed, and that nothing therein contained shall be construed to prevent any person who, at the date of the passage of the ordinance, shall have acquired or possessed the right to occupy any building as a residence, place of abode or place of assembly from exercising such a right; that nothing contained in the ordinance shall prevent the owner of any building who, when the ordinance became effective, leased, rented, or occupied it as a residence, place of abode or place of public assembly for colored persons from continuing to rent, lease or occupy such residence, place of abode or place of assembly for such persons, if the owner shall so desire; but if such house should, after the passage of the ordinance, be at any time leased, rented or occupied as a residence, place of abode, or place of assembly for white persons, it shall not thereafter be used for colored persons, if such occupation would then be a violation of section one of the ordinance; that nothing contained in the ordinance shall prevent the owner of any building, who when the ordinance became effective leased, rented or occupied it as a residence, place of abode, or place of assembly for white persons from continuing to rent, lease or occupy such residence, place of abode or place of assembly for such purpose, if the owner shall so desire, but if such house should, after the passage of the ordinance, be at any time leased, rented or occupied as a residence, place of abode or place of assembly for colored persons, then it shall not thereafter be used for white persons, if such occupation would then be a violation of section two thereof.

The ordinance contains other sections and a violation of its provisions is made an offense.

The assignments of error in this court attack the ordinance upon the ground that it violates the Fourteenth Amendment of the Constitution of the United States, in that it abridges the privileges and immunities of citizens of the United States to acquire and enjoy property, takes property without due process of law, and denies equal protection of the laws.

* * *

We pass then to a consideration of the case upon its merits. This ordinance prevents the occupancy of a lot in the City of Louisville by a person of color in a block where the greater number of residences are occupied by white persons; where such a majority exists colored persons are excluded. This interdiction is based wholly upon color; simply that and nothing more. In effect, premises situated as are those in question in the so-called white block are effectively debarred from sale to persons of color, because if sold they cannot be occupied by the purchaser nor by him sold to another of the same color.

This drastic measure is sought to be justified under the authority of the State in the exercise of the police power. It is said such legislation tends to promote the public peace by preventing racial conflicts; that it tends to maintain racial purity; that it prevents the deterioration of property owned and occupied by white people, which deterioration, it is contended, is sure to follow the occupancy of adjacent premises by persons of color.

The authority of the State to pass laws in the exercise of the police power, having for their object the promotion of the public health, safety, and welfare is very broad as has been affirmed in numerous and recent decisions of this court. Furthermore the exercise of this power, embracing nearly all legislation of a local character, is not to be interfered with by the courts where it is within the scope of legislative authority and the means adopted reasonably tend to accomplish a lawful purpose. But it is equally well established that the police power, broad as it is, cannot justify the passage of a law or ordinance which runs counter to the limitations of the Federal Constitution; that principle has been so frequently affirmed in this court that we need not stop to cite the cases.

The Federal Constitution and laws passed within its authority are by the express terms of that instrument made the supreme law of the land. The Fourteenth Amendment protects life, liberty, and property from invasion by the States without due process of law. Property is more than the mere thing which a person owns. It is elementary that it includes the right to acquire, use, and dispose of it. The Constitution protects these essential attributes of property. Property consists of the free use, enjoyment, and disposal of a person's acquisitions without control or diminution save by the law of the land. 1 Blackstone's Commentaries (Cooley's Ed.), 127.

True it is that dominion over property springing from ownership is not absolute and unqualified. The disposition and use of property may be controlled in the exercise of the police power in the interest of the public health, convenience, or welfare. Harmful occupations may be controlled and regulated. Legitimate business may also be regulated in the interest of the public. Certain uses of property may be confined to portions of the municipality other than the resident district, such as livery stables, brickyards and the like, because of the impairment of the health and comfort of the occupants of neighboring property. Many illustrations might be given from the decisions of this court, and other courts, of this principle, but these cases do not touch the one at bar.

The concrete question here is: May the occupancy, and, necessarily, the purchase and sale of property of which occupancy is an incident, be inhibited by the States, or by one of its municipalities, solely because of the color of the proposed occupant of the premises? That one may dispose of his property, subject only to the control of lawful enactments curtailing that right in the public interest, must be conceded. The question now presented makes it pertinent to enquire into the constitutional right of the white man to sell his property to a colored man, having in view the legal status of the purchaser and occupant.

Following the Civil War certain amendments to the Federal Constitution were adopted, which have become an integral part of that instrument, equally binding upon all the States and fixing certain fundamental rights which all are bound to respect * * *.

The effect of these Amendments was first dealt with by this court in *The Slaughter House Cases,* 16 Wall. 36. The reasons for the adoption of the Amendments were elaborately considered by a court familiar with the times in which the necessity for the Amendments arose and with the circumstances which impelled their adoption. In that case Mr. Justice Miller, who spoke for the majority, pointed out that the colored race, having been freed from slavery by the Thirteenth Amendment, was raised to the dignity of citizenship and equality of civil rights by the Fourteenth Amendment, and the States were prohibited from abridging the privileges and immunities of such citizens, or depriving any person of life, liberty, or property without due process of law. While a principal purpose of the latter Amendment was to protect persons of color, the broad language used was deemed sufficient to protect all persons, white or black, against discriminatory legislation by the States. This is now the settled law. In many of the cases since arising the question of color has not been involved and the cases have been decided upon alleged violations of civil or property rights irrespective of the race or color of the complainant. In *The Slaughter House Cases* it was recognized that the chief inducement to the passage of the amendment was the desire to extend federal protection to the recently emancipated race from unfriendly and discriminating legislation by the States.

* * *

In giving legislative aid to these constitutional provisions Congress enacted in 1866, c. 31, § 1, 14 Stat. 27 [Rev.Stats., § 1978] that:

"All citizens of the United States shall have the same right in every State and Territory as is enjoyed by white citizens thereof to inherit, purchase, lease, sell, hold, and convey real and personal property."

And, in 1870, by c. 114, § 16, 16 Stat. 144 [Rev.Stats., § 1977] that:

"All persons within the jurisdiction of the United States shall have the same right in every State and Territory to make and enforce contracts, to sue, be parties, give evidence, and to the full and equal benefit of all laws and proceedings for the security of persons and property as is enjoyed by white citizens, and shall be subject to like punishment, pains, penalties, taxes, licenses and exactions of every kind, and no other."

In the face of these constitutional and statutory provisions, can a white man be denied, consistently with due process of law, the right to dispose of his property to a purchaser by prohibiting the occupation of it for the sole reason that the purchaser is a person of color intending to occupy the premises as a place of residence?

The statute of 1866, originally passed under sanction of the Thirteenth Amendment, 14 Stat. 27, and practically reenacted after the adoption of the

Fourteenth Amendment, 16 Stat. 144, expressly provided that all citizens of the United States in any State shall have the same right to purchase property as is enjoyed by white citizens. Colored persons are citizens of the United States and have the right to purchase property and enjoy and use the same without laws discriminating against them solely on account of color. *Hall v. DeCuir,* 95 U.S. 485, 508. These enactments did not deal with the social rights of men, but with those fundamental rights in property which it was intended to secure upon the same terms to citizens of every race and color. *Civil Rights Cases,* 109 U.S. 3, 22. The Fourteenth Amendment and these statutes enacted in furtherance of its purpose operate to qualify and entitle a colored man to acquire property without state legislation discriminating against him solely because of color.

The defendant in error insists that *Plessy v. Ferguson,* 163 U.S. 537, is controlling in principle in favor of the judgment of the court below. In that case this court held that a provision of a statute of Louisiana requiring railway companies carrying passengers to provide in their coaches equal but separate accommodations for the white and colored races did not run counter to the provisions of the Fourteenth Amendment. It is to be observed that in that case there was no attempt to deprive persons of color of transportation in the coaches of the public carrier, and the express requirements were for equal though separate accommodations for the white and colored races. In *Plessy v. Ferguson,* classification of accommodation was permitted upon the basis of equality for both races.

In the *Berea College Case,* 211 U.S. 45, a state statute was sustained in the courts of Kentucky, which, while permitting the education of white persons and negroes in different localities by the same incorporated institution, prohibited their attendance at the same place, and in this court the judgment of the Court of Appeals of Kentucky was affirmed solely upon the reserved authority of the legislature of Kentucky to alter, amend, or repeal charters of its own corporations, and the question here involved was neither discussed nor decided.

In *Carey v. City of Atlanta,* 143 Georgia 192, the Supreme Court of Georgia, holding an ordinance similar in principle to the one herein involved, to be invalid, dealt with *Plessy v. Ferguson,* and *The Berea College Case,* in language so apposite that we quote a portion of it:

* * *

"The effect of the ordinance under consideration was not merely to regulate a business or the like, but was to destroy the right of the individual to acquire, enjoy, and dispose of his property. Being of this character, it was void as being opposed to the due-process clause of the constitution."

That there exists a serious and difficult problem arising from a feeling of race hostility which the law is powerless to control, and to which it must give a measure of consideration, may be freely admitted. But its solution cannot be promoted by depriving citizens of their constitutional rights and privileges.

As we have seen, this court has held laws valid which separated the races on the basis of equal accommodations in public conveyances, and courts of high authority have held enactments lawful which provide for separation in the public schools of white and colored pupils where equal privileges are given. But in view of the rights secured by the Fourteenth Amendment to the Federal Constitution such legislation must have its limitations, and cannot be sustained where the exercise of authority exceeds the restraints of the Constitution. We think these limitations are exceeded in laws and ordinances of the character now before us.

It is the purpose of such enactments, and, it is frankly avowed it will be their ultimate effect, to require by law, at least in residential districts, the compulsory separation of the races on account of color. Such action is said to be essential to the maintenance of the purity of the races, although it is to be noted in the ordinance under consideration that the employment of colored servants in white families is permitted, and nearby residences of colored persons not coming within the blocks, as defined in the ordinance, are not prohibited.

The case presented does not deal with an attempt to prohibit the amalgamation of the races. The right which the ordinance annulled was the civil right of a white man to dispose of his property if he saw fit to do so to a person of color and of a colored person to make such disposition to a white person.

It is urged that this proposed segregation will promote the public peace by preventing race conflicts. Desirable as this is, and important as is the preservation of the public peace, this aim cannot be accomplished by laws or ordinances which deny rights created or protected by the Federal Constitution.

It is said that such acquisitions by colored persons depreciate property owned in the neighborhood by white persons. But property may be acquired by undesirable white neighbors or put to disagreeable though lawful uses with like results.

We think this attempt to prevent the alienation of the property in question to a person of color was not a legitimate exercise of the police power of the State, and is in direct violation of the fundamental law enacted in the Fourteenth Amendment of the Constitution preventing state interference with property rights except by due process of law. That being the case the ordinance cannot stand.

Reaching this conclusion it follows that the judgment of the Kentucky Court of Appeals must be reversed, and the cause remanded to that court for further proceedings not inconsistent with this opinion.

Reversed.

NOTES AND QUESTIONS

1. This is a unanimous Supreme Court opinion, written in the heyday of the *Lochner* era, applying the Fourteenth Amendment to restrictions on property rights. No justice, not even Oliver Wendell Holmes, dissented from this opinion.

2. The Court does not speak of the ordinance in this case as a "taking" of property, but rather as a denial of property without due process of law. That is consistent with the language of the era: The Bill of Rights was not literally "incorporated"—and certainly not through the Privileges or Immunities Clause, because of the *Slaughter-House Cases*—but instead certain principles, such as the requirement of just compensation for takings, were part of due process of law. It would be easy to recast the opinion in terms of the Takings Clause: The right to sell you property to whomever you please who has valid legal capacity to purchase is an important right of property, and the ordinance "took" that right, without paying the owner just compensation for it. Of course, even with just compensation, the ordinance would violate the anti-discrimination principles of the Fourteenth Amendment, but in the immediate wake of *Plessy v. Ferguson,* that principle was not given the scope that we see today. Hence its formulation as a denial of property without due process of law.

3. The law at issue in this case also violates the Civil Rights Act of 1866. Why didn't the Court rely on that statute? The Kentucky ordinance obviously not give African-Americans the same right to purchase, lease, sell, hold, and convey real property as is enjoyed by white citizens. White people can under this law buy real estate in white neighborhoods, but African-Americans cannot.

4. The stated goal of the ordinance, in keeping with the eugenics-influenced racism of the times, was to maintain racial purity by segregating housing patterns by law. The Court's opinion clearly rules out those segregating ordinances—and does so more than a century ago. Why is it, then, that the United States of America has more racial segregation in housing today than it had in 1917? We are not sociologists and will not venture a definitive answer to that question. But consider whether at least part of the answer can be found in the following opinion of the Supreme Court.

B. VILLAGE OF EUCLID V. AMBLER REALTY CO.

272 U.S. 365 (1926)

■ MR. JUSTICE SUTHERLAND delivered the opinion of the Court.

The Village of Euclid is an Ohio municipal corporation. It adjoins and practically is a suburb of the City of Cleveland. Its estimated population is between 5,000 and 10,000, and its area from twelve to fourteen square miles, the greater part of which is farm lands or unimproved acreage. It lies, roughly, in the form of a parallelogram measuring approximately three and one-half miles each way. East and west it is traversed by three principal highways: Euclid Avenue, through the southerly border, St. Clair Avenue, through the central portion, and Lake Shore Boulevard, through the northerly border in close proximity to the shore of Lake Erie. The Nickel Plate railroad lies from 1,500 to 1,800 feet north of Euclid Avenue, and the Lake Shore railroad 1,600 feet farther to the north. The three highways and the two railroads are substantially parallel.

Appellee is the owner of a tract of land containing 68 acres, situated in the westerly end of the village, abutting on Euclid Avenue to the south and the Nickel Plate railroad to the north. Adjoining this tract, both on the east and on the west, there have been laid out restricted residential plats upon which residences have been erected.

On November 13, 1922, an ordinance was adopted by the Village Council, establishing a comprehensive zoning plan for regulating and restricting the location of trades, industries, apartment houses, two-family houses, single family houses, etc., the lot area to be built upon, the size and height of buildings, etc.

The entire area of the village is divided by the ordinance into six classes of use districts, denominated U-1 to U-6, inclusive; three classes of height districts, denominated H-1 to H-3, inclusive; and four classes of area districts, denominated A-1 to A-4, inclusive. The use districts are classified in respect of the buildings which may be erected within their respective limits, as follows: U-1 is restricted to single family dwellings, public parks, water towers and reservoirs, suburban and interurban electric railway passenger stations and rights of way, and farming, non-commercial greenhouse nurseries and truck gardening; U-2 is extended to include two-family dwellings; U-3 is further extended to include apartment houses, hotels, churches, schools, public libraries, museums, private clubs, community center buildings, hospitals, sanitariums, public playgrounds and recreation buildings, and a city hall and courthouse; U-4 is further extended to include banks, offices, studios, telephone exchanges, fire and police stations, restaurants, theatres and moving picture shows, retail stores and shops, sales offices, sample rooms, wholesale stores for hardware, drugs and groceries, stations for gasoline and oil (not exceeding 1,000 gallons storage) and for ice delivery, skating rinks and dance halls, electric substations, job and newspaper printing, public garages for motor vehicles, stables and wagon sheds (not exceeding five horses, wagons or motor trucks) and distributing stations for central store and commercial enterprises; U-5 is further extended to include billboards and advertising signs (if permitted), warehouses, ice and ice cream manufacturing and cold storage plants, bottling works, milk bottling and central distribution stations, laundries, carpet cleaning, dry cleaning and dyeing establishments, blacksmith, horseshoeing, wagon and motor vehicle repair shops, freight stations, street car barns, stables and wagon sheds (for more than five horses, wagons or motor trucks), and wholesale produce markets and salesrooms; U-6 is further extended to include plants for sewage disposal and for producing gas, garbage and refuse incineration, scrap iron, junk, scrap paper and rag storage, aviation fields, cemeteries, crematories, penal and correctional institutions, insane and feeble minded institutions, storage of oil and gasoline (not to exceed 25,000 gallons), and manufacturing and industrial operations of any kind other than, and any public utility not included in, a class U-1, U-2, U-3, U-4 or U-5 use. There is a seventh class of uses which is prohibited altogether.

Class U-1 is the only district in which buildings are restricted to those enumerated. In the other classes, the uses are cumulative; that is to say, uses in class U-2 include those enumerated in the preceding class, U-1; class U-3 includes uses enumerated in the preceding classes, U-2 and U-1, and so on. In addition to the enumerated uses, the ordinance provides for accessory uses, that is, for uses customarily incident to the principal use, such as private garages. Many regulations are provided in respect of such accessory uses.

The height districts are classified as follows: In class H-1, buildings are limited to a height of two and one-half stories or thirty-five feet; in class H-2, to 4 stories or fifty feet; in class H-3, to eighty feet. To all of these, certain exceptions are made, as in the case of church spires, water tanks, etc.

The classification of area districts is: in A-1 districts, dwellings or apartment houses to accommodate more than one family must have at least 5,000 square feet for interior lots and at least 4,000 square feet for corner lots; in A-2 districts, the area must be at least 2,500 square feet for interior lots, and 2 000 square feet for corner lots; in A-3 districts, the limits are 1,250 and 1,000 square feet, respectively; in A-4 districts, the limits are 900 and 700 square feet, respectively. The ordinance contains, in great variety and detail, provisions in respect of width of lots, front, side and rear yards, and other matters, including restrictions and regulations as to the use of billboards, signboards and advertising signs.

A single family dwelling consists of a basement and not less than three rooms and a bathroom. A two-family dwelling consists of a basement and not less than four living rooms and a bathroom for each family; and is further described as a detached dwelling for the occupation of two families, one having its principal living rooms on the first floor and the other on the second floor.

Appellee's tract of land comes under U-2, U-3 and U-6. The first strip of 620 feet immediately north of Euclid Avenue falls in class U-2, the next 130 feet to the north, in U-3, and the remainder in U-6. The uses of the first 620 feet, therefore, do not include apartment houses, hotels, churches, schools, or other public and semi-public buildings, or other uses enumerated in respect of U-3 to U-6, inclusive. The uses of the next 130 feet include all of these, but exclude industries, theatres, banks, shops, and the various other uses set forth in respect of J-4 to U-6, inclusive.

Annexed to the ordinance, and made a part of it, is a zone map, showing the location and limits of the various use, height and area districts, from which it appears that the three classes overlap one another; that is to say, for example, both U-5 and U-6 use districts are in A-4 area districts, but the former is in H-2 and the latter in H-3 height districts. The plan is a complicated one and can be better understood by an inspection of the map, though it does not seem necessary to reproduce it for present purposes.

The lands lying between the two railroads for the entire length of the village area and extending some distance on either side to the north and south, having an average width of about 1,600 feet, are left open, with slight exceptions, for industrial and all other uses. This includes the larger part of appellee's tract. Approximately one-sixth of the area of the entire village is included in U-5 and U-6 use districts. That part of the village lying south of Euclid Avenue is principally in U-1 districts. The lands lying north of Euclid Avenue and bordering on the long strip just described are included in U-1, U-2, U-3 and U-4 districts, principally in U-2.

The enforcement of the ordinance is entrusted to the inspector of buildings, under rules and regulations of the board of zoning appeals. Meetings of the board are public, and minutes of its proceedings are kept. It is authorized to adopt rules and regulations to carry into effect provisions of the ordinance. Decisions of the inspector of buildings may be appealed to the board by any person claiming to be adversely affected by any such decision. The board is given power in specific cases of practical difficulty or unnecessary hardship to interpret the ordinance in harmony with its general purpose and intent, so that the public health, safety and general welfare may be secure and substantial justice done. Penalties are prescribed for violations, and it is provided that the various provisions are to be regarded as independent and the holding of any provision to be unconstitutional, void or ineffective shall not affect any of the others.

The ordinance is assailed on the grounds that it is in derogation of § 1 of the Fourteenth Amendment to the Federal Constitution in that it deprives appellee of liberty and property without due process of law and denies it the equal protection of the law, and that it offends against certain provisions of the Constitution of the State of Ohio. The prayer of the bill is for an injunction restraining the enforcement of the ordinance and all attempts to impose or maintain as to appellee's property any of the restrictions, limitations or conditions. The court below held the ordinance to be unconstitutional and void, and enjoined its enforcement. 297 Fed. 307.

Before proceeding to a consideration of the case, it is necessary to determine the scope of the inquiry. The bill alleges that the tract of land in question is vacant and has been held for years for the purpose of selling and developing it for industrial uses, for which it is especially adapted, being immediately in the path of progressive industrial development; that for such uses it has a market value of about $10,000 per acre, but if the use be limited to residential purposes the market value is not in excess of $2,500 per acre; that the first 200 feet of the parcel back from Euclid Avenue, if unrestricted in respect of use, has a value of $150 per front foot, but if limited to residential uses, and ordinary mercantile business be excluded therefrom, its value is not in excess of $50 per front foot.

It is specifically averred that the ordinance attempts to restrict and control the lawful uses of appellee's land so as to confiscate and destroy a great part of its value; that it is being enforced in accordance with its terms; that prospective buyers of land for industrial, commercial and residential uses in the metropolitan district of Cleveland are deterred from buying any part of this land because of the existence of the ordinance and the necessity thereby entailed of conducting burdensome and expensive litigation in order to vindicate the right to use the land for lawful and legitimate purposes; that the ordinance constitutes a cloud upon the land, reduces and destroys its value, and has the effect of diverting the normal industrial, commercial and residential development thereof to other and less favorable locations.

* * *

It is not necessary to set forth the provisions of the Ohio Constitution which are thought to be infringed. The question is the same under both Constitutions, namely, as stated by appellee: Is the ordinance invalid in that it violates the constitutional protection "to the right of property in the appellee by attempted regulations under the guise of the police power, which are unreasonable and confiscatory?"

Building zone laws are of modern origin. They began in this country about twenty-five years ago. Until recent years, urban life was comparatively simple; but with the great increase and concentration of population, problems have developed, and constantly are developing, which require, and will continue to require, additional restrictions in respect of the use and occupation of private lands in urban communities. Regulations, the wisdom, necessity, and validity of which, as applied to existing conditions, are so apparent that they are now uniformly sustained, a century ago, or even half a century ago, probably would have been rejected as arbitrary and oppressive. Such regulations are sustained, under the complex conditions of our day, for reasons analogous to those which justify traffic regulations, which, before the advent of automobiles and rapid transit street railways, would have been condemned as fatally arbitrary and unreasonable. And in this there is no inconsistency, for while the meaning of constitutional guaranties never varies, the scope of their application must expand or contract to meet the new and different conditions which are constantly coming within the field of their operation. In a changing world, it is impossible that it should be otherwise. But although a degree of elasticity is thus imparted, not to the *meaning,* but to the *application* of constitutional principles, statutes and ordinances which, after giving due weight to the new conditions, are found clearly not to conform to the Constitution, of course, must fall.

The ordinance now under review, and all similar laws and regulations, must find their justification in some aspect of the police power, asserted for the public welfare. The line which in this field separates the legitimate from the illegitimate assumption of power is not capable of precise delimitation. It varies with circumstances and conditions. A regulatory zoning ordinance, which would be clearly valid as applied to the great cities, might be clearly invalid as applied to rural communities. In solving doubts, the maxim *sic utere tuo ut alienum non laedas,* which lies at the foundation of so much of the common law of nuisances, ordinarily will furnish a fairly helpful clew. And the law of nuisances, likewise, may be consulted, not for the purpose of controlling, but for the helpful aid of its analogies in the process of ascertaining the scope of, the power. Thus the question whether the power exists to forbid the erection of a building of a particular kind or for a particular use, like the question whether a particular thing is a nuisance, is to be determined, not by an abstract consideration of the building or of the thing considered apart, but by considering it in connection with the circumstances and the locality. A nuisance may be merely a right thing in the wrong place,—like a pig in the parlor instead of the barnyard. If the validity of the legislative classification for zoning purposes be fairly debatable, the legislative judgment must be allowed to control.

There is no serious difference of opinion in respect of the validity of laws and regulations fixing the height of buildings within reasonable limits, the character of materials and methods of construction, and the adjoining area which must be left open, in order to minimize the danger of fire or collapse, the evils of over-crowding and the like, and excluding from residential sections offensive trades, industries and structures likely to create nuisances.

Here, however, the exclusion is in general terms of all industrial establishments, and it may thereby happen that not only offensive or dangerous industries will be excluded, but those which are neither offensive nor dangerous will share the same fate. But this is no more than happens in respect of many practice-forbidding laws which this Court has upheld although drawn in general terms so as to include individual cases that may turn out to be innocuous in themselves. The inclusion of a reasonable margin to insure effective enforcement, will not put upon a law, otherwise valid, the stamp of invalidity. Such laws may also find their justification in the fact that, in some fields, the bad fades into the good by such insensible degrees that the two are not capable of being readily distinguished and separated in terms of legislation. In the light of these considerations, we are not prepared to say that the end in view was not sufficient to justify the general rule of the ordinance, although some industries of an innocent character might fall within the proscribed class. It cannot be said that the ordinance in this respect "passes the bounds of reason and assumes the character of a merely arbitrary fiat." *Purity Extract Co. v. Lynch,* 226 U.S. 192, 204. Moreover, the restrictive provisions of the ordinance in this particular may be sustained upon the principles applicable to the broader exclusion from residential districts of all business and trade structures, presently to be discussed.

* * *

We find no difficulty in sustaining restrictions of the kind thus far reviewed. The serious question in the case arises over the provisions of the ordinance excluding from residential districts, apartment houses, business houses, retail stores and shops, and other like establishments. This question involves the validity of what is really the crux of the more recent zoning legislation, namely, the creation and maintenance of residential districts, from which business and trade of every sort, including hotels and apartment houses, are excluded. Upon that question this Court has not thus far spoken. The decisions of the state courts are numerous and conflicting; but those which broadly sustain the power greatly outnumber those which deny altogether or narrowly limit it; and it is very apparent that there is a constantly increasing tendency in the direction of the broader view * * *.

* * *

The decisions [broadly upholding zoning] * * * agree that the exclusion of buildings devoted to business, trade, etc., from residential districts, bears a rational relation to the health and safety of the community. Some of the grounds for this conclusion are—promotion of the health and security from injury of children and others by separating dwelling houses from territory devoted to trade and industry; suppression and prevention of disorder; facilitating the extinguishment of fires, and the enforcement of street traffic regulations and other general welfare ordinances; aiding the health and safety of the community by excluding from residential areas the confusion and danger of fire, contagion and disorder which in greater or less degree attach to the location of stores, shops and factories. Another ground is that the construction and repair of streets may be rendered easier and less expensive by confining the greater part of the heavy traffic to the streets where business is carried on.

* * *

The matter of zoning has received much attention at the hands of commissions and experts, and the results of their investigations have been set forth in comprehensive reports. These reports which bear every evidence of painstaking consideration, concur in the view that the segregation of residential, business, and industrial buildings will make it easier to provide fire apparatus suitable for the character and intensity of the development in each section; that it will increase the safety and security of home life; greatly tend to prevent street accidents, especially to children, by reducing the traffic and resulting confusion in residential sections; decrease noise and other conditions which produce or intensify nervous disorders; preserve a more favorable environment in which to rear children, etc. With particular reference to apartment houses, it is pointed out that the development of detached house sections is greatly retarded by the coming of apartment houses, which has sometimes resulted in destroying the entire section for private house purposes; that in such sections very often the apartment house is a mere parasite, constructed in order to take advantage of the open spaces and attractive surroundings created by the residential character of the district. Moreover, the coming of one apartment house is followed by others, interfering by their height and bulk with the free circulation of air and monopolizing the rays of the sun which otherwise would fall upon the smaller homes, and bringing, as their necessary accompaniments, the disturbing noises incident to increased traffic and business, and the occupation, by means of moving and parked automobiles, of larger portions of the streets, thus detracting from their safety and depriving children of the privilege of quiet and open spaces for play, enjoyed by those in more favored localities,—until, finally, the residential character of the neighborhood and its desirability as a place of detached residences are utterly destroyed. Under these circumstances, apartment houses, which in a different environment would be not only entirely unobjectionable but highly desirable, come very near to being nuisances.

If these reasons, thus summarized, do not demonstrate the wisdom or sound policy in all respects of those restrictions which we have indicated as pertinent to the inquiry, at least, the reasons are sufficiently cogent to preclude us from saying, as it must be said before the ordinance can be declared unconstitutional, that such provisions are clearly arbitrary and unreasonable, having no substantial relation to the public health, safety, morals, or general welfare.

It is true that when, if ever, the provisions set forth in the ordinance in tedious and minute detail, come to be concretely applied to particular premises, including those of the appellee, or to particular conditions, or to be considered in connection with specific complaints, some of them, or even many of them, may be found to be clearly arbitrary and unreasonable. But where the equitable remedy of injunction is sought, as it is here, not upon the ground of a present infringement or denial of a specific right, or of a particular injury in process of actual execution * * *, it cannot be said that the landowner has suffered or is threatened with an injury which entitles him to challenge their constitutionality * * *.

* * * Under these circumstances, therefore, it is enough for us to determine, as we do, that the ordinance, in its general scope and dominant features, so far as its provisions are here involved, is a valid exercise of authority, leaving other provisions to be dealt with as cases arise directly involving them.

And this is in accordance with the traditional policy of this Court. In the realm of constitutional law especially, this Court has perceived the embarrassment which is likely to result from an attempt to formulate rules or decide questions beyond the necessities of the immediate issue. It has preferred to follow the method of a gradual approach to the general by a systematically guarded application and extension of constitutional principles to particular cases as they arise, rather than by out of hand attempts to establish general rules to which future cases must be fitted. This process applies with peculiar force to the solution of questions arising under the due process clause of the Constitution as applied to the exercise of the flexible powers of police, with which we are here concerned.

Decree reversed.

■ MR. JUSTICE VAN DEVANTER, MR. JUSTICE MCREYNOLDS and MR. JUSTICE BUTLER, dissent.

NOTES AND QUESTIONS

1. As in *Buchanan,* the Court does not examine the zoning ordinance as a potential "taking" of private property; it applies the governing model of substantive due process—though the Court applies it in a fashion that seems more deferential than in some other applications. And as in *Buchanan,* it would not be hard to translate this case into the language of takings: The right to use your property in a fashion that does not amount to a nuisance is an important right, so if the government takes that right without just compensation, the action is unlawful. (If the government is stopping a use that would be a nuisance, it is not taking anything, since you never had the right to commit a nuisance.) The Court did not take that path, and developments since 1937 effectively close it off under modern law.

2. The Court's promise to look carefully at specific applications of zoning ordinances was fulfilled just a few years later in *Nectow v. City of Cambridge*, 277 U.S. 183 (1928). In that case, the ordinance was "of the same general character as that considered by this court in *Euclid v. Ambler Co.* In its general scope it is conceded to be constitutional within that decision." 277 U.S. at 185. As applied to the plaintiff's land, however, the trial court (through a special master) found as a fact "that the health, safety,

convenience, and general welfare of the inhabitants of the part of the city affected will not be promoted by the disposition made by the ordinance of the locus in question." *Id.*at 188. Because "the invasion of the property of plaintiff in error was serious and highly injurious * * * [and] a necessary basis for the support of that invasion is wanting, the action of the zoning authorities comes within the ban of the Fourteenth Amendment and cannot be sustained." *Id.* at 188–89. A decade later, however, *West Coast Hotel* and subsequent cases effectively put an end to review at that level of rigor, even in particular cases.

3. The Supreme Court's decision in *Euclid* was obviously a key blow to property rights, at a time when substantive due process was still in its heyday. The case, however, may also have had a deeper and subtler impact. There is an emerging body of scholarship for the (intuitively sensible) proposition that government policies have contributed to, if not dictated, patterns of housing segregation. *See, e.g.*, RICHARD ROTHSTEIN, THE COLOR OF LAW: A FORGOTTEN HISTORY OF HOW OUR GOVERNMENT SEGREGATED AMERICA (2017). *Buchanan v. Warley*, 245 U.S. 60 (1917), recall, invalidated overtly race-based local housing policies. Consider the potential effects of *Euclid*. The stated rationale for zoning ordinances such as those in *Euclid* was the classic Progressive-era celebration of expertise and planning. Smart, well-credentialed people could organize human activity to make it safer and better for everyone. The best and the brightest, rather than individuals in a market, would decide where the houses, the factories, and the apartments would be located. The predictable result was zoning ordinances, such as the one in *Euclid,* that insured that well-off neighborhoods would *only* be accessible to the well-off in perpetuity, as any property uses that might bring more affordable housing into the area was cordoned off by law. If one could use wealth as a plausible—far from perfect, but plausible—proxy for race, Euclidean zoning could accomplish much of the work of the ordinances banned by *Buchanan* without any mention of race anywhere in the law or its legislative history. Mr. Rothstein reports that in 1916 only eight cities in the country had zoning laws, but by 1936, thanks to *Euclid,* 1,246 had put such ordinances in place. Today, every major city except Houston has zoning ordinances, as does virtually every suburb. Whatever their motivation, the practical effect of residential zoning is often to segregate housing. Mr. Rothstein argues that American residential living patterns are actually more segregated today than they were 120 years ago.

4. Under *Washington v Davis,* effects alone do not constitute an equal protection violation, so even if one could prove a racially discriminatory effect from zoning (which will often not be difficult), that alone would not make it unconstitutional under current law, though an ordinance with a racially discriminatory purpose could be invalid if the purpose could be discerned. Because the right to use property in a fashion that is not a nuisance is an obvious "privilege or immunity," a revitalized Privileges or Immunities Clause could be a powerful tool against exclusionary zoning.

5. As we saw earlier, *see supra* pages 1118–1119, the core idea of a "taking" is an exercise of the power of eminent domain. Over the past century or more, courts have wrestled with ascertaining when regulations of property short of formal condemnation amount to a taking requiring just compensation. In one sense, all regulation that goes beyond the common law of nuisance "takes" something that the landowner previously had. Does that make every such action a taking of property? Some theorists think so (though also think that just compensation can sometimes be implicit in the regulatory scheme), *see* RICHARD A. EPSTEIN: TAKINGS: PRIVATE PROPERTY AND THE POWER OF EMINENT DOMAIN (1985), but the law has never approached that understanding. On the other hand, if you regulate away literally all uses of the property, it starts to look hard to distinguish from an exercise of eminent domain. How does the law handle that enormous

range of regulatory action between condemnation and common law nuisance? The law has two principal tracks. One treats certain actions as takings without need for further analysis. Physical occupations of property, even when temporary, are takings *per se.* Regulation that destroys substantially all of the value of property is also a taking *per se, see Lucas v. South Carolina Coastal Council,* 505 U.S. 1003 (1992), though destruction of *much,* or even *most,* of the property's value does not count. Apart from those small but important categories of action, regulation is evaluated under a multi-factor test, whose application is unpredictable in just about every way except the result: The government usually wins.

6. Suppose, however, that the government acquires rights to physical occupation of land (and easements counts as physical occupation) by "trading" regulatory approvals, such as building permits or zoning waivers. If the underlying regulatory schemes are valid under post-*Euclid,* post-*West Coast Hotel* law, can the government leverage those schemes into land acquisition without paying for it? The Court first suggested "no" in *Nollan v. California Coastal Comm'n,* 483 U.S. 825 (1987), The Court clarified and extended *Nollan* in *Dolan v. City of Tigard*, 512 U.S. 374 (1994), which expanded on the standards for evaluating when "exactions" demanded by government authorities as a condition for receiving development permits become a taking requiring just compensation. The key question is how close a relationship there must be between the exaction and the claimed burden that the government claims justifies the exaction:

> In some States, very generalized statements as to the necessary connection between the required dedication and the proposed development seem to suffice. We think this standard is too lax to adequately protect petitioner's right to just compensation if her property is taken for a public purpose.
>
> Other state courts require a very exacting correspondence, described as the "specifi[c] and uniquely attributable" test. The Supreme Court of Illinois first developed this test in *Pioneer Trust & Savings Bank v. Mount Prospect,* 22 Ill.2d 375, 380, 176 N.E.2d 799, 802 (1961). Under this standard, if the local government cannot demonstrate that its exaction is directly proportional to the specifically created need, the exaction becomes "a veiled exercise of the power of eminent domain and a confiscation of private property behind the defense of police regulations." *Id.,* at 381, 176 N.E.2d, at 802. We do not think the Federal Constitution requires such exacting scrutiny, given the nature of the interests involved.
>
> A number of state courts have taken an intermediate position, requiring the municipality to show a "reasonable relationship" between the required dedication and the impact of the proposed development. Typical is the Supreme Court of Nebraska's opinion in *Simpson v. North Platte,* 206 Neb. 240, 245, 292 N.W.2d 297, 301 (1980), where that court stated:
>
>> "The distinction, therefore, which must be made between an appropriate exercise of the police power and an improper exercise of eminent domain is whether the requirement has some reasonable relationship or nexus to the use to which the property is being made or is merely being used as an excuse for taking property simply because at that particular moment the landowner is asking the city for some license or permit."
>
> Thus, the court held that a city may not require a property owner to dedicate private property for some future public use as a condition of obtaining a

> building permit when such future use is not "occasioned by the construction sought to be permitted." *Id.*, at 248, 292 N.W.2d, at 302.
>
> Some form of the reasonable relationship test has been adopted in many other jurisdictions. Despite any semantical differences, general agreement exists among the courts "that the dedication should have some reasonable relationship to the needs created by the [development]."
>
> We think the "reasonable relationship" test adopted by a majority of the state courts is closer to the federal constitutional norm than either of those previously discussed. But we do not adopt it as such, partly because the term "reasonable relationship" seems confusingly similar to the term "rational basis" which describes the minimal level of scrutiny under the Equal Protection Clause of the Fourteenth Amendment. We think a term such as "rough proportionality" best encapsulates what we hold to be the requirement of the Fifth Amendment. No precise mathematical calculation is required, but the city must make some sort of individualized determination that the required dedication is related both in nature and extent to the impact of the proposed development.

512 U.S. at 389–91. Four justices dissented, finding this "nexus" requirement too constraining on local governments and too difficult to administer. *See, e.g., id.* at 405 (Stevens, J., dissenting) ("The Court has made a serious error by abandoning the traditional presumption of constitutionality and imposing a novel burden of proof on a city implementing an admittedly valid comprehensive land use plan. Even more consequential than its incorrect disposition of this case, however, is the Court's resurrection of a species of substantive due process analysis that it firmly rejected decades ago.").

7. The *Dolan* Court expressly linked its "nexus" requirement for exactions to the doctrine of "unconstitutional conditions," under which "the government may not require a person to give up a constitutional right—here the right to receive just compensation when property is taken for a public use—in exchange for a discretionary benefit conferred by the government where the benefit sought has little or no relationship to the property." 512 U.S. at 385. *Nollan* had conspicuously avoided any mention of the unconstitutional conditions doctrine. There is no unifying theory, across all context, to explain when the Court will find that an apparent "trade" of constitutional rights for a government favor is permissible. *See supra* page 671.

8. There is a very good argument that, in 1791, the Takings Clause referred *only* to exercises of the power of eminent domain. *See* William Treanor, *The Original Understanding of the Takings Clause and the Political Process*, 95 COLUM. L. REV. 782 (1995). For purposes of the Fourteenth Amendment, does that matter? Or do we care what the understanding of takings would have been in 1868? *See* Michael B. Rappaport, *Originalism and Regulatory Takings: Why the Fifth Amendment May Not Protect Against Regulatory Takings but the Fourteenth Amendment May*, 45 SAN DIEGO L. REV. 729 (2008).

[Assignment 79]

XIX. THE CONFRONTATION CLAUSE

We now move from property to criminal procedure. Much of the Bill of Rights concerns criminal procedure; the Fourth, Fifth, Sixth, and Eighth Amendments are primarily, and in some cases solely, concerned with the rights of criminal defendants.

An "incorporated" Bill of Rights has perhaps its greatest impact on state criminal law, and a substantial percentage of all federal constitutional cases since the last great wave of incorporation in the 1960s has involved state criminal trials and convictions. We are leaving most of that world to courses in Constitutional Criminal Procedure, but two aspects of the incorporated Bill of Rights deserve treatment here. The first is quite possibly the most important originalist Supreme Court decision of this millennium.

In courses on Evidence, you will learn about the hearsay rule, which presumptively makes inadmissible (subject to several dozen exceptions) statements made by anyone other than a witness testifying in court under oath and subject to cross-examination, if the purpose of introducing the statement is to help prove that the contents of the statement are true (such as a police officer testifying, "the informant told me that Silvio killed the victim," as evidence that Silvio killed the victim—the hearsay rule makes the informant testify in court for the evidence to be admissible). Now think about the language of the Sixth Amendment's Confrontation Clause: "In all criminal prosecutions, the accused shall enjoy the right * * * to be confronted with the witnesses against him." Suppose that some out-of-court statement falls under one of the many exceptions to the hearsay rule (perhaps the informant was making a so-called "excited utterance"), so that it will be admitted into evidence against the defendant unless the Constitution intervenes. What does the Confrontation Clause say about using out-of-court statements in criminal cases? A simple textual analysis of the clause shows that one must ask and answer two questions. The first is: What makes someone a "witness" in a criminal case? Is a "witness" only someone who actually shows up in court? (That would make the Confrontation Clause pretty pointless, as we will see, but it is a linguistically possible interpretation.) Anyone whose statement somehow gets used as evidence against a defendant? (That would make the Confrontation Clause apply to *every* out-of-court statement, which is also linguistically possible.) Or does the term refer only to a subset of persons whose statements are introduced? That is a crucial question that the text demands be asked and answered. The second question is: Once someone is flagged as a "witness" for purposes of the Sixth Amendment, what does it mean to "confront" them? Do you just have to see them in court? Do you have to be able to cross-examine them? Does it matter if they are dead and can't be "confronted" anymore, but you "confronted" them sometime in the past? These two sets of questions leap out from the words of the Sixth Amendment.

The Supreme Court first started systematically asking and answering those two sets of questions in *2004*. So, what was it doing and asking about for the 213 years between 1791 and 2004? For most of that time, the short answer is "almost nothing," because there were few occasions for the federal courts to deal with the Confrontation Clause. Until the 1960s, there were very few federal criminal laws. Some of us oldsters grew up with the saying, "Don't make a federal case out it"—implying that a "federal" case was a really big and rare deal. For most of the Nation's history, criminal law was almost entirely a state matter, and the Confrontation Clause was not incorporated against the States until 1965. *See Pointer v. Texas,* 380 U.S. 400 (1965). For almost 200 years, there was simply not much for the federal courts to address. Richard D. Friedman, *The Confrontation Clause Re-rooted and Transformed*, 2003–2004 CATO S. CT. REV. 439, 447 ("So long as the Confrontation Clause was a limitation only on the federal judicial system, its bounds, and its relationship to hearsay doctrine, did not matter very much."). The 1960s brought both the federalization of crime and the incorporation of the Confrontation Clause, opening the federal courts to claims arising from state criminal trials. Faced with a flood of Confrontation Clause cases, mostly from state court proceedings, the Supreme Court in 1980 tried to settle how the Confrontation Clause would interact with state (and federal) evidentiary hearsay rules. The Court in 1980 *did not* ask who was a constitutional "witness" and what it means to "confront[ ]" those witnesses. Instead, the Court's settlement was: "[W]hen a hearsay declarant is not present for cross-examination at trial * * *, his statement is admissible only if it bears adequate 'indicia of reliability.' Reliability can be inferred without more in a case where the evidence falls within a firmly rooted hearsay exception. In other cases, the evidence must be excluded, at least absent a showing of particularized guarantees of trustworthiness." *Ohio v. Roberts,* 448 U.S. 56, 66 (1980). What does this really mean? As one of us has put it:

> In other words: If evidence was admitted by virtue of a hearsay exception that the justices on the Court circa 1980 would have learned about in law school half a century earlier, it automatically counts as "reliable" and its admission therefore does not violate the Confrontation Clause. If it is admitted pursuant to some newfangled hearsay exception (for example, the "catch-all" exception represented by Federal Rule of Evidence 807 and included in some state rules of evidence), then the Court will decide case by case whether the evidence is sufficiently reliable to be admitted over a Confrontation Clause exception. In all instances, the clause is read to exclude unreliable or untrustworthy evidence and nothing more.
>
> This approach has the considerable virtue of largely merging constitutional and nonconstitutional law regarding out-of-court statements into a single inquiry. It also has the considerable virtue of leaving very few cases for the federal courts to decide, as most out-of-court statements will be admitted, if at all, pursuant to well-established hearsay exceptions, leaving no additional constitutional analysis to be done. It has the further virtue of sounding good as a matter of policy; who would want to admit unreliable evidence or exclude reliable evidence? And it has the additional virtue, if one inclines to pro-prosecution results, of letting relatively few guilty crooks walk because of this particular legal technicality. It has the decided vice, however, of bearing no plausible relationship to the words of the Confrontation Clause, which neither contains nor intimates the words "reliability" or "trustworthiness" (much less "indicia of"), or to the clause's context, which focused not on the reliability of evidence as such but on the subjection of evidence to a particular procedural mechanism.

Gary Lawson, *Confronting* Crawford: *Justice Scalia, the Judicial Method, and the Adjudicative Limits of Originalism,* 84 U. CHI. L. REV. 2265, 2275–76 (2017). A quarter century after *Ohio v. Roberts*, the Court started asking the textually obvious questions.

Crawford v. Washington

541 U.S. 36 (2004)

■ JUSTICE SCALIA delivered the opinion of the Court.

Petitioner Michael Crawford stabbed a man who allegedly tried to rape his wife, Sylvia. At his trial, the State played for the jury Sylvia's tape-recorded statement to the police describing the stabbing, even though he had no opportunity for cross-examination. The Washington Supreme Court upheld petitioner's conviction after determining that Sylvia's statement was reliable. The question presented is whether this procedure complied with the Sixth Amendment's guarantee that, "[i]n all criminal prosecutions, the accused shall enjoy the right . . . to be confronted with the witnesses against him."

I

On August 5, 1999, Kenneth Lee was stabbed at his apartment. Police arrested petitioner later that night. After giving petitioner and his wife *Miranda* warnings,[1] detectives interrogated each of them twice. Petitioner eventually confessed that he and Sylvia had gone in search of Lee because he was upset over an earlier incident in which Lee had tried to rape her. The two had found Lee at his apartment, and a fight ensued in which Lee was stabbed in the torso and petitioner's hand was cut.

Petitioner gave the following account of the fight:

"Q. Okay. Did you ever see anything in [Lee's] hands?

"A. I think so, but I'm not positive.

"Q. Okay, when you think so, what do you mean by that?

"A. I could a swore I seen him goin' for somethin' before, right before everything happened. He was like reachin', fiddlin' around down here and stuff . . . and I just . . . I don't know, I think, this is just a possibility, but I think, I think that he pulled somethin' out and I grabbed for it and that's how I got cut . . . but I'm not positive. I, I, my mind goes blank when things like this happen. I mean, I just, I remember things wrong, I remember things that just doesn't, don't make sense to me later." App. 155 (punctuation added).

Sylvia generally corroborated petitioner's story about the events leading up to the fight, but her account of the fight itself was arguably different—particularly with respect to whether Lee had drawn a weapon before petitioner assaulted him:

"Q. Did Kenny do anything to fight back from this assault?

"A. (pausing) I know he reached into his pocket . . . or somethin' . . . I don't know what.

"Q. After he was stabbed?

"A. He saw Michael coming up. He lifted his hand . . . his chest open, he might [have] went to go strike his hand out or something and then (inaudible).

---

1 *[Editors' Note: The "Miranda" warning tells an arrestee that anything he or she says can and will be used against them in a court of law. That is permissible as a matter of hearsay law, because the biggest exception to the rule against hearsay is statements of the opposing party: You can always use the other party's out-of-court statements against them.]*

"Q. Okay, you, you gotta speak up.

"A. Okay, he lifted his hand over his head maybe to strike Michael's hand down or something and then he put his hands in his . . . put his right hand in his right pocket . . . took a step back . . . Michael proceeded to stab him . . . then his hands were like . . . how do you explain this . . . open arms . . . with his hands open and he fell down . . . and we ran (describing subject holding hands open, palms toward assailant).

"Q. Okay, when he's standing there with his open hands, you're talking about Kenny, correct?

"A. Yeah, after, after the fact, yes.

"Q. Did you see anything in his hands at that point?

"A. (pausing) um um (no)." Id., at 137 (punctuation added).

The State charged petitioner with assault and attempted murder. At trial, he claimed self-defense. Sylvia did not testify because of the state marital privilege, which generally bars a spouse from testifying without the other spouse's consent. See Wash. Rev.Code § 5.60.060(1) (1994). In Washington, this privilege does not extend to a spouse's out-of-court statements admissible under a hearsay exception, see *State v. Burden*, 120 Wash.2d 371, 377, 841 P.2d 758, 761 (1992), so the State sought to introduce Sylvia's tape-recorded statements to the police as evidence that the stabbing was not in self-defense. Noting that Sylvia had admitted she led petitioner to Lee's apartment and thus had facilitated the assault, the State invoked the hearsay exception for statements against penal interest, Wash. Rule Evid. 804(b)(3) (2003).

Petitioner countered that, state law notwithstanding, admitting the evidence would violate his federal constitutional right to be "confronted with the witnesses against him." Amdt. 6. According to our description of that right in *Ohio v. Roberts*, 448 U.S. 56 (1980), it does not bar admission of an unavailable witness's statement against a criminal defendant if the statement bears "adequate 'indicia of reliability.' " *Id.*, at 66. To meet that test, evidence must either fall within a "firmly rooted hearsay exception" or bear "particularized guarantees of trustworthiness." *Ibid.* The trial court here admitted the statement on the latter ground, offering several reasons why it was trustworthy: Sylvia was not shifting blame but rather corroborating her husband's story that he acted in self-defense or "justified reprisal"; she had direct knowledge as an eyewitness; she was describing recent events; and she was being questioned by a "neutral" law enforcement officer. The prosecution played the tape for the jury and relied on it in closing, arguing that it was "damning evidence" that "completely refutes [petitioner's] claim of self-defense." Tr. 468 (Oct. 21, 1999). The jury convicted petitioner of assault.

The Washington Court of Appeals reversed. It applied a nine-factor test to determine whether Sylvia's statement bore particularized guarantees of trustworthiness, and noted several reasons why it did not: The statement contradicted one she had previously given; it was made in response to specific questions; and at one point she admitted she had shut her eyes during the stabbing. The court considered and rejected the State's argument that Sylvia's statement was reliable because it coincided with petitioner's to such a degree that the two "interlocked." The court determined that, although the two statements agreed about the events leading up to the stabbing, they differed on the issue crucial to petitioner's self-defense claim: "[Petitioner's] version asserts that Lee may have had something in his hand when he stabbed him; but Sylvia's version has Lee grabbing for something only after he has been stabbed."

The Washington Supreme Court reinstated the conviction, unanimously concluding that, although Sylvia's statement did not fall under a firmly rooted hearsay exception, it bore guarantees of trustworthiness: " '[W]hen a codefendant's confession is virtually identical [to, i.e., interlocks with,] that of a defendant, it may be deemed reliable.' " 147 Wash.2d 424, 437, 54 P.3d 656, 663 (2002) * * *.

We granted certiorari to determine whether the State's use of Sylvia's statement violated the Confrontation Clause.

II

The Sixth Amendment's Confrontation Clause provides that, "[i]n all criminal prosecutions, the accused shall enjoy the right . . . to be confronted with the witnesses against him." We have held that this bedrock procedural guarantee applies to both federal and state prosecutions. *Pointer v. Texas*, 380 U.S. 400, 406 (1965). As noted above, *Roberts* says that an unavailable witness's out-of-court statement may be admitted so long as it has adequate indicia of reliability—*i.e.*, falls within a "firmly rooted hearsay exception" or bears "particularized guarantees of trustworthiness." 448 U.S., at 66. Petitioner argues that this test strays from the original meaning of the Confrontation Clause and urges us to reconsider it.

A

The Constitution's text does not alone resolve this case. One could plausibly read "witnesses against" a defendant to mean those who actually testify at trial, cf. *Woodsides v. State*, 3 Miss. 655, 664–665 (1837), those whose statements are offered at trial, see 3 J. Wigmore, Evidence § 1397, p. 104 (2d ed.1923) (hereinafter Wigmore), or something in-between. We must therefore turn to the historical background of the Clause to understand its meaning.

The right to confront one's accusers is a concept that dates back to Roman times. The founding generation's immediate source of the concept, however, was the common law. English common law has long differed from continental civil law in regard to the manner in which witnesses give testimony in criminal trials. The common-law tradition is one of live testimony in court subject to adversarial testing, while the civil law condones examination in private by judicial officers. See 3 W. Blackstone, Commentaries on the Laws of England 373–374 (1768).

Nonetheless, England at times adopted elements of the civil-law practice. Justices of the peace or other officials examined suspects and witnesses before trial. These examinations were sometimes read in court in lieu of live testimony, a practice that "occasioned frequent demands by the prisoner to have his 'accusers,' *i.e.* the witnesses against him, brought before him face to face." 1 J. Stephen, History of the Criminal Law of England 326 (1883). In some cases, these demands were refused. See 9 W. Holdsworth, History of English Law 216–217, 228 (3d ed.1944); *e.g.*, *Raleigh's Case*, 2 How. St. Tr. 1, 15–16, 24 (1603); *Throckmorton's Case*, 1 How. St. Tr. 869, 875–876 (1554).

Pretrial examinations became routine under two statutes passed during the reign of Queen Mary in the 16th century, 1 & 2 Phil. & M., c. 13 (1554), and 2 & 3 id., c. 10 (1555). These Marian bail and committal statutes required justices of the peace to examine suspects and witnesses in felony cases and to certify the results to the court. It is doubtful that the original purpose of the examinations was to produce evidence admissible at trial. See J. Langbein, Prosecuting Crime in the Renaissance 21–34 (1974). Whatever the original purpose, however, they came to be used as evidence in some cases, see 2 M. Hale, Pleas of the Crown 284 (1736), resulting in an adoption of continental procedure. See 4 Holdsworth, *supra*, at 528–530.

The most notorious instances of civil-law examination occurred in the great political trials of the 16th and 17th centuries. One such was the 1603 trial of Sir Walter Raleigh for treason. Lord Cobham, Raleigh's alleged accomplice, had implicated him in an examination before the Privy Council and in a letter. At Raleigh's trial, these were read to the jury. Raleigh argued that Cobham had lied to save himself: "Cobham is absolutely in the King's mercy; to excuse me cannot avail him; by accusing me he may hope for favour." 1 D. Jardine, Criminal Trials 435 (1832). Suspecting that Cobham would recant, Raleigh demanded that the judges call him to appear, arguing that "[t]he Proof of the Common Law is by witness and jury: let Cobham be here, let him speak it. Call my accuser before my face . . . ." 2 How. St. Tr., at 15–16. The judges refused, *id.*, at 24, and, despite Raleigh's protestations that he was being tried "by the Spanish Inquisition," *id.*, at 15, the jury convicted, and Raleigh was sentenced to death.

One of Raleigh's trial judges later lamented that " 'the justice of England has never been so degraded and injured as by the condemnation of Sir Walter Raleigh.' " 1 Jardine, *supra*, at 520. Through a series of statutory and judicial reforms, English law developed a right of confrontation that limited these abuses. For example, treason statutes required witnesses to confront the accused "face to face" at his arraignment. *E.g.*, 13 Car. 2, c. 1, § 5 (1661); see 1 Hale, *supra*, at 306. Courts, meanwhile, developed relatively strict rules of unavailability, admitting examinations only if the witness was demonstrably unable to testify in person. See *Lord Morley's Case*, 6 How. St. Tr. 769, 770–771 (H.L.1666); 2 Hale, *supra*, at 284; 1 Stephen, *supra*, at 358. Several authorities also stated that a suspect's confession could be admitted only against himself, and not against others he implicated.

One recurring question was whether the admissibility of an unavailable witness's pretrial examination depended on whether the defendant had had an opportunity to cross-examine him. In 1696, the Court of King's Bench answered this question in the affirmative, in the widely reported misdemeanor libel case of *King v. Paine*, 5 Mod. 163, 87 Eng. Rep. 584. The court ruled that, even though a witness was dead, his examination was not admissible where "the defendant not being present when [it was] taken before the mayor . . . had lost the benefit of a cross-examination." *Id.*, at 165, 87 Eng. Rep., at 585. The question was also debated at length during the infamous proceedings against Sir John Fenwick on a bill of attainder. Fenwick's counsel objected to admitting the examination of a witness who had been spirited away, on the ground that Fenwick had had no opportunity to cross-examine. See *Fenwick's Case*, 13 How. St. Tr. 537, 591–592 (H.C. 1696) (Powys) ("[T]hat which they would offer is something that Mr. Goodman hath sworn when he was examined . . .; sir J.F. not being present or privy, and no opportunity given to cross-examine the person; and I conceive that cannot be offered as evidence . . ."); *id.*, at 592 (Shower) ("[N]o deposition of a person can be read, though beyond sea, unless in cases where the party it is to be read against was privy to the examination, and might have cross-examined him . . . . [O]ur constitution is, that the person shall see his accuser"). The examination was nonetheless admitted on a closely divided vote after several of those present opined that the common-law rules of procedure did not apply to parliamentary attainder proceedings—one speaker even admitting that the evidence would normally be inadmissible. See *id.*, at 603–604 (Williamson); id., at 604–605 (Chancellor of the Exchequer); id., at 607; 3 Wigmore § 1364, at 22–23, n. 54. Fenwick was condemned, but the proceedings "must have burned into the general consciousness the vital importance of the rule securing the right of cross-examination." *Id.*, § 1364, at 22.

Paine had settled the rule requiring a prior opportunity for cross-examination as a matter of common law, but some doubts remained over whether the Marian statutes prescribed an exception to it in felony cases * * *. Nevertheless, by 1791 (the year the Sixth Amendment was ratified), courts were applying the cross-examination rule even to examinations by justices of the peace in felony cases. See *King v. Dingler*, 2 Leach 561, 562–563, 168 Eng. Rep. 383, 383–384 (1791); *King v. Woodcock*, 1 Leach 500, 502–504, 168 Eng. Rep. 352, 353 (1789). Early 19th-century treatises confirm that requirement. When Parliament amended the statutes in 1848 to make the requirement explicit, see 11 & 12 Vict., c. 42, § 17, the change merely "introduced in terms" what was already afforded the defendant "by the equitable construction of the law." *Queen v. Beeston*, 29 Eng. L. & Eq. R. 527, 529 (Ct.Crim.App.1854) (Jervis, C. J.).

B

Controversial examination practices were also used in the Colonies. Early in the 18th century, for example, the Virginia Council protested against the Governor for having "privately issued several commissions to examine witnesses against particular men *ex parte*," complaining that "the person accused is not admitted to be confronted with, or defend himself against his defamers." A Memorial Concerning the Maladministrations of His Excellency Francis Nicholson, reprinted in 9 English Historical Documents 253, 257 (D. Douglas ed.1955). A decade before the Revolution, England gave jurisdiction over Stamp Act offenses to the admiralty courts, which followed civil-law rather than common-law procedures and thus routinely took testimony by deposition or private judicial examination. See 5 Geo. 3, c. 12, § 57 (1765); Pollitt, The Right of Confrontation: Its History and Modern Dress, 8 J. Pub.L. 381, 396–397 (1959). Colonial representatives protested that the Act subverted their rights "by extending the jurisdiction of the courts of admiralty beyond its ancient limits." Resolutions of the Stamp Act Congress § 8th (Oct. 19, 1765), reprinted in Sources of Our Liberties 270, 271 (R. Perry & J. Cooper eds.1959). John Adams, defending a merchant in a high-profile admiralty case, argued: "Examinations of witnesses upon Interrogatories, are only by the Civil Law. Interrogatories are unknown at common Law, and Englishmen and common Lawyers have an aversion to them if not an Abhorrence of them." Draft of Argument in Sewall v. Hancock (Oct. 1768–Mar. 1769), in 2 Legal Papers of John Adams 194, 207 (L. Wroth & H. Zobel eds.1965).

Many declarations of rights adopted around the time of the Revolution guaranteed a right of confrontation. See Virginia Declaration of Rights § 8 (1776); Pennsylvania Declaration of Rights § IX (1776); Delaware Declaration of Rights § 14 (1776); Maryland Declaration of Rights § XIX (1776); North Carolina Declaration of Rights § VII (1776); Vermont Declaration of Rights Ch. I, § X (1777); Massachusetts Declaration of Rights § XII (1780); New Hampshire Bill of Rights § XV (1783), all reprinted in 1 B. Schwartz, The Bill of Rights: A Documentary History 235, 265, 278, 282, 287, 323, 342, 377 (1971). The proposed Federal Constitution, however, did not. At the Massachusetts ratifying convention, Abraham Holmes objected to this omission precisely on the ground that it would lead to civil-law practices: "The mode of trial is altogether indetermined; . . . whether [the defendant] is to be allowed to confront the witnesses, and have the advantage of cross-examination, we are not yet told . . . . [W]e shall find Congress possessed of powers enabling them to institute judicatories little less inauspicious than a certain tribunal in Spain, . . . the *Inquisition*." 2 Debates on the Federal Constitution 110–111 (J. Elliot 2d ed. 1863). Similarly, a prominent Antifederalist writing under the pseudonym Federal Farmer criticized the use of "written evidence" while objecting to the omission of a vicinage right: "Nothing can be more essential than the cross examining [of] witnesses, and generally before the triers of the facts in question . . . . [W]ritten evidence . . . [is] almost useless; it must be frequently taken ex parte, and but very seldom leads to the proper discovery of truth." R. Lee, Letter IV by the Federal Farmer (Oct. 15, 1787), reprinted in 1 Schwartz, *supra*, at 469, 473. The First Congress responded by including the Confrontation Clause in the proposal that became the Sixth Amendment.

Early state decisions shed light upon the original understanding of the common-law right. *State v. Webb*, 2 N.C. 103 (Super. L. & Eq. 1794) (*per curiam*), decided a mere three years after the adoption of the Sixth Amendment, held that depositions could be read against an accused only if they were taken in his presence. Rejecting a broader reading of the English authorities, the court held: "[I]t is a rule of the common law, founded on natural justice, that no man shall be prejudiced by evidence which he had not the liberty to cross examine." *Id.*, at 104.

Similarly, in *State v. Campbell*, 30 S.C.L. 124, 1844 WL 2558 (App.L.1844), South Carolina's highest law court excluded a deposition taken by a coroner in the absence of the accused. It held: "[I]f we are to decide the question by the established rules of the common law, there could not be a dissenting voice. For, notwithstanding the death of the witness, and whatever the respectability of the court taking the depositions, the solemnity of the occasion and the weight of the testimony, such depositions are *ex parte*, and, therefore, utterly incompetent." *Id.*, at 125. The court said that one of the "indispensable conditions" implicitly guaranteed by the State Constitution was that "prosecutions be carried on to the conviction of the accused, by witnesses confronted by him, and subjected to his personal examination." *Ibid.*

Many other decisions are to the same effect. Some early cases went so far as to hold that prior testimony was inadmissible in criminal cases *even if* the accused had a previous opportunity to cross-examine. Most courts rejected that view, but only after reaffirming that admissibility depended on a prior opportunity for cross-examination. Nineteenth-century treatises confirm the rule.

III

This history supports two inferences about the meaning of the Sixth Amendment.

A

First, the principal evil at which the Confrontation Clause was directed was the civil-law mode of criminal procedure, and particularly its use of *ex parte* examinations as evidence against the accused. It was these practices that the Crown deployed in notorious treason cases like Raleigh's; that the Marian statutes invited; that English law's assertion of a right to confrontation was meant to prohibit; and that the founding-era rhetoric decried. The Sixth Amendment must be interpreted with this focus in mind.

Accordingly, we once again reject the view that the Confrontation Clause applies of its own force only to in-court testimony, and that its application to out-of-court statements introduced at trial depends upon "the law of Evidence for the time being." 3 Wigmore § 1397, at 101. Leaving the regulation of out-of-court statements to the law of evidence would render the Confrontation Clause powerless to prevent even the most flagrant inquisitorial practices. Raleigh was, after all, perfectly free to confront those who read Cobham's confession in court.

This focus also suggests that not all hearsay implicates the Sixth Amendment's core concerns. An off-hand, overheard remark might be unreliable evidence and thus a good candidate for exclusion under hearsay rules, but it bears little resemblance to the civil-law abuses the Confrontation Clause targeted. On the other hand, *ex parte* examinations might sometimes be admissible under modern hearsay rules, but the Framers certainly would not have condoned them.

The text of the Confrontation Clause reflects this focus. It applies to "witnesses" against the accused—in other words, those who "bear testimony." 2 N. Webster, An American Dictionary of the English Language (1828). "Testimony," in turn, is typically "[a] solemn declaration or affirmation made for the purpose of establishing or proving some fact." *Ibid.* An accuser who makes a formal statement to government officers bears testimony in a sense that a person who makes a casual remark to an acquaintance does not. The constitutional text, like the history underlying the common-law right of confrontation, thus reflects an especially acute concern with a specific type of out-of-court statement.

Various formulations of this core class of "testimonial" statements exist: "*ex parte* in-court testimony or its functional equivalent—that is, material such as affidavits, custodial examinations, prior testimony that the defendant was unable to cross-examine, or similar pretrial statements that declarants would reasonably expect to be used prosecutorially," Brief for Petitioner 23; "extrajudicial statements . . . contained in formalized testimonial materials, such as affidavits, depositions, prior testimony, or confessions," *White v. Illinois*, 502 U.S. 346, 365 (1992) (THOMAS, J., joined by SCALIA, J., concurring in part and concurring in judgment); "statements that were made under circumstances which would lead an objective witness reasonably to believe that the statement would be available for use at a later trial," Brief for National Association of Criminal Defense Lawyers et al. as *Amici Curiae* 3. These formulations all share a common nucleus and then define the Clause's coverage at various levels of abstraction around it. Regardless of the precise articulation, some statements qualify under any definition—for example, *ex parte* testimony at a preliminary hearing.

Statements taken by police officers in the course of interrogations are also testimonial under even a narrow standard. Police interrogations bear a striking resemblance to examinations by justices of the peace in England. The statements are not *sworn* testimony, but the absence of oath was not dispositive. Cobham's examination was unsworn, see 1 Jardine, Criminal Trials, at 430, yet Raleigh's trial has long been thought a paradigmatic confrontation violation. Under the Marian statutes, witnesses were typically put on oath, but suspects were not. See 2 Hale, Pleas of the Crown, at 52. Yet Hawkins and others went out of their way to caution that such unsworn confessions were not admissible against anyone but the confessor. *See supra*, at 1360.

That interrogators are police officers rather than magistrates does not change the picture either. Justices of the peace conducting examinations under the Marian statutes were not magistrates as we understand that office today, but had an essentially investigative and prosecutorial function. England did not have a professional police force until the 19th century, so it is not surprising that other government officers performed the investigative functions now associated primarily with the police. The involvement of government officers in the production of testimonial evidence presents the same risk, whether the officers are police or justices of the peace.

In sum, even if the Sixth Amendment is not solely concerned with testimonial hearsay, that is its primary object, and interrogations by law enforcement officers fall squarely within that class.

B

The historical record also supports a second proposition: that the Framers would not have allowed admission of testimonial statements of a witness who did not appear at trial unless he was unavailable to testify, and the defendant had had a prior opportunity for cross-examination. The text of the Sixth Amendment does not suggest any open-ended exceptions from the confrontation requirement to be developed by the courts. Rather, the "right . . . to be confronted with the witnesses against him," Amdt. 6, is most naturally read as a reference to the right of confrontation at common law, admitting only those exceptions established at the time of the founding. As the English authorities above reveal, the common law in 1791 conditioned admissibility of an absent witness's examination on unavailability and a prior opportunity to cross-examine. The Sixth Amendment therefore incorporates those limitations. The numerous early state decisions applying the same test confirm that these principles were received as part of the common law in this country.

We do not read the historical sources to say that a prior opportunity to cross-examine was merely a sufficient, rather than a necessary, condition for admissibility of testimonial statements. They suggest that this requirement was dispositive, and not merely one of several ways to establish reliability * * *.

IV

Our case law has been largely consistent with these two principles * * *.

* * *

* * * Testimonial statements of witnesses absent from trial have been admitted only where the declarant is unavailable, and only where the defendant has had a prior opportunity to cross-examine.

V

Although the results of our decisions have generally been faithful to the original meaning of the Confrontation Clause, the same cannot be said of our rationales. *Roberts* conditions the admissibility of all hearsay evidence on whether it falls under a "firmly rooted hearsay exception" or bears "particularized guarantees of trustworthiness." 448 U.S., at 66. This test departs from the historical principles identified above in two respects. First, it is too broad: It applies the same mode of analysis whether or not the hearsay consists of *ex parte* testimony. This often results in close constitutional scrutiny in cases that are far removed from the core concerns of the Clause. At the same time, however, the test is too narrow: It admits statements that *do* consist of *ex parte* testimony upon a mere finding of reliability. This malleable standard often fails to protect against paradigmatic confrontation violations.

Members of this Court and academics have suggested that we revise our doctrine to reflect more accurately the original understanding of the Clause * * *.

* * *

A

Where testimonial statements are involved, we do not think the Framers meant to leave the Sixth Amendment's protection to the vagaries of the rules of evidence, much less to amorphous notions of "reliability." Certainly none of the authorities discussed above acknowledges any general reliability exception to the common-law rule. Admitting statements deemed reliable by a judge is fundamentally at odds with the right of confrontation. To be sure, the Clause's ultimate goal is to ensure reliability of evidence, but it is a procedural rather than a substantive guarantee. It commands, not that evidence be reliable, but that reliability be assessed in a particular manner: by testing in the crucible of cross-examination. The Clause thus reflects a judgment, not only about the desirability of reliable evidence (a point on which there could be little dissent), but about how reliability can best be determined. Cf. 3 Blackstone, Commentaries, at 373 ("This open examination of witnesses . . . is much more conducive to the clearing up of truth"); M. Hale, History and Analysis of the Common Law of England 258 (1713) (adversarial testing "beats and bolts out the Truth much better").

The *Roberts* test allows a jury to hear evidence, untested by the adversary process, based on a mere judicial determination of reliability. It thus replaces the constitutionally prescribed method of assessing reliability with a wholly foreign one. In this respect, it is very different from exceptions to the Confrontation Clause that make no claim to be a surrogate means of assessing reliability. For example, the rule of forfeiture by wrongdoing (which we accept) extinguishes confrontation claims on essentially equitable grounds; it does not purport to be an alternative means of determining reliability. *See Reynolds v. United States*, 98 U.S. 145, 158–159 (1879).

The Raleigh trial itself involved the very sorts of reliability determinations that *Roberts* authorizes. In the face of Raleigh's repeated demands for confrontation, the prosecution responded with many of the arguments a court applying *Roberts* might invoke today: that Cobham's statements were self-inculpatory, 2 How. St. Tr., at 19, that they were not made in the heat of passion, *id.*, at 14, and that they were not "extracted from [him] upon any hopes or promise of Pardon," *id.*, at 29. It is not plausible that the Framers' only objection to the trial was that Raleigh's judges did not properly weigh these factors before sentencing him to death. Rather, the problem was that the judges refused to allow Raleigh to confront Cobham in court, where he could cross-examine him and try to expose his accusation as a lie.

Dispensing with confrontation because testimony is obviously reliable is akin to dispensing with jury trial because a defendant is obviously guilty. This is not what the Sixth Amendment prescribes.

B

The legacy of *Roberts* in other courts vindicates the Framers' wisdom in rejecting a general reliability exception. The framework is so unpredictable that it fails to provide meaningful protection from even core confrontation violations.

Reliability is an amorphous, if not entirely subjective, concept. There are countless factors bearing on whether a statement is reliable; the nine-factor balancing test applied by the Court of Appeals below is representative * * *.

The unpardonable vice of the *Roberts* test, however, is not its unpredictability, but its demonstrated capacity to admit core testimonial statements that the Confrontation Clause plainly meant to exclude * * *.

To add insult to injury, some of the courts that admit untested testimonial statements find reliability in the very factors that *make* the statements testimonial. As noted earlier, one court relied on the fact that the witness's statement was made to police while in custody on pending charges—the theory being that this made the statement more clearly against penal interest and thus more reliable. *Nowlin, supra,* at 335–338, 579 S.E.2d, at 371–372. Other courts routinely rely on the fact that a prior statement is given under oath in judicial proceedings. That inculpating statements are given in a testimonial setting is not an antidote to the confrontation problem, but rather the trigger that makes the Clause's demands most urgent. It is not enough to point out that most of the usual safeguards of the adversary process attend the statement, when the single safeguard missing is the one the Confrontation Clause demands.

C

Roberts' failings were on full display in the proceedings below. Sylvia Crawford made her statement while in police custody, herself a potential suspect in the case. Indeed, she had been told that whether she would be released "depend[ed] on how the investigation continues." In response to often leading questions from police detectives, she implicated her husband in Lee's stabbing and at least arguably undermined his self-defense claim. Despite all this, the trial court admitted her statement, listing several reasons why it was reliable. In its opinion reversing, the Court of Appeals listed several *other* reasons why the statement was *not* reliable. Finally, the State Supreme Court relied exclusively on the interlocking character of the statement and disregarded every other factor the lower courts had considered. The case is thus a self-contained demonstration of *Roberts*' unpredictable and inconsistent application.

Each of the courts also made assumptions that cross-examination might well have undermined. The trial court, for example, stated that Sylvia Crawford's statement was reliable because she was an eyewitness with direct knowledge of the events. But Sylvia at one point told the police that she had "shut [her] eyes and . . . didn't really watch" part of the fight, and that she was "in shock." The trial court also buttressed its reliability finding by claiming that Sylvia was "being questioned by law enforcement, and, thus, the [questioner] is . . . neutral to her and not someone who would be inclined to advance her interests and shade her version of the truth unfavorably toward the defendant." The Framers would be astounded to learn that *ex parte* testimony could be admitted against a criminal defendant because it was elicited by "neutral" government officers. But even if the court's assessment of the officer's motives was accurate, it says nothing about Sylvia's perception of her situation. Only cross-examination could reveal that.

* * *

We readily concede that we could resolve this case by simply reweighing the "reliability factors" under *Roberts* and finding that Sylvia Crawford's statement falls short. But we view this as one of those rare cases in which the result below is so improbable that it reveals a fundamental failure on our part to interpret the Constitution in a way that secures its intended constraint on judicial discretion. Moreover, to reverse the Washington Supreme Court's decision after conducting our own reliability analysis would perpetuate, not avoid, what the Sixth Amendment condemns. The Constitution prescribes a procedure for determining the reliability of testimony in criminal trials, and we, no less than the state courts, lack authority to replace it with one of our own devising.

We have no doubt that the courts below were acting in utmost good faith when they found reliability. The Framers, however, would not have been content to indulge this assumption. They knew that judges, like other government officers, could not always be trusted to safeguard the rights of the people; the likes of the dread Lord Jeffreys were not yet too distant a memory. They were loath to leave too much discretion in judicial hands. By replacing categorical constitutional guarantees with open-ended balancing tests, we do violence to their design. Vague standards are manipulable, and, while that might be a small concern in run-of-the-mill assault prosecutions like this one, the Framers had an eye toward politically charged cases like Raleigh's—great state trials where the impartiality of even those at the highest levels of the judiciary might not be so clear. It is difficult to imagine *Roberts* providing any meaningful protection in those circumstances.

* * *

Where nontestimonial hearsay is at issue, it is wholly consistent with the Framers' design to afford the States flexibility in their development of hearsay law—as does *Roberts*, and as would an approach that exempted such statements from Confrontation Clause scrutiny altogether. Where testimonial evidence is at issue, however, the Sixth Amendment demands what the common law required: unavailability and a prior opportunity for cross-examination. We leave for another day any effort to spell out a comprehensive definition of "testimonial." Whatever else the term covers, it applies at a minimum to prior testimony at a preliminary hearing, before a grand jury, or at a former trial; and to police interrogations. These are the modern practices with closest kinship to the abuses at which the Confrontation Clause was directed.

In this case, the State admitted Sylvia's testimonial statement against petitioner, despite the fact that he had no opportunity to cross-examine her. That alone is sufficient to make out a violation of the Sixth Amendment. *Roberts* notwithstanding, we decline to mine the record in search of indicia of reliability. Where testimonial statements are at issue, the only indicium of reliability sufficient to satisfy constitutional demands is the one the Constitution actually prescribes: confrontation.

The judgment of the Washington Supreme Court is reversed, and the case is remanded for further proceedings not inconsistent with this opinion.

It is so ordered.

■ CHIEF JUSTICE REHNQUIST, with whom JUSTICE O'CONNOR joins, concurring in the judgment. [Omitted.]

NOTES AND QUESTIONS

1. The complex—and one might even say convoluted—developments post-*Crawford* cannot readily be summarized here. Suffice it to say that the seeming consensus of 2004—seven justices joined Justice Scalia's majority opinion—disappeared once the consequences of the *Crawford* framework began to manifest. Most notably, formalized laboratory reports, identifying substances as drugs or relaying blood alcohol levels, are clearly "testimonial" statements under *Crawford*. So the Constitution require the government to put the laboratory technicians (who may not make the best witnesses) on the stand in order to introduce those reports into evidence? "Yes, of course," said the Court. *See Melendez-Diaz v. Massachusetts,* 557 U.S. 305, 310–11 (2009):

> There is little doubt that the documents at issue in this case fall within the "core class of testimonial statements" thus described. Our description of that category mentions affidavits twice. See also *White v. Illinois*, 502 U.S. 346, 365 (1992) (THOMAS, J., concurring in part and concurring in judgment) ("[T]he Confrontation Clause is implicated by extrajudicial statements only insofar as they are contained in formalized testimonial materials, such as affidavits, depositions, prior testimony, or confessions"). The documents at issue here, while denominated by Massachusetts law "certificates," are quite plainly affidavits: "declaration [s] of facts written down and sworn to by the declarant before an officer authorized to administer oaths." Black's Law Dictionary 62 (8th ed.2004). They are incontrovertibly a " 'solemn declaration or affirmation made for the purpose of establishing or proving some fact.' " *Crawford, supra*, at 51 (quoting 2 N. Webster, An American Dictionary of the English Language (1828)). The fact in question is that the substance found in the possession of Melendez-Diaz and his codefendants was, as the prosecution claimed, cocaine—the precise testimony the analysts would be expected to provide if called at trial. The "certificates" are functionally identical to live, in-court testimony, doing "precisely what a witness does on direct examination." *Davis v. Washington*, 547 U.S. 813, 830 (2006) (emphasis deleted).
>
> Here, moreover, not only were the affidavits " 'made under circumstances which would lead an objective witness reasonably to believe that the statement would be available for use at a later trial,' " *Crawford, supra*, at 52, but under Massachusetts law the sole purpose of the affidavits was to provide "prima facie evidence of the composition, quality, and the net weight" of the analyzed substance, Mass. Gen. Laws, ch. 111, § 13. We can safely assume that the analysts were aware of the affidavits' evidentiary purpose, since that purpose—as stated in the relevant state-law provision—was reprinted on the affidavits themselves. See App. to Pet. for Cert. 25a, 27a, 29a.
>
> In short, under our decision in *Crawford* the analysts' affidavits were testimonial statements, and the analysts were "witnesses" for purposes of the Sixth Amendment. Absent a showing that the analysts were unavailable to testify at trial and that petitioner had a prior opportunity to cross-examine them, petitioner was entitled to " 'be confronted with' " the analysts at trial. *Crawford, supra*, at 54.

"NO!" said Justices Kennedy, Breyer, Alito, and Roberts. *See id.* at 343–46, 349, 351 (Kennedy, J., dissenting):

> The Court's fundamental mistake is to read the Confrontation Clause as referring to a kind of out-of-court statement—namely, a testimonial statement—that must be excluded from evidence. The Clause does not refer to kinds of statements. Nor does the Clause contain the word "testimonial." The text, instead, refers to kinds of persons, namely, to "witnesses against" the defendant. Laboratory analysts are not "witnesses against" the defendant as those words would have been understood at the framing. There is simply no authority for this proposition.
>
> * * *
>
> The Framers were concerned with a typical witness—one who perceived an event that gave rise to a personal belief in some aspect of the defendant's guilt. There is no evidence that the Framers understood the Clause to extend to unconventional witnesses * * *.
>
> * * *
>
> The Court today expands the Clause to include laboratory analysts, but analysts differ from ordinary witnesses in at least three significant ways. First, a conventional witness recalls events observed in the past * * *. [A]n analyst making a contemporaneous observation need not rely on memory; he or she instead reports the observations at the time they are made * * *. The Court cites no authority for its holding that an observation recorded at the time it is made is an act of "witness[ing]" for purposes of the Confrontation Clause.
>
> Second, an analyst observes neither the crime nor any human action related to it. Often, the analyst does not know the defendant's identity, much less have personal knowledge of an aspect of the defendant's guilt. The analyst's distance from the crime and the defendant, in both space and time, suggests the analyst is not a witness against the defendant in the conventional sense.
>
> Third, a conventional witness responds to questions under interrogation. But laboratory tests are conducted according to scientific protocols; they are not dependent upon or controlled by interrogation of any sort * * *. There is no indication that the analysts here—who work for the State Laboratory Institute, a division of the Massachusetts Department of Public Health—were adversarial to petitioner. Nor is there any evidence that adversarial officials played a role in formulating the analysts' certificates.
>
> * * *
>
> In addition to lacking support in historical practice or in this Court's precedent, the Court's decision is also contrary to authority extending over at least 90 years, 35 States, and six Federal Courts of Appeals.
>
> * * *
>
> The modern trend in the state courts has been away from the Court's rule and toward the admission of scientific test results without testimony—perhaps because the States have recognized the increasing reliability of scientific testing * * *. Today the Court strips that authority from the States by carving the minority view into the constitutional text.

Shortly thereafter, those four dissenting justices all but called for *Crawford* to be overruled when the Court again applied it to a laboratory report (in this instance a blood-alcohol test). *See Bullcoming v. New Mexico,* 564 U.S. 647, 684 (2011) (Kennedy, J., dissenting) ("Seven years after its initiation, it bears remembering that the *Crawford* approach was not preordained.") Justice Scalia cobbled together a coalition of himself and

Justices Thomas, Ginsburg, Kagan, and Sotomayor to keep the *Crawford* framework intact. Justice Thomas, however, has consistently adhered to a definition of a "witness" that is substantially narrower than Justice Scalia, or any other justice, had in mind, and he has sometimes been the swing vote in 4–1–4 decisions. *See Williams v. Illinois,* 567 U.S. 50 (2012) (plurality opinion) (the Confrontation Clause does not bar testimony by expert witnesses who read and rely on otherwise testimonial lab reports); *id.* at 103 (Thomas, J., concurring the judgment) (disagreeing with almost everything in the plurality's opinion, but agreeing with the conclusion because the private lab report was not formalized enough to be testimonial); *id.* at 118 (Kagan, J., dissenting) (expert testimony based on constitutionally inadmissible evidence is itself constitutionally inadmissible). Justices Scalia and Kennedy have been replaced by Justices Gorsuch and Kavanaugh. It is safe to assume that Justice Gorsuch will support *Crawford.* Justice Kavanaugh has yet to speak on that subject.

2. *Crawford* is monumentally important for two reasons. First, its impact on the administration of criminal justice is hard to overstate. Second, even more than *Heller, see supra* pages 1045–1059, it stands as perhaps the premier instance of originalist methodology in the face of an ambiguous text. Almost all of Justice Scalia's argument concerns the 1791 Sixth Amendment, but we are not aware of good reasons to think that confrontation rights would have been seen as narrower (or broader) in 1868.

[Assignment 80]

XX. THE DEATH PENALTY

Amendment VIII:

Excessive bail shall not be required, nor excessive fines imposed, nor cruel and unusual punishments inflicted.

Amendment XIV, Section 1:

All persons born or naturalized in the United States, and subject to the jurisdiction thereof, are citizens of the United States and of the state wherein they reside. No state shall make or enforce any law which shall abridge the privileges or immunities of citizens of the United States; nor shall any state deprive any person of life, liberty, or property, without due process of law; nor deny to any person within its jurisdiction the equal protection of the laws.

In 1972, in *Furman v. Georgia,* 408 U.S. 238 (1972), the Supreme Court put a temporary halt to all executions in the United States. *Furman* was a 5–4 decision, and each of the five justices in the majority wrote a separate opinion, so it is difficult to distill a "holding" from the case, despite (because of?) the almost 250 pages of opinions filling the *United States Reports.* There was not a majority of justices willing to declare categorically that capital punishment was always unconstitutional (though a few justices took that view); the concern was about arbitrariness in the administration of the penalty. *See, e.g., id.* at 309–10 (Stewart, J., concurring) ("These death sentences are cruel and unusual in the same way that being struck by lightning is cruel and unusual * * *. [T]he Eighth and Fourteenth Amendment cannot tolerate the infliction of a sentence of death under legal systems that permit this unique penalty to be so wantonly and so freakishly imposed."); *id.* at 313 (White, J., concurring) ("there is no meaningful basis for distinguishing the few case in which it is imposed from the many cases in which it is not"). Accordingly, every State that had capital punishment needed to re-work its statutes in order to comply with the (uncertain) requirements indicated in *Furman* and, in some fashion, make the administration of the death penalty less capricious (but not *too much* less capricious, because a mandatory death penalty, with no opportunity for a jury to impose a lesser sentence, was not going to pass muster either). Four years later, those "second-generation" statutes reached the Supreme Court.

A. GREGG V. GEORGIA

428 U.S. 153 (1976)

■ Judgment of the Court, and opinion of MR. JUSTICE STEWART, MR. JUSTICE POWELL, and MR. JUSTICE STEVENS, announced by MR. JUSTICE STEWART.[2]

The issue in this case is whether the imposition of the sentence of death for the crime of murder under the law of Georgia violates the Eighth and Fourteenth Amendments.

The petitioner, Troy Gregg, was charged with committing armed robbery and murder. In accordance with Georgia procedure in capital cases, the trial was in two stages, a guilt stage and a sentencing stage. The evidence at the guilt trial established that, on November 21, 1973, the petitioner and a traveling companion, Floyd Allen, while hitchhiking north in Florida were picked up by Fred Simmons and Bob Moore. Their car broke down, but they continued north after Simmons purchased another vehicle with some of the cash he was carrying. While still in Florida, they picked up another hitchhiker, Dennis Weaver, who rode with them to Atlanta, where he was let out about 11 p.m. A short time later, the four men interrupted their journey for a rest stop along the highway. The next morning the bodies of Simmons and Moore were discovered in a ditch nearby.

On November 23, after reading about the shootings in an Atlanta newspaper, Weaver communicated with the Gwinnett County police and related information concerning the journey with the victims, including a description of the car. The next afternoon, the petitioner and Allen, while in Simmons' car, were arrested in Asheville, N.C. In the search incident to the arrest a .25-caliber pistol, later shown to be that used to kill Simmons and Moore, was found in the petitioner's pocket. After receiving the warnings required by *Miranda v. Arizona,* 384 U.S. 436 (1966), and signing a written waiver of his rights, the petitioner signed a statement in which he admitted shooting, then robbing Simmons and Moore. He justified the slayings on grounds of self-defense. The next day, while being transferred to Lawrenceville, Ga., the petitioner and Allen were taken to the scene of the shootings. Upon arriving there, Allen recounted the events leading to the slayings. His version of these events was as follows: After Simmons and Moore left the car, the petitioner stated that he intended to rob them. The petitioner then took his pistol in hand and positioned himself on the car to improve his aim. As Simmons and Moore came up an embankment toward the car, the petitioner fired three shots and the two men fell near a ditch. The petitioner, at close range, then fired a shot into the head of each. He robbed them of valuables and drove away with Allen.

---

2 *[Editors' Note; Justices White and Rehnquist would have upheld the death penalty on broader grounds than those stated in the plurality opinion. There were thus five votes to uphold everything the plurality upheld.]*

A medical examiner testified that Simmons died from a bullet wound in the eye, and that Moore died from bullet wounds in the cheek and in the back of the head. He further testified that both men had several bruises and abrasions about the face and head which probably were sustained either from the fall into the ditch or from being dragged or pushed along the embankment. Although Allen did not testify, a police detective recounted the substance of Allen's statements about the slayings and indicated that directly after Allen had made these statements the petitioner had admitted that Allen's account was accurate. The petitioner testified in his own defense. He confirmed that Allen had made the statements described by the detective, but denied their truth or ever having admitted to their accuracy. He indicated that he had shot Simmons and Moore because of fear and in self-defense, testifying they had attacked Allen and him, one wielding a pipe and the other a knife.

* * * The jury found the petitioner guilty of two counts of armed robbery and two counts of murder.

At the penalty stage, which took place before the same jury, neither the prosecutor nor the petitioner's lawyer offered any additional evidence. Both counsel, however, made lengthy arguments dealing generally with the propriety of capital punishment under the circumstances and with the weight of the evidence of guilt. The trial judge instructed the jury that it could recommend either a death sentence or a life prison sentence on each count. The judge further charged the jury that in determining what sentence was appropriate the jury was free to consider the facts and circumstances, if any, presented by the parties in mitigation or aggravation.

Finally, the judge instructed the jury that it "would not be authorized to consider [imposing] the penalty of death" unless it first found beyond a reasonable doubt one of these aggravating circumstances;

> "One—That the offense of murder was committed while the offender was engaged in the commission of two other capital felonies, to-wit the armed robbery of [Simmons and Moore].
>
> "Two—That the offender committed the offense of murder for the purpose of receiving money and the automobile described in the indictment.
>
> "Three—The offense of murder was outrageously and wantonly vile, horrible and inhuman, in that they [*sic*] involved the depravity of [the] mind of the defendant."

Finding the first and second of these circumstances, the jury returned verdicts of death on each count.

The Supreme Court of Georgia affirmed the convictions and the imposition of the death sentences for murder. 233 Ga. 117, 210 S.E.2d 659 (1974). After reviewing the trial transcript and the record, including the evidence, and comparing the evidence and sentence in similar cases in accordance with the requirements of Georgia law, the court concluded that, considering the nature of the crime and the defendant, the sentences of death had not resulted from prejudice or any other arbitrary factor and were not excessive or disproportionate to the penalty applied in similar cases. The death sentences imposed for armed robbery, however, were vacated on the grounds that the death penalty had rarely been imposed in Georgia for that offense and that the jury improperly considered the murders as aggravating circumstances for the robberies after having considered the armed robberies as aggravating circumstances for the murders. *Id.* at 127, 210 S.E.2d at 667.

We granted the petitioner's application for a writ of certiorari limited to his challenge to the imposition of the death sentences in this case as "cruel and unusual" punishment in violation of the Eighth and the Fourteenth Amendments.

Before considering the issues presented it is necessary to understand the Georgia statutory scheme for the imposition of the death penalty. The Georgia statute, as amended after our decision in *Furman v. Georgia,* 408 U.S. 238 (1972), retains the death penalty for six categories of crime: murder, kidnaping for ransom or where the victim is harmed, armed robbery, rape, treason, and aircraft hijacking. The capital defendant's guilt or innocence is determined in the traditional manner, either by a trial judge or a jury, in the first stage of a bifurcated trial.

If trial is by jury, the trial judge is required to charge lesser included offenses when they are supported by any view of the evidence. After a verdict, finding, or plea of guilty to a capital crime, a presentence hearing is conducted before whoever made the determination of guilt. The sentencing procedures are essentially the same in both bench and jury trials. At the hearing:

> "[T]he judge [or jury] shall hear additional evidence in extenuation, mitigation, and aggravation of punishment, including the record of any prior criminal convictions and pleas of guilty or pleas of nolo contendere of the defendant, or the absence of any prior conviction and pleas: Provided, however, that only such evidence in aggravation as the State has made known to the defendant prior to his trial shall be admissible. The judge [or jury] shall also hear argument by the defendant or his counsel and the prosecuting attorney . . . regarding the punishment to be imposed." § 27–2503 (Supp. 1975).

The defendant is accorded substantial latitude as to the types of evidence that he may introduce. Evidence considered during the guilt stage may be considered during the sentencing stage without being resubmitted.

In the assessment of the appropriate sentence to be imposed the judge is also required to consider or to include in his instructions to the jury "any mitigating circumstances or aggravating circumstances otherwise authorized by law and any of [10] statutory aggravating circumstances which may be supported by the evidence. . . ." § 27–2534.1(b) (Supp. 1975). The scope of the non-statutory aggravating or mitigating circumstances is not delineated in the statute. Before a convicted defendant may be sentenced to death, however, except in cases of treason or aircraft hijacking, the jury, or the trial judge in cases tried without a jury, must find beyond a reasonable doubt one of the 10 aggravating circumstances specified in the statute. The sentence of death may be imposed only if the jury (or judge) finds one of the statutory aggravating circumstances and then elects to impose that sentence. If the verdict is death, the jury or judge must specify the aggravating circumstance(s) found. In jury cases, the trial judge is bound by the jury's recommended sentence.

In addition to the conventional appellate process available in all criminal cases, provision is made for special expedited direct review by the Supreme Court of Georgia of the appropriateness of imposing the sentence of death in the particular case. The court is directed to consider "the punishment as well as any errors enumerated by way of appeal," and to determine:

"(1) Whether the sentence of death was imposed under the influence of passion, prejudice, or any other arbitrary factor, and

(2) Whether, in cases other than treason or aircraft hijacking, the evidence supports the jury's or judge's finding of a statutory aggravating circumstance as enumerated in section 27.2534.1(b), and

(3) Whether the sentence of death is excessive or disproportionate to the penalty imposed in similar cases, considering both the crime and the defendant." § 27–2537 (Supp. 1975).

If the court affirms a death sentence, it is required to include in its decision reference to similar cases that it has taken into consideration.

A transcript and complete record of the trial, as well as a separate report by the trial judge, are transmitted to the court for its use in reviewing the sentence. The report is in the form of a 6 1/2-page questionnaire, designed to elicit information about the defendant, the crime, and the circumstances of the trial. It requires the trial judge to characterize the trial in several ways designed to test for arbitrariness and disproportionality of sentence. Included in the report are responses to detailed questions concerning the quality of the defendant's representation, whether race played a role in the trial, and, whether, in the trial court's judgment, there was any doubt about the defendant' guilt or the appropriateness of the sentence. A copy of the report is served upon defense counsel. Under its special review authority, the court may either affirm the death sentence or remand the case for resentencing. In cases in which the death sentence is affirmed, there remains the possibility of executive clemency.

We address initially the basic contention that the punishment of death for the crime of murder is, under all circumstances, "cruel and unusual" in violation of the Eighth and Fourteenth Amendments of the Constitution. In Part IV of this opinion, we will consider the sentence of death imposed under the Georgia statutes at issue in this case.

The Court on a number of occasions has both assumed and asserted the constitutionality of capital punishment. In several cases that assumption provided a necessary foundation for the decision, as the Court was asked to decide whether a particular method of carrying out a capital sentence would be allowed to stand under the Eighth Amendment. But until *Furman v. Georgia,* 408 U.S. 238 (1972), the Court never confronted squarely the fundamental claim that the punishment of death always, regardless of the enormity of the offense or the procedure followed in imposing the sentence, is cruel and unusual punishment in violation of the Constitution. Although this issue was presented and addressed in *Furman,* it was not resolved by the Court. Four Justices would have held that capital punishment is not unconstitutional *per se*; two Justices would have reached the opposite conclusion; and three Justices, while agreeing that the statutes then before the Court were invalid as applied, left open the question whether such punishment may ever be imposed. We now hold that the punishment of death does not invariably violate the Constitution.

The history of the prohibition of "cruel and unusual" punishment already has been reviewed at length [in *Furman*]. The phrase first appeared in the English Bill of Rights of 1689, which was drafted by Parliament at the accession of William and Mary. The English version appears to have been directed against punishments unauthorized by statute and beyond the jurisdiction of the sentencing court, as well as those disproportionate to the offense involved. The American draftsmen, who adopted the English phrasing in drafting the Eighth Amendment, were primarily concerned, however, with proscribing "tortures" and other "barbarous" methods of punishment.[17]

In the earliest cases raising Eighth Amendment claims, the Court focused on particular methods of execution to determine whether they were too cruel to pass constitutional muster. The constitutionality of the sentence of death itself was not at issue * * *.

But the Court has not confined the prohibition embodied in the Eighth Amendment to "barbarous" methods that were generally outlawed in the 18th century. Instead, the Amendment has been interpreted in a flexible and dynamic manner. The Court early recognized that "a principle to be vital must be capable of wider application than the mischief which gave it birth." *Weems v. United States,* 217 U.S. 349, 373 (1910). Thus the Clause forbidding cruel and unusual" punishments "is not fastened to the obsolete but may acquire meaning as public opinion becomes enlightened by a humane justice. *Id.* at 378. *See also Furman v. Georgia,* 408 U.S. at 429–430 (POWELL, J., dissenting); *Trop v. Dulles,* 356 U.S. 86, 100–101 (1958) (plurality opinion).

* * *

It is clear from the foregoing precedents that the Eighth Amendment has not been regarded as a static concept. As Mr. Chief Justice Warren said, in an oft-quoted phrase, "[t]he Amendment must draw its meaning from the evolving standards of decency that mark the progress of a maturing society." *Trop v. Dulles, supra* at 101. Thus, an assessment of contemporary values concerning the infliction of a challenged sanction is relevant to the application of the Eighth Amendment. As we develop below more fully, this assessment does not call for a subjective judgment. It requires, rather, that we look to objective indicia that reflect the public attitude toward a given sanction.

But our cases also make clear that public perceptions of standards of decency with respect to criminal sanctions are not conclusive. A penalty also must accord with "the dignity of man," which is the "basic concept underlying the Eighth Amendment." *Trop v. Dulles, supra* at 100 (plurality opinion). This means, at least, that the punishment not be "excessive." When a form of punishment in the abstract (in this case, whether capital punishment may ever be imposed as a sanction for murder), rather than in the particular (the propriety of death as a penalty to be applied to a specific defendant for a specific crime) is under consideration, the inquiry into "excessiveness" has two aspects. First, the punishment must not involve the unnecessary and wanton infliction of pain. Second, the punishment must not be grossly out of proportion to the severity of the crime.

Of course, the requirements of the Eighth Amendment must be applied with an awareness of the limited role to be played by the courts. This does not mean that judges have no role to play, for the Eighth Amendment is a restraint upon the exercise of legislative power * * *.

---

[17] This conclusion derives primarily from statements made during the debates in the various state conventions called to ratify the Federal Constitution * * *.

But, while we have an obligation to insure that constitutional bound are not overreached, we may not act as judges as we might as legislators * * *.

Therefore, in assessing a punishment selected by a democratically elected legislature against the constitutional measure, we presume its validity. We may not require the legislature to select the least severe penalty possible so long as the penalty selected is not cruelly inhumane or disproportionate to the crime involved. And a heavy burden rests on those who would attack the judgment of the representatives of the people.

This is true in part because the constitutional test is intertwined with an assessment of contemporary standards and the legislative judgment weighs heavily in ascertaining such standards. "[I]n a democratic society legislatures, not courts, are constituted to respond to the will and consequently the moral values of the people." *Furman v. Georgia, supra* at 383 (BURGER, C.J., dissenting). The deference we owe to the decisions of the state legislatures under our federal system is enhanced where the specification of punishments is concerned, for "these are peculiarly questions of legislative policy." *Gore v. United States,* 357 U.S. 386, 393 (1968). Caution is necessary lest this Court become, "under the aegis of the Cruel and Unusual Punishment Clause, the ultimate arbiter of the standards of criminal responsibility . . . throughout the country." *Powell v. Texas,* 392 U.S. 514, 533 (1968) (plurality opinion). A decision that a given punishment is impermissible under the Eighth Amendment cannot be reversed short of a constitutional amendment * * *.

In the discussion to this point we have sought to identify the principles and considerations that guide a court in addressing an Eighth Amendment claim. We now consider specifically whether the sentence of death for the crime of murder is a *per se* violation of the Eighth and Fourteenth Amendments to the Constitution. We note first that history and precedent strongly support a negative answer to this question.

The imposition of the death penalty for the crime of murder has a long history of acceptance both in the United States and in England. The common-law rule imposed a mandatory death sentence on all convicted murderers. *McGautha v. California,* 402 U.S. 183, 197–198 (1971). And the penalty continued to be used into the 20th century by most American States, although the breadth of the common-law rule was diminished, initially by narrowing the class of murders to be punished by death and subsequently by widespread adoption of laws expressly granting juries the discretion to recommend mercy.

It is apparent from the text of the Constitution itself that the existence of capital punishment was accepted by the Framers. At the time the Eighth Amendment was ratified, capital punishment was a common sanction in every State. Indeed, the First Congress of the United States enacted legislation providing death as the penalty for specified crimes. C. 9, 1 Stat. 112 (1790). The Fifth Amendment, adopted at the same time as the Eighth, contemplated the continued existence of the capital sanction by imposing certain limits on the prosecution of capital cases:

> "No person shall be held to answer for a capital, or otherwise infamous crime, unless on a presentment or indictment of a Grand Jury . . .; nor shall any person be subject for the same offense to be twice put in jeopardy of life or limb; . . . nor be deprived of life, liberty, or property, without due process of law. . . ."

And the Fourteenth Amendment, adopted over three-quarters of a century later, similarly contemplates the existence of the capital sanction in providing that no State shall deprive any person of "life, liberty, or property" without due process of law.

For nearly two centuries, this Court, repeatedly and often expressly, has recognized that capital punishment is not invalid *per se* * * *. And in *Trop v. Dulles*, 356 U.S. at 99, Mr. Chief Justice Warren, for himself and three other Justices, wrote:

> "Whatever the arguments may be against capital punishment, both on moral grounds and in terms of accomplishing the purposes of punishment . . ., the death penalty has been employed throughout our history, and, in a day when it is still widely accepted, it cannot be said to violate the constitutional concept of cruelty."

Four years ago, the petitioners in *Furman* and its companion cases predicated their argument primarily upon the asserted proposition that standards of decency had evolved to the point where capital punishment no longer could be tolerated. The petitioners in those cases said, in effect, that the evolutionary process had come to an end, and that standards of decency required that the Eighth Amendment be construed finally as prohibiting capital punishment for any crime regardless of its depravity and impact on society. This view was accepted by two Justices. Three other Justices were unwilling to go so far; focusing on the procedures by which convicted defendants were selected for the death penalty rather than on the actual punishment inflicted, they joined in the conclusion that the statutes before the Court were constitutionally invalid.

The petitioners in the capital cases before the Court today renew the "standards of decency" argument, but developments during the four years since *Furman* have undercut substantially the assumptions upon which their argument rested. Despite the continuing debate, dating back to the 19th century, over the morality and utility of capital punishment, it is now evident that a large proportion of American society continues to regard it as an appropriate and necessary criminal sanction.

The most marked indication of society's endorsement of the death penalty for murder is the legislative response to *Furman*. The legislatures of at least 35 States have enacted new statutes that provide for the death penalty for at least some crimes that result in the death of another person. And the Congress of the United States, in 1974, enacted a statute providing the death penalty for aircraft piracy that results in death. These recently adopted statutes have attempted to address the concerns expressed by the Court in *Furman* primarily (i) by specifying the factors to be weighed and the procedures to be followed in deciding when to impose a capital sentence, or (ii) by making the death penalty mandatory for specified crimes. But all of the post-*Furman* statutes make clear that capital punishment itself has not been rejected by the elected representatives of the people.

In the only statewide referendum occurring since *Furman* and brought to our attention, the people of California adopted a constitutional amendment that authorized capital punishment, in effect negating a prior ruling by the Supreme Court of California in *People v. Anderson,* 6 Cal.3d 628, 493 P.2d 880, cert. denied, 406 U.S. 958 (1972), that the death penalty violated the California Constitution.

The jury also is a significant and reliable objective index of contemporary values because it is so directly involved * * * At the close of 1974 at least 254 persons had been sentenced to death since *Furman,* and by the end of March 1976, more than 460 persons were subject to death sentences.

As we have seen, however, the Eighth Amendment demands more than that a challenged punishment be acceptable to contemporary society. The Court also must ask whether it comports with the basic concept of human dignity at the core of the Amendment. Although we cannot "invalidate a category of penalties because we deem less severe penalties adequate to serve the ends of penology," *Furman v. Georgia, supra,* at 451 (POWELL, J., dissenting), the sanction imposed cannot be so totally without penological justification that it results in the gratuitous infliction of suffering.

The death penalty is said to serve two principal social purposes: retribution and deterrence of capital crimes by prospective offenders.

In part, capital punishment is an expression of society's moral outrage at particularly offensive conduct. This function may be unappealing to many, but it is essential in an ordered society that asks its citizens to rely on legal processes rather than self-help to vindicate their wrongs * * *. "Retribution is no longer the dominant objective of the criminal law," *Williams v. New York,* 337 U.S. 241, 248 (1949), but neither is it a forbidden objective nor one inconsistent with our respect for the dignity of men. Indeed, the decision that capital punishment may be the appropriate sanction in extreme cases is an expression of the community's belief that certain crimes are themselves so grievous an affront to humanity that the only adequate response may be the penalty of death.

Statistical attempts to evaluate the worth of the death penalty as a deterrent to crimes by potential offenders have occasioned a great deal of debate. The result simply have been inconclusive. As one opponent of capital punishment has said:

> "[A]fter all possible inquiry, including the probing of all possible methods of inquiry, we do not know, and for systematic and easily visible reasons cannot know, what the truth about this 'deterrent' effect may be. . . .
>
> "The inescapable flaw is . . . that social conditions in any state are not constant through time, and that social conditions are not the same in any two states. If an effect were observed (and the observed effects, one way or another, are not large), then one could not at all tell whether any of this effect is attributable to the presence or absence of capital punishment. A 'scientific'—that is to say, a soundly based—conclusion is simply impossible, and no methodological path out of this tangle suggests itself." C. Black, Capital Punishment: The Inevitability of Caprice and Mistake 226 (1974).

Although some of the studies suggest that the death penalty may not function as a significantly greater deterrent than lesser penalties, there is no convincing empirical evidence either supporting or refuting this view. We may nevertheless assume safely that there are murderers, such as those who act in passion, for whom the threat of death has little or no deterrent effect. But for many others, the death penalty undoubtedly is a significant deterrent. There are carefully contemplated murders, such as murder for hire, where the possible penalty of death may well enter into the cold calculus that precedes the decision to act. And there are some categories of murder, such as murder by a life prisoner, where other sanctions may not be adequate.

The value of capital punishment as a deterrent of crime is a complex factual issue the resolution of which properly rests with the legislatures, which can evaluate the results of statistical studies in terms of their own local conditions and with a flexibility of approach that is not available to the courts. Indeed, many of the post-*Furman* statutes reflect just such a responsible effort to define those crimes and those criminals for which capital punishment is most probably an effective deterrent.

In sum, we cannot say that the judgment of the Georgia Legislature that capital punishment may be necessary in some cases is clearly wrong. Considerations of federalism, as well as respect for the ability of a legislature to evaluate, in terms of its particular State, the moral consensus concerning the death penalty and its social utility as a sanction, require us to conclude, in the absence of more convincing evidence, that the infliction of death as a punishment for murder is not without justification and thus is not unconstitutionally severe.

Finally, we must consider whether the punishment of death is disproportionate in relation to the crime for which it is imposed * * *. [W]hen a life has been taken deliberately by the offender, we cannot say that the punishment is invariably disproportionate to the crime. It is an extreme sanction, suitable to the most extreme of crimes.

We hold that the death penalty is not a form of punishment that may never be imposed, regardless of the circumstances of the offense, regardless of the character of the offender, and regardless of the procedure followed in reaching the decision to impose it.

We now consider whether Georgia may impose the death penalty on the petitioner in this case.

While *Furman* did not hold that the infliction of the death penalty *per se* violates the Constitution's ban on cruel and unusual punishments, it did recognize that the penalty of death is different in kind from any other punishment imposed under our system of criminal justice. Because of the uniqueness of the death penalty, *Furman* held that it could not be imposed under sentencing procedures that created a substantial risk that it would be inflicted in an arbitrary and capricious manner * * *.

Furman mandates that where discretion is afforded a sentencing body on a matter so grave as the determination of whether a human life should be taken or spared, that discretion must be suitably directed and limited so as to minimize the risk of wholly arbitrary and capricious action.

* * *

Jury sentencing has been considered desirable in capital cases in order "to maintain a link between contemporary community values and the penal system—a link without which the determination of punishment could hardly reflect 'the evolving standards of decency that mark the progress of a maturing society.'" But it creates special problems. Much of the information that is relevant to the sentencing decision may have no relevance to the question of guilt, or may even be extremely prejudicial to a fair determination of that question. This problem, however, is scarcely insurmountable. Those who have studied the question suggest that a bifurcated procedure—one in which the question of sentence is not considered until the determination of guilt has been made—is the best answer * * *.

But the provision of relevant information under fair procedural rules is not alone sufficient to guarantee that the information will be properly used in the imposition of punishment, especially if sentencing is performed by a jury. Since the members of a jury will have had little, if any, previous experience in sentencing, they are unlikely to be skilled in dealing with the information they are given. To the extent that this problem is inherent in jury sentencing, it may not be totally correctible. It seems clear, however, that the problem will be alleviated if the jury is given guidance regarding the factors about the crime and the defendant that the State, representing organized society, deems particularly relevant to the sentencing decision.

* * *

In summary, the concerns expressed in *Furman* that the penalty of death not be imposed in an arbitrary or capricious manner can be met by a carefully drafted statute that ensures that the sentencing authority is given adequate information and guidance. As a general proposition these concerns are best met by a system that provides for a bifurcated proceeding at which the sentencing authority is apprised of the information relevant to the imposition of sentence and provided with standards to guide its use of the information.

* * *

* * * Georgia's new sentencing procedures require as a prerequisite to the imposition of the death penalty, specific jury findings as to the circumstances of the crime or the character of the defendant. Moreover, to guard further against a situation comparable to that presented in *Furman,* the Supreme Court of Georgia compares each death sentence with the sentences imposed on similarly situated defendants to ensure that the sentence of death in a particular case is not disproportionate. On their face these procedures seem to satisfy the concerns of *Furman.* No longer should there be "no meaningful basis for distinguishing the few cases in which [the death penalty] is imposed from the many cases in which it is not." 408 U.S. at 313 (WHITE, J., concurring).

The petitioner contends, however, that the changes in the Georgia sentencing procedures are only cosmetic, that the arbitrariness and capriciousness condemned by *Furman* continue to exist in Georgia—both in traditional practices that still remain and in the new sentencing procedures adopted in response to *Furman.*

First, the petitioner focuses on the opportunities for discretionary action that are inherent in the processing of any murder case under Georgia law. He notes that the state prosecutor has unfettered authority to select those persons whom he wishes to prosecute for a capital offense and to plea bargain with them. Further, at the trial, the jury may choose to convict a defendant of a lesser included offense rather than find him guilty of a crime punishable by death, even if the evidence would support a capital verdict. And finally, a defendant who is convicted and sentenced to die may have his sentence commuted by the Governor of the State and the Georgia Board of Pardons and Paroles.

The existence of these discretionary stages is not determinative of the issues before us. At each of these stages an actor in the criminal justice system makes a decision which may remove a defendant from consideration as a candidate for the death penalty. *Furman,* in contrast, dealt with the decision to impose the death sentence on a specific individual who had been convicted of a capital offense. Nothing in any of our cases suggests that the decision to afford an individual defendant mercy violates the Constitution. *Furman* held only that, in order to minimize the risk that the death penalty would be imposed on a capriciously selected group of offenders, the decision to impose it had to be guided by standards so that the sentencing authority would focus on the particularized circumstances of the crime and the defendant.

* * *

Finally, the Georgia statute has an additional provision designed to assure that the death penalty will not be imposed on a capriciously selected group of convicted defendants. The new sentencing procedures require that the State Supreme Court review every death sentence to determine whether it was imposed under the influence of passion, prejudice, or any other arbitrary factor, whether the evidence supports the findings of a statutory aggravating circumstance, and "[w]hether the sentence of death is excessive or disproportionate to the penalty imposed in similar cases, considering both the crime and the defendant." * * *.

It is apparent that the Supreme Court of Georgia has taken its review responsibilities seriously * * *.

The provision for appellate review in the Georgia capital-sentencing system serves as a check against the random or arbitrary imposition of the death penalty. In particular, the proportionality review substantially eliminates the possibility that a person will be sentenced to die by the action of an aberrant jury. If a time comes when juries generally do not impose the death sentence in a certain kind of murder case, the appellate review procedures assure that no defendant convicted under such circumstances will suffer a sentence of death.

The basic concern of *Furman* centered on those defendants who were being condemned to death capriciously and arbitrarily. Under the procedures before the Court in that case, sentencing authorities were not directed to give attention to the nature or circumstances of the crime committed or to the character or record of the defendant. Left unguided, juries imposed the death sentence in a way that could only be called freakish. The new Georgia sentencing procedures, by contrast, focus the jury's attention on the particularized nature of the crime and the particularized characteristics of the individual defendant. While the jury is permitted to consider any aggravating or mitigating circumstances, it must find and identify at least one statutory aggravating factor before it may impose a penalty of death. In this way the jury's discretion is channeled. No longer can a jury wantonly and freakishly impose the death sentence; it is always circumscribed by the legislative guidelines. In addition, the review function of the Supreme Court of Georgia affords additional assurance that the concerns that prompted our decision in *Furman* are not present to any significant degree in the Georgia procedure applied here.

For the reasons expressed in this opinion, we hold that the statutory system under which Gregg was sentenced to death does not violate the Constitution. Accordingly, the judgment of the Georgia Supreme Court is affirmed.

It is so ordered.

■ MR. JUSTICE WHITE, with whom THE CHIEF JUSTICE and MR. JUSTICE REHNQUIST join, concurring in the judgment.

* * *

Petitioner's argument that there is an unconstitutional amount of discretion in the system which separates those suspects who receive the death penalty from those who receive life imprisonment, a lesser penalty, or are acquitted or never charged, seems to be in final analysis an indictment of our entire system of justice. Petitioner has argued, in effect, that no matter how effective the death penalty may be as a punishment, government, created and run as it must be by humans, is inevitably incompetent to administer it. This cannot be accepted as a proposition of constitutional law. Imposition of the death penalty is surely an awesome responsibility for any system of justice and those who participate in it. Mistakes will be made and discriminations will occur which will be difficult to explain. However, one of society's most basic tasks is that of protecting the lives of its citizens and one of the most basic ways in which it achieves the task is through criminal laws against murder. I decline to interfere with the manner in which Georgia has chosen to enforce such laws on what is simply an assertion of lack of faith in the ability of the system of justice to operate in a fundamentally fair manner.

* * *

■ MR. JUSTICE BLACKMUN, concurring in the judgment. [Omitted.]

■ MR. JUSTICE BRENNAN, dissenting.

* * *

In *Furman v. Georgia*, 408 U.S. 238, 257 (1972) (concurring opinion), I read "evolving standards of decency" as requiring focus upon the essence of the death penalty itself and not primarily or solely upon the procedures under which the determination to inflict the penalty upon a particular person was made. I there said:

> "From the beginning of our Nation, the punishment of death has stirred acute public controversy. Although pragmatic arguments for and against the punishment have been frequently advanced, this longstanding and heated controversy cannot be explained solely as the result of differences over the practical wisdom of a particular government policy. At bottom, the battle has been waged on moral grounds. The country has debated whether a society for which the dignity of the individual is the supreme value can, without a fundamental inconsistency, follow the practice of deliberately putting some of its members to death. In the United States, as in other nations of the western world, 'the struggle about this punishment has been one between ancient and deeply rooted beliefs in retribution, atonement or vengeance on the one hand, and, on the other, beliefs in the personal value and dignity of the common man that were born of the democratic movement of the eighteenth century, as well as beliefs in the scientific approach to an understanding of the motive forces of human conduct, which are the result of the growth of the sciences of behavior during the nineteenth and twentieth centuries.' It is this essentially moral conflict that forms the backdrop for the past changes in and the present operation of our system of imposing death as a punishment for crime." Id., at 296.

That continues to be my view. For the Clause forbidding cruel and unusual punishments under our constitutional system of government embodies in unique degree moral principles restraining the punishments at our civilized society may impose on those persons who transgress its laws * * *.

* * *

■ MR. JUSTICE MARSHALL, dissenting.

In *Furman v. Georgia*, 408 U.S. 238, 314 (1972) (concurring opinion), I set forth at some length my views on the basic issue presented to the Court in these cases. The death penalty, I concluded, is a cruel and unusual punishment prohibited by the Eighth and Fourteenth Amendments. That continues to be my view.

* * *

In *Furman* I concluded that the death penalty is constitutionally invalid for two reasons. First, the death penalty is excessive. And second, the American people, fully informed as to the purposes of the death penalty and its liabilities, would in my view reject it as morally unacceptable.

Since the decision in *Furman*, the legislatures of 35 States have enacted new statutes authorizing the imposition of the death sentence for certain crimes, and Congress has enacted a law providing the death penalty for air piracy resulting in death. I would be less than candid if I did not acknowledge that these developments have a significant bearing on a realistic assessment of the moral acceptability of the death penalty to the American people. But if the constitutionality of the death penalty turns, as I have urged, on the opinion of an *informed* citizenry, then even the enactment of new death statutes cannot be viewed as conclusive. In *Furman*, I observed that the American people are largely unaware of the information critical to a judgment on the morality of the death penalty, and concluded that if they were better informed they would consider it shocking, unjust, and unacceptable. A recent study, conducted after the enactment of the post-*Furman* statutes, has confirmed that the American people know little about the death penalty, and that the opinions of an informed public would differ significantly from those of a public unaware of the consequences and effects of the death penalty.

* * *

NOTES AND QUESTIONS

1. In the wake of *Furman*, more than thirty States adopted new death penalty laws that added procedural protections to protect against the arbitrary and capricious application of the death penalty. In *Gregg v. Georgia*, which you have just read, the Supreme Court held that the imposition of capital punishment, with these added procedural safeguards, is generally constitutional.

2. The Supreme Court has stuck by this decision down to the present day except for holding the death penalty unconstitutional as a punishment for rape, *Coker v. Georgia*, 433 U.S. 584 (1977); holding it unconstitutional to execute people with intellectual disabilities, *Atkins v. Virginia*, 536 U.S. 304 (2002); and holding it unconstitutional for those who committed murder under the age of 18, *Roper v. Simmons*, 543 U.S. 551 (2005). The latter case is especially interesting, as it raises some jurisprudential issues that go beyond the debate over the death penalty. That case is a fitting conclusion to this chapter.

B. ROPER V. SIMMONS

543 U.S. 551 (2005)

■ JUSTICE KENNEDY delivered the opinion of the Court.

This case requires us to address, for the second time in a decade and a half, whether it is permissible under the Eighth and Fourteenth Amendments to the Constitution of the United States to execute a juvenile offender who was older than 15 but younger than 18 when he committed a capital crime. In *Stanford v. Kentucky*, 492 U.S. 361 (1989), a divided Court rejected the proposition that the Constitution bars capital punishment for juvenile offenders in this age group. We reconsider the question.

I

At the age of 17, when he was still a junior in high school, Christopher Simmons, the respondent here, committed murder. About nine months later, after he had turned 18, he was tried and sentenced to death. There is little doubt that Simmons was the instigator of the crime. Before its commission Simmons said he wanted to murder someone. In chilling, callous terms he talked about his plan, discussing it for the most part with two friends, Charles Benjamin and John Tessmer, then aged 15 and 16 respectively. Simmons proposed to commit burglary and murder by breaking and entering, tying up a victim, and throwing the victim off a bridge. Simmons assured his friends they could "get away with it" because they were minors.

The three met at about 2 a.m. on the night of the murder, but Tessmer left before the other two set out. (The State later charged Tessmer with conspiracy, but dropped the charge in exchange for his testimony against Simmons.) Simmons and Benjamin entered the home of the victim, Shirley Crook, after reaching through an open window and unlocking the back door. Simmons turned on a hallway light. Awakened, Mrs. Crook called out, "Who's there?" In response Simmons entered Mrs. Crook's bedroom, where he recognized her from a previous car accident involving them both. Simmons later admitted this confirmed his resolve to murder her.

Using duct tape to cover her eyes and mouth and bind her hands, the two perpetrators put Mrs. Crook in her minivan and drove to a state park. They reinforced the bindings, covered her head with a towel, and walked her to a railroad trestle spanning the Meramec River. There they tied her hands and feet together with electrical wire, wrapped her whole face in duct tape and threw her from the bridge, drowning her in the waters below.

By the afternoon of September 9, Steven Crook had returned home from an overnight trip, found his bedroom in disarray, and reported his wife missing. On the same afternoon fishermen recovered the victim's body from the river. Simmons, meanwhile, was bragging about the killing, telling friends he had killed a woman "because the bitch seen my face."

The next day, after receiving information of Simmons' involvement, police arrested him at his high school and took him to the police station in Fenton, Missouri. They read him his *Miranda* rights. Simmons waived his right to an attorney and agreed to answer questions. After less than two hours of interrogation, Simmons confessed to the murder and agreed to perform a videotaped reenactment at the crime scene.

The State charged Simmons with burglary, kidnaping, stealing, and murder in the first degree. As Simmons was 17 at the time of the crime, he was outside the criminal jurisdiction of Missouri's juvenile court system. See Mo.Rev.Stat. §§ 211.021 (2000) and 211.031 (Supp.2003). He was tried as an adult. At trial the State introduced Simmons' confession and the videotaped reenactment of the crime, along with testimony that Simmons discussed the crime in advance and bragged about it later. The defense called no witnesses in the guilt phase. The jury having returned a verdict of murder, the trial proceeded to the penalty phase.

The State sought the death penalty. As aggravating factors, the State submitted that the murder was committed for the purpose of receiving money; was committed for the purpose of avoiding, interfering with, or preventing lawful arrest of the defendant; and involved depravity of mind and was outrageously and wantonly vile, horrible, and inhuman. The State called Shirley Crook's husband, daughter, and two sisters, who presented moving evidence of the devastation her death had brought to their lives.

In mitigation Simmons' attorneys first called an officer of the Missouri juvenile justice system, who testified that Simmons had no prior convictions and that no previous charges had been filed against him. Simmons' mother, father, two younger half brothers, a neighbor, and a friend took the stand to tell the jurors of the close relationships they had formed with Simmons and to plead for mercy on his behalf. Simmons' mother, in particular, testified to the responsibility Simmons demonstrated in taking care of his two younger half brothers and of his grandmother and to his capacity to show love for them.

During closing arguments, both the prosecutor and defense counsel addressed Simmons' age, which the trial judge had instructed the jurors they could consider as a mitigating factor. Defense counsel reminded the jurors that juveniles of Simmons' age cannot drink, serve on juries, or even see certain movies, because "the legislatures have wisely decided that individuals of a certain age aren't responsible enough." Defense counsel argued that Simmons' age should make "a huge difference to [the jurors] in deciding just exactly what sort of punishment to make." In rebuttal, the prosecutor gave the following response: "Age, he says. Think about age. Seventeen years old. Isn't that scary? Doesn't that scare you? Mitigating? Quite the contrary I submit. Quite the contrary."

The jury recommended the death penalty after finding the State had proved each of the three aggravating factors submitted to it. Accepting the jury's recommendation, the trial judge imposed the death penalty.

* * *

The trial court found no constitutional violation by reason of ineffective assistance of counsel and denied the motion for postconviction relief. In a consolidated appeal from Simmons' conviction and sentence, and from the denial of postconviction relief, the Missouri Supreme Court affirmed. The federal courts denied Simmons' petition for a writ of habeas corpus.

After these proceedings in Simmons' case had run their course, this Court held that the Eighth and Fourteenth Amendments prohibit the execution of a mentally retarded person. *Atkins v. Virginia*, 536 U.S. 304 (2002). Simmons filed a new petition for state postconviction relief, arguing that the reasoning of Atkins established that the Constitution prohibits the execution of a juvenile who was under 18 when the crime was committed.

The Missouri Supreme Court agreed. *State ex rel. Simmons v. Roper*, 112 S.W.3d 397 (2003) (en banc). It held that since *Stanford*,

> "a national consensus has developed against the execution of juvenile offenders, as demonstrated by the fact that eighteen states now bar such executions for juveniles, that twelve other states bar executions altogether, that no state has lowered its age of execution below 18 since *Stanford*, that five states have legislatively or by case law raised or established the minimum age at 18, and that the imposition of the juvenile death penalty has become truly unusual over the last decade." 112 S.W.3d, at 399.

On this reasoning it set aside Simmons' death sentence and resentenced him to "life imprisonment without eligibility for probation, parole, or release except by act of the Governor." *Id.*, at 413.

We granted certiorari, and now affirm.

II

The Eighth Amendment provides: "Excessive bail shall not be required, nor excessive fines imposed, nor cruel and unusual punishments inflicted." The provision is applicable to the States through the Fourteenth Amendment * * *.

The prohibition against "cruel and unusual punishments," like other expansive language in the Constitution, must be interpreted according to its text, by considering history, tradition, and precedent, and with due regard for its purpose and function in the constitutional design. To implement this framework we have established the propriety and affirmed the necessity of referring to "the evolving standards of decency that mark the progress of a maturing society" to determine which punishments are so disproportionate as to be cruel and unusual. *Trop v. Dulles*, 356 U.S. 86, 100–101 (1958) (plurality opinion).

In *Thompson v. Oklahoma*, 487 U.S. 815 (1988), a plurality of the Court determined that our standards of decency do not permit the execution of any offender under the age of 16 at the time of the crime * * *.

* * * With JUSTICE O'CONNOR concurring in the judgment on narrower grounds, the Court set aside the death sentence that had been imposed on the 15-year-old offender.

The next year, in *Stanford v. Kentucky*, 492 U.S. 361 (1989), the Court, over a dissenting opinion joined by four Justices, referred to contemporary standards of decency in this country and concluded the Eighth and Fourteenth Amendments did not proscribe the execution of juvenile offenders over 15 but under 18. The Court noted that 22 of the 37 death penalty States permitted the death penalty for 16-year-old offenders, and, among these 37 States, 25 permitted it for 17-year-old offenders. These numbers, in the Court's view, indicated there was no national consensus "sufficient to label a particular punishment cruel and unusual." *Id.*, at 370–371. A plurality of the Court also "emphatically reject[ed]" the suggestion that the Court should bring its own judgment to bear on the acceptability of the juvenile death penalty. *Id.*, at 377–378 (opinion of SCALIA, J., joined by REHNQUIST, C.J., and White and KENNEDY, JJ.).

The same day the Court decided *Stanford*, it held that the Eighth Amendment did not mandate a categorical exemption from the death penalty for the mentally retarded. *Penry v. Lynaugh*, 492 U.S. 302 (1989). In reaching this conclusion it stressed that only two States had enacted laws banning the imposition of the death penalty on a mentally retarded person convicted of a capital offense. According to the Court, "the two state statutes prohibiting execution of the mentally retarded, even when added to the 14 States that have rejected capital punishment completely, [did] not provide sufficient evidence at present of a national consensus." *Ibid.*

Three Terms ago the subject was reconsidered in *Atkins*. We held that standards of decency have evolved since *Penry* and now demonstrate that the execution of the mentally retarded is cruel and unusual punishment. The Court noted objective indicia of society's standards, as expressed in legislative enactments and state practice with respect to executions of the mentally retarded. When *Atkins* was decided only a minority of States permitted the practice, and even in those States it was rare. 536 U.S., at 314–315. On the basis of these indicia the Court determined that executing mentally retarded offenders "has become truly unusual, and it is fair to say that a national consensus has developed against it." *Id.*, at 316.

The inquiry into our society's evolving standards of decency did not end there. The *Atkins* Court neither repeated nor relied upon the statement in *Stanford* that the Court's independent judgment has no bearing on the acceptability of a particular punishment under the Eighth Amendment. Instead we returned to the rule, established in decisions predating *Stanford*, that " 'the Constitution contemplates that in the end our own judgment will be brought to bear on the question of the acceptability of the death penalty under the Eighth Amendment.' " 536 U.S., at 312 (quoting *Coker v. Georgia*, 433 U.S. 584, 597 (1977) (plurality opinion)). Mental retardation, the Court said, diminishes personal culpability even if the offender can distinguish right from wrong. The impairments of mentally retarded offenders make it less defensible to impose the death penalty as retribution for past crimes and less likely that the death penalty will have a real deterrent effect. Based on these considerations and on the finding of national consensus against executing the mentally retarded, the Court ruled that the death penalty constitutes an excessive sanction for the entire category of mentally retarded offenders, and that the Eighth Amendment " 'places a substantive restriction on the State's power to take the life' of a mentally retarded offender." *Id.*, at 321.

Just as the *Atkins* Court reconsidered the issue decided in *Penry*, we now reconsider the issue decided in *Stanford*. The beginning point is a review of objective indicia of consensus, as expressed in particular by the enactments of legislatures that have addressed the question. These data give us essential instruction. We then must determine, in the exercise of our own independent judgment, whether the death penalty is a disproportionate punishment for juveniles.

III

A

The evidence of national consensus against the death penalty for juveniles is similar, and in some respects parallel, to the evidence *Atkins* held sufficient to demonstrate a national consensus against the death penalty for the mentally retarded. When *Atkins* was decided, 30 States prohibited the death penalty for the mentally retarded. This number comprised 12 that had abandoned the death penalty altogether, and 18 that maintained it but excluded the mentally retarded from its reach. By a similar calculation in this case, 30 States prohibit the juvenile death penalty, comprising 12 that have rejected the death penalty altogether and 18 that maintain it but, by express provision or judicial interpretation, exclude juveniles from its reach. *Atkins* emphasized that even in the 20 States without formal prohibition, the practice of executing the mentally retarded was infrequent. Since *Penry*, only five States had executed offenders known to have an IQ under 70. In the present case, too, even in the 20 States without a formal prohibition on executing juveniles, the practice is infrequent. Since *Stanford*, six States have executed prisoners for crimes committed as juveniles. In the past 10 years, only three have done so: Oklahoma, Texas, and Virginia. In December 2003 the Governor of Kentucky decided to spare the life of Kevin Stanford, and commuted his sentence to one of life imprisonment without parole, with the declaration that " '[w]e ought not be executing people who, legally, were children.' " Lexington Herald Leader, Dec. 9, 2003, p. B3, 2003 WL 65043346. By this act the Governor ensured Kentucky would not add itself to the list of States that have executed juveniles within the last 10 years even by the execution of the very defendant whose death sentence the Court had upheld in *Stanford v. Kentucky*.

There is, to be sure, at least one difference between the evidence of consensus in *Atkins* and in this case. Impressive in *Atkins* was the rate of abolition of the death penalty for the mentally retarded. Sixteen States that permitted the execution of the mentally retarded at the time of *Penry* had prohibited the practice by the time we heard *Atkins*. By contrast, the rate of change in reducing the incidence of the juvenile death penalty, or in taking specific steps to abolish it, has been slower. Five States that allowed the juvenile death penalty at the time of *Stanford* have abandoned it in the intervening 15 years—four through legislative enactments and one through judicial decision.

Though less dramatic than the change from *Penry* to *Atkins* ("telling," to borrow the word *Atkins* used to describe this difference), we still consider the change from *Stanford* to this case to be significant. As noted in *Atkins*, with respect to the States that had abandoned the death penalty for the mentally retarded since *Penry*, "[i]t is not so much the number of these States that is significant, but the consistency of the direction of change." 536 U.S., at 315. In particular we found it significant that, in the wake of *Penry*, no State that had already prohibited the execution of the mentally retarded had passed legislation to reinstate the penalty. The number of States that have abandoned capital punishment for juvenile offenders since *Stanford* is smaller than the number of States that abandoned capital punishment for the mentally retarded after *Penry*; yet we think the same consistency of direction of change has been demonstrated. Since *Stanford*, no State that previously prohibited capital punishment for juveniles has reinstated it * * *.

The slower pace of abolition of the juvenile death penalty over the past 15 years, moreover, may have a simple explanation. When we heard *Penry*, only two death penalty States had already prohibited the execution of the mentally retarded. When we heard *Stanford*, by contrast, 12 death penalty States had already prohibited the execution of any juvenile under 18, and 15 had prohibited the execution of any juvenile under 17. If anything, this shows that the impropriety of executing juveniles between 16 and 18 years of age gained wide recognition earlier than the impropriety of executing the mentally retarded * * *.

* * *

As in *Atkins*, the objective indicia of consensus in this case—the rejection of the juvenile death penalty in the majority of States; the infrequency of its use even where it remains on the books; and the consistency in the trend toward abolition of the practice—provide sufficient evidence that today our society views juveniles, in the words *Atkins* used respecting the mentally retarded, as "categorically less culpable than the average criminal." 536 U.S., at 316.

B

A majority of States have rejected the imposition of the death penalty on juvenile offenders under 18, and we now hold this is required by the Eighth Amendment.

Because the death penalty is the most severe punishment, the Eighth Amendment applies to it with special force. Capital punishment must be limited to those offenders who commit "a narrow category of the most serious crimes" and whose extreme culpability makes them "the most deserving of execution." * * *

Three general differences between juveniles under 18 and adults demonstrate that juvenile offenders cannot with reliability be classified among the worst offenders. First, as any parent knows and as the scientific and sociological studies respondent and his *amici* cite tend to confirm, "[a] lack of maturity and an underdeveloped sense of responsibility are found in youth more often than in adults and are more understandable among the young. These qualities often result in impetuous and ill-considered actions and decisions." *Johnson, supra*, at 367 * * *. In recognition of the comparative immaturity and irresponsibility of juveniles, almost every State prohibits those under 18 years of age from voting, serving on juries, or marrying without parental consent.

The second area of difference is that juveniles are more vulnerable or susceptible to negative influences and outside pressures, including peer pressure * * *.

The third broad difference is that the character of a juvenile is not as well formed as that of an adult. The personality traits of juveniles are more transitory, less fixed.

These differences render suspect any conclusion that a juvenile falls among the worst offenders. The susceptibility of juveniles to immature and irresponsible behavior means "their irresponsible conduct is not as morally reprehensible as that of an adult." *Thompson, supra*, at 835 (plurality opinion) * * *.

In *Thompson,* a plurality of the Court recognized the import of these characteristics with respect to juveniles under 16, and relied on them to hold that the Eighth Amendment prohibited the imposition of the death penalty on juveniles below that age. We conclude the same reasoning applies to all juvenile offenders under 18.

Once the diminished culpability of juveniles is recognized, it is evident that the penological justifications for the death penalty apply to them with lesser force than to adults. We have held there are two distinct social purposes served by the death penalty: " 'retribution and deterrence of capital crimes by prospective offenders.' " As for retribution, we remarked in *Atkins* that "[i]f the culpability of the average murderer is insufficient to justify the most extreme sanction available to the State, the lesser culpability of the mentally retarded offender surely does not merit that form of retribution." 536 U.S., at 319. The same conclusions follow from the lesser culpability of the juvenile offender. Whether viewed as an attempt to express the community's moral outrage or as an attempt to right the balance for the wrong to the victim, the case for retribution is not as strong with a minor as with an adult. Retribution is not proportional if the law's most severe penalty is imposed on one whose culpability or blameworthiness is diminished, to a substantial degree, by reason of youth and immaturity.

As for deterrence, it is unclear whether the death penalty has a significant or even measurable deterrent effect on juveniles, as counsel for petitioner acknowledged at oral argument. Tr. of Oral Arg. 48. In general we leave to legislatures the assessment of the efficacy of various criminal penalty schemes. Here, however, the absence of evidence of deterrent effect is of special concern because the same characteristics that render juveniles less culpable than adults suggest as well that juveniles will be less susceptible to deterrence * * *.

In concluding that neither retribution nor deterrence provides adequate justification for imposing the death penalty on juvenile offenders, we cannot deny or overlook the brutal crimes too many juvenile offenders have committed. Certainly it can be argued, although we by no means concede the point, that a rare case might arise in which a juvenile offender has sufficient psychological maturity, and at the same time demonstrates sufficient depravity, to merit a sentence of death. Indeed, this possibility is the linchpin of one contention pressed by petitioner and his *amici*. They assert that even assuming the truth of the observations we have made about juveniles' diminished culpability in general, jurors nonetheless should be allowed to consider mitigating arguments related to youth on a case-by-case basis, and in some cases to impose the death penalty if justified. A central feature of death penalty sentencing is a particular assessment of the circumstances of the crime and the characteristics of the offender. The system is designed to consider both aggravating and mitigating circumstances, including youth, in every case. Given this Court's own insistence on individualized consideration, petitioner maintains that it is both arbitrary and unnecessary to adopt a categorical rule barring imposition of the death penalty on any offender under 18 years of age.

We disagree. The differences between juvenile and adult offenders are too marked and well understood to risk allowing a youthful person to receive the death penalty despite insufficient culpability. An unacceptable likelihood exists that the brutality or cold-blooded nature of any particular crime would overpower mitigating arguments based on youth as a matter of course, even where the juvenile offender's objective immaturity, vulnerability, and lack of true depravity should require a sentence less severe than death. In some cases a defendant's youth may even be counted against him. In this very case, as we noted above, the prosecutor argued Simmons' youth was aggravating rather than mitigating. While this sort of overreaching could be corrected by a particular rule to ensure that the mitigating force of youth is not overlooked, that would not address our larger concerns.

It is difficult even for expert psychologists to differentiate between the juvenile offender whose crime reflects unfortunate yet transient immaturity, and the rare juvenile offender whose crime reflects irreparable corruption * * *. If trained psychiatrists with the advantage of clinical testing and observation refrain, despite diagnostic expertise, from assessing any juvenile under 18 as having antisocial personality disorder, we conclude that States should refrain from asking jurors to issue a far graver condemnation—that a juvenile offender merits the death penalty.

When a juvenile offender commits a heinous crime, the State can exact forfeiture of some of the most basic liberties, but the State cannot extinguish his life and his potential to attain a mature understanding of his own humanity.

Drawing the line at 18 years of age is subject, of course, to the objections always raised against categorical rules. The qualities that distinguish juveniles from adults do not disappear when an individual turns 18. By the same token, some under 18 have already attained a level of maturity some adults will never reach. For the reasons we have discussed, however, a line must be drawn * * *. The age of 18 is the point where society draws the line for many purposes between childhood and adulthood. It is, we conclude, the age at which the line for death eligibility ought to rest.

These considerations mean *Stanford v. Kentucky* should be deemed no longer controlling on this issue * * *.

* * *

IV

Our determination that the death penalty is disproportionate punishment for offenders under 18 finds confirmation in the stark reality that the United States is the only country in the world that continues to give official sanction to the juvenile death penalty. This reality does not become controlling, for the task of interpreting the Eighth Amendment remains our responsibility. Yet at least from the time of the Court's decision in *Trop*, the Court has referred to the laws of other countries and to international authorities as instructive for its interpretation of the Eighth Amendment's prohibition of "cruel and unusual punishments." 356 U.S., at 102–103 (plurality opinion) ("The civilized nations of the world are in virtual unanimity that statelessness is not to be imposed as punishment for crime").

As respondent and a number of *amici* emphasize, Article 37 of the United Nations Convention on the Rights of the Child, which every country in the world has ratified save for the United States and Somalia, contains an express prohibition on capital punishment for crimes committed by juveniles under 18. United Nations Convention on the Rights of the Child, Art. 37, Nov. 20, 1989, 1577 U.N.T.S. 3, 28 I.L.M. 1448, 1468–1470 (entered into force Sept. 2, 1990). No ratifying country has entered a reservation to the provision prohibiting the execution of juvenile offenders. Parallel prohibitions are contained in other significant international covenants. See ICCPR, Art. 6(5), 999 U.N.T.S., at 175 (prohibiting capital punishment for anyone under 18 at the time of offense) (signed and ratified by the United States subject to a reservation regarding Article 6(5), as noted, supra, at 1194); American Convention on Human Rights: Pact of San Jose, Costa Rica, Art. 4(5), Nov. 22, 1969, 1144 U.N.T.S. 146 (entered into force July 19, 1978) (same); African Charter on the Rights and Welfare of the Child, Art. 5(3), OAU Doc. CAB/LEG/ 24.9/49 (1990) (entered into force Nov. 29, 1999) (same).

Respondent and his *amici* have submitted, and petitioner does not contest, that only seven countries other than the United States have executed juvenile offenders since 1990: Iran, Pakistan, Saudi Arabia, Yemen, Nigeria, the Democratic Republic of Congo, and China. Since then each of these countries has either abolished capital punishment for juveniles or made public disavowal of the practice. Brief for Respondent 49–50. In sum, it is fair to say that the United States now stands alone in a world that has turned its face against the juvenile death penalty.

Though the international covenants prohibiting the juvenile death penalty are of more recent date, it is instructive to note that the United Kingdom abolished the juvenile death penalty before these covenants came into being * * *.

It is proper that we acknowledge the overwhelming weight of international opinion against the juvenile death penalty, resting in large part on the understanding that the instability and emotional imbalance of young people may often be a factor in the crime. The opinion of the world community, while not controlling our outcome, does provide respected and significant confirmation for our own conclusions.

Over time, from one generation to the next, the Constitution has come to earn the high respect and even, as Madison dared to hope, the veneration of the American people. See The Federalist No. 49, p. 314 (C. Rossiter ed.1961). The document sets forth, and rests upon, innovative principles original to the American experience, such as federalism; a proven balance in political mechanisms through separation of powers; specific guarantees for the accused in criminal cases; and broad provisions to secure individual freedom and preserve human dignity. These doctrines and guarantees are central to the American experience and remain essential to our present-day self-definition and national identity. Not the least of the reasons we honor the Constitution, then, is because we know it to be our own. It does not lessen our fidelity to the Constitution or our pride in its origins to acknowledge that the express affirmation of certain fundamental rights by other nations and peoples simply underscores the centrality of those same rights within our own heritage of freedom.

The Eighth and Fourteenth Amendments forbid imposition of the death penalty on offenders who were under the age of 18 when their crimes were committed. The judgment of the Missouri Supreme Court setting aside the sentence of death imposed upon Christopher Simmons is affirmed.

It is so ordered.

■ JUSTICE STEVENS, with whom JUSTICE GINSBURG joins, concurring.

Perhaps even more important than our specific holding today is our reaffirmation of the basic principle that informs the Court's interpretation of the Eighth Amendment. If the meaning of that Amendment had been frozen when it was originally drafted, it would impose no impediment to the execution of 7-year-old children today. See *Stanford v. Kentucky*, 492 U.S. 361, 368 (1989) (describing the common law at the time of the Amendment's adoption). The evolving standards of decency that have driven our construction of this critically important part of the Bill of Rights foreclose any such reading of the Amendment. In the best tradition of the common law, the pace of that evolution is a matter for continuing debate; but that our understanding of the Constitution does change from time to time has been settled since John Marshall breathed life into its text. If great lawyers of his day—Alexander Hamilton, for example—were sitting with us today, I would expect them to join JUSTICE KENNEDY's opinion for the Court. In all events, I do so without hesitation.

■ JUSTICE O'CONNOR, dissenting.

The Court's decision today establishes a categorical rule forbidding the execution of any offender for any crime committed before his 18th birthday, no matter how deliberate, wanton, or cruel the offense. Neither the objective evidence of contemporary societal values, nor the Court's moral proportionality analysis, nor the two in tandem suffice to justify this ruling.

* * *

* * * [T]he rule decreed by the Court rests, ultimately, on its independent moral judgment that death is a disproportionately severe punishment for any 17-year-old offender. I do not subscribe to this judgment. Adolescents *as a class* are undoubtedly less mature, and therefore less culpable for their misconduct, than adults. But the Court has adduced no evidence impeaching the seemingly reasonable conclusion reached by many state legislatures: that at least *some* 17-year-old murderers are sufficiently mature to deserve the death penalty in an appropriate case. Nor has it been shown that capital sentencing juries are incapable of accurately assessing a youthful defendant's maturity or of giving due weight to the mitigating characteristics associated with youth.

On this record—and especially in light of the fact that so little has changed since our recent decision in *Stanford*—I would not substitute our judgment about the moral propriety of capital punishment for 17-year-old murderers for the judgments of the Nation's legislatures. Rather, I would demand a clearer showing that our society truly has set its face against this practice before reading the Eighth Amendment categorically to forbid it.

* * *

* * * [T]he Court adduces no evidence whatsoever in support of its sweeping conclusion that it is only in "rare" cases, if ever, that 17-year-old murderers are sufficiently mature and act with sufficient depravity to warrant the death penalty. The fact that juveniles are generally *less* culpable for their misconduct than adults does not necessarily mean that a 17-year-old murderer cannot be *sufficiently* culpable to merit the death penalty. At most, the Court's argument suggests that the average 17-year-old murderer is not as culpable as the average adult murderer. But an especially depraved juvenile offender may nevertheless be just as culpable as many adult offenders considered bad enough to deserve the death penalty. Similarly, the fact that the availability of the death penalty may be *less* likely to deter a juvenile from committing a capital crime does not imply that this threat cannot *effectively* deter some 17-year-olds from such an act. Surely there is an age below which no offender, no matter what his crime, can be deemed to have the cognitive or emotional maturity necessary to warrant the death penalty. But at least at the margins between adolescence and adulthood—and especially for 17-year-olds such as respondent—the relevant differences between "adults" and "juveniles" appear to be a matter of degree, rather than of kind. It follows that a legislature may reasonably conclude that at least *some* 17-year-olds can act with sufficient moral culpability, and can be sufficiently deterred by the threat of execution, that capital punishment may be warranted in an appropriate case.

Indeed, this appears to be just such a case * * *.

* * *

■ JUSTICE SCALIA, with whom THE CHIEF JUSTICE and JUSTICE THOMAS join, dissenting.

In urging approval of a constitution that gave life-tenured judges the power to nullify laws enacted by the people's representatives, Alexander Hamilton assured the citizens of New York that there was little risk in this, since "[t]he judiciary . . . ha[s] neither FORCE nor WILL but merely judgment." The Federalist No. 78, p. 465 (C. Rossiter ed.1961). But Hamilton had in mind a traditional judiciary, "bound down by strict rules and precedents which serve to define and point out their duty in every particular case that comes before them." *Id.*, at 471. Bound down, indeed. What a mockery today's opinion makes of Hamilton's expectation, announcing the Court's conclusion that the meaning of our Constitution has changed over the past 15 years—not, mind you, that this Court's decision 15 years ago was *wrong*, but that the Constitution *has changed.* The Court reaches this implausible result by purporting to advert, not to the original meaning of the Eighth Amendment, but to "the evolving standards of decency" of our national society. It then finds, on the flimsiest of grounds, that a national consensus which could not be perceived in our people's laws barely 15 years ago now solidly exists. Worse still, the Court says in so many words that what our people's laws say about the issue does not, in the last analysis, matter: "[I]n the end our own judgment will be brought to bear on the question of the acceptability of the death penalty under the Eighth Amendment." The Court thus proclaims itself sole arbiter of our Nation's moral standards—and in the course of discharging that awesome responsibility purports to take guidance from the views of foreign courts and legislatures. Because I do not believe that the meaning of our Eighth Amendment, any more than the meaning of other provisions of our Constitution, should be determined by the subjective views of five Members of this Court and like-minded foreigners, I dissent.

I

In determining that capital punishment of offenders who committed murder before age 18 is "cruel and unusual" under the Eighth Amendment, the Court first considers, in accordance with our modern (though in my view mistaken) jurisprudence, whether there is a "national consensus" that laws allowing such executions contravene our modern "standards of decency," *Trop v. Dulles*, 356 U.S. 86, 101 (1958) * * *. As in *Atkins v. Virginia*, 536 U.S. 304, 312 (2002), the Court dutifully recites this test and claims halfheartedly that a national consensus has emerged since our decision in *Stanford*, because 18 States—or 47% of States that permit capital punishment—now have legislation prohibiting the execution of offenders under 18, and because all of 4 States have adopted such legislation since Stanford.

Words have no meaning if the views of less than 50% of death penalty States can constitute a national consensus * * *.

* * *

In an attempt to keep afloat its implausible assertion of national consensus, the Court throws overboard a proposition well established in our Eighth Amendment jurisprudence. "It should be observed," the Court says, "that the *Stanford* Court should have considered those States that had abandoned the death penalty altogether as part of the consensus against the juvenile death penalty . . .; a State's decision to bar the death penalty altogether of necessity demonstrates a judgment that the death penalty is inappropriate for all offenders, including juveniles." * * * Consulting States that bar the death penalty concerning the necessity of making an exception to the penalty for offenders under 18 is rather like including old-order

Amishmen in a consumer-preference poll on the electric car. Of *course* they don't like it, but that sheds no light whatever on the point at issue * * *.

* * * [T]he Court says a legislative change in four States is "significant" enough to trigger a constitutional prohibition. It is amazing to think that this subtle shift in numbers can take the issue entirely off the table for legislative debate.

I also doubt whether many of the legislators who voted to change the laws in those four States would have done so if they had known their decision would (by the pronouncement of this Court) be rendered irreversible. After all, legislative support for capital punishment, in any form, has surged and ebbed throughout our Nation's history * * *.

* * *

Of course, the real force driving today's decision is not the actions of four state legislatures, but the Court's " ' "own judgment" ' " that murderers younger than 18 can never be as morally culpable as older counterparts. The Court claims that this usurpation of the role of moral arbiter is simply a "retur[n] to the rul[e] established in decisions predating *Stanford*." That supposed rule—which is reflected solely in dicta and never once in a *holding* that purports to supplant the consensus of the American people with the Justices' views—was repudiated in *Stanford* for the very good reason that it has no foundation in law or logic. If the Eighth Amendment set forth an ordinary rule of law, it would indeed be the role of this Court to say what the law is. But the Court having pronounced that the Eighth Amendment is an ever-changing reflection of "the evolving standards of decency" of our society, it makes no sense for the Justices then to *prescribe* those standards rather than discern them from the practices of our people. On the evolving-standards hypothesis, the only legitimate function of this Court is to identify a moral consensus of the American people. By what conceivable warrant can nine lawyers presume to be the authoritative conscience of the Nation?

* * *

Today's opinion provides a perfect example of why judges are ill equipped to make the type of legislative judgments the Court insists on making here. To support its opinion that States should be prohibited from imposing the death penalty on anyone who committed murder before age 18, the Court looks to scientific and sociological studies, picking and choosing those that support its position. It never explains why those particular studies are methodologically sound; none was ever entered into evidence or tested in an adversarial proceeding * * *.

We need not look far to find studies contradicting the Court's conclusions * * *.

* * *

That "almost every State prohibits those under 18 years of age from voting, serving on juries, or marrying without parental consent" is patently irrelevant * * *. As we explained in *Stanford*, 492 U.S., at 374, it is "absurd to think that one must be mature enough to drive carefully, to drink responsibly, or to vote intelligently, in order to be mature enough to understand that murdering another human being is profoundly wrong, and to conform one's conduct to that most minimal of all civilized standards." Serving on a jury or entering into marriage also involve decisions far more sophisticated than the simple decision not to take another's life.

* * *

III

Though the views of our own citizens are essentially irrelevant to the Court's decision today, the views of other countries and the so-called international community take center stage.

* * *

It is interesting that whereas the Court is not content to accept what the States of our Federal Union *say*, but insists on inquiring into what they *do* (specifically, whether they in fact *apply* the juvenile death penalty that their laws allow), the Court is quite willing to believe that every foreign nation—of whatever tyrannical political makeup and with however subservient or incompetent a court system—in fact *adheres* to a rule of no death penalty for offenders under 18. Nor does the Court inquire into how many of the countries that have the death penalty, but have forsworn (on paper at least) imposing that penalty on offenders under 18, have what no State of this country can constitutionally have: a *mandatory* death penalty for certain crimes, with no possibility of mitigation by the sentencing authority, for youth or any other reason. I suspect it is most of them. See, e.g., R. Simon & D. Blaskovich, A Comparative Analysis of Capital Punishment: Statutes, Policies, Frequencies, and Public Attitudes the World Over 25, 26, 29 (2002). To forbid the death penalty for juveniles under such a system may be a good idea, but it says nothing about our system, in which the sentencing authority, typically a jury, always can, and almost always does, withhold the death penalty from an under-18 offender except, after considering all the circumstances, in the rare cases where it is warranted. The foreign authorities, in other words, do not even speak to the issue before us here.

More fundamentally, however, the basic premise of the Court's argument—that American law should conform to the laws of the rest of the world—ought to be rejected out of hand. In fact the Court itself does not believe it. In many significant respects the laws of most other countries differ from our law—including not only such explicit provisions of our Constitution as the right to jury trial and grand jury indictment, but even many interpretations of the Constitution prescribed by this Court itself. The Court-pronounced exclusionary rule, for example, is distinctively American. When we adopted that rule in *Mapp v. Ohio*, 367 U.S. 643, 655 (1961), it was "unique to American jurisprudence." Since then a categorical exclusionary rule has been "universally rejected" by other countries, including those with rules prohibiting illegal searches and police misconduct, despite the fact that none of these countries "appears to have any alternative form of discipline for police that is effective in preventing search violations." England, for example, rarely excludes evidence found during an illegal search or seizure and has only recently begun excluding evidence from illegally obtained confessions. Canada rarely excludes evidence and will only do so if admission will "bring the administration of justice into disrepute." The European Court of Human Rights has held that introduction of illegally seized evidence does not violate the "fair trial" requirement in Article 6, § 1, of the European Convention on Human Rights.

The Court has been oblivious to the views of other countries when deciding how to interpret our Constitution's requirement that "Congress shall make no law respecting an establishment of religion. . . ." Amdt. 1. Most other countries—

including those committed to religious neutrality—do not insist on the degree of separation between church and state that this Court requires * * *.

And let us not forget the Court's abortion jurisprudence, which makes us one of only six countries that allow abortion on demand until the point of viability. Though the Government and *amici* in cases following *Roe v. Wade*, 410 U.S. 113 (1973), urged the Court to follow the international community's lead, these arguments fell on deaf ears.

* * *

The Court should either profess its willingness to reconsider all these matters in light of the views of foreigners, or else it should cease putting forth foreigners' views as part of the reasoned basis of its decisions. To invoke alien law when it agrees with one's own thinking, and ignore it otherwise, is not reasoned decisionmaking, but sophistry.

The Court responds that "[i]t does not lessen our fidelity to the Constitution or our pride in its origins to acknowledge that the express affirmation of certain fundamental rights by other nations and peoples simply underscores the centrality of those same rights within our own heritage of freedom." To begin with, I do not believe that approval by "other nations and peoples" should buttress our commitment to American principles any more than (what should logically follow) disapproval by "other nations and peoples" should weaken that commitment. More importantly, however, the Court's statement flatly misdescribes what is going on here. Foreign sources are cited today, not to underscore our "fidelity" to the Constitution, our "pride in its origins," and "our own [American] heritage." To the contrary, they are cited to set aside the centuries-old American practice—a practice still engaged in by a large majority of the relevant States—of letting a jury of 12 citizens decide whether, in the particular case, youth should be the basis for withholding the death penalty. What these foreign sources "affirm," rather than repudiate, is the Justices' own notion of how the world ought to be, and their diktat that it shall be so henceforth in America. The Court's parting attempt to downplay the significance of its extensive discussion of foreign law is unconvincing. "Acknowledgment" of foreign approval has no place in the legal opinion of this Court unless it is part of the basis for the Court's judgment—which is surely what it parades as today.

* * *

CHAPTER 6

THE PROGRESSIVE ERA AMENDMENTS

[Assignment 81]

The Progressive Era ran from roughly the 1880s through the start of the New Deal in the 1930s. During that time, six constitutional amendments were ratified—all in the last two decades of that period between 1913 and 1933. One of those amendments was a technical but important tweak to Congress and the presidency, and one was a repeal of a prior Progressive Era amendment, but the other four were transformative. Just as the three Reconstruction Amendments fundamentally altered the U.S. Constitution, so too did those four Progressive Era Amendments fundamentally alter the U.S. Constitution as well: 1) the Sixteenth Amendment authorizing the progressive, unapportioned income tax; 2) the Seventeenth Amendment providing for direct popular election of U.S. senators; 3) the Eighteenth Amendment prohibiting "the manufacturing, sale, or transportation of intoxicating liquors" within the United States; and 4) the Nineteenth Amendment assuring women the right to vote. Those four amendments were all ratified within an *eight-year span,* from 1913–1920. Taken together they produced a vast increase in the size and activities of the federal government the scope of which is difficult to convey adequately.

One major difference between the Progressive and the Reconstruction Amendments is that the former were presaged by substantial state approval prior to their being proposed by Congress to the States for ratification, while the Fourteenth and Fifteenth Amendments radically changed state practice and law once they were enacted. The Progressive Movement, with its advocacy for initiatives and referenda, especially in the Western States, was largely a populist movement, whereas the Fourteenth and Fifteenth Amendment were characterized by massive elite-driven changes imposed from the national level upon some more-then-recalcitrant States. Notwithstanding that the Progressive amendments continued on a path that had been building nationwide for decades beforehand, their articulation as supreme law led to massive social change.

That story is historical, political, and sociological more than it is strictly "legal," but the legal effects of these amendments cannot be understood apart from the social and political changes that they wrought (or at least accelerated). One well known discussion of this subject, from seven decades ago, comes from journalist/historian Frederick Lewis Allen. *See* FREDERICK LEWIS ALLEN, THE BIG CHANGE: AMERICA TRANSFORMS ITSELF: 1900–1950 (1952). Consider the "big change" noted by Allen over the first half of the twentieth century:

> It is hard for us, today, to realize how small the government was in 1900, and how limited in its functions and powers. It spent roughly half a billion dollars a year, about one-eightieth of what it was destined to spend half a century later (even before the Korean war stepped up the budget). In fact, the federal government in 1900 spent considerably less than New York

> State did in 1950. The national debt amounted to only a little over a billion and a quarter dollars—about one two hundredth of the 1950 debt of 257 billions. Even when one makes allowance for the diminished value of the dollar and for the way in which federal expenses have been swollen since 1900 by wars, and defense expenditures, those are incredibly small figures by today's standards.

Id. at 82. The comparison between 1900 and 2020 is even more shocking: In 1900, the federal government, spent half a billion dollars a year. In 2019, the federal government spent $3.422 trillion dollars. In 1900, the national debt was a little over $1.25 billion dollars. As of June 2019, the national debt was $16.17 trillion dollars (or substantially higher, depending on how you count it). Many factors drove this development, but there is no doubt that the Progressive Era amendments played a large role. The short version is: The Sixteenth Amendment gave the federal government a previously unavailable, and even previously unimaginable, revenue stream; the Seventeenth and Nineteenth Amendments fundamentally changed the representative character of government; and the Eighteenth Amendment required a federal administrative state more than a decade before the New Deal. Let us now look at these amendments and their impact.

I. THE FOUR TRANSFORMATIVE PROGRESSIVE ERA AMENDMENTS

A. THE SIXTEENTH AMENDMENT

> **The Congress shall have power to lay and collect taxes on incomes, from whatever source derived, without apportionment among the several States, and without regard to any census or enumeration.**

As we saw earlier, *see supra* pages 653–659, the Sixteenth Amendment formally overturned *Pollock v. Farmers' Loan & Trust Co.,* 158 U.S. 601 (1895). Given the momentum of the Progressive Era, an income tax was inevitable by 1913. Indeed, "[a]fter *Pollock* was decided many members of Congress wanted to go ahead and enact an income tax law anyway—not so much as a gesture of defiance but because they were convinced that the Court would not adhere to *Pollock*." DAVID A. STRAUSS, THE LIVING CONSTITUTION 137 (2010). To be safe, the Congress—with the endorsement of President Taft, who was the most conservative political figure on the scene—proposed the Sixteenth Amendment, and it was easily ratified.

The effects of the income tax were not felt immediately, but World War I gave the necessary push. By 1920, the income tax "was contributing ten times as much money [to the federal government] as the customs; and that was only the beginning of the rise of graduated income tax to a predominant place in the financing of a hugely expanded government, and to an important place among the instruments for the redistribution of wealth in America." ALLEN, *supra,* at 107. In 1900, the federal government had neither the power nor the inclination to engage in the redistribution of wealth. By 1937, it had both. The outflow side was handled by seminal Supreme Court opinions like *Steward Machine Co. v. Davis* 301 U.S. 548 (1937) (upholding the constitutionality of the unemployment compensation provisions of the Social Security Act) and *Helvering v. Davis*, 301 U.S. 619 (1937) (upholding the old age compensation features of the Social Security Act), which gave broad scope to the federal spending power. *See supra* pages 291, 669–670. The inflow came from the income tax, which was the only means by which the federal government could pay for its redistributionist program. Prior to the income tax, the federal government was funded largely by tariffs (or "customs"). There are limits to how much money you can raise with tariffs; at some point, people simply stop buying the taxed imported goods; and if other countries respond to tariffs with a trade war, the collateral effects on the domestic economy can be grim. Funding the federal government on tariff revenue strictly limited its scope. The Sixteenth Amendment did not single-handedly cause the federal government to grow, but it very substantially freed it to do so.

The federal government's expanded resources also allow it to control the States, as the federal government "returns" the money it acquires through the income tax to the States, to be spent on federally approved programs under federally prescribed conditions. *See supra* pages 678–684. The Sixteenth Amendment thus transformed the character of American federalism. Much of the constitutional law from the past century would not exist if not for the Sixteenth Amendment.

B. THE SEVENTEENTH AMENDMENT

The Senate of the United States shall be composed of two Senators from each state, elected by the people thereof, for six years; and each Senator shall have one vote. The electors in each state shall have the qualifications requisite for electors of the most numerous branch of the state legislatures.

When vacancies happen in the representation of any state in the Senate, the executive authority of such state shall issue writs of election to fill such vacancies: Provided, that the legislature of any state may empower the executive thereof to make temporary appointments until the people fill the vacancies by election as the legislature may direct.

This amendment shall not be so construed as to affect the election or term of any Senator chosen before it becomes valid as part of the Constitution.

In one sense, the Seventeenth Amendment is among the most momentous of all constitutional amendments. It changes a fundamental feature of the Constitution: After the Seventeenth Amendment, the Senate no longer represents the States directly, no more than does the House of Representatives. The States' control over the selection of senators was, along with the equal representation of States in the Senate, integral to the design of the Constitution of 1788. Introducing the direct election of senators is like introducing the designated hitter: It is still sort of the Constitution (or baseball), but not really.

In reality, however, the Seventeenth Amendment may not have been quite as momentous as it seems. Steps towards popular election of senators had started decades before the Seventeenth Amendment. The electorate became increasingly impatient with and unwilling to tolerate un-democratic forms of election. This process had already manifested itself with respect to state legislatures' power to choose the method for selecting presidential electors. By 1830, in every State, the legislature had given up its power directly to pick presidential electors in favor of the voters choosing the winner of each State's electoral votes in a majoritarian statewide election. Much the same process happened gradually as to Senate elections in the years leading up to 1913:

> The direct election of Senators [began] as early as the 1830's. Until that time, candidates for the U.S. Senate typically did not campaign in any significant way until their state legislature was elected * * *. Beginning in the 1830's, however, people who wanted to be elected to the Senate began appealing directly to the voters of the state to vote, in state legislative elections, for candidates who pledged to support them for the Senate.

STRAUSS, *supra,* at 133. An early harbinger of change was Illinois's 1858 senate election between Democratic incumbent Stephen Douglas and Republican challenger Abraham Lincoln. Lincoln was nominated by a State Republican Convention, and he challenged Douglas, who was nominated by the State Democratic election, to a series of famous statewide debates before the ordinary voters of Illinois, who were electing a state legislature that would then select a U.S. Senator. These debates were well attended, and they effectively de-localized the 1858 election of the Illinois state legislature, so that voters chose candidates pledged either to Douglas or Lincoln as senator. The end result was *de facto* state election by a majority of the voters statewide of a senatorial candidate. *See* AKHIL REED AMAR, AMERICA'S CONSTITUTION: A BIOGRAPHY 401–11 (2005). This process expanded in other States. Once party primaries selected candidates, the primary winners would effectively be chosen by primary voters, especially in one-party States. *See* STRAUSS, *supra,* at 133–34.

By the first decade of the twentieth century, twenty-eight of the forty-six States were holding Democratic and Republican primary elections in which the Democratic or the Republican candidate for the U.S. Senate was being picked directly by the voters. The state legislatures still picked the final winner, but state legislative discretion was greatly curtailed by these direct primary elections. In 1908, Oregon provided for a statewide majority vote to pick U.S. senators, and it " 'instructed" the state legislature to go with the people's choice. Thus, "[b]y early 1913, more than half the states had already committed themselves to a form of direct election—either the direct-primary approach in one-party states or some version of the Oregon Plan. Thus, when senators and state legislatures from these states supported the Direct Senate Election Amendment, they were voting to constitutionalize rules that were already largely in place or about to be in place." AMAR, *supra,* at 412.

C. THE EIGHTEENTH AMENDMENT

Section 1

After one year from the ratification of this article the manufacture, sale, or transportation of intoxicating liquors within, the importation thereof into, or the exportation thereof from the United States and all territory subject to the jurisdiction thereof for beverage purposes is hereby prohibited.

Section 2

The Congress and the several states shall have concurrent power to enforce this article by appropriate legislation.

Section 3

This article shall be inoperative unless it shall have been ratified as an amendment to the Constitution by the legislatures of the several states, as provided in the Constitution, within seven years from the date of the submission hereof to the states by the Congress.

One of the greatest and most uniquely American experiments with social moralism was the advent of nationwide Prohibition, accomplished by the adoption of the Eighteenth Amendment. The same moral groups and churches that had supported the abolition of slavery, the abolition of polygamy, and women's suffrage ironically also supported Prohibition. Prohibition was a great moral cause to end the power of the saloons and of sin itself. The saloons were especially vilified because, in many company towns, the company owned the saloon. Workers, when they got their paychecks, would go to the saloon and pay for a round of drinks, which they could not afford. Those workers would then go back to their families penniless. The saloon was thus seen as an immoral institution which especially hurt women and children. When Prohibition was accomplished, Billy Sunday preached to an audience of 10,000 and a national radio audience much larger that:

> "The reign of tears is over. The slums will soon be a memory. We will turn our prisons into factories and our jails into storehouses and corncribs. Men will walk upright now; women will smile and the children will laugh. Hell will be forever rent."

JAMES A. MORONE, HELLFIRE NATION: THE POLITICS OF SIN IN AMERICAN HISTORY 325 (2003). Instead, the homicide rate soared by 30 percent "to some of the highest levels in American history," *id.*, at 327—and, as we will see, federal governmental power exploded. Nonetheless, Prohibition was hardly a total failure by its own standards. "No other social movement lasted as long, promised as much, or stirred up so much trouble. Temperance organized modern feminism. It fired progressive imaginations and roused men and women to better themselves. Some historians even score Prohibition a success. Americans may have scrapped the program in 1933 (it took effect in January 1920), but by then Prohibition had shut down the noxious saloons, sobered up the working class, and slashed liquor consumption." *Id.* at 281.

By 1916, twenty-three States out of forty-eight had enacted some form of prohibition of alcohol. When the Eighteenth Amendment came up for a vote in Congress, it was approved by a vote of 65 to 20 in the Senate and 282 to 128 in the House of Representatives. Forty-six States ratified the amendment. Only Rhode Island and Connecticut were holdouts. Prohibition of alcohol was a popular mass movement, and as with the Sixteenth and Seventeenth Amendments, Congress in passing the Eighteenth Amendment was merely keeping up with the times.

The Eighteenth Amendment's prohibition on "the manufacture, sale, or transportation of intoxicating liquors" and the "importation thereof into, or the exportation thereof from the United States," however, marked a huge increase in the role of the federal government in policing criminal law matters, which had previously been almost wholly in the domain of the States. Prohibition led in 1930 to the creation of the Bureau of Alcohol, Tobacco, and Firearms (BATF) within the Department of Justice. BATF continues to exist in the Department of Justice (now as the Bureau of Alcohol, Tobacco, Firearms and Explosives) as a kind of federal police force, even though Prohibition ended in the 1930s. Prohibition of alcohol breathed life, funds, and a sense of mission into the Federal Bureau of Investigation, which grew enormously in power between 1924 and 1972 under the leadership of J. Edgar Hoover. The FBI was and is a part of the U.S. Department of Justice, and it is, along with the BATF, a type of federal police force. The FBI first used wiretapping to go after bootleggers during Prohibition, and its role grew in the face of events such as the St. Valentine's Day massacre, in which gangsters during Prohibition fought one another over control of the sale of illegal alcohol. For an account of how the Eighteenth Amendment spawned a significant increase in federal power over criminal and administrative law, and further changed the structure of American federalism, see Robert Post, *Federalism, Positive Law, and the Emergence of the American Administrative State: Prohibition in the Taft Court Era,* 48 WM. & MARY L. REV. 1 (2006).

> In sum, Prohibition pushed federal power into the nooks and crannies of American crime-fighting. The consequences included federal plea bargaining, a boom in prison construction, and voluminous legal precedents guiding searches, seizures, wiretaps, judicial process, and more. The dry effort integrated federal, state, and local law enforcement. And once again it drafted government into the nation's cultural conflicts. It constructed institutional and legal precedents for almost every aspect of the war on drugs (still fought in many ways by the same rules).

MORONE, *supra,* at 343.

D. THE NINETEENTH AMENDMENT

> **The right of citizens of the United States to vote shall not be denied or abridged by the United States or by any state on account of sex.**
>
> **Congress shall have power to enforce this article by appropriate legislation.**

The Nineteen Amendment was ratified in 1920, as the last of the four amendments that defined the Progressive Era. As with the income tax, direct election of senators, and Prohibition, the movement for women's suffrage gained substantial success at the State and Territorial level prior to the passage of the federal Nineteenth Amendment granting women the right to vote in all national and state elections. While seeking to amend the U.S. Constitution, the women's suffrage movement also waged a state-by-state campaign. *See supra* pages 1379–1380. By the time the Nineteenth Amendment was approved by the Congress, women could vote in all elections in fifteen States and in presidential elections in another twelve States. Here is a list of the States in which women could vote prior to the passage of the Nineteenth Amendment.

States granting women the right to vote prior to the Nineteenth Amendment:

1. Wyoming 1890
2. Colorado 1893
3. Utah 1896
4. Idaho 1896

5. Washington 1910
6. California 1911
7. Arizona 1912
8. Kansas 1912
9. Oregon 1912
10. Montana 1914
11. Nevada 1914
12. New York 1917
13. Michigan 1918
14. Oklahoma 1918
15. South Dakota 1918

Full Voting Rights before Nineteenth Amendment and before statehood:

1. Territory of Wyoming 1869
2. Territory of Utah 1870
3. Territory of Washington 1883
4. Territory of Montana 1887
5. Territory of Alaska 1913

Could vote for President prior to the Nineteenth Amendment:

1. Illinois 1913
2. Nebraska 1917
3. Ohio 1917
4. Indiana 1917
5. North Dakota 1917
6. Rhode Island 1917
7. Iowa 1919
8. Maine 1919
9. Minnesota 1919
10. Missouri 1919
11. Tennessee 1919
12. Wisconsin 1919

Gained Voting Rights after passage:

1. Vermont
2. New Hampshire
3. Massachusetts
4. Connecticut
5. Pennsylvania
6. New Jersey

7. Delaware
8. Maryland
9. West Virginia
10. Virginia
11. North Carolina
12. South Carolina
13. Georgia
14. Alabama
15. Florida
16. Mississippi
17. Louisiana
18. Arkansas
19. Texas
20. New Mexico
21. Kentucky

Professor Calabresi believes (over Professor Lawson's dubiety) that the Nineteenth Amendment worked a fundamental change in U.S. constitutional law beyond giving women the right to vote. When the Nineteenth Amendment is synthesized with the constitutional text that preceded it, its fundamentally radical nature is made clear. For example, the original Constitution refers to the President, to U.S. senators, and to U.S. representatives as "he," using the male pronoun. Does this mean that the Nineteenth Amendment gave women the right to vote but not to run for federal offices? Of course not! When the Nineteenth Amendment is synthesized with the original Constitution's use of "he," it becomes clear that those words of the Constitution should be read to mean "he or she." This was a permissible use of the male pronoun in 1787 (which is why Professor Lawson does not think that one needs a retroactive "synthesis" to see that the male pronouns in the Constitution were always generic). The King James Bible uses the pronoun "he" to mean "he or she." (Yep, says Professor Lawson.) The Nineteenth Amendment nails down the fact that the pronoun "he" was used in the Constitution in a latitudinarian way to mean "he or she." (GSL: Again, yep. Don't need a "synthesis" for that.)

The Nineteenth Amendment also suggests—and here both editors are speaking—that the rights to serve on criminal and civil juries must be open to both men and women. The right to vote includes the right to vote on a jury. *See supra* page 1267.

The Nineteenth Amendment also makes it clear—as should have been clear from the start—that the no-discrimination-on-account-of-caste rule of Section 1 of the Fourteenth Amendment applies to sex as a form of caste. The Nineteenth Amendment gives women the right to vote for president, senator, representative, or governor. It would be unthinkable that the very same amendment allowed women to have lesser contractual capacity or property rights than men.

The Sixteenth, Seventeenth, Eighteenth, and Nineteenth Amendments greatly added to the power of the national government, they validated the principle that the federal government could legitimately engage in the redistribution of wealth, further democratized the political process, and significantly altered the structure and practical operation of federalism. In their own way, these four constitutional amendments were as important to the balance of federal and state power as were the three Reconstruction Amendments.

E. THE TWENTIETH AMENDMENT

Section 1

The terms of the President and Vice President shall end at noon on the 20th day of January, and the terms of Senators and Representatives at noon on the 3d day of January, of the years in which such terms would have ended if this article had not been ratified; and the terms of their successors shall then begin.

Section 2

The Congress shall assemble at least once in every year, and such meeting shall begin at noon on the 3d day of January, unless they shall by law appoint a different day.

Section 3

If, at the time fixed for the beginning of the term of the President, the President elect shall have died, the Vice President elect shall become President. If a President shall not have been chosen before the time fixed for the beginning of his term, or if the President elect shall have failed to qualify, then the Vice President elect shall act as President until a President shall have qualified; and the Congress may by law provide for the case wherein neither a President elect nor a Vice President elect shall have qualified, declaring who shall then act as President, or the manner in which one who is to act shall be selected, and such person shall act accordingly until a President or Vice President shall have qualified.

Section 4

The Congress may by law provide for the case of the death of any of the persons from whom the House of Representatives may choose a President whenever the right of choice shall have devolved upon them, and for the case of the death of any of the persons from whom the Senate may choose a Vice President whenever the right of choice shall have devolved upon them.

Section 5

Sections 1 and 2 shall take effect on the 15th day of October following the ratification of this article.

Section 6

This article shall be inoperative unless it shall have been ratified as an amendment to the Constitution by the legislatures of three-fourths of the several states within seven years from the date of its submission."

The next Progressive Era constitutional amendment is the Twentieth Amendment, which was adopted on January 23, 1933 and which went into effect in 1937. This amendment makes several modest "good government" reforms. The Amendment shortens the period of time during which lame duck presidents serve by providing that newly elected presidents shall take office on January 20th rather than on March 4th. This promoted the cause of democracy, but it also shortens the time in which new presidents can assemble a staff and Cabinet.

Second, the Twentieth Amendment provides that the newly elected Senate and House of Representatives shall take office on January 3rd, seventeen days earlier than the President. This guarantees that any elections not resolved by voting in the Electoral College will be resolved by the newly elected House of Representatives and Senate and not by their lame duck predecessors in office, as occurred in 1801 when a lame-duck House resolved the tie between Thomas Jefferson and Aaron Burr. The new system is obviously much more democratic and well thought out than the old one it replaced.

The other changes made by the Twentieth Amendment are minor and technical but are all improvements. This final Progressive Era amendment shows the good-government tinkering side of the Progressive Movement.

F. THE TWENTY-FIRST AMENDMENT

Section 1

The eighteenth article of amendment to the Constitution of the United States is hereby repealed.

Section 2

The transportation or importation into any state, territory, or possession of the United States for delivery or use therein of intoxicating liquors, in violation of the laws thereof, is hereby prohibited.

Section 3

This article shall be inoperative unless it shall have been ratified as an amendment to the Constitution by conventions in the several states, as provided in the Constitution, within seven years from the date of the submission hereof to the states by the Congress.

The Twenty-First Amendment repealed the Eighteenth Amendment, but the damage done to American federalism and criminal law was irreparable. Institutions which acquired great power as a result of Prohibition like the Bureau of Alcohol, Tobacco, and Firearms and the FBI never surrendered the powers they usurped from the States.

The Twenty-First Amendment leaves States with unique powers over alcohol. This can lead to interesting questions about the relationship between the States' power and the Commerce Clause. The Supreme Court addressed that difficult topic in 2019. *See Tennessee Wine & Spirits Retailers Ass'n v. Thomas,* 139 S.Ct. 2449 (2019); Braden H. Boucek, *That's Why I Hang My Hat in Tennessee: Alcohol and the Commerce Clause,* 2018–19 CATO SUP. CT. REV. 119.

CHAPTER 7

MODERN ERA CONSTITUTIONAL AMENDMENTS

[Assignment 82]

The Modern Era began with the end of World War II and the outbreak of the Cold War between the United States and the former Soviet Union. There was a widespread perception in August 1945 that a recent global problem had been the emergence of strong men with a cult of personality built around them like Adolf Hitler, Benito Mussolini, Prime Minister Tojo of Japan, and Joseph Stalin. Mao Ze Dong soon joined this list after he became dictator of the People's Republic of China.

Many American opponents of President Franklin D. Roosevelt thought he had overstepped his bounds by breaking the two-term tradition for presidential service established by George Washington and continued by Presidents Jefferson, Madison, Monroe, Jackson, Grant, Cleveland, Theodore Roosevelt, and Woodrow Wilson. On March 24, 1947, the Twenty-Second Amendment was passed by Congress, and it was ratified on February 27, 1951. The amendment formally limits a President to ten years of service as President and two fully elected terms. Under the terms of the amendment, Franklin D. Roosevelt would not have been able to run for and win a third and a fourth term.

The text of the Amendment reads as follows:

I. THE TWENTY-SECOND AMENDMENT

Section 1

No person shall be elected to the office of the President more than twice, and no person who has held the office of President, or acted as President, for more than two years of a term to which some other person was elected President shall be elected to the office of President more than once. But this Article shall not apply to any person holding the office of President when this Article was proposed by Congress, and shall not prevent any person who may be holding the office of President, or acting as President, during the term within which this Article becomes operative from holding the office of President or acting as President during the remainder of such term.

Section 2

This article shall be inoperative unless it shall have been ratified as an amendment to the Constitution by the legislatures of three-fourths of the several States within seven years from the date of its submission to the States by the Congress.

In considering the arguments in favor of the adoption of this amendment, one point that comes quickly to mind is the enormous growth in the size and personnel of the executive branch from 1789 down to the present day. George Washington had perhaps 1,000 or 2,000 men who were under his control. Modern presidents, by contrast, have two million civil service employees and more than one million military employees. Moreover, modern presidents have control over U.S. nuclear weapons and a nearly unlimited ability to start wars with foreign powers. All of these features of the modern presidency make it a much more dangerous threat to liberty than was the original President. For that reason alone, codifying a 160-year precedent of presidents limiting themselves to two terms in office made a lot of sense. The two-term limit has kept personal charisma from allowing one person, with one set of ideas, from dominating national life for an entire generation.

Moreover, presidential democracy in Latin America, Russia, South Korea, the Philippines, and Indonesia has at times degenerated into hyper-presidential dictatorship. *See* THE FAILURE OF PRESIDENTIAL DEMOCRACY: COMPARATIVE PERSPECTIVES (Juan J. Linz ed., 1994) THE FAILURE OF PRESIDENTIAL DEMOCRACY: THE CASE OF LATIN AMERICA (Juan J. Linz & Arturo Valenzuela eds., 1994); Bruce Ackerman, *The New Separation of Powers*, 113 HARV. L. REV. 634 (2000). While the U.S. presidential system has not suffered from this problem and has lasted for 230 years, the vast increase in the power and personnel of the executive branch make it reasonable to guard against such an eventuality in the United States. The two-term limit on U.S. presidential power is thus probably a wise precaution.

The two-term limit has not been achieved, however, without Americans paying a price for it. All second-term presidents are now lame ducks and have less ability to get legislation passed by Congress than was the case before the adoption of presidential term limits. Many second-term presidents credibly threatened to run for third terms, like Ulysses S. Grant, Grover Cleveland, and Theodore Roosevelt. This helped these presidents to get things done in their second terms, which modern presidents are simply unable to do.

The fact that the President is term-limited while senators and representatives are not helps redress the enormous flow in political power from the legislative branch to the executive branch which has occurred since the New Deal. Even Joseph Story in the Jacksonian era worried about the danger of presidential dictatorship, as did critics of Abraham Lincoln and of both Roosevelts. Theodore Roosevelt, in particular, held the very dangerous belief that a President could do anything the Constitution did not affirmatively prevent him from doing. The adoption of the two-term limit on presidents is a necessary constitutional affirmation of what had been a long-standing practice once the New Deal greatly strengthened presidential power.

II. THE TWENTY-THIRD AMENDMENT

Section 1

The District constituting the seat of government of the United States shall appoint in such manner as the Congress may direct:

A number of electors of President and Vice President equal to the whole number of Senators and Representatives in Congress to which the District would be entitled if it were a state, but in no event more than the least populous state; they shall be in addition to those appointed by the states, but they shall be considered, for the purposes of the election of President and Vice President, to be

electors appointed by a state; and they shall meet in the District and perform such duties as provided by the twelfth article of amendment.

Section 2

The Congress shall have power to enforce this article by appropriate legislation.

The Twenty-Third Amendment is one of two civil rights amendments adopted in the 1960s as the nation struggled to give African-Americans the same civil rights as were enjoyed by white Americans and to redeem the promise of the Reconstruction Amendments. The Twenty-Third Amendment gave the heavily African-American capital city of Washington, D.C. three votes in the Electoral College that picks the President of the United States. The amendment was ratified on March 29, 1961 and reflected national embarrassment over the fact that residents of Washington, D.C. could not vote in federal elections.

Congress later proposed a constitutional amendment giving Washington, D.C. two Senators and a voting member of the House of Representative, but this amendment was not ratified by three quarters of the States. Today, Washington D.C. sends a non-voting member to the House of Representatives, who currently caucuses with the Democratic Party and can vote in that caucus.

III. THE TWENTY-FOURTH AMENDMENT

Section 1

The right of citizens of the United States to vote in any primary or other election for President or Vice President, for electors for President or Vice President, or for Senator or Representative in Congress, shall not be denied or abridged by the United States or any state by reason of failure to pay any poll tax or other tax.

Section 2

The Congress shall have power to enforce this article by appropriate legislation.

The Twenty-Fourth Amendment abolishing the use of poll taxes in federal elections was ratified by three quarters of the States on January 23, 1964—months after Dr. Martin Luther King's "I have a Dream" speech given from the steps of the Lincoln Memorial. It eliminated the use of poll taxes, which heavily disadvantaged African-Americans, in all federal elections. This amendment comes from the same time period as do the Civil Rights Act of 1964 and the Voting Rights Act of 1965. The Twenty-Fourth Amendment led to the following important U.S. Supreme Court opinion.

Harper v. Virginia Board of Elections

383 U.S. 663 (1966)

■ MR. JUSTICE DOUGLAS delivered the opinion of the Court.

These are suits by Virginia residents to have declared unconstitutional Virginia's poll tax.[1] The three-judge District Court, feeling bound by our decision in *Breedlove v. Suttles,* 302 U.S. 277, dismissed the complaint. The cases came here on appeal and we noted probable jurisdiction.

While the right to vote in federal elections is conferred by Art. I, § 2, of the Constitution (*United States v. Classic,* 313 U.S. 299, 314–315), the right to vote in state elections is nowhere expressly mentioned. It is argued that the right to vote in state elections is implicit, particularly by reason of the First Amendment and that it may not constitutionally be conditioned upon the payment of a tax or fee. We do not stop to canvass the relation between voting and political expression. For it is enough to say that once the franchise is granted to the electorate, lines may not be drawn which are inconsistent with the Equal Protection Clause of the Fourteenth Amendment. That is to say, the right of suffrage "is subject to the imposition of state standards which are not discriminatory and which do not contravene any restriction that Congress, acting pursuant to its constitutional powers, has imposed." *Lassiter v. Northampton Election Board,* 360 U.S. 45, 51. We were speaking there of a state literacy test which we sustained, warning that the result would be different if a literacy test, fair on its face, were used to discriminate against a class. *Id.* at 53. But the *Lassiter* case does not govern the result here, because, unlike a poll tax, the "ability to read and write . . . has some relation to standards designed to promote intelligent use of the ballot." *Id.* at 51.

We conclude that a State violates the Equal Protection Clause of the Fourteenth Amendment whenever it makes the affluence of the voter or payment of any fee an electoral standard. Voter qualifications have no relation to wealth nor to paying or not paying this or any other tax. Our cases demonstrate that the Equal Protection Clause of the Fourteenth Amendment restrains the States from fixing voter qualifications which invidiously discriminate. Thus without questioning the power of a State to impose reasonable residence restrictions on the availability of the ballot, we held in *Carrington v. Rash,* 380 U.S. 89, that a State may not deny the opportunity to vote to a bona fide resident merely because he is a member of the armed services * * *. Previously we had said that neither homesite nor occupation "affords a permissible basis for distinguishing between qualified voters within the

---

1 Section 173 of Virginia's Constitution directs the General Assembly to levy an annual poll tax not exceeding $1.50 on every resident of the State 21 years of age and over (with exceptions not relevant here). One dollar of the tax is to be used by state officials 'exclusively in aid of the public free schools' and the remainder is to be returned to the counties for general purposes. Section 18 of the Constitution includes payment of poll taxes as a precondition for voting. Section 20 provides that a person must 'personally' pay all state poll taxes for the three years preceding the year in which he applies for registration. By § 21 the poll tax must be paid at least six months prior to the election in which the voter seeks to vote. Since the time for election of state officials varies (Va.Code §§ 24–136, 24–160, 24–168; id., at § 24–22), the six months' deadline will vary, election from election. The poll tax is often assessed along with the personal property tax. Those who do not pay a personal property tax are not assessed for a poll tax, it being their responsibility to take the initiative and request to be assessed. Va.Code § 58–1163. Enforcement of poll taxes takes the form of disenfranchisement of those who do not pay, § 22 of the Virginia Constitution providing that collection of delinquent poll taxes for a particular year may not be enforced by legal proceedings until the tax for that year has become three years delinquent.

State." *Gray v. Sanders,* 372 U.S. 368, 380. We think the same must be true of requirements of wealth or affluence or payment of a fee.

Long ago in *Yick Wo v. Hopkins,* 118 U.S. 356, 370, the Court referred to "the political franchise of voting" as a "fundamental political right, because preservative of all rights." Recently in *Reynolds v. Sims,* 377 U.S. 533, 561–562, we said, "Undoubtedly, the right of suffrage is a fundamental matter in a free and democratic society. Especially since the right to exercise the franchise in a free and unimpaired manner is preservative of other basic civil and political rights, any alleged infringement of the right of citizens to vote must be carefully and meticulously scrutinized." There we were considering charges that voters in one part of the State had greater representation per person in the State Legislature than voters in another part of the State. We concluded:

> "A citizen, a qualified voter, is no more nor no less so because he lives in the city or on the farm. This is the clear and strong command of our Constitution's Equal Protection Clause. This is an essential part of the concept of a government of laws and not men. This is at the heart of Lincoln's vision of 'government of the people, by the people, [and] for the people.' The Equal Protection Clause demands no less than substantially equal state legislative representation for all citizens, of all places as well as of all races." *Id.* at 568.

We say the same whether the citizen, otherwise qualified to vote, has $1.50 in his pocket or nothing at all, pays the fee or fails to pay it. The principle that denies the State the right to dilute a citizen's vote on account of his economic status or other such factors by analogy bars a system which excludes those unable to pay a fee to vote or who fail to pay.

It is argued that a State may exact fees from citizens for many different kinds of licenses; that, if it can demand from all an equal fee for a driver's license, it can demand from all an equal poll tax for voting. But we must remember that the interest of the State, when it comes to voting, is limited to the power to fix qualifications. Wealth, like race, creed, or color, is not germane to one's ability to participate intelligently in the electoral process. Lines drawn on the basis of wealth or property, like those of race (*Korematsu v. United States,* 323 U.S. 214, 216), are traditionally disfavored. See *Edwards v. California,* 314 U.S. 160, 184–185 (Jackson, J., concurring); *Griffin v. Illinois,* 351 U.S. 12; *Douglas v. California,* 372 U.S. 353. To introduce wealth or payment of a fee as a measure of a voter's qualifications is to introduce a capricious or irrelevant factor. The degree of the discrimination is irrelevant. In this context—that is, as a condition of obtaining a ballot—the requirement of fee paying causes an "invidious" discrimination (*Skinner v. Oklahoma,* 316 U.S. 535, 541) that runs afoul of the Equal Protection Clause. Levy "by the poll," as stated in *Breedlove v. Suttles, supra,* at 281, is an old familiar form of taxation; and we say nothing to impair its validity so long as it is not made a condition to the exercise of the franchise. *Breedlove v. Suttles* sanctioned its use as "a prerequisite of voting." *Id.* at 283. To that extent the *Breedlove* case is overruled.

We agree, of course, with Mr. Justice Holmes that the Due Process Clause of the Fourteenth Amendment "does not enact Mr. Herbert Spencer's Social Statics" (*Lochner v. New York,* 198 U.S. 45, 75). Likewise, the Equal Protection Clause is not shackled to the political theory of a particular era. In determining what lines are unconstitutionally discriminatory, we have never been confined to historic notions of equality, any more than we have restricted due process to a fixed catalogue of what was at a given time deemed to be the limits of fundamental rights. Notions of what constitutes equal treatment for purposes of the Equal Protection Clause do change. This Court in 1896 held that laws providing for separate public facilities for white and Negro citizens did not deprive the latter of the equal protection and treatment that the Fourteenth Amendment commands. *Plessy v. Ferguson,* 163 U.S. 537. Seven of the eight Justices then sitting subscribed to the Court's opinion, thus joining in expressions of what constituted unequal and discriminatory treatment that sound strange to a contemporary ear. When, in 1954—more than a half-century later—we repudiated the "separate-but-equal" doctrine of *Plessy* as respects public education we stated: "In approaching this problem, we cannot turn the clock back to 1868 when the Amendment was adopted, or even to 1896 when *Plessy v. Ferguson* was written." *Brown v. Board of Education,* 347 U.S. 483, 492.

In a recent searching re-examination of the Equal Protection Clause, we held, as already noted, that "the opportunity for equal participation by all voters in the election of state legislators" is required. *Reynolds v. Sims, supra,* at 566. We decline to qualify that principle by sustaining this poll tax. Our conclusion, like that, in *Reynolds v. Sims,* is founded not on what we think governmental policy should be, but on what the Equal Protection Clause requires.

We have long been mindful that, where fundamental rights and liberties are asserted under the Equal Protection Clause, classifications which might invade or restrain them must be closely scrutinized and carefully confined.

Those principles apply here. For to repeat, wealth or fee paying has, in our view, no relation to voting qualifications; the right to vote is too precious, too fundamental to be so burdened or conditioned.

Reversed.

■ MR. JUSTICE BLACK, dissenting.

* * *

The Court denies that it is using the "natural-law-due-process formula." It says that its invalidation of the Virginia law "is founded not on what we think governmental policy should be, but on what the Equal Protection Clause requires." * * * The Court gives no reason at all to discredit the long-standing beliefs that making the payment of a tax a prerequisite to voting is an effective way of collecting revenue and that people who pay their taxes are likely to have a far greater interest in their government. The Court's failure to give any reasons to show that these purposes of the poll tax are "irrational," "unreasonable," "arbitrary," or "invidious" is a pretty clear indication to me that none exist. I can only conclude that the primary, controlling, predominate, if not the exclusive reason for declaring the Virginia law unconstitutional is the Court's deep-seated hostility and antagonism, which I share, to making payment of a tax a prerequisite to voting.

The Court's justification for consulting its own notions rather than following the original meaning of the Constitution, as I would, apparently is based on the belief of the majority of the Court that for this Court to be bound by the original meaning of the Constitution is an intolerable and debilitating evil; that our Constitution should not be "shackled to the political theory of a particular era," and that to save the country from the original Constitution the Court must have constant power to renew it and keep it abreast of this Court's more enlightening theories of what is best for our society. It seems to me that this is an attack not only on the great value of our Constitution itself but also on the concept of a written constitution which is to survive through the years as originally written unless changed through the amendment process which the Framers wisely provided. Moreover, when a "political theory" embodied in our Constitution becomes outdated, it seems to me that a majority of the nine members of this Court are not only without constitutional power but are far less qualified to choose a new constitutional political theory than the people of this country proceeding in the manner provided by Article V.

* * *

■ MR. JUSTICE HARLAN, whom MR. JUSTICE STEWART joins, dissenting.

The final demise of state poll taxes, already totally proscribed by the Twenty-Fourth Amendment with respect to federal elections and abolished by the States themselves in all but four States with respect to state elections, is perhaps in itself not of great moment. But that fact that the *coup de grace* has been administered by this Court instead of being left to the affected States or to the federal political process should be a matter of continuing concern to all interested in maintaining the proper role of this tribunal under our scheme of government.

* * *

Property and poll-tax qualifications, very simply, are not in accord with current egalitarian notions of how a modern democracy should be organized. It is of course entirely fitting that legislatures should modify the law to reflect such changes in popular attitudes. However, it is all wrong, in my view, for the Court to adopt the political doctrines popularly accepted at a particular moment of our history and to declare all others to be irrational and invidious, barring them from the range of choice by reasonably minded people acting through the political process. It was not too long ago that Mr. Justice Holmes felt impelled to remind the Court that the Due Process Clause of the Fourteenth Amendment does not enact the *laissez-faire* theory of society, *Lochner v. People of State of New York,* 198 U.S. 45, 75–76. The times have changed, and perhaps it is appropriate to observe that neither does the Equal Protection Clause of that Amendment rigidly impose upon America an ideology of unrestrained egalitarianism.

* * *

NOTES AND QUESTIONS

1. To the extent that this decision is based on the Equal Protection Clause of the Fourteenth Amendment, it is impossible square with the Constitution's original meaning, because Section 1 of the Fourteenth Amendment addresses only equality of civil rights and not equality of political rights like the right to vote. For the same reason, voting is not a "privilege or immunity" under the Privileges or Immunities Clause. Equality of political rights is, however, address by the Fifteenth, Nineteenth, and Twenty-Sixth Amendments. The Fifteenth Amendment, most pertinently, provides: "The right of citizens of the United States to vote shall not be denied or abridged by the United States or by any State on account of race, color, or previous condition of servitude." U.S. CONST. amend. XV. Six Southern States had poll taxes when this case was decided. Those taxes, as with Virginia's, were neutral on their face, but had—and were obviously designed to have—disparate racial impact. Even if there no "disparate impact" cause of action under

the Fourteenth Amendment, could there be a "disparate impact" claim under the Fifteenth Amendment? Given the history of using seemingly neutral devices to discriminate on the basis of race, it seems at least plausible to think that the Fifteenth Amendment can reach voting practices with different racial impacts. If that is right, what factual findings would a court need to make in order to conclude that a voting practice, neutral on its face, actually violates the Fifteenth Amendment? Did the Court in this case make such findings? Did the Court in this case need to make such findings? And if the Fifteenth Amendment has a disparate impact component, does it mean that disabling felons from voting violates the Fifteenth Amendment if it has a disparate impact on African-Americans?

IV. THE TWENTY-FIFTH AMENDMENT

Section 1

In case of the removal of the President from office or of his death or resignation, the Vice President shall become President.

Section 2

Whenever there is a vacancy in the office of the Vice President, the President shall nominate a Vice President who shall take office upon confirmation by a majority vote of both Houses of Congress.

Section 3

Whenever the President transmits to the President pro tempore of the Senate and the Speaker of the House of Representatives his written declaration that he is unable to discharge the powers and duties of his office, and until he transmits to them a written declaration to the contrary, such powers and duties shall be discharged by the Vice President as Acting President.

Section 4

Whenever the Vice President and a majority of either the principal officers of the executive departments or of such other body as Congress may by law provide, transmit to the President pro tempore of the Senate and the Speaker of the House of Representatives their written declaration that the President is unable to discharge the powers and duties of his office, the Vice President shall immediately assume the powers and duties of the office as Acting President.

Thereafter, when the President transmits to the President pro tempore of the Senate and the Speaker of the House of Representatives his written declaration that no inability exists, he shall resume the powers and duties of his office unless the Vice President and a majority of either the principal officers of the executive department or of such other body as Congress may by law provide, transmit within four days to the President pro tempore of the Senate and the Speaker of the House of Representatives their written declaration that the President is unable to discharge the powers and duties of his office. Thereupon

Congress shall decide the issue, assembling within forty-eight hours for that purpose if not in session. If the Congress, within twenty-one days after receipt of the latter written declaration, or, if Congress is not in session, within twenty-one days after Congress is required to assemble, determines by two-thirds vote of both Houses that the President is unable to discharge the powers and duties of his office, the Vice President shall continue to discharge the same as Acting President; otherwise, the President shall resume the powers and duties of his office.

The Twenty-Fifth Amendment was adopted on February 10, 1967 and was a response to concerns about what might have happened when President John F. Kennedy, after being assassinated, had lived but in a permanent coma. Senator Birch Bayh persuaded Congress that this was a sufficiently serious problem to require passage of a constitutional amendment.

The Twenty-Fifth Amendment accomplishes several things. First, it makes it clear that when the presidency is vacant, the Vice President actually *becomes* the President, and he does not merely "act as president." This is the interpretation of the Constitution that was followed by Presidents John Tyler, Andrew Johnson, Chester B. Arthur, Theodore Roosevelt, Calvin Coolidge, Harry S Truman, and Lyndon Johnson, but the Twenty-Fifth Amendment in Section 1 makes the point unarguably part of the Constitution. When the presidency is vacant, the Vice President actually *becomes* the President.

Second, the Twenty-Fifth Amendment imposes on presidents the duty, when the vice presidency is vacant, to "nominate a Vice President who shall take office upon confirmation by a majority vote of both Houses of Congress." This Clause was followed in 1973 when President Nixon nominated, and both Houses of Congress confirmed, Rep. Gerald R. Ford to fill the vacancy in the vice presidency occasioned by former Vice President Spiro Agnew resigning from office after not contesting bribery charges against him. When President Nixon was compelled to resign from office in August 1974, President Ford nominated, and both Houses of Congress confirmed, Nelson A. Rockefeller to be the new Vice President.

Amendment Twenty-Five, Section 2 thus increases the likelihood that the presidential succession statute will not be used. This statute has provided since 1947 that if there are vacancies in both the presidency and the vice presidency, the line of succession to the presidency shall be as follows: 1) the Speaker of the House of Representatives; 2) the President Pro Tempore of the Senate; and 3) the Cabinet officers starting with the Secretary of State and proceeding down to the most recently created Cabinet Department. *See* 3 U.S.C. § 19 (2012).

Article II, Section 1, Paragraph 6 provides that when both the presidency and the vice presidency become vacant, "the Congress may by Law [declare] what Officer shall then act as President, and such Officer shall act accordingly, until the Disability be removed, or a President shall be elected." Article I, Section 6 provides that "no person holding any Office under the United States, shall be a member of either House [of Congress] during his Continuance in Office.

These clauses read in tandem suggest, as James Madison believed, that the current presidential succession law is unconstitutional insofar as it puts the Speaker of the House and the President pro tempore of the Senate in the line of succession to the presidency. A Speaker of the House acting as President could not be a member of either House of Congress and if she resigned from Congress to satisfy the Incompatibility Clause, she would no longer be eligible to act as president under the presidential succession clause! Steven G. Calabresi, *The Political Question of Presidential Succession*, 48 STAN. L. REV. 155 (1995).

Moreover, the first duty of any person who "act[s] as President" when there is a vacancy in both the presidency and the Vice Presidency is to nominate a new Vice President for congressional confirmation. That person, once confirmed, would then become Vice President and then President under the Twenty-Fifth Amendment, bumping out of office the Acting President who had nominated the individual in question to be Vice President.

These complexities of the 25th Amendment pale in comparison with situations where a majority of the principal officers in the Cabinet declare a president either temporarily or permanently unfit to serve as president. Suffice it to say that the Twenty-Fifth Amendment took an area of law that was already a mess and in some ways made it worse.

NOTES AND QUESTIONS

1. How would you recommend that Congress revise the presidential succession statute in light of the difficulties mentioned above?

2. Would it be appropriate to have a special election to fill out a stub term whenever there is at least two years left in the president's term to run?

3. Are Cabinet Secretaries picked by the President and from his political party more appropriate replacements for a President than the Speaker of the House of Representatives or the President Pro Tempore of the Senate who may be from an opposing political party?

4. Is the question of the constitutionality of the presidential succession act justiciable or does it raise a political question?

V. AGE-BASED VOTING RULES

During the political controversy over the U.S. War in Vietnam, which became bitterly unpopular, many people argued, quite reasonably, that if 18-year-old men were old enough to be drafted to fight a war in Vietnam, they should be old enough to vote as well. The difficulty was that voting ages were set State by State, and most States had set the voting age at 21. In response to these concerns, Congress passed a federal statute, which purported to lower the voting age to 18 in all federal as well as state elections. This led to the decision of the following famous case—a case which, although now partially moot on its facts, raises fascinating questions of federalism. There was no majority opinion.

Oregon v. Mitchell

400 U.S. 112 (1970)

■ MR. JUSTICE BLACK, announcing the judgments of the Court in an opinion expressing his own view of the cases.

In these suits certain States resist compliance with the Voting Rights Act Amendments of 1970, Pub.L. 91–285, 84 Stat. 314, because they believe that the Act takes away from them powers reserved to the States by the Constitution to control their own elections. By its terms, the Act does three things. First: It lowers the minimum age of voters in both state and federal elections from 21 to 18. Second: Based upon a finding by Congress that literacy tests have been used to discriminate against voters on account of their color, the Act enforces the Fourteenth and Fifteenth Amendments by barring the use of such tests in all elections, state and national, for a five-year period. Third: The Act forbids States from disqualifying voters in national elections for presidential and vice-presidential electors because they have not met state residency requirements.

For the reasons set out in Part I of this opinion, I believe Congress can fix the age of voters in national elections, such as congressional, senatorial, vice-presidential and presidential elections, but cannot set the voting age in state and local elections. For reasons expressed in separate opinions, my Brothers DOUGLAS, BRENNAN, WHITE, and MARSHALL join me in concluding that Congress can enfranchise 18-year-old citizens in national elections, but dissent from the judgment that Congress cannot extend the franchise to 18-year-old citizens in state and local elections. For reasons expressed in separate opinions, my Brothers THE CHIEF JUSTICE, HARLAN, STEWART, and BLACKMUN join me in concluding that Congress cannot interfere with the age for voters set by the States for state and local elections. They, however, dissent from the judgment that Congress can control voter qualifications in federal elections. In summary, it is the judgment of the Court that the 18-year-old vote provisions of the Voting Rights Act Amendments of 1970 are constitutional and enforceable insofar as they pertain to federal elections and unconstitutional and unenforceable insofar as they pertain to state and local elections.

For the reasons set out in Part II of this opinion, I believe that Congress, in the exercise of its power to enforce the Fourteenth and Fifteenth Amendments, can prohibit the use of literacy tests or other devices used to discriminate against voters on account of their race in both state and federal elections. For reasons expressed in separate opinions, all of my Brethren join me in this judgment. Therefore the literacy-test provisions of the Act are upheld.

For the reasons set out in Part III of this opinion, I believe Congress can set residency requirements and provide for absentee balloting in elections for presidential and vice-presidential electors. For reasons expressed in separate opinions, my Brothers THE CHIEF JUSTICE, DOUGLAS, BRENNAN, STEWART, WHITE, MARSHALL, and BLACKMUN concur in this judgment. My Brother HARLAN, for the reasons stated in his separate opinion, considers that the residency provisions of the statute are unconstitutional. Therefore the residency and absentee balloting provisions of the Act are upheld.

Let judgments be entered accordingly.

I

The Framers of our Constitution provided in Art. I, § 2, that members of the House of Representatives should be elected by the people and that the voters for Representatives should have "the Qualifications requisite for Electors of the most numerous Branch of the State Legislature." Senators were originally to be elected by the state legislatures, but under the Seventeenth Amendment Senators are also elected by the people, and voters for Senators have the same qualifications as voters for Representatives. In the very beginning the responsibility of the States for setting the qualifications of voters in congressional elections was made subject to the power of Congress to make or alter such regulations if it deemed it advisable to do so. This was done in Art. I, § 4, of the Constitution, which provides:

> "The Times, Places and Manner of holding Elections for Senators and Representatives, shall be prescribed in each State by the Legislature thereof; *but the Congress may at any time by Law make or alter such Regulations,* except as to the Places of chusing Senators." (Emphasis supplied.)

Moreover, the power of Congress to make election regulations in national elections is augmented by the Necessary and Proper Clause. *See McCulloch v. Maryland,* 4 Wheat. 316 (1819). In *United States v. Classic,* 313 U.S. 299 (1941), where the Court upheld congressional power to regulate party primaries, Mr. Justice Stone speaking for the Court construed the interrelation of these clauses of the Constitution, stating:

> "While, in a loose sense, the right to vote for representatives in Congress is sometimes spoken of as a right derived from the states . . . this statement is true only in the sense that the states are authorized by the Constitution, to legislate on the subject as provided by § 2 of Art. I, to the extent that Congress has not restricted state action by the exercise of its powers to regulate elections under § 4 and its more general power under Article I, § 8, clause 18 of the Constitution 'to make all laws which shall be necessary and proper for carrying into execution the foregoing powers.' " 313 U.S. at 315.

The breadth of power granted to Congress to make or alter election regulations in national elections, including the qualifications of voters, is demonstrated by the fact that the Framers of the Constitution and the state legislatures which ratified it intended to grant to Congress the power to lay out or alter the boundaries of the congressional districts. In the ratifying conventions speakers argued that the power given Congress in Art. I, § 4, was meant to be used to vindicate the people's right to equality of representation in the House, *Wesberry v. Sanders,* 376 U.S. 1, 16 (1964), and that Congress would " 'most probably . . . lay the state off into districts.' " And in *Colegrove v. Green,* 328 U.S. 549 (1946), no Justice of this Court doubted Congress' power to rearrange the congressional districts according to population; the fight in that case revolved about the judicial power to compel redistricting.

Surely no voter *qualification* was more important to the Framers than the *geographical qualification* embodied in the concept of congressional districts. The Framers expected Congress to use this power to eradicate "rotten boroughs," and Congress has in fact used its power to prevent States from electing all Congressmen at large. There can be no doubt that the power to alter congressional district lines is vastly more significant in its effect than the power to permit 18-year-old citizens to go to the polls and vote in all federal elections.

* * *

In short, the Constitution allotted to the States the power to make laws regarding national elections, but provided that if Congress became dissatisfied with the state laws, Congress could alter them. A newly created national government could hardly have been expected to survive without the ultimate power to rule itself and to fill its offices under its own laws. The Voting Rights Act Amendments of 1970 now before this Court evidence dissatisfaction of Congress with the voting age set by many of the States for national elections. I would hold, as have a long line of decisions in this Court, that Congress has ultimate supervisory power over congressional elections. Similarly, it is the prerogative of Congress to oversee the conduct of presidential and vice-presidential elections and to set the qualifications for voters for electors for those offices. It cannot be seriously contended that Congress has less power over the conduct of presidential elections than it has over congressional elections.

On the other hand, the Constitution was also intended to preserve to the States the power that even the Colonies had to establish and maintain their own separate and independent governments, except insofar as the Constitution itself commands otherwise. My Brother HARLAN has persuasively demonstrated that the Framers of the Constitution intended the States to keep for themselves, as provided in the Tenth Amendment, the power to regulate elections. My major disagreement with my Brother HARLAN is that, while I agree as to the States' power to regulate the elections of their own officials, I believe, contrary to his view, that Congress has the final authority over federal elections. No function is more essential to the separate and independent existence of the States and their governments than the power to determine within the limits of the Constitution the qualifications of their own voters for state, county, and municipal offices and the nature of their own machinery for filling local public offices. Moreover, Art. I, § 2, is a clear indication that the Framers intended the States to determine the qualifications of their own voters for state offices, because those qualifications were adopted for federal offices unless Congress directs otherwise under Art. I, § 4. It is a plain fact of history that the Framers never imagined that the national Congress would set the qualifications for voters in every election from President to local constable or village alderman. It is obvious that the whole Constitution reserves to the States the power to set voter qualifications in state and local elections, except to the limited extent that the people through constitutional amendments have specifically narrowed the powers of the States. Amendments Fourteen, Fifteen, Nineteen, and Twenty-four, each of which has assumed that the States had general supervisory power over state elections, are examples of express limitations on the power of the States to govern themselves. And the Equal Protection Clause of the Fourteenth Amendment was never intended to destroy the States' power to govern themselves, making the Nineteenth and Twenty-fourth Amendments superfluous. My Brother BRENNAN's opinion, if carried to its logical conclusion, would, under the guise of insuring equal protection, blot out all state power, leaving the 50 States as little more than impotent figureheads. In interpreting what the Fourteenth Amendment means, the Equal Protection Clause should not be stretched to nullify the States' powers over elections which they had before the Constitution was adopted and which they have retained throughout our history.

Of course, the original design of the Founding Fathers was altered by the Civil War Amendments and various other amendments to the Constitution. The Thirteenth, Fourteenth, Fifteenth, and Nineteenth Amendments have expressly authorized Congress to "enforce" the limited prohibitions of those amendments by "appropriate legislation." The Solicitor General contends in these cases that Congress can set the age qualifications for voters in state elections under its power to enforce the Equal Protection Clause of the Fourteenth Amendment.

Above all else, the framers of the Civil War Amendments intended to deny to the States the power to discriminate against persons on account of their race. While this Court has recognized that the Equal Protection Clause of the Fourteenth Amendment in some instances protects against discriminations other than those on account of race, it cannot be successfully argued that the Fourteenth Amendment was intended to strip the States of their power, carefully preserved in the original Constitution, to govern themselves. The Fourteenth Amendment was surely not intended to make every discrimination between groups of people a constitutional denial of equal protection. Nor was the Enforcement Clause of the Fourteenth Amendment intended to permit Congress to prohibit every discrimination between groups of people. On the other hand, the Civil War Amendments were unquestionably designed to condemn and forbid every distinction, however trifling, on account of race.

* * *

As broad as the congressional enforcement power is, it is not unlimited * * *. Congress may only "enforce" the provisions of the amendments and may do so only by "appropriate legislation." * * *

* * *[I]n *South Carolina v. Katzenbach,* the Court upheld the literacy test ban of the Voting Rights Act of 1965. That Act proscribed the use of the literacy test in all elections in certain areas. But division of power between state and national governments, like every provision of the Constitution, was expressly qualified by the Civil War Amendments' ban on racial discrimination. Where Congress attempts to remedy racial discrimination under its enforcement powers, its authority is enhanced by the avowed intention of the framers of the Thirteenth, Fourteenth, and Fifteenth Amendments. *Cf. Harper v. Virginia Board of Elections,* 383 U.S. 663, 670 (1966) (BLACK, J., dissenting).

In enacting the 18-year-old vote provisions of the Act now before the Court, Congress made no legislative findings that the 21-year-old vote requirement was used by the States to disenfranchise voters on account of race. I seriously doubt that such a finding, if made, could be supported by substantial evidence. Since Congress has attempted to invade an area preserved to the States by the Constitution without a foundation for enforcing the Civil War Amendments' ban on racial discrimination, I would hold that Congress has exceeded its powers in attempting to lower the voting age in state and local elections. On the other hand, where Congress legislates in a domain not exclusively reserved by the Constitution to the States, its enforcement power need not be tied so closely to the goal of eliminating discrimination on account of race.

To invalidate part of the Voting Rights Act Amendments of 1970, however, does not mean that the entire Act must fall or that the constitutional part of the 18-year-old vote provision cannot be given effect. In passing the Voting Rights Act

Amendments of 1970, Congress recognized that the limits of its power under the Enforcement Clauses were largely undetermined, and therefore included a broad severability provision:

> "If any provision of this Act or the application of any provision thereof to any person or circumstance is judicially determined to be invalid, the remainder of this Act or the application of such provision to other persons or circumstances shall not be affected by such determination." 84 Stat. 318.

In this case, it is the judgment of the Court that Title III, lowering the voting age to 18, is invalid as applied to voters in state and local elections. It is also the judgment of the Court that Title III is valid with respect to national elections. We would fail to follow the express will of Congress in interpreting its own statute if we refused to sever these two distinct aspects of Title III * * *. Here, of course, the enforcement of the 18-year-old vote in national elections is in no way dependent upon its enforcement in state and local elections.

II

In Title I of the Voting Rights Act Amendments of 1970 Congress extended the provisions of the Voting Rights Act of 1965 which ban the use of literacy tests in certain States upon the finding of certain conditions by the United States Attorney General * * *. The constitutionality of Title I is not raised by any of the parties to these suits.

In Title II of the Amendments Congress prohibited until August 6, 1975, the use of any test or device resembling a literacy test in any national, state, or local election in any area of the United States where such test is not already proscribed by the Voting Rights Act of 1965. The State of Arizona maintains that Title II cannot be enforced to the extent that it is inconsistent with Arizona's literacy test requirement, Ariz.Rev.Stat.Ann. §§ 16–101.A.4, 16–101.A.5 (1956). I would hold that the literacy test ban of the 1970 Amendments is constitutional under the Enforcement Clause of the Fifteenth Amendment and that it supersedes Arizona's conflicting statutes under the Supremacy Clause of the Federal Constitution.

In enacting the literacy test ban of Title II Congress had before it a long history of the discriminatory use of literacy tests to disfranchise voters on account of their race. Congress could have found that as late as the summer of 1968, the percentage registration of nonwhite voters in seven Southern States was substantially below the percentage registration of white voters. Moreover, Congress had before it striking evidence to show that the provisions of the 1965 Act had had in the span of four years a remarkable impact on minority group voter registration. Congress also had evidence to show that voter registration in areas with large Spanish-American populations was consistently below the state and national averages. In Arizona, for example, only two counties out of eight with Spanish surname populations in excess of 15% showed a voter registration equal to the state-wide average. Arizona also has a serious problem of deficient voter registration among Indians. Congressional concern over the use of a literacy test to disfranchise Puerto Ricans in New York State is already a matter of record in this Court. *Katzenbach v. Morgan, supra.* And as to the Nation as a whole, Congress had before it statistics which demonstrate that voter registration and voter participation are consistently greater in States without literacy tests.

Congress also had before it this country's history of discriminatory educational opportunities in both the North and the South. The children who were denied an equivalent education by the "separate but equal" rule of *Plessy v. Ferguson,* 163 U.S. 537"] 163 U.S. 537 (1896), overruled in 163 U.S. 537 (1896), overruled in *Brown v. Board of Education,* 347 U.S. 483 (1954), are now old enough to vote. There is substantial, if not overwhelming, evidence from which Congress could have concluded that it is a denial of equal protection to condition the political participation of children educated in a dual school system upon their educational achievement. Moreover, the history of this legislation suggests that concern with educational inequality was perhaps uppermost in the minds of the congressmen who sponsored the Act. The hearings are filled with references to educational inequality. Faced with this and other evidence that literacy tests reduce voter participation in a discriminatory manner not only in the South but throughout the Nation, Congress was supported by substantial evidence in concluding that a nationwide ban on literacy tests was appropriate to enforce the Civil War amendments.

Finally, there is yet another reason for upholding the literacy test provisions of this Act. In imposing a nationwide ban on literacy tests, Congress has recognized a national problem for what it is—a serious *national* dilemma that touches every corner of our land. In this legislation Congress has recognized that discrimination on account of color and racial origin is not confined to the South, but exists in various parts of the country. Congress has decided that the way to solve the problems of racial discrimination is to deal with nationwide discrimination with nationwide legislation.

III

In Title II of the Voting Rights Act Amendments Congress also provided that, in presidential and vice-presidential elections, no voter could be denied his right to cast a ballot because he had not lived in the jurisdiction long enough to meet its residency requirements. Furthermore, Congress provided uniform national rules for absentee voting in presidential and vice-presidential elections. In enacting these regulations, Congress was attempting to insure a fully effective voice to all citizens in national elections. What I said in Part I of this opinion applies with equal force here. Acting under its broad authority to create and maintain a national government, Congress unquestionably has power under the Constitution to regulate federal elections. The Framers of our Constitution were vitally concerned with setting up a national government that could survive. Essential to the survival and to the growth of our national government is its power to fill its elective offices and to insure that the officials who fill those offices are as responsive as possible to the will of the people whom they represent.

IV

Our judgments today give the Federal Government the power the Framers conferred upon it, that is, the final control of the elections of its own officers. Our judgments also save for the States the power to control state and local elections which the Constitution originally reserved to them and which no subsequent amendment has taken from them. The generalities of the Equal Protection Clause of the Fourteenth Amendment were not designed or adopted to render the States impotent to set voter qualifications in elections for their own local officials and agents in the absence of some specific constitutional limitations.

■ MR. JUSTICE DOUGLAS.

I dissent from the judgments of the Court insofar as they declare § 302 of the Voting Rights Act, 84 Stat. 318, unconstitutional as applied to state elections and concur in the judgments as they affect federal elections, but for different reasons. I rely on the Equal Protection Clause and on the Privileges and Immunities Clause of the Fourteenth Amendment.

I

The grant of the franchise to 18-year-olds by Congress is in my view valid across the board.

I suppose that, in 1920, when the Nineteenth Amendment was ratified giving women the right to vote, it was assumed by most constitutional experts that there was no relief by way of the Equal Protection Clause of the Fourteenth Amendment. In *Minor v. Happersett,* 21 Wall. 162, the Court held in the 1874 Term that a State could constitutionally restrict the franchise to men. While the Fourteenth Amendment was relied upon, the thrust of the opinion was directed at the Privileges and Immunities Clause with a subsidiary reference to the Due Process Clause. It was much later, indeed not until the 1961 Term—nearly a century after the Fourteenth Amendment was adopted—that discrimination against voters on grounds *other than race* was struck down.

The first case in which this Court struck down a statute under the Equal Protection Clause of the Fourteenth Amendment was *Strauder v. West Virginia,* 100 U.S. 303, decided in the 1879 Term. In the 1961 Term we squarely held that the manner of apportionment of members of a state legislature raised a justiciable question under the Equal Protection Clause, *Baker v. Carr,* 369 U.S. 186. That case was followed by numerous others, *e.g.*: that one person could not be given twice or 10 times the voting power of another person in a state-wide election merely because he lived in a rural area or in the smallest rural county; that the principle of equality applied to both Houses of a bicameral legislature; that political parties receive protection under the Equal Protection Clause just as voters do.

The reapportionment cases, however, are not quite in point here, though they are the target of my Brother HARLAN's dissent. His painstaking review of the history of the Equal Protection Clause leads him to conclude that "political" rights are not protected though "civil" rights are protected. The problem of what questions are "political" has been a recurring issue in this Court from the beginning, and we recently reviewed them all in *Baker v. Carr, supra,* and in *Powell v. McCormack,* 395 U.S. 486. *Baker v. Carr* was a reapportionment case and *Powell v. McCormack* involved the exclusion from the House of Representatives of a Congressman. The issue of "political" question versus "justiciable" question was argued *pro* and *con* in those cases; and my Brother HARLAN stated in *Baker v. Carr,* 369 U.S. at 330 *et seq.*, and on related occasions (*Gray v. Sanders,* 372 U.S. 368, 382; *Wesberry v. Sanders,* 376 U.S. 1, 20; *Reynolds v. Sims,* 377 U.S. 533, 589) his views on the constitutional dimensions of the "political" question in the setting of the reapportionment problem.

Those cases involved the question whether legislatures must be so structured as to reflect with approximate equality the voice of every voter. The ultimate question was whether, absent a proper apportionment by the legislature, a federal court could itself make an apportionment. That kind of problem raised issues irrelevant here. Reapportionment, as our experience shows, presented a tangle of partisan politics in which geography, economics, urban life, rural constituencies, and numerous other nonlegal factors play varying roles. The competency of courts to deal with them was challenged. Yet we held the issues were justiciable. None of those so-called "political" questions are involved here.

This case, so far as equal protection is concerned, is no whit different from a controversy over a state law that disqualifies women from certain types of employment, *Goesaert v. Cleary,* 335 U.S. 464, or that imposes a heavier punishment on one class of offender than on another whose crime is not intrinsically different. *Skinner v. Oklahoma,* 316 U.S. 535. The right to vote is, of course, different in one respect from the other rights in the economic, social, or political field which, as indicated in the Appendix to this opinion, are under the Equal Protection Clause. The right to vote is a civil right deeply embedded in the Constitution. Article I, § 2, provides that the House is composed of members "chosen . . . by the People" and the electors "shall have the Qualifications requisite for Electors of the most numerous Branch of the State Legislature." The Seventeenth Amendment states that Senators shall be "elected by the people." The Fifteenth Amendment speaks of the "right of citizens of the United States to vote"—not only in federal but in state elections * * *

This "right to choose, secured by the Constitution," *United States v. Classic,* 313 U.S. 299, 315, is a civil right of the highest order. Voting concerns "political" matters; but the right is not "political" in the constitutional sense. Interference with it has given rise to a long and consistent line of decisions by the Court; and the claim has always been upheld as justiciable. Whatever distinction may have been made, following the Civil War, between "civil" and "political" rights, has passed into history. In *Harper v. Virginia Board of Elections,* 383 U.S. 663, 669, we stated: "Notions of what constitutes equal treatment for purposes of the Equal Protection Clause *do* change." * * *

Since the right is civil and not "political," it is protected by the Equal Protection Clause of the Fourteenth Amendment which in turn, by § 5 of that Amendment, can be "enforced" by Congress.

* * *

Congress might well conclude that a reduction in the voting age from 21 to 18 was needed in the interest of equal protection. The Act itself brands the denial of the franchise to 18-year-olds as "a particularly unfair treatment of such citizens in view of the national defense responsibilities imposed" on them. § 301(a)(1), Voting Rights Act, 84 Stat. 318. The fact that only males are drafted while the vote extends to females as well is not relevant, for the female component of these families or prospective families is also caught up in war and hit hard by it. Congress might well believe that men and women alike should share the fateful decision.

It is said, why draw the line at 18? Why not 17? Congress can draw lines and I see no reason why it cannot conclude that 18-year-olds have that degree of maturity which entitles them to the franchise * * *.

* * *

Equality of voting by all who are deemed mature enough to vote is certainly consistent "with the letter and spirit of the constitution." Much is made of the fact that Art. I, § 4, of the Constitution gave Congress only the power to regulate the "Manner of holding Elections," not the power to fix qualifications for voting in elections. But the Civil War Amendments—the Thirteenth, Fourteenth, and

Fifteenth—made vast inroads on the power of the States. Equal protection became a standard for state action and Congress was given authority to "enforce" it. The manner of enforcement involves discretion; but that discretion is largely entrusted to the Congress, not to the courts. If racial discrimination were the only concern of the Equal Protection Clause, then across-the-board voting regulations set by the States would be of no concern to Congress. But it is much too late in history to make that claim, as the cases listed in the Appendix to this opinion show. Moreover, election inequalities created by state laws and based on factors other than race may violate the Equal Protection Clause, as we have held over and over again. The reach of § 5 to "enforce" equal protection by eliminating election inequalities would seem quite broad. Certainly there is not a word of limitation in § 5 which would restrict its applicability to matters of race alone. And if, as stated in *McCulloch v. Maryland,* the measure of the power of Congress is whether the remedy is consistent "with the letter and spirit of the constitution," we should have no difficulty here * * *.

* * *

I would sustain the choice which Congress has made.

II

I likewise find the objections that Arizona and Idaho make to the literacy and residence requirements of the 1970 Act to be insubstantial.

* * *

We took a * * * step toward sustaining the present type of law in *Gaston County v. United States,* 395 U.S. 285 * * *.

> "It is only reasonable to infer that among black children compelled to endure a segregated and inferior education, fewer will achieve any given degree of literacy than will their better-educated white contemporaries. And on the Government's showing, it was certainly proper to infer that Gaston County's inferior Negro schools provided many of its Negro residents with a subliterate education, and gave many others little inducement to enter or remain in school." *Id.* at 295–296.

By like reasoning Congress in the present legislation need not make findings as to the incidence of literacy. It can rely on the fact that most States do not have literacy tests; that the tests have been used at times as a discriminatory weapon against some minorities, not only Negroes, but Americans of Mexican ancestry, and American Indians; that radio and television have made it possible for a person to be well informed even though he may not be able to read and write. We know from the legislative history that these and other desiderata influenced Congress in the choice it made in the present legislation; and we certainly cannot say that the means used were inappropriate.

Residence. The residency requirements of § 202 relate only to elections for President and Vice President. Section 202 abolishes durational residency and provides for absentee voting provided that registration may be required 30 days prior to the election. The effect of § 202 is to reduce all state durational residency requirements to 30 days.

* * *

The Fourteenth Amendment provides that: "No State shall make or enforce any law which shall abridge the privileges or immunities of citizens of the United States."

Durational residency laws of the States had such effect, says Congress. The "choice of means" to protect such a privilege presents "a question primarily addressed to the judgment of Congress." *Burroughs v. United States, supra,* at 547. The relevance of the means which Congress adopts to the condition sought to be remedied, the degree of their necessity, and the extent of their efficacy are all matters for Congress. *Id.* at 548.

The judgment which Congress has made respecting the ban of durational residency in presidential elections is plainly a permissible one in its efforts under § 5 to "enforce" the Fourteenth Amendment.

■ MR. JUSTICE HARLAN, concurring in part and dissenting in part.

From the standpoint of this Court's decisions during an era of judicial constitutional revision in the field of the suffrage, ushered in eight years ago by *Baker v. Carr,* 369 U.S. 186 (1962), I would find it difficult not to sustain all three aspects of the Voting Rights Act Amendments of 1970, Pub.L. 91–285, 84 Stat. 314, here challenged. From the standpoint of the bedrock of the constitutional structure of this Nation, these cases bring us to a crossroad that is marked with a formidable "Stop" sign. That sign compels us to pause before we allow those decisions to carry us to the point of sanctioning Congress' decision to alter state-determined voter qualifications by simple legislation, and to consider whether sound doctrine does not in truth require us to hold that one or more of the changes which Congress has thus sought to make can be accomplished only by constitutional amendment.

* * *

* * *Except for those who are willing to close their eyes to constitutional history in making constitutional interpretations or who read such history with a preconceived determination to attain a particular constitutional goal, I think that the history of the Fourteenth Amendment makes it clear beyond any reasonable doubt that no part of the legislation now under review can be upheld as a legitimate exercise of congressional power under that Amendment.

* * * Nothing in the original Constitution controlled the way States might allocate their political power except for the guarantee of a Republican Form of Government, which appears in Art. IV, § 4 No relevant changes in the constitutional structure were made until after the Civil War.

* * *

* * * [T]he framers of the Amendment expected the most significant portion of § 1 to be the clause prohibiting state laws "which shall abridge the privileges or immunities of citizens of the United States." These privileges were no doubt understood to include the ones set out in the first section of the Civil Rights Act. To be prohibited by law from enjoying these rights would hardly be consistent with full membership in a civil society.

The same is not necessarily true with respect to prohibitions on participation in the political process. Many members of Congress accepted the jurisprudence of the day, in which the rights of man fell into three categories: natural, civil, and political. The privileges of citizens, being "civil" rights, were distinct from the rights arising from governmental organization, which were political in character. Others no doubt relied on the experience under the similar language of Art. IV, § 2, which had never been held to guarantee the right to vote. The remarks of Senator Howard of

Michigan, who as spokesman for the Joint Committee explained in greater detail than most why the Amendment did not reach the suffrage, contain something of each view.

Since the Privileges and Immunities Clause was expected to be the primary source of substantive protection, the Equal Protection and Due Process Clauses were relegated to a secondary role, as the debates and other contemporary materials make clear. Those clauses, which appear on their face to correspond with the latter portion of § 1 of the Civil Rights Act and to be primarily concerned with person and property, would not have been expected to enfranchise the freedmen if the Privileges and Immunities Clause did not.

* * *

The 40th Congress, not content with enfranchisement in the South, proposed the Fifteenth Amendment to extend the suffrage to northern Negroes. This fact alone is evidence that they did not understand the Fourteenth Amendment to have accomplished such a result. Less well known is the fact that the 40th Congress considered and very nearly adopted a proposed amendment which would have expressly prohibited not only discriminatory voter qualifications but discriminatory qualifications for office as well. Each House passed such a measure by the required two-thirds margin. Cong. Globe, 40th Cong., 3d Sess., 1318, 1428 (1869). A conference committee, composed of Senators Stewart and Conkling and Representatives Boutwell, Bingham, and Logan, struck out the office-holding provision, *id.* at 1563, 1593, and with Inauguration Day only a week away, both Houses accepted the conference report. *Id.* at 1564, 1641. While the reasons for these actions are unclear, it is unlikely that they were provoked by the idea that the Fourteenth Amendment covered the field; such a rationale seemingly would have made the enfranchising provision itself unnecessary.

* * *

The history of the Fourteenth Amendment with respect to suffrage qualifications is remarkably free of the problems which bedevil most attempts to find a reliable guide to present decision in the pages of the past. Instead, there is virtually unanimous agreement, clearly and repeatedly expressed, that § 1 of the Amendment did not reach discriminatory voter qualifications. In this rather remarkable situation, the issue of the bearing of the historical understanding on constitutional interpretation squarely arises.

I must confess to complete astonishment at the position of some of my Brethren that the history of the Fourteenth Amendment has become irrelevant. In the six years since I first set out much of this history, I have seen no justification for such a result which appears to me at all adequate * * *.

* * *

Judicial deference is based not on relative factfinding competence, but on due regard for the decision of the body constitutionally appointed to decide. Establishment of voting qualifications is a matter for state legislatures. Assuming any authority at all, only when the Court can say with some confidence that the legislature has demonstrably erred in adjusting the competing interests is it justified in striking down the legislative judgment. This order of things is more efficient and more congenial to our system, and, in my judgment, much more likely to achieve satisfactory results than one in which the Court has a free hand to replace state legislative judgments with its own. *See Ferguson v. Skrupa,* 372 U.S. 726 (1963).

The same considerations apply, and with almost equal force, to Congress' displacement of state decisions with its own ideas of wise policy. The sole distinction between Congress and the Court in this regard is that Congress, being an elective body, presumptively has popular authority for the value judgment it makes. But since the state legislature has a like authority, this distinction between Congress and the judiciary falls short of justifying a congressional veto on the state judgment. The perspectives and values of national legislators on the issue of voting qualifications are likely to differ from those of state legislators, but I see no reason *a priori* to prefer those of the national figures, whose collective decision, applying nationwide, is necessarily less able to take account of peculiar local conditions. Whether one agrees with this judgment or not, it is the one expressed by the Framers in leaving voter qualifications to the States. The Supremacy Clause does not, as my colleagues seem to argue, represent a judgment that federal decisions are superior to those of the States whenever the two may differ.

* * *

The only constitutional basis advanced in support of the lowering of the voting age is the power to enforce the Equal Protection Clause, a power found in § 5 of the Fourteenth Amendment. For the reasons already given, it cannot be said that the statutory provision is valid as declaratory of the meaning of that clause. Its validity therefore must rest on congressional power to lower the voting age as a means of preventing invidious discrimination that is within the purview of that clause.

The history of the Fourteenth Amendment may well foreclose the possibility that § 5 empowers Congress to enfranchise a class of citizens so that they may protect themselves against discrimination forbidden by the first section, but it is unnecessary for me to explore that question. For I think it fair to say that the suggestion that members of the age group between 18 and 21 are threatened with unconstitutional discrimination, or that any hypothetical discrimination is likely to be affected by lowering the voting age, is little short of fanciful. I see no justification for stretching to find any such possibility when all the evidence indicates that Congress—led on by recent decisions of this Court—thought simply that 18-year-olds were fairly entitled to the vote and that Congress could give it to them by legislation.

I therefore conclude, for these and other reasons given in this opinion, that in § 302 of the Voting Rights Act Amendments of 1970 Congress exceeded its delegated powers. For reasons already stated, neither the power to regulate voting qualifications in presidential elections * * * nor the power to declare the meaning of § 1 of the Fourteenth Amendment * * * can support § 202 of the Act. It would also be frivolous to contend that requiring States to allow new arrivals to vote in presidential elections is an appropriate means of preventing local discrimination against them in other respects, or of forestalling violations of the Fifteenth Amendment * * *.

* * *

The remaining provision of the Voting Rights Act Amendments involved in these cases is the five-year suspension of Arizona's requirement that registrants be able to read the Constitution in English and to write their names. Although the issue is not free from difficulty, I am of the opinion that this provision can be sustained as a valid means of enforcing the Fifteenth Amendment.

Despite the lack of evidence of specific instances of discriminatory application or effect, Congress could have determined that racial prejudice is prevalent throughout the Nation, and that literacy tests unduly lend themselves to discriminatory application, either conscious or unconscious. This danger of violation of § 1 of the Fifteenth Amendment was sufficient to authorize the exercise of congressional power under § 2.

* * *

■ MR. JUSTICE BRENNAN, MR. JUSTICE WHITE, and MR. JUSTICE MARSHALL dissent from the judgments insofar as they declare § 302 unconstitutional as applied to state and local elections, and concur in the judgments in all other respects, for the following reasons.

* * *

In short, there is no question but that Congress could legitimately have concluded that the use of literacy tests anywhere within the United States has the inevitable effect of denying the vote to members of racial minorities whose inability to pass such tests is the direct consequence of previous governmental discrimination in education * * *. Five years of experience with the 1965 Act persuaded Congress that a nationwide ban on literacy and other potentially discriminatory tests was necessary to prevent racial discrimination in voting throughout the country. That conclusion is amply supported in the legislative record and § 201 of the 1970 Amendments is accordingly well within the scope of congressional power.

* * *

Whether or not the Constitution vests Congress with particular power to set qualifications for voting in strictly federal elections, we believe there is an adequate constitutional basis for § 202 in § 5 of the Fourteenth Amendment. For more than a century, this Court has recognized the constitutional right of all citizens to unhindered interstate travel and settlement. From whatever constitutional provision this right may be said to flow, both its existence and its fundamental importance to our Federal Union have long been established beyond question.

By definition, the imposition of a durational residence requirement operates to penalize those persons, and only those persons, who have exercised their constitutional right of interstate migration * * *.

* * *

We believe there is serious question whether a statute granting the franchise to citizens 21 and over while denying it to those between the ages of 18 and 21 could, in any event, withstand present scrutiny under the Equal Protection Clause. Regardless of the answer to this question, however, it is clear to us that proper regard for the special function of Congress in making determinations of legislative fact compels this Court to respect those determinations unless they are contradicted by evidence far stronger than anything that has been adduced in these cases. We would uphold § 302 as a valid exercise of congressional power under § 5 of the Fourteenth Amendment.

* * *

■ MR. JUSTICE STEWART, with whom THE CHIEF JUSTICE and MR. JUSTICE BLACKMUN join, concurring in part and dissenting in part. [Omitted.]

NOTES AND QUESTIONS

1. It is hard to dispute Justice Harlan's (massively long) discussion of why Section 1 of the Fourteenth Amendment does not address voting and thus does not give Congress Section 5 power to regulate age or residency requirements.

2. The opinions in these cases are confusing, even (especially?) in their full, unedited forms. If you have no idea what is going on in this case, you have been in good company for half a century.

3. At least with respect to the age requirement, the case became the fourth Supreme Court opinion in American history to be overruled by a constitutional amendment when the Twenty-Sixth Amendment to the Constitution was ratified on July 1, 1971. That Amendment provides that:

Section 1

> **The right of citizens of the United States, who are 18 years of age or older, to vote, shall not be denied or abridged by the United States or any state on account of age.**

Section 2

> **The Congress shall have the power to enforce this article by appropriate legislation.**

VI. THE TWENTY-SEVENTH AMENDMENT

> **No law, varying the compensation for the services of the Senators and Representatives, shall take effect, until an election of Representatives shall have intervened.**

The Twenty-Seventh Amendment was proposed by Congress to the States on September 25, 1789, along with the original Bill of Rights. While ten of the twelve amendments Congress proposed then were ratified by 1791, the Twenty-Seventh Amendment did not receive the support of three quarters of the States right away. The Amendment lay largely forgotten until 1982 when a student paper on the subject turned into a national campaign to get the amendment ratified. The amendment finally received the support of three quarters of the States on May 5, 1992—more than 202 years after it had been approved by Congress. On May 18, 1992, Don Wilson, the archivist of the United States, certified that the amendment had been validly ratified. It was then printed in the Federal Register. On May 20, 1992, Congress passed a concurrent resolution agreeing that the Twenty-Seventh Amendment had been validly ratified notwithstanding the fact it had lain before the States for more than 202 years. The vote was 99 to 0 in the Senate; and 414 to 3 in the House of Representatives. The congressional vote ended any uncertainty about the status of the Amendment.

The ultimate proof of the fact that Americans today accept the unity of our Constitution over the last 230 years came with the complete acceptance of the validity of the ratification of the Twenty-Seventh Amendment over a 203-year time period. An amendment which was approved by Congress in 1789 was deemed by an almost unanimous vote in Congress to have been validly ratified over a time period of more than 202 years. Nothing like this has ever happed or could ever happen in France. France really has had five constitutions since 1789, while the United States has had one. We think this casebook and the nearly unanimous acceptance of the Twenty-Seventh Amendment prove as much.

INDEX

References are to Pages